Praise for *Acts: An Exegetical Commentary*

"This is the most expansive treatment of Acts in modern scholarship. Keener offers the reader a sweeping tour of the relevant ancient material and modern scholarship on Acts. He takes Acts seriously as a work of ancient history; at the same time, he is aware of the literary and rhetorical dimensions of the text."

—**Gregory E. Sterling**,
Yale Divinity School

"Somewhat surprisingly, a socio-historical approach to Acts still needs to be defended and its value demonstrated. No one does this better—is more informed about ancient literature, parallels, and precedents, and more interactively and fruitfully engaged with contemporary literature and issues—than Craig Keener. For anyone wanting to appreciate how Acts 'worked' in its original context and to get into the text at some depth, Keener will be indispensable and 'first off the shelf.'"

—**James D. G. Dunn**,
University of Durham

"Keener takes very seriously the claim of the book of Acts to be historiography. His encyclopedic knowledge of ancient literature and his intelligent skill as an exegete make this a magisterial commentary."

—**Richard Bauckham**, University of St. Andrews; Ridley Hall, Cambridge

"Keener's incredibly detailed mega-commentary on Acts is a scholarly achievement that is unlikely to be surpassed in the foreseeable future. The author has an enviable mastery over an amazing number of primary and secondary sources, and he provides in-depth discussions of various critical approaches to the major interpretive issues, revealing the strength and weakness of each position while carefully arguing his own position. Every serious student of Acts owes it to herself or himself to carefully work their way through this significant contribution to scholarship."

—**David E. Aune**,
University of Notre Dame

"Craig Keener, a master of primary and secondary sources, has crafted another meticu-

lous commentary that is a joy to read. It is full of information that shows Keener's unusual industriousness and precision. Highly recommended."

—**James H. Charlesworth**,
Princeton Theological Seminary

"Craig Keener has provided us with a rich gem of a commentary on Acts. One can use it and get a real sense of what this key work is all about."

—**Darrell L. Bock**, research professor of New Testament studies, Dallas Theological Seminary

"Over the course of the last decade, Craig Keener has proved himself to be one of the greatest living commentators on the New Testament. This [commentary]—packed with an incredible amount of contextual information as well as wisdom about the text itself—is bound to become a standard reference work for many years to come."

—**Ben Witherington III**, Asbury Theological Seminary; doctoral faculty, St. Andrews University

"Acts has now taken a new step forward . . . the starting point for all Acts scholarship from now on!"

—**Scot McKnight**, professor of New Testament, Northern Seminary

"Perhaps the largest commentary on any single biblical writing. . . . It will be consulted frequently in coming years to draw upon [Keener's] commendable dedication to providing the results of his extensive acquaintance with the historical context of the NT."

—**Larry Hurtado**, University of Edinburgh

"As one has come to expect from Keener, there is thorough knowledge and use of the best and most important secondary literature and abundant utilization of a wide range of ancient sources. This is a commentary that will continue to serve as a detailed resource for both scholars and students wishing to explore the book of Acts."

—**Stanley E. Porter**,
McMaster Divinity College

"A magnificent achievement. Without any shadow of doubt, an indispensable reference work for all students of Acts and early Christianity."

—**Christopher Tuckett**, Pembroke College, University of Oxford

"The author proffers a very detailed and nuanced analysis of the text's exegetical problems while also paying close attention to the Greco-Roman environment that shaped Luke's narrative. Scholars of the New Testament, theologians, and classicists, but also laypersons, will want to consult and will benefit from Keener's erudite, impressive work."

—**Andreas Bendlin**, Department of Classics, University of Toronto

"This commentary is so thorough and comprehensive that it can truly be said to 'leave no stone unturned.' Keener has single-handedly wrought an encyclopedic work, the likes of which only whole teams of scholars have been able to produce in multivolume compendia. It therefore will be the first commentary to which scholars, students, and pastors will turn with any question on the text of Acts."

—**Seyoon Kim**, School of Theology, Fuller Theological Seminary

"This commentary sets Acts in its ancient social and historical setting. Keener shows convincingly how broadly and deeply Acts participates in ancient Hellenistic and Jewish thinking. This meticulous reconstruction fits well with his deep insights on Lukan theology in Acts. Keener's wide reading of scholarly discussion is stupendous. A marvelous, impressive, and inspiring commentary!"

—**Manfred Lang**, Martin Luther University, Halle-Wittenberg

"Keener's scholarship and personal experience give a distinctive cross-cultural perspective to his commentary. His excurses are treasure troves of cultural information. This detailed commentary will deservedly be a major resource on Acts in many libraries—personal and public—for years to come."

—**John J. Pilch**, Johns Hopkins University

"This promises to be the most comprehensive commentary on Acts to date. Keener presents a socio-historical reading of the text with meticulous precision, and his knowledge of scholarly research is impressive. The book of Acts is read as a historiographical work in which its author rewrites traditions; the documentation from ancient Jewish literature is exceptionally rich. Keener treats hermeneutical issues and the historical reliability of the text astutely and clearly. From now on, any exegesis of Acts will need to take into account this major work."

—**Daniel Marguerat**, University of Lausanne, Switzerland

"This book is a monumental exegetical commentary thanks to the amount of literary and social-historical information in it. Scholars and readers of the Acts of the Apostles will find it a precious source for consultation."

—**Fr. G. Claudio Bottini**, Faculty of Biblical Sciences and Archaeology (Studium Biblicum Franciscanum), Jerusalem

"Craig Keener's academic commentaries are among the most important in print, because they not only summarize former scholarship but also add so many new insights from primary literature of the time."

—**David Instone-Brewer**, Tyndale House, Cambridge

"Keener's commentary on Acts is a tour de force. One might be daunted by such hefty volume(s) on one book of the New Testament, but be reassured: this commentary may be all that you will ever need on Acts. It is not only exhaustive in its historical detail, it is rich in inspiring interpretation."

—**David E. Garland**, George W. Truett Theological Seminary, Baylor University

"Keener's massive commentary on the book of Acts is a gold mine of valuable information. His socio-historical reading of the text demonstrates the crucial importance of interpreting Acts in the context of Greek and Roman historiography. In addition, the vast amount of references to ancient sources and literature will be helpful for anyone interested in doing serious research on Acts."

—**Samuel Byrskog**, Centre for Theology and Religious Studies, Lund University

"Rich and detailed chapters, designed to immerse contemporary readers into the location of ancient readers, are the primary substance of this first of four volumes. . . . For anyone looking for a useful discussion of important features of 'introduction' to the Book of Acts, Keener's 600-page introduction is extraordinary. And for one looking for 'deep background' or 'thick description' of details behind, and assumed by, the text, Keener's work is without peer or parallel."

—**J. Bradley Chance**, *Interpretation*

"Keener's finished commentary will dwarf other modern commentaries, if measured by the quantity of either ink spilled or of citations of Greco-Roman texts. Beyond such metrics, Keener's magnum opus is a rich resource that will serve Acts scholars for years to come. . . . A scholar with extensive knowledge of Jewish and Greco-Roman materials, Keener brings this expertise to his commentary, introducing scores of relevant citations to subsequent scholars of Acts. . . . This volume is the result of the careful, balanced work of a senior scholar. Any serious scholar will want to have this valuable commentary ready-to-hand."

—**Daniel L. Smith**, *Review of Biblical Literature*

"This commentary is in a class by itself, not only because of its mega-size . . . but also because of its thoroughness and the meticulous scholarship it displays. Keener . . . summarizes past and current scholarly opinion on the historical and theological dimensions of Luke's account [and includes] numerous and informative excurses on various aspects of the Jewish and Greco-Roman cultural and social context contemporary with Luke's work. For those desiring an encyclopedic analysis of the Acts of the Apostles, this is definitely the resource to turn to."

—**Donald Senior, CP**, *The Bible Today*

"Those who have followed Keener's career have come to expect learned comment and extensive bibliography undergirding his research. . . . The detail of historical inquiry involved in this commentary is quite fantastic and stimulating. . . . Great appreciation must be expressed to Professor Keener for what may well be his *magnum opus!*"

—**Aaron W. White**, *Journal of the Evangelical Theological Society*

"By almost any measure, Craig Keener's commentary on Acts is a remarkable achievement. . . . He is thoroughly engaged with a wide range of critical studies of Acts and related writings. Keener also brings to the study of Acts a deep and extensive acquaintance with ancient Greco-Roman and Jewish literature, and the result is a rich, detailed commentary packed with abundant and useful information. . . . I am unable to agree with many of his convictions about Acts but am compelled to admire his well-conceived and well-documented arguments and interpretations."

—**Joseph Tyson**, *Review of Biblical Literature*

"Recent years have seen a steady stream of Acts commentaries but, by its sheer size and scope, Keener's contribution . . . promises to be a marker around which subsequent scholarly currents will be required to navigate. . . . In content and approach his work will stimulate further readings and rereadings of Acts. As such, I welcome it for its rejuvenation of what pedagogy calls the 'threshold concepts' informing our engagement with Acts. Keener's work will prove to be excursive and recursive, inviting readers into new liminal spaces behind, within, and in front of the text."

—**Matthew Sleeman**, *Expository Times*

"Written for academics, this work is equally accessible to pastors because of Keener's clear and flowing style. . . . Its major contribution lies precisely in taking readers from questions and data through the reasoning process to probable answers."

—**C. Anthony Ziccardi**, *Catholic Biblical Quarterly*

"Magisterial, meticulous, comprehensive, precise, impressively researched—these descriptors of Craig Keener's commentary are by almost anyone's standards not hyperbole. . . . Keener's refusal to dismissively reject, as well as his ability to cull insights from, those with whom he disagrees is a helpful model for all biblical scholars. . . . Keener is not short on presenting creative insights regarding the purpose and theology of Acts. . . . Keener's commentary is indeed an incredible contribution and will undoubtedly repay dividends to those who use it carefully."

—**Joshua W. Jipp**,
Bulletin for Biblical Research

"The references to primary and secondary sources mean that the research behind this book is positively encyclopedic. Keener's work stands apart from other Acts commentaries because of its size, magnitude, and weight and is therefore more of a reference resource on Acts in commentary form. . . . If you want a one-stop shop for a thorough overview of issues, interpretation, and exegesis of the text of Acts, this is the way to go."

—**Michael Bird**, *Euangelion* blog

"Keener's massive commentary on Acts is certainly impressive. . . . It will probably be the most comprehensive commentary on Acts available for some time."

—**Joseph D. Fantin**, *Bibliotheca Sacra*

"[Keener] has authored what may prove to be the lengthiest and most thorough commentary on the Acts of the Apostles in the English language. . . . Keener's scholarship is replete with citations both of secondary literature and of ancient sources. As a result, many of his introductory discussions are encyclopedic in scope and will enrich one's understanding not only of Acts but also of the world of the first century. . . . [This volume] paint[s] a rich tapestry of the world within which Luke lived and to which he wrote. Keener's work therefore helps students of the Scriptures undertake the work of exegesis in living color."

—**Guy Prentiss Waters**, *Themelios*

"A massive gold mine of information. . . . This is the go-to commentary on Acts. Keener amazingly combines attention to great detail with verve and clarity in writing."

—**Ray Van Neste**, *Preaching* (The Best in Bibles & Bible Reference for 2014)

"The great and enduring strength of the work is Keener's encyclopedic knowledge of the ancient world. He adduces not only many of the commonly referenced, but also a host of lesser-known yet relevant, passages and works. . . . In his commentary, Keener often highlights intertextual links between Acts and the Scriptures on which Luke so often drew, providing helpful and insightful analysis of this important aspect of Luke's writing and theology. He also displays more consideration for non-Western perspectives than do many Anglo commentators. . . . An invaluable resource for scholars and advanced students."

—**Peter H. Rice**, *Stone-Campbell Journal*

"One gains a new understanding of the word 'comprehensive' in commentary writing when this work of Craig Keener's on Acts is consulted. . . . This commentary is best treated as more of an encyclopedia of information about almost any topic that is raised in Acts and related to the ancient world than an exegetical commentary. For scholars of Acts, Keener's encyclopedia is indispensable!"

—**Alan J. Thompson**, *Credo*

ACTS
AN EXEGETICAL COMMENTARY

VOLUME 4

~~~~~~~~~~~~~~~

24:1–28:31

~~~~~~~~~~~~~~~

CRAIG S. KEENER

BakerAcademic
a division of Baker Publishing Group
Grand Rapids, Michigan

Published by Baker Academic
a division of Baker Publishing Group
P.O. Box 6287, Grand Rapids, MI 49516-6287
www.bakeracademic.com

Printed in the United States of America

Library of Congress Cataloging-in-Publication Data
Keener, Craig S., 1960–
    Acts : an exegetical commentary / Craig S. Keener.
      p. cm.
    Includes bibliographical references.
    ISBN 978-0-8010-4839-5 (cloth)
    1. Bible. N.T. Acts—Commentaries. I. Title.
BS2625.53.K446 2012
266.6'077—dc22   2011048744

Unless noted otherwise, all translations of Scripture are those of the author.

15   16   17   18   19   20   21   7   6   5   4   3   2

CONTENTS

ABBREVIATIONS

Ancient Sources

Note: Works are listed under their traditional authors for the sake of locating them, not to stake out a position regarding authorship claims.

General

abs.	*absoluti*, acquitted
amb.	*ambusti*, undecided
ap.	*apud*, in (quoted in)
Bk.	Book
damn.	*damnati*, condemned
DSS	Dead Sea Scrolls
ed. princ.	*editio princeps*
epil.	epilogue
ext.	external
frg(s).	fragment(s)
intro.	introduction
LCL	Loeb Classical Library
LXX	Septuagint
MS(s)	manuscript(s)
MT	Masoretic Text
Murat. Canon	Muratorian Canon
NT	New Testament
Or.	*Orations* (except in *Sib. Or.*)
OT	Old Testament
par.	parallel
pr.	*principium*
praef.	*praefatio*
pref.	preface
prol.	prologue
Q	Quelle (hypothetical common source for Matthew and Luke)
rec.	recension
Sp.	Spell
Sup.	Supplement(s)
v./vv.	verse/verses

Old Testament

Gen	Genesis
Exod	Exodus
Lev	Leviticus
Num	Numbers
Deut	Deuteronomy
Josh	Joshua
Judg	Judges
Ruth	Ruth
1–2 Sam	1–2 Samuel
1–2 Kgs	1–2 Kings
1–2 Chr	1–2 Chronicles
Ezra	Ezra
Neh	Nehemiah
Esth	Esther
Job	Job
Ps(s)	Psalm(s)
Prov	Proverbs
Eccl	Ecclesiastes
Song	Song of Songs/Song of Solomon
Isa	Isaiah
Jer	Jeremiah
Lam	Lamentations
Ezek	Ezekiel
Dan	Daniel
Hos	Hosea
Joel	Joel
Amos	Amos
Obad	Obadiah
Jonah	Jonah
Mic	Micah
Nah	Nahum
Hab	Habakkuk
Zeph	Zephaniah
Hag	Haggai
Zech	Zechariah
Mal	Malachi

New Testament

Matt	Matthew
Mark	Mark
Luke	Luke
John	John
Acts	Acts
Rom	Romans
1–2 Cor	1–2 Corinthians
Gal	Galatians
Eph	Ephesians
Phil	Philippians
Col	Colossians
1–2 Thess	1–2 Thessalonians
1–2 Tim	1–2 Timothy
Titus	Titus
Phlm	Philemon
Heb	Hebrews
Jas	James
1–2 Pet	1–2 Peter
1–3 John	1–3 John
Jude	Jude
Rev	Revelation

Septuagint (LXX)

1–4 Kgdms	1–4 Kingdoms
Ode(s)	Ode(s)

Old Testament Apocrypha

Add Esth	Additions to Esther
Bar	Baruch
Bel	Bel and the Dragon
Ep Jer	Epistle of Jeremiah
1–2 Esd	1–2 Esdras
Jdt	Judith
1–4 Macc	1–4 Maccabees
Pr Man	Prayer of Manasseh
Sg Three	Song of the Three Young Men
Sir	Sirach/Ecclesiasticus
Sus	Susanna
Tob	Tobit
Wis	Wisdom of Solomon

Old Testament Pseudepigrapha

OTP	*The Old Testament Pseudepigrapha*. Edited by James H. Charlesworth. 2 vols. Garden City, N.Y.: Doubleday, 1983–85.
Ahiq.	*Ahiqar*
Apoc. Ab.	*Apocalypse of Abraham*
Apoc. Adam	*Apocalypse of Adam*
Apoc. Elij.	*Apocalypse of Elijah*
Apoc. Ezek.	*Apocalypse of Ezekiel*
Apoc. Mos.	*Apocalypse of Moses*
Apoc. Sed.	*Apocalypse of Sedrach*
Apoc. Zeph.	*Apocalypse of Zephaniah*
As. Mos.	*Assumption of Moses*
Asc. Is.	*Ascension of Isaiah*
2–4 Bar.	*2–4 Baruch*
1–3 En.	*1–3 Enoch* (*2 En.* has recensions A and J)
Gr. Ezra	*Greek Apocalypse of Ezra*
Hist. Rech.	*History of the Rechabites*
Jan. Jam.	*Jannes and Jambres*

Jos. Asen.	*Joseph and Aseneth*[1]
Jub.	*Jubilees*
L.A.B.	Pseudo-Philo *Biblical Antiquities*
L.A.E.	*Life of Adam and Eve*
Lad. Jac.	*Ladder of Jacob*
Let. Aris.	*Letter of Aristeas*
Liv. Pr.	*Lives of the Prophets*[2]
Mart. Is.	*Martyrdom of Isaiah*
Odes Sol.	*Odes of Solomon*
Pr. Jac.	*Prayer of Jacob*
Pr. Jos.	*Prayer of Joseph*
Ps.-Eup.	Pseudo-Eupolemus
Ps.-Phoc.	Pseudo-Phocylides
Pss. Sol.	*Psalms of Solomon*
Sent. Syr. Men.	*Sentences of the Syriac Menander*
Sib. Or.	*Sibylline Oracles*
Sim.	*Similitudes of Enoch*
Syr. Men. Epit.	*Epitome of the Syriac Menander*
Test.	*Testament of*
Ab.	*Abraham (recensions A and B)*
Adam	*Adam*
Ash.	*Asher*
Benj.	*Benjamin*
Dan	*Dan*
Gad	*Gad*
Iss.	*Issachar*
Jac.	*Jacob*
Job	*Job*[3]
Jos.	*Joseph*
Jud.	*Judah*
Levi	*Levi*
Mos.	*Moses*
Naph.	*Naphtali*
Reub.	*Reuben*
Sim.	*Simeon*
Sol.	*Solomon*
Zeb.	*Zebulun*
Tr. Shem	*Treatise of Shem*

Dead Sea Scrolls and Related Texts

DJD	*Les grottes de Murabbaʿât*. Edited by P. Benoit, J. T. Milik, and R. de Vaux. 2 vols. Discoveries in the Judaean Desert 2. Oxford: Clarendon, 1961.
DSSNT	*The Dead Sea Scrolls: A New Translation*. By Wise, Abegg Jr., and Cook. San Francisco: HarperSanFrancisco, 1999.
1Qap Gen^ar	*Genesis Apocryphon*
1QH^a	*Hodayot* or *Thanksgiving Hymns*
1QpHab	*Pesher Habakkuk*
1QM	*Milḥamah* or *War Scroll*
1QS	*Serek Hayaḥad* or *Rule of the Community* or *Manual of Discipline*
1QSa	*Rule of the Congregation* (App. A to 1QS)
4Q285	*Sefer ha-Milḥamah*
11QT	*Temple Scroll*
CD	Cairo Genizah copy of the *Damascus Document*

1. The citations give double enumerations where the *OTP* translation (listed first) and the standard Greek text differ.

2. The citations first give the *OTP* reference, then the enumeration in Schermann's Greek text.

3. Where editions diverge, I cite the enumeration in both Spittler (in *OTP*) and Kraft.

Josephus and Philo

Jos.	Josephus
Ag. Ap.	Against Apion
Ant.	Antiquities of the Jews
Life	Life
War	Jewish War
Philo	
Abr.	On Abraham
Agr.	On Husbandry/Agriculture
Alleg. Interp.	Allegorical Interpretation (1–3)
Cher.	On the Cherubim
Conf.	On the Confusion of Languages
Contempl.	On the Contemplative Life
Creation	On the Creation
Decal.	The Decalogue
Dreams	On Dreams, That They Are God-Sent (1–2)
Drunkenness	On Drunkenness
Embassy	Embassy to Gaius
Eternity	On the Eternity of the World
Flacc.	Flaccus
Flight	On Flight and Finding
Giants	On the Giants
Good Person	Every Good Person Is Free
Heir	Who Is the Heir of Divine Things?
Hypoth.	Hypothetica
Jos.	Joseph
Migr.	The Migration of Abraham
Mos.	Life of Moses (1–2)
Names	On the Change of Names
Plant.	Concerning Noah's Work as a Planter
Posterity	On the Posterity of Cain and His Exile
Prelim. St.	Preliminary Studies
Prov.	On Providence (1–2)
QE	Questions and Answers on Exodus (1–2)
QG	Questions and Answers on Genesis (1–4)
Rewards	On Rewards and Punishments
Sacr.	On the Birth of Abel and the Sacrifices Offered by Him and His Brother Cain
Sobr.	On Sobriety
Spec. Laws	Special Laws (1–4)
Studies	On Mating with the Preliminary Studies
Unchangeable	Unchangeableness of God
Virt.	On Virtues
Worse	That the Worse Is Wont to Attack the Better

Targumic Texts

Tg.	Targum (+ biblical book)
Tg. Jon.	Targum Jonathan
Tg. Neof.	Targum Neofiti
Tg. Onq.	Targum Onqelos
Tg. Ps.-J.	Targum Pseudo-Jonathan
Tg. Rishon	Targum Rishon
Tg. Šeni	Targum Šeni

Mishnah, Talmud, and Related Literature

Soncino	The Babylonian Talmud. Edited by Isidore Epstein. 35 vols. London: Soncino, 1935–52.
b.	Babylonian Talmud
bar.	baraita (with rabbinic text)

m.	Mishnah
t.	Tosefta
y.	Jerusalem (Yerushalmi, Palestinian) Talmud
'Ab.	'Abot
'Abod. Zar.	'Abodah Zarah
'Arak.	'Arakin
B. Bat.	Baba Batra
B. Meṣi'a	Baba Meṣi'a
B. Qam.	Baba Qamma
Bek.	Bekorot
Ber.	Berakot
Beṣah	Beṣah (= Yom Ṭob [in the Tosefta])
Bik.	Bikkurim
Demai	Demai
'Ed.	'Eduyoth
'Erub.	'Erubin
Giṭ.	Giṭṭin
Ḥag.	Ḥagigah
Ḥal.	Ḥallah
Hor.	Horayot
Ḥul.	Ḥullin
Kelim	Kelim
Ker.	Kerithot
Ketub.	Ketubbot
Kil.	Kil'ayim
Kip.	Kippurim
Ma'aś.	Ma'aśerot
Ma'aś. Š.	Ma'aśer Šeni
Mak.	Makkot
Makš.	Makširin
Meg.	Megillah
Me'il.	Me'ilah
Menaḥ.	Menaḥot
Mid.	Middot
Miqw.	Miqwa'ot
Mo'ed Qaṭ.	Mo'ed Qaṭan
Naz.	Nazir
Ned.	Nedarim
Neg.	Nega'im
Nid.	Niddah
'Ohal.	'Ohalot (Ahilot in the Tosefta)
'Or.	'Orlah
Parah	Parah
Pe'ah	Pe'ah
Pesaḥ.	Pesaḥim
Qidd.	Qiddušin
Roš Haš.	Roš Haššanah
Šabb.	Šabbat
Sanh.	Sanhedrin
Šeb.	Šebi'it
Šebu.	Šebu'ot
Šeqal.	Šeqalim
Soṭah	Soṭah
Sukkah	Sukkah
Ta'an.	Ta'anit
Tamid	Tamid
Ṭehar.	Ṭeharot
Tem.	Temurah
Ter.	Terumot
Yad.	Yadayim
Yebam.	Yebamot
Yoma	Yoma
Zabim	Zabim
Zebaḥ.	Zebaḥim

Other Rabbinic Works

'Abot R. Nat.	'Abot de Rabbi Nathan (recensions A and B)
Der. Er. Rab.	Derek Ereṣ Rabbah
Der. Er. Zuṭ.	Derek Ereṣ Zuṭa
Deut. Rab.	Deuteronomy Rabbah
Eccl. Rab.	Ecclesiastes (Qoheleth) Rabbah
Esth. Rab.	Esther Rabbah
Exod. Rab.	Exodus Rabbah
Gen. Rab.	Genesis Rabbah
Jer. Tg.	Jerusalem Targum
Lam. Rab.	Lamentations Rabbah
Lev. Rab.	Leviticus Rabbah
Mek.	Mekilta (ed. Lauterbach)
Am.	Amalek
Bah.	Bahodesh
Besh.	Beshallah
Kaspa	Kaspa
Nez.	Nezikin
Pisha	Pisha
Shab.	Shabbata
Shir.	Shirata
Vay.	Vayassa
Midr. Pss.	Midrash on Psalms (Tehillim)
Num. Rab.	Numbers Rabbah
Pesiq. Rabb.	Pesiqta Rabbati
Pesiq. Rab Kah.	Pesiqta de Rab Kahana
Pirqe R. El.	Pirqe Rabbi Eliezer
Ruth Rab.	Ruth Rabbah
S. Eli. Rab.	Seder Eliyahu Rabbah
S. Eli. Zut.	Seder Eliyahu Zuta
Sem.	Semaḥot
Sipra	
A.M.	'Aḥarê Mot
Behuq.	Behuqotai
Emor	Emor
Mes.	Mesora
Neg.	Neg'aim
par.	parashah
pq.	pereq
Qed.	Qedošim
Sav	Sav
Sav M.d.	Sav Mekhilta deMiluim
Sh.	Shemini
Sh. M.d.	Shemini Mekhilta deMiluim
Taz.	Tazria
VDDeho.	Vayyiqra Dibura Dehobah
VDDen.	Vayyiqra Dibura Denedabah
Sipre Deut.	Sipre on Deuteronomy
Sipre Num.	Sipre on Numbers
Song Rab.	Song of Solomon Rabbah
Sop.	Soperim
Tanḥ.	Midrash Tanḥuma
Yalquṭ Isa.	Yalquṭ on Isaiah
Yalquṭ Pss.	Yalquṭ Psalms

Apostolic Fathers

AF	The Apostolic Fathers: Greek Texts and English Translations of Their Writings. Translated by J. B. Lightfoot and J. R. Harmer. Edited and revised by Michael W. Holmes. 2nd ed. Grand Rapids: Baker, 1992.
Barn.	Epistle of Barnabas
1–2 Clem.	1–2 Clement
Did.	Didache
Diogn.	Epistle to Diognetus
Herm.	Shepherd of Hermas
Mand.	Mandates
Sim.	Similitudes
Vis.	Visions
Ign.	Ignatius of Antioch
Eph.	Epistle to the Ephesians
Magn.	Epistle to the Magnesians
Phld.	Epistle to the Philadelphians
Pol.	Epistle to Polycarp
Rom.	Epistle to the Romans
Smyrn.	Epistle to the Smyrnaeans
Trall.	Epistle to the Trallians
Mart. Pol.	Martyrdom of Polycarp
Poly. Phil.	Polycarp Letter to the Philippians

Patristic and Other Early Christian Sources

ANF	Ante-Nicene Fathers: Translations of the Writings of the Fathers down to A.D. 325. Edited by A. Roberts and J. Donaldson. Revised by A. Cleveland Coxe. 10 vols. Grand Rapids: Eerdmans, 1975.
FC	Fathers of the Church
NPNF	Nicene and Post-Nicene Fathers. Edited by Philip Schaff. 14 vols. 1886–89. Repr., Peabody, Mass.: Hendrickson, 1994.
Ambrosiaster	
Comm.	**Ambrosiaster *Commentary on Paul's Epistles***
Aphrahat *Dem.*	**Aphrahat *Demonstrations***
Arator *Acts*	**Arator *On the Acts of the Apostles***
Aristides *Apol.*	**Aristides the Philosopher *Apology to Hadrian***
Athanas.	**Athanasius**
Fest. Let.	Festal Letters
Inc.	On the Incarnation
Vit. Ant.	Vita Antonii/On the Life of Anthony
Athenag. *Plea*	**Athenagoras *A Plea for Christians***
Aug.	**Augustine**
Bapt.	De baptismo contra Donatistas
C. du. ep. Pelag.	Contra duas epistulas Pelagianorum/ Against Two Letters of the Pelagians
City	City of God
Conf.	Confessions
Ep.	Epistles
Harm. G.	Harmony of the Gospels
Retract.	Retractations
Serm.	Sermons
Tract. Jn.	Tractates on John
Basil	**Basil of Caesarea (the Great)**
Holy Sp.	On the Holy Spirit
Hom. Hex.	Homilies on the Hexaemeron
Chrys.	**John Chrysostom**
Hom. Acts	Homilies on Acts
Hom. 1 Cor.	Homilies on the First Epistle of Paul to the Corinthians
Hom. 2 Cor.	Homilies on the Second Epistle of Paul to the Corinthians
Hom. Gen.	Homilies on Genesis
Hom. Jn.	Homilies on John

Hom. Matt.	Homilies on Matthew
Hom. Rom.	Homilies on Romans
Pan. Ign.	Panegyrics of Saint Ignatius
Clem. Alex.	**Clement of Alexandria**
Instr.	Instructor
Misc.	Miscellanies
Protr.	Protrepticus
Strom.	Stromata
Cyprian *Ep.*	**Cyprian *Epistles***
Cyril Jer. *Cat. Lect.*	**Cyril of Jerusalem *Catechetical Lectures***
Ephrem Syr. *Hom.*	**Ephrem the Syrian *Homily on Our Lord***
Epiph.	**Epiphanius**
De mens.	De mensuris et ponderibus
Her.	Refutation of All Heresies/Panarion
Euseb.	**Eusebius**
Chron.	Chronicle/Chronicon
Comm. Is.	Commentary on Isaiah
H.E.	Historia ecclesiastica/Ecclesiastical History
P.E.	Praeparatio evangelica/Preparation for the Gospel
Firm. Matern.	
Math.	**Firmicus Maternus *Matheseos libri VIII***
Greg. Naz. *Or.*	**Gregory of Nazianzus *Orations***
Greg. Nyssa *Greg.*	
Thaum.	**Gregory of Nyssa *Vita Gregorii Thaumaturgi***
Hippol. *Ref.*	**Hippolytus *Refutation of Heresies***
Iren. *Her.*	**Irenaeus *Against Heresies***
Jerome	
Comm. Gal.	Commentary on the Epistle to the Galatians
Dial. Pelag.	Dialogues against the Pelagians
Ep.	Epistles
Ruf.	Adversus Rufinum
Vigil.	Adversus Vigilantium
Vir. ill.	De viris illustribus/On Famous Men
Vit. Hil.	Vita S. Hilarionis eremitae/Life of St. Hilarion
Justin Martyr	
1–2 Apol.	1–2 Apology
Dial.	Dialogue with Trypho
Exhort.	Exhortation to the Greeks
Lact. *Div. Inst.*	**Lactantius *Divine Institutes***
Mac. Magn.	
Apocrit.	**Macarius Magnes *Apocriticus***
Malalas *Chronogr.*	**John Malalas *Chronographia***
Mart. *Just.*	**Martyrdom of Justin**
Mart. *Pion.*	**Martyrdom of Pionius**
Origen	
Cels.	Against Celsus
Comm. 1 Cor.	Commentary on 1 Corinthians
Comm. Matt.	Commentary on Matthew
Comm. Rom.	Commentary on Romans
Hom. Exod.	Homilies on Exodus
Hom. Luke	Homilies on Luke
Orosius *Hist.*	**Paulus Orosius *Historiarae adversus paganos***
Pass. Perp.	**Passion of Perpetua and Felicitas**
Pelagius	
Comm. 2 Cor.	Commentary on 2 Corinthians
Comm. Rom.	Commentary on Romans
Photius *Bibl.*	**Photius *Bibliotheca***
Ps.-Clem.	**Pseudo-Clementines**
Hom.	Homilies
Rec.	Recognitions

Ps.-Const. *Rom.*	**Pseudo-Constantius *The Holy Letter of St. Paul to the Romans***
Sulp. Sev. *Chron.*	**Sulpicius Severus *Chronica***
Tatian *Or. Gks.*	**Tatian *Oration to the Greeks***
Tert.	**Tertullian**
Adv. Jud.	Adversus Judaeos
Apol.	Apology
Bapt.	On Baptism
Cor.	De corona militis
Fasting	On Fasting, against the Psychics
Fug.	De fuga in persecutione/On Flight in Persecution
Marc.	Adversus Marcionem
Mart.	Ad martyras/To the Martyrs
Nat.	Ad nationes/To the Heathen
Pall.	De pallio
Pat.	De patientia
Praescr.	De praescriptione haereticorum/Prescription against Heretics
Scap.	Ad Scapulam
Scorp.	Scorpiace
Spec.	De spectaculis/The Shows
Test. an.	De testimonio animae/The Soul's Testimony
Wife	To His Wife
Theodoret	**Theodoret of Cyrrhus**
Comm. 1 Cor.	Commentary on 1 Corinthians
Comm. 2 Cor.	Commentary on 2 Corinthians
Hist. Rel.	Historia religiosa
Interp. Rom.	Interpretation of Romans
Theoph.	**Theophilus of Antioch *To Autolycus***

Nag Hammadi Texts

NHL	The Nag Hammadi Library in English. Edited by J. M. Robinson. San Francisco: Harper & Row, 1977.
Hyp. Arch.	Hypostasis of the Archons
Orig. World	Origin of the World
Sent. Sext.	Sentences of Sextus
Zost.	Zostrianos

New Testament Apocrypha and Pseudepigrapha

Acts John	Acts of John
Acts Paul	Acts of Paul
Acts Pet.	Acts of Peter
Acts Phil.	Acts of Philip
Acts Thom.	Acts of Thomas
Ap. John	Apocryphon of John
Apoc. Paul	Apocalypse of Paul
Apoc. Pet.	Apocalypse of Peter
Apost. Const.	Apostolic Constitutions
G. Eb.	Gospel of the Ebionites
G. Nic.	Gospel of Nicodemus
G. Pet.	Gospel of Peter
G. Thom.	Gospel of Thomas
G. Jms.	Gospel of James
Paul Thec.	Acts of Paul and Thecla
Prot. Jas.	Protevangelium of James

Other Greek and Latin Works and Authors

Ach. Tat. Achilles Tatius *Leucippe and Clitophon*

Ael. Arist. **Aelius Aristides**
  Def. Or. Defense of Oratory
  Leuct. Or. Leuctrian Orations
  Or. Orations
  Panath. Panathenaic Oration
  Sacr. Sacred Tales

Aelian (Claudius Aelianus)
  Farmers Letters of Farmers
  Nat. An. Nature of Animals
  Var. hist. Varia historia

Aeschines
  Ctes. Ctesiphon
  Embassy False Embassy
  Tim. Timarchus

Aeschylus
  Ag. Agamemnon
  Eum. Eumenides
  Lib. Libation-Bearers (Choephori)
  Pers. Persians
  Prom. Prometheus Bound
  Seven Seven against Thebes
  Suppl. Suppliant Women

Alciph. **Alciphron**
  Court. Courtesans
  Ep. Epistulae/Letters
  Farm. Farmers
  Fish. Fishermen
  Paras. Parasites

Amm. Marc. **Ammianus Marcellinus** *Res gestae*
Anacharsis *Ep.* [Ps.]-Anacharsis *Epistles*
Andocides *Myst.* **Andocides** *De mysteriis*
Ant. Diog. *Thule* **Antonius Diogenes** *Wonders beyond Thule*
Antiph. *Her.* **Antiphon** *Murder of Herodes*
Ap. Rhod. **Apollonius of Rhodes** *Argonautica*
Aphth. *Progymn.* **Aphthonius** *Progymnasmata*
Apoll. K. Tyre **Apollonius King of Tyre**
Apollod. **Apollodorus**
  Bib. Bibliotheca/Library
  Epit. Epitome

Appian
  Bell. civ. Bella civilia/Civil Wars
  Hist. rom. Historia romana/Roman History

Apul. **Apuleius**
  Apol. Apology
  De deo Socr. De deo Socratis
  Metam. Metamorphoses

Aratus *Phaen.* **Aratus** *Phaenomena*

Arist. **Aristotle**
  Breath On Breath
  Const. Ath. Constitution of Athens/Athēnaiōn politeia
  E.E. Eudemian Ethics
  Gen. Anim. Generation of Animals
  Heav. On the Heavens
  Hist. An. History of Animals
  Mem. Concerning Memory and Recollection
  Mete. Meteorology
  Mir. ausc. De mirabilibus auscultationibus
  N.E. Nicomachean Ethics
  Parv. Parva naturalia
  Poet. Poetics

  Pol. Politics
  Rhet. Art of Rhetoric
  Soul On the Soul
  V.V. Virtues and Vices

Aristob. **Aristobulus** *Fragments* (in Eusebius *H.E.*)

Aristoph. **Aristophanes**
  Acharn. Acharnians
  Birds Birds
  Ec. Ecclesiazusae
  Frogs Frogs
  Lys. Lysistrata
  Plut. Plutus/Rich Man
  Thesm. Thesmophoriazusae
  Wasps Wasps

Arius Did. *Epit.* **Arius Didymus** *Epitome of Stoic Ethics*

Arrian
  Alex. Anabasis of Alexander
  Ind. Indica
  Peripl. Periplus maris Euxini

Artem. *Oneir.* **Artemidorus Daldianus** *Oneirocritica*
Athen. *Deipn.* **Athenaeus** *Deipnosophists*
Aul. Gel. **Aulus Gellius** *Attic Nights*
Aur. Vict. *Epit. Caes.* **Aurelius Victor** *Epitome de Caesaribus*
Babr. **Babrius** *Fables*

Caesar **Julius Caesar**
  Afr. W. African War
  Alex. W. Alexandrian War
  C.W. Civil War
  Gall. W. Gallic War
  Sp. W. Spanish War

Callim. *Epig.* **Callimachus** *Epigrammata*
Callistr. **Callistratus**
  Descr. Descriptions
  Dig. In Digest of Justinian

Cato **Dionysius Cato**
  Coll. Dist. Collection of Distichs
  Distichs Distichs

Cato E. **Cato the Elder**
  Agr. De agricultura (De re rustica)

Catull. *Carm.* **Catullus** *Carmina*
Char. *Chaer.* **Chariton** *Chaereas and Callirhoe*

Cic. **Cicero**
  Acad. Academica
  Ag. Caec. Against Caecilius
  Agr. De lege agraria
  Amic. De amicitia
  Arch. Pro Archia
  Att. Letters to Atticus
  Balb. Pro Balbo
  Brut. Brutus, or De claris oratoribus
  Caecin. Pro Caecina
  Cael. Pro Caelio
  Cat. In Catilinam
  Clu. Pro Cluentio
  De or. De oratore
  Deiot. Pro rege Deiotaro
  Div. De divinatione
  Fam. Epistulae ad familiares/Letters to Friends
  Fat. De fato
  Fin. De finibus
  Flacc. Pro Flacco
  Font. Pro Fonteio
  Handb. Elec. Handbook of Electioneering
  Inv. De inventione
  Invect. Sall. Invective against Sallust

Leg.	De legibus
Leg. man.	Pro lege manilia
Lig.	Pro Ligario
Marcell.	Pro Marcello
Mil.	Pro Milone
Mur.	Pro Murena
Nat. d.	De natura deorum
Off.	De officiis
Opt. gen.	De optimo genere oratorum
Or. Brut.	Orator ad M. Brutum
Parad.	Paradoxa Stoicorum
Part. or.	De partitione oratoria
Phil.	Orationes philippicae
Pis.	In Pisonem
Prov. cons.	De provinciis consularibus
Quinct.	Pro Quinctio
Quint. fratr.	Epistulae ad Quintum fratrum
Rab. Perd.	Pro Rabirio Perduellionis Reo
Rab. Post.	Pro Rabirio Postumo
Resp.	De re publica
Rosc. Amer.	Pro Sexto Roscio Amerino
Rosc. com.	Pro Roscio comoedo
Scaur.	Pro Scauro
Senect.	De senectute
Sest.	Pro Sestio
Sull.	Pro Sulla
Top.	Topica
Tull.	Pro Tullio
Tusc.	Tusculan Disputations
Vat.	In Vatinium
Verr.	In Verrem
Colum.	**Columella**
Arb.	De arboribus/On Trees
Rust.	De re rustica/On Agriculture
Corn. Nep.	**Cornelius Nepos Generals**
Cornutus Summ.	**Cornutus Summary of Greek Theology**
Crates Ep.	**Pseudo-Crates Epistles**
Demet. Style	**Demetrius Phalereus On Style/De elocutione**
Demosth.	**Demosthenes**
Andr.	Against Androtion
Aphob. 1–3	Against Aphobus
Aristocr.	Against Aristocrates
Aristog. 1–2	Against Aristogeiton
Boeot. 1–2	Mantitheus against Boeotus
Chers.	On the Chersonese
Con.	Against Conon
Cor.	De corona/On the Crown
Ep.	Epistulae/Letters
Ep. Philip	Epistula Philippi/Letter of Philip
Epitaph.	Epitaphius/Funeral Speech
Eub.	Euxitheus against Eubulides
Exord.	Exordia (Prooemia)
Fals. leg.	De falsa legatione/False Embassy
Lacr.	Against Lacritus
Leoch.	Against Leochares
Lept.	Against Leptines
Mid.	In Midiam/Against Meidias
Navy	On the Navy-Boards
Neaer.	Against Neaera
Olymp.	Against Olympiodorus
Olynth. 1–3	Olynthiaca 1–3
Pant.	Against Pantaenetus
Philip. 1–3, [4]	Philippic Orations 1–3, 4
Steph. 1[–2]	Against Stephanus 1–2
Theocr.	Against Theocrines
Tim.	Against Timotheus

Timocr.	Against Timocrates
Zenoth.	Against Zenothemis
Dig.	**Digest of Justinian**
Dio Cass.	**Dio Cassius Roman History**
Dio Chrys. Or.	**Dio Chrysostom Orations**
Diod. Sic.	**Diodorus Siculus Library of History**
Diogenes Ep.	**[Ps.-]Diogenes Epistle**
Diog. Laert.	**Diogenes Laertius Lives of Eminent Philosophers**
Dion. Hal.	**Dionysius of Halicarnassus**
1–2 Amm.	1–2 Epistle to Ammaeus
Anc. Or.	On Ancient Orators
Ant. rom.	Antiquitates romanae/Roman Antiquities
Demosth.	Demosthenes
Din.	Dinarchus
Epid.	On Epideictic Speeches
Isaeus	Isaeus
Isoc.	Isocrates
Lit. Comp.	Literary Composition
Lysias	Lysias
Pomp.	Letter to Gnaeus Pompeius
Thuc.	Thucydides
Epict.	**Epictetus**
Diatr.	Diatribai
Encheir.	Encheiridion
Epicurus Let. Men.	**Epicurus Letter to Menoeceus**
Euhemerus Sacr.	
Hist.	**Euhemerus Sacred History**
Eunapius Lives	**Eunapius Lives of the Philosophers and Sophists**
Eurip.	**Euripides**
Alc.	Alcestis
Andr.	Andromache
Bacch.	Bacchanals
Cycl.	Cyclops
Dict.	Dictys
El.	Electra
Hec.	Hecuba
Hel.	Helen
Heracl.	Children of Heracles
Herc. fur.	Hercules furens/Madness of Heracles
Hipp.	Hippolytus
Hyps.	Hypsipyle
Iph. Aul.	Iphigeneia at Aulis
Iph. Taur.	Iphigeneia at Tauris
Med.	Medea
Oed.	Oedipus
Orest.	Orestes
Phoen.	Phoenician Maidens
Rhes.	Rhesus
Suppl.	Suppliants
Tro.	Troades/Daughters of Troy
Ezek. Trag. Exag.	**Ezekiel the Tragedian Exagōgē**
Florus Carm.	**Florus Carmina**
Frontin. Str.	**Frontinus Strategemata**
Fronto	**Marcus Cornelius Fronto**
Ad am.	Ad amicos
Ad Ant. imp.	Ad Antoninum imperatorem
Ad Ant. Pium	Ad Antoninum Pium
Ad M. Caes.	Ad Marcum Caesarem
Ad verum imp.	Ad verum imperatorem
Bell. parth.	De bello parthico
Eloq.	Eloquence
Ep. graec.	Epistulae graecae
Fer. als.	De feriis alsiensibus
Nep. am.	De nepote amisso
Pr. Hist.	Preamble to History

Gaius	
Dig.	In *Digest* of Justinian
Inst.	*Institutes*
Galen *N.F.*	**Galen *On the Natural Faculties***
Gorg. *Hel.*	**Gorgias *Encomium of Helen***
Gr. Anth.	**Greek Anthology**
Grattius *Cyneg.*	**Grattius *Cynegeticon***
Hdn.	**Herodian *History***
Hdt.	**Herodotus *Histories***
Heliod. *Eth.*	**Heliodorus *Ethiopian Story***
Heracl. *Ep.*	**Heraclitus *Epistles***
Heracl. *Hom. Prob.*	**Heraclitus *Homeric Problems***
Hermog.	**Hermogenes**
Inv.	*Invention*
Issues	*Issues*
Method	*Method in Forceful Speaking*
Progymn.	*Progymnasmata*
Hesiod	
Astron.	*Astronomy*
Cat. W. E.	*Catalogues of Women and Eoiae*
Sh. Her.	*Shield of Heracles*
Theog.	*Theogony*
W.D.	*Works and Days*
Hierocles	**Hierocles (the Stoic)**
Fatherland	*On Duties: How to Conduct Oneself toward One's Fatherland*
Gods	*On Duties: How to Conduct Oneself toward the Gods*
Love	*On Duties: On Fraternal Love*
Marr.	*On Duties: On Marriage*
Parents	*On Duties: How to Conduct Oneself toward One's Parents*
Hippocr.	**Hippocrates**
Aff.	*Affections*
Airs	*Airs, Waters, Places*
Aph.	*Aphorisms*
Barr. Wom.	*On Barren Women*
Dis.	*Diseases*
Ep.	*Epistles*
Epid.	*Epidemics*
Fleshes	*Fleshes*
Glands	*Glands*
Nat. Man	*Nature of Man*
Pl. Man	*Places in Man*
Progn.	*Prognostic*
Prorr.	*Prorrhetic*
Reg. Ac. Dis.	*Regimen in Acute Diseases*
Superf.	*On Superfetation*
Hom.	**Homer**
Il.	*Iliad*
Od.	*Odyssey*
Hom. Hymns	**Homeric Hymns**
Hor.	**Horace**
Ars	*Ars poetica*
Carm. saec.	*Carmen saeculare*
Ep.	*Epistles*
Epodes	*Epodes*
Odes	*Odes*
Sat.	*Satires*
Iambl.	**Iamblichus Chalcidensis**
Myst.	*Mysteries*
V.P.	*De vita pythagorica/On the Pythagorean Life/Life of Pythagoras*
Iambl. (nov.)	
Bab. St.	**Iamblichus (novelist) *Babylonian Story***
Isaeus	
Apollod.	*Estate of Apollodorus*
Aristarch.	*Aristarchus*
Astyph.	*Astyphilus*
Ciron	*Ciron*
Cleon.	*Cleonymus*
Demes.	*Against the Demesmen*
Dicaeog.	*Estate of Dicaeogenes*
Eumath.	*On Behalf of Eumathes*
Euphil.	*On Behalf of Euphiletus*
Hagnias	*Hagnias*
Hagnoth.	*Against Hagnotheus*
Menec.	*Menecles*
Nicost.	*Nicostratus*
Philoct.	*Philoctemon*
Pyrr.	*Pyrrhus*
Isoc.	**Isocrates**
Ad Nic.	*Ad Nicoclem/To Nicocles (Or. 2)*
Antid.	*Antidosis (Or. 15)*
Areop.	*Areopagiticus (Or. 7)*
Demon.	*To Demonicus (Or. 1)*
Ep.	*Epistles*
Nic.	*Nicocles/Cyprians (Or. 3)*
Panath.	*Panathenaicus (Or. 12)*
Paneg.	*Panegyricus (Or. 4)*
Peace	*On the Peace (Or. 8)*
Soph.	*Against Sophists (Or. 17)*
Julian Ap.	**Julian the Apostate**
Let.	*Letters*
Or.	*Orations*
Justin.	**Justinian**
Cod.	*Codex*
Dig.	*Digest*
Inst.	*Institutes*
Juv. *Sat.*	**Juvenal *Satires***
Libanius	
Anecdote	*Anecdote*
Comp.	*Comparison*
Declam.	*Declamations*
Descr.	*Description*
Encomium	*Encomium*
Invect.	*Invective*
Maxim	*Maxim*
Or.	*Orations*
Refutation	*Refutation*
Speech in Character	*Speech in Character*
Thesis	*Thesis*
Topics	*Common Topics*
Livy	**Livy *Ab urbe condita***
Longin. *Subl.*	**Longinus *On the Sublime***
Longus	**Longus *Daphnis and Chloe***
Lucan *C.W.*	**Lucan *Civil War***
Lucian	
Affairs	*Affairs of the Heart/Amores*
Alex.	*Alexander the False Prophet*
Amber	*Amber, or The Swans*
Anach.	*Anacharsis, or Athletics*
Astr.	*Astrology*
Book-Coll.	*The Ignorant Book-Collector*
Career	*The Dream, or Lucian's Career*
Carousal	*The Carousal (Symposium), or The Lapiths*
Charid.	*Charidemus*
Charon	*Charon, or The Inspectors*
Cock	*The Dream, or The Cock*
Critic	*The Mistaken Critic*
Cynic	*The Cynic*
Dance	*The Dance*
Dem.	*Demonax*
Demosth.	*In Praise of Demosthenes*
Dial. C.	*Dialogues of Courtesans*

Dial. D.	Dialogues of the Dead
Dial. G.	Dialogues of the Gods
Dial. S-G.	Dialogues of Sea-Gods
Dipsads	The Dipsads
Dion.	Dionysus
Disowned	Disowned
Downward Journey	Downward Journey
Eunuch	The Eunuch
Fisherman	The Dead Come to Life, or The Fisherman
Fly	The Fly
Fun.	Funerals
Hall	The Hall
Harm.	Harmonides
Hermot.	Hermotimus, or Sects
Hipp.	Hippias, or The Bath
Hist.	How to Write History
Icar.	Icaromenippus, or The Sky-Man
Indictment	Double Indictment
Judg. G.	Judgment of the Goddesses
Lex.	Lexiphanes
Lover of Lies	The Lover of Lies
Lucius	Lucius, or The Ass
Men.	Menippus, or Descent into Hades
Nero	Nero
Nigr.	Nigrinus
Oct.	Octogenarians
Par.	The Parasite: Parasitic an Art
Parl. G.	Parliament of the Gods
Patriot	The Patriot (Philopatris)
Peregr.	The Passing of Peregrinus
Phal.	Phalaris
Phil. Sale	Philosophies for Sale
Portr.	Essays in Portraiture
Portr. D.	Essays in Portraiture Defended
Posts	Salaried Posts in Great Houses
Prof. P.S.	A Professor of Public Speaking
Prom.	Prometheus
Prom. in Words	To One Who Said "You're a Prometheus in Words"
Runaways	The Runaways
Sacr.	Sacrifices
Sat.	Saturnalia/Conversation with Cronus
Ship	The Ship, or The Wishes
Slander	Slander
Slip	A Slip of the Tongue in Greeting
Soph.	The Sham Sophist, or The Solecist
Syr. G.	Syrian Goddess
Tim.	Timon, or The Misanthrope
Tox.	Toxaris, or Friendship
True Story	A True Story
Tyr.	The Tyrannicide
Z. Cat.	Zeus Catechized
Z. Rants	Zeus Rants
Lucret. Nat.	Lucretius De rerum natura
Lycophron Alex.	Lycophron of Chalcis Alexandra
Lysias Or.	Lysias Orationes
Macrob.	Macrobius
Comm.	Commentary on the Dream of Scipio
Sat.	Saturnalia
Manetho Aeg.	Manetho Aegyptiaca
Marc. Aur.	Marcus Aurelius Meditations
Mart. Epig.	Martial Epigrams
Max. Tyre	Maximus of Tyre Orationes
Men. Rhet.	Menander Rhetor (of Laodicea) Treatises
Min. Fel. Oct.	Minucius Felix Octavius
Modestinus Dig.	Herennius Modestinus in Digest of Justinian
Mus. Ruf.	Musonius Rufus
Musaeus Hero	Musaeus Hero and Leander
Nicolaus Progymn.	Nicolaus the Sophist Progymnasmata
Nin. Rom.	Ninus Romance
Orph. H.	Orphic Hymns
Ovid	
Am.	Amores
Ars	Ars amatoria
Con. Liv.	Consolatio ad Liviam
Her.	Heroides
Metam.	Metamorphoses
Pont.	Epistulae ex Ponto
Parth. L.R.	Parthenius Love Romance
Paulus	Julius Paulus
Dig.	In Digest of Justinian
Sent.	Sententiae/Opinions
Paus.	Pausanias Description of Greece
Pers. Sat.	Persius Satires
Petron. Sat.	Petronius Satyricon
Perv. Ven.	Pervigilium Veneris
Phaedrus	Phaedrus Fables
Philod.	Philodemus
Crit.	On Frank Criticism
Household	On Household Management
Piety	On Piety
Philost.	Flavius Philostratus (the Athenian)
Ep.	Epistulae/Love Letters
Ep. Apoll.	Epistles of Apollonius
Hrk.	Heroikos
Vit. Apoll.	Vita Apollonii/Life of Apollonius
Vit. soph.	Vitae sophistarum/Lives of the Sophists
Philost. Elder	
Imag.	Philostratus the Elder Imagines
Philost. Younger	
Imag.	Philostratus the Younger Imagines
Pindar	
Dith.	Dithyrambs
Isthm.	Isthmian Odes
Nem.	Nemean Odes
Ol.	Olympian Odes
Pyth.	Pythian Odes
Plato	
Alcib.	Alcibiades (1–2)
Apol.	Apology
Charm.	Charmides
Clitophon	Clitophon
Cratyl.	Cratylus
Ep.	Epistles
Epin.	Epinomis
Gorg.	Gorgias
Hipp. maj.	Hippias major
Hipp. min.	Hippias minor
Hipparch.	Hipparchus
Lach.	Laches
Laws	Laws
Menex.	Menexenus
Parm.	Parmenides
Phaedo	Phaedo
Phaedr.	Phaedrus
Phileb.	Philebus
Pol.	Politicus/Statesman
Prot.	Protagoras
Rep.	Republic
Soph.	Sophist
Symp.	Symposium

Theaet.	*Theaetetus*
Theag.	*Theages*
Tim.	*Timaeus*
Plaut.	**Plautus**
Bacch.	*Bacchides*
Cas.	*Casina*
Men.	*Menaechmi*
Miles glor.	*Miles gloriosus*
Most.	*Mostellaria*
Rud.	*Rudens*
Truc.	*Truculentus*
Pliny	**Pliny the Younger**
Ep.	*Epistles*
Panegyr.	*Panegyricus*
Pliny E. *N.H.*	**Pliny the Elder** *Natural History*
Plot. *Enn.*	**Plotinus** *Ennead*
Plut.	**Plutarch**
Adv. K. Well	*Advice about Keeping Well*
Aem. Paul.	*Aemilius Paulus*
Ag. Pleasure	*Against Pleasure (frgs.)*
Ages.	*Agesilaus*
Alc.	*Alcibiades*
Alex.	*Alexander*
Apoll.	*Letter of Consolation to Apollonius*
Arist.	*Aristides*
Borr.	*On Borrowing (That We Ought Not to Borrow)*
Br. Love	*On Brotherly Love*
Br. Wom.	*Bravery of Women*
Bride	*Advice to Bride and Groom*
Brut.	*Brutus*
Busybody	*On Being a Busybody*
C. Mar.	*Caius Marius*
Caes.	*Caesar*
Cam.	*Camillus*
Cat. Min.	*Cato Minor*
Chance	*Chance*
Cic.	*Cicero*
Cim.	*Cimon*
Cleverness	*Cleverness of Animals*
Cleom.	*Cleomenes*
Comm. Conc.	*Against the Stoics on Common Conceptions*
Comp. Alc. Cor.	*Comparison of Alcibiades and Coriolanus*
Comp. Arist. Cato	*Comparison of Aristides and Marcus Cato*
Comp. Lys. Sull.	*Comparison of Lysander and Sulla*
Comp. Thes. Rom.	*Comparison of Theseus and Romulus*
Compliancy	*On Compliancy*
Consol.	*Consolation to Wife*
Contr. A.	*On the Control of Anger*
Coriol.	*Coriolanus*
Crass.	*Crassus*
Demetr.	*Demetrius*
Demosth.	*Demosthenes*
Dial. L.	*Dialogue on Love*
Dinner	*Dinner of Seven Wise Men*
Div. V.	*Delays of Divine Vengeance*
E Delph.	*E at Delphi*
Eating Fl.	*Eating of Flesh*
Educ.	*On the Education of Children*
Envy	*On Envy and Hate*
Eum.	*Eumenes*
Exile	*On Exile*
Face M.	*Face on the Moon*
Fame Ath.	*Fame of the Athenians*
Fate	*On Fate*
Flatt.	*How to Tell a Flatterer from a Friend*
Fort. Alex.	*On the Fortune or the Virtue of Alexander*
Fort. Rom.	*Fortune of Romans*
Galba	*Galba*
Gen. of Soul	*Generation of the Soul in the "Timaeus"*
Gk. Q.	*Greek Questions*
Isis	*Isis and Osiris*
L. Wealth	*Love of Wealth*
Lect.	*On Lectures*
Love St.	*Love Stories*
Luc.	*Lucullus*
Lyc.	*Lycurgus*
Lys.	*Lysander*
M. Ant.	*Marc Antony*
M. Cato	*Marcus Cato*
Mal. Hdt.	*Malice of Herodotus*
Many Friends	*On Having Many Friends*
Marc.	*Marcellus*
Mor.	*Moralia*
Nat. Phen.	*Causes of Natural Phenomena*
Nic.	*Nicias*
Numa	*Numa*
Obsol.	*Obsolescence of Oracles*
Old Men	*Old Men in Public Affairs*
Or. Delphi	*Oracles at Delphi No Longer Given in Verse*
Otho	*Otho*
Par. St.	*Greek and Roman Parallel Stories*
Pel.	*Pelopidas*
Per.	*Pericles*
Phil. Power	*That a Philosopher Ought to Converse Especially with Men in Power*
Phoc.	*Phocion*
Plat. Q.	*Platonic Questions*
Pleas. L.	*Epicurus Actually Makes a Pleasant Life Impossible*
Poetry	*How the Young Man Should Study Poetry*
Pomp.	*Pompey*
Praising	*Praising Oneself Inoffensively*
Profit by Enemies	*How to Profit by One's Enemies*
Progr. Virt.	*How One May Become Aware of One's Progress in Virtue*
Publ.	*Publicola*
Pyrr.	*Pyrrhus*
R. Col.	*Reply to Colotes*
Rom.	*Romulus*
Rom. Q.	*Roman Questions*
S. Kings	*Sayings of Kings and Commanders*
S. Rom.	*Sayings of Romans*
S. Sp.	*Sayings of Spartans*
S. Sp. Wom.	*Sayings of Spartan Women*
Sert.	*Sertorius*
Sign Soc.	*Sign of Socrates*
Solon	*Solon*
St. Poets	*Stories and Poets*
Statecraft	*Precepts of Statecraft*
Stoic Cont.	*Stoic Self-Contradictions*
Sulla	*Sulla*
Superst.	*Superstition*
Table	*Table Talk*
Ten Or.	*Ten Orators*
Themist.	*Themistocles*
Thes.	*Theseus*
Tib. Gracc.	*Tiberius Gracchus*
Tim.	*Timoleon*
Uned. R.	*To an Uneducated Ruler*
Virt.	*Virtue and Vice*
W.V.S.C.U.	*Whether Vice Is Sufficient to Cause Unhappiness*

Polyb.	Polybius *History of the Roman Republic*
Porph.	Porphyry
Abst.	*De abstinentia*
Antr. nymph.	*De antro nympharum*
Ar. Cat.	*On Aristotle's Categories*
Isag.	*Isagoge sive quinque voces*
Marc.	*To Marcella*
Porphyry's	*Porphyry's Against the Christians: The Literary Remains.* Edited and translated by R. Joseph Hoffmann. Amherst, N.Y.: Prometheus, 1994.
V.P.	*Vita Pythagorae/Life of Pythagoras*
Prop. *Eleg.*	**Propertius *Elegies***
Ps.-Callisth. *Alex.*	**Pseudo-Callisthenes *Alexander Romance***
Ps.-Chion *Ep.*	**Pseudo-Chion of Heraclea *Epistulae***
Ptolemy	
Geog.	*Geography*
Tetrab.	*Tetrabiblos*
Publ. Syr.	**Publilius Syrus *Sentences***
Pyth. Sent.	***Pythagorean Sentences***
Quint.	Quintilian
Decl.	*Declamations*
Inst.	*Institutes of Oratory*
Quint. Curt.	**Quintus Curtius Rufus *History of Alexander***
Res gest.	***Res gestae divi Augusti***
Rhet. Alex.	***Rhetorica ad Alexandrum***
Rhet. Her.	***Rhetorica ad Herennium***
Sall.	Sallust
Catil.	*War with Catiline*
Ep. Caes.	*Epistulae ad Caesarem/Letters to Caesar*
Invect. M. Tull.	*Invective against Marcus Tullius*
Hist.	*Historiae*
Jug.	*War with Jugurtha*
Mith.	*Mithridates*
Philip.	*Speech of Philippus*
Pomp.	*Letter of Gnaeus Pompeius*
Sp. Caes.	*Speech to Caesar*
Sp. G. Cotta	*Speech of Gaius Cotta*
Sallustius *Gods*	**Sallustius *On the Gods and the Universe***
Sen. E.	**Seneca the Elder**
Controv.	*Controversiae*
Suas.	*Suasoriae*
Sen. Y.	**Seneca the Younger**
Ag.	*Agamemnon*
Apocol.	*Apocolocyntosis*
Ben.	*On Benefits*
Clem.	*De clementia*
Consol.	*Consolation to Marcia*
Const.	*De constantia*
Dial.	*Dialogues*
Ep. Lucil.	*Epistles to Lucilius*
Herc. fur.	*Hercules furens*
Herc. Ot.	*Hercules Otaeus*
Ira	*De ira*
Med.	*Medea*
Nat. Q.	*Natural Questions*
Phaed.	*Phaedra*
Phoen.	*Phoenician Women*
Prov.	*De providentia*
Tranq.	*De tranquillitate animi*
Troj.	*Trojan Women*
Vit. beat.	*De vita beata*

Servius *Comm. in Verg. Aen.*	**Maurius Servius Honoratus *Commentarius in Vergilii Aeneida***
Sext. Emp.	**Sextus Empiricus**
Eth.	*Against the Ethicists*
Math.	*Adversus mathematicos/Against the Professors*
Pyr.	*Outlines of Pyrrhonism*
Sil. It.	**Silius Italicus *Punica***
Soph.	**Sophocles**
Ajax	*Ajax*
Antig.	*Antigone*
El.	*Electra*
Oed. Col.	*Oedipus at Colonus*
Oed. tyr.	*Oedipus the King*
Philoc.	*Philoctetes*
Wom. Tr.	*Women of Trachis*
Soranus *Gynec.*	**Soranus *Gynecology***
Stad.	***Stadiasmus maris magni***
Statius	
Ach.	*Achilleid*
Silv.	*Silvae*
Theb.	*Thebaid*
Stob.	**Stobaeus**
Anth.	*Anthology*
Ecl.	*Eclogae*
Flor.	*Florilegium*
Strabo	**Strabo *Geography***
Suet.	**Suetonius**
Aug.	*Augustus*
Calig.	*Caligula*
Claud.	*Claudius*
Dom.	*Domitian*
Galba	*Galba*
Gramm.	*Grammarians*
Jul.	*Julius*
Nero	*Nero*
Rhet.	*Rhetoricians*
Tib.	*Tiberius*
Tit.	*Titus*
Vergil	*Vergil*
Vesp.	*Vespasian*
Vit.	*Vitellius*
Tac.	**Tacitus**
Agr.	*Agricola*
Ann.	*Annals*
Dial.	*Dialogus de oratoribus*
Germ.	*Germania*
Hist.	*History*
Terence	
Andr.	*Lady of Andros*
Brothers	*The Brothers*
Eun.	*Eunuch*
Moth.	*The Mother-in-Law*
Phorm.	*Phormio*
Self-T.	*Self-Tormentor*
Themistius *Or.*	**Themistius *Orationes***
Theod.	**Theodotion**
Theon *Progymn.*	**Aelius Theon *Progymnasmata*** (citing the Butts edition except where otherwise noted)
Theon of Smyrna	
Exp. Rer. Math.	*Expositio rerum mathematicarum*
Theophr.	**Theophrastus**
Caus. plant.	*De causis plantarum*
Char.	*On Characters*

Thucyd.	Thucydides *History of the Peloponnesian War*
Ulp. *Dig.*	Ulpian in *Digest* of Justinian
Val. Flacc.	Valerius Flaccus *Argonautica*
Val. Max.	Valerius Maximus *Memorable Deeds and Sayings*
Varro	
L.L.	*On the Latin Language*
Rust.	*De re rustica*
Veg. *Mil.*	Vegetius *De re militari*
Vell. Paterc.	Velleius Paterculus *Compendium of Roman History*
Vett. Val.	Vettius Valens *Anthology*
Virg.	Virgil
Aen.	*Aeneid*
Catal.	*Catalepton*
Ecl.	*Eclogues*
Georg.	*Georgics*
Priap.	*Priapea*
Vit. Aes.	*Vita Aesopi/Life of Aesop/Aesop Romance*
Vitruv. *Arch.*	Vitruvius *On Architecture*
Xen.	Xenophon
Ages.	*Agesilaus*
Anab.	*Anabasis*
Apol.	*Apologia Socratis*
Cav. Com.	*Cavalry Commander*
Cyr.	*Cyropaedia*
Hell.	*Hellenica*
Lac.	*Constitution of Lacedemonians*
Mem.	*Memorabilia*
Oec.	*Oeconomicus*
Symp.	*Symposium*
Xen. Eph. *Anthia*	Xenophon of Ephesus *Anthia and Habrocomes*

Other Ancient and Medieval Sources

ANET	*Ancient Near Eastern Texts Relating to the Old Testament*. Edited by James B. Pritchard. 2nd ed. Princeton: Princeton University Press, 1955.
ARMT	*Archives royales de Mari: Transcriptions et traductions*
ARS	*Ancient Roman Statutes*. Translated by Allan Chester Johnson, Paul Robinson Coleman-Norton, and Frank Card Bourne. Austin: University of Texas Press, 1961.
BCH	*Bulletin de correspondance hellénique*
Bede *Comm. Acts*	Venerable Bede *Commentary on the Acts of the Apostles*
BGU	*Ägyptische Urkunden aus den Königlichen Staatlichen Museen zu Berlin, Griechische Urkunden*. 15 vols. Berlin, 1895–1983.
Book of Dead	*Book of the Dead* (Egyptian)
Bray, *Corinthians*	*1–2 Corinthians*. Edited by Gerald Bray. ACCS: New Testament 7. Downers Grove, Ill.: InterVarsity, 1999.
Bray, *Romans*	*Romans*. Edited by Gerald Bray. ACCS: New Testament 6. Downers Grove, Ill.: InterVarsity, 1998.
CAGN	*Collected Ancient Greek Novels*. Edited by B. P. Reardon. Berkeley: University of California Press, 1989.
Cat. Act.	*Catena in Acta ss. apostolorum*. Edited by J. A. Cramer. Oxford: E Typographeo Academico, 1838 (Martin, *Acts: Catena on the Acts of the Apostles*).
Cat. Cor.	*Catenae in sancti Pauli epistolas ad Corinthios*. Edited by J. A. Cramer. Oxford: E Typographeo Academico, 1841 (Bray, *Corinthians: Catenae on Paul's Epistles to the Corinthians*).
CCSL	Corpus Christianorum: Series latina. Turnhout, 1935–.
CER	Origen. *Commentarii in Epistulam ad Romanos*. Edited by T. Heither. 5 vols. New York: Herder, 1990–95.
CMG	Corpus medicorum graecorum
CSEL	Corpus scriptorum ecclesiasticorum latinorum
Cod. theod.	*Codex theodosianus*
Confuc. *Anal.*	Confucius *Analects*[4]
Corp. herm.	*Corpus hermeticum*
CTH	*Catalogue des textes hittites*. By Emmanuel Laroche. Paris: Klincksieck, 1971.
Cyn. Ep.	*The Cynic Epistles: A Study Edition*. Edited by Abraham J. Malherbe. SBLSBS 12. Missoula, Mont.: Scholars Press, 1977.
Diehl	*Anthologia lyrica graeca*. Edited by E. Diehl. 2 vols. Leipzig: Teubner, 1925.
Düring	*Chion of Heraclea: A Novel in Letters*. Edited by Ingemar Düring. Göteborg, Sweden: Wettergren & Kerber, 1951.
ENPK	*Ein neuer Paulustext und Kommentar*. Edited by H. J. Frede. 2 vols. Freiburg im Breisgau: Herder, 1973–74.
Epicurea	*Epicurea*. Edited by H. Usener. Leipzig: Teubner, 1887.
Eshn.	Laws of Eshnunna
Eustath. *Com. Il.*	Eustathius of Thessalonica *Commentary on Iliad*
FIRA	*Fontes iuris romani antejustiniani*. Edited by S. Riccobono et al. 3 vols. 2nd ed. Florence: Barbèra, 1940–43.
GBP	*The Greek Bucolic Poets*. Translated by J. M. Edmonds. LCL. Cambridge, Mass.: Harvard University Press; London: Heinemann, 1912.
GCS	Die griechische christliche Schriftsteller der ersten [drei] Jahrhunderte
GGM	*Geographi graeci minores*. Edited by C. Müller. 3 vols. Paris: Didot, 1855–61.
Gilg.	Epic of Gilgamesh
Gnom. Vat.	*Gnomologium Vaticanum*
GVSGM	*Geographiae veteris scriptores graeci minores*. Edited by John Hudson. 4 vols. Oxford: E Theatro Sheldoniano, 1698–1712.
Hamm.	Code of Hammurabi
Incant. Text	Incantation text from *Corpus of the Aramaic Incantation Bowls*. By Charles D. Isbell. SBLDS 17. Missoula, Mont.: Scholars Press, 1975.
Just, *Luke*	*Luke*. Edited by Arthur A. Just Jr. ACCS: New Testament 3. Downers Grove, Ill.: InterVarsity, 2003.

4. Chai's enumeration followed parenthetically by the original enumeration.

KBo — *Keilschrifttexte aus Boghazköi.* Leipzig and Berlin, 1916–.

KUB — *Keilschrifturkunden aus Boghazköi*

LKA — *Literarische Keilschrifttexte aus Assur.* Edited by Erich Ebeling. Berlin: Akademie-Verlag, 1953.

LSAM — *Lois sacrées de l'Asie Mineure.* By Franciszek Sokolowski. Paris: E. de Boccard, 1955.

LSCG — *Lois sacrées des cités grecques.* By Franciszek Sokolowski. Paris: E. de Boccard, 1969.

MAMA — *Monumenta Asiae Minoris antiqua.* Edited by William M. Calder et al. Manchester, U.K.: Manchester University Press; London: Longmans, Green, 1928–.

Martin, *Acts* — *Acts.* Edited by Francis Martin, with Evan Smith. ACCS: New Testament 5. Downers Grove, Ill.: InterVarsity, 2006.

MOT — *The Montanist Oracles and Testimonia.* Edited by Ronald E. Heine. Macon, Ga.: Mercer University Press, 1989.

Oden and Hall, *Mark* — *Mark.* Edited by Thomas C. Oden and Christopher A. Hall. ACCS: New Testament 2. Downers Grove, Ill.: InterVarsity, 1998.

Pauluskommentare — *Pauluskommentare aus der griechischen Kirche.* Edited by K. Staab. Neutestamentliche Abhandlungen 15. Münster: Aschendorff, 1933 (Bray, *Corinthians*, and Bray, *Romans: Pauline Commentary from the Greek Church*).

Petav. — Synesius. *Opera quae extant omnia.* Edited by Dionysius Petavius (Denis Pétau). 2nd ed. Paris: D. Bechet, 1640.

PG — *Patrologia graeca.* [= *Patrologiae cursus completus: Series graeca*]. Edited by J.-P. Migne. 166 vols. Paris: J.-P. Migne, 1857–86.

PL — *Patrologia latina* [= *Patrologiae cursus completus: Series latina*]. Edited by J.-P. Migne. 217 vols. Paris: J.-P. Migne, 1844–46.

Pleket — H. W. Pleket, ed. *Texts on the Social History of the Greek World.* Vol. 2 of *Epigraphica.* Leiden: Brill, 1969.

Rev. Laws — *Revenue Laws of Ptolemy Philadelphus.* Edited by B. P. Grenfell. Oxford: Clarendon, 1896 (cited in *SPap*).

RG — *Rhetores graeci.* Edited by Leonhard von Spengel. 3 vols. Bibliotheca scriptorum graecorum et romanorum Teubneriana. Leipzig: Teubner, 1853–56.

Rhet. Gr. — *Rhetores graeci.* Edited by Christian Walz. 9 vols. in 10. Stuttgart: Cotta, 1832–36.

SB — *Sammelbuch griechischer Urkunden aus Ägypten.* Edited by F. Preisigke et al. Strassburg, 1915–.

SHA — *Scriptores Historiae Augustae*

SSGF — *The Sunday Sermons of the Great Fathers.* Translated and edited by M. F. Toal. 4 vols. Swedesboro, N.J.: Preservation, 1996.

Syncellus "Temple Program" — George Syncellus *Ecloga chronographica* "Temple Program for the New Year's Festivals at Babylon"

TUGAL — Texte und Untersuchungen zur Geschichte der altchristlichen Literatur

UPZ — *Urkunden der Ptolemäerzeit (ältere Funde).* Edited by U. Wilcken. 2 vols. Berlin: de Gruyter, 1927–57.

UT — Cyrus H. Gordon, *Ugaritic Textbook* I–III (Rome: Pontifical Biblical Institute, 1965)

Zonaras — John Zonaras *Epitome historiarum*

Papyri, Inscriptions, and Fragment Collections

AE — *L'année épigraphique*

CIG — *Corpus inscriptionum graecarum.* Edited by A. Boeckh et al. 4 vols. Berlin: Riemer, 1828–77.

CIJ — *Corpus inscriptionum judaicarum.* Edited by Jean-Baptiste Frey. 2 vols. Rome: Pontificio Istituto di Archeologia Christiana, 1936–52.

CIL — *Corpus inscriptionum latinarum.* Berlin: Riemer, 1862–.

CIS — *Corpus inscriptionum semiticarum.* Paris, 1881–.

CMRDM — *Corpus monumentorum religionis dei Menis.* Edited by Eugene Lane. 4 vols. Leiden: Brill, 1971–78.

CPJ — *Corpus papyrorum judaicarum.* Edited by Victor A. Tcherikover, Alexander Fuks, and Menahem Stern. 3 vols. Cambridge, Mass.: Harvard University Press for Magnes Press, 1957–64.

Diels-Kranz — Hermann Diels. *Die Fragmente der Vorsokratiker, griechisch und deutsch.* Edited by Walther Kranz. 3 vols. 9th ed. Berlin: Weidmann, 1959–60.

Eph. Ep. — *Ephemeris epigraphica: Corporis inscriptionum latinarum supplementum.* Edited by Wilhelm Henzen et al. 9 vols. Rome: Institutum Archaeologicum Romanum; Berlin: Riemer, 1872–1913.

Epid. inscr. — Epidaurus inscription

FGH — *Fragmente der griechischen Historiker.* Edited by F. Jacoby. 3 vols. in 15. Leiden: Brill, 1954–64.

GEF — *Greek Epic Fragments from the Seventh to the Fifth Centuries BC.* Translated by Martin L. West. LCL. Cambridge, Mass.: Harvard University Press, 2003.

I. Eph. — *Die Inschriften von Ephesos.* Edited by Hermann Wankel. 8 vols. in 10. Inschriften griechisher Städte aus Keinasien 11–17. Bonn: Rudolph Habelt, 1979–84.

I. Ital. — *Inscriptiones Italiae.* Edited by V. Bracco et al. Rome: Libreria dello Stato, 1931–.

IC — *Inscriptiones creticae.* Edited by M. Guarducci. 4 vols. Rome: Libreria dello Stato, 1935–50.

IG — *Inscriptiones graecae.* Berlin, 1873–.

IGBulg — *Inscriptiones graecae in Bulgaria repertae.* Edited by G. Mikhailov. Sofia: Academia Litterarum Bulgarica, 1956–.

IGLS	Inscriptions grecques et latines de la Syrie. Edited by L. Jalabert et al. Paris: Geuthner, 1929–.
IGRR	Inscriptiones graecae ad res romanas pertinentes. Edited by R. Cagnat et al. Paris: Leroux, I, 1911; III, 1906; IV, 1927.
ILS	Inscriptiones latinae selectae. Edited by H. Dessau. 3 vols. in 5. Berlin: Weidmann, 1892–1916.
KSB	Koptisches Sammelbuch. Edited by M. R. M. Hasitzka. Vienna: Brüder Hollinek, 1993–.
Nauck	Tragicorum graecorum fragmenta. Edited by A. Nauck. 2nd ed. Leipzig: Teubner, 1889.
OGIS	Orientis graeci inscriptiones selectae. Edited by W. Dittenberger. 2 vols. Leipzig: S. Hirzel, 1903–5.
P.Amh.	The Amherst Papyri. Edited by B. P. Grenfell and A. S. Hunt. London, 1900–1901.
P.Beatty	Chester Beatty Biblical Papyri. Edited by F. G. Kenyon. London, 1933–41.
P.Bour.	Les Papyrus Bouriant. Edited by P. Collart. Paris, 1926.
P.Cair.	Die demotischen Denkmäler. Edited by W. Spiegelberg. Catalogue général des antiquités égyptiennes du Musée du Caire. Leipzig, etc., 1904–32.
P.Cair.Masp.	Papyrus grecs d'époque byzantine. Edited by J. Maspero. 3 vols. in 6. Catalogue général des antiquités égyptiennes du Musée du Caire. Cairo: Institut Français d'Archéologie Orientale, 1911–16.
P.Cair.Zen.	Zenon Papyri. Edited by C. C. Edgar, O. Guéraud, and P. Jouguet. 5 vols. Catalogue général des antiquités égyptiennes du Musée du Caire. Cairo: Institut Français d'Archéologie Orientale, 1925–40.
P.Col.	Columbia Papyri. New York: Columbia University Press; Missoula, Mont.; and Atlanta: Scholars Press, 1929–.
P.Coll.Youtie	Collectanea papyrologica. Edited by A. E. Hanson et al. Bonn, 1976.
P.Duk.	Duke University papyrus collection
P.Egerton	Fragments of an Unknown Gospel and Other Early Christian Papyri. Edited by H. I. Bell and T. C. Skeat. London, 1935.
P.Eleph.	Elephantine-Papyri. Edited by O. Rubersohn. Berlin: Weidmann, 1907.
P.Enteux.	ΕΝΤΕΥΞΕΙΣ: Requêtes et plaintes adressées au roi d'Égypte au IIIe siècle avant J.-C. Edited by O. Guéraud. Cairo, 1931–32.
P.Fam.Theb.	A Family Archive from Thebes. Edited by M. El-Amir. Cairo, 1959.
P.Fay.	Fayum Towns and Their Papyri. Edited by B. P. Grenfell, A. S. Hunt, and D. G. Hogarth. London, 1900.
P.Flor.	Papyri greco-egizii, Papiri Fiorentini. Edited by G. Vitelli and D. Comparetti. Milan, 1906–15.
P.Fouad	Les Papyrus Fouad I. Edited by A. Bataille et al. Cairo, 1939.
P.Giss.	Griechische Papyri im Museum des Oberhessischen Geschichtsvereins zu Giessen. Edited by E. Kornemann, O. Eger, and P. M. Meyer. Leipzig and Berlin: Teubner, 1910–.
P.Giss.Univ.	Mitteilungen aus der Papyrussammlung der Giessener Universitätsbibliothek. Edited by H. King et al. 6 vols. Giessen: Töpelmann, 1924–39.
P.Grad.	Griechische Papyri der Sammlung Gradenwitz. Edited by G. Plaumann. Heidelberg, 1914.
P.Graux	Nos. 1–8: Sammelbuch griechischer Urkunden aus Ägypten. Vol. 4, nos. 7461–68. Edited by H. Henne. Heidelberg, 1931. Nos. 9–31: Papyrus Graux. Edited by S. Kambitsis. Geneva: Droz, 1995–2004.
P.Grenf.	Greek Papyri. Edited by B. P. Grenfell and A. S. Hunt. Catalogue général des antiquités égyptiennes du Musée du Caire. Oxford: Oxford University Press, 1903.
P.Gur.	Greek Papyri from Gurob. Edited by J. G. Smyly. Dublin: Hodges, Figgis, 1921.
P.Hal.	Dikaiomata: Auszüge aus alexandrischen Gesetzen und Verordnungen in einem Papyrus des Philologischen Seminars der Universität Halle (Pap.Hal. 1) mit einem Anhang weiterer Papyri derselben Sammlung. Edited by the Graeca Halensis. Berlin: Weidman, 1913.
P.Hamb.	Griechische Papyruskunden der Hamburger Staats- und Universitätsbibliothek. Leipzig, etc., 1911–98.
P.Heid.	Veröffentlichungen aus der Heidelberger Papyrussammlung. Edited by E. Siegmann et al. Heidelberg, 1956–.
P.Hib.	The Hibeh Papyri. Edited by B. P. Grenfell et al. London, 1906–55.
P.Köln	Kölner Papyri. Edited by B. Kramer et al. Opladen: Westdeutscher Verlag, 1976–.
P.Lips.	Griechische Urkunden der Papyrussammlung zu Leipzig. Vol. 1: Edited by L. Mitteis. Leipzig: Teubner, 1906. Vol. 2: Edited by R. Duttenhöfer. Archiv für Papyrusforschung und verwandte Gebiete, Beiheft 10. Munich: Saur, 2002.
P.Lond.	Greek Papyri in the British Museum. Edited by F. G. Kenyon et al. London: Printed by Order of the Trustees, 1893–.
P.Meyer	Griechische Texte aus Aegypten. Edited by P. M. Meyer. Berlin, 1916.
P.Mich.	Michigan Papyri. 19 vols. in 20. Ann Arbor, etc., 1931–99.
P.Mil.Vogl.	Papiri della R. Universitá di Milano; Papiri della Universitá degli Studi di Milano. Edited by A. Vogliano et al. 8 vols. in 9. Milan, 1937–2001.
P.Murabba'ât	Les grottes de Murabba'ât. Edited by P. Benoit, J. T. Milik, and R. de Vaux. Discoveries in the Judaean Desert 2. Oxford, 1961.
P.Oslo	Papyri Osloenses. Edited by S. Eitrem and L. Amundsen. Oslo, 1925–36.
P.Oxy.	The Oxyrhynchus Papyri. London: British Exploration Fund; Egypt Exploration Society, 1898–.
P.Panop.Beatty	Papyri from Panopolis in the Chester Beatty Library, Dublin. Edited by T. C. Skeat. Dublin, 1964.
P.Paris	Notices et textes des papyrus grecs (p. par.) du Musée du Louvre et de la Bibliotheque impériale. Edited by M. (A.-J.) Letronne,

	W. Brunet de Presle, and E. Egger. Paris: Imprimerie Impériale, 1865.
P.Petr.	*The Flinders Petrie Papyri.* Edited by J. P. Mahaffy and J. G. Smyly. Dublin, 1891–1905.
P.Rein.	*Les Papyrus Théodore Reinach.* Edited by P. Collart. Cairo, 1940.
P.Ryl.	*Catalogue of the Greek Papyri in the John Rylands Library, Manchester.* Edited by A. S. Hunt, J. de M. Johnson, and V. Martin. 4 vols. Manchester, U.K.: Manchester University Press, 1911–52.
P.Sakaon	*The Archive of Aurelius Sakaon.* Edited by G. M. Parássoglou. Bonn, 1978.
P.Stras.	*Griechische Papyrus der Kaiserlichen Universitäts- und Landes-bibliothek zu Strassburg.* Edited by F. Priesigke. Leipzig, 1912–.
P.Tebt.	*The Tebtunis Papyri.* Edited by B. P. Grenfell et al. London: H. Frowde, etc., 1902–.
P.Thead.	*Papyrus de Théadelphie.* Edited by P. Jouguet. Paris: Fontemoing, 1911.
P.Turner	*Papyri Greek and Egyptian.* Edited by P. J. Parsons et al. London, 1981.
P.Yale	*Yale Papyri in the Beinecke Rare Book and Manuscript Library.* Edited by J. F. Oates. New Haven, etc., 1967–.
P.Wash.Univ.	*Washington University Papyri.* Edited by V. B. Schuman, K. Maresch, and Z. M. Packman. Missoula, Mont.; Oplanden, Ger., 1980–90.
P.Wisc.	*The Wisconsin Papyri.* Edited by P. J. Sijpesteijn. Leiden; Zutphen, Neth.,1967–77.
PDM	*Papyri demoticae magicae.* Demotic texts in the *PGM* corpus as collated in *The Greek Magical Papyri in Translation, Including the Demotic Spells.* Edited by Hans Dieter Betz. 2nd ed. Chicago: University of Chicago Press, 1992–.
Pearson	*The Fragments of Sophocles.* Edited by A. C. Pearson. 3 vols. Cambridge: Cambridge University Press, 1917.
PGM	*Papyri graecae magicae: Die griechischen Zauberpapyri.* Edited by K. Preisendanz et al. 2 vols. Leipzig and Berlin: Teubner, 1928–31.
PSI	*Papiri della Società Italiana.* Edited by G. Vitelli et al. Florence, Felice le Monnier, etc., 1912–.
RECAM	*Regional Epigraphic Catalogues of Asia Minor*
SEG	*Supplementum epigraphicum graecum.* Amsterdam, etc., 1923–.
SPap	*Select Papyri.* Edited by A. S. Hunt, C. C. Edgar, and D. L. Page. 5 vols. LCL. Cambridge, Mass.: Harvard University Press, 1932–41.
SIG^2	*Sylloge inscriptionum graecarum.* Edited by W. Dittenberger. 3 vols. 2nd ed. Leipzig: S. Hirzel, 1898–1901.
SIG^3	*Sylloge inscriptionum graecarum.* Edited by W. Dittenberger. 4 vols. 3rd ed. Leipzig: S. Hirzel, 1915–24.
SVF	*Stoicorum veterum fragmenta.* Edited by H. von Arnim. 4 vols. Leipzig: Teubner, 1903–24.
TrGF	*Tragicorum graecorum fragmenta.* Edited by Bruno Snell et al. Göttingen: Vandenhoeck & Ruprecht, 1971–.
von Arnim	*Hierokles: Ethische Elementarlehre (Papyrus 9780).* Edited by H. von Arnim with W. Schubart. Berlin: Weidman, 1906.
W.Chrest.	*Grundzüge und Chrestomathie der Papyruskunde.* Edited by U. Wilcken and L. Mitteis. 2 vols. in 4. Leipzig and Berlin: Teubner, 1912.

Modern Sources

General

ad loc.	*ad locum,* at the place discussed
B.C.E.	before the Common Era
C.E.	Common Era
ca.	circa
ch(s).	chapter(s)
col.	column
e.g.	*exempli gratia,* for example
ed(s).	edition, editor(s), edited by
enl.	enlarged
esp.	especially
ET	English translation
fig.	figure
ft.	foot/feet
Gk.	Greek
Heb.	Hebrew
i.e.	*id est,* that is
impv.	imperative
in.	inch(es)
inv.	inventory number
kg.	kilogram(s)
km.	kilometer(s)
lit.	literally
m.	meter(s)
mi.	mile(s)
n(n).	note(s)
n.d.	no date
n.p.	no place/no publisher/no pages
n.s.	new series
no(s).	number(s)
p(p).	page(s)
par.	parallel
pl.	plural
R.	Rabbi
rev.	revised
s.v.	*sub verbo,* under the word
sect.	section
ser.	series
sing.	singular
sq.	square
trans.	translator(s), translated by
vs.	versus

Bible Translations

GNB	Good News Bible
GOODSPEED	E. J. Goodspeed, *The Complete Bible: An American Translation*
JB	Jerusalem Bible
MOFFATT	James Moffatt, *The New Testament: A New Translation*
NASB	New American Standard Bible
NEB	New English Bible
NIV	New International Version
NKJV	New King James Version
NLT	New Living Translation
NRSV	New Revised Standard Version
RSV	Revised Standard Version
RV	Revised Version
TWENTIETH CENTURY	Twentieth Century New Testament

Journals, Series, and Other Reference Works

AAAH	Acta Academiae Aboensis, Humaniora
AAAM	American Anthropological Association Monographs
AAAPSS	*Annals of the American Academy of Political and Social Science*
AARAS	American Academy of Religion Academy Series
AARTRSS	American Academy of Religion Teaching Religious Studies Series
AASF	Annales Academiae scientiarum fennicae
AB	Anchor Bible
ABD	*Anchor Bible Dictionary.* Edited by David N. Freeman. 6 vols. New York: Doubleday, 1992.
ABIG	Arbeiten zur Bibel und ihrer Geschichte
ABPRSSS	Association of Baptist Professors of Religion Special Studies Series
ABR	*Australian Biblical Review*
ABRL	Anchor Bible Reference Library
AbrN	*Abr-Nahrain*
ABW	*Archaeology in the Biblical World*

ACCS	Ancient Christian Commentary on Scripture
ACl	*Acta Classica*
ACQ	*American Church Quarterly*
ACR	*Australasian Catholic Record*
ADPV	Abhandlungen des Deutschen Palästina-Vereins
Advance	*Advance*
Aeg	*Aegyptus*
AfCrit	*Affirmation & Critique*
AfCS	*African Christian Studies*
AfET	*Africa Journal of Evangelical Theology (=EAfrJET)*
Africa	*Africa: Journal of the International African Institute, London*
AfSR	*African Studies Review*
AfSt	African Studies
AfThJ	*Africa Theological Journal*
AGP	*Archiv für Geschichte der Philosophie*
AGSU	Arbeiten zur Geschichte des Spätjudentums und Urchristentums
AHB	*Ancient History Bulletin*
AIPHOS	*Annuaire de l'Institut de philologie et d'histoire orientales et slaves*
AJA	*American Journal of Archaeology*
AJAH	*American Journal of Ancient History*
AJBA	*Australian Journal of Biblical Archaeology*
AJBI	*Annual of the Japanese Biblical Institute*
AJEC	Ancient Judaism and Early Christianity
AJP	*American Journal of Philology*
AJPS	*Asian Journal of Pentecostal Studies*
AJPSS	Asian Journal of Pentecostal Studies Series
AJSR	*Association for Jewish Studies Review*
AJT	*Asia Journal of Theology*
Alfinge	*Alfinge*
ALGHJ	Arbeiten zur Literatur und Geschichte des Hellenistichen Judentums
Altertum	*Das Altertum*
ALUOS	*Annual of Leeds University Oriental Society*
ALW	*Archiv für Liturgiewissenschaft*
AmAnth	*American Anthropologist*
AmAntiq	*American Antiquity*
AmBenRev	*American Benedictine Review*
AMECR	AME (African Methodist Episcopal) Church Review
AmEthn	*American Ethnologist*
AMEZQR	A.M.E. Zion (African Methodist Episcopal Zion) Quarterly Review
AmJPsyc	*American Journal of Psychiatry*
AmJSocPsyc	*American Journal of Social Psychiatry*
AmPsyc	*American Psychologist*
AmSocMissMonS	American Society of Missiology Monograph Series
AmSocMissS	*American Society of Missiology Series*
AmSocRev	*American Sociological Review*
Anám	*Anámnesis*
AnBib	Analecta Biblica
AnBrux	*Analecta Bruxellensia*
AnCrac	*Analecta cracoviensia*
AncSoc	*Ancient Society*
ANES	*Ancient Near Eastern Studies*
Angelicum	*Angelicum*
Annala	*Annala*
Annales	*Annales*
ANQ	*Andover Newton Quarterly*
ANRW	*Aufstieg und Niedergang der römischen Welt: Geschichte und Kultur Roms im Spiegel der neueren Forschung.* Edited by H. Temporini and W. Haase. Berlin and New York: de Gruyter, 1972–.
AnSt	*Anatolian Studies*
ANTC	Abingdon New Testament Commentaries
AnthConsc	*Anthropology of Consciousness*
AnthHum	*Anthropology and Humanism*
Anthrop	*Anthropos*
AnthrQ	*Anthropological Quarterly*
Antiquity	*Antiquity*
Antonianum	*Antonianum*
ANZJPsyc	*Australian and New Zealand Journal of Psychiatry*
ANZSTR	Australian and New Zealand Studies in Theology and Religion
AOAT	Alter Orient und Altes Testament
APAP	*Analytic Psychotherapy and Psychopathology*
APB	*Acta Patristica et Byzantina*
Apeiron	*Apeiron*
APOT	*The Apocrypha and Pseudepigrapha of the Old Testament in English.* Edited by R. H. Charles. 2 vols. Oxford: Clarendon, 1913.
APsPSAL	*Acta Psiquiatrica y Psicologica de America Latina*
Apuntes	*Apuntes*
AramSt	*Aramaic Studies*
ARAnth	*Annual Review of Anthropology*
ArbInt	Arbeiten zur Interkulturalität
Archaeology	*Archaeology*
ArchOd	*Archaeology Odyssey*
ArchRep	*Archaeological Reports*
Arethusa	*Arethusa*
ArIntHI	Archives Internationales d'histoire des idées
ARJ	*Annual of Rabbinic Judaism*
ASAMS	Association of Social Anthropologists Monograph Series
ASDE	*Annali di storia dell' esegesi*
AsEthn	*Asian Ethnology*
AshTJ	*Ashland Theological Journal*
ASNU	Acta Seminarii Neotestamentici Upsaliensis
ASocR	*American Sociological Review*
ASP	*American Studies in Papyrology*
AsSeign	*Assemblées du Seigneur*
ASSR	*Archives de sciences sociales des religions*
ASTI	*Annual of the Swedish Theological Institute*
AsTJ	*Asbury Theological Journal*
ATANT	Abhandlungen zur Theologie des Alten und Neuen Testaments
ATDan	Acta Theologica Danica
AThR	*Anglican Theological Review*
'Atiqot	*'Atiqot*
ATLABS	American Theological Library Association Bibliography Series
ATSSWCRMPCS	Asbury Theological Seminary Series in World Christian Revitalization Movements in Pentecostal/Charismatic Studies
AugCNT	Augsburg Commentary on the New Testament
AuOr	*Aula Orientalis*
AUSS	Andrews University Seminary Studies
AUSt	American University Studies
AYBRL	Anchor Yale Bible Reference Library

BA	Biblical Archaeologist
BAGB	Bulletin de l'Association Guillaume Budé
BAIAS	Bulletin of the Anglo-Israel Archaeological Society
BangTF	Bangalore Theological Forum
BapRT	Baptist Review of Theology/Revue baptiste de théologie
BAR	Biblical Archaeology Review
BASOR	Bulletin of the American Schools of Oriental Research
BASP	Bulletin of the American Society of Papyrologists
BBB	Bonner Biblische Beiträge
BBR	Bulletin for Biblical Research
BCompAW	Blackwell Companions to the Ancient World
BCompRel	Blackwell Companions to Religion
BDAG	Bauer, W., F. W. Danker, W. F. Arndt, and F. W. Gingrich. Greek-English Lexicon of the New Testament and Other Early Christian Literature. 3rd rev. ed. Chicago: University of Chicago, 1999.
BDV	Bulletin Dei Verbum
BECNT	Baker Exegetical Commentary on the New Testament
BEFAR	Bibliothèque des Écoles françaises d'Athènes et de Rome
BegChr	The Beginnings of Christianity: The Acts of the Apostles. Edited by F. J. Foakes-Jackson and Kirsopp Lake. 5 vols. London: Macmillan, 1920–33; repr., Grand Rapids: Baker Book House, 1979.
BehBrSc	Behavioural and Brain Sciences
BeO	Bibbia e Oriente
BETL	Bibliotheca Ephemeridum Theologicarum Lovaniensium
BETS	Bulletin of the Evangelical Theological Society (later = JETS)
BEURU	Bibliotheca Ekmaniana Universitatis Regiae Upsaliensis
BHMTSNABR	The Bishop Henry McNeal Turner Studies in North American Black Religion
BHT	Beiträge zur historischen Theologie
BI	Biblical Illustrator
Bib	Biblica
BiBh	Bible Bhashyam (Biblebhashyam)
BibInt	Biblical Interpretation
BibLeb	Bibel und Leben
BIBMS	BIBAL Monograph Series
BibOr	Biblica et Orientalia
BibRev	Biblia Revuo
BibSham	Bibliotheca Shamanistica
BibSp	Bible and Spade
BibT	The Bible Today
BibTh	Biblical Theology
BibUnt	Biblische Untersuchungen
Bijdr	Bijdragen
BIOSCS	Bulletin of the International Organization for Septuagint and Cognate Studies
BIS	Biblical Interpretation Series
BJGS	Bulletin of Judaeo-Greek Studies
BJPhilSc	British Journal for the Philosophy of Science
BJRL	Bulletin of the John Rylands University Library
BJS	Brown Judaic Studies
BJSoc	British Journal of Sociology
BK	Bibel und Kirche
BL	Bibel und Liturgie
BLE	Bulletin de Littérature Ecclésiastique
BK	Bibel und Kirche
BMedJ	British Medical Journal
BMik	Beth Mikra
BN	Biblische Notizen
BNTC	Black's New Testament Commentaries
BO	Bibliotheca orientalis
BollS	Bollingen Series
BPN	Bibliotheca Psychiatrica et Neurologica
BR	Biblical Research
BRev	Bible Review
BrillPauly	Brill's New Pauly, Encyclopaedia of the Ancient World: Antiquity. Edited by Hubert Cancik, Helmuth Schneider, and Christine F. Salazar. Leiden and Boston: Brill, 2002–.
BSac	Bibliotheca Sacra
BSClinPsyc	British School of Clinical Psychology
BSGA	Blackwell Studies in Global Archaeology
BSL	Biblical Studies Library
BTB	Biblical Theology Bulletin
BTCB	Brazos Theological Commentary on the Bible
BTr	Bible Translator
BTZ	Berliner Theologische Zeitschrift
BullCorrHell	Bulletin de Correspondance hellénique
BurH	Buried History
BWANT	Beiträge zur Wissenschaft vom Alten und Neuen Testament
ByF	Biblia y Fe
BZ	Biblische Zeitschrift
BZNW	Beihefte zur Zeitschrift für die neutestamentliche Wissenschaft
BZNWK	Beihefte zur Zeitschrift für die neutestamentliche Wissenschaft und die Kunde der älteren Kirche
CaÉ	Cahiers Évangile
CAH	Cambridge Ancient History
CahJos	Cahiers de Joséphologie
CahRB	Cahiers de la Revue Biblique
CanJBehSc	Canadian Journal of Behavioural Science
Cathedra	Cathedra
CathW	Catholic World
CBC	Cambridge Bible Commentary
CBET	Contributions to Biblical Exegesis and Theology
CBQ	Catholic Biblical Quarterly
CBQMS	Catholic Biblical Quarterly Monograph Series
CBR	Currents in Biblical Research
CBull	Classical Bulletin
C&C	Cross & Crown
CC	Continental Commentaries
CCER	Cahiers du Cercle Ernest-Renan
CCl	Civiltà Cattolica
CCRMS	Cross-Cultural Research and Methodology Series
CCSS	Catholic Commentary on Sacred Scripture
CCWJCW	Cambridge Commentaries on Writings of the Jewish and Christian World 200 BC to AD 200
CE	Coptic Encyclopedia. Edited by Aziz S. Atiya. 8 vols. New York: Macmillan, 1991.
CEC	The Context of Early Christianity
CGB	Church Growth Bulletin

CH	Church History
CHB	Christian History & Biography (formerly Christian History)
ChH	Christian History (continued as Christian History & Biography)
ChicSt	Chicago Studies
Chm	Churchman
ChongTJ	Chongshin Theological Journal
ChrÉg	Chronique d'Égypte
Christus	Christus
CHSC	Center for Hellenic Studies Colloquia
CHSP	Center for Hermeneutical Studies Protocol
ChuenKLS	Chuen King Lecture Series
CJ	Classical Journal
CJP	Canadian Journal of Philosophy
CJT	Canadian Journal of Theology
ClAnt	Classical Antiquity
ClassO	Classical Outlook
CMPsy	Culture, Medicine, and Psychiatry
CNS	Cristianesimo nella Storia
CNT	Commentaire du Nouveau Testament
Coll	Collationes
CollLat	Collection Latomus
Colloq	Colloquium
ColT	Collectanea Theologica
CommCog	Communication and Cognition
Commentary	Commentary
Communio	Communio
ComPsy	Comprehensive Psychiatry
ConBNT	Coniectanea biblica: New Testament Series
ConBOT	Coniectanea biblica: Old Testament Series
Concilium	Concilium
ConcJ	Concordia Journal
ConnCMon	Connecticut College Monographs
ConsJud	Conservative Judaism
CP	Classical Philology
CQ	Classical Quarterly
CR	Classical Review
CRBR	Critical Review of Books in Religion
CrisTR	Criswell Theological Review
Criterion	Criterion
CSHJ	Chicago Studies in the History of Judaism
CSHSMC	Comparative Studies of Health Systems and Medical Care
CSSH	Comparative Studies in Society and History
CT	Christianity Today
CTAfS	Christian Theology in African Scholarship
CTJ	Calvin Theological Journal
CTM	Concordia Theological Monthly
CTQ	Concordia Theological Quarterly
CTSR	Chicago Theological Seminary Register
CuadTeol	Cuadernos de Teología
CulRel	Culture and Religion
CurBS	Currents in Research: Biblical Studies
CurTM	Currents in Theology and Mission
CV	Communio Viatorum
CW	Classical World
DACB	Dictionary of African Christian Biography. New Haven: Overseas Ministries Study Center. Online: http://www.dacb.org.
Dados	Dados
DaughSar	Daughters of Sarah
DavLog	Davar Logos
DBM	Deltion Biblikon Meleton

DCDBCN	The Development of Christian Doctrine Before the Council of Nicaea
DécHell	Décrets hellénistiques
DeutsArcIns	Deutsches Archäologisches Institut
DeuUn	Deutsche Universitätszeitung
DiabMed	Diabetic Medicine
Diakonia	Diakonia
Dial	Dialog
Didaskalia	Didaskalia
Diogenes	Diogenes
Discovery	Discovery
Divinitas	Divinitas
DivThom	Divus Thomas
Diwa	Diwa: Studies in Philosophy and Theology
DLNTD	Dictionary of the Later New Testament and Its Developments. Edited by Ralph P. Martin and Peter H. Davids. Downers Grove, Ill.: InterVarsity, 1997.
DNTB	Dictionary of New Testament Background. Edited by Craig A. Evans and Stanley E. Porter. Downers Grove, Ill.: InterVarsity, 2000.
Dor le Dor	Dor le Dor
DOTHB	Dictionary of the Old Testament: Historical Books. Edited by Bill T. Arnold and H. G. M. Williamson. Downers Grove, Ill.: InterVarsity, 2005.
DOTP	Dictionary of the Old Testament: Pentateuch. Edited by T. Desmond Alexander and David W. Baker. Downers Grove, Ill.: InterVarsity, 2003.
DPCM	Dictionary of Pentecostal and Charismatic Movements. Edited by Stanley M. Burgess, Gary B. McGee, and Patrick H. Alexander. Grand Rapids: Zondervan, 1988.
DPL	Dictionary of Paul and His Letters. Edited by Gerald F. Hawthorne, Ralph P. Martin, and Daniel G. Reid. Downers Grove, Ill.: InterVarsity, 1993.
DRev	The Downside Review
DSD	Dead Sea Discoveries
DSt	Dutch Studies
DTT	Dansk Teologisk Tidsskrift
DVerb	Dei Verbum
EAfrJET	East African Journal of Evangelical Theology
EAfSt	Eastern African Studies
East Asian PastRev	East Asian Pastoral Review
ÉcBib	École biblique
EcRev	Ecumenical Review
EdF	Erträge der Forschung
EfMex	Efemerides Mexicana
ÉgT	Église et Théologie
EHPR	Études d'Histoire et de Philosophie Religieuses
EHRel	Études d'Histoire des Religions
EKKNT	Evangelisch-katholischer Kommentar zum Neuen Testament
EkkPhar	Ekklesiastikos Pharos
ELKZ	Evangelisch-Lutherische Kirchenzeitung
EMC	Echos du Monde Classique/Classical Views
Emmanuel	Emmanuel
Enc	Encounter
EncJud	Encyclopaedia Judaica. 16 vols. Jerusalem: Keter, 1972.
Enr	Enrichment
EphLit	Ephemerides Liturgicae
EphMar	Ephemerides Mariologicae

ÉPROER	Études préliminaires aux religions orientales dans l'empire romain	HABES	Heidelberger althistorische Beiträge und epigraphische Studien
EpwRev	Epworth Review	HBT	Horizons in Biblical Theology
Eranos	Eranos	HCPsy	Hospital and Community Psychiatry
ErAuf	Erbe und Auftrag	HDBull	Harvard Divinity Bulletin
ErIsr	Eretz-Israel (Erets-Yisrael)	HDR	Harvard Dissertations in Religion
ERT	Evangelical Review of Theology	HekRev	Hekima Review
ESEC	Emory Studies in Early Christianity	Helios	Helios
EspV	Esprit et Vie	Hen	Henoch
EstAg	Estudio Agustiniano	Herm	Hermathena
EstBib	Estudios Bíblicos	Hermeneia	Hermeneia—A Critical and Historical Commentary on the Bible
EstEcl	Estudios Eclesiásticos		
EtBib	Études Bibliques	Hermenêutica	Hermenêutica
Ethnology	Ethnology	Hesperia	Hesperia: Journal of the American School of Classical Studies at Athens
Ethos	Ethos		
EthRacSt	Ethnic and Racial Studies	Hesperia Sup	Hesperia Supplements
ETL	Ephemerides Theologicae Lovanienses	HeyJ	Heythrop Journal
ETR	Études Théologiques et Religieuses	HibJ	Hibbert Journal
ÉtudClass	Les Études Classiques	HisJBehSc	Hispanic Journal of Behavioral Sciences
Études	Études	Historia	Historia
EunDoc	Euntes Docete	HistTh	History and Theory
EurH	Europäische Hochschulschriften	HistW	History Workshop
EurSCO	European Studies on Christian Origins	HMFT	Health/Medicine and the Faith Traditions
EUSTS	European University Studies, Theology Series	HNT	Handbuch zum Neuen Testament
		HNTC	Harper's New Testament Commentaries
EvJ	Evangelical Journal	Hok	Hokhma
EvQ	Evangelical Quarterly	HolNTC	Holman New Testament Commentary
EvT	Evangelische Theologie	HR	History of Religions
Exp	Expositor	HS	Hebrew Studies
ExpBC	The Expositor's Bible Commentary	HSCP	Harvard Studies in Classical Philology
Explor	Explorations	HSM	Harvard Semitic Monographs
ExpT	Expository Times	HSS	Harvard Semitic Studies
FaithFreed	Faith and Freedom	HT	History Today
FCNTECW	Feminist Companion to the New Testament and Early Christian World	HTKNT	Herders theologischer Kommentar zum Neuen Testament
FemTheol	Feminist Theology	HTR	Harvard Theological Review
FF	Foundations and Facets	HTS	Harvard Theological Studies
FIAEC	Fédération Internationale des Associations d'Études Classiques	HTS/TS	HTS Teologiese Studies/Theological Studies
		HUCA	Hebrew Union College Annual
FidHist	Fides et Historia	HumDev	Human Development
FilNeot	Filología Neotestamentaria	HvTS	Hervormde Teologiese Studies
F&M	Faith & Mission	IBC	Interpretation: A Bible Commentary for Teaching and Preaching
FO	Folia Orientalia		
FoiVie	Foi et Vie	IBMR	International Bulletin of Missionary Research
ForKathTheol	Forum Katholische Theologie	IBRB	Institute for Biblical Research Bibliographies
Forum	Forum		
FourR	The Fourth R	IBS	Irish Biblical Studies
FPhil	Faith and Philosophy	IBT	Interpreting Biblical Texts
FreiRund	Freiburger Rundbrief	IC	Inscriptiones creticae. Edited by M. Guarducci. 4 vols. Rome, 1939–50.
FRLANT	Forschungen zur Religion und Literatur des Alten und Neuen Testaments		
		ICC	International Critical Commentaries
FSCS	Faith and Scholarship Colloquies Series	ICS	Illinois Classical Studies
FZPhTh	Freiburger Zeitschrift für Philosophie und Theologie	IEJ	Israel Exploration Journal
		IGSK	Inschriften Griechischer Städte aus Kleinasien
GBWW	Great Books of the Western World		
GCAJS	Gratz College Annual of Jewish Studies	IgViv	Iglesia viva
GDT	Global Dictionary of Theology: A Resource for the Worldwide Church. Edited by William A. Dyrness et al. Downers Grove, Ill.: InterVarsity, 2008.	IJAC	International Journal for the Advancement of Counselling
		IJAHS	International Journal of African Historical Studies
		IJComSoc	International Journal of Comparative Sociology
GNC	Good News Commentaries		
GNS	Good News Studies	IJSocLang	International Journal of the Sociology of Language
GOTR	Greek Orthodox Theological Review		
GR	Greece & Rome	IJSocPsyc	International Journal of Social Psychiatry
GRBS	Greek, Roman and Byzantine Studies	IKaZ	Internationale Katholische Zeitschrift
Greg	Gregorianum	ImBSt	Immersion Bible Studies
GTJ	Grace Theological Journal		

Imm	*Immanuel*
IndCHR	*Indian Church History Review*
InnTStud	*Innsbrucker theologische Studien*
Interchange	*Interchange: Papers on Biblical and Current Questions*
Interpretation	*Interpretation*
IntRevMiss	*International Review of Mission*
ISBE	*International Standard Bible Encyclopedia.* Rev. ed. Edited by Geoffrey W. Bromiley. 4 vols. Grand Rapids: Eerdmans, 1979–88.
IsLN	*Israel—Land and Nature*
IsNumJ	*Israel Numismatic Journal*
IsNumR	*Israel Numismatic Research*
ITQ	*Irish Theological Quarterly*
ITS	*Indian Theological Studies*
IVPNTC	InterVarsity Press New Testament Commentary
JAAR	*Journal of the American Academy of Religion*
JAAS	*Journal of Asia Adventist Seminary*
JAbnPsy	*Journal of Abnormal Psychology*
JAC	*Jahrbuch für Antike und Christentum*
JAfrHist	*Journal of African History*
JAM	*Journal of Asian Mission*
JAMA	*Journal of the American Medical Association*
JAmFolk	*Journal of American Folklore*
JANER	*Journal of Ancient Near Eastern Religions*
JANESCU	*Journal of the Ancient Near Eastern Society of Columbia University*
JAnthRes	*Journal of Anthropological Research*
JAOS	*Journal of the American Oriental Society*
JapRel	*Japanese Religions*
JAramB	*Journal for the Aramaic Bible (now = Aramaic Studies)*
JAS	*Journal of Asian Studies*
JASA	*Journal of the American Scientific Affiliation*
JATS	*Journal of the Adventist Theological Society*
JBL	*Journal of Biblical Literature*
JBLMS	Journal of Biblical Literature Monograph Series
JBPRes	*Journal of Biblical and Pneumatological Research*
JBPsi	*Jornal Brasileiro de Psiquiatria*
JBQ	*Jewish Bible Quarterly*
JCounsDev	*Journal of Counseling and Development*
JDharm	*Journal of Dharma*
JEA	*Journal of Egyptian Archaeology*
Jeev	*Jeevadhara*
JerPersp	*Jerusalem Perspective*
JerSJT	*Jerusalem Studies in Jewish Thought*
JECS	*Journal of Early Christian Studies*
JES	*Journal of Ecumenical Studies*
JESHO	*Journal of the Economic and Social History of the Orient*
JEthS	*Journal of Ethiopian Studies*
JETS	*Journal of the Evangelical Theological Society*
JEurPentTA	*Journal of the European Pentecostal Theological Association*
JExpPsyc	*Journal of Experimental Psychology*
JFSR	*Journal of Feminist Studies in Religion*
JGES	*Journal of the Grace Evangelical Society*
JGPSSS	*Journal of Gerontology Series B: Psychological Sciences & Social Sciences*
JGPsyc	*Journal of General Psychology*

JGRCJ	*Journal of Greco-Roman Christianity and Judaism*
JHC	*Journal of Higher Criticism*
JHI	*Journal of the History of Ideas*
JHistPhil	*Journal of the History of Philosophy*
JHistS	*Journal of Historical Studies*
JHistSex	*Journal of the History of Sexuality*
JHLT	*Journal of Hispanic/Latino Theology*
JHom	*Journal of Homosexuality*
JHS	*Journal of Hellenic Studies*
Jian Dao	*Jian Dao*
Jian Dao DS	Jian Dao Dissertation Series
JIHist	*Journal of Interdisciplinary History*
JITC	*Journal of the Interdenominational Theological Center*
JJS	*Journal of Jewish Studies*
JJTP	*Journal of Jewish Thought and Philosophy*
JLH	*Jahrbuch für Liturgik und Hymnologie*
JLR	*Journal of Law and Religion*
JMBeh	*Journal of Mind and Behavior*
JMenSc	*Journal of Mental Science*
JMFam	*Journal of Marriage and Family*
JMS	*Journal of Mithraic Studies*
JNES	*Journal of Near Eastern Studies*
JNSL	*Journal of Northwest Semitic Languages*
JÖAI	*Jahreshefte des Österreichischen archäologischen Instituts*
JPastCare	*Journal of Pastoral Care*
JPFC	*The Jewish People in the First Century: Historical Geography; Political History; Social, Cultural, and Religious Life and Institutions.* Edited by S. Safrai and M. Stern with D. Flusser and W. C. van Unnik. 2 vols. Compendia rerum iudaicarum ad Novum Testamentum 1. Vol. 1: Assen: Van Gorcum, 1974; vol. 2: Philadelphia: Fortress, 1976.
JPJ	*Journal of Progressive Judaism*
JPOS	*Journal of the Palestine Oriental Society*
JPsycHist	*Journal of Psychohistory*
JPsyChr	*Journal of Psychology and Christianity*
JPsyTE	*Journal of Psychiatric Treatment and Evaluation*
JPsyTh	*Journal of Psychology and Theology*
JPT	*Journal of Pentecostal Theology*
JPTSup	Journal of Pentecostal Theology Supplement
JQR	*Jewish Quarterly Review*
JR	*Journal of Religion*
JRA	*Journal of Roman Archaeology*
JRASS	Journal of Roman Archaeology Supplementary Series
JRefJud	*Journal of Reform Judaism*
JRelAf	*Journal of Religion in Africa*
JRelHealth	*Journal of Religion and Health*
JRelS	*Journal of Religious Studies*
JRH	*Journal of Religious History*
JRS	*Journal of Roman Studies*
JRT	*Journal of Religious Thought*
JSAlc	*Journal of Studies on Alcohol*
JSCE	*Journal of the Society of Christian Ethics*
JSHJ	*Journal for the Study of the Historical Jesus*
JSJ	*Journal for the Study of Judaism in the Persian, Hellenistic, and Roman Periods*
JSNT	*Journal for the Study of the New Testament*
JSNTSup	Journal for the Study of the New Testament: Supplement Series

JSocI	Journal of Social Issues	LUOSM	Leeds University Oriental Society Monograph
JSOT	Journal for the Study of the Old Testament	LVit	Lumen Vitae
JSOTSup	Journal for the Study of the Old Testament: Supplement Series	MAAR	Memoirs of the American Academy in Rome
JSP	Journal for the Study of the Pseudepigrapha	Maarav	Maarav
JSPSup	Journal for the Study of the Pseudepigrapha Supplement Series	MaisD	Maison Dieu
JSQ	Jewish Studies Quarterly	Man	Man
JSS	Journal of Semitic Studies	Manresa	Manresa
JSSR	Journal for the Scientific Study of Religion	MAP	Monographs on Ancient Philosophy
JStRel	Journal for the Study of Religion	Marianum	Marianum
JS/TS	Journal for Semitics/Tydskrif vir Semitistiek	Mayéutica	Mayéutica
JTC	Journal for Theology and Church	MBPS	Mellen Biblical Press Series
JTheol	Journal of Theology	McMJT	McMaster Journal of Theology
JTS	Journal of Theological Studies	MCom	Miscelánea Comillas
JTSA	Journal of Theology for Southern Africa	MdB	Le monde de la Bible
Judaism	Judaism	MedQ	Mediterranean Quarterly
JValInq	Journal of Value Inquiry	MelT	Melita Theologica
Kairos	Kairos	Meroitica	Meroitica
Kairós	Kairós	MFC	Message of the Fathers of the Church
KathKomNT	Katholischer Kommentar zum Neuen Testament	MHR	Mediterranean Historical Review
KBANT	Kommentare und Beiträge zum Alten und Neuen Testament	MHRC	Mental Health, Religion and Culture
		Midstream	Midstream
KEKNT	Kritisch-exegetischer Kommentar über das Neue Testament, begründet von H. A. W. Meyer	MilS	Milltown Studies
		Mishkan	Mishkan
		Missiology	Missiology: An International Review
Kerux	Kerux	Missionalia	Missionalia
Klio	Klio	MissSt	Mission Studies
KuI	Kirche und Israel	MissT	Mission Today
LangSc	Language Sciences	MJCSL	Michigan Journal of Community Service Learning
LangSoc	Language in Society		
Laós	Laós	MM	Moulton and Milligan
Latomus	Latomus	Mnemosyne	Mnemosyne
Laur	Laurentianum	MNTC	Moffatt New Testament Commentary
LCBI	Literary Currents in Biblical Interpretation	Moment	Moment
		Monist	Monist
LCL	Loeb Classical Library	Moralia	Moralia
LCQ	Lutheran Church Quarterly	MounM	Mountain Movers
LCR	Lutheran Church Review	MScRel	Mélanges de Science Religieuse
LD	Lectio Divina	MSJ	The Master's Seminary Journal
LebSeel	Lebendige Seelsorge	MTZ	Münchener Theologische Zeitschrift
LEC	Library of Early Christianity	Mus	Muséon: Revue d'études orientales
Leš	Lešonénu	NABPRSS	National Association of the Baptist Professors of Religion Special Studies Series
Levant	Levant		
Ling	Linguistics	NAC	New American Commentary
List	Listening: Journal of Religion and Culture	NBf	New Blackfriars
Listener	The Listener	NCamBC	New Cambridge Bible Commentary
LivL	Living Light	NCBC	New Century Bible Commentary
LNTS	Library of New Testament Studies	NCCS	New Covenant Commentary Series
LOS	London Oriental Series	NCS	Noyes Classical Studies
LouvS	Louvain Studies	NDST	Notre Dame Studies in Theology
LPSt	Library of Pauline Studies	NEA	Near Eastern Archaeology
LQ	Lutheran Quarterly	NEAEHL	New Encyclopedia of Archaeological Excavations in the Holy Land. Edited by M. Stern. 4 vols. Jerusalem: Israel Exploration Society & Carta; New York: Simon & Schuster, 1993.
LRB	Library of Religious Biography		
LSEMSA	London School of Economics Monographs on Social Anthropology		
LSJ	Liddell, Henry George, and Robert Scott. A Greek-English Lexicon. Revised by Henry Stuart Jones and Roderick McKenzie. Oxford: Clarendon, 1968.		
		NEASB	Near East Archaeological Society Bulletin
		NedTT	Nederlands Theologisch Tijdschrift
		Neot	Neotestamentica
LTJ	Lutheran Theological Journal	NESTTR	Near East School of Theology Theological Review
LTP	Laval Théologique et Philosophique		
LTPM	Louvain Theological and Pastoral Monographs	NFTL	New Foundations Theological Library
		NHL	The Nag Hammadi Library in English. Edited by James M. Robinson. San Francisco: Harper & Row, 1977.
LTQ	Lexington Theological Quarterly		
LumVie	Lumière et Vie		

NIB	*The New Interpreter's Bible*. Edited by Leander E. Keck. 12 vols. Nashville: Abingdon, 1994–2004.
NIBCNT	New International Biblical Commentary on the New Testament
NICNT	New International Commentary on the New Testament
NICOT	New International Commentary on the Old Testament
NIDB	*The New Interpreter's Dictionary of the Bible*. Edited by Katharine Doob Sakenfeld. 5 vols. Nashville: Abingdon, 2006–9.
NIDNTT	*The New International Dictionary of New Testament Theology*. Edited by Colin Brown. Grand Rapids: Zondervan, 1978.
NIGTC	New International Greek Testament Commentary
NIVAC	NIV Application Commentary
NortCE	Norton Critical Edition
NotesT	*Notes on Translation*
NovT	*Novum Testamentum*
NovTSup	Supplements to Novum Testamentum
NRTh	*La Nouvelle Revue Théologique*
NTA	New Testament Abstracts
NTAbh	Neutestamentliche Abhandlungen
NTD	Das Neue Testament Deutsch
NTG	New Testament Guides
NTIC	New Testament in Context
NTL	New Testament Library
NTM	New Testament Message: A Biblical-Theological Commentary
NTMon	New Testament Monographs
NTOA	Novum Testamentum et Orbis Antiquus
NTS	*New Testament Studies*
NTT	Norsk Teologisk Tidsskrift
NTTS	New Testament Tools and Studies
NumC	*Numismatic Chronicle*
Numen	*Numen: International Review for the History of Religions*
NV	*Nova et Vetera*
OBT	Overtures to Biblical Theology
OCD³	*Oxford Classical Dictionary*. Edited by Simon Hornblower and Antony Spawforth. 3rd rev. ed. Oxford: Oxford University Press, 2003.
Oceania	*Oceania*
OEANE	Oxford Encyclopedia of Archaeology in the Near East. Edited by Eric M. Meyers. 5 vols. New York: Oxford University Press, 1997.
OiC	*One in Christ*
OJRS	*Ohio Journal of Religious Studies*
ÖKTNT	Ökumenischer Taschenbuchkommentar zum Neuen Testament
OLA	Orientalia Lovaniensia Analecta
OLD	*Oxford Latin Dictionary*. Edited by P. G. W. Glare. Oxford: Clarendon, 1982.
Or	*Orientalia*
OrChr	Oriens Christianus
OrChrAn	Orientalia Christiana Analecta
Orientierung	*Orientierung*
Orpheus	*Orpheus*
OTP	*The Old Testament Pseudepigrapha*. Edited by James H. Charlesworth. 2 vols. Garden City, N.Y.: Doubleday, 1983–85.
PAAJR	*Proceedings of the American Academy for Jewish Research*
Pacifica	*Pacifica*
Parab	*Parabola*
PAST	Pauline Studies (Brill)
PastPsy	*Pastoral Psychology*
PastRev	*Pastoral Review*
PBMon	Paternoster Biblical Monographs
PBSR	*Papers of the British School at Rome*
PCNT	Paideia Commentaries on the New Testament
PEFQS	*Palestine Exploration Fund Quarterly Statement*
PentEv	*Pentecostal Evangel*
PEQ	*Palestine Exploration Quarterly*
PerMS	*Perceptual and Motor Skills*
Personalist	*The Personalist*
PerTeol	*Perspectiva Teológica*
PFES	Publications of the Finnish Exegetical Society
Phil	*Philologus*
PhilAnt	Philosophia Antiqua
Philosophy	*Philosophy*
PhilPA	*Philosophy and Public Affairs*
Phoenix	*Phoenix*
PHR	*Problèmes d'Histoire des Religions*
Phronesis	*Phronesis*
PIBA	*Proceedings of the Irish Biblical Association*
PillNTC	Pillar New Testament Commentary
PJBR	*Polish Journal of Biblical Research*
PNAS	*Proceedings of the National Academy of Sciences*
Pneuma	*Pneuma*
PolSt	*Political Studies*
Pom	*Pomegranate*
PopSt	*Population Studies*
POTTS	Pittsburgh Original Texts and Translations Series
P&P	*Priests & People*
P&Pres	*Past & Present*
Prism	*Prism*
ProcArisSoc	*Proceedings of the Aristotle Society*
ProcC	Proclamation Commentaries
ProEccl	*Pro Ecclesia*
ProtMon	*Protestantische Monatshefte*
PrRR	Princeton Readings in Religions
PRSt	*Perspectives in Religious Studies*
PrTMS	Princeton Theological Monograph Series
Prudentia	*Prudentia*
PSB	*Princeton Seminary Bulletin*
PSCC	Protocol Series of the Colloquies of the Center for Hermeneutical Studies
Psychosomatics	*Psychosomatics*
PsycRep	*Psychological Reports*
PsycRes	*Psychiatry Research*
PsycTRPT	*Psychotherapy: Theory, Research, Practice, Training*
PTMS	Pittsburgh Theological Monograph Series
PWS	Pietist and Wesleyan Studies
PWSup	Supplement to *Realencyclopädie der classischen Altertumswissenschaft*. Edited by Georg Wissowa, Kurt Witte, and Wilhelm Kroll. 15 vols. Stuttgart: J. B. Metzler, 1903–80.
PzB	*Protokolle zur Bibel*
Qad	*Qadmoniot*
QC	*Qumran Chronicle*
QDisp	Quaestiones Disputatae
QF	*Quatres Fleuves*

Ramus	Ramus	SAJPsyc	South African Journal of Psychology
RB	Revue Biblique	Salm	Salmanticensis
RBL	Review of Biblical Literature	SANT	Studien zum Alten und Neuen Testaments
RBPH	Revue Belge de Philologie et d'Histoire	SAnthM	Studies in Anthropological Method
RCB	Revista de Cultura Bíblica	SAOC	Studies in Ancient Oriental Civilizations
RCT	Revista Catalana de Teología	SBB	Stuttgarter Biblische Beiträge
RdT	Rassegna di teologia	SBEC	Studies in the Bible and Early Christianity
REA	Revue des Études Anciennes	SBET	Scottish Bulletin of Evangelical Theology
Readings	Readings: A New Biblical Commentary	SBFLA	Studii Biblici Franciscani Liber Annuus
REAug	Revue des Études Augustiniennes	SBL	Society of Biblical Literature
REB	Revista Eclesiástica Brasileira	SBLABib	SBL Academia Biblica
RechBib	Recherches bibliques	SBLBMI	Society of Biblical Literature The Bible and Its Modern Interpreters
Reconstructionist	Reconstructionist		
RefR	Reformed Review	SBLBSNA	Society of Biblical Literature Biblical Scholarship in North America
REG	Revue des Études Grecques		
REJ	Revue des Études Juives	SBLCP	Society of Biblical Literature Centennial Publications
RelBiog	Religion und Biographie		
RelHHeal	Religion, Health and Healing	SBLDS	Society of Biblical Literature Dissertation Series
Religion	Religion		
RelIntL	Religion and Intellectual Life	SBLEJL	Society of Biblical Literature Early Judaism and Its Literature
RelS	Religious Studies		
RelSRev	Religious Studies Review	SBLMS	Society of Biblical Literature Monograph Series
RelT	Religious Traditions		
RésCon	Résister et Construire	SBLRBS	Society of Biblical Literature Resources for Biblical Study
ResQ	Restoration Quarterly		
RevAg	Revista Agustiniana	SBLSBL	Society of Biblical Literature Studies in Biblical Literature
RevAgEsp	Revista Agustiniana de Espiritualidad (= RevAg)		
		SBLSBS	Society of Biblical Literature Sources for Biblical Study
RevExp	Review and Expositor		
ReVision	ReVision: A Journal of Consciousness and Transformation	SBLSCS	Society of Biblical Literature Septuagint and Cognate Studies
		SBLSemS	Society of Biblical Literature Semeia Studies
RevistB	Revista Biblica		
RevMet	Review of Metaphysics	SBLSemSup	Society of Biblical Literature Semeia Supplements
RevPhil	Revue de Philologie		
RevQ	Revue de Qumran	SBLSP	Society of Biblical Literature Seminar Papers
RevRel	Review for Religious		
RevScRel	Revue des Sciences Religieuses	SBLSymS	Society of Biblical Literature Symposium Series
RevThéol	Revue de Théologie		
RGRW	Religions in the Graeco-Roman World	SBLTT	Society of Biblical Literature Texts and Translations
Rhetorica	Rhetorica		
RHPR	Revue d'Histoire et de Philosophie religieuses	SBLWGRW	Society of Biblical Literature Writings from the Greco-Roman World
RHR	Revue de l'histoire des religions		
RivB	Rivista Biblica	SBLWGRWSup	Society of Biblical Literature Writings from the Greco-Roman World Supplement Series
RivSAnt	Rivista storica dell'Antichita		
RMPhil	Rheinisches Museum für Philologie		
RNT	Regensburger Neues Testament		
RocT	Roczniki Teologiczne	SBS	Stuttgarter Bibelstudien
RocTK	Roczniki Teologiczno-Kanoniczne (= RocT)	SBT	Studies in Biblical Theology
		ScC	La Scuola Cattolica
RomPhil	Romance Philology	ScEs	Science et Esprit
RQ	Römische Quartalschrift	SCEthn	Series in Contemporary Ethnography
RR	Review of Religion	SCHNT	Studia ad Corpus Hellenisticum Novi Testamenti
RRéf	Revue Réformée		
RRJ	Review of Rabbinic Judaism	SChrJud	Studies in Christianity and Judaism
RSLR	Rivista di Storia e Letteratura Religiosa	SCI	Scripta Classica Israelica
RSPT	Revue des Sciences Philosophiques et Théologiques	SCJ	Stone-Campbell Journal
		SCR	Studies in Comparative Religion
RSR	Recherches de Science Religieuse	ScrB	Scripture Bulletin
RSSSR	Research in the Social Scientific Study of Religion	Scriptura	Scriptura
		Scripture	Scripture
RStMiss	Regnum Studies in Mission	ScrJudCr	Scripta Judaica Cracoviensia
R&T	Religion and Theology	ScrTh	Scripta Theologica
RThom	Revue Thomiste	ScSoc	Science and Society
RTL	Revue Théologique de Louvain	SE	Studia Evangelica
RTP	Revue de Théologie et de Philosophie	SEÅ	Svensk Exegetisk Årsbok
RTR	Reformed Theological Review	SEAJT	South East Asia Journal of Theology
RuBL	Ruch Biblijny i Liturgiczny	SecCent	Second Century
SacEr	Sacris Erudiri		

Sefarad	*Sefarad*
SEHT	Studies in Evangelical History and Thought
Sem	*Semitica*
SémBib	*Sémiotique et Bible*
Semeia	*Semeia*
SGRR	Studies in Greek and Roman Religion
Shamanism	*Shamanism*
SHBC	Smyth & Helwys Bible Commentary
SHCM	Studies in the History of Christian Mission
SHR	Studies in the History of Religions (Supplements to Numen)
SICHC	Studies in the Intercultural History of Christianity
SIFC	*Studi Italiani di Filologia Classica*
Signs	*Signs*
SJFWJ	Studia Judaica: Forschungen zur Wissenschaft des Judentums
SJLA	Studies in Judaism in Late Antiquity
SJOT	*Scandinavian Journal of the Old Testament*
SJT	*Scottish Journal of Theology*
SJTOP	Scottish Journal of Theology Occasional Papers
SK	*Skrif en Kerk*
SkI	*Skeptical Inquirer*
SLJT	*Saint Luke's Journal of Theology*
SMedJ	*Southern Medical Journal*
SNTA	Studiorum Novi Testamenti auxilia
SNTSMS	Society for New Testament Studies Monograph Series
SNTSU	*Studien zum Neuen Testament und seiner Umwelt*
SO	*Symbolae Osloenses*
SocAnal	*Sociological Analysis*
SocG	*Sociologische Gids*
SocRes	*Social Research*
Sophia	*Sophia*
SP	Sacra Pagina
SpCh	*The Spirit & Church*
SPCI	Studies in Pentecostal and Charismatic Issues
SPhilA	*Studia Philonica Annual (Studia Philonica)*
SPhilMon	Studia Philonica Monographs
Spiritus	*Spiritus*
SPNT	Studies on Personalities of the New Testament
SR/SR	*Studies in Religion/Sciences religieuses*
SSAMD	Sage Series on African Modernization and Development
SSCS	SUNY Series in Classical Studies
SSMed	*Social Science & Medicine*
ST	*Studia Theologica*
StanHR	*Stanford Humanities Review*
StBibLit	Studies in Biblical Literature (Lang)
StBibSlov	*Studia Biblica Slovaca*
STDJ	Studies on the Texts of the Desert of Judah
StHistMiss	Studies in the History of Missions
STJ	*Stulos Theological Journal*
STK	*Svensk Teologisk Kvartalskrift*
StMkRev	*St Mark's Review*
StOv	*Studium Ovetense*
StPat	*Studia patavina*
StPB	*Studia Post-Biblica*
STRev	*Sewanee Theological Review*
StSpir	*Studies in Spirituality*
StTheolInt	Studies in Theological Interpretation
StThSt	Stellenbosch Theological Studies
Studies	*Studies: An Irish Quarterly Review*
SubBi	Subsidia Biblica
SUNT	Studien zur Umwelt des Neuen Testaments
Supplément	*Supplément*
SUSIA	Skrifter Utgivna av Svenska Institutet I Athen
SvMT	*Svensk Missionstidskrift*
SVTQ	*Saint Vladimir's Theological Quarterly*
SWJA	*Southwestern Journal of Anthropology*
SWJT	*Southwestern Journal of Theology*
SyllClass	*Syllecta Classica*
TA	*Tel Aviv*
TANZ	Texte und Arbeiten zum neutestamentlichen Zeitalter
TAPA	*Transactions of the American Philological Association*
Tarbiz	*Tarbiz*
TBC	Torch Bible Commentaries
TBei	*Theologische Beiträge*
TD	*Theology Digest*
TDNT	*Theological Dictionary of the New Testament.* Edited by Gerhard Kittel and Gerhard Friedrich. Translated by Geoffrey W. Bromiley. 10 vols. Grand Rapids: Eerdmans, 1964–76.
Telema	*Telema*
Teresianum	*Teresianum*
Teubner	Bibliotheca scriptorum graecorum et romanorum teubneriana
Textus	*Textus*
TGl	*Theologie und Glaube*
Them	*Themelios*
Theo	*Theologika*
Theof	*Theoforum*
TheolEv	*Theologia Evangelica*
Théologiques	*Théologiques*
Theology	*Theology*
THKNT	Theologischer Handkommentar zum Neuen Testament
Thought	*Thought*
ThQ	*Theologische Quartalschrift*
ThTo	*Theology Today*
TijSW	*Tijdschrift voor Sociale Wetenschappen*
TJ	*Trinity Journal*
TJT	*Toronto Journal of Theology*
T&K	*Texte & Kontexte*
TLG	*Thesaurus linguae graecae.* Online: http://www.tlg.uci.edu.
TLZ	*Theologische Literaturzeitung*
TNTC	Tyndale New Testament Commentaries
TOTC	Tyndale Old Testament Commentaries
TP	*Theologie und Philosophie*
TPAPA	*Transactions and Proceedings of the American Philological Association* (later = *TAPA*)
TPQ	*Theologisch-Praktische Quartalschrift*
Tradition	*Tradition*
TranscPsyc	*Transcultural Psychiatry*
TranscPsycRR	*Transcultural Psychiatric Research Review*
Transversalités	*Transversalités*
TRu	*Theologische Rundschau*
TS	*Theological Studies*
TSAJ	Texts and Studies in Ancient Judaism

TSHP	Texts and Studies in the History of Philosophy
TSJTSA	Texts and Studies of The Jewish Theological Seminary of America
TTCABS	T&T Clark Approaches to Biblical Studies
TTEd	*Teaching and Teacher Education*
TTKi	*Tidsskrift for Teologi og Kirke*
TTZ	*Trierer Theologische Zeitschrift*
TynBul	*Tyndale Bulletin*
TZ	*Theologische Zeitschrift*
UCPLA	Unidade Científico-Pedagógica de Letras e Artes
UCPP	University of California Publications in Philosophy
UJT	Understanding Jesus Today
UltRM	*Ultimate Reality and Meaning*
UNDCSJCA	University of Notre Dame Center for the Study of Judaism and Christianity in Antiquity
UnS	*Una Sancta*
USFISFCJ	University of South Florida International Studies in Formative Christianity and Judaism
USQR	*Union Seminary Quarterly Review*
VC	*Vigiliae Christianae*
VD	*Verbum Domini*
VE	*Vox Evangelica*
VerbEc	*Verbum et Ecclesia*
VFVRUL	Veröffentlichungen des Forschungsinstituts für vergleichende Religionsgeschichte an der Universität Leipzig
Vid	*Vidyajyoti*
VidJTR	*Vidyajyoti Journal of Theological Reflection*
VitIndRel	Vitality of Indigenous Religions
VR	*Vox Reformata*
VS	*Vox Scripturae*
VSpir	*Vie Spirituelle*
VT	*Vetus Testamentum*
VTSup	Vetus Testamentum Supplements
WAfJES	*West African Journal of Ecclesial Studies*
WArch	*World Archaeology*
WBC	Word Biblical Commentary
WD	*Wort und Dienst*
WestBC	Westminster Bible Companion
WJBlSt	*Western Journal of Black Studies*
WLQ	*Wisconsin Lutheran Quarterly*
WMANT	Wissenschaftliche Monographien zum Alten und Neuen Testament
WMQ	*William & Mary Quarterly*
WomSt	*Women's Studies*
Worship	*Worship*
WPJ	*World Policy Journal*
WPR	*World Press Review*
WSCM	World Studies of Churches in Mission (World Council of Churches)
WSPL	Warwick Studies in Philosophy and Language
WTJ	*Westminster Theological Journal*
WUNT	Wissenschaftliche Untersuchungen sum Neuen Testament
WW	*Word and World*
YCS	*Yale Classical Studies*
YJS	Yale Judaica Series
YonsJT	*Yonsei Journal of Theology*
YonsRTC	*Yonsei Review of Theology & Culture*
YPR	Yale Publications in Religion
YSMT	York Studies in Medieval Theology
ZAC/JAC	*Zeitschrift für Antikes Christentum/Journal of Ancient Christianity*
ZAW	*Zeitschrift für die Alttestamentliche Wissenschaft*
ZDMG	*Zeitschrift der Deutschen Morgenländischen Gesellschaft*
ZDPV	*Zeitschrift des Deutschen Palästina-Vereins*
ZECNT	Zondervan Exegetical Commentary on the New Testament
Zion	*Zion*
ZKG	*Zeitschrift für Kirchengeschichte*
ZKT	*Zeitschrift für Katholische Theologie*
ZKWKL	*Zeitschrift für kirchliche Wissenschaft und kirchliches Leben*
ZNT	*Zeitschrift für Neues Testament*
ZNW	*Zeitschrift für die Neutestamentliche Wissenschaft*
ZPE	*Zeitschrift für Papyrologie und Epigraphik*
ZRGG	*Zeitschrift für Religions- und Geistesgeschichte*
ZSNT	Zacchaeus Studies: New Testament
ZTK	*Zeitschrift für Theologie und Kirche*
Zyg	*Zygon: Journal of Religion and Science*
ZZ	*Der Zeichen der Zeit*

PART 6

TO ROME VIA JERUSALEM (20:1–28:31)

(CONTINUED)

PAUL'S DEFENSE BEFORE AUTHORITIES (24:1–26:32)

Luke's audience may be embarrassed not only by—or perhaps not even primarily by—Jesus's crucifixion but also by the captivity and ultimate execution of the apostle to the Gentiles. Luke's answer to such concerns is to show that only political enemies and corruption, not respectable justice, achieved Paul's condemnation. Luke sometimes employs the standard judicial defense technique of returning charges against accusers.

Paul's just case is subverted by political interests and a corrupt governor. Luke reports the heart of the Jerusalem elite's case as the charge that Paul subverts the Roman order (ironic in view of 23:2–15, esp. 23:12–15), whereas Paul reduces the opposition's motives (as in 22:30–23:10) to theological disagreement. Far from being subversive, Paul proves morally superior to the judge who fails to release him (24:24–27).

1. Introduction

Although the introductions, above, to Acts 22 and, below, to Acts 24:2–8 and 24:10–21 treat some relevant introductory questions, it is helpful here to raise some overarching questions of relevance to this narrative. First, the question of why Luke does not report supporters of Paul from the Jerusalem church is addressed. Then literary and historical observations are provided; because trial records would preserve a précis of each speech, chances are improved that Luke would have access to this information in a manner not available for many other kinds of speeches. Finally, brief comments are offered regarding the speeches' rhetoric (although this question is treated more fully at the introduction to Acts 22 and in the relevant verses in the speeches).

a. Paul's Supporters?

Where are members of the Jerusalem church?[1] According to ancient friendship ideals, friends (which could include recipients of benefactions) should not desert one another in hardship, when friendship was most needed.[2] Second-century Christians might visit their imprisoned leader, bring food, bribe guards to let them stay with him at night, read Scripture, and so forth.[3] Why do we not read of such activity here?

Although the narrative does not inform us that James or other Jerusalemite believers traveled to Caesarea to defend Paul, the idea that they "abandoned" Paul "concludes far

---

1. For discussions of this question, see further comment at Acts 21:22–24. For Jerusalem's importance for Luke, see also Keener, *Acts*, 1:698–702; now also, e.g., Areeplackal, "Symbolism."

2. Val. Max. 4.7.praef.; Fronto *Ad Ant. Pium* 3.4. They should remain loyal to death (e.g., Val. Max. 4.7.2, 6; Epict. *Diatr.* 2.7.3) and refuse to abandon their honor (Val. Max. 4.7.1, 4).

3. Lucian *Peregr.* 12 (perhaps exaggerating). Lucian focuses on the poor (perhaps mocking Christians' low-class appeal); the Jewish community in Caesarea was better endowed at this point.

too much from Luke's silence"; they "had no influence with either the chief priests or the Romans."[4] Whatever they did for Paul, they would have probably done privately. Although the majority of the Jerusalem church had heard negative rumors about Paul (Acts 21:21), the apparent lack of support in this narrative does not render implausible their leaders' earlier hospitable reception of Paul (21:17).[5] Paul may have had some support in Jerusalem, but those who welcomed him in Jerusalem had no reason to make the journey to Caesarea.[6] Friends in Caesarea surely did visit (21:8–9; 24:23), but Luke does not have reason to elaborate on this point; we should use his silence to condemn neither the Caesarean believers nor the Jerusalem church. For that matter, Luke is not explicit about his own presence, despite surely remaining on hand (21:18; 27:1).

Still, the chief priests likely believed that some of Paul's supporters *could* have come; presumably unaware of available witnesses in Caesarea, they may have expected that Paul could call some from Jerusalem. This could explain why, in the narrative world, Paul's opponents offer no false witnesses here, in contrast to Stephen's opponents in 6:13. (That the Romans would cross-examine witnesses less sympathetically than hearers did in 6:13–14 might have also provided a significant deterrent for potential witnesses.)

b. Literary and Historical Considerations

Paul's trials in Acts parallel those of Jesus in the Gospel of Luke;[7] the last 24 percent of Acts deals with Paul's detention, just as the last 23 percent of the Gospel deals with Jesus's passion.[8] More specifically, Paul's three trials in this section of Acts—two before governors and one before a Herodian ruler—parallel Jesus's three trials in Luke's passion narrative, two before the governor and one before Herod Antipas (Luke 23:3–4, 8–11, 14–16).[9] There is also a preliminary hearing before the Sanhedrin in both (Luke 23:66–71; Acts 23:1–10). Paul's speeches fulfill Jesus's promises in Luke 12:11–12 and 21:12–15, just as Stephen's wisdom does in Acts 6:10.[10]

Nevertheless, Luke's literary purpose does not obviate the value of his historical information, any more than the edifying purpose of most ancient historians requires the dismissal of their historical data.[11] Dibelius is, for example, too skeptical when he compares Josephus's similar arguments between Antipater and Nicolaus, which also end in adjournment.[12] Granted, Josephus likely lacked a transcript for the speeches,

---

4. Bauckham, "James," 478–79.

5. This is not to say that they would have approved of his public advocacy of the Gentile mission in Acts 22:21, in apparent disregard of their instructions and sensitivity to the local situation. But regarding Paul as indiscreet, or even preaching something that made their job more difficult, would not necessarily make them enemies.

6. Paul certainly also had his detractors among believers who seem to have been emboldened by his imprisonment (Phil 1:14–15), though they do not appear to be "Judaizers" (cf. Phil 1:17–18 with 3:2).

7. E.g., Witherington, *Acts*, 5; Omerzu, "Verhältnis." On Paul's trials and custody, see esp. Tajra, *Trial*; Rapske, *Custody*; and Omerzu, *Prozess*.

8. E.g., Witherington, *Acts*, 7.

9. One might contrast perhaps Peter's three denials of Jesus (Luke 22:61) and Pilate's three protests of Jesus's innocence (23:22), along with the people's continuing demands for Jesus's death (23:23). Rhetoricians preferred three illustrations to support a thesis (Quint. *Inst.* 4.5.3; Pliny *Ep.* 2.20.9; in early rabbinic texts, see Keener, *Matthew*, 207), but this is less relevant here.

10. Rapske, *Custody*, 398–401, demonstrates how Luke 21:12–19 anticipates *especially* Paul's defense speeches in Acts. Pagans also understood the attribution to deities of wise answers in court (Pliny *Ep.* 1.5.5).

11. Certainly Paul finds himself in court more than three times in Acts. As in other historical and biographical literature, parallels among characters guide authors rhetorically but do not control all the material (see my introduction, Keener, *Acts*, 1:568–74).

12. Dibelius, *Studies in Acts*, 7 (citing Jos. *War* 2.26–38; *Ant.* 17.230–49).

but not all writers would (see discussion below); historians could invent speeches, but they could also reproduce key themes of historical speeches where they had these available.[13] Further, officials had the genuine freedom to deliberate, and so reports of such deliberation tell us nothing about the nature of historical sources. Although Luke does report the speeches, like everything else in Acts, especially for his audience, the trial's adjournment (which is plausible given the political considerations involved) is not simply a literary fiction.[14]

This is not to deny that writers invented defense speeches. Many writers after Socrates's execution in 399 B.C.E., and through the fourth century C.E., practiced writing defenses of Socrates. Besides the well-known apologies of Plato and Xenophon, we have the declamations by Maximus of Tyre (*Or.* 3) and Libanius (*Declam.* 1.13–21; 2.127–47), and many were offered that have not remained extant.[15] Later generations of Socrates's apologists, however, were typically orators and moralists, and few would lend such speeches the historical credence offered to key information (albeit not entire speeches) in earlier writers such as Xenophon and even Plato (though these too adapted what they knew).

More important, Luke writes not as an orator (his summary speeches could not pass muster in this regard) but, rather, in the stream of ancient historiography. Here, too, rhetorical training was useful for writing speeches in character, but a more sober Hellenistic historical writer, as Luke consistently shows himself to be, could work from genuine traditions about what was spoken where these were available.[16] How available would some memories of these speeches be?

There is no reason to assume that Luke and other supporters could not be present for the speeches in Acts 24 (the status of guests probably would have prevented their presence in 25:23), although this is an initial hearing only.[17] Yet even if we could prove Luke's detailed accuracy, it would not require his presence: speakers could write out speeches beforehand or after a speech, and those skilled with words and legal rhetoric (as Luke is) could have helped the defendant prepare his case. Luke (through the defendant) could also have had access to the court summary of the prosecution speech (see the introduction, below, to Acts 24:2–8). Any such means would have provided Luke with many of his details even without his presence being necessary. In my view that Luke was Paul's traveling companion,[18] he could also have obtained a fairly good summary from Paul, who, of course, was present and whose letters display a sharp mind and hence probably a generally keen memory. Visitors were permitted (24:23), and the we-narrator is still with Paul in Acts 27:1. (It is hardly likely that the we-narrator sojourned most of this time back in the Aegean region or Antioch and merely happened to arrive back in Caesarea for Paul's voyage to Rome!)

13. See discussion in Keener, *Acts*, 1:271–319; for the preservation of key elements of court speeches, see Winter, "Official Proceedings"; discussion at Acts 24:2–9, below.

14. Judean embassies often got their way in Rome (McKechnie, "Embassies"); one would not wish to enter such a political minefield without good cause. The sort of "parallel" that Pervo, *Acts*, 602–3, provides to a novel (i.e., a hearing before a governor in Xen. Eph. *Anthia* 4.2.10–4.4.1) simply mimics reality; besides governors and kings hearing cases in Josephus, see the abundant documentation from a range of genres below. Nor was Paul a socially unimportant prisoner, as a "leader" of the Nazarenes (Acts 24:5).

15. Including those attributed to Crito (*Suda*, s.v. "Crito"), Lysias (Plut. *Mor.* 836b; Cic. *De or.* 1.231), and others (Trapp, *Maximus*, 24).

16. See discussion in Keener, *Acts*, 1:271–319.

17. Paul's companions would quickly learn of the transfer to Caesarea, and sufficient time had elapsed for them to make their way there (Acts 24:1, 11). Certainly the Gentiles among them had little incentive to tarry in Jerusalem without him.

18. See Keener, *Acts*, 1:402–16, and esp. 3:2350–74.

At the same time, this is a standard public trial before the governor's tribunal, following the usual format of prosecution and defense speeches. Hearings were usually open to the public;[19] thus Seneca the Elder warned that declamation students were unprepared for the real world of the courts (*Controv.* 9.pref. 4), where interruptions were common (9.pref. 3) and speakers had to be loud so that the judges could hear them over competing noise (9.pref. 5). Courtrooms were crowded and noisy, often with spectators along the walls, benches, and galleries (Pliny *Ep.* 6.33.3–4). Written documents would also be kept, summarizing the speeches and the proceedings, and the defendant would be among those with access to these.[20] A *notarius*, or scribe, would record the critical elements of the hearing.[21]

In addition to the probability of firsthand sources for Luke's detailed account here (on the usual dating of Acts), we may note that what he reports fits the pattern of Roman provincial trials. Acts approximates so closely the procedure of Roman law, in fact, that many Roman historians have treated it as the clearest illustration of how governors in the provinces conducted such trials.[22] A. N. Sherwin-White, a noted Roman historian who has written on the matter with particular expertise, has adequately demonstrated the legal accuracy of Luke's accounts, sufficiently challenging the unwarranted skepticism of Haenchen and others.[23] Although an author could certainly acquaint himself with Roman provincial hearings without having attended Paul's, the accuracy remains consistent with the picture that generally emerges from careful examination of the evidence, namely, a picture of Luke as an author interested in events of real history.

c. Rhetorical Observations

The forensic rhetoric of the speeches in Acts 24–26 is appropriate; although rhetoricians in practice mixed genres, they insisted on using the rhetorical style appropriate to their subject, including forensic rhetoric for judicial subjects (see, e.g., Hermog. *Issues* 34.21–35.2). Although good orators did not follow the prescribed examples of rhetorical textbooks precisely, ancient forensic petitions that have survived indicate that the handbooks accurately report the basic conventions of these speeches.[24] For a more detailed introduction to the defense speeches, see the introduction at Acts 22[25] (a speech not given in court but nevertheless provided with apologetic intent). For further rhetorical observations, see discussion in the following sections.

2. Charges against Paul (24:1–9)

It was customary in ancient rhetoric to add to the original charges other offenses, slandering a person's character to render the prosecution's overall case more plausible.

---

19. With Witherington, *Acts*, 703. We find Apollonius's disciple Damis present even in a private hearing in Philost. *Vit. Apoll.* 7.31, but this may be the way for Philostratus to account for his source of "information."

20. Winter, "*Captatio benevolentiae*," 505–6, 526–28; see discussion of Acts 24:2–9, below.

21. Witherington, *Acts*, 703.

22. Sherwin-White, "Trial," 101 (followed by many others, e.g., Jewett, *Chronology*, 40; Cassidy, *Politics*, 15; Yamauchi, *Stones*, 120–21). Some comparisons appear below.

23. Sherwin-White, *Society*, 48–70. Pervo, *Acts*, 592, argues against this position but cites as other advocates for it Mommsen, "Rechtverhältnisse"; Heusler, *Kapitalprozesse*; Winter, "Official Proceedings"; Rapske, *Custody*, 158–64; Omerzu, *Prozess*; and comments by Hemer and Tajra. Luke has apologetic and theological agendas, but these were not, as shown in the commentary introduction (esp. Keener, *Acts*, 1:148–65), incompatible with historians using genuine information.

24. See Winter, "*Captatio benevolentiae*," 506–7.

25. Keener, *Acts*, 3:3195–200; cf. 3159–60.

The heart of the charges against Paul is sedition, a capital offense, and profanation of the temple, an offense for which Jerusalemites themselves should have been permitted to execute the offender.

That Luke takes these charges seriously is clear from his elaborate narrative refutation of them: riots are associated with Paul through much of Acts but are caused not by Paul but instead by his enemies; Luke also gives an alternative reading (or, counting Lysias's version, two alternative readings) of Paul's seizure in the temple.

a. Bringing a Case against Paul (24:1–2a)

The five days (Acts 24:1) will have allowed both sides a short time to prepare their case. Prisoners were usually warned to have their case ready before their hearing occurred, but sometimes they had no advance warning of when this would be. It could be difficult to prepare a case (gathering evidence, witnesses, etc.) while in prison, though one could obtain legal counsel whether inside or outside prison.[26] Paul's friends, whether they traveled with him in 23:31–32 or followed afterward, could have contacted witnesses, especially those in Caesarea who could confirm how recently Paul had left for Jerusalem (24:11). Normally cases would remain on the docket for a longer period of time than this case does (cf. 24:21, 27), but the status of the litigants would have moved this case to the top of the list as soon as the accusers arrived (23:35; 24:1).[27]

i. CORRECT PROCEDURE

The prosecutor here presents the case against Paul[28] in the presence of the governor (24:1) before the accused is summoned to trial (24:2a). This was the correct Roman legal procedure.[29] Although the term used here (ἐμφανίζω) has a more general sense of clarifying or explaining, it often means presenting a formal report in a judicial sense, as here.[30] As noted above, Acts approximates so closely the procedure of Roman law[31] that many Roman historians have treated it as the clearest illustration of how governors in the provinces conducted such trials.[32]

Paul presumably has already been anticipating the hearing at least briefly when he is summoned (24:2a); the governor's aides would not simply send word to Paul's keepers unexpectedly, thereby risking keeping the governor and the accusers waiting.[33] The term for "summoned" here, by itself, could simply mean "invite" or "call" but, in

26. Rapske, *Custody*, 329.

27. Lentz, *Luke's Portrait*, 115, contends that Luke regularly portrays Paul's accusers as Jews of low status. This description may fit Paul's opponents in Acts often, but it does not fit them here; although both parallels with Jesus and the need to explain delays in Paul's trial provide reason to report such opposition, it departs from the pattern earlier in the book. If rhetoricians could use accusers' low status against them, Luke might also seek to make the best of a known situation with accusers of high social status (but negative moral status from the standpoint of Roman hearers) giving attention to Paul yet failing to persuade the governor. Yet Luke would probably not invent them: for those knowledgeable of Judean affairs (or who had spent some time in Judea around the time that Paul was in custody there, as Luke had), having such enemies might paint Paul well, but Luke's audience probably would not know the names and antics of these high priests.

28. Among the various meanings of ἐμφανίζω is to bring a report in a judicial setting or to bring charges (BDAG cites P.Hib. 72.4 [third century B.C.E.]; *PSI* 400.2; 2 Macc 3:7; *1 En.* 22:12; Jos. *Ant.* 10.166; 14.226), as in Acts 24:1; 25:2, 15.

29. Witherington, *Acts*, 703, following Mommsen, "Rechtverhältnisse."

30. BDAG cites Xen. *Mem.* 4.3.4; Diod. Sic. 14.11.2; Esth 2:22; Jos. *Ant.* 4.43; for bringing formal charges, *Ant.* 10.166.

31. Sherwin-White, *Society*, 48–70.

32. Sherwin-White, "Trial," 101.

33. Still, a summons can be quite sudden, as in Philost. *Vit. Apoll.* 7.31 (though he had unofficial advance notice the night before, he is taken out suddenly and without immediate warning).

this context, must mean "summon before a court" (cf. 4:18).[34] Although the accusers summarized their charges before the magistrate privately first, the case itself would have to be in Paul's presence (24:2a), allowing his response (25:16). The case likely began early in the morning or at least was docketed into a schedule of hearings that started early in the morning.[35] (The involvement of the high priests would demand priority for the hearing.) Governors normally held court in the morning.[36]

The relative status of the accusers and defendants constituted a major factor in trials in this period.[37] If someone of low status or respectability brought charges, a case might be considered suspect (Cic. *Verr.* 2.2.38.94). The accusers here, however, are of the highest possible local status, and their corporate presence is probably intended to weight the case in their favor.[38] Paul's sole clear social advantage is his Roman citizenship,[39] but some of his accusers (and the orator Tertullus) may share this advantage, though the charge that Paul is a ringleader among Nazarenes (Acts 24:5) probably also inadvertently suggests a constituency and makes Felix more cautious.

Luke clarifies for his readers that if the case is adjourned without conclusion (Acts 24:22), it is not for want of good arguments on Paul's side. Indeed, Luke depicts Paul as faring quite well, considering the forces arrayed against him. Given ancient politics, we may be certain that had the evidence against Paul proved compelling, Felix would have quickly convicted him and handed him over to the priestly leaders instead of letting his case languish so long.

II. TERTULLUS

Was Tertullus Jewish or Roman? Some scholars doubt that he was Jewish because the name is nowhere else attested for a Jew,[40] but this is an argument from silence; though Jews used Roman names less often than Greek ones, Roman names for Jewish people do randomly appear—such as "Paul" in the NT. Some argue that Tertullus may be Jewish, since he pleads in the first person plural (24:3, 6).[41] Others reasonably counter that a lawyer would identify with his clients anyway,[42] and claim (unconvincingly) that 24:5 distinguishes him from Jews (in fact, a first-person pronoun would not have sufficiently clarified the sense).[43]

As in Paul's own case, however, the dichotomy between Jewish and Roman is forced-choice logic (16:20–21). Where would the chief priests find a supportive lawyer in a mere five days except in Judea? And if he is Judean, he is likelier than not Jewish; he apparently comes with the elders from Jerusalem (24:1). Even had Luke not indicated that Tertullus came with them, it is implausible that they would hire their pleader in Caesarea (and a Syrian rather than a Jew) only after their arrival.[44]

34. See BDAG, citing esp. Jos. *Ant.* 14.169; also Barrett, *Acts*, 1094 (noting Plato *Laws* 11.937A; Demosth. *Fals. leg.* 211); cf. Conzelmann, *Acts*, 198.

35. Cf., e.g., Philost. *Vit. Apoll.* 8.1.

36. Cf., e.g., Cic. *Verr.* 2.4.66.147; John 18:28. On morning schedules, see Keener, *John*, 1098–99, and sources there; cf. also Symm. *Ep.* 1.23.3.

37. Rapske, "Prison," 827; Garnsey, *Status and Privilege*, 279–80. Papyrus appeals illustrate how even those of lower social station depended on those who had power (Meeks, *Moral World*, 35, citing, e.g., P.Oxy. 2852).

38. Witherington, *Acts*, 704.

39. Rapske, *Custody*, 158–59.

40. Williams, "Names," 112 (conceding that the name applies to a God-fearer in Aphrodisias).

41. Rapske, *Custody*, 160; Bruce, *Acts¹*, 421; cf. the possibility in Weiser, *Apostelgeschichte*, 627–28.

42. Barrett, *Acts*, 1093. In earlier centuries, Greek advocates usually wrote speeches for presenters in the latter's person (e.g., Demosthenes or Isaeus passim; although this practice is less relevant for a first-century Roman court).

43. Barrett, *Acts*, 1093 (in the final analysis, Barrett thinks the evidence uncertain either way [1094]).

44. Caesarean Jews apparently diverged in their perspectives (Jos. *Ant.* 20.178).

(They may have chosen Tertullus as an orator who had pleaded before Felix before and hence was familiar to him.)[45] In an earlier period, a provincial of rank would acquire a native provincial rather than a Roman citizen as an advocate (Cic. *Verr.* 2.2.43.106–7). Yet a well-educated, Jewish Roman citizen would best be able to counter Paul's status, and some high-ranking Jerusalemites were citizens (even equestrians, Jos. *War* 2.308). Aside from a speaker's opportunity to earn limited fees (see comment on Acts 24:10), those who shared high-status Roman values felt that an orator could accept a legal case for friendship, for generosity to the destitute, or for establishing a strategic precedent.[46]

If Tertullus is not a Roman citizen, he comes from a family sympathetic enough with Roman interests to provide its son a Roman name; such a name might subtly help the prosecution counter Paul's Roman connections. But it appears likelier than not that he, like Paul, is a Jewish Roman citizen. What is deeply ironic on the literary-theological level is that leaders supporting those angry with Paul for collaborating with Gentiles (cf. Acts 21:28; 22:21–22) apparently appeal to their own connections to use the Roman system in their favor. Indeed, they were earlier prepared to collaborate with assassins, the bane of the pro-Roman aristocracy (Acts 23:14–15; cf. 21:38).

III. Ananias and the Elders

Luke underlines both the political strength and the hypocrisy of Paul's accusers by naming the most influential among them—that is, Ananias. That he was high priest signifies his influence, but the previous occasion on which Luke named him signifies his hypocrisy. He had Paul struck, taking his guilt as a foregone conclusion (23:2); Paul publicly reproved him, inviting this powerful leader's implacable hostility (23:4); the high priest would view such a challenge as an affront to his honor.[47] If Luke's audience was accustomed, as many powerless (and not a few powerful) people in the ancient Mediterranean were, to unjust exploitation of power, they could easily enough identify with Paul here.

Ananias's hostility raises the stakes for Paul's case. A particularly informed reader might know that Felix became governor precisely because his predecessor lost a case against this Ananias (Jos. *War* 2.243–47). Ananias was not a legal opponent to take lightly. But Ananias might also not be Felix's favorite person. Although Ananias and Jonathan advocated Felix's appointment, Felix allegedly had Jonathan assassinated for reproving him too much afterward.[48] Felix's relationship with Ananias was likely less than ideal at this point.

Moreover, the leading priests seem to have had a vendetta against some early Christian leaders; perhaps two years after the events depicted here, a high priest (who served only three months in office) executed James, head of the Jerusalem church.[49] If elements of the priestly aristocracy viewed with such hostility James, who identified with the most pious elements of Jerusalem's culture, it is by no means historically

---

45. Rapske, *Custody*, 159.

46. Pliny *Ep.* 6.29.1–2; he then adds a fourth motivation of his own—namely, for achieving greater fame (6.29.3). The advocate in Quint. *Decl.* 333.5, 16, claims that his role compelled him to accept the case (but in context argues this point to evade a charge).

47. Like Jesus (Luke 22:67–70; 23:9), Paul refuses to be intimidated by unjust officials.

48. Jos. *Ant.* 20.162–63 (Le Cornu, *Acts*, 1296; Spangenberg in Chung-Kim and Hains, *Acts*, 325). One wonders how Josephus would know this, but it is plausible, at least, that the friction between Jonathan and Felix was known and hence a source of the rumor. Further, if Josephus knew the rumor, which presumably originated at some time near the assassination, Ananias would probably be no less privy to it.

49. Jos. *Ant.* 20.200.

implausible that the perceived leader of the movement's Diaspora mission would have generated potentially mortal hostility as well.

Luke's ideal reader, perhaps less accustomed to harmonized passion narratives than are most modern Christians, would probably also notice that Paul faces opposition from the high priest just as did Jesus (Luke 22:54),[50] the Twelve (Acts 4:6; 5:17; cf. Luke 3:2), and Stephen (Acts 7:1); Paul confronts the Jerusalem elite he once served (9:1–2).

That Ananias brings "some elders" might be significant. Although he obviously could not bring a large number, given the distance between Jerusalem and Caesarea, it is possible that even five days after Paul's arrest, the Sanhedrin is not yet unified (contrast perhaps 25:2, two years later; but even this may simply be generalizing summary).[51] It is possible that some of the elders who accompany the high priest are Pharisees (cf. 24:15), but he would hardly bring them as the majority or dominant members of the delegation.

The high priest may select the elders whom he trusts to be most committed to his cause (the Sadducean elite seem to have been the early Christian movement's primary opponents before 70 C.E.; cf. 4:1; 5:17; 6:12; 23:6–9). If detractors remained (23:9), the prosecution could likely pass over their view in silence; few in the Sanhedrin would think Paul's case significant enough to travel to Caesarea and publicly dispute with their high priest before the Romans, given the potential repercussions of such division.[52]

IV. THE RHETOR

In classical Greek, the term ῥήτωρ meant a skilled orator, but in this period, though it continued to mean an orator (e.g., Lucian *Prof. P.S.* 1; so also the Latin *rhetor*), it often carried the narrower sense, in view here, of a legal advocate.[53] Advocates for either the prosecution or the defense or both were common practice (see comment on Acts 24:10–21). "Rhetors" and professors of rhetoric normally grew up in wealthy families and increased their prestige by office holding and civic benefactions.[54]

Nevertheless, advocates were not experts in the law in this period so much as they were orators.[55] True lawyers—that is, jurists (*iuris prudentes*)—were legal scholars and did not need to argue cases; this was more commonly the domain of orators.[56] Orators, by contrast, were not legal experts but rhetorical experts.[57] Although orators regularly demonstrated their talents in court (indeed, under the empire, this became their primary venue), the accusers' use of an orator contrasts starkly with Paul's defense of himself (Acts 24:10–21).

50. In this case, the high priest's involvement is emphasized less than in Mark's passion narrative, though only to distribute it among all the priestly elite (cf. Luke 22:66–67, 70–71 with Mark 14:61–63).

51. Peer solidarity was important (cf. Avidov, "Peer Solidarity"), but we do know that the municipal elite of Jerusalem also fractured into numerous competing special interests in this period (see comment on Acts 23:6–10), though uniting when necessary. The Sanhedrin could disapprove of a high priest acting solely on his own initiative (Jos. *Life* 309).

52. A minority best reserved its political capital for more essential matters, and Jerusalem's elders could not afford to present a disunited front before the governor, in any case.

53. Witherington, *Acts*, 703n266 (citing, e.g., Jos. *Ant.* 17.226); Parsons, *Acts*, 324; BDAG cites Dio Chrys. *Or.* 76.4; P.Oxy. 37.1.4 (49 C.E.); 237.7.25; BGU 969.1.8.

54. Maclean and Aitken, *Heroikos*, xlvii (on sophists).

55. Crook, *Advocacy*, 175. They were not legal advisors or protectors (13, 196); what brought about juridical training later was the technicality of jurisprudence (197).

56. Honoré, "Lawyers," 836.

57. With Ferguson, *Backgrounds*, 51 (contrasting legal experts). Some ancients opined that orators made their living in law courts from others' wrongdoing (Tac. *Dial.* 41).

Luke may inform his audience that Tertullus is an orator to warn that his speech will be pure rhetoric, not truth. Philosophers often complained that orators were inferior in truth content to philosophers.[58] Thus, for example, when his oratorical instructor advised the twenty-five-year-old Marcus Aurelius to practice debating both sides of a legal case (Fronto *Ad M. Caes.* 5.27 [42]), the latter replied that he was now leaning toward philosophy and therefore could not debate both sides (4.13). Some moralist-leaning orators shared philosophers' concerns; Dio Chrysostom warned that many orators acted only for personal advantage, filling the void left by philosophers' silence.[59] Sophists and orators often simply gave audiences what they wanted.[60]

Not only do Paul's opponents have high status as a group; Paul faces a professional speaker.[61] (This could function as a literary equivalent of orators' warnings about opponents' cunning; see comment below.) This danger builds narrative suspense and invites the reader to recall God's promise that he will provide the wisdom to speak (Luke 21:15). There is no surprise that the case is adjourned without Paul's being released; under such circumstances, the surprise is that evidence for Paul's innocence is so compelling that Felix, in the face of such accusers, does not simply convict him.

It is not clear that the accusers use a formal advocate in Acts 25:7. Parties to cases apparently could plead cases either with (e.g., Pliny *Ep.* 6.31) or without (4.22) advocates, as they wished.[62] We cannot be certain because the account in Acts 25:7 is more compressed, in summary fashion, than the opening hearing here. In classical Athens, orators such as Isaeus and Demosthenes could write speeches for defendants to present,[63] but a Roman court at this level would often expect the Roman method of direct advocacy (as in, e.g., Cic. *Sest.*).[64] Sometimes in the papyri, advocates seem to know nothing about their case's circumstances apart from what appear in the brief; they were hired simply so that the case could be presented professionally.[65] Tertullus, however, will have been more fully briefed, representing such important clients.[66]

b. Introduction to the Prosecution Speech (24:2–8)

As any perplexed introductory student of Greek will attest, Tertullus's speech is full of flowery rhetoric, just what one would expect from an elite rhetor. His *captatio* abounds with special language calculated to create an impression, but Luke's audience will recognize that it lacks facts, whereas Paul's speech focuses instead on facts and argument. Before examining Tertullus's speech in detail, we should note some rhetorical features; the fact that a précis of prosecution speeches was normally a matter

---

58. E.g., Plato *Theaet.* 164CD; *Hipp. maj.*; Mus. Ruf. 8, pp. 62.40–64.4; Epict. *Diatr.* 3.23.20, 28; Max. Tyre 26.2; Marc. Aur. 1.7; cf. Tac. *Dial.* 32; Aul. Gel. 5.3.7; in Plato, see Kennedy, *Classical Rhetoric*, 42–60; in Galen, see Pearcy, "Galen."

59. Winter, "Philo among Sophists," 48–49 (citing Dio Chrys. *Or.* 32.19). For arguing both sides of a case, see, e.g., Quint. *Decl.* 331.14.

60. Winter, "Philo among Sophists," 53–54 (citing Dio Chrysostom and others).

61. Though Bruce, *Acts¹*, 424, views Tertullus's rhetoric as "ineffective."

62. So Hemer, *Acts in History*, 129 (following Sherwin-White). Many upper-class persons spoke for themselves (Crook, *Advocacy*, 123). Multiple persons might speak for either side in particularly important cases (Hermog. *Method* 27.444).

63. Also in the Hellenistic period; e.g., Theophr. *Char.* 17.8.

64. On this difference between Athenian and Roman systems, see esp. Crook, *Advocacy*, 30–31. In the Greek ideal, one spoke for oneself, but in practice unpaid advocates often helped, speaking along with them (Thür, "Synegoros").

65. Crook, *Advocacy*, 118.

66. On the basic level, Roman advocacy was supposed to be free (Crook, *Advocacy*, 34), particularly to those in need (125, 130, 186); but Crook (129–31) deals with fees. Routine advocacy was much lower on the social scale (124) than what Tertullus would provide; cf., e.g., the cheap public advocate in Lucian *Indictment* 15.

of legal record and hence available to the defense team; and evidence concerning the language of the proceedings.

Although Luke writes popular and not elite, rhetorical history, he displays notable rhetorical skills in this speech. Thus even a modern writer who is skeptical of much rhetorical ingenuity elsewhere in Acts acknowledges that Tertullus's speech makes good use of rhetoric.[67] A feasible rhetorical outline for the speech is as follows:

1. *Exordium* (Acts 24:2–4)
2. A brief *narratio*, encapsulating also the charges (24:5–6)
3. *Peroratio*, inviting the governor to investigate directly (24:8)[68]

The speech lacks formal proofs relevant to the "facts" of the *narratio*, but this fits what we find in the summaries of ancient forensic petitions in the papyri.[69] Still, the omission of proofs also serves a Lukan literary purpose: Paul points out that his opponents cannot prove their charges against him (24:13; 25:7).

Whereas scholars have more substantial reason to question the precision of Luke's sources for many earlier speeches in Acts, there is little reason to question the public speeches in Acts 24–26, during Luke's very likely sojourn near Paul in Judea (see discussion above and at the introduction to Acts 22).[70] Even if Luke could not be present for the trial (which is unlikely)[71] or his shorthand was inadequate, these speeches (unlike many earlier speeches in Acts) would have been preserved, probably in the same sort of summary fashion in which he presents them. Court transcripts, in the form of brief minutes summarizing trials, are quite common in extant papyri.[72] Against Haenchen's skepticism about Luke's speeches here, records of official proceedings were roughly the length Luke provides, and all these records were simply summaries.[73]

How would such notes be taken? Shorthand is at least a possibility. Our evidence for the recording of Greek shorthand (most relevant to this trial) is less firm, but clear evidence exists for Latin by about 50 C.E.[74] Although orators often elaborated at length

---

67. Jervell, "Future," 121; for numerous rhetorical devices here, see Keener, "Rhetorical Techniques," 224–34 (submitted in 2002, though published only in 2008). Contrast Bruce, *Acts*[1], 424, who views Tertullus's rhetoric as "ineffective."

68. With Witherington, *Acts*, 704–5, and others. Contrast Rapske, *Custody*, 162, who sees Acts 24:6, 8 as the *confirmatio*.

69. Winter, "Official Proceedings," 320–21; Witherington, *Acts*, 705 (who also treats other rhetorical features on 705); and others.

70. This reconstruction assumes a first-century date for these narratives, but the evidence of Acts is fully consistent with that and with the we-narrator being a genuine eyewitness (see the discussion in Keener, *Acts*, 1:402–16, and esp. 3:2350–74).

71. If Luke was present, he could have taken his own notes, and his summary could emphasize elements different from the précis provided by the court; see Judge, *First Christians*, 380–83, who compares what he believes to be a similar situation in P.Fouad 21 with P.Yale inv. 1528. Given the Caesarean hearings' outcome and the importance of precedent, however, any eyewitness summary of Luke's would not likely differ radically from that of official documents. Ancient historians usually had to depend on oral history (Walton and Sandy, *World*, 100), so both their presence and their access to primary documents were highly valuable.

72. E.g., P.Oxy. 37 (49 C.E.); 237, col. 7.19–29 (133 C.E.); P.Ryl. 75.1–12 (150 C.E.); P.Stras. 22.10–24 (207 C.E.); P.Thead. 15 (280–81 C.E.); P.Bour. 20 (after 350 C.E.) (and others in *SPap* 2:194–221, §§257–63).

73. Winter, "Official Proceedings," 307n7. Pervo objects partly on the basis of what Luke lacks (*Acts*, 593–95), but no narrative writer was obligated to include all the data at his or her disposal.

74. Winter, "*Captatio benevolentiae*," 526. One might expect governors' staffs to incorporate shorthand recorders soon after their emergence in Rome, which is probably earlier than our earliest extant samples. In the East, these would need to work especially in Greek, perhaps as predecessors of the Greek shorthand that is better attested later. Qualifying the procedure that Winter summarizes, shorthand was probably not yet always available (cf. Richards, *Letter Writing*, 92–93, 110); this deficiency here would not affect Winter's point, however, since a basic summary, which was all that was called for, would not require competence in shorthand.

(though cf. comment on Acts 24:4), records of official proceedings were kept brief.[75] After the court scribe copied the proceedings in shorthand, he summarized them as *oratio recta*; these records were brief, in précis form (like Luke's other speeches), but treated as verbatim and hence "certified copies."

Subsequent changes to such copies were severely punished; one governor had an offender for this crime whipped (in the period 43–48 C.E.), threatening death if the offense was repeated.[76] Such reports were not hidden away as private records. "Official papers, including records of proceedings . . . would have to be forwarded to the highest court of appeal" with a cover memo (25:26). Probably for 24:1–21, "as in any narrative in the first century purporting to summarize litigation before a Roman court, legal documents were used as sources."[77]

As Winter notes, there also remain "extant 'N' documents which appear to have been actual briefs prepared by a νομικός for his rhetor. Some of them contain a summary of the facts of the case in the wide margin in which the rhetor could write notes."[78] Orators also kept notes or transcripts of their speeches (though Tertullus's would not be available to Luke). Sometimes they revised them and published them later in improved form (e.g., Demosthenes and Cicero). Given his limited presentation time, Cicero delivered only two of his *Verrine Orations* but published all seven (Plut. *Cic.* 7.4).

Paul's trial had to be conducted either in Latin or in Greek,[79] but although some Latin was known in Palestine[80] and it was used by the provincial administration,[81] Paul's trial was almost certainly in Greek. We have many Latin inscriptions from Caesarea (especially after it later became a colony), but in this period, most relate to the Roman provincial administration; the most common language in the city was Greek.[82]

Courts used the language shared by the participants, and when this was impossible, they sought to provide translation.[83] The chief priests could afford a Latin-speaking lawyer, but most of them would not be able to understand Latin proceedings well enough to join in (Acts 24:9). Paul likely would have learned more Latin in Corinth in preparation for visiting Rome (cf. Acts 19:21; Rom 1:15; 15:23–24, 28–29),[84] but he would certainly be at a disadvantage if he had to respond to accusations leveled against him in Latin and give a fluent oration in that language.[85]

Claudius expected Roman citizens, even if high-status Greeks, to speak Latin (Suet. *Claud.* 16.2), but this was not the norm[86] (see comment on Acts 18:1–11). In the eastern Mediterranean world, especially outside a Roman colony[87] (i.e., in contrast to

75. Winter, "Official Proceedings," 307.
76. Winter, "*Captatio benevolentiae*," 527; idem, "Official Proceedings," 307.
77. Winter, "*Captatio benevolentiae*," 528.
78. Ibid., 506 (though noting that the *captatio*, such as Acts 24:2–4, was omitted from these). In traditional Egyptian law, each side had to present its case, and rebuttal of the opponents, in writing (Diod. Sic. 1.75.6–7).
79. See Winter, *Left Corinth*, 24n99.
80. Porter, "Latin Language."
81. Aune, "Latin," 335.
82. See Isaac, "Latin and Greek."
83. Winter, "*Captatio benevolentiae*," 526n104 (for translation citing P.Thead. 14). Greeks might even request Greek judges (Momigliano and Spawforth, "Cyrene"), but Paul was a Roman citizen.
84. Given the expense of writing a letter the length of Romans (Richards, *Letter Writing*, 167–68; cf. Dewey, "Oral-Aural Event," 146–47), which was nearly unheard of, Paul was certainly serious about visiting the believers there in the future. But the Christian assemblies in Rome, like the majority of synagogues there, were primarily Greek-speaking.
85. It is likewise doubtful that Luke was fluent in that language, though years in Philippi, at least, should have given him some familiarity.
86. See Adams, "*Romanitas*."
87. Even Caesarea, the immediate venue of the hearing, became a colony only later, under Vespasian (Smallwood and Rajak, "Caesarea").

Acts 18:12–17), the governor would likely expect a trial in Greek. Felix was not born an equestrian, but he was thoroughly competent in Greek, as suggested by his marriage to an Easterner (24:24). His counselors (cf. 25:12) would certainly know it as well, and Felix's later conversations with Paul (24:24–25) were undoubtedly in Greek.

c. Complimentary exordium (24:2b–3)

Once the public session began (24:2a, in contrast to 24:1), the prosecution would almost invariably speak first (24:2b);[88] any exceptions to this procedure were counted as highly irregular.[89] Conveniently for literary purposes, it was also the case that in paired declamations, the second often represented the preferred side (e.g., Max. Tyre 15–16; 23–24); that is, the second presenter held the rhetorical advantage (cf. Prov 18:17). One carefully arranged the *exordium* to anticipate the main speech, emphasizing one's strongest points.[90]

I. Praising the Governor

Orators could devote entire speeches to praising a governor. In an "address" (προσφωνητικός), an individual would praise the governor (Men. Rhet. 2.10, 414.31–418.4; for the title, see 414.32–415.1).[91] It would especially emphasize the governor's deeds (415.4), though the speaker would not elaborate in full detail unless he intended to provide a full encomium (416.28–417.4). Although praise of the governor dominates the beginning of this speech, it does so no more than was conventional in normal speeches to a governor.[92]

Tertullus's speech opens with a standard *captatio benevolentiae*, an *exordium* meant to secure the magistrate's favor by flattery.[93] Scholars often point out that the *captatio benevolentiae* reflects standard style.[94] His *exordium* closely resembles *exordia* in official legal petitions (e.g., P.Fouad 26).[95] Whereas the rest of the speech is summarized, the *exordium* is about the length found in other petitions[96] (though those, too, are likely summaries of longer praises delivered; a spokesman for the high priest might well have more time than the average petitioner).

Making a good impression on a judge had long been an important element of forensic rhetoric.[97] One should praise judges or jurors for their attention to justice (*Rhet. Alex.* 36, 1442a.14–16). A classical Athenian orator points out, "You are ... naturally more clever than other men," and so "it is not surprising that you pass most excellent laws" (Aeschines *Tim.* 178).[98] In the Roman republic, Cicero warns his

---

88. E.g., Lysias *Or.* 19.2, §152; Char. *Chaer.* 5.4.9; Terence *Eunuch* 10–13; Tac. *Ann.* 3.13; Apul. *Metam.* 10.7; *t. Sanh.* 6:3. The prosecution speech was typically called a κατηγορία (Porph. *Ar. Cat.* 55.3–4).

89. See Cicero's complaints in *Quinct.* 2.9; 9.33. Apparently, Jewish law usually made an exception in capital cases (*t. Sanh.* 7:2; cf. *m. Sanh.* 4:1).

90. Thus, in his *exordium*, Apuleius in his *Apologia* emphasizes the least damaging charges against himself (see Asztalos, "Apologia").

91. It was an encomium, though lacking some elements of the normal encomium (Men. Rhet. 2.10, 415.1–2).

92. Trajan, not much given to flattery, disapproves of Byzantium expending funds to send delegates to greet and honor himself and the governor of Moesia each year (Pliny *Ep.* 10.44, responding to 10.43.1–3).

93. Aune, *Environment*, 126; cf. idem, *Dictionary of Rhetoric*, 89, 176. See fuller comment on Acts 17:22. Securing audience favor was one of the first steps in normal speeches (*Rhet. Alex.* 29, 1436b.17–19; Cic. *De or.* 1.31.143; Men. Rhet. 2.3, 378.4–9; cf. Calboli Montefusco, "Exordium," 272); for some specific examples, see comment on Acts 17:22.

94. E.g., Conzelmann, *Acts*, 198 (citing Lucian *Indictment* 17).

95. Winter, "Official Proceedings," 315.

96. Ibid., 320.

97. E.g., Arist. *Rhet.* 2, esp. 2.1.1–9, 1377b–1378a. See further comment on Acts 7:51–53; 17:22.

98. Trans. C. D. Adams, LCL, 143.

audience that his opponents are exploiting them, "the best men" (Cic. *Sest.* 1.2).[99] In another case, he addresses the judge as "distinguished . . . by integrity, virtue, dignity, and authority" (*Rosc. com.* 3.7).[100] In a proem, he notes that his suffering client "has taken refuge in your integrity, uprightness, and compassion" (*Quinct.* 2.10).[101]

A petition from about three centuries after Cicero begins by praising the prefect's concern for justice (P.Ryl. 114.3–5). Not limiting flattery to his introduction, Apuleius regularly praises his judge's fairness,[102] good sense and education,[103] expeditious handling of the case,[104] and so forth.[105] "I rely on your impartiality and my innocence," he begins (Apul. *Apol.* 3). He tries to avoid appearing to flatter the judge, he explains, "But I cannot help praising you for your cleverness in questioning" (48). He name-drops a mutual friend of himself and the judge whose letter supports Apuleius's case (95–96). He trusts the judge's decision, he concludes, since he is "such a good and blameless man" (103). (For a discussion of flattery, see comment on Acts 4:13, where I note its frequent contrast, in ancient sources, with frank speech.)

Increasing the judge's favor was an essential goal of rhetoric (Quint. *Inst.* 4.1.20, 23); if this approach failed, one could even threaten judges that one would not hesitate to prosecute them for bribery (4.1.21). Flattery appears even in greetings that are not designed purely for persuasion (e.g., *Let. Aris.* 1–2).[106] Indeed, even later rabbis recognized the importance of appropriate flattery to Roman dignitaries. A rhetor (לוטייר) hired by a client would begin not with his client's case but with praising the king for his just rule; after raising his client's issue, he would again praise the king (*Sipre Deut.* 343.1.2).[107]

ii. Peace and Foresight (24:2)

The use of "much" (πολύς) is common in opening praises, often appearing at the beginning of a speech (Thucyd. 1.80.1; 2.35.1; 3.37.1); it is applicable, for example, to kings who provided "many advantages" for their people (Dion. Hal. 5.1.4).[108] "Through you" (διὰ σοῦ) resembles the language of honorary inscriptions, which often praise the benefits the state has received through a particular benefactor (e.g., *CIL* 5.875, from 105 C.E.).[109]

The issues praised (peace and stability; providence or foresight; and reforms) are characteristic in complimentary *exordia* or speeches. Thus one might praise a ruler for giving peace (*otia*, leisure) to the world (Sil. It. 14.686); the claim of the Pax Romana was central to Augustus's honor.[110] A governor who had dispersed

---

99. Trans. R. Gardner, LCL, 12:39.
100. Trans. J. H. Freese, LCL, 6:281.
101. LCL, 6:17. He repeats the substance of this appeal at the conclusion of his *narratio* (Cic. *Quinct.* 9.34).
102. Apul. *Apol.* 25, 102.
103. Apul. *Apol.* 36, 41, 60. Here he usually connects the judge with himself as a fellow educated person.
104. Apul. *Apol.* 84 (emphasizing the judge's foresight).
105. He complains that his accuser is wasting this noble judge's time with nonsense (Apul. *Apol.* 25, 46).
106. Cf. the persistent flattery in Apul. *Flor.* 9, an epideictic speech: "I seek the approval of no one more than the man of whom I approve more than all others" (9.31); "Now I declare openly that I am your admirer" (9.32); cf. also 9.33–34; 16.31; 17.3; and esp. 17.20: "the most excellent of all proconsuls."
107. Also in Goodman, *State*, 166 (citing it [394] as *Sipre Deut.* 343), comparing Apul. *Apol.* 36, 48. That I independently found the same rabbinic reference (and no others) probably suggests that that example is not common in rabbinic literature.
108. Conzelmann, *Acts*, 198. Cf. the repetition of πολυ- in Heb 1:1 (useful to its alliteration, Jewett, *Hebrews*, 9); cf. "many" in Sir 1:1; Luke 1:1 (cf. 2 Macc 2:24–25; Jos. *Ant.* 1.1; 20.154; Arrian *Alex.* 1.pref. 3; Nicolaus *Progymn.* 1.pref. 1; cf. also Moffatt, *Hebrews*, 2).
109. In Sherk, *Empire*, 158–59, §116.
110. *Res gest.* heading; 3.1; 25.1; 26.2–3; 27.2; cf. Gilbert, "Propaganda," 237–42; Benko, "Early Empire," 39; Fears, "Ideology of Power"; Horsley, "Assembly," 386; Bowley, "Pax." Haacker, *Theology*, 117–18, argues

robbers was praiseworthy, especially if there was peace throughout his province (Plut. *Cic.* 36.5, πάντων εἰρήνην); for example, as a good governor, Quintus had reduced thieves and robbers in rural areas and towns alike (Cic. *Quint. fratr.* 1.1.8.25).[111] One might praise a ruler when commodities were plentiful, when farmers could work the soil and sailors traverse the sea in peace, when barbarians and other enemies aroused no fear.[112] Praising a ruler for bringing "much peace" thus employed a stock phrase.[113]

Foresight (πρόνοια)[114] was common grounds for praising administrators (cf. 2 Macc 14:9).[115] It applies to benefactors[116] but, more relevant, appears in the *captatio* of some forensic papyri.[117] A related cause for praise was a ruler's ability to anticipate all needs.[118]

Whether the *captatio* in Tertullus's full speech was more detailed we cannot say; as already noted, Felix would be more patient with Ananias's agent than with the average petitioner. Laudatory titles were common, such as identifying a governor as "savior" (bringer of prosperity).[119] Related issues command attention; where necessary, one might appeal to the clemency characteristic of the judges (Cic. *Deiot.* 15.43).

More commonly, as noted above regarding judges, justice was a major theme.[120] Thus it reflects well on an emperor if he sends out just governors who guard the laws instead of accumulating wealth (Men. Rhet. 2.1–2, 375.18–21); a governor could be praised for his attentiveness to individuals' judicial cases (2.4, 389.6–7).[121] If we fill in information from later sources, orators praising a governor may have often worked with the four categories of virtue commonly accepted since Aristotle (2.3, 380.31):[122] one should praise the new governor's justice (379.19–20; 380.32–381.1),[123] his courage (379.25; 381.1), his sound self-control (379.32; 381.2),[124] and his insight

---

that Nero's reign revived this epideictic subject; Nero's propaganda on the subject invited Seneca's critique (Huttner, "Zivilisationskritik").

111. Likewise, no one would be impressed with a governor who claimed to keep peace (Cic. *Verr.* 2.5.1.2) if there were no threats of its disruption (2.5.2.5–2.5.4.9), and everyone would think ill of a governor who aggravated instability (2.5.4.9–2.5.6.14).

112. Men. Rhet. 2.1–2, 377.10–15, on the epilogue of an encomium for the emperor; an epilogue would typically drive home the most important points.

113. Witherington, *Acts*, 706n277 (citing Plut. *Alc.* 14.2; Jos. *Ant.* 7.20).

114. When used for humans, it especially signified concern or preparation for matters; see BDAG and sources listed there. It is praised in honorary inscriptions (e.g., *OGIS* 339.31, in Danker, *Corinthians*, 132).

115. Cf. perhaps also 2 Macc 4:6 (where peace depends on the king's providence; cf. Bruce, *Commentary*, 464). It might provide implicit commentary on Tertullus, however, that Jewish documents used this praise particularly for God (Wis 14:3; 3 Macc 4:21; 4 Macc 17:22; cf. Marcus, "Names and Attributes," 48), sometimes in explicit contrast to wicked rulers (3 Macc 5:30; 4 Macc 9:24; cf. Wis 6:7; Dan 11:37).

116. For inscriptions, see Harrison, "Benefaction Ideology," 109–16. Cf. even the wise "caring for" (προνοεῖν) the foolish (Dio Chrys. *Or.* 3.62).

117. See P.Fouad 26; P.Ryl. 114.5 in Winter, "*Captatio benevolentiae*," 517; Witherington, *Acts*, 706.

118. Winter, "Official Proceedings," 316, cites P.Oxy. 2131. See also, e.g., Nero's "foresight" in sending an excellent governor (*OGIS* 666.4–7, in Danker, *Corinthians*, 133).

119. Winter, "Official Proceedings," 315, cites P.Fouad 26.25, 49–50.

120. Philosophers and moralists also emphasized the need for kings to be just (e.g., Mus. Ruf. 8, p. 62.8–9; Dio Chrys. *Or.* 4.24).

121. By this standard, Felix fares poorly (Acts 24:26–27), though it must be said that he does not completely succumb to political expediency (cf. 25:15).

122. For the emperor, see Men. Rhet. 2.1–2, 373.7–8; in times of peace, one might omit "courage" (375.7–8). For these virtues in Aristotle (and Plato), cf. also Hippol. *Ref.* 1.17.

123. When applied to an emperor, this includes making just laws and appointing just governors (Men. Rhet. 2.1–2, 375.8–376.2).

124. Applied to an emperor, this leads to sound morals for the whole society (Men. Rhet. 2.1–2, 376.2–13; this is partly from his example, 376.8–9).

(380.1–3; 381.2).[125] One also discussed a governor's specific actions in terms of these four categories (385.8–9).[126]

One might recount the governor's deeds (379.5), but if they were not available, one could praise his home city or country (379.6–8), the deeds of his family (379.10), and so forth. One could "predict" how well he would do as a new governor (379.18). Praises could include analogies to earlier positive figures (2.14, 426.23–24) or contrasts with frequent bad examples.[127] Complaining about the difficulties existing before the current governor makes him look more competent (2.3, 378.18–26), although one might choose to omit this step and simply confess the governor's benefactions (378.26–379.2, esp. 378.27). It is no surprise that Seneca the Younger must warn a governor to protect himself from flatterers (Nat. Q. 4A.pref. 3) and advises him to remind flatterers that their compliments are transferred from old magistrates to new ones whenever they arrive (4A, pref. 13).

Like the invitation to cross-examine Paul in Acts 24:8, these praises express confidence in the governor's ability to make just decisions, and imply that the speaker presents an obviously just cause. It was common to encourage a hearer or reader that the writer trusted the reader to do what the writer asked,[128] including in early Christian exhortation.[129] This was particularly useful in a plea before judges or jury. One might claim that the opponent engaged in unethical means of winning the case but that one trusted in the gods and in the judges, whose justice would not be perverted.[130]

Such praises were also appropriate in appeals to pathos after concluding one's proofs.[131] Thus Cicero, finishing his argument, entreats the judge, on the basis of his client's age and suffering, "simply to follow the dictates of your natural goodness of heart" (Quinct. 30.91);[132] Cicero assures the judge that many of Cicero's fears were allayed as soon as he realized the judge's identity (30.92). Many scholars contend that Tertullus's lavish captatio contrasts starkly with Paul's boldness (Acts 24:10), raising suspense: will Felix succumb to empty rhetoric without proof?[133]

III. RELEVANT BUT INACCURATE FLATTERY

How accurate were Tertullus's praises? Most scholars recognize that Felix had crucified robbers and sought to suppress disorder;[134] but many doubt that Felix had earned sincere praise on these counts.[135] Because the content of a captatio was determined partly by rhetorical convention, many doubt that the present one needs to refer to Felix's specific activities here.[136] If any of Luke's audience had heard of Felix's

125. For an emperor, this involves administrative wisdom and wise evaluation of advice (Men. Rhet. 2.1–2, 376.13–23), including more foresight than a mantic (376.21–22).

126. Justice (Men. Rhet. 2.3, 385.9–22), temperance (385.22–28), wisdom (385.28–386.6), and courage (386.7–10).

127. Thus Sil. It. 14.684–88 contrasts a "just" ruler (probably Domitian!, 14.686–88) with the commonly exploitive provincial governors whom he has checked.

128. Cf., e.g., Cic. Fam. 2.4.2; 13.44.1; Phaedrus 3.epil. 20–21; Olson, "Expressions of Confidence."

129. E.g., 2 Cor 2:3; 7:4, 16; 8:22; 9:4; Gal 5:10; Phil 1:6; 1 Thess 4:9; 2 Thess 3:4; Heb 6:9; Phlm 8, 21.

130. E.g., Aeschines Ctes. 1.

131. Aristotle urged use of rational arguments to generate pathos (Kraftchick, "Πάθη," 48–50), but Romans used pathos as an appeal to stir or sway audience emotion (52–53, 56). On Aristotle's emphasis on emotion in rhetoric, see Hall, "Delivery," 232. On ἦθος and πάθος, see also Lampe, "Einsichten."

132. Trans. J. H. Freese, LCL, 6:101; the pathos section is Cic. Quinct. 30.91–31.99.

133. Johnson, Acts, 416.

134. Jos. War 2.253, 260, 263; Ant. 20.161.

135. Long after Felix's demise, Josephus also credits Felix (accurately or not) with having helped incite the violence (Ant. 20.162–66).

136. Haenchen, Acts, 652; Conzelmann, Acts, 198; Tajra, Trial, 120; Johnson, Acts, 410; Larkin, Acts, 337; Fitzmyer, Acts, 733.

administration (perhaps most easily from Judean travelers or fugitives), they may well have heard that it was under Felix that violent unrest spiraled out of control, partly through his brutal but inefficient attempts to crush it.[137]

Although these concerns about Felix's corrupt administration are accurate, other scholars also point accurately to a different perspective that an equally corrupt high priest, Ananias, may have felt appropriate. Tertullus does not offer idle praise; his clients supported the appointment of Felix to begin with, despite his freed status. Likewise, his suppression of many brigands (alluded to in 21:38) did testify that whatever his ultimate failings, he was concerned to maintain order, the point at issue here (24:5–6). The Sanhedrin could have argued that they appreciated these efforts and wanted him to establish order in this case as well (24:5–6).[138]

Tertullus's praises are not purely incidental to the issues at hand; the praises in a *captatio* should match the situation addressed and indicate the judge's competence for the matter under discussion in the case.[139] Rhetoricians advised a speaker to secure the audience members' goodwill by praising them, "and whenever possible this should be done in such a manner as to advance his case" (Quint. *Inst.* 3.7.23–24).[140] One would win the judge's favor not merely by tactful praise but by connecting the praise precisely to the case at hand (4.1.16). Thus, for example, a speaker in a novel praises his judge as "just and benevolent" (δίκαιος καὶ φιλάνθρωπος) and pleads for attention to his claims (Char. *Chaer.* 5.7.1).

A *captatio* should prepare for the charges, and Tertullus's *captatio* does so.[141] If Felix has brought peace, he ought to punish Paul, who disturbs public order (Acts 24:5–6).[142] "Reforms" might refer to revising the laws or using them flexibly; Tertullus could raise this matter to suggest that a governor wise in his use of law ought to quell Paul's rebellion.[143] Orators sometimes complained that their opponents dishonored the judges[144] or thought that they could take unfair advantage of the judges' indulgence or, worse yet, of their low morality.[145] Tertullus does not claim that Paul directly dishonored Felix, but he does imply that Paul's agenda was to undercut the very peace and reforms for which Felix had labored (24:2, 5).

Although the praises thus seem appropriate within the narrative world, they would probably read differently to any members of Luke's audience who were informed about earlier Judean politics or who had already heard the rest of Acts. Luke, in any case, would know of Felix's corruption first- or secondhand and reveals some of it to his audience (24:26–27). Luke (who sojourned for more than a year in Judea) would know, and some of his first audience might know, that Felix's misadministration helped lead to the Judean revolt, which, in contrast to Paul's preaching of concern for Gentiles (22:21; cf. Luke 6:35), would lead to Jerusalem's destruction (Luke 21:20–24).

For those who knew better, Tertullus's words would not only ring hollow; they would sound a note of irony.[146] On the level of Luke's (but not Tertullus's) message,

---

137. Commentators noted above cite esp. Tac. *Ann.* 12.54; cf. Jos. *Ant.* 20.161–82; less explicitly (perhaps for political reasons), *War* 2.252–71.

138. Winter, "*Captatio benevolentiae,*" 515–16; followed by Rapske, *Custody,* 161–62; and others.

139. See at length Winter, "*Captatio benevolentiae,*" 506–15. Note also *Rhet. Her.* 1.8 and the example (Livy 28.44.6–18) from a speech in a history (28.43.2–28.44.18) in Laird, "Rhetoric," 206.

140. Trans. H. E. Butler, LCL, 1:475.

141. With esp. Winter, "*Captatio benevolentiae,*" 321–22; also others, e.g., Rapske, *Custody,* 159.

142. With Witherington, *Acts,* 705.

143. Ibid., 706.

144. E.g., Cic. *Verr.* 2.4.40.86–2.4.41.90 (Verres dishonored Marcellus's name; Marcellus is one of the judges, 2.4.42.90).

145. E.g., Cic. *Verr.* 2.3.96.223.

146. With Pervo, *Story,* 82. Cf. Spangenberg 219v–220r (Chung-Kim and Hains, *Acts,* 325).

the irony might resemble Cicero's sarcastic condemnation of the corrupt governor Verres: "The prudence, the care, the watchfulness, with which he looked after and protected his province, have been put before you" (*Verr.* 2.5.10.25 [LCL]).

A clearer irony in the narrative itself, presupposing no extrinsic information, resides in what the speaker praises. Tertullus and his clients praise Felix for establishing "peace," so that they can convict Paul as a stirrer of unrest (Acts 24:5). Yet ironically, it is Paul's accusers who have breached the peace (21:26–31; 24:12, 18), as Felix might well surmise from Lysias's urgent report (23:27–30, 33); they rejected what brought peace (Luke 19:42). By contrast, Paul stands in continuity with those who announced good news of peace for the world (Acts 10:36; cf. 7:26; Luke 1:79; 2:14; 10:5–6).[147]

IV. MOST EXCELLENT, UNIVERSALLY PRAISED (24:3)

"Most excellent" (κράτιστε)[148] is not flattery but the appropriate title for the governor (Acts 23:26; 26:25). It was an appropriate address for an equestrian[149] (which Felix was not)[150] or for any governor (who by virtue of office exercised a normally equestrian prerogative).[151] "Everywhere and in every way" (πάντη τε καὶ πανταχοῦ) provides good rhetorical alliteration, supplemented further by the use of "all" (πάσης; NRSV: "utmost") later in the sentence.[152] Such alliteration was fitting for the opening of a speech or work,[153] and the very phrase is attested in other legal petitions.[154] Even without alliteration, writers might couple πανταχοῦ with other expressions of plenitude to reinforce the sense of sufficiency.[155] "Everywhere" hyperbole appears in rhetorically trained Latin as well: "Everywhere in the whole world at every hour."[156]

In fact, however, Judeans did not acknowledge Felix's supposed peace and reforms everywhere, and Felix knew that they did not. But this "everywhere" forms a nice contrast with the allegation in 24:5, that Paul foments trouble throughout the world. "Gratitude" (εὐχαριστίας) is the appropriate response to a benefactor,[157] applied elsewhere in Acts to Paul's response to God (27:35; 28:15).

147. Narrative ironies could be used to indicate guilt: thus Verres spared the pirates but slew the citizens (Cic. *Verr.* 2.5.29.73–74; 2.5.30.77); Saul spared the Amalekites but practiced *herem* against the priests (1 Sam 22:19; cf. earlier against Saul's Benjaminite people, in Judg 20:48). For various types of irony in ancient sources, see, e.g., Ray, *Irony*, 34–49; Duke, *Irony*, 8–12; and esp. now the excellent work of Berg, *Irony*, 25–99 (particularly 79–99).

148. The NRSV moves this to Acts 24:2, to begin Tertullus's address.

149. Hemer, *Acts in History*, 129. See comment on Acts 1:1 (the discussion on Theophilus).

150. Free birth was a prerequisite for equestrian status (Millar and Burton, "Equites," 551), though Felix's brother Pallas received the praetorian insignia (Pliny *Ep.* 8.6.4).

151. Still, it might not be coincidence that Luke, who may write with at least one equestrian in mind (Luke 1:3) and probably knew Felix's status, could not bring himself to include the title in Paul's address to Felix, although Paul used it for Festus (Acts 26:25).

152. Witherington, *Acts*, 706. Cf. Acts 17:30; 1 Cor 4:17; 9:22; 10:33; 12:6; 15:28; Eph 1:23; Col 3:11; perhaps Sir 50:22. Cf. the practice of reusing a term in different compound forms in one context (Hermog. *Method* 15.432).

153. See, e.g., Heb 1:1 (as often noted, e.g., Thurén, "Writings," 589; Lane, *Hebrews*, 6; Aune, *Dictionary of Rhetoric*, 212). It also appears elsewhere (e.g., Mus. Ruf. frg. 38, p. 136.2; Fronto *Ad Ant. imp.* 1.3; CD IV, 14; cf. Black, "Oration at Olivet," 86; van der Horst, "Cornutus," 170, citing Cornutus *Summ.* 17 [Lang, 26, lines 7–8]; in the LXX, see Lee, "Translations: Greek," 778). Any accumulation of similar sounds, consecutive or not, provided rhetorical παρήχησις (see Hermog. *Inv.* 4.7.194, citing Xen. *Hell.* 7.1.41; Hom. *Od.* 24.465; *Il.* 6.201–2). Some authors were said to overuse this device (Dion. Hal. *Demosth.* 26).

154. Conzelmann, *Acts*, 198.

155. E.g., Mus. Ruf. 9, p. 72.32 (ἀεὶ . . . πανταχοῦ); frg. 34 (using a negation), perhaps polemicizing against rhetorical overkill. The expression is thus pleonastic.

156. Pliny E. *N.H.* 2.5.22 (trans. H. Rackham, LCL, 1:183).

157. See, e.g., Sen. E. *Controv.* 9.1.intro.; 9.1.9; Pliny *Ep.* 2.13.9; 7.15.3; 7.31.7; further comment on Acts 23:17–18.

d. Plea for a Patient Hearing (24:4)

Some of the language of 24:4 (ἐπὶ πλεῖον and συντόμως) has been compared to an "administrative style."[158] One particularly noteworthy feature, however, is Tertullus's promise to be brief and the consequent abrupt end of his praise. Presumably the praise went on at somewhat greater length than in Luke's summary, and the remainder of the speech is also longer than the précis in our text. But requests for hearers' patience were common (cf. comment on Acts 26:3).

I. THE VIRTUE OF BREVITY

After extensive praise, a writer or speaker might halt, pleading the danger of what earlier Greeks called κόρος, praise so excessive that it annoys the audience and hence distracts from true achievements.[159] The promise of brevity appeared commonly in prefaces, and those writing digests made natural use of it (e.g., Val. Max. 1.pref.).[160] Concise speech was pleasant in conversation (Philost. *Hrk.* 29.6) and among moralists (e.g., Val. Max. 7.2.ext. 4, on a saying of Plato);[161] it was also valued in letters.[162]

Orators likewise valued brevity;[163] even those who disdained the principle themselves recognized that it was the usual opinion.[164] Classical Athenian orators might promise to communicate "in the fewest possible words" (Isaeus *Philoct.* 19) or might announce that they would not need much time to prove a particular case (Lysias *Or.* 23.1, §166). Cicero also praised brevity (*Or. Brut.* 40.139), though it is not surprising, given our knowledge of his own practice, that he counted this virtue "difficult" (*Brut.* 43.158).

Of course, one should not be so concise as to obscure one's point (Dion. Hal. 2 *Amm.* 2). One should be copious where necessary, Tacitus opines, but brief whenever possible (*Dial.* 23). (His friend Pliny apparently agreed,[165] but he lamented that the usual desire for brevity forced the omission of too much that was important.)[166] Some orators who were philosophically minded rejected undue time restrictions (Dio Chrys. *Or.* 12.38). Further, one who wished to attack another's case could assault its brevity, pointing out that had the opponent possessed genuinely strong arguments, he would have run out of time rather than out of words (Cic. *Rosc. Amer.* 32.89).[167]

---

158. Conzelmann, *Acts*, 198.

159. Pindar *Ol.* 2.95 (W. H. Race in LCL, 73n5, cites also Pindar *Pyth.* 1.82; 8.32; *Nem.* 10.20).

160. Wardle, *Valerius Maximus*, 67, notes also Vitruv. *Arch.* 5.pref. 3 as another preface, and Frontin. *Str.* 1.pref. among other digests. In other prologues, see Artem. *Oneir.* 1.pref.; Sen. E. *Controv.* 1.pref. 24; *Let. Aris.* 8.

161. See Jas 1:19; cf. Prov 10:19; 17:28; Eccl 5:2–3, 7; Eurip. *Aeolus* frg. 28 (Stob. 3.35.3); also the emphasis on brevity in Johnson, "Taciturnity," 331–32.

162. E.g., Pliny *Ep.* 2.5.13; 3.9.27; 4.5.3; 9.13.26 (though Pliny, in fact, considers longer letters a sign of affection, 9.20.1; 9.32). Papyrus letters averaged only eighty-seven words (and could be as few as eighteen; Richards, *Letter Writing*, 163); Paul's letters flout epistolary convention (Anderson, *Rhetorical Theory*, 113).

163. E.g., Aeschines *Embassy* 51; Dion. Hal. *Thuc.* 55; Lysias 5; Tac. *Dial.* 25; Fronto *Ad Ant. imp.* 1.2.4; Max. Tyre 18.6; 25.2; Philost. *Vit. soph.* 2.4.569. Johnson, *Acts*, 410, adds Lucian *Indictment* 20–21; Quint. *Inst.* 8.3.82; Longin. *Subl.* 9.14; 42.1–2. For the rhetorical principle, see Anderson, *Glossary*, 30, 112–13 (esp. for conciseness in narration, citing esp. *Rhet. Her.* 1.14; 4.68; Cic. *Inv.* 1.28; *De or.* 2.326–28; Theon *Progymn.* [*RG* 2:83, line 14, to 2:84, line 17]; Quint. *Inst.* 2.31–32, 40–51; 4.2.42); later, Nicolaus *Progymn.* 3, "On Narrative," 14.

164. E.g., Pliny *Ep.* 1.20.1 (quoting another); 6.33.7–8.

165. Pliny *Ep.* 4.5.4.

166. Pliny *Ep.* 1.20.2–3; 5.6.44. He felt that laziness drove many to brevity (1.20.23; 4.16.3; 6.2.5).

167. When convenient, however, Cicero claimed that he could speak briefly because the case was already spelled out in an earlier trial and because he was prone to brevity personally (*Quinct.* 10.34)! Cf. Macrinus's similar claim for brevity, based on the hearer's knowledge of the facts, in Hdn. 5.1.2; or Aeschines's eschewing of repeating facts, except in summary, in *Embassy* 118.

Lest an advocate protest this against Cicero, the latter insisted that he would use every hour and minute legally permitted him (*Verr.* 2.1.9.24–25).

Some orators were most convincing when most concise (Tac. *Dial.* 31); some forms of speeches were meant to be brief (Men. Rhet. 2.7, 405.15–16, 29). Failure to state one's point concisely could call for criticism (Dion. Hal. *Demosth.* 18); redundancy was inappropriate (*Demosth.* 24). When a speaker stated his point too lavishly rather than concisely, it was harder to hold the hearers' attention (*Demosth.* 20). A speech that was too long could stir prejudice, although one could counter this by protesting that there were many facts to cover (*Rhet. Alex.* 29, 1437b.29–30).[168]

Writers often sought to honor the virtue of conciseness. Protestations of the need for brevity could accompany transition from an old to a new point—for example, when leaving the prologue (Artem. *Oneir.* 1.pref.).[169] One could explain that one had many more available examples but must use restraint (Val. Max. 3.8.ext. 1) or focus only on the best examples (2.7.5; 3.7.ext. 5).[170] This limitation might be employed for the sake of brevity (Jos. *Ag. Ap.* 1.251) or to prevent one's writing from being "tedious."[171] One might claim to limit the praise, implying that far more could be said,[172] or even complain about the impossibility of exhausting the subject.[173]

A rhetorical critic might point out that he avoids quoting in full in order to save space (Dion. Hal. *Isaeus* 14)[174] or the reader's time (Dion. Hal. *Demosth.* 40; cf. Heb 11:32).[175] He could furnish countless examples, but to prevent inordinate length, he stops with those adequate to demonstrate his point (Dion. Hal. *Thuc.* 55). To continue would risk writing a textbook rather than an essay (Dion. Hal. *Demosth.* 46). One might promise to examine an issue more fully in a separate work "if time permits" (*Demosth.* 32).[176] Poets, too, might complain that time constraints forced them to omit much.[177] One could also claim, toward the end of one's work, to have written "briefly."[178] A sage might claim to be concise and to the point, avoiding frivolous rhetorical devices (Philost. *Vit. Apoll.* 1.17). Some claims about brevity, however, reflected mock humility.[179]

168. Denouncing others' crimes openly could also offend one's audience (Ps.-Cic. *Invect. Sall.* 8.22) if it was not handled judiciously.

169. So also speakers (Dio Chrys. *Or.* 18.5).

170. Cf. Polyb. 2.56.4; Dion. Hal. *Demosth.* 42; Men. Rhet. 2.4, 393.25–30; Plut. *Alex.* 1.1, 3; John 20:30; 21:25; cf. Arist. *Poet.* 8.1.3, 1451a; Mus. Ruf. 10, p. 78.22; Phaedrus 3.epil. 6–7; Diog. Laert. 6.7.98. The need, opines Musonius, is not for multiple proofs but for strong ones (Mus. Ruf. 1, p. 32.5–17).

171. Dion. Hal. *Lit. Comp.* 11; Sen. E. *Controv.* 1.pref. 24. Some subjects, however, a teller might never weary of (Val. Max. 3.7.1g), generating, by such comments, enthusiasm for the subjects.

172. Lysias *Or.* 2.2, §190; 2.54, §195; Philost. *Vit. soph.* 2.17.597.

173. E.g., Lysias *Or.* 2.1, §190; Vell. Paterc. 2.29.2; 2.46.1; 2.89.1, 5–6 (cf. also 2.54.1; 2.96.2–3; 2.119.1; 2.124.1; 2.126.1); Plut. *Mal. Hdt.* 1, *Mor.* 854F; Iambl. *V.P.* 28.135; Philo *Abr.* 1; 1 Macc 9:22; *Pesiq. Rab.* 3:2; *Song Rab.* 1:3, §1.

174. Cf. Dion. Hal. *Thuc.* 55; *Isaeus* 19–20; *Demosth.* 42, 46, 58; *Lit. Comp.* 11.

175. One might also stop short for the sake of credibility (Diod. Sic. 4.8.2) or abbreviate for the sake of readability (2 Macc 2:24–25; cf. Iambl. *V.P.* 27.128; 28.135).

176. Within the same work, see Heb 6:3.

177. Pindar *Pyth.* 4.247–48; *Nem.* 4.33–34; *Ol.* 2.95; cf. Diog. Laert. 6.2.69. See esp. the hyperbole in Hom. *Od.* 3.113–17.

178. E.g., Sall. *Ep. Caes.* 13.8; Heb 13:22; 1 Pet 5:12; at the beginning, *Barn.* 1.5. Given the (mock) apologies in Pliny *Ep.* 3.9.26–27, 37; 9.13.26, Hebrews can hardly have been thought brief if we take it as a letter (though Pliny claimed to prefer long letters, 9.20.1; 9.32). For Hebrews as a sermon, see, e.g., Goppelt, *Theology*, 2:240; Lane, *Hebrews*, lxix–lxxv; Hagner, *Hebrews*, xxiii; Aune, *Environment*, 213; as (overlapping with the sermonic suggestion) homiletic midrash, Buchanan, *Hebrews*, xix, 246; Fuller, "Hebrews," 10; Bruce, *Message*, 74; a sort of essay, Deissmann, *Studies*, 49; Kee, *Origins*, 150. A letter-essay (cf., e.g., Dionysius of Halicarnassus *1 Epistle to Ammaeus*; Cicero *Orator ad M. Brutum*; 2 Maccabees; cf. Reed, "Epistle," 173, noting the title λόγος) seems likeliest (with, e.g., Erdman, *Hebrews*, 11).

179. See, e.g., Symm. *Ep.* 1.14.1 (for a more genuine claim about brevity, cf. 1.15.1).

II. Speeches' Claims to Conciseness

More important, orators' speeches also illustrate this practice abundantly. An orator might protest that he could say more but must move ahead (Demosth. *Cor.* 266). He could claim, as Cicero often does when denouncing Verres, that he must pass over an opponent's numerous villainies for lack of time,[180] thereby implying many more than he could relate. Likewise, he could note that all eternity would be insufficient to finish praising his subjects, thereby excusing the need to cut the praise off somewhere.[181]

Many writers and orators undoubtedly had more information; others probably simply used brevity as a convenient excuse to imply the existence of more information than they had. This sometimes resembles paralipsis, the technique of mentioning something in the process of disclaiming opportunity to mention it (e.g., Phlm 19).[182] In an extreme case, one could apologize for speaking at inordinate length—after one had finished what one wanted to say (Ael. Arist. *Def. Or.* 73, §23D).[183] Apparently some ancients would also pretend that they were more concise than they actually had been; hence an advocate might promise to be brief, needing few words, yet speak as long as the accuser (who also claimed not to like long speeches; Lucian *Indictment* 20–21).

To make speeches shorter, orators could employ shorter words and recapitulate only at the conclusion (as an earlier writer suggested, *Rhet. Alex.* 22, 1434b.11–18);[184] Tertullus has been choosing words for their effect, not their conciseness. One could also omit whatever was not directly relevant to one's point, retaining only what was essential for clarity (30, 1438a.38–41).

Some orators liked to speak at length,[185] but in the law courts by this period, there were limits.[186] Although, in earlier times, people could listen to someone speak all day (cf. Tac. *Dial.* 19), probably already by Paul's day forensic orators were limited to about one or two hours for their speeches (*Dial.* 38), or perhaps a total of nine hours for the advocates' defense speeches in an important trial (Pliny *Ep.* 4.9.9).[187] Cicero, who liked the freedom to speak extensively,[188] complained that the new *lex Pompeia* in 52 B.C.E. allowed Roman speakers for the defense only three hours per speaker (*Brutus* 93.324); elsewhere he notes that previously the trial judges fixed the time allotted each party (*Quinct.* 9.33). In a proem, as here, one must be careful not to "weary" the judge (Quint. *Decl.* 338.3).

180. Cic. *Verr.* 2.2.1.1–2; 2.4.26.57; 2.4.46.102; 2.4.47.105; cf. similarly *Flacc.* 5.12. Isoc. *Antid.* 140, 310, 320 feigned inability to complete all his thoughts on a matter within the required time. See other examples at Acts 24:5.

181. E.g., Lysias *Or.* 2.1, §190; 2.54, §195 (cf. 2.2); cf. John 21:25; Max. Tyre 25.2.

182. On paralipsis, see, e.g., *Rhet. Her.* 4.27.37; Demosth. *Cor.* 268 (18.3); Hermog. *Method* 7.419–20; *Inv.* 2.5.117; Anderson, *Glossary*, 88–89. For further examples, see comment on Acts 24:19.

183. Cf. Cic. *Verr.* 2.4.49.109 (trans. L. H. G. Greenwood, LCL, 8:417): "I will weary you no further with this description" but come straight to my point. But often even those who offered to stop wanted the audience to encourage them to continue (Sen. Y. *Ep. Lucil.* 95.2; cf. Heb 5:11).

184. One could also expand speeches by including more recapitulation (*Rhet. Alex.* 20, 1433b.29–1434a.17).

185. For orators speaking at length, see, e.g., Winter, "Official Proceedings," 307. This is also illustrated in "N" documents (320; these may have been the advocate's ad hoc summaries of prospective arguments; so Crook, *Advocacy*, 117). A Roman aristocratic trial might require two days to listen to both sides, with the sentence rendered on the third (Val. Max. 5.8.3; cf. Pliny *Ep.* 2.11.18; cf. five days in Tac. *Ann.* 3.13), though some plaintiffs might have only minutes each in imperial assize districts in Egypt (cf. comment on Acts 18:14).

186. E.g., Pliny *Ep.* 1.23.2; 3.20.3 (noted for its breach). That the law permits speech at fuller length (1.20.11) probably refers to nonforensic speech (cf. Sen. E. *Controv.* 7.pref. 8).

187. The prosecution received six hours (Pliny *Ep.* 4.9.9), and Pliny notes that he spoke for the prosecution nearly five hours (2.11.14). Pliny worked hard at another, seven-hour speech (4.16.3); speaking or writing at length was fine so long as one *seemed* brief by sticking to the point (5.6.42–43).

188. Cicero could denounce a bill at length (Plut. *Cic.* 12.5).

III. REQUESTS FOR MORE TIME OR PATIENCE

Speakers could appeal for additional time (approval of which would automatically grant it to the opponents as well; Pliny *Ep.* 6.2.3), and judges could grant this request at their discretion (6.2.7–8). One useful way of reducing long orations was to require each side to address, one at a time, each of the main points in question.[189]

Classical Athens used a water clock to regulate speeches' length, though it was turned off during readings of depositions and laws;[190] the practice continued in this period.[191] Though administrators listened to minor cases quickly (or subordinates handled them; see comment on Acts 18:14), a case against a Roman citizen brought by the high priest Ananias, who had secured Felix's position, would require more extensive consideration.

Like Tertullus, many speakers begged their hearers to continue to listen to them, whether in the classical period,[192] the republic,[193] or the empire.[194] In a speech written by Demosthenes, a speaker begs his audience to hear him silently as they have heard out his opponent.[195] This was the standard convention advised in rhetorical handbooks, as a Hellenistic rhetorician points out (Dion. Hal. *Lysias* 24). (The invitation to hear was common outside forensic rhetoric as well; see comment on Acts 2:14–15.) A rhetorically trained writer might also promise readers not to delay them further, often at the end of a preface (Sen. E. *Controv.* 1.pref. 24; *Let. Aris.* 8). The basis for Tertullus's appeal to hear the case is yet more flattery—that is, based on Felix's ἐπιείκεια (clemency, indulgence, or tolerance; see BDAG).[196]

e. The Charges (24:5–6a)

Tertullus now moves from deceptively praising a corrupt governor to deceptively denouncing Christ's apostle.[197] Tertullus's charges might strike the members of Luke's ideal audience as deeply ironic. If they knew of Claudius's decree or similar language in its aftermath, they might find ironic the charges against the "pestilence" of Jewish unrest applied to Paul, who was, in fact, one of its targets (Acts 23:14–15). His ac-

189. See Suet. *Nero* 15; Pliny *Ep.* 6.22.2.
190. E.g., Isaeus *Menec.* 34; Lysias *Or.* 23.4, §166; classical Athens in Max. Tyre 3.8. On water clocks, see, e.g., Dohrn-van Rossum, "Clocks," 462–63; Lucian *Hipp.* 8.
191. Lucian *Fisherman* 10 (speaking of the defendant's allotted "water"), 28; *Indictment* 15, 16, 19; Apul. *Apol.* 28, 37, 94; Philost. *Vit. Apoll.* 8.2 (where the secretary offers to give Apollonius the water in the water clock that he needs); 8.4 (where the accuser demands the right to set the water clock to avoid Apollonius's talking too long); Libanius *Topics* 4.12. Commentators (Conzelmann, *Acts*, 198; Johnson, *Acts*, 410) often cite Lucian *Indictment* 15, 19, 26.
192. E.g., Aeschines *Embassy* 44 (cf. 24); Isaeus *Menec.* 2 (toward the beginning); *Cleonymus* 48 (beginning his final summation); Lysias *Or.* 19.2, §152.
193. Cic. *Verr.* 2.4.47.105; Quinct. 6.22.
194. Conzelmann, *Acts*, 198–99, cites Lucian *Indictment* 16; *Acta Isidori*.
195. Demosth. *Eub.* 1. Cf. similarly a request, combating prejudice, that the jury treat both parties impartially (Lysias *Or.* 15.1, §144).
196. The term connotes a virtue (e.g., Dio Chrys. *Ep.* 1, to Rufus) that sometimes appears in conjunction with πραΰτης (considerateness; Lucian *Alex.* 61; 2 Cor 10:1). It naturally suits one of superior rank, e.g., a master's treatment of workers (Dio Chrys. *Or.* frg. 5 [Stob. *Flor.* 4, 19.46 {Hense, 430}; 62.46 {Meineke}]) or a gentle, caring ruler (Dio Chrys. *Or.* 3.41). Stoics could criticize this indulgence (Arius Did. *Epit.* 2.7.11d, pp. 66–67.32–34).
197. Ancient hearers might have imagined (and lectors may have often reenacted) a typical gesture for denunciation at this point: stretching out "a slightly drooped index finger, with the two outer fingers curved" (Shiell, *Reading Acts*, 56). Cf. also gestures for reproach and refutation (extending the hand firmly and rapidly, 69–71); gestures of aversion (turning away the face, 76–77); gestures and the tone for indignation (62–65, 88), perhaps relevant for however much of Acts 24:6–7 is original. When debating or contending, one might extend or otherwise move the arm quickly, pace back and forth, and sometimes stamp one's foot (Hall, "Delivery," 225; cf. 224, citing *Rhet. Her.* 3.27). For gestures in ancient Israel, cf. Matthews, "Making Your Point."

cusers' claim that Paul spread dissension (in contrast to Felix spreading peace, 24:2) throughout the world (in contrast to Felix's praise everywhere, 24:3) would also prove ironic. Paul had not spread his message throughout the Roman "world" or even to its capital; but their instigation will help propel Paul to Rome, to the court of Caesar himself (27:24). And by following the conventional defense procedure of reversing the prosecution charges, Luke's larger narrative effectively shows that the source of the riots was Paul's enemies (albeit not always Jewish and not usually the Sanhedrin), not Paul.[198]

i. Ēthos and Broad-Based Guilt (24:5)

"Finding" guilt in someone is a common expression in Luke-Acts (Luke 23:2, 4, 14, 22; Acts 13:28; 23:9, 29; 24:20) and elsewhere (e.g., John 18:38; 19:4; see further BDAG). For Tertullus, Paul's alleged defilement of the temple (Acts 24:6) offered simply the most recent and representative example of a larger category of seditious acts (24:5). Forensic oratory was notoriously feisty and "warlike" (Pliny *Ep.* 7.9.7).

It was common to paint one's opponent's wickedness with a broad brush, emphasizing that one could offer, at most, samples of his crimes (cf. the protest of brevity in Acts 24:4).[199] Thus a classical Athenian orator complained that his problem in prosecuting his opponent, Eratosthenes, was not in knowing how to begin the accusation but in knowing where to end it (Lysias *Or.* 12.1, §120). So many were one man's crimes "that not even were he put to death a number of times" could he provide satisfaction for them (28.1, §179).[200]

Another orator warned that simply recounting all his opponent's crimes would take too long, squandering his hearers' time, and so he had to content himself with a few brief examples (Aeschines *Tim.* 109). In the republic, Cicero notes that the example he recounts is part of a much larger pattern of abuses (*Verr.* 2.2.47.118) but that if he does not stop listing the accused's crimes, his speech will never finish (2.2.48.118). Hearers expected such exaggerations in forensic rhetoric; one speaker complains that his accuser has gone beyond all others in shamelessness (Lysias *Or.* 24.13, §524). Rhetorical paralipsis could also become more specific, for example, beginning a speech by noting that one could additionally have charged the defendant with murder but settled for merely the charge at hand (Hermog. *Inv.* 1.3.104).

Judges and juries decided cases partly on the basis of *ēthos*—that is, character (*Rhet. Her.* 4.50.63; see further discussion at Acts 24:11, 14–17, 16).[201] In rhetorical theory, the speaker's character was important for persuasion.[202] Orators and judges could infer probable *ēthos* from a person's status (see comment on Acts 24:1) or past behavior (see comment on Acts 23:1). Thus one might examine the character of

---

198. A point not lost on Acts' ancient readers; thus Chrys. *Hom. Acts* 50 finds irony here in that it is Paul's very accusers who have stirred unrest.

199. Orators could elaborate on the crimes to eliminate sympathy (Hermog. *Progymn.* 6, "On Commonplace," 14). They also associated crimes with particular character types, on which they could then elaborate at length (cf. Nicolaus *Progymn.* 7, "On Commonplace," 36–37, 41)—assuming, of course, they had time (Acts 24:4)!

200. Trans. W. R. M. Lamb, LCL, 589.

201. The rational concept of *ēthos* formulated by Aristotle and the terminology were less in use by Paul's day (Aune, *Dictionary of Rhetoric*, 169–73, esp. 170–71; cf. Anderson, *Glossary*, 61–63; for ambiguity in Aristotle's use, cf. Woerther, "Origines"; for ἦθος and emotion in Aristotle, see also Hall, "Delivery," 232), but character remained a crucial issue in forensic rhetoric (Crook, *Advocacy*, 34); Perdue, "Rhetoric," 191, finds it emphasized even in Wisdom of Solomon. Ἦθος was especially important early in the speech, just as πάθος was useful for the rousing conclusion (Aune, *Dictionary of Rhetoric*, 171).

202. McTavish, "Priest."

respective claimants in the final part of a speech (Isaeus *Nicost.* 27)[203] or open a speech with comments on a person's character (Sallust *Catil.* 5.1). It was helpful to begin establishing the character of the claimants already in the proem (Quint. *Decl.* 338.4).

Denouncing opponents' character was standard forensic rhetoric.[204] Vilifying opponents' behavior toward a city would play well with earlier civic assemblies (e.g., Isaeus *Dicaeog.* 46); it was helpful to portray an opponent's actions as harmful to the people (*Rhet. Alex.* 4, 1426b.29–35). Describing shameful behavior was better than using insulting titles, which could create a backlash (35, 1441b.16–20); in public, one might even resort to sarcasm rather than direct attack (1441b.24–28). In Paul's day, however, courts were vicious, with no holds barred, especially when the accusers were of such distinguished rank as here (Acts 24:1). Paul can thus be denounced directly as a "pest" (24:5).

It was, indeed, customary not only to attack on the basis of the charges but to smear the accused person's character in other ways, slandering him or her as viciously as possible.[205] When Fronto learns that the person he must prosecute is a friend of Caesar's, he therefore promises to stick to the charges and not invent other accusations, but normally, shocking charges demanded prosecution with shocking tactics (*Ad M. Caes.* 3.3).[206] When Josephus wishes to counter Apion's anti-Jewish history, he also attacks his lexical work as a γραμματικός, since this will help undermine the scholar's credibility.[207]

Inventing additional offenses to prejudice the audience against an adversary's character was apparently common enough to warrant parody; the discourse of a losing speaker in a debate degenerates into insult: "Don't we know who your father was, and how your mother was a courtesan, and that you strangled your brother. . . ?"[208] In another case, an angry man threatens punishment for his opponent's burning the Acropolis. Informed that the Acropolis has not been burned, he replies that the offense, then, was stealing from the treasury. When informed that the treasury has not been violated, he charges that it will be.[209]

Accepted forms of legal polemic included attacks on the opponent's friends, witnesses, and so forth; "muckraking and fabrication" were commonplace.[210] People respected Roman politicians not just for their patriotism or benevolence but also for *inimicitiae*, which included pursuing their honor by shaming their enemies; this was a mandatory step in gaining more *dignitas*.[211] Cicero claims that he condescends to

203. The principle, the importance of examining the claimants' character, is laid out explicitly in Isaeus *Nicost.* 27.

204. Dion. Hal. *Isaeus* 3, 9; Cic. *Scaur.* 13.29; Demosth. *Or.* 21.1 (cited in Hermog. *Method* 5.418); Quint. *Decl.* 252.10; Apul. *Apol.* 1, 25; Hermog. *Inv.* 1.1.99. Ideally, one could attack both character in general and specific acts (Hermog. *Inv.* 1.2.102–3).

205. Isaeus passim, e.g., *Astyph.* 16; Lucian *Runaways* 18; Tac. *Ann.* 3.12 (cf. the attack on a defendant's previous career in 3.10). Had the defendant accused me of merely killing his father rather than mine, one complained, I would not be taking him to court (Lysias *Or.* 10.2, §116). Rhetoricians also learned to multiply existing charges by subdividing them into component elements (Hermog. *Inv.* 1.2.101–2).

206. Marcus Aurelius replied that this would win Fronto more favor from those sympathetic to the accused (Fronto *Ad M. Caes.* 3.5). An advocate might have to knowingly charge someone falsely but might manage to reduce harshness to the level necessary to his role (Quint. *Decl.* 333.8).

207. See Dillery, "Apion Historian." Character assassination offered a simple "argument," and Apion made an easy target (Jones, "Apion").

208. Lucian *Z. Rants* 52 (trans. A. M. Harmon, LCL, 2:167, 169).

209. Lucian *Tim.* 52–53. Likewise, a Cynic, angry at the last speaker, denounces him with many malicious reports in *Peregr.* 31.

210. Winter, *Left Corinth*, 66. For attacks on a person's friends, see, e.g., Aeschines *Tim.* 54–57. For denouncing opposing witnesses and supporters, see, e.g., Apul. *Apol.* 57–60; for praising a supporting witness, 61.

211. Winter, *Left Corinth*, 74.

attack Vatinius not because anyone would grant credence to such a worthless person but only to crush his arrogance (*Vat.* 1.1–2). Cicero presumes, or pretends to presume, his audience's knowledge of another's wickedness but lavishly expands what the category of that person's wickedness involved (*Pis.* 27.66). Apuleius notes that the misbehavior of Rufinus, who supports Apuleius's opponent, has been known for years: he is "the deviser of all falsehoods, the architect of all pretences, the breeding-ground of all evils, yes, the place, the haunt, the brothel of licence and gluttony" (*Apol.* 74). But, of course, Rufinus is not alone in his wickedness: "his whole house is that of a pimp, his whole household corrupt. He himself is infamous, his wife a whore, and his sons are of the same calibre" (75). Orators could stir an audience's passions by considering what the victims or their survivors had suffered[212]—quietly sidestepping the question of the defendant's guilt.

For Luke's audience, Tertullus is a cunning orator, fitting the worst stereotypes of seductive sophists.[213] Ancients understood the principle that falsehood appears more credible when mixed with some truth (Polyb. 34.2.2). The charges against Paul can seem plausible precisely because they are not the first such charges against him (Acts 16:20–21; 17:7; 18:13; 19:26–27, though Luke shows the implausibility or rejection in each case). One who had led a life above reproach was difficult to convict (e.g., Dion. Hal. *Ant. rom.* 7.58.2). Someone who has never had to be in court before or be charged with a scandal before is more likely to be innocent;[214] when necessary, a defender could admit that accusations had been made against his client in the past but protest that they never resulted in a conviction.[215] Speakers sometimes contended that the burden of proof rested more heavily on someone who was frequently charged than on someone who had rarely been brought to court.[216] If the defendant had a bad reputation, one orator charges, it was his own fault; a truly honorable person ought to live in such a manner as to be above suspicion.[217] Negative character made charges believable,[218] whereas positive character made them difficult to accept.[219] Defending himself based on his character, Apuleius avers, "Consistency of character with regard to virtue or wickedness . . . formed sure proof of embracing or spurning crime" (*Apol.* 90).[220]

ii. Paul the "Pest"

Tertullus not only dismisses Paul with the derisive "this man" (instead of naming him)[221] but lambasts him as a dangerous "plague." Denouncing Paul as a "pest" was

212. E.g., Lysias *Or.* 13.46, §134; Tac. *Ann.* 2.71; stirring anger in Libanius *Topics* 1.1, 14, 22; 3.2; 4.20. Stirring audience feeling against the defendant was an ideal conclusion to a prosecution speech (*Rhet. Alex.* 36, 1443b.16–21).

213. For Philo's Hellenistic Jewish critique of the abuse of sophistry for deception, see Winter, *Philo and Paul*, 91–94 (more generally, 83–98).

214. Sus 27; Isaeus *Aristarch.* 1 (though pleading especially that he is a less experienced speaker); *Cleon.* 35; Lysias *Or.* 5.2–3, §§102–3; 16.10, §146; Dio Chrys. *Or.* 46.7; Char. *Chaer.* 5.7.2. Lucian likes to parody this claim (*Phal.* 1.14; *Par.* 56). Prosecutors looked for past wrongdoing to cite a pattern (Hermog. *Inv.* 2.5.117–19).

215. Fronto *Ad am.* 2.7.5.

216. Cf., e.g., Isaeus *Aristarch.* 1; Lysias *Or.* 5.2–3, §§102–3; 7.24–29, §§110–11; 16.12, §146; Cic. *Sest.* 30.64. Apuleius charged that his accuser had "already been convicted of lying before the city prefect in a highly important case" (*Apol.* 3).

217. Aeschines *Tim.* 49. One who was above reproach would prove difficult to convict (Dion. Hal. *Ant. rom.* 7.58.2). The prosecutor might imaginatively depict the defendant's progressive moral deterioration through a series of crimes eventuating in the climactic accusation at hand (Libanius *Topics* 1.24–25; 2.18).

218. E.g., Quint. *Decl.* 313.15; 322.3; 331 intro; 331.21–22.

219. E.g., Quint. *Decl.* 314.2; 322.3; 351.8; 377.2–3.

220. Trans. Hunink, pp. 108–9.

221. With Horton, *Acts*, 374. On damning an enemy with anonymity, see comment on Acts 22:22.

strategic. The term λοιμός meant "pestilence" (as in Luke 21:11, where λοιμοί is conjoined with the similar-sounding λιμοί, "famines"). But it also applied to scoundrels who were contagious, moral "plagues," the most common use by far in the LXX.[222] Discord (στάσις, also Acts 24:5; 23:7) could also be described as a societal sickness (*Rhet. Alex.* 1, 1422b.33–36). Demosthenes used λοιμός for someone who subverted the good of the state (*Or.* 25.80);[223] someone being a "civic affliction" was a familiar expression for political unrest (Plato *Prot.* 322D).[224]

Perhaps even more relevant is that this charge closely echoes the phrase that the emperor Claudius had employed to describe Jews in 41 C.E.: "stirring up a plague everywhere, throughout the world."[225] (Cf. also Acts 17:6.) The context of Claudius's complaint was Jewish agitation for greater rights in Alexandria, such as Alexandrian citizenship (permitted only to Greeks).[226] Claudius warned Jews in Alexandria not to join with those in Syria or Egypt as if plotting against the entire world. He also warned that Alexandrians should stop denying local Jews the rights to practice their customs, granted by emperors (P.Lond. 1912.82–88); if, however, the Jews continued to agitate for further rights (such as Alexandrian citizenship), he would punish them as those "stirring a widespread plague [νόσον] infecting all the world [οἰκουμένης]" (P.Lond. 1912.98–100; CPJ 1.153.99–100). Being a "pest" encouraging unrest may have been the most damaging charge to level against a Jew in the decades between Claudius's decree and Jerusalem's revolt.[227] How better could the Jerusalem elite demonstrate their fidelity to Rome against stirrers of this well-known Jewish unrest, Tertullus argued, than by opposing one of its agents—namely, Paul?[228] (The tribune had quickly been disabused of precisely this notion in Acts 21:38.)

Would Luke's audience be aware of an earlier emperor's decree in Alexandria? Claudius's later policies regarding Judaism probably affected them more directly (18:2), but in Roman colonies such as Philippi and Corinth, the decree may have been known, and Corinth's Jewish community undoubtedly discussed and remembered it. It is possible that the language even passed into common usage. (A substantially later pagan anti-Jewish work might echo it, albeit in Alexandria.)[229] Whether Luke and his audience knew it or not, however, the decree would surely have been known to Felix, to Ananias, and to Tertullus.

III. THE NEW CHARGE OF *SEDITIO*

Whether or not Luke's audience might think of the anti-Jewish libel best attested in Claudius's decree, Roman rhetorical handbooks emphasized that the charge of agitation (στάσις) or sedition was the most effective charge;[230] this charge was dangerous under Claudius and Nero, though no more so than under Tiberius (as in Luke 23:2–5) and some other rulers. An ideal ruler should suppress unrest (στάσις, Mus.

---

222. E.g., 1 Sam 1:16; 2:12; 30:22; 2 Chr 13:7; Prov 19:25; 21:24; 22:10; 24:9; 29:8; 1 Macc 10:61; 15:3, 21.

223. BDAG; Fitzmyer, *Acts*, 733.

224. Riesner, *Early Period*, 100.

225. P.Lond. 1912.82–100; CPJ 2:36–55, §153.

226. Claudius, who was generous with Roman citizenship where convenient (see comment on Acts 22:28), probably guarded Alexandrian citizenship less out of conviction than to maintain order.

227. Sherwin-White, *Society*, 51 (emphasizing the narrative's contemporary language); Rapske, *Custody*, 161; cf. Riesner, *Early Period*, 100; Witherington, *Acts*, 707.

228. "The accusers of Paul were putting themselves on the side of the government" (Sherwin-White, *Society*, 52–53). Paul's accusers may intend a deliberate echo (with, e.g., Jeffers, *World*, 167).

229. CPJ 2:78–79, §156c (the Jews are "wishing to stir up the entire world [ὅλην τὴν οἰκουμένην]").

230. Neyrey, "Forensic Defense Speech," 215–26 (citing *Rhet. Her.* 2.3.3–4; Cic. *Inv.* 2.5.16–2.8.28); followed by Winter, "Official Proceedings," 320; Witherington, *Acts*, 707.

Ruf. 8, p. 64.13),²³¹ as Felix had attempted to do (Acts 24:2); now, Tertullus implies, Felix has the opportunity to demonstrate his justice again. The Romans dealt harshly with all cases of στάσις (see Luke 23:19, 25; Acts 19:20; cf. Mark 15:7). Ironically, Paul's case had generated στάσις among Jews recently; Luke uses this term to describe the Sanhedrin's own division over Paul's case (Acts 23:7, 10) and hence to underline the divisions that already existed between Pharisees and Sadducees there.

The primary charge is thus *seditio*, as in 17:6–7 and 18:12, an extremely dangerous offense with which to be charged;²³² this is a new charge not previously noted. The case against Paul has quietly dropped the original religious charges and accusers, rephrasing charges as political complaints important to a Roman court.²³³ Rhetoricians did sometimes cloud the real issues at hand, focusing on points not directly related to the case.²³⁴ Yet changing charges invited denunciation for having invented charges during withering cross-examination,²³⁵ and Felix had already heard a report of the outcome of the first hearing (23:28–29; see comment on Acts 24:20–21, the climax of Paul's argument). Were it not for weighty political considerations, Luke suggests, Felix might have thrown the case out of court.

Readers would know that Jesus faced the same charge of *seditio* in Luke 23:2 and was executed.²³⁶ He also faced multiple components in the charges against him before Pilate;²³⁷ the parallel with Jesus's execution thus builds suspense for Paul here. The chief priests told Pilate that Jesus was leading the people astray, forbidding taxes to Caesar and claiming to be a king (23:2), but also (most relevant here) that he stirred up the people from Galilee to Judea (23:5). Luke apparently invites members of his ideal audience who already view Jesus favorably to view favorably Paul's custody in the same terms.²³⁸

The flexible charge of *maiestas* against Paul could appear plausible; Nock emphasizes that "whatever Paul might say for himself, there had been riots in many places where he had been, and the Roman government did not like riots."²³⁹ That Luke makes no attempt to conceal such unrest in his narratives is telling; that Luke blames it fairly often on Jewish opposition fits the rhetorical technique of returning charges against one's opponents. Luke is undoubtedly historically correct that Paul's opponents associated him with unrest (leading to his Roman custody)²⁴⁰ and that, contrary to their claims, Paul was not politically seditious. Given the agendas of the historical Paul revealed in his letters, it is unthinkable that his aim was destabilization of the Roman order (cf. esp. Rom 13:1–7); it is also clear that he faced considerable opposition.²⁴¹

231. Philosophers such as Musonius made much of their view of the ideal ruler (e.g., Mus. Ruf. 8, p. 66.11; cf. Dio Chrys. *Or.* 1.21; 3.112; symposium in *Letter of Aristeas*), usually with minimal practical effect.

232. With Conzelmann, *Acts*, 199; Johnson, *Acts*, 411; Fitzmyer, *Acts*, 732.

233. Hemer, *Acts in History*, 129; Rapske, *Custody*, 160 (on prisonable charges, see 41–46). Paul was still accused of "attempting" to profane the temple (Acts 24:6), but this was a considerable scaling back of the original charge (21:28).

234. See La Bua, "*Obscuritas*" (citing Cicero's obfuscation).

235. E.g., Lysias *Or.* 7.2, §108; Cic. *Att.* 2.24. The defendant could easily charge that the plaintiff forgot the original complaint once it became necessary to prove and not simply allege a crime (Apul. *Apol.* 2). Failure to have raised a charge at an earlier hearing or occasion was suspicious (Quint. *Decl.* 301.19; Hermog. *Inv.* 3.5.148).

236. Mark 14:2–3 includes the "king of the Jews" charge but, while mentioning other charges, does not specify forbidding to pay taxes, which Luke may have from passion tradition or infer from Mark 12:13–15.

237. Noted, e.g., by Bruce, *Commentary*, 464n4.

238. With Padilla, *Speeches*, 222, Tertullus's charge is hostile within the narrative but, through dramatic irony, appears positive for Luke's ideal audience. On Luke's apologetic for Paul's innocence, see, e.g., Keener, "Apologetic."

239. Nock, *Paul*, 140.

240. The charges in Acts are not likely Luke's creation; see Keener, "Apologetic."

241. E.g., Rom 3:8; 15:31; 1 Cor 4:11–13; 2 Cor 1:8–10; 4:8–11; 6:5; 11:23–26; Gal 5:11; 6:12; Eph 3:1; 4:1; Phil 1:14–17; 1 Thess 2:2; 2 Thess 3:1–2; Phlm 9.

Inciting others to a crime was itself considered a crime only if the offense was treason.[242] *Maiestas*, or treason, was a very broad category of offense that could include even executing hostages without the emperor's permission;[243] more specifically, "internal treason or sedition" included "assembling a mob, armed or otherwise, against the interests of the state, or occupying temples or other places."[244] Sedition was a lesser charge, but when *maiestas* was hard to demonstrate, *seditio*, or stirring up the people, proved more suitable.[245] No clear line of demarcation separated treason from sedition, and they might share the same penalties.[246]

iv. Paul's Cumulative History with Riots

Tertullus presents a potentially damning and cumulative case against Paul; that Luke must mount an extensive (and, from our knowledge of Paul, virtually convincing) refutation of it throughout Acts indicates that the charges Luke reports were certainly leveled against Paul historically.[247]

The claim that he had stirred such unrest "among all Jews throughout the world" resembles, as noted above, Claudius's charge against the Jewish people as a whole (i.e., Paul's accusers charge that if there is Jewish unrest, Paul is one of its instigators).[248] It also fits conventional forensic hyperbole (also noted above).[249] Offenses "throughout the world" were incomparably terrible offenses.[250] It was possible to prove more hyperbolic than this: "Was there ever any riot [*seditio*]," Cicero demands, in which the object of his polemic "was not the leader? any rioter with whom he was not intimate? any disorderly meeting where he was not the ringleader?" (*Sest.* 52.1). Cicero's additional language was, however, exceptional; the charge against Paul reflects, in itself, quite strong forensic hyperbole. But once the hyperbole is taken into account, the charge likely reflects knowledge that Paul has been active over a wide geographic range. Acts itself attests that Paul had impacted a substantial number of Jewish communities in the eastern Mediterranean region, excluding Egypt.

Paul's arrest in Jerusalem, rather than in all these other places of alleged troublemaking, might seem more than coincidence, and the other claims would be questionable unless supported by evidence. Had there been time for research before this hearing (there was not, Acts 24:1), Paul's opponents might have listed riots with which Paul was associated instead of simply accusing him in a general way (probably on the basis of the Asian Jewish accusers' reports). Given sufficient warning, some Jews from Asia could have collected reports from other cities, though few would have been willing

242. Robinson, *Criminal Law*, 19.
243. Ibid., 76; as a broad category, 74–78.
244. Ibid., 76.
245. Ibid., 78–80.
246. Ibid., 80.
247. See Keener, "Apologetic." Wallace and Williams, *Acts*, 18–20, note six scenes in Acts where mobs are stirred against Paul, and observe that other sources from the period confirm that mobs were easily "manufactured."
248. Luke can hardly have thought this plausible, and if he had, he might have suppressed it the way he omitted the alleged association of Christ with unrest in Rome, if he knew the tradition we have in Suetonius (see comment on Acts 18:2).
249. Imperial propaganda also used "all the world" freely (e.g., *omnia* in Ovid *Tristia* 2.324; Vitruv. *Arch.* 1.pref. 1; Pliny E. *N.H.* 3.5.67; Dio Chrys. *Or.* 3.7; Men. Rhet. 2.12, 422.9–10; Jos. *War* 2.361; negatively, *4 Ezra* 11:1), applicable also to earlier Rome or other kingdoms (Xen. *Cyr.* 8.6.20; Polyb. 1.1; 1.64; 6.2.3; 6.50.6; 39.8.7; Corn. Nep. 18 [Eumenes], 3.3–4; 23 [Hannibal], 8.3; Sall. *Catil.* 36.4; Men. Rhet. 2.3, 388.8–9; Ps.-Callisth. *Alex.* 1.15, 23; Jdt 6:4; 11:1, 7; 3 Macc 6:5; cf. Aeschylus *Pers.* 74). One could also apply such hyperbole to a favorite teacher (οἰκουμένην in Eunapius *Lives* 493; cf. *Test. Mos.* 11:8).
250. E.g., those of Caligula in Jos. *Ant.* 19.1, 14; see comment on Acts 17:6. During the Roman civil war, Cicero lamented that the entire world was flaming (*Fam.* 4.1.2).

to travel around to various cities soliciting reports of unanswered charges that never[251] produced a conviction. Josephus shows that Jews in Asia carefully preserved, over the course of many generations, legal precedents and reports on matters important to their survival and rights.

Undoubtedly Paul's Asian Jewish adversaries had supplied the chief priest with their report from Ephesus and others they may have heard of, but these would have been only oral; they had not expected to find Paul, or an opportunity to accuse him, in Jerusalem, and hence would not have gathered documents and certainly would not have brought them to the festival. (Indeed, Paul had avoided Ephesus en route to Jerusalem, and many of these pilgrims would have left before the Ephesian elders returned from Miletus.) Even these oral reports are now secondhand, the original accusers having left (24:19), probably without offering formal affidavits (which might be effective but might also move Roman authorities sympathetic to Paul to invite these "witnesses" to appear).[252] They might not wish to remain so long after a festival (24:11), but they might also not wish to be accountable for their charges. If these Asian Jews believe that Paul retains powerful patrons in Ephesus (19:31), they might not wish to come into open conflict with his patrons, weakening their own status in Ephesus.

Luke himself provides a substantial list of potential incidents, but in each case, he refutes the potential charges:[253]

Acts Passage	Luke's Perspective	Jewish Involvement?
9:23–25	Paul meets opposition in Damascus	Jewish opposition
13:12	Paul and Barnabas receive a positive response from the proconsul	Despite a Jewish opponent
13:50	Aristocrats in Pisidian Antioch drive Paul and Barnabas out (perhaps forgotten by now; cf. 14:21–23)	Jewish instigation
14:5	Paul and Barnabas flee a mob in Iconium	Jewish instigation
14:19	Mob in Lystra nearly kills Paul	Jewish instigation
16:22–23	Paul and Silas are beaten in Philippi but vindicated (16:37–40)	Because of anti-Semitism
17:10	Paul escapes without responding to charges (but these expire once the politarchs have left office)	Jewish instigation
17:14	Paul is chased out of Beroea	Jewish instigation
17:32–34	Paul receives an acceptable response in Athens	No trouble from synagogue
18:12–17	Governor rejects the charges against Paul as purely religious	Jewish legal opposition
19:23	Riot erupts in Ephesus	No Jewish instigation, but it embarrasses the Jewish community (19:33–34)
21:28	Riot erupts in the Jerusalem temple	Jewish instigation

Where Roman officials appear, they are favorable, and the legal precedents positive (18:12–17; cf. 13:12); a favorable impression also results from intellectual dialogue

251. With the possible but unlikely exception of Ephesus; see comments at Acts 19:23–41; 20:16. Paul's worst troubles there probably became political rather than legal.

252. Witnesses could be arraigned (Apul. *Apol.* 44–45, for slaves, and 46, for others).

253. It seems a likely surmise that we can reconstruct one line of charge against Paul here, as Josephus's replies to Apion inadvertently preserved the latter's anti-Semitic claims. Cf. similarly the apologetic in 1–2 Samuel against considering David a usurper (e.g., 1 Sam 16:13–14; 19:5, 11–17; 23:16–18; 24:4–22; 27:8–10; 29:4–11; 2 Sam 1:14–15; 3:28; 4:11; 16:8; on royal spinmeisters, cf., e.g., Philost. *Hrk.* 31.5 or, more relevant [and more consistently favorable than Samuel–Kings], Assyrian annals; on ancient Near Eastern royal apologetic, see Long, "Samuel," 270) or Philostratus's apologetic against considering Apollonius as a magician (*Vit. Apoll.* 1.2; 5.12; 7.17, 39; 8.7). Cf. also Luke preempting charges against Jesus, e.g., by explaining that the swords were only so that Jesus could fulfill the prophecy about being considered a transgressor (Luke 22:36–38).

(17:32–34; 19:9–10). But Jewish instigation appears in the vast majority of these instances where trouble occurred.[254]

Luke's account is clearly ironic on this point: it is Paul's opponents who stirred the riots, rather than Paul himself. Paul, on the other hand, has some legal precedents in his favor, especially the Achaian governor's dismissal of frivolous religious charges brought by local synagogue leaders. Such official precedents could be concretely documented and would not dare be falsified.

The cumulative pattern of riots following Paul's preaching would appear problematic,[255] especially the one that resulted in his flight without exoneration in 17:10 (though the decree against him would be expired, it might still be remembered by local enemies and a matter of local record) and, most seriously, the riot in Ephesus. Ephesus was a major city, and historically the riot's aftermath apparently left Paul mostly unwelcome there (see comment on Acts 20:16). Luke emphasizes that even in Ephesus there were no real grounds against Paul (19:40) and that the frivolous charge never came to court (19:38–39). For his own audience, Luke is probably defending Paul as the founder of a large circle of Diaspora churches, even as Paul's detractors continued to contest his legacy. In locations such as Ephesus, some Christians may have come to see Paul's reputation as hurtful baggage no less than his non-Christian Jewish detractors there apparently had (19:33–34; cf. 2 Tim 1:15). Although Luke's interests may be primarily apologetic, he also makes good theological capital of the opposition: Jesus's message does bring division (Luke 12:51–53), as Paul's preaching has proved in synagogues (Acts 18:5–8; 19:8–9) and, in a sense, before the Sanhedrin (23:7, 10).

v. Reversal of Charges

Such a reversal of charges fits ancient forensic rhetoric,[256] but it is also central to Luke's own apologetic. First-century Jews' responses to riots were often to show, when possible, that their enemies caused the riots and therefore that Rome should reaffirm Jewish rights.[257] If Luke can argue that Paul's Jewish opponents, rather than Paul himself, incited many of these riots, he can contend that Christians should not be punished as authors of unrest.[258] (Perhaps for this reason, in 18:2 he also omits the unrest in Rome that Suetonius attributes to one "Chrestus.")

Of course, in the real world, extremists militantly hostile to some other people, including on religious grounds, do sometimes stir unrest, often inciting charges and countercharges between otherwise relatively peaceful communities.[259] Paul's letters do speak of experiencing considerable conflict, including with many Jewish leaders (cf. esp. 2 Cor 11:24), but hardly reveal him as one promoting sedition (cf. Rom 13:1–7); we can notice the rhetoric without dismissing the history. That people were sometimes in trouble through others' enmity was well recognized (e.g., Dio Chrys. *Ep.* 1, to Rufus), and people often charged opponents with maliciously twisting the

254. Paul's own letters testify of conflicts with his own people (2 Cor 11:24, 26), although he had them with Gentiles as well.

255. On the problematic character of Paul's association with tumults for Roman readers, see esp. Cassidy, "Opponents."

256. See Keener, *John*, 753; also Anderson, *Glossary*, 72 (citing Cic. *Orat.* 137). See fuller discussion below.

257. See Stoops, "Riot," 78–80.

258. Cf. ibid., 81.

259. The months that I spent in Plateau State, Nigeria, in the summers of 1998–2000 helped shape my thinking in this regard (cf. Keener, "Mayhem"). In more recent years the newer group Boko Haram has made evident the polarizing strategy already at work from some jihadists in the 1990s, but at that time some Western (and even some southern Nigerian) critics doubted the accuracy of my information.

truth (Philost. *Vit. Apoll.* 7.35). Luke knows that Paul was vilified even within parts of the church (Acts 21:21).

VI. NAZARENE SECT

Although Tertullus speaks pejoratively of the "Nazarenes," it is not clear that his designation of the movement as a "sect" (αἵρεσις) would bear automatically pejorative connotations. Greeks used this term for "sect" to refer to various philosophic schools, such as Epicureans, Peripatetics, and Stoics (Epict. *Diatr.* 2.19.20),[260] and possibly Skeptics.[261] In the first and second centuries C.E., it could also mean a "voluntary association";[262] different schools of medical thought were also so described before the Christian period.[263] The use of the term as referring to philosophic schools specifies groups with distinctive ideologies and justifies its application to Jewish "sects" (Acts 5:17; 15:5; 26:5). Josephus, who often applies the term to what he regards as the key movements within Palestinian Judaism,[264] may be thinking of philosophic sects.[265] Still, Tertullus is clearly hostile, and Paul reframes the language of "sect" to speak instead of the true "Way" in 24:14.[266]

Some scholars have suggested that the name "Nazarene" derives from the *nezer* ("branch") title of Isa 11:1, as probably in Matt 2:23.[267] More likely, the title derives from Jesus's own title "Nazarene" and was probably originally applied to the disciples, as was the term "Christians" (Acts 11:26; 26:28), with derisive intent. The term "Nazarene" (in its two Greek forms) appears nineteen times in the NT (including six other times in Acts and three times in Luke's Gospel), all of them (excepting this one and possibly Matt 2:23) designating Jesus by his place of origin. The title is by no means generally pejorative, but sometimes it is used in a pejorative manner (Acts 6:14)—perhaps related to Nazareth's size (cf. John 1:46),[268] though this is unclear.[269] It was apparently as orthodox a city as any.[270]

260. Cf. the (Stoic) sect of Chrysippus and Cleanthes (Hierocles p. 37, cols. 8, 10 [in van der Horst, "Hierocles," 157]); Arius Did. *Epit.* 2.7.6a, pp. 38–39.4; 6b, pp. 38–39.19; 7, pp. 42–43.26; 11m, pp. 86–87.22; pp. 90–91.16; the sect of Platonists (Macrob. *Comm.* 2.14.6–7, in van der Horst, "Macrobius," 226). See also discussion at Acts 5:17; 15:5.

261. Diog. Laert. 1.prol. 19–20 defines Skeptics as a sect only if it includes those who follow a principle and not just a doctrine.

262. See Desjardins, "Αἵρεσις in Christian Era."

263. See Staden, "Hairesis and Heresy."

264. Jos. *Ant.* 13.171, 288, 293; 20.199; *War* 2.118, 122, 137, 142, 162; *Life* 10, 12, 191, 197.

265. Cf. Jos. *Ant.* 15.371 (without the term). He also, however, applied the term politically (15.6).

266. See discussion on the meaning of "way" at Acts 9:2 (Keener, *Acts*, 2:1626–27). Similarly, some philosophic schools viewed their own ways as true. Cf. Stoic rejection of mere "opinion" (e.g., Arius Did. *Epit.* 2.7.11m, p. 94.5, 13–18; cf. 2.7.10b, p. 58.18, 27–30); so also in Pythagoreanism in Philost. *Ep. Apoll.* 52.

267. Pritz, *Nazarene Christianity*, 13–14; cf. Ulfgard, "Bibelutläggning"; on Matthew, cf., e.g., Keener, *Matthew*, 113–15.

268. Meyers and Strange, *Archaeology*, 56, suggest 1,600–2,000 inhabitants, based on the tombs; cf. p. 27. More recent estimates suggest below 500 (Stanton, *Gospel Truth?*, 112; Horsley, *Galilee*, 193; roughly 500 in Strange, "Nazareth," 113). People sometimes evaluated others based on the size or significance of their place of origin (e.g., Dio Chrys. *Or.* 32.22; Libanius *Invective* 3.2; *Comparison* 1.2; 2.2).

269. That many other Galilean villages were about the same size or smaller (Horsley, *Galilee*, 193; cf. Lewis, *Life*, 67–68) may argue against this thesis (Keener, *John*, 483–84). Cf. Chung-Kim and Hains, *Acts*, 326.

270. That one of the priestly courses reportedly settled here after 70 C.E. indicates that the priesthood found the town "clean" (Meyers and Strange, *Archaeology*, 27), but for questions on the tradition, see Trifon, "Msmrwt." Johanan ben Zakkai seems to have settled not far from Nazareth before 70 C.E. (Vermes, *Jesus the Jew*, 72, citing *y. Ber.* 7c; *b. Ber.* 34b). Still, even nearby Sepphoris (which later includes more pagan imagery; see, e.g., Dunbabin, "Dionysus") was strongly Jewish in character before the Judean-Roman war (see, e.g., Chancey and Meyers, "Jewish"; Chancey, "Milieu"; Reich, "Baths"; Evans, *World*, 24–26; Reed, *Archaeology*, 135), and Nazareth was more traditional than Sepphoris (Dark, "Landscapes"; Reed, *Archaeology*, 134–35, 138). On ancient Israelite pottery before resettlement in the Hellenistic period, see Horsley, *Galilee*, 193; on

Luke undoubtedly preserves a genuine Judean usage here. Although the usage originally arose probably from outsiders,[271] Jewish believers adopted it just as Gentile believers adopted the equally hostile "Christian" title; Tertullian and Eusebius know this as a title of early Christians, and it is unlikely that they derived the title solely from Tertullus's denunciation in Acts 24:5.[272] By calling Paul a ringleader of the Nazarenes, Tertullus forces him to defend all of the Judean Jewish movement;[273] this is, naturally, what both Luke and Luke's Paul would prefer (Luke 12:11–12; 21:12–13), as Paul's earlier "defense" speech in Acts 22:3–21 demonstrates.[274]

Tertullus's primary point is to denigrate Paul, recognizing that the Nazarenes are a minority sect favored by the poor and much less represented among the elite (cf. 21:20). By following a "messiah" executed for treason by the Romans, Nazarenes were easily associated with sedition (though more in rhetoric than in reality; in contrast to the groups mentioned in 21:38, Nazarenes do not appear to be persecuted or viewed as threatening in these years).[275] Moreover, a purveyor of ideas could not easily produce change by violence unless he had many followers.[276]

VII. PAUL AS A RINGLEADER

Ringleaders bore special responsibility for crimes committed by their movements.[277] But by pointing out that Paul is a leader in this movement and a stirrer of dissension elsewhere, it is just possible (though no more than that) that Tertullus intends to warn Felix that Paul is a commanding speaker and so Felix should not be taken in by what Paul says. Speakers would sometimes pretend to fear opponents' eloquence or authority (to keep the judge skeptical of the opponents' intentions; Quint. *Inst.*

the proper Hebrew form of the name, see Rüger, "ΝΑΖΑΡΕΘ." Later rabbis told of individual *minim* there (*t. Ḥul.* 2:24) but do not provide details for an entire Jewish Christian community (Miller, "*Minim*").

271. Bede *Comm. Acts* 24.5 (L. Martin, 177; Martin, *Acts*, 284) distinguishes Luke's use for Judean believers from the later use of the title for a specific sort of Jewish Christian movement (cf. Aug. *Ep.* 75.4.13 [from Jerome]; 82.2.16; Jerome *Vir. ill.* 3; *Dial. Pelag.* 3.2), arguing (probably rightly) that Christians were originally called "Nazarenes" as an insult (cf. Acts 11:26).

272. Pritz, *Nazarene Christianity*, 16. Pliny the Elder's reference to Nazerini stems from a pre-Christian source and hence cannot refer to believers in Jesus (Pritz, *Nazarene Christianity*, 17–18). Jewish followers of Jesus retained the title at least into the fourth century (Bagatti, *Church*, 12–13), as is evident both from later forms of the *Birkath ha-Minim* and from independent attestation of that malediction in Jerome (*Ep.* 112.13; *In Amos* 1.11–12; *In Isa.* 5.18–19; 49.7; 52.4–6) and Epiphanius (Flusser, *Judaism*, 638; Pritz, *Nazarene Christianity*, 104–5; cf. discussion in Urbach, "Self-Isolation," 288; Moore, "Canon," 111–12; Carroll, "Exclusion," 22; Jocz, *People*, 54–57; Keener, *John*, 211). (The *Birkath* may have cursed Jewish Jesus followers before the specification of "Nazarenes"; for Justin *Dial.* 16.4 [and possibly 93; 95; 96; 98; 123; 133], see Barnard, "Old Testament," 400; Horbury, "Benediction," 19; Shotwell, *Exegesis*, 83–84; Bauer, *Orthodoxy*, 274; Schiffman, "Crossroads," 151; *pace* Kimelman, "Evidence," 235–36; further discussion in Keener, *John*, 207–14.) Cf. later Gentile patristic discussions about them cited in Daniélou, *Theology*, 56 (Epiph. *Her.* 29; Jerome *Vir. ill.* 3). The idea that the post-first-century Jewish Christian movement originated in the later Gentile church (Munck, "Jewish Christianity," 114) is unfounded. Archaeological evidence in Palestine shows that Jewish Christianity persisted at least well into the Byzantine period (Meyers, "State," 134–35; cf. Saldarini, *Community*, 18–26; Mancini, *Discoveries*). Evidence remains "for a continuous Jewish-Christian or Christian presence for seven centuries" (Meyers, "Judaism and Christianity," 77).

273. Conzelmann, *Acts*, 199.

274. Through Paul's various hearings (esp. the later one before Agrippa), Paul, as an articulate spokesperson for the movement, a citizen and conciliatory toward the empire, probably increases tolerance for Palestinian Jewish Christianity, dissociating it from politically subversive revolutionary elements by defining the movement in wholly theological terms. This is part of God's plan for Paul, who was to reach kings (Acts 9:15). Moreover, it was amplified by his captivity, as is shown by the contrast with his previous stay in Caesarea, in Philip's house, with no contact with the Roman authorities or local elite.

275. Even in Acts, Christianity itself is not yet a legal charge, a circumstance that does not precede Nero (Molthagen, "Konflikte"; cf. 1 Pet 4:16). Cf. Acts 24:22; 25:22.

276. See this defense of Socrates, who used persuasion rather than force, in Xen. *Mem.* 1.2.10.

277. E.g., Dion. Hal. *Ant. rom.* 3.40.3; 5.43.2; 'Abot R. Nat. 40 A; Urbach, *Sages*, 1:465.

4.1.11), presenting opponents as cleverer speakers than themselves (Isaeus *Astyph.* 35; *Aristarch.* 1). Nicolaus of Damascus neutralized the effects of a defendant's pathos by warning of his craftiness (Jos. *War* 1.637). Cicero again provides examples: he warns that the opposing orator is more eloquent than himself (*Quinct.* 1.1–4; 24.77), but concludes with such a clinching argument (25.78–80) that no amount of sophistry could challenge it (26.80–27.85).[278] Apuleius's accuser began his case by warning of Apuleius's eloquence (Apul. *Apol.* 4).

Judges or juries might need to be reminded not to let a person's influence (Suet. *Tib.* 33)[279] or his advocate's eloquence (Val. Max. 8.9.3) sway the case in his favor, a caution that Paul might have also had reason to urge in view of his opponents' status (Acts 24:1). It was helpful to note where one's opponent held advantages, to keep the judge vigilant against them (*Rhet. Alex.* 36, 1442a.16–18). It was always wise to anticipate an opponent's objections,[280] and Paul's persuasiveness (and probably training) was known. Thus an accuser, after declaring an opponent's evils (Aeschines *Tim.* 70), could warn that the opponent would soon deny the charges (*Tim.* 71).[281]

By claiming that Paul is influential in the Nazarene sect (more so than he actually is, cf. Acts 21:21), Tertullus may unwittingly give Felix a cause to tread carefully regarding Paul. If Ananias and his sect of Sadducees were politically powerful though small, the Nazarene sect was, though politically powerless, influential with the people and probably larger even than the Pharisaic sect. (Pharisaism itself had a similar populist appeal, though it was of higher economic and educational status, on average, than the Nazarenes; see comment on Acts 21:20.) Given the social networks of Mediterranean cities (and especially Roman society), prosecuting or condemning a person incurred the enmity of his supporters.[282]

Even if the Nazarenes were currently not a threat, they were numerous, and what Felix would least want to do, given the insurrection throughout Judea, was to provoke an urban group to join in insurrection. (He had, however, been provoking peasants in the countryside.) More likely, Felix, who knows about the Nazarenes (24:22), simply does not believe them subversive but recognizes that much of the Jerusalem elite disagrees. In other words, he finds himself in virtually the same situation with Paul and the Nazarenes that Pilate had with Jesus two and a half to three decades earlier.

VIII. DEFILING THE TEMPLE (24:6A)

Denouncing categories of people (such as "adulterers" or "fathers"), though useful, allows only generalizations about behavior,[283] and so it is more strategic rhetorically to address a specific person's behavior (Hermog. *Issues* 29–30). Calling Paul a "pest" in

278. Lowering audience expectations was a common rhetorical practice (e.g., Lysias *Or.* 2.1, §190; 12.3, §120; *Rhet. Alex.* 29, 1436b.34–36; Sall. *Jug.* 85.31; Dio Chrys. *Or.* 1.9; 12.16; 32.39; 42.1; 46.7; 47.1, 8; Men. Rhet. 2.4, 391.14–15).

279. Cf. Val. Max. 8.1.abs.12 (where jurors sometimes showed mercy to a defendant of lower status; the reverse was, however, more common and even written into law).

280. See (on *prokatalepsis*, or anticipating opponents' objections) *Rhet. Alex.* 18, 1432b.11–1433b.16; 33, 1439b.2–14; 36, 1442b.4–6; 1443a.6–1443b.14; Hermog. *Inv.* 3.4.134; 4.13.206; *Method* 23.438–39; 27.444; in a wider range of sources, see Anderson, *Glossary*, 104; the forensic original sense in Plath, "Prolepsis"; in Paul's own writings, Anderson, *Rhetorical Theory*, 235. Quint. *Decl.* 338.6 warns against assuming what the opponent will say (perhaps to avoid reinforcing his argument), though with no aversion to countering arguments (e.g., 339.3).

281. Aeschines also notes that someone could accuse him, like his opponent, of sleeping with men, but he counters in advance that sleeping with men is not the problem but, rather, charging money for it (Aeschines *Tim.* 136–37). One might anticipate an opponent's appeal to pity (Libanius *Topics* 2.20).

282. Winter, *Left Corinth*, 67.

283. These could be useful for pathos but left themselves open to the response that it was a person, not a vice in general, that was on trial, and the person had not been proved guilty of such a vice (Cic. *Cael.* 12.29).

a general way is useless without a concrete illustration, and the only case his accusers can try to prove is that Paul "attempted" to profane the temple—behavior that they will argue is consistent with his past (alleged) activity and that he (and Luke) will argue is inconsistent with it.

The one charge concrete enough to prove effective against Paul is this charge of attempting to profane the temple; it assumes eyewitnesses (who are not, however, present for the trial, Acts 24:19). Although Lysias's description of Paul's seizure sounds less civil than does their own account, they might wish to construe Lysias's words in 23:27 (presumably now part of the public record) as an arrest, the impression they wish to leave about their own behavior here (although κρατέω also means "seize").[284] The impression of an arrest, or at least a coordinated seizure based on Jewish law, sounds orderly and deliberate, an impression naturally conveyed by the currently unified legal front against Paul. The informed reader, of course, knows that this implication is false. On the historical level, it also contradicts what Luke believes happened, because, had he believed that Jewish authorities first arrested Paul and then delivered him to the Romans, he could have used it to confirm his parallel with Jesus (as in Agabus's prophecy, 21:11). The temple police closed the temple doors (21:30) and may have been advancing through the crowd; but they had discernible clothing, and if they, rather than the mob, had been in control, it is unlikely that Lysias would have intervened and "rescued" Paul (23:27).[285] Knowing Lysias's report, Felix may greet the Jerusalem elders' claim with controlled skepticism.

Gentiles could be executed (perhaps even directly, Jos. *War* 6.126) for violating the temple,[286] but whereas Paul's supposed Gentile companion could have been killed had he been apprehended, no clear precedent existed for Paul's own conviction. It was clear, however, that massive protests could secure the execution of a Roman (or at least an auxiliary soldier) who disturbed the peace by desecrating something sacred to the Jewish people.[287]

Unfortunately for Paul's accusers, they cannot prove the claim offered in Acts 21:28; the Gentile was never found (otherwise he, too, would have been arraigned). Had the Asian Jews named Trophimus (21:29), the latter probably would have had eyewitnesses attesting his presence elsewhere at the time (i.e., an alibi), since he belonged to a group and, as a foreigner, would not likely be wandering alone in the city.[288] False witnesses (6:13) would be problematic if there were counterwitnesses, and most would not want to risk the penalty for false witness in a capital case if the judge might prove unsympathetic (in contrast to 6:12–15). It might be more difficult to secure the death sentence for the more modest charge that Paul's accusers must settle for—that he *attempted* to profane the temple—a charge that, most tellingly, they likewise cannot prove (24:13; cf. 25:7)![289] It is the sort of charge difficult to falsify but also to verify, because it addresses intention. Probable intention could be

284. As Bruce, *Acts¹*, 422, notes, the accusers' implication that they "arrested" Paul was "an excessively refined description of an attempt at lynching!" They grasped him to kill him on the spot, not to try him according to rules of evidence.

285. Witherington, *Acts*, 708, suggests that in order to be able to "claim jurisdictional rights to judge Paul under Jewish law," the accusers implied that "the temple police," rather than common Jews, seized Paul.

286. Bruce, *Commentary*, 116; see more fully comment at Acts 21:28.

287. Jos. *Ant.* 20.115–17; though cf. 20.108, 112.

288. Possibly, however, Trophimus left the city and did not show up for the trial, given the risk to him; cf. such behavior under duress in Acts 9:29–30; 17:10. Although the chief priests themselves would be more interested in Paul and might not want to specify how Paul "desecrated" the temple, Trophimus would risk more, as the Gentile "defiler" and probably not a Roman citizen, than Paul if put on trial.

289. Many concur that Tertullus has reduced the charge to "attempt" because of inadequate evidence (e.g., Foakes-Jackson, *Acts*, 214; Walaskay, *Came to Rome*, 54).

established only by the claims of 24:5 about Paul's long history as a rabble-rouser, claims that at this point they also could not prove.

Moreover, the same alleged background (24:5) does not fit the concrete charge: if Paul stirs Diaspora Jews to sedition, like a Judean revolutionary gone abroad, one would associate him more naturally with those who thought the temple authorities too lax in their administration of the temple's sanctity, not someone who would profane the temple itself. That such a person would have sought to bring a Gentile into the temple would seem even less compelling; it might also imply a pro-Gentile attitude, not the impression that Tertullus would want to offer before Felix.[290] Thus even the concrete charge is vague (at least in Luke's summary): Paul sought to desecrate the temple, but the means of his desecration are left unclear. Perhaps Tertullus hopes that Paul will attempt to explain, providing evidence against himself in the process. If the historical speech behind Luke's summary expanded the charge in greater detail, it is hard to know how Tertullus could have made the charge sound compelling.

f. Lysias's Interference (24:6b–8)

The textual problem of 24:6b–8a remains a matter of dispute. Textually, the addition is certainly suspect, and its genuineness is highly unlikely.[291] The earliest manuscripts favor its omission, although the geographic evidence is more divided (with Syriac, and also Armenian and Ethiopic, support for its inclusion but Coptic, and also Western and Georgian, support for its omission). Certainly the natural referent of οὗ in 24:8 should be Paul, not Lysias.[292] At the same time, the addition makes some sense,[293] whether because it reflects tradition or (more likely) because it reflects a logical inference from the text. It therefore merits comment, even if only by way of exploring the inferences drawn by ancient commentators closer to the culture than are their modern counterparts.

Whereas in 18:15 a Roman governor, against their petition, wanted synagogue leaders themselves to deal with internal religious law, here the petitioners want to judge Paul themselves (on a capital charge) or induce Felix to condemn him for sedition. Because the charge against Paul is that of profaning the temple, the Jerusalem authorities ideally want the Romans to hand Paul over to them, in contrast to the fate of Jesus, who was handed over to Rome by the Jerusalem leaders.[294] In their private view, plots to assassinate Paul (23:12–15; 25:3) would simply be exercising the right that was wrongly taken from them in the beginning. Jews' escape from Jewish punishment through appeal to Roman governors probably often frustrated Jewish courts,[295] but this would be especially the case where Roman policy explicitly granted Jewish courts jurisdiction.[296]

---

290. As Rapske, *Custody*, 162, suggests, "the explicit mention of Gentile uncleanness might have offended the governor." He probably preferred more adaptable Jews (cf. comment on Acts 24:24). Tertullus also replaces κοινόω (21:28) with βεβηλόω, which is more intelligible for a Gentile (Walaskay, *Came to Rome*, 54).

291. Cf. more cautiously Metzger, *Textual Commentary*, 490. Chance, *Acts*, 445, suggests that Tertullus's blatant falsehood fits the anti-Jewish tendency of the Western text.

292. If one accepts the interpolation as valid, it may read more easily as applying to Lysias (Metzger, *Textual Commentary*, 490; Conzelmann, *Acts*, 199).

293. So, e.g., Kistemaker, *Acts*, 838.

294. On the figurative level, Pilate "hands Jesus over" to the will of the chief priests and rulers (Luke 23:25; cf. Mark 15:15; Matt 27:26; most explicit in John 19:16); the literal action, however, is carried out by Roman agents.

295. See Safrai, "Self-Government," 408 (listing as examples offenses not punishable by Romans, such as intercourse with a Gentile woman and prostitution; cf. *b. Ber.* 58a).

296. For emphasis on the jurisdiction question here, see Winter, *Trial*, 77 (though temple defilement is a special case); Pervo, *Acts*, 597. (Pervo thinks Luke's presentation of Tertullus's case absurd; yet even granting

Whereas Lysias claimed to have "rescued" Paul from Jewish violence (23:27), Paul's accusers now attribute the only real violence to Lysias.[297] Therefore Felix should now put this offense right.[298] The textual variant at this point may be wrong, but its inference that Paul's enemies complained about Lysias is not impossible;[299] once Lysias's letter is public knowledge (as it might have become at the initial hearing in 24:1), the chief priests cannot win their case without challenging his credibility, and their relations with Roman administrators were often adversarial in any case. Their alleged claim is bold but unlikely to succeed; Lysias's action was public, and his soldiers could attest that they intervened in the face of violence.

The momentary bilingual confusion of the mob situation, however, might render plausible a Roman misunderstanding of the real situation, and the chief priests could well expect Lysias to prove unable to explain the least plausible claim in his letter—namely, that he knew Paul to be a Roman citizen before he intervened (23:27). How could Lysias have known that? If someone else knew and reported this to him, where was that witness? Tertullus could not cross-examine Lysias, but Felix could. In Roman (and Greek) courts, as noted above, those who took a defendant's side as witnesses or supporters could themselves become targets of the prosecution.[300] (Likewise, the prosecutor could be attacked by defendants' friends.)[301] Paul's opponents could also charge that Lysias, by allowing Paul to speak in 21:40, even after subduing him, was careless in controlling a dangerous riot (22:22–24).

Further, Jerusalem's aristocracy posed more of a political threat to Felix than one of his subordinates would.[302] Lysias could be expected to continue to support Paul; once a person used his influence to back another, failure brought him a corresponding measure of shame.[303] If we reject the authenticity of 24:7 (and we probably should), we should do so on textual grounds, not because the claim is too dramatic.

Lysias's letter does not specify for Felix exactly what group seized Paul (23:27 simply says, "the Jews"), but it certainly implies that the Sanhedrin was part of his opposition (23:28–29); now Ananias and the elders confirm the connection, even taking responsibility for the "arrest" (24:6a). Felix might be inclined to believe Lysias[304] and would not likely want to leave his own representative in Jerusalem open to charges without good reason. Nevertheless, Ananias and his allies posed a far more potent political threat if they were dishonored as if untruthful,[305] and they were far more useful allies if Felix put them in his debt by granting another favor. Josephus does not portray Felix as particularly sensitive to the Jerusalem aristocracy's

---

this verdict, I am aware of many absurd claims in some cultures today that prevail simply because of political weight or well-orchestrated propaganda.)

297. The incident with Paul is probably not the first conflict with Lysias; the relationship seems less than serene (Acts 22:30; 23:10), and Lysias is naturally far more concerned with keeping Felix happy than with appeasing the Sanhedrin.

298. Cf. Tajra, *Trial*, 123–24.

299. Witherington, *Acts*, 709, doubts that a rhetor would risk this claim before the governor.

300. E.g., Aeschines *Tim.* 54–57. Friends could also attack the prosecutor (Pliny *Ep.* 3.9.25).

301. Pliny *Ep.* 3.9.25, though he regained his audience by responding that allowing him to finish speaking would not affect the defendants' innocence.

302. As noted earlier, Felix's predecessor lost his position in conflict with the current high priest (Jos. *War* 2.245–46; *Ant.* 20.134–36).

303. See, e.g., Pliny *Ep.* 6.6.9, though the occasion there is political.

304. Would the latter have risked his position merely to spite the leaders of the city where he was stationed? Lysias also seems to treat Felix, who, like him, achieved equestrian rank without equestrian birth, as a patron.

305. "Lying" was a standard charge and countercharge in legal polemic (see Keener, *John*, 761–62). Josephus shows that Judean embassies usually got their way in Rome (McKechnie, "Embassies"); it was foolish to cross such powerful interests unnecessarily.

concerns[306] (which Josephus often plausibly portrays as Jewish attempts to keep peace against incompetent governors' provocation), and this independence may be a factor contributing to why he does not simply hand Paul over; but neither would Felix desire to provoke Ananias deliberately over what Felix would view as a relatively small matter.

If Lysias somehow learned about the plot (as revealed in his letter to Felix), the chief priests might suspect the possibility that he also learned about their cooperation with it. In case he had spoken ill of them to Felix, they could use the standard Greco-Roman forensic practice of counterattacking accusers (or, in this case, potential accusers; on the practice, see comment on Acts 24:19). Felix may partly protect Lysias in 24:22 (although Lysias's note did not implicate the chief priests, their own hostility toward Paul, demonstrated in 24:1–8, might suggest their common cause with the assassins). It was standard practice in forensic rhetoric to attack those likely to be supporters of one's opponents (e.g., Aeschines *Tim.* 193–95). The text of Acts 24:6b–8a is rightly suspect, yet its substance is, at the least, a later scribe's plausible inference, rooted in understanding the character of ancient forensic rhetoric.

g. Assertions (24:8–9)

It was conventional forensic rhetoric to assert that one spoke the truth and that one's enemy lied and to imply confidence that the very prudent judges in charge of the case certainly would recognize this.[307] Thus a speaker could plead that if his judges would only hear him objectively, he would readily persuade them that he was "guilty of no crime."[308] A speaker could imply his opponent's lack of integrity by claiming that it was knowledge already common to the jurors.[309] Each side could claim to present the genuine facts, inviting a verdict on its behalf;[310] many repeated charges more strenuously than evidence warranted,[311] perhaps to compensate for its lack. Cicero announces that his account corresponds precisely with the facts, even where what we would regard as a more balanced extant account disagrees.[312] A prosecutor could allege something without proof, and when another denied it under oath, the prosecutor could note that he expected this denial, since the man is a liar.[313]

Orators often urged judges (most frequently in their conclusions) to render verdicts conforming to justice,[314] with the implication that the orators found their own case persuasive and just. Thus, for example, again Cicero urges the jury to vote with its convictions, so honoring those who wisely chose the bravest and wisest jurors.[315] Rhetorical employment of impudence and volume sometimes succeeded in court more effectively than calm reason.[316]

Because the governor had freedom to judge *extra ordinem*,[317] accusers with high

---

306. E.g., Jos. *Life* 13; *Ant.* 20.162; *War* 2.270; but cf. *Ant.* 20.178. Felix had Jewish friends, but not of reputable character (*Ant.* 20.142; cf. 20.163); he married a Jewess, but only after seducing her to leave her husband (20.142–43); and he certainly never adopted Judaism (see comment on Acts 24:24).

307. For a simple appeal to the justice of one's case as a rhetorical strategy, see also Anderson, *Glossary*, 36.

308. Dion. Hal. *Ant. rom.* 9.29.3 (trans. E. Cary, LCL, 6:19).

309. Isaeus *Pyrr.* 40 (though in this case he goes on to provide evidence).

310. Isaeus *Cleon.* 41; cf. *Menec.* 19.

311. E.g., Isaeus *Aristarch.* 23.

312. Cic. *Mil.* 11.30, with N. H. Watts in LCL, 14:38 n. *a*.

313. Isaeus *Astyph.* 19.

314. E.g., Isaeus *Nicost.* 31; Lysias *Or.* 9.21, §116; 14.47, §144; 16.21, §147; Lucian *Indictment* 20 (toward the end).

315. Cic. *Mil.* 38.105 (the closing lines).

316. So Lucian *Tim.* 11.

317. The phrase applies to hearings where the magistrate exercises his full authority, or *imperium*, without needing recourse to regular Roman judicial procedure; see, e.g., Sohm, *Institutes*, §43 (p. 212).

status could simply allege "facts" without evidence, inviting the governor to exercise his own right to investigate.[318] On the rhetorical level, the request for an impartial investigation again implied (by *insinuatio*) that the truth of their cause was self-evident.[319]

That "the Judeans" (i.e., the high priest and elders of Acts 24:1) "joined the attack"[320] recalls insistent cries for Jesus's condemnation in Luke's passion narrative (Luke 23:18, 21, 23), including by the chief priests (23:5, 10).[321] Perhaps they acted as if they were witnesses, but while some (like the high priest) may well have been in the temple during the events at issue, it is unlikely that they dared claim to be eyewitnesses to the alleged attempted desecration, since they could face cross-examination (Acts 24:13, 19). In any case, the elders' contributions to Tertullus's claim would rhetorically reinforce their cause: the weight of high-status plaintiffs stands behind the charge.

Luke's audience faces suspense:[322] the rhetorical and political strength of Paul's opposition seems impossible to surmount, especially for readers recalling Jesus's condemnation by Pilate. But through his conversion, Paul became one of the earliest church's few public voices with significant status, and his counterargument is critical. If any Christian can defend himself in court, it will be Paul; the stakes are therefore high, since his vindication could help the rest of the movement (cf. Phil 1:7).

Although Luke has greatly abbreviated Tertullus's case (the promise of brevity in Acts 24:4 is conventional), 24:9 allows Luke to imply that much more was said on this occasion than the précis he has provided (see comment on Acts 2:40).

3. Paul's Defense (24:10–21)

Paul responds to Tertullus's argument skillfully. His opponents cannot prove their case or even dignify its plausibility; the true vendetta against him is purely theological. Luke also illustrates God's promises: probably at least partly because Paul is empowered by the promised Spirit, Paul speaks for himself instead of depending on a hired orator like Tertullus (Luke 12:11–12; 21:13–15). Not surprisingly, Luke narrates much more of the substance of Paul's speech than that of Tertullus. In contrast to Tertullus's proem in Acts 24:2–3, followed by assertions in 24:5–6, Paul's proem (24:10) consumes a much briefer proportion of his reported speech, which focuses on evidence, procedure, and content (24:11–21).

Various rhetorical strategies include Paul's conceding and confessing what is not a crime (24:14); emphasizing Paul's practice of virtue, the antithesis of the charges (24:17); possibly reversing the charges by innuendo (24:18); underlining the relevant legal observation that the proper plaintiffs have not appeared (24:19; this should close the case); and finally, pointing out that the real issue is purely theological (24:20–21; as in 24:14–15). For further rhetorical observations, see discussion on the particular verses in this section.

318. Witherington, *Acts*, 703, 710.
319. Thus a classical orator avoids calling as witnesses the wives of other men with whom Timarchus slept (allegedly to avoid shaming them) but offers, "I leave it to you to investigate this matter" (Aeschines *Tim.* 107 [trans. C. D. Adams, LCL, 87]).
320. See, e.g., συνεπιτίθημι in the LXX (Ps 3:6; Obad 13; perhaps Zech 1:15); see BDAG. Often the term has military connotations (Barrett, *Acts*, 1100; cf., e.g., Jos. *Ant.* 10.116).
321. Cf. also Johnson, *Acts*, 412.
322. Trial scenes were useful for suspense (e.g., Char. *Chaer.* 5.6.11).

a. Introduction

Before examining the speech in more detail, it is helpful to survey some features of Paul's strategy, to come to an understanding of why he speaks for himself, and to survey a proposed rhetorical outline.

i. Paul's Strategy

Despite the suspense generated by Tertullus's rhetorical skill and the status of Paul's opponents, Paul has his adversaries in a situation where he needs them to be legally. First, the original accusers are not present (24:19), and so the case ought to be thrown out of court. Second, accusers in this sort of trial bear the burden of proof,[323] and these accusers can offer none (24:13; cf. 25:7). Third, their motives for bringing charges are clearly suspect. The only charge addressed in the Sanhedrin's preliminary hearing (which Lysias's own letter attested in 23:28–29) is a doctrinal difference within Judaism itself (24:20–21)—no offense actionable in a Roman court. Indeed, *most* of Paul's defense draws attention to Jewish questions that no Roman governor would admit as actionable in a Roman court (24:14–21).

Paul's ultimate objective, however, is not self-defense; rather, as Luke 21:12–13 urges in such situations, it is to testify about Christ (Acts 24:24–25; 26:27–29). The present speech does focus on self-defense, as Paul's life hangs in the balance; he must establish that the case is purely theological and not political.[324] Yet in making his argument, he is also vindicating the Christian movement against its accusers. Once the new governor has publicly announced his opinion that Paul is innocent (25:24–25) and he is simply "seeking assistance in formulating the requisite memorandum to be forwarded to Rome for the appeal," Paul seeks to persuade an influential ruler to turn to Christ (26:26–29).[325]

Paul does not try to explain specific cases of past riots in order to show that they were caused by his enemies rather than by himself. Luke does this skillfully enough in narratives since Paul's conversion (and especially from Acts 14 forward), and so there is no need to provide it for Luke's audience again in Paul's speech. But specific cases are probably missing in Paul's speech for another reason as well. In five days of preparation and without time or even a compelling interest to procure witnesses from Diaspora cities against this one person, Tertullus perhaps could have done no more than asserted that Paul was guilty of causing riots. If so, at this point Paul does not even need to offer the concession that riots have surrounded him, apart from the riot in question, which he can show was directed against him. Conceding a pattern of riots at this point would unnecessarily arouse suspicion and require a detailed defense—with the onus of proof on Paul—rather than a vigorous refutation of the central charges.

ii. Speaking for Himself

Why does Paul not have an advocate aiding him as the high priest does? Although some wanted defendants to make their case in their own words, without an advocate (the emperor in Suet. *Claud.* 16.2), this was not the general expectation. Advocates for the prosecution and/or the defense were common practice.[326] In classical times,

323. Following the "accusatorial" rather than "inquisitional" mode of investigation (Witherington, *Acts*, 703). For analysis of Paul's rhetorical argument, see Keener, "Rhetorical Techniques," 234–51.

324. See Sherwin-White, *Society*, 51; Winter, "Official Proceedings," 326.

325. Winter, "Official Proceedings," 330–31. Luke's reports of these defenses may also provide us a summary of the sorts of arguments Paul later used before Caesar's tribunal (cf. Cazeaux, *Actes*, 338).

326. Winter, "*Captatio benevolentiae*," 505 (among his examples from roughly this period are P.Flor. 61; P.Fam.Teb. 19; P.Mil.Vogl. 25). They were well enough known to generate figurative uses (see Keener, *John*, 956–61).

orators usually wrote speeches for their clients to present in the clients' first person; sometimes, however, friends could function as advocates for others (e.g., Isaeus *Nicost.* 1).[327] Advocates were common in the Roman republic (e.g., Plut. *Cic.* 5.2; 39.5) and remained so in this era. Still, high-status speakers might argue their own case; women, children, slaves, and some others would need advocates (Hermog. *Method* 21.436–37).

Perhaps Paul lacked an advocate because it would be difficult to procure an orator of high caliber (to compete with the sort of orator the high priest would hire) in the five days since his arrival (Acts 24:1).[328] The Roman practice was originally (in the republic) for patrons, who had rhetorical training, to represent their clients in court.[329] Once playing an unpaid role, advocates eventually received fees.[330] Although the senate may have waived official fees for advocates early in Nero's reign (Tac. *Ann.* 13.5), this would have little effect in the provinces, and Nero seems to have repealed the restriction anyway, albeit limiting the price (Suet. *Nero* 17).[331] Unless Paul's collection was rejected (which, as argued above, was unlikely), Paul may have limited funds at his disposal (though Felix must have thought otherwise, Acts 24:26). Even if it were rejected, Paul would not likely feel free to employ the donations of Diaspora churches for Jerusalem in this manner.

Paul probably would have sufficient friends and supporters, however, to hire an advocate if he expected it to help. Instead, Paul apparently chooses to represent himself because he knows his case best and can do so.[332] Paul's rhetoric is good,[333] as one might expect for a person engaged for years in public speaking;[334] many upper-class persons, trained in rhetoric, spoke for themselves.[335] Yet Luke probably expects us to think especially of Paul's relying on the facts rather than on rhetorical skills (see comment on orators at Acts 24:1). Regardless of how much time Paul may or may not have had to prepare, Luke emphasizes Paul's making a case boldly, depending on the same Holy Spirit promised in the Gospel (Luke 12:12; 21:15). Xenophon denies that Socrates sought to prepare a defense (*Apol.* 1ff.), though Socrates acted from motives very different from Paul's; when he tried to write it out, his guardian deity

327. Cf. the contrast between advocates (though figuratively applied to laws) and prosecutors in Aeschines *Ctes.* 37.

328. One also needed a trustworthy advocate, not one easily corrupted into supporting the prosecution (*Lev. Rab.* 5:6).

329. Lintott, "Cliens," 451; Crook, *Advocacy*, 31–32; cf. Hor. *Sat.* 1.1.9–10. For the persistence of this perspective, see Crook, *Advocacy*, 122.

330. Paulus, "Advocatus." People disapproved when expedient (e.g., Tac. *Ann.* 11.5, in Claudius's reign; Claudius limited the fee to ten thousand sesterces [11.7]).

331. Nero certainly later paid well those who prosecuted his enemies (Tac. *Ann.* 16.33). Debate about similar legislation arose in Pliny the Younger's day (*Ep.* 5.9.3–5; 5.13.8–10). Ideally, orators undertook cases for friendship (6.29.1; 9.13.3) and waived fees (5.13.8, 10; 6.23.1–2), but those who merely taught rhetoric were sometimes thought more honest than their courtroom counterparts (2.3.5–6).

332. Rapske, *Custody*, 330, emphasizes Paul's "God-given confidence," "the strength of his case," and "his expertise in forensic discourse" (all of which fit the consistent portrayal in Acts).

333. Various possible rhetorical strategies (such as returning charges or insinuating guilt) are noted below (see also Keener, "Rhetorical Techniques," in detail). I find far fewer rhetorical *devices* in the Acts speeches, however, than in most of Paul's letters. Such devices were often considered inappropriate in letters, but some ancients also considered them inappropriate in forensic rhetoric, though they were popular. Anderson, *Glossary*, 127, points out that Quintilian (*Inst.* 4.1.9; 4.3.2) disapproves of the fact that such ostentatious display popular in declamations had leaked into judicial rhetoric in the courts, but the crowds enjoyed it (12.8.3; Pliny *Ep.* 2.14). "Quintilian himself cautions that when strong emotions are called for, artificial figures are quite out of place (*Inst.* 9.3.100–102)." Luke's major reason for omitting them, however, is probably space; each speech is only a précis.

334. Luke apparently does think of Paul as capable even in a forensic setting, according with the rhetorical competence evident in Paul's letters (Hock, "Paul and Education," 215–16).

335. Crook, *Advocacy*, 123. Still, even one able to speak for himself might find an advocate more advantageous (Quint. *Decl.* 260.2).

would not allow it (Xen. *Mem.* 4.8.5). That was because, in Socrates's case, it was his appropriate time to die (4.8.6).[336]

Although the stakes are high, Paul has some reason for confidence. In the narrative so far, Paul has had some bad experiences with local authorities (Acts 16:19–23;[337] 17:7) but generally good experiences with Roman governors and officers (18:14–16;[338] 21:32–33; 22:29; 23:24). It may also bear mention that the historical Paul's letters also suggest an appreciation for government when it fulfills its proper function (Rom 13:1–7; cf. also 1 Pet 2:13–15; 4:15–16). Felix may prove unworthy of such approbation (Acts 24:26–27), but Paul would not necessarily know this yet.

III. Suggested Forensic Structure

The structure of this speech differs notably from the "kerygmatic" outline often attributed to evangelistic speeches earlier in Acts (though Luke does include Jesus's resurrection). Although some scholars debate whether this is a genuine forensic defense speech[339] and although actual speeches need not follow the standard genres or the narrow outlines of rhetorical handbooks, forensic features are prominent in this speech as in the one it answers (24:2–8).[340] Bruce Winter suggests a structure for this speech that closely parallels the Roman defense speech found in Quintilian:[341]

1. *Prooemium* (i.e., the *exordium*): 24:10b
2. *Narratio*: 24:11
3. *Probatio* (proof): summarized in 24:12–13 (namely, that his accusers lack proof)
4. *Refutatio*: 24:14–18 (implying that the difference between himself and his accusers is theological)[342]
5. *Peroratio*: 24:19–21

One might outline this section differently[343] (in practice, speeches could mix narration with proofs; 24:17–18 is also narrative; refutation occurs throughout 24:13–21),[344] but the ideas are certainly compatible with a forensic argument.

b. Paul's exordium (24:10)

The governor nods[345] to signal his permission for Paul to speak; figures with authority could use a nod for various purposes, such as to express assent or to confirm a

---

336. Max. Tyre 3 went further, denying that Socrates even offered a defense, but this claim is unusual (Trapp, *Maximus*, 24–25).

337. This was, however, later mitigated by his Roman citizenship (Acts 16:35–38).

338. Paul may be assured of not being accused successfully of ἀδίκημα (Acts 24:20) because of his previous vindication from such (18:14, Luke's other use; cf. 25:10); he knew what Romans expected.

339. E.g., Porter, *Paul in Acts*, 151n1.

340. See esp. Neyrey, "Forensic Defense Speech"; for rhetorical elements (without a focus on the structure), see also Keener, "Rhetorical Techniques."

341. Winter, "Official Proceedings," 323. Quintilian claims that this is the most common view (*Inst.* 3.9.1; Winter also compares P.Ryl. 114).

342. On refutation, see, e.g., briefly Anderson, *Glossary*, 40; Smith, "Function of Refutation," 104–6; Hermog. *Progymn.* 5, "On Refutation and Confirmation," 11; Aphth. *Progymn.* 5, "On Refutation," 27–28S, 10R; Nicolaus *Progymn.* 6, "On Refutation and Confirmation," 30. For gestures for refutation, see Shiell, *Reading Acts*, 69–71 (esp. 69, citing Quint. *Inst.* 11.3.92, on thrusting the hand forward energetically and vehemently).

343. Cf. Aune, *Environment*, 126 (*captatio* in Acts 24:10, *narratio* in 24:11, and *propositio* in 24:12). Narration continues in 24:12, but it does function effectively as a proposition.

344. Luke's speeches often conveniently emphasize narrative (e.g., Acts 10:34–42; 22:3–21), which will appeal to the same audience for whom he writes his larger work in the narrative genre.

345. On this sense of νεύω, see BDAG (citing, e.g., Lucian *Downward Journey* 15; *BGU* 1078.9).

promise.[346] Even a bold prospective martyr might wait for permission before speaking (4 Macc 5:14–15), and we should not be surprised that Paul would address a Roman official respectfully (the Paul of the letters exhorts this very sort of behavior in Rom 13:7). Paul's *exordium* in Acts 24:10 contains some of the most elegant Greek in Acts, appropriately beginning the defense with the best rhetorical foundation.[347]

I. MANY YEARS

Paul recognizes that Felix has been for "many years" a judge for the nation. It is possible that the phrase is simply conventional, as it appears to be in one text that commentators regularly cite: Claudius notes that he had long entertained goodwill toward Alexandria's citizens, when, in fact, he had been emperor only one year (P.Lond. 6.1912.22).[348]

Nevertheless, the suggestion that Felix had been judge for only two years at this time[349] is unlikely. Most scholars argue that Felix had governed since 52 C.E. (cf. Jos. *Ant.* 20.137; *War* 2.247),[350] but some argue for as early as 49.[351] It is quite possible (if Tacitus's sources are reliable here) that Felix did rule Samaria from an earlier period, while the governor Cumanus ruled Judea (so Tac. *Ann.* 12.54).[352] Though Tacitus's reconstruction raises the question of why Josephus notes Felix's being "sent" only after Cumanus's fall, it is clear that Felix had to return to Rome with Cumanus; although he was exonerated, all sources agree that he was in Rome at the time of his appointment.

How "many years" intervened between his appointment and this hearing depends on when we date this narrative; a common view is that it was about 57 C.E., but dates range later and earlier (see discussion at Acts 21:38). If either the scene occurs as late as 57 or Felix governed a few years earlier than 52, "many years" would represent a minimum of five; even a handful of years might require little exaggeration. It was helpful for a case whenever a judge was already acquainted with the issues surrounding both sides of a case (Phaedrus 3.13.4). For the dates of Felix's tenure, see also the discussion at Acts 23:24.

II. IMPLIED CONFIDENCE IN FELIX'S UNDERSTANDING

Acknowledging Felix's long tenure as a judge as a basis for his confidence[353] is tantamount to the convention mentioned above (on Acts 24:8) of expressing confidence in the judge's discernment and the rightness of one's cause.[354] Isocrates concludes to a jury that he trusts that their judgment will be for his good, and encourages its

---

346. E.g., a deity (Callim. *Hymns* 3 [to Artemis], lines 39–40; 5 [on Pallas's bath], 131–36; Catull. *Carm.* 64.202–6; Max. Tyre 4.8; 41.2); a proud person to his freedmen (Tac. *Ann.* 13.23); an officer's implicit permission or commands (Libanius *Anecdote* 2.19). Cf. Malina and Rohrbaugh, *John*, 271 (citing Zeus in Hom. *Hymns* 222 [to Aphrodite]); Prescendi, "Numen," 894. Shiell, *Reading Acts*, 151–53, suggests that other gestures may have usually accompanied the nod of approval, such as "the thumb touching the knuckle of the index finger" (p. 152, citing a picture; Quint. *Inst.* 11.3.101–3). Quint. Curt. 3.3.27 claims that Alexander's soldiers would respond not only to a signal but to his very nod (*nutus*).

347. With, e.g., Bruce, *Acts*[3], 66–67.

348. E.g., Conzelmann, *Acts*, 199; Hanson, *Acts*, 228; also Porter, *Paul in Acts*, 155 (though he agrees that Felix had probably served as governor for five years, in addition to three or four prior years under Cumanus). Cf. the prayer for "many years [lit., "periods," as in P.Lond. 1912]" of one's rule in Men. Rhet. 2.10, 417.29–30.

349. E.g., Hanson, *Acts*, 228.

350. E.g., Fitzmyer, *Acts*, 734.

351. Riesner, *Early Period*, 219–21.

352. E.g., Hemer, *Acts in History*, 129, 172; Rapske, *Custody*, 162n57; also Conzelmann, *Acts*, 199 (though he thinks the phrase merely conventional "flowery language"); more tentatively Johnson, *Acts*, 405; Witherington, *Acts*, 709; cf. D. Williams, *Acts*, 394.

353. "Cheerfully" (εὐθύμως) suggests confidence (cf. cognates in Acts 27:22, 25, 36; Jas 5:13; 2 Macc 11:26). Winter, "Official Proceedings," 324, rightly points out that Paul in 24:10 displays "the confidence that a rhetor was encouraged to display" (citing Quint. *Inst.* 5.21.51).

354. It was helpful to express confidence that one's hearers would not be swayed by arguments (Anderson, *Glossary*, 14).

members to vote as they feel best (*Antid.* 323); he does not pause to point out that, naturally, they would do so with or without his permission! Cicero claims that if truth remains in the land, the judge will hear him (*Quinct.* 1.5), but he has full confidence, he insists, in the judge's integrity (2.1).[355] He has worked so hard against corruption that everyone now recognizes that not in the past decade has a jury "of such illustrious and acknowledged merit" been chosen (*Verr.* 2.1.7.18).[356] Another speaker is depicted as inviting his jurors to play prosecutor also, so sure is he of having more than sufficient evidence for his acquittal (Lucian *Fisherman* 9). Rhetoricians advised praising judges or jurors for their competence,[357] and it was common practice.[358] Flattery might be superfluous for a well-disposed audience (*Rhet. Alex.* 29, 1436b.19–29), but it would be important for a neutral audience (1436b.30–38).

Although Paul's *captatio* is likely a summary, it might be significant that it omits any compliments about Felix establishing peace, justice, and so forth.[359] If so, Paul's boldness here fits Luke's portrait of apostolic παρρησία, which would appeal to those who respected philosophers.[360] If this is too much to infer from a summary (and it may be), it is not too much to infer from Paul's subsequent behavior (Acts 24:25). Certainly, Paul does not fit the negative portrait of flattery common in ancient literature but instead merely expresses appropriate respect.[361] Given that Luke knows the kind of person Felix proved to be in the end (24:27), he may feel no obligation to portray him favorably or emphasize positive remarks from Paul.

Paul's *captatio* fits the issue under discussion—namely, Felix's competence in knowing Jewish culture and hence his ability to apprehend the theological character of a debate about the resurrection.[362] Felix's marriage to a Jewess (24:24) provided him additional knowledge (cf. 24:22); although portrayed by Josephus as hardheaded, on occasion he had been persuaded by argument (Jos. *Ant.* 20.178).[363]

c. Arrival for Worship Twelve Days Earlier (24:11)

In Luke's summary, Paul finishes his proem (24:10) more concisely than Tertullus does (24:2–3) and focuses (in 24:11–21) on evidence and procedure, unlike Tertullus's assertions (24:5–6). Paul already offers an argument in his defense in his introductory *narratio*, or narration of events leading up to the present situation. Because Luke provides us only a summary of Paul's speech, there are several possibilities about how the "twelve days" figures into his argument. That he came to worship probably increases his *ēthos*.

I. THE *NARRATIO*

Most scholars find the summary of the *narratio* in Acts 24:11;[364] a *narratio* would be necessary when the events around which the case revolved were in dispute.[365] A

---

355. Cicero could also write letters of recommendation while claiming that the person did not need one (*Fam.* 13.16.3; in 13.16.4, he finds himself recommending the person and hence "apologizes" and closes the letter).

356. Trans. L. H. G. Greenwood, LCL, 7:139.

357. E.g., *Rhet. Alex.* 36, 1442a.14–16; see comments on Acts 7:51; 24:2.

358. E.g., Cic. *Quinct.* 2.10; 9.34; see comments on Acts 7:51; 24:2. Cf. Antisthenes's version of the judgment of Odysseus and Ajax, where the former flatters the judges and the latter (who will lose, of course) insults them.

359. Tajra, *Trial*, 125, contends that Paul's *captatio* "was considerably less servile in tone than the rhetor's"; cf. Bruce, *Commentary*, 468; Dunn, *Acts*, 312.

360. Johnson, *Acts*, 416.

361. Distant cultures also distinguished between flattery and conciliatory respect; see, e.g., Confuc. *Anal.* 63 (13.23).

362. Winter, "*Captatio benevolentiae*," 523; idem, "Official Proceedings," 324.

363. Dunn, *Acts*, 312.

364. Winter, "Official Proceedings," 323; Aune, *Environment*, 126; Witherington, *Acts*, 710.

365. Quint. *Inst.* 4.2.4–5 (cited by Winter, "*Captatio benevolentiae*," 324n76; Witherington, *Acts*, 710).

narratio often included the length and sequence of events. Prosecutors could usually make most of the "sequence of events" in a narration (Hermog. *Issues* 47.8–11), analyzing "the sequence of events alleged by one or other party . . . in order to establish its coherence and plausibility and to highlight its implications."[366] If Tertullus's *narratio* included more than what our summary of his speech indicates (a reasonable guess), it is possible (though not certain) that Paul counters his claims here. Paul returns to the narration of events in Acts 24:17–18; speakers could divide the *narratio* and use some of it in proofs[367] (or summarize it in their conclusion).

Even were this *narratio* not a summary, we should not be surprised by its comparative brevity. Aside from the general value of conciseness (see comment on Acts 24:4), we should note that some Hellenistic rhetoricians thought it best to keep the *narratio* as concise as possible, using it meanwhile to convince hearers without their awareness (subliminally, so to speak; Dion. Hal. *Lysias* 18). That Luke elsewhere often prefers a long *narratio* befits his own preference for communicating a narrative message.

ii. The Twelve Days

The twelve days since entering Jerusalem apparently include only the time before Paul's arrival before Felix in Caesarea (Acts 23:33), usually delineated as follows (with the five more recent days added in the table's final line):[368]

Count of Days	Reference in Acts	Activity
First day	21:17	Arrival in Jerusalem
Second day	21:18	Meeting with James and elders
Third through ninth days	21:27	Seven days of purification (they may have been somewhat fewer: they were "nearly" up)
Tenth day	22:30	Sanhedrin hearing
Eleventh day*	23:11–12	The plot
Twelfth day	23:31–33	Transfer (escape) to Caesarea
Seventeenth day	24:1	Hearing after five days

*The passage of time in this case might be debated. Luke's ἐπιούσῃ in 23:11 (elsewhere always referring to the following day; 7:26; 16:11; 20:15; 21:18; cf. LXX Prov 3:28; 27:1) could refer to the night connected to the following day (so perhaps "the following night" in, e.g., RSV, NIV, NKJV, ESV, NET; "the night following," KJV, ASV; "the next night," NEW CENTURY). But it might also refer, as I have taken it (see also Bock, *Acts*, 674, Schnabel, *Acts*, 932; Witherington, *Acts*, 693), to the night adjacent to (thus immediately following) the day of the hearing (so NRSV, GNT, NLT, "that night"; NASB, "the night immediately following"), which also fits the Jewish reckoning of days from sundown. The plot is thus either two mornings after the Sanhedrin hearing or, as our count above tentatively presumes, one day after it.

The five days since Paul came to Caesarea (24:1) and three of the twelve days (spent in Roman custody) would not count toward days he could have spent making trouble. Luke records carefully these days in his own narrative to demonstrate how strong Paul's case was, just as he also reports potential witnesses on whom Paul could have called if necessary (Mnason, James, or, in Caesarea itself, where the hearing was being held, Philip and others who could attest how recently he had left for Jerusalem, presumably for Pentecost and in the company of other pilgrims). Some from Caesarea had even accompanied him part of the way (21:16); they could become useful as witnesses (cf. 11:12).[369]

366. Heath, *Hermogenes*, 84.

367. Hughes, "Rhetoric," 252; Amador, "Revisiting," 110–11; cf. deSilva, *Credentials*, 76. To put it differently, genuine speeches did not always follow handbooks' conventions.

368. Haenchen, *Acts*, 654n2; Johnson, *Acts*, 412; Witherington, *Acts*, 710; Schnabel, *Acts*, 957; this reading allows more ambiguity than many translations. Instead of trying to calculate the days, Pervo, *Acts*, 598, treats them as mere "rhetoric, like the 'many years' of vv. 10 and 17." Yet Luke specifies a number here (in contrast to Acts 24:10, 17), presumably inviting his audience to consider the events that he has narrated.

369. Defendants could not force the attendance of witnesses (Pliny *Ep.* 6.5.2) and usually could not summon witnesses from distant provinces (6.5.1); for the delays involved (not always granted), see, e.g., Tac. *Ann.* 13.53 (witnesses against a governor).

The particular reasons offered for Luke's mentioning the twelve days reflect less consensus. One view argues plausibly that the events are so recent that the supposed witnesses should be available.[370] In this case, Paul appeals, as Tertullus did in 24:8, to Felix's right (*extra ordinem*) to investigate the matter.[371] Now that the festival was presumably over, Paul's Asian Jewish accusers, who actually witnessed nothing directly, have probably gone home, but some of Paul's supporting witnesses may have remained. Another possibility, though not a likely one, is that Paul's recently shaved hair is external evidence that he recently completed his vow in Jerusalem (18:18; 21:26). But aside from our own uncertainty as to how he completed the vow, nothing in the text (admittedly condensed) suggests to us that Felix has sufficient information to understand this sense, though long-term defendants normally let their hair grow long.[372]

Another view is that Paul's mere nine days of freedom in Jerusalem hardly offered "time to foment a rebellion!"[373] How, then, was he accused of inciting all the political turmoil his opponents attributed to him? This would have been an argument from probability. Centuries earlier, Aristotle allowed that when no witnesses were available, an argument might be decided by probability (*Rhet.* 1.15.17, 1376a). Such arguments were already standard in classical rhetoric,[374] and they often remained useful in the Hellenistic[375] and Roman periods (see also comment at Acts 26:8). When Cicero could not refute a charge based on facts, he could resort to the probability argument, favored by Greek orators.[376]

Given the mere twelve days, the argument of Paul's opponents does not cohere well with the evidence or their own claims. Discrepancies in an opposing argument helped undermine the opponent's case,[377] and even an opponent's own arguments could be exploited to serve one's side.[378] For example, Cicero protests the unlikelihood that a man who genuinely believed another had cheated him would then enter a business partnership with him (*Quinct.* 24.76).[379] The same method obtained in other genres as well; thus historians and biographers could evaluate claims on the basis of internal consistency[380] or other matters of probability.[381] Josephus uses the same method in his apologetic against Apion, showing inherent self-contradictions in the

370. Winter, "*Captatio benevolentiae*," 324; similarly Conzelmann, *Acts*, 199 (Paul's "stay is easily reviewed"). One could also use the shortness of time to complain that the charges were too sudden to have collected full evidence for the defense (Apul. *Apol.* 1, four or five days).

371. Witherington, *Acts*, 710.

372. Pliny *Ep.* 7.27.14. Prisoners also might grow long hair, though the example (of long hair shaved) in Philost. *Vit. Apoll.* 7.34, 36; 8.7 relates to philosophy. Both growing hair long (Diod. Sic. 36.15.2; Sen. E. *Controv.* 4.1 excerpt; Lucan *C.W.* 2.375–76; Plut. *Cic.* 30.4; 35.4; *Apoll. K. Tyre* 7, 28; *y. Šabb.* 1:2, §2) and shaving it (see comment on Acts 18:18) were common expressions for mourning.

373. E.g., Gwalther 821 in Chung-Kim and Hains, *Acts*, 327. Dunn, *Acts*, 313. Conzelmann, *Acts*, 199, notes this view but regards it as less probable. A long delay could have also been used by the defense in its favor; a person failing to prosecute immediately could be accused, for that reason, of making up the charges (Lysias *Or.* 3.39, §99; Aeschines *Embassy* 122–23; Max. Tyre 18.6; cf. Hermog. *Issues* 69.3–13).

374. E.g., Lysias *Or.* 4.5–6, §101; 7.12–18, §§109–10; 12.27–28, §122; 19 passim (e.g., 19.24, §154); Isaeus *Astyph.* 14–15; *Pyrr.* 27; Demosth. *Fals. leg.* 120; *Pant.* 23; cf. Eurip. *Cretans* frg. 472e.11. See further discussion in Kennedy, *Classical Rhetoric*, 20–21.

375. E.g., *Rhet. Alex.* 7, 1428a.19–23; Dion. Hal. *Ant. rom.* 11.34.1–6. See also Anderson, *Glossary*, 37.

376. Lord, "Introduction," 358.

377. E.g., *Rhet. Alex.* 5, 1427b.12–30; 10, 1430a.26–27; Dion. Hal. *Lysias* 15; Cic. *Vat.* 1.3.

378. Ael. Arist. *Def. Or.* 311, §101D (cf. 340, §112D; 343–44, §114D; 446, §150D).

379. Cf. earlier, e.g., Lysias *Or.* 29.7, §182 (if Ergocles was really Philocrates's enemy, why did the former honor the latter with a high position?).

380. E.g., Dion. Hal. *Ant. rom.* 3.35.5–6. Dio Chrys. *Or.* 11 uses internal contradictions to discredit Homer (albeit probably as a rhetorical exercise).

381. E.g., Plut. *Arist.* 19.5–6 (against Hdt. 9.85); Arrian *Alex.* 3.3.6.

logic of Judaism's critics.[382] Once one discovered any inconsistencies in an opposing position, undiscerning hearers would usually mistrust everything in the opponent's speech (*Rhet. Alex.* 9, 1430a.14–21).[383] (See further comment at Acts 26:8.)

Lest anyone doubt Paul's arrival date (which could be confirmed by witnesses, including some in Caesarea itself), Paul also had good reason to be going up to Jerusalem when he did. Paul may appeal to Felix's knowledge of Judean customs in Acts 24:10 precisely because an allusion in 24:11 may take it for granted. Although it is not clear that Felix came to Jerusalem himself on this occasion, he could not but have known (and undoubtedly dispatched additional troops for) the recent festival. Paul had hoped to be in Jerusalem in time for Pentecost (20:16), and Luke's chronology in the travel narrative suggests that he almost certainly succeeded. Felix will recognize that if Paul came to Jerusalem only twelve days before his detention in Caesarea (a fact verifiable, as noted above, by witnesses even in Caesarea itself), he came in peace at the same time and for the same reason as most other Jews were coming.[384] Thus Paul points out that he came to Jerusalem "to worship."[385]

III. ARGUMENT BASED ON *ĒTHOS*

Paul could also be offering a particular sort of argument from probability, namely, one based on his *ēthos*: how plausible is it that someone would go up to the temple only for the festival (24:11)[386] and to bring alms (24:17) yet would merit the sort of denunciations the chief priests gave him? He was instead framed because of his theological convictions, which his accusers rejected (24:5c, 14–15).

This form of probability argument, based on the respective claimants' character or behavior, was common (see also discussion at Acts 24:14–16). Thus a case was hardly probable if a strong man charged a weaker one with assault, a poor man claimed that a rich man had seized his wealth, or a man known for violence charged a man with a reputation for peace.[387] Likewise, defendants could show that neither they nor anyone of their class or circle had ever committed the crimes of which they were accused.[388]

Examples abound. If Fannius was a rogue and Roscius an honorable person, is it really likely that the latter cheated the former (Cic. *Rosc. com.* 7.21)? One of noble character would not be guilty of such crimes, and so Sulla must be innocent (Cic. *Sull.* 24.68);[389] could his hearers think of any deed he has done compatible with such charges (26.72)? The accuser is a habitual liar (Cic. *Cael.* 29.69).[390] If the testator was our constant benefactor, surely this reveals his intention better than an old will made

---

382. E.g., Jos. *Ag. Ap.* 1.219–20, 267 (though some arguments in 1.267 are less implausible than he pretends); 2.8–27 (rightly), 148; cf. similarly *Life* 350.

383. Because finite presentations cannot declare all possible evidence, they can inevitably be deconstructed (cf. Keener, *John*, 38–39, 901). Even accurate cases can sometimes be charged with such "discrepancies"; modern critics charge them against Luke, and others charge Luke's critics with the same.

384. Since a rabble-rouser might have found Passover more suitable for exploiting liberationist sentiment (cf. Jos. *Ant.* 20.106; *War* 2.10–13; Jeremias, *Eucharistic Words*, 256–57 and n. 3), it may have turned out for the better that Paul could not arrive in time for Passover as he had probably originally hoped (Acts 20:3).

385. Luke depicts worship in Jerusalem with this same verb, προσκυνέω, in Acts 8:27; Luke 24:52; cf. Isa 27:13; 66:23 LXX; Zech 14:16–17; Tob 5:14; with a different spelling of Jerusalem, John 4:20–21.

386. Of course, one could argue that festivals were strategic opportunities to stir unrest and that Jewish nationalists kept them as well; some arguments could be turned either way (cf., e.g., the probably specious arguments in Thucyd. 2.39.1; 2.89.1–2 [cf. the disastrous inaccuracy of the latter in 2.90.4–6]).

387. *Rhet. Alex.* 36, 1442a.29–32; cf. also 1442a.32–37.

388. *Rhet. Alex.* 7, 1428b.34–36 (also that it would not have profited them to have committed these actions).

389. Cicero develops this argument further in *Sull.* 24.69–28.77. A defendant could appeal to good deeds preceding the trial to confirm his positive character (Hermog. *Inv.* 2.5.118–19).

390. The argument in Cicero's *Pro Flacco* also hinges on probability regarding the character of both the defendant and the prosecution witnesses (Lord, "Introduction," 358).

in haste (Isaeus *Cleon.* 12.36; 27.37). The charge that one withheld much property contradicts his character, illustrated, for example, in his expenditures on the city's welfare (Lysias *Or.* 19.24, §154). Claiming that alleged acts are out of keeping with one's character could help refute a probability argument based on such actions being profitable to one (*Rhet. Alex.* 36, 1443b.34–38).

Rather than defend himself against a charge he regarded as absurd, Scipio refused to stoop so low; he simply recounted his irreproachable life and so silenced his accusers (Appian *Hist. rom.* 11.7.40–41). Likewise, Xenophon claims that Socrates viewed his whole life as his defense (*Mem.* 4.8.4; *Apol.* 3). For arguments based on *ēthos*, see further comment on Acts 23:1.

d. The Prosecution Lacks Evidence (24:12–13)

Paul points out that Tertullus could not cite any testimony of Paul's seditious activity anywhere in Jerusalem (Acts 24:12)—testimony that might be rendered suspicious, in any case, by the recent character of Paul's arrival (24:11). Not only in this matter but in any at all, Tertullus cannot offer (and apparently has not offered) any proof (24:13). A defendant would sometimes briefly rebut the charges, in order, and then refute them more extensively, again—barring good reason to the contrary—in their sequence.[391] If Luke is summarizing any such procedure here, it is not impossible that Paul may have historically responded in sequence to the charges in 24:5–6. Paul begins by answering the sedition charge in 24:12, then perhaps turns to complaints about his Nazarene faith in 24:14–16, and finally addresses the temple desecration charge in 24:17–19.

i. No Debates in Jerusalem (24:12)

Paul responds immediately to the accusations of stirring unrest among Jerusalemites, especially in the temple (24:5–6). Starting with an opponent's accusation was an acceptable method in traditional forensic speech (Dion. Hal. *Lysias* 17); commonly one would summarize the opponent's argument, then refute it (*Lysias* 26).[392] (The denial here of making ἐπίστασις—that is, of stirring people up—directly responds to the dangerous charge of στάσις in Acts 24:5.) Proving events in Ephesus and distant cities would be difficult; since Paul, as the defendant, speaks after the prosecution, he wisely focuses on the only time for which evidence is easily available, that is, the time in Jerusalem. This focus also protects him from charges that might gain credibility by their frequent repetition in other cities.

That Paul had come to the city by no means proved that he had come to stir unrest. Indeed, in the city itself, the sphere of his accusers' own observation, he had barely been present long enough to do so (24:11). His mention of a lack of disputes in the synagogues could refer to his alleged Diaspora activity, but this would be inaccurate (since he *did* dispute there) and does not fit the sequence of nouns in the sentence (which are built up as rhetorical accumulation). It refers instead to debates in Jerusalem's synagogues, which probably numbered many[393] (cf. 26:11). His accusers did not even find Paul dialoguing or disputing (διαλεγόμενον) with anyone on this

391. Apuleius briefly refutes charges in *Apol.* 27 and elaborates in 28–65; in 61 he notes that he has been responding to the charges "one by one" (trans. V. Hunink, p. 83).

392. One could also compare one's arguments with those of the opponents when recapitulating (Anderson, *Glossary*, 22); Paul more explicitly addresses his opponents' case in Acts 24:18–21.

393. With Riesner, "Synagogues in Jerusalem," 204. Other cities with large Jewish populations, such as Salamis, could have multiple synagogues (Acts 13:5); the proximity of the temple would not eliminate these (see comment on Acts 6:9).

occasion, as would be common in schools of scribes, or debating with speakers in the temple (as Paul may have done on earlier occasions; contrast 9:29; the same term, διαλέγομαι, in 17:2, 17; 18:4, 19; 19:8–9; cf. 20:7, 9).[394] Specification of temple and synagogues alongside the city may reflect the sort of elaboration expected in a *narratio* (see Hermog. *Inv.* 2.7.120–21).

Romans were accustomed to academicians' debates, but they might show little tolerance if these debates ended up disturbing public order. Even had Paul been carrying on discussions in Jerusalem, this practice would not guarantee his guilt; advocates emphasized that simply engaging in an activity in which criminals also sometimes engaged did not make the activity itself criminal (Hermog. *Issues* 51.16–22; 52.1–4). But Paul can go beyond such a defense and argue that he was not debating in even the synagogues of the chief Jewish city, a place more vulnerable to Jewish unrest—a defense that would cast doubt on the claims of more distant unrest in places where Paul had been debating, claims that Tertullus would not be prepared to prove. By conjoining three locations (although separating the first syntactically and using the third in a different case) Paul's summary leaves the rhetorical impression of covering everywhere.[395]

Paul's controversial speech in the temple could not count against him, since it followed a riot already in process, was permitted by the tribune as an attempt to calm the crowd, and might have some witnesses who could testify that it was Paul's pro-Gentile stance that triggered the riot's resumption.[396] Paul also had maneuvered the discussion in the Sanhedrin in such a way as to make his views about the resurrection, rather than anything political, the clear issue of debate.

Some interpreters view Acts 24:12 as the speech's *propositio*,[397] or statement of the case, and others view it as a summary of the proofs.[398] It is feasible to view it as the former standing in for the latter in Luke's précis. One would offer a preview of arguments (to be developed in the proofs section) in the statement of the case (πρόθεσις), helping the audience to follow (Dion. Hal. *Lysias* 17).[399] In Acts 24:18, Paul returns to the central claim offered here.

II. THE DEMAND FOR PROOF (24:13)

Many speakers claimed to provide facts (see comment on Acts 24:9),[400] but genuinely providing evidence was another matter. A speaker who lacked direct evidence might argue that the veracity of his claim could be inferred indirectly from the evidence.[401]

One might offer a strong claim with "many proofs" (Isaeus *Aristarch.* 6), though some thinkers felt that strong proofs mattered more than multiple ones (Mus. Ruf. 1,

---

394. On earlier occasions (not mentioned here), Paul was evangelizing; on this more relevant occasion, by contrast, his errand has been purely one of reconciliation.

395. Cf. comment on Acts 23:8, where accumulation may function like polysyndeton.

396. Paul's Ephesian accusers apparently did not know Aramaic (making their charges more embarrassing to themselves), but much of the crowd would have, and it may have included Paul's Nazirite dependents and some other informed believers in the temple.

397. Aune, *Environment*, 126.

398. Winter, "Official Proceedings," 323.

399. See discussion of thesis and hypothesis in the section "An Outline for Acts?" at Acts 1:8 (Keener, *Acts*, 1:708–10).

400. E.g., Isaeus *Cleon.* 41; *Menec.* 19; Cic. *Mil.* 11.30. An orator's job was to prove points and then amplify them (Theon *Progymn.* 1.180–84).

401. So Aeschines *Tim.* 123–26 (pointing out that one could expect no witnesses to come forward in a matter that would incriminate themselves). Aeschines *Embassy* passim defends Aeschines himself against Demosthenes's inference (without evidence) that Philip bribed Aeschines.

p. 32.5–17). Proofs could often be stated tersely, the appropriate tone for the logically argumentative section of a speech (Dion. Hal. *Lysias* 9).[402] One should provide arguments against what is debatable but not against matters that are obviously wrong.[403]

Paul denies that his opponents can prove their claims against him. Such an insistence was standard in forensic rhetoric (and often true).[404] One could complain that one's opponent has ruined the opponent's own case,[405] or even explicitly accuse the opposing side of deception.[406] Most commonly, however, one could demand proof. Classical orators provide an abundance of examples: Isaeus complains that his opponents keep offering accusations without proving anything (*Cleon.* 49). Someone accused of a crime can demand that his accusers demonstrate his guilt or convict him.[407] Someone who makes a claim that violates logic can be challenged to explain it and be told that he cannot (Lysias *Or.* 4.5–6, §101). Apparent eloquence without arguments was simply verbosity (Pliny *Ep.* 5.20.4–5); one who resorts to depending solely on pathos rather than offering proof as much as admits one's guilt (Lysias *Or.* 27.12–13, §178–79).[408] A Hellenistic rhetorician explains that one must provide a demonstration and not simply assert what one cannot prove (Dion. Hal. *Lit. Comp.* 3).[409]

The claim that an opponent has not produced proof continued in Roman-period forensic rhetoric. On one occasion, Cicero charges that it is undignified for the prosecutor to attack his client on the basis of street gossip, "without proof" (*Mur.* 6.13). On another, the prosecution witness provided "no proof" and "brought no witnesses" (Cic. *Flacc.* 15.34).[410] The charge is false, Cicero insists on yet another occasion, and the accuser's attorney is "unable to prove" his case (*Rosc. Amer.* 29.79). In a second-century writer, a deity being punished by other deities demands proof of his guilt (Lucian *Prom.* 13, 19). Apuleius complains that his opponents have chosen a charge "easier to insinuate than to prove" (*Apol.* 2); they fail to support their allegation with proof, their case being "weak in facts but so strong in noise" (25). By such standards, he points out, anyone could be accused and almost any action become grounds for suspicion (54). A late second-century rhetorical writer explains that legal debate regularly includes a demand for evidence (Hermog. *Issues* 45.1–2). After that time, a writer could still present a defendant as winning his case by demanding that reliable

402. One might not require a long time to prove some cases (Lysias *Or.* 23.1, §166).

403. E.g., Polyb. 12.25K.9; Mus. Ruf. 1, p. 32.17.

404. It also appears in other rhetorical logic, e.g., in the second-century C.E. orator Aelius Aristides, *Def. Or.* 242, §75D (challenging those who fail to prove their point); cf. Quint. *Decl.* 351.6.

405. *Rhet. Alex.* 36, 1444a.28–34.

406. Dion. Hal. *Lysias* 33 (quoting Lysias *Or.* 34); Cic. *Quinct.* 6.22; see Theon *Progymn.* 17, 112P. For the frequent use of false testimony, see comment on Acts 6:11–13 (Keener, *Acts*, 2:1311–15).

407. Lysias *Or.* 24.24, §170; 25.14, §172; John 8:46. Such rhetorical boldness resembles epitrope or *permissio* (see Rowe, "Style," 147). Later handbooks continue to teach the demand for proof (see Hermog. *Inv.* 3.4.132; 3.5.141–42).

408. An appeal to pathos could secure unwarranted mercy in the short term (Pliny *Ep.* 2.11.2–3), but reasoned judgment carried much longer-term persuasiveness (2.11.6).

409. Proof would help an innocent defendant (Lucian *Fisherman* 17); as suggested above, some philosophers contended that strong proofs were better than numerous ones (Mus. Ruf. 1, p. 32.3, 5). For proofs, see, e.g., *Rhet. Alex.* 1, 1421b.24–26; Aristotle's three traditional kinds of proof (the speaker's ἦθος, πάθος appealing to the audience, and content-oriented demonstration, ἀπόδειξις) in Winter, *Philo and Paul*, 153–55 (at least some later writers followed Aristotle regarding demonstration: Porph. *Isag.* 1.6–7; cf. *Marc.* 8.142–43; cf. Robertson and Plummer, *First Corinthians*, 33). On logical demonstration, see also Mus. Ruf. frg. 44, p. 138.26–28; Iambl. *V.P.* 18.82; Anderson, *Glossary*, 23–24. In Paul's extant letters, he at least once may use the rhetorical sense of "demonstration" (1 Cor 2:4–5; Winter, *Philo and Paul*, 159–60; Witherington, *Corinthians*, 125; cf. Anderson, *Rhetorical Theory*, 265–66), though he probably does not use πίστις (in 1 Cor 2:5) in its rhetorical sense (Witherington, *Corinthians*, 125n19).

410. Cicero conveniently ignores the difficulty of the long journey from Greece to Rome for anyone wishing to testify.

witnesses be able to confirm the accusations against him (Philost. *Vit. Apoll.* 8.5). This form of defense was standard enough that Lucian could offer a mock defense of a tyrant, challenging the accuser's competence on the basis of lack of direct knowledge (*Phal.* 2.6).

This claim of lack of proof was especially useful for the defense, since the burden of proof rested with the accuser and suspects had to be freed if there was reasonable doubt (Cic. *Rosc. Amer.* 23.64–65).[411] A skillful rhetorician could seek to shift this burden,[412] but he would have to do so before the defense began speaking, since the defense spoke after the prosecution.[413] (Of course, if the prosecution offered much proof of the defendant's guilt and the defendant offered no proof of innocence, he would be convicted, as in the case of Herod's son Antipater.)[414] At the least, Paul's knowledge of standard rhetorical arguments would serve notice to Felix that he was no uneducated provincial easily dispensed with.

e. Admitting Piety (24:14)

In Acts 24:14 (and throughout 24:14–17), Paul "confesses" his Jewish piety, demonstrating that he is not the sort of person who would profane the temple. (Luke has elsewhere provided supporting evidence for this argument [e.g., 16:3; 18:18], though we could quickly draw the same conclusion even from several of Paul's own letters.) Paul's "confession" thereby paves the way for what he asserts is the real charge against him in 24:20–21.[415] Paul thus shows this to be an internal religious argument among Jews.

I. THE ISSUE OF *ĒTHOS* IN 24:14–17

In 24:14–17, Paul reinforces his *ēthos* as a pious worshiper of Israel's God, undermining, as already mentioned, the probability that he is the sort of person who would desecrate Israel's temple.

Whereas Tertullus's case argues that Paul is guilty of sedition and desecrating the temple, Paul points out the lack of evidence for his opponents' position (24:11) and countercharges that their case is motivated by other issues. He shows that his only "crime" is a religious position well within the bounds of Jewish faith (24:14) and that his opponents themselves admitted in a different setting the religious character of the charge (24:20–21). The real issues here are religious, not political, and so Felix should dismiss the case.[416]

In 24:14–18, Paul also further establishes his *ēthos*, arguing that the deeds attributed to him are inconsistent with his demonstrated character. He has attempted this argument before, at 23:1 (see comment there; also at 24:11); for him (and for many others), a consistently pious life is the strongest argument. This strategy also answers the attempt to portray his character badly in 24:5. Establishing *ēthos* was important

411. In classical Athens, too, a case was dismissed if the claimants could not prove their claims (Isaeus *Nicost.* 9). Conzelmann, *Acts*, 199, suggests that Paul invokes "the fundamental legal principle that one is innocent until proven guilty," but offers no documentation (cf. Deut 22:23–27). A defendant who was pardoned, however, also needed to be able to prove this (Pliny *Ep.* 10.58.3).

412. E.g., Lysias *Or.* 29.5, §181 (since some of Ergocles's money is missing and Philocrates is charged with holding it, the latter must prove that it is held by others).

413. Ancients also were alert to orators seeking to redefine the issues (cf. Solon's law in Aeschines *Tim.* 35).

414. Jos. *Ant.* 17.131; *War* 1.638.

415. For a structural connection between Acts 24:14–16 and 24:20–21, see also Talbert, *Acts*, 201 (who treats 24:11–13 as replying to the sedition charge in 24:5, and 24:17–19 as replying to the desecration charge in 24:6a).

416. Cf. also Hemer, *Acts in History*, 129; Witherington, *Acts*, 712.

in a defense or prosecution;[417] thus, after answering a charge with some documentary evidence, Lysias focuses on Mantitheus's positive life (*Or.* 16 passim).[418] Jurors indeed looked away from the accounts used to prosecute Metellus for extortion, because they "believed that they should read the proofs of upright administration" in his life, not in "a little wax and a few letters of the alphabet" (Val. Max. 2.10.1).[419] Cicero dismisses a slander against himself by claiming that witnesses know better because they know his character (*Verr.* 2.1.6.17).[420]

Among examples of appeals to *ēthos* are claims that one is not the kind of person who would commit sacrilege (Lysias *Or.* 7.41, §112). Given his piety (Acts 24:14–18), would Paul have really desecrated the temple (24:6)?[421] Some of Paul's detractors have doubted his loyalty to the law, but Luke portrays him as loyal (16:3; 18:18; 21:26), and his own letters suggest that, however novel his interpretations appear to be, he viewed himself as faithful to his ancestral faith.[422]

The defense speeches in Acts 24–26 focus more on God the Father than on Jesus, in contrast to 22:3–21.[423] Romans might misunderstand as misplaced loyalty that could lead to treason an emphasis on a human executed for claiming to be Israel's king. By contrast, a national deity was for them a purely religious matter, worthy of respect and not Roman interference. Jesus appears more in Acts 26 than in Acts 24, since Paul can expect Agrippa to have more understanding of the issues.

II. Confessing a Noncrime

In 24:14, Paul confesses (ὁμολογέω)[424] his real "crime," foreshadowing his conclusion that the real case against him is purely theological (24:20–21).[425] Those who admitted guilt could either defend their honorable intention (*purgatio*) or simply beg pardon (*deprecatio*; Cic. *Inv.* 2.31.94).[426] The guilty sometimes gained pardon by confessing (Phaedrus 3.epil. 22);[427] under a wicked dictator, even the innocent might gain more mercy by confessing than by denying a crime of which they were accused (Pliny *Ep.* 4.11.4–13). One could sometimes be cleared of a worse charge by confessing a lighter one (Val. Max. 8.1.abs.12); one who was clearly guilty of a lesser offense had to confess it to gain credibility in denying other charges (Pliny

---

417. E.g., Isaeus *Nicost.* 27. On a speaker's use of ἦθος and πάθος, see also Lampe, "Einsichten."

418. Also much of Lysias *Or.* 18 and many other speeches. One who has always displayed good character is more likely deemed innocent (7.30–33, §111), keeping the burden of proof on the accuser.

419. LCL, 1:221. Valerius, like his contemporaries and successors, often idealized earlier Rome.

420. For other arguments of Cicero based on character, see, e.g., *Sull.* 24.68–28.77.

421. Even those who disapproved of the temple hierarchy, such as the Essenes, did not go so far as to desecrate the temple. The Samaritans, however, did (Jos. *Ant.* 18.30); later revolutionaries did defile the temple (*War* 2.424; 4.171, 201, 242; 5.10, 18; 6.126), but it is highly unlikely that its defilement was their objective.

422. See, e.g., Rom 3:21, 31; 4:3; 9–11; 15:4; R. Williams, *Acts*, 155. More fully, see comments on Acts 16:3; 18:18; 21:24–26. Group loyalty was highly valued in the ancient Mediterranean world (Malina and Neyrey, *Portraits*, 164–69; the exception, of course, being when another loyalty conflicted with that to one's own group).

423. With, e.g., Porter, *Paul in Acts*, 157, 164.

424. For judicial settings for confessing wrongdoing, see *Dig.* 80.1; cf. *Mart. Pol.* 6.1; 9.2 and other sources in BDAG. This is more relevant here than confession of sin to God (Jos. *Ant.* 6.151; 1 John 1:9; see fuller comment at Acts 7:60).

425. With, e.g., Malina and Neyrey, *Portraits*, 83–84.

426. For definitions, see Cic. *Inv.* 1.11.15. For arguments that acts were due to errors or misfortune rather than injustice, see *Rhet. Alex.* 4, 1427a.27–31. For agreement on an act being committed yet dispute over whether it was wrong, see, e.g., *Rhet. Her.* 1.10.17 (taking Orestes's matricide as an example); Quint. *Decl.* 250.9. For confessing what became a crime only after its commission (here, loyalty to Sejanus before his fall), see, e.g., Tac. *Ann.* 6.5.

427. For the value of such confession, see Hermog. *Method* 32.447–48, citing as examples Hom. *Il.* 3.164; Hdt 1.35ff. Cicero warns, however, that *deprecatio* can prove dangerous in a trial (*Inv.* 2.34.104).

Ep. 4.9.6–7). One who would not confess committing the crime might concede the alleged crime's awfulness (Xen. *Hell.* 2.3.37).

Paul, however, tactically confesses what is not yet a crime under Roman law[428] and therefore offers no grounds for his conviction; he confesses to merely holding a theological conviction that is the real basis for the accusations (Acts 24:20–21). Paul "serves" (λατρεύω; also 27:23) his ancestral deity (cf. Israel "serving" God in 26:7; cf. Luke 1:74; for "ancestral," cf. Acts 22:3; 28:17; for Paul's affirmations of his orthodoxy, see, e.g., 23:6; 26:22); Romans generally respected nations' rights to practice their own ethnic, ancestral religions.[429] Far from acting "against the law" (25:8), Paul depended on it (just as Luke argues that the entire Jesus movement does, e.g., Luke 24:44).

Confessing an "offense" that was inoffensive to the judges was a common rhetorical strategy.[430] Thus Josephus divides his audience by first confessing that, according to its understanding, he is guilty (*Life* 139) and hence accepts even death if they think this penalty just (*Life* 141),[431] but then "confessing" that the money was to help a city strongly represented in his audience (*Life* 142)—thereby securing the support of some of his audience (*Life* 143). This is an example of "confessing" what turned out to be in hearers' interests, a particular form of the larger category of confessing noncrimes (see further examples under Acts 24:17). Other ancients also would admit what was not really a crime[432] or was even a benefit (see comment on Acts 24:17).[433]

Rhetorical training included instruction that one should admit any charges not dangerous to one's case (Aul. Gel. 12.12.1);[434] one should reserve one's credibility for where it was needed.[435] The technical Greek and Latin terms for the technique are συγχώρησις and *concessio*, admitting an opposing claim while one shows that it does not damage one's own case.[436] Of course, this rhetorical strategy was common enough that rhetorically proficient hearers could point it out and challenge it: when Regulus apologized for an inoffensive offense, his rival Pliny raised the real issue of contention, putting Regulus on the defensive (Pliny *Ep.* 1.5.11–14).

An older handbook advised showing that the law supported what one confessed. For example, one could confess killing, but in self-defense, or claim that the law performed the killing, since the law orders such an act.[437] A later handbook could likewise

428. Had it been, Paul's strategy would not have worked, just as Socrates could not hope to appease his Athenian judges by confessing to the practice of philosophy (Max. Tyre 3.4).

429. See discussion in Keener, *Acts*, 1:450–55.

430. See the discussion in Anderson, *Glossary*, 92. Such a strategy may have invited a tone of irony (on which see Shiell, *Reading Acts*, 84–85).

431. See comment on Acts 25:11.

432. E.g., Xen. *Hell.* 1.7.16–17; Quint. *Decl.* 300.9 (something praiseworthy); 301.3, 14; Apul. *Apol.* 55. Rhetorically trained writers could employ the figure in nonpolemical settings as well (Pliny *Ep.* 5.19.1; 7.28.1–2).

433. See, e.g., Cic. *Sest.* 69.145–46. Anything that could be said truly against philosophers they would "rather defend than deny" (Apul. *Apol.* 28, trans. p. 53).

434. This was, the same passage observes, so that if one was charged with something undeniable, one could deflect it with wit.

435. Likewise in fiction; by denying knowledge about the veracity of some legends, the gardener in Philost. *Hrk.* 8.8 acquires more credibility for the matters of which he claims to have eyewitness knowledge.

436. Rowe, "Style," 146–47 (citing Demosth. *Fals. leg.* 235; Cic. *Cael.* 4.10); Anderson, *Rhetorical Theory*, 224, speaks of παρομολογία, or partial admission (citing Rutilius Lupus *De figuris sententiarum et elocutionis* 1.19; Rom 5:7). Porter, "Paul and Letters," 582, proposes that Phil 1:15–18 is an example, but Acts 24:14 is much clearer. The technique has been recognized independently in Parsons, *Acts*, 327, and Keener, "Rhetorical Techniques" (published in 2008 but submitted in 2002).

437. *Rhet. Alex.* 36, 1444b.9–20. Making clear distinctions between acts for which one was responsible and those for which one was not was important. Much later an orator portrays some wanting to prosecute a poor man because his tears had driven the crowd to stone his enemy; he has the poor man object that weeping is not a crime (Libanius *Declam.* 36.28).

suggest the argument that the undisputed act was not a legally actionable offense.[438] Paul is quick here to affirm that his confession does not contradict, but rather flows from, his allegiance to the law of his people (Acts 24:14).

iii. Common Jewish Faith

What Paul calls the "Way" (see comment on Acts 9:2),[439] his opponents have just called a "sect"—that is, one sect among several (24:5). Despite his opponents' characterization of this "sect," Paul emphasizes that he and his movement share central features common to mainstream Judaism (24:14–15).[440] (If Ananias and others wished to deny the resurrection [24:15], Felix knew enough about Judean Judaism to recognize that it was in fact not Paul but Ananias's faction, the Sadducees, that held the minority position.)

Forensic oratory often focused on definition and counterdefinition of offenses or other matters (see Hermog. *Issues* 59.17–60.8). By drawing attention to his opponents' own characterization of his movement (which he considered the "Way," not merely one sect among many), Paul prepares to show how their prejudice against his theological views colored their prosecution.

By speaking of "the God of *our* fathers," Paul emphasizes his solidarity with his people's faith (see comment on Acts 3:13). He affirms all that is in the law and the prophets (see comments on Acts 16:3; 18:18; 21:24–26), and so he has not taken even a step toward apostasy (and hence would not have desecrated the temple in Acts 24:6).[441] Although Luke and Paul's letters both support Paul's claim here, rhetorical strategy provides the proximate cause for its mention at this point. Under other circumstances, an apostate might appeal to Rome to evade the enforcement of Jewish religious law; given the punishable charge of having desecrated the temple, however, emphasizing one's Jewish piety would prove more effective. It is also more consistent with Paul in both Acts and Paul's letters (cf., e.g., 2 Cor 11:24).

f. The Jewish Resurrection Hope (24:15)

Against accusations that Paul's views are totally idiosyncratic and not truly part of Judaism, Paul points out that the Jesus movement shares the most fundamental Jewish beliefs (24:14). These include hope in the future resurrection—a doctrine fundamental to the movement's understanding of Jesus, but a doctrine at which those who would balk are his Sadducean detractors (4:1–2), themselves the minority Palestinian position on this fundamental tenet of common Judaism.

Jewish sources often emphasized "hope in God" (e.g., *Let. Aris.* 261), and Palestinian

438. Hermog. *Issues* 38.12–17. Perhaps the victim merited the defendant's action, or some other party was responsible (39.1–5); or when the conceded behavior was only circumstantial evidence for guilt, one could advance plausible noncriminal reasons for it (49.7–24, with word, 49.9–14; acts, 49.15–19; and feelings, 49.20–24).

439. Ironically, modern comparisons of this title focus especially (and naturally) on Qumran's usage (see Fitzmyer, "Christianity in Light of the Scrolls," 240–41; Pao, *Isaianic Exodus*, 65–67), which is clearly sectarian by modern definitions. Yet by its self-definition, each group claimed to represent the true remnant of Israel; Qumran and Christians shared a common exclusivism, but Christians (at least in Luke's circle) did not withdraw from society.

440. Cf. Rapske, *Custody*, 163: it is not a sect because Paul's opponents share similar convictions. Luke often addresses what seem to be suspicions of Paul's loyalty to the law (Acts 21:21, 28; 23:29; 25:8; 28:17; Carras, "Observant Jews," 698). This approach could fit an apologetic to Israel such as Jervell envisions, but could also fit an apologetic to Rome, for whom the Christian movement's Jewish (and thus ancient) credentials would matter (see Keener, *Acts*, 1:448–57).

441. Some others held a contrary opinion of Paul (see comment on Acts 21:21), which both Paul and Luke are diligent to refute.

sources associated such hope especially with the resurrection (2 Macc 7:14).[442] Paul had employed this language at Acts 23:6 (and will allude to it again in 26:6–7; 28:20); see comment at Acts 23:6. From the start, Jesus's mission had included the objective of Israel's eschatological resurrection (Luke 2:34, ἀνάστασις).[443]

I. THE RESURRECTION AND PAUL'S ACCUSERS

Paul has been emphasizing that he and his accusers share faith in the same ancestral God and ancestral laws (Acts 24:14); now he points to their common faith in the resurrection.[444] Emphasizing solidarity with accusers was a good strategy; one could show that the real issue behind the charge should not be controversial, and this approach sometimes allowed one to paint accusers as sharing the "offense" with which one was accused.[445] (In this case, if Felix regards with disdain Paul's affirmation of the resurrection, he would have to hold in the same disdain the shared affirmation of some members of the Sanhedrin.)[446] An argument from probability also works well if the audience members will understand it because they share the same desires and objectives;[447] would anyone who was pious really want to desecrate the temple?

Did Paul's accusers, however, really share his faith in the resurrection or any form of eschatological hope? Luke has already informed us that the Sadducees, to whom the high priest Ananias (5:17; 24:1) belongs, do not affirm these views (Luke 20:27; Acts 4:1–2; 23:8). It is unlikely that all the elders whom Ananias brings (Acts 24:1) are Pharisees, the group that defended Paul a few days earlier (23:7–9); even if some of them are, would not others object to Paul's depiction of his accusers as sharing this hope? Paul may refer to the fact that some of the Sanhedrin share his position, a point he will suggest more forcefully at 24:21. If this is the point of his allusion, he might allude to the fact that some of the very body now accusing him took his side in 23:9.

Even if few of Paul's accusers share his position, however, the group's public disavowal of the position would hurt their case more than his. (Paul does later imply this disavowal for them, 24:20–21.) As already noted, affirmation of the resurrection was likely the majority view in early Judean Judaism, and the aristocratic priesthood could hardly claim to accuse all its people of apostasy or sedition. Felix would likely know (cf. 24:10, 24) that the high priest held a minority position on this doctrine, on which Paul's viewpoint was more representative. (Felix's Jewish wife, a valuable source for his knowledge of Judaism, may not have affirmed an eschatological resurrection either but, like him, undoubtedly found Paul an articulate exponent of this position, 24:24–25.) Paul and the Nazarenes may hold minority, "sectarian" views on some issues; on others they are closer to mainstream Judean faith than are the Sadducees (whom Luke also calls a "sect," 5:17). Paul's view of who constituted the righteous and wicked at the resurrection

---

442. Rhetoricians used concise definition, or ὁρισμός, as a technique (Anderson, *Glossary*, 84); Paul's defining hope in terms of the resurrection, however, is probably simply specifying the content.

443. For the "acceptance" or "awaiting" (προσδέχονται, Acts 24:15) of this hope, cf. Luke 2:25, 38; 12:36; 23:51.

444. For Luke, this would also provide "the basis of any possible rapprochement between Christians and Pharisees" (Dunn, *Acts*, 305).

445. Hermog. *Issues* 69.12–13.

446. As it is, Felix understands the issues (Acts 24:22) and has at least some sympathy for Jewish matters (24:24). Paul may use the same strategy to show Festus that even King Agrippa shares some of his views (26:24–27).

447. *Rhet. Alex.* 7, 1428a.26–30.

might well differ from theirs,[448] but any Gentile observer would view the essential doctrine as the same.

II. Future Judgment

Paul also apparently expects the judgment to happen soon (μέλλω need not mean this [see BDAG], but it is the most common sense in Luke-Acts),[449] which might sound subversive to the Romans were it not for how widespread the view was in early Palestinian Judaism; surely Felix would know the difference between passive eschatological expectations and activist revolutionaries.

Some denied even immortality, such as the Sadducees (see comment on Acts 23:8), but this view was more common in Judaism two centuries earlier[450] than in this period; others, deeply influenced by Hellenism, affirmed immortality without the resurrection.[451] The dominant view, however, was resurrection.[452] Given the acceptance of Daniel as canonical by most Jews, denial of a future resurrection of some sort, for both the righteous and the wicked, could prove difficult to maintain (Dan 12:2).[453]

Paul's expectation of a resurrection for judgment here may go further than many of his contemporaries. Some denied a resurrection for the wicked (2 Macc 7:14, unless it refers only to a resurrection "to life"). Some either restricted or only explicitly applied this resurrection promise to Israel or the saints[454] whereas others applied it also to the unrighteous.[455] Likewise, not all who affirmed a resurrection for judgment expected eternal torment to follow; the wicked could be resurrected to face the sentence of annihilation or tormented for a period of time before annihilation. In some views the wicked were not killed on the day of judgment or resurrected, but their souls remained in hell (1 En. 22:13).[456] The day of judgment would contrast their coming torment with the coming bliss of the righteous (4 Ezra 7:36–38, 47), but the torment might be temporary, a burning that annihilates (perhaps 7:61). In another view, their resurrection bodies might be fitted especially for suffering torment (2 Bar. 51:1–2; cf. Mark 9:43, 45, 47–48; Matt 5:29–30; 18:8).

448. Much of Judaism would probably share the ethical component of Luke's criterion (Luke 14:14). Paul's letters would equate believers with the righteous here (1 Cor 15:22–23; Phil 3:21; cf. 2 Cor 5:8; 1 Thess 4:14, 16–17). For the category of "the righteous," see, e.g., 1 En. 99:3; 100:5; 102:6, 10; 103:1.

449. See Mattill, Last Things, 43–45 (esp. 44, on Acts and Paul), 47 (suggesting Luke's reversion to classical usage with the future infinitive).

450. Cf. Sir 17:27–28; 30:17; 37:26; 44:8–15; 46:19; cf. 39:9.

451. Osborne, "Resurrection," 932–33, cites 4 Maccabees; Wis 2:23–24; 3:1–4; Philo Creation 135; Giants 14; possibly 1 En. 103:4.

452. E.g., 1 En. 61:5. See further comment below.

453. Puech, "Messianisme," also thinks that Qumran accepted the resurrection of both righteous and unrighteous. For discussion of afterlife hope in the OT, see, helpfully, Raharimanantsoa, Mort.

454. Osborne, "Resurrection," 933, cites 1 En. 22:13; 46:6; 51:1–2; Pss. Sol. 3:11–16; 13:9–11; 14:4–10; 15:12–15. Certainly the wicked would share no part in the "resurrection to life" (2 Macc 7:14); many Jewish writings more explicitly affirmed permanent destruction for the wicked, whether following or without a resurrection (e.g., Pss. Sol. 3:11–12; 13:11; 1QS IV, 13–14; Gen. Rab. 6:6; most sinners in t. Sanh. 13:3, 4; Pesiq. Rab Kah. 10:4; Pesiq. Rab. 11:5; cf. 2 Macc 12:43–45).

455. E.g., 2 Bar. 51:1–2; cf. t. Ber. 6:6; for distinction after death, see 1 En. 22:9–11. Osborne, "Resurrection," 933, cites 4 Ezra 4:41–43; 7:32–38; 2 Bar. 49:2–51:12; 85:13. He notes the very literal understanding of resurrection in 2 Macc 7:10–11; 14:46; Sib. Or. 4.179–82. Cf. sources in Keener, Matthew, 129, on Gehinnom (for various views of its duration); and in ibid., 710–11, on the resurrection of the dead. It appears in most streams of NT tradition and is denied in none: John 5:29; 2 Cor 5:10; Rev 20:4–6; Matt 25:46; cf. 5:29–30; 10:28; Luke 11:32. No one doubted that God would judge both righteous and wicked works (Ps 62:12; Prov 24:12; Sir 16:12, 14; Matt 16:27; Rom 2:6; 2 Cor 11:15; Rev 22:12; Pesiq. Rab. 8:2; cf. Rhet. Her. 3.2.3).

456. For the souls of the wicked remaining in hell on the day of judgment, see also 1 En. 61:5; 4 Macc 9:9; 12:12; t. Sanh. 13:5; probably L.A.B. 38:4; Asc. Is. 1:2; 3 En. 44:3; t. Ber. 5:31. Because 1 En. 108:6 refers to the spirits of sinners, it might not constitute evidence either way.

Like views regarding the resurrection, views on the (related) fate of the wicked varied. Josephus portrays the Pharisees as affirming eternal suffering for the wicked (Jos. *War* 2.163),[457] but among later rabbis, specific views also varied.[458] Many passages list various views side by side. Thus R. Akiba, followed by the majority school, denied that the flood generation would share in the coming world; another rabbi expected them to be neither raised nor judged; and another, that they would continue to suffer in Gehinnom after the righteous were raised (*b. Sanh.* 108a, bar.). Rabbi Ishmael (second century) denied a resurrection for at least some of the wicked; some other rabbis expected only a future day that would incinerate the wicked; the majority view argued for Gehinnom, but a substantial minority of named rabbis demurred (*Gen. Rab.* 26:6).

According to one common view, the wicked would suffer in Gehinnom for twelve months.[459] Some believed that the worst sinners, such as Pharaoh, would face eternal torment (a third-century rabbi in *Gen. Rab.* 26:2). Thus a common combination of views was that most wrongdoers would be tormented for twelve months and then annihilated, but the especially wicked[460] would endure eternal torment in Gehinnom (*b. Roš Haš.* 17a). Some insisted that the nations who persecuted Israel must be raised so that God could avenge Israel (*Pesiq. Rab.* 48:2).

Many Jewish sources affirm that Gehinnom was eternal for at least the worst sinners.[461] But in the most common early Jewish view, most sinners endure hell only temporarily and are then destroyed[462] or released;[463] as suggested above, twelve months is a familiar duration.[464] Early Christian sources tend toward the harsher image.[465] A few samples illustrate that later rabbis lacked a single position on the subject. The wicked would walk in darkness in Gehinnom (*Tg. Jon.* on 1 Sam 2:9). Some doubted a Gehinnom for the future age, claiming that the sun would punish the wicked instead.[466] Gentiles' children, who had done neither righteous nor unrighteous deeds, would not be resurrected but would not be punished either.[467]

Luke apparently believes in torment for the wicked in the intermediate stage of the afterlife (Luke 16:23–24);[468] he follows his sources in affirming a punishment that is

---

457. This may be equivalent to the Greek Tartarus (cf. postmortem torment in, e.g., Lucian *Downward Journey* 8); Josephus sometimes adapts the beliefs of Jewish schools to sound like Greek equivalents.

458. See also, e.g., Bonsirven, *Judaism*, 230; Davies, *Paul*, 84; see discussion below. Cf. Gehinnom for physicians in *m. Qidd.* 4:14 (R. Judah); for talking too much with women in *m. ʾAb.* 1:5; the wicked in 5:19, 20; more generally, the slaying of murderers in the messianic era (purportedly third-century tradition in *Deut. Rab.* 2:25).

459. *M. ʿEd.* 2:10 (attributed to R. Akiba); *b. Šabb.* 33b; *Lam. Rab.* 1:11/12, §40.

460. Such as those who denied the resurrection (e.g., Sadducees) or withdrew from the community (*minim*, or schismatics, probably including Jewish Christians). Not all *minim* were Nazarenes (cf., e.g., *b. Ber.* 29a), but many or most of them were (Dalman, *Jesus-Jeshua*, 36–37; Abrahams, *Studies* [2], 63; Herford, *Christianity*, 137–45, 365–81, 388; Schiffman, "Crossroads," 149; Pritz, *Nazarene Christianity*, 103; Keener, *John*, 198–99).

461. 4 Macc 9:9; 12:12; *t. Sanh.* 13:5; probably *1 En.* 108:5–6; *L.A.B.* 38:4; *Asc. Is.* 1:2; *3 En.* 44:3; *t. Ber.* 5:31; *b. Roš Haš.* 17a; *y. Ḥag.* 2:2, §5; *Sanh.* 6:6, §2; cf. Diod. Sic. 4.69.5; Plut. *Div. V.* 31, *Mor.* 567DE. For Gehinnom's vast size, note *b. Pesaḥ.* 94a; *Taʿan.* 10a; *Song Rab.* 6:9, §3; cf. Virg. *Aen.* 6.577–79. Many Jewish storytellers conflated Gehinnom with the Greek Tartarus (e.g., *Sib. Or.* 1.10, 101–3, 119; 4.186; 5.178; 11.138; cf. *Gr. Ezra* 4:22; *b. Giṭ.* 56b–57a; *y. Ḥag.* 2:2, §5; *Sanh.* 6:6, §2; *Apoc. Pet.* 5–12).

462. Cf. 1QS IV, 13–14; *Gen. Rab.* 6:6; most sinners in *t. Sanh.* 13:3, 4; *Pesiq. Rab Kah.* 10:4; *Pesiq. Rab.* 11:5; cf. 2 Macc 12:43–45.

463. *Num. Rab.* 18:20; some other texts are unclear, e.g., Sir 7:16; *Sipre Num.* 40.1.9; *Sipre Deut.* 311.3.1; 357.6.7; *ʾAbot R. Nat.* 16 A; 32, §69 B; 37, §95 B.

464. E.g., *b. Šabb.* 33b; *Lam. Rab.* 1:11–12, §40.

465. Matt 3:11; 25:41; Mark 9:43, 48; Jude 7; *Mart. Pol.* 11.2. Although Luke does not reject future eschatology in his effort to contextualize for Greek readers (Acts 17:31–32; 23:6; 24:15; contrast, e.g., Jos. *Ant.* 18.14, 18; *War* 2.163; Philo *Sacr.* 5, 8), Matthew's emphases retain more of their original Jewish flavor (cf. Milikowski, "Gehenna"; Goulder, *Midrash*, 63).

466. *B. ʿAbod. Zar.* 3b–4a; *Eccl. Rab.* 1:5, §2, citing third- and purportedly second-century traditions.

467. Earlier tradition in *Ruth Rab.* 3:2; *Eccl. Rab.* 9:4, §1.

468. For the torment of the wicked after death, see, e.g., *1 En.* 22:9–11; *4 Ezra* 7:36, 76–87.

apparently unending ("unquenchable" in 3:17; Q material shared with Matt 3:12),[469] but does not focus on it. His primary emphases in preaching the resurrection of the wicked are Paul's notably conservative Jewish orthodoxy and the moral demands of such a doctrine (Acts 24:25).[470]

Why would Paul emphasize not only his continuity with mainstream Judean Judaism but his orthodoxy according to stricter versions of the faith? Although early Christianity seems to have widely affirmed the resurrection of the damned,[471] Paul's extant letters (admittedly, occasional documents) speak of their eternal destruction without specifying (or, for that matter, disclaiming) the intermediate step of resurrection.[472] The Paul of this passage has particular reason to emphasize a strict position with this audience, however. Identifying with a more orthodox position further emphasizes that Paul is a *religious* Jew, not the sort of person known to desecrate the Jerusalem temple. Those who believed in an afterlife were also normally thought more inclined toward positive moral behavior than those who doubted any future accounting for their deeds (see comments on Acts 17:18; 24:16). By means of *ēthos*, the burden of proof thus favors Paul's righteousness (24:14, 20).

This emphasis on even the most rigorous (on one point) view of the resurrection also meets the accusers on the level of their claim to be religious spokesmen for their people. Regarding resurrection, Paul is closer to the dominant Judean view than are his Sadducean opponents; he is also more religiously conservative, not an apostate temple-defiler. Thus, for example, Plato's famous apology for Socrates emphasizes that although Socrates is accused of disbelieving the gods, he in fact believes in them more than do any of his accusers (*Apol.* 35D). Luke also serves on Felix (and anyone who identifies with him) notice of views that he will hear from Paul in more detail later (Acts 24:25).[473]

g. Paul's Blameless Conscience (24:16)

Paul claims here to exercise[474] a blameless[475] conscience before God and humans. In 24:14–15, Paul provides evidence that supports his claim to positive character in

---

469. One could question whether the sinner is as unending as the fire, but this seems to be the point in the Jesus tradition (cf. Mark 9:43, 48; Matt 5:29–30; 25:41, 46; probably Rev 14:11; 20:10). Most second-century Christians believed in a resurrection for immortal torment (Tatian *Or. Gks.* 13; cf. *1 Clem.* 11.1; *2 Clem.* 6.7; *Mart. Pol.* 2.3; 11.2; *Barn.* 20.1; *Diogn.* 10.7). Nevertheless, even some fairly conservative scholars have suggested that the meaning behind the NT language may point to annihilation (see Stott, "Response").

470. In early Christian literature the "unrighteous" (ἄδικος) is a recognizably Lukan (Luke 16:10–11; 18:11) and Pauline (Rom 3:5; 1 Cor 6:1, 9) term, though it appears elsewhere (Heb 6:10; 1 Pet 3:18; *2 Clem.* 20.1; Poly. *Phil.* 6.1; *Mart. Pol.* 3.1; 19.2; *Barn.* 3.3; *Herm.* 35.1–2; *Diogn.* 9.2; esp. *1 Clem.* 3.4; 5.4; 45.3–4; 56.11), even coupled with the "righteous" (Matt 5:45; 2 Pet 2:9), a common contrast (cf., e.g., *1 En.* 1:1; 62:13; 102:6, 9–10; 103:5; *2 Bar.* 48:48; *m. 'Ab.* 4:19; *Ahiq.* 8.29). The idea, but not the wording, reflects Dan 12:2.

471. Mark 9:42–48; Matt 5:29–30; John 5:29; Rev 20:4–5; cf. Luke 16:22–23.

472. Rom 2:5; 9:22; Phil 1:28; 3:19; 1 Thess 1:10; 5:9; 2 Thess 1:9; 2:10. Witherington, *Acts*, 711, suggests that Paul probably believed it, if 2 Cor 5:10 includes unbelievers at the judgment. (For the resurrection of believers in Paul's theology, see, e.g., Ware, *Synopsis*, §§89–90, pp. 162–67.) A resurrection of the unrighteous (to eternal shame, although not necessarily to continuous suffering) presumably is inevitable if one accepts Dan 12:2 as authoritative, as Paul undoubtedly did.

473. Acts 24:15 also includes the note of imminence probably implied in the use of μέλλειν. Although it is not rhetorically prudent for Paul to denounce the respected plaintiffs as "unrighteous" (contrast his implication for the original accusers in 24:19), Luke suggests that his message of a coming judgment brings discomfort even to the immoral judge (24:25).

474. C. Williams, *Acts*, 254–55, overemphasizes the athletic connotations of the term; although Paul often uses athletic metaphors in his letters (and in Acts, see 20:24), ἀσκέω had a much broader range of meaning by this period (cf. BDAG). Still, the verb and its cognates did sometimes supply figurative comparisons (e.g., Dio Chrys. *Or.* 18.6; Arius Did. *Epit.* 2.7.5b4, pp. 16–17.34–35; 2 Macc 15:4; 4 Macc 12:11; 13:22).

475. A term (ἀπρόσκοπος) that Paul uses for himself (1 Cor 10:32) and his ideal for his churches (Phil 1:10); elsewhere in biblical Greek, only at 3 Macc 3:8; Sir 32:21.

24:16, a claim that basically repeats Paul's affirmation to the Sanhedrin in 23:1 (see comment there). Paul was earlier interrupted in 23:2; Luke allows him to finish the argument here, and the allusion to the earlier passage invites the reader to consider the contrasting responses: whereas the high priest ordered Paul struck in contravention of the law (23:2), the Roman official does not hand him over to his accusers (though he also fails to release him).

Paul's positive character in 24:14–18 will contrast starkly with the illegalities and deception that Paul implies (by innuendo)[476] against his opponents in 24:19–21.[477] Indeed, even accusing someone of known virtuous character can reflect badly on the accuser.[478] Once convicted of terrible behavior, enemies ought not to be permitted to prosecute someone else (Aeschines *Tim.* 1–3).

Paul's claim to strive to live blamelessly in Acts 24:16 rests directly (ἐν τούτῳ) on the resurrection hope in 24:15. Those who believed in an afterlife were normally thought more inclined toward positive moral behavior than those who doubted any future accounting for their deeds.[479] Paul, who affirmed a resurrection of the unrighteous (ἀνάστασιν . . . ἀδίκων, 24:15) for damnation, was far less apt to commit unrighteousness (ἀδίκημα, 24:20; cf. 25:10–11) than those who did not so affirm (such as the Sadducees, 23:8; Luke 20:27).

Others could perceive Paul as a great sage (cf. Acts 26:24), but sages were honorable only if they lived according to what they taught.[480] Character delineation was a common rhetorical device for making a case (e.g., *Rhet. Her.* 4.50.63). For example, one noble testified that he knew nothing of the defendant except that when they encountered each other on a narrow road, the man "refused to get off his horse." The jurors considered this action so disrespectful that they inferred from it pervasively bad character and hence convicted him of the unrelated charges (Val. Max. 8.5.6). Portraying someone such as Socrates as a brothel keeper is an example of what legal theorists would call an implausible case (Hermog. *Issues* 33).

If Paul has genuinely sought to live with a clear conscience, an argument from this character trait would refute the prosecution's implications of evil motives and character. Felix apparently recognizes that Paul's character is sincere (more so than his own, Acts 24:25). On character, see further comments at Acts 23:1; 24:5, 11, 14–17 (this commentary divides the examples among these passages to prevent overly long sections). Referring to God as well as people in 24:16 is not precisely an oath (oaths were employed frequently in trials; see comment on Acts 23:12), but it accomplishes a similar purpose by implying God's witness and implicitly invoking God's punishment if Paul has misrepresented him. "God and people" was a common pairing (see comment on Acts 5:29).

If Paul here engages in a form of "boasting," it is under the circumstances for which Greco-Roman rhetoric permitted it.[481] Certainly a trial on a capital offense would have counted as grounds for being "compelled" to boast.[482] Paul in his letters brings

---

476. On rhetorical means of exciting suspicion, see Anderson, *Glossary*, 24.

477. On antithesis in rhetoric (often at the sentence level), see, e.g., *Rhet. Alex.* 26, 1435b.25–39; Dion. Hal. *Lysias* 14; Fronto *Ad Ant. imp.* 2.6.1; Rowe, "Style," 142; Lee, "Translations: Greek," 780; Black, "Oration at Olivet," 87; Anderson, *Glossary*, 21–22.

478. Cic. *Vat.* 10.25–26; cf. Apul. *Apol.* 9.4–5; the case of Socrates posthumously in Xen. *Mem.* 4.8.9–10.

479. See, e.g., Plut. *Pleas. L.* 23, *Mor.* 1103D; Wis 2:1–9.

480. See, e.g., Mus. Ruf. 1, p. 36.4–5, 9–12; comment on Acts 27:21.

481. For the principle, see, e.g., Quint. *Inst.* 11.1.17–19; Plut. *Praising, Mor.* 539A–547F; for an example of the practice, Cic. *Fam.* 5.12.8. On Plutarch's justifications for boasting, see, e.g., Forbes, "Self-Praise"; Smit, "Self-Praise," 347–52.

482. For boasting and necessity, see, e.g., 2 Cor 12:1, 11; Quint. *Inst.* 11.1.18; *Decl.* 262.2, 5; Pliny *Ep.* 1.8.4–6; Hermog. *Issues* 77.6–7; Apul. *Apol.* 11; cf. also Anderson, *Glossary*, 17.

forth his religious credentials when he needs to do so (2 Cor 11:22–33; Phil 3:4–6), though his criteria for boasting differ from those of his challengers.

h. Alms and Offerings for Israel (24:17–18)

Paul's being away "many years" may refer to six years (Acts 18:22)[483] or simply to the fact that he had not lived in his home city of Jerusalem (22:3) for many years. Having arrived only twelve days earlier (24:11) after many years' absence, he was certainly no rabble-rouser targeting Jerusalem.

i. Gifts and ēthos (24:17)

Still establishing his *ēthos*, Paul emphasizes that he came to bring alms and sacrifices. "Alms for my people" (cf. 10:2) probably echoes the righteous deeds of Tobit in the LXX (Tob 1:3, 16). Coming to bring offerings[484] presumably alludes to the offerings in Acts 21:26 (the only other use of the term προσφορά in Luke-Acts), perhaps funded by a portion of the collection from the Gentile churches. (The term's one use in the undisputed epistles of Paul applies to his priestly offering regarding the Gentiles, in the context of the Gentile churches' offerings.)[485]

Thus, Paul came for Jerusalem's benefit, not to cause it trouble. A bringer of offerings would not violate a temple (24:6); similarly, one accused of inciting a riot would hardly be easily thought guilty if he had been a benefactor for the city[486] (see comment on Acts 24:16). One possible rhetorical technique was the argument by contraries (*Rhet. Her.* 4.18.25); if Paul has come to serve his people and act piously, he ought not to be viewed as one who came to stir conflict. Failure to find any possible motives for a defendant's alleged actions cast doubt on charges against him.[487] Toward the end of a forensic speech, a speaker could remind the audience members that he had done kindnesses to them or to the very people who now seek the speaker's hurt, hence inviting compassion (*Rhet. Alex.* 36, 1444b.35–1445a.12); and a speaker could discredit opponents by using the opposite method (1445a.12–26).[488] Citing one's virtuous deeds, one could protest that one expected to be rewarded, not placed on trial (Hermog. *Inv.* 1.3.105). Arguing that one's opponents rewarded one's benefaction with false accusations was meant to shame the accusers (e.g., Apul. *Apol.* 103).

Paul's claim that he came as a benefactor is analogous to Peter's claim that he and John were being tried for a benefaction done to an infirm beggar (Acts 4:9). This argument could prove effective rhetorically. For example, if a defendant was forced to admit (ὁμολογεῖν, as in 24:14) an offense, he should endeavor to demonstrate that the act in question was legal, just, or beneficial to the public (συμφέρον).[489] One accused of acting against someone can claim in his defense that he acted on the victim's own behalf.[490] Even in classical rhetoric, a person could defend his actions by arguing that they had proved beneficial to the state (Xen. *Hell.* 5.11.32). One general reportedly

---

483. Larkin, *Acts*, 340.

484. This second verb and object roughly echo the point of the first (cf. Anderson, *Glossary*, 35–36, on *disiunctio* in *Rhet. Her.* 4.37–38)—namely, Paul's demonstrations of piety. But it is somewhat different.

485. Rom 15:16, 26–27. In both cases, Paul wants the offering to be "acceptable" (εὐπρόσδεκτος, Rom 15:16, 31). The term for offering here also appears in Eph 5:2, where the "aroma" implies also that it pleases God.

486. Libanius *Declam.* 36.1–3 (this could be coupled with a denial that the man did stir strife, as in 36.20–27 or Acts 24:12–13).

487. E.g., Apul. *Apol.* 48; 90; and (in the peroration) 102.

488. One should appeal to friendly feelings that already exist or should generate them; see *Rhet. Alex.* 34, 1439b.15–1440b.3. Similarly but facetiously, someone protests about being condemned when he is really his opponents' most faithful defender (Lucian *Fisherman* 5).

489. *Rhet. Alex.* 4, 1427a.24–30, esp. (for the advantage) 26–27.

490. Hermog. *Issues* 73.6–7.

invited his judges to punish him, provided they would publicly concede that he had been executed for acting for his country's good.[491]

Other examples abound. A much later rhetorician presents an argument in which a person confesses to having done what his accusers claimed but argues that it was not illegal and was in his hearers' interests (Libanius *Declam.* 44.57–59). Cicero, defending those who helped him in his hardship (*Sest.* 69.146), asks what crime Rome found in him when he protected the state (69.145). "And yet, if it is a crime to love one's country," he urges, "I have been punished enough for it," since an enemy of the state pulled down his house and caused other hardships.[492] Likewise here, should Paul be punished for the pious act of bringing alms to help his people (Acts 24:17)?[493] Paul's letters can employ this method of argument (2 Cor 12:13; Gal 4:16).

II. ALMS FOR THE JERUSALEM CHURCH (24:17)

Although the collection was specifically for, and distributed through, the church, it was indeed for (some of) the poor among Paul's people.[494] Only the wealthiest of benefactors (like the rulers of Adiabene)[495] could have claimed to sponsor *all* the poor in a city, and food distribution was often for one's own community first (see comment on Acts 6:1).

Certainly, even alms for the people as a whole would not contradict Luke's theology (Luke 6:32–35). Although Luke presents Paul as a clever speaker, Paul's love for his people is not feigned anywhere in Acts (see comments on Acts 18:18; 21:24–26). Likewise, the Paul of the letters expresses deep devotion to his people, in Rom 9:1–3 noting his continual sorrow and desire to sacrifice himself for his people.[496] Although it is true that missionaries in the process of acculturation often react against their cultures of origin,[497] eventually they typically integrate an appreciation for both cultures.[498] By the period in which Paul wrote Romans (before his Roman custody, Rom 15:25), he was mature in his cross-cultural identity as an apostle to the Gentiles concerned for his own people (11:13–14). The Paul of the letters, like the Paul of Acts, expects judgment on his people as Jewish prophets did, but differences of perspective between Luke and Paul are matters of emphasis, not the former's misrepresentation of the latter.

491. Appian *Hist. rom.* 11.7.41 (noting that the judges, shamed, then left him).

492. Cic. *Sest.* 69.145 (trans. R. Gardner, LCL, 12:237).

493. In Paul's case as in Cicero's, this appeal also invokes *pathos*, inviting compassion. Later rhetoricians continued to use this technique; the very matter for which they are accused is a benefaction (e.g., the commentary on Hermogenes's *Issues* by the fifth-century C.E. Platonist philosopher Syrianus, 2.68.3–5 in Heath, *Hermogenes*, 90).

494. With, e.g., Witherington, *Acts*, 712 (noting references to the poor in Rom 15:26; Gal 2:10). "The poor" may have been used as a special expression of piety (cf. 1QM XI, 9, 13; XIII, 14; XIV, 7; 1QpHab XII, 3, 6, 10; 4Q171 1–2 II, 9, 15; 1 + 3–4 III, 10; Israel in *Pesiq. Rab.* 9:2) for the needy Jerusalem church (cf. Dupont-Sommer, *Writings*, 397; Fitzmyer, "Christianity in Light of the Scrolls," 244; Hengel, *Property*, 34; idem, *Acts and History*, 118), though this is disputed (Keck, "Poor"). Whatever else may be involved, however, the offering is certainly for the poor (Reyes, "Remembering"). On "the poor," see discussion at Acts 3:2.

495. Cf. Jos. *Ant.* 3.320–21; 20.51–53, 101.

496. This may call to mind texts such as Jer 9:1 but esp. Moses's intercession in Exod 32:32.

497. Some sources on reverse culture or reentry shock, supplied to me by Prof. Warren Newberry, include Gullahorn and Gullahorn, "Extension"; idem, "Students Abroad"; Chen and Starosta, *Foundations*, esp. 174–75; Dodd, *Dynamics*, 167–71; Austin, *Readings in Reentry*; cf. also the nontechnical discussion in Pirolo, *Reentry Team*, 33–48. In addition to studies on missionary "reentry shock," cf. Grunlan and Mayers, *Cultural Anthropology*, 24–26, 85–88; Mayers, *Christianity Confronts Culture*, 188; Luzbetak, *Church and Cultures*, 96–103; among students returning from abroad, see Seiter and Waddell, "Reentry Process"; Lerstrom, "Transitions."

498. Cf., e.g., Grunlan and Mayers, *Cultural Anthropology*, 85–86; on acculturation, see, e.g., Nash and Schaw, "Achievement"; Frey and Roysircar, "Acculturation and Worldview," and sources cited there (also cited at Acts 21:26).

Luke's reference, however, must be to Paul's collection for the Jerusalem church, abundantly attested in his letters (see comment at Acts 20:4).[499] Christians were to put aside resources on the first day of each week (1 Cor 16:1). Honorary inscriptions, like Paul's instructions in 2 Cor 8–9, deliberately employ a variety of circumlocutions.[500] See further discussion at Acts 11:30; 20:4.

III. WHY LUKE'S SILENCE ELSEWHERE?

Why does Luke refer to this collection only here? Given Luke's abundant emphasis on caring for the poor,[501] Paul's reference to alms here is understandable; what is surprising is Luke's total lack of explicit mention of the collection elsewhere.[502] Perhaps one collection (Acts 11:29–30) was sufficient to make his point; Luke may expect us to infer more about this collection (alms for his people in Jerusalem) by analogy with the former one (a "ministry" for the siblings in Judea, 11:29). Both limited space and audience limitations could require a writer to maintain focus. If social ministry characterized early Christianity, Luke may not privilege one example above others and may have other points to emphasize on Paul's final journey to Jerusalem.

Still, why is there almost total silence about a matter so central historically to the trip described in detail at points in Acts, especially when Luke clearly cares about the unity of the Diaspora and the Jerusalem churches?

Suggested reasons for Luke's general silence fall into the following basic categories:[503]

1. Luke knew little about the collection and hence was not a companion of Paul. Yet his passing reference to the collection here (24:17) suggests that he knew more than he otherwise reports, and so this is the least plausible suggestion.[504]
2. Some embarrassment or other factors warranted Luke suppressing it. Proposals include the following:
   a. The Jerusalem church rejected the offering, tainted by Gentiles. But Gal 2:9–10 appears to contradict this.
   b. The collection symbolized reconciliation whereas Luke never mentions the *need* for reconciliation. But whereas Luke emphasizes unity (Acts 15:25), he also notes the need to achieve and renew it (15:5; 21:21–26).
   c. The collection was never delivered. But 24:17 itself suggests otherwise.
   d. The delegates delivered the offering, but it did not achieve reconciliation between the majority of the Jerusalem church and Paul's Gentile mission. This proposal is plausible.
3. From the advantage of hindsight or the needs of his audience, the collection was less important than it had been for Paul. After Jerusalem's destruction, the reconciling purpose of the offering was no longer relevant; Luke's interest is in Paul's arrest.

499. Although this is the nearly universal consensus, there are detractors, who can treat Luke's silence as thoroughgoing (Downs, "Collection").

500. Dahl, *Studies*, 37–38; Harrison, *Grace*, 300; Matera, *II Corinthians*, 181. On λογεία (1 Cor 16:1–2), see Thiselton, *Corinthians*, 1318; Garland, *1 Corinthians*, 751; in guilds, Deissmann, *Studies*, 142–43.

501. See, e.g., Hoyt, "Poor in Luke-Acts," 97–225. In early Christianity, see Grant, *Christianity and Society*, 124–45.

502. Das, *Galatians*, 163–64 (following Barrett, "Titus," 2), plausibly suggests that Luke's omission of Titus may be related to Titus's association with the collection.

503. Cf. Barrett, *Acts*, 1108 (apparently preferring the suppressing option); Witherington, *Acts*, 646.

504. Others also argue for the implausibility of this view (e.g., Thrall, *2 Corinthians*, 517, noting that Luke knows of the meeting with James and the elders; see also Morgan-Wynne, "Traditionsgrundlage").

There may be a gradual continuum between "suppressing" an embarrassing idea and failing to report it because it was no longer of interest. That the collection no longer remained a matter of great interest more than a decade afterward may be safely assumed; that it was also a matter of embarrassment is possible, though one wonders whether, at this remove, Luke had reason to focus on it even if it was not embarrassing. If it failed to achieve the high hopes Paul had for it—which is entirely plausible in view of Luke's report of the antagonism of some in the Jerusalem church (Acts 21:21; cf. Rom 15:25–27, 31)—it might not appear relevant. (Luke might have still chosen to report it as part of the hostile reaction to Paul in Jerusalem, but F. C. Baur totally aside, Luke had no reason to air the church's past dirty laundry more than necessary.) Below are some of the specific suggestions (from along the range between suppression and lack of interest), several of which may constitute factors in Luke's not recording the matter.

Some measure of "suppression" would be natural; it was appropriate compositional technique to pass over quickly whatever would displease one's audience and to elaborate whatever would be useful to them (Theon *Progymn.* 5.52–56). Some scholars think that the collection was embraced enthusiastically by the Jerusalem church,[505] but we lack sufficient evidence to support such an optimistic reading, given the social pressures the church faced (see comment on Acts 21:17–26). A failure of the offering in Macedonia or Achaia (cf. 2 Cor 8:11–12; 9:3–5) might have silenced Luke, but during Paul's three months in Corinth, he attests that these churches are indeed participating (Rom 15:26); if there was a conflict with any church, the evidence points to the church in Jerusalem (15:31).

Some contend that the Jerusalem church failed to welcome, and perhaps even rejected, Paul's collection.[506] As already argued above,[507] it is extremely unlikely that the collection was rejected out of hand; the Jerusalem "pillars" had commissioned it (Gal 2:10), even if only one of them remained in Jerusalem to accept it. It is possible, however, that it failed to achieve the full reconciliation Paul hoped for; Paul himself knew that this conclusion was possible (Rom 15:31).[508]

Historically, Paul intended his collection to signify a unity between Gentile churches and the Jerusalem church[509] (Rom 15:27; as well, perhaps, as among all the participating churches).[510] After 70 C.E., the Jerusalem church as such was no longer an issue; the voice of the mixed Diaspora churches was more dominant, and Jewish-Gentile reconciliation in the mixed churches had to progress by other means. Likewise, a great offering to a central location that would soon cease to exist might seem a shortsighted investment (although Paul would probably still have valued it himself for salvation-historical reasons).

505. Nickle, *Collection*, 145–46.

506. Wedderburn, "Collection"; Dunn, *Acts*, 266, 284; Park, *Jew or Gentile*, 70; cf. Johnson, *Acts*, 357; Thrall, *2 Corinthians*, 518, allows the possibility. Hengel and Schwemer, *Between Damascus and Antioch*, 255, suggest that James and the elders instead proposed redirecting the funds to sponsor the Nazirites, but this suggestion probably underestimates the money raised.

507. See introduction, above, to Acts 21:17–26 (Keener, *Acts*, 3:3113–16).

508. Haacker, *Theology*, 16, argues that in precisely the period preceding the war, some Jerusalemites wanted to reject Gentile offerings, perhaps making the offering more of an embarrassment to the Jerusalem church.

509. With, e.g., Hill, *Hellenists*, 173–78 (against Baur); Park, *Jew or Gentile*, 65–67; cf. Donaldson, *Paul and Gentiles*, 252; Everts, "Support," 299. Jerome *Vigil.* 13 (Martin, *Acts*, 286) suggested that Paul wanted to give the funds not just to anyone poor but to those in the holy land. John Knox thought that Luke omits the peace offering because he never describes the genuine friction between Jerusalem and the Diaspora churches, yet this perspective (shaped by Baur) flies in the face of the conflict in Acts 15, however domesticated.

510. Harrison, *Grace*, 308. Certainly Paul also was concerned about status issues (with, e.g., Theissen, *Setting*) and with the poor (cf. 2 Cor 8–9; see esp. Longenecker, *Remembering the Poor*); the Jewish-Gentile issue is just one facet of his approach.

Some scholars also suggest that Paul's offering was too far beyond what the pillars envisioned for the Jerusalem church's comfort, and that because too great a gift could overwhelm the beneficiary in the ancient reciprocity system, the Jerusalem church felt crushed under the weight of obligation.[511] Had they felt this way momentarily, however, they could have found theological justification to feel otherwise—justification such as Paul himself offered to some Gentile Christians (Rom 15:27) and could have reiterated for the Jerusalem church, directly or through intermediaries, if necessary.[512]

Even if the Jerusalem church responded positively, Paul's embarrassing detention soon afterward, the hostile environment toward Gentiles in the city, and the imminent war with Rome all undoubtedly prevented Paul's offering from achieving permanent significance in the relations between the Jerusalem and Diaspora churches.

Luke's overriding apologetic concern offers another reason for "suppressing" mention of the collection. Perhaps Luke is circumspect about the collection because of the role it plays in Paul's defense here; some readers might find less compelling an offering "for his nation" if its specific recipients were limited to members of Paul's own sect. A related suggestion (and probable factor) is that Luke mostly omits the collection because, to Romans, it may have seemed illegal or subversive.[513] Romans were nervous enough about local associations; any movement spreading throughout their empire and raising funds without government approval could seem subversive. By contrast, Romans did not oppose mere alms for Jerusalem,[514] although a century earlier even Asian Jews exporting gold for the Jerusalem temple could appear involved in a "barbaric superstition" (Cic. *Flacc.* 28.66–67).[515]

Still, Romans were happy enough to continue and reroute the temple tax to their own interests after Jerusalem's fall.[516] If any of Paul's colleagues used the temple tax analogy to help justify their collection,[517] Luke's churches would certainly know better than to offer that analogy after 70 C.E.[518] And if the Jerusalem church viewed the collection in light of biblical promises about an eschatological pilgrimage and/or eschatological gifts/tribute from the nations[519] (although Paul does not employ

---

511. Harrison, *Grace*, 19–20.

512. Texts about eschatological offerings of the Gentiles could also achieve this purpose. Paul himself defines reciprocity in terms of a debt of gratitude to God rather than to the human givers in 2 Cor 9:8–14 (see Keener, *Corinthians*, 214–15). But he also speaks elsewhere of obligation to the Jewish people (Rom 15:27); others could employ the language of debt to a people (Cic. *Quint. fratr.* 1.1.9.28; *Fam.* 11.10.1; 11.11.1; Val. Max. 5.6.ext. 2; cf. Rom 1:14).

513. Nickle, *Collection*, 148–51. Barrett, *Acts*, 559, thinks that Nickle may well be right on this point.

514. Thus Acts 11:28–30 would probably be seen as praiseworthy rather than problematic, as a response to famine.

515. For the temple tax in Asia Minor in general, see Trebilco, *Communities*, 13–16.

516. *CPJ* 1:80–81; 2:119–36, §§160–229; Dio Cass. *R.H.* 65.7.2; Hemer, "Ostraka"; Carlebach, "References." Appian *Hist. rom.* 11.8.50 claims that Jews paid a higher poll tax because they rebelled so often.

517. See Nickle, *Collection*, 74–99 (note esp. the comparison on 87–89); cf. (both parallels and contrasts) Panikulam, *Koinōnia*, 36ff.; (as one factor) Laing, "Collection"; (as a partial but not full analogy) Everts, "Support," 297. Nickle believes that if it were packaged as some other way than the temple tax, it would be viewed as illegal (*Collection*, 88–89); this view may overestimate Roman concern before 70 C.E., but it might well be a reason for Luke not to mention it *after* 70. On the temple tax, see, e.g., Safrai, "Relations," 188–91; the Qumran sect, unlike others, believed that the tax need be paid only once in a person's life (4Q159 1 II, 7).

518. Many doubt Nickle's analogy, noting that Paul's collection was voluntary (Witherington, *Corinthians*, 426n62) or simply that we lack explicit support in Paul's letters (Kruse, *Romans*, 546). Yet even if Nickle overstates the relationship, the analogy remains valuable in terms of comparisons that some contemporaries may have offered.

519. See, e.g., Isa 45:14; 60:5–17; 61:6; Tob 13:11 (more explicitly conquest in Mic 4:13; 1QM XII, 13–15); Nickle, *Collection*, 129–42; Martin, *Corinthians*, 258; Sanders, *Jesus and Judaism*, 93. Dunn, *Romans*, 874, notes that whereas Paul reinterpreted these texts to apply to equals (as he viewed other prophecies in a transformed way), those in Jerusalem may have seen it differently, which difference would generate some conflict.

these texts in describing the collection),[520] it was thinking of the kingdom's restoration to Israel (cf. Acts 1:6). Luke would have more sense than to let Paul strike this chord to the Roman governor.

If Luke writes after 70 C.E., as this commentary suggests, proposed factors explaining the irrelevance of Paul's collection grow in importance. Some of these suggestions concern the Jerusalem church. Some scholars think that Luke says so little about the collection because he has little sympathy for the Jerusalem church, which so abused his hero, Paul.[521] Against this suggestion is the impression of deep respect for the Jerusalem church that we gather from reading Acts 1–4 (and probably implied in 21:20, despite Luke's disagreements).

A much more plausible suggestion is that Luke lacked interest in the Jerusalem church's reception simply because there remained no "Jerusalem church" in Luke's day.[522] Those who associate the collection, in Paul's theology, with God's eschatological purpose for Jerusalem also believe that Luke lacked reason to emphasize the point after 70 C.E.[523] But the collection may have become less important long before 70; Paul neglects it in his own later letters, including Philippians.[524] If Paul did not emphasize the collection after its completion, Luke should hardly be faulted for analogous silence.

In the end, a variety of factors may be at play. If the Jerusalem church did not respond enthusiastically, if the collection could be misconstrued by Rome, and if many years had passed and the Jerusalem church no longer existed as such, Luke had every reason to mention the offering at most in passing. He might well have retained this one remaining reference, in 24:17, because of his concern for the poor (2:44–45; 11:29–30) and its value for the character element of Paul's apologetic in this speech.

IV. APPREHENDED WHILE WORSHIPING (24:18)

That Paul was "purified" (see comments on Acts 21:24, 26) suggests that his real intentions in the temple were quite the opposite of desecrating it (against 24:6). Paul is refuting his opponents' charges by demonstrating that he did, in fact, the opposite of what they charged: they accused him of profaning the temple (24:6), but he was making an offering there (21:26). If Paul's hair was long or shaved because of a vow (18:18; 21:24–26), that they found him "purified in the temple" might be evident simply from looking at him, but we cannot be sure of this evidence, since the nature and completion (cf. 21:27) of the vow is unclear in these texts. In any case, a temple was a place of sanctuary, an inviolable refuge,[525] yet Paul had been seized there.

Likewise, his "without crowd or tumult" refutes the charge of stirring unrest (against 24:5). Paul has been the victim of "tumult" (θόρυβος) twice in Luke's narrative, in the Ephesus temple riot (20:1; cf. the "crowd" in 19:33–35) and (most relevant here) in the Jerusalem temple riot (21:34; cf. the "crowd" in the same verse);[526] but Luke's audience knows that he did not start the unrest in either instance.

520. See Harrison, *Grace*, 305.

521. Ramsay, *Pictures*, 248.

522. Nickle, *Collection*, 147, thinks that the Jerusalem church's exclusion from the holy city forfeited their special role. Whatever its direct theological impact, it certainly had such an impact in terms of communication from Judean churches to the Diaspora.

523. Bauckham, "James," 479–80. Like most ancient Jews, however, Luke might maintain belief in an eschatological future for Jerusalem (cf. Acts 1:6–7; 3:19–21; Luke 22:30).

524. Matera, *II Corinthians*, 183.

525. Cf., e.g., 1 Kgs 1:50; Plut. *Alex.* 42.1; Tac. *Hist.* 1.43; and much fuller documentation at Acts 19:29.

526. Stoics applied θόρυβος to fear and confusion, along with noise (Arius Did. *Epit.* 2.7.10b, pp. 60–61.4; 2.7.10c, pp. 60–61.28), but while Luke sometimes adapts language of moralists (e.g., Acts 24:25), he employs the term more broadly here.

If someone argued that Paul's arrival, whatever his motives, precipitated the unrest, he could offer the standard response to such a charge: people could not be responsible for genuinely unforeseen consequences of their decisions.[527] Pliny the Younger laments that, in practice, people often unfairly judge by outcomes rather than by intentions (*Ep.* 5.9.7); an advocate would be always ready, however, to point out the unfairness of such an evaluation. Likewise, if it is argued that Paul's preaching precipitated hearers' hostility, Paul could argue that there was no law against his preaching of religious ideas unrelated to sedition.[528] But Paul had not been carrying on dialogues anyway (Acts 24:12).

Paul is about to imply who did start the riot; thus he begins the next clause (24:19a or, in some versions, the final line of 24:18) with the adversative function of the conjunction δέ: "Thus: 'It was not I who stirred up the tumult, but rather some Jews from Asia.'"[529] Classical Greek orators often retorted that accusers, being guilty themselves, ought not to bring charges. Paul follows a similar line of argument in 24:19.

i. Insinuating His Accusers' Guilt (24:19)

Returning the charges was standard fare in ancient rhetoric; Paul, by contrast, more subtly insinuates his accusers' guilt. They have illegally abandoned the case—which should require its dismissal—most likely because they have good reason to fear appearing in court themselves. No unrest surrounded Paul in Jerusalem (24:18)—until his accusers arrived (24:18–19). They were in fact thus prudent not to show themselves now.

i. Returning the Charges

Why does Paul start a sentence ("But [there were] certain Jews from Asia") that he fails to finish, omitting a verb? Writers and speakers sometimes affected intense emotion by leaving sentences incomplete;[530] this practice was expected at times in forensic speeches.[531] This practice is consistent with the Paul we know from his letters; he does this in Galatians, which, as largely a letter of reproof, displays the heat of passion (Gal 2:2–4, 6; cf. 5:12).[532] It is not difficult to reconstruct the implied but formally omitted words of the ellipsis.[533]

527. E.g., Hermog. *Issues* 68.10–69.21 (esp. the argument from mitigation, 69.15–17; cf. 39.10–16); Libanius *Declam.* 36.42; 44.50–52, 61; Quint. *Decl.* 301.16.
528. For the argument refuting the fallacy of affirming the consequent (as well as the standard counterargument to such a plea), see Hermog. *Issues* 48.15–23; Heath, *Hermogenes*, 87.
529. Rightly Conzelmann, *Acts*, 199. Admittedly ἀλλά would have been stronger.
530. See Anderson, *Glossary*, 41; cf. *Rhet. Her.* 4.30.41; Rowe, "Style," 149; Porter, "Paul and Letters," 583; Anderson, *Glossary*, 24. Dibelius's recourse to probable textual corruption here (*Studies in Acts*, 92) is most implausible.
531. So esp. Fronto in Naber, 211 (LCL, 1:40–41); see also Cic. *Verr.* 2.5.66.170. Some other kinds of speeches could also display intense emotion by disrupting normal rhetorical patterns (Men. Rhet. 2.9, 413.12–14).
532. Often noted though variously explained (e.g., Orchard, "Ellipsis"); though cf. Blommerde, "Ellipsis." Pliny begins complaining about someone in a letter, then breaks off in midsentence, deciding to be more gracious (*Ep.* 8.22.4); since the offender remains anonymous, however, it is a case of casual epistolography (as in 1 Cor 1:16), not *insinuatio*. Still, in the heat of anger, one could forget one's intended words (*'Abot R. Nat.* 1 A). On letters of admonition and blame, see, e.g., Stowers, *Letter Writing*, 85–90 ("letters of reproach" were even harsher; 139–41).
533. In true ellipsis, the words as well as the meaning can be reconstructed (Plath, "Ellipsis"); on ellipsis, see also Rowe, "Style," 135. The present case is closer to aposiopesis (see Rowe, "Style," 149, citing Demosth. *Cor.* 3; Cic. *Phil.* 12.2.4; Black, "Oration at Olivet," 87, citing *Rhet. Her.* 4.30.41; 4.54.67; Quint. *Inst.* 9.2.54–57; 9.3.60–61). Aposiopesis could be linked with paraleipsis, arousing suspicion by implication (Hermog. *Method* 7.419–20), as probably here.

The incompleteness here probably suggests a forceful point, namely, that his original accusers are the very ones who started the riot (as Luke's narrative claims, Acts 21:27–29, and Paul virtually claims later in 26:21). This would also explain, Paul implies, why they do not wish to be present for the hearing.[534] Paul speaks obliquely (on reasons for this practice, see discussion below on "insinuating guilt"), yet even the phrasing, "certain [τινὲς] Jews from Asia," can indicate that Paul intends to imply something with more forensic significance than a mere summary of events. From his experience in Asia, Paul probably knew those who had accused him (19:8–9; cf. 21:29), but "certain persons" was often the language of polemic.[535] Although Luke's audience would not know the names of these persons (excepting perhaps Alexander, if he was among them, 19:33), "non-naming" sometimes functioned as a polemical device.[536]

Rhetorical handbooks had long suggested that it was ideal to shift to one's adversaries, whenever possible, the very charges of which one was accused.[537] The handbooks simply reflected ancient practice; returning charges was good rhetoric.[538] Thus one might concede that an offense was deathworthy, then explain that it was one's accuser, and not oneself, who was guilty of such an offense.[539] Sometimes a classical orator would express surprise at the audacity of an accuser charging a client with the very offense of which the accuser was guilty.[540] The orator Aeschines, charged by Demosthenes with taking bribes, counters that Demosthenes is the real bribe taker (Aeschines *Embassy* 3; *Ctes.* 113, 156, 259) and that Demosthenes offers them as well (*Ctes.* 69).[541] Having presented evidence, Aeschines questions "whether . . . it is [he] whom Demosthenes has accused, or whether on the contrary he has accused himself in [Aeschines's] name."[542] When a man named Peithias was acquitted, he charged his accusers with a different offense and had them all convicted (Thucyd. 3.70.3–4). Although the prospect of returned accusations did not always deter frivolous prosecutions, those who entered litigation voluntarily often did so at their own peril.

Romans likewise would go on the offensive, attacking the character of those who charged their clients.[543] If, for example, Sestius's abusers now charge him with the violence they inflicted on him, they so charge him only "because he is alive. But that

534. If they could be shown to have started the riot, they would be punished; they had undoubtedly not reckoned on Roman intervention in the Jerusalem temple or the need to answer to Rome for their denunciation of Paul, though he was a Roman citizen (most of them probably were not, though they may have been citizens of Ephesus).

535. E.g., Aeschines *Ctes.* 1; Dio Chrys. *Or.* 12.36; Gal 2:4, 12; 1 Tim 1:3. Luke does sometimes name critics unknown to his audience where it would not create problems for local churches (e.g., Acts 4:6; 18:17 [on some views]; 19:33; 23:2; 24:1–2), though not always, and sometimes he probably simply lacked their names.

536. See Marshall, *Enmity*, 341–48.

537. E.g., *Rhet. Alex.* 36, 1442b.6–9; Cic. *Or. Brut.* 40.137; *De or.* 3.204; cf. *Cat.* 2.3; turning an opponent's argument against him in Hermog. *Inv.* 3.3.138.

538. Eurip. *Cretans* frg. 472e.33–35; Thucyd. 3.61.1; Dion. Hal. *Lysias* 24 (advising that this be done "at the outset" [trans. S. Usher, LCL, 1:67]). Another form of counteraccusation was to admit an offense but blame the victim for deserving it (Hermog. *Issues* 39.1–5).

539. Xen. *Hell.* 2.3.37.

540. Lysias *Or.* 3.1, §96. At least in declamations, those guilty of some kinds of offenses could not bring suit against anyone else (Quint. *Decl.* 250 intro.; 265 intro.).

541. Likewise, Philocrates (convicted of treason) used not Aeschines but Demosthenes as his advocate (Aeschines *Embassy* 14), and Demosthenes, rather than Aeschines, was his business partner (*Embassy* 56). Aeschines elsewhere objects to this frequent practice of countercharging accusers (*Tim.* 179) but does it himself. For views concerning bribes, see comment on Acts 24:26.

542. Aeschines *Embassy* 69 (LCL, 211).

543. E.g., Cic. *Quinct.* 3.11–9.33 (i.e., the entire *narratio*); *Rosc. Amer.* 30.82–45.132; Pliny *Ep.* 3.9.29; 4.9.20; 6.22.2, 4; 7.33.7. Although Apuleius gets around to denouncing his accuser (e.g., *Apol.* 56), he initially excuses himself from this necessity by pointing out that his accuser was so obscure, lowly, and worthless that Apuleius had never had occasion to get to know him (*Apol.* 16).

is not his fault."[544] Counterclaims could involve *ēthos*; thus, when Cicero prosecuted Verres, Verres tried to circulate a story that Cicero had taken a bribe to falsify his prosecution (Cic. *Verr.* 2.1.6.17). In Nero's reign, when a false accuser denounced Seneca, the latter effectively returned the charge against his accuser (Tac. *Ann.* 14.65). The practice of returning charges also appears in Jewish Christian reports or interpretations of Judean debates (Matt 12:43–45; John 8:37–51).

ii. Insinuating Guilt

Can Paul be returning the charges? If so, why does he not make this reversal explicit by finishing his sentence? He is probably employing an even more familiar rhetorical technique of insinuating guilt.[545] Speakers sometimes even explicitly claimed to pass over a matter even as they instead summarized it or at least hinted at it; Paul is more subtle but may well point in the same direction.

As noted above (with reference to the grammar), Paul addresses the issue obliquely; rhetoricians sometimes found it more appealing to audiences to stop short (or pretend to do so) rather than recount all the crimes, in order to avoid sounding too hostile.[546] This was especially the case if the defendants were relatives[547] or if, as in this case, the opponents were members of one's own people before a foreign judge (cf. Acts 28:19). Not mentioning one's mistreatment could be counted honorable.[548] Paul had nothing to lose: it was clear that someone had started the riot, and if it was not he, it was clear that it was his accusers. By not stating this more explicitly, he could avoid appearing vindictive while hinting enough to imply the truth.

Rhetoricians sometimes ostentatiously "passed over" a matter, pretending that it could not be discussed (the technique called *praeteritio*).[549] They could also claim more directly to omit subjects, while mentioning them in passing.[550] The technique also appears outside forensic rhetoric,[551] and Paul himself uses the technique in his letters (Phlm 19; cf. 2 Cor 9:1).[552] But it is especially well known in the rhetoric of the courts. Some classical orators claim that they could mention far more offenses than they do, thereby implying offenses that they do not need to recount.[553]

Cicero was happy to slander an accuser even as he claimed to avoid doing so, making frequent use of insinuation. Cicero sometimes did not denounce individuals by name, thus avoiding the impression of harshness while denouncing them by insinuation instead.[554] Without directly accusing Piso of gaining his office unethically, Cicero

544. Cic. *Sest.* 37.80 (trans. R. Gardner, LCL, 12:145).
545. On *insinuatio*, see Bower, "*Ephodos* and *insinuatio*." Perhaps (though not necessarily) Luke's audience could imagine a gesture of denunciation (on which see Shiell, *Reading Acts*, 56)? For examples besides those below, see, e.g., Quint. *Decl.* 331.22; 335.13; Hermog. *Inv.* 4.13.206, 208–9.
546. Cic. *Invect. Sall.* 8.22.
547. Dion. Hal. *Lysias* 24.
548. Val. Max. 2.2.5 praises envoys who delivered their message faithfully, without adding complaints about how they had been treated (including being spattered with urine).
549. Rutherford, "Silence"; cf., e.g., Cic. *Verr.* 2.2.48.118; 2.4.46.102; 2.4.47.105.
550. E.g., Demosth. *Cor.* 268; Cic. *Invect. Sall.* 5.13; Quint. *Decl.* 252.10. See παραλείψις in *Rhet. Alex.* 21, 1434a.25–26; *Rhet. Her.* 4.27.37; Fronto *Ad Ant. imp.* 1.2.4; Rowe, "Style," 149 (citing as examples Basil *Against Drunks* 125A; Aug. *Ep.* 125.4); Anderson, *Glossary*, 88–89 (citing, e.g., *Rhet. Her.* 1.9; 4.37; Heb 11:32). Fronto *Ad Ant. imp.* 1.2.9 gives a notably lengthy example of παραλείψις (shifting to Greek only for this rhetorical term, 1.2.9–10).
551. Cic. *Fam.* 13.5.3; 13.16.4; Mus. Ruf. 10, p. 78.22; Pliny *Ep.* 1.14.9 (cf. 1.19.3); Ael. Arist. *Def. Or.* 408, §§138D–139D; Fronto *Ad verum imp.* 2.3; Max. Tyre 24.1; Men. Rhet. 2.14, 429.1–4; Libanius *Encomium* 3.2; cf. Cic. *Fam.* 2.6.1.
552. On 2 Cor 9:1, see Amador, "Revisiting," 107.
553. E.g., Lysias *Or.* 3.44–45, §100; 31.20, §188.
554. E.g., Cic. *Agr.* 24.63–64. He also can describe briefly matters that he claims to pass over (*Sest.* 26.56).

insinuates his guilt: "But as to *how* each of us was elected I prefer to say nothing."[555] In many cases he even goes on to specify what he claims to merely insinuate (unlike some other orators). He assures one opponent, "[I have attacked only your tribunate,] for why question you about your misdeeds and shameful robberies [as governor] in Spain?"[556]

Likewise, Cicero comments that Clodia, who has charged his client, is sexually notorious: "of whom I will say no more than what is necessary" (*Cael.* 13.31).[557] Cicero then charges her through much of his speech; at one point he implies her guilt for her husband's earlier death, then claims that he must return to answering her charge, since he is tearful at that memory (24.60). He accuses another man of murdering his wife and then adding a crime that Cicero refuses to describe, in order to avoid undermining public morality by allowing that "the enormity of so great a crime has either existed in this state or has escaped punishment."[558] He further passes "over in silence" the defendant's other private vices to focus on public ones (*Cat.* 1.6.14).[559]

Cicero has much to say against Verres that he must pass over quickly (*Verr* 2.2.1.1, 2), in the process indicating (without a doubt accurately) that the evidence he can present is only the tip of the iceberg. He poses a question that he claims at some length not to ask (at the end of the claim, mentioning in passing what this unasked question is; 2.5.5.11). He promises to skip various facts, all of which he mentions (including some to stir pathos; 2.5.8.20–21). He claims to say nothing, for the moment, of matters that he addresses elsewhere—then recounts them.[560] He likewise claims to pass over Verres's "minor" offenses (which he then recounts, such as specific items he plundered from sacred buildings; 2.4.59.131).[561] Others were also happy to insinuate guilt; thus, for example, Apuleius notes that it was only his opponent raising an issue that forced Apuleius to expose "everyone's tacit suspicions" about his opponent (*Apol.* 98).[562]

Paul at the least implies that the original accusers are lying. This was a common charge against malicious accusers,[563] though Paul's response is worded more delicately, not employing the expression.

III. WITNESSES

The only genuine supposed witnesses were those who first claimed that Paul had brought a Gentile into the temple (Acts 21:27–28); the high priest and elders are of high status but are not genuine eyewitnesses. If they have brought forward a charge without being able to produce the original witnesses, they are ignoring the laws. In fact, Paul will argue, they are not the legitimate plaintiffs at all, and the original plaintiffs have abandoned the case.

555. Cic. *Pis.* 2.3 (trans. N. H. Watts, LCL, 14:147).
556. Cic. *Vat.* 5.13 (trans. R. Gardner, LCL, 12:257); he then returns immediately to the tribunate, having slipped this accusation in.
557. Trans. R. Gardner, LCL, 13:445.
558. Cic. *Cat.* 1.6.14 (trans. L. E. Lord, LCL, 10:27); he similarly avoids repeating other accusations because they are obscene and violate public propriety (*Verr.* 1.5.14; *Flacc.* 15.34).
559. Trans. L. E. Lord, LCL, 10:27.
560. Cic. *Verr.* 2.4.52.116; more briefly, 2.3.24.59.
561. On the horror that ancients felt at the plundering of temples, see discussion at Acts 19:37.
562. Trans. Hunink, p. 116.
563. E.g., Lysias *Or.* 3.39, §99; 4.13, §101; Dion. Hal. *Lysias* 33; Cic. *Quinct.* 6.22; *Rosc. com.* 16.46; *Mur.* 6.13; Apul. *Apol.* 3; 52; 69; 74; 83; 89; cf. Isaeus *Astyph.* 19. Writers against Jews tell "lies" about them (Jos. *Ag. Ap.* 2.79, 147, 289); Apion is a prime example of such a liar (2.85, 90, 98, 111, 115, 121, 122). Perkins, "John," 966, points out that Qumran's opponents are misled "by the Man of Lies . . . (1QpHab 2:2; 5:11; CD 20:15; 1QH 2:13–14; 4:10)." Perjury was punishable (Apul. *Apol.* 60; 89; Völkl, "Perjury").

Witnesses were important to trials; thus, in one long trial, after three days of speakers the court spent the fourth day examining witnesses (Pliny *Ep.* 4.9.15). Classical forensic speeches reveal that witnesses unwilling to testify could be compelled to do so (or to produce affidavits);[564] their unwillingness could be cited as evidence that they had something to conceal.

Legal debate regularly included a demand for evidence (Hermog. *Issues* 45.1–2); if no witnesses are available, "the defendant will demand them" (45.21).[565] Thus one might invite witnesses to come forward if indeed (the challenger mocks) there *are* any (Libanius *Declam.* 44.17).[566] Had an opponent simply produced witnesses, one might complain, this would have left one defenseless (Lysias *Or.* 7.20, §110), but he has failed to do so (7.23, §110). Lack of witnesses was, not surprisingly, a frequent cause for denunciation.[567] In one particularly unjust example of this kind of charge, refusal to hand over slaves for torture (the conventional means for securing slaves' testimony)[568] could also be construed as hiding something[569] (one making this charge would not stop to take account of humanitarian considerations).

Those who lacked witnesses would also seek to turn this deficiency to their advantage.[570] Cicero kindly spares his audience in one case the inconvenience of witnesses, he points out, because their words "can be so readily manipulated," as opposed to solid arguments based on probability and facts (*Cael.* 9.22).[571] The prosecutor who lacked witnesses would insist "that proof from facts is more trustworthy than that from witnesses: 'For facts cannot be persuaded'" (Hermog. *Issues* 46.4–8).[572] Because the very same orators used witnesses when it was to their advantage, however, ancient audiences, like their opponents, would not necessarily be convinced. Thus a speaker for the defense complains, "If he had produced witnesses, he would have expected you to believe them, but as he has none, he thinks that this also should count to my detriment."[573]

The high priest may have avoided calling Asian Jews to appear because he by this point knew that they could not prove their charges under cross-examination.[574] Testifying in a Roman court where they could be refuted under cross-examination was risky business. People heeded the testimony of honorable men, but if the case went against them, their testimony would be deemed false and they would lose their

564. Affidavits had long been used (e.g., Aeschines *Tim.* 45). If the person providing the affidavit was nearby, however, an opposing speaker could complain that they should have come in person, where they could be cross-examined (Apul. *Apol.* 59). For summoning witnesses, see, e.g., Apul. *Apol.* 44–46.

565. Heath, 37 (see at greater length Hermog. *Issues* 45.21–46.8; *Inv.* 3.5.141–42).

566. One might need to further establish that this was the sort of case that would produce many witnesses if the charges were true (Libanius *Declam.* 44.20–24). Sometimes demands for witnesses ignored the fact that the offense was not public and would have produced few witnesses (Lysias *Or.* 7.43, §112). But one could also cite the accusers' ignorance on key points as inconsistent with their assured claims (e.g., Apul. *Apol.* 53–54, 61).

567. E.g., Isaeus *Hagnias* 6; *Cleon.* 31–32, §37; Lysias *Or.* 7.19–23, §110; Cic. *Flacc.* 15.34.

568. Not everyone considered this method reliable (see discussion in sect. 11, "Torture," in the excursus "Slaves and Slavery" at Acts 12:13 [Keener, *Acts*, 2:1920–22]).

569. E.g., Lysias *Or.* 4.10–12, §101; 7.34–40, §111; see further discussion in sect. 11, "Torture," in the excursus "Slaves and Slavery" at Acts 12:13 (Keener, *Acts*, 2:1920–22). When (in a hypothetical case) the slave witness had died during torture, leaving no witness, the opposition contended that the torturer could be simply inventing the claims (Quint. *Decl.* 328.9–10).

570. One might also claim that someone had made a statement "in the hearing of all" without providing the witnesses (Isaeus *Cleon.* 11.36), admittedly more easily requested than produced even when the claim was true.

571. Trans. R. Gardner, LCL, 13:433.

572. Heath, 37; for an earlier example of this method, see Demosth. *Fals. leg.* 120; Hermog. *Inv.* 3.5.142–43. One could also discredit opposing witnesses by arguing that even lawgivers did not trust witnesses and hence established laws against false ones (*Rhet. Alex.* 15, 1431b.42–1432a.3).

573. Lysias *Or.* 7.23, §110 (trans. W. R. M. Lamb, LCL, 157).

574. With Bruce, *Commentary*, 470.

honor.[575] Not only opponents who brought lawsuits but also their witnesses were subjected to slanders against their character to discredit them.[576] Harsh treatment of those who brought frivolous lawsuits was frequent enough to serve as a deterrent in many cases.[577] The emperor Augustus had thrown out old accusations and allowed them to be renewed, provided the accuser would face the penalty due the accused if the accuser lost the suit (Suet. *Aug.* 32.2);[578] if such a rule were observed in Paul's case, the penalty would have been death. Domitian punished Josephus's Jewish accusers (Jos. *Life* 429).

Similar disincentives existed for testifying about earlier riots (cf. Acts 24:5). If Paul's accusers had been able to bring forward witnesses claiming his involvement in the Ephesian riot (19:23–40; cf. 24:5),[579] Paul could in principle[580] counter with testimony that it was the synagogue leaders, not he, who were publicly shouted down by Artemis's worshipers (19:33–34). More to the point, the value of testimony was weighed according to the status of those who offered it;[581] if Paul's supporters included Asiarchs (19:31) and members of their class (cf. 19:35, 37), his version of the riot would be held more acceptable. The Asiarchs might want Paul out of Ephesus and out of trouble, but once their previous connection with him was known, their reputation was better served by defending him (if they personally believed his case more defensible than not) than by joining his accusers. Whether or not it was likely that Paul would appeal to such witnesses, the simple possibility of the case causing more trouble to their own community in Ephesus was reason enough for Paul's accusers from Ephesus to be unwilling to pursue the matter in a Roman court. Luke's narrative thus makes good sense as it stands here.

IV. ABANDONING THE CASE

If changing charges could raise suspicion, so could changing plaintiffs.[582] That the original accusers from Asia are not present may be used to imply that they have something to hide.[583] One who fled trial could be presumed guilty; one who stood trial could claim that he did so because he knew himself innocent (Aeschines *Embassy* 6). Thus one could mock the status of a defendant who has not appeared: "Has he come at last? If not yet come, is he, at all events, near? If not yet near, has he at least

---

575. Cic. *Quinct.* 23.75.

576. E.g., Cic. *Scaur.* 17.38; *Flacc.* 15.34.

577. On laws addressing false accusations, see, e.g., Robinson, *Criminal Law*, 37.

578. This was normal procedure in the case of deliberately false accusations (Ferguson, *Backgrounds*, 51). The Sadducees interpreted the law as not allowing false witnesses to be executed unless the defendant had already been executed (*Sipre Deut.* 190.5.1).

579. It is unlikely, without advance preparation (impossible at this early juncture), that they would be able to bring much evidence concerning the pattern of riots in other cities, although they may have known of some (i.e., they could offer what they had heard from travelers, but this was hearsay and might not stand well under interrogation).

580. In practice this might be difficult if Tychicus and Trophimus (Acts 20:4), potential witnesses, had left Judea because of the charge (21:37–39); Timothy had not been present during the Ephesian riot (19:22).

581. E.g., Juv. *Sat.* 3.140–46 (satirically); Rapske, "Prison," 827; idem, *Custody*, 56–62; Winter, *Left Corinth*, 62–64; see comment on Acts 24:1. Thus, e.g., courts valued men's testimony above women's (e.g., Justin. *Inst.* 2.10.6; Jos. *Ant.* 4.219; *Sipra VDDeho. pq.* 7.45.1.1), with rare exceptions (Plut. *Publ.* 8.4; Wegner, *Chattel*, 120–23; for a nuanced treatment, see Maccini, *Women as Witnesses*, 63–97); so also that of slaves (e.g., Prop. *Eleg.* 3.6.20; Justin. *Inst.* 2.10.6; Jos. *Ant.* 4.219) and minors (Justin. *Inst.* 2.10.6; cf., e.g., Sen. E. *Controv.* 7.5).

582. See, e.g., Apul. *Apol.* 2, who contends that his accuser tried to transfer the plaintiff role to a minor "to avoid punishment for bringing a false accusation" (trans. V. Hunink, p. 26).

583. Accusers could be said to be admitting the defendant's innocence on matters about which they had remained silent (Cic. *Rosc. Amer.* 19.54). On the failure of these witnesses to appear, see Keener, "Rhetorical Techniques," 247–50.

set out from Asia? If he has not yet set out . . ."[584] The same principle could be applied to witnesses, who had less to lose (though also less incentive to participate).

More important, the original accusers' nonappearance constitutes *destitutio*, abandoning the case, if they are the legally appropriate plaintiffs, as Paul here charges. (Unfortunately for Paul's accusers, Paul was well educated and knew Roman law; he knew the privileges to which his Roman citizenship entitled him.) Under Roman law, the failure of plaintiffs to appear was a serious offense (Appian *Bell. civ.* 3.54); the recent emperor, Claudius, had proposed deciding such cases against plaintiffs, and in 61 C.E. (perhaps a year after Paul's trial), the proposed laws passed.[585] About a half century after Paul's hearing, some of those who had brought charges pleaded with the emperor that their coplaintiffs be forced to appear with them or that they be released from the case (Pliny *Ep.* 6.31.10); the emperor ordered all to appear and make their case, explain why they were dropping it, or be declared guilty of bringing false charges (6.31.12). Even classical Athens had added penalties for frivolous prosecutors who dropped cases after initiating them or whose cases proved too weak to persuade even a fifth of the jury.[586] When a province wished to drop its charge against a former governor, it sent a separate delegation to do so (7.6.1–6).

One could not convict an absent party unless the latter's absence was deliberate, and deciding capital cases against an absent defendant was illegal (Paulus *Sent.* 5.5.9; *Dig.* 48.19.5.pr.). Judges could punish unexcused absences as *contumacia*,[587] making impossible any appeal of sentence, though this specific term applied only to defendants in this era (probably introduced under Claudius; applied to plaintiffs only under Justinian).[588] We know of serious cases delayed because of the defendant's absence;[589] naturally, such a situation is not pertinent here, since Paul has no choice but to be present.

More relevant here is that the accuser's absence can stop the judicial process (Justin. *Cod.* 9.2.4).[590] In legal *absentia*, the court would sometimes dismiss the case or judge in favor of the defendant by default (*Dig.* 5.1.71).[591] At the very least, a person's absence could dispose the judge against him, sometimes (though not ideally) even if the person's absence was beyond his control.[592] When accusers did not appear, the recent emperor, Claudius, sometimes decided the case against them in their absence (Suet. *Claud.* 15; Dio Cass. 60.28.6).[593]

Lysias consulted the Sanhedrin only to discover the nature of the charges (Acts 23:28–29) and perhaps instructed its members to accuse Paul (23:30). But they lack witnesses, and they did not initiate the charges that led to the Sanhedrin meeting that had functioned as a preliminary hearing. They themselves could attest only

584. Marcus Aurelius in Fronto *Ad M. Caes.* 1.6.4 (trans. C. R. Haines, LCL, 1:159).

585. Suet. *Claud.* 15.2; Dio Cass. 60.28.6; see Sherwin-White, *Society*, 52–53 (widely followed: Hemer, *Acts in History*, 129–30; Fitzmyer, *Acts*, 737; Winter, "Official Proceedings," 326; Rapske, *Custody*, 163; Witherington, *Acts*, 712–13; Barrett, *Acts*, 1109).

586. MacDowell, "Sycophants"; see esp. Thür, "Epobelia," 1158. The fees were paid to the defendant.

587. Gizewski, "*Absentia*," 35.

588. Schiemann, "Contumacia" (citing *Dig.* 5.1.73.3 on the lack of appeal).

589. E.g., Pliny *Ep.* 2.11.9, 24. An arrogant person with imperial protection might refuse a summons (Tac. *Ann.* 2.34). Classical Athenian law allowed a defendant's conviction by default if he failed to appear despite attested notification (Thür, "Prosklesis," 49; idem, "Pseudokleteias graphe," 116).

590. Gizewski, "*Absentia*," 35.

591. Ibid. For cases usually being dropped if accusers did not pursue them, Witherington, *Acts*, 791, cites *Dig.* 38.14.8. For judgment by default against absent parties, cf. also Lucian *Parl. G.* 18.

592. The practice of Claudius in Suet. *Claud.* 15.2; in one case, a summoned witness failed to appear because he was dead (15.3).

593. Ramsay, *Teaching*, 366–67, admits that this sounds more unusual to Suetonius than to Dio Cassius.

Paul's theological position (24:20–21). Procedural matters were important, and one important method in judicial rhetoric was to challenge whether a case "should be allowed to come to trial" (Hermog. *Issues* 42.5–7).[594] Paul's objection is sound and should result in the dismissal of the case; that it does not suggests the political weight of his current opponents' status.

j. The Theological Charge (24:20–21)

Concluding words could include a final summation;[595] if Paul offered such a summation, Luke may omit it because his report of the speech is already a concise summary, or it may be implied in his denial of genuine wrongdoing (ἀδίκημα, Acts 24:20; cf. denial of the cognate verb ἀδικέω in the summary of 25:10–11).

Concluding words sometimes also included a final blow so decisive that it virtually closed the case as well as the speech (or the proofs section).[596] Thus, in one speech, after Cicero has consistently lowered expectations by comparing his own speaking ability unfavorably vis-à-vis that of his opponents,[597] he concludes his proofs by noting that the entire case turns on whether his client could have made a seven-hundred-mile trip in two to three days; since this was impossible, his case is irrefutable (*Quinct.* 25.78–80). Once the discussion was framed in such terms, it was difficult to dispute; Cicero knew when he had a compelling argument.[598]

In the same way, Paul reserves his ultimate argument for the end: his opponents already showed their hand in the preliminary hearing, and now they want to change their charges to provide a case more suitable for the governor.[599] As already noted, changing charges during a trial was highly suspect behavior.[600] Paul challenges his accusers to demonstrate that they had offered any other charge in the preliminary hearing except the theological one.[601] He appeals to his accusers' own knowledge[602] of the only matter of dispute in the hearing, recognizing that they could not deny their public behavior (especially given Lysias's presence and testimony; cf. Acts 23:29).[603]

---

594. Trans. Heath, p. 35; see also Hermog. *Inv.* 3.5.141.

595. E.g., *Rhet. Alex.* 22, 1434b.11–18; 36, 1443b.15–16; 37, 1445b.21–23; Apul. *Apol.* 103; see also Montefusco, "Epilogue"; discussion in the section "Recapitulating Earlier Themes" at Acts 28:16–31.

596. Apuleius saves some of his strongest arguments for late in the case (e.g., *Apol.* 8; 96) and a minor but irrefutable point, attested by witnesses, just before his peroration (101).

597. Cic. *Quinct.* 1.1–2, 4; 24.77.

598. Reading between the lines of some of his other speeches, one sometimes wonders if his case is sound; in this case, however, there appears little doubt, and Cicero seems utterly confident himself. Speeches could also build toward an emotional climax; see, e.g., Hermog. *Inv.* 3.13.162–63; 4.4.189, 191. One could also proceed from simpler to more complex material; Epictetus *Diatr.* 1.26.3.

599. Deconstructing and discrediting an opponent's position was a frequent forensic exercise (see, e.g., Heath, "Invention," 93–94); so also turning the opponent's own evidence against his position in favor of one's own (synoeciosis, or *conciliatio*, in Rowe, "Style," 145–46, citing Lysias *Or.* 24.23 [*On Behalf of a Cripple*]; Cic. *Rosc. Amer.* 29.80).

600. Lysias *Or.* 7.2, §108; Cic. *Att.* 2.24; Quint. *Decl.* 301.19.

601. Challenging one's opponents to refute one's position was what some would call epitrope (Rowe, "Style," 147) as well as displaying rhetorical παρρησία (see comment on Acts 4:13); cf. hypophora in *Rhet. Her.* 4.23.33–4.24.33; for examples, see Cic. *Verr.* 2.3.30.71; Rev 22:11; cf. Dion. Hal. *Lysias* 20; Cic. *Verr.* 2.2.31.76; Epict. *Diatr.* 1.12.21–22. Had Paul feigned not, in fact, knowing what other charge they might raise, pretending to ask for advice, that could be aporia (Rowe, "Style," 140–41); but in this context it would be highly sarcastic, and a challenge fits much better. For language such as "Let someone show," cf. Epict. *Diatr.* 1.4.13; 1.11.8; 4.13.23–24; Jas 2:18.

602. Since one could gesture toward those present (Shiell, *Reading Acts*, 57–62), ancient auditors would probably imagine such a gesture here. A gesture of insistence or emphasis (on which see 74–76, noting pointing toward the ground with one's index finger) is additionally possible here, though more difficult to infer; or perhaps indignation (on which see 63).

603. Nor would they wish to emphasize the truncation of their debate by Lysias's intervention, since the Sanhedrin's behavior on the occasion, as reported by Luke, would hardly appear praiseworthy.

The original accusers have abandoned the case (24:19), and the only charge that the new accusers can support is a theological one—namely, Paul's view of the resurrection (on which he happens to hold the majority Jewish opinion).[604] What is more, the official document submitted by the governor's own representative attests as much (23:29). If the real basis for the charge is theological, Paul is suffering for his faith in Christ. His own letters, incidentally, also articulate this understanding of his custody (Phil 1:13).

The initial hearing before the Sanhedrin provided a precedent that in turn influences the case here.[605] The reader knows that this outcome of the preliminary hearing was a result of Paul's cleverness and anticipation of subsequent hearings (just as his partial vindication in Philippi may have been won, on one reading, by his calculated silence about his Roman citizenship during a flogging; see comments on Acts 16:22, 37). Many narratives portrayed a protagonist's cleverness (e.g., that of Odysseus or Solomon) as a virtue. But clever rhetoric aside, the reader also knows that Paul is innocent of all the charges leveled against him.

By shifting the discussion from political to theological grounds for the accusations, Paul suggests that his accusers act disingenuously and that it is not Paul's behavior but their hostility that has produced the current conflict. Defendants commonly raised the concern of malicious accusers;[606] it was prudent to examine the motives of others, not just the one on trial (Hermog. *Issues* 47.1–6).[607] Cicero thus sought to put the motives of his client's accusers in a bad light (e.g., *Rosc. Amer.* 2.6).[608] Even a later historian could doubt an earlier source's information if it could be held to stem from malice.[609] Rhetoricians also sought to make their client "appear more fair-minded than his opponent," thereby securing goodwill; the impression that opponents have wronged the client generates sympathy for him.[610]

As noted above, one could transfer the accusers' charges back to the accusers and imply or even state that they were liars (see comment on Acts 24:19). Paul refrains from calling his high-status opponents liars, but if he is telling the truth, they are not, and the light he sheds on their motives suggests that their deception is deliberate. And Felix would have had enough experience with Ananias and his colleagues to know better than to assume that truth constituted their primary motivation.

4. Felix's Procrastination (24:22–27)

From Luke's portrayal of the case, Paul clearly has the upper legal hand: despite Tertullus's rhetoric, Paul has all the legal evidence in his favor. Even a governor with more

604. They might well feel certain that they knew the truth from reports that they had, but lacked firsthand evidence; they were certain that he should be executed under their law, and perhaps thinking Felix corrupt, they may have seen no other recourse except for a "lynching," as in Acts 25:3. But Paul's legal argument, as presented in Acts, is clearly stronger.

605. Classical Athens even provided to a defendant who requested it a preliminary hearing to prove whether the charge against him was contrary to the law (MacDowell, "*Paragraphē*"), though the present Roman hearing is quite different in form from Athenian practice. Paul also knows that it is Felix rather than the Sanhedrin whose "judgment" counts (Acts 24:10, 21).

606. E.g., Libanius *Declam.* 36.1–2, 10; 44.70. Plaintiffs had to head off this accusation (Hermog. *Inv.* 1.1.95–96). On the frequency of Roman cases stemming from personal enmity, see, e.g., Winter, *Left Corinth*, 65.

607. DeSilva, *Credentials*, 73, notes that Arist. *Rhet.* 2.23.24; 3.15.10; 3.16.6 advises one to show not only the falseness of an opponent's accusation but also the motives for such false accusation.

608. It was also standard procedure, as Cicero notes, for prosecutors to try to explain a credible motive (*Rosc. Amer.* 22.61–62).

609. Plut. *Alc.* 3.1; cf. *Mal. Hdt.* passim.

610. Dion. Hal. *Lysias* 24 (trans. Usher, LCL, 1:69). I use the masculine pronoun in the quotation because the source does, but in any case the vast majority of litigants (though not all) in the above cases were male.

integrity than Felix, however, would have serious political considerations in such a case—so serious, in fact, that had Paul not been a Roman citizen (see comment on Acts 16:37), he surely would have been handed over.

Moreover, Felix was hardly known as a paragon of integrity. Thus, Luke points out, Paul's imprisonment results not only from false accusations but also from political inertia in a notoriously difficult province. (Lest we suppose that the accumulation of delays reveals Luke to be guilty of special pleading,[611] such miscarriages of justice were frequent in the provinces, and Paul did survive for a surprising length of time under the circumstances.)

a. Felix Acts from Knowledge (24:22)

Felix's knowledge of Paul's movement helps explain why he adjourns the case for the moment instead of handing Paul over to his politically influential adversaries. (Neither Paul nor his accusers have mentioned Jesus,[612] but "Nazarenes" in Acts 24:5 would have alerted Felix to this connection.) Felix had a "more accurate" understanding of "the Way," perhaps meaning "more accurate than Paul's accusers expected."[613] Felix could know about "the Way" from his Jewish wife, Drusilla (24:24),[614] but his role as administrator would bring the Nazarenes to his attention more directly. Many in Jerusalem belonged to the Jesus movement (21:20), as did some in Caesarea (8:40; 21:8–9, 16), probably including some of his own auxiliaries stationed there (10:1–7, 24).

i. Knowledge versus Politics

Felix's knowledge about the Way is meant to explain his reaction to Paul's claim that the basis of the opposition was the doctrine of the resurrection (24:21); the governor already knew from Lysias that it was an intra-Jewish religious debate (23:29) and from Paul's accusers that he belonged to the minority sect of Nazarenes (24:5). Felix knew enough about the Way to recognize that, contrary to its characterization by its enemies (such as Paul's accusers), it was not a political threat to the province's stability.[615]

It also helps Luke's apologetic for Luke to explain that Felix acts out of political

611. Though to my knowledge no one portrays Paul as inciting sedition against Rome. Paul's letters are not compatible with the portrait painted by his accusers, and so it is historically implausible for us to concede this case against him. But this is more easily said today, when his letters weigh more heavily for his supporters than does the shadow of his execution by a powerful state.

612. Josephus apparently regarded Jesus as innocent and as a wonder-worker in *Ant.* 18.63 but, as in this speech, says little about him. Confronted with claims of miracles in his "name," some other members of the elite may have chosen not to make an issue out of Jesus himself.

613. Witherington, *Acts*, 713, suggests that Felix had a more accurate view than Paul's accusers held, because Felix recognized "that the Nazarenes were not rabble-rousers." It was helpful whenever a judge was already acquainted with the issues surrounding both sides of a case (Phaedrus 3.13.4). For ἀκριβῶς and its cognates, see, with regard to the law, Acts 22:3; 26:5; the message of Jesus, Luke 1:3; Acts 18:25–26; and legal inquiries, Acts 23:15, 20.

614. There being few, if any, Nazarenes in her class, she might know of it through family associations (her father had sought to execute Peter, Acts 12:2–4; but she might not have been exposed to such affairs directly). Still, her brother, Agrippa II, is presumed well informed; as Paul suggests, the movement was not hidden (26:26), a point that Luke exploits apologetically. In contrast to Luke's portrayal, the Western text, known for its antifeminist and anti-Judaic tendencies, blames her for Felix's refusal to release Paul (treated as clearly secondary in Metzger, *Textual Commentary*, 492; Pervo, *Acts*, 602, astonishingly, "might suspect" that the later addition reflects Luke's intention).

615. Its massive numbers had produced no signs of sedition (in contrast to the many resistance movements during Felix's tenure); here, moreover, was an articulate, educated Diaspora Jew, a (freeborn) Roman citizen who in a different setting might have conversed with Felix (a freedman) as a peer and was academically his superior (cf. Acts 24:24–26).

rather than juridical considerations: Felix realizes that Paul is attacked on religious, not legal, grounds, but he wants to offend neither a minority sect of significant size (21:20) nor, more important, the leading priests. It was politically indiscreet to offend the local elite "merely to do justice to a single person."[616]

The previous Roman governor's conflict with the current high priest and his allies (see comment on Acts 23:2) led to the banishment of that governor (Jos. *War* 2.245–46) and to Felix's becoming the current governor (2.247). Felix did not now need unnecessary trouble. Later a Jewish delegation from Caesarea accused him before Nero, and only his brother Pallas's intervention spared him punishment (*Ant.* 20.182). Further, it was possible to cooperate with the current high priest, Ananias, who was notably pro-Roman (see comment on Acts 23:2); offending an important local ally over a trivial case was imprudent.

At the same time, Felix was no friend of the Jerusalem aristocracy. Josephus claims that he funded the assassination of Ananias's colleague in the high priesthood, Jonathan, because the latter gave him too much meddlesome advice (*Ant.* 20.162–63). Even if Josephus's information is untrue (if it could be substantiated beyond mere gossip, it should have been raised at Felix's misconduct hearing in Rome in 20.182), it suggests an appearance of conflict between them.

Further, he has some political incentive not to convict Paul, entirely aside from the likely perception of his innocence. If Paul is genuinely a leader in an influential sect (Acts 24:5), then he has a "political" constituency that it would be better not to politicize or provoke against Roman authority. Because Paul is a Roman citizen, complaints on his behalf to Rome could perhaps obtain a hearing or at least contribute to any dossier eventually assembled against Felix. Although Felix committed atrocities (cf. Jos. *Ant.* 20.177, 182; *War* 2.270) and was ready to discipline even respectable people (e.g., Jos. *Life* 13), he apparently preferred to have pretexts even in circumstances in which Josephus (admittedly no fan of Felix's) claims that his violence was premeditated (*War* 2.319, 325).

Some Roman governors familiar with early Christians also recognized that Christians thrived, instead of buckling under, when their leaders were martyred; in the second century a governor in this region allegedly released a prominent Christian without even scourging him, to prevent creating a martyr.[617] It appears that Paul's eloquent and informed defense has earned Felix's respect (Acts 24:24–25), and Felix probably does not wish to harm this fellow Roman; but Luke hardly views Felix's politically driven distortion of justice in a positive light (24:26–27).[618]

II. DEFERRING THE CASE

The term ἀναβάλλω (a NT hapax legomenon), when used in legal contexts (the only sense relevant here), means "adjourn";[619] such adjourned trials could be picked up at later sessions (Livy 43.2.6, 10). The term for "deciding" the case here,

616. Ramsay, *Pictures*, 291; cf. also others, e.g., Nunnally, "Acts," 386. Readers in late antiquity could infer the same: John Chrysostom (*Hom. Acts* 51; *NPNF* 11:304) points out that the governors seek pretexts to defer justice so that they can avoid offending the Jewish leaders; Felix defers the case "not from ignorance . . . but knowing it." Some thought Claudius an incompetent judge because he was too good-natured (Suet. *Claud.* 15.3).

617. Lucian *Peregr.* 14.

618. Narratives could recount good deeds as exemplary even if their doers were primarily negative characters (e.g., Val. Max. 4.2.7; 4.7.1). Rapske, *Custody*, 111–12, suggests that the status tension between Paul's high status as an educated citizen and low status as a manual laborer helps explain why he is treated neither better nor worse than he is in some judicial situations. In the current setting, however, it is not his laborer status (which he would not volunteer) but his opponents' high status that balances the dispute.

619. See, e.g., Jos. *Ant.* 14.177; P.Tebt. 22.9 (from BDAG); Conzelmann, *Acts*, 200. Its few LXX uses are not forensic.

διαγινώσκω, is the same as at Acts 23:15, where it probably means "investigate"; both meanings (see BDAG) probably connote careful consideration. The "you" is plural, involving the plaintiffs as well as the defendant, but the plural simply specifies that Felix will decide the case in favor of one side; it does not imply that he will punish faulty accusers.[620] From the Roman standpoint, Lysias is the only independent witness of significant rank;[621] he would certainly come if Felix summoned him, but Felix offers no timetable for the summons, which he could easily have provided.

Like other Roman governors of Judea, Felix apparently kept many in prison; Albinus later freed prisoners of earlier procurators (Jos. *War* 2.273; cf. *Ant.* 20.215).[622] It would be evident to all parties that Felix was stalling. He earlier promised to decide the case once the accusers came (Acts 23:35); from the standpoint of Ananias, this has been done, and from the standpoint of Paul (24:19), it will never be done. Moreover, Felix has now sufficient evidence to throw the case out of court; Paul's accusers thus can hardly complain too loudly if Felix, though reluctant to convict, nevertheless fails to release the object of their concern.

At any rate, adjourning a case without a verdict was within his juridical authority, and the litigants could not do anything about it.[623] Roman officials generally left to local courts minor matters irrelevant to public order, but a governor's *imperium* (the authority of the state vested in him)[624] allowed him freedom to decide cases *extra ordinem*; outside Italy and the colonies, Roman law did not automatically apply. This was the governor's power of *coercitio*.[625] Some governors abused this freedom (Cic. *Verr.* 2.3.3.6), but deferring a case would not run much risk of later political consequences in Rome.[626]

Paul is not such a major issue for the chief priests (despite Luke's focus) that they are willing to fight the governor over the delay; they will try again with the next governor (Acts 25:2) but will not pursue the matter to Rome, where, given the records of the case, they probably have no chance of winning (28:21). Once Paul was in Rome, Rome would not accept these Judean leaders' complaints about Paul as threatening unrest, the primary potent political charge available; nor would the pro-Jewish sentiment of Poppaea Sabina, Nero's possibly involuntary mistress,[627] necessarily help Judean leaders against the equally Judean, but culturally savvy and articulate, apostle. If Nero's court later condemns Paul, it will have to be for other reasons.

620. Such a threat of punishment, which would not likely be carried out, would have had to have been communicated more specifically to make that point. Language such as "judging between you" or "judging concerning you" (e.g., 2 Sam 14:8) indicates deciding that one side is correct, but as best as I can ascertain need not always imply a penalty for one side. The expression καθ᾽ ὑμᾶς is especially Lukan in earliest Christian literature (Acts 17:18; 18:15; 24:22; also Eph 1:15; in the LXX, only Job 12:3; 16:4; in Philo, only *Names* 119).

621. Sherwin-White, *Society*, 53. Cestius Gallus later weighed the corrupt Florus's testimony more heavily than that of Judeans' complaints (Jos. *War* 2.333–35).

622. Rapske, *Custody*, 166; cf. Wikenhauser, *Apostelgeschichte*, 262.

623. With Rapske, *Custody*, 164. Keeping Paul in custody would leave his innocence in question, which would help Paul's enemies if he remained in custody when the next governor arrived (Le Cornu, *Acts*, 1345).

624. Cf. Derow, "*Imperium*."

625. See Ferguson, *Backgrounds*, 50–51; Treves and Lintott, "Coercitio."

626. Laws regulated postponements in Roman private lawsuits (see Metzger, *Outline*, 10–13, on *lex Irnitana* tablet 10, col. A, chs. 90–91), with notice given to the judge and adversary (*Outline*, 56); part of the point may be to prevent judges from delaying (pp. 60, 91). This would not restrict provincial governors from judging matters of public order, however.

627. Historians and biographers of the early second century viewed her much less favorably than did Josephus. They emphasized her own immorality; see Suet. *Otho* 3.1–2; Tac. *Hist.* 1.13 (cf. *Ann.* 13.46); Plut. *Galba* 19.4–5.

Some scholars are skeptical that many "good" officials in Acts would keep exonerating Christians as innocent; where then did the persecutions come from, they ask?[628] But Luke's apologetic focus makes him selective, not wrong; further, his portrayal is not as one-sided as his critics suggest. Paul's letters to Corinth (where Acts depicts Gallio's refusal to hear a case against him) show that Corinthian believers did not face regular persecution; indeed, some even went to pagan courts for justice (1 Cor 6:1–8). By contrast, Paul's letters to Philippi and Thessalonica (where Acts depicts Paul facing conflict) reveal harsher conflict. Paul's letters do not address the current passage, but it is noteworthy that Felix does not exonerate Paul; he merely defers the problem for his successor (Acts 24:27).

We should not read the Roman administrator's willingness to retain Paul in custody as if he doubted Lysias's claims (23:27–30); had he found the case for Paul's innocence demonstrably ambiguous, he would likely have handed him over to Jerusalem's municipal assembly for punishment.[629]

b. Light Custody (24:23)

Felix's generous treatment of the prisoner[630] probably implies for Luke's audience what the rest of the narrative's direction does: that Felix recognizes Paul's innocence though, for political reasons, he dares not simply acquit him.

i. Lighter Confinement

Given the lack of compelling evidence against him that would warrant harsher custody, it seems most likely that Paul continued in the praetorium.[631] The likely site of this palace was about four hundred meters from the inner harbor and close to the theater and the amphitheater.[632] The palace was large enough to hold a number of prisoners, and Paul could be conveniently "sent for and dismissed" from that location (24:24–26).[633] Certainly, given the known hostility against Paul (esp. 23:30) and the embarrassment that losing a Roman citizen in custody would cause the administration, Felix needed to keep him in a secure place.

Places of confinement varied in severity, usually according to the prisoner's status or the nature of the crime alleged.[634] That Paul should be allowed some ἄνεσις indicates that his custody is limited; when applied to detention, the term indicates a degree of freedom and the relaxing of custodial arrangements (see BDAG). This arrangement may suggest that Felix believed Paul to be innocent; if we may accept either the substance of the forensic speeches or the testimony of 24:24–25 (or, more likely, both), he surely did believe him innocent. Paul's was not, however, the lightest

628. Pervo, *Profit*, 38 (comparing Philost. *Vit. Apoll.* 1.15; 4.8; 6.38).
629. I observed similar situations in northern Nigeria during particular administrations, where sufficient documentation could establish particular casualty or atrocity claims to a significant degree, but the government moved deliberately to avoid antagonizing a militant segment of a religious community (cf., e.g., "Ethno Religion Violence"; Keener, "Mayhem," 63; and a variety of reports in my possession). International diplomacy today likewise takes into account political sensitivities.
630. Obvious by way of contrast to the many prisoners detained in Caesarea under harsher conditions (see Jos. *War* 2.273; *Ant.* 20.215; Rapske, *Custody*, 166).
631. See Burrell, Gleason, and Netzer, "Seaside Palace"; fuller discussion at Acts 23:35. The nature of surviving evidence may bias us in this direction (there were likely many places of detention in Caesarea; Jos. *War* 2.273); nevertheless, it seems most plausible. Nearby secure accommodations are possible, though more dangerous for Paul's periodic summons to Felix.
632. Holum, "Caesarea," 400. Herod situated his palace between the hippodrome (to its north) and the theater (to its south); see Weiss, "Buildings," 105 (also noting possible Roman and other models).
633. Rapske, *Custody*, 170.
634. See ibid., 9.

form of custody; yet it was better for Paul's safety, and Felix, like Lysias, does not take chances on being embarrassed. Staying in a citizen's house or renting one's own quarters (28:16), the sort of custody to which ἄνεσις sometimes applied (Jos. Ant. 18.235), would be too risky given the threats against him.

Even light custody could be difficult if the keeper was harsh;[635] in Caesarea, military guards would be auxiliaries, especially recruited from the local Syrian population, which was at odds with local Jews.[636] But Paul's keepers would undoubtedly keep in mind the governor's apparent favor (Acts 24:24–25), and Felix specifically appointed a centurion, who would have already proved himself and might have career concerns.[637] The keepers would not need to observe or sanction all Paul's activities when his visitors came;[638] regardless of activities, Paul would not be able to escape or be harmed. In contrast to Lysias, the governor had *imperium* to hold a Roman citizen in chains; even the freest forms of military custody included chains (cf. 26:29).[639]

As already noted, custody in a private house would be risky, given the threats against Paul. Some scholars point to the rising ethnic tensions in Caesarea, where Jews constituted half the city (see comments on Acts 10:1; 21:8).[640] The center of Paul's opposition is clearly Jerusalem, and it is not clear that despite the ethnic tensions, Caesarean Jews, whose contacts with Gentiles were more abundant than those of Jerusalemites, would see Paul as an enemy for preaching to Gentiles.[641] But radicals could easily enough journey from Jerusalem, and they could also circulate reports against Paul that would probably allow them to radicalize and recruit at least some assassins if Paul were known to be kept in a vulnerable location.

II. Plausibility

Those who view Acts as purely novelistic think the portrayal of Paul's custody too light. They note that in a later, largely fictitious work, Apollonius of Tyana found a good biographer (Philost. *Vit. Apoll.* 7.16), conversed with people of status (7.17–33), and enjoyed "a kind of relaxed custody after initial interrogation (7.40)."[642] The chief jailer was ordered to supply Apollonius's wants, though Apollonius observes that he has few of them.[643] One may also note that after Domitian acquitted Apollonius, he wanted to question him privately (cf. Acts 24:24), but then (in contrast to Paul in Acts) Apollonius vanished (Philost. *Vit. Apoll.* 8.5). (And one may note that not all of Apollonius's final custody was spent in lighter custody [7.34].)

This approach, however, casts the net for parallels too narrowly, since even novelists often constructed scenes that reflected legal realities. Thus, for example, Vespasian

---

635. Ibid., 34.

636. See comment on Acts 10:1; also Le Cornu, *Acts*, 1329.

637. The assignment of a centurion to arrange Paul's custody probably simply delegates a single assignment (centurions were sometimes delegated to special assignments, along with a small attachment of soldiers; Campbell, "Centurio," 127; but if centurions remained involved (cf. Acts 27:1), this reflects Paul's high status and probable favor with the governor (as in 24:24–25), perhaps as well as the security risk encountered in holding and protecting him. "The" centurion might suggest one of the centurions already with him (23:17, 23) but presumably simply refers to a centurion to whom Felix delegated the responsibility (just as he gave orders to someone in 23:35).

638. Rapske, *Custody*, 169.

639. Ibid.

640. Ibid., 169–70.

641. Coastal and inland cultures in Judea diverged significantly; see, rightly, Rosenfeld, "Culture."

642. Pervo, *Profit*, 155n163; the lighter custody in Philost. *Vit. Apoll.* 7.40 follows the fettered prison. Not all imprisonments in this novel were so comfortable (cf. Musonius in 4.35); Apollonius dared not visit Musonius, for the sake of the safety of both of them, but they corresponded (4.46). But lighter custody without bonds allowed for relaxed conversation (7.22).

643. Philost. *Vit. Apoll.* 7.28. Paul depends not on the jailer here but on his friends (Acts 24:23).

gave a captive (Josephus) expensive gifts even while the latter remained in custody, out of spiritual respect (Jos. *War* 3.408). Moreover, if either writer influenced the other, Luke indisputably wrote earlier than Philostratus; the latter, unlike Luke, also wrote in the primary heyday of novels.[644] For various reasons, Luke's portrait here is much more plausible than his detractors allow.

First, as noted above, Luke's perspective fits legal realities and is entirely plausible. A ruler who acted for political reasons rather than certainty of a defendant's guilt might, for example, give him an unusually light banishment (cf., e.g., the case of Otho's treatment of Dolabella, Tac. *Hist.* 1.88; Plut. *Otho* 5.1).[645] Second, as will be noted below, the access of friends to provide for him was not an unusual arrangement, although the governor's specifically ordering it would probably eliminate corrupt guards from profiting from it. Third, we should not exaggerate the ease of his arrangements; they could have been better.[646] Finally, we also know from Paul's own undisputed correspondence that even at what was probably a later stage in his custody, Paul had access to and influence with members of Caesar's household (Phil 4:22),[647] probably members of the Praetorian Guard (1:13).[648] At that time Paul also received gifts from outside without anything being confiscated (4:14, 18).

III. Support by Friends

Access to prisoners was not unusual, though had Felix not mandated it, it would have been at the discretion of the guards (who sometimes required bribes).[649] A Roman audience would consider a governor cruel if he denied a man imprisoned without trial visits from his aged father or young son (Cic. *Verr.* 2.5.8.21). Greek custom expected that women relatives, including wives, sisters, mothers, and others, could visit a man in prison.[650] A superior could arrange for a well-to-do prisoner's freedpersons and friends to have access to him (Jos. *Ant.* 18.202).

Although access was not unusual, Felix's command to allow support was important. Without such instructions, guards could prove harsh even to those who brought help to prisoners, sometimes confiscating, for personal gain or mockery, part of what the visitors

644. See discussion in Keener, *Acts*, 1:332–33. Novels existed in the first century but flourished especially in the late second and early third centuries (Bowie, "Readership," 443; Stephens, "Who Read Novels?," 414).
645. Cf. also Antipas's reluctance to punish John more harshly in Mark 6:17–20.
646. As Conzelmann notes (*Acts*, 200), we should not overestimate Paul's freedom as "idyllic" (comparing Constantine, *Cod. theod.* 11.7.3, on "free" military custody); Rapske, *Custody*, 171, points out that Paul's chains show that he did not have *custodia libera* ("free or open custody") but had merely *custodia liberior* (lightened custody); cf. G. Diodati in Chung-Kim and Hains, *Acts*, 329.
647. Referring to his clients, especially slaves and freedpersons (Beare, *Philippians*, 158; Craddock, *Philippians*, 81–82; Judge, *Pattern*, 34). Nevertheless, imperial slaves often wielded great power (deSilva, *Honor*, 192), and to outsiders, anyone of "Caesar's house" was important (Epict. *Diatr.* 4.6.31). By Domitian's time the gospel may have touched even Caesar's literal relatives (cf. Reicke, *Era*, 280).
648. Lightfoot, *Philippians*, 99–104; Knox, *Gentiles*, 179; Michael, *Philippians*, 30; Johnston, *Ephesians*, 37; Beare, *Philippians*, 57; Reicke, *Era*, 247–48; idem, "Caesarea," 285; Krentz, "Games," 360; cf. Jones, "Army," 198; Meeks, *Urban Christians*, 63. For their prominence to outsiders, see O'Rourke, "Law," 168–69; Epict. *Diatr.* 3.24.117. (By contrast, Duncan, *Ephesian Ministry*, 108–11, seeks to explain how these passages could fit an Ephesian imprisonment.)
649. For guards requiring bribes for admission, see Lucian *Peregr.* 12; Philost. *Vit. Apoll.* 7.36 (though the alleged briber was actually an informant); on bribery more generally, see comment on Acts 24:26. *Apost. Const.* 5.1.1 figures bribery into the cost assumed for helping prisoners (Rapske, *Custody*, 383; on limited access, see in general 381–83); eventually Christians pragmatically called these "wages" so that they could help the prisoners (p. 261). For inquiries into prisoners' affairs, see Ulp. *Dig.* 4.6.10 (Conzelmann, *Acts*, 224). Among the free, of course, visitors (especially unexpected ones) held a much greater role than in modern Western urban society (see Balch, "Paul, Families, and Households," 260, 265).
650. Lysias *Or.* 13.39–40, §133; in a later novel, Anthia visited her husband in prison whenever she could persuade the guards to allow it (Xen. Eph. *Anthia* 2.7).

brought.[651] In one story, a man had to beg a jailer to admit him to visit the prison and then shared his clothes with his close friend;[652] after this, he used some of his own earnings to gain the keeper's favor, and the rest to provide for his friend, also sleeping in front of the prison.[653] Later, however, a prisoner's death led to a lockdown, which made entrance difficult.[654] Once guards were manacled to some prisoners, the prisoner's associates might need the guard's permission to converse with him.[655] See also comment on Acts 23:16.

Someone must have provided for Paul, unless we should think of friends willing to endure the voyage to Rome with him (Acts 27:2) who nevertheless abandoned him to severe deprivation in detention. The purpose of prison rations was to prevent a captive from starving in custody, not to sustain health.[656] Such rations could also be withheld to punish or even kill[657] (although this would not happen to Paul given Felix's favorable instructions). Prisoners were responsible for securing their own resources,[658] but friends from the outside were able to supply food or drink.[659] As Brian Rapske points out, "Far from being an exceptional privilege as many would argue, such a provision relieved the prison system of responsibility for Paul's ongoing physical maintenance and care and could even be considered the usual arrangement."[660]

Some scholars suggest that Paul's supporters might be his sister and nephew in Jerusalem,[661] but this would demand a difficult commuting distance if practiced regularly. More likely, we should think of Christians present in Caesarea, among whom Paul had friends who knew his innocence (21:8–9, 16; cf. 21:11–14). Helpers might want to visit a prisoner out of affection or as the prisoner's servant; out of political solidarity; or out of philosophic or religious solidarity.[662] Early Christians often sought access to prisoners to help them (Phil 2:25; 4:18; 2 Tim 4:13; Heb 13:3; Matt 25:36).[663] Despite ethnic tensions in Caesarea, most Christians there would not have problems with Paul's Gentile mission, given the history of the church there (cf. Acts 8:40; 10:1).

Certainly Paul's associates, such as the narrator and Aristarchus (27:2), would be among those who would visit him. Presumably, they would lodge with Christians in Caesarea; some probably worked a trade while there to help pay for long-term accommodations after the trial failed to be resolved quickly.[664] This would have given Luke more opportunity to interview Philip (see comment on Acts 21:8) and might help

651. Rapske, *Custody*, 388. On harsher jail conditions, see comment on Acts 16:23–24.

652. Lucian *Tox.* 30.

653. Lucian *Tox.* 31.

654. Lucian *Tox.* 32 (the friend circumvented this by having himself imprisoned; both were finally released in *Tox.* 33 after coming to the prefect's attention and demanding trial).

655. Jos. *Ant.* 18.196; Rapske, *Custody*, 31.

656. Rapske, "Prison," 829. At least the early fifth-century C.E. *Codex theodosianus* provided for prisoners with no other means (*Cod. theod.* 9.3.7; Rapske, *Custody*, 209).

657. Rapske, "Prison," 829, cites Dio Cass. 58.3.5–6; Tert. *Fasting* 12; Heliod. *Eth.* 8.6.2; Cyprian *Ep.* 21.2; 33.2. See further Rapske, *Custody*, 212.

658. See Rapske, *Custody*, 209 (on obtaining food and drink in prison, see most fully 209–16).

659. Rapske, "Prison," 828–29, cites Jos. *Ant.* 18.204; *Life* 13–14; Lucian *Peregr.* 12; Tert. *Fasting* 12; *b. Mo'ed Qaṭ.* 3:1–2; *'Erub.* 21b. Paul would also need clothing, especially if some of what he had been wearing since the riot was torn (Le Cornu, *Acts*, 1331).

660. Rapske, *Custody*, 171.

661. Fitzmyer, *Acts*, 739. Providing for an imprisoned relative would be considered a pious duty and should not have run the same risk of retaliation as having betrayed the assassination plot (cf. Acts 23:22 and comment there).

662. Rapske, *Custody*, 370–72.

663. Lucian later claims that Christians tried to have one of their prominent teachers released, and failing that, served him in prison, bringing fancy foods and reading Scripture, visiting him or waiting nearby from morning through night (*Peregr.* 12).

664. Normal hospitality was not expected to last for more than a week, much less for two years; see Hock, *Social Context*, 29–31; discussion at Acts 16:15; 18:2. On the view that Luke the physician (Col 4:14) was

account for the repeated importance of Caesarea in Luke's account (though, apart from Jerusalem, it would naturally feature as Judea's most important city to Gentiles who knew the coast best).

Still, Paul's friends must have exercised some measure of courage. It was sometimes dangerous to be close to a prisoner;[665] sometimes one's supporters dwindled in the face of potential danger (Philost. *Vit. Apoll.* 4.37).[666] Even if visitors could be certain that Paul was the accusers' only target, chains were a matter of humiliation, sometimes deterring association with the prisoner (2 Tim 1:8, 16). Any kind of imprisonment bore associations with shame.[667] (In some cases, however, people visited famous prisoners just to see what they looked like or to assuage their jealousy with the captive's hardship.)[668]

IV. PAUL'S ACTIVITIES

What was Paul doing while in detention (besides occasionally preaching to Felix, Acts 24:24–26)? Ancient literature provides a range of possibilities, although only some seem relevant to what we know of Paul. Prisoners could engage in various activities; those attested include playing games,[669] reading, or conversing.[670] They also were known to pray, sing (cf. 16:25), and fast[671] and to write to,[672] or speak with,[673] others about philosophic or religious matters. We have letters from Paul's detention, possibly from Caesarea but more likely (in my view) from Rome—namely, Philippians, Philemon, probably Colossians, and (in my possibly minority view) probably also Ephesians. But Paul was probably also using visitors to disseminate his views.

It may have been because Paul stayed active that he remained a target of Jerusalem leaders' accusations (25:1–3) after "two years" (24:27; in practice this could mean less than two but more than one; see comment there). He could appear influential in Caesarea's Christian community, given his past experience with the city (9:30; 18:22) and his relationship with Philip (21:8), who had evangelized Gentiles (8:26–40) and settled there (8:40; 21:8).[674] Socrates, Apollonius, R. Akiba, and later Christian martyrs all applied themselves to teaching while in prison;[675] Paul may well have done the same for local visitors.

c. Educating Felix about the Faith (24:24)

The delay allows Paul to speak further with the governor in a different venue, continuing to fulfill Luke 21:12–15.[676] A private venue with a person of rank was

Paul's companion at this point (as well as in Col 4), we may note that physicians would be able to find ready employment almost anywhere (cf. Suet. *Jul.* 42.1; *Aug.* 42.3).

665. Rapske, *Custody*, 388–90. Those who sided with a prisoner could become suspects themselves if the case went against him (Winter, *Welfare*, 95).

666. Rapske, *Custody*, 388; cf. the temptation for dissociation in Quint. *Decl.* 307.6. Talbert, *Acts*, 211, cites the loyalty of one friend of the accused in the face of danger in Lucian *Tox.* 18.

667. Rapske, *Custody*, 298; cf. Phil 1:20.

668. Corn. Nep. 18 (Eumenes), 11.2; cf. Phil 1:16–17.

669. Rapske, "Prison," 829 (citing Sen. Y. *Tranq.* 14.6–7).

670. Rapske, "Prison," 829 (citing Plato *Phaedo* 61B; Suet. *Tib.* 61.4; Epict. *Diatr.* 2.6.27; Lucian *Peregr.* 12). For corresponding with letters, see Philost. *Vit. Apoll.* 4.46.

671. Rapske, "Prison," 829 (citing Plato *Phaedo* 60DE; 61AB; 117BC; Philost. *Vit. Apoll.* 7.31, 38; Tibullus 2.6.25–26).

672. Rapske, "Prison," 829 (citing Plato *Phaedo* 60DE; Cic. *Verr.* 2.5.112; Tac. *Ann.* 6.39; Philost. *Vit. Apoll.* 4.46; Poly. *Phil.* 13.2; Ign. passim).

673. Rapske, "Prison," 829 (citing Plato *Crito*; *Phaedo*; Philost. *Vit. Apoll.* 7.26–42; *m. Git.* 6:7).

674. Rapske, *Custody*, 357.

675. Ibid., 358.

676. Skinner, *Locating Paul*, 137–38, emphasizes how Paul's custody in Caesarea allows him to speak with the highest authorities in Judea. Judicial delays narrated in literary works (such as novels) normally served a

normally reserved for people of status and importance,[677] and so these meetings augment Luke's portrayal of Paul's status in the narrative.[678] Nevertheless, a ruler might well be interested in hearing from a famous sage (see comment below).

I. PRIVATE MEETINGS

When one sent for an apparently innocent prisoner for a private interview, in ideal justice it would be to confirm the prisoner's innocence and to free him (e.g., Xen. Eph. *Anthia* 4.4, with gifts). Given the rampant corruption of provincial officials, however (see comment on Acts 24:26), it was sometimes for the official's benefit,[679] with no intention of freeing the captive (cf. Mark 6:20). It was a crime to try and condemn someone in a dining room rather than a public hall (Sen. E. *Controv.* 9.2.4),[680] but corrupt governors were known to have prisoners marched even into their house (Cic. *Verr.* 2.3.23.56; cf. Luke 22:54).

Felix may desire to become further informed about "the Way" (Acts 24:22) for political reasons. Beyond this motive, Felix, even more than Lysias (21:37), has heard Paul and recognized that he is not merely a Roman citizen but an educated person, a sage more educated, indeed, than either Lysias or Felix. (He would be valued especially as a moralist, but his rhetorical skills matched Tertullus's in forensic rhetoric, and Paul might be his superior in deliberative rhetoric.)

Such teachers could be used as dinner entertainment at banquets for educated guests,[681] and Felix might count listening to Paul a leisure activity[682]—so long as the discourse remained at an intellectual rather than a moral level (24:25). It is possible that Drusilla views Paul similarly or (fitting a parallel with John the Baptist that Luke omits) as a prophet. In any case, Felix is no Sergius Paulus (13:12), though he expresses more interest than Gallio did (18:14–16).

II. DRUSILLA

Luke may mention Felix's Jewish wife partly to emphasize that the governor does know enough about Judaism to understand that Paul's message is within the range of Jewish beliefs (24:22).[683] That Luke explains her identity as Felix's wife (cf. 5:1, 7; 18:2) and points out that she is Jewish suggests that he does not expect most of his audience to already know who she is.

Still, it is tempting to suppose that some members of Luke's ideal audience may know of the circumstances of her marriage to Felix;[684] certainly, this assumption fits

---

narrative purpose; Schwartz, "Trial Scenes," 130, argues that the purpose here is talking with the governor. Within the narrative world, of course, up to two years must have seemed difficult for such a fruitless endeavor (but cf. Ezek 2:4–7; 3:7).

677. See, e.g., discussion of the morning salutation in Chow, *Patronage*, 75.

678. On Paul's high status in Acts, see esp. Lentz, *Luke's Portrait*, although he is less convinced that Luke's portrait is accurate.

679. Cf. the hypothetical case in Sen. E. *Controv.* 9.2.intro., where a proconsul had a criminal beheaded at a banquet to entertain a prostitute (cf. Mark 6:25–28; for analogous beheadings for entertainment, see Val. Max. 2.9.3; Livy 39.42; Plut. *M. Cato* 17.2–3; cf. Suet. *Calig.* 32.1; Jos. *Ant.* 13.380). The private interview in Jer 37:17–21 at least benefits Jeremiah; cf. 38:14–16.

680. Cf. also Jewish law in Cohn, *Trial*, 98 (citing *b. 'Abod. Zar.* 8b; *Sanh.* 41b; *Šabb.* 15a).

681. E.g., Slater, "Introduction," 2–3. Lower-quality entertainment included actors, fools, and jesters (see Schäfer, "Entertainers," 998–99).

682. Some intellectuals preferred listening to a philosopher to busy public life judging cases (Pliny *Ep.* 1.10.9–11; cf. 1.9.2–4).

683. See Dunn, *Acts*, 315.

684. Many scholars think that Luke presumes his audience's knowledge of it here (Rapske, *Custody*, 356; Johnson, *Acts*, 418–19; Fitzmyer, *Acts*, 740). In the historical information behind Luke's narrative, certainly Paul, Felix, and Drusilla knew of it, and it is therefore likely that Luke would as well. Luke might suppose that his audience knows of Felix's dishonorable recall, since he does not trouble himself to narrate it in Acts 24:27

Felix's response in 24:25. Judean refugees and those educated in the affairs of the eastern Mediterranean might know the story of Felix's marriage to Drusilla. Felix's marriages were widely known among those who knew anything of Felix (this might be a minority of Luke's audience even if we date Acts early, but clearly some accounts of the Judean royal family were widely known).[685] Moreover, it would take only some members of the audience to inform others of what it might be indiscreet for Luke to report about Paul's judge explicitly. Josephus provides the story in the greatest detail, but Suetonius (*Claud.* 28) notes that Felix married three queens,[686] and Tacitus (*Hist.* 5.9) names Drusilla as a princess.[687] Roman custom viewed negatively governors' sexual interest in locals, especially those already married to Rome's subjects.[688] Luke, who lived in Judea, undoubtedly knew of it, but one wonders why he leaves it unmentioned if it is of interest for his narrative (it is possible that it was not). Perhaps further discrediting the couple[689] might have weakened his apologetic (Luke presents this governor as more interested than Gallio or any governor since Sergius Paulus, after all),[690] or perhaps mentioning it explicitly might have courted trouble.[691]

Agrippa I (see comment on Acts 12:1) had two sons (of whom only Agrippa II survived childhood) and three daughters, Berenice, Mariamne, and the youngest, Drusilla (Jos. *Ant.* 18.132). Drusilla was born in about 38 C.E.[692] and hence may be about twenty here;[693] Agrippa named her after the favorite sister of his patron, Gaius Caligula.[694] She was six when her father died (19.354), and if Felix took office in 52, Drusilla was only about fourteen years old at his accession.[695] She was betrothed to Epiphanes, son of Antiochus, king of Commagene; but he broke his promise to her father to convert to Judaism (i.e., be circumcised), and so the betrothal was dissolved. When she was about age fifteen (in 53), her brother, Agrippa II, married her

and could not but have known of it himself (cf. 27:1; but Romans could have considered such a narration indecorous, especially if Felix or Pallas retained supporters). Paul presupposes that Corinthian believers knew of Damascus, and he mentions Aretas as king (2 Cor 11:32), but perhaps he had told them this story before. After Augustus (cf. Suet. *Aug.* 24), Roman governors and generals could take wives with them (cf. Tac. *Ann.* 1.40; 2.55; 3.33–35; 15.10; Matt 27:19; contrast Severus in Hdn. 3.2.5).

685. For unfortunate slanders about Berenice, see, e.g., Juv. *Sat.* 6.156–60; Jos. *Ant.* 20.145; cf., on the household, Pers. *Sat.* 5.180.

686. Perhaps a partial compensation for his limited birth rank as a freedman? Meanwhile, Drusilla might view marriage to a governor sent by Rome as improved status or simply have believed his promise to make her happy (Jos. *Ant.* 20.142).

687. He counts her, however, the granddaughter of Cleopatra and Marc Antony; unless this was through a different mother, there seems to be some confusion. Harmonizing, Lake and Cadbury, *Commentary*, 304, suggest that two of them (!) were named Drusilla (so also Bennett, "Drusilla regina"), but it is much likelier that Tacitus confuses two wives; or perhaps he confuses his source regarding Cleopatra and Herod (Jos. *Ant.* 15.97–98) or, more likely, Herod's wife Cleopatra of Jerusalem (*Ant.* 17.21; *War* 1.562). If any of Felix's wives descended from Cleopatra VII (which is uncertain), she would need to be a great-granddaughter, not granddaughter (Brenk and Canali De Rossi, "Felix").

688. See Williams, *Homosexuality*, 117–18.

689. Surely, from many points of view, it was a scandalous union ("Skandalheirat," Jervell, *Apostelgeschichte*, 575).

690. Cf. Bruce, *Acts¹*, 427, on Luke's fairly positive view of Felix. I do not consider Luke's view, in fact, positive, but it may be more positive than some of Felix's behavior (Acts 24:26) would lead us to anticipate.

691. Yet Josephus, usually positive (and politically prudent) toward the surviving family of Agrippa II, is not reticent in his description of the failings of this couple.

692. See Jos. *Ant.* 19.354 (she was six in 44 C.E.). The same passage suggests that Berenice was born ca. 28 C.E. and Agrippa I ca. 27 C.E., and hence were close to the age of thirty when Paul appeared before them.

693. She apparently married Felix at about sixteen years of age; Hemer, *Acts in History*, 173, suggests that if Luke's narrative occurs in 57, she is about nineteen at this time. She had been traumatized at her father's death; soldiers in Caesarea and Sebaste who hated her father seized images of herself and her sisters and placed them in a brothel (Jos. *Ant.* 19.356–57), as was widely known (19.363).

694. Williams, "Names," 100; she is the only Jewess we know to be so named (ibid.).

695. The estimate in Schürer, *Time of Jesus*, 229.

to Azizus, king of Emesa in Syria, who did take the step of circumcision to marry her (20.138–39).[696]

Despite his sacrifice, however, the union was quickly dissolved (20.141) because of Felix. Roman policy disapproved of governors marrying women from provinces under their jurisdiction,[697] but Felix for the moment held special favor, especially through his brother, in the imperial court. Drusilla was noted for extraordinary beauty, and Felix sent a Jewish Cypriot magician to persuade her to leave her husband and marry Felix instead (20.142). Thus Josephus remarks that she broke the law of her ancestors and married Felix; they named their son Agrippa (20.143). Perhaps meaning to underscore God's disfavor for their adultery and her abandoning the circumcised king for a Roman who never adopted Judaism, Josephus emphasizes that their son later died at the eruption of Mount Vesuvius (20.144).[698]

Felix's recall must have been traumatic to Drusilla (especially if she saw marriage to a Roman official as advantageous); sometimes the wife of an indicted governor could be suspected of complicity in his crimes,[699] though it would be highly unlikely in her case, and Pallas did manage to save her husband.

It is interesting that Felix listens to Paul as Antipas listened to John in earlier gospel tradition (Mark 6:20) and that both Felix and Antipas stole the wives of others (Herodian women in both cases).[700] Since Luke omits that section of Mark (and does not mention Felix's immorality), it is not likely that he intends a parallel, unless he simply forgot that he failed to include it. (Josephus confirms the immorality of both, and for him it is part of the larger saga of immorality in much of the Herodian royal family.) Although Felix listens to Paul as Antipas listened to John, Drusilla is not like Herodias here (6:19) or even like youthful Salome (6:22–25). If anything, her role resembles that of her sister Berenice with Agrippa in Acts 25:23; 26:30.[701] Just as Paul seeks to evangelize the couple, Luke (who probably did know the notorious account from his contemporary sojourn in Judea) welcomes everyone (e.g., Luke 5:8–10, 20, 30–32; 7:39–50; 15:1–2).

d. Fearing Ethical Admonition (24:25)

Paul here continues his role as a sage intelligible to Gentiles (see comment on Acts 19:9; cf. 17:22–31; 26:24); Felix's fear reinforces the portrait of his unethical conduct in keeping Paul prisoner.

i. Reasons for Paul's Opportunity

Remembering Jesus's commission to use detention as an opportunity to evangelize leaders, Paul appears unrelenting in his attempts to convert Felix. Although Luke's narration of this point would honor Paul among Luke's Christian hearers, it would not win Paul favor with Roman officials.[702] Not everyone in Rome appreciated Jewish

---

696. See Jos. *Ant.* 20.139 for the marriage, 20.138 for the date.

697. O'Rourke, "Law," 181; Schiemann, "Concubinatus," 682 (noting that concubinage was different; but no princess—whose status was higher than Felix's—would accede to such a role); cf. Williams, *Homosexuality*, 117–18.

698. Most attributed Vesuvius's eruption to deities (Statius *Silvae* 5.3.205–8); some Jews may have viewed it as divine judgment for Jerusalem's destruction (cf. Shanks, "Destruction"). Apparently Agrippa II, who appears in Acts 25–26, did not give official sanction to the union (Stern, "Province," 365).

699. Mart. *Epig.* 2.56; Pliny *Ep.* 3.9.19; cf. perhaps Tac. *Ann.* 3.33.

700. See also Dunn, *Acts*, 311; cf. Pervo, *Acts*, 603–4.

701. Luke pairs both genders where possible (see the commentary introduction, Keener, *Acts*, 1:599).

702. At best they might be amused, understanding how Paul had generated much antipathy and considering the ancient stereotype of Jewish proselytism. In Rome, however, where proselytism was often successful, it also often elicited a backlash; see Keener, *Acts*, 3:2475–76.

attempts to convert Romans; Nero's mistress from 58 C.E., Poppaea Sabina, was pro-Jewish, but this scene may depict events too early for that consideration to help Paul historically.[703] Historically, it is not impossible that Felix's wife, Drusilla, despite her having broken Jewish law and having married a Gentile, might have welcomed the influence of a Jew on her husband. It was not every Jewish sage in Caesarea who knew Greco-Roman moral and rhetorical discourse well enough to attract Felix's attention to traditional Jewish matters. Other entertainments were available in Caesarea,[704] but speakers provided entertainment at some banquets;[705] one may compare how Antipas treated John the Baptist (Mark 6:20).[706] What may have begun as intellectual stimulation for Felix (Acts 24:24), however, appears to have touched on his own personal life too uncomfortably.

Although Paul had learned how to use the Roman system well, Luke emphasizes that Paul did not compromise his message to secure favor. In the early empire, an era often criticized (at least by its second-century successors) for sycophancy, being unintimidated would be viewed as honorable (albeit also dangerous), characteristic of "frank speech" (see comment on Acts 4:13). Although wealthy people liked to dabble in philosophy and listen to sages, many Stoic and all Cynic sages warned against watering down their message to accommodate materialistic tastes. Felix might feel uncomfortable with Paul's moral pronouncements, but Felix had access to a cultural category that rendered them intelligible. Someone like Demetrius the Cynic would have provoked Felix more, and we need not think that Felix would treat Paul more harshly because of his preaching (provided it is not public knowledge).[707] So long as it remained a matter of purely objective, academic interest and did not touch on his own life, he could enjoy listening. He simply did not want to think about what Paul was saying.[708]

Although Paul converts neither the Roman administrators nor the king before whom he testifies in these chapters (cf. 9:15), he gains practice for his final testimony before Caesar's court (27:24).[709] Although Paul's moral formation is mainly Jewish and biblical, Luke's summary of Paul's moral exhortation here coheres well with Paul's letters in illustrating how effectively he learned to couch his message in the language of moralists and moral philosophers.[710]

II. JUSTICE, SELF-CONTROL, AND JUDGMENT

As is clear in 24:25, preaching "faith in Jesus" (24:24) is shorthand for an apostolic message that when fleshed out also implies the one true God's standards

703. On the dates for Poppaea Sabina, see, e.g., Cadoux and Griffin, "Poppaea Sabina"; for her pro-Jewishness, see Jos. *Ant.* 20.195; *Life* 16 (though cf. *Ant.* 20.252). Seneca the Younger, who was hardly pro-Jewish (*Ep. Lucil.* 95.47), exercised more influence at this time (Riesner, *Early Period*, 105).

704. A governor in Caesarea had access to considerable public entertainment, given Herod's hippodrome (cf. Patrich, "*Carceres*"), the theater, etc.

705. Such as lectures (Max. Tyre 22; Slater, "Introduction," 2–3; Pogoloff, *Logos*, 264–71) or recitations and readings (Corn. Nep. 25 [Atticus], 14.1; Val. Max. 2.1.10; Mart. *Epig.* 3.45; Iambl. *V.P.* 21.98; Stambaugh, *City*, 207).

706. Though Luke neglects this parallel; nevertheless, in keeping with Antipas's interest in being entertained by prophets, Luke does report that Antipas wanted to see Jesus (Luke 9:9; 23:8).

707. On sages being sometimes annoying but nearly always politically innocuous, see Keener, *John*, 1114; idem, "Truth."

708. Responses to moral preaching are sometimes similar in Bible Belt areas where harsh moral challenges appear culturally acceptable and taken for granted even to churchgoers who find them personally difficult.

709. Nevertheless, not how often but how well one spoke developed rhetorical fluency (Pliny *Ep.* 6.29.5–6).

710. Although Rome provided most of Felix's education, he may have proved interested in some other local sages in Caesarea; at least some Caesareans had interest in philosophers (cf. Gersht, "Statues"). But Paul offered the most ready access in Felix's leisure time, with no appointments needed.

and moral transformation (cf. 2:38; 20:21; 26:18). Of the three moral terms here, modern readers are most familiar with "righteousness" (as the term is usually translated into English in Paul's letters, although the Greek sense employed here is probably closer to "justice").[711] Although rhetoricians and philosophers often lectured on "justice," it is easy enough historically to see why the topic would disturb Felix.

The term ἐγκράτεια[712] (and its cognates, which in this case share the same semantic domain) is more difficult for modern readers but was in common use for self-control—that is, restraint of passions or emotions (especially the "baser" ones). It appears in Xenophon, noting that God gave both genders equally the authority to practice self-control (*Oec.* 7.27) and praising a general who restrains physical pleasures thereby (*Hell.* 4.8.22).[713] The classical orator Isocrates calls for self-control so that the soul will not be ruled by "gain, temper, pleasure, and pain" (*Demon.* 21).[714] Orators included this virtue in their arsenal of potential elements for epideictic speeches.[715]

The usage among philosophers is especially striking.[716] Xenophon reports that Socrates taught his friends to maintain such self-control in eating, drinking, intercourse, sleep, and enduring cold, heat, and work (*Mem.* 2.1.1). Pythagoras is said to have tested prospective disciples regarding self-control, especially of the tongue (Iambl. *V.P.* 17.72). Stoic philosophers also urged self-control of the tongue, belly, and sexual activity (Mus. Ruf. 16, p. 104.18–21);[717] for them it involved knowledge that kept one's behavior "in accord with correct reasoning."[718] Even Epicureans praised self-control (*temperantia*), though only because it produced peace of soul (Cic. *Fin.* 1.14.47). In philosophic literature this virtue of ἐγκράτεια is closely related to and overlaps substantially with σωφροσύνη,[719]—that is, rational moderation, temperance, or sound judgment (see discussion of this virtue at Acts 26:25). Because in

711. E.g., *Rhet. Alex.* 35, 1440b.17–19; 35, 1441b.4–5; Dion. Hal. *Isoc.* 15; Mus. Ruf. 8, p. 62.8–9; 14, p. 92.32; 17, p. 108.10; Arius Did. 2.7.5a, p. 10.8; 2.7.5b2, pp. 14–15.18–20; 2.7.5b5, pp. 18–19.34–35; 2.7.5b12, pp. 26–27.17–18; Men. Rhet. 1.3, 361.14–15, 17–22; 2.5, 397.22; Iambl. *V.P.* 30.167–86; cf. *Rhet. Alex.* 1, 1421b.28, 36–37; 6, 1427b.39–1428a.2; Mus. Ruf. 3, p. 40.25; 4, p. 44.12–16; p. 48.13; 6, p. 52.17; 7, p. 58.25; 8, p. 66.8; 9, p. 74.25; 14, p. 92.25; Dio Chrys. *Or.* 32.37. A governor's "justice" could be praised (Men. Rhet. 2.3, 379.19–20; 2.10, 415.25; for kings, Dio Chrys. *Or.* 3.7; 4.24; Men. Rhet. 2.1–2, 375.8; Philost. *Vit. Apoll.* 5.35; cf. Mus. Ruf. 8, p. 62.1–9).

712. The term could be listed among virtues alongside justice, δικαιοσύνη, as above (Philost. *Vit. Apoll.* 1.20). Self-control appears in a eulogy of Alexander (Arrian *Alex.* 7.28.2)—for whom the claim is incredible. For this emphasis in Greco-Roman and Diaspora Jewish literature (and, in Stowers's view, Paul's letters), see Stowers, *Rereading of Romans,* 42–82 (mentioning this passage, 79–80).

713. Sexual self-control could be a basis for praise of a person's character in later epideictic, e.g., Men. Rhet. 2.5, 398.18–21.

714. Trans. G. Norlin, LCL, 1:17.

715. E.g., Dio Chrys. *Or.* 29.14 (demanding the same of the bereaved, 29.22).

716. For Aristotle, undivided virtue was better than needing self-control for passions, but the latter was better than being uncontrolled (Engberg-Pedersen, *Paul and Stoics,* 52, citing *N.E.* 1.13.17, 1102b26–28; 7.8.4, 1151a11–20). Cf. also discussion in Stowers, "Self-Mastery," 525–34 passim.

717. See also the emphasis on self-control in Epict. *Diatr.* 2.10.18; Arius Did. *Epit.* 2.7.11i, pp. 78–79.13; cf. Galen *Grief* 79b; see also Jewish works influenced by Stoicism (4 Macc 5:34; *Let. Aris.* 278; the more common equivalent in 4 Maccabees is σωφροσύνη). It is equivalent to wisdom in Epict. *Diatr.* 2.21.9; Wis 8:21; and (via the law) 4 Macc 5:34–35.

718. Arius Did. *Epit.* 2.7.5b2, pp. 16–17.1–3 (Pomeroy).

719. For the relationship, see, e.g., Mus. Ruf. 5, p. 50.22–26; 18A, p. 112.6–7; Iambl. *V.P.* 31.195; *Letter* 3, frg. 5 (Stob. *Anth.* 3.5.48; see esp. comments of Dillon and Polleichtner on Iamblichus's adaptation of Xen. *Mem.* 1.5.4); Philost. *Vit. Apoll.* 1.20; in moral rhetoric, Dio Chrys. *Or.* 1.56; 23.11; 29.14 (cf. 3.58, where ἐγκράτεια substitutes for σωφροσύνη in the normal formulation); Men. Rhet. 2.3, 385.22–23; 2.10, 416.18–23; cf. also Titus 1:8. See esp. Arius Did. *Epit.* 2.7.5b2, pp. 14–15.15–16, where ἐγκράτεια is a category of the virtue σωφροσύνη.

sexual contexts the term can have sexual connotations, some scholars associate this exhortation with what we know of Felix and Drusilla.[720]

Like "justice" and "judgment," however, ἐγκράτεια was also important for how rulers or other leaders should conduct themselves;[721] indeed, a ruler ought to have more ἐγκράτεια than anyone else.[722] Such self-restraint regarding pleasures and merriment was particularly praiseworthy in a provincial governor (Men. Rhet. 2.10, 416.19). Although Paul would not likely make the connection explicit, this virtue might be particularly relevant to the sort of ruler who abused power by holding clearly innocent prisoners and summoning them periodically for personal entertainment.[723]

Felix, who sits as Paul's (corrupt) judge, now hears that he himself must answer to a greater judge.[724] Paul was "judged" by the Sanhedrin (24:21), and Felix presumed to decide the case (24:22), but ultimate judgment belongs to God (24:25). (On such ironic, inverted expectations for judgment in some ancient literature, see comment on Acts 7:55–56.) The judgment[725] is imminent,[726] which undoubtedly increases its fearfulness[727] for Felix. Gentiles also had traditions about matters being made right in the afterlife,[728] although some doubted that the gods acted in vengeance or punishment.[729] But the resurrection that Paul has been preaching (Acts 24:15, 21) and eternal judgment were certainly part of early Christianity's Jewish legacy (Heb 6:2), and Luke, presumably, expects us to infer that Paul's preaching of imminent judgment resembles what it means elsewhere in Luke-Acts: the risen Jesus is the judge (Acts 10:42; 17:31; cf. 7:35); he will pour out his fiery wrath (Luke 3:7, 9, 16–17); and even the religious elite will face his sentence (20:47).[730]

As should be clear to Felix in Acts 24:25 if not before, Paul clearly does have ethics grounded in Christ (24:24), verifying his claim in 24:14–16; Felix, by contrast, does not have the same ethical commitments (see comments on Acts 24:24, 26–27). In his letters, too, Paul could lecture on morality and judgment (Rom 1:18; 2:6–11),

720. Johnson, *Acts*, 419 (citing *Test. Naph.* 8:8; *Paul Thec.* 4–6), but recognizing that the narrator does not supply this information. Stowers, *Rereading of Romans*, 80, is understandably skeptical about reading Tacitus and Josephus into Luke here; but if some members of Luke's audience know of Felix at all, they might well know features widely known and assumed about him (at least that he was a corrupt imperial freedman).

721. E.g., Dio Chrys. *Or.* 3.85.

722. Dio Chrys. *Or.* 62.7. This statement belongs to Dio's larger discussion (*Or.* 62) of the virtuous versus the pleasure-seeking ruler. Philosophers often lectured on the philosopher as a king; for Stoics, see, e.g., Cic. *Fin.* 3.22.75; Sen. Y. *Ep. Lucil.* 108.13; Mus. Ruf. 8, p. 66.1–6, 13–26; Arius Did. *Epit.* 2.7.11g, p. 74.1; 2.7.11m, p. 88.26–29; p. 92.18 (see also Grant, *Paul*, 30, citing *SVF* 3.597, 588, 600, 603, 617–22); for Cynics, see, e.g., Epict. *Diatr.* 3.22.49; Max. Tyre 36.5; for Pythagoreans, cf. Iambl. *V.P.* 27.129. Many others ridiculed such notions (e.g., Hor. *Sat.* 1.3.125).

723. Philost. *Vit. Apoll.* 8.5 does make such a connection explicit: when Domitian acquitted Apollonius but sought to detain him to discuss matters irrelevant to the case, Apollonius then denounced him.

724. Cf. Schwartz, "Trial Scenes," 130: "Paul discusses an alternate form of justice with the judge (Acts 24:25)." For Paul confronting unjust power here, see also Walton, "Mission," 555. Luke's ideal audience already understands that God may be compared with an unjust judge (Luke 18:2, 4, 6) only *qal vahomer*—God is greater and just.

725. Cf. Luke 20:47. This relativizes the value of human examples of κρίμα, "condemnation," such as Luke 23:40; 24:20. Robinson and Wall, *Called*, 258–59, argue that the apostles speak as prophets, relativizing earthly authority in light of God's. Judgment is a Pauline theme both in Acts (17:31) and the letters (e.g., Rom 2:2–5; 14:10; 1 Cor 11:29–32, 34; Gal 5:10).

726. The usual use of μέλλω in Acts (Mattill, *Last Things*, 43–44).

727. Luke elsewhere employs ἔμφοβος for terror at suprahuman apparitions (Luke 24:5, 37; Acts 10:4). Cf. Pilate's fear of dealing with divine factors in John 19:7–8.

728. E.g., Dunand, *Religion en Égypte*, 139; see comment on Acts 10:42.

729. Cf. Max. Tyre 22.7; for other reasons, the Epicureans (see at Acts 17:18; Keener, "Epicureans").

730. Judgment appears in many other texts, especially in the Gospel, e.g., Luke 13:3, 5, 9; 17:29–30, 37. Fiery or wrathful eschatological judgment also appears in Paul's letters (e.g., Rom 2:5, 8; 9:22; 1 Thess 1:10; 2 Thess 1:7–8).

including for Gentiles (2:14–16; 1 Thess 1:9–10). Δικαιοσύνη ("righteousness" or "justice"; the latter sense would be especially appropriate for a governor) is a pervasive term in Pauline literature (more than fifty times, about 84 percent of them in the undisputed letters). He mentions ἐγκράτεια, or self-restraint, as a fruit of the Spirit (Gal 5:23) and uses cognates in 1 Cor 7:9 (for sexual self-control, relevant to what we know of Felix from Josephus) and 9:25 (cf. Titus 1:8); the term in Acts 24:25 for judgment (κρίμα) is used by Paul for divine judgment, especially in the eschatological time, in Rom 2:2–3; 3:8; 5:16; Gal 5:10.[731]

Those who have heard of Felix might well know that he "practised every kind of cruelty and lust" (Tac. *Hist.* 5.9)[732] and be familiar with the lurid tale of his seduction of Drusilla later reported by Josephus.[733] Many commentators think that Luke presumes this knowledge here;[734] whether or not he presumes it for all or (more likely) some of his readers, it was nevertheless known historically to the parties he reports here. Historically, we know that some believed that Felix also resented being given advice on how to conduct the affairs of the state. Perhaps he would tolerate it from an impractical moralist in his custody,[735] but he allegedly hired someone to kill Jonathan the high priest (Jos. *Ant.* 20.163–64) for giving too much meddlesome advice (20.162). In Luke's own narrative, one of Felix's explicit vices becomes obvious in Acts 24:26: greed and corruption.[736]

III. PUTTING PAUL OFF

Felix tells Paul in 24:25 that he will have to wait for further consideration, as he delays dealing further with the leaders in 24:22; he acts in character with the persona that the narrative has already portrayed for him.[737] He does call for Paul, but not to free him. Governors could become so busy (see comment on Acts 18:15) that, at one point, many letters from the office of Asia's governor were written by others until one governor at least had his freedman read through them to weight them for equity before sending them out (Cic. *Quint. fratr.* 1.2.3.8).[738]

With sufficient staff, governors might enjoy more leisure in most provinces, away from the bustle of daily politics in Rome (Sen. Y. *Nat. Q.* 4A.pref. 1). But governors normally had small staffs; Rome kept its bureaucracy to a minimum,[739] and presumably, if a governor wanted additional staff, he had to be able to afford them himself. A ruler might put people off by sending them away and telling them that when the appropriate time comes, he will send for them.[740] He might in fact have no intention

---

731. Probably also in Rom 13:2; 1 Cor 11:29, 34; perhaps Rom 11:33.

732. Trans. C. H. Moore, LCL, 2:191, 193. E.g., after promising a brigand safe conduct, he betrayed him (Jos. *Ant.* 20.161); he allegedly paid for an assassination by brigands, then failed to punish the brigands, encouraging more brigandage (20.162–65).

733. Jos. *Ant.* 20.142–43; such a report would not have gone over well in Rome (see Williams, *Homosexuality*, 117; comment on the punishment of governors at Acts 24:27).

734. E.g., Rapske, *Custody*, 356; Johnson, *Acts*, 418–19; Fitzmyer, *Acts*, 740.

735. For some Roman perceptions of "harmless" and impractical philosophers, see Keener, *John*, 1114; idem, "Truth."

736. Emphasized by Wall, "Acts," 322. Flessen, *Man*, 155–56, contrasts Felix with a more positive Lukan model in Caesarea, Cornelius.

737. Cf. also Peterson, *Acts*, 641: "He puts off making a personal decision about Christ, even as he puts off making a decision about Paul the prisoner." This is not, of course, the only time in Luke's narrative that Paul's hearers put him off (e.g., Acts 17:32; Jervell, *Apostelgeschichte*, 575).

738. In *Acts Paul* 3.17 (*Paul Thec.* 17), Paul is led off to prison until a governor has more time to hear him.

739. Garnsey and Saller, *Empire*, 21.

740. *Apoll. K. Tyre* 21. Cf. Caesar's difficult schedule, which reduces time for correspondence, in Fronto *Ad Ant. imp.* 2.3, 4. In Philost. *Vit. Apoll.* 7.22, the emperor says that he will send for Apollonius when he has leisure; such delays underline not only a ruler's schedule but also his superior status (which Philostratus inverts, as here).

of sending for them[741] but simply use this promise as a more polite way of refusing them. One might also postpone a case as long as needed if its obvious outcome is not to one's preference.[742]

e. Seeking a Bribe (24:26)

Although Felix apparently prevents Paul's guards from taking unfair economic advantage of his situation (Acts 24:23), he is not above hoping[743] to profit from it himself. This interest does not negate the less base interest already mentioned in 24:24–25 but is additional to it.[744] Under some circumstances, a person awaiting trial might be allowed to go free on bail until the case is called, and be held in the interim only if lacking sufficient funds to post bond.[745] But Paul cannot safely leave custody in any case (23:30),[746] and Luke's description of the desire for bribery is clear enough. Perhaps Felix is aware that the "alms" mentioned in 24:17 are substantial and assumes that the movement that provided them can also provide the bribe.

I. VIEWS OF BRIBERY AND CORRUPTION

Luke's portrayal of Felix here, though not wholly negative in the context, is not designed to commend him to the audience's sympathies.[747] Greek vocabulary uses many neutral terms for bribery (e.g., "persuade by gifts"),[748] but bribery became a very damaging charge in a forensic context. It is prominent in Attic orators because proof of bribery was essential to sustaining a charge of treason.[749] Despite the pervasiveness of bribery, Greek and Roman sources regularly portray bribes (by which they may have meant the more abusive examples of receiving gifts) as negative.[750] Judges who take bribes cannot weigh truth, Horace complains (*Sat.* 2.2.8). The gods cannot be bribed, Socrates allegedly opined, even by sacrifices.[751]

Romans were certain that other nations had worse practitioners of bribery than they had; during the republic, some were appalled that the Egyptian king used bribery openly to counter the Romans (Cic. *Fam.* 1.1.1); both Carthaginians (Polyb. 6.56.1–4) and Greeks (6.56.13–15) were supposed far more corrupt and addicted

741. *Apoll. K. Tyre* 21.

742. Tac. *Ann.* 13.33.

743. Although Luke employs ἐλπίζω in a purely "secular" sense here (as in Acts 16:19), in the context it might contrast with the resurrection hope (24:15) that Felix compromises partly for the sake of this one (24:25).

744. With Bruce, *Acts¹*, 427. In view of Paul's remaining prisoner despite Felix's apparent intellectual interest (24:24), it would be natural and probably accurate for Paul and his allies to infer typical pecuniary (24:26) and political (24:27) motives, but Luke may have also known cases of people freed via bribes, and Felix may have also dropped hints. For other examples of Luke's knowledge of corruption, including 23:27, see observations in Muñoz-Larrondo, *Postcolonial Reading*, 154.

745. Lewis, *Life*, 187–88.

746. For the protective element of custody, see, e.g., Rapske, "Prison," 827; discussion at Acts 23:16.

747. Constructing a person's *ēthos* negatively was a means for rhetorical assault (*Rhet. Alex.* 36, 1442a.13–14). That Luke's portrait is so much like Josephus's indicates that it rests on fact, but this does not reduce the negativity of the portrait. (Josephus's portrait is quite negative, but Rinaldi, "Note prosopografiche," thinks his portrayal "indulgent" compared with those by Tacitus, Suetonius, and Luke.)

748. Hornblower, "Bribery," 259.

749. Ibid., 260.

750. E.g., Hesiod *W.D.* 221; Sall. *Philip.* 6; *Speech of Macer* 5; Max. Tyre 5.7 (among evil professions); Tac. *Ann.* 2.34; 16.18 (a slave bribed to accuse his holder), 32 (a client bribed to accuse his patron); cf. Pliny the Younger's teasing in *Ep.* 1.7.5; massive corruption in Quint. Curt. 6.2.10; the importance of officials' freedom from corruption in Iambl. *Letter* 1, frg. 2 (Stob. *Anth.* 4.5.77). Earlier, see, e.g., Hamm. 5 (*ANET* 166); "The Instruction of Amen-em-opet" 20 (*ANET* 424); Exod 23:8; Mic 3:11; for a positive example of resisting corruption, see Dan 6:4; for biblical ethics against corruption, see, e.g., Arnold, *Vivre l'éthique*, 297–300.

751. Plato *Alcib.* 2.150A. Likewise, God (and Moses) could not be bribed (Jos. *Ant.* 4.46).

to bribes than gods-fearing Romans.[752] But even in the republic, many bought their offices by bribery,[753] including the governor's office.[754] Some protected others from legal charges, hoping in return to secure a province (which they could then exploit financially; Cic. *Sest*. 8.18). Even regarding voting, Cicero laments "the open bribery of the people tribe by tribe before the elections" (*Att*. 4.19).[755] Romans deplored the outright buying of votes, although cultivating favor through gifts had become widely accepted.[756] Finally Augustus decreed that anyone who bribed another to achieve office should be excluded from public office for five years (Dio Cass. 54.16.1); the senate and the emperor further limited campaign expenditures on gifts and dinners a century later (Pliny *Ep*. 6.19.1, 4).

Bribery occurred in many settings,[757] but the exercise of bribery and corruption was perhaps nowhere so rampant as in the judicial system.[758] Some bribed others to induce them make false accusations,[759] or to corrupt their perspectives as members of the jury[760] or judges.[761] In some periods of antiquity, the innocent had to pay bribes to spare their lives;[762] on other occasions the guilty either secured[763] or attempted to secure[764] acquittal through bribing jurors. Shameful leaders might release prisoners if they were given sufficient bribes.[765] As in Paul's case, matters could be delayed over money; one praetor kept guilty captives in prison to secure their money, promising to consider their case when he had time (Plut. *Caes*. 2.4).[766]

Such behavior was not legal; it was simply that those who did it discreetly (or sometimes openly) more often than not avoided the consequences. The *lex Iulia de*

752. Accepting bribes from neighboring kingdoms was horrendous (Plut. *Sulla* 5.6).

753. Suet. *Jul*. 13 (*pontifex maximus*); Cic. *Verr*. 2.2.49.122 (admitting underage officials); *Sest*. 49.105 ("Friends of the People"); cf. also other shifts of political allegiance due to bribes (Vell. Paterc. 2.48.4). Bribery was condemned but often happened (e.g., Cic. *Sest*. 66.139). Cf. also Wilson, "Bribery," 221.

754. Cf., e.g., Cic. *Sest*. 25.55; 30.66.

755. Cic. *Att*. 4.17 in another enumeration; trans. E. O. Winstedt, LCL, 22:333.

756. Lintott, "Ambitus" (despite the disdain attached where traditional lines of patronage were adversely affected); cf. idem, "Cliens," 451; Eder, "Elections," 897; the political implications of benefaction in Spawforth, "Euergetism." Cicero viewed as bribery excessive funds spent on public entertainments while the spender was a candidate (*Mur*. 2.3; 3.5; 23.46; 32.67–68; 36.77), but the same texts show that others interpreted these instead as public benefits. Though a crime particularly of the republic, election corruption continued in imperial times (Robinson, *Criminal Law*, 84).

757. "Buying" victories (Dion. Hal. *Epid*. 7.291); as noted above, guards demanded bribes (Rapske, *Custody*, 259–61, 383; Lucian *Tox*. 31); Phrygians wanted to bribe Philoctetes to desert to the Trojans (Dio Chrys. *Or*. 59.4); even a failed attempt to bribe the Delphic oracle (Corn. Nep. 6 [Lysander], 3.2). Demosthenes also took bribes (Aeschines *Embassy* 3; *Ctes*. 69, 113, 156, 259; Plut. *Demosth*. 14.2; 25.4), angering his people (Plut. *Demosth*. 25.5), though he was remembered for *not* taking them from Philip (Libanius *Maxim* 3.1; *Encomium* 5.12; cf. *Invect*. 3.5; 4.13). One person killed another because of a bribe (Cic. *Fam*. 8.15.2).

758. E.g., Lucian *Fisherman* 9; Tac. *Ann*. 4.31 (extortion); Quint. *Decl*. 313.15 (a prosecutor expressly *not* charged with accepting bribes); for governors, cf. Tac. *Ann*. 13.32; for the collusion of prosecutors, e.g., 14.41 (here punished with exile). For bribes, abuse of power for intimidation, and related forms of corruption, see at length Rapske, *Custody*, 62–67; briefly, see idem, "Prison," 827 (regarding corruption and detention arrangements).

759. Suet. *Jul*. 12; 20.5; a false charge of such bribery in Cic. *Verr*. 2.1.6.17 (circulated by the defendant); the charge in Apul. *Apol*. 58–59, 74 ("the buyer of witnesses," trans. V. Hunink, p. 95).

760. Val. Max. 9.1.7 (the bribes here were sexual favors); Suet. *Dom*. 8.1 (leading to the jurors being degraded).

761. E.g., Longin. *Subl*. 44.9.

762. Lysias *Or*. 12.9–11, §120–21; Cic. *Verr*. 2.3.28.69. These examples may reflect hostile prosecutorial rhetoric.

763. Clodius in Sen. Y. *Ep. Lucil*. 97.2 (Seneca considered this atrocious); 2 Macc 4:45.

764. Verres, thwarted by Cicero, in Cic. *Verr*. 1.6.16; 1.8.23–1.9.25; 1.12.36; 1.13.38.

765. Polyb. 38.18.4–5; Cic. *Verr*. 2.1.4.9 (pirate chiefs); Jos. *War* 2.273.

766. Caesar then expedited matters by crucifying all the prisoners (Plut. *Caes*. 2.4). Buying survival also occurred in military situations (e.g., Jer 41:8).

pecuniis repetundis made it illegal to take bribes from prisoners.[767] Political reforms included Pompey's law against bribery in 52 B.C.E. (Appian *Bell. civ.* 2.3.23); prosecutions for bribery occurred (2.4.24). Bribery was a crime against the Roman state[768] and was to be punished.[769]

Punishments against bribery were sometimes harsh. A moralizing tale about the Persian ruler Cambyses claimed that he had a corrupt judge flayed alive and the man's skin pulled over the chair on which the judge's son would sit when judging cases (Val. Max. 6.3.ext. 3). Bribery was a punishable offense in classical Athenian law (e.g., Lysias *Or.* 21 passim);[770] prosecutors could ask for the death sentence against it.[771] During the republic, Roman law also apparently decreed death as the penalty for it (Polyb. 6.56.1–4). Some laws were, however, honored more in the breach than in the observance.

ii. Governors' Corruption

Governors were not supposed to make themselves rich at provincials' expense (Catull. *Carm.* 10.7–13), but the practice nevertheless continued in the empire.[772] Provincials provided governors with many gifts and protection from charges of misadministration; from a different perspective, these could be viewed as bribes.[773] Technically, Roman law prohibited governors from accepting such gifts, although it was such a common practice that it could rarely be punished harshly.[774] Within the Roman context, though the worst abuses had to be checked, bribes probably did not bear the harsh negative connotations we think of today. Unsalaried officials may have viewed the payment of reasonable fees as both income and a logical way to reduce excess "demands on their time."[775] Nevertheless, serious abuses apparently abounded, and sometimes governors had to be indicted for receiving bribes[776] (see comment on trials of governors at Acts 24:27).

Even aside from the disproportionate benefits of government to the rich, abuses were endemic in such a system.[777] During Paul's lifetime, a freedman of Caligula became wealthy by taking bribes (Jos. *Ant.* 19.65). Closer in time to this hearing, the Syrians of Caesarea are said to have induced Caesar—by bribing Nero's tutor Burrhus with much money—to annul long-held Jewish citizen privileges in Caesarea (20.183). A few decades after Felix's Judean office, a proconsul was exploiting the wealthy province of Asia (Tac. *Agr.* 6), simply following a pattern already established centuries earlier.

---

767. Fitzmyer, *Acts*, 740; Witherington, *Acts*, 716 (following Tajra, *Trial*, 131–32). For Roman laws against bribery, see, e.g., Livy 40.19.11; cf. Robinson, *Criminal Law*, 20, 82; Wilson, "Bribery," 221 (reportedly a capital offense in Rome's Twelve Tables, but not so enforced later). Against corruption, Rapske, "Prison," 827, cites *Dig.* 48.11.7.prol.; see also extortion in Robinson, *Criminal Law*, 81.

768. Cic. *Sest.* 8.18; *Fam.* 3.11.2. Greeks felt that betraying one's nation for a bribe (Corn. Nep. 1 [Miltiades], 7.5) warranted severe punishment (7.6).

769. E.g., Cic. *Cael.* 32.78.

770. Leaders accepting bribes hurt all the people (Lysias *Or.* 25.19, §173; Aeschines *Tim.* 107), and those who received bribes were the sort of people who would betray the state (Lysias *Or.* 28.11, §180).

771. Lysias *Or.* 28.17, §181; 29.11, §182; Aeschines *Tim.* 87.

772. See, e.g., Crawford, "Debt," 143. Whatever improvements may have occurred, the claim that under Tiberius magistrates no longer oppressed provinces (Vell. Paterc. 2.126.4) is propaganda; for one example of corruption not long before, note the governor of Syria in Vell. Paterc. 2.117.2.

773. Garnsey and Saller, *Empire*, 152 (noting that one who discouraged a prosecution of the governor received many gifts in *CIL* 13.3162).

774. Pliny *Ep.* 4.9.6, 17–18 (based on the *lex Iulia repetundarum*, 59 B.C.E.). Given the cultural offensiveness of refusing gifts (e.g., Cicero *Fam.* 14.3.1), this standard was difficult.

775. Kelly, "Corruption," 402. Themistocles avoided personal corruption (Plut. *Themist.* 5.4), but for the state's good, he bribed a corrupt man to stay out of office (6.1).

776. E.g., Pliny *Ep.* 2.11.2 (a particularly serious case); 4.9.6–7; cf. 6.5.2.

777. Not only provincial administrators but agents of the imperial court received bribes (Suet. *Tit.* 7.1; Jos. *Ant.* 20.183–84).

The ancient precedents for governors' corruption were numerous. In 171 B.C.E., the senate had to set right the extortion of money by Roman officials in Spain (Livy 43.2.1–12). In the late republic, Cicero's predecessor had ruined the province of Cilicia before Cicero came (Cic. *Att.* 6.1), extracting poll taxes so ruthlessly that people had to sell property to pay it (5.16). A later writer also testifies that Cicero fought the corruption of the earlier administration, making restitution for what was embezzled (Plut. *Cic.* 36.4). Cicero can describe figuratively an official's exploitations as robberies (*rapinas, Phil.* 2.25.62).

Cicero's denunciations of Verres provide a stark (if occasionally hyperbolic) portrait of how dangerous a governor's corruption could be. Verres acted "like a pirate" in exploiting a city, and like a plague in exploiting the province of Sicily (Cic. *Verr.* 1.1.2); he had ruined Sicily's prosperity, and it would take many just governors to restore it (1.4.12). He levied unjust fines through violent intimidation (2.3.22.55) and had some people flogged so hard that they handed over their property to have their lives spared (2.3.28.69); allegedly, he even made parents purchase the right of burying their executed children (2.1.3.7). His corruption invited the flourishing of unjust accusations (2.2.38.94). He provoked Rome's allies unfairly to satisfy his lusts (2.1.27.70). He granted illegal favors for bribes (2.5.20.51).

Writers warned against engaging in corruption. Dio insisted that statesmen should not be corrupted by accepting bribes (Dio Chrys. *Or.* 22.5). Socrates rebuked those granting acquittals in return for bribes (34.10). Impartiality remained the ideal,[778] though it was often ignored.

Such warnings applied to governors, among others. Cicero advises a governor in Asia not to let his underlings take bribes (*Quint. fratr.* 1.1.4.13).[779] Some tax collectors were greedy, but a governor who was not greedy himself could restrain them (1.1.2.7). A later novelist complained that Greeks were often happy even if the Roman governors merely would not "sell justice," but this was like praising someone for not stealing (Philost. *Vit. Apoll.* 3.25).

Governors who resisted corruption were praiseworthy.[780] Plutarch praises Cicero because he refused to profit from the people (*Cic.* 8.1), refused gifts, and governed at his own expense (36.2; cf. Neh 5:14–19). By living thriftily, Lucilius, as governor of Sicily, managed to resist bribes and similar temptations (Sen. Y. *Nat. Q.* 4.pref. 18). Tacitus praises his father-in-law, a provincial administrator, for avoiding corruption and for rooting out the previous administration's corruption (*Agr.* 19).[781] Epideictic speeches to governors celebrated their incorruptibility in justice, including their rejection of bribes.[782]

III. CORRUPT GOVERNORS OF JUDEA

Some corruption certainly occurred in "backwater" provinces such as Judea. As Rapske notes, "Distance from the imperial capital also encouraged the abuse of

778. See fuller discussion at Acts 10:34 (Keener, *Acts*, 2:1796–97).

779. It was important for governors to avoid bribery (Cic. *Fam.* 3.11.2). When defending a governor rather than indicting one, Cicero claims that provincial governorships are a thankless task (*Flacc.* 35.87).

780. Cf. also much earlier magistrates who refused to grant inappropriate favors (Plut. *Themist.* 5.4), and officials who resisted bribery (Corn. Nep. 15 [Epaminondas], 4.1–3); cf. also Dan 6:4–5.

781. Tacitus also praises other earlier efficient governors (*Ann.* 16.23).

782. Men. Rhet. 2.10, 416.5–12, esp. 8–10, 15 (bribes, 15). Other earlier leaders were also praiseworthy for resisting corruption; Cato was so incorruptible that sums of money could be deposited with him (Pliny E. *N.H.* pref. 9). While auditing army accounts, Pliny the Younger was shocked with the abuses, but he praised Pollio's accounts (*Ep.* 7.31.2).

power."[783] Josephus accused Felix's predecessor Cumanus of having accepted bribes to avoid punishing the Samaritans (Jos. *Ant.* 20.118–19);[784] Judeans then accused Cumanus of being corrupted by Samaritans' gifts (20.127). Josephus thought that Felix bribed a high priest's friend to murder him (20.163). Felix's successor, Festus, appears to have been fairly just (see comment on Acts 24:27), but he was quickly succeeded by corrupt Albinus. Josephus accuses Albinus of practicing every form of wickedness (*War* 2.272), including taking bribes: receiving "ransoms" from relatives, he freed robbers imprisoned by local councils or earlier officials, retaining only those who could not pay (2.273; *Ant.* 20.215). The aristocratic priest Ananias hoarded money and deployed it to secure friendship with both Albinus and the current high priest (*Ant.* 20.205).

Albinus's successor, however, was even worse (Jos. *War* 2.277; *Ant.* 20.253–54), driving many to leave Judea (*War* 2.279; *Ant.* 20.256). Gessius Florus, who, through his wife's friendship with Nero's mistress, later obtained the province of Judea in 64 C.E.,[785] allegedly despoiled entire cities (*War* 2.278), robbed the temple treasury (2.293–95), and plundered homes in Jerusalem (2.305). His abuse of power helped fan the Judean resistance into flame (*War* 2.293, 296; *Ant.* 18.25) and provoke the Judean war (*War* 2.282–83; *Ant.* 20.257).[786] Most relevant here, he allegedly cared about nothing except receiving bribes (*War* 2.287). That Felix, though less rapacious than his successors, was also eager to take advantage of bribes is not only plausible but probable.[787] Luke's audience ideally might also think of the corruption of another governor who betrayed the innocent to satisfy other people's favor (Luke 23:24–25).

From a Jewish perspective, such behavior was unconscionable, a perversion of divine justice.[788] God rejects bribes[789] and commands his judges and servants to reject bribes lest they pervert justice.[790] God will curse those who accept bribes to do injustice (Deut 27:25; Sir 40:12–13), but bless those who refrain (Ps 15:5; Prov 15:27; Isa 33:15).[791] Josephus claims that his colleagues succumbed to bribery (*Life* 73) but that he himself did not (*Life* 79), though some were bribed to oppose him (*Life* 196).[792] He even claims that God's law requires that any judge who takes bribes be executed (*Ag. Ap.* 2.207), a view shared with some other Judean pietists (11QT LI, 16–18). Some later rabbis announced that corrupt judges would not share in the

---

783. Rapske, *Custody*, 69; so also idem, "Prison," 827. One example may be the waste of resources in Nicomedia (Pliny *Ep.* 10.37.1–2), which Trajan wanted investigated to make certain no one profited from it (10.38).

784. Although this may well be rumor based on inference from Cumanus's inaction, it is not an implausible guess.

785. See further Scullard, "Gessius Florus."

786. Allegedly, he nearly even killed Queen Berenice during his slaughters (Jos. *War* 2.312)! But he was a poor military leader (cf. *Life* 23–24).

787. *Pace* the reticence of Pervo, *Acts*, 605. At the very least the expectation of bribes, in Paul's case as otherwise, is consistent with Felix's known character (Whittaker, *Jews and Christians*, 142). More generally, were it not impolitic, I could name some locations in the world where I have encountered severe corruption that was almost outright thievery; encountering such practices first in ancient sources at least diminished my surprise; scholars dare not read these texts naively from the mere standpoint of our own limited cultural experience.

788. Cf., e.g., Job 6:22; Ps 26:10; Prov 17:23; 29:4; Eccl 7:7; Isa 1:23; 5:23; Ezek 22:12; Amos 5:12; Mic 3:11; 7:3; condemnation of judges corrupted by bribes also in *Tg. Isa.* 5:23; *Tg. Jon.* on 2 Sam 14:14.

789. Deut 10:17; Sir 35:14; Jos. *Ant.* 4.46.

790. Exod 23:8; Deut 16:19; 2 Chr 19:7; Jos. *Ant.* 4.216. *Tg. Ps.-J.* on Exod 23:8 expands the reasons for prohibiting bribes.

791. Judges who take bribes bring judgment on the world (*b. B. Bat.* 9b). Giving bribes when necessary (for purposes that are not unjust) seems less objectionable than receiving them (Prov 17:8; 21:14). Whereas the decisions of judges who accepted bribes are nullified, it is acceptable to pay a judge or witness for his time (*t. Bek.* 3:8).

792. Laws against bribes need not eradicate them; Samuel's sons took bribes (1 Sam 8:3; Jos. *Ant.* 6.34).

world to come.[793] Nevertheless, we do hear of Jewish judges accepting bribery.[794] A later rabbinic account complains repeatedly that the Roman government does nothing without payment, that is, bribes (*Eccl. Rab.* 11:1, §1).

iv. Felix and Paul

Small bribes would not interest Felix, and any anticipated bribe would need to be considerable to make it worth his political risk. He must assume that Paul is a person of substantial means[795] or at least has the social network to raise them. Paul has come to Jerusalem with considerable funds for alms for his people (Acts 24:17); he is also a leader in a large movement (24:5).[796] In fact, even if he were penniless, Felix would reason, surely other Nazarenes could raise funds for him; if the Jerusalem church is unable or unwilling to help, Paul's associates can recruit money from Diaspora churches.[797]

Would they raise money, however, for a bribe? It appears to be not lack of funds but conviction that prevents the payments.[798] Happily, though Felix may want money to free Paul, his reasons for not handing him over to his accusers are not exclusively pecuniary (the high priest surely could have afforded more inducements than Paul could have).

Paul's noncompliance with the expectation of a bribe appears courageous. It would also stir sentiments of justice on his behalf, whether in a Roman court[799] or among the ideal Greek audience of Luke's finished work. It would normally be indiscreet to challenge the corruption of a governor (who held more credibility with Rome than did Paul), but after Felix's humiliating recall, Luke's credibility might be the greater for challenging him (especially with those who knew anything about Felix). On discovering a person's innocence, a good governor would free the person and possibly even reward him or her.[800]

f. From Felix to Festus (24:27)

Our other historical sources confirm that Festus replaced Felix as governor of Judea and that Festus was a less corrupt administrator. Given the circumstances under which

---

793. *'Abot R. Nat.* 36 A (on judges who judge in their own towns; presumably this means that they are not impartial).

794. E.g., *Pesiq. Rab Kah.* 15:9.

795. It is perhaps assumed as befits a citizen of Tarsus (Pervo, *Story*, 83–84) or at least an educated traveler from there (not all Tarsians shared in the city's prosperity). At one time Paul apparently had substantial income (Acts 20:34). Given other hints of Paul's resources in this period, when he lived in rent quarters yet perhaps could not as readily support himself (cf. Acts 28:30), some argue that he had some means. Aside from possible contributions from Christians, Paul presumably did come from a wealthy family (cf. 9:1–2; 22:3) that was not wholly alienated from him (23:16); perhaps he had even come into a substantial inheritance, perhaps as the eldest male son. These are merely speculations. Our strongest evidence for why Felix might *expect* him to have means, however, appears in 24:5, 17 (treated below).

796. See Rapske, *Custody*, 106, 167; Johnson, *Sharing Possessions*, 24. If the Jerusalem church rejected the offering, Paul's associates still retained it (Dunn, *Acts*, 316), but this assumption is both unlikely and unnecessary; Felix would assume that Paul could raise more funds from his original source. Assumptions about rich friends can drive up prices; one may observe this dynamic today in poorer nations' marketplaces: local friends who accompany a foreigner from a wealthier nation may well have to pay more than usual because of their foreign guest.

797. By some means, Paul still has funds to rent a dwelling in Acts 28:30 (Johnson, *Sharing Possessions*, 24); after the shipwreck, however, it is possible that the initial funds were raised by Roman Christians.

798. Although this may have been the sort of situation for which the OT might not have forbidden giving (as opposed to receiving) payment (Prov 17:8; 21:14). Perhaps it would have simply whetted Felix's greed. In view of Paul's austere piety in Acts 24:25, John Chrysostom may be right that Felix should have known better (in *Cat. Act.* 24.25–26 [Martin, *Acts*, 287]).

799. The audience for which, some scholars think, Luke may have first compiled the abundant evidence of this section as a sort of legal dossier.

800. Lucian *Tox.* 33.

history shows that Felix was recalled, it made sense for Felix to provide Felix's accusers with any political favors possible without also risking other causes of accusation against himself (such as handing over an unconvicted Roman citizen for execution).

1. Felix's Recall

If Felix releases Paul, he will not help his own political situation vis-à-vis Felix's accusers; if he hands Paul over to Paul's enemies, Paul's allies might offer incriminating evidence that he handed over an innocent Roman citizen. Although Paul may be personally innocent of stirring riots, his enemies' likely reaction to his release would serve as a catalyst for instability, perhaps proving unsafe to Paul and, even more likely, to public order. To leave the matter to his successor is the safest choice politically for Felix.

When Nero decided to send Porcius Festus as Felix's successor,[801] Felix's accounting came due for the enemies he had made. He had so alienated the Jewish community in Caesarea, where he had openly sided with the Syrians against the Jews, that its leaders traveled to Rome to charge Felix before Nero.[802] He was spared only by the intercession of Pallas, who still held Nero's favor (Jos. Ant. 20.182).[803]

Luke himself recalls this practice of sending delegations to oppose choices for local leadership (Luke 19:14), although he does not waste words on the events of Felix's recall. Even in classical Athens, the conduct and accounts of a person leaving office would be carefully examined.[804] Roman law also permitted the conviction of former provincial governors in the interests of the empire, although such prosecutions were more often than not unsuccessful.[805] When Judean leaders accused Felix's predecessor, Cumanus, the emperor found him guilty and banished him (Jos. Ant. 20.136).[806] Josephus even claims that Florus (a Judean governor several years after Felix's recall) provoked the Judeans to war so that he would not have to answer their charges against him after his governorship ended (Jos. War 2.283).[807] About half a century after Felix's recall, Pliny's letters attest many trials of former governors accused by their provinces, trials in which Pliny often either defended or prosecuted governors.[808]

Given the pending accusations, Felix had good reason to do the Jerusalem authorities "a favor" just before his departure (Acts 24:27).[809] Favors invited reciprocation; to

---

801. A governor who refused to hand over his province when his successor arrived would be charged with treason (Robinson, *Criminal Law*, 76).

802. Provincials normally could not appeal a governor's decisions, but they could accuse him, in Rome, of extortion (O'Rourke, "Law," 175), and Jews were known for charging unjust governors (cf. Jos. *War* 2.240–46; *Ant.* 20.127–36; even outside the land, Philo *Flacc.* 103; Samaritans in Jos. *Ant.* 18.88–89).

803. The usual prayer for a good governor's long tenure (Men. Rhet. 2.10, 417.29–30) may have been offered early in Felix's office (cf. Acts 24:10), but he had engendered more enmity than support.

804. Gomme and Rhodes, "*Euthyna*"; cf. MacDowell, "Stratēgoi," 1448.

805. See Badian and Lintott, "Repetundae"; as a more general legal principle, cf. Zimmermann, "Restitution."

806. Felix's rank as a freedman could count against him; the tribune under Cumanus was gruesomely executed (*Ant.* 20.136; *War* 2.246). Blaming subordinates was politically expedient even for emperors (Wardle, "Blame Game").

807. Josephus, of course, is as ready to criticize Florus as Suetonius or Tacitus is eager to reproduce any negative reports about Nero and Domitian.

808. E.g., Africa in Pliny *Ep.* 2.11.2; 10.3A.2. The Baeticans (3.4.2, 8; 3.9.5, 17; 7.37.4–9) and Bithynians (4.9.2–3; 5.20.1–2; 6.13.1–2; but cf. their retraction in 7.6.1–6; 7.10.2) proved especially litigious. Of course, some governed well and won respect (3.7.3). The Pompeian law stipulated reasons for senators' being removed from office (10.114.1). Later a governor of Bithynia who employed his capital-jurisdiction right too freely was removed (Philost. *Vit. soph.* 2.24.607). Earlier governors were also at times accused and condemned (Tac. *Ann.* 3.38, 66–69, 70; 4.15; 13.30, 33, 43; 14.18, 28, 46; 16.21; cf. 16.30), and sometimes acquitted (4.36; 13.52), and some accused of misadministration could be driven to suicide (6.29).

809. As commentators regularly observe (Tajra, *Trial*, 133; Hemer, *Acts in History*, 130; Johnson, *Acts*, 419; Witherington, *Acts*, 714; Fitzmyer, *Acts*, 741). Of course, even Herod Agrippa I, who did not need to curry such favor, did so in Acts 12:3.

be ungrateful was to dishonor the obligation that one incurred by receiving a favor.[810] Felix could not conceivably offer sufficient favors to compensate for the damages he had done, but at this point it would be worth offering what he could, especially if his brother Pallas no longer held office (see discussion below). The extrabiblical evidence thus is consistent with Luke's portrait of Felix's concern here.

Even before this situation, however, Felix has left Paul in detention, and afterward Festus also will seek to do the authorities "a favor" (25:9; cf. 25:3). Both must consider the political dangers of denying the Sanhedrin's leaders what they want, and would have much bigger concerns than Paul to fight for.[811] Roman justice was not always consistent and was as much to set an example for public morality as to render justice to individuals. Individuals could be sacrificed to maintain public order.[812] Judicial corruption was also rampant, as noted in the comment on Acts 24:26 (and Luke's audience would, in view of 24:26, view this act as judicial corruption). Further, it was customary to take into account the relative social rank of both plaintiff and defendant (see comment on Acts 24:1). Paul was not the only Jewish Roman citizen; indeed, some Jewish aristocrats were equestrians (Jos. *War* 2.306–8).

II. DATE

Scholars debate in what year the transition from Felix to Festus occurred, a debate informed by various opinions on other aspects of the narrative's dating. Despite the interest the discussion generates, we should keep in mind that the divergence between the earliest and the latest standard datings is no more than five years (much less significant, for example, than many chronological questions that OT scholars face). The majority of scholars date Felix's recall to 59[813] or 60[814] C.E.; many, however, prefer about 55 or 56.[815]

Some argue that Felix could have been helped by Pallas only before Pallas's fall in 55 C.E.: "If Felix were recalled in early spring of 55, Pallas would just have had time to protect him."[816] Although Pallas lost his administrative position in 55 (Tac. *Ann.* 13.14), however, he retained power and influence. In 56, Pallas still indicated his wishes to servants and freedmen with only gestures lest he dishonor his voice by using it with those of lower status. When indicted in that year, he not only was proved innocent; the prosecutor was banished for his political ineptitude (13.23). When Nero finally allegedly poisoned Pallas in 62, it was hardly because Pallas had

---

810. See, e.g., deSilva, *Honor*, 109–10; for gratitude, see comment on Acts 23:17–18. For reciprocity expectations, see, e.g., Xen. *Cyr.* 5.5.33; 6.1.47; Publ. Syr. 71; Cic. *Fam.* 1.1.4; 1.9.9; 12.30.3; 13.3.1; Sen. E. *Controv.* 9.1.intro.; 9.1.9; Pliny *Ep.* 2.13.1; 4.1.5; 4.9.7; 5.2.1–2; 6.6.3; 7.19.10; 7.31.7; Statius *Silv.* 4.9; Alciph. *Fish.* 7 (Thalassus to Pontius), 1.7; Fronto *Ep. graec.* 4.3; 5.8; Jos. *Ant.* 19.184; Harrison, *Grace*, 15 (on the Greek East).

811. As Chow, *Patronage*, 78–79, notes, Gallio could be fairer to Paul than Felix and Festus were because Corinth had a smaller and less influential Jewish community than Judea.

812. E.g., Mucianus orders the execution of Vitellius's son to reduce discord (Tac. *Hist.* 4.80). Likewise, Cumanus had a soldier (admittedly guilty) beheaded to quiet the crowds that were agitating against him (Jos. *Ant.* 20.115–17; cf. 20.108–11).

813. E.g., Bruce, *Documents*, 88; idem, *Acts*¹, 428–29; Riesner, *Early Period*, 221–27; Rapske, *Custody*, 315. Some allow for either 59 or 60, while preferring the former (Jewett, *Chronology*, 43; idem, *Romans*, 20; Witherington, *Acts*, 78) or the latter (Stern, "Chronology," 74–76). Ananias's tenure ended by 59, but he does not appear in Acts after 24:1, i.e., up to two years before Felix's recall on this chronology.

814. Thompson, *Archaeology*, 290; Reicke, *Era*, 208; Yoo, "Paul et Festus" (on the date of Paul's trial before Festus).

815. E.g., Lake, "Chronology," 466; cf. Bunine, "Félix." Jerome's Latin rendering of Eusebius's *Chronicle* favors 56 C.E., but some argue that it contradicts earlier evidence (Green, "Festus," 795).

816. Lake, "Chronology," 466 (though allowing that Festus may not have arrived until 56; this delay would not, however, suit a smooth transition in a time of national unrest, a problem that Josephus almost surely would have added to his list of grievances). Bruce, *Commentary*, 474, notes the chronological difficulty.

lost his estates; it was rumored that he died for having retained his wealth too long by living into old age (14.65). The fall of Pallas in 55 cannot, therefore, be used to date Felix's recall before 55.[817]

Those who support a date for the transition around 59 or 60 C.E. point out that in 64 Josephus was still trying to free priests arrested by Felix (Jos. *Life* 13–16); this situation would make more sense if Felix remained procurator until 59 rather than 55.[818] The disappearance of Paul from history about 55 also makes little sense of early Christian tradition connecting Paul's execution in Rome with Nero's persecution, which began after the fire in 64.[819] Further, Josephus's report of Festus's tenure is much briefer than that concerning Felix or Festus's successors, suggesting to some that Festus's tenure itself, intervening between Felix's "many years" (Acts 24:10) and the crimes of Albinus and Florus before the war, was brief.[820] These are, however, arguments based on probability and relative chronology, and they would have to give way in the face of secure evidence for redating the transition.[821]

The numismatic evidence is more problematic. Coins mentioning Felix do not appear past 54/55 C.E. Others reply that a large number of new coins from 58/59 suggests a new procurator at that time, and hence they date the transition from Felix to Festus there;[822] we do not seem to have clear evidence of a new procurator before that time. Some have cited microletters on one coin, however, as appearing to place Festus's accession in 56, which fits the evidence of Eusebius's *Chronicle* exactly.[823] (It could also count in favor of Paul's release after the two years of 28:30 and might allow more time for the journeys presupposed in the Pastorals, though this could be at most a subsidiary argument; those journeys are workable even with the later chronology, and some deem them fictitious even with the earlier chronology.) If this evidence should prove compelling, its dating would place Felix's recall three years earlier than the often-proposed 59. Still, because "two years" (24:27) can include parts of two years, this would require an adjustment of the common Pauline chronology by (at minimum) only about two years.[824]

Up to the present, however, the supposed microletters remain elusive and not adequately documented or available to the scholarly world.[825] Some claims based

817. With Jewett, *Chronology*, 42; Robinson, *Redating*, 45; Riesner, *Early Period*, 221–22; Green, "Festus," 795.

818. Riesner, *Early Period*, 226. (Earlier, Lightfoot, *Acts*, 189, 323, suggested 60 C.E.) But others (Reicke, *Era*, 208) date the release to 62 C.E. (the earliest possible date, since Josephus calls Poppaea Nero's "wife," although this could be a retrospective honor to his benefactress). The captives Ismael and Helcias, however, were taken during Festus's tenure (Jos. *Ant.* 20.194–95).

819. See Riesner, *Early Period*, 226–27.

820. As Haenchen, *Acts*, 661, points out, Josephus's report may be brief simply because Festus presented few targets for scandal. See Jos. *Ant.* 20.182–97; *War* 2.271–72; clearly Festus died in office (*Ant.* 20.197, 200).

821. The false prophet of Jos. *Ant.* 20.169–72; *War* 2.261–63 also must be dated before Acts 21:38, itself up to two years before 24:27 (Green, "Festus," 795), if we take 21:38 as an exact report (see comment there).

822. Bruce, *Documents*, 88; Riesner, *Early Period*, 223; Green, "Festus," 795.

823. See McRay, "Archaeology and NT," 98, citing Vardaman as his source but not noting a publication; idem, *Archaeology*, 227, noted that Vardaman's work was as yet unpublished. Finegan, *Apostles*, 14, also cites Vardaman, again as an unpublished source (citing [in endnotes at 237n27] Vardaman, "Solution," 13; and personal correspondence).

824. If Paul was arrested shortly after Pentecost, the time of year for the accession of a new governor would be only a little more than a year after.

825. Not surprisingly, some thus express skepticism about Vardaman's "micro-graphic letters" (most harshly, yet understandably in this case, Carrier, "Pseudohistory"). Because Vardaman's claimed evidence is not available for public examination (e.g., legible photographs with clear markings), it so far remains difficult to take it into account in scholarly work (Riesner, e.g., ignores it), not unlike Morton Smith's alleged "Secret Mark" (against its authenticity, see, e.g., Carlson, *Hoax*; Jeffery, *Secret Gospel*; in favor of its authenticity, e.g., Hedrick, "Stalemate"; idem, "Secret Mark"; Stroumsa, "Testimony" [noting that he also saw the manuscript];

on supposed microletters are clearly incompatible with our other evidence,[826] and the microletters are so small that one wonders if they do not involve the imaginative reading of nonalphabetic marks, however well intentioned.[827] Until this evidence has been fully evaluated (and either decisively accepted or rejected) by experts, many scholars will continue to prefer a date about 59 C.E. on the basis of multiple (yet also not absolutely certain) sources of other evidence.

III. DELAYING PAUL

A governor was not supposed to leave office before his successor arrived (Suet. *Jul.* 18.1).[828] More important, he was supposed to diligently continue his work, including administering justice, until his successor arrived.[829] No one, however, could force a governor to speed up his cases, and even some notable defendants were detained for years without trial.[830] Prisoners could secure scribes to help them file petitions to expedite their cases or secure release, but a petition would have done Paul little good if his delayed captivity was deliberate.[831] If he was not condemned in two years, some scholars argue that Roman law might technically mandate his release;[832] but Luke can be referring to simply parts of two years (i.e., probably not a full two years), and again, provincial governors were not bound by laws applying in Rome. Even if Rome's law applied here, Paul's accusers could cause Felix more trouble than Paul's supporters could.

Once a person was convicted, his confinement might last a matter of days,[833] but the time could stretch much longer.[834] Delays before trial could take years, as Egyptian, Greek, and Roman evidence all attest.[835] Although imprisonment was not a formal legal punishment for free persons, long delays often had this practical effect.[836] The sources provide various reasons for the delays: "the sheer volume of court business,"[837] a change in magistrates,[838] magistrates' misbehavior or procrastination,[839] and litigants'

---

neutral but skeptical, Ehrman, "Response to Stalemate"; however scholars conclude these debates, the source is not first-century and is too tenuous for reconstructing the Jesus tradition). I admit my skepticism regarding the microletters, and because Vardaman passed away over a decade ago, publication appears unlikely.

826. E.g., Vardaman, "Life," 70–71, citing "REX JESUS" on a Damascus coin of 15 C.E. (cf. also Smith, "Chronology," 133–34, following him); aside from the date, Latin used "I," not the later "J." This is again the case on p. 74 (a coin of Agrippa I, from 43/44 C.E.). Likewise shockingly (though at least somewhat less implausibly), Vardaman must also shift the date of Pilate significantly earlier (pp. 78–79) to fit his redating of Jesus's chronology to 12 B.C.E. to 21 C.E. (e.g., pp. 56–57, 81; cf. Vardaman, "Chronology," 315–16); but Pilate's coins appear especially in 29 to 32 C.E. (Evans, "Excavating," 333). (It is the 21 C.E. part of this dating that is most problematic; for Jesus's birth in 12 B.C.E., only a few years earlier than many other scholars, see in more detail the careful work in Vardaman, "Lectures," 1:4–22.)

827. See, e.g., the drawings on Vardaman, "Life," 60, 70–71, 74; his drawings also appear in Smith, "Chronology," 134–36.

828. His assisting quaestor would take over for him if he did (Kierdorf, "Propraetor"; cf. idem, "Proquaestor"). For how judges were chosen and when delays before their appointment were appropriate, see Metzger, *Outline*, 61–76.

829. *Dig.* 1.16, citing Ulp. 10 (in Jones, *Empire*, 183).

830. E.g., Witherington, *Acts*, 703.

831. Rapske, *Custody*, 326–28.

832. Fitzmyer, *Acts*, 740 (following Dupont); see discussion at Acts 28:30.

833. Rapske, *Custody*, 12, cites Dio Cass. 58.27.5; Sen. Y. *Tranq.* 14.6–7.

834. Rapske, *Custody*, 12, cites Gaius in *Dig.* 48.19.29 (kept alive for torture to secure evidence against others).

835. Rapske, *Custody*, 316.

836. Rapske, "Prison," 828.

837. Rapske, *Custody*, 317–18. A plaintiff whose case could not be heard during a magistrate's visit might have to wait for the next year's visit (317).

838. Ibid., 318 (in this instance, it works in Paul's favor).

839. Ibid., 319. One operative principle was to avoid responsibility for a bad decision for which one could later be called to account (on avoiding responsibility, see Malina, *Windows*, 137; note also how Pliny defers all uncertain matters to Trajan, e.g., *Ep.* 10.74.3).

delays.[840] Paul's refusal to pay a bribe (Acts 24:26) and the political expediency of granting a favor to his accusers (24:27) account for the delays in Paul's case.[841]

After executing the most clearly guilty, Albinus emptied the prisons when he left, to show favor to the people of Jerusalem; Josephus complains that he thereby increased the number of robbers in the countryside.[842] But Albinus's action of releasing prisoners rather than leaving a case pending is portrayed as unusual;[843] such a release was probably more common during a governor's tenure.[844] Governors often efficiently dispatched a backlog when they needed to clear jails quickly; prisoners who appeared innocent would then be released, and those who appeared guilty could be summarily executed.[845] Josephus praises the swift justice of Philip, Herod's brother, who did not delay his tribunal but, whenever anyone needed judgment, offered it on the spot, punishing the guilty and pronouncing in favor of those wrongly accused (*Ant.* 18.107). Whether or not such quick decisions were in fact just, they appeared efficient.

IV. FESTUS

By leaving Paul prisoner after an initial hearing, Felix left his successor no indication of Paul's innocence, although the court records (similar to the précis that Luke provides us), with information that should have had obvious implications, would remain available whenever his case came up.[846] No one could predict how Festus would handle the case. Roman criminal law did not assign many specifics, and magistrates held considerable freedom to decide cases (though circumscribed somewhat in the case of Roman citizens).[847] Even if Felix had left Paul sentenced for a crime instead of leaving his case pending, Festus had legal authority to veto Felix's decree.[848] Indeed, had Felix been convicted in Rome, his earlier decrees could even have been annulled.[849]

Ironically, had it not been for the intervention of Paul's enemies (Acts 25:2–3), Paul could have languished in custody in Caesarea much longer. The accession of a new procurator meant new administrative priorities and a new shuffling of cases. Rapske notes that prisoners were often "'lost' in the bureaucratic machinery, spending months or years longer in custody awaiting 'discovery.'"[850]

Porcius Festus was presumably an equestrian belonging to the well-known *gens Porcia*, probably from the Porcii in Tusculum.[851] Whereas Josephus's *War* describes the procuratorships of Festus's predecessor, Felix (*War* 2.247–70), and Festus's successor, Albinus (2.272–76), at length, he describes Festus's in a paragraph (2.271). The description is short either because Josephus preferred to focus on causes of the war in this volume, or because Festus's tenure was fairly brief, or (most likely) both.[852] Josephus does, however, report more in his *Antiquities* (*Ant.* 20.182–97). Festus was effective in suppressing unrest (*War* 2.271; *Ant.* 20.188), and most relevant for

---

840. Rapske, *Custody*, 319–20.

841. Ibid., 320–21.

842. Jos. *War* 2.273; *Ant.* 20.215.

843. Sherwin-White, *Society*, 53; Jeffers, *World*, 168.

844. Governors apparently released many prisoners (Pliny *Ep.* 10.31.4), but when documentation proved inadequate, the release could be viewed as corruption (10.32.1–2).

845. Rapske, *Custody*, 328.

846. For the transfer of governors' records to their successors, see Vössing, "Archive," 1026.

847. Berger, Nicholas, and Lintott, "Law and Procedure," 833.

848. This was true of all peers or superiors (see Lewis, "Intercessio").

849. See Pliny *Ep.* 4.9; 10.56.4.

850. Rapske, *Custody*, 321.

851. Boismard and Lamouille, *Actes*, 2:257.

852. How brief is currently impossible to determine, since we do not know when his successor began and the debate about when Felix was recalled continues. But Festus died in office (Jos. *Ant.* 20.197, 200).

our passage, he showed some degree of tolerance for Jewish customs with which he disagreed (*Ant.* 20.193–94). But even here, his own tenure seems to encompass few events,[853] and he died in office (20.197).

In whatever year Festus became governor, he would have begun his office on July 1 (see comment on Acts 18:12–17); while this was the official starting date, however, with Felix gone, Judeans would have looked to him on whatever date he arrived. Paul was earlier detained in Caesarea in early summer, shortly after Pentecost (Acts 20:16; 24:11). Luke's "two years" can mean parts of two years (see comments on Pauline chronology at the beginning of Acts 9) and hence, if Luke uses the phrase loosely, could refer simply to the slightly more than one year between Felix's acceptance of the case and Festus's arrival.[854] One could assume a longer estimate, but in this shorter reading, even the lower chronology proposed for Festus's accession (56 C.E.) would fit all the data in Acts and the Pauline correspondence (with Paul being arrested in 55, shortly after the Egyptian's revolt; see comment on Acts 21:38).

5. Paul's Appeal to Caesar (25:1–12)

Luke emphasizes here that Paul's famous—or infamous—custody in Rome does not suggest his genuine guilt. A different governor finds no proof against Paul; rather, his very accusers are the true subverters of order and justice (25:3). (As already noted, reversing charges against accusers was standard defense procedure, and Luke employs it abundantly in these narratives.) Paul is compelled to go to Rome as a prisoner not because of misconduct but because of messy provincial politics, specifically in Judea, a province notorious to the Romans (even more so after the war of 66–73 C.E.) for its resistance to Roman order.

Paul's defense in Acts 25–26 continues the pattern already noted in Acts 24—namely, that Paul's trials in Acts resemble those of Jesus in Luke's passion narrative—and fulfills Jesus's prophecies about Christians testifying before courts.[855] O'Toole lists twelve similarities between Acts 25–26 and Luke 23:1–25, most of them persuasive when taken cumulatively:[856]

1. Both sections are structured as hearings.
2. There are four main characters in each (the Roman governor, a Herodian prince, Jewish accusers, the defendant).
3. The hearings are held at the procurator's instigation (Luke 23:6–7; Acts 25:22ff.).
4. The defendant is "led in" (Luke 23:1; Acts 25:6; cf. 25:22ff.).

853. It appears to be at least long enough to allow a delegation to travel to Rome (Jos. *Ant.* 20.193–94) and return (20.195–97; though the appointment in 20.196 could occur after Festus's death but before Caesar learns of it).

854. A creative allusion to two of Joseph's years in prison (Gen 41:1) is unlikely not only because Joseph was in prison before that period began (40:1) but because "two years" is only one of several lengths of detention in Scripture. Luke elsewhere rounds time periods to two years (Acts 19:10; 28:30) except when other estimates are closer (e.g., 11:26; 18:11; 19:8; 20:3; 28:11; cf. 20:31).

855. See esp. O'Toole, "Notion of 'Imitators.'" Cf. Gwalther 844–45 in Chung-Kim and Hains, *Acts*, 338.

856. See esp. O'Toole, *Acts 26*, 22–23; cf. also his suggested parallel outline (p. 24), although it does not add much to the pattern (introduction in Luke 23:1; Acts 25:1; hearing before the governor, Luke 23:2–3; Acts 25:2–12; introduction to the appearance before the Herodian prince, Luke 23:6–7; Acts 25:13–17; hearing before the Herodian prince, Luke 23:8–11[12]; Acts 26:1–23; dialogue, Luke 23:13–23; Acts 26:24–29; conclusion, Luke 23:24–25; Acts 26:30–32). Some points (e.g., the Suffering Servant motif) are less obvious.

5. The authorities find God's agent innocent (Luke 23:4, 14–15, 22; Acts 25:18, 25a; 26:31).
   a. Each governor thinks the defendant innocent, both before and after the trial.
   b. Each governor three times pronounces the defendant innocent.
   c. Agrippa II concurs with Festus, and Antipas (at least de facto) concurs with Pilate.
6. The defendant is accused by the high-priestly elite (Luke 23:2, 5, 10; Acts 25:2, 7, 11, 15–17; 26:2), who demand death (Luke 23:18, 21, 23; Acts 25:24) for acts against Israel and Caesar (Luke 23:2; Acts 25:8).
7. Antipas and Agrippa II happen to be in town (albeit both with good historical reasons) and want to see the prisoners (Luke 23:8; Acts 25:22).
8. The defendant appears before a Herodian ruler.
9. Although the defendant is innocent, he cannot be freed (Luke 23:16–25; Acts 26:32; cf. 28:18).
10. The Suffering Servant motif: the defendant is "led" (Isa 53:7–8), "handed over" (53:6, 12), and so forth.
11. Some apparently illogical aspects appear in both accounts (where, e.g., are Paul's accusers?).[857]
12. Both sections could be omitted without interrupting their surrounding context.

Most of these parallels, especially the first nine, are compelling. They reveal Paul imitating Jesus's sufferings, as Stephen did in Acts 7:56–60.

The very parallels, however, reveal asymmetry in Luke's treatment, particularly the much greater length of Paul's speech before Agrippa II than that of Jesus's appearance before Antipas (Luke 23:8–11; Acts 26:1–23). To some extent this asymmetry probably results from Luke's more complete source for Paul's trials than for Jesus's, but not entirely. Most noticeably, Acts 25 includes a lengthy dialogue between the procurator and the Herodian king (25:14–22). Moreover, the content of the dialogue does not appear to reflect any obvious historical source (who would have reported its content to Luke?), though most of its basic substance could be inferred from 25:24–27, amplified according to the customs of rhetoric used in most ancient historiography. Why does Luke elaborate so much on this section whereas he condenses so much material in earlier chapters?

Dunn suggests that one reason is suspense. Although earlier Roman officials favored Paul (13:12; 18:12–17; cf. 16:35–40; 19:31, 35–41), Felix did not. Though initially resisting (25:4–5) a plan potentially deadly to Paul (25:3), Festus is finally on the verge of accommodating the opposition's proposal (25:9).[858] The chapter, however, is not all suspense; once Paul has appealed to Caesar, the matter of his destination is decided (25:12). After this, the narrative provides no suspense about whether Paul will be going to Rome but only about how he will present his defense of the gospel, perhaps a foreshadowing of his later (unnarrated) defense before Caesar's tribunal.

There are likely other reasons for the extensive detail. These chapters (Acts 24–27) are particularly detailed as part of the material where Luke ("we") was nearby. But they are also detailed because they reflect Luke's apologetic for Paul and hence for the legal status of the Gentile Christian movement he had advanced. Although Christians did

---

857. By the time the appeal is made, Festus has already found no serious guilt (Acts 25:25) and merely needs to formulate his letter for Caesar's tribunal (25:26), though not inviting the accusers to contribute to the formulation of the charges (25:27) seems a reflection of Festus's bias toward Paul.

858. Dunn, *Acts*, 317–18.

follow a Lord crucified for sedition, Roman representatives recognized his innocence (Luke 23:4, 14, 22, 47). Moreover, the most noteworthy leader of the Gentile Christian mission movement was not only innocent but himself a Roman citizen. Both were condemned not because of Roman justice but because leaders acceded to the political demands of a hostile Jerusalem elite, now discredited by the Judean war. Roman officials suspicious of Jewish sedition should look not to the Christian followers of a Jewish Messiah but to these followers' accusers! It may have been difficult to persuade critics of this case, but it was the best apologetic available, and from Luke's perspective (as both a Christian and a loyal citizen of the Roman Empire), it was the truth.[859]

Luke may also elaborate the dialogue between a mostly just procurator and a reasonable king to highlight these characters. Yes, there were unjust procurators such as Pilate and Felix, and unjust Herodians such as Antipas and Herod Agrippa I; but Luke can make clear that he does not oppose all authority, Roman rule, or the rule of Rome's client kings. Further, he draws attention to their roles so that he can show that Paul's trials are not tragedy but God's sovereign plan to grant opportunities for his gospel in elevated settings (Luke 21:12–15). If the gospel must go to the ends of the earth before Israel's restoration (Acts 1:6–8), reaching the nations at least representatively through their rulers (4:27) showed that, in a representative way, this eschatological mission was already in the process of being fulfilled.

Why was Paul not simply released? Local politics sometimes impeded ideal Roman justice. Rome ruled through local elites, and so cooperation with the local leaders was important. Given ancient reciprocity conventions, Festus could win favors for his policies by granting favors where he could afford them, and was obligated by favors from the Jerusalem elite to offer favors in return.[860] These political realities collide with Roman ideals of justice for Roman citizens, and the tightrope Festus walks in this narrative probably resembles the tightrope he had to walk in history. Paul was too small an issue in the larger scheme of Judea's administration to be allowed to simply go free at the expense of the local leaders' annoyance, yet not guilty or inconsequential enough to be summarily convicted.

a. Authorities in Jerusalem Denounce Paul (25:1–5)

A new governor offers the leading Sadducees a fresh opportunity to revisit some cases on which Felix proved intractable (24:27); these include Paul's case, which some apparently prefer to be resolved extrajudicially. But while Festus may be eager to establish cordial relations with the leaders, he is not ready to begin his tenure by creating exceptions to normal protocol. Given the accumulation of political favor for Paul's enemies, it is only the promise of divine favor by which Luke can theologically account for his survival (23:11).

i. The Ardent Administrator (25:1)

That Festus takes only three days to commence contact with the Jerusalem leaders after his arrival shows that he is an efficient administrator (cf. the greater delay in 25:13), in contrast to Felix (24:27); perhaps he also knows of the damage done to Rome's relationship with Judea by his predecessor.[861]

---

859. See further Keener, *Acts*, 1:223–24, 441–57; idem, "Apologetic."

860. With Witherington, *Acts*, 719–20. Granted that Luke shapes the material for his work, the extreme skepticism of Pervo, *Acts*, 609, toward Luke's material seems unwarranted.

861. An efficient administrator might set immediately to investigating anomalies and correcting corruption (Pliny *Ep.* 10.17A.3; 10.18.3); one who judged swiftly was considered praiseworthy (Jos. *Ant.* 18.107). Stoics also emphasized acting immediately and avoiding delay (Arius Did. *Epit.* 2.7.11s, pp. 100–101.24–35).

Visiting the local ruling class upon one's arrival (25:1) was a prudent act for any new governor, just as it was a prudent political courtesy for Agrippa and Berenice to visit the new procurator (25:13). But this gesture would be all the more important because of the unrest of which he would have been apprised before his arrival, whether or not he knew of Felix's misadministration. Festus probably would not have known how deeply most of Judean society had become alienated from its ruling class, which was corrupt, was exploiting poorer priests (Jos. *Ant.* 20.181), and was too pro-Roman for the masses.[862]

ii. Plans against Paul (25:2–3)

The official chief priest is no longer Ananias (Acts 23:2; 24:1) but now Ishmael son of Phabi (Jos. *Ant.* 20.179),[863] appointed by Agrippa II (see Acts 25:13) probably shortly before Festus's accession (Jos. *Ant.* 20.182). The chief priests and other leaders were on very strained (sometimes even violent) terms during this period (20.180), but the condemnation of Paul seems to have been a matter on which the elite could agree, or at least not find sufficient cause to disagree. Whether the "leading people" (οἱ πρῶτοι; on this usage, cf. comments on Acts 13:50; 17:4; 28:7, 17) now included those Pharisees who had temporarily supported Paul (Acts 23:9) or not, all of Paul's critics here would be well-to-do and members of the elite, most likely belonging to the Sanhedrin or the families that supplied it with members.

The authorities apparently gave up on moving Paul's case so long as Felix remained procurator (though Felix refused to provoke them by simply releasing him).[864] Perhaps because Paul has been still influencing Judeans through his visitors during confinement (24:23) or perhaps because this is a small favor compared with the major redresses from Felix's time that required correction (cf. Jos. *War* 2.271), Paul remains high on their agenda as an initial favor to request of Festus (cf. also Acts 25:6). The issue of Paul may have been kept alive by his continued ministry in Caesarea, albeit through visitors disseminating his views (24:22) and perhaps through influence on the former governor, who favored tolerance toward Paul's movement (24:24).[865]

Revisiting the case would not prove difficult. Even had Felix closed Paul's case (and he had not), a case could be reopened if the accusers claimed "fresh evidence" (Pliny *Ep.* 7.6.10). Moving the case could be more complicated. His accusers may know that under Roman law, the citizen of one place who has a legal residence (*domicilium*) in another can be tried in either place, at the plaintiff's discretion (Gaius *Dig.* 50.1.29).[866] But it is doubtful that they can use this to make their case for Paul to be arraigned in Jerusalem; although he grew up there (Acts 22:3), he has not lived there for years, and his *domicilium*, if anywhere, would be Antioch (or perhaps, for

---

862. Witherington, *Acts*, 718, following Goodman, *Ruling Class*, ch. 6.

863. As commentators regularly point out (Conzelmann, *Acts*, 202; Johnson, *Acts*, 420). In Jos. *Ant.* 18.34 Ishmael son of Phabi precedes Caiaphas; is Josephus confused, or did the same high priest hold office twice (not unheard of in itself) some thirty-five to forty years apart? (The latter seems much harder to imagine, though it is not impossible that Agrippa might have reckoned an aged former high priest a logical choice for the office.) The high priests of this time were seizing the tithes belonging to the poorer priests, causing some of the latter even to starve (20.181). Agrippa later (after Festus's death) deposes Ananus, after three months in office, for acting illegally against the leader of the Jerusalem church and others (20.203).

864. Ehrhardt, *Acts*, 117, suggests that the strained relations between Felix and these leaders toward the end of his tenure (Jos. *Ant.* 20.182) made it impossible for them to approach him even with a bribe. This is possible, though he seems to have been more cooperative toward the very end (Acts 24:27; cf. Jos. *Ant.* 20.178).

865. Most Jerusalemites would oppose only the uncircumcised Gentile Christian movement, but the high priest's martyrdom of James (Jos. *Ant.* 20.200) suggests that even the Judean Nazarenes faced Sadducean hostility.

866. Apathy, "Domicilium."

various brief periods, Corinth and Ephesus).[867] His citizenship, of course, remains in Tarsus, where he was born (21:39). Sometimes a case had to be discontinued and later renewed—for example, when a prosecutor died.[868] But the accusers most likely rely on simply Festus's legal authority to make a decision independent of Felix (see comment on Acts 25:9), and they offer the new (and perhaps unseasoned) governor the opportunity to provide them an early favor (perhaps one among several, although Luke would have reason to infer and mention only one in particular).

Their desire for a "favor" (25:3) reflects a theme running throughout this context (χάρις, 24:27; 25:3, 9; χαρίζομαι, 25:11, 16).[869] It reinforces Luke's point that Paul's troubles with the Roman authorities stem wholly from accommodation to the Jerusalem elite's complaints. Certainly this is Paul's view within the narrative (25:11) and retrospectively the view that the narrative's Festus takes (25:16), when, like Lysias, he portrays his own initial behavior as more generous toward Paul than it actually had been in Luke's narrative of the initial hearing (25:9; cf. 21:32–38; 23:27).

Given the many revolutionaries in prison, Paul's case may come up here only because the Jerusalem authorities are less optimistic about securing his condemnation than they are about securing that of the revolutionaries (cf. Luke 23:18–19). Given the history of precedents in the case, they may have despaired of obtaining "justice" even from the new governor and hence hoped to execute their "right" of killing Paul directly, which Lysias had earlier seized from them (see comment at Acts 24:6). This might provide another reason for dealing with Paul at the beginning of Festus's tenure: it would not take many "accidents" en route to Jerusalem before Festus would refuse to send defendants there for trial.[870] They might hope that Festus would deal with genuine revolutionaries anyway (eventually he did, much more effectively than Felix, Jos. War 2.271; Ant. 20.185–88).

How would Luke know about the ambush? It is not impossible that the same source had surreptitiously revealed to him information as had done so before (Acts 23:16), but ancient historians also narrated motives on the basis of what they felt were reasonable inferences. If mostly the same people remained in power; if they insisted on sending Paul to Jerusalem rather than simply accuse him in Caesarea, where Paul was already being held; and if Luke had reason to believe that they had been party to such a plot on a previous occasion (23:14–15), it was a reasonable inference to assume that the motives had not changed.

Admittedly, a change of venue to Jerusalem would also be more convenient for the Jerusalem authorities and exert more pressure on the new governor; the latter point may be one factor in Festus's reluctance. They could present this venue as more convenient for the governor, who is already in Jerusalem, but he is about to return to Caesarea (25:4). They could otherwise succeed only by convincing Festus that Paul's case is a matter of Jewish and not Roman law, but given Paul's Roman custody for as much as two years under Felix, Festus would not likely be persuaded by that appeal.

The narrative here does not presuppose the Sanhedrin's right to judge capital cases under Roman rule.[871] Profanation of the temple (24:6) was the one capital offense

---

867. One could have multiple domiciles (Dig. 50.1.6.2; Apathy, "Domicilium," 630), but Paul does not appear to have had more than one at a time.

868. Schiemann, "Abolitio."

869. Tannehill, Acts, 306. Favor (χάρις) could distort justice (Rhet. Alex. 15, 1431b.40); it was understood that it might justifiably mitigate punishment on some occasions (Lucian Men. 13).

870. Others in this period used "accidents" as a cover for assassination (see, e.g., Tac. Ann. 14.3, 8, 11).

871. Pace Winter, Trial, 85.

allowed to be tried by locals, a custom that applied also to some other temples in the empire (e.g., in Eleusis; see comment on Acts 21:28). Further, the procurator might still maintain control of the trial (25:9), though the change of venue would help the accusers and any witnesses they might wish to call. Rome certainly did not grant Judeans capital jurisdiction in this period; the exceptions were under the client rulers, such as Herod, Agrippa I, and even the tetrarch Antipas, not under the Sanhedrin, Jerusalem's municipal council, during the tenure of procurators.[872] But this situation could have appeared to be potentially the very sort of case for which Rome originally withheld from locals the right of capital punishment: it would be inappropriate use of the right if local aristocracies used it to eliminate citizens loyal to Rome (in this instance, a Roman citizen).[873]

iii. Festus's Arrangement (25:4–5)

Various factors may influence Festus's refusal (25:4). Some scholars suggest that he felt that a prisoner whose loyalty to Judaism was questioned would be safer in Caesarea.[874] Although he would not yet have heard the report of the earlier plot (which appeared in a court document, 23:30, but presumably one among hundreds of documents awaiting his staff in Caesarea), he was probably informed of the general security situation before his arrival. But Festus traveled the road himself, albeit with a larger entourage, and this journey would be during daylight, in any case. If security concerned him, it was more likely concern that the Sanhedrin's Levite guards would provide less security than his own soldiers would.

Festus's concern, however, is probably less with security than with convenience and propriety. First, since Festus is about to leave for Caesarea (25:4), there is no point in sending for Paul to bring him to Jerusalem for trial. To send messengers by horseback to Caesarea (which would take one day) and bring Paul to Jerusalem (presumably another day), or to take perhaps two days each way (settling securely for the intervening night) if infantry accompanied the riders (because of bandits in the hills), would make little sense if Festus is leaving soon anyway (though "soon" is as many as eight to ten days, depending on when during his visit the leaders broached the request, 25:6).[875] Second, when in town, the procurator might hear cases, but on this occasion Festus has come only to visit; perhaps he does not even have his full *consilium* (25:12) with him, having left some important subordinates in Caesarea to run matters until his return.[876] (If he arrived in Judea slightly early, which is not impossible, he might also be more willing to make courtesy calls than to issue decisions before July 1.)

Third and most important, it was not prudent for a new official to begin his tenure with irregularities, which could constitute an informal precedent in his relations with locals. Rome specifically made the mixed coastal city of Caesarea Judea's capital, rather than the holy city preferred by the Judeans. Giving in to the request would likely invite further concessions toward Judean nationalism down the road. He might be willing

---

872. Although councils of subject territories could pronounce a death sentence, they had to bring their sentence before the governor for ratification (Blinzler, *Trial*, 164–68; Ramsay, *Church*, 293); most scholars thus currently recognize that the Sanhedrin lacked the legal authority to execute prisoners in this period (Jos. *Ant.* 20.200; Sherwin-White, *Society*, 32–43; Benoit, *Jesus*, 1:135; Stewart, "Procedure"; Sanders, *Jesus to Mishnah*, 17; Bruce, "Trial," 12–13; Keener, *John*, 1107–9).

873. Cf. Morris, *Luke*, 319.

874. Foakes-Jackson, *Acts*, 219.

875. "Eight days" appears in Luke 2:21; 9:28; but no allusion is evident, and this text says "eight or ten."

876. The *consilium* would consist of both his higher officials and young men who had accompanied him from Rome to learn provincial administration (see Bruce, *Commentary*, 479).

to consider such a concession (25:9), but not so quickly as to make it appear that it would be a regular sort of concession.

How would Festus, who has been in the country only three days, know that Paul is in Caesarea? Perhaps he does have some of his advisors with him (25:12), including some individuals from the previous administration; as a "leader of the Nazarenes" (24:5), Paul might be a particularly noteworthy prisoner. More likely, Paul's accusers may have said so; if not, it would be obvious from their request, since he has to be brought to Jerusalem (25:3) from somewhere and Felix's prisoners would be in Caesarea. By welcoming some of the Jerusalem leaders to travel with him (25:5), Festus shows them deference and respect. As here, so in general, prosecutors were not appointed by the state but were personal accusers.[877]

b. Paul Defends Himself before Festus (25:6–9)

Festus acts quickly and efficiently, in contrast to his predecessor (25:6); he is also politically astute enough to wish to accommodate local leadership if possible (25:9). Paul, however, makes such a compromise impossible: his opponents continue to produce baseless charges they cannot prove (25:7), and so Festus's readiness to accommodate them at this point is blatantly political rather than an act of justice ("as you well know," 25:10). Paul's only hope of obtaining a hearing not influenced by Judean political considerations is to appeal to Caesar (25:11). His appeal also expresses his confidence in his innocence before Caesar (25:8, 11).

i. Festus's Efficiency (25:6)

Whereas Festus greeted Jerusalem's leaders more quickly (25:1) than Agrippa and Berenice would visit him (25:13; but they could not well visit him in Caesarea before he had returned there), the latter stayed longer for their visit ("many days," 25:14). "Not more than eight or ten days," however, does not emphasize its brevity as a snub to Jerusalem's elite but perhaps is intended to explain what Festus meant by "shortly" (25:4). Perhaps more important for the narrative, "eight or ten days" serves as an emphatic contrast to Felix's "two years" (24:27). Festus took at most two weeks after his arrival before dealing with Paul's case, on the day after his return to Caesarea from the trip where the case was brought to his attention (25:1, 6). Luke thereby clarifies for the attentive reader that no backlog of cases justified Felix's procrastination and nothing questionable about Paul's case explained his long period in custody. One would "go down" to Caesarea or to almost any other Judean town from Jerusalem (see comment on Acts 11:27).

Given the likely backlog of cases (see comment on Acts 24:27), however, Paul's case is probably addressed this quickly only because of the Jerusalem opposition; ironically, his enemies expedite his case for him. (It is likewise their insistence that leads to Paul's opportunities to preach to Agrippa and Berenice [cf. 25:14–22].) Festus's quick action on any cases may be intended to clear all leftover business from the preceding administration, but it also reinforces for Luke's audience the point that Felix's delay was not because he lacked opportunity (24:25) but because he acted unjustly toward his notorious prisoner (24:26–27).

"Taking his seat on the tribunal"[878] means that he is ready to judge.[879] Luke's narrative reflects the basic elements of Roman judicial procedure. First, private plaintiffs

877. Cf. Cic. *Verr.* 2.2.38.94; Ferguson, *Backgrounds*, 51.
878. For the expression, see also Acts 25:17; 12:21; John 19:13; for a discussion of the tribunal platform (cf. Neh 8:4; 1 Esd 9:42; 2 Macc 13:26), see comments on Acts 18:12, 16–17.
879. In a capital case, a governor could issue a formal condemnation only *pro tribunali*, from the judgment seat (Blinzler, *Trial*, 240; Sherwin-White, *Society*, 47).

advance the complaint (25:2). Then "the governor appears formally on his tribunal, *pro tribunali*" (25:6), and his *consilium* advises him at his discretion (25:12).[880] The tribunal indicates that this is an official hearing, offering a contrast to Felix's informal visits for personal purposes (24:24–25).

II. Baseless Charges (25:7)

The collective barrage of accusations here resembles those against Jesus in Luke 23:10. In contrast to Acts 24:1, where the aristocrats depended on a rhetor, here they apparently all accuse Paul not so much in the form of a trial as of a "forceful display of political status" that will move Festus (25:9).[881] (The use of advocates was optional.)[882] Yet in this way they also fail to provide a carefully developed case, which does not help them in terms of persuading Festus.[883]

Luke claims that the opposition could not prove the charges. Apparently they also made charges based on Judean customs, some of which must have intrigued the governor, unable to understand them (25:19; cf. 24:20–21), but the capital charges (hinted at in 25:8; cf. 25:25) could not be proved. A case against defendants could be reopened if the prosecutors claimed new evidence (Pliny *Ep.* 7.6.10), but if the prosecutor's speech yielded no new evidence, it was to be thrown out of court.[884] Pliny responded to one such speech by simply pointing out that the prosecution had failed to offer fresh evidence, then ending his own response (7.6.12–13); the case was thrown out. Claims of lack of proof were standard responses to charges; when the claims were viewed as accurate, the case was won (see comment on Acts 24:13).

If the accusers had sent investigators on long journeys to perform research, they could have documented a trail of riots where Paul had preached (see comment on Acts 24:5); this would explain why Paul is not released. Such wide-ranging research was, however, rarely done for such a comparatively minor case as this. As much as his enemies wanted his case advanced on the docket, and as central as Paul's case is for Luke's own story, Paul was not a governor like Felix being tried in Rome but a mere troublemaker being accused before a new governor.

What if some enterprising enemy of Paul with sufficient leisure undertook such investigation, even simply securing written documentation[885] where oral reports led him? More easily than traveling, some members of the elite could have solicited reports from visiting Diaspora Jews,[886] though the presence of such witnesses at a trial, possibly demanded by the defense, would be difficult to secure.[887] Luke's contrary explanation of each of these riots, available to us in Acts, suggests that Paul would have had a plan of defense ready against these charges had he needed them. But that Luke mentions assertions without proof suggests that (at least from his apologetic perspective) the

880. Sherwin-White, *Society*, 48–49; followed, e.g., by Fitzmyer, *Acts*, 731.

881. Rapske, *Custody*, 184.

882. See Hemer, *Acts in History*, 129.

883. Rapske, *Custody*, 184. For a petition reopening the same case, see Winter, "Official Proceedings," 327.

884. This is in principle; in practice, the new governor could afford opportunity to start the case afresh (cf. Lewis, "Intercessio"; see comment at Acts 24:27). Prosecutors charged that those seeking to avoid trial had something to conceal (Quint. *Decl.* 250.8–9).

885. Cf. the use of affidavits, e.g., in Aeschines *Tim.* 45; Apul. *Apol.* 59–60.

886. Most would visit the temple without formally announcing the cities from which they hailed, but given Paul's notoriety in some cities and the number of servants available to some members of the priestly aristocracy, some witnesses might have been found.

887. They could be summoned (Apul. *Apol.* 46), but it was more difficult when witnesses were further away (44). That the first witnesses had disappeared (cf. Acts 24:18–19) did not speak well for the case dependent on witnesses; Paul probably had influential patrons and allies in Ephesus that his Ephesian Jewish accusers would not wish to challenge.

accusers apparently depended largely on their status rather than research. Paul was an issue for them, but apparently not one pressing enough to require lengthy work.

The "many and serious charges" would include those in Acts 24:5–6 (stirring dissension, trying to profane the temple) and acts against the law and against Caesar (see comment on Acts 25:8).

III. PAUL'S REFUTATION SUMMARIZED (25:8)

Paul again speaks without an advocate (see comment on Acts 24:10). The summary of the charges that Paul refutes here suggests that he follows a common and logical procedure—namely, summarizing the opponent's argument and then refuting it.[888]

Paul's response in 25:8 must be only a terse summary, as is the presentation of the charges in 25:7.[889] Paul succeeds not only in denying the charges mentioned here but in defining the case in terms of religious controversy. He provided the same definition for Felix (24:14–15, 20–21); whether or not Festus has reviewed the records of the previous hearings,[890] Luke presents Festus as persuaded by Paul's presentation of this matter (25:18–19).

The charge against the temple harks back to 21:28 and 24:6. The claim that Paul violated the Jewish law also recalls 21:28, though this was a charge in which Rome would have little interest (cf. 18:13–15). This charge would count in favor of the Jerusalem authorities' case for having Paul brought to Jerusalem to judge him by their own laws (25:20); for Luke's apologetic, however, it is what the entire issue amounted to (24:14; 25:18–19; cf. 21:21) and represents an offense that Roman officials would reject as worthy of consideration (18:15). If Christians were *apostate* from Judaism, this status might affect their assumed exemption from participation in the imperial cult; but Christians did not claim to be apostates, and Roman governors would hardly want to sort out Jewish theological matters.[891] Luke has been emphatic that Paul was not against the law (e.g., 21:24; for the movement more generally, cf. 21:20; Luke 2:22–27, 39).

The charge of speaking against Caesar, or *maiestas*, is new (contrast 24:5–6);[892] on the charge of *maiestas*, see also comment on Acts 17:7. It may have been brought by any disgruntled Ephesian Jewish leaders visiting the past year's festivals; they could have heard rumors from other traveling Diaspora Jews that Paul opposed Caesar (17:5–7), though they could not prove such rumors (25:7; cf. 24:13). Some may have cited his opposition to venerating the emperor or others besides the God of Israel, but such an accusation would carry little weight when offered by Paul's fellow Jews. Jews and Christians in the Diaspora did honor the emperor, though not as a deity.[893] The Jerusalem temple offered sacrifices on the emperor's

---

888. Dion. Hal. *Lysias* 26; Apul. *Apol.* 27–28 (with elaboration in 29–65), 61, 67. Soards, *Speeches*, 119, sees judicial rhetoric in Acts 25:8 and a combination of judicial and deliberative rhetoric in 25:10–11, but this may divide genres in the latter verses too finely, since the context is that of judicial speech (though cf. 26:28, regarding a theoretically judicial speech).

889. Perhaps something like Acts 25:8 served as a *propositio* for Paul's refutation of claims concerning his violation of both Jewish and Roman law. Rhetoricians sometimes offered and then refuted alternatives (Anderson, *Glossary*, 36, on διλήμματον; Hermog. *Inv.* 4.6.192).

890. Felix's records would have been left for him (see Vössing, "Archive," 1026).

891. Besides, participation in cults, including local imperial cults, was normally voluntary; Pliny required it of Christians, but these were people accused to him, not people he was hunting down. On abuse of the imperial cult in some NT scholarship, see recently, e.g., Galinsky, "Cult" (originally brought to my attention by Jason Myers); for various views, cf. Keener, *Acts*, 3:2553n2559.

892. As generally observed (Lake and Cadbury, *Commentary*, 308; Haenchen, *Acts*, 666; Johnson, *Acts*, 421; Dunn, *Acts*, 320).

893. See Harland, *Associations*, 213–37; cf. 1 Pet 2:13.

behalf,[894] and synagogues presumably also offered prayers for the emperor's well-being.[895] Again, without proving Paul an apostate from Judaism, they could not use Paul's failure to worship Caesar as proof of disloyalty or opposition to Caesar.

From a literary standpoint, the charge of opposing Caesar recalls the false charge that Jesus forbade payment of taxes to Caesar (Luke 23:2). Despite Jesus's support for appropriate loyalty to Caesar in front of many witnesses (20:22–25), his accusers charged him with the offense that they had wanted to use against him, depending (in that case, successfully) partly on their high status; unlike Paul, Jesus did not defend himself. Paul's confidence that the charge against him is false is reflected in his appeal to Caesar himself (Acts 25:11–12, 21; 26:32; 27:24; 28:19). The charge also informs the reader that Paul's opponents keep adding charges. As noted above (see comments on Acts 24:6, 21), changing the charges against a defendant during the trial was considered a sign that the accusers had invented them.[896] After more than a year, new charges might well surface, but one would expect that if the charges were credible, evidence would have surfaced with them. (Surely at least someone from the synagogue in Ephesus would have visited Jerusalem at least for festivals and brought at least affidavits?) Nevertheless, the charge may also represent a further extrapolation of the sedition charge of *maiestas* in 24:5: riots following Paul implied that he was seditious, and any act of sedition ultimately challenged Caesar.[897]

iv. Festus's Favor for the Elite (25:9)

Haenchen finds the sequence of events suspicious. Why does Festus merely offer to change the venue instead of pronouncing a verdict (25:9)?[898] Further, why should Paul appeal to Caesar instead of simply protesting a possible change of venue?[899] But as Tannehill notes, Haenchen's confusion stems from his "failure to take seriously the indications that Festus is a biased judge and recognized as such by Paul."[900] (In my view, Festus is not primarily hostile toward Paul; he is one of the fairer judges in Acts. Yet he is politically predisposed to accommodate the Sanhedrin insofar as possible;[901] see discussion below.) Festus may avoid a verdict because the current setting is akin to a preliminary hearing, but he may also do so because there are not yet sufficient grounds to condemn Paul and he wants to humor the local leaders insofar as possible by offering them further opportunity to make their case.

One could claim a venue to be hostile, seeking to reduce prejudice, but one normally could not alter it (Cic. *Balb.* 1.1–2); Festus, in fact, shows Paul generosity (perhaps based on how well Paul's defense has succeeded) by asking if he is willing to accept

---

894. E.g., Philo *Embassy* 232; Jos. *War* 2.197, 409; *Ant.* 18.257–59; *Ag. Ap.* 2.77; cf. Moore, *Judaism*, 2:115; Rabello, "Condition," 703–4; for earlier models, see, e.g., 1 Esd 6:31; 1 Macc 7:33; *Let. Aris.* 45; less relevant, 2 Macc 3:32. Others sacrificed to the emperor (Sen. Y. *Dial.* 9.14.9; Jos. *Ant.* 18.258) in addition to offering sacrifices and prayers on his behalf (*Res gest.* 9.1; Pliny *Ep.* 10.35–36, 52, 100; Fronto *Ad M. Caes.* 3.10; 5.25 [40]; *Ad Ant. imp.* 1.2.1; Apul. *Metam.* 11.17; Men. Rhet. 2.1–2, 377.20–22); for prayers for the governor, cf. Men. Rhet. 2.10, 417.29–30.

895. Cf. Bar 1:11; 1 Tim 2:2; Poly. *Phil.* 12.3; Abrahams, *Studies* (1), 64.

896. Lysias *Or.* 7.2, §108.

897. Cf. Dunn, *Acts*, 320: an "attempt to bring home . . . the fundamentally subversive character of Paul's work as seen by the plaintiffs (cf. 16.21; 17.7)." One could expand a charge by dividing its components (Hermog. *Inv.* 1.2.101, though not referring to subsequent hearings).

898. Haenchen, *Acts*, 668.

899. Ibid., 669. For further skepticism here, see Pervo, *Acts*, 611–12.

900. Tannehill, *Acts*, 307. Pervo, *Acts*, 612, concurs with this negative assessment of Tannehill, Cassidy (*Society*, 107–9), and Witherington but still regards Luke's narrative as implausible.

901. As today, politics entails compromises, sometimes at the expense of moral conviction, and many debate about where to draw the lines. He would also naturally trust the elite more than one of a different class and has not yet heard Paul's articulate speech.

the change. By appealing to Caesar, Paul can escape not only a move to Jerusalem but further hearings in Judea, and thus any location in which political pressures are likely to influence his case (just as these pressures kept him in custody, Acts 24:27).

Festus's offer to provide a favor to the Jerusalem elite[902] stems not from animus toward Paul but from an attempt to offer conciliatory gestures toward the leaders of a notoriously unstable province. This overture does not portray him as perfect, but it also does not depict him to be as corrupt as Felix.[903] (Ancient historians and biographers usually preferred "round" characters with a mixture of positive and negative traits.)[904] Festus has not promised to condemn Paul in Jerusalem and does not even promise to try him there without Paul's approval.[905]

Unlike Felix, Festus probably does not know of the plot against Paul (and if Festus were to learn of it only after its success, this knowledge would not benefit Paul); the only record of it from Felix's administration would be the brief mention in Lysias's letter (23:30), which may not have been reviewed by Festus himself. (The possible echoes of Lysias's letter in 25:16, 19, if not merely Lukan stylistic flourishes or apologetic connections, could suggest that Luke intends us to know otherwise, but Paul or others probably also would have brought this piece of the case file to Festus's attention during or after the hearing.) Further, the change of venue might seem to him, after continued insistence from the local leaders (he resisted temporarily in 25:3–4), but a small concession; he may have assumed that perhaps it was for any witnesses' convenience. It would also aid his insufficient understanding of local customs (25:20; contrast 24:22, 24). From Festus's standpoint, it might seem odd that if Paul's case were as clear-cut as Paul claimed, Felix had not freed him already. That meant either that there were problems with Paul's case or that it was extraordinarily politically sensitive. Although Festus would know that Felix was recalled on the charge of misadministering the province, he may have followed the likely Roman presumption that the Judeans were probably more at fault for this charge than the governor, and recognized the importance of avoiding alienating them unnecessarily.

We should not be surprised that Festus might wish to accommodate political pressures insofar as possible, given Josephus's portrait of him. One of Festus's primary objectives seems to have been the suppression of bandits (Jos. *War* 2.271; *Ant.* 20.188), and Paul stood accused by the local rulers[906] of stirring unrest (Acts 25:7; 24:5).[907] Whereas Felix had reason to grant the Jerusalem elite a favor to "buy off" their hostility (see comment on Acts 24:27), Festus wants to grant them a favor to establish a good working relationship with his new subjects.[908]

902. Sometimes Jewish people used the phrase "the Jews" negatively against other Jews; see comment on Acts 28:19; cf. Saldarini, *Community*, 34–36; Keener, *John*, 218.

903. On Festus as imperfect but significantly better than Felix, see, e.g., Walton, "Trying Paul," 138–39.

904. By reporting both sides sympathetically, a writer could increase suspense and praise for the victor, while augmenting tragic pathos in the impending defeat of noble characters on the other side (e.g., the Albans in Dion. Hal. *Ant. rom.* 3; plebeians and patricians in 9.39.1–6; Romans and Carthaginians in Livy 21.1.3; cf. Homer's even greater evenhandedness with Greek and Trojan heroes). Lucian critiques historians who praise only their own leaders and slander the other side (*Hist.* 7); Plutarch critiques one for malice (*Mal. Hdt.* 3, *Mor.* 855C). Cf. the greatest general of one era, nevertheless portrayed with fatal character flaws (Dion. Hal. *Ant. rom.* 8.60.1–2; 8.61.1–3). For biographies including both "flat" and "round" characters, see Burridge, *Gospels*, 182–84. Even one of Penelope's suitors, destined for death (Hom. *Od.* 18.155–56), was not wholly bad (18.119–56, 412–21). Aristotle advises portraying characters consistently, but this consistency could include portraying the characters' known inconsistencies (*Poet.* 15.6, 1454a).

905. This fits his character in Jos. *Ant.* 20.193–94.

906. Who seem to have worked peacefully with Festus (Jos. *Ant.* 20.193–94).

907. Suggested also by Witherington, *Acts*, 717–18.

908. Dunn, *Acts*, 320; cf. Spangenberg 226v–227r in Chung-Kim and Hains, *Acts*, 333.

Given the troubles that Judeans believed Felix had caused and how this affected Judean sentiments toward Rome (Jos. *Ant.* 20.182),[909] Festus would want to start offering favors as quickly as possible after his arrival. Some matters were nonnegotiable, so it was best to grant whatever favors were negotiable. Given the conventional practice of reciprocity in Mediterranean antiquity,[910] Festus could expect local aristocrats to repay his favors by lending their support to his mandate where possible.

In view of the need to be a politically astute governor as well as a judge, his newness as governor, and what he would consider the "unusually intractable native population," Festus deserves some credit for considering Paul's rights in the case.[911] Festus was not proposing to simply hand Paul over to his accusers; he would hear the case himself.[912] (Given the substantial element of local Judean law in question, he might also consent to using the local Sanhedrin as his advisory council,[913] as Lysias had attempted in Acts 22:30.) But he wanted to simplify matters and show his support for Paul's elite opponents by accommodating their preferred venue.

Festus also may have wanted to accommodate the local leaders by offering a new preliminary hearing, starting over again, instead of simply relying on the records of Felix's preliminary hearing.[914] This approach would be more time consuming than building on previous documents, which revealed the special interests at work that were hostile to Paul.[915] Nevertheless, such a decision was within his prerogatives as governor; indeed, even if Felix had left Paul sentenced for a crime instead of leaving his case pending, Festus had legal authority to veto Felix's decree.[916]

Repeating the preliminary hearing and disregarding the previous administration's documents could be disastrous for Paul, even without a change in venue. Paul had built his case for the prosecution's real motives being religious disagreement on Lysias's report of the Sanhedrin's dispute (23:28–29; 24:20–21); his ploy now obvious, the Sanhedrin was unlikely to play into his hands a second time and would be happy for the opportunity to revisit the case and recoup honor lost to Paul's craftiness.

Further, Paul had noted that his opponents lacked witnesses and proof, but what if they had concocted some since then, to be elaborated at a further hearing?[917] Memories had faded, and presumably most of the delegates who had come with Paul (excepting Aristarchus and Luke, 27:2) had long since returned to their cities (although he

909. Josephus's sequence of events suggests that whatever else Festus may have learned of in his eight to ten days in Jerusalem (Acts 25:6; and whatever else he may have known before sailing from Rome), he certainly would have been informed by local leaders of how much they hated his predecessor.

910. See comment on Acts 23:17–18.

911. Barrett, *Acts*, 1121.

912. This necessity is reinforced not least by the charge of speaking against Caesar (Acts 25:8), which is not a purely Jewish religious affair (Haenchen, *Acts*, 669).

913. Jeffers, *World*, 169. They would not replace his own *consilium*; grounds for selecting a *consilium* remained flexible in this period (Balsdon and Levick, "*Consilium principis*"), but a governor typically constituted a *consilium* from "citizens and senators" (Voss, "Consilium," 702).

914. Witherington, *Acts*, 721.

915. The governor would have these documents available, likely including Lysias's letter, as well as a précis of prosecution and defense speeches (with Le Cornu, *Acts*, 1359, who adds also possible reports of Felix from his conversations with Paul; but these were extralegal and would not have been recorded, at least not in the official records).

916. This was true of all peers or superiors (see Lewis, "Intercessio").

917. It was not impossible that some of the original Ephesian accusers retained sufficient hostility against Paul to collect written reports from other synagogues where Paul was associated with trouble (e.g., Thessalonica, Beroea, and Corinth). It still remained unlikely that any accusers visiting for festivals would wish to remain for hearings (especially if, as Luke's own account suggests, no local convictions resulted and the blame for unrest at least sometimes appeared to lie with the accusers), but the details of riots may well have become part of the official accusations against Paul at some point, since Luke must refute them (see comment on Acts 24:5).

would still presumably have local witnesses concerning the timing and purpose of his arrival). (For that matter, if Festus began with this concession, he might make other concessions, and the Sanhedrin could exploit his relative ignorance of the Judean situation in a way they had not been able to do with Felix.)[918] A change in venue offered the worse problem of the plot (unlike Paul, the new procurator, inexperienced in Judean affairs, presumably did not know how dangerous a move to Jerusalem could be, 23:16; 25:3). Given such factors, it is not difficult to understand Paul's appeal to Caesar in 25:10–11.

The narrative as it stands makes good sense historically, but what Luke reports also mirrors the theological direction of Acts as a whole. The Roman governor offers justice at Jerusalem (25:9), where Paul knows he cannot receive it; Paul instead appeals to Rome (25:10–12). The entire book of Acts emphasizes the movement from Jerusalem to Rome and often the development beyond the purely Jewish mission to a Gentile mission most immediately served—from the standpoint of peoples living in the empire—by targeting Rome itself.

Thus Paul's appeal, which much of Luke's later Christian audience might have regarded as misguided[919] in light of Nero's eventual persecution of Christians, appears instead as part of his broader strategy in the Gentile mission. It offered a model of boldness and aimed to instill a confidence that God offered Christians a future in a pagan empire (cf. Jer 29:7). From a broader historical horizon unavailable to Luke, although Luke's strategic vision was ultimately realized, many generations of Christians encountered hostility from the empire (as they often had in Jerusalem) until the time of that vision's realization.

c. Paul Appeals to Caesar (25:10–12)

After two years in custody, Paul recognizes that the political situation in Judea is too difficult and the Jerusalem elite will continue requesting his deportation to Jerusalem, with the possible consequence of his assassination (cf. 23:12–15; 25:3). Felix would have deferred the case indefinitely, neither handing Paul over to his enemies nor providing a hearing in which Paul could appeal. Paul avails himself of the opportunity presented now.

i. No Wrongdoing (25:10–11)

Paul suspects the political bias against him ("a favor," 25:11). There is no need for a new trial; one was already held, and Festus knows its outcome ("you know," 25:10). (For that matter, Festus *does* know Paul's innocence [explicit in 25:25], but if he stated it openly at the trial, he would be forced to acquit him.)[920] Whereas careful attention to individuals' trials was one criterion for praising a governor,[921] prejudiced jurors and

---

918. Bruce, *Commentary*, 477.

919. Hence perhaps not Spirit-led (cf. criticism of Paul's failure to keep to an original plan in 2 Cor 1:17, answered in 1:18–2:4). Although rhetoricians recommended that political leaders emphasize their inability to prophetically foresee the outcome of an action (cf., e.g., Demosth. *Pant.* 23; Hermog. *Issues* 68.10–69.21, esp. 69.15–17; Libanius *Declam.* 36.42; 44.50–52, 61), some may have proved skeptical of this argument from an apostle (hence perhaps Luke's apologetic; but Scripture nowhere attributed to prophets complete knowledge, e.g., 2 Kgs 4:27; 1 Cor 13:9; Matt 11:3//Luke 7:19). Cf. fuller comment on Acts 19:21.

920. Tannehill, *Acts*, 307, who therefore concludes that Festus is an unreliable judge, like Felix. But as suggested above, he is of more mixed character than Felix (though, from Verres onward, Romans were well aware of the character type of abusive provincial governors, and provincials had experience with it, albeit more so now in minor provinces such as Judea [treated as part of the larger province of Syria] than in major ones such as Macedonia, Asia, or Achaia).

921. Men. Rhet. 2.4, 389.6–7.

judges were the bane of defendants.[922] No defendant wants a juror who fails "to allow both sides to make their case on equal terms" (Max. Tyre 16.1).[923] When opponents had more political or rhetorical clout, a defendant could protest that he was vulnerable and at a disadvantage and that the stakes were much higher for himself than for his adversaries (Dion. Hal. *Lysias* 17).[924] Pleading for impartiality (with the implication that an impartial judge would favor the speaker) was a common forensic strategy.[925]

"As you know" implies that the previous documents of the case are available and their information has been at least summarized for Festus.[926] Paul's language here might sound too forward, but if there was risk of a judge's hostile bias, it was appropriate to demand that the judge render justice in accordance with the laws[927] or even to threaten judges (though not usually governors) that one would not hesitate to prosecute them for bribery if they judged wrongly (Quint. *Inst.* 4.1.21).[928] Cicero warns Verres's jury that the Roman people's confidence in the courts will be restored only if they convict Verres, who is boasting that his wealth will protect him from conviction (*Verr.* 1.1.1; 2.1.2.5). Paul has been submissive, respectful, and patient, but at this point the stakes are higher. Felix had neither freed Paul nor handed him over to his accusers, but the risk of being handed over to accusers appeared higher now (25:9).

Even a governor judging *extra ordinem* would take laws into consideration (as respectable customs and conventions of justice) if he was a fair judge. Ideally, this meant, among other things, that the same charge was not to be tried twice;[929] Festus would not think that he is doing so (since Felix never resolved the case conclusively, Acts 24:27), but from the standpoint of Luke and Paul, enough evidence has accumulated favoring Paul to render the case justly closed.

Paul's mention of his lack of fear about dying (25:11) implies that if transferred to Jerusalem, he will unjustly face a death he would not face before a Roman law court (justifying his appeal before a verdict). Even most philosophers who warned against lamenting sufferings noted that one should not crave them.[930] Defendants would often note that they were not afraid to die if found guilty, often as a way of expressing indignation against the charge or expressing certainty that they were innocent.[931] Thus one defendant concurred that an offense was worthy of death, but claimed that it was his accuser, not himself, who was guilty of the offense (Xen. *Hell.* 2.3.37); another claimed that if his acts had proved harmful to the state (here Sparta), he should be punished, but not if he had acted to the state's advantage (5.11.32). Josephus told his accusers that he did not refuse death if justice required it (*Life* 141), then convinced them that it did not (142).[932] Later a model speech offers, "If . . . then I [as a

---

922. Rhetors were trained how to deal with prejudiced juries (e.g., Hermog. *Issues* 34.10–14).

923. Trapp, 142.

924. For warnings about opponents' superior oratory, see, e.g., Isaeus *Astyph.* 35; *Aristarch.* 1; Cic. *Quinct.* 1.1–4.

925. E.g., Lysias *Or.* 15.1, §144; comment on Acts 24:10.

926. Roman administrations kept good records (see Rapske, *Custody*, 250). When in Caesarea, Luke likely had access to such documents himself (see Winter, "Official Proceedings"; comment on Acts 24:2–8).

927. *Rhet. Alex.* 19, 1433b.19–23.

928. "As you know" was also a rhetorical move to recruit judges or jury as witnesses (see, e.g., Aeschines *Tim.* 55–56, 65, 80, 89; further comment on Acts 26:5).

929. Hermog. *Issues* 42.15–19 (cf. the principle of double jeopardy).

930. E.g., Sen. Y. *Ep. Lucil.* 67.3–4. For the philosophically disposed, however, doing wrong was worse than suffering it (e.g., Mus. Ruf. 3, p. 40.30).

931. E.g., Xen. *Hell.* 2.3.37, 49; cf. Aeschines *Embassy* 5; *Tim.* 122; *Vit. Aes.* 128; the idea is not limited to Greek rhetoric (cf. Ps 7:3–5). Socrates counts it his appropriate time to die in Xen. *Mem.* 4.8.6; cf. Plato *Apol.* 37, which others cite. A first-century audience might suppose a gesture of indignation, such as pointing one's fingers together toward the mouth (as described in Shiell, *Reading Acts*, 63).

932. Noticed also by others (Conzelmann, *Acts*, 203; Fitzmyer, *Acts*, 745).

lawbreaker] should be punished, convict me," but insists that the evidence does not support the charge.[933] Offering that one assesses one's just penalty as death if found guilty was a standard rhetorical strategy for protesting one's innocence (*Rhet. Alex.* 29, 1437a.14–17).[934] Yet Paul also counters that the punishment is wrong if, as he pointed out in 25:10, he is innocent. Granting a concession and then taking it back given contrary conditions also fits rhetorical logic (Hermog. *Inv.* 3.10.158).

11. PAUL'S APPEAL (25:11)

Paul says that he stands before Caesar's tribunal. The term for Caesar's "tribunal" in 25:10 recalls that of Festus in 25:6. Festus is not the final authority but rather Caesar's representative in the system of appeal (cf. Luke 7:8, where the centurion exercises authority because he is "under authority").[935] Therefore, if Festus cannot safely handle the case for political reasons, he should refer it to Caesar (Acts 25:11), whose court would be under no such pressures.[936] Paul has been waiting long to go to Rome anyway (19:21), and he is so certain that he has not offended "against Caesar" (25:8) that he is ready to appeal to him.[937] When Paul speaks, he is literally "standing" before the tribunal (although ἵστημι can simply mean "appearing" before the tribunal); whoever was speaking at a given time would stand (25:18).[938]

The emperor to whom Paul appeals here is Nero; whether or not readers were familiar with Felix and Festus, they were probably familiar enough with the period of Paul's ministry to infer that the current emperor was Nero. Probably to Paul's detriment at some later hearing, Nero proved to be vicious against Christians in 64 C.E., but his approach then was driven by the need for a political scapegoat. In 54–59, he remained under the moderating influence of Seneca the philosopher and Burrus the praetorian prefect.[939] Paul's confidence fits the historical context of Paul's time better than when Luke is writing, by which time Christian readers would think only of Nero's evil.[940] It is also possible that Paul might have heard of Seneca's influence and might know that Seneca was a brother of Gallio, who dismissed the case against Paul in 18:14–16.[941]

---

933. Libanius *Declam.* 44.42 (trans. Heath, *Hermogenes,* 168).

934. It also helped distinguish hearers' natural moral outrage against the charges from the person who may not have committed them (cf. Cic. *Cael.* 12.29).

935. Commentators cite Ulp. *Dig.* 1.19.1: "Whatever Caesar's procurator performs and accomplishes is approved by Caesar as if he himself carried them out" (Conzelmann, *Acts,* 203; Fitzmyer, *Acts,* 745; cf. comments on agents in Keener, *John,* 310–15). The emperor (or his aides) approved appointments even in senatorial provinces (see Badian, "*Provincia,*" 1267).

936. Some also point out that Paul's release in Judea might expose him to assassination (Chance, *Acts,* 464, citing Barrett, *Shorter Commentary,* 375); although this may be true, if Festus released him publicly (as he probably would; or if privately, without public announcement of the timing), he would probably be safe initially in Caesarea (and perhaps led on his way by Philip's circle).

937. Luke elsewhere employs the verb ἐπικαλέω for "calling on" the Lord (e.g., Acts 2:21; 22:16), and it also answers nicely to ἐγκαλέω, "accuse," in these chapters (23:28–29; 26:2, 7). But ἐπικαλέω is also standard judicial terminology (see BDAG, citing Plut. *Marc.* 2.7; *Tib. Gracc.* 16.1), so that Luke's lexical options were limited and the apparent connections might be coincidental.

938. E.g., Xen. *Anab.* 5.1.2; 6.4.12; Pliny *Ep.* 4.9.18; 9.13.18; 'Abot R. Nat. 6 A; 1 Cor 14:30; cf. Pliny *Ep.* 2.19.3; see further comment at Acts 1:15. This allowed better visual contact for the court and the speaker's voice projection.

939. With Bruce, *Commentary,* 479; Witherington, *Acts,* 726.

940. See, e.g., Dio Chrys. *Or.* 3.134; 21.6; Epict. *Diatr.* 1.1.19–20; 1.25.22; 4.5.17; Plut. *Div. V.* 32, *Mor.* 567F; Pliny *Ep.* 1.5.1; 3.5.5; 5.5.3; 6.31.9; Juv. *Sat.* 4.136–39; 8.211–30; 10.15–18; 12.129; Suet. *Nero* passim (e.g., 38); Tac. *Hist.* 1.72; Lucian *Nero* 10; Paus. 10.7.1; Marc. Aur. 3.16; Dio Cass. 62.16.2; 62.18.1; though, for mixed views persisting outside the Roman elite, see, e.g., Tac. *Hist.* 1.4; Jos. *Ant.* 20.154. Later emperors also used Nero for negative propaganda (Kragelund, "Nero's *luxuria*"). Further on Nero, see Momigliano, "Nero"; Griffin, *Nero.*

941. Paul may have expected a turn for the worse in Roman imperial claims (cf. 2 Thess 2:3–12; I take this as authentic because no pseudepigrapher after 70 C.E. would invent 2 Thess 2:4) but would not necessarily anticipate it in Nero.

III. SENT TO ROME FOR TRIAL

Roman governors sometimes sent prisoners on to Rome for trial. For example, Felix had put aristocratic priests in bonds for a minor matter, then sent them to Rome to defend themselves before Caesar (Jos. *Life* 13); he also sent some prominent bandits to Rome for punishment (and perhaps to draw attention to his own diligence in having captured them; *War* 2.253). Before Felix's accession, the Syrian legate sent the leaders of Jewish and Samaritan factions to Rome to argue their respective cases (2.243; cf. *Ant.* 20.131). This practice may have particularly characterized high-profile or (as in Paul's case) politically sensitive cases—though it should be noted that Judea's governors did not refer most politically sensitive cases.

On this basis, one could surmise that Festus sent Paul to Rome even without the appeal Luke here describes;[942] this could sufficiently explain the connection between his detention in Caesarea and the later detention in Rome. What such an approach would fail to explain is the coincidence between Paul's destination in Rome while in Roman custody and his explicit earlier hope to visit Rome after Jerusalem (Rom 15:23–28). This "coincidence" suggests that Paul may have had something to do with his Roman destination (albeit providentially with the procurator's cooperation), just as depicted in Luke's narrative (Acts 25:10–11). It also independently coheres with Luke's narrative that Paul in his letters expected trouble from unbelievers in Judea (Rom 15:30–31) and elsewhere had conflicts with some leaders of his own people (2 Cor 11:24; cf. 1 Thess 2:15) and that in Phil 1:13 we next find him in Roman custody.

Moreover, Roman citizens would have been sent to Rome for trial more frequently than others. By the second century, it is possible that they were even routinely sent to Rome for trial (Pliny *Ep.* 6.31).[943] Pliny mentions a leading citizen of Ephesus who, having stirred his fellow citizens' envy, had to appeal to Trajan (and was acquitted; 6.31.3). When Pliny detained Christians who were Roman citizens, he sent them to Rome for trial (10.96.4) instead of simply executing them as he did the others (10.96.3).[944]

The early Valerian laws (especially 300 B.C.E.)[945] and Porcian laws (early second century B.C.E.)[946] allowed Roman citizens the right of appeal to the people, preventing execution without trial.[947] Eventually this privilege of appeal was extended to Roman citizens abroad as well.[948] The Porcian laws heavily penalized anyone who scourged

942. Certainly those who doubt Paul's Roman citizenship (but see discussion at Acts 16:37) must doubt his appeal (e.g., Alvarez Cineira, "Pablo," doubting even his transfer in custody to Rome); provincials who were not Roman citizens could not appeal a corrupt governor's decision to Rome except to charge him for extortion or if the emperor granted an exception (O'Rourke, "Law," 175).

943. Radice, LCL, 2:286n2, hypothesizes that perhaps all citizens were forwarded to Rome whether they appealed or not; but of course, in a capital case, it might be assumed that citizens with the option of appeal would nearly always exercise it.

944. Cf. also Winter, *Trial*, 84. Talbert, *Acts*, 204, cites also Lucian *Tox.* 17 (where Asia's governor forwards a prisoner to the emperor on a capital charge) and notes, nearer Paul's day, a Roman citizen who was imprisoned by Asia's proconsul but released by Nero (Tac. *Ann.* 16.10). Another person needing retrial was sent to Rome in Pliny *Ep.* 10.57.2, presumably because he was a Roman citizen (Radice, LCL, 2:236n1, comparing Paul's case). In some uncertain cases, Pliny sent a prisoner on (*Ep.* 10.74.3), but in others, he avoided the expense of sending the accused and sent merely the petitions (10.59). One operative principle was to avoid responsibility for a bad decision for which one could later be called to account.

945. The historicity of the earlier supposedly relevant Valerian laws, reportedly 509 and 449 B.C.E., is seriously disputed (Crawford, "Lex," 852).

946. Although the *leges Porciae* clearly addressed *provocatio*, their exact content is known only indirectly (cf. Crawford, "Lex," 851).

947. Derow, "*Imperium*," 752; cf. Staveley and Lintott, "*Provocatio*"; Lintott, *Romans*, 18; see (for different interpretations of this *provocatio ad populum*) esp. Berger, Nicholas, and Lintott, "Law and Procedure," 833.

948. Derow, "*Imperium*," 752; cf. Stambaugh, *City*, 93–94; Robinson, *Criminal Law*, 49.

or executed a citizen (Livy 10.9.4); the Valerian laws decreed it an evil act to scourge or behead a citizen who appealed, and later laws assessed heavy penalties for such a breach of propriety (10.9.5).

IV. TYPES OF APPEAL

Some have argued that in the era of the Roman Republic, two forms of appeal existed. The first was the *provocatio*, the right to appeal to the Roman people (*populus romanus*), protesting a magistrate's decision. This appeal was called the *provocatio ad populum*; in the empire, it became instead the *provocatio ad Caesarem*, the appeal to Caesar.[949] The second was the *appellatio*, appealing to an official to veto a colleague's decision; by the empire, this also became a prerogative of the emperor and hence largely merged with the *provocatio*.[950] Thus, during the empire, we should think of a general form of appeal rather than any strict boundaries between these two older forms.[951] Many now argue, in fact, against any boundaries between these terms.[952]

In the late republic, Romans used the *provocatio* to appeal above a private judge's head to the officials who appointed the judge, and by the empire these appeals could reach as high as Caesar.[953] Protecting Roman citizens in the provinces from exploitive governors (such as the earlier Verres), Augustus confirmed this right in his *lex Iulia de vi publica seu privata*.[954] The *lex Iulia de vi* "protected the Roman citizen who invoked the ancient right of *provocatio*, from summary punishment . . . without trial, . . . and from actual trial by magistrates outside Italy."[955] By the time of Trajan, such citizenship rights seem to have led to automatically sending to the emperor citizens charged with certain offenses.[956]

Roman citizens could appeal local courts' decisions to the governor and even to the emperor.[957] Roman citizens could claim the right to be judged by the emperor, especially in capital cases,[958] although, given the logistics of the empire, this usually meant simply the emperor's tribunal; by Nero's day, most of this case load was delegated.[959] To reduce potential appeals to manageable proportions, perhaps the governor might need to approve the grounds for the appeal (thus requiring the wording in Acts 25:26–27; but the need for explanation may suffice to account for this cover letter).

During the republic, the *provocatio* was not meant to intervene in a trial currently in progress, but during the empire, the emperor was often willing "to grant extraordinary

949. Bruce, *Commentary*, 478. On *provocatio*, see further Cadbury, "Law and Trial," 313–15. The three titles regularly used of Nero were "Caesar," "Augustus," and "Lord" (cf. Acts 25:26).

950. Bruce, *Acts¹*, 432 (emphasizing the emperor's adoption of tribunes' authority); Hemer, *Acts in History*, 130. On *appellatio*, see further Cadbury, "Law and Trial," 315–16.

951. Rapske, *Custody*, 186–88. Witherington, *Acts*, 723, views Acts 25:11 as *provocatio* and not *appellatio*.

952. Against boundaries between these terms at all, Rowe, *World*, 82, following Garnsey, "Criminal Jurisdiction," makes a strong case that the two terms could be roughly interchangeable (see Tac. *Ann.* 14.28); see also Schnabel, *Acts*, 992.

953. Fitzmyer, *Acts*, 746. Although our evidence concerns especially citizens, cf. the foreigner in *CIL* 1².583 (cited in Libero, "Provocatio").

954. Fitzmyer, *Acts*, 746.

955. Sherwin-White, *Society*, 58. This would not de facto exclude trial by the Roman governor, who, though outside Italy, functioned as Caesar's representative ("Caesar's tribunal," Acts 25:10).

956. Sherwin-White, *Society*, 60. For a full discussion of laws and historic precedents informing the practice of appeals, see Rapske, *Custody*, 48–56 (including probably an appeal against imprisonment, 50–51).

957. Hansen, "Galatia," 388, following Macro, "Cities," 670–71. For appeals of local decisions to higher courts, even to the emperor, Meeks, *Moral World*, 32, cites Ael. Arist. *Or.* 26.38–39; also Diaspora Jewish communities' appeal of local decisions to Roman authorities (Jos. *Ant.* 14.223–27, 234, 235, 241–46).

958. See further Garnsey, "Lex Iulia and Appeal." Whether governors generally could execute Roman citizens is debated, though it appears that, by Nero's time, some governors could do so (O'Rourke, "Law," 174).

959. O'Rourke, "Law," 177; Paulus, "Appellatio," 894 (citing Suet. *Aug.* 33.3; *Nero* 17). Many exceptions we cite are later, from Trajan's reign.

legal assistance upon request," a privilege that "was gradually institutionalized" and could occur during any stage of the trial.[960] Schnabel notes that defendants' right to appeal to the emperor is well attested in the early empire[961] and that such appeals could precede the verdict.[962] An appeal was particularly logical earlier in a trial if the conduct of the trial would likely incur danger or display prejudice.[963] Those who were not convicted could request a further hearing if they had sufficient reason: when some plaintiffs wished to drop a case before the emperor, the defendants asked for a trial to remove any suspicion (Pliny *Ep.* 6.31.11); the emperor wryly asked his *consilium* for advice, since "these people want to complain about being let off the charge against them" (6.31.12).[964]

v. An Irregular Appeal

Although an appeal before the verdict was not illegal, it was irregular.[965] People in provinces appealed first to the governor before appealing to the emperor (*Dig.* 49.1.21.pr.),[966] but this is irrelevant for Paul's trial, which is before the governor; moreover, a governor might refer a powerful plaintiff's difficult case to the emperor (Pliny *Ep.* 6.31.4).[967] More important, people *normally* appealed only after final verdicts.[968] Not everyone worried about regularity: dissatisfied with the outcome of their suit before the senate, provincial representatives appealed to the emperor (who referred them back to the senate; 6.13.1–2). The emperor might also agree to hear complaints that were not appeals of verdicts at all; someone who was wronged by another also complained to the emperor, who ordered a more efficient method of proceeding to abbreviate the hearing (6.22.1–2). Similarly, emperors could pardon people during a trial (Modestinus *Dig.* 48.16.17) no less than wait for its conclusion.[969]

Because Paul's appeal before a complete trial and sentence is unusual, scholars debate as to whether Festus had discretion over whether to grant it (hence his consultation in Acts 25:12).[970] Some think that Festus was legally bound by the *lex Iulia de vi publica* of Augustus's era to grant the appeal request.[971] It could have been difficult and perhaps potentially dangerous politically for a governor to deny any Roman citizen's appeal to the emperor.[972] Sherwin-White suggests that the charges against Paul were either *extra ordinem* or a particular kind of *ordo* whereby he could still

960. Conzelmann, *Acts*, 204; cf. likewise Bruce, *Commentary*, 478.

961. Schnabel, *Acts*, 993, citing (in n. 27) Dio Cass. 59.8.5; Suet. *Nero* 17; Tac. *Ann.* 14.28.1; 16.8.3; *I.Cos* 26; and noting Horsley, *New Documents* 1:51.

962. Schnabel, *Acts*, 993, citing (in n. 28) a case from 69 C.E. in Dio Cass. 64.2.3. He notes (on 993) that "available evidence suggests that the *appellatio* was not fully regulated" in the first century (citing esp. Omerzu, *Prozess*, 107–8, 489–91).

963. Hemer, *Acts in History*, 130 (following Schürer, *Age of Jesus Christ*, 1:369; against Haenchen).

964. Trans. B. Radice, LCL, 1:473. Their request was granted.

965. See Jones, *Empire*, 289. Jones's approach has, however, been challenged by Peter Garnsey and Fergus Millar; our information from the period remains too scanty for evaluating Luke's narrative on this point (Wallace and Williams, *Acts*, 122–23).

966. Paulus, "Appellatio," 894.

967. In that case, however, even Trajan, who seems to have heard many cases, asked that such matters (here adultery) not be referred to him (Pliny *Ep.* 6.31.6).

968. Paulus, "Appellatio," 894; see Rowe, *World*, 82 (following the critique of pre-sentence appeals and mandatory granting of appeals in Garnsey, "Criminal Jurisdiction," 53–55).

969. Schiemann, "Indulgentia," 793.

970. Cf., e.g., the brief discussion in Stambaugh and Balch, *Environment*, 31; Fitzmyer, *Acts*, 746.

971. See Foakes-Jackson, *Acts*, 219–20; Sherwin-White, *Society*, 63–64; Barrett, *Acts*, 1131. For the relevant part of the *lex Iulia*, scholars cite Ulp. *Dig.* 48.6.7, noting also additions in *Pauli sententiae* 5.26.1.

972. Cf. Conzelmann, *Acts*, 204. Tajra, *Trial*, 151, argues that the governor could reject some sorts of appeal, but not this kind.

appeal;[973] he contends that the governor had to approve Roman citizens' appeals in such cases.[974] Indeed, it was illegal to deny normal appeals, and such denials (which did happen) could be punished.[975] In this case, Festus might consult his advisors (25:12) only to ascertain whether this was the sort of *extra ordinem* case in which he must honor the appeal.[976]

Whether such requirements were in force in the first century remains open to question.[977] Pragmatism led governors to reject some appeals, but it helped if the defendant had marks of higher social status in addition to Roman citizenship.[978] That Paul appeared to be a prominent sage with a large constituency may have helped provide additional status; moreover, that he was articulate revealed his education. Whereas governors might try offenses such as murder and adultery without allowing appeals to Rome (given the growing number of citizens in the empire),[979] appeal was allowed in cases of treason,[980] which is relevant here (24:5; 25:8). A governor in Judea "could probably have ignored Paul's appeal with no one the wiser";[981] one of his successors crucified equestrians, who no doubt protested in vain (Jos. *War* 2.308).

Still, Festus is the one governor Josephus portrays from this period who seems to have honored official Roman policy (*War* 2.271–72). Acts and Josephus seem to agree on this portrayal; whether Festus had any obligation to grant Paul's request or not, Festus's concern for protocol would have proved fortunate or providential for Paul.

Whereas some scholars believe that granting Paul's appeal would have been mandatory, others believe that the irregularity of the appeal before a verdict probably moved it beyond such a strict obligation on Festus's part.[982] Luke himself tells us that Festus consulted with his *consilium* (Acts 25:12); perhaps he consulted to ascertain whether Roman policy required him to grant the appeal, but he may have done so because he had authority to decide what to do with the appeal.[983] This possibility may make better sense of Festus's public claim to have decided (ἔκρινα; in this case, as a judge) to honor the appeal (25:25). (Here refusal to retract the appeal after the conclusion of 26:32 is a matter of honor and propriety; Festus had already publicly decided to refer the case, and it would dishonor both Festus and the emperor not to follow through.)[984]

If Festus did have discretion to decide whether to grant this appeal (which I think

---

973. Sherwin-White, *Society*, 62. Black, "Law," 216–17 (following A. H. M. Jones), suggests that governors could ignore appeals for crimes within the *ordo* but accepted appeals for crimes *extra ordinem*.

974. Sherwin-White, *Society*, 63–64. See also Jones, *Roman Government*, 53–65, cited in Witherington, *Acts*, 723.

975. Rapske, *Custody*, 56.

976. Witherington, *Acts*, 723.

977. Schnabel, *Acts*, 993n30, noting lack of concrete evidence for this claim (citing Litewski, "Appellation," 86–87; Omerzu, *Prozess*, 89, 100, 494).

978. See Rapske, *Custody*, 56–62; Lentz, *Luke's Portrait*, 139–70, esp. 168–70; on the importance of status in Roman courts (though written into law only in the second century), see further Lentz, *Luke's Portrait*, 110–11, 115–17. Lentz argues (124–30) that governors possessed considerable latitude in making decisions, allowing exceptions to the rights of Roman citizens, and that (125) laws protecting citizens were more useful to those of high status.

979. In Pliny *Ep.* 6.31, the emperor hears a case of adultery but (6.31.6) wishes not to have such cases referred to him.

980. Jeffers, *World*, 199.

981. Johnson, *Acts*, 422.

982. Rapske, *Custody*, 188; idem, "Citizenship," 217; cf., e.g., Garnsey, "*Lex Iulia*," 184–85.

983. Rapske, *Custody*, 188; idem, "Citizenship," 217.

984. Some think that it could also appear to circumvent the emperor's authority (Jeffers, *World*, 169); this might prove less relevant in the case of strong grounds for an acquittal, but it is reasonable that Festus would not take the risk.

more likely), he had every reason to grant Paul's request (and even pretend to the local authorities that it would be inadvisable for him not to grant it). This decision would quickly remove a political complication from Festus's hands without his having to condemn an innocent Roman citizen or enrage the local elite.[985]

VI. REFUSING JUDEAN JURISDICTION

Paul's concern is not Roman but Jewish jurisdiction; Paul could demand his right as a citizen to be judged without interference from local laws.[986] Paul may refuse the implicit jurisdiction of an incompetent tribunal, the Sanhedrin[987] (even though the final judge was Festus himself, 25:9). Thus a Roman administrator prosecuted in Greece for corruption appealed to Rome's tribunes during the late republic, complaining "that he could not have a fair trial in Greece against Greeks" (Plut. *Caes.* 4.2).[988] Where local laws (such as the chief priests' interpretation of Judean laws, Acts 25:7–8) conflicted with Roman law, a Roman citizen could be referred to the emperor, though the latter often "decided in favour of local law."[989] (Provincial citizens of Rome or of free cities could choose between the jurisdiction of the local courts and that of Roman courts.)[990]

When possible, Paul had apparently submitted to Jewish courts (2 Cor 11:24); for a Jew to appeal to Romans to be delivered from Jewish punishments was to break from solidarity with one's Jewish community.[991] Earlier in Acts, Paul was "rescued" from a Jewish mob (Acts 21:30–32; 23:27) and Jewish accusers (18:14–15) without denying Jewish jurisdictions. Here, however, he denies the highest-ranking leaders of his people rightful jurisdiction over his case. He has already argued that what is at stake is a purely Jewish religious issue (24:20–21), but he uses his Roman citizenship to keep the trial under completely Roman auspices. He probably does so because he recognizes that his life is at stake (25:3), just as he avoided a beating because it was potentially deadly (22:25). Historically, Paul did appeal to his advantages when necessary, even boasting when "forced" to do so.[992]

It is, however, too much to view this as a rupture between "Judaism" and "Christianity," which must be tried as a new religion.[993] Why then would Luke focus so much of his work on the continuity between the church and its heritage in Israel? Why would Paul explain this continuity to Jewish leaders in Rome (28:20, 23), and that he was forced to appeal not to accuse his nation but to defend his life (28:19)? Why do his speeches emphasize his solidarity with his Jewish heritage (24:14–17, 21; 26:4–7, 22, 27)? The point is less theological; Paul wishes to save his life and perhaps also to establish positive legal precedents testifying that Christians are protected—as a legitimate form of the ancient faith of Israel.

985. Cf. Stambaugh and Balch, *Environment*, 31–32; Johnson, *Acts*, 423; Rowe, *World*, 83.

986. Only a severe situation demanding the restoration of public order (as in Jos. *War* 2.229–31; and this soldier was undoubtedly an auxiliary, in any case) would override this right. Garnsey thinks that Paul simply rejects Festus's proposal (Acts 25:9) as unjust (using the ancient principle of *reiectio*; "Criminal Jurisdiction," 56–57); but while this principle may play a part, by itself it does not explain the need to appeal to Caesar (see Rapske, *Custody*, 187, with Lintott, "Provocatio," 264–65).

987. Fitzmyer, *Acts*, 745. Certainly Paul has reason to distrust the Sanhedrin (Acts 23:16–22).

988. Trans. B. Perrin, *Lives*, LCL, 7:449.

989. Honoré, "Law and Procedure," 829.

990. Hence the governor or emperor (Stambaugh and Balch, *Environment*, 31). The bipartite system of local Egyptian courts and Greek-speaking circuit judges that was used in Egypt was abandoned in the mid-first century C.E. (Lewis, *Life*, 186–87).

991. Cf. Riesner, *Early Period*, 150. For the Jewish community's frustration over such appeals (even by those who were not Roman citizens), see, e.g., Safrai, "Self-Government," 408.

992. According to convention, although he inverts some of the substance of boasting (see, e.g., Keener, *Corinthians*, 221–22).

993. Cf. Tajra, "Appel à César."

Luke uses Paul's appeal to Caesar to reinforce the picture of his high status;[994] it was important for the Gentile Christian movement, as a mostly marginal minority in a status-conscious society, to be able to point to a leader who was of status. Eventually Paul, like Jesus, was unjustly executed; but both were exonerated by Roman judges, and Paul was of significant status (certainly not less than most of Luke's target audience in places such as Philippi and Corinth, where many of the Christians would have been Roman citizens).[995] That Luke so employs Paul's appeal, however, no more requires that Luke invented the appeal than that he invented Paul's Roman citizenship or that he invented the character of Paul.

VII. HISTORICAL CONCLUSIONS

Whatever one makes of the details of Luke's narrative here, those skeptical that Paul was a Roman citizen (or that his citizenship played a part in the trials) have a harder time explaining how Paul ended up in Roman (as opposed to local) custody and, very likely, how he ended up in custody in Rome itself (cf. Phil 4:22, though not all take this as custody in Rome).[996] Luke surely did not invent a Roman custody of up to two years in Caesarea, since Luke consistently portrays earlier Roman courts exonerating Paul;[997] inventing additional captivity would undercut Luke's own apologetic.[998] Yet we know that Paul expected potential conflict in Judea (Rom 15:31).

If Paul faced conflict with Judeans, how did this conflict eventuate in a protracted Roman detention, followed at some point by Paul's detention in Rome, without his being either released or handed over to local authorities to be punished according to local laws? Does not his Roman citizenship help explain such historical details (see comment on Acts 16:37)?

Further, in a document still extant but probably not read by Luke, Paul already had expressed his hope to travel to Rome after Jerusalem, in any case (Rom 15:22–25). Is it not therefore plausible that his interest had something to do with him reaching that destination (as here in Acts 25:10–11)? Any proposed legal anomalies make sense in terms of a governor's *extra ordinem* ruling and the political sensitivities of the current Judean situation. Luke's basic narrative seems plausible and consistent with other evidence. Thus, given his access to reliable information here (the "we" narrative), the work's historical genre, and the work's correspondence with major details of Paul's life (such as churches founded in particular regions) in Paul's letters, we have every reason to take Luke's claims on the matter seriously. Certainly we should take them more seriously than we should take modern speculation offered without corresponding evidence (which too often counts skepticism of Luke's narrative as itself the only necessary evidence for a contrary position).

VIII. FESTUS'S CONSILIUM (25:12)

Scholars generally recognize that the term συμβούλιον refers here to Festus's *consilium*, or advisory council, consisting of his *consiliarii* or *assessores*, his legal advisors.[999]

---

994. Neyrey, "Location of Paul," 278, following Lentz, *Luke's Portrait*, 139–53.

995. If Luke contrasts the status of Jesus as a Galilean artisan-sage with that of Paul as a rhetorically trained Roman citizen artisan-sage (while praising both), he could have found OT precedent in the inversion of Joseph (from slave to prince of Egypt) in Moses (from prince of Egypt to identifying with slaves).

996. With Riesner, *Early Period*, 155–56.

997. Such precedents are useful for Luke's apologetic, and Luke certainly does not amplify Paul's public punishments (2 Cor 11:23, 25).

998. See further discussion of this apologetic in, e.g., Keener, "Apologetic."

999. E.g., Sherwin-White, *Society*, 48–49; Haenchen, *Acts*, 668; Bruce, *Commentary*, 479; Fitzmyer, *Acts*, 731. On the *consilium*, see, e.g., Crook, *Advocacy*, 66–67, 99; Buckland, *Roman Law*, 635. In later centuries

The term applied to any ruling or advisory body,[1000] including the advisors of a ruler,[1001] of a general,[1002] or of governors.[1003] Because a judge would consult his *consilium* on legal matters (Cic. *Quinct.* 10.1), Cicero could appeal to the *consilium* as well as to the judge (1.4; 2.1; 6.1; 30.91). The emperor might choose for his own *consilium* members experienced in case law, for a fixed period of time (e.g., Pliny *Ep.* 6.31.1); naturally, any advisors taken to the provinces with governors would retain this capacity for a longer period. In the case of a governor, these would be his higher officials in addition to younger men who had come with him to learn effective provincial administration.[1004] The *assessores* (members of the *consilium*) might share the official's dinner table and entertainments.[1005]

Legal expertise was not a prerequisite for the office of governor, hence the need for consulting those more informed in the laws;[1006] magistrates thus often depended on advice of their councils, though making the final decisions themselves.[1007] Thus Josephus observes that those high in government had to be accompanied by counselors knowledgeable in their laws (*Ag. Ap.* 2.177), but notes that the Jewish people as a whole are very skilled in their laws (2.178). Paul's appeal is the sort of case for which a magistrate would surely consult his *consilium*; the emperor Trajan consulted his in an analogous case of defendants who rejected the dropping of their trial without official vindication (Pliny *Ep.* 6.31.11–12).

When judging cases *extra ordinem*, the governor was not bound by laws observed in Rome, but he would still consult with advisors and (in the case of more diligent governors) render justice as carefully as possible. In Paul's case, news of a denial of his appeal might reach Rome if he was thought to have many supporters (Acts 24:5); but the more important issue was that sending Paul to Rome relieved Festus of responsibility in a politically difficult situation. As Ajith Fernando puts it, Festus "must have been relieved by Paul's appeal to Caesar, for he could now wash his hands of the case."[1008]

Festus's concise "To Caesar you appealed, to Caesar you will go" might be intended as a direct quote of the educated governor; it is rhetorically balanced, with almost the same beginning in both clauses (except that ἐπί is necessary for the second) and similar-sounding verb endings (-σαι and -ση).[1009]

---

a *consilium* would include even a genuine jurist, but this resource was probably not available in this period (Crook, *Advocacy*, 193).

1000. Elsewhere in the NT, only for the Sanhedrin (Mark 3:6; 15:1; Matt 12:14; 22:15; 27:1, 7; 28:12), but nowhere in Luke-Acts and certainly not here.

1001. E.g., 4 Macc 17:17; Jos. *Ant.* 16.163; Philo *Spec. Laws* 4.175; *Embassy* 203–4, 206; cf. *Migr.* 136.

1002. E.g., Livy 44.34.2 (*consilium*). For the *consilium* more generally, including the use of family councils, see Lacey, "*Patria potestas*," 137–40; Voss, "Consilium."

1003. E.g., Philo *Embassy* 254; cf. *Flacc.* 18. See O'Rourke, "Law," 175.

1004. Bruce, *Commentary*, 479.

1005. Pliny *Ep.* 6.31.13–14 (on Trajan's generosity; but the relationships might grow even closer in a foreign province).

1006. Ferguson, *Backgrounds*, 51. Roman laws were not standardized or even collected in this period, making sufficient mastery of them difficult.

1007. See, e.g., O'Rourke, "Law," 174; Stambaugh and Balch, *Environment*, 32.

1008. Fernando, *Acts*, 593. Fernando's image of washing hands could remind modern readers of Pilate in Matt 27:24, though it functioned more widely as a repudiation of responsibility for innocent blood in Jewish tradition (see Deut 21:6–7; Ps 26:6; Isa 1:15–16; *Let. Aris.* 306; cf. G. Pet. frg. 1.1; for pagan usage, see Hom. *Il.* 6.266–68; Virg. *Aen.* 2.719; Soph. *Ajax* 654; Hdt. 1.35; in Blinzler, *Trial*, 217–18; Brown, *Death*, 834).

1009. The repetition of opening words is anaphora (albeit incomplete here because of the ἐπί; yet even this ἐπί serves a rhetorical function by balancing the beginning of ἐπικαλέω). End rhyme is homoeoteleuton (or, if the case had been the same here, homoeoptoton); see Rowe, "Style," 138; Porter, "Paul and Letters," 581; Lee, "Translations: Greek," 779; Black, "Oration at Olivet," 85–86; Anderson, *Glossary*, 78; cf., e.g., Mus. Ruf. 6, p. 54.12–13). These two verbs appear together in Hos 7:11 LXX, but in synthetic parallelism; given the application to sin there, an allusion here is extremely unlikely.

6. Festus Discusses Paul's Case with Agrippa (25:13–22)

In this private scene (though even more so in the private scene in 26:30–32), Luke shows us what the Roman governor really thinks about Paul's case once political considerations can be laid aside. Paul's accusers are not eager to follow Roman procedure (25:15–16), and Festus knows that the charges are simply theological disagreements (25:18–19), as Paul has been insisting.

a. Introduction

Although Agrippa's appearances frame the scene (25:13, 22), its heart is Festus's sharing his own opinion of the case (particularly Paul's innocence with respect to Roman law, 25:14–21). This scene raises two important introductory questions, the first more historical and the second more literary. First, what, if anything, is Luke's source for this private scene? Second, how do we make sense of Festus's apparent conviction of Paul's innocence in the logic of the larger narrative, in which he sends him to Rome as a prisoner?

i. Luke's Source?

What is Luke's source for the information in this scene?[1010] His potential "inside sources" for earlier matters in the Herodian family (Luke 8:3; Acts 13:1) might well be deceased and, in any case, certainly were no longer members of that circle. Some biblical prophets were able to supernaturally recount details to which they were not naturally privy (2 Kgs 6:12),[1011] and it is not impossible that Luke, who believes that the era of the Spirit and prophetic empowerment has come (Acts 2:17–18), believes himself guided by the Spirit. Josephus himself indicates that the belief in narrators with inspired insights remained current and available as a potential paradigm for pious writers.[1012]

If, however, Luke simply constructs this scene on the basis of inference from what he knows from public events in 25:24–27 and what could be expected of local advisors to incoming procurators, he acts within the bounds of most Hellenistic and Roman historiography.[1013] The event of the meeting and the substance of conversa-

1010. Various discussions of these issues appear, including (besides sources cited below) Yoo, "Entretien." That ancients sometimes considered sources for "inside information" is suggested by occasions where they supply it, including in fiction (e.g., Philost. *Vit. Apoll.* 3.27).

1011. Jos. *Ag. Ap.* 1.37 believes that biblical prophets wrote accounts wholly from inspiration. Greeks also believed that the Muses could provide information to an omniscient narrator whose information was otherwise lacking (e.g., Hom. *Il.* 2.484–92; 11.218; *Od.* 1.1; sources in Gordon, *Civilizations*, 224–25); in another culture, Nagy, "Prologue," xxxiii–xxxiv, cites a ninth-century Irish epic supposedly recounted to the poet by the deceased hero Fergus. When Odysseus recounts part of his own story, conversations of the gods and anything else he could not know naturally depend on superhuman beings such as Calypso, who heard the information from Hermes (Hom. *Od.* 12.389–90). I myself sometimes dream parts of biblical narrative in my sleep; in principle, someone prone to believe their dreams or even (in poetically engaged states) daydreams as revelatory might appeal to such experiences to reconstruct events. Normally, however, they would state this sort of source (since it would be considered authoritative for relevant genres), which does not normally appear to be employed in composing historical narratives.

1012. Many scholars contend that Josephus viewed himself as a prophetic historian (Hill, *Prophecy*, 27; Braun, "Prophet"; Mason, *Josephus and New Testament*, 20–21). On Josephus, *Jubilees*, and inspired history, see Hall, "History," 13–46; idem, *Histories*.

1013. Cf., e.g., Tac. *Ann.* 14.57; 15.59; Quint. Curt. 3.2.11–16 (the speaker dies in 3.2.17, and Darius, whom he addressed, soon after); cf. also speeches for opposing armies, e.g., Tac. *Ann.* 14.35. Polybius is more rigorous than most, insisting on accurate sources rather than mere plausibility (Polyb. 3.33.17–18, esp. 17) or imagining probable utterances (2.56.10). Omniscient narrators in their fullest form were better reserved for epic poetry (e.g., Sil. It. 9.66–177, 340–45; Judg 5:28–30), though they also appear in fiction (Char. *Chaer.* 1.12.2–4; Ach. Tat. 6.17) and elsewhere; in Jewish texts, see, e.g., Judg 3:24–25; Tob 5:16; Jdt 12:16; 1 Macc

tion might be safely inferred, and a good historian could develop this substance into an interesting dialogue scene. Historians regularly composed speeches; the less information historians had concerning the actual speech offered on the occasion, the greater the need for their creativity, according to the rhetorical canon of appropriate speech in character, would be necessary.[1014] The author of 1 Maccabees offers Antiochus's lament to his friends (1 Macc 6:10–13), even though the author could not have known this and presumably would not have pretended to know it.[1015] On the basis of what happened in public, Josephus can infer (or guess) what was said in private (e.g., *War* 2.319). Even Tacitus, perhaps the historian of the early empire most respected today, sometimes indulges in reporting characters' thoughts and fears (e.g., *Hist.* 2.74); he probably does so more often than Luke, precisely because Tacitus is more rhetorically sophisticated than is Luke.

This historical approach is not defective, just different from our own; modern historians simply take account of it when reading ancient historians, so as to reproduce the latter's essential information in ways more amenable to modern approaches. As Ben Witherington points out, although Luke normally edits genuine sources, this section is "not the sort of material Luke would likely have access to"; thus he "may be following the advice of his predecessors in making the speakers say what was appropriate to the occasion."[1016] Or as Barrett puts it (with regard to Festus's summary of the heart of the debate in Acts 25:19), "Luke can only have guessed at the contents of any conversation between Agrippa and Festus; but it was a good guess."[1017]

II. Festus's Perspective

At some points in the dialogue, Festus's description of events differs from Luke's prior narrative. Thus, whereas Festus claims that he would not "grant" Paul over to his adversaries without trial (25:16), Luke earlier says that Festus had planned to "grant" Paul to them at some level (cf. 25:9, 11).[1018] This is not a matter of rewording the basic substance (as in Luke 24:48–51 with Acts 1:8–9) or of prophetic license (as in Acts 21:11, 30–33) but more like a slight shading of the truth in one's favor, as in Lysias's report in 23:27. Festus is not a completely reliable character here, though he is also not a hostile one like Paul's accusers.

In this section Festus indicates that he needs to understand Jewish politics better so that he can frame his letter to the emperor most knowledgeably; unlike Felix,

---

6:10–13; 2 Macc 3:37–39. Sheeley finds Luke's asides for general information closest to historical narratives, though he finds disclosures of inside views only in romances (*Asides*, 179; he concludes that genres overlapped too much for these diverging pointers to tell us Luke's genre; probably they suggest a more popular, less sophisticated level of historiography). But most historians did construct scenes based on inference; Josephus reports private conversations in direct discourse in *Ant.* 19.38–45, 53–58, 78–83, even though most of his potential witnesses for the scenes died soon after the scenes that he recounts.

1014. Fornara, *Nature of History*, 167–68; more fully, this commentary's introductory chapter concerning speeches (Keener, *Acts*, 1:258–319). The Greek in Festus's speech (Acts 25:14–20) is fairly polished (with two optatives in 25:16), fitting a conversation between two highly educated Greek-speakers (Witherington, *Acts*, 729n401).

1015. Similarly, 2 Macc 3:37–39 reports Heliodorus's conversation with the king of Syria. In pure fiction, cf. the similar reporting of inaccessible speech (Ach. Tat. 6.17) or thoughts (Char. *Chaer.* 1.12.2–4); in epic, cf. the frequent scenes on Olympus, and even what one Thracian was dreaming before he was slain in his sleep (Hom. *Il.* 10.496–97)!

1016. Witherington, *Acts*, 119–20. The vast majority of scholars do believe that Luke constructed the scene (e.g., Jervell, *Apostelgeschichte*, 586; see this commentary's introductory chapter on speeches [Keener, *Acts*, 1:258–319]).

1017. Barrett, *Acts*, 1139.

1018. See Tannehill, *Acts*, 309–11, emphasizing (*pace* Haenchen) that Festus speaks as an unreliable character here, contradicting the reliable narrator's voice. Witherington, *Acts*, 729, concurs.

he lacks understanding of the relevant issues (24:22, 24), as both he (25:20) and the defendant (26:24–26) recognize. How can he explain to the emperor why he is forwarding an appeal of a person who appears innocent yet cannot simply be freed?[1019] He needs the advice—or perhaps the clear approval—of the Jewish king. If the ruling priestly families oppose Paul (25:2), Festus can go "over their head," from a Roman perspective, by appealing to Agrippa II, who is authorized by Rome to appoint high priests (Jos. *Ant.* 20.179, 196). This also secures Festus politically vis-à-vis Rome; Nero himself had recently expanded Agrippa's territories (20.159).

Festus, however, is already convinced that Paul is innocent of any crimes that could warrant death (Acts 25:18–19, 25). Some scholars therefore suggest that the logic appears fragile but appears so because Luke is pointing to Festus's political motives. Festus's request of advice for a letter to Caesar (25:26) is a ploy; his real audience will be the Jerusalem aristocrats. Agrippa and Berenice were hellenized and romanized, "perfectly sound spokespersons for the Jews who mattered"; if they could publicly concur with Festus's suspicion that this was a purely intra-Jewish religious affair,[1020] Festus could send Paul on with a letter to that effect while everyone saved face. Although the Jerusalem leaders might complain, Paul's appeal rescues Festus from the blame. "And the Emperor would respect the judgment of a 'Jewish king' that Paul's troubles stemmed from disputes over a superstition and that it was only his stubborn appeal that forced his delivery to the higher court (26:32)."[1021]

Whether these political motives supply Festus's whole motivation is debatable, but at the least they suggest some of the shrewd calculations necessary to address the politics of the situation. With Agrippa's support, Festus can achieve what he needs without unnecessarily alienating his new constituency. (Josephus's support of Festus's procuratorship suggests that whatever the response to his sending away of Paul, much of Jerusalem's aristocracy was mostly pleased with his performance.)

Luke has special interest in the Herod family,[1022] although the earlier sources available for historical information about what Herods said in their courts (Luke 8:3; Acts 13:1) would not be available here. Luke also parallels these Herodians with predecessors in his narrative: earlier Herod Antipas and Pilate became political allies through Jesus (Luke 23:12) as Agrippa II and Festus here do through Paul. But the contrast is more important (see comment on Acts 25:13). Agrippa and Berenice are especially important here as the highest-ranking officials to show openness to Paul and his mission, the first Jewish rulers to receive God's new messengers positively (previous Herods opposed John, Jesus, and Peter; Luke 3:20; 9:9; 13:31–32; 23:11; Acts 4:27; 12:1–23).

b. The Visit of Agrippa and Berenice (25:13)

Following appropriate protocol, Agrippa and his sister Berenice visit the new procurator. These two figures played a prominent role in Judean politics not only during this hearing of Paul but after the Judean war, and they may have been known

1019. Cf. Witherington, *Acts,* 726.
1020. He could hand Paul over to their judgment for these purely religious matters so long as they would relinquish the capital sentence; but Paul's appeal to Rome provided an easier alternative, taking matters off his hands.
1021. Johnson, *Acts,* 427. The imperial court might well dismiss the case with a warning against frivolous appeals!
1022. Cf. Luke 1:5; 3:1, 19; 9:7, 9; 13:31; 23:7–12, 15; Acts 4:27; 12:1–23. By contrast, Matthew includes only two major scenes with Herods, one borrowed from Mark's only major scene (which Luke strangely omits!). On Luke's approach to the Herod family, in light of his approach toward Rome, see Horn, "Haltung," 215–24.

to better-educated or better-traveled members of Luke's audience. (As members of the Judean royal family, who continued to play significant roles, they were probably better known than Felix or Festus, who were two among many local governors.)

I. AGRIPPA II IN HISTORY

Agrippa I (Acts 12:1) had two sons (Drusus, who died in childhood, and Agrippa II), and three daughters (Berenice, Mariamne, and Drusilla; Jos. *Ant.* 18.132). Marcus Julius Agrippa (Agrippa II) was born in 27 C.E. to King Agrippa I and his wife Cyprus (Jos. *War* 2.220). Agrippa II was seventeen when his father died (Jos. *Ant.* 19.354), an event reported in Acts 12:23.[1023] Claudius was ready to send Agrippa II to replace Agrippa I, but because his advisors persuaded him that the son was as yet too young to rule such a troubled province, he sent Cuspius Fadus as procurator (Jos. *Ant.* 19.360–63). When Agrippa II's uncle, Herod of Chalcis, died in 48 C.E., Claudius appointed Agrippa ruler of his territory, and Cumanus took the rest of the land (Jos. *War* 2.223).[1024]

Later, after Agrippa had demonstrated his administrative competence and loyalty to Rome, Claudius withdrew Chalcis and gave Agrippa the larger territories of Herod Philip and Lysanias (*War* 2.247; *Ant.* 20.138–39; cf. Luke 3:1).[1025] Nero further entrusted him with Tiberias, Taricheae, and part of Perea (Jos. *Ant.* 20.159).[1026] Agrippa II honored Nero by renaming Caesarea Philippi "Neronias," although the name reverted after Nero's disgraceful death.[1027] Agrippa II apparently had his own palace at Caesarea Philippi.[1028] Although Agrippa I was also a king (Acts 12:1), as was Herod the Great (Luke 1:5), Luke emphasizes the much smaller kingship of Agrippa II much more (Acts 25:13–14, 24, 26; 26:2, 7, 13, 19, 26–27, 30), perhaps partly because this appearance offers one fulfillment of Jesus's promise of his servants testifying before kings (Luke 21:12), and because Agrippa II also offers a more positive response.

II. BERENICE IN HISTORY

Although she lacks distinct public speaking parts, Luke includes references to Berenice as a prominent figure (one perhaps known to Diaspora Jews in his own day because of how close, some Jews believed, she came to becoming empress);[1029] she also participates in the positive verdict in Acts 25:30–31. This suggests Luke's continued interest in balancing genders as well as his primary interest of recruiting a number of prominent voices for positive verdicts on Paul. He seems to presuppose that his audience has heard of her, which would not be surprising given her role in major events that transpired after this narrative.

1023. For his sister Drusilla, see discussion at Acts 24:24.

1024. For the date, see Jos. *Ant.* 20.103–4.

1025. This happened the same year that Claudius installed Felix as governor of Judea (Jos. *Ant.* 20.137–38).

1026. This was in Nero's first year (Jos. *Ant.* 20.158), i.e., in the year starting in 54 C.E.

1027. Bruce, *Commentary*, 481.

1028. For a suggestion of its discovery, see Wilson and Tzaferis, "Banias Dig." Caesarea Philippi was famous for its grotto for Pan worship, attested in its earlier name "Paneas" (which has persisted even in its modern Arabic name, "Baniyas," in various sources styled also Banias or Banyas); cf. Pliny E. *N.H.* 5.15.71; Jos. *War* 1.404; *b. B. Bat.* 74b; Cornfeld, *Josephus*, 458. Christian tradition claimed that public pagan rites continued there until a later Christian miraculously demonstrated that Jesus was more powerful (Euseb. *H.E.* 7.17). On pagan worship there, see most fully Tzaferis, "Cults"; Tzaferis and Avner, "Hpyrwt." Pan was worshiped especially by pastoralists (e.g., Longus 2.26–31; 4.39) and honored at other caves (e.g., Paus. 1.32.7) and wooded areas (e.g., 8.38.5); nevertheless, caves (10.32.6) and wooded areas (5.10.1) could also be sacred to other deities (cf. also the second- and third-century C.E. pagan temple in Upper Galilee in Magness, "Observations"; for caves and deities, see also discussion in Keener, "Cave").

1029. Her status would also be evident if she was on Vespasian's imperial *consilium* temporarily (as in Young-Widmaier, "Representation").

Although Luke prefers the abbreviated form Βερνίκη (25:13, 23; 26:30) and is not the only writer to employ this form (Jos. *War* 2.217), Josephus usually employs the fuller name Βερενίκη, which is followed in this commentary.[1030] (It was a common name in Macedonian royal families, latinized as "Veronica.")[1031] Berenice was born in 28 C.E.,[1032] the sister of Agrippa II (Jos. *War* 2.220; *Life* 343). She married Marcus, brother of Tiberius Julius Alexander, in 41 C.E., around the age of thirteen (*Ant.* 19.276). Her husband apparently died soon after their marriage (19.276–77); her father, Agrippa I, then married her to her uncle Herod, king of Chalcis (19.277, 354).[1033] Her father died in 44 C.E., when she was sixteen years old (19.354), and her new husband-uncle died in 48 or possibly 49.[1034] That she was unprepared to marry immediately afterward is not surprising.[1035]

After this event she stayed with her brother, Agrippa II, for several years. This stay unfortunately led to suspicions of incest, almost certainly false;[1036] in the ancient world even more than today, many people mistrusted powerful women unattached to a husband. The gossip about her was widespread, even outside Judea; Juvenal mocks the renowned diamond that "barbarian" Agrippa gave his "impure" (*incestae*) sister (*Sat.* 6.156–60, esp. 158).[1037] One scholar who doubts that the report is creditable nevertheless thinks it likely that "a Hellenistic philadelphic marriage" would not have horrified her or Agrippa.[1038] Even such a concession is improbable. Although the Egyptian practice of sibling marriage[1039] may have influenced Ptolemaic Egypt, the usual Greek custom allowed only paternal half-sisters.[1040] Otherwise, intercourse with one's sister was highly dishonorable.[1041] Berenice was Agrippa's full sister, born from the same mother (Jos. *War* 2.220).

To quell the rumors of incest, in 53/54 C.E. she married Polemon, a ruler in Cilicia, after her wealth apparently persuaded him to accept circumcision as a tolerable price for the marriage (Jos. *Ant.* 20.145–46; contrast comment on Drusilla at Acts 24:24). Yet the marriage did not prove tolerable; she quickly deserted him, and he immediately abandoned his pretense of Jewish conversion (*Ant.* 20.146).[1042] She may

1030. Manuscript C changes Luke's abbreviated form to the longer one (matching Jos. *Ant.* 20.145; Fitzmyer, *Acts*, 749). Some view Josephus's portrayals of Berenice as unduly tendentious (Krieger, "Schwester").
1031. Bruce, *Acts¹*, 434. In the Macedonian royal house and among the Ptolemies, see Ameling, Strothmann, and Pahlitzsch, "Berenice, 1–9."
1032. This date is based on her being sixteen when her father died in 44 C.E. (Jos. *Ant.* 19.354).
1033. Smallwood and Griffin, "Berenice," suggest 46 C.E., but Hemer, *Acts in History*, 173, rightly dates this earlier. Her father arranged the marriage, and it was in effect when he died (Jos. *Ant.* 19.277, 354).
1034. For the date, in the eighth year of Claudius's reign, see Jos. *Ant.* 20.104. The death of Herod of Chalcis also appears in *War* 2.221–23; that he was both husband and uncle, in *Ant.* 20.145; *War* 2.217 (cf. Lev 18:14).
1035. Events surrounding her father's death surely also traumatized her, as soldiers in Caesarea and Sebaste who hated her father seized images of her and her sisters and placed them in a brothel (Jos. *Ant.* 19.356–57), as was widely known (19.363). Photius inferred that the daughters themselves were raped; although it is possible that Josephus euphemizes here, he elsewhere calls her a virgin at marriage (19.277).
1036. Omitted by Suetonius, Tacitus, and Dio Cassius and not credited by Josephus; Juvenal, who supports it, was anti-Jewish and exploited any available rumors for satire. See the several studies by classicists that are adduced by L. H. Feldman in *Josephus*, LCL, 10:81 n. *d*; the most important of these are summarized by O'Toole, *Acts 26*, 17n5. This is not to deny her later affair with Titus (see comment below), a matter raised by some in this connection; but the issues would not likely be deemed comparable; Titus was not her sibling.
1037. On this rumor, see, e.g., Macurdy, "Julia Berenice"; Whittaker, *Jews and Christians*, 33.
1038. Macurdy, "Julia Berenice," 251.
1039. E.g., Paus. 1.7.1; Diod. Sic. 1.27.1; Sext. Emp. *Pyr.* 1.152; see comment on Acts 15:20.
1040. Ach. Tat. 1.3.1–2; Corn. Nep. 5 (Cimon), 1.2; cf. Corn. Nep. pref. 4.
1041. E.g., Plut. *Cic.* 29.4; Diod. Sic. 10.31.1; Gaius *Inst.* 1.61. On incest, cf. Keener, "Adultery," 12–14; idem, *Acts*, 3:2272–73.
1042. See summary of many of these points also in Smallwood and Griffin, "Berenice."

have remained with her brother Agrippa as late as 65–66;[1043] they apparently had close and possibly even adjoining palaces in Jerusalem (*War* 2.426).

Berenice was pious by the standards of the Herodian family (*War* 2.313) and in 66 C.E. vainly risked her life to protect the lives of her people (2.310–12, 314). She joined Jerusalem leaders in protesting Florus's massacres to the Syrian legate (2.333).[1044] Nevertheless, she suffered the resentment of revolutionaries retaliating against all symbols of their oppression; soon after her attempted intervention for peace, they burned both the homes of the wealthy, including hers, and the records of their debts (2.426–27). Later she secured her brother's mercy toward one Justus, condemned to death for his part in the revolt (*Life* 343, 355).[1045]

Berenice had a well-known love affair with Titus, the son of the general sent to suppress the Judean revolt and himself the general who finished it. He was about eleven years her junior, but even at about forty, Berenice was said to retain all her charm. When Titus turned back from his mission to Rome because of the emperor Galba's unexpected death, some wrongly thought that he turned back only because of longing for Berenice (Tac. *Hist.* 2.2). He apparently promised her marriage, though his love for Berenice engendered suspicions of his unchastity along with his alleged use of "catamites and eunuchs" (Suet. *Tit.* 7.1). After their love affair in Judea, Titus and Berenice lived together openly when she visited Rome (starting in 75 C.E.), but out of deference to Roman opinion he dared not marry her.

When Titus became emperor in 79 C.E., he observed the higher standard expected of his new status; he sent her from Rome against the wishes of both.[1046] When she visited Rome again, he refused to see her;[1047] imperial duty came before personal affection.[1048] Although Josephus protests that the temple's destruction was not Titus's fault (*War* 6.254–66),[1049] later Jewish sources blame him for it and seethe with hatred for him.[1050] The contrary destinies of two peoples inexorably rent apart by their respective ethnic histories doomed the couple's romance. With tragic consequences for individual lives enmeshed in Jewish or Roman society, nothing quickly erased the momentous collision of competing nationalisms, whether the ethnic reconciliation in Christ that Paul preached, Roman tolerance for loyal subjects, or Jewish teachings on love of neighbor.

There is no reason to think that Agrippa II and his sister Berenice were disappointed to see Felix replaced (Acts 24:27), convenient as it may have been to have a brother-in-law as procurator. Berenice reportedly had been jealous of her sister Drusilla's beauty

1043. Hemer, *Acts in History*, 173, interprets Jos. *War* 2.310–12 and *Life* 48 thus (which texts at least suggest their close cooperation).

1044. Agrippa was in Alexandria at that point (Jos. *War* 2.335).

1045. Theissen, *Gospels*, 88, notes as relevant the knowledge that she influenced legal proceedings (or even served as a judge; Quint. *Inst.* 4.1.19).

1046. Suet. *Tit.* 7.2; Dio Cass. 65.15.3–5. A later source, intensifying the pathos, claims that she had already publicly called herself Titus's wife (Dio Cass. 65.15), and still later it was said that Titus punished anyone suspected of intercourse with her (Aur. Vict. *Epit. Caes.* 10; Schürer, *Time of Jesus*, 243).

1047. See Dio Cass. 66.18.1; Reicke, *Era*, 286; Smallwood and Griffin, "Berenice"; Schürer, *Time of Jesus*, 243.

1048. Cf. Crook, "Titus and Berenice."

1049. Tac. *Hist.* frg. 2 disagrees. The Flavian dynasty probably appreciated Josephus's apologetic on its behalf (the soldiers made an easy scapegoat; cf. Tac. *Hist.* 3.70–71; 1 Sam 15:21), in view of the offense of destroying shrines and the large number of Jews remaining in the empire. Romans praised Titus's defeat of Jerusalem as heroic (Val. Flacc. 1.12–14; Suet. *Titus* 5.2).

1050. E.g., *Sipre Deut.* 328.1.1–5; *ʾAbot R. Nat.* 1 A; 7, §§20–21 B; *b. Giṭ.* 56b; *Lev. Rab.* 20:5; 22:3; *Num. Rab.* 18:22; *Eccl. Rab.* 5:8–9, §4. We may compare his supposed intercourse with prostitutes on a law scroll in the holiest place (*Lev. Rab.* 22:3; *Num. Rab.* 18:22) with rabbis' prohibition of intercourse even in a room with a Torah scroll (*b. Ber.* 25b).

(Jos. *Ant.* 20.143). The circumstances of Felix's marriage to Drusilla were also scandalous, contravening Jewish laws (20.143).[1051] The king of Emesa had been circumcised to marry Drusilla, but she left him for Felix, who never adopted Judaism himself; Jewish people were enraged, and so far as we can tell Agrippa II never granted the marriage official approval.[1052] By contrast, Agrippa and Festus apparently worked together on fairly good terms (20.193–96). (Unlike Festus, Felix, with his local experience, Jewish wife, and possible tensions with Agrippa, had never introduced Paul to Agrippa, though it is not impossible that the latter could have heard of Paul [cf. Acts 25:22].)

III. CHARACTERS IN LUKE'S NARRATIVE AND EXTRINSIC WORLDS

Why does Luke call Agrippa I only "Herod," reserving the name "Agrippa" for his son Agrippa II? Uninformed members of Luke's first audience might well blend the ill-fated oppressor of the apostles in Acts 12 with John the Baptist's wicked executioner in the Gospel (like the other Gospels, Luke calls Herod Antipas only "Herod"; Luke 3:19; 9:7–9; 13:31; 23:7–12; Acts 4:27). But Luke wants to portray Agrippa II very differently, and associations generated by a shared name "would run counter to the needs of the narrative," as Tannehill notes, "for the two kings play quite different roles." Herod is a persecutor whereas Agrippa supports Paul.[1053]

Luke has another reason for emphasizing the younger Agrippa's name with positive associations. He follows gospel tradition in designating Herod Antipas only "Herod" and wishes to associate Herod Agrippa I, who caters to Judean nationalists (Acts 12:3), with him.[1054] But even the first-century reader in Luke's especially northeastern Mediterranean world who was least knowledgeable in Judean affairs would recognize that Agrippa was a Roman name.[1055] The most famous bearer of this Roman cognomen was Marcus Vipsanius Agrippa, Augustus's son-in-law; by adopting this name, members of the Herodian family demonstrated their close connections with the members of the Julio-Claudian imperial family as their patrons.[1056] Those who knew more about Judea would know that Agrippa II remained a Jewish leader influential with and respected by Rome even during the period when Luke was writing; Luke, like Josephus, has good reason to portray this living figure favorably (in addition to Agrippa's apparently conciliatory character).

Berenice and Agrippa would not be offensive figures to pro-Roman readers; they clearly opposed the revolt and were pro-Roman to the end.[1057] Naturally, Festus would find Agrippa's company more congenial than that of the Jerusalem municipal elite, who, from his perspective, might seem intransigent, corrupt, and ungrateful for Rome's benefits toward their class. Further, if Festus found an ally in Agrippa, the high priests would have much less to say about the case.

1051. Berenice had her own affairs with Gentiles later (cf. already Jos. *Ant.* 20.146–47 and her later relationship with Titus), perhaps reflecting her younger sister's behavior.

1052. Stern, "Province," 365.

1053. Tannehill, *Acts*, 315; cf. Witherington, *Acts*, 738. See esp. here Dicken, *Herod*, who argues that from a narrative standpoint the three "Herods" in Luke-Acts function as a composite character (e.g., 145–48), whereas Agrippa II fulfills a very different role. Despite Paul's hearing before Agrippa II in (presumably still) Herod's praetorium (Acts 23:35; see Dicken, *Herod*, 153, 156–61, noting also other parallels), the outcome differs (see 155), in that Paul, unlike John the Baptist, Jesus, and James, is not executed here, because the good news cannot be stopped (165).

1054. For discussion of Luke's "Herods," see Keener, *Acts*, 2:1868–69. Josephus sometimes calls Antipas "Herod" (*Ant.* 18.104–6, 243–55).

1055. E.g., the famous baths of Agrippa in Rome (Mart. *Epig.* 3.20.15; 3.36.6).

1056. Williams, "Names," 100. Besides Agrippa I and II, see also Jos. *Ant.* 18.137; 20.143–44; and an Agrippinus (20.147).

1057. Smallwood and Griffin, "Berenice."

The chief priests would have to concede that Agrippa II, for all his Roman affinities, was a benefactor. When the chief priests' ambassadors to Caesar requested the return of priestly vestments, Agrippa, who was then in Rome, interceded on their behalf (Jos. *Ant.* 20.9). Caesar granted the request, informing the ambassadors that they had Agrippa to thank (20.10). Likewise, Claudius's "freedmen" and "friends" supported Cumanus and the Samaritans against the Jews (including the high priest Ananias, sent to Rome in 20.131), and the Judeans' opponents would have succeeded against them had not Agrippa, then still in Rome, persuaded the empress Agrippina in favor of the Jews (Jos. *Ant.* 20.135).

Still, Agrippa II probably had a better relationship with Festus than with some of the high priests. Agrippa had a conflict with Ishmael, the new high priest, over Agrippa's palace view of the temple courts (*Ant.* 20.189–93), which led him to replace Ishmael as high priest (20.196).[1058] For reasons of military security, Festus took Agrippa's side against Ishmael (20.193). Agrippa freely exercised his legal authority from the Romans to replace high priests (20.179, 195–96, 203, 223).

Significantly, Agrippa at some point was titled a "friend of Caesar" (*OGIS* 419). Educated in Rome (Jos. *Ant.* 19.360), he maintained his pro-Roman posture throughout his life (cf., e.g., Jos. *Life* 340).[1059] When Florus massacred Jerusalemites, Agrippa publicly reproved the elite among his own people to dissuade them from escalating the violence (*War* 2.337–38). Accusing Florus seemed too dangerous, but so was neglecting the Judean unrest (2.343); thus he and Berenice calmed the people and temporarily secured peace with Rome (2.344–406).

The Roman sympathies of Agrippa and Berenice would not have endeared them to everyone. When rioters destroyed the house of Ananias in the upper city, they also destroyed the palaces of Agrippa and Berenice (*War* 2.426). Agrippa struck a coin in 89 C.E. portraying Nike (goddess of victory), commemorating the Roman victory over Judea.[1060] For Luke, Agrippa II would be a character relating to Israel in an ambivalent manner, somewhat analogously to Paul (though Paul would never have commemorated Jerusalem's destruction): they were not always appreciated, but they pointed the way to the future by supporting peaceful coexistence with Rome and the Gentiles.[1061]

After 70 C.E., the mostly Pharisaic sages of Yavneh still recognized the legitimacy of Agrippa's dynasty,[1062] but when he finally died childless about 92 C.E., the Herodian ruling dynasty ended.[1063] He thus remained alive and widely respected during the period when Luke was probably writing. Luke does not portray as honorable the demise of Agrippa II's father, but neither does Josephus (see comment on Acts

1058. Agrippa himself had appointed Ishmael near the end of Felix's tenure (Jos. *Ant.* 20.179), as he appointed his successor (20.196). On the conflict, see further Goodman, *Ruling Class*, 141–42; Witherington, *Acts*, 719; cf. Fitzmyer, *Acts*, 749.

1059. Though he also defended the Jews against Cumanus and the Samaritans (Jos. *War* 2.245; *Ant.* 20.135). Josephus (and if Josephus, certainly many more conservative Jews) attributes divine judgment in part to Agrippa's "progressive" stance on Levitical attire (*Ant.* 20.216–18, with the cooperation of a Sanhedrin, perhaps Jerusalem's, 20.216).

1060. Meyshan, "Coin Type of Agrippa." For Agrippa's loyalty to Rome during the war, some scholars cite also the later summary of Photius *Bibl.* 33 (Bock, *Acts*, 709).

1061. He may have been less conservative religiously than Paul, but the point is that neither was a nationalist, Agrippa partly from pragmatic political realism but both out of genuine appreciation for and relationships with some Gentiles.

1062. Trifon, "Qt' mmsnh," thinks that they recognized Agrippa II's rule as legitimate, on the basis of *m. Soṭah* 7:8 (a text that at least indicates his father's, hence likely his own, legitimacy).

1063. Fitzmyer, *Acts*, 749; Bruce, *Commentary*, 482n14 (with a slightly later date). Further on Agrippa, see Stern, "Herod," 1:300–305; Eckey, *Apostelgeschichte*, 538–39.

12:23), who owed much to the benevolence of Agrippa II.[1064] Whatever many Judeans may have thought of Agrippa's policies during the war, he had clearly emerged as a popular voice for moderation and was well respected in the era in which Luke was probably writing, after voices for Jewish resistance were largely discredited (at least outside Judea and North Africa). His openness to Paul therefore provided Luke with one of his climactic examples of people of status (in this case, even much higher than Theophilus's possibly equestrian rank) respecting Paul's message.

IV. ROYAL CONGRATULATIONS TO THE NEW GOVERNOR

Hospitality and greetings were part of the fabric of politeness in Greek and Roman society (see comment on greetings in Acts 21:7). As governor, Cicero daily received at dawn "those who came to pay him their respects" (Plut. *Cic.* 36.3).[1065] Offering congratulations was part of the culture as well,[1066] including congratulations to new officials or governors.[1067] Thus, for example, when Alexander became a leader, other leaders among the Greeks allegedly came to congratulate him (Plut. *Alex.* 14.1); Titus was on his way to congratulate Galba for his accession (but stopped in Corinth when he learned that Galba had died and others vied for power; Tac. *Hist.* 2.1). To breach protocol by not properly welcoming visitors of high social status risked insulting them and generating enmity (cf. Plut. *Caes.* 60.3).[1068] One who had good reason might request permission to be excused.[1069]

We know that Agrippa II took seriously the obligation of congratulating new rulers.[1070] A few years after the events that Luke describes here, Agrippa was in Alexandria congratulating Alexander for receiving the governorship of Egypt from Nero (Jos. *War* 2.309).[1071] Agrippa also met Cestius Gallus, legate of Syria,[1072] at Antioch (2.481),[1073] and Vespasian (3.29). He also accompanied Titus when he went to congratulate Galba; Titus stopped when he learned of Galba's assassination, as noted above, but Agrippa continued so that he could congratulate whoever became emperor (4.498–501). (At Berenice's urging, however, he returned to take the oath of allegiance to Vespasian [Tac. *Hist.* 2.81].)[1074] "The conclusion to be drawn from all of these visits," Robert O'Toole notes, is that "we would expect the visit of Agrippa II and Bernice to the newly appointed Festus in Acts 25:13ff."[1075] Agrippa and Berenice would visit Festus

---

1064. Agrippa also allegedly appreciated Josephus's account in the *Jewish War* (so *Ag. Ap.* 1.51–52); Foakes-Jackson, *Acts*, 221, suggests his patronage.

1065. Trans. B. Perrin, *Lives*, LCL, 7:173.

1066. E.g., Statius wrote a congratulatory poem to a friend who had recovered from an illness (*Silv.* 1.4, to Rutilius Gallicus); another offers congratulations on a new prospective son-in-law (Pliny *Ep.* 6.26.1). Agrippa I entertained visiting dignitaries (Jos. *Ant.* 19.338–39) and went out to greet Syria's governor (19.340).

1067. See, e.g., Dio Chrys. *Or.* 40.13 (to the emperor); Pliny *Ep.* 4.8.1; 10.43.3; Friedländer, *Life*, 1:211. See comment on ἀπάντησις at Acts 28:15.

1068. Caesar's refusal to rise to greet the senators in that passage would have been appropriate, however, if he was of much higher social station (Plut. *Caes.* 60.5).

1069. E.g., Pliny *Ep.* 9.37.1–5.

1070. Likewise, the high priests and powerful Jerusalemites met Agrippa II to congratulate him on his safe return before entreating a favor (Jos. *War* 2.336).

1071. Tiberius Alexander was an apostate from Judaism (Jos. *Ant.* 20.100), to whom Alexandrian Jews responded ambivalently, though the elite seem to have favored him (*War* 2.492–93); he immediately pledged his support to Vespasian in the civil war following Nero's death (4.616–17).

1072. See Jos. *War* 2.280; cf. *Life* 214.

1073. Cestius Gallus soon after marched the twelfth legion from Antioch to suppress Judean unrest (Jos. *War* 2.499–500).

1074. See discussion of each of these passages in O'Toole, *Acts 26*, 16. Vespasian knew Berenice's loyalty; later he apparently had Berenice on his imperial *consilium*, at least temporarily, when she was in Rome (75–79 C.E.; so Young-Widmaier, "Representation," from Quint. *Inst.* 4.1.19).

1075. O'Toole, *Acts 26*, 17.

in "Herod's praetorium" (Acts 23:25)—that is, a palace built initially by their own famous ancestor.[1076]

Historically, Agrippa and Festus probably established a good working relationship (Jos. *Ant.* 20.193–96);[1077] given both the problems of Festus's predecessor, Felix, and the helpfulness of Agrippa's being more romanized than most of the Jerusalem elite, it is reasonable to suppose that they sought to establish a good relationship from the first visit. In Luke's narrative, Festus and Agrippa use the case of Paul to "bond": Festus requests the favor of Agrippa's counsel; Agrippa responds affirmatively; and according to Roman reciprocity conventions, they establish *amicitia*, friendship.[1078] In a similar way, Luke suggests that Pilate and Herod Antipas used Jesus as a political pawn to establish their own relationship. Formerly at enmity, they established a friendship relationship by showing respect to each other on Jesus's account (Luke 23:12).[1079]

Because Agrippa was likely still alive and in favor when Luke wrote,[1080] it would be precarious for Luke to invent Agrippa's presence at Paul's hearing if Agrippa was not in fact present. To publish a document one hoped to circulate widely yet include false information about important persons whose enmity such publication could earn was hubris—not impossible, but neither is it the likeliest hypothesis. Josephus, probably writing later than Luke, likewise notes that he dares not have falsified information while witnesses such as Agrippa remain alive (*Ag. Ap.* 1.50–51); he complains about his rival who waited until after eyewitnesses were dead to publish his rival side of the story (*Life* 359–60).

c. Festus's Proposal (25:14–21)

Festus broaches the matter of Paul with Agrippa, apparently in the course of conversation. Recognizing Agrippa's romanization, he can ask for counsel about how to deal with a case for which he is culturally ill prepared: local Judean authorities want to condemn Paul on grounds completely unacceptable to Roman law. Festus needs to uphold Roman law but does not wish to exacerbate conflict with local leaders. Paul, the Roman citizen, prefers appealing to Rome to being tried in Jerusalem; although this relieves Festus of partial responsibility, he still needs to know what to write in a letter that will become publicly accessible (Acts 25:26).

i. Broaching Paul's Case (25:14–15)

Agrippa and Berenice's stay of "many days" is apparently longer than Festus's stay of eight to ten days in Jerusalem (25:6).[1081] Festus went to Jerusalem almost immediately (25:1); the royal siblings' courtesy visit is about two weeks after Festus's

---

1076. Possibly they or some other wealthy members of the Herod family had a country villa near Caesarea (on one such villa, see Hirschfeld and Vamosh, "Estate"), but their main residence was in Caesarea Philippi.

1077. Also suggested by O'Toole, *Acts 26*, 17.

1078. See Keener, "Friendship," 381.

1079. On the nature of such relationships among political peers (especially in Roman culture), see, e.g., Plut. *Ages.* 23.6; *Pomp.* 70.4; *Statecraft* 13, *Mor.* 806F–809B; *Phil. Power* 1, *Mor.* 776AB; *Old Men* 6, *Mor.* 787B; Ach. Tat. 4.6.1–3. Even Aristotle, who notes friendships based on goodness, pleasure, or utility (*E.E.* 7.2.9–13, 1236a; 7.10.10, 1242b; *N.E.* 8.13.1, 1162ab), assigns most to utility (*E.E.* 7.2.14, 1236a).

1080. Agrippa II may have died in 93 c.e.; some even argue for 100 c.e. (Hoehner, "Herod," 698). Some have advanced arguments that Acts postdates this period (see most influentially and persuasively Tyson, "Date of Acts," and esp. Pervo, *Dating Acts*), although, with the majority of scholars at the time of my writing, I believe that a date before 100 and even before 90 is more likely (see the argument in Keener, *Acts*, 1:383–401).

1081. Entertaining royal guests was an important diplomatic courtesy (cf., e.g., Jos. *Ant.* 19.339). One of the tasks of the provincial governor was diplomacy, given his limited staff; Millar, *Empire and Neighbours*, 63–64, views Acts 25:13 in this light. Luke's ambiguous "many days" may seek to avoid needless details distracting from the point (cf. 27:7, 20), but in view of his details elsewhere may simply indicate that he did not know the period's exact duration (cf. the phrase in 9:23; 18:18). Although only comparison of 9:23 with Galatians

arrival, but after he has finished in Jerusalem and has more leisure to receive them properly. Presumably briefed before sailing from Rome, Festus would expect a positive relationship with the romanized Agrippa but would also see the need to work on a relationship with Jerusalem's elite.

Festus may consider Paul's matter mostly resolved (25:12), not a pressing enough issue to raise early in the meeting, or perhaps he is restrained by the propriety of developing a friendly relationship first. Possibly both considerations are at work. In any case, he does not raise Paul's case initially, but only after some time, perhaps in the course of conversation.

Recognizing Agrippa's sensitivity to both cultures, he solicits his opinion. Since Agrippa also had troubles with the Jerusalem aristocracy (partly because he was more pro-Roman, partly because he was less traditional in his views), it is not surprising that the issue of a Roman citizen condemned by Jerusalem's elite would arise (25:15–16). (Had the case remained more important to Festus, he undoubtedly could have solicited local advice sooner, as Lysias did in 22:30; Agrippa has been there for many days.)[1082] Paul's appeal is already granted, but Agrippa can provide advice how to frame the letter (25:26), providing Festus with a favor and so solidifying their working "friendship" (see above; cf. Luke 23:12). Perhaps no less important, Agrippa's verdict will help provide Festus a cover against charges of insensitivity to local Judean demands.

ii. Local Demands versus Roman Law (25:16–18)

Retellings of events sometimes supplement details omitted earlier, so that Luke does not need to recount each detail in both versions (cf., e.g., the "forty days" of 1:3 with Luke 24:36–51). Festus may therefore have earlier appealed explicitly to Roman custom, as he suggests in Acts 25:16. Nevertheless, the pattern here is that Festus includes especially the details that present him in a good light.[1083]

Although Festus wants to be diplomatic with the Jerusalem elite, they know very well the Roman custom of not handing someone over without a defense (Acts 25:16; central to Roman law; cf. 23:30, 35);[1084] even Felix refused to simply hand Paul over without trial. (Indeed, Felix, despite offering a related favor under political duress [24:27], did not hand Paul the citizen over to his accusers even afterward.)[1085] Romans prided themselves in *aequitas romana*, Roman fairness; accusations could not be anonymous (cf. 24:19; Pliny *Ep.* 10.97), and defendants must have the opportunity to make their case before the judge and accusers.[1086] This was thought all the more

---

shows us that Luke's "many days" there could include years, such phrases could include such a duration elsewhere (e.g., Exod 2:23; 1 Kgs 2:38–39 [though not LXX]; perhaps Gen 21:34; 37:34; Deut 1:46–2:1).

1082. Still, the delay might be simply a sign of respect; whereas in my culture people tend to "get to the point" directly, some cultures respectfully reserve the request until the proper relational groundwork has been laid.

1083. Cf., e.g., Acts 23:27–30; Gen 3:10–12; Exod 32:22–24; Judg 20:5; and human nature.

1084. Even many educated Jerusalemites interested primarily in Jewish law may have known the basics of Roman law; in their later forms, indeed, much overlap exists (see esp. Cohen, *Law*, passim). Due process already characterized both Jewish and Roman law (with Pelikan, *Acts*, 268). Stating that something was "not the custom" locally could imply moral pride in one's people's mores (e.g., the Persian in Quint. Curt. 10.2.26). In contrast to the present passage, Luke usually applies the term to Jewish customs (Luke 1:9; 2:42; Acts 15:1; 16:21; 26:3), which Paul claims not to violate (28:17; cf. 6:14; 21:21).

1085. Factors such as Lysias's report and Festus's interrogation of Paul would have made Paul's innocence clear; political factors such as potential Nazarene support or knowledge of Paul's political connections elsewhere (cf. Acts 19:31) may have made inaction the least risky course.

1086. Ulp. *Dig.* 48.17.1; Appian *Bell. civ.* 3.8.54 (3.54.222). Commentators (e.g., Conzelmann, *Acts*, 206; Bruce, *Commentary*, 482; Johnson, *Acts*, 426; Fitzmyer, *Acts*, 750; Bock, *Acts*, 710; Parsons, *Acts*, 334; also Ferguson, *Backgrounds*, 51) widely cite these as explicit examples; see also Justin *1 Apol.* 3; cf. Athenag. *Plea* 3; Tert. *Apol.* 1.3; 2.2. Our passage is itself cited as such an example (Lewis and Reinhold, *Empire*, 550, noted

pressing if the stakes were serious (Pliny *Ep.* 2.11.9), as is the case here.[1087] When some were executed without this due process, it revealed corruption in the system (Tac. *Hist.* 1.6; Pliny *Ep.* 4.11.6).[1088] The system did not always work (as Luke recognized, Acts 16:20–23), but when it did not, the officials knew that it should have worked and were worried about the consequences (16:38–39).[1089]

Festus initially resisted a relocation of the venue to Jerusalem (25:3, 5), even though the request was probably not for a Jewish trial without Festus judging but rather, more likely, simply for relocation (with Festus judging but the local elite advising). In any case, he portrays his own role here positively for Agrippa, who would approve of his stated reason for noncompliance, and omits his later willingness to grant a change of venue to Jerusalem. Even in that case, Festus would remain the judge (25:9), and so he has not at any point capitulated to handing Paul over. Neither, however, has he simply freed him in view of the lack of concrete evidence against him on relevant charges (25:7). On his lack of delay, see comments on Acts 25:1, 6.

In 25:18, Festus confesses that he was expecting crimes for which the sentence of death could be executed (25:25) but found only debates about Jewish laws (25:19). Presumably Paul's accusers did offer capital charges (25:7–8); but they could not prove these (25:7), and Paul succeeded in demonstrating that the debate fell back to matters of theology (24:14–15, 20–21). Now Festus needs an expert in these laws who is also conversant with Roman thought and can interpret their relevance for him (25:26). "Crimes such as I was expecting" might also be rendered "crimes which I could recognize as such," reflecting the Latin legal formula *de quibus cognoscere volebam*; that is, these were not crimes he could accept as such under Roman law.[1090] As elsewhere in Luke-Acts, the Christian movement's accusers lacked proper "cause" or basis for prosecution (e.g., Luke 23:4; Acts 13:28; cf. 22:24; 25:27).

iii. Merely Religious Disputes (25:19)

Paul's accusers failed to prove the sedition charges (Acts 24:5; 25:8–9). The dispute was an intra-Jewish one, as previous Roman investigations or hearings had concluded (18:14–15; 23:29). The term for "disagreement" (ζήτημα) appears only in Acts in the NT;[1091] it does not imply that the matters must have been unimportant (cf. 15:2; 26:3), but it does indicate that they were not relevant to the jurisdiction of a Roman court (18:15; 23:29), the only court authorized to execute a death sentence. Every use in Acts applies to Jewish (or, in 15:2, specifically Jewish-Christian) issues. Paul himself would have agreed in viewing the debate as an intra-Jewish one; not only in his speeches in Acts but in Paul's extant letters, it is clear that he viewed his faith as genuinely Jewish, the epitome and fulfillment of OT expectations.[1092]

When Festus speaks of "religious" disagreements, he employs δεισιδαιμονία, the noun cognate of the adjective that Paul applies to Athenian paganism in 17:22. It is often, though not always, pejorative in Greek; its Latin equivalent, *superstitio*, was

---

by Winter, "Official Proceedings," 309n17). The terms for prosecution and defense in Acts 25:16 are standard (Porph. *Ar. Cat.* 55.3–4).

1087. On cases deferred until parties are present, see discussion at Acts 24:19.

1088. In Herod's court, see also Jos. *Ant.* 16.258.

1089. Viviano, "State" (esp. 238), shows that Festus's claim here, generally approved by Luke, is consistent with Paul's general affirmation of Roman government in Rom 13.

1090. Sherwin-White, *Society*, 50; Hemer, *Acts in History*, 131.

1091. The related sense of the cognate ζήτησις appears in Acts 25:20 (also 15:2, 7; John 3:25; 1 Tim 6:4; 2 Tim 2:23; Titus 3:9; differing from earlier usage in Eccl 3:15; Sir 33:26).

1092. With Barrett, *Acts*, 1139. On Paul's letters and Judaism, see, e.g., Davies, *Paul*; Sanders, *Paul and Judaism*; idem, *Law and People*.

nearly always negative. Because Festus is speaking with a Jew, some scholars argue that he cannot employ the term in a derogatory manner;[1093] others argue that because he views Agrippa as hellenized and "progressive," he can be derogatory and expect Agrippa to agree.[1094] But while Agrippa may have viewed some of the priests' views as superstitious, he would not have concurred, nor would Festus have expected him to concur, with the view that his Jewish faith as a whole (which seems to be the ground of overlap between Paul and the Jerusalem elite) was a superstition! (For Luke's usage, see comment on Acts 17:22.)

This is not the first time Luke presents someone with a benignly tolerant skepticism toward the claim that Jesus had risen (Luke 24:23). Festus does not agree with the resurrection notion, but to himself, Felix, and Agrippa, it is not a legal issue or an issue affecting the stability of the state. No one disagreed with the statement that Jesus was human (Acts 2:22; 17:31). Festus is undoubtedly aware of traditions of dying and rising gods[1095] but sees Jesus as a man, in terms quite different from those gods. Perhaps he would think of posthumous apparitions[1096] or a simple disagreement about whether Jesus had indeed actually died. In any case, he demonstrates that he misunderstands this notion of resurrection (like the philosophers in Acts 17:18).[1097] The issue must have been covered in the events summarized in 25:7–8, but Festus, unlike Felix (24:22), lacks the grasp of the Jewish categories needed to comprehend the point.

The issue has shifted from profaning the temple (a false and unprovable charge) to the theological question of whether the Christian movement remains part of Judaism. Festus may lack patience for such questions (cf. Gallio in 18:15), but this question could determine whether the movement should be viewed as part of a tolerated ethnic religion or as a rapidly growing, uncontrolled, and subversive cult.[1098] For Luke, whose Christian circles include many ethnic Gentiles, the relationship of the Christian movement to Judaism was a live question.[1099] The failure to persuade some synagogues and officials in cities and provinces about the Jewishness of the Christian movement sometimes led to persecution in those places, probably within two decades of Luke's writing.[1100]

IV. PREFERRING ROME TO JERUSALEM (25:20–21)

That Paul prefers Rome to Jerusalem serves the larger narrative's geographic direction (from Jerusalem to Rome) and also enables the preservation of Paul's life. Jewish Roman citizens could escape local Jewish jurisdiction by appealing to Roman

1093. E.g., Conzelmann, *Acts*, 206; Horton, *Acts*, 383n17; Schnabel, *Acts*, 997.

1094. Witherington, *Acts*, 730; cf. Villiers and Germiquet, "*Religio*." For Judaism as a superstition in Gentile eyes, Rowe, *World*, 228–29n217 cites Tac. *Hist.* 5.8; Jos. *Ant.* 14.228–32; and other sources (there following Stern, *Authors*), applicable to Christians in Tac. *Ann.* 15.44; Suet. *Nero* 16.2; Pliny *Ep.* 10.96. Roman procurators could negatively view Judaism as a superstition (Jos. *War* 2.174, on Pilate), but the term could be used positively as well (*Ant.* 10.42).

1095. This tradition does predate early Christianity (*ANET* 52–57, 108, 126–42, 149–55; Burkert, *Religion*, 160); Greeks seem to have been most familiar with Egyptian accounts of dying and rising deities (Max. Tyre 2.5; cf. Plut. *Isis* passim). Nevertheless, the Christian idea, rooted in the Jewish eschatological bodily resurrection and effected in history, is quite different by the standards of comparative religions (see the full argument in Keener, *John*, 1169–77, esp. 1172–77; idem, *Historical Jesus*, 332–37, esp. 335–37; idem, "Parallel Figures").

1096. See comment on Acts 1:3. But his wording may also reflect educated wit (e.g., with reference to life and death in Quint. *Decl.* 388.2).

1097. Ancient readers and auditors understood that the speech of unreliable characters did not necessarily reflect the views of an author (Proclus *Poet.* 6.1, K110.8–9).

1098. Cf. Gilchrist, "On What Charge?"

1099. See the discussion of "Israel's Story" in Keener, *Acts*, 1:459–77.

1100. See Keener, *John*, 176–79.

authorities; in a case of evading internal Jewish law, this appeal might be viewed as an act of apostasy (something that Paul denies in Acts [28:19–20] and that his letters also attest he had long avoided [2 Cor 11:24]), but in a capital case where the local authorities could not be trusted for fairness, it was thoroughly understandable.

Festus's admission that he is not competent to adjudicate the matter properly (Acts 25:20) reinforces Luke's essential point that an internal Jewish dispute is in view.[1101] The "question" or "issue" (ζήτησις, also 15:2, 7) probably functions as the equivalent of the Latin legal use of *quaestio*, a matter needing to be examined by judicial inquiry.[1102]

Festus's claim that he merely wanted to obtain good advice from the Jerusalem leaders (as his *consilium*; see comment on Acts 25:12), however, paints his motives differently than does Luke (25:9) or Luke's usually reliable protagonist, Paul (25:11).[1103] Although Festus states matters more positively, it is probably true that he did want local advice, and he is implying to Agrippa at this point his desire for it (25:14, 22).[1104] Some Roman officials would have simply deferred to the high priest to evaluate disputes about Jewish customs (Julius Caesar in Jos. *Ant.* 14.195). Deferring a politically difficult case to other properly constituted authorities could be helpful (Luke 23:6–7; Acts 23:34).

In the NT, only Luke uses διαπορέω, and he uses it to indicate perplexity (Luke 9:7; Acts 2:12; 5:24; 10:17); it can apply to officials debating their options—for example, Cicero being perplexed (διαποροῦντος) as to whether he should execute the criminals or show mercy (Plut. *Cic.* 20.1). But the cognate ἀπορέω (used here, in Acts 25:20) appears elsewhere (Mark 6:20; John 13:22; 2 Cor 4:8; Gal 4:20; Luke 24:4; cf. 1 Macc 3:31; Sir 18:7).[1105] Dio Chrysostom also invites his audience to give advice (*Or.* 47.12, 13, 14, 19, 20), using ἀπορέω (47.18). When Festus states that he is at a loss, he is soliciting advice, but not merely as a rhetorical device.

The Greek term Σεβαστός in Acts 25:21 (cf. also 25:25; 27:1) applied to the emperor and was equivalent to "Augustus," the "august one" (Luke 2:1, where it is employed in its narrower sense for Octavian).[1106] Apart from Tiberius, Octavian's successors adopted "Augustus" as a generic imperial title. The term διάγνωσις was used in legal settings for a legal decision or for a judicial inquiry culminating in one (Latin *cognitio*).[1107] The term for "sending" to Caesar (ἀναπέμπω) also had a common technical sense of sending to one higher in authority.[1108]

d. Agrippa's Interest (25:22)

Agrippa was probably eager to offer his expertise to Festus, solidifying their working relationship, and he could best help Festus describe the case (Acts 25:20, 26)

1101. Johnson, *Acts*, 426.

1102. Fitzmyer, *Acts*, 751.

1103. See Tannehill, *Acts*, 306. Witherington, *Acts*, 731, notes that Festus interprets Paul's appeal for his own political convenience, since acquittal would have served justice better.

1104. That is, probably both Acts 25:9 and 25:20 provide Luke's perspective on what happened and are best evaluated together on the narrative level.

1105. On aporia, see further Anderson, *Glossary*, 24; Rowe, "Style," 140–41; cf., e.g., Isoc. *Antid.* 140, 310, 320; Cic. *Or. Brut.* 40.137; *Verr.* 2.5.1.2; Pliny *Ep.* 10.2.1; 10.10.1; Dio Chrys. [Favorinus] *Or.* 37.9; Apul. *Flor.* 16.34; perhaps Val. Max. 3.2.2; cf. examples in Cicero's letters (*Fam.* 2.4.1; 2.11.1; *Att.* 3.5), though these are not feigned. For perplexity, e.g., Gen 32:8 LXX (32:7 ET).

1106. The Greek term would have lent itself easily to the imperial cult (cf. the cognates related to piety in Acts 13:43, 50; 16:14; 17:4, 17, 23; 18:7, 13; 19:27).

1107. See BDAG (citing, e.g., Plato *Laws* 9.865C; Wis 3:18 [for God's tribunal]; Jos. *Ant.* 8.133; 15.358). For "the emperor's decision," note *a cognitionibus Augusti* (Le Cornu, *Acts*, 1377).

1108. BDAG cites Plut. *C. Mar.* 17.3; Jos. *War* 2.571; *OGIS* 329.51; P.Hib. 1.57; P.Tebt. 7.7; for sending one to the proper person, see Jos. *Ant.* 4.218; Luke 23:7.

if he heard Paul. But Agrippa may also have further interest in the case; Festus has mentioned that the religious dispute concerns Jesus, whom Paul claims to be alive (25:19), and Agrippa already knows of the sect (26:26–28). Agrippa's interest in hearing Paul himself recalls Antipas's earlier interest in hearing Jesus himself (Luke 9:9; 23:8).[1109]

This hearing will fulfill part of Luke's nearer eschatology; before the wars, earthquakes, and so forth (Luke 21:10–12a), imprisoned disciples would be brought before kings and governors (21:12; one of each in this case), with opportunity to testify in a way that no one could refute (21:14–15). The tradition of Paul's testimony before rulers was not soon forgotten (*1 Clem.* 5.7).

A provincial governor could have a busy schedule, but Festus has made building relationships with the local elite a priority (Acts 25:1–2, 9, 13–14) and hence schedules a hearing for Paul the next day (cf. also 25:6). He is deliberate in his efficiency (in 25:17, he notes that he made no delay), a clear enough contrast with Felix (24:22, 27).

7. Paul before Agrippa (25:23–26:32)

Paul's defense speeches (before Jerusalem's crowds, the Sanhedrin, governors, and now Agrippa) may climax his earlier ministry, but the speech before Agrippa certainly climaxes the defense speeches. Paul is a citizen of both the Jewish and the Roman worlds, and he now addresses a hearer competent to understand both, as he himself does. Paul's rhetoric and message are geared toward persuasiveness; he seeks to persuade Agrippa that the faith is true, but if he succeeds even in showing it plausible and pious, he will serve the cause of continuing tolerance for it.[1110]

a. Introducing the Hearing (25:23–26:1a)

This paragraph sets the stage for Paul's speech before Agrippa (along with Berenice and Festus), including Festus's public summary that he found nothing worthy of death (25:25). The goal of hearing Paul's speech is to provide what to write to Rome (25:26–27); Paul's speech will confirm that his own interests are theological, not directly political (26:2–29), leading to the consent of all three evaluators that Paul is not worthy of death or even prison (25:31), even though he will go to Rome in Roman custody. All of this serves well Luke's apologetic for Paul, although it is an apologetic (for Paul's interests as being theological rather than politically subversive) to which readers of Paul's letters would generally give assent.

i. A Prominent Audience (25:23)

In a world where social status proved highly influential both in courts and in public opinion, Paul's exalted audience here is significant. Even if Paul might have preferred to devote his time to larger numbers of people, he now had the rare opportunity to

---

1109. Also noted by others (e.g., Munck, *Acts*, 238; Witherington, *Acts*, 731; Le Cornu, *Acts*, 1377; Gangel, *Acts*, 420; O'Toole, *Acts 26*, 22–24). On Luke 23:8, cf. Luke's use of the Q tradition in 10:24. If Luke based part or all of one scene on the other, it is likelier that he would construct the scene in Luke 23:6–12 on the basis of his knowledge of Paul's examination (to which he had fuller access) than the reverse (see rightly Omerzu, "Verhältnis"), though we should also keep in mind contrasts between the scenes and that both are culturally plausible.

1110. From the early Christian perspective, Nero's persecution, even if some treated it as establishing precedent, was an idiosyncratic expression of Nero's own wickedness whereas previous Roman precedents had favored tolerance for Christians.

expose his message to prominent people who would have a bearing on the tolerance accorded the movement.[1111]

(1) Pomp and Prominence

The elite's earthly pomp[1112] contrasts starkly with Paul's chains (26:29); the true king's honorable ambassador (cf. 2 Cor 5:20; Eph 6:20) arrives in humiliation before an earthly court (though he succeeds in his presentation).[1113] As Garnsey and Saller point out: "Romans paraded their rank whenever they appeared in public, and nowhere more conspicuously than at public spectacles in theatre, amphitheatre and circus. In Rome, Augustus confirmed and extended late Republican arrangements that allocated special seats or rows of seats to senators, equestrians and citizens."[1114] Cities in general also maintained distinctions in seating, visually reinforcing structure;[1115] of course, in the procurator's court in Herod's old palace, only people of rank (other than guards or servants) would be present. Jewish leaders could also display pomp (1 Macc 11:6); Luke's audience may well think of Agrippa II's father, who displayed his pomp in Acts 12:21.[1116] Yet it proved futile and empty before God (12:23; cf. Ps 49:12, 20; Isa 14:11).[1117] A biblically informed hearer might think of the pomp of Israel's and Judah's kings when Micaiah the prophet was brought before them (1 Kgs 22:10).

That Festus's tribunes (χιλίαρχοι) are in attendance provides a display of Roman military power; the Judean governor until 66 had six cohorts (Jos. *Ant.* 19.364) with one tribune each, all citizens no less than Paul, normally drawn from the equestrian order (see comments on Acts 10:1; 22:28). (Most of Judea's Roman troops—five cohorts—were stationed in Caesarea.) The tribune of the cohort stationed in Jerusalem[1118] would not be present; as many as five tribunes, however, might be present on this occasion.[1119] Presumably, any military activities in Caesarea (such as regular training exercises), if any were going on, could be directly supervised by the centurions. Festus may have his tribunes, men of honorable Roman rank, present to honor Agrippa's visit.

In addition to Roman military leaders, Caesarea's prominent men are in attendance; as Johnson notes, inviting many officials was a familiar practice.[1120] Herod the Great invited the Syrian legate Varus to consult on the issue of Antipater; to their council were also invited friends and relatives, including the king's sister Salome (Jos. *Ant.* 17.93; cf. *War* 1.620). Marcus Agrippa in Ionia had officials and kings present to hear

---

1111. For Paul's captivity as serving purposes for the gospel, see Skinner, *Locating Paul*, 137–38.

1112. BDAG compares the pomp and pageantry in Polyb. 15.25.22; 16.21.1; Diod. Sic. 12.83.4; Vett. Val. 38.26. It is possible that in addition to this standard usage, Luke's audience might recall the idea of vanity in Hab 2:18–19 LXX; the common idea in both uses of the phrase is "appearance" (Wis 18:17; Zech 10:1).

1113. Cf. the contrast, implied in Luke 2:1–14, between Caesar's pomp and the humility of the true king.

1114. Garnsey and Saller, *Empire*, 117 (citing Suet. *Aug.* 44; cf. Dio Cass. 60.7; Suet. *Claud.* 21; Tac. *Ann.* 15.32).

1115. Garnsey and Saller, *Empire*, 117.

1116. Josephus emphasizes Agrippa I's splendor even more than does Luke; see comment on Acts 12:21.

1117. Some Gentile thinkers also rejected pomp (Philost. *Vit. Apoll.* 3.26).

1118. Lysias would not likely belong to the Jerusalem cohort by this point, given the passage of possibly two years, the recall of Felix (Acts 24:27), and, most important, Lysias's office. The office of tribune was often a political stepping-stone (cf. Franke, "Tribunus militum," 903), and given conflicts there, Lysias would not likely have requested permanent duty in Jerusalem.

1119. Witherington, *Acts*, 732, suggests that the tribunes present could perhaps include Lysias. Lysias could well have been rotated to Caesarea by this time, but he could also have been moved elsewhere; senatorial tribunes (which he was not) held the tribune post for only a year, and though other tribunes held it longer, their military career often included at least two different positions (Campbell, "*Tribuni militum*").

1120. Thaumastus, one of Agrippa's most prominent servants, was inherited from Agrippa I; he was steward over both of Agrippa's estates (Jos. *Ant.* 18.192–94). But because Luke mentions only local officials and not an entourage of Agrippa and Berenice, Thaumastus is probably not present.

an appeal (*Ant.* 16.30).[1121] Paul's case was not as noteworthy as these, but the presence of leading citizens from Caesarea itself is in no way surprising.

It might appear that the prominent guests had short notice (Acts 25:22), but in fact they are doing what any client would do for his patron during the patron's court sessions. It was also prudent for local leaders to establish ties with a new governor early in his tenure; this would be especially the case in a city such as Caesarea, where Jews and Gentiles each vied for the governor's favor (though Gentiles would have the upper hand politically and are presumably dominant here, 25:24). The previous governor's apparent favoring of Gentiles over Jews in this very city led to a Jewish delegation's accusing him before the emperor.[1122]

(2) The Assembly's Significance

Still, the assembly seems unduly elevated for normal daily hearings; it was likely Agrippa's presence on this day (and perhaps some previous days, accompanying his host) that drew an additional crowd. Even if Agrippa had accompanied his host to his hearings fairly regularly during the visit, this day's presentation was specifically in honor of Agrippa (so 25:23), with him as the primary audience (25:24–26:1).[1123] Paul also recognizes this focus (26:2–3, 19, 26–27), though he also welcomes the other hearers (26:29). Festus presents this case as a special one meriting a wide hearing—ironically, as the direct result of the status of Paul's accusers and the priority they have attributed to him (24:5c; 25:2; esp. 25:24). It is not surprising that Berenice would also be welcome: she was a royal figure prominent in these years and in years that followed; some scholars, indeed, argue that she even served on Vespasian's *consilium* for a time afterward.[1124] (Paul follows accepted custom in addressing Agrippa more directly than his sister, especially since she does not speak publicly here.)[1125]

For Luke's purposes, however, the large entourage demonstrates again the opportunity Paul's detention afforded him to proclaim Christ to influential persons in society (Luke 21:12–13).[1126] For Festus, Agrippa is the guest of honor; for Luke, it is Paul who gains most in honor. Paul's social status allowed him a significant earthly audience (comparable to Jesus's appearances, with less social status, before Pilate, Antipas, and Jerusalem's municipal elite). Against his detractors (cf. already perhaps Phil 1:15, 17), Paul's detention was no accident, tragedy, or divine judgment; it was a divine opportunity (cf. already 1:12–18).

Although Paul's not being anti-Roman might impress the tribunes stationed in Caesarea (which had a significant movement of Jesus's followers, Acts 21:8, 12, 16), Luke's audience might envision some of these tribunes as involved in the war that broke out in 66 C.E. (although, given the intervening years—the number depending on whether we date this hearing as early as 56 or as late as 60—most would not be).[1127] The reader should not think of Cornelius, a Roman centurion converted in Caesarea nearly two decades earlier. If Cornelius was not retired already in Acts 10, he certainly would have been long retired by now; the normal tenure of a soldier's service was

1121. Johnson, *Acts*, 428.

1122. Jos. *Ant.* 20.177–78, 182; cf. *War* 2.270.

1123. Although all are invited to participate in formulating the charge, everyone will understand that this is especially Agrippa's role (Acts 25:26; 26:30–32); no one would compete with his established and hereditary rank.

1124. Young-Widmaier, "Representation."

1125. As a person of rank, however, she probably would not be wearing any traditional head covering (cf. Thompson, "Hairstyles"; Keener, "Head Coverings").

1126. Noted also by Johnson, *Acts*, 428.

1127. Tribunes could be moved and also take other positions (see Campbell, "*Tribuni militum*").

two decades,[1128] and centurions promoted from the ranks[1129] (as Cornelius may have been) could take many years to achieve that position.

Given the prominent guests present (25:23) and the lack of any mention of the presence of Paul's accusers (Festus simply summarizes their voice in 25:24), it is clear that the purpose of this hearing is only to give Agrippa the opportunity to offer his opinion, not to provide another genuine trial of Paul.[1130] Paul is thus explaining his gospel rather than defending his life here (thereby, however, also reinforcing his positive *ethos* and keeping the focus on the theological question, according to his strategy throughout the case). Given the high status of the audience, it is not likely that Luke or any of Paul's other companions would be here as in a formal trial. Luke would, however, have an abundance of opportunity to secure the summary of the events from Paul (27:1–2).

II. FESTUS'S PUBLIC EXPLANATION (25:24–27)

Having explained Paul's situation privately to Agrippa and Berenice (25:14–21), Festus now rehearses it for all the officials present as he holds court concerning Paul's case.

(1) The Jewish Complaint (25:24)

Festus's "all the Jewish multitude"[1131] (25:24) is dramatic hyperbole, though perhaps some local Caesarean Jews have now joined in the Jerusalemite charge ("both in Jerusalem and here").[1132] The chief priests who had presented the charges spoke for elite families in Jerusalem (25:1–3) and were certainly outnumbered by the Nazarenes (21:20). For Luke, the summary declaration that Paul should no longer live echoes the cry of the crowds in 22:22. The hyperbolic summary of the accusers here also serves to remind Luke's audience that only God's providence (through Felix and especially Festus) kept Paul from being handed over to such powerful political interests.

Festus may raise the stakes for dramatic effect, but he also portrays Paul's situation as a Jewish-Roman issue, so that if even the Jewish king exonerates Paul, the case may be regarded as settled. The Jewish-Roman way of presenting the case would have fit Festus's perceptions (a Roman citizen versus local officials in the Judean province), but it also ironically supports Luke's message: wrongly accused of having taken a Gentile into the temple (21:27–29), Paul did, indeed, bring uncircumcised Gentiles into Judaism; did, indeed, represent a ministry to Gentiles rejected by his nationalist siblings (22:21–22); and planned to bring his message even to Rome itself (28:16–31). In view of the temple's destruction, Luke can present Paul's way (welcoming and converting Gentiles instead of nationalist resistance) as the right way for Israel's future.

(2) Festus's Perspective (25:25)

In 25:25, Festus openly declares his own sentiments about the case, quite usefully for Luke. Just as the Roman governor and the Herodian ruler three times declare

---

1128. Friedländer, *Life*, 1:192; Stevenson, "Army," 227.

1129. E.g., Stevenson, "Army," 226; Jones, "Army," 203; Friedländer, *Life*, 1:194. It could take as many as twenty years for a common soldier to become a centurion (Thompson, "Military," 993).

1130. So also others; see, e.g., Barrett, *Acts*, 2:1145–46; Padilla, *Speeches*, 224–25.

1131. Perhaps Luke uses πλῆθος for the nation's "legal representatives" (Luke 23:1), as Witherington, *Acts*, 732, argues, but this is far from his (or others') usual usage. Festus thus may simply employ hyperbole, hyperbole dramatically useful in Luke's report given his narrative direction (cf. 28:25–28, although Luke's direct narration in that context is more nuanced; cf. 28:24).

1132. Alternatively and perhaps more likely, he refers to Paul's critics at the Caesarea hearing in 25:7; in this case his flourish appears even more hyperbolic.

Jesus not guilty (Luke 23:4, 15, 22; cf. also 23:47), so the Roman governor and the Herodian king three times declare Paul not guilty (Acts 23:29; 25:25; 26:31).[1133] If Paul had committed any crimes, they were crimes under Jewish law for which the Romans (who controlled the death penalty in the provinces, except in client kingdoms) would not allow the death sentence (cf. Luke 23:15; Acts 23:29; 25:11, 25; 26:31).

(3) Needing Agrippa's Counsel (25:26–27)

It is precisely the irregularity of the case that requires Festus to exercise wisdom to know what to write (Acts 25:26).[1134] Paul made an appeal without being condemned, yet it is to Festus's advantage to find grounds to honor the request and have the touchy political situation off his own hands. Given the irregularity, he needs wisdom to word the accompanying letter properly lest he be accused of frivolously sending work to Rome (which sometimes happened, cf. Pliny *Ep.* 6.31.6). Even a person of the highest status laid his honor on the line when making a recommendation to the emperor (2.9.2).

Nero himself, as well as his subordinates who perhaps would handle the case, would value no Jewish interpretation of the case more highly than Agrippa's.[1135] Festus seeks Agrippa's advice "especially"[1136] because of Agrippa's expertise in Jewish customs (as Paul notes, Acts 26:3), an expertise rare not among Judeans but among Judeans trusted by Rome and able to articulate Judean views in a manner intelligible to Romans. Because Festus asks Agrippa's advice so publicly, he undoubtedly intends to follow it[1137] (though he is legally free to decide as he chooses); if Agrippa could bear the responsibility for the decision, Festus would be saved from any cause for early friction with the Jerusalem elite (cf. Luke 23:4–7). But by stating his own view (Acts 25:25), he also makes it easier for Agrippa to provide favorable counsel.

That Festus calls Nero his "lord" (25:26; cf. the similar τὸν Σεβαστόν in 25:25) reflects common usage from the reigns of Claudius and especially Nero and later emperors[1138] (although this text is rare in using the absolute "the lord").[1139] Augustus may have avoided the title (Suet. *Aug.* 53.1),[1140] but inscriptions show its frequent

1133. As often noted (e.g., Conzelmann, *Acts*, 207; Witherington, *Acts*, 733). In Luke's passion narrative, the threefold pattern of Pilate's claim to find no guilt, however, may well be traditional, since it appears probably independently in John (Luke 23:4, 14, 22; John 18:38; 19:4, 6; Keener, *John*, 1115; Matson, "Death").

1134. On judges writing letters, see, e.g., Pliny *Ep.* 1.10.9–10. Few governors would trouble their emperors with the range of questions (some apparently trivial) about which Pliny (who may have hoped to publish his correspondence) writes Trajan, but Pliny's letters (e.g., 10.17A.3; 10.23.1–2; 10.70.1–3) nevertheless underline the importance of governors' correspondence with the imperial court.

1135. For Agrippa representing the emperor's power and thus using dominant-culture rhetoric here, see Robbins, *Beyond*, 312.

1136. Although μάλιστα is not an uncommon term, Luke employs it only three times in Luke-Acts, and the uses in Acts 25:26 and 26:3 are in close proximity, both with reference to Agrippa.

1137. Better not to seek the advice if one's mind was already made up (Pliny *Ep.* 9.13.6). For the value of Agrippa as advisor, given his Roman credibility, see also Rowe, *World*, 83.

1138. Cf., e.g., Foerster, "Κύριος," 1054–55; Conzelmann, *Acts*, 207; Johnson, *Acts*, 427; D. Williams, *Acts*, 423. It appears for Claudius in, e.g., P.Oxy. 37.6; for Nero in, e.g., P.Oxy. 246.30, 34, 37 (Fitzmyer, *Acts*, 752).

1139. Haenchen, *Acts*, 677, therefore suggests a Domitianic anachronism; although I date Acts before Domitian's reign, it is possible that Luke would use the language of his own era (he was not likely present for a hearing in such august company but could have updated the language, in any event). But Neronian uses such as "Nero Kyrios" and "lord of the world" (Deissmann, *Light*, 354, citing, e.g., SIG² 376.31; SIG³ 814.31, 55) seriously weaken the significance of Haenchen's concern in any case. A more serious objection to Luke's literary verisimilitude here would be that the title in this period (as opposed to Domitian's, Suet. *Dom.* 13.2; cf. Mart. *Epig.* 9.66.3; 10.72.3) would belong to the Greek East; but though Festus is a Roman, he is speaking Greek in the East, and so even this objection to Luke's verisimilitude of language is not compelling.

1140. This did not prevent some in the East from applying it to him (P.Oxy. 1143.4).

use for the emperor. Although "lord" appears in papyri as a title for kings from the Ptolemaic period, it began to flourish especially under Nero.[1141] Deissmann points out that in Egypt, "everywhere, down to the remotest village, the officials called Nero *Kyrios*."[1142] The Armenian king Tiridates even honored Nero as his master (δεσπότης) and god (Dio Cass. 62.5.2).[1143] "Lord" meant "ruler" and probably bears no direct religious connotations here (notwithstanding its divine connotations in the East)[1144] despite the prevalence of the imperial cult[1145] in Gentile regions of the eastern Mediterranean world.

In Acts 25:27, Festus may understate the matter when he suggests that it is "unreasonable" (ἄλογον) to send the prisoner without specifying the charges.[1146] Sending a report along with the prisoner (such reports were called *litterae dimissoriae sive apostoli*) was a mandatory procedure (Ulp. *Dig.* 49.6.1).[1147] It was intended as "a covering memorandum explaining the legal aspects of the case."[1148] To simply send Paul without explaining why he was referring rather than dismissing this case would at least annoy the court and might suggest the new governor's incompetence.[1149] The accuser's and defendants' petitions presumably would be part of the file (Pliny *Ep.* 10.59), but a cover letter would be necessary, normally summarizing the facts of the case in a way that displayed some investigation.[1150]

Nevertheless, Festus has to be more discreet than to spell out the political complications of the case, since the document would be public record. He needs a sensitive way to word the Jewish charges without unnecessarily compromising Roman justice. Whereas the Sanhedrin apparently proposed that he use it as his *consilium* (Acts 25:3, 9), Festus will use Agrippa as his *consiliarius* to advise Festus on Jewish questions.[1151] (Felix did not need one [24:22, 24].) As Sherwin-White emphasizes:

> The complication and prolongation of the trial of Paul arose from the fact that the charge was political—hence the procurators were reluctant to dismiss it out of hand—and yet the evidence was theological, hence the procurators were quite unable to understand it. Not surprisingly, Festus called in King Agrippa as an assessor, to help him draft the explanation which had to be sent with the prisoner to Rome.[1152]

1141. See Hemer, *Acts in History*, 180; cf. 131.

1142. Deissmann, *Light*, 353.

1143. Bruce, *Acts¹*, 438.

1144. The connotations are noted by Bruce, *Commentary*, 485n24 (though these were not yet relevant in Festus's Rome). Although Luke uses κύριος about one hundred times in Acts, he does not use it for Jesus in this immediate context (the nearest uses, in fact, are Acts 23:11; 26:15; 28:31), as if to draw an obvious contrast. ("My Lord" applies to Jesus in Luke 1:43; 20:42; Acts 2:34; Festus here speaks literally of "the Lord," which Luke often applies to Jesus.)

1145. Or, "cults"; so Galinsky, "Cult," 3, citing Beard, North, and Price, *Religions*, 348.

1146. Ἄλογος was often applicable to beasts or to people like them (Plato *Prot.* 324B; Xen. *Hiero* 7.3; Mus. Ruf. 18A, p. 112.31; Plut. *Statecraft* 5, *Mor.* 802E; Wis 11:15; 4 Macc 14:14, 18; *Test. Zeb.* 5:1; 2 Pet 2:12); such language often appealed to the philosophically minded (cf., e.g., Dio Chrys. *Or.* 3.3; Diogenes *Ep.* 28; Porph. *Marc.* 23.362).

1147. Bruce, *Commentary*, 438; Conzelmann, *Acts*, 207; Fitzmyer, *Acts*, 748, 753; Schnabel, *Acts*, 1001. The later codification of laws may include regulations not always followed, but they provide our best guide.

1148. Winter, "Official Proceedings," 309. Probably few decisions would generate as much paperwork as Pliny's later inquiries to Trajan, deferring to imperial discretion wherever firm precedent was lacking (e.g., Pliny *Ep.* 10.65.1–10.66.2; 10.72–73).

1149. With Rapske, *Custody*, 185.

1150. E.g., Pliny *Ep.* 6.31.4; 10.74.3; 10.96.3–4. The cover letters could also tacitly illustrate the political and status issues inherent in the case.

1151. With Fitzmyer, *Acts*, 753. The phrases προάγω and ἐφ' ὑμῶν appear in legal settings (Haenchen, *Acts*, 677), though, of course, not exclusively (see BDAG).

1152. Sherwin-White, *Society*, 51.

Agrippa's visit offers Festus a possible political escape, which Agrippa proves willing to provide. Paul's defense before Agrippa is not technically a trial (given his appeal to Caesar, already effective), but it will be important for framing how Paul is described to Rome—both inside the narrative world and for Luke's audience.[1153] For Luke, as well as for Festus, Agrippa provides a significant Jewish verdict, by which Luke can counter as bias and misunderstanding the Jewish objections to Paul that his narrative records.[1154]

III. AGRIPPA ADDRESSES PAUL (26:1A)

Agrippa acts the part of the benevolent ruler, permitting Paul to speak for himself; but for Luke's Christian audience, Paul in fact holds the higher status as God's ambassador (cf. 2 Cor 5:20; Eph 6:20).[1155] Paul awaits permission to speak, as was customary; even a bold prospective martyr waits for permission before speaking (4 Macc 5:15).

As in the other defense speeches, Paul does not have a human defense attorney (cf. Acts 24:1) to help him but trusts the Holy Spirit (Luke 12:11–12; 21:12–15; cf. John's "Paraclete," possibly "Advocate");[1156] Agrippa's phrase "speak concerning yourself" may underline this point again for the reader. Although Agrippa invites Paul to speak concerning himself (περὶ σεαυτοῦ),[1157] Paul uses his own story to speak also about Christ, the focus of most of his defense, as Jesus promised (Luke 21:13). His "innocence" rests on the integrity of his message; hence his speech, though judicial in setting, is able to pursue also a deliberative goal (Acts 26:28–29).[1158]

b. Proem and Paul's Background (26:1b–11)

Paul uses the speech's proem and the beginning of its *narratio* to emphasize his *ēthos*: although he has appealed to Caesar, he remains faithful to Judaism. He contends that the charges against him are entirely theological, emphasizing that he remains within Judaism, and has clear evidence (by direct revelation) that Jesus fulfills the true hope of Judaism.

Why then would he be concerned to avoid having to defend himself before the Jerusalem elite?[1159] Paul has reason to mistrust the leading priests (26:10, 12) and is a firsthand witness to the subversive repression of the Jesus movement that has probably been politely ignored among the Roman administration that needed to maintain peace with the movement's oppressors (26:9–12).

1153. Cf. O'Toole, *Acts 26*, 16.

1154. Cf. Agrippa's role in ibid., 16. Because the charge is an internal Jewish affair, Paul addresses Agrippa (Acts 26:2, 19; with Dunn, *Acts*, 325).

1155. Mistreating legates, envoys, or messengers of any sort was reprehensible and merited punishment (e.g., Eurip. *Heracl.* 272; Xen. *Anab.* 5.7.18–19, 34; Polyb. 2.8.12; 20.10.10; 38.10.5; Diod. Sic. 36.15.1–2; 40.1.1; Dion. Hal. *Ant. rom.* 8.43.4; Val. Max. 6.6.3–4; Dio Chrys. *Or.* 76.5; Dio Cass. 19.61; Hdn. 6.4.6; Ps.-Callisth. *Alex.* 1.35, 37). Mistreating a ruler's agents was a grave insult to the ruler (Diod. Sic. 4.10.3–4; Jos. *Ant.* 8.220–21).

1156. See Keener, *John*, 956–61, 1030–35.

1157. With verbs of petitioning, περί can function as the equivalent of ὑπέρ, hence "on behalf of" (thus "speak for yourself" in most translations), but the term's broader semantic range allows exploration of the "concerning" nuance as well (as the following speech, primarily *narratio* about Paul and his mission, illustrates).

1158. Porter, *Paul in Acts*, 151n1, resists imposing classical rhetorical categories on Paul's defense speeches. Rhetorical genres were often mixed in practice (see, e.g., Aune, *Dictionary of Rhetoric*, 307, 419).

1159. Aside from his private knowledge of the previous conspiracy presumably involving them (Acts 23:14–15), and the reasonable assumption that their insistence on relocating the trial venue (25:3) indicated continuing involvement. On this occasion, the chief priests are not present because Festus is inviting only Agrippa's perspective. (It is not likely that many are out of the country, although some leading Jewish inhabitants of Caesarea had sailed to Rome to accuse Felix; Jos. *Ant.* 20.182.)

1. INTRODUCTION TO PAUL'S SPEECH

In 26:2–29, Paul proclaims Christ to a king, fulfilling Jesus's promise (Luke 12:11–12; 21:12–13; Acts 9:15).[1160] Thus, whereas the king and other hearers within the narrative world may view Paul as a defendant, Luke's audience will view Paul as fulfilling his divinely ordained destiny.[1161] This version of Paul's conversion and call emphasizes Paul's mission to turn people to eternal life (Acts 26:18), just as Paul is now hoping to persuade King Agrippa (26:28–29).

(1) Paul's Climactic Defense Speech

Foakes-Jackson is probably right to argue that this speech, given its distinguished audience and its location as the final speech of this length in Acts (though cf. 28:17–20, 25–28), climaxes the thrust of the book's major apologetic speeches.[1162] Its point is that Paul, far from being a criminal, preaches in obedience to divine revelation and that his message is grounded in the historic hope of Israel and the Scriptures.[1163]

Whereas Paul makes a defense (ἀπολογέομαι) in the temple (22:1); to Felix (24:10); and to Festus (25:8; cf. Festus's use of the noun in 25:16), this term appears more often in the context of his speech before Agrippa (26:1, 2, and 24).[1164] "Consequently," O'Toole argues, "the high point of Paul's defense, to judge from Luke's stress on *apologeisthai* . . . , stands in the hearing before Festus and Agrippa II."[1165]

Speaking before both a king and a governor, Paul addresses his most socially elevated audience in Acts so far (the appearance before Caesar's tribunal [27:24] is not narrated).[1166] Jesus promised that soon after his ministry (before the wars, earthquakes, etc.; Luke 21:10–12), his disciples would be persecuted and held in synagogues and prisons, and brought before kings and governors (21:12) with the opportunity to testify about him (21:13), and that they would often gain their lives (21:18–19). More clearly than in Acts 24 and 25 (where Paul's life was directly in danger), Paul's defense speech in 26:2–29 focuses on explaining and arguing for the truth of his message about the risen Christ.[1167] Such preaching was central to Paul's ministry (Rom 15:18–20; 1 Cor 2:1–4; Gal 4:13), though naturally only letters to churches have been preserved.

This speech represents not only the climax of Paul's defense speeches but also the third account of his conversion in the book of Acts (Acts 9:1–8; 22:2–21). For this reason, some of the material below will be addressed only cursorily if it has been addressed in more detail in comments on the earlier passages. But one should not for this reason suppose that Luke's material is less important here; Luke employs repetition to reinforce it all the more.

As was rhetorically appropriate, Luke and Paul present Paul's story differently for different audiences, yet with a consistent nucleus of events.[1168] Each account

---

1160. Luke does not see a conflict between depending on the Spirit (Luke 12:11–12; 21:15) and using rhetorical and legal argumentation (see Kurz, *Acts*, 361–62). From an apologetic standpoint, it is notable that this king finds no political threat in Paul's preaching of "another king" (Acts 17:7; cf. Luke 19:38; 23:2–3, 38), understanding the Jewish messianic doctrine.

1161. See Padilla, *Speeches*, 225.

1162. See Foakes-Jackson, *Acts*, 223–24; cf. Witherington, *Acts*, 735.

1163. O'Toole, *Acts 26*, 160, sees its principal aim as defending the Christian claim of resurrection in Christ.

1164. With ibid., 35.

1165. Ibid., 36.

1166. Perhaps, though not certainly, because of its outcome; see discussion of Paul's possible second imprisonment at Acts 28:30–31.

1167. Cf. Philost. *Vit. Apoll.* 8.2, where Apollonius discusses philosophy more than he defends his life.

1168. Perhaps this is comparable to how the central event of Jesus's resurrection remains fairly constant in the different evangelistic speeches (in Acts 2:24–32; 3:15; 13:30–37; 17:31; for the resurrection as

presents some different features but functions as complementary to the other accounts.[1169] Given the OT allusions in distinctively defining Paul's mission in 26:16–18, this passage links Paul with the OT prophets.[1170] Understood in this manner, his revelation from God (26:13–18)[1171] is in continuity with his ancestral faith (revealed through Moses and the prophets, 26:22), an ethnic religion that Rome tolerates.[1172] This may be why Paul asks Agrippa if he believes the prophets (26:27).

Although Paul uses forensic rhetoric, this is not a "defense" speech in the same sense as the speeches in 24:10–21 or (as a summary) 25:8; Paul speaks not as a defendant answering charges but as a witness in his own defense[1173] and, more strangely from a Roman standpoint, a witness for Christ (which may help explain why Festus impatiently interrupts him in 26:24).[1174] This is not technically a trial but a hearing to decide the charges to be forwarded to Rome. Whereas other Christians before and after Paul may have been arraigned on their enemies' false charges, casting their movement in a bad light, Paul is articulate enough to respond to the charges. In a legal system that favors the powerful, Paul's eloquent voice offers a defense not only for himself but for the movement he represents.

(2) Rhetoric and Structure

The style is fairly elegant, with subtlety of syntax, paronomasia, some classical usages and Atticisms, and even the language of a Greek proverb. This style suits the speech's primary audience, a king highly educated in Greek rhetoric.[1175]

Bligh suggests the following chiastic outline:[1176]

> A Agrippa is familiar with Jewish ways (26:2–3a).
> B Paul requests a patient hearing and speaks of Pharisaic training (26:3b–5).
> C Paul defends faith in the resurrection (26:6–8).
> D Paul persecuted Christians (26:9–11a).

the central summary, cf. 1:22; 4:33), as in other early Christian preaching (1 Cor 15:3–4). See Witherington, "Editing," 335–44; idem, *Acts*, 309; further discussion at Acts 9:20, 23–25. As Witherington, *Acts*, 311, notes about the differences, "ancient historians were not nearly so concerned as we are today about minute details."

1169. Hedrick, "Paul's Conversion/Call," 432 (arguing for more traditional material in Acts 9 and 22); cf. Humphrey, *Voice*, 97–99.

1170. Fitzmyer, *Acts*, 755, thinks that this passage presents Paul as a prophet through allusions to Ezek 2:1–6; Jer 1:8; Isa 35:5; 42:7; 61:1.

1171. Given the repetition of θεός in four cases in Acts 26:6–8, 18–22, Parsons, "*Progymnasmata*," 58, identifies God as the subject of the speech (though, given Luke's Christology, it would seem forced-choice logic to lay this theocentric reading against O'Toole's christocentric reading). Cheng, *Characterisation*, 133, concludes that all seven of Paul's Lukan speeches are fundamentally theocentric.

1172. For the significance of this claim for Lukan apologetic, see this commentary's introduction, Keener, *Acts*, 1:449–56.

1173. Winter, "Official Proceedings," 330–31; Witherington, *Acts*, 736.

1174. Presumably those within the narrative world, even Festus (cf. Acts 25:19), are aware that Jesus himself was executed on a treason charge, but Paul (who in Acts tends to emphasize the resurrection more anyway) is more prudent than to emphasize Jesus's execution, which would require explanatory digression, in this speech.

1175. Johnson, *Acts*, 431, 440; Witherington, *Acts*, 736–37, both suggesting that this may be Paul's "most elegant" speech in Acts. I find this sophistication even in the *narratio*. Bruce, *Acts³*, 66–67, finds Atticisms in Acts 26:2, 4, 5, 13, 26, 29 (though he notes [67n6] some "awkward constructions" in 26:3, 20). Witherington, *Acts*, 736–37, notes that Paul had more opportunity to prepare than for the speech in Acts 22. Of course, Acts 22 is meant to be translation Greek, not following the rules of Greek rhetoric; and even here (though Paul had had up to two years to prepare a case in general) Paul had at most a day's advance notice of a hearing before Agrippa (25:22). On rhetoric in the defense speeches in general, see introduction to them in Keener, *Acts*, 3:3195–200, esp. 3199–200; also commentary on these speeches, passim.

1176. Bligh, *Galatians*, 99.

      E He did so in foreign cities and Damascus (26:11b–12a).
         F He had authority from the high priest; he saw a light (26:12b–13).
            G All fell; Christ said, "Why do you persecute me?" (26:14–15a).
               H Jesus disclosed himself (26:15b).
            G′ Paul was told to stand; Christ promised protection (26:16–17a).
         F′ Christ gave Paul authority to lead Gentiles to the light (26:17b–18).
      E′ Paul preached in Damascus and among Gentiles (26:19–20).
    D′ Jews persecuted Paul, but God protected him (26:21–22a).
  C′ Moses and the prophets foretold Jesus's death and resurrection (26:22b–23).
 B′ Festus grows impatient and interrupts, mocking Paul's learning (26:24–25).
A′ Agrippa understands (26:26a).

Some points may be emphasized or deemphasized to fit the chiastic structure, but this outline at least calls attention to some repeated themes. The emphasis that the above outline ignores, that Paul's resurrection message is grounded in Israel's heritage, is a major point toward the beginning (26:5–7) and end (26:22–23) of his speech, but in a genuine and complete speech, this would simply reflect the *narratio* preparing for the *propositio* and proofs, which was common.

Bruce suggests the following outline based on content:[1177]

1. *Exordium* (26:2–3)
2. Paul's Pharisaic resurrection hope (26:4–8)
3. His former persecuting zeal (26:9–11)
4. The heavenly vision (26:12–18)
5. His preaching in obedience to the vision (26:19–20)
6. His arrest (26:21)
7. The substance of his preaching (26:22–23)

Because speeches delivered before audiences did not always break down into the ideal outlines and classifications offered in ancient rhetorical handbooks,[1178] the function of sections may overlap, and scholars have offered various plausible rhetorical outlines. A few suggestions are noted below, but virtually all of them concur in identifying the *exordium* in 26:2–3 and the *narratio* from 26:4 to at least 26:18; that is, they agree in recognizing a disproportionately long *narratio*. Michel Quesnel suggests the following rhetorical structure:[1179]

1. *Exordium* (26:2–3)
2. *Refutatio* (26:4–8)
3. *Narratio* (26:9–18), in two parts (26:9–14; 26:15–18)
4. *Propositio* (26:19–20)
5. *Peroratio* (26:21–23)

1177. Bruce, *Acts*[1], 440; idem, *Commentary*, 488.
1178. With, e.g., Porter, *Paul in Acts*, 113; despite less flexible handbooks (cf. Carcopino, *Life*, 114–21).
1179. Quesnel, "Analyse rhétorique," 173–74. Differently but plausibly, Parsons, *Acts*, 338, regards Acts 26:1–8 as the *exordium*, identifying elements characteristic of one (Quint. *Inst.* 4.1.6–11).

Bruce Winter proposes a similar structure:[1180]

1. *Exordium* (26:2–3)
2. *Narratio* (26:4–18)
3. *Confirmatio* (26:19–20)
4. *Refutatio* (26:21), refuting the earlier charge of 24:6
5. *Peroratio* (26:22–23)

Some agree on the structure through the end of the *narratio* but see all of 26:19–23 as part of Paul's *argumentatio* or *probatio*.[1181]

One could argue against one aspect of these outlines by noting that the chronological narrative form of this section (following immediately what precedes) suggests that even 26:19–20 (or as far as 26:23) remains part of the *narratio*. Given the interruption and Luke's preference for recounting the *narratio* of speeches elsewhere, it is entirely possible that, apart from the *exordium* and *propositio*, most of Paul's speech is *narratio*.[1182] Since it is his behavior that is under dispute, a lengthy narrative is appropriate.[1183] Like most speeches in Acts, this ends incomplete, in this case barely after it has started.

Given an extended *narratio* (at least as far as 26:20), 26:21–23 or 26:22–23 might well be Paul's *propositio*. On this view, he is interrupted after his *propositio*, before he can advance proofs (26:24), but the reader loses nothing; Luke has provided the proofs for this proposition (26:22–23) throughout his own narrative and especially in earlier speeches (7:2–53; 13:16–47; 15:15–18).[1184] (If one chooses the shorter *narratio*, one could view 26:21 as the *propositio*.[1185] One could then view 26:22–23 as part of the proofs, but they must have included more elaborate development from OT Scripture, which Luke can simply presuppose from the earlier speeches mentioned above, as in Luke 24:44–45. Scripture proofs would have completely bewildered Festus in Acts 26:24.)

Against any of the outlines being conclusive, speeches did not, in fact, as already noted, always break down as easily as rhetorical handbooks might suggest. But the varied rhetorical approaches share enough common elements (especially on most of the *narratio* and what some implied proofs would have been) to assist the analysis here.

II. BEGINNING THE SPEECH (26:1B–3)

Stretching out the hand (26:1b) could express a variety of sentiments—for example, authority or compassion (4:30; Luke 5:13), seizing (Luke 22:53) or doing violence (Exod 7:5; 1 Esd 6:33; 1 Macc 6:25) to someone, oath formulas (Num 14:30), or supplication (1 Esd 8:73; 4 Macc 4:11; Sir 4:31). Motions with the hand

---

1180. Winter, "Official Proceedings," 330.

1181. Aune, *Environment*, 126.

1182. So also Witherington, *Acts*, 737–38, though he points out that Luke also provides Paul with a *refutatio* (Acts 26:25–26) and *peroratio* (26:27, 29), despite interruptions (26:24, 28); whether they function thus in the narrative world, Luke can employ them with this function. Witherington rightly notes that the intended proofs are alluded to in the *narratio* and *propositio* and suggests (perhaps too specifically) that they appear in earlier speeches in Acts 22–25.

1183. E.g., Cic. *Quinct.* 3.11–9.33 (though this is briefer than the proofs, 11.37–27.85). Ideally a *narratio* was brief (e.g., Dion. Hal. *Lysias* 9), but Luke is writing narrative and focuses on the narrative element in speeches, perhaps abbreviating it less than other elements. Here, however, a lengthy narrative is necessary, since Paul's case rests mainly on the divine commission he has received.

1184. O'Toole, *Acts 26*, 19–20, argues that the speech has features intended for Luke's audience more than for Agrippa or Festus (he acknowledges traditional material, but presented from a Lukan perspective [156]).

1185. As in Quesnel, "Analyse rhétorique," 173–74; or with Acts 26:21 as the *refutatio*, Winter, "Official Proceedings," 330.

are used elsewhere in Acts to invite attention (Acts 12:17; 19:33; 21:40; cf. 13:16), but they were also standard rhetorical gestures.[1186] The rhetorical gesture must be in view here,[1187] but a careful listener who has heard the story more than once may visualize with a dimension of pathos that gesture encumbered with "his chain-laden right hand" (cf. 26:29).[1188]

The *captatio benevolentiae* (26:2–3) is honest, more extensive, and more forceful (including μακάριον, though not in its usual LXX sense)[1189] than that for Felix (24:10). (In terms of Luke's own strategy in what information he chooses to narrate, it may be relevant that by the time Luke writes, Agrippa remains respected, in contrast to Felix.) Luke is also more explicit here about Paul's direct address than in 24:10,[1190] although Paul must have also addressed Felix with a title. Counting oneself fortunate to be heard by a fair or knowledgeable judge was a suitable rhetorical claim for opening praise (see, e.g., Apul. *Apol.* 1). Agrippa knows not only Jewish customs (see comment on Acts 6:14) but also about the "questions" or "debates" among the Jewish people (26:3; see comment on Acts 25:19; cf. 6:9), including therefore about "sects" such as the Nazarenes (24:5, 14; 26:28). He is therefore well qualified to attest that Paul is accused only on theological grounds, on "questions" or "debates" about the law (18:15; 23:29; 25:19). Those pleading cases often expressed special confidence in the judges' ability.[1191]

Paul's assumption that Agrippa was knowledgeable in Jewish affairs (26:3) has occasioned some discussion. Later rabbis reported the piety of Agrippa's steward[1192] and the piety of a King Agrippa, although there is debate as to whether the reference is to the father (Agrippa I) or to the son (Agrippa II, as here).[1193] (More likely, the reference is to the father but with implications for how the son would be viewed. Both had some popularity as descendants partly from the Hasmonean line and as rulers whose benefits to Judea had Roman sanction.) After the war, Judeans ready to accept Roman rule were welcome to live in Agrippa's realm.[1194]

1186. See, e.g., Ap. Rhod. 1.344; Philost. *Vit. soph.* 1.25.541; see further comment on Acts 13:16. Hall, "Delivery," 224, notes that speakers often began with dignified, gentle movement of the arm (*Rhet. Her.* 3.26), distinct from the more vigorous movement characterizing more emotional phases of the speech (3.27). Orators would emphasize points with an outstretched hand (including extended index and middle finger; Hurschmann, "Gestures," 832; but Shiell, *Reading Acts*, 74–75, says that, for emphasis, the orator pointed toward the ground). Quintilian offers the most detailed extant survey of rhetorical gestures but probably preserves or refines broader practice (see Hall, "Delivery," 226–27; idem, "Cicero and Quintilian"). A statue shows a Roman orator holding his toga or text with the left hand, keeping the right hand free for gestures (Shiell, *Reading Acts*, 41).

1187. With, e.g., Conzelmann, *Acts*, 209 (noting Apul. *Metam.* 2.21 and two statues). Bruce, *Commentary*, 488, envisions merely a salutation here (contrasting Acts 13:16; 21:40). But Shiell, *Reading Acts*, 153–54, is undoubtedly right in identifying the gesture with the beginning of a judicial speech's *exordium*, a motion that he identifies (154) as pressing together the ends of the thumb and the middle finger, the other fingers spread out, while "moving the arm gently from right to left."

1188. Rapske, *Custody*, 309; at 26:29, Padilla, *Speeches*, 210.

1189. The secular sense of μακάριος as "fortunate" (see at length sources in BDAG) reflects the high level of Greek here (Johnson, *Acts*, 431). Another sign of rhetorical elegance is "the classical use of the perfect ἥγημαι as a present" (Witherington, *Acts*, 737). Not flattery, Paul's *captatio* connects with the message (Kurzinger, *Apostelgeschichte*, 90).

1190. Because one could gesture toward persons in the audience (Shiell, *Reading Acts*, 57–62), it is possible that Luke's audience would envision Paul gesturing toward Agrippa, although this would need to be expressed in a particularly respectful manner.

1191. E.g., Isoc. *Antid.* 323; Cic. *Quinct.* 2.1; 30.92; *Verr.* 2.1.7.18; P.Ryl. 114.3–5 (from ca. 280 C.E.); see fuller comment at Acts 24:2, 10.

1192. O'Toole, *Acts 26*, 17 (with two talmudic references).

1193. Ibid. (with eight talmudic references), noting that if these refer to Agrippa, they corroborate his interest in the law.

1194. Ibid., 18.

Luke himself describes Agrippa's father as catering to conservative elements (12:3), and Josephus portrays Agrippa's sister Berenice as observing piety (*War* 2.313), though we lack this specific information about Agrippa II.[1195] Josephus does note that the priests did not think him very pious: he had built a dining and reclining area in an elevated Hasmonean palace he used, from which he could watch the activities of the priests in the sanctuary (*Ant.* 20.189–90), angering Jerusalem's leaders (20.191). Yet Agrippa's more liberal attitudes (cf. also 20.218), conjoined with his Roman upbringing and his consequent independence from Jerusalem's leaders, do work to Paul's advantage in terms of Roman tolerance.

The point here, however, is not Agrippa's personal piety but his knowledge of his people and their customs, a matter on which there is no dispute. Paul may implicitly contrast his hearing before Agrippa with those before Felix and Festus. It was naturally counted helpful when a judge was already acquainted with the issues surrounding both sides of a case (Phaedrus 3.13.4). Paul also respectfully echoes the introduction that Festus provided for Agrippa, not only with "King Agrippa" (26:2; 25:26) but with his term for "especially" (26:3; 25:26; two of the three uses in Luke-Acts).

The request for the judge or audience to listen patiently was conventional in ancient speeches;[1196] see comment on Acts 24:4, with its promise of brevity. Paul uses the respectful request δέομαι also in Acts 21:39. Ironically, however, Paul's request for them to hear him patiently so he can finish the speech is not granted (26:24, 28). His judges hear enough to decide his case but are not willing to accommodate his desire to persuade them about his message.

III. PAUL'S PIOUS BACKGROUND (26:4–5)

Paul begins the narration of his background by insisting that his Pharisaic piety is well known in Jerusalem, where he spent most of his life until Jesus revealed himself to Paul on the road to Damascus.

(1) Rhetorical Character

Paul begins his *narratio* in 26:4–5 with sentences including elegant, classical forms (ἴσασι; ἀκριβεστάτην), displaying his educated Greek (cf. 21:37), though he also employs less impressive forms.[1197] Although other uses of the word may turn up, it is also interesting (given the presence of the Jewish ruler) that Paul uses βίωσιν, a term found in this period particularly in Jewish sources (Sir prol. 14; a Jewish inscription from ca. 60–80 C.E.).[1198] Paul also rhetorically piles up phrases with overlapping meaning ("from my youth," "from the beginning," "for a long time")[1199] that reinforce how deep his Jewish, even Jerusalemite, upbringing goes (cf. Acts 22:3).[1200] (The Hellenistic part of his education cannot count against him with Agrippa.)

1195. Cf. Porter, *Paul in Acts*, 159.
1196. E.g., Aeschines *Embassy* 44; Cic. *Verr.* 2.3.5.10; *Mil.* 2.4; *Quinct.* 1.5; Apul. *Apol.* 13; 91 (plus the praise for his patience in 35); see further comment on Acts 7:2.
1197. Conzelmann, *Acts*, 209–10; Witherington, *Acts*, 737. Perhaps this was just the right admixture for such an audience (in view of Luke 1:1–4, it is not the case that Luke can construct nothing more elegant).
1198. Both these sources are cited in BDAG; Bruce, *Acts¹*, 441, both following Ramsay on the inscription (which is partly reconstructed, [βί]ωσιν). Bruce notes no other use before the sixth century C.E.
1199. Conzelmann, *Acts*, 210, compares Lucian *Peregr.* 8, which also engages apologetic biography. Luke employs ἄνωθεν as in Luke 1:3, his other use (quite different from Johannine usage).
1200. E.g., Malina and Neyrey, *Portrait*, 81. Commentators recognize the claim for Jerusalemite upbringing whether they agree with it (van Unnik, *Tarsus*, 46) or not (Haenchen, *Acts*, 682). The hypothesis that "this people" refers to Cilicia (Lake and Cadbury, *Commentary*, 315) is forced.

Encomia typically emphasized the subject's background,[1201] but this topic was also important in defense speeches, where it helped establish *ēthos* (see discussions at Acts 24:11, 14–17, 16). Others also spoke of behavior "from my youth up."[1202] A speech praising a person would use their background to show that they had made good use of it; conversely, one criticizing a person would use the person's background to show that their advantages stemmed wholly from nature and not from anything praiseworthy in their volition.[1203]

If it is known that the defendant misbehaved in the past, he may plead his youth or other reason for the behavior and note that he learned from the experience (*Rhet. Alex.* 7, 1428b.37–40). This approach could be relevant to Paul's confession, in Acts 26:10–11, of behavior that was illegal from a Roman standpoint. But such a confession was not ideal; many ancients believed that character was inborn and not easily changed (e.g., Pindar *Ol.* 11.19–20; 13.12), and so it was far better for one's own defense to be able to claim that one had not misbehaved. Socrates allegedly claimed that his whole life was his defense (Xen. *Mem.* 4.8.4).

The Paul of the letters notes that his past was blameless from a technical, legal standpoint (under Jewish, not Roman, law), though not right before God (Gal 1:13–14; Phil 3:4–9). Autobiography was often used apologetically (e.g., Jos. *Life* passim)[1204] and, like other biographies, often surveyed early life quickly to move to the relevant part (usually the political, military, philosophic, or other career). It was natural to employ autobiographic narrative this way in a judicial speech.

(2) Potential Witnesses

It was important to be able to produce witnesses in forensic rhetoric,[1205] including those to one's character.[1206] Testimony was especially effective when one could appeal to something done in public, noting (or implying) that there were many witnesses.[1207]

Paul here appeals to common knowledge, a frequent rhetorical technique.[1208] Thus someone can cite a fact to which "all Greece" testifies (Eurip. *Heracl.* 219). Demosthenes suggests that his hearers must know of Meidias's crimes, familiar to all other citizens (*Mid.* 1; cf. also 80; the later allusion in Hermog. *Inv.* 1.1.99). While recalling a past event in the public assembly, Aeschines claims his audience as his witnesses (*Embassy* 123). That Socrates could have suffered death already because of his stand for what was right, concerning this "you can have many witnesses" (Plato *Apol.* 32E).[1209] Cicero charges that everyone everywhere knows the wicked deeds of Verres.[1210]

Often such statements included the direct claim that the audience themselves knew (or, by implication, ought to have known) such matters (cf. Acts 2:22; 10:28, 37; 20:18, 34).[1211] Aeschines particularly exploits this method in denouncing Timarchus. If you were not the judges, exclaims Aeschines, I would summon all of you as witnesses,

1201. E.g., Men. Rhet. 2.1–2, 371.17–372.9; 2.3, 385.5–6; 2.11, 420.11, 18–21; Hermog. *Issues* 46.14–17.
1202. Apul. *Apol.* 5 (trans. Hunink, p. 29).
1203. *Rhet. Her.* 3.6.14. If someone lacked an illustrious heritage, the speaker could emphasize that virtues and education were what really showed a person's value (as in Apul. *De deo Socr.* 174–75).
1204. On apologetic autobiography, see also Lyons, *Autobiography*; for an example, see Jos. *Life* 336–67.
1205. E.g., Isaeus *Cleon.* 31–32, §37; Lysias *Or.* 3.14, §97; see comments on Acts 10:39–42; 24:19.
1206. E.g., Fronto *Ad am.* 1.1; see further comment on Acts 24:14–17.
1207. E.g., Isaeus *Cleon.* 11.36; Lysias *Or.* 3.27, §98 (claiming more than two hundred witnesses, though it is doubtful that all testify).
1208. E.g., Aeschines *Embassy* 14; Philost. *Ep. Apoll.* 37. See also comment on Acts 26:26.
1209. Trans. H. N. Fowler, LCL, 1:119 (πολλοὶ μάρτυρες).
1210. Cic. *Verr.* 1.5.15; 2.1.40.103.
1211. E.g., Isaeus *Pyrr.* 40. Matters of public knowledge were grounds for citizen votes (Aeschines *Tim.* 77–78).

since you know the truth of my claims (*Tim.* 89)! You are probably surprised that I have not yet mentioned Hegesandrus (*Tim.* 55), since you already know him (and his misdeeds with Timarchus) "better than I" (*Tim.* 56). You all know that what I am speaking is true (*Tim.* 65). Aeschines can appeal to their own memories (*Tim.* 44), though he adds affidavits because it is a court (*Tim.* 45). The audience's laughter at some of Timarchus's words that could carry sexual connotations revealed that they knew his reputation (*Tim.* 80).

Such claims were also relevant in apologetic autobiography or self-defense. I grew up among you, Aeschines contends; you know my ways and my integrity (*Embassy* 182, seeking his own acquittal). Rather than merely two or three witnesses, Josephus points to the support of all the Galilean multitude as witnesses on his behalf (*Life* 257); they could testify to how he has lived (*Life* 258). A Roman cried, "From early youth I have passed my life before your eyes[1212] both as a private citizen and in office; those who needed my voice, my counsel, my purse, have had them."[1213] Jesus in John's Gospel appeals to those who have heard him (John 18:21). Paul invokes the witness of the Thessalonians to how he has behaved (1 Thess 2:10). See comment on Acts 20:18 for related ideas.

Sometimes witnesses could be reluctant to testify, whether because of the inconvenience (e.g., Pliny *Ep.* 3.9.29) or out of personal sentiments (e.g., a husband reluctant to charge his wife with adultery, 6.31.5–6). Under duress, one might even appeal to the knowledge of witnesses whom one could not induce to testify: "That this story is true," Isaeus assures us, "many of the Araphenians . . . would probably testify for me, but I could not find anyone to give positive evidence in so grave a matter."[1214]

Although they may not be literally present, Paul effectively invites his accusers to "appear as witnesses for the defence."[1215] He is not harsh with them because discrediting adversaries gently (cf. also Acts 26:21) was a more prudent method than doing so severely (*Rhet. Alex.* 37.1445b.17–19), at least if one's judge might sympathize with one's adversaries as much as with oneself.

(3) Paul's Pharisaism (26:5)

Paul's claim that he "lived [ἔζησα, aorist tense] as a Pharisee" does not mean that he has since abandoned Pharisaism, at least from his understanding of the good that constituted the heart of that movement (cf. Acts 23:6);[1216] he is simply describing his orthodoxy "from the beginning." On the meaning of "sect," see comments at Acts 5:17; 15:5; Josephus already applied it to some Jewish movements, and it was especially relevant to Pharisees.[1217] Whereas some used the designation negatively when denouncing the group to which they applied the title (24:5, 14; 28:22), Paul employs it in its less prejudiced sense here. Both his language of "sect" and use of the term "religion" (θρησκεία) would be appropriate in a hearing aimed toward outsiders.[1218]

1212. *In ore vostro*; rhetoricians liked to recreate scenes before their audience's eyes (e.g., Quint. *Inst.* 9.2.40; Theon. *Progymn.* 7.53–55; see discussion in Keener, *Acts*, 1:135).

1213. Sall. *Sp. G. Cotta* 4 (trans. J. C. Rolfe, LCL, 409, 411).

1214. Isaeus *Astyph.* 18 (trans. E. S. Forster, LCL, 337).

1215. Van Unnik, *Tarsus*, 46.

1216. Witherington, *Acts*, 740, emphasizes the aorist (attributing the present tense in Acts 23:6 only to Paul's resurrection belief). For Dunn, *Acts*, 326, this text still counts Paul as a strict Pharisee. To the extent that Pharisees belonged to "associations" (as *haberim*; see comment on Acts 23:6), Paul could not have continued as one; but he regarded his beliefs as consistent with, and indeed the natural outgrowth of, the culturally open form of Pharisaism that he had learned (see Davies, *Paul*, passim). On Pharisaism, see comment on Acts 5:34–39.

1217. See Jos. *Life* 10, 12, 191, 197; *Ant.* 13.171, 293; 20.199; *War* 2.118, 122, 137, 142, 162; Alexander, "IPSE DIXIT," 123. It already designated philosophical schools (e.g., Epict. *Diatr.* 2.19.20), to which Josephus compared Jewish schools (*Life* 12).

1218. Gaventa, *Acts*, 341. For "religion," cf. the outside perspective also in 4 Macc 5:7, 13.

Paul underlines his Pharisaic orthodoxy (cf. 22:3; 23:6): he lived according to the "strictest" (ἀκριβεστάτην) sect. Some scholars have suggested that the Qumran scrolls call the Pharisees "speakers of smooth things,"[1219] since they were not strict from the perspective of monastic wilderness Essenes.[1220] But even if this is true, the Pharisees were the most meticulous observers of the law in mainstream society, the society that any of Paul's hearers might come in contact with. This expression (ἀκριβεστάτην) praises the Pharisees (and thereby Paul's Jewish piety in this respect). In general, one could praise a city whose laws were "precise"—that is, carefully and consistently spelled out;[1221] a city should also observe its laws meticulously or "with exactness."[1222] Most relevant is that Josephus employs the term to describe the Pharisees' careful treatment of their people's laws.[1223] Paul probably uses the phrase to mean "most accurate" as well as most meticulous in interpretation (cf. Luke's other uses of the term and its cognates in Luke 1:3; Acts 18:25–26; 22:3; 23:15, 20; 24:22).

Plato presents Socrates responding to the charge of disbelieving in the gods by arguing that he believes in them more than any of his accusers does (*Apol.* 35D). By emphasizing his fidelity to the law, Paul defends himself even against the non-capital charges of breaching Jewish law (his first claim in Acts 25:8). Given the diversity of opinion on Jewish interpretation of the law in Paul's day, and given Paul's conviction that his zeal for Jesus was the natural fruition of his now better-informed zeal for the law, it would be hard to deny his loyalty to it, though even the vast majority of Pharisees would have found his treatment of uncircumcised Gentiles troublesome if they understood this as making these new believers proselytes rather than God-fearers.

Certainly his central theological tenet that could be controversial, the resurrection, was a good Pharisaic notion and widely held in Palestinian Judaism. Pharisaism was tolerated, yet it rejected the denial of resurrection on which Paul claimed his accusers based their enmity toward him (24:20–21). Having mentioned his tolerated Pharisaism, he can now speak of the centrality of Israel's hope (26:6–7) that climaxed in the resurrection (26:8). If Pharisaism is tolerated, the charges against him based on that hope (26:6) should be dismissed.

IV. ON TRIAL FOR HIS JEWISH FAITH (26:6–7)

Because it is Pharisaic belief in resurrection in general that makes faith in Jesus's resurrection intelligible and because Paul has portrayed Sadducean opposition to this tenet as the true basis for opposition (23:6; 24:20–21), Paul can argue that he is on trial basically for sharing the resurrection hope of Judaism. Before a Jewish king, this portrayal of the charge would resemble being charged for performing a benefaction (4:9; cf. 24:17), a portrayal meant to shame the accusers.

(1) The Hope concerning the Promise (26:6)

The language of "promise" here reflects themes that run through Luke-Acts, but Luke-Acts may reveal the influence of Pauline theology of the promise (fulfilled

---

1219. Roth, "Subject Matter of Exegesis"; Kugel and Greer, *Interpretation*, 79; but others demur (Meier, "*Halaka*").

1220. Abegg, "Introduction to 4Q251." Certainly the Pharisees were more lenient regarding capital sentences than Sadducees were.

1221. Men. Rhet. 1.3, 363.7 (ἀκριβέσι); 364.10–14 (ἀκριβῶς).

1222. Men. Rhet. 1.3, 360.12–13 (Russell and Wilson, 61; ἀκριβῶς).

1223. Jos. *War* 1.110; 2.162; *Life* 191; cf. *Ant.* 13.297. But different Jewish groups apparently debated appropriate degrees of strictness (in the rabbis, cf., e.g., Lieberman, "Light," 396–400, though these examples need not oppose Qumran as he thinks).

in Christ, e.g., Rom 15:8; 2 Cor 1:20; Gal 3:14–29; Eph 3:6).[1224] The theme of a promise made to the ancestors evokes the promise that all Abraham's seed would be blessed (Acts 3:25; through repentance, 3:26), a promise available in the present through the eschatological Spirit (2:38–39). The epistolary Paul also speaks of the blessing of Abraham being available in the promise of the Spirit (Gal 3:14; cf. Eph 1:3).

Luke usually associates the divine "promise" either with the future inheritance of God's people (Acts 7:5, 17), including the resurrection that allows them to attain it (13:32–35; cf. 13:23),[1225] or with the present possession of the Spirit (Luke 24:49; Acts 1:4; 2:33, 39), the Spirit being a foretaste or (in Pauline terms) a down payment for the inheritance.

Here the focus of the promise is the "hope" for which the tribes seek (Acts 26:7), namely, the resurrection from the dead (26:8); this claim reflects a frequent use of "hope" in Acts (2:26; cf. 28:20), especially in these defense speeches (23:6; 24:15).[1226] For Luke, as for Paul, the present experience of the Spirit is the down payment of future resurrection (Rom 8:23; 2 Cor 1:22; 5:5; Eph 1:13–14). Luke has a future eschatology, expecting the resurrection of all and apparently also the restoration of Israel (occurring especially in the apostolic preaching), although his realized eschatology (Christ has risen and the Spirit has come) is more foregrounded in his narrative in Acts.[1227]

The "promise" theme is central to "Paul's first and last major speeches" (Acts 13:32; 26:6); this theme connects with the Jewish expectation of political freedom (Luke 1:69–75)[1228] and with the reign of the Davidic Messiah (Acts 13:23). Luke's focus on the resurrection might appear to fixate on a minor theme in early Judaism, but not when it is combined with the broader hope of which it is a part.[1229] The eschatological hope encompassed both personal resurrection for the righteous and Israel's corporate restoration (cf. the "twelve tribes" of 26:7).[1230] Further, the theme was no minor one for the Pharisees, whose conflicts with Sadducees often focused on this issue (see comment on Acts 23:6–9).

1224. Emphasis on the promise was widespread in early Jewish Christianity—e.g., in Hebrews. Through unbelief, Israel failed to achieve the promise of rest (Heb 4:1), but those who believe and persevere will inherit the promises (6:12), related to the promise to Abraham (6:13) of blessing and multiplying (6:14), received through waiting (6:15). Waiting in faith is rewarded by God's promise at his coming (10:36; 11:40), which even OT heroes did not yet receive (11:13, 39; probably related to resurrection, 11:35). God's promise to Abraham and his promise of the Melchizedek priesthood are both confirmed by God swearing by himself (6:17–18).

1225. Ezek 37 portrays Israel's restoration as resurrection; those who affirmed literal resurrection could connect the images (Sipre Deut. 306.28.3; y. Šeqal. 3:3; Exod. Rab. 48:4; cf. the Dura-Europos mural of Ezek 37:1–14, e.g., in Philonenko, "Ossements desséchés").

1226. Cf. the "eternal hope" promised to Jacob through Isaac's blessing in Jub. 31:32.

1227. After the initial enthusiasm for a completely realized eschatology (opposed by some, e.g., Morris, Judgment, 57–60), most scholars, including C. H. Dodd himself, moved toward the view that eschatology was inaugurated yet awaited a future consummation (see Cullmann, State, 87–88; Hunter, Predecessors, 147; Perrin, Kingdom, 58–78, esp. [on Dodd's change] 67; Ladd, Theology, 59). For some realized eschatology in the OT prophets, see Morris, Apocalyptic, 63 (in contrast, he argues, with apocalyptists, on 67); at Qumran, see Sanders, Judaism, 368–70; Aune, Cultic Setting; in Egyptian eschatology, the nature of time may yield something analogous (Book of Dead Spell 17, part S-3 [p. 27]).

1228. Tannehill, Acts, 320. Western readers currently have the luxury of spiritualizing such hopes away more than do some other readers; Luke seems to accept both the spiritual and the political hope, albeit only the first for this age (happily for his apologetic; cf. Acts 17:7).

1229. Tannehill, Acts, 319; followed also by Peterson, Acts, 661.

1230. For Israel's restoration, see, e.g., Isa 40:9–11; Jer 32:42–44; Ezek 37:21–28; Hos 11:9–11; 14:4–7; Amos 9:11–15. On one level Luke would see preliminary fulfillment in the Messiah's first coming, but he also expected a fuller completion in the future (Acts 1:6–7; 3:19–21; the limitation of the "times of the Gentiles" in Luke 21:24).

(2) The Tribes' Continual Worship (26:7)

Although many other sedentary nations also were divided into "tribes,"[1231] sometimes even twelve tribes,[1232] the phrase "our twelve tribes" refers to Israel,[1233] for which Luke sees a future hope when restored under apostolic leadership (Luke 22:30 [= Q Matt 19:28]). Scripture already associated the image of resurrection (see comment on Acts 26:6) with the reuniting of regathered Judah and Israel (Ezek 37:12–23). Even more prominently in Jewish tradition, the lost tribes would be restored in the eschatological time.[1234] Paul's particular compound form, δωδεκάφυλον, probably reflects an elevated style (only here in biblical Greek; cf. λαὸς ὁ δωδεκάφυλος, *Sib. Or.* 11.36, possibly late first-century B.C.E. Egypt).[1235]

The call to "serve" or "worship" (λατρεύω) God belonged to Israel (Luke 1:74; 4:8; Acts 7:7) and the language often bears a cultic sense (Luke 2:37; 4:8; cf. Acts 7:42); Paul also described his own service to God with this verb (Acts 24:14; 27:23).[1236] Serving "night and day" might evoke temple service (1 Chr 9:33; Ps 134:1, albeit neither with this verb; Rev 7:15);[1237] Luke's ideal example of this lifestyle is Anna the prophetess, who worshiped God in the temple night and day (Luke 2:37). Paul's

---

1231. E.g., Rome (Polyb. 6.14.7; Val. Max. 2.3.9b; 6.3.4; Tac. *Ann.* 3.4; Suet. *Jul.* 13; *Aug.* 56.1; 57.2; 101.2; *Tib.* 3.2; cf. Rapske, "Citizenship," 215, noting that it functioned as "a political and legal fiction"; Galsterer, "Tribus," 912, noting it was rarely used outside Rome); Athens (Lysias *Or.* 23.2, §166; Aeschines *Tim.* 33; Ael. Arist. *Panath.* 382, in 314D) and Attica (Graf, "Eponymus," 1166; about ten tribes); Corinth (Winter, *Left Corinth*, 190n19, notes ten tribes known from inscriptions); an estimated 118 tribes in India (Arrian *Ind.* 7.1); see further Smarczyk, "Phyle" (on Greek usage, starting among Ionians and Dorians but spreading [210]). Egypt had five "peoples" (Manetho *Aeg.* frg. 2.1). Alexander conquered twenty-two non-Greek nations and fourteen tribes of Greeks (Ps.-Callisth. *Alex.* 3.35), and Cyrus more tribes (Xen. *Cyr.* 1.1.5); Trajan's rule over innumerable tribes (Dio Chrys. *Or.* 3.6) was equivalent to ruling the world (3.7). On the "tribes" in cities of the Greek East, see MacMullen, *Social Relations*, 131–32; cf. Philost. *Vit. soph.* 1.11.495.

1232. So Persia in Xen. *Cyr.* 1.2.5; cf. its "twelve nations" in Quint. Curt. 3.3.13; cf. also the league of twelve Etruscan cities (Eder, "Cities").

1233. As in, e.g., Exod 24:4; 39:14; Deut 1:23; Josh 3:12; 4:4–5; Ezra 6:17; Ezek 47:13; Sir 44:23; *Sib. Or.* 3.249; 1QM II, 2–3; Philo *Sobr.* 66; *Prelim. St.* 168; *Flight* 185; *Mos.* 1.189, 221, 306; 2.160, 175, 178; *Spec. Laws* 1.79; 2.161; *Rewards* 57; *2 Bar.* 77:2; 78:4; 84:3; *Test. Naph.* 5:8; *Gen. Rab.* 68:11; 70:18. Awareness of the phrase continues much later (e.g., Qur'an 5.12; 7.160). Many scholars think that the phrase in Jas 1:1 refers to the church (Ropes, *James*, 118–19; Moffatt, *General Epistles*, 6; Dibelius, *James*, 66; Laws, *James*, 47–48; Kee, *Origins*, 149; Sloyan, "James," 29; Barth, *People of God*, 14; Davids, *James*, 63; tentatively, Sidebottom, *James*, 26); others think that it applies to messianic Jews (Martin, *James*, 9) or to Diaspora Jews more generally (Mayor, *James*, 29–30). (It is possible that James addressed a primarily Jewish audience but the edited letter was circulated and applied more widely.) The same division of opinion occurs at Rev 7:4–8, with many viewing the tribes as all Christians (Schlier, *Principalities*, 70; Barth, *People of God*, 14; Mounce, *Revelation*, 168–70; Johnson, *Revelation*, 85; Bauckham, *Climax*, 215–16, 399; Keener, *Revelation*, 230–22) and others only as ethnically Jewish followers of Jesus (González and González, *Revelation*, 55; Geyser, "Tribes"; Tenney, *Revelation*, 78; Walvoord, *Revelation*, 143).

1234. E.g. *Test. Benj.* 9:2 (though preceding a clear Christian interpolation); *Pesiq. Rab Kah.* 24:9; Jeremias, *Theology*, 235; Sanders, *Jesus and Judaism*, 96–97; Wright, *Paul*, 139–63. Speculations on the current location of the "lost" tribes varied (*4 Ezra* 13:40–43; *Gen. Rab.* 73:6; *Pesiq. Rab.* 31:10). Some rabbis affirmed the ten tribes' wickedness (*Gen. Rab.* 28:5) and doubted that they would return (*m. Sanh.* 10:5) or be saved (*t. Sanh.* 13:12; a minority view in *b. Sanh.* 110b, bar.). For Israel's eschatological regathering, see, e.g., Bar 4:37; 5:5; 2 Macc 2:18; Tob 13:6; *Pss. Sol.* 8:28; *Pesiq. Rab Kah.* Sup. 5:3; *Gen. Rab.* 98:9.

1235. In BDAG, cf. Hdt. 5.66.2; *Sib. Or.* 2.171. The only occurrence in the Apostolic Fathers is *1 Clem.* 55.6, but BDAG compares the adjective in *G. Jms.* 1:3. The idea, of course, is common (e.g., among Christians, Jas 1:1; Rev 21:12; *1 Clem.* 31.4; 43.2; *Barn.* 8.3; *Herm.* 94.1–2).

1236. Paul's letters also use it in the cultic sense in Rom 1:25; Phil 3:3 (cf. 2 Tim 1:3) and for Paul (Rom 1:9; cf. 2 Tim 1:3); also the noun cognate for Israel's (Rom 9:4) and the church's (12:1) worship. It stands for worship frequently in its many LXX uses. Rhetorically, "God" is emphasized in Acts 26:6–8, 18–22 (Parsons, "Progymnasmata," 58; idem, *Acts*, 339).

1237. Cf. Neh 1:6; Esth 4:16; Pss 22:2 (21:3 LXX); 77:2 (76:3); 87:2 LXX; Jdt 11:17; 2 Macc 13:10; 2 Tim 1:3; contrast Jer 16:13; Rev 14:11.

recognition that Israel worships God night and day compliments Israel's zeal[1238] (as the historical Paul did even when critiquing Israel, Rom 10:2). The verb καταντάω is common in Acts (nine of thirteen times in the NT), but the other NT uses are in Pauline literature and parallel the sense more closely, especially Phil 3:11 (attaining the resurrection).

Ironically, it is this very hope[1239] of the resurrection for which Paul now stands accused by leaders of a nation that mostly shared the same hope (Acts 26:7, end; cf. 26:6a; see comment on Acts 24:15); he will explain the opposition more specifically in 26:21. Paul remains consistent with his earlier claim that the genuine basis for opposition is a disagreement over the fact and nature of the resurrection (23:6; 24:21–22). A defendant might link his case with a higher (and sometimes widely accepted) cause, so that (for example) the attack on the defendant was an attack on the city and what it stood for.[1240] Paul is attacked by his people for defending the very heritage of his people. An argument from probability (see comment on Acts 26:8) also works better if the desire that the defendant articulates is one shared and understood by his audience—for example, the prosperity of his people.[1241]

v. God Can Raise the Dead (26:8)

The central objection to Paul's position was (especially among Greeks and those influenced by them, 17:32) the resurrection; but resurrection is not a problem for an omnipotent God. Although the term is frequent in Acts (roughly 21 times), Paul's "*judged* unbelievable" may echo his "I stand being *judged* for the promise" (26:6): Paul makes his case rise or fall with Jesus's resurrection, affording opportunity for him to focus on that question. His actions rest on his faith, and their theological defensibility (and his reliability as a witness) rests on its truth.

(1) Believing the Resurrection

If the logic of the flow of thought in the context seems tenuous to us, it is partly because Luke's summary is terse; but it is not hard to follow. The promise of Israel's restoration (26:6–7) is intimately connected with the hope of the resurrection (26:8; cf. Ezek 37:12–14; Dan 12:1–2), for which Paul is on trial (Acts 26:6). The concrete historical expression of this hope already fulfilled is in Jesus (26:9; cf. 4:2; in more detail 26:23); only disbelief in the resurrection of the body could be used to justify rejecting the eyewitness claims of those who have encountered the risen Christ (26:13–20). Yet those who accept the existence of an omnipotent God need not deny resurrection (26:8)—something Festus has been inclined to do (cf. 25:19).

Jesus's resurrection (26:9) is part of the eschatological resurrection hope (26:6–8) and need not be rejected by those who affirm resurrection logic: if the general category of resurrection is tenable, why not the specific example of Jesus's resurrection? And even those who do not regard it as tenable ought to regard it as tolerable: how could Paul be persecuted for affirming a resurrection of one person when the respected Pharisaic sect that nurtured him affirms a resurrection of many?

1238. "Night and day" often indicates zeal (e.g., Ps 1:2; Men. Rhet. 2.3, 384.29–30).
1239. The repetition of the noun after the cognate verb ἐλπίζει resembles διλογία, in which a word not strictly necessary is repeated for clarity (Anderson, *Glossary*, 37). The repetition, found in some translations (e.g., NRSV; NASB), of "promise" in Acts 26:6–7, however, is the translators' addition for clarity, not Luke's.
1240. E.g., Aeschines *Tim.* 1–2; similarly, a prosecutor could call all who love the senate to hate the defendant (*Rhet. Her.* 4.35.47). Not only Agrippa but the Gentile Romans present would regard love of country as a very high virtue (e.g., Val. Max. 2.2.1a).
1241. So *Rhet. Alex.* 7, 1428a.26–30.

When Paul uses the plural form of "among you" (παρ' ὑμῖν), he avoids sounding as though he is accusing Agrippa himself, although Agrippa, as a hellenized and romanized Jew, is perhaps more likely to accept the immortality of the soul[1242] (or, much less likely, Sadducean annihilation) than the Pharisaic doctrine of the resurrection. "Among you" would refer not to Judeans in general, many of whom did share the hope (26:6–7), but to those present, most of whom would not share it (see the list in 25:23).

(2) Countering the Usual Probability Argument

Although Luke (Luke 9:41; 12:46) and other NT writers tend to use ἄπιστος to mean "unbelieving,"[1243] it can also mean "incredible," "unbelievable," as here; this was, in fact, the more common classical usage (fitting the audience of this speech).[1244] Forensic orators dealing with past events sometimes treated witnesses as less credible than arguments from probability (see comment below).[1245] Acts follows the Isaianic emphasis on witnesses (see comment on Acts 1:8), and here (in contrast to some other passages) Paul counters the probability argument. He cannot argue, on the basis of common occurrence, that the resurrection is a probable event,[1246] but he can argue that, given God's power and promises, it is not improbable.

Arguments from probability were important in ancient rhetoric, including arguments against the consistency of the opposing position.[1247] When he lacks witnesses, Demosthenes builds an argument from inference and claims that his witnesses are the facts (*Fals. leg.* 120).[1248] Elsewhere he shows a charge to be absurd because it wrongly assumes his foreknowledge of events (*Pant.* 23). Another orator complains that the opponents propose something that violates probability: "Could anything be more incredible [ἀπιστότερα] than this?" (Isaeus *Cleon.* 22.37).[1249] Josephus refutes a charge of Apion by claiming that it is simply unbelievable (*Ag. Ap.* 2.82);[1250] he produces not only documents supporting his own case (*Life* 342) but logic refuting his challenger's (*Life* 350).[1251]

1242. Whether temporary, like the Stoics (Klauck, *Context*, 358; cf. Sen. Y. *Dial.* 11.9.3; 12.11.7; *Ep. Lucil.* 57.9), or permanent, like the Platonists (e.g., Plato *Phaedo* 64CE; Max. Tyre 10.5; Porph. *Marc.* 12.212–15; Philo *Creation* 135). See, e.g., brief discussion in Keener, *Corinthians*, 177–78.

1243. Unbelief (or unfaithfulness) was a moral failing (Luke 12:46), sometimes corporate (9:41). Luke, like some other early Christian writers, may understand unbelief as a moral failing in the face of contrary evidence, though "ignorance" (Acts 3:17; 17:23; this could include being uninformed and, further, being enmeshed in the corporate sin of alternative cultural plausibility structures) may reduce the degree of culpability vis-à-vis those who most should have known better.

1244. BDAG cites Bacchylides *Carmina* 17.117; Xen. *Cyr.* 3.1.26; Plato *Theag.* 130; *Corp. herm.* 9.10; *Let. Aris.* 296; Philo *Creation* 114 (and passim); Jos. *Ant.* 6.198; Justin *Dial.* 73.5–6; Athenag. *Plea* 30.3; and, as a closer parallel to the language here, Jos. *Ant.* 18.76.

1245. See, e.g., Hermog. *Inv.* 3.5.142. Classical rhetorical handbooks favored probability over direct evidence, though later orators used personality, motivation, and hard evidence as a basis for probability more than did earlier rhetoricians (Kennedy, *Classical Rhetoric*, 20–21).

1246. Cook, *Interpretation*, 55–58, esp. 59–61, notes that Celsus (esp. in Origen *Cels.* 3.22, 42, on p. 58) attacks as impossible the notion of resurrection from a Hellenistic perspective (comparing the apotheosis of Greek heroes). But (59–61) Celsus relied especially on the philosophic argument (see also comment on Acts 17:18).

1247. E.g., *Rhet. Alex.* 9, 1430a.14–21, 26–27; Hermog. *Inv.* 3.5.142–43, 146; 3.15.167; 4.14.211. See further Anderson, *Glossary*, 37. For one example (the improbability of a release having been by lower, unauthorized officials), see Pliny *Ep.* 10.31.4.

1248. For the method, see later Hermog. *Issues* 46.4–8.

1249. Trans. E. S. Forster, LCL, 18–19. Isaeus offers other arguments from probability (e.g., *Cleon.* 12.36; *Astyph.* 14–15; *Pyrr.* 27).

1250. Josephus challenges an account's probability on the basis of intrinsic inconsistencies (*Ag. Ap.* 1.267, 286; 2.8–27, 148).

1251. Here he asks how he, rather than Justus, could have caused the problem.

Historians and biographers also often evaluated their sources on the basis of probability;[1252] one could dismiss ancient claims, such as particular herbs restoring persons to life, as unbelievable.[1253] Standard rhetorical criteria for developing refutations include an argument's implausibility or impossibility;[1254] by contrast, defending an argument might entail contending for its possibility.[1255] See further discussion at Acts 24:11.

Sometimes, however, writers warned that what might otherwise sound improbable or exaggerated is true.[1256] Rhetoricians explained that one's support for what appears improbable might not seem unbelievable (ἀπίστως) if we provide supporting arguments (*Rhet. Alex.* 30, 1438b.2–4).[1257] Others recognized the contingency of plausibility structures; those schooled in only one philosophic system would find it internally consistent, but this approach ignored external realities.[1258] Most relevant here was the intelligibility of Paul's point: what is humanly impossible is not impossible for God (as for the resurrection, so also for miraculous births; Luke 1:37; cf. 18:27).[1259] The early stories about Dionysus are hard to believe, one biographer opines, but what would normally be improbable cannot be dismissed when one is dealing with a divine element (Arrian *Alex.* 5.1.2). If some could affirm this about created or begotten gods, how much more could anyone affirm it of the supreme Creator of the universe?

Technical rhetoricians distinguished among various kinds of rhetorical questions. One kind was a brief question that the speaker then proceeded to answer.[1260] Paul's question here, however, appears to require no direct answer; it assumes the unstated premise that nothing is impossible to God.[1261]

vi. Former Persecutor of Christians (26:9–11)

Paul both establishes his credibility in testifying for Christ (since it cannot be the result of his original presuppositions) and tarnishes the credibility of his accusers (Acts 26:10).

(1) Rhetoric

Paul's account of persecuting the saints (26:10–11) as the context for his revelation (26:12) is rhetorically sound. The support for opinion B by a character whom one would instead expect to hold opinion A carries much more weight in favor of opinion B than the support of someone whom one would expect to support it.[1262] One earlier rhetorical handbook expresses this principle in the case of witnesses:

1252. E.g., Polyb. 3.20.1–5; 3.47.6; 3.48.7–9; Dion. Hal. *Ant. rom.* 3.35.5–6; Plut. *Themist.* 25.1–2; 27.1. Also religious novelists (Philost. *Hrk.* 48.13; Maclean and Aitken, *Heroikos*, lxiv).
1253. So Pliny E. *N.H.* 25.5.13–14.
1254. Hermog. *Progymn.* 5, "On Refutation and Confirmation," 11; *Inv.* 4.12.202; Aphth. *Progymn.* 5, "On Refutation," 27–28S, 10R; Nicolaus *Progymn.* 6, "On Refutation and Confirmation," 30.
1255. Cf. Aphth. *Progymn.* 7, "On Commonplace," 35S, 20R; Nicolaus *Progymn.* 7, "On Commonplace," 44.
1256. E.g., Thucyd. 2.35.2–3 (on war exploits recounted at the funeral, when epideictic license was expected).
1257. Cf. also Hermog. *Inv.* 4.12.202–3 (offering the example of Hom. *Od.* 9.481). What seems too improbable is saved for the end (*Rhet. Alex.* 30, 1438b.4–10), as in Acts 17:31; but because Paul's hearers will already be aware of his view (and his defense is based on his affirming this particular view), he introduces it earlier here.
1258. So Lucian *Hermot.* 75.
1259. Pliny E. *N.H.* 2.5.27 would have objected that not even God could raise the dead, but this is a less powerful conception of God than in Judaism. Various deities proved unable to raise their beloved ones (e.g., Ovid *Metam.* 2.617–18; 4.247–49), though mythology paradoxically granted this power to others, such as Asclepius.
1260. Anderson, *Glossary*, 14.
1261. See Luke 1:37; Mark 10:27; Matt 19:26. See similar ideas in Callim. frg. 586; Iambl. *V.P.* 28.139, 148; cf. Philo *Mos.* 1.174; on Wisdom, Wis 7:27. For nothing being impossible to God except what violates his character by lying, see, e.g., *1 Clem.* 27.2 (cf. Hermog. *Issues* 33).
1262. See Heath, "Invention," 91; fuller comment at Acts 15:13–21.

Another thing to consider is whether the witness is a friend of the man for whom he is giving evidence, or in some way connected with his act, or whether he is an enemy of the person against whom he is giving evidence, or a poor man; because witnesses in these circumstances are suspected of giving false testimony, from motives in the one case of favor, in the other of revenge, and in the other of gain.[1263]

Paul, who now testifies for the risen Christ, had not been predisposed to listen to the Christian interpretation, and nothing less concrete than a divine epiphany transformed his cause. In the process, Paul also exposes the nasty underbelly of how the earliest Jesus movement had been treated, publicly confronting with truth an entire elite (25:23) who had political reasons to ignore it.

In 26:9, Paul introduces by way of summary the list of persecutions against Jesus's followers that he will develop in 26:10–11:[1264] he closed many of them up in prisons, voted against them at executions (26:10), punished them in synagogues, sought to make them blaspheme, and pursued them even to foreign cities (26:11). Paul's use of both the first-person pronoun (grammatically superfluous because implied in the verb) and the reflexive pronoun graphically highlights Paul's personal activity and responsibility.[1265]

(2) Imprisoning Saints

Paul's first action here was to shut[1266] many of the saints up in prisons (8:3; 22:4, 19). Since Paul himself is in custody, his confession of imprisoning others invites his persecutors to identify with him; if he (whose acts of coercion exceeded theirs, at least given his relative rank) was a candidate for conversion, so are they. Such detention appears as a frequent danger for God's servants in Luke-Acts,[1267] which reduces for Luke's audience the stigma otherwise attached to Paul's detention.

By speaking of members of the Way as "saints," "holy ones," Paul indicates at the outset that he was acting against God (26:14); see comment on those "sanctified" ("set apart," "consecrated as holy") at Acts 26:18 (also 20:32).[1268] "Saints" here may be shorthand for the saints in Jerusalem (Acts 9:13; Rom 15:26; 1 Cor 16:1; 2 Cor 9:1), apparently a common name or even a technical label for themselves.[1269] But it had broader applicability (Acts 9:32, 41), even to Gentile believers (26:18; see comment there).

Paul could lock up the "saints" not by his own license but precisely because he had received "authority" from the high priests (26:10; so also 9:14; 26:12).[1270] By

---

1263. *Rhet. Alex.* 15, 1431b.37–41 (trans. H. Rackham, LCL, 345). Many philosophers recommended dwelling more on positive memories of the past (Sorabji, *Emotion*, 231), but some also found valuable use for unpleasant memories in context (233).

1264. Cf. the rhetorical use of headings or summaries to introduce or conclude topics (cf. Isaeus *Cleon.* 48; Arius Did. *Epit.* 2.7.5b2, pp. 14–15.24; Fronto *Ad M. Caes.* 2.3.3).

1265. Note here Schnabel, *Acts*, 1005. If δεῖ suggests a divine passive, as elsewhere in Luke-Acts, it here belongs to Paul's former, mistaken notion of God's will (see Kurz, *Acts*, 357).

1266. Luke (and the NT) elsewhere uses the verb only for Antipas (Agrippa's relative) imprisoning John (Luke 3:20); it applies to chains (3 Macc 3:25) but especially to confinement (Jer 32:3; 2 Macc 13:21; Jos. *War* 4.327; *OGIS* 669.17; BDAG).

1267. For John (Luke 3:20), all believers (21:12), the apostles (Acts 5:19–25), Peter (12:4–10, 17), and Paul himself (16:23–40). The apostles, Peter, and Paul are released.

1268. Perhaps an ancient auditor would imagine a gesture of abhorrence (turning away the face; on the gesture, Shiell, *Reading Acts*, 76–77) or, less likely here, of memory (plucking the ear, cf. Sen. Y. *Dial.* 7.10.3). The text, however, gives us no clear guidance to this extent.

1269. Perhaps because they expected eschatological events there (cf. Dan 7:18, 21–22, 25, 27). On Luke's usual application to those in Judea, see Trebilco, "Self-Designations," 45–49.

1270. Contrast Jesus's gift of authority for benevolent activity (Luke 9:1; 10:19; cf. Acts 8:19) and promise of future authority (Luke 19:17).

mentioning the high priests (and the corporate decision-making perhaps suggested by "cast my vote"), Paul implicates his own accusers (underlining this point again in 26:12).[1271] (He had already incriminated their class in 22:5, and it is possible that silencing or at least discrediting his testimony is one concern in the case.) Rome did not grant local leaders the right to execute anyone, but Paul is about to mention people being put to death.[1272]

The very leadership that now accuses Paul, after he has quit acting criminally, acted criminally along with him.[1273] One rhetorical device was for a defendant or a politician to implicate his audience; its members shared in the decision for which he was now assigned responsibility.[1274] But it was far more common to reverse charges against one's accusers (see comment on Acts 24:19); Paul here implies that the chief priests approved of and sponsored these illegal acts.[1275] The implication may also be that if they now oppose Paul, it is because he has departed from such unethical activity whereas they continue in it (cf. 23:14–15; 25:3; and, more ambiguously but possibly as part of the court record, 23:30).

(3) Paul's "Vote"[1276]

Second, Paul "voted" against Christians at their executions (cf. Saul's agreement with Stephen's death, 8:1; 22:20). (Dividing up a charge into multiple components was a way to amplify it; Hermog. *Inv.* 1.2.101.) Casting his vote against "them" could mean that more than Stephen were put to death, which may fit the summary of 22:4 (though summaries strove more for the general sense than for precision in detail; see comments on Acts 2:41–47; 6:7). It might, however, be a generalizing plural, which would allow the possibility that his intentions were fulfilled in only one concrete case;[1277] analogously in his rhetoric, in 26:11 he claims to have pursued Christians to "foreign cities" whereas the only one we know of was Damascus (9:2; 22:5; 26:12).

Against some scholars,[1278] it is extremely unlikely that Paul was a member of the

1271. Cf. Witherington, *Acts*, 742 (following Keener, *Background Commentary*, 399). Of course, although this argument works rhetorically, it is "high priests" more generally, not the specific ones now accusing him (who probably were not the same leaders who commissioned him), who were complicit. Catchpole, *Trial*, 250, thinks that Acts 26:10 attests the Sanhedrin's authority to pass capital sentences but (against Winter) not to execute them without Roman approval; although this might be true, the present text indicates people (or, if a generalizing plural for Stephen, a person) being executed.

1272. Luke employs the verb ἀναιρέω especially for Jesus (Luke 22:2; 23:32; Acts 2:23; 10:39; 13:28) and Paul (Acts 9:23–24, 29; 23:15, 21, 27; 25:3); also for the apostles (5:33), including James (12:2). But Stephen (22:20) is the most relevant example here.

1273. Roman law did not regard mere advice or exhortation as creating liability; a request or an order to act illegally would be liable (Robinson, *Criminal Law*, 19–20). Most of those originally involved would now be deceased or could claim ignorance of the illegal part of Paul's activity. Conversely, involvement in such activity could be viewed as the forerunner of the current assassins (Acts 23:12–14). By implying the involvement in subversive activity of members of the elite (an implication borne out in some cases in Josephus), Paul could have offered the rhetorical strategy of pleading for the opposite of what the state's *enemies* would want (Hermog. *Inv.* 1.1.100).

1274. E.g., Libanius *Declam.* 36.42; 44.50–52, 61.

1275. If we construe "casting pebbles" literally, a majority approved of condemnation (Romans counted a tie vote as acquittal, Dion. Hal. *Ant. rom.* 7.64.6).

1276. I have used material here in Keener, "Vote."

1277. Paul's letters mention persecution but not execution, even in 1 Thess 2:15. One cannot argue from silence that no one or few were executed, but neither need one press the plural so as to be certain that it happened on multiple (still less, many) occasions. For a literal plural, see Peterson, *Acts*, 663–64; for its being rhetorical, see Marshall, *Acts*, 393.

1278. E.g., Blaiklock, *Acts*, 86; Rapske, *Custody*, 103; LaSor, *Knew*, 91–92; cf. Talbert, *Acts*, 193, who allows the possibility that Luke portrays Paul thus in Acts 22:5; Pervo, *Acts*, 630, thinking that Luke so portrays him (absurdly) here. Others rightly demur (e.g., Witherington, *Acts*, 742; Bock, *Acts*, 715; Lenski, *Acts*, 1033).

Sanhedrin. Granted, he came from a wealthy family;[1279] but it was also a Hellenist family (see comment at Acts 6:9), and most of the elders of the Sanhedrin came from aristocratic Judean (and very often priestly) families. He was too young (7:58) to hold such a respected position[1280] and was probably not yet married,[1281] and his occasions of being forced to boast about his background do not list this qualification (although one notes that he was advancing far in his age-group, Gal 1:14).

It is also unlikely that the "voting" is literal here. Some think that the juridical context and the frequent metonymy of "pebble" for "vote" in such contexts suggests a literal vote.[1282] The frequent use of "pebbles" in voting historically[1283] allowed for this metonymy, though other "ballots" were also employed.[1284] But the metonymy could stand for other means of corporate approval than a vote as well.[1285]

Johnson shows why literal voting is unlikely here: the present participle suggests condemnation roughly simultaneous with (rather than preceding) the execution; no voting is suggested in Acts 7:57–58; and for all Luke's emphasis on Paul's high status, Luke never portrays him as a member of the Sanhedrin (the only group in Israel that would even claim legitimate capital jurisdiction, had Rome granted it).[1286]

Most relevant (but often not noted by commentators) is the widespread figurative use of "ballots."[1287] Sometimes the phrase is used figuratively for expressing an opinion.[1288] When deciding the authenticity of a reputed speech of Lysias, Dionysius of Halicarnassus finds one criterion that casts the final "vote" (ψῆφον, *Lysias* 11).[1289]

1279. Rapske, *Custody*, 103, notes that many Pharisaic members were scribes (following Jeremias, *Jerusalem*, 236) and that only the wealthiest of the Pharisees, now moving into the bourgeoisie, would be admitted (citing Jos. *War* 2.411). See discussion on Paul's family background at Acts 22:3 (esp. Keener, *Acts*, 3:3217).

1280. Though Libanius *Anecdote* 3.13 might allow it for the educated, elders were more respected (cf. Aeschines *Ctes.* 4; *Tim.* 23, 25; 1 Tim 4:12); classical Athenians disallowed men below age thirty from sitting on the council (Xen. *Mem.* 1.2.35). See fuller discussion at Acts 7:58.

1281. The rule (*b. Sanh.* 36b) dates from after Jerusalem's destruction (Longenecker, *Ministry and Message*, 23–24), but it probably reflects mainstream Jewish expectations for leaders (see the excursus "Why Mention Their Virginity?" in Keener, *Acts*, 3:3094–102, here 3100). Many in antiquity considered ruling a family an important qualification for demonstrating ability to rule a city or others; Isoc. *Nic.* 41 (*Or.* 3.35); *Ad Nic.* 19; *Demon.* 35; Sen. Y. *Ben.* 4.27.5; cf. Plut. *Dinner* 12, *Mor.* 155D; Marc. Aur. *Med.* 1.16.4; Verner, *Household*, 152; Malherbe, *Social Aspects*, 99n21.

1282. Rapske, *Custody*, 102–3. The term ψῆφος usually applied to a voting pebble but came into "rabbinic literature as a loan word for a voting tablet or verdict" (Le Cornu, *Acts*, 1397, rightly noting Jastrow, *Dictionary*, 1196, on *Lam. Rab.* 2:1, §3). For metonymy, see, e.g., *Rhet. Her.* 4.32.43; Anderson, *Glossary*, 77 (citing Quint. *Inst.* 8.6.23–27 and other sources); Rowe, "Style," 126; Porter, "Paul and Letters," 578; Black, "Oration at Olivet," 85; Caird, *Language*, 136–37; Mickelsen, *Interpreting*, 186.

1283. E.g., Iambl. *V.P.* 35.260. White pebbles were used for acquittal, black ones for condemnation (Plut. *Alc.* 22.2; cf. Hemer, *Letters*, 97; Ford, *Revelation*, 399; Beasley-Murray, *Revelation*, 88); potsherds could be used to ostracize (Corn. Nep. 2 [Themistocles], 8.1; 5 [Cimon], 3.1). The traditional Roman oath was to hold a stone while swearing that the violator should be cast away like the stone, then hurling away the stone (Polyb. 3.25.7–9).

1284. E.g., a hollow disk for conviction and a solid-stem one for acquittal (Aeschines *Tim.* 79).

1285. Some scholars thus allow its application to "unofficial action" (Lake and Cadbury, *Commentary*, 317; Bruce, *Acts*[1], 443) or a figurative sense (Witherington, *Acts*, 742), such as siding with those so voting (Fitzmyer, *Acts*, 758). Cognates shifted accordingly; despite its etymology, ψήφισμα usually applied to a decree (Rhodes, "Psephisma," 110).

1286. Johnson, *Acts*, 434 (suggesting that the phrase could be used to emphasize the Sanhedrin's responsibility and Paul as their agent).

1287. E.g., ψῆφος in Xen. *Symp.* 5.8 (in a jest); figuratively cooperating (he uses συμψήφους, which has a broader semantic range [LSJ]) with God's decree in Mus. Ruf. frg. 38, p. 136.4–5; an analogy in Max. Tyre 16.3–4; evaluating truth in 33.1; Libanius *Encomium* 3.19; *Speech in Character* 6.1; 23.7. This usage probably retained a figurative element instead of becoming a standard part of the term's meaning; the term continued to mean voting (for its literal usage, see, e.g., Rhodes, "Katacheirotonia").

1288. Ael. Arist. *Def. Or.* 1, 1D; Libanius *Invective* 6.1; Symm. *Ep.* 1.96.

1289. When deciding whether to publish a speech, one could ask a friend to cast his vote (*calculam* [pebble], Pliny *Ep.* 1.2.5).

Lucian tells his patron that no matter what the vote (ψῆφον) of others on his work, his patron's carries far more weight and is decisive (*Harm.* 3).

Paul likely speaks of "casting his pebble" as a pun: as Stephen was being stoned to death, Paul cast his own pebble.[1290] This sense, granted, cannot be inferred simply from the idiom "cast"; jurors "casting" their pebble was idiomatic (cf. φέρειν τὴν ψῆφον, Plut. *Cic.* 7.4).[1291] But it makes excellent sense in this context. Some scholars object that this "seems an unlikely bit of gallows humor that does not suit the tenor of this speech."[1292] Puns were not, however, meant to be funny; they were displays of rhetorical skill or wit and sometimes were even used in arguments.[1293] Further, Luke would not have been the only writer in antiquity to conceive or report such a Greek wordplay. Compare one fragment of Hipponax (frg. 89): "by public vote . . . / Pebbled with stones she may die, an evil death to the evil."[1294] Likewise, when some accusers agree to drop their stones and vote as jurors instead, the defendant says, "Keep your stones [λίθους], however, . . . for you will need them presently at court."[1295]

(4) Discipline to Compel Renunciation of Christ

Third, Paul disciplined many Christians in the synagogues (perhaps hyperbolically, "all the synagogues"; cf. Acts 22:19); other texts mention only his going to the synagogues (9:2; 22:19) or punishing them in Jerusalem (22:5), and so this statement offers specific new information. This claim involved a very public matter, for which surviving witnesses could no doubt still be found (cf. 26:4–5, 26).[1296] We have evidence that early Christians did in fact face discipline in synagogues (Mark 13:9; Luke 12:11; 21:12; Matt 10:17; 23:39),[1297] including Paul himself once he became a follower of Christ (2 Cor 11:24).[1298]

That the purpose of the punishment was to compel the Nazarenes to "blaspheme" is also new information in Acts, negative information about Paul's prior behavior not shared earlier. The term here for "punish" (τιμωρέω) appears twice in the NT, both referring to Paul's activity against Christians (Acts 22:5). Although the term can refer to divine punishment,[1299] it also appears in Jewish martyr literature for the torture to which tyrants subjected Jewish martyrs (2 Macc 7:7).

1290. With Johnson, *Acts*, 434.

1291. For the idiom, BDAG adds Philo *Unchangeable* 75; Jos. *Ant.* 2.163; 10.60.

1292. Witherington, *Acts*, 742. Admittedly, Luke is not particularly fond of wordplays (unlike John); their occasional use might, however, suit the elevated rhetoric of this speech. (Elevated rhetoric avoided excessive puns, however; Anderson, *Glossary*, 93, 127; esp. idem, *Rhetorical Theory*, 283–85; cf. Sen. Y. *Ep. Lucil.* 108.12.)

1293. E.g., *Rhet. Her.* 4.21.29–4.22.31; Suet. *Jul.* 50.2; Lucian *True Story* 2.20; Ps.-Callisth. *Alex.* 1.35; *Jub.* 26:30; cf. Rowe, "Style," 132; homonyms in Porph. *Ar. Cat.* 61.10–68.3. On the word "head," see, e.g., Fronto *Ad M. Caes.* 2.3.3; CD VIII, 10–11; 1 Cor 11:3.

1294. *Herodes, Cercidas, and the Greek Choliambic Poets* (trans. A. D. Knox, LCL, 60–61 [ψηφῖδι]).

1295. Lucian *Fisherman* 11 (trans. A. M. Harmon, LCL, 3:19).

1296. If later sources are accurate, a person would be bound to a post and beaten, presumably outside the synagogue proper (*m. Mak.* 3:12; or lying on the ground, *Sipre Deut.* 286.4.1). There—if later records, again, reflect earlier procedure (or if there was a single, universally observed procedure)—a servant of the synagogue would stand on a stone behind the condemned person and strike with multiple straps of animal hide (*m. Mak.* 3:12) as hard as possible, one-third on the chest and two-thirds on the shoulder (*m. Mak.* 3:13; *Sipre Deut.* 286.5.1).

1297. Matthew adapts the language to parallel Jesus's experience (Matt 20:19, using μαστιγῶσαι) but probably appreciates this particular parallel because it belongs to the experience of his community. Warning of beatings in the synagogue likely derives from the earliest stratum of gospel tradition, when (or before) disciples remained in submission to the discipline of their synagogue communities (Anderson, *Mark*, 293). This is the period when the Jesus tradition would have been transmitted most reliably (Keener, *Matthew*, 322–23). Cf. also John 16:2.

1298. Fitzmyer, *Acts*, 758, also suggests synagogue floggings like Paul's own.

1299. Ezek 5:17; 14:15; 4 Macc 9:24; 12:18; 17:21; 18:5; Wis 12:20; 18:8.

The term generally translated "blaspheme" (βλασφημέω) can mean simply "speak against," but when applied technically, it is speech against God (Luke 12:10) or another deity (Acts 19:37); the strictest Jewish circles applied the presumable Hebrew equivalent of the term to abuse of the divine name (*m. Sanh.* 7:5), but it probably bore a more general sense in popular usage (Luke 5:21).[1300] It could mean speaking against or reviling Christ (22:65; 23:39), but given Christ's special association with the divine, it probably means more here (Acts 13:45; 18:6). The irony is that when some Jews persecuted Christians for "blaspheming" God (6:11), they were in fact urging them to truly blaspheme!

The language of compulsion (ἀναγκάζω),[1301] when applied to persecution of a group, need not specify the degree of its success toward all the individuals.[1302] When Antiochus offered a pig on the altar, he "compelled" (ἠνάγκασε) the Jewish people to stop worshiping their God (Jos. *Ant.* 12.253), but many did not comply (12.255). Likewise, his agent who was "compelling" them to sacrifice was killed by one of them (1 Macc 2:25).[1303] The same pattern appears elsewhere regarding Maccabean persecutions (2 Macc 6:1, 7, 18; 7:1; 4 Macc 4:26; 5:2, 27; 8:2; 18:5). Herod likewise placed Judeans under compulsion (ἀνάγκης; Jos. *Ant.* 16.2) to follow his laws even where those laws contradicted those of Judeans' ancestors.[1304] Josephus admiringly notes that captors could not force any of the captured Sicarii (or even their children) in Egypt to confess, or even pretend to confess, Caesar as their lord (*War* 7.418–19). Later the governor of Bithynia claimed (Pliny *Ep.* 10.96.5–6) that whereas former Christians offered to the emperor's image and reviled Christ (*maledicere Christo*), true Christians could not be forced to do so (*quorum nihil cogi posse dicuntur*).[1305] As Tertullian still later complained, officials tortured other prisoners to solicit confession of their activities, but only Christians to make them deny them (*Apol.* 2.10).

(5) Pursuit to Diaspora Cities

Fourth, Paul madly pursued Christians to distant cities. The language is graphic: Paul was "maddened with rage," just as he was "breathing murder" in Acts 9:1. He depicts his rage against them with the verb ἐμμαίνομαι, which means "be filled with such anger that one appears to be mad" (BDAG; cf. Jos. *Ant.* 17.174); by way of wordplay, this claim anticipates in Luke's narrative Festus's charge that Paul is now, as a Christian, "mad" (Acts 26:24, μαίνῃ, from μαίνομαι). For Paul, his only madness was *before* his belief in Jesus's resurrection. The verb διώκω means "persecute" (Luke 11:49; 21:12; Acts 7:52; 9:4–5; 22:4–8; 26:14–15) or "pursue" (Luke 17:23), both of which nuances are probably relevant here, though the emphasis on movement focuses on pursuit.

1300. See comment on Acts 6:11; cf. Brown, *Death*, 522–23. There were other ways to "profane" God's name (e.g., *y. Ta'an.* 3:10, §1).

1301. Paul's attempt to "compel" (ἠνάγκαζον, 26:11) them might contrast with the compulsion of evangelism (Luke 14:23; cf. Paul himself being compelled to appeal in Acts 28:19); Paul applies the term to "Judaizing" in Gal 2:3, 14; 6:12. Stoics, with their emphasis on freedom, despised such compelling or being compelled (Arius Did. *Epit.* 2.7.11g, pp. 72–73.26).

1302. D. Williams, *Acts*, 417 (arguing that the imperfect suggests repeated attempts). Conzelmann, *Acts*, 210, prefers a descriptive imperfect rather than a conative imperfect ("tried to make them blaspheme") but notes, "Nothing is said about the results of this effort" (cf. also Bruce, *Acts¹*, 443, comparing the imperfect συνήλλασσεν in Acts 7:26; Horton, *Acts*, 387).

1303. Philo chooses words carefully lest he be compelled to utter what would appear blasphemous (*Embassy* 141). But usually the activity of "compulsion" was successful (e.g., 1 Esd 4:6; Jdt 8:30; Philo *Embassy* 61).

1304. Josephus here exploits Stoic ideals of freedom to follow reason (e.g., Mus. Ruf. 16, p. 106.6–8, esp. 8; see further Keener, *John*, 750–51).

1305. So also Lake and Cadbury, *Commentary*, 317; Conzelmann, *Acts*, 210.

Diaspora ("outside," ἔξω) "cities" might be a generalizing plural[1306] for Damascus (Acts 9:2; 22:5); although it is likely that Damascus was not the only place where the fugitives fled, and Paul may have had in mind other missions elsewhere, Luke provides no indication that Paul in fact went to the other cities (cf. also Gal 1:13, 17, 22–23). A generalizing plural, however, would serve to intensify the tone of his hostility, represented by his intentions. Luke's language also contrasts for his audience Paul's activity as a persecutor with Paul's subsequent, narrated activity as a proclaimer: traveling to synagogues even in distant lands to honor Christ (e.g., 9:20; 13:5; 17:1–3, 10–12, 17; 18:4; 19:8; 28:23).

c. Paul's Divine Commission (26:12–18)

One defense argument in ancient rhetoric was the argument from necessity; a divine commission would certainly constitute necessity. Yet far from Paul using this divine necessity to justify wrongdoing, he appeals to it to justify his turning from wrongdoing to righteousness, confessing a noncrime (see comment on Acts 24:14).

i. A Light en route to Damascus (26:12–13)

Paul emphasizes again that he was authorized by the high priest; now, however, he was intercepted by Jesus and would ultimately become his agent instead (26:16–18). The light that shone on the travelers fits biblical depictions of divine glory. It also prepares for Paul's commission to turn others to light (26:18), using Paul's conversion in light as a particularly graphic model.

(1) Agent of the High Priests (26:12)[1307]

Paul again emphasizes that he acted as an agent of the high priesthood (26:10); Paul, who has repented,[1308] cannot be convicted without also calling into question the behavior of the high-priestly families, who might accuse him now precisely because his repentance threatens them. Previous participation of the aristocratic priests in Paul's persecuting activity casts their current requests for trial irregularities in a suspicious light. For Luke, who has apparently inherited the sentiments of Paul and/or the Jerusalem church, the high priesthood is not interested in justice in this sort of case but satisfied with lynchings (25:3). Who then, Paul and Luke appear to ask, is the real threat to peace and stability? (On the rhetorical strategy of returning charges, see comment on Acts 24:19.) Especially if Luke writes after 70 c.e., this case could appear compelling to many in the Roman world.

Simply denying Paul's claims might be precarious. For all that Paul's accusers know, the letters that Paul carried might still exist if he handed them over to the Christian community in Damascus. These would not count against the standing high priest or his associates, who were not personally involved, but would cast a shadow over their "class" by revealing that it harbored elements sympathetic with revolutionary-like aims.

Even according to Luke's version, the initiative to persecute came from Paul (9:1), but he apparently found a ready hearing and received the authorization (9:2); this may be why he could expect cooperation against the Nazarenes from the synagogues in Damascus. This also would help account for why the epistolary Paul can speak of

---

1306. That is, for rhetorical effect. On the possibility of generalizing plurals in some sense, see Wallace, *Grammar*, 402–6.

1307. Although the thought of Acts 26:12 fits the preceding context, I have kept it with 26:13 to avoid dividing the sentence; it provides the setting for what follows.

1308. Rome accepted Josephus when he switched sides against its enemies; Paul now appears more pro-Roman than the priests.

persecution from "the Judeans" even apart from his own activity and continuing after his own conversion and call (1 Thess 2:14–15; cf. Acts 9:29; though cf. also 9:31).

In Acts 9:1, Saul approached only the high priest, but here he notes the commission of plural high priests. This might be another "generalizing plural," but Paul could well reason that the high-priestly family had acted in concert, as they commonly did (4:6); or Luke may have simply emphasized the most prominent high-priestly ally of Paul earlier. Josephus also often uses the plural for the priestly aristocrats' families (see comment on Acts 4:6).[1309] That Paul was backed by their authority suggests that he acted as their agent.[1310] Agency was a wider Mediterranean concept intelligible to all of Paul's hearers, not exclusively to later rabbis.[1311] Thus Paul was once an "apostle of men," seeking to please them, before being an apostle of God (cf. Gal 1:1, 10). Some people in ancient courts, no less than in modern trials for war crimes, argued that their offense was not indictable if they were simply carrying out their orders (Pliny *Ep.* 3.9.14–15).[1312]

(2) Travel at Midday (26:13)

Why does Paul mention that the vision occurred at midday (also in Acts 22:6)? That the light was "brighter than the sun" at noon highlights how bright the vision was.[1313] Less relevant is that Philo suggested that midday, being the brightest time of day, was the best time for a vision;[1314] Luke at least would have agreed that it was an acceptable time for visions (cf. 10:9), but he apparently valued other times no less (10:3; 16:9; 18:9). A skeptic could have complained that Paul and Peter (who had another revelation about Gentiles in 10:9) both hallucinated at noon because of sunstroke.[1315] Luke mentions a "light from heaven" in 9:3 and 22:6 as well as here. To avoid confusion, it is therefore important for Luke to mention that others fell with Paul (a point not specified in 9:4; 22:7)[1316] and that the light was brighter than the sun.[1317] (For the light around Paul, see comment on Acts 9:3; on λαμπρότητα, "shining," see comment on the cognate λαμπρᾷ in Acts 10:30.)

The light was around him in 9:3 and 22:6 but here is also around those with him. (The blindness in earlier accounts [9:8; 22:11] also coheres with a vision, but it is compatible with sunstroke as well.) It was also assumed that people saw phantoms

---

1309. In contrast to OT usage, the NT (e.g., Mark 2:26; 14:55; 15:11; Acts 5:24; 23:14; 25:15; cf. 4:6), other early Christian texts (e.g., the agraphon in Jeremias, *Sayings*, 51), Josephus (e.g., *War* 2.243, 316, 318, 320, 322, 336, 342, 410–11; 4.314), and probably the Dead Sea Scrolls (1QM II, 1) apply "high priests" in the plural to the members or leaders of the priestly aristocracy, not to the chief priest alone (see Stern, "Aspects," 601, 603; Reicke, *Era*, 147–48; Feldman in *Josephus*, LCL, 10:157). The rapid transition of officeholders under the Romans may have rendered the usage more fluid as well.

1310. For the *shaliach* acting on the sender's authority, see, e.g., *m. Ber.* 5:5; *t. Taʿan.* 3:2; *b. Naz.* 12b; *y. Giṭ.* 1:1, §1. This commissioned authority was effective even when the *shaliach*'s status was low (*b. Ketub.* 99b–100a) or even when the *shaliach* was a slave (*b. Giṭ.* 23a; cf. *y. Giṭ.* 2:6, §1). This was also true for other envoys or messengers in the ancient Mediterranean world (Diod. Sic. 40.1.1; Dion. Hal. *Ant. rom.* 6.88.2; 2 Macc 1:20; Jos. *Life* 65, 72–73, 196–98; *Ant.* 18.1, 265).

1311. See Keener, *John*, 310–11, and sources there (including in ancient Israel, Prov 10:26; 13:17; 22:21; 25:13; 26:6; cf. 2 Macc 1:18).

1312. Tyrants were often ready, however, to dispose of those who carried out their crimes (e.g., Tac. *Ann.* 14.62, albeit without his execution).

1313. Gaventa, *Acts*, 342, rightly.

1314. O'Toole, *Acts 26*, 57, cites Philo *QG* 4.1 (on Gen 18:1–2); cf. *Abr.* 119.

1315. Ellens, *Light*, 109–10, suggests the possibility of something like a sunstroke, albeit not from a skeptical perspective (he believes that Paul encountered God through it).

1316. So also Haenchen, *Acts*, 685.

1317. Everyone recognized that the sun was brighter than anything natural (e.g., Philost. *Vit. soph.* 2.8.580). For revelations like the sun, see *1 En.* 14:18, 20; *2 En.* 1:5; Rev 1:16; probably Christian material in *Test. Levi* 18:4.

more often at night, and midday was the least likely time to encounter them (Philost. *Hrk.* 8.16). This was also no secretive, unverifiable revelation (see comment on Acts 26:26). Not only were others present during Paul's experience; it came at midday, not a time for secret activity.[1318]

Perhaps most relevant is what Paul's midday travel reveals about his commitment. Everyone was well aware that the sun was hottest around noon (Sir 43:3);[1319] the heat could be so terrible then that a Gentile poet could compare it hyperbolically with Zeus's lightning,[1320] and it could prove dangerous.[1321] Conversation out in the open then would be unpleasant (Heliod. *Eth.* 2.21), and people normally took shelter then under trees, in homes, or elsewhere.[1322] People broke for meals then[1323] and especially (often after meals)[1324] for a midday siesta.[1325] Sometimes attackers even found guards napping at midday, which rendered them susceptible to attack.[1326] On midday rest, see further discussion at Acts 8:26; see also discussions at Acts 10:9–10; 19:9. If Saul was traveling at midday, it was because he was "so intent on his errand to persecute Christians."[1327] That is, Luke notes the time of day not to explain the character of Paul's vision but to amplify his persecuting zeal already mentioned.

11. Jesus Confronts Saul (26:14–15)

Jesus challenges Saul for persecuting him through persecuting his followers. New elements in Paul's description here include both that the voice came in a Semitic language and the use of a Greek saying recognizable to Agrippa.

(1) The Revelation

Paul mentions here that all fell to the ground (more specific than in the other two accounts in Acts 9:4; 22:7).[1328] This reaction is consistent with responses to divine or angelic revelations in the OT (Ezek 1:28; 3:23; 43:3; 44:4; Dan 8:17–18; 10:9) and Jewish literature.[1329] It also resembles prostration for worship[1330] or falling backward in awe.[1331]

1318. Cf. the Pythagorean claim that respectable women went out at midday, i.e., when nothing was hidden (Lefkowitz and Fant, *Life*, 105, §107).

1319. Also, e.g., Sen. Y. *Nat. Q.* 4.2.18; Dio Chrys. *Or.* 35.23–24; for plants, cf. Philost. *Hrk.* 3.2.

1320. Aeschylus *Seven* 430–31.

1321. E.g., to boxers (Cic. *Brut.* 69.243; cf. Philost. *Hrk.* 15.6). Virgil reportedly died from sunstroke (Suet. *Vergil* 35).

1322. E.g., Gen 18:1; *Jos. Asen.* 3:2/3; Alciph. *Farm.* 9 (Pratinas to Epigonus), 3.12, ¶1.

1323. E.g., Suet. *Claud.* 34.2.

1324. E.g., Catull. *Carm.* 32.10; *Test. Ab.* 5:2 A; probably also in Dio Chrys. *Or.* 1.29.

1325. E.g., Sil. It. 13.637–38; Plut. *Themist.* 30.1; Suet. *Aug.* 78.1; *Vesp.* 21; *Vit. Aes.* 6; Heliod. *Eth.* 4.8; Philost. *Hrk.* 11.7; 16.3; Pliny *Ep.* 1.3.1; 7.4.4; 9.36.5 (though Pliny omitted his during the winter, when nights were longer, 9.40.2).

1326. E.g., Thucyd. 6.100.1; Polyb. 9.17.3; perhaps Xen. Eph. *Anthia* 1.13; Dio Chrys. *Or.* 36.15; cf. 2 Kgs 20:16–18 (feasting unprepared at midday). Also because of midday exhaustion from thirst and heat (Jos. *Ant.* 18.365); cf. some trained to endure the heat of the midday sun (Lucian *Anach.* 25).

1327. Yamauchi, *Stones*, 113.

1328. The use of καταπίπτω is unique to Luke in the NT (Luke 8:6; Acts 28:6), though it occurs in the later LXX (Neh 8:11; Ps 144:14 [145:14 ET]; 3 Macc 2:20; Wis 7:3; 13:16; 17:15); none of these uses is close in sense here, but compare another response to an encounter with the heavenly host in 4 Macc 4:11 (perhaps from the first century C.E.).

1329. E.g., Tob 12:16; *1 En.* 14:13–14; 60:3; 71:2, 11; *2 En.* 21:2; 22:4; *4 Ezra* 4:12; 10:30; *Jos. Asen.* 14:10–11; *Test. Job* 3:4/5; *Apoc. Zeph.* 6:9–10; Rev 1:17. Cf. fear in Gen 15:12; *1 En.* 89:30–31; 102:1; Ach. Tat. 1.3.4–5.

1330. E.g., 2 Chr 20:18; 29:30; 1 Esd 9:47; Jdt 6:18; 9:1; 1 Macc 4:40, 55; 3 Macc 5:50–51; Sir 50:21; *Sib. Or.* 3.716, 725; *L.A.B.* 4:5; *Test. Ab.* 20:12 A; 4:4 B.

1331. E.g., John 18:6; cf. 1 Sam 4:18. This may be a response to the divine name (Artapanus in Euseb. *P.E.* 9.27.24–26; *Sipra Sh. M.D.* 99.5.12); Talbert, *John*, 233, adds later traditions in which priests fell on their faces when hearing the divine name (*b. Qidd.* 71a; *Eccl. Rab.* 3:11, §3).

Most details here resemble those in the earlier accounts[1332] (for those details, see comments on the earlier accounts), but the divergences are significant.

Why does Paul mention here that the voice spoke in Hebrew or Aramaic (on the latter, see comments on Acts 21:40; 22:2)? One might have expected the emphasis on Semitic speech in Acts 22:7 (where the entire speech is Semitic), but the language is explicitly specified in neither 9:4 nor 22:7. Perhaps it appears here for Agrippa's benefit; use of a holy language ("Hebrew," though in fact it is likely Aramaic) would make sense for a revelation. The use of Aramaic explains the form Σαούλ in the call narratives in Acts;[1333] on this occasion, it may also explain why the voice calls him "Saul" when Paul's audience knows him as "Paul."[1334] It is unlikely, however, that Paul repeats Jesus's whole message in Aramaic (unless he translates afterward), since it would be no more intelligible to most of his audience than to Luke's; he most likely simply mentions the language in which Jesus addressed him.[1335]

Many considered Hebrew a holy language, as is evident from the comments of later rabbis, even when they wrote in Aramaic.[1336] Certainly it remained as a scribal language, as the majority of the Dead Sea Scrolls exemplify.[1337] Even rabbis who allowed other languages for various purposes valued Hebrew most highly.[1338] Some thought that God created the world in Hebrew[1339] and that, before Babel, everyone spoke it,[1340] but some Babylonian Amoraim insisted that the first man spoke Aramaic.[1341] Some rabbis discussed whether the Torah could be debated in any language or only in the holy tongue,[1342] but they could acknowledge that some Aramaic appeared throughout the Scriptures;[1343] further, Aramaic paraphrases were already in vogue long before this period (and before our current Targumim; cf. Neh 8:8).[1344] God reportedly spoke to Israel's prophets in Hebrew, the language of the holy angels.[1345] But the heavenly voice was sometimes thought to come in Aramaic rather than Hebrew.[1346] (For the repetition of Saul's name, see comment on Acts 9:4.)

(2) Kicking against the Goads

"Persecuting me" refers to persecuting Jesus's followers in Acts 26:10–12 (see comment on Acts 9:4); Paul's acts against Jesus's name in 26:9 are expressed in

---

1332. For example, Acts 26:15 is the same as 9:5 and 22:8 (except that 22:8 adds "the Nazarene").

1333. Conzelmann, *Acts*, 210; on this as the Aramaic (and not Hebrew) form, see Bruce, *Acts*[1], 444.

1334. Johnson, *Acts*, 435.

1335. Witherington, *Acts*, 743, thinks that Agrippa and Berenice would understand. They probably had learned some Aramaic but, having grown up in Rome, should not be supposed fluent in it; Paul would hardly quote the saying in Aramaic, then add a Greek proverb to contextualize. One might speak in Hebrew to prevent outsiders from understanding (4 Macc 16:15; the speech in 16:16–23 is given only in Greek), but Paul lacks any such motive here.

1336. E.g., *b. Ber.* 40b; *B. Qam.* 83a (distinguished from both Aramaic and Greek); *Meg.* 17b; *Gen. Rab.* 18:4; 74:13.

1337. See Abegg, "Hebrew Language."

1338. *Y. Meg.* 1:9, §2. But some rabbis thought that even secular matters could be spoken in the holy language (*b. Šabb.* 41a).

1339. E.g., fourth-century teachers in *Gen. Rab.* 18:4; 31:8.

1340. *Y. Meg.* 1:9, §1.

1341. *B. Sanh.* 38b.

1342. *B. Ber.* 13a, bar.

1343. *Gen. Rab.* 74:14 (R. Samuel bar Nahman, third-century Palestinian rabbi).

1344. Some thought that God exiled Israel to Babylonia because the language was similar to that of Torah (*b. Pesaḥ.* 87b). Others (probably later) welcomed the law in any language, or at least in Greek (*Deut. Rab.* 1:1).

1345. *Gen. Rab.* 52:5. In rabbinic polemic, angels did not understand even Aramaic (Yahalom, "Angels," citing *b. Soṭah* 33a; *b. Šabb.* 12b).

1346. E.g., *b. Soṭah* 33a; *Song Rab.* 8:9, §3. God addressed the Israelites in Egyptian because this was their language in Egypt (*Esth. Rab.* 4:12, attributed to a fourth-century source). Le Cornu, *Acts*, 1399, argues that most examples of the *bat qol* are in Hebrew, even when in Aramaic contexts, so that those who heard it in Aramaic (*t. Soṭah* 13:6) were on a lesser level.

26:10–12.[1347] "Kicking against the goads" appears only in this third recounting of the story, but Paul was apparently doing so by persecuting Jesus and his followers.[1348] Most commentators point out that Paul here uses a Greek proverb;[1349] this is Luke's only use of κέντρον and λακτίζω (as well as of σκληρός),[1350] and λακτίζω is a biblical hapax legomenon (while κέντρον appears only nine times, e.g., 4 Macc 14:19; Sir 38:25; Hos 5:12; 13:14). The proverb was widely used and by no means limited to Euripides.[1351]

More often emphasized than the other occurrences, however, are the closely parallel and widely known lines in Eurip. *Bacch*. 794–95.[1352] Significantly, this text in Euripides (along with cognate verbs in *Bacch*. 45, 325, 1255) provides the ultimate (though not necessarily the proximate) literary source for Luke's use of θεομάχοι in Acts 5:39.[1353] It is quite possible, given 5:39 and some other passages, that Luke knew Euripides's work directly,[1354] but many scholars argue that it is more likely that if he knows these words from Euripides, he does so through an anthology from which he studied and memorized when younger in school.[1355] School exercises included developing maxims and anecdotes into moral essays; although, technically, maxims, unlike anecdotes, were "not explicitly attributed, . . . in fact their source was usually known."[1356]

Since Luke presents Jesus's wording in more than one form elsewhere (Luke 24:47–49; Acts 1:4–8), it would not be surprising if "kicking against the goads" is an example of Luke's "literary freedom," Paul's explanation to his hearers rather than

1347. For the latter suggestion, see O'Toole, *Acts 26*, 47.

1348. Because the Greek proverb emphasizes future conduct, some apply it to the futility of Paul's future resistance (Fitzmyer, *Acts*, 759); "from now on you will have no discharge" from Christ's service (Munck, *Salvation*, 20; cf. idem, *Acts*, 242). This proposal may, however, import too much of the proverb's usual application into a context that applies it differently. Paul's current activity is futile, and so sooner or later he must submit to his owner (Dibelius, *Studies in Acts*, 189).

1349. Dibelius, *Studies in Acts*, 188–89; Munck, *Acts*, 48–49; Renehan, "Quotations," 22; Conzelmann, *Acts*, 210–11; Witherington, *Acts*, 743; Fitzmyer, *Acts*, 758; Barrett, *Acts*, 1158; Talbert, *Acts*, 207; Gilbert, "Acts," 248.

1350. Luke does use σκληροτράχηλος (Acts 7:51) and σκληρύνω (19:9) for hard hearts. Here the sense is "difficult" because it is "unpleasant"; cf. BDAG. Σκληρός can also mean "harsh" (e.g., Dio Chrys. *Or*. 32.26; BDAG, s.v. σκληρός, 2, 4).

1351. Scholars cite Pindar *Pyth*. 2.94–95 (the earliest reference, with the singular); frg. *Iambi adesp*. 13 Diehl; Aeschylus *Prom*. 323–25; *Ag*. 1624; Julian Ap. *Or*. 8.246B (where it is a παροιμία, or "proverb"); in Latin, Terence *Phorm*. 1.2.27–28; Plaut. *Truc*. 4.741; cf. the divine goad against a temple robber in Quint. *Decl*. 325.9. BDAG also lists additional sources (including an inscription from Asia Minor published in 1887).

1352. Similar references elsewhere in Euripides appear (scholars cite *Iph. Taur*. 1396; *Peliades* frg. 604 Nauck, from Stob. 3.3.22; LCL compares Pindar *Pyth*. 2.94–96, Aeschylus *Ag*. 1624, Eurip. *Bacch*. 794–95).

1353. Renehan, "Quotations," 22–23 (comparing also Eurip. *Iph. Aul*. 1408 if genuine); most recently, MacDonald, "Poetry," 480–81. By itself, the term and its cognates could apply to deities battling each other (as in Proclus *Poet*. 6, bk. 1, K149.5).

1354. Besides Acts 5:39, Luke may also likely evoke Euripides in Luke 4:23 (see Nolland, "Parallels to 'Physician,'" even more persuasively than he claims); on Acts 5–12, see Lang, *Kunst*, 201–50. Euripides was a common part of the core curriculum in antiquity (Hock, "Paul and Education," 203; Jeffers, *World*, 254); Dio recommends him most highly among tragedians (*Or*. 18.6; some will complain that he is too basic, but really he is most useful, 18.7). Although Luke's internal literary connection with Acts 5:39 suggests his own deliberate allusion, Paul himself might employ Euripidean language (see Stowers, *Rereading of Romans*, 260–63; Tobin, *Rhetoric in Contexts*, 232–34, 242; Bryan, *Preface*, 143–44; cf. Renehan, "Quotations," 24–26; Bendemann, "Diastase"; but contrast Jewett, *Romans*, 463). If Luke and/or Paul knew Euripides, it might be in written rather than acted form; most theater performances were consecrated to local deities and available inexpensively at their festivals (Cary and Haarhoff, *Life*, 153); R. Levi regarded attendance as sinful, perhaps for moral reasons (*Gen. Rab*. 67:3). On quotations, see comment on Acts 17:28.

1355. See Malherbe, *Social Aspects*, 42; idem, *Moral Exhortation*, 115. Euripides was one of the most excerpted poets in gnomologies at the primary level (Padilla, "Παιδεία," 430), and the play was widely known (cf. Schäfer, "Funktion," arguing for Luke's interpretive use of the allusions).

1356. Heath, *Hermogenes*, 13–14; quotation, 14. Paul is not developing a moral essay around the saying, but the educated Agrippa inside the narrative world and Theophilus outside it may have caught the allusion.

Jesus's original wording.[1357] The idea of Jesus's compelling summons is in any case not foreign to Paul; Paul's letters hint of his being "seized by Christ" (Phil 3:12) and undergoing a "compulsion" to preach (1 Cor 9:15–18).[1358] Whether Paul's or Luke's adaptation,[1359] it is particularly fitting in addressing King Agrippa, who had a Hellenistic education.[1360]

The point of the proverb, fitting in this context, is the futility for a human to strive against fate or the will of deity,[1361] precisely what Paul's hostility to the Christian movement is doing (cf. Acts 5:39). But whereas King Pentheus (in Euripides) and King Antiochus (in 2 Macc 7:19) reaped destruction for battling a deity, here the Lord's mercy turns Paul to the right way (cf. 1 Tim 1:12–16).

Most members of Luke's audience would probably have heard the Greek proverb, though they might not have gathered that it ultimately came in this form from Euripides. Although Euripides is the closest form, much of Luke's target audience may have also been able to supply secondary resonances that could theologically inform the claim. Those who were biblically informed and knew the Hebrew text may have thought of Israel's corrupt leaders (1 Sam 2:29) "kicking" against God, although the connection is not clear in the LXX. Clearer is that the same Hebrew verb applies to Israel "kicking" against God in Deut 32:15, where the LXX employs ἀπελάκτισεν, a cognate to our present term.[1362] Those who were biblically literate only in Greek might have also thought of Prov 26:3 LXX, where a κέντρον, or goad,[1363] for donkeys offers an analogy for a rod to punish wrongdoers (i.e., fools). Ironically, just as Paul seeks to "punish" believers in Jesus (cf. Acts 26:10–11), he now confronts Jesus's sharp goads against himself.

A goad was "a sharp pointed stick used to move cattle in the desired direction," like a modern "cattle prod."[1364] Goads had long been applied figuratively (though applied literally often enough for the figures to retain their allusive force)—for example, for anger[1365] or conscience.[1366] One pre-Christian Jewish writer compares the teachings of sages with oxgoads (βούκεντρα, Eccl 12:11). The gods might use adversities like "spurs" to provoke virtue;[1367] a pre-Christian Jewish source also claims that God

1357. Longenecker, *Paul*, 100; Witherington, *Acts*, 311, 743n487.

1358. Munck, *Salvation*, 20 (also citing Jer 20:7); Fitzmyer, *Acts*, 759.

1359. Redford, "Contextualization," 291–92, treats such adaptation as a model for contextualization.

1360. Jos. *Life* 359. Hellenism was even more dominant with Agrippa's ancestor Herod I, although not every example attributed to him is clear (see, e.g., the debate in Jacobson, "Colors"; Brenner, "True to Form").

1361. With Conzelmann, *Acts*, 211; Longenecker, *Acts*, 348; idem, *Paul*, 99; idem, *Ministry and Message*, 32. Lentz, *Luke's Portrait*, 85, associates "kicking against the goads" with rage against a deity, and hence with madness, in Eurip. *Bacch.* 795, and thus views it as appropriate to prepare for Acts 26:24; but in 26:24, Paul is considered mad in his converted rather than preconverted state.

1362. For this term's use for "kicking," see further BDAG.

1363. The LXX uses κέντρον for a bee sting (4 Macc 14:19); more relevantly, for discipline to make a horse move (Prov 26:3; see also *Pss. Sol.* 16:4) or to motivate an ox with a plow (Sir 38:25). For the semantic range, see also Thiselton, *Corinthians*, 1300; esp. BDAG.

1364. Johnson, *Acts*, 435. It has a long history; nineteenth-century Palestinian peasants used a goad that "was a strong pole, eight or ten feet long, with a pointed prick" to strike the oxen (Abbott, *Acts*, 110; cf. Judg 3:31). Mesopotamians also knew something like goads for horses (Gilg. 6.46ff. [*ANET* 84]). Oxen were "prodded to pull steadily or to make a straight furrow" (Dunn, *Acts*, 328).

1365. Val. Max. 9.3.2 (*stimuli*); but Sen. Y. *Dial.* 5.2.1 is not relevant.

1366. Val. Max. 9.11.3 (*stimulis*); cf. Philo *Decal.* 87 (though not using the same term); perhaps verbal encouragement in Pliny *Ep.* 1.8.1; 3.7.15; *calcar* as a stimulus in Symm. *Ep.* 1.62 (though it might be already a dead metaphor). Dunn, *Acts*, 328, doubts pangs of conscience here (cf. Acts 23:1; 24:16). The LCL translation of Lucian *Nigr.* 6 (quoting Hom. *Il.* 8.293) does not seem to be literal here (the context in Homer mentions horses, 8.290, but not relevantly); likewise, although Philod. *Crit.* col. 8b illustrates painful correction, it lacks the term κέντρον.

1367. Sen. Y. *Dial.* 1.4.6 (*stimulos*).

afflicts his servants to restore them to the way, spurring them like horses (*Pss. Sol.* 16:3–4), and Philo applies the image to punishments to teach the wicked (*Dreams* 2.294). Philo regularly uses κέντρον figuratively,[1368] whether for the affliction of reproof;[1369] the sting of the passions, pleasure, or pain;[1370] or philosophy stimulating attention to what was appropriate.[1371] Later rabbis, whose range of uses for metaphors typically proved less diverse, employed goads as a stock metaphor for the words of Torah, based on Eccl 12:11.[1372] The image of kicking against the owner's correction might recall, for some, OT images of Israel's disobedience to its master (Isa 1:3). Most obviously, it reflects the familiar experience of rebellious donkeys kicking hard and painfully (Babr. 122.11–12).[1373]

Whether or not most of Luke's audience would have caught the Euripides allusion (Theophilus may well have), they likely saw the connection with Acts 5:39 (which may draw from precisely the same possibly anthologized and ultimately Euripidean verse, referring to fighting God).[1374] Gamaliel warns that one cannot fight the Jesus movement without fighting God (5:39); fighting it is precisely what Gamaliel's student Saul does (26:10–11), and fighting God is precisely what the heavenly voice informs him that he has been doing.[1375]

III. Appointed as a Witness (26:16–17)

Paul's testimony shifts more fully to his calling—a calling that would incidentally explain, should anyone challenge him further with having started riots, why he was preaching on the occasions when riots were raised against him. Although his hearers do not share his self-evaluation (26:24), Paul is within their tolerance range (26:31–32).

(1) Paul's Commission in 26:16–18

Although Luke's audience already knows Paul's calling to the Gentiles, Luke has reserved his fullest account of Paul's call at the Damascus road revelation for the final, climactic narration of Paul's conversion—at one of the prominent occasions where the call is being fulfilled. This call was already implied in 9:15 (Jesus's words to Ananias) and in 22:21 (Jesus's words to Paul after his conversion),[1376] but only here do we find Jesus speaking it directly to Paul at his conversion. We know, and perhaps Luke's audience knew, that Paul's calling and conversion happened roughly simultaneously (Gal 1:13–16).

Paul's commissioning in 26:16–18 evokes the call of OT prophets or agents of the Lord.[1377] Cumulatively, these echoes portray Paul's experience as prophetic, like

1368. E.g., Philo *Embassy* 169; for alienation of mind in *Conf.* 5.

1369. Philo *Prelim. St.* 158 (a spear better than a mere "goad" for such unruly horses).

1370. Philo *Worse* 46; BDAG mentions also *PGM* 4.2911. This image draws on the other use of the noun, for animal stings (e.g., Rev 9:10).

1371. Philo *Prelim. St.* 74. He uses the verb κεντρίζω for spurring one (Joshua) to action (*Virt.* 69).

1372. E.g., *'Abot R. Nat.* 18 A; b. *Ḥag.* 3b; *Pesiq. Rab.* 3:2 (some adding also the words of the scribes); *Lev. Rab.* 29:7 (against the evil impulse); *Num. Rab.* 14:4.

1373. People often associated donkeys with folly and sluggishness (Raepsaet, "Donkey," 669). An ass might kick against an abusive owner more justly (cf. Lucian *Lucius* 31); horses and oxen kick when grieved (apparently goaded; Libanius *Encomium* 8.12).

1374. Those who destroyed temples fought not only against people but against God (Polyb. 32.15.13); see further discussion at Acts 5:39.

1375. Cf. Spencer, *Acts*, 227, who also connects Acts 26:14 with 5:38–39. Lang, "Self," 163–64, also makes the connection.

1376. Perhaps as much as three years after, given the chronology of Gal 1:18; but Luke's audience would not know this.

1377. With, e.g., Dupont, *Salvation*, 30; Munck, *Salvation*, 27; Stendahl, *Paul*, 10; Witherington, *Acts*, 745; Fitzmyer, *Acts*, 755; Crowe, *Acts*, 187.

prophetic callings in the OT; Paul thus asks Agrippa if he believes in the prophets (26:27).[1378] To disobey the call would be true rebellion against Israel's God; obedience to it has led to his being falsely accused of violating God's law. Refusing to heed God's message could be as consequential as refusing to heed biblical prophets; by implication, rejecting Paul's divine message would be tantamount to rejecting the prophetic message (26:22, 27).

Scholars often find in "delivering you" a recollection of God's promise to Jeremiah at his call (Jer 1:7–8).[1379] Jeremiah's ἐξαιρεῖσθαί σε (1:8; cf. also 1:19) by itself is hardly a sufficient connection to Luke's ἐξαιρούμενός σε (Acts 26:17),[1380] but we may factor in ἐξαποστείλω σε (Jer 1:7; cf. ἀποστέλλω σε in Acts 26:17)[1381] and Jeremiah's call as a "prophet to the nations" (Jer 1:5; cf. Acts 26:17) as well as to Israel.[1382] Acts 18:9–10 recounts a vision to Paul in which the Lord tells him not to be afraid because the Lord is with Paul, possibly echoing especially Jer 1:8; there is another possible allusion in Acts 9:15. Paul's letters also allude to his call in language at times reminiscent of Jeremiah's calling (see comment on Acts 9:15). There might also be a fainter echo of Ezek 2:1–6[1383] in "I am sending you" (ἐξαποστέλλω ἐγώ σε, 2:3) and the command to rise up (2:1), though neither phrase is rare by itself (e.g., the command to stand in Dan 10:11; sending in Exod 3:12; Ezek 3:6; the verb may evoke also Isa 61:1, quoted in Luke 4:18).

In Acts 26:18, Paul turns people to light as in Isa 42:6 and opens their eyes as in 42:7;[1384] this Isaiah passage easily connects midrashically with another, since both mention a "light for the nations" (49:6, as in 42:6), an Isaian phrase that applied to Paul's mission in Acts 13:47.[1385] The servant whom Isaiah addresses (Israel's righteous remnant) is also the same as the "witnesses" in Isa 43:10, 12 and 44:8, the primary background for the apostolic commission in Acts 1:8.

Paul's own writings emphasize his special revelations (2 Cor 12:1–4, 7; cf. 1 Cor 14:37; Rom 16:25–26; perhaps Gal 2:2; Eph 2:20; 3:2–9).[1386] Jesus, in himself, also revealed to his disciples special matters not seen by earlier prophets (Luke 10:21–24).

1378. Fitzmyer, *Acts*, 755.

1379. Many scholars find echoes of Jeremiah (e.g., Le Cornu, *Acts*, 1403, who notes that Paul himself connected his call with Jeremiah in Gal 1:13; in Acts, Schnabel, *Acts*, 1010; in Galatians, Das, *Galatians*, 131).

1380. The verb ἐξαιρέω appears more than 130 times in the LXX. Apart from Acts 23:27, most of the uses in Acts are biblical allusions (7:10; probably 12:11) or quotations (7:34)—none from Jeremiah.

1381. This conjunction of the verbs is much more significant statistically; the verbs ἐξαιρέω and ἀποστέλλω appear together in only three verses, none possibly relevant; ἐξαιρέω appears with ἐξαποστέλλω in Ps 143:7 (144:7 ET), also irrelevant. Broadened to paragraphs (as in Jer 1:7–8) or chapters, there are about seventeen examples, of which only Jer 1:7–8 is relevant.

1382. On the level of Luke's narrative, cf. perhaps Jeremiah as a "youth" (Jer 1:6–7); but this was a logical way for Luke to describe Paul in Acts 7:58, and had Luke intended a connection, he would have used Jeremiah's νέος (νεώτερος instead of νεανίας).

1383. Stendahl, *Paul*, 10; Fitzmyer, *Acts*, 755; Crowe, *Acts*, 187.

1384. Some scholars connect the opening of the eyes also with Isa 35:5 in the messianic era; although the idiom of opened eyes is frequent (as noted above), this would be a natural midrashic connection. With light to darkness, some connect Isa 42:16 in the immediate context of the dominant allusion (Dupont, *Salvation*, 30; Mufwata, *Extrémités*, 11–13; Marshall, "Acts," 599). Kim, *New Perspective*, 101–2, acknowledges Isa 42:7, 16 (with Isa 61:1) here and argues for hints of Isa 42 in Paul's call even in his letters (2 Cor 4:4–6, alluding to Isa 42:6–7; 49:6; Gen 1:3). Kim finds (102n4) several parallels between Acts 26:6–8 and 2 Cor 4:4–6, suggesting that Luke intentionally echoes Pauline language.

1385. Riesner, *Early Period*, 236, also notes the connection. See Luke 2:32, where Jesus is the salvific light for the Gentiles (as well as glory to Israel). DeSilva, *Galatians*, 80, suggests possible allusions to Isa 49:6 both here and in Gal 1:15.

1386. It is possible that Paul's "revelation" in Eph 3:3 is the same revelation of Christ in Gal 1:12, 16, fitting the link between Paul's conversion and commission (Acts 9:15; 26:17). In this case, it would suggest that much of his gospel was implicit in his first encounter with Jesus (for which thesis see Kim, *Origin*, passim).

A number of scholars argue that Paul's description of his calling in Acts 26:16–18 corresponds well with descriptions in his letters.[1387]

(2) Witness of What He Sees (26:16)

The command to "rise" or "stand" or not to fear was common after a theophany (e.g., Ezek 2:1; Matt 17:7) because mortals experiencing the theophany were generally felled to the ground.[1388] For example, an angel tells Aseneth, "Rise and stand on your feet, and I will tell you what I have to say" (*Jos. Asen.* 14:8).[1389] Luke sometimes elsewhere applies ὁράω (here both for the past appearance and the promise of future ones) to theophanies (Acts 7:2, 30, 35; cf. 2:3, 17; 7:44; 13:31; 16:9).

Paul is also told to arise in 9:6 and 22:10, but those texts tell Paul to enter Damascus for further instructions (presumably for Ananias's message in 9:15; 22:14–16). Here, however, Paul receives the message from the Lord directly. Luke might simply abbreviate by omitting Ananias here,[1390] but Paul's own account in Gal 1:12–16 probably suggests that Paul viewed his turning to Christ and his call to the Gentiles as part of the same event, as Luke does here.[1391] Paul insists that he received it without human mediation (1:12), and he wraps the call and conversion together as God's sovereign act of ironic grace (1:16).[1392] (For Ananias's role regarding Paul's calling being confirmatory, see comment on Acts 9:17.)

Luke uses προχειρίζομαι for Paul's calling also in Acts 22:14 (as well as seeing and hearing; and for Jesus's mission in 3:20, the only other NT use).[1393] Although the term does not appear in the biblical prophets,[1394] the idea may appear in Jer 1:5, 10 ("appointed") and Isa 42:6 ("appointed," lit., "gave").[1395] Luke elsewhere uses ὑπηρέτης for an honorable office in the Jewish community (Luke 4:20; Acts 5:22, 26), but it can imply subordination (Acts 13:5; Prov 14:35; Wis 6:4) as well as service for the Christian message (Luke 1:2; 1 Cor 4:1).[1396]

To be a "witness" (μάρτυς) in the context of Acts includes being an eyewitness (see Acts 1:22); this is part of Paul's commission in keeping with the resurrection appearance from which it derives. "Seen" recalls the larger "seen and heard" motif in Luke-Acts (see 2:33; 4:20; 22:14–15). What he has seen[1397] presumably involves the

---

1387. E.g., Kim, *New Perspective*, 101–2; Hengel and Schwemer, *Between Damascus and Antioch*, 47–50. Considering that Luke is a distinct writer, the correspondences appear noteworthy.

1388. E.g., Ezek 2:1–2; Dan 8:18; 10:11–12; Matt 17:7; Rev 1:17; Tob 12:17; 1 En. 60:4; 71:3; 2 En. 1:8; 20:2; 21:3; 22:5; 3 En. 1:7–9; 4 Ezra 5:15; 2 Bar. 13:1–2; Jos. Asen. 14:11; cf. PGM 1.77–78.

1389. Trans. Burchard, *OTP* 2:225; in the Greek text, the enumeration is 14:7 (Philonenko, 178). This text may echo biblical texts such as Ezek 2:1; Dan 10:11.

1390. Despite Ananias's importance to his narrative (noted in, e.g., Hounsa, *Figure*, 40–42). For telescoping the narrative to suit the audience (although the revelation remains from Jesus, in any case), see Witherington, "Editing," 342. Such abbreviation by omitting intermediaries probably appears in Matt 8:5; 9:18 (cf. Luke 7:3; Mark 5:35). Spotlighting a specific character and so condensing a narrative was not unusual; the technique also appears in Plutarch's biographies (Licona, "Plutarch's Biographies").

1391. Cf., e.g., Park, "Berufung"; Dupont, *Salvation*, 30.

1392. Cf. Fitzmyer, *Acts*, 430. Paul claims that he saw Jesus (1 Cor 9:1) in a sort of belated resurrection appearance (15:8).

1393. Cf. the similar term προχειροτονέω in Acts 10:41, also a NT hapax legomenon.

1394. Despite the many evocations of Scripture in the context, LXX uses of this term (Dan 3:22; 2 Macc 3:7; 8:9; 14:12) appear irrelevant; the cognate in Josh 3:12 is only a little better.

1395. "Grasp your hand" in the same verse could suggest Luke's term, but Luke's terminology here is more likely suggested by his own earlier usage (Acts 3:20; 22:14) than by the LXX.

1396. BDAG amply documents both the official and the serving nuances that can attach to the term. For the serving nuance, cf. also, e.g., Mus. Ruf. 3, p. 42.7–8; *Test. Job* 15:1; Thiselton, "Semantics," 81; as a Jewish title, usually in synagogues, see *CIJ* 1:xcix; 1:124, §172; Leon, *Jews of Rome*, 190.

1397. More generally, inviting one to recount not merely a message but what one has seen reflects biblical idiom in which Luke and his audience would be steeped (see, e.g., Gen 45:13, though most immediately Jesus's invitation in Q Luke 7:22//Matt 11:4).

vision being narrated, just as the Lord will appear to him further; Luke's audience, knowing that Paul was blinded (9:8), may hear some irony here. The Lord Jesus notes here that Paul will have some additional revelations; some of these appear in Acts, including another promise of deliverance (18:9–10) and other encouragements relating to deliverance so that he can fulfill his calling among the Gentiles in Rome (23:11; 27:24), or the giving of specific directions relevant for his call to Gentiles (16:7–10; 22:17). These experiences are consistent with the visions and dreams that Luke depicts as normal in the new age of the Spirit (2:17).

The term for "servant" or "minister" here, conjoined with the idea of (though with a different term for) "witness," probably evokes Luke's preface in Luke 1:2: just as Jesus's original apostles testified about what Jesus began to do and teach, so Paul was among those who testified of his continuing experience with Christ.

(3) Deliverance and the Gentile Mission (26:17)

Luke often likes to couple Israel ("the people") and the Gentiles, as here (Luke 2:32; Acts 4:25, 27; 15:14),[1398] and he will do so in describing Jesus's mission in 26:23 and, by implication, Paul carrying out his commission in Acts 26:20.[1399] Toward the end of Acts, Paul evokes again the calling in 26:17 by mentioning that God's salvation has been "sent" to "the Gentiles" (28:28, one of only two other verses in the NT that use both ἀποστέλλω and ἔθνος).[1400] (Here Paul is sent both to "the people," Israel, and to the Gentiles, since the relative pronoun ὅς occurs in the masculine accusative plural form οὕς rather than the neuter accusative plural form ἅ; "people," unlike "Gentiles," is masculine.)[1401] Paul in his letters also regards the Gentile mission as a task especially appointed for him (Rom 11:13; Gal 2:7–9; cf. Eph 3:1–8, esp. 3:8; Col 1:25–27).[1402]

There are numerous examples of Paul's "deliverances" in Acts (cf. Acts 9:16)—from Jews (9:23–25, 29–30; 18:12–16; 20:19; 21:27, 32), from Gentiles for non-Jewish or anti-Jewish reasons (16:38–39; 19:30–31, both parts of longer stories),[1403] and from Gentiles stirred by Jews (14:19–20; 17:8–10, 13–14; cf. 13:51). Perhaps in connection with his linking of various figures in salvation history, Luke elsewhere applies the present term (ἐξαιρέω) to Joseph (7:10), Israel (7:34), and Peter (12:11; cf. Paul in 23:27);[1404] in this context, as noted above, an allusion to Jeremiah's calling is likely (Jer 1:8).[1405]

IV. Darkness to Light (26:18)

Paul proclaims the light (Acts 26:23) as part of his commission (26:18) and his experience (26:13). If Paul's claims sound grandiose here, they are no more grandiose

1398. Although the LXX also uses the terms otherwise, it often enough employs them as here, e.g., Isa 62:10; 1 Macc 1:13; 4:58; 5:19, 43; 2 Macc 13:11; 14:15; Wis 10:15. For the church sometimes differentiated from both (cf. 1 Cor 10:32), see Minear, *Images*, 71.

1399. Despite Paul's commitment to both groups, the language is likely Luke's; in his letters, Paul combines the terms only in his quotations in Rom 15:10–11. In this passage, Paul's primary audience includes both Jews (Agrippa and Berenice) and a Gentile (Festus), and many other Gentiles are present.

1400. The other is Matt 10:5 (making the opposite point); after that, the first instance in extant early Christian literature is *Diogn.* 11.3.

1401. The same situation occurs in Acts 15:17, where "humanity" supplies the masculine to the neuter "Gentiles."

1402. In Eph 3:2–3, it was specially revealed to him and was his special call; cf. also 1 Tim 2:7.

1403. Jewish opposition in Ephesus had already occurred (Acts 20:19), but in this case Luke makes no direct connection with the Gentile persecution afterward.

1404. Deliverance from wicked nations (employing these terms) appears in 1 Chr 16:35; 2 Chr 32:17 (though we should not envision *allusions* to these passages or even to the exodus narrative). The LXX employs the verb for delivering his "people" rather than delivering from the "people" (Exod 18:10).

1405. For Jer 1:5 in Acts 26:17, see, e.g., Mufwata, *Extrémités*, 10–11.

than in undisputed (Rom 1:5, 13–14; 11:13; 16:4; Gal 2:7) as well as disputed (Eph 3:1–5, 8; Col 1:24–26) Pauline letters; indeed, in historical retrospect, Paul had a larger effect than he lived to see or than even his immediate successors would have realized. For biblical allusions here, see most fully the introduction, above, to Acts 26:16–18. There are probable signs of rhetorical elegance, including a genitive with an articular infinitive (Acts 26:18) and litotes (26:19).[1406]

(1) Opened Eyes

Others used the metaphor of opening eyes; Marcus Aurelius's teacher "opened" Marcus's "eyes."[1407] The expression applies to revealed insight about reality (Luke 24:16, 31; Gen 21:19),[1408] including perception of the spiritual realm (2 Kgs 6:17)[1409] and, most relevant here, God's truth (Ps 119:18; Eph 1:18),[1410] which the eyes of many could not see (Acts 28:27, quoting Isa 6:10). As noted above, the primary biblical allusion informing this image is probably the servant's mission in Isa 42:7, which contextually includes turning people to light (42:6); but this occurrence recalls a wider Isaian theme of opening eyes.[1411]

Vision was a frequent analogy for knowing[1412] and was often used for spiritual sight.[1413] Plato emphasized the vision of the mind that could see ideal forms;[1414] the physical senses were deceitful, and so the soul should depend only on itself and "see" invisible abstractions perceptible only to the mind.[1415] Eventually many writers emphasized the mind's or soul's ability to see;[1416] Philo speaks repeatedly of the "eyes" of the soul.[1417] Stoics such as Epictetus[1418] and Marcus Aurelius[1419] viewed the ignorant masses as "blind"; likewise, Seneca the Younger believed that only the pure mind could comprehend God.[1420]

1406. Witherington, *Acts*, 737; on litotes, see Rowe, "Style," 128; Porter, "Paul and Letters," 579. But Blass, Debrunner, and Funk, *Grammar*, 206, §400.6, think that the articular infinitive is used to clarify the grammar and appears only in NT passages reflecting OT language. Articular infinitives also appear, e.g., in Matt 2:13; Phil 3:10 (Dana and Mantey, *Grammar*, 284).

1407. Fronto *Ad M. Caes.* 3.18 (*oculos*). For the soul's vision without use of eyes, cf., e.g., Marc. Aur. 10.26; 11.1.1.

1408. Cf. also Luke 2:30; 19:42.

1409. In Jewish sources, see, e.g., *1 En.* 1:2 (cited by O'Toole, *Acts 26*, 72); *3 En.* 1:12; 4Q424 3 3; *4 Bar.* 9:3; cf. *t. B. Meṣiʿa* 2:30; *Hor.* 2:5; *y. Moʿed Qaṭ.* 3:7, §5; *Meg.* 1:5, §3; *Gen. Rab.* 15:2; in philosophy, e.g., Max. Tyre 10.6; Marc. Aur. 4.29; Iambl. *V.P.* 32.228. It applies to Israel's receiving spiritual vision in *1 En.* 89:41 and to eschatological vision in 90:35.

1410. Cf. Gen 3:5, 7; Num 22:31; see also 4Q434 1 II, 3–4; Philo *Spec. Laws* 3.6.

1411. For spiritually blind eyes, see Isa 6:10; 29:10; 43:8; 44:18; perhaps 59:10; for spiritual perception, 6:5; 30:20; 33:17; for healing blind eyes in the messianic era, 29:18; 32:3; 35:5. (The unity of Isaiah is a modern question that would not have affected ancient readings.)

1412. E.g., Max. Tyre 6.1.

1413. I adapt most of the background information here from Keener, *John*, 247–50.

1414. E.g., Plato *Phaedo* 65E; 66A; noted also by subsequent writers, e.g., Diog. Laert. 6.2.53; Justin *Dial.* 2; 4.1. On Plato and the vision of God, see Kirk, *Vision*, 16–18.

1415. Plato *Phaedo* 83A. Cf. also Iambl. *V.P.* 6.31; 16.70; 32.228. Later writers continued to find in Plato's Socrates an appeal for intellectual vision into the invisible world (Lucian *Phil. Sale* 18).

1416. E.g., Cic. *Tusc.* 1.19.44; Marc. Aur. 11.1.1 (cf. 10.26).

1417. For the opening of the soul's eyes, O'Toole, *Acts 26*, 72, cites Philo *QG* 1.39. Philo also speaks of the soul's eyes in *Spec. Laws* 1.37; 3.4, 6; *Unchangeable* 181; *Sacr.* 36, 69, 78; *Posterity* 8, 118; *Worse* 22; *Plant.* 22; *Drunkenness* 44; *Sobr.* 3; *Conf.* 92; *Migr.* 39, 48, 165, 191; *Heir* 89; *Prelim. St.* 135; *Names* 3, 203; *Abr.* 58, 70; *Dreams* 1.117; 2.160; *Mos.* 1.185, 289; *Rewards* 37; elsewhere, e.g., *Rhet. Alex.* pref. 1421a.22–23.

1418. Epict. *Diatr.* 1.18.4, 6; 2.20.37; 2.24.19; cf. 4.6.18.

1419. Marc. Aur. 4.29.

1420. Sen. Y. *Ep. Lucil.* 87.21, cited in Cary and Haarhoff, *Life*, 335. *Ep. Lucil.* 115.6 uses physical vision as an analogy for the mind's seeing virtue. Even a mythographer could speak of Numa seeing the heavenly deities through his mind (Ovid *Metam.* 15.62–64).

Such views flourished, however, particularly among those most deeply engaged with Platonic tradition. In the mid-second century C.E., the eclectic Platonist orator Maximus of Tyre stressed vision by the intellect (Max. Tyre 11.9; 38.3).[1421] He noted that at death those who love God will see him, ideal Beauty and pure Truth (9.6; 10.3; 11.11).[1422] In the meantime, one can strip off the layers of sense perception in the world's beauty to see God (11.11).[1423] The soul can recall only vaguely its prenatal vision of divine beauty (21.7); whereas such beauty remains perfect in the unchanging heavens, it grows faint in the lower realms of the senses (21.7–8). The third-century founder of Neoplatonism sought such vision: Plotinus allegedly "experienced in a trance actual visions of the transcendent God."[1424] Developing his views according to the Platonic model, Plotinus declared that the soul's vision, a sort of inner sight, contemplated the beauty of the Good in the realm of Ideas.[1425] His followers, however, retained older popular mythology alongside such views.[1426]

Early in the first century, the eclectic Jewish Platonist Philo reflects analogous notions. True knowledge is available through seeing transcendent reality, not depending on the body and its senses.[1427] Like other philosophers, he condemns blindness of soul,[1428] an image utilized for centuries even in popular drama.[1429] Wisdom can enable the soul to see; vision, the swiftest of senses, is preferable to hearing, and so inspiration is preferable to mere lectures.[1430] Because Philo's God is absolutely transcendent, seekers can know God only through ecstatically experienced mystical vision.[1431] Only the pure soul may envision God.[1432] Thus Abraham perceived God not with physical eyes but with those of the soul;[1433] the prophets were "seers" because of the active eyes of their souls;[1434] "Israel" means "the one who sees God."[1435]

Following biblical tradition, Philo states that divine vision depends on God's revelation: God is too transcendent to be perceived apart from his revelation.[1436] As in the OT, God is invisible;[1437] Philo allows that one can come to the Logos but warns that God is so transcendent over creation that even here one cannot fully perceive God.[1438] The present vision of deity is necessarily incomplete; mortals can perceive

1421. He allegorized Odysseus's travels as a visionary tour of the cosmos (similar to apocalyptic texts) by his soul (Max. Tyre 26.1).

1422. Cf. Philost. *Hrk.* 7.3; 1 Cor 13:12.

1423. Those unable to see God himself could be satisfied with worshiping his offspring (stars, *daimones*, etc.), below him in the cosmic hierarchy (Max. Tyre 11.12).

1424. Case, *Origins*, 93–94; cf. also Osborn, *Justin*, 72. Josephus expects his readers to understand (and perhaps react negatively) when he declares that an Egyptian ruler wished to "see the gods" (*Ag. Ap.* 1.232–34).

1425. Plot. *Enn.* 1.6, esp. 1.6.9.

1426. Case, *Origins*, 94. For his disciple Porphyry, by contrast, the wise person's soul continually "beholds" God (*Marc.* 16.274).

1427. E.g., Philo *Flight* 19.

1428. Philo *Worse* 22; *Dreams* 1.164.

1429. E.g., Soph. *Oed. tyr.* 371, 375, 402–3, 419, 454, 747, 1266–79.

1430. Philo *Sacr.* 78; cf. *Abr.* 57–58; also the citation of *Mos.* 1.66 in Aune, *Prophecy*, 148. In later Platonism, see Proclus *Poet.* 6.2, K182.19–20. For accessibility of divine vision through mystical encounter or intermediaries, see Mackie, "Seeing God."

1431. Isaacs, *Spirit*, 50; Dillon, "Transcendence in Philo"; Hagner, "Vision," 89–90. On parallels to ecstatic vision, see also Kirk, *Vision*, 23.

1432. Philo *Conf.* 92.

1433. Philo *Names* 3–6; cf. *Posterity* 8–21 (summarized in LCL introduction to *Posterity*).

1434. Philo *QG* 4.138.

1435. Philo *Conf.* 92, 146; *Dreams* 1.171; *Abr.* 57.

1436. Philo *Abr.* 80.

1437. Frequently, e.g., Philo *Spec. Laws* 2.165; *Cher.* 101; *Planter* 18; *Abr.* 75; *Migr.* 183; *Names* 14; *Dreams* 1.72; *Decal.* 60; 120; for the Logos as invisible, see *Creation* 31.

1438. Philo *Dreams* 1.66; contrast *QE* 2.39 (where the Logos is a vantage point for envisioning God).

only that God is, not what he is;[1439] only God can "apprehend God."[1440] The soul's eye is overwhelmed by God's glory,[1441] yet seeking God remains a blessed endeavor, "just as no one blames the eyes of the body because when unable to see the sun itself they see the emanation of its rays. "[1442] One should progress toward clearer vision; the ultimate vision of God is a reward for attaining perfection.[1443]

Neither Paul nor Luke engages the Platonic tradition deeply; Scripture offers a more proximate source here. Thus it should be noted that the motif of spiritual sight and blindness in the Jesus tradition (e.g., Mark 4:12; 8:18; Matt 13:13–16; 15:14; 23:16) flows especially and often explicitly from biblical tradition.[1444] The motifs of eschatological vision[1445]—spiritual blindness and sight representing straying from or following God's way,[1446] and spiritual sight representing spiritual insight into God's character and mysteries[1447]—persisted in "intertestamental" Palestinian Judaism. Later Jewish sources continued to employ this language.[1448] The rabbis had to explain biblical passages referring to Israel seeing God;[1449] they commented on the rare persons who, in some sense, "beheld" God's presence in the present time,[1450] but they especially focused on the eschatological vision of God.[1451] According to some later rabbis, obedience to the law produced nearness to—and, in some sense, the vision of—God;[1452] Merkabah literature stressed the mystical vision of God.[1453]

Regarding explicit sources for Luke's audience, Paul's opening people's eyes and turning them to light may reflect the Isaian servant's mission, emulating the path of Paul's Lord (Luke 4:18; cf. 1:78–79). Paul's hearers in the narrative world know nothing of Paul's experience of blindness, but Luke's audience knows that the very one called to open others' eyes (Acts 26:18) was first struck blind, and his eyes were opened when God's servant came to baptize him and report his commission (9:8, 17–18; 22:13–16).[1454] Such narrative symbolism also fits this context: Paul would turn others' eyes to the light just as he had encountered a light brighter than the midday sun in 26:13.

1439. Philo Rewards 39; Hagner, "Vision," 89, cites both this and Names 62.

1440. Philo Rewards 40 (LCL, 8:335). Cf. 1 Cor 2:11.

1441. Philo Spec. Laws 1.37.

1442. Philo Spec. Laws 1.40 (LCL, 7:121).

1443. Philo Rewards 36; cf. Dreams 72. Conzelmann, Corinthians, 228, contrasts the eschatological vision in 1 Cor 13:12 with Philo's usual mystical, ecstatic vision; Hagner, "Vision," 86, contrasts John and Philo's σῶμα-σῆμα conception.

1444. Esp. Isa 6:9–10; see also Deut 29:4; Isa 29:9–10; 35:5; 42:7, 16, 18–20; 43:8; 44:18; Jer 5:21; Ezek 12:2; cf. Dan 5:23.

1445. 1 En. 90:35; 4 Ezra 7:98 (after death); Asc. Is. 9:38 (though this is probably Christian).

1446. E.g., Wis 2:21; 1 En. 89:33, 41, 54; 93:8; 99:8; cf. Test. Dan 2:2, 4; Test. Jos. 7:5; Test. Benj. 4:2 (the last may be interpolated). Vision apparently functions as a symbol for knowing more of God in 1 En. 89:28.

1447. E.g., 1QS X, 10–11; XI, 5–6.

1448. E.g., Gen. Rab. 97 MSV, on Jacob's prophetic sight.

1449. E.g., 'Abot R. Nat. 1 A; Pesiq. Rab Kah. 26:9; Pesiq. Rab. 15:8.

1450. Cf. b. Sukkah 45b.

1451. 'Abot R. Nat. 1 A; Sipra Behuq. pq. 3.263.1.5; Sipre Deut. 310.6.1; Pesiq. Rab. 12:9; 37:2; cf. also Tanḥ. 4.18 and Agadath Bereshith 73.48 in Marmorstein, Anthropomorphism, 95; and discussion, 96–99; Kirk, Vision, 14–15.

1452. Marmorstein, Anthropomorphism, 105–6; this was also the prerequisite for the eschatological vision of God (96, 101).

1453. Chernus, "Visions"; Kirk, Vision, 11–13.

1454. Cf. Hamm, "Blindness and Healing." That Luke employs the event symbolically need not mean, of course, that he did not believe that it happened literally; otherwise we should expect to find much more creative narrative symbolism than we do. Luke uses narrative symbolism, but sparingly (certainly far less than John), as a Hellenistic historian, not as an epic poet.

(2) Turning to God

Isaiah's servant would turn (ἐπιστρέψαι) Israel back to God, and God would make the servant a "light" for salvation to the earth (Isa 49:6); salvation would come to all those on the earth who would turn (ἐπιστράφητε) to God (45:22).[1455] John the Baptist was already active in this calling (Luke 1:16–17);[1456] evoking the language of Isa 9:2, he would prepare for the one who would shine in darkness (Luke 1:79). Peter (Acts 3:19; 9:35) and the Hellenists (11:20–21) would also "turn" people to God. Paul has also effectively demonstrated this calling (14:15; 15:19; cf. 28:27), as he goes on to point out (26:20).[1457]

Satan's "authority" or "dominion"[1458] may include the world system (Luke 4:6).[1459] Judaism was unanimous that God is the ruler of the world;[1460] nevertheless, the (Gentile) human sphere could lie under God's dominion (1 John 5:19). The Qumran scrolls contrast the Prince of Lights (שר האורים)[1461] with Belial, prince of the wicked realm,[1462] and they present Belial as ruler of the army of the Kittim.[1463] Clearly, early Christians adopted the apocalyptic worldview in which God allowed the devil and his forces considerable activity among the nations in the present age (2 Cor 4:4; Eph 2:2; cf. Mark 3:22).[1464]

In Luke's theology, however, God's authority through the kingdom often crushes that of Satan (e.g., Luke 4:36; 9:1; 10:19; 11:18–20).[1465] On God's kingdom, see discussion at Acts 1:3, 6. Forgiveness of sins is a theme in Luke-Acts (Luke 3:3; 7:47–48; Acts 2:38; 22:16); whereas Pauline literature mentions "forgiveness" only occasionally, it mentions sin regularly (ἁμαρτία appears more than fifty times) and emphasizes how to be "justified." Paul's mission to lead people to "turn" and hence receive forgiveness of sins is none other than the apostolic (and, by extension, the church's) mission to lead people to repentance for forgiveness of sins (Luke 24:47).

1455. For this verb for turning to God in Isaiah, see also Isa 6:10 (significant in Acts 28:27); 19:22 (concerning Egypt); 31:6; 44:22; 55:7; cf. also Hos 3:5; 5:4; 6:1; 7:10; 11:5; 12:6; 14:1–2; Amos 4:6, 8–11; Joel 2:12–13; Sir 5:7; 17:25, 29; 18:13; 21:6. Luke is influenced by the LXX rendering of the Hebrew *shub* (Dupont, *Salvation*, 79).

1456. Cf. Mal 4:6 (3:23 LXX) for the idea but Sir 48:10 for the wording.

1457. For "turning" as repentance, cf. also Luke 17:4; 22:32. Paul uses ἐπιστρέφω for Jews (2 Cor 3:16) and Gentiles (1 Thess 1:9) turning to Christ, as well as for Christians falling away (Gal 4:9).

1458. Fitzmyer, *Acts*, 760, rightly compares "Belial's dominion" in the Qumran scrolls (1QS I, 18, 23; II, 19; 1QM XIV, 9) or (relevant to the "lot" or "inheritance" in Acts 26:18) "Belial's lot" (1QS II, 5, versus God's in II, 2).

1459. Unless Satan there exaggerated his delegated authority, as Luke might have surmised in light of Dan 4:32; but at least some authority was permitted to Satan (Luke 22:53). Human "authority" could be used negatively (Luke 20:20; 23:7; Acts 9:14), but many interpreters understand it as a delegated sphere distinct from spiritual authority (Luke 7:8; 20:25, on Caesar; Acts 5:4; see Walaskay, *Came to Rome*, 66).

1460. E.g., *Sipre Deut.* 27.2.1; *'Abot R. Nat.* 24, §51 B; cf. *Jub.* 25:23 ("Lord of the age"). Satan assumes this role (κοσμοκράτωρ) only in some later texts (e.g., Hoskyns, *Gospel*, 426, cites *Exod. Rab.* on 24:7, following Strack and Billerbeck, *Kommentar*). Some gnostics later argued that the Jewish God was the lord of the world, whom they identified with Satan, inviting apologetic (Marmorstein, *Names*, 64, 99).

1461. CD V, 18; "the prince of light" in 1QM XIII, 10 (Israel's helper).

1462. 1QM XVII, 5–6; Perkins, "John," 972, cites 1QM I, 1, 5, 13; IV, 2; XI, 8; 1QS I, 18; II, 19; III, 20–21. Cf. repeatedly "Prince Mastema," though his rule is specifically over the evil angels (*Jub.* 11:5, 10; 17:16; 18:9, 12; 48:2, 9, 12, 15; cf. 10:8; 19:28; 49:2); the "Prince of Darkness" (*Pesiq. Rab.* 20:2; 53:2).

1463. 1QM XV, 2–3. Pagans applied titles such as "ruler of the world" to prominent deities (Lucan *C.W.* 6.742–43; Segal, "Ruler," 248–49; the demiurge in Iren. *Her.* 1.5.4; cf. demonic "world rulers" in Eph 6:12; *Test. Sol.* 8:2–7; in the magical papyri, see Arnold, *Power*, 65; later astrological powers in MacGregor, "Principalities"; Lee, "Powers," 60) as well as the emperor (Ovid *Metam.* 15.758–59, 859–60; cf. other rulers in *y. 'Abod. Zar.* 3:1, §3; *Exod. Rab.* 5:14).

1464. On the apocalyptic image, see, e.g., Segal, "Ruler," 247. *Asc. Is.* 2:4 presents Beliar as the angel of sin who rules the world; but whereas Knibb thinks *Asc. Is.* 1–3 pre-Christian, I am doubtful.

1465. In this context, it seems possible that Paul links Satan's authority with that which the chief priests exercised to persecute Christians (Acts 26:10, 12; cf. 9:14), but the shared term may be simply coincidental.

Paul makes a shockingly universal and somewhat exclusive truth claim (for Gentiles as well as Jews) in a world where, apart from Jewish affirmation of one God, tolerance of most cults was often confused with accepting at least their partial validity. The universal benefit of his message and mission provides justification for his total zeal in pursuing it.

(3) Darkness to Light

Luke sometimes uses light, connected with seeing eyes (Luke 11:34), as a metaphor (8:16; 11:33–36); this image was, however, more common among many of his contemporaries, including Paul.[1466] Paul uses light-and-darkness imagery for spiritual or moral awareness, often through the gospel;[1467] as here, he can apply it to contrasts with Satan's kingdom[1468] and to conversion (2 Cor 4:6; esp. Col 1:12–13). This transition from darkness to light at a believer's conversion also appears in some Christian texts outside Paul's letters and Acts' speeches (1 Pet 2:9).

Luke's biblical canon often uses "light" figuratively,[1469] as does the early gospel tradition dependent on the OT.[1470] A variety of Jewish sources employ darkness and light figuratively for evil and good respectively[1471] or with reference to enlightenment in wisdom;[1472] "light/darkness" dualism is especially common in the Qumran scrolls.[1473]

Jewish teachers applied light and darkness imagery to a variety of specific occasions, all of which reflect a common appreciation for the goodness of light and a common disdain for the dangers of darkness (e.g., Job 18:5, 18; 24:13, 16). The image applied to the primeval light before or from the creation;[1474] in Gen 1:3, the light emerged through God's word, and this tradition continued to be developed.[1475] Because this

---

1466. For figurative darkness in Luke, see Luke 1:79; 11:34–35; 22:53. The power of darkness (probably including acting under the cloak of night, but cf. also John 13:30) in Luke 22:53 was involved in arranging Jesus's crucifixion; but even here, God remains sovereign over the outcome (Acts 2:23).

1467. See Rom 2:19; 13:12; 2 Cor 4:4, 6, 17; 6:14; Eph 1:18; 3:9; 5:8–9, 11, 13; 6:12; Col 1:12–13; 1 Thess 5:4–5; cf. 1 Cor 4:5; 2 Cor 11:14; 1 Tim 6:16; 2 Tim 1:10.

1468. Eph 6:12; Col 1:13; cf. 2 Cor 4:4; 6:14–15; 11:14; 1 Thess 5:5.

1469. E.g., 2 Sam 22:29; Pss 18:28; 27:1; 36:9; 43:3; 119:105, 130; Isa 2:5; 5:20; 9:2; 42:6; 49:6; 51:4. For the figurative use of "light" conjoined with opening eyes, see, e.g., Isa 42:6–7. For this background material, I am adapting Keener, *John*, 382–85.

1470. E.g., Matt 4:16 (Isa 9:1); 5:14 (Ps 27:1; I would cite here esp. Isa 42:6; 49:6); Luke 2:32 (Isa 42:6; 49:6), as noted by Painter, *John*, 33. In Platonic metaphysics, see Meyer-Schwelling, "Light"; e.g., Apul. *De deo Socr.* 124.

1471. E.g., 1QS III, 3 and passim; 1Q27 1 I, 5–6; 4Q183 II, 4–8 (and perhaps 4Q185 1–2 II, 6–8); *Test. Job* 43:6/4; *Sib. Or.* frg. 1.26–27 (*OTP* 2:377); cf. *1 En.* 108:12–14.

1472. E.g., Sir 31:17.

1473. E.g., 1QS III, 19–22; 1QM XIII, 5–6, 14–15. They also employ "day" figuratively with "light," and "night" with "darkness" (1QS X, 1–2). The scrolls added dualism to the OT images (Brown, *John*, 1:340; cf. Charlesworth, "Comparison"). Though acknowledging OT influence, Treves, "Date," 421, thinks that the imagery is "ultimately of Iranian origin," but Hebrew emphasis on contrasting opposites (e.g., "day" and "night") to represent a whole (cf. Gordon, *Near East*, 35n3) allows that the image's Jewish roots lay in the OT, despite exilic Persian influence accentuating the dualism (cf. similarly Manson, *Paul and John*, 118–19).

1474. It existed before visible things (*2 En.* 24:4, A, J; cf. *Exod. Rab.* 50:1) or appeared on the first day (e.g., *b. Ḥag.* 12a; *Gen. Rab.* 42:3; see fuller discussion in Urbach, *Sages*, 1:208–10), and by it one could see from one end of the world to the other (*3 En.* 5:3; *b. Ḥag.* 12a; *y. Ber.* 8:6, §5; *Gen. Rab.* 42:3; *Lev. Rab.* 11:7; *Num. Rab.* 13:5; *Ruth Rab.* proem 7; *Pesiq. Rab.* 23:6). Hengel, *Judaism and Hellenism*, 1:169, points to the "way Jewish-Palestinian and Pythagorean-Platonic and Stoic conceptions are intermingled in Aristobulus" on the primeval light; cf. perhaps the sun's scattering of chaos in Men. Rhet. 2.17, 438.20–24. Cf. the Yozer Or ("The Creator of Light") prayer in later synagogue liturgy (Bowman, *Gospel*, 68); Philo *Creation* 30–35.

1475. E.g., 2 Cor 4:6; the first-century C.E. pagan writer Longinus (*Subl.* 9.9) also attributes it to Moses. Cf. the Memra and the creation of light in *Tg. Neof.* 1 on Gen 1:3–5; God distinguished light from darkness for humanity's sake in 4Q392 frg. 1.

light would be restored,[1476] it also was connected with OT images of eschatological light and glory.[1477] Other Jewish teachers regularly called particularly righteous sages or other persons lights (cf. Matt 5:14; John 5:35),[1478] including Adam,[1479] Abraham,[1480] Jacob,[1481] Moses,[1482] David,[1483] R. Johanan ben Zakkai,[1484] and ultimately the Messiah;[1485] the designation also could be applied to Israel,[1486] Jerusalem,[1487] the temple,[1488] and to God himself.[1489] Moreover, Jewish literature portrays both Wisdom[1490] and Torah[1491]

1476. Because of human sin, it was hidden until the eschatological time (cf. *b. Ḥag.* 12a; *Gen. Rab.* 11:2; 42:3; *Exod. Rab.* 18:11; *Lev. Rab.* 11:7; *Num. Rab.* 13:5; *Pesiq. Rab.* 23:6; 42:4).

1477. E.g., *1 En.* 1:8; 5:7; 108:11–14; 1QM XVII, 6–7; 4Q541 9 I, 4–5; *Sib. Or.* 2.316 (probably in Christian redaction); *'Abot R. Nat.* 37, §95 B; *b. Ḥag.* 12b; *Pesaḥ.* 50a; *Sanh.* 91b; *Ta'an.* 15a; *Pesiq. Rab Kah.* 21:3–5; *Pesiq. Rab Kah.* Sup. 5:1; *Exod. Rab.* 14:3; 18:11; *Lev. Rab.* 6:6; *Song Rab.* 1:3, §3; *Eccl. Rab.* 11:7, §1; *Pesiq. Rab.* 36:1; 42:4; Matt 13:43; Rev 22:5.

1478. Simon ben Onias in Sir 50:6–7; possibly Samuel in *L.A.B.* 51:4; R. Eliezer in *'Abot R. Nat.* 13, §32 B; Honi the Circle-Drawer in *y. Ta'an.* 3:9, §4; Daniel's three friends in *Exod. Rab.* 15:6; the patriarchs in *Pesiq. Rab.* 8:4; possibly priests in 4Q504–506; cf. the righteous in general in *'Abot R. Nat.* 24 A and *Tg. Ps.-J.* on Exod 40:4; righteous deeds in *Gen. Rab.* 1:6. The expression must have been a fairly widespread one; Anna considers her son Tobias "the light of my eyes" (Tob 10:5); a source may have been 2 Sam 21:17 (cf. 1 Kgs 11:36; 15:4; 2 Kgs 8:19). In the eschatological time, see Wis 3:7–8 (cf. 5:6); Matt 13:43; Rev 22:5; *L.A.B.* 26:13; *4 Ezra* 7:97; *2 En.* 65:11 A; *Sipre Deut.* 47.2.1–2; *b. Sanh.* 100a; *Lev. Rab.* 30:2; *Eccl. Rab.* 1:7, §9; Abelson, *Immanence*, 89, cites *Yal. Pss.* 72. Cf. a pagan metaphor for a skillful sophist (Eunapius *Lives* 495), heroes (Men. Rhet. 2.11, 419.18–20; Philost. *Hrk.* 44.5; 45.5), or any great and beloved person (Fronto *Ad M. Caes.* 4.7).

1479. *'Abot R. Nat.* 9, §25 B; *y. Šabb.* 2:6, §2.

1480. *Test. Ab.* 7:14 B; *Gen. Rab.* 2:3; 30:10; *Pesiq. Rab.* 20:2.

1481. *Ruth Rab.* 2:12 (probably fourth century).

1482. *Sipre Num.* 93.1.3; *b. Soṭah* 12a; 13a; *Exod. Rab.* 1:20, 22, 24; *Pesiq. Rab.* 15:4; cf. *L.A.B.* 12:1.

1483. 11Q5 XXVII, 2; *b. Sanh.* 95a (following 2 Sam 21:17).

1484. *'Abot R. Nat.* 25 A; *b. Ber.* 28b.

1485. *1 En.* 48:4 (from the Similitudes, alluding to Isa 42:6; 49:6); the eschatological high priest in 1QSb IV, 27; and Amoraic sources in *Pesiq. Rab Kah.* Sup. 6:5; *Gen. Rab.* 1:6; 85:1; *Pesiq. Rab.* 36:1–2; 37:2; kingship in general in *Tg. 1 Chr.* 8:33.

1486. E.g., Sir 17:19; *Pesiq. Rab Kah.* Sup. 5:1; uses of Isa 60:3 in the late *Song Rab.* 1:3, §2; 1:15, §4; 4:1, §2. For the association with Israel more generally, cf. *b. Pesaḥ.* 103b; 104a; *Ḥul.* 26b.

1487. *Pesiq. Rab Kah.* 21:4 (citing Isa 60:3); *Gen. Rab.* 59:5 (citing Isa 60:3). Some see Jerusalem in Matt 5:14 (cf. Campbell, "Jerusalem," 346; Jeremias, *Promise*, 66; idem, *Sermon*, 33; idem, *Parables*, 217). A great city could be called a light (Pliny E. *N.H.* 5.31.120, on Ephesus and Smyrna).

1488. *Pesiq. Rab Kah.* 21:5, bar.; *Gen. Rab.* 2:5 (the temple in the messianic era; citing Isa 60:1); 3:4 (fifth century, citing Jer 17:12; Ezek 43:2).

1489. 1QH^a VII, 24–25; *4 Bar.* 9:3; *L.A.B.* 12:9; *L.A.E.* 28:2; *Test. Zeb.* 9:8 (paraphrasing Mal 4:2); PGM 4.1219–22; perhaps 4Q451 24 7; cf. *Sib. Or.* 3.285; *b. Menaḥ.* 88b (late second century); *Gen. Rab.* 3:4 (third century, citing Ps 104:2; also in *Exod. Rab.* 50:1); 59:5 (citing Isa 60:19); *Num. Rab.* 15:2; *Pesiq. Rab.* 8:5 (citing Pss 27:1; 119:105); 21:5 (citing Isa 60:19); Rev 21:23. In rabbinic texts, this often alludes to the Shekinah (e.g., *Sipre Num.* 41.1.1; *b. Ber.* 60b); the Shekinah of the first exodus is also depicted as light (e.g., Wis 17; 18:1–3; *b. Menaḥ.* 86b; *Exod. Rab.* 14:3). Later, Allah's truth is portrayed as light (Qur'an 9.32).

1490. Wis 6:12; 7:26, 29–30; 1QS II, 3; XI, 5–6; 1QM I, 8; 4 Ezra 14:20–21; cf. Sir 22:11; Tatian *Or. Gks.* 13; Philo *Alleg. Interp.* 3.45 (the Logos). Cf. the light of knowledge in both LXX and Qumran readings of Isa 53:11, perhaps adding light to what became the MT (cf. Seeligmann, "Phōs"). For light representing wisdom and law in the OT, see the references in Malatesta, *Interiority*, 99–102; Boismard, *Prologue*, 114 (esp. Pss 19:9; 119:105; Prov 4:18–19; 6:23; Eccl 2:13).

1491. Bar 4:2; 4Q511 1 7–8; 18 7–8; *CIJ* 1:409, §554; *L.A.B.* 9:8; 11:1–2; 15:6; 19:4, 6; 23:10; 33:3 end; 51:3; *2 Bar.* 17:4; 18:1–2; 59:2; *Sipre Num.* 41.1.2; *y. B. Meṣiʿa* 2:5, §2; *Hor.* 3:1, §2; *Sukkah* 5:1, §7; *Gen. Rab.* 26:7; *Pesiq. Rab.* 8:5; 46:3; cf. *L.A.B.* 37:3; *Sipre Deut.* 343.7.1; *Gen. Rab.* 3:5; *Exod. Rab.* 36:3; *Num. Rab.* 14:10; *Deut. Rab.* 4:4; 7:3; *Eccl. Rab.* 11:7, §1; *Pesiq. Rab.* 17:7. Torah also appears as fire (*m. 'Ab.* 2:10; *Sipre Deut.* 343.11.1; *'Abot R. Nat.* 43, §121 B, citing Deut 33:2; *b. Beṣah* 25b; *Ta'an.* 7a; *Pesiq. Rab Kah.* Sup. 3:2, citing Jer 23:29; *Song Rab.* 5:11, §6; the Ten Commandments as lightnings in *Tg. Neof.* 1 on Exod 20:2–3; *Tg. Ps.-J.* on Exod 20:2–3; *Tg. Neof.* 1 on Deut 5:6–7) or summons heavenly fire (*y. Ḥag.* 2:1, §9; *Song Rab.* 1:10, §2), and specific commandments, such as the Sabbath, appear as light (*Pesiq. Rab.* 8:4). God's words shine the light of understanding on the willing heart (4Q511 1 7–8; 18 7–8). Later, Islamic tradition claimed that Jesus's gospel contains light, confirming Torah (so Qur'an 5.46).

as light (e.g., Ps 119:105, 130; Prov 6:23). Many ancients used darkness as an image of ignorance.[1492] Death also was associated with darkness.[1493] And the punishment of the wicked in the afterlife could be associated with darkness.[1494]

Antithesis was a standard rhetorical device,[1495] displayed here in the antithesis between light and darkness, on the one hand, and Satan and God, on the other. Like Jewish writers noted above, Gentile writers commonly employed the contrast between light and darkness for good and evil.[1496] The opposition between light and darkness offered a natural metaphor for the incompatibility of good and evil.[1497] This moral imagery is frequent in the Qumran scrolls.[1498] The presence of light banishes darkness (1Q27 I, 5–6);[1499] this triumph of light would especially characterize the activity of the eschatological deliverer (John 1:5; 4Q541 9 I, 4–5).

Like others, Paul in his letters often employs the contrast between spiritual light (day) and darkness (Rom 2:19; 13:12–13; 1 Cor 4:5; 2 Cor 4:6; 6:14; Eph 5:8; 1 Thess 5:5; cf. Col 1:13). Other early Christians also taught that God called his people from darkness to light (1 Pet 2:9; cf. 1 John 2:8–9), perhaps reflecting Isaianic imagery (Isa 9:2; 42:16; 58:10). The same language appears in Jos. Asen. 8:9/10; this suggests some common source for the image (perhaps an interpretive tradition on Isa 9:2; 42:16; 50:10; or 58:10).[1500] Both Joseph and Aseneth and the NT references suggest conversion language;[1501] the passage in 1 Peter applies to Gentiles experiencing a spiritually Jewish identity in Christ (1 Pet 2:9–10). Also very possibly relevant is the Passover tradition that in the exodus God redeemed his people and brought them from darkness to light (m. Pesah. 10:5).[1502]

The immediate contextual connection here with light offers a concrete illustration: Paul was turned to a bright light (Acts 26:13) and now is called to summon others to the same light (26:18). (A vision of God would naturally emphasize light; in addition to biblical accounts of God's "glory," Jewish sources often depict light around God's throne.)[1503] Thus Paul's conversion becomes a paradigm for turning both Jews and Gentiles from their former understanding to a new relationship with God in Christ (that Paul intends his own conversion paradigmatically is explicit in 26:29). More broadly, this light may evoke that in Luke 2:32, which (as in Acts 26:17) applies to both Israel and the Gentiles.

1492. E.g., Val. Max. 7.2.ext. 1a (Socrates); Max. Tyre 29.5.

1493. E.g., Hom. Il. 4.503, 526; Lycophron Alex. 705–6; Sil. It. 7.586 (because those in the netherworld could no longer see the light of the world). See also discussion of "black" and death at Acts 1:10.

1494. E.g., Matt 8:12; 2 Pet 2:4; Jude 6; 1 En. 103:8; cf. 10:4–6; 63:6, 11; 92:5; 108:14. Cf. other sources in Keener, Matthew, 269.

1495. See, e.g., Anderson, Glossary, 21–22.

1496. E.g., Max. Tyre 34.1. Orators also praised the brilliance of deities (e.g., Men. Rhet. 2.17, 438.12–13, 20–24); writers also used light to symbolize the divine nature or care (Iambl. Myst. 1.9, 13).

1497. E.g., 2 Cor 6:14–16; Max. Tyre 34.1.

1498. See, e.g., the contrast between light and darkness in 1QS III, 3, 19, 25; X, 2; 1QM I, 1, 11; XIII, 5, 15; XIV, 17; 4Q462 1 9–10; 4Q548 1 10–16; 11Q11 V, 7; cf. 1QHᵃ XVII, 26; XX, 9; XXI, 15; 4Q257 III, 5; 4Q299 5 2; 4Q392 1 4–6; 11Q5 XXVI, 11; 11Q17 X, 5.

1499. Cf. Apollo as the sun god appearing to destroy darkness in Men. Rhet. 2.17, 438.20–24.

1500. Or perhaps a midrash on creation (2 Cor 4:6); or liturgical language (Pss 18:28; 112:4).

1501. With Conzelmann, Acts, 211. Whether Joseph and Aseneth includes Christian influence remains debated.

1502. The material might be unattributed or stem from Gamaliel II, but the tradition would be especially relevant if it could be attributed to Gamaliel I, who is early enough and also Paul's teacher (see Nunnally, "Acts," 396, noting b. Pesah. 116b); Rabban Gamaliel is the last-named rabbi, though anonymous material could follow Gamaliel's material.

1503. See, e.g., 1 Tim 6:16; 2 En. 25:4; cf. 1QM XII, 2; 2 En. 1a:6; 20:4; 42:5; Num. Rab. 14:3; Pesiq. Rab Kah. 21:5; also the "throne of glory" or "glorious throne" in 1 En. 9:4; 47:3; 60:2; 71:7; 3 En. 2:3–4; Test. Levi 5:1; b. Hag. 13a; Menah. 43b; Tg. Ps.-J. on Gen 27:1.

(4) Inheritance among Those Set Apart

As in Acts 20:32, the "inheritance" is among the "sanctified"—that is, God's people set apart for his promises (Paul has already applied "saints" to the persecuted believers in Jerusalem in 26:10). (For "inheritance," see comment on Acts 20:32.) Israel was God's sanctified inheritance (μερίδος ἡγιασμένης, 3 Macc 6:3). (On forgiveness of sins, see comment on Acts 2:38.)

"Saints" also referred to angels (4Q403 1 I, 31). Some scholars have suggested that when Pauline literature speaks of believers sharing the "inheritance of the saints" (Eph 1:18; Col 1:12), it refers to angels;[1504] such a usage, however, fits neither those letters' usage of "saints"[1505] nor the probable sense of "by faith" here in Acts 26:18. For fuller discussion of "saints" (and their inheritance), see comment on Acts 20:32.

That Gentile believers (26:17) are included in this designation implies that (using language from Pauline letters) they have been grafted in (Rom 11:17–19, 23–24), or made part of, the Messiah's empire (Eph 2:12–13). Including Gentile believers in this category would surprise Paul's hearers but probably not offend them (mostly Agrippa, Berenice, and Gentiles) the way it would have offended some other audiences in Acts (cf. Acts 22:21–22).

The language of Acts 26:18 resembles Col 1:12–14 in many respects, both texts probably imitating or (in my opinion, more likely) reflecting Pauline language (though for Luke this cannot be verbatim): God enables believers to share in the inheritance (κλῆρος, in both cases) of the holy or set-apart ones (in Col 1:12, ἁγίων) in light, having delivered them from the authority (ἐξουσία, in both cases) of darkness; in Christ they have forgiveness of sins (1:14).[1506]

d. Paul's Gospel (26:19–23)

Paul develops his argument from *ēthos* and protests against his accusers even further here. Jesus commissioned Paul to preach (Acts 26:16–18), and Paul, having always pursued the way he thought was pious (26:4–12), then carried out this commission (26:19–20). It was such preaching of righteousness and good behavior that provoked the attack in the temple (26:21), but by God's help, Paul survived and has continued to testify (26:22), as he is continuing to do even this day, to the message of Christ's resurrection (26:23).

i. Obeying Jesus's Commission (26:19–20)

Paul now carries out the commission given by Jesus in 26:16–18. Paul preached repentance from Damascus to Jerusalem, Judea, and to the Gentiles.

(1) Obeying the Heavenly Vision (26:19)

Paul now predicates (ὅθεν) all his behavior on the divine call of 26:16–18; the *narratio* up to this point provides the explanation for his otherwise controversial behavior.[1507] Paul obeys ("not disobey" is Lukan litotes) the heavenly vision,[1508] fitting the pattern of his predecessors in Luke-Acts. Jesus obeys the Father's heavenly call

---

1504. Lohse, *Colossians*, 36 (also noting Acts 20:32; 26:18).

1505. See Eph 1:1, 4, 15; 2:19; 3:5, 8, 18; 4:12; 5:3; 6:18; Col 1:2, 4, 22, 26; 3:12.

1506. Although Luke often uses ἄφεσις and ἁμαρτία together (Luke 1:77; 3:3; 24:47; Acts 2:38; 5:31; 10:43; 13:38; and here) as in Mark 1:4 and Matt 26:28, this is the only use in Pauline literature.

1507. Winter, "Official Proceedings," 330, notes that ὅθεν is appropriate for opening a *confirmatio* (P.Oxy. 2131; P.Fouad 26.13). It is relevant, however, for any transition predicated on what precedes (see the abundant sources in BDAG).

1508. Cf. also *1 En.* 93:2, where Enoch speaks of his "heavenly vision." In the NT, only Paul (in a summary of his visionary experiences, 2 Cor 12:1) and Luke (Luke 1:22; 24:23) employ the term ὀπτασία (in the Apostolic Fathers, *Mart. Pol.* 5.2; 12.3); for the idea of visions, see comment on Acts 2:17.

in Luke 3:21–22; Peter also obeys a vision from heaven (Acts 11:5) and points out that he had to obey God (11:17). Paul now obeys this initial vision (26:16) instead of kicking further against the goads (26:14). Obedience to the heavenly vision contrasts with his acting on the delegated authority of the priestly elite (26:10). That the vision was "heavenly" may mean that Paul experienced it as coming from the sky (cf. 11:5),[1509] or it may mean just that it was from the God associated with heaven.[1510] (Luke employs the same adjective in Luke 2:13, which could be construed as either "visible in heaven" or "having come from heaven," depending on how the scene is envisioned; cf. 2:15.) It may at least be noted that in this telling of Paul's call, he did experience a light "from heaven" (οὐρανόθεν, 26:13).[1511]

One could hardly be expected to disobey a heavenly vision.[1512] Paul's defense at this point is a defense from divine necessity (see comment on Acts 11:17). Necessity could justify actions otherwise more easily questioned.[1513] An act could not be condemned—even a wife's pregnancy by someone other than her husband—if it was genuinely by a god.[1514] Ancient rhetoric often considered divine activity the most persuasive form of testimony, a motif to which appeal is made regularly in Luke-Acts.[1515]

(2) Preaching Repentance (26:20)

Paul's mention of his widespread preaching not only provides a motive that explains his critics' false accusations (Acts 26:21) but also implicitly answers the claim that he was stirring unrest throughout the world (24:5). Paul will soon ground this pattern in Jesus's example of ministry to Jews and Gentiles alike (26:23). The geographic pattern of 26:20 closely follows the paradigm of 1:8 (cf. Luke 24:27), except that it starts where Paul found himself just after his conversion.[1516] Paul's "Gentiles" take the place of the "ends of the earth," just as Rome will ultimately fill this role in Luke's larger narration.

Fitting the narrative of Acts (Acts 9:19–20), which was likely constrained by Paul's own experience (cf. Gal 1:17), Paul preaches to Damascus before starting to do so in Jerusalem. Paul's preaching in Jerusalem appears in Acts 9:28–30; Judea may be

---

1509. So Dunn, *Jesus and Spirit*, 115. Some ancient sources speak of visions in the heavens (e.g., Jos. *War* 6.298–99; cf. Livy 21.62.4–5; Plut. *Themist.* 15.1), which fits one use of the adjective (cf. Jos. *Ant.* 1.69, 158; *War* 3.374; 5.214; *Ag. Ap.* 1.14, 255; Philo *Creation* 117) and Stephen's vision (Acts 7:55–56; cf. Luke 21:27), but the term can apply to anything heavenly or originating in heaven (e.g., 1 Esd 6:15; 2 Macc 7:34; see comment below).

1510. Outside Luke 2:13, the only other NT use is in Matthew (seven times for the heavenly Father); it appears in later portions of the LXX (1 Esd 6:15; 2 Macc 7:34; 9:10; 3 Macc 6:18; 4 Macc 4:11; 9:15; 11:3), but never describing a "vision." Cf. Luke 11:13. Many regarded the heavenly realm as purer and closer to the divine (e.g., Plato *Phaedr.* 248A–249A; Cic. *Resp.* 6.15.15; 6.17.17; 6.19.20; 6.26.29; *Tusc.* 1.19.43–44; 1.31.75; Sen. Y. *Nat. Q.* 1.pref. 6, 11–13; *Dial.* 5.6.1; 11.9.3; 12.8.5; 12.11.6; Max. Tyre 9.6; 11.10; 41.3; Diog. Laert. 8.1.27, 31; Philo *Spec. Laws* 1.66; 3.1–2; *Flight* 62; QG 3.45; *Test. Job* 33:3; 36:3; 41:4–5; 48–50 passim; cf. 1QM X, 12; discussion in Aune, *Revelation*, 318; idem, "Duality," 228–30).

1511. This adjective, appropriate for Hellenistic hearers, does imply a celestial origin, as in Acts 14:17; 4 Macc 4:10; Philo *Dreams* 1.112.

1512. Talbert, *Acts*, 208 (citing Livy 2.36; Plut. *Coriol.* 24). Paul recognizes in 1 Cor 9:17 that his calling is mandatory if he does not accept it voluntarily. An agent who failed to fulfill his commission could be penalized (*b. B. Qam.* 102ab, bar.). The "disobedient" in Luke-Acts are hostile toward God and his ways (Luke 1:17; Acts 14:2; 19:9; cf. John 3:36; Rom 2:8; 15:31; Eph 2:2; 5:6; Col 3:6; 1 Pet 3:20; 4:17; Sir 2:15; 16:6; *1 Clem.* 57.4; 58.1; 59.1; Poly. *Phil.* 2.1; Ign. *Magn.* 8.2; *Barn.* 12.4).

1513. See Anderson, *Glossary*, 17 (though especially on the deliberative, rather than judicial, use; he also notes its use in *refutatio*); more fully in *refutatio*, see ibid., 40.

1514. Ps.-Callisth. *Alex.* 1.9; Jos. *Ant.* 18.73 (though both these examples concern mortals merely pretending to be a god).

1515. See now helpfully and in detail McConnell, *Testimony*.

1516. Cf. also Hengel, "Geography of Palestine," 69n124 (noting the inclusion of Damascus and the omission of Samaria, fitting Luke's earlier narrative).

implied as a corollary of Jerusalem, making it formulaic here to fit the pattern in 9:31 and 1:8. One of Paul's own letters tells us about his trip to Jerusalem (Gal 1:18–19), which apparently somehow sooner or later had an impact on the churches of Judea through the report of his conversion (1:22–24); even here, Judea seems grammatically linked with Jerusalem (τε... τε, whereas other components are linked by καί)[1517] and is expressed irregularly.[1518] It might precede the Gentiles logically but not chronologically[1519] (cf. Acts 15:3; 18:22; 21:7–16; though Luke distinguishes Samaria and Caesarea from Judea, cf. 21:10). In any case, it may offer a contrast between the Judeans and the Gentiles, whom Paul also names and to whom he also preached (e.g., 13:7). Most important for Luke is how the claim fits his own narrative-theological pattern: Jerusalem, Judea, and beyond (cf. 1:8).[1520]

By preaching deeds appropriate to repentance (ἄξια τῆς μετανοίας), Paul closely echoes John's preaching in Luke 3:8 (ἀξίους τῆς μετανοίας), offering continuity between these prophets.[1521] The verb for "practicing" such deeds does not appear in Luke 3:8 but might allow for a contextual contrast with the forensic "practicing deeds deserving death" in Luke 23:15, 41; Acts 25:11, 25; 26:31. The exhortation to "turn to God" recalls the Lord's commission to Paul in Acts 26:18. Paul's manner of summarizing his message would not offend anyone present; Romans did not oppose public advocacy of morality.[1522] Naturally, by the label "repentance," Paul's message advocated some specific content (see comment on Acts 2:38), but the summary here is not inaccurate, or unusual for Luke, for whom not only John (Luke 3:3, 8) but Jesus (5:32; 10:13; 11:32; 13:3–5; 15:7, 10) and Peter (Acts 2:38; 3:19; 5:31; 8:22; 11:18) preached repentance. This was part of the summary of the apostolic commission (Luke 24:47); though Paul sometimes summarizes it as John's message (Acts 13:24; 19:4), he shares it himself toward both Gentiles and Jews, as here (17:30; 20:21).[1523]

ii. Paul Threatened for Piety (26:21)

Signs of rhetorical elegance appear in 26:21–23, including a form of the Attic πειράομαι in 26:21 (a NT hapax legomenon), the classical οὐδὲν... λέγων in 26:22, and the classical παθητός as "subject to suffering" in 26:23 (a NT hapax legomenon).[1524] Paul reiterates that the real basis for the charge against him is prejudice against his theological position and implies that this prejudice is itself impious.

1517. See BDAG, s.v. τε 2b and examples there; in the immediate context, see Acts 26:10, 16.
1518. "All the region of Judea" is accusative, in contrast to the other places being named in the dative; this might be the accusative of extent (Witherington, *Acts*, 746; on this use of the accusative, see, e.g., Robertson, *Grammar*, 469; Blass, Debrunner, and Funk, *Grammar*, 88, §161; Wallace, *Grammar*, 201–3). Schnabel, *Missionary*, 286, argues plausibly that Paul did indeed preach "in some of the smaller towns (and perhaps villages) of Judea." He probably did not do so in very many, however, or it would be difficult to understand Gal 1:22 (despite its hyperbole; cf. also Gal 1:19). Greater Judea could include Galilee (as in Acts 10:37; Pliny E. *N.H.* 5.15.70), but there is no reason to extend the sense here far outside Jerusalem.
1519. Witherington, *Acts*, 746.
1520. See Kurz, *Acts*, 359.
1521. Michaels, "Paul and Baptist," doubts that the echoes are deliberately Lukan; if correct, this observation would suggest that they preserve Paul's way of preaching. For Paul's preaching to those who were not yet believers, see again 1 Thess 1:9.
1522. Although "repentance" was especially a Jewish category (see comment on Acts 17:30), others would understand the moral point here.
1523. Although Paul's epistles employ the concept (using ἐπιστρέφω, as noted above on Acts 26:18), the specific term is relatively rare (Rom 2:4; for Christians, 2 Cor 7:9–10; 12:21; cf. 2 Tim 2:25); it appears in Petrine literature only at 2 Pet 3:9; Mark applies it once each for John (Mark 1:4), Jesus (1:15), and the disciples (6:12).
1524. Witherington, *Acts*, 737.

Seeking to kill Paul for his obedience to the divine commission was a heinous act of impiety. Paul claims in 26:21 that 26:20 offers the reasons (ἕνεκα τούτων) some of his own people wanted to kill him: because (26:20) he was preaching works appropriate to repentance (i.e., unobjectionably upright behavior) and/or because he was preaching to the Gentiles. This seems to insinuate that Paul's enemies do not favor upright behavior and/or that they are unwilling to communicate God's gifts to Gentiles. (This resembles the argument that one is, ironically, on trial for a benefaction or piety; see comments on Acts 4:9; 26:6–7.) That they tried to kill him (a Roman citizen) is itself a serious offense, since (as Paul argues) they, and not he, were in the wrong. Thus Paul is reversing the charges, as perhaps in 24:19 (see comment there). (Paul's wording about the attempt on his life fits Luke's narrative but also avoids explicitly contradicting Lysias's official version in 23:27, where the same verb appears.)

Thus, having completed his story, Paul begins to recount his thesis for which his *narratio* prepared (26:6–8): the Jewish opposition he faces (26:21; cf. 26:6–7) stems precisely from his commitment to the resurrection hope (26:23; cf. 26:8) rooted in the Scriptures (26:22; cf. 26:6–7). Whether this is (as some scholars hold) the *peroratio* repeating an earlier theme or (as I think) the *propositio* of an unfinished speech (again repeating an earlier theme, and paving the way for its further development), it serves the same literary function, namely, to frame the speech proper (after the *exordium*) and drive home the point.

Paul's encounter with the risen Christ (26:13–18) was simply the continuing experience of OT prophetic revelation and the outworking of OT promises. If the Christian faith did not spring from the OT hope, neither did Pharisaism or the dominant Judean belief in the resurrection; and no public spokesperson for Judaism in the presence of Gentiles would dare take intolerance so far as to condemn all these views. If, by contrast, the God of the OT remained active, Paul's revelation was consistent with the OT message and ought to be embraced like the revelations of earlier prophets. The early Christians believed that they lived in the era of OT fulfillment, and hence expected continuity with OT miracles and revelations.[1525]

Paul here accuses "some Jews" of trying to kill him because he obeyed the Jewish God, believed Jewish religion, and preached good deeds. That is, he summarizes his "crime" as something that is not a criminal offense, a common rhetorical technique (see comment on Acts 24:14). Further, he summarizes his crime as in fact a benevolent and good act (cf. 4:9); in forensic rhetoric, it strengthened the pathos of one's case if one could present one's opponents as doing evil in spite of or because of one's benevolence (see comment on Acts 24:17). If his opponents wanted to kill him simply for preaching morality and conversing with Gentiles, then they are the true lawbreakers; returning charges against one's accusers was conventional in forensic rhetoric (see comment on Acts 24:19). In 26:21, then, Paul begins to drive home the point of his *narratio*,[1526] at the same time revisiting for readers convincing themes elaborated in earlier speeches.

Paul's summary of his own activity is so benevolent[1527] that Festus would be unable

---

1525. This phenomenon tends to continue among Christian renewal movements today that expect continuing revelations because they believe that they continue to live in "biblical" times, instead of relegating biblical experiences to a past era. Although such movements often need more careful discernment measures (as also suggested in Acts), their openness to the Spirit's activity seems more consistent with the early Christian view of salvation history than does the extreme cessationist attribution of such activities to a bygone era, generally with postbiblical (or, at best, very tenuous biblical) explanations.

1526. Winter, "Official Proceedings," 330, takes this as the *refutatio*, which is plausible, though it might also be the *propositio*, or part of it, depending on the rest of the outline.

1527. Undoubtedly, Luke and Paul genuinely saw it as benevolent, but Paul's way of summarizing it would look more benevolent to the current court than would his opponents' way of summarizing the same information.

to grasp how 26:20 provided the basis for 26:21; Paul basically accuses "some Jews" of trying to kill him for honorable behavior. Agrippa, however, knows enough about the conflicts of Jewish sects in this period, including the Nazarenes, to comprehend the conflict: Paul was preaching the same message to Gentiles as to Jews (26:20), welcoming them all alike into God's kingdom and into the inheritance of the set-apart people (26:18).[1528] Naturally, such a message would conflict with Judean nationalism and the most common reading of Scripture in Paul's day. And, as Paul would know, neither Agrippa nor Festus approved of such Judean nationalism.

Paul judiciously omits the question of circumcision; Romans were unhappy about the proselytization of Romans to be circumcised, and Jews were unhappy about treating Gentile God-fearers as full converts without their first undergoing circumcision. But Agrippa will have heard enough to understand why some want to kill Paul; being more liberal-minded himself, however, he would likely have disapproved of what he would have seen as the fanatic fringe wanting to have Paul killed.

iii. Paul's Biblical Message (26:22–23)

On the view that 26:22–23 is Paul's *peroratio* (i.e., he was interrupted in 26:24 only when he was basically finished with the complete speech), it is interesting that Paul expresses his dependence on God's help instead of making a petition for help, a petition often offered to officials in a forensic *peroratio* (but also in an opening *exordium*).[1529] Some scholars also note parallels to the end of Jesus's final speech in Luke 24:44–48: Scripture is fulfilled; its substance is that Jesus is the Messiah and will suffer and rise.[1530] If Luke does not expect his audience to perceive this as the intended conclusion of Paul's speech (as I think more likely), it nevertheless fulfills an analogous function for Luke's narrative, and so these suggestions remain noteworthy.

(1) Testifying, Helped by God (26:22)

The connection in Paul's thought would not be obscure to ancient hearers. "Having obtained help" is probably a causal participial clause[1531]—that is, "because I obtained help." Any benefit rendered by a benefactor or patron obligated a dependent to respond with gratitude. Paul could not fail to testify of God's benevolence; otherwise, he would be an ungrateful beneficiary. The ingratitude of clients was highly offensive, though it was unlikely that anyone would prosecute Paul on that charge.[1532] Ingratitude to a deity for his or her favors was considered even worse and merited punishment from the deity.[1533] Paul's letters may reveal similar thoughts (cf., e.g., Rom 8:12; 2 Cor 5:14–15; Gal 2:20; Eph 2:8–10).[1534]

By "helped by God," Paul might refer specifically to his deliverance from the danger of the previous verse (Acts 26:21)—that is, through Roman intervention—though he could also have in mind (perhaps in addition to this) previous deliverances that he does

---

1528. See also Bruce, *Commentary*, 493.

1529. Winter, "Official Proceedings," 330 (comparing P.Oxy. 2131.8, 17–18 [*exordium* and *peroratio*]; *peroratio* in P.Fouad 26.55–56; cf. τυγχάνοντες, "obtaining," in the *exordium* in Acts 24:2). The term for "help," ἐπικουρία, was appropriate for answers to supplications, i.e., something granted by an official (Jos. *Ant.* 2.94, ἐπικουρίας τυγχάνειν), though it most often connoted "aid as an ally" (BDAG); one petitions a deity for ἐπικουρία in Wis 13:18, the only other use in biblical Greek.

1530. O'Toole, *Acts 26*, 159; expanded in Witherington, *Acts*, 747.

1531. On this usage, see, e.g., Blass, Debrunner, and Funk, *Grammar*, 215, §418.1; Dana and Mantey, *Grammar*, 227, §201.3; Wallace, *Grammar*, 631–32.

1532. See, e.g., Buckland, *Roman Law*, 88, 130; cf. Xen. *Cyr.* 1.2.6; Val. Max. 2.6.6; Jos. *Ant.* 19.361; as the worst of offenses, Cic. *Att.* 8.4; Sen. Y. *Ben.* 1.10.4; fuller comment on Acts 23:17–18.

1533. Cf. ʾAbot R. Nat. 46, §128 B; Rom 1:21; Harrison, *Grace*, 349–50. On gratitude due deities, see, e.g., Ael. Arist. *Panath.* 21, 161D–162D; Men. Rhet. 2.17, 437.7–9, 13–15; Diog. Laert. 8.1.24.

1534. See deSilva, *Honor*, 145–46.

not recount but that Paul and Luke's audience understood occurred during the ministry related in 26:20.[1535] One might contrast Paul's "help" from God with his opponents' sycophantic claim that they were "helped" by the previous governor, Felix (24:2).

Paul's "testifying" reflects the apostolic commission throughout Acts as well as the present court setting (see comment on Acts 1:8; cf. Luke 24:48). Paul offers testimony about Jesus to the court because this is part of what Jesus called all his followers to do (Luke 21:12–15), including specifically Paul (Acts 22:15), especially in the visionary commission he has just recounted (26:16).[1536]

Paul testifies to both small and great; the "great" are before him this day, but he testifies regularly to the small as well (as Luke would insist that any follower of Jesus must, Luke 9:48). The phrase "small and great" (also in Acts 8:10) was a standard idiom used often in the OT[1537] and early Judaism[1538] to mean "all" (by some definitions, a merism, like "heavens and earth" and "day and night").

The appeal to "the prophets and Moses" evokes the pairing elsewhere in Luke-Acts (Luke 16:29, 31; 24:27, 44; cf. Acts 28:23)[1539] as well as the use of other global references to signify a much larger array of texts than Luke provides at any one time (see, e.g., Acts 3:18, 21).[1540] Paul's claim of solidarity with the biblical message and hence with his Jewish heritage is so key to his presentation that he seeks to return to this issue in 26:27. Luke's Paul, like the Paul we meet in the letters, is utterly convinced that he can demonstrate that the Scriptures point to and confirm the reality of his message. Showing that the Christian movement remains part of Judaism and that the conflicts are purely theological also invites the protection normally afforded by Roman religious tolerance.

(2) Christ's Mission (26:23)

Paul proclaims Christ's mission, so that his own is an extension of Christ's (as indeed the parallel character of the narratives in Luke-Acts also suggests for Peter, Stephen, and other disciples). Paul here defines the prophetic promise (26:22) in terms of the gospel.[1541] Luke has explained earlier that Moses and the prophets testify to Christ's suffering (Luke 24:26, 46) and resurrection (16:31; 24:27, 44–46) and has provided the proofs in earlier speeches (for suffering, see comment on Acts 7:35–37; for resurrection, Acts 2:24–35; 13:33–37).[1542] Similarly, in Luke 24:44–47, the message of Christ's suffering and death (24:46) and its audience among all nations (24:47) seem to be grounded in Scripture (24:44–46); at least part of the biblical background here must be Isaiah's emphasis on the salvation of the Gentiles (see

---

1535. Cf. perhaps also τυχούσας in Acts 19:11; but this most likely reflects part of an idiom for "extraordinary" (see comment there).

1536. It is possible that ἕστηκα (from ἵστημι) also reflects a play on the command to "stand" in Acts 26:16, but the verb is so common (about sixty times in Luke-Acts) that no secure conclusion can be drawn.

1537. Esp. Gen 19:11; Deut 1:17; 1 Sam 20:2; 30:2, 19; 1 Kgs 22:31; 2 Kgs 23:2; 1 Chr 25:8; 26:13; 2 Chr 18:30; 34:30; Esth 1:5; Job 3:19; Pss 104:25; 115:13; Jer 16:6; Jonah 3:5.

1538. Jdt 13:4, 13; Wis 6:7; Bar 1:4; 1 Macc 5:45; 4 Macc 5:20; 1 Esd 1:54; 4Q266 1 18; 2 En. 61:4; Rev 11:18; 13:16; 19:5, 18; 20:12.

1539. In contrast to the more common phrase "the law and prophets" (as in Acts 13:15; 24:14; 28:23; cf. Matt 5:17; 7:12; 11:13; 22:40; John 1:45; Rom 3:21; also 4 Macc 18:10; synthetic parallelism in Zech 7:12; Test. Levi 16:2), the phrase "Moses and the prophets" is particularly Lukan in the NT (cf. later 1 Clem. 43.1; cf. m. 'Ab. 1:1).

1540. With Bruce, Commentary, 493–94, Luke offers the categories but not the specific testimonia or texts that Paul employed.

1541. Cf. the use of ὁρισμός, "definition," in rhetoric (on which see Anderson, Glossary, 84). Technically, Paul may here employ a conditional construction ("if . . . then he would"; Parsons, Acts, 343).

1542. That Jesus's suffering and resurrection were central to Paul's evangelistic preaching, and that he believed that he found these in the Scriptures, is impossible to dispute (1 Cor 15:3–4).

comment below).[1543] For Paul, this Gentile audience was nonnegotiable as part of his message (Acts 22:21). As darkness helped to facilitate the engineering of Jesus's crucifixion (Luke 22:53; cf. 23:44), so here light is associated with his resurrection.

That Christ is the "first" to proclaim light suggests that others should do so after him, making the mission in Luke-Acts paradigmatic for continuing Christian mission.[1544] Paul's own mission follows that of Jesus, who was a light to the Gentiles (Luke 2:32).[1545] Paul's mission of preaching light to the Gentiles (Acts 26:18) clearly echoes Isa 42:6–7 (and hence implies Isa 49:6) earlier in this speech (Acts 26:16–18), strongly suggesting the connection here. (Thus the biblical foundation for this proclamation [26:22] at least includes Isaiah's emphasis on the salvation of the Gentiles; see comment on Acts 1:8.) Paul earlier describes his mission as the servant who brings light in 13:47, but Jesus is the servant in Luke 4:18–21. Paul's mission is thus modeled after Jesus, which explains how he, like Jesus, embodies the mission of the Suffering Servant (see discussion of this background in the introduction to Acts 26:16–18, above). As in the larger story of Luke-Acts (Luke 2:32; 7:8–10), Paul's mission to Jew and Gentile alike, already noted (Acts 26:17), is therefore grounded in Jesus's mission to both alike (26:20). In keeping Luke's apologetic for Paul in the final quarter of Acts, Luke emphasizes that Christians who accepted Jesus's mission ought also to accept Paul's.

The term παθητός, "subject to suffering," is a biblical hapax legomenon, though it appears in Ignatius (*Eph.* 7.2; *Pol.* 3.2); it is another likely indication of this speech's elegance.[1546] Because few expected a suffering Messiah at this time, some commentators have asserted that Paul cannot be arguing for Jesus's death from Scripture but is merely countering arguments against the Messiah's death.[1547] But the early Christian concept of messiahship, defined by Jesus's ministry, departed in significant respects from contemporary expectations, and early Christians did believe that Scripture predicted Jesus's death (Acts 3:18; 1 Cor 15:3; 1 Pet 1:11). Luke's portrait of the rejected deliverer in Acts 7 is undoubtedly one of the approaches that he and his circle of believers had in mind.[1548]

The part of his speech that Paul is able to finish uninterrupted climaxes by summarizing his message (Jesus's suffering and resurrection) and (in its final word) that Jesus pioneered the mission to the Gentiles.

e. Paul's Desire to Convert His Audience (26:24–29)

Charged by Festus with madness, Paul responds by affirming both his sanity and the common knowledge (of both the events and the prophecies) on which he bases

1543. Note also Pao, *Isaianic Exodus*, 86, arguing that Acts 26:23 includes the same three elements as Luke 24:46–47, but with the third element of mission to Gentiles phrased as a "light to the nations" (evoking Isa 42:6; 49:6; and 51:4; but Isa 49:6 is the verse that Luke has quoted).

1544. Dupont, *Salvation*, 29, rightly argues that Paul carries forward this mission in Acts, but he overstates the case here: "Through him the work of Christ is carried on to the end, and the history of salvation is brought to completion." Paul himself becomes a model for the church's (and, more particularly, apostles' [albeit not in the Lukan sense of the term]) continuing mission. Paul's letters emphasize Christ's primacy, though especially with regard to resurrection itself (Rom 8:29; 1 Cor 15:20, 23; Col 1:18), on which Christ's primacy of proclamation here is predicated, though Paul often respects primacy more generally (Rom 1:16; 2:9–10; 11:16; 16:5; 1 Cor 16:15; 2 Cor 10:14).

1545. On Luke 2:32 and Luke-Acts, see Radl, "Beziehungen," 305–6.

1546. The NT always uses the noun πάθος for passion, but the verb πάσχω (in the form παθεῖν) is often used for Christ's suffering in Luke-Acts; see comment on Acts 1:3.

1547. Lake and Cadbury, *Commentary*, 321.

1548. On the concept of the "suffering Messiah" in later Jewish sources, probably stemming from the failed Bar Kokhba revolt, see the section "Views of Messiahship" in the excursus on messiahship at Acts 2:23 (Keener, *Acts*, 1:964–68).

his argument. His response to Agrippa, however, admits that he seeks his conversion, which Paul views as beneficial to Agrippa.

i. PAUL'S "MADNESS" (26:24)

Paul's biblically grounded announcement of resurrection (26:22–23) seems madness to Festus (26:24; cf. 25:19; 1 Cor 1:18, 23). Luke has elsewhere exemplified the difficulty of persuading those educated in conflicting paradigms (Acts 17:32); like Paul, he recognizes that his message is a stumbling block to educated Greeks (1 Cor 1:21–25), even if they prove more tolerant (in terms of outright persecution) than the street mobs he reports. As Johnson points out, neither Festus nor Agrippa is persuaded, and Festus even views Paul's talk as madness.[1549] Johnson concedes, however, that the speech is successful insofar as they believe Paul innocent; for Luke, this is a significant success, and it fits his own apologetic interest.[1550]

(1) Interruptions in Court Scenes

This interruption allows Luke to provide a more complete finale; at this point, the last lengthy speech in Acts parallels the first, where an interruption (Acts 2:37) functions similarly. This interruption fits Luke's pattern of frequently interrupted speeches more broadly[1551] (see comment on Acts 2:37; for a "loud voice," cf. comment on Acts 7:57).

Although the interruption serves Luke's literary purposes, one should not suppose that a judge would not interrupt Paul's speech. It is not an interruption in this speech but its rareness that appears unusual for a defendant presenting his case. Magistrates could interrupt with questions to the defendant or witnesses.[1552] Such interruptions in a court could be hostile.[1553] Thus friends of one defendant kept interrupting a prosecutor with hostility (Pliny *Ep.* 3.9.25–26); on another occasion the emperor, when judging Philiscus's case, repeatedly interrupted his self-defense with remarks and sudden questions (Philost. *Vit. soph.* 2.30.623).[1554]

Charges of madness would fit this pattern.[1555] Festus could mean "madness" in one of several ways, as could Luke. Most likely Festus thinks of Paul's visions of Jesus, on which he bases his behavior (Acts 26:8, 13–20), as a form of temporary insanity, perhaps mixed with the insanity of inspiration, rhetoric, and probably philosophy (given Paul's "learning"); Luke would lay emphasis on the elements of inspiration and philosophy, though correcting the insanity verdict with the assertion of Paul's

---

1549. Johnson, *Acts*, 443. Haenchen, *Acts*, 688, thinks that Luke employs Festus to exemplify the Roman government's inability to address the theological questions.

1550. Failure to persuade hearers could be judged as rhetorical failure (cf., e.g., Litfin, *Theology*, 191), but Luke is more interested here in political and legal apologetic; in an era when most Christians endured some marginalization, that people of such status *listened* to Paul could encourage much of Luke's audience. (Luke can also portray as legitimate rhetorical success accurate refutation without full persuasion; Acts 6:10.)

1551. With Haenchen, *Acts*, 688; see discussion in Aune, *Environment*, 127; esp. Smith, *Rhetoric of Interruption*; and discussion at Acts 2:37. Pervo, *Acts*, 635, helpfully notes the parallel with Acts 22:21–22: Paul's narration is ended once he brings up the subject of the Gentile mission.

1552. Crook, *Advocacy*, 66 (though noting [67] that some were able to complete their speeches—at least so far as we can tell from the records); see, e.g., Apul. *Apol.* 61.

1553. Hostile interlocution proved more precarious once the speaker held the primary audience's favor (Lucian *Prof. P.S.* 20).

1554. An accuser interrupted Apollonius's defense by clarifying the charge, and Apollonius continued (Philost. *Vit. Apoll.* 8.7).

1555. For a brief survey of the history of the interpretation of madness, including in classical Greece, see Leme Lopes, "Diagnostico"; for historical descriptions of what is now called schizophrenia, Jeste et al., "Schizophrenia"; more fully from Homer to Plato, see la Croce, "Concepto" (focusing on possession). The Furies could drive one such as Orestes mad (Juv. *Sat.* 14.285; Pers. *Sat.* 3.118; madness is also attributed to Furies elsewhere, e.g., in Quint. *Decl.* 314.17).

sobriety in 26:25. (Philosophers did not share the world's opinion of them; see discussion below.)

(2) Charges of Madness

Making one's adversary in a debate look foolish often drew derisive laughter and might, on rare occasions, even make the butt of the joke smile,[1556] but criticisms usually shamed their receiver.[1557] One person so abused responded that he would have been more disturbed by the abuse had he considered it deliberate instead of the result of an unstable mind.[1558] One could charge an opponent in court with madness.[1559] In other cases, a hearer might conclude that the teller of wild tales was either insane or a fraud.[1560] Unlike some interlocutors, Festus is not necessarily hostile (he praises Paul's learning), but he finds Paul's beliefs irrational.

In another court scene, the emperor tells one Appianus that he has lost his senses, and Appianus denies it.[1561] The wording is so close that it might reflect the diffusion of Christian tradition in the late empire. But both accounts may reflect an earlier tradition of Jewish martyr stories, where some persecutors charged Jewish martyrs with insanity (μαίνομαι and μανία, in both 4 Macc 8:5 and 10:13). Mockers who thought the righteous to suffer from insanity (μανίαν, from μανία) would eventually find the verdict of folly reversed (Wis 5:4). (Some may have counted Jesus as mad at his hearing.)[1562]

(3) Logical or Rhetorical Madness?

To Festus, the logic of Paul's defense is difficult to follow. Granted, Paul has established that he merely preaches a variation of Judaism, but what is the point of elaborating his beliefs after he has established this point? Roman thought could not accommodate the resurrection any more than Greek thought could (cf. Acts 17:32).[1563] More disconcertingly, Paul's argument does not sound like a logical defense; 26:22–23 sounds more like a deliberative thesis than a forensic one—as if Paul is trying to persuade his hearers of his irrelevant views. One form of defense in antiquity was the insanity defense,[1564] but this is not a plausible construal of Paul's point here.

Paul may have been forceful in his rhetoric, as orators sometimes were known to become.[1565] Cicero felt that a good orator would sometimes "fly into a passion

---

1556. Xen. *Cyr.* 2.2.16.

1557. See, e.g., Plut. *Demosth.* 11.4; *Cic.* 5.4; 27.1; 38.2–6; 39.1; 40.3.

1558. Sall. *Invect. M. Tull.* 1 (opening words).

1559. E.g., Apul. *Apol.* 52–53. Senility could be associated with madness (Apul. *Apol.* 53), but an older person who thoroughly refuted the charge could leave the court thinking the accuser mad instead (*Apol.* 37).

1560. Lucian *Lover of Lies* 5. One might rebuke someone as "mad" for an act of mortal folly (e.g., Quint. Curt. 7.2.6). Other signs of madness could include, e.g., jeering (Quint. *Decl.* 364 intro.) and misbehavior (367.1).

1561. Munck, *Acts*, 244–45, citing *Acta Appiani*, P.Yale. inv. 1536, col. 4.9–15; Conzelmann, *Acts*, 212, citing *Acta Appiani* in P.Oxy. 33.4.9–15; also cited in Pervo, *Acts*, 635.

1562. See Meggitt, "Madness," with considerable documentation regarding ancient madness. I would explain the same data in light of Pilate's viewing Jesus as a harmless sage (Keener, *John*, 1113–14; idem, "Truth"; briefly, "John," 425), although, as we shall see, the charge of madness overlapped with some characteristic sage behavior.

1563. Dunn, *Acts*, 331, suggests that Festus may have reacted against "the thought of the same national religion for all the diverse nations" (in Acts 26:23); although this is possible, it might overestimate the degree of success that Festus will have attributed to Paul.

1564. E.g., Hermog. *Issues* 58.19–59.3; Schiemann, "Furor" (citing Gaius *Inst.* 3.106); Libanius *Invect.* 5.18; cf. Eurip. *Herc. fur.*; Libanius *Descr.* 20.3; 23.1. An insane person was not legally liable but might be subject to physical restraint (Robinson, *Criminal Law*, 16), sometimes by his or her own family (Libero, "Disability," 535). Insane persons were not supposed to contract marriages (Paulus *Sent.* 2.1–9, in Lefkowitz and Fant, *Life*, 193, §196). Coupled with drugs, insanity could impair the senses (Isaeus *Astyph.* 37).

1565. See Dio Chrys. *Or.* 18.11; Hermog. *Progymn.* 8, "On Syncrisis," 20; Fredrickson, "Tears," 175. Paul was often forceful in his letters, more than in his personal dealings with the Corinthians (2 Cor 10:9–10; Fredrickson, "Tears," 167–72; Winter, *Philo and Paul*, 207; Savage, *Power*, 65).

and protest violently" (*Or. Brut.* 40.138),[1566] but although intensity of passion was important in rhetoric (Plut. *Cic.* 5.3), some condemned others who shouted too much as not understanding the appropriate ways to use passion (5.4). One rhetorician complains about a speaker who pretended insanity as a mark of genius (note the "insanity" of philosophy below) until he did indeed drive himself mad (Sen. E. *Controv.* 2.1.25). The philosophically inclined, of course (as Paul will claim to be in 26:25), eschewed such passions in rhetoric.[1567]

(4) Madness, Ecstasy, and Inspiration

Earlier in Acts those inspired by the Spirit were thought drunk (Acts 2:13), requiring Peter's rebuttal (2:15); early Christian inspiration by the Spirit sometimes appeared to outsiders as madness (1 Cor 14:23;[1568] 2 Cor 5:13[1569] [cf. 12:2–4]), as was typical for prophetic ecstasy (2 Kgs 9:11; Hos 9:7–8). In one early Jewish portrayal, Noah, although not necessarily ecstatic, was considered insane for speaking truth (*Sib. Or.* 1.172). In Christian experience, too, speaking the truth about God's unusual acts could be construed as madness (Acts 12:15).[1570] Various ancient texts portray prophetic "madness."[1571] In connection with the poets, for example, later Platonists spoke of the "madness" of inspiration,[1572] a madness that was superior to a "sound mind"[1573] and whose inspiration was superior to the reasoning of a sound mind.[1574]

Valerius Maximus reports that during the bacchanals' secret nocturnal rituals in Rome, men and women mingled and went insane (*furerentque*, Val. Max. 1.3.1), a very derogatory evaluation from a Roman perspective.[1575] Sometimes madness could even be a punishment for insulting the gods (Apollod. *Bib.* 2.2.2),[1576] such as trying to restrain those inspired by Dionysus.[1577]

Madness could be associated with inspiration or irrational frenzy of various sorts (less positive to Romans than to Greeks; discussed below), and it is not the first occasion in Acts where inspiration has passed for something less savory (inebriation in

1566. Trans. G. L. Hendrickson, LCL, 5:413.

1567. See Sen. Y. *Ep. Lucil.* 108.7; Anderson, *Rhetorical Theory*, 61; Kennedy, *Classical Rhetoric*, 30–31. I refer to the Stoics; some philosophers, such as Cynics, were less concerned about such restraint.

1568. Unfamiliar with glossolalia, outsiders could view it as μανία (Smit, "Tongues"; Forbes, *Prophecy*, 180); see further comment on Acts 2:13.

1569. Hubbard, "Out of Mind," applies Paul's claim in 2 Cor 5:13 to poor rhetorical skill (cf. similarly Fredrickson, "Tears," 174–76, noting that some ancients associated rhetorical emotional outbursts with being out of one's mind); but in the context of 2 Cor 3:13 and 12:2–4, it better fits a private experience with God (see Keener, *Corinthians*, 183–84). Bede *Comm. Acts* 26.24 applies it here.

1570. Cf. also the insanity charge against Jesus in John 10:20.

1571. E.g., Ovid *Metam.* 2.640–41. For a link between madness and spirit possession in some cultures, see, e.g., Firth, *Ritual*, 296–97.

1572. Proclus *Poet.* 6.1, K157.25–26; 6.2, K166.20–21; K180.29–30; K181.1–2. Cf. Homer "possessed" by the Muses in K198.30–199.1.

1573. *Poet.* 6.2, K178.24.

1574. *Poet.* 6.2, K182.17–19. Poetry without this sort of madness was "imperfect" (K182.16–20). In K180.11–12, Proclus cites as his authority Plato *Phaedrus* 245A.

1575. On ecstasy, sometimes in various cults, including that of Dionysus (see, e.g., Plut. *Rom. Q.* 112, *Mor.* 291AB; Artem. *Oneir.* 2.37), see discussion in Keener, *Acts*, 1:852–53, 858–59, 887, 898–905. On traditional Roman mistrust of frenzied cults, see, e.g., Livy 39.15.2–3; for unsoundness of mind and frenzy, see Cic. *Tusc.* 3.5.11; for the madness of the Galli, see Ovid *Fasti* 4.236, 243, 245–46. Magical spells could allegedly mar their victims' sanity (Apul. *Apol.* 80).

1576. Cf. also Hermog. *Inv.* 2.5.117. Normally madness was attributed to the gods (Quint. *Decl.* 314.17–19; Libanius *Speech in Character* 6.1) or Furies (Quint. *Decl.* 314.17). Insanity could also come from emotional trauma such as loss of sons (Val. Max. 1.1.20; for lesser loss of mind due to emotion, see, e.g., Men. Rhet. 2.9, 413.13–14). Cf. also the insanity of Ben Zoma, from beholding too much of God's glory in a *merkabah* vision (*b. Ḥag.* 14b, bar.).

1577. Soph. *Antig.* 955–65.

Acts 2:13). This is why Paul will counter with an emphasis on his sobriety in 26:25. Some scholars do see an allusion to the madness of inspiration here.[1578]

"Madness" (μανία) is associated with prophets in the LXX of Hos 9:7–8; its verb cognate μαίνομαι is associated with pagan celebration and possibly prophecy in Wis 14:28, and critics use the verb to denigrate prophetic "madness" in Jer 36:26 (29:26 ET). A second-century author claims that the Pythian priestesses prophesied ecstatically (Ael. Arist. *Def. Or.* 34–35, §11D; see comment on Acts 16:16).[1579] Some ancient readers might construe Festus as ironically speaking truth: Paul was "mad" in the sense of "inspired."[1580]

(5) Philosophic Madness

Festus mentions Paul's "letters" (τὰ ... γράμματα) as the source of his madness. Commentators are nearly all agreed that Festus here implies not mere literacy but higher education, as the term sometimes meant.[1581] This observation fits Luke's characterization of Paul as a sage (17:22–31; 19:9; 24:24–26) and is not inconsistent with Paul's pastoral role in his letters.[1582] Festus's remark fits Luke's apologetic: other respectable persons may differ with Paul, but they do not dismiss his intellect. This is better treatment than some ancient philosophers received.

The attribution of Paul's "madness" to learning qualifies it (contrast Peter and John as ἀγράμματοι in Acts 4:13), but it may also qualify the particular kind of "madness" in view. The masses would consider a Cynic sage such as Diogenes mad (Dio Chrys. *Or.* 6.3.82; 8.36; 9.8; 34.2),[1583] but truth, Dio Chrysostom opined, was sometimes viewed as madness by those embracing different plausibility structures (12.8).[1584] An orator could use *reductio ad absurdum* to make philosophic objections to rhetoric appear insane.[1585] Philostratus claims that Apollonius predicted Domitian's death and was accused of insanity (*Vit. Apoll.* 8.26).

One newly converted to philosophy depicts himself as maddened (lit. "divinely possessed") and drunk with philosophy (Lucian *Nigr.* 5), to which his companion retorts that this is not drunkenness but sobriety (σωφρονεῖν, *Nigr.* 6). But only those predisposed to it are so "divinely possessed" (*Nigr.* 37).

1578. Foakes-Jackson, *Acts*, 226–27 (applying it to Paul's oratory); Johnson, *Acts*, 438–39 (as one lexical option, citing Hdt. 4.79). Witherington, *Acts*, 748n520, opposes this view; elsewhere, however, he associates the noun cognate with ecstasy (as opposed to hysteria or insanity; idem, *Corinthians*, 278–79).

1579. On "prophetic" madness in ecstasy, see further discussion in Keener, *Acts*, 1:887, 898–905.

1580. So Bede *Comm. Acts* 26.24 (L. Martin, 184; Martin, *Acts*, 297), on Paul's spiritual madness.

1581. Commentators (Johnson, *Acts*, 439; Fitzmyer, *Acts*, 763) cite *Let. Aris.* 121; Xen. *Cyr.* 1.2.6; Plato *Apol.* 26D. The issue is not knowledge but the arduous study that it required (Haenchen, *Acts*, 688n3) or perhaps too much study of Jewish Scripture (Witherington, *Acts*, 749, tentatively; but while Paul so employs γράμμα, Luke does not). Much study produces weariness (Eccl 12:12), in the context of the teachings of sages being goads (12:11; cf. Acts 26:14). Boundaries between orality and literacy were not decisive; see, e.g., Goldhill, "Anecdote"; Habinek, "Literacy"; Parker, "Books," esp. 215–17. Although writing literacy was not widespread over the entire ancient population, reading literacy was probably significantly higher in urban settings; see, e.g., Hurtado, "Fixation," esp. 330–34 (cf. inscriptions from Roman Britain in Woolf, "Literacy," 54–56; public inscriptions in Ephesus in Burrell, "Reading"; and esp. Virgil in Pompeii's graffiti in Milnor, "Literacy"). People were literate on various levels and for various purposes (e.g., basic "name literacy" in Thomas, "Writing," 18–24, on classical Athens) without being able to compose literature (ibid., 41). Judging from his letters, Paul's literacy was much higher than average even in urban settings.

1582. Noted by Malherbe (*Philosophers*) and others.

1583. See further discussion of the attribution of madness to Cynics in Malherbe, *Philosophers*, 159 (adding Socrates *Ep.* 6.1; 9.3; Dio Chrys. *Or.* 66.25; 77/78.41; Lucian *Cynic* 5).

1584. Nevertheless, he also opined it "madness" to confront the hostile masses too directly (Dio Chrys. *Or.* 32.28) and wondered if it was madness for him to address a crowd that despised Cynics (34.4). Calling sane persons "insane" long enough will make them lose their mind (35.7).

1585. Ael. Arist. *Def. Or.* 339, §112D.

Many philosophers believed that the nonphilosophic masses were "mad," not thinking soundly.[1586] A foolish person, opined the Stoics, is insane.[1587] Dio Chrysostom observes that some would call him mad for confronting Alexandria's vices (*Or.* 32.24),[1588] but in reality it is the Alexandrians who act mad, pursuing entertainment like a narcotic (32.41), taking days to regain their senses (32.42).[1589] Likewise, when they hear the lyre, they lose their senses (32.65). Their sexual immorality is moral insanity.[1590] Excessive pride could also generate a form of moral insanity, compared to the frenzied rites of the mother goddess.[1591] For Paul, his madness belonged only to his preconversion persecution of believers (see comment on Acts 26:11).

Philosophic "madness," in the eyes of the masses, could be compared to the "madness" of inspiration (Dio Chrys. *Or.* 34.4). Middle Platonist philosophers, at least as early as Philo, began to seek visionary experiences of the divine through divine inspiration, a pattern that developed fully in later Platonism. Such philosophic ecstasy might help explain, from an uncommitted Gentile's perspective, the visionary experiences of the educated and articulate Paul (Acts 26:13, 16). A complication is that such Platonism (and similar ideas in Gnosticism) becomes pervasive especially in the second century and later; Stoicism remained the dominant philosophic school in this period. The ideas are probably this early, but would the Roman Festus (even with a respectable Greek education) have known them, and would Luke have expected him (and his audience) to know them? Even with these caveats, the possibility remains, especially given the reapplication of prophetic madness in Plato's *Phaedrus* itself.[1592]

A display of learning could suggest a prosperous background and high status, which often prejudiced judges in one's favor. Paul's "great learning" was perhaps more evident to the Roman officials who met him (21:37–38 and here) than to the average hearer of Luke's accounts. Despite Luke's rhetorical skill in the speeches (see various comments on the speech's special "elegance" above), it is probable that Paul could display his learning even more eloquently than Luke could present in his précis. Paul's letters exhibit a level of rhetorical proficiency (in argumentation, not in delivery), albeit not that of a rhetorician; this was supplemented by familiarity with Greek intellectual thought and his greater strength in the Scriptures. It is the last that matters most, however, for Festus's language may imply *documents*, namely, the prophets to whom Paul appeals (26:22; though not the specific sense in 28:21; Luke 16:6–7). Thus Paul now appeals to Agrippa, to whom his speech is particularly addressed, to attest the content of the prophets (26:27).

ii. Paul's Sobriety (26:25)

Although Paul is later ready to embrace King Agrippa's response (26:28–29), he now corrects that of Festus (26:24–25). It was rhetorically prudent not to rebuke members of the court even if they protested one's words, lest one risk stirring their

1586. E.g., Epict. *Diatr.* 1.12.9 (μαινόμενος); 1.21.4 (μαινομένων); Arius Did. *Epit.* 2.7.5b13, pp. 26–27.28–30; 2.7.5b13, p. 28.1–2; cf. Quint. *Decl.* 283.1; Lucian *Nigr.* 38; Diog. Laert. 1.87.

1587. Cic. *Parad.* 27–32; Mus. Ruf. 20, p. 126.2–3; Diog. Laert. 7.1.124; cf. Cic. *Tusc.* 3.5.10. Cf. Sen. Y. *Ep. Lucil.* 28, even regarding an ecstatic prophetess (in Virg. *Aen.* 6.78–79). Ignorance is madness in *Pyth. Sent.* 28.

1588. Malherbe, *Philosophers*, 160, notes that Dio Chrysostom appeals to the association of madness with inspiration when he is accused of madness, and in *Or.* 45.1 denies madness.

1589. He claims that Anacharsis the Scythian viewed Greek love of athletics in general as madness (Dio Chrys. *Or.* 32.44). Any nonsensical behavior could lead to one's appearing out of his or her mind (Dion. Hal. *Isoc.* 17; Dio Chrys. *Or.* 17.21; Alciph. *Fish.* 12 [Charopê to Glaucippê], 3.2, ¶1; cf. *Test. Job* 35:1–38:6, where Job's comforters test his sanity).

1590. Dio Chrys. *Or.* 32.91, using γυναιμανεῖς, "crazed for women."

1591. Philost. *Ep.* 69 (15). The heat of anger also produced temporary insanity (*Ep. Apoll.* 86).

1592. On which, see Evans, "Mad Ritual."

anger (*Rhet. Alex.* 18, 1433a.20–24). Paul responds respectfully. No one will accuse Luke of untidiness for allowing an interruption and response here; after a defense speech in a history was interrupted, it was possible for the speaker to conclude with final words.[1593]

Paul's term for "utter" (ἀποφθέγγομαι), used in the earliest extant Christian literature only in Acts, is associated with inspired speech in at least one (Acts 2:4) and possibly both (2:14) other uses (see comment on these passages).[1594] In that very context in Acts 2, such inspiration appeared to some as drunkenness (2:13). Paul's inspiration, however, ought not to be confused with madness (26:24), for he speaks soberly (26:25). "Words of truth and sobriety" here may be a hendiadys, hence, "words of sober truth."[1595] Such sobriety could be contrasted with madness, as here.[1596] Less relevant, some people in antiquity also spoke of a divinely inspired μανία that was superior to a "sound mind" (σωφροσύνης, Ael. Arist. *Def. Or.* 53, §17D).[1597]

(1) Philosophic Sobriety

Philosophers were widely known to extol this virtue of σωφροσύνη,[1598] extolled at length by Plato's Socrates.[1599] Following Aristotelian categories,[1600] the dominant Stoic philosophy of the era, including among Roman Stoics, made sobriety (σωφροσύνη)[1601] one of its central virtues;[1602] it regularly appears among the traditional four virtues.[1603] It means especially self-control over the passions, the baser emotions.[1604] It should

1593. A bystander interrupts (Quint. Curt. 6.10.36) after a speech (6.10.1–35), and the speaker concludes with final words (6.10.37).

1594. In the LXX, the term applies to inspiration positively in 1 Chr 25:1; negatively in Mic 5:12; Ezek 13:9, 19; Zech 10:2; and possibly to other speech in Ps 58:8 (59:7 ET); cf. also inspired speech in Philo *Heir* 259; *Joseph* 117; *Mos.* 2.253, 263. A cognate is oracular in Philo *Joseph* 95; Jos. *War* 2.159. Cf. Dupont, *Salvation*, 51.

1595. Johnson, *Acts*, 439.

1596. Commentators cite, e.g., Xen. *Mem.* 1.1.16; 3.9.6–7; cf. also Dio Chrys. *Or.* 32.28 (cf. 77/78.26); Lucian *Nigr.* 5–6; Arius Did. *Epit.* 2.7.5b13, pp. 26–27.30–31; Libanius *Descr.* 23.1–2 (explicit in 23.1). The full semantic range of the cognate σωφρονέω includes both self-control and sanity (BDAG; for the latter, against insanity, BDAG cites, e.g., Plato *Phaedr.* 22, 244A; *Rep.* 1.331C; Philo *Cher.* 69); in Luke-Acts, Luke 8:35.

1597. Also, e.g., Proclus *Poet.* 6.2, K178.24; K182.18–19.

1598. See, e.g., Mus. Ruf. 18B, p. 116.20; Arius Did. *Epit.* 2.7.5f, pp. 30–31.23; 2.7.11g, pp. 72–73.15; Lucian *Icar.* 30 (Zeus complaining that they were not living accordingly). Cf. also the moralist Plutarch in *Poetry* 11, *Mor.* 32C.

1599. See esp. Plato *Charm.* 159B–176C (LCL, 4:26–89); cf. Xen. *Mem.* 1.2.23; Iambl. *Letter* 3, frg. 5 (Stob. *Anth.* 3.5.48); also, in Irwin, *Philosophy*, 328, §§494–95, note Plato *Gorgias* 504E–507E. Plato related it to self-knowledge (though perhaps through a logical inconsistency in Plato; Rosen, "Sophrosyne"); especially moderation related to self-knowledge (Schmid, "Moderation"). On Socrates's view of σωφροσύνη in *Charmides*, see, e.g., Kosman, "Definition"; McKim, "Self-Knowledge"; but the *Charmides* dialogue drops this subject early on (so Van der Ben, *Charmides*). Socrates finds it incompatible with injustice (Eisenstadt, "Teaching"; cf. further McKirahan, "Protagoras").

1600. Ultimately said to go back to Socrates (Plato *Rep.* 4.428–34).

1601. I include in the discussion the adjective cognate, which usage demonstrates is normally related (at least in the many sources surveyed). Given the period and Festus's being a Roman speaking Greek, I focus on Musonius as an example, but other sources are also fruitful.

1602. As a summary of virtue in Mus. Ruf. 5, p. 50.22–26.

1603. E.g., Mus. Ruf. 4, p. 44.10–22, esp. 16–22; p. 48.1, 4, 8, 13, esp. 4; 6, p. 52.15, 17, 19, 21, esp. 15; 7, p. 58.25–26 (minus "courage"); 8, pp. 60.22–64.9, esp. 62.10–23; p. 66.7–8, esp. 8; 17, p. 108.9–10; Marc. Aur. 3.6; 8.1 (σώφρονα); Arius Did. *Epit.* 2.7.5a, pp. 10–11.7–9 (Zeno's views); 2.7.5b1, pp. 12–13.13–22 (and their converse in lines 22–29; as *samples* of virtues and vices; see lines 29–30); 2.7.5b2, pp. 14–15.1–4, esp. 3; 2.7.5b5, pp. 18–19.27–31 (with lines 21–26, 32–35). Cf. Mus. Ruf. 7, p. 58.25–26, esp. 26; 16, p. 104.32–34, esp. 33; frg. 38, p. 136.3; Libanius *Thesis* 3.3. See discussion in Lutz, "Musonius," 27, including n. 113. Cf. lists of virtues including at least three of these, e.g., Arius Did. *Epit.* 2.7.5b, pp. 10–11.16–21 (esp. 17); 2.7.11e, pp. 68–69.12–16; Philost. *Vit. Apoll.* 1.20. Apart from "justice" and funerary use of sobriety, the four virtues figure little in epigraphic sources in Ephesus and presumably similar cities (Judge, *First Christians*, 374–75).

1604. E.g., cf. Mus. Ruf. 3, p. 40.20–22; 4, p. 44.18–22; 6, p. 52.15–17; 8, p. 62.14–17; 16, p. 104.33–35; 17, p. 108.11–14; frg. 24, p. 130; Arius Did. *Epit.* 2.7.5b2, pp. 14–15.6; cf. Libanius *Anecdote* 4.8. Against

characterize the reign of the ideal ruler,[1605] might be applied even to a city as well as to an individual,[1606] and, of course, should characterize the philosopher.[1607] In a woman, the virtue is associated with chastity and avoiding unlawful relations.[1608] The virtue was also widespread in Greek philosophy in general[1609]—for example, among Pythagoreans.[1610] Outsiders might doubt the sobriety of one who abandons all for philosophy, but this person is truly wise (Dio Chrys. *Or.* 80.1). Given Luke's depiction of Paul as a sage and Festus's remark about Paul's education (Acts 26:24), the philosophic usage seems relevant, particularly given its linkage with "truth" here.

(2) General Usage

The ideal extended far beyond philosophers, however.[1611] A historian could, for example, praise young men able to demonstrate σωφροσύνη (Polyb. 31.25.2), which included avoiding sexual laxity, lavish banqueting, and other Greek excess (31.25.4).[1612] It was also a welcome female virtue connected with modesty, sexual self-control, and so forth.[1613] A Spartan declared that this virtue was central to self-respect, which was the prerequisite for courage (Thucyd. 1.84.3). Others used it to depict hardworking farmers (Libanius *Encomium* 7.5; *Comparison* 5.8).

Although Paul mentions it only briefly, this virtue appears more widely in speeches. For orators, σωφροσύνη or its synonyms functioned as one of the virtues

---

sexual indulgence, see, e.g., Mus. Ruf. 12, p. 86.13–16; against gluttony, e.g., 18A, p. 112.6–7 (cf. 112.29); 18B, p. 116.4–22, esp. 19–20; p. 118.4–7, esp. 5; p. 120.2–7, esp. 6–7; against grief, e.g., Arius Did. *Epit.* 2.7.5 L, pp. 36–37.3–5. See further Lutz, "Musonius," 28 (noting esp. Mus. Ruf. 6, p. 54.2–25). For the fullest definition, see Arius Did. *Epit.* 2.7.5b1, pp. 12–13.18–19; 2.7.5b2, pp. 14–15.15–16, 31–35; p. 16–17.1–3; cf. also 2.7.5b, pp. 10–11.21–25 (esp. 23); p. 12.1–2. For remaining within realistic limits and avoiding hubris, see Jewett, *Romans*, 739–40 (on Rom 12:3).

1605. Mus. Ruf. 8, p. 60.10–23; p. 62.10–21; Dio Chrys. *Or.* 3.7; Philost. *Vit. Apoll.* 5.35, 36. It was precisely the need for this virtue among those who governed that made democracy impracticable (Dio Chrys. *Or.* 3.47). A civic official might supervise this virtue (51.6).

1606. So Eisenberg, "*Sophrosune*" (on Plato *Rep.* 4.432A).

1607. E.g., Mus. Ruf. 8, p. 66.8; Dio Chrys. *Or.* 35.2. Roman men more generally apparently tried to control expression of emotion (see Clark, "Poetics"; e.g., Val. Max. 4.1.13); cf. Rives, *Religion*, 186, on educated persons of status.

1608. E.g., Mus. Ruf. 3, p. 40.17–18, 20; 4, p. 44.16–18; Libanius *Narration* 37. For the virtue as appropriate for women, see also Mus. Ruf. 4, p. 48.4; for philosophy teaching women this virtue, see also 3, p. 42.26–28. See more broadly North, "Mare." Eurip. *Oed.* frg. 545 links the adjective with wifely obedience.

1609. Commentators cite Plato *Rep.* 4.430E–431B; *Phaedr.* 244D; *Prot.* 323B; *Symp.* 196C; Diog. Laert. 3.91; Justin *Dial.* 39.4 (e.g., Johnson, *Acts*, 439; Larkin, *Acts*, 364; Witherington, *Acts*, 749). Cf. even Epicureans in Cic. *Fin.* 1.14.47 (*temperantiam*), a concession that Stoics exploited (Mus. Ruf. frg. 24, p. 130, with Lutz's note, p. 131).

1610. Cf., e.g., Philost. *Vit. Apoll.* 6.11; Iambl. *V.P.* 1.1; ruling the tongue, 31.195; concerning the temptations of youth, 8.41; 31.195 (sexual); overcoming passions in Iambl. *Letter* 3, frg. 2–3 (Stob. *Anth.* 3.5.45–46); the supreme virtue in *Letter* 3, frg. 5–6 (Stob. *Anth.* 3.5.48–49). Among a variation on the four virtues, see Iambl. *V.P.* 30.167–33.240, esp. 31.187–213.

1611. For a more detailed treatment, see North, *Sophrosyne*; idem, "'Sophrosyne' in Criticism"; Marshall, *Enmity*, 190–94 (especially in opposition to ὕβρις, arrogantly overstepping bounds). Wojciechowski, "Vocabulary," doubts that moral philosophy shaped much NT language; this observation holds true for most of Luke-Acts (and still more the other Gospels), but there are exceptions (and many exceptions in Pauline literature).

1612. Also in novels (e.g., Ach. Tat. 1.5.6; Philost. *Hrk.* 11.8; 26.1). Some ancients, however, thought that this virtue among the young (perhaps younger than Scipio, to whom Polybius refers?) reflected more on those who raised them than on themselves (*Rhet. Alex.* 35, 1441a.16–19, esp. 18–19). On self-control among young men, see, e.g., Men. Rhet. 2.3, 385.22–28, esp. 22–23; Libanius *Speech in Character* 10.2; 17.4 (cf. 4.1; *Invect.* 5.14); for the diverse standards for self-control (especially sexual) of the young in various Greek cities, see Men. Rhet. 1.3, 363.28–364.9. Some held that marriage conferred the virtue of temperance on the young (Dion. Hal. *Epid.* 2.263).

1613. E.g., Mus. Ruf. 3, p. 40.17–22, esp. 17; p. 42.26; 4, p. 44.22; Dio Chrys. *Or.* 32.56; Lucian *Hall* 7; *Sent. Sext.* 237; Libanius *Speech in Character* 18 (esp. 18.3); *Thesis* 1.13, 26–27; perhaps 1 Tim 2:9, 15; cf. Winter, *Wives*, 101–3.

useful in an encomium.[1614] Like others, epideictic orators utilized the four traditional categories of virtues, which sometimes provided convenient topics for extended ethical treatments,[1615] including, for example, what became recommended topics for praising the emperor,[1616] the governor,[1617] or a friend.[1618] In such praises this virtue could include restraint not only in baser pleasures but even in laughter, as a sign of dignity,[1619] though others allowed their heroes to laugh as well as to display self-control.[1620]

In contrast to the expectations of ecstasy noted above, one praises even a mantic who spoke with such self-control (Dio Chrys. *Or.* 1.56)—thereby illustrating the contrast between sobriety and "mad" inspiration. One who led a life of such self-control would be difficult to convict in court (Dion. Hal. *Ant. rom.* 7.58.2).

(3) Jewish Uses

Jewish sources in Greek display a range of meaning analogous to the non-Jewish uses. Those influenced by Stoic thought hail the virtue and its power to subdue harmful passions (4 Macc 1:30–31; 2:18; 3:17, 19; 5:23), including gluttony (1:3) and lust (1:3; 2:2, 16; *Test. Jos.* 4:1–2).[1621] In some instances it clearly appears among the four traditional virtues (4 Macc 1:6, 18; 2:23; 15:10; Wis 8:7).[1622] Only God could dispose one's mind toward this virtue (*Let. Aris.* 237, 248). The virtue appears fairly commonly in Hellenistic Jewish sources.[1623] Σωφροσύνη appears in some early Christian writers.[1624] It is not at all surprising here, especially in response to Festus's suggestion of undignified (perhaps ecstatic or philosophic) madness informing Paul's speech.

III. NOT IN A CORNER (26:26)

In response to Festus's failure to be persuaded, Paul calls Agrippa as a witness to the veracity of Paul's claims about Jewish matters, the very purpose for which Festus called this hearing (Acts 25:26–27). This appeal may be, as Witherington suggests, "a masterful rhetorical move."[1625] For Paul's speaking "boldly" (cf. 9:27–28; 13:46; 14:3; 19:8; 28:21), see comment on Acts 4:13. In trusting that nothing has escaped

---

1614. E.g., *Rhet. Alex.* 35, 1440b.17–19, esp. 19 (with Rackham, LCL, 405 n. *a*, noting the synonym). This is conformed to the four traditional virtues (prudence being doubled) in the spurious addition in *Rhet. Alex.* 38, 1447b.5–6. It is linked with "virtue" (ἀρετή) in Dio Chrys. *Or.* 39.2; with "orderliness" in 33.48.

1615. E.g., *Rhet. Alex.* 35, 1440b.17–19 (with slightly different wording; cf. also the spurious addition in 38, 1447b.5–6); Ael. Arist. *Def. Or.* 235, §72D; 382, §128D; Men. Rhet. 1.3, 361.14–17, esp. 15. Cf. these virtues in Dio Chrys. *Or.* 3.58 (adapting the wording slightly); 29.8, 14 (two elements); Lucian *Hermot.* 22 (three elements). It is linked with other virtues in Lucian *Portr.* 11, 12.

1616. Men. Rhet. 2.1–2, 373.7–8, esp. 8; 375.7–376.23, esp. 375.7–8 and 376.2–13. The emperor's example of self-control affected sexual chastity in the empire (376.5–6).

1617. Men. Rhet. 2.3, 379.19–380.3, esp. 379.32; 380.31–381.2, esp. 381.2; 385.8–386.10, esp. 385.8–9, 22–28; 2.10, 415.24–416.28, esp. 415.24–26, 416.18–23.

1618. Men. Rhet. 2.5, 397.21–24, esp. 22–23; cf. Pliny *Ep.* 3.2.2. The orator naturally adds to the four a fifth, "excellence in speaking ability" (Men. Rhet. 2.5, 397.23–24).

1619. Men. Rhet. 2.10, 416.19. For the impropriety of dignified persons laughing in public settings, see Aeschines *Tim.* 84.

1620. E.g., Philost. *Hrk.* 11.4.

1621. Elsewhere in Judaism, see, e.g., 2 Macc 4:37; and a Greek-speaking Jew who named his son Sophronios (Σωφρόνιος, *CIJ* 1:37, §55, with a menorah).

1622. Regularly in Philo: *Creation* 73; *Alleg. Interp.* 1.63, 65; *Cher.* 5; *Sacr.* 27, 84; *Worse* 18; *Posterity* 128; *Agr.* 18; *Drunkenness* 23; *Heir* 209; *Names* 197; *Abr.* 219; *Mos.* 2.185; 2.216; *Spec. Laws* 2.62; *Rewards* 160; *Good Person* 67, 70, 159. Cf. also Feldman, "Jehu."

1623. E.g., Jos. *Ag. Ap.* 2.176, 186, 195 (Josephus employs the noun twenty-one times); Ps.-Phoc. 76; *Test. Jos.* 4:2; 9:2; 10:2–3.

1624. *1 Clem.* 62.2; 64.1; Ign. *Eph.* 10.3.

1625. Witherington, *Acts*, 749.

the king's notice, Paul speaks respectfully to the king concerning what is expected of kings[1626] and, indeed, what philosophers expect of the ideal wise person.[1627]

(1) Appeals to Common Knowledge

When Paul appeals to Agrippa, his basis for assuming Agrippa's knowledge is that the events he recounts (or at least the reports about them, especially regarding Jesus, 26:23) are common knowledge within Judea. Appeals to common knowledge were standard in forensic rhetoric;[1628] such appeals to agreed-on knowledge do not require specific proofs (*Rhet. Alex.* pref. 1421a.4–6). Cicero appeals to his hearers' knowledge that Syracuse is the most beautiful of all cities (*Verr.* 2.4.52.117), and ironically demands of his opponent, "Conceal if you can your certainty of what all Sicily saw clearly."[1629] Defending himself, Apuleius regularly appeals to common knowledge:[1630] "All of you who were present must have seen" (*Apol.* 76); "The whole town heard about this" (94). Like Paul appealing to Agrippa's knowledge, Apuleius also appeals to his judge's knowledge (28; 98–99).

This practice spilled over into other disciplines besides forensic rhetoric; thus, for example, Xenophon reported Agesilaus's deeds "done before a crowd of witnesses" and hence undeniable (*Ages.* 3.1).[1631] Likewise, one rhetorician writing on literary criticism claims, "I need not say, when all educated people know it as well as I, that this passage does not consist of . . ."[1632] Although Seneca prefers to use Stoic argumentation rather than the popular argument that he may take for granted any point on which all agree, he attests to the pervasiveness of the latter view.[1633] Writing apologetic in which he contends against an accuser of Judaism, Josephus explicitly appeals to public knowledge, what is known by all the people (*Ag. Ap.* 2.107). He also offered his histories to the emperors while they and other eyewitnesses remained alive, when the information he reported was virtually "under their eyes" (*Life* 361).

Appeals to common knowledge or publicly available evidence also appear in novels, where the evidence may be fictitious; it is, however, presented as genuine evidence within the narrative world, reinforcing the point that such claims were normally made only when something like such evidence existed.[1634] Since Luke is writing a historical monograph resting on genuine sources and not a novel and is writing in a period when some witnesses and evidence remain available (Luke 1:2–4), he apparently believes that the basic claims he makes (such as the existence of a circle of eyewitnesses claiming to have met the risen Jesus) were publicly known events. Elsewhere, too, Luke emphasizes the public nature of the events, such as Jesus's crucifixion (known to all in Jerusalem at that time, 24:18), although a much smaller body of witnesses attested to the resurrection (Acts 10:41).

1626. Cf. 2 Sam 18:13; 1 Kgs 10:3; Prov 25:2.

1627. Arius Did. *Epit.* 2.7.11m, pp. 94–95.16–18.

1628. E.g., Aeschines *Embassy* 14; *Tim.* 44, 55–56, 65, 77–78, 80, 89; Isaeus *Pyrr.* 40; Cic. *Verr.* 1.5.15; 2.1.40.103. See discussion at Acts 24:8; 26:5.

1629. Cic. *Verr.* 2.3.30.71 (trans. Greenwood, LCL, 8:85). This rhetorical method resembles what some rhetoricians meant by *epitrope* or *permissio* (see Rowe, "Style," 147; but the definition differs in Anderson, *Glossary*, 54, following *Rhet. Her.* 4.39).

1630. E.g., Apul. *Apol.* 28; 59. Apuleius can also appeal to common knowledge in other rhetorical genres, e.g., Apul. *Flor.* 17.4; *De deo Socr.* 150.

1631. The less widely known something was, Xenophon opines, the more one ought to be skeptical (*Ages.* 5.6).

1632. Dion. Hal. *Lit. Comp.* 22 (trans. S. Usher, LCL, 2:187); likewise, there was no need to demonstrate what all acknowledged, that Demosthenes was the greatest orator (*Isaeus* 20).

1633. Sen. Y. *Ep. Lucil.* 117.6–7 (the popular view is in 117.6; his shift to a Stoic approach appears in 117.7).

1634. See Philost. *Hrk.* 8.12, 14, 17; cf. Maclean and Aitken, *Heroikos*, lxiii–lxiv.

We may object that today we have little reference to these events in first-century non-Christian Judean sources, but here Luke, much closer to the events than are his modern objectors, is more likely to be correct than are our objections. The only first-century non-Christian Judean historical source extant is Josephus; although his interests lie elsewhere, he mentions Jesus in connection with his brother James[1635] and, very likely, Jesus himself as a popular teacher.[1636] (The passage on the latter point, Jos. *Ant.* 18.63–64, has been disputed, but most scholars today accept it as authentic with spurious additions. All the 42 Greek and 171 Latin manuscripts of Josephus extant contain the disputed passage;[1637] but the earliest Christian citations omit the supernatural elements,[1638] and Josephus attributes belief in Jesus's messiahship only to others.)[1639] People may recall various public events years later without assigning them prominent roles as historical causes; Josephus gives Jesus no more space than he allots other popular prophets not directly part of his action. What seems unexpected is Josephus's silence about Jesus's movement (which cannot but have existed); that omission seems deliberate (see comment on Acts 21:20).

(2) "Not in a Corner" and Secret Teachings

Not only Paul's appeal to common knowledge but even his language ("these things were not done in a corner") would have been familiar.[1640] Commentators regularly cite very similar expressions in other authors, arguing that Paul here employs a common proverb, "in a corner" referring to whatever is secretive or private.[1641] Malherbe points to the commonly cited expression in Plato *Gorg.* 485D: one interlocutor charges that an old man will simply whisper his views in a corner. Malherbe notes that Aul. Gel. 10.22.17–24 quotes this passage and applies it to those who focus on trifles rather than what helps society; later Themistius *Or.* 22.265bc[1642] applies it to "those who withdraw from society."[1643] Thus, for more than seven hundred years, speaking in a corner was pejorative for those, especially philosophers, who withdrew from public

1635. Jos. *Ant.* 20.200. James fits Josephus's purview, as someone popular in Jerusalem martyred by the corrupt priesthood in the years just before the Judean-Roman war. The same priestly family was involved in both Jesus's and James's executions (Bock, "Blasphemy," 608, citing *Ant.* 20.197–203, M. Hengel, and R. Brown). See further discussion at Acts 21:23–24.

1636. Jos. *Ant.* 18.63–64, minus the Slavonic additions and some others not found in the Arabic version (see, e.g., Thackeray, *Josephus*, 125; Klausner, *Jesus of Nazareth*, 55ff.; Cornfeld, *Josephus*, 510; Meier, "Jesus in Josephus"; idem, "Testimonium"; Whealey, "Josephus"; Gramaglia, "*Testimonium*"; Paget, "Observations"; Vermes, *Jesus the Jew*, 79; Sanders, *Figure*, 50; Dubarle, "Témoignage"; Victor, "Testimonium"). That Josephus, despite his interest in revolutionaries, does not class Jesus with the revolutionaries suggests that most people could see the difference (cf. Acts 5:36–39; 24:22–23) and that the Sadducean priests were disingenuous in claiming otherwise.

1637. The surviving Greek manuscripts begin in the eleventh century, and the Latin in the sixth (Feldman, "Methods," 591), which is not unusual for manuscripts of the period.

1638. Feldman, "Methods," 591, cites here Jerome *Vir.* 13; the tenth-century writer Agapius, in Arabic; and others. On the Arabic omission of precisely the elements scholars often believed to be interpolated, see also Charlesworth, *Jesus within Judaism*, 95–96; idem, "Jesus, Literature, and Archaeology," 191–92; Evans, "Non-Christian Sources," 468; Eddy and Boyd, *Legend*, 193–94.

1639. See Feldman, "Methods," 591; Meier, "Jesus in Josephus"; idem, "Testimonium."

1640. Romans did have a private, more secretive space in their house (the *cubiculum*), but even part of their house was "public" space (Riggsby, "'Public' and 'Private'"), and this was honorable (Vell. Paterc. 2.14.3).

1641. Commentators (e.g., Conzelmann, *Acts*, 212; Longenecker, *Acts*, 350; Johnson, *Acts*, 439; Witherington, *Acts*, 749; Fitzmyer, *Acts*, 764; Peterson, *Acts*, 674) cite Plato *Gorg.* 485D; Epict. *Diatr.* 2.12.17; Plut. *Busybody* 2, *Mor.* 516b; cf. Plut. *Mor.* 777b; Terence *Brothers* 5.2.10. On the use of gnomes, see, e.g., Rowe, "Style," 148 (for proverbs, Anderson, *Glossary*, 91); they could be added, as perhaps here, as a "finishing touch" (some rhetoricians gave this use a technical name, ἐπιφώνημα; Anderson, *Glossary*, 55).

1642. Cf. also Themistius *Or.* 23.284b; 28.341d; 34.12; 26.322b.

1643. Malherbe, *Philosophers*, 155.

life.[1644] Whether or not the phrase's use had become idiomatic,[1645] it would be intelligible. Although the language was not limited to philosophers, it appeared often enough among them to suggest in this context that Paul maintains his role as a sage, one whose "learning" Festus has already acknowledged (Acts 26:24).[1646]

If we may judge by second-century apologists, some outsiders found Christians' private activity a natural target for this sort of criticism.[1647] Further, secretive meetings were viewed as subversive;[1648] by disclaiming any secretive activity, Paul thus reinforces his case that he and the Christian movement are no threat to the empire's stability.

It was understood that some private matters were shared in confidence only among trustworthy friends;[1649] to conceal secrets from one's in-group was offensive.[1650] More problematic were secret venues for teachings that could prove subversive, although, again, many secrets were acceptable if publicly understood to be apolitical. Greeks had mystery cults, in which a secret was not to be revealed to outsiders;[1651] Rome did not oppose these, though it had a tradition of suspicion toward unapproved cults stemming from second-century B.C.E. abuses by the Dionysus cult in Rome.

Some Jewish groups often spoke of spiritual mysteries revealed to a select group.[1652] Jewish sages also had a small collection of topics considered too esoteric for popular consumption and given out only very selectively to disciples.[1653] Luke emphasizes that the mysteries of the kingdom were not being held by a small group but being revealed. He speaks of the mysteries of the kingdom being revealed to a select group (Luke 8:10; Mark 4:11) but soon after notes that what is spoken in secret will be revealed (Luke 8:17; cf. Mark 4:22).[1654] Some later rabbis (perhaps combating something like gnostics) warned that false teachers work in secret but true wisdom is proclaimed openly.[1655]

iv. Seeking Agrippa's Conversion (26:27–29)

Paul's attempt to appeal to Agrippa as a witness (Acts 26:27), combined with Paul's earlier claims based on his revelations, moves Agrippa to the witty observation that

1644. Ibid., 155–56. This criticism may have proved especially effective against Epicureans, who did withdraw.

1645. Barrett, *Acts*, 1169, denies that "done in a corner" was an idiom, but acknowledges the similarity of some of these texts.

1646. See Malherbe, *Philosophers*, 159–60; Witherington, *Acts*, 750.

1647. Later, Celsus scoffed at any truth in Judaism or Christianity, since they occurred in a corner of obscure Palestine (Origen *Cels.* 4.36); Eusebius later countered that, far from being limited to a corner, Christians were scattered everywhere (*H.E.* 1.4.1–2; Pelikan, *Acts*, 277–78).

1648. See Malherbe, "Not in a Corner," 203; cf., e.g., Livy 39.15.11; 39.18.9; Tac. *Hist.* 2.54. Wonderworkers who acted in private were also thought to employ dangerous magic (Theissen, *Miracle Stories*, 61).

1649. E.g., Isoc. *Demon.* 24–25; Sir 6:9; 22:22; 27:17; Philo *Sobr.* 55; Jos. *Ag. Ap.* 2.207; Mitchell, "Friends by Name," 259; Keener, *John*, 1010.

1650. Among Epicureans, see Philod. *Crit.* frg. 40–42, esp. 41.

1651. Eurip. *Bacch.* 472; Lysias *Or.* 6.51, §107; Callim. *Aetia* 3.75.8–9; Dion. Hal. *Lit. Comp.* 25; Hor. *Odes* 3.2.25–29; Plut. *Educ.* 14, *Mor.* 10F; *Alcib.* 19.1; Heracl. *Ep.* 8; Aelian *Farmers* 1 (Euthycomides to Blepaeus); Paus. 1.14.3; 2.3.4; Lucian *Fisherman* 33; *Men.* 2; Apul. *Metam.* 3.15; Diog. Laert. 7.7.186; Tert. *Apol.* 7.6; Burkert, *Mystery Cults*, 7–9, 42; Mylonas, *Eleusis*, 224–29; Klauck, *Context*, 94. For punishments, see, e.g., Thucyd. 6.53.1–2; Ovid *Metam.* 3.710–20; Livy 39.13.1–8, 18.

1652. E.g., 1QpHab VII, 4–5, 13–14; 1QHᵃ II, 13–14; IX, 23–24; XI, 9–10, 16–17; XII, 11–13; 1QS VIII, 1–2, 12; IX, 13, 17–19; 4 Ezra 14:45–47; cf. Dan 2:18, 19, 22–23, 27–30, 47; 4:9; Wis 2:22; *Test. Levi* 2:10; *Test. Jud.* 16:4; *t. Qidd.* 5:21; *Exod. Rab.* 19:6; *Esth. Rab.* 2:4; all of rabbinic Judaism in *Pesiq. Rab.* 5:1; see further discussion in Nock, *Christianity*, 30; Gibbard, "Mystery," 109; Caragounis, *Mysterion*, 126; Casciaro Ramírez, "Misterio"; Keener, *Matthew*, 378–79; esp. Brown, "*Mysterion*"; idem, *Mystery*.

1653. E.g., *m. Ḥag.* 2:1; *t. Ḥag.* 2:1, 7; *'Abot R. Nat.* 39 A; *b. Ḥag.* 13a; 15a, bar.; *Pesaḥ.* 119a; *Šabb.* 80b; *y. Ḥag.* 2:1, §15, 63–64; *Gen. Rab.* 1:5, 10; 2:4; *Pesiq. Rab Kah.* 21:5; *2 En.* 24:3.

1654. One could read this promise solely eschatologically, but cf. Luke 8:15–16.

1655. *Sipre Deut.* 87.2.2, citing Prov 1:20–21.

Paul seeks his conversion (26:28). Consonant with Paul's mission (26:16–18), Paul gladly admits that he does indeed desire this outcome (26:29).

(1) Appeal to the Prophets (26:27)

Rhetoricians sometimes practiced the rhetorical device of apostrophe: shifting from addressing the entire audience to focusing on a particular member or group.[1656] Here, however, Agrippa has remained a central focus throughout (see esp. 26:2–3, 7, 13, 19). Festus interrupted Paul's address to Agrippa (26:24–25), and so Paul's appeal to Agrippa returns, in a sense, to his original primary audience; but he does so at this moment partly to respond to Festus.[1657] Festus has already claimed that he invited Agrippa's presence precisely to appeal to his expertise (25:26), and so he cannot complain that Paul appeals to it here (26:26); Paul's direct appeal to Agrippa also fits his other appeals to him in this context (26:2, 7, 13, 19).[1658] Paul's experience coheres with that of the biblical prophets, as Agrippa, who is biblically knowledgeable, can testify, and hence is not "madness" in any negative sense.

By asking if Agrippa believes the prophets, Paul is inquiring whether he accepts their testimony that Paul has been citing (26:22). This is a leading question in a context where "faith" in Jesus is the object (26:18). Paul implies that one who believes the prophets will consequently believe in Jesus; this implication presupposes a larger argument that Luke does not need to flesh out here, because he has illustrated the prophetic testimony to Jesus elsewhere (e.g., 3:24; 8:32–33; 13:34, 41). If Paul cited specific references, these could contribute to his *probatio*, or proofs, to which he can now appeal. As intimated above, he may also appeal to the prophets to suggest that his visionary experience stands in continuity with them (26:13, 16). Claiming that he knows that Agrippa is aware of common information (26:26) and believes the prophets (26:27) is complimentary (learning being positive, 26:24).[1659] He is tightening his case to make his conclusion of the truth of Christ's revelation difficult to evade (26:28).[1660]

(2) Evading Paul's Logical "Trap" (26:28)

Agrippa intelligently, publicly, and explicitly exposes Paul's not-so-subtle attempt to convert him: Paul is explaining his gospel on the basis of the prophets in 26:20–23, with Agrippa in view (26:19); after being interrupted, Paul seeks to return to the same point (26:27).[1661] Paul is not merely defending himself; he is trying to persuade his hearers about his faith (per Jesus's instructions, Luke 21:12–13). Paul's audacity in seeking to convert a person of Agrippa's status may offend (or amuse) Agrippa, but it also makes clear that Paul is no temple desecrator or leader of revolutionaries: he

1656. *Rhet. Her.* 4.15.22; Rowe, "Style," 139 (citing Rom 2:1; Tert. *Mart.* 1); Porter, "Paul and Letters," 581.

1657. Digressing from one's speech to address someone else is what some rhetoricians called apostrophe (*Rhet. Her.* 4.15.22; Men. Rhet. 2.16, 435.30–436.1, esp. 435.30; Rowe, "Style," 139; cf. Porter, "Paul and Letters," 581; Anderson, *Glossary*, 25).

1658. A speaker could appeal to a judge's expertise or knowledge, as in, e.g., Apul. *Apol.* 25; 36; 38 (all of which also thereby praise the judge).

1659. This may be especially complimentary in view of some conservatives—even Josephus—thinking Agrippa too "liberal" on some points (Jos. *Ant.* 20.189–91, 216–18, esp. 218).

1660. Those who view this as a *peroratio* can note that this was the place to elaborate and reiterate points in one's favor (Cic. *De or.* 1.31.143) and, ideally, to include emotional appeal (cf. Anderson, *Rhetorical Theory*, 181–82).

1661. Agrippa's conversion would have repercussions for Israel's conversion as a whole, a goal of the earliest Christians (cf. Acts 3:19–21), including the historical Paul (Rom 11:13–27). As Agrippa might know from his sister Drusilla (Acts 24:24), Paul had already sought to convert Felix (24:24–25; Agrippa and Felix were not on favorable terms). For Paul, of course, seeking conversion was not the frequent modern notion of recruiting more allies to one's "side" but the sharing of a great benefit with the recipient.

is a politically innocuous Nazarene, whose apolitical but evangelical fanaticism has led him into trouble with the already troublesome Jerusalem priesthood. Sharing Rome's ideals regarding religious tolerance (ideals the support of which Luke seeks to encourage), Agrippa would hardly find legal fault here (Acts 26:31–32).

How should we understand Agrippa's reply? One could read it as indicative (e.g., NASB): "In a short [time?] you will persuade me to be a Christian." In this case Luke presents Paul's case as so compelling that he nearly converts King Agrippa himself or at least as showing that Jews who care about their tradition must take Paul's message seriously. "It is not 'madness' but what the prophets spoke about in their writings."[1662] This would be consonant with Luke's apologetic, would fit Agrippa's being impressed with Paul (26:32), and would be, even if an exaggeration, an expression of praise for Paul's skill.[1663] Still, Agrippa would find it politically next to impossible, humanly speaking, to openly align himself with a minority sect extremely unpopular with the ruling elite. Indeed, it would work against his purpose in visiting Festus to begin with, which was undoubtedly to impress him favorably and build a stronger political connection than had been possible with Agrippa's corrupt brother-in-law, Felix. On any first-century dating of Acts, Agrippa (50–ca. 100 C.E.) was likely still alive when Luke wrote; Luke would hardly dare co-opt him as a "believer" or seriously misrepresent what he professed on the occasion.[1664] The majority of scholars and translations, however, read Agrippa's reply as interrogative (e.g., NRSV), on the basis of how they understand the context: "Will you persuade me, in so short [a time?], to be a Christian?"

In either case, Agrippa's intent may be ironic.[1665] Many scholars argue that "be a Christian" here refers to "play the part of a Christian"[1666] (cf., e.g., 1 Kgs 20:7 LXX [21:7 ET], ποιεῖς βασιλέα);[1667] certainly ποιέω is not the normal way to say "become a Christian."[1668] Agrippa can hardly deny the prophets, but if he answers, "Yes, I believe the prophets," he could be construed by some of his hearers as taking Paul's side. Thus, on this view, he objects (whether in the form of a question or in that of a statement), "So you want me to play the part of a Christian by agreeing with what you are saying!"[1669] (Others argue that the grammar supports only "about to make me a Christian" or "try to make me a Christian," noting that the verb applied to "playing" a part only in later patristic writers.)[1670] "Christian" is probably not a friendly term (see Acts 11:26), though it shows that Agrippa well understands what movement Paul's articulate defense represents.

1662. See O'Toole, *Acts 26*, 145.

1663. The best rhetoric was supposed to be able to sway a judge (Cic. *Brut.* 93.322). Dunn, *Acts*, 323, suggests a parallel with "the thief on the cross" in Luke 23:40–43, but he was converted, unlike Agrippa, and their status is too divergent to represent a convincing parallel.

1664. This would prove even more problematic than using Sergius Paulus's conversion (see comment on Acts 13:12). Writers hoping to gain a hearing could not afford to misrepresent matters of public interest on which they could be readily challenged (see, e.g., the comments of Judge, *First Christians*, 379–80, regarding the Gallic Romans publishing their own version of Claudius's speech).

1665. Cf. Malherbe, *Philosophers*, 161, who notes that many philosophers allowed for instantaneous conversion; he also notes that some told conversion accounts (as Paul has) inviting imitation but that the anticipated responses to such accounts were often ironic or sarcastic.

1666. C. Williams, *Acts*, 265; Conzelmann, *Acts*, 212; Johnson, *Acts*, 440; Dunn, *Acts*, 332.

1667. Several (C. Williams, *Acts*, 265; Conzelmann, *Acts*, 212; Johnson, *Acts*, 440) cite this verse, though the parallel is uncertain.

1668. Some MSS (including E, P, Ψ, and many minuscules; italic texts) thus prefer γενέσθαι, reflecting Paul's favorable twist on Agrippa's words in the next verse (Acts 26:29).

1669. As Bruce, *Commentary*, 495–96, puts this, "In short, you are trying to make me play the Christian" (cf. also idem, *Acts¹*, 449).

1670. E.g., Fitzmyer, *Acts*, 764 (against Haenchen, Conzelmann, and Schneider); Bock, *Acts*, 723.

The Greek verb for "persuade" here probably belongs to the irony. If we take "persuade" as conative, we could read it as "try to persuade," but the likelihood of this reading, which is not obvious, is questionable.[1671] (Agrippa's "persuade" might echo Paul's own use of the term in 26:26: Paul is persuaded that these matters are public record, but Agrippa is not yet persuaded to become a Christian on that account.)

Another vexing question is the meaning of ὀλίγῳ (usually translated "in so short a time"); does it refer to length of time or brevity of arguments (cf. 24:5)? Some argue for a nontemporal sense because, they claim, Paul's sense is not temporal in 26:29.[1672] This argument is questionable, since the meaning in 26:29 could be temporal instead of referring to people of high and low status. One could argue that Paul refers to his hearers "small or great" (ὀλίγῳ ... μεγάλῳ) in 26:29, echoing his own words about his audience in 26:22 (μικρῷ ... μεγάλῳ); in this case the "great" might be Agrippa and Festus, but would the small be the other officials (25:23) or guards and servants whom Luke has not mentioned? Unless he refers to the embarrassment of a public conversion, Agrippa in 26:28 cannot mean, "Do you hope to persuade me among the lowly present?" (thereby risking offense among the local officials). Agrippa could be asking, "Do you persuade me with so few arguments?" and Paul could respond in 26:29, "Whether my arguments are few or many . . ."[1673] Or Agrippa could be saying, "You are persuading me to play the Christian [assuming that this reading is defensible, which is debated] a little!"[1674] In this case Agrippa dismisses him with humor, and Paul accomplishes little (insofar as he seeks the king's conversion).[1675] But the neuter use of ὀλίγος with prepositions was indeed suitable to express "a short time," "quickly," and this is the likeliest sense in both 26:28 and 26:29.[1676] It may be relevant that some people ridiculed the idea of instant conversion claimed by some others.[1677]

Is Agrippa teasing Paul? Rejoinders could be harsh but were often meant to make people laugh (e.g., Plut. *Demosth.* 11.4). Banter and making fun of others were common in speeches and entertained the audience, although one obtained the reputation for being malicious if one overdid it (Plut. *Cic.* 5.4; 27.1; 39.1).[1678] Banter could be playful; for example, Seneca the Elder could claim that he wanted to stop his work and go back to enjoying his old age, when he had every intention of continuing the work (*Controv.* 10.pref. 1).

That Agrippa employs "Christian" rather than "Nazarene" may have been significant, but at this remove, the data being what it is, it is difficult to be certain what the significance was. Because "Christian" perhaps began as a title of ridicule but was adopted by followers of the Way themselves (Acts 11:26), perhaps it sounds less harsh than "Nazarene," used by Paul's prosecutor in 24:5. But "Christian" would also sound harsh when coupled with a legal charge (1 Pet 4:16), and believers may have adopted "Nazarene" no less than "Christian." It is also possible that Agrippa is being less than respectful with the title. Most likely, however, Agrippa prefers a term that

1671. Johnson, *Acts*, 440. Conative force seems more convincing in Acts 26:11.

1672. E.g., Johnson, *Acts*, 440. Cf. Calvin's various options in Chung-Kim and Hains, *Acts*, 345.

1673. Witherington, *Acts*, 751; cf. O'Toole, *Acts 26*, 144.

1674. Johnson, *Acts*, 440.

1675. Ibid., 443.

1676. See BDAG, citing, e.g., Plato *Apol.* 22B; Jos. *Ant.* 18.145; Lucian *Tox.* 24; cf. Blass, Debrunner, and Funk, *Grammar*, 104, §195. Turner, *Grammatical Insights*, 98–99, cites classical parallels and argues that Agrippa warns, "You are trying to persuade me that you have made me a Christian in a short time (or easily)."

1677. Talbert, *Acts*, 209, cites Lucian *Nigr.* 1; Plut. *Progr. Virt., Mor.* 75CE. Parsons, *Acts*, 346, suggests that Agrippa sides with those skeptical of instant conversion (citing also Albinus *Epitome doctrinae platonicae* 30.2). Certainly he is skeptical of the possibility of his own.

1678. For Cicero's incessant jesting, see Plut. *Cic.* 38.2–6 (the examples in 38.3–6 reveal that Cicero had perfected the art of witty cynicism, used for sarcastic insults); 40.3.

has gained broader Greek usage[1679] whereas "Nazarene" reflects a more local Judean coinage.[1680] Because "Christian" may be a title of derision, Agrippa may protest that Paul is asking him to lower his status.

In any case, Agrippa acts in character here with what little we know externally concerning his relationship with the Christian movement. He did not become a Christian, but neither did he actively persecute Christians (in contrast to Luke's report about his father). When, after Festus's death, the high priest Ananus illegally executed some individuals, including James, leader of the Jerusalem church, Agrippa, acting in concert with the new governor, removed Ananus from office (Jos. *Ant.* 20.201–3).[1681] Simply because Paul appears in a Christian document rather than in Josephus is no reason to doubt that he, like James, held a significant role that could invite Agrippa's attention; perhaps Paul's testimony even helped the hellenistically educated Agrippa to be more favorably disposed toward Christians.

(3) Wanting All to Share His Faith (26:29)

Paul's exclamatory interjection is rhetorically appropriate.[1682] Paul wants all his hearers to be "Christians";[1683] what Agrippa may mean as a term of levity Paul embraces positively.[1684] If Agrippa takes "Christian" as a title of derision in 26:28, Paul rejects that idea, finding no shame in his own role except for the chains. Paul balances Agrippa's "short time" with "long time"[1685] and the implication of Agrippa as his primary audience ("not only you [singular]") with "but rather all those listening to me today." The balance is euphonic, but it also communicates significant meaning. Paul is ready to pay a greater price ("a long time"), and his mission is to all, both Jews (e.g., Agrippa and Berenice) and Gentiles (e.g., most of the others present, Acts 25:23), as Paul has already noted (26:20).

In the larger context of Luke's narrative about Paul's trials, Paul's willingness to speak a long time probably means that he is ready to talk further with Agrippa, as with Felix before (24:24–25). Malherbe also notes that some philosophers debated whether conversion was instantaneous or gradual and suggests that in response to Agrippa's objection to expecting his sudden conversion, Paul declares that he welcomes Agrippa's conversion whether suddenly or gradually.[1686] That Paul wants others to be like him presents as an example his own faith in the preceding narration, just as his commission to call others to light (26:18) relates to his own encounter with light (26:13).

1679. A Latin construction, it may also have been gaining some currency in Roman circles (1 Pet 4:16; Tac. *Ann.* 15.44; Suet. *Nero* 16.2; but cf. Suet. *Claud.* 25.4). Nevertheless, it started among Greek-speakers in Antioch, and Festus was not familiar with the movement before meeting Paul (Acts 25:19).

1680. So also Tajra, *Trial*, 169.

1681. James was not the only individual executed, but he is the only one whom Josephus specifically names (*Ant.* 20.200) and hence was presumably a prominent target.

1682. This figure (called ἐμβόησις by some who used technical terms) was particularly appropriate in apostrophe (Anderson, *Glossary*, 41), hence here. On *exclamatio*, see Rowe, "Style," 143 (citing Greg. Naz. *Or.* 8.14; Cic. *Cat.* 1.2); Porter, "Paul and Letters," 582 (on Paul); Thurén, "Writings," 603n70 (on Jude 11).

1683. Fitzmyer, *Acts*, 765: "the only place in the NT where the potential optative with *an* occurs in a main clause, expressing an attainable wish (BDF [Blass, Debrunner, and Funk, *Grammar*] §§359.2; 385.1)."

1684. Cf. Justin *Dial.* 8, where Justin wishes all to share his devotion to Christ. For Paul wishing all his hearers to be like him, cf. Gal 4:12; for identification with others, see, e.g., Cic. *Quint. fratr.* 1.3.3; *Or. Brut.* 31.110; Pliny *Ep.* 6.30.1; 2 Kgs 3:7; especially in a plea, Suet. *Galba* 20.1. Some (Shiell, *Reading Acts*, 200) suggest that Paul is being wry and humorous here; at the least, he responds to Agrippa's wit with witty banter appropriate to an intellectual, while remaining nonthreatening.

1685. Whether the reference is, indeed, temporal is debated, though the temporal meaning is suitable; see discussion on Acts 26:28.

1686. Malherbe, *Philosophers*, 162.

Although addressing most of the speech to Agrippa, he appeals here not only to Agrippa but to all who hear him (he is called, after all, to everyone, 26:17). When a judge's advisors might influence the outcome of the case, it was natural to appeal to them as well as to the judge (Cic. *Quinct.* 2.1, expressing confidence in them); but while others might comment on Paul's case (cf. Acts 26:30–31), Paul's interest in them is less judicial than evangelistic (cf. "small and great" in 26:22, though most of his hearers here would have been considered "great").

(4) Except for His Chains (26:29)

Paul concludes the comparison with "except for these chains." This is *epidiorthōsis* or *epanorthōsis*, "the correction or improvement of a remark immediately recognized by the speaker as unsuitable."[1687] He wants the hearers to be like him[1688] in following Christ, which he presents as of benefit to them (26:18), but not like him with regard to his chains. Although Paul embraces "Christian" positively rather than as a term of derision, he does not wish the humiliating status of chains on his hearers.[1689]

Because chains are a shame and humiliation in this culture,[1690] failure to qualify his wish that they be like him could risk insulting the dignity of these people of high status.[1691] (For a prisoner to be in bonds could indicate that the outcome of the trial was virtually predetermined,[1692] but they do appear in relatively light custody as well,[1693] as probably here.) Even associates felt considerable social pressure to abandon prisoners,[1694] perhaps even exemplified in Agrippa's reluctance to directly agree with Paul in 26:28. One need not be lame to be a philosopher, a lame philosopher granted (Epict. *Diatr.* 1.8.14).

This concluding exception is not, however, a mere accidental afterthought, for it deliberately highlights some points. It serves various rhetorical functions: it builds rapport with his audience members by showing concern for them; it draws attention to the matter where Paul genuinely experiences shame; and it underlines the pathos of his condition. The pathos function was especially appropriate at the end of a speech,[1695] and Paul, winding down, appears to offer his *peroratio*;[1696] although this might not be Paul's intended *peroratio* within the narrative world, it functions thus at least on the level of Luke's narrative. His chains suited custom; Roman citizens

---

1687. Rowe, "Style," 141 (citing as examples Basil *Hom. Hex.* 9.7.63C; Aug. *Serm.* 339 c. 1); cf. Porter, "Paul and Letters," 581 (on Rom 3:5). For correction as a rhetorical device, see further *Rhet. Her.* 4.26.36; Hermog. *Inv.* 4.12.203–4; also Anderson, *Rhetorical Theory*, 162, 170–71, on metabole in Gal 3:4; 4:9. One could provide for correction deliberately rather than as an afterthought.

1688. This is again a positive projection of *ēthos*; Paul is confident of his moral rectitude.

1689. If he were presumed guilty, his testimony also would not be taken seriously, since many regarded the testimony of certain classes of criminals as invalid (e.g., *b. Sanh.* 26b).

1690. Polyb. 20.10.7–9; 38.17.2; cf. 2 Tim 1:16; Heb 11:36; Rapske, "Prison," 829; for punishment in general, Dio Chrys. *Or.* 76.4. See further comment on Acts 16:39; 22:29. Some (e.g., Ach. Tat. 4.9) also used them for those who were "mad" (Acts 26:24); in Polyb. 32.3.6–8, one so treated (though with the addition of a neck collar) eventually went insane.

1691. Rapske, *Custody*, 309. Chains even functioned as a form of torture; see idem, "Prison," 828, and sources there; comment on Acts 22:29.

1692. Quint. Curt. 6.9.26 (cf. 6.9.25); cf. LCL, 2:84 n. *a* (Rolfe): "Hence not *sine praeiudicio*."

1693. E.g., Jos. *Ant.* 18.233; perhaps Pliny *Ep.* 10.57.2.

1694. Rapske, "Prison," 829 (citing, e.g., Sen. Y. *Ep. Lucil.* 9.9; Philost. *Vit. Apoll.* 4.37; Lucian *Tox.* 18, 28–29).

1695. E.g., Isaeus *Menec.* 44, 47; Cic. *Quinct.* 30.91–31.99; *Rab. Post.* 17.47–48; Quint. *Decl.* 267.12–13; 270.25–29; 291.7–8; 298.16; 315.24–25; 322.31; 328.7; 331.14; 338.3; 339.29–32. Sumney, "Πάθος," 147, notes that despite ancient handbooks placing it especially at the end, pathos could be used anywhere in a speech.

1696. See Witherington, *Acts*, 751. On pathos, see comment on Acts 20:31; it was used anywhere, but especially in the *peroratio*.

could be kept in chains while being tried or being brought to Rome.[1697] But in light of other customs, they could still evoke sympathy. Chains could indicate a more severe detention,[1698] and they were sometimes forgone for higher-status prisoners unlikely to attempt escape (Polyb. 32.3.5). That Paul is still in them (even as late as Acts 28:20)[1699] invites sympathy.[1700] It fits the larger rhetorical implication that he should be freed.

The nature of Paul's chaining was probably that his right wrist was manacled to his guard's left wrist; this practice allowed a (right-handed) guard the advantage in the event of need to use force against or on behalf of a prisoner.[1701] Other chains (both wrists; more severely, legs, neck, or each part of the body) were possible,[1702] but we need not suppose they were used in Paul's case. Sometimes chains even outweighed a prisoner, but more often they were about ten to fifteen pounds of iron.[1703] Those left in chains even overnight in damp prisons would find their chains eventually rusting on their sweaty limbs, providing extreme discomfort; some scholars have even suggested chains' becoming attached to prisoners' limbs.[1704] Again, however, Paul's lighter detention need not presuppose these harsher scenarios.

For Luke's ideal audience, Paul remains the consummate sage. Stoics emphasized the soul over the body and hence the relative unimportance of the body's fettering so long as the soul remained free (Cic. *Fin.* 3.22.75). Indeed, a Roman Stoic points out that exiles and fugitives often become famous, rather than dishonored, by exile (Mus. Ruf. 9, p. 72.12, 18, 20–21). Paul notes his chains but also suggests that his life is otherwise favored in what matters most.

Far from being intimidated by those he addresses, Paul speaks respectfully as a respectable person to other respectable people, people who would not have listened patiently to Christians who were less educated and articulate. And far from being put off by Paul's presumption, members of the elite are apparently sufficiently impressed as to treat him as an honorable person (26:30–32). Luke's audience would also appreciate Paul's forthrightness.[1705]

f. The Verdict (26:30–32)

It is no coincidence or literary error that Luke concludes the defense speeches, and Paul's ministry before the voyage to Rome, with these brief verses. Whatever his judges' opinion of him in other respects (such as "madness" in Acts 26:24), it is the legal verdict that counts most. The defense speeches of Acts 22–26 close with this final relevant verdict:[1706] Paul is not worthy of death or imprisonment. On this com-

---

1697. See Conzelmann, *Acts*, 212 (citing, e.g., the second edict of Augustus from Cyrene); Rapske, *Custody*, 27. Apparently, chaining was employed even for house arrest (Jos. *Ant.* 18.237; Rapske, *Custody*, 31). Those tried for offenses such as treason might "plead their case in chains" (Quint. *Decl.* 303 intro., Bailey, LCL).

1698. See Rapske, *Custody*, 9, 25–26, 28; idem, "Prison," 828; further discussion at Acts 21:33; 22:29.

1699. This apparently remained true historically; given the cultural humiliation associated with them, it is unlikely that later tradition invented them (Eph 4:3; 6:20; 2 Tim 1:16) for his Roman detention (Phil 1:7, 13–17; Phlm 1, 9–10, 13, 23; Eph 3:1; 4:1; Col 4:3, 10, 18; cf. 2 Tim 1:8; 2:9). Luke would hardly retroject this shame for his hero earlier than he believed authentic, in view of his pro-Roman *Tendenz*.

1700. Sufferings (including a person's past life) were often used to generate public sympathy in court (e.g., Pliny *Ep.* 4.9.22).

1701. Rapske, *Custody*, 31.

1702. Ibid., 206–7. For the neck, see, e.g., Quint. Curt. 7.5.36; for the feet, Apul. *Flor.* 17.7.

1703. Rapske, *Custody*, 207.

1704. Ibid., 207–8.

1705. Thus a philosopher could address a tyrant without fear (Apul. *False Preface* 2.106; Diog. Laert. 2.68); see further comment on Acts 4:13. Here Jones, "Holds Power," 168, uses communication theory to identify power positioning and highlights the prisoner Paul's surprising lack of "subservience" to Agrippa the king.

1706. Except the implied favor of Acts 28:31; the verdict of Caesar's own tribunal is not recorded.

mentary's suggested date for Acts, Luke's audience probably knows that Paul faced both, but the most socially qualified voices here deny that he should have faced either.

The combined verdict of Festus, Berenice, and especially Agrippa, who is a representative of Israel acceptable to Rome (and still respected after the Judean war), is that Paul does not deserve death or imprisonment. In an empire where Roman power had executed both Jesus and Paul, the latter after a long imprisonment, this assurance would be important for edification and evangelism as well as for a legal apologetic for Christians that could address apparently negative precedents. (Although governors were not bound by precedents in any case, the state was reluctant to reverse long precedents, conceding long-standing error.) The verdict is climactic, directly before the storm and serpent incidents provide divine verdicts on Paul's behalf.

1. INTRODUCTION

Here, as in 25:14–22, Luke recounts a scene where neither he nor a reliable source was likely present.[1707] Given the letter that must have accompanied Paul to Rome, however (25:26–27), something quite close to the events briefly narrated here is a safe inference. Although the officials recognize that Paul is innocent and are unwilling to hand him over to his accusers, they are also "constrained" by political "realities." Sending Paul to Rome lets them off the hook. Now that they are relieved from the political responsibility, they can freely declare his innocence.[1708]

As Tannehill notes, the chapter (and hearing) that concludes with these verses "presents a climactic summary of Paul's mission as the narrator wants it to be remembered": as a witness, Paul is linked with prophets and sent to Jews and Gentiles alike.[1709] The pronouncement of innocence here fits Luke's public apologetic, climaxing a series of such pronouncements in Paul's ministry and paralleling the declarations of Luke's passion narrative (see Acts 23:29; 25:25; cf. 16:36–39; 28:18; esp. comment at Acts 18:14–15). Pilate likewise pronounced Jesus innocent (Luke 23:4, 14, 22), forced only by political considerations to hand Jesus over (23:20, 23); Herod also found him innocent of the charges against him (23:15).[1710] The centurion at the cross also declared Jesus's innocence (23:47,[1711] probably Luke's application of a more encompassing statement in Mark 15:39), perhaps paralleling Lysias's observation in Acts 23:29.

Luke reports even Jesus's arrest in such a way as to forestall accusations: although the disciples had swords (Luke 22:36), they had them only in order that Jesus could be condemned as a transgressor (22:37). Further, they did not have *many* swords (22:38), and Jesus opposed their use (22:51). In good forensic fashion, Jesus offered a valid countercharge against those who arrested him (22:52–53). The cumulative force of Luke's defense is compelling: Jesus's followers, including those in the Gentile Christian movement, of which the Jewish missionary Paul was the most visible leader, are not seditious and should not be persecuted or repressed.

1707. Poets could act as omniscient narrators with such scenes (e.g., Sil. It. 9.66–177, 340–45), but stricter historians frowned on them when written by laxer historians (Polyb. 2.56.10). Luke offers very few of them (see esp. Acts 25:14–22), but where he does, he fleshes them out no more than most historians did (his expanded portrayal is mostly speech material in 25:14–22 and 26:31–32, which historians could flesh out) and bases them on reasonable inference from his perspective of the events.

1708. Cf. Tannehill, *Acts*, 329. On the principle of avoiding taking responsibility, see Malina, *Windows*, 137.

1709. Tannehill, *Acts*, 329.

1710. Most scholars see the connection (e.g., C. Williams, *Acts*, 266; Johnson, *Acts*, 440; Dunn, *Acts*, 323). The connections between innocence statements for Jesus and Paul were also not lost on earlier interpreters (John Chrysostom in *Cat. Act.* 23.28–30 [Martin, *Acts*, 282]).

1711. Doble, *Paradox*, 93–160, contends that the meaning is "righteous," including in Luke 23:47, rather than (with many scholars; cf. 70–92) "innocent." Although "righteous" does fit Luke's larger usage best, righteousness should, presumably, include the relevant nuance of innocence here.

II. PAUL'S INNOCENCE (26:30–31)

Gentiles conclude that Paul's offense does not merit death or imprisonment; the respected Jewish figure Agrippa, who understands Paul's teaching better than any of the Gentiles present and knows that the Nazarenes are politically innocuous, clinches this recognition by noting (in Acts 26:32) that Paul could have simply been acquitted altogether. Luke's forensic language here is significant: having "practiced nothing worthy of death" is a familiar Lukan apologetic refrain (Luke 23:15, 41; Acts 25:11, 25; elsewhere in the NT only Rom 1:32); Paul had preached only "practicing" works "worthy of" repentance (Acts 26:20).

"King and governor" in 26:30 recalls the opportunity to witness to kings and governors in Luke 21:12–13 (together only here in Luke-Acts, and in the same sequence; elsewhere in the NT, but not in the same sequence, Mark 13:9; Matt 10:18). Presumably, the group conversing in Acts 26:31 includes the members of 26:30, hence the officials of 25:23.[1712] At the very least, they are present and thus party to the conversation, but their input is probably solicited as Festus sought the advice of his *consilium* in 25:12. If for Festus Paul's "much learning" reveals him as a sort of philosopher or sage (see comment on 26:24–25) Festus will view him as politically innocuous.[1713]

Luke was not privy to the conversation among the elite in 26:31–32 (presumably including the entire company mentioned in 26:30),[1714] but he can safely infer from the outcome that Agrippa II did not think Paul guilty.[1715] Had Agrippa sided with the Sanhedrin, Paul might have been handed over to the Sanhedrin, the more politically convenient course. One could instead argue that, given Paul's appeal to Caesar, sending him to Rome was the more expedient course now, in any case, and Paul was not released instead because Agrippa was offended by his attempt to convert him (26:27–29). But Festus's letter, based partly on and undoubtedly explicitly appealing to Agrippa's recommendations, would be public record for Paul's case in Rome, and hence Agrippa's opinions might be safely inferred. Although Luke's scenario seems much more plausible than the opposite inference, what matters most from a literary perspective is the confirmation again of Paul's innocence. As Jesus was twice pronounced innocent by a Roman governor and once by a Herodian prince, so likewise is Paul twice pronounced innocent by a Roman governor and once by a Herodian prince.

III. AGRIPPA'S FINAL WORD (26:32)

Other hearers may have concluded that Paul did nothing worthy of death or imprisonment, and one could well expect Agrippa, a "progressive" Jew unhappy with the divisions in Judaism that would soon lead to war with Rome, to concur. (Indeed, Agrippa would soon have conflict with the new high priest he himself appointed; see Jos. *Ant.* 20.179, 189–96.)[1716] But Agrippa does more than concur; the one hearer who

1712. With Witherington, *Acts*, 752.
1713. Cf. the same principle regarding the Johannine Pilate in Keener, "Truth."
1714. Dicken, *Herod*, 162, argues that since the only chiliarch who features previously in Luke's narrative, Lysias, is favorable toward Paul and helps him (Acts 23:10, 19–31), we should infer the same regarding the composite character of chiliarchs here (25:23).
1715. Luke would need to be fairly certain about this point to include it, since Agrippa II remained alive and influential when (according to the range of dates assigned Acts by the majority of Acts scholars) Luke wrote. Although Luke was not privy to the conversation, Agrippa's support for Paul could, if known to prominent Gentiles from Caesarea (Acts 25:23; 26:30), come up in some conflicts with Caesarean Jewish leaders (who apparently opposed Paul, 25:24, although this could refer hyperbolically to Jerusalemite envoys speaking in Caesarea) in that period of tension. But Luke would no longer be in Caesarea (27:1–2) and hence would not have access to this information unless travelers from the church in Caesarea brought news of the rumor.
1716. See Goodman, *Ruling Class*, 141–42.

understands the arguments among the Jewish sects states openly his opinion that Paul could well have been set free.

(1) Politically Irrevocable Appeal

The complication is that Paul has appealed to Caesar; the pluperfect ἐπεκέκλητο implies that the appeal is now irrevocable. But whereas a governor could not scourge or mistreat a Roman citizen who had appealed, he certainly could acquit one. The impossibility of his doing so here is not legal but political.[1717] Refusing to retract the appeal after the conclusion of Acts 26:32 is a matter of honor and propriety;[1718] Festus has already publicly announced that he is referring the case, and it would dishonor both Festus and the emperor for Festus not to follow through.[1719] To appear to decide a case already appealed to Caesar could seem a usurpation of the emperor's *auctoritas*. If word reached Rome, this could risk hurting a governor's career opportunities.[1720] (This situation did not arise very often in practice, since the appeal usually followed the public verdict; Paul's appeal was unusual, creating an unusual—but for the officials, a politically expedient—situation.) If we wonder why word might reach Rome of Festus's acquitting rather than referring Paul to the emperor, we need think only of Paul's accusers.[1721] The conflict between the former high priest and the governor Cumanus led to the latter's banishment; at some point in time near the events described in these narratives, the conflict between the chief priests and Felix was playing out in Rome. Agrippa could afford to call Paul innocent, but Festus could not afford to simply release him.

Thus, canceling such an appeal could appear to be a usurpation of the prerogatives of Caesar's court and also would put Festus back in the political situation he was in before. To mention the latter is not discreet, and so it is the former that is emphasized; the political constraints of Rome, rather than those of the Sanhedrin, will control the surface direction of the narrative from this point forward. Behind that surface, however, Luke sees not merely false accusations but more fundamentally God's providence, fulfilling the mission that God has already given Paul (19:21; 23:11; cf., later, 27:24), even if, as in the case of Jesus, this mission led to the fulfillment of his passion (Luke 9:51; cf. 9:31).

Luke's point here is not to make Paul's appeal look foolish. Luke's audience already knows that Paul was forced to appeal to avoid being killed (Acts 25:3; cf. 23:30; 28:19), a situation about which Agrippa has no knowledge. Even if Paul eventually dies in Rome, he has gained more years than he would have had if sent to Jerusalem. Luke records the verdict merely to show that all precedents in Paul's case and all verdicts

---

1717. Cf. the irrevocability of royal decrees in Esth 1:19; 8:8; Dan 6:8, 12, 15, 17; many think that these cases refer not to a law (for which we lack significant extrabiblical evidence, e.g., Sprinkle, "Law," 647; we admittedly lack relevant contemporary Persian sources) but to the king's honor (cf., e.g., Walton, Matthews, and Chavalas, *Background Commentary*, 485, 490, 635, 739; *pace*, e.g., Baldwin, *Daniel*, 128).

1718. On the importance of honor (and shame), see, e.g., Hom. *Il.* 5.471–93, 529–32; 8.145–50, 167–71; Isaeus *Cleon.* 39 (§37); Publ. Syr. 211–12; Pliny *Ep.* 3.4.1; 5.11.2; 6.6.4, 9; Suet. *Jul.* 11; 19.2; Arius Did. *Epit.* 2.7.10c, pp. 60–61.19; 2.7.11i, pp. 78–79.25–29; Lucian *Critic* 4; Philost. *Hrk.* 45.8; Hermog. *Issues* 76.5–6; 78.22–79.6; Nicolaus *Progymn.* 7, "On Commonplace," 44; deSilva, "Honor and Shame"; idem, "Wisdom"; idem, "Shame"; Jewett, "Shame"; Delaney, "Seeds," 16; Brandes, "Reflections," 121–23; Barton, *Honor*; idem, "Moment"; Malina and Neyrey, *Portrait*, 176–82. Christian and Islamic tradition have likely reinforced some traditional Mediterranean values on this point (cf. Brandes, "Reflections," 126). It remains important in many cultures and ethical discussions today (e.g., Park, *Hurt to Healing*, 37–44).

1719. Cf. Rapske, *Custody*, 188.

1720. Sherwin-White, *Society*, 65; Hemer, *Acts in History*, 132; D. Williams, *Acts*, 423; Witherington, *Acts*, 752–53; Jeffers, *World*, 169. Offenses that seriously detracted from the emperor's honor were treasonous (Robinson, *Criminal Law*, 77–78).

1721. Perhaps they would not protest (cf. Acts 28:21), but this could not be taken for granted.

from those truly qualified to pronounce them vindicated Paul. If he eventually died in Rome in Nero's persecution, the cause was Nero's well-known depravity (albeit less acknowledged in Greece, possibly Luke's primary target audience), not any deficiency in the persuasiveness of Paul's case.

(2) Usefulness of Agrippa's Opinion

Nevertheless, Agrippa's statement in 26:32, an opinion specifically solicited to help Festus frame Paul's letter of introduction to the imperial court (25:26–27), would undoubtedly become part of the record sent on to Rome.[1722] It was to Festus's advantage to explicitly attribute the opinion to Agrippa, demonstrating that he had done the necessary research by consulting an expert on Judean issues recognized as such by Rome. He could well quote Agrippa and then add something like this: "Here is Agrippa's opinion; it may well be correct, but given the insistence of the leaders of Jerusalem's Sanhedrin, I thought it best not to act without consulting Your Majesty. I have sent the prisoner to you for a decision."

Even under the most favorable of emperors, it was wiser to ask procedural questions than to take matters for granted, if any possibility of later negative evaluations of the judgments was conceivable.[1723] This report would help explain Paul's favorable treatment in 28:16, 30–31.[1724] It would also help explain Luke's ability to infer the essential content of the officials' meeting.[1725]

1722. With Witherington, *Acts*, 753 (following Cassidy, *Society*, 113); D. Williams, *Acts*, 423. For records of decisions of official bodies, see Rüpke, "Commentarii," 628; this occasion may be more informal, but then it must take the place of an official decision in Festus's notes. Normally, the defendant's and accusers' petitions would also be forwarded (Pliny *Ep.* 10.59, though the defendant in this example is not sent); we do not know whether this is the case here (Acts 28:21 addresses synagogues, not Caesar's court).

1723. See, e.g., Pliny *Ep.* 10.96–97, where Trajan basically confirms all of Pliny's judgments. (Pliny, however, may have had the added incentive of seeking to collect as much correspondence with the emperor as possible, which could be subsequently published to his own honor. Cf. similarly Noreña, "Economy," who notes that Pliny's letters honor both himself and Trajan by offering an illusion of closeness that the letters do not, in fact, indicate was possible.)

1724. One could argue the contrary, namely, that after Luke's (convenient) ending, Nero confirms Festus's death sentence (Omerzu, "Fallstudie"), and that Luke is simply careful so as to portray neither Paul nor the Roman administration in a bad light (idem, "Angeklagter," 137). This argument is plausible, but Luke, who does not hesitate to portray Felix's corruption, appears (on my view) more favorable concerning Festus; I believe that the Lukan evidence points more easily to favored treatment reflecting Festus's positive, or at least neutral, appraisal of Paul's honor (see comment on Acts 28:30–31). On my view, Luke does not provide even a semblance of legitimate grounds for Paul's later execution; but of course one could respond plausibly that providing such a semblance would not serve Luke's apologetic purpose. Nero's court could also disregard a positive recommendation (see comment below), but the recommendation would remain in the case records (if not burned in the fire of 64).

1725. Although the declaration fits Luke's purpose, one should not conclude from Paul's later execution that Luke simply invented it. Given what we know of Nero and his persecution of Christians (Tac. *Ann.* 15.44), it is plausible that he disregarded Agrippa's verdict (and also possible that Paul was released and rearrested later). For an example of a fictitious account, see Philost. *Vit. Apoll.* 8.5, where Domitian acquits Apollonius but wishes to detain him further, and so the latter vanishes.

VOYAGE TO ROME (27:1–28:15)

To Paul's recent legal success, Luke now adds divine vindication through storm, shipwreck, and snakebite. Paul's destiny is to testify before Caesar in Rome (19:21; 23:11; 27:24), and nothing will prevent him from fulfilling his calling. On the way, he manages to save many other lives through his obedience and prayer to the true God. Whatever the ultimate outcome of the hearing before Caesar, the hearer of Acts will understand that Paul has been divinely vindicated.

Luke's Gospel arranged probably chronologically disparate material about Jesus's ministry around his final, fateful journey to Jerusalem (Luke 9–19). Paul likewise undertakes many journeys (although their geographic details allow Luke a firmer chronology here than in the Gospel) in Acts 13:4–14:28; 15:36–18:1; 18:18–19:1; 20:1–21:16.[1] But Paul's final voyage in the work is 27:1–28:16, a voyage that not only organizes dramatic elements but is dramatic in its own right.[2] Earlier voyages may foreshadow this one for Luke's audience; everyone knew that storms and shipwrecks were frequent, so Paul might face one sooner or later.[3] The disaster in Acts 27 can serve Luke's apologetic[4] for Paul's Roman mission: Paul would surely have perished before reaching the imperial court had God not planned for him to testify there (23:11; 27:24). Whatever the outcome of Paul's hearing, then, Paul's testimony there was God's will, despite the claims of his critics.[5]

Luke addresses Paul's final voyage in special detail. This section merits such detail for Luke because of the adventure (useful for the same audience to whom the narrative genre appealed), because Luke was present (and hence had access to more detail), and because Paul was finally en route to Rome, the heart of the empire (19:21; cf. 1:8), toward which Acts has been moving for some time (e.g., 2:10; 10:1–2; 13:12; 16:21, 37–38; 18:2–3, 12–17; 19:21). Any ancient auditor embarrassed by Paul's Roman captivity (cf. Eph 3:1, 13; Phil 1:17; 2 Tim 1:8, 12, 16–17) should remember that he was able to reach Rome only by divine care.

The section also further develops Paul's ἦθος. Paul warns (27:9–10); he reassures, having gained God's favor for all (27:21–26); he gives instructions to protect everyone (27:31, 33–35). He also helps others practically (28:3), survives miraculously (28:5–6), and brings healing to the sick (28:8–9). Consequently, his honor keeps growing both within the narrative (27:31–32, 43; 28:10) and for Luke's audience.

---

1. Johnson, *Acts*, 10.

2. Others note this chapter's role as a literary climax, including in its depiction of Paul (Börstinghaus, *Sturmfahrt*).

3. It might also not be coincidence that Paul chose passage on his earlier voyages, whereas here his participation is at others' discretion. But in contrast to Greek tales of heroes who avoided doomed voyages, Luke never emphasizes Paul's earlier prophetic avoidance of shipwrecks. (Such a portrayal would not have fit well the widely traveled historical Paul; 2 Cor 11:25.)

4. More generally, cf. Salmeier, *Restoring*, 187: "Even a shipwreck has its necessity (27:26) since God uses it to demonstrate the divine protection under which Paul exists."

5. See discussion in Keener, *Acts*, 1:445–47; idem, "Apologetic."

1. Introduction

Various issues in this narrative invite introductory treatment. Of these, particularly important is a comparison with other sea voyage narratives, with a bearing on Luke's literary models and perhaps a discussion of the narrative's historical substance. We must also survey the account's function for Luke and the paradigm it could offer for his audience.[6]

a. Sea Travel Narratives

Literary artfulness and historical tradition are by no means incompatible; historians who also proved adept at recounting their stories were not for that reason any less historians. F. F. Bruce long ago argued that Luke drew on the literary tradition of storms and shipwrecks established as early (in extant sources) as the *Odyssey*, while noting that this observation did not detract from the historical substance of Luke's report.[7] This compatibility has, however, been debated, and it will be explored more fully below.

i. Various Genres

Scholars have traced the development of various kinds of sea travel narratives, which appear in a variety of genres. In one form of travel narrative, early Greek ethnographers used sea travels to frame their accounts of different peoples encountered on such voyages; these evolved into *periploi*, a genre describing lands from the standpoint of ships voyaging along their coasts.[8] Such accounts were distinct from historical descriptions (e.g., Arrian *Ind.* 18–42), myths (Dion. Hal. *Ant. rom.* 1.49–53), epics (Hom. *Od.* 9–12), and novels (Lucian *True Story*).[9] Luke's interests are not, of course, geographic (although his geography proves accurate),[10] nor does he write of ancient myths or compose novels for entertainment. Certainly one cannot simply identify a single Hellenistic "sea-voyage genre."[11]

Susan Marie Praeder notes that most ancient travelogues are longer than Acts 27–28.[12] Although most *periploi* focused on coastal geography, quite unlike Luke,[13]

6. For one concise bibliography of relevant sources on Acts 27, see Jervell, *Apostelgeschichte*, 602.

7. Bruce, *Commentary*, 498; idem, *Acts¹*, 450. MacDonald, "Shipwrecks," finds Homer's *Odyssey* the sole model (esp. *Od.* 5, 12), which he thinks Luke christianizes. Direct dependence on Homeric language or even allusions is not impossible, but it cannot be exclusive (see Talbert, *Acts*, 213). Although Luke's ideal reader may be familiar with the *Odyssey*, we know from many quotations in Luke-Acts that he expects familiarity with the LXX as a more primary subtext and hence would expect familiarity with, e.g., Jonah. Herodotus imitates Homer's style (see Woodman, *Rhetoric*, 1–3); we need not for this reason doubt the historical genre of Herodotus's work, though what this meant in his day differs from what historiography became (Woodman might go too far in his skepticism on account of the imitation [4–5]). For the *Odyssey*'s influence on early Roman historiography, see discussion in Leigh, "Early Roman Epic." Naturally, novels also appropriated Homeric literary conventions (cf. Telò, "Gaze").

8. Koester, *Introduction*, 1:114. See more extensively Davis, "Navigation," 161–75 (a work brought to my attention by Mark Wilson).

9. Aune, *Environment*, 123. Cf. Davis, "Navigation," 162: "Nearly all of the extant versions are prose works devoid of literary pretensions, although many go beyond the formula and insert historical, mythological or paradoxographical vignettes."

10. *Periploi* normally required "impersonal style" and "interest in coastal peoples, places, and imports and exports," unlike Acts (Praeder, "Acts 27:1–28:16," 687).

11. *Pace* Robbins, "Land and Sea." Cf. Haenchen, *Acts*, 710, who doubts a "standard account of sea voyages" in antiquity, noting that shipwrecks in novels are samples among countless other adventures and that such travel reports do not always lead to catastrophe.

12. Praeder, "Acts 27:1–28:16," 687, noting that sea itineraries could be short (e.g., Hom. *Od.* 9.82–84), only a little longer (Virg. *Aen.* 3.266–77), or much longer but travelogues were longer.

13. Praeder, "Acts 27:1–28:16," 687.

travelogues do appear in a range of genres: Cic. *Fam.* 16.9.2 is similar in length and interests to Acts' account; other accounts appear in "poems, factual itineraries and fictional, fantastic adventures. . . . Thus the fact that Acts 27:1–8 and 28:11–16 are travelogues is no guarantee of their literary genre, reliability or unreliability."[14]

Although sea storms and shipwrecks appear in a wide variety of genres, many scholars have identified them as constituting a literary type scene with its own set conventions; that is, in whatever genre one was writing, certain details would normally be emphasized in such scenes.[15] As Praeder points out, "By the first century A.D. storm scenes were part of literary tradition and part of rhetorical training."[16] Naturally, some such details were necessary simply to address the very situations involved in confronting storms or shipwrecks,[17] and so we will need to evaluate the reported conventions more closely to see which are genuinely significant as conventions. Some later writers used Homer's sea storms (*Od.* 5.291–473; 12.402–25) as models for their own narratives, including Virg. *Aen.* 1.34–179 (which became the Roman model).[18] Such literary models affected "everything from navigators' notes to pure fiction."[19]

Scholars emphasizing parallels with fictitious storms often neglect contrasts, such as "stylized descriptions of waves piling up like mountains, the battle of opposing winds, thunder and lightning," and the like.[20] Luke employs a broad nautical vocabulary (such as his term for "ship" in 27:41; though cf. 1 Kgs 9:26–27; 10:11, 22; 2 Chr 9:21; Prov 30:19; 31:14; Wis 5:10; 4 Macc 7:1; twenty-seven times in Josephus) to exhibit his rhetorical skill, and it is plausible that he may have derived some of his vocabulary from Greek literary tradition as well as sailing. Nevertheless, the narrative employs nautical language in the correct ways.[21]

II. Exploiting Literary Conventions

Some scholars are convinced, however, that Paul's sea voyage depicted by Luke must be fictitious. Certainly, literary comparisons with novels are appropriate. Similar storm scenes appear in novels,[22] often conjoined with shipwrecks.[23] Storms and shipwrecks indeed appeared so often in novels that satirists ridiculed[24] or parodied[25] the literary conventions. Pervo rightly points out that Luke contributes to a vast ancient

14. Ibid., 688. Cicero also summarizes his recent travels, including contrary winds, elsewhere (*Att.* 5.12–13).

15. For parallels with other sea voyages, including suspense-building, see esp. Praeder, "Acts 27:1–28:16."

16. Ibid., 693. Cf. similarly battle scenes; reflecting a common rhetorical curriculum, they were similar in most ancient historians, but of course ancient battles did have similar characteristics (Laistner, *Historians*, 57, 95), and some historians (such as Thucydides, vs. Livy, on the siege of Syracuse; Caesar, vs. average historians; and sometimes Sallust) could get even military details quite accurate (ibid., 58).

17. With, e.g., Porter, "'We' Passages," 552; Schnabel, "Reading Acts," 254.

18. Aune, *Environment*, 129 (citing Livy 21.58.3–11; Sen. Y. *Ag.* 465–578; Lucan *C.W.* 4.48–120). Some overemphasize Virgil allusions here (e.g., Shea, "Pieces of Epic"), although comparisons are instructive. Reardon, "Homing to Rome," compares the emphasis on a voyage to Rome in both Virgil and Acts. But by this period, there was a sense in which all roads did lead to Rome (Ramsay, "Roads and Travel," 376)—particularly for prisoners sent there for trial.

19. Pervo, *Profit*, 51, rightly.

20. Schnabel, "Reading Acts," 254, following Reiser, "Charakter," 53, and citing Petron. *Sat.* 114.1–3; Ach. Tat. 3.2.2; 3.2.8.

21. On this last point, see Schnabel, "Reading Acts," 254, also noting (with qualification) Kratz, *Rettungswunder*, 336–37.

22. Aune, *Environment*, 129 (citing Char. *Chaer.* 3.3.10–18; Xen. Eph. *Anthia* 3.2.11–15; Heliod. *Eth.* 1.22.3–5; Ach. Tat. 3.1–5 [see esp. 3.2]).

23. Johnson, *Acts*, 451, compares later *Ps.-Clem. Hom.* 12.9.3–12.10.4. See also, e.g., *Apoll. K. Tyre* 11 (with a description pieced together from Virgil and elsewhere); Xen. Eph. *Anthia* 3.4, 12 (in contrast to Luke, *most* of Xenophon's ships are wrecked!); the hypothetical setting in Sen. E. *Controv.* 8.6.

24. Johnson, *Acts*, 451, cites Juv. *Sat.* 12.17–82; Lucian *Posts* 1–2.

25. Johnson, *Acts*, 451, cites Lucian *True Story* 1.6.

literature on nautical adventures and that Luke intended his work to be enjoyed.[26] But as noted in this commentary's introduction, historians sought their readers' enjoyment in addition to their instruction (unenjoyable works were hardly marketable in the patron-centered world of ancient "publishing"). Historians used the same narrative techniques as fiction,[27] and as Loveday Alexander notes, "romance does not have a monopoly on voyage-narratives."[28] After all, voyages, storms, and even shipwrecks happened in the real world.

"Historians had no need to liven up their material with a shipwreck," Pervo protests, "but composers of fiction did, often enough to inspire parodies."[29] Yet historians and biographers do include shipwrecks and storms when available and relevant,[30] especially if they were themselves present (cf. 2 Cor 11:25).[31] Admittedly, they rarely develop scenes of storms at length, but neither did most novels,[32] despite the literary interest, and some historical writers did provide more detail than others. It is noteworthy that, for example, a second-century C.E. sophist depicts a genuine sea storm with language borrowed from the *Odyssey*.[33] "Thus," Aune notes, "ancients could conceptualize real experiences with traditional literary *topoi*."[34] Luke could evoke ancient adventure scenes, but his story takes place in the real first-century world of Paul, under real storm conditions, without sirens, clashing rocks, and the like from the mythical past.[35] Writers also employed accounts of real storms at sea for moralistic purposes[36]—for example, to address the behavior of philosophers.[37]

Others note a source with which Luke's audience would be familiar from readings of the prophets—namely, Jonah.[38] For readers in the Aegean, stories of shipwrecks would be familiar even apart from older literary traditions. Nevertheless, such

26. Pervo, *Story*, 91. We may note that some seafarers invented fictitious stories about these perils themselves (Lucian *Posts* 1–2), but because such perils did occur (commonly enough for those who sailed often, 2 Cor 11:25). Pervo, *Acts*, 645, finds parallels between Acts 27 and novels (noting others, including Pokorny, "Romfahrt"; Weiser, *Apostelgeschichte*, 2:659); for a literary but not historical shipwreck, see also Seul, *Rettung*.

27. See, e.g., Keener, *Acts*, 1:53–54, 63, 66–67, 70–72, 81, 125n72, 131–33, 146, 160; cf. 119, 126, 134n162, 148, 264, 279; here, also Johnson, *Acts*, 457.

28. Alexander, *Context*, 85. So also Marguerat, *Histoire*, 368; idem, *Historian*, 256, noting various genres and preferring especially exploration narratives and narratives about the settlement of colonies.

29. Pervo, *Profit*, 51. More recently, Pervo has clarified his argument, recognizing that Acts is a work of ancient historiography (*Acts*, 15) but arguing that popular genres, including popular historiography, could include elements that we would call fictitious. Certainly no one will disagree that at many points ancient historians employed standards different from those observed in the guild today. Comparisons with novels are, moreover, helpful. But these comparisons are most fruitfully undertaken alongside fuller attention to ancient historical works, an endeavor not as fully developed by Pervo (as even a survey of his commentary's index of ancient sources will reveal), despite his noteworthy contributions in many other areas; see Keener, "Review of Pervo."

30. E.g., Suet. *Jul.* 25.2; *Claud.* 17.2; see further comment below.

31. E.g., Jos. *Life* 14–15; Lucian *Peregr.* 43 (a storm); Dio Chrys. *Or.* 7.1–2 (a shipwreck, *if* we accept his claim that the story is authentic [though undoubtedly adapted]; he reports that these were common, 7.6, 51–52, 55). See further comment and sources below.

32. Praeder, "Acts 27:1–28:16," 694–95.

33. Aune, *Environment*, 129, citing Ael. Arist. *Or.* 48.65–68.

34. Aune, *Environment*, 129.

35. Of course, novels set in the real world also lacked these, but Luke's voyage approximates known weather conditions at various locations (see discussion ad loc. below) in ways that novels would not care to research, if the novelists could even collect such information (certainly not by voyaging under such conditions!).

36. Johnson, *Acts*, 451, cites, for the fidelity of friendship, Lucian *Tox.* 19–20; for the efficacy of prayer, *y. Ber.* 9:1.

37. Johnson, *Acts*, 451, cites Diog. Laert. 2.71; also a novelistic adaptation of this pattern in Lucian *Peregr.* 43–44. See further comment on Acts 27:21–26, with citations from a range of genres.

38. Noted, e.g., by Bruce, *Commentary*, 498; idem, *Acts¹*, 451; also Pervo, *Acts*, 645 (who, like Bruce, also notes the *Odyssey*); extensive discussion in Börstinghaus, *Sturmfahrt*, 183–209 (also noting Ps 107, pp.

traditions would affect the elements that one emphasized and how one described them. Some scholars have suggested Jonah typology here; it is not very prominent, but one might be able to construct the climax of a very minor Jonah subtext in Luke-Acts. The Ninevites repented at Jonah's preaching (Luke 11:29–30, 32) and would condemn Israel (11:32); the gospel will be received in Rome even if Paul's Jewish audience proves ambivalent (Acts 28:23–28, esp. 28:28). Jonah's westward travel in a ship led to the conversion of his fellow travelers, though in the prophetic book it was because of Jonah's judgment for disobedience (a stark contrast with Paul's obedience here). This allusion has a more explicit basis in the text of Luke-Acts (in Luke 11) than allusion to the *Odyssey* does, though it cannot supply all the details.[39]

If there is a Jonah allusion here, it could belong to a larger subtext in this chapter:

Jonah	Paul
Jonah went west (to Tarshish; Jonah 1:3)	Paul went west to Rome
Wind and storm; ship about to break up (1:4)	Similarly; cf. Acts 27:41
Sailors were afraid, cried out to gods, threw cargo into the sea to lighten the ship (1:5)	They threw out the cargo to lighten the ship (27:18, 38)
Meanwhile Jonah slept (1:5)	If any connection at all, perhaps Paul prayed instead of slept (27:23; but this is at most implicit; cf. Luke 8:23–24)*
Jonah is exhorted to call on his God to bring deliverance (1:6) but is not reported to have done so	Paul apparently prayed, as noted above (probably implied in Acts 27:23–24, but Luke does not make this explicit)
Jonah was the cause of the storm (1:7–10, 12, 14–15)	Paul was the cause of the rescue (27:24)

*Jesus's sleep in Luke 8 is probably not relevant here; Luke does little with Jonah allusions beyond some basic elements, explicitly applying the Jonah analogy only to Jesus (11:29–32; following Q, Matt 12:39–41).

Overall, the parallels are not very compelling if we are trying to demonstrate Jonah as the narrative's single literary grid, since many of the parallels fit sea scenes in general. Certainly, key elements of Jonah's narrative, such as ingestion by a hefty marine organism, do not recur. There may be some value, however, especially in contrasts, so long as we do not make literary imitation of Jonah Luke's primary purpose.

III. GENUINE SHIPWRECKS

Both histories[40] and biographies[41] included an abundance of sea storms and shipwrecks, attesting that seafarers commonly faced them.[42] Some scholars suggest that one-fifth of travelers by sea could expect serious danger on their voyages.[43] Paul was not the only frequent sea voyager to experience or be involved in multiple storms or

209–24; Ezek 27, on 224–28; and extrabiblical sources). Jonah was one of the most popular figures in later Christian art, though especially because of the comparison with Jesus (see discussion in Ferguson, "Jonah").

39. The predication of aspects of the brief Jonah story on the more adventuresome Greek Argonautica (Hamel, "Argo to Nineveh") is chronologically problematic, and sea-travel lore was widespread.

40. Johnson, *Acts*, 451, cites Thucyd. 2.6.26; 6.20.104; 8.24.31, 34; Hdt. 3.138; 7.188; Talbert, *Acts*, 212, cites Tac. *Ann.* 2.23–24. See also Vell. Paterc. 1.1.2 (albeit legendary); 2.79.3–4; Jos. *War* 3.425, 530; Tac. *Ann.* 15.18 (two hundred ships destroyed by a storm in the harbor), 46.

41. Johnson, *Acts*, 451, cites Jos. *Life* 15; Diog. Laert. 7.3; Ael. Arist. *Sacr.* 2.11–12, 65–67; 4.35–37. See also Suet. *Jul.* 25.2; *Claud.* 17.2; *Nero* 40.3. A liar's appeal to the dangers of the sea, however, can sound implausible (Jos. *Ant.* 17.335).

42. Finding parallels in accounts of genuine sea voyages, see also Schnabel, "Reading Acts," 254–55, who notes the fuller argument in Reiser, "Charakter," 53–61, and Lucian *Navigium* 7–9; Ael. Arist. *Sacred Tales* 2.65–68; 4.32–36; Arrian *Peripl.* 4.1–5.2; and esp. Plutarch *Dion* 25.1–5.

43. Toner, *Culture*, 48. Not all will accept Toner's basis in extrapolations from oracular responses, but these at least inform us that dangers were encountered often.

shipwrecks (2 Cor 11:25). For example, Octavian suffered shipwreck with the army at a young age (Suet. *Aug.* 8.1); a different storm later destroyed his fleets (16.2); still later, he ran into two more storms, losing more ships (17.3). Some people drowned at sea.[44] Lucian notes that the huge ship *Isis* had already nearly been wrecked by a storm on that voyage (*Ship* 7).

Sailors were also known for courage because they faced potential death for their work;[45] even if sailing could yield more income than small farming, many regarded it as far more dangerous.[46] Who would happily undertake a sea voyage, one Jewish writer asks, without confidence that they "can reach a harbor?" (*2 Bar.* 22:3). Asked what kind of boat was safest, one critic replied, "Those which are safely moored."[47] Marine archaeology attests that shipwrecks were frequent. "Over 1,000 ancient shipwreck sites are known from the Mediterranean," and more are likely to turn up.[48] That Paul himself, before his Roman custody, already wrote of being shipwrecked three times is not very surprising, given the frequency of his travel.[49]

Historians used the same stereotypical literary motifs as novelists when depicting sea storms and shipwrecks, precisely because Greeks often undertook sea voyages, faced storms, and suffered shipwrecks.[50] At the same time, Praeder argues, "contrary to an often repeated opinion, storm scenes are not all that characteristic of ancient novels. Nor are the storm and shipwreck in Acts 27:9–28:10 that much like the storm and shipwrecks in ancient novels."[51] The only two *lengthy* storms and shipwrecks in novels (in Petronius and Achilles Tatius) reveal more about the authors' rhetorical training than about a novelistic literary tradition.[52]

Further, the parallels with other examples of the genre are often exaggerated. Whereas 27:9–12 may follow literary models for storms, it appears that 27:13–20 does not do so.[53] Despite "traces of literary tradition and rhetorical training" in 27:13–20, Praeder points out, "it is not a storm scene in the epic style. It omits a number of the characteristic elements of storm scenes in that style, e.g., the release and the riot of storm winds, thunder and lightning, swelling of waves to the sky, sinking of waves to the depths of the sea, and the surrender of the pilot to the winds and the waves."[54] Although many of Luke's descriptions reflect familiarity with elements conventional

44. E.g., Suet. *Terence* 5 (one report); *Jul.* 89; *Aug.* 27.4; Philost. *Vit. soph.* 1.10.494 (Protagoras). This happens in modern times in this region as well (e.g., Cavarnos, *St. Methodia*, 61).

45. Alciph. *Fish.* 3 (Glaucus to Galateia), 1.3, esp. ¶3. For fatal sea storms, see also, e.g., Philost. *Hrk.* 31.6; various dangers, Libanius *Thesis* 1.28; *Anecdote* 3.25; *Comparison* 4.12–13; *Narration* 13.

46. Aelian *Farmers* 18 (Demylus to Blepsias); Libanius *Comparison* 4.1, 3; for the risks of seeking profit by sea trade, see also Sen. Y. *Nat. Q.* 4A.pref. 7. Some conceded the danger but argued that it was worth the risk (Libanius *Thesis* 3.7).

47. Athenaeus *Deipn.* 8.350b (trans. C. B. Gulick, LCL, 4:85); cf. preference for remaining on land in Eurip. *Philoctetes* frg. 789a (= 793 N).

48. Parker, "Shipwrecks"; cf. Konen, "Shipwrecks." Shipwrecks were common enough for shipwreck epitaphs to constitute a specific category of epigrams (see Di Nino, "Posidippus' Shipwrecks").

49. Also observed by Ambrosiaster *Commentary on Paul's Epistles* (Vogels, 293; Bray, *Corinthians*, 298).

50. Johnson, *Acts*, 450, noting that Luke includes but compresses these motifs. On the danger of storms at sea, see, e.g., Ovid *Metam.* 11.474–569 (ending in one's death); Sen. Y. *Ep. Lucil.* 53.1–5; Philost. *Hrk.* 1.2; for the difficulties of sea travel, e.g., Sen. Y. *Ep. Lucil.* 57.1; and its dangers in 2 Cor 11:25–26; hypothetical shipwrecks in declamations, e.g., Quint. *Decl.* 259 intro.; 259.8.

51. Praeder, "Acts 27:1–28:16," 694. Cf. also Peterson, *Acts*, 686.

52. Praeder, "Acts 27:1–28:16," 694–95.

53. Ibid., 693.

54. Ibid., 694 (with many examples of each of these elements). Praeder thinks that Luke composed with literary models in mind and possibly some tradition but that he does not follow "the epic model for storm scenes" (694). She thinks that Luke's rhetorical training helps him fill in here, as in the speeches (695). Elements such as lightning were known to occur during some sea storms (Libanius *Anecdote* 3.25).

in literary descriptions of storms, Luke does not simply adopt formulas or strive for a standard literary effect.[55]

Certainly novels emphasized heroes and heroines surviving various perils, including shipwreck,[56] but Paul's letters depict him surviving far more perils, including shipwrecks, than Luke does. (Luke omits the night and day in the sea of 2 Cor 11:25, preferring to narrate in more detail "we" material. On my view, this is both because the chronological placement of the storm in Acts 27 fits Luke's narrative purposes and because he was present to experience the details firsthand, thereby etching them well in his memory.)

A key element of most ancient novels (the heroine or other romantic partners) is also missing; even later apocryphal acts that imitated our canonical Acts sometimes included a (celibate) heroine (e.g., Thecla). The nautical portion of novels nearly always included pirates, but Luke omits these; if one argues that Rome had mainly suppressed pirates by Luke's day, the same was true for the days of the extant novelists, nearly all of whom wrote after he did. Had Luke been writing pure fiction, would he not have followed through more thoroughly on his parallels with Jesus and simply had Paul still the storm (Luke 8:24–25) instead of enduring it?[57] (It is even possible to construe 8:25 as Jesus expecting his disciples to be able to still storms, though it appears more likely that he simply expected them to trust that the boat would not sink with him in it and leave his mission unfulfilled. Paul does match up to Jesus's storm-stilling standard [Acts 27:24].)

Luke does not narrate Paul's earlier shipwrecks (2 Cor 11:25), and he does not mind recounting voyages concisely without such adventure (e.g., Acts 16:11–12; 20:14–15; 21:1–2). Why would he invent a shipwreck here? His audience might already know that the narrator accompanied Paul to Rome, but there was no need to enliven this particular voyage when other scenes (healings in Malta or difficulties in Rome) could have commanded more attention.[58]

Whereas a storyteller (for example, a composer of one of the later apocryphal gospels and acts) added supernatural and hagiographic elements, Luke includes nothing distinctively supernatural except an angelic communication (narrated only by Paul, 27:23–26), and Paul offers only what could be construed as sensible advice (27:10, 31) rather than any explicit prophecy apart from that angelic communication.[59] Luke is more interested in Paul's character (as in historically genuine accounts of philosophers during sea storms) and in the obstacles that God surmounts so that Paul can safely reach Caesar's court.[60] An ancient skeptic could have cited the storm and the ship's consequent destruction to challenge Paul's virtue (contrasting the survival of Jonah's ship and especially the boat of Jesus's disciples), but Luke, who does not invent a miracle to save the ship, nevertheless argues for an opposite reading of the event he witnessed.

55. See Witherington, *Acts*, 764–65 (following Praeder, "Acts 27:1–28:16," 689).

56. Cf. the same theme in a mosaic in Whitehouse, "Shipwreck on Nile."

57. Cf. Johnson, *Acts*, 457 (though his added point that the details are not necessary for the parallels is easily answered whether the narrative is novelistic or historical).

58. Of course, apart from the storm, the entire stay in Malta (including details such as Luke's naming of Publius) might be presumed fictitious, but the same sort of skepticism with regard to other ancient historical works would leave little of ancient history accessible (especially since this section purports to derive from an eyewitness himself).

59. See Dunn, *Acts*, 335.

60. Cf. ot patriarchal narratives, regarded by most early Jews and Christians as historical; in these God surmounted obstacles to his promise of seed, such as repeated challenges to the matriarchs' chastity (Gen 12:15–20; 20:2–18; 26:7–11) or their infertility (21:7; 25:21; 30:22) and also the patriarchs' and matriarchs' putative ages (17:17; 21:5; less difficult, cf. 25:20, 26).

IV. FIRST-PERSON NARRATION

If it is asked why this scene is more detailed than other voyages even in Luke's "we" material,[61] one answer seems obvious enough (in addition to this voyage to Rome climaxing Paul's travels): a suspense-filled storm and shipwreck (which also serve Luke's moralistic and apologetic purposes) are much more interesting, and offer much more detail worth reporting, than would elaborating further on the various ports into which his ship put. This is the deadliest sea storm Paul has faced where Luke is an eyewitness; it makes a good story, and Luke knows the details. Attention to storms and shipwrecks in novels and other narratives reveals that this was a favorite interest for ancient readers, and this would invite Luke's focus.[62] What storyteller even today, who is writing a genuine account and has had an eyewitness experience of such drama, would omit it from the story?[63]

Luke's details here, absent at some other points in his narrative, support the suggestion of historical memories. Dunn emphasizes the names of the centurion, the cohort, and Paul's associates (27:1–2); the details of his itinerary, "including lesser known place names like Cnidus, Salmone and Cauda" (27:7, 16); nautical terminology and the name of the wind (27:14), easily derived from sailors aboard; and the numbers (27:37).[64] These details are not only specific but, wherever we can test them (especially regarding weather conditions, locations, distances, and other information gathered from sailors on such a voyage), accurate.[65] The classicist Arthur Darby Nock, responding to Dibelius's protest that 27:11 reflects naiveté, indicates, "Personally, I regard this as an authentic transcript of the recollections of an eyewitness, with the confusion and coloring which so easily attach themselves to recollections."[66]

Greek historians valued authorial participation in at least some of the events reported; by giving such detail, Luke can substantiate his claim to have participated and been close enough to Paul to write the work.[67] Historians, like other narrators, also valued painting scenes carefully;[68] Luke is less rhetorical and less interested in developing scenes than higher-class writers,[69] but he can do so here where the details underline the dramatic character of his story.[70] Moreover, it builds suspense here: will Paul reach Rome to fulfill his calling? Paul, at least, is certain.

61. Johnson, *Acts*, 456 (though he rejects [457] skepticism about its core). Again, histories did not flesh out most storm scenes to this extent, but neither did most novels. But eyewitness material was often more detailed.
62. See, e.g., Gaventa, *Acts*, 349.
63. E.g., when retelling my wife's or my stories (as in one forthcoming book), I often prefer to focus on the true adventures of chief interest to our audience, even though some less exciting elements of the story are naturally of greater personal importance to my wife and myself.
64. Dunn, *Acts*, 335; cf. idem, *Beginning*, 998. For nautical terminology, see, e.g., Robertson, *Luke*, 206ff., though a study of these terms in the *TLG* today would undoubtedly change commentators' understanding of numerous details. Moreover, whereas most elements of Acts 21–28 relate directly to the rejection in Jerusalem that impels Paul to Rome, this voyage reports details that could have been used elsewhere in the book if their sole purpose was dramatic effect.
65. Hemer, *Acts in History*, 329. On Luke's details and their correspondence with extrinsic sources, see esp. and more recently Reynier, *Recherches*, an important work (also noting the emphasis that Acts' structure gives to this final voyage).
66. Nock, *Essays*, 823 (citing also several Acts scholars agreeing with his position).
67. Witherington, *Acts*, 755–56, emphasizing Hellenistic αὐτοψία. Luke could offer this only toward the end of his work, where he participated and can compensate for the less detailed descriptions of earlier parts of the book (ibid., 756).
68. Cf., e.g., Dion. Hal. *Lysias* 7; Fronto *Ad Ant. imp.* 2.6.4–15 (on Sallust).
69. With Witherington, *Acts*, 757, Luke keeps the story "germane to the plot"—namely, the gospel's progress from Jerusalem to Rome—while holding the reader's interest along the way.
70. Cf., e.g., the attention to details in Gen 22:1–19 (in contrast with the summary action of much of the surrounding narrative), meant to heighten pathos.

A few scholars, however—most notably the skilled and thorough sociorhetorical critic Vernon Robbins—have proposed that Luke's "we," far from a mark of historical authenticity, was a generic convention common to ancient sea voyages.[71] Despite Robbins's brilliance and command of ancient sources, this claim has been widely (although not universally) criticized.[72] (See at length the comment on and excursus at Acts 16:10, which treats most fully the "we" narratives in general.)[73] As noted above, sea voyages appear in a variety of genres, but even if we substitute "type scene" for "genre," Robbins's claim remains problematic. Others have argued that many of Robbins's sources do not support his case, and that he omits many that would challenge his case. Thus his many parallels are not representative of the larger evidence and hence are "highly selective."[74] As one scholar complains regarding his parallels from novels, "not one of the sources he cites has all of the features that Acts does, so his model of the shipwreck is clearly his own reconstruction of this type, not one found in the ancients in the kind of detail that he claims."[75]

Robbins has responded to many of the criticisms raised against his argument.[76] He points out, for example, that his argument was always that we-narratives begin on the sea, not that all sea voyages are we-narratives.[77] One cannot then count sea-voyage narratives without the first person plural against the use of a "we" convention in some sea voyages. A remaining problem, however, is that "we" can appear in both Acts and other ancient literature both on sea and on land. Luke's sea voyages do not all include "we," nor is "we" limited to sea voyages[78] (see fuller discussion at 16:10). Robbins questions whether travel on land genuinely disqualifies the cases in Acts as sea voyages, since these travels began at sea.[79] Given the limited material available to us in Acts, however, this distinction seems too fine. Most journeys of significant length in the Mediterranean world were more easily undertaken by sea, and a genuine traveling companion mentioning his presence without highlighting his action would naturally surface especially in travel narratives.

What is most significant for understanding Acts, however (even if not the center of Robbins's argument), is that first-person narration for sea voyages does not occur in novels any more than in historical works.[80] Robbins's most reasonable example, some argue, is from Josephus's *Life* (14–16), but this is "an acknowledged historical account."[81] Ancient parallels do not support the idea of first-person narration being

71. Robbins, "We-Passages and Sea Voyages"; idem, "Land and Sea." Worse, MacDonald, "Shipwrecks," thinks that Luke uses the third person to indicate the real world and the first to narrate folktales. Cf. discussion of various positions in Seul, *Rettung*, 340–46 (addressing arguments for "we" as indicating a written source), 347–48 (arguments treating the voyage reports as integral parts of the itinerary), 349–51 (treating the historical reliability of the voyage reports); he concludes that Luke himself inserted the "we" (527).

72. E.g., Praeder, "First Person Narration," 210–14; Rapske, "Travel and Trade," 1249; Hemer, "First Person Narrative"; idem, *Acts in History*, 317–19; Witherington, *Acts*, 640–41; Porter, *Paul in Acts*, 20–24. Robbins does note, however, supporters (Robbins, *Beyond*, 83–84) and cites Eduard Norden's work before his own (64).

73. Keener, *Acts*, 3:2350–74.

74. Porter, "'We' Passages," 554.

75. Ibid., 552.

76. See esp. Robbins, *Beyond*, 82–113.

77. Ibid., 84–85.

78. See, e.g., Praeder, "First Person Narration," 216.

79. Robbins, *Beyond*, 104.

80. Ibid. Plümacher, *Geschichte*, 85–108, notes that Luke's use of "we" would appeal to historians' valuing direct knowledge (with sea voyages being important for this).

81. Porter, "'We' Passages," 557. Gnuse, "*Vita apologetica*," rightly notes that *Life* is an apologetic biography, resembling Luke's portrayal of Paul. But within this genre, Josephus normally exploits and adapts experiences that he did have instead of fabricating them.

used to falsely imply companionship with a narrative's protagonist;[82] it was characteristic specifically neither of ancient history writing nor of sea voyages.[83] Cicero includes "we" in a sea-travel narrative that is inescapably autobiographic (*Fam.* 16.9.1–2).

It seems far more likely that "we" means what it normally does in a historical document—namely, that the author was present.[84] It is natural, when one has boarded a ship, to speak of "we" when something is experienced by all who are aboard;[85] often "we" appears in sea voyages "because they recall personal experience."[86] As F. C. Burkitt expressed it about a century ago, "The voyage of Paul, with the shipwreck, reads like what no doubt it really is, an account written by an eye-witness."[87]

Since nearly all scholars agree that Paul went to Rome and since it is far likelier that he sailed there than that he traveled by land, a sea voyage by Paul to Rome at this point seems historically secure. Because the features of the voyage during a storm fit nautical evidence too well to be pure imagination apart from a genuine voyage, these features of the voyage also appear historical. There seems little remaining for more skeptical scholars to challenge—except to argue that Luke has conflated Paul's voyage with a separate shipwreck account that came into his possession, which also followed the same Rome-ward course and hence appeared useful for his story.

v. A Real Storm without Paul?

Knowing that Paul earlier faced other shipwrecks (2 Cor 11:25), it is not impossible that Luke could have saved narrating one for here and then created the story's details here based on someone else's Rome-ward voyage. The minimalist methodology this approach assumes is not, however, the best way to reconstruct historical probabilities. If one can accept only those claims in antiquity for which external evidence remains, we would need to dismiss most claims based on the remaining silence. But is this the likeliest way to treat a first- or even second-generation source that fits a historical genre and is independently confirmed by external evidence as often as Luke is? A source that can often be corroborated is itself evidence for an ancient event, although the evidence is not as strong as it would be if corroborated by other independent sources.[88]

Scholars often point back to the research of a Mediterranean mariner using an older sort of craft, whose voyages confirmed both Paul's route and many details of the narration.[89] As Barrett remarks, the author of Acts 27 clearly knew Mediterranean and

---

82. See Praeder, "First Person Narration," 215.

83. Ibid., 217–18. Thus, Praeder argues, ancient literary conventions shed no light on Luke's use of first-person narration (218). Against the convention in ancient historiography in general, see Nock, *Essays*, 828 (widely cited).

84. With, e.g., Hemer, "First Person Narrative"; Dunn, *Acts*, 335. Given the many volumes of ancient historiography surviving, I do not rule out the possibility of any exceptions; but the rule normally observed among ancient histories is certainly that the writer uses the first person within the narrative only when present (and historical writers normally were not distinct from narrators). See full discussion of the meaning of "we" at Acts 16:10 (Keener, *Acts*, 3:2350–74, esp. 2361–62, 2367–69, 2371–73).

85. Porter, "'We' Passages," 557.

86. Hemer, *Acts in History*, 319.

87. Burkitt, *Sources*, 16.

88. For many events in antiquity, many of our sources may ultimately depend on a single source, so accepting in any source only the events that can be verified "independently" would leave very little room for textually based historical reconstruction. Of course, the biases of subsequent generations often determine what is preserved, though even the dictum that history is always written by the winners is overstated (cf., e.g., Xenophon, Thucydides, and Josephus).

89. Smith, *Voyage*, passim (first published in 1848; cited already by Lightfoot, *Acts*, 59, 215, 262, 277, 306, yet still in use in recent studies of Mediterranean navigation, such as Davis, "Navigation," e.g., 228, 338). Bruce, *Documents*, 89–90, also cites Holtzmann, *Synoptiker-Apostelgeschichte*, 421. Smith's experiences will not provide exact figures for the voyage depicted in this chapter, but they do offer approximations close enough to dismiss the view that the voyage so depicted was coincidentally composed by imagination.

Adriatic conditions and locations.[90] Luke is no more elaborate than other historians in describing sea storms and shipwrecks, and he correctly identifies all the ports and locations.[91] Indeed, he proves more accurate than Pliny the Elder and Ptolemy on the location of Cauda, the difference being that whereas they were encyclopedic in their information, Luke had been at the location.[92] At the very least, Luke had to have "an actual voyage to serve as model,"[93] one undertaken in such a storm as he describes.

Luke cannot have simply invented the story; it reflects a real voyage, storm, and shipwreck, whether one wishes to believe that Paul was on board or not. Some scholars indeed acknowledge it as a genuine voyage (even of Paul himself) but regard the scenes where Paul is mentioned (27:9–11, 21–26, 31, 33–36, 43) as interpolations into the genuine narrative.[94] But we cannot expect passengers (as opposed to sailors and the weather) to be the major focus of action in descriptions of a storm at sea,[95] and the only criterion for deleting verses here—namely, Paul's presence—assumes what it hopes to prove (i.e., that Paul's presence can be deleted, leaving the account of a storm).

If the narrative rests on a real sea voyage (as Haenchen thinks), is it likelier that Luke coincidentally found another authentic account of a voyage from Sidon to Italy or that he authored the narrative as a whole on the basis of Paul's voyage, which historically must have proceeded from the east to Rome?[96] If Paul sometimes survived storms at sea (earlier ones in 2 Cor 11:25), and if the present narrative accurately depicts such a storm, why should we assume that Paul's presence here is fictitious? If the narrative rests on reminiscences of Paul's voyage (as many who favor the interpolations contend), one could argue that Luke has inserted Paul's speeches and leadership,[97] but would it not be in keeping with the historical Paul that he did speak out and, as an educated person often engaged in persuasion and leadership, did so with at least some persuasiveness? I have suggested earlier that, if one follows usual historiographic approaches, in Luke's "we" material even speeches would likely have a higher claim to genuine eyewitness tradition than in many earlier parts of his story.

More scholars today recognize the literary improbability of assuming that Luke simply interpolated his Pauline material into a genuine but mostly non-Pauline story.[98] If one applied this minimalist approach to Thucydides, one would dismiss as slanted

90. Barrett, *Acts*, 1178 (in view of Smith's work).

91. Johnson, *Acts*, 451 (citing Thucyd. 8.24.34; Ael. Arist. *Sacr.* 2.68, on the timing fitting storms); Hemer, "First Person Narrative."

92. Hemer, *Acts in History*, 331; see comment on Acts 27:16.

93. Hemer, *Acts in History*, 329. Gilchrist, "Shipwreck," argues that Luke's account stems from an eyewitness (including the "we" material and the location where the ship ran aground).

94. Most often cited are Dibelius, *Studies in Acts*, 107, 204–5, 213–14; Haenchen, *Acts*, 709; Schneider, *Apostelgeschichte*, 2:387; Conzelmann, *Acts*, 216–21; Conzelmann and Lindemann, *Interpreting*, 241. Others rightly regard this solution as implausible (e.g., Jervell, *Apostelgeschichte*, 612–14; followed by Schnabel, "Reading Acts," 255–56n35).

95. Witherington, *Acts*, 757 (also complaining that removing Paul material sometimes interrupts larger sentences, e.g., Acts 27:43–44).

96. See also Witherington, *Acts*, 757–58.

97. Cf. Haenchen, *Acts*, 709–11. For challenges of Haenchen's skepticism, see, e.g., Hemer, *Acts in History*, 138–39n110.

98. See, e.g., Porter, *Paul in Acts*, 26; Witherington, *Acts*, 757–58; Barrett, *Acts*, 1178–80. Barrett, *Acts*, 1180, thinks that Paul and his companions probably experienced the storm, with some details being added from traditional shipwreck stories (though we might well wonder whether traditional shipwreck stories included such details because they often accompanied shipwrecks). One creative and extensively argued approach that differs from most scholars is that of Seul, *Rettung*: he accepts 27:1–8 and 28:11–16 as authentic reports of Paul's journey to Rome but Paul's captivity and the "we" material as Luke's creation. I have already argued extensively, however, for Paul's Roman custody before he reached Rome.

or legendary a voyage accepted as genuine, even in detail, by virtually all classicists (Thucyd. 6.1–61).[99] One could retain the overall expedition while deleting all the scenes that include the activity of Nicias, yet there is no historical reason to delete such scenes.[100] Certainly Luke's narrative makes sense as it stands, as a coherent literary whole,[101] and all of it is in Luke's style (despite the nautical terms).

That Paul was on board is the only item of the story left for skeptics to challenge, because it is the most obvious item that cannot, strictly speaking, be either verified or falsified by external means. (We can test the locations and weather conditions; Paul, who is dead and gone, is no longer available for experiment.) Yet it seems methodologically suspect to support a skepticism so thoroughgoing that one must acknowledge the narrative to be accurate wherever we can test it, yet rule out of court its veracity on those points where its data cannot be tested.[102] Luke could not know that later readers would be able to test any of his claims, and so it would seem much more objective to accept that the historical character of what we cannot test is likely comparable to what we can test. Rejecting Paul's presence or activity appears to me the last desperate attempt to salvage some refuge for skeptical assumptions, but because this approach lacks concrete supporting evidence, it should be judged an act of skeptical fideism.

b. The Account's Function

The account emphasizes Paul's final voyage to Rome. Far from Paul going to Rome to face merited judgment, the results of his folly, or sheer tragedy, Paul goes in God's providence, just as Jesus went to the cross. God protected Paul from storm, shipwreck, and snakebite to fulfill his purpose in Rome.

I. LUKE'S PROBABLE PURPOSES

In addition to emphasizing that God sent Paul to Rome, the account serves moralistic ("Heed God's servant") and apologetic purposes.[103] Luke's apologetic is not for a legendary divine man; Paul does not still the storm.[104] But the account portrays Paul's character persevering through testing (see comment on Acts 27:21–26), as well as speaking wisely and rescuing his fellow passengers by God's power. Paul wins over the centurion, Rome's chief representative on the voyage[105] (cf. Luke 23:47). Paul's gracious concern for others also continues to establish his

99. Hanson, "Journey of Nikias," 318 (as summarized in Hemer, *Acts in History*, 330).

100. Hanson, "Journey of Nikias," 319 (as summarized in Hemer, *Acts in History*, 330).

101. See esp. Tannehill, *Acts*, 330–33 (with Paul intervening in the drama at strategic moments, 331–33). For literary variation in terminology for sailing, see Parsons, *Acts*, 353.

102. That is, such an inconsistent suspicion should itself be methodologically suspect, as I maintain throughout this commentary.

103. Tannehill, *Acts*, 338–39, sees Luke applying it to political salvation, requiring that the voice of Christians like Paul be heeded. Cf. Spangenberg and Gwalther in Chung-Kim and Hains, *Acts*, 350.

104. Johnson, *Acts*, 458. Stilling storms by prayer appears in Jewish sources (Theissen, *Miracle Stories*, 65, citing Jonah 1:14; *b. B. Meṣiʿa* 59b; *y. Ber.* 9:1; see also Ps 107:28–29). For nature miracle reports in more recent times, see, e.g., Yung, "Integrity," 174; Eskridge, *Family*, 32, 80–81; McGee, "Regions Beyond," 70; idem, "Miracles," 253; Ising, *Blumhardt*, 215; Heim, *Transformation*, 195–98; Koschorke, Ludwig, and Delgado, *History*, 223–24; Sanneh, *West African Christianity*, 181–83; Kinnear, *Tide*, 60–62, 92–96; Anderson, *Pelendo*, 43–47; Peckham, *Sounds*, 106–7, 113, 225; Koch, *Revival*, 143–44, 155–58, 208–17; idem, *Gifts*, 106–7; idem, *Zulus*, 151, 158, 238, 243, 278, 288–96; Crawford, *Miracles*, 75; Tari, *Wind*, 24–25, 32–33, 44–49, 78–84, 100–101; idem, *Breeze*, 6, 16–17, 42–43, 85, 91, 97–98, 117–18, 154–56; Wiyono, "Timor Revival," 285–86; Laurentin, *Miracles*, 4–5, 49, 95–97, 110–12; Wilson, "Miracle Events," 276–77; Crump, *Knocking*, 13; Dunkerley, *Healing Evangelism*, 112; Castleberry, "Impact," 111–12; King, *Mountains*, 16, 20, 38, 42, 46; Chavda, *Miracle*, 9–10, 128–29; Numbere, *Vision*, 130, 206–7, 213, 266; Pytches, *Come*, 108–9; Khai, "Pentecostalism," 268–69; Bush and Pegues, *Move*, 54–55, 59, 64, 192; McClenon, *Events*, 144; see Keener, *Miracles*, 579–99.

105. Cf. Johnson, *Acts*, 459. The assumption that the centurion evokes memory of the *Aeneid* specifically (cf. Shea, "Pieces of Epic"), rather than Rome in general, is excessive, despite parallels with Virgil elsewhere.

positive *ēthos*, reinforcing Luke's apologetic for Paul, who was in Roman custody because of false accusations.

Paul's very survival in such a deadly storm could underscore his innocence for Luke's ancient audience. It was considered much safer to sail with pious companions than with those thought to have acted impiously (Xen. *Cyr.* 8.1.25). Once, when a ship on which a philosopher sailed confronted a storm, some impious men aboard began to cry out to the gods to rescue them. He ordered them to be quiet lest the gods "hear and become aware that you are here in the ship" (Diog. Laert. 1.86).[106] Many ancients thought that injustice (Hom. *Od.* 3.133), impiety (Aeschylus *Seven* 602–4; Dio Chrys. *Or.* 32.80), or pollution (Eurip. *El.* 1355; Antiph. *Her.* 82) brought about shipwrecks; they would have expected Paul's guilt on any of these points to render him susceptible to trouble at sea.[107] Luke's biblically informed ideal audience need have thought no further than Jonah for this principle (Jonah 1:8–10). Forensic orators could even use a person's survival during a sea voyage as divine attestation of the defendant's innocence.[108] In the event that people doubted the vindication of the storm, they should be convinced by Paul's immunity to the snakebite (Acts 28:3–6; see comment there).

Perhaps Luke's most important purpose, however, fits a larger apologetic agenda. Through the details of the storm Luke lavishly portrays the obstacles God surmounts to allow Paul to speak before Caesar and bring the gospel to Rome.[109] For those who questioned why Paul, if truly innocent of sedition, would have been tried in Rome, Luke offers a compelling and consistent response: it was God's will for Paul to go to Rome, just as it was God's will for Jesus to go to the cross. If the narrative's movement from heritage to mission and Jerusalem to Rome leads to an implied martyrdom (admittedly a matter of some debate), believers in the cross regarded martyrdom in Christ as not the end but an opportunity for God to bring transformation. Ancient narratives could attribute sea storms to either natural or divine causes; they could likewise attribute the outcomes to either natural (or human) or divine causes.[110] This ship's danger involves natural causes (at least failure to heed Paul's warning), but the deliverance is clearly divine.[111]

God could demonstrate his power by stilling the storm (as in Luke 8:24–25) but also by preserving his servant through it and using his servant to bring the other passengers safely through it as well. Ancients who spent much time on the seas recognized

106. Trans. Hicks, LCL, 1:89.

107. Aune, *Environment*, 130. For divine vindication here, see also Talbert and Hayes, "Theology of Sea Storms"; Talbert, *Mediterranean Milieu*, 175–95 (comparing Jesus's facing the storm in Luke 8:22–25). For impiety leading to a fleet's destruction, see, e.g., Val. Max. 1.1.ext. 1; see further comment at Acts 28:4. Cf. Satan accusing people during dangerous times, such as sea travel, *Eccl. Rab.* 3:2, §2.

108. See Ladouceur, "Shipwreck and Pollution," pointing to Andocides *Myst.* 137–39 (which he regards as more explicit than Antiph. *Her.* 82–83).

109. See Quesnel, "Naufrage"; Walaskay, *Came to Rome*, 60.

110. Talbert, *Acts*, 212–13, lists (1) those with divine causes and outcomes (Jonah 1:3–17; Hom. *Od.* 4.499–511; 5.291–453; Aeschylus *Ag.* 647–66; Hdt. 7.188–92; Eurip. *Tro.* 77–86; *Iph. Taur.* 1391–1489; Ap. Rhod. 2.1093–1121; Virg. *Aen.* 1.122–252; Sen. Y. *Ag.* 456–578; Statius *Theb.* 5.360–421; Val. Flac. 1.614–58; Sil. It. 17.244–90; Char. *Chaer.* 3.3); (2) those with divine causes but outcomes reflecting human choices (Eurip. *Hel.* 400–413; Plaut. *Rud.* 62–78); (3) those with natural causes but divine outcomes (*Herpyllis*; Virg. *Aen.* 3.253–75; Ovid *Tristia* 1.2.1–110; Jos. *Life* 13–16; Ael. Arist. *Sacr.* 2.12–14; Lucian *Posts* 1–2; *Ship* 7–9; Ach. Tat. 1.1; 3.1–5; *Test. Naph.* 6:1–10); (4) those with natural causes and natural (or human) outcomes (Ap. Rhod. 4.1228–47; Polyb. 1.37; *Nin. Rom.* C; Virg. *Aen.* 5.14–43; Ovid *Metam.* 11.472–574; Phaedrus 4.23; Lucan *C.W.* 5.560–677; 9.319–47; Petron. *Sat.* 114; Jos. *War* 1.279–80; Quint. Curt. 4.3.16–18; Dio Chrys. *Or.* 7.2–7; Tac. *Ann.* 2.23–24; Ael. Arist. *Sacr.* 2.64–68; Lucian *Tox.* 19–21; *True Story* 1.5–6; 2.47; Xen. Eph. *Anthia* 2.11; 3.2, 12; Apoll. K. *Tyre* 11–12; Heliod. *Eth.* 1.22; 5.27).

111. So rightly Talbert, *Acts*, 215.

that they could not control their own safety there, and hence they sought the protection of greater powers. Some viewed Isis as protectress from storms and dangers (Apul. *Metam.* 11.25);[112] for other such protection, see comment on Acts 28:11. Monotheists recognized that God rather than merchants controlled the outcome of all expeditions (cf. Jas 4:13–16).[113]

Although Luke does not allegorize the account to produce his moral applications, there were others who did so with such accounts. Philosophers used nautical metaphors,[114] sometimes extensive, in which the soul faced storms.[115] Sometimes they allegorized literary accounts accordingly; for example, Odysseus's wanderings became the trials and storms of the soul.[116] Nautical metaphors are frequent in other kinds of sources as well.[117] Governors,[118] other leaders of the state,[119] and philosophers[120] were sometimes compared to helmsmen, as were orators,[121] reason,[122] and God.[123] Orators naturally compared oratory with sailing.[124] The difficulties of the state were like being tossed on the sea;[125] political assemblies provided "storms and tempests";[126] and one following the whims of the masses was like a pilot obeying the whims of passengers, leading to shipwreck (Dio Chrys. *Or.* 34.16, 32, 37).[127] Those who started their life or career well but ended badly could be compared to shipwrecks.[128] Such images appear

112. Hence the twin figures of Isis on her namesake ship in Lucian *Ship* 5 (Casson, *Travel*, 159).

113. Cf. *1 En.* 97:8–10; *Exod. Rab.* 52:3; see further comment on God's sovereignty in the excursus at Acts 2:23 (Keener, *Acts*, 1:933–38).

114. E.g., Sen. Y. *Ep. Lucil.* 70.2–4; 96.5; Philo *Flight* 27; cf. figurative storms in, e.g., 1QH^a III, 8; XV, 7–8.

115. E.g., Sen. Y. *Ben.* 7.1.3 (using Demetrius the Cynic; see Grant, *Paul*, 49); Max. Tyre 11.10–11; 25.5; Philost. *Vit. Apoll.* 3.35; 4.9; Philo *Agr.* 89; cf. Sen. Y. *Ep. Lucil.* 104.27; Sir 33:2 [36:2]; 4 Macc 15:32. Storms also could represent war (Heracl. *Hom. Prob.* 5.3–4) or tyranny (5.5–6, 8).

116. E.g., Sen. Y. *Ep. Lucil.* 88.7; Max. Tyre 7.5; 10.7; 11.6; 21.8.

117. E.g., Xen. *Anab.* 5.8.20; Ovid *Pont.* 1.5.39; Dio Chrys. *Or.* 40.12; Plut. *Themist.* 2.6; *Or. Delphi* 21, *Mor.* 404E (one depiction of inspiration); *Table* 1.4.3, *Mor.* 622B (drinking parties facing shipwreck); Apul. *Flor.* 23.1–5 (for health); Philost. *Hrk.* 34.5 (playing on sea voyage imagery from the *Odyssey*); 53.2–3 (but the dialogue partner is a ship captain); Wis 5:10; *Test. Job* 18:7; storms in Vell. Paterc. 2.72.5; Quint. *Decl.* 321.14.

118. E.g., Dio Chrys. *Or.* 34.16, 32; Men. Rhet. 2.3, 379.28–29; cf. Dio Chrys. *Or.* 77/78.7.

119. E.g., Soph. *Antig.* 993–94; Xen. *Mem.* 1.2.9; Cic. *Sest.* 9.20; *Inv.* 1.3.4; *Off.* 1.22.77; military leaders in Xen. *Anab.* 5.8.20; Quint. Curt. 5.9.3; kings in Dio Chrys. *Or.* 1.29; Israel's leaders (such as Moses, Joshua, and Samuel) in *Pesiq. Rab.* 47:4.

120. E.g., Sen. Y. *Ep. Lucil.* 108.37 (cf. 85.35–37; comments by Lang, "Self," 172); Mus. Ruf. 2, p. 36.29–32; 5, p. 50.10–14; 16, p. 104.7; Max. Tyre 15.2, 8; 16.3; 30.1–2; a Stoic argues that philosophers make the best pilots and navigators for the state (Lucian *Hermot.* 29).

121. E.g., Dio Chrys. *Or.* 12.38; Pliny *Ep.* 9.26.4.

122. Plut. *Plat. Q.* 9.1, *Mor.* 1008A; Max. Tyre 13.7; Philo *Cher.* 36; 4 Macc 7:1; cf. the soul in Iambl. *Soul* 3.16, §371; 6.33, §382.

123. Max. Tyre 4.9; *Let. Aris.* 251; Philo *Creation* 46. Lucian *Indictment* 2 also compares Zeus with a κυβερνήτης; cf. Pindar *Pyth.* 5.122–23; the first god in Dio Chrys. *Or.* 40.36. Noting the religious uses of κυβέρνησις, Roberts, "Seers," views it in 1 Cor 12:28 as a subtype of prophecy.

124. Pliny *Ep.* 6.23.10; Fronto *Ad Ant. imp.* 1.2.3.

125. Dion. Hal. *Ant. rom.* 11.9.1. Medieval sources continued the use of a ship as an allegory for the state (Evans, *Wycliffe*, 234); for the church, see Spangenberg in Chung-Kim and Hains, *Acts*, 358.

126. Cic. *Mil.* 2.5 (trans. Watts, LCL, 14:11); cf. Dio Chrys. *Or.* 34.37; other trials to the state in Dion. Hal. *Ant. rom.* 11.9.1. Cf. the shipwreck of the state in Cic. *Sest.* 6.15.

127. Cf. also the importance of the concord of κυβερνήτης and sailors as an illustration for the state (Dio Chrys. *Or.* 39.6).

128. Val. Max. 3.6.praef. (*naufragia*). Independently, Pervo, *Acts*, 649–51, cites examples of ancient nautical symbolism; he treats them as more relevant to Acts 27 than most scholars (including myself) think plausible (most concrete, lengthy *narratives* such as Acts 27 made only limited use of symbolism). But his symbolic link with Jesus's passion (648–53; complaining about Luke's historiography, idem, "Dying") does make sense; many commentators do see Acts 27 as parallel to Jesus's passion in the Gospel (see Wright, *People of God*, 375; Goulder, *Type and History*, 61; Horton, *Death*, 56–59 [noting, e.g., Acts 27:20 with Luke 23:44–45 and citing as still more extensive Radl, *Paulus*, 227–49]; brief discussion in Keener, *Acts*, 1:560–61, 565). At the same time, Luke narrates neither Paul's literal death nor (obviously) his raising (cf. discussion in Schnabel,

in early Christian texts as well (Eph 4:14; Heb 6:19; 1 Tim 1:19; Jas 1:6; *Barn.* 3.6). But rarely did such metaphors constitute entire narratives; authors might interpret earlier narratives, but rarely did they compose narratives with such allegorical purposes in view. None of these other texts, then, authorizes us to read Luke's dramatic narrative in that manner.

ii. Theology and Applicability

Luke's primary interest in the sea voyage narrative is to attest Paul as God's servant and show that God would bring him to Rome regardless of all obstacles. The gospel must reach Rome, and the apparent defeat that the gospel suffered in Paul's later execution was clearly part of the plan of the God who brought Paul to Rome and protected and used him all the way. That is, whether by Paul's living or by his dying, the gospel would gain a new hearing and spread all the more (cf. Phil 1:20).

Luke's interest in Paul as a central character stems from Paul's role as an agent of the gospel and his particular mission of bringing the gospel to the Gentiles. His interest in Paul's vindication is therefore an interest in the vindication of the Gentile mission, especially in the gospel that saves Gentiles without requiring them to adopt Jerusalem culture or Jewish strictures. The message of this voyage narrative, then, is of a piece with the message of the rest of Acts: "Nothing can stop the gospel." Also, it reiterates that the gospel is for all peoples; through God's providence and his servants' obedience and sacrifice, it will penetrate even the heart of the empire. This mission will require suffering, but the suffering itself becomes an opportunity to show what God's servants are made of (a pattern also recognized by ancient philosophers) and hence to glorify God all the more.

What could subsequent audiences do with such an account after Paul's innocence no longer remained an apologetic issue? I have argued that defending Paul's legacy remained crucial for Luke.[129] Nevertheless, those wishing to learn from and apply Luke's wisdom here in a manner consistent with Luke's theology could recommunicate the intensity of his dramatic point through rehearsing the narrative. They could point out how God protects the divinely initiated mission and how God's servants are called to sacrifice obediently for this mission (not, as in much of modern Western Christendom, focusing on their personal fulfillment).[130] They could point out that God's servants should expect testing[131] and how the kinds of suffering that God's servants share with other people can provide opportunities for spiritual leadership. When Christians and non-Christians are suffering, they share in their common humanity, but Christians' hope for God's purpose in the midst of their suffering can help provide others with meaning and courage. A strong testimony of faith in God (whether, as in Paul's case, for short-term deliverance for his calling, which God had spoken, or simply for the long-range fulfillment of God's purposes when God has not spoken beyond those broader purposes) can lead others to faith.

"Reading Acts," 274–75, against the symbolic reading). Acts 28 is not easily construed as resurrection and proves much briefer than Luke 24. Where parallelism occurs in ancient sources, it need not imply lack of historical information; see discussion in Keener, *Acts*, 1:564–74.

129. Keener, "Apology"; idem, *Acts*, 1:223–24, 441–50.

130. This is not to rule out any value in personal fulfillment (some NT writers certainly emphasize personal transformation at least) but to say that Luke, like most other NT writers, would find a self-focus utterly astonishing as the *priority* for people who call Christ their "Lord." His narrative is, of course, about the spread of the gospel, and so he tells us about private aspects of spiritual formation only a bit more than he tells us about the apostles' diet (though he undoubtedly takes for granted the necessity of both).

131. God does not stop the contrary winds (Chrys. *Hom. Acts* 53); escaping the court, Paul faces storm and shipwreck (John Chrysostom in *Cat. Act.* 27.4–5 [Martin, *Acts*, 300]).

Luke would assert that God is able to do miracles. He does not promise that God will do miracles, or the same miracles, on every occasion: Paul does not still the storm here as Jesus does in the Gospels. But God does astonishingly save everyone aboard the ship, fulfilling Paul's words and confirming Paul as a spiritual leader to those aboard.[132] Faith that God's purposes will be fulfilled, and that God can fulfill them miraculously in answer to prayer and in confirmation of the explicit divine calling and purposes, fits Luke's narrative theology here.

2. The Voyage Begins (27:1–8)

The beginning of Paul's voyage portends what will come, both in terms of hospitality (Acts 27:3; cf. 28:7, 10, 14–15) and in terms of hostile weather (27:4, 7–8).

a. Julius of the Augustan Cohort (27:1)

When Paul and—presumably because of Festus's favor shown toward Paul—his companions are to sail for Rome (evidently after some delay, given Festus's apparently quick scheduling of Paul's case after his arrival and the later chronological note in 27:9), they are assigned to a centurion, here introduced because of his significance as a character in the following scenes. By this point Luke's audience will think of other positive centurions in Luke-Acts.

i. The Military Escort

Governors sometimes assigned centurions, along with some soldiers (27:31–32, 42), to special duties.[133] (Here they are probably a small number of soldiers; we should not infer from the presence of a centurion that he brought sixty or more soldiers with him.)[134] Notable prisoners might be under the supervision of centurions, sometimes in deference to the prisoner's rank (Jos. *Ant.* 18.202). Paul's access to centurions (cf. Acts 23:17; 27:9–11) probably suggests his status; a centurion might even become friendly with a high-status captive (Jos. *Ant.* 18.230–31), although he would suffer if this led to dereliction of duty (cf. 18.231–33). Luke also reports other "good" centurions playing major roles in his stories (Luke 7:2; 23:47; Acts 10:1).

Some older commentators thought that the soldiers were *frumentarii*, escorting the Roman grain fleet; but this role started in the early second century, and we lack evidence that the soldiers here were responsible for escorting the fleet.[135] Others suggest that they were *speculatores*, a distinct unit of imperial guards (but not part of the Syrian Augustan cohort mentioned below).[136] They need not derive from a "special" unit, however; routine peacetime duties for soldiers included guard duty, being sent by the governor in a security function, and so forth.[137]

132. Western readers for whom Hume's definition of miracles as violations of nature obtains might balk, but most believers in God's activity would see God's work in preserving 276 people in an ancient shipwreck even without the stilling of a storm.

133. See Campbell, "Centurio," 127; idem, *Army*, 47. Soldiers borrowed from their original unit could be returned to it after fulfilling their assignment (cf. Campbell, "Equites," 5, for temporary use in elite units).

134. See, e.g., Pliny *Ep.* 10.21.1 (ten soldiers); 10.27–28 (six additional soldiers); 10.77.1 (a legionary centurion; but this is exceptional, 10.78.1–2). A special assignment could include one centurion, two horsemen, and ten elite soldiers (10.21.1). For mere guard duty, however, as few soldiers as possible would be used (10.19.1–2; 10.20.1–2).

135. Longenecker, *Acts*, 353–54 (citing, for their date under Trajan, Aurelius Victor *Liber de Caesaribus* 13.5–6); Witherington, *Acts*, 760.

136. Longenecker, *Acts*, 354.

137. Thompson, "Military," 995.

From the name "Julius," some suggest that the centurion was already a Roman citizen, not simply a provincial auxiliary hoping to achieve citizenship on his retirement.[138] A Roman supervisor for the Roman Paul made sense; the subordinate soldiers, by contrast, were probably not yet citizens.[139] (If their willingness to kill the prisoners targeted Paul in Acts 27:42, it might allow Syrian anti-Jewish prejudice; but it probably does not [cf. 27:31–32].) Some suggest that the nomen "Julius" (without his other names) would fit only "an older man in the Julio-Claudian setting."[140] Others note that Luke and Paul often use praenomens or cognomens for non-Latins, but Luke uses the nomen for both auxiliary centurions he mentions (cf. 10:1).[141] Some citizens were eventually allowed in auxiliary units,[142] and soldiers could be moved to and from legions;[143] some equestrians also entered the army with the rank of centurion,[144] so it is not surprising if some Roman citizen legionaries chose to become centurions even among auxiliaries.[145]

ii. The Augustan Cohort

Roman legions had distinctive standards and names.[146] It was natural to name both legions and cohorts for the first *princeps* of Rome; in addition to his renown for other matters, Augustus had made major changes in the Roman army.[147] It is possible that he conferred the name *Augusta* officially on some units.[148] Entire legions bore the title of *Augustus*.[149] The "Second" and "Third Augustan" legions each used an ibex, and the "Eighth Augustan" legion used a bull.[150] Auxiliary units could be named for the kinds of weapons they used, earlier commanders, or a region or people; sometimes the name could be combined with that of the emperor (e.g., *I Augusta Thracum*).[151]

Scholars frequently note that "Augustan cohort" was a title for some auxiliary troops, attested in the Transjordan in the time of Agrippa II (*OGIS* 421).[152] Perhaps more important, we know that the *Cohors Augusta I* resided in Syria in 6 C.E., and a prefect of the "Au[gustan]" cohort appears just east of Galilee during the time of Agrippa II—that is, in the second half of the first century (*ILS* 1.2683; *CIL*

138. Rapske, *Custody*, 269. Auxiliary recruits might take a Roman name when enlisting, but at retirement they took the emperor's nomen (Jeffers, *World*, 203–4). But Julius is in active duty, not retired; Tiberius (whose name included "Julius") died in 16 C.E.; Gaius Caligula (also Julius) died in 41. Pervo, *Acts*, 655, suggests that Luke's "use of a single name is characteristic of popular literature"; this may often be correct, but in the East, even a more elite historian such as Josephus normally called mere centurions by single names: "Antonius" (*War* 3.333), "Arius" (*Ant.* 17.282; *War* 2.63, 71), "Capito" (*War* 2.298), "Fabius" and "Furius" (*Ant.* 14.69), "Gallus" (*War* 4.37), "Julian" (*War* 6.81), "Liberalius" (*War* 6.282), and "Priscus" (*War* 6.175). The double name in *Ant.* 19.307 appears in an official decree, not ordinary narrative.

139. Rapske, *Custody*, 270.

140. Hemer, *Acts in History*, 180.

141. Jeffers, *World*, 204, 206. Roman citizen soldiers used each other's nomens "well into the first century" (206); regular use of cognomens in the army stems only from the time of Claudius, much later than in the general population (202–3).

142. Southern, *Army*, 143.

143. Ibid., 130.

144. Ibid.

145. Campbell, personal correspondence, June 19, 2006.

146. Le Bohec, "Ensigns," 993–95.

147. On these, see Stevenson, "Army," 218–28.

148. See Rapske, *Custody*, 268–69.

149. For the *Legio II Augusta*, see Campbell, "Legio," 363 (noting its uses in Europe, e.g., from Tac. *Hist.* 3.44); and for the *Legio VIII Augusta*, 366 (used in the Balkans and Moesia and helping Vespasian in 69 C.E.).

150. Le Bohec, "Ensigns," 993–94.

151. Campbell, "Auxilia," 420.

152. E.g., Bruce, *Commentary*, 500; Conzelmann, *Acts*, 215; Johnson, *Acts*, 445; Witherington, *Acts*, 758; Dunn, *Acts*, 337.

3.6687).[153] (If there was only one "Augustan cohort" in the area, Luke need not specify the number;[154] his audience probably would not have known the difference, in any case.) Thus a centurion from a cohort with such a name, presumably from this region, is not at all surprising.

Some scholars also mention that Josephus speaks of σεβαστηνοί ("august ones"; cf. *Ant.* 19.356, 361) before the death of Agrippa I;[155] but this is probably irrelevant, since the title likely simply means "those from Sebaste" (19.365–66; *War* 2.52). It could apply to the same cohort that Luke intends here only if Luke mistook the name, which is unlikely both because of his good Greek and because he would have spent enough time (on my premises that the narrative's "we" includes him) on board ships with Julius to have the information correct.[156]

Luke rarely names soldiers' cohorts, but the two units that he does may be named in part because providing their titles can also serve Luke's literary purposes. If the "Italian cohort" (Acts 10:1) offers a symbolic hint toward Rome, the "Augustan cohort" does the same, adding interest in Caesar himself (cf. 27:24).

III. OTHER VOYAGERS

Other prisoners accompanied Paul. Military custody, developed during the empire, was less severe than imprisonment,[157] but prisoners transported under military guard undoubtedly had diverse experiences.[158] Although some Roman citizens were, like Paul, undoubtedly transported to Rome for trial, most criminals shipped to Rome were probably already convicted and were intended for the *venationes*, the bloody games to amuse the Roman people at the expense of the condemned prisoners' lives.[159] Although most of the prisoners (and most other passengers) would have been men (as were most prisoners), it is not impossible that a few were women (cf. 8:3; 9:2; 22:4; comment on Acts 8:3). Until the era of Constantine, women shared the same cells with men, predictably often leading to their sexual abuse.[160] Needless to say, most of the prisoners would not be eager to see Rome.[161]

For "we" in this narrative, see discussion at the introduction to this section (and much more fully at Acts 16:10); contrary to the assertions of some NT scholars, "we" in historical narratives did imply the narrator's presence. Certainly the relative distribution of details here supports the suggestion of an eyewitness; Acts is most detailed in the "we" sections. Some doubt that Luke would have remained with Paul for two years in Caesarea, given the dangers to a Gentile Christian in Judea after the accusation of 21:29.[162] The danger, however, would be in Jerusalem, not in Caesarea, where Paul was held in custody. Luke could well have even been traveling in parts of Judea, col-

---

153. E.g., Bruce, *Commentary*, 500n9; Munck, *Acts*, 249; Conzelmann, *Acts*, 215; Johnson, *Acts*, 445; Witherington, *Acts*, 758; Rapske, *Custody*, 269. Rabbi Isaac (second century C.E.) spoke of an Augustan legion (*Gen. Rab.* 94:9).

154. Rapske, *Custody*, 269.

155. Cf. Johnson, *Acts*, 445; Witherington, *Acts*, 758 (not preferring this explanation).

156. Even if the term referred to an "Augustan cohort," this could be relevant only if these were Roman troops at Agrippa I's disposal; Agrippa died in 44 C.E., and Julius is a Roman under the governor's authority.

157. Rapske, *Custody*, 9, 28 (citing *Dig.* 48.3.12, 14; 48.22.7.1; and esp. 48.3.1).

158. Rapske, *Custody*, 29–30.

159. Ramsay, "Roads and Travel," 397; followed by Witherington, *Acts*, 758n17 (via Keener, *Background Commentary*, 400). On the *venationes*, see, e.g., Suet. *Claud.* 34.1–2; *Nero* 12.1; further comment at Acts 19:29.

160. Rapske, *Custody*, 279–80; he suggests the possibility that women could be among the prisoners here (281). We cannot be sure, since we do not know how many prisoners are involved, and women were capital prisoners less often than men.

161. The later Ignatius, seeking martyrdom, was an exception.

162. Hengel, "Geography of Palestine," 77 (though, curiously, he does believe that Luke accompanied Paul to Rome, p. 78).

lecting and confirming information for the project that eventually became his Gospel;[163] Diaspora Christians would appreciate his access to Judean Christians' accounts about Jesus. But that the "we" resumes here after leaving off in 21:18 need not imply his travels by itself;[164] it could simply mean that he did not participate in the direct action of his narrative (surrounding Paul). Luke rarely uses "we" except in travel narratives, where his participation in the main actor's action is inescapable. What is much more difficult to credit is the idea that Luke left Judea after 21:18 and then returned coincidentally in time for the voyage to Rome. Probably Paul and the companions who remained with him kept hoping for a speedy resolution to his case (cf. 24:23, 25–26). For the named companion of Paul, Aristarchus, see comment on Acts 27:2.

b. Embarking with Aristarchus (27:2)

Luke's details here (such as the Adramyttian ship) fit an eyewitness report, and the mention of Aristarchus (and the narrator, presumably Luke) matches Paul's own letters.

i. Aristarchus and Luke

Luke reveals that Aristarchus the Thessalonian (19:29; 20:4) is among the members of the "we" group in 27:1. We know from Paul's captivity epistles (probably sent from Rome) that Aristarchus (Col 4:10; Phlm 24)[165] and Luke (Col 4:14; Phlm 24) were among Paul's companions when he was in custody, probably in Rome, and so the present report is not surprising.

Paul even calls Aristarchus his "fellow prisoner" in Col 4:10; this description, however, may be figurative,[166] since he uses the same title for Epaphras while in prison (Phlm 23) and for Andronicus and Junia in a letter written when he was free (Rom 16:7). It could, however, imply that these colleagues shared his captivity (Andronicus and Junia an earlier one, and the others later) by participating in his suffering (cf. Phil 1:7). In principle, Trophimus might have been sent for trial if available (cf. Acts 21:27–29), but there is no reason to assume the same for Aristarchus (the earlier riot in Ephesus notwithstanding, 19:29).[167] It is possible, however, that Aristarchus and Luke were allowed to accompany Paul as potential witnesses for the defense, though the state would not be burdened with the cost or delay of sending for such witnesses.[168]

People of status sometimes brought servants with them on voyages; they prepared food in the galley and sometimes erected tents for sleeping on deck.[169] Ramsay argues that Luke and Aristarchus performed duties for Paul normally performed by slaves and must have passed as Paul's servants to be allowed to travel with the prisoner.[170] But Romans at least sometimes did not permit even slaves to accompany masters, and the (possibly refused) request that we know of for servants pertained to a high-ranking senator (Pliny *Ep.* 3.16.8–9).[171]

---

163. See Luke 1:3. Because Luke's geographic knowledge is most precise in Jerusalem and along the coast, we may suspect that he traveled in these areas, which makes the best sense for a Greek-speaking Gentile accustomed to cities and coastal areas. Informants could supply his other information without his travel to each location. But he probably spent more time, and gathered more information from older disciples, in Caesarea.

164. Dunn, *Acts*, 337, suggests that he was simply occupied with other business, while remaining on hand.

165. Others also note these texts (Conzelmann, *Acts*, 215; Hemer, *Acts in History*, 188; Dunn, *Acts*, 337).

166. So Rapske, *Custody*, 372–73.

167. Aristarchus was also apparently Jewish; see Col 4:10–11.

168. On the latter point, cf. Pliny *Ep.* 6.5.1–2.

169. Casson, *Mariners*, 193. The six hundred passengers on Josephus's ship slept on deck, perhaps because it was a grain ship (Hirschfeld, "Ship of Paul," 28).

170. Ramsay, *Letters*, 33; idem, *Traveller and Citizen*, 316.

171. See also Rapske, *Custody*, 374, though he is more optimistic that the servants might have been allowed to accompany the senator.

Probably Paul's friends were simply allowed to accompany him and continue ministering to him, as in Acts 24:23,[172] especially in view of the elite characters' apparent expectation of his legal exoneration (26:32). Since the decision was made that "we" should sail, the orders apparently came from Festus or his aides, not Julius, but they would help remind Julius of the favor his charge Paul had, leading to his special treatment (e.g., 27:3).[173] Paul might also be the only Roman citizen among the prisoners, allowing him higher status and favors.[174] That he was not already condemned (presumably unlike most of the other prisoners) cannot have hurt his standing.

Because ships transported cargos and only incidentally carried passengers, they did not provide services. Passengers brought their own food, which servants might prepare in the galley; passengers slept in the open on deck or in tents set up at night.[175] (During the coming storm they might seek to find space below deck; see discussion below.) Undoubtedly, the centurion transports and billets both the prisoners and the soldiers guarding them by requisition.[176] Exercising his delegated authority, he could secure passage (cf. 27:2, 6; 28:11) and probably acquire food.[177] Centurions and other Roman military agents could requisition or "impress" supplies or service from ships or others.[178] Prisoners in custody received minimal sustenance to prevent starvation in captivity,[179] but their needs would be supplied by friends when prisoners had friends (see comments on Acts 24:23; 27:3).

Presumably, the centurion would expect Paul's traveling companions to supply Paul's needs; the centurion would not be responsible for providing their food, and he would be happy to relinquish the need to provide for Paul's (particularly since the act of requisitioning often provoked dissatisfaction from those required to accommodate it). As mentioned, most ships' primary function was to transport cargo, and so "passengers provided their own mattresses, blankets, clothes, materials for

---

172. With Rapske, *Custody*, 378. Shame was associated with custody (298), and so they valued Paul more than status.

173. If the narrator was a physician (Col 4:14), he might be allowed to accompany Paul if the latter suffered any chronic ailments (of which Acts would hardly inform us; but cf. Gal 4:13); a physician would have been welcome on board, in any event (cf., e.g., the scalpels found in a shipwreck, likely indicating a doctor who was a passenger, Casson, *Mariners*, 173).

174. See Dunn, *Acts*, 337.

175. Casson, *Mariners*, 192–93 (noting [193] that ships did provide "water, which was stored in a large wooden tank in the hold"); Adkins and Adkins, *Life*, 188; Branch and Schoville, "Ships," 195. The hold included "a large wooden tank" for drinking water (Adkins and Adkins, *Life*, 188); after any length of time, however, drinking water aboard the ship would not be fresh (Libanius *Comparison* 4.10). Apparently most people slept on deck (Libanius *Maxim* 1.13; 2.8), a practice perhaps deterred later in this voyage by the storm (even before, *some* slept in the hold, *Maxim* 1.13).

176. Rapske, *Custody*, 272. On requisition to transport persons, see esp. Llewelyn, *Documents*, 7:58–92, §4 ("The Provision of Transport for Persons"); governors had to check abuses in this system (80–85).

177. Rapske, *Custody*, 273. A general could impress horses (Val. Max. 7.3.3; cf. 1 Sam 11:7).

178. To supplement what tax revenues could not cover, soldiers could requisition what they needed (Lewis, *Life*, 172–73; *Dig.* 50.4.18.4; 50.5.10.2–3; 50.5.11; *Cod. theod.* 8 passim in Rapske, "Travel and Shipwreck," 14; Sall. *Jug.* 75.4; cf. Lintott, *Romans*, 8–9; the tax in D'Andrea, "*Hospitium militum*") and require local inhabitants to supply forced labor (Mark 15:1). (On the Roman administration's use of local transport services, see, e.g., the *kanon* in Horsley, *Documents*, 1:36–45; most fully, Llewelyn, *Documents*, 7:58–92.) Soldiers were known to sometimes abuse this privilege, often annoying the senate as well as local residents (Livy 43.7.11; 43.8.1–10; Apul. *Metam.* 9.39; Hdn. 2.3.4; 2.5.1; Sherk, *Empire*, 89, 136 [citing P.Lond. 3.1171; *IGLS* 5.1998 = *SEG* 17.755]; *PSI* 446; Jones, *Empire*, 197; Llewelyn, *Documents*, 7:80–85; cf. P.Hal. 1.166–85); later rabbis told of Romans forcing Jews to carry burdens on the Sabbath (*y. Ḥag.* 2:1, §8). I borrow this information from Keener, *Matthew*, 199 (on Matt 5:41). Requisition for a few travelers was not comparable to securing supplies for a legion, the feeding of which could require the equivalent of an acre of produce every week (Southern, *Army*, 220–21).

179. Rapske, "Prison," 829.

washing, food, and cookware."[180] Ships often had facilities for cooking and catering for those with means; but some smaller ships (less relevant to this case, 27:37) would not, and all passengers would need to bring their own food.[181] Even one small ship that was examined "had cooking facilities far more sophisticated than, for example, on Columbus's ships, which had no more than a firebox protected from the wind by a hood."[182] But ships often included dinnerware only for the crew.[183]

Such needs make all the more relevant the benevolence of local believers in 27:3; 28:14. The traveling party would have probably brought clothing appropriate to the season among its resources; those who could afford it would bring one kind of cape for mild weather, another kind for rainy weather, and still another kind for cold weather.[184]

11. Embarking in an Adramyttian Ship

The party found its ship in the artificial harbor of Caesarea, which was one of the best in the region (see comment on Acts 10:1). Archaeology shows that the designers built two breakwaters 1,500 feet into the sea, one being 150 and the other 200 feet in width. Where these breakwaters met northwest of the harbor, they formed an entrance 60 feet wide. Although most of Josephus's description is accurate, some of the blocks are even larger than what he describes, weighing more than fifty tons.[185] Reminders of imperial power and the pervasiveness of pagan worship were not far away. Three large colossi stood on pillars at the north entrance to Caesarea's harbor (Jos. *War* 1.413), perhaps in imitation of the fallen Colossus of Rhodes; not far away, above the harbor, stood a Caesar temple with a colossus of Caesar inside.[186]

"Ship of Adramyttium" means "a ship with its home port Adramyttium," not that the party boarded it there.[187] Adramyttium was near Assos and Lesbos and also near Troas, to Troas's southeast (Strabo 13.1.2, 51); some writers included it in the Troad (though others did not; 13.1.4), but it was near Troy's famous Mount Ida (13.1.51).[188] A famous temple of Apollo lay in the territory of Adramyttium, and the river from Mount Ida flowed past it (13.1.62). Athenians originally colonized it, and it hosted a noteworthy port (13.1.51). It is mentioned alongside Assos as a notable city; a famous "Asiatic" rhetor of an earlier era hailed from there (13.1.66). Most relevant here, Adramyttium had an important artificial harbor that improved safety in the Troad, like that at Assos (but not comparable to the better one at Troas).[189] At some point it moved inland (to a site at modern Edremit), but it probably remained on the coast during Paul's (and Luke's) day (at Ören).[190]

---

180. Stambaugh and Balch, *Environment*, 39.

181. Rapske, *Custody*, 223–24 (noting that this was also true of prisoners in general; see comment on Acts 24:23; and also suggesting that some ships may have provided catering for people of means); Casson, *Mariners*, 193 (for passengers in general).

182. Casson, *Mariners*, 175. The seventh-century C.E. ship in question was about "70 feet (20.52 meters) long and 17 feet (5.22 meters)" across; the cooking area on this ship was "11 feet by 4 feet and 6 feet high, covered by a tiled roof; it housed an ample firebox of tiles surmounted by an iron grill." If I understand Casson correctly, the cooking area would thus take up more than 15 percent of the deck's surface on that ship.

183. Davis, "Navigation," 204 (following Swiny and Katzev, "Shipwreck," 345), noting such items as "plates, bowls, saucers, drinking cups and wooden spoons."

184. Rapske, *Custody*, 219.

185. McRay, *Archaeology*, 140 (also noting [140, 142] massive vaults for trade there; see comment on Acts 12:19–20).

186. Such monuments were common in ancient harbors; see Höckmann, "Harbours," 1138.

187. Agreeing with Haenchen, *Acts*, 698.

188. The Gulf of Adramyttium was also near Ida (Strabo 13.1.6).

189. Hemer, "Alexandria Troas," 92 (citing Leaf's work on Strabo 13.1.65).

190. Mitchell, "Archaeology," 142–43. On Adramyttium, see further Schnabel, *Mission*, 1147, and resources that he cites.

The ship was headed north toward Asia Minor; the party took it only to find a larger ship headed west from a larger port (Acts 27:3). Only the largest ships ventured into the open sea, and this route north was standard for northbound ships in the East.[191] Like most ships in antiquity, this one was fairly small; only a few exceeded 250 tons, since the wooden keels of heavier ships were easily shattered in turbulent seas.[192] This vessel was a "coaster," hugging the coast and putting in at ports in Asia as land breezes allowed; because they depended on uncertain breezes, progress could be tedious on such vessels.[193] Although such voyages often led to Rhodes (21:1),[194] Lycia (27:5) was another common destination, where the travelers would surely find Alexandrian grain ships bound for Rome.[195]

c. Hospitality in Sidon (27:3)

Because unloading and loading cargo consumed considerable time, most passengers would go ashore during such freight movements.[196] Prisoners would normally be kept in custody, but Julius shows Paul exceptional "kindness"; he probably either trusts Paul considerably, on the basis of information from Festus, or sends a guard or two with him (even sending only a single guard would suggest a measure of trust; if Julius expected that he would need to detain more guards, he probably would not have allowed Paul to go; cf. comment on Acts 27:42). Then again, if Paul has friends who can supply the needs of some or all of the party voluntarily, reducing the need to requisition supplies, Julius may have found this beneficial (see discussion below).

i. Julius's Benevolence

Julius's treating Paul and his companions "kindly" (the adverb φιλανθρώπως) reflects the language of Hellenistic-Roman ethics; although it is a NT hapax legomenon, a cognate noun appears in 28:2 (describing the benevolence offered by Maltese residents) and Titus 3:4 (offered by God). Although it is tenuous to conclude with certainty on the basis of two examples, it is possible that Luke focuses on a capacity for kindness among non-Christians;[197] what is clear is that it is a form of benevolence. It was certainly praiseworthy and hence appropriate for encomia.[198] Others used the noun and its cognates to depict the emperor's kindness;[199] it was a helpful virtue for leaders.

That the term is used of Julius reveals again a positive view of a Roman official, including centurions (cf. Luke 7:2; 23:47; Acts 10:1).[200] But while the "Augustan"

191. Witherington, *Acts*, 759; Branch and Schoville, "Ships," 195.

192. Cary and Haarhoff, *Life*, 135. Private coastal traders owned such vessels (known as *orariae naves*, Rapske, *Custody*, 375).

193. Ramsay, "Roads and Travel," 380 (noting Dio Chrys. *Or.* 34.36).

194. Ramsay, "Roads and Travel," 380.

195. Hemer, *Acts in History*, 133. For the proximity of Lycia to Rhodes, see, e.g., Menander *Aspis* 37, 79–80; for their historic relationship, see comment on Acts 21:1.

196. Marshall, *Acts*, 404. Hirschfeld, "Ship of Paul," 28, points out that "texts and representations indicate grain was loaded or unloaded by means of sacks carried by porters."

197. Stoics felt that nature provided a sense of common humanity among people (Cic. *Fin.* 3.19.63). If some scholars argue that Luke writes an apologetic for Rome (so Walaskay), an apologetic for some good in non-Christians (against an apocalyptic dualism such as one might construe from some Johannine language) is not impossible (though reconstructing a particular redactional background for it would be speculative).

198. Men. Rhet. 2.11, 420.22; see fuller discussion at Acts 28:2.

199. Dio Chrys. *Or.* 40.15; 45.2–3; Men. Rhet. 2.1–2, 375.10; 2.13, 423.7; cf. Mus. Ruf. 8, p. 66.11 (on the ideal); Dio Chrys. *Or.* 4.24–25 (on ideal rulers); Paus. 1.23.1 (rulers).

200. With, e.g., Barrett, *Acts*, 1183. Spencer, *Acts*, 232, portrays the centurion as Paul's patron (undoubtedly in the broadest sense). For noble models of Romans, see, e.g., Jos. *Ant.* 18.282, 305.

centurion may exercise benevolent authority, Paul remains the center of divine activity in the narrative, just as Augustus apparently set events in motion in Luke 2:1–3 but Jesus (portrayed in terms deliberately contrasting with the emperor) is the real center of God's activity there (2:1–14).

Julius's favor toward Paul also implies a high status for Paul, a fairly consistent emphasis of Luke.[201] Rome also treats Paul with respect for his status. Perhaps the centurion also respects Paul's age or his status in his movement.[202] Certainly his observation that members of this movement appear in many cities, knowing and ready to provide for Paul, would bolster Julius's conviction that Paul holds high status in the movement. Luke also adds pathos and underlines Paul's *ēthos* by the response of others who know him well. Everywhere he goes, Christians lament his departure (Acts 20:37–38; cf. 21:5); he is an object of affection (except among those who want to kill him!).

ii. Sidon and Paul's Friends

The ship probably stopped at Sidon for trade; Sidon had a good harbor (Strabo 16.2.22).[203] Sidon was about sixty-nine nautical miles from Caesarea and hence could be reached in a day, as here, under good sailing conditions.[204] It had been a "free" city since 111 B.C.E.[205] An earthquake had demolished two-thirds of the original Phoenician Sidon (though most of the people escaped; Strabo 1.3.16). The city had been known since Homer's day for its beautiful art and craftsmanship.[206] Religiously, it was still known in this period for the healing temple of Eshmun and the throne of Astarte.[207] Nevertheless, it had a Jewish community.[208]

It may not be coincidence that, for Luke, Sidon was not only where Paul received hospitality but the chief city in the region where God sent Elijah to receive hospitality from a widow (Luke 4:26).[209] Like the other famous Phoenician city, Tyre, Sidon was also less inhospitable to Jesus than was his homeland (6:17; 10:13–14;[210] see comments on Acts 11:19; 12:20). Luke reports further about the gospel's reception in Phoenicia more generally. Paul also had friends in nearby Tyre (perhaps a day's walk, and a briefer coastal voyage),[211] who had warned him not to go to Jerusalem (Acts 21:3); churches appear in Phoenicia as early as 11:19, and Paul ministered there in 15:3 with reports of Gentile conversions that encouraged believers there. Paul could also have met Sidonian believers in the journey of 11:29–30 and 12:25,

201. With, e.g., Witherington, *Acts*, 759; more generally in Acts, Lentz, *Luke's Portrait*.

202. A public slave, sent to kill a renowned old man, refused to do so (Val. Max. 2.10.6).

203. Bruce, *Acts¹*, 453, notes its "double harbour" from Ach. Tat. 1.1. Sometimes Alexandrian ships attempting to move north toward Cyprus could also be driven east toward Sidon by a strong wind from the west (Davis, "Navigation," 218, citing the *Isis* in Lucian *Ship* 7).

204. Marshall, *Acts*, 404; cf. Bruce, *Commentary*, 453; Conzelmann, *Acts*, 215. Progress was normally very slow on a ship's first day from Alexandria (Davis, "Navigation," 216), but those sailing the open sea could often reach Cyprus after several days (218).

205. Fitzmyer, *Acts*, 770.

206. Hom. *Il*. 6.289–91; Strabo 1.2.33; 16.2.24. For astronomy and mathematics, see Strabo 16.2.24. For glass manufacture, see Pliny E. *N.H.* 5.17.76; also brief notice in Schoville, "Glass," 212. In this period, glass had become a geographically wide industry, including in Jerusalem (Kahn, "Herodian Innovation").

207. Khalifeh, "Sidon," 40.

208. See Stern, "Diaspora," 142 (citing Jos. *Ant*. 17.324; *War* 2.479).

209. Sarepta (Zarephath), which both Luke 4:26 and 1 Kgs 17:9–10 LXX specify, was also well known (Khalifeh, "Sarepta").

210. Material from Mark (Mark 3:8) and Q (Matt 11:21–22).

211. Tyre, Sidon, and Aradus formed a three-city unity, hence Tripolis (Strabo 16.2.15); Tyre was less than 30 mi. to the south. Tyre and Sidon rivaled each other in fame and size (16.2.22).

in 18:22, in 9:30, or at some time that Luke does not record; like Tyre, Sidon was on the way between Caesarea and Antioch.

Allowing Paul to visit "friends"[212] could portray them as benefactors or patrons (since they supply his needs; see comment on Acts 19:31), but more likely the emphasis is on peers, a common Greek sense of the term φίλος.[213] When used formally, patronage was a long-term relationship with prescribed obligations; Paul accepted hospitality from congregations without accepting long-term patronage (Rom 15:24; 1 Cor 16:6).[214] The Christian movement, more than any idealist philosophic sect, is a movement of "friends";[215] its expansion has allowed Christians to find hospitality anywhere.[216] Indeed, the apostle to the Gentiles has many places in the Diaspora that welcome him (see Acts 28:15).

That Paul obtains care for his needs there fits the custom of friends providing for prisoners (24:23).[217] If the high-status prisoner can be cared for without Julius having to requisition supplies, this was to the latter's as well as the former's advantage. The term for their "care" for him, ἐπιμελείας, could include care for the sick (cf. the cognate verb in Luke 10:34–35), but it was broader than this (1 Tim 3:5); it could suggest that they spared no effort in diligently caring for his need (cf. 1 Esd 6:10). Siding with a known prisoner could make people suspects themselves if the case went against the prisoner;[218] but it was often emphasized that true "friends" were ready to suffer and die for each other (also relevant at Acts 28:13–15).[219] Moreover, Paul would have explained the special circumstances of his case.

As in 28:14–15, however, an important reason for Luke's narrating the support of Paul's friends is to confirm that, despite the usual practice of friends withdrawing from someone charged by the state, Paul's friends were not ashamed of his chains (cf. 2 Tim 1:16). In the language of ancient forensic rhetoric, they thus function as character witnesses in support of Paul, reinforcing Luke's apologetic on his behalf.

d. Past Cyprus to Myra (27:4–5)

Some modern readers (particularly in landlocked areas) are not interested in nautical details, but such details would have proved more interesting to an ancient audience,[220] certainly in the Aegean region, where we have postulated a major part of Luke's audience and where ports were common. Analysis of Luke's narrative by a meteorologist shows the correspondence of Luke's description with known meteorological phenomena in the relevant parts of the Mediterranean.[221]

212. Rightly emphasized here by Bock, *Acts*, 732, as significant in antiquity. On friendship in antiquity, see discussion at Acts 19:31; also Fitzgerald, *Friendship*; Gehrke, "Friendship"; Reibnitz, "Friendship"; Keener, "Friendship"; idem, *John*, 1004–15.

213. Cf., e.g., Hom. *Il.* 18.81–82; Plato *Laws* 8.837AB; Arist. *E.E.* 7.9.1, 1241b; Diog. Laert. 5.31; Iambl. *V.P.* 29.162; 30.167; *Let. Aris.* 228; Thom, "Equality"; Keener, "Friendship," 382.

214. Witherington, *Acts*, 761.

215. Cf. esp. Epicureans, in Diog. Laert. 10.1.10; Culpepper, *School*, 101; Stowers, *Letter Writing*, 66; Meeks, *Moral World*, 57; Stambaugh and Balch, *Environment*, 143. See further discussion on friendship groups at Acts 2:44–45. Some, comparing 3 John 15, thus see "the friends" here as a title (Arrington, *Acts*, 255), although it could also mean "his friends" (cf. Malherbe, *Social Aspects*, 112).

216. An ideal among Pythagoreans, Jewish travelers, and others, which Luke portrays as widely realized among early Christians.

217. See more fully Rapske, "Prison," 829; comment on Acts 24:23.

218. Winter, *Welfare*, 95.

219. See, e.g., Diod. Sic. 10.4.4–6; Val. Max. 2.6.11; 4.7 passim; Mus. Ruf. 7, p. 58.23; Epict. *Diatr.* 2.7.3; Keener, "Friendship," 383–84.

220. They appear in historical works and even in novels (Char. *Chaer.* 1.11).

221. See White, "Meteorological Appraisal" (a former professional meteorologist, p. 407), supplying more details on weather patterns in Acts 27:5–26.

1. Passing Crete with Contrary Winds (27:4)

Contrary winds often delayed sailing;[222] one means of extrapolation suggests that roughly half of all sea voyages suffered delays.[223] "Contrary" winds here means those hindering the ship's progress to the northwest (from Syria toward Myra, Acts 27:5). The usual winds, for a period generally of at least six weeks toward the end of the sailing season,[224] are from the northwest to the northeast, which were precisely contrary to the ship's northwestern direction.[225] (Such winds were more helpful for travel to the west or southwest.)[226] Ancient ships' square rigs made it much more difficult for them to sail into the winds.[227] In the second century B.C.E., Athens fell behind in trade especially because the Etesian winds made northward travel more difficult.[228]

Ideally, the shortest distance would have been to sail from the southwestern tip of Cyprus (for which see comment on Acts 13:4) directly toward Myra,[229] but this route was impossible in view of the winds. (A ship from Myra to Syria, by contrast, could simply sail across the open sea west of Cyprus, a voyage that Luke may have remembered by now with some appreciation [21:1–3].) Other reports from antiquity illustrate the difficulty of this voyage. Although Myra is roughly due north of Alexandria, contrary winds drove a ship sailing from Alexandria to Rome east to Sidon (Lucian *Ship* 7).[230]

Instead the travelers sailed on the east of Cyprus (the shape of which forced them ever further east) to shield them from this wind, leaving them a briefer voyage due north (or northeast) toward Cilicia, then a long coasting voyage along the south of Asia Minor (Cilicia and Pamphylia)[231] until they reached Myra.[232] ("Under the shelter of" [also Acts 27:7] probably means the leeward side, as in the NRSV.)[233] Westward currents on the southern coast of Asia Minor would help the latter part of the voyage;

---

222. Casson, *Mariners*, 164, 196, 207; in ancient literature, see, e.g., Cic. *Att.* 5.12; Caesar *C.W.* 3.107; Pliny *Ep.* 10.15.1; 10.17A.1. Problems with winds here may foreshadow the narrative's coming gale (Green, "Acts," 766).

223. Toner, *Culture*, 48, reasoning from the proportion of oracular responses. Although such extrapolations are tenuous, they offer one of our few concrete ways of estimating at least order of magnitude. For fear of weather delays, cf. also Symm. *Ep.* 1.9.

224. Rapske, "Travel and Shipwreck," 35. Many commentators mention "summer" winds here, but it is quite late in the season, since delays due to the winds have them leaving Crete in September or October (perhaps past Oct. 5; see comment on Acts 27:9).

225. Bruce, *Acts*[1], 453; Hemer, *Acts in History*, 133; Witherington, *Acts*, 761. Most nautical sources here follow Smith, *Voyage*, 67–68; but some helpfully add *Sailing Directions for the Mediterranean* (U.S. Navy Hydrographic Office Nr 154A, 1942), 32–33 (Conzelmann, *Acts*, 215n5).

226. Cicero appreciated the "Etesian winds," which moved ships and cooled the summer heat (*Nat. d.* 2.53.131).

227. Casson, *Mariners*, 196.

228. Ibid., 164.

229. Cf. Conzelmann, *Acts*, 215. Davis, "Navigation," 78–81, notes that ships did not have to hug the coasts in eastern Mediterranean sailing, though he recognizes (78) that Luke's ship did so. Alexandrian grain ships headed for Rome would often depend on diurnal, offshore winds when they lacked the rarer southeast wind, later called a khamsin (208).

230. Lake and Cadbury, *Commentary*, 327, noting that this Adramyttian ship may have also been coming north from Alexandria. (It was probably too small, however, to be a grain vessel headed for Rome; see Acts 27:6.)

231. United by one article because Luke views them from the standpoint of the voyage (a single coast) rather than provincially (Hemer, *Acts in History*, 133). For coasting along Lycia and Pamphylia, see also, e.g., Tac. *Ann.* 2.79. Some ancients thought the Pamphylians descended from Trojans (Strabo 14.4.1), including Herodotus (Strabo 14.4.3, citing Hdt. 7.91). On Pamphylia, see further Martini, "Pamphylia"; comment on Acts 13:13.

232. Hemer, *Acts in History*, 133; Bruce, *Commentary*, 502; idem, *Acts*[1], 453. Mark Wilson (correspondence, Nov. 25, 2011) estimates a voyage of 657 mi. (1060 km.) from Caesarea to Myra.

233. So BDAG. Moulton and Milligan, *Vocabulary*, cite Philost. *Imag.* p. 365.1 (ed. Kayser) from Herwerden, *Lexicon*.

the land breeze blowing at a right angle from the shore (offshore at night, onshore during the day) also offered an improvement to winds blowing from the west.[234]

Even in good weather, however, ships typically sailed north to Asia before turning west. Alexandrian grain ships normally "headed for the southern coast of Asia Minor on a port tack, there turned west and, on a starboard tack, coasted along to Rhodes," then headed for the south of Crete.[235] The route, then, would have been familiar to the sailors, in any case.

II. MYRA IN LYCIA (27:5)

The winds caused many delays; the Western text offers either tradition or, more likely, a plausible educated guess that the voyage took fifteen days from Cyprus to Myra.[236] The Etesian winds were east winds in Asia; when they were blowing as east winds (generally from about July 19 to August 19[237] and for a few days during the winter), they blew during the day and stopped at night.[238] But given the temporal note of 27:9, they seem to be past the time Pliny assigns to the helpful Etesian winds.

The Adramyttian ship was probably returning to its home port after Myra, necessitating a change of ships for the travelers (27:6).[239] Myra in Lycia was apparently a common destination for Alexandrian grain ships.[240] Myra's port was Andriace (Ἀνδριάκη, sometimes spelled as Andriaca); the city proper lay two or three miles inland from its harbor (Strabo 14.3.7).[241] That Hadrian later built a granary at Andriace attests its commercial importance.[242] Myra's later Christian bishop Nicolaus (ca. 303 C.E.) took the place of Poseidon for sailors and became their patron saint as well as that of children (Western tradition transformed him into "Saint Nicholas").[243] Like most ancient cities, Myra in this period had its own famous pagan shrines. A spring of Apollo there was known for its fish that, when invited three times by a pipe, supposedly came and offered oracular responses (Pliny E. *N.H.* 32.8.17).

Myra was a prominent Lycian city in the Hellenistic era; in the time of the empire, it appears in inscriptions as a μητρόπολις.[244] Of the twenty-three cities in the Lycian league, Myra was among the six noted to be the largest (Strabo 14.3.3); it was just after Patara (14.3.6; see comment on Acts 21:1). The city was elevated, lying twenty stadia above sea level on a high hill (Strabo 14.3.7). Mountainous forests offered timber for building ships; goats' hair provided fabric for robes. But while the mountains provided

234. Bruce, *Commentary*, 502; idem, *Acts*[1], 453; Conzelmann, *Acts*, 215; Hemer, *Acts in History*, 133. Dependence on offshore breezes was unreliable (Dio Chrys. *Or.* 34.37); Pliny E. *N.H.* 2.48.127 says that Etesian winds stopped at night. Davis, "Navigation," 219, notes that during warmer seasons "onshore winds from the southerly quarter govern in the morning and afternoon" along the western leg of Asia Minor's southern coast, "then shift offshore as northerlies in the late afternoon and evening. These conditions permitted sailing ships to push westward with the current on a prolonged series of tacks lasting from a half to a full day." Yet shipwrecks along the rocky coast indicate the dangers here (see ibid., following Parker, *Shipwrecks*, map 1).

235. Casson, *Mariners*, 208; see also Le Cornu, *Acts*, 1450.

236. Witherington, *Acts*, 761n39; D. Williams, *Acts*, 428; Arnold, "Acts," 469.

237. Pliny E. *N.H.* 2.47.123–24. He writes that south winds dominated the summer, after May 10 (2.47.123), especially from August 19 until about forty days before the autumnal equinox (2.47.124). Cf. waiting for these winds in summer in Galen *Grief* 23a (with 21).

238. Pliny E. *N.H.* 2.48.127.

239. Finegan, *Apostles*, 189.

240. See Ramsay, "Roads and Travel," 380; also many commentaries, e.g., Bruce, *Commentary*, 502. On Myra, see further Fant and Reddish, *Sites*, 254–59. It is known for, among other things, its sea necropolis and river necropolis (Fant and Reddish, *Sites*, 257).

241. Bruce, *Commentary*, 502; Witherington, *Acts*, 761; Zimmermann, "Myra," 412 (5 km.).

242. Mitchell, "Myra," noting also that "a civic ferry service linked the city with Limyra to the east (*OGI* [*OGIS*] 572)."

243. Finegan, *Apostles*, 189.

244. Mitchell, "Myra." The city is attested by the fifth century B.C.E. (Zimmermann, "Myra," 412).

resources for commerce, they also isolated Lycia except along the coast and left less arable land for prosperity than some of their neighbors possessed.[245] Fisheries on the islands off the coast provided income, and some ancients counted as a delicacy Lycian sponges.[246] The Taurus mountain range separated Lycia from the Cibyrans to the north.[247]

If for no other reason, because Attalia in southwest Pamphylia (Acts 14:25) adjoined Lycia, it is reasonable to surmise that Paul knew something of Lycia.[248] Paul would also have known something of Pamphylia, probably even before visiting Attalia; as this text implies, Pamphylia was also close to Cilicia.[249] The "coast of Cilicia" would be particularly familiar to Paul (9:11, 30; 11:25; 21:39; cf. 15:41). The "coast of Pamphylia" was potentially dangerous;[250] the waters were sometimes very rough where the Pamphylian and Lycian seas met (Lucian *Ship* 8).

In Greek myth, the Cyclopes came from Lycia (Strabo 8.6.11). Lycians were allies of Troy in the legendary Trojan War,[251] and Homer claimed that Lycians were Trojans (Strabo 10.2.10),[252] though Lycians also purportedly appeared in other locations (12.8.5). In more recent times, Lycians united under the Lycian League in the early second century B.C.E., under a Lyciarch.[253] Later, Rome rewarded Rhodes's loyalty (cf. comment on Acts 21:1) by granting it control over Lycia, a grant that provoked tensions between Rhodes and Lycia (Polyb. 22.5.1–10), but Lycia still later achieved freedom from Rhodes (30.31.4; 31.4.3). Most recently the emperor Claudius, annoyed with the Lycians' feuding, removed this freedom and restored them to Rhodes (Suet. *Claud.* 25.3). Lycia had been hellenized for several centuries, and it experienced a building boom soon after under Vespasian, which included "aqueducts and bathhouses."[254]

Under Greek influence, the Lycians equated their mother goddess with Leto, and in the period of the empire, Lycia worshiped Leto and her twin children, Apollo and Artemis, as the national gods. Lycians held festivals at the center of this cult, the Letoon. Perhaps in association with Apollo (see comment on Acts 16:16), Lycia was known for its oracular centers, most famously Apollo's oracle at Patara.[255] Myra's most notable cult was (Artemis) Eleuthera.[256] Some Jews lived in Lycia and nearby Caria;[257] for Lycia, Samos, and Pamphylia, see 1 Macc 15:23.[258]

---

245. Harrill, "Asia Minor," 132–33.

246. Ibid., 133.

247. Strabo 14.2.1. On the Cibyratic Convention, see Lightfoot, *Colossians*, 6–7.

248. On their proximity, see further Pliny E. *N.H.* 5.27.97; Quint. Curt. 3.1.1 (in Alexander's day); Tac. *Ann.* 2.79. Sometime in the reign of Claudius (Levick, *Roman Colonies*, 163) or Nero (pp. 227–28) or Vespasian (74 C.E.; Zimmermann, "Lycia"), Pamphylia was administratively joined to Lycia; but either Nero or Galba may have rejoined Pamphylia to Galatia (so Levick, *Roman Colonies*, 164), and so it is difficult to determine the status of administrative links at the time of Paul's voyage. For further treatment of Lycia, see, e.g., Pliny E. *N.H.* 5.28.100–102 (including on its cities and rivers; on nearby Caria, *N.H.* 5.29.103–9); briefly Carroll, "Lycia"; Zimmermann, "Lycia"; Schnabel, *Mission*, 1090–91; for summary of 1990s archaeological work on "the Cibyratis and Lycia," see Mitchell, "Archaeology," 164–70.

249. Pliny E. *N.H.* 5.23.94; 5.26.96.

250. For a near shipwreck there, see Jos. *War* 1.280; *Ant.* 14.377.

251. Hom. *Il.* 2.876–77; possibly a Lycia closer to Troy in 5.105, 173. Their heroes in the legendary Trojan War were remembered centuries later (Philost. *Hrk.* 39.1).

252. Some also claimed that Trojan Cilicians settled in Pamphylia (Strabo 14.4.1).

253. Bryce, "Lycia," 386–87. This league continued in imperial times (Behrwald, "Lycian League").

254. Mitchell, "Lycia," 895; on its hellenization, see also Mitchell, *Anatolia*, 1:85. Greek supplanted the local language (on which see Melchert, "Lycian Language") in the late fourth century B.C.E. (so Mitchell, "Lycia," 895; it had vanished, at least in written form, by the second century B.C.E., idem, *Anatolia*, 1:172).

255. Bryce, "Lycia," 386.

256. Mitchell, "Myra."

257. See Stern, "Diaspora," 148 (for Caria, 148–49). Lycia is also among the sample regions listed for divine judgment in *Sib. Or.* 3.514.

258. Luke might mention sailing past Cilicia for pathos, remembering Paul's homeland (Acts 9:11, 30; 21:39), but far more likely includes it as part of his emphasis on geographic horizons of interest to his audience.

e. Transfer to an Alexandrian Ship (27:6)

Julius transfers them at Myra to an Alexandrian grain ship bound for Italy.

I. WHY THE TRANSFER?

It is possible that Julius had originally planned to take his party north to Smyrna, Troas, and Neapolis, employing the same land route later followed by Ignatius from Smyrna.[259] But instead he transships so as to continue by sea, and this approach may well have been planned or even standard (note the similar arrangement in Patara, Acts 21:1–2).[260] The Adramyttian ship (27:2) would soon reach its home port, and so the voyagers would need to transfer to another vessel at some point.

Because Myra (27:5) was a regular port for many Egyptian grain ships sailing toward Rome (such as the *Isis* mentioned by Lucian; see also comment on Acts 27:5), it was also a good port to find an Alexandrian ship heading for Rome.[261] A later (Hadrianic) granary attests Myra's importance (like Patara's, 21:1) for the transport of grain.[262]

Certainly, transport on vessels of the Alexandria-Rome grain fleet, known for its efficiency, could secure the fastest access to Rome.[263] Luke displays some firsthand knowledge of the prominence of Alexandrian ships on the sea route to Rome (also 28:11; for other aspects of Alexandria, see comment on Acts 18:24).[264]

II. EGYPT'S GRAIN AND ROME

Even by the end of the republic, most of Rome's male citizens received the monthly grain dole, and the lower classes grew dependent on it.[265] The average number of the dole's recipients that ancient records report for the early empire is 200,000.[266] Rome may have imported as many as 200,000 to 400,000 tons of wheat every year;[267] some regions produced a sufficient surplus for other regions, but Rome was taken care of first.[268] (This helped ensure political stability in the emperor's capital; limited grain in Rome led to riots.)[269] Of the eight important grains exploited today, the ancient Mediterranean world used only wheat and barley.[270] Romans usually bought their bread in the form of loaves that were flat and round.[271]

259. Ramsay, "Roads and Travel," 385.

260. Foakes-Jackson, *Acts*, 229.

261. See Conzelmann, *Acts*, 215–16.

262. Hemer, *Acts in History*, 134.

263. Casson, *Travel*, 150. Of several different routes (the others including land travel), this was the swiftest (Ramsay, "Roads and Travel," 377–78).

264. Keener, *Acts*, 3:2801–5.

265. Shelton, *Romans*, 133; see also Suet. *Aug.* 40.2; 42.1–3; Dio Cass. 62.18.5; discussion of urban poverty at Acts 3:2. Further on Rome's grain trade, see Sallares, "Grain Trade," 979–81.

266. Casson, *Mariners*, 207. Some estimate that only a small percentage of Rome's population received the dole (Robinson, *Criminal Law*, 89).

267. Garnsey and Saller, *Empire*, 84 (including all sources); on the higher end, Kraybill, *Cult and Commerce*, 107; Eckey, *Apostelgeschichte*, 559. For a lower estimate of 150,000 tons, see Garnsey, "Grain," 118; for 135,000, see Casson, *Mariners*, 207. For the transport of grain in the empire, see Llewelyn, *Documents*, 7:112–27, §6; for the grain fleet, Hirschfeld, "Ship of Paul." Scheidel and Friesen, "Size," estimate the gross income of the empire at fifty million tons of wheat annually (roughly twenty billion sesterces).

268. Garnsey and Saller, *Empire*, 98–99; cf. Bauckham, *Climax*, 362–63.

269. E.g., Appian *Bell. civ.* 5.8.67; Tac. *Ann.* 6.13; 12.43; Stambaugh, *City*, 143. Toner, *Culture*, 169, views protest, most frequently involving food, as a form of popular resistance against "elite misrule." The population could also riot when deprived of theater entertainment (because of the strike of a low-paid actor; Dio Cass. 56.47.2).

270. Rapske, "Travel," 25; cf. wheat and millet in Stambaugh, *City*, 144. See further discussion of wheat in Sallares, "Grain," 966–67; on food access, see now Wilson, *Hungry*.

271. Stambaugh, *City*, 146 (citing Pliny E. *N.H.* 19.53).

Most Romans knew Egypt especially for its wheat;[272] everyone knew that Egypt paid particularly heavy tribute (Strabo 17.1.12), undoubtedly an unfortunate penalty for its fertility. From the time that Augustus annexed Egypt, this province supplied perhaps 135,000 tons; some ancients estimated Egypt as the source of one-third of the grain eaten in Rome (Jos. *War* 2.386).[273] Although productive Sicily, Sardinia, and Africa were nearer, simplifying the transportation, most of Rome's grain came from Egypt.[274] Much of the grain came as tribute or rents paid by tenants working the land of imperial estates.[275]

Egypt's grain was politically sensitive: anything willfully delaying the arrival of grain in Rome was legally punishable.[276] The emperor's representatives managed the province, and Roman nobles could enter Egypt only with the emperor's permission.[277] Rome kept three legions there (Strabo 17.1.12). Soon after the events depicted in our narrative, the strategic value of these legions became widely apparent; because Vespasian controlled Egypt, he could cut off Rome's grain to force its surrender (Tac. *Hist.* 3.4.8).[278] Others also knew that Alexandria was one of the most obvious places to purchase grain.[279]

Egypt had both good sea harbors and good transport by river (the Nile; Strabo 17.1.13). Earlier Egyptian transport on the Nile and the Red Sea was a precursor for the Roman grain fleet.[280] Grain also had to be transported within Egypt,[281] and Nile grain boats varied from small bound-papyrus skiffs to ships 20 meters long that carried up to 500 tons.[282] Metropolites (higher-status citizens of capitals of the nomes, or administrative districts), rather than the skippers, generally owned the boats.[283] Egyptian travel was sophisticated; the 328-foot (100 m.) lighthouse on the Pharos island,[284] built about 300–280 b.c.e., illumined seven or eight miles around it on Egypt's dangerous coastline and was counted among the Seven Wonders of the Ancient World.[285] Egyptian pilots had the best reputation, and hence ships

272. E.g., Polyb. 9.11a.1–4; Max. Tyre 23.5. For the Egypt-Rome grain trade in the empire, see Charlesworth, *Trade Routes*, 16–34.

273. Lewis, *Life*, 165. Casson, *Travel*, 129, estimates 150,000 tons; but in idem, *Mariners*, 207, he estimates 135,000 tons. Most bread eaten in Rome used grain from Egypt or North Africa (198).

274. Ramsay, "Roads and Travel," 378. Italy produced inadequate wheat and could not compete economically with imported wheat (378). For Libyan grain, see, e.g., Martial *Epig.* 13.12.

275. Garnsey, "Grain," 120.

276. Robinson, *Criminal Law*, 89.

277. Tac. *Ann.* 2.59; Ramsay, "Roads and Travel," 378.

278. For concern over Italy's vulnerability based on dependence for outside food supplies, see Tac. *Ann.* 3.54.

279. Thus Helena sent her servants to buy grain there during famine in Judea (Jos. *Ant.* 20.51).

280. Cadbury, *Acts in History*, 28. Before Rome's conquest of the East, Alexandria and Rhodes monopolized the grain trade (Casson, *Mariners*, 164).

281. E.g., P.Giss. 11 (118 c.e., a letter from an intra-Egypt transporter of government grain); P.Col. 1, recto 4, col. 1 (155 c.e., a receipt from the government grain trade).

282. Lewis, *Life*, 142 (noting also larger vessels' square sails for moving north and oars for moving south against the current).

283. Ibid., 143.

284. Pharos was "close to the mainland, and forms with it a harbour with two mouths," but Caesar devastated the island in his war with Alexandria (Strabo 17.1.6 [trans. Jones and Sterrett, LCL, 8:23]). It had the best weather in Egypt (17.1.7). The island lighthouse continued to stand during the empire (Pliny E. *N.H.* 5.34.128; Lucian *Hist.* 62).

285. Friedländer, *Life*, 1:352; Purcell, "Lighthouses." This wonder appears only in some lists (Brodersen, "Seven Wonders"); "lamps portraying Isis of Pharos" celebrated this lighthouse (Frankfurter, *Religion in Egypt*, 54; on the lighthouse further, see also Davis, "Navigation," 214–16). Alexandrian documents concerned with mercantile economies are naturally also concerned about ships (e.g., *Tr. Shem* 4:5; cf. 6:16; 11:6).

coveted them most;[286] it is likely that the Alexandrian ship here has some Egyptian crewmembers.[287]

III. ROME'S GRAIN SHIPS

Earlier scholars often argued that the Roman government ran the grain fleet,[288] and this allowed Julius to secure passage on any ship and even take charge.[289] Although this may have been true in a later period, Rome in this period worked with private ship owners, who speculated in Alexandrian grain.[290] Greeks, Phoenicians, and Syrians owned and ran nearly all mercantile ships, including Alexandrian grain ships; Rome merely provided the organization that kept the grain fleet efficient.[291] Julius secures passage and takes charge of relevant matters the way he would with any private enterprise; as Rome's highest authorized representative present, he could commandeer whatever he needed to execute his commission. He would not control the ship's ultimate destination, but he could requisition what he needed along the way. Although there were no passenger ships in antiquity, the large grain vessels of the Alexandrian fleet offered the best passenger service available.[292]

Presumably, many of the grain ships normally traveled in fleets,[293] but individual ships also loaded and sailed at separate times.[294] Often an owner possessed a single ship, though owning five ships instead of one would increase the profit.[295] Ships normally sailed from Alexandria in April, May, or June, but they could face long administrative delays in ports such as Puteoli; ships that could not return to Alexandria before late August might face winter weather if they attempted a second trip,[296] but given the financial pressure, freelance vessels must have often gambled on the time to make a second trip.[297]

Shipowners' profit, rather than sailors' interests, often dictated whether a ship would make a second run. Although the timing was risky (see comment on Acts 27:9) and ships might need to winter somewhere along the way, they could make more profit if they succeeded.[298] The *Isis* reportedly made at least seventy-two thousand drachmas per year (ten Attic talents; Lucian *Ship* 13).[299] The wealthy financed ships; although

286. Friedländer, *Life*, 1:351.
287. During the empire, even Roman warships (which carried Roman soldiers) often used foreign crews (Burckhardt, "Epibatai").
288. E.g., Bruce, *Commentary*, 503; more cautiously, Cadbury, *Acts in History*, 59 (Rome "controlled, if it did not actually own, the merchant marine"). On the Roman commercial marine, see Friedländer, *Life*, 1:189–90.
289. Cf. Dunn, *Acts*, 337–38 (hoping he could "combine his escort duty with that of supervising a grain shipment").
290. Rapske, "Travel," 26; Stambaugh, *City*, 145; Conzelmann, *Acts*, 217; Witherington, *Acts*, 760; Andreau, "Negotiator," 613; on grain ships, see also Seul, *Rettung*, 46–49. The Alexandrian fleet continued to supply Rome until the completion of Constantinople in 330; after this time, Egypt supplied the eastern capital while North Africa fed those still in Rome (Casson, *Mariners*, 212).
291. Casson, *Mariners*, 212.
292. Ibid., 209. Thus, although Vespasian could have taken any naval vessel, he chose one from this fleet (Jos. *War* 7.21; cf. Philo *Flacc.* 26).
293. Rapske, "Travel," 27; Ramsay, "Roads and Travel," 379 (citing Sen. Y. *Ep.* 77.1); Hirschfeld, "Ship of Paul," 26.
294. Ramsay, "Roads and Travel," 379.
295. Lucian *Ship* 13–14, esp. 14.
296. The harvest ended in May; threshed grain would presumably remain ready to ship out at profit. On administrative delays, see, e.g., Hirschfeld, "Ship of Paul," 29.
297. Davis, "Navigation," 208, argues that most ships would have attempted a second trip in late summer, advancing "as far as possible before the fierce depressions of autumn began"; he offers "Paul's ship and Lucian's *Isis*" as examples that had to seek winter havens along the way.
298. Casson, *Mariners*, 210–11 (explicitly mentioning the example of Paul's ship). That ships had a sort of insurance urged some to more risky behavior for profit (cf. Philost. *Vit. Apoll.* 4.32, accusing some of deliberately wrecking unprofitable ships).
299. Rapske, "Travel," 28.

most ship owners were of lower status, the urban elite lent them money and hence presumably controlled a large share of profits.[300] The risk of large losses limited the profitability of such ventures.[301]

Good weather usually allowed the voyage from Rome to Alexandria in ten to thirteen days (nine was exceptional, Pliny E. *N.H.* 19.3);[302] in worse weather the voyage to Alexandria might take up to three weeks.[303] By contrast, the voyage from Alexandria to Rome (as here) was more difficult, in rough weather requiring forty-five days.[304] Working from ancient sources, Ramsay even estimated fifty days: six days from Alexandria to Cyprus, three more to Myra, ten to Rhodes, fifteen to the western end of Crete, thirteen to the Strait of Messina plus a day there, and two more to Puteoli.[305] Others estimate that exceptionally bad weather might require a voyage of two months or more.[306] The Etesian winds, blowing from the northwest to the northeast, helped ships sailing south to achieve four to six knots per hour, but these very winds could more than double the maximum length of the voyage in the opposite direction; a ship could not head straight toward Rome but kept tacking.[307]

Given the number of crewmembers and passengers it carried (Acts 27:37), this was a sizable ship. Scholars often refer to Lucian's *Isis*, which was 180 feet long, at least 45 feet wide, and 40 to 44 feet deep.[308] Seafaring ships varied from 800 to 1,500 tons, with some estimating the *Isis* at even 1,575 tons.[309] Underwater archaeology and other sources have provided considerable information about the construction and design of large ships.[310] Although nothing just like the *Isis* has yet turned up, a first-century merchant ship wrecked near Caesarea measures 147.5 feet (45 m.) in length, which is reasonably close.[311] If possible, the highest end of ship size might have even resembled the massive imperial barges, the largest known of which was some 239 feet (73 m.) long by 79 feet (24 m.) wide.[312] The most common range, however, was between 50 and 120 feet (15–37 m.) long.[313] On the lower end, another measure of the size of such vessels is Claudius's minimum required tonnage for participation in the grain fleet: at least 68 tons.[314]

f. Near Cnidus, Salmone, and Lasea (27:7–8)

Winds made the voyage west difficult and foreshadowed (both for participants within the narrative world and for Luke's story) the greater dangers to come.

300. Pleket, "Elites and Business," 137–38.
301. See MacMullen, *Social Relations*, 100.
302. Rapske, "Travel," 36; Casson, *Mariners*, 207; cf. Davis, "Navigation," 80.
303. Rapske, "Travel," 36; Casson, *Travel*, 151–52; cf. Moore, "Life," 229 (with shorter minimum and longer maximum estimates).
304. Riesner, *Early Period*, 315; Casson, *Mariners*, 208.
305. Ramsay, "Roads and Travel," 381. The estimate to Myra seems low (perhaps from the west of Cyprus), and to Rhodes too long.
306. E.g., Casson, *Travel*, 151–52; Stambaugh and Balch, *Environment*, 39.
307. Rapske, "Travel," 35–36; Casson, *Mariners*, 196.
308. Using the slightly differing figures of Friedländer, *Life*, 1:351; Casson, *Travel*, 158–59; the comparison with the *Isis* is old (e.g., Abbott, *Acts*, 247). Lucian's figures are 120 cubits long and a maximum of 29 deep (*Ship* 5); but Lucian notes that this ship was exceptionally large, so that some came to Athens just to see it (*Ship* 1).
309. Friedländer, *Life*, 1:351. Estimates of the *Isis*'s cargo capacity range from 1,000 to 3,500 tons (Rapske, "Travel," 31); Casson, *Mariners*, 209, probably most realistically suggests 1,000–1,300 tons.
310. See Fitzgerald, "Ship of Paul," 32–38.
311. Rapske, "Travel," 31.
312. Adkins and Adkins, *Life*, 188.
313. Ibid., 187, giving a range of 150 to 350 long tons.
314. Later 340 tons or fleets with ships each carrying at least 68 tons (Rapske, "Travel," 31).

I. WEATHER AND THE VOYAGE

The ship probably left Lycia in the more favorable weather that came between the several-day storms typical of this season. Such conditions account for westerly winds and slow progress and for later winds shifting to a north or northeast wind.[315] It would take two to three days from Cnidus to Salmone, and by then another storm could move east through the Aegean.[316]

The same wind blowing from the northwest that made the voyage to Myra difficult remained a challenge en route to Cnidus.[317] The travelers could have sailed to Rhodes (21:1),[318] south along its lee, and then across the sea toward Crete; but perhaps they preferred to sail south from farther north (given the winds blowing south), or perhaps they had originally hoped to cross the Aegean to Corinth or a port easier to reach in the south of Greece.

They may have sailed north of Rhodes (cf. 21:1) because they were hoping for a route different from the one they finally were compelled to take.[319] From Cnidus a favorable wind could allow them to sail west to Cythera, an island off Cape Malea in southern Greece. So long as winds were blowing from the northwest, however, a voyage to Malea would be difficult, and given the impending change of season, they may have preferred to sail southeast to Crete, which they could reach, instead of awaiting more favorable sailing.[320] Unable to sail adequately into the strong wind, they tacked toward the south; had they sailed from somewhat farther east than Cnidus, they would have risked being driven by the west wind into Rhodes's eastern shore.[321]

II. CNIDUS (27:7)

Cnidus had two harbors, the eastern one being particularly large, able to hold triremes and harboring twenty naval ships.[322] For centuries it had been visited by ships from distant shores, including Egypt (Thucyd. 8.24.35).[323] Cnidus was significant enough as a port to appear in Pliny the Elder's list of distances.[324] It was Sostratus of Cnidus who dedicated the Pharos lighthouse in Alexandria's harbor[325] besides designing some of Cnidus.[326] Whereas Caesarea Maritima required advanced construction techniques, even early methods of construction could exploit "natural features such as sheltered bays and headlands, as at Cnidus."[327]

Cnidus lay on a peninsula in southwestern Asia Minor, in Caria, but many of its

315. White, "Meteorological Appraisal," 404.
316. Ibid.
317. With, e.g., Hemer, *Acts in History*, 134; Bruce, *Commentary*, 503 (following Smith, *Voyage*, 75–76); Dunn, *Acts*, 338.
318. A common port along the eastern part of the Alexandria-to-Rome route (Casson, *Mariners*, 208; Davis, "Navigation," 220–22).
319. See Ramsay, "Roads and Travel," 380. Literary itineraries often mention sailing by Cnidus in the vicinity of Cos and Rhodes (e.g., Xen. Eph. *Anthia* 1.11; cf. Pliny E. *N.H.* 5.36.133); Rhodes was apparently stronger than Cnidus (Polyb. 31.5.1–5).
320. Bruce, *Commentary*, 503–4.
321. Hanson, *Acts*, 244–45.
322. Strabo 14.2.15; cf. Bruce, *Commentary*, 503. Wilson (correspondence, Nov. 25, 2011) estimates that Cnidus was 130 mi. (210 km.) past Myra (Acts 27:5).
323. Bruce, *Acts¹*, 454; idem, *Commentary*, 503; Johnson, *Acts*, 446; Witherington, *Acts*, 761; Parsons, *Acts*, 354; for Egyptian cults there, see Koester, *Paul and World*, 148.
324. Pliny E. *N.H.* 2.112.245, placing Cnidus 86.5 mi. from Rhodes and 25 mi. from Cos.
325. Strabo 17.1.6; Pliny E. *N.H.* 36.18.83; Lucian *Hist.* 62.
326. Pliny E. *N.H.* 36.12.18; Lucian *Hist.* 62; *Hipp.* 2; *Affairs* 11. For the writer Ctesias, see Lucian *Lover of Lies* 2.
327. Souza, "Harbours," 667.

people lived on a high island, about seven stadia around, connected to the mainland by moles (Strabo 14.2.15). It was founded about 900 B.C.E. and identified itself as Dorian, claiming a Spartan heritage.[328] Cnidus's people were located on a peninsula in the Gulf of Cos (see comment on Acts 21:1) in southwestern Asia Minor. Cnidus was a "free city" (*civitas libera*) under Rome.[329] It boasted notable intellectuals in its heritage and had a well-known medical school and fine wines.[330] Ancients noted some famous marble statues there (Pliny E. *N.H.* 36.4.20–22).

Aphrodite was a particular object of worship in Cnidus, which dedicated sanctuaries to her (Paus. 1.1.3). One Aphrodite temple there was particularly famous, containing a famous naked statue of Aphrodite by Praxiteles.[331] The temple precincts included a sacred grove of luxurious trees and hosted many visitors; it was particularly crowded with people from the city during sacred festivals.[332] Shells allegedly used to castrate some noble youths were venerated in Cnidus's shrine of Aphrodite (Pliny E. *N.H.* 9.41.80). Excavations have revealed not only this famous Aphrodite sanctuary but also other temples (one of Apollo) and a Hellenistic theater adapted in the Roman period.[333]

III. CRETE AND SALMONE (27:7)

Salmone was the first place the travelers would likely reach in Crete, since it was on the island's northeast tip, toward Rhodes.[334] It was Crete's eastern cape, estimated at a thousand stadia from Rhodes and double that figure to Criumetopon on the western end of Crete (Strabo 2.4.3). Some scholars suggest that the name is Phoenician (like many south Cretan names), meaning a place of refuge from the wind;[335] Paul's ship was certainly not the first to benefit from Cretan topography.

The voyagers' reaching Cape Salmone fits the situation in which the wind was blowing from the northwest (which was expected in late summer),[336] but this may have also been the normal route (or at least a common one; see Lucian *Ship* 9).[337] Whereas a north wind could dash a ship onto Crete's northern coast, which had few harbors, the southern coast of Crete could provide shelter from the northern wind.[338] The southern coast had more harbors, and the south winds around Crete are usually gentler than the northern ones.[339] Whereas Luke and other passengers unfamiliar

328. As in Rhodes, Halicarnassus, and Cos (Strabo 14.2.6). Archaeologists have found both Doric and Ionic temple structures (Finegan, *Apostles*, 191).

329. Strabo 14.1.15; Pliny E. *N.H.* 5.29.104.

330. Strabo 14.1.15; see also Cook and Sherwin-White, "Cnidus."

331. Lucian *Portr.* 6; *Portr. D.* 8; 18; 22–23; *Affairs* 11. *Affairs* 13 claims that it was of Parian marble; *Z. Rants* 10 has Pentelic marble. Philost. *Vit. Apoll.* 6.40 tells the story of a passion-crazed youth sacrificing to the statue in hopes of securing marriage to it. On Aphrodite of Cnidus, see further Havelock, *Aphrodite*; Lesswing, "Aphrodite."

332. Lucian *Affairs* 12.

333. Finegan, *Apostles*, 191.

334. Strabo 10.4.2; Pliny E. *N.H.* 4.12.58; *Stad.* 318, 355 (Conzelmann, *Acts*, 216; Johnson, *Acts*, 446; Davis, "Navigation," 222; contrast the different Salmone in Eurip. *Aeolus* frg. 14). It was presumably modern Cape Sidero (Cochrane, "Salmone," 285; H. Rackham in *Pliny: Natural History*, LCL, 2:161 n. *a*; though Lake and Cadbury, *Commentary*, 327, were uncertain), Ákra Sídheros. Cf. the Samonium shrine in northeast Crete (Sanders, *Crete*, 138).

335. Hemer, *Acts in History*, 135–36.

336. Bruce, *Acts*¹, 454 (following Smith, *Voyage*, 454); Hemer, *Acts in History*, 134–35. But it seems to be later than late summer by this point (see Acts 27:9; 28:11).

337. Conzelmann, *Acts*, 216; Hemer, *Acts in History*, 134. A ship moving north from Egypt to Sidon and beyond (Lucian *Ship* 7) would head toward Lycia (*Ship* 8–9; especially in contrary winds) before sailing west; if keeping south of Crete, the ship could have reached Malea instead of Athens (*Ship* 9).

338. Ramsay, "Roads and Travel," 380.

339. Ibid. (contrasting the Adriatic).

with the route may have thought it unusual to sail under Crete, the captain would not have planned otherwise this late in sailing season.[340]

Everyone knew Crete as one of the largest islands (with Sardinia, Sicily, and Cyprus; Strabo 14.2.10); voyagers might find temporary safety from a storm there.[341] In contrast to the Pontic seas, the "Cretan sea" (like that of Sicily and Sardinia) was considered very deep (1.3.4).[342] Educated people in the Roman Empire still recalled the naval prowess of ancient Crete, though they were also aware that it had been lost (10.4.17).[343] Agriculture (for both consumption and export) probably dominated Crete's economy in this period.[344] Augustus joined together Crete and Cyrenaica as a Roman province (17.3.25), with Gortyna as the capital.[345] Crete was less crucial to and less integrated into the empire than the wealthy province of Asia. One influential Cretan Roman citizen of this era, Claudius Timarchus, incurred the displeasure of the Roman senate by insisting that he controlled local popular expressions of gratitude to the Roman proconsuls (Tac. *Ann.* 15.20).

Cretans had preserved some ancient traditions, allegedly including mystic rites related to the Phrygian mother goddess[346] in connection with Zeus's famous rearing in Crete (Strabo 10.3.7, 13).[347] They especially were reputed to practice orgiastic worship reenacting Zeus's birth (10.3.11). Foreign trade spread the Egyptian cults of Isis and Serapis here, especially in port cities; evidence comes from many cities with or near ports, including Lasea (Acts 27:8; *IC* 1.15.2) and Phoenix (Acts 27:12; *IC* 2.20.7).[348] An Alexandrian helmsman (perhaps relevant to Paul's Alexandrian ship) set up the dedication at Phoenix; it mixes devotion to Serapis with devotion to the emperors and other gods.[349] In Greek mythology, the bronze man Talos guarded Crete;[350] more persistent was the idea that its early king Minos and his brother Rhadamanthus judged the dead in the afterlife.[351]

---

340. Casson, *Mariners*, 211; cf. Davis, "Navigation," 222. Alexandrian grain ships usually sailed west from Rhodes to the south of Crete, then sought to remain on westward course to Syracuse (Casson, *Mariners*, 208).

341. E.g., Heliod. *Eth.* 5.22.7 (in Johnson, *Acts*, 446).

342. Its boundaries appear somewhat ambiguous (see Strabo 2.5.21; 7.7.4; 10.5.13).

343. On the Minoans, cf., e.g., Bennet, "Minoan Civilization"; Hiesel, "Minoan Culture"; and sources there. For Late Bronze and Early Iron archaeology there, see Betancourt, "Crete," 71–72.

344. Sanders, *Crete*, 35. For the economy in Roman Crete in general, see 32–35.

345. See Sonnabend, "Crete," 937 (citing Plut. *Pomp.* 29); nevertheless, Cyrene exerted little cultural influence on Crete (Sanders, *Crete*, 133). For Roman urban life, see Sanders, *Crete*, 13–15; for settlement patterns in this period, 16–31; for art, 47–56; for architecture, 57–88; for Rome's subjugation of Crete, Vell. Paterc. 2.34.1; for some key cities, see concisely Schnabel, *Mission*, 1284–85. Gortyna was 9 mi. (15 km.) east on the main road from Phaistos, which was 7.5 mi. (12 km.) due north of Fair Havens (Finegan, *Apostles*, 192).

346. For Dionysiac rites connected with this, see Strabo 10.3.11–15. Some believed that ancient Cretans accepted homosexual practice more than did others (Sext. Emp. *Pyr.* 3.199–200).

347. On Zeus being reared in Crete, see Hesiod *Theog.* 479–80; Eurip. *Hyps.* frg. 752g.23; Apollod. *Bib.* 1.1.6; Lucian *Sacr.* 5, 10; Philost. *Vit. Apoll.* 4.34; harmonizing, Diod. Sic. 3.61.1–3 claims that it was a different Zeus; Arcadians, who claimed Zeus's birthplace for themselves, referred to a local "Crete" instead of the island (Paus. 8.38.2). (For the cave where he was supposed to have been born, see Sonnabend, "Ida"; cf. Max. Tyre 10.1.) Cretans also claimed his tomb there; so Callim. *Hymns* 1 (to Zeus), line 9; Philost. *Vit. soph.* 2.4.569. For this, Callim. *Hymns* 1.8 calls them liars; others mock the story (Lucian *Parl. G.* 6; *Tim.* 4; *Z. Rants* 45; *Lover of Lies* 3; *Sacr.* 10), even as late as the Byzantine Lucian *Patriot* 10. Most outsiders took the tomb tradition no more seriously than did non-Corinthians took the Corinthian claim that Corinth's eponymous founder was a son of Zeus (cf. Paus. 2.1.1), but it was useful for Euhemerus (*Sacr. Hist.* 6, in Grant, *Religions*, 76) and for Jewish polemic (*Sib. Or.* 8.45–49).

348. Sanders, *Crete*, 36–37. Isis proved less popular than Serapis, perhaps because she was too distinct from the indigenous mother goddess to be assimilated to her (37). The imperial cult was apparently quite popular (37–38); for Cretan religion in this period in general, see 36–46. Tac. *Ann.* 3.63 probably also suggests devotion to the imperial cult.

349. Sanders, *Crete*, 37.

350. Kearns, "Talos."

351. E.g., Lucian *Z. Cat.* 18; *Men.* 11–13; see further detail at Acts 10:42.

Some ancients claimed (on the basis of a fallacious etymology; Tac. *Hist.* 5.2) that the Jewish people were originally exiled from Crete. A fairly small number of funerary inscriptions testify to a Jewish presence in Crete from the first century B.C.E. to the fifth century C.E.[352] One indicates that a Sophia of Gortyna was "an Elder and leader of the synagogue at Kissamos."[353] Philo insists that Crete, like Euboea and Cyprus, had a significant Jewish presence (*Embassy* 282).[354] The few literary references suggest that Jews in Crete were fairly prosperous; Josephus's third wife was a Cretan from a quite prominent family (Jos. *Life* 427). Sometimes, however, the Jewish community was exploited: in the early empire, a Sidonian impostor pretending to be a son of Herod induced them to give him money (*Ant.* 17.327; *War* 2.103);[355] in 431 C.E., a false prophet claiming to be Moses allegedly led many over a cliff.[356]

According to tradition, Paul later returned to Crete[357] with Titus, whom he left there to appoint elders (Titus 1:5), but the claim, citing Acts 27:7, that Paul installed Titus as Gortyna's first bishop in 58 C.E.[358] cannot be verified in Acts.[359] The next attestation of Christianity there appears a century later, in a letter of Dionysius of Corinth (in Euseb. *H.E.* 4.21), in which Gortyna is preeminent but Knossos also has a bishop (Pinytus).[360]

iv. Fair Havens and Lasea (27:8)

That the travelers reached Fair Havens "with difficulty" is not surprising. The eastern cape of Crete would be difficult to pass, especially given the northwest wind.[361]

Καλοὶ Λιμένες (Fair Havens) retains the same name in modern Greek today and is a small bay.[362] The site (with two adjoining sheltered areas for ships) and that of nearby Lasea are amply attested in ancient sources, but they are, beyond their local function, insignificant sites that we would not normally expect to appear in an account unless it depended on someone who had traveled there.[363] Lasea appears in other ancient writers with various permutations of the name (this was common in south Cretan names), especially "Lasos" in Pliny E. *N.H.* 4.12.59.[364]

352. Sanders, *Crete*, 43 (noting Bandy, *Inscriptions of Crete*, appendix, 140; *IC* 4.211 and perhaps 2.13.8); Laidlaw, Nixon, and Price, "Crete," 409. Some Diaspora Jews also expected divine judgment on Crete (*Sib. Or.* 3.504–5), among many other places; we also have some evidence of trade with Herodian Caesarea (Sussman, "Oil-Lamp").

353. Sanders, *Crete*, 43 (following Bandy, *Inscriptions of Crete*, B3).

354. Noted also in Schnabel, *Missionary*, 121.

355. Caesar accepted their losses as sufficient punishment for following a false king (Jos. *Ant.* 17.338).

356. Sanders, *Crete*, 43, citing, for the last, Socrates Ecclesiasticus 38 (and the *Anglo-Saxon Chronicle* for that year).

357. Would the earlier unplanned visit depicted in Acts 27 have stirred Paul to reach Crete later?

358. Sonnabend, "Crete," 937; more relevant sources, but later and less reliable, are Euseb. *H.E.* 3.4 and *Acts of Titus* (Finegan, *Apostles*, 192). Finegan (192) points out that the 6 mi. (10 km.) from Fair Havens to Lebena, and then the main road to Gortyna, was not a great distance. But while Paul was there for a period of time (Acts 27:9), he was a prisoner.

359. It should, however, be noted that if Titus did remain with them through Acts 27:8, Luke's omission of the fact would fit his apparent omission of Titus's role elsewhere, despite his prominence in Paul's writings. The omission may be deliberate, though we can only speculate concerning the reason.

360. Sanders, *Crete*, 43, 45. For significant evidence over the next few centuries, see p. 45. Knossos was traditionally known for the minotaur (Philost. *Vit. Apoll.* 4.34); in this period it was becoming increasingly cosmopolitan (see Sweetman, "Knossos").

361. Hemer, *Acts in History*, 135. Even the southern coast of Crete experienced turbulence in July through October (Davis, "Navigation," 223).

362. Bruce, *Commentary*, 504.

363. Hemer, *Acts in History*, 136; Riesner, *Early Period*, 224.

364. Hemer, *Acts in History*, 136; Bruce, *Commentary*, 504. (The denial in Johnson, *Acts*, 446–47, may stem from the difference in name.)

Fair Havens is a bay east of Cape Lithinon and 1.25 miles (2 km.) west of Lasea; an inland journey of 7.5 miles (12 km.) would bring one to the famous Minoan city of Phaistos (Phaestus). The bay would protect a ship from any of the four winds experienced in southern Crete "except perhaps a gentle *Euros*."[365] Some offshore islands help protect the bay from winds, though even the largest island is no more than a quarter of a mile (1.6 km.) in length.[366] The bay forms a triangle, the top of which leads to a slender valley lodged between two hills.[367] It had at least some inhabitants; many Roman sherds have been found near the chapel of Saint Paul, "early and late, with further Roman occupation NW of the modern village."[368] But Fair Havens served mostly as the harbor for Lasea, which flourished through trade[369] (on Lasea, see comment below).

The term λιμήν meant "harbor" (as in Acts 27:12),[370] though it could also be applied to other havens, even of figurative character (4 Macc 7:3; 13:6–7).[371] But as Tannehill notes, "Good Harbors" proves an "ironic name," since it was "not a good harbor for spending the winter (v. 12)."[372] An important function of harbors was to provide shelter from storms (Sen. Y. *Nat. Q.* 6.1.6).

Fair Havens was the best available shelter the travelers had found since Salmone, and they could go no farther unless the wind changed. About 6 miles (10 km.) beyond Fair Havens lay Cape Matala, after which Crete's southern coast turns sharply north, offering little protection against a northwester.[373] Yet Fair Havens, although sheltered against northwest winds and somewhat protected from the sea by nearby islets, was open to nearly "half the compass," suggesting the value of finding a better winter harbor if possible.[374] There was also no significant settlement at Fair Havens, which belonged to Lasea, about 5 miles to its east.[375] Such conditions (especially the long commute between the ship and the town for those who would guard the ship during the winter) made it seem highly undesirable for those accustomed to the ports of the East and Rome.

The town of Lasea, near which Luke places Fair Havens, was 5 miles (8 km.) from Lebena, a site especially devoted to the worship of Asclepius.[376] An island named Nissos Traphos lay across from Lasea, which stood on a headland and had bays on either side; a mole extending nearly to the island protected vessels from wind on either side,

---

365. White, "Meteorological Appraisal," 404; cf. Finegan, *Apostles*, 195. White (405) argues that the problem was not the harbor but that the sailors (and probably soldiers) would prefer a livelier urban area to winter in over a "quiet fishing village." On the undesirability of wintering at most sites on Crete's southern coast, see Davis, "Navigation," 223 (though it "was probably safe" there, 226).

366. Finegan, *Apostles*, 192 (noting that the largest is ironically called Megalonisi; another is "St. Paul's Island").

367. Ibid. On the Platanos Valley and the mountains and their role in the narrative's weather conditions, see White, "Meteorological Appraisal," 406.

368. Sanders, *Crete*, 160. The site includes both St. Paul's chapel and a cave where legend claims (probably fictitiously) that Paul stayed (Fant and Reddish, *Sites*, 76).

369. Fant and Reddish, *Sites*, 74.

370. E.g., Ps 107:30; 1 Esd 5:55; 1 Macc 14:5; 2 Macc 12:6, 9; 14:1.

371. Limenia (Λιμενία) was a city in the *interior* of Cyprus (Strabo 14.6.3).

372. Tannehill, *Acts*, 331 (noting that this and the explicit comment of Acts 27:9 inform the reader of the value of Paul's advice [27:10], although participants in the story world do not recognize it).

373. Bruce, *Commentary*, 504; Hemer, *Acts in History*, 136. See the map in Sanders, *Crete*, fig. 64. The purpose of harbors, whether natural or artificial, was precisely to protect ships from stormy weather (Vitruv. *Arch.* 5.12.1–2).

374. Hemer, *Acts in History*, 136; Bruce, *Commentary*, 507, following Smith, *Voyage*, 85n.

375. Hemer, *Acts in History*, 136.

376. Sanders, *Crete*, 159–60; Lebena was one of Gortyna's two ports (Finegan, *Apostles*, 192). On this cult at Lissos, see Sanders, *Crete*, 84. A famous sanctuary of Asclepius lay on Mount Ida (Philost. *Vit. Apoll.* 4.34).

depending on the wind's direction.[377] The town itself, though not excavated, seems to cover a significant area; surveys indicate Hellenistic tombs, pottery, inscriptions (*IC* 1.15), walls, and possibly an aqueduct system.[378] It appears to have been continuously occupied from the early Minoan until the late Roman period, its Roman period being its most prosperous.[379] An aqueduct supplied Lasea with water that it conducted from a spring located about half a mile (ca. 1 km.) distant.[380] Archaeologists have excavated a later, significant Christian basilica at Lasea.[381]

3. Ignoring Paul's Warning (27:9–13)

Paul advises the ship not to leave in the current weather conditions; the centurion trusts more in the counsel of those in charge of the ship than in Paul. He will soon discover, however, that God can give his servants wisdom about the sea that even the nautical experts lack (as in Luke 5:4–9).

a. A Prisoner's Advice?

Paul's role as God's prophet does not surprise us, but that anyone unaware of this role would entertain his opinion (albeit rejecting it) probably suggests some social status as well. Luke's interest here, however, seems less in explaining Paul's status (although he is happy to imply it) and more in revealing his general accuracy in speaking about the future.

i. Paul's Input

That Paul is permitted to provide any input at all to the centurion is striking. Passengers typically lived on deck, whether in the open or in small shelters they raised for the occasion.[382] Important people could have chairs on the poop and could chat with the skipper; those who could afford books often spent time reading;[383] others gambled.[384]

The situation was, however, far different for prisoners. They could be detained in darkness below deck or tied to the ship's crossbeams (3 Macc 4:10). Like other prisoners, Paul may well have been transported in chains, but being of higher status he was apparently permitted much more freedom and even respect.[385] As noted above, this may stem from the apparent support of the governor and the king implied in their letter (Acts 25:26; 26:31–32; though this would have been sealed, Julius probably has corresponding verbal instructions). Especially sailors, but also higher-class passengers, could express their views regarding travel plans.[386] If Paul was sent (and thought innocent) by the government,[387] was a Roman citizen, and had attendants

377. Finegan, *Apostles*, 192.
378. Sanders, *Crete*, 160.
379. Finegan, *Apostles*, 192.
380. Ibid.
381. Sanders, *Crete*, 114.
382. Rapske, *Custody*, 205.
383. Casson, *Travel*, 156.
384. Ibid., 157.
385. Rapske, *Custody*, 205 (citing, on the chains, Livy 29.15.5; 29.21.12; Jos. *Ant.* 20.131; *War* 7.449). Rapske thinks that Paul may have been chained to the centurion; but this is not clear (though it would explain Paul's presence at a council in Acts 27:9–12 if he was present), and in 27:3 at least, it seems more likely that he was chained to another guard.
386. Praeder, "Acts 27:1–28:16," 691n18, citing Ael. Arist. *Or.* 50.32–37; Cic. *Fam.* 16.9.4. Even in some earlier Greek military settings, everyone could express their views (Xen. *Anab.* 1.3.13).
387. He had spoken eloquently before Agrippa, and Agrippa's favor toward him had probably dictated the orders that Festus issued for the centurion.

representing a movement that he apparently led (an appearance confirmed by the honored treatment accorded him by its members in various locations), he might hold more status (at least on land) than the ship's officers.[388]

Some scholars suggest that it "is inconceivable" that Paul, a prisoner, would offer advice at a council of those deciding the course of the ship.[389] If Paul was chained to the centurion,[390] he may have come to such a meeting precisely as a prisoner; but this chaining arrangement is unclear (27:3), and even if he was chained to the centurion at times, it would also be possible for him to be chained elsewhere during an important meeting. If the report of 27:9–12 is condensed, Paul may not be at the same meeting where the majority of leaders decided to set out (27:11–12); perhaps he communicates his view to the others indirectly, by telling the centurion, who later reports the decision of the others back to him. That he urges "them" (27:9) and not just the centurion (27:11) sounds more active, however, as does the address, "Men," and if this is the case, he is not relegated to the normal role of prisoners in this narrative.

Luke, however, need not feel that he strains his first-century audience's credulity (even if some modern readers demur). It is quite possible that a number of persons were present and not simply the four who were named; such discussion was probably not on board the ship and need not have been private. The centurion's respect for Paul's status will allow Paul to speak, even if Julius's respect is not sufficient for Julius to trust Paul more than the ship's most experienced personnel.

Others think that the centurion or someone else may have included Paul in this informal council because of his extensive travel experience.[391] Careful pilots sometimes solicited the counsel of others aboard a ship with knowledge of sea travel (Sen. Y. *Ep. Lucil.* 14.8); Luke does not indicate that those in charge here solicited or even welcomed it, but there seems little reason to doubt that they permitted it.[392] Those who were widely traveled gained experience and wisdom (Sir 31:9–12), and even if one counts only the sea travels specifically indicated in Acts, Paul traveled about three thousand miles by sea over a span of nearly thirty years.[393] Paul had no experience in this region (perhaps in contrast to some aboard the ship), but he probably had experience with winter travel (and we know, though Luke does not tell us, that he had considerable experience with shipwrecks, 2 Cor 11:25). The Paul of the letters, like Paul here, was appropriately cautious in this regard, usually wintering in secure locations (1 Cor 16:6; Titus 3:12; cf. 2 Tim 4:21; Acts 20:2–3).[394]

11. PAUL'S SPIRITUAL PROMINENCE

People consulted omens before undertaking voyages; Greeks also welcomed portents but in general respected also ecstatic prophecy. Religious advice could be taken seriously (see comment on Acts 27:10). Some doubt the authenticity of Acts 27:9–11 in part because the "owner" and "captain" do not reappear later, even at the shipwreck.[395] This is, however, a weak argument from silence; Paul is Luke's focus, and these characters make their appearance only in passing and where necessary. (Most of the 276

388. This might be the case especially if the captain was a slave (see this possibility in Casson, *Mariners*, 195–96). But in any case it is nautical expertise that concerns the centurion, and Paul's many voyages would count with him less than the captain's profession.

389. Conzelmann, *Acts*, 216.

390. Rapske, *Custody*, 205.

391. Foakes-Jackson, *Acts*, 230; Witherington, *Acts*, 763; cf. Schnabel, "Reading Acts," 255.

392. See Rapske, *Custody*, 377.

393. Witherington, *Acts*, 754 (adding the figures in Haenchen, *Acts*, 702–3).

394. See also Riesner, *Early Period*, 308–9.

395. Conzelmann, *Acts*, 216.

people aboard do not appear individually at all. The centurion appears more often, both because he is more closely involved in Luke's story of Paul—the only places he appears [27:1, 3, 6, 11, 31, 43]—and because he is a representative of Rome, Luke's long-range and by now immediate goal.) Further, from Luke's perspective, it is Paul who, by the end of the voyage, commands greater respect from passengers, who by then are concerned with their survival rather than with the ship and its cargo.

The theological point seems clearer than the details of how Paul made his opinion known. The man of God knew better what would happen than those specialized in the trade (cf. Luke 5:4–10; comment on Acts 27:9). A later writer, Philostratus, makes an analogous point about his hero Apollonius, who is (unlike Paul) a θεῖος ἀνήρ (divine man) in the sense in which scholars usually employ the phrase: Apollonius leaves a ship, warning of the danger (*Vit. Apoll.* 4.13, 18); the ship afterward sinks.[396] The point there is that "inattention to the θεῖος ἀνήρ is revenged."[397] Ancient intellectuals recognized that people should not be condemned for not knowing how a decision would turn out,[398] but the leadership of Paul's voyage had fair warning and were responsible for their own loss of cargo and ship (Acts 27:21).

b. Late in Sailing Season (27:9)

Luke is explicit that the sea was becoming dangerous; if it is Paul (27:10), rather than the captain and pilot (27:11), who discerns the character of the sea, the informed reader might remember the rabbi who knew more about fish than did fishermen (Luke 5:4–10).[399] Luke's description of a fall departure fits; the new governor may have assumed office in July (see comment on Acts 18:12–17), heard Paul's case quickly, and, after some time (presumably after some other prisoners' cases were heard, Acts 27:1), ordered that Paul and other prisoners be sent to Rome. The ship's further delays bring it closer to the early-winter weather.

i. Wintering

Winter travel could be difficult and dangerous.[400] It is not surprising that the Greek term for being tossed in a storm (χειμάζω, 27:18) is closely related in its origin to the term for winter weather (χεῖμα). Most people considered winter's cold unpleasant[401]

---

396. Later he warns his disciple Damis to travel by land, and a storm destroys some ships and scatters others (Philost. *Vit. Apoll.* 7.41); in 5.18, Apollonius told his companions that it was better to change ships but did not warn others aboard; the ship that they left sank.

397. Theissen, *Miracle Stories*, 102. Schnabel, *Acts*, 1038, views Paul's words not "as a prophecy or a prediction" but as an expression of "common sense"; this could be correct, but others who knew his words would probably view them as divine prediction after the fact. Paul later suggests that they should have "obeyed" him (27:21), though God has now granted him the lives of the others aboard (27:24), despite the warning of 27:10. We may debate whether Paul's initial concern was misplaced or an initial divine warning was conditional and changed in answer to Paul's prayer, but many apparently did see prophecies as conditional (21:4, 12).

398. E.g., Hermog. *Issues* 68.10–69.21, esp. 69.15–17.

399. That Paul, rather than Peter with his nautical experience on the lake of Galilee, is the hero here may be instructive but probably simply reflects the character of Luke's information; Peter, who relocates to Jerusalem in Acts, is never associated with fishing in Acts (at most, some scholars suggest a sail allusion in Acts 10:11).

400. As often noted, e.g., Hock, *Social Context*, 78 (noting Ps.-Chion *Ep.* 12 [p. 62.21–22 Düring]; Char. *Chaer.* 3.5.1; Lucian *Dem.* 35; also noting Dio Chrys. *Or.* 36.1 for preferring summer travel); for avoiding winter travel, see also Symm. *Ep.* 1.20.3. Even for nontravelers, death declarations became increasingly more common through autumn and winter, reaching a peak in February, followed by a decline in March; but this is in warmer Egypt, and the reasons are uncertain (Scheidel, "Death Declarations"; though cf. Wiesehöfer, "Mortality," 214: in Egypt, mortality doubled during summer). In North Africa, winter may have been easier for local travel due to desert heat (see Apul. *Apol.* 72). In some locations the climate has changed (e.g., Masada was apparently cooler and more humid two millennia ago; Issar and Yakir, "Isotopes").

401. E.g., Sen. Y. *Ep. Lucil.* 107.7; cf. the brazier in Jer 36:22 and shelter in John 10:23. Winter was harder on health (Symm. *Ep.* 1.100) and difficult for those with hardships (4Q179 1 I, 6; Matt 24:19–20).

and preferred lands with shorter winters (and summers).[402] Undesirable rainstorms were common during the winter, the rainy season.[403] Rivers sometimes overflowed during winter,[404] and bodies of water too shallow during summer might even become navigable in winter (Pliny *Ep.* 5.6.12). In some regions cold weather kept men from field work during winter;[405] winter compelled many to stay indoors and spend time with their spouses.[406] Cold winter rains could bury roads deep in mud,[407] and the usually dry creek beds (wadis) were filled with water and difficult to cross.[408] Deep winter snow in some locations also hindered travel.[409] Some winters (perhaps including this one) were particularly severe, crippling communications.[410]

As a long-term member of the Roman military, the centurion would be well aware of winter travel's dangers. Although there were exceptions for strategic reasons,[411] even armies often chose not to move during winter, unable to accomplish much safely;[412] snow normally deterred armies from attacking (Xen. *Anab.* 4.4.8),[413] and a winter rainstorm could make it difficult for an army to see or hear (Tac. *Hist.* 3.69). Winter could thus, indeed, slow down a war (Polyb. 35.1.5) and was hard on armies.[414] A march in cold mountains with winter-like conditions could cause soldiers to lose their hands and feet.[415] In one famous Greek expedition through the snow (marching in northern country), many people and animals died in the snow (Xen. *Anab.* 4.5.4) while others survived the night by burning fires (4.5.5). Some fell behind on the march, their eyes blinded or their toes lost from the cold (4.5.12). A large army, too, would find provision difficult during winter in some regions.[416]

Thus people would typically "spend the winter" in some location instead of moving

402. Men. Rhet. 1.2, 348.4–7; cf. 347.31–33; 351.2, 10–11.

403. Hesiod *W.D.* 450; Theophr. *Caus. plant.* 2.2.1; 3.4.3; 3.23.2; Pindar *Pyth.* 5.10; Pliny E. *N.H.* 17.2.17; Song 2:11; cf. stormy winds in autumn in Pindar *Pyth.* 5.120. The cold winter rains often made land travel more difficult (cf., e.g., *Num. Rab.* 3:6). More positively, rains watered plants (late autumn, in Philost. *Hrk.* 3.2). For winter as the rainy season in Greece, see also Rackham, "Greece (Geography)."

404. Tac. *Hist.* 3.50; cf. Paus. 9.43.3; Zech 14:8. They also flooded in spring with the melting of mountain snows (e.g., Arrian *Alex.* 7.21.2–3; cf. Hdn. 8.4.2–3).

405. Hesiod *W.D.* 494; cf. 504–5 (late January and early February).

406. Men. Rhet. 2.7, 408.19–23. For warmer winter garments, see Croom, *Clothing*, 24 (citing Juv. *Sat.* 14.185–88; *P.Oxy.* 16, 1901; *m. Ketub.* 5:8).

407. E.g., *m. Ta'an.* 1:3; Jeremias, *Jerusalem*, 58.

408. Cf. Hom. *Il.* 5.87–88; 13.137; *Od.* 19.205–7; Ap. Rhod. 1.9; Livy 44.8.6–7; Appian *Hist. rom.* 12.11.76; Hdn. 3.3.7.

409. Alciph. *Farm.* 27 (Ampelion to Euergus), 3.30, ¶1; Paus. 4.72.5; cf. Longus 3.3; Babr. 45.2–3.

410. Cic. *Fam.* 2.14.1; 12.5.1.

411. E.g., Dion. Hal. *Ant. rom.* 9.25.1; Livy 43.18.1; 44.1.1; Arrian *Alex.* 4.21.10; but some proved disastrous (Hdn. 6.6.3). Augustus traveled north in winter to mourn over Drusus's death (Tac. *Ann.* 3.5).

412. 2 Sam 11:1 (with also comment in Long, "2 Samuel," 457); Suppiluliuma 1.74 (tablet 7, frg. 28, KBo 5.6, A.1.40); Xen. *Cyr.* 6.1.14; Polyb. 10.40; Diod. Sic. 14.17.12; 15.73.4; 20.113.3; 29.2.1; Livy 5.2.1; 21.58.1–2; 22.22.21; 23.18.9–10; 25.11.20; 32.4.7; 32.32.1; 37.39.2; 38.27.9; 38.32.2; 43.7.11; 43.9.3; 44.16.2; 45.8.8; 45.9.1; Sall. *Jug.* 61.2; 97.3; Corn. Nep. 14 (Datames), 6.1; 17 (Agesilaus), 3.4; 18 (Eumenes), 5.7; 8.1, 4; Lucan *C.W.* 2.648; Appian *Hist. rom.* 7.7.43; 11.3.16; 12.15.101; Heracl. *Hom. Prob.* 9.10–11; Arrian *Alex.* 3.6.1; Tac. *Ann.* 13.35–36; Suet. *Jul.* 35.1; *Aug.* 24.1; Hdn. 5.5.3; *BGU* 696.3; Jos. *War* 4.442; *Ant.* 18.262; Dio Cass. 55.24.2. Winter might invite an armistice (Diod. Sic. 15.73.4).

413. Mountain snow in Persia made passage difficult in Quint. Curt. 5.4.18.

414. E.g., Arrian *Alex.* 4.21.10. Quint. Curt. 8.4.1 says that Alexander started a winter march prematurely and the army was caught in a terrible storm (8.4.3–8); the members of his army warmed themselves with bonfires (8.4.11–12), but two thousand died from the storm (8.4.13). In one region, terrible snow and cold (7.3.11–12) killed some, blinding others and causing frostbite (7.3.13). Some lay down, but others forced them on, since moving forward was the only solution (7.3.14).

415. Hdn. 6.6.3. This was reported to happen even for some working around the camp during a freezing winter (Tac. *Ann.* 13.35). Winter made the Alps nearly impassible (Vell. Paterc. 2.105.3).

416. Quint. Curt. 3.8.8 (supply lines over the mountains being problematic).

around.[417] Armies generally wintered somewhere (true in biographies[418] and novels[419] but especially in histories, which fairly often had or included a military focus);[420] though often in encampments, they sometimes were quartered in private homes.[421] A general could leave garrisons in freshly constructed outposts and withdraw the rest of the army to a city (Diod. Sic. 14.17.12). Earlier Roman armies had usually spent winters at home; but about 403 B.C.E., the tribunes had them build forts in the territories of their enemies, and these functioned as winter quarters.[422] Troops needed to obtain supplies before winter, especially if withdrawing into forts.[423] During this time they could work on building and repairing ships or other duties.[424] Armies set out again in spring,[425] but if they set out too early they could imperil themselves (Livy 21.58.1–2). The Roman military season ran from March to October,[426] suiting the same weather conditions that dictated sailing season.[427] Sometimes they did fight during winter, but usually this was noted as exceptional.[428]

11. Winter Voyages for Ships

Travel by sea could prove even more difficult by winter, which often delayed sailing.[429] Chilly northern winds stirred the seas in winter,[430] and many ancients noted the dangers of the winter sea and winter sea travel.[431] Most thus avoided travel by sea during the winter,[432] and ships usually wintered somewhere (cf. Acts 27:12).[433] (For the many exceptions, see further discussion below.) Throughout antiquity, normal sailing season ran mostly from April through October.[434] Friends sometimes warned

417. E.g., Cic. *Fam.* 7.17.3; see discussion in Ramsay, "Roads and Travel," 377. Novels imitated reality here (Ach. Tat. 8.19.3). Shepherds also preferred lowlands for grazing (Cary and Haarhoff, *Life*, 110) and used sheep pens (Virg. *Georg.* 3.295–96; Ap. Rhod. 2.123–25) during winter (for heavy snows delaying spring pasturing, see Longus 3.3); families with fewer sheep might admit them to the home in inclement weather (Bailey, "Shepherd Poems," 5–6).

418. Corn. Nep. 17 (Agesilaus), 3.4; 18 (Eumenes), 5.7; 8.1, 4; Caesar *Gall. W.* 5.26; Plut. *Alex.* 37.3; Suet. *Aug.* 17.3; Philost. *Vit. soph.* 2.1.562.

419. In one of the rarer "historical" novels, see Ps.-Callisth. *Alex.* 2.17.

420. E.g., Polyb. 2.64.1; 2.65.1; 3.92.9; 3.99.9; 3.100.1; 5.57.1; 5.66.3, 5; 10.40; 14.6.7; 27.18.1; Diod. Sic. 20.113.3; 29.2.1; Sall. *Jug.* 61.2; 97.3; Livy 22.22.21; 23.18.9–10; 25.11.20; 32.4.7; 32.32.1; 37.39.2; 38.27.9; 45.8.8; Appian *Hist. rom.* 7.7.43; 11.3.16; 12.15.101; Tac. *Ann.* 2.57, 79; 15.8, 17; Vell. Paterc. 2.110.1; 2.111.4; 2.113.3; 2.114.5; 2.120.2; Dio Cass. 55.24.2; Hdn. 5.5.3. For documentary sources, e.g., *BGU* 696.3 (156 C.E.).

421. Livy 43.9.3; cf. in various cities in Livy 45.9.1. It was offensive, however, to stay beyond winter (Livy 43.7.11), and bad generals sometimes plundered some of the goods of cities where they stayed (Caesar *C.W.* 3.31).

422. Livy 5.2.1; Plut. *Cam.* 2.5; cf. such winter fortresses in 22 C.E. in Tac. *Ann.* 3.74. Others also could send troops home for winter (e.g., Philip in Polyb. 4.87.13, also early). Roman winter forts were constructed of wood (Jeffers, *World*, 172).

423. Xen. *Cyr.* 6.1.15; Livy 44.16.2; more generally, cf. Prov 6:8. It was especially hard to fight in winter without provisions (Suet. *Jul.* 35.1).

424. Caesar *Gall. W.* 5.1.

425. Arrian *Alex.* 3.6.1; 2 Sam 11:1.

426. Dupont, *Life*, 199.

427. Cf., e.g., Paus. 1.6.6, where people sail for war in the spring.

428. Dion. Hal. *Ant. rom.* 9.25.1; Livy 43.18.1; 44.1.1; Arrian *Alex.* 1.24.5. Cf. Xen. *Hell.* 1.2.16, where armies staying in one place for winter (1.2.15) could sally out on nearby expeditions.

429. E.g., Marcus Aurelius in Fronto *Ad M. Caes.* 2.10.3.

430. Pindar *Partheneion* 2.16–20.

431. E.g., Virgil [*Ciris*] 480; Longus 2.19, 21. Rain was troublesome for sea voyagers (*Song Rab.* 8:6, §3).

432. Dion. Hal. *Ant. rom.* 7.2.1; Livy 38.41.15; Tac. *Agr.* 10; Macrob. *Sat.* 1.12.14 (in van der Horst, "Macrobius," 227); Ach. Tat. 8.19.3; Apul. *Metam.* 11.5; Hdn. 5.5.3; Jos. *War* 1.279–80; 2.203; 4.499; *Eccl. Rab.* 3:2, §2; 2 Tim 4:21; Ramsay, "Roads and Travel," 376–79; Cary and Haarhoff, *Life*, 136; Charlesworth, *Trade Routes*, 226 (and sources there). For limitations on travel in antiquity, see, e.g., Liefeld, "Preacher," 11–16.

433. E.g., Livy 38.41.15; Appian *Bell. civ.* 5.8.76 (Marc Antony's fleet).

434. Casson, *Mariners*, 40.

against sailing during winter; one warned the philosopher Demonax that if he voyaged during winter, the fish might eat him. (The philosopher simply replied that it would be fair, since he had eaten many fish.)[435]

Ships caught sailing in this season, like Paul's ship in this account, often either were delayed or stopped to winter (e.g., Jos. *War* 2.203; 4.499). After facing a storm, a ship wintered in Sicily before returning to Italy (Dion. Hal. *Ant. rom.* 7.2.1). Like armies, ships would set out again as soon as winter had passed.[436] These general conditions clearly affected the region in question. Leaving Italy by the sea to its south was too dangerous in winter (and so Cicero fled by the northern one, what we call the Adriatic; Cic. *Att.* 9.3). A severe winter also could detain grain ships bound for Rome, leading to unrest in the capital (Tac. *Hist.* 4.38).

Why would a grain ship leave in this season? Not many years earlier, the emperor Claudius responded to Roman unrest over grain shortages by inviting merchants to transport grain even in winter. He promised to make good any loss due to storms (Suet. *Claud.* 18.2) and offered incentives (such as Roman citizenship to Latins) if they brought grain to Rome (18.3).[437] Claudius's offer of improved status to these *navicularii*, or private ship owners, constituted an important objective for many of the freedmen engaged in the trade.[438]

Many ships did make such calculated gambles, though with varying degrees of success.[439] Individual examples abound of commercial vessels plying the seas even in winter,[440] their owners apparently finding that overall rates of profit remained high. In earlier times, because of haste, some Spartans sailed home in mid-winter (Xen. *Ages.* 2.31). Needing supplies, Sulla sent an officer to Egypt and Libya to procure ships though it was the worst part of winter (Plut. *Luc.* 2.2–3). In urgent conditions, Caesar escaped an enemy naval blockade by moving in winter, but another of his winter naval escapades proved dangerous (Suet. *Jul.* 58.2). He also voyaged to Sicily in winter to prepare for battle (Plut. *Caes.* 52.1). Another risked his life by often traveling at sea in winter on behalf of Cicero's safety (Cic. *Fam.* 13.60.2). In emergencies, others had set out for Rome and reached it during the stormy season.[441] Not all expeditions, however, proved so fortunate,[442] and for most in normal circumstances, the risks would outweigh potential benefits. Those who sailed in winter were well aware that it was not the preferred season (e.g., Virg. *Aen.* 4.309). Sailors facing such a voyage often did so with dread.[443]

Sea travel was considered safe (in terms of seasons) during the period from about May 27 to September 14; the periods from March 10 to May 26 and September 14

435. Lucian *Dem.* 35.

436. E.g., Apul. *Metam.* 11.5.

437. Cf. also Cadbury, *Acts in History*, 60 (in 83n3 noting Claudius's promise of citizenship to shipbuilders, Gaius *Inst.* 1.32c); Ramsay, "Roads and Travel," 376; Johnson, *Acts*, 446; Schnabel, *Acts*, 1035. Would Rome also pay better for grain in the off-season?

438. Rathbone, "*Navicularii*"; cf. Suet. *Claud.* 19. Petronius portrays the freedman Trimalchio as having gained wealth through his ships (Petronius mocks Trimalchio's pretension and low-class background throughout chs. 26–78 of his *Satyricon*).

439. See Rapske, "Travel," 4–6, 22–29, on exceptions; more widely in pre-Roman sources, apart from coastal travel, Tammuz, "*Mare clausum*?"; cf. Virg. *Aen.* 4.309. In the late republic, pirates apparently remained active during winter (Suet. *Jul.* 4). Pliny the Elder wryly observes that pirates first compelled winter travel but avarice has now replaced pirates as the cause (*N.H.* 2.47.125).

440. Davis, "Navigation," 65–76, argues that winter commercial navigation was not even exceptional but routine. Although winter clearly curtailed much travel, as Davis acknowledges, he is able to adduce various cases of such travel (esp. 69–76), most notably (on 70) P.CairoZenon 59029; P.Mich.Zenon 10; P.Lond. 1979.

441. E.g., Cic. *Verr.* 2.2.38.95.

442. In Jos. *War* 1.279–80, some are nearly shipwrecked off Pamphylia; cf. Tac. *Ann.* 15.46.

443. Dio Chrys. *Or.* 32.11 (for a brief voyage); cf. Hesiod *W.D.* 618–30.

to November 11 were considered risky; and the period from November 11 to March 10 was considered very dangerous.[444] The discussion nearest Paul's voyage narrows the restrictions to November 11 to February 8, probably in view of the increased demand for commercial traffic.[445]

With merely "the fast" being past, the travelers are not in the most dangerous season, but they are in a potentially risky season, and it is likely to become only riskier as the voyage proceeds farther. (In literature, including historical writing, writers sometimes introduce warnings of storms or shipwrecks by noting seasons or weather.)[446]

III. Suggested Dates

Because we cannot know for sure the year of Paul's voyage, we cannot be certain of the dates for the fast or other details. Those who favor 59 C.E. note an advantage for their position here, however, in that the Day of Atonement fell later that year than in any other year from 55 to 62 C.E. and hence would allow the final voyage to Rome in February (when it was possible though not always safe) instead of January (when it would be impossible and not attempted apart from emergencies).[447] Jewett provides the following chronology:[448]

58 C.E.	59 C.E.	Events in Acts 27–28
Sept. 16	Oct. 5	Day of Atonement
Sept. 19	Oct. 8	Before Tabernacles (27:9–10; estimated midway between the two festivals)
Sept. 26	Oct. 15	Terminus ad quem for a departure with a gentle south wind (27:13)
Sept. 29	Oct. 18	Three-day period of 27:14–19
Oct. 13	Nov. 1	End of 14 days (27:27, 33)
Oct. 14	Nov. 2	Ashore on Malta (27:39–44)
Oct. 17	Nov. 5	End of three days in Publius's home (28:7)
Jan. 17	Feb. 5	End of three months on Malta (28:11)

Although three months (Acts 28:11) could mean parts of three months and hence be shorter, abbreviating the months in this case would render the final voyage problematic. To most commentators, Luke's mentioning only "the fast" suggests that the Feast of Tabernacles (starting five days later; Lev 23:27, 34) has not yet happened; this was the limit that later rabbis used for safe sailing season.[449]

IV. The Day of Atonement

It is possible, however, that Luke, instead of implying that it is the most recent event on the Jewish calendar, chooses the fast as a chronological marker because

444. Scholars (Rapske, "Travel," 3, 22; Lake and Cadbury, *Commentary*, 328; Bruce, *Commentary*, 506; Fitzmyer, *Acts*, 175; cf. Lohse, *Environment*, 211) cite Veg. *Mil.* 4.39; Pliny E. *N.H.* 2.47.122 (on winter, see esp. 2.47.125); Tac. *Hist.* 4.81; cf. Hesiod *Theog.* 616–21, 663–82. For slightly different calculations from these sources, see Ramsay, "Roads and Travel," 376 (May 26 to September 14; March 11 to May 26; September 15 to November 10), but it is doubtful that everyone observed the dates exactly from one year to another. Weather could vary and was not determined by dates (cf. Pliny E. *N.H.* 18.56.205).

445. Davis, "Navigation," 71–72, on Pliny E. *N.H.* 2.47.122–25.

446. Praeder, "Acts 27:1–28:16," 689 (citing numerous sources, including Polyb. 1.37.4; Callim. *Epig.* 18; Lucan *C.W.* 5.539–59). In addition, Aratus lists the constellation Altar as a sign of coming storms (*Phaen.* 410); clouds clearing in the Manger foretell storms abating (994–96); and early-flying cranes portend early winters (1077–79).

447. Jewett, *Chronology*, 52; Bruce, *Commentary*, 506; Hemer, *Acts in History*, 137–38; Witherington, *Acts*, 762; Riesner, *Early Period*, 225. Most scholars credit Workman, "Date."

448. Jewett, *Chronology*, 51–52.

449. Bruce, *Commentary*, 506 (following Ramsay, *Traveller and Citizen*, 322); Rapske, "Travel," 23; Riesner, *Early Period*, 225. The rabbinic sources usually cited are *Gen. Rab.* 6:5, 44–45; see also *Song Rab.* 7:2, §2; *Eccl. Rab.* 3:2, §2 (noting that travelers risk death after Sukkoth and then even prayers will not help!). On Tabernacles, see, e.g., *m. Sukkah* passim; Safrai, "Temple," 866–67, 894–95; Keener, *John*, 703–4, 722–24.

Paul kept it (as a prisoner on a ship, keeping Tabernacles would be more difficult). In this case the voyage may be placed slightly later (though just a few weeks later, even the ship's council would not have consented to sail in Acts 27:11–12). In any case, it seems most likely that the travelers disembarked again in mid-October or later and were on Malta most of November through January.[450] The dates could be moved forward a few more weeks if Luke uses a Syrian-Jewish calendar as Josephus did, moving Tishri 10 (the Day of Atonement) to October 28,[451] though this does not seem to fit the geographic range of most of Luke's audience.

That Luke expects his ideal audience to know "the fast" is not surprising; like his expositions of Scripture, this allusion suggests a biblically informed ideal audience familiar with the synagogue. Yet it may imply more than simple mention of a festival would; Luke calculates time by festivals (20:6, 16), as does Paul (1 Cor 16:8).[452] Many Christians today are familiar with various Jewish festivals from Scripture, but unless they live in an area with many observant Jews, they may not know the Jewish calendar (e.g., when Tishri occurred) so as to use such festivals as chronological markers. By contrast, it seems likely that many early Christians, including in the Pauline circle, continued to celebrate or at least respect Jewish festivals, even if some of these had taken on new, retrospective associations for Christians (cf., e.g., 1 Cor 5:7; 11:23–25). Luke certainly had no objection to leaving this impression (cf. Acts 18:18; 21:26).[453]

Although Yom Kippur (the Day of Atonement) was a fast, most Jews also celebrated it as a festival (despite *Jub.* 34:18–19).[454] That is, it was counted as a festival despite its solemnity (Philo *Spec. Laws* 2.193–94). According to later rabbis, after the fast girls would dance in the vineyards to find husbands, and the fast itself was one of Israel's happiest days in the year.[455]

c. Paul's Warning (27:10)

Not all sailing during this season was destructive (or the ship would never have set out), and so Paul's insight here (in light of his activity elsewhere in Acts) may be viewed, on the level of Luke's larger story, as divinely given, not merely intuition based on weather.[456] Paul speaks confidently here as in the rest of Acts; this confidence is consistent with Luke's character portrayal of him elsewhere as God's agent. For his address, "Men," see comment on Acts 2:14.

I. LATER CORRECTION

Paul's warning about loss of life builds suspense for the narrative.[457] That it is "corrected" in Acts 27:24 does not mean that Luke thinks that Paul lacks divine insight

---

450. With Bruce, *Commentary*, 506.

451. Conzelmann, *Acts*, 216.

452. Paul's chronological reckoning by festivals is not controversial even among those who tend to stress the Greek setting more (e.g., Deissmann, *Paul*, 97).

453. Cf. Sandmel, *Judaism*, 480n57, who thinks that Paul meant to leave this impression.

454. The Qumran sect also celebrated it with more remorse than did the Pharisees (Baumgarten, "Yom Kippur"); for the Qumranites' augmented emphasis on self-affliction, see Körting, "Theology of Atonement"; for some prayers for that day, see 1Q34 + 1Q34bis 1–2 6; 4Q508 2 3.

455. See Safrai, "Religion," 812, and sources there. On the Day of Atonement, see further *m. Yoma* passim; Safrai, "Temple," 897–98; Wright, "Day of Atonement" (esp. 75–76, on early Jewish sources, including 11QT XXV, 10–XXVII, 10); in the OT, Hartley, "Atonement." Some pagans considered Jewish concern for the timing of their fast superstitious (Fronto *Ad M. Caes.* 2.7).

456. Countering the notion of fate here, Ammonius in *Cat. Act.* 27.10 (Martin, *Acts*, 301) attributes Paul's prediction to his being a prophet.

457. For suspense as a rhetorical technique, see Dion. Hal. *Lysias* 13; Cic. *Verr.* 2.5.5.10–11; Sen. E. *Controv.* 4.pref. 1.

here;[458] biblical prophecies were often conditional, and God sometimes relented of a warning in view of repentance (Jer 18:7–10; Jonah 3:10) or prayer (Exod 32:10–14; Job 42:8), though this was not guaranteed (Jer 7:16; 11:14; 14:11; Ezek 14:20). The cargo (Acts 27:18, 38) and ship (27:41–44) are ultimately lost just as Paul warns.

Because Paul later instructs his fellow voyagers about the island (27:26; cf. 27:39–40), encourages them to eat before swimming (27:34), and warns against a maneuver that would lead to most of their deaths (27:31–32), Luke implies that were Paul not on board, most of the people would have perished. He seems to imply in 27:24 that it was especially Paul's prayers that averted this fate; the angel indicates that the rest of the people were spared for his sake. His presence also spares the other prisoners (27:42–43).

ii. Deities, Prophets, and Sailing

Although many ancients sought to predict the weather on the basis of natural signs,[459] men of God and divine men also could be thought to warn of impending dangers. Thus one accurately predicted that a ship would sink (Iambl. *V.P.* 28.136). As noted above, a ship sank as Apollonius warned (Philost. *Vit. Apoll.* 4.13–18).[460] Long before Paul, an inspired poet was reportedly warned in a dream not to sail; he stayed behind whereas the others who sailed were drowned in a storm (Val. Max. 1.7.ext. 3). As Lionel Casson notes, unfavorable omens or bad dreams could detain a ship's sailing, provided "the ship's officers took them seriously."[461] Some ancients, however, appeared more skeptical, if often selectively and conveniently so. Hannibal reportedly (the source is likely a detractor) insisted that his own favorable advice was better than the diviners' negative warnings (Val. Max. 3.7.ext. 6).

Many even consulted oracles before voyages.[462] Some did not want to sail against the wind without a good omen or divine guidance (Philost. *Hrk.* 1.2; 6.5). Those sailing across the Adriatic (cf. Acts 27:27) might first seek a favorable omen (Iambl. *V.P.* 35.257). Sages also often advised proper safety precautions; if one ignored such precautions, one ought not to blame Fortune (Babr. 49).[463] Fishermen reportedly knew to avoid the sea during a terrible storm.[464]

Petition was also important.[465] A Stoic philosopher observed that no one left "a harbour without first sacrificing to the gods and invoking their aid" (Epict. *Diatr.* 3.21.1).[466] Those leaving a sacred island would pour a libation before leaving it, even with favorable winds (Philost. *Hrk.* 58.5). The Jewish perspective recognized God's sovereignty over the waters (*1 En.* 101:6; cf. Ps 107:23–30; Jonah 1:4); God might use them to destroy sinners (*1 En.* 101:5–6; cf. 1 Kgs 22:48–49; Ps 48:7; Isa 2:16;

458. Although this present text is not a prophecy, Paul certainly positioned himself as in continuity with the prophets as recently as Acts 26:16–19, 27. Divinely guided wisdom might better express how Luke's audience would understand Paul's counsel here.

459. Pliny E. *N.H.* 18.85.359. For some accurate meteorological understanding in early Jewish sources, see Alpert and Neumann, "Correlation." Cf. Luke 12:54–55; the variant reading in Matt 16:2–3.

460. In Philost. *Vit. Apoll.* 6.11, Apollonius could discern people's hearts and know the future because he had great wisdom.

461. Casson, *Travel*, 155; cf. further 156. See further Hübner, "Weather Portents."

462. E.g., Tac. *Hist.* 2.4; Toner, *Culture*, 48. Other cultures have also used fortune-telling before voyages; see, e.g., King, *Believer*, 48.

463. Whereas fools gave way to fear, sages preferred caution (Aug. *City* 14.8, first paragraph, on Stoic views).

464. Alciph. *Fish.* 10 (Cephalus to Pontius), 1.10; they also allegedly checked shores for corpses from wrecked ships afterward, to bury them as a good deed (1.10, paragraph 4).

465. Romans usually started journeys with sacrifice or prayer; Rüpke, "Religion," 5.

466. Trans. Oldfather, LCL, 2:127. Lucian mocks the idea of prayer in which some sailors pray for a north wind while others pray for the south (*Icar.* 25; cf. 26).

23:1, 14; Rev 8:9). God ultimately controlled not only rain[467] but also lightning, thunder, and storm.[468]

Pythagoras's presence on a boat reportedly provided good sailing conditions (Iambl. *V.P.* 3.16); he could stop hostile winds and storms (28.135).[469] (In some Jewish accounts, God saved a Gentile ship because of a Jewish boy aboard.)[470] If some hearers expected such feats from Paul, they might, in view of the storm and the loss of the ship, question Paul's virtue (though, for more sympathetic hearers, the miracle of everyone's survival might counter that suspicion adequately); this concern would provide Luke with incentive to report this scene. At the same time, Luke is always happy to report Paul's wisdom,[471] especially in "we" narratives, where Luke includes additional detail. (Luke himself is also presumably no more concerned by the loss of the ship than he would be by the loss of the pigs in Luke 8:33–37; the new faith of some was an incomparably greater gift.[472] Additionally, the officers were responsible for the loss of their own ship [Acts 27:21].)[473]

In ancient literature, "forecasts of storm and shipwreck . . . are followed by storms and/or shipwrecks";[474] there was little reason for reporting them otherwise. Because Paul is a reliable character, the reader will expect his prediction to come true;[475] this warning therefore builds suspense.

d. Heeding the Ship's Officers (27:11)

The professional mariners naturally prove more persuasive to Julius than does Paul. Preferring their counsel to Paul's is a mistake that Julius will not repeat later in the narrative (27:31–32).

i. Ignoring Warnings

So urgent was Rome's grain supply that maliciously delaying a grain ship could result in a fine;[476] likewise, warnings against shipwreck could be taken badly if they

---

467. E.g., *Jub.* 12:4, 18; *Pss. Sol.* 5:11/9; *2 Bar.* 21:7–8; later rabbis affirmed that God alone holds the "key" of rain (*b. Sanh.* 113a; *Ta'an.* 2a; *Gen. Rab.* 73:4; *Pesiq. Rab.* 42:7; *Tg. Neof.* 1 on Gen 30:22; *Tg. Ps.-J.* on Deut 28:12). As a sign of God's beneficence, see *Jub.* 20:9; *b. Ber.* 33a; *Ta'an.* 2ab, 7a; *y. Ta'an.* 1:1, §2; *Lev. Rab.* 35:8; Flusser, *Judaism*, 482; God could also withhold rains for judgment (e.g., *1 En.* 101:2).

468. E.g., 1 Sam 12:17–18; Ps 107:29; Jonah 1:4; *1 En.* 41:3; *Sib. Or.* 1.32; 2.15; 4.113; 5.302–3. Greeks called Zeus "the high-thunderer" (e.g., Hom. *Od.* 5.4; Paus. 10.9.11; Pindar *Ol.* 8.44), who produced thunder and lightning (Hom. *Il.* 7.443, 454; 8.2–3, 75–77, 133; 9.236–37; 10.5; 13.624; Aristoph. *Lys.* 773; Ap. Rhod. 1.510–11, 730–31; Paus. 5.22.5; 5.24.9; Apollod. *Bib.* 1.2.1; Pindar *Pyth.* 4.23; 6.24; *Ol.* 4.1; 9.7; 13.77; Plut. *Alex.* 28.2; Sil. It. 17.474–78; differently, Paus. 8.29.1; Pliny E. *N.H.* 2.18.82). Greeks and Romans shared with Jews the conception of the highest deity ruling storms (Brown, "Elements"). See further discussion in Keener, *John*, 877.

469. Although Pythagoras was very early, many of the miracle claims about him come, admittedly, from a post-NT era hailing divine men, a factor to be taken into account (see Keener, *John*, 268–70; Kee, *Miracle*, 37). Blackburn, "ΑΝΔΡΕΣ," 192, notes that traditions report Pythagoras and Apollonius preserving ships by their presence, not miraculously saving them from storms as in Mark 4:35–41.

470. *Pesiq. Rab Kah.* 18:5; *Pesiq. Rab.* 32:3/4. These are not the same as stories about a miracle worker, but Jewish sources do claim God's stilling storms in answer to prayer (cf. Theissen, *Miracle Stories*, 65, citing Jonah 1:14; *b. B. Meṣi'a* 59b; *y. Ber.* 9:1; on Jewish miracle workers producing and stopping rain, see, e.g., Jos. *Ant.* 14.22; *m. Ta'an.* 3:8; *b. Ta'an.* 19b–20a; 23ab; *y. Ta'an.* 3:9, §§6–8; Vermes, *Jesus the Jew*, 70, 76; Moore, *Judaism*, 1:377–78). On God's sparing others for one's sake, see Gen 18:26 (Bruce, *Acts¹*, 462); 2 Macc 3:33.

471. Both prophets (1 Kgs 17:14; 2 Kgs 2:21–22; 4:3–4, 41) and later semidivine heroes (Philost. *Hrk.* 4.10) could offer divinely given wisdom concerning matters of nature.

472. Luke has an incomparably higher value for people than for possessions (e.g., Acts 2:44–45; Luke 3:11; 10:4; 17:31–32).

473. Whether anyone would have made good the loss, as in Claudius's reign, is less certain.

474. Praeder, "Acts 27:1–28:16," 690. Some go to sea against all sense, despite predictions (p. 690, citing Ael. Arist. *Or.* 50.32–37; Hom. *Od.* 3.139).

475. With Praeder, "Acts 27:1–28:16," 690.

476. Robinson, *Criminal Law*, 89.

harmed commerce.[477] Here Paul may not be taken seriously enough to merit any indignation. The weather has, after all, been hostile (and so, what would one expect of some overcautious landlubber?). Moreover, the prisoner might be thought to harbor personal motives for being in no hurry to reach Rome.

In ancient literature, fellow passengers or sailors usually ignore predictions of storm or shipwreck, just as they do here. This characteristic appears in various genres,[478] though naturally it is most emphasized in works relishing suspense and adventure. Heeded warnings offer little adventure and hence do not make for interesting accounts. Unheeded warnings are not, however, limited to adventurous novels. In one history, the captains warned Roman leaders not to sail on the rough coast of Sicily facing toward Libya (Polyb. 1.37.4), but Romans, accustomed at the time to relying purely on valor, failed to heed the counsel (1.37.7–8). Polybius felt that their folly yielded history's costliest naval catastrophe (1.37.3), one that he felt would be repeated until Romans learned to avoid some locations and seasons (1.37.10).

Perhaps two decades after Paul sailed to Rome, a helmsman urged Pliny the Elder, then sailing toward Mount Vesuvius, to turn back from approaching the land near the mountain (Pliny *Ep.* 6.16.11); he ignored the advice and later died from the fumes there (6.16.19).[479] Most relevant for Luke is that his audience may remember Jesus's disciples and, still more, outsiders misunderstanding or disbelieving his warnings about his impending passion or other matters.

ii. Impatience to Sail

Even before Claudius's invitation for winter shipping (Suet. *Claud.* 18.2–3), it was known that many put out to sea impatiently despite bad weather and hence were shipwrecked (Cic. *Fam.* 16.9.1). "Sailors are apt to hurry things with an eye to their own gain," Cicero warned, but one should be more cautious than that (16.9.4).[480] Some regarded captains who sailed as soon as favorable winds arose, despite compelling reason to do otherwise, as slaves to their ships and the winds (Philost. *Hrk.* 53.2).

The ship would winter in Crete, in any case, and a better harbor would better protect the ship; but profit may have also influenced some of those deciding. The fewer the repairs required in spring, the faster the shippers might reach Rome with their cargo, discharge it, and return to Alexandria for more. Or, on the view that Fair Havens was an adequate harbor, those in charge may have been concerned with the sailors' and soldiers' discontent at wintering at this fishing village instead of a livelier urban area such as Phoenix.[481] (The sailors may have even been giving advice contrary

---

477. Hermog. *Issues* 65.17–22 (hypothetical). The accused might object that he intended the warning to apply only to sailing at dangerous times (67.6–8), an argument hard to refute both in that case and here in Luke's narrative (Acts 27:9).

478. Praeder, "Acts 27:1–28:16," 690, mentions Chion of Heraclea (mocked by sailors on his vessel), Roman fleet pilots, Calchas, etc. (citing Ps.-Chion *Ep.* 4.1; *Herpyllis* 7–11; Lucan *C.W.* 5.539–93; Philost. *Vit. Apoll.* 5.18; Polyb. 1.37.3–6; Quintus of Smyrna *Posthomerica* 14.360–69).

479. Since Pliny the Younger has many details of his uncle's final days, presumably the scene is based on recollections from others present (it sounds as if many of them did escape) and not simply on the author's inference. Pliny *Ep.* 9.13.6 warned against asking advice if one would not consider what was given.

480. Trans. W. G. Williams, LCL, 27:337. Citing the same text, Praeder, "Acts 27:1–28:16," 690–91, notes that it was prudent to sail with someone who could restrain his haste.

481. White, "Meteorological Appraisal," 405. Sailors usually spent most of the winter at home in taverns (Libanius *Comparison* 4.9, though from an anti-sailing perspective). Local entertainments and the availability of sexual encounters may have been among the considerations, given reports about some young sailors in antiquity (cf., e.g., Corinth in Dio Chrys. *Or.* 8.5; Mart. *Epig.* 10.70.11–12). Although women in pre-Christian Crete may have been less segregated than in some other parts of the Greek world (cf. Westgate, "House"; for women's same-gender social ties in modern Crete, see, e.g., Pizzuto-Pomaco, "Shame," 42), most girls in a traditional fishing village would not be "available" whereas mercantile centers could offer more activity.

to Paul's.) Moreover, in either case, the farther they were on their voyage, the sooner they might reach Rome once sailing season opened.[482]

The shippers might not naturally invite audience sympathy; the poor would not identify with them,[483] and, profitable though shipping was, the landed elites despised it.[484] Roman aristocrats viewed traders as dishonest for selling products at higher prices than those at which they had bought them (without augmenting their value).[485] By the empire, however, aristocrats found that they could enrich themselves by hiring others to trade on their behalf.[486]

Audience sympathy, however, is not the issue here. Luke elsewhere challenges such elite-status biases—for example, by making shepherds the first human witnesses of Jesus's birth besides Mary and Joseph (Luke 2:8–18; shepherding was a despised profession).[487] Luke's interest here is to exploit not any audience prejudices of these people's status but the failure of the shippers' expertise vis-à-vis Paul's divinely led wisdom.

III. THE OFFICERS DESIGNATED

The term ναύκληρος (a biblical hapax legomenon) can mean "shipowner."[488] Although there were apparently a few Jewish shipowners (cf. *m. B. Bat.* 5:1), most were wealthy Gentiles.[489] But would the shipowner be sailing, and with this single ship? Most shipowners would not trust all their goods to the fate of a single ship at sea (Hesiod *W.D.* 689–91).

The term ναύκληρος, however, can also refer to a captain or other officer.[490] Because a helmsman (perhaps a κυβερνήτης) was normally the captain, many scholars argue that ναύκληρος refers to the shipowner here.[491] Owners of fleets and those who bankrolled merchants would not travel with their ships, but inscriptions show that a smaller businessman with only one ship often traveled with it as its captain.[492] Still, it might seem odd that a merchant owning only a single ship could afford such a massive one (Acts 27:37).[493] Some, citing Plut. *Statecraft* 13, *Mor.* 807b; Jos. *Ant.* 9.209, note that when the two terms ναύκληρος and κυβερνήτης are conjoined, ναύκληρος can refer to the ship's owner, who chooses its master.[494] But Josephus is no clearer than Acts (again, the supposed "owner" is aboard during the storm), and Plutarch, too,

482. With Finegan, *Apostles*, 195–96.

483. Other nonelites who were land based also could have little understanding of, hence little sympathy for, mariners.

484. Stambaugh and Balch, *Environment*, 69 (citing Trimalchio in Petronius *Satyricon*); Bauckham, *Climax*, 373; see also Philod. *On Death* 33.25–36 (with sources noted by Henry, including Jocelyn, "Lucretius," 50).

485. Jeffers, *World*, 184. For traders as greedy, see, e.g., Sall. *Jug.* 64.6; Libanius *Comparison* 4.6–7; Sir 26:29–27:2. They might need to either escape the ship naked or sink with their wealth (Libanius *Comparison* 4.12).

486. Jeffers, *World*, 184.

487. On shepherds' being despised, see, e.g., Appian *Hist. rom.* 1.2 (fragments); Livy 39.29.9; Xen. Eph. *Anthia* 3.12; *b. Sanh.* 25b; MacMullen, *Social Relations*, 2; Koester, *Symbolism*, 17; Tooley, "Shepherd," 23; Malina and Rohrbaugh, *John*, 118; Keener, *John*, 799–800.

488. So, e.g., NRSV; Hanson, *Acts*, 245; Bruce, *Commentary*, 507.

489. Applebaum, "Economic Life," 688–89, citing other evidence.

490. So BDAG.

491. Barrett, *Acts*, 1190 (citing, for the steersman, Plato *Rep.* 1.341CD). One often found such shipowners (Latin *navicularii*) buying and selling at the ports (Bauckham, *Climax*, 373); on their offices in Ostia, see Caird, *Revelation*, 226.

492. Haenchen, *Acts*, 700; Bruce, *Commentary*, 507. In practice this meant that merchants often sailed (Libanius *Anecdote* 3.24). Although most effective ownership belonged to the wealthy, boats could also be effectively sold in the form of a long lease (e.g., P.Lond. 1164, from 212 C.E.; *SPap* 1:112–17).

493. Though this was the case with the even larger *Isis* (Lucian *Ship* 14); the owner staked everything on the single ship. Starting in the first century B.C.E., ναύκληροι united in "corporations to ship larger quantities of grain and to share the risks" (Schmitz, "Naukleros").

494. BDAG (s.v. κυβερνήτης).

can be read differently.⁴⁹⁵ In classical usage, ναύκληρος could refer to a shipowner "or also a captain"; in Ptolemaic Egypt it could apply to the shipowner or one leasing the ship but especially to "the cargo carrier, who bore the financial risk."⁴⁹⁶ Although ναύκληρος was distinct from both κυβερνήτης and, sometimes, "shipowner," the same person could fulfill two or more of these functions.⁴⁹⁷

The term's semantic range may be broad; sometimes the κυβερνήτης could hold the higher authority, and ναύκληρος could refer to the pilot.⁴⁹⁸ Often shipowners used slaves as sailors, and so they might "own" not only the ship but the crew and pilot as well.⁴⁹⁹ Traditional titles could also conceal a variety of functions. Even on Athenian triremes, a κυβερνήτης was not only navigator; he could also do steering in storms or battles (a duty otherwise delegated to quartermasters). But he also would replace a captain under duress and, in practice, exercised effective command (the τριήραρχος being only a political appointee).⁵⁰⁰ Sometimes a κυβερνήτης might be a captain who would need to reason with his crew.⁵⁰¹

A κυβερνήτης was thought to enjoy his toil (Dio Chrys. Or. 3.56); yet he had to be on guard continually day and night to protect the ship against hidden reefs (3.64), and so he might sleep less than the night watchman (3.65).⁵⁰² He was the most important person on the ship, responsible for its safety (Philo Creation 88).

Although the sense of ναύκληρος differed somewhat in the Hellenistic period, the sense of the two titles was apparently more regular in the Roman period. In this period the ναύκληρος (equivalent to the Latin navicularius) normally hired someone to arrange cargo, crew, and so forth. Although sometimes such a person accompanied and ran the ship, usually he would delegate this task to the κυβερνήτης (equivalent to the Latin gubernator), who, as in the Hellenistic period, exercised authority "as sailing master and gave orders to the crew while underway—Give sail! Correct your course! Wear off! Come about! Make way against the head wind! Take in all sail!"⁵⁰³

Although most people slept on deck, larger merchant ships normally had a cabin toward the stern, large enough only for the captain and sometimes other prominent persons.⁵⁰⁴ The conversation here, however, is probably taking place on land (Acts 27:9).

Those who worked on Alexandrian grain ships were often Greeks, Syrians, or Phoenicians.⁵⁰⁵ But even many in Rome's own navy were Egyptians, as we know from letters that they wrote home, found among the Egyptian papyri; one letter from a boy

495. Conzelmann, Acts, 216, reads Plut. Statecraft 13, Mor. 807b, as the captain choosing the pilot (κυβερνήτης) and the pilot choosing the sailors. He controls the ship in Libanius Anecdote 3.24, but no distinction is offered between captains and owners (except that someone different owns the merchandise).

496. Schmitz, "Naukleros."

497. Ibid.

498. Cf. Dio Chrys. Or. 34.16; Johnson, Acts, 447, cites Plut. Dinner 18, Mor. 162A; Jos. Ant. 9.209 (comparing also Petron. Sat. 101). Josephus is again ambiguous.

499. Casson, Mariners, 195–96; cf. Davis, "Navigation," 201. The captain and mates were the likeliest to belong to the shipowner, since he could rent the other slave crew members (Casson, Mariners, 196). That the pilot here belongs to the decision-making process need not mean that he is not a slave, given managerial roles for many ancient slaves, but on the whole, it could seem likelier that he was not.

500. Casson, Mariners, 86.

501. Lucian Alex. 56 (the κυβερνήτης in this case being sixty years old); cf. Libanius Anecdote 2.19.

502. See also Libanius Maxim 1.13; 2.8. On a pilot needing help after days without sleep (perhaps a hypothetical situation), see Dio Chrys. Or. 77/78.7; on a κυβερνήτης not being able to sleep or get drunk like others aboard, see Lucian Indictment 2.

503. Davis, "Navigation," 204 (see more fully 202–4, tracing usage from the classical era).

504. Casson, Mariners, 192.

505. Ibid., 212.

in a small village even attests that he met in the navy others from his hometown.[506] On one Egyptian grain ship, the shipwright himself is Egyptian, as is a boy working on board (Lucian *Ship* 2);[507] a pilot of an Egyptian ship navigating the coast of Greece could also be Egyptian.[508]

iv. The Centurion's Decision?

That the centurion believes the shippers rather than Paul is not surprising. He is kind to Paul (Acts 27:3) but does not yet accept him as a prophet. Later he continues to show Paul special favor under duress (27:43), and by that point he heeds him (27:31–32); Paul certainly does prove to be a prophet (27:26, 34). It was understood that people were most apt to obey those they believed most competent in the matter at hand—for example, a doctor when one was sick, or a pilot when one was aboard a ship (Xen. *Mem.* 3.3.9).

Some scholars complain that Luke portrays the centurion as being in charge of the ship, a circumstance not true either during the voyage or in Luke's own day.[509] This view may react against earlier claims that Roman officers would exercise authority on imperial grain ships.[510] But Luke, in fact, presents the decision as made by a "majority" (Acts 27:12), presumably of people of rank. The centurion does not command the ship in 27:11, but he can decide whether his own group will wait out the winter in Lasea for another ship in the spring, whether to make a case for the ship's staying, or whether to disregard Paul and follow the majority decision.[511] Luke's point may be simply "that all of the important people on the ship disagreed with Paul,"[512] which raises suspense.

Whether ναύκληρος refers to a captain or other officer or to a shipowner, he may well have solicited the advice of other persons of influence who had chartered passage.[513] Certainly this would at least include the centurion, and the centurion's voice could be influential. In some Egyptian papyri, peasants petitioned centurions as the most accessible agents of Rome; in Apuleius, a peasant who crosses a soldier[514] seeking to seize his animal loses his life. Julius's opinion would have been among those solicited, and perhaps Paul's would have been solicited as well (see comment above). Later in the voyage the centurion does act autonomously from the captain (27:32), but this may be because he and his soldiers are armed and can use emergency force in the service of survival or because the right of requisition has given him a measure of authority.

v. Why the Gamble?

The captain might want advice even if no lives are at risk; in the end, he is probably responsible for any goods he is transporting, as in freight boats on the Nile in

506. Ibid., 188–89.
507. In addition, the old man controlling the rudders is said to have curly hair (Lucian *Ship* 6), though his ethnicity is not specified.
508. Philost. *Vit. Apoll.* 3.23 (referring to an earlier period).
509. E.g., Haenchen, *Acts*, 700.
510. As in, e.g., Ramsay, "Roads and Travel," 379; idem, *Traveller and Citizen*, 324. In Egyptian villages, where a visiting centurion might be the highest representative of the Roman government available (cf. also *CIJ* 2:132, §920; *Sipre Deut.* 309.1.1; Lewis, *Life*, 22, 24), a centurion might even take some functions as a magistrate, but he would not take command of a ship (the soldiers take emergency action in 27:31–32 not because of rank but because they are armed).
511. See Rapske, *Custody*, 377.
512. Conzelmann, *Acts*, 216.
513. Aside from the question of advice, a κυβερνήτης might be happy to talk with nonsailors about his ship (Lucian *Ship* 7).
514. The soldier in Apul. *Metam.* 9.39 may be simply an ordinary soldier, but the "vine-rod" he carries was normally carried by centurions; see Lindsay, *Golden Ass*, 209n1.

this period (P.Oxy. 3250, from 63 c.e.) and in earlier times (P.Hib. 2.198.5.111–22).[515] Then again, if the captain does not own the boat, he might be more likely to gamble its contents on beating the storm, provided he expects survival: those renting boats agreed in contracts to return them undamaged *except* for acts of God such as storms (or attacks by pirates).[516]

Although everyone would be eager to sail if at all possible,[517] they would not risk their lives if they genuinely believed that they would soon face a deadly storm. How did such seamen, presumably experienced, fail to foresee the likelihood of the storm? For one thing, mountains more than a thousand meters high and only a kilometer or two from Fair Havens obstructed their vision to the north and east.[518] But "a low-index weather pattern" may have also led them to underestimate the danger. During such a period, storms move "west to east along a relatively fixed track," in this case, across the northern Mediterranean Sea; thus a fairly constant "bubble" of good weather could lie directly south of the storm route.[519] The winds shifted every few days, and pleasant weather was sandwiched between storms.[520] The gamble these shippers made would have succeeded on most occasions, but over the course of time some such gambles were bound to prove fatal.

e. Trying to Reach Phoenix (27:12–13)

The pilot and captain (Acts 27:11) are more concerned about keeping the ship in good condition or, alternatively, about keeping the sailors happy for the winter than about immediate safety, at least so long as safety appears to them significantly more probable than not.[521] (Fair Havens was perhaps not the best harbor, but at least the nearby islands offered some shelter whereas, if the ship faced a storm outside the harbor, they risked being driven out to sea.)[522] Ultimately this decision will cause them to lose the ship (27:41).[523]

i. Hoping to Reach Phoenix (27:12)

Presumably no one was arguing that the ship should try to reach Rome before winter; most would have agreed had Paul's objection been merely to this. But most thought that they could find a better harbor in Crete to spend the winter; they had ventured across the Aegean to Crete, and sailing a little farther if calmer winds arose seemed a fairly safe gamble. The ship itself would seem safer in a better harbor. Ancients could evaluate harbors according to wind conditions.[524] One wind direction, χῶρος, means "northwest," equivalent to the Latin *caurus/corus*.[525] The term λίψ probably means

515. Horsley, *Documents*, 2:74, §25.
516. Llewelyn, *Documents*, 6:82–83, §12.
517. Including the centurion, who would rather not requisition homes in which to quarter his soldiers and prisoners for more of the winter than necessary. A larger city with a greater Roman presence and appreciation for Rome would be more useful in every respect.
518. White, "Meteorological Appraisal," 405–6.
519. Ibid., 406 (noting, "This allowed the heat from the Sahara Desert to slide northward and fuel the storms, while keeping them on track as they slid eastward").
520. Ibid.
521. Concern for safety precautions appears both in sages (perhaps Prov 14:16; 22:3; 27:12) and in laws concerning negligence (e.g., Exod 21:29, 32–34, 36; Deut 22:8; Eshn. 5, 53–58; Hamm. 229–37, 244–52).
522. Bruce, *Commentary*, 507 (following Smith, *Voyage*, 85n), though also noting the site's weaknesses.
523. Cf. Luke 21:21, where it is better to abandon the city than to lose life (though the point is clearer in Mark and Matthew).
524. Conzelmann, *Acts*, 217, citing Arrian *Peripl.* 4.
525. Conzelmann, *Acts*, 217 (noting Pliny E. *N.H.* 2.119 for west-northwest). Seamen hybridized Latin and Greek weather terms, including *corus* (*IGRR* 1.177 = *IG* 14.1308 in Hemer, *Acts in History*, 140–41; cf. also BDAG).

"west" or (conjoined with χῶρος here) "southwest." It usually meant "southwest" in classical Greek, "south"[526] and very rarely "west"[527] in the LXX, and (probably most important for a report perhaps overheard from Egyptian sailors) "west" in the papyri.[528]

Most of the southwest coast of Crete is extremely "steep and inhospitable," but it has some "fertile coastal plains and at the western end, several very hospitable valleys leading up into the mountains."[529] Coastal cities included Lissos, with its Asclepius sanctuary, and, to its east, "ancient Phoenix, with its excellent harbour" in the vicinity of modern Loutro; Phoenix had two sister cities inland: Aradena, "above on a mountain plain,"[530] and Anopolis, "600 meters above Loutro"[531] and across "a spectacular gorge" from Aradena.[532] Other inland sites less than ten kilometers from Phoenix reveal habitation in the Roman period. Thus Phoenix was a strategic destination, among fairly few.[533]

Strabo notes that Phoenix (Φοῖνιξ) lay on the southern side of a Cretan isthmus and that Phoenix belonged to the Lampians (Strabo 10.4.3). Notwithstanding our uncertainty concerning its precise location, its general location is not in dispute. Commentators estimate that it was as much as 50 miles west of Fair Havens, about 34 to 36 miles west of Cape Matala,[534] and probably (Ptolemy *Geog.* 3.15 [3.17.3]) about 34 miles from the west end of Crete.[535] A straight line from Cape Matala to Phoenix would be shorter, but since the ship would hug to the coast rather than sail straight for Phoenix, it was more than 80 kilometers (ca. 50 mi.) past Cape Matala.[536]

The exact location of ancient Phoenix is disputed today; seismic activity has changed the topography, reducing certain correlations with ancient descriptions.[537] Near Phoenix is the rocky peninsula Cape Mouros, extending almost a mile (1.6 km.) into the sea and surrounded by two bays.[538] The best harbor is the eastern one, where the small, modern fishing village of Loutro[539] lies, but this harbor looks southeast whereas the winds Luke mentions indicate a harbor that looked west.[540] Some, including Smith, have argued for the eastern bay.[541] Most, however, argue that the right site is the west-facing harbor

526. Gen 13:14; 20:1; 24:62; 28:14; Exod 27:9; 37:7; 38:9; Num 2:10; 3:29; 10:6; 34:3–4; 35:5; Deut 1:7; 3:27; 33:23; Josh 15:1–4, 7–8, 10; 17:9–10; 18:5, 13–16, 19; 19:9; 2 Chr 28:18; Ps 77:26; Isa 43:6; Ezek 47:19; 48:28.

527. 2 Chr 32:30; 33:14.

528. Conzelmann, *Acts*, 217. Even unprotected, the winds would not push them seaward, and Crete itself still protected them from the worst northern winds.

529. Sanders, *Crete*, 29.

530. Ibid.

531. Ibid., 165.

532. Ibid., 29. Limited remains at Anopolis (Hellenistic) and Aradena (a later basilica, 165) leave some uncertainty about the level of habitation in this period.

533. There were coastal cities with Roman habitation before Phoenix in present-day Ayios Savvas, Ayios Photia, Cape Melissa, and Ayia Galini (Sanders, *Crete*, 164), though a wrecked ship not far from Ayia Galini (165) might testify to the difficulty of the harbor. Closer is probably Matala, though Roman evidence is incomplete and the harbor may have been difficult, as illustrated by a wreck north of the bay (161).

534. Bruce, *Commentary*, 508; Witherington, *Acts*, 765.

535. Barrett, *Acts*, 1192. Ramsay, "Roads and Travel," 379, 381, surmises that Phoenix was probably a common winter harbor.

536. See Sanders, *Crete*, fig. 64.

537. For significant evidence supporting uplift in western Crete and the rise in water level around the island during the medieval and modern periods, see Sanders, *Crete*, "Appendix III: Sea Level Functions," 181–82. For earthquake destruction levels from fourth-century Crete, see pp. 30, 172. On the city of Phoenix, see further Sonnabend, "Phoenix."

538. The description of the location for Phoenix in Ptolemy *Geog.* 3.15.3 places it near Cape Mouros (Finegan, *Apostles*, 196).

539. Located with Phoenix in Sanders, *Crete*, fig. 64; not to be confused with Loutra on the interior (fig. 64).

540. Barrett, *Acts*, 1192. Because Ptolemy's list moves from west to east, the Phoinikos Harbor (Phoenix Harbor) was west of Phoenix proper, on the western bay; further, sailors view Loutro as unsafe during winter (Finegan, *Apostles*, 197).

541. Smith, *Voyage*, 87–92.

across from Loutro, still called Phonika (or Phineka) Bay, which faces southwest and is open to westerly winds. Its anchorage is not good today, but this situation stems from geologic changes in Crete in the past two millennia, possibly with silting from the two streams flowing nearby. In antiquity it was likely safer.[542] This western bay is about 150 feet, or 25 fathoms (46 m.), deep and lacks reefs; although it is not used for a harbor today, it probably was in antiquity.[543] This bay has two inlets: the one facing northwest has mostly filled in, but the other facing southwest remains 42 to 48 feet (7–8 fathoms; 13–15 m.) deep.[544] This topography fits Luke's claim that the harbor faced both southwest and northwest, a claim that seems unlikely on the southern coast of Crete but is supported by archaeological evidence. The line of seashells shows that the northwest area was once fourteen feet lower—that is, at the sea.[545]

Some scholars suggest "that Luke confused the two bays," one facing east and the other facing west, since Ptolemy (*Geog.* 3.17.3) uses "Phoenix" for both the western bay (Φοινικοῦς λιμήν) and the city to its east (Φοίνιξ πόλις).[546] Although this assumption is hardly necessary, there is no reason to believe that Luke traveled there or knew much about the site apart from what he heard sailors discuss, since the ship never reaches there. For this same reason, in the final analysis, knowledge of the site has little bearing on Luke's narrative.[547]

Some ancients could relate the name "Phoenix" to the bird of that name, which was reborn every five centuries.[548] Although the bird could be used to symbolize resurrection,[549] there is probably no thought of such a symbolic connection here (well as it would work). Phoenix was, after all, a genuine city; the term refers even more to the date palm;[550] and more important, one would expect a city to be named Phoenix because it was founded much earlier by the widely seafaring Phoenicians.[551] Luke does not normally avail himself of opportunities to exploit potential allegorical associations of place names.

II. THE DECEPTIVE FAVORABLE WIND (27:13)

Calm before storms often appears in narratives of sea voyages in various genres.[552] Sailors took advantage of favorable winds,[553] and sometimes excessive optimism about

542. Bruce, *Commentary*, 508; Haenchen, *Acts*, 700n7; Arrington, *Acts*, 254; Hemer, *Acts in History*, 139; Witherington, *Acts*, 764; Barrett, *Acts*, 1192 (viewing this site as "virtually certain"). On the changes of topography due to earthquakes, Finegan, *Apostles*, 197.

543. Finegan, *Apostles*, 196 (noting also the bay's two inlets, one mostly filled up).

544. Ibid.

545. Kistemaker, *Acts*, 923, following Ogilvie, "Phoenix," and noting other results of seismic activity in southern Crete.

546. Conzelmann, *Acts*, 217.

547. With Johnson, *Acts*, 447.

548. E.g., Ovid *Metam.* 15.391–407 (claiming that this is its Assyrian name, 15.393); *Am.* 2.6.54 (on its longevity); Sen. Y. *Ep. Lucil.* 42.2; Pliny E. *N.H.* 10.2.4 (540 years); 13.9.42; Philost. *Vit. Apoll.* 3.49 (living in India but visiting Egypt every 500 years); Ach. Tat. 3.25 (without resurrection); cf. one view in Tac. Ann. 6.28; a speaker in Lucian *Peregr.* 27; see further Van den Broek, *Myth of Phoenix*; idem, "Phoenix"; Käppel, "Phoenix." On its rare appearance, see, e.g., Ael. Arist. *Def. Or.* 426, §144D; Philost. *Letters* 8 (46). The depiction of the Ethiopian and Indian phoenix in Pliny E. *N.H.* 10.2.3–5 resembles Asia's golden pheasants (trans. H. Rackham, LCL, 3:292 n. *a*). In Jewish sources, see *3 Bar.* 6:9–10; 7:5; Ezek. Trag. *Exag.* 254–69 (on which cf. Heath, "Visuality"); in the rabbis, see *Gen. Rab.* 19:5; Niehoff, "Phoenix." In Tac. *Ann.* 6.28, Tacitus doubts that it has appeared (see discussion in Keitel, "Non-appearance").

549. In early Christian literature, see *1 Clem.* 25.2; in art, Latourette, *First Five Centuries*, 324.

550. E.g., John 12:13; Rev 7:9; *Herm.* 68.1; often in the LXX (e.g., 2 Macc 10:7; 14:4; Sir 24:14; 50:12); Josephus (e.g., *Ant.* 3.9, 102, 113, 124, 154, 183, 245); and Philo (e.g., *Alleg. Interp.* 3.74; *Unchangeable* 137; *Agr.* 112; *Flight* 183, 186–87).

551. On the name, cf. Tsirkin, "Canaan."

552. Praeder, "Acts 27:1–28:16," 691 (citing Ap. Rhod. 4.1223–25; Arrian *Peripl.* 5; Ps.-Chion *Ep.* 4.1–2; *Herpyllis* 17; Quintus of Smyrna *Posthomerica* 14.403–18; Sen. Y. *Ag.* 431–55; Tac. *Ann.* 2.23.2).

553. Cic. *Att.* 16.4–5 (on the Etesian winds [*etesiis*]).

current calm weather could breed danger.[554] A south wind, mentioned here (νότου), would keep them close to shore, as opposed to winds from the north;[555] west winds would hinder their progress.[556] A south wind would help them stay with the coast as they rounded Cape Matala, four miles to the west, but then they may have sought to move west-northwest, across the Bay of Messara (Mesará), for some thirty-four or more miles toward Phoenix.[557] Unfortunately, south winds in this region can easily "back suddenly to a violent northeaster, the well-known *gregale*."[558] For centuries, this kind of easterly gale, or gregale, had driven other ships in similar ways, and it remains a cause for concern today as well.[559]

Although mountains obstructed vision to the north and east as long as the voyagers remained in the harbor of Fair Havens,[560] once the ship had moved into the Bay of Messara, those on board could view the shift in weather coming from the east, from the Platanos Valley, and from the north, from Mount Ida.[561] They had seen such conditions before but did not anticipate the severity: the Platanos Valley generated unexpected conditions.[562] This narrow, vegetated valley lay between two mountain ranges, each more than 1,200 meters high; this formation made the valley an ideal conduit for harsh gusts of air. The mountains constrict cool air flows, decreasing atmospheric pressure and raising the speed of the wind.[563] Waiting just one or two more days in the harbor would have prevented their being blasted out to sea by such a wind.[564]

Sailors typically, as noted above, sought the favor of the gods; thus those in charge may have seen the wind as a providential benefaction from their deities. The whims of Greek and Roman deities, however, were often arbitrary.[565] Once caught in the storm, the voyagers could only submit to it (Acts 27:15, 17); they would lose hope (27:20), except for the more modest hope of seeing day (27:29), until Paul offered them new hope (27:33).

They "weighed anchor"; the more general term Luke uses for this activity was widely used with this sense.[566] A few miles of sailing brought them past the shelter of Cape Matala, keeping cautiously close to shore (as Luke observes). Now they would have only about thirty-four to thirty-six miles to Phoenix, a voyage they might normally

554. Dio Chrys. *Or.* 34.53 speaks of swimmers who swim out too far in fine weather, unaware that a storm will come.

555. This south wind resembled what one might expect during summer (Pliny E. *N.H.* 2.47.123). Odysseus's ship was detained twelve days in Crete by a strong north wind (Hom. *Od.* 19.199–202, fictitious but perhaps nautically informed regarding Crete).

556. Cf. the advantage of a south wind for northward travel in Acts 28:13; the hot southern wind in Luke 13:29 reflects Palestinian conditions (though, in general, south winds brought hot air and north ones brought cold air; so Vitruv. *Arch.* 8.2.5–6; *1 En.* 34:2; cold north wind in Plut. *Bride* 12, *Mor.* 139DE).

557. Hemer, *Acts in History*, 141.

558. Ibid. In Casson, *Mariners*, 211, this is an east-northeaster. More generally (not specifically on this region), Hünemörder, "Notos," notes that the νότος proper "blew from various directions in winter (from November) and is described as rain-bringing, stormy and bringing obscured visibility."

559. See Casson, *Mariners*, 73, 211; also Finegan, *Apostles*, 197 (noting the use of *gregale* on Malta and the "low" over Libya). In the story in Hdt. 4.152, this wind blew a Greek ship all the way to Spain; Paul's ship happily reached Malta first (Casson, *Mariners*, 211).

560. White, "Meteorological Appraisal," 405–6. For a readily accessible photograph of mountains along the southern Cretan coast, see Chance, *Acts*, 497.

561. White, "Meteorological Appraisal," 406.

562. Ibid. Crete normally has a mild climate (Pliny E. *N.H.* 4.12.58).

563. White, "Meteorological Appraisal," 406.

564. Ibid., 407.

565. See discussion on deities' immorality at Acts 14:15; for deities granting "benefactions" that were harmful or that they later regretted, see Ovid *Metam.* 2.44–102; 3.287–98, 308–9; 11.100–105; 14.129–53; Apollod. *Bib.* 3.4.3.

566. See BDAG (citing, e.g., Philo *Mos.* 1.85; Jos. *Ant.* 7.97; 9.229; 13.86).

complete the same day.[567] The favorable wind could help them cross the broad Bay of Messara.[568] This was the most precarious part of the voyage, requiring a favorable wind; once they had passed the shelter of Cape Matala, they lay unprotected in the wide bay.[569] Unfortunately, it was at precisely this juncture that their gambit failed: the gale struck while they lay most exposed to it.

4. Disaster at Sea (27:14–20)

The narrative builds suspense as the situation grows hopeless (27:20). This situation provides the context for Paul's assurance of God's intervention (27:21–26), which appears all the more conspicuous for its contrast with the situation and the attitude of others on board.

a. Euraquilo (27:14)

Luke displays some interest in meteorology elsewhere,[570] but such interest would be inevitable when one was confronting a storm at sea. "Not long after,"[571] they encountered the "typhoon" called Euraquilo. What was Euraquilo?

1. A Dangerous Northeast Wind

Sailors knew four major winds, which together could be subdivided into twelve;[572] the terminology for particular winds, however, varied among writers.[573] Luke's Εὐρακύλων is not difficult to account for; the Aquilo was normally north-northeast[574] or northeast,[575] known for driving rain from Italy to Africa,[576] and the Eurus can appear as a southeast wind[577] or sometimes an east wind.[578] Together they may be east by northeast, or "north-one-third-east."[579] Sailing was a multicultural business,

567. Conzelmann, *Acts*, 217. With favoring winds, ships could cover roughly 50 nautical mi. in an average daylight period, or 90 mi. in twenty-four hours; this was hardly surpassed until the eighteenth century (Cary and Haarhoff, *Life*, 136).

568. Bruce, *Commentary*, 508.

569. With, e.g., Finegan, *Apostles*, 197.

570. On Luke 12:54–56 (on the south and the west winds), see Bovon, *Studies*, 38–50. Biblical idiom (both in Hebrew and in the LXX) labels winds differently from their direction (e.g., hot "east" winds being from the south), but Luke's perspective is not Palestinian (see Theissen, *Gospels*, 252–54). For ancient meteorology, addressing anything above the earth (including atmosphere and stars), see Fritscher, "Meteorology" (for Aristotle, 797–98; for Hellenistic and Roman sources, 798–99; for further sources, including books, see the bibliography, 800).

571. On litotes, see Rowe, "Style," 128.

572. On these, see Sen. Y. *Nat. Q.* 5.16.1–5.17.2; cf. Hünemörder, "Winds," 653–54. Williams, "Winds," thinks that Seneca includes a moralizing perspective in discussing winds, but a verdict on this thesis will not affect the information applied here.

573. Johnson, *Acts*, 447 (citing Strabo 1.2.21). For wind titles, see, e.g., Pliny E. *N.H.* 2.46.119–2.48.127; see esp. the wider discussion of twelve- and eight-wind roses in Davis, "Navigation," 92–106 (concluding on 106 that the twelve-wind pattern prevailed starting no later than the first century B.C.E.).

574. Sen. Y. *Nat. Q.* 5.16.6.

575. Pliny E. *N.H.* 2.46.119–20; 2.47.123. This was opposite the African wind from the southwest (cf. 18.77.336). The winter Aquilo, starting Nov. 11, is northeast (2.47.125).

576. Sen. Y. *Nat. Q.* 5.18.2; Lucan *C.W.* 9.422–23.

577. LSJ. *OLD* 628 gives the Latin as east or (parenthetically) southeast wind (with supporting references). Eurus and Aquilo appear together in Sen. Y. *Nat. Q.* 5.16.2.

578. The *eurus* is between *aquilo* (northeast) and *volturnus* (the southeast wind; *OLD* 2100) in Aul. Gel. 2.22.11 (but Pliny E. *N.H.* 2.46.119; 18.77.338 identifies *volturnus* with *eurus*). Praeder, "Acts 27:1–28:16," 691, views *eurus* as the east and *aquilo* as the north in other sources (Hom. *Od.* 5.295–96; Hor. *Epodes* 10.5–8; Lucan *C.W.* 5.597–612; Ovid *Metam.* 11.481; Petron. *Sat.* 114.3).

579. Smith, *Voyage*, 103, 161; Bruce, *Commentary*, 509.

especially on Alexandrian ships voyaging to Rome, and so the mixing of Greek and Latin titles was not unusual. Seneca the Younger accepted the Greek title "Eurus" as already latinized (*Nat. Q.* 5.16.4). The apparent hybrid *euroaquilo* is attested on a twelve-point North African wind rose using Latin wind names.[580]

A northeaster was considered the most dangerous wind.[581] Pleasant as the southern wind typically was, such winds in this region often unexpectedly back into a violent gregale, or northeaster.[582] Mount Ida was eight thousand feet high, and perhaps the northeaster rushed down from there unobstructed across the Plain of Messara.[583] It would have then caught them at their most vulnerable location, while they were past the shelter of Cape Matala and crossing the wide Bay of Messara.[584] Despite what Luke would have heard from the sailors, this may not have been technically the Euraquilo normally experienced in this region of Crete.[585] It may well have been a more specific, unusual phenomenon related to the structure of the valley north of Fair Havens;[586] but because it was blowing them to the southwest, the sailors could well have used this name. For those wishing to sail northwest toward Phoenix, a sudden wind from the north would blow them out to sea; a persistent northeaster (what they apparently faced at greater length) could blow them toward the dangerous Syrtis (see comment on Acts 27:17). An ἄνεμος τυφωνικός involved "swirling clouds and sea caused by the meeting of opposing air currents."[587]

II. Winds and Theologies

Luke's audience may surmise that the sudden wind at this most vulnerable location is more than coincidence. Ancients generally attributed the winds to deities. For example, Juno unbars the winds and points to the fleet, so that the winds prevent their advance (Val. Flacc. 8.322–27).[588] But in Acts 27:4, 7, 13–15, 40, the winds are God's instrument to provide Paul with an opportunity to testify.[589]

Although ancient writers frequently used storms and winds figuratively, this was not their primary application in narratives, particularly historical narratives (see introduction, above, to Acts 27). The literary setting and genre indicate literal disaster (with theological, moral, and apologetic applications), not an allegorical one. If there are any connections with figurative uses of such language in Luke-Acts, however, Paul is more like John the Baptizer, who was not a reed "shaken by the wind" (Luke 7:24), than like the Twelve, terrified by wind (8:23–25); Paul, unshaken, trusts God (Acts 27:21–25). A contrast with the positive "violent" wind of Pentecost (2:2; cf.

---

580. Hemer, *Acts in History*, 141; Davis, "Navigation," 104; Luke likely heard it from the sailors (Hemer, *Acts in History*, 142). It is a northeast wind (*CIL* 8.26652 [*OLD* 628]).

581. Witherington, *Acts*, 765.

582. Hemer, *Acts in History*, 141; Bruce, *Commentary*, 509 (following Smith, *Voyage*, 102).

583. Witherington, *Acts*, 765. For Roman-period habitation of this plain, see Sanders, *Crete*, 20–24. Philost. *Hrk.* 31.9 speaks of a wind that swept down from Mount Ida every morning, but he refers to the namesake mountain in the Troad.

584. Hemer, *Acts in History*, 141.

585. The four winds experienced in southern Crete included the Euraquilo, "a severe northeasterly wind associated with passage of a cold front or similar trough of low pressure usually associated with a storm centre to the north in the Aegean Sea" (White, "Meteorological Appraisal," 403). Shipwrecks near Crete do appear in ancient sources (e.g., the myth in Vell. Paterc. 1.1.2).

586. White, "Meteorological Appraisal," 406–7, arguing that the ship could have succeeded against a Euraquilo.

587. Witherington, *Acts*, 765; see also Bruce, *Commentary*, 509.

588. For some further comment on winds, see comment on Acts 2:2; on wind deities, see also Mussies, "Wind-Gods."

589. The wind's more positive narrative function in Acts 28:13 is to explain the group's later, quicker progress, after the sufferings of the storm and shipwreck.

27:41) is also possible;[590] both 2:2 and 27:15 use forms of φέρω with the wind. In both cases the "wind" plays a role in leading God's agents for the spread of his message among the nations.

b. Driven past Cauda (27:15–16)

Unable to control the ship against such a coercive wind, the voyagers were driven by it. The best the sailors could do, when momentarily sheltered by the island of Cauda, was to haul the ship's boat aboard. This boat will later prove important to the story (27:30–31).

I. DRIVEN ALONG (27:15)

Those driven off course by northerly winds sometimes had to settle for destinations farther south. Thus one novel tells of a ship headed for Italy that was driven to Sicily and from there embarked again to Italy from Syracuse (Xen. Eph. *Anthia* 5.1; cf. Acts 28:12).[591] Being at the mercy of the winds was a common feature of stories about storms at sea,[592] perhaps because the most dangerous storms at sea typically included this peril (although often explicitly articulated for narrative suspense). Repetition of the point in the circumstances of 27:17 reinforces the portrait of their helplessness.

Most ships had just one mast and mainsail, "sometimes supplemented" by two smaller sails.[593] Because ancient ships' mainsails were cut square, they could not easily face into a headwind and hence had "to make very wide tacks, or to wait for a change in the wind. If caught in a storm, they might not be able to keep their head to the wind, and would remain exposed to heavy seas on their broadside."[594] Although ancient ships could (against some earlier writers) with effort sail against a wind,[595] this was no ordinary wind. Luke's ship was larger (though smaller than Lucian's three-mast *Isis*) and hence had a second mast carrying the foresail (mentioned in Acts 27:40). The foresail projected forward and was used for driving and steering; it was likely so employed as the ship gave way to the wind (27:15), and was "hoisted to the wind" in 27:40.[596]

II. RESCUING THE BOAT NEAR CAUDA (27:16)

The probable location of Cauda (modern Gavdos),[597] considered the southernmost Greek island, is more than twenty miles west-southwest of where the storm

590. Especially if it is viewed as realized eschatology along with the eschatological fire of Acts 2:3 (cf. the possible eschatological cast of 6:48–49, though this is a flood more than Matthew's storm; Matt 7:24–27).

591. One voyager to Italy was supposedly blown off course to the outer sea (Paus. 1.23.5); the peoples depicted in 1.23.6 are mythical, but this narrative illustrates that Aegean peoples knew about winds blowing people off course.

592. Johnson, *Acts*, 448, cites Hom. *Od.* 9.82–84; Heliod. *Eth.* 5.27.2; Ach. Tat. 3.1–2; Petron. *Sat.* 114; Lucian *Tox.* 19; *A True Story* 1.6; 2.46; *Ship* 7.

593. Cary and Haarhoff, *Life*, 135. These were the mainsail, usually also a foresail, and on larger ships also a topsail above the mainsail, and on some Hellenistic ships also a mizzen (Casson, *Mariners*, 190, 194). For more detail on the mainsail (probably with "two smaller triangular" sails above it), foresail (*artemon*), and mizzen (at the stern), see Fitzgerald, "Ship of Paul," 31–32.

594. Cary and Haarhoff, *Life*, 135 (comparing [n. 3] Acts 27). Luke's ἀντοφθαλμέω, for facing, appears a figurative adaptation of the term (BDAG), employed more literally in Acts 6:10 D; Wis 12:14; 1 *Clem.* 34:1; *Barn.* 5:10 (see other texts in Bruce, *Acts¹*, 458–59), although some have suggested an allusion to the ancient practice of eyes sometimes painted on either side of the ship's prow (Smith, *Voyage*, 98n2; Witherington, *Acts*, 765). In the 1440s ships better able to tack against wind than their predecessors facilitated Portuguese involvement in Africa (Irvin and Sunquist, *History*, 37).

595. Cf. Casson, *Mariners*. See Pliny E. *N.H.* 2.48.128, mentioning the method of "slacking sheets" (trans. Rackham, LCL, 1:269). For sailing into a wind, using maneuvers such as tacking, see also Wallinga, "Poseidonios" (noting *FGH* 87F46 and other passages).

596. Rapske, "Travel," 33. Sails could be pulled down in view of an impending storm (Petron. *Sat.* 114).

597. Many MSS have Κλαῦδα or variations thereof, perhaps partly because it sounded more familiar (cf. "Claudius"); Cassiodorus and Ψ (eighth–ninth centuries) have Γαύδην, closer to the modern name. All these

likely struck the travelers in the Bay of Messara, after they had passed Cape Matala.[598] This is precisely where the trajectory of a northeaster should have carried them, and it is not the sort of information someone would have inferred without having been blown there.[599] Cauda provides an anchorage, but not on the part of the island (eastnortheast) they would have been passing.[600] Although they were unable to secure the ship near Cauda, the brief respite that its leeward side provided from the wind gave them momentary opportunity for maneuvers.

The island was inhabited in this period,[601] although this would have made no difference for the voyagers unable to land there. It was much smaller than islands where ships that Paul used usually put into port;[602] at much less than fifty square kilometers (20 sq. mi.), less than a tenth the size of Samothrace, it appears as a geographic marker.[603]

Sailors would use the dinghy, a small boat, for landings or for pulling the ship's head in the right direction during tacking.[604] Normally the ship would tow its dinghy behind the stern,[605] usually with a sailor in it.[606] In a storm, however, this practice risked the smaller boat's loss,[607] and so it was safer to haul it on board. At times during a storm a shipmaster could board the skiff—which was attached to the boat with a rope—to pull the ship in the right direction.[608] The present storm, however, was too severe for this maneuver to succeed.

Luke's "we" (27:17) suggests that he participated in hauling in the boat; in contrast to some technical tasks that only sailors could do, passengers could be drafted (or could volunteer, as in 28:3) to help.[609] Because it was now full of water, it would be heavy,

---

variants were already in use for the same island: Greek writers (such as Hierocles and Ptolemy) use Κλαῦδος whereas Latin writers omit the *l* (Pliny the Elder uses "Gaudos"; Mela uses "Caudos"; Bruce, *Acts¹*, 459; Finegan, *Apostles*, 198). Pliny E. *N.H.* 4.12.61 places Gaudos not too far from the western cape of Crete. The Venetians called it Gozzo, not to be confused with a similarly named site near Malta.

598. Cauda is also said to be ca. 25 mi., or ca. 40 km., south of Phoenix (Conzelmann, *Acts*, 218, cites Pliny E. *N.H.* 4.61; *Stad.* 328; Ptolemy *Geog.* 3.17.11); online sources place Cauda slightly less distant than this from Loutro. Cauda is more than 35 mi. (more than 50 km.) west of Cape Matala. Sanders, *Crete*, 172, locates "Gavdhos" ca. 20 km. south of Crete.

599. With Hemer, *Acts in History*, 142. That the variants in the textual tradition match contemporary variants of the island's name, however, suggests that it was not unknown.

600. Bruce, *Commentary*, 509 (following Smith, *Voyage*, 113n). Various internet sources note that the island is triangular and fairly rocky but with beaches and many pines and cedars; fairly dry, it does not experience frequent rainstorms. Some modern writers (sometimes appealing to Callimachus) link it with Ortygia, Calypso's island in Homer's *Odyssey*.

601. For habitation attested in the Roman period, see Sanders, *Crete*, 10, fig. 2; p. 128. Christianity is also attested fairly early on the island, though obviously much later than our narrative (128). Today the island is said to have less than fifty (perhaps about forty) permanent inhabitants.

602. Larger, however, than other islands near Crete; see, e.g., Sanders, *Crete*, 11, fig. 3; 12, fig. 4.

603. One source lists it as 27 km. in area.

604. Lake and Cadbury, *Commentary*, 332; see Casson, *Travel*, 157. The term σκάφη (Acts 27:16, 30, 32) is good Greek (BDAG cites, e.g., Polyb. 1.23.7; *BGU* 1157.8; 1179; though the only LXX use, Dan 14:33, means "bowl"; a related term applies to boats over twenty times in Josephus), though Hemer, *Acts in History*, 143, suggests here the Latin loanword *scapha*, which applied to the sort of boat that Luke mentions (Caesar *Gall. W.* 4.26.4). Bede *Comm. Acts* 27.16–17 thinks of a light skiff (*scapha*) covered with hide (following Isidore), but further reading later convinced him (Bede, *Retractatio in Actus apostolorum* 27) that it could refer to a boat hollowed from a single tree (Martin, *Bede*, 191n).

605. Johnson, *Acts*, 448, cites Heliod. *Eth.* 5.27.6 (so also Parsons, *Acts*, 356).

606. Casson, *Mariners*, 195; Davis, "Navigation," 215n64 (citing Petron. *Sat.* 102.5). It is not clear from the narrative that anyone is inside, but if someone is, this would be another reason to bring the dinghy on board as quickly as possible.

607. Apart from being torn loose and swept away, it could be smashed against the ship's hull (cf., e.g., Finegan, *Apostles*, 198; Larkin, *Acts*, 370).

608. Davis, "Navigation," 215n64, quoting Cic. *Inv.* 2.154.

609. Luke's proximity to one or more sailors by volunteering at times may have also helped him acquire his specific nautical information of parts of the narrative.

and hence they were "scarcely" (μόλις) able to retrieve it.[610] Luke's audience will soon hear of this boat again, when it will prove better surrendered to the sea (27:30–32).

c. Avoiding the Syrtis (27:17)

Conzelmann wonders if Luke's transition to the third person here is a careless slip.[611] Instead, it reflects Luke's precision; only the sailors (or at least others who did not include Luke) performed the activities noted here. In the same way, in the next verse (27:18), all those aboard (hence "we") were tossed by the storm, but only the crew (hence "they") tossed cargo overboard. As in the "we" material more generally, Luke reserves "we" exclusively for activities in which he (along with others) participated, rarely intruding himself into the narrative's action.

i. The Danger of the Syrtis

The ship would in fact ultimately "run aground" (the same term appears in 27:26; for nautical usage, see BDAG), but not in a location as dangerous as the voyagers feared. The shoals of the Syrtis could ground a ship, but too far from land for the passengers to have any hope for safety.

Ships often followed a south wind between Cyrene and western Crete (Strabo 17.3.21), but the danger lay in the unusually expansive area of shallows and shoals to Cyrene's west. Strabo noted that the Syrtes (the Greater and the Lesser) were near Cyrenaea and the Libyan and Sicilian seas (2.5.20).[612] The area in general was thought difficult for sailors: Romans had found the area of the sea between Sicily and Libya particularly dangerous (Polyb. 1.37.1–3), the Libyan coast was thought to have fewer inlets and bays than any other coast (Pliny E. N.H. 5.1.1), and many feared death on "the Libyan (sea)" (Philodemus On Death 33.7).

The Greater Syrtis was not far west of Cyrene (Polyb. 3.39.2), and its head was the southernmost part of the Mediterranean (Strabo 2.5.25), some 600 miles (1,000 km.) from Carthage.[613] The modern Gulf of Sidra (Sirte) stretches roughly from Benghazi to Tripoli (Arabic Ṭarābulus).[614]

According to ancient estimates, the Lesser Syrtis was estimated to be about 1,600 stadia around, with the islands of Meninx[615] and Cercina at its mouth. The Greater Syrtis was much larger, sometimes estimated at 5,000 stadia around and 1,800 across or, more conservatively, 4,000 and 1,500 stadia respectively (2.5.20).[616] It was the Greater Syrtis, rather than the *Syrtis minor* (farther west than their trajectory), toward which the vessel's trajectory was driving them.[617]

610. Bruce, *Commentary*, 509; idem, *Acts¹*, 459; Hemer, *Acts in History*, 143. Luke has a greater predilection for this term than most early Christian writers and employs it especially regarding the storm (the NT uses are Acts 14:18; 27:7, 8, 16; Rom 5:7; 1 Pet 4:18; it is absent in the Apostolic Fathers and appears in the LXX only in the later parts, Prov 11:31; Wis 9:16; Sir 21:20; 26:29; 29:6; 32:7; 3 Macc 1:23; 5:15).

611. Conzelmann, *Acts*, 218.

612. For the Syrtis's association with Libya, see, e.g., Hdt. 2.32; 2.150; 4.174; the myth of the Psylli in Hdt. 4.173; Aul. Gel. 16.11. Purcell, "Syrtes," defines the area as "from Cyrenaica . . . through Tripolitania to Tunisia."

613. Strabo 17.3.18 estimates more than 5,000 stadia from the start of the Greater Syrtis to Carthage. Pliny E. N.H. 5.4.26, following Polybius, estimates the distance from the Lesser Syrtis to Carthage as 300 mi.

614. See Fitzmyer, *Acts*, 776, citing Pliny E. N.H. 5.4.27.

615. Homer's lotus-eaters supposedly continued to live on Meninx (Polyb. 1.39.2; 34.3.12; Strabo 3.4.3; 17.3.17), though they may be a past phenomenon in Pliny E. N.H. 5.4.28. On this island, see further Huss, "Meninx" (who also comments on Syrtis in idem, "Syrtis").

616. Strabo 17.3.20, perhaps preferring the more conservative or another source, estimates it as 3,930 stadia around and 1,500 across. Pliny E. N.H. 5.4.26, following Polybius, estimates the width of the Lesser Syrtis as 100 mi. and its circumference as 300 mi. Pliny E. N.H. 5.4.27 estimates 250 mi. between the two Syrtes, and the circumference of the Greater Syrtis as 625 mi., with an entrance 312 mi. wide.

617. Lake and Cadbury, *Commentary*, 333; Bruce, *Commentary*, 510.

Towns did lie on the land adjoining these shoals,[618] but the Syrtis rendered use of local bays problematic (Pliny E. *N.H.* 5.4.26). Strabo 17.3.20 notes that some ancients took these risks. It appears that despite these dangers, maritime trade prospered with "the Three Cities of Sabratha, Lepcis Magna, and Oea, which also functioned as outlets for the semi-arid hinterland and trans-Saharan trade; and the ports of south Tunisia, such as Tacape, were of some importance."[619] Yet even sailors who knew the region would scarcely want to face it at the mercy of the gale, unable to navigate their own course.

The Syrtis was known as a terrifying place[620] and a hazard for sailors to avoid.[621] The danger of the Syrtis was shallow waters at places, leading to boats becoming stuck in the shallows during the ebb and flow of tides (Strabo 17.3.20).[622] An early Roman fleet, unaccustomed to this region, grounded on shoals at low tide in the Lesser Syrtis, though the Romans escaped when they lightened their vessels and the tide rose.[623] Storytellers could depict the Syrtis as a three days' voyage inland but warned that once a boat had entered, it would be trapped and destroyed there (Dio Chrys. *Or.* 5.8–9).[624] Locals who knew the shoals were said to plunder the ships stranded there (Quint. Curt. 4.7.19).

The nearer Syrtis was the Greater Syrtis, at this point still nearly 400 miles (over 600 km.) away; by forcing the ship in a southwestern direction, however, the wind was driving Paul's company toward the Syrtis.[625] It was to avoid this very danger that Alexandrian ships en route to Rome preferred sailing north to Lycia (Acts 27:5–6) instead of west, too close to the Libyan coast.[626] Sources from this period reflect "an obsessional fear" of the Syrtis.[627] Thus sailors off the coast stayed as far as possible from the Syrtis, "taking precautions not to be caught off their guard and driven by winds into these gulfs," one even traveling thirty days by land to go around it.[628] So terrifying were the Syrtes that western Mediterranean literature regularly linked them with the mythical dangers of Scylla and Charybdis.[629] (In historical times,

618. Pliny E. *N.H.* 5.3.25 (on the Lesser Syrtis); Berenice (modern Benghazi), one of the five prominent cities of Cyrenaica, is "at the tip of the horn of the Syrtis" (5.5.31 [trans. Rackham, LCL, 2:241]).

619. Purcell, "Syrtes."

620. E.g., Ps.-Tibullus 3.4.92 (*horrendave Syrtis*); Jos. *War* 2.381.

621. Commentators (Conzelmann, *Acts*, 218; Johnson, *Acts*, 448) cite Dio Chrys. *Or.* 5.8–11; Pliny E. *N.H.* 5.26. Cf. the early nineteenth-century explorations in Cella, *Narrative*; Beechey and Beechey, *Proceedings*.

622. Hemer, *Acts in History*, 144, describes it as "an extensive zone of shallows and quicksands."

623. Polyb. 1.39.3–4. When they foolishly attempted the voyage again, however, their fleet was destroyed (1.39.5–6). Josephus flatters Roman valor as unstopped by the Syrtis (*War* 2.381). Speaking more technically from a modern perspective, the Mediterranean Sea has, for those familiar with oceans, relatively low tidal variation. In some locations this can be as little as 14 cm. (Genoa), though in other locations (such as Gibraltar) up to 1.2 m. or even more (Davis, "Navigation," 27).

624. Dio Chrys. *Or.* 5.10 compares the "porous," sandy bottom of the sea there with the sand dunes of the Libyan landscape.

625. Marshall, *Acts*, 409; Rapske, "Travel," 39; Witherington, *Acts*, 766. To ancient mariners, it might well seem closer than it was; Pliny E. *N.H.* 4.12.60 estimates 80 mi. from Crete to Malea (Morea in southern Greece) and just 125 mi. from Crete's Cape Crio to Cyrene (beyond which lay the Greater Syrtis). Elsewhere Pliny opines that the Cyrenian coast (well before the Syrtes) juts into Cretan Sea 224 mi. from Crete (*N.H.* 5.5.32). Libyans crossed the sea to visit a shrine in Crete (Philost. *Vit. Apoll.* 4.34).

626. Ramsay, "Roads and Travel," 380.

627. Hemer, *Acts in History*, 144, cites, e.g., Virg. *Aen.* 1.111, 146; Ps.-Tibullus 3.4.91; Prop. *Eleg.* 2.9.33.

628. Strabo 17.3.20 (trans. H. L. Jones, LCL, 8:197).

629. Catull. *Carm.* 64.156; Ps.-Tibullus 3.4.90–92; Ovid *Am.* 2.16.21–26 ("the Libyan Syrtes," 2.16.21–22; Scylla and Charybdis, 2.16.23–26). For the dangers of Scylla and Charybdis, see also Hom. *Od.* 12.85, 103–13, 125–26, 245, 426–46; Virg. *Aen.* 3; Ovid *Her.* 12.123–25; *Metam.* 13–14; Apul. *De deo Socr.* 178; Libanius *Speech in Character* 25.5; cf. Lucan *C.W.* 1.547–48; Lucian *Critic* 27. Cf. Harris, *Scylla*; more recently, the developmental interpretation of the myth in Hopman, *Scylla*.

though, most associated Scylla and Charybdis geographically with the Strait of Messina off Sicily.)[630]

Even Greek writers could speak of a Scylla-like monster lurking near the Syrtis. Dio Chrysostom tells (or invents) the myth of an African kind of monster preying on animals and people near the Syrtis (*Or.* 5.6–7). Each of these monsters looked like an exquisitely beautiful woman on top (5.12); the rest was a snake, with a snake's head (5.13).[631] Whereas they would catch other creatures by speed, they would seduce men (5.14). Once a man came close for intercourse, the concealed serpent (ὄφις) part would sting and kill him, then eat him (5.15, 27).[632] One traveler from Libya to Egypt went by land, avoiding the dangers of the Syrtis at sea, and discovered a monster's tomb (Lucian *Dipsads* 6). For sailors who had never navigated these waters, such stories may have provided supplemental terrors; but the dangers of such land creatures could not be realized if, as seemed likely, they might never even reach land. Again, though there were figurative uses of these images,[633] Luke's narrative at this point is primarily literal, and those aboard the ship would know stories of grave dangers ahead. Luke's point is the dangers through which God preserved his message for Rome.

II. SURVIVAL MANEUVERS

The sailors' particular maneuvers are more difficult to reconstruct. It is clear that mariners sometimes girded a ship with a rope to help it withstand the hard sea (e.g., Ap. Rhod. 1.367–70); the verb ὑποζώννυμι is elsewhere used of bracing ships.[634] In rough waters, frapping cables were used "around the outside of the hull, and in the case of merchantmen, under it" (BDAG, s.v. ὑποζώννυμι). Older Athenian triremes had employed "bracing cables" called ὑποζώματα, what one employed to accomplish the bracing implied in Luke's cognate verb in 27:17.[635] What is much less clear is the method used for this vessel.[636] Egyptian art nearly two millennia before Luke apparently illustrates a method of stretching a rope above deck between the stern and the prow to hold them together and prevent the ship from breaking up.[637] More likely, the crew used these cables to brace the hull and protect the keel.[638] Perhaps sailors accomplished this by wrapping the cables around prow or stern, then from either side of the deck slackening and pulling them back around the hull until they were ideally

---

630. Thucyd. 4.24.4; Polyb. 34.3.9–12, esp. 10; Cic. *Verr.* 2.5.55.146; Pliny E. *N.H.* 3.8.87 (in light of 3.5.73); cf. Cic. *Sest.* 8.18. See also Rose and Hornblower, "Charybdis"; cf. Griffiths, "Scylla"; Harder, "Scylla"; Ovid reconciling two traditions in Lowe, "Scylla."

631. Dio notes here that they were not winged like sphinxes and made no sound except like a dragon.

632. Offering a more sober perspective, Pliny the Elder notes that the land swarmed with serpents (*N.H.* 5.4.26). Paul encounters one instead in Malta (Acts 28:3), but snakes of various sorts were widespread.

633. The twin dangers of Scylla and Charybdis were sometimes used for comparisons with supposedly greater dangers, such as debt (Cic. *Sest.* 8.18); squandering money on a harp-girl (Alciph. *Fish.* 21 [Euploüs to Thalasserôs], 1.18, ¶3); luxury and shamelessness (Heracl. *Hom. Prob.* 70.10–11; cf. the Sirens, 70.9); an opponent's big and offensive mouth (Lucian *Critic* 27); Verres (Cic. *Verr.* 2.5.55.146); and someone else evil (Catull. *Carm.* 64.156). Likewise, the Syrtes could be a danger worth facing for love (Ovid *Am.* 2.16.21–22).

634. Sources (BDAG; Bruce, *Acts¹*, 460) cite Polyb. 27.3.3; Athen. *Deipn.* 5.204A; *IG* 1².73.9. After an extensive examination, Cadbury, "ὑποζώματα," also concludes (352) that Luke probably refers to the hogging truss. Ropes on ships were made from "flax, hemp, papyrus, or esparto grass" (Casson, *Mariners*, 193). Admittedly, our archaeological sources for understanding the process remain quite limited (Fitzgerald, "Ship of Paul," 34).

635. Rapske, "Travel," 35, though noting that extant parallels so far address only warships (but as Hirschfeld, "Ship of Paul," 26–27, notes, so far we lack "records of gear for commercial vessels" though archaeological evidence for this gear is also lacking). Bruce, *Acts¹*, 460, notes the noun in Plato *Rep.* 10.616C; *Laws* 12.945C; and elsewhere.

636. Frapping was normally attempted when a ship was beached (D. Williams, *Acts*, 433).

637. C. Williams, *Acts*, 271 (noting Cadbury, *Acts in History*, 10; the illustration in Cadbury, "ὑποζώματα," 351n28).

638. Cf. similarly Abbott, *Acts*, 252: "around the middle of the ship, at right angles to its length."

positioned and could be fastened in place.[639] As commentators note, Luke's use of βοήθεια fits common nautical usage for such supports, though his verb's allusion to the cognate ὑποζώματα is more explicit.[640] Pliny the Elder mentions that one danger of typhoons (see Acts 27:14) is that they could shatter not only spars but even the hull (*N.H.* 2.132).

Such undergirding was in fact routine before steel hulls came into use. In his dissertation on ancient Mediterranean navigation, Danny Davis points out that whereas "long, narrow warships employed these long cables longitudinally to prevent the stresses of hogging and sagging in moderate and heavy seas," merchant ships like Paul's "rigged them around the hull laterally to prevent plank joinery from splitting and seams from opening as a result of the twisting and flexing of the hull in exceptionally harsh sea states."[641]

More difficult is the "vessel" (σκεῦος, an unfortunately very generic designation, like the English "object" or "thing"; cf. Luke 8:16; 17:31; Acts 9:15) that the sailors "loosen" or "lower" (χαλάσαντες).[642] Some scholars suggest that it refers to a sail, perhaps a mainsail (cf. the same term in Acts 10:11, 16; 11:5); this would prevent the wind from driving the ship as quickly.[643] (But surely they would have taken down all rigging before passing Cauda [27:16]?) They would seek to tack as far against the wind as possible to counter the drift southwest toward the Syrtis.[644]

During severe storms, sailors would "clear the decks of unnecessary gear,"[645] "lower the yard to drop the ship's center of gravity,"[646] "shorten the sail(s) or replace the mainsail with a smaller *nothos* ('bastard') sail to maintain headway,"[647] and so forth. Thus Luke may refer here to lowering the "yard, the mainsail lashed to it and the fair-weather topsail (*supparum*)" to prevent "the mast from cracking" and allow sailors to set up "a storm sail closer to the deck . . . for maintaining steerageway."[648]

Others suggest attempts to mitigate the wind's force by using anchors and cables. The anchors had nothing to catch on here (in contrast to 27:29) but functioned as drags.[649] Stone anchors appear as early as the Bronze Age,[650] with wooden anchors

639. So Bruce, *Commentary*, 509; apparently R. Williams, *Acts*, 162 (though rightly noting our uncertainty); the fourth and likeliest option in Conzelmann, *Acts*, 218. The ferocity of the waves would make this procedure difficult until it had been accomplished. After its success, those hit by waves on deck might also find such additional ropes helpful.

640. For βοήθεια, sources (BDAG; Bruce, *Commentary*, 509) cite Arist. *Rhet.* 2.5.18, 1383a; Diod. Sic. 3.8.5; Philo *Jos.* 33.

641. Davis, "Navigation," 228n107, commenting on Acts 27:17 and also noting the similar strategy (with different words) in Synesius *Ep.* 4.198. Davis suggests (229n109) that grain ships' hulls may "have been double-planked," like a first-century B.C.E. "large wine-carrier" found by marine archaeologists off the French coast (citing for that ship Parker, *Shipwrecks*, 249–50).

642. Luke's other uses refer to "letting down," usually (Luke 5:4–5, fishing nets; Acts 27:30, the dinghy) but not quite always (Acts 9:25; cf. 2 Cor 11:33) into water.

643. Johnson, *Acts*, 448. Hemer, *Acts in History*, 143, suggests that the sailors retained for the ship "only a minimal storm-sail," for steadying the ship.

644. Hemer, *Acts in History*, 143.

645. Davis, "Navigation," 227, citing Xen. *Oec.* 8.15–16.

646. Davis, "Navigation," 228, citing here (228n105) Acts 27:17, pointing out that χαλάω refers to "slackening, loosening, or unstringing (e.g., a bow), and in Greek nautical contexts, σκεῦος typically means equipment, gear or naval stores and does not typically include anchors (see *LSJ*, s.v.)."

647. Davis, "Navigation," 228 (citing Synesius *Ep.* 4.164–65).

648. Davis, "Navigation," 228n105 (noting also James Smith's earlier treatment).

649. One of the views in Conzelmann, *Acts*, 218 (citing Plut. *Talkativeness, Mor.* 507a; Lucian *Tox.* 19); the view in Bede *Comm. Acts* 27.15, comparing a similar activity in the "British sea."

650. Wachsmann and Haldane, "Anchors," 137–38. For stone anchors at Ugarit, usually 220–400 pounds (but up to half a ton, for 70 ft. ships of 200 tons or more), see Craigie, *Ugarit*, 39.

by the seventh century B.C.E. (Romans giving them lead cores, and Greeks stone);[651] iron anchors, noted as early as Herodotus (Hdt. 9.74), appear commonly from the first century C.E. forward (as attested in shipwrecks).[652] The Seleucids had employed the anchor as a dynastic symbol, found on Judean coins.[653]

Meanwhile the voyagers were being "driven" along, the wind against their starboard, drifting at an estimated mile and a half each hour, "about eight degrees north of west," toward what appeared possible destruction.[654]

d. Discarding Cargo and Equipment (27:18–19)

Life matters more than possessions (Luke 17:31–32), and reduced to desperation, the crew is now ready to abandon the precious cargo for which they initially risked sailing late in the season.

i. Throwing Cargo Overboard (27:18)

Emergency conditions require jettisoning part of the cargo. The term χειμάζω, used only here in the NT, is related to a term for winter weather (χεῖμα) and appears in ancient literature both for difficult storms at sea (as here) and for figurative ones (see examples in BDAG). The specific activities Luke reports in Acts 27:18–19 are not borrowed from prototypical storm scenes, but such scenes normally do report operations undertaken to attempt to save the ship.[655]

Alexandrian grain ships were normally full when they set out on their voyage to Rome.[656] Merchants and shipowners, chronically underfunded, frequently borrowed money to purchase cargoes, then repaid the loans after selling the cargo. The high-risk insurance caveat in this arrangement was that if the ship was destroyed, the loan would not need to be repaid; this justified expensive loans (with interest of sometimes up to 30 percent of the price).[657] To jettison the cargo is a drastic act unless they expect to lose the ship in any case (27:10)—or view it as necessary to save their lives, whatever the owner's loss. Many members of Luke's audience, whatever their status, might have little sympathy toward shipowners, *navicularii*, who often belonged to the municipal elite and were often nouveau riche freedmen.[658]

In the face of a rough storm, a crew might lighten the ship, reducing the likelihood of being sunk, by throwing unnecessary objects overboard. To throw overboard instead the expensive cargo[659]—the transport of which constituted the reason for the long voyage—demonstrates the extent of the crew's current desperation to save

---

651. Wachsmann and Haldane, "Anchors," 138; for some lead ones, cf. Casson, *Mariners*, 173; cf. Adkins and Adkins, *Life*, 189–90. A Herodian anchor found near the Dead Sea consists of wood and lead (Hadas, "Routes").

652. Wachsmann and Haldane, "Anchors," 138–39. For various smaller anchors, as found on the sort of fishing boat that Peter may have used, see Nun, "Fishing," 317; see also sources on anchors in Rapske, "Travel," 33n149.

653. Jacobson, "Anchor." For other symbolic uses, see Heb 6:19; Montefiore, *Hebrews*, 116; Lane, *Hebrews*, 153; cf. perhaps Heb 2:1 (Lane, *Hebrews*, 35, 37).

654. Bruce, *Commentary*, 510.

655. Praeder, "Acts 27:1–28:16," 691 (citing Ach. Tat. 3.1.1–2; *Herpyllis* 25–30; Heliod. *Eth.* 5.27.3–4; Ovid *Metam.* 11.482–91; Tac. *Ann.* 2.23.4–5).

656. Casson, *Mariners*, 208.

657. Millett, "Maritime Loans"; Krampe, "Fenus nauticum," 381; idem, "Naufragium," 541 (citing *Dig.* 4.9.3.1); Toner, *Culture*, 45 (estimating 20 percent); cf. Schmitz, "Loan," 759; Andreau, "Maritime Loans," 362. The interest rate was not limited (cf. Paulus *Sent.* 2.14.3) until Justinian (Justin. *Cod.* 4.32.26.2; Krampe, "Fenus nauticum," 381). Sometimes the arrangement may have invited entrepreneurs with unprofitable ventures to commit insurance fraud (Philost. *Vit. Apoll.* 4.32). Meanwhile, lenders who lent to sailors worried about winds and wrecks (so Gregory of Nyssa, as cited in Toner, *Culture*, 24).

658. Rathbone, "Navicularii."

659. A large ship's cargo could be quite lucrative (Lucian *Ship* 13–14); hence "this great loss" in Acts 27:21.

their lives.[660] Aristotle remarks that sometimes discarding the cargo is necessary; no one would discard his property under normal circumstances, "but to save his life and that of his shipmates any sane man would do so" (*N.E.* 3.1.5, 1110a).[661] Comparing a political crisis, Cicero notes that in a storm one must throw everything else overboard (*Quint. fratr.* 3.8.1). At a helmsman's order, desperate passengers in a storm might throw overboard even gold and silver, and merchants might discard their own goods in which they had hoped for profit (Ach. Tat. 3.2.9). In other settings, Luke also valued preserving one's life at the expense of one's property (Luke 17:31–32; cf. 1 Macc 2:28).

Some scholars argue that the jettison of cargo in Jonah 1:5 LXX is Luke's closest verbal model.[662] (On proposed Jonah background, see the discussion, above, at the beginning of Acts 27.) Yet jettisons are typical for storm scenes (and, undoubtedly, storm experiences) in ancient literature.[663] This is true of storm scenes in histories as well as in other genres.[664] They happened commonly enough for later laws to regulate the practice.[665] Later rabbis told a story that a crew threw one of Nicanor's doors for the temple overboard during a storm, and when they prepared to discard the second one, Nicanor begged them to throw him in with it. As the story went, the sea then calmed and the other door was also recovered (*b. Yoma* 38a, bar.). Luke may have derived two words from Jonah's phrase ἐκβολὴν ἐποιήσαντο, though even here we cannot be sure that Luke thought of a specific source; ἐκβολή is a recognized term for the activity depicted,[666] and the phrase appears elsewhere.[667]

II. Not All the Cargo (27:18)

The imperfect ἐποιοῦντο (contrast Jonah's aorist) allows for the action to be completed later (Acts 27:38), although, given the surrender of even (apparently) the ship's tackle in 27:19, one could suppose that the wheat discarded in 27:38 could be food kept for their own needs—that is, only a small part of the cargo. Then again, the participation of at least some passengers as well as crew in 27:38 (cf. 27:36–37) may suggest that more effort was needed, but this could simply reflect the access of all aboard to the wheat (since they were eating it, 27:36) or the physically weakened condition of those aboard (27:33).

Even had Luke said nothing about some cargo remaining, however, we should not imagine that the entire cargo was discarded on the first day that the sailors began to do it. Some of the largest ships—and this must be one of them (27:37)—could carry

---

660. As Casson notes (*Travel*, 157), "The alternative to keeping the ship afloat was death." For losing a cargo to escape alive, cf. also Jos. *Ant.* 14.377; *War* 1.280; for jettisoning some things to save others, Quint. Curt. 5.9.3.

661. Trans. Rackham, LCL, 19:119. Conzelmann, *Acts*, 220, compares *1 En.* 101:4–5, where frightened sailors will hurl their goods into the sea. A shipwreck survivor who lost his possessions at sea could, with special skills, acquire his living afresh afterward (Phaedrus 4.23); cf. similarly a sage who was a refugee (Val. Max. 7.2.ext. 3). Galen praises Zeno for reportedly remaining content after losing all in a shipwreck (*Grief* 48).

662. Cf. C. Williams, *Acts*, 271–72; Bruce, *Commentary*, 511n42; idem, *Acts¹*, 460; Praeder, "Acts 27:1–28:16," 691; cf. Jos. *Ant.* 9.211–12. Wall, "Acts," 348, suggests that Luke may have chosen σκευή because of its similarity to Jonah's σκεῦος (cf. BDAG), also thrown overboard.

663. Praeder, "Acts 27:1–28:16," 691 (citing Ach. Tat. 3.2.9; Juv. *Sat.* 12.30–53); Johnson, *Acts*, 448, adds other sources (including Heliod. *Eth.* 5.27.7).

664. E.g., Polyb. 1.39.3–4; Jos. *War* 1.280.

665. Davis, "Navigation," 229, citing *Nomos Rhodiōn Nautikos* 9: the captain should consult passengers with goods and allow them to vote. Someone should record the items being thrown overboard for the sake of later compensation.

666. Conzelmann, *Acts*, 218 (citing Jonah 1:5 LXX; Lucian *Posts* 1; Ach. Tat. 3.2.9; Jos. *War* 1.279–80).

667. BDAG cites Pollux *Onomasticon* 1.99.

more than 250 tons;[668] ships carrying government cargos often ran to 340 tons, and some grain vessels to 1,200 tons.[669] Grain ships bound for Rome carried a minimum of 68 tons in this period, and the massive *Isis* carried at least 1,000 tons.[670]

A second- or third-century C.E. letter indicates that dockside unloading took about twelve days.[671] Unloading might take less for ships like this one than for some others: Josephus's ship had more than twice as many passengers as Luke's vessel (Jos. *Life* 15; Acts 27:37); fitting all (?) the sailors into a single boat (Acts 27:30) suggests a much smaller ship than the *Isis* with its massive crew.[672] But it was still no easy enterprise, nor would it be accomplished all in a single day, especially without the equipment used in the docks. It has been suggested that the crew here jettisoned only the upper cargo, perhaps above deck or in the upper levels of storage.[673]

Throwing items overboard would consume less time than carefully unloading them, but the speed would still depend on how the grain was stored. Such ships held partitions in their hold to separate individuals' lots so that the owners could be compensated if their merchandise was lost. Probably the grain, at least the grain they began discarding this day, was stored in sacks.[674] Grain piled six feet high exerts a vertical pressure of close to 240 pounds per square foot. But "if not sacked or binned it could 'flow' in rough seas, exerting sudden lateral pressure upon the hull of up to 160 lbs. per square foot at places and threatening breach or capsize."[675] Even if it was in sacks, however, sacks of such weight were not easily moved. It is not surprising that some of the task remains in 27:38.[676]

III. DISCARDING EQUIPMENT (27:19)

Keeping track of the number of days at sea was probably common[677] and could well be particularly likely in such a dramatic situation. That the crew acted "with their own hands" (αὐτόχειρες) is emphatic, perhaps ominously implying the "increasing danger."[678]

Scholars debate the precise meaning of the claim that the voyagers "cast down" (ἔρριψαν) the "object" (σκευήν; the term may be more specific than its cognate in 27:17, but that is not saying much).[679] Some have suggested (with the Old Latin

668. Souza, "Ships." One first-century B.C.E. wreck was carrying between 225 and 390 tons of wine amphoras; another from this period carried 500 to 600 tons (Casson, *Mariners*, 172). Another, carrying blocks of stone, contained 350 tons (p. 173). Even as early as ancient Ugarit, scholars estimate some ships of 200 tons (Craigie, *Ugarit*, 39).

669. Casson, *Mariners*, 191 (noting one case ca. 40 C.E. with 1,300 tons).

670. Rapske, "Travel," 31. Casson, *Mariners*, 209, estimates between 1,000 and 1,300 tons, noting that only eighty ships so massive would have been required to supply Egypt's 135,000 tons for Rome each year. This ship was probably unusual, however; Lucian *Ship* 5 notes the report that the huge ship *Isis*, bound for Rome, carried sufficient grain "to feed all Attica for a year" (LCL, 6:437). One third-century B.C.E. ship later mentioned in Athenaeus has been estimated as holding nearly 2,000 tons (Hirschfeld, "Ship of Paul," 27).

671. Rapske, "Travel," 31.

672. Ibid., 32. The *Isis* had virtually an army's worth of sailors according to Lucian *Ship* 6.

673. Cf. Rapske, "Travel," 32–33. Any grain accessible to water because of leakage would be ruined and swelling by this point, in any case.

674. Ibid., 32. Hirschfeld, "Ship of Paul," 28–29, presents partitions and sacks as separate ways of compartmentalizing the cargo.

675. Rapske, "Travel," 35.

676. In Acts 27:38, it is possible that the crew also has help, if the subject of the verbs remains the same throughout that sentence. Here, however, Luke does distinguish "we" from "they." Aside from sacks, large clay vessels would also be difficult to move (on their size, see, e.g., Casson, *Mariners*, 170; Docter, "Pithos," 306).

677. E.g., Acts 21:1; 27:19, 27, 33; Philost. *Hrk.* 6.3.

678. Bruce, *Acts*[1], 461. The term is not a Lukan coinage; see Jos. *War* 7.393; *Ant.* 13.363; and other sources in BDAG.

679. Some suggest anything left on deck (D. Williams, *Acts*, 434, but exempting the passengers' luggage if it remained secured, in view of the third- rather than first-person pronoun). This could include the yard (noted below) without being limited to it (Bock, *Acts*, 736).

version) the use of another anchor as a brake. More likely Luke refers to "the yard, an enormous spar which could be almost as long as the vessel itself" and which needed "to be lowered to the deck and either secured properly or cast adrift." This was a difficult task requiring many workers.[680] A mast could be jettisoned when "it de-socketed itself with the rolling, yawing and heaving of the ship in rough seas and high winds,"[681] or because it was a quick way "to lighten the ship . . . with a few swings of the axe."[682] Such an extreme measure left only the artemon (foresail),[683] but it was frequent enough for later Roman law to address monetary issues surrounding accidental or deliberate demasting of ships.[684]

e. Surrendering Hope (27:20)

Circumstances became so grave (particularly the inability to see sun or stars), Luke emphasizes, that those aboard lost hope.[685] This loss of hope excepts Paul (27:21–26), whose faith the contrast highlights. This loss of hope also climaxes the description of the terrible situation, thereby dramatically underlining the reality of the miracle that follows.

i. NEITHER SUN NOR STARS

"Many days" highlights the danger;[686] "no small storm" is litotes, a literary way to say "a great storm."[687] Sailing at night, with diminished visibility, raised the chance of shipwreck (Diod. Sic. 31.45.1); this was all the more the case when nothing was visible both night and day.[688] Some descriptions of particularly dangerous storms at sea mention that no stars were visible (Ovid *Metam.* 11.520–21).[689] Sailors in the Mediterranean normally could use the stars for navigation, but not during this long-term storm; a meteorologist notes that this problem characterizes "autumnal storms that ravage the Mediterranean during the time of low-index weather patterns."[690]

The obscuring of both sun and stars[691] was particularly terrifying (Isa 13:10;

---

680. Casson, *Travel*, 157 (who thinks that the passengers were drafted to help here, as may have happened in other storms). Cf. also Bruce, *Commentary*, 510 (following Smith, *Voyage*, 111–12); for rigging, see Finegan, *Apostles*, 199. Johnson, *Acts*, 448, who notes the extremity of cutting down the mast in Juv. *Sat.* 12.52–60, rightly points out that it is satire. Even in severe twentieth-century storms, sailors would jettison expensive equipment to try to preserve the ship (Braun, *Here*, 95–96; Braun, *Way*, 13).

681. Davis, "Navigation," 229, citing Hom. *Od.* 12.409–13.

682. Davis, "Navigation," 230.

683. Ibid., citing Juv. *Sat.* 12.30–69.

684. Davis, "Navigation," 230, citing Papinianus *Dig.* 14.2.3; Hermogenianus *Dig.* 14.2.5 pr. 1; *Nomos Rhodiōn Nautikos* 35.

685. This may include Luke himself, although the first-person-plural pronoun is directly connected here with deliverance rather than with the loss of hope (*pace* the NIV, trying to circumvent a passive construction).

686. Storms could lengthen voyages (cf. the *Isis*'s seventy days from Alexandria to the Piraeus; Lucian *Ship* 9).

687. On litotes, see, e.g., Rowe, "Style," 128; comment on Acts 1:5. The term χειμών can imply a winter storm (cf. the season in Acts 27:9), but the sense had extended to storms in general (see BDAG). That this "tempest" "pressed" (ἐπικειμένου) on them reflects its force due to the low-pressure zone, but the analogous sound links it rhetorically with χειμῶνος.

688. Some also considered breezes on "sunny days" healthier, with winter chills increasing pain (Symm. *Ep.* 1.100); winter also decreased the hours of sunlight, of course (1.20.3).

689. Such storms could be held to affect only the lower heavens; the stars themselves, being in the upper heavens, were unaffected (so Sen. Y. *Dial.* 5.6.1). For some, the nonappearance of heavenly bodies could indicate that they were astrologically impotent at this time (cf. *Gen. Rab.* 25:2), but the navigational meaning is far more dominant in sea voyage passages.

690. White, "Meteorological Appraisal," 407.

691. Praeder, "Acts 27:1–28:16," 692, notes Virg. *Aen.* 3.203–4 (where sun and stars were obscured for three days in a storm near Crete). Even trees' shrouding stars in the forest could terrify soldiers (Quint. Curt.

Ezek 32:7; Joel 2:10; 3:15); see discussion of darkness at Acts 2:20.[692] Stars enabled one to determine the hour of the night (Polyb. 9.15.7); but more important here, they were necessary to plot location[693] and determine if Paul's ship was still at risk of being driven to the Syrtis (Acts 27:17). That they were obscured illustrates the storm's intensity. Indeed, one reason for avoiding winter travel was the difficulty storms posed to navigation.[694] The obscuring of the sun invited observers' attention both in eschatological descriptions (Acts 2:20; Luke 21:25) and in historic judgment miracles (Luke 23:45; Acts 13:11). Perhaps it similarly invites attention to Paul's message here (cf. Jonah 1:15–16). Many Gentiles considered the sun and stars to be deities (Acts 7:42–43; see comment there); but the true God is sovereign over them.

Miracle stories often build suspense by emphasizing the grave danger that precedes the relief;[695] the same was true of sea rescue stories.[696] Sea voyages in general often mention the disappearance of hope;[697] of course, in the circumstances Luke describes, such a disappearance is intrinsically probable, in any case,[698] but mentioning it adds suspense. Sometimes in ancient texts storms even function as omens of impending doom.[699] By now the crew undoubtedly realized that they would drift too far south to reach Sicily, but they could not hope to survive being driven onto the Tunisian coast in a storm.[700]

11. No Hope for Deliverance

In this context Luke regularly uses σωτηρία (Acts 27:34), σῴζω (27:20, 31), or διασῴζω (27:43, 44; 28:1, 4) for deliverance from a storm. God's power to save physically provides a suitable metaphor for his power to save spiritually (e.g., 4:9, 12; Luke 8:36, 48, 50; 17:19; 18:42). Luke's description of their plight—terror over the obscuring of sun and stars—suits a foretaste of eschatological trauma:[701] signs in the sun, stars, sea, and waves (Luke 21:25) would lead to people fainting from fear (21:26). But believers should show courage and not abandon it (21:28)—fitting Paul's role in the following paragraph (Acts 27:21–26).

5.4.25; the snow in 5.4.18 renders deciduous tree leaves unlikely, but perhaps he thinks of tall conifers). For common ancient veneration of the sun as a deity, see note on Acts 2:20 (Keener, *Acts*, 1:918–19n630); for later dedications to Sol Invictus, see discussion in Carbó García, "Sol Invictus."

692. It may appear tempting to parallel Paul's testing toward the end of Acts with Jesus's passion on this point (Luke 23:44), or to envision it as a sort of proleptic eschatological fulfillment (Acts 2:20). Had this been Luke's intention, however, he could have worded the parallel much more clearly (mentioning either the moon here, as in 2:20, or darkness, as in both other texts; Luke 23:44 does not mention the sun, and neither other text mentions stars). But the other texts share some of the associations mentioned below.

693. With Hanson, *Acts*, 248; Conzelmann, *Acts*, 218. Phoenicians (best known for sailing) were held to be skilled in this (Lucian *Icar.* 1). For the use of nautical astronomy, see esp. discussion in Davis, "Navigation," 120–57; for wind roses, see 90–119. For the ancient use of astronomy to calculate dates, see Robinson, "Ardua."

694. Souza, "Navigation"; Casson, *Mariners*, 195. For the constellations and named stars in Greek sources, see Toomer, "Constellations" (note also the "barbarian" tradition, 383).

695. Theissen, *Miracle Stories*, 52 (citing, e.g., Lucian *Lover of Lies* 11).

696. Theissen, *Miracle Stories*, 52 (citing, e.g., Mark 4:37; *Hom. Hymns* 33.11–12 [to the Dioscuri]).

697. Praeder, "Acts 27:1–28:16," 692 (noting Ach. Tat. 5.9.2; Arrian *Ind.* 35.7; Eurip. *Iph. Taur.* 1413; Lucan *C.W.* 5.636–37; Ovid *Tristia* 1.2.23; a related image in Lucan *C.W.* 5.453–55). Johnson, *Acts*, 449, adds other sources (Hom. *Od.* 5.297–304; 12.277–79; Ael. Arist. *Or.* 2.12; Ach. Tat. 3.2.4; Lucian *Tox.* 20; Thucyd. 1.2.65).

698. Cf. also Johnson, *Acts*, 448–49.

699. E.g., Sil. It. 12.623–26; 1 Sam 7:10. When such omens were not to their advantage, generals sometimes explained them away (Sil. It. 12.627–29; Plut. *Alex.* 60.2).

700. Hemer, *Acts in History*, 145. Cf. Acts 27:17.

701. In some apparently special Lukan material, though the material is closely related to Matt 24:29 rather than possibly simply composed from whole cloth.

Luke's wording was also natural language for physical deliverances[702] or safety,[703] including in childbirth,[704] military situations,[705] and, as here, at sea.[706] This designation appears frequently for deliverances in ancient sea voyage literature.[707] Luke often uses "hope" in a natural sense as well (Luke 6:34; 23:8; Acts 16:19; 24:26). It is not impossible that, as in the case of deliverance, natural hope could offer a useful analogy for the hope of Christ (Luke 24:21; Acts 2:26; 23:6; 24:15; 26:6–7; 28:20), as in the "hope" for eschatological "salvation" in Pauline literature;[708] but even when "hope" and "deliverance" terms are conjoined, they can refer to natural circumstances.[709]

Deaths at sea were counted particularly tragic (e.g., Pliny *Ep.* 5.21.3).[710] Some ancients believed that those who died at sea never descended to Hades but that their souls wandered endlessly above the waters where they died (Ach. Tat. 5.16.1–2). What was most terrible about death at sea was the impossibility of burial,[711] and what some may have dreaded most about lack of burial was the tradition that the unburied could not enter Hades.[712] It was also believed that the unavenged ghosts of those who died violently could wander or haunt places;[713] thus, burying a deceased person's remains might appease a spirit and end its haunting.[714] (Romans called the dead who were not buried *Lemures*, and believed that they haunted areas, disturbing the living.)[715] In addition to such considerations, of course, drowning was a hideous way to die.[716]

702. E.g., Apul. *Metam.* 6.28; Char. *Chaer.* 2.7.6; 2.8.1; *Pss. Sol.* 16:5; *Let. Aris.* 18; 4 Macc 17:21–22; Jos. *Ant.* 11.282; *War* 5.415; 6.310; *Test. Job* 19:2/1; Ramsay, *Teaching*, 94–95; from demons in Incant. Text 17.1–2; 19.2; 34.1, 6; 47.1; probably eschatological, nationalistic deliverance in Jos. *Ant.* 20.189.

703. E.g., Aeschines *Embassy* 74; Plut. *Statecraft* 32, *Mor.* 824D; Jdt 11:3; Philo *Decal.* 53, 60, 155; 4 Macc 15:8; cf. Dio Chrys. *Or.* 40.36; civic security in Proclus *Poet.* 5, K49.1–2.

704. E.g., Terence *Andr.* 473; perhaps 1 Tim 2:15 (cf. Winter, *Wives*, 109–10; Keener, *Paul*, 118–20); for medical help more generally, e.g., Men. Rhet. 2.17, 443.27 (of Apollo).

705. Xen. *Anab.* 5.2.24; Lysias *Or.* 2.66, §196; Demosth. *Cor.* 324; *Epitaph.* 10, 23; *Ep.* 1.2; by the Lord in Sir 46:1; 1 Macc 4:25; Jdt 8:17; Jos. *Ant.* 2.339; 3.1; cf. Plut. *Themist.* 9.4.

706. Diod. Sic. 4.43.1; 11.24.2; Dion. Hal. *Ant. rom.* 11.9.1; Ach. Tat. 3.5; Libanius *Comparison* 4.4–5.

707. With Praeder, "Acts 27:1–28:16," 692–93.

708. Rom 8:24; 1 Thess 5:8; cf. 1 Tim 1:1; 4:10; Titus 2:13; also 2 *Clem.* 1.7; Ign. *Phld.* 5.2; *Barn.* 1.3; 12.3, 7. For abandoned hope, see, e.g., *Herm.* 75.4.

709. Repeatedly in LXX Psalms and Job; Bar 4:22; 1 *Clem.* 16.16; *Barn.* 17.1; esp. 2 Macc 3:29, mentioning loss of hope as here; Libanius *Comparison* 4.4 (marginal hope of safety at sea). Still, sometimes even such usage can lend itself to eschatological analogies (cf. 1 *Clem.* 11.1). But the allegorization by some to suggest a theology of universal spiritual salvation (based on the non-Christian passengers) inappropriately confuses distinguishable nuances of the term at the expense of Luke's explicit theology elsewhere (e.g., Acts 4:12; see Schnabel, "Reading Acts," 264).

710. Cf. the honors for Ajax, lost at sea in Philost. *Hrk.* 31.8–9. For fear of death at sea, see, e.g., Philodemus *On Death* 32.31–34; 33.34–36 (where such fear is rejected).

711. E.g., Ach. Tat. 23.3; Prop. *Eleg.* 3.7.7–26; Libanius *Comparison* 4.14 (eaten by fish instead); *Eccl. Rab.* 3:2, §2; cf. Hermog. *Issues* 39.15–16; on a lake in Sil. It. 6.12–13; in a river in Val. Max. 1.4.2; Philost. *Hrk.* 19.7. Even if a ship was safe, it would not retain a corpse on board (*Apoll. K. Tyre* 25), but tombs could be erected for those lost at sea, even if their bodies were not recovered (*Gr. Anth.* 7.397) or only half-recovered (7.506; corpses washed up from the sea could be unrecognizable, Quint. *Decl.* 388.17). Despite the possible attempt to evade final judgment by being scattered over the seas (*b. Giṭ.* 56b), God would restore even those lost at sea for that day (1 *En.* 61:5; *Sib. Or.* 2.233).

712. Hom. *Il.* 23.70–74; Virg. *Aen.* 6.365–66; Heliod. *Eth.* 6.15; for this belief also in the ancient Near East, Monson, "Kings," 62, cites Abusch, "Ghost"; van der Toorn, *Religion*, 55, 60–61; cf. also Provan, "Kings," 150. Those who died beforehand in Crete would have easily been inhumed (for the local custom, see Sanders, *Crete*, 40–43).

713. Lucan *C.W.* 1.11; Pliny *Ep.* 7.27.5–11; Plut. *Cim.* 1.6; 6.5–6; Johnston, "Dead, Cult of," 114; cf. similarly, in some other traditional religion, Mbiti, *Religions*, 109.

714. Lucian *Lover of Lies* 31. The only other traditional complication would be the one obol needed for entry (*Dial. D.* 423 [2/22, Charon and Menippus 1]).

715. Garland and Scheid, "Death"; cf. Rüpke, *Religion*, 130.

716. *Test. Ab.* 17:16; 19:11–12 A. Romans employed it as one of the most terrible punishments; see Val. Max. 1.1.13; Livy 1.51.9 (drowned with a crate full of stones); 27.37.5–7 (newborn hermaphrodite); Suet.

5. Paul Shares the Angel's Message (27:21–26)

After setting the dramatic stage of deadly peril and others' loss of hope (Acts 27:14–20), Luke reports Paul's faith and encouragement stemming from an angelic revelation (27:21–26).

a. Introduction

Because many individual elements of Paul's speech appear straightforward but particular questions apply to the pericope as a whole, it is helpful to survey these questions in an introductory manner here: the literary character of this pericope as an indirect revelation report (unusual for Luke); the question of whether Paul's voice could be heard during a storm; whether other passengers would heed him and the nature of his speech; and Luke's positive portrayal of Paul's courage in the face of danger.

i. Indirect Revelation Report

Why does Luke recount only Paul's report of the vision rather than the vision itself? Luke normally reports visions directly (7:55–56; 9:3–5, 10–16; 10:3–6, 10–16; 18:9–10; 23:11), but he diverges from that pattern here. This divergence could serve the purpose of literary variation, but it may also point to Luke's historiographic method. Where his sources report visions, he follows their reports.[717] In the more detailed "we" material, where he himself was present, however, he can recount more credibly Paul's report of the vision than an experience to which he himself was not privy.[718] The one exception to this pattern is 16:9, but in this case Luke was apparently directly involved in the discussion and interpretation of the dream (16:10). That this difference in narrative texture accounts for the character of the secondary report here seems to me likelier than not, though one dare not insist on it as certain (the "we" material does cover less space than the rest of the narrative, offering fewer examples for comparison).

ii. Paul's Voice in a Storm

Most scholars doubt that Paul could have addressed his companions during a storm.[719] It has been noted that such speeches fit a literary convention of storm scenes.[720] Some draw from this observation the conclusion that Luke composes the account according to literary convention; although such a conclusion is plausible, we should also keep in mind that the ancients knew sailing conditions on their own vessels better than do most modern critics. If such scenes were impossibilities, would the

---

Aug. 67.2; Modestinus Dig. 48.9.9; cf. weasels in Babr. 27. See also Luke 17:2; Mark 9:42; Matt 18:6; Rev 18:21. This method also prevented burial (cf. Derrett, "Mylos onikos"; Cic. Phil. 11.2.5).

717. Visions are a critical element in Luke's theological epistemology; see, e.g., Acts 2:17; 11:5 (on the latter, see, e.g., Nguyen, Peter, 137–38, 163).

718. Why Luke omits the first person here is unclear, since he has not gone temporarily overboard. Perhaps historically (given the layout of the ship, especially if they are below deck) Paul addressed only a group of those aboard; the third person plural in the preceding context seems to refer to the ship's crew (27:17–19), although Luke casually mentions his participation where it occurs in the same scenes (27:16, 18). Certainly Paul's message is directed toward those who made a wrong decision, not his companions (27:21), though his prediction extends beyond the crew (27:22, 24).

719. Haenchen, Acts, 704; Conzelmann, Acts, 218; Praeder, "Acts 27:1–28:16," 696.

720. Praeder, "Acts 27:1–28:16," 696, helpfully cites Hom. Od. 5.299–312; Lucan C.W. 5.653–71; Sen. Y. Ag. 510–27; Sil. It. 17.260–67; Val. Flacc. 1.626–33; Virg. Aen. 1.92–101. Chance, Acts, 500, rightly points out that some of these "speeches" are prayers and hence do not reveal a convention of people aboard a ship listening to speeches.

incongruity never have occurred to ancient writers?[721] Or did such accounts implicitly praise the speakers' ability to project their voices? Rhetoric highly valued this ability to project the voice.[722]

Given literary freedoms concerning speeches, it is certainly possible that Luke has dramatized the account.[723] Alternatively, we may consider that the storm's intensity would vary from day to day, and Paul may have chosen to speak out during a lull in its noise. (For noise other than the storm being audible at some point, see comment on Acts 27:27.)

Another possibility also merits consideration, although it more debatable than the possibility of a lull in the sound of the storm. Given the weather, perhaps not everyone aboard would be on deck all the time, and the scene could be envisioned as being below deck.[724] (If a grain ship's cargo required hundreds of passengers to sleep on deck,[725] the situation might be somewhat different after a difficult storm and with some of the grain discarded; 27:18.) Paul's "standing among them" in 27:21 implies that the rest were seated; perhaps especially the crew worked on deck during much of the storm whereas many others would be beneath the deck.[726]

Because most remains of vessels are from their bottoms, ships' superstructures are difficult to reconstruct.[727] Nevertheless, from what we know, under normal circumstances most people would not *want* to stay below deck; when prisoners were transported there, this experience was depicted as enduring continuous darkness and listed among their torments.[728] Because grain was stored below deck and water-swelled grain could rupture the ship's hull, a watertight hatch sealed off the grain below, and the crew would want to continue to protect it.[729] Paul was obviously above deck in 27:30–31.[730]

But while there would likely be "tight hatches, planking and bulkheads" below deck to prevent the flowing of grain (whether it was sacked or poured in), there could

721. Cf. the similar concern of Witherington, *Acts*, 767. He suggests (767–68) that there were surely times when ancients tried to "rally crew and passengers," as in modern times.

722. See Hall, "Delivery," 220; cf. voice training (and sometimes a herald) on 230 (Quint. *Inst.* 11.3.19; Suet. *Aug.* 84).

723. As Soards points out (*Speeches*, 128), Luke has Paul stand "in their midst," like a Greek orator and in keeping with Luke's depiction of some other speeches (Acts 1:15; 17:22, 33; cf. 4:7; 23:10).

724. Some people even in normal circumstances slept below deck (Libanius *Maxim* 1.13). Perhaps in special circumstances using torches, but probably more often smaller lamps, for some light; in any case, the lighting would be weak, but the voyagers would by now be accustomed to this problem. A low ceiling would not provide good acoustics for a large crowd, although, in much of the Majority World today, pastors do manage to address hundreds of people in relatively small spaces without a sound system.

725. See, e.g., Hirschfeld, "Ship of Paul," 28.

726. Witherington, *Acts*, 768. For the phrase "stand" (or "be stood," "placed") "in the midst," see also 4:7; 17:22; Luke 24:36 (similarly Acts 1:15); four other times in the NT; for speeches, Jos. *Ant.* 7.278; 9.169; 10.63; 11.168.

727. Personal correspondence, Justin Leidwanger, Oct. 7, 2014.

728. 3 Macc 4:9–10, apparently envisioning quite a large number of prisoners. Although novels normally played on social reality, it is possible that the author of this one lacked genuine knowledge of ships; his contemporary knowledge, however, seems likelier than our modern guesses. See also the below-deck torment in *Mart. Felix appendix* (in Rapske, *Custody*, 205).

729. Mark Wilson, personal correspondence, Oct. 13, 2014. During a storm, Davis, "Navigation," 227, notes, the crew would "shut and secure cabin doors and cargo hatches to prevent swamping" (while warning in n. 103 that archaeological remains provide no information regarding "decks, hatches and cabins," since only the lower parts of ships have survived). Given the danger of wet grain swelling, grain ships' hatches must have been watertight, and *Nomos Rhodiōn Nautikos* 38 shows that sailors must bail water; if the cargo gets wet, the sailors are liable (Davis, "Navigation," 228n108). Citing the *Nomos Rhodiōn Nautikos*, Wilson (correspondence, Oct. 13, 2014) notes that because the pilot, owner, and sailors all received shares in the profit, they would be reluctant to risk the grain's security.

730. With Rapske, *Custody*, 205.

well be some room where people could huddle there in emergency conditions.[731] This could especially be the case if some of the discarded cargo in 27:18 had been from below deck.[732] Justin Leidwanger, a specialist in maritime archaeology teaching at Stanford, remarks that while passengers normally stayed above deck, "I suppose I don't have any trouble imagining passengers huddling below deck fore or aft in a pinch. . . . I'm consistently amazed at how many people can fit in small spaces in the holds of ships these days, particularly when (unfortunately) quite desperate, so 276 might be doable in a pinch," especially given that Josephus shows that some ships could transport more than double that number.[733] There was even sometimes accommodation below deck in steerage, though the number who could fit there would be limited.[734]

Even if Paul speaks below deck, however, we do not know how many people would hear him. People could hear Paul more easily below deck than above it, but would all 276 people (27:37) be able to gather in a single place? (One must consider particularly the limitations imposed by bulkheads that compartmentalized different batches of grain sacks.)[735] This was, presumably, not a rowing ship,[736] but on older triremes, officers could communicate with their 170 rowers[737] (though presumably the rhythm was often managed through expedients such as drums rather than voices).[738] Perhaps not all people were, in fact, present, including even Luke himself; although Luke has just used the first person plural (27:15–16, 20; and revisits it immediately afterward, in 27:37), in 27:17–19, 21 and 27:33–36 he uses the third person.[739] (Luke is not above using hyperbole even when explicitly saying "all" [cf. 19:10], as later in 27:33.) In 27:33–36 he may have even addressed primarily the soldiers just mentioned in 27:32 (or perhaps also sailors in 27:30, 38–40), although the repetition of "all" in 27:37 (from 27:33, 35–36) might suggest that Luke intends to depict all the voyagers at least on the latter occasion (but see comment there). On the latter occasion, the weather may have been more suitable for hearing above deck (see comment on Acts 27:27). In that instance, the imperfect form παρακάλει could allow for Paul moving

731. Justin Leidwanger, personal correspondence, Oct. 7, 2014. Cf. a sailor guarding the hold in Paulinus of Nola *Ep*. 49.1–3 (cited in Davis, "Navigation," 226–27).

732. Brian Rapske, personal correspondence, Oct. 13, 2014, allows for the possibility that this was on-deck cargo. For the sorts of reasons provided, both Rapske and Mark Wilson (personal correspondence, Oct. 13, 2014) think the scene more likely on deck than below it.

733. Personal correspondence, Oct. 7, 2014; Prof. Leidwanger also consulted with Prof. Elizabeth Greene.

734. Rapske, Oct. 13, 2014, citing Casson. Leidwanger, personal correspondence, Oct. 7, 2014, suggests that such accommodations were normally for voyagers who could pay more.

735. Mentioned in Justin Leidwanger, personal correspondence, Oct. 7, 2014.

736. Triremes remained the choice warships through the fourth century C.E. (Souza, "Triremes"), but this is not a warship. Though "merchant galleys" with rowers did exist in this period (Casson, *Mariners*, 192; plate 44), most merchant ships of the period did not employ them (Schneider, "Rigging"), and the dependence on winds and failure to mention rowers during the storm count against this likelihood here. George Bass (founder of the Institute of Nautical Archaeology) and Frederick van Doorninck Jr., both emeritus professors of the Nautical Archaeology Program at Texas A&M University, kindly confirmed for me the unlikelihood that Paul's vessel included rowers; Dr. van Doorninck added, "The use of a galley to transport grain would only occur for some special, unusual reason, where speed and certainty of delivery were important considerations. It is quite safe to assume that St. Paul was not on a galley" (Bass and van Doorninck, personal correspondence, Feb. 27, 2007).

737. The call of the κελευστής (boatswain) kept time for the rowers; Karanika, "Songs," suggests that Orpheus may have held this role in Apollonius Rhodius's *Argonautica*.

738. For the number, see Casson, *Mariners*, 85. Supergalleys with up to 4,000 rowers (Casson, *Mariners*, 130; it "never saw action") would have been more problematic. The heyday of galleys was earlier (see the focus on classical Greek vessels in Tilley, "Trireme").

739. Although the disjunction could result from Luke's already knowing the revelation and hence not needing to be addressed. Some suggest that even if Paul offered such a speech, only a few of the passengers would have heard him (Chance, *Acts*, 500).

around and exhorting people in smaller clusters (27:33), although his movement would be limited if he remained chained.[740]

Nevertheless, whether Paul was above or below deck, we may imagine analogous acoustic problems with a general addressing tens of thousands of troops before battle; yet such scenes are so pervasive in ancient literature[741] that we dare not doubt that generals offered such addresses[742] (though certainly not everyone heard them).[743] (In more recent times, John Wesley spoke to thousands; similarly, Ben Franklin performed an experiment showing that more than thirty thousand could hear Whitefield preaching at one time.)[744]

If Demosthenes practiced projecting his voice against the waves (Val. Max. 8.7.ext. 1) and a regular speaker knew how to project his voice (see comment on Acts 21:40), it is possible that Paul could make himself heard among some or many of those on deck or gathered in the largest area below deck. Luke in any case thought the scene plausible, and he or (on other views) his source was on the ship.

In any case, both the circumstances and literary effectiveness suggest this location for such a speech. In other literature, such speeches typically occur "at a high point in the storm and at a low point in the fortunes of the sea travelers."[745]

III. PAUL'S SPEECH

How likely is it that Paul would be able to command his fellow passengers' attention? Concern for plausibility on this point is less pressing than concerns about volume or accommodating most people in one location on board. Danger weakens convention[746] and allows natural leaders to rise to rapid prominence; stories are told of such events in more recent times.[747] Then as now, leaders whose plans brought disaster faced criticism;[748] presumably most of the passengers would by this point be angry with those who made the decision to set out to sea, and Paul's contrary wisdom, once known, would earn respect.

Paul had considerable practice leading and speaking to voluntary followers (as

740. If he was chained to Julius, the latter would have to be very receptive to Paul to have accommodated this; but cf. 27:31–32.

741. With Anson, "Exhortation," rightly. This is not to deny historians' frequent creativity in composing the speeches, expanding according to appropriate expectations; see, e.g., Iglesias-Zoido, "Speeches."

742. E.g., Thucyd. 2.86.6–2.88.1; 4.9.4–4.11.1; Polyb. 15.10; Dion. Hal. *Ant. rom.* 6.6.1–6.9.6 (esp. 6.8.1); Quint. Curt. 4.14.1–6, 9–26; 5.8.6–17; 6.3.1–18; Appian *Hist. rom.* 8.7.42; 8.17.116; *Bell. civ.* 4.16.126; Arrian *Alex.* 3.9.5–7; Tac. *Hist.* 2.32; *Ann.* 3.46; 14.36; *Agric.* 30–32, 33–34; Deut 20:2–8, esp. 20:3–4; 1QM X, 2–5; Jos. *Ant.* 3.44–45; in other genres, cf. Hom. *Il.* 13.95–124; *Battle of Frogs and Mice* 110–21, 132–59; Xen. *Cyr.* 2.1.14–18; Dion. Hal. *Demosth.* 32; Sil. It. 9.184–216; 17.292–337. Granted, even many of these speeches in histories are elaborated, but they reveal the standard expectation of prebattle speeches.

743. When there was much noise, armies could not hear (e.g., Quint. Curt. 4.9.20; 4.13.38; Tac. *Ann.* 6.35), except for leaders and those nearby (Quint. Curt. 4.14.7); thus those farther away might be thought to misunderstand gestures (Suet. *Jul.* 33). Some suggest that behind the historiographic convention generals simply rode in front of the army, delivering more concise exhortations (Marincola, "Speeches," 128); if that is the case, however, we could postulate something similar for this scene.

744. Noll, *History*, 93; see further discussion at Acts 2:14–15. Modern sound systems, of course, are not comparable, allowing one to address even a million people; see Stanley, *Diffusion*, 71, following Martin, *Prophet*, 418.

745. Praeder, "Acts 27:1–28:16," 696.

746. Even status could adjust normal expectations regarding prisoners; even some people sent to execute speakers were restrained at least temporarily by their status and eloquence (Appian *Bell. civ.* 1.8.72; Val. Max. 8.9.2; cf. similarly 2.10.6).

747. See, e.g., the account of the Liberian boy Samuel Morris in the late nineteenth century, whose faith is said to have affected the crew on a long voyage (for popular versions, see, e.g., Baldwin, *Samuel Morris*, 40, 78; Whalin, *Samuel Morris*, 77–95, 169–70).

748. Leaders' response was often that they could not foreknow the future; see Quint. *Decl.* 301.16; Hermog. *Issues* 68.10–69.21 (esp. 69.15–17); Libanius *Declamation* 36.42–43; 44.50–52, 61.

opposed to, e.g., the centurion's experience with direct subordinates), perhaps more than anyone else aboard. Especially if Paul's Roman citizenship, his special treatment by Julius, and, most important for religiously sensitive ancients, his previous warning against setting out were widely known, he could command a hearing. Undoubtedly people had been crying out to their gods[749] (at least until they gave up hope in Acts 27:20), since human effort could no longer help them.

It is doubtful that the setting calls for a rhetorically polished speech, but to the extent that anyone would have sought to classify the speech, it would be more deliberative than anything else.[750] But Paul's speech is unlike the many more literary speeches cited as parallels among storm speeches (most of which concern preparation for death).[751] Words of assurance are common in miracle stories, including accounts about Jesus[752] as well as those about divine men or others.[753]

iv. Paul's Courage

Although Paul was presumably afraid at times,[754] his own lists of sufferings also reveal a character determined to accomplish his mission regardless of the cost, and this is the side of his character on which Luke here focuses. Luke emphasizes Paul's fearlessness in a manner comporting with expectations for a sage. The Stoic wise man could exercise caution but not its negative counterpart, fear, which was considered irrational.[755] A philosopher should remain unafraid when facing dangers.[756] Even the fear of death was deemed irrational[757]—a belief shared by Stoics[758] and Epicureans[759]

749. As was usual in storms at sea (Jonah 1:5–6; Ach. Tat. 3.5; Apoll. K. Tyre 39). Juvenal (Sat. 12) praises the gods for rescuing his friend from death during a shipwreck (joking that he is serious, since his friend already has heirs); a Jewish inscription likewise praises God for saving its writer at sea (Horsley, Documents, 4:113, §26). Deities could supposedly prevent mobility (Athen. Deipn. 15.672C) or grant instantaneous mobility (John 6:21); Pythagoras could provide speed in sailing (Iambl. V.P. 3.16; 28.135).
750. Witherington, Acts, 767.
751. Ibid.
752. E.g., Mark 2:5; 5:36; 6:50; 7:29; 9:23; 10:49; Luke 7:13; John 11:23.
753. Theissen, Miracle Stories, 59, cites Philost. Vit. Apoll. 3.38; 4.10, 45; 7.38; Lucian Lover of Lies 11; Hymn of Isyllus in IG 4.128.
754. 1 Cor 2:3 (interpreted literally by Chrys. Hom. 1 Cor. 6.2, who emphasizes Paul's humanity); 2 Cor 7:5; cf. 2 Cor 11:3; 12:20.
755. Engberg-Pedersen, Paul and Stoics, 73, 311n32; also noted in Aug. City 14.8, first paragraph (about Stoics); cf. Winter, Left Corinth, 54; Attridge, "Stoic Tradition," 89, on the Fourth Gospel's portrayal of Jesus. Learning to be free from fear was treated as a basic matter of philosophy (e.g., Epict. Diatr. 2.1.21). In a distant culture, cf. the ideal of the calm, unafraid, and nonanxious wise person in Confuc. Anal. 11 (9.28); 59 (7.36); 61 (12.4); 71 (14.30) (though righteousness is more important than courage, 75 [17.23]); or the virtuous person, who fears only that which truly matters, in 70 (16.8).
756. Mus. Ruf. 8, p. 66.10; cf. Iambl. V.P. 32.224–25; Stowers, "Resemble Philosophy?," 93. On philosophers against fear, see further Val. Max. 3.3.ext. 1; Sen. Y. Ben. 4.27.1; Ep. Lucil. 13; 98.6; Dio Chrys. Or. 1.13; 3.34; Crates Ep. 7; Arius Did. Epit. 2.7.5a, p. 10.11; 2.7.5b, pp. 12–13.6; 2.7.5b1, pp. 12–13.27–29; 2.7.5c, pp. 28–29.14–15; Philost. Vit. Apoll. 1.23. Stoics valued tranquility and peace of mind (Sen. Y. Dial. 4.12.6; 4.13.2; 5.6.1; 9 passim; Ep. Lucil. 75.18; Mus. Ruf. frg. 38, p. 136.1–3; Epict. Diatr. 1.4.1; Arius Did. Epit. 2.7.5b1, p. 12.31–33; 2.7.5k, p. 34.1–4; 2.7.11s, p. 100.7), as did Epicureans (Lucret. Nat. 5.1198–1206; Cic. Fin. 1.14.47; Lucian Alex. 47; Diog. Laert. 10.131; 10.144.17) and others (Iambl. V.P. 2.10; cf. Cic. Amic. 22.84; Hossenfelder, "Ataraxia").
757. E.g., Cic. Leg. 1.23.60; Diogenes Ep. 28; Max. Tyre 11.11; 36.2; Iambl. V.P. 32.228. Cf. Val. Max. 9.13. praef.; 9.13.3; Plut. Poetry 14, Mor. 37A; Sir 40:2, 5; Heb 2:14–15; Mart. Pol. passim.
758. Sen. Y. Ep. Lucil. 80.6; 82 passim; 98.10; Nat. Q. 1.pref. 4; 2.58.3; 6.32.12; Dial. 9.11.4–5; Mus. Ruf. 1, p. 34.31–33; 3, pp. 40.35–42.1; p. 42.3; 4, p. 48.5–6; 17, p. 110.1, 12–13; Epict. Diatr. 1.17.25; 2.1.13; 2.18.30; Marc. Aur. 9.3; 12.35; cf. Marc. Aur. 8.58. But even philosophers could admit to struggling with this fear (Mus. Ruf. 6, pp. 54.35–56.7, esp. 56.2). Cf. Trelenberg, "Märtyrer," for possible Stoic influence on ancient Christian martyr narrations.
759. Perhaps especially Epicureans; see, e.g., Lucret. Nat. passim (esp. 1.102–26; 3.1–30, 87–93; cf. O'Keefe, "Lucretius"; Warren, "Lucretius"); Cic. Fin. 1.18.60; 4.5.11; Nat. d. 1.20.56; Diog. Laert. 10.125.

alike. How bravely a philosopher dies, ancient observers often maintained, is a real test of his beliefs and character.[760] Cicero praises one who faced hardship "with the serenity of a philosopher" (*Fam.* 6.14.3).[761]

This general expectation applied to sea voyages as well; the courageous man who does not fear death would remain serene on a wind-whipped sea in a furious storm.[762] How a philosopher acted in a storm at sea was considered a real test of his genuineness (Aul. Gel. 1.2.11).[763] Epictetus thus takes to task those who claim philosophy when lecturing but fear death during shipwreck or other dangers.[764] If a ship goes down, a philosophically minded person's responsibility is to "drown without fear, neither shrieking nor crying out against God, but recognizing that what is born must also perish."[765] Lucian cites Peregrinus's fear during a storm to prove his inauthenticity as a philosopher (*Peregr.* 42–44).[766] By contrast, Pyrrho the Skeptic (ca. 360–270 B.C.E.) allegedly remained unperturbed during a storm at sea that unnerved the others aboard (Diog. Laert. 9.11.68). (Even if such depictions were conventional in antiquity, some such accounts were firsthand,[767] and those whose convictions protected them from being visibly shaken during a storm have also impressed subsequent generations.)[768]

Thus a truly great philosopher would not be shaken or terrified by things that terrified others.[769] Philosophic literature abounds with examples of philosophers' virtuous perseverance.[770] Pythagoras kept philosophizing calmly regardless of circumstances, unafraid even of death (Iambl. *V.P.* 32.220). The most commonly offered example was Socrates, refusing to compromise at his trial or flee before his execution. If a steersman faced death bravely at sea, refusing to jump ship, how could Socrates fear death (Max. Tyre 3.7)? Socrates's endurance of various hardships, some argued, demonstrated that he was a sincere teacher (Xen. *Mem.* 1.2.1).

The Stoic and Epicurean ideal of tranquility under duress (even torture) was hardly universal; Aristotle, for example, counted it absurd.[771] Honest Stoics might also admit that even philosophers struggle with the fear of death, though they must overcome it.[772] In practice, many philosophers fell short. Some who acknowledged that many or most fell short praised "genuine" philosophers all the more who displayed endurance (e.g., Pliny *Ep.* 3.11.5–6). As the story went, when Aristippus (ca. 435–350 B.C.E.) became anxious during a storm, others aboard, not afraid, mocked

760. E.g., Cic. *Fin.* 2.30.96–98; cf. tested bravery in Sen. Y. *Ep. Lucil.* 66.50.
761. Other philosophers, too, are praised for maintaining tranquility, avoiding emotional disturbances (e.g., Iambl. *V.P.* 2.10), and living by what they taught (Diod. Sic. 9.9.1).
762. Sen. Y. *Nat. Q.* 6.32.4 (on Seneca's expectation of courage when facing death, see Nietmann, "Seneca"); cf. Lucian *Dem.* 35.
763. Mus. Ruf. 8, p. 66.10; Diog. Laert. 1.86; 2.71; 9.11.68; Aul. Gel. 1.2.11; 19.1.4–6, 11–21; cf. Brawley, *Luke-Acts and Jews*, 56.
764. Epict. *Diatr.* 2.19 (e.g., 2.19.19). Philost. *Vit. Apoll.* 1.23 denies that one who fears is yet a philosopher. Lucian writes that Socrates and most other philosophers feared when facing the underworld (*Dial. D.* 421 [4/21, Menippus and Cerberus 1–2]) but Cynics did not (422 [4/21, Menippus and Cerberus 1–2]); others, however, emphasized Socrates's fearlessness concerning death (Max. Tyre 3.7).
765. Epict. *Diatr.* 2.5.12 (trans. Oldfather, LCL, 1:241).
766. Brawley, *Luke-Acts and Jews*, 56. "This wondrous person who was thought to be superior to death," Lucian complains, "fell to wailing along with the women!" (*Peregr.* 43 [trans. Harmon, LCL, 5:49]).
767. E.g., Lucian *Peregr.* 42–44. One notes the same interest in Aul. Gel. 19.1.4–6, although the philosopher here fails the test.
768. Chance, *Acts*, 508, cites how the Moravians' faith during a storm at sea impressed John Wesley.
769. Eunapius *Lives* 504; cf. Galen *Grief* 48.
770. Stowers, "Resemble Philosophy?," 93.
771. Ibid. (citing Arist. *N.E.* 7.1153b19).
772. Mus. Ruf. 6, pp. 54.35–56.7, esp. 56.2. Cf. Galen's limits in *Grief* 72a, 73–74, 78b.

his comparative cowardice. "The lives at stake in the two cases are not comparable," he replied.[773] When, during a storm at sea in the second century c.e., Aulus Gellius found a Stoic philosopher as pale as everyone else (though not screaming), he discovered that the philosopher was afraid (Aul. Gel. 19.1.4–6). The philosopher explained that many Stoics allow initial fear as long as one overcomes it (19.1.11–21).[774] Most relevant for Luke's Paul here, however, might be Jesus's ability to sleep during a storm (Luke 8:23–24), though Luke might not make a direct parallel (Paul is not asleep here, despite reference to a nocturnal revelation in Acts 27:23, and Luke's depiction of Jesus appears less emphatic about him sleeping during the storm than is the language of Mark 4:37–38).

b. Paul's Message of Hope (27:21–26)

Paul does not still a storm like Jesus (Luke 8:24), but he does trust that it will not prevent the fulfillment of his calling (Acts 27:24), exceeding the confidence of the disciples in Luke 8:24 (they are reproved in 8:25).[775]

i. Paul's Assurance (27:21–22)

In the face of the others' hopelessness, Paul reminds them that he spoke the unhappy truth before (Acts 27:21) and therefore ought now to be believed as he speaks a happier message of assurance (27:22). Their failure to eat (27:21a) stems not from having thrown all food overboard (cf. 27:33–36)[776] but, rather, from seasickness,[777] mortal anxiety (see esp. 27:36),[778] or both.[779] Not eating here sets the stage for how Paul later encourages them to eat and causes them to take heart (27:33–38).[780]

For the address "men," see comment on Acts 2:14; Luke employs the interjection "O" (ὦ), introducing addressees, far more rarely than the address "men" and nowhere else conjoins it with "men."[781] Although Luke uses it to address Theophilus, whom he honors (1:1), all his other references appear in rebukes (13:10; cf. 18:14), including—perhaps relevant here—rebukes to those slow to believe God's truth (Luke 9:41

773. Diog. Laert. 2.71 (LCL, 1:201).
774. Seneca viewed such initial fear as merely a bodily reaction, not counting it as true emotion until one has rationally considered and chosen it (Sen. Y. Ira 2.2.1–2.4.2 [on such initial fear, see esp. 2.3.3; cf. 2.2.1], in Sorabji, Emotion, 73–74). For an analogy from a different culture, cf. Confucius's sudden "change of countenance" during thunder or strong winds, in Confuc. Anal. 334 (10.16), despite his teachings on calmness noted above.
775. On the challenge of faith versus fear in the passage about Jesus's stilling the storm (Mark 4:35–41), cf., e.g., Wallace, Miracles, 59–62.
776. In contrast to etymological expectation, ἀσιτία and ἄσιτος (Acts 27:33) refer to only lack of appetite and eating (see BDAG).
777. With Conzelmann, Acts, 218; Fernando, Acts, 612; cf. Bruce, Commentary, 461. This is common "on a rough voyage, even when there is no thought of shipwreck" (Lake and Cadbury, Commentary, 334); it is doubtful, however, that experienced sailors would have been as susceptible under normal circumstances. For the physical and emotional trauma, see, e.g., Ps 107:26–27.
778. Tannehill, Acts, 334 (noting their loss of hope in Acts 27:20); cf. Brenz 233 in Chung-Kim and Hains, Acts, 354. Grief or anger might keep people from eating (Philost. Hrk. 31.7; see fuller comment on Acts 9:9).
779. Rapske, Custody, 359. More speculatively, some (Hemer, Acts in History, 145; Bruce, Commentary, 461) suggest that seawater spoiled the food or that cooking was impossible (during normal voyages passengers remained on deck, and cooking facilities were extremely limited); Rapske, Custody, 359, is probably right to doubt this suggestion in view of Acts 27:33–36. (Seawater would not only spoil the grain but expand it; see idem, "Travel," 35.) Some passengers may have also run low on food, or preserved what little they had, because of the unexpected length of time without the ship's being able to make port.
780. With Tannehill, Acts, 334.
781. E.g., Epict. Diatr. 2.1.23; in Latin, Fronto Ad M. Caes. 2.3.1. It appears often in the LXX, but especially in the later parts, and pervasively in 4 Maccabees (4 Macc 5:6; 6:22; 7:6–7, 10, 15; 8:5, 17; 9:1, 17; 10:10; 11:4, 12, 20–21; 14:2–3, 7; 15:1, 4, 13, 16–17, 29–30; 16:6–10, 14, 16; 17:2, 4; 18:1, 20). For Luke's uses, see comment on Acts 1:1.

[cf. Mark 9:19]; 24:25). Pauline literature also employs the interjection in various ways[782] but usually in rebukes (Rom 2:1, 3; 9:20; Gal 3:1).[783]

To the extent that the speech follows any rhetorical conventions, Paul does offer in Acts 27:21 a brief survey of events leading up to the current situation, functioning as a *narratio*.[784] Retroactive criticism of sailors' folly in setting out under dangerous conditions was not unique to Paul (e.g., Polyb. 1.37.10), but he had warned them in advance.[785] "Gaining" injury and "loss" may be an ironic touch,[786] attracting attention like an oxymoron.[787] The loss of the ship, perhaps previously viewed as disastrous, now appears as a small price in an assurance of their survival (Acts 27:22).

ii. Angelic Appearance (27:23)

Perhaps in view of the amount of his scroll remaining, Luke now introduces an incident through Paul's speech without having recounted it first. Such retrospectives were common enough in literature; one could hark back to unrecorded events of the preceding day that were now necessary to be reported.[788] Given claims of divine deliverances by other deities in antiquity (see comment on Acts 28:11), Paul is careful to indicate that he serves "God"—that is, the highest God (for the majority who would by now know him, this would mean the true God, the only one worshiped by the Jewish people).[789] As in other passages, when Paul speaks to those who do not know Israel's God, he begins with monotheism (14:15–17; 17:23; 1 Thess 1:9; cf. Rom 1:19). It is also clear, however, that when people are in need, Paul is ready to help in God's name without requiring prior faith in his God (cf. also 28:3, 8–9).

Whether Paul was asleep or not during the revelation is not clear,[790] especially if it is the same night when he is addressing others on board, as might be suggested by "this night."[791] The agents of revelation in dreams or night visions vary in Acts: a man in 16:9, the Lord in 18:9 and 22:18, and an angel here. Angelic revelations are promi-

---

782. As a pure interjection in Rom 11:33 (cf. also *1 Clem.* 53.5; *Diogn.* 9.5); positively in 1 Tim 6:11, 20 (cf. also 1 Esd 3:24; 4:2, 12, 32; 4 Macc 6:22; 7:6–7, 10, 15; 14:2–3, 7; 15:13, 29–30; 16:14; 17:2, 4; 18:1).

783. Cf. also, e.g., 2 Macc 7:34; 4 Macc 9:1, 17; 10:10; 11:4, 12, 21; Jas 2:20; *1 Clem.* 23.4.

784. Witherington, *Acts*, 767.

785. Luke also implies that Paul is their spiritual benefactor, a claim that would invite reciprocity (cf., e.g., Publ. Syr. 71).

786. Witherington, *Acts*, 767.

787. On oxymoron, see Rowe, "Style," 143; Aune, *Dictionary of Rhetoric*, 327; Porter, "Paul and Letters," 582. The specific term, however, is not yet extant prior to the fourth century C.E. (Anderson, *Rhetorical Theory*, 227).

788. E.g., Ach. Tat. 2.7. Heliod. *Eth.* 1, indeed, picks up partway through a story.

789. Fitzmyer, *Acts*, 777; Johnson, *Acts*, 449 (comparing Ael. Arist. *Or.* 2.12; Plut. *Br. Wom.* 8–9, *Mor.* 247E–248A; Petron. *Sat.* 105); on divine epiphanies rescuing at sea, see Theissen, *Miracle Stories*, 101. Luke's placement of "angel" after the clause designating the genitive for "of God" underlines that Paul is God's (not the angel's) servant.

790. For ancients, epiphanies remained valid in either case (Proclus *Poet.* 6.1, K110.24).

791. Cf. Luke 12:20; Mark 14:30; Gen 19:33–34; 30:15; Ruth 3:2; Jdt 8:33; 11:3, 5; 13:14; Tob 6:16; the expression appears emphatic (shared with me by Stanley Porter, personal correspondence, Dec. 9, 2012) and characterizes the Septuagint much more than, say, the more polished Greek of Josephus, Philo, or the Apostolic Fathers. When not referring to the current night, these references often refer to the impending night (cf. also BDAG: "this very night," citing *Test. Ab.* 7A; *Jos. Asen.* 24:13; *Apoc. Mos.* 2), but Paul narrates a matter past rather than impending. Many commentators, however, envision Paul speaking the next day; he could be referring simply to "last night" (Bruce, *Acts¹*, 461; cf. also Marshall, *Acts*, 410; Fitzmyer, *Acts*, 777; Peterson, *Acts*, 689; NRSV). This proposal makes sense especially if Paul reckons a day as beginning from sundown—less so if he expects his audience to think from sunrise. More consideration might be allowed the possibility that Paul speaks the same night, the "marker of close proximity" simply suggesting that the vision (perhaps while awake) had just happened (as noted by Cynthia Long Westfall, personal correspondence, Dec. 9–10, 2012). What the normal sleep routine was in such conditions (27:20) and whether Paul would address many others while it remained night are legitimate questions for which Luke's sparse description offers few answers. The next scene occurs at night (27:27), but not the same one.

nent in Luke's infancy narratives, which are unique among the extant sources (Luke 1:11–20, 26–38; 2:9–15),[792] and appear in the resurrection narratives (24:4–7, 23; cf. Matt 28:2, 5; John 20:12). They also bring divine messages in Acts 1:10–11 (to the disciples), 8:26 (to Philip), and 10:3 (to Cornelius); elsewhere they bring deliverance (e.g., 5:19; 12:7–9). An angel brings encouragement in testing (as here) to Jesus in Gethsemane (Luke 22:43). The language is familiar: an angel stands (παρέστη), as in Luke 1:11 (ἑστώς), and encourages the recipient not to be afraid, as in 1:13, 30 (μὴ φοβοῦ in all three cases, as also in the risen Lord's words in Acts 18:9).[793]

Communications from angels appear common in early Christianity, although they are reported according to their genre; in Revelation (e.g., Rev 1:1; 17:1; 21:9) they function as we would expect in a typical apocalypse, whereas in Acts they are closer to their role in most OT narratives (Gen 31:11; 1 Kgs 19:5; Zech 4:1) and other early Christian narratives (Matt 1:20; 2:13, 19). Revelations from angels are also common in other early Jewish sources,[794] and they sometimes appear in night visions.[795] Often God sends them in response to prayers.[796] Gentiles also affirmed the reality of divine messengers,[797] some of whom communicated with mortals in dreams.[798] Even later Platonists, for whom the divine was invisible to mortal sight, allowed δαίμονες as intermediary messengers.[799]

If there is any Jonah allusion in this chapter, as many scholars think, its focus here would be a contrast. Whereas in Jonah, a prophet sailing to the west, was running from his God and endangering all the Gentiles with him (Jonah 1:6–10), here one who serves God and goes west in obedience to God saves the lives of those with him. (For "serve" or "worship" [λατρεύω], see comment on Acts 26:7.)

III. God's Promise (27:24)

Not only will God fulfill Paul's mission; his fellow voyagers' lives will be protected on his account (which is of greater interest to Paul's audience in the narrative world).[800] (The fulfillment of this promise would certainly commend appreciation for Paul's

792. Matthew has angelic instructions in dreams but does not recount the same incidents as reported in Luke.

793. For Jesus in the Gospels, see Mark 5:36; Luke 5:10; 8:50; 12:32; the risen Jesus in Rev 1:17; an oracle of Scripture in John 12:15. The exact expression appears thirty-five times in the LXX, often God (Gen 15:1; 26:24; 28:13; 46:3) or his angel (Gen 21:17; Dan 10:12, 19; cf. Judg 6:23) speaking; also in oracles (Isa 7:4; 10:24; 41:10, 13; 43:1, 5; 44:2; 54:4; Jer 26:28 [46:28 ET]).

794. E.g., *1 En.* 1:2; 10:1; 19:1; 22:3; 23:4; 27:1; 33:3; 40:2, 8–9; 43:3–4; 46:2–3; 52:5; 74:2; 75:3–4; 78:10; 79:6; 82:7; 108:5–6; *Jub.* 2:1; 17:11; 32:21; *4 Ezra* 5:20, 31; 7:1; 10:29; *2 Bar.* 55:3; *3 Bar.* 1:8; 2:5; 4:5, 7; *4 Bar.* 6:15 (a message of encouragement, as here); *Test. Reub.* 3:15; 5:3; *Test. Levi* 2:9; 5:1, 3; 9:6; *Test. Jud.* 15:5; *b. Ber.* 51a; *Ned.* 20a; perhaps 4Q529; see also comment on Acts 8:26. On angels in apocalyptic literature, see also Morris, *Apocalyptic*, 35; in later sources, see Blau and Kohler, "Angelology," 587. The first part of Daniel includes angels as deliverers (3:28; 6:22; as in Acts 5:19; 12:7–11), though only in characters' comments rather than direct narration, but the later part also includes them as revealers (Dan 8:15–19; 9:21–23), as in apocalyptic and elsewhere (e.g., Gen 16:7–12; Judg 13:3–5; esp. Zech 1:9–19; 2:3; 4:5; 5:5; 6:5). Some later sources taught that an angel could perform only one errand per mission (*Gen. Rab.* 50:2, bar.; cf. *b. B. Meṣiʿa* 86b). Angels as messengers differs from the Promethean tradition of angels revealing divine secrets without authorization (cf. Gal 1:8; *b. Šabb.* 88a; *Gen. Rab.* 50:9; 68:12; 78:2; cf. even Elijah once, in *b. B. Meṣiʿa* 85b).

795. 4Q537 frg. 1, introductory line.

796. See Johnson, *Prayer*, 63–65.

797. See, e.g., Iris (Hom. *Il.* 2.786–87; 4.121–24; Virg. *Aen.* 5.618–20); Hermes (Cornutus *Summ.* 16 [Lang, 20, lines 18–19], in van der Horst, "Cornutus," 169).

798. Cf. "someone who looked like an angel," sent by Diana, in Apoll. K. Tyre 48 (*CAGN* 769; but the final version is from the fifth or sixth century C.E.). On apparitions in dreams, see comment on Acts 16:9–10.

799. E.g., Max. Tyre 8.8; 9.2; cf. Iambl. *Myst.* 2.10. Later Platonists allowed angels to appear as generic "humans" (Proclus *Poet.* 6.1, K114.9–10). Philosophers did not depend on such revelations, however; Socrates based his divine leading on internal intuition, not any direct external revelation (Rapske, *Custody*, 395).

800. Contrast Jonah 1:12. For God saving some on behalf of others' merits, Jerome *Against Jovinianus* 2.24 (Martin, *Acts*, 304) cites Acts 27 (and God sparing Sodom for ten righteous or Zoar for Lot's sake).

God to his hearers, although they might simply regard this deity as a particularly powerful one among many.) The irony of a prisoner aboard saving all by his divinely mandated upcoming trial is hard to miss, perhaps suggesting a theological narrative parallel with Jesus's execution as a means of salvation.

The angel addresses Paul by name, as was common in OT assurance oracles[801] (cf. also the angelic revelation in Acts 10:3; Luke 1:13, 28). "Fear not" also appears in Luke's first angelic revelations (Luke 1:13, 30); this is his final one. For Luke, the divine message in Acts 27:24 provides a reliable theological perspective on the events in the narrative.[802] The message fits a triple affirmation of divine necessity in Paul's trip to Rome, divinely revealed in three different ways in or close to times of crisis. By the Spirit, Paul decided that he "must" (δεῖ) see Rome (19:21); the Lord promised that Paul "must" (δεῖ) testify in Rome (23:11; and hence would survive his current hardship); now, at another time of hardship, an angel reaffirms that Paul "must" (δεῖ) stand before Caesar (27:24).[803] In the larger plan of Luke-Acts, such a hearing provides a further opportunity to fulfill the promise of testimony before royal courts in Luke 21:12–13.[804]

"Before Caesar" presumably means before his tribunal.[805] By Nero's day most of the cases were in fact delegated to others.[806] Nero himself apparently avoided personal jurisdiction of cases before 62 C.E., and it is not clear that even then he chose regular involvement in them.[807] Paul nevertheless will bring the Christian message before the Roman government, seeking, presumably, its cognizance and approval (cf. Phil 1:7, 12–13; 4:22).[808] Whether or not he would succeed in gaining its approval, his long detention raised the visibility of the movement in the heart of the empire, and Paul may have reasoned, like some modern marketers, that even negative publicity was publicity that could promote the movement in the long run (Phil 1:12–14). Publicity is also Luke's own strategy through the writing of Acts; he probably thinks that he is carrying further Paul's wisdom. Paul may not have guessed that this approach would take a few centuries to prevail, but even during Nero's subsequent persecution in Rome, high-intensity publicity probably helped propagate the movement, albeit at the cost of many of its adherents' lives.

The angel in Acts 27:24 corrects Paul's words in 27:10, where Paul expected many lives to be lost. Although Paul might have been simply mistaken on this detail in 27:10, there is no need to view his words in 27:10 negatively even had he prophesied. Scripture already used the language of God changing his mind in view of repentance (see comment on Acts 27:10; cf. 1 Kgs 21:27–29; Jer 18:7–11; Jonah 3:9–10) or prayer (Exod 32:10–14; Jer 26:19; Amos 7:3, 6; cf. Gen 18:26–32; 2 Sam 24:16). That God has "granted" Paul the lives of those aboard means, at the very least, that God has altered the natural expectation of the situation.

801. Aune, Prophecy, 268 (contrasting the relative scarcity in analogous Greco-Roman oracles).
802. Rapske, "Travel," 46, even treats it as "the hermeneutical tool" for interpreting the rest of the narrative.
803. See Tannehill, Acts, 292. Schröter, "Modell," 75, approaches Acts' widely agreed open ending with consideration of 19:21 and 23:11.
804. In context, this seems to occur before Jerusalem's conquest (Luke 21:20–24) and/or before Jesus's return (21:25–28).
805. Only the elite might view Caesar as accessible personally as, for example, media-saturated U.S. residents sometimes view their president or celebrities today.
806. O'Rourke, "Law," 177; see comment on Acts 25:10.
807. See Sherwin-White, Society, 110.
808. Luke may expect us to infer that Paul's later arguments before Caesar's tribunal reflect the sorts of arguments found in his defense speeches in Acts 24–26 (cf. Cazeaux, Actes, 338). The tradition of Paul's testimony before rulers outlived him (see 1 Clem. 5.7).

That God has "granted" (perfect tense, already settled) Paul's fellow voyagers could be an answer to Paul's prayers (cf. Luke 1:13).[809] (Compare 2 Macc 3:31–33, where God "granted" [κεχάρισται, 3:33, as here] Heliodorus's life in answer to Onias's prayers.)[810] The verb, common for benefactions in honorary inscriptions, need not imply an answer to a request, but it sometimes does bear this connotation.[811] If we should infer that Paul's prayers were involved (Luke is not quite explicit here), Gentiles also believed that prayers for safety at sea could be answered (e.g., Ach. Tat. 3.5; cf. Jonah 1:14–16). Ships endangered at sea were often believed to be rescued by divine intervention.[812]

Gentiles also believed that a pious or blessed person's presence could protect a ship, and so they will know how to apply Paul's words. For example, Caesar was said to have instructed his fellow travelers not to fear, for they carried not only him but his luck.[813] Apollonius reportedly preserved the ship he was traveling on (Philost. *Vit. Apoll.* 4.13);[814] as mentioned earlier, Pythagoras's presence on a boat reportedly provided good sailing conditions (Iambl. *V.P.* 3.16). Also as mentioned above, in some Jewish accounts, God saved a Gentile ship because of a Jewish boy aboard.[815] This narrative offers a stark contrast to the *Odyssey*, where Odysseus tragically lost all his companions, mostly at sea,[816] but given the great variety of sea stories (with varying rates of survivors),[817] there is no reason to infer that the contrast is deliberate.

iv. Paul's Faith (27:25)

Paul expresses the sort of faith praised in Luke 1:45, trusting that matters will turn out as God has spoken (cf. Luke 2:20; 22:13; contrast 1:18).[818] For Paul's faith in the midst of danger, see comment on ancients' philosophic "heroes" in the introduction, above, to Acts 27:21–26. Paul encourages his fellow travelers as the angel has encouraged him ("Do not fear," Acts 27:24), twice repeating his exhortation to courage (εὐθυμέω appears in both 27:22 and 27:25 and only once elsewhere in the NT, the LXX, and the Apostolic Fathers, i.e., in Jas 5:13).

v. Aground on an Island (27:26)

Paul's final words might seem like bad news but, in the context of the promise of survival, are simply anticlimactic. Almost everyone believed that deities who worked

809. Cf. Dan 10:12, different term; the aorist for "received" in Mark 10:24.
810. This is the only LXX use of the verb in precisely this form, but the verb does not by itself necessarily imply prayer (e.g., 3 Macc 5:11; 4 Macc 5:8). Nor is it a necessary inference from Luke's theology (Acts 11:18, different term; nor even Paul's, e.g., Phil 1:29).
811. BDAG cites, e.g., Diod. Sic. 13.59.3.
812. Johnson, *Acts*, 449 (citing Ps 106:28–29 LXX; *Test. Naph.* 6:8–9; Plut. *Dinner* 18, *Mor.* 161F; Lucian *Ship* 9; *Posts* 1; Ach. Tat. 3.5; cf. further discussion of Ps 107 [106 LXX] in Börstinghaus, *Sturmfahrt*, 209–24). Neptune also calmed the sea for the *Argo* in Val. Flacc. 1.651–52; Apollo helped sailors in a storm (Apollod. *Bib.* 1.9.26); see further comment at Acts 28:11.
813. Theissen, *Miracle Stories*, 102, citing Plut. *Caes.* 38; Dio Cass. 41.46.
814. See comment in Theissen, *Miracle Stories*, 102.
815. *Pesiq. Rab Kah.* 18:5; *Pesiq. Rab.* 32:3/4. Theissen, *Miracle Stories*, 102, cites *y. Ber.* 9:1. These examples are not the same as a miracle worker, but such workers do appear in Jewish sources as well (emphasized especially by Vermes, *Jesus and Judaism*; cf. summary in Keener, *John*, 270–72). On God's sparing others for one's sake, see Gen 18:26 (Bruce, *Acts¹*, 462); 2 Macc 3:33. If 4Q541 7 3 refers to the eschatological priest (as Cook, "Words of Levi," 259–60, argues), it notes the sea being quieted because of him (but is this figurative for eschatological peace? and does it imply his direct authority?).
816. Cf. the later portrait of Odysseus "alone and naked and shipwrecked" (Mus. Ruf. 9, p. 72.1).
817. Sometimes few survived (Dio Chrys. *Or.* 7.55; cf. Jos. *Life* 15).
818. Johnson, *Acts*, 449 (who also cites, for the view that a shipwreck was guided by divine purpose, Ael. Arist. *Or.* 2.12–13; for one's fate at sea fulfilling prophecy, Hom. *Od.* 5.300–302).

deliverance (including the biblical YHWH; e.g., Exod 10:13; 14:21; Num 11:31) could do so through means within creation.

An island was sometimes a storm-tossed ship's final hope. In a great storm, Apollo was said to have sent lightning so that mariners could see an island and reach it quickly (Apollod. *Bib.* 1.9.26). The necessity (δεῖ; as often in Acts, presumably divine necessity) of grounding on an island would seem frightening, but coupled with the promise of their survival, it would become (provided an island confirmed Paul's prediction by appearing!) their only plan for survival (Acts 27:39).

Given the difficulty of even bringing the ship's boat under control (27:16), it is by no means certain that the crew had sufficient opportunity to attempt to ground their ship near Cauda, and had they been able to do so, it might not have appeared survivable. Nevertheless, it is possible that they could have done so but did not want to risk the ship, its cargo, and many of the lives on board. Desperate to avoid the Syrtis (27:17, the alternative place to run aground [ἐκπίπτω]),[819] they now have no alternative but to try to ground themselves near an island first, provided they find one.

Some commentators note that Paul's words are inexact, as in 27:10, since the ship is grounded on a reef rather than the island itself.[820] It is not likely that anyone would have complained, however. Indeed, some hearers may have even suspected such a scenario, since the reef was attached to the island below the water, and it would be hard to run "aground" and so lose the ship all the way out of the water anyway. Moreover, Luke's audience will be accustomed to inexact yet fully authoritative prophecies (e.g., Gen 37:9–10 [cf. 35:18–19]; Isa 37:29, 36–37; see comment on Acts 21:11).

6. Paul's Leadership Approaching Land (27:27–38)

Throughout the narrative Paul's influence has increased, until now the soldiers (Acts 27:31–32) and passengers (27:34–36) are heeding him.

a. Spying Land in the Sea of Adria (27:27)

That many of the sailors were awake at midnight implies the dramatic intensity of the situation (see comment on Acts 16:25); the time would have to be estimated from the last light seen through the clouds (see comment on Acts 27:39).

How did the sailors surmise the approach of land? Was there now sufficient moonlight (without the moon itself being visible) to make out land projecting above waves in the distance?[821] Some crew members were normally assigned to watch from the prow and stern (Philost. *Vit. Apoll.* 4.9).

More often scholars suggest that the crew noticed a change in sound, hearing the breakers battering land over the sound of the wind and earlier waves.[822] If they were

---

819. Elsewhere in Luke-Acts only at Acts 12:7; 27:29. Although the term had a range of meaning, this is the likeliest sense here given the present context and nautical usage (see BDAG, citing Eurip. *Hel.* 409; Thucyd. 2.92.3; Diod. Sic. 1.31.5; 2.60.1).

820. Witherington, *Acts*, 770. Cf. sometimes similar complaints about Jesus's hyperbole in Mark 13:2; Luke 21:6; cf. Danker, *New Age*, 198; Kaufman, "Eastern Wall," 115.

821. One could discern the time of night from the moon on nights too cloudy for observing the zodiac (Polyb. 7.16.3; 9.15.12; Virg. *Aen.* 7.9; Ovid *Fasti* 2.697; Sil. It. 15.616; cf. Plut. *Alc.* 20.5; contrast Plut. *Nat. Phen.* 24, *Mor.* 917F).

822. Bruce, *Commentary*, 515; Fitzmyer, *Acts*, 778. Conzelmann, *Acts*, 219, allows either this or the sea anchors dragging; 30 m. is too deep for this, but he doubts Luke's knowledge of the depth (see comment on Acts 27:28).

on a westward trajectory toward Malta's Saint Paul's Bay, they would have "passed within a quarter of a mile of the low rocky point of Koura, where the breakers are particularly violent in an easterly gale. They would have seen the breaking foam, but nothing of the shore or its configuration."[823] If the wind was not currently at gale strength, a ship approaching from the east could have heard the breakers at Koura Point from a mile and a half away.[824] Rocks near the surface would normally indicate land somewhere near, as opposed to the deepest seas.

If a strong northeast wind kept driving the ship leeward, minimizing its advance as it tacked starboard,[825] fourteen days would be just about right to bring the ship to about this location.[826] A nineteenth-century mariner estimated that to traverse the roughly 470 nautical miles[827] from Cauda to Koura (see comment on Acts 27:28), under conditions described in the narrative and at a drift of about one and a half miles per hour, would take 13 days, 1 hour, and 21 minutes. (We should allow some variation for the size of the vessel, our lack of precise knowledge of the wind speed, and so forth, but the margins for error on various points tend to cancel each other out.)

Given the ship's persistent attempts to tack north to avoid the Syrtis (and a possible shift of wind allowing the ship to make more progress northward), the ship could have approached Malta toward Saint (or Sant) Paul's Bay; a ship that passed Cauda in an evening would be within three miles of this bay by the midnight of the fourteenth day.[828] Luke's description here is not the work of an active imagination but recounts, directly or indirectly, the observation of someone who survived the storm that Luke depicts.

Some modern readers have complained that Luke's use of "the Adriatic Sea" (τῷ Ἀδρίᾳ) is imprecise, since our Adriatic does not extend south of Italy. This objection has led some to favor an Adriatic site, the island of Mljet, for Luke's "Malta" (Μελίτη) (see comment on Acts 28:1), though this is an impossible location for a ship driven by a northeast wind.

That premise about the Adriatic, however, rests on an anachronistic reading of current language into ancient texts. Just as some ancient literature extended the Ionian Sea across the entire east-west length of the Mediterranean, some ancient texts described the seas from as far north as Venice to as far south as North Africa as the Adriatic.[829] Ptolemy describes all of the region as far south as Sicily and Crete as the Adriatic Sea (distinct from the Adriatic Gulf to the north).[830] Other geographers include the Ionian Sea in the Adria (Strabo 2.5.20, though including the region from Crete to

---

823. Hemer, *Acts in History*, 146.

824. Lake and Cadbury, *Commentary*, 338.

825. Wallinga, "Poseidonios," argues that διαφερομένων here refers not to being "driven" but to zigzagging, including tacking.

826. Lake and Cadbury, *Commentary*, 335. The lack of sun (Acts 27:20) does not mean that days could not be calculated; day may have offered at least hazy light at times whereas night offered none. Chrys. *Hom. Acts* 53 opines that the storm's long duration proved providential, so that Paul could teach them longer; certainly Paul has gained the centurion's full respect (27:43; cf. 28:7).

827. By air (Conzelmann, *Acts*, 219). Bruce, *Commentary*, 514, following Smith, notes 476.6 mi. The figure may be higher if they traveled not straight but northward from a southward drift as the northern wind weakened, allowing them to reach Malta instead of the Syrtis.

828. Smith, *Voyage*, 126–28; followed by Bruce, *Commentary*, 514–15; Hemer, *Acts in History*, 145; Witherington, *Acts*, 771.

829. Lake and Cadbury, *Commentary*, 335 (following the more extensive study of Treidler, "Ionische Meer," esp. 86–91), noting that some ancients would have labeled this region Ionian, others Adriatic. For the entire sea east of Italy, see also Cary and Murray, "Adriatic Sea."

830. Ptolemy *Geog.* 3.4.1 (the sea east of Sicily); 3.15.1 (west of Crete). These texts are often noted (e.g., Lake and Cadbury, *Commentary*, 335; Conzelmann, *Acts*, 219; Schille, *Apostelgeschichte*, 466; Nunnally, "Acts," 408).

Sicily in the "Sicilian Sea") and include the Strait of Messina (across from Rhegium, Paus. 5.25.2), between Italy and Sicily, as the meeting of the Adriatic and Tyrrhenian seas (5.25.3).[831] Various additional texts are explicit about a boundary farther south than the modern Adriatic,[832] and most scholars concur that these larger boundaries include Malta.[833] Josephus also, in a voyage toward Rome, was shipwrecked in the "Adriatic" (κατὰ μέσον τὸν Ἀδρίαν, *Life* 15)—which is as implausible as Luke's claim would be unless we use the definition of that sea then current.[834]

b. Approaching Land (27:28–29)

As evidence reveals that they are approaching closer to land, anxiety increases about the danger of landfall at night, with barely any visibility.

I. SOUNDINGS (27:28)

The term βολίζω (here the aorist active participle βολίσαντες) was the normal nautical "term for taking soundings"—that is, for determining the depth of the water.[835] Pliny the Elder assumes the typical practice of soundings when he notes that soundings have never reached the deepest part of the sea.[836] Archaeologists have recovered some lead weights used for such soundings; the undersides of these leads contained a hollow area smeared with grease or tallow so as to pull up samples from the sea floor below (cf. Hdt. 2.5).[837]

Conzelmann thinks that the depth of "twenty fathoms" here is just for effect: "Luke hardly stood by and counted as they were taking soundings!"[838] Yet standing by and counting (or rather, listening to the sailors do so) might be exactly what a good historian would do, not to mention anyone on deck highly invested in knowing the voyagers' progress (for survival's sake) and competent to understand what was happening. (Even our brief "we" narratives reveal that the narrator had lived near north Aegean seaports and had voyaged before.)

In fact, the soundings fit external data. A mariner's observations suggest that only about half an hour would pass between the soundings of twenty and fifteen fathoms. Twenty fathoms fits the location where they surmised land, and as they proceeded further to prepare to anchor (Acts 27:29), they would reach a location about fifteen fathoms deep in about half an hour.[839] As one expert in ancient sea travel notes, the soundings in 27:28 show that "the water was shoaling dangerously fast."[840]

831. Rapske, "Travel," 41; Bruce, *Acts*[1], 462. Ramsay, "Roads and Travel," 380, attributes this title to influence from winds from the Adriatic (in its narrower original and modern senses).

832. Rapske, "Travel," 40 (citing, e.g., Livy 5.33.7; Strabo 2.5.29; 7.5.9–10; Lucan *C.W.* 2.613–15). Strabo 7.5.9 notes the extension of the narrower, technical usage, though still linking it with the Illyrian seaboard; some referred to the northern Adriatic as simply the "upper sea" (Cic. *Att.* 16.8). In Pliny E. *N.H.* 3.26.150, only the northern Adriatic (the "upper sea") is Adriatic, the southern waters being "Ionian."

833. Rapske, "Travel," 40–41; Ramsay, *Pictures*, 312–13; Bruce, *Commentary*, 515; Conzelmann, *Acts*, 219; Hemer, *Acts in History*, 145–46; Witherington, *Acts*, 770.

834. Josephus is soon after in Puteoli (*Life* 16); cf. Acts 28:13.

835. Hemer, *Acts in History*, 147 (followed by BDAG; Witherington, *Acts*, 771).

836. Pliny E. *N.H.* 2.105.224 (contrasting this unmeasured depth with opinions that the deepest sea is 2 mi. deep; but his claim of fresh water bubbling up there [2.105.225] does not suggest firsthand acquaintance).

837. Casson, *Mariners*, 173, 195; Hemer, *Acts in History*, 147 (following Casson, *Ships*, 246).

838. Conzelmann, *Acts*, 219. A Greek "fathom" was about 6.1 ft. or 1.85 m., so the figure here should be some 120 ft. or 37 m.

839. Bruce, *Commentary*, 516; idem, *Acts*[1], 463 (following Smith); Hemer, *Acts in History*, 147; cf. similarly Lake and Cadbury, *Commentary*, 339.

840. Casson, *Mariners*, 211.

II. Trying to Delay until Morning (27:29)

Although Paul warned his hearers that the ship would run aground (24:26) and the voyagers would survive (24:24), the crew fears[841] to run aground on the "rough places" (τραχεῖς τόπους) so far from shore.[842] Rugged terrain near land without established harbors could wreck incoming ships,[843] and sailing in the dark increased the risk of a fatal collision with rocks (Philost. *Hrk.* 31.6). In the morning light, when they can see well enough to navigate better, they will try to reach the bay (Acts 27:39) but will be grounded on a reef instead (27:41).

They are shoaling too quickly (27:28), and so they throw out anchors to prevent being driven onto rocks they cannot see.[844] (That anchors did not always prevent shipwreck is attested by the number of anchors found in shipwrecks from the first century C.E. forward.)[845] Some sailors might be designated as normally in charge of anchors (Philost. *Vit. Apoll.* 4.9), although they may have needed some other sailors' help for this more complex operation. Normally the sailors would not throw out anchors from the stern. Modern ships cast anchors from the bow; this was also the usual ancient practice, but they were also able to cast from the stern.[846] Here they face a special sort of situation, seeking to drive the ship aground in the morning; unlike ships anchoring in harbor, they plan to resume course once visibility permits.[847] Had they anchored from the bow, the ship could have been driven around so that its stern would crash against the rocks.[848]

Meanwhile they "prayed" (or perhaps "wished"; εὔχομαι can mean either; see BDAG) for daylight, when (able to see more clearly) they would try to steer the ship as close as possible to land. This experience echoes what was now traditional literary language (especially since Hom. *Od.* 9.151, 306, 436, though these occasions are not at sea per se),[849] but it was probably also common practice.

c. Retaining the Sailors' Expertise (27:30–32)

In Acts 27:30–32, Luke emphasizes both Paul's insight (recognizing both that the sailors will abandon the ship and that it cannot be saved if the sailors abandon it) and his increased status. By this point, Julius and his soldiers, who have had close contact with Paul, trust him more than they trust the maritime experts (cf. 27:9–11). This is not to dismiss the sailors' value: Paul's reason for retaining them is undoubtedly to keep their expertise in bringing the ship close enough to shore (cf. 27:39–41) for others to survive, and these sailors will do this only if they are aboard with their lives,

841. Tannehill, *Acts*, 333, suggests that they doubt Paul's words. On the portrayal of fear, contrast Paul's confidence and the comment on philosophers' ideal courage in the introduction, above, to Acts 27:21–26. But historically, even Paul did have fears (2 Cor 7:5).

842. Luke elsewhere uses τραχύς only figuratively (following Isa 40:4 LXX), for John preparing the road for the king's coming (for rough roads, see also Bar 4:26; *Pss. Sol.* 8:17). On the expected Syrtis, see comment on Acts 27:17.

843. Conzelmann, *Acts*, 219, cites as an example Dio Chrys. *Or.* 7.2 (and for a smoother island surf, Lucian *True Story* 1.6).

844. With, e.g., Casson, *Mariners*, 211. For information on ancient anchors, see comment on Acts 27:17.

845. Wachsmann and Haldane, "Anchors," 138. Anchors could, however, at least symbolize safety (Appian *Hist. rom.* 11.9.56). Paulinus of Nola *Ep.* 49.1–3 (cited in Davis, "Navigation," 226) tells of a ship casting anchors in an island's lee, but the winds soon sundered the anchors' cables.

846. Bruce, *Acts*[1], 463, cites a figure in Smith; also Appian *Hist. rom.* 8.18.123 (where Romans anchored by the stern) and (in the modern period) Lord Horatio Nelson (who followed the example of Acts 27; Abbott, *Acts*, 254).

847. Smith, *Voyage*, 135 (followed by Witherington, *Acts*, 771, who also notes that ancient ships were shaped similarly in the bow and the stern).

848. Hemer, *Acts in History*, 147; Bruce, *Acts*[1], 463.

849. Bruce, *Acts*[1], 463; Witherington, *Acts*, 764.

too, at stake. Only by abandoning the lifeboat, a hope for just a few, are the many ultimately saved through obedience to Paul's God.

i. THE ESCAPE PLAN (27:30)

Often sailors had little stake in a ship.[850] In some cases, they might not even be sailors voluntarily; in many cases, sailors were the shipowner's slaves or were rented from other slaveholders for the voyage.[851] The sailors here more likely signed on to make a living, but in any case, saving their own lives could take precedence over the ship and its other passengers. Several sailors ought to have been sufficient for the supposed maneuvers, but loading the dinghy with a significant proportion of the crew necessarily looked more suspicious, since one would not expect the entire crew to be needed for the maneuvers.[852]

Many scholars think that Luke's suspicion of the sailors' motives is unfounded, though we can infer this conclusion only because Luke correctly reports the incident. Some argue that the dinghy could not fit the entire crew (though we know the size of neither)[853] and any attempt to reach shore in such a small boat would be precarious after dark.[854] Given the strong wind, some argue, the sailors would indeed have to cast anchors from the bow by boat.[855] Certainly anchors from the bow were normal and would be safe now that the stern had been secured. Certainly, also, such large ships were not easily maneuvered, and the skiff was used for maneuvers, including "to tow or push the ship into and out of berths and through confined waters."[856] But the bow was conveniently also in the direction of land, and it is questionable whether the boat needed most or all of the crew.

Although maneuvers might be necessary, it is possible that the passage rightly construes these sailors' motives. If these sailors expected that the ship might not reach land the next day, it made more sense to try to steal away in the boat (which risked capsizing but not grounding) at the only time they could do so undetected—at night. (If they had reached the shallows of the Syrtis that they feared in 27:17, they may have held out little hope for the ship itself.) The very possibility that such maneuvers

850. This may not be true in all cases. In some cases, it seems, they received as pay a portion of the profit (Wilson, personal correspondence Oct. 13, 2014, citing the *Nomos Rhodiōn Nautikos*).

851. Casson, *Mariners*, 195–96; cf. Davis, "Navigation," 201. In at least hypothetical cases, one remaining aboard a ship that others have abandoned during a storm may become its owner (Hermog. *Issues* 40.20–41.13); but such an action is futile if the ship is doomed.

852. Often a single skillful person could be sufficient; see the hypothetical example in Cic. *Inv.* 2.154 in Davis, "Navigation," 215. We might also allow for the possibility that Luke's language is simply imprecise and not all the sailors belonged to the conspiracy; but their being needed to save the ship suggests that at least those who knew sailing adequately belonged to it.

853. A crew could be large, given the size of this ship (cf. Casson, *Mariners*, 209, citing Lucian, though concerning a much larger ship), but this objection against Luke's interpretation is not very convincing. Davis, "Navigation," 204, estimates "two dozen or more sailors" for one ship twice this size (noting four or five sailors for much smaller ships; cf. the limited number on 205n28, concerning Demosth. *Or.* 34.10), so the crew here includes perhaps a dozen hands (cf. thirteen for the midsize vessel on 205, noting Synesius *Ep.* 3.20–23). The dinghy's size is harder to predict, but the fleeing sailors would not want to overload it. Perhaps Luke means skilled sailors as opposed to other hands (cf. Acts 27:27), speaking inexactly (as he often does). In an account in Paulinus of Nola *Ep.* 49.1–3, 12 (cited in Davis, "Navigation," 226–27), however, a grain ship's entire crew (save one, by accident) crowded into the skiff to escape. Presumably the "we" narrator knew the approximate number of hands, and he surely knew the size of the boat; but he does not supply sufficient details for us to resolve their relative sizes with any certainty.

854. Cf., e.g., the many fatalities when some tried to swim toward an unseen shore after dark (Livy 28.36.12).

855. E.g., Hanson, *Acts*, 249; Conzelmann, *Acts*, 219. Lake and Cadbury, *Commentary*, 336, suggest that cutting off the boat "was the direct cause of the shipwreck," since without it they could have ferried people to shore when the weather improved. But 276 people would also require much ferrying with much risk.

856. Davis, "Navigation," 215 (also noting the use of tugboats at major ports).

were at times attempted would lend plausibility to their claim that they were departing only temporarily, while they could use this departure as a ruse to attempt escape in the likeliest means possible.[857] The nocturnal trip was hardly safe,[858] but a mariner provides modern examples of sailors risking such attempts when the alternatives to such risks appeared worse.[859] Luke has already implied that those aboard are not certain that the anchors will hold until daybreak.[860]

If they waited for day and the dinghy was the only means of reaching land, there could be conflict over who would come to use it, and the soldiers, being fully armed, presumably would win.[861] One novel illustrates the competition that could ensue for places on a dinghy once a helmsman gave up the ship. Calling for the other sailors, he climbed down the ladder into the boat:[862]

> They jumped in close after him, and then was confusion worse confounded and a hand-to-hand fight ensued. They who were already in the boat began to cut the rope which held her to the ship, while all the passengers made preparations to jump where they saw the helmsman holding on to the rope; the boat's crew objected to this, and, being armed with axes and swords, threatened to attack any who leaped in.

Better to escape before others clamored for the same boat! With land nearby, another approach might have saved more lives: individual sailors or small groups of sailors could ferry passengers to land in successive trips.[863] Nevertheless, ferrying 276 people would have required an enormous number of trips, and if the trip proved too dangerous, the boat might survive only so many trips.[864] (Even a single attempted trip, laden with crew during a severe storm, could prove fatal.)[865] These sailors, by escaping together, might improve their own chances of survival—while unfortunately reducing that of others.

It is difficult to know to what degree the account would match ancient stereotypical expectations of sailors; it does not necessarily conform to expectations for a particular genre. Some (probably mainly of the leisured class)[866] viewed sailors as untrustworthy (Plut. *Dinner* 18, *Mor.* 161C) or as incompetent in emergencies (Ael. Arist. *Or.* 2.12, 65–67).[867] It is not clear that everyone would have shared this opinion. (Other stereotypes included foolhardy exposure to danger—a view held

857. So also Hemer, *Acts in History*, 148.

858. Davis, "Navigation," 231, cites a fictitious account of survivors escaping in a boat swept terrifyingly through the night until it reached shore (Plaut. *Rud.* 2.3.36–41). Reading the text as depicting desperate measures for desperate circumstances, see, e.g., Marshall, *Acts*, 412; Bock, *Acts*, 739.

859. Smith, *Voyage*, 137, with examples; followed by Witherington, *Acts*, 771n85.

860. See Tannehill, *Acts*, 333. He complains (334) that Haenchen's skepticism on this point creates "a new story more to" his liking.

861. The contingent of soldiers is probably fairly small (such assignments might include about ten; Pliny *Ep.* 10.27). But escape without conflict would be preferred to conflict, in any case.

862. Ach. Tat. 3.3.1–2 (trans. S. Gaselee, LCL, 141). Those in the boat began striking at those trying to enter, lest it be swamped by too many people (3.3.4).

863. Lake and Cadbury, *Commentary*, 336, suggest that this was the best means of escape once the gale ended. But they may overestimate the strength of the anchors and may have estimated the duration of the gale more modestly than the sailors, who, after days being driven by it, had little hope of its swift diminution. The weather has been unpleasant for days (Acts 27:4, 7–8) and, now further into the dangerous sailing season, does not seem inclined to improve soon (28:2).

864. Modern readers may think of the failure to make optimal use of lifeboats on the Titanic: in emergency situations, many people rank personal survival or safety over that of others.

865. See Paulinus of Nola *Ep.* 49.1–3, 12 (cited in Davis, "Navigation," 226–27, 231).

866. Mariners derived especially from a "low social stratum" (Davis, "Navigation," 200), and sailors and even captains could be tortured in the course of investigating shipwrecks (201). Unlike shipowners and shipbuilders, sailors and even navigators lacked their own guild, even in major commercial centers such as Ostia (202).

867. Johnson, *Acts*, 454.

by some afraid of the sea—and the sexual activity of visitors in local ports.)[868] Beyond stereotypes, however, criminal elements apparently abounded, and sailors were known for violent behavior, including robbing passengers on board.[869] Some even suggest that "most if not all participated in the seedy underworld that characterized the waterfronts of ancient harbor cities."[870]

Flight in ships' boats is not a regular novelistic motif, but it does appear (Petron. *Sat.* 102; 114.7; Ach. Tat. 3.3.1–4).[871] That some would flee before a ship could sink, however, is reasonable (presumably a reason for novelists to have sometimes thought of it).[872] If Luke presents these motives for the sailors, he presumably believed his presentation correct; he is certainly not glorifying Paul's ability to persuade everyone on the ship[873] (though he is portraying a natural level of confusion and fear aboard, which maintains a level of suspense). Still, Luke's description will not put off his audience; sailors did not have the best reputation, as noted above, and Luke writes for hearers who can respect Rome's soldiers.

Whether Luke understands or misunderstands the motives of the sailors, what is most striking is that the boat, which could save only a few and seemed the best means for survival,[874] was not necessary to save anyone. God (cf. Acts 27:24) allowed everyone to reach land safely (27:43–44), even those who could not swim (27:44). Only by abandoning the slim natural hope posed by the boat for a few were the many ultimately saved by God.

11. Paul's Warning (27:31)

Paul's earlier promise of survival for all (27:22–24) is now seen to be a conditional prophecy, but Paul is continuing to listen to God and is ready for the condition (27:31).

Paul's concern about the sailors' departure could have been right whether or not the assumption of 27:30 is correct; whether the sailors would abandon the ship (so 27:30), would endanger their own lives, or would execute a maneuver in a fatally wrong way, their act could have endangered others aboard, who had no idea how to guide the ship forward in the morning (27:39–41).[875] (By not specifying the sailors' plan as Luke himself does in 27:30, Luke allows Paul's words within the narrative to avoid openly shaming the sailors.)[876]

868. Courtesans served rich shipowners, e.g., Lucian *Dial. C.* 7 (Musarium and Her Mother ¶2), 296; 12 (Joessa, Pythias, and Lysias ¶1), 311; also ship's officers, *Dial. C.* 14 (Dorio and Myrtale 2), 320; and other sailors, *Dial. C.* 14 (Dorio and Myrtale 3), 320.

869. Davis, "Navigation," 201, noting that the later *Nomos Rhodiōn Nautikos* stipulates "penalties against predatory sailors for robbing other ships or merchants and passengers on board, for fighting against other sailors (with fist, stone and ax!), for killing other crew members, and more." Ancient religion often involved offerings and rituals more than morality, but many people in antiquity did expect the gods to punish the wicked.

870. Davis, "Navigation," 201–2, following Rauh, *Merchants*, 161–62.

871. Praeder, "Acts 27:1–28:16," 701 (emphasizing the few references, against Conzelmann; cf. Pervo, *Acts*, 662).

872. With also Witherington, *Acts*, 772n85. Petronius wrote shortly before Luke and was probably unknown to him; Achilles Tatius may depend on Petronius. Whether it was a motif before Petronius is impossible to know.

873. Cf. Hemer, *Acts in History*, 148n138.

874. A dinghy often promised at best a narrow hope for survival, yet also the only one (Davis, "Navigation," 231).

875. Cf. Tannehill, *Acts*, 333; Hemer, *Acts in History*, 148; Witherington, *Acts*, 772. The principle that one who remains aboard an abandoned ship during a storm becomes the new owner (Hermog. *Issues* 40.20; 41.1–13) suggests the value of someone knowledgeable remaining aboard. Alternatively, Soards, *Speeches*, 129, thinks that the prohibition concerns unbelief: because God had already promised safety to those aboard (Acts 27:22–25), leaving the ship demonstrated unbelief. But is their faith necessary to fulfill the promise of 27:22–25, and is such faith generated under compulsion?

876. That Luke, through time spent with sailors that is suggested as a possibility above, could have learned of the plot is not impossible, but inference would seem likelier in this case, since they would not likely confide in anyone for whom there would be no room in the boat.

Paul's warning could involve any of these possibilities and remain plausible, and it is not surprising that the centurion at this point would follow his counsel.[877] Paul has warned against setting out (cf. 27:10–12, 21) and accurately predicted the island that they now approach (27:26); as one now likely viewed as a prophet or divine agent (the centurion knew Paul's religious commitment from the first), he would now have more credibility than personnel who chose to set out. Further, Paul has probably been the only voice offering hope (27:20, 22–24), and thus his counsel would seem the only hope the voyagers have.

On one level, Paul may appear to have achieved virtual command of the ship,[878] but such an appearance should not be exaggerated; not everyone necessarily shares the centurion's sentiments (the sailors, most obviously, do not). Moreover, Paul remains vulnerable to abuse as a prisoner (27:42). How may the reader balance 27:31–32 with the danger in 27:42? It is important to remember that the centurion values Paul as a divine spokesman;[879] the soldiers may accept Paul's accuracy yet not wish to risk incurring punishment if he escapes (27:42). Indeed, as a divine spokesman he might be all the more able to escape, and such an incident would not always turn out well for the guards (cf. 12:19). Yet ancient tales are also full of deities defending and avenging their agents (just as nations did), and so the centurion will wisely seek to preserve Paul's life, in any event (27:43). Another way of balancing these scenes is also possible; perhaps the soldiers are thinking only of killing other prisoners in 27:42, but the centurion (27:43) knows that their inconsistency might be difficult to justify in retrospect.

III. The Soldiers' Faith (27:32)

Although there is no necessary thought of exclusive monotheistic faith here (or even personal allegiance; see comment on Acts 27:31), the soldiers do believe that Paul speaks divine truth. As elsewhere in his work, Luke portrays soldiers with at least partial faith (Luke 3:14; 7:2, 9; 23:47; Acts 10:1–7).[880]

In a later story, a crew escaping in a boat cut it loose from the ship and tried to escape while the passengers, left behind, tried to sink it (Ach. Tat. 3.4.2).[881] Paul did not in fact command the cutting off of the boat here but only implied the demand that the sailors stay on board; cutting loose the boat would, however, prevent the sailors from escaping in it (and hence from removing their needed expertise along with the boat) without the need to threaten them directly and risk more aggressive confrontation. It would not require a great deal of speculation to suppose that the sailors resented this action (though they might have expected the soldiers to seize the boat for themselves in the morning otherwise); but in any case, their own lives now depend on the same factors as the lives of the rest of the people on board, and so their expertise will help drive the ship as close as possible to the shore.

What is most significant here is the reverence that Paul now commands. All on

877. Polyb. 1.32.1–9 reports that when a Spartan complained about Carthaginian strategy, the generals summoned him and, being convinced of his knowledge, put him in charge of the troops (who cheered). (They won this battle; 1.34.1–12.)

878. Lentz, *Luke's Portrait*, 94 (regarding this portrait as fictitious). Thomas, "Upside-Down," may have a point in viewing Paul's being in charge as part of Luke's use of irony to subvert the social order.

879. Vespasian gave Josephus expensive gifts even while the latter remained in custody, out of respect for his prophetic gift (Jos. *War* 3.408). Cf. fear of a prophet (a divine agent) in Gen 20:7–8, although this was not always the response.

880. Luke's verb for "letting down" can be used for acts of faith (Luke 5:4–5; Mark 2:4) but does not bear such connotations exclusively (cf. Acts 9:25), including in this context (27:17).

881. For cutting off such a boat during a storm, Johnson, *Acts*, 454, cites also Heliod. *Eth.* 5.27.6.

board would recognize that the boat could be useful in ferrying people to shore should they draw near land too rugged for harboring. By cutting off this limited hope, in obedience to Paul, Julius and, apparently (or at least by obedience to Julius), his soldiers ultimately stake everything on the promise of Paul's God. Even in captivity, God might favor his servant (cf. Gen 39:4, 21–22; Dan 1:19–20).

d. Encouraging Others to Eat (27:33–38)

Paul remains calm and in control like a genuine philosopher,[882] the sort of intellectual hero Luke's audience could readily respect. Storms, shipwrecks, and pirates were frequent settings for verifying philosophers' true character;[883] this was why philosophers used catalogues of their hardships.[884] Meanwhile Paul pastorally cares for all those aboard, helping to ensure their survival.

I. INTRODUCTION

Susan Marie Praeder finds in sea voyage literature no parallels to Luke's account in Acts 27:33–38. There are no invitations to share meals under such conditions in other literature; the obvious parallels instead are to Christian meals in Luke-Acts.[885] Likewise, earlier in Luke's work, Jesus, after a crisis has passed, also urged one to eat (Luke 8:55).

Some scholars find in this passage a type of the Eucharist,[886] especially since the food is for their "preservation" or "salvation" ($\sigma\omega\tau\eta\rho\acute{\iota}\alpha\varsigma$) in Acts 27:34 and similar language appears in Luke 22:19. "Salvation" in Acts 27:34, of course, refers to physical survival (the term's most common meaning in normal Greek and in this context), but Luke is ready to use it for double entendres elsewhere (4:9–12). Other scholars respond with skepticism toward a Eucharist here. Witherington offers several objections:[887]

1. The Lord's Supper is not dominant in Luke-Acts, and certainly we lack indication of salvation by it.
2. "Take," "break," and "thank" are not specifically eucharistic but derive from thanksgiving at all Jewish meals (cf. Luke 9:16; 24:30).[888] "The Lord's Supper was indebted to this earlier Jewish practice, not the other way around."
3. The passage lacks wine and the interpretation of elements.
4. Paul does not distribute the bread.
5. The bread satisfies hunger (Acts 27:38)—more like the feeding of the five thousand than like Luke 22.
6. Pagans remain pagans after they have eaten.
7. The focus here is not ecclesiology but Paul's heroism to rescue others.

. Witherington, *Acts*, 772 (citing Diog. Laert. 2.71; Lucian *Peregr.* 43–44; and Keener, *Background Commentary*, 402). See further comment in the introduction, above, to Acts 27 and esp. at Acts 27:21–26.

883. Johnson, *Acts*, 455 (citing Epict. *Diatr.* 4.1.92; 4.1.174; Diog. Laert. 2.71, 77; 2.130; 4.50; 6.74; 7.2; 9.68; cf. Hom. *Od.* 12.270–300; Lucian *Tox.* 20). See further comment in the introduction, above, to Acts 27.

884. On which see esp. Fitzgerald, *Cracks*, passim.

885. Praeder, "Acts 27:1–28:16," 696–97.

886. More often, and plausibly, some think that Luke styles the meal to evoke (albeit not constitute) the Eucharist (cf., e.g., Tannehill, *Acts*, 335; idem, *Shape*, 231; Praeder, "Acts 27:1–28:16," 699; Heil, *Meal Scenes*, 293–305; Pervo, *Acts*, 664; Jipp, *Visitations*, 35; cf. my view below). F. Martin, in Martin, *Acts*, 306, doubts a Eucharist here but notes that the church fathers' application to that agenda is not surprising, since (306–7) they were often preaching homilies; without viewing this meal as the Eucharist, John Chrysostom draws lessons for the church (307).

887. Witherington, *Acts*, 772–73. Cf. Barrett, *Acts*, 2:1208–10; Jervell, *Apostelgeschichte*, 609 (also listing some commentators on both sides).

888. See also Dunn, *Acts*, 341. For thanksgiving at meals, see, e.g., *Jub.* 22:6; *Sib. Or.* 4.25–26; Jos. *War* 2.131; *m. Ber.* 6:1–6; Safrai, "Religion," 802–3; Slater, "Kiddush"; after meals, cf. also *Pesiq. Rab Kah.* 28:2; *b. Ber.* 34b; *y. Ter.* 1:6; Finkelstein, *Making*, 333–84; Troster, "Quest"; perhaps at Qumran, Weinfeld, "Grace."

The cumulative force of most of these arguments is sufficient to establish that this is not a eucharistic meal within the narrative world; such a claim does not, however, imply that Luke's audience would see no connection or instruction for their practice of the Lord's Supper. The Lord's Supper is part of a broader pattern of eating together in Luke-Acts, and this broader pattern in turn affects how we read the Lord's Supper (cf. Luke 22:17, 19; Acts 27:35).[889] The symposia with tax collectors and sinners in Luke's Gospel also indicate that the fellowship meals are open to everyone, not exclusively for the righteous. (See further comment on Acts 27:35–36.)

ii. Encouraging Them to Eat (27:33–34)

Luke continues to emphasize Paul's *ēthos*, displaying his care for all, whether believers or not.[890] Such a persona would commend Paul in a forensic context or any other and does appear consistent with the warm, pastoral relationship Paul's letters suggest that he had with many congregations and with those he guided into the faith.[891]

(1) Their Failure to Eat (27:33)

Fourteen days is a long time without food but, under the circumstances (see comment on Acts 27:20), believable.[892] Eating after so long a time[893] would be hard on their digestion, but even with the ship somewhat more stable than usual (Acts 27:29), the voyagers would probably eat only lightly. Nevertheless, they would need some short-term energy for the struggle ahead (27:43–44). Passengers may have feared to finish the limited rations they had brought for the voyage, uncertain how long their drifting would last. But while the cargo wheat was neither prepared nor belonged to them, survival could have taken precedence over such considerations. More critically, their lack of eating may reflect both seasickness and anxiety (see comment on Acts 27:21–22); the latter may be occasioned by the threat of death (27:36) and exacerbated by the cultural horror of death unburied (see comment on Acts 27:20). In the face of anxiety,[894] they also may not be sleeping much in anticipation of the approaching dawn, when Paul addresses them (cf. 16:25).

If we press the imperfect force of παρεκάλει, it might mean that Paul was exhorting passengers regularly, probably individually and in small groups (cf. 20:20) rather than all together as depicted in his previous speech (27:21–26). Perhaps many are now on deck. Although Paul is doing this before dawn, most of the passengers are apparently

---

889. Cf. Heil, *Meal Scenes*, 293–305, 312; Hamm, *Acts*, 118. As Kurz, *Acts*, 370–71, notes regarding echoes of the Lord's Supper, "Luke's purpose is to hint at the salvific effect of Paul's example, not to claim that Paul actually celebrated the Eucharist with hundreds of non-Christians on a ship while waiting out a storm."

890. Those who think that the historical Paul cared only for believers may have a harder time explaining how he converted nonbelievers; his extant writings, though occasional letters to churches, also betray a concern for outsiders at points (e.g., 1 Cor 14:24; 1 Thess 4:12).

891. Incidentally, in terms of application, it may also offer a model for caring engagement with nonbelievers as fellow human beings, an insight that has sometimes been in unduly short supply in some religious circles with which some readers may be familiar.

892. Aelius Aristides also speaks of his ship "being adrift for fourteen days, with no one on board being able to eat during that time (2:68 [*Sacr.* 2.68])" (Johnson, *Acts*, 455; also in Parsons, *Acts*, 358). This is a true account, written in the second century, long after Luke (i.e., the accounts must be independent). Some argue that most poor people in antiquity normally ate only one or, at most, two meals daily (Schneider, "Nutrition," 919). Hyperbole is not impossible (allowed for in Parsons, *Acts*, 358); Arrington, *Acts*, 261, suggests that Paul's words are a forceful way of saying that they have "not eaten properly," rather than that they were without food altogether.

893. Keeping count of days at sea (as also in Acts 21:1; 27:19, 27) was apparently a common practice (Philost. *Hrk.* 6.3).

894. On anxiety among the causes for lack of sleep that are noted in ancient sources, see, on Acts 2:15, Keener, *Acts*, 1:872n111.

awake; anxiety is likely a factor for most,[895] but in his case he serves them pastorally, trying to make certain that all survive (cf. his labors day and night in 20:31). Such an image of Paul is consonant with Luke's emphasis on social ministry (e.g., 2:44–45; 11:29–30) and Luke's respectful approach to the empire.[896] Paul has presumably embraced these people, even without their conversion, as part of his "shepherdly" responsibility (cf. 20:28 for the converted).[897] He does not discharge his "ministerial duty" only at expected professional moments but uses every opportunity in his life to serve others. Non-Christian Gentiles would also view this activity as virtuous. It was good for citizens of a city to work for the common good, just as all those in a ship must work together for the common safety (Dio Chrys. Or. 48.7). Paul cares about others in the ship, fitting ancient ideals of virtue.

(2) Eating Necessary (27:34)

That none of the voyagers would die, and that food was necessary for their survival, suggests the tension between divine sovereignty and human obedience in the rest of the narrative (the unconditional promise of Acts 27:22–24 has a condition in 27:31). Perhaps, in Luke's view, the prophecy was conditional from the start; or perhaps the conditions must be met, yet in this case God's larger promise takes into account God's knowledge that the conditions will be met.

In this context Luke frequently uses σωτηρία (27:34), σῴζω (27:20, 31), and διασῴζω[898] (27:43, 44; 28:1, 4) for physical deliverance; this was the most common usage of such words. On a less theological level, the claim of divine deliverance would be intelligible to Paul's fellow voyagers. "Save" could mean "preserve"[899] and could apply to salvation (deliverance or protection) of the state[900] or deliverance in battle.[901] Gods were called "saviors," especially Zeus.[902] Most relevant is that "gods" were thought to "save" people at sea.[903] This appears equally in Jewish sources.[904] "Soteria" also became the title of "a sacrifice or festival celebrating deliverance from danger."[905] (See fuller discussion at Acts 27:20.)

But for Luke, God's saving acts for individuals in the present foreshadow God's greater plan of eschatological salvation in Christ. Thus the traditional biblical notion of salvation from enemies (Luke 1:71) both is literal (1:74, probably at Israel's restoration; cf. Acts 1:6–7) and includes present salvation by forgiveness (Luke

---

895. On causes of sleeplessness in ancient literature, see Keener, *John*, 841; fuller comment at Acts 2:14–15.

896. As opposed to the more "sectarian" worldview of churches under persecution (see John 15:18–25; Keener, *John*, 149–52, 1017–18; cf. also apocalyptic sources protesting the oppression of God's people), Luke (like, e.g., many Jews in Asia) is comfortable with much Greco-Roman culture (see comment on Acts 19:31).

897. This is also plausible for one who has cultivated pastoral skills in nurturing and leading people. As one example, when Emmanuel Itapson, a Nigerian pastor, came as a student to Eastern Seminary in Philadelphia in 1996, I regularly found seminarians in his room baring their hearts to him simply because relating to people in a pastoral way was second nature to him.

898. Seventy-five percent of all NT uses of this final verb are Lukan, and of these, two-thirds appear in this context. All uses in earliest Christianity are physical (Acts 23:24; Luke 7:3; Matt 14:36; 1 Pet 3:20; *1 Clem.* 9.4, echoing 1 Pet 3:20; *1 Clem.* 12.5–6; *Mart. Pol.* 8.2).

899. *Let. Aris.* 45.

900. E.g., Mus. Ruf. 20, p. 126.8; Aeschines *Embassy* 74 (the city); Lysias *Or.* 2.66, §196 (soldiers fought for their people's deliverance); Hermog. *Inv.* 1.1.98–99.

901. Xen. *Anab.* 5.2.24.

902. Aeschylus *Suppl.* 26.

903. E.g., Diod. Sic. 4.43.1; Ach. Tat. 3.5; Lucian *Dial. G.* 287; cf. a Jewish inscription praising God for deliverance at sea in Horsley, *Documents*, 4:113. Isis was "Lord" of rainstorms (a second-century C.E. aretalogy in Grant, *Religions*, 133, employing the masculine form for "Lord").

904. Noah and his family were also "saved" in relation to water (Wis 10:4; Jos. *Ant.* 1.77, 79; 1 Pet 3:20).

905. Jameson, "Soteria."

1:77).[906] A paralytic's healing through Jesus's name (Acts 4:9) becomes evidence that Jesus's name is the exclusive means of salvation (4:12).

Going without food was vain (cf. 23:14) unless it was fasting conjoined with prayer (13:2; 14:23), as perhaps it had been in Paul's case (cf. 27:24). Food will provide the voyagers strength for what is ahead (27:43–44; cf. 9:19) and, in such circumstances, is preferable to fasting (1 Sam 14:26–31).[907] Thus, for example, Odysseus urged the people to stop fasting (from mourning), lest they be too weak to fight (Hom. *Il.* 19.156–70, 231–33). Luke's audience may recall Jesus's compassionate concern that people be able to eat (Luke 9:13–17; cf. Mark 8:3).

As the least significant and smallest part of the body, a hair was the most dispensable;[908] to promise that not a hair would be lost was a graphic Semitic (including OT) way of promising survival.[909] Likewise, "not a hair on the head" of Daniel's three friends had been burned when they emerged from the fire, nor was the smell of smoke on them (Dan 3:27; 3 Macc 6:6). The most immediate allusion for Luke's readers is Jesus's promise about persecution (Luke 21:18, in the context of 21:16–19),[910] although, if physical, it must be hyperbolic (21:16; cf. 12:4). The text here depicts a different situation, but Luke can still draw on Jesus's principle. Paul's favor with God is sufficient to carry all of his fellow passengers to safety, even though most of them are not worshipers of his God. If none of them would perish, they could release their despair enough to eat and cooperate with their promised survival. They had food available before but lacked courage to eat (27:36).

iii. Paul and His Hearers Eat (27:35–36)

Paul's example encourages others to eat, in a scene that might remind Luke's audience of other fellowship meals in Luke-Acts (though the circumstances here are quite different).

Given the urgency of the situation, it is not likely that 276 people aboard could access the cooking area and prepare food. Probably some had food (such as bread,[911] dried figs, and so forth) available that would require minimal preparation; passengers without much money would need to bring their own food on a ship.[912] Whether most people still had some food of their own or whether some shared their bread, the setting and Paul's exhortation seem to underline that the passengers shared their situation in common. It could seem reasonable to construe 27:38 as if it was especially grain they were eating, since only after they finished did they discard the grain into the sea. In this case the issue is emergency strength in the face of hunger (cf. Luke 6:1). But while people can eat raw wheatberries, raw and unprepared wheat can be difficult to

906. Cf. deliverance from present spiritual oppressors in Luke 8:36; liberation from them in 13:16; Acts 10:38.

907. Cf. weakness for battle among those who had missed breakfast (Polyb. 3.71.11–3.72.6); eating could help a weakened person regain strength (*y. Ber.* 2:7, §3). Accustoming oneself to deprivation, however, was often considered healthful (Val. Max. 2.5.6; Mus. Ruf. 9, p. 70.13–22; 20, p. 126.6–7, helping courage; Dio Chrys. *Or.* 6.8; Lucian *Tim.* 33; Max. Tyre 36.5; on rigor, see further comment at Acts 2:44–45).

908. Cf. *b. B. Qam.* 50a: God judges those close to him "for matters as light as a single hair" (Soncino). Publ. Syr. 186: "Even one hair has a shadow of its own" (trans. J. W. Duff, LCL, 39).

909. 1 Sam 14:45; 2 Sam 14:11; 1 Kgs 1:52; cf. Matt 10:30; *b. B. Bat.* 16a. Allison, "Hairs," thinks that the passage in Matthew alludes to the omniscient God counting hairs (Pss 40:12; 69:4), thus knowing rather than protecting; there is some tension with the context, but some measure of protection may be in view even in that text (see Keener, *Matthew,* 327).

910. See also Luke 12:7 (Q, also in Matt 10:30), which emphasizes the large number of hairs (cf. Pss 40:12; 69:4). It is not clear that Luke 21:18 is meant to be harmonized fully with 21:16.

911. Perhaps originally wrapped to prevent its getting moldy or stale, and hence now still edible.

912. Rapske, *Custody,* 223–24; Casson, *Mariners,* 193.

digest, especially if it has not been soaked overnight (though Luke knows that it is edible; see again Luke 6:1).[913] Paul's food here, however, is plainly bread (Acts 27:35).

Although this meal is not the Lord's Supper, it belongs to Luke's fellowship meal theme, of which the Lord's Supper is one part (see the introduction, above, to Acts 27:33–38). The occasion here is closer to Jesus's eating with "sinners" in the Gospel (Luke 5:30; 7:34; 15:2; 19:7; cf. 7:36–37; 11:37–38; 14:1), inviting all to God's banquet (14:13–14, 21–24), which the Lord's Supper also foreshadows (22:18).[914] Like Jesus, Paul also assumes something like the role of host,[915] although unlike Jesus he does not provide most of the bread (Luke 9:13–17). Presumably Paul, like Jesus in the Gospel (15:1), spoke openly about God among the voyagers, at least after they landed (Acts 28:9). But even in the highlights described, he glorified the name of his God (27:23, 35) among these Gentiles.

People poured libations to deities at the beginning of banquets,[916] so Paul's thanksgiving in 27:35 would be intelligible in a Gentile context. Paul gives thanks publicly, demonstrating public faith in the midst of hardship, as in 16:25 (cf. 28:15).[917] As is probably also implied in 16:28, his response to hardship has made him the de facto spiritual leader of the ad hoc community of which he has become a part. This picture praises Paul, but it also suggests that part of Luke's ideal for the expansion of Jesus's movement is that God's agents should view every encounter with others in need as a potential opportunity for ministry to them. As in the case of Jesus at times in Luke's Gospel, this ministry was often most effective when the minister shared the same sufferings or outsider status.

Giving thanks for food (Luke 22:17, 19; 1 Cor 10:30; 11:24) was a standard Jewish meal custom.[918] Indeed, 1 Tim 4:3–5 and, still more clearly, *Did.* 9.2–3; 10.3 recall the usual Jewish benediction over a meal.[919] Bread was a standard staple of the ancient Mediterranean world.[920] Although people generally honored their deities when beginning meals, it will be clear that Paul's God, whom he thanks, is the one to whom he has already attributed their coming deliverance.

This is Paul's fourth intervention; although he was unheeded during his initial attempt, everyone obeys him by this time (Acts 27:36).[921] Given the events Luke has narrated, this submission is the response we would expect. Nevertheless, this response does not suggest that everyone has faith, even with the ship's having approached land;

---

913. Wheat normally is processed (e.g., into bread) before being preserved and eaten, especially helpful for the digestive systems of persons who have not eaten for two weeks.

914. The historical Paul apparently knew the tradition of Jesus's eating with sinners (see Dunn, *Theology of Paul*, 192, on Gal 2:12, 14–15). On the motif in the Gospels, see, e.g., Keener, *Historical Jesus*, 211–12; and esp. Powell, "Table Fellowship," 928–30, and sources discussed there.

915. So Jipp, *Visitations*, 255–56.

916. See Harland, *Associations*, 77; Boring, Berger, and Colpe, *Commentary*, 147; cf., e.g., Iambl. *V.P.* 21.98–99.

917. Apparently it was customary to "offer sacrifices in thanks for a safe return"—upon *arrival* (Casson, *Mariners*, 194). Here Paul expresses faith; his thanksgiving is for food, but it calls attention to faith in the God who will help them.

918. As also noted by others, including Haenchen, *Acts*, 707; Peterson, *Acts*, 694; Gilbert, "Acts," 250–51; Schnabel, *Acts*, 1046.

919. Cf. *Apost. Const.* 7.26.4; Ambrosiaster *Commentary on Paul's Epistles* (Vogels, 118; Bray, *Corinthians*, 102); *Jub.* 22:6; *Sib. Or.* 4.25–26; Jos. *War* 2.131; *m. Ber.* 3:3; 6:1–8:8.

920. Safrai, "Home," 747; Neusner, *Beginning*, 23; cf. Pliny E. *N.H.* 22.68.138; in more detail, Lewis, *Life*, 68. Ancients typically regarded wheat as the most important kind of food besides wine (e.g., Diod. Sic. 4.3.5). Likewise, most of the ancient Near Eastern diet was cereals (Hopkins, "Cereals," 479).

921. With Johnson, *Acts*, 455. That they were "encouraged" or "fortified" fits Paul's earlier exhortation in 27:22, 25 (using the cognate verb; cognates appear elsewhere in the NT only at 24:10; Jas 5:13; in the LXX only at 2 Macc 11:26, but thirteen times in Josephus and thirty times in Philo).

eventually approaching land somewhere was one thing, and everyone on board making it safe to shore another (and even Paul himself regarded the promise as conditional, though he helped ensure that the condition was met, 27:31).

iv. Throwing Wheat Overboard (27:37–38)

The large number of people aboard (highlighting the miracle) could require a massive amount of food, but they might make use of the grain on board.

(1) Many Passengers (27:37)

Why Luke includes the number of passengers precisely here, in the midst of the feeding report, is unclear; perhaps the people had to be numbered before being fed (cf. Luke 9:14),[922] or perhaps Luke simply wanted to narrate the initial response to Paul's speech before turning to the number of those whose survival Paul had just predicted. Some scholars point out that the number 276 is triangular (with a base of 23);[923] Pythagoreans made much of significant numbers[924] such as triangular numbers, and they appear at some other points in the NT (John 21:11; Rev 13:18).[925] Had Luke said "about" (as in some MSS; but "ὡς with an exact statement of number is inappropriate"),[926] we might have expected that he rounded to the nearest "significant" number (cf. Acts 19:7; perhaps Luke 8:42) although he or his sources usually rounded to the nearest multiple of ten, fifty, or a hundred (cf. Acts 2:41; 4:4; 5:36; 13:18, 19; Luke 3:23; 9:14). But he omits such a qualification (and even had he included it, he might simply have left a margin for error, having counted as accurately as possible).[927] Moreover, one wonders why the triangle of twenty-three would have been deemed particularly significant and how quickly his hearers would have recognized it.[928] Given Luke's lack of interest in symbolic numbers (or most Pythagorean themes) elsewhere, the triangular number is likely a coincidence.[929] The crew may well have had an exact count, especially given the current circumstances.

Some scholars are skeptical of the number,[930] but the literal estimate is by no means problematic;[931] we know, indeed, of many ships much larger.[932] Although Josephus is known for his unverifiable, exaggerated estimates in Judea, he expects his claim of

922. Schnabel, *Acts*, 1046, suggests this or possibly an early morning roll call (27:33, 39). Normally passengers were responsible for their own food, but the circumstances of bread distribution may have dictated otherwise in this case.

923. Colson, "Triangular Numbers," 72 (who Praeder, "Acts 27:1–28:16," 699n48, suggests may be the sole advocate of this position; though cf. C. Williams, *Acts*, 272–73); now also Pervo, *Acts*, 665; Twelftree, *Paul*, 267.

924. See Laroche, "Numbers"; on ancient theories about symbolic numbers, see Menken, *Techniques*, 27–29. Lucian *Phil. Sale* 4 parodies the Pythagorean emphasis on triangular numbers.

925. The occurrence in John 21:11 might be coincidental (see discussion in Keener, *John*, 1231–33); on the possibly more significant occurrence in Rev 13:18, see Rissi, *Time*, 76; Caird, *Revelation*, 176; esp. Bauckham, *Climax*, 390–94, 403–4.

926. Metzger, *Textual Commentary*, 499.

927. Dunn, *Acts*, 341, suggests a morning (Acts 27:33) roll call, in case some had been lost during the rough voyage and fasting.

928. Twenty-three is a prime number, but no more significant than seventeen or nineteen. There are sixteen square and more than twenty triangular numbers up to 276; given the various figures offered in Acts, the odds are fairly high of one randomly being triangular or having some other distinctive feature. Luke shows no discernible pattern of such numbers—that is, such explanations do not account for the rougher estimates in 2:41; 4:4; 19:19; or 21:38 or for the closer figures in 23:23; 27:28; or 27:33. The case is not like that of the doubly triangular number in Rev 13, which belongs to a work full of symbols.

929. As most concur (e.g., Conzelmann, *Acts*, 220; cf. C. Williams, *Acts*, 272–73).

930. Packer, *Acts*, 214, preferring the manuscripts saying "76." This variant is improbable (see Metzger, *Textual Commentary*, 499–500).

931. Even Foakes-Jackson, *Acts*, 232, who prefers the unlikely variant "76," concedes that the larger number is credible (citing Josephus).

932. Cf. Cary and Haarhoff, *Life*, 135; see comment on Acts 27:6, 18.

six hundred voyagers aboard his ship (of whom eighty were fast swimmers) to be credible (*Life* 14–15).[933] (The ship in Josephus's account wrecked only a few years after the one in Luke's narrative.)[934] On the massive *Isis* (Lucian *Ship* 5), which may have carried 1,000 to 1,300 tons, and other large ships, see further comment on Acts 27:18. Transatlantic European and American ships were not as large as the *Isis* until "the beginning of the nineteenth century."[935] Scholars specialized in the study of ancient navigation typically accept Josephus's number here, and some suggest that Paul's ship would have held more had they not been sailing off-season.[936]

(2) A Final Meal (27:38)

"When they had eaten enough" (κορεσθέντες) recalls everyone's being filled after Jesus supplied food (Luke 9:14, 17).[937] Unlike Jesus's meal, the present meal is not miraculous, but it constitutes an act of faith in what God is accomplishing. After eating, the voyagers were free to discard what they could of the rest, acknowledging that they would not need it anymore: they would have one chance at survival and no more.

Some scholars suggest that the grain here jettisoned was kept back from Acts 27:18 as ballast or for food,[938] but the amount needed for food would be negligible in terms of such a ship's weight.[939] A grain ship bound for Rome could carry hundreds of tons of wheat,[940] and so it is highly unlikely that they could have already finished the job started in 27:18[941] (whether to retain ballast or simply from sheer exhaustion and inability). (Normally ballast was sand or stone,[942] necessary only on the route back to Alexandria, when the ship lacked grain.) It is unlikely that they are able to discard all the grain even now; each sack was an average load that a man could carry, but disposing of a typical grain ship's cargo required the disposal of some 7,500 sacks,[943] probably impossible during the few remaining hours of the night.[944]

Discarding the grain might show faith that the voyage was nearing its completion; it also may constitute an important factor in getting the ship close enough to land to allow the passengers to swim or float ashore (27:39–44). The grain in the hold could weigh the ship down, making it more likely that the ship would ground on rocks before reaching shore. If the hull ruptured, the immediate problem would be water filling the ship, but even if the breach was contained, wetted grain in one part of the ship would have eventually caused disaster. A long-term risk in grain becoming wet was "germination, infestation or rotting," but a more immediate problem was that it could swell to even double its original volume, potentially rupturing the plates of

933. Casson, *Mariners*, 211, thinks that Paul's ship sailed below capacity in passenger numbers (which might make the proportion of crew higher); given the lateness of sailing season, this is possible (though not certain).

934. Schnabel, *Acts*, 1046, has four years.

935. Casson, *Mariners*, 209. On the massive tonnage of Roman cargo ships, see further pp. 172–73, 191.

936. Cf. Hemer, *Acts in History*, 149, following Casson here. Hundreds could be aboard (Casson, *Travel*, 156).

937. With Tannehill, *Acts*, 335. The specific verb differs, here being rare in the NT (1 Cor 4:8; cf. Deut 31:20 LXX).

938. Bruce, *Commentary*, 517; Johnson, *Acts*, 455 (comparing Luke 12:42, which uses a NT hapax legomenon; but cf. instead Luke 3:17; 12:18; 16:7).

939. With Lake and Cadbury, *Commentary*, 337.

940. See Rapske, "Travel," 31–32; fuller comment on Acts 27:18.

941. See Lake and Cadbury, *Commentary*, 337; Rapske, "Travel," 32–33.

942. Casson, *Mariners*, 193.

943. Rapske, personal correspondence, Oct. 13, 2014.

944. Even assuming passengers helping the crew in passing up the sacks in "bucket-brigade" style, if one were to guess eight minutes from hold to sea for each bag nearest the deck, the process would require fifteen or sixteen hours; carriers working at multiple hatches would reduce this figure accordingly, but sacks stored deeper in the hold would also take longer to transport. As noted earlier, unloading a vessel in more orderly fashion sometimes took twelve days (Rapske, "Travel," 31).

even the ships of our own era.[945] The primary and urgent problem now, however, was to avoid grounding the ship too far from shore. Excessive water on the decks could seep through their boards to lower compartments. Eventually, as "force or chain pumps" could no longer remove all the water, "the crew and the passengers" could reduce excess weight only by discarding "part or all of the cargo."[946] The cargo, once so precious (see comment on Acts 27:12), has now become completely expendable (see comment on Acts 27:18).[947]

7. Reaching Land Safely (27:39–44)

The sailors manage to bring the ship close enough to shore to provide hope of passengers reaching it safely, but the ship itself can go no further. Despite the urgent situation, Julius saves Paul and, on his account, the other prisoners from the soldiers' fears about escapees. In the end, despite the circumstances, all 276 persons aboard the ship reach shore safely.

a. Grounding the Ship (27:39–41)

Attempting to ground the ship proves partially successful in that the voyagers move closer to the beach (27:39–40), but the ship ultimately wrecks perilously before reaching shore (27:41), which maintains suspense.

i. Spying a Beach (27:39)

Even if they could still not see the sun (27:20), this limitation would not impose zero visibility; storms can obscure the sun without shrouding all its light. An island could mean salvation to a storm-tossed ship at sea (e.g., Apollod. *Bib.* 1.9.26). Their attempt to reach the beach is what we would expect, and might even fulfill Paul's warning that they would "run aground" on an island (Acts 27:26); it turns out, however, that the running aground occurs at a reef before the beach (27:41). Luke employs different nautical terms in both cases; the prophecy to Paul does not specify where they will run aground, nor does it obviate the importance of human effort and cooperation along the way (27:31).

Malta has a number of natural bays, including a large bay on the southeast and a number further north on the eastern coast. One is a place of two harbors, with modern Valletta between them; 7.5 miles (12 km.) farther north is "St. Paul's Bay."[948] The three fairly large northern bays on Malta, toward the northwest, are (moving northward) Salina Bay, Saint Paul's Bay, and Mellieha Bay.[949]

Today Saint Paul's Bay on northeast Malta lacks a good beach;[950] also, the sea level may now be three to five feet (1–1.5 m.) higher at places than in Paul's day.[951] But on

---

945. Rapske, "Travel," 35, following esp. Rickman, "Grain Trade," 261, 265; cf. Hirschfeld, "Ship of Paul," 28 (also citing Rickman). On methods for keeping grain dry on ancient ships, see Fitzgerald, "Ship of Paul," 37–38.

946. Davis, "Navigation," 229.

947. When ships were destroyed, the creditors who underwrote the loans had to assume responsibility (Millett, "Maritime Loans"; Krampe, "Fenus nauticum," 381). Some even willfully sabotaged unprofitable ships to escape the debt (Philost. *Vit. Apoll.* 4.32). In some sources, however, the pilot and owner received shares of the profit (Wilson, personal correspondence, Oct. 13, 2014).

948. Finegan, *Apostles*, 200.

949. Ibid., 202.

950. Conzelmann, *Acts*, 220. Topographic changes may account for this, but we do not know much about the condition of the beach even in the narrative.

951. Finegan, *Apostles*, 202 (noting that possible approaches to the bay nevertheless cohere fairly well with the soundings of Acts 27:28).

the whole the topography fits Luke's description, and the vast majority of scholars currently accept this identification.[952] (Some have argued this especially from the place of two seas in 27:41,[953] but some other data, such as the proximity of Kouros to Saint Paul's Bay, seem stronger.) Some point to "a flat strand on the southwestern side of the bay" as where the sailors may have attempted to run the ship aground, "and a sandbank just inside the entrance, locally called St. Paul's Bank, could be where the ship" grounded.[954] Luke's audience might recall the beach in 21:5, where Christians knelt with Paul to send him off to face danger; here the narrative recalls that he has survived many dangers. It is possible that a beach appears in both passages, however, simply because some places where sea and land meet have beaches, including these two locations.

Malta was a common stopping point for Alexandrian grain ships,[955] but even if some of the sailors might have recognized the main harbor in good weather, they were approaching the island from a very different direction and not coming to a major port.[956]

II. Trying to Reach Shore (27:40)

To reach shore safely required maximum effort all at once, with nothing held back in reserve; they would have at most one opportunity to bring the ship to land, and if they failed, there would not be another. The sailors attempted three complex maneuvers together: releasing the stern anchors, releasing the rudder, and raising a sail.[957]

First, they had to release the anchors on both sides of the stern. They apparently simply cut them and released them into the sea, perhaps for the sake of urgency; at this point there could be no concern about preserving them for reuse at a later time.[958] Another first-century Mediterranean shipwreck reveals that the crew dropped five identical anchors in a straight line. On the basis of this evidence, one analyst (who thinks that Luke's other details sound authentic) suggests that Paul's ship likewise dropped the anchors in succession, intending to hold the ship in place until they could save even the ship. On this view, the problem was that through the night, three of the four anchor ropes gave way, requiring the sailors to release the final one during daybreak.[959] Although Luke was not a sailor and could have easily conflated some details (he sometimes does this on land as well),[960] he was aware of the general anxiety of those on board, eager for day (27:29).[961] Since Luke

952. E.g., Packer, *Acts*, 214; Schnabel, *Acts*, 1044; note the summary of opinion in R. Williams, *Acts*, 164; this is the case, apparently, even with Haenchen (*Acts*, 707). An underwater survey for wrecks along the Maltese coast might provide more objective data, but this ship's remains could have been swept out to sea (with much of its cargo having been discarded), especially over the centuries; and if a first-century ship were found, we could not be certain that it was Paul's.

953. Heutger, "Paulus auf Malta," argues for Mellieha Bay (the bay just north of the traditional Saint Paul's Bay and not far south of the South Comino Channel separating Malta from the island of Comino) especially from διθάλασσον in Acts 27:41, but the sense of the term remains disputed; see comment on Acts 27:41.

954. Finegan, *Apostles*, 202.

955. See Friedländer, *Life*, 1:352; Casson, *Mariners*, 208. This is true even if it was not part of "the normal shipping route" (Haenchen, *Acts*, 707). Malta and Sicily were major targets for Alexandrian ships sailing from Crete, but reaching either by accident or mere coincidence would be difficult; together they comprised only roughly 5 percent "of the horizon as viewed from the western end of Crete" (Davis, "Navigation," 224).

956. With Larkin, *Acts*, 376.

957. Cf. Hemer, *Acts in History*, 150–51; Conzelmann, *Acts*, 220; Johnson, *Acts*, 455–56.

958. Barrett, *Acts*, 1212, suggests that the anchors were released from the ropes, but simply releasing the ropes would be the simpler maneuver.

959. Throckmorton, "Shipwrecks, Anchors, and Paul," 80.

960. If there would be confused and forgotten details in his eyewitness account, this could be the place to look for them: Luke might well have stowed any notes in a waterproof container by this point (though this action could also come after it is clear the ship is sinking in Acts 27:41).

961. See Rapske, "Travel," 34n150.

(or, according to other views, his source) was there and we were not, he may be correct even on this detail: they did not trust the anchors to hold indefinitely and preferred to attempt reaching land by day. A prophet (Paul) had also mentioned grounding on an island (27:26), which they might construe as reason for this attempt to come closer.

Second, they unbound the rudders, which had been tied to prevent unwelcome movement. Now they would need the rudders to steer as best they could toward the beach, a difficult maneuver. Ancient ships used "steering-paddles" or oars as rudders and had two, joined by a crossbar but controlled by one helmsman.[962] The helmsman would pull the long tiller toward him or push it away to control the two steering oars.[963] The sailors may have removed these paddles from the water when they were not being used and lashed them to the hull with ropes.[964] Some scholars think that here instead they dismantled the steering, allowing the wind to drive the ship.[965] Although this would be an interesting point theologically (cf. the design of the "arks" in Gen 6–8 and Exod 2:3, depending completely on God), it is a far less likely way to construe the words.[966]

Third, they hoisted a sail,[967] undoubtedly a foresail (see BDAG, s.v. ἀρτέμων),[968] to catch wind toward the beach and enable them to maneuver. The ship probably had two masts; the second, the smaller foresail (the artemon) at the bow, was used for both steering and driving.[969] When a ship was slowing down, as when it was approaching harbor, the artemon might be removed;[970] here, however, they need all possible speed to reach land while they can.

III. Grounded Perilously (27:41)

Luke displays his literary skill by directly evoking Greek literary traditions. Although Luke uses πλοῖον in all his other fourteen references to vessels on the voyage to Rome, his term for the ship here, ναῦς, may well evoke older usage,[971] and the verb ἐπικέλλω was poetic. Neither term appears elsewhere in the NT or in the Apostolic Fathers, but they appear together in Hom. Od. 9.148, 546 (cf. also 13.113–14), as

962. BDAG, s.v. πηδάλιον (following Casson, Ships [1971 ed.], 224n2). On control by the κυβερνήτης, see, e.g., Lucian Indictment 2; on more than one rudder, see, e.g., Dio Chrys. Or. 75.10; Lucian Ship 6; on two rudders per ship controlled by the κυβερνήτης, see, e.g., Dio Chrys. Or. 77/78.7.

963. Casson, Mariners, 194; for the steering oars as early as the sixth century B.C.E., see p. 77. The irony of one person keeping the ship safe through a single tiller was not lost on ancients (e.g., Lucian Ship 6; Indictment 2; cf. Jas 3:4); on failure to use the rudder to steer the ship, leading to shipwreck, see, e.g., Apul. Flor. 23.2 (for the danger of an oversize rudder, see Apul. Apol. 19). One improvement in the Middle Ages was the replacement of the steering oars with a "handier stern rudder" (Casson, Mariners, 218).

964. Rapske, "Travel," 33; the ropes used on ships were made of "flax, hemp, papyrus, or esparto grass" (Casson, Mariners, 193). Ships that lost their rudders might still survive except in a storm (Dio Chrys. Or. 75.10), but merchant ships probably had additional oars for emergencies (Casson, Mariners, 192).

965. Cf. Barrett, Acts, 1212.

966. Cf. Johnson, Acts, 455–56.

967. Casson, Mariners, 193, notes, "Sails were chiefly of linen, usually of oblong blocks of cloth sewn together . . . ; the edges were secured by a boltrope . . . and the corners reinforced by leather patches." In earlier times, too, the sails were made of linen (40).

968. The artemon, which projected over the ship's bows, was the foresail (Casson, Mariners, 194); although first explicitly attested in Roman times, it undoubtedly goes back to Hellenistic times (p. 190; cf. 79, 158). Most sails were square, but the foresail was triangular (195) and slightly smaller than the mainsail (79).

969. Rapske, "Travel," 33. Large grain vessels could include two square sails (the large mainsail and a smaller sail); the foremast was slanted at an angle (Jeffers, World, 38). Bruce, Commentary, 467, compares Juv. Sat. 12.68–69.

970. Casson, Mariners, 194.

971. Aune, Environment, 129, calls it "obsolete," but it recurs in contemporary texts (BDAG cites Philo Eternity 138; Jos. Life 165; Sib. Or. 8.348). Padilla, "Παιδεία," 430, cites its usage in papyri.

scholars widely note.[972] The verb for the prow's[973] "sticking fast," ἐρείδω, also appears in Homer.[974] Ancient writers liked to describe ships crashing into rocky land,[975] perhaps the way modern action viewers are enamored of spectacular explosions. Apparently, however, many relished the literary opportunity more than Luke did. For example: "Our vessel . . . drove unexpectedly on to a rock hidden under water, and was utterly broken in pieces; as she slipped off the rock the mast fell on one side, breaking up part of her and carrying the rest beneath the water."[976]

To claim that Luke borrows appropriate literary language to describe an event is not to claim that he invented the event itself; he simply recognizes it as a good story that merits worthy telling. His account here is plausible, though the details remain obscured by the debate over the exact path through which they drove the ship (i.e., which proposal is *more* plausible), an uncertainty fueled by two millennia of geological change.[977] Is διθάλασσον here a flow of water between land masses or a strip of land between water? Despite James Smith's careful examination of the topography, the term more likely indicates the latter, something like a sandbar.[978]

Smith viewed it as a channel, no more than a hundred yards wide, between the island of Salmonetta, which shelters Saint Paul's Bay on the northwest, and Malta's mainland.[979] (The "two seas" might then mean the place where the Mediterranean Sea meets the bay, although this seems an odd way to describe the bay.) A ship entering this channel would strike mud graduating into clay, which could explain the prow's being immobilized.[980] But why would any crew try to navigate their ship through such a narrow passage, given their efforts to bring the ship under control (Acts 27:40)?[981]

The place of two seas is probably a sandbar, shoal, promontory, or some other ridge dividing the water.[982] This could be Saint Paul's Bank; the shoal is twelve meters underwater but was probably more substantial two millennia ago.[983] In any case, instead of reaching the island's shore they struck another body, wedging in the front of the ship so that they could not advance. Meanwhile, the stern lay exposed to the full force of the waves, which at this location are particularly violent. If the ship could

---

972. Aune, *Environment*, 129; Conzelmann, *Acts*, 221; Praeder, "Acts 27:1–28:16," 701; Witherington, *Acts*, 764. Padilla, "Παιδεία," 430, questions whether it is a deliberate imitation of Homer or simply reflects familiarity with the term used there. For the verb, BDAG adds Ap. Rhod. 1.1362; 2.352.

973. Some prows were rounded whereas others projected forward (Casson, *Mariners*, 192, 195), but most were rounded and, like sterns, "curved upward in graceful arcs" (192; for earlier versions of prows and sterns, see 76–77).

974. Conzelmann, *Acts*, 221 (comparing also the Latin phrase in Virg. *Aen.* 5.206, where a prow stuck fast). BDAG provides many references; perhaps most relevant is Pindar *Pyth.* 10.51–52.

975. Johnson, *Acts*, 449–50, cites Dio Chrys. *Or.* 7.2; Lucian *Posts* 2; *True Story* 1.6; Ach. Tat. 3.4. In Lucian *Posts* 1–2, sailors spin yarns of ships breaking up and survivors swimming ashore.

976. Ach. Tat. 3.4.3 (LCL, 143).

977. Fitzmyer, *Acts*, 782, notes that there are five proposals, though he favors "the northwest side of the strait near St. Paul's Islands."

978. See BDAG (viewing it as a point of land jutting out with the sea on either side; BDAG notes that it occurs in, e.g., Strabo 1.1.8; 2.5.22; Dio Chrys. *Or.* 5.9; *Sib. Or.* 5.334). The context in Dio Chrys. *Or.* 5.9, where the LCL translates διθάλαττα as "cross-currents" (LCL, 1:239), refers to shoals (*Or.* 5.8–10, esp. 5.9), as probably here.

979. Smith, *Voyage*, 143–47; followed by Bruce, *Commentary*, 518.

980. Smith, *Voyage*, 144; followed by Bruce, *Commentary*, 518; Hemer, *Acts in History*, 151. The beach did not quite fit, but Smith could explain this as due to erosion (Hemer, *Acts in History*, 150).

981. Witherington, *Acts*, 774.

982. Munck, *Acts*, 251; Conzelmann, *Acts*, 220; Johnson, *Acts*, 456; Larkin, *Acts*, 376–77; Witherington, *Acts*, 774; earlier, cf. Bede *Comm. Acts* 27:41a.

983. Witherington, *Acts*, 774; cf. Conzelmann, *Acts*, 220. Fitzmyer, *Acts*, 780, suggests that instead the term means "a place subject to crosswinds, rather than a geographical spot."

not advance to shore, those on board would have to do so without the ship if they hoped to survive (27:42–44).

As for the fate of the ship, some of its planks disappeared immediately (27:44); at lower sea level and in a less rainy season, local inhabitants might have salvaged some of the wood, since the ship was not far from shore.

b. All Survive (27:42–44)

Not only does Julius spare the prisoners for Paul's sake; as God promised, God spares all aboard for Paul's sake, making Paul a benefactor par excellence.[984] The survival of many this close to shore might be likely, in any case, but the survival of all without exception (including the aged, the infirm, and perhaps children), especially in their weakened state (27:33), is utterly extraordinary apart from divine intervention, just as Paul promised. In contrast to tragic narratives, Luke's storm scene has a happy upturn at the end.

i. Killing the Prisoners (27:42)

The prisoners could hardly escape if chained;[985] but neither could they swim to shore if chained, and so the alternative to killing them would be either to let them drown (and hope that none could break free unsupervised)[986] or to unchain them and risk their escape. Obviously no one could accompany them to shore and keep them under guard during the flight. If prisoners drowned and their bodies were not recovered, they would still be considered unaccounted for, risking the suspicion that they might have escaped (and presumably, by now the centurion, at least, trusts Paul's expectation that all will survive, 27:24). The reader may recall that Paul's influence apparently prevented an escape before (16:28), but the soldiers in the narrative world would not know about that.

Luke knows that some soldiers might seek their own interests (Luke 3:14). The soldiers' plan to kill the prisoners[987] may have seemed reasonable to them if most of the prisoners were slated to be fed to beasts in Rome anyway; death by sword might seem more merciful. But they were not taking Paul into consideration.[988] Though charged with a capital offense, he had not been convicted, may have been sent with instructions for generous treatment (cf. Acts 24:23; 26:31–32), may have appeared to hold significant status, was not a likely escape threat (he had, after all, appealed to Caesar), and had said that his God wanted him to appear before Caesar. But consistency might suggest treating all the prisoners the same way; Julius may have a difficult time explaining why he spared one prisoner while killing the others. Thus

---

984. That this portrayal has apologetic value need not be doubted; reliable characters in Luke's narrative portray as immoral their arraignments for benefactions (Acts 4:9; 24:17; cf. 26:6–7).

985. See the objection of Haenchen, *Acts*, 708.

986. Soldiers could be beaten if a captive committed suicide; if the death was by accident, as could happen when one was swimming to shore, this must be proved by witnesses (Rapske, *Custody*, 32). Given the public and potentially deadly circumstances, they would need only prove that the prisoners died; but death by sword was counted more merciful than death by drowning (on the horror of capital punishment by drowning, see, e.g., Val. Max. 1.1.13; Livy 1.51.9; further discussion at Acts 27:20).

987. Ambrosiaster *Commentary on Paul's Epistles* (Vogels, 294–95; Bray, *Corinthians*, 298) reads this danger into Paul's earlier ministry (2 Cor 11:26).

988. Like the centurion (though not as close to Paul), the soldiers apparently respected Paul as a divine agent (Acts 27:31–32); on the religious interests of many soldiers, see comment on Acts 10:2. But even if they appreciated the hope that he provided, his prophecy of survival remained to be tested, and even if they were grateful, they might value their own lives more than his. Or they might have excepted Paul, but the centurion recognized that, once in Rome, they might not be able to readily explain the inconsistency.

Paul is indirectly responsible for preserving (or at least prolonging) the lives of his fellow prisoners.[989]

Guards might prefer suicide to court-martial for the charge of dereliction of duty (Acts 16:27; Petron. *Sat.* 112); most commentators note the Roman custom of the guard's responsibility for his prisoners, a custom that Luke's attentive readers in particular will surely recall (cf. Acts 12:18–19).[990] Justinian's later code formalized the principle that a guard whose prisoner escaped would fulfill the prisoner's sentence (Justin. *Cod.* 9.4.4).[991] The degree of penalty was, however, connected with the measure of the guard's culpability[992] and the significance of the prisoner(s). Thus, for example, if a slave escaped, the guard simply had to compensate the slaveholder for the loss.[993] The shipwreck and storm would probably be sufficient to absolve the soldiers of legal liability for any of the prisoners escaping, but if they failed to prove this, they could be executed for negligence.[994] Given such stakes and given the unpredictability and political considerations of superiors, it could appear safer to kill the prisoners.

They could do so, however, only if the centurion acquiesced; moreover, they may have felt that they could not justify sparing prisoners selectively;[995] unlike higher magistrates, even the centurion was not technically authorized to make such choices. Even the centurion apparently did not value the other prisoners enough to spare them if Paul were not there.[996] Again, this concern is understandable; although they might evade punishment for an escaped prisoner under the circumstances, there was no point taking such a risk with potentially arbitrary officials, given the stakes. Julius is ready to venture the minimal risk to their lives, however, to protect Paul.[997] Knowing what he now knows about Paul, he might count angering Paul's powerful deity a more proximate risk. His recognition of Paul's special spiritual status here contrasts with his neglect of Paul's counsel in 27:11.[998]

ii. Swimming Ashore (27:43)

The centurion wishes to "save" (διασῶσαι) Paul; ironically, Paul is the cause of all those aboard being "saved" (the same verb) as well (Acts 27:44; 28:1). By sparing Paul, the centurion becomes an agent fulfilling God's promise to Paul (27:24), just as some other Roman officers have been (21:32; 23:24).

Julius acts courageously. Centurions who crossed their soldiers in emergency situations sometimes incurred grave hostility. Centurions had the responsibility for discipline in the Roman army and could beat soldiers; many soldiers therefore hated them and, in mutinies, sometimes killed them.[999] These soldiers, however, seem to

989. As also he is the agent of preserving all those aboard in Acts 27:24, 31–32 (Abbott, *Acts*, 257).

990. E.g., Munck, *Acts*, 114; Ramsay, "Roads and Travel," 386; Bruce, *Commentary*, 519; Dunn, *Acts*, 342. When an entire unit was blamed for a military failure, the majority might be required to club to death a small percentage of the unit, selected by lot (Le Bohec, "Decimatio").

991. Fitzmyer, *Acts*, 780. Cf. an analogous idea in 1 Kgs 20:39–40.

992. People were not criminally liable for accidents (Robinson, *Criminal Law*, 16); intention was necessary for a crime (16–17, 49).

993. Rapske, *Custody*, 30. A guard lacked custodial liability if an object was destroyed by an "act of god" ("Custodia," 1029, though addressing the law of obligations, not prisoners).

994. Rapske, *Custody*, 271.

995. Ibid.

996. Ibid.

997. A centurion who befriended a prisoner might rejoice at his survival (Jos. *Ant.* 18.231) so long as this did not risk the centurion's own life (18.232–33). Luke contrasts the centurion's "purpose" (27:43) with that of the soldiers by employing a noun and participle that are both cognate to the noun in 27:42.

998. Agreeing with Lang, "Self," 171.

999. Le Bohec, "Disciplina," 538 (citing Tac. *Ann.* 1.17.4; 1.18.1; 1.23.3–4; 1.32.1); for wanting to kill their leaders, e.g., Tac. *Hist.* 4.36; for killing the strictest centurions, Tac. *Hist.* 1.80. For mutinies and near

be on better terms with their centurion, and may even concur with his decision (cf. 27:31–32).[1000]

The soldiers could not well carry the prisoners to land in the water, even if they trusted them to come voluntarily. (The proposed view that some escaped not on "things from the ship" but "people from the ship"[1001] in 27:44 is implausible;[1002] "from the ship" here is extraneous if Luke refers to people.) Once some soldiers had reached land (27:43), it might be difficult for prisoners emerging from the water to get past them (27:42)—though admittedly not at all impossible, given the number of passengers (27:37) and likely reduced visibility (cf. 28:2; earlier, 27:20). The soldiers presumably could not have brought their swords if trying to swim instead of floating on wood,[1003] but they perhaps could count on other passengers cooperating with them rather than with the prisoners.[1004]

Although the centurion's orders here respond to the concern of the soldiers in 27:42 (and hence address soldiers and prisoners), Luke may also depict him as issuing these orders to everyone on board (since "in this way," οὕτως—through the people's swimming or paddling or riding wave-propelled planks to shore—"all" came safely to land in 27:44; perhaps relevant even if the advice narrowly concerns the prisoners, as some might infer from the third person). The pilot and the captain once wielded the most authority on board (27:11), but Paul's advice, executed through the centurion, now proves the primary political force on board. As noted above, a centurion would not control a ship's nautical matters; he would, however, control the only fully armed contingent on board and would thus wield considerable power in such an emergency. Julius is now exercising his emergency authority in the service of one whom he regards as giving God's instructions (27:24), as already in 27:31–32. The survival of everyone vindicates this wisdom (27:44). Luke's point seems to be that God made his agent known and that even a worldly authority could have the sense to act on the truth that agent offered. Julius's own initiative may also serve a function in fulfilling the divine purpose here.

Swimming, especially in such waters, could demonstrate physical prowess,[1005] but

---

mutinies, see, e.g., Vell. Paterc. 2.125.2; Quint. Curt. 4.10.4; 6.2.4; 7.2.31 (averted in 6.6.12; 7.1.4); Appian *Bell. civ.* 5.13.127–29; Tac. *Hist.* 1.80; 2.30, 44, 68; 3.21; 4.46, 56; *Agr.* 16; see also Campbell, "Mutiny." Syrian auxiliaries, some of whom may be present in this mission from Caesarea, may have been particularly prone to mutiny (Fronto *Pr. Hist.* 12). For complaints, see, e.g., Sherk, §67, pp. 107–8 (P.Fouad 1.21; P.Yale 1528; from 63 C.E.). But money could help secure soldiers' loyalty (Polyb. 11.25.8–10; Hdn. 4.7.4; 6.8.8; Jos. *Ant.* 19.129; cf. Appian *Hist. rom.* 7.1.2; Pliny *Ep.* 7.31.2; Suet. *Jul.* 67–69; Jos. *Life* 78); their own financial need sometimes generated their unrest (Xen. *Anab.* 7.6.11–22; 7.7.48; Polyb. 5.50.1; Diod. Sic. 33.22.1; Appian *Hist. rom.* 3.1.2; *Bell. civ.* 5.3.18; Tac. *Hist.* 4.19). On soldiers' pay, see discussion at Acts 10:2. Centurions and tribunes also made special targets for enemies (e.g., Tac. *Ann.* 12.17). Suetonius may depict the current emperor, Nero, as indulging the military more than did his successor (Suet. *Nero* 8; 10; 43; *Vesp.* 8; cf. Luke, "Ideology").

1000. Soldiers could also prove loyal to their centurions (see, e.g., Tac. *Hist.* 2.60).

1001. E.g., Hanson, *Acts*, 251; Barrett, *Acts*, 1215 (the μέν . . . δέ construction he cites does not affect the question of whether the "others" from the ship are human); cf. Haenchen, *Acts*, 708n8; Witherington, *Acts*, 774n103 (who regards this view as "less likely").

1002. Modern forms of lifesaving do not appear to have been widely known. Stories of boys or others riding dolphins' backs (e.g., Hdt. 1.24) are not relevant to human lifesaving; one could definitely not go on another's back (Ael. Arist. *Def. Or.* 376, §125D); a lover might be able to rescue only his beloved's body (Xen. Eph. *Anthia* 3.2).

1003. In Lucian *True Story* 2.47, the survivors of shipwreck managed to swim out with their weapons, but as a parody, this description may not pretend realism on this matter. Preparing to swim or fight, Caesar stripped but "bound a dagger to his thigh" (Vell. Paterc. 2.43.2, LCL).

1004. Vulnerable shipwreck survivors would not be inclined to trust potential criminals (cf. Phaedrus 4.23.16, depicting robbers looting what shipwreck survivors had salvaged).

1005. E.g., Jos. *Life* 15; Hom. *Od.* 5.388–89, 399, 438–41; 7.276–77, 280–81; 23.23–38; Keener, *John*, 1230; idem, "Vigor," 564 (and cf. 567–68). Le Cornu, *Acts*, 1473, notes that the rabbis required fathers to

it would prove too difficult for many. Soldiers at sea sometimes had to swim; in one naval battle, only those Athenians who swam ashore escaped alive (Thucyd. 2.90.5).[1006] Survival for those swimming to safety could be viewed as providential. When a ship was going down, those in it who were wise should throw themselves overboard and swim to safety (Corn. Nep. 12 [Chabrias], 4.3), leaving behind anything that could weigh them down (Phaedrus 4.23.11–15).[1007] In one probably true account,[1008] a friend jumped into the sea to save his friend who fell overboard; through most of the night they floated on corks, but toward daybreak they found the gangplank, then floated on that to land.[1009] Although those who were shipwrecked had to try to swim, they often drowned instead.[1010] Perhaps Julius expects the healthier people to swim ashore first so that they can help to receive others coming ashore, or intends to keep the waters less congested with bodies aiming for the same stretch of land. (Survival would appear much easier here, however, with waves washing people ashore, than were they in the deep sea.)

III. FLOATING ASHORE (27:44)

Some would be unable to swim, if for no other reason than that they are weakened from hunger (27:33). Most have also had little sleep, likely including during the night they have just endured (if we may read παρεκάλει in Acts 27:33 with its full force, Paul has been exhorting them before dawn). They had eaten nothing for fourteen days (27:33) and needed strength even to digest the food they had eaten that night (27:36, 38). The ability to struggle at all underlines the miracle contained in everyone surviving. That people could make such an effort, however, is believable.[1011]

After weeks of uncertainty about survival and inability to eat, the survivors are undoubtedly quite traumatized and their nerves on edge.[1012] But no one could help but marvel that even the weakest have survived (out of 276 persons, 27:37) or that Paul predicted this survival (27:24). By this point, presumably nearly everyone aboard would regard Paul as a hero with special power from God (cf. his favor with God in 27:23–24). Thus it is not surprising that only the locals suspect him of being an object of divine vengeance (28:4), that Julius would share hospitality extended to himself with Paul and his companions (28:7), or that word would spread quickly about Paul's supernatural abilities (28:8–9).

---

teach their sons swimming (b. Qidd. 29a; 30b; Eccl. Rab. 9:9, §1). Given Paul's age, he may have floated on something instead, but he did have some water survival experience (2 Cor 11:25). Swimming was rarely done as a sport, but it was a skill for fishing and other activities and, apparently, often done like the modern crawl, with alternating strokes (Decker, "Swimming").

1006. For a later escape from battle by diving (here into a river) and swimming, see Val. Max. 3.2.11; the British auxiliaries, living near the sea, had notable facility in swimming (Tac. Agr. 18). Swimmers were sometimes preserved in the sea (Dio Chrys. Or. 64.10); sometimes those who fell overboard have made it safely to land (e.g., Dio Chrys. [if genuine] Or. 63.4).

1007. In Lucian True Story 2.47, the shipwrecked people carried whatever they could while swimming, but it is not clear that this is intended to be realistic.

1008. Lucian Tox. 21 claims that the swimmers remained alive in Athens when he wrote. In another likely true account, Agrippina, though injured, swam to the safety of some small boats in Tac. Ann. 14.5.

1009. Lucian Tox. 20–21. Cf. Paul's night in the sea in 2 Cor 11:25.

1010. E.g., Hom. Od. 23.233–38 (most died); Livy 28.36.12; Prop. Eleg. 2.26.1–2; Longus 1.30; Xen. Eph. Anthia 3.2. For the dangers of swimmers' drowning, see the story of Hero and Leander (e.g., in Musaeus Hero; alluded to, e.g., in Fronto Ad M. Caes. 3.13.3).

1011. My wife, who fled war as a refugee, informs me that she saw weakened people muster a final burst of strength if they were fleeing death.

1012. In today's language, we would expect them all to be suffering from post-traumatic stress syndrome for some time afterward.

Presumably neither the swimmers nor the paddlers had to dive from deck (for all the narrative's action, Luke offers no explicit indication that the ship was sinking rapidly in 27:41); more likely, they climbed down ropes into the frigid waters. Assuming that the ship grounded in a shoal, the swimmers would be moving from shallow to deep to shallow water again, but in poor weather conditions. Presumably the planks were from the ship. Wreckage from the stern would fit other narratives but reduce the certainty of all paddlers having access to them;[1013] the other possibility is wood deliberately taken from the ship before descending. These might be pieces of a mast or other items,[1014] but this is not the usual sense of σανίς (board);[1015] some scholars have suggested that they were boards used in the cargo hold for storing grain.[1016]

Those who survived shipwrecks, both in fact and in fiction, sometimes remained afloat by holding on to timbers from their broken ships.[1017] Such timbers were notoriously flimsy, however (e.g., *Apoll. K. Tyre* 12), so that a weak argument in court was compared to a piece of a broken ship (Val. Max. 8.1.abs.12). After a shipwreck near shore, it could be expected that many things would be washed ashore; this was common enough to merit mention in law.[1018]

Despite the disadvantages of the rough weather, waves would help propel people toward the shore. The Mediterranean Sea lacks tides in the technical sense applied to oceans, but storms can generate swells that today are used even for surfing off some parts of the coast of Malta, including Mellieha Bay. Especially given its modern topography, Saint Paul's Bay would not be useful for surfing, but floating would be a different matter. The momentum of waves propels to shore whatever rides them.[1019]

iv. Luke's Notes? (27:44)

Some scholars have reasonably argued that any of Luke's notes taken in Judea would have been lost during the attempt to reach shore.[1020] Papyrus is not waterproof,[1021] and preserving it would require putting the document in a waterproof container "such as

1013. Certainly, ancients envisioned shipwrecks in which only some could have access to planks (note the philosophic debate regarding which of two swimmers should retain the one plank in Berthelot, "Problem," 171–83).

1014. In a false story of Odysseus, he survived ten days in the sea by clinging to his destroyed ship's mast (Hom. *Od.* 14.310–15).

1015. See the cognates in lxx Exod 27:8; 2 Kgs 12:9; 3 Macc 4:10; Song 8:9; Ezek 27:5. One relevant sense is a ship's deck (as in 3 Macc 4:10), though tearing boards loose may have been difficult unless some had already been battered; wooden writing tablets would be too small for help.

1016. BDAG (citing Breusing, *Nautik*, 203).

1017. E.g., Hom. *Od.* 5.371; Ovid *Metam.* 11.559–61; Xen. Eph. *Anthia* 2.11; Lucian *Tox.* 20 (an apparently true story); *Apoll. K. Tyre* 12 (though most who grasped timbers nevertheless perished). Praeder, "Acts 27:1–28:16," 701, cites some of the same texts and also Ach. Tat. 3.4.6–5.3 (Conzelmann, *Acts*, 221, also cites Xen. Eph. *Anthia* 2.11.10; to this, Johnson, *Acts*, 456, adds *Test. Naph.* 6:6).

1018. Stealing during the confusion of shipwreck was a more severe crime than looting things washed up on shore (Robinson, *Criminal Law*, 35; this differs from robbing shipwreck survivors, as in Phaedrus 4.23.16). In severe shipwrecks, however, even the wood might prove unsalvageable (Dio Chrys. *Or.* 7.51–52).

1019. Jennifer A. Miskov, personal correspondence, May 22–23, 2014 (Miskov's PhD is in history, but she has extensive earlier experience as a surfer). Googling "surfing" + "Malta" yields information about sites (e.g., http://www.yourcarhiremalta.com/water-sports/surfing-malta/). Miskov adds (May 22, 2014), "Unless there is an undertow in a certain part, which is unlikely, the high surf will push people to shore and build momentum for them to get there. Also, sandbar means shallow water which also means bigger and more powerful waves breaking in that spot."

1020. Cf. Porter, *Paul in Acts*, 38 (though this would also undermine Porter's own thesis of the source).

1021. Though it is durable. Papyrus in book collections lasted, on average, for "a useful life of between one hundred and two hundred years" (Houston, "Evidence," 251), and some were used for more than five centuries (250).

a jar with a cork lid, sealed with tar or wax."[1022] Had he carried papyrus with him on the voyage, it would become moldy if it became damp. People recycled papyrus by washing its surface with a sponge.[1023] If Luke used papyrus, he could have employed the sort of papyrus, developed in Claudius's era, that was superior to most of our ordinary papyri,[1024] but it was still not waterproof.[1025]

For several reasons, however, it is better to argue that Luke had notes and that they survived. One argument is an analogy that is at best inconclusive: Caesar is said to have preserved papers while swimming away from the enemy to the nearest ship. He supposedly preserved the papers by holding up his left hand all the way, at the same time pulling his cloak in his teeth lest it fall into enemy hands (Suet. *Jul.* 64).[1026] Even assuming that the water was calm, however, and noting the short distance (two hundred paces), this was an extraordinary maneuver;[1027] challenges to its plausibility[1028] are reasonable. It is possible that the story depends on a genuine core amplified by Caesar's typical boasting and others' praises; at the least, it is another example of someone swimming to safety (or waiting until it arrived). But (assuming a prone position rather than lying on one's back) even staying afloat in still water while awaiting help appears difficult with one hand kept above water.[1029]

There are stronger arguments. First, although much of Luke's account is general enough to simply reflect his memory, his "we" itineraries are more detailed and seem to serve no other purpose than a factual one.[1030] This probably includes even the details of the voyage in Acts 27, although it is possible that he could simply reconstruct these from memory because they were recent when he had occasion to record them again afterward. This first argument is the most important because,

---

1022. Porter, *Paul in Acts*, 38–39n95. Casson, *Mariners*, 170, writes of amphoras used for transporting liquids, sometimes sealed by a cork stopper but more frequently one of "fired clay, set in mortar" (see also Docter, "Transport Amphorae," 860–61, noting airtight containers much earlier than this period; for vast numbers of amphoras of oil imported to Rome, see also Lobell, "Talk"). In the ancient Near East (Wartke, "Pitch," 304, from the fifth or fourth millennium B.C.E.) and widely in the Greco-Roman world (Burford-Cooper, "Pitch," 305, including on "ship-timber"), pitch was used to seal substances against water. Even those stopped with cork, however, could not be used by Luke (even if they were dry inside): most were more than 3 ft. (1 m.) high; made of clay, the most common size weighed 50 or more pounds (23–24 kg.) even empty (Casson, *Mariners*, 170; Greeks' "largest clay storage vessel" could exceed a man's height, Docter, "Pithos," 306). These were too big, too heavy, too wet on the inside, and too hard to reseal. Luke's container would thus have to be smaller (see discussion below), but these amphoras do illustrate that watertight containers existed.

1023. Porter, *Paul in Acts*, 38–39n95. For the danger of dampness to papyrus, see, e.g., Galen *Grief* 19. Papyrus was available mainly from Egypt (Pliny E. *N.H.* 13.22.71; Ps.-Callisth. *Alex.* 1.8; for some elsewhere, see Pliny E. *N.H.* 13.22.72); on its manufacture, see Pliny E. *N.H.* 13.23.74–13.24.82 (esp. 13.23.74–77); Dimarogonas, "Pliny on Papyrus"; Aune, *Dictionary of Rhetoric*, 328. For writing on it with a reed pen, see, e.g., Milligan, *Thessalonians*, 121–24; Cary and Haarhoff, *Life*, 168; Bruce, *Books*, 13; Richards, *Letter Writing*, 29. Papyrus was also thought to have medicinal use (Pliny E. *N.H.* 24.51.88).

1024. See Pliny E. *N.H.* 13.24.79 (noting that the inferior kind dominant in Augustus's reign was still used for ordinary correspondence, 13.24.80; most surviving papyri from Egypt would be the latter). Luke might have used the superior material for a book draft (though regular papyrus for mere notes).

1025. Dampness caused a wealthy second-century writer's papyri to decompose and stick together; see Galen *Grief* 19.

1026. Sometimes, if one needed to swim, one would entrust one's short tunic to a servant (Theophr. *Char.* 25.2), and so the idea of pulling a heavier cloak in water (especially if it was wool) is startling.

1027. Plutarch, recounting the same story, allows that "it is said" that Caesar protected the papers, claiming that arrows were falling around him (*Caes.* 49.4).

1028. E.g., Porter, *Paul in Acts*, 38n95.

1029. Nevertheless, Jennifer A. Miskov, who has considerable experience as a swimmer and surfer, informs me that holding one hand high in deep water is easily possible for a person who knows how to swim or even dog-paddle. At my request, she even carried out the maneuver to demonstrate that it was not difficult (personal correspondence, Oct. 19, 2014). How dry one could keep papers, between waves and splashing, is a different question (Oct. 20, 2014).

1030. See Keener, *Acts*, 3:2350–74.

whereas other arguments establish only the possibility of such notes, this one makes them likely.

Second, Luke has had a couple weeks (27:33) to consider the possibility of (at best) a difficult landing, and at least a night to consider it seriously. He could have obtained a watertight container if he did not have one (there would be sealable containers for other purposes on board, though most in the hold would be too heavy to try to take to shore),[1031] and once the stern started breaking up (27:41), he could have secured his most important documents in the container before climbing down into the sea.[1032] Mark Wilson suggests that "waterproof skins" could be "used to store and transport fragile documents of papyrus or parchment." He notes the likelihood of documents transported by sea when great libraries such as those at Alexandria or Pergamum were being collected.[1033] The very tendency of papyrus to grow moldy if damp suggests that Luke would have brought a container for a long voyage or that he would have employed some other substance of stronger quality than papyrus, perhaps parchment or vellum.[1034] Wood and wax would be more durable but would not contain all of Luke's notes or be easily carried to shore. In any case, that most writing materials used on ships utilized more waterproof materials than papyrus[1035] suggests that Luke would have undertaken this voyage better prepared.[1036] (Luke would hardly need notes for the details of the shipwreck itself, which were too graphic and traumatic for a typical survivor of the events to easily forget.)

Third, Luke could be among those floating and swept in on pieces of wood, with his light container on top of the wood; the container's surface would become wet, but at least it would not be fully submerged for more than a few moments at a time. The distance to shore would not be far. Fourth, even if the papyrus was damaged somewhat in the process, the author might well recall enough of the details of the recent voyage to transcribe, based on whatever may have remained.

Finally and most important, he would likely have back in Syro-Palestine, probably left with Christians in Caesarea, a backup copy (which he could either consult if this

1031. Smaller ones were probably available on board. Justin Leidwanger (personal correspondence, Oct. 9, 2014) notes the existence of "small bottles in the Roman world that could have been plugged the same way" one would "plug an amphora with a cork or ceramic stopper fitted with clay" or the like; "the common wares we traditionally find in galleys could have been stoppered with organic materials that did not survive"; unlike "the larger stoppered amphoras," smaller containers with less density might not sink. Finding materials to seal the container would be a second issue if one did not come prepared. Certainly some materials (such as lead and resin) within the ship itself were used to keep out water (see Fitzgerald, "Ship of Paul," 37–38), but these would be less accessible than the "planks" (Acts 27:44).

1032. Cf. Rapske, "Travel," 34n151 (against Pervo and others); followed by, e.g., Le Cornu, *Acts*, 1471.

1033. Wilson, personal correspondence, Oct. 13, 2014.

1034. A parchment (μεμβράνας in 2 Tim 4:13, where they could be notebooks or Christian writings; cf. Ferguson, *Backgrounds*, 93; Skeat, "Parchments"; Lee, "Parchments"; Donfried, *Thessalonica*, 294, 298–99) could consist of papyrus or animal skins (BDAG; the latter usage more closely suits the term's Latin origin). The latter were, however, more expensive (Kelly, *Pastoral Epistles*, 215; Watson, "Education," 311), complicating matters if Luke had many notes beyond details of travels and basic notes supporting Paul's legal innocence. Animal skins finally supplanted papyrus only in the fourth century (Aune, *Dictionary of Rhetoric*, 336), but they existed earlier. Galen had both some papyri (*Grief* 19) and parchment codices (31–36, esp. 33–35). On leather parchments, see Forbes, *Technology*, 5:61–64.

1035. Justin Leidwanger (personal correspondence, Oct. 9, 2014), notes that "most records we have … of writing on ships involve things like wax tablets or lead letters, obviously meant to be durable against water in that tough environment." Also, there is evidence that not only the author of Luke's "we" narratives but a number of others wrote at sea, at least compiling itineraries (see esp. Davis, "Navigation," 189–97); list literacy was one of the most basic forms of literacy (Thomas, "Writing," 28–30).

1036. Mark Wilson, personal correspondence, Oct. 13, 2014, suggests that Paul, given prior shipwreck experiences (2 Cor 11:25), could have advised Luke accordingly even had Luke not been aware of this himself. The voyages in the "we" material suggest that Luke would have known of Paul's travel experiences as well as had some of his own.

one was damaged, or depend on entirely if this one was lost) of his most important notes[1037] before the voyage. It was customary to keep multiple copies of important or lengthy works.[1038] Cicero left records of his accounts in two cities.[1039] Luke would certainly be able to regain access to these before the two-year period in 28:30 ended, and even more certainly before he began writing the book of Acts. This is not strictly an argument for the survival of a manuscript that he had with him, but it does counter the skepticism that the narrator of the storm scene could have also authored the rest of the "we" narrative. Again, in such a situation he could reconstruct the storm narrative from what survived of his notes or from memory; trauma often reinforces memory more deeply.[1040]

v. Luke's Point

Thus, Luke celebrates, they all came safely to land.[1041] God's favor toward Paul eliminates casualties (27:24), and the voyagers' obedience to God's message through Paul plays a role in this survival (27:42–44). A careful hearer of Luke-Acts might recall that heeding Jesus's words also leads to surviving a flood (albeit a figurative kind, Luke 6:47–49). When one who escaped a battle dove from a bridge into a river, then swam safely to land, others might conclude that the gods were with him (Val. Max. 3.2.1). The survival of all 276 passengers against all odds vindicated Paul's status as a divine messenger and hence (a fortiori) could have also been used to vindicate Paul's innocence toward those skeptical about it.[1042]

8. Ministry in Malta (28:1–10)

One could group the entire ministry in Malta together (Acts 28:1–10) or divide it into two paragraphs: Paul's surviving a snakebite (28:1–6), and healings and hospitality (28:7–10). God vindicates Paul when Paul is confronted with a snakebite as God vindicated him at sea, for Paul must see Caesar. Both initial verdicts of the "barbarians" miss the mark: Paul is neither being punished by deity nor a

---

1037. On notebooks, see, e.g., Richards, *Letter Writing*, 55–57. See comments on notes in Keener, *Acts*, 1:287–90 (for notebooks, see 1:198n235, 288n256, 289n258; 3:2541n2439).

1038. Even for letters; see Cic. *Ad Brut.* 3.1 (2.2.1); *Fam.* 3.3.2; *Att.* 13.29; Sen. Y. *Ep. Lucil.* 99; esp. Cic. *Fam.* 7.25.1. In rare emergencies, two copies of a letter might be sent by different means to make sure that at least one reached its destination; Brutus notes that he received both (Cic. *Fam.* 11.11.1). Cf. duplicate copies in Galen *Grief* 22–23a (though those in 21–22 were specifically requested).

1039. Cic. *Att.* 6.7 (though these are official records, because he was governor).

1040. See Bauckham, *Eyewitnesses*, 331–32; Elliott, *Feelings*, 44–45 (citing, e.g., Izard, "Relationships," 22); Redman, "Eyewitnesses," 184; note limitations in Allison, *Jesus*, 7n40; and the exception cited in Woodman, *Rhetoric*, 18–22.

1041. Johnson, *Acts*, 456, compares Ael. Arist. *Or.* 2.12 (a later work). That Luke omits "we" here is curious, unless he emphasizes the safety of the prisoners (Acts 27:42). That all (out of 276) should have survived seems remarkable (cf. Num 31:49), but some incidents in modern times render it plausible (e.g., Harriet Tubman's never losing a slave or any of the eight hundred Union troops whom she guided on later raids, Sterling, *Sisters*, 259). Some of my wife's refugee escape accounts also astonish me, though with fewer persons involved; for accounts of protection miracles, cf., e.g., Balcombe, *Door*, 68–69; see further Keener, *Miracles*, 274–75n68; even (not noted there) reports of assailants suddenly becoming unable to see their prospective victims, from Pastor Massamba of Madouma parish, interviewed by Dr. Médine Moussounga, June 26, 1999; a different (larger-scale but secondhand) incident reported to Médine Moussounga on Sept. 14, 1999; and Józef Bałuczyński, provided for me by Dr. Rob Starner, Sept. 1 and 14, 2014.

1042. Cf. Miles and Trompf, "Luke and Antiphon"; *pace* Rapske, "Travel," 43–44; see comment on Acts 28:4–6. Even today, many regard the survival of nearly all people in a major accident as "miraculous" (see Vivian Sequera, "'Miracle' in Colombia Crash: Woman Dies, 130 Live," Associated Press, http://news.yahoo.com/s/ap/20100816/ap_on_re_la_am_ca/lt_colombia_plane_crash; cf. http://www.bbc.co.uk/news/world-asia-pacific-11187166).

deity himself; rather, God vindicates him as his agent. Their faulty understanding in 28:1–6, however, is no doubt corrected through Paul's continuing ministry in 28:7–10. Paul ultimately endears himself to the hospitable people of the island through benefactions of healing as he had endeared himself to the people aboard the ship by speaking as God's agent.

a. Some Introductory Issues

Many ancients believed that gods punished malefactors at sea (often destroying innocent seafarers who were with them); this was true not only in Greek but also in Jewish texts (Jonah 1:1–2:1). Paul's survival at sea and from the snakebite showed that Paul was not only innocent but divinely vindicated.[1043] From the most important perspective—the divine one—Luke's audience recognizes Paul's vindication whatever the later outcome of his trial before Nero's court. (By the time Luke likely writes, Nero is not well thought of, anyway, though he is much better liked in Greece, where I locate Luke's central audience, than in Rome.) Paul may have been criticized after his death for his Roman custody and execution, as Jesus was; thus it is important for Luke to reiterate how often God did in fact deliver Paul before Paul finally died (even that death fulfilling God's will). This is also an important reason for the parallels between Jesus and Paul: both suffered for God's purposes, and God vindicated both of them.[1044]

Some commentators have observed traces of medical terminology in Acts 28:1–10; some of the suggestions are more defensible than others. Dioscorides uses καθάπτομαι (nowhere else attested in the NT, the LXX, or the Apostolic Fathers) for toxins entering the body;[1045] πίμπρημι is likewise a rare term,[1046] employed most often (though not exclusively) in medical texts, for a swelling.[1047] (The other sense listed in BDAG, to "burn with fever," might be particularly relevant here: the snake does not cause Paul to "burn" [28:6], but he drops it into the fire [28:5] and cures someone else who is "[aflame with] fever" [28:8].)[1048] Other terms, such as καταπίπτω (Acts 28:6; 26:14; Luke 8:6),[1049] are simply not rare enough or medical enough to suggest a specifically medical connection.[1050] Even if the cumulative use of particularly medical terminology in Luke-Acts is consistent with the tradition that Luke was a doctor (without its proving so),[1051] we may presume that his general sense remains intelligible to his audience.[1052]

1043. See Witherington, *Acts*, 769; and others (see comment below, on Acts 28:4–5).

1044. See also, e.g., Puskas, "Conclusion: Investigation," 151–52. Thus some compare the entire storm sequence with Jesus's passion; Clabeaux, "Viper," argues that Paul's snakebite offers even closer parallels. For Luke's apologetic for Paul, see Keener, "Apologetic"; such apologetic was important as early as 2 Cor 2:14–7:4, where (in ch. 3) Paul uses *synkrisis* to compare apostolic ministry with Moses (treated in Keener, *Corinthians*, 168–69, and many other sources).

1045. Bruce, *Commentary*, 470 (citing Galen *Si quis optimus medicus est* 13; following Hobart, *Medical Language*, 288–89).

1046. Cf. πρήθω in Num 5:21, 22, 27 LXX; Jos. *Ant.* 3.271.

1047. Hobart, *Medical Language*, 50; see, e.g., SIG 1179.15; BDAG.

1048. For "burn," see also, e.g., Jos. *Ant.* 17.274, 291; the single Euripides fragment (from his *Syleus*) cited in Philo *Alleg. Interp.* 3.202; Jos. 78; *Good Person* 99 (though Philo employs the term elsewhere for swelling in *Spec. Laws* 3.62, with reference to Num 5, as in Jos. *Ant.* 3.271).

1049. Hobart, *Medical Language*, 50.

1050. In the LXX, Neh 8:11; 3 Macc 2:20; 4 Macc 4:11; Ps 144:14; Wis 7:3; 13:16; 17:15; cf. also *Test. Job* 30:1; Jos. *War* 6.64; *Ant.* 5.27 (BDAG). The term θηρίον is pervasive (thirty-eight NT uses, esp. in Revelation; 131 times in the LXX; though Hobart, *Medical Language*, 51, who emphasizes its medical application to serpents).

1051. See Witherington, *Acts*, 779n129 (noting Horsley, *Documents*, 2:20ff., §2); see discussion of authorship in Keener, *Acts*, 1:402–22, esp. 414–16. Today, see esp. discussion in Weissenrieder, *Images*.

1052. Today's medical terminology is probably more apt to be technical than in antiquity.

b. Malta (28:1)

Paul's sea travels left him with many experiences on islands (e.g., Acts 20:15; 21:1; cf. 16:11).[1053] Malta is called Μελίτη (as here) in a range of ancient sources;[1054] in Latin it was Melite Africana.[1055] Again Luke is dealing with the real world, not fictitious geography.[1056]

i. Mljet or Kefallinía?

As early as the eighth century c.e., an interpreter suggested the island today called Mljet (earlier Melita Illyrica [Latin], Meleda [Italian]) as an alternative to Malta, and it remains an alternative today.[1057] This interpretation of a Dalmatian island near modern Dubrovnik rests on a narrower construal of "Adria" (27:27) as what we call the Adriatic today, but usage was wider in Luke's day. This Dalmatian site is unlikely. A northeaster would hardly blow a ship from Crete and Cauda to Mljet in the north, especially if the sailors feared the Syrtis in the south (27:17).[1058] Further, a ship bound for Rome from Mljet would sail to Italy's western coast, not (as from Malta) to Syracuse (28:12).[1059]

Most scholars therefore reject this identification in favor of Malta.[1060] Granted, Ptolemy (*Geog.* 2.16.9) apparently called it Μελιτήνη, but it was far less known than the Maltese Μελίτη. Pliny the Elder calls it Melite and attributes Maltese terriers to this location, probably confusing it with the better-known Malta,[1061] but he speaks of a thousand islands in this Illyrian region.[1062] Simply bearing this name no more makes Mljet the right site than Samothrace in the north Aegean (Acts 16:11), which some ancients claimed once bore the name Μελίτη because of its wealth,[1063] or another Melite among many towns of Magnesia adjoining Thessaly.[1064]

Similar problems hold for the proposal of Kefallinía (Cephalonia),[1065] which again is usually rejected in favor of Malta.[1066] In its favor, this would be a way to fit the events presupposed in the Pastorals into the narrative of Acts (though the fit is not very persuasive, since 1 Timothy and Titus offer no real hint of Roman custody). It was

1053. Spencer, "Odyssey in Acts," emphasizes Paul's development and challenges on islands; but of course, a seafarer would necessarily visit islands.

1054. BDAG cites Diod. Sic. 15.12.2; Strabo 6.2.11; 17.3.16; Ps.-Scylax *Periplum maris interni* 94 (Fabricius, 34); and inscriptions.

1055. Fitzmyer, *Acts*, 782.

1056. Contrast the islands that Greeks report in the Adriatic (*in mari Hadriatico*) that are called the Electrides—which do not exist (Pliny E. *N.H.* 37.11.32); on the island of lotus-eaters, see comment on Acts 27:17; for real versus novelistic geography, cf. again Keener, "Official."

1057. E.g., Acworth, "Where Was Paul Shipwrecked?"; Meinardus, "Shipwrecked in Dalmatia." Cf. the argument against this site already in Abbott, *Acts*, 257.

1058. With, e.g., Barrett, *Acts*, 1219–20.

1059. Witherington, *Acts*, 775, also notes that Malta, unlike Mljet, was on the grain route for Alexandrian ships. Although this observation fits the vessel's trajectory, we should remember that the ship did not end up in Malta voluntarily!

1060. E.g., Hemer, "Euraquilo and Melita"; Pesch, *Apostelgeschichte*, 2:297; Rapske, "Travel," 37–43; Lake and Cadbury, *Commentary*, 340; Bruce, *Commentary*, 520–21; idem, *Acts¹*, 469; Fitzmyer, *Acts*, 782; Peterson, *Acts*, 698.

1061. Pliny E. *N.H.* 3.26.152 (see LCL, 2:115 n. *b*). For the other Malta (Melite), see 3.8.92 (in the section on Sicily, 3.8.86–3.9.94, fitting Luke's location, Acts 28:12).

1062. Pliny E. *N.H.* 3.26.151.

1063. Strabo 7, frg. 50a; 10.3.19.

1064. Pliny E. *N.H.* 4.9.32.

1065. Not as far north as Mljet but still far north of Crete. This position is favored (and extensively and carefully argued) by Warnecke, *Romfahrt des Paulus*; Suhl, "Seeweg" (on the normal sea route for Alexandrian ships, but as noted, this is not completely relevant here).

1066. E.g., Schwank, "Nacht"; idem, "Spurensuche auf Kefalonia"; Sant and Sammut, "Doch auf Malta"; Wehnert, "Gestrandet"; idem, "Insel Kephallenia."

a free island off the coast of Greece.[1067] But this island was never clearly known as Melite.[1068] Ancient Cephallenia (if it is the same Kefallinía) lacked sufficient drinking water, creating difficulty for the many goats there for half of every year[1069] (though this is the rainy season).[1070] It will hardly do to press "Adriatic" in its narrowest sense (Acts 27:27) while ignoring the island's name in 28:1.

II. MALTA

Malta is about 58 miles south of Sicily,[1071] 180 miles east of Tunisia, and 220 miles north of the Libyan coast. Malta is 16 to 18 miles long (northwest to southeast) and 8 to 9 miles wide at its widest point, for a total of fewer than 100 square miles (considerably larger than Cauda, though closer to one-tenth the size of Sicily). This is therefore no small island. (Today it supports a population of more than 400,000.) Saint Paul's Bay, the most commonly proposed site of landfall, is 3 to 4 miles (ca. 5 km.) from the northeast tip of the island.[1072]

Malta was known for its temple of Juno (Val. Max. 1.1.ext. 2) in the town "also called Melita" (Cic. *Verr.* 2.4.46.103), which Verres reportedly looted while governor of Sicily (2.4.46.104).[1073] The island was also known for its small dogs (Strabo 6.2.11),[1074] and it "prospered from olive-oil and textile production."[1075] Collections of Jewish catacombs on the island are estimated to be from the second to the fifth centuries C.E.[1076]

It may seem odd that the sailors had recognized the much smaller Cauda (Acts 27:16) more quickly than Malta (27:39), but they recognized Cauda by its location south of Crete before they lost their bearings, and even apart from the dim morning light and current rain, the approach to a northern bay was not the usual approach of ships to this island. Because Phoenicians named the island Melita for the Canaanite word for "refuge," some scholars have suggested that 28:1 means that "after we were all safe, we understood 'Melita' to be well-named."[1077] But Luke and his companions do

1067. Pliny E. *N.H.* 4.12.54.

1068. Rapske, "Travel," 42.

1069. They allegedly drink by facing the windy sea with their mouths open (Val. Max. 1.8.ext. 18; Wardle, *Valerius Maximus*, 286, compares Arist. *Mir. ausc.* 9 and notes the claim in Aelian *Nat. An.* 3.32 that they do not "drink for six months").

1070. The proximity of the modern island of Kefallinía, in the Ionian Sea, to the Greek coast would make nonsense of the narrative, and its proximity to Ithaca would make lack of more explicit identification (which could be helpful for Homeric allusions) at least unusual.

1071. The standard encyclopedia distance, presumably referring to the shortest distance from Malta's northernmost point to Sicily. Strabo 17.3.16 places Malta (Μελίτη) 500 stadia from Cossurus, which is the island opposite the Selinus River in Sicily. For Pliny the Elder's coordinates, see *N.H.* 3.8.92.

1072. Supposed relics of St. Paul in Malta drew seventeenth-century travelers' attention (Freller, "Evasissemus," unfortunately rooting this approach in Luke's narrative), but the traditions about Paul on Malta are much older than this.

1073. Excavations have likely confirmed the site (Wardle, *Valerius Maximus*, 128; Trump, "Malta," 403). Cicero stayed in Malta but had to leave there during his banishment (*Att.* 3.4), and he went to Malta during part of the civil war (10.9). Cicero claims that the Phoenicians had never bothered the site; Phoenicians had their own goddesses, however (e.g., Hdn. 5.6.4), and so Juno is probably simply the Roman identification. On ancient Malta, see also Sagona, Gregory, and Bugeja, *Antiquities*; Sagona, *Archaeology*; Sammut, *Monuments*; Lewis, *Ancient Malta*; idem, *Paths*; Goulder, *Pavements*; Mahoney, *History*; earlier, Boisgelin de Kerdu, *Malta* (focused on a later period); Caruana, *Pottery*. With respect to medical practices on Malta, with possible relevance to the illnesses described below, see Savona-Ventura, *Medicine in Malta*.

1074. Lake and Cadbury, *Commentary*, 340, compare the island's dogs in the modern era.

1075. Salmon, Boardman, and Potter, "Melita."

1076. Goodenough, *Symbols*, 2:57. Apparently, the Jewish presence was not large, but the Jewish people there spoke Greek (see *CIJ* 1:471, §655).

1077. Bruce, *Commentary*, 521, entertaining a suggestion by J. R. Harris from 1909–10 (rightly rejected by Lake and Cadbury, *Commentary*, 340).

not know the local language (28:2), and a Greek might well think the island named for honey (μέλι) or sweetness.

c. Barbarian Benevolence (28:2)

In this passage, "barbarians" (possibly meaning here those not conversant in Greek) display the highly regarded virtue of kindness toward other people, and in the following context, they will prove extremely receptive to Paul's ministry. A book emphasizing the good news for all peoples (1:8) might here subvert a particular Greek stereotype possibly held by some of Luke's audience (cf. analogously Luke 10:29–37).[1078]

I. HOSPITALITY

Ancient Mediterranean culture was notably hospitable (see comment on Acts 16:15),[1079] and this was probably truer of sedentary traditional areas than of faster-paced cities. One basis for praising a location in antiquity was its hospitality (Men. Rhet. 2.3, 384.22),[1080] and by that criterion the "barbarians" of Malta fare far better than elite Philippi, cultured Athens, or sacred Jerusalem.[1081] Sharing one's food and drink was considered particularly kind (Xen. Cyr. 8.2.2).

Such hospitality was particularly necessary to victims of shipwreck.[1082] Receiving shipwrecked strangers hospitably was a widespread human law (Eurip. Cycl. 299–301). Helping a shipwrecked person was an act of kindness comparable to showing the right path to a wanderer or sharing bread with the hungry (Sen. Y. Ep. Lucil. 95.51). Thus Dio Chrysostom reports local, rural hospitality when he experienced shipwreck (Or. 7.5–6, 55–58).[1083] Locals did not always receive survivors so hospitably, however. Thus, in one novel a shipwrecked doctor had to beg for clothing and funds (Xen. Eph. Anthia 3.4); in other settings, too, because the shipwrecked lacked possessions, they might need to beg for their living (Phaedrus 4.23.24–25). Survivors of war could be compared to someone rescued "from a shipwreck, in nakedness and destitution" (Plut. Cam. 31.5).[1084]

II. BENEVOLENT KINDNESS

Orators also praised cities on the basis of their φιλανθρωπία (the term Luke uses here),[1085] and Luke's narrative reveals his gratitude. Such praises most often appear when a speaker is honoring benefactors or potential benefactors—that is, those in a superior position for providing aid. Those needing an official's favor would praise his φιλανθρωπία;[1086] one should praise a governor's φιλανθρωπία to his subjects as

1078. See esp. Jipp, Visitations, 257–60 (for the stereotype, see 40–42). Greeks held both positive and negative views of barbarian character; although Luke's view of their religious perspective may be open to more debate (Acts 28:4, 6, though such sentiments appear among other peoples in his writings, e.g., 14:11; Luke 13:2, 4), he certainly provides a favorable view of their kindness here, using the same language as for that of Julius. Luke thus seems to lie toward the positive side of the Greek spectrum on the question.
1079. Readings from many Asian and other cultures today grasp the importance of hospitality more quickly than do many Western readings; see, e.g., Nguyen, "Asian View."
1080. Pindar Ol. 13.3; in the ancient Near East, see Gordon, Near East, 200.
1081. See also this emphasis in Jipp, Visitations, 40–42, esp. 41.
1082. Scholars (e.g., Gaventa, Acts, 356) cite various examples of such hospitality (e.g., Dio Chrys. Or. 7.4–6; Petron. Sat. 114; Lucian True Story 1.28–29; 2.46); Hock, "Ethnography," 109, cites as an example of taking in a shipwreck victim Xen. Eph. Anthia 3.4.3. It appears in various genres because here, as often, novels imitated reality.
1083. He claims this as a genuine experience (Dio Chrys. Or. 7.1, 81); even if embellished, it probably reflects a genuine encounter.
1084. Trans. B. Perrin, Lives, LCL, 2:173. Toner, Culture, 155, suggests texts (Cic. Sest. 93; Hor. Ars. 20) that might imply the shipwrecked begging, although he also provides an alternative explanation.
1085. E.g., Men. Rhet. 1.3, 363.6. Philanthropy could include hosting banquets and aiding those in distress (Parsons, Acts, 367, pointing to Diog. Laert. 3.98).
1086. E.g., Men. Rhet. 2.13, 423.7–10 (esp. 8–9; to the emperor).

part of his justice (Men. Rhet. 2.10, 416.5–12, esp. 416.6). Deities were also known for their φιλανθρωπία, or love of humanity;[1087] this was also true of the supreme deity (Mus. Ruf. 17, p. 108.14),[1088] who set the example for humans (p. 108.14–16).[1089] This virtue[1090] was characteristic of those who would show kindness when wronged (10, p. 78.33), like (in principle) philosophers (p. 78.34) and in contrast to beasts (p. 78.28). See further discussion at Acts 27:3.

Here again Luke provides an example of nonbelievers' kindness (cf. Luke 10:33–35; see comment on Acts 27:3).[1091] It is possible that Luke might concede to John's radical moral dualism (cf. John 15:18–25) in principle (cf. Luke 11:23; 16:13), but he certainly qualifies such dualism in practice (as even John does, to an extent; cf., e.g., John 7:12, 31, 43, 51). That they are Gentiles provides a fitting climax to Luke's paradox regarding the Gentile mission: rejected by Israel's leaders (Luke 22–23; Acts 21–26), both Jesus (Luke 23:47) and Paul are esteemed by strangers. But while the local people are Paul's benefactors here, he more than returns the kindness (as befits ancient reciprocity conventions) in Acts 28:8–9,[1092] in turn becoming something like *their* benefactor (and hence receiving their honor, 28:10).[1093]

Though "philanthropy" was a more conventional Greek virtue, Greeks sometimes applied their virtues to barbarians (27:3), even projecting on them virtues in which they felt themselves wanting.[1094] Though Persians were "barbarians" and enemies of Greeks, Musonius pointed out, they treated Themistocles kindly.[1095] Of course, "barbarian" could have harsher moral connotations; some recounted the cruelty of barbarians[1096] or spoke of cruel behavior as barbarous.[1097] Romans praised the emperor for subduing "barbarians."[1098] One might expect to find "barbarous" peoples in a remote area, away from (Greco-Roman) "civilization."[1099]

iii. "Barbarians"

Ancient writers sometimes categorized humanity into two groups,[1100] Greeks and barbarians,[1101] so that the mention of both groups together comprised all humanity,

1087. Dio Chrys. *Or.* 3.82 (inviting imitation); Philost. *Hrk.* 16.5.

1088. For the Jewish God, in Hellenistic terms, see, e.g., *Let. Aris.* 257; Marcus, "Names and Attributes," 48.

1089. See, in Judaism, *Let. Aris.* 208 (and Hadas, *Aristeas*, 181, 183).

1090. As a Stoic virtue, see, e.g., Mus. Ruf. 14, p. 92.31; cf. Marc. Aur. 7.31; among other philosophers, e.g., Lucian *Dem.* 11; among others in general, *Portr.* 11.

1091. Stoics believed that nature provided a sense of common humanity that made people feel akin to each other (Cic. *Fin.* 3.19.63).

1092. On reciprocity regarding gifts, see, e.g., Pliny *Ep.* 6.6.3; Herman, "Gift"; Highet, "Reciprocity"; Harrison, *Grace*, 1, 15, 40–43, 50–53; further comment on Acts 23:17–18. Chrys. *Hom. Acts* 54 also views Paul's healing ministry here as returning Publius's benefaction.

1093. For healings understood at least in some way as benefactions in antiquity, see comment on Acts 4:9 and sources cited there.

1094. Johnson, *Acts*, 461 (citing Philost. *Vit. Apoll.* 2.26, 30; 3.24–25); cf. Libanius *Narration* 37. Contrast Cadbury, *Acts in History*, 25: "Their alien speech foreboded to any Greek unfriendly treatment" (though he may be right that their benefaction adds to the picture of providential circumstances surrounding Paul's voyage).

1095. Mus. Ruf. 9, p. 72.4–6. On the Greek and Roman concept of some "noble" barbarians, see, e.g., Anacharsis *Ep.* 9; Strabo 7.3.7; cf. *Gr. Anth.* 7.92. For the introduction, above, to Acts 8:26–40, in Keener, *Acts*, 2:1538, 1557.

1096. Val. Max. 9.3.ext. 10 (*barbari*), though he also recounts others' cruelty.

1097. Philost. *Hrk.* 19.6 (where Hector speaks a "barbarian" language but his violence was justifiable rather than barbarous); 48.18 (justifying Achilles's barbarous act). Cf. also 57.9 (not employing the term; Philostratus is post-NT).

1098. Men. Rhet. 2.1–2, 377.15–16; 2.12, 422.24–27.

1099. Dio Chrys. *Or.* 36.25 (on some barbarous, merely nominal Greeks). People in major urban centers of the empire were sometimes surprised to discover "civilization" elsewhere (Pliny *Ep.* 9.11.2).

1100. Philosophers tended to divide humanity differently, into wise and foolish (Arius Did. *Epit.* 2.7.11g, pp. 72–73.5–8); Jews, into Jew and Gentile.

1101. For "barbarians" as all non-Greeks, see, e.g., Aeschylus *Ctes.* 259; Isoc. *Helen* (*Or. 10*) 67–68; Corn. Nep. 5 (Cimon), 2.3; 7 (Alcibiades), 7.4; 8 (Thrasybulus), 4.3; 9 (Conon), 5.2; Dion. Hal. *Ant. rom.* 1.16.1;

whether in philosophers,[1102] rhetoricians,[1103] historians,[1104] or elsewhere.[1105] Thus Greeks could consider wholly "civilized" groups such as Trojans[1106] and Persians[1107] "barbarians." Although this dichotomy was originally Greek, Romans[1108] and Jews[1109] often simply adapted it as conventional language. Even Greeks did not always use it in a derogatory sense; after advising that one distinguish between Greeks and barbarians,[1110] a rhetorician explains how to praise barbarians.[1111] The basis for the contrast was often (though not by any means always) primarily linguistic.[1112]

Some scholars think that Luke's designation of the indigenes as "barbarians" reflects Greek cultural snobbery,[1113] and Greeks could certainly so employ "barbarian" at times.[1114] (That was in fact the most common usage after the Persian Wars.)[1115] But

1.24.4; 1.28.4; Lucian *Dem.* 34; Paus. 10.32.3; Athen. *Deipn.* 10.457F; 11.461B. Thucyd. 1.3.3 notes that the distinction is absent in Homer because it postdates him.

1102. Plato *Alcib.* 2.141C; *Theaet.* 175A; *Laws* 9.870AB; 10.887E; Arist. *Heav.* 1.3.270b; Sext. Emp. *Eth.* 1.15; Diog. Laert. 6.1.2.

1103. Isoc. *Nic.* 50 (*Or.* 3.37); *Paneg.* 108; Isaeus *Menec.* 24; Demosth. *Lacr.* 2; *Chers.* 6, 67; *Cor.* 202, 270; *Fals. leg.* 268; *Rhet. Alex.* pref. 1420b.16; Dio Chrys. *Or.* 1.14; 9.12; 12.11, 27–28; 31.20; 32.35; 36.43; Ael. Arist. *Def. Or.* 331, §109D; *Panath.* 1, 150D; Max. Tyre 11.5; Men. Rhet. 1.3, 364.24–25.

1104. Diod. Sic. 1.4.5–6; 1.9.3, 5; 3.73.6; 11.13.2; 11.32.1; 14.23.3–4; 14.30.5–6; 14.102.1; Dion. Hal. *Ant. rom.* 3.11.10; 3.23.19; 4.23.2; 4.25.3; 6.8.2; 6.80.1; 6.84.3; 7.70.3; 11.1.2; Appian *Hist. rom.* 12.16.113.

1105. See, e.g., Strabo 6.1.2; 13.1.1; 15.3.23; Plut. *Ages.* 10.3; *Tim.* 28.2; *Eum.* 16.3; *Bride* 21, *Mor.* 141A; Philost. *Hrk.* 54.10; Rom 1:14; *Diogn.* 5.4; Tatian *Or. Gks.* 1, 21, 29.

1106. E.g., *Cypria* 10; Libanius *Invect.* 2.1; *Speech in Character* 15.2, 5 (less surprisingly, Medea in 16.1); Philost. *Hrk.* 23.12; 31.2. Yet Achilles's anti-Trojan behavior could be negatively "barbarous" (Philost. *Hrk.* 48.18).

1107. E.g., Isoc. *Paneg.* 108; Lysias *Or.* 2.57, §195; 2.59, §196; Sext. Emp. *Eth.* 1.15; Strabo 15.3.23; Mus. Ruf. 9, p. 72.4; Plut. *Themist.* 6.2; Arrian *Alex.* 1.18.1; Ps.-Callisth. *Alex.* 1.38; Parthians in Jos. *Ant.* 18.47; Asia in Val. Max. 4.6.ext. 3. In Aeschylus *Pers.* 391–93, even Persians are depicted as calling their own people barbarians (391) in contrast to the Greeks (393).

1108. Cic. *Inv.* 1.24.35; Sen. Y. *Dial.* 5.2.1; cf. Cic. *Off.* 3.26.99. Some other Roman texts add Romans as a third category (Juv. *Sat.* 10.138; Quint. *Inst.* 5.10.24). Polybius had portrayed Romans partly as barbarians, partly as "honorary Greeks" (Champion, "Romans").

1109. Although Jews sometimes classified themselves differently (cf. Philo *Spec. Laws* 2.165), Greeks included Jews among "barbarians" (Strabo 16.2.38; some considered them the worst of barbarians, Apollonius in Jos. *Ag. Ap.* 2.148), and some Jews followed suit (*War* 1.preamble 3). Jewish writers in Greek often summarized humanity as "Greeks and barbarians" (5.17; *Ant.* 1.107; 15.136; 18.20; *Ag. Ap.* 1.201; 2.39; Philo *Cher.* 91; *Drunkenness* 193; *Abr.* 267; *Mos.* 2.20; *Decal.* 153; *Spec. Laws* 2.18, 20, 44, 165; 4.120; *Good Person* 94, 98; *Contempl.* 21; *Embassy* 145, 292). They also wrote of Jews versus Greeks where relevant (Jos. *Ant.* 19.278; see comment on Acts 14:1).

1110. Men. Rhet. 1.2, 353.31–354.1; cf. also Dion. Hal. *Epid.* 3.268.

1111. The most ancient or kingly of barbarians will be easiest to praise for their heritage (Men. Rhet. 1.2, 354.1–8; e.g., Phrygians for their antiquity, 354.2).

1112. E.g., Plato *Cratyl.* 409DE; 421D; 425E–426A; Plut. *Educ.* 6, *Mor.* 4A; Sext. Emp. *Pyr.* 3.267; Max. Tyre 8.8; Philost. *Hrk.* 19.6; the Isis aretalogy in Grant, *Religions*, 132; Philo *Conf.* 6, 190; *Sib. Or.* 3.516, 528; 1 Cor 14:11. The term βάρβαρος originated as onomatopoeia (on which see *Rhet. Her.* 4.31.42; Anderson, *Glossary*, 82–84; Flury, "Onomatopoeia," noting this term on 142); non-Greek language sounded like "bar-bar" to Greeks (Bruce, *Corinthians*, 131; McCoskey, *Race*, 54 ["evidently"]).

1113. Cadbury, *Acts in History*, 32; cf. Judge, *Pattern*, 60–61.

1114. E.g., Demosth. *Philip.* 1.40; 3.31; Paus. 8.22.6; Philost. *Ep. Apoll.* 21; esp. Diog. Laert. 1.33 (thanking gods for being Greek rather than barbarian); on their superstition, Plut. *Superst.* 2, *Mor.* 166AB; Char. *Chaer.* 6.7.12; Xen. Eph. *Anthia* 3.11; Philost. *Hrk.* 23.16; on their stupidity, Dion. Hal. *Ant. rom.* 5.4.3; Ps.-Callisth. *Alex.* 3.2; on their inferior cultural virtues or character, Eurip. *Heracl.* 130–31; *Orest.* 485–86; Paus. 9.16.4 (normally); Max. Tyre 19.4; on their inferior beauty, Xen. Eph. *Anthia* 2.2; on being like beasts, Libanius *Invect.* 2.1; *Topics* 2.6. In Philost. *Hrk.* 28.12, where it applies to Scythians but not Cyrus, it approximates "savages" (cf. the Roman use in Suet. *Galba* 6.3). Sometimes morally uncivilized, "barbaric" behavior denigrated ethnic Greeks rather than barbarians (Dio Chrys. *Or.* 36.25; Diogenes *Ep.* 28). For regions called Barbaria, see Goldenberg, "Barbaria." Greeks could even look down on Romans at times (e.g., Lucian *Dem.* 40); not everyone took kindly to their arrogance (e.g., *Sib. Or.* 3.171, 732; 4.70; Jos. *Ag. Ap.* 1.15–18, 58). The snobbery dominates in pre-Hellenistic sources and after the Greek cultural revival of the second century.

1115. See McCoskey, *Race*, 54 (noting stereotypes on 56; in Greek comedy, 152). Apul. *Flor.* 3.6 uses the Latinized form to depict an unkempt Phrygian from mythical times.

Luke portrays them as benevolent (28:2) and at least some people there as elite (28:7) and hence might think primarily of linguistic barbarism—that is, those who do not speak Greek.[1116] (Romans adapted the nomenclature for their own purposes.)[1117] Granted, Greeks could contrast themselves with barbarians in terms of genuine (Greek) education;[1118] in earlier times, they could also protest that barbarians ought not to rule Greeks[1119] but, rather, Greeks barbarians.[1120] But the linguistic difference may be the primary point of the term in this context (cf. discussion of the Maltese language below) and would be sufficient by itself to merit the title. Those lacking Greek language normally also lacked its culture as well.

Some find it odd that Luke would regard Paul as a nonbarbarian, distinct from the Maltese locals; after all, he was Jewish and not Greek.[1121] But if we think of the language only, the differentiation makes good sense: Paul's Greek was notably fluent (21:37),[1122] and those who voyaged on the ship from the East were also Greek-speakers, in contrast to the Maltese.

It is also possible, however, that Luke does call attention to traditional Greek expectations about "barbarians." He does not apply this label to peoples in respected Asia Minor, even when they do not speak Greek (or at least not as a primary language, 14:11). If Luke does evoke Greek sentiments about Greek versus barbarian culture, he quickly subverts them by underlining the Maltese people's virtue of hospitality, part of the repertoire of Greek virtues.[1123]

IV. THE MALTESE PEOPLE

Carthaginians controlled Melita from the sixth century B.C.E., and "Punic traditions remained strong throughout the Roman period."[1124] The Maltese descended from Phoenician settlers, and their indigenous language in Paul's day remained a

1116. With, e.g., Bruce, *Commentary*, 521; idem, *Acts*¹, 470; Arrington, *Acts*, 264; Johnson, *Acts*, 461 (noting Hdt. 2.57; and for ignorance of Greek customs, Char. *Chaer.* 6.3.7); BDAG ("certainly without derogatory tone"). For accidental barbarisms in speaking Greek, see Rowe, "Style," 122; Anderson, *Glossary*, 30; Polyb. 39.1.1–9; in terms of accent, Philost. *Vit. soph.* 1.8.490. Greeks could mock foreigners who made slips in their Greek (Appian *Hist. rom.* 3.7.2); translation into Greek was also typically a "barbarian" initiative (Görgemanns, "Translations," 850–51). Plut. *Educ.* 6, *Mor.* 4A, wants to avoid Greek children's exposure to barbarian language and character.

1117. Quint. *Inst.* 1.5.5–33 applies the loanword *barbarismus* (barbarism) to the use of foreign terms in Latin (1.5.8; also to cruel language, 1.5.9). The Greek historian Dionysius of Halicarnassus (*Ant. rom.* 1.90.1), who wishes to praise Rome, divides all languages into Greek or barbarian but claims that Latin is a mixture of the two.

1118. E.g., Diod. Sic. 1.2.6; Iambl. *V.P.* 8.44. Sometimes we read of people protesting that they were not "barbarian," i.e., lowly assimilated into Greek culture or language (P.Oxy. 1681.4–7, esp. 5; Fronto *Ad M. Caes.* 1.8.7; *Ep. graec.* 1.5). The "noble barbarian" tradition sometimes countered this claim (Anacharsis *Ep.* 2.1–2).

1119. Demosthenes *Against Theocrines*, pre-Roman. Barbarians' nature is more servile (Arist. *Pol.* 3.9.3, 1285a), and unlike Greeks, they are fit to be enslaved (1.2.18, 1255a; Eurip. *Iph. Aul.* 1401).

1120. Eurip. *Iph. Aul.* 1400–1401; Demosth. *Olynth.* 3.24 (cf. also *Philip.* 3.45); Arist. *Pol.* 1.1.4, 1252b; Tullius in Dion. Hal. *Ant. rom.* 4.26.2 (insisting that Latins are Greeks). Greeks and barbarians are natural enemies (Plato *Rep.* 5.470C).

1121. Cadbury, *Acts in History*, 32 (pointing out that Jews such as Philo and Josephus admit that they are barbarians, he regards this as Greek "superiority," as in Acts 21:37–39). See further, e.g., Strabo 16.2.38; Jos. *War* 1.3; *Ag. Ap.* 2.148; but cf. Philo *Embassy* 215; Jos. *Ant.* 18.47.

1122. Indeed, if we take into account the difference between rhetorical expectations for letters and those for (more demanding) historical narrative, Paul's Greek, on average, compares favorably in some ways to Luke's!

1123. See Jipp, *Visitations*, 24, 40–42, 103–5, 258–59. For the image of what came to be called "noble barbarians," see 43–44; also my comments above and Keener, *Acts*, 2:1538, 1557.

1124. Salmon, Boardman, and Potter, "Melita"; cf. Casson, *Mariners*, 66. Melite fell to Rome in 218 B.C.E. (Kalcyk and Niemeyer, "Melite").

Punic (Carthaginian) variety of the ancestral Phoenician tongue.[1125] Bilingual inscriptions from Malta in this period include Punic (*CIS* 1.124; *CIG* 3.5753), which was apparently the sole language of the majority of people.[1126] (Aristocratic Romans would not have approved.)[1127] Their ethnic identity was also Phoenician, like that of the descendants of Phoenicians in North Africa;[1128] Punic culture continued for at least two centuries after the Roman conquest.[1129] (Even today Malta's location and history lead to linguistic fusion. The modern Maltese language fuses Arabic from North Africa with a Sicilian dialect of Italian; though considered a Semitic language, it is written with Latin script.)[1130]

The dominant Punic language of the Maltese would not have created a barrier for the communication occurring in Acts 28:7–10.[1131] Finding Latin-speakers who could interpret for the less educated locals would not have been difficult. Publius (28:7) would speak Latin, as would others. Because Caesar settled veterans there, a number of families on the island would have spoken Latin as a first language, even if none are here on the beach.[1132] (Prominent Romans had stayed on Malta; e.g., Cic. *Att.* 10.9.)

This was not unusual in the West. In contrast to Rome's pro-Greek policy in the East,[1133] Rome used Latin for the cities it founded in the West, "ignoring all local languages, whether Iberian, Celtic, Punic, or Libyan."[1134] These societies included a romanized elite, some who retained indigenous culture fully, and others (ideally many) who were partially romanized.[1135] Roman-period texts in Punic are sometimes bilingual (with Latin) and use Latin loanwords.[1136] First-century Malta produced inscriptions with both Greek and Latin, and excavators have found distinctly Roman architectural remains (such as baths and villas).[1137]

Still, the "barbarian" linguistic claim of Acts 28:2 is entirely probable. On Malta (as on the other proposed island), educated people spoke Greek and/or Latin whereas most of the inhabitants could not, as both inscriptions and literary sources attest.[1138] Because most first-century inscriptions there are bilingual with Punic and Greek (the latter perhaps because of the Eastern grain traffic), some scholars suggest that the

1125. Trump, "Malta," 404; Lake and Cadbury, *Commentary*, 340 (citing Strabo 17.3.15–16; Diod. Sic. 5.12; Cic. *Verr.* 4.46–47; following Zahn, *Apostelgeschichte*, 841ff., for fuller documentation); see other sources in Hemer, *Acts in History*, 152n149.

1126. Haenchen, *Acts*, 713 (citing Zahn, *Apostelgeschichte*, 842); Conzelmann, *Acts*, 223; Fitzmyer, *Acts*, 783. For interaction of Latin, Punic, and other languages in nearby Sicily, see Tribulato, *Language*.

1127. Note the disdain in Apul. *Apol.* 98. By Apuleius's day, Latin and Punic bilingualism was probably common in Carthage (Hilton, "Introduction," 126), at least among the educated.

1128. Many North African indigenes still called themselves "Canaanites" in their Punic language much later (Aug. *Ep.* 209.2–3; Greene, "North Africa," 155). Their local identities also asserted themselves against Rome in the Donatist controversies (e.g., Mandouze, "Donatisme," 366).

1129. Trump, "Malta," 404. On the Punic period, see Trump, "Malta," 403–4. Punic religion also persisted (Scheid, "Africa: Religion").

1130. It became one of Malta's official languages in 1934. But the Semitic character of the language (which González, *Acts*, 275, compares with Phoenician) primarily reflects Arabic.

1131. Malina and Pilch, *Acts*, 175, suggest that Paul's knowledge of Aramaic would help with communication. Even if Semitic connections were helpful, however, mutual intelligibility would surely be limited.

1132. See Haenchen, *Acts*, 713; Barrett, *Acts*, 1220.

1133. Garnsey and Saller, *Empire*, 189.

1134. Ibid., 186 (citing, e.g., *CIL* 2.4319).

1135. Bénabou, "Résistance," 374 (on Roman Africa, contending that romanized peasants and townspeople were probably the majority; but the degree of romanization was undoubtedly higher where Rome had more interests, such as grain). Webster, "Creolizing," argues that outside the elites, Roman provinces were more accurately "creolized" than "romanized." Local cultures even affected Roman culture; on Gaul, see Woolf, "Romans and Natives."

1136. Amadasi Guzzo, "Phoenician-Punic," 324.

1137. Barrett, *Acts*, 1220.

1138. Ibid., 1221 (noting Diod. Sic. 5.12; Cic. *Verr.* 2.4.46, mentioned above).

islanders likely spoke Punic with one another but Greek to their shipwrecked guests.[1139] Probably most of the nonelite persons present did not even speak Greek (hence the label "barbarians"; but cf. their apparent intelligibility in 28:4, 6), but only a few of those present would need to know some for communication and interpretation to occur. Once the voyagers made contacts of higher status (28:7), communication would be more fluent.

v. Starting a Fire

As noted above, orators praised cities for their hospitality and philanthropy; when possible, they also liked to praise them for their good weather,[1140] an option that Luke does not have for this narrative! The rain is expected during this season (see comment on Acts 27:9) and reflects the same hostile weather that kept skies continually overcast for days (27:20).[1141] Commentators suggest that the temperature in Malta during this time of year is normally about 50° F.[1142] Modern websites suggest an average closer to 60° F (about 15° C),[1143] but in any case the temperature would be lower and would feel cooler in the rain, especially to those who had come ashore in their barest garments and now had nothing dry to wear.[1144] Everyone would recognize that those soaked with water would feel cold (cf. Polyb. 3.71.11–3.72.6).[1145] The first attempts to bring the ship to land, and hence probably the arrival of the first swimmers ashore, came in the early morning light (Acts 27:27, 33, 39), and even normal mornings were cool.[1146]

Once they were on land, the first act of those drenched during a storm at sea might be to start a fire (Virg. *Aen.* 1.174–76). It is possible (though no more than that) that Luke's audience might recall another fireside scene: whereas Peter denied Jesus at a fireside (Luke 22:56–57), Paul here honors Jesus. The fire itself is not unusual, and readers of Acts would not necessarily think of Luke 22 (both indicate cool weather, but Luke words them differently);[1147] still, these are the only two explicit fireside scenes, and both events are roughly parallel in literary location, placed near the ends of their respective books. The cock reveals Peter's failure (22:60–61) whereas the viper in Acts 28:5 reveals Paul's "power."

d. Paul Survives a Snakebite (28:3–6)

When a viper bites Paul, locals apparently expect him to die from the bite, offering the popular association of divine vengeance as the cause. Paul's survival of the bite,

---

1139. Witherington, *Acts*, 776.

1140. Men. Rhet. 1.2, 347.13–351.2; 351.10–11.

1141. It fits the gregale in contrast to the warm southeastern winds (Hemer, *Acts in History*, 153, comparing the sirocco).

1142. See Witherington, *Acts*, 777. He cites Haenchen, *Acts*, 713n3; Haenchen in fact follows Zahn in suggesting an October average of 22° C, i.e., over 70° F, with a low of 12°, i.e., some 54° F, during a northeasterly storm and unbearable heat during a southeasterly storm.

1143. According to http://www.holiday-weather.com/malta/averages/december, Malta has an average of 57° F (14° C) in December, the island's wettest month; 63° F (17° C) in November; 55° F (13° C) in January. The average low for December is 52° F (11° C). According to http://en.wikipedia.org/wiki/Climate_of_Malta, Malta averages 59–61° F (15–16° C) in winter and 63° F (17° C) during the periods of spring to March and autumn to December.

1144. If one reasons from average temperatures rather than the rain, the cooler temperatures of the proposed Adriatic site would seem more likely at this point (as Barrett, *Acts*, 1221, notes). Haenchen, *Acts*, 713n3, notes that those "soaked to the skin" would freeze in the wind.

1145. Ambrosiaster *Commentary on Paul's Epistles* (Vogels, 295–96; Bray, *Corinthians*, 299) applies Paul's experience of cold and exposure (2 Cor 11:27) to Malta, but Paul wrote 2 Corinthians before this experience.

1146. Dio Chrys. *Or.* 52.1 compares early summer mornings to autumn weather.

1147. The warming scene is also not distinctively Lukan (Mark 14:54; John 18:18).

however, convinces them of something more positive but with them erring in the opposite direction, that he is divine instead. Here, as elsewhere in Acts, signs testify to God's power; apart from the gospel message, however, signs can be misinterpreted (cf. 14:11–13). Some scholars view this passage as a power encounter, with the serpent representing evil forces (cf. Luke 10:19; discussion below); a literal serpent, however, still allows the usual point of signs in Acts.

I. THE SETTING (28:3)

Paul's snakebite occurs when he is helping gather sticks[1148] for a fire, a menial task perhaps considered more appropriate for those of inferior status. Paul, however, is willing to work with his hands (as in Acts 20:34 and in Paul's own letters; see discussion at Acts 18:3). Paul cares for others' needs throughout the voyage (27:10, 22, 31, 34), drawing no distinction between Christians and non-Christians in his service.[1149]

When stiff from cold, snakes can easily be mistaken for twigs until revived by heat.[1150] (Egyptian snake charmers had long exploited this characteristic of snakes.)[1151] Some ancients told a fable about a farmer who warmed a viper nearly dead from the cold (Babr. 143.1–2), as Paul inadvertently does here. The viper then stretched itself out, fastened to his hand, and bit the farmer fatally (143.3–4). As the man was dying, he realized his story's moral: never show mercy to the wicked (143.5–6).[1152]

II. HARMFUL SNAKEBITES AND CURES

Snakebites appear as a frequent cause of suffering in antiquity,[1153] and they sometimes proved fatal.[1154] In Dioscorides's *De materia medica*, bites and stings appear frequently: scorpion stings account for 11.9 percent of cases; rabies, 10.42 percent; spider bites, 7.36 percent; and snakebites, 7.66 percent.[1155] An island snakebite on the foot lamed the legendary Philoctetes, who was abandoned because of his cries;[1156] Jewish teachers also viewed serpents as dangerous (e.g., *t. B. Qam.* 1:4).[1157]

1148. BDAG has for φρύγανον, in the plural, "pieces of dry wood / brushwood especially for making fires" and provides documentation. Le Cornu, *Acts*, 1478, suggests an open bonfire using brushwood, which, as undergrowth, was perhaps less wet, and suggests that Malta had experienced less of the storm. With the ship's breakup and swimmers using boards, plenty of wood might lie on the shore, but it would still be too wet for kindling. On bonfires for warmth after a storm, see, e.g., Quint. Curt. 8.4.11–12.

1149. With Johnson, *Acts*, 461, who also points out that Jesus modeled service (Luke 22:24–27). Cf. the model of helping others in practical labor in 2 Kgs 4:39; 6:2–7.

1150. Bruce, *Commentary*, 521 (following Lawrence, *Revolt*, 107).

1151. See esp. Currid, *Egypt*, 86–95, esp. 95.

1152. The fable is also attested in Phaedrus 4.20.

1153. E.g., Philost. *Hrk.* 4.4. Pliny E. *N.H.* 25.55.99 calls snakebite "the worst ill of all" (LCL, 7:209).

1154. Apollod. *Bib.* 1.3.2; 3.6.4; Diod. Sic. 20.42.2; Ovid *Metam.* 11.775–76 (a nymph!); cf. Hierocles *Elements of Ethics* 2.12–15; for the expectation that they would be fatal, see Libanius *Comparison* 5.10. Vipers' poison was thought to be toxic on arrows (Ovid *Pont.* 1.2.16; Sil. It. 1.322).

1155. Touwaide, "Disease," 548 (including also in the toxicological category mushroom poisoning, 10.56 percent). Various texts naturally linked serpents with scorpions as venomous creatures, as in Luke 10:19 (Pliny E. *N.H.* 11.62.163; 20.71.182; 23.80.155; 27.98.124; Plut. *Div. V.* 20, *Mor.* 562C; Deut 8:15 [cf. Grelot, "Étude"]; *t. Šabb.* 7:23; *Sipre Deut.* 172.1.1; *y. Šabb.* 14:1, §2; *Exod. Rab.* 10:1; *Eccl. Rab.* 5:8–9, §4); for the danger posed by scorpions, including pain and sometimes death, see, e.g., Xen. *Mem.* 1.3.12; Pliny E. *N.H.* 11.30.86–88; Fronto *Ad M. Caes.* 5.8 (23); 5.9 (24). For treatments (according to some sources), see Pliny E. *N.H.* 20.51.133; 20.63.171; 20.71.182; 24.66.108; 27.98.124; 27.104.127; 28.42.155; to keep them away, 20.52.145; 23.80.155; 25.72.119; 28.5.24; to attract them, 20.48.120.

1156. Hom. *Il.* 2.721–23; Soph. *Philoc.* passim, esp. 632; Dio Chrys. *Or.* 59.3; Philost. *Hrk.* 28.2; Philost. Younger *Imag.* 17. Snakes were known particularly for biting feet (Aeschylus *Suppl.* 896–97; Ovid *Metam.* 11.775–76; Gen 3:15; 49:17; cf. *Sib. Or.* 1.59–64), and so accidentally stepping on one could be dangerous (Diod. Sic. 20.42.2; Virg. *Aen.* 2.379–81).

1157. In Scripture, e.g., Prov 23:32 (of wine); Eccl 10:8, 11. Rabbis sometimes mentioned snakebites alongside dog bites (*y. Roš Haš.* 3:9, §4; cf. *y. Ter.* 8:7, §6).

Even piety did not always protect from snakebites,[1158] but extraordinary piety was thought to sometimes have that effect.[1159] When once a poisonous reptile bit R. Hanina ben Dosa while he was praying,[1160] he did not interrupt his prayers, and only the reptile died.[1161] In a later version, R. Hanina deliberately provoked a hostile reptile to bite him, so that the reptile died; he then lectured, "It is not the lizard that kills, it is sin that kills!"[1162]

Greeks told wonder stories about snakes and associated them with particular cults.[1163] Thus, if the snake in a frieze at Eleusis is intended literally, Eleusinian initiates ideally needed not to fear snakes (to whatever extent such an ideal was realized).[1164] Snakes could be associated with Asclepius (and hence healing);[1165] with Apollo slaying the serpent Python (see comment on Acts 16:16), the Furies, or other terrifying monsters with snake "hair";[1166] and perhaps with Orphic or Dionysiac rites in older Macedonia.[1167] In mythology, killing snakes even caused one man a magical transgender experience.[1168]

Snakebites were among maladies not easily cured.[1169] Many cures and preventions reflect folk traditions. For example, Lemnian soil supposedly cured one's snakebite (Philost. *Hrk.* 28.5); stag's tooth or stag's testicles protected against snakebite;[1170] Egyptian priests provided spells against them from the pharaonic period to late antiquity.[1171]

1158. E.g., *y. Ter.* 8:5, §6 (here because one left wine susceptible to uncleanness as well as to venom); *Pesiq. Rab Kah.* 26:2 (a young man whose father was pious and had pious guests). See esp. R. Eleazar ben Dama in *t. Ḥul.* 2:22 (Smith, *Parallels*, 82).

1159. Brawley, *Luke-Acts and Jews*, 57, cites *b. Šabb.* 156b on protection for Israelites with merit; later, cf. Antony of Choziba *Life of Saint George* 5.22. The point of the story is deliverance from astrology and fate. Greek heroes such as Heracles conquered serpents, but differently (Paus. 1.24.2).

1160. One should not interrupt prayer even if a snake coiled around one's heel (*m. Ber.* 5:1; *Exod. Rab.* 9:3).

1161. See *m. Ber.* 5:1; *t. Ber.* 3:20 (2:20 in some versions). Hanina appears as a "charismatic" sage elsewhere (cf. *m. Ber.* 5:5; *Soṭah* 9:14–15; *b. Ber.* 34b; *Yoma* 53b; *Taʿan.* 24a; 24b–25a; *Yebam.* 121b; *Soṭah* 49ab; *B. Qam.* 50a; *B. Meṣiʿa* 106a; *B. Bat.* 74b; *Ḥul.* 86a); see further Vermes, *Jesus the Jew*, 73–74 (citing also *b. Ber.* 33a; *y. Ber.* 9a; cf. Urbach, *Sages*, 1:109); he is portrayed as respected by rabbis (*b. Ber.* 61b) and demons (*b. Pesaḥ.* 112b). Others cite the same text for Acts (Cadbury, *Acts in History*, 25; idem, *Making*, 343; following Cadbury, see also Kanda, "Form," 299).

1162. *B. Ber.* 33a, bar. (Soncino).

1163. For snakes in Greek myth and religion, see, e.g., Kauppi, *Gods*, 107–10; most fully Charlesworth, *Serpent* (esp. 125–87). Athena could be portrayed sporting a deadly snake (Libanius *Descr.* 22.8), and the infant Heracles slew them (e.g., Apollod. *Bibl.* 2.4.8; Libanius *Narration* 23; 24.2). In ancient Middle Eastern religion, see Hendel, "Serpent," 744–45.

1164. Burkert, *Mystery Cults*, 94. Rousselle, "Snake-Handling," provides some information on Hellenistic women snake handlers, but the study is marred by its excessive Freudian grid.

1165. Statius *Silv.* 3.4.25; Paus. 2.27.2; Lucian *Alex.* 14; cf. Koester, *Introduction*, 1:182; Klauck, *Context*, 165. Serpents were sacred to Athena (Plut. *Isis* 71, *Mor.* 379D) and also appear in connection with Egyptian traditional religion (cf., e.g., the Isis iconography in Brenk, "Image," 223).

1166. E.g., Pindar *Pyth.* 10.46–47; Ovid *Metam.* 4.454, 475, 491–99; *Her.* 2.119; *Tristia* 4.7.11–12; Tibullus 1.3.69; Sen. Y. *Herc. fur.* 88, 100–103; Statius *Theb.* 1.103; 8.762–64; Sil. It. 2.546–47; 9.442–43; Lucian *Dial. G.* 250 (23/19, Aphrodite and Eros 1); Paus. 1.28.6 (on Aeschylus); Ach. Tat. 1.3.4; cf. (often with serpent parts elsewhere) Hom. *Il.* 6.179–82; Apollod. *Bib.* 1.6.3; 3.14.1; Ovid *Metam.* 4.481–84, 617–20; *Fasti* 3.799–800; Sen. Y. *Ep. Lucil.* 113.9; Dio Chrys. *Or.* 5.13; 66.29; Paus. 8.42.4; Philost. *Hrk.* 8.7–8; *PGM* 4.2614; *Apoc. Zeph.* 6:8; with scorpion parts, Pliny E. *N.H.* 8.30.75; Rev 9:7–10. Cf. Bremmer, "Gorgo," 938.

1167. Pomeroy, *Goddesses*, 122, citing Plut. *Alex.* 2.4–5.

1168. See, e.g., Hesiod *Melampodia* 3 (from scholiast on Hom. *Od.* 10.494); Ovid *Metam.* 3.316–38; Lucian *Dial. D.* 445 (9/28, Menippus and Tiresias 1).

1169. Arrian *Ind.* 15.11 claims that Greek physicians could not cure Indian snakebites but Indians knew how to.

1170. Pliny E. *N.H.* 28.42.150. For remedies and prophylaxis against snakebites, 28.42.149–54; against scorpions, 28.42.155; plants useful for curing snakebites are listed in 25.55.99–25.71.119 passim. For further protection against snakebites, see 29.22.71. Among medicinal testicles, those of beavers were among the most highly valued (Hierocles *Elements of Ethics* 3.12–16). Ancient medical superstitions more generally included bloodletting (Nutton, "Phlebotomy"; see more generally sources in Keener, *Acts*, 1:417–18).

1171. Frankfurter, *Religion in Egypt*, 211. For charms against snakes, see Pliny E. *N.H.* 28.4.19; in Jewish texts, see Ps 58:5; Eccl 10:11; Sir 12:13; cf. Jer 8:17.

The Asclepius temple in Cos recommended a particular mixture to cure all venomous wounds except that caused by the asp.[1172] Remedies also included the following:[1173]

- "Fresh dung of sheep boiled down in wine and applied, and mice cut in two and placed on the wound" are cures.[1174]
- Turnip seed is rubbed into the skin or mixed with wine and then drunk to prevent snakebite; according to some, this could be mixed with wine and oil as a cure.[1175]
- Cultivated radishes in water and vinegar, rubbed into the skin, are a cure.[1176]
- Rue cures snakebites.[1177]
- A rubdown with three leaves and a special kind of oil serves as a serpent repellant.[1178]
- Roman coriander mixed with honey and vinegar cures serpent wounds; burning it keeps serpents away.[1179]
- Pounded mustard, applied with vinegar, counteracts serpent bites and scorpion stings.[1180]
- Anything from the phalangitis plant helps treat serpent, scorpion, or spider wounds.[1181]
- Although serpents like fennel to cure their eyesight,[1182] a similar substance cures snake and scorpion wounds.[1183]
- Others view hippomarathum as the most effective cure for snakebites.[1184]
- For vipers, some recommend placing a viper head on the bite.[1185]
- Eating a sort of grape cures serpent bites;[1186] bayberries cause venomous animals to stay away and, if drunk, can help cure their wounds.[1187]
- Pliny the Elder warns, however, that the best protection against serpents is a fasting person's saliva.[1188]

1172. Pliny E. *N.H.* 20.100.264. Asclepius oracles supposedly revealed the useful herbs (Philost. *Vit. Apoll.* 3.44).

1173. Most of these are reported in Pliny, never one to suffer folly unchecked—except, apparently, in cases such as these.

1174. Pliny E. *N.H.* 29.15.59 (trans. W. H. S. Jones, LCL, 8:221), also listing other cures; cf. the decoctions in 24.93.150; 24.99.157; 27.34.57.

1175. Pliny E. *N.H.* 20.9.18.

1176. Pliny E. *N.H.* 20.13.23.

1177. Pliny E. *N.H.* 20.51.132 (clear, Pliny assures us, because weasels eat rue before battling snakes).

1178. Pliny E. *N.H.* 20.63.171. This herb also healed scorpion stings and snakebites (20.65.173) in case someone had failed to use it as a prevention. For rubdown with another substance, see 24.92.148.

1179. Pliny E. *N.H.* 20.71.182; another substance, when burned, also keeps them away or intoxicates them into harmlessness (24.92.148). My wife informs me that in Congo, a particular herb planted around a home is believed to keep snakes at a distance (to those who use it, it appears efficacious, but empirical studies are so far lacking).

1180. Pliny E. *N.H.* 20.87.236. Ground pines cure scorpion stings (24.20.29) and, when mixed with honey, can cure serpent bites (24.20.30); wine mixed with a particular kind of leaf also cures snakebites (24.35.52); so also agnus castus (24.38.61).

1181. Pliny E. *N.H.* 27.98.124.

1182. Pliny E. *N.H.* 20.95.254.

1183. Pliny E. *N.H.* 20.96.256.

1184. Pliny E. *N.H.* 20.96.258.

1185. Pliny E. *N.H.* 29.21.69. See other cures for viper bites in 29.21.69–70.

1186. Pliny E. *N.H.* 23.11.14.

1187. Pliny E. *N.H.* 23.80.155 (noting that they serve as a prophylaxis if drunk with wine). Some ancients prescribed exactly ten berries for scorpion stings (23.80.156).

1188. Pliny E. *N.H.* 28.7.35. The tradition of the potentially curative properties of fasting saliva (see further 28.7.35–37; 28.22.76) apparently remained in later eras (Rack, "Healing," 140–41).

One folk cure, then viewed as religious, for snakebite in Jewish sources would also be viewed as sympathetic magic from a modern vantage point.[1189]

III. AUTHORITY OVER SNAKES

Slightly closer to this narrative might be claims of people immune to snakes. Pliny the Elder claims that some people have magical powers—for example, those who can scare away serpents and, by touch or suction, can cure those bitten by them. Sometimes this property ran in the family; to test this claim empirically, Romans threw one of these people into a container with snakes, which did not harm him; the drawback of this gift is that these people emit a foul odor during the spring.[1190]

Greeks and Jews, however, had other accounts that, like Jewish stories about R. Hanina ben Dosa, are much closer to this narrative; they emphasize a holy person's divine protection from or power over animals. Pythagoras allegedly subdued snakes and sent them away pacified (Iambl. *V.P.* 28.142), as part of his ability to soothe (13.60) and persuade (13.61–62) animals. He believed that all creatures were linked in "brotherhood" because they were composed of the same elements; thus, rather than harm animals, he sought to educate them (24.108). Beasts were also supposedly harmless to other "divine men."[1191] The Pythagorean Apollonius was said to tame fierce dogs (Philost. *Vit. Apoll.* 6.43; 8.30). Some writers could also romanticize about the devout being safe from animals (Hor. *Odes* 1.22.1–16, noting the retreat of a wolf).

A plausible biblical background is Moses's divinely given authority over serpents, and divine protection against (or healing for) the bites of serpents (Exod 4:3; 7:9–12; Num 21:6–9; cf. Deut 8:15).[1192] Somewhat less likely, Paul's authority over the viper might also evoke humanity's original authorization over all creatures, including "creeping things" (Gen 1:28).[1193] Jewish traditions sometimes viewed this mandate as continuing after the fall; thus, for example, God's people would subdue all wild animals so long as they followed God (*Test. Iss.* 7:7).[1194] In some Jewish traditions, creatures of the earth still obeyed Adam after the fall (*Apoc. Mos.* 29:13–14), although this is not a permanent arrangement (24:4). Adam's son Seth orders the beast (a serpent; cf. *L.A.E.* 37:1–3) to stand back from himself, God's image (39:1–2), and it obeys (39:3; cf. also *Apoc. Mos.* 12:1–2).

Other Jewish texts refer to human rule over animals. In an earlier text, crows obey Abram (*Jub.* 11:20).[1195] Human peace with animals would be restored in the

---

1189. See Bar-Ilan, "Magic and Religion."

1190. Pliny E. *N.H.* 28.6.30 (he notes people on one island who have similar effectiveness against crocodiles, 28.6.31).

1191. Conzelmann, *Acts*, 223, cites Plut. *Cleom.* 39; Lucian *Lover of Lies* 11. Cf. later stories about Saint Francis. Strelan, *Strange Acts*, 291, suggests that here Paul, like Heracles, defeats the netherworld creature by fire; this connection, however, reads too much into the fire here and overlooks the vast repertoire of closer potential parallels.

1192. For the Egyptian background for this motif, see Currid, *Egypt*, 83–103, 146–55, esp. 87–88, 148–49.

1193. The LXX uses a term here for reptiles, often applied to snakes (see BDAG). These creatures were to obey human commands (Philo *Abr.* 45), worship Adam (*Creation* 83), or follow Adam (cf. *Gen. Rab.* 63:13); Adam named them (Gen 2:19–20; Philo *Creation* 149) and was to rule them (Gen 1:26–28; Ps 8:6–8; Sir 17:4; Philo *Creation* 148; cf. 1 Esd 4:2; Wis 10:2). If Jesus evokes Adam in Luke 3:38, Adam typology (cf. Acts 17:26; Neyrey, *Passion*) might be in the background here, though I believe that it is unlikely. Epict. *Diatr.* 1.16.5 believed that nature equipped animals to serve people (though he refers especially to sheep).

1194. Because the context is about prevailing over sin, this passage in the *Testament of Issachar* could be understood in a manner analogous to Luke 10:19, but other parallel lines suggest that the two passages relate on the general principle of authority rather than on their specific object. Cf. Joseph's immunity to love potion in *Test. Jos.* 6:1–8, esp. 7–8.

1195. For cooperative animals, see also *Test. Job* 40:10/11; for creatures' fear of humans, the purportedly Tannaitic tradition in *Gen. Rab.* 34:12 (but this applies only before people sin, *Song Rab.* 3:7, §5, bar.).

eschatological era of Isa 11:6–9 (see, e.g., *Sib. Or.* 3.788–95); regarding snakes in particular, some rabbis expounded Isa 11:8 (children unharmed by snakes) as children pulling the poison from adders' mouths (*Sipra Behuq. pq.* 2.262.1.3). Christian tales about the apostles also gave them remarkable authority,[1196] such as John's authority over obedient bedbugs (*Acts John* 60–61). More important than such sources would be the widely known story of God protecting Daniel from lions (Dan 6:22) and especially the psalmist's confidence of safety with regard to lions and serpents (Ps 91:13).[1197] Some ancient interpreters treated Paul's victory here as a model, arguing that holiness or faith could protect the virtuous from snakebites, as they protected Paul.[1198]

At least some early Christians viewed picking up serpents (presumably unintentionally, as here) without suffering harm as a sign of divine power (Mark 16:18).[1199] Luke curiously omits a Markan statement, which he could have developed into a parallel for Acts 28:3–9 (Mark 1:13), about safety among animals. Luke earlier presents Jesus as authorizing the Seventy or Seventy-Two to tread on serpents and scorpions uninjured (Luke 10:19); although that text uses this image symbolically for power over evil spirits (10:17–18, 20), it implies that Paul shares the same measure of authority delegated from Jesus.[1200]

Some scholars thus suggest a corresponding allusion to Satan's work here.[1201] Luke does not always employ the image of a serpent thus; probably the image in Luke 3:7 evokes parent murder.[1202] Although there is no thought that the viper represents a demon, Luke's audience could easily believe that its fixing on Paul (who alone is bitten, as the observers notice, Acts 28:4) constitutes an attack from Satan, who is a very personal character in Luke-Acts (Luke 4:2–13; 8:12; 10:18) and can cause physical suffering (13:16; Acts 10:38).[1203] What would be the coincidence that the

1196. Conzelmann, *Acts*, 223, compares *Act Thom.* 106; *Acts Pet.* 5.29.

1197. The latter text is noted by Basil *Hom. Hex.* 9.6 (Martin, *Acts*, 312).

1198. See Theodoret in *Cat. Act.* 28.3; Basil *Hom. Hex.* 9.6, citing Ps 91:13 (Martin, *Acts*, 312). This approach continues the similar Jewish model noted above.

1199. Not necessarily dependent on Luke here. Malina and Pilch, *Acts*, 175, note that snake handling without suffering harm is documented for some experiencing altered states of consciousness.

1200. Thus the reader of Acts 28:4 knows better than to accept the verdict of the outsiders (Klauck, *Magic*, 114). Serpents may be associated with demons in *1 En.* 69:12 (possibly, but not necessarily, in *t. Šabb.* 7:23), but they are under Gabriel's control in the earlier *1 En.* 20:7. They are associated with casting spells in *Sipre Deut.* 172.1.1; with snake-charming magic in *ANET* 326; Iambl. (nov.) *Bab. St.* 10 (Photius *Bibl.* 94.75b); perhaps with magic in Ps.-Callisth. *Alex.* 1.10; with paganism in Hom. *Il.* 12.208–9 (a portent of Zeus); Simpson, *Literature of Egypt*, 45–53; Albright, *Biblical Period*, 13; Kaiser, "Pantheon," 42–43. Southern Semites apparently associated serpents (like some other animals) with jinn (Alexander, *Possession*, 15–16); for other wild beasts (especially hyenas) associated with jinn in Somalia, see Lewis, "Possession," 191 (for hyenas, see also Tubiana, "Zar," 19).

1201. E.g., Gaventa, *Acts*, 358; Thomas, *Deliverance*, 290–93, esp. 292; Jipp, *Visitations*, 46, 261 (following Susan Garrett, a noted expert on Lukan demonology, in advancing the concept of a "turf battle" here). Some ancient interpreters compared the viper here with unclean spirits (Bede *Comm. Acts* 28.3b [L. Martin, 193]) or the devil (Arator *Acts* 2 [Schrader, 91–92; Martin, *Acts*, 311–12]). Cf. various negative portrayals of snakes in mythology (e.g., in Bremmer, "Snake"; idem, "Gorgo"; Benson, "Dragon"). Augustan iconography might also use a serpent to depict threats (Knox, "Serpent"). For Genesis's serpent as the devil, see Wis 2:24; *3 Bar.* 9:7; cf. *Acts John* 94; as Sammael, *Tg. Ps.-J.* on Gen 3:6 (McNamara, *Targum*, 121); the devil utilized the serpent in *Apoc. Mos.* 16:1, 5. For the association of serpents or dragons with witchcraft, see Hor. *Sat.* 1.8.33–35; *PGM* 4.662–64, 2426–28, 2614.

1202. See Keener, "Brood of Vipers." In addition to sources cited there (including Eurip. *Orestes* 479; Hdt. 3.109; Aelian *Animals* 1.24 [cf. 15.16]; Pliny E. *N.H.* 10.82.170; Plut. *Div. V.* 32, *Mor.* 567F), see also Apul. *Apol.* 85; though doubt about the tradition is expressed in Philost. *Vit. Apoll.* 2.14. This may be a reason for vipers being sewn into a parricide's sack (Modestinus *Dig.* 48.9.9), although the practice may belong to a later period (Robinson, *Criminal Law*, 47). For "viper" or "serpent" as an insult more generally, see, e.g., Menander *Dyskolos* 480; Cic. *Vat.* 2.4; Plut. *Them.* 29.1; Apul. *Apol.* 8; Apoll. K. *Tyre* 32.

1203. This point would appear intelligible in many cultures. Several of my informants from rural Africa, including some Westerners who have lived there, have similarly viewed unusually targeted snake attacks as

narrative's hero, the one on whose behalf all the voyagers were preserved, would be the one bitten?

IV. The Viper in Malta (28:3–6)

There are no poisonous snakes in Malta today[1204] (an argument that some have used for the island being Kefallinía, where snakes include a poisonous viper).[1205] Of Malta's four varieties of snakes, only one is common, the nonpoisonous western whip snake. The other three are likewise not poisonous, though they look something like vipers.[1206] Some scholars thus suggest that the viper in the narrative was a nontoxic snake, such as *Coronella austriaca*, which resembles a viper and can fasten on to its victim as Acts 28:3–4 suggests.[1207] It is attested in Sicily and surrounding islands, and one was once identified on Malta in modern times. It also is known to irritate easily and fastens its teeth on people,[1208] but it can be easily pulled off without much damage to the skin.[1209] We could readily forgive Luke, not being from Malta, for not knowing local snakes (or understanding the conversation in 28:4–6).

Since even gestures and expressions might imply the responses of 28:4–6, it seems that the locals expected the viper to be toxic,[1210] but many people in snake-infested areas may simply avoid all snakebites instead of developing expertise in distinguishing similar forms of snakes from one another. In popular belief, even among the educated, all snakes were poisonous (Pliny E. *N.H.* 8.35.85).[1211] Luke reports the incident without passing verdict on the toxicity of the snakebite (though presumably Luke values it as a miracle example, in addition to valuing the opportunity to report the Maltese audience's response; ἔχιδνα also is normally viewed as a *poisonous* snake).

Nevertheless, would locals assume toxicity if *no* snakes on their island were known to be poisonous? Commentators often note that there may have been more kinds of

---

ultimately propelled by demonic attacks (cf. association with sorcery in Mbiti, *Religions*, 261–62). An even larger number of informants have affirmed divine protection in the face of snake attacks (e.g., Thomas, *Walls*, 33–34, 42–43; likely the point in Braun, *Way*, 54; Braun, *Here*, 248). For healing, see, e.g., Sithole, *Voice*, 56 (an African example); Ebenezer Perinbaraj (interview, Dec. 25, 2012, regarding Jharkand in India).

1204. See, e.g., Haenchen, *Acts*, 713n4; Twelftree, *Paul*, 266.

1205. Warnecke, *Romfahrt des Paulus*, 145–56.

1206. Le Cornu, *Acts*, 1479, citing Sultana and Falzon, *Wildlife*, 199, 202.

1207. Hemer, *Acts in History*, 153; Pesch, *Apostelgeschichte*, 2:298 (cf. Peterson, *Acts*, 699, though including n. 11). Le Cornu, *Acts*, 1479 (following Sultana and Falzon, *Wildlife*, 199, 202), writes of the "leopard snake," the *Coronella leopardinus*, which averages 3 ft. in length and is yellow or ash gray (with many "reddish-brown spots" bordered by black). Living especially "among stones and vegetation," it might be found in brushwood, as likely here. Although NT commentators often speak of the leopard snake (the European ratsnake) as the *Coronella leopardinus*, other sources usually call it *Zamenis situla* (usually today), *Coluber leopardinus*, or *Elaphe situla* (cf. The Reptile Database [http://www.reptile-database.org/]). On various snake species in ancient sources, see Hünemörder, "Snake."

1208. Conzelmann, *Acts*, 223, argues that "poisonous snakes do not bite and then hang on" (my wife, who grew up around snakes, said they would hold on if the alternative was to fall into flames). Bruce, *Commentary*, 522, simply says that vipers do not coil. Le Cornu, *Acts*, 1479, notes that these kinds of snake do cling as well as bite, though vipers only bite; their saliva is venomous, but they cannot inject it. Because such snakes strike only when threatened, it may have viewed Paul or the heat as a threat.

1209. Ramsay, *Luke the Physician*, 64 (also comparing two similar species found there, the *Coronella leopardinus* most resembling a viper in color).

1210. It is also true that some ancients believed that snakes harmless to locals could kill foreigners (Pliny E. *N.H.* 8.84.229); Luke does not explicitly indicate that the snake was deadly but only that the locals believed it to be. Charlesworth, *Serpent*, 330, apparently suggests that Paul was not actually bitten, or at least that the viper failed to inject much poison.

1211. Hemer, *Acts in History*, 153; Johnson, *Acts*, 462. The rabbis also expected snakebite to kill quickly (Le Cornu, *Acts*, 1482, cites *Exod. Rab.* 31:6; *b. Yebam.* 16:6; *y. Roš Haš.* 3.8.59a). For widely believed but erroneous views about vipers in antiquity, see Keener, *Matthew*, 123nn146, 148; idem, "Brood of Vipers," 6–8. Nevertheless, we read of tame pet snakes (Suet. *Tib.* 72, on Tiberius; Philost. *Hrk.* 31.3, on the legendary Ajax), and Pliny the Elder, cited above, believed asps deadlier than other kinds of serpents (*N.H.* 29.18.65).

snakes in Malta two millennia ago than are there today.[1212] Malta is heavily inhabited (with some 400,000 residents), and the forest cover is now gone.[1213]

Since humans are poisonous snakes' enemies, we should not be surprised if such snakes went extinct here; this has commonly occurred in many parts of the world as human expansion displaced snakes from their natural habitat. (Ancient capture of elephants for Roman spectacles, for example, drove North African elephants extinct.)[1214] Likewise, during my stays in Africa, locals have sometimes informed me about the disappearance of some snakes and dangerous animals in their region over the previous generation or two, as humans have expanded their settlement and eliminated possible dangers and competitors; killing snakes was often considered a duty.

v. Snakebite as Divine Vengeance? (28:4)

Cadbury catalogues some of the events implying divine providence in the narrative: Paul escapes from Judean demands for his execution; from the soldiers' judgment that they should kill the prisoners; from the Syrtis; from shipwreck; "from the savages, dreaded as pillagers of shipwrecks";[1215] and from harm from the snakebite.[1216] Many scholars today argue that Luke presents Paul's survival as vindicating his innocence.[1217] A survivor of shipwreck could be viewed as having divine favor.[1218] Although the local people draw the wrong conclusion from Paul's immunity to the snakebite in Acts 28:6, they rightly reverse their negative verdict in 28:4. This reversal underscores an implicit theme of Luke in these final chapters: Paul is vindicated by a justice greater than that of the Sanhedrin, Felix, Festus, Agrippa, or even the emperor before whom Paul is destined to appear.[1219]

Ancients would not view as a coincidence one's death by snakebite after escaping from shipwreck. Shipwrecks were often viewed as signs of divine punishment,[1220] a perspective that could be raised even in court.[1221] Indeed, some viewed it as just that the gods sink an entire ship, drowning all aboard, to punish a single impious person on board (Babr. 117). But an impious person who survived a shipwreck was not therefore guaranteed survival. Whoever suffered shipwreck more than once was said to blame Neptune wrongly; the fault lay with the person who invited such calamity.[1222]

Novels developed this expectation. Pirates who sold a pious captive and then faced terrible storms might realize that they had experienced fair sailing only for their

---

1212. Barrett, *Acts*, 1222; Bruce, *Commentary*, 522 (comparing tradition about early Ireland); Witherington, *Acts*, 777; Bock, *Acts*, 743. Fossil remains might be too early.

1213. Hemer, *Acts in History*, 153. This was pointed out already in Abbott, *Acts*, 257. Certainly Saint Paul's Bay in Malta is heavily urbanized today, with a residential population of more than 20,000 and rising to some 60,000 during the summer months, with a population density of 1,400 per sq. km. (3,700 per sq. mi.).

1214. Bauckham, *Climax*, 357; Weeber, "Environment," 1007; Schneider, "Ivory."

1215. This description is probably a misinterpretation of Luke's "barbarians"; see comment on Acts 28:2. But locals in Libya were thought to plunder shipwrecks (Quint. Curt. 4.7.19), and seizing flotsam was common enough to warrant legal measures, potentially even as harsh as capital punishment (Krampe, "Naufragium," 541, citing *Dig.* 47.9.3.8; 48.8.3.4).

1216. Cadbury, *Acts in History*, 25.

1217. See, e.g., Aune, *Environment*, 130; Talbert and Hayes, "Sea Storms."

1218. Val. Max. 1.8.ext. 7; Lucian *Phal.* 2.4 (ironically in this case); *Posts* 1 (again reflecting Lucian's skepticism). Any escape from tragedy was only by God's power (*Let. Aris.* 268).

1219. With Dunn, *Acts*, 347.

1220. Brawley, *Luke-Acts and Jews*, 56 (citing Jonah 1:4–8; *b. B. Meṣiʿa* 59b); Aune, *Environment*, 130; also, e.g., *1 En.* 101:5; Val. Max. 1.1.ext. 1 (destruction of a fleet); Sen. E. *Controv.* 7.1.4 (punishment for parricide); Iambl. *V.P.* 18.88; 34.247 (a Pythagorean who revealed a sacred mystery); see further the introduction, above, to Acts 27.

1221. E.g., Cic. *Verr.* 2.1.18.46 (the ship carrying divine statues that Verres had stolen was destroyed by a storm). Others, however, recognized that shipwreck, like being robbed, was not one's fault (Quint. *Decl.* 320.12).

1222. Publ. Syr. 331; also cited in Aul. Gel. 17.14.4. Perhaps like some other frequent seafarers, Paul would not agree; see 2 Cor 11:25.

captive's sake (Char. *Chaer.* 3.3.9–11). A survivor might be viewed as pious unless he survived only for a worse fate. One pirate claimed that he was spared death at sea only because of his piety (3.4.9); he was, in fact, spared for his impiety, however (3.4.10), so that he might face a worse fate (3.4.18).[1223] Evildoers who seemed to escape death in the short run would suffer their just deserts afterward.[1224]

Mere change in means of death would likewise simply signal that vengeance was inevitable, coming by one means or another (see discussion on Acts 28:4–5).[1225] This very circumstance of someone escaping shipwreck to die of snakebite is attested in an epitaph in *Gr. Anth.* 7.290, as commentators widely observe;[1226] the principle of escaping one trouble to face another is even older.[1227] Biblically literate readers might think more immediately of the more distant but better-known image in Amos 5:19, where one who escapes from a lion suffers divine judgment through a serpent.[1228]

It was often assumed, however, that those who genuinely survived and prospered must not be guilty of murder, for otherwise the gods would have taken advantage of their sea voyage to punish them (e.g., Antiph. *Her.* 82–84;[1229] cf. also Andocides *Myst.* 137–39).[1230] (It was not, therefore, surprising that many ancients preferred to sail with virtuous rather than with impious comrades [Xen. *Cyr.* 8.1.25].) In one novel, the Nile twice rescued Habrocomes from death, persuading onlookers and the prefect that the gods favored him and he might be innocent (Xen. Eph. *Anthia* 4.2).[1231] A person could appeal to how well the gods were treating him, to defend his character.[1232] Naturally, speakers for the defense and prosecution would interpret the same events quite differently.[1233] One could argue in court that another's sufferings at sea testify to his wickedness,[1234] a good reason for Luke not to invent the storm and shipwreck to begin with. One could also compare the joy of an acquitted person to that of someone who had escaped from a storm at sea (Max. Tyre 3.4). Helpfully for Luke's apologetic, Paul's survival of snakebite as well as storm attested his innocence.[1235]

1223. Though innocent, Apollonius (wrongly) feared that Neptune had spared him death at sea so that he could die another way (*Apoll. K. Tyre* 12). Pervo, *Acts*, 674, compares the robber's death by snakebite in Heliod. *Eth.* 2.20.

1224. Ant. Diog. *Thule* 109b–110a, 112a.

1225. The verdict, however, depends on the rhetorical perspective; thus one could generate pathos with the image of a person surviving a storm only to face shipwreck at the harbor (Dio Chrys. *Or.* 40.12).

1226. Conzelmann, *Acts*, 223 (who therefore jumps to the conclusion that Luke's account is "based on a literary motif"); Brawley, *Luke-Acts and Jews*, 56; Bruce, *Commentary*, 522n11; Johnson, *Acts*, 462; Polhill, *Acts*, 532; Witherington, *Acts*, 778. Klauck, *Magic*, 114, thinks that *Gr. Anth.* 9.269 (also cited by Johnson and Witherington) is closer, though the slayer is a seal. For snakes' association with justice and vengeance in Greek sources, see also Kauppi, *Gods*, 108–10. In a Middle Egyptian story two millennia earlier, by contrast, a large serpent befriended and prophesied to a shipwreck survivor ("The Shipwrecked Sailor," starting to speak in lines 57–68; see Simpson, *Literature of Egypt*, 45–53).

1227. Note Mesopotamian proverbs, e.g., *ANET* 425 (Akkadian proverb I [40:5]; Sumerian proverb 3).

1228. Not Luke's term for "viper" here, though he knows the LXX term that Amos uses (Luke 10:19; 11:11). Snakebite for a murderer who escaped from a lion appears in a papyrus in Grenfell and Hunt, *Fragments*, 133–34 (noted by Brawley, *Luke-Acts and Jews*, 57). For God's slaying through scorpion sting, see *b. Ned.* 41a; *Gen. Rab.* 10:7; through various creatures including serpents and scorpions, *Gen. Rab.* 10:5.

1229. Cited by Brawley, *Luke-Acts and Jews*, 56–57; esp. and originally by Miles and Trompf, "Luke and Antiphon," esp. 262–64. Ladouceur, "Shipwreck and Pollution," 436–39, shows that some evildoers did escape shipwreck.

1230. Cited by Ladouceur, "Shipwreck and Pollution," as a better parallel.

1231. Cf. the persistent survival of Polycarp's body in *Mart. Pol.* 15.1–16.2.

1232. E.g., Dion. Hal. *Ant. rom.* 8.33.1–3; Char. *Chaer.* 8.4.2 (war as an impartial judge!).

1233. E.g., regarding the hypothetical Vestal priestess who survived being thrown from the Tarpeian Rock for adultery (Sen. E. *Controv.* 1.3.1–6), whom only some defended as divinely vindicated (1.3.7).

1234. So Lysias *Or.* 6.21–32, §§105–6, regarding Andocides (disregarding his survival).

1235. With, e.g., Tannehill, *Acts*, 341; Miles and Trompf, "Luke and Antiphon"; Ladouceur, "Shipwreck and Pollution." Jipp, *Visitations*, 46, 262n31, contrasts with this the view that Paul here overcomes demonic opposition; but the approaches can be complementary.

This survival would confirm that Paul, unlike Jonah (Jonah 1:7–9), was not the cause of his ship's calamity, even though prisoners might be the first voyagers to whom critics would want to assign the guilt.

Jewish people viewed beasts as one divine means of judgment,[1236] and this included snakes.[1237] Greeks and Romans could view snakes similarly (cf. perhaps *Gr. Anth.* 7.290, above);[1238] even Pliny the Elder viewed snakes as executing revenge on anyone who killed their mates (*N.H.* 8.35.86).[1239] A snakebite on the hand might seem poetic justice for a "murderer" who used his hand for evil.[1240]

The "barbarians" (Acts 28:2) viewed Paul as a murderer facing justice. (On their view at this point, he would thus have been responsible for the shipwreck rather than for its passengers' survival.) Ironically, he had once been a murderer at least indirectly (26:10) but had become an agent of life (13:46, 48; 27:24). From Luke's perspective, murderers in fact sometimes escaped justice in this life (3:14–15), but Jesus's resurrection provided the paradigm (albeit not always the schedule) for divine vindication. This narrative at least obliquely critiques the assumption that one can infer sin from tragedies.[1241]

VI. PERSONIFIED JUSTICE (28:4)

Most scholars argue that by "justice" the Maltese residents refer to a goddess of justice.[1242] Justice was often personified, for example, alongside the Fates (Hor. *Odes* 2.17.15–16) or in a picturesque manner as a female deity (Chrysippus in Aul. Gel. 14.4).[1243] One facing unjust death at others' hands could depend on Justice to favor him (Philost. *Hrk.* 33.37). Commentators cite numerous examples of Justice as a goddess personifying revenge;[1244] perhaps most relevant is that Justice watches "over all that happens at sea" (Plut. *Dinner* 18, *Mor.* 161F).[1245] The Roman equivalent of the

---

1236. E.g., Wis 11:15–16 (if one had worshiped beasts); *t. Sanh.* 8:3 (purportedly about Simeon ben Shetah). Cf. the common formula in the prophets (e.g., Jer 16:4; Ezek 5:17; 14:21; serpents in Jer 8:17; Amos 9:3) and the example in Num 21:5–9.

1237. Boring, Berger, and Colpe, *Commentary*, 333–34, cite *Mek. Kaspa* 3.78.12; see esp. Silberman, "Paul's Viper" (adding other sources, e.g., *Lam. Rab.* 2:2, and emphasizing that Acts 28 shows Paul as specially favored by God). That Paul is even bitten might challenge, from a Lukan perspective, the idea that such bites should be viewed as punishments.

1238. Jipp, *Visitations*, 262n31, may be correct, however, that this text emphasizes instead fate's "unpredictability."

1239. Hemer, *Acts in History*, 153.

1240. Suggested by Cadbury, *Acts in History*, 26. On punishments (including those from deities) fitting crimes, see comment on Acts 3:2.

1241. A lesson also illustrated in Job's comforters (Job 4–25); cf. ancient Near Eastern wisdom in *ANET* 434–35; KRT C (vi) (*ANET* 149); Kramer, "Variation"; idem, "Literature," 281.

1242. Lake and Cadbury, *Commentary*, 341; R. Williams, *Acts*, 167; Bruce, *Acts¹*, 471; Schnabel, *Acts*, 1050. The term δίκη in other early Christian sources refers to divine vengeance or judgment (2 Thess 1:9; Jude 7; *Herm.* 27.5; 96.3; cf. *Did.* 1.5; 2 Macc 8:11, 13; 4 Macc 4:13, 21; 6:28; 8:14, 22; 9:9, 15, 32; 11:3; 12:12; 18:22; other LXX references).

1243. As a virgin in Dio Chrys. *Or.* 75.5; alongside Truth in Max. Tyre 10.1 (interpreting allegorically); Zeus's daughter in Eurip. *Andromeda* frg. 151 (Stob. 1.3.23). Phrygians worshiped the twin deities "Holy and Just" (Mitchell, *Anatolia*, 2:25) and—more relevant—a goddess of Justice (2:18). The Greek Dike was one of the three Horae from an ancient period (cf. Hom. *Il.* 5; Hesiod *Theog.* 901–2; *W.D.* 220–24); further on Dike, see van der Horst, "Dike" (on 252 noting the contemporary rather than classical perspective in Acts 28:4); distinct from Dike, cf. Themis (Käppel, "Themis," 424). On personified abstractions as deities, see Rives, *Religion*, 17.

1244. E.g., Johnson, *Acts*, 462; Fitzmyer, *Acts*, 783; citing Hesiod *Theog.* 902 (born alongside the Fates); Soph. *Antig.* 538; Arrian *Alex.* 4.9.7. She reported to Zeus and he executed justice in Hesiod *W.D.* 239, 256 (Larkin, *Acts*, 380). Cf. also Stenger, "Nemesis," on personified retribution. For the alleged view of the Persians, see Philost. *Vit. Apoll.* 1.25. Some resented as superstitious views of personified punishment (Pliny E. *N.H.* 2.5.14).

1245. Johnson, *Acts*, 462. Justice also could see in darkness (e.g., Eurip. *Oed.* frg. 555) and witnessed concealed misdeeds to punish them (Eurip. *Archelaus* frg. 255.2–6; *Phrixus* frg. 835; cf. *Melanippe* frg.

Greek Dike was Justitia; she appears primarily in poetry, but she also had a temple, and Augustus celebrated her as a virtue.[1246]

In Jewish thought, of course, justice was subordinate to God; when God brings judgment, evildoers face "terrifying justice" (δίκης, *Sib. Or.* 3.634).[1247] But along with mercy, justice was often personified as one of God's chief attributes.[1248] As among Greeks, so in Hellenistic Jewish sources, Justice pursued sinners and executed vengeance (Wis 1:8; 4 Macc 18:22).[1249]

Although syncretism and the blending of deities were common (see comment on Acts 8:10), these local residents, outside major harbors or cities, were probably minimally hellenized or romanized themselves.[1250] Punic religion persisted in Punic areas in the Roman period.[1251] Would the Maltese here have spoken of anything like a Greek goddess? Although Lake and Cadbury, for example, envision a Semitic deity of the Maltese that Luke has translated,[1252] Conzelmann doubts the need to seek "a Punic equivalent" to the Greek deity Justice.[1253] Since Luke would not likely know any Punic, Conzelmann's skepticism is understandable here. Nevertheless, sources indicate that the Phoenicians did have a divine or semidivine Justice; in Philo of Byblos, Sydyk (Justice) was a sort of demigod.[1254] Even had this not been the case, however, Luke could have presented in a more Hellenistic way a more abstract justice executed by a larger pantheon.[1255]

If Luke does report the locals' intention accurately, how would he know what they were saying?[1256] He could probably extrapolate the basic ideas (though more in Acts 28:4 than in 28:6) from their gestures and expressions; historians could use inference to fill in dialogue and speeches. Probably some of the locals knew rudimentary Greek or Latin; but they probably communicated to one another in Malta's Punic dialect (see comment on Acts 28:2), and so Luke might gain a more precise idea of their discussion only if he asked or was later (perhaps after 28:8–9) informed.

506.7–8), and the sufferings of the wicked were thought to vindicate the existence of deities (Eurip. *Oenomaus* frg. 577).

1246. Rose and Scheid, "Iustitia." Citing Ovid *Pont.* 3.6.25, Wright, *Paul*, 270, notes that this temple was consecrated in 13 C.E. Following Dihle, Jewett, *Romans*, 276, notes her association with the imperial cult. Vengeance was likewise a deity (Tac. *Ann.* 3.18).

1247. Gentiles, too, could attribute justice to the chief deity (e.g., Sil. It. 6.467).

1248. E.g., *3 En.* 31:1; *Tg. Rishon* on Esth 3:1; on these contrasting attributes more generally, see *Sipra VDDeho. par.* 12.65.2.4; *Sipre Num.* 8.8.2; *Sipre Deut.* 26.5.1; 323.4.1; *b. 'Abod. Zar.* 3b; *Ber.* 7a; *y. Ta'an.* 2:1, §12; *Gen. Rab.* 12:15; 21:7; 26:6; 33:3; 73:3; *Exod. Rab.* 6:1, 3; 45:6; *Lev. Rab.* 23:2; 29:4, 6, 9; *Num. Rab.* 9:18; *Eccl. Rab.* 4:1, §1; 8:1, §1; *Song Rab.* 2:17, §1; *Pesiq. Rab.* 10:9; 15:17; 40:2; see further Urbach, *Sages,* 1:448–61; Naeh, "Ποτήριον."

1249. See esp. the comments about Philonic usage in Lake and Cadbury, *Commentary*, 341 (the term appears 145 times in the Philonic corpus). Cf. δίκη in Jos. *War* 1.84 (Gaventa, *Acts*, 357; Josephus employs the term 157 times).

1250. Despite Roman pretensions with urban elites (Garnsey and Saller, *Empire*, 186), Punic remained dominant in North Africa even "six centuries after the Roman conquest" (Garnsey and Saller, *Empire*, 193; cf. 203).

1251. See Scheid, "Africa: Religion." In this period, locals often gave Punic deities Roman names (Rives, *Religion*, 71).

1252. Lake and Cadbury, *Commentary*, 341 (comparing Acts 14:12). Ramsay, *Luke the Physician*, 11, also thinks that Luke hellenizes their language.

1253. Conzelmann, *Acts*, 223.

1254. At least as understood by Euseb. *P.E.* 1.10 (Larkin, *Acts*, 380), who may have interpreted the source through a Christian grid when he was preserving it. Certainly, a Punic inscription from second-century B.C.E. Malta indicates the continuing worship of Canaanite/Phoenician goddesses at that time (for discussion of the precise translation, see Frendo, "Inscription").

1255. Cadbury, *Acts in History*, 25, notes that everyone in antiquity would have accepted the concept of avenging justice, even if only Greeks and Romans personified it.

1256. A question rightly raised, e.g., by Dunn, *Acts*, 347.

(Publius and other members of the island's elite certainly would have spoken Latin and probably, in many cases, Greek.)

VII. VIEWING PAUL AS A GOD (28:6)

Paul does not merely escape being bitten, suggesting innocence; rather, he fails to suffer the expected effects of a bite, suggesting special divine protection. Mistaking a mortal for a divinity appears commonly enough in ancient sources, especially novels (see comments on Acts 10:26; 14:11). Supernatural power bestowed by a god would make one appear as a god.[1257] Sometimes it is portrayed as humorous—for example, when Dionysius thinks that his slave Callirhoe is Aphrodite (Char. *Chaer.* 2.3.6–7), just as, on another occasion, some others thought that she was Aphrodite (1.14.1).

When the "barbarians," seeing Paul's immunity to the snakebite, change their mind from thinking that he is a murderer to thinking that he is a god (Acts 28:6), Luke offers some comic relief at the "barbarians'" expense. Whereas he was not making fun of them in 28:2, he is making fun of them here. This would be especially the case if his humor plays on Greek stereotypes of barbarians;[1258] Greek writers could portray barbarians as "superstitious by nature" (Xen. Eph. *Anthia* 3.11)[1259] or non-Greeks as too ready to worship mortals.[1260] (When it was useful for their purposes, however, Romans could also portray Greeks as fickle,[1261] a vice relevant to the radical change of mind here.[1262] The elite also could view the "masses" as superstitious and fickle.)[1263]

If Luke views the "barbarians" as superstitious or credulous (esp. in Acts 28:6), however, he does so no more than he views the people of Lystra (a Roman colony!) in 14:11 as such (and as fickle "masses" in 14:19).[1264] The change of mind here is precisely the opposite of what is encountered in 14:11–19: from wrongdoer to deity in this case, and from deity to wrongdoer in the other.[1265] If Luke displays any prejudice, it could be along the lines of rural versus urban;[1266] but the Maltese here are kind, and his only real complaint is most likely anti-pagan instead (cf. 17:18; 19:32).[1267] A chief reliable character in his narrative detests paganism in cultured Athens no less (17:16). The anti-pagan humor touches on a motif running throughout Acts.[1268] Whereas Jesus does receive adoration of sorts in the Gospel, it is inappropriate for other mortals. Peter rejects it (10:26), as do Paul and a companion on an earlier occasion (14:11). By contrast, Simon claims it (8:9–10), and Herod Agrippa I accepts it (12:22) with disastrous consequences (12:23). The only approved human recipient of veneration in Luke-Acts is Jesus (Luke 24:52, according to the best-attested reading; cf. 5:8;

1257. So *PGM* 1.190–91, promising the angel-helper's guidance in achieving this.

1258. On ethnic stereotypes in antiquity, see Malina and Neyrey, *Portraits*, 169–72, esp. 171–72.

1259. Anderson, 153; cf. Plut. *Superst.* 2, *Mor.* 166AB; Char. *Chaer.* 6.7.12. The portrayal of the superstition here is not hostile. Romans could disdain "barbaric" Spanish reception of a Roman general with incense and altars (Val. Max. 9.1.5); they were much more favorable toward Asia's imperial cult.

1260. See Persians in Quint. Curt. 6.6.2; 8.5.11, 14; Indians in 8.10.1. Cf. perhaps Dan 2:46 (with 3:5).

1261. Cic. *Flacc.* 11.24 (though he is anti-Greek here only because Greeks are prosecution witnesses). More often they portrayed Egyptians as fickle (Quint. Curt. 4.1.30; Pliny *Panegyr.* 31.2).

1262. On fickleness, see, e.g., Cic. *Fam.* 1.9.11; 5.2.10; *Quint. fratr.* 1.2.2.4; Vell. Paterc. 2.80.1; Apul. *Apol.* 77; fuller discussion at Acts 2:47.

1263. E.g., Quint. Curt. 4.10.7.

1264. For the apostles' enemies manipulating the crowds there, see Bechard, *Walls*, 431.

1265. As pointed out by Bruce, *Commentary*, 523n12; Gaventa, *Acts*, 358. The change of mind here might suggest some humbling, though not on the dramatic level of the apostles' actual competitors such as Simon (Acts 8:24), Elymas (13:11), or Sceva's sons (19:16).

1266. For these prejudices in antiquity, see the discussion in Keener, *Acts*, 1:589–96, esp. 592–96.

1267. Or perhaps viewing nonbelievers in general as too credulous (since he makes fun of the Sanhedrin also; cf. Acts 23:9–10). This would be returning a popular pagan perception of early Christians.

1268. For Jewish ridicule of idolatry, see discussion at Acts 14:15–17, esp. Keener, *Acts*, 2:2158–64.

17:16). Luke does not narrate Paul's response to the perspective here (he does not appear even cognizant of it), but the competent reader will infer his expected response from the previous occasion (Acts 14:14–18).

Recently Joshua Jipp has offered a strong argument concerning how Luke's first-century audience would have construed the "barbarians'" understanding of Paul as divine in connection with the hospitality offered before and after this turn in the narrative.[1269] Ancient narratives about theoxenies—unwitting hospitality or inhospitality toward a deity, with appropriate rewards or punishments following—were common; sometimes in Greek circles and regularly in Jewish circles analogous narratives also apply to divine agents, which Paul is here.[1270] Jipp notes that Jesus, too, was recognized in a setting of hospitality (Luke 24:29–32).[1271] He argues that in contrast to Jewish rejection in 28:17–25, Paul's last major scene of ministry among Gentiles in Acts is one of welcome, suggesting the trajectory for the continuing Gentile mission.[1272]

e. Healings and Hospitality (28:7–10)

Paul is exalted even in his continuing captivity; such exaltation within hardship reflects a common feature of biblical narratives. Joseph was exalted in Potiphar's house (Gen 39:2–6) and in prison (39:20–23); David was exalted as a bandit leader (1 Sam 22:2) or mercenary for the Philistines (27:5–7) even while fleeing King Saul.

Just as Greeks might praise Poseidon for fair weather after a winter storm,[1273] Luke implicitly praises God's providential care for the anticlimax that reduces the dramatic intensity by which the storm has dominated the narrative. God, who has watched over every point in the spread of the gospel to the Gentiles (e.g., Acts 10–11), has preserved the apostle for his witness in Rome; in the West God uses him first in Malta. From the standpoint of Acts 28:8–10, it is evident that the storm was no disaster, as it first appeared (and might well continue to appear from the standpoint of the owner's or underwriter's losses), but God's plan to lead Paul to such open people.[1274]

i. Publius's Hospitality (28:7)

Luke says that Publius lived in the vicinity of the shipwreck. Although he does not specify the "neighborhood" in view, we do have some details about Malta's habitation. Most prominent among such details is that one major inland city, founded by Carthaginians, was Melita, which Muslims later named Medina, with a suburb named Rabat.[1275] From Roman times until 1570 (when Valetta became the capital), Malta's

1269. Although they are mistaken about Paul being a god, Jipp, *Visitations*, 45–46, argues that they correctly perceive him as connected with the divine (a divine agent).
1270. Jipp, *Visitations*, 24, in his work clearly demonstrating the connection with theoxenies, on which see 77–95, 122–26 (for divine agents, e.g., 81–88; in Luke-Acts, 219–35); more briefly, Keener, *Acts*, 2:2148–49. These include Telemachus hosting Athena (Jipp, *Visitations*, 77–81); Dionysus in the *Bacchae* (a story to which Luke elsewhere alludes, 88–95). Jipp places the motif in the larger context of hospitality in Jipp, *Visitations*, 59–170 (including in Roman literature, 112–26; in Jewish sources, including the OT, 131–70; in Luke-Acts, 171–218); on which subject see also Arterbury, *Hospitality*; briefly, Keener, *Acts*, 3:2414–20.
1271. Jipp, *Visitations*, 25, 234–35.
1272. Ibid., 25, 29, 274–81 (cf. more broadly 247–52); see fuller discussion of the idea at Acts 28:17–31. Jipp connects Luke's motif of hospitality to his larger plot theme of Gentile reception. See my positive review of Jipp's work in Keener, "Review of Jipp."
1273. E.g., Pindar *Isthm.* 7.38–39.
1274. For Luke's emphasis on God's providence, see comment on Acts 2:23. Here too Luke may present Paul as like a good sage, making the best of what he faces (see comment on Acts 27:21–26).
1275. Finegan, *Apostles*, 200, 202.

capital was Medina/Rabat.[1276] The area around modern Valetta (today's capital) was also inhabited in the Punic and Roman periods.[1277]

Although most of the people who first helped the wrecked seafarers were poor, probably peasants, Luke indicates that many of the nearby estates belonged to Publius, who (wherever on the island his main residence was located) owned much of the nearby land. His name suggests, as does his status as the "first" citizen (see comment below), that he was a Roman citizen,[1278] as were many members of local elites in the western empire. Whether or not the "barbarians" who first welcomed the voyagers were his clients, Publius surely had many tenant farmers working his land and probably many clients in something closer to the more traditional urban sense as well. Word about Paul would therefore spread quickly. The system of landowners and tenants characterized most of the ancient Mediterranean world (e.g., Mark 12:1–2; see discussion of rural poverty at Acts 3:2).

Luke calls Publius the "first" man of the island—that is, one of its most influential citizens (see Luke's usage of πρῶτος in Acts 13:50; 28:17). The phrase "first" for a "leading citizen" is common in Latin[1279] and in Greek.[1280] When Augustus chose the fictively innocuous self-designation *princeps* ("first"), he borrowed a title from the republic (still used in the empire) for people of rank (see, e.g., Suet. *Aug.* 66; *Res gest.* 12).[1281] Officials in Asia employed the title "first,"[1282] as did those in Achaia;[1283] *princeps* is also a chief man in a town in Sicily (Cic. *Verr.* 2.3.23.56). It is also attested in inscriptions from Malta itself for the chief (πρῶτος, *IG* 14.601 = *IGRR* 1.512), and perhaps the foremost, citizen (*primus, CIL* 10.7495 = *ILS* 5415) of the Maltese.[1284]

Some scholars suggest that the title might mean that Publius was the praetorian legate (the administrator of Malta), since the legate's title was *Melitensium primus omnium*;[1285] but probably by now a procurator governed Malta (*CIL* 10.7494).[1286] Luke would not normally refer to a Roman official by his praenomen alone (Publius);[1287] and the question arises whether a legate would own so much of the local land. (That his father is present suggests that Publius is from Malta, since Roman officials did not bring their parents on such administrative assignments.)[1288]

1276. Ibid., 200.

1277. Ibid.

1278. Certainly it was a common Latin name (e.g., Mart. *Epig.* 7.87.3; 10.98.11).

1279. E.g., *princeps* in Vell. Paterc. 2.30.6; 2.53.2; 2.74.4 ("a leading man of the place," LCL); 2.90.1; Pliny *Ep.* 3.2.2; 6.31.3. For praises of individuals as among the "first" of their groups, see Symm. *Ep.* 1.2.4; 1.79; cf. 1.2.3.

1280. E.g., for one of the most prominent people in Pontus, Lucian *Alex.* 45 (πρῶτος).

1281. Balsdon and Griffin, "*Princeps*." For analogous uses, see Balsdon and Levick, "*Princeps iuventutis*"; Badian, "*Princeps senatus*."

1282. Strabo 14.42 (πρωτεύοντες); πρῶτος in *OGIS* 528, 544–45, 549, 652.

1283. The high priest of the Achaian imperial cult as *primus* (West, *Inscriptions*, no. 68.9, pp. 50–51).

1284. Wikenhauser, *Apostelgeschichte*, 283; Conzelmann, *Acts*, 223; Weiser, *Apostelgeschichte*, 669; Ramsay, *Pictures*, 313; Hemer, *Acts in History*, 153. The latter text (*CIL* 10.7495) may simply indicate the first to make some benefactions and so may not be an official title (Barrett, *Acts*, 1224). Because the designation also appears in Asia Minor, its occurrence on Malta cannot by itself establish the case for Malta (with Suhl, "Titel," arguing for Kefallinía).

1285. Fitzmyer, *Acts*, 783 (apparently speaking of the legate of Sicily's praetor, but possibly referring to the *legatus pro praetore*, an ex-consul who governed a province with a praetor's authority); cf. Lake and Cadbury, *Commentary*, 342 (positively—noting Luke's usual "correct local nomenclature"—but tentatively); Gasque, "Acts and History," 56; Bruce, *Commentary*, 523.

1286. Barrett, *Acts*, 1224. Before Paul's period, Melita belonged to the Roman province of Sicily, but it held municipal status by the early second century C.E. under an imperial procurator (Salmon, Boardman, and Potter, "Melita").

1287. Barrett, *Acts*, 1224. Some, however, compare Polybius's regular abbreviation of Publius Cornelius Scipio Aemilianus to Πόπλιος, noting that Luke, as a Greek, might write like Polybius or by how he heard peasants speak of Publius (Bruce, *Acts¹*, 472; idem, *Commentary*, 523n16; Witherington, *Acts*, 780n135).

1288. In an earlier period, they did not even bring their wives; after Augustus (cf. Suet. *Aug.* 24) Roman governors could take wives with them (cf. Tac. *Ann.* 1.40; 2.54–55; 3.33–34; Matt 27:19; contrast Severus in Hdn. 3.2.5).

In any case, we perhaps should not make too much of Luke's usage, as if the designation is uniquely superlative; although the singular and the article make sense this way, Luke might simply rank him among the foremost citizens, as in Acts 13:50, 17:4, and (in the nearer context) 28:17.[1289] These examples are plural, but Luke uses an articular singular in 16:12, where he also probably means "first" loosely.

Luke surely does not mean that Publius welcomed all 276 persons to his table; rather, he invited the people of rank. The most prominent of the seafarers would include the centurion (showing hospitality to a representative of the Roman military was showing respect to Rome; cf. Luke 7:8) and perhaps Paul as a Roman citizen. But by now Paul's status is so secure with the centurion (and everyone else on board) that, citizen or not, he would likely be invited, and his companions with him.[1290] If conversation included the events leading up to their arrival on Malta (as it surely would; cf. Odysseus's accounts of his travels to hosts), the topic of Paul's divine favor and abilities would arise. This in turn could raise the issue of Publius's sick father (although this matter could have come up in conversation anyway), in Acts 28:8 (cf. Mark 1:30).

It is unlikely that for three days Publius would have considered, or been able to accommodate, Paul's Jewish purity regulations, which were required for a kosher diet as strictly interpreted.[1291] Attentive readers of Luke-Acts, sensitive to normal Jewish dietary constraints, could have recognized in this passage Luke's emphasis on table fellowship with Gentiles.[1292] If Jesus ate with sinners (Luke 5:29; 15:1–2),[1293] then Jewish Christians could eat with Gentiles (Acts 11:3–12; 15:20, 29; 16:4). Following the principles of Jesus (though Luke omits Mark 7:1–23) and the Spirit's revelation in Acts, Paul could (from Luke's perspective)[1294] honor building relationships for the gospel's sake (Acts 28:8–10) as a higher value than attending to his diet.[1295]

Most of the survivors would lack immediate means to pay for their lodgings;[1296] finding temporary employment during this rainy season might be more difficult than usual. (Ancient customs of hospitality would have probably smoothed their transition, however. Hospitality to strangers of shipwreck was not unusual.)[1297] But the centurion could "impress" locals to provide lodging for his soldiers and prisoners (see comment on Acts 27:2)[1298] after Publius's three days of full hospitality had ended (on temporal limits to hospitality expectations, see comment on Acts 16:15). Given Paul's ministry, however, the local people seem eager to serve them (28:8–10); Julius

1289. Thus, similarly, one of Pontus's chief citizens is τοῦ Πόντου πρῶτος (Lucian *Alex.* 45).

1290. Cf. also Calvin. The centurion was responsible for acquiring food for his prisoners, and voluntary hospitality was preferable to needing to requisition supplies from unwilling locals. Prisoners and even ordinary soldiers might not dine with the centurion and his host, but Paul is a citizen with status and leader of a movement. Dining with one's prisoner violated protocol (see comment on Acts 16:34 at Keener, *Acts*, 3:2514), but in this case the custodial orders are presumably more favorable (cf. Acts 24:23; 26:31–32) than they were in 16:23, and Paul's keeper now respects him as an agent of deity (27:31–32).

1291. Though, given the respect Paul commanded as a miracle worker, he could undoubtedly have avoided meat without offense provided he offered explanation, just as Pythagoreans could be generally respected for their distinctive dietary practices.

1292. For the significance of table fellowship in antiquity, see, e.g., Jipp, *Visitations*, 105–11 (on guest-friendship in the historians); briefly, Keener, *Acts*, 1:1005. The significance of table fellowship may be more readily intelligible in cultures with similar approaches; see, e.g., Adewuya, "Revisiting"; cf. also Kim, *Bread*; Velankanni, "Eucharist."

1293. For discussion of this issue, see, e.g., Powell, "Table Fellowship."

1294. And probably Paul's as well; see Gal 2:11–14, though the character of the food itself is not specified.

1295. Cf. Rapske, *Custody*, 214–15.

1296. Cf. Dunn, *Acts*, 348 (stressing the need of the 276 to pay for lodgings).

1297. See Hock, *Social Context*, 79 (n. 28, comparing Sen. Y. *Ben.* 4.11.3; 37.1; Dio Chrys. *Or.* 7.2–20, 55–58; Ach. Tat. 6.9.3).

1298. See also Rapske, *Custody*, 273.

the centurion cannot help but note that Paul achieves voluntarily what Rome would have to achieve compulsorily by requisition.

II. HEALING PUBLIUS'S FATHER (28:8)

Although Publius is the patron of the company in 28:7, Paul becomes his benefactor in 28:8, healing his father. Luke's ideal audience might think here of Luke 4:38–39, where Simon welcomes Jesus and Jesus heals Simon's mother-in-law (cf. Mark 1:29–31). (These two Lukan passages contain Luke's only two uses of πυρετός.) Jesus is Simon's guest; Paul is Publius's guest. In both cases, the healing apparently leads to many crowds seeking healing for themselves (Luke 4:40; Acts 28:9).[1299]

Reciprocity relationships were standard for benefaction in antiquity, and Luke here demonstrates his view that they were appropriate between Christians and non-Christians.[1300] Paul's expression of his apostolic authorization also differs starkly from the Roman imperial authority; whereas Romans may impress services (Luke 23:26), Paul works within the networks of Christian love (Acts 27:3; 28:14) and Mediterranean hospitality (Luke 9:4; 10:7; Acts 28:7). Although Rome saw itself as providing roads, law, and (to most cultures apart from Greeks) civilization,[1301] it imposed its will by power; Paul simply offers benefaction to those willing to receive it. Thus, whereas Julius probably requisitions for his group housing and food from locals, Paul becomes an object of voluntary gratitude and gifts (Acts 28:10).

Paul heals by laying on hands, as did Jesus (Luke 4:40; 13:13; cf. Mark 5:23; 6:5; 8:23, 25) and others (Acts 9:12, 17);[1302] the Spirit was also bestowed this way (8:17–19; 9:17; 19:6; cf. 6:6; 13:3). This benevolent use of hands may be contrasted with the hostile hands of those who persecuted God's servants in the Gospel (Luke 20:19; 21:12; 22:53) and Acts (Acts 4:3; 5:18; 12:1; 21:27). In the immediate context, it also contrasts with the snake dangling harmlessly from Paul's hand (28:4).[1303] Prayer often accompanied the laying on of hands (6:6; 13:3) and healings (9:40). On beds, see comment on Acts 9:34.

III. FEVERS

Not only did Paul not "burn with fever" (a possible meaning of a verb in 28:6) when the snake bit him, but God used him to cure another's fever (28:8, albeit a

1299. Also Johnson, *Acts*, 466; Chance, *Acts*, 516; Pervo, *Acts*, 675; Jipp, *Visitations*, 50, 266–67; Zimmermann, "Hinführung," 515; for a different approach, cf. Kirchschläger, "Fieberheilung." In Luke 4:39, Jesus "rebuked" the fever as he would a demon (note 4:35; 9:42; cf. the variant reading in 9:55; 4Q560 I, 4; though cf. also Luke 8:24); cf. interpretations of Lev 26:16; Deut 28:22. Some scholars thus think that a spirit was involved in Luke 4:38–39 (e.g., Pilch, *Healing*, 99, 106). For fever demons, see also, e.g., Dickie, "Headless Demons"; cf. Levene, "Heal." The probably deliberate parallel does not require us to suppose that Luke invented either event (one with a source in Mark 1:30–31, the other in a "we" section; on parallels and history, see discussion at Keener, *Acts*, 1:562–74, esp. 569–74).

1300. With Tannehill, *Acts*, 340; Witherington, *Acts*, 776. Tannehill's doubt that evangelism was involved, however, is questionable: by this point, Luke can expect his audience to know that apostles heal by Jesus's name (Acts 3:6; 16:18; 19:13), although, of course, Paul's Greek would be of more limited kerygmatic benefit on Malta (cf. comment on Acts 28:2). Just as baptism, faith, or repentance is not mentioned with every conversion but other passages allow us to infer this pattern of Lukan soteriology, we should expect some evangelism (spiritual benefaction) arising out of the physical benefaction here.

1301. Cf. Niang, "Seeing," 170, on Rome's belief in its divine mission to "civilize" barbarians.

1302. Fitzmyer, *Acts*, 784, notes the practice for exorcism in 1Qap Gen[ar] XX, 21–22, 28–29. Cf. also *Jos. Asen.* 8:9; 21:6; 2 Kgs 5:11 LXX.

1303. With Weissenrieder, *Images*, 345. Nevertheless, her connection of that image with images of physicians with serpents in the hand seems less compelling, since Luke does not connect the serpent with healing here (despite the common image, e.g., Quint. Curt. 9.8.26–27; Statius *Silv.* 3.4.25; Paus. 2.27.2; Lucian *Alex.* 14; Ramsay, *Letters*, 286; Koester, *Introduction*, 1:182; Klauck, *Context*, 165; earlier, Kaiser, "Pantheon," 42).

different term).[1304] Understanding the depth of danger potentially involved in fever and dysentery can help us appreciate the degree to which the present healing would be valued as a sign of God's working.[1305] Fever, most commonly due to malaria (but sometimes typhoid), was widespread in Mediterranean antiquity.[1306] Malaria includes a variety of febrile diseases spread by the anopheles mosquito.[1307] Of diseases appearing in ancient medical literature, malaria and tuberculosis are the most common.[1308] (In citing ancient medical literature, I am not preferring it to modern empirical medicine but using it to provide the context for how ancient audiences likely viewed such ailments.)[1309] In biblical Greek, only Luke (and only in this passage) employs a plural form of πυρετός—that is, "fevers."[1310] The plural frequently appears this way for a single person and is especially noteworthy in medical writers.[1311] Presumably Luke means that the father's fevers were intermittent, coming and going, as fevers often were (and as malaria commonly is in its earlier stages).[1312]

One form is nocturnal malaria; one ancient physician wrote of someone with a fever that occurred on and off for fifty-two days, delirious and unable to sleep at night but sleeping the rest of the time.[1313] Others had their worst fever attacks at midday.[1314] (Again, in this section I am concerned primarily with ancient views of sickness possibly familiar to Luke and his audience, not with empirical diagnoses. Ancient reports of observations remain useful, though they often address concerns different from medical interests today.)[1315] In a winter fever[1316] (the season, at least, depicted here), the fever would usually abate if the patient lost consciousness, but

1304. One may also note that instead of falling sick from the rain and "cold" in 28:2, Paul healed another's fever.

1305. I treated these following matters in Keener, "Fever."

1306. Touwaide, "Disease," 550. In most cities, some people had fever, but only in unusual epidemics did most people have it (Dio Chrys. Or. 32.92). Snakebite (Acts 28:3–4) could also cause fever (cf. perhaps "fiery" serpents in the wilderness, Num 21:6; Deut 8:15), but the connection is not strong enough (given the wider variety of associations both with snakebite and with fever) to emphasize a connection in Luke's narrative. "Fever" usually designated a particular class of illness (Nutton, "Fever," 409).

1307. Touwaide, "Malaria," 195. Touwaide notes (195–96) that it spread from Africa to Mesopotamia, impacted Greece more noticeably especially ca. 430 B.C.E. and later, but spread farther in the Hellenistic period, peaking in the second century C.E. and then declining in late antiquity and the Byzantine era. For ancient mosquito plagues and local efforts to eradicate them, see Hünemörder, "Mosquito."

1308. Sallares, "Disease"; especially malaria (Nutton, "Fever," 410).

1309. This may be especially relevant for those who find much medical imagery in Luke-Acts (see esp. and helpfully Weissenrieder, Images). Ordinary papyri might tell us more about popular views than do medical texts, although Luke's ideal audience would have been urban and often more educated than those who typically dictated extant Egyptian papyrus documents; one of my doctoral students, Thomas Grafton, has been collecting some observations regarding sickness and health in the papyri. Nevertheless, medical texts at least provide an ancient context, as I suggested in Keener, "Fever."

1310. The singular appears in Matt 8:15; Mark 1:31; Luke 4:38–39; John 4:52; and Deut 28:22 LXX; never in the Apostolic Fathers.

1311. Hobart, Medical Language, 52; Ramsay, Luke the Physician, 16. That malarial (and "sand-fly") attacks were intermittent, of course, requires no specialist knowledge (Lake and Cadbury, Commentary, 343), and Luke's Mediterranean audience would grasp his point readily.

1312. With, e.g., Lake and Cadbury, Commentary, 343. Sallares, "Disease," speaks of malarial fevers recurring "every two or three days." No one would assume that one who had recovered from fever only a few days before had necessarily been cured (Dio Chrys. Or. 34.17). For continuous fever, see, e.g., Hippocr. Epid. 2.2.6; 5.1, 16.

1313. Hippocr. Epid. 7.2. My wife and son both experienced frequent nocturnal malarial attacks in Central Africa.

1314. Hippocr. Dis. 2.40 (recommending withholding medicine until the ninth day, after the patient had finished being "cleaned out").

1315. Various writers' ideas are preserved under Hippocrates's name; although I list most works under their purported authors' names for the sake of consistency (since degree of certainty about the authenticity of documents varies), probably most of the Hippocratic corpus belongs to Hippocrates's successors.

1316. Sallares, "Disease," suggests that malaria was most common in summer and fall; but fall had transitioned into winter here.

it might afterward return dangerously.[1317] Many physicians treated winter fever with water and perhaps juices, but they significantly reduced food.[1318] Sponging a fevered person to cool him or her was also a useful treatment; in urgent cases, this could take precedence over observing the Sabbath.[1319]

Fevers could be seasonal, and ancient writers often distinguished four types.[1320] "Quartan" fevers, though milder than some others, were the longest,[1321] but they were said not to last more than a year.[1322] Although usually striking men between the ages twenty-five and forty-five (given Publius's status, his father is surely older), such a fever was said to come most often in autumn and persist only if accompanied by another sickness.[1323] In a quartan fever's early stages, one had no appetite, but one regained it; the sufferer produced white mucous and sometimes a noisy stomach and bloody stool; after the fever, one remained weak and light-headed (Hippocr. *Epid.* 7.45). Another kind of fever was "semitertian";[1324] still another category consisted of "summer fevers." On the seventh through the ninth days, rough bite-like (yet not itchy) bumps appeared on the skin; sometimes the person became comatose and often was sleepy through the summer. This form of fever was rarely fatal, but no treatment was effective (2.3.1).[1325] "Tertian" fevers were accompanied by nightmares, hemorrhages, and sometimes delirium (4.20); the night preceding an attack was usually more difficult than the night afterward (6.2.10).

Fevers proved fatal to some, but others survived; some fevers were milder than others (Hippocr. *Progn.* 20.1–3). In the most dangerous cases, a person would die on the fourth day or earlier (20.4–5). The assault of some fevers decreased at the fourth day, but the second bout would run until the seventh day, the third until the eleventh, and so on, up to twenty days (20.5–18). They could also last longer, through sixty days (20.19–22).

Ancient medical writers described "fever" in various ways. Some writing in the Hippocratic tradition depicted fevers as coming in various colors, feeling different to those touching the afflicted.[1326] Quartan fever could produce a coma (Hippocr. *Epid.* 4.13). The various speculations about causes and cures suggest how uncontrollable these maladies were. Excess wine or exhaustion could produce winter fever, but it could become other diseases (Hippocr. *Aff.* 12). As one might guess from the etymology of πυρετός, many connected it, at least figuratively, with an internal fire (πῦρ). Thus fever may be "kindled" and glands "inflamed,"[1327] and a sick person burns with a heavenly fire (*b. Ned.* 41a). Some opined that excess phlegm produced the fever by swelling tissues;[1328] they believed that one could treat this condition by warming the body for three or four days (so that sweat would relieve the fever), not cooling the

1317. Hippocr. *Reg. Ac. Dis.* 24.
1318. Hippocr. *Aff.* 12; (more severely) *Reg. Ac. Dis.* 24. Drink and gruel also helped summer fevers (*Aff.* 14).
1319. For a mother caring for her child (*t. Šabb.* 12:13 [R. Simeon ben Gamaliel]; *y. Ma'aś. Š.* 2:1, §4). Fever appears with chills in Deut 28:22 LXX and subsequent incantations (4Q560 and elsewhere; see Lincicum, "Fever").
1320. See Hippocr. *Nat. Man* 15.1–40. Sallares, "Disease," notes three types: (1) falciparum, the most harmful; (2) vivax, the most common; and (3) quartan.
1321. See Hippocr. *Epid.* 1.24; also *Nat. Man* 15.22–40, on quartans.
1322. Hippocr. *Epid.* 6.6.11. On quartan fever (τεταρταῖος), see further 4.13; 6.6.5.
1323. Hippocr. *Nat. Man* 15.22–40. Four-day (*quadrini circuitus*) fevers did not start in the winter (Pliny E. *N.H.* 7.50.170).
1324. Hippocr. *Epid.* 5.89; 7.43, 95, 96.
1325. Hippocr. *Aff.* 14 prescribes drink and gruel for violent summer fevers, with recovery expected on the seventh or ninth day.
1326. Hippocr. *Epid.* 6.14.
1327. Φλογιῶσιν, Hippocr. *Glands* 2. Fevers are καῦσοι in *Airs* 3.27–29.
1328. Hippocr. *Pl. Man* 27. *Dis.* 1.23 views the heating of bile or phlegm as the cause of fever.

person until the fourth day.[1329] It was a good sign when jaundice and chills relieved a fever before the seventh day, but if jaundice occurred without chills and at a different time, the patient would likely die.[1330] Some opined that quartan fever was incompatible with epilepsy and that it even cured it (Hippocr. *Epid.* 6.6.5).[1331]

IV. TREATMENTS FOR FEVER

Treatments of malaria focused on symptoms, especially the fever itself and the spleen.[1332] Aulus Cornelius Celsus lists many different Greek medical opinions on how to treat fever and so suggests "trying them all (*De medicina* 3.14)."[1333] Ancients proposed various treatments of fever's attendant chills, such as agaric mixed with hot water, or (in the case of tertian fevers) siderite (a mineral) with oil.[1334] Some physicians sought to treat some kinds of fever by keeping the patient awake.[1335] Other alleged cures included the following:

- Deer flesh[1336]
- A wolf's salted right eye, used as an amulet (recommended by magi)[1337]
- Cat feces with a horned owl's claw, used as an amulet (also recommended by the magi for quartans)[1338]
- One substance that cures tertians and quartans, as a cure also for the bite of rabid dogs[1339]
- Suggested by one writer, sexual intercourse as a cure for quartan fever so long as menstruation is beginning[1340]

Elsewhere Pliny the Elder notes that medicines afford little help against quartans; thus he notes some remedies proposed by magicians, starting with recommended amulets.[1341] Some who recovered also undoubtedly claimed supernatural cures; Lucian complains that, given all the ignoramuses in circulation, it would not be surprising if some claimed healing through a revelation of the deceased charlatan Peregrinus (*Peregr.* 28).

V. DYSENTERY

Hippocratic writings sometimes mention fever and dysentery together.[1342] Dysentery sometimes accompanied other symptoms,[1343] including fever and pain, and

1329. Hippocr. *Pl. Man* 27. One should not, however, heat the head lest one add to the fever and produce delirium (33).
1330. Hippocr. *Reg. Ac. Dis.* 36.
1331. See the occasional beneficial effects of dysentery that Hippocratics supposed, noted below.
1332. Touwaide, "Malaria," 195.
1333. Stambaugh, *City*, 136–37 (the source is probably from the first century c.e.).
1334. Pliny E. *N.H.* 26.71.115; another remedy in 26.71.116.
1335. Dossey, "Greeks," 237, noting that some Roman physicians such as Caelius objected.
1336. Pliny E. *N.H.* 28.66.228 (in a larger list in 28.66.228–29).
1337. Pliny E. *N.H.* 28.66.228. Pliny reports with healthy cynicism such cures proposed by magi (28.66.229); he notes that they specify the necessary details of the cures so precisely that no one can obtain such things (29.12.53)! According to the magi, mixing the head and tail of a dragon with lion's forehead hair and other substances makes one invulnerable (29.20.68).
1338. Pliny E. *N.H.* 28.66.228 (the amulet must be worn for seven of the fever's periods to prevent relapse).
1339. Pliny E. *N.H.* 28.23.82.
1340. Pliny E. *N.H.* 28.23.83.
1341. Pliny E. *N.H.* 30.30.98. For traditional magical cures for quartan fevers, see 30.30.98–104.
1342. Hippocr. *Epid.* 2.6.26; 7.3; Hobart, *Medical Language*, 52; see esp. Weissenrieder, *Images*, 342 (who notes connections with this illness in ancient medical texts, especially Luke's depiction of the father's age, the season, and the climate, pp. 343–44). BDAG cites Hippocrates (CMG 1.1:57, lines 27–28; 1.1:60, line 27. Josephus attributes the affliction of Ashdod partly to dysentery (*Ant.* 6.3).
1343. Hippocr. *Prorr.* 1.143; *Epid.* 1.17.5–13.

in such cases could lead to death.[1344] In one case, a patient had dysentery, fever, and bloody stool, with pain in the belly growing from the thirtieth to the fortieth day, but the patient eventually recovered.[1345] Often this combination of symptoms occurred during the hot summer, when dysentery was most common.[1346] Summer fevers (see the brief discussion above) could be linked with diarrhea (Hippocr. *Epid.* 7.39);[1347] in summer, drinking water often sickened with dysentery, diarrhea, and quartan fever those living near marshes.[1348] Dysentery and fever were most common in summer after a particularly rainy spring.[1349] But the father of wealthy Publius would probably not live near a marsh, and the weather is now cold. It is possible that the symptoms have continued since the summer or that one ailment has weakened his body to another.

One writer described dysentery as accompanied by pain and colic inside, ulcerated intestines, with the passing of phlegm and bloody stools; "The disease is long, painful, and usually mortal" (Hippocr. *Aff.* 23).[1350] Some did recover from dysentery,[1351] but others died; one patient swelled up, had diarrhea, and died.[1352] Hippocrates reportedly claimed that one would die from dysentery if the bile was black but usually not if it was yellow (Galen *N.F.* 2.9.131).[1353] Despite the relative silence of ancient physicians about childhood sickness, "enteric diseases such as infantile viral diarrhoea and amoebic dysentery probably accounted for most of the high infant mortality observed in cemeteries."[1354] Presumably dysentery was also hard on older persons, as here.

Hippocratic writers supposed that dysentery sometimes had beneficial effects. Painless dysentery with fever could help relieve intestinal blockage (Hippocr. *Epid.* 2.6.26); fevers (1.20.1) might be finally "cured" by diarrhea and dysentery that ended the sickness (1.20.4); and fever might be rare when the bowels were loose (Hippocr. *Airs* 3.27–29). Likewise, another text concludes that dysentery could cure some diseases by passing them off in the stools (Hippocr. *Prorr.* 2.22).[1355] But they recognized that dysentery normally weakened patients rather than helped them.[1356]

Various folk cures for dysentery existed:[1357]

- Navew seed with some warm water[1358]
- Holly leaves, which are also helpful for cholera and menstruation and, when mixed with wine, prevent diarrhea[1359]

1344. Hippocr. *Prorr.* 2.22. So painful was dysentery that later rabbis assigned it atoning efficacy, forgiving all of the sufferer's sins (Le Cornu, *Acts,* 1486, citing *b. 'Erub.* 41b).

1345. Hippocr. *Epid.* 7.3. Cicero had dysentery for ten days (*Fam.* 7.26; Shelton, *Romans,* 86).

1346. Hippocr. *Epid.* 1.15.16–18.

1347. Fevers made digestion worse (Galen *N.F.* 2.8.119); thin excretions from the bowels often accompanied dysentery (Hippocr. *Epid.* 1.17.1–4).

1348. Hippocr. *Airs* 7.27–29. (On climate conditions for dysentery, cf. also 3.24.) Although not understanding malaria's transmission by mosquitoes, ancients recognized that malaria prevailed especially in swampy regions (Heracl. *Hom. Prob.* 11.5; Touwaide, "Malaria," 195).

1349. Hippocr. *Airs* 10.13.

1350. Trans. P. Potter, LCL, 5:43 (noting that one should treat it by cleaning the head and providing medicine to clean out bile; doing so while the patient remained strong was his or her only hope).

1351. E.g., Hippocr. *Epid.* 4.38, 41; 7.3. In one unusual account, a woman had dysentery and bloody stool until she gave birth, then became healthy (5.90; 7.99).

1352. Hippocr. *Epid.* 5.30.

1353. See also sources cited by Weissenrieder, *Images,* 341.

1354. Sallares, "Disease."

1355. Cf. Hippocr. *Epid.* 4.38, where a patient's health improved in general after the dysentery ended.

1356. After dysentery ended, the patient would have "an abscess or some swelling" (Hippocr. *Reg. Ac. Dis.* 35 [trans. Potter, LCL, 6:301]).

1357. Pliny E. *N.H.* 28.58.202–10 deals with cures for the bowels in general.

1358. Pliny E. *N.H.* 20.11.21.

1359. Pliny E. *N.H.* 24.72.116. Basil rubbed into the skin also helped diarrhea associated with cholera (20.48.121–22).

- A tree fruit[1360]
- Veal broth[1361]
- Mallow (also useful against epilepsy);[1362] cultivated sorrel;[1363] beeswax mixed with gruel;[1364] juice from pounded vine leaves;[1365] and a decoction of white myrtle in wine[1366]

One supposed cure proposed for dysentery and that Paul and Luke certainly would have rejected was unbridled sexual activity (πορνείη, Hippocr. *Epid.* 7.122). Traditional magical cures also existed.[1367]

VI. Healing the Fever Here (28:8)

Scholars have often linked the specific fever here with a kind traditionally associated with Malta and known as "Malta fever." In 1887 scientists discovered its cause, a microorganism called *Micrococcus melitensis*, found in the milk of goats on the island. The recurrent and intestinal character of the ailment fits this description.[1368] Untreated, it usually lasts about four months, but it could last two to three years.[1369] Barrett's caution is prudent: this proposal is plausible and may be accurate, but it is not completely certain because "there are other causes of fever."[1370] Wilkinson is more skeptical: Luke mentions dysentery, which is not part of Malta fever;[1371] rather, the real diagnosis is "acute bacillary dysentery with fever and diarrhoea with blood and mucus in the stool, the result of his consumption of infected food or contaminated water."[1372]

Although ancient writers describe occasional miracle workers who healed by means of prayer,[1373] they also report other religious remedies (in addition to the medical treatments noted above). Old Romans worshiped Febris, goddess of Fever (to reduce her malevolence); three temples to Fever continued to exist in Paul's day in Rome (Val. Max. 2.5.6).[1374] Undoubtedly a fever that often concerned Romans was malaria; apparently the sick used charms that touched their bodies, which they afterward deposited in her sanctuaries.[1375] People used incantations against fever and fever demons;[1376] because erotic magic was thought to cause "burning,"[1377] fever

1360. Pliny E. *N.H.* 24.79.129.
1361. Pliny E. *N.H.* 28.58.204.
1362. Pliny E. *N.H.* 20.84.227–28.
1363. Pliny E. *N.H.* 20.86.234.
1364. Pliny E. *N.H.* 22.55.116.
1365. Pliny E. *N.H.* 23.3.3. So also *omphacium*, from vines (23.4.7), and ground-up grape stones (23.9.13).
1366. Pliny E. *N.H.* 23.81.162.
1367. Pliny E. *N.H.* 30.19.55–58.
1368. Hemer, *Acts in History*, 153–54; Bruce, *Commentary*, 523n17.
1369. Larkin, *Acts*, 381.
1370. Barrett, *Acts*, 1226.
1371. Wilkinson, *Healing*, 160; cf. Malina and Pilch, *Acts*, 176 ("dysenteric symptoms in only 7 percent of cases").
1372. Wilkinson, *Healing*, 160–61; idem, *Health*, 87.
1373. See Theissen, *Miracle Stories*, 65.
1374. People brought remedies to these shrines, which they then applied to the afflicted (Val. Max. 2.5.6). Cf. also Graf, "Healing Gods." In the second and third centuries C.E., those with malaria also invoked "Tertiana or Quartana (*CIL* 7.99; 12.3129); in Cicero's day they were not yet deified (*Nat. d.* 3.24)" (Graf, "Healing Gods"; see also Nutton, "Fever," 410); on personified Febris, see also Schaffner, "Febris," 376. Pliny the Elder regarded the temple to Febris as base superstition (*N.H.* 2.5.15–16, esp. 16).
1375. Scheid, "Febris."
1376. See Dickie, "Headless Demons"; Levene, "Heal."
1377. E.g., *PGM* 36.69, 80–84, 102, 110–14, 199–200, 295–311, 340–41, 346, 355–59; 62.1–24; 101.32–33.

might also originate from such sources.[1378] Hero cults also offered healings in answers to prayer, including for "quartan fever" (Philost. *Hrk.* 16.1).[1379] Here, however, the true God provides healings through his agent, just as he has provided healings elsewhere in Acts.[1380]

Some scholars have argued (probably at least partly for theological and apologetic reasons) that signs gradually decreased after Pentecost, contending for their cessation at the end of the apostolic or subapostolic era.[1381] Such a position cannot, however, be argued from Acts (or, in my opinion, from any first- or second-century Christian texts).[1382] One dissertation charts signs in Paul's ministry as follows and observes that, if anything, Paul's signs increased rather than decreased in Acts:[1383]

Location in Acts	General Period in Paul's Ministry	Activity	Signs	Estimated Date
13–14	"First Missionary Journey"	Evangelism, church planting	Elymas blinded; paralytic at Lystra walks (and those summarized in 14:3)	47–48 C.E.
16:1–18:23	"Second Missionary Journey"	Evangelism, church planting	Exorcism; miracles in Corinth*	49–52 C.E.
19:1–21:15	"Third Missionary Journey"	Evangelism, church planting	Extraordinary miracles (19:11–12); Eutychus raised	52–57 C.E.
21:16–28:31	Voyage to Rome	Ministry as a prisoner†	Publius's father and numerous others	57–60 C.E.

*The miracles in Corinth are from 2 Cor 12:12, not mentioned by Luke.
†Though still in the context of his witness.

Paul naturally had less opportunity to perform signs while in detention in Caesarea (Acts 22–26;[1384] though Luke does not report his signs in every location, even when we may infer from other sources that they happened, 2 Cor 12:12; cf. Rom 15:19), but the voyage to Rome demonstrates that he had not "lost his touch." Even had he not provided this demonstration, Luke did not need to repeat signs in every location to leave his readers with the impression that they remained a regular occurrence in

1378. Cf. esp. LiDonnici, "Burning." In third-century C.E. Jewish sources, cf. *Test. Sol.* 8:5–7 (brought to my attention by an anonymous reviewer of my article Keener, "Fever," for the *Bulletin for Biblical Research*).

1379. This source derives from a later period when hero cults were more common, but the hero cult with which healing was most associated—that of Asclepius—was quite prominent by Paul's day. See Keener, *Acts*, 1:326–29.

1380. Although most of my African informants have suffered malaria and used medicine, there are reports of some instant and permanent healings from severe forms of malaria (e.g., Thomas, *Walls*, 84; cf. Chevreau, *Turnings*, 142). People report many other immediate healings from fevers in the context of prayer, although these did not ordinarily provide permanent immunity from subsequent cases of fevers of any sort (e.g., in Keener, *Miracles*, 230, 275–76, 282, 283n123, 284n125, 295, 335, 346, 346n236, 347–50, 364, 367, 373, 383n210, 386, 388, 408n427, 411–12, 418, 419n518, 431n26, 448, 452, 504n506, 546–47, 569, 641; for dysentery, see ibid., 279).

1381. See, e.g., Derickson, "Cessation," arguing partly from Paul's not healing Epaphroditus (Phil 2:26–27), Timothy (1 Tim 5:23), and Trophimus (2 Tim 4:20). But not everyone was healed earlier in Paul's ministry, either, including Paul himself (Gal 4:13). See the brief discussion concerning signs in this commentary's introduction (Keener, *Acts*, 1:537–49, esp. 539–41). Some allow that healings continued but suggest that they were no longer appropriately called "signs"; but see comment in Keener, *Acts*, 3:2239n319.

1382. Certainly signs and charismatic activity are still emphasized in later books, such as Revelation (e.g., Rev 11:3–6; 19:10) and the Pastorals (1 Tim 1:18; 4:14).

1383. Dollar, "Theology of Healing," 46, for the table; for the conclusion, 47.

1384. They seem to predominate in missionary church-planting settings, breaking fresh ground in evangelism (with Wagner, *Acts*, 536); this remains true both in earlier history and in many modern accounts (see, e.g., Keener, *Miracles*, 226, 240n159, 241, 265, 277–79, 288, 367–68; Yung, "Integrity," 173–75; Moreland, *Triangle*, 166–67). One would not expect as many during a period of detention, even if it is depicted in great detail, but Paul's continuing charismatic speech, at least, is assumed (cf. Luke 12:11–12).

Paul's ministry. As one narrative critic points out, repetition provides an "aggregative" effect;[1385] "new information does not negate earlier information; it is added to it."[1386]

VII. HEALINGS AND HONORS (28:9–10)

The paragraph opens with Publius's hospitality (Acts 28:7), then narrates Paul's benefaction (28:8–9), then returns to the kindness of the Maltese to Paul and his companions (28:10). By portraying a people so open and charitable, Luke may subvert some cultural expectations set up by his use of "barbarians" in 28:2, 4.[1387] It was also recognized that sages or those with other education might lose other possessions at sea but could quickly begin anew once on land.[1388]

Later tradition claims that Paul's stay led to the conversion of Malta's people.[1389] Although Luke is not specific about evangelism, he normally presents signs as a result of the message (14:3), and so he probably expects us to infer that Paul proclaimed Christ alongside performing healings. That the island was converted so quickly as later tradition suggests is highly doubtful; that a number of those experiencing or witnessing healings would have responded to Paul's message with faith[1390] seems likely. Language barriers would have limited the extent to which Paul could communicate (cf. the need for translation in 14:14), but given the eagerness of the local people to help him, some probably tried to translate for him.

Luke's claim here should be approached with the same degree of confidence a majority of interpreters accord to other claims in the "we" material, without prejudice against claims involving healing. Regardless of one's presuppositions regarding supernatural or divine activity, an abundance of modern global analogies suggest frequent cures in faith contexts, however explained.[1391] In his comments on this passage, William S. Kurz notes that one of his former doctoral students reported his experience of large-scale evangelism in India and Africa, made "particularly persuasive" by "the many healings that occur through their preaching and prayer with the sick. I was surprised to be reminded that numerous healings like those of Paul on Malta are still occurring, often" in parts of the world where people recognize "their need for God's help and have not raised rationalist barriers to divine intervention."[1392]

One seasoned scholar has recently expressed skepticism regarding a number of Luke's reports about Paul's healings in Acts,[1393] although the scholar emphasizes that he has sought merely a historical minimum and is not claiming that none of the

1385. See Dewey, "Oral-Aural Event," 149.

1386. Ibid., 150, specifically arguing that the emphasis on persecution later in Mark does not negate the earlier emphasis on miracles but adds to it. The frequent parallelisms in Luke-Acts (noted by, e.g., Goulder, Talbert, and Tannehill) suggest that, if Luke's repetition diverges from the common aggregative function of repetition at all, it is only to make it more emphatic.

1387. Though, as already noted, the "noble barbarian" tradition already existed, as did other more nuanced perspectives. Luke's perspective is friendly but is not unique to him.

1388. E.g., Phaedrus 4.23; Vitruv. *Arch.* 6.pref. 1–2; cf. similarly in the case of a refugee from war (Val. Max. 7.2.ext. 3).

1389. Finegan, *Apostles*, 202, citing Chrys. *Hom. Acts* 54. Third- to sixth-century C.E. catacombs in the proximity of Rabat point to a strong Christian presence at least in that period (Kalcyk and Niemeyer, "Melite").

1390. Many would have at least regarded his God as particularly powerful, and the strict monotheism of Paul's message would have invited a more specific faith content for those who embraced it.

1391. See Keener, *Acts*, 1:362–77, and other sources noted there.

1392. Kurz, *Acts*, 378–79. Other recent commentators on various books have also begun to take account of Majority World testimony to extraordinary healing and the like (e.g., Das, *Galatians*, 300).

1393. Twelftree, *Paul*, 229–71. One should note that he treats many of the individual accounts in just one or two pages. I address this work here because it appeared too recently for treatment in this commentary's introduction.

other data is reliable.[1394] That what the scholar does find as reliable corroborates what he already noted in Paul's letters[1395] is not surprising, given his method throughout. Consistency with what he had already found in Paul's letters functioned as a major criterion for what he would accept. Yet Paul addresses the topic in such a cursory manner that excluding Luke's reports based on such limited data will undoubtedly exclude genuine material rather than highlight it. By contrast, some other recent scholars continue to recognize various reasons for the two authors' different emphases and do not screen out Luke's claims that differ from Paul's.[1396] Again, Paul seems to have expected signs and wonders where he preached the gospel, including in places that Luke does not mention them (Rom 15:19; 2 Cor 12:12).

Because Luke claims that the Maltese highly honored "us" (28:10), some scholars have argued that Luke (i.e., Luke the physician of Col 4:14) practiced his medical art alongside Paul's supernatural healing.[1397] Although we cannot rule out such medical practice, nothing in the text suggests it.[1398] Paul's companions were honored as a group because they were with him. Moreover, those who were coming in Acts 28:9 undoubtedly did so in response to Paul's sign in 28:8.

The argument that ἰάσατο in 28:8 refers to Paul's activity whereas ἐθεραπεύοντο in 28:9 refers to Luke's[1399] has nothing to commend it. Granted, the former term appears for miraculous healings, both those performed by Jesus (Luke 5:17; 6:18–19; 7:7; 8:47; 9:11, 42; 14:4; 17:15; 22:51; Acts 10:38) and those performed through his agents (Luke 9:2; Acts 9:34)—though nowhere else for Paul. But θεραπεύω also applies to divine healing, through Jesus (Luke 4:40; 5:15; 6:7, 18; 7:21; 8:2; 13:14; 14:3) and his disciples (9:1, 6; 10:9; Acts 4:14; 5:16; 8:7). It applies to physicians only once (Luke 8:43), and there as a contrast between their inability to provide a cure and Jesus's success.[1400]

Honoring benefactors was of paramount importance and was, indeed, beneficiaries' primary responsibility in most transactions.[1401] Grateful healed patients sometimes honored Asclepius by dedicating models of their healed parts at some of his sanctuaries;[1402] undoubtedly Paul and his companions received more useful honors.

1394. Twelftree, *Paul*, 270. The minimum, however, seems to me a very bare minimum, and on grounds that I believe are often far less dependable than would be considering Luke's general reliability where we can test him. Twelftree rejects both Luke and "we" as eyewitnesses. Twelftree's argument pertains only to Luke's reports, however; Twelftree does not deny the possibility or reality of miracles (see, e.g., Twelftree, *Miracle Worker*, 41–42; idem, "Historian and Miraculous").

1395. Twelftree, *Paul*, 271.

1396. See, e.g., Gonzalez, "Healing" (published in the same year as Twelftree). For my own approach to Luke's miracle reports, see more extensively Keener, *Acts*, 1:320–82; idem, "Miracle Reports: Perspectives"; "Raising"; "Reports and Analogy"; "Reports Today"; "Miracles"; "Miracles: Dictionary." Because I find Luke generally reliable where he can be tested, including in the claim that miracles were believed to have happened through Paul's ministry (Rom 15:19; 2 Cor 12:12), I accept the core of his reports as historical evidence as I would any other ancient historical source so otherwise credible (see Keener, *Acts*, 1:166–257). This means not that such sources did not elaborate, mix information (accidentally or deliberately), and the like but that historical reports are themselves evidence to be considered with or without specific external corroboration.

1397. Ramsay, *Luke the Physician*, 16.

1398. Roman armies also had medical staff (see Southern, *Army*, 233–37), but there is no reason to believe that Julius's small band of soldiers included one.

1399. Ibid., citing also Harnack. Knowling, "Acts," 541–42, cites Holtzmann to this effect but treats the matter only as possible, not certain.

1400. Both terms also have their figurative uses (Luke 4:23; Acts 28:27). See likewise the critique by Wilkinson, *Healing*, 164.

1401. See comments on honor and shame at Acts 13:44–45 and 26:32; cf. comment on gratitude at 23:17–18. Even Stoics allowed honor as a contingent good (though not an intrinsic one; Arius Did. *Epit.* 2.7.5 L, pp. 34–35.17–20).

1402. See, e.g., Klauck, *Context*, 165. Suggestions that this image informs 1 Cor 12:12–27 (cf. Hill, "Temple"; Garner, "Temple of Asklepius"; Murphy-O'Connor, *Corinth*, 165) are unlikely in view of closer Stoic language.

Indeed, Luke likely means something more substantive than abstract "honors"; he always uses τιμή in the monetary sense (Acts 4:34; 5:2–3; 7:16; 19:19).[1403] Still, the notion of honor is likely present, since the verb τιμάω, also used here, normally means "honor" (Luke 18:20); our conception of "valuing" may connect the concepts (see BDAG).

These "honors" or gifts are complemented by the supplying of Paul's and his companions' needs when they travel[1404]—that is, by sending them off with provision.[1405] Undoubtedly Julius the centurion could only wonder at his prisoner being sent away with such honors, helping to explain his openness to others supporting Paul in Acts 28:14. (For the departure here, see comment on Acts 28:11.) The narrative has moved from Paul and others receiving expected hospitality as shipwreck survivors (28:2) to Paul receiving honors and gifts as a benefactor.

9. Final Voyage to Rome (28:11–15)

Brief travelogues (27:1–8; 28:11–16) frame the shipwreck story[1406] because Luke must summarize how Paul and his companions came to undergo the storm and how they reached Rome afterward. Luke also uses some of the stops, however, to show the unity of Diaspora Christians with Paul and his mission (27:3; 28:14–15).

Despite the considerable distance remaining, most of the rest of the voyage to Rome, proving relatively uneventful, is summarized in the usual manner of Luke's travel itineraries. That the believers in Rome come to meet and welcome Paul a considerable distance from the city does, however, reinforce Paul's *ēthos* by reminding us how well loved Paul was by many of his contemporaries (see comment on Acts 20:36–38).[1407]

a. Departing on Another Pagan Vessel (28:11)

The travelers return to their objective of reaching Rome as soon as possible. The ship has a figurehead of deities that were supposed to provide protection at sea; Luke's audience knows, however, from the foregoing narrative that it is really Paul's God who provides protection at sea, here especially to protect his agent for his purposes in history.

i. After Three Months

If Luke begins counting the three months after the events of 28:8–9 (or at least 28:8), a greater margin is available for calculating their winter stay, but Luke may mean three months after the shipwreck (and the difference may be slight in any case,

1403. With Witherington, *Acts*, 780; Bruce, *Commentary*, 524. One could "honor" physicians financially (Sir 38:1) and hence a healer such as Paul; this need not suggest Luke's medical skill here (a possibility suggested, e.g., by Bruce, *Commentary*, 524n18). Pervo, *Acts*, 671, finds implausible Luke's "neglect" of Paul's prisoner status in this section, but Luke has supplied plausible reasons for his favored treatment, treatment that could also be given to other honorable prisoners on occasion (e.g., Jos. *Ant.* 18.203).

1404. Johnson, *Acts*, 463, thinks "honors" more likely in the first phrase because the second phrase is monetary; but the first phrase may refer to honors or gifts during the many weeks that Paul spent with the people of Malta, and the second to parting gifts (though the Greek is not fully clear). In Symm. *Ep.* 1.20.2, pupils should honor their teachers with gifts.

1405. Cf. Rom 15:24; 1 Cor 16:6; Meeks, *Urban Christians*, 66.

1406. Witherington, *Acts*, 783.

1407. Neither in Acts nor in Paul's letters did everyone appreciate Paul (see, e.g., Phil 1:15, 17; Keener, "Apologetic"), but emphasizing the affection of many who knew or knew of Paul functions as a narrative means of praising Paul's character, thus supporting the narrative's overall apologetic agenda. It also fits the expressions of affection, often mutual, in Paul's letters (e.g., 1 Cor 4:14–15; 2 Cor 1:6–7; 6:11–13; 7:2–4; 12:14–15, 19; Gal 4:12–20; Phil 1:7–8; 2:17; 1 Thess 2:7–12; 3:5–12).

if 28:8 occurs during the "three days" of 28:7). The three months on Malta presumably would correspond roughly to the three winter months most difficult for sailing. Even the most urgent business could be detained at sea for three months (Jos. *War* 2.203).[1408] Determining precise dates is impossible, but general considerations allow an estimate. Sailing season opened fully around March 10 (Veg. *Mil.* 4.39),[1409] but this date for renewed sailing starts the preceding three months on Malta too late (especially given the custom of counting part of a period of time as the whole). Even if the "fast" (Acts 27:9) began late in autumn,[1410] December 10 is too late for their arrival on Malta. Sailing could begin as early as the west winds began blowing, usually around February 7 or 8 (Pliny E. *N.H.* 2.47.122),[1411] a date that some think even more common in this period.[1412] In some years west winds might blow earlier than in others, and a winter that started early and with undue severity would not necessarily persist with that character. The variation between the proposed dates may depend on the economic urgency and daring of the captains and on the weather in a given year. Given the "extra initiatives" offered by Claudius and Nero, a ship bound for Rome might leave as soon as weather allowed.[1413]

Sailors could celebrate once winter was past and sailing became possible again (Apul. *Metam.* 11.5, on the dedication of a ship in Isis's name). For the general avoidance of winter travel, duration of the season, and exceptions, see the extended discussion at Acts 27:9.

II. The Voyage

The travelers sailed on an "Alexandrian ship," probably a late-season[1414] grain ship that had wintered in Malta rather than risk the seas (or more of the seas) that wrecked Paul's previous vessel.[1415] (On Alexandrian grain ships, see comment on Acts 27:6.) It is surely too early in the season for the ship to have come directly from Alexandria immediately beforehand.

Some commentators suggest that the company sailed from Malta's primary port, near what is now Valletta.[1416] Valletta is some ten miles (17 km.) south of Saint Paul's Bay and perhaps closer to where they spent much of their sojourn on the island; today Valletta is Malta's capital and the ideal port for ships traveling to nearby Syracuse in Sicily.[1417] The area around modern Valletta was also inhabited in the Punic and Roman periods.[1418]

Considering the distance they had come, Syracuse (Acts 28:12) was not far from Malta,[1419] and if the weather was reasonably good, they might set out. Presumably

1408. Lake and Cadbury, *Commentary*, 343.
1409. Fitzmyer, *Acts*, 784, suggests this sailing date. Sailing season opened in Corinth one year on March 5 (Apul. *Metam.* 11.5, 17; Conzelmann, *Acts*, 223).
1410. The fast was later (Oct. 5) in 59 C.E., and so they possibly reach Malta as late as late October (Hemer, *Acts in History*, 154); see comment on Acts 27:9. Luke does not specify how long the fast had been over.
1411. Lake and Cadbury, *Commentary*, 343; Bruce, *Commentary*, 525; Hemer, *Acts in History*, 154; Rapske, "Travel," 24–25; cf. also Conzelmann, *Acts*, 223. Libanius *Descr.* 7.5 has ambiguously "spring."
1412. See Davis, "Navigation," 71–72.
1413. Witherington, *Acts*, 781. On incentives, see comment on Acts 27:9.
1414. Ramsay, "Roads and Travel," 379, thought that these vessels often sailed in a body (Sen. Y. *Ep. Lucil.* 77.1), but admitted that there were exceptions such as this one and that in Acts 27:6.
1415. Ships that wintered in or near Italy might have a better voyage back to Alexandria in the spring than the reverse (cf. Casson, *Mariners*, 210).
1416. E.g., Bruce, *Acts¹*, 473; Witherington, *Acts*, 781. Valletta was built in 1565; its heart is on the Mount Sceberras promontory, between the east and west harbors.
1417. A much larger town, Sliema, with some 15,000 residents, is in Valletta's immediate proximity.
1418. Finegan, *Apostles*, 200.
1419. Though, for ancient ships, "a rather wide and dangerous stretch of the sea" separated Malta from Sicily (Cic. *Verr.* 2.4.46.103 [LCL, 8:409]; cf. the story of a shipwreck en route to Sicily in Libanius *Narration* 13).

Paul has no premonitions of danger on this voyage (in contrast to 27:10); the previous ship's experience would not be relevant to any reservations of the new captain, and Julius might depend on this captain's assurances (along with Paul's lack of objection) that weather patterns were less risky here than in late-autumn Crete. Once in Italy, Julius seems in no hurry (28:14), but he may have felt a greater urgency about reaching Italy. One possible reason could be that in Malta they were dependent on requisitioned hospitality and reciprocated benefaction (to Paul) whereas in Italy Julius, at least, might be less likely to feel "stranded."

Julius could requisition passage on a vessel to Italy,[1420] and once he reached Rome he would no longer require it; even once in Italy, Paul's friends there (28:14), from whom nothing needed to be requisitioned, allowed an excuse to stay without the inconvenience of requisitioning. Granted, Paul's ministry may provide equivalent signs of hospitality in both Malta and at Puteoli, but the stay in Puteoli was well within the normal bounds of ancient hospitality whereas the stay in Malta stretched far beyond it (on the normal expected duration of ancient hospitality, see comment on Acts 16:15).

III. Dioscuri and Protection at Sea

This ship was dedicated to "the Twin Brothers"—that is, Castor[1421] and Polydeuces (in Latin, Pollux).[1422] Most translations and commentators take Luke's term παράσημος as "figurehead,"[1423] though Luke does not specify whether this image was literally carved to constitute the beak of the prow (difficult, since there were two of them),[1424] was simply figures set up at the prow,[1425] or was even more simply figures painted on both sides of the prow (as in the *Isis* depicted by Lucian).[1426] The term can mean that the prow was "marked" by the Twins, and it probably functions as the equivalent[1427] for τὸ παράσημον, the "insignia" or "emblem" found on both sides of a ship's prow.[1428] Most scholars note that ships, like inns, were named for their figureheads.[1429] Figureheads' implied religious patronage was significant; the first Athenian to capture a Persian ship severed its figurehead and consecrated it to Apollo (Plut. *Themist.* 15.2).

Some point to the ancient function of these brothers as vindicators of truth and argue that Luke thereby implies for Hellenistic readers Paul's authenticity or even

1420. See Rapske, *Custody*, 272–73; comment on Acts 27:3.

1421. Bede *Comm. Acts* 28.11 rightly corrects the Latin *insigne Castrorum* ("standard of fortified camps"; see comment on Acts 28:16) to *insigne Castorum* ("standard of the Castores"), based on Διοσκούροις in Acts' Greek manuscripts.

1422. An old ship dedicates herself to the Dioscuri in the image in Catull. *Carm.* 4.25–27; sailors often dedicated their rudders to sea deities as well (Max. Tyre 2.1). In a novel, Clitophon has heard sailors claim that ships may be sacred (Ach. Tat. 5.16.8), perhaps referring to their dedication to deities on their figureheads. On the Dioscuri, note also the brief discussion in Keener, *Miracles,* 584–85; Dowden, "Dioskouroi," 258.

1423. E.g., NRSV; Bruce, *Acts¹,* 473.

1424. Greeks favored these literal figureheads far less than did their Phoenician predecessors (Casson, *Mariners,* 79); the prows often extended forward like battering rams, though not for that purpose (192). Ancient Homeric prows did have "fish-shaped or bird-shaped" ensigns on top (42); the cult image in Philost. *Hrk.* 9.6 might be attached to the prow. The upright beam on the prow often included a relief relevant to the ship's name (Casson, *Mariners,* 193), such as a deity (ibid., plate 42).

1425. Cf. the head of a deity in the niche on the prow in Casson, *Mariners,* plate 38.

1426. Lucian *Ship* 5. For how they may have been portrayed, see Bredow, "Dioscuri: Iconography."

1427. BDAG suggests a textual corruption, but Luke's wording might reflect Jewish anti-pagan influence (the adjective παράσημος is used for a pagan brand in 3 Macc 2:29).

1428. BDAG, citing, e.g., Plut. *Mor.* 162a; P.Lond. 2.256a, 2 p. 99; P.Tebt. 486; *CIL* 3 = *ILS* 4395.

1429. Bruce, *Acts¹,* 473; Longenecker, *Acts,* 362; Johnson, *Acts,* 463 (citing Plut. *Dinner* 18, *Mor.* 162B; *Br. Wom.* 9, *Mor.* 248A; also the *Isis* in Lucian *Ship* 5).

the Twin Brothers' favor on the voyage.[1430] Suiting this association with truth, sailors may have often sworn by the Dioscuri.[1431] But while it is possible that this insignia reinforces the notion of Paul's authenticity, it is not likely; the Dioscuri were far more often associated with safety at sea (see discussion below). No such insignia is mentioned on earlier voyages, and a major point of the storm narrative is that only the true God brings protection, partly through his loyal servant.

Given the anti-pagan polemic in Acts (Acts 7:43; 14:15; 17:16, 29; cf. 8:9–11; 19:26), Luke's theological point[1432] in mentioning the Dioscuri is, if anything, ironic: after God wrought a great deliverance, Paul's company sails on another ship that trusts in false gods. The practical offshoot of such irony is theological realism: no matter what the initial triumphs (such as in 27:43–28:10), most of the world remains unconvinced and perhaps even unaware of the truth (cf. 1 Kgs 19:1–4), yet God accomplishes his purposes nonetheless. Moreover, there was a wide range of associations with the Dioscuri (the most obvious and relevant here being sailors' dependence on them for protection), not a single one (see the discussion below).

Naturally, voyagers invoked divine help before sailing.[1433] Often they invoked deities such as Isis, considered a protectress from storms and dangers (Apul. *Metam.* 11.25); thus a ship could be consecrated in her name (11.5) or even be named for her, with a figure of her on either side of the prow (Lucian *Ship* 5).[1434] But the Dioscuri (a pagan designation that Luke does not hesitate to use), also known as the Twins, were more prominent. Navigators could be associated with the Dioscuri as easily as with Poseidon and the Nereids.[1435]

Commentators often note that sailors viewed the Dioscuri as providing protection at sea.[1436] From an early period, they were thought to subdue the sea's raging, which wrecked ships.[1437] They were considered "saviors" at sea;[1438] someone who denied their help during a storm at sea would frighten his hearers.[1439] Thus sailors invoked them in storms or other troubles at sea.[1440] Poets claimed that both brothers (as "stars") helped ships facing storms.[1441]

The Twins were thought to intervene and appear in desperate situations (cf. *Hom. Hymns* 33.12 [to the Dioscuri]), and some claimed to have seen them as stars during a

---

1430. With various nuances, see Ladouceur, "Shipwreck and Pollution," 443–47; Brawley, *Luke-Acts and Jews*, 57; Witherington, *Acts*, 770.

1431. Lucian *Dial. C.* 14 (*Dorio and Myrtale* 4), 321.

1432. It could be mere description, but that he mentions only this insignia and not those of other ships suggests that he does have a point here and that he is well aware of the association of the Dioscuri with sea voyages.

1433. E.g., Epict. *Diatr.* 3.21.12; Fronto *Ad M. Caes.* 3.9.2; for superstition and sailing, see Casson, *Travel*, 155; for specifically astrological superstition and sailing, see Manilius *Astrology* (*Astronomica*) (ca. 14 C.E.) in Friedländer, *Life*, 1:189.

1434. Given grain ships sailing to and from Alexandria, association with an Egyptian goddess (Isis) is not surprising.

1435. Ael. Arist. *Def. Or.* 148, §46D. They work for Poseidon in Lucian *Dial. G.* 287 (25/26, Apollo and Hermes).

1436. E.g., Bruce, *Acts¹*, 474; Johnson, *Acts*, 463 (citing Epict. *Diatr.* 2.18.29; Lucian *Ship* 9; Ael. Arist. *Or.* 4.35–37); cf. Gradl, "Glaube," 260.

1437. Eurip. *El.* 1240–42.

1438. E.g., Diod. Sic. 4.43.1–2; Artem. *Oneir.* 2.37; Lucian *Dial. G.* 287 (25/26, Apollo and Hermes); *Alex.* 4 (cf. Casson, *Travel*, 178); cf. Libanius *Topics* 3.7 (comparing the role of physicians for the sick). Helen joins them as a "savior" of sailors in Eurip. *Orest.* 1636–37 (she was their sister even in the earliest sources; Hom. *Il.* 3.237–38; she secured immortality for them in Lucian *Charid.* 6).

1439. Plut. *Pleas. L.* 23, *Mor.* 1103C. Alexander scorning the Dioscuri (Dio Chrys. *Or.* 64.20) is an example of his hubris (64.21).

1440. E.g., Sil. It. 15.82–83; Catull. *Carm.* 68A.65; Epict. *Diatr.* 2.18.29.

1441. E.g., Ovid *Fasti* 5.720. They are depicted with stars on their heads in Lucian *Dial. G.* 282 (25/26, Apollo and Hermes).

storm;[1442] this conception may have originated in "the sudden appearance of the stars when the clouds and storm have cleared."[1443] Sailors believed that the Dioscuri came to their aid during storms also when lights settled on the sails (Sen. Y. *Nat. Q.* 1.1.13), presumably the phenomenon of corona discharge (a luminous discharge caused by increased electrical activity from the storm) that later European sailors called Saint Elmo's fire.[1444] Sometimes in antiquity, seafarers might claim that this appearance of a star on the masthead during a storm guided their ship safely to port.[1445] One might claim that the Dioscuri, appearing on the sails to bring deliverance, commanded him to compose an encomium about them.[1446] In dreams they symbolized bad weather but also safety in the midst of it.[1447] They also allegedly appeared as stars on both sides of a Spartan ship destined for victory in battle.[1448]

IV. Background of the Dioscuri

In ancient mythology, the Dioscuri were sons of Leda (e.g., Sil. It. 15.82–83). They were noted for their participation in the voyage of the *Argo*, and in some traditions, they sojourned in the region of Colchis.[1449] Although their title, "Dioscuri," implies that they were both sons of Zeus, only Pollux was genuinely born from him; thus Castor was mortal.[1450] When Castor was slain (Ovid *Fasti* 5.709–10),[1451] Pollux avenged him (5.711–12), then prayed that he would not be deified without his brother. Rather they should let their heaven be shared (5.715–18); thus the brothers alternated in heaven (5.719–20).[1452] Their love for each other became proverbial.[1453] The Dioscuri continued to sail the seas after their mortality because they had done so in life (Max. Tyre 9.7).

In any case, both Greeks and Romans in this period believed that the Twins were deified.[1454] Like other deities, they had sanctuaries[1455] and altars[1456] and received

1442. Max. Tyre 9.7 (Trapp, *Maximus*, 83n23, compares Alcaeus frg. 34; *Hom. Hymns* 33 [to the Dioscuri]; Theoc. 22.8–22).
1443. Theissen, *Miracle Stories*, 101.
1444. Corcoran in LCL, 1:21n2. "Saint Elmo" is an Italian corruption of "Saint Erasmus" of Formia (died ca. 303 C.E.), one of sailors' patron saints. Sailors also endured nearby lightning during storms (Libanius *Anecdote* 3.25).
1445. Lucian *Ship* 9. Lucian regards many claims of their appearing on the masthead as fabricated (*Posts* 1).
1446. Lucian *Charid.* 3.
1447. Artem. *Oneir.* 2.37.
1448. Plut. *Lys.* 12.1 (the stars disappeared before another battle that the Spartans lost, 18.1). They also reportedly appeared in the Forum so as to symbolize a victory (Plut. *Coriol.* 3.4) and allegedly appeared at the lake of Juturna (Val. Max. 1.8.1). For their association with Sparta, see also, e.g., Robbins, "Kastoreion."
1449. Appian *Hist. rom.* 12.15.101, 103. Euhemerus extolled them among the Argonauts and noted that they appear as helpers of those in danger (*Sacr. Hist.* 6, in Grant, *Religions*, 76).
1450. E.g., *Cypria* frg. 9, from Clem. Alex. *Protr.* 2.30.5 (*GEF* 89).
1451. *Cypria* frg. 17, from Philod. *Piety* B 4833 Obbink (*GEF* 97). He was killed in the course of the brothers' stealing cattle (*Cypria* 3)! Elsewhere, they plundered Athens (*Cypria* frg. 12, from scholiast D on Hom. *Il.* 3.242 [*GEF* 93]).
1452. On the alternation, see also, e.g., Sil. It. 9.295; 13.804–5; Lucian *Dial. D.* 328–29 (1/1, Diogenes 1). Many ancients seem to have assumed six months in heaven apiece annually, but Hom. *Od.* 11.304 has both living every other day (so also *Cypria* 3; Lucian *Dial. G.* 276 [4/24, Hermes and Maia 1]; 281 [25/26, Apollo and Hermes]). Some thought that Castor received the better end of the deal (Suet. *Jul.* 10.1); others joked that the alternation was a foolish way to express love, since they would not manage to see each other (Lucian *Dial. G.* 286 [25/26, Apollo and Hermes]).
1453. Ovid *Tristia* 4.5.30; *Pont.* 1.7.32; Val. Max. 5.5.3.
1454. E.g., Hor. *Odes* 3.3.9–10 (Pollux); 4.5.35–36 (Castor); *Epodes* 17.40–44; Quint. Curt. 8.5.8 (a Roman probably creating dialogue for earlier Greeks); Arrian *Alex.* 4.8.2–3. Some people had identified them with Samothracian gods (e.g., Varro *Latin Language* 5.10.58). On their role in religion, see, e.g., Scheer, "Dioscuri."
1455. E.g., Paus. 1.18.2.
1456. E.g., Paus. 3.13.6; 5.15.5.

votive offerings.[1457] As constellations (Gemini), they affected fate;[1458] their appearance in a storm was considered a favorable sign.[1459] It was thought that they sometimes slew those who insulted them.[1460] Although some ancients apparently doubted the beneficence of deified or heroized mortals (Babr. 63.7–12), most thought otherwise.[1461] The cult of the Dioscuri was ancient among Greeks, who hailed them as "saviors."[1462]

Castor and Pollux also were highly honored in Rome after their alleged intervention in 484 B.C.E.[1463] Similarly, they were thought to watch over Rome,[1464] and all Romans knew the temple of Castor in their forum,[1465] with its statue of mounted Castor,[1466] restored and rededicated several decades before Paul's voyage.[1467] Their importance for Rome may be gauged from their utility for imperial veneration: the mad emperor Caligula allegedly seated himself between Castor and Pollux in their temple,[1468] and Augustus's adopted sons were assimilated to these twins in statuary.[1469] These associations may also be involved in Luke's mention of them: Paul was now heading to the center of Roman paganism. Nevertheless, the associations with the sea are far more prominent and would require little specific knowledge of Rome itself to fathom.[1470]

Not only in Rome but closer to the region where Paul's company encountered this vessel, the Dioscuri were well known.[1471] The Dioscuri were popular on coins at Rhegium,[1472] though this was not the ship's home port, since it spent no time there (Acts 28:13) and is expressly Alexandrian (28:11). An island near southern Italy and Sicily—that is, in this region—was apparently dedicated to these deities as well.[1473]

1457. So, apparently, Gr. Anth. 6.149.

1458. Pers. Sat. 5.49. Both Greeks and Romans included them in the zodiac (Hübner, "Constellations," 1189); this constellation also appears in Jewish astrological texts (e.g., 4Q318 2 II, 9). For astrology in seafaring, see, e.g., Friedländer, Life, 1:189.

1459. Bruce, Commentary, 474, citing Hor. Odes 1.3.2; 3.29.64.

1460. Pausanias (reporting local stories) in 3.16.2–3; 4.3.1. This fits the behavior of immortal "heroes" in Philost. Hrk. passim.

1461. E.g., using heroes as patron deities (e.g., Philost. Hrk. 14.4) or sacrificing to them when passing through their regions (17.6; 18.2).

1462. See Parker, "Dioscuri."

1463. Purcell, "Castor." Cf., e.g., Symm. Ep. 1.95.3; and Salzman's list of other versions in Symmachus, 174n6 (Val. Max. 1.8.1; Ovid Fasti 1.708; Latin Panegyrics 2.39.4).

1464. Val. Max. 1.8.1.

1465. Cic. Sest. 15.34; 37.79; 38.83; 39.85; Quinct. 4.17; Phil. 6.5.13; Verr. 2.1.50.130; 2.1.51.133; Res gest. 4.20. It was visible from the venue of Verres's trial (Verr. 2.3.16.41).

1466. Statius Silv. 1.1.53–54 ("Leda's son").

1467. Suet. Tib. 20.

1468. Suet. Calig. 22.2.

1469. Vanderpool, "Portraiture," 376–77 (her examples are from Corinth, and Paul may have seen them). For use in imperial propaganda, cf. also Purcell, "Castor"; Kauppi, Gods, 113–14. Unlike cultures fearful of twins, Romans celebrated them (in the imperial family, see Tac. Ann. 2.84); some ancient authorities attributed twins' birth to superfetation ("Twins," 50; Pindar Pythian 9.84–86; Apollod. Bib. 3.10.7; Sen. Y. Ben. 7.1.3; Pliny E. N.H. 7.11.48–49; for superfetation generally, see Remus, Conflict, 31–34; Pliny E. N.H. 10.83.182).

1470. Occasionally the Dioscuri are portrayed as riding on horseback, a fairly distinctive posture among Greek and Roman deities (Oppermann, "Rider-gods"; they ride white horses in Lucian Dial. G. 283 [25/26, Apollo and Hermes]); Castor was also an old patron deity of chariot racing (Pindar Pyth. 5.9; much earlier, Homer linked him with horses, Il. 3.237; Od. 11.300; for their charioteers, see Pliny E. N.H. 6.5.16, who assumes them to be historical figures; cf. Robbins, "Kastoreion"). This claim is, however, of no relevance to Luke's narrative; the more prominent associations are more relevant.

1471. That another pair of twin deities was native to Sicily as early as the sixth century B.C.E. and continued to be venerated into this period (Lamboley, "Palici," 386) might have also facilitated the early welcome of the Dioscuri in Sicily, Paul's next stop.

1472. See Kee, Every Nation, 294.

1473. Pliny E. N.H. 3.10.96.

Outside the region, they were widely known;[1474] even in Judea, the hellenistically educated would know of them.[1475] Luke's audience understands from the preceding narrative, however, that it is not the Dioscuri but Paul's God who stands watch over the voyage and protects his servant.

b. From Syracuse to Puteoli (28:12–13)

The voyage from Malta to Syracuse to Rhegium and Puteoli appears uneventful, summarizing the progress of Paul and his companions to Rome. Apparently there are not yet known believers there, since Luke likes to emphasize that local churches in diverse parts of the empire knew of and welcomed Paul (27:3; 28:14–15).

Educated romanized readers in Corinth or Philippi would appreciate Luke's mention of Syracuse, Rhegium, and Puteoli in 28:12–13; not only were they important in current east-west trade, but two of these cities figured prominently in Greeks' history. There can be little doubt historically that Paul was transported from Malta via these cities to Rome, where he remained in custody;[1476] these cities belonged to the expected route (though Malta was not always one stop).[1477] Following a frequent route, Alexandrian grain ships would work "south of Crete and then, tacking continuously, beat their way to Syracuse in Sicily, with perhaps a stop at Malta en route."[1478] Everyone recognized that Syracuse was a major port;[1479] a ship sailing for Italy but blown off course to Sicily would disembark there (Xen. Eph. *Anthia* 5.1).[1480]

i. Syracuse (28:12)

The voyage to Syracuse, on Sicily's[1481] southeast, was close to one hundred miles. Luke does not explain the three days' delay there; since the ship had left Malta early in the season, as if the voyage was urgent, there may have been a weather delay.[1482] Unexpectedly good weather had presumably allowed sailing from Malta; but the season remained dangerous, and perhaps they needed to await good weather again. A ship with time to spare might wait at Syracuse for a southerly wind to help the voyage northward.[1483] An Alexandrian ship bound for Rome but wintered on Malta

---

1474. Mitchell, *Anatolia*, 2:28, notes what are thought to be the Dioscuri on reliefs in south Pisidia, where Paul has also traveled.

1475. Some evidence cited in support of this (Jacobson, "Colors"; cf. idem, "Helmet"), however, does not seem compelling (Brenner, "True to Form").

1476. Lüdemann, *Christianity*, 265.

1477. Although the voyage from Malta to Syracuse was roughly half that from Cephallenia, Barrett, *Acts*, 1229, considers neither suggestion implausible.

1478. Casson, *Mariners*, 208.

1479. E.g., Philost. *Vit. Apoll.* 8.15 (in transit from Italy to the east).

1480. Sicily is en route to western Italy in Philost. *Vit. Apoll.* 7.10; it also appears on or near that route in Lucian *True Story* 1.34 (one of the account's few resemblances with reality).

1481. On Sicily, see Pliny E. *N.H.* 3.8.86–3.9.94 (including volcanoes in 3.9.93–94); Olshausen, "Sicily"; Finley, *Sicily*; Goldsberry, "Sicily"; Wilson, *Sicily*; Scramuzza, *Sicily*; Guido, *Sicily*; Messineo and Borgia, *Ancient Sicily*; Tribulato, *Language*; earlier, Freeman, *Story of Sicily*; for recent excavations, see De Angelis, "Archaeology"; for archaeology of Syracuse, Günther, "Syracusae," 51–52; Olshausen, "Sicily." Given Greek history in Syracuse, educated Greeks also knew that Syracuse lay in Sicily (e.g., Philost. *Vit. Apoll.* 8.14–15); its capture by Rome in 212 B.C.E. allowed Rome to make Sicily a Roman province (Vell. Paterc. 2.38.2).

1482. So Hemer, *Acts in History*, 154, who suggests a north or northwest wind hindering "the passage of the Straits of Messina." A delay for unloading is very unlikely, since this Alexandrian ship was undoubtedly carrying grain for Rome.

1483. Casson, *Mariners*, 208 (noting that ships in a hurry might press ahead against northwesterly winds anyway). A Roman writer says that southerly winds were dominant in summer (Pliny E. *N.H.* 2.47.123–24); for Italy, the south and southwest winds are damp (2.48.126; Pliny held the south wind to be especially unhealthy when dry, 2.48.127); Pliny also held that the south wind generates higher waves on average than the northeast wind (2.48.128).

would not need to stop in Sicily to unload grain; Sicily had enough of its own, but Rome depended on imports.

Syracuse was huge, about a quarter the size of Rome.[1484] Its beauty was well known; Cicero calls it "the loveliest of all cities" and expects his audience to have heard this claim before.[1485] He describes Syracuse in his day as the combination of four cities (*Verr.* 2.4.53.118).[1486] The heart of Syracuse was an island partly sheltering a bay on the Sicilian mainland. The island city was well fortified, with strong walls, and it easily controlled the harbor (2.5.38.98). This island had two harbors and hosted the Roman governors, temples of Diana and Minerva, and a spring called Arethusa (2.4.53.118).[1487]

The second constituent town was Achradina, holding a marketplace, a senate house, a temple of Jupiter, and houses. The third town, Tycha, had athletic grounds and temples, and the fourth, Neapolis, was the newest part, with a theater and temples of Ceres and Libera (2.4.53.119). Syracuse was known for bronze work, ship construction, and fishing.[1488] Syracuse also had gladiatorial games;[1489] a small Roman theater remains, probably from the first century C.E., and many stone quarries are evident.[1490]

Greeks from Corinth, led by one Archias, colonized Syracuse in about 734 B.C.E., establishing great wealth but reducing indigenes of the area to serfdom.[1491] Syracuse ruled an empire of its own for a time, allied itself with the Carthaginians, and under the Roman Republic became the governor's seat for Sicily. Augustus established a colony of Roman veterans there (Strabo 6.2.4; as well as at five other Sicilian cities).[1492] Greek settlers had long before brought many Greek cults to Greek colonies in Sicily,[1493] including Syracuse.[1494] Jews in Sicily not only maintained their distinctive identity and Jewish traditions but also interacted with Greco-Roman culture.[1495]

ii. Rhegium (28:13)

Rhegium, on Italy's southwest coast (at the tip of Italy's boot), was about seventy miles beyond Syracuse. It was just six to seven miles across from Sicily,[1496] but because the waters of two seas met in a strait between Messene in Sicily and Rhegium in mainland Italy, the narrow passage from Sicily to Italy had long been counted dangerous

1484. Cary and Haarhoff, *Life*, 103, estimate a quarter million for Syracuse.
1485. Cic. *Verr.* 2.4.52.117 (trans. L. H. G. Greenwood, LCL, 8:427); the claim suits his purpose of emphasizing Verres's wickedness against it. That Augustus called his private study "Syracuse" (Suet. *Aug.* 72.2) may reflect Roman aesthetic appreciation for the city; cf. Gowers, "Syracuse."
1486. Finegan, *Apostles*, 206, lists five districts.
1487. On Arethusa (and its supposed subterranean link with Greece), see Pliny E. *N.H.* 2.106.225; cf. 3.8.89.
1488. Finegan, *Apostles*, 206.
1489. Tac. *Ann.* 13.49.
1490. Finegan, *Apostles*, 207.
1491. On Corinth, Archias, and the wealth, see Strabo 6.2.4; for the date, see Bruce, *Commentary*, 526. The harbor contributed to Syracuse's wealth (Clarke, "Italy," 479).
1492. See also Woodhead and Wilson, "Syracuse," 1464; Jameson, "Sicily," 1402. For Syracuse's history, especially the Greek period, see Günther, "Syracusae," 40–51 (though the Roman period is treated only briefly, 50–51); Cartledge, *Ancient Greece*; Champion, *Tyrants*; Favorito, *Coinage*.
1493. Jameson, "Sicily Cults."
1494. Woodhead and Wilson, "Syracuse." On Persephone worship in Syracuse, see Zuntz, *Persephone*, passim.
1495. See Rutgers, "Interaction." See at length Simonson, *Jews in Sicily*.
1496. Pliny the Elder estimated the Strait of Messina, between Italy and Sicily, at ca. 1.5 mi. (12 stadia; *N.H.* 3.5.73; also noted in 3.8.86); in fact, the strait is 8 mi. (13 km.) wide at the south and 2 mi. (3 km.) wide at the north (Finegan, *Apostles*, 208). Rhegium was estimated by Pliny at 11.5 mi. (93 stadia) from that tip. (Most sources either identify ancient Columna Regia, on the strait, with—or locate it near—the modern Reggio di Calabria [e.g., H. Rackham in LCL, 2:54 n. *a*, on *N.H.* 3.8.86]. A recent source brought to my attention by Joseph Carey places Columna Regia somewhat further, about 15 km. north, between Porticello and Punta Pezzo.)

(Thucyd. 4.24.4), even closely linked with the legendary Charybdis (see comment on Acts 27:17).[1497] Although late spring through autumn winds were calmer in this strait,[1498] the current season was less predictable.[1499] Ships could often ride a current northward through the strait, but if it slackened before they reached Italy's Tyrrhenian Sea beyond the strait,[1500] they could enter safe ports at Messina or Rhegium or wait near either the Sicilian or Italian coast for some slower northerly currents.[1501] Rhegium remained an important stop between Rome and Sicily.[1502]

The geographically informed understood that both Rhegium and Puteoli lay on the route between Rome and the East, important points for the Alexandrian grain trade.[1503] Those approaching Rome from the east could reach Rhegium and then Puteoli en route to Rome (Suet. *Tib.* 5.3). Roman ships traveling west could also spend time at Rhegium (Polyb. 5.110.3).

In earlier times Rhegium was a powerful city in its region (Strabo 6.1.6); it was founded in the late eighth century B.C.E. to guard the Strait of Messina from Italy's side.[1504] An ancient Greek colony, it retained much of its Greek character despite its loyalty to Rome, with some Greek institutions and religious cults surviving until the second century C.E.[1505] Although Rome subdued it in 271 B.C.E., it remained a strategic, hence coveted, location, and the Carthaginians under Hannibal nearly captured it afterward (Polyb. 9.7.10; 9.9.4). Long before Paul, the citizens of Rhegium (*Regini*) were already Roman citizens (Cic. *Verr.* 2.4.60.135); nevertheless, it was one of the few areas near Sicily to retain their Greek roots (Strabo 6.1.2).

Although the sea route northward was faster (once the south wind began blowing again, Acts 28:13), Rhegium was also well connected with the rest of Italy by a road northward into Campania, where the road joined the Appian Way (Strabo 6.3.7). Since the voyage from Rhegium to Puteoli covers more than two hundred miles (ca. 350 km.), the travelers' arrival on the second day with a favorable wind suggests "an average speed of five knots," about right for ships of that era.[1506]

III. Puteoli (28:13)

Paul's ship, the Twin Brothers, made extraordinarily good time to Puteoli, able to take advantage of winds from the south that blew early in the spring.[1507] Puteoli was on the northern side of the Bay of Naples, only about twenty kilometers west of Naples (Neapolis) on the most sheltered part of its bay. A ship coming from the south

1497. On navigating Scylla and Charybdis here, see Davis, "Navigation," 232–33.

1498. Ibid., 231, citing *Med Pilot* 2.560.

1499. Heavy winds required greater caution, having destroyed ships in this area (see Davis, "Navigation," 232, following James Smith in n. 122).

1500. Davis, "Navigation," 231, notes (at least with respect to the calmer seasons) that ships would normally "enter the southern end of the strait at mid-channel in the morning at or near the onset of . . . the northerly flood current which averages approximately 5 kts," propelling the ship north. Ships always navigated the passage by daylight.

1501. Ibid., 231–32.

1502. Lomas, "Rhegium." The emperor Gaius Caligula had built places for receiving Alexandrian grain ships in Sicily and Rhegium (Jos. *Ant.* 19.205).

1503. For the Alexandrian route, cf. Friedländer, *Life*, 1:352; Ramsay, "Roads and Travel," 377; Moore, "Life," 229.

1504. Clarke, "Italy," 479. Messene was founded at about the same time on the Sicilian side (Finegan, *Apostles*, 208).

1505. Lomas, "Rhegium." Rhegium produced the great sculptor Pythagoras (Pliny E. *N.H.* 34.19.59, 60). Further on Rhegium, see also Muggia, "Regium"; earlier, Vallet, *Rhégion*.

1506. Conzelmann, *Acts*, 224. The voyage from a comparable point in Italy south to Messene took about three days in Philost. *Vit. Apoll.* 8.15.

1507. For this leg of the voyage, early spring was much more favorable than summer or autumn (Davis, "Navigation," 233).

into the Bay of Naples would pass the island of Capri;[1508] 4,000 feet (1,220 m.) high, Mount Vesuvius would be visible there.[1509] Naples was founded in the mid-seventh century B.C.E. Puteoli, the commercial port, was not far from Cumae, a political center, and Misenum, a Roman naval base.[1510] Puteoli's exports included sulfur, pottery, iron utensils, and a mortar composed partly of volcanic ash.[1511] Archaeologists have found the city's market, about 125 by 118 feet (38 by 36 m.), with porches and shops around it,[1512] and also a modest Augustan amphitheater, 427 by 312 feet (130 by 95 m.).[1513]

Puteoli was a strategic location for Italy's trade; rumors about Egypt would normally reach there before Rome (Cic. *Att.* 4.10), and its location near Rome and on the sea was well known (e.g., Philo *Embassy* 185, employing the earlier Greek name). Commentators often note the importance of Puteoli to the Alexandrian grain traffic (see Acts 28:11).[1514] Before Claudius improved Rome's harbor in Ostia at the mouth of the Tiber (Suet. *Claud.* 20), Puteoli was the Alexandrian grain fleet's primary maritime destination.[1515] Paul arrives during the reign of Nero, Claudius's successor, but even then Puteoli remained the most important western Italian port for trade outside Italy during this season; it took time for Ostia to surpass it (Titus later used it, Suet. *Tit.* 5.3).[1516] Even when cargoes continued on to Ostia, passengers might disembark at Puteoli.[1517] In Paul's day, Puteoli's crowds would stand along the docks watching for the sails of the first Alexandrian ships (Sen. Y. *Ep. Lucil.* 77.1).

Puteoli, built on a hill, was earlier a port or naval base for the Cumeans, but Rome controlled it from about 338 B.C.E., and when battling Hannibal, Rome established a colony there (Strabo 5.4.6). Because of the wells (*putei*) there (or possibly the sulfurous odor of the waters; *puteo* means "stink"), Rome also changed its name to Puteoli (5.4.6).[1518] Nero apparently granted Puteoli greater colony status (Tac. *Ann.* 14.27). The port city could be extremely hot at noon (Fronto *Ad M. Caes.* 2.6.3) but would normally be much cooler during this season. Inscriptions show "a flourishing civic life" there; it was also a prominent resort area, and many wealthy Romans "owned villas there."[1519]

1508. Finegan, *Apostles*, 208, noting that it had twelve villas and Tiberius lived there from 26/27 to 37 (described in Tac. *Ann.* 4.67).

1509. Finegan, *Apostles*, 208. Vesuvius, which erupted violently in 79 C.E., was ca. 30 km. from Puteoli.

1510. Ibid., 209.

1511. Ibid., 210.

1512. Ibid., 211.

1513. Ibid. (noting that the amphitheater was expanded to seat forty thousand under the Flavians, making it one of Italy's largest; this in turn suggests its prominence already in Paul's day). Already in 1851 scholars had counted thirteen structures in Puteoli's harbor (Abbott, *Acts*, 259).

1514. Cf. Cadbury, *Acts in History*, 60; Lake and Cadbury, *Commentary*, 13; Clarke, "Italy," 479; Casson, *Mariners*, 210. Ships from western Sicily sailed northeast toward Puteoli or other Roman ports, a trajectory confirmed by a cluster of shipwrecks in the Sicilian Channel; see Davis, "Navigation," 84, following McCann and Oleson, *Shipwrecks*; cf. also McCann and Freed, *Archaeology*.

1515. Casson, *Travel*, 129; idem, *Mariners*, 199–200. In the late republic, Puteoli was known for its granaries (Cic. *Fin.* 2.26.84).

1516. Conzelmann, *Acts*, 224 (citing, for Ostia's later ascendancy, Sen. Y. *Ep. Lucil.* 77; for Puteoli's corresponding decline, *OGIS* 595); cf. Strabo 5.4.6. Based on dental enamel, some argue for heavy first-century youthful immigration to Ostia-Portus (Prowse et al., "Isotopic Evidence"); some criticize that study's methodology (Bruun, "Isotopes"), but others defend it as the simplest explanation of the data (Killgrove, "Response"). On Ostia (and Claudius's lighthouse there), see further, e.g., Meiggs, Gallina, and Claridge, *Roman Ostia*; Bakker, *Mills-Bakeries*; Olssen, Mitternacht, and Brandt, *Synagogue*; Davis, "Navigation," 234–36; Bédoyère, *Cities*; Stöger, *Rethinking Ostia*; Laurence and Newsome, *Rome, Ostia, Pompeii*; van der Meer, *Ostia Speaks*. Further on Puteoli, see Zevi and Jodice, *Puteoli*; Jones, *Bankers*; Ostrow, "Problems"; earlier, see, e.g., Dubois, *Pouzzoles*.

1517. Johnson, *Acts*, 464; Hemer, *Acts in History*, 154–55; Dunn, *Acts*, 350.

1518. Those from the Greek East sometimes used the name "Dicearchia" (or "Dicaearchia") (Jos. *Life* 16).

1519. Lomas, "Puteoli."

Although the maritime voyage was complete, the journey to Rome was not; even directly as the crow flies, Puteoli remained more than 120 miles (ca. 200 km.) from Rome, and by road farther still. Normally those traveling on to Rome would follow "the Via Campana to Capua, and from there the Via Appia."[1520] Shortly before Puteoli the group would reach the Appian Way, so named because it was planned when Appius Claudius was censor (312 B.C.E.).[1521] The Via Appia, or Appian Way, was the major thoroughfare from Rome toward the south of Italy.[1522] It crossed the Pontine (or Pomptine) Marshes.[1523] The land route to Rhegium (Acts 28:13), which Paul's company had not taken, was not technically the Via Appia but also often went by that name.[1524]

c. Believers' Hospitality (28:14–15)

The group's hearty reception in Italy merited Luke's attention and reveals several points of interest: the Christian movement was already noticeable in Italy, even outside Rome; the movement was loving and hospitable (positive virtues that would commend it in Luke's Greco-Roman setting); and Paul was loved and welcomed (supporting Luke's characterization of his *ēthos*).[1525]

i. Christians in Puteoli (28:14)

Given Puteoli's importance as an Italian port, the appearance of Christians there (28:14) is hardly surprising if Christians were in Rome (as Paul's letter to the Romans makes clear they were; cf. earlier Luke's report in 18:2).[1526] Other groups from the East settled there and often propagated their cults. An influential Tyrian colony there (*IG* 14.830) spread its cult of Baal of Sarepta;[1527] Puteoli had a temple of the Egyptian god Serapis by 105 B.C.E.[1528] It also had one of Italy's oldest synagogues outside Rome and apparently a sizable Jewish community (Jos. *Ant.* 17.328; *War* 2.104).[1529]

Some scholars have suggested pre-79 C.E. evidence of Christians in nearby Herculaneum (ca. 25 km.) because of cross marks on a wall there;[1530] this evidence is not very compelling (was the cross necessarily used as a Christian symbol here?), but with attestation of a sizable Christian community in Rome (e.g., Tac. *Ann.* 15.44; Rom 1:7; cf. Suet. *Nero* 16.2), it is intrinsically likely that some Christians had settled near a major conduit to Rome.

Some suggest that Luke contrasts the heroes of Acts 28:11 (whose brotherhood was well known) with the real and more genuinely helpful "brothers" of 28:14.[1531] This

1520. Conzelmann, *Acts*, 224. The first road may have been rough (Rapske, "Travel," 20).
1521. Allen, "Appius, Forum of"; Bruce, *Commentary*, 527.
1522. Salmon and Potter, "Via Appia"; "Italy's most famous road" (Rathmann, "Via Appia," 368).
1523. Salmon and Potter, "Via Appia"; idem, "Pomptine Marshes."
1524. Salmon and Potter, "Pomptine Marshes."
1525. Paul did have enemies in Rome (Phil 1:15–17) but seemed to have more friends (Phil 1:14–16; Rom 16:3–15).
1526. Also Witherington, *Acts*, 784.
1527. Grant, *Gods*, 30–32; Hemer, *Acts in History*, 155.
1528. Grant, *Gods*, 29.
1529. Clarke, "Italy," 480; Bruce, *Acts*¹, 474; idem, *Commentary*, 527; Hemer, *Acts in History*, 155; for Jews in Italy outside Rome, see, e.g., Goodenough, *Symbols*, 2:51–55; Stern, "Diaspora," 160–70. Exaggerating Rome's greatness, some rabbis told of late first-century sages hearing Rome's "traffic from as far away as Puteoli, a hundred and twenty *mil* away" (*Sipre Deut.* 43.3.7 [Neusner, 1:139]).
1530. Finegan, *Apostles*, 212–13, tentatively suggesting that the cross be construed as a Christian symbol and allowing that its removal might relate to the owner's martyrdom under Nero. (Alternatively, the owner might have removed it during Nero's persecution to prevent such martyrdom.) The Pompeian Rotas-Sator Square is not specifically Christian (Hofmann, "Square"; cf. Baines, "Square").
1531. Spencer, *Acts*, 236; cf. Hamm, *Acts*, 123.

is possible, but if Luke intends such a contrast, he certainly does not go out of his way to emphasize it; although the brotherhood of the Dioscuri was well known, Luke does not explicitly call the Dioscuri "brothers" in 28:11 (despite some translations).

How did they "find" the brothers? (The language contrasts with 28:15, where other brothers, having heard advance news from Puteoli, come to meet them.) Presumably they looked for them in Puteoli, perhaps using some logic to find them (cf. 16:13) or simply inquiring about them, possibly at a synagogue (cf. Matt 10:11).[1532] Paul may have also heard about Christians in Puteoli from travelers (e.g., Phoebe, Rom 16:1) or correspondents in Rome (Rom 16). It is also not unlikely historically that many Christians in Italy knew of Paul; even aside from his friends in Rome, he had written his extraordinarily long letter (by ancient standards) to the Roman believers a few years before. A letter of that length was an expensive undertaking intended for wide readership, and its preservation suggests that it had circulated widely. Although Paul may have intended only a friendly visit,[1533] the hospitable Christians[1534] strongly "urged" or "exhorted" (παρεκλήθημεν, Acts 28:14) the group to stay, presumably revealing their appreciation of Paul (of which Luke approves).

II. PERMITTED A WEEK'S STAY (28:14)

Seven days is a fairly lengthy stay (20:6; 21:4; contrast 21:7; 27:3–4), which allows Luke to emphasize (as in 28:15) that his protagonist was loved throughout the Diaspora and by partly Gentile churches (despite some antipathy in Jerusalem). This is all the clearer when we consider that Paul was a prisoner; although chains were generally a matter of shame (see comments on Acts 21:33–34; 26:29), Paul's hosts welcomed both him and his official (but well-disposed) captors.[1535] (In view of their lack of embarrassment in front of Julius, it is clear that they were not at this point expecting imperial persecution.) The sorts of scruples that Jerusalem Christians once had regarding Cornelius are obviously not in effect among such Diaspora believers.

Given struggles, evident in Paul's letters, against Paul's interpretation of Christianity, Luke's report of his positive reception in various places may serve a partly apologetic function for Pauline Christianity.[1536] Luke also emphasizes, for the sake of any outsiders, that the Christian movement was like an extended family (see Luke 18:29–30; Mark 10:29–30): one could expect to find hospitality wherever one traveled (also the ideal for Jews and some other minorities; see comment on Acts 16:15).

Given what potentially awaited him in Rome, Paul himself may have been happy to visit and pray with Christians before proceeding; Acts 28:15 hints that he still needed to be encouraged. But why would the centurion allow it? One suggestion is that he left a guard with Paul but Julius himself and his other prisoners, whose arrival in Rome he would wish to expedite, traveled on to Rome.[1537] Yet leaving few guards with Paul, when he was surrounded by so many friends, was an act of great trust—one that could risk his own life if he was charged with negligence for Paul's escape.[1538] Although he

---

1532. On locating people by inquiry, see Ling, "Stranger in Town"; cf. 1 Sam 9:11, 18.

1533. But then where were Julius and his other prisoners?

1534. Hospitality was a Christian virtue (Rom 12:13; 1 Tim 3:2; 5:10; 1 Pet 4:9), but also one pervasive and widely respected in antiquity (see comment on Acts 16:15) and hence one profitable for Luke to report.

1535. Cf. Plut. *Cic.* 32.1: respecting Cicero, most people disregarded Clodius's order that no one provide him shelter (later they were rewarded, 33.4).

1536. After Paul's custody in Rome had lasted for some time, he had both supporters and detractors in the Christian community there; see Phil 1:16–17 (on the assumption that Philippians refers to a Roman detention). For Acts as partly an apologetic for Paul after his execution, see also Keener, "Apologetic."

1537. Dunn, *Acts*, 350.

1538. Although Leptines, because he was eager to stand trial in Rome, was counted a low enough security risk to be sent to Rome without chains or guard (Polyb. 32.3.5).

may have trusted Paul this much by this point (cf. already 27:3), another complication existed. Arriving without one of the prisoners (who would come later) would leave Julius with questions to answer. Although Julius may trust Paul enough by this point, it is unlikely that Luke would have let such an extraordinary evidence of trust pass unmentioned. Given the delays so far, a few more days would hardly matter, and Julius and the others had undoubtedly remained dependent on hospitality in Malta until their very recent voyage.

Although Julius previously approved Paul's receiving hospitality (27:3), he likely did so without any expense of unnecessary delay. That he now grants a delay of an entire week allows Luke to demonstrate the transformation of Paul's status on the journey to Rome. We can speculate on the reasons, but paramount among those that the narrative itself implies is the respect that Julius now has for his prisoner.[1539] Paul was not only a Roman citizen but also a prominent person with friends in various parts of the empire (27:3; 28:14–15). More important, Julius has seen the miracles (28:8–9) and gifts or honors (28:10), and he was already heeding Paul as a prophet by the end of the voyage (27:31–32); he is in no hurry to see his prisoner, already vindicated in his eyes, brought to detention in Rome.[1540] Far from the narrative being implausible as it stands, it is unlikely that Julius would refuse Paul's request (or perhaps be eager to deliver him to further custody) after what Luke narrates he has observed (27:10, 26, 31–32, 34, 41, 44; 28:5, 8–9); it may be that some modern readers who object to Julius's delay may do so largely because they are skeptical of these prior elements in the narrative.

In addition, the group is ahead of schedule for travelers in the spring, leaving early in spring from Malta instead of from Judea, Asia, or Crete. Another factor or reason for Julius's approving the delay could be the discomfort of the sea voyage, which might invite a rest stop before continuation of the journey to Rome (the road they would need to take was reportedly "rough and flinty").[1541] The journey of about 120 to 130 miles could take up to a week; some of the journey ran through hill country and, as mentioned, the Pontine Marshes,[1542] although travelers could avoid the latter.[1543]

Further, the hospitality of Paul's friends would help Julius. Whereas prisoners might need to supply their own food while awaiting trial in Rome (Jos. Life 14), Julius can requisition what he needs for them (see comment on Acts 27:3). But especially because of its abuses, requisitioning caused much tension, and hospitality would prove much more convenient.[1544] Although Ignatius's guards (unlike Paul's) were not impressed with him, they accepted hospitality while journeying to Rome (Ign. Rom. 5.1); he spent enough time in Smyrna to receive delegations and send four long letters.[1545] Likewise, private hospitality was generally preferable to boardinghouses

1539. Further, a centurion might do what he could for his prisoner with whom he had become friends, *if* he anticipated his soon release (Jos. *Ant.* 18.230–33). As noted earlier, the narrative leads the reader to understand that Paul was sent with the favor of both Festus and Agrippa.

1540. Despite what appears to be an early departure from Malta (see comment on Acts 28:11 for reasons).

1541. Rapske, "Travel," 20–21, citing *Acts Pet.* 2.6. Rapske notes (21) that billeting facilities closer to Rome would be more prioritized, provincial soldiers with prisoners constituting a lower priority (one wonders, however, whether supply would increase as well as demand).

1542. Witherington, *Acts*, 786.

1543. Salmon and Potter, "Pomptine Marshes." Malaria was known to be more common in swampy areas (Heracl. *Hom. Prob.* 11.5; Touwaide, "Malaria," 195). The Pontine Marshes offered the main body of water between Lake Avernus and the Tiber (Tac. *Ann.* 15.42).

1544. Rapske, *Custody*, 273–74; idem, "Travel," 20. Requisitioning was sometimes abused and often generated resentments; see, e.g., Sherk, *Empire*, 89, 136; further comment on Acts 27:2.

1545. Rapske, *Custody*, 275. Rapske argues that "the venue and offer" of hospitality may have proved sufficient even apart from Julius's respect for Paul (though I believe that the latter is Luke's literary emphasis).

and inns available along the way,[1546] and the closer one came to Rome, the heavier the competing demands would be for billeting.[1547]

Another possibility is that someone in the company had fallen too sick to travel; if anyone's sickness provided reason for the delay, Luke may have felt it incongruous to mention this after the dramatic healings of Acts 28:8–9 if this one was not accompanied by an instant recovery. But no evidence directly points to this solution, and there are reasons enough for Julius to have accommodated Paul's friends.

"Thus we came to Rome" does not imply that the seven-day "sojourn" with these Christians means that they walked with Paul to Rome (though it could be a seven-day journey). Luke would hardly write that they "implore" Paul to "sojourn" with them if what he meant was that they wanted to travel with him. Rather, Luke is saying, "This is the manner in which we came to Rome," a manner continued in 28:15 (with its honorary delegation meeting him) and completed with arrival at Rome in 28:16. Paul travels to Rome not like a prisoner but like an honored official.

Undoubtedly the party proceeded to Capua, 20 miles (32 km.) beyond Puteoli, to connect with the Via Appia, the primary land conduit to Rome.[1548] The journey from Capua to Rome would take 131 miles (211 km.); the Via Appia went to Sinuessa on the coast, then inland to Minturnae, back to the coast at Formiae, then down to the coast again at Tarracina, where the Via Appia became Tarracina's *decumanus*, or "main longitudinal street." Tarracina was roughly halfway to Rome from Capua, leaving 64 more miles (103 km.) to travel.[1549]

III. ROMAN CHRISTIANS WELCOME PAUL (28:15)

"Brothers" (as in Puteoli, 28:14) from Rome came to meet Paul on his way to the city. Among Luke's theological reasons for emphasizing this "sibling" support is the notion of spiritual family as a reward for faithful sacrifice: one who leaves behind family and possessions for God's kingdom has many more of both in God's kingdom (Luke 18:29–30). Some scholars think that Luke wants even to emphasize Paul as the Roman church's founder here,[1550] but the fact that the "siblings" are already Christians and Luke mentions the church as early as Acts 18:2 counters this suggestion.[1551]

What Luke does show is that the Christians of the empire's prestigious capital honor and receive Paul—much more than the Jerusalem church had. In Acts, the gospel (which for Luke includes the Pauline gospel of the Gentile mission) has moved from Jerusalem to Rome, the heart of the empire. If Luke were addressing the more global situation today, he would likely insist that no one region maintains an eternal privilege in the gospel; as one region is turning from it, it is spreading to others. For Luke's audience, however, how the gospel reached even to the imperial household (cf. Phil 4:22) in the prestigious heart of the empire serves an analogous function.[1552]

1546. Ibid.

1547. Ibid., 276. Rapske also suggests (276) the value of waiting in Puteoli if Julius wanted a vehicle; a centurion could requisition a cart, three mules, or six donkeys cheaply (idem, "Travel," 18, citing Horsley, *Documents*, 1, §9.21). But finding one of suitable size may have been difficult.

1548. Finegan, *Apostles*, 213 (noting, however, that modern Capua is 3 mi. [5 km.] closer to Rome than the ancient town).

1549. Ibid.

1550. Haenchen, *Acts*, 720; Conzelmann, *Acts*, 224. Paul himself hopes to supply a theological foundation of some sort (Rom 1:11, 15) yet delays visiting the Roman Christians precisely because he is occupied with territories genuinely needing evangelism (15:20–24).

1551. See also Franklin, *Interpreter*, 132, rightly noting that Luke could have omitted mention of other Christians there.

1552. For Christians within the empire, Rome did eventually (long after Luke's death, whenever one dates him) become a center of Christian faith, as did Constantinople. Quite different, almost antithetical, is

Luke does not explain how the Christians in Rome knew of Paul's approach or how they recognized each other. To call him a "storyteller" for this reason,[1553] however, is to infer too much from silence and not enough from the facts that he and Paul provide us. Paul spent seven days in Puteoli (28:14); even had Christians there not deliberately sent word ahead to Rome, travelers would be passing from one place toward the other daily and would carry both messages and news.

That Roman Christians historically knew of Paul is certain.[1554] His letter to "the consecrated ones" there (Rom 1:7) must have circulated widely in Rome through the approval of house church leaders named in Rom 16.[1555] Some of Paul's coworkers in Corinth visited Rome (most clearly, Phoebe in 16:1–2), and the contact between the congregations (Corinth being a Roman colony) was significant (as 1 Clement attests). When the winds were favorable, a person could reach Rome from Corinth in about a week, and so travelers (such as Phoebe) were probably frequent.[1556] That Paul knew so much about the issues in the Roman churches when he wrote his letter to them suggests a solid source of information.

Moreover, many Roman Christians knew Paul by face.[1557] In the early empire, heavy provincial immigration sustained the Roman population despite the high mortality rate,[1558] and so it is not surprising that many of Paul's mobile urban contacts would eventually find themselves there. From Paul's own letter to the Romans[1559] we learn that Prisca and Aquila now led a house church there (Rom 16:3–5), and we discover many of his former colaborers already at work there (16:3–15, esp. 16:7, 9). Prisca and Aquila were with Paul in Ephesus during the height of his ministry there (1 Cor 16:8–9, 19) but were in Rome by the time of Paul's last visit to Corinth (Rom 16:3; cf. Acts 20:3). According to tradition, they finally left Rome only later, probably during the Neronian persecution (2 Tim 4:19).[1560] They would have spoken much about Paul, although it is uncertain that they would be expecting his arrival (would word

Revelation's approach to Rome, which contemporary Jewish thinkers usually identified with Daniel's fourth and final predicted kingdom; for Augustine, the ultimate city of God lay elsewhere.

1553. Fitzmyer, Acts, 787. Of course, it is possible (even quite likely) for Luke to be a good "storyteller" without insisting that he invented the story; Fitzmyer himself accepts the "we" narrative as an eyewitness account (98–103).

1554. With, e.g., Foakes-Jackson, Acts, 234; Faw, Acts, 292.

1555. Gaventa, "Believers," 106, does warn that Luke may not have known of the letter and hence allows that it may not have been influential. But given the brevity of Luke's account, it is too much to infer from Luke's silence whether he knew about the letter; if Luke authored the "we" source, Luke visited Rome with Paul and presumably had a more important firsthand acquaintance with believers there.

1556. Riesner, Early Period, 316–17.

1557. Paul would have met many of the Jewish Christian leaders in Corinth and elsewhere in the East after Claudius's expulsion (cf. Jewett, Romans, 59–60, 968), though Paul probably did not know all of them (cf., e.g., ibid., 970). Some early Christians believed that even Peter was there before Paul's arrival; see (in Bray, Romans, 23–24) Ps.-Constantius Holy Letter of St. Paul to the Romans (ENPK 22); Theodoret Interpretation of Romans (IER, PG 82:56). We lack, however, any genuinely early attestation for this idea. Although Luke could ignore Peter to focus on the importance of Paul reaching Rome, it is likelier that later Roman Christians' emphasis on their Petrine foundation led them to place it before Paul's arrival (see also comment on Acts 12:17). This emphasis may have arisen through their earlier connections with the Jerusalem church, which was originally led by Peter (Hengel, Peter, 94).

1558. Garnsey and Saller, Empire, 99.

1559. This is assuming the integrity of Rom 16, the greetings at least being part of the original letter; so most scholars today, e.g., Lung-Kwong, Purpose, 24–35; Lönnermark, "Frågan"; Donfried, "Note"; Morris, Romans, 28; Haacker, Theology, 12; Donfried, "Note on Romans 16," 57; Hultgren, Romans, 22–23; pace Manson, "Letter"; Richards, "Chronological Relationship." Esp. influential has been Gamble, Textual History.

1560. Some commentators read Heb 13:24 as referring to them, perhaps implying that they remain in Italy (Montefiore, Hebrews, 254), but I believe that this interpretation is unlikely (preferring the understanding that Heb 13 is written from Italy).

of his appeal have reached Rome before Paul himself did?).[1561] There was reason to believe, however, that Paul hoped to visit eventually (Rom 1:10; 15:23–24).[1562]

Given those greeted in Rom 16, the majority of members in the Roman church by this time were probably Gentiles (1:5, 13; 11:13)[1563] of originally non-Roman extraction,[1564] and a large proportion were probably of slave or freed backgrounds[1565] (like many Roman Jews in an earlier generation; see comment on Acts 28:17). Paul knew many of them already.[1566] Some leaders were Jewish (Aquila and Priscilla; Andronicus and Junia; Herodion),[1567] as were a minority of the members (possibly including Aristobulus's household in Rom 16:10).[1568] Indeed, if one may infer anything from the content of Paul's letter to the Roman Christians, the Roman church's originally Jewish background also remains heavily influential theologically. There may have even been some Christians of high status, especially if the "foreign superstition" with which Pomponia Graecina was charged (Tac. Ann. 13.32.3–5) was Christianity.[1569] Women played a prominent role in the church (cf. Rom 16:3–7, 12, 15).[1570]

In view of later Christian housing in Rome, many of the believers were undoubtedly located in Transtiberinum (modern Trastevere),[1571] where also a large number of Jewish people lived (see fuller treatment at Acts 28:17). That this area across the Tiber remained unscathed by the conflagration of 64 C.E. may help to partly explain Nero's using Christians as scapegoats.[1572] Their likely second most dominant location was a low-class area around Porta Capena, where much traffic entered the city and many immigrants lived.[1573]

1561. Certainly, if they did know of Paul's appeal, his failure to arrive before now would not have caused consternation; people would more readily assume that his ship had wintered somewhere than that it had been lost.
1562. These texts show that he planned to come after visiting Jerusalem; his custody in Judea had delayed this, but it could be assumed that he would come if and when the custody was resolved.
1563. See, e.g., Nanos, Mystery, 77–84; Dunn, Romans, liii, 900; Moo, Romans, 9–13; Das, Paul and Jews, 60, 64; idem, "Audience"; Tobin, Rhetoric in Contexts, 37, 408; Haacker, Theology, 12; Jewett, Romans, 59, 70; Kruse, Romans, 2; earlier, cf. Schlatter, Romans, 11.
1564. Cf. Dunn, Romans, 900.
1565. Ibid.
1566. Some of the groups apparently lacked leaders known to Paul, perhaps because their original leaders had been expelled in 49 C.E. (Jewett, Romans, 61; see comment on Acts 18:2); but would not new leaders have arisen in the groups? Paul, however, may know many of the leaders precisely because, between the expulsion and their return, he met them in the East (Jewett, Romans, 59–60).
1567. Many suspect that Herodion was a slave or freedman of the Herodian household (Rom 16:11; see Dunn, Romans, 896; Stuhlmacher, Romans, 250; Jewett, Romans, 967).
1568. It was a common name, but many cite Jos. War 2.221; e.g., Sanday and Headlam, Romans, 425; Hunter, Romans, 132; Dunn, Romans, 896; Jewett, Romans, 72–73n485, 966. Josephus does not, however, indicate whether Aristobulus would remain alive in Rome in the late 50s; if he was not, it seems unclear that his former household would continue to be called by his name.
1569. Whittaker, Jews and Christians, 147, argues that it was (noting catacombs and customs). A short generation later, some suggest Flavius Clemens and his wife, Domitilla (see Dio Cass. 67.14.1–2; cf. Suet. Dom. 15), fitting later Christian tradition (Euseb. Chron. 96 [Helm, 192]; H.E. 3.18.4; Ramsay, Church in Empire, 261; Chadwick, Early Church, 26; Mattingly, Christianity, 35; Parkes, Conflict, 87; Caird, Revelation, 20–21; allowing for somewhat more varied possibilities, Robinson, Redating, 232; Reicke, Era, 295–97).
1570. With Dunn, Romans, 900; Venetz, "Frauen." From 1 Clem. 21.7, Dunn, Romans, 900, surmises that the church later became more hierarchical; but even then, 1 Clement, though more hierarchical than the Pastorals, is more egalitarian than many of Clement's contemporaries (see Keener, "Woman," 1211–12). Women had more freedom in Rome than in many other parts of the empire (see Keener, Acts, 1:605–37, esp. 606, 608–9), perhaps including in synagogues (White, "Synagogue in Ostia," 32), although, at least in the late republic, men probably outnumbered women in Rome (Stambaugh, City, 89).
1571. Jewett, Romans, 62 (noting the high density of apartment buildings there).
1572. Ibid., 63.
1573. Ibid., 62–63. On the basis of later material, Jewett also assigns (63) Christians to the Campus Martius and the Aventine Hill, but Christians may have expanded there later as the church won more Latin-speaking Roman citizens.

Nor should we question whether the Roman church was already large enough to send such a delegation.[1574] Paul addresses not the entire Roman church in Rom 16 but those he knew personally, many of whom were leaders.[1575] Further, a few years before his arrival, the "whole world" knew of the faith of the Roman saints (Rom 1:8); while this universal claim is partly hyperbole (cf. Col 1:23; 1 Thess 1:8; perhaps Rom 10:18) and partly because Rome was the imperial capital, it would scarcely have made sense to apply such words to a small and struggling church. Finally, Nero found hundreds, possibly thousands (given the number of "torches" he would need), of Christians to persecute starting in 64 (Tac. *Ann.* 15.44), probably no more than half a decade after this narrative.[1576] Further suggesting the Roman church's numerical strength, it apparently remained strong after this persecution (cf. *1 Clement* title).[1577]

IV. HONORARY DELEGATIONS

The nature of Paul's entry is noteworthy. The disciples came from far away to "meet" him, offering the sort of welcome appropriate to a royal emissary or official[1578] (cf., e.g., 1 Thess 4:17),[1579] a practice that is widely attested. The Latin *adventus* was the Roman equivalent for the Greek παρουσία, applicable to the arrival of emperors, cult statues, generals, and others of importance.[1580] People of rank were to even come out of retirement on their estates to Rome to hail a new emperor (Pliny *Ep.* 3.7.6–7).[1581] The Judean king Agrippa I went out to meet Syria's Roman governor to show the Romans the highest respect (Jos. *Ant.* 19.340).

Greeks might receive a victorious general with applause, then conduct him to his house in triumph (Dion. Hal. *Ant. rom.* 7.7.2);[1582] Romans likewise would go out to "meet" a returning general (even a defeated one, Sil. It. 10.634). To come to congratulate a leader or other person who had won success was an expected social convention.[1583] When Cicero returned from exile, cities came out to meet (ἀπάντησιν) him (Plut. *Cic.* 33.5); he claimed that no town failed to "send official deputations to congratulate [him]" (Cic. *Pis.* 22.51).[1584]

1574. Luke omits the church's founding (though cf. Acts 2:10) because his narrative is focused on Paul (with Johnson, *Acts*, 464).

1575. Tobin, *Rhetoric in Contexts*, 39, infers "at least five different house churches" in Rom 16:3–16; cf. also Jewett, *Romans*, 62. Perhaps going too far, Judge, *First Christians*, 442–43, infers no "church" there, but merely immigrants Paul knew from the East.

1576. See further Tobin, *Rhetoric in Contexts*, 35; Jewett, *Romans*, 61–62.

1577. Rome remained a center of persecution in the views of early Christians (cf. Ign. *Eph.* 1.2; 21.2; *Rom.* 5.1; 10.2).

1578. Although the LXX lacks this technical usage, going out to meet someone to honor them appears (Judg 11:31, 34; 1 Sam 13:10; 30:21; 2 Sam 6:20; 19:26; Jer 41:6 [48:6 LXX]). For generals and rulers, see Vespasian in Jos. *War* 3.459 (at Tiberias); 7.70–71 (at Rome; Talbert, *John*, 118); for officials or prominent persons, see further Milligan, *Thessalonians*, 62 (citing P.Tebt. 43.7; Polyb. 5.26.8).

1579. On the imagery in 1 Thess 4:17, see Best, *Thessalonians*, 199; Bruce, *Thessalonians*, 102–3; Marshall, *Thessalonians*, 131; Ladd, *Hope*, 91; Donfried, *Thessalonica*, 34; Harrison, *Authorities*, 59–60 (emphasizing imperial connections).

1580. Gizewski, "Adventus."

1581. In this case, Trajan permitted the freedom not to do so, but (at least in Pliny's view, and probably more generally) he proved an unusually generous emperor. Not being permitted to come to welcome the emperor indicated the latter's displeasure (a death sentence under Nero, Tac. *Ann.* 16.24). Even cities from Asia sent delegations to congratulate the emperor (Dio Chrys. *Or.* 40.13–14). Pliny sought to greet Trajan on a later occasion (Pliny *Ep.* 10.10.2). One should run to meet a king (*b. Ber.* 58a), although this action might otherwise be thought undignified.

1582. Those in Ashkelon met (συνάντησιν) Jonathan to honor him (1 Macc 10:86; cf. 11:60), but probably in lieu of being captured (cf. 10:84–85).

1583. E.g., Alexander in Plut. *Alex.* 14.1; generally, Friedländer, *Life*, 1:211; see discussion at Acts 25:13. For athletes, see, e.g., Pliny *Ep.* 10.118.1.

1584. Trans. N. H. Watts, LCL, pp. 201, 203. People put out torches and lamps to honor him as he passed, as one who had achieved a great triumph (Plut. *Cic.* 22.3–4).

Orators from delegations sent to meet a new governor would laud him with lavish praise: "We have come out to meet [προαπηντήκαμεν] you, all of us, in whole families, children, old men, adults, priestly clans,"[1585] hailing "you our saviour and fortress, our bright star."[1586] The governor's arrival was the most pleasurable of days, and now the people's sun shines brighter![1587] When a town viewed some prominent person as its patron, they would celebrate his arrivals (*adventus*, Pliny *Ep.* 4.1.4).

Failure to display this honor could offend a prominent person. Claudius was angry with the people of Ostia for not sending a delegation to meet him, though he forgave them (Suet. *Claud.* 38.1). One of the reasons Cicero gave for divorcing his wife was that when he was returning from a long absence, she failed to come out to meet him (Plut. *Cic.* 41.2). Those whose friends did not meet them in person to congratulate or welcome them could, however, offer excuses that their friends might accept (Pliny *Ep.* 6.28.1). A generous friend might even request that someone who was physically weak not come out to meet him or his agent (7.23.1).

The term ἀπάντησις was not at all limited to this technical usage (see, e.g., Matt 25:6),[1588] but given the city that Paul was entering, readers in Roman colonies in the East might[1589] well think of the custom in which triumphant Roman generals (in this period, the emperor) would enter the city in triumph, leading humiliated captives.[1590] Ironically, Paul, in chains, in this case would enter Rome with a different kind of triumph;[1591] early Christians evoked the Roman triumph to illustrate victory in sufferings (2 Cor 2:14–16).[1592] In the larger context of Luke-Acts, Paul's entrance would thus parallel Jesus's "triumphal entry" into Je-

1585. Men. Rhet. 2.3, 381.7–10 (Russell and Wilson, 101).

1586. Men. Rhet. 2.3, 381.11–12 (Russell and Wilson, 101).

1587. Men. Rhet. 2.3, 381.15–17.

1588. Common in the LXX (Judg 4:18; 14:5; 15:14; 19:3; 20:25, 31; 1 Sam 4:1; 6:13; 9:14; 13:15; 15:12; 16:4; 21:2; 25:32, 34; 1 Chr 12:18; 14:8; 19:5; 2 Chr 12:11; 15:2; 19:2; 20:17; 28:9; 1 Esd 1:23; Add Esth 16:9; Jdt 5:4; 1 Macc 12:41; 2 Macc 12:30; 14:30; 15:12; 3 Macc 1:19; Sir 19:29; Jer 28:31 [51:31 ET]; 34:3 [27:3 ET]); most of the seventy LXX uses of συνάντησις have this technical meaning; other cognate nouns would add up to twenty-six more references. Cf. even more the cognate verb (Mark 14:13; Luke 17:12; *Herm.* 23.3), but it seems to bear a wider semantic range.

1589. Admittedly, Luke could allude to Paul's celebrity status among Christians without referring to the Roman triumph (so Witherington, *Acts*, 787). Paul does not, of course, enter the Porta Triumphalis, and though ἀπάντησις (in Acts 28:15) can be applied to a triumphal entry, nothing in the term itself requires this specific interpretation. It is the connection between Jesus's kingly triumphal entry and Paul's welcome into Rome that might lend credibility to this image in both cases.

1590. E.g., Dion. Hal. *Ant. rom.* 9.26.9; 11.50.1; Cic. *Verr.* 2.5.26.65–67; Sall. *Jug.* 114.3; Livy 3.29.4–5; 31.49.3; 35.8.9; 40.43.4–6; Val. Max. 2.8.1, 6, 7; 4.4.5; 5.2.6; Vitruv. *Arch.* 1.1.5; Sil. It. 17.173–74; Appian *Hist. rom.* 12.17.116; Plut. *Cam.* 7.1; *Caes.* 55.2; 56.4; cf. further Hafemann, "Triumph"; idem, *Suffering*, 12–34; Thomas, *Revelation 19*, 21–45; here, e.g., Horton, *Acts*, 404; for pre-Roman analogies, see, e.g., the Assyrian custom in Monson, "Kings," 86. Augustus tried to reserve the image for himself and his successor (see Hickson, "Augustus *triumphator*"; Eder, "Triumph," 947–48; for some public response to Augustus's victory in 13 C.E., cf. Billows, "Procession"); late in his reign, women could participate more than during the republic (Flory, "Integration"). By Luke's day, Rome may have celebrated some three hundred triumphs since its founding (Talbert, *Corinthians*, 140, citing Orosius *Hist.* 7.9.8). Although the exact date of the custom's origin is debated (e.g., Rüpke, "Triumphator"; Versnel, "Herring?"), it is pre-Christian by several centuries. For other triumph-like greetings in Rome that were not technically triumphs (technically closer to Paul's entry here), see, e.g., Vell. Paterc. 2.45.5; 2.59.6; 2.89.1; *Res gest.* 2.12.

1591. Chrys. *Hom. Acts* 55 also compares Paul's entrance to the imperial triumphal entries, emphasizing the victory of martyrdom.

1592. See 2 Cor 2:14–16 (see various approaches in, e.g., Williamson, "Triumph"; Marshall, "Shame"; Breytenbach, "Proclamation"; Duff, "Metaphor" [cf. also idem, "Suffering"]; Scott, "Triumph"; Thrall, *2 Corinthians*, 191–95), where I understand Paul to be a captive awaiting execution, sharing Christ's suffering and resurrection power (Keener, *Corinthians*, 164; cf. Hafemann, *Suffering*; Barnett, *Corinthians*, 150; Witherington, *Corinthians*, 368–69); Tert. *Apol.* 50.3. Cf. perhaps Ambrosiaster *Commentary on Paul's Epistles* (Vogels, 209–10; Bray, *Corinthians*, 209); Euseb. *H.E.* 6.41. Some find allusions to triumphs in other Pauline texts, such

rusalem (Luke 19:37–38),[1593] though both presage suffering at the hands of the local establishment. The connection with Jesus's entry is probably the point most in favor of this suggestion; Jews, like other peoples, understood the principle of celebrating victory or of hailing returning victors (1 Sam 18:6–7; 1 Macc 13:51).

Whereas a connection with triumphal entries is uncertain, it is clear that the magnificent reception depicted here portrays Paul as a highly respected figure. The popularity of an Eastern teacher in Italy immediately on his arrival could be viewed as a sign of the teacher's greatness.[1594] Romans were gravely concerned about new Eastern cults[1595] and hence could have viewed Paul's popularity less favorably. (This would be especially the case if they viewed his παρουσία as competition with the emperor's; but the practice of greeting an honorable person was widespread, and no one concerned with the emperor's honor would view a prisoner as much competition, particularly in this period, when the Christian movement was not a serious concern.)[1596] But that the greetings were in the open[1597] (and in the presence of a Roman officer) should have defused such concerns. Luke's portrayal here is apologetic only by way of being epideictic: he defends the Pauline mission by showing how widely respected Paul was and how Christian love united most of the early Christian movement across geographic lines.

Because this is a delegation, it probably included some of the prominent leaders of the Roman church,[1598] including some of those Paul names in Rom 16:3–15 (though probably many, presumably belonging to the working class, could not have left their work for so long).

That Paul took "courage" does not mean that he was "depressed" before (*pace* some interpreters), but it could easily suggest anxiety or fear (cf. Acts 23:11).[1599] Although approaching Rome as a prisoner could be a matter of concern by itself, Paul also may have had some reason to be concerned about his reception in the Roman church,[1600] over which he had taken such care a few years earlier in his letter to the Romans; indeed, not all local believers proved supportive during his detention (Phil 1:15–17). The delegation's coming to meet him relieved any concerns of Paul's that Christians might avoid him because of his chains, a mark of shame.[1601] Ancient sources reveal that

as Eph 1:20–21; 4:8; Phil 2:9–10; and most clearly Col 2:15 (see Barth, *Ephesians*, 1:170; Ramsay, *Letters*, 388; idem, *Luke the Physician*, 297; cf. Kreitzer, "Rome").

1593. Likewise a peaceful one not truly analogous to Roman triumphs, since donkeys (Luke 19:30–35) characterized civil processions (Judg 10:4; 1 Kgs 1:33; cf. Hdn. 4.1.3); asses were of lower status than horses (Babr. 76.18–19). (Others also contrast Jesus's triumphal entry with Roman triumphs, noting the irony, e.g., Graves and May, *Matthew*, 83–84, 89.) If one were to view Luke 21:24 as alluding to a Roman triumph (as in Thomas, *Revelation 19*, ch. 2; cf. Brent, "Cult"), one might contrast this with Luke 19:37–38; but the language in Luke 21:24 is probably more general than that.

1594. E.g., Iambl. *V.P.* 6.29–30 (though some think 6.29 an interpolation).

1595. See, e.g., Keener, *Paul*, 140–42. Earlier cults such as those of Asclepius (in 293 B.C.E.) and Cybele (in 204 B.C.E.; Grant, *Gods*, 32–33) had become naturalized. Egyptian Mysteries became especially popular under Caligula (Dunand, "Mystères," 38), but they faced serious challenges.

1596. Luke, however, does probably contrast the true Savior-King, laid in a manger, with the mighty Augustus in Luke 2:1, 8–14.

1597. See comment on Acts 26:26.

1598. Rapske, *Custody*, 378–81, argues that this is the primary sense of "brothers" here (based on parallels with Ignatius, Peregrinus, and some Pauline usage). This is not, however, Luke's usage (Luke 8:21; Acts 1:15–16; 9:17, 30; 10:23; 11:1, 12, 29; 12:17; 14:2; 15:1, 3, 7, 13; 16:2, 40; 17:6, 10, 14), and so his emphasis is on Christians' spiritual unity, not the "rank" of the delegates.

1599. Ibid., 225; cf. 2 Cor 2:13; 7:5. The related idea of courage included a variety of components (in Stoic anthropology, see Arius Did. *Epit.* 2.7.5b2, pp. 14–15.16–18).

1600. See Tobin, *Rhetoric in Contexts*, 5, 101, 207, 418; cf. Dahl, *Studies*, 77.

1601. See Rapske, *Custody*, 310. See further comment on Acts 21:33–34; 26:29. Many believe that Paul had some detractors in Rome when he wrote his letter (cf., e.g., Rom 3:8; Stuhlmacher, *Romans*, 6, 8–9, 50).

the presence and visits of friends often encouraged prisoners.[1602] Whereas Paul earlier thanked God (Acts 27:35) after encouraging others to take courage (27:22, 25), here he is encouraged himself and thanks God again.[1603] Once shunned by believers in Jerusalem (9:26), Paul is now an honored dignitary of the growing Diaspora church movement (cf. also 27:3).

v. The Journey (28:15)

The Roman Christians had come a long way, more than a day's journey along the Appian Way, to meet him. The Forum of Appius (Forum Appii)[1604] was 43 Roman miles (39.5 mi.; 63.5 km.) southeast of Rome (for the forty-third milestone, see *CIL* 10.6825), and the Three Taverns was 33 Roman miles (30 mi.; 49 km.) southeast of Rome.[1605] Both sites were ancient stations along the Appian Way by the time of Paul's arrival, lined with both "monuments above ground and columbaria for graves below ground."[1606] That believers met him at both sites may be a special indication of honor for Paul (as Luke may intend it) or simply reflect disconnected house churches (or, less likely, different work schedules, with individuals coming as they were able). Other scholars have plausibly even suggested that it reflects the Roman church's Jewish-Gentile division that many believe is addressed in Paul's earlier letter to the Romans,[1607] perhaps with both sides contending for the apostle's support. In any case, both groups (if we should think of different groups here) respected and valued Paul.

A canal ran from the Forum of Appius[1608] to near Tarracina (62 Roman mi. from Rome); mules normally pulled the canal boats at night through the Pontine Marshes.[1609] The forum lay at the northern part of the marshes, near the termination of the most recent failed attempt to construct a canal for draining the marsh.[1610] Not surprisingly, the site's discomforts included gnats, frogs, and poor drinking water.[1611] Horace (*Sat.* 1.5.3) also complained that the Forum of Appius was "crammed with boatmen and stingy tavern-keepers."[1612] Unpleasant as it may have seemed, anything would seem anticlimactic after the traumatic voyage to Malta, and Luke mentions the site only in passing and only because of the encounter there. The group may have traveled by barge, or they may have continued their trek on foot, as they usually did.[1613]

"Three Taverns" (Tres Tabernae) was a more favored stopping place and may have originated because it stood "at the crossroads of the road from Antium to Norba and the Appian Way."[1614] Settlements often grew up around solitary inns, often bearing

1602. Rapske, *Custody*, 385–88.

1603. Johnson, *Acts*, 465. Although rabbinic sources were written later, they provide a wide sampling of the sorts of thanksgivings, including blessings recited when meeting wise persons, friends, etc. (Le Cornu, *Acts*, 1499, citing *m. Ber.* 9:3–4).

1604. On the forum in Roman towns (which generated the name of this market town and others such as Forum Julii), see DeLaine, "Forum" (on Forum Julii specifically, see Stevens and Drinkwater, "Forum Iulii").

1605. Lake and Cadbury, *Commentary*, 345; Haenchen, *Acts*, 718n4; Conzelmann, *Acts*, 224; Hemer, *Acts in History*, 156.

1606. Cadbury, *Acts in History*, 60.

1607. Lung-Kwong, *Purpose*, 254–55 (inferring two groups from the grammar, following Newman and Nida, *Acts*, 507), though others doubt that these groups, if they existed, met separately in Rome (Das, *Debate*, 49–51).

1608. Luke's Ἀππίου Φόρου reflects the Latin Appii Forum; even with respect to Roman colonies, Luke elsewhere speaks of a forum (a Latin term missing also in the LXX, Philo, and Josephus) as an ἀγορά, but here he transliterates a place name.

1609. Allen, "Appius, Forum of" (citing Strabo 5.3.6); Finegan, *Apostles*, 213.

1610. Witherington, *Acts*, 787; cf. Strabo 5.3.6 (Hemer, "Three Taverns," 843).

1611. Allen, "Appius, Forum of."

1612. Conzelmann, *Acts*, 224.

1613. Finegan, *Apostles*, 214.

1614. Hemer, "Three Taverns," 844; Clarke, "Italy," 481; Uggeri, "Tres Tabernae." Cicero's friend Curio met him when he had just left the road to Antium for the Via Appia, at Tres Tabernae (*Att.* 2.12); he sent the letter

the names of these inns, which explains such Roman settlements as Three Taverns, Rufini Taberna ("Rufinus's Inn," a North African hamlet), and Ad Stabulam ("By the Country Inn," in southern France).[1615] Sturdy travelers could make the trip from Three Taverns to Rome in a single day.[1616]

Both sites mentioned in Acts 28:15 were regular stopping places along the Via Appia,[1617] and so it is likely that the delegates spent either the coming night or (awaiting him) the preceding one there. Regular stopping places along the way made a journey feel much shorter than did deserted roads (Demet. *Style* 2.47). The more-than-120-mile journey from Puteoli to Rome would require as many as five overnight rest stops, at which points Julius could requisition food and beds in inns or government hostels, where available.[1618] (Military travelers carried *diplomata*, papers providing them with access to lodging on the way.[1619] Local communities maintained stopping locations available to any travelers but offering priority to the imperial post.)[1620] Given Luke's emphasis here, it seems more likely than not that he would have mentioned it had further Christian hospitality been available at stops along the way. Probably few Christians had yet settled in smaller Italian communities; Eastern Christians would tend to settle first in urban areas with Greek-speaking immigrant communities.

The journey from Puteoli would be full of sights for a Roman citizen aware of much of Rome's history; on the Via Domitiana from Puteoli to Neapolis, for example, Paul would have passed Virgil's tomb.[1621] These sites are not, however, of direct importance to Luke, may have been unknown to his Eastern audience, and possibly may not have mattered much to Paul, given his circumstances.

from Tres Tabernae and moved on shortly afterward (2.13). The crossroads made it a likelier place for chance encounters, unlike the meeting depicted in Acts 28:15.

1615. Casson, *Travel*, 201.
1616. Clarke, "Italy," 481.
1617. Cic. *Att*. 2.10 (Lake and Cadbury, *Commentary*, 345; Witherington, *Acts*, 787). From Rome to the Forum of Appius on the Appian Way, see, e.g., Hor. *Sat*. 1.5.1–8.
1618. Rapske, *Custody*, 206.
1619. E.g., Tac. *Hist*. 2.54. Presumably, had Julius lost his in the shipwreck, he could have acquired the necessary documents from appropriate officials in Syracuse or probably even in Malta.
1620. Rapske, "Travel," 14–15, noting also that the more basic rest stops were *mutationes* and the more complete, *mansiones*.
1621. Longenecker, *Acts*, 363.

CONTINUING MINISTRY
IN ROME (28:16–31)

Luke directs the trajectory of his second volume toward the "ends of the earth" (Acts 1:8), which is fulfilled in a proleptic way (promising future success) with the arrival of the apostle to the Gentiles in the (Roman) world's capital. On my view of the work's date, Luke could have narrated Paul's eventual execution in Rome (perhaps after an initial release and a period of continuing ministry), but, in keeping with a pattern through most of his work, he chooses to end the narrative on a happier note that reveals the trajectory that he expects for the gospel's spread. Despite obstacles and sufferings, the gospel that reached Rome will continue its success to the ends of the earth.

1. Introduction

This volume ends relatively abruptly, but it recapitulates some of the work's major themes, including the Gentile mission, the importance of evangelizing Rome (and hence, in principle, all peoples), and the obduracy of God's own people. Against many interpreters, however, it does not teach a final rejection of Israel.

a. Luke's Surprising Closing

Ancient writers were more comfortable with "open" endings than are modern readers (see discussion at Acts 28:30–31). Yet there is a reason Luke ends with Paul in Rome.

Many real hearers, including Theophilus, may have known that Luke narrated the mission's movement from Jerusalem to Rome, but we should also consider how the ending would have sounded to less-prepared auditors. A first-time reader can expect that the gospel will reach the ends of the earth, in light of 1:8; throughout Luke's narrative, the reader will simply question how that will be fulfilled. For an uninformed first-time reader, 28:16–31 is a surprise ending; Paul fulfills the mission (or, in my reading, provides the proleptic conclusion pointing to a greater future fulfillment) as a captive.[1] This ending would be all the more striking in a setting where many wanted to dissociate themselves from the memory of Paul's imprisonment and execution.[2] Yet Paul's custody in Rome is an occasion not of tragedy (or for viewing Paul negatively)[3] but of triumph; the gospel has reached Rome. As Jesus triumphs through his own unjust execution, so do his agents accomplish God's purposes in the very face of their

---

1. See Parsons, *Departure*, 155. For a survey of the history of research on Acts 28:16–31, see Puskas, *Conclusion: Significance*, 1–32.
2. See Keener, "Apologetic."
3. For Luke's defense of Paul's legacy, probably challenged in light of Paul's detention and execution, see Keener, "Apologetic," and sources cited there.

unjust treatment.[4] As Spivey, Smith, and Black observe, "Though some might regard Paul's imprisonment and journey to Rome as the result of the work of evil men or the quirk of a cruel fate, for Luke they are the fulfillment of God's will."[5] And if the gospel has reached the heart of the empire, it will also reach the ends of the earth.

That Luke leaves off his story of Paul at a literarily unexpected point[6] draws attention to his concluding scenes and summary. Luke's use of "narrative suspension" fits ancient models and allows him to emphasize major themes.[7] This suspension allows Luke to reiterate emphatically his primary themes: expected heirs of God's promises reject the message of those promises' fulfillment; good news about Israel's king is offered to the Gentiles (in a movement from heritage to mission, without rejecting the former); "pagan" Rome is not the enemy but, in fact, offers positive legal precedents for Christians' "religious freedom"; and nothing can stop the gospel or God's purpose for its expansion. This narrative conclusion may also allow Luke to reframe the church's memory of Paul and his martyrdom, thereby supporting the expansion of the Pauline (noncircumcisionist) Gentile mission.[8]

Luke leads readers to expect Paul's acquittal,[9] his condemnation, or perhaps both.[10] But in 28:30–31, Luke offers a positive, surprise ending, an almost comic upturn, just as his Gospel concludes with resurrection and Jesus's ascension.[11] Although an uninformed audience, on its initial hearing, expected Acts to end with Paul's execution, Luke ends with Paul's relative freedom even in custody, showing that Roman law was favorable to Paul's case and contending that Nero's tyranny and repression of the church was legally anomalous, not an appropriate precedent for others in the empire to follow. Luke also ends with the tension that pervades his two volumes: because God's own people do not, as a whole, embrace his new work, it is right for his agents to share God's promise also with the Gentiles (28:23–28).

b. Recapitulating Earlier Themes

That Luke's conclusion would revisit earlier themes in his work is not surprising.[12] A closing summary was frequent in speeches and rhetorical essays[13]—for example, "I will now sum up what I have said, and I beg the close attention of you all."[14] Some

4. Like Jesus, Paul was accused by his own people's leaders and consequently oppressed (however reluctantly) by the Mediterranean world's dominant kingdom. Both endured, however, with ironic confidence in the triumph of the greater kingdom of God that they served.

5. Spivey, Smith, and Black, *Anatomy*, 267. Cf. the argument of Skinner, *Locating Paul*.

6. This does not, of course, mean that Acts is "incomplete," any more than Homer's *Iliad* is incomplete for not depicting Achilles's death (Fitzmyer, *Acts*, 792) and for ending anticlimactically.

7. Marguerat, "Enigma of Closing," 304.

8. Cf. ibid. For Luke's emphasis on the mission to all peoples in Luke-Acts, see Keener, *Acts*, 1:437–40, 505–11; and now also Marguerat and Steffek, "Naissance."

9. Witherington, *Acts*, 793.

10. His favorable treatment from Rome suggests acquittal (as does Acts 28:30–31), but hints in the narrative and (on the probable later date) the audience's knowledge of Paul's martyrdom suggest a later condemnation under Nero.

11. Luke offers hope even in his depiction of conflict with Roman Jewish leaders (Acts 28:24; see Tannehill, "Rejection," 98–99). For Luke's motives for a positive ending, cf. Trompf, *Retributive Justice*, 78–90, esp. 83, 89.

12. *Inclusio* can cover entire books (e.g., John 1:1, 18; 20:28–31; Rom 1:5; 16:25; see also examples in Harvey, *Listening*, 66–67, 104–6, 111–12, with Hom. *Il.* 1, 24), including in histories (see Xen. *Hell.* in Brown, *Historians*, 92).

13. E.g., Aeschines *Tim.* 177 (albeit before the closing illustration), 196; Dion. Hal. *Thuc.* 55; *Demosth.* 32; Cic. *Quinct.* 19.60 (concluding a section); 28.85–29.90 (for the entire proofs section, immediately before the conclusion); Ael. Arist. *Leuct. Or.* 5.43–44; Gorg. *Hel.* 20 (cf. *Hel.* 21).

14. Isaeus *Cleon.* 48 (trans. Forster, LCL, 31), out of fifty-one paragraphs.

rhetorical handbooks emphasized the value of recapitulation (παλιλλογία)[15] as a form of reminder (ἀνάμνησις)[16] at the end of a division of a speech and finally at the entire speech's conclusion;[17] after finishing a speech, one should normally "conclude by giving a concise repetition, recalling what [one has] said to . . . hearers' memory."[18] The longer the speech, the more important the recapitulation.[19] Indeed, epilogues in speeches often recapitulated the arguments of a speech in sequence or reverse sequence; they also could be used to arouse emotion.[20] Conclusions did not always summarize,[21] but it was not unusual for them to do so.

Because Luke writes narrative, he does not have sequential arguments to revisit,[22] but we can expect themes to recur in this closing section. (Books of history could also include closing summaries;[23] they did not need to include explicit summaries, however, and Luke does not offer one. Other genres also often included closing summaries.)[24] The concluding section of Acts revisits some themes developed during Paul's defense in Acts 21–26, including references to Paul's chains, the hope of Israel, Jewish accusations or unbelief, and Paul's fidelity to his heritage.[25]

Underlining its importance for recapitulating many of Luke's most prominent themes, this closing section of Acts recalls numerous key points in Luke-Acts. Charles Puskas examines some of the obvious locations: the introduction and conclusion of Luke's Gospel (Luke 1–3; 23–24), the programmatic section of the Gospel (Luke 4), and the introduction to Acts (Acts 1). He compares Acts 28 with Luke 1–3[26] regarding references to the Spirit speaking through prophets (Luke 1:67; 2:25–27; Acts 28:25),[27] opposition to Christ and his followers (ἀντιλέγω in Luke 2:34; Acts 28:19, 22),[28] and σωτήριον for the Gentiles, using the language of Isaiah LXX (Luke 2:30, 32, echoing Isa 40:5; 42:6; 49:6; Luke 3:6, quoting Isa 40:5; Acts 28:28, quoting Isa 40:5).[29]

Although Acts 1 is not "parallel" with Acts 28 in the same way that some other

15. *Rhet. Alex.* 20, 1433b.29–1434a.17; 36, 1444b.21–35. On recapitulation, cf. also Anderson, *Rhetorical Theory*, 181–82.

16. *Rhet. Alex.* 20, 1433b.29; cf. 37, 1445b.21–23.

17. *Rhet. Alex.* 20, 1433b.30–31; see summaries, κεφαλαίοι, in 1433b.32. It was useful for every kind of speech and every part of the speech (36, 1444b.23); for repeating the charge, see 36, 1443b.15–16. See also Hermog. *Method* 12.427 (where Kennedy adds Anonymous Seguerianus 203, 206, and 236; Apsines 10.54); for summarizing points just after making them, see, e.g., Quint. *Decl.* 249.14.

18. *Rhet. Alex.* 37, 1445b.21–23 (LCL, 441); Quint. *Decl.* 338.2 (refreshing the judge's memory at the end).

19. *Rhet. Alex.* 22, 1434b.1–11 (1434b.5–8 for each division, and 1434b.8–11 at the speech's end).

20. Montefusco, "Epilogue"; cf. Anderson, *Rhetorical Theory*, 181–82. Cf. also closing exhortations (e.g., Fronto *Ad M. Caes.* 3.16.2; 2 Cor 13:11–12). For epilogues arousing pathos, see, e.g., Quint. *Decl.* 338.3; comment on Acts 26:29. For epilogues seeking to please hearers and invite favor, see Quint. *Decl.* 338.1, 3.

21. See, e.g., Arius Did. *Epit.* 2.7.12, pp. 102–3.1–11, though noting that he has covered his topic.

22. Even in speeches, if one was abbreviating rather than expanding, one could skip recapitulation at the ends of sections and reserve it for the very end (*Rhet. Alex.* 22, 1434b.11–18, esp. 15–17).

23. E.g., Polyb. 2.71.7–10, esp. 7–8 (summarizing the preliminary section of Polybius's history, i.e., Polyb. 1–2); 39.8.3–6 (he announces his closing summary in 39.8.3, provides it in 39.8.4–6, then offers closing comments in 39.8.7–8). On Luke's own use of summaries, see comments on Acts 2:41–47; 6:7.

24. E.g., philosophic essays, as in Cic. *Fin.* 5.32.95–96; Mus. Ruf. 3, p. 42.23–29 (summarizing all of Mus. Ruf. 3); 6, pp. 54.26–56.11 (esp. ἐν κεφαλαίῳ in 54.26), with a summary of the summary in p. 56.7–11; Hippol. *Her.* bk. 10, esp. 10.1.

25. Cf. Puskas, "Conclusion: Investigation," 74–77. Puskas updated this work in idem, *Conclusion: Significance,* including, on this point, 66–73.

26. Puskas, "Conclusion: Investigation," 111–12; idem, *Conclusion: Significance,* 96–103. Cf. further Dupont, "Rapport," 380–402; the extensive work of Flichy, *Oeuvre de Luc,* offering literary connections, including between the two-volume work's beginning and end.

27. Though the Gospel refers to a current phenomenon.

28. Elsewhere in Luke-Acts only at Acts 13:45; perhaps Luke 20:27 (a less likely variant).

29. This form, σωτήριον, appears in Luke-Acts only at Luke 2:30; 3:6; and Acts 28:28 (and elsewhere in the NT only at Eph 6:17, echoing Isa 59:17).

texts are, both include διδάσκω (1:1; 28:31); the Holy Spirit (1:2, 8; 28:25); four of Acts' eight uses of βασιλεία (1:3, 6; 28:23, 31); knowledge (withheld in 1:7 and given in 28:28);[30] and witness (1:8; 28:23).[31] Most important is that the concluding passage allows the completion of the mission from Jerusalem (1:8) to Rome (28:16) and presents the worldwide mission as Luke's last reported words of Jesus (1:8) and Paul (28:28).[32] That an ending would recall a beginning would not surprise an ancient audience.[33]

In more detail, Puskas offers ten comparisons (some much more significant than others, and some reflecting a consistent pattern in Luke-Acts) between this passage and Luke 4:[34]

1. Luke opens each with location and time (Luke 4:16; Acts 28:16, 23).
2. Each contains an evangelistic setting involving Jewish hearers (Luke 4:16; Acts 28:17, 23).
3. In each, there is a division into two scenes, the first with a favorable response and the second speaking of the Gentile mission (Luke 4:16–22, 23–30; Acts 28:17–22, 23–28).
4. Jewish hearers are initially politely interested (Luke 4:22; Acts 28:22).
5. Each contains terms such as κηρύσσω (Luke 4:18–19; Acts 28:31).
6. There is a response of unbelief from God's people (Luke 4:28; Acts 28:24–25).
7. Each expresses spiritual perception concerning salvation, using LXX language (Luke 4:18; Acts 28:26–27).
8. Each uses ἀποστέλλω (Luke 4:18; Acts 28:28).
9. Current events fulfill Scripture (Luke 4:18–19 [Isa 61:1–2]; Acts 28:26–27 [Isa 6:9–10]).
10. Gentiles receive God's favor (Luke 4:25–27; Acts 28:28).

Puskas suggests nine parallels of Acts 28 with Luke 23–24:[35]

1. Both contain accusations that the protagonists lead others astray (Luke 23:14; Acts 28:17).[36]
2. The protagonists are "handed over" to the Romans (Luke 24:7; Acts 28:17), alluding to Isaiah's Suffering Servant (Isa 53:6, 12 LXX).
3. They are "examined" by Romans (Luke 23:14; Acts 28:18), who want to release them (Luke 23:20; Acts 28:18) because there is "no cause for death" (Luke 23:27; Acts 28:18).
4. Jewish opposition leads to the problem in both cases (Luke 23:18–25; Acts 28:19).
5. A similar structure pervades both Luke 24:36–53 and Acts 28:17–31 (including two corresponding scenes and an epilogue).
6. Both expound the words of Moses and the prophets concerning Jesus (Luke 24:27, 44–46; Acts 28:23).

30. This comparison is too tenuous, since the nature of what is known differs substantially in the two cases.
31. Parsons, *Departure*, 156–58, likewise concurs with much of Puskas's work on Acts 1 and 28.
32. Puskas, "Conclusion: Investigation," 92–93; cf. idem, *Conclusion: Significance*, 82–86.
33. Josephus concludes his *Jewish Antiquities* by noting that he has fulfilled what he promised at the work's beginning (20.261); cf. Quint. *Decl.* 267.12.
34. Puskas, "Conclusion: Investigation," 103–5; idem, *Conclusion: Significance*, 91–96; see also Neirynck, "Luke 4,16–30," 387–95.
35. Puskas, "Conclusion: Investigation," 97–98; idem, *Conclusion: Significance*, 86–91.
36. Acts 28:17 is at most implicit on this point.

7. Both sections note unbelief (Luke 24:41; Acts 28:24) and hardness of heart (Luke 24:25; Acts 28:25–27).
8. Both sections emphasize preaching to the nations (Luke 24:47–48; Acts 28:28, 30–31).
9. Both end on a note of victory (Luke 24:50–53; Acts 28:30–31).

Certainly Acts 28:17–31 provides a fitting climax to Luke's work, and in a sense it interprets Paul's "passion" in light of that of Jesus. This both vindicates the Pauline mission and reinforces Jesus's warning that those who want to follow him must share his cross as well as the resurrection hope (Luke 9:23).

Jesus's model in the Gospel and especially his commission in Luke 24 and Acts 1 determine the direction of Acts' narrative. Jerusalem geographically frames Luke's Gospel, whereas the second volume moves from Jerusalem to Rome. The mission that begins with Jerusalem is recapitulated in Rome, as in many earlier cities, by starting with the Jewish people. Luke ends with Paul carrying on the mission, looking toward the future of the Gentile mission (28:28). The work thus ends with a prospective view toward the future, a future that, on my post-Pauline dating of the book, has already begun for Luke's audience. He expressly expects the Gentile mission to continue, presumably empowered by the same Spirit as from the beginning (2:38–39).

c. Rejecting Israel?

Not only does the passage echo many earlier themes of Luke-Acts; it recalls a conflict with some Diaspora Jews that was sounded from shortly after Paul's first full-length speech in Acts (13:45–46).[37] Some scholars suppose that this is a final repudiation of Israel, the "time of the Gentiles," climaxing the developments in Acts 13:46 and 18:6.[38] This argument, however, reads the conclusion of Luke-Acts against rather than in light of what precedes it; it probably also reads Luke-Acts anachronistically, in light of the duration of the subsequent schism between Jews and Gentile Christians, which proved far longer and more thoroughgoing than Luke (or Paul) could have imagined. Granted, the "time of the Gentiles" has come, but Luke sees this period as a temporary era (see ἄχρι in Luke 21:24), followed by a "redemption" (21:28) that includes Israel (1:68; 2:38). Moreover, it is unclear why the pronouncement of this passage constitutes a more decisive rejection of Israel than does the stronger language of Acts 13:46 and 18:6 (here Paul mentions the mission to the Gentiles; there he indicates turning from Jews in order to turn to Gentiles). A paradigmatic, continuing pattern during the "Gentile era," of ministry to Jewish people followed by ministry to more receptive Gentiles, seems more likely.[39]

This passage cannot function as a decisive and permanent rejection of God's plan for all Jews. Paul's Jewish audience remains divided; some are receptive (28:23–24),

---

37. Cf. Borgman, *Way*, 309, who treats Acts 13:16–41 and 28:25–28 as Paul's "Two Framing Speeches to Israel"; many others note the repetition of rejection (e.g., Langner, *Hechos*, 387).

38. Conzelmann, *Acts*, 227, contrasting the future conversion in Rom 9–11; cf. similarly Rese, "Second Thoughts," 201; Jervell, *Apostelgeschichte*, 628 (summarized in Marshall, "Acts," 600). Jervell, *Apostelgeschichte*, 116, believes that the Gentile mission continues beyond Rome but that the Jewish mission ends there. Sometimes rhetoricians would close a speech by stirring *indignatio* against antagonists, as a form of pathos (see Anderson, *Rhetorical Theory*, 181–82); such conflict could well be in view here, but that does not require permanent repudiation of the Jewish people.

39. Treating the text not as fully paradigmatic but as against those who see the "Gentile era" as a turning from Israel, Moessner, "End(s)ings," 219, argues that the gospel is offered to both Jew and Gentile (as in this passage), but "times of the Gentiles" means that Gentiles may hear without preaching to Israel first (arguing [218] from Diodorus that the conclusion of one narrative may usher in a divergent narrative).

and Paul keeps ministering to them, fitting the pattern of his earlier ministry.[40] Specifically, they were divided earlier in Acts (13:43–45; 14:1–2; 17:4–5, 10–14; 18:4–8) and presumably continued to be so after Paul's statement in 28:25–28. He continues welcoming "all" visitors, evidently both Jew and Gentile (28:30),[41] and preaching the "kingdom" (28:31), as he did with the synagogue leaders (28:23).[42] Paul and Luke express anguish not because there is no "remnant" but because a mere remnant cannot constitute "a satisfactory fulfillment of God's promises to Israel."[43]

Further, Paul's turning to the Gentiles is no more a decisive rejection of future opportunities for the Jewish people than his earlier turnings in 13:46–48, 18:6, 22:21, and 26:17–18—"no more final indeed than the words of Isa. 6.9–10 were for Isaiah's mission to his people."[44] Luke simply reiterates (like Paul in Rom 1:16; 9:24; 10:12)[45] that the gospel must always be offered to Israel first in each location, repeating the pattern.[46]

Luke wants to continue to affirm heritage while focusing on mission; it is highly improbable that he roots Jesus and the Jerusalem church so securely in the story of Israel throughout his work only to reject that heritage (and the people who maintained it) at the end.[47] Indeed, Paul speaks favorably of the ancestral customs (Acts 28:17), "my nation" (28:19), and "the hope of Israel" (28:20).[48] Tannehill argues that far from rejecting Judaism here, Luke reaffirms Paul's fidelity to his Jewish heritage. The focus of Luke's defense of Paul in 21:17–28:31 is "to defend Paul against the view that he has betrayed Judaism."[49] Paul elsewhere asserts his Jewish identity (21:39; 22:3) and his loyalty to his ancestral heritage (22:3; 23:6; 24:11–17; 25:8; 26:4–7; 28:17).[50] If, as most scholars argue, Luke writes after the destruction of Jerusalem, the question of mission is paramount, but the question of the identity of the heritage's true guardians has taken a fresh turn.[51]

40. Tannehill, *Acts*, 352; Dunn, *Partings*, 150; cf. Tannehill, *Shape*, 145–65.

41. Certainly, at the very least, those persuaded earlier (Dunn, *Partings*, 150–51). Acts 28:29 is probably a later addition to smooth the transition from 28:28, and so 28:30 follows directly on the affirmation of the Gentile mission in 28:28. For comment on the textual variant constituting 28:29, see discussion in, e.g., Hauser, *Strukturen*, 42–43; Metzger, *Textual Commentary*, 502.

42. Cf. also Dunn, *Partings*, 150–51; Witherington, *Acts*, 802–3 (noting that Acts 28:24 and 28:30 "frame the quotation").

43. Tannehill, "Story of Israel," 339; cf. Tyson, "Problem," 137 (who notes the inadequacy of partial acceptance but thinks that Luke views the Jewish mission as having failed and ended). Luke appears ambivalent, refusing "to decide on the future of the relation between church and synagogue" (Marguerat, "Enigma of Closing," 304). He wanted all, both Jewish and Gentile, to respond, but this did not fit what he saw happening (Tannehill, "Rejection," 101).

44. Dunn, *Partings*, 151; cf. Litwak, "Views," 239. Dunn's same arguments in *Partings* appear in idem, *Acts*, 353. Stagg, "Mission," 278, argues that this passage is less optimistic than Rom 9–11, suggesting that perhaps historically Paul had by this time grown disillusioned "because of the negative reception in Jerusalem." But this is unlikely both in Acts and in Paul (who already anticipated hostility in Jerusalem, Rom 15:31).

45. For the compatibility of Paul's speech here with Pauline theology in Romans, see esp. Litwak, "Views" (focusing on Rom 11); idem, *Echoes*, 241–48; cf. Watson, *Gentiles*, 81–82; Kruse, *Romans*, 68; Marshall, "Acts," 600, cites also Koet, *Studies*, 119–39; Larkin, *Acts*, 390–91; Wall, "Acts," 361–64.

46. Dunn, *Acts*, 182–83. Dunn (353) emphasizes that in this sense the passage is not a "final" scene so much as a "typical" scene. Marguerat, *Histoire*, 333; idem, *Historian*, 152–54, 230, argues that the narrative's open ending allows for varied Jewish responses. If starting with synagogues is a matter of strategy as well as of theology (see discussion at Acts 13:5), we might envision Luke allowing the pattern to be expanded to cover other groups that knew Scripture, but he would not repudiate ministry to the Jewish people.

47. See Bock, "Israel," 113: "Nothing suggests that the story has changed from the one told in the infancy material and the teaching of John, Jesus, and Peter"; "Gentile inclusion does not mean Israel's exclusion." Cf. also the hope of Israel's restoration as part of Luke's vision of the kingdom in Bird, *Gospel of the Lord*, 16.

48. With Dunn, *Partings*, 150.

49. Tannehill, "Story of Israel," 339 (also suggesting that Paul offers a model for continuing the appeal to Jewish hearers, despite increasing hostility).

50. Dunn, *Acts*, xii, arguing that the Christian movement's schism with the synagogue is nowhere final in Acts.

51. Israel had already known many radical transitions in its history, from the exodus to the monarchy to the exile to Roman rule. Some of these transitions were decisive and largely unanticipated by the people.

2. Paul Meets Jewish Leaders (28:16–22)

In each city, Paul begins with the Jewish community (see discussion at Acts 13:5), and he does the same in Rome despite a flourishing Christian community already there (cf. 28:15).[52] Luke also shows that Paul carries on his ministry openly under the nose of the Roman authorities, while in Roman custody. That is, despite the idiosyncratic activity of Nero, the Roman authorities, by and large, recognized that the Christian movement was a politically innocuous form of Judaism.

a. Entering Mighty Rome (28:16)

Since the Augustan era, Roman propaganda exalted the capital as "the eternal city" and divine.[53] Until London reached a million in the eighteenth century, no Western city grew so large again, and only the empire's infrastructure could support a capital so massive.[54] Rome imported at least two hundred thousand tons of food each year; other regions also had imports, but Rome was taken care of first, subsidized by its empire.[55] Some scholars estimate that Rome's annual income was 100 to 200 million denarii—somewhere close to 10 percent of the entire empire's product.[56]

Pliny the Elder boasts, "There has been no city in the whole world that could be compared to Rome in magnitude."[57] Earlier, Dionysius of Halicarnassus noted that by conquering the world, Rome seized the attention of all the world's cities.[58] Some later rabbis, despising Rome's paganism, hyperbolically envisioned its majesty: 365 sections of Rome with 365 palaces each, each having 365 stories, and each story holding enough to provide the whole world with food.[59]

i. Rome's Population

Some have estimated only two hundred thousand residents for ancient Rome, rejecting the usual consensus;[60] but concrete ancient census data seems to make this estimate problematic. Some others estimate that first-century C.E. Rome had about half a million inhabitants.[61] Some reach this estimate by extrapolating population density from Pompeii and Ostia.[62]

Packer extrapolates from housing in Rome. Later (fourth-century) building catalogues indicate some forty-five to forty-six thousand *insulae* in Rome;[63] estimating their

52. Nanos, *Mystery*, 242–44 (cf. 26, 28n13), connects this decision with Paul's theology expressed in Romans, though I believe that he may overstate the case (e.g., I doubt the necessity of this sequence—or even Paul's arrival—for an "apostolic foundation").

53. Last, "Social Policy," 456–58; cf., on the "eternal city," Kraybill, *Cult and Commerce*, 57 (citing *I. Eph.* 599; Jos. *War* 5.367). For polemic against the "eternal city," see Rev 18:7; perhaps *L.A.B.* 7:1; in *b. Ber.* 58a, see Zalcman, "Eternal City." On the divinity of Roma, see, e.g., Aune, *Revelation*, 922–23; Bauckham, *Climax*, 344; Reicke, *Era*, 231; Engels, *Roman Corinth*, 92; Beauvery, "Prostituée."

54. Garnsey and Saller, *Empire*, 83. Pliny E. *N.H.* 3.5.66 estimates that by 73 C.E., Rome's walls were 13 mi. and 200 yards around.

55. Garnsey and Saller, *Empire*, 84, 98–99.

56. Jeffers, *World*, 143.

57. Pliny E. *N.H.* 3.5.67 (trans. Rackham, LCL, 2:51). Cf. the famous, lengthier praise of Rome by Aelius Aristides in the second century C.E.

58. Dion. Hal. *Anc. Or.* 1.3.

59. *B. Pesah.* 118b. Rome's riches were incomparable (so *'Abot R. Nat.* 28 A).

60. Rohrbaugh, "Pre-industrial City," 133, citing "recent studies."

61. Watson, "Cities," 212.

62. See Storey, "Population." Lower estimates may be plausible within the city walls if the dole included those in outlying areas. But could parts of the popular capital (outside public spaces, which consumed much of the city) have a higher population density than Pompeii and Ostia, and (in view of ancient writers' complaints about toppling buildings) higher buildings?

63. Packer, "Housing," 83; cf. Wallace-Hadrill, "*Domus*," 7–9. But the meaning of *insulae* in the Regionary catalogues is disputed (Storey, "Insulae," argues for residential units, not the larger buildings).

population density along the lines of Ostia's (at 84.6 persons per *insula*, with 33.9 per the *insulae* that include luxury apartments),[64] he concludes that later Rome had half a million inhabitants and at its height, closer to Paul's day, Rome had less than a million.[65]

Others contend that more-concrete ancient sources support the traditional, higher estimate of a million,[66] a range that probably remains closer to the consensus.[67] Earlier census figures indeed yield fairly consistent numbers. A census in the early period of the consulate indicated 130,000 adult citizens (i.e., not including children, foreigners, or slaves);[68] around the seventieth Olympiad, there were 150,700 adult citizens;[69] and a census at the time of Menenius Agrippa's death in the fifth century B.C.E. lists 110,000 citizens,[70] as did a later one.[71] But the population grew in time. Although 320,000 householders were said to be receiving the grain dole before the civil wars of the first century B.C.E., the numbers were only 150,000 in Rome afterward (Suet. *Jul.* 41).[72] The population then steadily increased again.

Augustus reckoned (*Res gest.* 15) that his handouts went sometimes to 320,000, 250,000, or, at other times, 200,000 male citizens. This could imply a median estimate of about 670,000 free citizens and, in addition, an estimated slave population of 30 percent, resident free foreigners, and citizens of status either too high or too low to be figured into the grain dole.[73] (Many free foreigners lived in Rome in all periods.)[74] This could suggest in turn a population of no less than a million.

As Italian towns were romanized, more Italians migrated to Rome, and its population grew rapidly in the first century.[75] Because Rome's mansions and public buildings consumed more than half of the city's sixteen square miles, the population density must have been comparable to that of many crowded cities in our own era.[76] That the Circus Maximus was later expanded to hold about a quarter of a million spectators[77] suggests a high figure, since ancient theaters did not accommodate the majority of a city's residents.

64. Packer, "Housing," 85–86. Storey, "Units at Ostia," views *insulae* there also as residential units.

65. Packer, "Housing," 82–87, esp. 87.

66. E.g., Lintott, *Romans*, 85; Mattingly, *Christianity*, 10–11 (about a million, but admitting uncertainty); Clarke, "Italy," 465 (about a million); Cary and Haarhoff, *Life*, 103 (a million or more); Friedländer, *Life*, 4:17–28, esp. 24–25 (more than a million); Crawford, "Population" (more than a million); Ellison, *Mystery*, 23 (more than a million in less than 8 sq. mi.); Harrison and Yamauchi, "Census," 268; idem, "Cities," 301; even higher is the estimate of Carcopino, *Life*, 20–21, with some 1,700,000 residents (Friedländer, *Life*, 4:24–25, gives more than 1.5 million for the early second century). Stambaugh, *City*, 89, estimates (from the grain dole) 750,000 to a million; Gager, "Class," 106, accepts an estimate of 600,000 to a million.

67. Galinsky, "Continuity," 78, sees "upward of a million" as the consensus for Augustan Rome.

68. Dion. Hal. *Ant. rom.* 5.20.1.

69. Dion. Hal. *Ant. rom.* 5.75.3.

70. Dion. Hal. *Ant. rom.* 6.96.4.

71. Dion. Hal. *Ant. rom.* 9.15.2. The number later declined to (or the counting was refined to) 103,000 (9.36.3).

72. Plut. *Caes.* 55.3 implies that this was the census of all the people, but his generalization is probably less accurate.

73. Garnsey and Saller, *Empire*, 83. Packer, "Housing," 83, also notes that not all Rome's residents were direct beneficiaries of the grain dole (though also noting [p. 89] that grain imported to Rome would feed the entire metropolitan area). When earlier Rome had 110,000 citizens (Dion. Hal. *Ant. rom.* 9.15.2), other residents (including women, children, foreigners, and other noncitizens) outnumbered citizens at least three to one (hence at least quadrupling the number).

74. See Dresken-Weiland, "Fremde." On Rome's ethnic and religious diversity, see, e.g., Lung-Kwong, *Purpose*, 62–66; not all elite Romans, of course, viewed this favorably (see Meeks, *Moral World*, 25, citing Tac. *Ann.* 15.44.3).

75. White, "Development," 44. The dramatic increase in Roman census figures under Augustus may reflect many Roman citizens living abroad (Crawford, "Population").

76. Jeffers, *World*, 62; see esp. Stambaugh, *City*, 90, comparing Calcutta.

77. Packer, "Housing," 82.

Some disparity in figures may arise from what segment of the population one counts. Packer's estimate, based on *insulae*, reckons from the space enclosed in Rome's walls whereas the grain dole may have served the metropolitan area.[78] Romans might have included the city's population for a mile outside the city walls.[79] Emphasizing particular methods of calculation will produce somewhat different results, but all estimates (usually half a million to slightly more than a million) yield the same basic order of magnitude.

Drinking water for such a large population would not be a problem. Estimates of aqueducts importing 332,306,624 gallons of water every day by the early second century[80] show that they provided more than was necessary merely for a million people's drinking purposes.

II. ENTERING ROME

Traveling along the Appian Way, Paul would have been near the Aqua Claudia, the aqueduct built by Claudius. As with roads approaching many cities, monumental tombs lined the road approaching Rome. Rome's fourth-century B.C.E. wall had been falling into a somewhat ruined state, its relevance diminished by the city's spread beyond the wall (a situation remedied under duress only more than two centuries after Paul's arrival).[81]

Along this route, Paul undoubtedly entered Rome by the Porta Capena (the Porta Appia, farther out on the same route, is later, part of Aurelian's wall).[82] Thus he would have passed near Nero's palace[83] and the Circus Maximus. This was also one of the locations that probably held a larger-than-usual proportion of Christians.[84] Ahead lay the seven ancient hills,[85] famous in ancient sources.[86] Paul would have reached Rome early in the new year after his departure; thus, if Paul left Caesarea in 59 C.E., he would have reached Rome early in 60 (on the unresolved question of dating, see comment on Acts 24:27).

III. PAUL'S CUSTODY

That Paul was a prisoner in Rome was a strong tradition of early Christians;[87] although they might have wanted to invent a trip to Rome, they would not have invented

78. On the latter point, see ibid., 89.

79. Expanding the walls also added suburbs (Pliny E. *N.H.* 3.5.67); long before Paul's day, the city stretched well beyond its walls (Dion. Hal. *Ant. rom.* 4.13.4–5).

80. McRay, *Archaeology*, 49, contending that the lower estimate in Frontin. *De aquaeductibus* 65–73 reflects an earlier situation. Frontinus is closer to Paul's time, but his own estimate of 222,237,060 gallons is still more than enough for drinking (and probably bathing and sewage as well).

81. Finegan, *Apostles*, 214.

82. With, e.g., Lawrence, *Atlas*, 167. For the most part (with some significant exceptions), Rome's medieval roads basically follow the ancient road patterns (Wallace-Hadrill, "*Domus*," 7). Guards at Rome's gates apparently observed those who entered, but only stopped those appearing suspicious (Philost. *Vit. Apoll.* 4.39).

83. Fitzmyer, *Acts*, 788.

84. Jewett, *Romans*, 63. Many immigrants lived there (p. 62), fitting the Greek names and language of much of the congregation.

85. Finegan, *Apostles*, 218: on the left the Aventine, on the right the Caelian, directly ahead the Palatine, beyond it the Capitoline, and on to the north the Esquiline, Viminal, and Quirinal.

86. See, e.g., Varro *Latin Language* 5.7.41; Dion. Hal. *Ant. rom.* 4.13.2–3; Ovid *Tristia* 1.5.69–70; Pliny E. *N.H.* 3.5.66; Sil. It. 10.586; 12.608; Statius *Silv.* 2.3.21; 4.1.6–7; Suet. *Dom.* 4.5; Symm. *Ep.* 1.12.3; *Sib. Or.* 2.18; 11.113, 116; Caird, *Revelation*, 216 (citing, e.g., Virg. *Geor.* 2.535; *Aen.* 6.782–83; Hor. *Carm.* 7; Cic. *Att.* 6.5); Aune, *Revelation*, 944–45. Some other cities imitated this tradition (see Pisidian Antioch in Levick, *Roman Colonies*, 78); in fact, one could count more than seven (Langdon, "Hills"; cf. Pliny E. *N.H.* 36.24.122).

87. Some of the traditions are clearly later (see Chadwick, "Paul in Rome"), but others are early (*1 Clem.* 5.6–7); cf. also traditions of Peter's crucifixion in Rome (Tert. *Scorp.* 15; Euseb. *H.E.* 2.25.5–8; cf. Falasca, "Bones"; Keener, *John*, 1237–38). Tertullian seems to think that Rome's archives record the executions of

his prisoner status any more than they would have invented Jesus's crucifixion on the charge of treason. Paul is a prisoner in numerous Pauline and disputed Pauline passages (Eph 3:1; 6:20; Phil 1:7; Col 4:18; Phlm 10, 13; 2 Tim 4:16), some texts apparently pointing more specifically to detention in Rome (Phil 1:13;[88] 4:22; see comment below).[89] Going to Rome had been Paul's own intention all along (Rom 15:22–24, 28), and so, if he visited there without being detained at some point, why would the tradition have invented his imprisonment there, given the shame attached to detentions?[90]

As in Acts 27:2, Paul's own material shows that Luke and Aristarchus were with Paul during his detention (Col 4:10, 14; Phlm 24). The Pauline corpus, however, also supplies personal details missing in Acts—namely, that Mark (Col 4:10; Phlm 24), Epaphras (Phlm 23, as a fellow prisoner; Col 4:12), and Demas (Col 4:14; Phlm 24) were with him and later that Demas left him (2 Tim 4:10), that Luke remained (4:11), and that Mark needed to join him (4:11).

Who made the determination that Paul would be permitted (ἐπετράπη here indicates some official ruling) to stay by himself with a single guard?[91] Luke might even deliberately refuse to name the official out of discretion,[92] but the later Western text does not share his reticence, indicating a ruling by the στρατοπέδαρχος. If the Western text has a particular office in mind, its opinion could be useful whether it preserves reliable tradition (more readily available in the West, where the events occurred) or even merely speculation more historically informed than our own might be. The Western text could allude to the Praetorian prefect (the sense of the term in LSJ), since the Praetorian Guard was in charge of prisoners sent from the provinces (cf. Pliny *Ep.* 10.57.2).[93] Afranius

---

Peter and Paul (*Scorp.* 15); Tertullian appeals to such archives elsewhere (*Marc.* 4.7; *Apol.* 21; see Yamauchi, "Archives," 80).

88. On the premise of a Caesarean imprisonment, the praetorium is the governor's palace (mentioned in Acts 23:35), but it also suits the Roman Praetorian Guard (word circulating through their headquarters, also a *praetorium*).

89. Many do favor the Roman imprisonment, e.g., Barth, *Ephesians,* 1:3; Dodd, *New Testament Studies,* 99; Nock, *Paul,* 221; Knox, *Gentiles,* 179; Reicke, "Caesarea"; Fee, *Philippians,* 34–37; cf., without ruling out Ephesus, O'Brien, *Colossians, Philemon,* xlix–liv; Dunn, *Epistles,* 39–41; Moo, *Letters,* 41–46. Some others think that an Ephesian detention better accounts for Philippians (Duncan, *Ephesian Ministry,* 72–87; Engberg-Pedersen, *Paul and Stoics,* 312n2, following Hyldahl, *Chronologie,* 18–51; cf. Koester, "Ephesos in Literature," 122; Deissmann, *Light,* 237); an imprisonment in Ephesus is possible but (in contrast to Rome) hypothetical (see the introduction, above, to Acts 19:23–41; against an Ephesian imprisonment, see, e.g., Hemer, *Acts in History,* 272; Johnston, *Ephesians,* 2; against Philippians, but not some other letters, being written there, see Harrison, "Ephesian Theory," 260–61). Most detentions were brief, and banishment from Ephesus is much likelier than a long enough detention there to offer Philippians' statements about custody (Hemer, *Acts in History,* 272). Cousar, *Philippians,* 11, thinks an Ephesian provenance for Philippians somewhat likelier than a Roman one, but in n. 18 recognizes that "an increasing number of recent commentators opt for the Roman imprisonment as the place for writing the letter" (noting for the Roman provenance O'Brien, *Philippians,* 18–26; Fee, *Philippians,* 34–38; Bockmuehl, *Philippians,* 25–31; and Hooker, "Philippians," 473–75). Some cite the journey of Onesimus as an argument for an Ephesian provenance of Philemon (Phlm 10–18), but Onesimus likely fled for at least enough time for his hair to grow before meeting Paul (if Onesimus's head was shaved, as suggested for adult male slaves in Wilson, "Barbers," 142). A more substantive argument can be made for Rome: it is far likelier that Epaphroditus would have fallen deathly sick (Phil 2:27, 30) due to a voyage from Philippi to Rome than due to a much shorter journey from Philippi to Ephesus.

90. He also anticipated trouble in Judea (Rom 15:31), where Luke claims that Paul was arrested.

91. This could be in response to the assumption of his innocence suggested in the accompanying letter of 25:26–27; 26:31–32.

92. Haenchen, *Acts,* 718n5. Nero himself apparently avoided personal involvement with cases until 62 C.E. (Sherwin-White, *Society,* 110).

93. Sherwin-White, *Society,* 108–9; O'Rourke, "Law," 169; Jeffers, *World,* 170 (in Paul's day, the Praetorians intervened in Tac. *Ann.* 11.1); Conzelmann, *Acts,* 224; Blaiklock, *Acts,* 197; cf. Calvin. On the Praetorian prefect, see Campbell and Matthews, "*Praefectus praetorio*"; Gutsfeld, "Praefectus praetorio." On the praetorian guard, see Campbell, "Praetorians"; now most extensively, Bingham, *Praetorian Guard.*

Burrus filled this office by himself [94] from 51 until 62 C.E., when he died, possibly from poison (though Tacitus regards this suspicion as uncertain).[95] Because the Praetorian prefect's office was powerful, equestrians rather than senators filled the office to prevent rivalry with the emperor.[96]

The term, however, could also apply (at least etymologically, admittedly not a decisive argument) to a commander of a military camp or of an army (στρατόπεδον),[97] and in any case Burrus would probably have delegated the prisoners' respective assignments to a lesser official.[98] Another proposal is the *princeps peregrinorum*,[99] but this officer was originally in charge of grain (more relevant to Paul's ship), and his police duties are not clear before the second century C.E.[100]

A stronger proposal appears to be the *princeps castrorum*, head administrator of the *officium* of the Praetorian Guard.[101] There is, however, at present no certain record of this office before Trajan's time;[102] our sources are too incomplete to rule it out, but we cannot be certain. In any case, as already noted, Burrus could have delegated the detention of incoming prisoners (separating citizens on appeal from the larger numbers sent to satisfy the Roman public's thirst for bloody amusements) to any of his high-ranking subordinate officers. Each of the twelve cohorts under him was commanded by an equestrian tribune.[103]

The Praetorian Guard originally consisted of nine cohorts, but Claudius and Nero raised their number to twelve, with five hundred to a thousand soldiers each.[104] Traditionally the emperor's bodyguard, they maintained order for Italy as the legions did in the provinces,[105] though Rome also had an urban police force (the three or four *cohortes urbanae*, lesser paid than Praetorians) under the consular *praefectus urbi*.[106] In contrast to the freedmen used in the fire brigade and the night police, the Praetorians

94. Apart from Burrus and earlier Sejanus, there were normally two prefects; they were normally equestrians (Stevenson, "Army," 233). If this is the office in view, the Western text's language is strikingly accurate for the period in view (D. Williams, *Acts*, 448, citing Tac. *Ann*. 12.42; 14.51), but Luke could mean simply whatever prefect would supervise prisoners, regardless of whether he had a colleague (D. Williams, *Acts*, 448).

95. Tac. *Ann*. 12.42; 14.51; Momigliano and Griffin, "Burrus." Poison (as opposed to the alternative of sickness) was the sort of rumor that would have naturally spread in view of hatred of Nero. Along with Seneca, Burrus had helped restrain Nero's misdeeds (Tac. *Ann*. 13.2); Seneca also helped preserve Burrus for a time (13.20–21), and Burrus's death weakened Seneca's influence (14.52).

96. O'Rourke, "Law," 168–69. The case of Sejanus showed the office risky regardless of precautions.

97. Luke 21:20; 2 Macc 8:12; 9:9; 3 Macc 6:17; 4 Macc 3:13; Wis 12:8.

98. On the praetorian prefect's sometimes limited duties, see Gutsfeld, "Praefectus praetorio," 757. Burrus might have heard Paul's final case at the end of his first Roman detention (Schnabel, *Missionary*, 116); Burrus died in 62 C.E. (Momigliano and Griffin, "Burrus").

99. Bruce, *Commentary*, 528–29 (in addition to the possibility of Burrus); Barrett, *Acts*, 1233 (as a lesser possibility).

100. Tajra, *Trial*, 178–79.

101. Sherwin-White, *Society*, 110; followed by O'Rourke, "Law," 169; Tajra, *Trial*, 179; Barrett, *Acts*, 1233. Rapske, *Custody*, 174–76, suggests either the *princeps castrorum* or the *princeps praetorii*. The *princeps castrorum* was the highest centurion over the *frumentarii* in Rome, with little opportunity for promotion in this era (Gross-Albenhausen, "Princeps castrorum"); for the office of praefectus castrorum in Roman legions, normally after a tribunate, see Eck, "Praefectus castrorum."

102. Witherington, *Acts*, 788 (favoring the Praetorian prefect).

103. Ferguson, *Backgrounds*, 41.

104. Stevenson, "Army," 232; Ferguson, *Backgrounds*, 41.

105. Stevenson, "Army," 232–33.

106. Ibid., 234; on Rome's police force, see Campbell, "*Cohortes urbanae*"; Eck, "Urbanae cohortes" (noting that they shared the camp with the praetorians); Nippel, "Police" (questioning [463] to what extent they were involved in fighting crime); Gutsfeld, "Praefectus urbi"; Southern, *Army*, 119–20; on the city prefect of Rome, see Cadoux and Tomlin, "*Praefectus urbi*"; on the equestrian commander of the *vigiles*, sometimes promoted to praetorian prefect, see Eck, "Praefectus vigilum."

and the city cohorts were recruited exclusively from free persons.[107] Most of the re-cruits were from Central Italy, but some exceptions came from Asia or Macedonia.[108] Praetorians were the elite of the Roman military: they served sixteen years (versus a legionary's twenty), were paid two denarii a day (versus a legionary's ten asses), and received five thousand denarii on discharge (versus three thousand for a legionary).[109] It is possible that Paul's own correspondence reveals the involvement of Praetorians in his custody arrangements (Phil 1:13; 4:22),[110] as well as his influence on some of them.

Careful track would be kept of the location and length of the prisoner's custody; detailed data, including regular updates on the prisoner's status, would be available to the appropriate officials.[111] If Paul was not yet adequately conversant in Latin, translation of the decision was probably provided for him;[112] in any case, he and his companions saw it soon enough.

A prisoner was normally kept by two soldiers,[113] and so the assignment of a single guard[114] (per shift) confirms that the official saw little threat in this older Roman citizen from the East. This is his lightest form of custody since shortly after his arrest.[115] Use-ful as such a positive arrangement is for Luke's apologetic, Luke does not appear to be merely inventing information here. His foundation in genuine information seems confirmed in that Luke can no longer claim that Paul is guarded by a centurion; a regular soldier guards him. Because the rank of the guard corresponded with one's status and Paul's Roman citizenship is anything but unusual in Rome, he now has only a regular soldier guarding him.[116] Luke's mention of a single soldier suggests that Aristarchus was Paul's voluntary companion (and that "fellow prisoner" in Col 4:10 is figurative for, at most, Paul's companion during captivity), not a literal captive (see comment on Acts 27:2).

Luke's portrayal of Paul chained to a guard[117] meets his portrait of Paul ever eager to evangelize in Phil 1:13 and 4:22. Paul, with perhaps characteristic hyperbole (given the size of the Praetorian Guard in Rome), claims that his testimony of imprison-ment for Christ has become known throughout the entire Praetorian Guard (and everywhere else, 1:13!). He also claims that members of Caesar's household have become Christians (4:22), which could indicate imperial servants but which many

107. Friedländer, *Life*, 1:191.

108. Stevenson, "Army," 233.

109. Ibid., 234; cf. Friedländer, *Life*, 1:191; Jones, "Army," 198. It was important for the emperor to ensure their loyalty in particular.

110. Cf. Lightfoot, *Philippians*, 99–104; Knox, *Gentiles*, 179; Erdman, *Philippians*, 59; Michael, *Philippians*, 28–30; Jones, "Army," 198; Reicke, *Era*, 247–48; Johnston, *Philippians*, 37; Fee, *Philippians*, 113; Horton, *Acts*, 409; Krentz, "Games," 360; see comment above. I do not find persuasive here the alternative reconstruction of Duncan, *Ephesian Ministry*, 108–11. Among other means, the daily watchword kept the emperor in regular contact with the praetorian guard (Eaton, "Significance").

111. Rapske, *Custody*, 250 (noting prison records such as P.Oxy. 43.3104).

112. Cf. Winter, "*Captatio benevolentiae*," 526n104. Rapske, *Custody*, 330, suggests that Paul defended himself even in Rome; if so, however, he probably would have been at the disadvantage of using Greek (ac-cepted, but sometimes with prejudice; see Val. Max. 2.2.2; comment on Acts 18:14–50). Yet a few decades later Dio apparently delivered a speech in Rome (Dio Chrys. *Or.* 72).

113. Conzelmann, *Acts*, 224.

114. Correspondingly, note the single "chain" of Acts 28:20 (versus the plural "chains" in 21:33; 26:29).

115. Witherington, *Acts*, 788–89, noting that the duty was probably rotated every four hours (Jos. *Ant.* 18.169).

116. Rapske, *Custody*, 180–81. Witherington, *Acts*, 789–90, argues against any perceived diminution of Paul's status, suggesting instead that the case is viewed as less important on the basis of Paul's perceived innocence.

117. The usual custom (Acts 12:6; Sen. Y. *Ep. Lucil.* 5.7; Jos. *Ant.* 18.196; Conzelmann, *Acts*, 93). The "chains" appear also in Eph 6:20; 2 Tim 1:16, but Paul probably had been wearing chains for a long period (Acts 21:33; 22:29; 26:29; Johnson, *Acts*, 469).

apply to members of the Praetorian Guard.[118] (Of course, Paul is not the only one in Rome preaching [cf. 1:14–18].)

If some guards are converted,[119] why does Luke (who may have known of the Letter to the Philippians even if he knew of few others) not mention it? On an early dating of Acts (before Paul's execution), he might not yet know; a bit later, during the Neronian persecution, it might endanger the converts. Possibly (and more compatible with most proposed datings), he does not want to distract from the Jewish focus of the final scene. Luke has reported enough converts; he is nearing the end of the standardized scroll, and he cannot record every detail yet keep his work to two volumes.

IV. PAUL'S LENIENT TREATMENT

If either Burrus or any of his subordinates (exercising his delegated authority) treated Paul as leniently as Luke reports, Paul was not viewed as a threat.[120] Julius's favorable oral report about Paul, which could interpretively supplement or even temporarily replace Festus's likewise favorable letter,[121] no doubt helped in Paul's kindlier treatment. Certainly a Roman citizen accused by fellow Judeans who either were not citizens or had a history of problems with Roman authorities could be viewed favorably or even sympathetically (a matter that Luke, with his conciliatory emphasis toward Roman government, would readily report).

Festus presumably recommended the sort of custody appropriate for Paul as a citizen awaiting trial (cf. Acts 26:31).[122] Not all imprisonments were equally severe; much depended on the location of detention. The worst prison in Rome was the state prison, and its harshest chamber was "the Tullianum or death cell."[123] Even Rome's quarry prison, where prisoners quarried stone, was more bearable than this.[124] The corpses of criminals executed in Rome's state prison were normally hurled onto the stairs on the Capitoline Hill, then dragged by hooks into the Forum and discarded in the Tiber.[125] Military custody was lighter than imprisonment;[126] confinement in a barracks was a severer form of military custody than confinement to a private house,[127] and so Paul's arrangements are lighter than most, probably lighter than those of the other prisoners sent to Rome along with him.

One should nevertheless not overestimate Paul's freedom.[128] If the severest form of custody was imprisonment, the lightest was to be on one's own, without chains (e.g.,

118. See comment above on Phil 1:13 and 4:22.

119. As some other commentators suggest (e.g., Dunn, *Acts*, 351). The potential conversion of captors is not the exclusive realm of fiction; it is reported, for example, that a prison guard claimed to have been converted through Watchman Nee's testimony in a setting of a far harsher detention (Kinnear, *Tide*, 304).

120. Witherington, *Acts*, 788.

121. If the documents were lost at sea; copies could be sent for but would take months to arrive.

122. Tajra, *Trial*, 180, notes that the governor normally decided the form of custody on the basis of both the charge and the prisoner's status (*Dig.* 48.3.1).

123. Rapske, *Custody*, 9. See further comment below regarding the Mamertine prison. See also Fortini, *Carcer*; earlier, Gori, *Carcere Mamertino*; O'Reilly, *Victims*; Parker, *Prison*.

124. Rapske, *Custody*, 9, 20–25.

125. Ibid., 14 (citing a vast range of sources: Ovid *Ars* 271–82; Val. Max. 6.9.13; Sen. *Con.* 9.2.2–3; Pliny E. *N.H.* 8.145; Dio Cass. 58.1.3; 58.11.3–4; 59.18.3; 60.16.1; 61.35.4). On the horror of corpses remaining unburied, see comment on Acts 8:2.

126. Rapske, *Custody*, 28, noting that this form arose during the time of the empire (comparing *Dig.* 48.3.1, 12, 14; 48.22.7.1); cf. Hemer, *Acts in History*, 157. Still, some undoubtedly experienced better treatment than others (Rapske, *Custody*, 29–30).

127. Rapske, *Custody*, 9.

128. Pervo, *Profit*, 155n163, compares Apollonius's relaxed custody after his first interrogation (Philost. *Vit. Apoll.* 7.40).

entrusted to the supervision of a person of higher rank).[129] Because Paul stays in his own place, some scholars regard his detention as "free" or "open custody" (*custodia libera*), as opposed to *custodia militaris*,[130] but Paul's chains make this assumption questionable (26:29; 28:20). Nevertheless, on a spectrum of punishments, it would be *custodia liberior*: freer, or a lightened, form of custody.[131]

Chains were most characteristic of harsher forms but could also occur with lighter forms of custody; chains were normally waived for high status (which Paul would not have as a Roman Jew in Rome, in contrast to the East).[132] Military custody often entailed being manacled to guards, as here,[133] even for house arrest (Jos. *Ant.* 18.237).[134] (Nor did the waiving of fetters for a high-status person guarantee lenient treatment; one could be kept without chains [e.g., Plut. *Cic.* 19.2] yet sentenced to death [20.3; 21.3].)

Within the home, Paul would exercise considerable freedom. Some access to prisoners, at least for relatives to supply food, was common even in prisons (see comment at Acts 24:23); access would be easier for someone "under house arrest" but remained at the supervisors' discretion.[135] That large numbers of visitors (Acts 28:17, 23) had ready access to Paul, however, suggests not that each of his individual guards proved generous but that they had orders to allow it; "unhindered" (28:31) is a significant legal term.[136] Prisoners could engage in philosophic or religious conversation with guests and others.[137] The venue would not hinder this: philosophers sometimes taught students in their homes or rented quarters besides using public places or patrons' homes.[138]

Educated prisoners often read and wrote,[139] and we have many examples of ancient literary works written from prisons.[140] Given Paul's lighter custody, he would have ready access to writing materials through his visitors;[141] writing letters such as Philippians or Philemon would not have been problematic. Yet in Rome, Paul would have lacked the unusual status considerations that merited special treatment in the East; why then was his custody relatively light? Presumably it was light because the documentation from the procurator Festus demonstrated that the case against him was weak.[142] For Paul's use of Greek and possibly some Latin, see comment on Acts 18:12–13.[143]

v. Where Was Paul?

The Western text's "outside the barracks" could imply a place "in and later near the Praetorian barracks located at the Porta Viminalis just beyond the walls to the NE of

129. Rapske, "Prison," 828 (citing *Dig.* 48.3.1). For entrustment to sureties in the house of a citizen, see further Rapske, *Custody,* 32–34.
130. Barrett, *Acts,* 1232 (following Tajra, *Trial,* 179–81).
131. Rapske, *Custody,* 171.
132. Rapske, "Prison," 828.
133. Ibid. (citing Sen. Y. *Ep. Lucil.* 5.7; *Tranq.* 10.3; Jos. *Ant.* 18.189–237; Ign. *Rom.* 5.1).
134. For fuller discussion, see Rapske, *Custody,* 31; comment on Acts 26:29.
135. See Rapske, *Custody,* 381–83, esp. 382. Cf. the circumstances in *Mart. Just.* 3.3A (in Talbert, *Acts,* 230).
136. Rapske, *Custody,* 276.
137. See Rapske, "Prison," 829; fuller discussion at Acts 16:25; 24:23.
138. Malherbe, *Moral Exhortation,* 13.
139. Rapske, *Custody,* 332–33.
140. Ibid., 342–46.
141. Ibid., 347.
142. Ibid., 183. As noted above, Julius's oral report might have had to suffice temporarily if the documentation perished in the shipwreck and had to be replaced later. If the soldiers managed to preserve anything, however, this sort of documentation would have had priority.
143. Esp. at Keener, *Acts,* 3:2766–67.

the city."[144] Although technically outside the gates, the Praetorians' camp counts as part of larger Rome.[145] But the Western text here may be an inference from the use of a soldier; the Praetorian Guard was active throughout Rome, and Paul's housing situation does not appear unusual, nor do his visitors seem put off by it.[146]

Although the Vulgate suggests that Paul stayed in a boardinghouse in Rome, such lodgings tended to be cramped spaces that could not readily accommodate the description in 28:17, 23, 30. A secondary consideration is that a long-term prisoner chained to a guard might have seemed a threat to "business" at an inn or boardinghouse, and food would be unclean.[147]

An apartment is far more likely. Multioccupant apartment buildings were the norm in Rome.[148] Paul could have met with larger groups of people in the bottom-floor atrium or courtyard for the building, if one was available. This would not disturb neighbors, who used apartments mainly to sleep and store possessions.[149] Perhaps Paul had a third-story or higher apartment to control the cost,[150] but if his friends also stayed with him and they had any means of income, he may have had better accommodations closer to the ground floor. Because Paul already had friends in Rome, they could have located the accommodations for him or perhaps even allowed him (and his guard) to stay with them for a portion of rent.

Paul's accommodations function like house churches did, and local churches may have helped. This may indeed be Luke's primary point, connecting Paul's ministry with the usual form of local ministry in Luke-Acts (cf. Acts 5:42; 20:20–21): Luke emphasizes (in Rapske's words) "that *the prisoner Paul's entire two year ministry in Rome was house church-like.*"[151] Luke does not use the term "house," but this is because he is constrained by his historical data; in Rome, upstairs apartments were about all that was available, and these are not called houses (1:13; 9:36; 20:8).[152] Only a few aristocrats in Rome could afford a *domus*, or house; nearly all Rome's residents stayed in *insulae*, or tenements.[153]

VI. APARTMENTS IN ROME

How should we envision Paul's accommodations? Only about 3 percent of Rome's residents lived in a *domus*; most lived in multioccupant *insulae*.[154] Like many modern cities, Rome responded to urban crowding by expanding upward, with multiple-story apartment buildings.[155] The quality and size of apartments tended to decline as elevation increased.[156] Firms that made money by building quickly and cheaply often skirted building codes, leading to frequent collapses.[157] Poorer persons sometimes

144. Rapske, *Custody*, 177.
145. Pliny E. *N.H.* 3.5.67.
146. Cf. Witherington, *Acts*, 789n26.
147. Rapske, *Custody*, 237. On the disrepute associated with these, see p. 232; comment on Acts 16:15.
148. See Packer, "Housing," 80–81; Clarke, *Houses*, 26; Stambaugh, *City*, 157, 172–78; Owens, *City*, 156; Carcopino, *Life*, 24–30; Wallace-Hadrill, "*Domus*," 7–10; Höcker, "House," 546; McRay, *Archaeology*, 82–83; cf. Jewett, *Romans*, 53–55.
149. Rapske, *Custody*, 238–39. The claim that an apartment would allow him to prepare (kosher) meals (238), however, is questionable; because of their limited facilities, many apartment dwellers ate at taverns.
150. Ibid., 239.
151. Ibid., 365; emphasis Rapske's.
152. Ibid., 366. Even many of the wealthy lived in apartment buildings, albeit on the ground floor.
153. Ibid., 228; Packer, "Housing," 81.
154. Blue, "House Church," 155–56; cf. Packer, "Housing," 80; Harrison and Yamauchi, "Cities," 301.
155. Clarke, *Houses*, 26. For archaeological evidence for multistoried dwellings in Pompeii and especially Herculaneum, see Wallace-Hadrill, *Houses*, 74. Subletting was common for higher floors (Wallace-Hadrill, *Houses*, 110).
156. Stambaugh, *City*, 157, 172–73; cf. Clarke, "Italy," 477.
157. Höcker, "House," 546 (following Juv. *Sat.* 3.188–310); cf. idem, "Insula"; Carcopino, *Life*, 31; Packer, "Housing," 81–82.

shared apartments;[158] it is estimated that most people lived in one- or two-room apartments, sleeping and storing possessions there but conducting their life outside in public areas.[159]

Although there may be problems with the figures in the fourth-century Regionaries, those figures probably reflect statistics kept by the *praefectus urbi* and are the most objective numbers we have to work with. They indicate forty-four to forty-six thousand *insulae* in Rome.[160] Some scholars suggest that if we construe these as property units surveyed in the census (rather than as blocks), they could average about 250 square meters with (on average) twenty-two persons per unit, divided over four to five floors, not an exceptionally high urban-population density.[161] (The meaning of Rome's *insulae*, however, is a matter of great debate.)[162] Yet the average probably tells us little about specific social realities: some blocks had five stories, but others only two or three;[163] moreover, wealthier residents consumed more space, indicating severe crowding for poorer residents.

Many *insulae* had *tabernae*, or shops, on the outside ground floor, which sometimes included a mezzanine or back room for the family who ran the shop. Sometimes higher-class apartments facing the inside courtyard lay behind these *tabernae*; such wealthy apartments often contained multiple rooms, including space for servants, and could welcome a small number of guests. Even these "deluxe" apartments, however, rarely had kitchens or latrines.[164] At least well-to-do ground-floor apartment dwellers could dig cess trenches, but seepage could occur.[165] For excreting waste, there were chamber pots, the areas beneath stairs, or a walk to public latrines.[166] Although public latrines were inexpensive, the poor used especially the more convenient chamber pots, typically stored under the staircase (*CIL* 6.29791) and dumped on the nearest smelly dung heap (cf. Livy 39.44.5; Lucret. *Nat.* 4.1026).[167]

Most buildings contained between three and five floors of apartments (*cenacula*) above this ground floor; the cheaper, higher apartments were more flimsy, with one or two rooms.[168] The inside rooms, lacking access to fresh air or sunlight, served little purpose except for sleep. Each family might have its own inside sleeping room, but families would "share a common sitting room."[169] But even the common sitting room would accommodate too few people for much of a "house church"; where available,

158. Stambaugh, *City*, 175, notes that "separate tenants" sometimes "occupied the sleeping and sitting rooms opening off a shared medianum" (citing *Dig.* 9.3.5.2).

159. Blue, "House Church," 155–56n138.

160. Wallace-Hadrill, "*Domus*," 7–9; cf. Packer, "Housing," 83.

161. Wallace-Hadrill, "*Domus*," 9–10. Carcopino, *Life*, 29, suggests that "blocks of flats" typically looked the same from the outside. Some tenements were already perilously high by the late republic (pp. 24–25), and in imperial Rome, even some persons of the higher class found themselves on the third floor (26) in buildings that went much higher (26, citing Juv. *Sat.* 3.190–96). For their fragility, see pp. 30–32.

162. Owens, *City*, 54, 71, 156, is closer to the idea of housing blocks, as is Balch, "Families," 259. Storey, "Insulae," suggests residential units and also works with a lower population estimate than in Wallace-Hadrill, "*Domus*," 7–9. In any case, it seems to refer to a multioccupant unit (Stambaugh, *City*, 90).

163. Wallace-Hadrill, "*Domus*," 10.

164. Jeffers, "Families," 132; Stambaugh, *City*, 174.

165. Carcopino, *Life*, 40.

166. Jeffers, "Families," 132.

167. Carcopino, *Life*, 41–42 (noting that babies were sometimes also abandoned on such dung heaps). Emptying it out the window was a punishable offense, especially when it hit a pedestrian below (Juv. *Sat.* 3.269–72; Carcopino, *Life*, 42–43, 46).

168. Jeffers, "Families," 132; on the reduced cost of higher apartments, see also Rapske, *Custody*, 232. Owners built them as high as possible, renting out even the smallest spaces (231).

169. Jeffers, "Families," 132.

house churches in Rome may have met in the ground-floor apartments of some better-endowed members.[170]

Those who wished to cook could use portable stoves, typically charcoal braziers close to a window; these often led to residential fires.[171] Residents could and often did, however, resort to neighborhood restaurants for hot food.[172] Based on remains from nearby Ostia, Rome's apartments would lack heat, and upper floors would lack running water.[173] Summer heat in the upper stories would be stifling; residents of the top floor also might have to contend with leaky roofs.[174]

Seneca viewed apartment buildings as brittle, repeatedly employing images of such buildings collapsing or burning down.[175] Despite Nero's renovation of the city after the great fire of 64 C.E.,[176] similar complaints continued afterward.[177] In the early second century, Trajan established a height limit of 60 Roman feet to minimize such disasters,[178] but by the middle of that century, another writer could still attest the burning of an entire block of apartments, noting that such fires made them a bad investment.[179] For more discussion on apartment buildings in the empire, see comments on Acts 18:2–3; 20:9.

Housing in Rome, as in most urban areas today, was expensive. A house could cost up to 875,000 denarii (3.5 million sesterces), which few could afford; rent for the cheapest (upper-story) apartments (rooms) might run from 100 to 125 denarii (400–500 sesterces) annually, and much more for nicer apartments.[180] Considering that housing was much more expensive in Rome than elsewhere[181] and in view of average wages, life in Rome must have been difficult for most of its residents. The average person may have earned 200 denarii per year; soldiers in legions received 225 denarii, and auxiliaries 100 to 200.[182] Thus even the cheapest rent would consume half of one's wages, most of the rest being needed for food.[183] If this was the situation of the working poor, the chronically unemployed can have barely survived in the city. In this period, rich and poor often lived in close proximity, often with the wealthy living on the ground floor of multistory buildings.[184]

170. Ibid., 133. For *apartment* churches (not all of the well-endowed), see Jewett, *Romans*, 63, also noting that this fits the dominant form of housing in Trastevere.

171. Jeffers, "Families," 132; Rapske, *Custody*, 231.

172. Toner, *Culture*, 109–10; Jeffers, "Families," 132; Rapske, *Custody*, 231.

173. Rapske, *Custody*, 231.

174. Ibid.

175. Packer, "Housing," 81, citing Sen. Y. *Ben.* 4.6.2; 6.15.7; *Ira* 3.35.4–5.

176. Packer, "Housing," 81, citing Tac. *Ann.* 15.43; Suet. *Nero* 16.1. Nero's and Tigellinus's estates may have escaped conflagration partly because they were not tightly packed like the wooden housing of the poor.

177. Packer, "Housing," 81, citing Mart. *Epig.* 1.108.3; 1.117.6–7; 3.30.3; 4.37; 5.22; 6.27.1–2; 7.20.20; 8.14; Juv. *Sat.* 3.6ff., 166, 190–202, 223–25, 235, 268–77; 11.12–13.

178. Packer, "Housing," 82, citing Aur. Vict. *Epit. Caes.* 13.13.

179. Packer, "Housing," 82, citing Aul. Gel. 15.1.2–3. Fires continued (*SHA*, Antonius Pius 9; Ulp. *Dig.* 9.2.27.8).

180. Stambaugh, *City*, 154. Blue, "House Church," 156, estimates that most upper-story apartments rented for 2,000 sesterces a year, requiring most tenants to sublet.

181. Stambaugh, *City*, 154. As Talbert, *Acts*, 229, observes, Juvenal (a satirist who often does exaggerate) laments the high rent in Rome for inferior lodging (*Sat.* 3.164–66) and that one could buy a good house outside Rome for the cost of a year's rent of a chamber near the roof in Rome (3.223–25). The dole and perhaps prospects of better or easier wages presumably lured workers there.

182. Stambaugh, *City*, 356n41.

183. Ibid., 154, notes that earlier, during the republic, an average worker received two to four sesterces per day (Cic. *Rosc. com.* 28); thus, housing aside, five days' wages each month would be necessary to purchase grain for feeding an individual for the month (correspondingly higher with more people). The food situation was happily alleviated somewhat by the dole (noted above). For food needs generally, see Schneider, "Nutrition."

184. Stambaugh, *City*, 157; Wallace-Hadrill, *Houses*, 141, 183; Owens, *City*, 156.

The term μίσθωμα of Acts 28:30 normally means "contract price" or "rent" (BDAG),[185] but in the context the best sense is "rented quarters" or "at his own expense."[186] Since most Romans lived in rented accommodations, this translation makes sense.[187] As noted above, however, rent in Rome was expensive—in fact, about four times that in any other part of Italy.[188] How would Paul have paid for his room? Some suggest that he worked at his trade while in custody. But Paul's earning money by his trade during this period of his life is improbable; although Paul has reduced custody arrangements, they remain custody. Prisoners could sign business documents and so forth, but they could not work at a trade during imprisonment. They were also kept from barbers' knives and other dangerous utensils, which would likely include leatherworking tools (though Paul could have otherwise borrowed them from Prisca and Aquila). Storefront apartments were expensive, and it might be physically difficult to work leather or make tents while chained, even loosely, to a soldier.[189] Another possibly substantive factor is that there could be prejudice against buying from a prisoner (though perhaps Aquila and Prisca could have sold his products for him).

Paul may have had support from other local Christians (28:15–16).[190] If Paul's letter to the Philippians has a Roman provenance, he received a substantial gift from believers in Philippi during this period, one for which its carrier made a risky trip (perhaps during a season of difficult travel).[191] Given the circumstances of the shipwreck, we can hardly assume that he and his colleagues brought money with them[192] (which would be too heavy to swim with and which shipwreck survivors usually abandoned in the sea). If Luke "the physician" (Col 4:14) was one of his companions, Luke probably could have made and contributed significant earnings; Rome had earlier sought to recruit more Eastern physicians to relocate there.[193] Food would be less problematic. As a Roman citizen with a registered dwelling in the city, Paul qualified, as did other Romans, for the grain dole (which, as grain, would not be ritually impure).[194]

If he was staying in an apartment, his stay may have required special arrangements with the landlord. Because apartments were often paid for at the end of a period of tenancy, a landlord may not have easily welcomed a prisoner on a capital charge (who might be executed before payment was due); thus the lease would favor the landlord.[195]

185. See further *SIG* 1024, 1200; Philo *Spec. Laws* 1.280; Johnson, *Acts*, 472–73; discussion in Mealand, "Close and Vocabulary," 584–85. Cf. one sense of μίσθωσις in Thür, "Misthosis," 69–70. "Two years" (as a common length), "rented," and "unrestricted" all appear in ancient leases (Mealand, "Close and Vocabulary," 595).

186. With, e.g., NASB; NRSV; Witherington, *Acts*, 813; Pervo, *Acts*, 687; Schnabel, *Acts*, 1075. Haenchen, *Acts*, 726n2, notes that though the term normally designates "house-rent," it is equivalent to "καθ'ἑαυτόν in [Acts] 28.16 and ξενία in 28.23"; Pervo, *Acts*, 687, is probably right to explain it as a metonym. Inns for the poor had daily or other short-term leases, but apartments, especially lower ones, had long-term leases (Rapske, *Custody*, 235–36). Regarding prisoners in rented housing, Conzelmann, *Acts*, 224, cites Ulp. *Dig.* 48.2.3.

187. Rapske, *Custody*, 177–79, esp. 179.

188. Ibid., 234.

189. Ibid., 324–26.

190. Johnson, *Function*, 32, suggests that ἰδίῳ in Acts 28:30 implies that Paul is living from his own means rather than that of the Roman church, but could the term simply deny instead a cost to the Roman government?

191. See Phil 2:25–30; 4:10–19; on the likely economic sense of κοινωνία in Phil 1:5 (and cf. the cognate verb in 4:15), see Ogereau, "Κοινωνία," 371–74; Wansink, "Law," 990; Panikulam, *Koinōnia*, 83–85 (as both spiritual and material). The phrase sometimes applied to covering rent (Michael, *Philippians*, 11).

192. Even if, as I doubt, the collection was wholly rejected and thus left in Paul's hands.

193. See Suet. *Jul.* 42.1; cf. Suet. *Aug.* 42.3; Pliny *Ep.* 10.5.1; Sherk, *Empire*, 127–28.

194. Rapske, *Custody*, 239–42 (noting that the dole, distributed monthly, amounted to about ten gallons of free corn each year). Cf. Sen. Y. *Ben.* 4.28.2, who notes that every citizen receives the dole, even thieves (in Rapske, *Custody*, 241; Talbert, *Acts*, 230), though Seneca may not think of those actually in custody.

195. Rapske, *Custody*, 239. Paul's favorable treatment may have reduced the apparent likelihood of execution, but one might not wish to trust a potential criminal, guard or no guard, as much as someone else.

Owners sought as much profit as possible, gaining considerable money from their frequently flimsy structures, which often burned or collapsed.[196]

Luke's portrayal contrasts starkly with traditions, preserved later, of Paul's final detention in the Mamertine prison. On my view that Paul was released at least briefly, these portrayals need not conflict; the Mamertine was a death prison, in contrast to Paul's light custody portrayed at the end of Acts (and presupposed in texts such as Phil 1:13; 4:22). The Mamertine lay at the foot of the Capitoline, near the temple of Concord. The upper chamber is vaulted, with sides varying from twelve to sixteen feet (3.6–5 m.) long; the subterranean chamber beneath it, called the Tullianum, which people originally entered through an opening in its ceiling, is fairly round, with a diameter of more than twenty feet (7 m.). Notorious prisoners were detained there and sometimes were executed there.[197]

b. Inviting the Jewish Leaders (28:17)

Here as elsewhere in Acts, Paul starts his ministry in a new location first among his own Jewish people. In this case, Paul is immobile and hence invites the Jewish community leaders to visit him instead of him going to them. Because he is preaching to them in chains, he must also explain the circumstances of his custody.

I. Inviting the Leaders

Paul waits only three days to become acclimated to Rome before calling leaders of the local Jewish congregations; acting just three days after a long journey demonstrates efficiency in getting down to business quickly (as with Festus in Acts 25:1; cf. Luke 14:21–23). Aided by his knowledge of Roman culture,[198] motivated by his heart for his people (cf. Acts 24:11–17; Rom 9:3–5) and his long-standing desire to minister to Rome (Acts 19:21; Rom 1:10–11), and perhaps eager to compensate for the long delay of winter, Paul wastes no time in beginning his mission there. Paul must invite these congregational leaders because, in contrast to his earlier travels, he cannot visit the local synagogues this time.[199] There is also some irony in Paul as a prisoner inviting the Jewish community's *leaders*;[200] but Paul is recognized as a leader and an authority concerning the Nazarenes.

In addition to his evangelistic motives (the only ones relevant to Luke's presentation here), Paul's meeting with Jewish leaders could serve his case legally. Given the strength of the Jewish community in Rome and their political clout (attested in this period particularly when Poppaea Sabina was Nero's mistress), their support could help him if they would give it.[201] He could preempt any hostility by emphasizing that he would not be their enemy in court and that he remained faithful to his heritage despite the hostility of Judean authorities.[202] That Paul is willing to dispute with Jewish leaders over Jesus's identity, however, indicates that his primary concern is

---

196. Ibid., 229.

197. Finegan, *Apostles*, 224. Although the tradition itself is not implausible, one can also see why Roman tradition would associate Paul's final detention with this site.

198. Even had he lacked it before Corinth, he would certainly have learned it in new Corinth, which imitated Rome at every turn (see Winter, *Left Corinth*, 8–11).

199. So Fitzmyer, *Acts*, 792.

200. Dormeyer and Galindo, *Apostelgeschichte*, 389.

201. Rapske, *Custody*, 330–31. Poppaea Sabina's influence may come somewhat later (especially in 62 C.E.), but precedent may have rendered it more effective. On the question of historical tradition in the narrative, cf., e.g., Jervell, *Apostelgeschichte*, 631.

202. He might also need to explain his chains and his case to prevent these from reflecting badly on the Christian movement in the Roman Jewish estimation. Historically, perhaps some local Christians ultimately found his imprisonment too embarrassing to defend him, using it as an occasion to preach Jesus but distance

evangelistic rather than an interest in gaining legal allies. Here, as everywhere else, he preaches to the heirs of the ancestral promises first.

ii. Rome's Jewish Community

Rome had a sizable Jewish community, known to other Jewish communities in the empire (Philo *Embassy* 155–57).[203] This community had many synagogues, with different names reflecting their sponsors (such as Agrippa) or geographical origins (e.g., Tripoli).[204] (On their names, see further comment below.) Some scholars argue that these synagogues sometimes represented various Diaspora communities and hence were fairly diverse.[205] One early synagogue named "Hebrews" may stem from first-century b.c.e. immigrants.[206] Some Jews in Rome also descended from Jewish slaves freed there.[207] Scholars generally concur that each synagogue had its own leadership, and the Roman Jewish community, in contrast to that in Alexandria, lacked a single gerousiarch or other leader to speak for the entire community.[208] Many of the Jewish gatherings in this period may have met in homes.[209]

The majority of Jewish residences, and more than half the synagogues, were located in Transtiberinum (modern Trastevere)—that is, across the Tiber from Rome's center (Philo *Embassy* 155); this continued to be where most Jews lived into medieval times.[210] The Jewish community began especially here, spreading later to "the Campus Martius and the Subura," and by the first century b.c.e., they were found in the port town of Ostia;[211] but the majority remained in Transtiberinum.[212] Hundreds may have lived in each cramped building in an area with "narrow, crowded streets and towering apartment buildings thronged with poor, unassimilated immigrants."[213]

Probably many of the free Jewish residents found employment "at the nearby docks on the Tiber."[214] Because most of the first Christians in Rome were Jewish or poor Romans, many Christians would be in Transtiberinum as well.[215] This information gives us an idea about where many of Paul's Jewish visitors lived, however, rather than about where he himself was staying; Luke offers no indication that the sites

themselves from him, but his case may have simply provided increased opportunity for open conversation (Phil 1:14–17).

203. On Roman Judaism, see further Levinskaya, *Diaspora Setting*, 167–93; Leon, *Jews of Rome*; Nanos, *Mystery*, 42–75; Penna, "Juifs à Rome"; Kraabel, "Jews in Rome"; Ilan, "Torah"; for brief summary, e.g., Keener, *Romans*, 10–13; on the synagogues, Leon, *Jews of Rome*, 135–66; on burial places, see, e.g., *CIJ* 1:lvi–lxii; Pitigliani, "Catacombs"; Leon, *Jews of Rome*, 54–55. For the Jewish community in Ostia, see, e.g., *CIJ* 1:393, §533.

204. *CIJ* 1:lxxi–lxxxi. At least eleven are known, though not all from the same period; they appeared in the Campus Martius, near the Porta Capena, in Subura, but especially across the Tiber (Levinskaya, *Diaspora Setting*, 182–85; Clarke, "Italy," 466).

205. See Williams, "Structure Re-considered."

206. Lung-Kwong, *Purpose*, 97 (citing *CIJ* 1:230, §291; 1:288, §371; 1:373, §510; 1:397, §535).

207. See Levinskaya, *Diaspora Setting*, 169; the excursus on freedpersons at Acts 6:9 (Keener, *Acts*, 2:1304–6).

208. Leon, *Jews of Rome*, 170; Witherington, *Acts*, 794. Rome may well not have wished its resident-alien communities too united.

209. Nanos, "Churches," 15, suggesting hundreds of them and noting that our hard evidence for synagogue buildings in Rome is later.

210. Jeffers, "Families," 131; cf. Stambaugh, *City*, 95; Levinskaya, *Diaspora Setting*, 167–93; Clarke, "Italy," 466. Although Jewish people settled elsewhere, the majority still remained here.

211. Richardson, "Synagogues," 18–19.

212. Jeffers, "Families," 131.

213. Ibid.

214. Ibid.

215. Ibid., 132. The first Gentile followers of Jesus in Rome were mostly Greek-speaking and were influenced by Jesus's Jewish followers.

were related (Acts 28:16–17), although, if Paul could choose, he may have preferred a low-rent area with many Greek-speaking Jews and Christians.

Rome's synagogues could be named for their patrons, characteristics, founders' cities, or location within Rome.[216] Synagogues from the Augustan period that were named for Augustus and his lieutenant, Agrippa, probably took these names to honor the imperial family for relieving Jews' situation in Rome.[217] There may also be a synagogue "of the Herodians" (although the text is reconstructed), honoring Herod the Great as a patron who helped Diaspora Jews and "as king of all Jews everywhere."[218] Like most immigrant religious cults, synagogues generally adapted existing buildings when they first arrived;[219] some evidence suggests that even an early second-century synagogue in Ostia may have evolved from an *insula*.[220] Many synagogues in Rome, however, would by now have their own buildings.[221]

The fortunes of Rome's Jewish community, and possibly their population, had varied considerably in recent generations. Pompey's enslavement of Jews increased Rome's Jewish population significantly, but gradually some became free citizens.[222] Augustus had been personally benevolent toward Rome's Jews, influencing Roman tolerance during his reign.[223] After a scandal involving a Jewish charlatan raising funds from Roman women, Tiberius deported 4,000 Jews able to bear arms (Suet. *Tib.* 36; Jos. *Ant.* 18.81–84); in 4 B.C.E., 8,000 Roman Jews joined their concerns to a Judean delegation (Jos. *Ant.* 17.299–303; *War* 2.80).[224] From these figures some scholars have extrapolated a guess of 20,000 Roman Jews at the time of Paul's arrival.[225] Others suggest at least 30,000, a reasonable estimate.[226] Some have estimated higher, more than double the lowest figure;[227] Leon, for example, thinks that 40,000 to 50,000 would be a fair extrapolation of Josephus's 8,000 men, though he allows that Josephus's figure may be exaggerated.[228] Nevertheless, it is difficult to be precise even to the degree of such estimates. These varied estimates are based partly on Tiberius's expulsion of 19 C.E., yet that event must have reduced the Jewish community and further immigration augmented it. Further, if Claudius had expelled much of the Jewish community,[229]

216. Lung-Kwong, *Purpose*, 93–101, esp. 95–99.
217. Richardson, "Synagogues," 19–23.
218. Ibid., 23–28; quotation, 28. The plural could allow a later Herod, e.g., Agrippa I or II, permitting the "synagogue of the Agrippans" the same referent (28n48).
219. White, "Synagogue in Ostia," 33–34.
220. Ibid., 43–46, 49–50; though cf. also White, "Synagogue and Society"; Runesson, "Oldest Building." Inscriptions note that it was renovated through a patron's donations (White, "Synagogue in Ostia," 53–66; both donors were apparently Roman citizens, p. 62).
221. Most of the inscriptions concerning some thirteen Roman synagogues are two to three centuries after Paul, but at least three to five of the known ones probably precede him (Tobin, *Rhetoric in Contexts*, 22).
222. Richardson, "Synagogues," 18; Clarke, "Italy," 466.
223. Richardson, "Synagogues," 17. Rome treated their religious meetings as *collegia* (19).
224. Brändle and Stegemann, "Formation," 120.
225. Ibid.
226. Barclay, *Jews in Diaspora*, 295, citing Tac. *Ann.* 2.85.4, who includes Egyptians but limits the number to freedmen (citizens) and those of military age. Josephus claims that the majority of Jewish men refused conscription (*Ant.* 18.84).
227. Higher estimates often reach 50,000 (Jewett, *Chronology*, 37); the relative proportion of Rome's population varies with estimates of the total population. For 40,000–50,000, see, e.g., Cullmann, *Peter*, 79; Clarke, "Italy," 466. Levinskaya, *Diaspora Setting*, 182, notes that the estimates range from 10,000 to 60,000; Jewett, *Romans*, 55, estimates 15,000–60,000 in the mid-50s; Finegan, *Archeology of New Testament*, 208, mentions 20,000–60,000; Hultgren, *Romans*, 7, lists 20,000–50,000.
228. Leon, *Jews of Rome*, 135. Leon also cites (136) the 4,000 men aged 18 to 45, pressed into Tiberius's military service, as supporting 50,000. Yet this both seems a generous estimate and fails to reckon with a possible reduction in the local Jewish population in consequence. For a discussion of evidence concerning Roman Jews' longevity, see pp. 229–30.
229. See fuller comment on Acts 18:2; also Keener, "Edict."

Luke by Acts 28 assumes that it is again thriving, though auditors aware of the costs of moving might well infer that some Jews had not returned (and probably more had never left). Luke has mentioned only the expulsion, not the return, but though he does not explain the apparent incongruity in his narrative, inhabitants of the empire would understand that, with Claudius's death, the Jewish exiles had returned (see comment on Acts 18:2).[230]

The extent to which Roman Jews integrated into Roman culture seems to have varied. That most continued to speak Greek rather than Latin[231] (though apparently few used Hebrew or Aramaic as a major language)[232] suggests that members of this majority of the community retained their distinct cultural identities. (A large percentage of names in Rome's Jewish catacombs are Latin, but these may often indicate their freed status more than their linguistic preference.)[233] The Roman church likewise remained especially Greek-speaking through the mid-second century.[234] Although members of most immigrant groups lived near each other, this custom seems to have held particularly true for the Jewish residents.[235]

Jewish residents were culturally distinct from their neighbors. Jewish people contributed few iconographic symbols to Roman culture and, though using Roman decorations, preferred their own symbols to Roman ones.[236] After Paul's day, however, Christians, lacking their own distinctive iconography, adopted many Roman (but not many Jewish) symbols[237]—probably because of, in part, the large influx of Gentiles experienced by the churches.

Most Jews (and Christians) were probably among the city's poor: some poor Roman citizens but many ex-slaves, non-Roman free persons, and some "Greek-speaking slaves."[238] At the same time, evidence from the Ostian synagogue suggests an upwardly mobile Jewish community, highly acculturated to Italian social life.[239]

Given various anti-Jewish incidents (at least one probably partly in response to Jewish Christians; see comment on Acts 18:2)[240] and sentiments in Rome (see comment on Acts 16:20–21),[241] the Jewish community had considerable reason for caution in associating with potentially troublesome Christians. Jewish proselytism was a major

230. Esp. Keener, *Acts*, 3:2708.

231. Leon, *Jews of Rome*, 75–77; Lung-Kwong, *Purpose*, 105; Noy, "Writing"; Avi-Yonah, "Archaeological Sources," 54. For Greek inscriptions, see *CIJ* 1:6–143; for Latin, *CIJ* 1:143–97. Of 534 inscriptions, Leon, *Jews of Rome*, 75, reckons that 76 percent are in Greek, 23 percent in Latin, and only about 1 percent in other languages. The Appia catacomb was the most romanized, with 36.4 percent in Latin (63.6 percent in Greek); but Monteverde is 78.2 percent Greek; Nomentana, 92.6 percent Greek; and others, 87.7 percent Greek (Leon, *Jews of Rome*, 77). There was no distinctive Roman Jewish form of Greek or Latin (77–92, esp. 92). Some interchange occurred, however (cf. a Latin inscription in Greek letters, and a Greek one in Latin letters; Cappelletti, "Inscriptions"). Use of Greek was conventional for immigrants from the urban eastern Mediterranean world.

232. For some possible Aramaic, see Chilton, "Epitaph"; see more fully *CIJ* 1:228–32.

233. Stambaugh and Balch, *Environment*, 161–62 (suggesting that half the names are Latin, yet all but a quarter of the inscriptions are in Greek); Lung-Kwong, *Purpose*, 102–3.

234. Stambaugh and Balch, *Environment*, 164.

235. Jeffers, "Families," 131.

236. Snyder, "Interaction," 78–81. At least in later sources, however, their adaptation of Roman memorial customs suggests significant acculturation; see Williams, "Image and Text."

237. Snyder, "Interaction," 81–86 (though noting that Christians infused them with new meaning). Roman authorities viewed Christians as distinct from the larger Jewish community (Judge, *First Christians*, 431–41).

238. Jeffers, "Families," 129.

239. White, "Synagogue in Ostia," 67; idem, "Synagogue and Society"; but the arguments are disputed by Runesson, "Oldest Building."

240. Keener, *Acts*, 3:2697–711.

241. Esp. excursus at Keener, *Acts*, 3:2472–77. E.g., it was secretive, subversive, and unfriendly (Juv. *Sat.* 14.100–103; Tac. *Hist.* 5.5). Some may have also confused Jews with other Eastern groups from Syria (perhaps in Juv. *Sat.* 8.160). For one brief survey of views about Judaism in Rome, see Judge, *First Christians*, 427–30.

source of resentment,[242] and this new movement was notorious for proselytizing zeal.[243] Further, at least some Christians abandoned the circumcision, holy days, and food prescriptions for which other Jews sometimes suffered ridicule or ostracism.[244] This laxer new movement thus offered a welcome alternative for some Gentiles as well as competition for available proselytes.[245]

III. ROME'S SYNAGOGUE LEADERS

Who were these leaders? The titles of many of Roman Jewry's leaders over the centuries remain extant, although the duties of most remain unclear:[246]

1. ἀρχισυνάγωγος, appearing four or five times[247]
2. γερουσιάρχης, fourteen times[248]
3. ἄρχων, about fifty times[249]
4. γραμματεύς, twenty-five times[250]
5. ὑπηρέτης, once[251]
6. φροντιστής, twice[252]
7. προστάτης, twice[253]
8. πατὴρ συναγωγῆς, ten times, and μήτηρ συναγωγῆς, three times[254]
9. ἱερεύς, five times[255]

Luke speaks of the "first ones" among the Jewish people in Rome, a familiar expression for high-ranking citizens (e.g., Pliny *Ep.* 3.2.2) that he uses elsewhere (Acts 13:50), including shortly before this passage (28:7). Most scholars agree that Rome's synagogues, in contrast to those in some other locations (e.g., Alexandria), lacked a central leadership beyond leaders of individual synagogues.[256] This arrangement would be less apt to provoke concerns from Rome's own administration and was probably conducive to the gospel's spread. Evidence reflects a range in socioeconomic status among Roman Jews;[257] although a much larger proportion of the community belonged to

242. Gager, *Anti-Semitism*, 55–56; Tajra, *Trial*, 21–24; see comment on Acts 16:20–21. For Jewish proselytism in Rome, see also Leon, *Jews of Rome*, 250–56; Lung-Kwong, *Purpose*, 107–8.

243. Christian proselytism could thus have offered a secondary reason to withdraw (Walters, "Impact," 181–82).

244. On this ridicule and ostracism, cf., e.g., Sen. Y. *Ep. Lucil.* 95.47; Plut. *Table* 4.4.4, *Mor.* 669C; Jos. *Ag. Ap.* 2.137–38; Leon, *Jews of Rome*, 39; Sevenster, *Anti-Semitism*, 136–39; Gager, *Anti-Semitism*, 57; Sanders, *Figure*, 37; Rochette, "Juifs et Romains."

245. On Gentile sympathizers to Roman Judaism, see, e.g., Tobin, *Rhetoric in Contexts*, 23; Jewett, *Romans*, 57–58. For Gentile antipathy to proselytism in Rome, see comment above.

246. Levinskaya, *Diaspora Setting*, 185–92.

247. Ibid., 186–87. On this title elsewhere (where it may have sometimes involved patronage), see discussion at Acts 13:15; cf. also 18:8, 17.

248. Levinskaya, *Diaspora Setting*, 187. The gerousiarchs of Ostia's synagogue were "socially connected and upwardly mobile" (White, "Synagogue in Ostia," 66). Roman Jews displayed particularly high respect for old age (Leon, *Jews of Rome*, 230).

249. Levinskaya, *Diaspora Setting*, 187–90.

250. Ibid., 190.

251. Ibid.

252. Ibid.

253. Ibid., 190–91.

254. Ibid., 191.

255. Ibid., 192. Cf. also ἐξάρχων, possibly a liturgical title at some point in history (Williams, "Exarchon").

256. E.g., Clarke, "Italy," 467; Ferguson, *Backgrounds*, 454. For Alexandrian Jewish traditions, see, e.g., Schwemer, "Gründungslegenden"; further comment on Acts 18:24.

257. Leon, *Jews of Rome*, 235–36. For Jewish family life in Rome, see *CIJ* 1:cxii–cxviii; for social life, 1:lxii–lxviii. Unable to enter Roman associations because of idolatrous ceremonies, Roman Jews had their own associations (1:lxii–lxviii). Some suggest that most Christians before Nero were of low status, lacking even citizenship to protect them from Nero's persecution (Gray-Fow, "Why Christians?").

the lower end of that range,[258] most of the leaders depicted here presumably belonged to the higher end of the range. Many Roman Jews were apparently well educated,[259] with these leaders again representative of such elements.

iv. Jesus's Followers in Rome

The Christian movement in Rome started within Judaism, probably brought by Jewish immigrants.[260] The number of synagogues and their loose connection probably allowed for the rapid spread of the Christian movement; even if some congregations expelled Christians, others might welcome them.[261] A Jewish foundation seems necessary to account for the deep Jewishness of themes and argumentation in Paul's letter to the Romans.[262] Many make a strong argument, however, that by now most of the Roman believers are Gentiles;[263] at the least, separation from the synagogue may be inferred from the difference between Suetonius's and Tacitus's reports of the Roman Christians, two decades apart.[264]

The primary schism probably began or was completed in Claudius's time during events reported in Suetonius (*Claud.* 25.4; see comment on Acts 18:2).[265] Because this conflict invited imperial intervention, synagogues undoubtedly distanced themselves from the Jesus movement, forcing Jesus's followers into new house congregations.[266] During the absence of many or most Jewish believers who were not Roman citizens (Acts 18:2), Gentile Christians would have developed independent congregations.[267] The recent troubles in the Jewish community may have also inclined many Gentiles

258. With Clarke, "Italy," 467; see also the discussion above.

259. Leon, *Jews of Rome*, 236.

260. With Walters, "Impact," 176; Nock, *Paul*, 207; cf. Dunn, *Romans*, xlvi–l; Acts 2:10. They could even have come from Jerusalem (so Hengel and Schwemer, *Between Damascus and Antioch*, 257–58; Longenecker, *Introducing Romans*, 82–83, following Brown and Meier, *Antioch and Rome*, 103–4). Some scholars have even suggested that the movement grew primarily from immigration and experienced little public preaching before Paul's arrival (Judge and Thomas, "Origin"). On Eastern immigration to Rome, see Ramsay, "Roads and Travel," 376; Clarke, "Italy," 466; Carcopino, *Life*, 55; Nock, *Conversion*, 66–70; of Jews, *CIJ* 1:282, §362; 1:287–88, §370; 1:411, §556 (involuntarily); 1:365, §500; Leon, *Jews of Rome*, 238–40; on provincials in Rome, e.g., Friedländer, *Life*, 4:11; most thoroughly on the church in Rome, see Lampe, *Paul to Valentinus*.

261. Cf. Wiefel, "Community," 108.

262. Cf. Tobin, *Rhetoric in Contexts*, 45, 417; Simpson, "Investigation." Paul can articulate views in Judean ways (Davies, *Paul*), and Roman and Jerusalem Jews were kept in constant contact by travelers to the capital (cf. *m. 'Erub.* 4:1; *Sanh.* 4:7; *b. Sanh.* 32b; *Me'il.* 17ab; if Avi-Yonah, "Archaeological Sources," 54, is correct, some Roman synagogues might even be oriented toward Jerusalem). But while most Roman Jews had Judean backgrounds (Tobin, *Rhetoric in Contexts*, 23, citing Philo *Embassy* 155), their Judean ancestors had come more than a century earlier. (Still, many continued to come from Judea voluntarily, e.g., *CIJ* 1:282, §362; 1:287–88, §370; Leon, *Jews of Rome*, 240.) Some have argued that the Roman church in Paul's day remained predominantly Jewish (e.g., Fahy, "Romans"; Klausner, *Jesus to Paul*, 505), although this view is no longer widely held. Perhaps more plausibly the Roman church, while predominantly Gentile, retained ties with the Jerusalem church (Longenecker, *Introducing Romans*, 136, 146); Jewish concerns certainly figure prominently in Paul's letter to Jesus's followers in Rome.

263. Tobin, *Rhetoric in Contexts*, 37, citing Rom 1:5–6, 13; 15:16; Tobin's argument from names in 16:3–16, however (following Lampe, *Christen*, 124–53), is weak; see also Hunter, *Romans*, 26; Wiefel, "Community in Rome," 93; Hare, *Persecution*, 173; Fitzmyer, *Romans*, 33; Das, *Paul and Jews*, 64; idem, *Debate*, 54–70; Haacker, *Theology*, 12; Tobin, *Rhetoric in Contexts*, 408; Rodríguez, *Call Yourself*, 7–10. Some doubt that we can know which group predominated (Cranfield, *Romans*, 1:18).

264. Tobin, *Rhetoric in Contexts*, 35–36; cf. 40–41. Roman Jews did interact with Roman Gentiles (see Rutgers, "Evidence"). Some find Luke offering in Acts 28 a justification or reason for the break (cf. Hauser, *Strukturen*, 240).

265. Keener, *Acts*, 3:2697–711.

266. Das, *Paul and Jews*, 59; cf. Haacker, *Theology*, 13; for expulsion in 49 c.e., see Tobin, *Rhetoric in Contexts*, 40–41.

267. E.g., Harrington, *God's People*, 57. This may have simply completed a process begun earlier when Claudius prohibited Jewish meetings (41 c.e., in Dio Cassius; see comment on Acts 18:2; more briefly, Keener, "Edict").

to avoid associating with the synagogues.[268] Jewish believers who returned probably favored establishing their own congregations over joining existing synagogues.[269] (Many scholars think that Paul's earlier letter to the Romans was meant to reconcile Jewish and Gentile believers, and possibly house congregations, in Rome.)[270]

At this point most of the leaders do not paint all Christians alike (28:21), and though they have heard bad reports about Christians, they welcome dialogue with one of the sect's scribally trained leaders (28:22). The language suggests, however, that their recent contact with Christians is minimal, confirming the suspicion that most of the Jesus movement in Rome no longer belongs to the synagogues. That the schism occurred some time before would also explain Paul's offering his usual, initially conciliatory approach to a different Jewish community before turning to the Gentiles.

There may be five or more house churches represented in Rom 16:3–16,[271] and this might be only the tip of the iceberg. By 64 C.E., Nero's persecution uncovered massive numbers of Christians, enough that by burning those he caught he could light his imperial gardens at night and execute many others in different ways (Tac. Ann. 15.44).[272] Nevertheless, Nero's persecution failed to eradicate, and may have failed to even slow, the movement. With deadly persecution presumably lifted after Nero's death (and the publicity, albeit hostile, during Nero's reign), the movement probably grew in the following decades.[273]

Just as the synagogues of Rome lacked a centralized authority, the same was probably true for the first house churches there. Ignatius emphasizes the office of bishop in six of his seven letters to churches, the only exception being his letter to believers in Rome (ca. 110 C.E.).[274] Likewise, the Shepherd of Hermas (Vis. 2.4.3; 3.9.7) refers only to "elders who govern the church."[275] Centralization appears to have occurred later in Rome than in many other locations. Probably some house churches continued to observe traditional Jewish customs whereas others (perhaps the majority) did not.[276] Paul's dialogues about the law (cf. Acts 28:23) would be matters of great local interest in this context. Because Paul is an outsider to the local conflict and belongs to the same class as the synagogue leaders (and also had an excellent Jerusalem education in Torah), he can gain a hearing with synagogue leaders that local Christians probably cannot.

268. See Keesmat, "Capital," 48. Some xenophobic sensitivities to Jewish practices may have contributed another factor. Nanos suggests that most Roman anti-Judaism emerged later, in the backlash against the Judean war ("Churches," 17), but note the pre-70 evidence (such as Cicero, Horace, and the expulsions under Tiberius and Claudius) cited in my excursus on anti-Judaism at Acts 16:20 (Keener, Acts, 3:2472–77). Appreciation for and antipathy toward Judaism coexisted among Roman Gentiles in this period.

269. This contrasts with the probable situation envisioned for the later Johannine community (see Keener, John, 194–214, esp. 207–14). Some argue that only the most radical voices were expelled from Rome to begin with and the others had less knowledge of Christianity (see Lung-Kwong, Purpose, 256), but surely some of those expelled had by now returned (cf. Rom 16:3–5).

270. E.g., Lung-Kwong, Purpose, 413–14; Harrington, God's People, 57; Chilton, Approaches, 222–24; Haacker, Theology, 48–49; Watson, Gentiles, 175–91; cf. Keener, Romans, 11–16. The approach is not new; for example, note Origen Comm. Rom. on 16:3 (see Reasoner, Full Circle, xxv); cf. Nicholas of Lyra's preface to his Romans commentary (Levy, Krey, and Ryan, Romans, 53); further, in the nineteenth century, J. W. Colenso addressed multiethnic questions in Romans (see Draper, "Drama").

271. With Tobin, Rhetoric in Contexts, 39; for texts referring either to households or to ministry (though the ministries need not be limited to leading house churches), see Rom 16:5, 6, 7, 9, 10, 11, 15.

272. On Nero's persecution from a Christian perspective, see Euseb. H.E. 2.25; among Tacitus's contemporaries, more briefly see Suet. Nero 16.2. Tobin, Rhetoric in Contexts, 35, rightly emphasizes the large number of Christians, even allowing for exaggeration by Tacitus. Of course, some of those arrested may have also been falsely accused out of expediency.

273. Cf. 1 Clem. title; 65.2; Ign. Rom. title.

274. Lane, Hebrews, lx.

275. Ibid.

276. Tobin, Rhetoric in Contexts, 41.

v. Explaining His Innocence

The speeches in 28:17–20 and 28:25–28 structurally resemble other speeches in Acts.[277] (One may compare even the pattern in Luke's report of Paul's first major speech in Acts, 13:16–47.)[278] On the address, "men," see comment on Acts 2:14; on "brothers," see comment on Acts 9:17. This pairing of terms (ἄνδρες ἀδελφοί) appears frequently in Acts regardless of the speaker (1:16; 2:29, 37; 7:2, 26; 13:15, 26, 38; 15:7, 13; 22:1; 23:1, 6; 28:17); it does not appear in the Gospel or elsewhere in the NT, though it is not wholly unique to Luke (see, e.g., 4 Macc 8:19; *1 Clem.* 14.1; 37.1; 43.1; 62.1).

Before one could hope to gain a hearing for one's cause, it was necessary to show that one was not guilty of wrongdoing.[279] That Paul did nothing against his people or customs responds to the populist charge in Acts 21:28 (people, law, and temple; for customs, see also 21:21; 6:14). It also portrays him, like Jesus, as a faithful Judean wrongly prosecuted by hostile political interests.[280]

Paul speaks of not having offended against "our people" and uses λαός, a term Luke employs throughout his work for God's chosen people. (For "customs," see comment on Acts 6:14.) Paul's conciliatory approach at the beginning of this speech[281] and throughout (28:19–20) prepares the reader to view Paul's later warning (28:25–28) in its setting of rejected grace, not as hostility against his people.

That Paul was "delivered" as prisoner into "the hands of" the Romans would contradict the details of Luke's narrative if pressed so far, but we should not read too much into Luke's succinct wording here;[282] Luke is not so careless as to undermine the claim of his own narrative in his carefully designed final section. Yet Luke has an important narrative reason to employ this wording, which also fits Agabus's summary in 21:11: this language allows Paul to parallel Jesus's passion.[283] Jesus was "handed over" to the Romans by his own people (Luke 18:32; Acts 3:13; cf. Luke 9:44; 24:7). Puskas suggests that this is one of several echoes of Isaiah's Suffering Servant. (Although Jesus is the servant par excellence, Luke also applies the role to those who share Jesus's mission; Acts 13:47.) Puskas sees the following parallels between the servant and Paul:

1. The handing over (παραδίδωμι) motif (28:17; cf. 21:11; Isa 53:6, 12 LXX)
2. "Led" in (Acts 25:6, 23; Isa 53:7–8) and declared innocent (Acts 25:18, 25; 26:31–32; cf. Isa 50:9; 53:9)
3. Other servant motifs from Isa 42:1, 6–7 and 49:6 (Acts 9:15, ἐκλογῆς; 26:18; 13:47)

---

277. Puskas, "Conclusion: Investigation," 44; idem, *Conclusion: Significance,* 38–46, 54–58; see discussion of the unity of Luke's Acts speeches in Keener, *Acts,* 1:305–6, 499–500.

278. Chance, *Acts,* 525, compares initial openness to Paul's message (Acts 13:42–43; 28:21–22), a larger audience (13:44; 28:23) with less openness (though 13:45 is far more negative than 28:24–25), and a quote from Isaiah and announcement of turning to Gentiles (13:46–47; 28:26–28).

279. Cf. Mus. Ruf. frg. 32; further discussion in Keener, *John,* 762–63; comment on Acts 24:5.

280. Cf. Puskas, "Conclusion: Investigation," 135; idem, *Conclusion: Significance,* 117.

281. Witherington, *Acts,* 796–97, sees this designation as something of a *captatio benevolentiae,* though it is not part of a direct address.

282. Unless perhaps Paul is graciously avoiding implicating Jerusalemites (or other Jews) for the riot; even in Acts 24:18, addressing a Roman rather than a Jewish audience, he only implies his opponents' guilt and stops short of explicit accusation.

283. On the level of the narrative, his opponents claimed to have arrested him (Acts 24:6), and Lysias claims to have rescued him (23:27); that Paul's summary here agrees with the former perspective (against Luke's own account) underlines how conciliatory Paul is being.

These parallels with Isa 53 are not so compelling with regard to Paul, but Puskas notes the same motifs with regard to Jesus (handing over, as above; "led" to execution in Luke 22:59; 23:1; declared innocent in 23:4, 14–15, 22), who is explicitly called the "servant" (Acts 3:13, 26; 4:25, 27, 30) and identified with Isaiah's servant (8:32–33, 35).[284] Given the parallel between Paul and Jesus, these ideas therefore at least indirectly inform Paul's mission.

c. Paul's Defense (28:18–20)

Paul rehearses his innocence and the fact that Judeans objected to his release but emphasizes that he is offering no counteraccusation against his people. He is no apostate appealing to Rome to escape Jewish courts but a loyal follower of Jewish faith.

i. Romans Wanted to Release Him (28:18)

Paul's claim that Rome was willing to release him (28:18) until the Jerusalem leaders objected (28:19) either adds to our understanding of earlier narratives an element that Luke omitted or summarizes the narrative's tendency from an apologetic perspective.[285] Though Paul probably knows of a previous word of his innocence (from the chiliarch Lysias, 23:29), Festus's commitment to this view and his willingness to release him are not recounted before the Jerusalem leaders' objection to his release (possibly implied in 25:9). Yet Paul's "you know" in 25:10 probably implies the recognition that Festus does know Paul's innocence (a claim that he does not contest) and that Paul remains detained purely for political reasons. Further, in the logic of Luke's narrative, it was certainly only on the basis of Jerusalemite objections that Paul was detained even after Festus's public recognition of his innocence; that is, he was detained for political reasons.

The description in this passage is close enough for an apologetic summary, though it again illustrates that Luke's focus is more on the larger picture of Paul's innocence than on narrating all details. It also provides an echo of the passion narrative, where Pilate desired to release Jesus (Luke 23:15–18; Acts 3:13).[286] There was no "cause" for putting either Jesus or Paul to death (Acts 13:28; 26:31). Although biographers and historians had limited freedom to tamper with historical details in support of their parallels between characters, speech material could allow a bit more freedom.[287]

ii. Necessity, Not Counteraccusation (28:19)

Because the real basis for holding Paul was Judean politics, Paul appealed to Caesar (25:11) to escape the political situation and obtain a fair trial.[288] That he was "compelled" (ἠναγκάσθην) to appeal to Caesar is an argument from necessity,[289] hence an argument that his appeal should not be held against him. His purpose was not, however, to bring a countersuit or countercharges (a conventional practice), or to bring Jerusalem's internal "dirty laundry" before the world (an activity that could

---

284. Puskas, "Conclusion: Investigation," 141–43; idem, *Conclusion: Significance*, 124.

285. Regarding Jerusalem opposition, Luke 13:33 provides a theological template for persecution in Jerusalem. At the same time, Luke's theological interest suggests that he deployed information usefully, not that he fabricated it: Jesus's crucifixion historically was near Jerusalem; subsequent persecution occurred in that region (1 Thess 2:14–15); and Paul himself expected hostility there (Rom 15:31) and appears in history in Roman custody after this journey.

286. Tannehill, *Acts*, 346; Witherington, *Acts*, 797; Chance, *Acts*, 521.

287. See the discussion in Keener, *Acts*, 1:299–319.

288. Paul's persecution tried to "compel" Christians to blaspheme (Acts 26:11); persecution against Paul "compelled" him to appeal to Caesar (28:19).

289. E.g., Hermog. *Issues* 77.20–78.21; Anderson, *Glossary*, 17; examples include Pliny *Ep.* 1.8.6. See comment on Acts 11:17; cf. also comment on Acts 26:19.

feed some Romans' anti-Judaism and hence adversely affect the recently tenuous status of Roman Jews). If debates over the Messiah had led to political repercussions for Jews in Rome in 49 c.e. (see comment on Acts 18:2),[290] this reassurance may be particularly welcome.

Romans understood the concept of political revenge. In Roman politics, when others prevented one from achieving some glory, one might work to diminish their honor accordingly (Suet. *Jul.* 11; 19.2). More important, when seeking to discredit accusers, one could impugn the credibility of prosecution witnesses; if they all belonged to a single people, one might dismiss the credibility of that entire race (Cic. *Flacc.* 4.9–10; 5.11–9.20). Returning charges was, as noted, a standard defense strategy.[291] More concretely here, Paul implies that he could countersue (cf. *Dig.* 48.1.5) but allays his hearers' concerns that he might do so.[292] An orator could be more conciliatory with a politically powerful opponent whom he did not wish to alienate (e.g., Cic. *Mur.* 29.60).

Given the relatively recent expulsion under Claudius, the last thing that Roman Jewry would need was another scandal,[293] such as a Jewish Roman citizen accusing the nation or even renouncing his Judaism (as Paul certainly will not do).[294] Just as the behavior of a family member could shame one,[295] so could that of one's compatriot if prejudice against one's people already existed. Thus in a conflict between Jews and Samaritans, each side closed ranks and accused only the other (Jos. *Ant.* 20.127).[296] When Jews, even those who were not Roman citizens, appealed to Roman governors to complain about their Jewish judges, this could stir problems for the community as a whole. Especially problematic were instances where a Jewish court had sentenced someone for an offense not punishable under Roman law, such as intercourse with a Gentile or a Jewish woman serving as a prostitute.[297]

Still, even to his Jewish hearers, Paul must address his accusers' malice, though only by means of insinuation and implicitly contrasting his benevolent motives with the motives of his accusers.[298] He does, however, imply at least this much, and he cannot help but doing so if he defends himself; claiming that a charge against oneself was false would normally be construed as essentially claiming that one's accuser was a slanderer or liar.[299] Even so, it was helpful, when one was discrediting respected adversaries, to do so not in bitterness but gently; such responses seemed more plausible.[300] To be able to present oneself as forced to speak in a court in spite of one's inclination against

290. See Keener, *Acts*, 3:2708–11.

291. See, e.g., Lysias *Or.* 3.1, §96; Thucyd. 3.61.1; 3.70.3–4; at greater length, comment on Acts 24:18–21 (esp. 24:19).

292. With Rapske, *Custody*, 189.

293. Against Diaspora Jews' airing their community's dirty laundry, see, e.g., comments by Robertson and Plummer, *First Corinthians*, 110; Bruce, *Corinthians*, 59; for Christians, see 1 Cor 6:6. One should not accuse one's people, especially during persecution (Bonsirven, *Judaism*, 149).

294. Tiberius's expulsion involved a scandal of exploitation; the more recent one under Claudius may have even involved strife over Jesus's identity, making it closer to the present situation (see comment on Acts 18:2; though the leaders in Acts 28:22 sound less familiar with the sect).

295. E.g., Xen. *Symp.* 2.10; *Apol.* 31; Plut. *Themist.* 2.6; Mart. *Epig.* 2.56; Gaius *Inst.* 3.221; Diog. Laert. 2.114; Sir 42:11; 1 Cor 11:5.

296. For identity insults and aggression, cf. Korostelina, "Insults," 221. Witherington, *Acts*, 799, even cites 11QT LXIV, 6–8 to suggest that the strictest Jews regarded as treasonous presenting information damaging to the Jewish people to foreigners. This passage probably directly refers, however, only to betraying them directly.

297. Safrai, "Self-Government," 408.

298. For insinuation, see, e.g., Cic. *Cat.* 1.6.14; fuller comment at Acts 24:18–19.

299. E.g., Cic. *Mur.* 6.13; John 8:44; see further comment on Acts 24:18; Keener, *John*, 762.

300. *Rhet. Alex.* 37.1445b.17–19.

it was the rhetorically superior position.[301] For example, a person might claim that he had never before accused a fellow citizen but the accusation against him forced him to denounce the slanderer for the public good.[302]

"Jews" here can mean "Judeans,"[303] though (contrary to the proposals of some scholars) the term does not always have a geographic referent.[304] Writers could employ the term with neutral significance,[305] could call themselves "Israel" but describe themselves as "Jews" ("Judeans") when dealing with foreigners,[306] and at other times could apply the label to Jewish opponents without detracting from their own Jewishness.[307] (The term had various uses; some inscriptions employ it geographically, though more employ it ethnically or religiously, sometimes including Gentile adherents.)[308] Both in inscriptions and in Josephus, some Jewish people used this term for other Jewish people.[309] Given Paul's own identity (cf. Acts 16:3; 18:18; 22:3; 23:6) and audience (28:17), a geographic reference to "Judeans" seems likeliest in this context.[310] His hearers' reply suggests that they understand him to mean *Judeans* here (28:21).

Diaspora Jews would regard Paul's wording as honorable, like the appeal to a king by Onias not as an accuser (κατήγορος) of his fellow Jews but seeking their welfare (2 Macc 4:5). (Paul had insinuated the guilt of his Asian Jewish accusers in Acts 24:18–19, but even there he did not go beyond insinuation, did not attack his people [24:14, 17], and did not press countercharges against anyone.) Loyalty to one's country was a highly respected virtue among Romans;[311] they valued it even above parental authority.[312] They praised duty and respect toward one's people and relatives (a concept they enshrined in their own concept of Roman *pietas*).[313] Con-

301. Dion. Hal. *Isaeus* 10, 11. This reluctance was, of course, often genuine, but for orators' sometimes feigning reluctance to address matters that they, in fact, desired to prove, see Marshall, *Enmity*, 349.

302. Aeschines *Tim.* 1.

303. See Malina, *Windows*, xv, on general usage; elsewhere, cf. Robinson, "Destination," 129. For various uses of "Judea" in Luke-Acts, see Bechard, "Judaea," including the use for the Roman district (683–84); highlighting the diverse usage in light of the ambiguities of ethnicity, see Barreto, *Negotiations*, 81–90. This appears especially frequently in the Fourth Gospel (e.g., Cuming, "Jews"; Lowe, "IOYΔAIOI"; Meeks, "Jew," 181–82; cf. Geyser, "Israel"), though especially applied to the Jerusalem elite (with, e.g., Brown, *John*, 1:lxxi; Crossan, "Anti-Semitism," 199; Baum, *Gospel*, 111; Pereyra, "Significado"; Tsuchido, "Anti-Semitism"; Beutler, "Identity," 230–31). On the Johannine usage, see also discussions in Keener, *John*, 214–27; differently but extensively, White, "Jews" (for Jewish sources, 84–92).

304. See Williams, "*Ioudaios*"; Meeks, "Aliens," 290n2 (to p. 130); Barreto, *Negotiations*, 78–79; cf. recent discussions from varying perspectives in Baker, "Jew"; Miller, "*Ioudaios*"; idem, "Ethnicity"; Schwartz, "Judaisms." Although applicable in Palestine (e.g., *CIJ* 2:158, §972, from 197 C.E.), it could also apply to Diaspora Jews (e.g., *CPJ* 1:134–35, §9; 1:149–50, §18; *CIJ* 1:509, §697; 1:512, §709; 1:513, §710; 2:13–14, §746). It need not even be limited to descendants of Judah (and Benjamin); see, e.g., *Tg. Neof.* 1 on Gen 49:8; *Gen. Rab.* 98:6.

305. Cf., e.g., *CIJ* 1:495, §683; 1:509, §697; 2:13–14, §746 (Ephesus); 2:158, §972 (Palestine); *CPJ* 1:134–35, §9; 1:149–50, §18. Cf. also Overman, *Crisis*, 401. I am adapting two sentences here from Keener, *John*, 219–20.

306. See Tomson, "Israel" (citing a range of sources, including inscriptions, papyri, and coins); Ashton, *Understanding*, 153, citing, e.g., usage in 1 Maccabees.

307. Saldarini, *Community*, 34–36. Cf. Tomson, "Israel." Pervo, *Acts*, 682, complains that the term gives away Luke's parallel to Luke 23:15–20; although a parallel to Jesus's passion is not improbable, the term does not appear in that passage (though Jerusalemites appear included in 23:13). The label in Acts 12:3 cannot easily apply to all Jerusalemites (although conditions now differ from those reported in 2:47), but it may link Peter with Paul's accusers in 24:27, where it applies to members of Jerusalem's elite.

308. See Kraemer, "Meaning of 'Jew.'"

309. Overman, *Crisis*, 401.

310. Luke can use it of a specific group rather than of the people as a whole; e.g., it applies to just forty men in Acts 23:12–13.

311. E.g., Val. Max. 2.2.1a; 5.6 passim; see further comment on Acts 21:39 (there applying to Tarsus as one of Paul's two home cities, here to the other, Jerusalem).

312. Val. Max. 5.6.praef. (whether Romans' loyalty to Rome or Carthaginians' to their own).

313. On this concept among Romans, see Greene and Scheid, "*Pietas*."

cealing the shame of kin was a conventional Jewish value.[314] Rhetorical handbooks recommended that when the plaintiffs were the defendants' relatives, the plaintiffs should avoid appearing malicious;[315] the same would necessarily apply to a defendant's countercharges. Not mentioning one's mistreatment could be honorable; one writer praised some envoys who, though spattered with urine and otherwise dishonored, simply delivered their message faithfully (Val. Max. 2.2.5).

Nevertheless, this portrayal of Paul is not simply Luke's apologetic for his work or Paul's apologetic within the narrative (though it suits the purposes of both).[316] Paul did genuinely desire his people's welfare (Rom 9:1–5; 10:1). Historically, we know that Paul did not withdraw from his community by appealing to his Roman citizenship to escape synagogue scourgings (2 Cor 11:24–25).[317] The present situation was more dangerous, yet the closest Paul came to direct counteraccusations was *insinuatio* in Acts 24:18–19 and 26:10. Paul's love for his people appears also in his letters (e.g., Rom 9:3; 10:1).

III. Chained for Israel's Hope (28:20)

How did Paul "request" to speak with these Jewish leaders? He probably used some local Jewish Christians, who once belonged to, or were at least familiar with, local synagogues to make the contacts. The term for "request" here (a form of παρακαλέω) is strong enough to allow the sense "urge," which was appropriate for matters of supreme importance.[318] It was not dishonorable for a person of rank to employ even stronger language if the cause was urgent (see, e.g., Cicero's frequent explicit "begging" in letters of recommendation;[319] sometimes he even urged, "I earnestly beg of you again and again").[320]

Paul must explain his chains, normally a badge of dishonor;[321] he can turn them into a mark of honor instead by explaining that they are for the hope of Israel.[322] (This connection does comport with the Paul of the letters, who viewed himself as imprisoned for Christ [Phil 1:13], whom he would indeed have regarded as Israel's hope [Rom 11:26].)[323] If in Acts 26:29 Paul uses the chains as a mark of pathos, here he employs them as a mark of honor, following the Jewish martyr tradition.[324] Physically, chains could cause considerable suffering; a prisoner could wear chains weighing ten to fifteen pounds, but in cases of severe crimes, the weight could be as great as the

314. See deSilva, *Honor*, 171–72 (and his example in *Test. Jos.* 17:1–2).

315. Dion. Hal. *Lysias* 24, summarizing the recommendation of contemporary rhetorical handbooks.

316. Establishing that a defendant's character was such that the defendant would not commit such an offense was conventional rhetoric (e.g., Lysias *Or.* 7.41, §112; see fuller comment on Acts 24:14–17).

317. So also Riesner, *Early Period*, 150.

318. See Luke 7:4; 8:31–32, 41; 15:28; Acts 9:38; 13:42; 16:9, 15, 39; 19:31; 21:12; in pleas for a fair hearing, Acts 24:4; 25:2. For the semantic range, see BDAG. In letters, see Aune, *Environment*, 188; Stowers, *Letter Writing*, 24, 78. One could strengthen such entreaties through tears (Cic. *Sest.* 11.26) or through invoking deities in one's appeals (e.g., Isaeus *Menec.* 47; Rom 12:1).

319. E.g., Cic. *Fam.* 13.14.2; 13.20.1; 13.24.3; 13.26.2; 13.30.2; 13.32.2; 13.35.2; 13.54.1; 13.72.2; 13.74.1.

320. E.g., Cic. *Fam.* 13.28b.2 (LCL, 27:89); 13.41.2; 13.43.2; 13.45.1; 13.47.1; 13.73.2; 13.76.2. Cicero also uses this wording in a nonrecommendation letter, imploring his brother to stay well (*Quint. fratr.* 3.1.7.25).

321. See comments on Acts 21:33–34; 26:29; but the chain itself was used to ensure the defendant's appearance at trial, not as a legal penalty itself (O'Rourke, "Law," 174). Philosophers (especially Stoics) could view fetters as irrelevant to what mattered, one's soul (Cic. *Fin.* 3.22.75).

322. Such a claim might appeal to Judean nationalists rather than to Roman Jews, especially since many of the Jewish leaders meeting him may have been, like himself, Roman citizens; but he can explain it.

323. From a different perspective, given the charge against Paul in Acts 21:28, he would be a prisoner for the sake of Gentile Christians (Eph 3:1).

324. Though the enemy here is not a pagan tyrant but the Jerusalem elite, Jewish Maccabean literature also condemned some members of the priestly elite, especially pagan accommodationists.

prisoner's own.[325] Given the circumstances of Paul's custody and the apparent favor that he enjoys, his chains are probably lighter than this.[326] It was normal "security against escape in light custody."[327]

In light of Luke's usage, the "hope of Israel" to which Paul refers is the hope of resurrection (23:6; 24:15; 26:6–8),[328] a hope grounded in Israel's heritage and in God's promises to the Jewish people's ancestors.[329] Again Luke is faithful to the historical Paul, who was ready to sacrifice for his people (Rom 9:1–3; 10:1) and expressed confidence in God's faithfulness to his promises to them (9:4–5; 11:26–29), even if only a remnant had yet responded (11:5). How was Luke's Paul suffering for Israel's hope? Perhaps he viewed his suffering as for Israel because he went to Jerusalem in God's will despite the prophetic warnings of Acts 20:23 and 21:4, 11,[330] but more likely it is because Paul's belief in the resurrection (as an intrinsic part of his faith in the risen Christ) provided implacable political enemies of high rank (23:6).

d. Their Interest (28:21–22)

The Jewish leaders assure Paul, whom they treat as an intellectual and social peer, that they have not heard anything bad about him personally. They have, however, heard negative reports about the Christian movement and would appreciate his perspective as a learned Judean Jew and Roman citizen as well as a Christian. Although this group, as in many other local Jewish communities in Acts, is ultimately divided by Paul's message, the community is tolerant, and there is no thought of persecution (unless Luke expects his audience to presuppose later conflicts not mentioned in his narrative).

i. No Complaints against Paul (28:21)

Although Paul notes that Judean leaders had raised charges against him (28:17, 19), his hearers here note that they have not received the charges. Historically, their claim is plausible, indicating that not everyone was as familiar with Paul as his significance in Luke's narrative might lead one to expect. At the same time, the claim is significant for the narrative's apologetic, reminding Luke's audience that the charges against Paul were not universally known but came specifically from Judea.[331]

That no one in Rome had offered bad reports about Paul provides a significant contrast with Paul's experience in Jerusalem (21:21), on a narrative level reinforcing the tentative expectation that Paul's understanding of the gospel may face more success in Rome than in Jerusalem. (For the various senses of "brothers," see comment on Acts 9:17.) This open-mindedness is no guarantee of conversion (cf. 17:32), but it was better than closed-mindedness (cf. 17:11). Elsewhere Paul was spoken against by many Diaspora Jews (9:1–2, 29; 13:45, 50; 14:2, 19; 17:5, 13; 18:13; 20:19). But

325. Rapske, *Custody*, 206–9; idem, "Prison," 828; see further comments at Acts 12:6; 26:29.
326. Cf. lesser detentions in Rapske, *Custody*, 9, 25–27 (though normally only those of high status completely escaped chains in prison, p. 28; cf. Polyb. 32.3.5).
327. Rapske, *Custody*, 181. Thus even light custody could include some bonds (Jos. *Ant.* 18.233).
328. With more nuancing, see Anderson, *Raised*, 261–92. For Jewish uses of hope (e.g., *Jub.* 31:32) and being on trial for a higher cause, see comment on Acts 26:6–7. The Lord himself was Israel's hope (Jer 14:8; 17:13).
329. The hope fulfills the inaugural hopes of the first volume (Luke 2:25–28; 24:21; Pervo, *Story*, 95). Before the final fulfillment, much suffering would intervene, but Jesus had promised (and established) future hope beyond it (cf. Fusco, "Future of Israel"). Deutschmann, "Hoffnung," argues that the "hope of Israel" here enters an intra-Jewish dialogue and evokes Acts' major themes (cf. idem, *Synagoge*, 188–217).
330. Rapske, *Custody*, 411. Cf. Rom 15:25, 31.
331. On Luke's apologetic for Paul and its grounding in genuine historical events, see Keener, "Apologetic." Paul did experience Jewish accusations in some settings, but the potential charges that stand behind his experience in the final quarter of the book derive specifically from Jerusalem.

while Paul himself has not yet been the object of criticism, the messianic movement with which he is associated has been (28:22).

Not surprisingly, the strategic Roman Jewish community maintained connections with the Jewish people's mother city in Jerusalem.[332] Because Paul's ship left Malta early in the season (28:11), it is not unusual that he would have reached Rome before any hostile reports from Judea, most travelers having been delayed by winter.[333] Because it was always possible that such messengers[334] would come, it was prudent for Paul to make his case first (cf. the haste in 28:17). (Indeed, had travelers gone most of the way by land, they might have reached Rome already. But most would prefer the sea, and even land travel was more difficult in winter; see comment on Acts 27:9. Apparently potential accusers, if they deemed the case worthy of pursuit at all, had also not chosen to sail before Paul.)

It is unclear, however, whether the accusers ever appeared (see comment on Acts 28:30–31); they may have abandoned the case as hopeless (see comment on Acts 24:19). Judean priests often won their cases in Rome.[335] If they did not succeed before two Roman governors of Judea, however, there was little point of attempting the same before the emperor who received the governor's opinion, especially given the penalties for frivolous prosecution.[336] No one wanted to prosecute an unwinnable case; discovering in court the innocence of the person whom one was charging was shameful, a grave embarrassment (Suet. *Claud.* 16.3). If the chief priests know that Agrippa II himself supported Paul (though they were not likely privy to his private verdict in Acts 26:31, Festus presumably included it in his official letter, 25:26), they lack incentive to pursue their case further; at the least, they will know that Agrippa approved sending Paul on to Rome, and Agrippa retains far more of Rome's favor than they would. In Luke's narrative, it is clear in fact that Paul's accusers did not believe that they could defeat him before a Roman judge, even in Judea; this was why they chose to resort to assassination (25:3).

One could not legally try a Roman citizen if no one had come forward to prosecute him (Cic. *Verr.* 2.5.54.141). When accusers initiated a case but did not finish it, it would be decided in favor of the defendant (see comment on Acts 24:19). Appeals to Caesar had to be settled, with both sides appearing, within a year and a

---

332. See, e.g., Dunn, *Romans*, xlvi–xlvii. Jerusalem's high priest would wield influence in the Diaspora (Sanders, *Jesus to Mishnah*, 255–57; cf. 2 Macc 1:1, 10, 18; *Let. Aris.* passim). Late first-century rabbis reportedly traveled to Rome (*Sipre Deut.* 43.3.7). Some argue that some of the Sanhedrin's pre-Herodian influence in the Diaspora was eventually acquired by the rabbinic movement (Safrai, "Relations," 204–9). Later rabbis applied some laws only to Eretz Israel (*t. 'Or.* 1:8) but articulated other rules also for the Diaspora (*m. Roš Haš.* passim, e.g., 1:4; *t. Sanh.* 2:6; *Sipre Deut.* 59.1.2; 188.1.2; *y. B. Qam.* 4:1, §3; *Giṭ.* 5:6, §3). Probably in the early period, however, few in the Diaspora knew rabbinic prescriptions, but leaders of Diaspora communities probably knew about major decisions among scribal leaders in Judea (cf., e.g., Katz, "Issues," 45–46).

333. Rapske, *Custody*, 323, sees only a seasonal travel delay here. On a narrative level, such correspondence between Jewish communities could evoke the letters that Paul carried in Acts 9:2 and 22:5; but Luke employs a different term (though the semantic range overlapped; see BDAG, s.v. γράμμα, 2.b). If documents regarding Paul's trial were lost in the shipwreck, securing duplicates would also require a new message to Judea and time for documents to arrive (Arrington, *Acts*, 269, citing the first edition of Blaiklock, *Acts*, 194).

334. It would be conceivable for the Sanhedrin to send official representatives or agents (on which cf. De Ridder, *Discipling*, 125–26) instead of simply entrusting documents to travelers. Cities accusing governors sent delegations (see comment on Acts 24:27); but Paul, though perceived as a serious nuisance, would merit neither this expenditure nor, apparently, the continuance of the case.

335. McKechnie, "Paul," 121–22.

336. Hemer, *Acts in History*, 157; Bruce, *Acts*[1], 477; idem, *Commentary*, 530; cf. Tajra, *Trial*, 187–88; Witherington, *Acts*, 799.

half; otherwise, the case would be decided by default in favor of the one present.[337] Technically, prosecutors had to appear or suffer penalty,[338] but since the case has been transferred from Judea, the reluctance of high-status accusers to make the voyage for this single case is both understandable and probable, and lesser representatives would carry accordingly less weight.

The accusers' apparent reluctance to address Paul's case after two years (Acts 28:30–31) would be significant for Luke's audience. The case of someone who delayed prosecution could, for example, also be questioned for that reason by opposing orators.[339] Likewise, if those who initiated a charge appear reluctant to prosecute and test their charge in court, they can be portrayed as having fabricated it.[340] That having no accuser was considered honorable[341] is helpful to Luke's portrayal (perhaps one reason he ends Acts where he does).

All these legal precedents in Paul's favor lead us to expect an acquittal,[342] which may indeed have happened (Nero's persecution in Rome cannot be dated before 64 C.E., and the current narrative cannot easily be dated later than 60).[343] Because Poppaea Sabina was favorable to Jewish interests and married Nero in 62,[344] the case against Paul might have taken a suddenly different turn after Luke's "two years" in 28:30–31, but it is not clear that the Roman Jewish community would have advocated against Paul (despite the earlier situation suggested by Suet. *Claud.* 25.4). If the Judeans had not taken up Paul's now-distant case seriously by then, they may have invested little further effort in it; other matters in Judea were far more pressing, and the local leader of Jesus's movement, his brother James, had been executed in a scandalous manner.

Some scholars also suggest that the deposition of the high priest Ishmael ben Phiabi, probably in 58 C.E., 59, or soon after, accounts for the dropping of the case.[345] Ishmael was in fact high priest only briefly (ca. 59 C.E.; Jos. *Ant.* 20.179, shortly before Festus's arrival in 20.182) before being deposed (20.195–96), and certainly not Paul's only high-priestly enemy. But it is not impossible that this change of high priests offers an additional factor for the failure of members of Jerusalem's council to follow through with Paul's prosecution. Depending on the version of Pauline chronology preferred, it is also possible that the deposing of Annas II in 62 C.E.—for executing the Nazarene leader James and others—may have led to the dropping of charges.[346]

---

337. Conzelmann, *Acts*, 240–41 (citing *BGU* 628), though he cites (p. 228) other texts that can be used against the view that Romans would automatically dismiss such a case.

338. Bruce, *Acts*³, 541–42.

339. E.g., Lysias *Or.* 3.39, §99; Max. Tyre 18.6; see comment on Acts 24:21.

340. See *Rhet. Alex.* 29, 1437a.18–21.

341. Sen. E. *Controv.* 2.1.7 (*accusatorem non habeo*); cf. John 8:46.

342. E.g., Bammel, "Activity," 363: the lack of accusations and the previous cases of Roman fairness point to acquittal.

343. Though not all agree (Bunine, "Félix"). Bede *Comm. Acts* 28.31b predicates Paul's release to preach in the West on Nero's not yet having become as evil as in his later years (citing Jerome *Vir. ill.* 5 [TU 14:10, 6/9]).

344. Cf. Bruce, *Commentary*, 530; on her respect for Judaism, see Das, *Debate*, 199–200; Barclay, *Jews in Diaspora*, 308; Grüll and Benke, "Graffito." But while some think that she diverted Nero's anger from Jews to Christians, there is no evidence for this (Walters, "Impact," 180); she may have viewed Christians as a Jewish sect and respected them for the same reasons she respected Judaism. Josephus, a high-class Judean like Paul's opponents, found her favorable, but she also secured the appointment of Gessius Florus, one of Judea's worst governors (Cadoux and Griffin, "Poppaea Sabina"). Goffin, "Poppaea," 614, regards her as smart but extravagant (citing Dio Cass. 62.28.1; Pliny E. *N.H.* 28.182–83; 11.238).

345. Riesner, *Early Period*, 225–26, citing *b. Yoma* 9a for his long tenure and Jos. *Ant.* 20.194–96 for his deposition (but the long tenure is more difficult to harmonize with Josephus; cf. 18.34).

346. Riesner, "Pauline Chronology," 22.

11. COMPLAINTS AGAINST THIS SECT (28:22)

The Jewish leaders' interest in hearing more does not guarantee commitment (cf. Acts 17:19; 28:24).[347] That the movement is "spoken against" (ἀντιλέγεται) may echo Paul's own words: he did not come to "speak against" his own people (28:19), but the movement he defends has been "spoken against."[348] In Acts, the movement does not face opposition from everyone; but it often confronts opposition within the Jewish community, and (given the frequency of travel to and from Rome) these leaders may have heard about incidents elsewhere. On "sect," see comments on Acts 5:17; 24:5; the phrase "this sect" merely specifies the movement and is not derogatory here.[349]

How is it possible that the local Jewish leaders did not know about the Christian movement firsthand?[350] If these events occur in 60 C.E., just a few years later the church in Rome is massive enough that Nero can use large numbers of accused Christians as torches in his imperial gardens, presumably requiring hundreds of Christians, especially if this spectacle continued for successive nights. He executed other Christians by other means (Tac. *Ann.* 15.44), yet when he finished, the Roman church apparently remained vigorous or quickly recovered (cf. *1 Clement*). This suggests a thriving church in Rome; we know that at least some of its leaders (e.g., Aquila and Priscilla, Andronicus and Junia, and Herodion [if a leader]; Rom 16:3–5, 7, 11) were Jewish.[351] Certainly this movement must have affected these synagogue leaders' congregations.

Various proposals offer a partial solution. Because Rome's Jewish community lacked a central organization or hierarchy, communication may have been limited.[352] If among Jesus's followers only the Jewish believers were expelled from Rome a decade earlier, leaving a primarily Gentile church, Roman synagogues' contact with Jewish Christians could have been minimal for a number of years.[353] Likewise, even if most Jews were expelled (and not only Jesus's followers among them), probably over the issue of Christ's identity (see comment on Acts 18:2),[354] Gentile Christians probably predominated in the church until recently.[355]

Further, messianic Jews would have remained an apparent liability to the community; whether all Jewish residents or only Jewish Christians were expelled, non-Christian Roman Jews, to protect their own standing, may have withdrawn from

347. With Barrett, *Acts*, 1242.

348. In view of Luke's apologetic, it might seem odd that he mentions complaints about the sect unnecessarily (see comment on Acts 18:2), but if (possibly) Paul was posthumously accused of making matters worse for Christians by his preaching, the note that such sentiments existed before his arrival (quite plausible, especially in view of Suet. *Claud.* 25.4; see Keener, "Edict") would serve a useful purpose.

349. E.g., "this sect" is used sympathetically for Stoics in Arius Did. *Epit.* 2.7.6b, pp. 38–39.19; 2.7.7, pp. 42–43.26.

350. Haenchen, *Acts*, 728, views their ignorance as historically implausible. Judge, *First Christians*, 450, counts their ignorance against Suet. *Claud.* 25 referring to Christians. Yet on 452–53, he suggests that the believers continued to meet "under the umbrella of the synagogues." On 431–41, he emphasizes that Rome's officials viewed Christians and Jews as distinct in all of our other sources.

351. Certainly the first Roman Christians were Jewish (Acts 2:10); according to a plausible tradition, they wanted Roman converts to keep the law (Ambrosiaster *Comm.*, on Rom 6, in Lane, "Social Perspectives," 203).

352. Rapske, *Custody*, 331.

353. Rutgers, "Policy," 106; Brändle and Stegemann, "Formation," 126; Das, *Paul and Jews*, 59; cf. Rapske, *Custody*, 331. Nanos, *Mystery* (e.g., 14, 384; esp. 72–74), believes that Gentile Christians remained in Roman synagogues, but this remains a minority view.

354. See Keener, *Acts*, 3:2708–11.

355. Rackham, *Acts*, 501. By this period the Roman church seems to have included both Gentiles (Rom 1:5–6; 11:13) and Jews (7:1; 16:3–4, 7, 11), perhaps divided along the lines of house churches (Brändle and Stegemann, "Formation," 123–25), but most scholars (e.g., Tobin, *Rhetoric in Contexts*, 37) argue that the majority were now Gentiles.

Christians after Claudius's edict.[356] Whereas Suetonius treats an intra-Jewish schism in 49 C.E., Christians by 64 are identified in Rome in a manner distinguishable from the rest of the Jewish community.[357]

None of these solutions, however, is fully satisfactory by itself, even if they help explain the apparently limited contact between these leaders and the Jesus movement. If my reading of Suetonius is correct (at Acts 18:2) and if the date of Claudius's expulsion is 49 (see comment on Acts 18:2),[358] then Jewish people in Rome were debating about this sect only about a decade earlier. Even if the entire community was expelled from Rome (which is unlikely; Roman citizens certainly would not have been affected), it is not likely that those who returned would have forgotten about Christians. If the debates about "Chrestus" concerned messianism in general and not the Christians specifically, the case for these leaders' limited knowledge of Christians might be easier. Yet even if only messianism was debated, they would have acquired some knowledge of this messianic sect. Luke does not mention the cause of the expulsion in Acts 18:2 and hence need not presuppose Roman Jewish knowledge of Christians, but if we ask historically how his claim here can be harmonized with Suetonius, the above solutions must be supplemented.

To read the text as if the Jewish leaders lack all knowledge of Christians is inaccurate. In fact they do know about the Christian movement from hearsay (that it is widely spoken against); Luke seems clear about that.[359] What they do not have is a fellow educated Jewish leader of status from whom they can learn what the movement teaches; they have come as leaders dialoguing with a leader, a member of their own class and a fellow Roman citizen of standing. Paul is scribally educated, and so he can give the best explanation for the movement. Aquila and Prisca are in Rome by this time (Rom 16:3–5), but they perhaps have little contact with the synagogue leaders (because, as some of the above suggestions propose, the church had already been separated from the synagogue by the events preceding Claudius's expulsion or by the growth of its Gentile element; the couple may have belonged to the original schism [Acts 18:2]; and even Aquila and Prisca may have targeted Gentiles, Rom 16:4). For the meaning of "sect," see comments on Acts 5:17; 24:5.

3. Recalcitrance of God's People Prophesied (28:23–28)

When Paul finds Rome's Jewish leaders divided, he appeals to Scripture to explain the unbelief of some (as he used it to warn of unbelief in Acts 13:40–41). Paul, once blind (9:8), now notes that others continue to be blind, maintaining a centuries-old pattern of recalcitrance among God's people.[360] This recalcitrance justifies the continuing offer of Israel's hope to the Gentiles.

356. Walters, "Impact," 181 (leaving Christians "exposed in 64 C.E."); Tobin, *Rhetoric in Contexts*, 35–36, argues that they were even expelled. Nanos, *Mystery*, 375, who doubts significant expulsion, argues that an expulsion over the issue of Christ should have produced greater hostility against the Christian movement than this passage suggests.

357. Tobin, *Rhetoric in Contexts*, 35, citing Tac. *Ann.* 15.44 (but cf. the interpretation in Lund, "Verbrennung," where they are part of the Jewish community).

358. See Keener, *Acts*, 3:2705–8.

359. Luke is also clear that Christians have been in Rome before (Acts 2:10; 18:2) and are there now (28:15), so it is not likely that he should be construed as implying that the movement was completely unknown there.

360. Incidentally, Christian history suggests that Christendom has displayed the same disappointing patterns as Israel's history did—as if to suggest that the problem is one endemic to human nature.

a. Paul Explains Jesus (28:23)

Although invited strictly to speak about the Nazarene sect (28:22), Paul (in Luke's summary) explains about the kingdom and Jesus, the source of the sect. Paul preached to many in Rome and was probably instrumental in the expansion of the church before Nero's persecution.

The summary of Paul's ministry here resembles the summary in 20:18–35, though it is much briefer: Paul "solemnly testifies" (20:21, 24; cf. 18:5; 23:11; for others, 2:40; 8:25; 10:42) and preaches about God's kingdom (20:25; cf. 14:22; 19:8; for others, e.g., 8:12; Luke 8:1; 9:2; Paul's "solemn testimony" in Rome fulfills Acts 23:11). (For Paul's use of "persuasion," see, for example, 18:4; 19:8, 26; 26:28.) Paul's preaching of the "kingdom" brackets the material from 28:23 to 28:31, explaining why the kingdom is offered to Gentiles as well as to Israel.[361] The global reference to preaching from the law and the prophets resembles the pattern in Acts 3:18, 21, 24 and Luke 24:27, 44 (cf. Luke 16:16, 29, 31; Acts 10:43; 13:27; esp. 24:14; 26:27).[362] Such preaching is summarized in Acts 7 and (for Paul's preaching) Acts 13:16–47; closing mention of Paul speaking from the law and prophets might evoke especially Luke's closing mention of Jesus doing so (Luke 24:27, 44).[363]

That "more" (πλείονες) were coming (in addition to those in 28:17) says nothing about the need for more biblically skilled reinforcements (i.e., more "experts"), as if refuting Paul were the primary objective.[364] The point instead is the interest that Paul's case and, if he continued after that day, his arguments generated. It is possible that all of 28:23–28 occurred on a single day (the day appointed in 28:23), but it is also possible that Luke has telescoped Paul's regular practice with the visitors thereafter, as hinted in the use of the imperfect ἐξετίθετο (as well as the imperfect verbs in 28:24). (Paul's words in 28:25–28 occurred on a single occasion, as suggested by the aorist participle εἰπόντος, but the continuation of his ministry afterward is probably suggested by the imperfect verb and the present participles in 28:30–31.)

Since we know explicitly of at least eleven ancient synagogues in Rome (at least four from the early empire) and that the Jewish community in Rome was large, the numbers of visitors could have been substantial.[365] Visitors were important in Roman society;[366] on Paul's accommodations allowing so many visitors, see comment on Acts 28:16.[367]

That Paul could dialogue from morning to evening is not in the least surprising, given his wealth of knowledge and the coming and going of different visitors and groups of visitors.[368] One might easily need to repeat oneself with new auditors arriving

361. The kingdom proclamation may also relativize Rome's authority (Burfeind, "*Muss* nach Rom") and surely does so eschatologically (see Acts 1:6; 3:21), but given Luke's apologetic, this is not likely Luke's emphasis (cf. 17:7).

362. For global references, see comment on Acts 3:18; such a summary serves the literary purpose of suggesting more than Luke has space to report (see Aune, *Environment*, 127–28, comparing Hellenistic historians; comment on Acts 2:40). Puskas, "Conclusion: Investigation," 140–41, argues that Luke shows Jesus and Paul to be prophets themselves.

363. For continuity between Jesus and the disciples in preaching the kingdom in Luke-Acts, see helpfully Siffer, "Proclamation du Royaume."

364. *Pace* Rapske, *Custody*, 361.

365. Ibid., 180.

366. Balch, "Paul, Families, and Households," 260, 265. At least in homes *without* guards, they could walk in uninvited (260).

367. The term ξενία could mean "hospitality" but also applied to a guest room (Phlm 22; other sources in BDAG) or to where hospitality was shown (cf. Jos. *Ant.* 1.200; 5.147; Witherington, *Acts*, 800–801), not necessarily "the inn in which he has rented a room" (Haenchen, *Acts*, 723).

368. By way of one simple illustration that I can recount firsthand (others could offer similar illustrations), as a professor I have taught intensive courses both in the United States and in Africa consisting primarily of forty hours of lecture over five days, sometimes for multiple weeks back to back. Admittedly, with the lecture

(Quint. *Decl.* 313.1). Nevertheless, "from morning to evening" suggests great effort (cf. Exod 18:14) and recalls Paul's ministry of "day and night" in Ephesus (Acts 20:11)[369] as well as occasions of his lengthy preaching and teaching (20:11).[370]

b. A Divided Audience (28:24)

A divided audience is common in Acts and is by no means a specifically Jewish problem (17:4–5, 12; 19:9; cf. 13:43; 17:32; 23:7).[371] The imperfect verbs here suggest a continuing division and response (one that probably continued in further discussions after Paul's speech in 28:25–28; note the imperfect ἀπεδέχετο in 28:30). That some were persuaded (as Paul desired, 28:23; in contrast to others who would not "believe")[372] indicates that some became followers of Jesus; Luke omits the proportions, since his emphasis is merely on the division.[373] This division and Paul's continuing ministry to Jewish people after other Jews rejected his message fit the pattern of Paul's ministry as a whole, including in 19:10 (after he left the synagogue).[374]

Against those who think that this passage constitutes a decisive rejection of the Jewish people or of a mission to them, the summary in 28:24 is less negative than many earlier summaries emphasizing Jewish unbelief (13:45, 50; 14:2, 19; 18:2;[375] though clearly Paul's ministry did reach many Jewish people, e.g., 18:7–8). The rejection here can be no more absolute than any other in Acts, especially in view of some believers being mentioned here.[376] Earlier prophets had also affirmed a remnant (as here) while denouncing those that were not part of the remnant.[377] But the pattern of repeated divisions in Jewish communities, and hence repeated rejections from many Jews, does suggest the disappointment of both Luke and Paul that Israel as a whole has not yet embraced the message.

Gentiles often held that active unbelief provoked the anger of deities.[378] But one also finds judgments for disbelieving divine agents in the OT (2 Kgs 9:7; Dan 9:6–7; Amos 7:12–17), some Jewish texts,[379] and Luke-Acts (Luke 1:20; Acts 13:11). Some

---

format I could continue at this pace only for a few weeks, and I was younger than Paul is in this narrative. Interactively, however, one can dialogue at significantly greater length; I debated with another academician for more than seven hours and have taught interactively for as long as fourteen continuous hours.

369. Language also applicable to worship and prayer (Luke 2:37; 18:7; Acts 26:7; cf. 1 Thess 3:10; 1 Tim 5:5; 2 Tim 1:3) and that Paul also applied to his ministry elsewhere (1 Thess 2:9; 2 Thess 3:8).

370. Peter also apparently preached a long sermon of at least a few hours (Acts 3:1; 4:3), though speeches of such length were common.

371. Nor only an ancient one, as Kisau, "Acts," 1347, illustrates by citing an Akamba proverb. Like a chorus in an ancient play that functioned as a single character (Arist. *Poet.* 18.19, 1456a) but could be divided, Luke can depict a group as unified, but he often emphasizes the divided opinions among hearers.

372. For "persuasion" suggesting adherence, see, e.g., Acts 17:4; 19:26; 26:28; for persuasion in a synagogue setting, 18:4; 19:8. The unbelief at the end of the Gospel (Luke 24:11, 41, Luke's only other uses of ἀπιστέω) differs in being temporary, applying to disciples (cf. Mark 16:11, 14, 16); but unbelief was culpable (Luke 9:41). Nevertheless, as in Paul's theology, the "unbelief" of some Jews would not negate God's faithfulness to his promise (Rom 3:3; cf. 11:20, 23).

373. Rapske, *Custody*, 362.

374. Tannehill, *Acts*, 352.

375. Cf. also Dunn, *Acts*, 354 (who mentions Acts 13:50; 14:4; 17:5; 18:12; 22:30; 23:12).

376. Soards, *Speeches*, 206; cf. Green, "Acts," 767. Contrast Wright, *People of God*, 375, for whom Paul's preaching in Rome redefines the meaning of Israel's restoration in Acts 1:6; in my opinion this approach overlooks the pattern of returning to Israel and also Luke's continuing expectation of the Jewish people's faith (in light of how the words would be understood in a first-century context, see 1:7; 3:19–21; 26:6–7; 28:20).

377. For judgment against Israel, see, e.g., Isa 2:1–3:26; Jer 4:6; 5:9, 29; 9:9; 15:1–9; Amos 2:6; 3:2; 5:5; 7:8–9; 9:4; Mic 1:6–16; for the righteous-minority idea, see, e.g., Ezek 9:4–6; Mal 3:16–17; Rom 9:27; 11:5.

378. E.g., Ovid *Metam.* 3.513–18; cf. Porph. *Marc.* 22.348–60. Philostratus recognizes that failing to believe a semidivine hero after sufficient evidence has been presented would be unjust (*Hrk.* 17.1). Yet one should neither believe too much (gullibility) nor disbelieve too much (skepticism; Plut. *Cam.* 6.4).

379. E.g., *b. B. Bat.* 75a; *Pesiq. Rab Kah.* 18:5; cf. *Tg. Ps.-J.* on Gen 25:29, 32.

ancients contended that their interlocutors' unbelief stemmed from envy (Lucian *Tox.* 56). Although Luke has repeated many disappointing responses from God's own people in his work, he may also contrast Jewish rejection here with the welcome Paul received as a divine messenger among Gentiles in Acts 28:1–10.[380]

c. Paul's Warning (28:25)

Whereas some visitors may treat the debate as an intellectual exercise, Paul, though ready to dialogue academically, concludes like a prophet.[381] If he has spoken from God, they will be judged if they reject his message. Luke is not following the particular modern academic approach that any position is acceptable provided one can make a case for it (useful as that approach is for teaching argumentation); he is convinced that Paul's case is genuinely true and will convince anyone with an open mind and hence that people are morally responsible to be persuaded by it.[382] Ultimately, though Paul may stand trial in a human court, it is his hearers who stand under Isaiah's judgment (Isa 6:9–10; Acts 28:25–27).[383] Whereas he may have no charge to bring against his people before Rome (Acts 28:19), he brings a prophetic charge from God against some of them here in 28:25–28.[384]

Unlike Mark, Luke in his Gospel does not offer the full text of this Isaiah passage in his parables section (he offers an abbreviated form in Luke 8:10; contrast Mark 4:12; Matt 13:13–15; John 12:39–40).[385] Why does Luke locate it here? Sometimes a summation or closing argument could include the strongest argument for one's case.[386] Yet by expanding the quotation that he provides in abbreviated form at Luke 8:10, Luke makes that hermeneutical key for the parables a key also for evaluating obduracy throughout his entire narrative. Paul's mission in the Diaspora can fit the paradigm of Jesus in Galilee, reflected in 8:5–8, 11–15[387] (from the Jesus tradition):[388]

380. Jipp, *Visitations*, 25, 29, 271 (emphasizing the pattern of Jewish leaders rejecting the message on 247–52, and in Acts 28:17–27 specifically, on 274–81).

381. For such competing views regarding the nature of the proclaimer's speech, see, e.g., Ezek 33:32–33; for Paul himself, Acts 24:25–26. For Paul speaking as a prophet here, see Litwak, *Echoes*, 181–200 (including as an example of those who prophesy in Acts 2:18, p. 198). Popkes, "Worte," argues that 28:25–28 is important for the portrayal of Paul in Acts (regarding the relation to Judaism, etc.).

382. That Luke believes his message's truth to be absolute and not simply relative does not mean that he would endorse social intolerance or persecution of those who reject his gospel, a different (political) form of absolutism often (conveniently?) conflated today with any affirmation of objective truth. Luke portrays dialogue in this passage and never in his entire work condones violence as a means of spreading the apostolic message. In Luke's world, Luke expected Christians to be objects of persecution at times, not its authors.

383. Marguerat, *Historian*, 219. On the theme of reversal of judgment in antiquity, see comment on Acts 7:51–53, 56; Keener, "Inverted Guilt."

384. Cf. Shiell, *Reading Acts*, 193 (following Soards, *Speeches*, 132), in seeing this as ironic.

385. Like Matt 13:15 and John 12:40, Luke also follows the LXX's "and I shall heal them" rather than Mark's mention of forgiveness (which may reflect an Aramaic interpretive tradition; see Evans, *World*, 61). Some dispute the usual interpretation of Mark's passage (Peisker, "Konsekutives"; Jeremias, *Parables*, 17), and some construe Matthew's point as different from that of Mark (Stern, *Parables in Midrash*, 201–2), but even if intended partly ironically, both likely have God's plan in view (Keener, *Matthew*, 380–81).

386. E.g., Isaeus *Hagnias* 50; Cic. *Quinct.* 25.78–80.

387. Cf. also Ehrhardt, *Acts*, 128. For a treatment of Acts 28:25–28 in light of Luke's larger use of Isaiah, see Pao, *Isaianic Exodus*, 101–9.

388. I have argued that even parabolic interpretations can derive from the tradition (Keener, *Matthew*, 381–82), as was standard with Jewish parables in general (Johnston, "Interpretations," 561–62, 565–66, 638; Vermes, *Religion*, 92–99; Stern, *Parables in Midrash*, 24). Contrary to many earlier scholars, the burden of proof rests with those who deny that Jesus—alone out of Jewish parable makers—would have sometimes supplied interpretations. Nor is there any historical reason to deny the authenticity of parable interpretations attributed to Jesus simply because of multiple extrinsic referents, since these were also common in rabbinic parables (Johnston, "Interpretations," 608, 638–39; Witherington, *Christology of Jesus*, 72; cf. Scott, *Parable*, 44; at greater length, see Blomberg, *Parables*).

some ignored the message or rejected it immediately; some received it but fell away through hardship (cf. Acts 14:22); some received it but fell away through lives of ease or pleasure (cf. 13:43, 45); but others persevered to bear good fruit. Like Luke's narrative in the Gospel, his narrative in Acts focuses on the first and fourth kinds of soil and hence a twofold division of response (the kind most evident in the sorts of individual scenes Luke narrates). Thus the rejection of Paul's message is part of the larger rejection of Jesus's message, and this, in turn, is part of the entire story of Israel's history (Isa 6:9–10; cf. 53:1–3).

Jesus spoke parables so that his less-committed hearers would not understand (Luke 8:10); Isaiah supported the expectation that many would resist the truth. Paul here employs Isaiah's words merely as a summons to repent[389] and a prediction whereas Isaiah's mission in the Hebrew text is to harden his hearers (Isa 6:9–10); but Paul follows the LXX rendering and interpretation of Isaiah closely.[390] Even apart from the LXX form, however, this prediction can represent wholesale and permanent rejection of Israel for Luke no more than it did for Isaiah. Predictions fulfilled within the narrative suggest that other predictions, too, will be fulfilled, including the restoration of the kingdom to Israel in God's time (Acts 1:6–7; 3:21; Luke 22:30).[391] That the "Holy Spirit" (as inspirer of prophecy and here of Scripture)[392] "spoke well" (καλῶς ... ἐλάλησεν) was to be expected; speaking "well" appears also in Luke 20:39,[393] but the gospel tradition known to Luke also applies the term to a prophecy of Isaiah (Mark 7:6; cf. Matt 15:7).[394]

Some Jews and Romans likely doubted the message's or the movement's Jewishness because so many Jews had rejected it (cf. Rom 3:3), but Luke is able to argue that this very rejection fits an expectation from the Jewish heritage and Scriptures (cf. similarly Isa 53:1 in Rom 10:16).[395] Rhetorically, it was prudent to turn everything possible to the advantage of one's argument;[396] Luke's (and other first-century Christians') use of Isaiah proves more apologetic[397] than in rabbinic (Isaiah promising ultimate forgiveness) or patristic (Isaiah proving predestination) interpretation.[398] But Luke has a much longer subtext in Israel's history to show that God's people often rejected their prophets (Acts 7:9, 35–37, 51–53), making this Isaiah quotation merely an

389. For the text's hortatory value (rather than spelling Israel's rejection), cf. Kilgallen, "Heal."
390. Cf. also Longenecker, *Acts*, 366–67; Witherington, *Acts*, 804–5; Bonnah, *Spirit*, 253. Although Ezek 2:3–5 and 3:4–5 expand the interpretive horizons of this text (van de Sandt, "No Salvation"), it is not clear that Luke's audience would note allusions to these texts.
391. Gaventa, *Acts*, 27, believes that Acts anticipates Paul's death and Jesus's parousia without narrating them; the same can be said of Jerusalem's fall in Luke's Gospel (Luke 19:43–44; 21:20–24).
392. See comment in Keener, *Acts*, 1:537. The major programmatic texts (Luke 4:18–19; 24:46–49; Acts 1:8; 2:17–18; cf. 10:38) mention the Spirit's equipping God's agents for ministry; the text that Luke cites here does not mention the Spirit explicitly, and so Luke may compensate by more explicitly attributing the text to the Spirit.
393. Cf. Mark 12:32. The sense in Luke 6:26 is different ("well" being attached to the object rather than to the speaker).
394. Bovon, *Studies*, 117, argues that καλῶς suggests a Christian way of reading Isaiah over against the synagogue way, comparing (117–18) Mark 7:6; Matt 15:7; *Barn.* 10.11. He argues that the aorist points to a particular past speaking and historical context but it can be reapplied for new settings (p. 119).
395. Luke presumably expected his audience to catch the irony (see Ray, *Irony*, passim).
396. E.g., Heath, "Invention," 97.
397. Cf. Lindars, *Apologetic*, 159: early Christians exploited Isa 6:9–10 as an apologetic response to Jewish unbelief.
398. See Evans, "Isaiah in Writings." Some take the apparent purpose of God to blind his people as irony (Ray, *Irony*, 55, following Hollenback, "Irony"); but it may reflect penal blindness (God handing them over to their choices), and in Luke's larger narrative it probably functions intertextually as God's way of enabling the Gentile mission so that all could have an opportunity (cf. Rom 11:32; Ray, *Irony*, 159).

apt concluding summary of the larger pattern.[399] Isaiah's addressing the "ancestors" reinforces the antiquity of the pattern of the disobedience and repudiation by "our" and "your ancestors" (7:39, 51–52; cf. Luke 6:26; 11:47–48).[400]

What the text cannot mean is that Paul was giving up on any future plan of God for his people. Despite Jesus's use of Isa 6 in Luke 8:10, Jesus continued his ministry to Israel.[401] The point is not the abandoning of ultimate hope for Israel (Acts 1:6) but focusing on the mission to the Gentiles until the Father's time for Israel's restoration (1:7–8). Luke still believes in "the hope of Israel," mentioned as recently as 28:20.[402] This becomes even clearer when we examine the Isaian context from which Luke derives the quotation.

Some intertextual observations are in order, since the nucleus of Luke's ideal audience is fairly biblically literate. Luke and his ideal audience surely knew (cf. 28:25) that these words first depicted Isaiah's inaugural call; Isaiah did not terminate his mission after receiving these words but rather began his public ministry.[403] Prophets and apostles came after Isaiah and preached to Israel (cf. Luke 11:49). After Isaiah saw the Lord's glory (Isa 6:1, 5), he was commissioned to tell Israel's people that they would not see with their eyes or hear with their ears (6:9–10)—that is, that they would be spiritually blind and deaf (cf. 29:9; 42:18–19; 43:8).[404] Paul himself had been blinded yet received sight through seeing the Lord Jesus's glory (Acts 9:3–4, 8); now he was called to open his people's eyes (26:18). Isaiah's proclamation to Israel also yields proclamation to Gentiles (e.g., Isa 56:3–8), as Paul's does here (Acts 28:28).

Historically, it is interesting that Isaiah played a special role in Paul's ministry to people in Rome; all Paul's explicit mentions of Isaiah are in Romans (Rom 9:27, 29; 10:16, 20; 15:12). But this is likely the text Luke would have used anyway (Luke 8:10).[405] More important, the Paul who wrote to believers in Rome also could use similar imagery for Israel's blindness, including from Isaiah.[406]

d. Blind and Deaf (28:26–27)

Although Luke does not compose the quotation, it is a key text that helps inform his theology and vocabulary elsewhere.[407] Isaiah's prophecy here quoted (Isa 6:9–10) is in the context of Isaiah's call (6:1–8) and the announcement of Israel's judgment

399. Cf. Fitzmyer, *Acts*, 791: the condemnation was not new; Luke used traditional language because they continued the obduracy of their ancestors.

400. Promises also came to the ancestors (Luke 1:55; Acts 3:13, 25; 13:17, 32; 26:6), but Isaiah's message here concerns disobedience. Like the OT prophets themselves, Luke includes both strands, with a noticeable shift from "our fathers" (Acts 28:17, applicable to all Jewish people) to "your fathers" (28:25, not applicable to members of the remnant). The pattern was not new and hence not surprising, and would presumably continue to repeat; there is no decisive change or rejection of ministry to Israel here.

401. With Soards, *Speeches*, 207–8n52.

402. On the relevance of Acts 28:20 for interpreting this paragraph, see Brawley, "Promises and Jews," 296. Given the mixed Jewish responses earlier in the Gospel, Brawley, "Borderlines," views the Jewish people's ultimate decision to Jesus as open-ended.

403. Cf. also Witherington, *Acts*, 802–3 (also noting the remnant of Isa 6:13).

404. Luke's contemporaries would read Isaiah as a unity (as in the Isaiah scroll; cf. 1QIsaᵃ).

405. Luke also explicitly mentions Isaiah at Acts 8:28, 30 and at programmatic, key points in Luke 3:4; 4:17; and strongly implies Isaianic material in Acts 1:8; see the discussion of Luke's programmatic use of Isaiah in Pao, *Isaianic Exodus*.

406. The blinded eyes of Rom 11:8 recall Isa 29:10; Deut 29:4. Although Paul often reads christocentrically, many of Paul's readings address the definition of God's people (Hays, *Conversion*, 187). For Israel's disobedience, Ware, *Synopsis*, §63, pp. 118–23, cites, e.g., Rom 9:1–5; 9:30–10:4; 10:19–21; 11:7–10, 11–32; 1 Cor 1:23–24; 1 Thess 2:14–16.

407. For a survey of scholarly interpretations of Luke's use of Isaiah here, see Lehnert, "Verstockung" (viewing Luke's use as positive toward God's promise).

and devastation (6:11–13). It would provide an appropriate end for Acts, recognizing that there were two paths,[408] one leading through Jesus to the Gentile mission, the other leading to resistance against Rome without divine sanction and to the holy city's devastation.

"Go" (here πορεύθητι) is a common command, including in Luke-Acts (e.g., Luke 5:24; 7:50; 8:48; esp. 7:8); nevertheless, it seems noteworthy here how frequently this verb appears in commands for ministry (cf. Acts 9:11, 15), both ministry to Israel (5:20) and cross-culturally (8:26; 10:20), including Paul's call to the Gentiles (22:21).[409] Healing offers a spiritual analogy elsewhere in Luke-Acts (e.g., Luke 5:31), as does blindness (see comment below).

The quotation in Acts 28:27[410] lists images of body parts (with synonymous semantic force)[411] chiastically:

A The heart has become dull
 B The ears are hard of hearing
  C They closed their eyes
  C′ Lest they see by means of their eyes
 B′ And hear with their ears
A′ And they understand with their hearts and turn

"And I heal them" (and perhaps the preceding phrase, "and they turn") stands outside the chiasmus proper. The chiasmus draws attention to the insensate moral and spiritual state of the people who fail to perceive God's true message. The chiasmus is Isaiah's, but Luke reproduces it fully for good reason.

The passage, placed in the context of Isaiah's call and mission, reflects themes pervasive in both Isaiah and other prophets.[412] Physical blindness offers a metaphor for spiritual obduracy elsewhere in the biblical prophets (e.g., Isa 29:9; 42:18–20; 43:8; 44:18; Jer 5:21; Ezek 12:2) as well as elsewhere in the culture (see comment on Acts 9:8).[413] Israel lacked both eyes to see and ears to hear (Deut 29:4). Thus writers

408. For the call to decide between two paths toward the end of a work, cf. Josh 24:15 (somewhat earlier, Deut 30:19). Elsewhere, see, e.g., the two ways in Sen. Y. *Ep. Lucil.* 8.3; 27.4; Diogenes *Ep.* 30; Ps 1:1; *m. ʾAb.* 2:9; *4 Ezra* 7:3–16, 60–61; 8:1–3; *Test. Ab.* 11:2–11 A; 8:10–16 B; *Test. Ash.* 1:3, 5; Matt 7:13–14 (cf. Luke 13:23–24); *Did.* 1.1–6.2; *Barn.* 18.1–21.9.

409. Admittedly, it is not in any way distinctively Lukan; Matthew employs the verb in the imperative seven times (without including this part of the Isaiah citation). But elsewhere in the NT, it appears only twice in John (and also once in an interpolated section [John 8:11, in 7:53–8:11]); in the Apostolic Fathers, it appears only six times, all in *Hermas* (35.2; 38.11; 46.2; 61.4; 66.6; 77.4). Luke-Acts employs it seventeen times (about 63 percent of NT uses); proportionately, only Matthew's uses (in half as much material as Luke-Acts) come close.

410. Luke's use of Greek is necessary for his audience but also appropriate here for Paul's audience in Rome, given the dominance of Greek use in the Roman Jewish community. Scripture citations appear at Rome in Greek (resembling the LXX or Aquila), Hebrew, and Latin versions (*CIJ* 1:lxvi).

411. For the figurative moralistic use of body parts (e.g., tongue, eyes, ears), in addition to OT uses see, e.g., Thucyd. 3.38.7; *Rhet. Her.* 4.49.62; Cic. *Vat.* 2.4; Livy 3.71.5; Val. Max. 6.2.praef.; Sen. Y. *Ep. Lucil.* 20.2; 40.4; Pliny E. *N.H.* 18.1.4; Plut. *Statecraft* 5, *Mor.* 802DE; Fronto *Ad M. Caes.* 1.8.3; Lucian *Dem.* 12; Max. Tyre 7.7; 25.6; Philost. *Hrk.* 34.4; Libanius *Declam.* 44.70, 79; 4QpNah 3–4 II, 8; *b. ʿArak.* 15a; perhaps most relevant, Paul's accumulation in Rom 3:13–18; cf. Porph. *Marc.* 33.506–7; *Gen. Rab.* 67:3; *Lev. Rab.* 16:4; *Song Rab.* 1:15, §2; 4:1, §2; 7:5, §2. For the figure synecdoche, where a part represents the whole, see *Rhet. Her.* 4.33.44–45; Rowe, "Style," 127; Porter, "Paul and Letters," 578; Black, "Oration at Olivet," 85 (citing Quint. *Inst.* 8.16.19); Anderson, *Glossary,* 112 (adding Cic. *De or.* 3.168).

412. Early Christian authors, such as Paul, also mined these other texts (see, e.g., Rom 11:8, which seems to mix Isa 29:10 with wording from the present text).

413. Renehan, "Quotations," 20, cites numerous classical "parallels" for Acts 28:26 (Hom. *Il.* 15.128–29; Aeschylus *Prom.* 447–48; *Ag.* 1623; Soph. *Oed. tyr.* 413; Soph. frg. 837 Nauck = frg. 923 Pearson; Demosth. *Aristog.* 1.89; Heracl. frg. 34 Diels-Kranz) but concedes that they are coincidence, because (p. 21) NT writers

spoke of those who, though physically blind, revealed great intellectual[414] or spiritual[415] vision. Stoics regarded all people as ignorant, and hence as blind[416] (sometimes as "deaf and blind");[417] some others also used blindness and deafness figuratively for ignorance.[418] Jewish writers also spoke of spiritual blindness and deafness (*1 En.* 90:7); for example, Potiphar's wife was "blinded by sin" (*Test. Jos.* 7:5).[419]

Paul was called to "turn" people and "open their eyes" (see Acts 26:18 and comment there), but he was not responsible for his hearers' obduracy (cf. Luke 9:5; 10:10–11; Acts 20:26).[420] Luke probably also links Paul's transformation from blindness to sight with the call to turn others from spiritual blindness to spiritual sight (compare Acts 26:18 with 9:8, 18).[421] Lack of understanding also characterized Moses's people (συνιέναι, 7:25) and even Jesus's disciples before the resurrection (Luke 18:34; 24:45; cf. 2:50).[422] Physical "eyes" are used for, or fail to achieve, spiritual perception in Luke 2:30; 10:23; 19:42; 24:16, 31; and Acts 26:18; "ears" are used the same way in Luke 8:8; 9:44; 14:35.[423] Already earlier in Acts, Stephen notably denounced Jewish opponents of his message for hard "hearts" and "ears" (Acts 7:51; cf. 7:57; see comment there); he also noted (as here in 28:25) that they continued their ancestors' resistance against the Spirit through the prophets (7:51–52). Jerusalem's blinded eyes to Jesus's mission (Luke 19:42) invited judgment (19:43–44); Luke would also know that judgment came on God's blinded people in Isaiah's context (relevant here to the outcome of the Judean-Roman war, in the wake of which Luke may be writing).

The term for "turn" here (ἐπιστρέφω) involves repentance or restoration in many Lukan texts (Acts 9:35; 11:21; 14:15; 15:19; cf. Luke 17:4; 22:32), sometimes with reference to Israel (Luke 1:16–17; Acts 3:19). Calling people to "turn" and opening their "eyes" were central to Paul's mission (Acts 26:18, 20); perhaps most relevant here is that ἐπιστρέφω could refer to Israel's eschatological turning (3:19).[424] The term for "heal" here appears fifteen times in Luke-Acts—elsewhere for physical healings performed by Jesus and his followers, the majority (except

---

depend here on the ᴏᴛ (Isa 6:9–10; cf. Jer 5:21; Ezek 12:2). Centuries later, some non-Jews used the earlier biblical prophetic tradition of Israel's being blind and deaf to God's messengers (cf., e.g., Qur'an 5.71).

414. E.g., Marcus Perperna in Val. Max. 8.13.5; cf. Democritus in Aul. Gel. 10.17.1.

415. E.g., Tiresias in Soph. *Oed. tyr.* 371, 375, 402–3, 419, 454, 747, 1266–79; Ovid *Metam.* 3.336–38, 525; Apollod. *Bib.* 3.6.7. Cf. Phineas in Ap. Rhod. 2.184.

416. Sen. Y. *Ep. Lucil.* 50.3; Epict. *Diatr.* 1.18.4, 6.

417. Epict. *Diatr.* 2.20.37; 2.24.19. A Skeptic portrays the ignorant accordingly in Lucian *Phil. Sale* 27. Cf. Heraclitus on the uselessness of eyes and ears to the unwise (frg. 107 Diels-Kranz, 22B, in Byrskog, *History*, 147).

418. E.g., Aeschylus *Prom.* 447–48; Val. Max. 7.3.6; Dio Chrys. *Or.* 32.26; Epict. *Disc.* 2.24.19. Receptivity to hear could be described poetically as offering "vacant ears" (*vacuas aures*, Val. Max. 2.4.4; cf. Philost. *Hrk.* 57.1; 2 Tim 4:3–4); one might persuade another by filling his "ears" (Quint. Curt. 10.1.36).

419. Cf. Isa 29:9; 42:18–19; 56:10; *1 En.* 99:8; 4Q424 1 3; 4Q434 1 I, 3–4; Wis 2:21; *Test. Levi* 13:7; *Exod. Rab.* 30:20; Mark 4:12; 8:17–18; John 9:39–41; 12:40; Rom 1:21; Eph 4:18.

420. The obduracy lay with the hearers, not with the message or the messenger (cf. Cassandra's inability to persuade with her mantic gift, Apollod. *Bib.* 3.12.5).

421. For Luke's use of blindness and healing, including Paul's, see also, e.g., Hartsock, "Blindness," 91. In other narrative, see, e.g., the argument of Kiel, "Blindness" (on Tobit).

422. Although some located understanding in the head (Philo *Dreams* 1.32 notes the debate), the "heart" was regularly associated with understanding and cognition, as in this quotation (cf., e.g., Luke 9:47; Deut 29:3 [29:4 ET]; ʟxx Prov 2:2; 14:33; 20:5; Philo *Flight* 123).

423. "Eyes to see" and "ears to hear" were familiar phrases (Deut 29:4; Eccl 11:7; Ezek 12:2; 40:4; 44:5; Mark 4:9, 23; Matt 11:15; Luke 8:8; 14:35; Rom 11:8; *2 En.* 65:2; cf. *Pesiq. Rab.* 21:2/3). Closed eyes could be associated with sleep (including spiritually, Isa 29:10) or with death (e.g., Gen 46:4; Ps 13:3; Val. Max. 2.6.8). On ears in Luke-Acts (esp. Luke 4:21), see Ulrichs, "Ears."

424. In his letters, Paul believed that God sovereignly delayed that wholesale turning (while allowing a present remnant) to allow time for Gentiles to be converted (Rom 11; cf. Acts 28:28).

for 9:34; 28:8)[425] in Israel.[426] In this climactic interpretation in Acts, Jesus's and his agents' signs to Israel become an offer of God's restoration. Biblical prophets had also played on both spiritual and physical nuances of healing, often employing the image figuratively (e.g., Isa 53:5; 57:18; Jer 3:22; 17:14; 33:6; Hos 11:3; 14:4), yet in some collections alongside eschatological physical healing (e.g., Isa 29:18; 32:3–4; 35:5–6).

Luke's ideal audience was biblically literate and might well think of Isaiah's context (see comment on Acts 8:32–33). Paul, like Isaiah (Isa 6:1), was privy to a divine revelation (Acts 9:3–4). Further, Luke's hearers might think of how the Isaiah text continued: until the land would be laid waste (Isa 6:11). For Luke's audience (probably) after 70 C.E., this would be a significant context to mine. But presumably Luke, like Isaiah, also expected a future restoration (Acts 1:6–7; 3:19–21).

e. Salvation for the Gentiles (28:28)

Acts ends by emphasizing not Israel's rejection but rather the more positive prospect of the message's continuing expansion among the Gentiles. An unacceptably mixed Jewish response has continued, but it justifies the continued offer of Israel's hope to the nations.

An emphasis on the worldwide mission, including the Gentiles, constitutes the final words of both Jesus before his ascension (1:8) and Paul (28:28) in Luke-Acts.[427] (Peter's last speech also defends the circumcision-free Gentile mission [15:7–11].) Paul's quotation of Isa 6:9–10 in Acts 28:26–27 also evokes the context of Isaiah's call (Isa 6:1–8); Isaiah's call offers a relevant model for the Gentile mission in Acts 28:28.[428] More explicitly, Isaiah's verdict of blindness applied only to "this people" (Acts 28:26–27), leaving the Gentiles free to respond.

This is not the first time Paul had warned that he would turn to the Gentiles (Acts 13:46–47; 18:6), yet went on to offer his message to Jewish communities in new venues (e.g., 14:1; 19:8).[429] Paul apparently continues his ministry to Jews and Gentiles alike immediately after this warning (28:30–31). For Luke, the "apostle to the Gentiles"[430] (Rom 11:13; cf. 15:18; Gal 2:7–9; Acts 22:21) was, in fact, called to both Jews and Gentiles (Acts 9:15; 26:17; cf. Rom 11:14; 1 Cor 9:20; 2 Cor 11:24, 26) and always goes to Jewish people first in any location (e.g., Acts 13:5, 14; 14:1; 17:1, 10; see comment on Acts 13:5) despite rejection in many (not all, 17:11–12) previous locations. Luke reiterates that Paul was called to both Jews and Gentiles (9:15; 22:15; 26:17–18, 23),[431] although it is his initially controversial Gentile mission that demanded the most attention for a first-century audience.

Far from Luke implying a final rejection of the Jewish people, Soards suggests, "the *expectation* created by the repetitions in the speeches and narrative of Acts is that Paul

425. Jipp, *Visitations*, 280, finds a contrast in the juxtaposed narratives of Gentile welcome in 28:1–10 and Jewish rejection here, including Gentiles in Malta receiving healing (28:8–9) that is here rejected.

426. The sudden shift from subjunctive to future indicative, though permissible in Koine, might "highlight the hope of salvation" (Peterson, *Acts*, 717). Mark 4:12 says "forgiven" instead of "healed," perhaps reflecting a Jewish interpretive tradition also found in the Targumim (see Chilton, "Targum," 246).

427. Puskas, "Conclusion: Investigation," 93; idem, *Conclusion: Significance*, 84; emphasizing the importance of 28:28 for Luke's conclusion, see also Kilgallen, "Acts 28,28." Similarly, the ascended Jesus sends Paul to Gentiles (Acts 22:21; 26:17–18) and to Rome (23:11) in his latest quoted statements.

428. Litwak, *Echoes*, 189, suggests verbal and conceptual resemblances with Ezek 3:7; these do not, however, appear very distinctive or obvious.

429. With, e.g., Soards, *Speeches*, 206; Witherington, *Acts*, 805–6; Le Cornu, *Acts*, xxxv, 1522; see the introduction, above, to Acts 28:17–31.

430. In Romans, technically, *an* apostle to the Gentiles (with, e.g., Dunn, *Romans*, 656; Kruse, *Romans*, 430).

431. With Tannehill, *Acts*, 352.

(and others?) will have increasing success among the Gentiles but that, as before, the preachers will certainly return to preach to the Jews. . . . While Luke writes Acts to explain an increasingly Gentile church to itself, through repetition he also created an *expectation* of an ongoing mission" to the Jewish people.[432]

If Israel's rejection of the message invited a focus on the Gentiles (Acts 13:46; 18:6; Luke 4:24–27; cf. 21:24), following the demands of Luke 10:10–14, the mission to both was God's plan from the start, not a pure by-product of Jewish disobedience (2:32; Acts 1:8).[433] What Israel's failure to fully embrace the gospel allowed was a simultaneous mission to Israel and the Gentiles instead of believers finishing the mission to Israel before believers could turn to the Gentiles (cf. Gentiles' conversion in response to Israel's exaltation in Isa 2:2; 60:1–14; 62:2; 66:12, 19–20). Paul does not say that the Gentiles *instead of* Israel will heed the message; rather, he claims that they will "also" (καί) listen.[434]

Paul's threat to turn to the Gentiles might also fit a rhetorical function of provoking Paul's people to "jealousy" by not taking their privilege for granted (Rom 11:14).[435] Although such a message may have remained intelligible to messianic Jewish communities in Judea and Galilee well into the second century, it became increasingly subject to distortion in the perceptions of Gentile Christians (by then numerically dominant) after the first century and has been tragically misunderstood by Gentile Christendom through most of its history.[436]

The phrase "salvation of God" evokes the theme of salvation for God's people (with the ingathering of the Gentiles) in Isaiah; this is clear because Luke's other clear reference to "the salvation of God" is his paraphrase of Isa 40:5 LXX (which adds "salvation" to the MT there) in Luke 3:6, which is for "all flesh" (cf. similarly Acts 2:17, 21).[437] The "salvation" "sent" to the Gentiles was first "sent" to Israel (Acts 13:26). Luke uses Paul's "let it be known to you" (γνωστὸν . . . ἔστω ὑμῖν) here for solemn

432. Soards, *Speeches*, 206–7. Likewise, from the perspective of both Luke and Paul, preaching to the Gentiles fulfills a "promise given to Israel by the prophets" (Le Cornu, *Acts*, xxxv).

433. See Nolland, "Salvation-History," 76–81; cf. the approaches of Eisen, *Poetik*; Deutschmann, *Synagoge*, 188–217; and others; on the compatibility of Rom 11 and Acts 28:16–31, see esp. Litwak, "Views." Apparently, both Paul (Rom 11:11–12, 15, 25–26) and Luke (Acts 3:19–21) believe that Jewish disobedience providentially delayed the consummation of the kingdom and hence allowed time for further evangelizing of Gentiles (cf. Acts 1:6–8).

434. See Litwak, "Views," 237–38.

435. See Lehnert, "Absage"; Litwak, "Views," 240. For the text's use as a reproof inviting conversion rather than rejection, see van de Sandt, "No Salvation." The subject of provocation could be Paul's success in the anticipated eschatological conversion of Gentiles (Nanos, *Mystery*, 18, 249–50).

436. The first-century Christian movement was part of middle Judaism (Boccaccini, *Judaism*, 16–19, 215; Meyers, "Judaism and Christianity," 69; earlier, though only on pre-Pauline Christianity, cf. Dibelius, *Tradition*, 29) and continued to be so viewed by some Gentile outsiders into the second century (Lucian *Peregr.* 11; though cf. Judge, "Judaism and Rise"). Both Jewish Jesus-followers' necessary repudiation of Bar Kokhba and the growth of Gentile Christianity probably facilitated the rejection of the Jewish Jesus-followers by most other Judeans (Schiffman, *Jew*, 75–78). (The earlier *Birkath ha-minim* may have simply made Jewish Jesus-followers uncomfortable; see Hare, *Persecution*, 56; Katz, "Issues," 51.) The earliest patristic sources often differentiated Jewish believers they considered faithful to Jesus from those they deemed heretical (see Pritz, *Nazarene Christianity*, 19–28, 75; Bagatti, *Church*, 31), but later Gentile writers rejected most (Jerome *Ep.* 112.13 and other sources cited in Bagatti, *Church*, 34–35; Finegan, *Records*, 59; though cf. more nuanced sources in Daniélou, *Theology*, 56). Nevertheless, popular Gentile Christian and Jewish piety continued to overlap at least as late as the end of the fourth century (see Kinzig, "Non-Separation"). As late as the tenth century, Jacob al-Kirkisani, an author from the Jewish Karaite sect, may have continued to view Jewish Christians as a Jewish sect analogous to Pharisees (though he may simply reflect earlier sources; see Simon, *Sects*, 131).

437. For "God's salvation," see, e.g., Ps 50:23; but God speaks often of "my salvation" in Isaiah (Isa 46:13; 49:6; 51:5–6, 8; 56:1; cf. "his [God's] salvation" in 25:9).

pronouncements (Peter in 2:14; 4:10; Paul in 13:38).[438] That the Gentiles will "hear" contrasts them with Israel in the Isaiah quotation in 28:26–27.

4. Continuing, Unhindered Ministry (28:30–31)

Most ancient works have some sort of conclusion, though the particulars vary according to genre.[439] Although Luke offers no formal, structured conclusion (and touches on themes less clearly here than in Acts' introduction), he does revisit some primary themes in these closing verses. (See also discussion at Acts 28:17–31 of ancient works' conclusions, including their value for summarizing major themes.)

Luke's collection of precedents and his positive ending offer hope of Roman toleration, but such hope was necessary precisely because the church in some places had experienced intolerance. The Jerusalem church was apparently no longer persecuted by the time of its closing mention in Acts and was probably dispersed by the time Luke wrote Acts. By contrast, Christians in Rome, the heart of the empire on which he has focused, faced severe persecution before (on the most likely view of Acts' date) Luke wrote.[440]

a. Introduction

Luke leaves the Pauline, Gentile mission open-ended because he remains optimistic that nothing could hinder the gospel from reaching the ends of the earth (1:8). What happened at the end of the "two years" (28:30) Luke mentions? Some signals within the narrative point to Paul's execution, and others to his exoneration; perhaps the likeliest solution is the one also suggested by early Christian tradition, namely, that Paul was released, then later rearrested and executed. If Luke's climax and goal are Rome, Paul's subsequent departure would be anticlimactic. If Luke desires a positive ending (and/or positive precedents), an execution in Rome later in Nero's reign was no better a place to end his account than an earlier execution if Paul died earlier. In any case, Acts is not a biography, and in Luke's literary milieu, writers in many genres could end where they wished.

i. OPEN ENDINGS

Scholars offer various explanations for Luke's abrupt ending.[441] Some scholars have argued that the book concludes as it does because Luke intended a third volume, tracing the gospel indeed to the ends of the earth.[442] (Some ancient writers were dissatisfied with the ending and added more, such as the gloss, which became part of Ethiopic

438. Occurring together nowhere else in the NT, the two terms appear together in this form in 1 Esd 2:18; Ezra 4:12, 13; 5:8 LXX; cf. similar language in *Test. Jud.* 20:1; *Test. Iss.* 6:1.

439. Cf. Roberts, "Closure."

440. On Nero's persecution, see, e.g., Tac. *Ann.* 15.44; Suet. *Nero* 16; Euseb. *H.E.* 2.25.5–7; cf. also Sulp. Sev. *Chron.* 2.29 (in Barrett, *Documents*, 17; Finegan, *Apostles*, 23); Goppelt, "Existence," 194; idem, *Times*, 106 (citing Euseb. *H.E.* 4.26.9); Koester, *Introduction*, 1:313. On the authenticity of Tacitus's report, see, e.g., Mattingly, *Christianity*, 31–32; Harris, "References," 348–50; *pace* Fau, "Authenticité." Some scholars suggest that Christians' apocalyptic perspective on the fire contributed to their function as scapegoats (Giovannini, "Incendium"); some suggest a delay between the fire and the persecution, dating the latter to 65 (Robinson, *Redating*, 145; idem, *Trust*, 66–67). Against some scholars (e.g., Smallwood, *Jews*, 217–18), it is unlikely that the Jewish community instigated this persecution (Hare, "Relationship").

441. For one detailed survey of explanations by category, see Omerzu, "Schweigen," 128–44.

442. Winandy, "Finale des Actes" (following T. Zahn on the third volume). For an exploration and evaluation of different solutions to why Acts, in contrast to later legends, does not narrate Paul's death, see Omerzu, "Schweigen" (with conclusions, 151–56).

versions of Acts, about Paul's later work in Rome.)[443] But even if Paul proceeded to Spain (Rom 15:24, 28; cf. *1 Clem.* 5.7), would Luke expect sufficient material for a third volume? Could the infrastructure of his narrative conceivably support the sort of parallelism found in the first two volumes into a third?[444] Others suggest that the end (Paul's martyrdom?) was later removed to allow further travels in the East.[445] But more surgery than a simple amputation of final verses would be necessary for such an adjustment: even if Paul's eventual martyrdom is implied (and this is debated), it certainly could not follow so abruptly upon all the positive indicators of Roman favor in the narrative as we have it.[446]

Some propose that Acts ends where it does because Luke finished it during the two years mentioned in Acts 28:30.[447] This view merits far more consideration than it is often accorded, but for reasons suggested in the commentary introduction,[448] I argue that it is less likely than a later date. Among my most important reasons for questioning this view is that, unless we date Mark's writing and widespread circulation before 62 C.E. (so that Luke could have used it in his Gospel) or deny that Luke used Mark, it is difficult to contend for such an early date.[449] Further, Luke does seem aware that Paul eventually has a hearing (27:24) and that *something* happened after two years (28:30).[450] Political considerations could have dictated omitting Paul's martyrdom,[451] but one would expect a persecuted church to need the sort of encouragement provided by the stark moral dualism of the Johannine corpus, rather than the culture-friendly vision of Luke-Acts.

Some suggest that the incomplete conclusion recalls the end of the so-called Deuteronomistic History (at 2 Kgs 25:29–30);[452] others suggest that Luke employs Mark (a major source in his Gospel) as a model.[453] If Luke uses Mark's model, he invites the reader to consider his earlier passages for clues to what follows.[454] (The invitation

443. Uhlig, "Actaschluss in Version." This was probably accidental, but ancient writers sometimes wished to "finish" or polish works regarded as incomplete (Suet. *Vergil* 41).

444. Proponents of a planned third volume could suggest this obstacle as one of the reasons the third volume never appeared; the frequency of open endings in antiquity, however, undercuts the necessity for such an appeal.

445. A view mentioned in C. Williams, *Acts*, 18–19.

446. Moreover, Acts is close to the length of the Gospel, and so such a conclusion would have had to be succinct, hardly a fitting parallel (especially without a resurrection) to the Gospel's passion narrative.

447. E.g., Mattill, "Purpose."

448. Keener, *Acts*, 1:383–401.

449. Admittedly the arguments currently advanced for dating Mark no earlier than 64 C.E. are less than satisfactory, but also unaware of satisfactory arguments to date it earlier I work within the consensus range of dates. Even if the consensus on Mark shifted earlier, other reasons exist for dating Luke after 70. Many arguments for dating the Gospels, however, are admittedly more speculative than our scholarly views that rest on more substantive ancient evidence.

450. Witherington, *Acts*, 807.

451. Cf. self-censorship due to political sensitivities in Cic. *Fam.* 2.4.1; 2.5.1; 2.12.1; 3.1.1; 4.4.2; *Quint. fratr.* 3.8.2; cf. also *Att.* 8.2 (where he burned Atticus's last letter to prevent it from falling into the wrong hands).

452. Litwak, *Echoes*, 197–98 (proposing a model, not echoes); the view is mentioned (but not followed) also by Aune, *Environment*, 118. The proposal that Luke models the conclusion of Acts on the conclusion of 2 Kings (2 Kgs 25:27–30), because the exiled king there epitomizes his people's hope (Davies, "Ending"; cf. Paul as a prisoner in the new Babylon in Schmidt, "Abkehr"), is questionable; Jehoiachin is too tangential a figure. Nevertheless, 2 Kings offers an example of Jewish narrative works that tended to prefer happy endings, in contrast to Greek tragedy; 2 Kings ends on a note of hope in captivity—as an implied promise for the future.

453. Brosend, "Means," 358–62, esp. 362. Some think that the original ending of Mark is missing, because the ending at Mark 16:8 proved a problem to later scribes. But as already noted, abrupt endings were common in antiquity; this ending appeared problematic to later scribes only because subsequent Gospels (at least our extant ones, especially the popular Gospel of Matthew) ended differently, redefining the concept of gospel genre and its appropriate ending.

454. Brosend, "Means," 360–61.

to read the future in view of what Luke does include is probable even if he does not follow Mark, just as the same invitation may be inferred in Mark without knowledge of Mark's models.)

But the question of specific models aside, "open" or unfinished endings were quite common in ancient literature.[455] Some works ended "unsatisfactorily" because their sources did so.[456] Some works ended abruptly because they were never finished.[457] Thucydides's history breaks off at a surprisingly incomplete point (Thucyd. 8.109.1);[458] although the work was preserved in that form, it troubled ancient rhetorical critics.[459] As one classical scholar notes, "Challenging, 'unresolved' endings are a specialty of classical historians, including Herodotus, Thucydides (unfinished), Xenophon (*Hellenica*), and Sallust (in both monographs)."[460]

In general, however, sudden endings also seem to have troubled ancient readers less than they trouble us. Some, for perhaps no particular reason, ended abruptly once the collection (as one might expect), story, or even topic was finished.[461] No less a rhetorician than Dionysius of Halicarnassus ends a rhetorical essay by simply noting that though he would have provided more examples, he does not wish to go on (*Demosth.* 58). Other rhetoricians also ended speeches suddenly (at least in their extant written form).[462] For other writers it was a stylistic habit.[463] Although most speeches included summaries or conclusions, even a speech (at least in its published, extant form) could end suddenly with some stark evidence that seized the hearer's attention.[464]

II. RHETORICAL FUNCTION

Some endings were deliberately "open" rather than unfinished. Narrative suspension could perform a standard rhetorical function in antiquity, leaving some matters open for the future, including in Hellenistic historiography.[465] Writers also could end an account while projecting further events within the narrative world: Homer never narrates Troy's fall in the *Iliad*, ending only with Hector's burial (*Il.* 24). But because Hector was Troy's last defender (emphasized already in 6.403; 22.506–7), this ending certainly implies the tragic fall of Troy.

The open-endedness of Acts may invite the audience to look beyond the closing

---

455. See Plut. *Fame Ath.* 8, *Mor.* 351B; *Fort. Alex.* 2.13, *Mor.* 345B; *Fort. Rom.* 13, *Mor.* 326C; *Uned. R.* 7, *Mor.* 782F; Isoc. *Demon.* 52; Demet. *Style* 5.304; Hdn. 8.8.8; *L.A.B.* (perhaps in this case the original end is missing?); Mark 16:8; see also discussion in Adams, *Genre*, 233–42; esp. Magness, *Sense*.

456. Aune, *Environment*, 118, on Philostratus *Vita Apollonii*.

457. Lucan's *Civil War* ends abruptly (at 10.542–46), possibly because he never finished it (book 10 is one of the shortest books in the *Civil War*). Schiffman, "Scroll," allows this possibility for Qumran's *Temple Scroll*.

458. It may have originally ended with Thucyd. 7.87.6, which sounds like a temporary ending; Thucydides then may have added Thucyd. 8 later, not finishing it (only Thucyd. 8 lacks speeches) because he intended to add another book after the war was resolved.

459. Dion. Hal. *Thuc.* 12 (complaining that Thucydides violates his stated intention in Thucyd. 5.26).

460. Moles, "Time," 113, citing Marincola, "Looking to End." Moles finds in Herodotus the most relevant model, noting the tension between his "unresolvedness" and "multiple closural devices" (citing also Dewald, "Kings"), as in Acts.

461. E.g., Men. Rhet. 1.3, 367.8.

462. Dio Chrys. *Or.* 13 (in 13.37); *Or.* 19 (at 19.5); *Or.* 34 (at 34.53); *Or.* 41 (at 41.14; it may have ended there, since he had made his point, though it lacks any formal summarizing conclusion); *Or.* 70; 71.

463. See Val. Max. 9.15.ext. 2; but also at the conclusions of earlier books, e.g., 1.8.ext. 19; see Wardle, *Valerius Maximus*, 289 (noting that Valerius offers transitions only in his prefaces and otherwise marks a division into books only at Val. Max. 9.15.1).

464. Isaeus *Pyrr.* 80. For brief conclusions, see, e.g., Lysias *Or.* 23.12, §167–23.16, §168.

465. See Marguerat, "Enigma of Closing," 304; idem, "Énigme"; idem, *Histoire*, 333; idem, *Historian*, 215–16.

words of the book,[466] to project the same unstoppable progress of the gospel into the long-range future. That an ancient reader competent in literary and rhetorical conventions could recognize this invitation is clear: John Chrysostom recognized that Acts, following rhetorical conventions, closes here to leave the auditor thirsty for more and to reflect on the message.[467] Acts' incomplete ending may even invite the audience to participate in spreading the gospel;[468] instead of writing an explicit third volume, Luke points to the continuing church as the continuation of his story.[469] Given Luke's Isaian backdrop for "ends of the earth" (1:8; 13:47; Isa 49:6), Acts clearly has not *literally* reached that goal.[470] Paul and Jerusalem's apostles have not reached the "ends of the earth" (1:8), so readers are invited to continue the mission.[471] Something like "open" endings appear earlier in Luke-Acts,[472] and Luke provides some closure by rehearsing persistent themes before his closing, hence pointing to the future "through circularity and parallelism."[473] By focusing on Paul's preaching and not his martyrdom,[474] Luke underlines his theme.

Though genuine, the open-endedness of the book should not be exaggerated. Whereas a biography without the subject's death would be unusual,[475] as would be a romance without a secure conclusion, a historical monograph treating a particular theme need not recount a primary protagonist's end. Paul's martyrdom or release is not Luke's primary concern; in God's providence, the gospel has reached the heart of the empire, which portends well for its future.[476] Acts "ends with a good Greek sentence terminating in an effective rhythmical phrase," an acceptable literary closing for a work in Greek.[477]

Moreover, Luke may wish to end where he does, or close to where he does, partly

466. Dunn, *Acts*, 278; both for carrying on the mission of the apostle to the Gentiles and for the future response of the Jewish people, Marguerat, *Histoire*, 333; idem, *Historian*, 152–54, 230; cf. Magness, *Sense*, 124–25, for Mark. The final scene occurs in a world much closer to that of the members of Luke's audience than did the opening scene, hence opening into their world (Alexander, *Context*, 228–29; idem, "Back to Front"), but with the overall effect of connecting them to the larger narrative of salvation history. See now esp. Troftgruben, "Ending," 187, 233, 243–44, noting both closure and openness and how this combination in epics provides links to a larger narrative of salvation history and continuing witness. (The feature shared with "epic" here is the character of foundation story [cf. Troftgruben's "narrative of beginnings," 236], not epic poetry or the nature of relation to extrinsic reality. Troftgruben's work does not argue regarding Acts' genre [235]; historiography has diverse endings [145].)

467. Chrys. *Hom. Acts* 55 (pointed out by Talbert, *Acts*, 231; also Adams, *Genre*, 231).

468. Rosner, "Progress," 232–33; cf. Willimon, *Acts*, 192; Backhaus, "Hörsaal"; Marguerat, *Historian*, 230; as an invitation to a nonbeliever, Lang, "Self," 173 (cf. Jeremias, *Parables*, 131–32; Goppelt, *Theology*, 1:136 on Luke 15:32). Cf. Schwartz, "Trial Scenes," 131, who contrasts novels' "happily-ever-after" endings, noting that these are inappropriate "if the narrator means to extend the narrative into the world of the implied audience."

469. Cayzer, "Ending." Or, in keeping with my discussion of Acts' focus, Luke points to the continuing *mission* as the continuation of his story.

470. Moles, "Time," 117, citing also the opinion of "Cyril, Theodoret, Chrysostom, and Ambrose" from Just, *Luke*, 114; Martin, *Acts*, 9–10. See also Jipp, *Visitations*, 286; further discussion of the phrase in Keener, *Acts*, 1:702–8, and sources cited there (esp. Pao).

471. Moles, "Time," 118, treating Paul in the closing scene as a model; "in continuing the Christian mission," Luke's audience "themselves will become apostles, 'sent-out ones,' like Jesus himself (Lk. 4:18, 43; 9:48; 10:16; Acts 3:20, etc.), like the twelve," and like Paul. See similarly Jipp, *Visitations*, 286–87.

472. "Open" ends also appear in Luke 22:47–53 (Tannehill, *Luke*, 298) and 24:44–53 (Dunn, *Acts*, 278), though ending a final volume would not be quite the same.

473. Tannehill, *Acts*, 354; see also Jipp, *Visitations*, 281–82, on "*both* elements of narrative closure and openness" (following Troftgruben, *Conclusion*, 144–78).

474. Marguerat, "Énigme" (also suggesting a reversal of expectations, in which Israel rather than Paul is judged in Rome).

475. See Burridge, *Gospels*, 146–47, 179–80. For evidence for open endings in collected (as opposed to individual) biographies, however, see Adams, *Genre*, 238–42 (for death in individual biographies, see 260).

476. Brosend, "Means," 356–57; Witherington, *Acts*, 808–9.

477. Hanson, *Acts*, 256.

to preserve a happy ending. Mark's abrupt ending involves witnesses afraid to speak; Acts ends with the model of continuing proclamation.[478] Acts is not a novel, but Luke was surely well aware of the popularity of happy endings, likely one of the reasons for which novels came to be widely read.[479] Similarly, whereas tragedy colored not only much Greek drama but also historiography[480] (e.g., Tacitus; comedy affected novels rather than historiography), traditional Jewish works, emphasizing a perspective of God's providence, more often preferred happy endings for those who obeyed God (e.g., the Joseph story; Esther; cf. even 2 Kings, for Israel).[481] (Richard Pervo helpfully draws comparisons with "upbeat" endings in various genres.)[482] Most commentators (including myself) think that Paul was probably dead when Luke wrote, but Luke ends on a hopeful note, showing that Paul's gospel continues to spread "unhindered."[483] Foakes-Jackson compared Acts' conclusion to that of 2 Maccabees, "which closes with the great victory of Judas Maccabeus over Nicanor, leaving the hero at the moment of triumph, so soon to be followed by his defeat and death."[484] At the same time, Acts is not triumphalistic; Paul preaches the Lord's kingdom but remains in the current human empire's custody.[485]

Luke is not denying Paul's eventual execution but pointing to the potential for legal vindication within the Roman system. Political considerations led to Jesus's execution (without preventing divine vindication), but Paul's articulate defense showed the possibility of different, more just outcomes, especially in hearings away from the political complications of pre-70 Judea. If Nero executed Paul and others, Luke believes that his tyranny was exceptional, not the norm for the Roman system. As Pheme Perkins points out, Acts ends not with Paul's death but with his preaching (Acts 28:23–31); Luke's focus is not biography but the gospel's spread.[486] Although Luke is aware of further events, his interest is not Paul's eventual trial (27:24) but the vindication of the mission to the Gentiles (28:28).[487] This mission has now extended to the very

478. Moles, "Time," 115, underlines this contrast.

479. See, e.g., Char. *Chaer.* 8 (ending happily for everyone involved). Repath, "*Leucippe*," argues that Achilles Tatius diverges from the standard convention of novels ending happily.

480. For the contrast, see Troftgruben, "Ending," 145, 232. Moles, "Time," 115, critiques those who view Luke's conclusion as tragic, arguing that they neglect 28:30–31.

481. Acts develops Luke's Gospel more fully than Joshua develops Deuteronomy, but might be compared with Joshua in some respects (though the movement's expansion in Acts is antithetical to conquest; see comment on Acts 16:9). As in the early narratives of Acts (esp. chs. 4–6), Israel faced various internal and external challenges in Joshua; although the work is clearly unfinished, Joshua focuses on positive summaries. Platonists mistrusted both tragedies and comedies, because they nurtured unhealthy emotions (Proclus *Poet.* 5, K42.12–17; K50.12–15).

482. Pervo, *Acts*, 689–90, 695–96, citing novels, biblical texts, epics, and Greco-Roman historiography, including 2 Kgs 25 (see discussion below) and, most beneficially, 2 Macc 15.

483. Spencer, *Acts*, 241; Aune, *Environment*, 118; see further, for aesthetic and other considerations, Trompf, "Death of Paul."

484. Foakes-Jackson, *Acts*, 236. On the death of Judas, see 1 Macc 9:18–22; for 2 Maccabees' positive ending, see 2 Macc 15:35–37 (followed by a literary conclusion in 15:38–39). Cf. Homer's *Iliad*, probably the most commonly read book of Greek antiquity; *Il.* 24 closes before Achilles's death, but announcements have foreshadowed it (21.110; 23.80–81); likewise the fall of Troy (12.15). Holloway, "Truths," shows that later church historians like Eusebius (423–25) and Theodoret of Cyr (426–29), as well as earlier Jewish sources like 2 Chronicles (429–30) and 2 Maccabees (430–32), like Luke, chose to end before particularly unpleasant events.

485. Contrast the *Aeneid*, the conclusion of which reinforces Augustan imperial ideology (even if in limited form; cf. the argument of Nickbackht, "*Aemulatio*").

486. Perkins, *Reading*, 258. Many who think that Acts implies Paul's execution recognize that Luke ends where he does because he has achieved his objective (which is not Paul's death) fully by Acts 28:30–31 (e.g., Conzelmann, *Acts*, 228; Spencer, *Acts*, 241; Johnson, *Acts*, 475).

487. Johnson, *Acts*, 476 (though I believe that he errs concerning the finality of rejection of the Jewish mission).

heart of the empire.[488] (Luke's audience need not be in Rome to appreciate the importance of the mission climaxing there; they need only be in the Roman Empire.)

So far I have written on the assumption that Paul was dead when Luke wrote. I think this view (and a post-70 C.E. dating for Luke-Acts) is likelier than not, but (unless we can date Mark with absolute certainty) it is not possible to be dogmatic on this point. Whether or not Luke writes after Paul is already dead, however, internal evidence within Luke's work could point to the expectation of his eventual martyrdom, an expectation that many commentators suggest. Before turning to whether Acts leads us to expect Paul's immediate death or release, we must digress to consider the common proposal of a two-year limit to cases.

III. A TWO-YEAR LIMIT?

Something apparently happened at the end of the two years (28:30); if after that point Paul merely continued what he was already doing in custody in 28:30–31, there is little reason for Luke to specify this limit.[489] Thus, at the end of two years, Paul could have been released, executed, or banished to an island.[490] Does Luke expect the audience to infer from Paul's two years of favor in custody (28:30) that he was released at the end of this time? The legal data is ambiguous enough to suggest that ancient readers, like modern ones, could not have assumed that such a release was demanded, but the data also suggests that given other cues in the narrative, Paul was not likely held indefinitely (and thus Luke's "two years" may point to the limit in Paul's own case).

Luke has other reasons to mention the two years (undoubtedly a round figure). Paul spent two years in Ephesus (19:10; cf. three years, i.e., parts of three different years, in 20:31), and Luke might positively evoke this successful period in Paul's ministry for his ministry while he was detained in Rome.[491] His two years in Caesarea (24:27) mirror this period of captivity even more closely,[492] suggesting a total of four rounded years (at least a period of more than two and probably three full years altogether). Two years was also a fairly common span of time specified in rental agreements (e.g., P.Mich. 9.563.19; see μισθώματι in Acts 28:30).[493]

Nevertheless, readers might well infer something about Paul's case from the duration of his detention in Rome. Ancient writers generally agreed that two years was a long time for detention (Philo *Flacc.* 128), but contrary to many commentators' assertions,[494] such ancient opinions do not amount to a legal limit to the period of detention.[495]

Some scholars cite evidence that appeals to Caesar had to be settled (and hence both sides had to appear before the court) within eighteen months; if only one side was present, the case might go in its favor.[496] This view rests especially on arguments of

488. Filson, "Journey Motif," 76–77, even argues that Luke wanted to emphasize that Paul, rather than Peter (who arrived later), was the Roman church's "apostolic sponsor" and hence his gospel is paramount there. This approach probably reads second-century church politics into a first-century source, however.

489. Except on the early-date view that Luke finished Acts at that time.

490. On banishment to an island as a frequent penalty, see, e.g., Plut. *Exile* 12, *Mor.* 604B; Pliny *Ep.* 3.9.34; 6.22.5; Tac. *Ann.* 1.3, 53; 3.68–69; Rev 1:9; further comment on Acts 18:2. For its role as a political strategy under Augustus, see Drogula, "Controlling Travel."

491. Chrys. *Hom. Acts* 55 suggests two years in Asia, three in Corinth, and two in Rome.

492. There Paul remained captive because he was a political problem, here perhaps because of bureaucracy, which may impinge on Paul's freedom but not so much that it prevents Luke from leaving the tone positive.

493. Mealand, "Close and Vocabulary," 588–89, 595; Witherington, *Acts*, 813.

494. Usually citing also Pliny *Ep.* 10.56.4 (a grace period for different reasons) and 10.57.2, which are even less relevant; see Fitzmyer, *Acts*, 796–97; cautiously, Bruce, *Acts¹*, 480.

495. With, e.g., Johnson, *Acts*, 473; Schnabel, *Acts*, 1076.

496. Bruce, *Commentary*, 534–35; Conzelmann, *Acts*, 240–41 (citing *BGU* 628), but cf. p. 228.

William Ramsay, who regarded eighteen months as the legal equivalent of two years,[497] concerning limits for cases in what he regarded as third-century C.E. sources.[498] In a noncapital case, the limit was six months for an appeal within Italy and "nine months if from the provinces";[499] in a capital case, the periods "were twelve and eighteen months respectively."[500] He argues that such limits stemmed from Claudius's acquittal of those long detained whose accusers failed to show up;[501] the problem is that his earlier, second-century source (Suet. *Claud.* 15) regards this acquittal as more unusual than his later source (Dio Cass. 60.28.6). Cadbury made the most widely cited case for a concrete "statute of limitations,"[502] but Sherwin-White later refuted it.[503]

Although such long delays were never desirable, automatic release for a two-year delay is not attested as an established law before 529 C.E.[504] Whatever the ideal, courts were congested, and people could be in prison longer than two years.[505]

IV. OTHER POSSIBILITIES OF RELEASE

Still, release need not be automatic in order for it to be granted. If accusers did not appear after two years, it is likely that Paul would be released;[506] the case could be decided against them or simply dropped (see, at some length, comment on Acts 24:19). Luke indicates that Paul's opponents did not get word to Rome before him (Acts 28:21) and offers no indication that they reached there in the two years of 28:30; given Festus's letter (25:26–27; 26:31–32), they may well have abandoned a hopeless case (see comment on Acts 28:21).

In this period historically, when Nero was under Seneca's influence (and Nero intervened little in the legal process),[507] laws would probably decide the outcome, and especially if Paul or his allies in Rome knew of the relation between Seneca and Gallio, Paul could have even appealed to Gallio's pronouncement as one of his favorable precedents (18:14–15). Before 62 C.E., Nero avoided involvement with cases, in deliberate contrast to his predecessor's policy (Tac. *Ann.* 13.4.2). Although this disinterest could have occasioned more delays,[508] it more likely simply allowed his authorized subordinates to decide the cases without him. In the year 62, by interceding with Poppaea, Josephus secured the release of some Jewish prisoners sent to Nero's court by Felix (*Life* 16).

Paul would be quite vulnerable to Jewish accusations in 64 C.E., and tradition does in fact point to his arrest during the persecution of Christians that began then (Tac.

---

497. Ramsay, *Teaching*, 352.

498. Admitting his lack of expertise, he was following the opinion of Cambridge scholar J. S. Reid.

499. The additional three months might factor in winter delays in travel, but the intervening length was doubled for capital charges.

500. Ramsay, *Teaching*, 365.

501. Ibid., 366.

502. Cadbury, "Law and Trial," 319–26. Robinson, *Criminal Law*, 21, notes that limits to how long an offense was prosecutable started under Augustus and varied by offense (e.g., five years for adultery but no limit for parricide); the general rule of twenty years was introduced much later under Diocletian.

503. Sherwin-White, *Society*, 108–19 (also refuting others in addition to Cadbury). This is not to deny that "old" crimes might invite leniency or dismissal in some cases; see below.

504. Barrett, *Acts*, 1251–52; Bruce, *Acts*³, 541–42; Schnabel, *Acts*, 1076; cf. already Abbott, *Acts*, 262.

505. Rapske, *Custody*, 322–23. Already in Claudius's era, court cases were innumerable, and this problem would hardly have decreased under Nero (Talbert, *Acts*, 230, citing Dio Cass. 60.28.6 on Claudius's era).

506. With, e.g., Witherington, *Acts*, 792. Barrett, *Acts*, 1251–52, thinks it possible that the "two years" means that the case was dropped, though he follows Sherwin-White in finding Cadbury's particular defense of this position inadequate; see also Omerzu, "Schweigen," 148–49. Sherwin-White, *Society*, 119, allows that Paul may have "secured a merely casual release," though he thinks this unclear from Acts.

507. Though Nero had some concern with law; Suet. *Nero* 15.1.

508. Jeffers, *World*, 170.

Ann. 15.44).[509] But it is difficult to date Luke's account of Paul's detention in Rome (perhaps beginning in 60) so late,[510] and four years would have been unusually long for a single detention in one place,[511] especially given Paul's apparent enjoyment of favor in our narrative.[512] Thus a release with subsequent rearrest (made easier by Paul's earlier detention, which clarified his status in the movement) seems plausible.

Admittedly, cases for the emperor's court could be backlogged (with or without Nero's personal interest in the cases), and Paul's case would hardly warrant priority from a Roman perspective.[513] But even given these considerations, such a long delay seems unusual and improbable.[514] Paul's case was not a complicated one to decide if no accusers arrived within a reasonable period of time. Moreover, Greeks and Romans alike disliked punishments long after the crimes were supposed to have been committed;[515] some kinds of actions had to be finished within a year, and so it was not good to delay bringing a suit or for magistrates to delay plaintiffs.[516] If delays went too long, a prisoner could use a scribe to file a petition for his hearing or his release; though this probably would not have worked in Rome and Paul did not risk it in Caesarea (where it could have offended Felix, whose justice was less predictable than that of Festus), the fact that it was sometimes done illustrates that officials were not unmindful of the impropriety of excessive delays.[517]

The system also would not lose track of its prisoners; careful and extensive records were kept, and they were reviewed regularly.[518] Though prisoners sometimes had no advance warning of when their case would come up, they were usually warned to have it ready.[519] (Although our present book of Acts is not a mere collection of legal precedents for use at Paul's trial, as some earlier scholars claimed, its many precedents may suggest that Luke or his sources deliberately collected such precedents for such an earlier occasion.)

Moreover, on the assumption here that Luke writes after Paul's death, would Luke end with two years' detention when the two years were followed by neither execution nor release but only *another* two years' detention (until Nero's persecution began)? As argued below, both tradition and the trajectory of Luke's narrative suggest Paul's eventual release—before his eventual martyrdom.

509. Some suggest that Eusebius dates Paul's execution even later, to 67, but where Eusebius's evidence is most clear is simply that Paul suffered under Nero (*H.E.* 2.25), who reigned from 54 to 68.

510. The debated options concerning the close of Felix's tenure in Judea range earlier, rather than later, than 60 C.E.; see comment on Acts 24:27. To dismiss the involvement of Felix, and hence to assume the invention of his and Festus's participation in the detailed "we" narrative, runs against the evidence surveyed above and is far less probable than a release and rearrest.

511. Periodically it was helpful to clear the jails of those thought probably innocent (Rapske, *Custody*, 326–28; cf. Jeffers, *World*, 171). Though Caesar claimed that long imprisonment was a harsher punishment than death (Cic. *Cat.* 4.4.7), scholars often argue that detention was not normally intended as a punishment (Aune, *Revelation*, 166; Hemer, *Letters*, 68; Caird, *Revelation*, 35), and it does not seem to be meant as such in Paul's case.

512. With, e.g., Kelly, *Pastoral Epistles*, 9; cf. Hemer, *Acts in History*, 175n28.

513. Le Cornu, *Acts*, 1526, suggests that some less important cases could even be dropped to reduce the backlog.

514. With others, including Bruce, *Commentary*, 535.

515. Cf. something like a statute of limitations in Lysias *Or.* 7.17, §109; Aeschines *Tim.* 39; Hermog. *Issues* 44.10–12 (not a statute of limitations). After long delays, some governors were also reluctant to enforce a sentence (Pliny *Ep.* 10.31.3); even Trajan was reluctant if the men were elderly, but only if the case dated back more than ten years (10.33.2); cf. those who claimed not to have been Christians for many years (10.96). Trajan ruled against making a man repay a forbidden grant, since twenty years had passed (10.110–11).

516. Metzger, *Outline*, 50.

517. See the information in Rapske, *Custody*, 326–28.

518. See esp. the detailed information in ibid., 250.

519. Ibid., 329.

v. Eventual Execution?

Most scholars believe that "two years" suggests that *something* happened at the end of that period, release or death. To which of these two alternatives does Luke's narrative more readily point, from a literary perspective? Here again commentators are divided. Some even suggest that perhaps the Roman church, which is not mentioned after Acts 28:15, did not prove supportive[520] (but given Luke's tight focus on the relationship between Israel and the Gentile mission in 28:17–28, this suggestion constitutes a classic argument from silence).

Many scholars think that the narrative points to Paul's eventual execution, a position that makes good sense.[521] Obviously, if the trial was unsuccessful and Luke is reporting positive legal precedents or focusing on the gospel's spread or simply wishes to end happily, he will want to end before narrating the trial.[522] Given his apologetic emphasis, one might have expected Luke to report a favorable verdict if one occurred.[523] But what if Paul was rearrested, tried, and executed within two or three years, as tradition suggests?[524] Narrating a temporary release might still serve Luke's purpose, but not if it took Paul away from Rome for a time, when Luke's objective was seeing Paul's gospel to Rome.

Scholars offer specific textual evidence for foreshadowings of Paul's martyrdom, but these suggestions are of varying weight: Luke's telling of the story does not suggest a return to Ephesus (20:25; cf. 20:29, 38), but the "imprisonment" that Paul faces (20:23) has been fulfilled for up to four years by the time Luke's narrative leaves off; the prediction that Jewish people would bind him and hand him over to the Gentiles (21:11) is fulfilled already in 21:30–33.[525] Paul's willingness to die fits Luke's model of discipleship (20:24; 21:13; cf. Luke 9:23; 11:49), but for all the suspense that his willingness offers, Luke offers no specific prediction of his death (in stark contrast to Jesus's passion predictions, e.g., Luke 9:22; 20:15). The last narrated plots against Paul's life that could parallel those against Jesus were in Acts 23:12–15 and 25:3—in Judea, far from Paul's spiritually fruitful custody in Rome (28:30–31). The promise that he would appear before Caesar (27:24) does not specify the outcome.[526]

Some scholars object that Roman officials earlier in Acts prefer "political expediency" to justice;[527] although this was true in the case of Pilate judging Jesus, it must be modified somewhat for Paul the Roman citizen. Luke provides several precedents where Roman officials protect Paul from Jewish hostility (18:14–15); even where they procrastinate (24:27) or consider following expediency (25:9), they do not hand Paul over to his accusers (25:4, 16), the most expedient course politically. Festus allows Paul's irregular appeal to Rome, and Luke suggests an official consensus on his innocence (26:31–32); the narrative suggests that, once removed from the

---

520. Barrett, *Acts*, 1250. Contrast the reception described by Luke in Acts 28:15.

521. E.g., Conzelmann, *Acts*, 228; Jewett, *Chronology*, 45; Tannehill, *Acts*, 353; Faw, *Acts*, 296; Omerzu, "Angeklagter," 136–37; Talbert, *Acts*, 231. Barrett, *Acts*, 1249, remains uncertain what happens after two years, but suggests that it might be omitted because it was unedifying.

522. Trompf, "Death of Paul"; Aune, *Environment*, 118; Spencer, *Acts*, 241; Dunn, *Acts*, 343 (who also notes [344, 346] that with Paul's vindication in Acts 28:1–7, Luke's audience need not await Caesar's verdict). Death without a resurrection does not provide a helpful parallel to Luke 23–24.

523. Barrett, *Acts*, 1252 (tentatively).

524. Witherington, *Acts*, 815–16n132.

525. With, e.g., Bammel, "Activity," 363n25.

526. Or that it would occur at the end of the two years, although, all other factors being equal, this inference seems the most obvious one (i.e., that it occurs on this visit to Rome preceded by the storm and not on another). Luke could have telescoped historically discrete events, but as in the case of Acts 20:25, this is not the most probable way to read the text unless other evidence invites this reading.

527. Tannehill, *Acts*, 355.

weight of excessive political considerations, Paul can expect better treatment from Roman justice. Historically, if the chief priests sent a delegation to Nero requesting Paul's execution, they might have obtained what they wished;[528] but travel to Rome demanded a significant investment of time, and most of our examples of successful delegations concerned major political issues in Judea. Luke's own focus on Paul's importance aside, would Paul have been worth such a delegation to them historically?[529] Normally when Josephus reports Judean delegations, they involve matters directly affecting the status of their people or the leaders.[530]

vi. Eventual Release?

Still, even if we find evidence pointing to Paul's eventual martyrdom (and at least 20:25 might point this way),[531] some commentators too easily confuse that expectation with the assumption that it is implied for the end of the two-year period in 28:30–31—a direction in which Luke's narrative probably does *not* point. If Luke writes after Paul's martyrdom, it is reasonable that he need not report what his audience can take for granted,[532] but it also need not follow that the execution happened immediately after the close of his narrative.

Many scholars believe that Luke's narrative points to "a positive outcome for Paul" after the specified two years.[533] Although not certain, this is probable for several reasons. First, as Luke's narrative closes, Paul is evangelizing without restriction under the very nose of Rome's elite Praetorian Guard, a matter that Luke deliberately emphasizes (28:16, 23, 30–31; cf. Phil 1:13; 4:22). Second, at the last explicit mention of the issue, no accusers have come forward to prosecute the case, and so Paul, as the appellant, is the only voice in the case (and retains, or has regained a copy of, presumably favorable documentation from Festus; Acts 25:25; 26:31–32). "Two years" suggests that no one is pressing for his urgent prosecution, and so far, delays in his case have always thwarted his enemies rather than helped them. Third, Luke's narratives render dubious the likelihood that the Judean authorities would follow the case to Rome (especially if assassination seemed a securer way to punish him than Roman condemnation, 25:3). Luke is emphatic that they could not prove their accusations (24:13; 25:7) and suggests that they and the government both recognize this fact (25:10).[534] Meanwhile,

528. McKechnie, "Embassies," noting a number of successful Judean delegations in Josephus.

529. Though they do bring the case up early with Festus, this could be partly because Paul was one of the few prisoners with whom they had not already succeeded (or, perhaps in some cases, decisively failed) under Felix.

530. They might get an opponent beheaded (e.g., Jos. *War* 2.246), but this was over a conflict with the Samaritans on which Rome would pronounce judgment.

531. The prediction need not point this way, but it does put Luke's details in tension with the thesis that Paul visited Ephesus after his release (a thesis that could provide a way to chronologically harmonize Acts with the tradition in the Pastorals). Luke may have deliberately heightened pathos, pointing to the execution and omitting consideration of a later journey irrelevant to his story. (Cf. Chariton's false cues that create suspense before his typically happy ending [Doulamis, "Ends Well"]; for concluding narratives modifying expectations generated by earlier narratives, cf. also Peirano, "Hellenized Romans.") Nevertheless, by itself the evidence of Acts 20:25 would lend more support against a later visit to Ephesus than in its favor. Alternatively, Paul's being unable to enter Ephesus (see comment on Acts 20:16) might suggest his leaving Timothy there without Paul entering himself (1 Tim 1:3), but this suggestion is speculative.

532. Karris, *Invitation*, 232 (comparing biographic movies today, which need not end with a subject's death).

533. Bammel, "Activity," 363; Rapske, *Custody*, 191; Longenecker, *Acts*, 368; Witherington, *Acts*, 618–20; Murphy-O'Connor, *Paul*, 218; Reicke, *Era*, 220 (noting Nero's release of other Jewish prisoners in 62 c.e.); Schnabel, *Acts*, 1076; very tentatively, Walaskay, *Acts*, 246; Arrington, *Acts*, 271–72.

534. Cf. Marshall, *Acts*, 426: "It is hard to see how Paul could have been condemned to death on the evidence offered in Acts" (though Marshall also thinks that Luke recognizes Paul's impending martyrdom).

according to Luke's perspective, Roman Jewish leaders were not hostile to Paul or all of one mind (28:21).[535]

Fourth, Paul's treatment by Festus, Julius, and those who approved his light custody in Rome points toward a positive resolution of his case and his release.[536] His custody is exceptionally light, allowing unhindered access and his own rented quarters. As Rapske puts it in light of such factors, "the evidence against Paul is not only weak, inconsistent and hence false from the Lukan perspective but apparently from the perspective of Roman officialdom as well."[537] Fifth, although Jesus was executed within the narrative, Luke emphasizes that both Jesus's and Paul's judges thought them innocent;[538] Paul, unlike Jesus, has escaped Judea, where there were political incentives to condemn Paul.[539] Sixth, from the standpoint of the Roman government before 64 C.E., Paul was politically and legally inconsequential unless he had enemies powerful enough to generate problems for him in Rome. Finally, Paul's letters probably written from Rome suggest his own expectation that it was more likely than not that he would be released (see comment below on Phil 1:24–26; Phlm 22).

VII. RELEASE, THEN EXECUTION

Luke need not explicitly report the acquittal or release because, for all Luke's apologetic interest, Paul's preaching in Rome is the narrative's appropriate climax.[540] If Paul proceeded briefly to Spain afterward (cf. Rom 15:24, 28; *1 Clem.* 5.7), this journey would be anticlimactic from the standpoint of Luke's purpose (though at the "ends of the earth"; see comment on Acts 1:8).[541] If he returned (then or later) to the East to strengthen older churches such as those in Ephesus (as the Pastorals could suggest), this mission would be even more anticlimactic (cf. the Ephesian elders in Acts 20:38). If matters suddenly turned for the worse and Paul was executed soon after his release, Luke has little reason to muddy up his closing portrait by explaining how this happened. His audience presumably knew that Paul was ultimately martyred under Nero; a brief release would make little difference in the basic account.

If Luke writes after Paul's martyrdom but suggests his release beforehand, we can account for both suggested trajectories of data in Acts;[542] scholarly arguments for both positions, then, could be correct. As noted below, this solution also makes the best sense of early Christian traditions. Luke may write in light of his audience's knowledge that Paul was released before his martyrdom.[543]

Other evidence supports this reading of the literary evidence. Tradition suggests that Paul was in fact released, then rearrested and martyred on his second visit to

---

535. See commentary at these verses; also, e.g., Ramsay, *Teaching*, 353–58.

536. With, e.g., ibid., 359–61, 367; Witherington, *Acts*, 618.

537. Rapske, *Custody*, 191.

538. Ramsay, *Teaching*, 361, noting the parallel.

539. One might expect Luke to narrate Paul's death to correspond to that of Jesus, but if Luke writes after Paul's decease, he disappoints our expectation whether Paul was executed at this time or later.

540. So also Ramsay, *Teaching*, 369, as well as the many scholars who give the same reason for Luke's not recounting Paul's martyrdom.

541. Perhaps also from Luke's narratorial vantage point, since Luke probably did not know enough Latin to venture farther west himself.

542. Scholars sometimes note both apparent trajectories (e.g., Marshall, *Acts*, 425–26).

543. Otherwise, if he sought to "surprise" the members of his audience with a happy ending, he would certainly surprise them, but he might confuse them as well—as much as he has confused modern scholars trying to determine where his evidence points! It is not impossible that such information is irrelevant to his purpose, and hence Luke leaves unanswered the tension between his positive ending and their knowledge of Paul's eventual martyrdom; but it seems likelier than not that at least the center of Luke's ideal audience had some more information.

Rome (Euseb. *H.E.* 2.22.1–7; probably implied earlier in *1 Clem.* 5.5–7).[544] If *1 Clem.* 5.7 (which almost certainly includes Paul's voyage to Spain) does not imply Paul's release yet reports accurate tradition,[545] Luke would have to have omitted a major period in Paul's life after the collection for Jerusalem (cf. Rom 15:24–28). For Luke to omit such a major portion of Paul's ministry before the close of Luke's narrative (and in what seems to be continuous "we" material) contrasts starkly with Luke's methodology elsewhere; by contrast, no one would expect Luke to recount events that occurred after the close of his narrative. Likewise, whether or not one accepts some level of Pauline authorship in the Pastorals, even some of those who believe that the Pastorals are wholly pseudepigraphic allow that they reflect genuine tradition about Paul's ministry in the East after his release.[546]

Historically, if Paul's "captivity epistles" come from a period of detention in Rome,[547] it is significant that Paul was cautiously optimistic about his release (Phil 1:19, 25) and anticipated seeing his friends in the East again (1:25–26; 2:24; Phlm 22).[548] If Paul's letters suggest as much reason for optimism as Luke's own account independently suggests, is it not more probable that the optimism was justified than that it was not? His apparent plan to return to western Asia Minor (Phlm 22) and, if possible, Macedonia (Phil 1:27) is compatible with the later itinerary implied in the Pastorals tradition (if in fact he was released).[549]

If Paul was released, his rearrest is plausible or even probable: hundreds or even thousands of Christians were martyred, and Paul's high visibility (especially given his first arrest) would have made him a particular target.[550] (Those previously charged on any grounds were more easily prosecuted on subsequent occasions; see, for example, Isaeus *Cleon.* 35; comment on Acts 24:5.) If two different Roman detentions (the first under house arrest, the second a genuine imprisonment) seem to stretch unduly the bounds of plausibility (the simplicity of Occam's razor) for some readers, we should recall how central Rome was; the saying that all roads lead to Rome was not without foundation. Many of Paul's friends ended up there (Rom 16:3–15),

544. Kelly, *Pastoral Epistles*, 10; R. Williams, *Acts*, 170–71; Witherington, *Acts*, 792; Peterson, *Acts*, 721; Schnabel, *Missionary*, 116–17; at length, see Lightfoot, *Acts*, 338–51; earlier, Chrys. *Hom. Acts* 55 (Martin, *Acts*, 318–19). Koester, *Paul and World*, 78, offers a plausible argument for Paul's martyrdom in Philippi after ministry in the East, dating the tradition of his final Roman imprisonment no earlier than *Acts of Paul*. Koester could be correct, but *1 Clem.* 5.5–7 *does* sound (*pace* Koester) as though Paul ended in the West, before the emperor; *1 Clement* has a pro-Rome bias, but it is early. Schnabel, *Missionary*, 117, doubts that *1 Clem.* 5 depends merely on Rom 15:24, since it speaks of the "limits of the west" rather than Spain.

545. Later the Muratorian Canon, lines 35–39, adds that Paul went from Spain to Rome (Kelly, *Pastoral Epistles*, 10; Schnabel, *Missionary*, 117). Talbert, *Acts*, 231, notes also *Acts Pet.* 3.1 and *Acts of Xanthippe, Polyxena, and Rebecca* but suggests that all these references reflect an inference from Rom 15:24, 28. The possibility of an inference may be increased by later Christians' probable reluctance to think that an inspired apostle's plans failed (already problematic to the Corinthians, though it should have been more obvious to Paul's later readers; cf. 2 Cor 1:17–24).

546. Koester, "Ephesos in Literature," 124–25 (though, conversely, uncertain about the widely attested tradition that Paul was martyred in Rome); idem, *Paul and World*, 77–78.

547. With many (e.g., Barth, *Ephesians*, 1:3; Dodd, *New Testament Studies*, 99; Nock, *Paul*, 221; Knox, *Gentiles*, 179; Reicke, "Caesarea"; Bruce, *Epistles*, 32–33, 193–96; Fee, *Philippians*, 34–37; Bence, *Acts*, 248–49), though many others demur; see further Keener, *Acts*, 4:3723n89.

548. With Kelly, *Pastoral Epistles*, 9; Longenecker, *Acts*, 368; Horton, *Acts*, 410. The language of "hope" normally suggests a positive expectation. The Pastorals and the traditions of Paul's martyrdom could both be read in light of the church's growing martyrology after Paul, in contrast to Paul's expectation of freedom.

549. Such words in Philemon and Philippians fit less easily with Paul's plans to evangelize Spain (Rom 15:24, 28); perhaps he simply lacks reason to mention those plans in these letters, or perhaps he abandoned them for logistical reasons.

550. Jeffers, *World*, 170, suggests that Nero, who avoided hearing cases earlier, may have tried cases of Christians from 64 C.E. forward.

and Paul himself desired to visit there (1:10–13; 15:22–29), so that he could have returned voluntarily.[551] Less likely, if Paul was arrested elsewhere, he might have been taken to Rome (though it is not clear that Nero's persecution extended beyond Rome,[552] an exception might be made for a prominent leader who had already been charged once).[553]

VIII. PAUL'S LATER MOVEMENTS?

Scholars diverge widely in their estimates of historical tradition in the Pastorals, but many do accept some tradition here, and these sources constitute at least some of our concrete ancient external evidence. Following is a summary of Paul's movements implied in the Pastorals. As noted at Acts 20:25, it is difficult to account for many of these movements within the narrative of Acts, which is why many scholars have preferred to view them as occurring after that narrative.[554]

Titus 1:5	Paul left Titus in Crete (in Acts 27:8?).*
1 Tim 1:3	Paul left Timothy in or near Ephesus (despite Acts 20:25) and told him to stay there.
1 Tim 1:3	Then Paul went on to Macedonia.
Titus 3:12	Having passed west of Macedonia, Paul was in Nicopolis with Tychichus and urged Titus to come to him there before winter.
1 Tim 3:14	Paul hoped to return to Asia.
2 Tim 4:13, 20	Paul then returned to Asia, leaving Trophimus in Miletus and Erastus in Corinth (2 Tim 4:20); he also passed Troas (4:13).
2 Tim 1:8, 16; 2:9; 4:16–17	He was in Rome again as a prisoner.
2 Tim 4:11	Luke was with him there (cf. Acts 28:16).
2 Tim 4:11, 21	Paul wanted Timothy to bring Mark with him and come to him before winter.
2 Tim 4:12	Paul had sent Tychichus (who had probably remained with Paul since Nicopolis) to Ephesus, where Timothy probably still remained (cf. 2 Tim 1:18; compare also 1 Tim 1:20 with 2 Tim 2:17).
Titus 3:12; 2 Tim 4:10	After Crete, Titus rejoined Paul, probably in Nicopolis as invited (Titus 3:12), and then went north to Dalmatia (2 Tim 4:10).

*Keeping in mind that Acts never names Titus, for whatever reason.

Apart from a Pauline tradition, it is fairly difficult to account for the complexity of these movements, their degree of internal consistency, and the record of so many details. Pseudepigraphers could include details irrelevant to their point for the purpose of prosopopoeia (writing speeches "in character"), but rarely would they include so many. Documents that presuppose so much "history" normally depended on a substantial body of traditions (even if they were mostly mythological and legendary traditions portraying centuries past, as in Homer or Ovid). The Pastorals at the least reflect some traditions of Paul's movements, but some can be reconciled with Acts

551. The voluntary submission of Polycarp and Ignatius to arrest (once discovered) might be rooted in earlier models.

552. See, e.g., Goppelt, "Existence," 194.

553. The same limitation of the pogrom to Rome might invite anyone wishing to try him to do so in Rome; his citizenship might have led to the same destination on appeal.

554. If the Pastorals are pseudepigraphic, as most think (e.g., Scott, *Pastoral Epistles*, xvi–xxiii; Zmijewski, "Pastoralbriefe"; Maloney, "Authorship"; Cook, "Fragments"; Rogers, "Pastoral Epistles"; Dunn, *Jesus and Spirit*, 347–50), some traditions that they reflect may be fitted into Acts without concern for the others. But if they are Pauline by an amanuensis (as a minority of scholars think, e.g., Kelly, *Pastoral Epistles*, 3–33; Fee, *Timothy*, xx; Ellis, "Authorship"; McRay, "Authorship"; Spencer, *Timothy*, 2–10) or even include substantial traditions edited by a close disciple of Paul (a common mediating position, including by some who classify them as pseudepigraphic), we must make more room for them. When comparing diverging sources that probably provide some historical information, it is methodologically more comprehensive to see if both can be accommodated somehow unless one or both sources can be completely dismissed out of hand.

only with difficulty unless they belong to a period after Paul's release.[555] If even some of these traditions are reliable, we may have additional support for Paul's release before his rearrest.[556]

One could argue that Luke invented Paul's capture in Jerusalem, and substitute the itinerary of the Pastorals (which omit the journey to Jerusalem). But Paul clearly did plan to go to Jerusalem before Rome and anticipated possible trouble there (Rom 15:24–25, 31), and so Acts' itinerary is likely. The Pastorals may also imply that Paul was in Rome earlier, then visited Ephesus before returning to Rome (2 Tim 1:16–18, if related to Phlm 10).[557]

Later tradition reports the deaths of Peter and Paul (Peter's martyrdom is reported as early as *1 Clem.* 5.4, and Paul's is suggested in 5.6). Finegan surveys some of the later evidence.[558] Tertullian implies (by comparison with John the Baptist), and *Acts of Paul* states, that Paul was beheaded;[559] this basic claim fits the claim of Paul's Roman citizenship in Acts (which I have taken to be accurate; see discussion at Acts 16:37).[560] One Roman presbyter toward the beginning of the third century seems to imply that the "trophies" (from the context, these were tombs or memorials) of Peter and Paul were at the Vatican and the Ostian Way, respectively (Euseb. *H.E.* 2.25.7).[561] Sulpicius Severus (363–420 c.e.) claims that many Christians under Nero were crucified or burned alive and that Paul was beheaded and Peter crucified.[562] His contemporary Jerome reports that both apostles died on the same day in Nero's fourteenth year (67/68 c.e.), but this tradition seems more open to question.[563] Finegan thinks that Peter was martyred about 64–65, and Paul in 67.[564] Paul's martyrdom could also be in 64; we do not know that Nero's persecution lasted over a period of years. But even if it was in 64, it seems unlikely that Luke's detention, which is depicted as having lasted for at least three years until, at the latest, 62, led directly to it (see discussion below).

b. Ministry in Custody (28:30–31)

Paul's ministry in custody repeats various emphases that run throughout Acts. As at Caesarea, Paul is free to have visitors (Acts 24:23; 28:17–28); this makes sense of his continuing bonds with visitors in his letters at this time (Phil 2:19, 25, 30; 4:18; Col 4:7–14; cf. 2 Tim 1:16–17).[565] Paul's welcoming his visitors suggests hospitality

555. The problem then is apparent doublets with material earlier from Paul's ministry, but most such "doublets" contain the sort of details most likely to recur (see the table in the excursus "Acts and the Pastorals" at Acts 20:25 [Keener, *Acts*, 3:3024–25]).

556. Clark, *Acts*, 390, makes the second imprisonment hinge on the genuineness of the Pastorals (and is uncertain about their genuineness). But the traditions in the Pastorals (whether they are attributed directly to Paul or not) are one argument among several, and not the only argument, for this position. Marshall, *Pastoral Epistles*, 68–71, who does not ultimately think Paul the direct author of the Pastorals (though the material is Pauline), rejects arguments that a second imprisonment is implausible, noting that a second imprisonment simply stems from our data (including the data in the Pastorals).

557. The sequence seems to be Rome, then Ephesus, but it is possible that he thinks of service in Ephesus before Rome (the sequence can be read this way if the other evidence requires it).

558. Finegan, *Apostles*, 22–25. For traditions on Paul's martyrdom, see briefly Talbert, *Acts*, 231–32 (citing Euseb. *H.E.* 2.22.1–2; 2.25.5–8; *Acts Paul* 10; *Acts Pet.* 3.1; Tert. *Praescr.* 36).

559. Finegan, *Apostles*, 24 (though *Acts of Paul* says that milk spurted out!).

560. Keener, *Acts*, 3:2517–27.

561. Finegan, *Apostles*, 24; Heid, "Romanness," 410 (more questionably suggesting this interpretation earlier in Ign. *Rom.* 4.2–3, and citing on 411 archaeological evidence from ca. 160 c.e.). On the Ostian Way, see Finegan, *Apostles*, 28–30. Finegan also explores (30–34) other evidence from catacombs (including the tradition that the apostles were buried there; but the traditions cannot *all* be correct).

562. Sulp. Sev. *Chron.* 2.29; cf. Tac. *Ann.* 15.44.

563. Finegan, *Apostles*, 23.

564. Ibid., 34.

565. With Johnson, *Acts*, 473 (who also cites 2 Tim 4:9–13, though it may refer to a different captivity).

(and perhaps expenditures additional to his rent); on ancient hospitality, see comment on Acts 16:15. (On his rented quarters, see comment on Acts 28:16.) Custody does not prevent his ministry; it redirects it to different and otherwise inaccessible venues.[566] Such barriers could not stop the gospel.[567]

1. Boldly Preaching the Kingdom

The phrase "boldly preaching the kingdom" evokes earlier themes in Luke-Acts. The "kingdom" (see comment on Acts 1:3) technically was associated with Israel (see comment on Acts 1:6),[568] but Dan 2:44–45 had announced that it would come to all the earth (relevant in most uses in Acts). In Dan 2, God's kingdom comes in the time of the fourth mortal kingdom (2:40–43), which was normally understood by Luke's contemporaries as Rome.[569] First-century interpreters would not trifle with a brief Median kingdom between Babylon and Persia (2:39)[570] and would understand the "Kittim" of 11:30 as the Romans.[571] For Daniel, this kingdom's arrival is future; for Luke, it is both future (Luke 1:33;[572] 11:2; 13:28–29; 19:12; 22:29–30; cf. 6:20; 12:32) and present (11:20; 17:21; 18:17; 22:25–26), often in the same contexts.[573] The mixture of present and future understandings of the kingdom in early Christianity stemmed from the understanding of two comings of the Christians' king, Jesus (see comment on Acts 1:4).

The "kingdom" appears about fifty times in Luke-Acts, especially in the preaching of Jesus in the Gospel.[574] It appears only eight times in Acts, twice from Jesus (Acts 1:3, 6), once from Philip (8:12, summarizing his teaching), and five times from Paul, though only two of these (14:22; 20:25) are direct speech (and even 14:22 is obvious summary). Two (40 percent) of Paul's uses (and two-thirds of the occasions that are pure summaries of his usage) appear in the concluding section of Acts, where they form an *inclusio* bracketing the final scene of Paul's contending with Israel (28:23, 31).[575] Though appearing only eight times in Paul's undisputed letters, βασιλεία (the term translated "kingdom") has strategic significance there.[576] Its role here in Acts, however, is particularly strategic. Not only does it bracket Paul's final scene; this kingdom preaching thus also brackets the book, connecting Jesus's teaching in 1:3,

566. Skinner, *Locating Paul*, 187, 194–95.

567. Ibid., 200; cf. Gwalther 905–6 in Chung-Kim and Hains, *Acts*, 370.

568. For Luke's view of the kingdom as in some way the expected Davidic kingdom, see Hahn, "Kingdom," 295 (because Jesus is king for the church, Hahn's article connects this kingdom with the church).

569. See the excursus on God's kingdom at Acts 1:3 (Keener, *Acts*, 1:671–74).

570. Though Dan 7:7–8, 19–27 is more ambiguous (the ten horns do not precisely fit Alexander and his four successor kingdoms), the description does sound like the desolation of the Seleucids in Dan 11. Perhaps the text would blend Greek and Roman kingdoms as "Western" invaders (cf. Caragounis, "Culture"). The Medes do appear in Vell. Paterc. 1.6.6 (treated by some as a gloss); cf. Mendels, "Five Empires"; *Gen. Rab.* 99:2; *y. Taʾan.* 2:5, §1.

571. Cf. Rabin, "Jannaeus"; Burrows, *Scrolls*, 123–42; idem, *More Light*, 194–203; Dupont-Sommer, *Writings*, 167–68; the excursus on God's kingdom at Acts 1:3 (Keener, *Acts*, 1:671–74).

572. Though, at this point, present and future are not yet distinguished.

573. E.g., Luke 17:21 is present, but the context in 17:22–37 and 18:7–8 is future; see esp. 13:18–21.

574. For "proclaiming" (usually one of two verbs) the "kingdom," see with κηρύσσω Luke 8:1; 9:2; Acts 8:12; 20:25; with εὐαγγελίζω Luke 4:43; 8:1; 16:16; Acts 8:12.

575. For *inclusio*, see, e.g., Catull. *Carm.* 52.1, 4; 57.1, 10; Plut. *Demosth.* 26.4; 28.5; Pliny *Ep.* 3.16.1, 13; Matt 5:3, 10; 19:30; 20:16; 1 Cor 12:31; 14:1; Rev 1:4, 8; comment in Aune, *Dictionary of Rhetoric*, 229; Harvey, *Listening*, 61–96 (esp. 66–67, 75–76), esp. 102–3; in narratives, see Hermog. *Inv.* 4.8.195, commenting on Demosth. *Or.* 20.73 (*Against Leptines*); in Luke-Acts, Luke 15:24, 32. Dupont, "Rapport," finds *inclusio* between Acts 28:16 and 30 (362–64); between 28:17a and 25a (364); and between 28:23 and 30–31 (364–65).

576. Thompson, "Paul in Acts," 435–36; Wright, *Paul*, 480.

6 and Paul's in 28:23, 31.[577] This theme binds Paul's preaching with the message of Jesus,[578] indicating that Luke expects his audience to apply to itself the demands and promises of God's reign announced by Jesus.[579]

Luke uses κηρύσσω ("preach") seventeen times;[580] the verb διδάσκω appears thirty-one times;[581] the various subjects demonstrate the same continuity as with the "kingdom" message. This emphasis on the message's kingdom content is especially clear where two verbs of proclamation appear together (e.g., κηρύσσω with εὐαγγελίζω, Luke 8:1; cf. Acts 10:42; or εὐαγγελίζω with διδάσκω, Luke 20:1; Acts 5:42; 15:35).[582]

Paul speaks openly with παρρησία (a term that Luke reserves for his second volume, along with the cognate verb παρρησιάζομαι), just like the Jerusalem apostles (Acts 2:29; 4:13, 29, 31) and Apollos (18:26).[583] Paul earlier "spoke boldly" publicly (13:46; 14:3; 19:8), including before rulers (26:26) and in the face of hostility from his own people (9:27, 28). In this context, Paul has no reason to fear Rome, which offers relative freedom for his preaching, but given Luke's portrayal of Paul elsewhere as a genuine sage, Paul would have spoken courageously and forthrightly here as elsewhere, no less than any Cynic sage (see comment on Acts 4:13).[584] Although chains were normally a matter of shame, Paul did historically display παρρησία despite them (Eph 6:19–20; Phil 1:20; 1 Thess 2:2).[585] He also apparently requested prayer that he might speak boldly or clearly during his custody (Eph 6:19–20; Col 4:3–4).[586]

II. Unhindered

Luke's two-volume work closes on the word "unhindered" (ἀκωλύτως). Stoics spoke of being "free"[587] and hence not "subject to hindrance,"[588] but because the sense here is different, it is probably only a fortuitous coincidence that Arrian ends Epictetus's discourses almost on that very note (Epict. *Diatr.* 4.13.24, τῶν ἀκωλύτων, close to the end). That "unhindered" can be a "legal term"[589] is significant in this context for

---

577. See also Moessner, "End(s)ings," 221; Pervo, *Acts*, 687. For a whole-book *inclusio*, see, e.g., John 1:1; 20:28 (cf. Falconer, "Prologue," 233; Keener, *John*, 426); Isa 1:13, 29; 66:3, 17, 23 (Harvey, *Listening*, 91–92); Hom. *Il.* 1; 24 (ibid., 111–12).

578. For continuity with Jesus, see also Siffer, "Proclamation du Royaume."

579. One should also note the irony of Rome's prisoner proclaiming the kingdom of an executed king titled "Lord" in 28:31; see Cassidy, "Proclamation."

580. For John (Luke 3:3; Acts 10:37), Jesus (Luke 4:18–19, 44; 8:1), disciples (Luke 8:39; 9:2; 24:47; Acts 10:42; cf. Luke 12:3), Stephen (Acts 8:5), and Paul (9:20; 20:25; here at 28:31; and, by outsiders' attribution, 19:13) and paralleled once with teaching Moses in the synagogues (15:21). On this verb, see also comment on Acts 8:5.

581. For Jesus (Luke 4:15, 31; 5:3, 17; 6:6; 11:1; 13:10, 22; 19:47; 20:1; 21:37; Acts 1:1 [where it summarizes half of his ministry]; by outsiders' attribution, Luke 13:26; 20:21; 23:5), the Holy Spirit (Luke 12:12), the Jerusalem apostles (Acts 4:2; 5:21, 42; in outsiders' words, 4:18; 5:25, 28), Paul and Barnabas (11:26; 15:35), false teachers (15:1), Apollos (18:25), and Paul (18:11; 20:20; outsiders' attribution, 21:21, 28). Paul is accused of teaching against Israel (21:21, 28) but instead teaches the kingdom (28:31; cf. 28:17–28).

582. For a discussion of meaning, see comment on Acts 5:42.

583. Some note that the phrase "with all boldness" was not uncommon (Jos. *Ant.* 16.379; Dion. Hal. *Ant. rom.* 9.53.7; Witherington, *Acts*, 814).

584. For comparison with philosophers here, see also Johnson, *Acts*, 473; Witherington, *Acts*, 814. The term was applicable to frank speech before a ruler (e.g., Men. Rhet. 2.3, 386.7–9; see further comment on Acts 4:13) and certainly to defiance of Rome had that proved necessary.

585. Rapske, *Custody*, 311–12, emphasizing that God's provision overcame the shame associated with chains.

586. Noted by Horton, *Acts*, 409.

587. See, e.g., Keener, *Corinthians*, 80; more fully idem, *John*, 746–51, esp. 750–51.

588. Cf. Arius Did. *Epit.* 2.7.11g, pp. 72–73.26–28, esp. 27.

589. See Dunn, *Acts*, 356; Mealand, "Close and Vocabulary"; BDAG (citing, e.g., P.Oxy. 502; BGU 917.14; P.Lips. 26.11; 30.9; and other sources). Some compare Socrates not being hindered in talking with his friends (Dupertuis, "Speech," 166, cites Plato *Apol.* 39E), which might be closer in sense to Acts 24:23. Although I do believe that Acts depicts Paul as a wise sage and sometimes uses the model of Socrates (see comments on Acts

what it says about Paul's status and, as argued above, about a positive outcome for Paul's immediate detention (or at the least a positive appraisal of what Luke considers *normal* Roman tolerance). The term could apply to freedom to practice Judaism without hindrance (cf. Jos. *Ant.* 16.41, 166).[590] It shows Roman toleration, and Luke concludes on this note, rather than on Paul's martyrdom, perhaps in part to invite Rome to continue this policy.[591] If imperial officials of his day recognize the weakness of Nero's discredited policies, they might find persuasive precedents before those of Nero.

What does Luke's own usage tell us about how he employs this term? Although the term certainly belongs to Luke's apologetic that was seeking Roman toleration,[592] it also reflects the theological message that pervades his work: the kingdom is God's doing, and whatever the obstacles and apparent setbacks along the way, God steadily advances it.[593] The cognate verb κωλύω appears twelve times in Luke-Acts, sometimes for hindering people from entering the kingdom (Luke 11:52; cf. 18:16)[594] or for God himself "hindering" ministry in some location (Acts 16:6). More significant here are the texts indicating (through implied answers to their questions) that nothing can hinder God's surprising work among the Gentiles (8:36; 10:47; 11:17).[595] God himself has established this work in the heart of the empire.

The closest formal parallel is 24:23, where Felix orders that none of Paul's friends be hindered from helping him in prison; both there and here the idea is Paul's legal freedom.[596] But in the largest context of Luke-Acts, this lack of hindrance merely fills out the picture of the unfettered message: nothing could hinder God's plan for the gospel, whether the prejudices of the church (Acts 10:47; 11:17; cf. 8:36; Luke 9:49–50; 18:16), the hostility of other religious teachers (Luke 11:52), or the power of Rome (Acts 24:23). Even through the very forms of suffering that appear to destroy the gospel—such as Jesus's crucifixion and Paul's imprisonment—the living God is at work to accomplish his purposes.

III. Luke's Expectations for the Future

"Unhindered" offers an apt closing word for the book of Acts. Luke's point is that though Paul is bound, God's message is not (2 Tim 2:9).[597] As one scholar summarizes the message of Acts: "*Nothing can stop the gospel*"! "The very last word of the Greek text is *akōlutōs*, without obstacle. God's plan has succeeded. The gospel has reached 'the

---

4:19–20; 5:29; 17:18–19), and I affirm that Socrates offers a model for martyrdoms (hence passion stories) in general, I believe that Socrates provides only one element of the wider context. (For a heavier emphasis on comparison with Socrates, suggesting even dependence on Plato and Xenophon, see MacDonald, "Categorization.") Certainly Luke did not invent Paul's martyrdom (which he does not narrate); Luke's apologetic fits other evidence that cumulatively suggests that Paul ultimately died in Roman custody, though of course Paul could not narrate that either (cf. Phil 1:7, 20–24; Phlm 10; Col 4:3, 18; Eph 6:20; 2 Tim 4:16–18; *1 Clem.* 5.5–7).

590. Johnson, *Acts*, 473 (noting also the usage for doing tasks uninterrupted, Jos. *Ant.* 12.104); Witherington, *Acts*, 814.

591. Haenchen, *Acts*, 726, 732; cf. Liefeld, *Acts*, 46: by this phrase Luke "does not so much summarize the past as he opens the future."

592. Chrys. *Hom. Acts* 55 notes the irony that Paul, though hindered in Judea, was now unhindered in Rome. But Luke here probably emphasizes Roman respect for Paul's religious freedom.

593. With, e.g., Stagg, *Acts*, 266.

594. Cf., for hindrances to the mission, also in Rom 1:13; 1 Thess 2:16. Luke uses the term four times as often as Mark (Mark 9:38, 39; 10:14).

595. That nothing could hinder God was long-standing Jewish theology (*1 En.* 41:9; cf. the adjective ἀκώλυτος, albeit in a different sense, describing Wisdom in Wis 7:23). Cf. Spencer, *Acts*, 241; Witherington, *Acts*, 815–16.

596. With Rapske, *Custody*, 182 (who also notes the Roman tolerance of preaching).

597. With Johnson, *Acts*, 473; Faw, *Acts*, 296. Cf. also Cassiodorus *Commentary on Acts* 72: although bound, Paul frees others from sin (Pelikan, *Acts*, 295).

uttermost part of the earth,' and there is boldly and effectively proclaimed."[598] Gamaliel's supposition in Acts 5:39 was confirmed: if the movement was of God, nothing could stop it, for as Paul the persecutor learned, one cannot fight against God (26:14).

Luke also provides indication that the gospel will reach the ends of the earth (1:8); if it has reached the heart of the Roman Empire, it will prevail despite the obstacles.[599] Far from being stamped out, it will continue to spread and multiply, whether by legal precedents, by successful debates, by signs and wonders, or by outsiders observing Christian unity. Luke celebrates this expectation; some Roman polytheists would have abhorred it.[600] In his narrative Luke highlights the trajectory from Jesus's concern for outsiders to the success of the Diaspora mission. It stemmed not from a single revelation but from the independent experiences of Philip (8:26, 29), Peter (10:9–22, 44–47; 11:5–17; 15:7–9), the Antioch church (11:20–24), and Saul of Tarsus (9:15; 22:17–21; 26:17–18), who would ultimately implement strategic elements of this vision. The Spirit guided the church across barriers it had taken for granted (8:29; 10:19; 13:2, 4; 15:28; cf. 28:25–28); obstacles arose, but Luke's interest is more in the trajectory of success.

Subsequent history may allow us to highlight the failings of Christians and often those of the church more than Luke chose to do; the terrible legacy of Christian anti-Semitism also deeply marred Luke's (and Paul's) hopes for the Christian witness to the Jewish people for much of at least eighteen of the past twenty centuries. Nevertheless, subsequent history also suggests that Luke's central insight about the Gentile mission's success was remarkably accurate. In his world, when Christians remained a small sect in a sea of polytheism, Luke had faith that the divine leaven of Jesus's kingdom message in the Christian movement would spread rather than be stamped out. He was convinced that centralizing the gospel in one culture or location, even in Jerusalem, was not the way of the future (a conviction most likely reinforced, before he wrote, by Jerusalem's fall); instead, the way was the worldwide, Gentile mission advocated by Paul. Nearly two millennia later, Jesus is known and revered (in different ways) by the two largest world religions, and his followers live in almost every nation and culture.

Luke might grieve over much of what he would see in much of modern Christendom—certainly, for example, in the materialism and consumerism of Christians in the secular West (cf. Luke 12:33; 14:33). He would undoubtedly express surprise that the parousia (the "delay" of which he already recognized, Acts 1:6–8) has been delayed for so long. But he would surely regard the international fellowship of Christians worldwide as a dramatic confirmation of Paul's calling and mission—a calling and mission that, at a deeper level, stemmed from Jesus's command and depended on the leading and power of God's own Spirit, for which believers are to pray. He might well ask why Christians in different cultures have not shared their lives and resources further for one another and for the objective of that mission.

---

598. R. Williams, *Acts*, 27, 170; cf. Barclay, *Acts*, 193; cf. also the title of Troftgruben, *Conclusion*. (I believe that Luke envisioned Rome's relation to the ends of the earth, however, as merely proleptic; see also Keener, *Acts*, 1:702–8.) This theme of God sovereignly surmounting obstacles also appears in Israel's Scripture, e.g., in Genesis, where God's purpose for Israel surmounts obstacles (threats from the promised land's inhabitants; closed matriarchal wombs; kings interested in the matriarchs; etc.).

599. Luke need not narrate it explicitly in a third volume (*pace*, e.g., Winandy, "Finale des Actes") because he implies it within the narrative world (starting from Acts 1:8). But (as factors such as the appearance of the African official in 8:26–40 suggest) the ends of the earth do remain as an objective beyond these ends' immediate and proleptic fulfillment in Rome (see Rosner, "Progress," 218; Gaventa, *Acts*, 65–66; comment on Acts 1:8).

600. Umurhan and Penner, "Crossroads," 192, follow Cadbury (*Acts in History*, 13) in citing Juv. *Sat.* 3.62.

POSTSCRIPT

During the course of this work's publication (2012–2015), numerous other works have been published. Although I have continued attempting to update the volumes that remained forthcoming, many works that would have been addressed in 2015 are naturally missing in the introduction published in 2012. For example, in 2015 a greater number of Acts scholars follow Richard Pervo's second-century date for Acts than was the case several years earlier. Dr. Pervo has made a consistent argument and drawn on a range of evidence.

For reasons already stated in my introduction, I remain persuaded of a first-century date. Nevertheless, in 2015 I would take into account the shift in opinion when summarizing the state of scholarship; although a second-century date for Acts undoubtedly remains a minority position, it is surely more prominent than it was even a mere decade ago. Because both my commentary, only now complete, and several forthcoming major works on Acts argue for a first-century date, I suspect that supporters of a first-century date will flourish more, but it is currently appropriate to speak of divided opinion. Scholars who cite only their own circles as representative of "critical" scholarship or consensus (a behavior characteristic neither of Dr. Pervo nor myself) display merely their own academic parochialism.

In light of this current discussion, I would argue my own case for a first-century date at slightly greater length, including by pointing out more strongly that the argument for a second-century date for Acts often depends on separating Acts chronologically from Luke's Gospel, as some of its key supporters do. Although I allow for some differences in extrinsic genre, I, with most Acts scholars, view Luke-Acts as a mostly cohesive narrative unity, a case I believe firmly established by Charles Talbert, Robert Tannehill, and others. I believe it is less plausible to date components with such literary unity decades apart, and I believe that evidence also continues to support a first-century date for Luke's Gospel (although some scholars also challenge this point).[1] I would also highlight again my intrinsic argument based on Luke's apologetic for Paul responding to specific local accusations that appear to remain live issues, as well as noting both internal and external evidence regarding authorship.[2]

---

1. Cf., e.g., Luke 6:36 (and other material evoking both Luke's and Matthew's likely adaptations of Q) in *1 Clem.* 13.2; Poly. *Phil.* 2.3; perhaps 1 Tim 5:18 (unless just a shared logion). Aside from what I still regard as the likely echo of Acts 2:24 in Poly. *Phil.* 1.2, echoes of Acts seem weaker, e.g., "judge of the living and the dead" in Acts 10:42 and Poly. *Phil.* 2.1; *2 Clem.* 1.1 (but also the verb in 1 Pet 4:5; 2 Tim 4:1; *Barn.* 7.2); Acts 20:35 in *1 Clem.* 2.1 (but both may echo an agraphon or Q); possibly Acts 14:22 in *Barn.* 7.11.

2. Again, I argue that ancient readers would understand the "we" as a claim that the author traveled with Paul (see comment on Acts 16:10 in Keener, *Acts*, 3:2350–74) and that other modern approaches ingeniously circumvent the obvious evidence. Early Christian tradition associates the work with the likeliest of the traveling companions named in Pauline literature.

Some newer studies would lead me to highlight some elements of a discussion more than before.[3] Recent publications with full translations of fragments of historians would also further inform my work and should inform the work of those who follow.[4] Contrary to what some scholar friends suggested with reference to the completion of this four-volume commentary, much more work remains to be done on Acts in light of its historical context. I have merely begun scratching the surface, hoping to whet students' appetite for further explorations.

Still, new information often simply reinforces existing information, for example, that historians were bound to sources in a way that epic poets were not;[5] that historians might be less careful on some details;[6] that it is important to take into account historians' perspectives;[7] and so forth. Although I could cite countless valuable new works that I did not discover or were not published in time to cite at appropriate places in the commentary proper—yet that I discovered before its completion—normally they would complement, augment, or qualify individual footnotes rather than major strands of argument.[8]

3. For example, although I acknowledged already the biographic element in Luke's historiography, the evidence provided for successive biographies of sages in Adams, *Genre*, invites further attention. Martin, "Topic Lists," argues that biographers used progymnastic topic lists in designing biographies. At the same time, both biography and history more generally used rhetoric in ways appropriate to the genre. Even when focusing on a person, historians valued description in ways that pure epideictic did not (cf. Farrington, "Action").

4. See, e.g., Cornell, *Fragments* (2,736 delicious pages); Nichols, *Ctesias*; Llewellyn-Jones and Robson, *Ctesias*. Cf. also Broggiato, "Artemon," for discussion of Artemon's likely research in the massive library of Pergamum.

5. Men. Rhet. 1.1.333.31–1.1.334.5. Dionysius contends that most historians were satisfied merely to report facts, whereas he also wanted to explore events' causes (Dion. Hal. *Ant. rom.* 5.56.1). Greek historians often had multiple sources (see, e.g., Muntz, "Diodorus Siculus"; Évrard, "Polybe," comparing Polyb. 26.1 and Livy 41.20), though these are not always easily reconstructed (Muntz, "Sources"), but considered it better to consult living sources than to depend solely on written ones (Schepens, "Aspects," 113–14). On some points in 2 Maccabees, see, e.g., Shanks, "Inscription"; Gera, "Olympiodoros."

6. Contrast, e.g., Jos. *Ant.* 18.252 (the fuller account) with *War* 2.183. Yet at times Josephus could also be more accurate than we expect (see Ben David, "Settlements"), and elsewhere he provides evidence that coheres with other evidence (cf., e.g., Kavanagh, "Identity," on Aquila in Jos. *Ant.* 19.110–11).

7. On Acts and historiography, see Uytanlet, *Historiography*. On the influence of *Tendenz* in ancient Jewish historiography, see Kelhoffer, "The Maccabees at Prayer" (cf. also Hellenistic influence on the prayers in 2 Maccabees in Simkovich, "Greek Influence"; for different outlooks among different Greek historians, see, e.g., Chaplin, "Conversations"; among Roman historians, e.g., Beneker, "Crossing"). Examining rhetorical aspects of event-focused literature remains appropriate (cf., e.g., Grillo, "*Scribam*"). For earlier periods (in this case legendary ones) shaped from the perspective of the present (in this case in epic), cf. Franke, "Truth in Time" (epics reshaped history fairly freely; see, e.g., Chiu, "Importance," on Lucan). With regard to speeches in Acts, Lightfoot, *Acts*, 311, notes the possible limitations of Luke's sources and the necessary presence of his own style; with regard to his sources, he suspects that some would be oral, e.g., from Philip the evangelist with whom Luke had lodged (321).

8. For some samples of newer or missed works (which could be multiplied): historians' narrative use of geography (Edwards, "Capri," on Tac. *Ann.* 4.67); novelists' frequent lack of concern for precision in geography (though cf. suggestion of a copyist error in Xen. Eph. *Anthia* 5.10.2 in Capra, "Detour"); not only did novels and histories share some narrative techniques, but novelists sometimes emulated historians (Trzaskoma, "Echoes"; idem, "Miletus") as well as dramatists (Scourfield, "Chaereas"); Greek respect for women physicians-midwives (Laes, "Midwives"); how Acts could be heard in a second-century setting (Dupertuis and Penner, *Engaging*; esp. the orienting approach in Penner, "Reading"); Acts' Aegean audience (Zeichmann, "Location"); changing thought on Lukan theology (Bottini, "Lukásova teológia"); the narrative unity of Luke-Acts (Morgan, "Luc-Actes"); the authorial unity of Luke-Acts (Parsons and Gorman, "Unity"); narrative clues to how Luke highlights ethnic universalism (García Serrano, "Origins"; cf. Marguerat and Steffek, "Naissance"); Luke's ecclesiology (Scaer, "Foundations"); the prophetic character of and connections with Luke-Acts (Johnson, *Prophetic Church*, an important work; see also Stronstad et al., "Review"; McWhirter, *Prophets*); suffering's role in God's present purposes in Luke-Acts (Tabb, "Salvation"); Luke's narrative development of Peter as a character (Schreiber, "Berufen"); Theophilus's proposed relationship with Paul (Nodet, "Théophile"); Luke's implicit homiletical guidance (Graves, "Paradigm"); Acts 1:4's implicit hermeneutical guidance (Wall, "Waiting"); reading Acts 1:6–8 like an ambiguous oracle (Bale, "Oracle"); fresh discussions of whether seating was ever segregated in ancient synagogues (relevant for the discussion at Acts 1:14; Spigel, "Reconsidering");

In addition to acknowledgments noted in volume 1, I am grateful to Asbury Theological Seminary for a sabbatical in fall 2012 allowing me to check the editing and perform the majority of indexing for volume 2, as well as checking nearly half the

discussion on the ascension (for 1:9–11; Bovon, "Ascension Stories"; Bracci, "Mistero"; cf. Kapic and Vander Lugt, "Ascension"; Acts 1:3 being postascension in de Jonge, "Chronology"); Pentecost as a Lukan evidence of the resurrection (Brink, "Proof"); theological reflections on glossolalia (for 2:4; Augustine, "Pentecost"); debates concerning Augustan "golden age" expectations (for 2:17; Zanker, "Lyric"); historians sometimes using numerical hyperbole (for 2:41; Hilbert, "Enemies"); the cultural distinctiveness and theological basis for the friendship activity depicted in 2:41–47 (Hume, *Community*); the salvation-historical shift in the temple's significance through Luke-Acts (for 2:46; García Serrano, "Temple"); Luke requiring faith in Christ for salvation (for 4:12; Barrett, "Pour Out," contesting other readings of 2:17 and 10:34–35; regarding 4:12, cf. discussion in Michel, "Annäherungen"); God's dangerously holy presence through the new community extending beyond the temple proper (Le Donne, "Offering"); probable Pentheus allusions even in Philostratus's *Life of Apollonius* (for Acts 5:39; Praet, Demoen, and Gyselinck, "Domitian"); Luke's interest in widows (for 6:1; Leineweber, *Witwen*); ancient Jewish Hellenists (for 6:1; Zugmann, "Judentum"); possible origination of ἐκκλησία among the Hellenists (Trebilco, "Call Themselves"; but contrast Kooten, "Church"); thoughts on the role of the Seven (Koet, "Díptico"); Luke's typological use of Joseph (for 7:9–14; Lunn, "Allusions"); speculation that Stephen baptized some uncircumcised Gentiles (Zehetbauer, "Stephanus"); a proposed parallel with Stephen's vision (7:55–56; Back, "Spirituelle Einsicht"); contrasts between the martyrdoms of Zechariah (2 Chr 24) and Stephen (for Acts 7:60; Kalimi, "Episoden"; cf. already idem, "Murders"); a narrative treatment of Philip (esp. Acts 8; Fabien, *Philippe*; Legrand, "Review"); Simon the tanner as marginal socially rather than ritually (for 9:43; Oliver, "Insignificance"); ancient dream-visions (esp. 1QapGen XIX) and Acts 10 (Miller, "Exploring"); apocalyptic elements in the rabbinic *bat qol* traditions (for 10:13; Costa, "Littérature apocalyptique"); Roman approaches to ritual purity (for 10:15; Lennon, "Pollution"); Christ as Lord challenging Caesar's hegemony (for 10:36; 17:7; Alexander, "Vision"); Galilee as part of Judea (for 10:37; from the perspective in Pliny E. *N.H.* 5.15.70); other discussions of Agrippa's self-serving and Roman character (for Acts 12:1–4; cf. Kerkeslager, "Agrippa"; coins in Schwentzel, "Images") and of Judean slaves (for 12:13; e.g., González Echegaray, "Esclavos"); Paul's implicit character development in Acts 13–14 (Schmidt, "Weg"); challenging Josephan evidence for the South Galatian theory (Koch, "Völkertafel"); information possibly relevant for ethnic neighborhoods yet cosmopolitan interaction in Antioch (for 13:1; cf. Eickelman, *Middle East*, 218, on pre-1975 Lebanon); some Gentiles viewing Moses as a magician (mentioned at 13:6; see Apul. *Apol.* 90); ancient name interpretation (for Acts 13:9; Zingerman, "Name"); Philo on the conquest (for 13:19, Cover, "Conquest"); public respect for the counsel of women only when they were elite, in times of crisis (for 13:50; Buszard, "Speech"), and even then sparingly (Stevenson, "Women in Livy," on Livy 1); expanded definitions of "Greeks" (for Acts 14:1; Ferrary, "Géographie"); moderate rabbinic approaches toward idolatry (for 14:15–17; 19:33–34; Furstenberg, "Views"); round characters even in epic (for 15:39; cf. Grillo, "Reflections"); Paul and ethnicity (for 16:1–3; the thorough work of Sechrest, *Jew*); complexities of ethnic hybridization (for 16:2–3; Scott, "Local Responses"); Samothracian mysteries or the Cabiri in Thessalonica (for 16:11 and 17:1; Dimitrova, *Theoroi*; Verhoef, "Reacted"; cf. also Maull, "Stream," though more speculatively); single women honored by freedpersons (for 16:15; Mueller, "Single Women"); church hospitality in contrast with inns (for 16:15; cf. Lau, "Gasthäuser"); suicide for love (for discussion at 16:27; Dutsch, "Genre"); challenges regarding Athens's intellectual priority (for 17:16–31; Roberto, "History"); Epicurus regarding the chief good as pleasure (for 17:18; Cic. *Fin.* 1.9.29) and anti-Epicurean tendencies (Cic. *Fin.* 2.12.35–2.13.43; Dyson, "Pleasure," on Sen. Y. *Vit. beat.* 11.1; Warren, "Pleasure"); a character's misunderstanding serving humor (for Acts 17:18; Aristoph. *Acharn.* 751–52), or ancient perceptions of Judaism as a philosophy (Bosch-Veciana, "Filosofia"); Epimenidean tradition and Acts 17 (esp. for 17:23, 28; Rothschild, *Paul in Athens*, including careful examination of the traditional attribution in 17:28 on 8–23; Epimenidea in the early empire, 37–49; skillful and relevant, though not all will press the analogy with Epimenides this far [e.g., 133]); some henotheistic trends (for 17:28; Gasparini, "Isis"); Luke's dependence on a genuine speech of Paul at Athens (Ramelli, "Discours"); early Christian citations of noncanonical sources (17:28; Billings, "Poets"); discussion of baths (at 18:8; Hoffman, "Baths"); an attempt to connect Gal 2 and Acts 18:22 (Konradt, "Datierung"); the Isis and Serapis cults in Alexandria (for 18:18, 24; Schmidt, "Sturz des Serapis"; Bommas, "Isis in Alexandria") and the scientific resources at Alexandria's library (for 18:24; Engster, "Alexandria"); conflict with the Artemis cult as fighting beasts (in view of connections between the huntress deity and animals; Hooker, "Artemis"); Roman antipathy toward plundering temples (for 19:37; e.g., Wells, "Impiety"); the offensiveness of rejecting gifts (for the discussion at 21:17–18; Mendels, "Rejection"); comparison of the Nazirite vow in Acts 21:23–27 and in Josephus and Philo (Chepey, "Timing"); how a Greek visitor would understand the temple's warning inscription (for 21:28; Llewelyn and Beek, "Reading"); the comparability of the Judean rioters (21:27–22:29) with the pagan ones in Ephesus (19:23–40; Golding, "Pagan Worship"); connection of meal scenes in 16:34; 20:7–12; 27:33–36 (Grappe, "Repas"); the Hebraism of followers being at one's feet (for Acts 22:3; see, e.g., MT Judg 4:10 [and LXX]; 8:5); and so forth.

editing for volume 3. I owe special thanks also to Tim West at Baker Academic. For good reason, almost no biblical scholars subscribe to the wooden view of inerrancy of the biblical narratives held by the most conservative popular readers; but Tim's careful and detailed work on the commentary is so superb that it could almost meet that unusual standard. I am grateful also to those who have contributed in proofreading and Scripture indexing, including those who did the largest amounts: Robert Banning, Jeremy Cunningham, Amy Donaldson, and Cal Robertson.

WORKS CITED

Primary Sources

Achilles Tatius. *Clitophon and Leucippe.* Translated by S. Gaselee. LCL. New York: G. P. Putnam's Sons; London: Heinemann, 1917.

Aelian. *On the Characteristics of Animals.* Translated by A. F. Scholfield. 3 vols. LCL. Cambridge, Mass.: Harvard University Press, 1958–59.

Aelius Aristides. Translated by C. A. Behr. 4 vols. LCL. Cambridge, Mass.: Harvard University Press, 1973.

Aeschines. *The Speeches.* Translated by Charles Darwin Adams. LCL. Cambridge, Mass.: Harvard University Press; London: Heinemann, 1919.

Aeschylus. LCL. 2 vols. Cambridge, Mass.: Harvard University Press; London: Heinemann, 1922–26.

Alciphron. See *Letters of Alciphron, Aelian, and Philostratus.*

Ambrosiaster. *Commentarius in epistulas Paulinas.* Edited by H. J. Vogels. 3 vols. CSEL 81. Vienna: Hoelder-Pichler-Tempsky, 1966–69.

Ancient Near Eastern Texts Relating to the Old Testament. Edited by James B. Pritchard. 2nd ed. Princeton: Princeton University Press, 1955.

Androtion and the Atthis: The Fragments Translated with Introduction and Commentary. By Phillip Harding. New York: Oxford University Press, 1994.

Ante-Nicene Fathers: Translations of the Writings of the Fathers down to A.D. 325. Edited by A. Roberts and J. Donaldson. Revised by A. Cleveland Coxe. 10 vols. Grand Rapids: Eerdmans, 1975.

Antonius Diogenes. *The Wonders beyond Thule.* Translated by Gerald N. Sandy. *CAGN* 775–82.

Antony of Choziba. *Life of Saint George of Choziba; and, the Miracles of the Most Holy Mother of God at Choziba.* Translated by Tim Vivian and Apostolos N.

Athanassakis. San Francisco: International Scholars, 1994.

Apocalypse of Elijah. Translated by Orval S. Wintermute. *OTP* 1:735–53.

Apocalypse of Zephaniah. Translated by Orval S. Wintermute. *OTP* 1:508–15.

Apocalypsis Esdrae. Pages 24–33 in *Apocalypses apocryphae.* Edited by Konstantin von Tischendorf. Hildesheim: Georg Olms, 1966. See also *Greek Apocalypse of Ezra.*

Apocalypsis Esdrae; Apocalypsis Sedrach; Visio beati Esdrae. Edited by O. Wahl. Pseudepigrapha Veteris Testamenti Graece 4. Leiden: Brill, 1977. See also *Greek Apocalypse of Ezra.*

The Apocrypha and Pseudepigrapha of the Old Testament in English. Edited by R. H. Charles. 2 vols. Oxford: Clarendon, 1913.

Apocryphon of Ezekiel. Translated by J. R. Mueller and S. E. Robinson. *OTP* 1:487–95.

Apollodorus. *Library; Epitome.* Translated by Sir James George Frazer. 2 vols. LCL. Cambridge, Mass.: Harvard University Press; London: Heinemann, 1921.

Apollonius King of Tyre. Translated by Gerald N. Sandy. *CAGN* 736–72.

Apollonius Rhodius. *The Argonautica.* Translated by R. C. Seaton. LCL. Cambridge, Mass.: Harvard University Press; London: Heinemann, 1912.

The Apostolic Fathers: Greek Texts and English Translations of Their Writings. Translated by J. B. Lightfoot and J. R. Harmer. Edited and revised by Michael W. Holmes. 2nd ed. Grand Rapids: Baker, 1992.

Appian. *Roman History; Civil Wars.* Translated by Horace White. 4 vols. LCL. Cambridge, Mass.: Harvard University Press, 1912–13.

Apuleius. *The Golden Ass.* Translated by W. Adlington. Revised by S. Gaselee. LCL. Cambridge, Mass.: Harvard University Press, 1915.

Arator. *On the Acts of the Apostles.* Edited and translated by Richard J. Schrader. Cotranslated by Joseph L. Roberts III and John F. Makowski. Atlanta: Scholars Press, 1987.

Aratus. *Phaenomena.* In *Callimachus: Hymns and Epigrams; Lycophron; Aratus.* Translated by G. R. Mair and A. W. Mair. Rev. ed. LCL. Cambridge, Mass.: Harvard University Press; London: Heinemann, 1955.

Aristeas to Philocrates; Letter of Aristeas. Edited and translated by Moses Hadas. New York: Harper & Brothers, 1951. Repr., New York: KTAV, 1973. See also *Letter of Aristeas.*

Aristobulus. "Fragments." Translated by A. Yarbro Collins. *OTP* 2:831–42 (introduction, 831–36; translation, 837–42).

Aristophanes. Translated by Benjamin Bickley Rogers. 3 vols. LCL. Cambridge, Mass.: Harvard University Press, 1924.

Aristotle. Translated by Philip H. Wicksteed et al. 23 vols. LCL. Cambridge, Mass.: Harvard University Press; London: G. P. Putnam's Sons, 1926–70.

Aristotle. *The Poetics.* (With Longinus and Demetrius in Loeb vol.) Rev. ed. LCL. London: Heinemann, 1932.

Arius Didymus. *Epitome of Stoic Ethics.* Edited by Arthur J. Pomeroy. SBLTT 44. Graeco-Roman Series 14. Atlanta: SBL, 1999.

Arrian. *Anabasis Alexandri.* Translated by P. A. Brunt. 2 vols. LCL. Cambridge, Mass.: Harvard University Press; London: Heinemann, 1976–83.

Artapanus. Translated by J. J. Collins. *OTP* 2:889–903.

Artemidori Daldiani. *Onirocriticon Libri.* V. Teubner. Lipsiae: B. G. Teubneri, 1963.

Artemidorus Daldianus. *The Interpretation of Dreams (Oneirocritica).* Edited and translated by Robert J. White. NCS. Park Ridge, N.J.: Noyes, 1975.

Athenaeus. *The Deipnosophists*. Translated by Charles Burton Gulick. 7 vols. LCL. New York: G. P. Putnam's Sons; London: Heinemann, 1927–41.

Augustine. *Concerning the City of God against the Pagans*. Translated by Henry Bettenson. Introduction by David Knowles. New York: Penguin, 1972.

Aulus Gellius. *The Attic Nights*. Translated by John C. Rolfe. 3 vols. Rev. ed. LCL. Cambridge, Mass.: Harvard University Press, 1927–52.

Babrius and Phaedrus. Translated by Ben Edwin Perry. LCL. Cambridge, Mass.: Harvard University Press, 1965.

The Babylonian Talmud. Edited by Isidore Epstein. 35 vols. London: Soncino, 1935–52.

2 Baruch. Translated by A. F. J. Klijn. *OTP* 1:615–52.

3 Baruch. Translated by H. E. Gaylord, Jr. *OTP* 1:653–79.

4 Baruch. Translated by S. E. Robinson. *OTP* 2:413–25. See also *Paraleipomena Jeremiou*.

Basil of Caesarea. *Sur le Saint-Esprit*. Edited by Benoît Pruche. 2nd ed. Sources chrétiennes 17 bis. Paris: Cerf, 1968.

Bede, Venerable. *Commentary on the Acts of the Apostles*. Edited and translated by Lawrence T. Martin. Kalamazoo, Mich.: Cistercian, 1989.

The Book of the Dead, or Going Forth by Day: Ideas of the Ancient Egyptians concerning the Hereafter as Expressed in Their Own Terms. Translated by Thomas George Allen. Prepared for publication by Elizabeth Blaisdell Hauser. SAOC 37. Chicago: University of Chicago Press, 1974.

[Caesar.] *Alexandrian, African, and Spanish Wars*. Translated by A. G. Way. LCL. Cambridge, Mass.: Harvard University Press, 1955.

Caesar. *The Civil Wars*. Translated by A. G. Peskett. LCL. Cambridge, Mass.: Harvard University Press, 1914.

Caesar. *The Gallic War*. Translated by H. J. Edwards. LCL. Cambridge, Mass.: Harvard University Press, 1917.

Callimachus. *Aetia, Iambi, Lyric Poems, Hecale, Minor Epic and Elegiac Poems, and other Fragments*. Translated by C. A. Trypanis. LCL. Cambridge, Mass.: Harvard University Press, 1958.

Catullus. Translated by Francis Warre Cornish. In *Catullus, Tibullus, Pervigilium Veneris*. Revised by G. P. Goold. 2nd rev. ed. LCL. Cambridge, Mass.: Harvard University Press, 1988.

Chariton. *Chaereas and Callirhoe*. Translated by Warren E. Blake. Ann Arbor: University of Michigan Press; London:

Humphrey Milford, Oxford University Press, 1939.

Chariton. *De Chaerea et Callirhoe amatoriarum narrationum libri octo*. Oxford: Clarendon; London: Humphrey Milford, 1938.

Die Chronik des Hieronymus. 2nd ed. Edited by R. Helm. Berlin: Akademie, 1956.

Chrysostom, John. *Homilies on the Acts of the Apostles*. Translated by J. Walker, J. Sheppard, and H. Browne. Revised by George B. Stevens. Pages 1–328 in vol. 11 of *Nicene and Post-Nicene Fathers*. Edited by Philip Schaff. 14 vols. 1886–89. Repr., Peabody, Mass.: Hendrickson, 1994.

Cicero. Translated by Harry Caplan et al. 29 vols. LCL. Cambridge, Mass.: Harvard University Press, 1913–.

Collected Ancient Greek Novels. Edited by B. P. Reardon. Berkeley: University of California Press, 1989.

Columella. *On Agriculture*. Translated by Harrison Boyd Ash, E. S. Forster, and Edward H. Heffner. 3 vols. LCL. Cambridge, Mass.: Harvard University Press, 1941–55.

[Confucius]. *The Sacred Books of Confucius and Other Confucian Classics*. Edited and translated by Ch'u Chai and Winberg Chai. Introduction by Ch'u Chai. New York: Bantam/University Books, 1965.

Cornutus. *Theologiae graecae compendium*. Edited by Carl Lang. Teubner. Leipzig: Teubner, 1881.

Corpus Inscriptionum Graecarum auctoritate et impensis Academiae Litterarum Regiae Borussicae, vol. 2. Edited by Augustus Boeckh. Berolini, 1843.

Corpus inscriptionum judaicarum. Edited by Jean-Baptiste Frey. 2 vols. Sussidi allo studio delle Antichità cristiane 1 and 3. Rome: Pontificio Istituto di Archeologa Cristiana, 1936–52.

Corpus of the Aramaic Incantation Bowls. By Charles D. Isbell. SBLDS 17. Missoula, Mont: Scholars Press, 1975.

Corpus papyrorum judaicarum. Edited by Victor A. Tcherikover, Alexander Fuks, and Menahem Stern. 3 vols. Cambridge, Mass.: Harvard University Press for Magnes Press, 1957–64.

The Cynic Epistles: A Study Edition. Edited by Abraham J. Malherbe. SBLSBS 12. Missoula, Mont.: Scholars Press, 1977.

The Dead Sea Scriptures, in English Translation. By Theodor H. Gaster. 3rd rev. and enl. ed. Garden City, N.Y.: Doubleday, 1976.

The Dead Sea Scrolls: A New Translation. By Michael Wise, Martin Abegg Jr., and Edward Cook. San Francisco: Harper SanFrancisco, 1999.

The Dead Sea Scrolls in English. Edited by Geza Vermes. 2nd ed. New York: Penguin, 1981.

Demetrius Phalereus. *On Style*. Translated by W. Rhys Roberts. Pages 255–487 in *Aristotle: The Poetics; Longinus: On the Sublime; Demetrius*. Translated by W. Hamilton Fyfe and W. Rhys Roberts. Rev. ed. LCL. Cambridge, Mass.: Harvard University Press, 1932.

Demetrius the Chronographer. Translated by J. Hanson. *OTP* 2:843–54.

Demosthenes. Translated by J. H. Vince et al. 7 vols. LCL. Cambridge, Mass.: Harvard University Press, 1926–49.

Diehl, Ernst. *Anthologia Lyrica Graeca*. Bibliotheca scriptorum graecorum et romanorum teubneriana. Leipzig: Teubner, 1949–52.

Dio Cassius. *Roman History*. Translated by Earnest Cary. 9 vols. LCL. Cambridge, Mass.: Harvard University Press, 1914–27.

Dio Chrysostom. Translated by J. W. Cohoon and H. Lamar Crosby. 5 vols. LCL. Cambridge, Mass.: Harvard University Press, 1932–51.

Diodorus of Sicily [Diodorus Siculus]. *The Library of History*. Translated by C. H. Oldfather et al. 12 vols. LCL. Cambridge, Mass.: Harvard University Press; London: Heinemann, 1933–67.

Diogenes Laertius. *Lives of Eminent Philosophers*. Translated by R. D. Hicks. 2 vols. LCL. Cambridge, Mass.: Harvard University Press, 1925.

Dionysius of Halicarnassus. *Critical Essays*. Translated by Stephen Usher. 2 vols. LCL. Cambridge, Mass.: Harvard University Press, 1974.

Dionysius of Halicarnassus. *On Epideictic Speeches*. See Pseudo-Dionysius of Halicarnassus.

Dionysius of Halicarnassus. *The Roman Antiquities*. Translated by Earnest Cary, following Edward Spelman. 7 vols. LCL. Cambridge, Mass.: Harvard University Press, 1937–45.

1 Enoch (Ethiopic Apocalypse). Translated by E. Isaac. *OTP* 1:5–89. See also *The Ethiopic Book of Enoch*.

2 Enoch (Slavonic Apocalypse). Translated by F. I. Anderson. *OTP* 1:91–221.

3 Enoch (Hebrew Apocalypse). Translated by P. Alexander. *OTP* 1:223–315.

Epictetus. *The Discourses and Manual together with Fragments of His Writings*. Translated by P. E. Matheson. 2 vols. Oxford: Clarendon, 1916.

Epictetus. *The Discourses as Reported by Arrian; the Manual; and Fragments*. Translated by W. A. Oldfather. 2 vols. LCL.

Cambridge, Mass.: Harvard University Press, 1926–28.

Epicurus: The Extant Remains. Edited by Cyril Bailey. Oxford: Oxford University Press, 1926; repr., Hildesheim: Olms, 1970.

The Epistles of Anacharsis. Translated by Anne M. McGuire. Pages 36–51 in *The Cynic Epistles: A Study Edition*. Edited by Abraham J. Malherbe. SBLSBS 12. Missoula, Mont.: Scholars Press, 1977.

The Epistles of Crates. Translated by Ronald F. Hock. Pages 54–89 in *The Cynic Epistles: A Study Edition*. Edited by Abraham J. Malherbe. SBLSBS 12. Missoula, Mont.: Scholars Press, 1977.

The Epistles of Diogenes. Translated by Benjamin Fiore. Pages 92–183 in *The Cynic Epistles: A Study Edition*. Edited by Abraham J. Malherbe. SBLSBS 12. Missoula, Mont.: Scholars Press, 1977.

The Epistles of Heraclitus. Translated by David R. Worley. Pages 186–215 in *The Cynic Epistles: A Study Edition*. Edited by Abraham J. Malherbe. SBLSBS 12. Missoula, Mont.: Scholars Press, 1977.

The Epistles of Socrates and the Socratics. Translated by Stanley Stowers and David R. Worley. Pages 218–307 in *The Cynic Epistles: A Study Edition*. Edited by Abraham J. Malherbe. SBLSBS 12. Missoula, Mont.: Scholars Press, 1977.

The Essene Writings from Qumran. By A. Dupont-Sommer. Translated by G. Vermes. Gloucester, Mass.: Peter Smith, 1973.

The Ethiopic Book of Enoch: A New Edition in the Light of the Aramaic Dead Sea Fragments. Edited by Michael A. Knibb, in consultation with Edward Ullendorff. 2 vols. Oxford: Clarendon, 1978. See also *1 Enoch*.

Eunapius. *The Lives of the Sophists*. Pages 319–565 in Philostratus and Eunapius, *The Lives of the Sophists*. Translated by Wilmer Cave Wright. LCL. New York: G. P. Putnam's Sons; London: Heinemann, 1922.

Eupolemus. Translated by F. Fallon. *OTP* 2:861–72.

Euripides. Translated by A. S. Way. 4 vols. LCL. Cambridge, Mass.: Harvard University Press, 1912.

Euripides. Translated by David Kovacs, Christopher Collard, and Martin Cropp. 8 vols. LCL. Cambridge, Mass.: Harvard University Press, 1994–2008.

Eusebius. *Church History*. Translated by Arthur Cushman McGiffert. Vol. 1 in *A Select Library of Nicene and Post-Nicene Fathers of the Christian Church*. Edited by Philip Schaff and Henry Wace. New York: Charles Scribner's Sons, 1904.

Eusebius. *Ecclesiastical History*. Translated by C. F. Cruse. Grand Rapids: Baker, 1955.

Ezekiel the Tragedian. Translated by R. G. Robertson. *OTP* 2:803–19.

4 Ezra. Translated by Bruce M. Metzger. *OTP* 1:516–59.

The Fathers according to Rabbi Nathan. Translated by Judah Goldin. YJS 10. New Haven: Yale University Press, 1955.

The Fathers according to Rabbi Nathan (Abot de Rabbi Nathan) Version B. Translation and commentary by Anthony J. Saldarini. SJLA 11. Leiden: Brill, 1975.

"Fragments of Pseudo-Greek Poets." Translated by Harold W. Attridge. *OTP* 2:821–30.

Fronto. *The Correspondence of Marcus Cornelius Fronto with Marcus Aurelius Antoninus, Lucius Verus, Antoninus Pius, and Various Friends*. Translated by C. R. Haines. 2 vols. Rev. ed. LCL. Cambridge, Mass.: Harvard University Press; London: Heinemann, 1928–29.

Fronto. *Epistulae M. Cornelii Frontonis et M. Aurelii imperatoris epistulae, L. Veri et T. Antonii Pii et Appiani epistularum reliquiae*. Edited by S. A. Naber. Leipzig: Teubner, 1867.

Gaius. *The Institutes*. Translated by W. M. Gordon and O. F. Robinson with the Latin text of Seckel and Kuebler. Texts in Roman Law. Ithaca, N.Y.: Cornell University Press, 1988.

Galen. *On the Avoidance of Grief*. Translated in Clare K. Rothschild and Trevor W. Thompson, "Galen: 'On the Avoidance of Grief.'" *Early Christianity* 2 (2011): 110–29.

Galen. *On the Natural Faculties*. Translated by Arthur John Brock. LCL. New York: G. P. Putnam's Sons; London: Heinemann, 1916.

Georgius Syncellus et Nicephorus. Edited by W. Dindorf. 2 vols. Bonn: Weber, 1829.

Gorgias. *Encomium of Helen*. Edited and translated by Douglas Maurice MacDowell. Bristol, U.K.: Bristol Classical Press, 1982.

The Gospel of Peter. Translated by Christian Maurer. Pages 179–87 in vol. 1 of *New Testament Apocrypha*. Edited by Edgar Hennecke, Wilhelm Schneemelcher, and R. McL. Wilson. 2 vols. Philadelphia: Westminster, 1963–65.

The Gospel of Thomas. Translated by T. O. Lambdin. Introduction by Helmut Koester. *NHL* 117–30.

The Greek Anthology. Translated by W. R. Paton. 5 vols. LCL. Cambridge, Mass.: Harvard University Press, 1916–17.

Greek Apocalypse of Ezra. Translated by M. E. Stone. *OTP* 1:561–79. See also *Apocalypsis Esdrae*.

The Greek Bucolic Poets. Translated by J. M. Edmonds. LCL. Cambridge, Mass.: Harvard University Press; London: Heinemann, 1912.

Greek Epic Fragments from the Seventh to the Fifth Centuries BC. Translated by Martin L. West. LCL. Cambridge, Mass.: Harvard University Press, 2003.

The Greek Magical Papyri in Translation, Including the Demotic Spells. Edited by Hans Dieter Betz. 2nd ed. Chicago: University of Chicago Press, 1992–.

Les grottes de Murabba'ât. Edited by P. Benoit, J. T. Milik, and R. de Vaux. 2 vols. DJD 2. Oxford: Clarendon, 1961.

Hallo and Younger, *Context of Scripture*. Hallo, William W., and K. Lawson Younger Jr., eds. *The Context of Scripture*. 3 vols. Leiden: Brill, 2003.

Heliodorus. *Ethiopian Story*. Translated by Sir Walter Lamb. Everyman's Library. New York: E. P. Dutton; London: J. M. Dent & Sons, 1961.

Heraclitus. *Homeric Problems*. Edited and translated by Donald A. Russell and David Konstan. SBLWGRW 14. Atlanta: SBL, 2005.

[Hermogenes]. *Invention and Method: Two Rhetorical Treatises from the Hermogenic Corpus*. Translated with introductions and notes by George A. Kennedy. SBLWGRW 15. Atlanta: SBL, 2005.

Hermogenes. *On Issues: Strategies of Argument in Later Greek Rhetoric*. Translated by Malcolm Heath. Oxford: Clarendon, 1995.

Herodes, Cercidas, and the Greek Choliambic Poets. Translated by A. D. Knox. LCL. Cambridge, Mass.: Harvard University Press, 1961.

Herodian. *History*. Translated by C. R. Whittaker. 2 vols. LCL. Cambridge, Mass.: Harvard University Press, 1969.

Herodotus. *Histories*. Translated by A. D. Godley. 4 vols. LCL. Cambridge, Mass.: Harvard University Press, 1920–25.

Hesiod. *Hesiod, The Homeric Hymns, and Homerica*. Translated by Hugh G. Evelyn-White. Rev. ed. LCL. Cambridge, Mass.: Harvard University Press; London: Heinemann, 1936.

Hierocles the Stoic: Elements of Ethics, Fragments, and Excerpts. Edited by Ilaria Ramelli (essay, translation, commentary). Translated (from Ramelli's work) by David Konstan. SBLWGRW 28. Atlanta: SBL, 2009.

Hippocrates. Translated by W. H. S. Jones et al. 8 vols. LCL. Cambridge, Mass.: Harvard University Press, 1923–95.

Hippocrates. *Opera omnia*. Edited by Heiberg et al. CMG 1. Leipzig, Berlin: Teubner, 1927–.

Hippolytus. *Refutatio omnium haeresium.* Edited by Paul Wendland. Vol. 3 of *Werke.* GCS 26. Leipzig: Hinrichs, 1916.

Homer. *The Iliad.* Translated by A. T. Murray. 2 vols. LCL. Cambridge, Mass.: Harvard University Press, 1924.

Homer. *The Odyssey.* Translated by A. T. Murray. Revised by George E. Dimock. 2 vols. 2nd ed. LCL. Cambridge, Mass.: Harvard University Press, 1995.

Horace. *The Odes and Epodes.* Translated by C. E. Bennett. LCL. Cambridge, Mass.: Harvard University Press; London: William Heinemann, 1914.

Horace. *Satires, Epistles, and Ars Poetica.* Translated by H. Rushton Fairclough. LCL. New York: G. P. Putnam's Sons; London: William Heinemann, 1926.

Iamblichus. *A Babylonian Story.* Translated by Gerald N. Sandy. *CAGN* 783–97.

Iamblichus. *De Anima: Text, Translation, and Commentary.* By John F. Finamore and John M. Dillon. PhilAnt 42. Leiden: Brill, 2002; repr., Atlanta: SBL, n.d.

Iamblichus of Chalcis: *The Letters.* Translation, introduction, and notes by John M. Dillon and Wolfgang Polleichtner. SBLW GRW 19. Atlanta: SBL, 2009.

Iamblichus. *On the Mysteries of the Egyptians, Chaldeans, and Assyrians.* Translated by Thomas Taylor. 3rd ed. London: Stuart & Watkins, 1968.

Iamblichus. *On the Pythagorean Way of Life: Text, Translation, and Notes.* Edited and translated by John Dillon and Jackson Hershbell. SBLTT 29. Graeco-Roman Religion Series 11. Atlanta: Scholars Press, 1991.

Die Inschriften von Ephesos. Edited by Hermann Wankel. 8 vols. in 10. IGSK 11–17. Bonn: Rudolf Habelt, 1979–84.

Inscriptions Reveal: Documents from the Time of the Bible, the Mishna, and the Talmud. Edited by Efrat Carmon. Translated by R. Grafman. Jerusalem: Israel Museum, 1973.

Isaeus. Translated by Edward Seymour Forster. LCL. Cambridge, Mass.: Harvard University Press, 1927.

The Isaiah Targum. Translated by Bruce Chilton. Aramaic Bible 11. Wilmington, Del.: Michael Glazier, 1987.

Isocrates. *Orations.* Translated by George Norlin and Larue van Hook. 3 vols. LCL. New York: G. P. Putnam's Sons; London: Heinemann, 1928–61.

Jannes and Jambres. Translated by A. Pietersma and R. T. Lutz. *OTP* 2:427–42.

Jerome. *Opera exegetica.* Vol. 1. Edited by P. de Lagarde, G. Morin, and M. Andriaen. CCSL 72. Turnhout, Belg.: Brepolis, 1959.

Joseph and Asenath. Translated by C. Burchard. *OTP* 2:177–247.

Joseph et Aséneth: Introduction, texte critique, traduction, et notes. Edited by Marc Philonenko. StPB 13. Leiden: Brill, 1968.

Josephus. Translated by H. St. J. Thackeray et al. 10 vols. LCL. Cambridge, Mass.: Harvard University Press, 1926–65.

Josephus. *The Jewish War.* Edited by Gaalya Cornfeld, with Benjamin Mazar and Paul L. Maier. Grand Rapids: Zondervan, 1982.

Justin Martyr. *First Apology.* Translated by Marcus Dods and George Reith. *ANF* 1:159–87.

Justinian. *Institutes.* Translated by Peter Birks and Grant McLeod, with the Latin text of Paul Krueger. Ithaca, N.Y.: Cornell University Press, 1987.

Juvenal. *Satires.* In *Juvenal and Perseus.* Translated by G. G. Ramsay. Rev. ed. LCL. Cambridge, Mass.: Harvard University Press, 1940.

The Ladder of Jacob. Translated by H. G. Lunt. *OTP* 2:401–11.

Letter of Aristeas. Translated by R. J. H. Shutt. *OTP* 2:7–34. See also *Aristeas to Philocrates; Letter of Aristeas.*

The Letters of Alciphron, Aelian, and Philostratus. Translated by Allen Rogers Benner and Francis H. Forbes. LCL. Cambridge, Mass.: Harvard University Press; London: Heinemann, 1949.

The Letters of Symmachus: Book 1. Translated by Michele Renee Salzman and Michael Roberts. Introduction and commentary by Michele Renae Salzman. SBLWGRW 30. Atlanta: SBL, 2011.

Libanius's Progymnasmata*: Model Exercises in Greek Prose Composition and Rhetoric.* Translation, introduction, and notes by Craig A. Gibson. SBLWGRW 27. Edited by Malcolm Heath. Atlanta: SBL, 2008.

Life of Aesop. Translated in Lawrence M. Wills, "The Aesop Tradition." Pages 222–37 in *The Historical Jesus in Context.* Edited by Amy-Jill Levine, Dale C. Allison Jr., and John Dominic Crossan. PrRR. Princeton: Princeton University Press, 2006.

The Literature of Ancient Egypt: An Anthology of Stories, Instructions, Stelae, Autobiographies, and Poetry. Edited by William Kelly Simpson. 3rd ed. New Haven: Yale University Press, 2003.

Lives of the Prophets. Translated by D. R. A. Hare. *OTP* 2:379–99.

Lives of the Prophets. Propheten und Apostellegenden nebst Jüngerkatalogen des Dorotheus und verwandter Texte. Edited by Theodor Schermann. TUGAL 31.3. Leipzig: J. C. Hinrichs, 1907. Greek text.

Livy. *Ab urbe condita.* Translated by B. O. Foster et al. 14 vols. LCL. Cambridge, Mass.: Harvard University Press, 1919–59.

[Longinus]. *On the Sublime.* Translated by W. Hamilton Fyfe. Pages 119–254 in *Aristotle: The Poetics; Longinus: On the Sublime; Demetrius.* Translated by W. Hamilton Fyfe and W. Rhys Roberts. Rev. ed. LCL. Cambridge, Mass.: Harvard University Press, 1932.

Longus. *Daphnis and Chloe.* Translated by George Thornley. Revised by J. M. Edmonds. Pages vii–xxiii, 1–247 in *Daphnis and Chloe by Longus; The Love Romances of Parthenius; and Other Fragments.* Translated by George Thornley and S. Gaselee. LCL. Cambridge, Mass.: Harvard University Press, 1916.

Lucan. *The Civil War.* Translated by J. D. Duff. LCL. Cambridge, Mass.: Harvard University Press, 1928.

Lucian. Translated by A. M. Harmon, K. Kilburn, and M. D. Macleod. 8 vols. LCL. Cambridge, Mass.: Harvard University Press, 1913–67.

Lucian. *A True Story.* Translated by B. P. Reardon. *CAGN* 619–49.

Lucretius. *De rerum natura.* Translated by W. H. D. Rouse. 3rd rev. ed. LCL. Cambridge, Mass.: Harvard University Press, 1937.

Lycophron. *Alexandra.* Translated by A. W. Mair. Pages 303–443 in *Callimachus: Hymns and Epigrams; Lycophron; Aratus.* Translated by G. R. Mair and A. W. Mair. Rev. ed. LCL. Cambridge, Mass.: Harvard University Press; London: Heinemann, 1955.

Lysias. Translated by W. R. M. Lamb. LCL. Cambridge, Mass.: Harvard University Press, 1930.

"3 Maccabees." Translated by H. Anderson. *OTP* 2:509–29.

"4 Maccabees." Translated by H. Anderson. *OTP* 2:531–64.

Manetho. Translated by W. G. Waddell. LCL. Cambridge, Mass.: Harvard University Press, 1940.

Marcus Aurelius. *The Communings with Himself.* Edited and translated by C. R. Haines. LCL. Cambridge, Mass.: Harvard University Press, 1916.

Martial. *Epigrams.* Translated by Walter C. A. Ker. 2 vols. LCL. London: Heinemann; New York: G. P. Putnam's Sons, 1919–20.

The Martyrdom and Ascension of Isaiah. Translated by M. A. Knibb. *OTP* 2:143–76.

Maximus of Tyre. *The Philosophical Orations.* Translated by M. B. Trapp. Oxford: Clarendon, 1997.

The Meaning of the Glorious Koran. Translated by Mohammed Marmaduke Pickthall. New York: New American Library, 1953.

Mekilta de-Rabbi Ishmael. Translated by Jacob Z. Lauterbach. 3 vols. Philadelphia: Jewish Publication Society of America, 1933–35.

Menander. Edited and translated by W. Geoffrey Arnott. 3 vols. LCL. Cambridge, Mass.: Harvard University Press; London: William Heinemann, 1979–2000.

Menander Rhetor. Edited and translated by D. A. Russell and N. G. Wilson. Oxford: Clarendon, 1981.

The Midrash Rabbah. Edited by H. Freedman and Maurice Simon. Translated by H. Freedman et al. Foreword by I. Epstein. 5 vols. London: Soncino, 1977.

Minor Latin Poets. Translated by J. Wight Duff and Arnold M. Duff. Rev. ed. LCL. Cambridge, Mass.: Harvard University Press, 1935.

The Mishnah. Translated by Herbert Danby. London: Oxford University Press, 1933.

The Mishnah. Edited and translated by Philip Blackman. 7 vols. 2nd ed. New York: Judaica, 1963.

Monumenta Asiae Minoris antiqua. Edited by William M. Calder et al. 7 vols. Manchester, U.K.: Manchester University Press; London: Longmans, Green, 1928–56.

Musaeus. *Hero and Leander.* Translated by Cedric Whitman. Introduction by Thomas Gelzer. LCL. Cambridge, Mass.: Harvard University Press, 1975.

"Musonius Rufus: The Roman Socrates." Translated by Cora E. Lutz. *YCS* 10 (1947): 3–147.

The Nag Hammadi Library in English. Edited by J. M. Robinson. San Francisco: Harper & Row, 1977.

Nepos, Cornelius. *On Great Generals; On Historians.* Translated by John C. Rolfe. LCL. Cambridge, Mass.: Harvard University Press, 1984.

New Testament Apocrypha. Edited by Edgar Hennecke, William Schneemelcher, and R. McL. Wilson. 2 vols. Philadelphia: Westminster, 1963–65.

The Odes of Solomon. Translated by James H. Charlesworth. *OTP* 2:725–71.

The Odes of Solomon. Translated by James H. Charlesworth. Oxford: Clarendon, 1973.

The Old Testament Pseudepigrapha. Edited by James H. Charlesworth. 2 vols. Garden City, N.Y.: Doubleday, 1983–85.

Die Oracula sibyllina. Edited by Johannes Geffcken. GCS 8. Leipzig: Hinrichs, 1902. See also *Sibylline Oracles.*

The Orphic Hymns: Text, Translation and Notes. Translated by Apostolos N. Athanassakis. SBLTT 12. Graeco-Roman Religion Series 4. Missoula, Mont.: Scholars Press, 1977.

Orphica. Translated by M. Lafargue. *OTP* 2:795–801.

Ovid. *The Fasti.* Translated by Sir James George Frazer. LCL. Cambridge, Mass.: Harvard University Press, 1931.

Ovid. *Heroides; Amores.* Translated by Grant Showerman. LCL. Cambridge, Mass.: Harvard University Press, 1914.

Ovid. *Metamorphoses.* Translated by Frank Justus Miller. 2 vols. LCL. Cambridge, Mass.: Harvard University Press; London: Heinemann, 1916–21.

Ovid. *Tristia; Ex Ponto.* Translated by Arthur Leslie Wheeler. LCL. Cambridge, Mass.: Harvard University Press; London: Heinemann, 1924.

Paraleipomena Jeremiou. Edited and translated by Robert A. Kraft and Ann-Elizabeth Purintun. SBLTT 1. Pseudepigrapha Series 1. Missoula, Mont.: SBL, 1972. See also *4 Baruch.*

Parthenius. *The Love Romances; Fragments.* Translated by S. Gaselee. Pages 251–373 in *Daphnis and Chloe by Longus; The Love Romances of Parthenius; and Other Fragments.* Translated by George Thornley and S. Gaselee. LCL. Cambridge, Mass.: Harvard University Press, 1916.

Pausanias. *Description of Greece.* Translated by W. H. S. Jones and H. A. Ormerod. 5 vols. LCL. Cambridge, Mass.: Harvard University Press, 1918–35.

Pelagius. *Pelagius's Commentary on St. Paul's Epistle to the Romans.* Translated and edited by Theodore de Bruyn. Oxford: Oxford University Press, 1993.

Persius. *Satires.* In *Juvenal and Persius.* Translated by G. G. Ramsay. Rev. ed. LCL. Cambridge, Mass.: Harvard University Press, 1940.

Pervigilium Veneris. Translated by J. W. Mackail. In *Catullus, Tibullus, Pervigilium Veneris.* Revised by G. P. Goold. 2nd rev. ed. LCL. Cambridge, Mass.: Harvard University Press, 1988.

Pesikta de-Rab Kahana: R. Kahana's Compilation of Discourses for Sabbaths and Festival Days. Translated by William G. Braude and Israel J. Kapstein. Philadelphia: Jewish Publication Society of America, 1975.

Pesikta Rabbati. Translated by William G. Braude. 2 vols. YJS 18. New Haven: Yale University Press, 1968.

Petronius. *Satyricon.* Translated by Michael Heseltine. Pages 1–324 in *Petronius; Seneca: Apocolocyntosis.* Translated by Michael Heseltine and W. H. D. Rouse. LCL. New York: Macmillan; London: Heinemann, 1913.

Petronius. *The Satyricon.* With Seneca, *The Apocolocyntosis.* Translated by J. P.

Sullivan. Rev. ed. New York: Penguin, 1986.

Philo. Translated by F. H. Colson, G. H. Whitaker, and R. Marcus. 12 vols. LCL. Cambridge, Mass.: Harvard University Press, 1929–62.

Philo the Epic Poet. Translated by H. Attridge. *OTP* 2:781–84.

Philodemus. *On Death.* Translation, introduction, and notes by W. Benjamin Henry. SBLWGRW 29. Atlanta: SBL, 2009.

Philodemus. *On Frank Criticism.* Edited and translated by David Konstan et al. SBLTT 43. Graeco-Roman Series 13. Atlanta: Scholars Press, 1998.

Philodemus, On Property Management. Translated with an introduction and notes by Voula Tsouna. SBLWGRW 33. Atlanta: SBL, 2012.

Philostratus, Flavius. *Heroikos.* Edited and translated by Jennifer K. Berenson Maclean and Ellen Bradshaw Aitken. Prologue by Gregory Nagy. Epilogue by Hemut Koester. SBLWGRW 1. Atlanta: SBL, 2001.

Philostratus, Flavius. *The Life of Apollonius of Tyana.* Translated by F. C. Conybeare. 2 vols. LCL. Cambridge, Mass.: Harvard University Press, 1912.

Philostratus, Flavius, and Eunapius. *The Lives of the Sophists.* Translated by Wilmer Cave Wright. LCL. New York: G. P. Putnam's Sons; London: Heinemann, 1922.

Philostratus the Elder. *Imagines;* Callistratus, *Descriptions.* Translated by Arthur Fairbanks. LCL. New York: G. P. Putnam's Sons; London: Heinemann, 1931.

Pindar. *Odes.* Translated by William H. Race. 2 vols. LCL. Cambridge, Mass.: Harvard University Press, 1997.

Plato. Translated by Harold North Fowler et al. 12 vols. LCL. Cambridge, Mass.: Harvard University Press, 1914–26.

Pliny the Elder. *Natural History.* Translated by H. Rackham, W. H. S. Jones, and D. E. Eichholz. 10 vols. LCL. Cambridge, Mass.: Harvard University Press, 1938–62.

Pliny the Younger. *Letters and Panegyricus.* Translated by Betty Radice. 2 vols. LCL. Cambridge, Mass.: Harvard University Press, 1969.

Plotinus. *Enneads.* Translated by A. H. Armstrong. 7 vols. LCL. Cambridge, Mass.: Harvard University Press, 1966–88.

Plutarch. *Lives.* Translated by Bernadotte Perrin et al. 11 vols. LCL. Cambridge, Mass.: Harvard University Press, 1914–26.

Plutarch. *Moralia.* Translated by Frank Cole Babbitt et al. 17 vols. in 18. LCL. New York: G. P. Putnam's Sons; Cambridge,

Mass.: Harvard University Press; London: Heinemann, 1927–2004.

Polybius. *The Histories*. Translated by W. R. Paton. 6 vols. LCL. Cambridge, Mass.: Harvard University Press, 1922–27.

Polybius. *The Rise of the Roman Empire*. Edited by F. W. Walbank. Translated by Ian Scott-Kilvert. New York: Penguin, 1979.

Porphyry. *Against the Christians: The Literary Remains*. Edited and translated by R. Joseph Hoffmann. Amherst, N.Y.: Prometheus, 1994.

Porphyry. *On Aristotle's Categories*. Translated by Steven K. Strange. Ithaca, N.Y.: Cornell University Press, 1992.

Porphyry. *Porphyry the Philosopher to Marcella*. Edited and translated by Kathleen O'Brien Wicker. SBLTT 28. Graeco-Roman Religion Series 10. Atlanta: Scholars Press, 1987.

Porphyry the Phoenician. *Isagoge*. Edited and translated by Edward W. Warren. Toronto: Pontifical Institute of Mediaeval Studies, 1975.

Prayer of Joseph. Translated by J. Z. Smith. OTP 2:699–714.

Proclus the Successor on Poetics and the Homeric Poems: Essays 5 and 6 of His Commentary on the Republic of Plato. Translated with an introduction and notes by Robert Lamberton. SBLWGRW 34. Atlanta: SBL, 2012.

Progymnasmata: Greek Textbooks of Prose Composition and Rhetoric. Edited and translated by George A. Kennedy. SBLWGRW 10. Atlanta: SBL, 2003.

Propertius. *The Elegies*. Translated by H. E. Butler. LCL. Cambridge, Mass.: Harvard University Press, 1912.

Psalmi Salomonis. Pages 471–89 in vol. 2 of *Septuaginta id est Vetus Testamentum Graece*. Edited by Alfred Rahlfs. 2 vols. Stuttgart: Deutsche Bibelgesellschaft, 1979.

Psalms of Solomon. Translated by R. B. Wright. OTP 2:651–70.

Pseudo-Callisthenes. *The Alexander Romance*. Translated by Ken Dowden. CAGN 650–735.

Pseudo-Dionysius of Halicarnassus. *On Epideictic Speeches*. Pages 362–81 in *Menander Rhetor*. Edited and translated by D. A. Russell and N. G. Wilson. Oxford: Clarendon, 1981.

Pseudo-Eupolemus. Translated by R. Doran. OTP 2:873–82.

Pseudo-Hecataeus. Translated by R. Doran. OTP 2:905–19.

Pseudo-Philo. Translated by Daniel J. Harrington. OTP 2:297–377.

Pseudo-Philo. *Liber antiquitatum biblicarum*. Edited by Guido Kisch. Publications in Mediaeval Studies 10. Notre Dame, Ind.:

University of Notre Dame Press, 1949. Latin text.

Pseudo-Phocylides. Pages 95–112 in *Theognis, Ps.-Pythagoras, Ps.-Phocylides, Chares, Anonymi aulodia, Fragmentum teliambicum*. Edited by Ernst Diehl and Douglas Young. 2nd ed. Teubner. Leipzig: Teubner, 1971. Greek text.

Pseudo-Phocylides. Translated by P. W. van der Horst. OTP 2:565–82.

Pseudo-Scylax of Caria. *Periplum maris interni*. Edited by B. Fabricius [H. T. Dietrich]. Leipzig: Teubner, 1878.

Ptolemy. *Geographia*. Edited by K. F. A. Nobbe. 3 vols. in 2. Leipzig: K. Tauchnitz, 1843–45.

Ptolemy. *Tetrabiblos*. Translated by F. E. Robbins. LCL. Cambridge, Mass.: Harvard University Press, 1940.

Publilius Syrus. *Sententiae*. Pages 14–111 in *Minor Latin Poets*. Translated by J. Wight Duff and Arnold M. Duff. Rev. ed. LCL. Cambridge, Mass.: Harvard University Press, 1935.

Quintilian. *The Institutio oratoria*. Translated by H. E. Butler. 4 vols. LCL. Cambridge, Mass.: Harvard University Press; London: Heinemann, 1920–22.

[Quintilian] *The Lesser Declamations*. Edited and translated by D. R. Shackleton Bailey. 2 vols. LCL. Cambridge, Mass.: Harvard University Press, 2006.

Quintus Curtius. *History of Alexander*. Translated by John C. Rolfe. 2 vols. LCL. Cambridge, Mass.: Harvard University Press; London: Heinemann, 1946.

Rhetorica ad Alexandrum. Translated by H. Rackham. Pages 258–449 in vol. 2 of Aristotle, *Problems*. Translated by W. S. Hett. 2 vols. LCL. Cambridge, Mass.: Harvard University Press; London: Heinemann, 1936–37.

Rhetorica ad Herennium. Translated by Harry Caplan. Vol. 1 of *Cicero*. Translated by Harry Caplan et al. 29 vols. LCL. Cambridge, Mass.: Harvard University Press, 1954.

Sallust. Translated by J. C. Rolfe. LCL. Cambridge, Mass.: Harvard University Press, 1931.

Select Papyri. Vol. 1: *Non-literary Papyri: Private Affairs*. Vol. 2: *Non-literary Papyri: Public Documents*. Vol. 3: *Literary Papyri: Poetry*. Translated by A. S. Hunt, C. C. Edgar, and D. L. Page. 3 vols. in 5. LCL. Cambridge, Mass.: Harvard University Press, 1932–41.

Seneca the Elder. *Declamations* [*Controversiae* and *Suasoriae*]. Translated by M. Winterbottom. 2 vols. LCL. Cambridge, Mass.: Harvard University Press; London: Heinemann, 1974.

Seneca the Younger. *Ad Lucilium epistulae morales*. Translated by Richard M. Gummere. 3 vols. LCL. Cambridge, Mass.: Harvard University Press, 1920–34.

Seneca the Younger. *Moral Essays*. Translated by John W. Basore. 3 vols. LCL. Cambridge, Mass.: Harvard University Press, 1928–35.

Seneca the Younger. *Naturales quaestiones*. Translated by Thomas H. Corcoran. 2 vols. LCL. Cambridge, Mass.: Harvard University Press, 1971–72.

Seneca the Younger. *Tragedies*. Translated by John G. Fitch. LCL. Cambridge, Mass.: Harvard University Press, 2002.

The Sentences of Sextus. Edited and translated by Richard A. Edwards and Robert A. Wild. SBLTT 22. Early Christian Literature Series 5. Chico, Calif.: Scholars Press, 1981.

Sentences of the Syriac Menander. Translated by T. Baarda. OTP 2:583–606.

Septuaginta id est Vetus Testamentum Graece. Edited by Alfred Rahlfs. 2 vols. Stuttgart: Deutsche Bibelgesellschaft, 1979.

Sextus Empiricus. Translated by R. G. Bury. 4 vols. LCL. Cambridge, Mass.: Harvard University Press, 1933–49.

Sibylline Oracles. Translated by J. J. Collins. OTP 1:317–472. See also *Die Oracula sibyllina*.

Sifra: An Analytical Translation. Translated by Jacob Neusner. 3 vols. BJS 138–40. Atlanta: Scholars Press, 1988.

Sifra de-ve Rav. Edited by I. H. Weiss. Vienna, 1862.

Sifre to Deuteronomy: An Analytical Translation. Translated by Jacob Neusner. 2 vols. BJS 98, 101. Atlanta: Scholars Press, 1987.

Sifré to Numbers: An American Translation and Explanation. Translated by Jacob Neusner. 2 vols. BJS 118–19. Atlanta: Scholars Press, 1986.

Silius Italicus. *Punica*. Translated by J. D. Duff. 2 vols. LCL. Cambridge, Mass.: Harvard University Press, 1927–34.

Sophocles. Translated by Hugh Lloyd-Jones. 3 vols. LCL. Cambridge, Mass.: Harvard University Press, 1994–96.

Soranus. *Gynecology*. Translated by Owsei Temkin, with the assistance of Nicholson J. Eastman, Ludwig Edelstein, and Alan F. Guttmacher. Baltimore: Johns Hopkins University Press, 1956.

Statius. Translated by J. H. Mozley. 2 vols. Rev. ed. LCL. Cambridge, Mass.: Harvard University Press; London: Heinemann, 1928–55.

Stobaeus. *Eclogarum physicarum et ethicarum libri duo*. Edited by Augustus Meineke. 2 vols. Leipzig: Teubner, 1860–64.

Stobaeus. *Florilegium.* In *Anthologium.* Edited by Otto Hense. 5 vols. Berlin: Weidmann, 1884–1912.

Strabo. *Geography.* Translated by Horace Leonard Jones and John Robert Sitlington Sterrett. 8 vols. LCL. Cambridge, Mass.: Harvard University Press, 1917–32.

Suetonius. Translated by J. C. Rolfe. 2 vols. LCL. New York: Macmillan; Cambridge, Mass.: Harvard University Press; London: Heinemann, 1914.

Suetonius. *The Twelve Caesars.* Translated by Robert Graves. Baltimore: Penguin, 1957.

Symmachus. See *The Letters of Symmachus.*

Tacitus. *The Annals of Imperial Rome.* Rev. ed. Translated by Michael Grant. Baltimore: Penguin, 1959.

Tacitus. *The Complete Works.* Edited by Moses Hadas. Translated by Alfred John Church and William Jackson Brodribb. New York: Modern Library, 1942.

Tacitus. *Dialogus; Agricola; Germanica.* Translated by William Peterson and Maurice Hutton. LCL. New York: G. P. Putnam's Sons, 1914.

Tacitus. *The Histories.* Translated by Clifford H. Moore. 2 vols. LCL. London: Heinemann; Cambridge, Mass.: Harvard University Press, 1937–48.

Talmud of the Land of Israel: A Preliminary Translation and Explanation. Edited by Jacob Neusner. 35 vols. Chicago: University of Chicago Press, 1982–94.

Targum Jonathan of the Former Prophets. Translated by Daniel J. Harrington and Anthony J. Saldarini. Aramaic Bible 10. Wilmington, Del.: Michael Glazier, 1987.

Targum Neofiti 1: Deuteronomy. Translated by Martin McNamara. Aramaic Bible 5A. Collegeville, Minn.: Liturgical Press, 1997.

Targum Neofiti 1: Exodus. Translated by Martin McNamara, with notes by Robert Hayward. With *Targum Pseudo-Jonathan: Exodus.* Translated by Michael Maher. Aramaic Bible 2. Collegeville, Minn.: Liturgical Press, 1994.

Targum Neofiti 1: Genesis. Translated by Martin McNamara. Aramaic Bible 1A. Collegeville, Minn.: Liturgical Press, 1992.

Targum Neofiti 1: Leviticus. Translated by Martin McNamara, with notes by Robert Hayward. With *Targum Pseudo-Jonathan: Leviticus.* Translated by Michael Maher. Aramaic Bible 3. Collegeville, Minn.: Liturgical Press, 1994.

Targum Neofiti 1: Numbers. Translated by Martin McNamara. With *Targum Pseudo-Jonathan: Numbers.* Translated by Ernest G. Clarke, with Shirley Magder. Aramaic Bible 4. Collegeville, Minn.: Liturgical Press, 1995.

The Targum of Ezekiel. Translated by Samson H. Levy. Aramaic Bible 13. Wilmington, Del.: Michael Glazier, 1987.

The Targum of Jeremiah. Translated by Robert Hayward. Aramaic Bible 12. Wilmington, Del.: Michael Glazier, 1987.

The Targum of Job. Translated by Céline Mangan. With *The Targum of Proverbs.* Translated by John F. Healey. And *The Targum of Qohelet.* Translated by Peter S. Knobel. Aramaic Bible 15. Collegeville, Minn.: Liturgical Press, 1991.

The Targum of Ruth. Translated by D. R. G. Beattie. With *The Targum of Chronicles.* Translated by J. Stanley McIvor. Aramaic Bible 19. Collegeville: Liturgical Press, 1994.

The Targum of the Minor Prophets. Translated by Kevin J. Cathcart and Robert P. Gordon. Aramaic Bible 14. Wilmington, Del.: Michael Glazier, 1989.

The Targum Onqelos to Deuteronomy. Translated by Bernard Grossfeld. Aramaic Bible 9. Wilmington, Del.: Michael Glazier, 1988.

The Targum Onqelos to Exodus. Translated by Bernard Grossfeld. Aramaic Bible 7. Wilmington, Del.: Michael Glazier, 1988.

The Targum Onqelos to Genesis. Translated by Bernard Grossfeld. Aramaic Bible 6. Wilmington, Del.: Michael Glazier, 1988.

The Targum Onqelos to Leviticus and to Numbers. Translated by Bernard Grossfeld. Aramaic Bible 8. Wilmington, Del.: Michael Glazier, 1988.

Targum Pseudo-Jonathan: Deuteronomy. Translated by Ernest G. Clarke. Aramaic Bible 5B. Collegeville, Minn.: Liturgical Press, 1998.

Targum Pseudo-Jonathan: Exodus. See entry for *Targum Neofiti 1: Exodus.*

Targum Pseudo-Jonathan: Genesis. Translated by Michael Maher. Aramaic Bible 1B. Collegeville, Minn.: Liturgical Press, 1992.

"Temple Program for the New Year's Festivals at Babylon." Translated by A. Sachs. Pages 331–34 in *ANET.* Edited by J. B. Pritchard. 2nd ed. Princeton: Princeton University Press, 1955.

The Temple Scroll: An Introduction, Translation, and Commentary. By Johann Maier. JSOTSup 34. Sheffield, U.K.: JSOT Press, 1985.

Terence. Translated by John Sargeaunt. 2 vols. LCL. Cambridge, Mass.: Harvard University Press, 1912.

Tertullian. *Apology; De spectaculis.* Translated by T. R. Glover. LCL. Cambridge, Mass.: Harvard University Press, 1931.

Testament of Abraham. Translated by E. P. Sanders. *OTP* 1:882–902.

The Testament of Abraham: The Greek Recensions. Translated by Michael E. Stone.

SBLTT 2. Pseudepigrapha Series 2. Missoula, Mont.: SBL, 1972.

Testament of Adam. Translated by S. E. Robinson. *OTP* 1:993–95.

Testament of Isaac. Translated by W. F. Stinespring. *OTP* 1:903–11.

Testament of Job. Translated by R. P. Spittler. *OTP* 1:839–68.

The Testament of Job according to the SV Text. Edited by Robert A. Kraft, with Harold Attridge, Russell Spittler, and Janet Timbie. SBLTT 5. Pseudepigrapha Series 4. Missoula, Mont.: Scholars Press, 1974.

Testament of Moses. Translated by J. Priest. *OTP* 1:919–34.

Testament of Solomon. Translated by D. C. Duling. *OTP* 1:935–87.

The Testament of Solomon. Edited by Chester Charlton McCown. Leipzig: J. C. Hinrichs, 1922. Greek text.

Testaments of the Twelve Patriarchs. The Greek Versions of the Testaments of the Twelve Patriarchs, Edited from Nine MSS together with the Variants of the Armenian and Slavonic Versions and Some Hebrew Fragments. Edited by R. H. Charles. Oxford: Clarendon, 1908.

Die Texte aus Qumran. Vol. 1. Edited by Eduard Lohse. 2nd ed. Munich: Kösel, 1971.

Theodotus. Translated by F. Fallon. *OTP* 2:790–93.

Theognis, Ps.-Pythagoras, Ps.-Phocylides, Chares, Anonymi aulodia, Fragmentum teliambicum. Edited by Ernst Diehl and Douglas Young. 2nd ed. Teubner. Leipzig: Teubner, 1971.

Theon, Aelius. "The Progymnasmata of Theon the Sophist: A New Text with Translation and Commentary." By James R. Butts. PhD diss., Claremont Graduate School, 1987.

Theophrastus. *Characters.* Translated by J. M. Edmonds. LCL. Cambridge, Mass.: Harvard University Press, 1929.

Theophrastus. *De causis plantarum.* Translated by Benedict Einarson and George K. K. Link. 3 vols. LCL. Cambridge, Mass.: Harvard University Press, 1976–90.

Thucydides. *History of the Peloponnesian War.* Translated by Charles Forster Smith. 4 vols. Rev. ed. LCL. Cambridge, Mass.: Harvard University Press, 1921–30.

Tibullus. Translated by J. P. Postgate. In *Catullus, Tibullus, Pervigilium Veneris.* Revised by G. P. Goold. 2nd rev. ed. LCL. Cambridge, Mass.: Harvard University Press, 1988.

The Tosefta. Translated by Jacob Neusner et al. 6 vols. New York: KTAV, 1977–86.

Treatise of Shem. Translated by J. H. Charlesworth. *OTP* 1:481–86.

Tripartite Tractate (I, 5). Translated by H. W. Attridge and Dieter Mueller. Introduction by H. W. Attridge and E. Pagels. *NHL* 54–97.

The Two Targums of Esther. Translated by Bernard Grossfeld. Aramaic Bible 18. Collegeville, Minn.: Liturgical Press, 1991.

Valerius Flaccus. *Argonautica*. Translated by J. H. Mozley. Rev. ed. LCL. Cambridge, Mass.: Harvard University Press, 1936.

Valerius Maximus. *Memorable Deeds and Sayings*. Edited and translated by D. R. Shackleton Bailey. 2 vols. LCL. Cambridge, Mass.: Harvard University Press, 2000.

Valerius Maximus. *Memorable Deeds and Sayings, Book 1*. Edited and translated by D. Wardle. Oxford: Clarendon, 1998.

Varro. *On the Latin Language*. Translated by Roland G. Kent. 2 vols. LCL. Cambridge, Mass.: Harvard University Press, 1938.

Velleius Paterculus. *Compendium of Roman History. Res Gestae Divi Augusti*. Translated by Frederick W. Shipley. LCL 152. Cambridge, Mass.: Harvard University Press, 1924.

Vettius Valens. *Anthologiarum libri*. Edited by W. Kroll. Berlin: Weidmann, 1908.

Vettius Valens. *Anthologiarum libri novem*. Edited by David Pingree. Teubner. Leipzig: Teubner, 1986.

Virgil. Translated by H. Rushton Fairclough. 2 vols. Rev. ed. LCL. Cambridge, Mass.: Harvard University Press, 1934–35.

Vitruvius. *On Architecture*. Translated by Frank Granger. 2 vols. New York: G. P. Putnam's Sons; London: William Heinemann, 1931–34.

Xenophon. *Cyropaedia*. Translated by Walter Miller. 2 vols. LCL. Cambridge, Mass.: Harvard University Press, 1914.

Xenophon. *Hellenica; Anabasis*. Translated by Carleton L. Brownson. 3 vols. LCL. Cambridge, Mass.: Harvard University Press, 1918–22.

Xenophon. *Memorabilia; Oeconomicus*. Translated by E. C. Marchant. LCL. Cambridge, Mass.: Harvard University Press, 1923.

Xenophon. *Scriptura minora*. Translated by E. C. Marchant. LCL. Cambridge, Mass.: Harvard University Press, 1925.

Xenophon. *Symposium; Apology*. Translated by O. J. Todd. LCL. Cambridge, Mass.: Harvard University Press, 1922.

Xenophon of Ephesus. *An Ephesian Tale*. Translated by Graham Anderson. *CAGN* 125–69.

Secondary Sources

Aalen, "Chapters." Aalen, Sverre. "St Luke's Gospel and the Last Chapters of I Enoch." *NTS* 13 (1, 1966): 1–13.

Aalen, "Reign." Aalen, Sverre. "'Reign' and 'House' in the Kingdom of God in the Gospels." *NTS* 8 (3, 1962): 215–40.

Aarde, "Houses." Aarde, Andries G. van. "'The Most High God Does Live in Houses, but Not Houses Built by Men . . .': The Relativity of the Metaphor 'Temple' in Luke-Acts." *Neot* 25 (1, 1991): 51–64.

Aarde, "Methods." Aarde, Andries G. van. "Methods and Models in the Quest for the Historical Jesus: Historical Criticism and/or Social Scientific Criticism." *HTS/TS* 58 (2, 2002): 419–39.

Aasgaard, "Role Ethics." Aasgaard, R. "'Role Ethics' in Paul: The Significance of the Sibling Role for Paul's Ethical Thinking." *NTS* 48 (4, 2002): 513–30.

Abasciano, "Diamonds." Abasciano, B. J. "Diamonds in the Rough: A Reply to Christopher Stanley concerning the Reader Competency of Paul's Original Audiences." *NovT* 49 (2, 2007): 153–83.

Abbott, *Acts.* Abbott, Lyman. *The Acts of the Apostles: With Notes, Comments, Maps, and Illustrations.* New York: A. S. Barnes, 1876.

Abdalla, "Friend." Abdalla, Ismail H. "Neither Friend nor Foe: The *malam* Practitioner–*yan bori* Relationship in Hausaland." Pages 37–48 in *Women's Medicine: The zar-bori Cult in Africa and Beyond.* Edited by I. M. Lewis, Ahmed Al-Safi, and Sayyid Hurreiz. Edinburgh: Edinburgh University Press for the International African Institute, 1991.

Abegg, "4QMMT." Abegg, Martin, Jr. "Miqsat Ma'asey ha-Torah (4QMMT)." *DNTB* 709–11.

Abegg, "Hebrew Language." Abegg, Martin, Jr. "Hebrew Language." *DNTB* 459–63.

Abegg, "Hope." Abegg, Martin, Jr. "Messianic Hope and 4Q285: A Reassessment." *JBL* 113 (1, 1994): 81–91.

Abegg, "Introduction to 1Q29." Abegg, Martin, Jr. Introduction to "Tongues of Fire (1Q29, 4Q376)." *DSSNT* 178–79.

Abegg, "Introduction to 4Q251." Abegg, Martin, Jr. Introduction to "A Commentary on the Law of Moses (4Q251)." *DSSNT* 271–72.

Abegg, "Introduction to 4Q265." Abegg, Martin, Jr. Introduction to "Portions of Sectarian Law (4Q265)." *DSSNT* 278.

Abegg, "Introduction to 4Q276–277." Abegg, Martin, Jr. Introduction to "The Ashes of the Red Heifer (4Q276–277)." *DSSNT* 283–84.

Abegg, "Introduction to 4Q285." Abegg, Martin, Jr. Introduction to "The War of the Messiah (4Q285, 11Q14)." *DSSNT* 291–92.

Abegg, "Introduction to 4Q369." Abegg, Martin, Jr. Introduction to "The Inheritance of the Firstborn, the Messiah of David (4Q369)." *DSSNT* 328–29.

Abegg, "Liturgy: Qumran." Abegg, Martin, Jr. "Liturgy: Qumran." *DNTB* 648–50.

Abegg, "Messiah." Abegg, Martin, Jr. "The Messiah at Qumran: Are We Still Seeing Double?" *DSD* 2 (2, 1995): 125–44.

Abegg, "Pseudo-prophets." Abegg, Martin, Jr. "Pseudo-prophets (4Q385–388, 390–391)." *DNTB* 869–70.

Abell, *Experience.* Abell, Troy D. *Better Felt Than Said: The Holiness-Pentecostal Experience in Southern Appalachia.* Waco: Markham, 1982.

Abelson, *Immanence.* Abelson, Joshua. *The Immanence of God in Rabbinical Literature.* 2nd ed. New York: Hermon, 1969.

Aberbach, "Hzqyhw." Aberbach, Moses. "Hzqyhw mlk yhwdh wrby yhwdh hsny': hqsrym msyhyym." *Tarbiz* 53 (3, 1984): 353–71.

Abogunrin, "Search." Abogunrin, Samuel O. "The Modern Search of the Historical Jesus in Relation to Christianity in Africa." *AfThJ* 9 (3, 1980): 18–29.

Abraham, "Good News to Poor." Abraham, M. V. "Good News to the Poor in Luke's Gospel." *BangTF* 19 (1987): 1–13.

Abrahams, *Studies* (1). Abrahams, I. *Studies in Pharisaism and the Gospels.* 1st ser. Cambridge: Cambridge University Press, 1917. Repr., with prolegomenon by Morton S. Enslin. Library of Biblical Studies. New York: KTAV, 1967.

Abrahams, *Studies* (2). Abrahams, I. *Studies in Pharisaism and the Gospels.* 2nd ser. Cambridge: Cambridge University Press, 1924.

Abrahamsen, "Reliefs." Abrahamsen, Valerie Ann. "The Rock Reliefs and the Cult of Diana at Philippi." ThD diss., Harvard University, May 1986.

Abrahamsen, "Rock Reliefs." Abrahamsen, Valerie Ann. "Christianity and the Rock Reliefs at Philippi." *BA* 51 (1, 1988): 46–56.

Abrahamsen, "Women at Philippi." Abrahamsen, Valerie Ann. "Women at Philippi: The Pagan and Christian Evidence." *JFSR* 3 (2, 1987): 17–30.

Abrams, "Boundaries." Abrams, Daniel. "The Boundaries of Divine Ontology: The Inclusion and Exclusion of Metatron in the Godhead." *HTR* 87 (3, 1994): 291–321.

Abri, "Meaning of Pentecost." Abri, J. "The Theological Meaning of Pentecost." [In Japanese.] *Kator shin* (1, 1965): 133–51. (Abstract: *NTA* 10:53.)

Abusch, "Ghost." Abusch, Tzvi. "Ghost and God: Some Observations on a Babylonian Understanding of Human Nature." Pages 373–77 in *Self, Soul and Body in Religious Experience.* Edited by Albert I. Baumgarten with Jan Assmann and Guy G. Stroumsa. SHR 68. Leiden: Brill, 1998.

Accoroni, "Healing Practices." Accoroni, Dafne. "Healing Practices among the Senegalese Community in Paris." Pages 3–17 in *Studies in Witchcraft, Magic, War, and Peace in Africa*. Edited by Beatrice Nicolini. Lewiston, N.Y.: Edwin Mellen, 2006.

Achebe, "Ogbanje Phenomenon." Achebe, Chinwe C. "The Ogbanje Phenomenon—An Interpretation." Pages 24–43 in *Healing and Exorcism—The Nigerian Experience: Proceedings, Lectures, Discussions, and Conclusions of the First Missiology Symposium on Healing and Exorcism, Organised by the Spiritan International School of Theology, Attakwu, Enugu, May 18–20, 1989*. Edited by Chris U. Manus, Luke N. Mbefo, and E. E. Uzukwu. Enugu, Nigeria: Snapp, 1992.

Achtemeier, "Light." Achtemeier, Elizabeth R. "Jesus Christ, the Light of the World: The Biblical Understanding of Light and Darkness." *Interpretation* 17 (1963): 439–49.

Achtemeier, *Miracle Tradition*. Achtemeier, Paul J. *Jesus and the Miracle Tradition*. Eugene, Ore.: Cascade, 2008.

Achtemeier, "Miracle Workers." Achtemeier, Paul J. "Jesus and the Disciples as Miracle Workers in the Apocryphal New Testament." Pages 149–86 in *Aspects of Religious Propaganda in Judaism and Early Christianity*. Edited by Elisabeth Schüssler Fiorenza. UNDCSJCA 2. Notre Dame, Ind.: University of Notre Dame Press, 1976.

Achtemeier, "Perspective on Miracles." Achtemeier, Paul J. "The Lucan Perspective on the Miracles of Jesus: A Preliminary Sketch." *JBL* 94 (4, 1975): 547–62. Repr., pages 153–67 in *Perspectives on Luke-Acts*. ABPRSSS 5. Edited by Charles H. Talbert. Danville, Va.: Association of Baptist Professors of Religion; Edinburgh: T&T Clark, 1978.

Ackerman and Lee, "Communication." Ackerman, Susan E., and Raymond L. M. Lee. "Communication and Cognitive Pluralism in a Spirit Possession Event in Malaysia." *AmEthn* 8 (4, 1981): 789–99.

Ackroyd, *1 Samuel*. Ackroyd, Peter R. *The First Book of Samuel*. CBC. Cambridge: Cambridge University Press, 1971.

Acworth, "Where Was Paul Shipwrecked?" Acworth, Angus. "Where Was St. Paul Shipwrecked? A Re-examination of the Evidence." *JTS* 24 (1, 1973): 190–93.

Adam with Vercoutter, "Importance of Nubia." Adam, S., with J. Vercoutter. "The Importance of Nubia: A Link between Central Africa and the Mediterranean." Pages 226–43 in *Ancient Civilizations of Africa*. Edited by G. Mokhtar. General History of Africa 2. Berkeley: University of California Press; London: Heinemann Educational; Paris: United Nations Educational, Scientific and Cultural Organization, 1981.

Adamo, *Africa*. Adamo, David Tuesday. *Africa and Africans in the Old Testament*. International Scholars Publications. San Francisco: Christian Universities Press, 1998.

Adamo, "Africa." Adamo, David Tuesday. "The Place of Africa and Africans in the Old Testament and Its Environment." PhD diss., Baylor University, 1986.

Adams, "Citizenship." Adams, Sean A. "Paul the Roman Citizen: Roman Citizenship in the Ancient World and Its Importance for Understanding Acts 22:22–29." Pages 309–26 in *Paul: Jew, Greek, and Roman*. Edited by Stanley Porter. PAST 5. Leiden: Brill, 2008.

Adams, *Genre*. Adams, Sean A. *The Genre of Acts and Collected Biography*. SNTSMS 156. Cambridge: Cambridge University Press, 2013.

Adams, *Nubia*. Adams, William Y. *Nubia: Corridor to Africa*. Princeton: Princeton University Press, 1977.

Adams, *Period*. Adams, Alice Dana. *The Neglected Period of Anti-Slavery in America (1808–1831)*. Radcliffe College Monographs 14. Gloucester, Mass.: Peter Smith, 1964.

Adams, "Placing." Adams, Edward. "Placing the Corinthian Communal Meal." Pages 22–37 in *Text, Image, and Christians in the Graeco-Roman World: A Festschrift in Honor of David Lee Balch*. Edited by Aliou Cissé Niang and Carolyn Osiek. PrTMS 176. Eugene, Ore.: Pickwick, 2012.

Adams, "Preface." Adams, Sean A. "Luke's Preface and Its Relationship to Greek Historiography: A Response to Loveday Alexander." *JGRCJ* 3 (2006): 177–91.

Adams, "Romanitas." Adams, James N. "'Romanitas' and the Latin Language." *CQ* 53 (1, 2003): 184–205.

Adams, "Sources." Adams, Sean A. "On Sources and Speeches: Methodological Discussions in Ancient Prose Works and Luke-Acts." Pages 389–411 in *Christian Origins and Greco-Roman Culture: Social and Literary Contexts for the New Testament*. Edited by Stanley Porter and Andrew W. Pitts. Vol. 1 of Early Christianity in Its Hellenistic Context. Vol. 9 in Texts and Editions for New Testament Study. Leiden: Brill, 2013.

Adams, *Stars*. Adams, Edward. *The Stars Will Fall from Heaven: "Cosmic Catastrophe" in the New Testament and Its World*. LNTS 347. New York: T&T Clark, 2007.

Adamsheck, *Pottery*. Adamsheck, Beverly. *The Pottery*. Vol. 4 of *Kenchreai, Eastern Port of Corinth: Results of Investigations by the University of Chicago and Indiana University for the American School of Classical Studies at Athens*. Leiden: Brill, 1979.

Adeniyi, "Interaction." Adeniyi, M. O. "Interaction Through Medicine, Charms, and Amulets: Islam and the Yoruba Traditional Religion." Pages 58–62 in *Religion, Medicine, and Healing*. Edited by Gbola Aderibigbe and Deji Ayegboyin. Lagos: Nigerian Association for the Study of Religions and Education, 1995.

Adewuya, "Reading." Adewuya, J. Ayodeji. "Reading Ephesians 6:10–18 in the Light of African Pentecostal Spirituality." Pages 83–93 in *Global Voices: Reading the Bible in the Majority World*. Edited by Craig Keener and M. Daniel Carroll R. Foreword by Edwin Yamauchi. Peabody: Hendrickson, 2013.

Adewuya, "Revisiting." Adewuya, J. Ayodeji. "Revisiting 1 Corinthians 11.[1]7–34: Paul's Discussion of the Lord's Supper and African Meals." *JSNT* 30 (1, 2007): 95–112.

Adeyemi, "Approach." Adeyemi, M. E. "A Sociological Approach to the Background of Pauline Epistles." *DBM* 10 (1, 1991): 32–42.

Adeyemi, "Θέσεις." Adeyemi, M. E. "Οι θέσεις του Απ. Παύλου για τη σωτηρία από τις δυνάμεις του κακού." *DBM* 20 (1, 2001): 82–96.

Adeyemo, "Dreams." Adeyemo, Tokunboh. "Dreams." Page 993 in *Africa Bible Commentary*. Edited by Tokunboh Adeyemo. Grand Rapids: Zondervan; Nairobi: WordAlive, 2006.

Adinolfi, "Autorità romane." Adinolfi, Marco. "San Paolo e le autorità romane negli Atti degli apostoli." *Antonianum* 53 (3–4, 1978): 452–70.

Adinolfi, "Tarso." Adinolfi, Marco. "Tarso, patria di stoici." *BeO* 19 (5, 1977): 185–94.

Adkin, "Underwear." Adkin, Neil. "Did the Romans Keep Their Underwear on in Bed?" *CW* 93 (6, 2000): 619–20.

Adkins, *Merit*. Adkins, Arthur W. *Merit and Responsibility: A Study in Greek Values*. Oxford: Clarendon, 1960.

Adkins and Adkins, *Life*. Adkins, Lesley, and Roy A. Adkins. *Handbook to Life in Ancient Rome*. New York: Oxford University Press, 1994.

Adler, "Adjacent." Adler, Yonathan. "Second Temple Period Ritual Baths Adjacent to Agricultural Installations: The Archaeological Evidence in Light of Halakhic Sources." *JJS* 59 (1, 2008): 62–72.

Adler, "Anti-Roman." Adler, Eric. "Who's Anti-Roman? Sallust and Pompeius Trogus on Mithridates." *CJ* 101 (4, 2006): 383–407.

Adler, "Baths." Adler, Yonathan. "The Ritual Baths near the Temple Mount and Extra-purification before Entering the Temple Courts: A Reply to Eyal Regev." *IEJ* 56 (2, 2006): 209–15.

Adler, "Pathogenesis." Adler, Shelley R. "Ethnomedical Pathogenesis and Hmong Immigrants' Sudden Nocturnal Deaths." *CMPsy* 18 (1994): 23–59.

Adler, *Pfingstfest.* Adler, Nikolaus. *Das erste christliche Pfingstfest: Sinn und Bedeutung des Pfingstberichtes Apg 2:1–13.* Münster: Aschendorff, 1938.

Adler, *Taufe.* Adler, Nikolaus. *Taufe und Handauflegung: Eine exegetisch-theologische Untersuchung von Apg 8:14–17.* Münster: Aschendorff, 1951.

Adler, "Tombs." Adler, Yonathan. "Ritual Baths Adjacent to Tombs: An Analysis of the Archaeological Evidence in Light of the Halakhic Sources." *JSJ* 40 (1, 2009): 55–73.

Adler, "Virgin." Adler, Rachel. "The Virgin in the Brothel and Other Anomalies: Character and Context in the Legend of Beruriah." *Tikkun* 3 (6, 1988): 28–32, 102–5.

Ådna, "Herrens." Ådna, Jostein. "Herrens tjener i Jesaja 53 skildret som triumferende Messias: Profettargumens gjengivelse og tolkning av Jes 52,13–53,12." *TTKi* 63 (2, 1992): 81–94.

Adogbo, "Pollution." Adogbo, Michael P. "A Comparative Study of Pollution in African and Biblical Traditions." *AJT* 20 (1, 2006): 103–13.

"Aetiology." "Aetiology: Roman Literature." *BrillPauly* 15: 982–84.

Ager, "Civic Identity." Ager, Sheila L. "Civic Identity in the Hellenistic World: The Case of Lebedos." *GRBS* 39 (1, 1998): 5–21.

Ager, "Familiarity." Ager, Sheila L. "Familiarity Breeds: Incest and the Ptolemaic Dynasty." *JHS* 125 (2005): 1–34.

Agnew, "Adversary." Agnew, Francis H. "Paul's Theological Adversary in the Doctrine of Justification by Faith: A Contribution to Jewish-Christian Dialogue." *JES* 25 (4, 1988): 538–54.

Agosto, "Conventions." Agosto, Efrain. "Paul's Use of Greco-Roman Conventions of Commendation." PhD diss., Boston University Graduate School, 1996.

Agosto, "Paul and Commendation." Agosto, Efrain. "Paul and Commendation." Pages 101–33 in *Paul in the Greco-Roman World: A Handbook.* Edited by J. Paul Sampley. Harrisburg, Pa.: Trinity Press International, 2003.

Agosto, "Publics." Agosto, Efrain. "Who Is It For? The Publics of Theological Research." *Theological Education* 43 (2, 2008): 11–20.

Agosto, "Social Analysis." Agosto, Efrain. "Social Analysis of the New Testament and Hispanic Theology: A Case Study." *JHLT* 5 (4, 1998): 6–29.

Agouridis, "Ἀντιμετωπιση." Agouridis, S. "ἡ ἀντιμετωπιση της Μαγειας τῶν ἑλληνιστικῶν χρονῶν ἀπο το Βιβλιῳ τῶν Πραξεων τῶν ἀποστολων." *DBM* 5 (2–3, 1977–78): 119–35. (Abstract: *NTA* 23:166.)

Agouridis, "Δεσμά του Παύλου." Agouridis, S. "Τὰ δεσμά του Παύλου κατά τις Πράξεις των Αποστόλων (Πραξ. 21, 27–28, 31)." *DBM* 18 (1, 1989): 5–29. (Abstract: *NTA* 34:324.)

Agouridis, "Son of Man." Agouridis, S. "The Son of Man in Enoch." *DBM* 2 (6, 1973): 130–47.

Aharoni, *Archaeology.* Aharoni, Yohanan. *The Archaeology of the Land of Israel.* Translated by Anson F. Rainey. Philadelphia: Westminster, 1982.

Aitken, "Rhetoric." Aitken, J. K. "Rhetoric and Poetry in Greek Ecclesiastes." *BIOSCS* 38 (2005): 55–77.

Ajibade, "Hearthstones." Ajibade, George Olusola. "Hearthstones: Religion, Ethics, and Medicine in the Healing Process in the Traditional Yorùbá Society." Pages 193–213 in *Studies in Witchcraft, Magic, War, and Peace in Africa.* Edited by Beatrice Nicolini. Lewiston, N.Y.: Edwin Mellen, 2006.

Aker, "Gifts." Aker, Benny C. "Charismata: Gifts, Enablements, or Ministries?" *JPT* 11 (1, 2002): 53–69.

Aker, "Tongues." Aker, Benny C. "The Gift of Tongues in 1 Corinthians 14:1–5." *Paraclete* 29 (1, 1995): 13–21.

Akinwumi, "Babalola." Akinwumi, Elijah Olu. "Babalola, Joseph Ayodele." No pages. *DACB.* Online: http://www.dacb.org/stories/nigeria/babalola2_joseph.html.

Akinwumi, "Idahosa." Akinwumi, Elijah Olu. "Idahosa, Benson Andrew." No pages. *DACB.* Online: http://www.dacb.org/stories/nigeria/idahosa_bensona.html.

Akinwumi, "Orimolade." Akinwumi, Elijah Olu. "Orimolade Tunolase, Moses." No pages. *DACB.* Online: http://www.dacb.org/stories/nigeria/orimolade_moses.html.

Akinwumi, "Oschoffa." Akinwumi, Elijah Olu. "Oschoffa, Samuel Bilewu." No pages. *DACB.* Online: http://www.dacb.org/stories/nigeria/oschoffa_samuelb.html.

Alamino, *Footsteps.* Alamino, Carlos. *In the Footsteps of God's Call: A Cuban Pastor's Journey.* Translated by Osmany Espinosa Hernández. Edited by David Peck and Brian Stewart. Mountlake Terrace, Wash.: Original Media Publishers, 2008.

Alarcón Sainz, "Vocables." Alarcón Sainz, Juan J. "Vocables griegos y latinos en los Proemios (Petihôt) de Lamentaciones Rabbah." *Sefarad* 49 (1, 1989): 3–10.

Albani and Glessmer, "Instrument de mesures." Albani, Matthias, and Uwe Glessmer. "Un instrument de mesures astronomiques à Qumrân." *RB* 104 (1, 1997): 88–115.

Albarella et al., *Pigs.* Albarella, Umberto, Keith Dodney, Anton Ervynck, and Peter Rowley-Conwy, eds. *Pigs and Humans: 10,000 Years of Interaction.* New York: Oxford University Press, 2008.

Albl, *Scripture.* Albl, Martin C. *"And Scripture Cannot Be Broken": The Form and Function of the Early Christian Testimonia Collections.* NovTSup 96. Leiden: Brill, 1999.

Albrecht, *Iamblichus.* Albrecht, Michael von, ed. and trans. *Iamblichus, Pythagoras: Legende, Lehre, Lebensgestaltung.* Zurich: Artemis, 1963.

Albrecht, "Thecla." Albrecht, Ruth. "Thecla." *BrillPauly* 14: 420.

Albright, *Biblical Period.* Albright, William Foxwell. *The Biblical Period from Abraham to Ezra.* New York: Harper & Row, 1963.

Albright, *Horizons.* Albright, William Foxwell. *New Horizons in Biblical Research.* London: Oxford University Press, 1966.

Albright, "Simon Magus." Albright, William Foxwell. "Appendix 7: Simon Magus as 'the Great Power of God.'" Pages 305–8 in *The Acts of the Apostles.* By Johannes Munck. Revised by William Foxwell Albright and C. S. Mann. AB 31. Garden City, N.Y.: Doubleday, 1967.

Albright, *Stone Age.* Albright, William Foxwell. *From the Stone Age to Christianity: Monotheism and the Historical Process.* Baltimore: Johns Hopkins University Press, 1946.

Albright, *Yahweh.* Albright, William Foxwell. *Yahweh and the Gods of Canaan.* Jordan Lectures, 1965. Garden City, N.Y.: Doubleday, 1968.

Albright and Mann, *Matthew.* Albright, William Foxwell, and C. S. Mann. *Matthew.* AB 26. Garden City, N.Y.: Doubleday, 1971.

Albright and Mann, "Qumran and Essenes." Albright, William Foxwell, and C. S. Mann. "Qumran and the Essenes: Geography, Chronology, and Identification of the Sect." Pages 11–25 in *The Scrolls and Christianity: Historical and Theological Significance.* Edited by Matthew Black. London: SPCK, 1969.

Albrile, "Colore." Albrile, Ezio. "Il colore dei Magi." *Antonianum* 81 (2, 2006): 323–38.

Albrile, "*Sigilla*." Albrile, Ezio. "*Sigilla anuli Salomonis:* Mito e leggenda nella tradizione magica su Salomone." *Antonianum* 82 (2, 2007): 351–72.

Alcorta, "Music." Alcorta, Candace S. "Music and the Miraculous: The Neurophysiology of Music's Emotive Meaning." Pages 230–52 in *Parapsychological Perspectives*. Vol. 3 of *Miracles: God, Science, and Psychology in the Paranormal*. Edited by J. Harold Ellens. Westport, Conn.; London: Praeger, 2008.

Aldred, *Egypt*. Aldred, Cyril. *Egypt to the End of the Old Kingdom*. New York: McGraw-Hill; London: Thames & Hudson, 1965.

Aleixandre, "Mujeres." Aleixandre, Dolores. "Sara, Raquel, y Miriam: Tres mujeres en la tradición profética y en el *midrás*." *MCom* 54 (105, 1996): 317–38.

Aletheia, "Localización." Aletheia, Xabier. "Localización de la comunidad de Lucas." *EstBib* 69 (3, 2011): 289–300.

Aletti, "*Dispositio*." Aletti, Jean-Noel. "La *dispositio* rhétorique dans les épîtres pauliniennes: Propositions de méthode." *NTS* 38 (3, 1992): 385–401.

Aletti, "Evangelizzare." Aletti, Jean-Noel. "Evangelizzare o testimoniare? Il caso di Paolo negli *Atti degli Apostoli*." *EunDoc* 61 (2, 2008): 179–91.

Aletti, "Rhetoric." Aletti, Jean-Noël. "Rhetoric in the Letters of Paul." Pages 232–47 in *The Blackwell Companion to Paul*. Edited by Stephen Westerholm. BCompRel. Oxford: Blackwell, 2011.

Aletti, "Testimoni." Aletti, Jean-Noel. "Testimoni del Risorto: Spirito Santo e testimonianza negli *Atti degli apostoli*." *Rivista di teologia dell'evangelizzazione* 2 (4, 1998): 287–98.

Alexander, "Action." Alexander, Paul. "Nonviolent Direct Action in Acts 2: The Holy Spirit, the Early Church, and Martin Luther King, Jr." Pages 114–24 in *Trajectories in the Book of Acts: Essays in Honor of John Wesley Wyckoff*. Edited by Paul Alexander, Jordan Daniel May, and Robert G. Reid. Eugene, Ore.: Wipf & Stock, 2010.

Alexander, "Back to Front." Alexander, Loveday C. A. "Reading Luke-Acts from Back to Front." Pages 419–46 in *The Unity of Luke-Acts*. Edited by Joseph Verheyden. BETL 142. Leuven: Leuven University Press, 1999.

Alexander, "Biography." Alexander, Loveday C. A. "Acts and Ancient Intellectual Biography." Pages 31–63 in *The Book of Acts in Its Ancient Literary Setting*. Edited by Bruce W. Winter and Andrew D. Clarke. Vol. 1 of *The Book of Acts in Its First Century Setting*. Edited by Bruce W. Winter. Grand Rapids: Eerdmans; Carlisle, U.K.: Paternoster, 1993.

Alexander, "Book Production." Alexander, Loveday C. A. "Ancient Book Production and the Circulation of the Gospels." Pages 71–112 in *The Gospels for All Christians: Rethinking the Gospel Audiences*. Edited by Richard Bauckham. Grand Rapids: Eerdmans, 1998.

Alexander, "Chronology." Alexander, Loveday C. A. "Chronology of Paul." *DPL* 115–23.

Alexander, "Conscience." Alexander, Kimberly Ervin. "Matters of Conscience, Matters of Unity, Matters of Orthodoxy: Trinity and Water Baptism in Early Pentecostal Theology and Practice." *JPT* 17 (1, 2008): 48–69.

Alexander, *Context*. Alexander, Loveday C. A. *Acts in Its Ancient Literary Context: A Classicist Looks at the Acts of the Apostles*. Early Christianity in Context; LNTS 298. London: T&T Clark, 2005.

Alexander, "Dreambook." Alexander, Philip S. "Bavli Berakhot 55a–57b: The Talmudic Dreambook in Context." *JJS* 46 (1–2, 1995): 230–48.

Alexander, "Ἐκκλησιολογία." Alexander, Loveday. "Ἡ εκκλησιολογία των Πράξεων. Κέντρο και περιφέρεια." *DBM* 24 (1, 2006): 55–75.

Alexander, "Exhortation." Alexander, T. C. "Paul's Final Exhortation to the Elders from Ephesus: The Rhetoric of Acts 20:17–38." PhD diss., Emory University, 1990.

Alexander, "Fiction and Genre." Alexander, Loveday C. A. "Fact, Fiction, and the Genre of Acts." *NTS* 44 (3, 1998): 380–99.

Alexander, *Fire*. Alexander, Estrelda Y. *Black Fire: One Hundred Years of African American Pentecostalism*. Downers Grove, Ill.: InterVarsity, 2011.

Alexander, "Formal Elements." Alexander, Loveday C. A. "Formal Elements and Genre: Which Greco-Roman Prologues Most Closely Parallel the Lukan Prologues?" Pages 9–26 in *Jesus and the Heritage of Israel: Luke's Narrative Claim upon Israel's Legacy*. Edited by David P. Moessner. Luke the Interpreter of Israel 1. Harrisburg, Pa.: Trinity Press International, 1999.

Alexander, *Healing*. Alexander, Kimberly Ervin. *Pentecostal Healing: Models in Theology and Practice*. JPTSup. Blandford Forum, Dorset, U.K.: Deo, 2006.

Alexander, "Hellenism." Alexander, Philip S. "Hellenism and Hellenization as Problematic Historiographical Categories." Pages 63–80 in *Paul beyond the Judaism/Hellenism Divide*. Edited by Troels Engberg-Pedersen. Louisville: Westminster John Knox, 2001.

Alexander, "Imago mundi." Alexander, Philip S. "Notes on the 'Imago Mundi' of the Book of Jubilees." *JJS* 33 (1–2, 1982): 197–213.

Alexander, "Introduction." Alexander, Philip S. Introduction to "3 (Hebrew Apocalypse of) Enoch." *OTP* 1:223–53.

Alexander, "IPSE DIXIT." Alexander, Loveday C. A. "IPSE DIXIT: Citation of Authority in Paul and in the Jewish Hellenistic Schools." Pages 103–27 in *Paul beyond the Judaism/Hellenism Divide*. Edited by Troels Engberg-Pedersen. Louisville: Westminster John Knox, 2001.

Alexander, "Luke's Preface." Alexander, Loveday C. A. "Luke's Preface in the Context of Greek Preface-Writing." *NovT* 28 (1, 1986): 48–74.

Alexander, "Mapping." Alexander, Loveday C. A. "Mapping Early Christianity: Acts and the Shape of Early Church History." *Interpretation* 57 (2, 2003): 163–73.

Alexander, "Memory." Alexander, Loveday. "Memory and Tradition in the Hellenistic Schools." Pages 113–53 in *Jesus in Memory: Traditions in Oral and Scribal Perspectives*. Edited by Werner H. Kelber and Samuel Byrskog. Waco: Baylor University Press, 2009.

Alexander, "Omphalos." Alexander, Philip S. "Jerusalem as the *Omphalos* of the World: On the History of a Geographical Concept." *Judaism* 46 (2, 1997): 147–58.

Alexander, "Oral Variants." Alexander, T. Desmond. "The Wife/Sister Incidents of Genesis: Oral Variants?" *IBS* 11 (1, 1989): 2–22.

Alexander, *Possession*. Alexander, William Menzies. *Demonic Possession in the New Testament: Its Historical, Medical, and Theological Aspects*. Edinburgh: T&T Clark, 1902. Repr., Grand Rapids: Baker Book House, 1980.

Alexander, *Preface*. Alexander, Loveday C. A. *The Preface to Luke's Gospel: Literary Convention and Social Context in Luke 1.1–4 and Acts 1.1*. SNTSMS 78. Cambridge: Cambridge University Press, 1993.

Alexander, "Preface." Alexander, Loveday C. A. "The Preface to Acts and the Historians." Pages 73–103 in *History, Literature, and Society in the Book of Acts*. Edited by Ben Witherington III. Cambridge: Cambridge University Press, 1996.

Alexander, "Septuaginta." Alexander, Loveday C. A. "*Septuaginta, Fachprosa, imitatio*: Albert Wifstrand and the Language of Luke-Acts." Pages 1–26 in *Die Apostelgeschichte und die hellenistische Geschichtsschreibung: Festschrift für Eckhard Plümacher zu seinem 65. Geburtstag*. Edited by Cilliers Breytenbach and Jens Schröter. Leiden: Brill, 2004.

Alexander, *Signs*. Alexander, Paul. *Signs and Wonders: Why Pentecostalism Is the World's Fastest Growing Faith*. Foreword by Martin E. Marty. San Francisco: Jossey-Bass, 2009.

Alexander, "Sons of God." Alexander, Philip S. "The Targumim and Early Exegesis of 'Sons of God' in Genesis 6." *JJS* 23 (1, 1972): 60–71.

Alexander, "This Is That." Alexander, Loveday C. A. "'This Is That': The Authority of Scripture in the Acts of the Apostles." *PSB* 25 (2, 2004): 189–204.

Alexander, "Variants." Alexander, T. Desmond. "Are the Wife/Sister Incidents of Genesis Literary Compositional Variants?" *VT* 42 (1992): 145–53.

Alexander, "Vision." Alexander, Loveday. "Luke's Political Vision." *Interpretation* 66 (3, 2012): 283–93.

Alexander and Yong, *Daughters*. Alexander, Estrelda, and Amos Yong, eds. *Philip's Daughters: Women in Pentecostal-Charismatic Leadership*. PrTMS 104. Eugene, Ore.: Pickwick, Wipf & Stock, 2009.

Alföldy, "Tiberiéum." Alföldy, G. "Pontius Pilate und das Tiberiéum von Caesarea Maritima." *SCI* 18 (1999): 85–108.

Allan, "Formula." Allan, John A. "The 'in Christ' Formula in the Pastoral Epistles." *NTS* 10 (1, 1963): 115–21.

Allegro, "Cryptic Document." Allegro, John M. "An Astrological Cryptic Document from Qumran." *JSS* 9 (2, 1964): 291–93.

Allegro, "Light." Allegro, John M. "Further Light on the History of the Qumran Sect." *JBL* 75 (2, 1956): 89–95.

Allegro, "References." Allegro, John M. "Further Messianic References in Qumran Literature." *JBL* 75 (3, 1956): 174–87.

Allegro, *Scrolls*. Allegro, J. M. *The Dead Sea Scrolls*. Baltimore: Penguin Books, 1959.

Allély, "Enfants malformés." Allély, Annie. "Les enfants malformés et handicapés à Rome sous le principat." *REA* 106 (1, 2004): 73–101.

Allen, "Appius, Forum of." Allen, G. H. "Appius, Forum of." *ISBE* 1:214.

Allen, *Death of Herod*. Allen, O. Wesley, Jr. *The Death of Herod: The Narrative and Theological Function of Retribution in Luke-Acts*. SBLDS 158. Atlanta: Scholars Press, 1997.

Allen, *Pentecost*. Allen, Roland. *Pentecost and the World: The Revelation of the Holy Spirit in the "Acts of the Apostles."* London: Oxford University Press, 1917.

Allen, *Philosophy*. Allen, Reginald E., ed. and trans. *Greek Philosophy: Thales to Aristotle*. Readings in the History of Philosophy. New York: Free Press; London: Collier-Macmillan, 1966.

Allen, *Preaching*. Allen, Ronald J. *Preaching Luke-Acts*. Saint Louis: Chalice, 2000.

Allen, "Romans I–VIII." Allen, Leslie C. "The Old Testament in Romans I–VIII." *VE* 3 (1964): 6–41.

Allen and Richardson, "Reconstruction." Allen, William L., and James B. Richardson III. "The Reconstruction of Kinship from Archaeological Data: The Concepts, the Methods, and the Feasibility." *Am Antiq* 36 (1, Jan. 1971): 41–53.

Allen, Halliday, and Sikes, *Hymns*. Allen, Thomas W., W. R. Halliday, and E. E. Sikes. *The Homeric Hymns*. Oxford: Oxford University Press, 1936.

Allison, "Calf." Allison, Dale C., Jr. "Resurrecting a Calf: The Origin of *Testament of Abraham* 6:5." *JTS* 55 (1, 2004): 103–16.

Allison, "Doubt." Allison, Ralph B. "If in Doubt, Cast It Out? The Evolution of a Belief System Regarding Possession and Exorcism." *JPsyChr* 19 (2, 2000): 109–21.

Allison, "Elijah." Allison, Dale C., Jr. "Elijah Must Come First." *JBL* 103 (2, 1984): 256–58.

Allison, "Eschatology." Allison, Dale C., Jr. "A Plea for Thoroughgoing Eschatology." *JBL* 113 (4, 1994): 651–68.

Allison, "Hairs." Allison, Dale C., Jr. "'The Hairs of Your Head Are All Numbered.'" *ExpT* 101 (11, 1990): 334–36.

Allison, *Jesus*. Allison, Dale C., Jr. *Constructing Jesus: Memory, Imagination, and History*. Grand Rapids: Baker Academic, 2010.

Allison, "Land." Allison, Dale C., Jr. "Land in Early Christianity." *DLNTD* 642–44.

Allison, "Matt. 23:39 = Luke 13:35b." Allison, Dale C. "Matt. 23:39 = Luke 13:35b as a Conditional Prophecy." *JSNT* 18 (1983): 75–84.

Allison, *Moses*. Allison, Dale C., Jr. *The New Moses: A Matthean Typology*. Minneapolis: Fortress, 1993.

Allison, "Thallus." Allison, Dale C., Jr. "Thallus on the Crucifixion." Pages 405–6 in *The Historical Jesus in Context*. Edited by Amy-Jill Levine, Dale C. Allison Jr., and John Dominic Crossan. PrRR. Princeton: Princeton University Press, 2006.

Allison, "Tree." Allison, Dale C., Jr. "Abraham's Oracular Tree (T. Abr. 3:1–4)." *JJS* 54 (1, 2003): 51–61.

Allo, *Épître aux Corinthiens*. Allo, E. Bernard. *Seconde épître aux Corinthiens*. Paris: J. Gabalda, 1953.

Allport, *Prejudice*. Allport, Gordon W. *The Nature of Prejudice*. 25th anniv. ed. New York: Perseus, 1979.

Alonso-Núñez, "Economy." Alonso-Núñez, José Miguel. "Addenda: Economy: Classical Antiquity." *BrillPauly* 5:1174–79.

Alonso-Núñez, "Ethics." Alonso-Núñez, José Miguel. "Economical Ethics." *BrillPauly* 4:795–98.

Alpert and Neumann, "Correlation." Alpert, P., and J. Neumann. "An Ancient 'Correlation' between Streamflow and Distant Rainfall in the Near East." *JNES* 48 (1989): 313–14.

Alsup, "Type." Alsup, John E. "Type, Placement, and Function of the Pronouncement Story in Plutarch's *Moralia*." *Semeia* 20 (1981): 15–27.

Alvar, Gordon, and Rodríguez, "Mithraeum at Lugo." Alvar, Jaime, Richard Gordon, and Celso Rodríguez. "The Mithraeum at Lugo (*Lucus Augusti*) and Its Connection with *Legio VII Gemina*." *JRA* 19 (2006): 266–77.

Alvares, "Magus." Alvares, Jean. "A Hidden Magus in Chariton's 'Chaireas and Callirhoe.'" *Hermes* 128 (3, 2000): 383–84.

Álvarez Cineira, "Ciudadano." Álvarez Cineira, David. "Pablo ¿Un ciudadano romano?" *EstAg* 33 (3, 1998): 455–86.

Álvarez Cineira, "Pasos." Álvarez Cineira, David. "Los primeros pasos del cristianismo en Roma." *EstBib* 64 (2, 2006): 201–35.

Alvarez Valdés, "Espíritu Santo." Alvarez Valdés, Ariel. "Quando desceu o Espírito Santo sobre os apóstolos?" *REB* 62 (248, 2002): 913–18.

AMA Medical Guide. *American Medical Association Family Medical Guide*. Edited by Charles B. Clayman. 3rd rev. ed. New York: Random House, 1994.

Amadasi Guzzo, "Phoenician-Punic." Amadasi Guzzo, Maria Giulia. "Phoenician-Punic." *OEANE* 4:317–24.

Amadon, "Calendation." Amadon, Grace. "Ancient Jewish Calendation." *JBL* 61 (4, 1942): 227–31.

Amador, "Revisiting." Amador, J. D. H. "Revisiting 2 Corinthians: Rhetoric and the Case for Unity." *NTS* 46 (1, 2000): 92–111.

Amandry, *Mantique*. Amandry, Pierre. *La mantique apollinienne à Delphes*. Paris: E. de Boccard, 1950.

Amaru, "Prophets." Amaru, Betsy Halperin. "The Killing of the Prophets: Unraveling a Midrash." *HUCA* 54 (1983): 153–80.

Amaru, "Theology." Amaru, Betsy Halperin. "Land Theology in Josephus' *Jewish Antiquities*." *JQR* 71 (4, 1981): 201–29.

Amaru, "Women." Amaru, Betsy Halperin. "Portraits of Biblical Women in Josephus' Antiquities." *JJS* 39 (2, 1988): 143–70.

Ambühl, "Thanatos." Ambühl, Annemarie. "Thanatos." *BrillPauly* 14:365–66.

Ameling, "Lot." Ameling, Walter. "Lot, Election by: Ptolemaic and Roman Egypt." *BrillPauly* 7:816–17.

Ameling, "Sibling Marriage." Ameling, Walter. "Sibling Marriage." *BrillPauly* 13:410–11.

Ameling, "Strategos." Ameling, Walter. "Strategos: Hellenistic States." *BrillPauly* 13:872–73.

Ameling, Strothmann, and Pahlitzsch, "Berenice, 1–9." Ameling, Walter, Meret Strothmann, and Johannes Pahlitzsch. "Berenice, 1–9." *BrillPauly* 2:600–603.

Ames, "Fellowship." Ames, Tracy. "Fellowship, Pharisees, and the Common People in Early Rabbinic Tradition." *SR/SR* 34 (3–4, 2005): 339–56.

Amiran, "Centre." Amiran, Ruth. "Un centre économique et culturel." *MdB* 54 (May 1988): 18–21.

Amit, "*Miqveh* Complex." Amit, David. "A *miqveh* Complex near Alon Shevut." *'Atiqot* 38 (1999): 75–84.

Amitai, "Ash." Amitai, Pinchas. "Scorpion Ash Saves Woman's Eyesight." *BRev* 11 (2, 1995): 36–37.

Amitay, "Shim'on." Amitay, Ory. "Shim'on ha-Sadiq in His Historical Context." *JJS* 58 (2, 2007): 236–49.

Ammerman, "Sociology." Ammerman, Nancy T. "Sociology and the Study of Religion." Pages 76–88 in *Religion, Scholarship, Higher Education: Perspectives, Models, and Future Prospects*. Edited by Andrea Sterk. Notre Dame, Ind.: University of Notre Dame Press, 2001.

Amundsen, "Suicide." Amundsen, Darrel W. "Suicide and Early Christian Values." Pages 77–153 in *Suicide and Euthanasia: Historical and Contemporary Themes*. Edited by B. A. Brody. Dordrecht, Neth.: Kluwer, 1989.

Anderson, *Christology*. Anderson, Paul N. *The Christology of the Fourth Gospel: Its Unity and Disunity in the Light of John 6*. WUNT 2.78. Tübingen: Mohr Siebeck, 1996.

Anderson, "Exaltation." Anderson, Gary A. "The Exaltation of Adam and the Fall of Satan." *JJTP* 6 (1, 1997): 105–34.

Anderson, "Face." Anderson, Allan. "The Charismatic Face of Christianity in Asia." Pages 1–12 in *Asian and Pentecostal: The Charismatic Face of Christianity in Asia*. Edited by Allan Anderson and Edmond Tang. Foreword by Cecil M. Robeck. RSt Miss, AJPS 3. Oxford: Regnum; Baguio City, Philippines: APTS, 2005.

Anderson, *Glossary*. Anderson, R. Dean, Jr. *Glossary of Greek Rhetorical Terms Connected to Methods of Argumentation, Figures, and Tropes from Anaximenes to Quintilian*. Leuven: Peeters, 2000.

Anderson, "Joy." Anderson, Gary A. "The Expression of Joy as a Halakhic Problem in Rabbinic Sources." *JQR* 80 (3–4, 1990): 221–52.

Anderson, *Mark*. Anderson, Hugh. *The Gospel of Mark*. NCBC. London: Oliphants (Marshall, Morgan & Scott), 1976.

Anderson, *Pelendo*. Anderson, Alpha E. *Pelendo: God's Prophet in the Congo*. Chicago: Moody, 1964.

Anderson, *Pentecostalism*. Anderson, Allan. *An Introduction to Pentecostalism: Global Charismatic Christianity*. Cambridge: Cambridge University Press, 2004.

Anderson, *Philostratus*. Anderson, Graham. *Philostratus: Biography and Belles Lettres in the Third Century A.D.* London: Croom Helm, 1986.

Anderson, "Points." Anderson, Allan. "To All Points of the Compass: The Azusa Street Revival and Global Pentecostalism." *Enr* 11 (2, 2006): 164–72.

Anderson, *Psalms*. Anderson, A. A. *Psalms*. 2 vols. NCBC. Grand Rapids: Eerdmans; London: Marshall, Morgan & Scott, 1972.

Anderson, *Quest*. Anderson, Paul N. *The Fourth Gospel and the Quest for Jesus: Modern Foundations Reconsidered*. LNTS 321. London: T&T Clark, 2006.

Anderson, *Raised*. Anderson, Kevin L. *"But God Raised Him from the Dead": The Theology of Jesus' Resurrection in Luke-Acts*. PBMon. Milton Keynes, UK: Paternoster, 2006.

Anderson, "Reading Tabitha." Anderson, Janice Capel. "Reading Tabitha: A Feminist Reception History." Pages 108–44 in *The New Literary Criticism and the New Testament*. Edited by Edgar V. McKnight and Elizabeth Struthers Malbon. Valley Forge, Pa.: Trinity Press International; Sheffield, U.K.: JSOT Press, 1994. Repr., pages 22–48 in *The Feminist Companion to the Acts of the Apostles*. Edited by Amy-Jill Levine with Marianne Blickenstaff. Cleveland: Pilgrim; Edinburgh: T&T Clark, 2004.

Anderson, "Resurrection." Anderson, K. L. "The Resurrection of Jesus in Luke-Acts." PhD diss., Brunel University, 2000.

Anderson, *Rhetorical Theory*. Anderson, R. Dean, Jr. *Ancient Rhetorical Theory and Paul*. Rev. ed. CBET 18. Leuven: Peeters, 1999.

Anderson, "Sacrifice." Anderson, Gary A. "Sacrifice and Sacrificial Offerings: Old Testament." *ABD* 5:870–86.

Anderson, "Samaritan Literature." Anderson, Robert T. "Samaritan Literature." *DNTB* 1052–56.

Anderson, "Second Sophistic." Anderson, Graham. "Rhetoric and the Second Sophistic." Pages 339–53 in *A Companion to Roman Rhetoric*. Edited by William Dominik and Jon Hall. Oxford: Blackwell, 2007.

Anderson, *Shore*. Anderson, Courtney. *To the Golden Shore: The Life of Adoniram Judson*. Boston: Little, Brown, 1956. Repr., Valley Forge, Pa.: Judson, 1987.

Anderson, "Signs." Anderson, Allan. "Signs and Blunders: Pentecostal Mission Issues at 'Home and Abroad' in the Twentieth Century." *JAM* 2 (2, 2000): 193–210.

Anderson, "Socrates." Anderson, Albert. "Was Socrates Unwise to Take the Hemlock?" *HTR* 65 (1972): 437–52.

Anderson, "Temple." Anderson, Robert T. "The Elusive Samaritan Temple." *BA* 54 (2, 1991): 104–7.

Anderson, *Vision*. Anderson, Robert M. *The Vision of the Disinherited: The Making of American Pentecostalism*. New York: Oxford University Press, 1979.

Anderson, "Worship." Anderson, Paul N. "Authentic Worship in John and in Luke-Acts: Influence, Interfluence, and Resonance." Seminar paper for the Johannine Writings Seminar, Society for New Testament Studies, Bard College, Aug. 5., 2011.

Anderson, "Xenophon." Anderson, Graham. "Introduction" to *An Ephesian Tale* by Xenophon of Ephesus. Pages 125–28 (with further notes on 129–69) in *Collected Ancient Greek Novels*. Edited by B. P. Reardon. Berkeley: University of California Press, 1989.

Anderson and Hardie, "Lucanus." Anderson, William Blair, and Philip Russell Hardie. "Annaeus Lucanus, Marcus." *OCD*[3] 94–95.

Anderson, Ellens, and Fowler, "Way Forward." Anderson, Paul N., J. Harold Ellens, and James W. Fowler. "A Way Forward in the Scientific Investigation of Gospel Traditions: Cognitive-Critical Analysis." Pages 247–76 in *From Christ to Jesus*. Vol. 4 of *Psychology and the Bible: A New Way to Read the Scriptures*. Edited by J. Harold Ellens and Wayne G. Rollins. Westport, Conn.: Praeger, 2004.

Anderson-Stojanovic, "Leather." Anderson-Stojanovic, Virginia R. "Leather." *OEANE* 3:339–40.

Ando, "Interpretatio." Ando, Clifford. "Interpretatio romana." *CP* 100 (1, 2005): 41–51.

Andreau, "Banks." Andreau, Jean. "Banks." *BrillPauly* 2:484–88.

Andreau, "Maritime Loans." Andreau, Jean. "Maritime Loans." *BrillPauly* 8:360–62.

Andreau, "Negotiator." Andreau, Jean. "Negotiator." *BrillPauly* 9:612–14.

Andreau, "Wages." Andreau, Jean. "Wages: Classical Antiquity." *BrillPauly* 15:542–44.

Andrei, "430 Years." Andrei, O. "The 430 Years of Ex. 12:40, from Demetrius to Julius Africanus: A Study in Jewish and Christian Chronography." *Hen* 18 (1–2, 1996): 9–67.

Andrewes and Rhodes, "Four Hundred." Andrewes, Antony, and P. J. Rhodes. "Four Hundred, the." *OCD*³ 608.

Andrews, "Worship." Andrews, S. J. "The Worship of the Tabernacle Compared with That of the Second Temple." *JBL* 6 (June 1886): 56–68.

Aneshensel and Phelan, *Handbook.* Aneshensel, Carol S., and Jo C. Phelan. *Handbook of the Sociology of Mental Health.* New York: Kluwer Academic/Plenum, 1999.

Angus, *Mystery-Religions.* Angus, S. *The Mystery-Religions and Christianity.* New York: Scribner, 1925.

Annas, "Ethics." Annas, Julia. "Ethics in Stoic Philosophy." *Phronesis* 52 (1, 2007): 58–87.

Annen, "Heilige Geist." Annen, Franz. "'Der Heilige Geist und wir haben beschlossen . . .': Impulse aus der Apostelgeschichte für eine Spiritualität des Leitens." *Diakonia* 31 (3, 2000): 170–74.

Anson, "Assemblies." Anson, Edward Madden. "Macedonian Judicial Assemblies." *CP* 103 (2, 2008): 135–49.

Anson, "Exhortation." Anson, Edward M. "The General's Pre-Battle Exhortation in Graeco-Roman Warfare." *GR* 57 (2, 2010): 304–18.

Anspach, "Kinship and Divorce." Anspach, Donald F. "Kinship and Divorce." *JMFam* 38 (2, May 1976): 323–30.

Anthony, "Saying." Anthony, Peter. "What Are They Saying about Luke-Acts?" *ScrB* 40 (1, 2010): 10–21.

Antonaccio, "Hero Cult." Antonaccio, Carla M. "Contesting the Past: Hero Cult, Tomb Cult, and Epic in Early Greece." *AJA* 98 (3, 1994): 389–410.

Antoni, "Phoebe." Antoni, Silke. "Phoebe." *BrillPauly* 11:146–47.

Apathy, "Domicilium." Apathy, Peter. "Domicilium." *BrillPauly* 4:630–31.

Applebaum, "Economic Causes." Applebaum, Shim'on. "Josephus and the Economic Causes of the Jewish War." Pages 237–64 in *Josephus, the Bible, and History.* Edited by Louis H. Feldman and Gohei Hata. Detroit: Wayne State University Press, 1989.

Applebaum, "Economic Life." Applebaum, Shim'on. "Economic Life in Palestine." *JPFC* 631–700.

Applebaum, *Jews and Greeks in Cyrene.* Applebaum, Shim'on. *Jews and Greeks in Ancient Cyrene.* SJLA 28. Leiden: Brill, 1979.

Applebaum, "Legal Status." Applebaum, Shim'on. "The Legal Status of the Jewish Communities in the Diaspora." *JPFC* 420–67.

Applebaum, "Organization." Applebaum, Shim'on. "The Organization of the Jewish Communities in the Diaspora." *JPFC* 465–503.

Applebaum, "Social Status." Applebaum, Shim'on. "The Social and Economic Status of the Jews in the Diaspora." *JPFC* 701–27.

Applebaum, "Zealots." Applebaum, Shim'on. "The Zealots: The Case for Reevaluation." *JRS* 61 (1971): 155–70.

Appold, *Motif.* Appold, Mark L. *The Oneness Motif in the Fourth Gospel: Motif Analysis and Exegetical Probe into the Theology of John.* WUNT 2.1. Tübingen: J. C. B. Mohr, 1976.

Arafat, "Treasure." Arafat, Karim W. "Treasure, Treasuries and Value in Pausanias." *CQ* 59 (2, 2009): 578–92.

Arai, "Gemeindeethik." Arai, Sasagu. "Individual- und Gemeindeethik bei Lukas." *AJBI* 9 (1983): 88–127.

Arai, "Spirituality." Arai, Paula K. R. "Medicine, Healing, and Spirituality: A Cross-cultural Exploration." Pages 207–18 in *Teaching Religion and Healing.* Edited by Linda L. Barnes and Inés Talamantez. AARTRSS. Oxford: Oxford University Press, 2006.

Arai, "Stephanusrede." Arai, Sasagu. "Stephanusrede—gelesen vom Standpunkt ihrer Leser." *AJBI* 15 (1989): 53–85. (Abstract: *NTA* 34:323.)

Arav, "Straton's Tower." Arav, Rami. "Some Notes on the Foundation of Straton's Tower." *PEQ* 121 (2, 1989): 144–48.

Arbel, "Liturgy: Rabbinic." Arbel, Daphna V. "Liturgy: Rabbinic." *DNTB* 650–52.

Arbel, "Understanding." Arbel, Daphna V. "'Understanding of the Heart': Spiritual Transformation and Divine Revelations in the Hekhalot and Merkavah Literature." *JSQ* 6 (4, 1999): 320–44.

Archer, *Survey.* Archer, Gleason L. *A Survey of Old Testament Introduction.* Chicago: Moody, 1964.

Areeplackal, "Symbolism." Areeplackal, M. "The Symbolism of 'Jerusalem' in Luke-Acts." *Bible Bhashyam* 37 (2, 2011): 102–54.

Arena, "Invective." Arena, Valentina. "Roman Oratorical Invective." Pages 149–60 in *A Companion to Roman Rhetoric.* Edited by William Dominik and Jon Hall. Oxford: Blackwell, 2007.

Argyle, *Matthew.* Argyle, A. W. *The Gospel according to Matthew.* Cambridge: Cambridge University Press, 1963.

Argyle, "Philo." Argyle, A. W. "Philo and the Fourth Gospel." *ExpT* 63 (12, 1952): 385–86.

Argyle, "Semitism." Argyle, A. W. "An Alleged Semitism." *ExpT* 67 (8, 1956): 247.

Argyle, "University." Argyle, A. W. "The Ancient University of Alexandria." *CJ* 69 (4, 1974): 348–50.

Arlandson, "Lifestyles." Arlandson, James Malcolm. "Lifestyles of the Rich and Christian: Women, Wealth, and Social Freedom." Pages 155–70 in *The Feminist Companion to the Acts of the Apostles.* Edited by Amy-Jill Levine with Marianne Blickenstaff. Cleveland: Pilgrim; Edinburgh: T&T Clark, 2004.

Arlandson, *Women.* Arlandson, James Malcolm. *Women, Class, and Society in Early Christianity: Models from Luke-Acts.* Peabody, Mass.: Hendrickson, 1997.

Armenti, "Galileans." Armenti, Joseph R. "On the Use of the Term 'Galileans' in the Writings of Josephus Flavius: A Brief Note." *JQR* 72 (1, 1981): 45–49.

Armstrong, "Later Platonism." Armstrong, H. Hilary. "The Self-Definition of Christianity in Relation to Later Platonism." Pages 74–99 in *The Shaping of Christianity in the Second and Third Centuries.* Vol. 1 of *Jewish and Christian Self-Definition.* Edited by E. P. Sanders. Philadelphia: Fortress, 1980.

Arnaldich, "Sacerdocio." Arnaldich, Luis. "El sacerdocio en Qumran." *Salm* 19 (2, 1972): 279–322.

Arnold, "Acts." Arnold, Clinton E. "Acts." Pages 218–503 in vol. 2 of *Zondervan Illustrated Bible Backgrounds Commentary.* Edited by Clinton E. Arnold. Grand Rapids: Zondervan, 2002.

Arnold, "Ephesians." Arnold, Clinton E. "Ephesians, Letter to the." *DPL* 239–49.

Arnold, "Ephesus." Arnold, Clinton E. "Ephesus." *DPL* 249–53.

Arnold, "Festivals." Arnold, Irene Ringwood. "Festivals of Ephesus." *AJA* 76 (1, 1972): 17–22.

Arnold, "Magical Papyri." Arnold, Clinton E. "Magical Papyri." *DNTB* 666–70.

Arnold, *Power.* Arnold, Clinton E. *Ephesians—Power and Magic: The Concept of Power in Ephesians in Light of Its Historical Setting.* SNTSMS 63. Cambridge: Cambridge University Press, 1989.

Arnold, "Prayer." Arnold, Russell C. D. "Qumran Prayer as an Act of Righteousness." *JQR* 95 (3, 2005): 509–29.

Arnold, *Samuel.* Arnold, Bill T. *1 and 2 Samuel.* NIVAC. Grand Rapids: Zondervan, 2003.

Arnold, "Satan." Arnold, Clinton E. "Satan, Devil." *DLNTD* 1077–82.

Arnold, "Sceva." Arnold, Clinton E. "Sceva, Solomon, and Shamanism: The Jewish Roots of the Problem at Colossae." *JETS* 55 (1, 2012): 7–26.

Arnold, "Use of Old Testament in Acts." Arnold, Bill T. "Luke's Characterizing Use of the Old Testament in the Book of Acts." Pages 300–323 in *History, Literature, and Society in the Book of Acts*. Edited by Ben Witherington III. Cambridge: Cambridge University Press, 1996.

Arnold, *Vivre l'éthique*. Arnold, Daniel. *Vivre l'éthique de Dieu: L'amour et la justice au quotidien*. Saint-Légier, Switzerland: Editions Emmaüs, 2010.

Arnott, "Realism." Arnott, W. Geoffrey. "Longus, Natural History, and Realism." Pages 199–215 in *The Search for the Ancient Novel*. Edited by James Tatum. Baltimore: Johns Hopkins University Press, 1994.

Aron-Schnapper and Hanet, "Archives." Aron-Schnapper, Dominique, and Daniele Hanet. "Archives orales et histoire des institutions sociales." *Revue française de sociologie* 19 (2, 1978): 261–75.

Arowele, "Signs." Arowele, P. J. "This Generation Seeks Signs: The Miracles of Jesus with Reference to the African Situation." *AfThJ* 10 (3, 1981): 17–28.

Arrington, *Acts*. Arrington, French L. *The Acts of the Apostles: An Introduction and Commentary*. Peabody, Mass.: Hendrickson, 1988.

Arrington, *Aeon Theology*. Arrington, French L. *Paul's Aeon Theology in 1 Corinthians*. Washington, D.C.: University Press of America, 1978.

Arterbury, "Downfall." Arterbury, Andrew. "The Downfall of Eutychus." Pages 201–21 in *Contemporary Studies in Acts*. Edited by Thomas E. Phillips. Macon, Ga.: Mercer University Press, 2009.

Arterbury, "Hospitality." Arterbury, A. E. "The Ancient Custom of Hospitality, the Greek Novels, and Acts 10:1–11:18." *PRSt* 29 (1, 2002): 53–72.

Arterbury, *Hospitality*. Arterbury, Andrew. *Entertaining Angels: Early Christian Hospitality in Its Mediterranean Setting*. NTMon 8. Sheffield: Sheffield Phoenix, 2005.

Arthur, "Classics." Arthur, Marylin B. "Review Essay: Classics." *Signs* 2 (2, 1976): 382–403.

Arthur, "Early Greece." Arthur, Marylin B. "Early Greece: The Origins of the Western Attitude toward Women." Pages 7–58 in *Women in the Ancient World: The Arethusa Papers*. Edited by John Peradotto and J. P. Sullivan. SSCS. Albany: State University of New York Press, 1984.

Arzt, "Ägyptische Papyri." Arzt, Peter. "Ägyptische Papyri und das Neue Testament:

Zur Frage der Vergleichbarkeit von Texten." *PzB* 6 (1, 1997): 21–29.

Asamoah-Gyadu, "Hearing." Asamoah-Gyadu, Kwabena. "'Hearing in Our Own Tongues the Wonderful Works of God': Pentecost, Ecumenism and Renewal in African Christianity." *Missionalia* 35 (3, Nov. 2007): 128–45.

Ascough, "Associations." Ascough, Richard S. "Greco-Roman Philosophic, Religious, and Voluntary Associations." Pages 3–19 in *Community Formation in the Early Church and in the Church Today*. Edited by Richard N. Longenecker. Peabody, Mass.: Hendrickson, 2002.

Ascough, *Associations*. Ascough, Richard S. *Paul's Macedonian Associations: The Social Context of 1 Thessalonians and Philippians*. WUNT 2.161. Tübingen: Mohr Siebeck, 2003.

Ascough, "Civic Pride at Philippi." Ascough, Richard S. "Civic Pride at Philippi: The Text-Critical Problem of Acts 16.12." *NTS* 44 (1, 1998): 93–103.

Ascough, "Commensality." Ascough, Richard S. "Forms of Commensality in Greco-Roman Associations." *CW* 102 (1, 2008): 33–45.

Ascough, *Lydia*. Ascough, Richard S. *Lydia: Paul's Cosmopolitan Hostess*. Collegeville, Minn.: Liturgical, 2009.

Ascough, "Mission." Ascough, Richard S. "Redescribing the Thessalonians' 'Mission' in Light of Graeco-Roman Associations." *NTS* 60 (1, Jan. 2014): 61–82.

Ascough, "Recent Studies." Ascough, Richard S. "Recent Studies of Philippi." *TJT* 13 (1, 1997): 72–77.

Ascough, "Technique." Ascough, Richard S. "Narrative Technique and Generic Designation: Crowd Scenes in Luke-Acts and in Chariton." *CBQ* 58 (1, 1996): 69–81.

Ascough, Harland, and Kloppenborg, *Associations*. Ascough, Richard S., Philip A. Harland, and John S. Kloppenborg. *Associations in the Greco-Roman World: A Sourcebook*. Waco: Baylor University Press, 2012.

Asen, "Amos' Faith." Asen, Bernhard Arthur. "Amos' Faith: A Structural-Developmental Approach." PhD diss., Saint Louis University, 1980.

Ash, "John's Disciples." Ash, Anthony. "John's Disciples: A Serious Problem." *ResQ* 45 (1–2, 2003): 85–93.

Ash, "Tacitus." Ash, Rhiannon. "Tacitus and the Battle of Mons Graupius: A Historiographical Route Map?" Pages 434–40 in *A Companion to Greek and Roman Historiography*. Edited by John Marincola. 2 vols. Oxford: Blackwell, 2007.

Ashe, *Miracles*. Ashe, Geoffrey. *Miracles*. London: Routledge & Kegan Paul, 1978.

Ashkanani, "Zar." Ashkanani, Zubaydah. "Zar in a changing world: Kuwait." Pages 219–30 in *Women's Medicine: The zar-bori Cult in Africa and Beyond*. Edited by I. M. Lewis, Ahmed Al-Safi, and Sayyid Hurreiz. Edinburgh: Edinburgh University Press for the International African Institute, 1991.

Ashton, *Religion*. Ashton, John. *The Religion of Paul the Apostle*. New Haven: Yale University Press, 2000.

Ashton, *Understanding*. Ashton, John. *Understanding the Fourth Gospel*. Oxford: Clarendon, 1991.

Ashworth, "Hospitality." Ashworth, John. "Hospitality in Luke-Acts." *BibT* 35 (5, 1997): 300–304.

Asiedu, "Self." Asiedu, F. B. A. "Paul and Augustine's Retrospective Self: The Relevance of Epistula XXII." *REAug* 47 (1, 2001): 145–64.

Asirvatham, "Fervor." Asirvatham, Sulochana Ruth. "No Patriotic Fervor for Pella: Aelius Aristides and the Presentation of the Macedonians in the Second Sophistic." *Mnemosyne* 61 (2, 2008): 207–27.

Asmis, "Model." Asmis, Elizabeth. "A New Kind of Model: Cicero's Roman Constitution in De republica." *AJP* 126 (3, 2005): 377–416.

Asmis, "Order." Asmis, Elizabeth. "Lucretius' New World Order: Making a Pact with Nature." *CQ* 58 (1, 2008): 141–57.

Assmann, "Isis." Assmann, Jan. "Isis." Pages 456–58 in *Dictionary of Deities and Demons in the Bible*. 2nd rev. ed. Edited by Karel van der Toorn, Bob Becking, and Pieter W. van der Horst. Leiden: Brill; Grand Rapids: Eerdmans, 1999.

Assmann, "Justice." Assmann, Jan. "When Justice Fails: Jurisdiction and Imprecation in Ancient Egypt and the Near East." *JEA* 78 (1992): 149–62.

Assmann, "Magic and Theology." Assmann, Jan. "Magic and Theology in Ancient Egypt." Pages 1–18 in *Envisioning Magic: A Princeton Seminar and Symposium*. Edited by Peter Schäfer and Hans G. Kippenberg. SHR 75. Leiden: Brill, 1997.

Asso, "Raconter." Asso, Philippe. "Raconter pour persuader: Discours et narration des *Actes des apôtres*." *RSR* 90 (4, 2002): 555–71.

Astour, "Names in Semitic World." Astour, Michael C. "Greek Names in the Semitic World and Semitic Names in the Greek World." *JNES* 23 (3, 1964): 193–201.

Asztalos, "Apologia." Asztalos, Monika. "Apuleius' *Apologia* in a Nutshell: The *exordium*." *CQ* 55 (1, 2005): 266–76.

Atallah, "Milestone." Atallah, Nabil. "A New Milestone from Ishtafina, Ajlun Area, Jordan." *Levant* 35 (2003): 153–58.

Athenian Agora. The Athenian Agora: A Guide to the Excavations. Compiled by Mabel Lang and C. W. Eliot. Athens: American School of Classical Studies at Athens, 1954.

Atiat, "Sanctuary." Atiat, T. M. "A Nabataean Sanctuary at al-Mujib Nature Reserve: A Preliminary Notice." *Levant* 37 (2005): 163–68.

Atkinson, "Defining." Atkinson, Kenneth. "On Further Defining the First-Century CE Synagogue—Fact or Fiction? A Rejoinder to H. C. Kee." *NTS* 43 (4, 1997): 491–502.

Atkinson, "Herodian Origin." Atkinson, Kenneth. "On the Herodian Origin of Militant Davidic Messianism at Qumran: New Light from *Psalm of Solomon* 17." *JBL* 118 (3, 1999): 435–60.

Atkinson, "Luke-Acts." Atkinson, William. "Pentecostal Responses to Dunn's *Baptism in the Holy Spirit*: Luke-Acts." *JPT* 6 (1995): 87–131.

Atkinson, "Polemics." Atkinson, Kenneth. "Anti-Roman Polemics in the Dead Sea Scrolls and Related Literature: Their Later Use in John's Apocalypse." *QC* 12 (2–4, 2004): 109–22.

Atkinson, "Responses." Atkinson, William. "Pentecostal Responses to Dunn's *Baptism in the Holy Spirit*: Pauline Literature." *JPT* 7 (1995): 49–72.

Atkinson, "Women." Atkinson, Kenneth. "Women in the Dead Sea Scrolls: Evidence for a Qumran Renaissance during the Reign of Queen Salome Alexandra." *QC* 11 (1–4, 2003): 37–56.

Attridge, "Historiography." Attridge, Harold W. "Jewish Historiography." Pages 311–43 in *Early Judaism and Its Modern Interpreters.* Edited by Robert A. Kraft and George W. E. Nickelsburg. SBLBMI 2. Atlanta: Scholars Press, 1986.

Attridge, *History in Josephus.* Attridge, Harold W. *The Interpretation of Biblical History in the* Antiquitates judaicae *of Flavius Josephus.* HDR 7. Missoula, Mont.: Scholars Press, 1976.

Attridge, "Stoic Tradition." Attridge, Harold W. "An 'Emotional' Jesus and Stoic Tradition." Pages 77–92 in *Stoicism in Early Christianity.* Edited by Tuomas Rasimus, Troels Engberg-Pedersen, and Ismo Dunderberg. Grand Rapids: Baker Academic, 2010.

Aubert, *Motif.* Aubert, Bernard. *The Shepherd-Flock Motif in the Miletus Discourse (Acts 20:17–38) Against Its Historical Background.* StBibLit 124. New York: Peter Lang, 2009.

Aubin, "Reversing Romance." Aubin, Melissa. "Reversing Romance? The *Acts of Thecla* and the Ancient Novel." Pages 257–72 in *Ancient Fiction and Early Christian Narrative.* Edited by Ronald F. Hock, J. Bradley Chance, and Judith Perkins. SBLSymS 6. Atlanta: SBL, 1998.

Augoustakis, "*Nequaquam.*" Augoustakis, Antonios. "*Nequaquam historia digna*? Plinian Style in *Ep.* 6.20." *CJ* 100 (3, 2005): 265–73.

Augustine, "Pentecost." Augustine, Daniela C. "Pentecost, Empowerment and Glossolalia." *International Journal for the Study of the Christian Church* 11 (4, 2011): 288–304.

Auhagen, "Rhetoric." Auhagen, Ulrike. "Rhetoric and Ovid." Pages 413–24 in *A Companion to Roman Rhetoric.* Edited by William Dominik and Jon Hall. Oxford: Blackwell, 2007.

Aulie, "Movement." Aulie, H. Wilbur. "The Christian Movement among the Chols of Mexico, with Special Reference to Problems of Second-Generation Christianity." DMiss diss., Fuller Theological Seminary, 1979.

Aune, "Amulets." Aune, David E. "Amulets." *OEANE* 1:113–15.

Aune, "Biography." Aune, David E. "Greco-Roman Biography." Pages 107–26 in *Greco-Roman Literature and the New Testament: Selected Forms and Genres.* Edited by David E. Aune. SBLSBS 21. Atlanta: Scholars Press, 1988.

Aune, *Cultic Setting.* Aune, David E. *The Cultic Setting of Realized Eschatology in Early Christianity.* NovTSup 28. Leiden: Brill, 1972.

Aune, "Delay." Aune, David E. "The Significance of the Delay of the Parousia for Early Christianity." Pages 87–109 in *Current Issues in Biblical and Patristic Interpretation: Studies in Honor of Merrill C. Tenney Presented by His Former Students.* Edited by Gerald F. Hawthorne. Grand Rapids: Eerdmans, 1975.

Aune, *Dictionary of Rhetoric.* Aune, David E. *The Westminster Dictionary of New Testament and Early Christian Literature and Rhetoric.* Louisville: Westminster John Knox, 2003.

Aune, "Duality." Aune, David E. "Anthropological Duality in the Eschatology of 2 Cor 4:16–5:10." Pages 215–40 in *Paul beyond the Judaism/Hellenism Divide.* Edited by Troels Engberg-Pedersen. Louisville: Westminster John Knox, 2001.

Aune, *Environment.* Aune, David E. *The New Testament in Its Literary Environment.* LEC 8. Philadelphia: Westminster, 1987.

Aune, "Heracles." Aune, David E. "Heracles and Christ: Heracles Imagery in the Christology of Early Christianity." Pages 3–19 in *Greeks, Romans, and Christians: Essays in Honor of Abraham J. Malherbe.* Edited by David L. Balch, Everett Ferguson, and Wayne A. Meeks. Minneapolis: Fortress, 1990.

Aune, "Latin." Aune, David E. "Latin." *OEANE* 3:333–37.

Aune, *Literature.* Aune, David E., ed. *Greco-Roman Literature and the New Testament: Selected Forms and Genres.* SBLSBS 21. Atlanta: Scholars Press, 1988.

Aune, "Magic." Aune, David E. "Magic in Early Christianity." *ANRW* 23.1:1507–57. Part 2, *Principat,* 23.1. Edited by H. Temporini and W. Haase. Berlin: de Gruyter, 1980.

Aune, "Problem of Genre." Aune, David E. "The Problem of the Genre of the Gospels. A Critique of C. H. Talbert's *What Is a Gospel?*" Pages 9–60 in vol. 2 of *Studies of History and Tradition in the Four Gospels.* Edited by R. T. France and David Wenham. 2 vols. Gospel Perspectives 1–2. Sheffield, U.K.: JSOT Press, 1980–81.

Aune, "*Prooimion.*" Aune, David E. "Luke 1.1–4: Historical or Scientific *prooimion*?" Pages 138–48 in *Paul, Luke, and the Graeco-Roman World.* Edited by Alf Christophersen et al. JSNTSup 217. Sheffield, U.K.: Sheffield Academic, 2002; London: T&T Clark, 2003.

Aune, *Prophecy.* Aune, David E. *Prophecy in Early Christianity and the Ancient Mediterranean World.* Grand Rapids: Eerdmans, 1983.

Aune, "Προφήτης." Aune, David E. "The Use of προφήτης in Josephus." *JBL* 101 (3, 1982): 419–21.

Aune, "Publication." Aune, David E. "Publication." Pages 388–89 in *The Westminster Dictionary of New Testament and Early Christian Literature and Rhetoric.* By David E. Aune. Louisville: Westminster John Knox, 2003.

Aune, "Religion." Aune, David E. "Religion, Greco-Roman." *DNTB* 917–26.

Aune, *Revelation.* Aune, David E. *Revelation.* 3 vols. WBC 52, 52b, 52c. Dallas: Word, 1997.

Aune, "Use." Aune, David E. "Justin Martyr's Use of the Old Testament." *BETS* 9 (4, Fall 1966): 179–97.

Aurenhammer, "Sculptures." Aurenhammer, Maria. "Sculptures of Gods and Heroes from Ephesos." Pages 251–80 in *Ephesos, Metropolis of Asia: An Interdisciplinary Approach to Its Archaeology, Religion, and Culture.* Edited by Helmut Koester. HTS. Valley Forge, Pa.: Trinity Press International, 1995.

Aus, "Pillars." Aus, Roger D. "Three Pillars and Three Patriarchs: A Proposal concerning Gal 2:9." *ZNW* 70 (3–4, 1979): 252–61.

Aus, "Plans." Aus, Roger D. "Paul's Travel Plans to Spain and the 'Full Number of the Gentiles' of Rom. xi.25." *NovT* 21 (3, 1979): 232–62.

Austin, *Readings in Reentry*. Austin, Clyde N. *Readings in Cross-cultural Reentry*. Abilene, Tex.: Abilene Christian University Press, 1987.

Avalos, "Medicine." Avalos, Hector Ignacio. "Medicine." *OEANE* 3:450–59.

Avemarie, "Acta." Avemarie, Friedrich. "Acta Jesu Christi. Zum christologischen Sinn der Wundermotive in der Apostelgeschichte." Pages 539–62 in *Die Apostelgeschichte im Kontext antiker und frühchristlicher Historiographie*. Edited by Jörg Frey, Clare K. Rothschild, and Jens Schröter, with Bettina Rost. BZNWK 162. Berlin: de Gruyter, 2009.

Avemarie, "Aporien." Avemarie, Friedrich. "Aporien der Theodizee: Zu einem Schlüsselthema früher rabbinischer Märtyrererzählungen." *JSJ* 34 (2, 2003): 199–215.

Avemarie, "Erwählung." Avemarie, Friedrich. "Erwählung und Vergeltung: Zur optionalen Struktur rabbinischer Soteriologie." *NTS* 45 (1, 1999): 108–26.

Avemarie, "Sterben." Avemarie, Friedrich. "Sterben für Gott und die Tora. Das Martyrium im antiken Judentum." *Theologie der Gegenwart* 51 (3, 2008): 162–75.

Avemarie, *Tora und Leben*. Avemarie, Friedrich. *Tora und Leben: Untersuchungen zur Heilsbedeutung der Tora in der frühen rabbinischen Literatur*. TSAJ 55. Tübingen: Mohr, 1996.

Averbeck, "Tabernacle." Aberbeck, Richard E. "Tabernacle." *DOTP* 807–27.

Averna, "Suasoria." Averna, Daniela. "La suasoria nelle preghiere agli dei: percorso diacronico dalla commedia alla tragedia." *Rhetorica* 27 (1, 2009): 19–46.

Avery-Peck, "Charismatic." Avery-Peck, Alan J. "The Galilean Charismatic and Rabbinic Piety: The Holy Man in the Talmudic Literature." Pages 149–65 in *The Historical Jesus in Context*. Edited by Amy-Jill Levine, Dale C. Allison Jr., and John Dominic Crossan. PrRR. Princeton: Princeton University Press, 2006.

Aviam, "Topography." Aviam, Mordechai. "Topography, Josephus, and Jesus." Paper presented at the second Princeton-Prague Symposium on Jesus: Methodological Approaches to the Historical Jesus, Princeton, Apr. 19, 2007.

Avidov, "Peer Solidarity." Avidov, A. "Peer Solidarity and Communal Loyalty in Roman Judaea." *JJS* 49 (2, 1998): 264–79.

Avigad, "Burnt House." Avigad, Nahman. "The Burnt House Captures a Moment." *BAR* 9 (6, 1983): 66–72.

Avigad, "Flourishing." Avigad, Nahman. "Jerusalem Flourishing—A Craft Center for Stone, Pottery, and Glass." *BAR* 9 (6, 1983): 48–65.

Avigad, *Jerusalem*. Avigad, Nahman. *Discovering Jerusalem*. Nashville: Thomas Nelson, 1980.

Avioz, "Lot." Avioz, M. "Josephus's Portrayal of Lot and His Family." *JSP* 16 (1, 2006): 3–13.

Avioz, "Moses." Avioz, M. "Moses in the Passover Haggada." *HBT* 31 (1, 2009): 45–50.

Avioz, "Nathan's Oracle." Avioz, M. "Josephus' Retelling of Nathan's Oracle (2 Samuel 7)." *JSP* 20 (1, 2006): 9–17.

Avi-Yonah, "Archaeological Sources." Avi-Yonah, Michael. "Archaeological Sources." *JPFC* 46–62.

Avi-Yonah, "Geography." Avi-Yonah, Michael. "Historical Geography of Palestine." *JPFC* 78–116.

Avi-Yonah, *Hellenism*. Avi-Yonah, Michael. *Hellenism and the East: Contacts and Interrelations from Alexander to the Roman Conquest*. Ann Arbor: University Microfilms International for the Institute of Languages, Literature, and the Arts, Hebrew University, Jerusalem, 1978.

Avi-Yonah, "War." Avi-Yonah, Michael. "The 'War of the Sons of Light and Sons of Darkness' and Maccabean Warfare." *IEJ* 2 (1, 1952): 1–5.

Avner, "Account." Avner, Rina. "The Account of Caesarea by the Piacenza Pilgrim and the Recent Archaeological Discovery of the Octagonal Church in Caesarea Maritima." *PEQ* 140 (3, 2008): 203–12.

Ayles, "Credibility." Ayles, H. H. B. "The Credibility of Acts." *The Interpreter* 20 (1923–24): 25–34.

Azenabor, "Witchcraft." Azenabor, Godwin Ehi. "The Idea of Witchcraft and the Challenge of Modern Science." Pages 21–35 in *Studies in Witchcraft, Magic, War, and Peace in Africa*. Edited by Beatrice Nicolini. Lewiston, N.Y.: Edwin Mellen, 2006.

Azevedo, Prater, and Lantum, "Biomedicine." Azevedo, Mario J., Gwendolyn S. Prater, and Daniel N. Lantum. "Culture, Biomedicine, and Child Mortality in Cameroon." *SSMed* 32 (12, 1991): 1341–49.

Baarlink, "Bedeutung." Baarlink, Heinrich. "Die Bedeutung der Prophetenzitate in Lk 4,18–19 und Apg 2,17–21 für das Doppelwerk des Lukas." Pages 483–91 in *The Unity of Luke-Acts*. Edited by Joseph Verheyden. BETL 142. Leuven: Leuven University Press, 1999.

Bäbler, "Poseidon." Bäbler, Balbina. "Poseidon. II. Iconography." *BrillPauly* 11:677–78.

Bäbler, "Zeus." Bäbler, Balbina. "Zeus: Iconography." *BrillPauly* 15:925–26.

Bacchiocchi, "Rome and Christianity." Bacchiocchi, Samuele. "Rome and Christianity until A.D. 62." *AUSS* 21 (1, 1983): 3–25.

Bacchiocchi, *Sabbath to Sunday*. Bacchiocchi, Samuele. *From Sabbath to Sunday: A Historical Investigation of the Rise of Sunday Observance in Early Christianity*. Rome: Pontificial Gregorian University Press, 1977.

Bachmann, "Paulusperspektive." Bachmann, Michael. "J. D. G. Dunn und die Neue Paulusperspektive." *TZ* 63 (1, 2007): 25–43.

Bachmann, "Stephanusepisode." Bachmann, Michael. "Die Stephanusepisode (Apg 6,1–8,3): Ihre Bedeutung für die lukanische Sicht des jerusalemischen Tempels und des Judentums." Pages 545–62 in *The Unity of Luke-Acts*. Edited by Joseph Verheyden. BETL 142. Leuven: Leuven University Press, 1999.

Bachmann, "Verus Israel." Bachmann, Michael. "*Verus Israel*: Ein Vorschlag zu einer 'mengentheoretischen' Neubeschreibung der betreffenden paulinischen Terminologie." *NTS* 48 (4, 2002): 500–512.

Back, "Spirituelle Einsicht." Back, Frances. "Spirituelle Einsicht und geistliche Blindheit: Die Stephanusvision und Test Hiob 52." *Early Christianity* 3 (4, 2012): 419–34.

Backhaus, "Hörsaal." Backhaus, Knut. "Im Hörsaal des Tyrannus (Apg 19,9): Von der Langlebigkeit des Evangeliums in kurzatmiger Zeit." *TGl* 91 (1, 2001): 4–23.

Backhaus, "Kohelet." Backhaus, Franz Josef. "Kohelet und die 'Diatribe'—hermeneutische und methodologische Überlegungen zu einem noch ausstehenden Stilvergleich." *BZ* 42 (2, 1998): 248–56.

Bacon, *Introduction*. Bacon, Benjamin W. *An Introduction to the New Testament*. New York: Macmillan, 1900.

Badawy, *Architecture*. Badawy, Alexander. *A History of Egyptian Architecture: The Empire (1580–1085 B.C.)*. Berkeley: University of California Press, 1968.

Badian, "Acclamation." Badian, Ernst. "Acclamation." *OCD³* 4.

Badian, "Alexander." Badian, Ernst. "Alexander 'the Great.'" *BrillPauly* 1:469–75.

Badian, "Aquilius Manius." Badian, Ernst. "Aquilius (1) Manius." "Aquilius (2) Manius." *OCD³* 134.

Badian, "Princeps senatus." Badian, Ernst. "Princeps senatus." *OCD³* 1247.

Badian, "Provincia." Badian, Ernst. "Provincia/Province." *OCD³* 1265–67.

Badian, "Tabellarii." Badian, Ernst. "Tabellarii." *OCD³* 1467.

Badian, "Verres." Badian, Ernst. "Verres, Gaius." *OCD*[3] 1588–89.

Badian and Lintott, "Repetundae." Badian, Ernst, and Andrew William Lintott. "Repetundae." *OCD*[3] 1308–9.

Badian and Potter, "Canals." Badian, Ernst, and T. W. Potter. "Canals." *OCD*[3] 285.

Badian and Spawforth, "Inns." Badian, Ernst, and Antony J. S. Spawforth. "Inns, Restaurants." *OCD*[3] 759–60.

Badilita, "Exégèse." Badilita, S. "Philon d'Alexandrie et l'exégèse allégorique." *FoiVie* 107 (4, 2008): 63–76.

Baer, "Bodies." Baer, Jonathan R. "Perfectly Empowered Bodies: Divine Healing in Modernizing America." PhD diss., Yale University, 2002.

Baer, *Categories*. Baer, Richard A., Jr., *Philo's Use of the Categories Male and Female*. ALGHJ 3. Leiden: Brill, 1970.

Baer, *Heilige Geist*. Baer, Heinrich von. *Der Heilige Geist in den Lukasschriften*. BWANT 3. Stuttgart: W. Kohlhammer, 1926.

Bagalawis, "Power." Bagalawis, Manuel A. "'Power' in Acts 1:8: Effective Witnessing through Signs and Wonders." *JAM* 3 (1, 2001): 1–13.

Bagatti, *Church*. Bagatti, Bellarmino. *The Church from the Circumcision*. Jerusalem: Franciscan Printing Press, 1971.

Bagnall, "Beginnings." Bagnall, Roger S. "The Beginnings of the Roman Census in Egypt." *GRBS* 32 (3, 1991): 255–65 and plate 1.

Bagnall, *Books*. Bagnall, Roger S. *Early Christian Books in Egypt*. Princeton: Princeton University Press, 2009.

Bahat, "Down Under." Bahat, Dan. "Jerusalem Down Under: Tunneling along Herod's Temple Mount Wall." *BAR* 21 (6, 1995): 30–47.

Bahat, "Jerusalem." Bahat, Dan. "Jerusalem." *OEANE* 3:224–38.

Bahat, "Temple Mount." Bahat, Dan. "Jesus and the Herodian Temple Mount." Pages 300–308 in *Jesus and Archaeology*. Edited by James H. Charlesworth. Grand Rapids: Eerdmans, 2006.

Bailey, *Epicurus*. Bailey, Cyril, ed. *Epicurus: The Extant Remains*. Oxford: Oxford University Press, 1926. Repr., Hildesheim: Olms, 1970.

Bailey, "Matriarchs." Bailey, James L. "Josephus' Portrayal of the Matriarchs." Pages 154–79 in *Josephus, Judaism, and Christianity*. Edited by Louis H. Feldman and Gohei Hata. Detroit: Wayne State University Press, 1987.

Bailey, *Peasant Eyes*. Bailey, Kenneth Ewing. *Through Peasant Eyes: More Lucan Parables, Their Culture and Style*. Grand Rapids: Eerdmans, 1980.

Bailey, *Poet*. Bailey, Kenneth Ewing. *Poet and Peasant: A Literary-Cultural Approach to the Parables in Luke*. Grand Rapids: Eerdmans, 1976.

Bailey, "Portrayal." Bailey, James L. "Josephus' Portrayal of the Matriarchs." Pages 154–79 in *Josephus, Judaism, and Christianity*. Edited by Louis H. Feldman and Gohei Hata. Detroit: Wayne State University Press, 1987.

Bailey, *Prophets*. Bailey, Homer. *A Commentary on the Minor Prophets*. Grand Rapids: Baker, 1972.

Bailey, "Shepherd Poems." Bailey, Kenneth Ewing. "The Shepherd Poems of John 10: Their Culture and Style." *NESTTR* 14 (1, 1993): 3–21.

Bailey, "Song of Mary." Bailey, Kenneth Ewing. "The Song of Mary: Vision of a New Exodus (Luke 1:46–55)." *NESTTR* 2 (1, 1979): 29–35.

Bailey, "Thessalonians." Bailey, J. A. "Who Wrote II Thessalonians?" *NTS* 25 (2, 1979): 131–45.

Bailey, "Tradition." Bailey, Kenneth Ewing. "Informal Controlled Oral Tradition and the Synoptic Gospels." *AJT* 5 (1, 1991): 34–54.

Baines, "Square." Baines, William. "The Rotas-Sator Square: A New Investigation." *NTS* 33 (3, 1987): 469–76.

Baines and Málek, *Atlas*. Baines, John, and Jaromír Málek. *Atlas of Ancient Egypt*. New York: Facts on File, 1980.

Bainton, *Stand*. Bainton, Roland H. *Here I Stand: A Life of Martin Luther*. New York: Abingdon, 1950.

Baird, *Corinthian Church*. Baird, William. *The Corinthian Church—A Biblical Approach to Urban Culture*. New York: Abingdon, 1964.

Baker, *Identity*. Baker, Coleman A. *Identity, Memory, and Narrative in Early Christianity: Peter, Paul, and Recategorization in the Book of Acts*. Eugene, Ore.: Pickwick, 2011.

Baker, "Jew." Baker, Cynthia. "A 'Jew' by Any Other Name?" *Journal of Ancient Judaism* 2 (2, 2011): 153–80.

Baker, "Justin's Agraphon." Baker, Aelred. "Justin's Agraphon in the Dialogue with Trypho." *JBL* 87 (3, 1968): 277–87.

Baker, "Theatre." Baker, Murray. "Who Was Sitting in the Theatre at Miletos? An Epigraphical Application of a Novel Theory." *JSJ* 36 (4, 2005): 397–416.

Baker, *Visions*. Baker, H. A. *Visions beyond the Veil*. 12th ed. Minneapolis: Osterhus, n.d.; new ed. New Kensington, Pa.: Whitaker House, 2006.

Baker and Baker, *Enough*. Baker, Rolland, and Heidi Baker. *There Is Always Enough: The Story of Rolland and Heidi Baker's Miraculous Ministry among the Poor*. Kent, U.K.: Sovereign World; Grand Rapids: Baker, 2003.

Baker and Baker, *Miracles*. Baker, Heidi, and Rolland Baker. *Expecting Miracles: True Stories of God's Supernatural Power and How You Can Experience It*. Grand Rapids: Baker, 2007. Also published as *The Hungry Always Get Fed: A Year of Miracles*. West Sussex, U.K.: New Wine Ministries, 2007.

Bakke, *Urban Christian*. Bakke, Raymond. *The Urban Christian: Effective Ministry in Today's Urban World*. Downers Grove, Ill.: InterVarsity, 1987.

Bakker, *Mills-Bakeries*. Bakker, Jan Theo. *The Mills-Bakeries of Ostia: Description and Interpretation*. Amsterdam: J. C. Gieben, 1999.

Balch, "Accepting." Balch, David L. "Accepting Others: God's Boundary Crossing according to Isaiah and Luke-Acts." *CurTM* 36 (6, 2009): 414–23.

Balch, "Acts as Historiography." Balch, David L. "Acts as Hellenistic Historiography." Pages 429–32 in *SBL Seminar Papers, 1985*. Edited by K. H. Richards. SBLSP 24. Atlanta: Scholars Press, 1985.

Balch, "Ἀκριβῶς." Balch, David L. "Ἀκριβῶς . . . γράψαι (Luke 1:3): To Write the Full History of God's Receiving All Nations." Pages 229–50 in *Jesus and the Heritage of Israel: Luke's Narrative Claim upon Israel's Legacy*. Edited by David P. Moessner. Luke the Interpreter of Israel 1. Harrisburg, Pa.: Trinity Press International, 1999.

Balch, "Areopagus Speech." Balch, David L. "The Areopagus Speech: An Appeal to the Stoic Historian Posidonius against Later Stoics and the Epicureans." Pages 52–79 in *Greeks, Romans, and Christians: Essays in Honor of Abraham J. Malherbe*. Edited by D. L. Balch et al. Minneapolis: Fortress, 1990.

Balch, "Encomia." Balch, David L. "Two Apologetic Encomia: Dionysius on Rome and Josephus on the Jews." *JSJ* 13 (1–2, 1982): 102–22.

Balch, "Families." Balch, David L. "Paul, Families, and Households." Pages 258–92 in *Paul in the Greco-Roman World: A Handbook*. Edited by J. Paul Sampley. Harrisburg, Pa.: Trinity Press International, 2003.

Balch, "Friendship." Balch, David L. "Political Friendship in the Historian Dionysius of Halicarnassus, *Roman Antiquities*." Pages 123–44 in *Greco-Roman Perspectives on Friendship*. Edited by John T. Fitzgerald. SBLRBS 34. Atlanta: Scholars Press, 1997.

Balch, "Genre." Balch, David L. "The Genre of Luke-Acts: Individual Biography,

Adventure Novel, or Political History." *SWJT* 33 (1990): 5–19.

Balch, "Gospels: Forms." Balch, David L. "Gospels (Literary Forms)." *BrillPauly* 5:947–49.

Balch, "Household Codes." Balch, David L. "Household Codes." Pages 25–50 in *Greco-Roman Literature and the New Testament: Selected Forms and Genres.* Edited by David E. Aune. SBLSBS 21. Atlanta: Scholars Press, 1988.

Balch, "Houses." Balch, David L. "Rich Pompeiian Houses, Shops for Rent, and the Huge Apartment Building in Herculaneum as Typical Spaces for Pauline House Churches." *JSNT* 27 (1, 2004): 27–46.

Balch, "ΜΕΤΑΒΟΛΗ ΠΟΛΙΤΕΙΩΝ." Balch, David L. "ΜΕΤΑΒΟΛΗ ΠΟΛΙΤΕΙΩΝ—Jesus as Founder of the Church in Luke-Acts: Form and Function." Pages 139–88 in *Contextualizing Acts: Lukan Narrative and Greco-Roman Discourse.* Edited by Todd Penner and Caroline Vander Stichele. SBLSymS 20. Atlanta: SBL, 2003.

Balch, *Wives.* Balch, David L. *Let Wives Be Submissive: The Domestic Code in 1 Peter.* SBLMS 26. Chico, Calif.: Scholars Press, 1981.

Balcombe, *Door.* Balcombe, Dennis. *China's Opening Door.* Lake Mary, Fla.: Charisma House, 2014.

Baldwin, *Daniel.* Baldwin, Joyce G. *Daniel: An Introduction and Commentary.* TOTC. Leicester, U.K.: Inter-Varsity, 1978.

Baldwin, *Samuel Morris.* Baldwin, Lindley. *Samuel Morris: The African Boy God Sent to Prepare an American University for Its Mission to the World.* Reprint ed. Grand Rapids: Baker, 1987.

Bale, "Oracle." Bale, Alan. "The Ambiguous Oracle: Narrative Configuration in Acts." *NTS* 57 (4, 2011): 530–46.

Ballance, "Site." Ballance, M. "The Site of Derbe: A New Inscription." *AnSt* 7 (1957): 145–51.

Ballweg, "Extensions." Ballweg, John A. "Extensions of Meaning and Use for Kinship Terms." *AmAnth* 71 (1, 1969): 84–87.

Balsdon, "Women." Balsdon, John Percy Vyvian Dacre. "Women in Imperial Rome." *HT* 10 (1, 1960): 24–31.

Balsdon and Griffin, "*Princeps.*" Balsdon, John Percy Vyvian Dacre, and Miriam T. Griffin. "*Princeps.*" *OCD³* 1246–47.

Balsdon and Levick, "Claudius." Balsdon, John Percy Vyvian Dacre, and Barbara M. Levick. "Claudius (Tiberius Claudius Nero Germanicus)." *OCD³* 337–38.

Balsdon and Levick, "*Consilium principis.*" Balsdon, John Percy Vyvian Dacre, and Barbara M. Levick. "*Consilium principis.*" *OCD³* 377.

Balsdon and Levick, "*Damnatio memoriae.*" Balsdon, John Percy Vyvian Dacre, and Barbara M. Levick. "*Damnatio memoriae.*" *OCD³* 427.

Balsdon and Levick, "*Iuvenes.*" Balsdon, John Percy Vyvian Dacre, and Barbara M. Levick. "*Iuvenes* (or *iuventus*)." *OCD³* 791–92.

Balsdon and Levick, "*Princeps iuventutis.*" Balsdon, John Percy Vyvian Dacre, and Barbara M. Levick. "*Princeps iuventutis.*" *OCD³* 1247.

Balsdon and Lintott, "Acta." Balsdon, John Percy Vyvian Dacre, and Andrew William Lintott. "Acta." *OCD³* 10.

Balsdon and Lintott, "*Maiestas.*" Balsdon, John Percy Vyvian Dacre, and Andrew William Lintott. "*Maiestas.*" *OCD³* 913–14.

Baltussen, "Grief." Baltussen, Han. "Personal Grief and Public Mourning in Plutarch's Consolation to His Wife." *AJP* 130 (1, 2009): 67–98.

Balty, "Odeum." Balty, Jean-Charles. "Odeum." *OEANE* 4:177–78.

Baltzly, "Stoic Pantheism." Baltzly, Dirk. "Stoic Pantheism." *Sophia* 42 (2, 2003): 3–33.

Bamberger, "Philo and Aggadah." Bamberger, Bernard J. "Philo and the Aggadah." *HUCA* 48 (1977): 153–85.

Bamberger, "Prophet." Bamberger, Bernard J. "The Changing Image of the Prophet in Jewish Thought." Pages 301–23 in *Interpreting the Prophetic Tradition: The Goldman Lectures, 1955–1966.* Edited by Harry M. Orlinski. Cincinnati: Hebrew Union College Press; New York: KTAV, 1969.

Bamberger, *Proselytism.* Bamberger, Bernard J. *Proselytism in the Talmudic Period.* New York: KTAV, 1968.

Bamberger, *Story.* Bamberger, Bernard J. *The Story of Judaism.* New York: Union of American Hebrew Congregations, 1962.

Bammel, "Activity." Bammel, Ernst. "Jewish Activity against Christians in Palestine according to Acts." Pages 357–64 in *The Book of Acts in Its Palestinian Setting.* Edited by Richard Bauckham. Vol. 4 of *The Book of Acts in Its First Century Setting.* Edited by Bruce W. Winter. Grand Rapids: Eerdmans; Carlisle, U.K.: Paternoster, 1995.

Bammel, "Romans 13." Bammel, Ernst. "Romans 13." Pages 365–83 in *Jesus and the Politics of His Day.* Edited by Ernst Bammel and C. F. D. Moule. Cambridge: Cambridge University Press, 1984.

Bammel, "Text." Bammel, Ernst. "Der Text von Apostelgeschichte 15." Pages 439–46 in *Les Actes des apôtres: Traditions, rédaction, théologie.* Edited by Jacob Kremer.

BETL 48. Gembloux, Belg.: J. Duculot; Leuven: Leuven University Press, 1979.

Bammel, "Trial." Bammel, Ernst. "The Trial before Pilate." Pages 415–51 in *Jesus and the Politics of His Day.* Edited by Ernst Bammel and C. F. D. Moule. Cambridge: Cambridge University Press, 1984.

Bammer, *Architektur.* Bammer, Anton. *Die Architektur des jüngeren Artemision von Ephesos.* Wiesbaden: F. Steiner, 1972.

Bammer, "Ephesus." Bammer, Anton. "Ephesus." *OEANE* 2:252–55.

Bammer, *Heiligtum.* Bammer, Anton. *Die Heiligtum der Artemis von Ephesos.* Graz, Austria: Akademische Druck- und Verlagsanstalt, 1984.

Bampfylde, "Similitudes." Bampfylde, Gillian. "The Similitudes of Enoch: Historical Allusions." *JSJ* 15 (1, 1984): 9–31.

Bandy, *Inscriptions of Crete.* Bandy, Anastasios C. *The Greek Christian Inscriptions of Crete.* Athens: Christian Archaeological Society, 1970.

Banks, *Community.* Banks, Robert. *Paul's Idea of Community: The Early House Churches in Their Historical Setting.* Grand Rapids: Eerdmans, 1980.

Banks, "Kinship." Banks, David J. "Changing Kinship in North Malaya." *AmAnth* 74 (Oct. 1972): 1254–75.

Baptist, "Conversion." Baptist, A. J. "The Conversion/Call of Paul." *BiBh* 35 (1, 2009): 3–15.

Bar, "Aelia Capitolina." Bar, Doron. "Aelia Capitolina and the Location of the Camp of the Tenth Legion." *PEQ* 130 (1, 1998): 8–19.

Bar, "Intermarriage." Bar, Shaul. "Intermarriage in the Biblical Period." *BibT* 45 (2, 2007): 97–104.

Barag, "Castle." Barag, Dan. "King Herod's Royal Castle at Samaria-Sebaste." *PEQ* 125 (1, 1993): 3–18.

Baras, "*Testimonium.*" Baras, Zvi. "The *Testimonium flavianum* and the Martyrdom of James." Pages 338–48 in *Josephus, Judaism, and Christianity.* Edited by Louis H. Feldman and Gohei Hata. Detroit: Wayne State University Press, 1987.

Baratte, "Cutlery." Baratte, François. "Cutlery." *BrillPauly* 3:1030–32.

Baratte, "Table Utensils." Baratte, François. "Table Utensils." *BrillPauly* 14:88–89.

Barber, "Courage of Ananias." Barber, John L. "The Paradoxical Courage of Ananias." *RevRel* 56 (6, 1997): 571–77.

Barbi, "Use and Meaning." Barbi, Augusto. "The Use and Meaning of (Hoi) Ioudaioi in Acts." Pages 123–42, 243–45 in *Luke and Acts.* Edited by Gerald O'Collins and Gilberto Marconi. Translated by Matthew J. O'Connell. New York: Paulist, 1993.

Barc, "Taille." Barc, Bernard. "La taille cosmique d'Adam dans la littérature juive rabbinique des trois premiers siècles après J.-C." *RevScRel* 49 (3, 1975): 173–85.

Barceló, "Hispania." Barceló, Pedro. "Hispania, Iberia: Geography and History." *BrillPauly* 6:384–91.

Barclay, *Acts.* Barclay, William. *The Acts of the Apostles.* Rev. ed. Philadelphia: Westminster, 1976.

Barclay, "Acts ii.14–40." Barclay, William. "Acts ii.14–40." *ExpT* 70 (7, 1959): 196–99.

Barclay, "Jesus and Paul." Barclay, John M. G. "Jesus and Paul." *DPL* 492–503.

Barclay, *Jews in Diaspora.* Barclay, John M. G. *Jews in the Mediterranean Diaspora: From Alexander to Trajan (323 BCE–117 CE).* Berkeley: University of California Press, 1996.

Barclay, "New Man." Barclay, William. "The One, New Man." Pages 73–81 in *Unity and Diversity in New Testament Theology: Essays in Honor of George E. Ladd.* Edited by Robert A. Guelich. Grand Rapids: Eerdmans, 1978.

Barclay, "Paul among Jews." Barclay, John M. G. "Paul among Diaspora Jews: Anomaly or Apostate?" *JSNT* 60 (1995): 89–120.

Barclay, "Paul and Jewish People." Barclay, John M. G. "Paul, Judaism, and the Jewish People." Pages 188–201 in *The Blackwell Companion to Paul.* Edited by Stephen Westerholm. BCompRel. Oxford: Blackwell, 2011.

Barclay, "Thessalonica and Corinth." Barclay, John M. G. "Thessalonica and Corinth: Social Contrasts in Pauline Christianity." *JSNT* 47 (1992): 512–30.

Barclay, "Toughest." Barclay, J. M. G. "Who's the Toughest of Them All? Jews, Spartans and Roman Torturers in Josephus' Against Apion." *Ramus* 36 (1, 2007): 39–50.

Barclay, *Train a Child.* Barclay, William. *Train Up a Child: Educational Ideals in the Ancient World.* Philadelphia: Westminster, 1959.

Barclay, "Undermine." Barclay, J. M. G. "'Do We Undermine the Law?': A Study of Romans 14.1–15.6." Pages 287–308 in *Paul and the Mosaic Law.* Edited by James D. G. Dunn. The Third Durham-Tübingen Research Symposium on Earliest Christianity and Judaism (Durham, Sept. 1994). Grand Rapids/Cambridge: Eerdmans, 2001. (Without English translations of essays, the work originally appeared as Tübingen: J. C. B. Mohr, 1996.)

Bardski, "Intuitions parallèles." Bardski, Krzysztof. "Gen 22,1–14: Les intuitions parallèles des traditions juive et chrétienne dans le dialogue creative entre le texte biblique et la communauté de foi." *ColT* 71 (special issue, 2001): 5–13.

Bar-Ilan, "Magic and Religion." Bar-Ilan, Meir. "Between Magic and Religion: Sympathetic Magic in the World of the Sages of the Mishnah and Talmud." *RRJ* 5 (3, 2002): 383–99.

Barker, "Acoustics." Barker, Andrew D. "Acoustics." *OCD*³ 8–9.

Barker, "Census Returns." Barker, D. C. "Census Returns and Household Structures." Pages 87–93, §21, in *A Review of the Greek Inscriptions and Papyri Published in 1979.* By G. H. R. Horsley. Vol. 4 of *New Documents Illustrating Early Christianity.* North Ryde, N.S.W., Australia: Ancient History Documentary Research Centre, Macquarie University, 1987.

Barker, *Church's Neurosis.* Barker, C. Edward. *The Church's Neurosis and Twentieth-Century Revelations.* London: Rider, 1975.

Barker, "Golden Age." Barker, Duncan. "'The Golden Age Is Proclaimed'? The *Carmen saeculare* and the Renascence of the Golden Race." *CQ* 46 (2, 1996): 434–46.

Barker, "Music." Barker, Andrew D. "Music." *OCD*³ 1003–12.

Barkhuizen, "Proclus." Barkhuizen, J. H. "Proclus of Constantinople, Homily 17, 'Encomium of the Holy Stephen, First of the Martyrs': Translation and Analysis." *APB* 15 (2004): 1–21.

Barnard, "Judgment." Barnard, L. W. "The Judgment in 2 Peter iii." *ExpT* 68 (10, 1957): 302.

Barnard, *Justin Martyr.* Barnard, L. W. *Justin Martyr: His Life and Thought.* Cambridge: Cambridge University Press, 1967.

Barnard, "Logos Theology." Barnard, L. W. "The Logos Theology of St Justin Martyr." *DRev* 89 (295, 1971): 132–41.

Barnard, "Mark and Alexandria." Barnard, L. W. "St. Mark and Alexandria." *HTR* 57 (2, 1964): 145–50.

Barnard, "Matt. III.11" Barnard, L. W. "Matt. III.11//Luke III.16." *JTS* 8 (1, 1957): 107.

Barnard, "Old Testament." Barnard, L. W. "The Old Testament and Judaism in the Writings of Justin Martyr." *VT* 14 (4, 1964): 395–406.

Barnard, "Stephen and Alexandrian Christianity." Barnard, L. W. "Saint Stephen and Early Alexandrian Christianity." *NTS* 7 (1, 1960): 31–45.

Barnard, "Study." Barnard, L. W. "Justin Martyr in Recent Study." *SJT* 22 (2, 1969): 152–64.

Barnard, "Universal Systems." Barnard, Alan. "Universal Systems of Kin Categorization." *African Studies* 37 (1, 1978): 69–81.

Barnes, "Apostle on Trial." Barnes, Timothy D. "An Apostle on Trial." *JTS* 20 (2, 1969): 407–19.

Barnes, "Finishing." Barnes, Grace Preedy. "The Art of Finishing Well: Paul as Servant Leader, Acts 18:1–28 and 20:17–38." Pages 239–47 in *Mission in Acts: Ancient Narratives in Contemporary Context.* Edited by Robert L. Gallagher and Paul Hertig. AmSocMissS 34. Maryknoll, N.Y.: Orbis, 2004.

Barnes, "Introduction." Barnes, Linda L. "Introduction." Pages 3–26 in *Teaching Religion and Healing.* Edited by Linda L. Barnes and Inés Talamantez. AARTRSS. Oxford: Oxford University Press, 2006.

Barnes, "Monotheists." Barnes, Timothy D. "Monotheists All?" *Phoenix* 55 (2001): 142–62.

Barnes, "Parmenides." Barnes, Jonathan. "Parmenides and the Eleatic One." *AGP* 61 (1979): 1–21.

Barnes, "Paul and ben Zakkai." Barnes, Colin. "Paul and Johanan ben Zakkai." *ExpT* 108 (12, 1997): 366–67.

Barnes and Talamantez, *Religion and Healing.* Barnes, Linda L., and Inés Talamantez, eds. *Teaching Religion and Healing.* AARTRSS. Oxford: Oxford University Press, 2006.

Barnett, *Birth.* Barnett, Paul W. *The Birth of Christianity: The First Twenty Years.* Grand Rapids: Eerdmans, 2005.

Barnett, *Corinthians.* Barnett, Paul W. *The Second Epistle to the Corinthians.* NICNT. Grand Rapids: Eerdmans, 1997.

Barnett, "Eschatological Prophets." Barnett, Paul W. "The Jewish Eschatological Prophets." PhD diss., University of London, 1977.

Barnett, "Paul." Barnett, Paul W. "Appendix 1: Paul in the Book of Acts." Pages 392–95 in *All Things to All Cultures: Paul among Jews, Greeks, and Romans.* Edited by Mark Harding and Alanna Nobbs. Grand Rapids: Eerdmans, 2013.

Barnett, "Prophets." Barnett, Paul W. "The Jewish Sign Prophets—A.D. 40–70—Their Intentions and Origin." *NTS* 27 (5, 1981): 679–97.

Barnett, "Salvation." Barnett, Paul W. "Salvation." *DLNTD* 1072–75.

Barnouw, "Customs." Barnouw, Victor. "Eastern Nepalese Marriage Customs and Kinship Organization." *SWJA* 11 (1, 1955): 15–30.

Baron, *History of Jews.* Baron, Salo Wittmayer. *Social and Religious History of the Jews.* 2 vols. 2nd ed. New York: Columbia University Press, 1952.

Baroody, "Healing." Baroody, Naseeb B. "Spiritual Healing in Psychosomatic Disease." Pages 87–92 in *Faith Healing:*

Finger of God? Or, Scientific Curiosity? Compiled by Claude A. Frazier. New York: Thomas Nelson, 1973.

Bar-Oz et al., "Garbage." Bar-Oz, Guy, Ram Bouchnik, Ehud Weiss, Lior Weissbrod, Daniella E. Bar-Yosef Mayer, and Ronny Reich. "'Holy Garbage': A Quantitative Study of the City Dump of Early Roman Jerusalem." *Levant* 39 (2007): 1–12.

Barr, "Dependence." Barr, George K. "Literary Dependence in the New Testament Epistles." *IBS* 19 (4, 1997): 148–60.

Barr, "Impact." Barr, George K. "The Impact of Scalometry on New Testament Letters." *ExpT* 114 (1, 2002): 3–9.

Barr, "Paul and LXX." Barr, James. "Paul and the LXX: A Note on Some Recent Work." *JTS* 45 (2, 1994): 593–601.

Barr, *Physics and Faith*. Barr, Stephen M. *Modern Physics and Ancient Faith*. Notre Dame, Ind.: University of Notre Dame Press, 2003.

Barr, "Scale." Barr, George K. "Scale and the Pauline Epistles." *IBS* 17 (1, 1995): 22–41.

Barr, "Tent Makers." Barr, George K. "Romans 16 and the Tent Makers." *IBS* 20 (3, 1998): 98–113.

Barr, *Will of Zeus*. Barr, Stringfellow. *The Will of Zeus: A History of Greece from the Origins of Hellenic Culture to the Death of Alexander*. New York: Dell, 1961.

Barr and Wentling, "Biography and Genre." Barr, David L., and Judith L. Wentling. "The Conventions of Classical Biography and the Genre of Luke-Acts: A Preliminary Study." Pages 63–88 in *Luke-Acts: New Perspectives from the Society of Biblical Literature Seminar*. Edited by Charles H. Talbert. New York: Crossroad, 1984.

Barr, Leonard, Parsons, and Weaver, *Acts*. Barr, Beth Allison, Bill J. Leonard, Mikeal C. Parsons, and C. Douglas Weaver, eds. *The Acts of the Apostles: Four Centuries of Baptist Interpretation. The Baptists' Bible*. Waco: Baylor University Press, 2009.

Barreto, "Difference." Barreto, Eric D. "Negotiating Difference: Theology and Ethnicity in the Acts of the Apostles." *WW* 31 (2, 2011): 129–37.

Barreto, *Negotiations*. Barreto, Eric D. *Ethnic Negotiations: The Function of Race and Ethnicity in Acts 16*. WUNT 2.294. Tübingen: Mohr Siebeck, 2010.

Barrett, *1 Corinthians*. Barrett, C. K. *A Commentary on the First Epistle to the Corinthians*. New York: Harper & Row, 1968.

Barrett, *2 Corinthians*. Barrett, C. K. *A Commentary on the Second Epistle to the Corinthians*. HNTC 8. New York: Harper & Row, 1973.

Barrett, *Acts*. Barrett, C. K. *A Critical and Exegetical Commentary on the Acts of the Apostles*. 2 vols. Edinburgh: T&T Clark, 1994–98.

Barrett, "Acts and Corpus." Barrett, C. K. "Acts and the Pauline Corpus." *ExpT* 88 (1, 1976): 2–5.

Barrett, *Adam*. Barrett, C. K. *From First Adam to Last*. New York: Scribner's, 1962.

Barrett, "Address to Elders." Barrett, C. K. "Paul's Address to the Ephesian Elders." Pages 107–21 in *God's Christ and His People: Studies in Honour of Nils Alstrup Dahl*. Edited by Jacob Jervell and Wayne A. Meeks. Oslo: Universitets forlaget, 1977.

Barrett, "Anecdotes." Barrett, D. S. "'One-Up' Anecdotes in Jewish Literature of the Hellenistic-Roman Era." *Prudentia* 13 (2, 1981): 119–26.

Barrett, "Claudius, Gaius, and Kings." Barrett, Anthony A. "Claudius, Gaius, and the Client Kings." *CQ* 40 (1, 1990): 284–86.

Barrett, *Documents*. Barrett, C. K. *The New Testament Background: Selected Documents*. London: SPCK, 1956. Repr., New York: Harper & Row, 1961.

Barrett, "Eschatology." Barrett, C. K. "The Eschatology of the Epistle to the Hebrews." Pages 363–93 in *The Background of the New Testament and Its Eschatology: Essays in Honour of Charles Harold Dodd*. Edited by W. D. Davies and D. Daube. Cambridge: Cambridge University Press, 1964.

Barrett, "First Testament." Barrett, C. K. "The First Testament?" *NovT* 38 (1996): 94–104.

Barrett, *Gospel Tradition*. Barrett, C. K. *Jesus and the Gospel Tradition*. London: SPCK, 1967.

Barrett, "Historicity." Barrett, C. K. "The Historicity of Acts." *JTS* 50 (2, 1999): 515–34.

Barrett, "History." Barrett, C. K. "How History Should Be Written." Pages 33–57 in *History, Literature, and Society in the Book of Acts*. Edited by Ben Witherington III. Cambridge: Cambridge University Press, 1996.

Barrett, "Idols." Barrett, Rob. "Idols, Idolatry, Gods." Pages 351–55 in *Dictionary of the Old Testament Prophets*. Edited by Mark J. Boda and J. Gordon McConville. Downers Grove, Ill.: IVP Academic, 2012.

Barrett, "Imitatio." Barrett, C. K. "Imitatio Christi in Acts." Pages 251–62 in *Jesus of Nazareth, Lord and Christ: Essays on the Historical Jesus and New Testament Christology*. Edited by Joel B. Green and Max Turner. Grand Rapids: Eerdmans; Carlisle, U.K.: Paternoster, 1994.

Barrett, *John*. Barrett, C. K. *The Gospel according to St. John: An Introduction with Commentary and Notes on the Greek Text*. 2nd ed. Philadelphia: Westminster, 1978.

Barrett, "Κατέλαβεν." Barrett, C. K. "Κατέλαβεν in John i.5." *ExpT* 53 (9, 1942): 297.

Barrett, "Luke/Acts." Barrett, C. K. "Luke/Acts." Pages 231–44 in *It Is Written—Scripture Citing Scripture: Essays in Honour of Barnabas Lindars, SSF*. Edited by D. A. Carson and H. G. M. Williamson. Cambridge: Cambridge University Press, 1988.

Barrett, *Oil Lamp*. Barrett, D. G. *The Ceramic Oil Lamp as an Indicator of Cultural Change within Nabataean Society in Petra and Its Environs circa CE 106*. Gorgias Dissertations 32, Near Eastern Studies 8. Piscataway, N.J.: Gorgias, 2008.

Barrett, *Paul*. Barrett, C. K. *Paul: An Introduction to His Thought*. Louisville: Westminster John Knox, 1994.

Barrett, "Paul Shipwrecked." Barrett, C. K. "Paul Shipwrecked." Pages 51–64 in *Scripture—Meaning and Method: Essays Presented to Anthony Tyrrell Hanson for His Seventieth Birthday*. Edited by B. P. Thompson. Hull, U.K.: Hull University Press, 1987.

Barrett, "Pour Out." Barrett, Matthew. "'I Will Pour Out My Spirit on All Flesh': Are Acts 2 and 10 Proof-Texts for Inclusivism?" *Detroit Baptist Seminary Journal* 17 (2012): 79–98.

Barrett, *Shorter Commentary*. Barrett, C. K. *Acts: A Shorter Commentary*. London: T&T Clark, 2002.

Barrett, "Simon Magus." Barrett, C. K. "Light on the Holy Spirit from Simon Magus (Acts 8,4–25)." Pages 281–95 in *Les Actes des apôtres: Traditions, rédaction, théologie*. Edited by Jacob Kremer. BETL 48. Gembloux, Belg.: J. Duculot; Leuven: Leuven University Press, 1979.

Barrett, *Spirit*. Barrett, C. K. *The Holy Spirit and the Gospel Tradition*. London: SPCK, 1966.

Barrett, "Statistics." Barrett, David B. "Statistics, Global." *DPCM* 810–29.

Barrett, "Table." Barrett, David B. "Annual Statistical Table on Global Mission: 1997." *IBMR* 21 (Jan. 1997): 25.

Barrett, "Titus." Barrett, C. K. "Titus." Pages 1–14 in *Neotestamentica et Semitica: Studies in Honour of Matthew Black*. Edited by E. Earle Ellis and Max Wilcox. Edinburgh: T&T Clark, 1969.

Barrett, Johnson, and Crossing, "Missiometrics 2007." Barrett, David B., Todd M. Johnson, and Peter F. Crossing. "Missiometrics 2007: Creating Your Own Analysis of Global Data." *IBMR* 31 (1, Jan. 2007): 25–32.

Barrett-Lennard, *Healing*. Barrett-Lennard, R. J. S. *Christian Healing after the New Testament: Some Approaches to Illness in the Second, Third, and Fourth Centuries*. Lanham, Md.: University Press of America, 1994.

Barrington-Ward, "Spirit Possession." Barrington-Ward, Simon. "'The Centre Cannot Hold . . .': Spirit Possession as Redefinition." Pages 455–70 in *Christianity in Independent Africa*. Edited by Edward Fasholé-Luke, Richard Gray, Adrian Hastings, and Godwin Tasie. Bloomington: Indiana University Press, 1978.

Barrow, *Slavery*. Barrow, R. H. *Slavery in the Roman Empire*. 1928. Repr., New York: Barnes & Noble; London: Methuen & Co., 1968.

Barry, "Aristocrats." Barry, W. D. "Aristocrats, Orators, and the 'Mob': Dio Chrysostom and the World of the Alexandrians." *Historia* 42 (1, 1993): 82–103.

Barry, "Exposure." Barry, W. D. "Exposure, Mutilation, and Riot: Violence at the *Scalae Gemoniae* in Early Imperial Rome." *GR* 55 (2, 2008): 222–46.

Barry, "Roof Tiles." Barry, W. D. "Roof Tiles and Urban Violence in the Ancient World." *GRBS* 37 (1, 1996): 55–74.

Bartchy, "Community." Bartchy, S. Scott. "Community of Goods in Acts: Idealization or Social Reality?" Pages 309–18 in *The Future of Early Christianity: Essays in Honor of Helmut Koester*. Philadelphia: Augsburg Fortress, 1991.

Bartchy, "Power." Bartchy, S. Scott. "Divine Power, Community Formation, and Leadership in the Acts of the Apostles." Pages 89–104 in *Community Formation in the Early Church and in the Church Today*. Edited by Richard N. Longenecker. Peabody, Mass.: Hendrickson, 2002.

Bartchy, *Slavery*. Bartchy, S. Scott. ΜΑΛΛΟΝ ΧΡΗΣΑΙ: *First-Century Slavery and the Interpretation of 1 Corinthians 7:21*. SBLDS 11. Missoula, Mont.: SBL, 1973.

Bartel, "Role." Bartel, LeRoy R. "The Role of the Holy Spirit in Teaching Ministry." Pages 321–44 in *Trajectories in the Book of Acts: Essays in Honor of John Wesley Wyckoff*. Edited by Paul Alexander, Jordan Daniel May, and Robert G. Reid. Eugene, Ore.: Wipf & Stock, 2010.

Bartels, *Roots*. Bartels, F. L. *The Roots of Ghana Methodism*. Cambridge: Cambridge University Press, 1965.

Barth, "Descent." Barth, Frederik. "Descent and Marriage Reconsidered." Pages 3–19 in *The Character of Kinship*. Edited by Jack Goody. New York: Cambridge University Press, 1973.

Barth, *Dogmatics*. Barth, Karl. *Church Dogmatics: The Doctrine of Reconciliation*. 4.3. Edinburgh: T&T Clark, 1961.

Barth, *Ephesians*. Barth, Markus. *Ephesians*. 2 vols. AB 34, 34A. Garden City, N.Y.: Doubleday, 1974.

Barth, "Faith." Barth, Markus. "The Faith of the Messiah." *HeyJ* 10 (1969): 363–70.

Barth, *Justification*. Barth, Markus. *Justification: Pauline Texts Interpreted in the Light of the Old and New Testaments*. Translated by A. M. Woodruff III. Grand Rapids: Eerdmans, 1971.

Barth, "Law." Barth, Gerhard. "Matthew's Understanding of the Law." Pages 58–164 in *Tradition and Interpretation in Matthew*. Edited by Günther Bornkamm, Gerhard Barth, and Heinz Joachim Held. Philadelphia: Westminster; London: SCM, 1963.

Barth, *Letters*. Barth, Karl. *Letters 1961–1968*. Translated and edited by Geoffrey W. Bromiley. Grand Rapids: Eerdmans, 1981.

Barth, *People of God*. Barth, Markus. *The People of God*. JSNTSup 5. Sheffield, U.K.: JSOT Press, 1983.

Barthell, *Gods*. Barthell, Edward E., Jr. *Gods and Goddesses of Ancient Greece*. Coral Gables, Fla.: University of Miami Press, 1971.

Bartleman, *Azusa Street*. Bartleman, Frank. *Azusa Street*. Foreword by Vinson Synan. 1925. Repr., Plainfield, N.J.: Logos, 1980.

Bartlett, "Coming." Bartlett, W. "The Coming of the Holy Ghost according to the Fourth Gospel." *ExpT* 37 (2, 1925): 72–75.

Bartlett, *Jews*. Bartlett, John R. *Jews in the Hellenistic World: Josephus, Aristeas, the Sibylline Oracles, Eupolemus*. CCWJCW 1.1. Cambridge: Cambridge University Press, 1985.

Barton, "Approaches." Barton, Stephen C. "Social-Scientific Approaches to Paul." *DPL* 892–900.

Barton, "Audiences." Barton, Stephen C. "Can We Identify the Gospel Audiences?" Pages 173–94 in *The Gospels for All Christians: Rethinking the Gospel Audiences*. Edited by Richard Bauckham. Grand Rapids: Eerdmans, 1998.

Barton, *Honor*. Barton, Carlin A. *Roman Honor: The Fire in the Bones*. Berkeley: University of California Press, 2001.

Barton, "Missionary." Barton, Stephen C. "Paul as Missionary and Pastor." Pages 34–48 in *The Cambridge Companion to St Paul*. Edited by James D. G. Dunn. Cambridge: Cambridge University Press, 2003.

Barton, "Moment." Barton, Carlin A. "The 'Moment of Truth' in Ancient Rome: Honor and Embodiment in a Contest Culture." *StanHR* 6 (2, 1998): 16–30.

Barton, *Oracles*. Barton, John. *Amos's Oracles against the Nations: A Study of Amos 1.3–2.5*. Cambridge: Cambridge University Press, 1980.

Barton, "Origin." Barton, George A. "The Origin of the Names of Angels and Demons in the Extra-canonical Apocalyptic Literature to 100 A.D." *JBL* 31 (1912): 156–67.

Barton, "Sociology." Barton, Stephen C. "Sociology and Theology." Pages 459–72 in *Witness to the Gospel: The Theology of Acts*. Edited by I. Howard Marshall and David Peterson. Grand Rapids: Eerdmans, 1998.

Barton, "Values." Barton, Stephen C. "Social Values and Structures." *DNTB* 1127–34.

Barton and Horsley, "Cult Group." Barton, Stephen C., and G. H. R. Horsley. "A Hellenistic Cult Group and the New Testament Churches." *JAC* 24 (1981): 7–41.

Bartsch, "Inhalt." Bartsch, Hans W. "Inhalt und Funktion des urchristlichen Osterglaubens." *NTS* 26 (2, 1980): 180–96.

Baslez, "Martyrs." Baslez, Marie-Françoise. "Des martyrs juifs aux martyrs chrétiens." *EspV* 118 (194, 2008): 19–23.

Baslez, "Monde." Baslez, Marie-Françoise. "Le monde des Actes des apôtres: Approches littéraires et études documentaires." Pages 63–84 in *Les Actes des apôtres—Histoire, récit, théologie: XXe congrès de l'Association catholique française pour l'étude de la Bible (Angers, 2003)*. Edited by Michel Berder. LD 199. Paris: Cerf, 2005.

Bass, "Necessity." Bass, Kenneth. "The Narrative and Rhetorical Use of Divine Necessity in Luke-Acts." *JBPRes* 1 (Fall 2009): 48–68.

Bass and van Doorninck, personal correspondence. Bass, George F., and Frederick van Doorninck Jr. Personal correspondence to the author, Feb. 27, 2007.

Basser, "Allusions." Basser, Herbert W. "Allusions to Christian and Gnostic Practices in Talmudic Tradition." *JSJ* 12 (1, 1981): 87–105.

Basser, "Democratize." Basser, Herbert W. "The Rabbinic Attempt to Democratize Salvation and Revelation." *SR/SR* 12 (1, 1983): 27–33.

Basser, "Interpretations." Basser, Herbert W. "Superstitious Interpretations of Jewish Laws." *JSJ* 8 (2, 1977): 127–38.

Basser, "Merkavah Narrative." Basser, Herbert W. "Merkavah Narrative: Two Paradigmatic Examples." *RRJ* 2 (1999): 89–100.

Basser, "Practices." Basser, Herbert W. "Allusions to Christian and Gnostic Practices in Talmudic Tradition." *JSJ* 12 (1, 1981): 87–105.

Basser, "Priests." Basser, Herbert W. "Priests and Priesthood, Jewish." *DNTB* 824–27.

Bassler, "Cain." Bassler, Jouette M. "Cain and Abel in the Palestinian Targums. A Brief Note on an Old Controversy." *JSJ* 17 (1, 1986): 56–64.

Bassler, "Corinthians." Bassler, Jouette M. "1 Corinthians." Pages 321–29 in *The Women's Bible Commentary*. Edited by Carol A. Newsom and Sharon H. Ringe. London: SPCK; Louisville: Westminster John Knox, 1992.

Bassler, "Divine Impartiality." Bassler, Jouette M. "Divine Impartiality in Paul's Letter to the Romans." *NovT* 26 (1, 1984): 43–58.

Bassler, *Impartiality*. Bassler, Jouette M. *Divine Impartiality: Paul and a Theological Axiom*. SBLDS 59. Chico, Calif.: Scholars Press, 1982.

Bassler, "Luke on Impartiality." Bassler, Jouette M. "Luke and Paul on Impartiality." *Bib* 66 (4, 1985): 546–52.

Basso, "Music." Basso, Rebecca. "Music, Possession, and Shamanism among Khond Tribes." *CulRel* 7 (2, 2006): 177–97.

Bastomsky, "Nero." Bastomsky, S. J. "The Emperor Nero in Talmudic Legend." *JQR* 59 (4, 1969): 321–25.

Bastomsky, "View." Bastomsky, S. J. "The Talmudic View of Epicureanism." *Apeiron* 7 (1, 1973): 17–19.

Batch, "Littérature tannaïtique." Batch, C. "La littérature tannaïtique comme source historique pour l'étude du judaïsme du deuxième temple: Les questions méthodologiques de Jacob Neusner et de Peter Schäfer." *REJ* 166 (1–2, 2007): 1–15.

Bate, "Mission." Bate, Stuart C. "The Mission to Heal in a Global Context." *IntRevMiss* 90 (356/357, Jan./Apr. 2001): 70–80.

Bates, "Sons." Bates, M. W. "Why Do the Seven Sons of Sceva Fail? Exorcism, Magic, and Oath Enforcement in Acts 19,13–17." *RevBib* 118 (3, July 2011): 408–21.

Batey, *Imagery*. Batey, Richard A. *New Testament Nuptial Imagery*. Leiden: Brill, 1971.

Batstone, "Theory." Batstone, William W. "Postmodern Historiographical Theory and the Roman Historians." Pages 24–40 in *The Cambridge Companion to the Roman Historians*. Edited by Andrew Feldherr. Cambridge: Cambridge University Press, 2009.

Batten, "Acts 10." Batten, Jim. "Acts 10:36–43 and the Gospel of Mark." *AfCrit* 14 (1, 2009): 92–96.

Batten, "Moral World." Batten, Alicia. "The Moral World of Greco-Roman Associations." *SR/SR* 36 (1, 2007): 135–51.

Bauckham, *Acts in Setting*. Bauckham, Richard, ed. *The Book of Acts in Its Palestinian Setting*. Vol. 4 of *The Book of Acts in Its First Century Setting*. Edited by Bruce W. Winter. Grand Rapids: Eerdmans; Carlisle, U.K.: Paternoster, 1995.

Bauckham, "Acts of Paul." Bauckham, Richard. "The Acts of Paul as a Sequel to Acts." Pages 105–52 in *The Book of Acts in Its Ancient Literary Setting*. Edited by Bruce W. Winter and Andrew D. Clark. Vol. 1 of *The Book of Acts in Its First Century Setting*. Edited by Bruce W. Winter. Grand Rapids: Eerdmans; Carlisle, U.K.: Paternoster, 1993.

Bauckham, *Climax*. Bauckham, Richard. *The Climax of Prophecy: Studies on the Book of Revelation*. Edinburgh: T&T Clark, 1993.

Bauckham, "Colossians 1:24." Bauckham, Richard. "Colossians 1:24 Again: The Apocalyptic Motif." *EvQ* 47 (3, 1975): 168–70.

Bauckham, *Crucified*. Bauckham, Richard. *God Crucified: Monotheism and Christology in the New Testament*. Grand Rapids: Eerdmans, 1998.

Bauckham, "Earthquake." Bauckham, Richard. "The Eschatological Earthquake in the Apocalypse of John." *NovT* 19 (3, 1977): 224–33.

Bauckham, "East Rather Than West." Bauckham, Richard. "What If Paul Had Travelled East Rather Than West?" *BibInt* 8 (1–2, 2000): 171–84.

Bauckham, *Eyewitnesses*. Bauckham, Richard. *Jesus and the Eyewitnesses: The Gospels as Eyewitness Testimony*. Grand Rapids: Eerdmans, 2006.

Bauckham, "Eyewitnesses." Bauckham, Richard. "The Eyewitnesses and the Gospel Traditions." *JSHJ* 1 (1, 2003): 28–60.

Bauckham, "Gospels." Bauckham, Richard. "For Whom Were the Gospels Written?" Pages 9–48 in *The Gospels for All Christians: Rethinking the Gospel Audiences*. Edited by Richard Bauckham. Grand Rapids: Eerdmans, 1998.

Bauckham, *Gospels for Christians*. Bauckham, Richard, ed. *The Gospels for All Christians: Rethinking the Gospel Audiences*. Grand Rapids: Eerdmans, 1998.

Bauckham, "Historiographical Characteristics." Bauckham, Richard. "Historiographical Characteristics of the Gospel of John." *NTS* 53 (1, 2007): 17–36.

Bauckham, "James." Bauckham, Richard. "James and the Jerusalem Church." Pages 415–80 in *The Book of Acts in Its Palestinian Setting*. Edited by Richard Bauckham. Vol. 4 of *The Book of Acts in Its First Century Setting*. Edited by Bruce W. Winter. Grand Rapids: Eerdmans; Carlisle, U.K.: Paternoster, 1995.

Bauckham, "James and Gentiles." Bauckham, Richard. "James and the Gentiles (Acts 15.13–21)." Pages 154–84 in *History, Literature, and Society in the Book of Acts*. Edited by Ben Witherington III. Cambridge: Cambridge University Press, 1996.

Bauckham, *Jude*. Bauckham, Richard. *Jude, 2 Peter*. WBC 50. Waco: Word, 1983.

Bauckham, "Latin Names." Bauckham, Richard. "Paul and Other Jews with Latin Names in the New Testament." Pages 202–20 in *Paul, Luke, and the Graeco-Roman World*. Edited by Alf Christophersen et al. JSNTSup 217. Sheffield, U.K.: Sheffield Academic, 2002; London: T&T Clark, 2003.

Bauckham, "Liber antiquitatum." Bauckham, Richard. "The Liber antiquitatum biblicarum of Pseudo-Philo and the Gospels as 'Midrash.'" Pages 33–76 in *Studies in Midrash and Historiography*. Edited by R. T. France and David Wenham. Gospel Perspectives 3. Sheffield, U.K.: JSOT Press, 1983.

Bauckham, "Sequel." Bauckham, Richard. "The *Acts of Paul*: Replacement of Acts or Sequel to Acts?" Pages 159–68 in *The Apocryphal Acts of the Apostles in Intertextual Perspectives*. Edited by Robert F. Stoops. *Semeia* 80. Atlanta: Scholars Press, 1997.

Bauckham, "Spirit." Bauckham, Richard. "The Role of the Spirit in the Apocalypse." *EvQ* 52 (2, 1980): 66–83.

Bauckham, "Summaries." Bauckham, Richard. "Kerygmatic Summaries in the Speeches of Acts." Pages 185–217 in *History, Literature, and Society in the Book of Acts*. Edited by Ben Witherington III. Cambridge: Cambridge University Press, 1996.

Bauckham, *Testimony*. Bauckham, Richard. *The Testimony of the Beloved Disciple: Narrative, History, and Theology in the Gospel of John*. Grand Rapids: Baker Academic, 2007.

Bauckham, "Visiting." Bauckham, Richard. "Visiting the Places of the Dead in the Extra-canonical Apocalypses." *PIBA* 18 (1995): 78–93.

Bauckham, *Women*. Bauckham, Richard. *Gospel Women: Studies of the Named Women in the Gospels*. Grand Rapids: Eerdmans, 2002.

Baudry, "Péché chez Philon." Baudry, Gerard-Henry. "Le péché originel chez Philon d'Alexandrie." *MScRel* 50 (2, 1993): 99–115.

Baudry, "Péché dans pseudépigraphes." Baudry, Gerard-Henry. "Le péché originel dans les pseudépigraphes de l'Ancien Testament." *MScRel* 49 (3–4, 1992): 163–92.

Baudry, "Péché de Qoumrân." Baudry, Gerard-Henry. "Le péché originel dans les écrits de Qoumrân." *MScRel* 50 (1, 1993): 7–23.

Baudy, "Hermes." Baudy, Gerhard. "Hermes: Cult and Mythology." *BrillPauly* 6:214–19.

Baudy, "Parilia." Baudy, Gerhard. "Parilia." *BrillPauly* 10:531–32.

Baudy, "Tree Cult." Baudy, Gerhard. "Tree Cult." *BrillPauly* 14:886–87.

Bauer, "Friendship." Bauer, David R. "When Friendship Fails." Paper presented to the Faculty of Asbury Theological Seminary, Aug. 29, 2011.

Bauer, "Namen." Bauer, Johannes B. "'Literarische' Namen und 'literarische' Bräuche (zu Joh 2,10 und 18,39)." *BZ* 26 (2, 1982): 258–64.

Bauer, *Orthodoxy*. Bauer, Walter. *Orthodoxy and Heresy in Earliest Christianity*. Edited by Robert A. Kraft and Gerhard Krodel. Philadelphia: Fortress, 1971.

Bauer, "Tod." Bauer, Dieter. "Der Tod von Märtyrern und die Hoffnung auf die Auferstehung." *BK* 57 (2, 2002): 82–86.

Bauernfeind and Michel, "Beiden Eleazarreden." Bauernfeind, Otto, and Otto Michel. "Die beiden Eleazarreden in Jos. bell. 7,323–336; 7,341–388." *ZNW* 58 (3–4, 1967): 267–72.

Baugh, "Cult Prostitution." Baugh, Steven M. "Cult Prostitution in New Testament Ephesus: A Reappraisal." *JETS* 42 (3, 1999): 443–60.

Baugh, "Marriage." Baugh, Steven M. "Marriage and Family in Ancient Greek Society." Pages 103–31 in *Marriage and Family in the Biblical World*. Edited by Ken M. Campbell. Downers Grove, Ill.: InterVarsity, 2003.

Baugh, "Paul and Ephesus." Baugh, Steven M. "Paul and Ephesus: The Apostle among His Contemporaries." PhD diss., University of California, Irvine, 1990.

Baugh, "Phraseology and Reliability." Baugh, Steven M. "Phraseology and the Reliability of Acts." *NTS* 36 (2, 1990): 290–94.

Baugh, "World." Baugh, Steven M. "A Foreign World: Ephesus in the First Century." Pages 13–52 in *Women in the Church: A Fresh Analysis of 1 Timothy 2:9–15*. Edited by Andreas J. Köstenberger, Thomas R. Schreiner, and H. Scott Baldwin. Grand Rapids: Baker, 1995.

Baum, "Anonymity." Baum, Armin D. "The Anonymity of the New Testament History Books: A Stylistic Device in the Context of Greco-Roman and Ancient Near Eastern Literature." *NovT* 50 (2, 2008): 120–42.

Baum, *Gospel*. Baum, Gregory. *The Jews and the Gospel: A Re-examination of the New Testament*. London: Bloomsbury, 1961.

Baum, "Paulinismen." Baum, Armin D. "Paulinismen in den Missionsreden des lukanischen Paulus: Zur inhaltlichen Authentizität der *oratio recta* in der Apostelgeschichte." *ETL* 82 (4, 2006): 405–36.

Baum, "Sources." Baum, Armin D. "Matthew's Sources—Written or Oral? A Rabbinic Analogy and Empirical Insights." Pages 1–23 in *Built upon the Rock: Studies in the Gospel of Matthew*. Edited by Daniel M. Gurtner and John Nolland. Grand Rapids and Cambridge, U.K.: Eerdmans, 2007.

Baum, "Variation." Baum, Armin D. "Semantic Variation within the *Corpus paulinum*: Linguistic Considerations concerning the Richer Vocabulary of the Pastoral Epistles." *TynBul* 59 (2, 2008): 271–92.

Baum, "Wir- und Er-Stellungen." Baum, Armin D. "Autobiografische Wir- und Er-Stellungen in den neutestamentlichen Geschichtsbüchern im Kontext der antiken Literaturgeschichte." *Bib* 88 (4, 2007): 473–95.

Baumbach, "Sadducees." Baumbach, Günther. "The Sadducees in Josephus." Pages 173–95 in *Josephus, the Bible, and History*. Edited by Louis H. Feldman and Gohei Hata. Detroit: Wayne State University Press, 1989.

Baumbach, "Sadduzäerverständnis." Baumbach, Günther. "Das Sadduzäerverständnis bei Josephus Flavius und im Neuen Testament." *Kairos* 13 (1, 1971): 17–37.

Baumbach, "Zeloten." Baumbach, Günther. "Zeloten und Sikarier." *TLZ* 90 (10, 1965): 727–40.

Baumgarten, "4Q502." Baumgarten, Joseph M. "4Q502, Marriage or Golden Age Ritual?" *JJS* 34 (2, 1983): 125–35.

Baumgarten, "Citation." Baumgarten, Joseph M. "A 'Scriptural' Citation in 4Q Fragments of the Damascus Document." *JJS* 43 (1, 1992): 95–98.

Baumgarten, "Essene." Baumgarten, Albert I. "He Knew That He Knew That He Knew That He Was an Essene." *JJS* 48 (1, 1997): 53–61.

Baumgarten, "Exclusions." Baumgarten, Joseph M. "Exclusions from the Temple: Proselytes and Agrippa I." *JJS* 33 (1–2, 1982): 215–25.

Baumgarten, "Miracles." Baumgarten, Albert I. "Miracles and Halakah in Rabbinic Judaism." *JQR* 73 (3, 1983): 238–53.

Baumgarten, "Netinim." Baumgarten, Joseph M. "The Exclusion of 'Netinim' and Proselytes in 4QFlorilegium." *RevQ* 8 (29/1, 1972): 87–96.

Baumgarten, *Paulus und Apokalyptik*. Baumgarten, Jörg. *Paulus und die Apokalyptik*. Neukirchen-Vluyn: Neukirchener Verlag, 1975.

Baumgarten, "Pharisaic *paradosis*." Baumgarten, Albert I. "The Pharisaic *paradosis*." *HTR* 80 (1, 1987): 63–77.

Baumgarten, "Pharisees." Baumgarten, Albert I. "The Name of the Pharisees." *JBL* 102 (3, 1983): 411–28.

Baumgarten, "Problems." Baumgarten, Joseph M. "Some Problems of the Jubilees Calendar in Current Research." *VT* 32 (4, 1982): 485–89.

Baumgarten, "Qumran Studies." Baumgarten, Joseph M. "Qumran Studies." *JBL* 77 (1958): 249–57.

Baumgarten, "Seductress." Baumgarten, Joseph M. "The Seductress of Qumran." *BRev* 17 (5, 2001): 21–23, 42.

Baumgarten, "Unwritten Law." Baumgarten, Joseph M. "The Unwritten Law in the Pre-rabbinic Period." *JSJ* 3 (1, 1972): 7–29.

Baumgarten, "Yom Kippur." Baumgarten, Joseph M. "Yom Kippur in the Qumran Scrolls and Second Temple Sources." *DSD* 6 (2, 1999): 184–91.

Baumgarten and Mansoor, "Hodayot." Baumgarten, Joseph M., and Menahem Mansoor. "Studies in the New *Hodayot* (Thanksgiving Hymns)—II." *JBL* 74 (3, 1955): 188–95.

Bayer, "Eschatology in Acts 3:17–26." Bayer, Hans F. "Christ-Centered Eschatology in Acts 3:17–26." Pages 236–50 in *Jesus of Nazareth, Lord and Christ: Essays on the Historical Jesus and New Testament Christology*. Edited by Joel B. Green and Max Turner. Grand Rapids: Eerdmans; Carlisle, U.K.: Paternoster, 1994.

Bayer, "Preaching." Bayer, Hans F. "The Preaching of Peter in Acts." Pages 257–74 in *Witness to the Gospel: The Theology of Acts*. Edited by I. Howard Marshall and David Peterson. Grand Rapids: Eerdmans, 1998.

Baynes, "Transformation." Baynes, Leslie. "Philo, Personification, and the Transformation of Grammatical Gender." *SPhilA* 14 (2002): 31–47.

Baynham, *Alexander*. Baynham, Elizabeth. *Alexander the Great: The Unique History of Quintus Curtius*. Ann Arbor: University of Michigan Press, 1998.

Baynham, "Barbarians." Baynham, Elizabeth. "Barbarians I: Quintus Curtius' and Other Roman Historians' Reception of Alexander." Pages 288–300 in *The Cambridge Companion to the Roman Historians*. Edited by Andrew Feldherr. Cambridge: Cambridge University Press, 2009.

Baynham, "Quintus Curtius." Baynham, E. J. "Quintus Curtius Rufus on the 'Good King': The Dioxippus Episode in Book 9.7.16–26." Pages 427–33 in *A Companion to Greek and Roman Historiography*. Edited by John Marincola. 2 vols. Oxford: Blackwell, 2007.

Bays, "Revival." Bays, Daniel H. "Christian Revival in China, 1900–1937." Pages 161–79 in *Modern Christian Revivals*.

Edited by Edith Blumhofer and Randall H. Balmer. Urbana: University of Illinois Press, 1993.

Bazin, "Past." Bazin, Jean. "The Past in the Present: Notes on Oral Archaeology." Pages 59–74 in *African Historiographies: What History for Which Africa?* Edited by Bogumil Jewsiewicki and David Newbury. SSAMD 12. Beverly Hills, Calif.; London; and New Delhi: Sage, 1986.

Bazzana, "Missionaries as Physicians." Bazzana, Giovanni B. "Early Christian Missionaries as Physicians: Healing and Its Cultural Value in the Greco-Roman Context." *NovT* 51 (3, 2009): 232–51.

Beale, "Descent." Beale, Gregory K. "The Descent of the Eschatological Temple in the Form of the Spirit at Pentecost, Part 1: The Clearest Evidence." *TynBul* 56 (1, 2005): 73–102.

Beale, *Revelation.* Beale, Gregory K. *The Book of Revelation: A Commentary on the Greek Text.* Grand Rapids: Eerdmans, 1999.

Beale, "Temple." Beale, Gregory K. "The Descent of the Eschatological Temple in the Form of the Spirit at Penecost, Part 2: Corroborating Evidence." *TynBul* 56 (2, 2005): 63–90.

Beall, "Essenes." Beall, Todd S. "Essenes." *DNTB* 342–49.

Bean, "Propontis." Bean, George Ewart. "Propontis." *OCD*[3] 1259.

Bean and Mitchell, "Cilicia." Bean, George Ewart, and Stephen Mitchell. "Cilicia." *OCD*[3] 330–31.

Beard, "Virgins." Beard, Mary. "The Sexual Status of Vestal Virgins." *JRS* 70 (1980): 12–27.

Beard, North, and Price, *Religions.* Beard, Mary, John North, and Simon Price. *Religions of Rome,* vol. 1, *A History.* Cambridge: Cambridge University Press, 1998.

Beardslee, "Inaccuracies." Beardslee, J. W. "Alleged Inaccuracies in Acts." *Bible Student* 7 (1903): 226–34.

Beare, *Matthew.* Beare, Francis Wright. *The Gospel according to Matthew.* San Francisco: Harper & Row, 1981.

Beare, *Peter.* Beare, Francis Wright. *The First Epistle of Peter: The Greek Text with Introduction and Notes.* 2nd rev. ed. Oxford: Blackwell, 1958.

Beare, *Philippians.* Beare, Francis Wright. *A Commentary on the Epistle to the Philippians.* 2nd ed. London: Adam & Charles Black, 1969.

Beare, "Spirit." Beare, Francis Wright. "The Risen Jesus Bestows the Spirit: A Study of John 20:19–23." *CJT* 4 (2, 1958): 95–100.

Beasley-Murray, *Baptism.* Beasley-Murray, George R. *Baptism in the New Testament.* Grand Rapids: Eerdmans, 1962.

Beasley-Murray, "Baptism." Beasley-Murray, George R. "Baptism." *DPL* 60–66.

Beasley-Murray, *John.* Beasley-Murray, George R. *John.* WBC 36. Waco: Word, 1987.

Beasley-Murray, "Kingdom." Beasley-Murray, George R. "The Kingdom of God and Christology in the Gospels." Pages 22–36 in *Jesus of Nazareth, Lord and Christ: Essays on the Historical Jesus and New Testament Christology.* Edited by Joel B. Green and Max Turner. Grand Rapids: Eerdmans; Carlisle, U.K.: Paternoster, 1994.

Beasley-Murray, *Revelation.* Beasley-Murray, George R. *The Book of Revelation.* NCBC. Greenwood, S.C.: Attic; London: Marshall, Morgan & Scott, 1974.

Beasley-Murray, "Romans 1:3f." Beasley-Murray, Paul. "Romans 1:3f: An Early Confession of Faith in the Lordship of Jesus." *TynBul* 31 (1980): 147–54.

Beattie, "Boanerges." Beattie, D. R. G. "Boanerges: A Semiticist's Solution." *IBS* 5 (1, 1983): 11–13.

Beattie, "Mediumship." Beattie, John. "Spirit Mediumship in Bunyoro." Pages 159–70 in *Spirit Mediumship and Society in Africa.* Edited by John Beattie and John Middleton. Foreword by Raymond Firth. New York: Africana, 1969.

Beattie and Middleton, "Introduction." Beattie, John, and John Middleton. Introduction. Pages xvii–xxx in *Spirit Mediumship and Society in Africa.* Edited by John Beattie and John Middleton. Foreword by Raymond Firth. New York: Africana, 1969.

Beattie and Middleton, *Mediumship.* Beattie, John, and John Middleton, eds. *Spirit Mediumship and Society in Africa.* Foreword by Raymond Firth. New York: Africana, 1969.

Beaujeu, "Cultes locaux." Beaujeu, Jean. "Cultes locaux et cultes d'empire dans les provinces d'occident aux trois premiers siècles de notre ère." Pages 433–43 in *Assimilation et résistance à la culture gréco-romaine dans le monde ancien: Travaux du VIe Congrès international d'études classiques.* Edited by D. M. Pippidi. FIAEC. Paris: Belles Lettres, 1976.

Beauregard and O'Leary, *Brain.* Beauregard, Mario, and Denyse O'Leary. *The Spiritual Brain: A Neuroscientist's Case for the Existence of the Soul.* New York: HarperCollins, 2007.

Beauvery, "Prostituée." Beauvery, Robert. "L'Apocalypse au risque de la numismatique: Babylone, la grande prostituée et le sixième roi Vespasien et la déesse Rome." *RB* 90 (2, 1983): 243–60.

Beauvoir, "Herbs." Beauvoir, Max-G. "Herbs and Energy: The Holistic Medical System of the Haitian People." Pages 112–33 in *Haïtian Vodou: Spirit, Myth, and Reality.* Edited by Patrick Bellegarde-Smith and Claudine Michel. Bloomington: Indiana University Press, 2006.

Beavis, "Kingdom." Beavis, Mary Ann. "The Kingdom of God, 'Utopia,' and Theocracy." *JSHJ* 2 (1, 2004): 91–106.

Beavis, "Origins." Beavis, Mary Ann. "Christian Origins, Egalitarianism, and Utopia." *JFSR* 23 (2, 2007): 27–49.

Beavis, "Therapeutae." Beavis, Mary Ann. "Philo's Therapeutae: Philosopher's Dream or Utopian Construction?" *JSP* 14 (1, 2004): 30–42.

Bebbington, *Dominance.* Bebbington, David W. *The Dominance of Evangelicalism: The Age of Spurgeon and Moody.* A History of Evangelicalism 3. Downers Grove, Ill.: InterVarsity, 2005.

Bechard, "Case." Bechard, Dean P. "The Disputed Case against Paul: A Redaction-Critical Analysis of Acts 21:27–22:29." *CBQ* 65 (2, 2003): 232–50.

Bechard, "Judaea." Bechard, Dean P. "The Theological Significance of Judaea in Luke-Acts." Pages 675–91 in *The Unity of Luke-Acts.* Edited by Joseph Verheyden. BETL 142. Leuven: Leuven University Press, 1999.

Bechard, "Rustics." Bechard, Dean P. "Paul among the Rustics: The Lystran Episode (Acts 14:8–20) and Lucan Apologetic." *CBQ* 63 (1, 2001): 84–101.

Bechard, *Walls.* Bechard, Dean P. *Paul outside the Walls: A Study of Luke's Socio-geographical Universalism in Acts 14:8–20.* AnBib 143. Rome: Editrice Pontificio Istituto Biblico, 2000.

Beck, "Anonymity." Beck, David R. "The Narrative Function of Anonymity in Fourth Gospel Characterization." *Semeia* 63 (1993): 143–58.

Beck, "Astrology." Beck, Roger. "Astrology." *OCD*[3] 195.

Beck, "Common Authorship." Beck, B. E. "The Common Authorship of Luke and Acts." *NTS* 23 (3, 1977): 346–52.

Beck, "Ecphrasis." Beck, Deborah. "Ecphrasis, Interpretation, and Audience in *Aeneid* 1 and *Odyssey* 8." *AJP* 128 (4, 2007): 533–49.

Beck, "Evangelism." Beck, David R. "Evangelism in Luke-Acts: More Than an Outreach Program." *F&M* 20 (2, 2003): 85–103.

Beck, "Mysteries." Beck, Roger. "The Mysteries of Mithras: A New Account of Their Genesis." *JRS* 88 (1998): 115–28.

Beck, *Paradigm*. Beck, David R. *The Discipleship Paradigm: Readers and Anonymous Characters in the Fourth Gospel*. Leiden: Brill, 1997.

Beck, "Ritual." Beck, Roger. "Ritual, Myth, Doctrine, and the Initiation in the Mysteries of Mithras: New Evidence from a Cult Vessel." *JRS* 90 (2000): 145–80 and plates 13–14.

Beck, "Roman Tradition." Beck, Hans. "The Early Roman Tradition." Pages 259–65 in *A Companion to Greek and Roman Historiography*. Edited by John Marincola. 2 vols. Oxford: Blackwell, 2007.

Beck, "Women." Beck, Rosalie. "The Women of Acts: Foremothers of the Christian Church." Pages 279–307 in *With Steadfast Purpose: Essays on Acts in Honor of Henry Jackson Flanders, Jr*. Edited by Naymond H. Keathley. Waco: Baylor University Press, 1990.

Beck, "Zodiac." Beck, Roger. "Interpreting the Ponza Zodiac." *JMS* 1 (1, 1976): 1–19.

Beck and Thomas, "Education." Beck, Frederick Arthur George, and Rosalind Thomas. "Education, Greek." *OCD³* 506–10.

Becken, "Healing Communities." Becken, Hans-Jürgen. "African Independent Churches as Healing Communities." Pages 227–39 in *Afro-Christian Religion and Healing in Southern Africa*. Edited by G. C. Oosthuizen, S. D. Edwards, W. H. Wessels, and I. Hexham. African Studies 8. Lewiston, N.Y.: Edwin Mellen, 1989.

Becker, "Camel." Becker, Cornelia. "Camel: Ancient Orient." *BrillPauly* 2:1019.

Becker, "Frohbotschaft." Becker, Jürgen. "Jesu Frohbotschaft und Freudenmahl für die Armen." *BK* 33 (2, 1978): 43–47.

Becker, "Moon Deities." Becker, Andrea. "Moon Deities: General." *BrillPauly* 9:199–200.

Becker, "Phylakterion." Becker, Andrea. "Phylakterion." *BrillPauly* 11:205–8.

Becker, "Scapegoat Rituals." Becker, Andrea. "Scapegoat Rituals." *BrillPauly* 13:48–49.

Beckwith, *Argument*. Beckwith, Francis J. *David Hume's Argument Against Miracles: A Critical Analysis*. Lanham: University Press of America, 1989.

Bedal, "Desert Oasis." Bedal, Leigh-Ann. "Desert Oasis: Water Consumption and Display in the Nabataean Capital." *NEA* 65 (4, 2002): 225–34.

Bedenbender, "Kampf." Bedenbender, A. "Kampf der Menschen, Kampf der Götter, 1. Teil: Die religiösen und ideologischen Auseinandersetzungen im Umfeld des jüdischen Krieges." *T&K* 28 (108, 2005): 26–48.

Bediako, "African Culture." Bediako, Kwame. "Jesus in African Culture: A Ghanaian Perspective." Pages 93–121 in *Emerging Voices in Global Christian Theology*. Edited by William A. Dyrness. Grand Rapids: Zondervan, 1994.

Bediako, *Christianity in Africa*. Bediako, Kwame. *Christianity in Africa: The Renewal of a Non-Western Religion*. Edinburgh: Edinburgh University Press; Maryknoll, N.Y.: Orbis, 1995.

Bédoyère, *Cities*. Bédoyère, Guy de la. *Cities of Roman Italy: Pompeii, Herculaneum and Ostia*. London: Bristol Classical Press, 2010.

Beecher, "Placebo." Beecher, Henry K. "Surgery as Placebo: A Quantitative Study of Bias." *JAMA* 176 (1961): 1102–7.

Beechey and Beechey, *Proceedings*. Beechey, Frederick William, and Henry William Beechey. *Proceedings of the expedition to explore the northern coast of Africa, from Tripoly eastward; in MDCCCXXI. and MDCCCXXII., comprehending an account of the Greater Syrtis and Cyrenaica; and of the ancient cities composing the pentapolis*. London: J. Murray, 1828.

Beer, "Lykwdm." Beer, Moshe. "'L lykwdm hhbrty sl hz'l" [On Solidarity among the Sages]. *Zion* 53 (2, 1988): 149–66.

Begg, "Abigail Story." Begg, Christopher T. "The Abigail Story (1 Samuel 25) according to Josephus." *EstBib* 54 (1, 1996): 5–34.

Begg, "Abimelech." Begg, Christopher T. "Abimelech, King of Shechem according to Josephus." *ETL* 72 (1, 1996): 146–64.

Begg, "Ahaz." Begg, Christopher T. "Ahaz, King of Judah according to Josephus." *JSP* 10 (1, 1996): 28–52.

Begg, "Altar." Begg, Christopher T. "The Transjordanian Altar (Josh 22:10–34) according to Josephus (*Ant.* 5.100–114) and Pseudo-Philo (*LAB* 22.1–8)." *AUSS* 35 (1, 1997): 5–19.

Begg, "Altar(s)." Begg, Christopher T. "The Cisjordanian Altar(s) and Their Associated Rites according to Josephus." *BZ* 41 (2, 1997): 192–211.

Begg, "Amaziah." Begg, Christopher T. "Amaziah of Judah according to Josephus (*Ant.* 9.186–204)." *Antonianum* 70 (1, 1995): 3–30.

Begg, "Ark." Begg, Christopher T. "The Ark in Philistia according to Josephus: *Ant.* 6,1–6." *ETL* 72 (4, 1996): 385–97.

Begg, "Assassination." Begg, Christopher T. "The Assassination of Ishbosheth according to Josephus." *Antonianum* 73 (2, 1998): 241–53.

Begg, "Athaliah's coup." Begg, Christopher T. "Athaliah's Coup and Overthrow according to Josephus." *Antonianum* 71 (2, 1996): 191–210.

Begg, "Battle." Begg, Christopher T. "Israel's Battle with Amalek according to Josephus." *JSQ* 4 (3, 1997): 201–16.

Begg, "Blanks." Begg, Christopher T. "Filling in the Blanks: Josephus' Version of the Campaign of the Three Kings, 2 Kings 3." *HUCA* 64 (1993): 89–109.

Begg, "Capture of Jebus." Begg, Christopher T. "David's Capture of Jebus and Its Sequels according to Josephus: *Ant.* 7,60b-70." *ETL* 74 (1, 1998): 93–108.

Begg, "Ceremonies." Begg, Christopher T. "The Ceremonies at Gilgal/Ebal according to Pseudo-Philo: *LAB* 21,7–10." *ETL* 73 (1, 1997): 72–83.

Begg, "Death of Ahab." Begg, Christopher T. "The Death of King Ahab according to Josephus." *Antonianum* 64 (2–3, 1989): 225–45.

Begg, "Demand for King." Begg, Christopher T. "Israel's Demand for a King according to Josephus." *Mus* 110 (3–4, 1997): 329–48.

Begg, "Disappearances of Enoch." Begg, Christopher T. "'Josephus's Portrayal of the Disappearances of Enoch, Elijah, and Moses': Some Observations." *JBL* 109 (4, 1990): 691–93.

Begg, "Dismissal by Philistines." Begg, Christopher T. "David's Dismissal by the Philistines according to Josephus." *TZ* 54 (2, 1998): 111–19.

Begg, "Elisha's Deeds." Begg, Christopher T. "Elisha's Great Deeds according to Josephus (*AJ* 9,47–94)." *Hen* 18 (1–2, 1996): 69–110.

Begg, "Execution." Begg, Christopher T. "The Execution of the Saulides according to Josephus." *Sefarad* 56 (1, 1996): 3–17.

Begg, "Fall." Begg, Christopher T. "Ahaziah's Fall (2 Kings 1): The Version of Josephus." *Sefarad* 55 (1, 1995): 25–40.

Begg, "First Sparing." Begg, Christopher T. "David's First Sparing of Saul according to Josephus." *Laur* 39 (1–3, 1998): 455–71.

Begg, "Gedaliah." Begg, Christopher T. "The Gedaliah Episode and Its Sequels in Josephus." *JSP* 12 (1994): 21–46.

Begg, "Illness" Begg, Christopher T. "Hezekiah's Illness and Visit according to Josephus." *EstBib* 53 (3, 1995): 365–85.

Begg, "Jehoahaz." Begg, Christopher T. "Jehoahaz, King of Israel, according to Josephus." *Sefarad* 55 (2, 1995): 227–37.

Begg, "Jehoshaphat" Begg, Christopher T. "Jehoshaphat at Mid-career according to *AJ* 9,1–17." *RB* 102 (3, 1995): 379–402.

Begg, "Jeremiah under Jehoiakim." Begg, Christopher T. "Jeremiah under Jehoiakim according to Josephus (*Ant.* 10.89–95)." *AbrN* 33 (1995): 1–16.

Begg, "Jeremiah under Zedekiah." Begg, Christopher T. "Jeremiah under King

Zedekiah according to *Ant.* 10.102–130." *REJ* 156 (1–2, 1997): 7–42.

Begg, "Jeroboam-Ahijah Encounter." Begg, Christopher T. "The Jeroboam-Ahijah Encounter according to Josephus." *AbrN* 34 (1996–97): 1–17.

Begg, "Joash and Elisha." Begg, Christopher T. "Joash and Elisha in Josephus, *Ant.* 9.177–185." *AbrN* 32 (1994): 28–46.

Begg, "Josiah." Begg, Christopher T. "The Death of Josiah: Josephus and the Bible." *ETL* 64 (1, 1988): 157–63.

Begg, "Jotham." Begg, Christopher T. "Jotham and Amon: Two Minor Kings of Judah according to Josephus." *BBR* 6 (1996): 1–13.

Begg, "Loss of Ark." Begg, Christopher T. "The Loss of the Ark according to Josephus." *SBFLA* 46 (1996): 167–86.

Begg, "Massacre." Begg, Christopher T. "The Massacre of the Priests of Nob in Josephus and Pseudo-Philo." *EstBib* 55 (2, 1997): 171–98.

Begg, "Nahum." Begg, Christopher T. "Josephus and Nahum Revisited." *REJ* 154 (1–2, 1995): 5–22.

Begg, "Putsch." Begg, Christopher T. "Josephus's Version of Jehu's Putsch (2 Kgs 8,25–10,36)." *Antonianum* 68 (4, 1993): 450–84.

Begg, "Rape of Tamar." Begg, Christopher T. "The Rape of Tamar (2 Samuel 13) according to Josephus." *EstBib* 54 (4, 1996): 465–500.

Begg, "Return of Ark." Begg, Christopher T. "The Return of the Ark according to Josephus." *BBR* 8 (1998): 15–37.

Begg, "Revolt." Begg, Christopher T. "The Revolt of Sheba according to Josephus." *Jian Dao* 9 (1998): 1–26.

Begg, "Royal Lottery." Begg, Christopher T. "The 'Royal Lottery' according to Josephus." *RCT* 21 (2, 1996): 273–88.

Begg, "Samuel Leader of Israel." Begg, Christopher T. "Samuel Leader of Israel according to Josephus." *Antonianum* 72 (2, 1997): 199–216.

Begg, "Samuel's Anointing." Begg, Christopher T. "Samuel's Anointing of David in Josephus and Pseudo-Philo." *RSLR* 32 (3, 1996): 491–529.

Begg, "Samuel's Discourse." Begg, Christopher T. "Samuel's Farewell Discourse according to Josephus." *JSP* 11 (1, 1997): 56–77.

Begg, "Saul's Start." Begg, Christopher T. "Saul's Royal Start according to Josephus." *SacEr* 37 (1997): 5–32.

Begg, "Saul's War." Begg, Christopher T. "Saul's War with Amalek according to Josephus." *Laur* 37 (3, 1996): 387–415.

Begg, "Second Sparing." Begg, Christopher T. "David's Second Sparing of Saul according to Josephus." *TynBul* 48 (1, 1997): 93–117.

Begg, "Service." Begg, Christopher T. "David's Philistine Service according to Josephus." *Jian Dao* 7 (1997): 1–16.

Begg, "Six Kings." Begg, Christopher T. "The Last Six Kings of Israel according to Josephus: *Ant.* 9,228–278." *ETL* 72 (4, 196): 371–84.

Begg, "Solomon's Apostasy." Begg, Christopher T. "Solomon's Apostasy (1 Kgs. 11,1–13) according to Josephus." *JSJ* 28 (3, 1997): 294–313.

Begg, "Solomon's Dreams." Begg, Christopher T. "Solomon's Two Dreams according to Josephus." *Antonianum* 71 (4, 1996): 687–704.

Begg, "Transfer of Ark." Begg, Christopher T. "David's Transfer of the Ark according to Josephus." *BBR* 7 (1997): 11–35.

Begg, "Two 'Satans.'" Begg, Christopher T. "Solomon's Two 'Satans' according to Josephus." *BN* 85 (1996): 44–55.

Begg, "Uzziah." Begg, Christopher T. "Uzziah (Azariah) of Judah according to Josephus." *EstBib* 53 (1, 1995): 5–24.

Begg, "Visit." Begg, Christopher T. "The Visit of the Queen of Sheba according to Josephus." *JS/TS* 15 (1, 2006): 107–29.

Begg, "Zedekiah." Begg, Christopher T. "Josephus's Zedekiah." *ETL* 65 (1, 1989): 96–104.

Begg, "Ziklag Interlude." Begg, Christopher T. "The Ziklag Interlude according to Josephus." *Teresianum* 48 (2, 1997): 713–36.

Behar, "Témoignages." Behar, C. "Les témoignages du culte de Sérapis dans la Palestine romaine et le traité *Abodah Zarah*." *REJ* 161 (3–4, 2002): 567–71.

Behr, "Church." Behr, John. "From Apostolic Church to Church Catholic, and Back Again." *ProEccl* 16 (1, 2007): 14–17.

Behrend and Luig, "Introduction." Behrend, Heike, and Ute Luig. "Introduction." Pages xiii–xxii in *Spirit Possession, Modernity and Power in Africa*. Edited by Heike Behrend and Ute Luig. Madison: University of Wisconsin Press, 1999.

Behrwald, "Lycian League." Behrwald, Ralf. "Lycian League." *BrillPauly* 7:915–16.

Beidelman, "Incest." Beidelman, T. O. "Some Kaguru Notions about Incest and Other Sexual Prohibitions." Pages 181–201 in *Rethinking Kinship and Marriage*. Edited by Rodney Needham. ASAMS 11. New York: Tavistock, 1971.

Bekken, *Word*. Bekken, Per Jarle. *The Word Is Near You: A Study of Deuteronomy 30:12–14 in Paul's Letter to the Romans in a Jewish Context*. BZNWK 144. Berlin: de Gruyter, 2007.

Belayche, "Actors." Belayche, Nicole. "Religious Actors in Daily Life: Practices and Related Beliefs." Pages 275–91 in *A Companion to Roman Religion*. Edited by Jörg Rüpke. BCompAW. Oxford: Blackwell, 2011.

Belfiore, "Plots." Belfiore, Elizabeth. "Aristotle's *muthos* and Narratological Plots." *CBull* 73 (2, 1997): 141–47.

Belke, "Iconium." Belke, Klaus. "Iconium." *BrillPauly* 6:706–7.

Belke, "Lycaonia." Belke, Klaus. "Lycaonia." *BrillPauly* 7:910–12.

Belke, "Lystra." Belke, Klaus. "Lystra." *Brill Pauly* 8:47–48.

Belkin, *Philo*. Belkin, Samuel. *Philo and the Oral Law: The Philonic Interpretation of Biblical Law in Relation to the Palestinian Halakah*. HSS 11. Cambridge, Mass.: Harvard University Press, 1940.

Bell, "Egypt." Bell, H. Idris. "Egypt under the Early Principate." Pages 284–315 in *The Augustan Empire: 44 B.C.–A.D. 70*. Edited by S. A. Cook, F. E. Adcock, and M. P. Charlesworth. CAH 10. Cambridge: Cambridge University Press, 1934. Repr., 1966.

Bell, "Teshubah." Bell, Richard H. "Teshubah: The Idea of Repentance in Ancient Judaism." *JPJ* 5 (1995): 22–52.

Bellemore, "Josephus, Pompey, and Jews." Bellemore, Jane. "Josephus, Pompey, and the Jews." *Historia* 48 (1, 1999): 94–118.

Belleville, *2 Corinthians*. Belleville, Linda L. *2 Corinthians*. IVPNTC. Downers Grove, Ill.: InterVarsity, 1996.

Belleville, *Glory*. Belleville, Linda L. *Reflections of Glory: Paul's Polemical Use of the Moses-Doxa Tradition in 2 Corinthians 3.1–18*. JSNTSup 52. Sheffield, U.K.: Sheffield Academic, 1991.

Belleville, *Leaders*. Belleville, Linda L. *Women Leaders and the Church: Three Crucial Questions*. Grand Rapids: Baker, 2000.

Bellinger, "Psalms and Acts." Bellinger, W. H., Jr. "The Psalms and Acts: Reading and Rereading." Pages 127–43 in *With Steadfast Purpose: Essays on Acts in Honor of Henry Jackson Flanders, Jr.* Edited by Naymond H. Keathley. Waco: Baylor University Press, 1990.

Bellinzoni, *Sayings*. Bellinzoni, A. J. *The Sayings of Jesus in the Writings of Justin Martyr*. NovTSup 17. Leiden: Brill, 1967.

Bellinzoni, "Source of Agraphon." Bellinzoni, Arthur J., Jr. "Source of the Agraphon in Justin Martyr's Dialogue with Trypho 47:5." *VC* 17 (1963): 65–70.

Bels, "Survie." Bels, J. "La survie de l'âme, de Platon à Posidonius." *RHR* 199 (2, 1982): 169–82.

Belt, "Petra." Belt, Don. "Petra: Ancient City of Stone." *National Geographic* 194 (Dec. 1998): 16–133.

Bénabou, "Résistance." Bénabou, Marcel. "Résistance et romanisation en Afrique du Nord sous le haut-empire." Pages 367–75 in *Assimilation et résistance à la culture gréco-romaine dans le monde ancien: Travaux du VIe Congrès international d'études classiques*. Edited by D. M. Pippidi. FIAEC. Paris: Belles Lettres, 1976.

Benario, "Recent Works." Benario, Herbert W. "Recent Works on Tacitus: 1974–1983." *CW* 80 (2, 1986): 73–147.

Benario, "Work." Benario, Herbert W. "Recent Work on Tacitus: 1994–2003." *CW* 98 (3, 2005): 251–336.

Benatar, "Obligation." Benatar, David. "Obligation, Motivation. and Reward: An Analysis of a Talmudic Principle." *JLR* 17 (1–2, 2002): 1–17.

Bence, *Acts*. Bence, Philip A. *Acts: A Bible Commentary in the Wesleyan Tradition*. Indianapolis: Wesleyan, 1998.

Benda, "Factors." Benda, B. B. "Factors Associated with Rehospitalization among Veterans in a Substance Abuse Treatment Program." *Psychiatric Services* 53 (2002): 1176–78.

Ben David, "Settlements." Ben David, Chaim. "Were There 204 Settlements in Galilee at the Time of Josephus Flavius?" *JJS* 62 (1, 2011): 21–36.

Bendemann, "Diastase." Bendemann, Reinhard von. "Die kritische Diastase von Wissen, Wollen und Handeln: Traditionsgeschichtliche Spurensuche eines hellenistischen Topos in Römer 7." *ZNW* 95 (1–2, 2004): 35–63.

Bendlin, "Intertextuality." Bendlin, Andreas. "Intertextuality." *BrillPauly* 6:873–75.

Benediktson, "First Silent Reader." Benediktson, D. Thomas. "The First Silent Reader of Latin Literature." *CW* 100 (1, 2006): 43–44.

Benediktson, "Madness." Benediktson, Dale Thomas. "Caligula's Madness: Madness or Interictal Temporal Lobe Epilepsy?" *CW* 82 (5, 1989): 370–75.

Beneker, "Chaste Caesar." Beneker, Jeffrey. "No Time for Love: Plutarch's Chaste Caesar." *GRBS* 43 (1, 2002–3): 13–29.

Beneker, "Crossing." Beneker, Jeffrey. "The Crossing of the Rubicon and the Outbreak of Civil War in Cicero, Lucan, Plutarch, and Suetonius." *Phoenix* 65 (1–2, 2011): 74–99.

Ben Eliyahu, "Polemic." Ben Eliyahu, Eyal. "The Rabbinic Polemic against Sanctification of Sites." *JSJ* 40 (2, 2009): 260–80.

Bengtsson, "Kvinnor." Bengtsson, Hakan. "Kvinnor i Qumran—en fråga om text eller kontext?" *SEÅ* 68 (2003): 135–53.

Benko, "Early Empire." Benko, Stephen. "The History of the Early Roman Empire." Pages 37–80 in *The Catacombs and the Colosseum: The Roman Empire as the Setting of Primitive Christianity*. Edited by Stephen Benko and John J. O'Rourke. Valley Forge, Pa.: Judson, 1971.

Benko, "Edict." Benko, Stephen. "The Edict of Claudius of A.D. 49 and the Instigator Chrestus." *TZ* 25 (6, 1969): 406–18.

Benko, *Rome and Christians*. Benko, Stephen. *Pagan Rome and the Early Christians*. Bloomington: Illinois University Press, 1984.

Bennema, "Conflict." Bennema, Cornelis. "The Ethnic Conflict in Early Christianity: An Appraisal of Bauckham's Proposal on the Antioch Crisis and the Jerusalem Council." *JETS* 56 (4, Dec. 2013): 753–63.

Bennema, *Power*. Bennema, Cornelis. *The Power of Saving Wisdom: An Investigation of Spirit and Wisdom in Relation to the Soteriology of the Fourth Gospel*. Tübingen: Mohr Siebeck, 2002. Repr., Eugene, Ore.: Wipf & Stock, 2007.

Bennet, "Minoan Civilization." Bennet, John. "Minoan Civilization." *OCD*³ 985–87.

Bennett, "Drusilla regina." Bennett, Chris. "Drusilla regina." *CQ* 53 (1, 2003): 315–19.

Bennett, "Hour." Bennett, Lerone, Jr. "When the Man and the Hour Are Met." Pages 7–39 in *Martin Luther King, Jr.: A Profile*. Edited by C. Eric Lincoln. Rev. ed. New York: Hill & Wang, 1984.

Bennett, *Not Afraid*. Bennett, Robert H. *I Am Not Afraid: Demon Possession and Spiritual Warfare; True Accounts from the Lutheran Church of Madagascar*. St. Louis: Concordia, 2013.

Benoit, "Angelology." Benoit, Pierre. "Pauline Angelology and Demonology: Reflexions on the Designations of the Heavenly Powers and on the Origin of Angelic Evil according to Paul." *Religious Studies Bulletin* 3 (1, 1983): 1–18.

Benoit, *Jesus*. Benoit, Pierre. *Jesus and the Gospel*. Translated by Benet Weatherhead. 2 vols. Vol. 1: New York: Herder & Herder; London: Darton, Longman & Todd, 1973. Vol. 2: New York: Seabury (Crossroad); London: Darton, Longman & Todd, 1974.

Benoit, "Mystères." Benoit, A. "Les mystères païens et le christianisme." Pages 73–92 in *Mystères et syncrétismes*. By F. Dunand et al. EHRel 2. Paris: Librairie Orientaliste Paul Geuthner, 1975.

Benoit, "Reconstitution." Benoit, Pierre. "La reconstitution archéologique de la Forteresse Antonia." *AJBA* 2 (2, 1973): 16–22.

Benson, "Dragon." Benson, Ivan M. "Revelation 12 and the Dragon of Antiquity." *ResQ* 29 (2, 1987): 97–102.

Benson, *Healing*. Benson, Herbert, with Marg Stark. *Timeless Healing: The Power and Biology of Belief*. New York: Scribner, 1996.

Bentley, *Relics*. Bentley, James. *Restless Bones: The Story of Relics*. London: Constable, 1985.

Ben Zeev, "Ambiguities." Ben Zeev, Miriam Pucci. "Josephus' Ambiguities: His Comments on Cited Documents." *JJS* 57 (1, 2006): 1–10.

Ben Zeev, "Capitol." Ben Zeev, Miriam Pucci. "Polybius, Josephus, and the Capitol in Rome." *JSJ* 27 (1, 1996): 21–30.

Ben Zeev, "Greek Attacks." Ben Zeev, Miriam Pucci. "Greek Attacks against Alexandrian Jews during Emperor Trajan's Reign." *JSJ* 20 (1, 1989): 31–48.

Ben Zeev, *Jewish Rights*. Ben Zeev, Miriam Pucci. *Jewish Rights in the Roman World: The Greek and Roman Documents Quoted by Josephus Flavius*. TSAJ 74. Tübingen: Mohr Siebeck, 1999.

Ben Zeev, "New Perspectives." Ben Zeev, Miriam Pucci. "New Perspectives on the Jewish-Greek Hostilities in Alexandria during the Reign of Emperor Caligula." *JSJ* 21 (2, 1990): 227–35.

Ben Zeev, "Position." Ben Zeev, Miriam Pucci. "Did the Jews Enjoy a Privileged Position in the Roman World?" *REJ* 154 (1–2, 1995): 23–42.

Ben Zeev, "Reliability." Ben Zeev, Miriam Pucci. "The Reliability of Josephus Flavius: The Case of Hecataeus' and Manetho's Accounts of Jews and Judaism: Fifteen Years of Contemporary Research (1974–1990)." *JSJ* 24 (2, 1993): 215–34.

Berends, "African Healing Practices." Berends, Willem. "African Traditional Healing Practices and the Christian Community." *Missiology* 21 (3, 1993): 275–88.

Berends, "Celebrate at Pentecost?" Berends, Bill. "What Do We Celebrate at Pentecost?" *VR* 63 (1998): 42–66.

Berg, *Irony*. Berg, InHee Cho. *Irony in the Matthean Passion Narrative*. Minneapolis: Fortress, 2014.

Bergendorff, *Lutheran Reformation*. Bergendorff, Conrad. *The Church of the Lutheran Reformation: A Historical Survey of Lutheranism*. St. Louis: Concordia, 1967.

Berger, "Faces." Berger, Peter L. "Four Faces of Global Culture." Pages 419–27 in *Globalization and the Challenges of a New Century: A Reader*. Edited by Patrick O'Meara, Howard D. Mehlinger, and Matthew Krain. Bloomington: Indiana University Press, 2000.

Berger, "Gattungen." Berger, Klaus. "Hellenistische Gattungen im Neuen Testament." *ANRW* 25.2:1031–1432. Part 2, *Principat*, 25.2. Edited by H. Temporini and W. Haase. Berlin: de Gruyter, 1984.

Berger, "Gerechtigkeit Gottes." Berger, Klaus. "Neues Material zur 'Gerechtigkeit Gottes.'" *ZNW* 68 (3–4, 1977): 266–75.

Berger, "Kaminiates." Berger, Albrecht. "Kaminiates, Iohannes." *BrillPauly* 7:14.

Berger, "Kollyrium." Berger, P. R. "Kollyrium für die blinden Augen, Apk. 3:18." *NovT* 27 (2, 1985): 174–95.

Berger, *Relativism*. Berger, Peter L., ed. *Between Relativism and Fundamentalism: Religious Resources for a Middle Position*. Grand Rapids: Eerdmans, 2010.

Berger, *Rumor*. Berger, Peter L. *A Rumor of Angels: Modern Society and the Rediscovery of the Supernatural*. Garden City, N.Y.: Doubleday, 1969.

Berger, "Themes." Berger, David. "Three Typological Themes in Early Jewish Messianism: Messiah Son of Joseph, Rabbinic Calculations, and the Figure of Armilus." *AJSR* 10 (2, 1985): 141–64.

Berger, "Women." Berger, Iris. "Women in East and Southern Africa." Pages 5–62 in *Women in Sub-Saharan Africa*, by Iris Berger and E. Frances White. Restoring Women to History. Bloomington: Indiana University Press, 1999.

Berger and Lintott, "Prison." Berger, Adolf, and Andrew William Lintott. "Prison." *OCD*[3] 1248.

Berger, Nicholas, and Lintott, "Law and Procedure." Berger, Adolf, Barry Nicholas, and Andrew William Lintott. "Law and Procedure, Roman: 3. Criminal Law and Procedure." *OCD*[3] 831–34.

Berger and Wyschogrod, *Jewish Christianity*. Berger, David, and Michael Wyschogrod. *Jews and "Jewish Christianity."* New York: KTAV, 1978.

Bergholz, *Aufbau*. Bergholz, Thomas. *Der Aufbau des lukanischen Doppelwerkes: Untersuchungen zum formalliterarischen Charakter von Lukas-Evangelium und Apostelgeschichte*. EurH, Reihe 23, Theologie 545. Frankfurt, Bern, and New York: Peter Lang, 1995.

Berghuis, *Fasting*. Berghuis, Kent D. *Christian Fasting: A Theological Approach*. Foreword by Scot McKnight. Richardson, Tex.: Biblical Studies Press, 2007.

Bergmeier, "Beobachtungen." Bergmeier, Roland. "Beobachtungen zu 4Q521 f 2, II, 1–13." *ZDMG* 145 (1, 1995): 38–48.

Bergmeier, "Erfüllung." Bergmeier, Roland. "Erfüllung der Gnadenzusagen an David." *ZNW* 86 (3–4, 1995): 277–86.

Bergmeier, "Gottesfreunde." Bergmeier, Roland. "Der Stand der Gottesfreunde:

Zu Philos Schrift 'Über die kontemplative Lebensform.'" *Bijdr* 63 (1, 2002): 46–70.

Bergquist, "Good News to Poor." Bergquist, James A. "'Good News to the Poor': Why Does This Lucan Motif Appear to Run Dry in the Book of Acts?" *BangTF* 18 (1986): 1–16.

Bergren, "Nehemiah." Bergren, Theodore A. "Nehemiah in 2 Maccabees 1:10–2:18." *JSJ* 28 (3, 1997): 249–70.

Bergunder, "Healing." Bergunder, Michael. "Miracle Healing and Exorcism: The South Indian Pentecostal Movement in the Context of Popular Hinduism." *IntRevMiss* 90 (356–357, 2001): 103–12.

Bergunder, "Miracle Healing." Bergunder, Michael. "Miracle Healing and Exorcism in South Indian Pentecostalism." Pages 287–305 in *Global Pentecostal and Charismatic Healing*. Edited by Candy Gunther Brown. Foreword by Harvey Cox. Oxford: Oxford University Press, 2011.

Bergunder, *Movement*. Bergunder, Michael. *The South Indian Pentecostal Movement in the Twentieth Century*. Studies in the History of Christian Missions. Grand Rapids: Eerdmans, 2008.

Berlin, "Life." Berlin, Andrea M. "Jewish Life before the Revolt: The Archaeological Evidence." *JSJ* 36 (4, 2005): 417–70.

Berlin, "Monarchy." Berlin, Andrea M. "From Monarchy to Markets: The Phoenicians in Hellenistic Palestine." *BASOR* 306 (May 1997): 75–88.

Bernabé Ubieta, "Asociaciones." Bernabé Ubieta, Carmen. "Asociaciones y familias en el mundo del cristianismo primitivo." *EstBib* 64 (1, 2006): 99–125.

Bernabé Ubieta, "Esposas." Bernabé Ubieta, Carmen. "Las esposas divinas en la cultura mediterránea." *EphMar* 46 (2, 1996): 223–57.

Bernal, *Athena*. Bernal, Martin. *Black Athena: The Afroasiatic Roots of Classical Civilization*. 3 vols. London: Free Association; New Brunswick, N.J.: Rutgers University Press, 1987–2006.

Bernard, "Discours." Bernard, Jacques-Emmanuel. "Du discours à l'épistolaire: Les échos du *Pro Plancio* dans la lettre de Cicéron à Lentulus Spinther (*Fam.* I, 9)." *Rhetorica* 25 (3, 2007): 223–42.

Bernard, "Historical Value." Bernard, J. H. "The Historical Value of the Acts of the Apostles." Pages 208–30 in *Criticism of the New Testament: St. Margaret's Lectures, 1902*. By W. Sanday et al. Edited by H. Hensley Henson. New York: Scribner; London: John Murray, 1902.

Bernard, "Miracle." Bernard, J. H. "Miracle." Pages 379–96 in vol. 3 of *A Dictionary of the Bible Dealing with Its Language, Literature, and Contents Including the Biblical Theology*. Edited by James Hastings. 5

vols. New York: Scribner's, 1898–1909. Vol. 3 is 1900.

Berndt, "Role." Berndt, Catherine H. "The Role of Native Doctors in Aboriginal Australia." Pages 264–84 in *Magic, Faith, and Healing: Studies in Primitive Psychiatry Today*. Edited by Ari Kiev. Foreword by Jerome D. Frank. New York: Free Press, 1964.

Bernstein, "Adoptees." Bernstein, Neil W. "Adoptees and Exposed Children in Roman Declamation: Commodification, Luxury, and the Threat of Violence." *CP* 104 (3, 2009): 331–53.

Bernstein, "Angels." Bernstein, Moshe J. "Angels at the Aqedah: A Study in the Development of a Midrashic Motif." *DSD* 7 (3, 2000): 263–91.

Bernstein, "*Puer*." Bernstein, Neil W. "Mourning the *puer delicatus*: Status Inconsistency and the Ethical Value of Fostering in Statius, *Silvae* 2.1." *AJP* 126 (2, 2005): 257–80.

Bernstein, "Study." Bernstein, Moshe J. "Ky qllt 'lhym tlwy (Deut. 21:23): A Study in Early Jewish Exegesis." *JQR* 74 (1, 1983): 21–45.

Bernstein, "Women." Bernstein, Moshe J. "Women and Children in Legal and Liturgical Texts from Qumran." *DSD* 11 (2, 2004): 191–211.

Berry, "Acculturation." Berry, J. W. "Acculturation as Varieties of Adaptation." Pages 9–25 in *Acculturation Theory, Models, and Some New Findings*. Edited by A. M. Padilla. Boulder, Colo.: Westview, 1980.

Berry et al., "Attitudes." Berry, J. W., et al. "Acculturation Attitudes in Plural Societies." *Applied Psychology: An International Review* 38 (1989): 158–206.

Berry and Heath, "Oratory and Declamation." Berry, D. H., and Malcolm Heath. "Oratory and Declamation." Pages 393–420 in *Handbook of Classical Rhetoric in the Hellenistic Period, 330 B.C.–A.D. 400*. Edited by Stanley E. Porter. Leiden: Brill, 1997.

Berschin, "Biography." Berschin, Walter. "Biography: Late Antiquity." *BrillPauly* 2:653–55.

Bertalotto, "Immersion." Bertalotto, P. "Immersion and Expiation: Water and Spirit from Qumran to John the Baptist." *Hen* 27 (1–2, 2005): 163–81.

Berthelot, "Conquest." Berthelot, Katell. "Philo of Alexandria and the Conquest of Canaan." *JSJ* 38 (1, 2007): 39–56.

Berthelot, "Idéologie maccabéenne." Berthelot, Katell. "L'idéologie maccabéenne: Entre idéologie de la résistance armée et idéologie du martyre." *REJ* 165 (1–2, 2006): 99–122.

Berthelot, "Infirmes." Berthelot, Katell. "La place des infirmes et des 'lépreux' dans les textes de Qumrân et les Évangiles." *RB* 113 (2, 2006): 211–41.

Berthelot, "Interprétation symbolique." Berthelot, Katell. "L'interprétation symbolique des lois alimentaires dans la Lettre d'Aristée: Une influence pythagoricienne." *JJS* 52 (2, 2001): 253–68.

Berthelot, "Poseidonios d'Apamée." Berthelot, Katell. "Poseidonios d'Apamée et les juifs." *JSJ* 34 (2, 2003): 160–98.

Berthelot, "Problem." Berthelot, Katell. "A Classical Ethical Problem in Ancient Philosophy and Rabbinic Thought: The Case of the Shipwrecked." *HTR* 106 (2, Apr. 2013): 171–99.

Berthelot, "Zeal." Berthelot, Katell. "Zeal for God and Divine Law in Philo and the Dead Sea Scrolls." *SPhilA* 19 (2007): 113–29.

Beskow, "Branding." Beskow, P. "Branding in the Mysteries of Mithra?" Pages 487–501 in *Mysteria Mithrae*. Edited by Ugo Bianchi. ÉPROER 80. Leiden: Brill, 1979.

Besnier, "Migration et *telos*." Besnier, Bernard. "Migration et *telos* d'après le *De migratione Abrahami*." *SPhilA* 11 (1999): 74–103.

Best, "Acts xiii.1–3." Best, Ernest. "Acts xiii.1–3." *JTS* 11 (2, 1960): 344–48.

Best, *Corinthians*. Best, Ernest. *Second Corinthians*. IBC. Atlanta: John Knox, 1987.

Best, "Exorcism." Best, Ernest. "Exorcism in the New Testament and Today." *BibTh* 27 (1977): 1–9.

Best, *Mark*. Best, Ernest. *Mark: The Gospel as Story*. Studies of the New Testament and Its World. Edinburgh: T&T Clark, 1983.

Best, *Peter*. Best, Ernest. *1 Peter*. NCBC. Greenwood, S.C.: Attic, n.d.; London: Marshall, Morgan & Scott, 1971.

Best, "Pneuma." Best, Ernest. "The Use and Non-use of Pneuma by Josephus." *NovT* 3 (3, 1959): 218–25.

Best, *Supernatural*. Best, Gary. *Naturally Supernatural: Joining God in His Work*. Cape Town: Vineyard International, 2005.

Best, *Temptation*. Best, Ernest. *The Temptation and the Passion: The Markan Soteriology*. SNTSMS 2. Cambridge: Cambridge University Press, 1965.

Best, *Thessalonians*. Best, Ernest. *A Commentary on the First and Second Epistles to the Thessalonians*. BNTC. London: Adam & Charles Black, 1977.

Betancourt, "Crete." Betancourt, Philip P. "Crete." *OEANE* 2:70–72.

Béteille, "Race." Béteille, André. "Race and Descent as Social Categories in India." *Daedalus* 96 (2, 1967): 444–63.

Bethge, "Fragmenta biblica Cantabrigiensis." Bethge, Hans-Gebhard. "Fragmenta biblica Cantabrigiensis—unbekannte Fragmente der Apostelgeschichte und anderer frühchristlicher Schriften in koptischer Sprache: Ein Werkstattbericht." Pages 333–43 in *Die Apostelgeschichte und die hellenistische Geschichtsschreibung: Festschrift für Eckhard Plümacher zu seinem 65. Geburtstag*. Edited by Cilliers Breytenbach and Jens Schröter. Leiden: Brill, 2004.

Betlyon, "Coinage." Betlyon, John Wilson. "Coinage." *ABD* 1:1076–89.

Betori, "Ricera." Betori, Giuseppe. "Alla ricera di un'articolazione per il libro degli Atti." *RivB* 37 (2, 1989): 185–205.

Betori, "Strutturazione." Betori, Giuseppe. "Strutturazione degli Atti e storiografia antica." *CNS* 12 (2, 1991): 251–63. (Abstract: *NTA* 36:194.)

Bettini, "*Mythos*." Bettini, Maurizio. "*Mythos/fabula*: Authoritative and Discredited Speech." *HR* 45 (3, 2006): 195–212.

Betty, "Evidence." Betty, Stafford. "The Growing Evidence for 'Demonic Possession': What Should Psychiatry's Response Be?" *JRelHealth* 44 (1, Spring 2005): 13–30.

Betz, "Christuserkenntnis." Betz, Otto. "Fleischliche und 'geistliche' Christuserkenntnis nach 2. Korinther 5,16." *TBei* 14 (4–5, 1983): 167–79.

Betz, *Corinthians*. Betz, Hans Dieter. *2 Corinthians 8 and 9: A Commentary on the Administrative Letters of the Apostle Paul*. Hermeneia. Philadelphia: Fortress, 1985.

Betz, "Fragmenta." Betz, Hans Dieter. "Fragmenta 21–23, 157–158, 176–178." Pages 317–24 in *Plutarch's Theological Writings and Early Christian Literature*. Edited by Hans Dieter Betz. SCHNT 3. Leiden: Brill, 1975.

Betz, "Fragments." Betz, Hans Dieter. "Fragments from a Catabasis Ritual in a Greek Magical Papyrus." *HR* 19 (1980): 287–95.

Betz, *Galatia*. Betz, Hans Dieter. *A Commentary on Paul's Letter to the Churches in Galatia*. Hermeneia. Philadelphia: Fortress, 1979.

Betz, "Hermetic Interpretation." Betz, Hans Dieter. "The Delphic Maxim GNOTAI SAUTON in Hermetic Interpretation." *HTR* 63 (4, Oct. 1970): 465–84.

Betz, *Jesus*. Betz, Otto. *What Do We Know about Jesus?* Philadelphia: Westminster; London: SCM, 1968.

Betz, "Jewish Magic." Betz, Hans Dieter. "Jewish Magic in the Greek Magical Papyri (*PGM* VII.260–71)." Pages 45–63 in *Envisioning Magic: A Princeton Seminar and Symposium*. Edited by Peter Schäfer and Hans G. Kippenberg. SHR 75. Leiden: Brill, 1997.

Betz, "John." Betz, Otto. "Was John the Baptist an Essene?" *BRev* 6 (6, 1990): 18–25.

Betz, "Kingdom." Betz, Otto. "Jesus' Gospel of the Kingdom." Pages 53–74 in *The Gospel and the Gospels*. Edited by Peter Stuhlmacher. Grand Rapids: Eerdmans, 1991.

Betz, *Magical Papyri*. Betz, Hans Dieter, ed. *The Greek Magical Papyri in Translation, Including the Demotic Spells*. 2nd ed. Chicago: University of Chicago Press, 1992–.

Betz, "Maxim in Papyri." Betz, Hans Dieter. "The Delphic Maxim 'Know Yourself' in the Greek Magical Papyri." *HR* 21 (2, Nov. 1981): 156–71.

Betz, "Miracles in Josephus." Betz, Otto. "Miracles in the Writings of Flavius Josephus." Pages 212–35 in *Josephus, Judaism, and Christianity*. Edited by Louis H. Feldman and Gohei Hata. Detroit: Wayne State University Press, 1987.

Betz, "Servant Tradition." Betz, Otto. "The Servant Tradition of Isaiah in the Dead Sea Scrolls." *Journal for Semitics* 7 (1, 1995): 40–56.

Betz, *Sokratische Tradition*. Betz, Hans Dieter. *Der Apostel Paulus und die sokratische Tradition*. Tübingen: Mohr Siebeck, 1972.

Betz, Dirkse, and Smith, "Numinis." Betz, Hans Dieter, Peter A. Dirkse, and E. W. Smith, Jr. "De sera numinis vindicta (Moralia 548–568A)." Pages 181–235 in *Plutarch's Theological Writings and Early Christian Literature*. Edited by Hans D. Betz. SCHNT 3. Leiden: Brill, 1975.

Beus, "Traditie." Beus, C. de. "Paulus en de traditie over de opstanding in I Cor. 15:3 vlg." *NedTT* 22 (3, 1968): 185–99.

Beutler, "Identity." Beutler, Johannes. "The Identity of the 'Jews' for the Readers of John." Pages 229–38 in *Anti-Judaism and the Fourth Gospel: Papers of the Leuven Colloquium, 2000*. Edited by R. Bieringer, D. Pollefeyt, and F. Vandecasteele-Vanneuville. Assen, Neth.: Royal Van Gorcum, 2001.

Bexley, "Rome." Bexley, Erica M. "Replacing Rome: Geographic and Political Centrality in Lucan's Pharsalia." *CP* 104 (4, 2009): 459–75.

Beyer, "ἐπίσκοπος." Beyer, Hermann W. "ἐπίσκοπος." *TDNT* 2:608–22.

Bhatia, "Booty." Bhatia, Shyam. "A War's Human Booty." *The Observer* (Apr. 9, 1995). Repr., *WPR* (Aug. 1995): 40.

Bhayro, "Status." Bhayro, Siam. "The Status of Non-Jews in the Eschaton: An Enochic Debate." *Jewish Culture and History* 6 (2, 2003): 1–10.

Bianchi, "Epilegomena." Bianchi, Ugo. "Epilegomena." Pages 873–79 in *Mysteria Mithrae*. Edited by Ugo Bianchi. ÉPROER 80. Leiden: Brill, 1979.

Bianchi, "Rédemption." Bianchi, Ugo. "La rédemption dans les livres d'Adam." *Numen* 18 (1, 1971): 1–8.

Bickerman, "Date." Bickerman, Elias J. "The Date of the Testaments of the Twelve Patriarchs." *JBL* 69 (3, 1950): 245–60.

Bickerman, "Inscriptions." Bickerman, Elias J. "The Warning Inscriptions from Herod's Temple." *JQR* 37 (1946–47): 387–405.

Bieberstein, "Freiheit." Bieberstein, Sabine. "Die Freiheit, die Tora, und die Gemeinden des Messias Jesus: Anfragen an das Konzept des 'gesetzesfreien Heidenchristentums.'" *BK* 57 (3, 2002): 139–44.

Bieberstein, "Ituraea." Bieberstein, Klaus. "Ituraea." *BrillPauly* 6:1028.

Bieder, "Kinship." Bieder, Robert E. "Kinship as a Factor in Migration." *JMFam* 35 (3, Aug. 1973): 429–39.

Bielecki, "Problems." Bielecki, T. "Some Research Problems concerning Caiaphas." *FO* 34 (1998): 65–70.

Bieringer, "Women." Bieringer, Reimund. "Women and Leadership in Romans 16. The Leading Roles of Phoebe, Prisca, and Junia in Early Christianity: Part I." *East Asian PastRev* 44 (3, 2007): 221–37.

Biers, *Bath*. Biers, Jane C. *The Great Bath on the Lechaion Road*. Vol. 17 of *Corinth: Results of Excavations Conducted by the American School of Classical Studies at Athens*. Princeton: American School of Classical Studies at Athens, 1985.

Biers, "Baths in Corinth." Biers, Jane C. "Lavari est vivere: Baths in Roman Corinth." Pages 303–19 in *Corinth: The Centenary, 1896–1996*. Edited by Charles K. Williams II and Nancy Bookidis. Vol. 20 of *Corinth: Results of Excavations Conducted by the American School of Classical Studies at Athens*. Princeton: American School of Classical Studies at Athens, 2003.

Bietak, "Problems." Bietak, Manfred. "Problems of Middle Bronze Age Chronology: New Evidence from Egypt." *AJA* 88 (1984): 471–85.

Bietenhard, "Dekapolis." Bietenhard, Hans. "Die Dekapolis von Pompeius bis Traian: Ein Kapitel aus der neutestamentlichen Zeitgeschichte." *ZDPV* 79 (1, 1963): 24–58.

Bietenhard, "ὄνομα." Bietenhard, Hans. "ὄνομα." *TDNT* 5:242–83.

Biguzzi, "Mc. 14, 58." Biguzzi, Giancarlo. "Mc. 14, 58: Un tempio *acheiropoiētos*." *RivB* 26 (3, 1978): 225–40.

Bikai, Kanellopoulos, and Saunders, "Beidha." Bikai, P. M., C. Kanellopoulos, and S. L. Saunders. "Beidha in Jordan: A Dionysian Hall in a Nabataean Landscape." *AJA* 112 (3, 2008): 465–507.

Bilde, "Causes." Bilde, Per. "The Causes of the Jewish War according to Josephus." *JSJ* 10 (2, 1979): 179–202.

Bilde, "Galilaea." Bilde, Per. "Galilaea og galilaeerne på Jesu tid." *DTT* 43 (2, 1980): 113–35.

Bilezikian, *Roles*. Bilezikian, Gilbert. *Beyond Sex Roles: What the Bible Says about a Woman's Place in Church and Family*. Grand Rapids: Baker, 1986.

Billigmeier and Turner, "Roles." Billigmeier, Jon-Christian, and Judy A. Turner. "The Socio-economic Roles of Women in Mycenaean Greece: A Brief Survey from Evidence of the Linear B Tablets." Pages 1–18 in *Reflections of Women in Antiquity*. Edited by Helene P. Foley. New York: Gordon & Breach Science, 1981.

Billings, "Poets." Billings, Bradly S. "'As Some of Your Own Poets Have Said': Secular and Non-canonical Literature in the New Testament and Some (Post)modern Parallels." *ExpT* 123 (10, 2012): 479–85.

Billows, "Procession." Billows, Richard. "The Religious Procession of the Ara Pacis Augustae: Augustus' *supplicatio* in 13 B.C." *JRA* 6 (1993): 80–92.

Bindemann, "Verkündiger." Bindemann, Walter. "Verkündigter Verkündiger: Das Paulusbild der Wir-Stücke in der Apostelgeschichte—seine Aufnahme und Bearbeitung durch Lukas." *TLZ* 114 (10, 1989): 705–20.

Binder, "Age(s)." Binder, Gerhard. "Age(s)." *BrillPauly* 1:331–35.

Binder, "Kiss." Binder, Gerhard. "Kiss." *BrillPauly* 7:54–62.

Binder, "Language Switching." Binder, Vera. "Language Switching." *BrillPauly* 7:222–23.

Binder and Niehoff, "Diglossia." Binder, Vera, and Johannes Niehoff. "Diglossia." *BrillPauly* 4:410–11.

Bing, "Cilicia." Bing, J. Daniel. "Cilicia." *ABD* 1:1022–24.

Bingham, *Praetorian Guard*. Bingham, Sandra. *The Praetorian Guard: A History of Rome's Elite Special Forces*. London: I. B. Tauris, 2012; Waco: Baylor University Press, 2013.

Binsbergen, *Change*. Binsbergen, Wim M. J. van. *Religious Change in Zambia: Exploratory Studies*. London: Kegan Paul, 1981.

Bird, "Dust." Bird, Michael F. "When the Dust Finally Settles: Coming to a Post–New Perspective Perspective." *CrisTR* n.s. 2 (2, 2005): 57–69.

Bird, "End." Bird, Phyllis A. "The End of the Male Cult Prostitute: A Literary-Historical and Sociological Analysis of Hebrew *qadesh-qedeshim*." Pages 37–80 in *Congress Volume: Cambridge 1995*. The Fifteenth Congress of the International

Organization for the Study of the Old Testament. Edited by J. A. Emerton. VTSup 66. Leiden: Brill, 1997.

Bird, *Gentile Mission*. Bird, Michael F. *Jesus and the Origins of the Gentile Mission*. LNTS 331. London: T&T Clark, 2006.

Bird, *Gospel of the Lord*. Bird, Michael F. *The Gospel of the Lord: How the Early Church Wrote the Story of Jesus*. Grand Rapids: Eerdmans, 2014.

Bird, "Justification." Bird, Michael F. "Justification as Forensic Declaration and Covenant Membership: A *via media* between Reformed and Revisionist Readings of Paul." *TynBul* 57 (1, 2006): 109–30.

Bird, *Paul*. Bird, Michael F., ed. *Four Views on the Apostle Paul*. Grand Rapids: Zondervan, 2012.

Bird, "Quest." Bird, Michael F. "Is There Really a 'Third Quest' for the Historical Jesus?" *SBET* 24 (2, 2006): 195–219.

Bird, "Rhetorical Approach." Bird, Michael F. "Reassessing a Rhetorical Approach to Paul's Letters." *ExpT* 119 (9, 2008): 374–79.

Bird, "Romans." Bird, Michael F. "The Letter to the Romans." Pages 177–204 in *All Things to All Cultures: Paul among Jews, Greeks, and Romans*. Edited by Mark Harding and Alanna Nobbs. Grand Rapids: Eerdmans, 2013.

Bird, "Unity." Bird, Michael F. "The Unity of Luke-Acts in Recent Discussion." *JSNT* 29 (4, 2007): 425–48.

Bird and Keener, "Generalist Scholars." Bird, Michael F., and Craig S. Keener. "Jack of All Trades and Master of None: The Case for 'Generalist' Scholars in Biblical Scholarship." *SBL Forum* (electronic), June 2009 (posted May 27, 2009). http://www.sbl-site.org/publica tions/article .aspx?ArticleID=820.

Bird and Sprinkle, *Faith*. Bird, Michael F., and Preston M. Sprinkle, eds. *The Faith of Jesus Christ: Exegetical, Biblical, and Theological Studies*. Foreword by James D. G. Dunn. Milton Keynes: Paternoster; Peabody, Mass.: Hendrickson, 2009.

Biscoe, *History*. Biscoe, Richard. *The History of the Acts of the Holy Apostles Confirmed from Other Authors*. 2 vols. London: C. Davis & S. Austen, 1742. Repr. with different pagination, Oxford: Clarendon, 1829. Repr., 2 vols. in 1. Oxford: Oxford University Press, 1840.

Bishop, *Apostles*. Bishop, Eric F. F. *Apostles of Palestine: The Local Background to the New Testament Church*. London: Lutterworth, 1958.

Bishop, "Bread." Bishop, Eric F. F. "'He That Eateth Bread with Me Hath Lifted Up His Heel against Me.'—Jn xiii.18 (Ps xli.9)." *ExpT* 70 (11, 1959): 331–33.

Bishop, *Healing*. Bishop, George. *Faith Healing: God or Fraud?* Los Angeles: Sherbourne Press, 1967.

Bishop, "Sleepless Nights." Bishop, Eric F. F. "The 'Why' of Sleepless Nights." *EvQ* 37 (1, 1965): 29–31.

Bittarello, "Construction." Bittarello, Maria Beatrice. "The Construction of Etruscan 'Otherness' in Latin Literature." *GR* 56 (2, 2009): 211–33.

Bivin, "Prayers." Bivin, David. "Prayers for Emergencies." *JerPersp* 5 (1992): 16–17.

Black, *Aramaic Approach*. Black, Matthew. *An Aramaic Approach to the Gospels and Acts*. Oxford: Clarendon, 1967.

Black, "Christological Use." Black, Matthew. "The Christological Use of the Old Testament in the New Testament." *NTS* 18 (1, 1971): 1–14.

Black, "Essenes." Black, Matthew. "The Account of the Essenes in Hippolytus and Josephus." Pages 172–75 in *The Background of the New Testament and Its Eschatology: Essays in Honour of Charles Harold Dodd*. Edited by W. D. Davies and D. Daube. Cambridge: Cambridge University Press, 1964.

Black, "Form of Sermon." Black, C. Clifton. "The Rhetorical Form of the Hellenistic Jewish and Early Christian Sermon: A Response to Lawrence Wills." *HTR* 81 (1, 1988): 1–18.

Black, "Language." Black, Matthew. "The Recovery of the Language of Jesus." *NTS* 3 (4, 1957): 305–13.

Black, "Law." Black, Mark. "Paul and Roman Law in Acts." *ResQ* 24 (4, 1981): 209–18.

Black, "Mark in Acts." Black, C. Clifton. "John Mark in the Acts of the Apostles." Pages 101–20 in *Literary Studies in Luke-Acts: Essays in Honor of Joseph B. Tyson*. Edited by Richard P. Thompson and Thomas E. Phillips. Macon, Ga.: Mercer University Press, 1998.

Black, "Oration at Olivet." Black, C. Clifton. "An Oration at Olivet: Some Rhetorical Dimensions of Mark 13." Pages 66–92 in *Persuasive Artistry: Studies in New Testament Rhetoric in Honor of George A. Kennedy*. Edited by Duane F. Watson. JSNTSup 50. Sheffield, U.K.: Sheffield Academic, 1991.

Black, "Parables." Black, Matthew. "The 'Parables' of Enoch (1 En 37–71) and the 'Son of Man.'" *ExpT* 88 (1, 1976): 5–8.

Black, "Presentation of Mark." Black, C. Clifton. "The Presentation of John Mark in the Acts of the Apostles." *PRSt* 20 (3, 1993): 235–54.

Black, *Rhetoric of Gospel*. Black, C. Clifton. *The Rhetoric of the Gospel: Theological Artistry in the Gospels and Acts*. Saint Louis: Chalice, 2001.

Black, *Scrolls*. Black, Matthew. *The Scrolls and Christian Origins*. London: Thomas Nelson, 1961.

Black and Tait, "Archives." Black, J. A., and W. J. Tait. "Archives and Libraries in the Ancient Near East." Pages 2197–209 in *Civilizations of the Ancient Near East*. Edited by Jack M. Sasson. 4 vols. New York: Scribner's, 1995.

Blackburn, "ΑΝΔΡΕΣ." Blackburn, Barry L. "'Miracle Working ΘΕΙΟΙ ΑΝΔΡΕΣ' in Hellenism (and Hellenistic Judaism)." Pages 185–218 in *The Miracles of Jesus*. Edited by David Wenham and Craig Blomberg. Gospel Perspectives 6. Sheffield, U.K.: JSOT Press, 1986.

Blackburn, "Miracles." Blackburn, Barry L. "The Miracles of Jesus." Pages 353–94 in *Studying the Historical Jesus: Evaluations of the State of Current Research*. Edited by Bruce Chilton and Craig A. Evans. NTTS 19. Leiden: Brill, 1994.

Blackman, "Purification." Blackman, Aylward M. "Purification (Egyptian)." Pages 476–82 in vol. 10 of *The Encyclopaedia of Religion and Ethics*. Edited by James Hastings. 13 vols. Edinburgh: T&T Clark, 1908–26.

Blaiklock, *Acts*. Blaiklock, E. M. *The Acts of the Apostles: An Historical Commentary*. Grand Rapids: Eerdmans, 1959.

Blaiklock, *Archaeology*. Blaiklock, E. M. *The Archaeology of the New Testament*. Rev. ed. Nashville: Thomas Nelson, 1984.

Blaiklock, *Cities*. Blaiklock, E. M. *Cities of the New Testament*. Westwood, N.J.: Fleming H. Revell, 1965.

Blaiklock, "Document." Blaiklock, E. M. "The Acts of the Apostles as a Document of First Century History." Pages 41–54 in *Apostolic History and the Gospel: Biblical and Historical Essays Presented to F. F. Bruce on His 60th Birthday*. Edited by W. Ward Gasque and Ralph P. Martin. Exeter, U.K.: Paternoster; Grand Rapids: Eerdmans, 1970.

Blanco Pacheco, "María y el Espíritu." Blanco Pacheco, S. "María y el Espíritu en los Hechos de los apóstoles." *EphMar* 48 (2, 1998): 223–30. (Abstract: *NTA* 43:281–82.)

Blank, "Mensch." Blank, Josef. "Der gespaltene Mensch: Zur Exegese von Röm 7,7–25." *BibLeb* 9 (1, 1968): 10–20.

Blank, "Schwört." Blank, Josef. "Schwört überhaupt nicht." *Orientierung* 53 (1989): 97–99.

Blank, "Texts." Blank, Debra Reed. "Little Known Rabbinic Texts on Women and Prayer." *ConsJud* 48 (1, 1995): 7–10.

Blänsdorf, "Archaism." Blänsdorf, Jürgen. "Archaism [Latin Literature]." *BrillPauly* 1:978–79.

Blanton, "Account-book." Blanton, Thomas R. "The Benefactor's Account-book: The Rhetoric of Gift Reciprocation according to Seneca and Paul." *NTS* 59 (3, July 2013): 396–414.

Blass, Debrunner, and Funk, *Grammar*. Blass, F., and A. Debrunner. *A Greek Grammar of the New Testament and Other Early Christian Literature*. Revised and translated by Robert W. Funk. Chicago: University of Chicago Press, 1961.

Blassingame, *Slave Testimony*. Blassingame, John W., ed. *Slave Testimony: Two Centuries of Letters, Speeches, Interviews, and Autobiographies*. Baton Rouge: Louisiana State University Press, 1977.

Blattenberger, *Rethinking*. Blattenberger, David E., III. *Rethinking 1 Corinthians 11:2–16 through Archaeological and Moral-Rhetorical Analysis*. SBEC 36. Lewiston, N.Y.: Edwin Mellen, 1997.

Blau, "Hebrew Language." Blau, Joshua. "Hebrew Language and Literature." *OEANE* 3:5–12.

Blau and Kohler, "Angelology." Blau, Ludwig, and Kaufmann Kohler. "Angelology." Pages 583–97 in vol. 1 of *The Jewish Encyclopedia*. Edited by Isidore Singer. 12 vols. New York: Funk & Wagnalls, 1901–6.

Blauw, *Missionary Nature*. Blauw, Johannes. *The Missionary Nature of the Church*. Grand Rapids: Eerdmans, 1962.

Blawatsky and Kochelenko, *Culte de Mithra*. Blawatsky, W., and G. Kochelenko. *Le culte de Mithra sur la côte septentrionale de la mer Noire*. ÉPROER 8. Leiden: Brill, 1966.

Bleeker, "Initiation." Bleeker, C. J. "Initiation in Ancient Egypt." Pages 49–58 in *Initiation: Contributions to the Theme of the Study-Conference of the International Association for the History of Religions Held at Strasburg, September 17th to 22nd 1964*. Edited by C. J. Bleeker. SHR 10. Leiden: Brill, 1965.

Bleich, "Abortion." Bleich, J. David. "Abortion and Jewish Law." Pages 405–19 in *New Perspectives on Human Abortion*. Edited by Thomas W. Hilgers, Dennis J. Horan, and David Mall. Frederick, Md.: University Publications of America, 1981.

Blenkinsopp, *Isaiah*. Blenkinsopp, Joseph. *Isaiah 40–55: A New Translation with Introduction and Commentary*. AB 19A. New York: Doubleday, 2002.

Blenkinsopp, *Pentateuch*. Blenkinsopp, Joseph. *The Pentateuch: An Introduction to the First Five Books of the Bible*. ABRL. New York: Doubleday, 1992.

Blenkinsopp, "Reproach." Blenkinsopp, Joseph. "The Prophetic Reproach." *JBL* 90 (Sept. 1971): 267–78.

Blidstein, "4QFlorilegium." Blidstein, Gerald J. "4QFlorilegium and Rabbinic Sources on Bastard and Proselyte." *RevQ* 8 (31/3, 1974): 431–35.

Blidstein, *Garden.* Blidstein, Gerald J. *In the Rabbis' Garden: Adam and Eve in the Midrash.* Northvale, N.J.: Aronson, 1997.

Bligh, *Galatians.* Bligh, John. *Galatians: A Discussion of St Paul's Epistle.* Householder Commentaries 1. London: St Paul, 1970.

Blinzler, *Trial.* Blinzler, Josef. *The Trial of Jesus: The Jewish and Roman Proceedings against Jesus Christ Described and Assessed from the Oldest Accounts.* Translated by Isabel and Florence McHugh. Westminster, Md.: Newman, 1959.

Bloch, "Concordia." Bloch, René. "Concordia." *BrillPauly* 3:681–82.

Bloch, "Elpenor." Bloch, René. "Elpenor." *BrillPauly* 4:929.

Bloch, "Elpis." Bloch, René. "Elpis." *Brill Pauly* 4:930.

Bloch, "Monotheism." Bloch, René. "Monotheism." *BrillPauly* 9:171–74.

Bloch, "Posidonian Thoughts." Bloch, René. "Posidonian Thoughts—Ancient and Modern." *JSJ* 35 (3, 2004): 284–94.

Bloch, "Pygmies." Bloch, René. "Pygmies." *BrillPauly* 12:238–39.

Blockley, "Truth." Blockley, R. C. "Ammianus and Cicero on Truth in Historiography." *AHB* 15 (1, 2001): 14–24.

Blomberg, *Gospels.* Blomberg, Craig L. *The Historical Reliability of the Gospels.* 2nd ed. Downers Grove, Ill.: InterVarsity, 2008.

Blomberg, "Law." Blomberg, Craig L. "The Christian and the Law of Moses." Pages 397–416 in *Witness to the Gospel: The Theology of Acts.* Edited by I. Howard Marshall and David Peterson. Grand Rapids: Eerdmans, 1998.

Blomberg, "Liberation Theology." Blomberg, Craig L. "'Your Faith Has Made You Whole': The Evangelical Liberation Theology of Jesus." Pages 75–93 in *Jesus of Nazareth, Lord and Christ: Essays on the Historical Jesus and New Testament Christology.* Edited by Joel B. Green and Max Turner. Grand Rapids: Eerdmans; Carlisle, U.K.: Paternoster, 1994.

Blomberg, *Matthew.* Blomberg, Craig L. *Matthew.* NAC 22. Nashville: Broadman, 1992.

Blomberg, *Parables.* Blomberg, Craig L. *Interpreting the Parables.* Downers Grove, Ill.: InterVarsity, 1990.

Blomberg, "Posesiones materiales." Blomberg, Craig L. "Las posesiones materiales en el cristianismo primitivo." *Kairós* 25 (1999): 7–27.

Blomberg, *Poverty.* Blomberg, Craig L. *Neither Poverty nor Riches: A Biblical Theology of Material Possessions.* Grand Rapids: Eerdmans, 1999.

Blomberg, "Reflections." Blomberg, Craig L. "Concluding Reflections on Miracles and Gospel Perspectives." Pages 443–57 in *The Miracles of Jesus.* Edited by David Wenham and Craig Blomberg. Gospel Perspectives 6. Sheffield, U.K.: JSOT Press, 1986.

Blomberg, *Reliability of John's Gospel.* Blomberg, Craig L. *The Historical Reliability of John's Gospel: Issues and Commentary.* Downers Grove, Ill.: InterVarsity, 2001.

Blomberg, "Thomas." Blomberg, Craig L. "Tradition and Redaction in the Parables of the Gospel of Thomas." Pages 177–205 in *The Jesus Tradition outside the Gospels.* Edited by David Wenham. Gospel Perspectives 5. Sheffield, U.K.: JSOT Press, 1984.

Blommerde, "Ellipsis." Blommerde, A. C. M. "Is There an Ellipsis between Galatians 2,3 and 2,4?" *Bib* 56 (1, 1975): 100–102.

Blomqvist, "Chryseïs." Blomqvist, Karin. "Chryseïs and Clea, Eumetis and the Interlocutress: Plutarch of Chaeronea and Dio Chrysostom on Women's Education." *SEÅ* 60 (1995): 173–90.

Bloomer, "Declamation." Bloomer, W. Martin. "Roman Declamation: The Elder Seneca and Quintilian." Pages 297–306 in *A Companion to Roman Rhetoric.* Edited by William Dominik and Jon Hall. Oxford: Blackwell, 2007.

Bloomfield, *Recensio.* Bloomfield, S. T. *Recensio Synoptica: Annotationis Sacrae; Being a Critical Digest and Synoptical Arrangement of the most important Annotations on the New Testament, exegetical, philological, and doctrinal: carefully collected and condensed, from the best commentators, both ancient and modern, and so digested as to form one consistent body of annotation, in which each portion is systematically attributed to its respective Author, and the foreign matter translated into English; the whole accompanied with a copious body of original annotations.* 8 vols. London: C. and J. Rivington, 1826–28.

Blue, "House Church." Blue, Bradley. "Acts and the House Church." Pages 119–222 in *The Book of Acts in Its Graeco-Roman Setting.* Edited by David W. J. Gill and Conrad Gempf. Vol. 2 of *The Book of Acts in Its First Century Setting.* Edited by Bruce W. Winter. Grand Rapids: Eerdmans; Carlisle, U.K.: Paternoster, 1994.

Blue, "Influence." Blue, Bradley. "The Influence of Jewish Worship on Luke's Presentation of the Early Church." Pages 473–98 in *Witness to the Gospel: The Theology of Acts.* Edited by I. Howard Marshall and David Peterson. Grand Rapids: Eerdmans, 1998.

Blume, "Hypokrites." Blume, Horst-Dieter. "Hypokrites." *BrillPauly* 6:638–41.

Blumenthal, "Wesen." Blumenthal, Elke. "Vom Wesen der altägyptischen Religion." *TLZ* 117 (1992): 889–96.

Blumhofer, personal correspondence. Blumhofer, Edith L. Personal correspondence with the author, Apr. 18, 2006.

Blumhofer, "Portrait." Blumhofer, Edith L. "Portrait of a Generation: Azusa Street Comes to Chicago." *Enr* 11 (2, 2006): 95–102.

Blumhofer, *Sister.* Blumhofer, Edith L. *Aimee Semple McPherson: Everybody's Sister.* Grand Rapids: Eerdmans, 1993.

Blumhofer and Balmer, *Revivals.* Blumhofer, Edith, and Randall H. Balmer, eds. *Modern Christian Revivals.* Urbana: University of Illinois Press, 1993.

Blunt, *Veracity.* Blunt, John James. *The Veracity of the Gospels and the Acts of the Apostles: Argued from the Undesigned Coincidences to Be Found in Them, When Compared, First, with One Another; Secondly, with Josephus.* Boston: Perkins & Marvin, 1829.

Blyth, "Cicero." Blyth, Dougal. "Cicero and Philosophy as Text." *CJ* 106 (1, 2010): 71–98.

Boatwright, "Imperial Women." Boatwright, Mary T. "The Imperial Women of the Early Second Century A.C." *AJP* 112 (4, 1991): 513–40.

Boatwright, "Theaters." Boatwright, Mary T. "Theaters in the Roman Empire." *BA* 53 (4, 1990): 184–92.

Bobzien, "Conception." Bobzien, Susanne. "The Inadvertent Conception and Late birth of the Free-Will Problem." *Phronesis* 43 (2, 1998): 133–75.

Bobzien, "Freedom." Bobzien, Susanne. "Freedom: Philosophical." *BrillPauly* 5:548–49.

Boccaccini, *Judaism.* Boccaccini, Gabriele. *Middle Judaism: Jewish Thought, 300 B.C.E. to 200 C.E.* Foreword by James H. Charlesworth. Minneapolis: Fortress, 1991.

Boccaccini, "Multiple Judaisms." Boccaccini, Gabriele. "Multiple Judaisms." *BRev* 11 (1, 1995): 38–41, 46.

Bock, *Acts.* Bock, Darrell L. *Acts.* BECNT. Grand Rapids: Baker Academic, 2007.

Bock, *Blasphemy.* Bock, Darrell L. *Blasphemy and Exaltation in Judaism and the Final Examination of Jesus.* WUNT 2.106. Tübingen: Mohr Siebeck, 1998. Reprinted as *Blasphemy and Exaltation in Judaism: The Charge against Jesus in Mark 14:53–65.* Grand Rapids: Baker, 2000.

Bock, "Blasphemy." Bock, Darrell L. "Blasphemy and the Jewish Examination of Jesus." Pages 589–667 in *Key Events in the Life of the Historical Jesus: A Collaborative Exploration of Context and Coherence.*

Edited by Darrell L. Bock and Robert L. Webb. Grand Rapids: Eerdmans, 2010.

Böck, "Commentary." Böck, Barbara. "'An Esoteric Babylonian Commentary' Revisited." *JAOS* 120 (4, 2000): 615–20.

Bock, "Israel." Bock, Darrell L. "Israel in Luke-Acts." Pages 103–15 in *The People, the Land, and the Future of Israel: Israel and the Jewish People in the Plan of God.* Edited by Darrell L. Bock and Mitch Glaser. Grand Rapids: Kregel, 2014.

Bock, *Luke.* Bock, Darrell L. *Luke.* 2 vols. BECNT. Grand Rapids: Baker, 1994.

Bock, *Proclamation.* Bock, Darrell L. *Proclamation from Prophecy and Pattern: Lucan Old Testament Christology.* JSNTSup 12. Sheffield, U.K.: JSOT Press, 1987.

Bock, "Scripture and Realisation of Promises." Bock, Darrell L. "Scripture and the Realisation of God's Promises." Pages 41–62 in *Witness to the Gospel: The Theology of Acts.* Edited by I. Howard Marshall and David Peterson. Grand Rapids: Eerdmans, 1998.

Bock, *Theology.* Bock, Darrell L. *A Theology of Luke and Acts.* Biblical Theology of the New Testament. Grand Rapids: Zondervan, 2012.

Bock, "Words." Bock, Darrell L. "The Words of Jesus in the Gospels: Love, Jive, or Memorex?" Pages 73–99 in *Jesus under Fire.* Ed. by Michael J. Wilkins and J. P. Moreland. Grand Rapids: Zondervan, 1995.

Bockmuehl, *Law.* Bockmuehl, Markus. *Jewish Law in Gentile Churches: Halakah and the Beginning of Christian Public Ethics.* Edinburgh: T&T Clark, 2000.

Bockmuehl, "Law." Bockmuehl, Markus. "Natural Law in Second Temple Judaism." *VT* 45 (1, 1995): 17–44.

Bockmuehl, "Let Acts Be Acts." Bockmuehl, Markus. "Why Not Let Acts Be Acts? In Conversation with C. Kavin Rowe." *JSNT* 28 (2, 2005): 163–66.

Bockmuehl, "Messiah." Bockmuehl, Markus. "A 'Slain Messiah' in 4Q Serekh Milhamah (4Q285)?" *TynBul* 43 (1, 1992): 155–69.

Bockmuehl, *Philippians.* Bockmuehl, Markus. *The Epistle to the Philippians.* BNTC. Grand Rapids: Baker Academic, 2013.

Bockmuehl, *Theology.* Bockmuehl, Klaus. *The Unreal God of Modern Theology—Bultmann, Barth, and the Theology of Atheism: A Call to Recovering The Truth of God's Reality.* Translated by Geoffrey W. Bromiley. Colorado Springs, Colo.: Helmers & Howard, 1988.

Boda, Falk, and Werline, *Development.* Boda, Mark J., Daniel K. Falk, and Rodney A. Werline, eds. *Seeking the Favor of God.* Vol. 2: *The Development of Penitential Prayer*

in Second Temple Judaism. SBLEJL 22. Atlanta: SBL, 2007.

Boda, Falk, and Werline, *Impact.* Boda, Mark J., Daniel K. Falk, and Rodney A. Werline, eds. *Seeking the Favor of God.* Vol. 3: *The Impact of Penitential Prayer beyond Second Temple Judaism.* SBLEJL 23. Atlanta: SBL, 2008.

Boddy, "Spirit Possession." Boddy, Janice. "Spirit Possession Revisited: Beyond Instrumentality." *ARAnth* 23 (1994): 407–34.

Boddy, "Spirits and Selves." Boddy, Janice. "Spirits and Selves in Northern Sudan: The Cultural Therapeutics of Possession and Trance." *AmEthn* 15 (1, 1988): 4–27.

Boddy, *Wombs.* Boddy, Janice. *Wombs and Alien Spirits: Women, Men, and the Zar Cult in Northern Sudan.* Madison: University of Wisconsin Press, 1989.

Bodel, "Caveat emptor." Bodel, John. "Caveat emptor: Towards a Study of Roman Slave-Traders." *JRA* 18 (2005): 181–95.

Bodel and Olyan, *Religion.* Bodel, John, and Saul M. Olyan, eds. *Household and Family Religion in Antiquity.* Ancient World: Comparative Histories. Oxford: Blackwell, 2008.

Bodel and Reid, "Dedicatory Inscription." Bodel, John, and Sara K. Reid. "A Dedicatory Inscription to the Emperor Trajan from the Small Temple at Petra, Jordan." *NEA* 65 (4, 2002): 249–50.

Bodendorfer, "Rechten." Bodendorfer, Gerhard. "Abraham zur Rechten Gottes: Der Ps 110 in der rabbinischen Tradition." *EvT* 59 (4, 1999): 252–66.

Bodinger, "'Hébreux' et 'hellénistes.'" Bodinger, M. "Les 'hébreux' et les 'hellénistes' dans le livre des *Actes des apôtres.*" *Hen* 19 (1, 1997): 39–58.

Bodnár, "Eleatic School." Bodnár, István. "Eleatic School." *BrillPauly* 4:891–93.

Bodnár, "Milesian School." Bodnár, István. "Milesian School." *BrillPauly* 8:879–80.

Bodoff, "Tragedy." Bodoff, Lippman. "The Tragedy of Jephthah." *JBQ* 28 (4, 2000): 251–55.

Bodzek, "Remarks." Bodzek, J. "Remarks on the Iconography of Samaritan Coinage: Hunting in *Paradeisos*?" *IsNumR* 2 (2007): 35–45 and plate 4.

Boer, *Decades of Blood.* Boer, Jan H. *Nigeria's Decades of Blood: 1980–2002.* Belleville, Ont.: Essence, 2003.

Boer, *Fatherhood.* Boer, P. A. H. de. *Fatherhood and Motherhood in Israelite and Judean Piety.* Leiden: Brill, 1974.

Boer, *Morality.* Boer, W. Den. *Private Morality in Greece and Rome: Some Historical Aspects.* Mnemosyne, bibliotheca classica batava: Supplementum 57. Leiden: Brill, 1979.

Boers, *Justification.* Boers, Hendrikus. *The Justification of the Gentiles: Paul's Letters to the Galatians and Romans.* Peabody, Mass.: Hendrickson, 1994.

Boersma, *Violence.* Boersma, Hans. *Violence, Hospitality, and the Cross: Reappropriating the Atonement Tradition.* Grand Rapids: Baker Academic, 2004.

Bogart and Montell, *Memory.* Bogart, Barbara Allen, and William Lynwood Montell. *From Memory to History: Using Oral Sources in Local History.* Nashville: American Association for State and Local History, 1981.

Bøgh, "Kybele." Bøgh, Birgitte. "The Phrygian Background of Kybele." *Numen* 54 (3, 2007): 304–39.

Bohak, "Impact." Bohak, Gideon. "The Impact of Jewish Monotheism on the Greco-Roman World." *JSQ* 7 (1, 2000): 1–21.

Bohak, "Theopolis." Bohak, Gideon. "Theopolis: A Single-Temple Policy and Its Singular Ramifications." *JJS* 50 (1, 1999): 3–16.

Bohannon and Middleton, "Introduction." Bohannon, Paul, and John Middleton. Introduction. Pages xi–xiii in *Kinship and Social Organization.* Edited by Paul Bohannan and John Middleton. Garden City, N.Y.: Natural History Press, 1968.

Böhl, "Verhältnis." Böhl, Felix. "Über das Verhältnis von Shetija-Stein und Nabel der Welt in der Kosmogonie der Rabbinen." *ZDMG* 124 (2, 1974): 253–70.

Böhlig, *Geisteskultur von Tarsos.* Böhlig, H. *Die Geisteskultur von Tarsos im augusteischen Zeitalter mit Berücksichtigung der paulinischen Schriften.* FRLANT 19. Göttingen: Vandenhoeck & Ruprecht, 1913.

Bohm, "Nero." Bohm, R. K. "Nero as Incendiary." *CW* 79 (6, 1986): 400–401.

Böhm, *Samarien.* Böhm, Martina. *Samarien und die Samaritai bei Lukas: Eine Studie zum religionshistorischen und traditionsgeschichtlichen Hintergrund der lukanischen Samarientexte und zu deren topographischer Verhaftung.* WUNT 2.111. Tübingen: Mohr Siebeck, 1999.

Bóid, "Transmission." Bóid, I. R. M. "The Transmission of the Samaritan Joshua-Judges." *DSt* 6 (1, 2004): 1–30.

Boisgelin de Kerdu, *Malta.* Boisgelin de Kerdu, Pierre Marie Louis de. *Ancient and modern Malta: containing a full and accurate account of the present state of the islands of Malta and Goza, the history of the knights of St. John of Jerusalem, also a narrative of the events which attended the capture of these islands by the French, and their conquest by the English: and an appendix, containing authentic state papers and other documents.* London: Printed for R. Phillips, 1805.

Boismard, *Prologue*. Boismard, Marie-Émile. *St. John's Prologue*. Translated by the Carisbrooke Dominicans. London: Blackfriars, 1957.

Boismard, "Review." Boismard, Marie-Émile. Review of J. W. Doeve, *Jewish Hermeneutics in the Synoptic Gospels and Acts*. *RB* 63 (1956): 291.

Boismard and Lamouille, *Actes*. Boismard, Marie-Émile, and A. Lamouille. *Les Actes des deux apôtres*. EtBib, nouvelle série. Paris: Lecoffre, 1990–.

Bokser, *Description*. Bokser, Baruch M. *Philo's Description of Jewish Practices*. PSCC 30. Berkeley, Calif.: Center for Hermeneutical Studies in Hellenistic and Modern Culture, 1977.

Bokser, "Justin and Jews." Bokser, Ben Zion. "Justin Martyr and the Jews." *JQR* 64 (2, 1973): 97–122; (3, 1974): 204–11.

Bokser, "Wonder-Working." Bokser, Baruch M. "Wonder-Working and the Rabbinic Tradition: The Case of Hanina ben Dosa." *JSJ* 16 (1, 1985): 42–92.

Bolotnikov, "War." Bolotnikov, Alexander. "The Theme of Apocalyptic War in the Dead Sea Scrolls." *AUSS* 43 (2, 2005): 261–66.

Bolt, "Daimons." Bolt, Peter G. "Jesus, the Daimons, and the Dead." Pages 75–102 in *The Unseen World: Christian Reflections on Angels, Demons, and the Heavenly Realm*. Edited by Anthony N. S. Lane. Grand Rapids: Baker; Carlisle, U.K.: Paternoster, 1996.

Bolt, "Mission." Bolt, Peter G. "Mission and Witness." Pages 191–214 in *Witness to the Gospel: The Theology of Acts*. Edited by I. Howard Marshall and David Peterson. Grand Rapids: Eerdmans, 1998.

Bolton, "Spaces." Bolton, M. Catherine. "Gendered Spaces in Ovid's Heroides." *CW* 102 (3, 2009): 273–90.

Bomann, *Faith in Barrios*. Bomann, Rebecca Pierce. *Faith in the Barrios: The Pentecostal Poor in Bogotá*. Boulder, Colo., and London: Lynn Rienner, 1999.

Bomann, "Salve." Bomann, Rebecca Pierce. "The Salve of Divine Healing: Essential Rituals for Survival among Working-Class Pentecostals in Bogotá, Colombia." Pages 187–205 in *Global Pentecostal and Charismatic Healing*. Edited by Candy Gunther Brown. Foreword by Harvey Cox. Oxford: Oxford University Press, 2011.

Bömer, *Kommentar*. Bömer, Franz., *Kommentar*. Vol. 2 of Publius Ovidius Naso [Ovid], *Die Fasten*. Edited and translated by Franz Bömer. Heidelberg: C. Winter, 1958.

Bommas, "Isis in Alexandria." Bommas, Martin. "Isis in Alexandria." *BN* 147 (2010): 25–47.

Bonfante, "Chiliarchos." Bonfante, Larissa. "Chiliarchos." *BrillPauly* 3:227.

Bonfante, "Naked Greek." Bonfante, Larissa. "The Naked Greek." *Archaeology* 43 (5, 1990): 28–35.

Bonnah, *Spirit*. Bonnah, George Kwame Agyei. *The Holy Spirit: A Narrative Factor in the Acts of the Apostles*. SBB 58. Stuttgart: Verlag Katholisches Bibelwerk GmbH, 2007.

Bonnard, "Esprit Saint." Bonnard, Pierre. "L'Esprit Saint et l'Église selon le Nouveau Testament." *RHPR* 37 (1957): 81–90.

Bonnard, *Matthieu*. Bonnard, Pierre. *L'Évangile selon Saint Matthieu*. CNT 1. Neuchâtel, Switz.: Delachaux & Niestlé, 1963.

Bonneau, "Achever." Bonneau, Guy. "'Pour y achever l'organisation' (Tite 1,5): L'institutionnalisation de l'Église au temps du Nouveau Testament." *ScEs* 52 (1, 2000): 87–107.

Bonner, *Education*. Bonner, Stanley F. *Education in Ancient Rome*. London: Methuen, 1977.

Bons, "Psaume 2." Bons, Eberhard. "Psaume 2: Bilan de recherche et essai de réinterprétation." *RevScRel* 69 (2, 1995): 147–71.

Bonsirven, *Judaism*. Bonsirven, Joseph. *Palestinian Judaism in the Time of Jesus Christ*. New York: Holt, Rinehart & Winston, 1964.

Bonwetsch, "Prophetie." Bonwetsch, Nathanael. "Die Prophetie im apostolischen und nachapostolischen Zeitalter." *ZKWKL* 5 (8–9, 1884): 408–24, 460–77.

Bony, "Ecclésiologie, II." Bony, Paul. "L'ecclésiologie paulinienne dans la recherche récente, II." *EspV* 115 (131, 2005): 12–16.

Bony, "Ecclésiologie, III." Bony, Paul. "L'ecclésiologie paulinienne dans la recherche récente, III." *EspV* 115 (132, 2005): 16–21.

Bonz, "Approaches." Bonz, Marianne Palmer. "Differing Approaches to Religious Benefaction: The Late Third-Century Acquisition of the Sardis Synagogue." *HTR* 86 (2, 1993): 139–54.

Bonz, "Best and Worst." Bonz, Marianne Palmer. "The Best of Times, the Worst of Times: Luke-Acts and Epic Tradition." ThD diss., Harvard Divinity School, 1996.

Bonz, "Inscriptions." Bonz, Marianne Palmer. "The Jewish Donor Inscriptions from Aphrodisias: Are They Both Third-Century, and Who Are the *theosebeis*?" *HSCP* 96 (1994): 281–99.

Bonz, *Past as Legacy*. Bonz, Marianne Palmer. *The Past as Legacy: Luke-Acts and Ancient Epic*. Minneapolis: Fortress, 2000.

Bookidis, "Religion." Bookidis, Nancy. "Religion in Corinth: 146 B.C.E. to 100 C.E." Pages 141–64 in *Urban Religion in Roman Corinth: Interdisciplinary Approaches*. Edited by Daniel N. Schowalter and Steven J. Friesen. HTS 53. Cambridge, Mass.: Harvard University Press, 2005.

Bookidis, "Sanctuaries of Corinth." Bookidis, Nancy. "The Sanctuaries of Corinth." Pages 247–59 in *Corinth: The Centenary, 1896–1996*. Edited by Charles K. Williams II and Nancy Bookidis. Vol. 20 of *Corinth: Results of Excavations Conducted by the American School of Classical Studies at Athens*. Princeton: American School of Classical Studies at Athens, 2003.

Boomershine and Bartholomew, "Technique." Boomershine, Thomas E., and Gilbert L. Bartholomew. "The Narrative Technique of Mark 16:8." *JBL* 100 (2, 1981): 213–23.

Borchert, "Ephesus." Borchert, Gerald L. "Ephesus." *ISBE* 2:115–17.

Borg, *Conflict*. Borg, Marcus J. *Conflict, Holiness, and Politics in the Teachings of Jesus*. SBEC 5. New York: Edwin Mellen, 1984.

Borg, "Disagreement." Borg, Marcus J. "An Appreciative Disagreement." Pages 227–43 in *Jesus and the Restoration of Israel: A Critical Assessment of N. T. Wright's Jesus and the Victory of God*. Edited by Carey C. Newman. Downers Grove, Ill.: InterVarsity, 1999.

Borg, *Jesus*. Borg, Marcus J. *Jesus: Uncovering the Life, Teachings, and Relevance of a Religious Revolutionary*. New York: HarperOne, 2006.

Borg, *Vision*. Borg, Marcus J. *Jesus, a New Vision: Spirit, Culture, and the Life of Discipleship*. San Francisco: Harper & Row, 1987.

Borg, "Zealot." Borg, Marcus J. "The Currency of the Term 'Zealot.'" *JTS* 22 (2, 1971): 504–12.

Borgeaud, "Excursions." Borgeaud, Philippe. "Trojan Excursions: A Recurrent Ritual, from Xerxes to Julian." *HR* 49 (4, 2010): 339–53.

Borgeaud, "Mother Goddesses." Borgeaud, Philippe Borgeaud, "Mother Goddesses." *BrillPauly* 9:237–39.

Borgen, "Agent." Borgen, Peder. "God's Agent in the Fourth Gospel." Pages 137–48 in *Religions in Antiquity: Essays in Memory of Erwin Ramsdell Goodenough*. Edited by Jacob Neusner. SHR 14. Leiden: Brill, 1968.

Borgen, "Eschatology." Borgen, Peder. "Eschatology and 'Heilsgeschichte' in Luke-Acts." PhD diss., Drew University, 1956.

Borgen, "Miracles." Borgen, Peder. "Miracles of Healing in the New Testament." *ST* 35 (2, 1981): 91–106.

Borgen, "Paul to Luke." Borgen, Peder. "From Paul to Luke: Observations toward Clarification of the Theology of Luke-Acts." *CBQ* 31 (1969): 168–82.

Borgen, "Reception." Borgen, Peder. "Jesus Christ, the Reception of the Spirit, and a Cross-national Community." Pages 220–35 in *Jesus of Nazareth, Lord and Christ: Essays on the Historical Jesus and New Testament Christology*. Edited by Joel B. Green and Max Turner. Grand Rapids: Eerdmans; Carlisle, U.K.: Paternoster, 1994.

Borgen, "Reviewing and Rewriting." Borgen, Peder. "Philo of Alexandria: Reviewing and Rewriting Biblical Material." *SPhilA* 9 (1997): 37–53.

Borgman, *Way*. Borgman, Paul. *The Way according to Luke: Hearing the Whole Story of Luke-Acts*. Grand Rapids: Eerdmans, 2006.

Boring, "Oracles." Boring, M. Eugene. "How May We Identify Oracles of Christian Prophets in the Synoptic Tradition? Mark 3:28–29 as a Test Case." *JBL* 91 (4, 1972): 501–21.

Boring, *Sayings*. Boring, M. Eugene. *Sayings of the Risen Jesus: Christian Prophecy in the Synoptic Tradition*. SNTSMS 46. Cambridge: Cambridge University Press, 1982.

Boring, Berger, and Colpe, *Commentary*. Boring, M. Eugene, Klaus Berger, and Carsten Colpe, eds. *Hellenistic Commentary to the New Testament*. Nashville: Abingdon, 1995.

Börner-Klein, "Killing." Börner-Klein, D. "Killing in Self-Defense in Rabbinical Law." *JSQ* 4 (2, 1997): 169–82.

Bornkamm, *Experience*. Bornkamm, Günther. *Early Christian Experience*. Translated by Paul L. Hammer. New York: Harper & Row; London: SCM, 1969.

Bornkamm, "Missionary Stance." Bornkamm, Günther. "The Missionary Stance of Paul in I Corinthians 9 and in Acts." Pages 194–207 in *Studies in Luke-Acts: Essays in Honor of Paul Schubert*. Edited by Leander E. Keck and J. Louis Martyn. Nashville: Abingdon, 1966.

Bornkamm, *Paul*. Bornkamm, Günther. *Paul*. Translated by D. M. G. Stalker. New York: Harper & Row, 1971.

Borowitz, *Christologies*. Borowitz, Eugene B. *Contemporary Christologies: A Jewish Response*. New York: Paulist, 1980.

Borowski, "Eat." Borowski, Oded. "Eat, Drink, and Be Merry: The Mediterranean Diet." *NEA* 67 (2, 2004): 96–107.

Borse, "Timotheus und Titus." Borse, Udo. "Timotheus und Titus, Abgesandte Pauli im Dienst des Evangeliums." Pages 27–43 in *Der Diakon: Wieder-entdeckung und Erneuerung seines Dienstes*. Edited by Josef G. Ploger and Herman J. Weber. Freiburg im Breisgau: Herder, 1980.

Börstinghaus, *Sturmfahrt*. Börstinghaus, Jens. *Sturmfahrt und Schiffbruch: Zur lukanischen Verwendung eines literarischen Topos in Apostelgeschichte 27,1–28,6*. WUNT 2.274. Tübingen: Mohr Siebeck, 2010.

Borza, "Samothrace." Borza, Eugene N. "Samothrace." *OCD*[3] 1352.

Borzì, "Accostamento." Borzì, S. "L'accostamento fra Apollonio di Tiana e Cristo." *Laós* 8 (1, 2001): 19–24.

Bos, "Philo." Bos, Abraham P. "Philo of Alexandria: A Platonist in the Image and Likeness of Aristotle." *SPhilA* 10 (1998): 66–86.

Bos, "Profeet." Bos, R. "Van wie segt de profeet dit? Een een-voudige vraag en een meervoudig antwoord." *HTS/TS* 61 (4, 2005): 1049–69.

Bosch-Veciana, "Filosofia." Bosch-Veciana, Antoni. "La 'filosofia' del judaisme alexandrí com a 'manera de viure.'" *RCT* 34 (2, 2009): 503–21.

Boshoff and van Aarde, "Apokaliptiek." Boshoff, H. J., and A. G. van Aarde. "Grieks-Romeinse apokaliptiek en die Christelike kerugma." *HTS/TS* 61 (4, 2005): 1131–48.

Bosman, "Athletes." Bosman, Philip R. "Meat, Muscle, and Mind: Diogenes and the Athletes." *Scriptura* 90 (2005): 660–69.

Bosman, "Conscience." Bosman, Philip R. "Conscience and Free Speech in Philo." *SPhilA* 18 (2006): 33–47.

Bosman, "Riddle Contest." Bosman, Philip R. "The Gymnosophist Riddle Contest (Berol. P. 13044): A Cynic Text?" *GRBS* 50 (2, 2010): 175–92.

Bosman, "Selling Cynicism." Bosman, Philip. "Selling Cynicism: The Pragmatics of Diogenes' Comic Performances." *CQ* 56 (1, 2006): 93–104.

Bostock, "Elisha." Bostock, D. Gerald. "Jesus as the New Elisha." *ExpT* 92 (2, 1980): 39–41.

Bosworth, "Beating." Bosworth, F. F. "Beating in Texas Follows Ministry to Blacks: F. F. Bosworth's 1911 Letter to His Mother, Dallas, Tex., Aug. 21, 1911." *Assemblies of God Heritage* 6 (2, Summer 1986): 5, 14.

Bosworth, "Historians and Sources." Bosworth, A. B. "Plus ça change: Ancient Historians and Their Sources." *ClAnt* 22 (2003): 167–97.

Bosworth, "Pseudo-Callisthenes." Bosworth, Albert Brian. "Pseudo-Callisthenes." *OCD*[3] 1270.

Bosworth, "Vespasian." Bosworth, Albert Brian. "Vespasian and the Slave Trade." *CQ* 52 (1, 2002): 350–57.

Botermann, "Heidenapostel." Botermann, Helga. "Der Heide napostel und sein Historiker: Zur historischen Kritik der Apostelgeschichte." *TBei* 24 (2, 1993): 62–84.

Botermann, *Judenedikt*. Botermann, Helga. *Das Judenedikt des Kaisers Claudius: Römischer Staat und Christiani im 1. Jahrhundert*. Stuttgart: Steiner, 1996.

Botermann, "Synagoge." Botermann, Helga. "Die Synagoge von Sardes: Eine Synagoge aus dem 4. Jahrhundert?" *ZNW* 81 (1–2, 1990): 103–21.

Botha, "Cognition." Botha, Pieter J. J. "Cognition, Orality-Literacy, and Approaches to First-Century Writings." Pages 37–63 in *Orality, Literacy, and Colonialism in Antiquity*. SBLSemS 47. Atlanta: SBL, 2004.

Botha, "Community." Botha, Pieter J. J. "Community and Conviction in Luke-Acts." *Neot* 29 (2, 1995): 145–65.

Botha, "Exploring Gesture." Botha, Pieter J. J. "Exploring Gesture and Nonverbal Communication in the Bible and the Ancient World: Some Initial Observations." *Neot* 30 (1, 1996): 1–19.

Botha, "Literacy." Botha, P. J. J. "Greco-Roman Literacy as Setting for New Testament Writings." *Neot* 26 (1, 1992): 195–215.

Botha, "Point of View." Botha, Pieter J. J. "History and Point of View: Understanding the Sadducees." *Neot* 30 (2, 1996): 235–80.

Botha, "Research." Botha, F. J. "Recent Research and the Lord's Prayer." *Neot* 1 (1967): 42–50.

Botha, "Rhetoric and Josephus." Botha, Pieter J. J. "History, Rhetoric, and the Writings of Josephus." *Neot* 31 (1, 1997): 1–20.

Bottari, *Free*. Bottari, Pablo. *Free in Christ: Your Complete Handbook on the Ministry of Deliverance*. Foreword by Carlos Annacondia. Lake Mary, Fla.: Creation House, Strang Communications, 2000.

Bottini, "Lukásova teológia." Bottini, G. Claudio. "Lukásova teológia, retrospektíva a aktuálne pozície." *StBibSlov* 4 (1, 2012): 1–19.

Bottini and Casalini, "Informazione." Bottini, G. Claudio, and Nello Casalini. "Informazione e ricostruzione in Atti degli apostoli: Note di lettura." *SBFLA* 52 (2002): 125–74.

Böttrich, "Astrologie." Böttrich, Christfried. "Astrologie in der Henoch Tradition." *ZAW* 109 (2, 1997): 222–45.

Böttrich, "Liturgie." Böttrich, Christfried. "Das 'Sanctus' in der Liturgie der hellenistischen Synagoge." *JLH* 35 (1994–95): 10–36.

Boudon, "Marges." Boudon, Véronique. "Aux marges de la médecine rationnelle: Médecins et charlatans à Rome au temps de Galien (IIe s. de notre ère)." *REG* 116 (1, 2003): 109–31.

Bouquet and Morzadec, *Sibylle*. Bouquet, Monique, and Françoise Morzadec, eds. *La Sibylle: Parole et représentation*. Rennes: Presses Universitaires de Rennes, 2004.

Bourgeois, "Spittle." Bourgeois, Sarah L. "Mark 8:22–26: Jesus and the Use of Spittle in a Two-Stage Healing." ThM thesis, Dallas Theological Seminary, 1999.

Bourgine, "Opfer." Bourgine, M. B. "Das Opfer Abrahams in jüdischer und christlicher Auslegung: Gen 22,1–19 im Midrasch Bereschit Rabba und in den Genesis-Homilien des Origenes." *UnS* 51 (4, 1996): 308–15.

Bourguignon, "Appendix." Bourguignon, Erika. "Appendix." Pages 359–76 in *Religion, Altered States of Consciousness, and Social Change*. Edited by Erika Bourguignon. Columbus: Ohio State University Press, 1973.

Bourguignon, "Assessment." Bourguignon, Erika. "An Assessment of Some Comparisons and Implications." Pages 321–39 in *Religion, Altered States of Consciousness, and Social Change*. Edited by Erika Bourguignon. Columbus: Ohio State University Press, 1973.

Bourguignon, "Distribution." Bourguignon, Erika. "World Distribution and Patterns of Possession States." Pages 3–34 in *Trance and Possession States: Proceedings of the Second Annual Conference, R. M. Bucke Memorial Society, March 4–6, 1966*. Edited by Raymond Prince. Montreal: R. M. Bucke Memorial Society, 1968.

Bourguignon, "Epilogue." Bourguignon, Erika. "Epilogue: Some Notes on Contemporary Americans and the Irrational." Pages 340–56 in *Religion, Altered States of Consciousness, and Social Change*. Edited by Erika Bourguignon. Columbus: Ohio State University Press, 1973.

Bourguignon, "Introduction." Bourguignon, Erika. "Introduction: A Framework for the Comparative Study of Altered States of Consciousness." Pages 3–35 in *Religion, Altered States of Consciousness, and Social Change*. Edited by Erika Bourguignon. Columbus: Ohio State University Press, 1973.

Bourguignon, "Multiple Personality." Bourguignon, Erika. "Multiple Personality, Possession Trance, and the Psychic Unity of Mankind." *Ethos* 17 (1989): 371–84.

Bourguignon, *Possession*. Bourguignon, Erika. *Possession*. Chandler & Sharp Series

in Cross-Cultural Themes. San Francisco: Chandler & Sharp, 1976.

Bourguignon, "Self." Bourguignon, Erika. "The Self, the Behavioral Environment, and the Theory of Spirit Possession." *Culture and Meaning in Cultural Anthropology*. Edited by Melford E. Spiro. New York: Free Press, 1965.

Bourguignon, "Spirit Possession Belief." Bourguignon, Erika. "Spirit Possession Belief and Social Structure." Pages 17–26 in *The Realm of the Extra-human: Ideas and Actions*. Edited by Agehananda Bharati. The Hague and Paris: Mouton, 1976.

Bourguignon, "World Distribution." Bourguignon, Erika. "World Distribution and Patterns of Possession States." Pages 3–34 in *Trance and Possession States: Proceedings of the Second Annual Conference, R. M. Bucke Memorial Society, March 4–6, 1966*. Edited by Raymond Prince. Montreal: R. M. Bucke Memorial Society, 1968.

Bousset, *Kyrios Christos*. Bousset, William. *Kyrios Christos: A History of the Belief in Christ from the Beginnings of Christianity to Irenaeus*. Translated by John E. Steely. Nashville: Abingdon, 1970.

Bouwman, "'Livre' et date." Bouwman, Gijs. "Le 'premier livre' (Act. I,1) et la date des Actes des apôtres." Pages 553–65 in *L'Évangile de Luc: The Gospel of Luke*. Edited by F. Neirynck. Rev. ed. BETL 32. Leuven: Leuven University Press, 1989.

Bouzek, "Scythians." Bouzek, Jan. "Scythians." *OEANE* 4:503–5.

Bovon, "Apostelakten." Bovon, François. "Die kanonische Apostelgeschichte und die apokryphen Apostelakten." Pages 349–79 in *Die Apostelgeschichte im Kontext antiker und frühchristlicher Historiographie*. Edited by Jörg Frey, Clare K. Rothschild, and Jens Schröter, with Bettina Rost. BZNWK 162. Berlin: de Gruyter, 2009.

Bovon, "Ascension Stories." Bovon, François. "The Lukan Ascension Stories." *Korean New Testament Studies* 17 (3, 2010): 563–95.

Bovon, "Canonical and Apocryphal Acts." Bovon, François. "Canonical and Apocryphal Acts of Apostles." *JECS* 11 (2, 2003): 165–94.

Bovon, "Études." Bovon, François. "Études lucaniennes: Rétrospective et prospective." *RTP* 125 (2, 1993): 113–35.

Bovon, "Reception." Bovon, François. "The Reception of the Book of Acts in Late Antiquity." Pages 66–92 in *Contemporary Studies in Acts*. Edited by Thomas E. Phillips. Macon, Ga.: Mercer University Press, 2009.

Bovon, "Saint-Esprit." Bovon, François. "Le Saint-Esprit, l'Église, et les relations humaines selon Actes 20,36–21,16." Pages

339–58 in *Les Actes des apôtres: Traditions, rédaction, théologie*. Edited by Jacob Kremer. BETL 48. Gembloux, Belg.: J. Duculot; Leuven: Leuven University Press, 1979.

Bovon, *Studies*. Bovon, François. *Studies in Early Christianity*. Tübingen: J. C. B. Mohr; Grand Rapids: Baker Academic, 2003.

Bovon, "Studies." Bovon, François. "Studies in Luke-Acts: Retrospect and Prospect." *HTR* 85 (1992): 175–96.

Bovon, *Theologian*. Bovon, François. *Luke the Theologian: Thirty-Three Years of Research (1950–1983)*. Translated by Ken McKinney. Allison Park, Pa.: Pickwick, 1987.

Bovon and Bouvier, "Étienne." Bovon, François, and Bertrand Bouvier. "Étienne le premier martyr: Du livre canonique au récit apocryphe." Pages 309–31 in *Die Apostelgeschichte und die hellenistische Geschichtsschreibung: Festschrift für Eckhard Plümacher zu seinem 65. Geburtstag*. Edited by Cilliers Breytenbach and Jens Schröter. Leiden: Brill, 2004.

Bowe, "Birth." Bowe, B. E. "The Birth of the Church." *BibT* 37 (5, 1999): 288–93.

Bower, "*Ephodos* and *insinuatio*." Bower, E. W. "*Ephodos* and *insinuatio* in Greek and Latin Rhetoric." *CQ* 8 (1958): 224–30.

Bowers, "Communities." Bowers, W. P. "Jewish Communities in Spain in the Time of Paul the Apostle." *JTS* 26 (2, 1975): 395–402.

Bowers, "Mission." Bowers, W. Paul. "Mission." *DPL* 608–19.

Bowers, "Nubian Christianity." Bowers, Paul. "Nubian Christianity: The Neglected Heritage." *East AfET* 4 (1, 1985): 3–23.

Bowers, "Propaganda." Bowers, Paul. "Paul and Religious Propaganda in the First Century." *NovT* 22 (4, 1980): 316–23.

Bowers, "Route through Mysia." Bowers, W. P. "Paul's Route through Mysia: A Note on Acts XVI.8." *JTS* 30 (2, 1979): 507–11.

Bowersock, *Arabia*. Bowersock, G. W. *Roman Arabia*. Cambridge, Mass.: Harvard University Press, 1983.

Bowersock, *Augustus*. Bowersock, G. W. *Augustus and the Greek World*. Oxford: Clarendon, 1965.

Bowersock, "Cult." Bowersock, G. W. "The Imperial Cult: Perceptions and Persistence." Pages 171–82 in *Self-Definition in the Greco-Roman World*. Edited by Ben F. Meyer and E. P. Sanders. Vol. 3 of *Jewish and Christian Self-Definition*. Edited by E. P. Sanders. Philadelphia: Fortress, 1982.

Bowersock, *Fiction as History*. Bowersock, G. W. *Fiction as History: Nero to Julian*.

Berkeley: University of California Press, 1994.

Bowersock, *Sophists in Empire*. Bowersock, G. W. *Greek Sophists in the Roman Empire*. Oxford: Clarendon, 1969.

Bowie, "Apollonius." Bowie, Ewen L. "Apollonius of Tyana: Tradition and Reality." *ANRW* 16.2:1652–99. Part 2, *Principat*, 16.2. Edited by H. Temporini and W. Haase. Berlin: de Gruyter, 1978.

Bowie, "Novel." Bowie, Ewen L. "Novel, Greek." *OCD*³ 1049–50.

Bowie, "Philostratus." Bowie, Ewen L. "Philostratus: Writer of Fiction." Pages 181–96 in *Greek Fiction: The Greek Novel in Context*. Edited by J. R. Morgan and R. Stoneman. London: Routledge, 1994.

Bowie, "Readership." Bowie, Ewen L. "The Readership of Greek Novels in the Ancient World." Pages 435–59 in *The Search for the Ancient Novel*. Edited by James Tatum. Baltimore: Johns Hopkins University Press, 1994.

Bowie, "Second Sophistic." Bowie, Ewen L. "Second Sophistic." *OCD*³ 1377–78.

Bowie, "Sophistic." Bowie, Ewen L. "Second Sophistic." *BrillPauly* 13:185–91.

Bowker, *Pharisees*. Bowker, John W. *Jesus and the Pharisees*. Cambridge: Cambridge University Press, 1973.

Bowker, "Proem and Yelammedenu Form." Bowker, John W. "Speeches in Acts: A Study in Proem and Yelammedenu Form." *NTS* 14 (1, 1967): 96–111.

Bowker, "Visions." Bowker, John W. "'Merkabah' Visions and the Visions of Paul." *JSS* 16 (2, 1971): 157–73.

Bowley, "Pax." Bowley, James E. "Pax Romana." *DNTB* 771–75.

Bowley, "Purification Texts." Bowley, James E. "Purification Texts (4Q274–279, 281–284, 512–514)." *DNTB* 873–74.

Bowman, *Documents*. Bowman, John, trans. and ed. *Samaritan Documents Relating to Their History, Religion, and Life*. POTTS 2. Pittsburgh.: Pickwick, 1977.

Bowman, *Drama*. Bowman, John Wick. *The First Christian Drama: The Book of Revelation*. Philadelphia: Westminster, 1968.

Bowman, *Gospel*. Bowman, John. *The Fourth Gospel and the Jews: A Study in R. Akiba, Esther, and the Gospel of John*. PTMS 8. Pittsburgh: Pickwick, 1975.

Bowman, *Intention*. Bowman, John Wick. *The Intention of Jesus*. Foreword by Walter Marshall Horton. Philadelphia: Westminster, 1943.

Bowman, "Prophets." Bowman, John. "Prophets and Prophecy in Talmud and Midrash." *EvQ* 22 (2, 1950): 107–14; (3, 1958): 205–20; (4, 1950): 255–75.

Bowman, "Samaritan and Pauline Theology." Bowman, John. "The Doctrine of Creation, Fall of Man, and Original Sin in Samaritan and Pauline Theology." *RTR* 19 (3, 1960): 65–72.

Bowman and Komoszewski, *Deity*. Bowman, Robert M., Jr., and J. Ed Komoszewski. *Putting Jesus in His Place: The Case for the Deity of Christ*. Foreword by Darrell L. Bock. Grand Rapids: Kregel, 2007.

Bowman and Rathbone, "Administration in Egypt." Bowman, Alan K., and Dominic Rathbone. "Cities and Administration in Roman Egypt." *JRS* 82 (1992): 107–27.

Bowman and Wilson, *Settlement*. Bowman, Alan, and Andrew Wilson, eds. *Settlement, Urbanization, and Population*. Oxford Studies on the Roman Economy. New York: Oxford University Press, 2012.

Boxall, "History and Spirit." Boxall, Ian. "History and the Spirit in Acts." *P&P* 18 (3, 2004): 129–33.

Boyd, "Model." Boyd, Gregory A. "The Ground-Level Deliverance Model." Pages 129–57 in *Understanding Spiritual Warfare: Four Views*. Edited by James K. Beilby and Paul Rhodes Eddy. Grand Rapids: Baker Academic, 2012.

Boyd, "Motivations." Boyd, Gregory A. "Two Ancient (and Modern) Motivations for Ascribing Exhaustively Definite Foreknowledge to God: A Historical Overview and Critical Assessment." *RelS* 46 (1, 2010): 41–59.

Boyd, *Sage*. Boyd, Gregory A. *Cynic Sage or Son of God?* Wheaton, Ill.: BridgePoint, 1995.

Boyd-Taylor, "Adventure." Boyd-Taylor, Cameron. "Esther's Great Adventure: Reading the LXX Version of the Book of Esther in Light of Its Assimilation to the Conventions of the Greek Romantic Novel." *BIOSCS* 30 (1997): 81–113.

Boyer, "Folk Psychiatry." Boyer, L. Bryce. "Folk Psychiatry of the Apaches of the Mescalero Indian Reservation." Pages 384–419 in *Magic, Faith, and Healing: Studies in Primitive Psychiatry Today*. Edited by Ari Kiev. Foreword by Jerome D. Frank. New York: Free Press, 1964.

Bracci, "Mistero." Bracci, Mario. "Il mistero dell'ascensione al cielo: Note intorno alla post-esistenza del Figlio." *EunDoc* 63 (1, 2010): 159–87.

Braden, "Study." Braden, Charles S. "Study of Spiritual Healing in the Churches." Pages 224–35 in *New Concepts of Healing: Medical, Psychological, and Religious*, by Alice Graham Ikin. Introduction by Wayne E. Oates. New York: Association Press, 1956. Reprinted from *Pastoral Psychology* (May 1954): 19–23.

Bradford, *Sabbath Roots*. Bradford, Charles E. *Sabbath Roots: The African Connection*. Silver Spring, Md.: Ministerial Association of the General Conference of Seventh-Day Adventists, 1999.

Bradley, "Apologia." Bradley, Keith R. "Law, Magic, and Culture in the *Apologia* of Apuleius." *Phoenix* 51 (2, 1997): 203–33.

Bradley, "Captives." Bradley, Keith R. "On Captives under the Principate." *Phoenix* 58 (3–4, 2004): 298–318 and plates 1–17.

Bradley, "Fullonica." Bradley, Mark. "'It All Comes Out in the Wash': Looking Harder at the Roman *fullonica*." *JRA* 15 (2002): 20–44.

Bradley, "Sentimental Education." Bradley, Keith R. "The Sentimental Education of the Roman Child: The Role of Pet-Keeping." *Latomus* 57 (3, 1998): 523–57.

Bradley, *Slaves*. Bradley, Keith R. *Slaves and Masters in the Roman Empire: A Study in Social Control*. Brussels: Latomus, 1984. Repr., New York: Oxford University Press, 1987.

Bradley, "Suetonius." Bradley, Keith R. "Suetonius (Gaius Suetonius Tranquillus)." *OCD*³ 1451–52.

Bradley, "Traffic." Bradley, Keith R. "'The Regular, Daily Traffic in Slaves': Roman History and Contemporary History." *CJ* 87 (2, 1992): 125–38.

Bradley, "Wet-Nursing." Bradley, Keith R. "Wet-Nursing at Rome: A Study in Social Relations." Pages 201–29 in *The Family in Ancient Rome: New Perspectives*. Edited by Beryl Rawson. Ithaca, N.Y.: Cornell University Press, 1986.

Bradley et al., *Tradition*. Bradley, S., et al. *The American Tradition in Literature*. 5th ed. New York: Random House, 1981.

Bragg, "Raids." Bragg, Edward. "Roman Seaborne Raids during the Mid-Republic: Sideshow or Headline Feature?" *GR* 57 (1, 2010): 47–64.

Bram, "Fate." Bram, Jean Rhys. "Fate and Freedom: Astrology vs. Mystery Religions." Pages 326–30 in *SBL Seminar Papers, 1976*. Edited by George MacRae. SBLSP 10. Missoula, Mont.: Scholars Press, 1976.

Branch, *Parting*. Branch, Taylor. *Parting the Waters: America in the King Years 1954–63*. New York: Simon & Schuster, 1988.

Branch and Schoville, "Ships." Branch, Robin Gallaher, and Keith N. Schoville. "Boats and Ships." Pages 190–98 in vol. 1 of *Dictionary of Daily Life in Biblical and Post-Biblical Antiquity*. Edited by Edwin M. Yamauchi and Marvin R. Wilson. Peabody, Mass.: Hendrickson, 2014.

Brand, *Perspectives*. Brand, Chad Owen. *Perspectives on Spirit Baptism: Five Views*. Nashville: Broadman & Holman, 2004.

Brandes, "Reflections." Brandes, Stanley. "Reflections on Honor and Shame in the

Mediterranean." Pages 121–34 in *Honor and Shame and the Unity of the Mediterranean*. Edited by David D. Gilmore. AAAM 22. Washington, D.C.: American Anthropological Association, 1987.

Brändle and Stegemann, "Formation." Brändle, Rudolf, and Ekkehard W. Stegemann. "The Formation of the First 'Christian Congregations' in Rome in the Context of the Jewish Congregations." Pages 117–27 in *Judaism and Christianity in First-Century Rome*. Edited by Karl P. Donfried and Peter Richardson. Grand Rapids: Eerdmans, 1998.

Brandon, *Zealots*. Brandon, S. G. F. *Jesus and the Zealots*. New York: Scribner's, 1967.

Brandt, "Retournement." Brandt, Pierre-Yves. "La conversion, retournement ou changement d'appartenance? Approche psychologique du parcours de Pierre dans l'ouvre lucanienne." *ETR* 84 (1, 2009): 1–22.

Branham, "Humor." Branham, R. Bracht. "Authorizing Humor: Lucian's *Demonax* and Cynic Rhetoric." *Semeia* 64 (1993): 33–48.

Brant, *John*. Brant, Jo-Ann A. *John*. PCNT. Grand Rapids: Baker Academic, 2011.

Brant, "Mimesis." Brant, Jo-Ann A. "Mimesis and Dramatic Art in Ezekiel the Tragedian's *Exagoge*." Pages 129–47 in *Ancient Fiction: The Matrix of Early Christian and Jewish Narrative*. Edited by Jo-Ann A. Brant, Charles W. Hedrick, and Chris Shea. SBLSymS 32. Atlanta: SBL, 2005.

Brashear, "Corpora." Brashear, William M. "Out of the Closet: Recent Corpora of Magical Texts." *CP* 91 (4, 1996): 372–83.

Bratcher, "Acts ix.7." Bratcher, Robert G. "*Akouō* in Acts ix.7 and xxii.9." *ExpT* 71 (8, 1960): 243–45.

Bratcher, "Jews." Bratcher, Robert G. "'The Jews' in the Gospel of John." *BTr* 26 (4, 1975): 401–9.

Bratcher and Nida, *Handbook on Mark*. Bratcher, Robert G., and Eugene A. Nida. *A Translator's Handbook on the Gospel of Mark*. Leiden: Brill, for the United Bible Societies, 1961.

Brathwaite, "Tongues." Brathwaite, Renea. "Tongues and Ethics: William J. Seymour and the 'Bible Evidence': A Response to Cecil M. Robeck, Jr." *Pneuma* 32 (2010): 203–22.

Braun, "Beobachtungen." Braun, Herbert. "Beobachtungen zur Tora-Vershärfung im häretischen Spätjudentum." *TLZ* 79 (6, 1954): 347–52.

Braun, *Here*. Braun, Willys K. *Here Am I: An Autobiography*. Wilmore, Ky.: Evangelism Resources, 2003.

Braun, *Jean*. Braun, François-Marie. *Jean le théologien et son évangile dans l'Église ancienne*. EtBib. Paris: Lecoffre, 1959.

Braun, "Prophet." Braun, M. "The Prophet Who Became a Historian." *Listener* 56 (1956): 53–57.

Braun, "Sacrifice d'Isaac." Braun, François-Marie. "Le sacrifice d'Isaac dans le quatrième évangile d'après le Targum." *NRTh* 101 (4, 1979): 481–97.

Braun, "Use of Amos." Braun, Michael A. "James' Use of Amos at the Jerusalem Council: Steps toward a Possible Solution of the Textual and Theological Problems." *JETS* 20 (2, 1977): 113–21.

Braun, *Way*. Braun, Thelma M. *On the Way: Joyful Jottings from a Missionary's Pen. A Devotional Autobiography*. Nappanee, Ind.: Evangel Publishing House, 2009.

Braund, "Misogamist." Braund, Susanna H. "Juvenal—Misogynist or Misogamist?" *JRS* 82 (1992): 71–86.

Bravo, "Antiquarianism." Bravo, Benedetto. "Antiquarianism and History." Pages 515–27 in *A Companion to Greek and Roman Historiography*. Edited by John Marincola. 2 vols. Oxford: Blackwell, 2007.

Brawley, "Abrahamic Traditions." Brawley, Robert L. "Abrahamic Covenant Traditions and the Characterization of God in Luke-Acts." Pages 109–32 in *The Unity of Luke-Acts*. Edited by Joseph Verheyden. BETL 142. Leuven: Leuven University Press, 1999.

Brawley, "Blessing." Brawley, Robert L. "For Blessing All Families of the Earth: Covenant Traditions in Luke-Acts." *CurTM* 22 (1, 1995): 18–26.

Brawley, "Borderlines." Brawley, Robert L. "Ethical Borderlines between Rejection and Hope: Interpreting the Jews in Luke-Acts." *CurTM* 27 (6, 2000): 415–23.

Brawley, *Centering on God*. Brawley, Robert L. *Centering on God: Method and Message in Luke-Acts*. Louisville: Westminster John Knox, 1990.

Brawley, "Commonwealth." Brawley, Robert L. "The Spirit, the Power, and the Commonwealth in Acts." *BibT* 37 (5, 1999): 268–75.

Brawley, *Luke-Acts and Jews*. Brawley, Robert L. *Luke-Acts and the Jews: Conflict, Apology, and Conciliation*. SBLMS 33. Atlanta: Scholars Press, 1987.

Brawley, "Paul in Acts." Brawley, Robert L. "Paul in Acts: Lucan Apology and Conciliation." Pages 129–47 in *Luke-Acts: New Perspectives from the Society of Biblical Literature Seminar*. Edited by Charles H. Talbert. New York: Crossroad, 1984.

Brawley, "Promises and Jews." Brawley, Robert L. "The God of Promises and the Jews in Luke-Acts." Pages 279–96

in *Literary Studies in Luke-Acts: Essays in Honor of Joseph B. Tyson*. Edited by Richard P. Thompson and Thomas E. Phillips. Macon, Ga.: Mercer University Press, 1998.

Brawley, "Social Identity." Brawley, Robert L. "Social Identity and the Aim of Accomplished Life in Acts 2." Pages 16–33 in *Acts and Ethics*. Edited by Thomas E. Phillips. NTMon 9. Sheffield, U.K.: Sheffield Phoenix, 2005.

Bray, "Ambrosiaster." Bray, Gerald. "Ambrosiaster." Pages 21–38 in *Reading Romans through the Centuries: From the Early Church to Karl Barth*. Edited by Jeffrey P. Greenman and Timothy Larsen. Grand Rapids: Brazos, 2005.

Bray, "Angel." Bray, Jasmine. "An Angel in the Ravine." *MounM* (July 1993): 16–17.

Bray, *Corinthians*. Bray, Gerald, ed. *1–2 Corinthians*. ACCS: New Testament 7. Downers Grove, Ill.: InterVarsity, 1999.

Bray, *Romans*. Bray, Gerald, ed. *Romans*. ACCS: New Testament 6. Downers Grove, Ill.: InterVarsity, 1998.

Brayer, "Psychosomatics." Brayer, Menahem M. "Psychosomatics, Hermetic Medicine, and Dream Interpretation in the Qumran Literature (Psychological and Exegetical Consideration)." *JQR* 60 (2, 1969): 112–27; 60 (3, 1970): 213–30.

Brayford, "Shame." Brayford, S. A. "To Shame or Not to Shame: Sexuality in the Mediterranean Diaspora." *Semeia* 87 (1999): 163–76.

Bredero, *Christendom*. Bredero, Adriaan H. *Christendom and Christianity in the Middle Ages*. Translated by Reinder Bruinsma. Grand Rapids: Eerdmans, 1994.

Bredow, "Dioscuri: Iconography." Bredow, Iris von. "Dioscuri: Iconography." *Brill Pauly* 4:520–22.

Bredow, "Neapolis." Bredow, Iris von. "Neapolis." *BrillPauly* 9:579–80.

Bredow, "Scythae." Bredow, Iris von. "Scythae." *BrillPauly* 13:149–60.

Brehm, "Significance of Summaries." Brehm, H. Alan. "The Significance of the Summaries for Interpreting Acts." *SWJT* 33 (1, 1990): 29–40.

Breiner, "Abuse Patterns." Breiner, Sander J. "Child Abuse Patterns: Comparison of Ancient Western Civilization and Traditional China." *APAP* 2 (1, 1985): 27–50.

Breitenbach, "Epos." Breitenbach, Alfred. "Epos." Pages 99–102 in vol. 1 of *Neues Testament und Antike Kultur*. Edited by K. Erlemann et al. 4 vols. Neukirchen-Vluyn: Neukirchener, 2004–5.

Brekus, "Catholics." Brekus, Catherine. "Catholics in America: The Test of 'Freedom of Religion.'" *ChH* 102 (2012): 12–15.

Bremback and Howell, *Persuasion*. Bremback, Winston L., and William S. Howell. *Persuasion: A Means of Social Influence*. 2nd ed. Englewood Cliffs, N.J.: Prentice-Hall, 1976.

Bremmer, "Attis." Bremmer, Jan N. "Attis: A Greek God in Anatolian Pessinous and Catullan Rome." *Mnemosyne* 57 (5, 2004): 534–73.

Bremmer, "Birth." Bremmer, Jan N. "The Birth of the Term 'Magic.'" *ZPE* 126 (1999): 1–12.

Bremmer, "Divination: Greek." Bremmer, Jan N. "Divination: Greek." *BrillPauly* 4:569–74.

Bremmer, "Gorgo." Bremmer, Jan N. "Gorgo." *BrillPauly* 5:937–38.

Bremmer, "Nymph." Bremmer, Jan N. "Nymph." Pages 635–36 in *Dictionary of Deities and Demons in the Bible*. 2nd rev. ed. Edited by Karel van der Toorn, Bob Becking, and Pieter W. van der Horst. Leiden: Brill; Grand Rapids: Eerdmans, 1999.

Bremmer, "Poseidon." Bremmer, Jan. "Poseidon. I. Myth and Cult." *BrillPauly* 11:673–77.

Bremmer, "Snake." Bremmer, Jan N. "Snake: Myth and Religion." *BrillPauly* 13:556–58.

Brenk, "Art." Brenk, Beat. "Art and *Propaganda fide*: Christian Art and Architecture, 300–600." Pages 691–725 in *Constantine to c. 600*. Edited by Augustine Casiday and Frederick W. Norris. Vol. 2 of *The Cambridge History of Christianity*. 9 vols. Cambridge: Cambridge University Press, 2007.

Brenk, "Doctrine." Brenk, Frederick E. "A Most Strange Doctrine: *Daimon* in Plutarch." *CJ* 69 (1973–74): 1–11.

Brenk, "Exorcism." Brenk, Frederick E. "The Exorcism at Philippi in Acts 16.11–40: Divine Possession or Diabolic Inspiration?" *FilNeot* 13 (25–26, 2000): 3–21.

Brenk, "Image." Brenk, Frederick. "Image and Religion: A Christian in the Temple of Isis at Pompeii." Pages 218–38 in *Text, Image, and Christians in the Graeco-Roman World: A Festschrift in Honor of David Lee Balch*. Edited by Aliou Cissé Niang and Carolyn Osiek. PrTMS 176. Eugene, Ore.: Pickwick, 2012.

Brenk and Canali De Rossi, "Felix." Brenk, Frederick E., and Filippo Canali De Rossi. "The 'Notorious' Felix, Procurator of Judaea, and His Many Wives (Acts 23–24)." *Bib* 82 (3, 2001): 410–17.

Brennan, "*Cursus honorum*." Brennan, T. Corey. "*Cursus honorum*." *OCD³* 415.

Brennan, "Epicurus." Brennan, Tad. "Epicurus on Sex, Marriage, and Children." *CP* 91 (4, 1996): 346–52.

Brennan, "Poets." Brennan, T. Corey. "The Poets Julia Balbilla and Damo at the Colossus of Memnon." *CW* 91 (4, 1998): 215–34.

Brennan, *Stoic Life*. Brennan, Tad. *The Stoic Life: Emotions, Duties, and Fate*. New York: Oxford University Press; Oxford: Clarendon, 2005.

Brennan, "Theory." Brennan, Tad. "The Old Stoic Theory of Emotions." Pages 21–70 in *The Emotions in Hellenistic Philosophy*. Edited by Juha Sihvola and Troels Engberg-Pedersen. TSHP 46. Dordrecht, Neth.: Kluwer Academic, 1998.

Brenner, "True to Form." Brenner, Charles Sandy. "Herod the Great Remains True to Form." *NEA* 64 (4, 2001): 212–14.

Brent, "Cult." Brent, Allen. "Luke-Acts and the Imperial Cult in Asia Minor." *JTS* 48 (2, 1997): 411–38.

Brentjes, "China." Brentjes, Burchard. "China." *BrillPauly* 3:229.

Brewer, "Group Dynamics." Brewer, Earl D. C. "How to Evangelize through Group Dynamics in the Local Church." In *A Year of Evangelism in the Local Church*. Edited by Gordon Pratt Baker and Edward Ferguson Jr. Nashville: Tidings, 1960.

Breytenbach, "Hypsistos." Breytenbach, Cilliers. "Hypsistos." Pages 439–43 in *Dictionary of Deities and Demons in the Bible*. 2nd rev. ed. Edited by Karel van der Toorn, Bob Becking, and Pieter W. van der Horst. Leiden: Brill; Grand Rapids: Eerdmans, 1999.

Breytenbach, "Proclamation." Breytenbach, Cilliers. "Paul's Proclamation and God's 'thriambos' (Notes on 2 Corinthians 2:14–16b)." *Neot* 24 (2, 1990): 257–71.

Breytenbach, *Provinz*. Breytenbach, Cilliers. *Paulus und Barnabas in der Provinz Galatien: Studien zu Apostelgeschichte 13f.; 16,6; 18,23 und den Adressaten des Galaterbriefes*. Leiden: Brill, 1996.

Breytenbach, "Reasons." Breytenbach, Cilliers. "Probable Reasons for Paul's Unfruitful Missionary Attempts in Asia Minor (A Note on Acts 16:6–7)." Pages 157–69 in *Die Apostelgeschichte und die hellenistische Geschichtsschreibung: Festschrift für Eckhard Plümacher zu seinem 65. Geburtstag*. Edited by Cilliers Breytenbach and Jens Schröter. Leiden: Brill, 2004.

Breytenbach, *Versöhnung*. Breytenbach, Cilliers. *Versöhnung: Eine Studie zur paulinischen Soteriologue*. WMANT 60. Neukirchen-Vluyn: Neukirchener Verlag, 1989.

Breytenbach, "Versöhnung." Breytenbach, Cilliers. "Versöhnung, Stellvertretung, und Sühne: Semantische und traditionsgeschichtliche Bemerkungen am Beispiel der paulinischen Briefe." *NTS* 39 (1, 1993): 59–79.

Breytenbach, "Zeus und Gott." Breytenbach, Cilliers. "Zeus und der lebendige Gott: Anmerkungen zu Apostelgeschichte 14.11–17." *NTS* 39 (3, 1993): 396–413.

Breytenbach and Day, "Satan." Breytenbach, Cilliers, and Peggy L. Day. "Satan." Pages 726–32 in *Dictionary of Deities and Demons in the Bible*. 2nd rev. ed. Edited by Karel van der Toorn, Bob Becking, and Pieter W. van der Horst. Leiden: Brill; Grand Rapids: Eerdmans, 1999.

Bricault, "Deities." Bricault, L. "Deities from Egypt on Coins of the Southern Levant." *IsNumR* 1 (2006): 123–36 and plates 17–19.

Brickhouse and Smith, "Sign." Brickhouse, Thomas C., and Nicholas D. Smith. "'The Divine Sign Did Not Oppose Me': A Problem in Plato's *Apology*." *CJP* 16 (1985): 511–26.

Briese, "Ostrich Eggs." Briese, Christoph. "Ostrich Eggs." *BrillPauly* 10:290–91.

Bright, "Augustine." Bright, Pamela. "Augustine." Pages 59–80 in *Reading Romans through the Centuries: From the Early Church to Karl Barth*. Edited by Jeffrey P. Greenman and Timothy Larsen. Grand Rapids: Brazos, 2005.

Bright, *History*. Bright, John. *A History of Israel*. 3rd ed. Philadelphia: Westminster, 1981.

Brighton, *Sicarii*. Brighton, Mark Andrew. *The Sicarii in Josephus's Judean War: Rhetorical Analysis and Historical Observations*. SBLEJL 27. Atlanta: SBL, 2009.

Brighton, "Sicarii." Brighton, Mark Andrew. "The Sicarii in Acts: A New Perspective." *JETS* 54 (3, Sept. 2011): 547–58.

Brin, "Uses." Brin, Gershon. "Concerning Some of the Uses of the Bible in the Temple Scroll." *RevQ* 12 (4, 1987): 519–28.

Brindle, "Census." Brindle, Wayne. "The Census and Quirinius: Luke 2:2." *JETS* 27 (1, 1984): 43–52.

Brindle, "Jew First." Brindle, Wayne A. "'To the Jew First': Rhetoric, Strategy, History, or Theology?" *BSac* 159 (634, 2002): 221–33.

Bringmann, "Tetraches." Bringmann, Klaus. "Tetraches, Tetrachia." *BrillPauly* 14:322–23.

Brink, "Proof." Brink, Laurie. "Luke's Narrative Proof of the Resurrection: The Coming of the Spirit." *New Theology Review* 23 (2, 2010): 77–79.

Brinks, "Artemis." Brinks, C. L. "'Great Is Artemis of the Ephesians': Acts 19:23–41 in Light of Goddess Worship in Ephesus." *CBQ* 71 (4, 2009): 776–94.

Brinsmead, *Galatians*. Brinsmead, Bernard Hungerford. *Galatians, Dialogical*

Response to Opponents. SBLDS 65. Chico, Calif.: Scholars Press, 1982.

Briquel, "Divination: Rome." Briquel, Dominique. "Divination: Rome." *Brill Pauly* 4:574–77.

Brisson, "Nature." Brisson, Luc. "Nature, Natural Philosophy." *BrillPauly* 9:529–36.

Brixhe, *Essai sur grec anatolien.* Brixhe, Claude. *Essai sur le grec anatolien au début de notre ère.* Travaux et mémoires: Études anciennes 1. Nancy: Presses Universitaires de Nancy, 1987.

Broadhead, "Priests." Broadhead, Edwin K. "Jesus and the Priests of Israel." Pages 125–44 in *Jesus from Judaism to Christianity: Continuum Approaches to the Historical Jesus.* Edited by Tom Holmén. EurSCO; LNTS 352. London: T&T Clark, 2007.

Brock, "Magdalene." Brock, Ann G. "Jesus, Mary Magdalene, and Other Women: Reflections on How to Work Historically in Light of an Open Canon." Paper presented at the second Princeton-Prague Symposium on Jesus: Methodological Approaches to the Historical Jesus, Princeton, Apr. 20, 2007.

Brock and Scott, *Criticism.* Brock, Bernard L., and Robert L. Scott. *Methods of Rhetorical Criticism: A Twentieth-Century Perspective.* 2nd ed. Detroit: Wayne State University Press, 1980.

Brocke, *Thessaloniki.* Brocke, Christoph vom. *Thessaloniki—Stadt der Kassander und Gemeinde des Paulus: Eine frühe christliche Gemeinde in ihrer heidnischen Umwelt.* WUNT 2.125. Tübingen: Mohr Siebeck, 2001.

Brockman, "Braide." Brockman, Norbert. "Braide, garrick Sokari Marian." No pages. *DACB.* Online: http://www.dacb.org /stories/nigeria/braide1_garrick.html.

Brockman, "Kimbangu." Brockman, Norbert. "Simon Kimbangu." No pages. *DACB.* Online: http://www.dacb.org /stories/demrepcongo/kimbangu1 _simon.html.

Brockman, "Kivuli." Brockman, Norbert. "Kivuli, David Zakayo." No pages. *DACB.* Online: http://www.dacb.org/stories /kenya/kivulidavidz1.html.

Brockmann, "Apostelkonzil." Brockmann, Thomas. "Luther und das Apostelkonzil (Apg 15)." *ZKG* 114 (3, 2003): 303–22.

Brodersen, "Seven Wonders." Brodersen, Kai. "Seven Wonders of the Ancient World." *OCD³* 1397.

Brodie, "2 Kgs 5 as Component." Brodie, Thomas L. "Towards Unraveling the Rhetorical Imitation of Sources in Acts: 2 Kgs 5 as One Component of Acts 8,9–40." *Bib* 67 (1986): 41–67.

Brodie, "Division and Reconciliation." Brodie, Thomas L. "Luke's Redesigning of Paul: Corinthian Division and Reconciliation (1 Corinthians 1–5) as One Component of Jerusalem Unity (Acts 1–5)." *IBS* 17 (3, 1995): 98–128.

Brodie, "Emulation." Brodie, Thomas L. "Luke-Acts as an Imitation and Emulation of the Elijah-Elisha Narrative." Pages 78–85 in *New Views on Luke and Acts.* Edited by Earl Richard. Collegeville, Minn.: Liturgical Press, 1990.

Brodie, "Imitation of Texts." Brodie, Thomas L. "Greco-Roman Imitation of Texts as a Partial Guide to Luke's Use of Sources." Pages 17–46 in *Luke-Acts: New Perspectives from the Society of Biblical Literature Seminar.* Edited by Charles H. Talbert. New York: Crossroad, 1984.

Brodie, "Stoning of Naboth." Brodie, Thomas L. "The Accusing and Stoning of Naboth (1 Kgs 21:8–13) as One Component of the Stephen Text (Acts 6:9–14; 7:58a)." *CBQ* 45 (3, 1983): 417–32.

Brodie, "Unravelling." Brodie, Thomas L. "Towards Unravelling Luke's Use of the Old Testament: Luke 7.11–17 as an *imitatio* of 1 Kings 17.17–24." *NTS* 32 (2, 1986): 247–67.

Broer, "Death." Broer, Ingo. "The Death of Jesus from a Historical Perspective." Pages 145–68 in *Jesus from Judaism to Christianity: Continuum Approaches to the Historical Jesus.* Edited by Tom Holmén. EurSCO; LNTS 352. London: T&T Clark, 2007.

Broggiato, "Artemon." Broggiato, Maria. "Artemon of Pergamum (FGrH 569): A Historian in Context." *CQ* 61 (2, 2011): 545–52.

Brondos, "Luther." Brondos, David A. "Did Paul Get Luther Right?" *Dial* 46 (1, 2007): 24–30.

Broneer, "Athens." Broneer, Oscar. "Athens, City of Idol Worship." *BA* 21 (1, 1958): 2–28.

Broneer, "Contests." Broneer, Oscar. "Where Athletic Contests Were Linked with Underground Vows and Burnt Sacrifices of Oxen: The Shrines of Corinth's Isthmian Games." *Illustrated London News* 234 (Feb. 28, 1959): 342–43.

Broneer, "Corinth." Broneer, Oscar. "Corinth: Center of Paul's Missionary Work in Greece." *BA* 14 (4, 1951): 78–96.

Broneer, "Crown." Broneer, Oscar. "The Isthmian Victory Crown." *AJA* 66 (3, 1962): 259–63.

Broneer, "Games." Broneer, Oscar. "The Apostle Paul and the Isthmian Games." *BA* 25 (1, 1962): 2–31.

Broneer, *Lamps Corinth.* Broneer, Oscar. *Terracotta Lamps.* Vol. 4, part 2, of *Corinth: Results of Excavations Conducted by the American School of Classical Studies at Athens.* Cambridge, Mass.: Harvard University Press, 1930.

Broneer, *Lamps Isthmia.* Broneer, Oscar. *Terracotta Lamps.* Vol. 3 of *Isthmia: Excavations by the University of Chicago under the Auspices of the American School of Classical Studies at Athens.* Princeton: American School of Classical Studies at Athens, 1977.

Broneer, *Temple of Poseidon.* Broneer, Oscar. *Temple of Poseidon.* Vol. 1 of *Isthmia: Excavations by the University of Chicago under the Auspices of the American School of Classical Studies at Athens.* Princeton: American School of Classical Studies at Athens, 1971.

Bronner, "Prophetesses through Rabbinic Lenses." Bronner, Leila L. "Biblical Prophetesses through Rabbinic Lenses." *Judaism* 40 (2, 1991): 171–83.

Brooke, "4Q174." Brooke, George J. "Florilegium (4Q174)." *DNTB* 378–80.

Brooke, "4Q175." Brooke, George J. "Testimonia (4Q175)." *DNTB* 1205–7.

Brooke, "Beatitudes." Brooke, George J. "The Wisdom of Matthew's Beatitudes (4QBeat and Mt. 5:3–12)." *ScrB* 19 (1989): 35–41.

Brooke, "Interpretation." Brooke, George J. "Eschatological Bible Interpretation in the Scrolls and in the New Testament." *Mishkan* 44 (2005): 18–25.

Brooke, "Pesharim." Brooke, George J. "Pesharim." *DNTB* 778–82.

Brooke, "Pesher." Brooke, George J. "Qumran Pesher: Towards the Redefinition of a Genre." *RevQ* 10 (4, 1981): 483–503.

Brooke, "Science." Brooke, John Hedley. "Science and Theology in the Enlightenment." Pages 7–27 in *Religion and Science: History, Method, Dialogue.* Edited by W. Mark Richardson and Wesley J. Wildman. Foreword by Ian G. Barbour. New York: Routledge, 1996.

Brookins, "Name." Brookins, Timothy A. "The (In)frequency of the Name 'Erastus' in Antiquity: A Literary, Papyrological, and Epigraphical Catalog." *NTS* 59 (4, Oct. 2013): 496–516.

Broom and Selznick, *Sociology.* Broom, Leonard, and Philip Selznick. *Sociology: A Text with Adapted Readings.* 3rd ed. New York: Harper & Row, 1963.

Brooten, "Paul and Law." Brooten, Bernadette J. "Paul and the Law: How Complete Was the Departure?" *PSB,* supplementary issue 1 (1990): 71–89.

Brooten, "Segregated." Brooten, Bernadette J. "Were Women and Men Segregated in Ancient Synagogues?" *Moment* 14 (7, 1989): 32–39.

Brooten, *Women Leaders*. Brooten, Bernadette J. *Women Leaders in the Ancient Synagogue: Inscriptional Evidence and Background Issues*. Chico, Calif.: Scholars Press, 1982.

Brosend, "Means." Brosend, William F., II. "The Means of Absent Ends." Pages 348–62 in *History, Literature, and Society in the Book of Acts*. Edited by Ben Witherington III. Cambridge: Cambridge University Press, 1996.

Broshi, "Credibility of Josephus." Broshi, Magen. "The Credibility of Josephus." *JJS* 33 (1–2, 1982): 379–84.

Broshi, "Date Beer." Broshi, Magen. "Date Beer and Date Wine in Antiquity." *PEQ* 139 (1, 2007): 55–59.

Broshi, "Dimensions." Broshi, Magen. "The Gigantic Dimensions of the Visionary Temple in the Temple Scroll." *BAR* 13 (6, 1987): 36–37.

Broshi, "Essenes." Broshi, Magen. "Essenes at Qumran? A Rejoinder to Albert Baumgarten." *DSD* 14 (1, 2007): 25–33.

Broshi, "Estimating." Broshi, Magen. "Estimating the Population of Ancient Jerusalem." *BAR* 4 (2, 1978): 10–15.

Broshi, "Population de l'ancienne Jérusalem." Broshi, Magen. "La population de l'ancienne Jérusalem." *RB* 82 (1, 1975): 5–14.

Broughton, "Asia Minor." Broughton, T. R. S. "Roman Asia Minor." Pages 499–918 in vol. 4 of *An Economic Survey of Ancient Rome*. Edited by T. Frank, et al. 6 vols. Baltimore: Johns Hopkins University Press, 1933–40.

Broughton, "Roman Army." Broughton, T. R. S. "The Roman Army." *BegChr* 5:427–41.

Broughton and Mitchell, "Pontus." Broughton, T. R. S., and Stephen Mitchell. "Pontus." *OCD³* 1220.

Brown, *Apostasy*. Brown, Schuyler. *Apostasy and Perseverance in the Theology of Luke*. Rome: Pontifical Biblical Institute Press, 1969.

Brown, "Aristarchus." Brown, Andrew L. "Aristarchus (3)." *OCD³* 159.

Brown, "Awakenings." Brown, Candy Gunther. "Global Awakenings: Divine Healing Networks and Global Community in North America, Brazil, Mozambique, and Beyond." Pages 351–69 in *Global Pentecostal and Charismatic Healing*. Edited by Candy Gunther Brown. Foreword by Harvey Cox. Oxford: Oxford University Press, 2011.

Brown, "'Baptism' and 'Baptism.'" Brown, S. "'Water Baptism' and 'Spirit-Baptism' in Luke-Acts." *AThR* 59 (1977): 135–51.

Brown, *Birth*. Brown, Raymond E. *The Birth of the Messiah: A Commentary on the Infancy Narratives in Matthew and Luke*. Garden City, N.Y.: Doubleday, 1977.

Brown, *Blood*. Brown, Michael L. *Our Hands Are Stained with Blood*. Shippensburg, Pa.: Destiny Image, 1992.

Brown, "Burial." Brown, Raymond E. "The Burial of Jesus (Mark 15:42–47)." *CBQ* 50 (1988): 233–45.

Brown, *Communication*. Brown, Jeannine K. *Scripture as Communication: Introducing Biblical Hermeneutics*. Grand Rapids: Baker Academic, 2007.

Brown, *Death*. Brown, Raymond E. *The Death of the Messiah—From Gethsemane to Grave: A Commentary on the Passion Narratives in the Four Gospels*. 2 vols. New York: Doubleday, 1994.

Brown, "Deliverance." Brown, Schuyler. "Deliverance from the Crucible: Some Further Reflexions on 1QH iii.1–18." *NTS* 14 (2, 1968): 247–59.

Brown, "Elements." Brown, John Pairman. "Yahweh, Zeus, Jupiter: The High God and the Elements." *ZAW* 106 (2, 1994): 175–97.

Brown, *Essays*. Brown, Raymond E. *New Testament Essays*. Garden City, N.Y.: Doubleday, 1968.

Brown, *Global Healing*. Brown, Candy Gunther, editor. *Global Pentecostal and Charismatic Healing*. Foreword by Harvey Cox. Oxford: Oxford University Press, 2011.

Brown, *Healer*. Brown, Michael L. *Israel's Divine Healer*. Studies in Old Testament Biblical Theology. Grand Rapids: Zondervan, 1995.

Brown, *Historians*. Brown, Truesdell S. *The Greek Historians*. Lexington, Mass.: D. C. Heath, 1973.

Brown, *Israel and Greece*. Brown, John Pairman. *Ancient Israel and Ancient Greece: Religion, Politics, and Culture*. Minneapolis: Fortress, 2003.

Brown, *John*. Brown, Raymond E. *The Gospel according to John*. 2 vols. AB 29, 29A. Garden City, N.Y.: Doubleday, 1966–70.

Brown, "Kingship." Brown, John Pairman. "From Divine Kingship to Dispersal of Power in the Mediterranean City-State." *ZAW* 105 (1, 1993): 62–86.

Brown, *Late Antiquity*. Brown, Peter. *The World of Late Antiquity*. London: Thames & Hudson, 1971.

Brown, "Messianism." Brown, Raymond E. "The Messianism of Qumran." *CBQ* 19 (1, 1957): 53–82.

Brown, *Miracles*. Brown, Colin. *Miracles and the Critical Mind*. Grand Rapids: Eerdmans; Exeter: Paternoster, 1984.

Brown, "Mysterion." Brown, Raymond E. "The Semitic Background of the New Testament *mysterion*." *Bib* 39 (1958): 426–48; 40 (1959): 70–87.

Brown, *Mystery*. Brown, Raymond E. *The Semitic Background of the Term "Mystery" in the New Testament*. Philadelphia: Fortress, 1968.

Brown, "Parallels." Brown, John Pairman. "Synoptic Parallels in the Epistles and Form-History." *NTS* 10 (1, 1963): 27–48.

Brown, "Parasite." Brown, Peter George McCarthy. "Parasite." *OCD³* 1112.

Brown, "Privatization." Brown, John Pairman. "The Privatization of Greek Specialties in the Hellenistic World: Drama, Athletics, Citizenship." *RB* 112 (4, 2005): 536–66.

Brown, "Prologues." Brown, Schuyler. "The Role of the Prologues in Determining the Purpose of Luke-Acts." Pages 99–111 in *Perspectives on Luke-Acts*. ABPRSSS 5. Edited by Charles H. Talbert. Danville, Va.: Association of Baptist Professors of Religion; Edinburgh: T&T Clark, 1978.

Brown, "Resonance Perspective." Brown, Warren S. "Tuning the Faith: The Cornelius Story in Resonance Perspective." *PRSt* 33 (4, 2006): 449–65.

Brown, "Scrolls." Brown, Raymond E. "The Dead Sea Scrolls and the New Testament." Pages 1–8 in *John and Qumran*. Edited by James H. Charlesworth. London: Geoffrey Chapman, 1972.

Brown, "Stichomythia." Brown, Andrew L. "Stichomythia." *OCD³* 1443.

Brown, "Syria." Brown, Peter. "Town, Village, and Holy Man: The Case of Syria." Pages 213–20 in *Assimilation et résistance à la culture gréco-romaine dans le monde ancien: Travaux du VIe Congrès international d'études classiques*. Edited by D. M. Pippidi. FIAEC. Paris: Belles Lettres, 1976.

Brown, "Tent Meetings." Brown, Candy Gunther. "From Tent Meetings and Store-Front Healing Rooms to Walmarts and the Internet: Healing Spaces in the United States, the Americas, and the World, 1906–2006." *CH* 75 (3, 2006): 631–47.

Brown, *Testing Prayer*. Brown, Candy Gunther. *Testing Prayer: Science and Healing*. Cambridge: Harvard University Press, 2012.

Brown, "Theory of Development." Brown, Raymond E. "J. Starcky's Theory of Qumran Messianic Development." *CBQ* 28 (1, 1966): 51–57.

Brown, *Thought*. Brown, Colin. *From the Ancient World to the Age of the Enlightenment*. Vol. 1 of *Christianity and Western Thought: A History of Philosophers, Ideas and Movements*. 3 vols. Downers Grove, Ill.: IVP Academic, 1990.

Brown and Meier, *Antioch and Rome*. Brown, Raymond E., and John P. Meier. *Antioch and Rome: New Testament Cradles of Catholic Christianity*. New York: Paulist, 1983.

Brown, Donfried, and Reumann, *Peter.* Brown, Raymond E., Karl P. Donfried, and John Reumann, eds. *Peter in the New Testament.* New York: Paramus; Toronto: Paulist; Minneapolis: Augsburg, 1973.

Brown, Mory, Williams, and McClymond, "Effects." Brown, Candy Gunther, Stephen C. Mory, Rebecca Williams, and Michael J. McClymond. "Study of the Therapeutic Effects of Proximal Intercessory Prayer (STEPP) on Auditory and Visual Impairments in Rural Mozambique." *SMedJ* 103 (9, Sept. 2010): 864–69.

Browne, *Michigan Collection.* Browne, Gerald M. *Documentary Papyri from the Michigan Collection.* ASP 6. Toronto: A. M. Hakkert, 1970.

Browning, "Greek Diglossia." Browning, Robert. "Greek Diglossia Yesterday and Today." *IJSocLang* 35 (1982): 49–68.

Brownlee, "Comparison with Sects." Brownlee, William H. "A Comparison of the Covenanters of the Dead Sea Scrolls with Pre-Christian Jewish Sects." *BA* 13 (3, 1950): 49–68.

Brownlee, *Habakkuk.* Brownlee, William H. *The Text of Habakkuk in the Ancient Commentary from Qumran.* JBLMS 11. Philadelphia: SBL, 1959.

Brownlee, "Interpretation." Brownlee, William H. "Biblical Interpretation among the Sectaries of the Dead Sea Scrolls." *BA* 14 (3, 1951): 54–76.

Brownlee, "Light." Brownlee, William H. "Light on the Manual of Discipline (DSD) from the Book of Jubilees." *BASOR* 123 (Oct. 1951): 30–32.

Brownlee, "Messianic Motifs." Brownlee, William H. "Messianic Motifs of Qumran and the New Testament." *NTS* 3 (1, 1956): 12–30; (3, 1957): 195–210.

Brownlee, "Servant." Brownlee, William H. "The Servant of the Lord in the Qumran Scrolls, I." *BASOR* 132 (Dec. 1953): 8–15.

Brownson, "Introduction to *Anabasis.*" Brownson, Carleton L. Introduction to *Anabasis.* Pages 231–38 in vol. 2 of *Xenophon.* Translated by Carleton L. Brownson, O. J. Todd, and E. C. Marchant. 4 vols. LCL. New York: G. P. Putnam's Sons, 1918–23.

Brownson, "Introduction to *Hellenica.*" Brownson, Carleton L. Introduction to *Hellenica.* Pages vii–xi in vol. 1 of *Xenophon.* Translated by Carleton L. Brownson, O. J. Todd, and E. C. Marchant. 4 vols. LCL. New York: G. P. Putnam's Sons, 1918–23.

Brox, "Notizen." Brox, Norbert. "Zu den persönlichen Notizen der Pastoralbriefe." *BZ* 13 (1, 1969): 76–94.

Bruce, *Acts¹.* Bruce, F. F. *The Acts of the Apostles: The Greek Text with Introduction and Commentary.* 1st ed. Grand Rapids: Eerdmans, 1951.

Bruce, *Acts³.* Bruce, F. F. *The Acts of the Apostles: The Greek Text with Introduction and Commentary.* 3rd rev. and enl. ed. Grand Rapids: Eerdmans; Leicester, U.K.: Apollos, 1990.

Bruce, "All Things." Bruce, F. F. "'All Things to All Men': Diversity in Unity and Other Pauline Tensions." Pages 82–99 in *Unity and Diversity in New Testament Theology: Essays in Honor of George E. Ladd.* Edited by Robert A. Guelich. Grand Rapids: Eerdmans, 1978.

Bruce, "Apologetic and Purpose." Bruce, F. F. "Paul's Apologetic and the Purpose of Acts." *BJRL* 69 (1986–87): 379–93.

Bruce, *Apostle.* Bruce, F. F. *Paul: Apostle of the Heart Set Free.* Grand Rapids: Eerdmans, 1977.

Bruce, "Apostolic Succession." Bruce, F. F. "The True Apostolic Succession: Recent Study of the Book of Acts." *Interpretation* 13 (2, 1959): 131–43.

Bruce, *Books.* Bruce, F. F. *The Books and the Parchments.* Rev. ed. Old Tappan, N.J.: Fleming H. Revell, 1963.

Bruce, *Choice.* Bruce, Steve. *Choice and Religion: A Critique of Rational Choice Theory.* Oxford: Oxford University Press, 2000.

Bruce, *Commentary.* Bruce, F. F. *Commentary on the Book of the Acts: The English Text with Introduction, Exposition, and Notes.* NICNT. Grand Rapids: Eerdmans, 1977.

Bruce, *Corinthians.* Bruce, F. F. *1 and 2 Corinthians.* NCBC 38. Greenwood, S.C.: Attic; London: Marshall, Morgan & Scott, 1971.

Bruce, "Date of Mark." Bruce, F. F. "The Date and Character of Mark." Pages 69–89 in *Jesus and the Politics of His Day.* Edited by Ernst Bammel and C. F. D. Moule. Cambridge: Cambridge University Press, 1984.

Bruce, *Documents.* Bruce, F. F. *The New Testament Documents: Are They Reliable?* 5th rev. ed. Grand Rapids: Eerdmans; Leicester, U.K.: Inter-Varsity, 1981.

Bruce, *Epistles.* Bruce, F. F. *The Epistles to the Colossians, to Philemon, and to the Ephesians.* NICNT. Grand Rapids: Eerdmans, 1984.

Bruce, "Exposition." Bruce, F. F. "Biblical Exposition at Qumran." Pages 77–98 in *Studies in Midrash and Historiography.* Edited by R. T. France and David Wenham. Gospel Perspectives 3. Sheffield, U.K.: JSOT Press, 1983.

Bruce, "First Church Historian." Bruce, F. F. "The First Church Historian." Pages 1–14 in *Church, Word, and Spirit: Historical and Theological Essays in Honor of Geoffrey W.*

Bromiley. Edited by J. E. Bradley and R. A. Muller. Grand Rapids: Eerdmans, 1987.

Bruce, "'Hebrews' or 'Essenes.'" Bruce, F. F. "'To the Hebrews' or 'To the Essenes'?" *NTS* 9 (3, 1963): 217–32.

Bruce, *History.* Bruce, F. F. *New Testament History.* Garden City, N.Y.: Doubleday, 1972.

Bruce, "History." Bruce, F. F. "The History of New Testament Study." Pages 21–59 in *New Testament Interpretation: Essays on Principles and Methods.* Edited by I. Howard Marshall. Grand Rapids: Eerdmans, 1977.

Bruce, "Holy Spirit in Acts." Bruce, F. F. "The Holy Spirit in the Acts of the Apostles." *Interpretation* 27 (2, 1973): 166–83.

Bruce, "Jesus." Bruce, F. F. "Jesus and the Gospels in the Light of the Scrolls." Pages 70–82 in *The Scrolls and Christianity: Historical and Theological Significance.* Edited by Matthew Black. London: SPCK, 1969.

Bruce, "Lycaonia." Bruce, F. F. "Lycaonia." *ABD* 4:420–22.

Bruce, "Lycus Valley." Bruce, F. F. "Colossian Problems, Part 1: Jews and Christians in the Lycus Valley." *BSac* 141 (561, 1984): 3–15.

Bruce, "Matthew." Bruce, Alexander Balmain. "Matthew." Pages 61–340 in vol. 1 of *The Expositor's Greek Testament.* Edited by W. Robertson Nicoll. 5 vols. New York: Hodder & Stoughton, 1897–1910. Repr., Grand Rapids: Eerdmans, 1979.

Bruce, *Message.* Bruce, F. F. *The Message of the New Testament.* Grand Rapids: Eerdmans, 1981.

Bruce, *Mind.* Bruce, F. F. *A Mind for What Matters.* Grand Rapids: Eerdmans, 1990.

Bruce, "Myth." Bruce, F. F. "Myth and History." Pages 79–99 in *History, Criticism, and Faith.* Edited by Colin Brown. Downers Grove, Ill.: InterVarsity, 1976.

Bruce, "Name of Felix." Bruce, F. F. "The Full Name of the Procurator Felix." *JSNT* 1 (1978): 33–36.

Bruce, "New Testament and Classical Studies." Bruce, F. F. "The New Testament and Classical Studies." *NTS* 22 (3, 1976): 229–42.

Bruce, "Paul." Bruce, F. F. "Paul in Acts and Letters." Pages 679–92 in *Dictionary of Paul and His Letters.* Edited by R. P. Martin et al. Downers Grove, Ill.: InterVarsity, 1993.

Bruce, "Paul and Athenians." Bruce, F. F. "Paul and the Athenians." *ExpT* 88 (1, 1976): 8–12.

Bruce, "Paul's Use of Old Testament." Bruce, F. F. "Paul's Use of the Old Testament in Acts." Pages 71–79 in *Tradition and Interpretation in the New Testament: Essays in Honor of E. Earle Ellis for His 60th*

Birthday. Edited by Gerald F. Hawthorne and Otto Betz. Grand Rapids: Eerdmans; Tübingen: J. C. B. Mohr, 1987.

Bruce, *Peter*. Bruce, F. F. *Peter, Stephen, James, and John: Studies in Early Non-Pauline Christianity*. Grand Rapids: Eerdmans, 1979.

Bruce, "Philip and Ethiopian." Bruce, F. F. "Philip and the Ethiopian." *JSS* 34 (2, 1989): 377–86.

Bruce, "Phrygia." Bruce, F. F. "Phrygia." *ABD* 5:365–68.

Bruce, "Powers." Bruce, F. F. "Paul and 'The Powers That Be.'" *BJRL* 66 (2, 1984): 78–96.

Bruce, "Presentation of the Spirit." Bruce, F. F. "Luke's Presentation of the Spirit in Acts." *CrisTR* 5 (1, 1990): 15–29.

Bruce, "Real Paul?" Bruce, F. F. "Is the Paul of Acts the Real Paul?" *BJRL* 58 (2, 1976): 282–305.

Bruce, "Record or Reconstruction?" Bruce, F. F. "The Acts of the Apostles: Historical Record or Theological Reconstruction?" *ANRW* 25.3:2569–603. Part 2, *Principat*, 25.3. Edited by H. Temporini and W. Haase. Berlin: de Gruyter, 1985.

Bruce, *Speeches in Acts*. Bruce, F. F. *The Speeches in the Acts of the Apostles*. London: Tyndale, 1942.

Bruce, "Speeches Thirty Years After." Bruce, F. F. "The Speeches in Acts—Thirty Years After." Pages 53–68 in *Reconciliation and Hope*. Edited by Robert Banks. Grand Rapids: Eerdmans, 1974.

Bruce, "Spirit in Apocalypse." Bruce, F. F. "The Spirit in the Apocalypse." Pages 333–44 in *Christ and Spirit in the New Testament: Studies in Honour of C. F. D. Moule*. Edited by Barnabas Lindars and Stephen S. Smalley. Cambridge: Cambridge University Press, 1973.

Bruce, "Spirit in Qumran Texts." Bruce, F. F. "Holy Spirit in the Qumran Texts." *ALUOS* 6 (1966): 49–55.

Bruce, *Thessalonians*. Bruce, F. F. *1 and 2 Thessalonians*. WBC 45. Waco: Word, 1982.

Bruce, *Thoughts*. Bruce, F. F. *Second Thoughts on the Dead Sea Scrolls*. Grand Rapids: Eerdmans, 1956.

Bruce, *Time*. Bruce, F. F. *The Time Is Fulfilled*. Grand Rapids: Eerdmans, 1978.

Bruce, "Trial." Bruce, F. F. "The Trial of Jesus in the Fourth Gospel." Pages 7–20 in vol. 1 of *Studies of History and Tradition in the Four Gospels*. Edited by R. T. France and David Wenham. 2 vols. Gospel Perspectives 1–2. Sheffield, U.K.: JSOT Press, 1980–81.

Brucker, "Wunder." Brucker, Ralph. "Die Wunder der Apostel." *ZNT* 4 (7, 2001): 32–45.

Bruckner, "History." Bruckner, L. I. "The History and Character of the Niasan People Movement in Indonesia." DMiss diss., Fuller Theological Seminary, 1979.

Brueggemann, "Amos IV 4–13." Brueggemann, Walter A. "Amos IV 4–13 and Israel's Covenant Worship." *VT* 15 (1, 1965): 1–15.

Brueggemann, "Intercessory Formula." Brueggemann, Walter A. "Amos' Intercessory Formula." *VT* 19 (4, 1969): 385–99.

Brueggemann, *Land*. Brueggemann, Walter. *The Land: Place as Gift, Promise, and Challenge in Biblical Faith*. 2nd ed. Minneapolis: Fortress, 2003.

Brug, "Lottery or Election?" Brug, John F. "Acts 1:26—Lottery or Election?" *WLQ* 95 (3, 1998): 212–14.

Brug, "Review." Brug, John F. Review of *The IVP Bible Background Commentary*. *WLQ* 92 (3, 1995): 237–38.

Bruggen, *Narratives*. Bruggen, Jakob van. *Christ on Earth: The Gospel Narratives as History*. Translated by Nancy Forest-Flier. Grand Rapids: Baker, 1998. Original Dutch edition, Kampen: J. H. Kok, 1987.

Bruner, *Theology*. Bruner, Frederick Dale. *A Theology of the Holy Spirit: The Pentecostal Experience and the New Testament Witness*. Grand Rapids: Eerdmans, 1970.

Bruni, "Spirito." Bruni, Giancarlo. "Lo Spirito Santo nella letteratura lucana." Pages 99–110 in *Le teologia narrativa di san Luca*. By Giovanni Leonardi et al. Credere oggi 119–20. Padua: Messaggero, 2000.

Bruns, *Art*. Bruns, J. Edgar. *The Art and Thought of John*. New York: Herder & Herder, 1969.

Brunt, "Cicero and Historiography." Brunt, P. A. "Cicero and Historiography." Pages 311–40 in ΦΙΛΙΑΣ ΧΑΡΙΝ: *Miscellanea di Studi Classici in Onore di Eugenio Manni*. Edited by M. José Fontana, Maria Teresa Piraino, and F. Paolo Rizzo. Rome: Bretschneider, 1980.

Brunt, "Romanization." Brunt, P. A. "The Romanization of the Local Ruling Classes in the Roman Empire." Pages 161–73 in *Assimilation et résistance à la culture gréco-romaine dans le monde ancien: Travaux du VIe Congrès international d'études classiques*. Edited by D. M. Pippidi. FIAEC. Paris: Belles Lettres, 1976.

Brusco, "Gender." Brusco, Elizabeth. "Gender and Power." Pages 74–92 in *Studying Global Pentecostalism: Theories and Methods*. Edited by Allan Anderson, Michael Bergunder, André Droogers, and Cornelis van der Laan. Anthropology of Christianity 10. Berkeley: University of California, 2010.

Brusco, *Machismo*. Brusco, Elizabeth E. *The Reformation of Machismo: Evangelical Conversion and Gender in Colombia*. Austin: University of Texas Press, 1995.

Bruun, "Isotopes." Bruun, Christer. "Water, Oxygen Isotopes, and Immigration to Ostia-Portus." *JRA* 23 (2010): 109–32.

Bryan, *Caesar*. Bryan, Christopher. *Render to Caesar: Jesus, the Early Church, and the Roman Superpower*. Oxford: Oxford University Press, 2005.

Bryan, "Hallel." Bryan, Christopher. "Shall We Sing Hallel in the Days of the Messiah? A Glance at John 2:1–3:21." *SLJT* 29 (1, 1985): 25–36.

Bryan, *Preface*. Bryan, Christopher. *A Preface to Romans: Notes on the Epistle in Its Literary and Cultural Setting*. New York: Oxford University Press, 2000.

Bryce, "Lycia." Bryce, Trevor R. "Lycia." *OEANE* 3:386–87.

Bryce, "Study." Bryce, David W. "'As in All the Churches of the Saints': A Text-Critical Study of 1 Corinthians 14:34,35." *LTJ* 31 (1, 1997): 31–39.

Bryce, "Terms." Bryce, T. R. "Two Terms of Relationship in the Lycian Inscriptions." *JNES* 37 (3, July 1978): 217–25.

Bryen, "Visibility." Bryen, Ari Z. "Visibility and Violence in Petitions from Roman Egypt." *GRBS* 48 (2, 2008): 181–200.

Bryen and Wypustek, "Evil Eyes." Bryen, Ari Z., and Andrzej Wypustek. "Gemellus' Evil Eyes (P.Mich. VI 423–424)." *GRBS* 49 (4, 2009): 535–55.

Bryson, "Angels." Bryson, Sue. "Angels among Us." *Guideposts* (July 1994): 46.

Buber, *Faith*. Buber, Martin. *The Prophetic Faith*. New York: Macmillan, 1949.

Buchanan, "Age." Buchanan, George Wesley. "The Age of Jesus." *NTS* 41 (2, 1995): 297.

Buchanan, *Consequences*. Buchanan, George Wesley. *The Consequences of the Covenant*. NovTSup 20. Leiden: Brill, 1970.

Buchanan, *Hebrews*. Buchanan, George Wesley. *To the Hebrews*. AB 36. Garden City, N.Y.: Doubleday, 1972.

Buchanan, "Office." Buchanan, George Wesley. "The Office of Teacher of Righteousness." *RevQ* 9 (2, 1977): 241–43.

Buchanan, "Purity." Buchanan, George Wesley. "The Role of Purity in the Structure of the Essene Sect." *RevQ* 4 (15/3, 1963): 397–406.

Bucher, "Evaluation." Bucher, Gregory S. "Toward a Literary Evaluation of Appian's Civil Wars, Book 1." Pages 454–60 in *A Companion to Greek and Roman Historiography*. Edited by John Marincola. 2 vols. Oxford: Blackwell, 2007.

Büchler, *Atonement*. Büchler, Adolf. *Studies in Sin and Atonement in the Rabbinic Literature of the First Century*. 1927. Repr., New York: KTAV, 1967.

Büchler, *Conditions*. Büchler, Adolf. *The Economic Conditions of Judaea after the Destruction of the Second Temple*. London: Jews' College Press, 1912.

Büchler, "Open Air." Büchler, Adolf. "Learning and Teaching in the Open Air in Palestine." *JQR* n.s. 4 (1913–14): 485–91.

Buchler and Selby, *Kinship*. Buchler, Ira R., and Henry A. Selby. *Kinship and Social Organization: An Introduction to Theory and Method*. New York: Macmillan, 1968.

Büchli, "Fides." Büchli, Jörg. "Fides: Christian." *BrillPauly* 5:417–18.

Büchner, "*Psh*." Büchner, Dirk. "*Psh*: Pass Over or Protect?" *BN* 86 (1997): 14–17.

Büchsel, *Geist*. Büchsel, D. Friedrich. *Der Geist Gottes im Neuen Testament*. Gütersloh: Bertelsmann, 1926.

Buckingham, *Daughter*. Buckingham, Jamie. *Daughter of Destiny: Kathryn Kuhlman... Her Story*. Plainfield, N.J.: Logos International, 1976.

Buckland, *Roman Law*. Buckland, W. W. *A Text-Book of Roman Law from Augustus to Justinian*. 3rd ed. Revised by Peter Stein. Cambridge: Cambridge University Press, 1963.

Buckland, *Slavery*. Buckland, W. W. *The Roman Law of Slavery: The Condition of the Slave in Private Law from Augustus to Justinian*. Cambridge: Cambridge University Press, 1908.

Buckwalter, *Christology*. Buckwalter, H. Douglas. *The Character and Purpose of Luke's Christology*. SNTSMS 89. Cambridge: Cambridge University Press, 1996.

Buckwalter, "Saviour." Buckwalter, H. Douglas. "The Divine Saviour." Pages 107–24 in *Witness to the Gospel: The Theology of Acts*. Edited by I. Howard Marshall and David Peterson. Grand Rapids: Eerdmans, 1998.

Budin, "Reconsideration." Budin, Stephanie L. "A Reconsideration of the Aphrodite-Ashtart Syncretism." *Numen* 51 (2, 2004): 95–145.

Buell, *Race*. Buell, Denise Kimber. *Why This New Race? Ethnic Reasoning in Early Christianity*. New York: Columbia University Press, 2005.

Bulgakov, *Relics*. Bulgakov, Sergius. *Relics and Miracles: Two Theological Essays*. Translated by Boris Jakim. Grand Rapids: Eerdmans, 2011.

Bull, "Caesarea." Bull, Robert J. "Caesarea Maritima—The Search for Herod's City." Pages 106–22 in *Archaeology in the World of Herod, Jesus and Paul*. Edited by Hershel Shanks and Dan P. Cole. Vol. 2 in Archaeology and the Bible: The Best of BAR. Washington, D.C.: Biblical Archaeology Society, 1990.

Bull, "Context." Bull, Robert J. "An Archaeological Context for Understanding John 4:20." *BA* 38 (1, 1975): 54–59.

Bull, "Mithraic Medallion." Bull, R. "A Mithraic Medallion from Caesarea." *IEJ* 24 (3–4, 1974): 187–90.

Bull, "Report XII." Bull, Robert J. "Field Report XII." *BASOR* 180 (Dec. 1965): 37–41.

Bull and Wright, "Temples." Bull, Robert J., and G. Ernest Wright. "Newly Discovered Temples on Mt. Gerizim in Jordan." *HTR* 58 (2, 1965): 234–37.

Bull et al., "Exorcism." Bull, Dennis L., et al. "Exorcism Revisited: Positive Outcomes with Dissociative Identity Disorder." *JPsyTh* 26 (2, 1998): 188–96.

Bullock, "Converted by Lightning?" Bullock, John D. "Was Saint Paul Struck Blind and Converted by Lightning?" *Survey of Opthalmology* 39 (2, 1994): 151–60.

Bultmann, *Christianity*. Bultmann, Rudolf. *Primitive Christianity in Its Contemporary Setting*. Translated by Reginald H. Fuller. New York: Meridian, 1956.

Bultmann, "Demythologizing." Bultmann, Rudolf. "On the Problem of Demythologizing (1952)." Pages 95–130 in *The New Testament and Mythology and Other Basic Writings*. Edited by Schubert Ogden. Philadelphia: Fortress, 1984.

Bultmann, "Exegesis." Bultmann, Rudolf. "Is Exegesis without Presuppositions Possible?" Pages 145–53 in *The New Testament and Mythology and Other Basic Writings*. Edited by Schubert Ogden. Philadelphia: Fortress, 1984.

Bultmann, "History and Eschatology." Bultmann, Rudolf. "History and Eschatology in the New Testament." *NTS* 1 (1, 1954): 5–16.

Bultmann, *Jesus and Word*. Bultmann, Rudolf. *Jesus and the Word*. Translated by Louise Pettibone Smith and Erminie Huntress Lantero. New York: Scribner's, 1958.

Bultmann, *John*. Bultmann, Rudolf. *The Gospel of John: A Commentary*. Translated by G. R. Beasley-Murray, R. W. N. Hoare, and J. K. Riches. Philadelphia: Westminster, 1971.

Bultmann, "Mythology." Bultmann, Rudolf. "New Testament and Mythology." Pages 1–43 in *The New Testament and Mythology and Other Basic Writings*. Edited by Schubert Ogden. Philadelphia: Fortress, 1984.

Bultmann, *Old and New Man*. Bultmann, Rudolf. *The Old and New Man in the Letters of Paul*. Translated by Keith R. Crim. Richmond, Va.: John Knox, 1967.

Bultmann, "Science." Bultmann, Rudolf. "Science and Existence." Pages 131–44 in *The New Testament and Mythology and Other Basic Writings*. Edited by Schubert Ogden. Philadelphia: Fortress, 1984.

Bultmann, *Second Corinthians*. Bultmann, Rudolf. *The Second Letter to the Corinthians*. Translated by Roy A. Harrisville. Minneapolis: Augsburg, 1985.

Bultmann, *Theology*. Bultmann, Rudolf. *Theology of the New Testament*. Translated by Kendrick Grobel. 2 vols. New York: Scribner's, 1951.

Bultmann, *Tradition*. Bultmann, Rudolf. *The History of the Synoptic Tradition*. Translated by John Marsh. 2nd ed. Oxford: Blackwell, 1968.

Bultmann, *Word*. Bultmann, Rudolf. *Jesus and the Word*. Translated by Louise Smith and Erminie Lantero. New York: Scribner's, 1958.

Bundy, "Irving." Bundy, D. D. "Irving, Edward." *DPCM* 470–71.

Bunine, "Félix." Bunine, Alexis. "Paul, Jacques, Félix, Festus, et les autres: Pour une révision de la chronologie des derniers procurateurs de la Palestine." *RB* 111 (3, 2004): 387–408; (4, 2004): 531–62.

Bunine, "Réception." Bunine, Alexis. "La réception des premiers païens dans l'Église: Le témoignage des Actes." *BLE* 108 (2, 2007): 259–88.

Bünker, "Disposition der Eleazarreden." Bünker, Michael. "Die rhetorische Disposition der Eleazarreden (Josephus, Bell. 7,323–388)." *Kairos* 23 (1–2, 1981): 100–107.

Burchard, *Dreizehnte Zeuge*. Burchard, Christoph. *Der dreizehnte Zeuge*. FRLANT 103. Göttingen: Vandenhoeck & Ruprecht, 1970.

Burchard, "Importance." Burchard, Christoph. "The Importance of Joseph and Aseneth for the Study of the New Testament: A General Survey and a Fresh Look at the Lord's Supper." *NTS* 33 (1, 1987): 102–34.

Burchard, "Introduction." Burchard, Christoph. Introduction to "Joseph and Asenath." *OTP* 2:177–201.

Burchard, "Note on 'PHMA." Burchard, Christoph. "A Note on 'PHMA in JosAs 17:1f.; Luke 2:15, 17; Acts 10:37." *NovT* 27 (4, 1985): 281–95.

Burckhardt, "Epibatai." Burckhardt, Leonhard. "Epibatai." *BrillPauly* 4:1038.

Buresch, *Klaros*. Buresch, Karl. *Klaros: Untersuchungen zum Orakelwesen des späteren Altertums*. Leipzig: Teubner, 1889. Repr., Allen: Scientia, 1973.

Burfeind, "*Muss* nach Rom." Burfeind, Carsten. "Paulus *muss* nach Rom: Zur politischen Dimension der Apostelgeschichte." *NTS* 46 (1, 2000): 75–91.

Burfeind, "Philippus." Burfeind, Carsten. "Wen hörte Philippus? Leises Lesen und lautes Vorlesen in der Antike." *ZNW* 93 (1–2, 2002): 138–45.

Burford, *Craftsmen*. Burford, Alison. *Craftsmen in Greek and Roman Society*. Aspects of Greek and Roman Life. London: Thames & Hudson; Ithaca, N.Y.: Cornell University Press, 1972.

Burford-Cooper, "Pitch." Burford-Cooper, Alison. "Pitch: II. Classical Antiquity." *BrillPauly* 11:304–5.

Burge, "Barnabas." Burge, Gary M. "Barnabas." *DPL* 66–67.

Burge, *Community*. Burge, Gary M. *The Anointed Community: The Holy Spirit in the Johannine Tradition*. Grand Rapids: Eerdmans, 1987.

Burgers, "Coinage." Burgers, P. "Coinage and State Expenditure: The Reign of Claudius, AD 41–54." *Historia* 50 (1, 2001): 96–114.

Burgess, "Evidence." Burgess, Stanley M. "Evidence of the Spirit: The Medieval and Modern Western Churches." Pages 20–40 in *Initial Evidence: Historical and Biblical Perspectives on the Pentecostal Doctrine of Spirit Baptism*. Edited by Gary B. McGee. Peabody, Mass.: Hendrickson, 1991.

Burgess, "Pandita Ramabai." Burgess, Ruth Vassar. "Pandita Ramabai: A Woman for All Seasons: Pandita Ramabai Saraswati Mary Dongre Medhavi (1858–1922)." *AJPS* 9 (2, 2006): 183–98.

Burgess, "Proclaiming." Burgess, Stanley M. "Proclaiming the Gospel with Miraculous Gifts in the Postbiblical Early Church." Pages 277–88 in *The Kingdom and the Power: Are Healing and the Spiritual Gifts Used by Jesus and the Early Church Meant for the Church Today?* Edited by Gary S. Greig and Kevin N. Springer. Ventura, Calif.: Regal, 1993.

Burgess, *Revolution*. Burgess, Richard. *Nigeria's Christian Revolution: The Civil War Revival and Its Pentecostal Progeny (1967–2006)*. RStMiss. Eugene, Ore.: Wipf & Stock, 2008.

Burgmann, "Lehrer." Burgmann, Hans. "Wer war der 'Lehrer der Gerechtigkeit'?" *RevQ* 10 (4, 1981): 553–78.

Burgmann, "Nordemigration." Burgmann, Hans. "Die Nordemigration hat stattgefunden." *FO* 28 (1991): 157–78.

Burian, "Itinerare." Burian, Jan. "Itinerare: Imperium Romanum." *BrillPauly* 6:1023–26.

Burke, "Adoption." Burke, Trevor. "Pauline Adoption: A Sociological Approach." *EvQ* 73 (2, 2001): 119–34.

Burkert, "Craft." Burkert, Walter. "Craft versus Sect: The Problem of Orphics and Pythagoreans." Pages 1–22 in *Self-Definition in the Greco-Roman World*. Edited by Ben F. Meyer and E. P. Sanders. Vol. 3 of *Jewish and Christian Self-Definition*. Edited by E. P. Sanders. Philadelphia: Fortress, 1982.

Burkert, *Mystery Cults*. Burkert, Walter. *Ancient Mystery Cults*. Carl Newell Jackson Lectures. Cambridge, Mass.: Harvard University Press, 1987.

Burkert, *Orphism*. Burkert, Walter, et al. *Orphism and Bacchic Mysteries: New Evidence and Old Problems of Interpretation*. Edited by W. Wuellner. PSCC 28. Berkeley, Calif.: Center for Hermeneutical Studies in Hellenistic and Modern Culture, 1977.

Burkert, *Religion*. Burkert, Walter. *Greek Religion*. Translated by John Raffan. Cambridge, Mass.: Harvard University Press, 1985.

Burkert, "Symposia." Burkert, Walter. "Oriental Symposia: Contrasts and Parallels." Pages 7–24 in *Dining in a Classical Context*. Edited by William J. Slater. Ann Arbor: University of Michigan Press, 1991.

Burkhardt, "Inspiration der Schrift." Burkhardt, Helmut. "Inspiration der Schrift durch weisheitliche Personalinspiration: Zur Inspirationlehre Philos von Alexandrien." *TZ* 47 (3, 1991): 214–25.

Burkitt, *Church and Gnosis*. Burkitt, F. Crawford. *The Church and Gnosis: A Study of Christian Thought and Speculation in the Second Century*. Morse Lectures for 1931. Cambridge: Cambridge University Press, 1932.

Burkitt, *Gospel History*. Burkitt, F. Crawford. *The Gospel History and Its Transmission*. Edinburgh: T&T Clark, 1907.

Burkitt, *Sources*. Burkitt, F. Crawford. *The Earliest Sources for the Life of Jesus*. Boston: Houghton Mifflin, 1910.

Burkitt, "Use of Mark." Burkitt, F. Crawford. "The Use of Mark in the Gospel according to Luke." *BegChr* 2:106–20.

Burnette-Bletsch, "Jael." Burnette-Bletsch, Rhonda. "At the Hands of a Woman: Rewriting Jael in Pseudo-Philo." *JSP* 17 (1998): 53–64.

Burney, *Aramaic Origin*. Burney, C. F. *The Aramaic Origin of the Fourth Gospel*. Oxford: Clarendon, 1922.

Burns, *Debate*. Burns, Robert M. *The Great Debate on Miracles: From Joseph Glanvill to David Hume*. Lewisburg, Pa.: Bucknell University Press, 1981.

Burns, "Hume and Miracles." Burns, Robert M. "David Hume and Miracles in Historical Perspective." PhD diss., Princeton University, 1971.

Burns, *Romans*. Burns, J. Patout, Jr., trans. and ed. *Romans: Interpreted by Early Christian Commentators*. The Church's Bible. Grand Rapids: Eerdmans, 2012.

Burrell, "Reading." Burrell, Barbara. "Reading, Hearing, and Looking at Ephesos." Pages 69–95 in *Ancient Literacies: The Culture of Reading in Greece and Rome*. Edited by William A. Johnson and Holt N. Parker. New York: Oxford University Press, 2009.

Burrell, Gleason, and Netzer, "Seaside Palace." Burrell, Barbara, Kathryn Gleason, and Ehud Netzer. "Uncovering Herod's Seaside Palace." *BAR* 19 (3, 1993): 50–57, 76.

Burridge, "Biography." Burridge, Richard A. "Biography." Pages 371–91 in *Handbook of Classical Rhetoric in the Hellenistic Period, 330 B.C.–A.D. 400*. Edited by Stanley E. Porter. Leiden: Brill, 1997.

Burridge, "Biography, Ancient." Burridge, Richard A. "Biography, Ancient." *DNTB* 167–70.

Burridge, "Genre of Acts." Burridge, Richard A. "The Genre of Acts—Revisited." Pages 3–28 in *Reading Acts Today: Essays in Honour of Loveday C. A. Alexander*. Edited by Steve Walton et al. LNTS 427. London: T&T Clark, 2011.

Burridge, *Gospels*. Burridge, Richard A. *What Are the Gospels? A Comparison with Graeco-Roman Biography*. SNTSMS 70. Cambridge: Cambridge University Press, 1992.

Burridge, "Gospels and Acts." Burridge, Richard A. "The Gospels and Acts." Pages 507–32 in *Handbook of Classical Rhetoric in the Hellenistic Period, 330 B.C.–A.D. 400*. Edited by Stanley E. Porter. Leiden: Brill, 1997.

Burridge, *New Earth*. Burridge, Kenelm. *New Heaven, New Earth*. Oxford: Blackwell, 1969.

Burridge, *One Jesus*. Burridge, Richard A. *Four Gospels, One Jesus? A Symbolic Reading*. Grand Rapids: Eerdmans, 1994.

Burridge, "People." Burridge, Richard A. "About People, by People, for People: Gospel Genre and Audiences." Pages 113–46 in *The Gospels for All Christians: Rethinking the Gospel Audiences*. Edited by Richard Bauckham. Grand Rapids: Eerdmans, 1998.

Burridge and Gould, *Jesus*. Burridge, Richard A., and Graham Gould, *Jesus Now and Then*. Grand Rapids: Eerdmans, 2004.

Burrows, *More Light*. Burrows, Millar. *More Light on the Dead Sea Scrolls*. New York: Viking, 1958.

Burrows, *Scrolls*. Burrows, Millar. *The Dead Sea Scrolls*. New York: Viking, 1955.

Burrus, "Acts." Burrus, Virginia. "The Gospel of Luke and the Acts of the Apostles." Pages 133–55 in *A Postcolonial*

Commentary on the New Testament Writings. Edited by Fernando F. Segovia and R. S. Sugirtharajah. London: T&T Clark, 2007.

Burstein, *African Civilizations.* Burstein, Stanley. *Ancient African Civilizations: Kush and Axum.* Princeton: Marcus Wiener, 1998.

Burton, *Blessing.* Burton, Keith Augustus. *The Blessing of Africa: The Bible and African Christianity.* Downers Grove, Ill.: InterVarsity, 2007.

Burton, "Commensality." Burton, Joan. "Women's Commensality in the Ancient Greek World." *GR* 45 (2, 1998): 143–65.

Burton, "*Immunitas.*" Burton, Graham Paul. "*Immunitas.*" *OCD*³ 749–50.

Burton, "Passover." Burton, William L. "The Passover." *BibT* 47 (2, 2009): 101–5.

Burton, "*Portoria.*" Burton, Graham Paul. "*Portoria.*" *OCD*³ 1228.

Burton, "State." Burton, Graham Paul. "The Roman Imperial State, Provincial Governors, and the Public Finances of Provincial Cities, 27 B.C.–A.D. 235." *Historia* 53 (3, 2004): 311–42.

Busch, "Presence." Busch, Austin. "Presence Deferred: The Name of Jesus and Self-Referential Eschatological Prophecy in Acts 3." *BibInt* 17 (5, 2009): 521–53.

Busenitz, "Understanding." Busenitz, Irvin A. "The Reformers' Understanding of Paul and the Law." *MSJ* 16 (2, 2005): 245–59.

Bush and Pegues, *Move.* Bush, Luis, and Beverly Pegues. *The Move of the Holy Spirit in the 10/40 Window.* Edited by Jane Rumph. Seattle: YWAM, 1999.

Buss, "Prophecy." Buss, Martin J. "Mari Prophecy and Hosea." *JBL* 88 (Sept. 1969): 338.

Buszard, "Speech." Buszard, Bradley. "The Speech of Greek and Roman Women in Plutarch's *Lives.*" *CP* 105 (1, 2010): 83–115.

Butcher, *Theory.* Butcher, S. H. *Aristotle's Theory of Poetry and Fine Art, with a critical text and translation of* The Poeticus. Preface on Aristotelian Literary Criticism by John Gassner. 4th ed. N.p.: Dover Publications, 1951.

Buth, "Aramaic Language." Buth, Randall J. "Aramaic Language." *DNTB* 86–91.

Buth, "ΒΟΝΕΡΕΓΕΜ." Buth, Randall. "Mark 3:17 ΒΟΝΕΡΕΓΕΜ and Popular Etymology." *JSNT* 10 (1981): 29–33.

Butler, *Dreams.* Butler, Sally A. L. *Mesopotamian Conceptions of Dreams and Dream Rituals.* AOAT 258. Münster: Ugarit, 1998.

Butler, "Materialization." Butler, Noah. "The Materialization of Magic: Islamic Talisman in West Africa." Pages 263–76 in *Studies in Witchcraft, Magic, War, and Peace in Africa.* Edited by Beatrice Nicolini. Lewiston, N.Y.: Edwin Mellen, 2006.

Butler, "Theory." Butler, Jon. "Theory and God in Gotham." *History and Theory* 45 (4, 2006): 47–61.

Butterweck, "Begegnung." Butterweck, Annelise. "Die Begegnung zwischen Esau und Jakob (Gen. 33,1–18) im Spiegel rabbinischer Ausdeutungen." *BN* 116 (2003): 15–27.

Butticaz, "Actes 3." Butticaz, Simon. "Actes 3,1–26. Le relèvement de l'infirme comme paradigme de la restauration d'Israël." *ETR* 84 (2, 2009): 177–88.

Butticaz, *Identité.* Butticaz, Simon David. *L'Identité de l'Église dans les Actes des apôtres: De la restauration d'Israël à la conquête universelle.* BZNW 174. Berlin: de Gruyter, 2011.

Butting, "Bedeutung." Butting, Klara. "Die Bedeutung der Rolle Rut im Judentum: Dem Messias die Tür öffnen." *BK* 54 (3, 1999): 113–16.

Butts, "Progymnasmata of Theon." Butts, James R., ed. "The Progymnasmata of Theon: A New Text with Translation and Commentary." PhD diss., Claremont Graduate School, 1987.

Buys and Nambala, "Hambuindja." Buys, Gerhard, and Shekutaamba Nambala. "Thusnelda Hambuindja." No pages. *DACB.* Online: http://www.dacb.org/stories/namibia/hambuindja_thusnelda.html.

Buys and Nambala, "Kanambunga." Buys, Gerhard, and Shekutaamba Nambala. "Alfeus Kanambunga." No pages. *DACB.* Online: http://www.dacb.org/stories/namibia/kanambunga_alfeus.html.

Buzzard, "Acts 1:6." Buzzard, Anthony. "Acts 1:6 and the Eclipse of the Biblical Kingdom." *EvQ* 66 (3, 1994): 197–215.

Buzzard, "Eclipse." Buzzard, Anthony. "Acts 1:6 and the Eclipse of the Biblical Kingdom." *Journal from the Radical Reformation* 16 (2, 2009): 3–21.

Byatt, "Population Numbers." Byatt, Anthony. "Josephus and Population Numbers in First Century Palestine." *PEQ* 105 (1, 1973): 51–60.

Byrne, "New Perspective." Byrne, Brendan. "Interpreting Romans: The New Perspective and Beyond." *Interpretation* 58 (3, 2004): 241–52.

Byrne, "Pre-existence." Byrne, Brendan. "Christ's Pre-existence in Pauline Soteriology." *TS* 58 (2, 1997): 308–30.

Byrne, *Romans.* Byrne, Brendan. *Romans.* SP 6. Collegeville, Minn.: Liturgical Press, 1996.

Byron, "Lineage." Byron, John. "Noble Lineage as a Response to Enslavement in the Testament of Naphtali 1.9–12." *JJS* 55 (1, 2004): 45–57.

Byron, "Paul and Background." Byron, John. "Paul and the Background of Slavery: The *status quaestionis* in New Testament Scholarship." *CBR* 3 (1, 2004): 116–39.

Byron, "Redrawing." Byron, Gay L. "Redrawing the Boundaries of Early Christianity: The Case of the Axumite Empire and Its Sources." Pages 135–41 in *A New Day: Essays on World Christianity in Honor of Lamin Sanneh.* Edited by Akintunde E. Akinade. Foreword by Andrew F. Walls. New York: Peter Lang, 2010.

Byrskog, "Co-senders." Byrskog, Samuel. "Co-senders, Co-authors, and Paul's Use of the First Person Plural." *ZNW* 87 (3–4, 1996): 230–50.

Byrskog, *History.* Byrskog, Samuel. *Story as History, History as Story: The Gospel Tradition in the Context of Ancient Oral History.* Tübingen: Mohr Siebeck, 2000. Repr., Boston: Brill, 2002.

Byrskog, "History." Byrskog, Samuel. "History or Story in Acts—A Middle Way? The "We" Passages, Historical Intertexture, and Oral History." Pages 257–83 in *Contextualizing Acts: Lukan Narrative and Greco-Roman Discourse.* Edited by Todd Penner and Caroline Vander Stichele. SBLSymS 20. Atlanta: SBL, 2003.

Caballero Cuesta, "Oración en Iglesia." Caballero Cuesta, J. M. "La oración en la Iglesia primitiva: Estudio sobre el libro de los Hechos de los apóstoles." *Burgense* 38 (1, 1997): 33–65.

Cabié, "Les 'sept.'" Cabié, R. "Quand les 'sept' deviennent des diacres." *BLE* 97 (3, 1996): 219–26.

Cadbury, *Acts in History.* Cadbury, Henry J. *The Book of Acts in History.* London: Adam & Charles Black, 1955.

Cadbury, "Commentary on Preface." Cadbury, Henry J. "Commentary on the Preface of Luke." *BegChr* 2:489–510.

Cadbury, "Dilemma." Cadbury, Henry J. "The Dilemma of Ephesians." *NTS* 5 (2, 1959): 91–102.

Cadbury, "Dust and Garments." Cadbury, Henry J. "Dust and Garments." *BegChr* 5:269–77.

Cadbury, "Eschatology." Cadbury, Henry J. "Acts and Eschatology." Pages 300–311 in *The Background of the New Testament and Its Eschatology: Essays in Honour of Charles Harold Dodd.* Edited by W. D. Davies and D. Daube. Cambridge: Cambridge University Press, 1964.

Cadbury, "Erastus." Cadbury, Henry J. "Erastus of Corinth." *JBL* 50 (2, 1931): 42–58.

Cadbury, "Features." Cadbury, Henry J. "Four Features of Lucan Style." Pages 87–102 in *Studies in Luke-Acts: Essays in*

Honor of Paul Schubert. Edited by Leander E. Keck and J. Louis Martyn. Nashville: Abingdon, 1966.

Cadbury, "Hellenists." Cadbury, Henry J. "The Hellenists." *BegChr* 5:59–74.

Cadbury, "Law and Trial." Cadbury, Henry J. "Roman Law and the Trial of Paul." *Beg Chr* 5:297–338.

Cadbury, "Lucius." Cadbury, Henry J. "Lucius of Cyrene." *BegChr* 5:489–95.

Cadbury, *Making*. Cadbury, Henry J. *The Making of Luke-Acts*. London: SPCK, 1968.

Cadbury, "Names for Christians." Cadbury, Henry J. "Names for Christians and Christianity in Acts." *BegChr* 5:375–92.

Cadbury, "Speeches." Cadbury, Henry J. "The Speeches in Acts." *BegChr* 5:402–27.

Cadbury, "Summaries." Cadbury, Henry J. "The Summaries in Acts." *BegChr* 5:392–402.

Cadbury, "Tradition." Cadbury, Henry J. "The Tradition." *BegChr* 2:209–64.

Cadbury, "ὑποζώματα." Cadbury, Henry J. "ὑποζώματα." *BegChr* 5:345–54.

Cadbury, "'We' in Luke-Acts." Cadbury, Henry J. "'We' and 'I' Passages in Luke-Acts." *NTS* 3 (2, 1957): 128–32.

Cadbury, Foakes-Jackson, and Lake, "Subsidiary Points." Cadbury, Henry J., F. J. Foakes-Jackson, and Kirsopp Lake. "Subsidiary Points." *BegChr* 2:349–59.

Cadbury, Foakes-Jackson, and Lake, "Writing History." Cadbury, Henry J., F. J. Foakes-Jackson, and Kirsopp Lake. "The Greek and Jewish Traditions of Writing History." *BegChr* 2:7–29.

Cadoux, "*Carcer*." Cadoux, Theodore J. "The Roman *carcer* and Its Adjuncts." *GR* 55 (2, 2008): 202–21.

Cadoux and Griffin, "Poppaea Sabina." Cadoux, Theodore John, and Miriam T. Griffin. "Poppaea Sabina." *OCD*³ 1221.

Cadoux and Rhodes, "Areopagus." Cadoux, Theodore John, and P. J. Rhodes. "Areopagus." *OCD*³ 151–52.

Cadoux and Tomlin, "*Praefectus urbi*." Cadoux, Theodore John, and R. S. O. Tomlin. "*Praefectus urbi*." *OCD*³ 1239.

Cagney, "Patrick." Cagney, Mary. "Patrick the Saint." *ChH* 60 (1998): 10–15.

Cagniart, "Attitude." Cagniart, Pierre. "Seneca's Attitude towards Sports and Athletics." *AHB* 14 (4, 2000): 162–70.

Caird, *Apostolic Age*. Caird, George B. *The Apostolic Age*. London: Gerald Duckworth, 1955.

Caird, "Expounding." Caird, George B. "Expounding the Parables, I: The Defendant (Matthew 5.25f.; Luke 12.58f.)" *ExpT* 77 (2, 1965): 36–39.

Caird, *Language*. Caird, G. B. *The Language and Imagery of the Bible*. Philadelphia: Westminster, 1980.

Caird, *Revelation*. Caird, George B. *A Commentary on the Revelation of Saint John the Divine*. HNTC. New York: Harper & Row, 1966.

Cairus, "Works-Righteousness." Cairus, Aecio E. "Works-Righteousness in the Biblical Narrative of Josephus." *ExpT* 115 (8, 2004): 257–59.

Calambrogio, "Saulo." Calambrogio, Leone. "Saulo: prima e dopo negli Atti degli Apostoli." *Laós* 16 (1, 2009): 41–44.

Calboli, "Asianism." Calboli, Gualtiero. "Asianism." *BrillPauly* 2:156–57.

Calboli, "Atticism." Calboli, Gualtiero. "Atticism." *BrillPauly* 2:324–25.

Calboli, "Genera." Calboli, Gualtiero. "Genera causarum." *BrillPauly* 5:749–51.

Calboli Montefusco, "Epilogue." Calboli Montefusco, Lucia. "Epilogue." *BrillPauly* 4:1110.

Calboli Montefusco, "Exercitatio." Calboli Montefusco, Lucia. "Exercitatio." *Brill Pauly* 5:265–66.

Calboli Montefusco, "Exordium." Calboli Montefusco, Lucia. "Exordium." *Brill Pauly* 5:272–73.

Calder, "Acts 14:12." Calder, William M. "Acts 14:12." *ExpT* 37 (11, 1926): 528.

Calder, "Cult of Homonades." Calder, William M. "A Cult of the Homonades." *CR* 24 (1910): 76–81.

Calder, "Introduction, 1." Calder, William M. Introduction. Pages ix–xxviii in vol. 1 of *Monumenta Asiae Minoris antiqua*. Edited by W. M. Calder et al. Manchester, U.K.: Manchester University Press; London: Longmans, Green, 1928–.

Calder, "Introduction, 7." Calder, William M. Introduction. Pages ix–xliii in vol. 7 of *Monumenta Asiae Minoris antiqua*. Edited by W. M. Calder et al. Manchester, U.K.: Manchester University Press; London: Longmans, Green, 1928–.

Calder, "Light on Baucis and Philemon." Calder, William M. "New Light on Ovid's Story of Baucis and Philemon." *Discovery* 3 (Aug. 1922): 207–11.

Calder, "Zeus and Hermes at Lystra." Calder, William M. "Zeus and Hermes at Lystra." *Exp* 7 (10, 1910): 1–6.

Calder and Mitchell, "Galatia." Calder, William Moir, and Stephen Mitchell. "Galatia." *OCD*³ 621.

Calder et al., "Ephesus." Calder, William Moir, et al. "Ephesus." *OCD*³ 528.

Calder, Gray, and Mitchell, "Asia." Calder, William Moir, Eric William Gray, and Stephen Mitchell. "Asia, Roman Province." *OCD*³ 189–90.

Calderón, "Lenguas." Calderón, Carlos. "¿Qué eran las lenguas en el pensamiento del apóstol Pablo? (Segunda de dos partes)." *Kairós* 42 (2008): 53–74.

Calderón, "Llenura." Calderón, Carlos. "¿Qué es la llenura del Espíritu Santo en Hechos?" *Kairós* 34 (2004): 27–41.

Caldwell, "Prayers." Caldwell, Debbie. "We Depend on Your Prayers." *MounM* (Nov. 1995): 5–6.

Callahan, "Witness." Callahan, Allen Dwight. "'Brother Saul': An Ambivalent Witness to Freedom." *Semeia* 83–84 (1998): 235–50.

Callahan and Horsley, "Resistance." Callahan, Allen Dwight, and Richard A. Horsley. "Slave Resistance in Classical Antiquity." *Semeia* 83–84 (1998): 133–51.

Callan, "Background of Decree." Callan, Terrance. "The Background of the Apostolic Decree (Acts 15:20, 29; 21:25)." *CBQ* 55 (2, 1993): 284–97.

Callan, "Preface and Historiography." Callan, Terrance. "The Preface of Luke-Acts and Historiography." *NTS* 31 (4, 1985): 576–81.

Callan, "Prophecy." Callan, Terrance. "Prophecy and Ecstasy in Greco-Roman Religion and in 1 Corinthians." *NovT* 27 (2, 1985): 125–40.

Callaway, "Reflections." Callaway, Philip R. "Reflections on the Language of the 'Historical' Dead Sea Scrolls." *QC* 12 (2–4, 2004): 123–26.

Calvin, *Acts*. Calvin, John. *Commentaries: The Acts of the Apostles, 1–13*. Translated by John W. Fraser and W. J. G. McDonald. Grand Rapids: Eerdmans, 1965.

Calvin, *Prophets*. Calvin, John. *Commentaries on the Twelve Minor Prophets*. Translated by John Owen. Grand Rapids: Eerdmans, 1950.

Cameron, "Achilles." Cameron, Alan. "Young Achilles in the Roman World." *JRS* 99 (2009): 1–22.

Cameron, "Anthology." Cameron, Alan Douglas Edward. "Anthology." *OCD*³ 101–2.

Cameron, "Black and White." Cameron, Averil. "Black and White: A Note on Ancient Nicknames." *AJP* 119 (1, 1998): 113–17.

Cameron, "Neither Male nor Female." Cameron, Averil. "'Neither Male nor Female.'" *GR* 27 (1, 1980): 60–68.

Camp, "Athens, Topography." Camp, John McKesson, II. "Athens, Topography." *OCD*³ 205–6.

Camp, "Reexamining Concord." Camp, Ashby L. "Reexamining the Rule of Concord in Acts 2:38." *ResQ* 39 (1, 1997): 37–42.

Campbell, "4QMMT^d." Campbell, Jonathan G. "4QMMT^d and the Tripartite Canon." *JJS* 51 (2, 2000): 181–90.

Campbell, "Anchor." Campbell, Douglas A. "An Anchor for Pauline Chronology: Paul's Flight from 'the Ethnarch of King Aretas' (2 Corinthians 11:32–33)." *JBL* 121 (2, 2002): 279–302.

Campbell, "Aquilius Regulus." Campbell, John Brian. "Aquilius Regulus, Marcus." *OCD*³ 133–34.

Campbell, *Army*. Campbell, John Brian. *The Roman Army, 31 BC–AD 337: A Sourcebook*. London: Routledge, 1994.

Campbell, "Attestation." Campbell, Douglas A. "Possible Inscriptional Attestation to Sergius Paul[l]us (Acts 13:6–12), and the Implications for Pauline Chronology." *JTS* 56 (1, 2005): 1–29.

Campbell, "Auxilia." Campbell, John Brian. "Auxilia." *BrillPauly* 2:420–21.

Campbell, "Auxilia." Campbell, John Brian. "Auxilia." *OCD*³ 224–25.

Campbell, "Camps." Campbell, John Brian. "Camps." *OCD*³ 283–84.

Campbell, "Canabae." Campbell, John Brian. "Canabae." *OCD*³ 284–85.

Campbell, "Cavalry." Campbell, John Brian. "Cavalry: Rome." *BrillPauly* 3:53–55.

Campbell, "Centuria: Military." Campbell, John Brian. "Centuria: Military." *Brill Pauly* 3:126–27.

Campbell, "Centurio." Campbell, John Brian. "Centurio." *BrillPauly* 3:127–28.

Campbell, "Cohortes urbanae." Campbell, John Brian. "Cohortes urbanae." *OCD*³ 356.

Campbell, *Deliverance*. Campbell, Douglas A. *The Deliverance of God: An Apocalyptic Rereading of Justification in Paul*. Grand Rapids: Eerdmans, 2009.

Campbell, "Diploma." Campbell, John Brian. "Diploma." *OCD*³ 485.

Campbell, "Donativum." Campbell, John Brian. "Donativum." *OCD*³ 494.

Campbell, "Elders of Church." Campbell, Alastair. "The Elders of the Jerusalem Church." *JTS* 44 (2, 1993): 511–28.

Campbell, "Equites." Campbell, John Brian. "Equites singulares." *BrillPauly* 5:4–5.

Campbell, "Exploratores." Campbell, John Brian. "Exploratores." *BrillPauly* 5:277–78.

Campbell, *Iconography*. Campbell, Leroy A. *Mithraic Iconography and Ideology*. ÉPROER 11. Leiden: Brill, 1968.

Campbell, "Jerusalem." Campbell, Kenneth M. "The New Jerusalem in Matthew 5.14." *SJT* 31 (1978): 335–63.

Campbell, "Journeys." Campbell, Thomas H. "Paul's 'Missionary Journeys' as Reflected in His Letters." *JBL* 74 (2, 1955): 80–87.

Campbell, "Judaizers." Campbell, William S. "Judaizers." *DPL* 512–16.

Campbell, "Legio." Campbell, John Brian. "Legio." *BrillPauly* 7:356–70.

Campbell, "Legion." Campbell, John Brian. "Legion." *OCD*³ 839–42.

Campbell, "Libri coloniarum." Campbell, John Brian. "Libri coloniarum." *OCD*³ 855.

Campbell, "Manipulus." Campbell, John Brian. "Manipulus (Maniple)." *OCD*³ 918.

Campbell, "Ministry." Campbell, Evvy Hay. "Holistic Ministry and the Incident at the Gate Beautiful." Pages 37–44 in *Mission in Acts: Ancient Narratives in Contemporary Context*. Edited by Robert L. Gallagher and Paul Hertig. AmSocMissS 34. Maryknoll, N.Y.: Orbis, 2004.

Campbell, "Mutiny." Campbell, John Brian. "Mutiny." *BrillPauly* 9:377–80.

Campbell, "Narrator." Campbell, William Sanger. "The Narrator as 'He,' 'Me,' and 'We': Grammatical Person in Ancient Histories and in the Acts of the Apostles." *JBL* 129 (2, 2010): 385–407.

Campbell, "Paul in Pamphylia." Campbell, Douglas A. "Paul in Pamphylia (Acts 13.13–14a; 14.24b–26): A Critical Note." *NTS* 46 (4, 2000): 595–602.

Campbell, personal correspondence. Campbell, John Brian. Personal correspondence with the author. June 16 and June 19, 2006.

Campbell, "Praetorians." Campbell, John Brian. "Praetorians." *BrillPauly* 11:773–75.

Campbell, "Praetorium." Campbell, John Brian. "Praetorium." *OCD*³ 1241.

Campbell, "Praetorium (Brill)." Campbell, John Brian. "Praetorium." *BrillPauly* 11:775–76.

Campbell, "Primipilus." Campbell, John Brian. "Primipilus." *OCD*³ 1246.

Campbell, "Scratching." Campbell, Susan. "Scratching the Itch: Paul's Athenian Speech Shaping Mission Today." *ERT* 35 (2, 2011): 177–84.

Campbell, "Tribuni militum." Campbell, John Brian. "Tribuni militum." *OCD*³ 1549.

Campbell, *Union*. Campbell, Constantine R. *Paul and Union with Christ: An Exegetical and Theological Study*. Grand Rapids: Zondervan, 2012.

Campbell, "Velites." Campbell, John Brian. "Velites." *OCD*³ 1584–85.

Campbell, "Veterans." Campbell, John Brian. "Veterans." *OCD*³ 1592.

Campbell, "Vexillum." Campbell, John Brian. "Vexillum." *OCD*³ 1594.

Campbell, "We" Passages. Campbell, William Sanger. *The "We" Passages in the Acts of the Apostles: The Narrator as Narrative Character*. SBLSBL 14. Atlanta: SBL, 2007.

Campbell and Matthews, "Praefectus praetorio." Campbell, John Brian, and John F. Matthews, "Praefectus praetorio." *OCD*³ 1238–39.

Campos Méndex. "Dios Mithra." Campos Méndex, Israel. "El dios Mithra en los nombres personales durante la dinastía persa aqueménida." *AuOr* 24 (2, 2006): 165–75.

Cancik, "Gattung." Cancik, Hubert. "Die Gattung Evangelium: Das Evangelium des Markus im Rahmen der antiken Historiographie." Pages 85–113 in *Markus-Philologie: Historische, literargeschichtliche, und stilistische Untersuchungen zum zweiten Evangelium*. Edited by Hubert Cancik. WUNT 33. Tübingen: Mohr Siebeck, 1984.

Cancik, "Institutions." Cancik, Hubert. "The History of Culture, Religion, and Institutions in Ancient Historiography: Philological Observations concerning Luke's History." *JBL* 116 (4, 1997): 673–95.

Cancik, "Institutionsgeschichte." Cancik, Hubert. "Das Geschichtswerk des Lukas als Institutionsgeschichte. Die Vorbereitung des Zweiten Logos im Ersten." Pages 519–38 in *Die Apostelgeschichte im Kontext antiker und frühchristlicher Historiographie*. Edited by Jörg Frey, Clare K. Rothschild, and Jens Schröter, with Bettina Rost. BZNWK 162. Berlin: de Gruyter, 2009.

Cancik-Lindemaier, "Allegoresis." Cancik-Lindemaier, Hildegard, et al. "Allegoresis." *BrillPauly* 1:511–16.

Cancik-Lindemaier, "Vestals." Cancik-Lindemaier, Hildegard. "Vestals." *Brill Pauly* 15:340–42.

Candiard, "Vision." Candiard, Adrien. "La vision de Pierre à Joppé (Ac 10,9–16): Esquisse d'histoire d'un commentaire dans l'Occident latin." *RB* 116 (4, 2009): 527–56.

Canevet, "Remarques sur l'utilisation." Canevet, Mariette. "Remarques sur l'utilisation du genre littéraire historique par Philon d'Alexandrie dans la *Vita Moysis*, ou Moïse général en chef-prophète." *RevScRel* 60 (3–4, 1986): 189–206.

Cangh, "Miracles." Cangh, Jean-Marie van. "Miracles de rabbins et miracles de Jésus: La tradition sur Honi et Hanina." *RTL* 15 (1, 1984): 28–53.

Cappelletti, "Inscriptions." Cappelletti, Silvia. "Latin Inscriptions in Greek Characters, Greek Inscriptions in Latin Characters: A Study of the Jewish Evidence in Rome." *BJGS* 39 (2006–7): 28–34.

Capper, "Context." Capper, Brian J. "The Palestinian Cultural Context of Earliest Christian Community of Goods." Pages 323–56 in *The Book of Acts in Its Palestinian Setting*. Edited by Richard Bauckham.

Vol. 4 of *The Book of Acts in Its First Century Setting*. Edited by Bruce W. Winter. Grand Rapids: Eerdmans; Carlisle, U.K.: Paternoster, 1995.

Capper, "Houses." Capper, Brian J. "Essene Community Houses and Jesus' Early Community." Pages 472–502 in *Jesus and Archaeology*. Edited by James H. Charlesworth. Grand Rapids: Eerdmans, 2006.

Capper, "Interpretation of Acts 5.4." Capper, Brian J. "The Interpretation of Acts 5.4." *JSNT* 19 (1983): 117–31.

Capper, "Monks." Capper, Brian J. "'With the Oldest Monks . . .': Light from Essene History on the Career of the Beloved Disciple?" *JTS* 49 (1, 1998): 1–55.

Capper, "Reciprocity." Capper, Brian J. "Reciprocity and the Ethic of Acts." Pages 499–518 in *Witness to the Gospel: The Theology of Acts*. Edited by I. Howard Marshall and David Peterson. Grand Rapids: Eerdmans, 1998.

Capps, *Village Psychiatrist*. Capps, Donald. *Jesus the Village Psychiatrist*. Louisville: Westminster John Knox, 2008.

Capra, "Detour." Capra, Andrea. "Detour en Route in the Aegean Sea? Xenophon of Ephesus 5.10.2." *CP* 107 (1, 2012): 70–74.

Caquot, "Livre." Caquot, André. "Le livre des Jubilés, Melchisedeq, et les dîmes." *RHR* 199 (2, 1982): 235–36.

Caquot, "Jubilés." Caquot, André. "Le livre des Jubilés, Melchisedeq, et les dîmes." *JJS* 33 (1–2, 1982): 257–64.

Caquot, "Secte et temple." Caquot, André. "La secte de Qumrân et le temple (essai de synthèse)." *RHPR* 72 (1, 1992): 3–14.

Caragounis, "Culture." Caragounis, Chrys C. "Greek Culture and Jewish Piety: The Clash and the Fourth Beast of Daniel 7." *ETL* 65 (4, 1989): 280–308.

Caragounis, "Dionysios Halikarnasseus." Caragounis, Chrys C. "Dionysios Halikarnasseus, the Art of Composition, and the Apostle Paul." *JGRCJ* 1 (2000): 25–54.

Caragounis, *Mysterion*. Caragounis, Chrys C. *The Ephesian Mysterion: Meaning and Content*. ConBNT 8. Lund, Swed.: C. W. K. Gleerup, 1977.

Caragounis, "Scholarship." Caragounis, Chrys C. "Scholarship, Greek and Roman." *DNTB* 1065–86.

Carandini, "Pottery." Carandini, Andrea. "Pottery and the African Economy." Pages 145–62 in *Trade in the Ancient Economy*. Edited by Peter Garnsey, Keith Hopkins, and C. R. Whittaker. Berkeley: University of California Press, 1983.

Carastro, "Tirésias." Carastro, Marcello. "Quand Tirésias devint un *mágos*: Divination et magie en Grèce ancienne

(Ve–IVe siècle av. n. è.)." *RHR* 224 (2, 2007): 211–30.

Carbó García, "Sol Invictus." Carbó García, Juan Ramón. "La problématique de Sol Invictus: Le cas de la Dacie Romaine." *Numen* 57 (5, 2010): 583–618.

Carcopino, *Life*. Carcopino, Jérôme. *Daily Life in Ancient Rome: The People and the City at the Height of the Empire*. Edited by Henry T. Rowell. Translated by E. O. Lorimer. New Haven: Yale University Press, 1940.

Carlebach, "References." Carlebach, A. "Rabbinic References to Fiscus judaicus." *JQR* 66 (1, 1975): 57–61.

Carlson, *Hoax*. Carlson, Stephen C. *The Gospel Hoax: Morton Smith's Invention of Secret Mark*. Waco: Baylor University Press, 2005.

Carlston, "Vocabulary." Carlston, Charles. "The Vocabulary of Perfection in Philo and Hebrews." Pages 133–60 in *Unity and Diversity in New Testament Theology: Essays in Honor of George E. Ladd*. Edited by Robert A. Guelich. Grand Rapids: Eerdmans, 1978.

Carmichael, "*Haggadah*." Carmichael, Calum. "The Passover *haggadah*." Pages 343–56 in *The Historical Jesus in Context*. Edited by Amy-Jill Levine, Dale C. Allison Jr., and John Dominic Crossan. PrRR. Princeton: Princeton University Press, 2006.

Carmignac, "Kittim." Carmignac, Jean. "Les Kittim dans la 'Guerre des fils de lumière contre les fils de ténèbres.'" *NRTh* 77 (7, 1955): 737–48.

Carmignac, "Melkisédeq." Carmignac, Jean. "Le document de Qumrân sur Melkisédeq." *RevQ* 7 (3, 1970): 343–78.

Carmignac, "Pré-pascal." Carmignac, Jean. "Pré-pascal et post-pascal: Sens et valeur de ces expressions." *EspV* 90 (28, 1980): 411–15.

Carmon, *Inscriptions*. Carmon, Efrat, ed. *Inscriptions Reveal: Documents from the Time of the Bible, the Mishna, and the Talmud*. Translated by R. Grafman. Jerusalem: Israel Museum, 1973.

Caron, "Divorce." Caron, Gerard. "Did Jesus Allow Divorce? (Mt. 5:31–32)." *African Ecclesial Review* 24 (1982): 309–16.

Carpenter, "Deuteronomy." Carpenter, Eugene E. "Deuteronomy." Pages 418–547 in vol. 1 of *Zondervan Illustrated Bible Backgrounds Commentary: Old Testament*. Edited by John Walton. 5 vols. Grand Rapids: Zondervan, 2009.

Carpinelli, "Memorial." Carpinelli, Francis Giordano. "'Do This as My Memorial' (Luke 22:19): Lucan Soteriology of Atonement." *CBQ* 61 (1, 1999): 74–91.

Carr, *Angels*. Carr, Wesley. *Angels and Principalities*. Cambridge: Cambridge University Press, 1981.

Carr, *Writing*. Carr, David M. *Writing on the Tablet of the Heart: Origins of Scripture and Literature*. New York: Oxford, 2005.

Carras, "Observant Jews." Carras, George P. "Observant Jews in the Story of Luke and Acts: Paul, Jesus, and Other Jews." Pages 693–708 in *The Unity of Luke-Acts*. Edited by Joseph Verheyden. BETL 142. Leuven: Leuven University Press, 1999.

Carreira Neves, "História e Espírito." Carreira Neves, Joaquim das. "História e Espírito Santo nos Actos dos apóstolos." *Didaskalia* 25 (1–2, 1995): 195–234.

Carrier, "Pseudohistory." Carrier, Richard C. "Pseudohistory in Jerry Vardaman's Magic Coins: The Nonsense of Micro Graphic Letters." *SkI* 26 (2, 2002): 39–41, 61.

Carroll, "Analysis." Carroll, Scott. "A Preliminary Analysis of the *Epistle to Rehoboam*." *JSP* 4 (1989): 91–103.

Carroll, "Chios." Carroll, Scott T. "Chios." *ABD* 1:910.

Carroll, "Exclusion." Carroll, Kenneth L. "The Fourth Gospel and the Exclusion of Christians from the Synagogues." *BJRL* 40 (1957–58): 19–32.

Carroll, *Looms*. Carroll, Diane Lee. *Looms and Textiles of the Copts: First Millennium Egyptian Textiles in the Carl Austin Rietz Collection of the California Academy of Sciences*. San Francisco: California Academy of Sciences; Seattle: University of Washington Press, 1988.

Carroll, "Lycia." Carroll, Scott T. "Lycia." *ABD* 4:422.

Carroll, "Mysia." Carroll, Scott T. "Mysia." *ABD* 4:940–41.

Carroll, "Pamphylia." Carroll, Scott T. "Pamphylia." *ABD* 5:138–39.

Carroll, "Portrayal of Pharisees." Carroll, John T. "Luke's Portrayal of the Pharisees." *CBQ* 50 (4, 1988): 604–21.

Carroll, *Response to End*. Carroll, John T. *Response to the End of History: Eschatology and Situation in Luke-Acts*. SBLDS 92. Atlanta: Scholars Press, 1988.

Carroll, "Rhodes." Carroll, Scott T. "Rhodes." *ABD* 5:719–20.

Carson, "Acts 8:37." Carson, Cottrel R. "Acts 8:37—A Textual Reexamination." *USQR* 51 (1–2, 1997): 57–78.

Carson, *Fallacies*. Carson, D. A. *Exegetical Fallacies*. Grand Rapids: Baker, 1984.

Carson, "Inconsistency." Carson, D. A. "Pauline Inconsistency: Reflections on I Corinthians 9.19–23 and Galatians 2.11–14." *Chm* 100 (1, 1986): 6–45.

Carson, *John*. Carson, D. A. *The Gospel according to John*. Leicester, U.K.: InterVarsity; Grand Rapids: Eerdmans, 1991.

Carson, "Matthew." Carson, D. A. "Matthew." Pages 3–599 in vol. 8 of *The Expositor's Bible Commentary*. Edited by Frank Gaebelein. Grand Rapids: Zondervan, 1984.

Carson, "Pseudonymity." Carson, D. A. "Pseudonymity and Pseudepigraphy." *DNTB* 857–64.

Carson, *Showing Spirit*. Carson, D. A. *Showing the Spirit: A Theological Exposition of 1 Corinthians 12–14*. Grand Rapids: Baker, 1987.

Carson, "Silent." Carson, D. A. "'Silent in the Churches': On the Role of Women in 1 Corinthians 14:33b–36." Pages 140–53 in *Recovering Biblical Manhood and Womanhood: A Response to Evangelical Feminism*. Edited by John Piper and Wayne Grudem. Wheaton, Ill.: Crossway, 1991.

Carson, *Sovereignty*. Carson, D. A. *Divine Sovereignty and Human Responsibility: Biblical Perspectives in Tension*. NFTL. Atlanta: John Knox, 1981.

Carson, "Sovereignty in Philo." Carson, D. A. "Divine Sovereignty and Human Responsibility in Philo: Analysis and Method." *NovT* 23 (2, 1981): 148–64.

Carson, *Triumphalism*. Carson, D. A. *From Triumphalism to Maturity: An Exposition of 2 Corinthians 10–13*. Grand Rapids: Baker, 1984.

Carson, Moo, and Morris, *Introduction*. Carson, D. A., Douglas J. Moo, and Leon Morris. *An Introduction to the New Testament*. Grand Rapids: Zondervan, 1992.

Carter, "Big Men." Carter, T. L. "'Big Men' in Corinth." *JSNT* 66 (1997): 45–71.

Carter, *Empire*. Carter, Warren. *The Roman Empire and the New Testament: An Essential Guide*. Nashville: Abingdon, 2006.

Carter, "Empire." Carter, Warren. "Paul and the Roman Empire: Recent Perspectives." Pages 7–26 in *Paul Unbound: Other Perspectives on the Apostle*. Edited by Mark D. Given. Peabody, Mass.: Hendrickson, 2010.

Carter and Earle, *Acts*. Carter, Charles W., and Ralph Earle. *The Acts of the Apostles*. Grand Rapids: Zondervan, 1973.

Cartledge, *Ancient Greece*. Cartledge, Paul. *Ancient Greece: A History in Eleven Cities*. New York: Oxford University Press, 2009.

Cartledge, "Freedmen." Cartledge, Paul A. "Freedmen: Greece." *BrillPauly* 5:439–41.

Cartledge, "Glossolalia." Cartledge, Mark J. "The Nature and Function of New Testament Glossolalia." *EvQ* 72 (2, 2000): 135–50.

Cartledge, "Helots." Cartledge, Paul A. "Helots." *BrillPauly* 6:117–19.

Cartledge, "Herodotus." Cartledge, Paul A. "Taking Herodotus Personally." *CW* 102 (4, 2009): 371–82.

Cartledge, "Industry." Cartledge, Paul A. "Industry." *OCD*[3] 756–57.

Cartledge, "Metoikos." Cartledge, Paul A. "Metoikos." *BrillPauly* 8:810–13.

Cartledge, "Rise and Fall." Cartledge, D. R. "The Rise and Fall of Simon Magus." *BRev* 21 (4, 2005): 24–36.

Cartledge, "Tongues-Speech." Cartledge, Mark J. "The Practice of Tongues-Speech as a Case Study: A Practical-Theological Perspective." Pages 206–34 in *Speaking in Tongues: Multi-disciplinary Perspectives*. Edited by Mark J. Cartledge. SPCI. Waynesboro, Ga., and Bletchley, Milton Keynes, U.K.: Paternoster, 2006.

Cartledge, "Vows." Cartledge, Tony W. "Were Nazirite Vows Unconditional?" *CBQ* 51 (3, 1989): 409–22.

Cartledge, Hodkinson, and Spawforth, "Sparta." Cartledge, Paul A., Stephen J. Hodkinson, and Antony J. S. Spawforth. "Sparta." *OCD*[3] 1431–33.

Cartledge and Sallares. "Earthquakes." Cartledge, Paul A., and J. Robert Sallares. "Earthquakes." *OCD*[3] 501.

Caruana, *Pottery*. Caruana, Adrian A. *Ancient pottery from the ancient pagan tombs and Christian cemeteries in the islands of Malta*. Malta: Govt. Print. Off., 1899.

Cary and Haarhoff, *Life*. Cary, M., and T. J. Haarhoff. *Life and Thought in the Greek and Roman World*. 4th ed. London: Methuen, 1946.

Cary and Hammond, "Dyrrhachium." Cary, Max, and Nicholas Geoffrey Lemprière Hammond. "Dyrrhachium." *OCD*[3] 499–500.

Cary and Murray, "Adriatic Sea." Cary, Max, and William M. Murray. "Adriatic Sea." *OCD*[3] 14.

Casalegno, "Espírito disse a Filipe." Casalegno, Alberto. "'O Espírito disse a Filipe': Reflexões sobre o Espírito nos Atos dos apóstolos a partir de 8,26–40." *PerTeol* 30 (80, 1998): 37–56.

Casalegno, "Espírito Santo." Casalegno, Alberto. "A ação do Espírito Santo na assembléia de Jerusalém (At 15)." *PerTeol* 37 (103, 2005): 367–80.

Casalegno, "Evangelização." Casalegno, Alberto. "Evangelização e práticas mágicas nos Atos dos apóstolos." *PerTeol* 24 (62, 1992): 13–28.

Casalini, "Nuovi commenti." Casalini, N. "Nuovi commenti agli Atti degli apostoli: Saggio bibliografico." *SBFLA* 52 (2002): 175–216.

Casas García, "Ambiente." Casas García, V. "Ambiente socio-político en el judaísmo contemporáneo de Jesús." *ByF* 4 (11, 1978): 136–50.

Casciaro Ramírez, "Himnos." Casciaro Ramírez, José M. "Los 'himnos' de Qumran y el 'misterio' paulino." *ScrTh* 8 (1, 1976): 9–56.

Casciaro Ramírez, "Misterio." Casciaro Ramírez, José M. "El 'misterio' divino en los escritos posteriores de Qumran." *ScrTh* 8 (1976): 445–75.

Casdorph, *Miracles*. Casdorph, H. Richard. *The Miracles: A Medical Doctor Says Yes to Miracles!* Plainfield, N.J.: Logos International, 1976.

Case, *Origins*. Case, Shirley Jackson. *The Social Origins of Christianity*. 1923. Repr., New York: Cooper Square, 1975.

Casey, "Μάρτυς." Casey, Robert P. "Μάρτυς." *BegChr* 5:30–37.

Casey, "Simon." Casey, Robert P. "Simon Magus." *BegChr* 5:151–64.

Casey, "'Son of Man' in Similitudes." Casey, Maurice. "The Use of the Term 'Son of Man' in the Similitudes of Enoch." *JSJ* 7 (1, 1976): 11–29.

Casiday, "Sin." Casiday, Augustine. "Sin and Salvation: Experiences and Reflections." Pages 501–30 in *Constantine to c. 600*. Edited by Augustine Casiday and Frederick W. Norris. Vol. 2 of *The Cambridge History of Christianity*. 9 vols. Cambridge: Cambridge University Press, 2007.

Cassidy, "Opponents." Cassidy, Richard J. "The Non-Roman Opponents of Paul." Pages 150–62 in *New Views on Luke and Acts*. Edited by Earl Richard. Collegeville, Minn.: Liturgical Press, 1990.

Cassidy, *Politics*. Cassidy, Richard J. *Jesus, Politics, and Society: A Study of Luke's Gospel*. Maryknoll, N.Y.: Orbis, 1979.

Cassidy, "Proclamation." Cassidy, Richard J. "Paul's Proclamation of *Lord* Jesus as a Chained Prisoner in Rome: Luke's Ending Is in His Beginning." Pages 142–53 in *Luke-Acts and Empire: Essays in Honor of Robert L. Brawley*. Edited by David Rhoads, David Esterline, and Jae Won Lee. PrTMS 151. Eugene, Ore.: Pickwick, 2011.

Cassidy, *Society*. Cassidy, Richard J. *Society and Politics in the Acts of the Apostles*. Maryknoll: Orbis, 1987.

Cassin, "Philosophia." Cassin, B. "*Philosophia enim simulari potest, eloquentia non potest*, ou: Le masque et l'effet." *Rhetorica* 13 (2, 1995): 105–24.

Casson, *Mariners*. Casson, Lionel. *The Ancient Mariners: Seafarers and Sea Fighters of the Mediterranean in Ancient Times*. 2nd ed. Princeton: Princeton University Press, 1991.

Casson, *Ships*. Casson, Lionel. *Ships and Seamanship in the Ancient World*. 2nd ed. Princeton: Princeton University Press, 1986.

Casson, *Travel.* Casson, Lionel. *Travel in the Ancient World.* London: George Allen & Unwin, 1974.

Cassuto, *Exodus.* Cassuto, Umberto. *A Commentary on the Book of Exodus.* Translated by Israel Abrahams. Jerusalem: Magnes, 1967.

Cassuto, *Hypothesis.* Cassuto, Umberto. *The Documentary Hypothesis and the Composition of the Pentateuch.* Translated by Israel Abrahams. Jerusalem: Magnes, 1961.

Cassuto, "Palace." Cassuto, Umberto. "The Palace of Baal." *JBL* 61 (1942): 51–56.

Castillo, "Possession." Castillo, R. J. "Spirit Possession in South Asia, Dissociation or Hysteria? Part I: Theoretical background." *CMPsy* 18 (1994): 1–21.

Castleberry, "Impact." Castleberry, Joseph Lee. "It's Not Just for Ignorant People Anymore: The Future Impact of University Graduates on the Development of the Ecuadorian Assemblies of God." Ed.D. diss., Teachers College, Columbia University, 1999.

Castro-Blanco, "Sensitivity." Castro-Blanco, David R. "Cultural Sensitivity in Conventional Psychotherapy: A Comment on Martínez-Taboas (2005)." *PsycTRPT* 42 (1, 2005): 14–16.

Catchpole, "Paul, James, and Decree." Catchpole, David R. "Paul, James, and the Apostolic Decree." *NTS* 23 (4, 1977): 428–44.

Catchpole, *Trial.* Catchpole, David R. *The Trial of Jesus: A Study in the Gospels and Jewish Historiography from 1770 to the Present Day.* StPB 18. Leiden: Brill, 1971.

Catchpole, "'Triumphal' Entry." Catchpole, David R. "The 'Triumphal' Entry." Pages 319–34 in *Jesus and the Politics of His Day.* Edited by Ernst Bammel and C. F. D. Moule. Cambridge: Cambridge University Press, 1984.

Catling, "Cyprus." Catling, Hector William. "Cyprus." *OCD³* 419–20.

Catling, "Delos." Catling, Hector William. "Delos." *OCD³* 442–44.

Catling, "Paphos." Catling, Hector William. "Paphos." *OCD³* 1108.

Catling, "Salamis." Catling, Hector William. "Salamis." *OCD³* 1347.

Cavaness, "Women." Cavaness, Barbara. "Women Used of God." *Assemblies of God Heritage* 25 (4, 2005–6): 24–29.

Cavarnos, *St. Methodia.* Cavarnos, Constantine. *St. Methodia of Kimolos, Remarkable Ascetic, Teacher of Virtue, Counselor, Comforter, and Healer (1865–1908): An Account of Her Life, Character, Miracles, and Influence, Together with Selected Hymns from the Akolouthia in Honor of Her, and a Letter to Her Sister Anna.* Modern Orthodox Saints 9. Belmont, Mass.: Institute for Byzantine and Modern Greek Studies, 1978.

Cavigneaux, "Herméneutique." Cavigneaux, A. "Aux sources du Midrash: L'herméneutique babylonienne." *AuOr* 5 (2, 1987): 243–55.

Cayzer, "Ending." Cayzer, J. "The Ending of Acts: Handing On the Baton." *StMkRev* 161 (1995): 23–25.

Cazeaux, *Actes.* Cazeaux, Jacques. *Les Actes des Apôtres: L'Église entre le martyre d'Étienne et la mission de Paul.* LD. Paris: Les Éditions du Cerf, 2008.

Cella, *Narrative.* Cella, Paolo della. *Narrative of an expedition from Tripoli in Barbary, to the Western frontier of Egypt, in 1817, by the bey of Tripoli. . . by Paolo della Cella. . . With an appendix containing instructions for navigating the Great Syrtis.* Translated by Anthony Aufrere. London: J. and A. Arch, 1822.

"Ceremony." "An Awe-Inspiring Ceremony." *ChH* 37 (1993): 41.

Cerfaux, *Church.* Cerfaux, L. *The Church in the Theology of St. Paul.* Translated by Geoffrey Webb and Adrian Walker. New York: Herder & Herder, 1959.

Cerro, "Hechos." Cerro, Gonzalo del. "Los hechos apócrifos de los apóstoles: Su género literario." *EstBib* 51 (2, 1993): 207–32.

Cha, "Virgins." Cha, Jung-Sik. "The Ascetic Virgins in I Corinthians 7:25–38." *AJT* 12 (1, 1998): 89–117.

Chadwick, "All Things." Chadwick, Henry. "'All Things to All Men' (I Cor. ix.22)." *NTS* 1 (4, 1955): 261–75.

Chadwick, "Defence." Chadwick, Henry. "Justin Martyr's Defence of Christianity." *BJRL* 47 (1964–65): 275–97.

Chadwick, *Early Church.* Chadwick, Henry. *The Early Church.* Pelican History of the Church 1. New York: Penguin, 1967.

Chadwick, "Paul in Rome." Chadwick, Henry. "St. Peter and St. Paul in Rome: The Problem of the Memoria Apostolorum ad Catacumbas." *JTS* 8 (1, 1957): 30–52.

Chadwick, *Reformation.* Chadwick, Owen. *The Reformation.* Pelican History of the Church 3. Baltimore: Penguin, 1964.

Chae, "Yeon." Chae, Y. S. "A Biblical Exegesis of the Korean Cultural Concept, 'Yeon' (Indirect Karma): A Test-Case of the Hermeneutics of Resonance." *AJT* 18 (2, 2004): 247–66.

Chambers, "Knock." Chambers, Kathy. "'Knock, Knock—Who's There?' Acts 12.6–17 as a Comedy of Errors." Pages 89–97 in *The Feminist Companion to the Acts of the Apostles.* Edited by Amy-Jill Levine with Marianne Blickenstaff.

Cleveland: Pilgrim; Edinburgh: T&T Clark, 2004.

Chamblin, "Freedom." Chamblin, J. Knox. "Freedom/Liberty." *DPL* 313–16.

Champion, "Aetolia." Champion, Craige B. "Polybius and Aetolia: A Historiographical Approach." Pages 356–62 in *A Companion to Greek and Roman Historiography.* Edited by John Marincola. 2 vols. Oxford: Blackwell, 2007.

Champion, "Romans." Champion, Craige. "Romans as BAPBAPOI: Three Polybian Speeches and the Politics of Cultural Indeterminacy." *CP* 95 (4, 2001): 425–44.

Champion, *Tyrants.* Champion, Jeff. *The Tyrants of Syracuse: War in Ancient Sicily.* Vol. 1, *480–367 BC.* Barnsley: Pen & Sword Military, 2010.

Chan, "Glossolalia." Chan, Simon K. H. "Evidential Glossolalia and the Doctrine of Subsequence." *AJPS* 2 (2, 1999): 195–211.

Chan, "Response." Chan, Simon K. H. "A Response to Max Turner." *AJPS* 2 (2, 1999): 279–81.

Chance, *Acts.* Chance, J. Bradley. *Acts.* SHBC. Macon, Ga.: Smyth & Helwys, 2007.

Chance, "Perspectives." Chance, J. Bradley. "Talbert's New Perspectives on Luke-Acts: The ABC's of Ancient Lives." Pages 181–201 in *Cadbury, Knox, and Talbert: American Contributions to the Study of Acts.* Edited by Mikeal C. Parsons and Joseph B. Tyson. SBLBSNA 18. SBLCP. Atlanta: Scholars Press, 1992.

Chance, "Prognostications." Chance, J. Bradley. "Divine Prognostications and the Movement of Story: An Intertextual Exploration of Xenophon's *Ephesian Tale* and the Acts of the Apostles." Pages 219–34 in *Ancient Fiction and Early Christian Narrative.* Edited by Ronald F. Hock, J. Bradley Chance, and Judith Perkins. SBLSymS 6. Atlanta: SBL, 1998.

Chancey, *Galilee.* Chancey, Mark. *Greco-Roman Culture and the Galilee of Jesus.* SNTSMS 134. New York: Cambridge University Press, 2006.

Chancey, "Milieu." Chancey, Mark. "The Cultural Milieu of Ancient Sepphoris." *NTS* 47 (2, 2001): 127–45.

Chancey and Meyers, "Jewish." Chancey, Mark, and Eric M. Meyers. "How Jewish Was Sepphoris in Jesus' Time?" *BAR* 26 (4, 2000): 18–33, 61.

Chandra shekar, "Possession Syndrome." Chandra shekar, C. R. "Possession Syndrome in India." Pages 79–95 in *Altered States of Consciousness and Mental Health: A Cross-cultural Perspective.* Edited by Colleen A. Ward. CCRMS 12. Newbury Park, Calif.: Sage, 1989.

Chandy, "Discipling." Chandy, V. "The Discipling of Muslims in Sri Lanka." MA thesis, Fuller Theological Seminary, 1981.

Chaplin, "Conversations." Chaplin, Jane D. "Conversations in History: Arrian and Herodotus, Parmenio and Alexander." *GRBS* 51 (4, 2011): 613–33.

Chapman, "Cannibalism." Chapman, Honora Howell. "Josephus and the Cannibalism of Mary (*BJ* 6.199–219)." Pages 419–26 in *A Companion to Greek and Roman Historiography*. Edited by John Marincola. 2 vols. Oxford: Blackwell, 2007.

Chapman, "Josephus." Chapman, Honora. "Josephus." Pages 319–31 in *The Cambridge Companion to the Roman Historians*. Edited by Andrew Feldherr. Cambridge: Cambridge University Press, 2009.

Chapman, "Marriage." Chapman, David M. "Marriage and Family in Second Temple Judaism." Pages 183–239 in *Marriage and Family in the Biblical World*. Edited by Ken M. Campbell. Downers Grove, Ill.: InterVarsity, 2003.

Chappell, "Healing Movement." Chappell, Paul Gale. "The Divine Healing Movement in America." PhD diss., Drew University, 1983.

Charette, "Tongues as of Fire." Charette, Blaine. "'Tongues as of Fire': Judgment as a Function of Glossolalia in Luke's Thought." *JPT* 13 (2, 2005): 173–86.

Charles, "Engaging the Mind." Charles, J. Daryl. "Engaging the (Neo)Pagan Mind: Paul's Encounter with Athenian Culture as a Model for Cultural Apologetics (Acts 17:16–34)." *TJ* 16 (1, 1995): 47–62.

Charles, *Jubilees*. Charles, R. H. *The Book of Jubilees, or The Little Genesis*. London: Adam & Charles Black, 1902.

Charles, "Testaments." Charles, R. H. "Testaments of the Twelve Patriarchs." Pages 282–367 in vol. 2 of *The Apocrypha and Pseudepigrapha of the Old Testament in English*. Edited by R. H. Charles. 2 vols. Oxford: Clarendon, 1913.

Charles, "Vice Lists." Charles, J. Daryl. "Vice and Virtue Lists." *DNTB* 1252–57.

Charlesworth, "Archaeology." Charlesworth, James H. "Jesus Research and Archaeology: A New Perspective." Pages 11–63 in *Jesus and Archaeology*. Edited by James H. Charlesworth. Grand Rapids: Eerdmans, 2006.

Charlesworth, "Astrology." Charlesworth, James H. "Jewish Astrology in the Talmud, Pseudepigrapha, the Dead Sea Scrolls, and Early Palestinian Synagogues." *HTR* 70 (3–4, 1977): 183–200.

Charlesworth, "Avenging." Charlesworth, M. P. "The Avenging of Caesar." Pages 1–30 in *The Augustan Empire: 44 B.C.–A.D. 70*. Edited by S. A. Cook, F. E. Adcock, and M. P. Charlesworth. CAH 10. Cambridge: Cambridge University Press, 1934. Repr., 1966.

Charlesworth, "Comparison." Charlesworth, James H. "A Critical Comparison of the Dualism in IQS III,13–IV,26 and the 'Dualism' Contained in the Fourth Gospel." *NTS* 15 (4, 1969): 389–418.

Charlesworth, "Consensus." Charlesworth, James H. "A Rare Consensus among Enoch Specialists: The Date of the Earliest Enoch Books." *Hen* 24 (1–2, 2002): 225–34.

Charlesworth, *Disciple*. Charlesworth, James H. *The Beloved Disciple: Whose Witness Validates the Gospel of John?* Valley Forge, Pa.: Trinity Press International, 1995.

Charlesworth, "Introduction to Fragments." Charlesworth, James H. "Editor's Introduction to Fragments of Lost Judeo-Hellenistic Works." *OTP* 2:775–76.

Charlesworth, "Jesus, Literature, and Archaeology." Charlesworth, James H. "Jesus, Early Jewish Literature, and Archaeology." Pages 177–98 in *Jesus' Jewishness: Exploring the Place of Jesus within Early Judaism*. Edited by James H. Charlesworth. Philadelphia: American Interfaith Institute; New York: Crossroad, 1991.

Charlesworth, *Jesus within Judaism*. Charlesworth, James H. *Jesus within Judaism: New Light from Exciting Archaeological Discoveries*. ABRL. New York: Doubleday, 1988.

Charlesworth, "Origin." Charlesworth, James H. "Conclusion: The Origin and Development of Resurrection Beliefs." Pages 218–31 in *Resurrection: The Origin and Future of a Biblical Doctrine*. By James H. Charlesworth et al. New York: T&T Clark, 2006.

Charlesworth, *Pesharim*. Charlesworth, James H. *The Pesharim and Qumran History: Chaos or Consensus?* Grand Rapids: Eerdmans, 2002.

Charlesworth, "Peter." Charlesworth, James H. "Has the Name 'Peter' Been Found among the Dead Sea Scrolls?" *QC* 2 (1993): 105–6.

Charlesworth, *Pseudepigrapha and New Testament*. Charlesworth, James H. *The Old Testament Pseudepigrapha and the New Testament: Prolegomena for the Study of Christian Origins*. SNTSMS 54. Cambridge: Cambridge University Press, 1985.

Charlesworth, *Pseudepigrapha and Research*. Charlesworth, James H. *The Pseudepigrapha and Modern Research with a Supplement*. Chico, Calif.: Scholars Press, 1981.

Charlesworth, "Psychobiography." Charlesworth, James H. "Psychobiography: A New and Challenging Methodology in Jesus Research." Pages 21–57 in *From Christ to Jesus*. Edited by J. Harold Ellens and Wayne G. Rollins. Vol. 4 of *Psychology and the Bible: A New Way to Read the Scriptures*. Westport, Conn.: Praeger, 2004.

Charlesworth, "Resurrection." Charlesworth, James H. "Resurrection: The Dead Sea Scrolls and the New Testament." Pages 138–86 in *Resurrection: The Origin and Future of a Biblical Doctrine*. By James H. Charlesworth et al. New York: T&T Clark, 2006.

Charlesworth, "Self-Definition in Additions." Charlesworth, James H. "Christian and Jewish Self-Definition in Light of the Christian Additions to the Apocryphal Writings." Pages 27–55 in *Aspects of Judaism in the Graeco-Roman Period*. Edited by E. P. Sanders with A. I. Baumgarten and Alan Mendelson. Vol. 2 of *Jewish and Christian Self-Definition*. Edited by E. P. Sanders. Philadelphia: Fortress, 1981.

Charlesworth, *Serpent*. Charlesworth, James H. *The Good and Evil Serpent: How a Universal Symbol Became Christianized*. AYBRL. New Haven: Yale University Press, 2010.

Charlesworth, "Sketch." Charlesworth, James H. "The Historical Jesus: Sources and a Sketch." Pages 84–128 in *Jesus Two Thousand Years Later*. Edited by James H. Charlesworth and Walter P. Weaver. FSCS. Harrisburg, Pa.: Trinity Press International, 2000.

Charlesworth, *Trade Routes*. Charlesworth, M. P. *Trade Routes and Commerce of the Roman Empire*. 2nd rev. ed. New York: Cooper Square, 1970.

Charlesworth and Evans, "Agrapha." Charlesworth, James H., and Craig A. Evans. "Jesus in the Agrapha and Apocryphal Gospels." Pages 479–533 in *Studying the Historical Jesus: Evaluations of the State of Current Research*. Edited by Bruce Chilton and Craig A. Evans. NTTS 19. Leiden: Brill, 1994.

Charlesworth and Sanders, "More Psalms." Charlesworth, James H., and J. A. Sanders. "More Psalms of David." *OTP* 2:609–24.

Charnov, "Shavuot." Charnov, Bruce H. "Shavuot, 'Matan Torah,' and the Triennial Cycle." *Judaism* 23 (3, 1974): 332–36.

Chase, *Credibility*. Chase, Frederic Henry. *The Credibility of the Book of the Acts of the Apostles*. London: Macmillan, 1902.

Chataway and Berry, "Experiences." Chataway, C. J., and J. W. Berry. "Acculturation Experiences, Appraisal, Coping, and Adaptation: A Comparison of Hong Kong Chinese, French, and English Students in Canada." *CanJBehSc* 21 (1989): 295–309.

Chavda, *Miracle*. Chavda, Mahesh, with John Blattner. *Only Love Can Make a Miracle:*

The Mahesh Chavda Story. Ann Arbor: Servant, 1990.

Cheesman, "Neopoioi." Cheesman, C. E. A. "Neopoioi." *BrillPauly* 9:648–49.

Chempakassery, "Cain." Chempakassery, Philip. "Cain in the Bible and Outside." *BiBh* 30 (2, 2004): 123–47.

Chempakassery, "Jerusalem Pentecost." Chempakassery, Philip. "Jerusalem Pentecost: An Indian Reinterpretation and Challenges." *Jeev* 34 (200, 2004): 108–21.

Chen, "Design." Chen, Doron. "The Design of the Ancient Synagogues in Judea: Masada and Herodium." *BASOR* 239 (1980): 37–40.

Chen, *Father*. Chen, Diane Grace. *God as Father in Luke-Acts*. StBibLit 92. New York: Peter Lang, 2006.

Chen, "Father." Chen, Diane Grace. "God as Father in Luke-Acts." PhD diss., Fuller Theological Seminary, 2004.

Chen and Starosta, *Foundations*. Chen, Guo-Ming, and William J. Starosta. *Foundations of Intercultural Communication*. Needham, Mass.: Allyn & Bacon, 1998.

Cheng, *Characterisation*.Cheng, Ling. *The Characterisation of God in Acts: The Indirect Portrayal of an Invisible Character*. PBMon. Milton Keynes, UK: Paternoster, 2011.

Cheon, "Plagues." Cheon, Samuel. "Josephus and the Story of the Plagues: An Appraisal of a Moralising Interpretation." *AJT* 18 (1, 2004): 220–30.

Chepey, "Samson." Chepey, Stuart D. "Samson the 'Holy One': A Suggestion regarding the Reviser's Use of ἅγιος in Judg 13,7; 16,17 LXX Vaticanus." *Bib* 83 (1, 2002): 97–99.

Chepey, "Timing." Chepey, Stuart. "Is the Timing Respecting Paul and the Four Men under a Vow in Acts 21:23–27 Plausible?" *CrisTR* 9 (2, Spring 2012): 69–75.

Chéreau, "Babel à la Pentecôte." Chéreau, Georgette. "De Babel à la Pentecôte: Histoire d'une bénédiction." *NRTh* 122 (1, 2000): 19–36.

Chernick, "Application." Chernick, Michael. "Internal Restraints on *Gezerah Shawah*'s Application." *JQR* 80 (3–4, 1990): 253–82.

Chernick, "Responses." Chernick, Michael. "Some Talmudic Responses to Christianity, Third and Fourth Centuries." *JES* 17 (3, 1980): 393–406.

Cherniss, "Introduction." Cherniss, Harold. Introduction to *Stoic Self-Contradictions*. Pages 369–411 in vol. 13, part 2, of Plutarch, *Moralia*. Translated by Frank Cole Babbitt et al. 17 vols. in 18. LCL. New York: G. P. Putnam's Sons; Cambridge, Mass.: Harvard University Press; London: Heinemann, 1927–2004.

Chernus, "Individual." Chernus, Ira. "Individual and Community in the Redaction of the Hekhalot Literature." *HUCA* 52 (1981): 253–74.

Chernus, "Visions." Chernus, Ira. "Visions of God in Merkabah Mysticism." *JSJ* 13 (1–2, 1982): 123–46.

Cherry, "Marriage." Cherry, David. "Marriage and Acculturation in Roman Algeria." *CP* 92 (1, 1997): 71–83.

Chesnut, *Born Again in Brazil*. Chesnut, R. Andrew. *Born Again in Brazil: The Pentecostal Boom and the Pathogens of Poverty*. New Brunswick, N.J.: Rutgers University Press, 1997.

Chesnut, "Exorcising." Chesnut, Andrew. "Exorcising the Demons of Deprivation: Divine Healing and Conversion in Brazilian Pentecostalism." Pages 169–85 in *Global Pentecostal and Charismatic Healing*. Edited by Candy Gunther Brown. Foreword by Harvey Cox. Oxford: Oxford University Press, 2011.

Chester, "Justification." Chester, Tim. "Justification, Ecclesiology, and the New Perspective." *Them* 30 (2, 2005): 5–20.

Chestnut, "Setting." Chestnut, R. D. "The Social Setting and Purpose of Joseph and Aseneth." *JSP* 3 (1988): 21–48.

Cheum, "Spirit and Mission." Cheum, David Chee Wai. "The Spirit and Mission in the Book of Acts." *JAM* 6 (2, 2004): 3–15.

Cheung, "Acts 14:27–15:35." Cheung, Alex T. M. "A Narrative Analysis of Acts 14:27–15:35: Literary Shaping in Luke's Account of the Jerusalem Council." *WTJ* 55 (1, 1993): 137–54.

Cheung, *Idol Food*. Cheung, Alex T. *Idol Food in Corinth: Jewish Background and Pauline Legacy*. JSNTSup 176. Sheffield, U.K.: Sheffield Academic, 1999.

Chevallier, *Ancien Testament*. Chevallier, Max-Alain. *Ancien Testament, hellénisme et judaïsme, la tradition synoptique, l'oeuvre de Luc*. Vol. 1 of *Souffle de Dieu: Le Saint-Esprit dans le Nouveau Testament*. Point théologique 26. Paris: Beauchesne, 1978.

Chevallier, *Esprit de Dieu*. Chevallier, Max-Alain. *Esprit de Dieu, parole d'hommes: Le rôle de l'Esprit dans les ministères de la parole selon l'apôtre Paul*. Neuchâtel: Delachaux et Niestlé, 1966.

Chevallier, *Esprit et le Messie*. Chevallier, Max-Alain. *L'Esprit et le Messie dans le bas-judaïsme et le Nouveau Testament*. EHPR 49. Paris: Presses Universitaires de France, 1958.

Chevallier, "Pentecôtes." Chevallier, Max-Alain. "'Pentecôtes' lucaniennes et 'Pentecôtes' johanniques." *RSR* 69 (2, 1981): 301–13.

Chevallier, "Souffle." Chevallier, Max-Alain. "Le souffle de Dieu dans le judaïsme, aux abords de l'ère chrétienne." *FoiVie* 80 (1, 1981): 33–46.

Chevreau, *Turnings*. Chevreau, Guy. *Turnings: The Kingdom of God and the Western World*. Foreword by Rolland Baker and Heidi Baker. Tonbridge, Kent, U.K.: Sovereign World, 2004.

Chew, "Focalization." Chew, Kathryn. "Focalization in Xenophon of Ephesos' *Ephesiaka*." Pages 47–59 in *Ancient Fiction and Early Christian Narrative*. Edited by Ronald F. Hock, J. Bradley Chance, and Judith Perkins. SBLSymS 6. Atlanta: SBL, 1998.

Chhuanliana, "Theocentricity." Chhuanliana, Ramsay Kawlni. "Lukan Theocentricity and the Understanding of Pathian in Mizo Christianity." *AJT* 23 (1, 2009): 92–110.

Chiat, *Handbook*. Chiat, Marilyn Joyce Segal. *Handbook of Synagogue Architecture*. BJS 29. Chico: Scholars, 1982.

Chibici-Revneanu, "Stehplatz." Chibici-Revneanu, Nicole. "Ein himmlischer Stehplatz: Die Haltung Jesu in der Stephanus-Vision (Apg 7.55–6) und ihre Bedeutung." *NTS* 53 (4, 2007): 459–88.

Chiera, *Clay*. Chiera, Edward. *They Wrote on Clay*. Chicago: University of Chicago Press, 1938.

"Child Laborers" "Child Laborers." *WPR* (Oct. 1992): 33.

Childs, *Canon*. Childs, Brevard. *The New Testament as Canon: An Introduction*. London: SCM, 1984.

Childs, *Political Black Minister*. Childs, John Brown. *The Political Black Minister: A Study in Afro-American Politics and Religion*. Reference Publications in Afro-American Studies. Boston: G. K. Hall & Co., 1980.

Childs and Herbert, "Metallurgy." Childs, S. Terry, and Eugenia W. Herbert. "Metallurgy and Consequences." Pages 276–300 in *African Archaeology*. Edited by Ann Brower Stahl. Blackwell Studies in Global Archaeology. Oxford: Blackwell, 2005.

Chilton, "Announcement." Chilton, Bruce. "Announcement in Nazara: An Analysis of Luke 4:16–21." Pages 147–72 in vol. 2 of *Studies of History and Tradition in the Four Gospels*. Edited by R. T. France and David Wenham. 2 vols. Gospel Perspectives 1–2. Sheffield, U.K.: JSOT Press, 1980–81.

Chilton, *Approaches*. Chilton, Bruce. *Judaic Approaches to the Gospels*. USFISFCJ 2. Atlanta: Scholars Press, 1994.

Chilton, "Development." Chilton, Bruce. "A Comparative Study of Synoptic Development: The Dispute between Cain and Abel in the Palestinian Targums and the Beelzebul Controversy in the Gospels." *JBL* 101 (4, 1982): 553–62.

Chilton, "Epitaph." Chilton, Bruce. "The Epitaph of Himerus from the Jewish Catacombs of the Via Appia." *JQR* 79 (2–3, 1988–89): 93–100.

Chilton, "Exorcism." Chilton, Bruce. "Exorcism and History: Mark 1:21–28." Pages 253–71 in *The Miracles of Jesus*. Edited by David Wenham and Craig Blomberg. Gospel Perspectives 6. Sheffield, U.K.: JSOT Press, 1986.

Chilton, "Gamaliel." Chilton, Bruce. "Gamaliel." *ABD* 2:903–6.

Chilton, *Rabbi Paul*. Chilton, Bruce. *Rabbi Paul: An Intellectual Biography*. New York: Doubleday, 2004.

Chilton, "Second Night." Chilton, Bruce. "Isaac and the Second Night: A Consideration." *Bib* 61 (1, 1980): 78–88.

Chilton, "Targum." Chilton, Bruce. "Targum, Jesus, and the Gospels." Pages 238–55 in *The Historical Jesus in Context*. Edited by Amy-Jill Levine, Dale C. Allison, Jr., and J. D. Crossan. PrRR. Princeton: Princeton University Press, 2006.

Chilton, "Transmission." Chilton, Bruce. "Targumic Transmission and Dominical Tradition." Pages 21–45 in vol. 1 of *Studies of History and Tradition in the Four Gospels*. Edited by R. T. France and David Wenham. 2 vols. Gospel Perspectives 1–2. Sheffield, U.K.: JSOT Press, 1980–81.

Chilton, Comfort, and Wise, "Temple." Chilton, Bruce, P. W. Comfort, and Michael O. Wise. "Temple, Jewish." *DNTB* 1167–83.

Chilton and Neusner, "Gamaliel." Chilton, Bruce, and Jacob Neusner. "Paul and Gamaliel." *BBR* 14 (1, 2004): 1–43.

Chilton and Neusner, "Paul and Gamaliel." Chilton, Bruce, and Jacob Neusner. "Paul and Gamaliel." *RRJ* 8 (2005): 113–62.

Chilton and Yamauchi, "Synagogues." Chilton, Bruce, and Edwin Yamauchi. "Synagogues." *DNTB* 1145–53.

Chinn, "Eyes." Chinn, Christopher M. "Before Your Very Eyes: Pliny *Epistulae* 5.6 and the Ancient Theory of Ekphrasis." *CP* 102 (3, 2007): 265–80.

Chinwokwu, "Localizing." Chinwokwu, Emmanuel Nlenanya. "Localizing the Global: Revisiting New Testament Christology in an African Context." Paper presented at the Society for New Testament Studies, Bard College, Aug. 5, 2011.

Chiquete, "Healing." Chiquete, Daniel. "Healing, Salvation, and Mission: The Ministry of Healing in Latin American Pentecostalism." *IntRevMiss* 93 (370–71, 2004): 474–85.

Chiu, "Importance." Chiu, Angeline. "The Importance of Being Julia: Civil War, Historical Revision and the Mutable Past in Lucan's Pharsalia." *CJ* 105 (4, 2010): 343–60.

Chmiel, "'Sociophonie' de la fête." Chmiel, J. "Une 'sociophonie' de la fête de Shavouot-Pentecôte." *AnCrac* 28 (1996): 219–24.

Cho, "Foundation." Cho, Sung Hyun. "A Theoretical Foundation for a Healing Ministry in the Context of the Korean Evangelical Holiness Church." ThM thesis, Fuller School of World Mission, 1995.

Cho, "Healing." Cho, Il-Koo. "Healing in the Context of Korean Pentecostalism, 1950s to the Present: Historical and Ethnographic Approaches." PhD diss., Claremont Graduate University, 2002.

Cho, *Spirit and Kingdom*. Cho, Youngmo. *Spirit and Kingdom in the Writings of Luke and Paul: An Attempt to Reconcile These Concepts*. Foreword by R. P. Menzies. PBMon. Waynesboro, Ga., and Milton Keynes, U.K.: Paternoster, 2005.

Cho, "Spirit and Kingdom." Cho, Youngmo. "Spirit and Kingdom in Luke-Acts: Proclamation as the Primary Role of the Spirit in Relation to the Kingdom of God in Luke-Acts." *AJPS* 6 (2, 2003): 173–97.

Choat and Nobbs, "Formulae." Choat, Malcolm, and Alanna Nobbs. "Monotheistic Formulae of Belief in Greek Letters on Papyrus from the Second to the Fourth Century." *JGRCJ* 2 (2001–5): 36–51.

Chock, "Kinship." Chock, Phyllis Pease. "Kinship and Culture: Some Problems in Ndembu Kinship." *SWJA* 23 (1, 1967): 74–89.

Choge, "Hospitality." Choge, Emily J. "Hospitality in Africa." Page 390 in *Africa Bible Commentary*. Edited by Tokunboh Adeyemo. Grand Rapids: Zondervan; Nairobi: WordAlive, 2006.

Choi, "Personality." Choi, Mun Hong. "The Personality of the Holy Spirit in the New Testament with Special Reference to Luke-Acts." PhD diss., University of Wales, 1999.

Chomsky, *Structures*. Chomsky, Noam. *Syntactic Structures*. The Hague: Mouton, 1966.

Chow, *Patronage*. Chow, John K. *Patronage and Power: A Study of Social Networks in Corinth*. JSNTSup 75. Sheffield, U.K.: JSOT Press, 1992.

Chow, "World." Chow, John K. "Christians in an Ever-Changing World: Lessons from I Clement and I Corinthians." *List* 32 (1, 1997): 39–47.

Chrétien, "Exchange." Chrétien, Jean-Pierre. "Confronting the Unequal Exchange of the Oral and the Written." Pages 75–90 in *African Historiographies: What History for Which Africa?* Edited by Bogumil Jewsiewicki and David Newbury. SSAMD 12. Beverly Hills, Calif.: Sage, 1986.

Christ, "Consuming Bodies." Christ, Alice. "Consuming Bodies in Early Imperial Rome." *AHB* 10 (3–4, 1996): 93–109.

Christensen, *Canon*. Christensen, Duane L. *Explosion of the Canon: The Greek New Testament in Early Church History*. North Richland Hills, Tex.: BIBAL Press, 2004.

Christes, "Artes liberales." Christes, Johannes. "Artes liberales." *BrillPauly* 2:71–73.

Christes, "Education." Christes, Johannes. "Education." *BrillPauly* 4:815–25.

Christes, "Education/Culture." Christes, Johannes. "Education/Culture." *Brill Pauly* 4:825–35.

Christes, "Grammaticus." Christes, Johannes. "Grammaticus." *BrillPauly* 5:986–87.

Christes, "School." Christes, Johannes. "School: Rome." *BrillPauly* 13:79–83.

Christol and Drew-Bear, "Sergii Pauli." Christol, M., and Thomas Drew-Bear. "Les Sergii Pauli et Antioche." Pages 177–92 in *Actes du Ier congrès international sur Antioche de Piside*. Edited by Thomas Drew-Bear, Mehmet Tashalan, and Christine M. Thomas. Collection archéologie et histoire de l'antiquité, Université Lumière-Lyon 2, vol. 5. Paris: Boccard, 2002.

Chroust, "Comments." Chroust, Anton-Hermann. "Some Comments on Philo of Alexandria, De aeternitate mundi." *LTP* 31 (2, 1975): 135–45.

Chroust, "Fragment." Chroust, Anton-Hermann. "A Fragment of Aristotle's On Philosophy in Philo of Alexandria, De opificio mundi I, 7." *DivThom* 77 (2, 1974), 224–35.

Chroust, "Myth." Chroust, Anton-Hermann. "The Myth of Aristotle's Suicide." *Modern Schoolman* 44 (1967): 177–78.

Chrupcala, "Disegno." Chrupcala, Leslaw D. "Il disegno di Dio e l'annuncio del regno alla luce di At 28,17–31." *SBFLA* 47 (1997): 79–96.

Chuen, "Acts 10." Chuen, Lim Yeu. "Acts 10: A Gentile Model for Pentecostal Experience." *AJPS* 1 (1, 1998): 62–72.

Chung-Kim and Hains, *Acts*. Chung-Kim, Esther, and Todd R. Hains, eds. *Acts*. Reformation Commentary on Scripture VI. Downers Grove, Ill.: IVP Academic, 2014.

Ciampa, "Decapolis." Ciampa, Roy E. "Decapolis." *DNTB* 266–68.

Ciampa, "Examined." Ciampa, Roy. "'Examined the Scriptures'? The Meaning of *anakrinontes tas graphas* in Acts 17:11." *JBL* 130 (3, Fall 2011): 527–41.

Ciampa and Rosner, *Letter*. Ciampa, Roy E., and Brian S. Rosner. *The First Letter to the Corinthians*. PillNTC. Grand Rapids: Eerdmans, 2010.

Cifrak, "Petrus." Cifrak, Mario. "Petrus und Jakobus bei dem sog. Apostelkonzil in Jerusalem (Apg 15)." *Antonianum* 85 (1, 2010): 9–18.

Citroni, "Dedications." Citroni, Mario. "Dedications." *OCD*³ 438–39.

Citroni, "Patronage, Literary." Citroni, Mario. "Patronage, Literary: Roman." *OCD*³ 1124–26.

Claasen, "Exile." Claasen, J. M. "Exile, Death, and Immortality: Voices from the Grave." *Latomus* 55 (3, 1996): 571–90.

Clabeaux, "Viper." Clabeaux, John. "The Story of the Maltese Viper and Luke's Apology for Paul." *CBQ* 67 (4, 2005): 604–10.

Cladis, "Modernity." Cladis, Mark S. "Modernity *in* Religion: A Response to Constantin Fasolt's 'History and Religion in the Modern Age.'" *History and Theory* 45 (4, 2006): 93–103.

Clara Rhodos. Clara Rhodos: Studi e materiali pubblicati a cura dell'Istituto storico-archeologico di Rodi. 10 vols. Rhodes, Greece: Istituto Storico-Archeologico, 1928–41.

Clark, *Acts*. Clark, Albert C. *The Acts of the Apostles: A Critical Edition with Introduction and Notes in Selected Passages*. Oxford: Clarendon, 1933.

Clark, "Childbirth." Clark, Edith Gillian. "Childbirth." *OCD*³ 321.

Clark, "Construction." Clark, David J. "A Not Infrequent Construction: Litotes in the Book of Acts." *BTr* 55 (4, 2004): 433–40.

Clark, *Early Church*. Clark, Elizabeth A. *Women in the Early Church*. MFC 13. Wilmington, Del.: Michael Glazier, 1983.

Clark, "Evidence." Clark, Mathew S. "Initial Evidence: A Southern African Perspective." *AJPS* 1 (2, 1998): 203–17.

Clark, *Impartation*. Clark, Randy. *There Is More: Reclaiming the Power of Impartation*. Foreword by Bill Johnson. Mechanicsburg, Pa.: Global Awakening, 2006.

Clark, "Miracles." Clark, David K. "Miracles in the World Religions." Pages 199–213 in *In Defense of Miracles: A Comprehensive Case for God's Action in History*. Edited by R. Douglas Geivett and Gary R. Habermas. Downers Grove, Ill.: InterVarsity, 1997.

Clark, *Parallel Lives*. Clark, Andrew C. *Parallel Lives: The Relation of Paul to the Apostles in the Lucan Perspective*. Carlisle, U.K.: Paternoster, 2001.

Clark, "Poetics." Clark, Christina A. "The Poetics of Manhood? Nonverbal Behavior in Catullus 51." *CP* 103 (3, 2008): 257–81.

Clark, "Role." Clark, Andrew C. "The Role of the Apostles." Pages 169–90 in *Witness to the Gospel: The Theology of Acts*. Edited by I. Howard Marshall and David Peterson. Grand Rapids: Eerdmans, 1998.

Clark, "Widows." Clark, Edith Gillian. "Widows." *OCD*³ 1621–22.

Clark, *Women in Antiquity*. Clark, Gillian. *Women in Late Antiquity: Pagan and Christian Lifestyles*. Oxford: Oxford University Press, 1993.

Clark, "Worship." Clark, Kenneth W. "Worship in the Jerusalem Temple after A.D. 70." *NTS* 6 (4, 1960): 269–80.

Clarke, "Alexandria." Clarke, Andrew D. "Alexandria." *DNTB* 23–25.

Clarke, "Alexandrian Library." Clarke, Andrew D. "Alexandrian Library." *DNTB* 25–26.

Clarke, "Alexandrian Scholarship." Clarke, Andrew D. "Alexandrian Scholarship." *DNTB* 27–29.

Clarke, "Brother." Clarke, Andrew D. "Equality or Mutuality? Paul's Use of 'Brother' Language." Pages 151–64 in *The New Testament in Its First Century Setting: Essays on Context and Background in Honour of B. W. Winter on His 65th Birthday*. Edited by P. J. Williams et al. Grand Rapids and Cambridge, U.K.: Eerdmans, 2004.

Clarke, "Erastus Inscription." Clarke, Andrew D. "Another Corinthian Erastus Inscription." *TynBul* 42 (1, 1991): 146–51.

Clarke, *Geography*. Clarke, Katherine. *Between Geography and History: Hellenistic Constructions of the Roman World*. Oxford: Clarendon, 1999.

Clarke, *Houses*. Clarke, John R. *The Houses of Roman Italy: 100 B.C.–A.D. 250*. Berkeley: University of California Press, 1991.

Clarke, "Imitators." Clarke, Andrew D. "'Be Imitators of Me': Paul's Model of Leadership." *TynBul* 49 (2, 1998): 329–60.

Clarke, "Italy." Clarke, Andrew D. "Rome and Italy." Pages 455–81 in *The Book of Acts in Its Graeco-Roman Setting*. Edited by David W. J. Gill and Conrad Gempf. Vol. 2 of *The Book of Acts in Its First Century Setting*. Edited by Bruce W. Winter. Grand Rapids: Eerdmans; Carlisle, U.K.: Paternoster, 1994.

Clarke, *Leadership*. Clarke, Andrew D. *A Pauline Theology of Church Leadership*. LNTS 362. London: T&T Clark, 2008.

Clarke, "Septuagint." Clarke, W. K. L. "The Use of the Septuagint in Acts." *BegChr* 2:66–105.

Clarke, "Spaces." Clarke, John R. "Constructing the Spaces of Epiphany in Ancient Greek and Roman Visual Culture." Pages 257–79 in *Text, Image, and Christians in the Graeco-Roman World: A Festschrift in Honor of David Lee Balch*. Edited by Aliou Cissé Niang and Carolyn Osiek. PrTMS 176. Eugene, Ore.: Pickwick, 2012.

Clarke, *Wrestlin' Jacob*. Clarke, Erskine. *Wrestlin' Jacob: A Portrait of Religion in the Old South*. Atlanta: John Knox, 1979.

Classen, "Analyse." Classen, Carl Joachim. "Zur rhetorischen Analyse der Paulusbriefe." *ZNW* 86 (1–2, 1995): 120–21.

Classen, "Poetry." Classen, Carl Joachim. "Poetry and Rhetoric in Lucretius." *TAPA* 99 (1968): 77–118.

Classen, "Rhetoric." Classen, Carl Joachim. "St. Paul's Epistles and Ancient Greek and Roman Rhetoric." *Rhetorica* 10 (4, 1992): 319–44.

Classen, *Rhetorical Criticism*. Classen, Carl Joachim. *Rhetorical Criticism of the New Testament*. Boston: Brill Academic, 2002.

Classen, "Rhetorik." Classen, Carl Joachim. "Paulus und die antike Rhetorik." *ZNW* 82 (1–2, 1991): 1–33.

Clay, *Epicurus*. Clay, Diskin. *Epicurus and Lucretius*. Ithaca, N.Y.: Cornell University Press, 1983.

Clayton, "Audience." Clayton, Edward W. "The Audience for Aristotle's *Rhetoric*." *Rhetorica* 22 (2, 2004): 183–203.

"Clean Water." "Clean Water for a Thirsty World." *World Vision Today* (Autumn 2000).

"Cleanser Used." "Was Cleanser Used to Clean the James Ossuary Inscription?" *BAR* 31 (1, 2005): 54.

Cleary, "Sanitation." Cleary, A. Simon Esmonde. "Sanitation." *OCD*³ 1354.

Cleave, *Satellite Atlas*. Cleave, R. L. W., ed. *The Holy Land Satellite Atlas*. 2 vols. Nicosia, Cyprus: Rohr Productions, 1999.

Clements, "Background." Clements, Ronald E. "The Old Testament Background of Acts 10:34–35." Pages 203–16 in *With Steadfast Purpose: Essays on Acts in Honor of Henry Jackson Flanders, Jr*. Edited by Naymond H. Keathley. Waco: Baylor University Press, 1990.

Clements, *Prophecy*. Clements, Ronald E. *Prophecy and Tradition*. Atlanta: John Knox, 1975.

Clerget, "Lumière." Clerget, Joël. "La lumière du nom ou le parcours subjectif dans un corps social, Actes 9, 1–19." *SémBib* 86 (1997): 31–38.

Clifford, "Tent." Clifford, Richard J. "Tent of El and Israelite Tent of Meeting." *CBQ* 33 (Apr. 1971): 221–27.

Clinebell, *Care*. Clinebell, Howard. *Basic Types of Pastoral Care and Counseling: Resources for the Ministry of Healing and Growth*. Rev. ed. Nashville: Abingdon, 1984.

Clines, *Approach*. Clines, David J. A. *I, He, We, and They: A Literary Approach to Isaiah 53*. JSOTSup 1. Sheffield, U.K.: JSOT Press, 1976.

Clines, "Image." Clines, David J. A. "Image of God." *DPL* 426–28.

Clinton, "Epiphany." Clinton, Kevin. "Epiphany in the Eleusinian Mysteries." *ICS* 29 (2004): 85–101.

Cloete and Smit, "Name Called Babel." Cloete, G. D., and D. J. Smit. "'Its Name

Was Called Babel . . .'" *JTSA* 86 (1994): 81–87.

Co, "Summaries in Acts." Co, Maria Anicia. "The Major Summaries in Acts—Acts 2, 42–47; 4, 32–35; 5, 12–16: Linguistic and Literary Relationship." *ETL* 68 (1, 1992): 49–85.

Cobet, "Miletus." Cobet, Justus. "Miletus." *BrillPauly* 8:886–95.

Cocchini, "Evoluzione della festa." Cocchini, Francesca. "L'evoluzione storica-religiosa della festa di Pentecoste." *RivB* 25 (3, 1977): 297–326.

Cochrane, "Salmone." Cochrane, Michael R. "Salmone." *ISBE* 4:285.

Cockerill, "Melchizedek." Cockerill, Gareth Lee. "Melchizedek or 'King of Righteousness.'" *EvQ* 63 (4, 1991): 305–12.

Cockle, "Leuce Come." Cockle, Walter Eric Harold. "Leuce Come." *OCD*³ 848.

Cody, *Sanctuary*. Cody, Aelred. *Heavenly Sanctuary and Liturgy in the Epistle to the Hebrews*. St. Meinrad, Ind.: Grail, 1960.

Coetzee, "Life." Coetzee, J. C. "Life (Eternal Life) in St. John's Writings and the Qumran Scrolls." *Neot* 6 (1972): 48–66.

Coffee, "Theseus." Coffee, Neil. "Statius' Theseus: Martial or Merciful?" *CP* 104 (2, 2009): 221–28.

Coffey, "Knowledge." Coffey, David M. "Natural Knowledge of God: Reflections on Romans 1:18–32." *TS* 31 (4, 1970): 674–91.

Coggins, *Samaritans*. Coggins, R. J. *Samaritans and Jews: The Origins of Samaritanism Reconsidered*. Atlanta: John Knox; Oxford: Blackwell, 1975.

Coggins, "Samaritans and Acts." Coggins, R. J. "The Samaritans and Acts." *NTS* 28 (3, 1982): 423–34.

Coggins, "Samaritans in Josephus." Coggins, R. J. "The Samaritans in Josephus." Pages 257–73 in *Josephus, Judaism, and Christianity*. Edited by Louis H. Feldman and Gohei Hata. Detroit: Wayne State University Press, 1987.

Cohen, "Asinaeus." Cohen, Naomi G. "Asinaeus and Anilaeus: Additional Comments to Josephus' Antiquities of the Jews." *ASTI* 10 (1975–76): 30–37.

Cohen, "Attitude and Reality." Cohen, Y. "The Attitude to the Gentile in the Halakhah and in Reality in the Tannaitic Period." *Imm* 9 (1979): 32–41.

Cohen, *Beginnings*. Cohen, Shaye J. D. *The Beginnings of Jewishness: Boundaries, Varieties, Uncertainties*. Berkeley: University of California Press, 1999.

Cohen, "Benjaminite." Cohen, K. L. "Paul the Benjaminite: Mystery, Motives and Midrash." *CHSP* 60 (1990): 21–28.

Cohen, "Ceremony." Cohen, Shaye J. D. "The Rabbinic Conversion Ceremony." *JJS* 41 (2, 1990): 177–203.

Cohen, "Conversion." Cohen, Shaye J. D. "Conversion to Judaism in Historical Perspective: From Biblical Israel to Postbiblical Judaism." *ConsJud* 36 (4, 1983): 31–45.

Cohen, "Criterion." Cohen, Avinoam. "Was Age the Decisive Criterion of Subordination among the Amoraim?" *JQR* 92 (3–4, 2002): 279–313.

Cohen, "Earliest Evidence." Cohen, Naomi G. "Earliest Evidence of the Haftarah Cycle for the Sabbaths between *y"z btmwz* and *swkwt* in Philo." *JJS* 48 (2, 1997): 225–49.

Cohen, "Evidence on Synagogue." Cohen, Shaye J. D. "Pagan and Christian Evidence on the Ancient Synagogue." Pages 159–81 in *The Synagogue in Late Antiquity*. Edited by Lee I. Levine. Philadelphia: American Schools of Oriental Research, 1986.

Cohen, "False Prophets." Cohen, Shaye J. D. "False Prophets (4Q339), Netinim (4Q340), and Hellenism at Qumran." *JGRCJ* 1 (2000): 55–66.

Cohen, "Fathers." Cohen, Shaye J. D. "Can Converts to Judaism Say 'God of Our Fathers'?" *Judaism* 40 (4, 1991): 419–28.

Cohen, "Josephus and Scripture." Cohen, N. G. "Josephus and Scripture: Is Josephus' Treatment of the Scriptural Narrative Similar throughout the *Antiquities* I–XI?" *JQR* 54 (4, 1964): 311–32.

Cohen, *Josephus in Galilee*. Cohen, Shaye J. D. *Josephus in Galilee and Rome: His Vita and Development as a Historian*. Leiden: Brill, 1979.

Cohen, "Julia." Cohen, Sarah T. "Augustus, Julia, and the Development of Exile *ad insulam*." *CQ* 58 (1, 2008): 206–17.

Cohen, *Law*. Cohen, Boaz. *Jewish and Roman Law: A Comparative Study*. 2 vols. New York: Jewish Theological Seminary of America Press, 1966.

Cohen, *Maccabees*. Cohen, Shaye J. D. *From the Maccabees to the Mishnah*. LEC 7. Philadelphia: Westminster, 1987.

Cohen, "Masada." Cohen, Shaye J. D. "Masada: Literary Tradition, Archaeological Remains, and the Credibility of Josephus." *JJS* 33 (1982): 385–405.

Cohen, "Matrilineal Principle in Perspective." Cohen, Shaye J. D. "The Matrilineal Principle in Historical Perspective." *Judaism* 34 (1, 1985): 5–13.

Cohen, "Meir." Cohen, Naomi G. "Rabbi Meir, a Descendant of Anatolian Proselytes: New Light on His Name and the Historic Kernel of the Nero Legend in Gittin 56a." *JJS* 23 (1, 1972): 51–59.

Cohen, "Missionize." Cohen, Shaye J. D. "Did Ancient Jews Missionize?" *BRev* 19 (4, 2003): 40–47.

Cohen, "Names of Translators." Cohen, Naomi G. "The Names of the Translators in the Letter of Aristeas: A Study in the Dynamics of Cultural Transition." *JSJ* 15 (1, 1984): 32–64.

Cohen, "Noahide Commandments." Cohen, Naomi G. "Taryag and the Noahide Commandments." *JJS* 43 (1, 1992): 46–57.

Cohen, "Origins of Matrilineal Principle." Cohen, Shaye J. D. "The Origins of the Matrilineal Principle in Rabbinic Law." *AJSR* 10 (1, 1985): 19–53.

Cohen, "Respect for Judaism." Cohen, Shaye J. D. "Respect for Judaism by Gentiles according to Josephus." *HTR* 80 (4, 1987): 409–30.

Cohen, "Shekhinta." Cohen, Norman J. "Shekhinta ba-Galuta: A Midrashic Response to Destruction and Persecution." *JSJ* 13 (1–2, 1982): 147–59.

Cohen, "Structural Analysis." Cohen, Norman J. "Structural Analysis of a Talmudic Story: Joseph-Who-Honors-the-Sabbaths." *JQR* 72 (3, 1982): 161–77.

Cohen, "Virtues and Laws." Cohen, Naomi G. "The Greek Virtues and the Mosaic Laws in Philo: An Elucidation of *De specialibus legibus* IV 133–135." *SPhilA* 5 (1993): 9–23.

Cohen, "Was Timothy Jewish?" Cohen, Shaye J. D. "Was Timothy Jewish (Acts 16:1–3)? Patristic Exegesis, Rabbinic Law, and Matrilineal Descent." *JBL* 105 (2, 1986): 251–68.

Cohen, "What Happened at Masada?" Cohen, Shaye J. D. "What Really Happened at Masada?" *Moment* 13 (5, 1988): 28–35.

Cohen, "Women." Cohen, Shaye J. D. "Women in the Synagogues of Antiquity." *ConsJud* 34 (2, 1980): 23–29.

Cohick, *Women*. Cohick, Lynn H. *Women in the World of the Earliest Christians: Illuminating Ancient Ways of Life*. Grand Rapids: Baker Academic, 2009.

Cohn, *Trial*. Cohn, Haim. *The Trial and Death of Jesus*. New York: KTAV, 1977.

Cohn-Sherbok, "Introduction." Cohn-Sherbok, Dan. "Introduction." Pages ix–xx in *Voices of Messianic Judaism: Confronting Critical Issues Facing a Maturing Movement*. Edited by Dan Cohn-Sherbok. Baltimore: Lederer, 2001.

Cohn-Sherbok, *Messianic Judaism*. Cohn-Sherbok, Dan. *Messianic Judaism*. New York, London: Cassell, 2000.

Cohn-Sherbok, "Paul and Exegesis." Cohn-Sherbok, Dan. "Paul and Rabbinic Exegesis." *SJT* 35 (2, 1982): 117–32.

Cole, *Mark*. Cole, R. A. *The Gospel according to St. Mark*. TNTC. Grand Rapids: Eerdmans, 1961.

Cole, "Model." Cole, Harold R. "A Model of Contextualized Deliverance Ministry: A Case Study: The Cordillera Rehabilitation Center." *JAM* 5 (2, Sept. 2003): 259–73.

Cole, "Numbers." Cole, R. Dennis. "Numbers." Pages 338–417 in vol. 1 of *Zondervan Illustrated Bible Backgrounds Commentary: Old Testament*. Edited by John Walton. 5 vols. Grand Rapids: Zondervan, 2009.

Cole, "Read." Cole, Susan Guettel. "Could Greek Women Read and Write?" Pages 219–45 in *Reflections of Women in Antiquity*. Edited by Helene P. Foley. New York: Gordon & Breach Science, 1981.

Cole, *Theoi megaloi*. Cole, Susan Guettel. *Theoi megaloi: The Cult of the Great Gods at Samothrace*. ÉPROER 96. Leiden: Brill, 1984.

Coleman, "Dynamic." Coleman, Robert E. "The Dynamic of the Holy Spirit in the Apostolic Church." *STJ* 7 (1–2, 1999): 27–35.

Collart, *Philippes*. Collart, Paul. *Philippes, ville de Macédoine*. Paris: Boccard, 1937.

Collected Novels. *Collected Ancient Greek Novels*. Edited by B. P. Reardon. Berkeley: University of California Press, 1989.

Colless, "Inscriptions." Colless, Brian E. "The Proto-alphabetic Inscriptions of Sinai." *AbrN* 28 (1990): 1–52.

Colleyn, "Horse." Colleyn, Jean-Paul. "Horse, Hunter and Messenger: The Possessed Men of the *Nya* Cult in Mali." Pages 68–78 in *Spirit Possession, Modernity and Power in Africa*. Edited by Heike Behrend and Ute Luig. Madison: University of Wisconsin Press, 1999.

Collins, "Apocalyptic Literature." Collins, John J. "Apocalyptic Literature." Pages 345–70 in *Early Judaism and Its Modern Interpreters*. Edited by Robert A. Kraft and George W. E. Nickelsburg. SBLBMI 2. Atlanta: Scholars Press, 1986.

Collins, "Aristobulus." Collins, A. Yarbro. Introduction to "Aristobulus." *OTP* 2:831–36.

Collins, "Artapanus." Collins, John J. Introduction to "Artapanus." *OTP* 2:889–96.

Collins, *Beginning*. Collins, Adela Yarbro. *The Beginning of the Gospel: Probings of Mark in Context*. Minneapolis: Fortress, 1992.

Collins, "Cause." Collins, Derek. "Nature, Cause, and Agency in Greek Magic." *TAPA* 133 (2003): 17–49.

Collins, *Corinthians*. Collins, Raymond F. *First Corinthians*. SP 7. Collegeville, Minn.: Liturgical Press, 1999.

Collins, *Diakonia*. Collins, John H. *Diakonia: Re-interpreting the Ancient Sources*. New York and Oxford: Oxford University Press, 1990.

Collins, "Eschatologies." Collins, John J. "Eschatologies of Late Antiquity." *DNTB* 330–37.

Collins, *Exorcism*. Collins, James M. *Exorcism and Deliverance Ministry in the Twentieth Century: An Analysis of the Practice and Theology of Exorcism in Modern Western Christianity*. Foreword by Ian Stackhouse. SEHT. Colorado Springs: Paternoster, 2009.

Collins, "Eyewitnesses." Collins, John N. "Re-thinking 'Eyewitnesses' in the Light of 'Servants of the Word' (Luke 1:2)." *ExpT* 121 (9, 2010): 447–52.

Collins, "Improvisation." Collins, Derek. "Improvisation in Rhapsodic Performance." *Helios* 28 (1, 2001): 11–27.

Collins, "Integrity." Collins, Raymond F. "A propos the Integrity of 1 Thes." *ETL* 55 (1, 1979): 67–106.

Collins, "*Joseph and Aseneth*." Collins, John J. "*Joseph and Aseneth*: Jewish or Christian?" *JSP* 14 (2, 2005): 97–112.

Collins, *Language of God*. Collins, Francis S. *The Language of God: A Scientist Presents Evidence for Belief*. New York: Free Press, 2006.

Collins, *Life of Jesus*. Collins, Adela Yarbro. *Is Mark's Gospel a Life of Jesus?* The Père Marquette Lecture in Theology 1990. Milwaukee: Marquette University Press, 1990.

Collins, "Mapping." Collins, Derek. "Mapping the Entrails: The Practice of Greek Hepatoscopy." *AJP* 129 (3, 2008): 319–45.

Collins, *Mark*. Collins, Adela Yarbro. *Mark: A Commentary*. Minneapolis: Fortress, 2007.

Collins, "Natural Theology." Collins, John J. "Natural Theology and Biblical Tradition: The Case of Hellenistic Judaism." *CBQ* 60 (1, 1998): 1–15.

Collins, "Oracles." Collins, John J. "Sibylline Oracles." *DNTB* 1107–12.

Collins, "Prince." Collins, John J. "Prince." Pages 662–64 in *Dictionary of Deities and Demons in the Bible*. 2nd rev. ed. Edited by Karel van der Toorn, Bob Becking, and Pieter W. van der Horst. Leiden: Brill; Grand Rapids: Eerdmans, 1999.

Collins, "Revolution." Collins, Andrew W. "The Palace Revolution: The Assassination of Domitian and the Accession of Nerva." *Phoenix* 63 (1–2, 2009): 73–106.

Collins, "Servant." Collins, John J. "The Suffering Servant at Qumran?" *BRev* 9 (6, 1993): 25–27, 63.

Collins, *Sibylline Oracles*. Collins, John J. *The Sibylline Oracles of Egyptian Judaism*. SBLDS 13. Missoula, Mont.: SBL, 1972.

Collins, "Sibylline Oracles." Collins, John J. Introduction to "Sibylline Oracles." *OTP* 1:317–26, 354–61, 381–83, 390–92, 406, 408–9, 415–17, 430–33, 443–44, 453, 459–60, 469.

Collins, "Son of God." Collins, John J. "A Pre-Christian 'Son of God' among the Dead Sea Scrolls." *BRev* 9 (3, 1993): 34–38, 57.

Collins, "Son of Man." Collins, John J. "The Son of Man in First-Century Judaism." *NTS* 38 (3, 1992): 448–66.

Collins, "Symbol." Collins, John J. "A Symbol of Otherness: Circumcision and Salvation in the First Century." Pages 163–86 in *"To See Ourselves as Others See Us": Christians, Jews, "Others" in Late Antiquity*. Edited by Jacob Neusner and Ernest S. Frerichs. Scholars Press Studies in the Humanities. Chico, Calif.: Scholars Press, 1985.

Collins, "Temptation." Collins, Raymond F. "The Temptation of Jesus." *MelT* 26 (1974): 32–45.

Collins, "Testamentary Literature." Collins, John J. "The Testamentary Literature in Recent Scholarship." Pages 268–85 in *Early Judaism and Its Modern Interpreters*. Edited by Robert A. Kraft and George W. E. Nickelsburg. SBLBMI 2. Atlanta: Scholars Press, 1986.

Collins, "Theories." Collins, Randall. "Functional and Conflict Theories of Educational Stratification." *AmSocRev* 36 (1971): 1002–19.

Collins, "Verses." Collins, Derek. "The Magic of Homeric Verses." *CP* 103 (3, 2008): 211–36.

Collins, "Vessels." Collins, M. F. "The Hidden Vessels in Samaritan Traditions." *JSJ* 3 (2, 1972): 97–116.

Collins, "Works." Collins, John J. "The Works of the Messiah." *DSD* 1 (1994): 98–112.

Collins, *Written*. Collins, Raymond F. *These Things Have Been Written: Studies on the Fourth Gospel*. LTPM 2. Louvain: Peeters; Grand Rapids: Eerdmans, 1990.

Colpe, "Essener." Colpe, C. "Die Essener und das Judenchristentum: Zu den Handschriftenfunden am Toten Meer." *DeuUn* 12 (5–6, 1957): 20–23; (7, 1957): 10–15.

Colson, "Possession." Colson, Elizabeth. "Central and South Africa: Spirit Possession among the Tonga of Zambia." Pages 69–103 in *Spirit Mediumship and Society in Africa*. Edited by John Beattie and John Middleton. Foreword by Raymond Firth. New York: Africana, 1969.

Colson, "Triangular Numbers." Colson, F. H. "Triangular Numbers in the New Testament." *JTS* 16 (1915): 67–76.

Colwell, "Defining Away." Colwell, Gary. "On Defining Away the Miraculous." *Philosophy* 57 (1982): 327–37.

Combet-Galland, "Expulsion." Combet-Galland, Corina. "L'expulsion du mal: Un acte de naissance de l'Église." *FoiVie* 104 (1, 2005): 43–61.

Combet-Galland, "Voyage." Combet-Galland, Corina. "Paul l'apôtre: Un voyage contrarié pour bagage." *ETR* 80 (3, 2005): 361–74.

Combrink, *Analysis*. Combrink, H. J. B. *Structural Analysis of Acts 6:8–8:3*. StThSt 4. Cape Town: Dutch Reformed Church, 1979.

Compton, "Census." Compton, Jared M. "Once More: Quirinius's Census." *Detroit Baptist Seminary Journal* 14 (2009): 45–54.

Concannon, "Archaeology." Concannon, Cavan W. "The Archaeology of the Pauline Mission." Pages 57–83 in *All Things to All Cultures: Paul among Jews, Greeks, and Romans*. Edited by Mark Harding and Alanna Nobbs. Grand Rapids: Eerdmans, 2013.

Conley, "Philo." Conley, Thomas M. "Philo of Alexandria." Pages 695–713 in *Handbook of Classical Rhetoric in the Hellenistic Period, 330 B.C.–A.D. 400*. Edited by Stanley E. Porter. Leiden: Brill, 1997.

Connolly, "Virtue." Connolly, Joy. "Virtue and Violence: The Historians on Politics." Pages 181–94 in *The Cambridge Companion to the Roman Historians*. Edited by Andrew Feldherr. Cambridge: Cambridge University Press, 2009.

Consani, "Koiné et dialectes." Consani, Carlo. "La koiné et les dialectes grecs dans la documentation linguistique et la réflexion métalinguistique des premiers siècles de notre ère." Pages 23–39 in *Une langue introuvable?* Vol. 1 of *La koiné grecque antique*. Edited by Claude Brixhe. Travaux et mémoires: Études anciennes 10. Nancy: Presses universitaires de Nancy, 1993.

Constant, "Psaume 16 dans discours." Constant, Pierre. "Forme textuelle et justesse doctrinale de l'Ancien Testament dans le Nouveau: La citation du Psaume 16 dans le discours d'Actes 2." *BapRT* 2 (1, 1992): 4–15.

Constantakopoulou, "Islander." Constantakopoulou, Christy. "Proud to Be an Islander: Island Identity in Multi-polis Islands in the Classical and Hellenistic Aegean." *MHR* 20 (1, 2005): 1–34.

Constantinides, "Zar." Constantinides, Pamela. "The History of *zar* in the Sudan: Theories of Origin, Recorded Observation, and Oral Tradition." Pages 83–99 in *Women's Medicine: The zar-bori Cult in Africa and Beyond*. Edited by I. M. Lewis, Ahmed Al-Safi, and Sayyid Hurreiz. Edinburgh: Edinburgh University Press for the International African Institute, 1991.

Conte and Most, "Genre." Conte, Gian Biagio, and Glenn W. Most. "Genre." *OCD*³ 630–31.

Conti, "Paolo ad Efeso." Conti, V. "Paolo ad Efeso." *RivB* 37 (3, 1989): 283–303.

Conway, "Gender." Conway, Colleen. "Gender and Divine Relativity in Philo of Alexandria." *JSJ* 34 (4, 2003): 471–91.

Conybeare, "Introduction." Conybeare, F. C. Introduction. Pages v–xv in vol. 1 of Philostratus, *The Life of Apollonius of Tyana*. Translated by F. C. Conybeare. 2 vols. LCL. Cambridge, Mass.: Harvard University Press, 1912.

Conybeare, "Stoning of Stephen." Conybeare, F. C. "The Stoning of St. Stephen." *Exp*, 8th ser., 6 (1913): 466–70.

Conzelmann, *Acts*. Conzelmann, Hans. *A Commentary on the Acts of the Apostles*. Edited by Eldon Jay Epp with Christopher R. Matthews. Translated by James Limburg, A. Thomas Kraabel, and Donald H. Juel. Hermeneia. Philadelphia: Fortress, 1987.

Conzelmann, "Areopagus." Conzelmann, Hans. "The Address of Paul on the Areopagus." Pages 217–30 in *Studies in Luke-Acts: Essays in Honor of Paul Schubert*. Edited by Leander E. Keck and J. Louis Martyn. Nashville: Abingdon, 1966.

Conzelmann, *Corinthians*. Conzelmann, Hans. *1 Corinthians: A Commentary on the First Epistle to the Corinthians*. Edited by George W. MacRae. Translated by James W. Leitch. Bibliography and references by James W. Dunkly. Hermeneia. Philadelphia: Fortress, 1975.

Conzelmann, *History*. Conzelmann, Hans. *History of Primitive Christianity*. Translated by John E. Steely. Nashville: Abingdon, 1973.

Conzelmann, "Luke's Place." Conzelmann, Hans. "Luke's Place in the Development of Early Christianity." Pages 298–316 in *Studies in Luke-Acts: Essays in Honor of Paul Schubert*. Edited by Leander E. Keck and J. Louis Martyn. Nashville: Abingdon, 1966.

Conzelmann, "Mädchen." Conzelmann, Hans. "Korinth und die Mädchen der Aphrodite: Zur Religionsgeschichte der Stadt Korinth." *Nachrichten der Akademie der Wissenschaften in Göttingen, Philologisch-historische Klasse* 8 (1967–68): 247–61.

Conzelmann, *Theology*. Conzelmann, Hans. *An Outline of the Theology of the New Testament*. New York: Harper & Row, 1969.

Conzelmann, *Theology of Luke*. Conzelmann, Hans. *The Theology of St. Luke*. Translated by G. Buswell. New York: Harper & Row; London: Faber & Faber, 1960.

Conzelmann and Lindemann, *Interpreting*. Conzelmann, Hans, and Andreas Lindemann. *Interpreting the New Testament: An Introduction to the Principles and Methods of New Testament Exegesis*. Translated by Siegfried S. Schatzmann. Peabody, Mass.: Hendrickson, 1988.

Cook, "4Q246." Cook, Edward M. "4Q246." *BBR* 5 (1995): 43–66.

Cook, "Aramaic Language." Cook, Edward M. "Aramaic Language and Literature." *OEANE* 1:178–84.

Cook, "Conversion." Cook, Edwin A. "On the Conversion of Non-agnates into Agnates among the Manga, Jimi River, Western Highlands District, New Guinea." *SWJA* 26 (2, 1970): 190–96.

Cook, *Dogma*. Cook, Michael. *Early Muslim Dogma: A Source-Critical Study*. Cambridge: Cambridge University Press, 1981.

Cook, "Exegesis." Cook, James I. "John 20:19–23—An Exegesis." *RefR* 21 (2, 1967): 2–10.

Cook, "Fragments." Cook, David. "The Pastoral Fragments Reconsidered." *JTS* 35 (1, 1984): 120–31.

Cook, *Interpretation*. Cook, John Granger. *The Interpretation of the New Testament in Greco-Roman Paganism*. Peabody, Mass.: Hendrickson, 2002; Tübingen: J. C. B. Mohr, 2000.

Cook, "Manticores." Cook, Robert. "Devils and Manticores: Plundering Jung for a Plausible Demonology." Pages 165–84 in *The Unseen World: Christian Reflections on Angels, Demons, and the Heavenly Realm*. Edited by Anthony N. S. Lane. Grand Rapids: Baker; Carlisle, U.K.: Paternoster, 1996.

Cook, "Mission." Cook, Michael J. "The Mission to the Jews in Acts: Unraveling Luke's 'Myth of the 'Myriads.'" Pages 102–23 in *Luke-Acts and the Jewish People: Eight Critical Perspectives*. Edited by Joseph B. Tyson. Minneapolis: Augsburg, 1988.

Cook, *Muhammad*. Cook, Michael. *Muhammad*. Past Masters Series. New York: Oxford University Press, 1983.

Cook, "Perspective on Women." Cook, Johann. "Ben Sira's Perspective on Women—Jewish and/or Hellenistic?" *JS/TS* 17 (1, 2008): 1–18.

Cook, "Philosophy." Cook, Johann. "Greek Philosophy and the Septuagint." *JNSL* 24 (1, 1998): 177–91.

Cook, "Plutarch's Use." Cook, Brad L. "Plutarch's Use of λέγεται: Narrative Design and Source in *Alexander*." *GRBS* 42 (4, 2001): 329–60.

Cook, "Titus and Berenice." Cook, J. A. "Titus and Berenice." *AJP* 72 (1951): 162–75.

Cook, "Weights." Cook, Edward M. "Weights and Measures." *ISBE* 4:1046–55.

Cook, "Words of Levi." Cook, Edward M. "The Words of Levi." *DSSNT* 250–60.

Cook, "Zenon Papyri." Cook, Rosalie R. E. "Zenon Papyri." *DNTB* 1300–1303.

Cook, *Zeus*. Cook, Arthur Bernard. *Zeus: A Study in Ancient Religion*. 3 vols. Cambridge: Cambridge University Press, 1914–40.

Cook and Sherwin-White, "Cnidus." Cook, John Manuel, and Susan Mary Sherwin-White. "Cnidus." *OCD*³ 354.

Cooper, "Crafts." Cooper, Alison Burford. "Crafts, Trade: Classical Antiquity." *Brill Pauly* 3:899–907.

Cooper, "Philosophers." Cooper, John M. "Greek Philosophers on Suicide." Pages 9–38 in *Suicide and Euthanasia: Historical and Contemporary Themes*. Edited by Baruch Alter Brody. Dordrecht, Neth.: Kluwer, 1989.

Cooper, "Posidonius." Cooper, John M. "Posidonius on Emotions." Pages 71–111 in *The Emotions in Hellenistic Philosophy*. Edited by Juha Sihvola and Troels Engberg-Pedersen. TSHP 46. Dordrecht, Neth.: Kluwer Academic, 1998.

Cooper, "Prophecies." Cooper, Jerrold. "Assyrian Prophecies, the Assyrian Tree, and the Mesopotamian Origins of Jewish Monotheism, Greek Philosophy, Christian Theology, Gnosticism, and Much More." *JAOS* 120 (3, 2000): 430–44.

Coote, *Amos*. Coote, Robert B. *Amos among the Prophets: Composition and Theology*. Philadelphia: Fortress, 1981.

Cope, *Scribe*. Cope, O. Lamar. *Matthew: A Scribe Trained for the Kingdom of Heaven*. CBQMS 5. Washington, D.C.: Catholic Biblical Association of America, 1976.

Cope, "Step." Cope, Lamar. "1 Cor 11:2–16: One Step Further." *JBL* 97 (3, 1978): 435–36.

Copestake, "How Neurotic?" Copestake, David R. "How Neurotic Was Paul?" *ExpT* 94 (7, 1983): 200–204.

Copher, "Presence in the Bible." Copher, Charles B. "Blacks/Negroes: Participants in the Development of Civilization in the Ancient World and Their Presence in the Bible." *JITC* 23 (1, 1995): 3–47.

Copher, *Studies*. Copher, Charles B. *Black Biblical Studies—An Anthology of Charles B. Copher: Biblical and Theological Issues on the Black Presence in the Bible*. Chicago: Black Light Fellowship, 1993.

Coppens, "Don." Coppens, J. "Le don de l'Esprit d'après les textes de Qumrân et le quatrième évangile." Pages 209–23 in *L'Évangile de Jean: Études et problèmes*. RechBib 3. Leuven: Desclée de Brouwer, 1958.

Coppens, "Imposition." Coppens, J. "L'imposition des mains dans les Actes des apôtres." Pages 404–38 in *Les Actes des apôtres: Traditions, rédaction, théologie*. Edited by Jacob Kremer. BETL 48. Gembloux, Belg.: J. Duculot; Leuven: Leuven University Press, 1979.

Cordier, "Circoncision." Cordier, P. "Les Romains et la circoncision." *REJ* 160 (3–4, 2001): 337–55.

Corley, "Caution." Corley, Jeremy. "Caution, Fidelity, and the Fear of God: Ben Sira's Teaching on Friendship in Sir 6:5–17." *EstBib* 54 (3, 1996): 313–26.

Corley, "Interpreting Paul's Conversion." Corley, Bruce. "Interpreting Paul's Conversion—Then and Now." Pages 1–17 in *The Road from Damascus: The Impact of Paul's Conversion on His Life, Thought, and Ministry*. Edited by Richard N. Longenecker. Grand Rapids: Eerdmans, 1997.

Corley, *Meals*. Corley, Kathleen E. *Private Women, Public Meals: Social Conflict in the Synoptic Tradition*. Peabody, Mass.: Hendrickson, 1993.

Cormack, "Funerary Monuments." Cormack, Sarah H. "Funerary Monuments: Hellenistic and Roman Periods." *OEANE* 2:347–50.

Cormack and Hammond, "Amphipolis." Cormack, James M. R., and Nicholas G. L. Hammond. "Amphipolis." *OCD*³ 76.

Cornell, "*Annales maximi*." Cornell, Tim J. "*Annales maximi*." *OCD*³ 98.

Cornell, "Annals." Cornell, Tim J. "Annals, Annalists." *OCD*³ 98–99.

Cornell, *Fragments*. Cornell, T. J., ed. *The Fragments of the Roman Historians*. Oxford: Oxford University Press, 2014.

Cornell, "*Tumultus*." Cornell, Tim J. "*Tumultus*." *OCD*³ 1564–65.

Cornfeld, *Josephus*. Cornfeld, Gaalya, ed., with Benjamin Mazar and Paul L. Maier. *Josephus: The Jewish War*. Grand Rapids: Zondervan, 1982.

Corrington, "Defense." Corrington, Gail Paterson. "The Defense of the Body and the Discourse of Appetite: Continence and Control in the Greco-Roman World." *Semeia* 57 (1992): 65–74.

Corrington, "Power." Corrington, Gail Paterson. "Power and the Man of Power in the Context of Hellenistic Popular Belief." *Helios* 13 (1, 1986): 75–86.

Corsten, *Inschriften von Kios*. Corsten, Thomas, ed. *Die Inschriften von Kios*. IGSK 29. Bonn: Rudolf Habelt, 1985.

Corvisier, "Pèlerinages." Corvisier, Jean-Nicolas. "Voyages et pèlerinages dans le monde grec antique." *MScRel* 66 (3, 2009): 31–40.

Corzo, *Wall Paintings*. Miguel Angel Corzo, ed., *Wall Paintings of the Tomb of Nefertari: Scientific Studies for Their Conservation*. Cairo: Egyptian Antiquities Organization, 1987.

Cosby, "Language." Cosby, Michael R. "Paul's Persuasive Language in Romans 5." Pages 209–26 in *Persuasive Artistry: Studies in New Testament Rhetoric in Honor of George A. Kennedy*. Edited by Duane F. Watson. JSNTSup 50. Sheffield, U.K.: Sheffield Academic, 1991.

Cosgrave, *History of Costume*. Cosgrave, Bronwyn. *The Complete History of Costume and Fashion from Ancient Egypt to the Present Day*. New York: Checkmark, 2000.

Cosgrove, "Divine ΔEI." Cosgrove, Charles H. "The Divine ΔEI in Luke-Acts: Investigations into the Lukan Understanding of God's Providence." *NovT* 26 (2, 1984): 168–90.

Costa, "Exorcisms." Costa, Tony. "The Exorcisms and Healings of Jesus Within Classical Culture." Pages 113–44 in *Christian Origins and Greco-Roman Culture: Social and Literary Contexts for the New Testament*. Edited by Stanley Porter and Andrew W. Pitts. Vol. 1 of Early Christianity in Its Hellenistic Context. Vol. 9 in Texts and Editions for New Testament Study. Leiden: Brill, 2013.

Costa, "Littérature apocalyptique." Costa, José. "Littérature apocalyptique et judaïsme rabbinique: Le problème de la bat qol." *REJ* 169 (1–2, 2010): 57–96.

Costa Grillo, "Discurso de Pedro." Costa Grillo, José Geraldo. "O discurso de Pedro em Pentecostes: Estudo do gênero literário em Atos 2:14–40." *VS* 7 (1, 1997): 37–52.

Cothenet, "Prière." Cothenet, Édouard. "La prière apostolique de Paul." *EspV* 118 (204, 2008): 10–15.

Cothenet, "Secte de Qumrân et la communauté chrétienne." Cothenet, Edouard. "La secte de Qumrân et la communauté chrétienne." *EspV* 99 (37, 1989): 488–94.

Cothenet, "Témoignage." Cothenet, Edouard. "Le témoignage selon saint Jean." *EspV* 101 (28, 1991): 401–7.

Cotter, "Miracle." Cotter, Wendy. "Miracle." *NIDB* 4:99–106.

Cotter, *Miracles*. Cotter, Wendy. *Miracles in Greco-Roman Antiquity: A Sourcebook for the Study of New Testament Miracle Stories*. CEC. London: Routledge, 1999.

Cotter, *Miracle Stories*. Cotter, Wendy J. *The Christ of the Miracle Stories: Portrait through Encounter*. Grand Rapids: Baker Academic, 2010.

Cotter, "Miracle Stories." Cotter, Wendy. "Miracle Stories: The God Asclepius, the Pythagorean Philosophers, and the Roman Rulers." Pages 166–78 in *The Historical Jesus in Context*. Edited by

Amy-Jill Levine, Dale C. Allison Jr., and John Dominic Crossan. PrRR. Princeton: Princeton University Press, 2006.

Cotton, "Gospel." Cotton, Roger D. "The Gospel in the Old Testament According to Paul in Acts 13." Pages 277–89 in *Trajectories in the Book of Acts: Essays in Honor of John Wesley Wyckoff*. Edited by Paul Alexander, Jordan Daniel May, and Robert G. Reid. Eugene, Ore.: Wipf & Stock, 2010.

Cotton, "Significance." Cotton, Roger D. "The Pentecostal Significance of Numbers 11." *JPT* 10 (1, 2001): 3–10.

Cotton and Geiger, "Yyn." Cotton, Hannah M., and Joseph Geiger. "Yyn lhwrdws hmlk." *Cathedra* 53 (1989): 3–12.

Cotton and Greenfield, "Property." Cotton, Hannah M., and Jonas C. Greenfield. "Babatha's Property and the Law of Succession in the Babatha Archive." *ZPE* 104 (1994): 211–24.

Cottrell, *Egypt*. Cottrell, Leonard. *Egypt*. London: Nicholas Vane, 1965.

Couch, "Rhodes." Couch, Aaron J. "Rhodes." *ISBE* 4:182–83.

Coulston, "Mercenaries." Coulston, Jonathan C. N. "Mercenaries." *OCD*[3] 961–62.

Court, "Right." Court, J. M. "Right and Left: the Implications for Matthew 25.31–46." *NTS* 31 (2, 1985): 223–33.

Court, "Rivals." Court, John M. "Rivals in the Mission Field." *ExpT* 113 (12, 2002): 399–403.

Courtney, "Epic." Courtney, Edward. "Epic: Roman Literature." *BrillPauly* 4:1051–57.

Cousar, *Galatians*. Cousar, Charles B. *Galatians*. IBC. Atlanta: John Knox, 1982.

Cousar, *Philippians*. Cousar, Charles B. *Philippians and Philemon: A Commentary*. NTL. Louisville: Westminster John Knox, 2009.

Cousland, "Athletics." Cousland, J. R. C. "Athletics." *DNTB* 140–42.

Cousland, "Dionysus *theomachos*?" Cousland, J. R. C. "Dionysus *theomachos*? Echoes of the *Bacchae* in 3 Maccabees." *Bib* 82 (4, 2001): 539–48.

Cousland, "Prophets and Prophecy." Cousland, J. R. C. "Prophets and Prophecy." *DNTB* 830–35.

Cousland, "Temples." Cousland, J. R. C. "Temples, Greco-Roman." *DNTB* 1186–88.

Couture, "Glossolalie et mantra." Couture, André. "Glossolalie et mantra." *Cahiers du CRSR (Centre de recherches en sociologie religieuse)* 3 (1980): 105–16.

Couturier, "Vision du conseil." Couturier, Guy. "La vision du conseil divin: Étude d'une forme commune au prophétisme et à l'apocalyptique." *ScEs* 36 (1, 1984): 5–43.

Covell, "Foreword." Covell, Ralph. "Foreword." Pages ix–xi in *Witnesses to Power: Stories of God's Quiet Work in a Changing China*, by Tetsunao Yamamori and Kim-kwong Chan. Waynesboro, Ga.: Paternoster, 2000.

Cover, "Conquest." Cover, Michael. "Reconceptualizing Conquest: Colonial Narratives and Philo's Roman Accuser in the Hypothetica." *SPhilA* 22 (2010): 183–207.

Cowen, "Study of Laws." Cowen, Shimon. "The Halachic Study of the Noahide Laws." *Journal of Judaism & Civilization* 6 (2004): 60–110.

Cowton, "Alms Trade." Cowton, Christopher J. "The Alms Trade: A Note on Identifying the Beautiful Gate of Acts 3.2." *NTS* 42 (3, 1996): 475–76.

Cox, *Fire*. Cox, Harvey. *Fire from Heaven: The Rise of Pentecostal Spirituality and the Reshaping of Religion in the Twenty-First Century*. Reading, Mass.: Addison-Wesley, 1995.

Cox, "Foreword." Cox, Harvey. "Foreword." Pages xvii–xxi in *Global Pentecostal and Charismatic Healing*. Edited by Candy Gunther Brown. Foreword by Harvey Cox. Oxford: Oxford University Press, 2011.

Cox, "Miracles." Cox, Harvey. "Into the Age of Miracles: Culture, Religion, and the Market Revolution." *WPJ* 14 (1, Spring 1997): 87–95.

Cox, "Purification." Cox, Steven. "Paul's Purification Rite: Compromise or Cultural Sensitivity?" *CrisTR* 6 (1, 2008): 81–96.

Cracknell and White, *Methodism*. Cracknell, Kenneth, and Susan J. White. *An Introduction to World Methodism*. Cambridge: Cambridge University Press, 2005.

Craddock, *Philippians*. Craddock, Fred B. *Philippians*. Interpretation: A Bible Commentary for Preaching and Teaching. Atlanta: John Knox, 1985.

Craffert, "Healer." Craffert, Pieter F. "Crossan's Historical Jesus as Healer, Exorcist, and Miracle Worker." *R&T* 10 (3–4, 2003): 243–66.

Crafton, "Vision." Crafton, Jeffrey A. "Paul's Rhetorical Vision and the Purpose of Romans: Toward a New Understanding." *NovT* 32 (4, 1990): 317–39.

Cragg, *Reason*. Cragg, Gerald R. *The Church and the Age of Reason, 1648–1789*. Rev. ed. Penguin History of the Church 4. Baltimore: Penguin, 1970.

Craghan, "Amos." Craghan, John F. "The Prophet Amos in Recent Literature." *BTB* 2 (3, 1972): 242–61.

Craghan, "Mari." Craghan, John F. "Mari and Its Prophets: The Contributions of Mari to the Understanding of Biblical Prophecy." *BTB* 5 (Feb. 1975): 32–55.

Craig, "Miracles." Craig, William Lane. "The Problem of Miracles: A Historical and Philosophical Perspective." Pages 9–48 in *The Miracles of Jesus*. Edited by David Wenham and Craig Blomberg. Gospel Perspectives 6. Sheffield, U.K.: JSOT Press, 1986.

Craig, "Resurrection." Craig, William Lane. "The Bodily Resurrection of Jesus." Pages 47–74 in vol. 1 of *Studies of History and Tradition in the Four Gospels*. Edited by R. T. France and David Wenham. 2 vols. Gospel Perspectives 1–2. Sheffield, U.K.: JSOT Press, 1980–81.

Craig, "Tomb." Craig, William Lane. "The Empty Tomb of Jesus." Pages 173–200 in *Studies of History and Tradition in the Four Gospels*. Edited by R. T. France and David Wenham. Gospel Perspectives 2. Sheffield: JSOT Press, 1981.

Craigie, *Ugarit*. Craigie, Peter C. *Ugarit and the Old Testament*. Grand Rapids: Eerdmans, 1983.

Crandall, *Raising*. Crandall, Chauncey W., IV. *Raising the Dead: A Doctor Encounters the Miraculous*. New York: FaithWords, 2010.

Crane, "Burying." Crane, Jonathan K. "Jews Burying Gentiles." *RRJ* 10 (2, 2007): 145–61.

Cranfield, "Name." Cranfield, C. E. B. "Giving a Dog a Bad Name: A Note on H. Räisänen's *Paul and the Law*." *JSNT* 38 (1990): 77–85.

Cranfield, "Response." Cranfield, C. E. B. "Has the Old Testament Law a Place in the Christian Life? A Response to Professor Westerholm." *IBS* 15 (2, 1993): 50–64.

Cranfield, *Romans*. Cranfield, C. E. B. *A Critical and Exegetical Commentary on the Epistle to the Romans*. 2 vols. ICC. Edinburgh: T&T Clark, 1975.

Cranfield, "Romans 1.18." Cranfield, C. E. B. "Romans 1.18." *SJT* 21 (3, 1968): 330–35.

Cranston, *Miracle*. Cranston, Ruth. *The Miracle of Lourdes: Updated and Expanded Edition by the Medical Bureau of Lourdes*. New York: Image Books, Doubleday, 1988.

Crapanzaro, "Introduction." Crapanzaro, Vincent. Introduction. Pages 1–40 in *Case Studies in Spirit Possession*. Edited by Vincent Crapanzaro and Vivian Garrison. New York: Wiley, 1977.

Crapanzaro, "Mohammed." Crapanzaro, Vincent. "Mohammed and Dawia: Possession in Morocco." Pages 141–76 in *Case Studies in Spirit Possession*. Edited by Vincent Crapanzaro and Vivian Garrison. New York: Wiley, 1977.

Crapanzaro and Garrison, *Case Studies*. Crapanzaro, Vincent, and Vivian Garrison, eds. *Case Studies in Spirit Possession*. New York: Wiley, 1977.

Crawford, "Citizenship." Crawford, Michael H. "Citizenship, Roman." *OCD*³ 334–35.

Crawford, "Debt." Crawford, Michael H. "Debt, Debt Redemption." *BrillPauly* 4:140–44.

Crawford, "Folly." Crawford, Sidnie White. "Lady Wisdom and Dame Folly at Qumran." *DSD* 5 (3, 1998): 355–66.

Crawford, "Healing." Crawford, Suzanne J. "Religion, Healing, and the Body." Pages 29–45 in *Teaching Religion and Healing*. Edited by Linda L. Barnes and Inés Talamantez. AARTRSS. Oxford: Oxford University Press, 2006.

Crawford, "Lex." Crawford, Michael H. "Lex." *OCD*³ 849–53.

Crawford, *Miracles*. Crawford, Don. *Miracles in Indonesia: God's Power Builds His Church!* Wheaton: Tyndale, 1972.

Crawford, "Money." Crawford, Michael H. "Money, Money Economy: Rome." *BrillPauly* 9:150–57.

Crawford, "Population." Crawford, Michael H. "Population, Roman." *OCD*³ 1223.

Crawford, "Promised Land." Crawford, Timothy G. "Taking the Promised Land, Leaving the Promised Land: Luke's Use of Joshua for a Christian Foundation Story." *RevExp* 95 (2, 1998): 251–61.

Crawford, *Shantung Revival*. Crawford, Mary K. *The Shantung Revival*. Shanghai: China Baptist Publication Society, 1933.

Crawford and Lipsedge, "Help." Crawford, Tanya A., and Maurice Lipsedge. "Seeking Help for Psychological Distress: The Interface of Zulu Traditional Healing and Western Biomedicine." *MHRC* 7 (2, June 2004): 131–48.

Creech, "Narratee." Creech, R. Robert. "The Most Excellent Narratee: The Significance of Theophilus in Luke-Acts." Pages 107–26 in *With Steadfast Purpose: Essays on Acts in Honor of Henry Jackson Flanders, Jr.* Edited by Naymond H. Keathley. Waco: Baylor University Press, 1990.

Crehan, "Confirmation of Eunuch." Crehan, Joseph H. "The Confirmation of the Ethiopian Eunuch (Acts 8:39)." Pages 187–95 in *The Heritage of the Early Church: Essays in Honor of the Very Reverend Georges Vasilievich Florovsky*. OrChrAn 195. Rome: Pontificium Institutum Studiorum Orientalium, 1973.

Crenshaw, *Affirmation*. Crenshaw, James L. *Hymnic Affirmation of Divine Justice: The Doxologies of Amos and Related Texts in the Old Testament*. SBLDS 24. Missoula, Mont.: Scholars Press, 1975.

Cribbs, "Agreements." Cribbs, F. Lamar. "The Agreements That Exist between John and Acts." Pages 40–61 in *Perspectives on Luke-Acts*. ABPRSSS 5. Edited by Charles H. Talbert. Danville, Va.: Association of Baptist Professors of Religion; Edinburgh: T&T Clark, 1978.

Cripps, *Amos*. Cripps, Richard S. *A Critical and Exegetical Commentary on the Book of Amos*. London: SPCK, 1969.

Crisler, "Acoustics." Crisler, B. Cobbey. "The Acoustics and Crowd Capacity of Natural Theaters in Palestine." *BA* 39 (1976): 128–41.

Croatto, "Prophet." Croatto, J. Severino. "Jesus, Prophet like Elijah, and Prophet-Teacher like Moses in Luke-Acts." *JBL* 124 (3, 2005): 451–65.

Crocetti, "Madre." Crocetti, Giuseppe. "La madre di Gesù e l'Eucaristia nella prospettiva lucana (Lc 1–2; At 1,14; 2,42–47)." *RivB* 48 (4, 2000): 401–34.

Crocker, "Corrupt Priests." Crocker, P. T. "Corrupt Priests—A Common Phenomenon." *BurH* 26 (1990): 36–43.

Crocker, "Meroe and Eunuch." Crocker, P. T. "The City of Meroe and the Ethiopian Eunuch." *BurH* 22 (3, 1986): 53–72.

Crocker, "Silversmiths." Crocker, P. T. "Ephesus: Its Silversmiths, Its Tradesmen, and Its Riots." *BurH* 23 (4, 1987): 76–78.

Croft, "Text Messages." Croft, Steven. "Text Messages: The Ministry of Women and Romans 16." *Anvil* 21 (2, 2004): 87–94.

Croke, "Historiography." Croke, Brian. "Late Antique Historiography, 250–650 CE." Pages 567–81 in *A Companion to Greek and Roman Historiography*. Edited by John Marincola. 2 vols. Oxford: Blackwell, 2007.

Cromhout, "Judeans." Cromhout, Markus. "Were the Galileans 'Religious Jews' or 'Ethnic Judeans'?" *HTS/TS* 64 (3, 2008): 1279–97.

Cromhout and van Aarde, "Judean Ethnicity." Cromhout, M., and A. G. van Aarde. "A Socio-cultural Model of Judean Ethnicity: A Proposal." *HTS/TS* 62 (1, 2006): 69–101.

Cronjé, "Περὶ ὕψους." Cronjé, J. V. "Longinus' Περὶ ὕψους and the New Testament." *APB* 5 (1994): 38–53.

Crook, *Advocacy*. Crook, J. A. *Legal Advocacy in the Roman World*. Ithaca, N.Y.: Cornell University Press, 1995.

Crook, *Law of Rome*. Crook, John. *Law and Life of Rome*. Ithaca, N.Y.: Cornell University Press, 1967.

Crook, "Loyalty." Crook, Zeba. "BTB Readers Guide: Loyalty." *BTB* 34 (4, 2004): 167–77.

Crook, "Titus and Berenice." Crook, John A. "Titus and Berenice." *AJP* 72 (2, 1951): 162–75.

Croom, *Clothing*. Croom, Alexandra T. *Roman Clothing and Fashion*. Charleston, S.C.: Tempus, 2000.

Crosby, "Introduction." Crosby, H. Lamar. Introduction to the Sixty-Second Discourse [*Or.* 62]. Page 23 in vol. 5 of *Dio Chrysostom*. Translated by J. W. Cohoon and H. Lamar Crosby. 5 vols. LCL. Cambridge, Mass.: Harvard University Press, 1932–51.

Cross, "Fragment." Cross, Frank M., Jr. "A New Qumran Biblical Fragment Related to the Original Hebrew Underlying the Septuagint." *BASOR* 132 (Dec. 1953): 15–26.

Cross, "Genres." Cross, Anthony R. "Genres of the New Testament." *DNTB* 402–11.

Cross, "Inscriptions from Sardis." Cross, Frank Moore. "The Hebrew Inscriptions from Sardis." *HTR* 95 (1, 2002): 3–19.

Cross, *Library*. Cross, Frank Moore. *The Ancient Library of Qumran and Modern Biblical Studies*. Rev. ed. Garden City, N.Y.: Doubleday, 1961. Repr., Grand Rapids: Baker, 1980.

Cross, "Manuscripts." Cross, Frank M., Jr. "The Oldest Manuscripts from Qumran." *JBL* 74 (3, 1955): 147–72.

Cross, *Myth*. Cross, Frank Moore. *Canaanite Myth and Hebrew Epic*. Cambridge, Mass.: Harvard University Press, 1973.

Cross, "Tabernacle." Cross, Frank Moore, Jr. "The Tabernacle: A Study from an Archaeological and Historical Approach." *BA* 10 (Sept. 1947): 45–68.

Cross, "Wrote." Cross, Frank Moore. "The Dead Sea Scrolls and the People Who Wrote Them." *BAR* 3 (1, 1977): 1, 23–32, 51.

Cross and Eshel, "Ostraca." Cross, F. M., and Esther Eshel. "Ostraca from Khirbet Qumrân." *IEJ* 47 (1–2, 1997): 17–28.

Cross and Livingstone, *Dictionary of Church*. Cross, F. L., and E. A. Livingstone, eds. *The Oxford Dictionary of the Christian Church*. 3rd ed. Oxford: Oxford University Press, 2005.

Cross and Talmon, *Qumran and History*. Cross, Frank Moore, and Shemaryahu Talmon, eds. *Qumran and the History of the Biblical Text*. Cambridge, Mass.: Harvard University Press, 1975.

Crossan, "Anti-Semitism." Crossan, Dominic M. "Anti-Semitism and the Gospel." *TS* 26 (2, 1965): 189–214.

Crossan, *Birth*. Crossan, John Dominic. *The Birth of Christianity: Discovering What Happened in the Years Immediately after the Execution of Jesus*. San Francisco: HarperCollins, 1998.

Crossan, *Jesus.* Crossan, John Dominic. *The Historical Jesus: The Life of a Mediterranean Jewish Peasant.* San Francisco: HarperSanFrancisco, 1991.

Crossan, "Moses." Crossan, John Dominic. "From Moses to Jesus: Parallel Themes." *BRev* 2 (1986): 18–27.

Crossan, "Necessary." Crossan, John Dominic. "Why Is Historical Jesus Research Necessary?" Pages 7–37 in *Jesus Two Thousand Years Later.* Edited by James H. Charlesworth and Walter P. Weaver. FSCS. Harrisburg, Pa.: Trinity Press International, 2000.

Crouzel, "Imitation." Crouzel, Henri. "L'imitation et la 'suite' de Dieu et du Christ dans les premiers siècles chrétiens, ainsi que leurs sources gréco-romaines et hébraïques." *JAC* 21 (1978): 7–41.

Crowe, *Acts.* Crowe, Jerome. *The Acts.* NTM 8. Wilmington, Del.: Michael Glazier, 1979.

Crown, *Samaritans.* Crown, Alan D. *The Samaritans.* Tübingen: J. C. B. Mohr, 1989.

Crown, "Schism." Crown, Alan D. "Redating the Schism between the Judaeans and the Samaritans." *JQR* 82 (1–2, 1991): 17–50.

Crown and Cansdale, "Settlement." Crown, Alan D., and Lena Cansdale, "Qumran: Was It an Essene Settlement?" *BAR* 20 (5, 1994): 24–35, 73–78.

Croy, "Epicureanism." Croy, N. Clayton. "Epicureanism." *DNTB* 324–27.

Croy, "Philosophies and Preaching." Croy, N. Clayton. "Hellenistic Philosophies and the Preaching of the Resurrection (Acts 17:18, 32)." *NovT* 39 (1, 1997): 21–39.

Croy, "Religion, Personal." Croy, N. Clayton. "Religion, Personal." *DNTB* 926–31.

Crump, *Jesus the Intercessor.* Crump, David. *Jesus the Intercessor: Prayer and Christology in Luke-Acts.* WUNT 2.49. Tübingen: Mohr Siebeck, 1992. Repr., BSL. Grand Rapids: Baker, 1999.

Crump, *Knocking.* Crump, David. *Knocking on Heaven's Door: A New Testament Theology of Petitionary Prayer.* Grand Rapids: Baker Academic, 2006.

Cruz, "Hermeneutics." Cruz, Roli G. dela. "Testimonial Hermeneutics of Filipino Pentecostal Preaching." Paper presented at the William Menzies Annual Lectureship, Asia Pacific Theological Seminary, Jan. 27, 2009.

Cruz, "Response." Cruz, Roli G. dela. "Salvation in Christ and Baptism in Spirit: A Response to Robert Menzies, 'Evidential Tongues: An Essay on Theological Method.'" *AJPS* 1 (2, 1998): 125–47.

Crystal, "Applied Sociolinguistics." Crystal, David. "Why Did the Crowd Think St Peter Was Drunk? An Exercise in Applied Sociolinguistics." *NBf* 79 (924, 1998): 72–76.

Cuellar, Harris, and Jasso, "Scale." Cuellar, I., L. C. Harris, and R. Jasso. "An Acculturation Scale for Mexican American Normal and Clinical Populations." *HisJBehSc* 2 (3, 1980): 199–217.

Cueva, "Longus and Thucydides." Cueva, Edmund P. "Longus and Thucydides: A New Interpretation." *GRBS* 39 (4, 1998): 429–40.

Cueva, "Texts." Cueva, Edmund P. "Recent Texts on the Ancient World and the Occult." *CBull* 82 (2, 2006): 181–207.

Cullen, "Euphoria." Cullen, Peter J. "Euphoria, Praise, and Thanksgiving: Rejoicing in the Spirit in Luke-Acts." *JPT* 6 (1995): 13–24.

Cullmann, *Baptism.* Cullmann, Oscar. *Baptism in the New Testament.* SBT 1. London: SCM, 1950.

Cullmann, *Christology.* Cullmann, Oscar. *The Christology of the New Testament.* Philadelphia: Westminster, 1963.

Cullmann, *Early Church.* Cullmann, Oscar. *The Early Church.* Edited by A. J. B. Higgins. London: SCM, 1956.

Cullmann, "Eschatology and Missions." Cullmann, Oscar. "Eschatology and Missions in the New Testament." Pages 409–21 in *The Background of the New Testament and Its Eschatology: Essays in honour of Charles Harold Dodd.* Edited by W. D. Davies and D. Daube. Cambridge: Cambridge University Press, 1964.

Cullmann, "Infancy Gospels." Cullmann, Oscar, trans. "Infancy Gospels." German translation translated into English by A. J. B. Higgins. Pages 363–417 in *Gospels and Related Writings.* Vol. 1 of *New Testament Apocrypha.* Edited by Edgar Hennecke, Wilhelm Schneemelcher, and R. McL. Wilson. Philadelphia: Westminster, 1963.

Cullmann, *Peter.* Cullmann, Oscar. *Peter: Disciple–Apostle–Martyr.* Philadelphia: Westminster, 1953.

Cullmann, "Qumran Texts." Cullmann, Oscar. "The Significance of the Qumran Texts for Research into the Beginnings of Christianity." *JBL* 74 (4, 1955): 213–26.

Cullmann, *State.* Cullmann, Oscar. *The State in the New Testament.* New York: Scribner's, 1956.

Cullmann, *Time.* Cullmann, Oscar. *Christ and Time.* Translated by by Floyd V. Filson. Philadelphia: Westminster, 1950.

Cullmann, *Worship.* Cullmann, Oscar. *Early Christian Worship.* Philadelphia: Westminster, 1953.

Culpepper, *Anatomy.* Culpepper, R. Alan. *Anatomy of the Fourth Gospel: A Study in Literary Design.* Philadelphia: Fortress, 1983.

Culpepper, *John.* Culpepper, R. Alan. *The Gospel and Letters of John.* IBT. Nashville: Abingdon, 1998.

Culpepper, *School.* Culpepper, R. Alan. *The Johannine School: An Evaluation of the Johannine-School Hypothesis Based on an Investigation of the Nature of Ancient Schools.* SBLDS 26. Missoula, Mont.: Scholars Press, 1975.

Culy, "Friend." Culy, Martin M. "Jesus—Friend of God, Friend of His Followers: Echoes of Friendship in the Fourth Gospel." PhD diss., Baylor University, 2002.

Cuming, "Jews." Cuming, G. J. "The Jews in the Fourth Gospel." *ExpT* 60 (10, 1949): 290–92.

Cumont, *After Life.* Cumont, Franz. *After Life in Roman Paganism: Lectures Delivered at Yale University on the Silliman Foundation.* New Haven: Yale University Press, 1922.

Cumont, "Mithraeum." Cumont, Franz. "The Dura Mithraeum." Pages 151–214 in vol. 1 of *Mithraic Studies: Proceedings of the First International Congress of Mithraic Studies.* Edited by John R. Hinnells. 2 vols. Manchester, U.K.: Manchester University Press, 1975.

Cunningham, "Categories." Cunningham, Clark E. "Categories of Descent Groups in a Timor Village." *Oceania* 37 (1, Sept. 1966): 13–21.

Cunningham, "Ekphrasis." Cunningham, Valentine. "Why Ekphrasis?" *CP* 102 (1, 2007): 57–71.

Cunningham, *Faith.* Cunningham, Mary. *Faith in the Byzantine World.* Downers Grove, Ill.: InterVarsity, 2002.

Cunningham, *Many Tribulations.* Cunningham, Scott. *"Through Many Tribulations": The Theology of Persecution in Luke-Acts.* JSNTSup 142. Sheffield, U.K.: Sheffield Academic, 1997.

Cunville, "Evangelization." Cunville, R. R. "The Evangelization of Northeast India." DMiss diss., Fuller Theological Seminary, 1975.

Curchin, "Literacy." Curchin, Leonard A. "Literacy in the Roman Provinces: Qualitative and Quantitative Data from Central Spain." *AJP* 116 (3, 1995): 461–76.

Curran, "Rape." Curran, Leo C. "Rape and Rape Victims in the *Metamorphoses.*" Pages 263–86 in *Women in the Ancient World: The Arethusa Papers.* Edited by John Peradotto and J. P. Sullivan. SSCS. Albany: State University of New York Press, 1984.

Curran, "War." Curran, J. R. "The Jewish War: Some Neglected Regional Factors." *CW* 101 (1, 2007): 75–91.

Currid, *Egypt*. Currid, John D. *Ancient Egypt and the Old Testament*. Foreword by Kenneth A. Kitchen. Grand Rapids: Baker, 1997.

Curry, "Diet." Curry, Andrew. "The Gladiator Diet." *Archaeology* 61 (6, 2008): 28–30.

Curtis, "Character." Curtis, Heather D. "The Global Character of Nineteenth-Century Divine Healing." Pages 29–45 in *Global Pentecostal and Charismatic Healing*. Edited by Candy Gunther Brown. Foreword by Harvey Cox. Oxford: Oxford University Press, 2011.

Curtis, *Faith*. Curtis, Heather D. *Faith in the Great Physician: Suffering and Divine Healing in American Culture, 1860–1900*. Baltimore: Johns Hopkins University Press, 2007.

Curtis, "Houses of Healing." Curtis, Heather D. "Houses of Healing: Sacred Space, Spiritual Practice, and the Transformation of Female Suffering in the Faith Cure Movement, 1870–90." *CH* 75 (3, 2006): 598–611.

Curtis, "Lord for Body." Curtis, Heather D. "The Lord for the Body: Pain, Suffering, and the Practice of Divine Healing in Late-Nineteenth-Century American Protestantism." ThD diss., Harvard University, 2005.

Curty, "Parenté." Curty, Olivier. "À propos de la parenté entre juifs et spartiates." *Historia* 41 (2, 1992): 246–48.

Cuss, *Cult*. Cuss, Domique. *Imperial Cult and Honorary Terms in the New Testament*. Paradosis 23. Fribourg: Fribourg University Press, 1974.

"Custodia." "Custodia." *BrillPauly* 3:1028–30.

Cuvigny, "Sens de *misthios*." Cuvigny, H. "Sens de *misthios* chez Flavius Josèphe, BJ 3.126 et 5.49." *RevPhil* 73 (1, 1999): 27–37.

Cyran, "Namaszczenie Jezusa." Cyran, W. "Namaszczenie Jezusa Duchem Świętym i mocą (Dz 10, 38) (Die Salbung mit dem Heiligen Geist und mit Kraft [APG 10, 38]." *RocT* 42 (1, 1995): 95–101.

Czachesz, *Commission Narratives*. Czachesz, István. *Commission Narratives: A Comparative Study of the Canonical and Apocryphal Acts*. Studies on Early Christian Apocrypha 8. Leuven: Peeters, 2007.

Czachesz, "Logic." Czachesz, István. "Narrative Logic and Christology in Luke-Acts." *CV* 37 (2, 1995): 93–106.

Czachesz, "Magic and Mind." Czachesz, István. "Magic and Mind: Toward a Cognitive Theory of Magic, with Special Attention to the Canonical and Apocryphal *Acts of the Apostles*." *Annali di storia dell'esegesi* 24 (2, 2007): 295–321.

Dafni, "Natürliche Theologie." Dafni, Evangelia G. "Natürliche Theologie im Lichte des hebräischen und griechischen Alten Testaments." *TZ* 57 (3, 2001): 295–310.

Dafni, "Septuaginta." Dafni, Evangelia G. "Septuaginta und Plato in Justins 'Dialog mit Tryphon.'" *Neot* 43 (2, 2009): 449–65.

Dagron and Calloud, "Récit." Dagron, Alain, and Jean Calloud. "Actes des Apôtres chapitre 6. Un récit peut en cacher un autre. . ." *SémBib* 134 (2009): 57–65.

Dahl, "Abraham." Dahl, Nils A. "The Story of Abraham in Luke-Acts." Pages 139–58 in *Studies in Luke-Acts: Essays in Honor of Paul Schubert*. Edited by Leander E. Keck and J. Louis Martyn. Nashville: Abingdon, 1966.

Dahl, "Creation." Dahl, Nils A. "Christ, Creation, and the Church." Pages 422–43 in *The Background of the New Testament and Its Eschatology: Essays in Honour of Charles Harold Dodd*. Edited by W. D. Davies and D. Daube. Cambridge: Cambridge University Press, 1964.

Dahl, "Factor." Dahl, Nils A. "The Neglected Factor in New Testament Theology." Pages 153–63 in *Jesus the Christ: The Historical Origins of Christological Doctrine*. Edited by Donald H. Juel. Minneapolis: Fortress, 1991.

Dahl, "Manndraperen." Dahl, Nils A. "Manndraperen og hans far (Joh 8:44)." *NTT* 64 (3, 1963): 129–62.

Dahl, *Studies*. Dahl, Nils A. *Studies in Paul: Theology for the Early Christian Mission*. Minneapolis: Augsburg, 1977.

Dahood, *Psalms*. Dahood, Mitchell. *Psalms I, Psalms 1–50*. AB 16. Garden City, N.Y.: Doubleday, 1966.

Dakin, "Belief." Dakin, Arthur. "The Belief in the Miraculous in New Testament Times." *ExpT* 23 (1911–12): 37–39.

Daley, "Confessions." Daley, Brian E. "The Acts and Christian Confessions: Finding the Start of the Dogmatic Tradition." *ProEccl* 16 (1, 2007): 18–25.

Dalin, "Tzedakah." Dalin, David G. "*Tzedakah* with Dignity: Jewish Charity and Self-Help in Rabbinic Tradition." *ConsJud* 51 (3, 1999): 3–22.

Dalman, *Jesus in Talmud*. Dalman, Gustaf. *Jesus Christ in the Talmud, Midrash, Zohar, and the Liturgy of the Synagogue*. Cambridge, U.K.: Deighton, Bell, 1893. Repr., New York: Arno, 1973.

Dalman, *Jesus-Jeshua*. Dalman, Gustaf. *Jesus-Jeshua: Studies in the Gospels*. New York: Macmillan, 1929.

Dalton, "Areopagus." Dalton, Russell W. "'Electronic Areopagus': Communicating the Gospel in Multimedia Culture." *Journal of Theology* 103 (1999): 17–33.

Dalton, "Interpretation." Dalton, William J. "The Interpretation of 1 Peter 3,19 and 4,6: Light from 2 Peter." *Bib* 60 (4, 1979): 547–55.

Dalton, "Proclamatio." Dalton, William J. "Proclamatio Christi spiritibus facta: Inquisitio in textum ex prima epistola S. Petri 3, 18–4, 6." *VD* 42 (5, 1964): 225–40.

Dalton, *Proclamation*. Dalton, William J. *Christ's Proclamation to the Spirits: A Study of 1 Peter 3:18–4:6*. Rome: Pontifical Biblical Institute Press, 1965.

Dalton, "Proclamation." Dalton, William J. "Christ's Proclamation to the Spirits (1 Peter 3:19)." *ACR* 41 (4, 1964), 322–27.

Dalton, "Victory." Dalton, William J. "Christ's Victory over the Devil and the Evil Spirits." *BibT* 1 (18, 1965), 1195–1200.

Daly-Denton, "Prophet." Daly-Denton, Margaret. "David the Psalmist, Inspired Prophet: Jewish Antecedents of a New Testament *datum*." *ABR* 52 (2004): 32–47.

Damgaard, "Brothers." Damgaard, Finn. "Brothers in Arms: Josephus' Portrait of Moses in the 'Jewish Antiquities' in the Light of His Own Self-Portraits in the 'Jewish War' and the 'Life.'" *JJS* 59 (2, 2008): 218–35.

Damgaard, "Brugen." Damgaard, F. "Brugen af Mosesfortaellingerne hos Paulus og Josefus: I lyset af antikkens politiske ideal om 'enighed.'" *DTT* 71 (2, 2008): 114–31.

Damon, "Rhetoric." Damon, Cynthia. "Rhetoric and Historiography." Pages 439–50 in *A Companon to Roman Rhetoric*. BCompAW. Edited by William Dominik and Jon Hall. Oxford: Blackwell, 2007.

Damon, "Source to *sermo*." Damon, Cynthia. "From Source to *sermo*: Narrative Technique in Livy 34.54.4–8." *AJP* 118 (2, 1997): 251–66.

Dana, *Holy Spirit*. Dana, H. E. *The Holy Spirit in Acts*. 2nd ed. Kansas City, Mo.: Central Seminary Press, 1943.

Dana and Mantey, *Grammar*. Dana, H. E., and Julius R. Mantey. *A Manual Grammar of the Greek New Testament*. Toronto: Macmillan, 1955.

Danby, *Mishnah*. Danby, Herbert, trans. *The Mishnah*. London: Oxford University Press, 1933.

Dandoy, Selinsky, and Voigt, "Celtic Sacrifice." Dandoy, Jeremiah R., Page Selinsky, and Mary M. Voigt. "Celtic Sacrifice." *Archaeology* 55 (1, 2002): 44–49.

D'Andrea, "Hospitium militum." D'Andrea, C. T. "La fiscalità nel mondo antico: Il caso dell'*hospitium militum*." *ZAC/JAC* 11 (3, 2007): 448–63.

Daneel, *Zionism*. Daneel, M. L. *Zionism and Faith-Healing in Rhodesia: Aspects of African Independent Churches*. Translated by V. A. February. Communications 2. The Hague and Paris: Mouton, 1970.

Danfulani, "Conflict." Danfulani, Umar Habila Dadem. "Religious Conflict on the Jos Plateau: The Interplay between Christianity and Traditional Religion During the Early Missionary Period." *SvMT* 89 (1, 2001): 7–40.

D'Angelo, "ANHP Question." D'Angelo, Mary Rose. "The ANHP Question in Luke-Acts: Imperial Masculinity and the Deployment of Women in the Early Second Century." Pages 44–69 in *A Feminist Companion to Luke*. Edited by A.-J. Levine, with M. Blickenstaff. FCNTECW 3. Sheffield, U.K.: Sheffield Academic, 2002.

D'Angelo, "Redactional View." D'Angelo, Mary Rose. "Women in Luke-Acts: A Redactional View." *JBL* 109 (3, 1990): 441–61.

Daniel, "Anti-Semitism." Daniel, Jerry L. "Anti-Semitism in the Hellenistic-Roman Period." *JBL* 98 (1, 1979): 45–65.

Daniel, "Labour." Daniel, Christopher G. "Indentured Labour and the Christian Movement in Sri Lanka." DMiss diss., Fuller Theological Seminary, 1978.

Daniel, "Prophètes." Daniel, Constantin. "'Faux prophètes': Surnom des esséniens dans le sermon sur la montagne." *RevQ* 7 (1, 1969): 45–79.

Daniel, "Signs and Wonders." Daniel, Christopher G. "Signs and Wonders in Sri Lanka." *CGB* (Jan. 1977): 103–8.

Daniélou, *Infancy Narratives*. Daniélou, Jean. *The Infancy Narratives*. Translated by Rosemary Sheed. London: Compass; Burns & Oates, 1968.

Daniélou, *Theology*. Daniélou, Jean. *The Theology of Jewish Christianity*. Edited and translated by John A. Baker. DCDBCN 1. London: Darton, Longman & Todd; Chicago: Henry Regnery, 1964.

Daniélou and Marrou, *Six Hundred Years*. Daniélou, Jean, and Henri Marrou. *The First Six Hundred Years*. Vol. 1 of *The Christian Centuries: A New History of the Catholic Church*. Translated by Vincent Cronin. New York: McGraw-Hill, 1964.

Daniels, "Army." Daniels, C. M. "The Role of the Roman Army in the Spread and Practice of Mithraism." Pages 249–74 in vol. 2 of *Mithraic Studies: Proceedings of the First International Congress of Mithraic Studies*. Edited by John R. Hinnells. 2 vols. Manchester, U.K.: Manchester University Press, 1975.

Daniels, "Differences." Daniels, David D., III. "God Makes No Differences in Nationality: The Fashioning of a New Racial/

Nonracial Identity at the Azusa Street Revival." *Enr* 11 (2, 2006): 72–76.

Daniels, "Scribes." Daniels, Peter T. "Scribes and Scribal Techniques." *OEANE* 4:500–502.

Danker, *Benefactor*. Danker, Frederick W. *Benefactor: Epigraphic Study of a Greco-Roman and New Testament Semantic Field*. Saint Louis: Clayton, 1982.

Danker, *Corinthians*. Danker, Frederick W. *II Corinthians*. AugCNT. Minneapolis: Augsburg, 1989.

Danker, "Debt." Danker, Frederick W. "Paul's Debt to the *De corona* of Demosthenes: A Study of Rhetorical Techniques in Second Corinthians." Pages 262–80 in *Persuasive Artistry: Studies in New Testament Rhetoric in Honor of George A. Kennedy*. Edited by Duane F. Watson. JSNTSup 50. Sheffield, U.K.: Sheffield Academic, 1991.

Danker, *Luke*. Danker, Frederick W. *Luke*. ProcC. Philadelphia: Fortress, 1976.

Danker, *New Age*. Danker, Frederick W. *Jesus and the New Age, according to St. Luke*. Saint Louis: Clayton, 1972.

Danker, "Purple." Danker, Frederick W. "Purple." *ABD* 5:557–60.

Danyun, *Lilies*. Danyun. *Lilies amongst Thorns*. Translated by Brother Dennis. Tonbridge: Sovereign World, 1991.

Dar, "Menorot." Dar, S. "Three *menorot* from Western Samaria." *IEJ* 34 (2–3, 1984): 177–79 and plate 20BC.

Dar and Applebaum, "Road." Dar, Shimon, and Shimon Applebaum. "The Roman Road from Antipatris to Caesarea." *PEQ* 105 (1973): 91–99.

Darbo-Peschanski, "Origin." Darbo-Peschanski, Catherine. "The Origin of Greek Historiography." Pages 27–38 in *A Companion to Greek and Roman Historiography*. Edited by John Marincola. 2 vols. Oxford: Blackwell, 2007.

Darcus, "Daimon." Darcus, S. M. "Daimon as a Force Shaping Ethos in Heraclitus." *Phoenix* 28 (1974): 390–407.

Darcus, "Logos." Darcus, S. M. "Logos of Psyche in Heraclitus." *RivSAnt* 9 (1979): 89–93.

Darcus, "Phren." Darcus, S. M. "*Daimon* Parallels the Holy *phren* in Empedocles." *Phronesis* 22 (1977): 175–90.

Dark, "Landscapes." Dark, Kenneth Rainsbury. "Roman-Period and Byzantine Landscapes between Sepphoris and Nazareth." *PEQ* 140 (2, 2008): 87–102.

Darko, "Response." Darko, Daniel K. "Response: Moral Standing as a Community or Individual Exorcism in Ephesians 6:10–20?" Pages 95–98 in *Global Voices: Reading the Bible in the Majority World*. Edited by Craig Keener and M. Daniel

Carroll R. Foreword by Edwin Yamauchi. Peabody: Hendrickson, 2013.

D'Arms, "Slaves." D'Arms, John H. "Slaves at Roman Convivia." Pages 171–83 in *Dining in a Classical Context*. Edited by William J. Slater. Ann Arbor: University of Michigan Press, 1991.

Darr, *Character Building*. Darr, John A. *On Character Building: The Reader and the Rhetoric of Characterization in Luke-Acts*. LCBI. Louisville: Westminster/John Knox, 1992.

Darr, "Irenic or Ironic?" Darr, John A. "Irenic or Ironic? Another Look at Gamaliel before the Sanhedrin (Acts 5:33–42)." Pages 121–39 in *Literary Studies in Luke-Acts: Essays in Honor of Joseph B. Tyson*. Edited by Richard P. Thompson and Thomas E. Phillips. Macon, Ga.: Mercer University Press, 1998.

Darr, "Watch How You Listen." Darr, John A. "'Watch How You Listen' (Luke 8.18): Jesus and the Rhetoric of Perception in Luke-Acts." Pages 87–107 in *The New Literary Criticism and the New Testament*. Edited by Edgar V. McKnight and Elizabeth Struthers Malbon. Valley Forge, Pa.: Trinity Press International; Sheffield, U.K.: JSOT Press, 1994.

Das, "Acts 8." Das, A. Andrew. "Acts 8: Water, Baptism, and the Spirit." *ConcJ* 19 (2, 1993): 108–34.

Das, "Audience." Das, A. Andrew. "The Gentile-Encoded Audience of Romans: The Church Outside the Synagogue." Pages 29–46 in *Reading Paul's Letter to the Romans*. Edited by Jerry L. Sumney. SBLRBS 73. Atlanta: SBL, 2012.

Das, "Covenantal Nomism." Das, A. Andrew. "Beyond Covenantal Nomism: Paul, Judaism, and Perfect Obedience." *ConcJ* 27 (3, 2001): 234–52.

Das, *Debate*. Das, A. Andrew. *Solving the Romans Debate*. Minneapolis: Fortress, 2007.

Das, *Galatians*. Das, A. Andrew. *Galatians*. Concordia Commentary: A Theological Exposition of Sacred Scripture. St. Louis: Concordia, 2014.

Das, *Paul and Jews*. Das, A. Andrew. *Paul and the Jews*. LPSt. Peabody, Mass.: Hendrickson, 2003.

Das, "Pressure Points." Das, A. Andrew. "Paul and the Law: Pressure Points in the Debate." Pages 99–116 in *Paul Unbound: Other Perspectives on the Apostle*. Edited by Mark D. Given. Peabody, Mass.: Hendrickson, 2010.

Dasuekwo, "Charms." Dasuekwo, L. S. "Charms and Amulets in Christian and Muslim Homes." Pages 13–18 in *Religion, Medicine, and Healing*. Edited by Gbola Aderibigbe and Deji Ayegboyin. Lagos:

Nigerian Association for the Study of Religions and Education, 1995.

Daube, "Concessions to Sinfulness." Daube, David. "Concessions to Sinfulness in Jewish Law." *JJS* 10 (1–2, 1959): 1–13.

Daube, "Enfant." Daube, David. "Enfant Terrible." *HTR* 68 (3–4, 1975): 371–76.

Daube, *Exodus Pattern.* Daube, David. *The Exodus Pattern in the Bible.* All Souls Studies 2. London: Faber & Faber, 1963.

Daube, "Gospel and Rabbis." Daube, David. "The Gospels and the Rabbis." *Listener* 56 (6, 1956): 342–46.

Daube, "Johanan ben Zaccai." Daube, David. "Three Notes Having to Do with Johanan ben Zaccai." *JTS* 11 (1, 1960): 53–62.

Daube, "Linguistics of Suicide." Daube, David. "The Linguistics of Suicide." *PhilPA* 1 (4, 1972): 387–437.

Daube, *New Testament and Judaism.* Daube, David. *The New Testament and Rabbinic Judaism.* London: University of London, Athlone Press, 1956. Repr., Peabody, Mass.: Hendrickson, n.d.

Daube, "Reform." Daube, David. "A Reform in Acts and Its Models." Pages 151–63 in *Jews, Greeks, and Christians: Religious Cultures in Late Antiquity: Essays in Honor of William David Davies.* Edited by Robert Hamerton-Kelly and Robin Scroggs. SJLA 21. Leiden: Brill, 1976.

Daube, "Responsibilities." Daube, David. "Responsibilities of Master and Disciples in the Gospels." *NTS* 19 (1, 1972): 1–15.

Daube, "Sadducees and Angels." Daube, David. "On Acts 23: Sadducees and Angels." *JBL* 109 (3, 1990): 493–97.

Daube, *Studies in Law.* Daube, David. *Studies in Biblical Law.* New York: KTAV, 1969.

Daube, "Typology in Josephus." Daube, David. "Typology in Josephus." *JJS* 31 (1, 1980): 18–36.

Daube, "Witnesses." Daube, David. "The Law of Witnesses in Transferred Operation." *JANESCU* 5 (1973): 91–93.

Dauphin, "Amulet." Dauphin, Claudine. "A Greco-Egyptian Magical Amulet from Mazzuvah." *'Atiqot* 22 (1993): 145–47.

Dauphin, "Apollo and Asclepius." Dauphin, Claudine. "From Apollo and Asclepius to Christ: Pilgrimage and Healing at the Temple and Episcopal Basilica of Dor." *SBFLA* 49 (1999): 397–430 and plates 1–4.

David, "Exclusion." David, Jonathan. "The Exclusion of Women in the Mithraic Mysteries: Ancient or Modern?" *Numen* 47 (2, 2000): 121–41.

Davids, "Healing." Davids, Peter H. "Healing, Illness." *DLNTD* 436–39.

Davids, "Homily." Davids, Peter H. "Homily, Ancient." *DNTB* 515–18.

Davids, *James.* Davids, Peter H. *The Epistle of James: A Commentary on the Greek Text.* NIGTC. Grand Rapids: Eerdmans, 1982.

Davids, "Miracles." Davids, Peter H. "Miracles in Acts." *DLNTD* 746–52.

Davids, "Signs." Davids, Peter H. "Signs and Wonders." *DLNTD* 1093–95.

Davidson, *Africa in History.* Davidson, Basil. *Africa in History: Themes and Outlines.* New York: Macmillan, 1968.

Davidson, "Patterns." Davidson, James E. "The Patterns of Salvation in Paul and in Palestinian Judaism." *JRelS* 15 (1–2, 1989): 99–118.

Davidson, "Polybius." Davidson, James. "Polybius." Pages 123–36 in *The Cambridge Companion to the Roman Historians.* Edited by Andrew Feldherr. Cambridge: Cambridge University Press, 2009.

Davies, "Aboth." Davies, W. D. "Reflexions on Tradition: The Aboth Revisited." Pages 129–37 in *Christian History and Interpretation: Studies Presented to John Knox.* Edited by W. R. Farmer, C. F. D. Moule, and R. R. Niebuhr. Cambridge: Cambridge University Press, 1967.

Davies, "Anatolian Languages." Davies, Anna Morpurgo. "Anatolian Languages." *OCD³* 81–82.

Davies, "Birthplace of Essenes." Davies, Philip R. "The Birthplace of the Essenes: Where Is 'Damascus'?" *RevQ* 14 (4, 1990): 503–19.

Davies, "Citizenship." Davies, John Kenyon. "Citizenship, Greek." *OCD³* 333–34.

Davies, "Ending." Davies, Philip. "The Ending of Acts." *ExpT* 94 (11, 1983): 334–35.

Davies, *Gospel and Land.* Davies, W. D. *The Gospel and the Land: Early Christianity and Jewish Territorial Doctrine.* Berkeley: University of California Press, 1974.

Davies, "Greek Language." Davies, Anna Morpurgo. "Greek Language." *OCD³* 653–56.

Davies, *Healer.* Davies, Stevan L. *Jesus the Healer: Possession, Trance, and the Origins of Christianity.* New York: Continuum, 1995.

Davies, *Introduction.* Davies, W. D. *Introduction to Pharisaism.* Philadelphia: Fortress, 1967.

Davies, *Invitation.* Davies, W. D. *Invitation to the New Testament: A Guide to Its Main Witnesses.* Garden City, N.Y.: Doubleday, 1966.

Davies, *Matthew.* Davies, Margaret. *Matthew.* Readings. Sheffield, U.K.: JSOT Press, 1993.

Davies, "Passover." Davies, Philip R. "Passover and the Dating of the Aqedah." *JJS* 30 (1, 1979): 59–67.

Davies, *Paul.* Davies, W. D. *Paul and Rabbinic Judaism: Some Rabbinic Elements in Pauline Theology.* 4th ed. Philadelphia: Fortress, 1980.

Davies, *Physics.* Davies, Paul. *God and the New Physics.* New York: Simon & Schuster, 1983.

Davies, "Preface." Davies, Paul. "Preface." Pages ix–xiv in *The Re-Emergence of Emergence: The Emergentist Hypothesis from Science to Religion.* Edited by Philip Clayton and Paul Davies. Oxford: Oxford University Press, 2006.

Davies, "Pronunciation, Greek." Davies, Anna Morpurgo. "Pronunciation, Greek." *OCD³* 1254–55.

Davies, "Prophet/Healer." Davies, Stevan L. "The Historical Jesus as a Prophet/Healer: A Different Paradigm." *Neot* 30 (1, 1996): 21–38.

Davies, "Pythios." Davies, John K. "*Pythios* and *Python*: The Spread of a Cult Title." *MHR* 22 (1, 2007): 57–69.

Davies, "Religion." Davies, Jason. "Religion in Historiography." Pages 166–80 in *The Cambridge Companion to the Roman Historians.* Edited by Andrew Feldherr. Cambridge: Cambridge University Press, 2009.

Davies, *Rhetoric.* Davies, Margaret. *Rhetoric and Reference in the Fourth Gospel.* JSNT Sup 69. Sheffield, U.K.: JSOT Press, 1992.

Davies, "Samaritan Inscription." Davies, Graham. "A Samaritan Inscription with an Expanded Text of the Shema.'" *PEQ* 131 (1, 1999): 3–19.

Davies, *Sermon.* Davies, W. D. *The Sermon on the Mount.* Cambridge: Cambridge University Press, 1966.

Davies, *Setting.* Davies, W. D. *The Setting of the Sermon on the Mount.* Cambridge: Cambridge University Press, 1964.

Davies, "Spirit in Mekilta." Davies, W. D. "Reflections on the Spirit in the Mekilta: A Suggestion." *JANESCU* 5 (1973): 95–105.

Davies, "Tabernacle." Davies, G. Henton. "Tabernacle." Pages 498–506 in vol. 4 of *Interpreter's Dictionary of the Bible.* Edited by George Arthur Buttrick. New York: Abingdon, 1962.

Davies, "Temple in Damascus Document." Davies, P. R. "The Ideology of the Temple in the Damascus Document." *JJS* 33 (1–2, 1982): 287–301.

Davies, *Torah.* Davies, W. D. *Torah in the Messianic Age and/or the Age to Come.* JBLMS 7. Philadelphia: SBL, 1952.

Davies and Allison, *Matthew.* Davies, W. D., and Dale C. Allison. *A Critical and Exegetical Commentary on the Gospel according to Saint Matthew.* 3 vols. ICC. Edinburgh: T&T Clark, 1988–97.

Davies and Taylor, "Testimony." Davies, Philip R., and Joan E. Taylor. "On the

Testimony of Women in 1QSa." *DSD* 3 (3, 1996): 223–35.

Davila, "4Q534." Davila, James R. "4QMessar (4Q534) and Merkavah Mysticism." *DSD* 5 (3, 1998): 367–81.

Davila, "Macrocosmic Temple." Davila, James R. "The Macrocosmic Temple, Scriptural Exegesis, and the Songs of the Sabbath Sacrifice." *DSD* 9 (1, 2002): 1–19.

Davila, "Pseudepigrapha as Background." Davila, James R. "The Old Testament Pseudepigrapha as Background to the New Testament." *ExpT* 117 (2, 2005): 53–57.

Davis, "Acts 2." Davis, Jud. "Acts 2 and the Old Testament: The Pentecost Event in Light of Sinai, Babel and the Table of Nations." *CrisTR* 7 (1, 2009): 29–48.

Davis, "Age." Davis, J. J. "The Age of Saint Joseph at the Time of His Marriage." *CahJos* 6 (1958): 47–66.

Davis, "Ascension-Myth." Davis, Whitney M. "The Ascension-Myth in the Pyramid Texts." *JNES* 36 (3, 1977): 161–79.

Davis, "Evaluations." Davis, P. J. "'Since My Part Has Been Well Played': Conflicting Evaluations of Augustus." *Ramus* 28 (1, 1999): 1–15.

Davis, "Navigation." Davis, Danny Lee. "Commercial Navigation in the Greek and Roman World." PhD diss., University of Texas at Austin, 2009.

Davis, *Proofs*. Davis, Stephen T. *God, Reason, and Theistic Proofs*. Grand Rapids: Eerdmans, 1997.

Davis, Kendall, and O'Collins, *Resurrection*. Davis, Stephen T., Daniel Kendall, and Gerald O'Collins. *The Resurrection: An Interdisciplinary Symposium on the Resurrection of Jesus*. Oxford: Oxford University Press, 1997.

Dawes, "Danger." Dawes, Gregory W. "The Danger of Idolatry: First Corinthians 8:7–13." *CBQ* 58 (1, 1996): 82–98.

Dawsey, "Folk-Epic." Dawsey, James M. "Characteristics of Folk-Epic in Acts." Pages 317–25 in *SBL Seminar Papers, 1989*. Edited by David J. Lull. SBLSP 28. Atlanta: Scholars Press, 1989.

Dawsey, "Luke's Positive Perception." Dawsey, James M. "The Origin of Luke's Positive Perception of the Temple." *PRSt* 18 (1981): 5–22.

Dawsey, "Questions of Style." Dawsey, James M. "The Literary Unity of Luke-Acts: Questions of Style—A Task for Literary Critics." *NTS* 35 (1, 1989): 48–66.

Dawsey, *Voice*. Dawsey, James M. *The Lukan Voice: Confusion and Irony in the Gospel of Luke*. Macon, Ga.: Mercer University Press, 1986.

Dawson, *Healing*. Dawson, George Gordon. *Healing: Pagan and Christian*. London: SPCK; New York: Macmillan, 1935.

Dawson, "Movements." Dawson, Lorne L. "Who Joins New Religious Movements and Why: Twenty Years of Research and What Have We Learned?" Pages 116–30 in *Cults and New Religious Movements: A Reader*. Edited by Lorne L. Dawson. Oxford: Blackwell, 2003.

Dawson, "Urbanization." Dawson, John. "Urbanization and Mental Health in a West African Community." Pages 305–42 in in *Magic, Faith, and Healing: Studies in Primitive Psychotherapy Today*. Edited by Ari Kiev. Introduction by Jerome D. Frank. New York: Free Press, 1964.

Dayagi-Mendels, "Hygiene." Dayagi-Mendels, Michal. "Personal Hygiene." *OEANE* 4:300–302.

Dayhoff, "Barros." Dayhoff, Paul S. "de Barros, Luciano Gomes." No pages. *DACB*. Online: http://www.dacb.org/stories/capeverde/barros_luciano.html.

Dayhoff, "Guiva." Dayhoff, Paul S. "Guiva, Esther Danisane." No pages. *DACB*. Online: http://www.dacb.org/stories/mozambique/guiva_esther.html.

Dayhoff, "Machava." Dayhoff, Paul S. "Machava, Sumão." No pages. *DACB*. Online: http://www.dacb.org/stories/mozambique/machava_simao.html.

Dayhoff, "Marais." Dayhoff, Paul S. "Marais, Christopher." No pages. *DACB*. Online: http://www.dacb.org/stories/southafrica/marais_christopher.html.

Dayhoff, "Mthethwa." Dayhoff, Paul S. "Mthethwa, Johanne Patisa." No pages. *DACB*. Online: http://www.dacb.org/stories/southafrica/mthethwa_johanne.html.

Dayhoff, "Mucavele." Dayhoff, Paul S. "Mucavele, Timoteo Umelwane Njanje." No pages. *DACB*. Online: http://www.dacb.org/stories/mozambique/mucavele_timoteo.html.

Dayhoff, "Vilakati." Dayhoff, Paul S. "Vilakati, Norman Magodzi." No pages. *DACB*. Online: http://www.dacb.org/stories/swaziland/vilikati_norman.html.

Dayton, *Theological Roots*. Dayton, Donald. *Theological Roots of Pentecostalism*. Metuchen, N.J.: Scarecrow, 1987. Repr., Peabody, Mass.: Hendrickson, 1994.

Deacon, "Emergence." Deacon, Terrence W. "Emergence: The Hole at the Wheel's Hub." Pages 111–50 in *The Re-Emergence of Emergence: The Emergentist Hypothesis from Science to Religion*. Edited by Philip Clayton and Paul Davies. Oxford: Oxford University Press, 2006.

De Angelis, "Archaeology." De Angelis, Franco. "Archaeology in Sicily, 2001–2005." *ArchRep* 53 (2007): 123–90.

De Boer, "Depiction." De Boer, Martinus C. "The Depiction of 'the Jews' in John's Gospel: Matters of Behavior and Identity." Pages 260–80 in *Anti-Judaism and the Fourth Gospel: Papers of the Leuven Colloquium, 2000*. Edited by R. Bieringer, D. Pollefeyt, and F. Vandecasteele-Vanneuville. Assen: Royal Van Gorcum, 2001.

Decharneux, "Cult." Decharneux, Baudouin. "Mithra's Cult: An Example of Religious Colonialism in Roman Times?" Pages 93–105 in *Orality, Literacy, and Colonialism in Antiquity*. SBLSemS 47. Atlanta: SBL, 2004.

Decharneux, "Interdits." Decharneux, Baudouin. "Interdits sexuels dans l'oeuvre de Philon d'Alexandrie dit 'le juif.'" *PHR* 1 (1990): 17–31.

Decker, "Isthmia." Decker, Wolfgang. "Isthmia." *BrillPauly* 6:988–89.

Decker, "Prizes." Decker, Wolfgang. "Prizes (games)." *BrillPauly* 11:889–90.

Decker, "Pythia." Decker, Wolfgang. "Pythia." *BrillPauly* 12:291–94.

Decker, "Swimming." Decker, Wolfgang. "Swimming." *BrillPauly* 13:978.

Decock, "Holy Ones." Decock, P. B. "Holy Ones, Sons of God, and the Transcendent Figure of the Righteous in 1 Enoch and the New Testament." *Neot* 17 (1983): 70–82.

Decock, "Isaiah 53:7–8." Decock, P. B. "The Understanding of Isaiah 53:7–8 in Acts 8:32–33." *Neot* 14 (1981): 111–33.

DeConick, *Recovering*. DeConick, April D. *Recovering the Original Gospel of Thomas: A History of the Gospel and Its Growth*. LNTS 286. London: T&T Clark, 2005.

Decopoulos, *Rhodes*. Decopoulos, John. *Rhodes*. Athens: Olympic Color, [1980].

Deehan, "Thorn." Deehan, John. "Year of Paul 11: Antioch—Paul's Thorn in the Flesh?" *PastRev* 5 (2, 2009): 29–34.

Deere, *Power of Spirit*. Deere, Jack. *Surprised by the Power of the Spirit*. Grand Rapids: Zondervan, 1993.

Deere, *Voice*. Deere, Jack. *Surprised by the Voice of God*. Grand Rapids: Zondervan, 1996.

De Giorgi, "Antioch." De Giorgi, Andrea U. "The Formation of a Roman Landscape: The Case of Antioch." *JRA* 20 (2007): 283–98.

Dehandschutter, "Persécution." Dehandschutter, B. "La persécution des chrétiens dans les Actes des apôtres." Pages 541–46 in *Les Actes des apôtres: Traditions, rédaction, théologie*. Edited by Jacob Kremer. BETL 48. Gembloux, Belg.: J. Duculot; Leuven: Leuven University Press, 1979.

Dehandschutter, "Proto-Martyr." Dehandschutter, Boudewijn. "Stephen the

Proto-Martyr in the Writings of John Chrysostom." *Sacra Scripta* 6 (2, 2008): 111–22.

Deissmann, *Light*. Deissmann, G. Adolf. *Light from the Ancient East*. Grand Rapids: Baker, 1978.

Deissmann, *Paul*. Deissmann, G. Adolf. *Paul: A Study in Social and Religious History*. New York: Harper, 1957.

Deissmann, *Studies*. Deissmann, G. Adolf. *Bible Studies: Contributions Chiefly from Papyri and Inscriptions to the History of the Language, the Literature, and the Religion of Hellenistic Judaism and Primitive Christianity*. Translated by Alexander Grieve. Edinburgh: T&T Clark, 1923. Repr., Winona Lake, Ind.: Alpha, 1979.

Deissmann, "Value." Deissmann, G. Adolf. "The Historical Value of the New Testament." *LCQ* 2 (1929): 257–70.

Deissmann-Merten, "Kinship." Deissmann-Merten, Marieluise. "Kinship: Rome." *BrillPauly* 7:52–54.

De Lacy, "Lucretius." De Lacy, P. H. "Lucretius and the History of Epicureanism." *TAPA* 79 (1948): 12–23.

Del Agua, "Evangelization." Del Agua, Agustín. "The Lucan Narrative of the 'Evangelization of the Kingdom of God': A Contribution to the Unity of Luke-Acts." Pages 639–63 in *The Unity of Luke-Acts*. Edited by Joseph Verheyden. BETL 142. Leuven: Leuven University Press, 1999.

DeLaine, "Baths." DeLaine, Janet. "Baths." *OCD³* 235–36.

DeLaine, "Forum." DeLaine, Janet. "Forum." *OCD³* 606.

DeLaine, "Tabularium." DeLaine, Janet. "Tabularium." *OCD³* 1468.

Delaney, "Seeds." Delaney, Carol. "Seeds of Honor, Fields of Shame." Pages 35–48 in *Honor and Shame and the Unity of the Mediterranean*. Edited by David D. Gilmore. AAAM 22. Washington, D.C.: American Anthropological Association, 1987.

Delaygue, "Grecs." Delaygue, M.-P. "Les Grecs connaissaient-ils les religions de l'Inde à l'époque hellénistique?" *BAGB* 54 (2, 1995): 152–72.

Del Colle, "Baptism." Del Colle, Ralph. "Spirit Baptism: A Catholic Perspective." Pages 241–79 in *Perspectives on Spirit Baptism: Five Views*. Edited by Chad Owen Brand. Nashville: Broadman & Holman, 2004.

Delcor, "Bundesfest und Pfingstfest." Delcor, Mathias. "Das Bundesfest in Qumran und das Pfingstfest." *BibLeb* 4 (3, 1963): 188–204.

Delcor, "Mythe." Delcor, Mathias. "Le mythe de la chute des anges et de l'origine des

géants comme explication du mal dans le monde, dans l'apocalyptique juive: Histoire des traditions." *RHR* 190 (1, 1976): 3–53.

Delcor, "Repas." Delcor, Matthias. "Repas cultuels esséniens et thérapeutes: Thiases et Haburoth." *RevQ* 6 (1968): 401–25.

Delebecque, *Actes*. Delebecque, Édouard. *Les Deux Actes des Apôtres*. EtBib, n.s., 6. Preface by Ceslas Spicq. Paris: Librairie Lecoffre, J. Gabalda, 1986.

Delia, "Population of Alexandria." Delia, Diana. "The Population of Roman Alexandria." *TAPA* 118 (1988): 275–92.

Delitzsch, *Isaiah*. Delitzsch, Franz. *Biblical Commentary on the Prophecies of Isaiah*. Translated by James Martin. 2 vols. 1873. Repr., Grand Rapids: Eerdmans, 1980.

Delitzsch, *Psalms*. Delitzsch, Franz. *Psalms*. Translated by Francis Bolton. 3 vols. Grand Rapids: Eerdmans, 1980.

Delling, "ἀρχηγός." Delling, Gerhard. "ἀρχηγός." *TDNT* 1:487–88.

Delmore, "Pratique." Delmore, J. "La pratique du baptême dans le judaïsme contemporain des origines chrétiennes." *LumVie* 6 (26, 1956): 165–204.

Delobel, "Text." Delobel, Joël. "The Text of Luke-Acts: A Confrontation of Recent Theories." Pages 83–107 in *The Unity of Luke-Acts*. Edited by Joseph Verheyden. BETL 142. Leuven: Leuven University Press, 1999.

Delville, "Prosélytisme juif." Delville, J.-P. "L'épître aux Hébreux à la lumière du prosélytisme juif." *RCT* 10 (2, 1985): 323–68.

Deman, "Mithras and Christ." Deman, A. "Mithras and Christ: Some Iconographical Similarities." Pages 507–17 in vol. 2 of *Mithraic Studies: Proceedings of the First International Congress of Mithraic Studies*. Edited by John R. Hinnells. 2 vols. Manchester, U.K.: Manchester University Press, 1975.

Dembski, *Design*. Dembski, William A. *Intelligent Design: The Bridge between Science and Theology*. Foreword by Michael Behe. Downers Grove, Ill.: InterVarsity, 1999.

Dembski, *Inference*. Dembski, William A. *The Design Inference*. Cambridge: Cambridge University Press, 1998.

Deming, *Celibacy*. Deming, Will. *Paul on Marriage and Celibacy: The Hellenistic Background of 1 Corinthians 7*. 2nd ed. Grand Rapids: Eerdmans, 2004.

Deming, "Indifferent Things." Deming, Will. "Paul and Indifferent Things." Pages 384–403 in *Paul in the Greco-Roman World: A Handbook*. Edited by J. Paul Sampley. Harrisburg, Pa.: Trinity Press International, 2003.

Deming, "Male Sexuality." Deming, Will. "Mark 9.42–10.12, Matthew 5.27–32, and B. Nid. 13b: A First Century Discussion of Male Sexuality." *NTS* 36 (1, 1990): 130–41.

Demoen, "Paradigm." Demoen, Kristoffel. "A Paradigm for the Analysis of Paradigms: The Rhetorical *exemplum* in Ancient and Imperial Greek Theory." *Rhetorica* 15 (2, 1997): 125–58.

Dempster, Klaus, and Petersen, *Globalization of Pentecostalism*. Murray W. Dempster, Byron D. Klaus, and Douglas Petersen, eds. *The Globalization of Pentecostalism: A Religion Made to Travel*. Foreword by Russell P. Spittler. Carlisle, U.K.: Paternoster; Oxford: Regnum, 1999.

Demsky, "Literacy." Demsky, Aaron. "Literacy." *OEANE* 3:362–69.

Denaux, "Theme." Denaux, Adelbert. "The Theme of Divine Visits and Human (In)Hospitality in Luke-Acts: Its Old Testament and Graeco-Roman Antecedents." Pages 255–79 in *The Unity of Luke-Acts*. Edited by Joseph Verheyden. BETL 142. Leuven: Leuven University Press, 1999.

Denaux, "Visie." Denaux, A. "De moderne joodse visie op Paulus van Tarsus." *Coll* 39 (1, 2009): 73–87.

Dench, *Asylum*. Dench, Emma. *Romulus' Asylum: Roman Identities from the Age of Alexander to the Age of Hadrian*. Oxford: Oxford University Press, 2005.

Dench, "Ethnography." Dench, Emma. "Ethnography and History." Pages 493–503 in *A Companion to Greek and Roman Historiography*. Edited by John Marincola. 2 vols. Oxford: Blackwell, 2007.

Dennison, "Revelation." Dennison, William D. "Natural and Special Revelation: Reassessment." *Kerux* 21 (2, 2006): 13–34.

Denova, *Things Accomplished*. Denova, Rebecca I. *The Things Accomplished among Us: Prophetic Tradition in the Structural Pattern of Luke-Acts*. JSNTSup 141. Sheffield, U.K.: Sheffield Academic, 1997.

Denzey, "Beast." Denzey, Nicola. "Facing the Beast: Justin, Christian Martyrdom, and Freedom of the Will." Pages 176–98 in *Stoicism in Early Christianity*. Edited by Tuomas Rasimus, Troels Engberg-Pedersen and Ismo Dunderberg. Grand Rapids: Baker Academic, 2010.

Denzey, "Enslavement." Denzey, Nicola. "'Enslavement to Fate,' 'Cosmic Pessimism,' and Other Explorations of the Late Roman Psyche: A Brief History of a Historiographical Trend." *SR/SR* 33 (3–4, 2004): 277–99.

Dequeker, "Saints." Dequeker, L. "The 'Saints of the Most High' in Qumran and Daniel." *Oudtestamentische Studiën* 18 (1973): 108–87.

Dequeker, "Zodiaque." Dequeker, Luc. "Le zodiaque de la synagogue de Beth Alpha et le midrash." *Bijdr* 47 (1, 1986): 2–30.

Derda, "Moses." Derda, T. "Did the Jews Use the Name Moses in Antiquity?" *ZPE* 115 (1997): 257–60.

Derda, "Reply." Derda, T. "The Jews and the Name of Moses in Antiquity—A Reply." *ZPE* 124 (1999): 210.

Derickson, "Cessation." Derickson, Gary W. "The Cessation of Healing Miracles in Paul's Ministry." *BSac* 155 (619, 1998): 299–315.

De Ridder, *Discipling*. De Ridder, Richard R. *Discipling the Nations*. Grand Rapids: Baker, 1971.

De Ridder, *Rejected*. De Ridder, Richard R. *God Has Not Rejected His People*. Grand Rapids: Baker, 1977.

Dermawan, "Study." Dermawan, Julia Theis. "A Study of the Nias Revival in Indonesia." *AJPS* 6 (2, 2003): 247–63.

De Roo, "4Q525." De Roo, Jacqueline C. R. "Beatitudes Text (4Q525)." *DNTB* 151–53.

DeRouchie, "Circumcision." DeRouchie, Jason S. "Circumcision in the Hebrew Bible and Targums: Theology, Rhetoric, and the Handling of Metaphor." *BBR* 14 (2, 2004): 175–203.

Derow, "*Imperium*." Derow, Peter Sidney. "*Imperium*." *OCD*³ 751–52.

Derow, "Magistracy, Roman." Derow, Peter Sidney. "Magistracy, Roman." *OCD*³ 911.

Derow, "*Tribuni plebes*." Derow, Peter Sidney. "*Tribuni plebes*." *OCD*³ 1549–50.

Derrett, "Akeldama." Derrett, J. Duncan. M. "Akeldama (Acts 1:19)." *Bijdr* 56 (2, 1995): 122–32.

Derrett, "Ananias, Sapphira." Derrett, J. Duncan M. "Ananias, Sapphira, and the Right of Property." Pages 193–201 in vol. 1 of *Studies in the New Testament* by J. Duncan M. Derrett. Leiden: Brill, 1977–.

Derrett, *Audience*. Derrett, J. Duncan M. *Jesus's Audience: The Social and Psychological Environment in Which He Worked*. New York: Seabury, 1973.

Derrett, "Co-rescuers." Derrett, J. Duncan M. "James and John as Co-rescuers from Peril (Lk. V 10)." *NovT* 22 (4, 1980): 299–303.

Derrett, "Homer." Derrett, J. D. M. "Homer in the New Testament." *ExpT* 121 (2, 2009): 66–69.

Derrett, *Law*. Derrett, J. Duncan M. *Law in the New Testament*. London: Darton, Longman & Todd, 1970.

Derrett, "*Mylos onikos*." Derrett, J. Duncan M. "*Mylos onikos* (Mk 9:42 par.)." *ZNW* 76 (3–4, 1985): 284.

Derrett, "Palingenesia." Derrett, J. Duncan M. "Palingenesia (Matthew 19.28)." *JSNT* 20 (1984): 51–58.

Derrett, "Shepherd." Derrett, J. Duncan M. "The Good Shepherd: St. John's Use of Jewish Halakah and Haggadah." *ST* 27 (1, 1973): 25–50.

Derrett, "Simon Magus." Derrett, J. Duncan M. "Simon Magus (Acts 8:9–24)." *ZNW* 73 (1982): 52–68.

DesCamp, "Women." DesCamp, Mary Therese. "Why Are These Women Here? An Examination of the Sociological Setting of Pseudo-Philo through Comparative Reading." *JSP* 16 (1997): 53–90.

deSilva, *Credentials*. deSilva, David A. *The Credentials of an Apostle: Paul's Gospel in 2 Corinthians 1–7*. BIBMS 4. North Richland Hills, Tex.: BIBAL Press, 1998.

deSilva, "Exaltation." deSilva, David A. "Exaltation, Enthronement." *DLNTD* 359–63.

deSilva, *Galatians*. deSilva, David A. *Global Readings: A Sri Lankan Commentary on Paul's Letter to the Galatians*. Eugene, Ore.: Cascade, 2011.

deSilva, *Honor*. deSilva, David A. *Honor, Patronage, Kinship, and Purity: Unlocking New Testament Culture*. Downers Grove, Ill.: InterVarsity, 2000.

deSilva, "Honor and Shame." deSilva, David A. "Honor and Shame." *DNTB* 519–21.

deSilva, *Introduction*. deSilva, David A. *An Introduction to the New Testament: Contexts, Methods, and Ministry Formation*. Downers Grove, Ill.: InterVarsity; Leicester, U.K.: Apollos, 2004.

deSilva, "Lies." deSilva, David A. "Judith the Heroine? Lies, Seduction, and Murder in Cultural Perspective." *BTB* 36 (2, 2006): 55–61.

deSilva, "Meaning." deSilva, David A. "The Meaning of the New Testament and the *Skandalon* of World Constructions." *EvQ* 64 (1, Jan. 1992): 3–21.

deSilva, "Patronage." deSilva, David A. "Patronage." *DNTB* 766–71.

deSilva, "Paul and Stoa." deSilva, David A. "Paul and the Stoa: A Comparison." *JETS* 38 (4, 1995): 549–64.

deSilva, "Reality." deSilva, David A. "Measuring Penultimate against Ultimate Reality: An Investigation of the Integrity and Argumentation of 2 Corinthians." *JSNT* 52 (1993): 41–70.

deSilva, *Shame*. deSilva, David A. *Despising Shame: Honor Discourse and Community Maintenance in the Epistle to the Hebrews*. SBLDS 152. Atlanta: Scholars Press, 1995.

deSilva, "Shame." deSilva, David A. "Honor and Shame." *DOTP* 431–36.

deSilva, *Teachers*. deSilva, David A. *The Jewish Teachers of Jesus, James, and Jude: What Earliest Christianity Learned from the Apocrypha and Pseudepigrapha*. New York: Oxford University Press, 2012.

deSilva, "Tools." deSilva, David A. "Using the Master's Tools to Shore Up Another's House: A Postcolonial Analysis of 4 Maccabees." *JBL* 126 (1, 2007): 99–127.

deSilva, "Wisdom." deSilva, David A. "The Wisdom of Ben Sira: Honor, Shame, and the Maintenance of the Values of a Minority Culture." *CBQ* 58 (3, 1996): 433–55.

deSilva, "Wisdom of Solomon." deSilva, David A. "Wisdom of Solomon." *DNTB* 1268–76.

Desjardins, "Αἵρεσις in Christian Era." Desjardins, Michel. "Bauer and beyond: On Recent Scholarly Discussions of αἵρεσις in the Early Christian Era." *SecCent* 8 (2, 1991): 65–82.

Deslauriers, "Difference." Deslauriers, Marguerite. "Sexual Difference in Aristotle's Politics and His Biology." *CW* 102 (3, 2009): 215–31.

Desmond, *Cynics*. Desmond, William. *Cynics*. Ancient Philosophies 3. Berkeley: University of California, 2008.

Desmond, *Praise*. Desmond, William D. *The Greek Praise of Poverty*. Notre Dame, Ind.: University of Notre Dame Press, 2006.

Desprez, "Groups." Desprez, Vincent. "Jewish Ascetical Groups at the Time of Christ: Qumran and the Therapeutae." *AmBenRev* 41 (3, 1990): 291–311.

Destrooper-Georgiades, "Coins." Destrooper-Georgiades, A. "Jewish Coins Found in Cyprus." *IsNumR* 1 (2006): 37–49.

Detienne, "Polythéisme." Detienne, Marcel. "Un polythéisme recrit: Entre Dionysos et Apollon—mort et vie d'Orphee." *ASSR* 30 (59/1, 1985): 65–75.

Deutschmann, "Hoffnung." Deutschmann, A. "Die Hoffnung Israels (Apg 28,20)." *BN* 105 (2000): 54–60.

Deutschmann, *Synagoge*. Deutschmann, Anton. *Synagoge und Gemeindebildung: Christliche Gemeinde und Israel am Beispiel von Apg 13,42–52*. BibUnt 30. Regensburg: Verlag Friedrich Pustet, 2001.

Devadason, "Missionary Societies." Devadason, Samuel. "Indian Missionary Societies." DMiss diss., Fuller Theological Seminary, 1978.

De Vaux, *Israel*. De Vaux, Roland. *Ancient Israel: Its Life and Institutions*. 2 vols. Translated by John MacHugh. New York: McGraw-Hill, 1961.

Dever, "Ashdod." Dever, William G. "Ashdod." *OEANE* 1:219–20.

Devine, "Birth-Rate." Devine, A. M. "The Low Birth-Rate in Ancient Rome: A

Possible Contributing Factor." *RMPhil* 128 (3–4, 1985): 313–17.

De Vries, "Fear of God." De Vries, S. J. "Note concerning the Fear of God in the Qumran Scrolls." *RevQ* 5 (2, 1965): 233–37.

Dewald, "Construction." Dewald, Carolyn. "The Construction of Meaning in the First Three Historians." Pages 89–101 in *A Companion to Greek and Roman Historiography*. Edited by John Marincola. 2 vols. Oxford: Blackwell, 2007.

Dewald, "Kings." Dewald, Carolyn. "Wanton Kings, Picked Heroes, and Gnomic Founding Fathers: Strategies of Meaning at the End of Herodotus' *Histories*." Pages 62–82 in *Classical Closure: Reading the End in Greek and Latin Literature*. Edited by Deborah H. Roberts, Francis M. Dunn and Don Fowler. Princeton: Princeton University Press, 1997.

De Weever, "Candace." De Weever, Jacqueline. "Candace in the Alexander Romances: Variations on the Portrait Theme." *RomPhil* 43 (1990): 529–46.

De Wet, "Signs." De Wet, Christiaan Rudolph. "Signs and Wonders in Church Growth." MA thesis, Fuller Theological Seminary, 1981.

Dewey, *Debate*. Dewey, Joanna. *Markan Public Debate: Literary Technique, Concentric Structure, and Theology in Mark 2:1–3:6*. SBLDS 48. Chico, Calif.: Scholars Press, 1980.

Dewey, "Oral-Aural Event." Dewey, Joanna. "The Gospel of Mark as an Oral-Aural Event: Implications for Interpretation." Pages 145–63 in *The New Literary Criticism and the New Testament*. Edited by Edgar V. McKnight and Elizabeth Struthers Malbon. Valley Forge, Pa.: Trinity Press International; Sheffield, U.K.: JSOT Press, 1994.

DeWitt, "Demosthenes." DeWitt, Norman W., and Norman J. DeWitt. Vol. 7 in *Demosthenes. Works*. Translated by J. H. Vince, C. A. Vince, A. T. Murray, N. W. DeWitt, and N. J. DeWitt. 7 vols. LCL. Cambridge, Mass.: Harvard University Press, 1926–49.

DeWitt, *Epicurus*. DeWitt, Norman W. *Epicurus and His Philosophy*. Minneapolis: University of Minnesota Press, 1954.

Dexinger, "Limits." Dexinger, Ferdinand. "Limits of Tolerance in Judaism: The Samaritan Example." Pages 88–114 in *Aspects of Judaism in the Graeco-Roman Period*. Edited by E. P. Sanders with A. I. Baumgarten and Alan Mendelson. Vol. 2 of *Jewish and Christian Self-Definition*. Edited by E. P. Sanders. Philadelphia: Fortress, 1981.

Dexinger, "Taheb-Vorstellung." Dexinger, Ferdinand. "Die Taheb-Vorstellung als

politische Utopie." *Numen* 37 (1, 1990): 1–23.

DeYoung, Emerson, Yancey, and Kim, *United*. DeYoung, Curtiss Paul, Michael O. Emerson, George Yancey, and Karen Chai Kim. *United by Faith: The Multiracial Congregation as an Answer to the Problem of Race*. New York: Oxford University Press, 2003.

De Zwaan, "Greek Language." De Zwaan, J. "The Use of the Greek Language in Acts." *BegChr* 2:30–65.

Dhennin, "Necropolis." Dhennin, Sylvain. "An Egyptian Animal Necropolis in a Greek Town." *Egyptian Archaeology* 33 (Fall 2008): 12–14.

Dibelius, "Initiation." Dibelius, Martin. "The Isis Initiation in Apuleius and Related Initiatory Rites." Pages 61–121 in *Conflict at Colossae: A Problem in the Interpretation of Early Christianity Illustrated by Selected Modern Studies*. Edited translated by Fred O. Francis and Wayne A. Meeks. SBLSBS 4. Missoula, Mont.: SBL, 1973.

Dibelius, *James*. Dibelius, Martin. *James: A Commentary on the Epistle of James*. Revised by Heinrich Greeven. Edited by Helmut Koester. Translated by Michael A. Williams. Hermeneia. Philadelphia: Fortress, 1976.

Dibelius, *Jesus*. Dibelius, Martin. *Jesus*. Translated by Charles B. Hedrick and Frederick C. Grant. Philadelphia: Westminster, 1949.

Dibelius, *Paul*. Dibelius, Martin. *Paul*. Edited and completed by Werner Georg Kümmel. Philadelphia: The Westminster Press, 1953.

Dibelius, *Studies in Acts*. Dibelius, Martin. *Studies in the Acts of the Apostles*. Edited by H. Greeven. Translated by M. Ling. New York: Scribner's, 1956.

Dibelius, *Tradition*. Dibelius, Martin. *From Tradition to Gospel*. Translated by Bertram Lee Woolf. Cambridge, U.K.: James Clarke; Greenwood, S.C.: Attic, 1971.

Dibelius and Conzelmann, *Pastoral Epistles*. Dibelius, Martin, and Conzelmann, Hans. *The Pastoral Epistles: A Commentary on the Pastoral Epistles*. Edited by Helmut Koester. Translated by Philip Buttolph and Adela Yarbro. Hermeneia. Philadelphia: Fortress, 1972.

Dibelius and Kümmel, *Paul*. Dibelius, Martin. *Paul*. Edited and completed by Werner Georg Kümmel. Philadelphia: Westminster, 1953.

Dicken, *Herod*. Dicken, Frank. *Herod as a Composite Character in Luke-Acts*. WUNT 2.375. Tübingen: Mohr Siebeck, 2014.

Dickey, "Κύριε." Dickey, Eleanor. "Κύριε, δέσποτα, *domine*: Greek Politeness in the Roman Empire." *JHS* 121 (2001): 1–11.

Dickey, "Latin Influence." Dickey, Eleanor. "Latin Influence on the Greek of Documentary Papyri: An Analysis of Its Chronological Distribution." *ZPE* 145 (2003): 249–57.

Dickey, "Terms." Dickey, Eleanor. "Literal and Extended Use of Kinship Terms in Documentary Papyri." *Mnemosyne* 57 (2, 2004): 133–76.

Dickie, "Evil Eye." Dickie, Matthew W. "Heliodorus and Plutarch on the Evil Eye." *CP* 86 (1, 1991): 17–29.

Dickie, "Headless Demons." Dickie, Matthew W. "Bonds and Headless Demons in Greco-Roman Magic." *GRBS* 40 (1, 1999): 99–104.

Dickie, "Kolossos." Dickie, Matthew W. "What Is a *kolossos* and How Were *kolossoi* Made in the Hellenistic Period?" *GRBS* 37 (3, 1996): 237–57.

Dickie, "Who Practised Love-Magic?" Dickie, Matthew W. "Who Practised Love-Magic in Classical Antiquity and in the Late Roman World?" *CQ* 50 (2, 2000): 563–83.

Dickie and Payne, "House." Dickie, Archibald Campbell, and J. Barton Payne. "House." *ISBE* 2:770–72.

Dickson, "Gospel as News." Dickson, John P. "Gospel as News: Εὐαγγελ- from Aristophanes to the Apostle Paul." *NTS* 51 (2, 2005): 212–30.

Dictionary of African Christian Biography. *Dictionary of African Christian Biography*. New Haven: Overseas Ministries Study Center. Online: http://www.dacb.org.

Diefenbach, "Sehen." Diefenbach, Manfred. "Das 'Sehen des Herrn' vor Damaskus: Semantischer Zugang zu Apg 9, 22 und 26." *NTS* 52 (3, 2006): 409–18.

Dietrich, "Suicide." Dietrich, Jessica Shaw. "Death Becomes Her: Female Suicide in Flavian Epic." *Ramus* 38 (2, 2009): 187–202.

Díez Macho, "Hijo del hombre." Díez Macho, Alejandro. "La cristología del hijo del hombre y el uso de la tercera persona en vez de la primera." *ScrTh* 14 (1, 1982): 189–201.

Dihle, "Biography." Dihle, Albrecht. "The Gospels and Greek Biography." Pages 361–86 in *The Gospel and the Gospels*. Edited by Peter Stuhlmacher. Grand Rapids: Eerdmans, 1991.

Dihle, "Liberté." Dihle, Albrecht. "Liberté et destin dans l'antiquité tardive." *RTP* 121 (2, 1989): 129–47.

Dihle, "Prose Rhythm." Dihle, Albrecht. "Prose Rhythm." *BrillPauly* 12:40–44.

Di Lella, "Health." Di Lella, Alexander A. "Health and Healing in Tobit." *BibT* 37 (2, 1999): 69–73.

Di Lella, "Likeness." Di Lella, Alexander A. "The One in Human Likeness and the Holy Ones of the Most High in Daniel 7." *CBQ* 39 (1, 1977): 1–19.

Dilke, *Maps*. Dilke, Oswald Ashton Wentworth. *Greek and Roman Maps*. Ithaca, N.Y.: Cornell University Press, 1985.

Dill, *Society*. Dill, Samuel. *Roman Society from Nero to Marcus Aurelius*. New York: Meridian, 1956.

Dillard and Longman, *Introduction*. Dillard, Raymond B., and Tremper Longman. *An Introduction to the Old Testament*. Grand Rapids: Zondervan, 1994.

Dillery, "Apion Historian." Dillery, John. "Putting Him Back Together Again: Apion Historian, Apion *grammatikos*." *CP* 98 (4, 2003): 383–90.

Dillery, "Historians." Dillery, John. "Greek Historians of the Near East: Clio's 'Other' Sons." Pages 221–30 in *A Companion to Greek and Roman Historiography*. Edited by John Marincola. 2 vols. Oxford: Blackwell, 2007.

Dillery, "Roman Historians." Dillery, John. "Roman Historians and the Greeks: Audiences and Models." Pages 77–107 in *The Cambridge Companion to the Roman Historians*. Edited by Andrew Feldherr. Cambridge: Cambridge University Press, 2009.

Dillery, "Sacred History." Dillery, John. "Greek Sacred History." *AJP* 126 (4, 2005): 505–26.

Dillmann, "Begegnungen." Dillmann, Rainer. "Begegnungen voller Spannung. Beobachtungen zum Mit- und Gegeneinander von Petrus und Paulus im Neuen Testament." *SNTSU* 33 (2008): 25–39.

Dillon, *Eye-Witnesses*. Dillon, Richard J. *From Eye-Witnesses to Ministers of the Word*. AnBib 82. Rome: Biblical Institute Press, 1978.

Dillon, "Ganymede as Logos." Dillon, John. "Ganymede as the Logos: Traces of a Forgotten Allegorization in Philo." *Studia philonica* 6 (1979–80): 37–40; *CQ* 31 (1, 1981): 183–85.

Dillon, *Middle Platonists*. Dillon, John M. *The Middle Platonists: 80 B.C. to A.D. 220*. Ithaca, N.Y.: Cornell University Press, 1977.

Dillon, "Philosophy." Dillon, John M. "Philosophy." *DNTB* 793–96.

Dillon, "Plato." Dillon, John M. "Plato, Platonism." *DNTB* 804–7.

Dillon, "Portraits." Dillon, Sheila. "The Portraits of a Civic Benefactor of 2nd-C. Ephesos." *JRA* 9 (1996): 261–74.

Dillon, "Reclaiming." Dillon, John M. "Reclaiming the Heritage of Moses: Philo's Confrontation with Greek Philosophy." *SPhilA* 7 (1995): 108–23.

Dillon, "Transcendence in Philo." Dillon, John M. "The Transcendence of God in Philo: Some Possible Sources." *CHSP* 16 (1975): 1–8.

Dillon and Hershbell, "Introduction." Dillon, John M., and Jackson Hershbell. Introduction. Pages 1–29 in Iamblichus, *On the Pythagorean Way of Life: Text, Translation, and Notes*. Edited and translated by John M. Dillon and Jackson Hershbell. SBLTT 29. Graeco-Roman Religion Series 11. Atlanta: Scholars Press, 1991.

Dillon and Polleichtner, *Iamblichus*. Dillon, John M., and Wolfgang Polleichtner. "Introduction." Pages xiii–xxv in Iamblichus of Chalcis: *The Letters*. SBLWGRW 19. Atlanta: SBL, 2009.

Dimant, "Pesharim." Dimant, Devorah. "Pesharim, Qumran." *ABD* 5:244–51.

Dimant, "Resurrection." Dimant, Devorah. "Resurrection, Restoration, and Time-Curtailing in Qumran, Early Judaism, and Christianity." *RevQ* 19 (76, 2000): 527–48.

Dimant and Strugnell, "Vision." Dimant, Devorah, and John Strugnell. "The Merkabah Vision in *Second Ezekiel* (4Q385 4)." *RevQ* 14 (3, 1990): 331–48.

Dimarogonas, "Pliny on Papyrus." Dimarogonas, Andrew D. "Pliny the Elder on the Making of Papyrus Paper." *CQ* 45 (2, 1995): 588–90.

Di Mattei, "Physiologia." Di Mattei, Steven. "Moses' Physiologia and the Meaning and Use of Physikôs in Philo of Alexandria's Exegetical Method." *SPhilA* 18 (2006): 3–32.

Dimitrova, *Theoroi*. Dimitrova, Nora Mitkova. *Theoroi and Initiates in Samothrace: The Epigraphical Evidence*. Hesperia Supplement 37. Princeton, N.J.: The American School of Classical Studies at Athens, 2008.

Dimont, *History*. Dimont, Max I. *Jews, God, and History*. New York: New American Library, 1962.

Di Nino, "Posidippus' Shipwrecks." Di Nino, M. M. "Posidippus' Shipwrecks." *MHR* 21 (1, 2006): 99–104.

Dinsmoor, *Architecture of Greece*. Dinsmoor, William Bell. *The Architecture of Ancient Greece: An Account of Its Historic Development*. New York: W. W. Norton, 1975.

Dinwiddy, "Missions." Dinwiddy, Hugh. "Missions and Missionaries as Portrayed by English-Speaking Writers of Contemporary African Literature." Pages 426–42 in *Christianity in Independent Africa*. Edited by Edward Fasholé-Luke et al. Bloomington: Indiana University Press, 1978.

Dion, "Vision de Pierre." Dion, Paul-E. "Dt. 12 et la vision de Pierre à Joppé." *ScEs* 36 (2, 1984): 207–10.

Dion and Pummer, "Synagogue." Dion, Paul E., and Reinhard Pummer. "A Note on the 'Samaritan-Christian Synagogue' in Ramat-Aviv." *JSJ* 11 (2, 1980): 217–22.

Dionne, "Épisode." Dionne, Christian. "L'épisode de Lystre (Ac 14,7–20a): Une analyse narrative." *ScEs* 57 (1, 2005): 5–33.

Dionne, "Figure de Dieu." Dionne, Christian. "La figure narrative de Dieu dans le discours à Lystre (Ac 14,15–17)." *ScEs* 57 (2, 2005): 101–24.

Dionson, "Doctrine." Dionson, Narciso C. "The Pentecostal Doctrine of Baptism in the Holy Spirit: A Pastoral Confession." *AJPS* 2 (2, 1999): 233–42.

Diop, "Origin." Diop, Cheikh Anta. "Origin of the Ancient Egyptians." Pages 35–63 in *Great African Thinkers: Cheikh Anta Diop*. Edited by Ivan Van Sertima. New Brunswick, N.J.: Journal of African Civilizations, 1986.

DiOrio, *Miracle*. DiOrio, Ralph A. *A Miracle to Proclaim: Firsthand Experiences of Healing*. Garden City, N.Y.: Image Books, Doubleday, 1984.

Di Sabatino, "Frisbee." Di Sabatino, David. "Appendix 3: Lonnie Frisbee." Pages 392–407 in *The Quest for the Radical Middle: A History of the Vineyard*, by Bill Jackson. Foreword by Todd Hunter. Cape Town: Vineyard International, 1999.

Di Segni, "Chapel of Paul." Di Segni, Leah. "A Chapel of St. Paul at Caesarea Maritima? The Inscriptions." *SBFLA* 50 (2000): 383–400.

Di Segni, "Giv'at Seled Cave." Di Segni, Leah. "A Fragmentary Greek Inscription from the Giv'at Seled Burial Cave." *'Atiqot* 20 (1991): 164–65.

Di Segni, "Palinode." Di Segni, Leah. "The Hadrianic Inscription from Southern Samaria (?)—A Palinode." *SBFLA* 53 (2003): 335–40.

Di Segni, "Toponym." Di Segni, Leah. "A New Toponym in Southern Samaria." *SBFLA* 44 (1994): 579–84.

Distelrath, "Prodigium." Distelrath, Götz. "Prodigium." *BrillPauly* 11:931–32.

DiTommaso, "Note." DiTommaso, Lorenzo. "A Note on Demetrius the Chronographer, Fr. 2.11 (= Eusebius, *PrEv* 9.21.11)." *JSJ* 29 (1, 1998): 81–91.

Dix, *Ministry*. Dix, Gregory. *The Apostolic Ministry*. Edited by Kenneth E. Kirk. London: Hodder & Stoughton, 1947.

Dixon, *Roman Mother*. Dixon, Suzanne. *The Roman Mother*. Norman: Oklahoma University Press, 1988.

Djomhoué, "Histoire." Djomhoué, Priscille. "Une histoire de rapprochement: Actes 10–11,18." *FoiVie* 104 (4, 2005): 71–82.

Dmitriev, "Grant." Dmitriev, Sviatoslav. "'Claudius' Grant of Cilicia to Polemo." *CQ* 53 (1, 2003): 286–91.

Dmitriev, "Observations." Dmitriev, Sviatoslav. "Observations on the Historical Geography of Roman Lycaonia." *GRBS* 41 (4, 2000): 349–75.

Dobbeler, "Geschichte." Dobbeler, Stephanie von. "Geschichte und Geschichten: Der theologische Gehalt und die politische Problematik von 1 und 2 Makkabäer." *BK* 57 (2, 2002): 62–67.

Dobbeler, *Philippus*. Dobbeler, Axel von. *Der Evangelist Philippus in der Geschichte des Urchristentums: Eine prosopographische Skizze*. TANZ 30. Tübingen: Francke, 2000.

Dobbin, *Dance*. Dobbin, Jay D. *The Jombee Dance of Montserrat: A Study of Trance Ritual in the West Indies*. Columbus: Ohio State University Press, 1986.

Doble, *Paradox*. Doble, Peter. *The Paradox of Salvation: Luke's Theology of the Cross*. SNTSMS 87. Cambridge: Cambridge University Press, 1996.

Dobson, "Centurion or Officer?" Dobson, Brian. "Legionary Centurion or Equestrian Officer? A Comparison of Pay and Prospects." *AncSoc* 3 (1972): 193–207.

Dobson, "Depiction." Dobson, Elizabeth Spalding. "Pliny the Younger's Depiction of Women." *CBull* 58 (6, 1982): 81–85.

Dobson and Hornblower, "*Epitaphios*." Dobson, John Frederic, and Simon Hornblower. "*Epitaphios (logos)*." *OCD*³ 547–48.

Dockx, "Compagnon de Paul?" Dockx, S. "Luc a-t-il été le compagnon d'apostolat de Paul?" *NRTh* 103 (3, 1981): 385–400.

Dockx, "Voyage." Dockx, S. "The First Missionary Voyage of Paul: Historical Reality or Literary Creation of Luke?" Pages 209–21 in *Chronos, Kairos, Christos: Nativity and Chronological Studies Presented to Jack Finegan*. Edited by Jerry Vardaman and Edwin M. Yamauchi. Winona Lake, Ind.: Eisenbrauns, 1989.

Docter, "Pithos." Docter, Roald Frithjof. "Pithos." *BrillPauly* 11:306–7.

Docter, "Transport Amphorae." Docter, Roald Frithjof. "Transport Amphorae." *BrillPauly* 14:860–64.

Dodd, "Background." Dodd, C. H. "The Background of the Fourth Gospel." *BJRL* 19 (1935): 329–43.

Dodd, *Bible and Greeks*. Dodd, C. H. *The Bible and the Greeks*. London: Hodder & Stoughton, 1935.

Dodd, *Dynamics*. Dodd, Carley H. *Dynamics of Intercultural Communication*. 5th ed. Boston: McGraw-Hill, 1998.

Dodd, "Fall." Dodd, C. H. "The Fall of Jerusalem and the 'Abomination of Desolation.'" *JRS* 37 (1947): 47–54.

Dodd, *Interpretation*. Dodd, C. H. *The Interpretation of the Fourth Gospel*. Cambridge: Cambridge University Press, 1965.

Dodd, *New Testament Studies*. Dodd, C. H. *New Testament Studies*. Manchester, U.K.: Manchester University Press, 1967.

Dodd, *Parables*. Dodd, C. H. *The Parables of the Kingdom*. London: Nisbet, 1936.

Dodd, *Preaching*. Dodd, C. H. *The Apostolic Preaching and Its Developments*. London: Hodder & Stoughton, 1936. Repr., Grand Rapids: Baker, 1980.

Dodd, *Problem*. Dodd, Brian. *The Problem with Paul*. Downers Grove, Ill.: InterVarsity, 1996.

Dodd, "Prologue." Dodd, C. H. "The Prologue to the Fourth Gospel and Christian Worship." Pages 9–22 in *Studies in the Fourth Gospel*. Edited by F. L. Cross. London: A. R. Mowbray, 1957.

Dodd, *Tradition*. Dodd, C. H. *Historical Tradition in the Fourth Gospel*. Cambridge: Cambridge University Press, 1965.

Dodson, "*Somniis*." Dodson, Derek S. "Philo's *De somniis* in the Context of Ancient Dream Theories and Classifications." *PRSt* 30 (3, 2003): 299–312.

Doeve, *Hermeneutics*. Doeve, J. W. *Jewish Hermeneutics in the Synoptic Gospels and Acts*. Assen, Neth.: Van Gorcum, 1954.

Doherty, "Figure." Doherty, Earl. "The Puzzling Figure of Jesus in John Dominic Crossan's Birth of Christianity: A Critical Discussion." *JHC* 6 (2, 1999): 216–58.

Dohrn-van Rossum, "Clocks." Dohrn-van Rossum, Gerhard. "Clocks." *BrillPauly* 3:461–64.

Dolfe, "'Blood' and Acts 20:28." Dolfe, Karl Gustav. "The Greek Word of 'Blood' and the Interpretation of Acts 20:28." *SEÅ* 55 (1990): 64–70.

Dölger, "*THEOU PHŌNĒ*." Dölger, Franz Joseph. "*THEOU PHŌNĒ*." *Antike und Christentum* 5 (1936): 218–23.

Dollar, *Exploration*. Dollar, Harold E. *A Biblical-Missiological Exploration of the Cross-cultural Dimensions in Luke-Acts*. San Francisco: Mellen Research University Press, 1993.

Dollar, "Theology of Healing." Dollar, Harold E. "A Cross-cultural Theology of Healing." DMiss diss., Fuller Theological Seminary, 1980.

Dombrowski, "Misfortune." Dombrowski, Bruno W. "On Misfortune, Fate, Destiny, and History according to 1QS and Relevant Words in Texts from Khirbet Qumran as well as Equivalents in the Hellenistic Environment." *QC* 6 (1–4, 1996): 47–63.

Domeris, "Confession." Domeris, William R. "The Confession of Peter according to John 6:69." *TynBul* 44 (1, 1993): 155–67.

Dominian, *Growth*. Dominian, Jack. *The Growth of Love and Sex*. Grand Rapids: Eerdmans, 1984.

Dominy, "Spirit, Church, and Mission." Dominy, Bert B. "Spirit, Church, and Mission: Theological Implications of Pentecost." *SWJT* 35 (2, 1993): 34–39.

Donahue, *Christ*. Donahue, John R. *Are You the Christ? The Trial Narrative in the Gospel of Mark*. SBLDS 10. Missoula, Mont.: SBL, 1973.

Donahue, "Decades on Rich and Poor." Donahue, John R. "Two Decades of Research on the Rich and Poor in Luke-Acts." Pages 129–44 in *Justice and the Holy: Essays in Honor of Walter Harrelson*. Edited by D. A. Knight and P. J. Paris. Atlanta: Scholars Press, 1989.

Donahue, "Iunia Rustica." Donahue, J. F. "Iunia Rustica of Cartima: Female Munificence in the Roman World." *Latomus* 63 (4, 2004): 873–91.

Donahue, "Redaction Criticism." Donahue, John R. "Redaction Criticism: Has the *Hauptstrasse* Become a *Sackgasse*?" Pages 27–57 in *The New Literary Criticism and the New Testament*. Edited by Edgar V. McKnight and Elizabeth Struthers Malbon. Valley Forge, Pa.: Trinity Press International; Sheffield, U.K.: JSOT Press, 1994.

Donaldson, "Bandits." Donaldson, Terence L. "Rural Bandits, City Mobs, and the Zealots." *JSJ* 21 (1, 1990): 19–40.

Donaldson, "Convert." Donaldson, Terence L. "Israelite, Convert, Apostle to the Gentiles: The Origin of Paul's Gentile Mission." Pages 62–84 in *The Road from Damascus: The Impact of Paul's Conversion on His Life, Thought, and Ministry*. Edited by Richard N. Longenecker. Grand Rapids: Eerdmans, 1997.

Donaldson, *Paul and Gentiles*. Donaldson, Terence L. *Paul and the Gentiles: Remapping the Apostle's Convictional World*. Minneapolis: Fortress, 1997.

Donaldson, "Riches." Donaldson, Terence L. "'Riches for the Gentiles' (Rom 11:12): Israel's Rejection and Paul's Gentile Mission." *JBL* 112 (1, 1993): 81–98.

Donaldson, "Royal Sympathizers." Donaldson, Terence L. "Royal Sympathizers in Jewish Narrative." *JSP* 16 (1, 2006): 41–59.

Donaldson, "Sectarian Nature." Donaldson, Terence L. "Moses Typology and the Sectarian Nature of Early Christian Anti-Judaism: A Study in Acts 7." *JSNT* 12 (1981): 27–52.

Donaldson, "Zealot and Convert." Donaldson, Terence L. "Zealot and Convert: The

Origin of Paul's Christ-Torah Antithesis." *CBQ* 51 (4, 1989): 655–82.

Donceel-Vouté, "Coenaculum." Donceel-Vouté, Pauline H. E. "'Coenaculum'—la salle à l'étage du *locus* 30 à Khirbet Qumrân sur la mer Morte." *Res orientales* 4 (1993): 61–84.

Donegani, "Procès." Donegani, Isabelle. "Ac 4,1–31 et le procès de l'énonciation (I): Arrestation de Pierre et Jean et déposition de Pierre au Sanhédrin (Ac 4,1–12)." *SémBib* 134 (2009): 23–44.

Donelson, "Cult Histories." Donelson, L. R. "Cult Histories and the Sources of Acts." *Bib* 68 (1, 1987): 1–21.

Donfried, "Christology and Salvation." Donfried, Karl P. "Attempts at Understanding the Purpose of Luke-Acts: Christology and the Salvation of the Gentiles." Pages 112–22 in *Christological Perspectives: Essays in Honor of Harvey K. McArthur*. Edited by R. F. Berkey and S. A. Edwards. New York: Pilgrim, 1982.

Donfried, "Cults." Donfried, Karl P. "The Cults of Thessalonica and the Thessalonian Correspondence." *NTS* 31 (3, 1985): 336–56.

Donfried, "Note." Donfried, Karl Paul. "A Short Note on Romans 16." *JBL* 89 (4, 1970): 441–49.

Donfried, "Note on Romans 16." Donfried, Karl P. "A Short Note on Romans 16." Pages 50–60 in *The Romans Debate*. Edited by Karl P. Donfried. Minneapolis: Augsburg, 1977.

Donfried, "Presuppositions." Donfried, Karl P. "False Presuppositions in the Study of Romans." Pages 120–48 in *The Romans Debate*. Edited by Karl P. Donfried. Minneapolis: Augsburg, 1977.

Donfried, "Rethinking." Donfried, Karl P. "Rethinking Paul: On the Way toward a Revised Paradigm." *Bib* 87 (4, 2006): 582–94.

Donfried, "Revisionists." Donfried, Karl P. "Paul and the Revisionists: Did Luther Really Get It All Wrong?" *Dial* 46 (1, 2007): 31–40.

Donfried, "Test Case." Donfried, Karl P. "Paul and Judaism: I Thessalonians 2:13–16 as a Test Case." *Interpretation* 38 (3, 1984): 242–53.

Donfried, *Thessalonica*. Donfried, Karl P. *Paul, Thessalonica, and Early Christianity*. Grand Rapids: Eerdmans; London: T&T Clark, 2002.

Doody, "Natural History." Doody, Aude. "Pliny's Natural History: Enkuklios Paideia and the Ancient Encyclopedia." *JHI* 70 (1, 2009): 1–21.

Doohan, *Acts*. Doohan, Leonard. *Acts of Apostles: Building Faith Communities*. San Jose, Calif.: Resource, 1994.

Dor, "Bobon." Dor, Joel. "Jean Bobon et la psychopathologie du langage." *Acta psychiatrica belgica* 83 (3, 1983): 197–206.

Doran, "Malchus." Doran, R. "Cleodemus Malchus." *OTP* 2:883–87.

Doran, "Narrative Literature." Doran, R. "Narrative Literature." Pages 287–310 in *Early Judaism and Its Modern Interpreters*. Edited by Robert A. Kraft and George W. E. Nickelsburg. SBLBMI 2. Atlanta: Scholars Press, 1986.

Dorandi, "Copy." Dorandi, Tiziano. "Copy." *BrillPauly* 3:774–78.

Dorandi, "Epicurean School." Dorandi, Tiziano. "Epicurean School." *BrillPauly* 4:1071–75.

Dorandi, "Publication." Dorandi, Tiziano. "Publication." *BrillPauly* 12:185–86.

Dorcey, *Silvanus*. Dorcey, Peter F. *The Cult of Silvanus: A Study in Roman Folk Religion*. New York: Brill, 1992.

Dorcey, "Women." Dorcey, Peter F. "The Role of Women in the Cult of Silvanus." *Numen* 36 (2, 1989): 143–55.

Doriani, "History." Doriani, Daniel M. "A History of the Interpretation of 1 Timothy 2." Pages 213–67 in *Women in the Church: A Fresh Analysis of 1 Timothy 2:9–15*. Edited by Andreas J. Köstenberger, Thomas R. Schreiner, and H. Scott Baldwin. Grand Rapids: Baker, 1995.

Doriani, "Review." Doriani, Daniel M. Review of Craig S. Keener, *A Commentary on the Gospel of Matthew*. *Presbyterion* 26 (1, 2000): 34–35.

Döring, "Cyrenaics." Döring, Klaus. "Cyrenaics." *BrillPauly* 4:4–6.

Dormeyer, *Evangelium*. Dormeyer, Detlev. *Evangelium als literarische und theologische Gattung*. EdF 263. Darmstadt: Wissenschaftliche Buchgesellschaft, 1989.

Dormeyer, "Gattung." Dormeyer, Detlev. "Die Gattung der Apostelgeschichte." Pages 437–75 in *Die Apostelgeschichte im Kontext antiker und frühchristlicher Historiographie*. Edited by Jörg Frey, Clare K. Rothschild, and Jens Schröter, with Bettina Rost. BZNWK 162. Berlin: de Gruyter, 2009.

Dormeyer, "Historii." Dormeyer, Detlev. "Pragmatyczne i patetyczne pisanie historii w historiografii greckiej, we wczesnym judaizmie i w Nowym Testamencie." *ColT* 78 (2, 2008): 81–94.

Dormeyer and Galindo, *Apostelgeschichte*. Dormeyer, Detlev, and Florencio Galindo. *Die Apostelgeschichte: Ein Kommentar für die Praxis*. Stuttgart: Katholisches Bibelwerk, 2003.

Dorries, "Irving and Spirit Baptism." Dorries, David W. "Edward Irving and the 'Standing Sign' of Spirit Baptism." Pages 41–56 in *Initial Evidence: Historical and Biblical

Perspectives on the Pentecostal Doctrine of Spirit Baptism*. Edited by Gary B. McGee. Peabody, Mass.: Hendrickson, 1991.

Dorsey, "Carts." Dorsey, David A. "Carts." *OEANE* 1:433–34.

Dorsey, "Roads." Dorsey, David A. "Roads." *OEANE* 4:431–34.

Dorsey, "Travel." Dorsey, David A. "Travel; Transportation." *ISBE* 4:891–97.

Dossey, "Greeks." Dossey, Leslie. "Watchful Greeks and Lazy Romans: Disciplining Sleep in Late Antiquity." *JECS* 21 (2, 2013): 209–39.

Dothan, "Acco." Dothan, Moshe. "Acco." *ABD* 1:50–53.

Dougherty, "Did Paul Fall?" Dougherty, Charles T. "Did Paul Fall off a Horse?" *BRev* 13 (4, 1997): 42–44.

Doughty, "Fictional History in Acts 18." Doughty, Darrell J. "Luke's Story of Paul in Corinth: Fictional History in Acts 18." *JHC* 4 (1, 1997): 3–54.

Douglas, "Abominations." Douglas, Mary. "The Abominations of Leviticus." Pages 202–5 in *Reader in Comparative Religion: An Anthropological Approach*. Edited by William A. Lessa and Evon Z. Vogt. 3rd ed. New York: Harper & Row, 1972.

Douglas, *Purity and Danger*. Douglas, Mary. *Purity and Danger*. London: Routledge & Kegan Paul, 1966.

Doukellis, "Panhellenion." Doukellis, P. N. "Hadrian's *Panhellenion*: A Network of Cities?" *MHR* 22 (2, 2007): 295–308.

Doulamis, "Ends Well." Doulamis, Konstantin. "All's Well That Ends Well: Storytelling, Predictive Signs, and the Voice of the Author in Chariton's Callirhoe." *Mnemosyne* 65 (1, 2012): 18–39.

Doumet, *Étude*. Doumet, Joseph. *Étude sur la couleur poupre ancienne: et tentative de reproduction du procédé de teinture de la ville de Tyr décrit par Pline l'Ancien. Study on the Ancient Purple Colour: and an attempt to reproduce the dyeing procedure of Tyre as described by Pliny the Elder*. Translated by Robert Cook. Beirut: Imprimerie Catholique, 1980.

Douyon, "Examen." Douyon, Emerson. "L'examen au Rorschach des vaudouisants haïtiens." Pages 97–119 in *Trance and Possession States: Proceedings of the Second Annual Conference, R. M. Bucke Memorial Society, March 4–6, 1966*. Edited by Raymond Prince. Montreal: R. M. Bucke Memorial Society, 1968.

Dover, "Attitudes." Dover, K. J. "Classical Greek Attitudes to Sexual Behavior." Pages 143–58 in *Women in the Ancient World: The Arethusa Papers*. Edited by John Peradotto and J. P. Sullivan. SSCS. Albany: State University of New York Press, 1984.

Dowd, "Ordination." Dowd, Sharyn. "'Ordination' in Acts and the Pastoral Epistles." *PRSt* 29 (2, 2002): 205–17.

Dowd, "Theology." Dowd, Sharyn E. "Toward a Johannine Theology of Prayer." Pages 317–35 in *Perspectives on John: Method and Interpretation in the Fourth Gospel.* Edited by Robert B. Sloan and Mikeal C. Parsons. NABPRSS 11. Lewiston, N.Y.: Edwin Mellen, 1993.

Dowden, "Aeneas." Dowden, Ken. "Aeneas." Pages 11–12 in *Dictionary of Deities and Demons in the Bible.* 2nd rev. ed. Edited by Karel van der Toorn, Bob Becking, and Pieter W. van der Horst. Leiden: Brill; Grand Rapids: Eerdmans, 1999.

Dowden, "Callisthenes." Dowden, Ken. "Introduction to Pseudo-Callisthenes, The Alexander Romance." Pages 650–54 in *Collected Ancient Greek Novels.* Edited by B. P. Reardon. Berkeley: University of California Press, 1989.

Dowden, "Daphne." Dowden, Ken. "Daphne." Pages 220–21 in *Dictionary of Deities and Demons in the Bible.* 2nd rev. ed. Edited by Karel van der Toorn, Bob Becking, and Pieter W. van der Horst. Leiden: Brill; Grand Rapids: Eerdmans, 1999.

Dowden, "Dioskouroi." Dowden, Ken. "Dioskouroi." Pages 258–59 in *Dictionary of Deities and Demons in the Bible.* 2nd rev. ed. Edited by Karel van der Toorn, Bob Becking, and Pieter W. van der Horst. Leiden: Brill; Grand Rapids: Eerdmans, 1999.

Dowden, "Jason." Dowden, Ken. "Jason." Pages 463–64 in *Dictionary of Deities and Demons in the Bible.* 2nd rev. ed. Edited by Karel van der Toorn, Bob Becking, and Pieter W. van der Horst. Leiden: Brill; Grand Rapids: Eerdmans, 1999.

Dowden, "Marsyas." Dowden, Ken. "Marsyas." *OCD*[3] 930.

Dowden, "Narration." Dowden, Ken. "Apuleius and the Art of Narration." *CQ* 32, (2, 1982): 419–35.

Dowden, "Silvanus." Dowden, Ken. "Silvanus." Pages 778–79 in *Dictionary of Deities and Demons in the Bible.* 2nd rev. ed. Edited by Karel van der Toorn, Bob Becking, and Pieter W. van der Horst. Leiden: Brill; Grand Rapids: Eerdmans, 1999.

Downey, *History of Antioch.* Downey, Glanville. *History of Antioch in Syria from Seleucus to the Arab Conquest.* Princeton: Princeton University Press, 1961.

Downing, "Actuality." Downing, F. Gerald. "Actuality versus Abstraction: The Synoptic Gospel Model." *Continuum* 1 (3, 1991): 104–20.

Downing, "Common Ground." Downing, F. Gerald. "Common Ground with Paganism in Luke and Josephus." *NTS* 28 (4, 1982): 546–59.

Downing, "Conventions" Downing, F. Gerald. "Compositional Conventions and the Synoptic Problem." *JBL* 107 (1, 1988): 69–85.

Downing, *Cynics.* Downing, F. Gerald. *Cynics, Paul and the Pauline Churches: Cynics and Christian Origins II.* London: Routledge, 1998.

Downing, "Law and Custom." Downing, F. Gerald. "Law and Custom: Luke-Acts and Late Hellenism." Pages 148–58, 187–91 in *Law and Religion: Essays on the Place of the Law in Israel and Early Christianity by Members of the Ehrhardt Seminar.* Edited by Barnabas Lindars. Cambridge, U.K.: James Clark, 1988.

Downing, "Pagan Theism and Speeches." Downing, F. Gerald. "Ethical Pagan Theism and the Speeches in Acts." *NTS* 27 (4, 1981): 544–63.

Downing, "Paul's Drive." Downing, F. Gerald. "Paul's Drive for Deviants." *NTS* 49 (3, 2003): 360–71.

Downing, "Philo on Wealth." Downing, F. Gerald. "Philo on Wealth and the Rights of the Poor." *JSNT* 24 (1985): 116–18.

Downing, "Relevance." Downing, F. Gerald. "A bas les aristos: The Relevance of Higher Literature for the Understanding of the Earliest Christian Writings." *NovT* 30 (3, 1988): 212–30.

Downing, "Resurrection." Downing, F. Gerald. "The Resurrection of the Dead: Jesus and Philo." *JSNT* 15 (1982): 42–50.

Downing, "Strands." Downing, F. Gerald. "Common Strands in Pagan, Jewish, and Christian Eschatologies in the First Century." *TZ* 51 (3, 1995): 196–211.

Downs, "Collection." Downs, David J. "Paul's Collection and the Book of Acts Revisited." *NTS* 52 (1, 2006): 50–70.

Dräger, "Iason." Dräger, Paul. "Iason." *Brill Pauly* 6:682–85.

Dräger, "Lemnian Women." Dräger, Paul. "Lemnian Women, Hypsipyle." *BrillPauly* 7:381–82.

Drane, "Background." Drane, John W. "The Religious Background." Pages 117–25 in *New Testament Interpretation: Essays on Principles and Methods.* Edited by I. Howard Marshall. Grand Rapids: Eerdmans, 1977.

Drane, "Romans." Drane, John W. "Why Did Paul Write Romans?" Pages 208–27 in *Pauline Studies: Essays Presented to Professor F. F. Bruce on His 70th Birthday.* Edited by Donald A. Hagner and Murray J. Harris. Exeter, U.K.: Paternoster; Grand Rapids: Eerdmans, 1980.

Draper, "Church-State Conflict." Draper, Jonathan. "Church-State Conflict in the Book of Acts: A South African Perspective." *JTSA* 97 (1997): 39–52.

Draper, "Didache." Draper, Jonathan. "The Jesus Tradition in the Didache." Pages 269–87 in *The Jesus Tradition outside the Gospels.* Edited by David Wenham. Gospel Perspectives 5. Sheffield, U.K.: JSOT Press, 1984.

Draper, "Drama." Draper, Jonathan A. "Hermeneutical Drama on the Colonial Stage. Liminal Space and Creativity in Colenso's *Commentary on Romans.*" *JTSA* 103 (1999): 13–32.

Draper, "Greek." Draper, H. Mude. "Did Jesus Speak Greek?" *ExpT* 67 (10, 1956): 317.

Draper, "Orality." Draper, Jonathan A. "Orality, Literacy, and Colonialism in Antiquity." Pages 1–6 in *Orality, Literacy, and Colonialism in Antiquity.* SBLSemS 47. Atlanta: SBL, 2004.

Dresken-Weiland, "Fremde." Dresken-Weiland, Jutta. "Fremde in der Bevölkerung des kaiserzeitlichen Rom." *RQ* 98 (1–2, 2003): 18–34.

Drexhage, "India." Drexhage, Hans-Joachim. "India, Trade with." *BrillPauly* 6:773–77.

Drijvers, "Inscriptions." Drijvers, H. J. W. "Inscriptions of the Hellenistic and Roman Periods." *OEANE* 3:165–68.

Drijvers and de Jong, "Mithras." Drijvers, Han J. W., and Albert F. de Jong. "Mithras." Pages 578–81 in *Dictionary of Deities and Demons in the Bible.* 2nd rev. ed. Edited by Karel van der Toorn, Bob Becking, and Pieter W. van der Horst. Leiden: Brill; Grand Rapids: Eerdmans, 1999.

Driver, *Amos.* Driver, S. R. *The Books of Joel and Amos.* Cambridge: Cambridge University Press, 1907.

Driver, *Scrolls.* Driver, G. R. *The Judaean Scrolls: The Problem and a Solution.* Oxford: Blackwell, 1965.

Droege, *Faith Factor.* Droege, Thomas A. *The Faith Factor in Healing.* Philadelphia: Trinity Press International, 1991.

Droge, "Anonymously." Droge, A. J. "Did 'Luke' Write Anonymously? Lingering at the Threshold." Pages 495–518 in *Die Apostelgeschichte im Kontext antiker und frühchristlicher Historiographie.* Edited by Jörg Frey, Clare K. Rothschild, and Jens Schröter, with Bettina Rost. BZNWK 162. Berlin: de Gruyter, 2009.

Droge, "*Mori lucrum.*" Droge, Arthur J. "*Mori lucrum*: Paul and Ancient Theories of Suicide." *NovT* 30 (3, 1988): 263–86.

Drogula, "Controlling Travel." Drogula, Fred K. "Controlling Travel: Deportation, Islands and the Regulation of Senatorial Mobility in the Augustan Principate." *CQ* 61 (1, May 2011): 230–66.

Drower, *Mandaeans*. Drower, E. S. *The Mandaeans of Iraq and Iran: Their Cults, Customs, Magic, Legends, and Folklore*. Leiden: Brill, 1962.

Drummond, "*Fasces*." Drummond, Andrew. "*Fasces*." *OCD*³ 587–88.

Drury, *Design*. Drury, John. *Tradition and Design in Luke's Gospel: A Study in Early Christian Historiography*. London: Darton, Longman & Todd, 1976.

D'Sa, "Salvation of Rich." D'Sa, T. "The Salvation of the Rich in the Gospel of Luke." *Vid* 52 (1988): 170–80.

D'Souza, "Sermons of Peter." D'Souza, A. "The Sermons of Peter in the Acts of the Apostles." *BiBh* 4 (2, 1978): 117–30.

Dubarle, "Témoignage." Dubarle, André-Marie. "Le témoignage de Josèphe sur Jésus d'après la tradition indirecte." *RB* 80 (4, 1973): 481–513.

Dubois, *Pouzzoles*. Dubois, Charles. *Pouzzoles antique (histoire et topographie)*. Paris: Albert Fontemoing, 1907.

Du Bois, *World and Africa*. Du Bois, W. E. Burghardt. *The World and Africa: An Inquiry into the Part Which Africa Has Played in History*. Enl. ed., with new writings on Africa, 1955–61. New York: International Publishers, 1965.

Dubourdieu, "Dead, Cult of." Dubourdieu, Annie. "Dead, Cult of: Roman." *BrillPauly* 4:114–16.

Dubourdieu, "Divinités de la parole." Dubourdieu, Annie. "Divinités de la parole, divinités du silence dans la Rome antique." *RHR* 220 (3, 2003): 259–82.

Dubuisson, "Procurateur." Dubuisson, Michel. "Le 'procurateur' de Judée." *RBPH* 77 (1, 1999): 131–36.

Dudley, *Civilization of Rome*. Dudley, Donald R. *The Civilization of Rome*. New York: New American Library, 1960.

Dudley, "Speeches." Dudley, Merle B. "The Speeches in Acts." *EvQ* 50 (3, 1978): 147–55.

Duff, *Freedmen*. Duff, A. M. *Freedmen in the Early Roman Empire*. Oxford: Clarendon, 1928. Reprinted with minor corrections, Cambridge: Heffer, 1958.

Duff, "Metaphor." Duff, Paul Brooks. "Metaphor, Motif, and Meaning: The Rhetorical Strategy behind the Image 'Led in Triumph' in 2 Corinthians 2:14." *CBQ* 53 (1, 1991): 79–92.

Duff, "Models." Duff, Timothy E. "Models of Education in Plutarch." *JHS* 128 (2008): 1–26.

Duff, "Socratic Suicide?" Duff, R. A. "Socratic Suicide?" *ProcArisSoc* 83 (1982–83): 35–48.

Duff, "Suffering." Duff, Paul Brooks. "Apostolic Suffering and the Language of Processions in 2 Corinthians 4:7–10." *BTB* 21 (4, 1991): 158–65.

Duff and Spawforth, "Anagnōstēs." Duff, John Wight, and Antony J. S. Spawforth. "Anagnōstēs." *OCD*³ 80.

Duffey, *Lessons*. Duffey, John M. *Lessons Learned: The Anneliese Michel Exorcism*. Eugene, Ore.: Wipf & Stock, 2011.

Duffield, *Cranmer*. Duffield, G. E. *The Work of Thomas Cranmer*. Introduction by J. I. Packer. Philadelphia: Fortress, 1965.

Duffin, *Miracles*. Duffin, Jacalyn. *Medical Miracles: Doctors, Saints, and Healing in the Modern World*. Oxford: Oxford University Press, 2009.

Dugan, "Ciceronianism." Dugan, John. "Preventing Ciceronianism: C. Licinius Calvus' Regimens for Sexual and Oratorial Self-Mastery." *CP* 96 (4, 2001): 400–428.

Duhaime, "Dualisme." Duhaime, Jean L. "Dualisme et construction de l'identité sectaire à Qumrân." *Théologiques* 13 (1, 2005): 43–57.

Duhaime, "Remarques." Duhaime, Jean L. "Remarques sur les dépôts d'ossements d'animaux à Qumrân." *RevQ* 9 (2, 1977): 245–51.

Duhaime, "Voies." Duhaime, Jean L. "Les voies des deux esprits (*1QS* iv 2–14): Une analyse structurelle." *RevQ* 19 (75, 2000): 349–67.

Duke, *Irony*. Duke, Paul D. *Irony in the Fourth Gospel*. Atlanta: John Knox, 1985.

Duling, "Introduction." Duling, Dennis C. Introduction to "Testament of Solomon." *OTP* 1:935–59.

Dumais, *Communauté*. Dumais, Marcel. *Communauté et mission: Une lecture des Actes des apôtres*. Rev. ed. Montreal: Bellarmin, 2000.

Dumais, "Langage." Dumais, Marcel. "Le langage des discours d'évangélisation des Actes: Une forme de langage symbolique?" Pages 467–74 in *Les Actes des apôtres: Traditions, rédaction, théologie*. Edited by Jacob Kremer. BETL 48. Gembloux, Belg.: J. Duculot; Leuven: Leuven University Press, 1979.

Dumais, "Ministères et Esprit." Dumais, Marcel. "Ministères, charismes, et Esprit dans l'oeuvre de Luc." *ÉgT* 9 (3, 1978): 413–53.

Dumais, "Salut." Dumais, M. "Le salut en dehors de la foi en Jésus-Christ? Observations sur trois passages des Actes des apôtres." *ÉgT* 28 (2, 1997): 161–90.

Dunand, "Mystères." Dunand, Françoise. "Les mystères égyptiens." Pages 11–62 in *Mystères et syncrétismes*. Edited by M. Philonenko et M. Simon. EHRel 2. Paris: Librairie Orientaliste Paul Geuthner, 1975.

Dunand, *Religion en Égypte*. Dunand, Françoise. *Religion populaire en Égypte romaine*. ÉPROER 77. Leiden: Brill, 1979.

Dunbabin, "Convivial Spaces." Dunbabin, K. M. D. "Convivial Spaces: Dining and Entertainment in the Roman Villa." *JRA* 9 (1996): 66–80.

Dunbabin, "Dionysus." Dunbabin, K. M. D. "Domestic Dionysus? Telete in Mosaics from Zeugma and the Late Roman Near East." *JRA* 21 (2008): 193–224.

Dunbabin, "Triclinium." Dunbabin, Katherine M. D. "Triclinium and Stibadium." Pages 121–48 in *Dining in a Classical Context*. Edited by William J. Slater. Ann Arbor: University of Michigan Press, 1991.

Dunbabin, Eliot, and Hornblower, "Long Walls." Dunbabin, Thomas James, Charles William John Eliot, and Simon Hornblower. "Long Walls, The." *OCD*³ 884.

Duncan, *Ephesian Ministry*. Duncan, George S. *St. Paul's Ephesian Ministry*. London: Hodder & Stoughton, 1929.

Duncker, "Viduae." Duncker, P.-G. "'. . . Quae vere viduae sunt' (1 Tim. 5, 3)." *Angelicum* 35 (2, 1958): 121–38.

Dunken, "Connection." Dunken, D. "The Corinthian Connection." *BibT* 35 (5, 1997): 294–99.

Dunkerley, *Healing Evangelism*. Dunkerley, Don. *Healing Evangelism: Strengthen Your Witnessing with Effective Prayer for the Sick*. Foreword by J. I. Packer. Grand Rapids: Chosen, 1995.

Dunn, *Acts*. Dunn, James D. G. *The Acts of the Apostles*. Narrative Commentaries. Valley Forge, Pa.: Trinity Press International, 1996.

Dunn, *Baptism*. Dunn, James D. G. *Baptism in the Holy Spirit: A Re-examination of the New Testament Teaching on the Gift of the Spirit in Relation to Pentecostalism Today*. SBT, 2nd ser., 15. London: SCM, 1970.

Dunn, "Baptism." Dunn, James D. G. "Baptism in the Spirit: A Response to Pentecostal Scholarship on Luke-Acts." *JPT* 3 (1993): 3–27.

Dunn, *Beginning*. Dunn, James D. G. *Beginning from Jerusalem*. Vol. 2 of Christianity in the Making. Grand Rapids: Eerdmans, 2009.

Dunn, "Demythologizing." Dunn, James D. G. "Demythologizing—The Problem of Myth in the New Testament." Pages 285–307 in *New Testament Interpretation: Essays on Principles and Methods*. Edited by I. Howard Marshall. Grand Rapids: Eerdmans, 1977.

Dunn, *Epistles*. Dunn, James D. G. *The Epistles to the Colossians and to Philemon: A Commentary on the Greek Text*. NIGTC. Grand Rapids: Eerdmans, 1996.

Dunn, "Gospel According to Paul." Dunn, James D. G. "The Gospel According to St. Paul." Pages 139–53 in *The Blackwell Companion to Paul*. Edited by Stephen Westerholm. BCompRel. Oxford: Blackwell, 2011.

Dunn, *Jesus and Spirit*. Dunn, James D. G. *Jesus and the Spirit: A Study of the Religious and Charismatic Experience of Jesus and the First Christians as Reflected in the New Testament*. London: SCM, 1975.

Dunn, "Justice." Dunn, James D. G. "The Justice of God: A Renewed Perspective on Justification by Faith." *JTS* 43 (1, 1992): 1–22.

Dunn, "Kingdom." Dunn, James D. G. "Spirit and Kingdom." *ExpT* 82 (2, 1970): 36–40.

Dunn, *New Perspective*. Dunn, James D. G. *The New Perspective on Paul*. Rev. ed. Grand Rapids: Eerdmans, 2008.

Dunn, *Partings*. Dunn, James D. G. *The Partings of the Ways: Between Christianity and Judaism and Their Significance for the Character of Christianity*. London: SCM; Philadelphia: Trinity Press International, 1991.

Dunn, *Perspective*. Dunn, James D. G. *A New Perspective on Jesus: What the Quest for the Historical Jesus Missed*. Grand Rapids: Baker, 2005.

Dunn, "Reconstructions." Dunn, James D. G. "Reconstructions of Corinthian Christianity and the Interpretation of 1 Corinthians." Pages 295–310 in *Christianity at Corinth: The Quest for the Pauline Church*. Edited by Edward Adams and David G. Horrell. Louisville: Westminster John Knox, 2004.

Dunn, *Remembered*. Dunn, James D. G. *Jesus Remembered*. Vol. 1 of *Christianity in the Making*. Grand Rapids: Eerdmans, 2003.

Dunn, *Romans*. Dunn, James D. G. *Romans*. 2 vols. WBC 38A, B. Dallas: Word, 1988.

Dunn, "Spirit." Dunn, James D. G. "Spirit. NT." *NIDNTT* 3:693–707.

Dunn, "Synagogue." Dunn, James D. G. "Did Jesus Attend the Synagogue?" Pages 206–22 in *Jesus and Archaeology*. Edited by James H. Charlesworth. Grand Rapids: Eerdmans, 2006.

Dunn, *Theology of Paul*. Dunn, James D. G. *The Theology of Paul the Apostle*. Grand Rapids: Eerdmans, 1998.

Dunn, "Theory." Dunn, James D. G. "Kenneth Bailey's Theory of Oral Tradition: Critiquing Theodore Weeden's Critique." *JSHJ* 7 (1, 2009): 44–62.

Dunn, *Unity*. Dunn, James D. G. *Unity and Diversity in the New Testament: An Inquiry into the Character of Earliest Christianity*. London: SCM, 1977.

Dunn, "Works of Law." Dunn, James D. G. "Yet Once More—'The Works of the Law': A Response." *JSNT* 46 (1992): 99–117.

Dunne, *Experiment*. Dunne, J. W. *An Experiment with Time*. New York: Macmillan, 1927.

Dunnill, "Whose Faith?" Dunnill, John. "Saved by Whose Faith?—The Function of πίστις Χριστοῦ in Pauline Theology." *Colloq* 30 (1, 1998): 3–25.

Dunning, "Perspective." Dunning, H. Ray. "A Wesleyan Perspective on Spirit Baptism." Pages 181–229 in *Perspectives on Spirit Baptism: Five Views*. Edited by Chad Owen Brand. Nashville: Broadman & Holman, 2004.

Dupertuis, "Socratizing Paul." Dupertuis, Rubén. "Socratizing Paul: The Portrait of Paul in Acts." *FourR* 22 (6, 2009): 11–15, 18, 28.

Dupertuis, "Speech." Dupertuis, Rubén R. "Bold Speech, Opposition, and Philosophical Imagery in the Acts of the Apostles." Pages 153–68 in *Engaging Early Christian History: Reading Acts in the Second Century*. Edited by Rubén R. Dupertuis and Todd Penner. Bristol, Conn.: Acumen, 2013.

Dupertuis, "Summaries." Dupertuis, Rubén R. "The Summaries of Acts 2, 4, and 5 and Plato's *Republic*." Pages 275–93 in *Ancient Fiction: The Matrix of Early Christian and Jewish Narrative*. Edited by Jo-Ann A. Brant, Charles W. Hedrick, and Chris Shea. SBLSymS 32. Atlanta: SBL, 2005.

Dupertuis and Penner, *Engaging*. Dupertuis, Rubén R., and Todd Penner, eds. *Engaging Early Christian History: Reading Acts in the Second Century*. Durham, UK: Acumen, 2013.

Duplantier, "Mort." Duplantier, Jean-Pierre. "La mort d'Ananie et Saphire: Actes 5, 1–11." *SémBib* 135 (2009): 5–24.

Du Plessis, "Rule." Du Plessis, I. J. "The Rule of Christ and the Rule in the Church," in "Ministry in the Pauline Letters: Proceedings of the Twelfth Meeting of 'Die Nawe-Testamentiese-Werkgemeenskap van Suid-Afrika.'" Special Issue, *Neot* 10 (1976): 20–30.

Du Plooy, "Author." Du Plooy, G. P. V. "The Author in Luke-Acts." *Scriptura* 32 (1990): 28–35.

Dupont, "Discours de Pierre et chapitre XXIV." Dupont, Jacques. "Les discours de Pierre dans les Actes et le chapitre XXIV de l'Évangile de Luc." Pages 239–84 in *L'Évangile de Luc: The Gospel of Luke*. Edited by F. Neirynck. Rev. ed. BETL 32. Leuven: Leuven University Press, 1989.

Dupont, "Don de l'Esprit." Dupont, Jacques. "Ascension du Christ et don de l'Esprit d'après Actes 2.33." Pages 219–27 in *Christ and Spirit in the New Testament: In Honour of Charles Francis Digby Moule*. Edited by Barnabas Lindars and Stephen S. Smalley. Cambridge: Cambridge University Press, 1973.

Dupont, *Life*. Dupont, Florence. *Daily Life in Ancient Rome*. Translated by Christopher Woodall. Oxford: Blackwell, 1992.

Dupont, "Peuple d'entre les nations." Dupont, Jacques. "Un peuple d'entre les nations (Actes 15.14)." *NTS* 31 (3, 1985): 321–35.

Dupont, "Question du plan." Dupont, Jacques. "La question du plan des Actes des apôtres à la lumière d'un texte de Lucien de Samosate." *NovT* 21 (3, 1979): 220–31.

Dupont, "Rapport." Dupont, Jacques. "La conclusion des Actes et son rapport à l'ensemble de l'ouvrage de Luc." Pages 359–404 in *Les Actes des apôtres: Traditions, rédaction, théologie*. Edited by Jacob Kremer. BETL 48. Gembloux, Belg.: J. Duculot; Leuven: Leuven University Press, 1979.

Dupont, *Salvation*. Dupont, Jacques. *The Salvation of the Gentiles: Essays on the Acts of the Apostles*. Translated by John R. Keating. New York: Paulist, 1979.

Dupont, *Sources*. Dupont, Jacques. *The Sources of the Acts: The Present Position*. Translated by Kathleen Pond. New York: Herder & Herder; London: Darton, Longman & Todd, 1964.

Dupont, "Structure oratoire." Dupont, Jacques. "La structure oratoire du discours d'Étienne (Actes 7)." *Bib* 66 (2, 1985): 153–67.

Dupont-Roc, "Tradition textuelle." Dupont-Roc, Roselyne. "La tradition textuelle des Actes des apôtres: Positions actuelles et enjeux." Pages 43–62 in *Les Actes des apôtres—Histoire, récit, théologie: XXe congrès de l'Association catholique française pour l'étude de la Bible (Angers, 2003)*. Edited by Michel Berder. LD 199. Paris: Cerf, 2005.

Dupont-Sommer, *Manuscrits*. Dupont-Sommer, André. *Les manuscrits de la mer Morte et la problème des origines chrétiennes*. Paris: Estienne, 1969.

Dupont-Sommer, *Writings*. Dupont-Sommer, André. *The Essene Writings from Qumran*. Translated by G. Vermes. Oxford: Blackwell, 1961. Repr., Gloucester, Mass.: Peter Smith, 1973.

Durand and Massey, *Miracles*. Durand, Jorge, and Douglas S. Massey. *Miracles on the Border: Retablos of Mexican Migrants to the United States*. Tucson: University of Arizona Press, 1995.

Duriez, *AD 33*. Duriez, Colin. *AD 33: The Year That Changed the World*. Downers Grove, Ill.: IVP Books, 2006.

Du Sablon, "Religiosité." Du Sablon, Vincent. "Religiosité hellénistique et accès au cosmos divin." *ÉtudClass* 74 (1, 2006): 3–23.

Du Toit, "Faith and Obedience." Du Toit, A. B. "Faith and Obedience in Paul." *Neot* 25 (1, 1991): 65–74.

Du Toit, "Swyggebod." Du Toit, A. B. "Die swyggebod van 1 Korintiërs 14:34–35 weer eens onder die loep (The *taceat mulier* of 1 Cor 14:34–35 Revisited)." *HvTS* 57 (1–2, 2001): 172–86.

Du Toit, "Tale." Du Toit, A. B. "A Tale of Two Cities: 'Tarsus or Jerusalem' Revisited." *NTS* 46 (3, 2000): 375–402.

Du Toit, "Vorstellung." Du Toit, David S. "Die Vorstellung eines Begleitdämons in Philostrats *Vita Apollonii*." *WD* 25 (1999): 149–66.

Dutsch, "Genre." Dutsch, Dorota. "Genre, Gender, and Suicide Threats in Roman Comedy." *CW* 105 (2, 2012): 187–98.

Dvorjetski, "Healing Waters." Dvorjetski, Esti. "Healing Waters: The Social World of Hot Springs in Roman Palestine." *BAR* 30 (4, 2004): 16–27, 60.

Dvorjetski, "Medical History." Dvorjetski, Esti. "The Medical History of Rabbi Judah the Patriarch: A Linguistic Analysis." *HS* 43 (2002): 39–55.

Dyer, *Athens*. Dyer, Thomas Henry. *Ancient Athens: Its History, Topography, and Remains*. London: Bell and Daldy, 1873.

Dyk, "Teologia." Dyk, S. "Teologia gloszenia slowa Bożego wedlug Dz 2." *RocT* 49 (6, 2002): 149–69.

Dyson, "Pleasure." Dyson, Henry. "Pleasure and the Sapiens: Seneca, *De vita beata* 11.1." *CP* 105 (3, 2010): 313–17.

Earl, "Prologue-Form in Historiography." Earl, Donald. "Prologue-Form in Ancient Historiography." *ANRW* 2:842–56. Part 1, *Republik*, 2. Edited by H. Temporini and W. Haase. Berlin: de Gruyter, 1976.

Earle, "Borders." Earle, Duncan. "The Borders of Distinctions: Dog Days." Paper read at the Society for Humanistic Anthropology Invited Session on Practice, Performance, and Participation, American Anthropological Association Annual Meeting, Chicago, Nov. 2003.

"Earliest Alphabet." "Earliest Alphabet: A Canaanite Invention—Preserved in Sinai Mines." *BAR* 10 (4, 1984): 26–54.

Earman, "Bayes." Earman, John. "Bayes, Hume, and Miracles." *FPhil* 10 (3, 1993): 293–310.

Earman, *Failure*. Earman, John. *Hume's Abject Failure: The Argument Against Miracles*. Oxford: Oxford University Press, 2000.

Earman, "Hume." Earman, John. "Bayes, Hume, Price, and Miracles." Pages 91–109 in *Bayes's Theorem*. Edited by Richard Swinburne. Oxford: Oxford University Press, 2005.

Easterling, "Canon." Easterling, Patricia E. "Canon." *OCD*³ 286.

Eastwell, "Voodoo Death." Eastwell, Harry D. "Voodoo Death and the Mechanism for Dispatch of the Dying in East Arnhem, Australia." *AmAnth* 84 (1, 1982): 5–18.

Eaton, "Significance." Eaton, Jonathan. "The Political Significance of the Imperial Watchword in the Early Empire." *GR* 58 (1, 2011): 48–63.

Ebner, "Incestus." Ebner, Constanze. "Incestus." *BrillPauly* 6:763–64.

Ebner, "Latrocinium." Ebner, Constanze. "Latrocinium." *BrillPauly* 7:295–96.

Echard, "Possession Cult." Echard, Nicole. "The Hausa *bori* Possession Cult in the Ader Region of Niger." Pages 64–80 in *Women's Medicine: The* zar-bori *Cult in Africa and Beyond*. Edited by I. M. Lewis, Ahmed Al-Safi, and Sayyid Hurreiz. Edinburgh: International African Institute, Edinburgh University Press, 1991.

Eck, "Claudius." Eck, Werner. "Claudius (3.1)." *BrillPauly* 3:405–9.

Eck, *Cursus Honorum* Inscriptions." Eck, Werner. "There Are No *cursus honorum* Inscriptions: The Function of the *cursus honorum* in Epigraphic Communication." *SCI* 28 (2009): 79–92.

Eck, "Praefectus castrorum." Eck, Werner. "Praefectus castrorum." *BrillPauly* 11:753–54.

Eck, "Praefectus vigilum." Eck, Werner. "Praefectus vigilum." *BrillPauly* 11:755.

Eck, "Spiegel." Eck, Werner. "Ein Spiegel der Macht: Lateinische Inschriften römischer Zeit in Iudaea/Syria Palaestina." *ZDPV* 117 (1, 2001): 47–63.

Eck, "Urbanae cohortes." Eck, Werner. "Urbanae cohortes." *BrillPauly* 15:122.

Eckey, *Apostelgeschichte*. Eckey, Wilfried. *Die Apostelgeschichte: Der Weg des Evangeliums von Jerusalem nach Rom*. 2 vols. Neukirchen-Vluyn: Neukirchener Verlag, 2000.

Ecklund, *Science*. Ecklund, Elaine Howard. *Science vs. Religion: What Scientists Really Think*. Oxford: Oxford University Press, 2010.

Eckstein, *Deathday*. Eckstein, Jerome. *The Deathday of Socrates—Living, Dying, and Immortality: The Theater of Ideas in Plato's Phaedo*. Frenchtown, N.J.: Columbia, 1981.

Edanad, "Spirit and Community." Edanad, Antony. "The Spirit and the Christian Community according to Acts of the Apostles." *Jeev* 28 (164, 1998): 98–108.

Eddinger, "Nabatean/Roman Temple." Eddinger, T. W. "A Nabatean/Roman Temple at Dhat Ras, Jordan." *NEA* 67 (1, 2004): 14–25.

Eddy, "Diogenes." Eddy, Paul Rhodes. "Jesus as Diogenes? Reflections on the Cynic Jesus Thesis." *JBL* 115 (3, 1996): 449–69.

Eddy, "Reality of Spirits." Eddy, Paul Rhodes. "The Reality of Spirits." Unpublished paper in the author's possession.

Eddy and Boyd, *Legend*. Eddy, Paul Rhodes, and Gregory A. Boyd. *The Jesus Legend: A Case for the Historical Reliability of the Synoptic Jesus Tradition*. Grand Rapids: Baker Academic, 2007.

Edelstein, "Villa outside Jerusalem." Edelstein, Gershon. "What's a Roman Villa Doing outside Jerusalem?" *BAR* 16 (6, 1990): 32–42.

Edelstein and Edelstein, *Asclepius*. Edelstein, Emma J., and Ludwig Edelstein. *Asclepius: A Collection and Interpretation of the Testimonies*. 2 vols. Baltimore: Johns Hopkins University Press, 1945.

Eder, "Cities." Eder, Walter. "Twelve Cities, League (Etruscan) of." *BrillPauly* 15:48–49.

Eder, "Elections." Eder, Walter. "Elections." *BrillPauly* 4:894–97.

Eder, "Envoys." Eder, Walter. "Envoys." *BrillPauly* 4:1008.

Eder, "Triumph." Eder, Walter. "Triumph, Triumphal Procession." *BrillPauly* 14:945–48.

Edersheim, *Life*. Edersheim, Alfred. *The Life and Times of Jesus the Messiah*. Reprint: N.p.: MacDonald, n.d.

Edgar, "Messianic Interpretation." Edgar, S. L. "The New Testament and Rabbinic Messianic Interpretation." *NTS* 5 (1, 1958): 47–54.

Edgar, "Respect." Edgar, S. L. "Respect for Context in Quotations from the Old Testament." *NTS* 9 (1, 1962): 55–62.

Edghill, *Amos*. Edghill, E. A. *The Book of Amos with Notes by Ernest Arthur Edghill, B.D.* Edited by G. A. Cooke. London: Methuen, 1914.

Edmunds, "Sick." Edmunds, P. K. "Is Any Sick among You." Pages 69–74 in *Faith Healing: Finger of God? Or, Scientific Curiosity?* Compiled by Claude A. Frazier. New York: Thomas Nelson, 1973.

Edo, "Cronologías." Edo, P. M. "Cronologías paulinas. Un estado de la cuestión." *ScrTh* 41 (1, 2009): 177–98.

Edson, "Cults of Thessalonica." Edson, Charles. "Cults of Thessalonica." *HTR* 41 (1948): 181–88.

Edson and Price, "Ruler-cult." Edson, Charles Farwell, and Simon R. F. Price. "Ruler-cult: Greek." *OCD*³ 1337–38.

Edwards, "Cappadocia." Edwards, Douglas R. "Cappadocia." *OEANE* 1:419–22.

Edwards, "Capri." Edwards, Rebecca. "Tacitus, Tiberius and Capri." *Latomus* 70 (4, 2011): 1047–57.

Edwards, "Crowns." Edwards, Laurence L. "Rabbi Akiba's Crowns: Postmodern Discourse and the Cost of Rabbinic Reading." *Judaism* 49 (4, 2000): 417–35.

Edwards, "Deformity." Edwards, Martha L. "The Cultural Context of Deformity in the Ancient Greek World." *AHB* 10 (3–4, 1996): 79–92.

Edwards, "Earliest Christianity." Edwards, O. C. "Earliest Christianity: The Period of the Book of Acts in Recent Literature." *STRev* 53 (1, 2009): 91–105.

Edwards, "Exorcisms." Edwards, M. J. "Three Exorcisms and the New Testament World." *Eranos* 87 (2, 1989): 117–26.

Edwards, "Healing." Edwards, F. S. "Healing: Xhosa Perspective." Pages 329–45 in *Afro-Christian Religion and Healing in Southern Africa*. Edited by G. C. Oosthuizen, S. D. Edwards, W. H. Wessels, and I. Hexham. AfSt 8. Lewiston, N.Y.: Edwin Mellen, 1989.

Edwards, "Miletus." Edwards, Douglas R. "Miletus." *OEANE* 4:26–28.

Edwards, "Numenius." Edwards, M. J. "Atticizing Moses? Numenius, the Fathers, and the Jews." *VC* 44 (1, 1990): 64–75.

Edwards, "Possession." Edwards, Felicity S. "Amafufunyana Spirit Possession: Treatment and Interpretation." Pages 207–25 in *Afro-Christian Religion and Healing in Southern Africa*. Edited by G. C. Oosthuizen, S. D. Edwards, W. H. Wessels, and I. Hexham. AfSt 8. Lewiston, N.Y.: Edwin Mellen, 1989.

Edwards, "Quoting Aratus." Edwards, M. J. "Quoting Aratus: Acts 17, 28." *ZNW* 83 (3–4, 1992): 266–69.

Edwards, "Reading." Edwards, Douglas R. "Pleasurable Reading or Symbols of Power? Religious Themes and Social Context in Chariton." Pages 31–46 in *Ancient Fiction and Early Christian Narrative*. Edited by Ronald F. Hock, J. Bradley Chance, and Judith Perkins. SBLSymS 6. Atlanta: SBL, 1998.

Edwards, "Satire." Edwards, M. J. "Satire and Verisimilitude: Christianity in Lucian's *Peregrinus*." *Historia* 38 (1, 1989): 89–98.

Edwards, *Savior*. Edwards, James R. *Is Jesus the Only Savior?* Grand Rapids: Eerdmans, 2005.

Edwards, "Tyre." Edwards, Douglas R. "Tyre in the Greco-Roman Period." *ABD* 6:690–92.

Edwards and Reasoner, "Rome." Edwards, Ruth B., and Mark Reasoner. "Rome: Overview." *DNTB* 1010–18.

Efroymson, "Connection." Efroymson, David P. "The Patristic Connection." Pages 98–117 in *AntiSemitism and the Foundations of Christianity*. Edited by Alan T. Davies. New York: Paulist Press, 1979.

Egelhaaf-Gaiser, "Sites." Egelhaaf-Gaiser, Ulrike. "Roman Cult Sites: A Pragmatic Approach." Pages 205–21 in *A Companion to Roman Religion*. Edited by Jörg Rüpke. BCompAW. Oxford: Blackwell, 2011.

Egger-Wenzel, "Terminology." Egger-Wenzel, Renate. "The Change of the Sacrifice Terminology from Hebrew into Greek in the Book of Ben Sira. Did the Grandson Understand His Grandfather's Text Correctly?" *BN* 40 (2009): 69–93.

Eggleston, "Wilderness." Eggleston, Chad L. "Wilderness, Desert." Pages 843–47 in *Dictionary of the Old Testament Prophets*. Edited by Mark J. Boda and J. Gordon McConville. Downers Grove, Ill.: IVP Academic, 2012.

Ego, "Ethnarchos." Ego, Beate. "Ethnarchos." *BrillPauly* 5:85–86.

Ego, "Gerousia." Ego, Beate. "Gerousia: Jewish." *BrillPauly* 5:819.

Ehling, "Anmerkungen." Ehling, Kay. "Zwei Anmerkungen zum ἀργύριον in Apg 19,19." *ZNW* 94 (3–4, 2003): 269–75.

Ehrensperger, *Encouraged*. Ehrensperger, Kathy. *That We May Be Mutually Encouraged: Feminism and the New Perspective in Pauline Studies*. New York: T&T Clark, 2004.

Ehrensperger, "Imitators." Ehrensperger, Kathy. "'Be Imitators of Me as I am of Christ': A Hidden Discourse of Power and Domination in Paul?" *LTQ* 38 (4, 2003): 241–61.

Ehrensperger, *Power*. Ehrensperger, Kathy. *Paul and the Dynamics of Power: Communication and Interaction in the Early Christ-Movement*. LNTS 325. New York: T&T Clark, 2007.

Ehrhardt, *Acts*. Ehrhardt, Arnold. *The Acts of the Apostles*. Manchester, U.K.: Manchester University Press, 1969.

Ehrhardt, "Construction and Purpose." Ehrhardt, Arnold. "The Construction and Purpose of the Acts of the Apostles." *ST* 12 (1958): 45–79.

Ehrlich, "Lending Shoulder." Ehrlich, Uri. "The Ritual of Lending a Shoulder: Distribution and Signification in Talmudic Times." *HUCA* 75 (2004): 23–35.

Ehrlich, "Rituals." Ehrlich, Uri. "Verbal and Non-verbal Rituals of Leave-Taking in Rabbinic Culture—Phenomenology and Significance." *JSQ* 8 (1, 2001): 1–26.

Ehrlich, "Tora." Ehrlich, Ernst Ludwig. "Tora im Judentum." *EvT* 37 (6, 1977): 536–49.

Ehrman, *Forged*. Ehrman, Bart D. *Forged: Writing in the Name of God—Why the Bible's Authors Are Not Who We Think They Are*. New York: HarperOne, 2011.

Ehrman, *Interrupted*. Ehrman, Bart D. *Jesus Interrupted: Revealing the Hidden Contradictions in the Bible (and Why We Don't Know About Them)*. New York: HarperOne, 2009.

Ehrman, *Introduction*. Ehrman, Bart D. *The New Testament: A Historical Introduction to the Early Christian Writings*. 3rd ed. New York and Oxford: Oxford University Press, 2004.

Ehrman, *Misquoting*. Ehrman, Bart D. *Misquoting Jesus: The Story behind Who Changed the Bible and Why*. San Francisco: HarperSanFrancisco, 2005.

Ehrman, *Prophet*. Ehrman, Bart D. *Jesus: Apocalyptic Prophet of the New Millennium*. Oxford: Oxford University Press, 1999.

Ehrman, "Response to Stalemate." Ehrman, Bart D. "Response to Charles Hedrick's Stalemate." *JECS* 11 (2, Summer 2003): 155–63.

Ehro, "Nature." Ehro, T. M. "The Ahistorical Nature of *1 Enoch* 56:5–8 and Its Ramifications upon the *Opinio Communis* on the Dating of the *Similitudes of Enoch*." *JSJ* 40 (1, 2009): 23–54.

Eichrodt, "Faith in Providence." Eichrodt, Walther. "Faith in Providence and Theodicy in the Old Testament." In *Theodicy in the Old Testament*. Edited by James L. Crenshaw. Philadelphia: Fortress, 1983.

Eickelman, *Middle East*. Eickelman, Dale F. *The Middle East: An Anthropological Approach*. 2nd ed. Englewood Cliffs, N.J.: Prentice Hall, 1989.

Eickstedt, "Piraeus." Eickstedt, Klaus-Valtin von. "Piraeus." *BrillPauly* 11:286–90.

Eigler, "Excursus." Eigler, Ulrich. "Excursus." *BrillPauly* 5:258–59.

Eigo, *Experience*. Eigo, Francis A., ed. *The Human Experience of Conversion: Persons and Structures in Transformation*. Proceedings of the Theology Institute of Villanova University 19. Villanova, Pa.: Villanova University Press, 1987.

Eilberg-Schwartz, "What Happens?" Eilberg-Schwartz, Howard. "What Happens When God Invents Language?" *Moment* 14 (5, 1989): 36–41.

Eilers, "Date of Edict." Eilers, Claude. "The Date of Augustus' Edict on the Jews (Jos. *AJ* 16.162–165) and the Career of C. Marcius Censorinus." *Phoenix* 58 (1–2, 2004): 86–95.

Eisen, *Poetik*. Eisen, Ute E. *Die Poetik der Apostelgeschichte: Eine narratologische Studie*. NTOA 58. Fribourg: Academic Press; Göttingen: Vandenhoeck & Ruprecht, 2006.

Eisen, "Streitwagen." Eisen, U. E. "'Ich vernichte die Streitwagen . . .'—Aspekte paulinischer Herrschaftskritik und ihre alttestamentlichen Wurzeln." *ZNT* 7 (14, 2004): 31–39.

Eisenbaum, "Polemics." Eisenbaum, Pamela. "Paul, Polemics, and the Problem of Essentialism." *BibInt* 13 (3, 2005): 224–38.

Eisenberg, *"Sophrosune."* Eisenberg, P. "Sophrosune, Self, and State: A Partial Defense of Plato." *Apeiron* 9 (2, 1975): 31–36.

Eisenman, *Maccabees.* Eisenman, Robert. *Maccabees, Zadokites, Christians, and Qumran: A New Hypothesis of Qumran Origins.* StPB 34. Leiden: Brill, 1983.

Eisenman, "Ossuary." Eisenman, Robert. "The James Ossuary—Is It Authentic?" *FO* 38 (2002): 233–36.

Eisenman, "Sicarii Essenes." Eisenman, Robert. "Sicarii Essenes, 'Those of the Circumcision,' and Qumran." *JHC* 12 (1, 2006): 17–28.

Eisenstadt, "Teaching." Eisenstadt, Michael. "Protagoras' Teaching in Plato's *Protagoras.*" *SO* 56 (1981): 47–61.

Eisman, "Dio and Josephus." Eisman, M. M. "Dio and Josephus: Parallel Analyses." *Latomus* 36 (3, 1977): 657–73.

Eitrem, Croon, and Dietrich, "Trees." Eitrem, Sam, Johan Harm Croon, and B. C. Dietrich. "Trees, Sacred." *OCD*[3] 1548–49.

Ejizu, "Exorcism." Ejizu, Christopher I. "Cosmological Perspective on Exorcism and Prayer-Healing in Contemporary Nigeria." Pages 11–23 in *Healing and Exorcism—The Nigerian Experience: Proceedings, Lectures, Discussions, and Conclusions of the First Missiology Symposium on Healing and Exorcism, Organised by the Spiritan International School of Theology, Attakwu, Enugu, May 18–20, 1989.* Edited by Chris U. Manus, Luke N. Mbefo, and E. E. Uzukwu. Enugu, Nigeria: Snapp, 1992.

Ekechi, "Factor." Ekechi, Felix K. "The Medical Factor in Christian Conversion in Africa: Observations from Southeastern Nigeria." *Missiology* 21 (3, 1993): 289–309.

Elbaum, "Sermon." Elbaum, Yaakov. "From Sermon to Story: The Transformation of the Akedah." *Prooftexts* 6 (2, 1986): 97–116.

Elbert, "Acts 2:38." Elbert, Paul. "Acts 2:38 in Light of the Syntax of Imperative-Future Passive and Imperative-Present Participle Combinations." *CBQ* 75 (1, Jan. 2013): 94–107.

Elbert, "Face to Face." Elbert, Paul. "Face to Face: Then or Now?" Paper presented at the seventh annual meeting of the Society for Pentecostal Studies, Springfield, Mo., Dec. 1–3, 1977.

Elbert, "Miletus Speech." Elbert, Paul. "Paul of the Miletus Speech and 1 Thessalonians: Critique and Considerations." *ZNW* 95 (2004): 258–68.

Elbert, "Observation." Elbert, Paul. "An Observation on Luke's Composition and Narrative Style of Questions." *CBQ* 66 (1, 2004): 98–109.

Elbert, "Spirit through Lukan Lens." Elbert, Paul. "Spirit, Scripture, and Theology through a Lukan Lens: A Review Article." *JPT* 13 (1998): 55–75.

Elbert, "Themes." Elbert, Paul. "Pentecostal/Charismatic Themes in Luke-Acts at the Evangelical Theological Society: The Battle of Interpretive Method." *JPT* 12 (2, 2004): 181–215.

Elder, "Question." Elder, Linda Bennett. "The Woman Question and Female Ascetics among Essenes." *BA* 57 (4, 1995): 220–34.

Elgvin, "Belial." Elgvin, Torleif. "Belial, Beliar, Devil, Satan." *DNTB* 153–57.

Elgvin, "Interpretation." Elgvin, Torleif. "The Individual Interpretation of the Servant." *Mishkan* 43 (2005): 25–33.

Elgvin, "Section." Elgvin, Torleif. "The Genesis Section of 4Q422 (4Q ParaGenExod)." *DSD* 1 (2, 1994): 180–96.

Eliade, *Rites.* Eliade, Mircea. *Rites and Symbols of Initiation: The Mysteries of Birth and Rebirth.* Translated by Willard R. Trask. New York: Harper & Row, 1958.

Eliade, *Shamanism.* Eliade, Mircea. *Shamanism: Archaic Techniques of Ecstasy.* Translated by Willard R. Trask. BollS 76. New York: Bollingen Foundation, 1964. Distributed by Pantheon Books.

Eliav, "Bath." Eliav, Yaron Z. "The Roman Bath as a Jewish Institution: Another Look at the Encounter between Judaism and the Greco-Roman Culture." *JSJ* 31 (4, 2000): 416–54.

El-Khouri, "Fertility." El-Khouri, Lamia. "Fertility as an Element in Late Nabataean Beliefs: The Archaeological Evidence Considered." *Levant* 39 (2007): 81–90.

Elkins, "Models." Elkins, Richard E. "Three Models of Western Bukidnon Manobo Kinship." *Ethnology* 7 (1968): 171–89.

Elkins, "Sacrifice." Elkins, Richard E. "Blood Sacrifice and the Dynamics of Supernatural Power among the Manobo of Mindanao: Some Missiological Implications." *Missiology* 21 (3, 1993): 321–31.

Elledge, "Eyes." Elledge, Casey D. "Josephus, Tacitus, and Suetonius: Seeing Jesus through the Eyes of Classical Historians." Pages 691–720 in *Jesus Research: New Methodologies and Perceptions; The Second Princeton-Prague Symposium on Jesus Research.* Edited by James H. Charlesworth. Grand Rapids: Eerdmans, 2014.

Elledge, "Sources." Elledge, Casey. "Critiquing Sources for Jesus: Josephus, Tacitus, and Suetonius." Paper presented at the second Princeton-Prague Symposium on

Jesus: Methodological Approaches to the Historical Jesus, Princeton, Apr. 20, 2007.

Ellens, *Light.* Ellens, J. Harold. *Light from the Other Side: The Paranormal as Friend and Familiar (Real Life Experiences of a Spiritual Pilgrim).* Eugene, Ore.: Resource Publications, 2011.

Eller, *Disciple.* Eller, Vernard. *The Beloved Disciple—His Name, His Story, His Thought: Two Studies from the Gospel of John.* Grand Rapids: Eerdmans, 1987.

Elliger, *Paulus in Griechenland.* Elliger, Winfried. *Paulus in Griechenland: Philippi, Thessaloniki, Athen, Korinth.* SBS 92–93. Stuttgart: Katholisches Bibelwerk, 1978.

Ellington, "Kissing." Ellington, John. "Kissing in the Bible: Form and Meaning." *BTr* 41 (4, 1990): 409–16.

Ellington, "Who's Who." Ellington, John. "Who's Who in Acts 16–17? Problems of Pronoun Reference." *BTr* 54 (4, 2003): 407–15.

Ellingworth, "Men and Brethren." Ellingworth, Paul. "Men and Brethren . . .' (Acts 1.16)." *BTr* 55 (1, 2004): 153–55.

Ellingworth, "'We' and 'I.'" Ellingworth, Paul. "'We' and 'I' in 2 Corinthians: A Question." *BTr* 34 (2, 1983): 246.

Ellingworth, "'We' in Paul." Ellingworth, Paul. "'We' in Paul." *BTr* 56 (4, 2005): 226–32.

Elliott, "Apocrypha." Elliott, J. L. "The Christian Apocrypha and Archaeology." Pages 683–91 in *Jesus and Archaeology.* Edited by James H. Charlesworth. Grand Rapids: Eerdmans, 2006.

Elliott, *Arrogance.* Elliott, Neil. *The Arrogance of Nations: Reading Romans in the Shadow of Empire.* Paul in Critical Contexts. Minneapolis: Fortress, 2008.

Elliott, "Criticism." Elliott, John H. "Social-Scientific Criticism of the New Testament and Its Social World: More on Method and Models." *Semeia* 35 (1986): 1–33.

Elliott, "Cunctator." Elliott, Jackie. "Ennius' 'Cunctator' and the History of a Gerund in the Roman Historiographical Tradition." *CQ* 59 (2, 2009): 532–42.

Elliott, "Fear." Elliott, John H. "The Fear of the Leer: The Evil Eye from the Bible to Li'l Abner." *Forum* 4 (4, 1988): 42–71.

Elliott, *Feelings.* Elliott, Matthew. *Faithful Feelings: Emotion in the New Testament.* Leicester, U.K.: Inter-Varsity, 2005.

Elliott, "Household and Meals." Elliott, John H. "Household and Meals vs. Temple Purity: Replication Patterns in Luke-Acts." *BTB* 21 (3, 1991): 102–8.

Elliott, "Israelite." Elliott, John H. "Jesus the Israelite Was neither a 'Jew' nor a 'Christian': On Correcting Misleading Nomenclature." *JSHJ* 5 (2, 2007): 119–54.

Elliott, *Liberating*. Elliott, Neil. *Liberating Paul: The Justice of God and the Politics of the Apostle.* Maryknoll: Orbis, 1994.

Elliott, "Patronage." Elliott, John H. "Patronage and Clientism in Early Christian Society. A Short Reading Guide." *Forum* 3 (4, 1987): 39–48.

Elliott, "Purity System." Elliott, John H. "Household and Meals versus the Temple Purity System: Patterns of Replication in Luke-Acts." *HTS/TS* 47 (2, 1991): 386–99.

Elliott, *Survivors*. Elliott, Mark Adam. *The Survivors of Israel: A Reconsideration of the Theology of Pre-Christian Judaism.* Grand Rapids: Eerdmans, 2000.

Elliott, "Temple." Elliott, John H. "Temple versus Household in Luke-Acts: A Contrast in Social Institutions." *HTS/TS* 47 (1, 1991): 88–120.

Ellis, "Authorship." Ellis, E. Earle. "The Problem of Authorship: First and Second Timothy." *RevExp* 56 (4, 1959): 343–54.

Ellis, "Christ and Spirit." Ellis, E. Earle. "Christ and Spirit in 1 Corinthians." Pages 269–77 in *Christ and Spirit in the New Testament: Studies in Honor of C. F. D. Moule.* Edited by Barnabas Lindars and Stephen S. Smalley. Cambridge: Cambridge University Press, 1973.

Ellis, "Coworkers." Ellis, E. Earle. "Coworkers, Paul and His." *DPL* 183–89.

Ellis, "End of Earth." Ellis, E. Earle. "'The End of the Earth' (Acts 1:8)." *BBR* 1 (1991): 123–32.

Ellis, *Eschatology*. Ellis, E. Earle. *Eschatology in Luke.* Philadelphia: Fortress, 1972.

Ellis, "Fonction de l'eschatologie." Ellis, E. Earle. "La fonction de l'eschatologie dans l'Évangile de Luc." Pages 51–65 in *L'Évangile de Luc: The Gospel of Luke.* Edited by F. Neirynck. Rev. ed. BETL 32. Leuven: Leuven University Press, 1989.

Ellis, *Genius*. Ellis, Peter F. *The Genius of John: A Composition-Critical Commentary on the Fourth Gospel.* Collegeville, Minn.: Liturgical Press, 1984.

Ellis, *Matthew*. Ellis, Peter F. *Matthew: His Mind and His Message.* Collegeville, Minn.: Liturgical Press, 1974.

Ellis, *Message*. Ellis, Peter F. *The Men and the Message of the Old Testament.* 3rd ed. Collegeville, Minn.: Liturgical Press, 1976.

Ellis, "Midrashic Features." Ellis, E. Earle. "Midrashic Features in the Speeches of Acts." Pages 303–12 in *Mélanges bibliques en hommage au R. P. Béda Rigaux.* Edited by A. Descamps and A. de Halleux. Gembloux, Belg.: J. Duculot, 1970.

Ellis, "New Testament Uses Old." Ellis, E. Earle. "How the New Testament Uses the Old." Pages 199–219 in *New Testament Interpretation: Essays on Principles and Methods.* Edited by I. Howard Marshall. Grand Rapids: Eerdmans, 1977.

Ellis, "Pastoral Letters." Ellis, E. Earle. "Pastoral Letters." *DPL* 658–66.

Ellis, *Paul and Interpreters*. Ellis, E. Earle. *Paul and His Recent Interpreters.* Grand Rapids: Eerdmans, 1961.

Ellison, *Mystery*. Ellison, H. L. *The Mystery of Israel: An Exposition of Romans 9–11.* Grand Rapids: Baker; Exeter, U.K.: Paternoster, 1966.

Ellison, *Prophets*. Ellison, H. L. *The Prophets of Israel from Ahijah to Hosea.* Grand Rapids: Eerdmans; Exeter, U.K.: Paternoster, 1969.

Elman, "Suffering." Elman, Yaakov. "The Suffering of the Righteous in Palestinian and Babylonian Sources." *JQR* 80 (3–4, 1990): 315–39.

Elnes and Miller, "Elyon." Elnes, Eric E., and Patrick D. Miller. "Elyon." Pages 293–99 in *Dictionary of Deities and Demons in the Bible.* 2nd rev. ed. Edited by Karel van der Toorn, Bob Becking, and Pieter W. van der Horst. Leiden: Brill; Grand Rapids: Eerdmans, 1999.

Elsdon, "Converted." Elsdon, Ron. "Was Paul 'Converted' or 'Called'? Questions of Methodology." *PIBA* 24 (2001): 17–47.

Elsner, "Geography." Elsner, John. "Hagiographic Geography: Travel and Allegory in the *Life of Apollonius of Tyana*." *JHS* 117 (1997): 22–37.

Eltester, "Gott und Natur." Eltester, Walther. "Gott und die Natur in der Areopagrede." Pages 202–27 in *Neutestamentliche Studien für Rudolf Bultmann.* 2nd ed. BZNW 21. Berlin: Alfred Töppelmann, 1957.

Elvers et al., "Acilius." Elvers, Karl-Ludwig, et al. "Acilius." *BrillPauly* 1:99–101.

Emanuele, "*Aes corinthium*." Emanuele, D. "*Aes corinthium*: Fact, Fiction, and Fake." *Phoenix* 43 (4, 1989): 347–58.

Ember, "Descent Groups." Ember, Melvin. "The Nonunilinear Descent Groups of Samoa." *AmAnth* 61 (4, Aug. 1959): 573–77.

Embry, "Solomon." Embry, Brad J. "The Name 'Solomon' as a Prophetic Hallmark in Jewish and Christian Texts." *Hen* 28 (1, 2006): 47–62.

Emilsson, "Plotinus." Emilsson, Eyjólfur Kjalar. "Plotinus on the Emotions." Pages 339–63 in *The Emotions in Hellenistic Philosophy.* Edited by Juha Sihvola and Troels Engberg-Pedersen. TSHP 46. Dordrecht, Neth.: Kluwer Academic, 1998.

Emmel, "Coptic Language." Emmel, Stephen. "Coptic Language." *ABD* 4:180–88.

Emmet, "Tradition." Emmet, C. W. "The Case for the Tradition." *BegChr* 2:265–97.

Emmons, *Ghosts*. Emmons, Charles F. *Chinese Ghosts and ESP: A Study of Paranormal Beliefs and Experiences.* Metuchen, N.J.: Scarecrow, 1982.

Empereur, "Diving." Empereur, Jean-Yves. "Diving on a Sunken City." *Archaeology* 52 (2, 1999): 36–43.

Encyclopaedia Judaica. 16 vols. Jerusalem: Keter, 1972.

Endres, *Interpretation*. Endres, John C. *Biblical Interpretation in the Book of Jubilees.* CBQMS 18. Washington, D.C.: Catholic Biblical Association of America, 1987.

Eneja, "Message." Eneja, M. U. "Goodwill Message from His Lordship Rt. Rev. Dr. M. U. Eneja, Bishop of Enugu." Pages 163–68 in *Healing and Exorcism—The Nigerian Experience: Proceedings, Lectures, Discussions, and Conclusions of the First Missiology Symposium on Healing and Exorcism, Organised by the Spiritan International School of Theology, Attakwu, Enugu, May 18–20, 1989.* Edited by Chris U. Manus, Luke N. Mbefo, and E. E. Uzukwu. Enugu, Nigeria: Snapp, 1992.

Engberg-Pedersen, *Beyond Divide*. Engberg-Pedersen, Troels, ed. *Paul beyond the Judaism/Hellenism Divide.* Louisville: Westminster John Knox, 2001.

Engberg-Pedersen, "Dream." Engberg-Pedersen, Troels. "Philo's *De vita contemplativa* as a Philosopher's Dream." *JSJ* 30 (1, 1999): 40–64.

Engberg-Pedersen, "Introduction." Engberg-Pedersen, Troels. "Introduction: Paul beyond the Judaism/Hellenism Divide." Pages 1–16 in *Paul beyond the Judaism/Hellenism Divide.* Edited by Troels Engberg-Pedersen. Louisville: Westminster John Knox, 2001.

Engberg-Pedersen, "Marcus." Engberg-Pedersen, Troels. "Marcus Aurelius on Emotions." Pages 305–37 in *The Emotions in Hellenistic Philosophy.* Edited by Juha Sihvola and Troels Engberg-Pedersen. TSHP 46. Dordrecht, Neth.: Kluwer Academic, 1998.

Engberg-Pedersen, *Paul and Stoics*. Engberg-Pedersen, Troels. *Paul and the Stoics.* Louisville: Westminster John Knox; Edinburgh: T&T Clark, 2000.

Engberg-Pedersen, "Relationship." Engberg-Pedersen, Troels. "The Relationship with Others: Similarities and Differences between Paul and Stoicism." *ZNW* 96 (1–2, 2005): 35–60.

Engberg-Pedersen, "Scene." Engberg-Pedersen, Troels. "Setting the Scene: Stoicism and Platonism in the Transitional Period in Ancient Philosophy." Pages 1–14 in *Stoicism in Early Christianity.* Edited by Tuomas Rasimus, Troels Engberg-Pedersen, and Ismo Dunderberg. Grand Rapids: Baker Academic, 2010.

Engberg-Pedersen, "Spirit." Engberg-Pedersen, Troels. "The Material Spirit:

Cosmology and Ethics in Paul." *NTS* 55 (2, 2009): 179–97.

Engberg-Pedersen, "Stoisk." Engberg-Pedersen, Troels. "Stoisk og paulinsk menneskesyn—ligheder og forskelle." *NTT* 104 (1, 2003): 29–34.

Engberg-Pedersen, "Vices." Engberg-Pedersen, Troels. "Paul, Virtues, and Vices." Pages 608–33 in *Paul in the Greco-Roman World: A Handbook.* Edited by J. Paul Sampley. Harrisburg, Pa.: Trinity Press International, 2003.

Engel, "Death." Engel, George. "Sudden and Rapid Death during Psychological Stress: Folklore or Folk Wisdom?" *Annals of Internal Medicine* 74 (1971): 771–82.

Engels, "Demography." Engels, Donald. "The Use of Historical Demography in Ancient History." *CQ* 34 (2, 1984): 386–93.

Engels, "Geography." Engels, Johannes. "Geography and History." Pages 541–52 in *A Companion to Greek and Roman Historiography.* Edited by John Marincola. 2 vols. Oxford: Blackwell, 2007.

Engels, "Infanticide." Engels, Donald. "The Problem of Female Infanticide in the Greco-Roman World." *CP* 75 (2, 1980): 112–20.

Engels, *Roman Corinth.* Engels, Donald W. *Roman Corinth: An Alternative Model for the Classical City.* Chicago: University of Chicago Press, 1990.

Englhofer, "Birthday." Englhofer, Claudia. "Birthday." *BrillPauly* 2:670–73.

Englhofer, "Ultima verba." Englhofer, Claudia. "Ultima verba." *BrillPauly* 15:89–91.

Engster, "Alexandria." Engster, Dorit. "Alexandria als Stadt der Forschung und Technik." *BN* 147 (2010): 49–66.

Enns, *Exodus.* Enns, Peter. *Exodus.* NIVAC. Grand Rapids: Zondervan, 2000.

Enns, "Interpretation." Enns, Peter. "Biblical Interpretation, Jewish." *DNTB* 159–65.

Enns, *Problem.* Enns, Peter. *Inspiration and Incarnation: Evangelicals and the Problem of the Old Testament.* Grand Rapids: Baker Academic, 2005.

Enslin, *Ethics.* Enslin, Morton Scott. *The Ethics of Paul.* New York: Abingdon, 1957.

Enz, "Exodus." Enz, Jacob J. "The Book of Exodus as a Literary Type for the Gospel of John." *JBL* 76 (3, 1957): 208–15.

Epp, *Junia.* Epp, Eldon Jay. *Junia: The First Woman Apostle.* Minneapolis: Fortress, 2005.

Epp, *Tendency.* Epp, Eldon Jay. *The Theological Tendency of Codex Bezae Cantabrigiensis in Acts.* SNTSMS 3. Cambridge: Cambridge University Press, 1966.

Epplett, "Capture." Epplett, Christopher. "The Capture of Animals by the Roman Military." *GR* 48 (2, 2001): 210–22.

Eppstein, "Excommunicated." Eppstein, Victor. "When and How the Sadducees Were Excommunicated." *JBL* 85 (2, 1966): 213–224.

Epstein, *Enmity.* Epstein, David F. *Personal Enmity in Roman Politics, 218–43 BC.* London: Routledge, 1989.

Erdkamp, "Agriculture." Erdkamp, P. "Agriculture, Underemployment, and the Cost of Rural Labour in the Roman World." *CQ* 49 (2, 1999): 556–72.

Erdman, *Galatians.* Erdman, Charles R. *The Epistle of Paul to the Galatians.* Philadelphia: Westminster, 1966.

Erdman, *Hebrews.* Erdman, Charles R. *The Epistle to the Hebrews.* Philadelphia: Westminster, 1966.

Erdman, *Philippians.* Erdman, Charles R. *The Epistle of Paul to the Philippians.* Philadelphia: Westminster, 1966.

Erichsen-Wendt, "Tabitha." Erichsen-Wendt, Friederike. "Tabitha—Leben an der Grenze: Ein Beitrag zum Verständnis von Apg 9,36–43." *BN* 127 (2005): 67–87.

Erker, "Voix dangereuses." Erker, Darja Sterbenc. "Voix dangereuses et force des larmes: Le deuil féminin dans la Rome antique." *RHR* 221 (3, 2004): 259–91.

Erlemann, Heiligenthal, and Vouga, "Urgemeinde." Erlemann, K., R. Heiligenthal, and F. Vouga. "Die Einheit der Urgemeinde—Fiktion oder Wirklichkeit." *ZNT* 3 (6, 2000): 40–53.

Erler, "Epicurus." Erler, Michael. "Epicurus." *BrillPauly* 4:1075–84.

Erler, "Irony." Erler, Michael. "Irony: Philosophy." *BrillPauly* 6:944–45.

Ernst, "Reich." Ernst, H. "Reich Gottes im rabbinischen Judentum Gegenwärtig in Israel und zukünftig in der Welt." *BK* 62 (2, 2007): 109–12.

Eron, "Mastery." Eron, Lewis John. "'That Women Have Mastery over both King and Beggar' (*TJud.* 15.5)—The Relationship of the Fear of Sexuality to the Status of Women in Apocrypha and Pseudepigrapha: 1 Esdras (*3 Ezra*) 3–4, Ben Sira, and the *Testament of Judah*." *JSP* 9 (1991): 43–66.

Errington, "Beroea." Errington, Robert Malcolm. "Beroea: Hellenistic and Roman Periods." *BrillPauly* 2:606.

Errington, "Macedonia." Errington, Robert Malcolm. "Macedonia, Macedones." *BrillPauly* 8:57–70.

Errington, "Philippi." Errington, Robert Malcolm. "Philippi." *BrillPauly* 11:23–24.

Erskine, "Cicero." Erskine, Andrew. "Cicero and the Shaping of Hellenistic Philosophy." *Herm* 175 (2003): 5–15.

Erskine, *Stoa.* Erskine, Andrew. *The Hellenistic Stoa: Political Thought and Action.*

Ithaca, N.Y.: Cornell University Press, 1990.

Erskine, *Troy.* Erskine, Andrew. *Troy between Greece and Rome: Local Tradition and Imperial Power.* New York: Oxford University Press, 2003.

Ervin, *Conversion-Initiation.* Ervin, Howard M. *Conversion-Initiation and the Baptism in the Holy Spirit.* Peabody, Mass.: Hendrickson, 1984.

Escobar, *Tides.* Escobar, Samuel. *Changing Tides: Latin America and World Mission Today.* AmSocMissMonS 31. Maryknoll, N.Y.: Orbis, 2002.

Escobedo, "Lens." Escobedo, Mario II. "Enlarging the Pentecostal Hermeneutical Lens: Luke's Use of Ecphrasis in Acts 2.1–4." Pages 125–45 in *Trajectories in the Book of Acts: Essays in Honor of John Wesley Wyckoff.* Edited by Paul Alexander, Jordan Daniel May, and Robert G. Reid. Eugene, Ore.: Wipf & Stock, 2010.

Eshel, "Exorcist." Eshel, Esther. "Jesus the Exorcist in Light of Epigraphic Sources." Pages 178–85 in *Jesus and Archaeology.* Edited by James H. Charlesworth. Grand Rapids: Eerdmans, 2006.

Eshel, "Mastema's Attempt." Eshel, Esther. "Mastema's Attempt on Moses' Life in the 'Pseudo-Jubilees' Text from Masada." *DSD* 10 (3, 2003): 359–64.

Eshel, "Rebukes." Eshel, Esther. "4Q477: The Rebukes by the Overseer." *JJS* 45 (1, 1994): 111–22.

Eshel, "Sny." Eshel, Hanan. "Sny hrbdym hhystwryym hmtw'dym bmgylt psr hbqwq." *Zion* 71 (2, 2006): 143–52.

Eshete, *Movement.* Eshete, Tibebe. *The Evangelical Movement in Ethiopia: Resistance and Resilience.* Waco: Baylor University Press, 2009.

Eshleman, "Affection." Eshleman, Kendra. "Affection and Affiliation: Social Networks and Conversion to Philosophy." *CJ* 103 (2, 2007–8): 129–40.

Eshleman, "Sophists." Eshleman, Kendra. "Defining the Circle of Sophists: Philostratus and the Construction of the Second Sophistic." *CP* 103 (4, 2008): 395–413.

Eskola, "Covenantal Nomism." Eskola, Timo. "Paul, Predestination, and 'Covenantal Nomism'—Re-assessing Paul and Palestinian Judaism." *JSJ* 28 (4, 1997): 390–412.

Eskola, *Messiah.* Eskola, Timo. *Messiah and the Throne: Jewish Merkabah Mysticism and Early Christian Exaltation Discourse.* WUNT 2.142. Tübingen: Mohr Siebeck, 2001.

Eskola, "Paul et judaïsme." Eskola, Timo. "Paul et le judaïsme du second temple:

La sotériologie de Paul avant et après E. P. Sanders." *RSR* 90 (3, 2002): 377–98.

Eskola, *Theodicy*. Eskola, Timo. *Theodicy and Predestination in Pauline Soteriology*. WUNT 2.100. Tübingen: Mohr Siebeck, 1998.

Eskridge, *Family*. Eskridge, Larry. *God's Forever Family: The Jesus People Movement in America*. Oxford: Oxford University Press, 2013.

Esler, *Community*. Esler, Philip Francis. *Community and Gospel in Luke-Acts: The Social and Political Motivations of Lucan Theology*. SNTSMS 57. Cambridge: Cambridge University Press, 1987.

Esler, *Conflict*. Esler, Philip Francis. *Conflict and Identity in Romans: The Social Setting of Paul's Letter*. Minneapolis: Fortress, 2003.

Esler, "Glossolalia and Admission." Esler, Philip Francis. "Glossolalia and the Admission of Gentiles into the Early Christian Community." *BTB* 22 (3, 1992): 136–42. Repr., pages 37–51 in *The First Christians in Their Social Worlds: Social-Scientific Approaches to New Testament Interpretation*. London: Routledge, 1994.

Esler, "Reply." Esler, Philip Francis. "A Reply to A. G. Van Aarde, 'The Most High God Does Live in Houses, but Not Houses Built by Men.'" *Neot* 25 (1991): 173–74.

Esler, *Worlds*. Esler, Philip Francis. *The First Christians in Their Social Worlds: Social-Scientific Approaches to New Testament Interpretation*. London: Routledge, 1994.

Espinosa, "Contributions." Espinosa, Gastón. "'The Holy Ghost Is Here on Earth?': The Latino Contributions to the Azusa Street Revival." *Enr* 11 (2, 2006): 118–25.

Espinosa, "Healing in Borderlands." Espinosa, Gastón. "Latino Pentecostal Healing in the North American Borderlands." Pages 129–49 in *Global Pentecostal and Charismatic Healing*. Edited by Candy Gunther Brown. Foreword by Harvey Cox. Oxford: Oxford University Press, 2011.

"Essene Origins." "Essene Origins—Palestine or Babylonia?" *BAR* 8 (5, 1982): 54–56.

Estrada, *Followers*. Estrada, Nelson P. *From Followers to Leaders: The Apostles in the Ritual of Status Transformation in Acts 1–2*. JSNTSup 255. London: T&T Clark, 2004.

"Ethno Religion Violence." "The Ethno Religion Violence in Plateau State as It Affects Wase Local Governments Area." A paper presented to Sultan Ibrahim Dasuki Miyatti Allah House Kaduna by the representative of the Wase Taroh community. Nigeria, Apr. 2003.

Etienne, "Diangienda." Etienne, Byaruhanga Kabarole. "Diangienda, Ku-ntima Joseph." No pages. *DACB*. Online: http://www.dacb.org/stories/demrepcongo/f-diangienda_joseph.html

Étienne et al., "Romanisation." Étienne, R., et al. "Les dimensions sociales de la romanisation dans la péninsule Ibérique des origines à la fin de l'empire." Pages 95–107 in *Assimilation et résistance à la culture gréco-romaine dans le monde ancien: Travaux du VIe Congrès international d'études classiques*. Edited by D. M. Pippidi. FIAEC. Paris: Belles Lettres, 1976.

Euskirchen, "Celts: Religion." Euskirchen, Marion. "Celts: Religion." *BrillPauly* 3:96–99.

Evans, "Apollonius." Evans, Craig A. "Apollonius of Tyana." *DNTB* 80–81.

Evans, "Caiaphas Ossuary." Evans, Craig A. "Caiaphas Ossuary." *DNTB* 179–80.

Evans, "Crafts." Evans, Jane DeRose. "Recent Research in Roman Crafts (1985–1995)." *CW* 91 (4, 1998): 235–72.

Evans, "Daniel's Visions." Evans, Craig A. "Defeating Satan and Liberating Israel: Jesus and Daniel's Visions." *JSHJ* 1 (2, 2003): 161–70.

Evans, "Excavating." Evans, Craig A. "Excavating Caiaphas, Pilate, and Simon of Cyrene: Assessing the Literary and Archaeological Evidence." Pages 323–40 in *Jesus and Archaeology*. Edited by James H. Charlesworth. Grand Rapids: Eerdmans, 2006.

Evans, "Exile." Evans, Craig A. "Jesus and the Continuing Exile of Israel." Pages 77–100 in *Jesus and the Restoration of Israel: A Critical Assessment of N. T. Wright's Jesus and the Victory of God*. Edited by Carey C. Newman. Downers Grove, Ill.: InterVarsity, 1999.

Evans, *Fabricating Jesus*. Evans, Craig A. *Fabricating Jesus: How Modern Scholars Distort the Gospels*. Downers Grove, Ill.: InterVarsity, 2006.

Evans, "Face." Evans, Craig A. "'He Set His Face': A Note on Luke 9, 51." *Bib* 63 (4, 1982): 545–48.

Evans, "Friendship." Evans, Katherine G. "Friendship in Greek Documentary Papyri and Inscriptions: A Survey." Pages 181–202 in *Greco-Roman Perspectives on Friendship*. Edited by John T. Fitzgerald. SBLRBS 34. Atlanta: Scholars Press, 1997.

Evans, "Function." Evans, Craig A. "The Function of the Elijah/Elisha Narratives in Luke's Ethic of Election." Pages 70–83 in *Luke and Scripture: The Function of Sacred Tradition in Luke-Acts*. Craig A. Evans and James A. Sanders. Minneapolis: Fortress, 1993.

Evans, "Holy Men." Evans, Craig A. "Holy Men, Jewish." *DNTB* 505–7.

Evans, "Isaiah in Writings." Evans, Craig A. "Isaiah 6:9–10 in Rabbinic and Patristic Writings." *VC* 36 (3, 1982): 275–81.

Evans, "Kingdom." Evans, Craig A. "Inaugurating the Kingdom of God and Defeating the Kingdom of Satan." *BBR* 15 (1, 2005): 49–75.

Evans, "Mad Ritual." Evans, Nancy. "From Mad Ritual to Philosophical Inquiry: Ancient and Modern Fictions of Continuity and Discontinuity." *R&T* 15 (3–4, 2008): 304–20.

Evans, "Messianic Apocalypse." Evans, Craig A. "Messianic Apocalypse (4Q521)." *DNTB* 695–98.

Evans, "Messianism." Evans, Craig A. "Messianism." *DNTB* 698–707.

Evans, *Narrative*. Evans, C. Stephen. *The Historical Christ and the Jesus of Faith: The Incarnational Narrative as History*. Oxford: Clarendon, 1996.

Evans, "Naturalism." Evans, C. Stephen. "Methodological Naturalism in Historical Biblical Scholarship." Pages 180–205 in *Jesus and the Restoration of Israel: A Critical Assessment of N. T. Wright's Jesus and the Victory of God*. Edited by Carey C. Newman. Downers Grove, Ill.: InterVarsity, 1999.

Evans, "Non-Christian Sources." Evans, Craig A. "Jesus in Non-Christian Sources." Pages 443–78 in *Studying the Historical Jesus: Evaluations of the State of Current Research*. Edited by Bruce Chilton and Craig A. Evans. NTTS 19. Leiden: Brill, 1994.

Evans, "Ossuary." Evans, Craig A. "On the Recently Discovered James Ossuary." *DavLog* 2 (1, 2003): 65–72.

Evans, "Pilate Inscription." Evans, Craig A. "Pilate Inscription." *DNTB* 803–4.

Evans, "Prayer of Enosh." Evans, Craig A. "Prayer of Enosh (4Q369 + 4Q458)." *DNTB* 820–21.

Evans, "Prophecy and Polemic." Evans, Craig A. "Prophecy and Polemic: Jews in Luke's Scriptural Apologetic." Pages 171–211 in *Luke and Scripture: The Function of Sacred Tradition in Luke-Acts*. Edited by Craig A. Evans and James A. Sanders. Minneapolis: Fortress, 1993.

Evans, "Prophetic Setting." Evans, Craig A. "The Prophetic Setting of the Pentecost Sermon." Pages 212–24 in *Luke and Scripture: The Function of Sacred Tradition in Luke-Acts*. Edited by Craig A. Evans and James A. Sanders. Minneapolis: Fortress, 1993.

Evans, "Prophets." Evans, Craig A. "Josephus on John the Baptist and Other Jewish Prophets of Deliverance." Pages 55–63 in *The Historical Jesus in Context*. Edited by Amy-Jill Levine, Dale C. Allison, Jr., and

John Dominic Crossan. PrRR. Princeton: Princeton University Press, 2006.

Evans, "Sanctuaries." Evans, Nancy A. "Sanctuaries, Sacrifices, and the Eleusinian Mysteries." *Numen* 49 (3, 2002): 227–54.

Evans, "Son." Evans, Craig A. "A Note on the 'First-Born Son' of 4Q369." *DSD* 2 (2, 1995): 185–201.

Evans, "Son of God Text." Evans, Craig A. "Son of God Text (4Q246)." *DNTB* 1134–37.

Evans, "Targum 2 Samuel 5.8." Evans, Craig A. "A Note on Targum 2 Samuel 5.8 and Jesus' Ministry to the 'Maimed, Halt, and Blind.'" *JSP* 15 (1997): 79–82.

Evans, *Texts*. Evans, Craig A. *Ancient Texts for New Testament Studies: A Guide to the Background Literature*. Peabody, Mass.: Hendrickson, 2005.

Evans, "Therapeutae." Evans, Craig A. "Therapeutae." *DNTB* 1230–31.

Evans, *World*. Evans, Craig A. *Jesus and His World: The Archaeological Evidence*. Louisville: Westminster John Knox, 2012.

Evans, *Wycliffe*. Evans, G. R. *John Wycliffe: Myth and Reality*. Downers Grove, Ill.: IVP Academic, 2005.

Evans-Pritchard, *Kinship*. Evans-Pritchard, E. E. *Kinship and Marriage among the Nuer*. Oxford: Clarendon, 1951.

Evans-Pritchard, *Religion*. Evans-Pritchard, E. E. *Nuer Religion*. Oxford: Clarendon, 1956.

Evans-Pritchard, *Witchcraft*. Evans-Pritchard, E. E. *Witchcraft, Oracles, and Magic among the Azande*. Foreword by C. G. Seligman. Oxford: Clarendon, 1937.

Eve, *Miracles*. Eve, Eric. *The Jewish Context of Jesus' Miracles*. JSNTSup 231. London: Sheffield Academic, 2002.

Evens, "Mind." Evens, T. M. S. "Mind, Logic, and the Efficacy of the Nuer Incest Prohibition." *Man*, n.s., 18 (1983): 111–33.

Everson, "Days of Yahweh." Everson, A. Joseph. "The Days of Yahweh." *JBL* 93 (3, 1974): 329–37.

Everts, "Support." Everts, Jane M. "Financial Support." *DPL* 295–300.

Everts, "Tongues or Languages?" Everts, Jenny. "Tongues or Languages? Contextual Consistency in the Translation of Acts 2." *JPT* 4 (1994): 71–80.

Everts and Baird, "Palmer." Everts, Janet Meyer, and Rachel Schutte Baird. "Phoebe Palmer and her Pentecostal Protégées: Acts 2.17–18 and Pentecostal Woman Ministers." Pages 146–59 in *Trajectories in the Book of Acts: Essays in Honor of John Wesley Wyckoff*. Edited by Paul Alexander, Jordan Daniel May, and Robert G. Reid. Eugene, Ore.: Wipf & Stock, 2010.

Every, "Jews and God-Fearers." Every, E. "Jews and God-Fearers in the New Testament Period." *Imm* 5 (1975): 46–50.

Évrard, "Polybe." Évrard, Étienne. "Polybe et Tite-Live, à propos d'Antiochus IV." *Latomus* 70 (4, 2011): 977–82.

Eya, "Healing." Eya, Regina. "Healing and Exorcism: The Psychological Aspects." Pages 44–54 in *Healing and Exorcism— The Nigerian Experience: Proceedings, Lectures, Discussions, and Conclusions of the First Missiology Symposium on Healing and Exorcism, Organised by the Spiritan International School of Theology, Attakwu, Enugu, May 18–20, 1989*. Edited by Chris U. Manus, Luke N. Mbefo, and E. E. Uzukwu. Enugu, Nigeria: Snapp, 1992.

Fabbro, "Prospettive." Fabbro, F. "Prospettive d'interpretazione della glossolalia paolina sotto il profilo della neurolinguistica." *RivB* 46 (2, 1998): 157–78.

Fabien, "Conversion de Simon." Fabien, Patrick. "La conversion de Simon le magicien (Ac 8,4–25)." *Bib* 91 (2, 2010): 210–40.

Fabien, "Interprétation." Fabien, Patrick. "L'interprétation de la citation d'Is 53,7–8 en Ac 8,32–33." *RB* 117 (4, 2010): 550–70.

Fabien, *Philippe*. Fabien, Patrick. *Philippe 'l'évangéliste' au tournant de la mission dans les Actes des apôtres: Philippe, Simon le magicien et l'eunuque éthiopien*. LD 232. Paris: Cerf, 2010.

Fàbrega, "War Junia(s)?" Fàbrega, Valentin. "War Junia(s), der hervorragende Apostel (Rom. 16,7), eine Frau?" *JAC* 27–28 (1984–85): 47–64.

Fabricius, "Παραχρῆμα." Fabricius, Cajus. "Zu παραχρῆμα bei Lukas." *Eranos* 83 (1–2, 1985): 62–66.

Fabry, "Jesaja-Rolle." Fabry, Heinz-Josef. "Die Jesaja-Rolle in Qumran: Älteste Handschriften und andere spannende Entdeckungen." *BK* 61 (4, 2006): 227–30.

Fabry, "Texte." Fabry, Heinz-Josef. "Neue Texte aus Qumran." *BK* 48 (1, 1993): 24–27.

Fabry, "Umkehr und Metanoia." Fabry, Heinz-Josef. "Umkehr und Metanoia als monastisches Ideal in der 'Mönchsgemeinde' von Qumran." *ErAuf* 53 (3, 1977): 163–80.

Fagan, "Bathing." Fagan, Garrett G. "Bathing for Health with Celsus and Pliny the Elder." *CQ* 56 (1, 2006): 190–207.

Fagan, "Genesis." Fagan, Garrett G. "The Genesis of the Roman Public Bath: Recent Approaches and Future Directions." *AJA* 105 (3, 2001): 403–26.

Fahy, "Note." Fahy, Thomas. "A Note on Romans 9:1–18." *ITQ* 32 (3, 1965): 261–62.

Fahy, "Romans." Fahy, Thomas. "St. Paul's Romans Were Jewish Converts." *ITQ* 26 (2, 1959): 182–91.

Faierstein, "Elijah." Faierstein, Morris M. "Why Do the Scribes Say That Elijah Must Come First?" *JBL* 100 (1, 1981): 75–86.

Faiman, "Hebrews." Faiman, David. "How Many Hebrews Left Egypt?" *JBQ* 18 (1989–90): 230–33.

Fairchild, "Associations." Fairchild, Mark R. "Paul's Pre-Christian Zealot Associations: A Re-examination of Gal 1.14 and Acts 22.3." *NTS* 45 (4, 1999): 514–32.

Faivre and Faivre, "Rhétorique." Faivre, Cecile, and Alexandre Faivre. "Rhétorique, histoire, et débats théologiques: À propos d'un ouvrage sur simon 'le magicien.'" *RevScRel* 73 (3, 1999): 293–313.

Faivre and Faivre, "Terre." Faivre, Alexandre, and Cécile Faivre. "'Sur la terre comme au ciel.' L'image des sept dans le mise en place d'un diaconat chrétien." *RevScRel* 82 (1, 2008): 91–105.

Falasca, "Bones." Falasca, Stefania. "Where Are Peter's Bones?" *30 Days* 3 (2, 1990): 38–45.

Falconer, "Prologue." Falconer, R. A. "The Prologue to the Gospel of John." *Exp*, 5th ser., 5 (1897): 222–34.

Falise and Loviny, "Soldiers." Falise, Thierry, and Christophe Loviny. "Child Soldiers of Myanmar." *WPR* (Oct. 1994): 25. (Reprinted from the *Eastern Express* [Hong Kong].)

Falk, "4Q393." Falk, Daniel K. "4Q393: A Communal Confession." *JJS* 45 (2, 1994): 184–207.

Falk, "4Q542." Falk, Daniel K. "Testament of Qahat (4Q542)." *DNTB* 1199–1200.

Falk, *Jesus*. Falk, Harvey. *Jesus the Pharisee: A New Look at the Jewishness of Jesus*. New York: Paulist, 1985.

Falk, "Law." Falk, Z. W. "Jewish Private Law." *JPFC* 1:504–34.

Falk, "Prayer Literature." Falk, Daniel K. "Jewish Prayer Literature and the Jerusalem Church in Acts." Pages 267–301 in *The Book of Acts in Its Palestinian Setting*. Edited by Richard Bauckham. Vol. 4 of *The Book of Acts in Its First Century Setting*. Edited by Bruce W. Winter. Grand Rapids: Eerdmans; Carlisle, U.K.: Paternoster, 1995.

Fallaize, "Purification." Fallaize, E. N. "Purification: Introductory and Primitive." Pages 455–66 in vol. 10 of *Encyclopedia of Religion and Ethics*. Edited by James Hastings. 13 vols. Edinburgh: T&T Clark, 1918.

Fant, *Miracles*. Fant, David J., ed. *Modern Miracles of Healing: Personal Testimonies of Well-Known Christian Men and Women to the Power of God to Heal Their Bodies*.

Harrisburg, Pa.: Christian Publications, 1943.

Fant and Reddish, *Sites*. Fant, Clyde E., and Mitchell G. Reddish. *A Guide to Biblical Sites in Greece and Turkey*. Oxford: Oxford University Press, 2003.

Fantuzzi, "Aratus." Fantuzzi, Marco. "Aratus of Soli." *BrillPauly* 1:955–59.

Fantuzzi, "Ekphrasis." Fantuzzi, Marco. "Ekphrasis: Greek." *BrillPauly* 4:872–75.

Fantuzzi, "Historical Epic." Fantuzzi, Marco. "Historical Epic." *BrillPauly* 6:409–11.

Fape, *Powers*. Fape, Michael Olusina. *Powers in Encounter with Power—Paul's Concept of Spiritual Warfare in Ephesians 6:10–12: An African Christian Perspective*. Fearn, U.K.: Christian Focus, 2003.

Farahian, "Vision." Farahian, Edmond. "Paul's Vision at Troas (Acts 16:9–10)." Pages 197–207 in *Luke and Acts*. Edited by Gerald O'Collins and Gilberto Marconi. Translated by Matthew J. O'Connell. New York: Paulist, 1993.

Faraone, "Curses." Faraone, Christopher A. "Curses and Blessings in Ancient Greek Oaths." *JANER* 5 (2005): 139–56.

Faraone, "New Light." Faraone, Christopher A. "New Light on Ancient Greek Exorcisms of the Wandering Womb." *ZPE* 144 (2003): 189–97.

Faraone, "Spells." Faraone, Christopher A. "When Spells Worked Magic." *Archaeology* 56 (2, 2003): 48–53.

Faraone, "Stopping Evil." Faraone, Christopher A. "Stopping Evil, Pain, Anger, and Blood: The Ancient Greek Tradition of Protective Iambic Incantations." *GRBS* 49 (2, 2009): 227–55.

Farber, *Kinship Systems*. Farber, Bernard. *Comparative Kinship Systems: A Method of Analysis*. New York: Wiley, 1968.

Faris, "Sibling Terminology." Faris, James C. "Sibling Terminology and Cross-Sex Behavior: Data from the Southeastern Nuba Mountains." *AmAnth* 71 (3, 1969): 482–88.

Farmer, "Judas." Farmer, William R. "Judas, Simon, and Athronges." *NTS* 4 (1958): 147–55.

Farmer, *Maccabees*. Farmer, William R. *Maccabees, Zealots, and Josephus*. New York: Columbia, 1956.

Farmer, "Peter and Paul." Farmer, William R. "Peter and Paul, and the Tradition concerning 'the Lord's Supper' in 1 Corinthians 11:23–26." Pages 35–55 in *One Loaf, One Cup—Ecumenical Studies of 1 Cor 11 and Other Eucharistic Texts: The Cambridge Conference on the Eucharist, August 1988*. Edited by Ben F. Meyer. New Gospel Studies 6. Macon, Ga.: Mercer University Press, 1993.

Farmer, *Synoptic Problem*. Farmer, William R. *The Synoptic Problem: A Critical Analysis*. New York: Macmillan, 1964.

Farmer, *Verses*. Farmer, William R. *The Last Twelve Verses of Mark*. SNTSMS 25. Cambridge: Cambridge University Press, 1974.

Farnell, *Cults*. Farnell, Lewis Richard. *The Cults of the Greek States*. 5 vols. Oxford: Clarendon, 1896–1909.

Farnell, "Perspective." Farnell, F. David. "The New Perspective on Paul: Its Basic Tenets, History, and Presuppositions." *MSJ* 16 (2, 2005): 189–243.

Farrar, *Life and Work*. Farrar, F. W. *The Life and Work of St. Paul*. London: Cassell, 1903.

Farrer, *Matthew and Luke*. Farrer, Austin. *St. Matthew and St. Luke*. London: Dacre, 1954.

Farrington, "Action." Farrington, Scott. "Action and Reason: Polybius and the Gap between Encomium and History." *CP* 106 (4, 2011): 324–42.

Farrington, *Faith of Epicurus*. Farrington, Benjamin. *The Faith of Epicurus*. New York: Basic Books, 1967.

Farris, "Semitic Sources." Farris, Stephen C. "On Discerning Semitic Sources in Luke 1–2." Pages 201–37 in vol. 2 of *Studies of History and Tradition in the Four Gospels*. Edited by R. T. France and David Wenham. 2 vols. Gospel Perspectives 1–2. Sheffield, U.K.: JSOT Press, 1980–81.

Fass, "Angels." Fass, David E. "How the Angels Do Serve." *Judaism* 40 (3, 1991): 281–89.

Fau, "Authenticité." Fau, G. "L'authenticité du texte de Tacite sur les chrétiens." *CCER* 19 (72, 1971): 19–24.

Faure, "Mystère." Faure, Patrick. "Le mystère d'Israël selon les textes Alexandrin et Occidental des Actes des apôtres." *NRTh* 127 (1, 2005): 3–17.

Faure, *Pentecôte*. Faure, Patrick. *Pentecôte et Parousie: Ac 1,6–3,26. L'Église et le Mystère d'Israël entre les Textes Alexandrin et Occidental des Actes des Apôtres*. EtBib, n.s., 50. Paris: Gabalda, 2003.

Fauth, "Metatron." Fauth, Wolfgang. "Tatrosjah-Totrosjah und Metatron in der jüdischen Merkabah-Mystik." *JSJ* 22 (1, 1991): 40–87.

Favez et al., "Isagogic literature." Favez, Charles, et al. "Isagogic Literature." *OCD*³ 767.

Favez, Williams, and Scheid, "Nenia." Favez, Charles, Gordon Willis Williams, and John Scheid. "Nenia." *OCD*³ 1034.

Favorito, *Coinage*. Favorito, Emilio N. *The Bronze Coinage of Ancient Syracuse: A Reference Manual on the Types of the Bronze Coins of Ancient Syracuse Including a Compilation of Specimens from the Collections of the Members of the Society Historia Numorum-Boston and Other Sources*. SHN 2. Boston: E. N. Favorito, 1990.

Favret-Saada, *Witchcraft*. Favret-Saada, Jeanne. *Deadly Words: Witchcraft in the Bocage*. Translated by Catherine Cullen. Cambridge: Cambridge University Press, 1980.

Faw, *Acts*. Faw, Charles E. *Acts: Believers Church Bible Commentary*. Scottsdale, Pa.: Herald, 1993.

Fears, "Ideology of Power." Fears, J. Rufus. "Rome: The Ideology of Imperial Power." *Thought* 55 (216, 1980): 98–109.

Feder, "Solomon." Feder, Theodore. "Solomon, Socrates, and Aristotle." *BAR* 34 (5, 2008): 32–36.

Fee, "Church Order." Fee, Gordon D. "Reflections on Church Order in the Pastoral Epistles, with Further Reflection on the Hermeneutics of *ad hoc* Documents." *JETS* 28 (2, 1985): 141–51.

Fee, "Conversion." Fee, Gordon D. "Paul's Conversion as Key to His Understanding of the Spirit." Pages 166–83 in *The Road from Damascus: The Impact of Paul's Conversion on His Life, Thought, and Ministry*. Edited by Richard N. Longenecker. Grand Rapids: Eerdmans, 1997.

Fee, *Corinthians*. Fee, Gordon D. *The First Epistle to the Corinthians*. NICNT. Grand Rapids: Eerdmans, 1987.

Fee, "*Eidōlothyta*." Fee, Gordon D. "*Eidōlothyta* Once Again: An Interpretation of 1 Corinthians 8–10." *Bib* 61 (2, 1980): 172–97.

Fee, *Gospel*. Fee, Gordon D. *Gospel and Spirit: Issues in New Testament Hermeneutics*. Peabody, Mass.: Hendrickson, 1991.

Fee, *Paul, Spirit, and People*. Fee, Gordon D. *Paul, the Spirit, and the People of God*. Peabody, Mass.: Hendrickson, 1996.

Fee, *Philippians*. Fee, Gordon D. *Paul's Letter to the Philippians*. NICNT. Grand Rapids: Eerdmans, 1995.

Fee, *Presence*. Fee, Gordon D. *God's Empowering Presence: The Holy Spirit in the Letters of Paul*. Peabody, Mass.: Hendrickson, 1994.

Fee, *Timothy, Titus*. Fee, Gordon D. *1 and 2 Timothy, Titus*. GNC. San Francisco: Harper & Row, 1984.

Fee and Stuart, *Worth*. Fee, Gordon D., and Douglas Stuart. *How to Read the Bible for All Its Worth: A Guide to Understanding the Bible*. 2nd ed. Grand Rapids: Zondervan, 1993.

Feeney, "History." Feeney, Denis. "The History of Roman Religion in Roman Historiography and Epic." Pages 129–42 in *A Companion to Roman Religion*. Edited by Jörg Rüpke. BCompAW. Oxford: Blackwell, 2011.

Feeney, "Silius Italicus." Feeney, Denis C. "Silius Italicus, Tiberius Catius Asconius." OCD³ 1407.

Feeney, "Time." Feeney, Denis. "Time." Pages 139–51 in *The Cambridge Companion to the Roman Historians*. Edited by Andrew Feldherr. Cambridge: Cambridge University Press, 2009.

Feig Vishnia, "Shadow Army." Feig Vishnia, R. "The Shadow Army—The *lixae* and the Roman Legions." *ZPE* 139 (2002): 265–72.

Feinberg, "Meaning." Feinberg, Paul D. "The Meaning of Inerrancy." Pages 267–306 in *Inerrancy*. Edited by Norman L. Geisler. Grand Rapids: Zondervan, 1979.

Feinberg, *Prophets*. Feinberg, Charles L. *The Minor Prophets*. Chicago: Moody, 1976.

Felber, "Hospitality." Felber, Heinz. "Hospitality: Ancient Orient and Egypt." *BrillPauly* 6:528–29.

Felder, *Race*. Felder, Cain Hope. *Race, Racism, and the Biblical Narratives*. Minneapolis: Augsburg Fortress, 2002.

Felder, "Racial Ambiguities." Felder, Cain Hope. "Racial Ambiguities in the Biblical Narratives." Pages 17–24 in *The Church and Racism*. Edited by Gregory Baum and John Coleman. Concilium 151. New York: Seabury; Edinburgh: T&T Clark, 1982.

Felder, *Waters*. Felder, Cain Hope. *Troubling Biblical Waters: Race, Class, and Family*. BHMTSNABR 3. Maryknoll, N.Y.: Orbis, 1989.

Feldherr, "Introduction." Feldherr, Andrew. "Introduction." Pages 1–8 in *The Cambridge Companion to the Roman Historians*. Edited by Andrew Feldherr. Cambridge: Cambridge University Press, 2009.

Feldherr, "Tacitus' Jews." Feldherr, Andrew. "Barbarians II: Tacitus' Jews." Pages 301–16 in *The Cambridge Companion to the Roman Historians*. Edited by Andrew Feldherr. Cambridge: Cambridge University Press, 2009.

Feldherr, "Translation." Feldherr, Andrew. "The Translation of Catiline." Pages 385–90 in *A Companion to Greek and Roman Historiography*. Edited by John Marincola. 2 vols. Oxford: Blackwell, 2007.

Feldman, "Ahab." Feldman, Louis H. "Josephus' Portrait of Ahab." *ETL* 68 (4, 1992): 368–84.

Feldman, "Ahasuerus." Feldman, Louis H. "Josephus' Portrait of Ahasuerus." *ABR* 42 (1994): 17–38.

Feldman, "*Antiquities* and Antiquities." Feldman, Louis H. "Josephus' *Jewish Antiquities* and Pseudo-Philo's *Biblical Antiquities*." Pages 59–80 in *Josephus, the Bible,*

and History. Edited by Louis H. Feldman and Gohei Hata. Detroit: Wayne State University Press, 1989.

Feldman, "Apologist of World." Feldman, Louis H. "Josephus as an Apologist of the Greco-Roman World: His Portrait of Solomon." Pages 69–98 in *Aspects of Religious Propaganda in Judaism and Early Christianity*. Edited by Elisabeth Schüssler Fiorenza. UNDCSJCA 2. Notre Dame, Ind.: University of Notre Dame Press, 1976.

Feldman, "'Aqedah." Feldman, Louis H. "Josephus as a Biblical Interpreter: The 'Aqedah." *JQR* 75 (3, 1985): 212–52.

Feldman, "Asa." Feldman, Louis H. "Josephus' Portrait of Asa." *BBR* 4 (1994): 41–59.

Feldman, "Balaam." Feldman, Louis H. "Philo's Version of Balaam." *Hen* 25 (3, 2003): 301–19.

Feldman, "Calf." Feldman, Louis H. "Philo's Account of the Golden Calf Incident." *JJS* 56 (2, 2005): 245–64.

Feldman, "Command." Feldman, Louis H. "The Command, according to Philo, Pseudo-Philo, and Josephus, to Annihilate the Seven Nations of Canaan." *AUSS* 41 (1, 2003): 13–29.

Feldman, "Concubine." Feldman, Louis H. "Josephus' Portrayal (*Antiquities* 5.136–174) of the Benjaminite Affair of the Concubine and Its Repercussions (Judges 19–21)." *JQR* 90 (3–4, 2000): 255–92.

Feldman, "Conversion." Feldman, Louis H. "Conversion to Judaism in Classical Antiquity." *HUCA* 74 (2003): 115–56.

Feldman, "Daniel." Feldman, Louis H. "Josephus' Portrait of Daniel." *Hen* 14 (1–2, 1992): 37–96.

Feldman, "David." Feldman, Louis H. "Josephus' Portrait of David." *HUCA* 60 (1989): 129–74.

Feldman, "Death of Moses." Feldman, Louis H. "The Death of Moses, according to Philo." *EstBib* 60 (2, 2002): 225–54.

Feldman, "Elijah." Feldman, Louis H. "Josephus' Portrait of Elijah." *JSP* 8 (1, 1994): 61–86.

Feldman, "Ezra." Feldman, Louis H. "Josephus' Portrait of Ezra." *VT* 43 (2, 1993): 190–214.

Feldman, "Hellenism." Feldman, Louis H. "How Much Hellenism in Jewish Palestine?" *HUCA* 57 (1986): 83–111.

Feldman, "Hellenizations: Abraham." Feldman, Louis H. "Hellenizations in Josephus' *Jewish Antiquities:* The Portrait of Abraham." Pages 133–53 in *Josephus, Judaism, and Christianity*. Edited by Louis H. Feldman and Gohei Hata. Detroit: Wayne State University Press, 1987.

Feldman, "Hezekiah." Feldman, Louis H. "Josephus's Portrait of Hezekiah." *JBL* 111 (4, 1992): 597–610.

Feldman, "Importance." Feldman, Louis H. "The Importance of Jerusalem as Viewed by Josephus." *International Rennert Guest Lecture Series* 2 (1998): 1–23.

Feldman, "Introduction." Feldman, Louis H. Introduction. Pages 17–49 in *Josephus, the Bible, and History*. Edited by Louis H. Feldman and Gohei Hata. Detroit: Wayne State University Press, 1989.

Feldman, "Isaac." Feldman, Louis H. "Josephus' Portrait of Isaac." *RSLR* 29 (1, 1993): 3–33.

Feldman, "Jacob." Feldman, Louis H. "Josephus' Portrait of Jacob." *JQR* 79 (2–3, 1988–89): 101–51.

Feldman, "Jehoshaphat." Feldman, Louis H. "Josephus' Portrait of Jehoshaphat." *SCI* 12 (1993): 159–75.

Feldman, "Jehu." Feldman, Louis H. "Josephus' Portrait of Jehu." *JSQ* 4 (1, 1997): 12–32.

Feldman, "Jeroboam." Feldman, Louis H. "Josephus' Portrait of Jeroboam." *AUSS* 31 (1, 1993): 29–51.

Feldman, "Jonah." Feldman, Louis H. "Josephus' Interpretation of Jonah." *AJSR* 17 (1, 1992): 1–29.

Feldman, "Joseph." Feldman, Louis H. "Josephus' Portrait of Joseph." *RB* 99 (2, 1992): 397–417; (3, 1992): 504–28.

Feldman, "Joshua." Feldman, Louis H. "Josephus's Portrait of Joshua." *HTR* 82 (4, 1989): 351–76.

Feldman, "Josiah." Feldman, Louis H. "Josephus' Portrait of Josiah." *LouvS* 18 (2, 1993): 110–30.

Feldman, "Levites." Feldman, Louis H. "The Levites in Josephus." *Hen* 28 (2, 2006): 91–102.

Feldman, "Manasseh." Feldman, Louis H. "Josephus' Portrait of Manasseh." *JSP* 9 (1991): 3–20.

Feldman, "Methods." Feldman, Louis H. "Josephus: Interpretive Methods and Tendencies." *DNTB* 590–96.

Feldman, "Moses." Feldman, Louis H. "Josephus' Portrait of Moses." *JQR* 82 (3–4, 1992): 285–328; 83 (1–2, 1992): 7–50.

Feldman, "Nehemiah." Feldman, Louis H. "Josephus' Portrait of Nehemiah." *JJS* 43 (2, 1992): 187–202.

Feldman, "Noah." Feldman, Louis H. "Josephus' Portrait of Noah and Its Parallels in Philo, Pseudo-Philo's *Biblical Antiquities*, and Rabbinic Midrashim." *PAAJR* 55 (1988): 31–57.

Feldman, "Omnipresence." Feldman, Louis H. "The Omnipresence of the God-Fearers." *BAR* 12 (5, 1986): 58–69.

Feldman, "Pharaohs." Feldman, Louis H. "Josephus' Portraits of the Pharaohs." *SyllClass* 4 (1993): 49–63.

Feldman, "Pro-Jewish Intimations." Feldman, Louis H. "Pro-Jewish Intimations in Anti-Jewish Remarks Cited in Josephus' *Against Apion*." *JQR* 78 (3–4, 1988): 187–251.

Feldman, "Reflections on Jews." Feldman, Louis H. "Reflections on Jews in Graeco-Roman Literature." *JSP* 16 (1997): 39–52.

Feldman, "Rehoboam." Feldman, Louis H. "Josephus' Portrait of Rehoboam." *SPhilA* 9 (1997): 264–86.

Feldman, "Roncace's Portraits." Feldman, Louis H. "On Professor Mark Roncace's Portraits of Deborah and Gideon in Josephus." *JSJ* 32 (2, 2001): 193–220.

Feldman, "Samuel." Feldman, Louis H. "Josephus' Portrait of Samuel." *AbrN* 30 (1992): 103–45.

Feldman, "Samson." Feldman, Louis H. "Josephus' Version of Samson." *JSJ* 19 (2, 1988): 171–214.

Feldman, "Saul." Feldman, Louis H. "Josephus' Portrait of Saul." *HUCA* 53 (1982): 45–99.

Feldman, "Solomon." Feldman, Louis H. "Josephus' Portrait of Solomon." *HUCA* 66 (1995): 103–67.

Feldman, "Sympathizers." Feldman, Louis H. "Proselytes and 'Sympathizers' in the Light of the New Inscriptions from Aphrodisias." *REJ* 148 (3–4, 1989): 265–305.

Feldman, "Version of 'Aqedah." Feldman, Louis H. "Philo's Version of the 'Aqedah." *SPhilA* 14 (2002): 66–86.

Feldman, "View of Birth." Feldman, Louis H. "Philo's View of Moses' Birth and Upbringing." *CBQ* 64 (2, 2002): 258–81.

Feldtkeller, *Identitätssuche*. Feldtkeller, Andreas. *Identitätssuche des syrischen Urchristentums: Mission, Inkulturation, und Pluralität im ältesten Heidenchristentum*. NTOA 25. Freiburg, Switz.: Universitätsverlag; Göttingen: Vandenhoeck & Ruprecht, 1993.

Fellows, personal correspondence. Fellows, Richard G. Personal correspondence to the author. June 5 and 7, 2007.

Fellows, "Renaming." Fellows, Richard G. "Renaming in Paul's Churches: The Case of Crispus-Sosthenes Revisited." *TynBul* 56 (2, 2005): 111–30.

Fellows, "Titus." Fellows, Richard G. "Was Titus Timothy?" *JSNT* 81 (2001): 33–58.

Felton, "Statues." Felton, D. "The Animated Statues of Lucian's *Philopseudes*." *CBull* 77 (1, 2001): 75–86.

Fensham, "Seventy." Fensham, F. Charles. "The Numeral Seventy in the Old Testament and the Family of Jerubaal, Ahab, Panammuwa, and Athirat." *PEQ* 109 (July–December 1977): 113–15.

Fenske, "Aspekte." Fenske, Wolfgang. "Aspekte biblischer Theologie dargestellt an der Verwendung von Ps 16 in Apostelgeschichte 2 und 13." *Bib* 83 (1, 2002): 54–70.

Fenton, *John*. Fenton, J. C. *The Gospel according to John in the Revised Standard Version*. New Clarendon Bible. London: Oxford University Press, 1970.

Fenton, "Order of Miracles." Fenton, John. "The Order of the Miracles Performed by Peter and Paul in Acts." *ExpT* 77 (12, 1966): 381–83.

Ferch, "Aeons." Ferch, Arthur J. "The Two Aeons and the Messiah in Pseudo-Philo, 4 Ezra, and 2 Baruch." *AUSS* 15 (2, 1977): 135–51.

Ferchiou, "Possession Cults." Ferchiou, Sophie. "The Possession Cults of Tunisia: A Religious System Functioning as a System of Reference and a Social Field for Performing Actions." Pages 209–18 in *Women's Medicine: The zar-bori Cult in Africa and Beyond*. Edited by I. M. Lewis, Ahmed Al-Safi, and Sayyid Hurreiz. Edinburgh: International African Institute, Edinburgh University Press, 1991.

Ferdinando, "Demonology." Ferdinando, Keith. "Screwtape Revisited: Demonology Western, African, and Biblical." Pages 103–32 in *The Unseen World: Christian Reflections on Angels, Demons, and the Heavenly Realm*. Edited by Anthony N. S. Lane. Grand Rapids: Baker; Carlisle, U.K.: Paternoster, 1996.

Ferguson, *Backgrounds*. Ferguson, Everett. *Backgrounds of Early Christianity*. Grand Rapids: Eerdmans, 1987.

Ferguson, *Demonology*. Ferguson, Everett. *Demonology of the Early Christian World*. Symposium Series 12. New York and Toronto: Edwin Mellen, 1984.

Ferguson, "Hellenists." Ferguson, Everett. "The Hellenists in the Book of Acts." *ResQ* 12 (4, 1969): 159–80.

Ferguson, "Jonah." Ferguson, Everett. "Jonah in Early Christian Art: Death, Resurrection, and Immortality." Pages 342–53 in *Text, Image, and Christians in the Graeco-Roman World: A Festschrift in Honor of David Lee Balch*. Edited by Aliou Cissé Niang and Carolyn Osiek. PrTMS 176. Eugene, Ore.: Pickwick, 2012.

Fernandey, "Brotherhood." Fernandey, James W. "Bantu Brotherhood: Symmetry, Socialization, and Ultimate Choice in Two Bantu Cultures." Pages 339–66 in *Kinship and Culture*. Edited by Francis L. K. Hsu. Chicago: Aldine, 1971.

Fernández-Garrido, "Stasis-theory." Fernández-Garrido, Regla. "Stasis-theory in Judicial Speeches of Greek Novels." *GRBS* 49 (3, 2009): 453–72.

Fernández Marcos, "Religión judía." Fernández Marcos, Natalio. "La religión judía vista por los autores griegos y latinos." *Sefarad* 41 (1, 1981): 3–25.

Fernando, *Acts*. Fernando, Ajith. *Acts*. NIVAC. Grand Rapids: Zondervan, 1998.

Ferrary, "Géographie." Ferrary, Jean-Louis. "La géographie de l'hellénisme sous la domination romaine." *Phoenix* 65 (1–2, 2011): 1–22.

Ferrary, "Philhellenism." Ferrary, Jean-Louis. "Philhellenism." *BrillPauly* 11:19–21.

Ferreira, "Plan." Ferreira, Johan. "The Plan of God and Preaching in Acts." *EvQ* 71 (3, 1999): 209–15.

Fesko, "Imputation." Fesko, J. V. "N. T. Wright on Imputation." *RTR* 66 (1, 2007): 2–22.

Fesko, "Works of Law." Fesko, J. V. "N. T. Wright and the Works of the Law." *F&M* 22 (1, 2004): 64–83.

Festugière, *Astrologie*. Festugière, A.-J. *L'astrologie et les sciences occultes*. Vol. 1 of *La révélation d'Hermès Trismégiste*. 2nd ed. Paris: Lecoffre, 1950.

Festugière, *Epicurus*. Festugière, A.-J. *Epicurus and His Gods*. Oxford: Blackwell, 1955; Cambridge, Mass.: Harvard University Press, 1956.

Festugière, "Lemerle." Festugière, A.-J. Review of Paul Lemerle, *Philippes et la Macédoine orientale à l'époque chrétienne et byzantine*. *RB* 54 (1947): 132–40.

Festugière, "Nouvelle édition du 'Vita.'" Festugière, A.-J. "Sur une nouvelle édition du 'De vita Pythagorica' de Jamblique." *REG* 50 (1937): 470–94.

Festugière, *Religion*. Festugière, A.-J. *Personal Religion among the Greeks*. Los Angeles: University of California Press, 1954.

Feuillet, "Affinités." Feuillet, André. "La doctrine des épîtres pastorales et leurs affinités avec l'oeuvre lucanienne." *RThom* 78 (2, 1978): 181–225.

Feuillet, "Antithèse." Feuillet, André. "L'antithèse péché-justice dans l'épître aux Romains." *NV* 58 (1, 1983): 57–70.

Feuillet, *Apocalypse*. Feuillet, André. *The Apocalypse*. Translated by Thomas E. Crane. Staten Island, N.Y.: Alba House, 1965.

Feuillet, "Deux references." Feuillet, André. "Deux références évangéliques cachées au Serviteur martyrisé (*Is* 52, 13–53, 12): Quelques aspects importants du mystère rédempteur." *NRTh* 106 (4, 1984): 549–65.

Fiedler, "Herkunft." Fiedler, Peter. "Zur Herkunft des gottesdienstlichen Gebrauchs von Psalmen aus dem Frühjudentum." *ALW* 30 (3, 1988): 229–37.

Fiedrowicz, "Rezeption." Fiedrowicz, Michael. "Die Rezeption und Interpretation der paulinischen Areopag-Rede in der patristischen Theologie." *TTZ* 11 (2, 2002): 85–105.

Fieger, *Schatten*. Fieger, Michael. *Im Schatten der Artemis: Glaube und Ungehorsam in Ephesus*. Bern: Peter Lang, 1998.

Field, "Possession." Field, Margaret J. "Spirit Possession in Ghana." Pages 3–13 in *Spirit Mediumship and Society in Africa*. Edited by John Beattie and John Middleton. Foreword by Raymond Firth. New York: Africana, 1969.

Field, *Search*. Field, Margaret J. *Search for Security: An Ethno-psychiatric Study of Rural Ghana*. London: Faber & Faber, 1960.

Fields, "Story." Fields, Leslie Leyland. "The Gospel Is More Than a Story." *CT* (July 2012): 38–43.

Fields and Merrifield, "Kinship." Fields, Harriet L., and William R. Merrifield. "Mayoruna (Panoan) Kinship." *Ethnology* 19 (Jan. 1980): 1–28.

Fiema, "Roman Petra." Fiema, Zbigniew T. "Roman Petra (A.D. 106–363): A Neglected Subject." *ZDPV* 119 (1, 2003): 38–58.

Fiensy, "Composition." Fiensy, David A. "The Composition of the Jerusalem Church." Pages 213–36 in *The Book of Acts in Its Palestinian Setting*. Edited by Richard Bauckham. Vol. 4 of *The Book of Acts in Its First Century Setting*. Edited by Bruce W. Winter. Grand Rapids: Eerdmans; Carlisle, U.K.: Paternoster, 1995.

Fikhman, "Appearance." Fikhman, I. "The Physical Appearance of Egyptian Jews according to the Greek Papyri." *SCI* 18 (1999): 131–38.

Filbeck, "Problems." Filbeck, David. "Problems in Translating First Person Plural Pronouns in 2 Corinthians." *BTr* 45 (4, 1994): 401–9.

Filson, "Analysis." Filson, William Robert. "An Analysis of the Relationship of Pre-Christian Beliefs of the Ibaloi Pentecostal Christians to Their Beliefs and Practices concerning the Verbal Gifts of 1 Corinthians 12:8–12." MDiv thesis, Asia Pacific Theological Seminary, 1993.

Filson, "Christians in Pompeii." Filson, Floyd V. "Were There Christians in Pompeii?" *BA* 2 (2, 1939): 13–16.

Filson, "Ephesus." Filson, Floyd V. "Ephesus and the New Testament." *BA* 8 (3, 1945): 73–80.

Filson, *History*. Filson, Floyd V. *A New Testament History*. Philadelphia: Westminster, 1964.

Filson, "Journey Motif." Filson, Floyd V. "The Journey Motif in Luke-Acts." Pages 68–77 in *Apostolic History and the Gospel: Biblical and Historical Essays Presented to F. F. Bruce on His 60th Birthday*. Edited by W. Ward Gasque and Ralph P. Martin. Exeter, U.K.: Paternoster; Grand Rapids: Eerdmans, 1970.

Filson, *Matthew*. Filson, Floyd V. *A Commentary on the Gospel according to St. Matthew*. New York and Evanston, Ill.: Harper & Row, 1960.

Filson, "Study." Filson, William R. "A Comparative Study of Contextualized and Pentecostal Approaches to Nominal Muslims in Indonesia." DMin diss., Asia Pacific Theological Seminary, 2006.

Finamore and Dillon, "Introduction." Finamore, John F., and John M. Dillon. "Introduction." Pages 1–25 in *Iamblichus De Anima: Text, Translation, and Commentary*. Philosophia Antiqua 42. Leiden: Brill, 2002; repr., Atlanta: SBL, n.d.

Finch, "Views of Ageing." Finch, Caleb Ellicott. "Evolving Views of Ageing and Longevity from Homer to Hippocrates: Emergence of Natural Factors, Persistence of the Supernatural." *GR* 57 (2, 2010): 355–77.

"Finds or Fakes." "Update—Finds or Fakes? The Other Shoe: Five Accused of Antiquities Fraud." *BAR* 31 (2, 2005): 58–69.

Fine, *Interaction*. *Jews, Christians, and Polytheists in the Ancient Synagogue: Cultural Interaction in the Greco-Roman Period*. Edited by Steven Fine. London: Routledge, 1999.

Fine and Meyers, "Synagogues." Fine, Steven, and Eric M. Meyers. "Synagogues." *OEANE* 5:118–23.

Finegan, *Apostles*. Finegan, Jack. *The Archeology of the New Testament: The Mediterranean World of the Early Christian Apostles*. Boulder, Col.: Westview; London: Croom Helm, 1981.

Finegan, *Archeology of New Testament*. Finegan, Jack. *The Archeology of the New Testament: The Life of Jesus and the Beginning of the Early Church*. Princeton: Princeton University Press, 1969.

Finegan, *Light from Past*. Finegan, Jack. *Light from the Ancient Past*. Princeton: Princeton University Press, 1946.

Finegan, *Records*. Finegan, Jack. *Hidden Records of the Life of Jesus*. Philadelphia: Pilgrim, 1969.

Finegan, *Religions*. Finegan, Jack. *The Archeology of World Religions*. Princeton: Princeton University Press, 1952.

Finger, *Meals*. Finger, Reta Halteman. *Of Widows and Meals: Communal Meals in the Book of Acts*. Grand Rapids: Eerdmans, 2007.

Fink, "Responses." Fink, Marion Michael, Jr. "The Responses in the New Testament to the Practice of Fasting." PhD diss., Southern Baptist Theological Seminary, 1974.

Fink, Hoey, and Snyder, "*Feriale Duranum*." Fink, R. O., A. S. Hoey, and W. F. Snyder. "The *Feriale Duranum*." *YCS* 7 (1940): 1–222.

Finkel, "Pesher." Finkel, Asher. "The Pesher of Dreams and Scriptures." *RevQ* 4 (3, 1963): 357–70.

Finkelberg, "*Cypria*." Finkelberg, Margalit. "The *Cypria*, the *Iliad*, and the Problem of Multiformity in Oral and Written Tradition." *CP* 95 (1, 2000): 1–11.

Finkelberg, "Parmenides." Finkelberg, Aryeh. "Parmenides: Between Material and Logical Monism." *AGP* 70 (1988): 1–14.

Finkelberg, "Regional Texts." Finkelberg, Margalit. "Regional Texts and the Circulation of Books: The Case of Homer." *GRBS* 46 (3, 2006): 231–48.

Finkelberg, "Virtue." Finkelberg, Margalit. "Virtue and Circumstances: On the City-State Concept of *arete*." *AJP* 123 (1, 2002): 35–49.

Finkelstein, *Akiba*. Finkelstein, Louis. *Akiba: Scholar, Saint, and Martyr*. New York: Atheneum, 1970.

Finkelstein, "Documents." Finkelstein, Louis. "Pre-Maccabean Documents in the Passover Haggadah." *HTR* 35 (4, 1942): 291–332; 36 (1, 1943): 1–38.

Finkelstein, *Making*. Finkelstein, Louis. *Pharisaism in the Making: Selected Essays*. New York: KTAV, 1972.

Finkelstein, *Pharisees*. Finkelstein, Louis. *The Pharisees: The Sociological Background of Their Faith*. 2 vols. 3rd ed. Philadelphia: Jewish Publication Society of America, 1962.

Finkler, "Religion." Finkler, Kaja. "Teaching Religion and Healing at a Southern University." Pages 47–57 in *Teaching Religion and Healing*. Edited by Linda L. Barnes and Inés Talamantez. AARTRSS. Oxford: Oxford University Press, 2006.

Finlay, *Columba*. Finlay, J. *Columba*. London: Victor Gollancz, 1979.

Finley, *Economy*. Finley, M. I. *The Ancient Economy*. Sather Classical Lectures 43. Berkeley: University of California Press, 1973.

Finley, *Sicily*. Finley, Moses I. *Ancient Sicily*. Totowa, N.J.: Rowman and Littlefield, 1979.

Finley, *Slavery*. Finley, M. I. *Ancient Slavery and Modern Ideology*. New York: Viking, 1980.

Finley, *Thucydides*. Finley, John H., Jr. *Thucydides*. Ann Arbor Paperbacks. Ann Arbor: University of Michigan,

the President and Fellows of Harvard College, 1942.

Finley and Treggiari, "Freedmen." Finley, M. I., and Susan M. Treggiari. "Freedmen, Freedwomen." *OCD³* 609.

Finn, "God-Fearers Reconsidered." Finn, Thomas M. "The God-Fearers Reconsidered." *CBQ* 47 (1, 1985): 75–84.

Finney, *Memoirs.* Finney, Charles G. *Memoirs of Rev. Charles G. Finney.* New York: A. S. Barnes & Company, 1876.

Finsterbusch, "Christologie als Blasphemie." Finsterbusch, K. "Christologie als Blasphemie: Das Hauptthema der Stephanusperikope in lukanischer Perspektive." *BN* 92 (1998): 38–54.

Fiore, "Cynicism." Fiore, Benjamin. "Cynicism and Skepticism." *DNTB* 242–45.

Fiore, "Exemplification." Fiore, Benjamin. "Paul, Exemplification, and Imitation." Pages 228–57 in *Paul in the Greco-Roman World: A Handbook.* Edited by J. Paul Sampley. Harrisburg, Pa.: Trinity Press International, 2003.

Fiore, "Theory." Fiore, Benjamin. "The Theory and Practice of Friendship in Cicero." Pages 59–76 in *Greco-Roman Perspectives on Friendship.* Edited by John T. Fitzgerald. SBLRBS 34. Atlanta: Scholars Press, 1997.

Firth, "Foreword." Firth, Raymond. Foreword. Pages ix–xiv in *Spirit Mediumship and Society in Africa.* Edited by John Beattie and John Middleton. New York: Africana, 1969.

Firth, *Ritual.* Firth, Raymond. *Tikopia Ritual and Belief.* Boston: Beacon, 1967.

Firth, *We, the Tikopia.* Firth, Raymond. *We, the Tikopia: A Sociological Study of Kinship in Primitive Polynesia.* 2nd ed. Preface by Bronislaw Malinowski. Boston: Beacon, 1963.

Fischer and Stein, "Marble." Fischer, Moshe L., and Alla Stein. "Josephus on the Use of Marble in Building Projects of Herod the Great." *JJS* 45 (1, 1994): 79–85.

Fischer and Tal, "Decoration." Fischer, Moshe, and Oren Tal. "Architectural Decoration in Ancient Israel in Hellenistic Times: Some Aspects of Hellenization." *ZDPV* 119 (1, 2003): 19–37.

Fischer and Tal, "Totenmahlrelief." Fischer, Moshe, and Oren Tal, "A Fourth-Century BCE Attic Marble *Totenmahlrelief* at Apollonia-Arsuf." *IEJ* 53 (1, 2003): 49–60.

Fishbane, *Interpretation.* Fishbane, Michael. *Biblical Interpretation in Ancient Israel.* Oxford: Clarendon, 1985.

Fisher, "Hubris." Fisher, Nick R. E. "Hubris." *OCD³* 732–33.

Fishwick, "Caesar." Fishwick, Duncan. "The Temple of Caesar at Alexandria." *AJAH* 9 (2, 1984): 131–34.

Fishwick, "Caesareum." Fishwick, Duncan. "The Caesareum at Alexandria Again." *AJAH* 12 (1, 1987): 62–72.

Fishwick, "Numen Augusti." Fishwick, Duncan. "Numen Augusti." *ZPE* 160 (2007): 247–55.

Fishwick, "Ossuaries." Fishwick, Duncan. "The Talpioth Ossuaries Again." *NTS* 10 (1, 1963): 49–61.

Fishwick, "Ovid." Fishwick, Duncan. "Ovid and Divus Augustus." *CP* 86 (1, 1991): 36–41.

Fisk, "Bible" Fisk, Bruce N. "Rewritten Bible in Pseudepigrapha and Qumran." *DNTB* 947–53.

Fisk, "Eating Meat." Fisk, Bruce N. "Eating Meat Offered to Idols: Corinthian Behavior and Pauline Response in 1 Corinthians 8–10 (A Response to Gordon Fee)." *TJ* 10 (1, 1989): 49–70.

Fisk, "Genesis Apocryphon." Fisk, Bruce N. "Genesis Apocryphon (1QapGen)." *DNTB* 398–401.

Fisk, "Offering Isaac." Fisk, Bruce N. "Offering Isaac Again and Again: Pseudo-Philo's Use of the Aqedah as Intertext." *CBQ* 62 (3, 2000): 481–507.

Fisk, "Scripture." Fisk, Bruce N. "Scripture Shaping Scripture: The Interpretive Role of Biblical Citations in Pseudo-Philo's Episode of the Golden Calf." *JSP* 17 (1998): 3–23.

Fitzgerald, "Affliction Lists." Fitzgerald, John T. "Affliction Lists." *DNTB* 16–18.

Fitzgerald, *Cracks.* Fitzgerald, John T. *Cracks in an Earthen Vessel: An Examination of the Catalogues of Hardships in the Corinthian Correspondence.* SBLDS 99. Atlanta: Scholars Press, 1988.

Fitzgerald, "Egnatius." Fitzgerald, John T. "Egnatius, the Breathalyzer Kiss, and an Early Instance of Domestic Homicide at Rome." Pages 119–31 in *Text, Image, and Christians in the Graeco-Roman World: A Festschrift in Honor of David Lee Balch.* Edited by Aliou Cissé Niang and Carolyn Osiek. PrTMS 176. Eugene, Ore.: Pickwick, 2012.

Fitzgerald, *Friendship.* Fitzgerald, John T., ed. *Greco-Roman Perspectives on Friendship.* SBLRBS 34. Atlanta: Scholars Press, 1997.

Fitzgerald, "Friendship." Fitzgerald, John T. "Paul and Friendship." Pages 319–43 in *Paul in the Greco-Roman World: A Handbook.* Edited by J. Paul Sampley. Harrisburg, Pa.: Trinity Press International, 2003.

Fitzgerald, "Hospitality." Fitzgerald, John T. "Hospitality." *DNTB* 522–25.

Fitzgerald, "Reconciliation." Fitzgerald, John T. "Paul and Paradigm Shifts: Reconciliation and Its Linkage Group." Pages

241–62 in *Paul beyond the Judaism/Hellenism Divide.* Edited by Troels Engberg-Pedersen. Louisville: Westminster John Knox, 2001.

Fitzgerald, "Ship of Paul." Fitzgerald, Michael. "The Ship of Saint Paul, Part II: Comparative Archaeology." *BA* 53 (1, 1990): 31–39.

Fitzgerald, "Slaves." Fitzgerald, John T. "The Stoics and the Early Christians on the Treatment of Slaves." Pages 141–75 in *Stoicism in Early Christianity.* Edited by Tuomas Rasimus, Troels Engberg-Pedersen, and Ismo Dunderberg. Grand Rapids: Baker Academic, 2010.

Fitzgerald, "Speech." Fitzgerald, Dale K. "Prophetic Speech in Ga Spirit Mediumship." Paper presented at the sixty-eighth annual meeting of the American Anthropological Association, New Orleans, Nov. 21, 1969.

Fitzmyer, *Acts.* Fitzmyer, Joseph A. *The Acts of the Apostles: A New Translation with Introduction and Commentary.* AB 31. New York: Doubleday, 1998.

Fitzmyer, *Apocryphon.* Fitzmyer, Joseph A. *The Genesis Apocryphon of Qumran Cave 1: A Commentary.* 2nd rev. ed. BibOr 18A. Rome: Biblical Institute Press, 1971.

Fitzmyer, "Christianity in Light of the Scrolls." Fitzmyer, Joseph A. "Jewish Christianity in Acts in Light of the Qumran Scrolls." Pages 233–57 in *Studies in Luke-Acts: Essays in Honor of Paul Schubert.* Edited by Leander E. Keck and J. Louis Martyn. Nashville: Abingdon, 1966.

Fitzmyer, "'Elect of God' Text." Fitzmyer, Joseph A. "The Aramaic 'Elect of God' Text from Qumran Cave IV." *CBQ* 27 (4, 1965): 348–72.

Fitzmyer, "Elijah." Fitzmyer, Joseph A. "More about Elijah Coming First." *JBL* 104 (2, 1985): 295–96.

Fitzmyer, *Essays.* Fitzmyer, Joseph A. *Essays on the Semitic Background of the New Testament.* 2nd ed. SBLSBS 5. Missoula, Mont.: Scholars Press, 1974.

Fitzmyer, "Essene." Fitzmyer, Joseph A. "The Qumran Community: Essene or Sadducean?" *HeyJ* 36 (4, 1995): 467–76.

Fitzmyer, *Luke.* Fitzmyer, Joseph A. *The Gospel according to Luke (I–IX).* AB 28. Garden City, N.Y.: Doubleday, 1981.

Fitzmyer, "Melchizedek." Fitzmyer, Joseph A. "Melchizedek in the MT, LXX, and the NT." *Bib* 81 (1, 2000): 63–69.

Fitzmyer, *One.* Fitzmyer, Joseph A. *The One Who Is to Come.* Grand Rapids: Eerdmans, 2007.

Fitzmyer, "Ossuary." Fitzmyer, Joseph A. "The James Ossuary and Its Implications." *TD* 52 (4, 2005): 323–39.

Fitzmyer, "Paul and Scrolls." Fitzmyer, Joseph A. "Paul and the Dead Sea Scrolls." Pages 599–621 in vol. 2 of *The Dead Sea Scrolls after Fifty Years*. Edited by Peter W. Flint and James C. Vanderkam. 2 vols. Leiden: Brill, 1999.

Fitzmyer, "Quotations." Fitzmyer, Joseph A. "The Use of Explicit Old Testament Quotations in Qumran Literature and in the New Testament." *NTS* 7 (4, 1961): 297–333.

Fitzmyer, "Role of Spirit." Fitzmyer, Joseph A. "The Role of the Spirit in Luke-Acts." Pages 165–83 in *The Unity of Luke-Acts*. Edited by Joseph Verheyden. BETL 142. Leuven: Leuven University Press, 1999.

Fitzmyer, *Romans*. Fitzmyer, Joseph A. *Romans: A New Translation with Introduction and Commentary*. AB 33. New York: Doubleday, 1993.

Fitzmyer, "Sacrifice." Fitzmyer, Joseph A. "The Sacrifice of Isaac in Qumran Literature." *Bib* 83 (2, 2002): 211–29.

Fitzmyer, "Son of God." Fitzmyer, Joseph A. "4Q246: The 'Son of God' Document from Qumran." *Bib* 74 (2, 1993): 153–74.

Fitzmyer, *Theologian*. Fitzmyer, Joseph A. *Luke the Theologian: Aspects of His Teaching*. New York: Paulist, 1989.

Fitzmyer, *Wandering Aramean*. Fitzmyer, Joseph A. *A Wandering Aramean: Collected Aramaic Essays*. SBLMS 25. Missoula, Mont.: Scholars Press, 1979.

Fitzpatrick, "Carneades." Fitzpatrick, Matthew P. "Carneades and the Conceit of Rome: Transhistorical Approaches to Imperialism." *GR* 57 (1, 2010): 1–20.

Flaig, "Gladiator." Flaig, Egon. "Gladiator." *BrillPauly* 5:855–57.

Flanagan, "Women." Flanagan, Neal M. "The Position of Women in the Writings of St. Luke." *Marianum* 40 (3–4, 1978): 288–304.

Flannery, *Anguish*. Flannery, Edward H. *The Anguish of the Jews: Twenty-Three Centuries of Anti-Semitism*. Preface by John M. Oesterreicher. New York: Macmillan, 1965.

Flattery, *Spirit*. Flattery, George M. *A Biblical Theology of the Holy Spirit*. 3 vols. Springfield, Mo.: Global University, 2009.

Fleischer, *Artemis von Ephesos*. Fleischer, Robert. *Artemis von Ephesos und verwandte Kultstatuen aus Anatolien und Syrien*. ÉPROER 35. Leiden: Brill, 1973.

Fleming, "Dames." Fleming, Thomas. "Des dames du temps jadis." *CJ* 82 (1986): 73–80.

Fleming, "Savoring." Fleming, Stuart J. "Savoring the Grape." *Archaeology* 54 (6, 2001): 26–27.

Flemming, *Contextualization*. Flemming, Dean. *Contextualization in the New Testament: Patterns for Theology and Mission*. Downers Grove, Ill.: InterVarsity, 2005.

Flemming, "Contextualizing." Flemming, Dean. "Contextualizing the Gospel in Athens: Paul's Areopagus Address as a Paradigm for Missionary Communication." *Missiology* 30 (2, 2002): 199–214.

Flemming, "Women and Medicine." Flemming, Rebecca. "Women, Writing, and Medicine in the Classical World." *CQ* 57 (1, 2007): 257–79.

Flender, *Theologian*. Flender, Helmut. *St Luke: Theologian of Redemptive History*. Translated by Reginald H. Fuller and Ilse Fuller. London: SPCK, 1967.

Flesher, "Dialect." Flesher, Paul V. M. "The Aramaic Dialect of the James Ossuary Inscription." *AramSt* 2 (1, 2004): 37–55.

Fless and Moede, "Music." Fless, Friederike, and Katja Moede. "Music and Dance: Forms of Representation in Pictorial and Written Sources." Pages 249–62 in *A Companion to Roman Religion*. Edited by Jörg Rüpke. BCompAW. Oxford: Blackwell, 2011.

Flessen, *Man*. Flessen, Bonnie J. *An Exemplary Man: Cornelius and Characterization in Acts 10*. Eugene, Ore.: Pickwick, 2011.

Fletcher, "Correction." Fletcher, Kristopher F. B. "Ovidian 'Correction' of the Biblical Flood?" *CP* 105 (2, 2010): 209–13.

Fletcher-Louis, "4Q374." Fletcher-Louis, Crispin H. T. "4Q374—A Discourse on the Sinai Tradition: The Deification of Moses and Early Christology." *DSD* 3 (3, 1996): 236–52.

Fletcher-Louis, *Angels*. Fletcher-Louis, Crispin H. T. *Luke-Acts: Angels, Christology, and Soteriology*. WUNT 2.94. Tübingen: J. C. B. Mohr, 1997.

Fletcher-Louis, "Reflections." Fletcher-Louis, Crispin H. T. "Some Reflections on Angelomorphic Humanity Texts among the Dead Sea Scrolls." *DSD* 7 (3, 2000): 292–312.

Flew, *God*. Flew, Antony, with Roy Abraham Varghese. *There Is a God: How the World's Most Notorious Atheist Changed His Mind*. New York: HarperOne, 2007.

Flichy, "État des recherches." Flichy, Odile. "État des recherches actuelles sur les Actes des apôtres." Pages 13–42 in *Les Actes des apôtres—Histoire, récit, théologie: XXe congrès de l'Association catholique française pour l'étude de la Bible (Angers, 2003)*. Edited by Michel Berder. LD 199. Paris: Cerf, 2005.

Flichy, *Oeuvre de Luc*. Flichy, Odile. *L'oeuvre de Luc: L'Évangile et les Actes des apôtres*. CaÉ 114. Paris: Cerf, 2000.

Flint, "Psalms and Hymns." Flint, Peter W. "Psalms and Hymns of Qumran." *DNTB* 847–53.

Flint, "Psalms in Light of Scrolls." Flint, Peter W. "The Book of Psalms in the Light of the Dead Sea Scrolls." *VT* 48 (4, 1998): 453–72.

Flohr, "*Fullones*." Flohr, M. "*Fullones* and Roman Society: A Reconsideration." *JRA* 16 (2003): 447–50.

Flokstra, "Sources." Flokstra, Gerald J., III. "Sources for the Initial Evidence Discussion: A Bibliographical Essay." *AJPS* 2 (2, 1999): 243–59.

Flory, "*Augusta*." Flory, Marleen B. "The Meaning of *Augusta* in the Julio-Claudian Period." *AJAH* 13 (2, 1988): 113–38.

Flory, "Deification." Flory, Marleen B. "The Deification of Roman Women." *AHB* 9 (3–4, 1995): 127–34.

Flory, "Family." Flory, Marleen B. "Family and 'familia': A Study of Social Relations in Slavery." PhD diss., Yale University, 1975.

Flory, "Integration." Flory, Marleen B. "The Integration of Women into the Roman Triumph." *Historia* 47 (4, 1998): 489–94.

Flory, "Livia and History." Flory, Marleen B. "Livia and the History of Public Honorific Statues for Women in Rome." *TAPA* 123 (1993): 287–308.

Flory, "Where Women Precede Men." Flory, Marleen B. "Where Women Precede Men: Factors Influencing the Order of Names in Roman Epitaphs." *CJ* 79 (3, 1984): 216–24.

Flower, "Alternatives." Flower, Harriet I. "Alternatives to Written History in Republican Rome." Pages 65–76 in *The Cambridge Companion to the Roman Historians*. Edited by Andrew Feldherr. Cambridge: Cambridge University Press, 2009.

Flower, *Theopompus*. Flower, Michael A. *Theopompus of Chios: History and Rhetoric in the Fourth Century B.C.* Oxford: Clarendon, 1994.

Flowers, "En pneumati." Flowers, Harold J. "En pneumati hagiō kai puri." *ExpT* 64 (5, 1953): 155–56.

Flury, "Onomatopoeia." Flury, Peter. "Onomatopoeia." *BrillPauly* 10:142–43.

Flusser, "Goddess of Samaria." Flusser, David. "The Great Goddess of Samaria." *IEJ* 25 (1, 1975): 13–20.

Flusser, *Judaism*. Flusser, David. *Judaism and the Origins of Christianity*. Jerusalem: Magnes, 1988.

Flusser, "Laying-On of Hands." Flusser, David. "Healing through the Laying-On of Hands in a Dead Sea Scroll." *IEJ* 7 (1957): 107–8.

Flusser, "Light on First Church." Flusser, David. "Ostracon from Qumran Throws

Light on First Church." *JerPersp* 53 (1997): 12–15.

Flusser, "Love." Flusser, David. "Jesus, His Ancestry, and the Commandment of Love." Pages 153–76 in *Jesus' Jewishness: Exploring the Place of Jesus within Early Judaism*. Edited by James H. Charlesworth. Philadelphia: American Interfaith Institute; New York: Crossroad, 1991.

Flusser, "Paganism." Flusser, David. "Paganism in Palestine." *JPFC* 1065–1100.

Flusser, "Roots." Flusser, David. "Jewish Roots of the Liturgical Trishagion." *Imm* 3 (1973–74): 37–43.

Flusser, *Sage*. Flusser, David, with R. Steven Notley. *The Sage from Galilee: Rediscovering Jesus' Genius*. Introduction by James H. Charlesworth. 4th ed. Grand Rapids and Cambridge: Eerdmans, 2007.

Flusser, "Salvation." Flusser, David. "Salvation Present and Future." *Numen* 16 (2, 1969): 139–55.

Flusser, "Upanishads." Flusser, David. "Abraham and the Upanishads." *Imm* 20 (1986): 53–61.

Flynn et al., "Dependence." Flynn, Patrick M., et al. "Looking Back on Cocaine Dependence: Reasons for Recovery." *American Journal on Addictions* 12 (5, 2003): 398–411.

Foakes-Jackson, *Acts*. Foakes-Jackson, F. J. *The Acts of the Apostles*. MNTC. London: Hodder & Stoughton, 1931.

Foakes-Jackson, *Criticism*. Foakes-Jackson, F. J. *St. Luke and a Modern Writer—A Study in Criticism: A Praelection Delivered before the Council of the Senate*. Cambridge: W. Heffer & Sons, 1916.

Foakes-Jackson, *Peter*. Foakes-Jackson, F. J. *Peter—Prince of the Apostles: A Study in the History and Tradition of Christianity*. New York: Doran, 1927.

Foakes-Jackson and Lake, "Background of Jewish History." Foakes-Jackson, F. J., and Kirsopp Lake. "Background of Jewish History." *BegChr* 1:1–34.

Foakes-Jackson and Lake, "Development." Foakes-Jackson, F. J., and Kirsopp Lake. "The Development of Thought on the Spirit, the Church, and Baptism." *BegChr* 1:321–44.

Foakes-Jackson and Lake, "Dispersion." Foakes-Jackson, F. J., and Kirsopp Lake. "The Dispersion." *BegChr* 1:137–68.

Foakes-Jackson and Lake, "Internal Evidence of Acts." Foakes-Jackson, F. J., and Kirsopp Lake. "The Internal Evidence of Acts." *BegChr* 2:121–204.

Foakes-Jackson and Lake, "Teaching." Foakes-Jackson, F. J., and Kirsopp Lake. "The Public Teaching of Jesus and His Choice of the Twelve." *BegChr* 1:267–99.

Foakes-Jackson and Lake, "Zealots." Foakes-Jackson, F. J., and Kirsopp Lake. "The Zealots." *BegChr* 1:421–25.

Focant, "Fils de l'homme." Focant, Camille. "Du fils de l'homme assis (Lc 22,69) au fils de l'homme debout (Ac 7,56): Enjeux théologique et littéraire d'un changement sémantique." Pages 563–76 in *The Unity of Luke-Acts*. Edited by Joseph Verheyden. BETL 142. Leuven: Leuven University Press, 1999.

Foerster, "Art." Foerster, G. "Art and Architecture in Palestine." *JPFC* 971–1006.

Foerster, "Geist." Foerster, Werner. "Der heilige Geist im Spätjudentum." *NTS* 8 (2, 1962): 117–34.

Foerster, "Κύριος." Foerster, Werner. "Κύριος." *TDNT* 3:1039–58.

Foerster, "Survey of Synagogues." Foerster, G. "A Survey of Ancient Diaspora Synagogues." Pages 164–72 in *Ancient Synagogues Revealed*. Edited by L. I. Levine. Jerusalem: Israel Exploration Society, 1981.

Fogel, "Friends." Fogel, Jerise. "Can Girls Be Friends? Talking about Gender in Cicero's de Amicitia." *CW* 103 (1, 2009): 77–87.

Fogel and Engerman, *Time*. Fogel, Robert William, and Stanley L. Engerman. *Time on the Cross: The Economics of American Negro Slavery*. Boston: Little, Brown, 1974.

Fogelin, *Defense*. Fogelin, Robert J. *A Defense of Hume on Miracles*. Princeton: Princeton University Press, 2003.

Fögen, *Tears*. Fögen, Thorsten, ed. *Tears in the Graeco-Roman World*. Berlin: de Gruyter, 2009.

Foley, "Conception." Foley, Helene P. "The Conception of Women in Athenian Drama." Pages 127–68 in *Reflections of Women in Antiquity*. Edited by Helene P. Foley. New York: Gordon & Breach Science, 1981.

Folwarski, "Point of Contact." Folwarski, Shirley. "Point of Contact." *Guideposts* (July 1994): 28–29.

Foner, *Reconstruction*. Foner, Eric. *Reconstruction: America's Unfinished Revolution, 1863–1877*. New York: Harper & Row, 1988.

Fontana, "Historians." Fontana, Benedetto. "Ancient Roman Historians and Early Modern Political Theory." Pages 362–79 in *A Companion to Greek and Roman Historiography*. Edited by John Marincola. 2 vols. Oxford: Blackwell, 2007.

Fontana, "Opera." Fontana, Raniero. "L'opera' di Luca: Storia dello Spirito e alchimia del'umano (At 1–15)." *BeO* 48 (4, 2001): 215–34.

Fontana, "Universalismo." Fontana, Raniero. "Universalismo noachide e religioni (osservazioni a margine di Atti 15)." *EstBib* 65 (1–2, 2007): 147–57.

Fontenrose, *Delphic Oracle*. Fontenrose, Joseph E. *The Delphic Oracle: Its Response and Operations*. Berkeley: University of California Press, 1978.

Forbes, "Books." Forbes, Clarence A. "Books for the Burning." *TAPA* 67 (1936): 114–25.

Forbes, "Comparison." Forbes, Christopher. "Paul and Rhetorical Comparison." Pages 134–71 in *Paul in the Greco-Roman World: A Handbook*. Edited by J. Paul Sampley. Harrisburg, Pa.: Trinity Press International, 2003.

Forbes, "Demonology." Forbes, Christopher. "Pauline Demonology and/or Cosmology? Principalities, Powers, and the Elements of the World in Their Hellenistic Context." *JSNT* 85 (2002): 51–73.

Forbes, "Inspired Speech." Forbes, Christopher. "Early Christian Inspired Speech and Hellenistic Popular Religion." *NovT* 28 (3, 1986): 257–70.

Forbes, "Paul." Forbes, Christopher. "Paul among the Greeks." Pages 124–42 in *All Things to All Cultures: Paul among Jews, Greeks, and Romans*. Edited by Mark Harding and Alanna Nobbs. Grand Rapids: Eerdmans, 2013.

Forbes, "Principalities." Forbes, Christopher. "Paul's Principalities and Powers: Demythologizing Apocalyptic?" *JSNT* 82 (2001): 61–88.

Forbes, *Prophecy*. Forbes, Christopher. *Prophecy and Inspired Speech in Early Christianity and Its Hellenistic Environment*. WUNT 2.75. Tübingen: J. C. B. Mohr, 1995. Repr., Peabody, Mass.: Hendrickson, 1997.

Forbes, "Self-Praise." Forbes, Christopher. "Comparison, Self-Praise, and Irony: Paul's Boasting and the Conventions of Hellenistic Rhetoric." *NTS* 32 (1, 1986): 1–30.

Forbes, *Technology*. Forbes, R. J. *Studies in Ancient Technology*. 9 vols. Leiden: Brill, 1955–64.

Forbes and Browning, "Glossa." Forbes, Peter B. R., and Robert Browning. "Glossa, Glossary: Greek." *OCD*³ 639–40.

Forbis, "Image." Forbis, Elizabeth P. "Women's Public Image in Italian Honorary Inscriptions." *AJP* 111 (4, 1990): 493–512.

Force, "Breakdown." Force, James E. "The Breakdown of the Newtonian Synthesis of Science and Religion: Hume, Newton, and the Royal Society." Pages 143–63 in *Essays on the Context, Nature, and Influence of Isaac Newton's Theology*, by James E. Force and Richard H. Popkin. IntArHistI 129. Dordrecht: Kluwer Academic, 1990.

Force, "Dominion." Force, James E. "Newton's God of Dominion: The Unity of Newton's Theological, Scientific, and Political Thought." Pages 75–102 in *Essays on the Context, Nature, and Influence of Isaac Newton's Theology*, by James E. Force and Richard H. Popkin. ArIntHistI 129. Dordrecht: Kluwer Academic, 1990.

Ford, *Abomination*. Ford, Desmond. *The Abomination of Desolation in Biblical Eschatology*. Washington, D.C.: University Press of America, 1979.

Ford, "Animal Symbolism." Ford, J. Massyngberde. "Jewish Law and Animal Symbolism." *JSJ* 10 (2, 1979): 203–12.

Ford, "Crucifixion." Ford, J. Massyngberde. "The Crucifixion of Women in Antiquity." *JHC* 3 (2, 1996): 291–309.

Ford, "Influence." Ford, J. Massyngberde. "Can We Exclude Samaritan Influence from Qumran?" *RevQ* 6 (1, 1967): 109–29.

Ford, *Revelation*. Ford, J. Massyngberde. *Revelation*. AB 38. Garden City, N.Y.: Doubleday, 1975.

"Forgotten Slaves." "Forgotten Slaves." *WPR* (Janury 1991): 57.

Forman, *Art*. Forman, Werner, and Bedřich Forman. *Egyptian Art*. Text by Milada Vilímková. Translated by Till Gottheiner. Preface by Mohammed H. Abu-ur-Rahman. London: Peter Nevill, 1962.

Fornara, *Nature of History*. Fornara, C. W. *The Nature of History in Ancient Greece and Rome*. Berkeley: University of California Press, 1983.

Fornberg, "Abraham." Fornberg, Tord. "Abraham in the Time of Christ." *SEÅ* 64 (1999): 115–23.

Fornberg, "Times." Fornberg, Tord. "Abraham in the Times of Christ." [In Arabic.] *Bayn al-Nahrayn* 26 (103–4, 1998): 250–57. (Abstract: *NTA* 43:544.)

Forrester, "Pentecost." Forrester, Duncan B. "The Perennial Pentecost." *ExpT* 116 (7, 2005): 224–27.

Förster, "Sprach Paulus." Förster, Niclas. "Sprach Paulus einen kilikischen Koine-Dialekt? Ein bisher übersehener Aspekt in der Biographie des Paulus." *ZNW* 88 (1997): 316–21.

Forsythe, *Livy*. Forsythe, Gary. *Livy and Early Rome: A Study in Historical Method and Judgment*. Historia, Einzelschriften 132. Stuttgart: Franz Steiner, 1999.

Forsythe, "Quadrigarius." Forsythe, Gary. "Claudius Quadrigarius and Livy's Second Pentad." Pages 391–96 in *A Companion to Greek and Roman Historiography*. Edited by John Marincola. 2 vols. Oxford: Blackwell, 2007.

Forte, "Echoes Revisited." Forte, A. J. "Book I of Josephus' 'Bellum iudaicum': Sources and Classical Echoes Revisited." *Didaskalia* 36 (2, 2006): 31–52.

Fortenbaugh, "Cicero." Fortenbaugh, William W. "Cicero as a Reporter of Aristotelian and Theophrastean Rhetorical Doctrine." *Rhetorica* 23 (1, 2005): 37–64.

Fortes, "Kinship." Fortes, Meyer. "Kinship and Marriage among the Ashanti." Pages 252–84 in *African Systems of Kinship and Marriage*. Edited by A. R. Radcliffe-Brown and Daryll Forde. New York: Oxford University Press, 1950.

Fortini, *Carcer*. Fortini, Patrizia. *Carcer tullianum: il carcere mamertino al Foro romano*. Guide Electa per la Soprintendenza archeologica di Roma. Milano: Electa; Roma: Soprintendenza archeologica di Roma, 1998.

Fossum, "Angel in Jude." Fossum, Jarl. "Kyrios Jesus as the Angel of the Lord in Jude 5–7." *NTS* 33 (2, 1987): 226–43.

Fossum, "Angel in Samaritanism." Fossum, Jarl. "The Angel of the Lord in Samaritanism." *JSS* 46 (1, 2001): 51–75.

Fossum, *Name*. Fossum, Jarl E. *The Name of God and the Angel of the Lord: Samaritan and Jewish Concepts of Intermediation and the Origin of Gnosticism*. Tübingen: Mohr, 1985.

Fossum, "Simon Magus." Fossum, Jarl E. "Simon Magus." Pages 779–81 in *Dictionary of Deities and Demons in the Bible*. 2nd rev. ed. Edited by Karel van der Toorn, Bob Becking, and Pieter W. van der Horst. Leiden: Brill; Grand Rapids: Eerdmans, 1999.

Fossum, "Son of God." Fossum, Jarl E. "Son of God." Pages 788–94 in *Dictionary of Deities and Demons in the Bible*. 2nd rev. ed. Edited by Karel van der Toorn, Bob Becking, and Pieter W. van der Horst. Leiden: Brill; Grand Rapids: Eerdmans, 1999.

Foster, "Continuity." Foster, Brian L. "Continuity and Change in Rural Thai Family Structure." *JAnthRes* 31 (Spring 1975): 34–50.

Foster, "Educating." Foster, Paul. "Educating Jesus: The Search for a Plausible Context." *JSHJ* 4 (1, 2006): 7–33.

Foster, "Introduction." Foster, B. O. Introduction. Pages ix–xxxv in vol. 1 of Livy, *Ab urbe condita*. Translated by B. O. Foster et al. 14 vols. LCL. Cambridge, Mass.: Harvard University Press, 1919–59.

Foster, "Rhetoric." Foster, Edith. "The Rhetoric of Materials: Thucydides and Lucretius." *AJP* 130 (3, 2009): 367–99.

Foucart, *Associations religieuses*. Foucart, P. *Des associations religieuses chez les Grecs: Thiases, Éranes, Orgéons*. Paris: Klincksieck, 1873. Repr., New York: Arno, 1975.

Fournier, *Episode*. Fournier, Marianne. *The Episode at Lystra: A Rhetorical and Semiotic Analysis of Acts 14:7–20a*. AUSt 7.197. New York: Lang, 1997.

Fowl, "Imitation." Fowl, Stephen E. "Imitation of Paul/of Christ." *DPL* 429–31.

Fowler, *Constructions*. Fowler, Don. *Roman Constructions: Readings in Postmodern Latin*. Oxford: Oxford University Press, 2000.

Fowler and Fowler, "Golden Age." Fowler, Peta G., and Don P. Fowler. "Golden Age." *OCD*³ 642.

Fox, "Dionysius." Fox, Matthew. "Dionysius, Lucian, and the Prejudice against Rhetoric in History." *JRS* 91 (2001): 76–93.

Fox, "Rhetoric." Fox, Matthew. "Rhetoric and Literature at Rome." Pages 369–81 in *A Companion to Roman Rhetoric*. Edited by William Dominik and Jon Hall. Oxford: Blackwell, 2007.

Fox, "Thucydides." Fox, Robin Lane. "Thucydides and Documentary History." *CQ* 60 (1, 2010): 11–29.

Fox, "Witchcraft." Fox, J. Robin. "Witchcraft and Clanship in Cochiti Therapy." Pages 174–200 in *Magic, Faith, and Healing: Studies in Primitive Psychiatry Today*. Edited by Ari Kiev. Foreword by Jerome D. Frank. New York: Free Press, 1964.

Foxe's Book of Martyrs. Foxe, John. *Foxe's Book of Martyrs*. Edited by W. Grinton Berry. Grand Rapids: Revell, 1998.

Foxhall, "Food Supply." Foxhall, Lin. "Food Supply: Greek." *OCD*³ 604.

Foxhall, "Tenant." Foxhall, Lin. "The Dependent Tenant: Land Leasing and Labour in Italy and Greece." *JRS* 80 (1990): 97–114 and plate 3.

Fraade, "Rhetoric." Fraade, Steven D. "Rhetoric and Hermeneutics in Miqsat Ma'ase ha-Torah (4QMMT): The Case of the Blessings and Curses." *DSD* 10 (1, 2003): 150–61.

Frahm, Jansen-Winkeln, and Wiesehöfer, "Historiography: Ancient Orient." Frahm, Eckart, Karl Jansen-Winkeln, and Josef Wiesehöfer. "Historiography: Ancient Orient." *BrillPauly* 6:415–18.

Frame, *Thessalonians*. Frame, James Everett. *A Critical and Exegetical Commentary on the Epistles of St. Paul to the Thessalonians*. ICC. Edinburgh: T&T Clark, 1912.

France, "Authenticity." France, R. T. "The Authenticity of the Sayings of Jesus." Pages 101–43 in *History, Criticism, and Faith*. Edited by Colin Brown. Downers Grove, Ill.: InterVarsity, 1976.

France, "Barnabas." France, R. T. "Barnabas—Son of Encouragement." *Them* 4 (1, 1978): 3–6.

France, "Exegesis." France, R. T. "Exegesis in Practice: Two Examples." Pages 252–81 in *New Testament Interpretation: Essays* on *Principles and Methods*. Edited by I. Howard Marshall. Grand Rapids: Eerdmans, 1977.

France, "God and Mammon." France, R. T. "God and Mammon." *EvQ* 51 (1, 1979): 3–21.

France, *Gospel of Matthew*. France, R. T. *The Gospel of Matthew*. NICNT. Grand Rapids: Eerdmans, 2007.

France, "Jesus the Baptist?" France, R. T. "Jesus the Baptist?" Pages 94–111 in *Jesus of Nazareth, Lord and Christ: Essays on the Historical Jesus and New Testament Christology*. Edited by Joel B. Green and Max Turner. Grand Rapids: Eerdmans; Carlisle, U.K.: Paternoster, 1994.

France, *Mark*. France, R. T. *The Gospel of Mark: A Commentary on the Greek Text*. NIGTC. Grand Rapids: Eerdmans, 2002.

France, *Matthew*. France, R. T. *Matthew*. TNTC. Grand Rapids: Eerdmans, 1985.

France, "Romans." France, R. T. "From Romans to the Real World: Biblical Principles and Cultural Change in Relation to Homosexuality and the Ministry of Women." Pages 234–53 in *Romans and the People of God: Essays in Honor of Gordon D. Fee on the Occasion of His 65th Birthday*. Edited by Sven K. Soderlund and N. T. Wright. Grand Rapids: Eerdmans, 1999.

Francis, "Graffiti." Francis, E. D. "Mithraic Graffiti from Dura-Europos." Pages 424–45 in vol. 2 of *Mithraic Studies: Proceedings of the First International Congress of Mithraic Studies*. Edited by John R. Hinnells. 2 vols. Manchester, U.K.: Manchester University Press, 1975.

Francis, "Humility." Francis, Fred O. "Humility and Angelic Worship in Col 2:18." Pages 163–95 in *Conflict at Colossae: A Problem in the Interpretation of Early Christianity Illustrated by Selected Modern Studies*. Edited and translated by Fred O. Francis and Wayne A. Meeks. SBLSBS 4. Missoula, Mont.: SBL, 1973.

Francis, "Maidens." Francis, James A. "Metal Maidens, Achilles' Shield, and Pandora: The Beginnings of 'Ekphrasis.'" *AJP* 130 (1, 2009): 1–23.

Francis, "Three Graces." Francis, Jane. "The Three Graces: Composition and Meaning in a Roman Context." *GR* 49 (2, 2002): 180–98.

Francis, "Truthful Fiction." Francis, James A. "Truthful Fiction: New Questions to Old Answers on Philostratus' *Life of Apollonius*." *AJP* 119 (3, 1998): 419–41.

Francisco, "Amos." Francisco, Clyde T. "Teaching Amos in the Churches." *Rev Exp* 63 (4, 1966): 413–25.

Franco, "Scale." Franco, Juan N. "An Acculturation Scale for Mexican-American Children." *JGPsyc* 108 (1983): 175–81.

Frank, *Aspects*. Frank, Tenney. *Aspects of Social Behavior in Ancient Rome*. Cambridge, Mass.: Harvard University Press, 1932.

Frank, "Devotion." Frank, Georgia. "Lay Devotion in Context." Pages 531–47 in *Constantine to c. 600*. Edited by Augustine Casiday and Frederick W. Norris. Vol. 2 of *The Cambridge History of Christianity*. 9 vols. Cambridge: Cambridge University Press, 2007.

Frank, *Persuasion*. Frank, Jerome D. *Persuasion and Healing: A Comparative Study of Psychotherapy*. Baltimore: Johns Hopkins, 1961.

Franke, "Tribunus militum." Franke, Thomas. "Tribunus militum." *BrillPauly* 14:903–4.

Franke, "Truth in Time." Franke, William. "On Doing the Truth in Time: The *Aeneid*'s Invention of Poetic Prophecy." *Arion* 19 (1, 2011): 53–63.

Frankemölle, "Apostoł Paweł." Frankemölle, H. "Apostoł Paweł i jego interpretacja śmierci Jezusa Chrystusa (Apostel Paulus und seine Interpretation des Todes Jesu Christi)." *ColT* 61 (2, 1991): 5–16.

Frankenberry, *Faith*. Frankenberry, Nancy K. *The Faith of Scientists in Their Words*. Princeton: Princeton University Press, 2008.

Frankforter, *History*. Frankforter, A. Daniel. *A History of the Christian Movement: The Development of Christian Institutions*. Chicago: Nelson-Hall, 1978.

Frankfurter, "Curses." Frankfurter, David. "Curses, Blessings, and Ritual Authority: Egyptian Magic in Comparative Perspective." *JANER* 5 (2005): 157–85.

Frankfurter, "Egyptian Response to Revolt." Frankfurter, David. "Lest Egypt's City Be Deserted: Religion and Ideology in the Egyptian Response to the Jewish Revolt (116–117 C.E.)." *JJS* 43 (2, 1992): 203–20.

Frankfurter, "Magic." Frankfurter, David. "The Magic of Writing and the Writing of Magic: The Power of the Word in Egyptian and Greek Traditions." *Helios* 21 (1994): 189–221.

Frankfurter, "Perils." Frankfurter, David. "The Perils of Love: Magic and Countermagic in Coptic Egypt." *JHistSex* 10 (3–4, 2001): 480–500.

Frankfurter, *Religion in Egypt*. Frankfurter, David. *Religion in Roman Egypt: Assimilation and Resistance*. Princeton: Princeton University Press, 1998.

Frankfurter, "Ritual Expertise." Frankfurter, David. "Ritual Expertise in Roman Egypt and the Problem of the Category 'Magician.'" Pages 115–35 in *Envisioning Magic: A Princeton Seminar and Symposium*. Edited by Peter Schäfer and Hans G. Kippenberg. SHR 75. Leiden: Brill, 1997.

Franklin, *Interpreter*. Franklin, Eric. *Luke: Interpreter of Paul, Critic of Matthew*. JSNTSup 92. Sheffield, U.K.: JSOT Press, 1994.

Franklin, "Literacy." Franklin, James L., Jr. "Literacy and the Parietal Inscriptions of Pompeii." Pages 77–98 in *Literacy in the Roman World*. Edited by M. Beard et al. JRASS 3. Ann Arbor: Journal of Roman Archaeology, University of Michigan, 1991.

Franklin, "Spirit-Baptism." Franklin, Lloyd David. "Spirit-Baptism: Pneumatological Continuance." *RevExp* 94 (1, 1997): 15–30.

Franz, "Daimons." Franz, Marie-Louise von. "Daimons and the Inner Companion." *Parab* 6 (4, 1981): 36–44.

Frateantonio, "Haruspices." Frateantonio, Christa. "Haruspices: Latin Records." *BrillPauly* 5:1154–56.

Frateantonio, "Miracles." Frateantonio, Christa. "Miracles, Miracle-workers: Greco-Roman." *BrillPauly* 9:52–53.

Frateantonio, "Promanteia." Frateantonio, Christa. "Promanteia." *BrillPauly* 12:4–5.

Frateantonio, "Promantis." Frateantonio, Christa. "Promantis." *BrillPauly* 12:5.

Frateantonio, "Superstitio." Frateantonio, Christa. "Superstitio." *BrillPauly* 13:952–54.

Frateantonio, "Votive Offerings." Frateantonio, Christa. "Votive Offerings: Classical Antiquity." *BrillPauly* 15:526–28.

Frede, "Fate." Frede, Dorothea. "Fate." *Brill Pauly* 5:366–68.

Frede, "Monotheism." Frede, Michael. "Monotheism and Pagan Philosophy in Later Antiquity." Pages 41–68 in *Pagan Monotheism in Late Antiquity*. Edited by Polymnia Athanassiadi and Michael Frede. Oxford: Oxford University Press, 1999.

Frede, "Pleasure." Frede, Dorothea. "Pleasure." *BrillPauly* 11:366–68.

Frede, "Theano." Frede, Michael. "Theano." *BrillPauly* 14:377–78.

Fredrickson, "Free Speech." Fredrickson, David E. "Free Speech in Pauline Political Theology." *WW* 12 (4, 1992): 345–51.

Fredrickson, "Hardships." Fredrickson, David E. "Paul, Hardships, and Suffering." Pages 172–97 in *Paul in the Greco-Roman World: A Handbook*. Edited by J. Paul Sampley. Harrisburg, Pa.: Trinity Press International, 2003.

Fredrickson, "No Noose." Fredrickson, David E. "No Noose Is Good News: Leadership as a Theological Problem in the Corinthian Correspondence." *WW* 16 (4, 1996): 420–26.

Fredrickson, "Tears." Fredrickson, David E. "'Through Many Tears' (2 Cor 2:4):

Paul's Grieving Letter and the Occasion of 2 Corinthians 1–7." Pages 161–79 in *Paul and Pathos*. Edited by Thomas H. Olbricht and Jerry L. Sumney. SBLSymS 16. Atlanta: SBL, 2001.

Freed and Freed, "Possession." Freed, S. S., and R. R. Freed. "Spirit Possession as an Illness in a North American Village." *Ethnology* 3 (1964): 152–97.

Freedman, "Jacob." Freedman, Harry. "Jacob and Esau: Their Struggle in the Second Century." *JBQ* 23 (2, 1995): 107–15.

Freedman, "Pottery." Freedman, David Noel. "Pottery, Poetry, and Prophecy: An Essay on Biblical Poetry." *JBL* 96 (1, 1977): 5–26.

Freedman and MacAdam, "Witness." Freedman, David Noel, and Henry I. MacAdam. "*Acts* 28:15–31: The Critical Witness to Early Dating of the Synoptic Gospels." *ScrJudCr* 6 (2008): 15–37.

Freeman, "Observations." Freeman, Derek. "Some Observations on Kinship and Political Authority in Samoa." *AmAnth* 66 (3, 1964): 553–68.

Freeman, *Story of Sicily*. Freeman, Edward A. *The Story of Sicily: Phoenician, Greek and Roman*. New York: G. P. Putnam's Sons; London: T. F. Unwin, 1892.

Frei, "Apologetics." Frei, Hans. "Apologetics, Criticism, and the Loss of Narrative Interpretation." Pages 45–64 in *Why Narrative? Readings in Narrative Theology*. Edited by Stanley Hauerwas and L. Gregory Jones. Grand Rapids: Eerdmans, 1989.

Freidzon, *Spirit*. Freidzon, Claudio. *Holy Spirit, I Hunger for You*. Lake Mary, Fla.: Charisma House, Strang, 1997.

Freller, "Evasissemus." Freller, Thomas. "'(. . .) Et cum evasissemus, tunc cognovimus quia Melita insula vocabatur': Der Schiffbruch des hl. Paulus auf 'Melita' und die Installation eines Kults." *ZKG* 115 (1–2, 2004): 117–63.

French, "Roads." French, David. "Acts and the Roman Roads of Asia Minor." Pages 49–58 in *The Book of Acts in Its Graeco-Roman Setting*. Edited by David W. J. Gill and Conrad Gempf. Vol. 2 of *The Book of Acts in Its First Century Setting*. Edited by Bruce W. Winter. Grand Rapids: Eerdmans; Carlisle, U.K.: Paternoster, 1994.

Frend, "Old Testament." Frend, W. H. C. "The Old Testament in the Age of the Greek Apologists, A.D. 130–180." *SJT* 26 (2, 1973): 129–50.

Frend, "Place of Miracles." Frend, W. H. C. "The Place of Miracles in the Conversion of the Ancient World to Christianity." Pages 11–21 in *Signs, Wonders, Miracles: Representations of Divine Power in the Life of the Church; Papers Read at the 2003 Summer Meeting and the 2004 Winter Meeting of the Ecclesiastical History Society*.

Edited by Kate Cooper and Jeremy Gregory. Rochester: Boydell & Brewer, for the Ecclesiastical History Society, 2005.

Frend, *Rise of Christianity*. Frend, W. H. C. *The Rise of Christianity*. Philadelphia: Fortress, 1984.

Frendo, "Inscription." Frendo, Anthony J. "A New Punic Inscription from Zejtun (Malta) and the Goddess Anat-Astarte." *PEQ* 131 (1, 1999): 24–35.

Frenschkowski, "Zauberworte." Frenschkowski, M. "Zauberworte: Linguistische und sprachpsychologische Beobachtungen zur spätantiken griechischen und römischen Magie." *Annali di storia dell'esegesi* 24 (2, 2007): 323–66.

Freston, "Transnationalisation." Freston, Paul. "The Transnationalisation of Brazilian Pentecostalism: The Universal Church of the Kingdom of God." Pages 196–215 in *Between Babel and Pentecost: Transnational Pentecostalism in Africa and Latin America*. Edited by André Corten and Ruth Marshall-Fratani. Bloomington: Indiana University Press, 2001.

Freud, *Interpretation*. Freud, Sigmund. *The Interpretation of Dreams*. Harmondsworth, U.K.: Penguin, 1977.

Freund, "Image." Freund, Richard. "'Created in the Image of God'—Graeco-Roman Jewish Art—New Perspectives from Archaeology." Pages 354–67 in *Text, Image, and Christians in the Graeco-Roman World: A Festschrift in Honor of David Lee Balch*. Edited by Aliou Cissé Niang and Carolyn Osiek. PrTMS 176. Eugene, Ore.: Pickwick, 2012.

Frey, "Fragen." Frey, Jörg. "Fragen um Lukas als 'Historiker' und den historiographischen Charakter der Apostelgeschichte: Eine thematische Annäherung." Pages 1–26 in *Die Apostelgeschichte im Kontext antiker und frühchristlicher Historiographie*. Edited by Jörg Frey, Clare K. Rothschild, and Jens Schröter, with Bettina Rost. BZNWK 162. Berlin: de Gruyter, 2009.

Frey, "Suicide?" Frey, R. G. "Did Socrates Commit Suicide?" *Philosophy* 53 (1978): 106–8.

Frey and Roysircar, "Acculturation and Worldview." Frey, Lisa L., and Gargi Roysircar. "Effects of Acculturation and Worldview for White American, South American, South Asian, and Southeast Asian Students." *IJAC* 26 (3, 2004): 229–48.

Freyne, "Archaeology." Freyne, Sean. "Archaeology and the Historical Jesus." Pages 64–83 in *Jesus and Archaeology*. Edited by James H. Charlesworth. Grand Rapids: Eerdmans, 2006.

Freyne, "Ethos." Freyne, Sean. "The Ethos of First-Century Galilee." *PIBA* 17 (1994): 69–79.

Freyne, *Galilean*. Freyne, Sean. *Jesus, a Jewish Galilean: A New Reading of the Jesus-Story*. London: T&T Clark, 2004.

Freyne, "Galileans." Freyne, Sean. "The Galileans in the Light of Josephus' *Vita*." *NTS* 26 (3, 1980): 397–413.

Freyne, *Galilee and Gospel*. Freyne, Sean. *Galilee and Gospel: Collected Essays*. WUNT 125. Tübingen: Mohr Siebeck, 2000.

Freyne, *Galilee, Jesus*. Freyne, Sean. *Galilee, Jesus, and the Gospels: Literary Approaches and Historical Investigations*. Philadelphia: Fortress, 1988.

Freyne, "Geography." Freyne, Sean. "The Geography, Politics, and Economics of Galilee and the Quest for the Historical Jesus." Pages 75–121 in *Studying the Historical Jesus: Evaluations of the State of Current Research*. Edited by Bruce Chilton and Craig A. Evans. NTTS 19. Leiden: Brill, 1994.

Freyne, "Jesus and Archaeology." Freyne, Sean. "The Historical Jesus and Archaeology." *Explor* 10 (2, 1996): 6.

Freyne, "Relations." Freyne, Sean. "Galilee-Jerusalem Relations according to Josephus' *Life*." *NTS* 33 (4, 1987): 600–609.

Freyne, "Religion." Freyne, Sean. "Galilean Religion of the First Century C.E. against Its Social Background." *PIBA* 5 (1981): 98–114.

Freyne, "'Servant' Community." Freyne, Sean. "Jesus and the 'Servant' Community in Zion: Continuity in Context." Pages 109–24 in *Jesus from Judaism to Christianity: Continuum Approaches to the Historical Jesus*. Edited by Tom Holmén. EurSCO. LNTS 352. London: T&T Clark, 2007.

Frick, "Means and Mode." Frick, Peter. "The Means and Mode of Salvation: A Hermeneutical Proposal for Clarifying Pauline Soteriology." *HBT* 29 (2, 2007): 203–22.

Frickenschmidt, *Evangelium als Biographie*. Frickenschmidt, Dirk. *Evangelium als Biographie: Die vier Evangelien im Rahmen antiker Erzählkunst*. TANZ 22. Tübingen: Francke, 1997.

Friedheim, "Relations judéo-samaritaines." Friedheim, Emmanuel. "Sur les relations judéo-samaritaines en Palestine du Ier au IVème siècle p. C. entre accommodement et éviction." *TZ* 60 (3, 2004): 193–213.

Friedheim, "Remarques." Friedheim, Emmanuel. "Quelques remarques sur l'évocation de Jérusalem dans la littérature Gréco-Latin non chrétienne." *RHPR* 90 (2, 2010): 161–78.

Friedländer, *Life*. Friedländer, Ludwig. *Roman Life and Manners under the Early*

Empire. Translated from the 7th rev. ed. by Leonard A. Magnus, J. H. Freese, and A. B. Gough. 4 vols. London: G. Routledge & Sons; New York: E. P. Dutton, 1908–13.

Friedman, "Features." Friedman, Theodore. "Some Unexplained Features of Ancient Synagogues." *ConsJud* 36 (3, 1983): 35–42.

Friedrichsen, "Agreements." Friedrichsen, Timothy A. "The Matthew-Luke Agreements against Mark: A Survey of Recent Studies, 1974–1989." Pages 335–91 in *L'Évangile de Luc: The Gospel of Luke.* Edited by F. Neirynck. Rev. ed. BETL 32. Leuven: Leuven University Press, 1989.

Frier, "Annuities." Frier, Bruce W. "Subsistence Annuities and Per Capita Income in the Early Roman Empire." *CP* 88 (3, 1993): 222–30.

Frier, "Fertility." Frier, Bruce W. "Natural Fertility and Family Limitation in Roman Marriage." *CP* 89 (4, 1994): 318–33.

Frier, *Landlords.* Frier, Bruce W. *Landlords and Tenants in Imperial Rome.* Princeton: Princeton University Press, 1980.

Frier, "Market in Rome." Frier, Bruce W. "The Rental Market in Early Imperial Rome." *JRS* 67 (1977): 27–37.

Friesen, "Cult." Friesen, Steven J. "The Cult of the Roman Emperors in Ephesos: Temple Wardens, City Titles, and the Interpretation of the Revelation of John." Pages 229–50 in *Ephesos, Metropolis of Asia. An Interdisciplinary Approach to Its Archaeology, Religion, and Culture.* Edited by Helmut Koester. HTS. Valley Forge, Pa.: Trinity Press International, 1995.

Friesen, "Demography." Friesen, Steven J. "Prospects for a Demography of the Pauline Mission: Corinth among the Churches." Pages 351–70 in *Urban Religion in Roman Corinth: Interdisciplinary Approaches.* Edited by Daniel N. Schowalter and Steven J. Friesen. HTS 53. Cambridge, Mass.: Harvard University Press, 2005.

Friesen, "Economics." Friesen, Steven J. "Paul and Economics: The Jerusalem Collection as an Alternative to Patronage." Pages 27–54 in *Paul Unbound: Other Perspectives on the Apostle.* Edited by Mark D. Given. Peabody, Mass.: Hendrickson, 2010.

Friesen, "Ephesus." Friesen, Steven J. "Ephesus: Key to a Vision in Revelation." *BAR* 19 (3, 1993): 24–37.

Friesen, "Poverty." Friesen, Steven J. "Poverty in Pauline Studies: Beyond the So-Called New Consensus." *JSNT* 26 (3, 2004): 323–61.

Friesen, "Wrong Erastus." Friesen, Steven J. "The Wrong Erastus: Ideology, Archaeology, and Exegesis." Pages 231–56 in

Corinth in Context: Comparative Studies on Religion and Society. Edited by Steven J. Friesen et al. NovTSup 134. New York: Brill, 2010.

Frisch, *Inschriften von Ilion.* Frisch, Peter, ed. *Die Inschriften von Ilion.* IGSK 3. Bonn: Rudolf Habelt, 1975.

Frisch and Schutz, "Analysis." Frisch, Jack A., and Noel W. Schutz. "Componential Analysis and Semantic Reconstruction: The Proto Central Yuman Kinship System." *Ethnology* 6 (3, July 1967): 272–93.

Fritsch, *Community.* Fritsch, Charles T. *The Qumran Community: Its History and Scrolls.* New York: Macmillan, 1956.

Fritscher, "Meteorology." Fritscher, Bernhard. "Meteorology: Classical Antiquity." *BrillPauly* 8:796–800.

Fritz, "Temple." Fritz, Volkmar. "What Can Archaeology Tell Us about Solomon's Temple?" *BAR* 13 (4, 1987): 38–49.

Frodsham, *Apostle.* Frodsham, Stanley. *Smith Wigglesworth: Apostle of Faith.* Springfield, Mo.: Gospel Publishing House, 1948.

Frost, "Apocalyptic." Frost, Stanley Brice. "Apocalyptic and History." Pages 134–47 in *The Bible in Its Literary Milieu.* Edited by Vincent L. Tollers and John R. Maier. Grand Rapids: Eerdmans, 1979.

Frost, "Attitudes toward Blacks." Frost, Peter. "Attitudes toward Blacks in the Early Christian Era." *SecCent* 8 (1, 1991): 1–11.

Frost, *Exits.* Frost, K. B. *Exits and Entrances in Menander.* Oxford: Clarendon, 1988.

Frost, *Healing.* Frost, Evelyn. *Christian Healing: A Consideration of the Place of Spiritual Healing in the Church of Today in the Light of the Doctrine and Practice of the Ante-Nicene Church.* Foreword by T. W. Crafer. London and Oxford: A. R. Mowbray, 1940.

Frost, "Preservation." Frost, Frank. "Sausage and Meat Preservation in Antiquity." *GRBS* 40 (3, 1999): 241–52.

Frost, *Revelation.* Frost, Henry W. *Matthew Twenty-Four and the Revelation.* New York: Oxford University Press, 1924.

Früchtel, *Vorstellungen.* Früchtel, Ursula. *Die kosmologischen Vorstellungen bei Philo von Alexandrien: Ein Beitrag zur Geschichte der Genesisexegese.* ALGHJ 2. Leiden: Brill, 1968.

Fry, *Spirits.* Fry, Peter. *Spirits of Protest: Spirit-Mediums and the Articulation of Consensus among Zezuru of Southern Rhodesia (Zimbabwe).* Cambridge: Cambridge University Press, 1976.

Fry et al., *Religions.* Fry, C. George, et al. *Great Asian Religions.* Grand Rapids: Baker, 1984.

Frye, "Faith Healing." Frye, Glenn R. "Faith Healing." Pages 12–18 in *Healing*

and Religious Faith. Edited by Claude A. Frazier. Philadelphia: United Church Press, 1974.

Frye, *Heritage.* Frye, Richard N. *The Heritage of Central Asia: From Antiquity to the Turkish Expansion.* Princeton: Markus Wiener, 1996.

Frye, *Persia.* Frye, Richard N. *The Heritage of Persia.* Cleveland: World, 1963.

Frye, "Problems." Frye, Roland Mushat. "The Synoptic Problems and Analogies in Other Literatures." Pages 261–302 in *The Relationships among the Gospels: An Interdisciplinary Dialogue.* Edited by William O. Walker Jr. San Antonio: Trinity University Press, 1978.

Fryer, "Congregational Renewal." Fryer, Kelly A. "The Book of Acts in Congregational Renewal." *WW* 25 (4, 2005): 448–52, 454–56, 458.

Fryer, "Reconciliation." Fryer, N. S. L. "Reconciliation in Paul's Epistle to the Romans." *Neot* 15 (1981): 34–68.

Frykenberg, "Globalization." Frykenberg, Robert Eric. "Gospel, Globalization, and Hindutva: The Politics of 'Conversion' in India." Pages 108–32 in *Christianity Reborn: The Global Expansion of Evangelicalism in the Twentieth Century.* Edited by Donald M. Lewis. SHCM. Grand Rapids: Eerdmans, 2004.

Frymer-Kensky, "Epic." Frymer-Kensky, Tikva. "The Atrahasis Epic and Its Significance for Our Understanding of Genesis 1–9." *BA* 40 (4, 1977): 147–55.

Frymer-Kensky, "Flood Stories." Frymer-Kensky, Tikva. "What the Babylonian Flood Stories Can and Cannot Teach Us about the Genesis Flood." *BAR* 4 (4, 1977): 32–41.

Fuchs, "Demography." Fuchs, Camil. "Demography, Literacy, and Names Distribution in Ancient Jerusalem—How Many James/Jacob Son of Joseph Brother of Jesus Were There?" *PJBR* 4 (1, 2004): 3–30.

Fuchs, "Techniques." Fuchs, Stephen. "Magic Healing Techniques among the Balahis in Central India." Pages 121–38 in *Magic, Faith, and Healing: Studies in Primitive Psychiatry Today.* Edited by Ari Kiev. Foreword by Jerome D. Frank. New York: Free Press, 1964.

Fuhrer, "Hymn." Fuhrer, Therese. "Hymn: The Latin Hymnus." *BrillPauly* 6:620–22.

Fuks, "Antagonistic Neighbours." Fuks, Gideon. "Antagonistic Neighbours: Ashkelon, Judaea, and the Jews." *JJS* 51 (1, 2000): 42–62.

Fuks, "Freedmen." Fuks, Gideon. "Where Have All the Freedmen Gone? On an Anomaly in the Jewish Grave-Inscriptions from Rome." *JJS* 36 (1, 1985): 25–32.

Fulco, "Lamp." Fulco, William J. "An Early Christian Lamp from Aswan Inscribed NEOΠICT." *RB* 110 (1, 2003): 86–88 and plate.

Fuller, "Baptized." Fuller, R. H. "Was Paul Baptized?" Pages 505–8 in *Les Actes des apôtres: Traditions, rédaction, théologie.* Edited by Jacob Kremer. BETL 48. Gembloux, Belg.: J. Duculot; Leuven: Leuven University Press, 1979.

Fuller, "Classics." Fuller, Reginald H. "Classics and the Gospels: The Seminar." Pages 173–92 in *The Relationships among the Gospels: An Interdisciplinary Dialogue.* Edited by William O. Walker, Jr. San Antonio: Trinity University Press, 1978.

Fuller, *Formation.* Fuller, Reginald H. *The Formation of the Resurrection Narratives.* New York: Macmillan, 1971.

Fuller, *Gospel.* Fuller, Daniel P. *Gospel and Law: Contrast or Continuum?* Grand Rapids: Eerdmans, 1980.

Fuller, "Harman." Fuller, Lois. "Harman, James Tswanya." No pages. *DACB.* Online: http://www.dacb.org/stories /nigeria/harman_james.html.

Fuller, "Hebrews." Fuller, Reginald H. "The Letter to the Hebrews." Pages 1–27 in *Hebrews–James–1 and 2 Peter–Jude–Revelation.* Edited by Gerhard Krodel. ProcC. Philadelphia: Fortress, 1977.

Fuller, "Jews." Fuller, Reginald H. "The 'Jews' in the Fourth Gospel." *Dial* 16 (1, Winter 1977): 31–37.

Fuller, *Restoration.* Fuller, Michael E. *The Restoration of Israel: Israel's Re-gathering and the Fate of the Nations in Early Jewish Literature and Luke-Acts.* BZNWK 138. Berlin: de Gruyter, 2006.

Fuller, "Taiwo." Fuller, Lois. "Taiwo, Paul." No pages. *DACB.* Online: http://www .dacb.org/stories/nigeria/taiwo_paul .html.

Fuller, "Theologia Crucis." Fuller, R. H. "Luke and the Theologia Crucis." Pages 214–20 in *Sin, Salvation, and the Spirit.* Edited by D. Durken. Collegeville, Minn.: Liturgical Press, 1979.

Fuller, "Theology." Fuller, Daniel P. "Biblical Theology and the Analogy of Faith." Pages 195–213 in *Unity and Diversity in New Testament Theology: Essays in Honor of George E. Ladd.* Edited by Robert A. Guelich. Grand Rapids: Eerdmans, 1978.

Fuller, "Tongues." Fuller, R. H. "Tongues in the New Testament." *ACQ* 3 (3, 1963): 162–68.

Fuller, "Tsado." Fuller, Lois. "Tsado, Paul Jiya." No pages. *DACB.* Online: http:// www.dacb.org/stories/nigeria/tsado _paul.html.

Fullmer, *Resurrection.* Fullmer, Paul M. *Resurrection in Mark's Literary-Historical Perspective.* LNTS 360. New York: T&T Clark, 2007.

Fumagalli, "Concezione." Fumagalli, Aristide. "La concezione biblica della coscienza morale. L'originalità di S. Paolo." *RdT* 50 (2, 2009): 195–216.

Fung, "Curse." Fung, Ronald Y. K. "Curse, Accursed, Anathema." *DPL* 199–200.

Furley, "Epicurus." Furley, David John. "Epicurus." *OCD*[3] 532–34.

Furley, *Formation.* Furley, David. *The Formation of the Atomic Theory and Its Earliest Critics.* Vol. 1 of *The Greek Cosmologists.* Cambridge: Cambridge University Press, 1987.

Furley, "Hymn." Furley, William D. "Hymn: The Greek Hymnos." *BrillPauly* 6:616–20.

Furley, "Protrepticus." Furley, David John. "Protrepticus." *OCD*[3] 1265.

Furnham and Wong, "Comparison." Furnham, Adrian, and Linda Wong. "A Cross-cultural Comparison of British and Chinese Beliefs about the Causes, Behaviour Manifestations, and Treatment of Schizophrenia." *PsycRes* 151 (1–2, 2007): 123–38.

Furnish, *II Corinthians.* Furnish, Victor Paul. *II Corinthians.* AB 32A. Garden City, N.Y.: Doubleday, 1984.

Furnish, *Theology.* Furnish, Victor Paul. *The Theology of the First Letter to the Corinthians.* New Testament Theology. Cambridge: Cambridge University Press, 1999.

Furstenberg, "Views." Furstenberg, Yair. "The Rabbinic View of Idolatry and the Roman Political Conception of Divinity." *JR* 90 (3, 2010): 335–66.

Fusco, "Future of Israel." Fusco, Vittorio. "Luke-Acts and the Future of Israel." *NovT* 38 (1, 1996): 1–17.

Fusco, "Sezioni-noi." Fusco, Vittorio. "Le sezioni-noi degli Atti nella discussione recente." *BeO* 25 (2, 1983): 73–86.

Fusillo, "Euhemerus." Fusillo, Massimo. "Euhemerus." *BrillPauly* 5:160–61.

Fusillo, "Novel." Fusillo, Massimo. "Novel: Greek." *BrillPauly* 9:837–42.

Fusillo, "Pseudo-Callisthenes." Fusillo, Massimo. "Pseudo-Callisthenes." *BrillPauly* 12:114.

Gabrielsen, "Brotherhoods." Gabrielsen, V. "Brotherhoods of Faith and Provident Planning: The Non-public Associations of the Greek World." *MHR* 22 (2, 2007): 183–210.

Gaca, "Declaration." Gaca, Kathy L. "Paul's Uncommon Declaration in Romans 1:18–32 and Its Problematic Legacy for Pagan and Christian Relations." Pages 1–33 in *Early Patristic Readings of Romans.* Edited by Kathy L. Gaca and L. L. Welborn. Romans through History and Culture Series. New York and London: T&T Clark, 2005.

Gaca, "Technology." Gaca, Kathy L. "The Reproductive Technology of the Pythagoreans." *CP* 95 (2, 2000): 113–32.

Gaca and Welborn, "Receptions." Gaca, Kathy L., and L. L. Welborn. "Romans in Light of Early Patristic Receptions." Pages i–vi in *Early Patristic Readings of Romans.* Edited by Kathy L. Gaca and L. L. Welborn. Romans through History and Culture Series. New York and London: T&T Clark, 2005.

Gaffin, *Perspectives.* Gaffin, Richard B., Jr. *Perspectives on Pentecost: Studies in New Testament Teaching on the Gifts of the Holy Spirit.* Phillipsburg, N.J.: Presbyterian and Reformed, 1979.

Gaffin, "View." Gaffin, Richard B., Jr. "A Cessationist View." Pages 25–64 in *Are Miraculous Gifts for Today? Four Views.* Edited by Wayne A. Grudem. Grand Rapids: Zondervan, 1996.

Gafni, "Josephus and Maccabees." Gafni, Isaiah M. "Josephus and 1 Maccabees." Pages 116–31 in *Josephus, the Bible, and History.* Edited by Louis H. Feldman and Gohei Hata. Detroit: Wayne State University Press, 1989.

Gagarin, "Thirty Tyrants." Gagarin, Michael. "Thirty Tyrants." *OCD*[3] 1513.

Gage and Beck, "Barren Women and Eunuch." Gage, Warren Austin, and John R. Beck. "The Gospel, Zion's Barren Woman, and the Ethiopian Eunuch." *Crux* 30 (2, 1994): 35–43.

Gager, *Anti-Semitism.* Gager, John G. *The Origins of Anti-Semitism: Attitudes toward Judaism in Pagan and Christian Antiquity.* New York: Oxford University Press, 1983.

Gager, "Class." Gager, John G. "Religion and Social Class in the Early Roman Empire." Pages 99–120 in *The Catacombs and the Colosseum: The Roman Empire as the Setting of Primitive Christianity.* Edited by Stephen Benko and John J. O'Rourke. Valley Forge, Pa.: Judson, 1971.

Gager, "Gentiles and Synagogues." Gager, John G. "Jews, Gentiles, and Synagogues in the Book of Acts." *HTR* 79 (1–3, 1986): 91–99.

Gager, *Kingdom.* Gager, John G. *Kingdom and Community.* Englewood Cliffs, N.J.: Prentice-Hall, 1975.

Gager, *Moses.* Gager, John G. *Moses in Greco-Roman Paganism.* SBLMS 16. Nashville: Abingdon, 1972.

Gager, "Moses the Magician." Gager, John G. "Moses the Magician: Hero of an Ancient Counter-culture?" *Helios* 21 (2, 1994): 179–88.

Gager, "Notes on Paul's Conversion." Gager, John G. "Some Notes on Paul's

Conversion." *NTS* 27 (5, 1981): 697–704.

Gager, "Outsiders." Gager, John G. "Judaism as Seen by Outsiders." Pages 99–116 in *Early Judaism and Its Modern Interpreters.* Edited by Robert A. Kraft and George W. E. Nickelsburg. SBLBMI 2. Atlanta: Scholars Press, 1986.

Gager, "Review." Gager, John G. Review of Robert M. Grant, *Early Christianity and Society: Seven Studies*; A. J. Malherbe, *Social Aspects of Early Christianity*; and Gerd Theissen, *Sociology of Early Palestinian Christianity. RelSRev* 5 (3, 1979): 174–80.

Gagnon, *Homosexual Practice.* Gagnon, Robert A. J. *The Bible and Homosexual Practice: Texts and Hermeneutics.* Nashville: Abingdon, 2001.

Gaines, "Handbooks." Gaines, Robert N. "Roman Rhetorical Handbooks." Pages 163–80 in *A Companion to Roman Rhetoric.* Edited by William Dominik and Jon Hall. Oxford: Blackwell, 2007.

Gaines, "Lilith." Gaines, Janet Howe. "Lilith, Seductress, Heroine, Murderer?" *BRev* 17 (5, 2001): 12–20, 43–44.

Gaiser, *Healing.* Gaiser, Frederick J. *Healing in the Bible: Theological Insight for Christian Ministry.* Grand Rapids: Baker Academic, 2010.

Gaiya, "Gindiri." Gaiya, Musa A. B. "Paul Gofo Gunen Gindiri." No pages. *DACB.* Online: http://www.dacb.org/stories/nigeria/gindiri_paul.html.

Gal, "T'syyt." Gal, Zvi. "T'syyt kly 'bn bglyl hthtwn." *'Atiqot* 20 (1991): 25–26.

Gale and Pruss, "Argument." Gale, Richard M., and Alexander Pruss. "A New Cosmological Argument." *RelS* 35 (1999): 461–76.

Gale and Pruss, *Existence.* Gale, Richard M., and Alexander Pruss. *The Existence of God.* Aldershot, U.K.: Ashgate/Dartmouth, 2003.

Galinsky, "Continuity." Galinsky, Karl. "Continuity and Change: Religion in the Augustan Semi-Century." Pages 71–82 in *A Companion to Roman Religion.* Edited by Jörg Rüpke. BCompAW. Oxford: Blackwell, 2011.

Galinsky, "Cult." Galinsky, Karl. "The Cult of the Roman Emperor: Uniter or Divider?" Pages 1–21 in *Rome and Religion: A Cross-Disciplinary Dialogue on the Imperial Cult.* Edited by Jeffrey Brodd and Jonathan L. Reed. Atlanta: SBL, 2011.

Gallagher, "Acts 4:22–31." Gallagher, Robert L. "From 'Doingness' to 'Beingness': A Missiological Interpretation, Acts 4:22–31." Pages 45–58 in *Mission in Acts: Ancient Narratives in Contemporary Context.* Edited by Robert L. Gallagher and Paul Hertig. AmSocMissS 34. Maryknoll, N.Y.: Orbis, 2004.

Gallagher, "Conversion and Community." Gallagher, Eugene V. "Conversion and Community in Late Antiquity." *JR* 73 (1, 1993): 1–15.

Gallagher, *Divine Man.* Gallagher, Eugene V. *Divine Man or Magician? Celsus and Origen on Jesus.* SBLDS 64. Chico, Calif.: Scholars Press, 1982.

Gallagher, "Hope." Gallagher, Robert L. "Hope in the Midst of Trial, Acts 12:1–11." Pages 157–66 in *Mission in Acts: Ancient Narratives in Contemporary Context.* Edited by Robert L. Gallagher and Paul Hertig. AmSocMissS 34. Maryknoll, N.Y.: Orbis, 2004.

Gallas, "Fünfmal." Gallas, Sven. "'Fünfmal vierzig weniger einen . . .': Die an Paulus vollzogenen Synagogalstrafen nach 2Kor 11,24." *ZNW* 81 (3–4, 1990): 178–91.

Galley, "Heilige." Galley, Susanne. "Jüdische und christliche Heilige—ein Vergleich." *ZRGG* 57 (1, 2005): 29–47.

Galli, *Francis of Assisi.* Galli, Mark. *Francis of Assisi and His World.* Downers Grove, Ill.: InterVarsity, 2002.

Galpaz-Feller, "Widow." Galpaz-Feller, Pnina. "The Widow in the Bible and in Ancient Egypt." *ZAW* 120 (2, 2008): 231–53.

Galsterer, "Tribus." Galsterer, Hartmut. "Tribus." *BrillPauly* 14:906–12.

Gamble, *Books and Readers.* Gamble, Harry Y. *Books and Readers in the Early Church: A History of Early Christian Texts.* New Haven: Yale University Press, 1995.

Gamble, "Formation." Gamble, Harry Y. "Canonical Formation of the New Testament." *DNTB* 183–94.

Gamble, "Literacy." Gamble, Harry. "Literacy and Book Culture." *DNTB* 644–48.

Gamble, *Textual History.* Gamble, Harry Y. *The Textual History of the Letter to the Romans: A Study in Textual and Literary Criticism.* Grand Rapids: Eerdmans, 1977.

Gane, *Leviticus.* Gane, Roy. *Leviticus, Numbers.* NIVAC. Grand Rapids: Zondervan, 2004.

Gane, "Leviticus." Gane, Roy E. "Leviticus." Pages 284–337 in vol. 1 of *Zondervan Illustrated Bible Backgrounds Commentary: Old Testament.* Edited by John Walton. 5 vols. Grand Rapids: Zondervan, 2009.

Gangel, *Acts.* Gangel, Kenneth O. *Acts.* HolNTC. Nashville: Broadman & Holman, 1998.

Gangloff, "Mythes." Gangloff, Anne. "Mythes, fables, et rhétorique à l'époque impériale." *Rhetorica* 20 (1, 2002): 25–56.

Gapp, "Universal Famine." Gapp, Kenneth Sperber. "The Universal Famine under Claudius." *HTR* 28 (4, 1935): 258–65.

Garbett, "Mediums." Garbett, G. Kingsley. "Spirit Mediums as Mediators in Valley Korekore Society." Pages 104–27 in *Spirit Mediumship and Society in Africa.* Edited by John Beattie and John Middleton. Foreword by Raymond Firth. New York: Africana, 1969.

García Martínez, "Samma'el." García Martínez, Florentino. "Samma'el in Pseudo-Jonathan and the Origin of Evil." *JNSL* 30 (2, 2004): 19–41.

García Martínez, "Sonship." García Martínez, Florentino. "Divine Sonship at Qumran and in Philo." *SPhilA* 19 (2007): 85–99.

García Martínez, "Textos." García Martínez, Florentino. "Nuevos textos mesiánicos de Qumrán y el Mesías del Nuevo Testamento." *Communio* 26 (1, 1993): 3–31.

García Recio, "Agarrar." García Recio, J. "Agarrar la orla del manto." *EstBib* 66 (1–4, 2008): 477–97.

García Serrano, "Origins." García Serrano, Andrés. "At the Origins of Christianity: From Division to Inclusion." *EstBib* 70 (4, 2012): 477–95.

García Serrano, "Temple." García Serrano, Andrés. "The Jerusalem Temple according to Luke." *EstBib* 71 (1, 2013): 37–56.

Gardner, "Adoption." Gardner, Jane F. "The Adoption of Roman Freedmen." *Phoenix* 43 (3, 1989): 236–57.

Gardner, *Healing Miracles.* Gardner, Rex. *Healing Miracles: A Doctor Investigates.* London: Darton, Longman & Todd, 1986.

Gardner, *Leadership.* Gardner, Jane F., ed. *Leadership and the Cult of the Personality.* The Ancient World: Source Books. London: Dent; Toronto: Hakkert, 1974.

Gardner, "Leadership and Benefaction." Gardner, Gregg. "Jewish Leadership and Hellenistic Civic Benefaction in the Second Century B.C.E." *JBL* 126 (2, 2007): 327–43.

Gardner, "Miracles." Gardner, Rex. "Miracles of Healing in Anglo-Celtic Northumbria as Recorded by the Venerable Bede and His Contemporaries: A Reappraisal in the Light of Twentieth Century Experience." *BMedJ* 287 (Dec. 24–31, 1983): 1927–33.

Gardner, "Mqbym." Gardner, A. E. "Mqbym g' wmqbym d' whmsbr bymy hmqbym." *Zion* 53 (2, 1988): 291–301. (Abstract: *NTA* 33:220.)

Gardner, *Women.* Gardner, Jane F. *Women in Roman Law and Society.* Bloomington: Indiana University Press, 1986.

Gargano, "Lectio divina." Gargano, Innocenzo. "Lectio divina" sugli Atti degli apostoli. 3 vols. Conversazioni bibliche. Bologna: Dehoniane, 1998–2000.

Garland, "Absence." Garland, David E. "The Absence of an Ordained Ministry in the

Churches of Paul." *PRSt* 29 (2, 2002): 183–95.

Garland, "Age." Garland, Robert S. J. "Age." *OCD*³ 38.

Garland, *1 Corinthians*. Garland, David E. *1 Corinthians*. BECNT. Grand Rapids: Baker, 2003.

Garland, *2 Corinthians*. Garland, David E. *2 Corinthians*. Nashville: Broadman & Holman, 1999.

Garland, "Delinquency." Garland, Robert. "Juvenile Delinquency in the Graeco-Roman World." *HT* 41 (10, 1991): 12–19.

Garland, "Dispute." Garland, David E. "The Dispute over Food Sacrificed to Idols (1 Cor 8:1–11:1)." *PRSt* 30 (2, 2003): 173–97.

Garland, *Greek Way of Death*. Garland, Robert. *The Greek Way of Death*. Ithaca, N.Y.: Cornell University Press, 1985.

Garland, *Piraeus*. Garland, Robert. *Piraeus*. 2nd ed. London: Duckworth, 2002.

Garland, "Piraeus." Garland, Robert. "Piraeus." *OCD*³ 1185.

Garland and Scheid, "Death." Garland, Robert, and John Scheid. "Death, Attitudes to." *OCD*³ 433–34.

Garlington, "Perspective." Garlington, Donald B. "The New Perspective on Paul: An Appraisal Two Decades Later." *CrisTR* n.s. 2 (2, 2005): 17–38.

Garner, "Temple of Asklepius." Garner, G. G. "The Temple of Asklepius at Corinth and Paul's Teaching." *BurH* 18 (4, 1982): 52–58.

Garner, "Temples." Garner, G. G. "The Temples of Mt. Gerizim: Tell er Ras—Probable Site of the Samaritan Temple." *BurH* 11 (1, 1975): 33–42.

Garnet, "Light." Garnet, Paul. "Qumran Light on Pauline Soteriology." Pages 19–32 in *Pauline Studies: Essays Presented to Professor F. F. Bruce on His 70th Birthday*. Edited by Donald A. Hagner and Murray J. Harris. Exeter, U.K.: Paternoster; Grand Rapids: Eerdmans, 1980.

Garnett, *Duma*. Garnett, Mary. *Take Your Glory, Lord: William Duma, His Life Story*. Roodepoort, South Africa: Baptist Publishing House, 1979.

Garnsey, "Criminal Jurisdiction." Garnsey, Peter. "The Criminal Jurisdiction of Governors." *JRS* 58 (1968): 51–59.

Garnsey, "Grain." Garnsey, Peter. "Grain for Rome." Pages 118–30 in *Trade in the Ancient Economy*. Edited by Peter Garnsey, Keith Hopkins, and C. R. Whittaker. Berkeley: University of California Press, 1983.

Garnsey, *Ideas of Slavery*. Garnsey, Peter. *Ideas of Slavery from Aristotle to Augustine*. Cambridge: Cambridge University Press, 1996.

Garsney, "*Lex Iulia* and Appeal." Garsney, Peter. "The *lex Iulia* and Appeal under the Empire." *JRS* 56 (1966): 167–89.

Garnsey, "Malnutrition." Garnsey, Peter. "Malnutrition, Famine." *BrillPauly* 8:204–9.

Garnsey, *Status and Privilege*. Garnsey, Peter. *Social Status and Legal Privilege in the Roman Empire*. Oxford: Oxford University Press, 1970.

Garnsey, "Stoics and Slavery." Garnsey, Peter. "The Middle Stoics and Slavery." Pages 159–74 in *Hellenistic Constructs: Essays in Culture, History, and Historiography*. Edited by P. Cartledge, P. Garnsey, and E. Gruen. Berkeley: University of California Press, 1997.

Garnsey and Saller, *Empire*. Garnsey, Peter, and Richard Saller. *The Roman Empire: Economy, Society, and Culture*. Berkeley: University of California Press, 1987.

Garrard-Burnett, "Demons." Garrard-Burnett, Virginia. "Casting Out Demons in Almolonga: Spiritual Warfare and Economic Development in a Maya Town." Pages 209–25 in *Global Pentecostalism: Encounters with Other Religious Traditions*. Edited by David Westerlund. New York: I. B. Taurus, 2009.

Garrett, *Demise*. Garrett, Susan R. *The Demise of the Devil: Magic and the Demonic in Luke's Writings*. Minneapolis: Fortress, 1989.

Garrett, *Rethinking Genesis*. Garrett, Duane. *Rethinking Genesis: The Sources and Authorship of the First Book of the Pentateuch*. Grand Rapids: Baker, 1991.

Garrett, "Weaker Sex." Garrett, Susan R. "The 'Weaker Sex' in the *Testament of Job*." *JBL* 112 (1, 1993): 55–70.

Garrison, "Metaphor." Garrison, Roman. "Paul's Use of the Athlete Metaphor in 1 Corinthians 9." *SR/SR* 22 (2, 1993): 209–17.

Garrison, "Syndrome." Garrison, Vivian. "The 'Puerto Rican Syndrome' in Psychiatry and *espiritismo*." Pages 383–449 in *Case Studies in Spirit Possession*. Edited by Vincent Crapanzaro and Vivian Garrison. New York: Wiley, 1977.

Garrison, *Theophilus*. Garrison, Roman. *The Significance of Theophilus as Luke's Reader*. SBEC 62. Lewiston, N.Y.: Edwin Mellen, 2004.

Garroway, "Heresy." Garroway, Joshua D. "The Pharisee Heresy: Circumcision for Gentiles in the Acts of the Apostles." *NTS* 60 (1, Jan. 2014): 20–36.

Garstad, "Belus." Garstad, Benjamin. "Belus in the *Sacred History* of Euhemerus." *CP* 99 (3, 2004): 246–57.

Garte, "Resurrection." Garte, Edna. "The Theme of Resurrection in the Dura-Europos Synagogue Paintings." *JQR* 64 (1973): 1–15.

Gärtner, *Areopagus*. Gärtner, Bertril. *The Areopagus Speech and Natural Revelation*. ASNU 21. Lund, Swed.: C. W. K. Gleerup, 1955.

Gärtner, "Gnome." Gärtner, Hans Armin. "Gnome." *BrillPauly* 5:884–91.

Gärtner, "Prooemium." Gärtner, Hans Armin. "Prooemium." *BrillPauly* 12:16–18.

Gärtner, "Synkrisis." Gärtner, Hans Armin. "Synkrisis." *BrillPauly* 14:28.

Gärtner, *Temple*. Gärtner, Bertril. *The Temple and the Community in Qumran and the New Testament: A Comparative Study in the Temple Symbolism of the Qumran Texts and the New Testament*. Cambridge: Cambridge University Press, 1965.

Gärtner and Eigler, "Epitome." Gärtner, Hans Armin, and Ulrich Eigler. "Epitome." *BrillPauly* 4:1153–56.

Garuti, "Melchisedek." Garuti, Paolo. "Melchisedek, figura chiave nelle dispute sulla legittimità del sacerdozio gerosolimitano ai tempi di Gesù: La Bibbia, Qumram, gli apocrifi." *Angelicum* 81 (1, 2004): 7–27.

Garver, "Aristotle." Garver, Eugene. "Aristotle on the Kinds of Rhetoric." *Rhetorica* 27 (1, 2009): 1–18.

Gaskin, *Philosophy*. Gaskin, J. C. A. *Hume's Philosophy of Religion*. London: Macmillan, 1978.

Gasparini, "Isis." Gasparini, Valentino. "Isis and Osiris: Demonology vs. Henotheism?" *Numen* 58 (5–6, 2011): 697–728.

Gasparro, *Soteriology*. Gasparro, Giulia Sfameni. *Soteriology and Mystic Aspects in the Cult of Cybele and Attis*. ÉPROER 103. Leiden: Brill, 1985.

Gasque, "Acts and History." Gasque, W. Ward. "The Book of Acts and History." Pages 54–72 in *Unity and Diversity in New Testament Theology: Essays in Honor of George E. Ladd*. Edited by Robert A. Guelich. Grand Rapids: Eerdmans, 1978.

Gasque, *Criticism*. Gasque, W. Ward. *A History of the Criticism of the Acts of the Apostles*. Grand Rapids: Eerdmans; Tübingen: Mohr Siebeck, 1975.

Gasque, "Cyrene." Gasque, W. Ward. "Cyrene." *ABD* 1:1230–31.

Gasque, "Iconium." Gasque, W. Ward. "Iconium." *ABD* 3:357–58.

Gasque, "Speeches." Gasque, W. Ward. "The Speeches of Acts: Dibelius Reconsidered." Pages 232–50 in *New Dimensions in New Testament Study*. Edited by Richard N. Longenecker and Merrill C. Tenney. Grand Rapids: Zondervan, 1974.

Gasque, "Tarsus." Gasque, W. Ward. "Tarsus." *ABD* 6:333–34.

Gaster, *Scriptures*. Gaster, Theodor H. *The Dead Sea Scriptures*. Garden City, N.Y.: Doubleday, 1976.

Gaster, *Studies*. Gaster, Moses. *Studies and Texts in Folklore, Magic, Mediaeval Romance, Hebrew Apocrypha, and Samaritan Archaeology*. 3 vols. New York: KTAV, 1971.

Gaston, "Anti-Judaism and Passion Narrative." Gaston, Lloyd. "Anti-Judaism and the Passion Narrative in Luke and Acts." Pages 127–53 in *Paul and the Gospels*. Vol. 1 of *Anti-Judaism in Early Christianity*. Edited by P. Richardson and D. Granskou. SChrJud 2. Waterloo, Ont.: Wilfred Laurier University Press, 1986.

Gaston, "Impact." Gaston, Lloyd. "The Impact of New Perspectives on Judaism and Improved Jewish-Christian Relations on the Study of Paul." *BibInt* 13 (3, 2005): 250–54.

Gaston, "Influence." Gaston, Thomas E. "The Influence of Platonism on the Early Apologists." *HeyJ* 50 (4, 2009): 573–80.

Gathercole, *Boasting*. Gathercole, Simon J. *Where Is Boasting? Early Jewish Soteriology and Paul's Response in Romans 1–5*. Grand Rapids: Eerdmans, 2002.

Gathercole, "Christology." Gathercole, Simon J. "Paul's Christology." Pages 172–87 in *The Blackwell Companion to Paul*. Edited by Stephen Westerholm. BCompRel. Oxford: Blackwell, 2011.

Gathercole, *Son*. Gathercole, Simon J. *The Pre-existent Son: Recovering the Christologies of Matthew, Mark, and Luke*. Grand Rapids: Eerdmans, 2006.

Gatti, "Eutyc(h)ius." Gatti, Paolo. "Eutyc(h)ius." *BrillPauly* 5:240.

Gatti, "Eutychius Proculus." Gatti, Paolo. "Eutychius Proculus." *BrillPauly* 5:241.

Gatumu, *Concept*. Gatumu, Kabiro wa. *The Pauline Concept of Supernatural Powers: A Reading from the African Worldview*. Foreword by D. G. Dunn. PBMon. Carlisle, U.K.: Paternoster; Eugene, Ore.: Wipf & Stock, 2008.

Gaventa, *Acts*. Gaventa, Beverly Roberts. *The Acts of the Apostles*. ANTC. Nashville: Abingdon, 2003.

Gaventa, "Believers." Gaventa, Beverly Roberts. "Paul and the Roman Believers." Pages 93–107 in *The Blackwell Companion to Paul*. Edited by Stephen Westerholm. BCompRel. Oxford: Blackwell, 2011.

Gaventa, "Comment(ary)ing." Gaventa, Beverly Roberts. "Comment(ary)ing on Acts." Paper presented at the annual meeting of the SBL, Philadelphia, Nov. 21, 2005.

Gaventa, *Darkness*. Gaventa, Beverly Roberts. *From Darkness to Light: Aspects of Conversion in the New Testament*. OBT. Philadelphia: Fortress, 1986.

Gaventa, "Daughters." Gaventa, Beverly Roberts. "What Ever Happened to Those Prophesying Daughters?" Pages 49–60 in *The Feminist Companion to the Acts of the Apostles*. Edited by Amy-Jill Levine with Marianne Blickenstaff. Cleveland: Pilgrim; Edinburgh: T&T Clark, 2004.

Gaventa, "Ecclesiology." Gaventa, Beverly Roberts. "Theology and Ecclesiology in the Miletus Speech: Reflections on Content and Context." *NTS* 50 (1, 2004): 36–52.

Gaventa, "Eschatology Revisited." Gaventa, Beverly Roberts. "The Eschatology of Luke-Acts Revisited." *Enc* 43 (1982): 27–42.

Gaventa, *Mary*. Gaventa, Beverly Roberts. *Mary: Glimpses of the Mother of Jesus*. SPNT. Columbia: University of South Carolina Press, 1995.

Gaventa, *Mother*. Gaventa, Beverly Roberts. *Our Mother Saint Paul*. Louisville: Westminster John Knox, 2007.

Gaventa, "Overthrown Enemy." Gaventa, Beverly Roberts. "The Overthrown Enemy: Luke's Portrait of Paul." Pages 439–49 in *SBL Seminar Papers, 1985*. Edited by K. H. Richards. SBLSP 24. Atlanta: Scholars Press, 1985.

Gaventa, "Witnessing." Gaventa, Beverly Roberts. "Witnessing to the Gospel in the Acts of the Apostles: Beyond the Conversion or Conversation Dilemma." *WW* 22 (3, 2002): 238–45.

Gavrilov, "Techniques." Gavrilov, Alexander K. "Techniques of Reading in Classical Antiquity." *CQ* 47 (1, 1997): 56–73.

Gawlina, "Paulus und Plato." Gawlina, Manfred. "Paulus und Plato: *Prosopon* gegen *idea*." *TP* 80 (1, 2005): 17–30.

Geagan, *Athenian Constitution*. Geagan, Daniel J. *The Athenian Constitution after Sulla*. Hesperia Sup 12. Princeton: American School of Classical Studies at Athens, 1967.

Gebauer, "Mission und Zeugnis." Gebauer, Roland. "Mission und Zeugnis: Zum Verhältnis von missionarischer Wirksamkeit und Zeugenschaft in der Apostelgeschichte." *NovT* 40 (1, 1998): 54–72.

Gebhard, "Rites." Gebhard, Elizabeth R. "Rites for Melikertes-Palaimon in the Early Roman Corinthia." Pages 165–203 in *Urban Religion in Roman Corinth: Interdisciplinary Approaches*. Edited by Daniel N. Schowalter and Steven J. Friesen. HTS 53. Cambridge, Mass.: Harvard University Press, 2005.

Geer, "Lucanisms." Geer, Thomas C. "The Presence and Significance of Lucanisms in the 'Western' Text of Acts." *JSNT* 39 (1990): 59–76.

Gehrke, "Ephebeia." Gehrke, Hans-Joachim. "Ephebeia." *BrillPauly* 4:1018–21.

Gehrke, "Euergetism." Gehrke, Hans-Joachim. "Euergetism." *BrillPauly* 5:154–56.

Gehrke, "Friendship." Gehrke, Hans-Joachim. "Friendship: Social History." *BrillPauly* 5:552–54.

Gehrke, "Leisure." Gehrke, Hans-Joachim. "Leisure." *BrillPauly* 7:374–77.

Geiger, "'Pyqwrws." Geiger, J. "ltwldwt hmynh ''pyqwrws.'" *Tarbiz* 42 (3–4, 1973): 499–500.

Geiger, "Weg." Geiger, Georg. "Der Weg als roter Faden durch Lk-Apg." Pages 663–73 in *The Unity of Luke-Acts*. Edited by Joseph Verheyden. BETL 142. Leuven: Leuven University Press, 1999.

Geivett and Habermas, *Miracles*. Geivett, R. Douglas, and Gary R. Habermas. *In Defense of Miracles: A Comprehensive Case for God's Action in History*. Downers Grove, Ill.: InterVarsity, 1997.

Gelfand, "Disorders." Gelfand, Michael. "Psychiatric Disorders as Recognized by the Shona." Pages 156–73 in *Magic, Faith, and Healing: Studies in Primitive Psychiatry Today*. Edited by Ari Kiev. Foreword by Jerome D. Frank. New York: Free Press, 1964.

Gelfand, *Religion*. Gelfand, Michael. *Shona Religion: With Special Reference to the Makorekore*. Foreword by M. Hannan. Cape Town: Juta, 1962.

Gelinas, "*Ex gradibus entium*." Gelinas, Luke. "The Stoic Argument *ex gradibus entium*." *Phronesis* 51 (1, 2006): 49–73.

Gempf, "Appropriateness." Gempf, Conrad. "Historical and Literary Appropriateness in the Mission Speeches of Paul in Acts." PhD diss., University of Aberdeen, 1989.

Gempf, "Athens." Gempf, Conrad. "Athens, Paul at." Pages 51–54 in *Dictionary of Paul and His Letters*. Edited by R. P. Martin et al. Downers Grove, Ill.: InterVarsity, 1993.

Gempf, "Before Paul Arrived." Gempf, Conrad. "Before Paul Arrived in Corinth: The Mission Strategies in 1 Corinthians 2:2 and Acts 17." Pages 126–42 in *The New Testament in Its First Century Setting: Essays on Context and Background in Honour of B. W. Winter on His 65th Birthday*. Edited by P. J. Williams et al. Grand Rapids and Cambridge, U.K.: Eerdmans, 2004.

Gempf, "God-Fearers." Gempf, Conrad. "Appendix 2: The God-Fearers." Pages 444–47 in *The Book of Acts in the Setting of Hellenistic History*, by Colin J. Hemer. Edited by Conrad H. Gempf. WUNT 49. Tübingen: Mohr Siebeck, 1989.

Gempf, "Neapolis." Gempf, Conrad. "Neapolis." *ABD* 4:1052–53.

Gempf, "Paphos." Gempf, Conrad. "Paphos." *ABD* 5:139–40.

Gempf, "Salamis." Gempf, Conrad. "Salamis." *ABD* 5:904–5.

Gempf, "Speaking." Gempf, Conrad. "Public Speaking and Published Accounts." Pages 259–303 in *The Book of Acts in Its Ancient Literary Setting*. Edited by Bruce W. Winter and Andrew D. Clarke. Vol. 1 of *The Book of Acts in Its First Century Setting*. Edited by Bruce W. Winter. Grand Rapids: Eerdmans; Carlisle, U.K.: Paternoster, 1993.

Gemünden, "Passionnelle." Gemünden, Petra von. "La femme passionnelle et l'homme rationnel? Un chapitre de psychologie historique." *Bib* 78 (4, 1997): 457–80.

Genuyt, "Écritures." Genuyt, François. "Écritures et résurrection de Jésus: Une lecture du premier discours de Pierre (Ac 2,14–36)." *LumVie* 51 (253, 2002): 55–66.

George, "Architecture." George, Michele. "Domestic Architecture and Household Relations: Pompeii and Roman Ephesos." *JSNT* 27 (1, 2004): 7–25.

George, "Beginnings." George, A. C. "Pentecostal Beginnings in Travancore, South India." *AJPS* 4 (2, 2002): 215–37.

George, "Israël." George, Augustin. "Israël dans l'oevre de Luc." *RB* 75 (4, 1968): 481–525.

Georgi, "Aeneas und Abraham." Georgi, Dieter. "Aeneas und Abraham: Paulus unter dem Aspekt der Latinität?" *ZNT* 5 (10, 2002): 37–43.

Georgi, *Opponents*. Georgi, Dieter. *The Opponents of Paul in Second Corinthians*. Philadelphia: Fortress, 1986.

Georgi, "Socioeconomic Reasons." Georgi, Dieter. "Socioeconomic Reasons for the 'Divine Man' as a Propagandistic Pattern." Pages 27–42 in *Aspects of Religious Propaganda in Judaism and Early Christianity*. Edited by Elisabeth Schüssler Fiorenza. UNDCSJCA 2. Notre Dame, Ind.: University of Notre Dame Press, 1976.

Gera, "Olympiodoros." Gera, Dov. "Olympiodoros, Heliodoros and the Temples of Koile Syria and Phoinike." *ZPE* 169 (2009): 125–55.

Geraghty, "Paul before Areopagus." Geraghty, G. "Paul before the Areopagus: A New Approach to Priestly Formation in the Light of *Ecclesia in Africa*." *AfCS* 12 (3, 1996): 32–41.

Gerberding, "Women." Gerberding, Kieth A. "Women Who Toil in Ministry, Even as Paul." *CurTM* 18 (4, 1991): 285–91.

Gerdmar, "Hebreer och hellenister." Gerdmar, Anders. "Hebreer och hellenister i urförsamlingen—ett receptions-kritiskt perspektiv" [Hebrews and Hellenists in the Jerusalem Church—A Reception-Critical Perspective]. *SEÅ* 67 (2002): 105–19.

Gerhardsson, *Memory*. Gerhardsson, Birger. *Memory and Manuscript: Oral Tradition and Written Transmission in Rabbinic Judaism and Early Christianity*. ASNU 22. Uppsala: C. W. K. Gleerup, 1961.

Gerhardsson, *Origins*. Gerhardsson, Birger. *The Origins of the Gospel Traditions*. Philadelphia: Fortress, 1979.

Gerhardsson, "Path." Gerhardsson, Birger. "The Path of the Gospel Tradition." Pages 75–96 in *The Gospel and the Gospels*. Edited by Peter Stuhlmacher. Grand Rapids: Eerdmans, 1991.

Gerhardsson, "Performance Criticism." Gerhardsson, Birger. "'Performance Criticism'—en ny exegetisk disciplin?" *SEÅ* 72 (2007): 95–108.

Gero, "Messiah." Gero, Stephen. "'My Son the Messiah': A Note on 4 Esr 7:28–29." *ZNW* 66 (3–4, 1975): 264–67.

Gero, "Polemic." Gero, Stephen. "Jewish Polemic in the Martyrium Pionii and a 'Jesus' Passage from the Talmud." *JJS* 29 (2, 1978): 164–68.

Geroussis, *Delphi*. Geroussis, Panayotis. *Guide to Delphi*. 2nd ed. N.p., 1967.

Gershenson, "Satan." Gershenson, Daniel E. "The Name Satan." *ZAW* 114 (3, 2002): 443–45.

Gersht, "Dionysiac Sarcophagi." Gersht, Rivka. "Dionysiac Sarcophagi from Caesarea Maritima." *IEJ* 41 (1–3, 1991): 145–56.

Gersht, "Reader of Scroll." Gersht, Rivka. "The Reader of the Scroll from Caesarea Maritima." *TA* 13–14 (1, 1986–87): 67–70 and plate 4.

Gersht, "Statues." Gersht, Rivka. "Three Greek and Roman Portrait Statues from Caesarea Maritima." *'Atiqot* 28 (1996): 99–113.

Gersht, "Tyche." Gersht, Rivka. "The Tyche of Caesarea Maritima." *PEQ* 116 (2, 1984): 110–14.

Gervers, "Iconography." Gervers, Michael. "The Iconography of the Cave in Christian and Mithraic Tradition." Pages 579–99 in *Mysteria Mithrae*. Edited by Ugo Bianchi. ÉPROER 80. Leiden: Brill, 1979.

Gessert, "Myth." Gessert, Genevieve. "Myth as *consolatio*: Medea on Roman Sarcophagi." *GR* 51 (2, 2004): 217–49.

Gessler-Löhr, "Mummies." Gessler-Löhr, Beatrix. "Mummies." *BrillPauly* 9:277–78.

Gesundheit, "Suicide." Gesundheit, Benjamin. "Suicide—A Halakhic and Moral Analysis of *Masekhet Semahot*, chapter 2, laws 1–6." *Tradition* 35 (3, 2001): 34–51.

Geva, "Searching." Geva, Hillel. "Searching for Roman Jerusalem." *BAR* 23 (6, 1997): 34–45, 72–73.

Geyser, "Israel." Geyser, Albert S. "Israel in the Fourth Gospel." *Neot* 20 (1986): 13–20.

Geyser, "Metodologiese vooronderstellings." Geyser, P. A. "Hermeneutiese uitgangspunte in historiese-Jesus navorsing: Metodologiese vooronderstellings (Hermeneutical Premises in Historical Jesus Research: Methodological Presuppositions)." *HTS/TS* 56 (4, 2000): 1146–70.

Geyser, "Tribes." Geyser, Albert. "The Twelve Tribes in Revelation: Judean and Judeo-Christian Apocalypticism." *NTS* 28 (3, 1982): 388–99.

Geyser, "Uitgangspunte." Geyser, P. A. "Hermeneutiese uitgangspunte in historiese-Jesus navorsing, Deel 1: Sosiaal-wetenskaplike vooronderstellings (Hermeneutical Premises in Historical Jesus Research, Part 1: Social-Scientific Presuppositions)." *HTS/TS* 56 (2–3, 2000): 527–48.

Ghéon, *Secret*. Ghéon, Henri. *The Secret of the Curé d'Ars*. London: Sheed & Ward, 1952.

Giangrande, "Dream." Giangrande, Giuseppe. "A Dream in Xenophon Ephesius." *Orpheus* 23 (1–2, 2002): 29–31.

Gibbard, "Mystery." Gibbard, S. M. "The Christian Mystery." Pages 97–120 in *Studies in Ephesians*. Edited by F. L. Cross. London: A. R. Mowbray, 1956.

Gibbs, *Creation*. Gibbs, John G. *Creation and Redemption: A Study in Pauline Theology*. NovTSup 26. Leiden: Brill, 1971.

Gibbs, "Launching of Mission." Gibbs, Eddie. "The Launching of Mission: The Outpouring of the Spirit at Pentecost, Acts 2:1–41." Pages 18–28 in *Mission in Acts: Ancient Narratives in Contemporary Context*. Edited by Robert L. Gallagher and Paul Hertig. AmSocMissS 34. Maryknoll, N.Y.: Orbis, 2004.

Gibert, "Invention." Gibert, Pierre. "L'invention d'un genre littéraire." *Lum Vie* 30 (153–54, 1981): 19–33.

Giblet, "Mouvement." Giblet, Jean. "Un mouvement de résistance armée au temps de Jésus?" *RTL* 5 (4, 1974): 409–26.

Gibson, "Inscriptions of Smyrna." Gibson, E. Leigh. "Jews in the Inscriptions of Smyrna." *JJS* 56 (1, 2005): 66–79.

Gibson, "Lost Cause." Gibson, Shimon. "A Lost Cause." *BAR* 30 (6, 2004): 55–58.

Gibson, "Notes." Gibson, Craig A. "Introduction and Notes." Introduction, pages xvii–xxv, and notes, passim, in *Libanius's Progymnasmata: Model Exercises in Greek Prose Composition and Rhetoric*. Translation, introduction, and notes by Craig A. Gibson. SBLWGRW 27. Edited by Malcolm Heath. Atlanta: SBL, 2008.

Gibson, "Testing." Gibson, Jeffrey B. "Testing and Trial in Secular Greek Thought." *DNTB* 1207–11.

Gibson, "Tychaion." Gibson, Craig A. "The Alexandrian Tychaion and the Date of Ps.-Nicolaus Progymnasmata." *CQ* 59 (2, 2009): 608–23.

Gielen, "Gefangener." Gielen, M. "Paulus—Gefangener in Ephesus?" *BN* 131 (2006): 79–103; 133 (2007): 63–77.

Giesen, *Herrschaft*. Giesen, Heinz. *Herrschaft Gottes—heute oder morgen? Zur Heilsbotschaft Jesu und der synoptischen Evangelien.* BibUnt 26. Regensburg: Pustet, 1995.

Giesen, "Verheissungen." Giesen, Heinz. "Gott steht zu seinen Verheissungen: Eine exegetische und theologische Auslegung des Pfingstgeschehens (Apg 2,1–13)." *SNTSU* 28 (2003): 83–120.

Gifford-Gonzalez, "Pastoralism." Gifford-Gonzalez, Diane. "Pastoralism and Its Consequences." Pages 187–224 in *African Archaeology*. Edited by Ann Brower Stahl. Blackwell Studies in Global Archaeology. Oxford: Blackwell, 2005.

"Gift of Tongues." "Gift of Tongues." *New Zealand Christian Record* (Apr. 14, 1881): 11.

Gil, "Decline." Gil, Moshe. "The Decline of the Agrarian Economy in Palestine under Roman Rule." *JESHO* 49 (3, 2006): 285–328.

Gilbert, "Acts." Gilbert, Gary. "Acts" (introduction and notes). Pages 197–252 in *The Jewish Annotated New Testament: New Revised Standard Version*. Edited by Amy-Jill Levine and Marc Zvi Brettler. New York: Oxford University Press, 2011.

Gilbert, "Administration." Gilbert, Gary. "Jews in Imperial Administration and Its Significance for Dating the Jewish Donor Inscription from Aphrodisias." *JSJ* 35 (2, 2004): 169–84.

Gilbert, "Civic Life." Gilbert, Gary. "Jewish Involvement in Ancient Civic Life: The Case of Aphrodisias." *RB* 113 (1, 2006): 18–36.

Gilbert, "Convert." Gilbert, Gary. "The Making of a Jew: 'God-Fearer' or Convert in the Story of Izates." *USQR* 44 (3–4, 1991): 299–313.

Gilbert, "École." Gilbert, Maurice. "À l'école de la sagesse: La pédagogie des sages dans l'ancien Israël." *Greg* 85 (1, 2004): 20–42.

Gilbert, "List." Gilbert, Gary. "The List of Nations in Acts 2: Roman Propaganda and the Lukan Response." *JBL* 121 (3, 2002): 497–529.

Gilbert, "Propaganda." Gilbert, Gary. "Roman Propaganda and Christian Identity in the Worldview of Luke-Acts." Pages 233–56 in *Contextualizing Acts: Lukan Narrative and Greco-Roman Discourse*. Edited by Todd Penner and Caroline Vander Stichele. SBLSymS 20. Atlanta: SBL, 2003.

Gilchrist, "Eyewitness Reporting." Gilchrist, Mike. "The 'We' Sections as Eyewitness Reporting: Some New Arguments." Paper presented to the Book of Acts Seminar, British New Testament Society, University of Aberdeen, Sept. 3–5, 2009.

Gilchrist, "On What Charge?" Gilchrist, J. M. "On What Charge Was St. Paul Brought to Rome?" *ExpT* 78 (9, 1967): 264–66.

Gilchrist, "Shipwreck." Gilchrist, J. M. "The Historicity of Paul's Shipwreck." *JSNT* 61 (1996): 29–51.

Gilders, "Blood." Gilders, William K. "Blood and Covenant: Interpretive Elaboration on Genesis 9.4–6 in the Book of *Jubilees*." *JSP* 15 (2, 2006): 83–118.

Giles, "Exponent." Giles, Kevin. "Is Luke an Exponent of 'Early Protestantism'?" *EvQ* 54 (4, 1982): 193–205; 55 (1, 1983): 3–20.

Giles, "Possession." Giles, Linda L. "Spirit Possession and the Symbolic Construction of Swahili Society." Pages 142–64 in *Spirit Possession, Modernity and Power in Africa*. Edited by Heike Behrend and Ute Luig. Madison: University of Wisconsin Press, 1999.

Giles, "Possession Cults." Giles, Linda L. "Possession Cults on the Swahili Coast: A Re-examination of Theories of Marginality." *Africa* 57 (2, 1987): 234–58.

Giles, "Present-Future Eschatology." Giles, Kevin. "Present-Future Eschatology in the Book of Acts." *RTR* 40 (1981): 65–71; 41 (1982): 11–18.

Giles, "Spirits." Giles, Linda. "The Role of Spirits in Swahili Coastal Society." Pages 61–85 in *Studies in Witchcraft, Magic, War, and Peace in Africa*. Edited by Beatrice Nicolini. Lewiston, N.Y.: Edwin Mellen, 2006.

Giles, *Woman*. Giles, Kevin. *Created Woman: A Fresh Study of the Biblical Teaching*. Canberra: Acorn, 1985.

Gill, "Achaia." Gill, David W. J. "Achaia." Pages 433–53 in *The Book of Acts in Its Graeco-Roman Setting*. Edited by David W. J. Gill and Conrad Gempf. Vol. 2 of *The Book of Acts in Its First Century Setting*. Edited by Bruce W. Winter. Grand Rapids: Eerdmans; Carlisle, U.K.: Paternoster, 1994.

Gill, "Character." Gill, Christopher John. "Character." *OCD*³ 317.

Gill, "Character-Development." Gill, Christopher. "The Question of Character-Development: Plutarch and Tacitus." *CQ* 33 (2, 1983): 469–87.

Gill, "Did Galen Understand?" Gill, Christopher. "Did Galen Understand Platonic and Stoic Thinking on Emotions?" Pages 113–48 in *The Emotions in Hellenistic Philosophy*. Edited by Juha Sihvola and Troels Engberg-Pedersen. TSHP 46. Dordrecht, Neth.: Kluwer Academic, 1998.

Gill, "Dionysios." Gill, David. "Dionysios and Damaris: A Note on Acts 17:34." *CBQ* 61 (3, 1999): 483–90.

Gill, "Élites." Gill, David W. J. "Acts and the Urban Élites." Pages 105–18 in *The Book of Acts in Its Graeco-Roman Setting*. Edited by David W. J. Gill and Conrad Gempf. Vol. 2 of *The Book of Acts in Its First Century Setting*. Edited by Bruce W. Winter. Grand Rapids: Eerdmans; Carlisle, U.K.: Paternoster, 1994.

Gill, "Erastus." Gill, David W. J. "Erastus the Aedile." *TynBul* 40 (2, 1989): 293–301.

Gill, "Galen and Stoics." Gill, Christopher. "Galen and the Stoics: Mortal Enemies or Blood Brothers?" *Phronesis* 52 (1, 2007): 88–120.

Gill, "Macedonia." Gill, David W. J. "Macedonia." Pages 397–417 in *The Book of Acts in Its Graeco-Roman Setting*. Edited by David W. J. Gill and Conrad Gempf. Vol. 2 of *The Book of Acts in Its First Century Setting*. Edited by Bruce W. Winter. Grand Rapids: Eerdmans; Carlisle, U.K.: Paternoster, 1994.

Gill, "Meat-Market." Gill, David W. J. "The Meat-Market at Corinth (1 Corinthians 10:25)." *TynBul* 43 (2, 1992): 389–93.

Gill, "Philosophy." Gill, Christopher. "Hellenistic and Roman Philosophy." *Phronesis* 53 (3, 2008): 303–13.

Gill, "Policy." Gill, David W. J. "Acts and Roman Policy in Judaea." Pages 15–26 in *The Book of Acts in Its Palestinian Setting*. Edited by Richard Bauckham. Vol. 4 of *The Book of Acts in Its First Century Setting*. Edited by Bruce W. Winter. Grand Rapids: Eerdmans; Carlisle, U.K.: Paternoster, 1995.

Gill, "Religion." Gill, David W. J. "Religion in a Local Setting." Pages 79–92 in *The Book of Acts in Its Graeco-Roman Setting*. Edited by David W. J. Gill and Conrad Gempf. Vol. 2 of *The Book of Acts in Its First Century Setting*. Edited by Bruce W. Winter. Grand Rapids: Eerdmans; Carlisle, U.K.: Paternoster, 1994.

Gill, "Roman Colony in Achaea." Gill, David W. J. "Corinth: A Roman Colony in Achaea." *BZ* 37 (2, 1993): 259–64.

Gill, "Structure of Acts 9." Gill, David. "The Structure of Acts 9." *Bib* 55 (1974): 546–48.

Gill, "Studies." Gill, Christopher. "Hellenistic and Roman Philosophy (and Some More General Studies)." *Phronesis* 54 (3, 2009): 286–96.

Gill, "Travels through Cyprus." Gill, David W. J. "Paul's Travels through Cyprus (Acts 13:4–12)." *TynBul* 46 (2, 1995): 219–28.

Gill and Gempf, "Preface." Gill, David W. J., and Conrad Gempf. Preface. Pages ix–xiii in *The Book of Acts in Its Graeco-Roman Setting*. Edited by David W. J. Gill and Conrad Gempf. Vol. 2 of *The Book of Acts in Its First Century Setting*. Edited by Bruce W. Winter. Grand Rapids: Eerdmans; Carlisle, U.K.: Paternoster, 1994.

Gillespie, *Dynamics*. Gillespie, V. Bailey. *The Dynamics of Religious Conversion*. Birmingham, Ala.: Religious Education Press, 1991.

Gillet-Didier, "*Paradosis*." Gillet-Didier, Veronique. "*Paradosis*: Flavius Josèphe et la fabrique de la tradition." *REJ* 158 (1–2, 1999): 7–49.

Gilliard, "More Silent Reading." Gilliard, Frank D. "More Silent Reading in Antiquity: *Non omne verbum sonabat*." *JBL* 112 (4, 1993): 689–96.

Gilliland, "Missionaries." Gilliland, Dean S. "For Missionaries and Leaders: Paul's Farewell to the Ephesian Elders, Acts 20:17–38." Pages 257–73 in *Mission in Acts: Ancient Narratives in Contemporary Context*. Edited by Robert L. Gallagher and Paul Hertig. AmSocMissS 34. Maryknoll, N.Y.: Orbis, 2004.

Gillman, "Hospitality in Acts 16." Gillman, John. "Hospitality in Acts 16." *LouvS* 17 (2–3, 1992): 181–96.

Gillman, "Jason." Gillman, Florence Morgan. "Jason." *ABD* 3:649.

Gillman, *Possessions and Faith*. Gillman, John. *Possessions and the Life of Faith: A Reading of Luke-Acts*. ZSNT. Collegeville, Minn.: Liturgical Press, 1991.

Gilman, "Miracles." Gilman, James E. "Reconceiving Miracles." *RelS* 25 (4, 1989): 477–87.

Gilmore, "Shame." Gilmore, David D. "Introduction: The Shame of Dishonor." Pages 2–21 in *Honor and Shame and the Unity of the Mediterranean*. Edited by David D. Gilmore. AAAM 22. Washington, D.C.: American Anthropological Association, 1987.

Gineste, "Trophime." Gineste, B. "'Èsan gar proeôrakotes' (Actes 21,29): Trophime a-t-il été 'vu' à Jérusalem?" *RThom* 95 (2, 1995): 251–72.

Ginsberg, "Cave Scrolls." Ginsberg, H. L. "The Cave Scrolls and the Jewish Sects: New Light on a Scholarly Mystery." *Commentary* 16 (1953): 77–81.

Ginsburg, *Kabbalah*. Ginsburg, Christian D. *The Essenes: Their History and Doctrines; The Kabbalah: Its Doctrines, Development, and Literature*. London: Routledge & Kegan Paul, 1955. (The Kabbalah section

is a reprint from 1863; that on the Essenes, from 1864.)

Giovannini, "Chastity." Giovannini, Maureen J. "Female Chastity Codes in the Circum-Mediterranean: Comparative Perspectives." Pages 61–74 in *Honor and Shame and the Unity of the Mediterranean*. Edited by David D. Gilmore. AAAM 22. Washington, D.C.: American Anthropological Association, 1987.

Giovannini, "Incendium." Giovannini, Adalberto. "Tacite, L''incendium Neronis,' et les chrétiens." *REAug* 30 (1–2, 1984): 3–23.

Gippert, "Language Contact." Gippert, Jost. "Language Contact." *BrillPauly* 7:214–15.

Girard, "Interpretatio romana." Girard, Jean-Louis. "Interpretatio romana: Questions historiques et problèmes de méthode." *RHPR* 60 (1, 1980): 21–27.

Giroud, "Propre." Giroud, Jean-Claude. "Le 'propre' et le 'commun.'" *SémBib* 134 (2009): 17–22.

Gispert-Sauch, "Upanisad." Gispert-Sauch, George. "Brhadaranyaka Upanisad 1.3.28 in Greek Literature?" *Vid* 40 (4, 1976): 177–80.

Gitay, "Criticism." Gitay, Yehoshua. "Rhetorical Criticism and the Prophetic Discourse." Pages 13–24 in *Persuasive Artistry: Studies in New Testament Rhetoric in Honor of George A. Kennedy*. Edited by Duane F. Watson. JSNTSup 50. Sheffield, U.K.: Sheffield Academic, 1991.

Gitler, "Amulets." Gitler, Haim. "Four Magical and Christian Amulets." *SBFLA* 40 (1990): 365–74.

Gizewski, "*Absentia*." Gizewski, Christian. "*Absentia*." *BrillPauly* 1:34–35.

Gizewski, "Acta." Gizewski, Christian. "Acta." *BrillPauly* 1:115–17.

Gizewski, "Adventus." Gizewski, Christian. "Adventus." *BrillPauly* 1:161.

Gizewski, "Aediles." Gizewski, Christian. "Aediles." *BrillPauly* 1:168–69.

Gizewski, "Comitia." Gizewski, Christian. "Comitia." *BrillPauly* 3:621–23.

Gizewski, "Cursus honorum." Gizewski, Christian. "Cursus honorum." *BrillPauly* 3:1020–22.

Gizewski, "Damnatio." Gizewski, Christian. "Damnatio memoriae." *BrillPauly* 4:60–61.

Gizewski, "Diploma." Gizewski, Christian. "Diploma." *BrillPauly* 4:528.

Gizewski, "Duoviri." Gizewski, Christian. "Duoviri, Duumviri." *BrillPauly* 4:739–40.

Gizewski, "Lictor." Gizewski, Christian. "Lictor." *BrillPauly* 7:543–44.

Gizewski, "Maiestas." Gizewski, Christian. "Maiestas." *BrillPauly* 8:185–87.

Glad, "Adaptability." Glad, Clarence E. "Paul and Adaptability." Pages 17–41 in *Paul in the Greco-Roman World: A Handbook*. Edited by J. Paul Sampley. Harrisburg, Pa.: Trinity Press International, 2003.

Glad, *Paul and Philodemus*. Glad, Clarence E. *Paul and Philodemus: Adaptability in Epicurean and Early Christian Psychagogy*. NovTSup 81. Leiden: Brill, 1995.

Gladstone, "Sign Language." Gladstone, Robert J. "Sign Language in the Assembly: How Are Tongues a Sign to the Unbeliever in 1 Cor 14:20–25?" *AJPS* 2 (2, 1999): 177–94.

Glancy, "Dialectic." Glancy, Jennifer A. "The Mistress-Slave Dialectic: Paradoxes of Slavery in Three LXX Narratives." *JSOT* 72 (1996): 71–87.

Glancy, "Obstacles." Glancy, Jennifer A. "Obstacles to Slaves' Participation in the Corinthian Church." *JBL* 117 (3, 1998): 481–501.

Glasson, *Advent*. Glasson, T. Francis. *The Second Advent: The Origin of the New Testament Doctrine*. 3rd rev. ed. London: Epworth, 1963.

Glasson, *Moses*. Glasson, T. Francis. *Moses in the Fourth Gospel*. SBT. Naperville, Ill.: Alec R. Allenson, 1963.

Glasson, "Son of Man Imagery." Glasson, T. Francis. "The Son of Man Imagery: Enoch XIV and Daniel VII." *NTS* 23 (1, 1976): 82–90.

Glatzer, "Study." Glatzer, Nahum Norbert. "A Study of the Talmudic Interpretation of Prophecy." *RR* 10 (2, 1946): 115–37.

Gleason et al., "Promontory Palace." Gleason, Kathryn L., et al. "The Promontory Palace at Caesarea Maritima: Preliminary Evidence for Herod's *praetorium*." *JRA* 11 (1998): 23–52.

Glenny, "Continence." Glenny, W. Edward. "1 Corinthians 7:29–31 and the Teaching of Continence in *The Acts of Paul and Thecla*." *GTJ* 11 (1, 1990): 53–70.

Glenny, "Septuagint." Glenny, W. Edward. "The Septuagint and Apostolic Hermeneutics: Amos 9 in Acts 15." *BBR* 22 (1, 2012): 1–26.

Glew, "Experience." Glew, Anne M. S. "Personal Experience in Faith Healing." Pages 81–86 in *Faith Healing: Finger of God? Or, Scientific Curiosity?* Compiled by Claude A. Frazier. New York: Thomas Nelson, 1973.

Glombitza, "Charakterisierung." Glombitza, Otto. "Zur Charakterisierung des Stephanus in Act 6 und 7." *ZNW* 53 (1962): 238–44.

Glover, *Paul*. Glover, T. R. *Paul of Tarsus*. London: Student Christian Movement, 1925. Repr., Peabody, Mass.: Hendrickson, 2002.

Glueck, *Rivers*. Glueck, Nelson. *Rivers in the Desert: A History of the Negev*. New York: Grove, 1960.

Gnilka, "Gemeinschaftsmal." Gnilka, Joachim. "Das Gemeinschaftsmal der Essener." *BZ* 5 (1961): 39–55.

Gnilka, *Jesus*. Gnilka, Joachim. *Jesus of Nazareth: Message and History*. Translated by Siegfried S. Schatzmann. Peabody, Mass.: Hendrickson, 1997.

Gnuse, "Dream Interpreter in Foreign Court." Gnuse, Robert. "The Jewish Dream Interpreter in a Foreign Court: The Recurring Use of a Theme in Jewish Literature." *JSP* 7 (1990): 29–53.

Gnuse, "Prison." Gnuse, Robert. "From Prison to Prestige: The Hero Who Helps a King in Jewish and Greek Literature." *CBQ* 72 (1, 2010): 31–45.

Gnuse, "Temple Experience." Gnuse, Robert K. "The Temple Experience of Jaddus in the *Antiquities* of Josephus: A Report of Jewish Dream Incubation." *JQR* 83 (1993): 349–68.

Gnuse, "Temple Theophanies." Gnuse, Robert. "The Temple Theophanies of Jaddus, Hyrcanus, and Zechariah." *Bib* 79 (4, 1998): 457–72.

Gnuse, "Vita apologetica." Gnuse, Robert. "*Vita apologetica*: The Lives of Josephus and Paul in Apologetic Historiography." *JSP* 13 (2, 2002): 151–69.

Gödde, "Hamadryads." Gödde, Susanne. "Hamadryads." *BrillPauly* 5:1121.

Godin, "Moi perdu." Godin, André. "Moi perdu ou moi retrouvé dans l'expérience charismatique: Perplexité des psychologues." *ASSR* 20 (40, 1975): 31–52.

Godron, "Healings." Godron, Gérard. "Healings in Coptic Literature." *CE* 4:1212–14.

Godwin, *Mystery Religions*. Godwin, Joscelyn. *Mystery Religions in the Ancient World*. San Francisco: Harper & Row, 1981.

Goergen, *Mission*. Goergen, D. J. *The Mission and Ministry of Jesus*. Wilmington, Del.: Michael Glazier, 1986.

Goette, "Athens." Goette, Hans Rupprecht. "Athens." *BrillPauly* 2:254–71.

Goetz and Blomberg, "Burden of Proof." Goetz, Stewart C., and Craig L. Blomberg, "The Burden of Proof." *JSNT* 11 (1981): 39–63.

Goff, *Fields*. Goff, James R., Jr. *Fields White unto Harvest: Charles F. Parham and the Missionary Origins of Pentecostalism*. Fayetteville, Ark.: University of Arkansas Press, 1988.

Goff, "Instruction." Goff, Matthew J. "Hellenistic Instruction in Palestine and Egypt: Ben Sira and Papyrus Insinger." *JSJ* 36 (2, 2005): 147–72.

Goff, "Theology of Parham." Goff, James R., Jr. "Initial Tongues in the Theology of Charles Fox Parham." Pages 57–71 in *Initial Evidence: Historical and Biblical Perspectives on the Pentecostal Doctrine of Spirit Baptism*. Edited by Gary B. McGee. Peabody, Mass.: Hendrickson, 1991.

Goffin, "Poppaea." Goffin, Bettina. "Poppaea (2)." *BrillPauly* 11:614–15.

Goforth, *Goforth*. Goforth, Rosalind. *Goforth of China*. Rev. ed. Minneapolis: Bethany, 1986. Original edition, 1937.

Goguel, *Life*. Goguel, Maurice. *The Life of Jesus*. Translated by Olive Wyon. New York: Macmillan, 1948.

Gökovali, *Guide*. Gökovali, Sadan. *The Complete Guide to Ephesus*. Izmir, Turkey: Ticaret Matbaacilik, n.d.

Golb, "Anomalies." Golb, Norman. "The Major Anomalies in the Qumran-Sectarian Theory and Their Resolution." *QC* 2 (3, 1993): 161–82.

Golb, "Manuscripts." Golb, Norman. "Khirbet Qumran and the Manuscripts of the Judaean Wilderness: Observations on the Logic of Their Investigation." *JNES* 49 (2, 1990): 103–14.

Golb, "Qadmoniot." Golb, Norman. "Qadmoniot and the 'Yahad' Claim." *QC* 7 (3–4, 1997): 171–73.

Golberg, "Choruses." Golberg, Shari. "The Two Choruses Become One: The Absence/Presence of Women in Philo's *On the Contemplative Life*." *JSJ* 39 (4–5, 2008): 459–70.

Gold, "Mosaic Map." Gold, V. R. "The Mosaic Map of Madeba." *BA* 21 (3, 1958): 50–71.

Gold, "She-Wolves." Gold, Barbara K. "How Women (Re)Act in Roman Love Poetry: Inhuman She-Wolves and Unhelpful Mothers in Propertius' *Elegies*." *Helios* 33 (2, 2006): 165–87.

Goldenberg, "Axis." Goldenberg, Robert. "The Broken Axis: Rabbinic Judaism and the Fall of Jerusalem." *JAAR* 45 (3, supplement, 1977): 869–82.

Goldenberg, "Ban." Goldenberg, Robert. "The Septuagint Ban on Cursing the Gods." *JSJ* 28 (4, 1997): 381–89.

Goldenberg, "Barbaria." Goldenberg, David M. "Geographica rabbinica: The Toponym Barbaria." *JJS* 50 (1, 1999): 53–73.

Goldenberg, "Scythian-Barbarian." Goldenberg, David M. "Scythian-Barbarian: The Permutations of a Classical Topos in Jewish and Christian Texts of Late Antiquity." *JJS* 49 (1, 1998): 87–102.

Goldhill, "Anecdote." Goldhill, Simon. "The Anecdote: Exploring the Boundaries between Oral and Literate Performance in the Second Sophistic." Pages 96–113 in *Ancient Literacies: The Culture of Reading in Greece and Rome*. Edited by William A. Johnson and Holt N. Parker. New York: Oxford University Press, 2009.

Goldin, "Magic." Goldin, Judah. "The Magic of Magic and Superstition." Pages 115–47 in *Aspects of Religious Propaganda in Judaism and Early Christianity*. Edited by Elisabeth Schüssler Fiorenza. UNDCS JCA 2. Notre Dame, Ind.: University of Notre Dame Press, 1976.

Golding, "Pagan Worship." Golding, Thomas A. "Pagan Worship in Jerusalem?" *BSac* 170 (679, 2013): 304–16.

Goldingay, "Comic Acts?" Goldingay, John. "Are They Comic Acts?" *EvQ* 69 (2, 1997): 99–107.

Goldingay, "Expounding." Goldingay, John. "Expounding the New Testament." Pages 351–65 in *New Testament Interpretation: Essays on Principles and Methods*. Edited by I. Howard Marshall. Grand Rapids: Eerdmans, 1977.

Goldman, "Roman Footwear." Goldman, Norma. "Roman Footwear." Pages 101–32 in *The World of Roman Costume*. Edited by Judith L. Sebesta and Larissa Bonfante. Madison: University of Wisconsin Press, 2001.

Goldsberry, "Sicily." Goldsberry, Mary A. "Sicily and Its Cities in Hellenistic and Roman Times." PhD diss., University of North Carolina, 1973.

Goldstein, "Acceptance." Goldstein, Jonathan A. "Jewish Acceptance and Rejection of Hellenism." Pages 64–87 in *Aspects of Judaism in the Graeco-Roman Period*. Edited by E. P. Sanders with A. I. Baumgarten and Alan Mendelson. Vol. 2 of *Jewish and Christian Self-Definition*. Edited by E. P. Sanders. Philadelphia: Fortress, 1981.

Goldstein, "Alexander." Goldstein, Jonathan A. "Alexander and the Jews." *PAAJR* 59 (1993): 59–101.

Goldstein and Pingree, "Almanacs." Goldstein, Bernard R., and David Pingree. "Astrological Almanacs from the Cairo Geniza." *JNES* 38 (3, 1979): 153–76; (4, 1979): 231–56.

Gomm, "Spirit Possession." Gomm, Roger. "Bargaining from Weakness: Spirit Possession on the South Kenya Coast." *Man* 10 (1975): 530–43.

Gomme, Cadoux, and Rhodes, "*Ekklēsia*." Gomme, Arnold Wycombe, Theodore John Cadoux, and P. J. Rhodes. "*Ekklēsia*." *OCD*³ 514–15.

Gomme and Hornblower, "*Dokimasia*." Gomme, Arnold Wycombe, and Simon Hornblower. "*Dokimasia*." *OCD*³ 490.

Gomme and Rhodes, "Astynomoi." Gomme, Arnold Wycombe, and P. J. Rhodes. "Astynomoi." *OCD*³ 198.

Gomme and Rhodes, "*Euthyna*." Gomme, Arnold Wycombe, and P. J. Rhodes. "*Euthyna, euthynai*." *OCD*³ 577.

Gomme and Rhodes, "Grammateis." Gomme, Arnold Wycombe, and P. J. Rhodes. "Grammateis." *OCD*³ 646.

Gonzales, "Oracle." Gonzales, Matthew. "The Oracle and Cult of Ares in Asia Minor." *GRBS* 45 (3, 2005): 261–83.

González, *Acts*. González, Justo L. *Acts: The Gospel of the Spirit*. Maryknoll, N.Y.: Orbis, 2001.

Gonzalez, "Healing." Gonzalez, Eliezer. "Healing in the Pauline Epistles: Why the Silence?" *JETS* 56 (3, Sept. 2013): 557–75.

González, *Months*. González, Justo L. *Three Months with the Spirit*. Nashville: Abingdon, 2003.

González Echegaray, "Esclavos." González Echegaray, Joaquín. "Los esclavos en la Palestina del tiempo de Jesús." *Salm* 56 (1, 2009): 85–112.

González and González, *Revelation*. González, Catherine Gunsalus, and Justo L. González. *Revelation*. WestBC. Louisville: Westminster John Knox, 1997.

Good, *King*. Good, Deirdre J. *Jesus the Meek King*. Harrisburg, Pa.: Trinity Press International, 1999.

Goodacre, "Scripturalization." Goodacre, Mark. "Scripturalization in Mark's Crucifixion Narrative." Pages 33–47 in *The Trial and Death of Jesus: Essays on the Passion Narrative in Mark*. Edited by Geert Van Oyen and Tom Shepherd. CBET 45. Leuven: Peeters, 2006.

Goodblatt, "Priestly Ideologies." Goodblatt, David. "Priestly Ideologies of the Judean Resistance." *JSQ* 3 (3, 1996): 225–49.

Goodblatt, "Suicide in Sanctuary." Goodblatt, David. "Suicide in the Sanctuary: Traditions on Priestly Martyrdom." *JJS* 46 (1–2, 1995): 10–29.

Goodenough, "Bosporus Inscriptions." Goodenough, Erwin R. "The Bosporus Inscriptions to the Most High God." *JQR* 47 (1957): 221–44.

Goodenough, *Church*. Goodenough, Erwin R. *The Church in the Roman Empire*. New York: Cooper Square, 1970.

Goodenough, *Introduction*. Goodenough, Erwin R. *An Introduction to Philo Judaeus*. 2nd ed. Oxford: Blackwell, 1962.

Goodenough, "Perspective of Acts." Goodenough, Erwin R. "The Perspective of Acts." Pages 51–59 in *Studies in Luke-Acts: Essays in Honor of Paul Schubert*. Edited by Leander E. Keck and J. Louis Martyn. Nashville: Abingdon, 1966.

Goodenough, *Symbols*. Goodenough, Erwin R. *Jewish Symbols in the Greco-Roman Period*. 13 vols. BollS 37. Vols.

1–12: New York: Pantheon, 1953–65. Vol. 13: Princeton: Princeton University Press, 1968.

Gooder, "Women." Gooder, Paula. "Year of Paul 12: Women in the Pauline Churches." *PastRev* 5 (3, 2009): 10–15.

Goodman, "Angels." Goodman, David. "Do Angels Eat?" *JJS* 37 (1986): 160–75.

Goodman, *Demons*. Goodman, Felicitas D. *How about Demons? Possession and Exorcism in the Modern World*. Bloomington: Indiana University Press, 1988.

Goodman, "Disturbances." Goodman, Felicitas D. "Disturbances in the Apostolic Church: A Trance-Based Upheaval in Yucatán." Pages 227–364 in *Trance, Healing, and Hallucination: Three Field Studies in Religious Experience*. By Felicitas D. Goodman, Jeannette H. Henney, and Esther Pressel. New York: Wiley, 1974.

Goodman, *Ecstasy*. Goodman, Felicitas D. *Ecstasy, Ritual, and Alternate Reality: Religion in a Pluralistic World*. Bloomington: Indiana University Press, 1988.

Goodman, "Essenes." Goodman, Martin. "A Note on the Qumran Sectarians, the Essenes, and Josephus." *JJS* 46 (1–2, 1995): 161–66.

Goodman, "Glossolalia." Goodman, Felicitas D. "Phonetic Analysis of Glossolalia in Four Cultural Settings." *JSSR* 8 (2, 1969): 227–39.

Goodman, *Michel*. Goodman, Felicitas D. *The Exorcism of Anneliese Michel*. Eugene, Ore.: Resource, 2005.

Goodman, "Nerva." Goodman, Martin. "Nerva, the *fiscus judaicus*, and Jewish Identity." *JRS* 79 (1989): 40–44.

Goodman, "Note." Goodman, Martin. "A Note on Josephus, the Pharisees, and Ancestral Tradition." *JJS* 50 (1, 1999): 17–20.

Goodman, "Proselytizing." Goodman, Martin. "Proselytizing in Rabbinic Judaism." *JJS* 40 (2, 1989): 175–85.

Goodman, *Rome and Jerusalem*. Goodman, Martin. *Rome and Jerusalem: The Clash of Ancient Civilizations*. New York: Vintage, 2008.

Goodman, *Ruling Class*. Goodman, Martin. *The Ruling Class of Judaea: The Origins of the Jewish Revolt against Rome, A.D. 66–70*. Cambridge: Cambridge University Press, 1987.

Goodman, *Speaking in Tongues*. Goodman, Felicitas D. *Speaking in Tongues: A Cross-cultural Study of Glossolalia*. Chicago: University of Chicago Press, 1972.

Goodman, *State*. Goodman, Martin. *State and Society in Roman Galilee, A.D. 132–212*. Oxford Centre for Postgraduate Hebrew Studies. Totowa, N.J.: Rowman & Allanheld, 1983.

Goodman, "Style of Discourse." Goodman, Felicitas D. "Altered Mental State vs. 'Style of Discourse': Reply to Samarin." *JSSR* 11 (3, 1972): 297–99.

Goodman, "Trajan." Goodman, Martin. "Trajan and the Origins of Roman Hostility to the Jews." *P&Pres* (182, 2004): 3–29.

Goodman, *Trance Journeys*. Goodman, Felicitas D. *Trance Journeys and Other Ecstatic Experiences*. Bloomington: Indiana University Press, 1990.

Goodman, "Workshop." Goodman, Felicitas D. "Experiential Workshop." Pages 112–15 in *Proceedings of the Fourth International Conference on the Study of Shamanism and Alternate Modes of Healing, Held at the St. Sabina Center, San Rafael, California, September 5–7, 1987*. Edited by Ruth-Inge Heinze. N.p.: Independent Scholars of Asia; Madison, Wis.: A-R Editions, 1988.

Goodman, Henney, and Pressel, *Trance*. Goodman, Felicitas D., Jeannette H. Henney, and Esther Pressel. *Trance, Healing, and Hallucination: Three Field Studies in Religious Experience*. New York: Wiley, 1974.

Goodrich, "Quaestor." Goodrich, John K. "Erastus, *Quaestor* of Corinth: The Administrative Rank of ὁ οἰκονόμος τῆς πόλεως (Rom 16.23) in an Achaean Colony." *NTS* 56 (1, Jan. 2010): 90–115.

Goodrich, "Responding." Goodrich, John K. "Erastus of Corinth (Romans 16.23): Responding to Recent Proposals on His Rank, Status, and Faith." *NTS* 57 (4, Oct. 2011): 583–93.

Goodspeed, "Gaius Titius Justus." Goodspeed, Edgar J. "Gaius Titius Justus." *JBL* 69 (1950): 382–83.

Gooley, "Deacons." Gooley, Anthony. "Deacons and the Servant Myth." *PastRev* 2 (6, 2006): 3–7.

Goppelt, "Existence." Goppelt, Leonhard. "The Existence of the Church in History according to Apostolic and Early Catholic Thought." Pages 193–209 in *Current Issues in New Testament Interpretation: Essays in Honor of Otto A. Piper*. Edited by William Klassen and Graydon F. Snyder. New York: Harper & Row, 1962.

Goppelt, *Judaism*. Goppelt, Leonhard. *Jesus, Paul, and Judaism*. Translated by Edward Schroeder. New York: Thomas Nelson, 1964.

Goppelt, *Theology*. Goppelt, Leonhard. *Theology of the New Testament*. Edited by Jürgen Roloff. Translated by John E. Alsup. 2 vols. Grand Rapids: Eerdmans, 1981–82.

Goppelt, *Times*. Goppelt, Leonhard. *Apostolic and Post-apostolic Times*. Translated by Robert Guelich. Grand Rapids: Baker, 1980.

Goppelt, "Τύπος." Goppelt, Leonhard. "Τύπος, ἀντίτυπος, τυπικός, ὑποτύπωσις." *TDNT* 8:246–59.

Goranson, "Inkwells." Goranson, Stephen. "Qumran—The Evidence of the Inkwells." *BAR* 19 (6, 1993): 67.

Gordis, "'Begotten' Messiah." Gordis, Robert. "The 'Begotten' Messiah in the Qumran Scrolls." *VT* 7 (1957): 191–94.

Gordon, *Civilizations*. Gordon, Cyrus H. *The Common Background of Greek and Hebrew Civilizations*. New York: W. W. Norton, 1965.

Gordon, "Egyptian Deities." Gordon, Richard L. "Egyptian Deities." *OCD*³ 512–13.

Gordon, "Incantations." Gordon, Cyrus H. "Two Aramaic Incantations." Pages 231–44 in *Biblical and Near Eastern Studies: Essays in Honor of William Sanford LaSor*. Edited by Gary A. Tuttle. Grand Rapids: Eerdmans, 1978.

Gordon, *Introduction*. Gordon, Cyrus H. *Introduction to Old Testament Times*. Ventnor, N.J.: Ventnor, 1953.

Gordon, "Ma." Gordon, Richard L. "Ma." *BrillPauly* 8:49–51.

Gordon, "*Mithraeum*." Gordon, Richard L. "The Sacred Geography of a *mithraeum*: The Example of Sette Sfere." *JMS* 1 (2, 1976): 119–65.

Gordon, "Mithraism." Gordon, Richard. "Institutionalized Religious Options: Mithraism." Pages 392–405 in *A Companion to Roman Religion*. Edited by Jörg Rüpke. BCompAW. Oxford: Blackwell, 2011.

Gordon, *Near East*. Gordon, Cyrus H. *The Ancient Near East*. New York: W. W. Norton, 1965.

Gordon, "Poseidon." Gordon, Richard L. "Poseidon." Pages 659–62 in *Dictionary of Deities and Demons in the Bible*. 2nd rev. ed. Edited by Karel van der Toorn, Bob Becking, and Pieter W. van der Horst. Leiden: Brill; Grand Rapids: Eerdmans, 1999.

Gordon, "Psalm 82." Gordon, Cyrus H. "History of Religion in Psalm 82." Pages 129–31 in *Biblical and Near Eastern Studies: Essays in Honor of William Sanford LaSor*. Edited by Gary A. Tuttle. Grand Rapids: Eerdmans, 1978.

Gordon, "Sarapis." Gordon, Richard L. "Sarapis." *OCD*³ 1355–56.

Gordon, "Sceptre." Gordon, Richard L. "Raising a Sceptre: Confession-Narratives from Lydia and Phrygia." *JRA* 17 (2004): 177–96.

Gordon, *Slavery*. Gordon, Murray. *Slavery in the Arab World*. New York: New Amsterdam, 1989.

Gordon, "Syncretism." Gordon, Richard L. "Syncretism." *OCD*³ 1462–63.

Gordon, "Vesta." Gordon, Richard L. "Vesta, Vestals." *OCD*³ 1591.

Görg, "Göttin." Görg, Manfred. "Die Göttin Isis und die heilige Maria: Gottesmütter im Vergleich." *UnS* 59 (4, 2004): 371–80.

Görg, "Ionien." Görg, Manfred. "Ionien und Kleinasien in früher ausserbiblischer Bezeugung." *BN* 127 (2005): 5–10.

Görg, "Wehen." Görg, Manfred. "Vom Wehen des Pneuma." *BN* 66 (1993): 5–9.

Görgemanns, "Biography." Görgemanns, Herwig. "Biography: Greek." *BrillPauly* 2:648–51.

Görgemanns, "Epistolography." Görgemanns, Herwig. "Epistolography." *Brill Pauly* 4:1144–48.

Görgemanns, "Translations." Görgemanns, Herwig. "Translations: Greek Sphere." *BrillPauly* 14:850–52.

Gori, *Carcere Mamertino*. Gori, Fabio. *Il carcere mamertino ed il robore Tulliano*. Rome: Tip. delle Scienze matematiche e fisiche, 1868.

Gorman, *Abortion*. Gorman, Michael. *Abortion and the Early Church: Christian, Jewish, and Pagan Attitudes in the Greco-Roman World*. Downers Grove, Ill.: InterVarsity, 1982.

Gorman, *Apostle*. Gorman, Michael J. *Apostle of the Crucified Lord: A Theological Introduction to Paul and His Letters*. Grand Rapids: Eerdmans, 2004.

Gorman, "*Aristeia*." Gorman, Vanessa B. "Lucan's Epic *Aristeia* and the Hero of the *Bellum civile*." *CJ* 96 (3, 2001): 263–90.

Gorman, "Pythagoras Palaestinus." Gorman, Peter. "Pythagoras Palaestinus." *Phil* 127 (1, 1983): 30–42.

Gornik, *Word*. Gornik, Mark R. *Word Made Global: Stories of African Christianity in New York City*. Foreword by Andrew F. Walls. Afterword by Emmanuel Katongole. Grand Rapids: Eerdmans, 2011.

Goshen-Gottstein, "God the Father." Goshen-Gottstein, Alon. "God the Father in Rabbinic Judaism and Christianity: Transformed Background or Common Ground?" *JES* 38 (3, 2001): 470–504.

Goss, *History*. Goss, Charles Chaucer. *Statistical History of the First Century of American Methodism, with a summary of the origin and present operations of other denominations*. New York: Carlton and Porter, 1866.

Gossmann, "Möglichkeit." Gossmann, Hans-Christoph. "Die Möglichkeit der literarischen Abhängigkeit des Josephus von Ovid: Dargestellt am Beispiel der Sintfluterzählung." *ZRGG* 41 (1, 1989): 83–86.

Goswell, "Hermeneutics." Goswell, Gregory. "The Hermeneutics of the Haftarot." *Tyn Bul* 58 (1, 2007): 83–100.

Goswell, "Order." Goswell, Greg. "The Order of the Books of the New Testament." *JETS* 53 (2, June 2010): 225–41.

Gotter, "*Origines*." Gotter, Ulrich. "Cato's *Origines*: The Historian and His Enemies." Pages 108–22 in *The Cambridge Companion to the Roman Historians*. Edited by Andrew Feldherr. Cambridge: Cambridge University Press, 2009.

Goudineau, "Marseilles." Goudineau, Christian. "Marseilles, Rome, and Gaul from the Third to the First Century BC." Pages 76–86 in *Trade in the Ancient Economy*. Edited by Peter Garnsey, Keith Hopkins, and C. R. Whittaker. Berkeley: University of California Press, 1983.

Gough, "Mappilla." Gough, Kathleen. "Mappilla: North Kerala." Pages 415–42 in *Matrilineal Kinship*. Edited by David M. Schneider and Kathleen Gough. Berkeley: University of California Press, 1973.

Gough, "Variation." Gough, Kathleen. "Variation in Preferential Marriage Forms." Pages 614–30 in *Matrilineal Kinship*. Edited by David M. Schneider and Kathleen Gough. Berkeley: University of California Press, 1973.

Gould, *Ethics*. Gould, John. *The Development of Plato's Ethics*. Cambridge: Cambridge University Press, 1955.

Gould, *Love*. Gould, Thomas. *Platonic Love*. London: Routledge & Kegan Paul, 1963.

Gould, *Philosophy of Chrysippus*. Gould, Josiah B., Jr. *The Philosophy of Chrysippus*. Leiden: Brill, 1970.

Gould, "Position in Athens." Gould, John. "Law, Custom, and Myth: Aspects of the Social Position of Women in Classical Athens." *JHS* 100 (1980): 38–59.

Goulder, *Competing Mission*. Goulder, Michael D. *Paul and the Competing Mission in Corinth*. LPSt. Peabody, Mass.: Hendrickson, 2001.

Goulder, "Letters." Goulder, Michael D. "Did Luke Know Any of the Pauline Letters?" *PRSt* 13 (2, 1986): 97–112.

Goulder, *Midrash*. Goulder, Michael D. *Midrash and Lection in Matthew*. Speaker's Lectures in Biblical Studies, 1969–71. London: SPCK, 1974.

Goulder, *Pavements*. Goulder, Tancred C. *The Mosaic Pavements in the Museum of Roman Antiquities at Rabat, Malta*. Malta: Dept. of Museums, 1983.

Goulder, *Type and History*. Goulder, Michael D. *Type and History in Acts*. London: SPCK, 1964.

Goulet-Cazé, "Hipparchia." Goulet-Cazé, Marie-Odile. "Hipparchia." *BrillPauly* 6:334–35.

Gounelle, "État de la recherche." Gounelle, Rémi. "Actes apocryphes des apôtres et Actes des apôtres canoniques: État de la recherche et perspectives nouvelles (I)." *RHPR* 84 (1, 2004): 3–30.

Gounelle, "Réception." Gounelle, Rémi. "Les Actes apocryphes des apôtres témoignent-ils de la réception des *Actes des apôtres* canoniques?" Pages 177–211 in *Les Actes des apôtres—Histoire, récit, théologie: XXe congrès de l'Association catholique française pour l'étude de la Bible (Angers, 2003).* Edited by Michel Berder. LD 199. Paris: Cerf, 2005.

Gourgues, "Dossier fermé?" Gourgues, Michel. "La literature profane dans le discours d'Athènes (*Ac* 17,16–31): Un dossier fermé?" *RB* 109 (2, 2002): 241–69.

Gourgues, "¿Expediente cerrado?" Gourgues, Michel. "La literature profana en el discurso de Atenas (He 17,16–31): ¿Expediente cerrado?" *Anám* 13 (2, 2003): 15–45.

Gowers, "Syracuse." Gowers, Emily. "Augustus and 'Syracuse.'" *JRS* 100 (2010): 69–87.

Gowing, "Republic." Gowing, Alain M. "The Imperial Republic of Velleius Paterculus." Pages 411–18 in *A Companion to Greek and Roman Historiography.* Edited by John Marincola. 2 vols. Oxford: Blackwell, 2007.

Gowing, "Tradition." Gowing, Alain M. "The Roman *exempla* Tradition in Imperial Greek Historiography: The Case of Camillus." Pages 332–47 in *The Cambridge Companion to the Roman Historians.* Edited by Andrew Feldherr. Cambridge: Cambridge University Press, 2009.

Gowler, *Host, Guest.* Gowler, David B. *Host, Guest, Enemy, and Friend: Portraits of the Pharisees in Luke and Acts.* ESEC 2. New York: Peter Lang, 1991.

Grabbe, "Sanhedrin." Grabbe, Lester L. "Sanhedrin, Sanhedriyyot, or Mere Invention?" *JSJ* 39 (1, 2008): 1–19.

Grabbe, "Synagogue." Grabbe, Lester L. "Synagogue and Sanhedrin in the First Century." Pages 1723–45 in vol. 2 of *Handbook for the Study of the Historical Jesus,* ed. Stanley E. Porter and Tom Holmén. 4 vols. Leiden: Brill, 2011.

Grabbe, "Tradition." Grabbe, Lester L. "The Jannes/Jambres Tradition in Targum Pseudo-Jonathan." *JBL* 98 (3, 1979): 393–461.

Gräbe, "Discovery." Gräbe, Peter J. "The Pentecostal Discovery of the New Testament Theme of God's Power and Its Relevance to the African Context." *Pneuma* 24 (2, 2002): 225–42.

Gräbe, "Δύναμις." Gräbe, Peter J. "Δύναμις (in the Sense of Power) as a Pneumatological Concept in the Main Pauline Letters." *BZ* 36 (2, 1992): 226–35.

Graburn, "Incest Taboos." Graburn, Nelson. "Introduction to 'Incest Taboos: Origins and Functions.'" Pages 324–25 in *Readings in Kinship and Social Structure.* Edited by Nelson Graburn. New York: Harper & Row, 1971.

Graburn, *Readings.* Graburn, Nelson, ed. *Readings in Kinship and Social Structure.* New York: Harper & Row Publishers, 1971.

Gradl, "Gebet." Gradl, Hans-Georg. "Alles liegt in deiner Hand: Ein Gebet der ersten Christen." *ErAuf* 82 (4, 2006): 436–39.

Gradl, "Glaube." Gradl, Hans-Georg. "Glaube in Seenot (Die Stillung des Sturms)—Mk 4,35–41 (Lk 8,22–25)." Pages 257–65 in *Die Wunder Jesu.* Edited by Ruben Zimmermann. Vol. 1 in *Kompendium der frühchristlichen Wundererzählungen.* München: Gütersloh, 2013.

Gradwohl, "Frau." Gradwohl, R. "'Jeder, der keine Frau hat, ist kein Mensch': Eva in der Tradition des Judentums." *BK* 53 (1, 1998): 35–38.

Graeser, *Plotinus and Stoics.* Graeser, Andreas. *Plotinus and the Stoics: A Preliminary Study.* PhilAnt 22. Leiden: Brill, 1972.

Graetz, "Miriam." Graetz, Naomi. "Miriam: Guilty or Not Guilty?" *Judaism* 40 (2, 1991): 184–92.

Graf, "Aphrodite." Graf, Fritz. "Aphrodite." Pages 64–68 in *Dictionary of Deities and Demons in the Bible.* 2nd rev. ed. Edited by Karel van der Toorn, Bob Becking, and Pieter W. van der Horst. Leiden: Brill; Grand Rapids: Eerdmans, 1999.

Graf, *Apollo.* Graf, Fritz. *Apollo.* Gods and Heroes of the Ancient World. London: Routledge, 2009.

Graf, "Archegetes." Graf, Fritz. "Archegetes." *BrillPauly* 1:980–81.

Graf, "Artemis." Graf, Fritz. "Artemis." *BrillPauly* 2:62–67.

Graf, "Asia Minor: Religion." Graf, Fritz. "Asia Minor: Religion: Graeco-Roman Period." *BrillPauly* 2:150–52.

Graf, "Athena." Graf, Fritz. "Athena." Pages 116–19 in *Dictionary of Deities and Demons in the Bible.* 2nd rev. ed. Edited by Karel van der Toorn, Bob Becking, and Pieter W. van der Horst. Leiden: Brill; Grand Rapids: Eerdmans, 1999.

Graf, "Cabiri." Graf, Fritz. "Cabiri." *BrillPauly* 2:860–64.

Graf, "Curse." Graf, Fritz. "Curse: Greece and Rome." *BrillPauly* 3:1018–20.

Graf, "Death." Graf, Fritz. "Untimely Death, Witchcraft, and Divine Vengeance: A Reasoned Epigraphical Catalog." *ZPE* 162 (2007): 139–50.

Graf, "Dionysus." Graf, Fritz. "Dionysus." Pages 252–59 in *Dictionary of Deities and Demons in the Bible.* 2nd rev. ed. Edited by Karel van der Toorn, Bob Becking, and Pieter W. van der Horst. Leiden: Brill; Grand Rapids: Eerdmans, 1999.

Graf, "Dodona." Graf, Fritz. "Dodona, Dodone: Oracle." *BrillPauly* 5:606–7.

Graf, "Ecstasy." Graf, Fritz. "Ecstasy: Greek and Roman Antiquity." *BrillPauly* 4:799–801.

Graf, "Ephesia Grammata." Graf, Fritz. "Ephesia Grammata." *BrillPauly* 4:1023.

Graf, "Epiphany." Graf, Fritz. "Epiphany." *BrillPauly* 4:1121–23.

Graf, "Eponymus." Graf, Fritz. "Eponymus." *BrillPauly* 4:1166–67.

Graf, "Exorcism." Graf, Fritz. "Exorcism." *BrillPauly* 5:270–72.

Graf, "Fortuna." Graf, Fritz. "Fortuna." *BrillPauly* 5:505–9.

Graf, "Healing Deities." Graf, Fritz. "Healing Deities, Healing Cults: Greece and Rome." *BrillPauly* 6:22–26.

Graf, "Healing Gods." Graf, Fritz. "Healing Gods." *OCD³* 670.

Graf, "Heracles: Cult." Graf, Fritz. "Heracles: Cult." *BrillPauly* 6:159–60.

Graf, "Hero Cult." Graf, Fritz. "Hero Cult." *BrillPauly* 6:247–51.

Graf, "Hieros Gamos: Greece." Graf, Fritz. "Hieros Gamos: Greece." *BrillPauly* 6:322.

Graf, "Hieros Gamos: Term." Graf, Fritz. "Hieros Gamos: Term." *BrillPauly* 6:321.

Graf, "Hispania." Graf, Fritz. "Hispania, Iberia: Religion." *BrillPauly* 6:396–98.

Graf, "Hypsistos." Graf, Fritz. "Hypsistos." *BrillPauly* 6:650–52.

Graf, "Incubation" (*BrillPauly*). Graf, Fritz. "Incubation." *BrillPauly* 6:766–67.

Graf, "Incubation" (*OCD³*). Graf, Fritz. "Incubation." *OCD³* 753–54.

Graf, "Initiation." Graf, Fritz. "The Magician's Initiation." *Helios* 21 (2, 1994): 161–77.

Graf, "Ionian Festivals." Graf, Fritz. "Ionian Festivals." *OCD³* 764.

Graf, *Magic.* Graf, Fritz. *Magic in the Ancient World.* Translated by Franklin Philip. Cambridge, Mass.: Harvard University Press, 1997.

Graf, "Nabateans." Graf, David F. "Nabateans." *OEANE* 4:82–85.

Graf, "Thargelia." Graf, Fritz. "Thargelia." *OCD³* 1492.

Graf, "Zeus." Graf, Fritz. "Zeus." Pages 934–40 in *Dictionary of Deities and Demons in the Bible.* 2nd rev. ed. Edited by Karel van der Toorn, Bob Becking, and

Pieter W. van der Horst. Leiden: Brill; Grand Rapids: Eerdmans, 1999.

Grafton, "Arabs." Grafton, David D. "The Arabs of Pentecost: Greco-Roman Views of the Arabs and Their Cultural Identity." *NESTTR* 30 (2, 2009): 183–201.

Grafton, "Eclipses." Grafton, Anthony T. "Eclipses." *OCD*³ 502.

Grafton, "Time-reckoning." Grafton, Anthony T. "Time-reckoning." *OCD*³ 1527–28.

Grainger, *Phoenicia*. Grainger, John D. *Hellenistic Phoenicia*. Oxford: Clarendon, 1991.

Grainger, *Syria*. Grainger, John D. *The Cities of Seleucid Syria*. Oxford: Clarendon, 1990.

Gramaglia, "*Testimonium*." Gramaglia, P. A. "Il *Testimonium Flavianum*: Analisi linguistica." *Hen* 20 (2, 1998): 153–77.

Grams, "Mission Theologians." Grams, R. G. "Paul among the Mission Theologians." *Missionalia* 33 (3, 2005): 459–79.

Granger-Taylor, "Toga." Granger-Taylor, Hero. "Toga." *OCD*³ 1533.

Grant, "Black Woman." Grant, Jacquelyn. "Black Theology and the Black Woman." Pages 323–38 in vol. 1 of *Black Theology: A Documentary History*. Edited by James H. Cone and Gayraud S. Wilmore. 2nd ed. rev. 2 vols. Maryknoll, N.Y.: Orbis, 1993.

Grant, *Black Women's Jesus*. Grant, Jacquelyn. *White Women's Christ and Black Women's Jesus: Feminist Christology and Womanist Response*. AARAS 64. Atlanta: Scholars Press, 1989.

Grant, "Christian and Roman History." Grant, Robert M. "Introduction: Christian and Roman History." Pages 15–26 in *The Catacombs and the Colosseum: The Roman Empire as the Setting of Primitive Christianity*. Edited by Stephen Benko and John J. O'Rourke. Valley Forge, Pa.: Judson, 1971.

Grant, *Christianity and Society*. Grant, Robert M. *Early Christianity and Society: Seven Studies*. San Francisco: Harper & Row, 1977.

Grant, "Dietary Laws." Grant, Robert M. "Dietary Laws among Pythagoreans, Jews, and Christians." *HTR* 73 (1–2, 1980): 299–310.

Grant, "Economic Background." Grant, F. C. "The Economic Background of the New Testament." Pages 96–114 in *The Background of the New Testament and Its Eschatology: Essays in Honour of Charles Harold Dodd*. Edited by W. D. Davies and D. Daube. Cambridge: Cambridge University Press, 1964.

Grant, *Gnosticism*. Grant, Robert M. *Gnosticism and Early Christianity*. 2nd ed. New York: Columbia University Press, 1966.

Grant, *Gods*. Grant, Robert M. *Gods and the One God*. LEC 1. Philadelphia: Westminster, 1986.

Grant, *Hellenism*. Grant, Frederick C. *Roman Hellenism and the New Testament*. New York: Scribner's, 1962.

Grant, *Historians*. Grant, Michael. *The Ancient Historians*. New York: Scribner's; London: Weidenfeld and Nicolson, 1970.

Grant, "Introduction to Tacitus." Grant, Michael. Introduction. Pages 7–26 in Tacitus, *The Annals of Imperial Rome*. Rev. ed. Translated by Michael Grant. Baltimore: Penguin, 1959.

Grant, *Judaism and New Testament*. Grant, Frederick C. *Ancient Judaism and the New Testament*. New York: Macmillan, 1959.

Grant, *Miracle*. Grant, Robert M. *Miracle and Natural Law in Graeco-Roman and Early Christian Thought*. Amsterdam: North-Holland, 1952.

Grant, *Paul*. Grant, Robert M. *Paul in the Roman World: The Conflict at Corinth*. Louisville: Westminster John Knox, 2001.

Grant, *Religions*. Grant, Frederick C., ed. *Hellenistic Religions: The Age of Syncretism*. Library of Liberal Arts. Indianapolis: Bobbs-Merrill; New York: Liberal Arts, 1953.

Grant, *Social History*. Grant, Michael. *A Social History of Greece and Rome*. New York: Scribner's; Oxford: Maxwell Macmillan International, 1992.

Grant, "Social Setting." Grant, Robert M. "The Social Setting of Second-Century Christianity." Pages 16–29 in *The Shaping of Christianity in the Second and Third Centuries*. Vol. 1 of *Jewish and Christian Self-Definition*. Edited by E. P. Sanders. Philadelphia: Fortress, 1980.

Grappe, "Intérêt." Grappe, Christian. "De l'intérêt de 4 Maccabées 17.18–22 (et 16.20–1) pour la christologie du NT." *NTS* 46 (3, 2000): 342–57.

Grappe, "Jésus." Grappe, Christian. "Jésus parmi d'autres prophètes de son temps." *RHPR* 81 (4, 2001): 387–411.

Grappe, "Récit de la Pentecôte." Grappe, Christian. "À la jonction entre Inter et Nouveau Testament: Le récit de la Pentecôte." *FoiVie* 89 (5, 1990): 19–27.

Grappe, "Repas." Grappe, Christian. "Repas nocturnes, fêtes et identité dans les Actes." *RHPR* 93 (1, 2013): 121–34.

Grasham, "Archaeology and Baptism." Grasham, Bill. "Archaeology and Christian Baptism." *ResQ* 43 (2, 2001): 113–16.

Grässer, *Forschungen*. Grässer, Erich. *Forschungen zur Apostelgeschichte*. WUNT 137. Tübingen: Mohr Siebeck, 2001.

Grässer, "Parusieerwartung." Grässer, Erich. "Die Parusieerwartung in der Apostelgeschichte." Pages 99–127 in *Les Actes des apôtres: Traditions, rédaction, théologie*. Edited by Jacob Kremer. BETL 48. Gembloux, Belg.: J. Duculot; Leuven: Leuven University Press, 1979.

Grassi, "Ezekiel xxxvii.1–14." Grassi, Joseph A. "Ezekiel xxxvii.1–14 and the New Testament." *NTS* 11 (2, 1965): 162–64.

Grassi, *Laugh*. Grassi, Joseph A. *God Makes Me Laugh: A New Approach to Luke*. GNS 17. Wilmington, Del.: Michael Glazier, 1986.

Grassi, "Matrix." Grassi, Joseph A. "Mary as Matrix in Luke's Response to Worship of Artemis/Diana, the Moon Mother Goddess (Acts 19:21–41)." *EphMar* 57 (1, 2007): 17–27.

Grassi, *World*. Grassi, Joseph A. *A World to Win: The Missionary Methods of Paul the Apostle*. Maryknoll, N.Y.: Maryknoll, 1965.

Graver, "Προπάθειαι." Graver, M. "Philo of Alexandria and the Origins of the Stoic προπάθειαι." *Phronesis* 44 (4, 1999): 300–325.

Graves, "Paradigm." Graves, Michael. "WWLD? The Writer of Luke-Acts as a Paradigm for Pastoral Prophetic Preaching." *RevExp* 109 (3, 2012): 397–412.

Graves, "Reading." Graves, Michael. "The Public Reading of Scripture in Early Judaism." *JETS* 50 (3, 2007): 467–87.

Graves and May, *Matthew*. Graves, Mike, and David M. May. *Preaching Matthew: Interpretation and Proclamation*. Saint Louis: Chalice, 2007.

Gray, "Athenian Curiosity." Gray, Patrick. "Athenian Curiosity (Acts 17:21)." *NovT* 47 (2, 2005): 109–16.

Gray, "Class and Classics." Gray, Bennison. "Class and Classics: The Social Basis of Ancient Bilingualism." *LangSc* 1 (1, 1979): 50–84.

Gray, "Cult." Gray, Robert F. "The Shetani Cult among the Segeju of Tanzania." Pages 171–87 in *Spirit Mediumship and Society in Africa*. Edited by John Beattie and John Middleton. Foreword by Raymond Firth. New York: Africana, 1969.

Gray, "Exorcism." Gray, John N. "Bayu Utarnu: Ghost Exorcism and Sacrifice in Nepal." *Ethnology* 26 (1987): 179–99.

Gray, *Figures*. Gray, Rebecca. *Prophetic Figures in Late Second Temple Jewish Palestine: The Evidence from Josephus*. New York: Oxford University Press, 1993.

Gray, "Implied Audiences." Gray, Patrick. "Implied Audiences in the Areopagus Narrative." *TynBul* 55 (2, 2004): 205–18.

Gray, *"Mimesis."* Gray, Vivienne. *"Mimesis* in Greek Historical Theory." *AJP* 108 (3, 1987): 467–86.

Gray, "Narrative Manner." Gray, Vivienne. "Narrative Manner and Xenopon's More Routine *Hellenica*." Pages 342–48 in *A Companion to Greek and Roman Historiography*. Edited by John Marincola. 2 vols. Oxford: Blackwell, 2007.

Gray, "Orontes." Gray, Eric William. "Orontes." *OCD*[3] 1077.

Gray-Fow, "Why Christians?" Gray-Fow, M. J. G. "Why the Christians? Nero and the Great Fire." *Latomus* 57 (3, 1998): 595–616.

Grayston, *Epistles.* Grayston, Kenneth. *The Johannine Epistles.* NCBC. Grand Rapids: Eerdmans; London: Marshall, Morgan & Scott, 1984.

Grayston and Herdan, "Authorship." Grayston, K., and G. Herdan, "The Authorship of the Pastorals in the Light of Statistical Linguistics." *NTS* 6 (1, 1959): 1–15.

Grayzel, *History of Jews.* Grayzel, Solomon. *A History of the Jews.* 2nd ed. Philadelphia: Jewish Publication Society of America, 1968.

Grazier, *Power Beyond.* Grazier, Jack. *The Power Beyond: In Search of Miraculous Healing.* New York: Macmillan, 1989.

Grebe, "Exile." Grebe, Sabine. "Why Did Ovid Associate His Exile with a Living Death?" *CW* 103 (4, 2010): 491–509.

Green, "Acts." Green, Joel B. "Acts." Pages 735–67 in *The New Interpreter's One Volume Commentary.* Edited by Beverly Roberts Gaventa and David Petersen. Nashville: Abingdon, 2010.

Green, "Anuncio." Green, Eugenio. "El anuncio del evangelio ante el poder imperial en Tesalónica." *Kairós* 39 (2006): 9–21.

Green, *Asian Tigers.* Green, Michael. *Asian Tigers for Christ: The Dynamic Growth of the Church in South East Asia.* Foreword by Datuk Yong Ping Chung. London: SPCK, 2001.

Green, "Claudius." Green, C. M. C. "Claudius, Kingship, and Incest." *Latomus* 57 (4, 1998): 765–91.

Green, "Cornelius." Green, Joel B. "Cornelius." *DLNTD* 243–45.

Green, "Crucifixion." Green, Joel B. "Crucifixion." *DPL* 197–99.

Green, "Death." Green, Joel B. "Death of Christ." *DPL* 201–9.

Green, "Demise of Temple." Green, Joel B. "The Demise of the Temple as 'Culture Center' in Luke-Acts: An Exploration of the Rending of the Temple Veil (Luke 23:44–49)." *RB* 101 (4, 1994): 495–515.

Green, "Diodorus." Green, Peter. "Diodorus Siculus on the Third Sacred War." Pages 363–70 in *A Companion to Greek and Roman Historiography.* Edited by John Marincola. 2 vols. Oxford: Blackwell, 2007.

Green, *Evangelism.* Green, Michael. *Evangelism in the Early Church.* Grand Rapids: Eerdmans, 1970.

Green, "Festus." Green, Joel B. "Festus, Porcius." *ABD* 2:794–95.

Green, "Good News." Green, Joel B. "Good News to Whom? Jesus and the 'Poor' in the Gospel of Luke." Pages 59–74 in *Jesus of Nazareth, Lord and Christ: Essays on the Historical Jesus and New Testament Christology.* Edited by Joel B. Green and Max Turner. Grand Rapids: Eerdmans; Carlisle, U.K.: Paternoster, 1994.

Green, "History/Writing." Green, Joel B. "The Book of Acts as History/Writing." *LTQ* 37 (3, 2002): 119–27.

Green, *Holy Spirit.* Green, Michael. *I Believe in the Holy Spirit.* 2nd ed. Grand Rapids: Eerdmans, 1989.

Green, "Interpretation." Green, Gene L. "Relevance Theory and Biblical Interpretation." Pages 217–40 in *The Linguist as Pedagogue: Trends in Teaching and Linguistic Analysis of the New Testament.* Edited by Stanley E. Porter and Matthew Brook O'Donnell. NTMon. Sheffield: Sheffield Phoenix, 2009.

Green, *Luke.* Green, Joel B. *The Gospel of Luke.* NICNT. Grand Rapids: Eerdmans, 1997.

Green, "Metarepresentation." Green, Gene L. "Relevance Theory and Theological Interpretation: Thoughts on Metarepresentation." *Journal of Theological Interpretation* 4 (2010): 75–90.

Green, "Monsters." Green, Anthony. "Monsters: Ancient East and Egypt." *BrillPauly* 9:182–83.

Green, "Patrón." Green, Eugenio. "¡Patrón! La clientela en Tesalónica romana." *Kairós* 43 (2008): 79–85.

Green, "Possession and *Pneuma.*" Green, Peter. "Possession and *Pneuma*: The Essential Nature of the Delphic Oracle." *Arion* 17 (2, 2009): 27–47.

Green, "Pragmatics." Green, Gene L. "Lexical Pragmatics and Biblical Interpretation." *JETS* 50 (4, 2007): 799–812.

Green, "Problem of Beginning." Green, Joel B. "The Problem of a Beginning: Israel's Scriptures in Luke 1–2." *BBR* 4 (1994): 61–85.

Green, "Pythagoras." Green, Elliot A. "Did Pythagoras Follow Nazirite Rules?" *JBQ* 20 (1, 1991): 35–42, 60.

Green, "Queen." Green, Elliott A. "The Queen of Sheba: A Queen of Egypt and Ethiopia?" *JBQ* 29 (3, 2001): 151–55.

Green, "Rabbinic Production." Green, Dennis. "4QIs[c]: A Rabbinic Production of Isaiah found at Qumran?" *JJS* 53 (1, 2002): 120–45.

Green, "Reaffirmation." Green, Joel B. "Luke-Acts, or Luke and Acts? A Reaffirmation of Narrative Unity." Pages 101–19 in *Reading Acts Today: Essays in Honour of Loveday C. A. Alexander.* Edited by Steve Walton et al. LNTS 427. London: T&T Clark, 2011.

Green, "Repentance and Forgiveness." Green, Joel B. "'Proclaiming Repentance and Forgiveness of Sins to All Nations': A Biblical Perspective on the Church's Mission." Pages 13–43 in *The World Is My Parish: The Mission of the Church in Methodist Perspective.* Edited by A. G. Padgett. StHistMiss 10. Lewiston, N.Y.: Edwin Mellen, 1992.

Green, "Repetition." Green, Joel B. "Internal Repetition in Luke-Acts: Contemporary Narratology and Lucan Historiography." Pages 283–99 in *History, Literature, and Society in the Book of Acts.* Edited by Ben Witherington III. Cambridge: Cambridge University Press, 1996.

Green, "Salvation." Green, Joel B. "Salvation to the Ends of the Earth: God as the Saviour in the Acts of the Apostles." Pages 83–106 in *Witness to the Gospel: The Theology of Acts.* Edited by I. Howard Marshall and David Peterson. Grand Rapids: Eerdmans, 1998.

Green, *Spirit.* Green, Michael. *I Believe in the Holy Spirit.* 2nd ed. Grand Rapids: Eerdmans, 1989.

Green, *Storm-God.* Green, Alberto R. W. *The Storm-God in the Ancient Near East.* Biblical and Judaic Studies from the University of California, San Diego 8. Winona Lake, Ind.: Eisenbrauns, 2003.

Green, "Syria and Cilicia." Green, E. M. B. "Syria and Cilicia—A Note." *ExpT* 71 (2, 1959): 52–53.

Green, *Thirty Years.* Green, Michael. *Thirty Years That Changed the World: The Book of Acts for Today.* Grand Rapids: Eerdmans, 2002.

Green, "Undeifying Tiberius." Green, Steven J. "Undeifying Tiberius: A Reconsideration of Seneca, *Apocolcyntosis* 1.2." *CQ* 60 (1, 2010): 274–76.

Green, "Will of God." Green, Gene L. "Finding the Will of God: Historical and Modern Perspectives, Acts 16:1–30." Pages 209–20 in *Mission in Acts: Ancient Narratives in Contemporary Context.* Edited by Robert L. Gallagher and Paul Hertig. AmSocMissS 34. Maryknoll, N.Y.: Orbis, 2004.

Green, *Word*. Green, Chris. *The Word of His Grace: A Guide to Teaching and Preaching from Acts*. Leicester: Inter-Varsity, 2005.

Green and McKeever, *Historiography*. Green, Joel B., and Michael C. McKeever. *Luke-Acts and New Testament Historiography*. IBRB 8. Grand Rapids: Baker, 1994.

Greenbaum, "Possession Trance." Greenbaum, Lenora. "Possession Trance in Sub-Saharan Africa: A Descriptive Analysis of Fourteen Societies." Pages 58–87 in *Religion, Altered States of Consciousness, and Social Change*. Edited by Erika Bourguignon. Columbus: Ohio State University Press, 1973.

Greenbaum, "Societal Correlates." Greenbaum, Lenora. "Societal Correlates of Possession Trance in Sub-Saharan Africa." Pages 39–57 in *Religion, Altered States of Consciousness, and Social Change*. Edited by Erika Bourguignon. Columbus: Ohio State University Press, 1973.

Greenberg, "Indications." Greenberg, Gillian. "Indications of the Faith of the Translator in the Peshitta to the 'Servant Songs' of Deutero-Isaiah." *AramSt* 2 (2, 2004): 175–92.

Greene, "Libya." Greene, Joseph A. "Libya." *OEANE* 3:357–58.

Greene, "North Africa." Greene, Joseph A. "North Africa." *OEANE* 4:154–64.

Greene and Scheid, "*Pietas*." Greene, William Chase, and John Scheid. "*Pietas*." *OCD*[3] 1182.

Greenfield, *Spirits*. Greenfield, Sidney M. *Spirits with Scalpels: The Culturalbiology of Religious Healing in Brazil*. Walnut Creek, Calif.: Left Coast Press, 2008.

Greenfield and Sokoloff, "Astrological Text." Greenfield, J. C., and M. Sokoloff, "An Astrological Text from Qumran (4Q318) and Reflections on Some Zodiacal Names." *RevQ* 16 (4, 1995): 507–25.

Greenfield and Sokoloff, "Omen Texts." Greenfield, J. C., and M. Sokoloff, "Astrological and Related Omen Texts in Jewish Palestinian Aramaic." *JNES* 48 (3, 1989): 201–14.

Greengus, "Gaps." Greengus, Samuel. "Filling Gaps: Laws Found in Babylonia and in the Mishna but Absent in the Hebrew Bible." *Maarav* 7 (1991): 149–71.

Greenhut, "Cave." Greenhut, Zvi. "Burial Cave of the Caiaphas Family." *BAR* 18 (5, 1992): 28–36, 76.

Greenhut, "Tomb." Greenhut, Zvi. "Discovery of the Caiaphas Family Tomb." *JerPersp* 4 (4–5, 1991): 6–12.

Greening and Stoppelbein, "Religiosity." Greening, L., and L. Stoppelbein. "Religiosity, Attributional Style, and Social Support as Psychosocial Buffers for African American and White Adolescents' Perceived Risk for Suicide." *Suicide and Life-Threatening Behavior* 32 (4, 2002): 404–17.

Greenspahn, "Prophecy." Greenspahn, Frederick E. "Why Prophecy Ceased." *JBL* 108 (1, 1989): 37–49.

Greenspan, "Blue." Greenspan, Art. "The Search for Biblical Blue." *BRev* 19 (1, 2003): 32–39, 52.

Greenspoon, "Mission." Greenspoon, Leonard J. "Mission to Alexandria: Truth and Legend about the Creation of the Septuagint, the First Bible Translation." *BRev* 5 (4, 1989): 34–37, 40–41.

Greenspoon, "Pronouncement Story." Greenspoon, Leonard J. "The Pronouncement Story in Philo and Josephus." *Semeia* 20 (1981): 73–80.

Greenstone, *Messiah*. Greenstone, Julius H. *The Messiah Idea in Jewish History*. Philadelphia: Jewish Publication Society of America, 1906.

Greenway, "Success." Greenway, Roger S. "Success in the City: Paul's Urban Mission Strategy, Acts 14:1–28." Pages 183–95 in *Mission in Acts: Ancient Narratives in Contemporary Context*. Edited by Robert L. Gallagher and Paul Hertig. AmSoc MissS 34. Maryknoll, N.Y.: Orbis, 2004.

Greenway, "Urban Church Planting." Greenway, Roger S. "Keys to Urban Church Planting." Pages 11–19 in *Guidelines for Urban Church Planting*. Edited by Roger S. Greenway. Grand Rapids: Baker, 1976.

Greeven, "Propheten." Greeven, Heinrich. "Propheten, Lehrer, Vorsteher bei Paulus: Zur Frage der 'Amten' im Urchristentum." *ZNW* 44 (1952–53): 1–43.

Gregor, "Abortigo." Gregor, Douglas B. "Abortigo en la antikva mondo." *BRev* 17 (4, 1981): 71–90.

Gregory, "Abraham." Gregory, Bradley C. "Abraham as the Jewish Ideal: Exegetical Traditions in Sirach 44:19–21." *CBQ* 70 (1, 2008): 66–81.

Gregory, "Galilee." Gregory, Andrew. "A Galilee Less Greek Than Before?" *ExpT* 118 (7, 2007): 337–38.

Gregory, "Irenaeus." Gregory, Andrew. "Irenaeus and the Reception of Acts in the Second Century." Paper presented at the annual meeting of the SBL, Washington, D.C., Nov. 19, 2006.

Gregory, *Reception*. Gregory, Andrew. *The Reception of Luke and Acts in the Period before Irenaeus: Looking for Luke in the Second Century*. WUNT 2.169. Tübingen: Mohr Siebeck, 2003.

Gregory, "Reception and Unity." Gregory, Andrew. "The Reception of Luke and Acts and the Unity of Luke-Acts." *JSNT* 29 (4, 2007): 459–72.

Gregory, "Reception of Acts." Gregory, Andrew. "Irenaeus and the Reception of Acts in the Second Century." Pages 47–65 in *Contemporary Studies in Acts*. Edited by Thomas E. Phillips. Macon, Ga.: Mercer University Press, 2009.

Gregory, "Secular Bias." Gregory, Brad S. "The Other Confessional History: On Secular Bias in the Study of Religion." *History and Theory* 45 (4, 2006): 132–49.

Greiner, "Eve." Greiner, Susan L. "Did Eve Fall or Was She Pushed?" *BRev* 15 (4, 1999): 16–23, 50–51.

Grelot, "Démonologie." Grelot, Pierre. "Miracles de Jésus et Démonologie Juive." Pages 59–72 in *Les Miracles de Jésus selon le Nouveau Testament*, by J.-N. Aletti et al. Edited by Xavier Léon-Dufour. Paris: Éditions du Seuil, 1977.

Grelot, "Étude." Grelot, Pierre. "Étude critique de Luc 10, 19." *RSR* 69 (1, 1981): 87–100.

Grelot, "Noms." Grelot, Pierre. "Les noms de parenté dans le livre de *Tobie*." *RevQ* 17 (65–68, 1996): 327–37.

Grelot, "Notes sur Testament." Grelot, Pierre. "Notes sur le Testament araméen de Levi." *RB* 63 (3, 1956): 391–406.

Grene, *Political Theory*. Grene, David. *Greek Political Theory: The Image of Man in Thucydides and Plato*. Chicago: University of Chicago Press, 1950.

Grenfell and Hunt, *Fragments*. Grenfell, Bernard, and Arthur Hunt, eds. *New Classical Fragments and Other Greek and Latin Papyri*. Oxford: Clarendon, 1897.

Grenz and Olson, *Theology*. Grenz, Stanley J., and Roger E. Olson. *Twentieth-Century Theology: God and the World in a Transitional Age*. Downers Grove, Ill.: InterVarsity, 1992.

Gresham, *Doctrine*. Gresham, John L., Jr. *Charles G. Finney's Doctrine of the Baptism of the Holy Spirit*. Peabody, Mass.: Hendrickson, 1987.

Grieb, *Story*. Grieb, A. Katherine. *The Story of Romans: A Narrative Defense of God's Righteousness*. Louisville: Westminster John Knox, 2002.

Grieshammer, "Isis." Grieshammer, Reinhard. "Isis: Egypt." *BrillPauly* 6:966.

Griffin, "Demetrius." Griffin, Miriam T. "Demetrius (19)." *OCD*[3] 450.

Griffin, *Nero*. Griffin, Miriam T. *Nero: The End of a Dynasty*. New Haven: Yale University Press, 1984.

Griffin, "Philosophy." Griffin, Miriam T. "Philosophy, Cato, and Roman Suicide." *GR* 33 (1986): 64–77, 192–202.

Griffin, "Suicide." Griffin, Miriam T. "Suicide." *OCD*[3] 1453.

Griffith, "Miracles." Griffith, Stephen. "Miracles and the Shroud of Turin." *FPhil* 13 (1, 1996): 34–49.

Griffith, "Mithras." Griffith, Alison B. "Mithras, Death, and Redemption in Statius, *Thebaid* I, 717–20." *Latomus* 60 (1, 2001): 108–23.

Griffith, "Women." Griffith, Alison B. "Completing the Picture: Women and the Female Principle in the Mithraic Cult." *Numen* 53 (1, 2006): 48–77.

Griffith and Sherwin-White, "Antiochus." Griffith, Guy Thompson, and Susan Mary Sherwin-White. "Antiochus IV." *OCD*³108–9.

Griffith, Young, and Smith, "Elements." Griffith, Ezra E., John L. Young, and Dorothy L. Smith. "An Analysis of the Therapeutic Elements in a Black Church Service." *HCPsy* 35 (5, May 1984): 464–69.

Griffiths, "Baucis." Griffiths, Alan H. "Baucis." *OCD*³ 236–37.

Griffiths, "Epimenides." Griffiths, Alan H. "Epimenides." *OCD*³ 546.

Griffiths, "Scylla." Griffiths, Alan H. "Scylla." *OCD*³ 1374.

Griffiths, "Xenoglossy." Griffiths, J. Gwyn. "Some Claims of Xenoglossy in the Ancient Languages." *Numen* 33 (1, 1986): 141–69.

Grigg, *Urban Poor*. Grigg, Viv. *Cry of the Urban Poor*. Monrovia, Calif.: MARC, World Vision International, 1992.

Grigoropoulos, "Population." Grigoropoulos, Dimitris. "The Population of the Piraeus in the Roman Period: A Reassessment of the Evidence of Funerary Inscriptions." *GR* 56 (2, 2009): 164–82.

Grillo, "Reflections." Grillo, Luca. "Leaving Troy and Creusa: Reflections on Aeneas' Flight." *CJ* 106 (1, 2010): 43–68.

Grillo, "*Scribam*." Grillo, Luca. "*Scribam ipse de me*: The Personality of the Narrator in Caesar's *Bellum Civile*." *AJP* 132 (2, 2011): 243–71.

Grindal, "Heart." Grindal, Bruce T. "Into the Heart of Sisala Experience: Witnessing Death Divination." *JAnthRes* 39 (1983): 60–80.

Grindheim, "Jødedommen." Grindheim, S. "Paulus og jødedommen: Et overblikk over nyere forskning." *TTKi* 77 (2, 2006): 102–16.

Grintz, "Hebrew." Grintz, Jehoshua M. "Hebrew as the Spoken and Written Language in the Last Days of the Second Temple." *JBL* 79 (1, 1960): 32–47.

Grintz, "Jubilees." Grintz, Yehoshua M. "Jubilees, Book of." *EncJud* 10:324–26.

Grisez, *Abortion*. Grisez, Germain. *Abortion: The Myths, the Realities, and the Arguments*. New York: Corpus, 1970.

Groenewald, "Mammon." Groenewald, E. P. "God and Mammon." *Neot* 1 (1967): 59–66.

Groenewegen-Frankfort and Ashmole, *World*. Groenewegen-Frankfort, H. A., and Bernard Ashmole. *The Ancient World*. Library of Art History 1. New York: New American Library, 1967.

Grof, "Potential." Grof, Stanislav. "Healing Potential of Spiritual Experiences: Observations from Modern Consciousness Research." Pages 126–46 in *Psychodynamics*. Vol. 3 of *The Healing Power of Spirituality: How Faith Helps Humans Thrive*. Edited by J. Harold Ellens. 3 vols. Santa Barbara, Calif.: Praeger, 2010.

Groh, "Jews and Christians." Groh, Dennis E. "Jews and Christians in Late Roman Palestine: Towards a New Chronology." *BA* 51 (2, 1988): 80–96.

Groh, "Meal." Groh, John E. "The Qumran Meal and the Last Supper." *CTM* 41 (1970): 279–95.

Gross-Albenhausen, "Princeps castrorum." Gross-Albenhausen, Kirsten. "Princeps castrorum." *BrillPauly* 11:858.

Grossfeld, "Torah." Grossfeld, Bernard. "Torah." *DNTB* 1241–45.

Grossman, "Figurine." Grossman, E. "The Bronze Figurine of the Goddess Minerva from Apollonia, Israel." *TA* 20 (2, 1993): 225–27.

Grossman, "Reading." Grossman, Maxine. "Reading for Gender in the Damascus Document." *DSD* 11 (2, 2004): 212–39.

Grubbs, "Marriage." Grubbs, Judith Evans. "'Marriage More Shameful Than Adultery': Slave-Mistress Relationships, 'Mixed Marriages,' and Late Roman Law." *Phoenix* 47 (2, 1993): 125–54.

Gruber-Miller, "Relationships." Gruber-Miller, John. "Exploring Relationships: *Amicitia* and *Familia* in Cicero's *de Amicitia*." *CW* 103 (1, 2009): 88–92.

Gruchy, "Mission." Gruchy, Steve de. "Mission in Acts 1–11: An Experiment in Bible Study." *IntRevMiss* 94 (373, 2005): 228–34.

Grudem, *Gifts*. Grudem, Wayne A., ed. *Are Miraculous Gifts for Today? Four Views*. Grand Rapids: Zondervan, 1996.

Grudem, *Prophecy*. Grudem, Wayne A. *The Gift of Prophecy in 1 Corinthians*. Lanham, Md.: University Press of America, 1982.

Grudem, *Theology*. Grudem, Wayne. *Systematic Theology: An Introduction to Biblical Doctrine*. Grand Rapids: Zondervan, 1994.

Gruen, *Diaspora*. Gruen, Erich S. *Diaspora: Jews amidst Greeks and Romans*. Cambridge, Mass.: Harvard University Press, 2002.

Grüll and Benke, "Graffito." Grüll, Tibor, and László Benke. "A Hebrew/Aramaic Graffito and Poppaea's Alleged Jewish Sympathy." *JJS* 62 (1, 2011): 37–55.

Grummond, "Pax Augusta." Grummond, Nancy Thomson de. "Pax Augusta and the Horae on the Ara Pacis Augustae." *AJA* 94 (4, 1990): 663–77.

Grundmann, "Decision." Grundmann, Walter. "The Decision of the Supreme Court to Put Jesus to Death (John 11:47–57) in Its Context: Tradition and Redaction in the Gospel of John." Pages 295–318 in *Jesus and the Politics of His Day*. Edited by Ernst Bammel and C. F. D. Moule. Cambridge: Cambridge University Press, 1984.

Grundmann, "δύναμαι/δύναμις." Grundmann, Walter. "δύναμαι/δύναμις." *TDNT* 2:284–317.

Grundmann, "Healing." Grundmann, Christoffer H. "Healing—A Challenge to Church and Theology." *IntRevMiss* 90 (356–57, 2001): 26–40.

Grundmann, *Jesus der Galiläer*. Grundmann, Walter. *Jesus der Galiläer und das Judentum*. Leipzig: G. Wigand, 1941.

Grunlan and Mayers, *Cultural Anthropology*. Grunlan, Stephen A., and Marvin K. Mayers. *Cultural Anthropology: A Christian Perspective*. Grand Rapids: Zondervan, 1979.

Guelich, *Sermon on Mount*. Guelich, Robert A. *The Sermon on the Mount: A Foundation for Understanding*. Waco: Word, 1982.

Guevin, "Saul." Guevin, Benedict. "'Saul, Saul, Why Are You Persecuting Me?' Augustine's Use of Acts 9:4 in His Enarrationes in Psalmos." *DRev* 127 (449, 2009): 261–68.

Guido, *Sicily*. Guido, Margaret. *Sicily: An Archaeological Guide; The Prehistoric and Roman Remains and the Greek Cities*. Praeger Archaeological Guides. New York: Praeger, 1967.

Guijarro Oporto, "Articulación literaria." Guijarro Oporto, Santiago. "La articulación literaria del libro de los Hechos." *EstBib* 62 (2, 2004): 185–204.

Guillaume, *Islam*. Guillaume, Alfred. *Islam*. New York: Penguin, 1956.

Guillemette, "Forme." Guillemette, Pierre. "La forme des récits d'exorcisme de Bultmann: Un dogme à reconsidérer." *ÉgT* 11 (1980): 177–93.

Guillet, "Récits évangéliques." Guillet, Jacques. "Les récits évangéliques de la résurrection." *QF* 15–16 (1982): 7–21.

Gulick, *Captured*. Gulick, Anna D. *Captured: An Atheist's Journey with God*. Lexington, Ky.: Emeth, 2012.

Gullahorn and Gullahorn, "Extension." Gullahorn, John T., and Jeanne E.

Gullahorn. "An Extension of the U-Curve Hypothesis." *JSocI* 19 (1963): 33–47.

Gullahorn and Gullahorn, "Students Abroad." Gullahorn, J. T., and Jeanne E. Gullahorn. "American Students Abroad: Professional versus Personal Development." *AAAPSS* 368 (1966): 43–59.

Gülzow, "Soziale Gegebenheiten." Gülzow, Henneke. "Soziale Gegebenheiten der altkirchlichen Mission." Pages 189–226 in *Die alte Kirche.* Edited by Heinzgünter Fröhnes and Uwe W. Knorr. Kirchengeschichte als Missionsgeschichte 1. Munich: Kaiser, 1974.

Gundry, "Ecstatic Utterance?" Gundry, Robert H. "'Ecstatic Utterance' (N.E.B.)?" *JTS* 17 (2, 1966): 299–307.

Gundry, "Frustration." Gundry, Robert H. "The Moral Frustration of Paul before His Conversion: Sexual Lust in Romans 7:7–25." Pages 228–45 in *Pauline Studies: Essays Presented to Professor F. F. Bruce on His 70th Birthday.* Edited by Donald A. Hagner and Murray J. Harris. Exeter, U.K.: Paternoster; Grand Rapids: Eerdmans, 1980.

Gundry, "Genre." Gundry, Robert H. "Recent Investigations into the Literary Genre 'Gospel.'" Pages 97–114 in *New Dimensions in New Testament Study.* Edited by Richard N. Longenecker and Merrill C. Tenney. Grand Rapids: Zondervan, 1974.

Gundry, *Matthew.* Gundry, Robert H. *Matthew: A Commentary on His Literary and Theological Art.* Grand Rapids: Eerdmans, 1982.

Gundry, "Physicality." Gundry, Robert H. "The Essential Physicality of Jesus' Resurrection according to the New Testament." Pages 204–19 in *Jesus of Nazareth, Lord and Christ: Essays on the Historical Jesus and New Testament Christology.* Edited by Joel B. Green and Max Turner. Grand Rapids: Eerdmans; Carlisle, U.K.: Paternoster, 1994.

Gundry, *Sōma.* Gundry, Robert H. *Sōma in Biblical Theology: With Emphasis on Pauline Anthropology.* Cambridge: Cambridge University Press, 1976.

Gundry, "Staying Saved." Gundry, Robert H. "Grace, Works, and Staying Saved in Paul." *Bib* 66 (1, 1985): 1–38.

Gundry, *Use.* Gundry, Robert H. *The Use of the Old Testament in St. Matthew's Gospel: With Special Reference to the Messianic Hope.* NovTSup 18. Leiden: Brill, 1975.

Gundry-Volf, "Gender." Gundry-Volf, Judith M. "Paul on Women and Gender: A Comparison with Early Jewish Views." Pages 184–212 in *The Road from Damascus: The Impact of Paul's Conversion on His Life, Thought, and Ministry.* Edited by Richard N. Longenecker. Grand Rapids: Eerdmans, 1997.

Gundry-Volf, "Pneumatics." Gundry-Volf, Judith M. "Celibate Pneumatics and Social Power: On the Motivations for Sexual Asceticism in Corinth." *USQR* 48 (3–4, 1994): 105–26.

Gundry-Volf, "Universalism." Gundry-Volf, Judith M. "Universalism." *DPL* 956–61.

Günther, "Gescheiterte Mission." Günther, Matthias. "Die gescheiterte Mission: Niemand weiss so recht etwas über das paulinische Werk in Ephesus zu sagen." *ZZ* 1 (7, 1998): 32–34.

Günther, "Syracusae." Günther, Linda-Marie. "Syracusae." *BrillPauly* 14:39–53.

Gurney, *Aspects.* Gurney, O. R. *Some Aspects of Hittite Religion.* Oxford: Oxford University Press, 1977.

Gurney, *Hittites.* Gurney, O. R. *The Hittites.* Baltimore: Penguin, 1972.

Gusella, "Therapeutae." Gusella, Laura. "The Therapeutae and Other Community Experiences of the Late Second Temple Period." *Hen* 24 (3, 2002): 295–329.

Gusmer, *Healing.* Gusmer, Charles W. *The Ministry of Healing in the Church of England: An Ecumenical-Liturgical Study.* Alcuin Club Collections 56. Great Wakering, U.K.: Mayhew-McCrimmon, 1974.

Gussler, "Change." Gussler, Judith D. "Social Change, Ecology, and Spirit Possession among the South African Nguni." Pages 88–126 in *Religion, Altered States of Consciousness, and Social Change.* Edited by Erika Bourguignon. Columbus: Ohio State University Press, 1973.

Gustafson, "Afflictions." Gustafson, Henry. "The Afflictions of Christ: What Is Lacking?" *BR* 8 (1963): 28–42.

Gustafsson, "Graffiti." Gustafsson, Berndt. "The Oldest Graffiti in the History of the Church?" *NTS* 3 (1, 1956): 65–69.

Guthrie, "Blast." Guthrie, Stan, with Obed Minchakpu. "'A Blast of Hell: 500,000 People Uprooted, Thousands Dead in Violence." *CT* (Oct. 7, 2002): 28.

Guthrie, "Breakthrough." Guthrie, Stan. "Muslim Mission Breakthrough." *CT* (Dec. 13, 1993): 20–26.

Guthrie, *Greeks and Gods.* Guthrie, W. K. C. *The Greeks and Their Gods.* Boston: Beacon, 1950.

Guthrie, *Introduction.* Guthrie, Donald. *New Testament Introduction.* 4th rev. ed. Downers Grove, Ill.: InterVarsity, 1990.

Guthrie, *Orpheus.* Guthrie, W. K. C. *Orpheus and Greek Religion: A Study of the Orphic Movement.* 2nd ed. New York: W. W. Norton, 1966.

Guthrie and Szanton, "Diagnosis." Guthrie, B., and D. Szanton. "Folk Diagnosis and Treatment of Schizophrenia: Bargaining with Spirits in the Philippines." Pages 147–63 in *Culture-Bound Syndromes,*

Ethno-Psychiatry, and Alternate Therapies. Edited by W. Lebra. Honolulu: University of Hawaii Press, 1976.

Gutierrez, *Milagros.* Gutierrez, Angel Luis. *Mujer de Milagros.* Guaynabo, Puerto Rico: Editorial Chari, 1991.

Gutierrez and Wallbrown, "Sensitivity." Gutierrez, Lalei E., and Fred H. Wallbrown. "Enhancing Nonverbal Sensitivity through Glossolalic Training." *JPsyTE* 5 (1, 1983): 9–13.

Gutman, "Gamala." Gutman, Shemariyahu. "Gamala." *NEAEHL* 2:459–63.

Gutmann, "Beth Alpha." Gutmann, Joseph. "Beth Alpha." *OEANE* 1:299–300.

Gutmann, "Paintings." Gutmann, Joseph. "The Dura Europos Synagogue Paintings: The State of Research." Pages 61–72 in *The Synagogue in Late Antiquity.* Edited by Lee I. Levine. Philadelphia: American Schools of Oriental Research, 1986.

Gutsfeld, "Beer." Gutsfeld, Andreas. "Beer: Greece and Rome." *BrillPauly* 2:575.

Gutsfeld, "Dishes." Gutsfeld, Andreas. "Dishes, Meals." *BrillPauly* 4:554–56.

Gutsfeld, "Praefectus praetorio." Gutsfeld, Andreas. "Praefectus praetorio." *BrillPauly* 11:757–60.

Gutsfeld, "Praefectus urbi." Gutsfeld, Andreas. "Praefectus urbi." *BrillPauly* 11:760.

Gutsfeld, "Wine." Gutsfeld, Andreas. "Wine: Classical Antiquity." *BrillPauly* 15:658–70.

Gutt, *Relevance Theory.* Gutt, Ernst-August. *Relevance Theory: A Guide to Successful Communication in Translation.* Dallas: Summer Institute of Linguistics; New York: United Bible Societies, 1992.

Guttmann, "Miracles." Guttmann, Alexander. "The Significance of Miracles for Talmudic Judaism." *HUCA* 20 (1947): 363–406.

Guyot, "Eunuchs." Guyot, Peter. "Eunuchs." *BrillPauly* 5:172–74.

Gzella, "Sprachsituationen." Gzella, Holger. "Das Aramäische in den römischen Ostprovinzen: Sprachsituationen in Arabien, Syrien, und Mesopotamien zur Kaiserzeit." *BO* 63 (1–2, 2006): 16–39.

Haacker, "Bild." Haacker, Klaus. "Das Bild der Kirche in der Apostelgeschichte des Lukas." *TBei* 32 (2, 2001): 70–89.

Haacker, "Erst." Haacker, Klaus. "Erst unter Quirinius? Ein Übersetzungsvorschlag zu Lk 2, 2." *BN* 38–39 (1987): 39–43.

Haacker, "Geist." Haacker, Klaus B. "Der Geist und das Reich im Lukanischen Werk: Konkurrenz oder Konvergenz zwischen Pneumatologie und Eschatologie?" *NTS* 59 (2013): 325–45.

Haacker, "Paul's Life." Haacker, Klaus. "Paul's Life." Pages 19–33 in *The Cambridge Companion to St Paul.* Edited by James D. G.

Dunn. Cambridge: Cambridge University Press, 2003.

Haacker, *Theology*. Haacker, Klaus. *The Theology of Paul's Letter to the Romans*. Cambridge: Cambridge University Press, 2003.

Haak, "Approach." Haak, Cornelius J. "The Missional Approach: Reconsidering Elenctics (Part 2)." *CTJ* 44 (2, 2009): 288–305.

Haar and Ellis, "Possession." Haar, Gerrie ter, and Stephen Ellis. "Spirit Possession and Healing in Modern Zambia: An Analysis of Letters to Archbishop Milingo." *African Affairs* 87 (347, 1988): 185–206.

Haas, "Sibling Terms." Haas, Mary R. "Sibling Terms as Used by Marriage Partners." *SWJA* 25 (3, 1969): 228–35.

Haase, "Aretalogies." Haase, Mareile. "Aretalogies." *BrillPauly* 15:1003–4.

Haber, *Purify*. Haber, Susan. *"They Shall Purify Themselves": Essays on Purity in Early Judaism*. Edited by Adele Reinhartz. SBLEJL 24. Atlanta: SBL, 2008.

Habermas, *Evidence*. Habermas, Gary R. *Ancient Evidence for the Life of Jesus: Historical Records of His Death and Resurrection*. Nashville: Thomas Nelson, 1984.

Habinek, "Literacy." Habinek, Thomas. "Situating Literacy at Rome." Pages 114–40 in *Ancient Literacies: The Culture of Reading in Greece and Rome*. Edited by William A. Johnson and Holt N. Parker. New York: Oxford University Press, 2009.

Hacham, *"Aristeas."* Hacham, Noah. "The *Letter of Aristeas*: A New Exodus Story?" *JSJ* 36 (1, 2005): 1–20.

Hacham, "Polemic." Hacham, Noah. "3 Maccabees: An Anti-Dionysian Polemic." Pages 167–83 in *Ancient Fiction: The Matrix of Early Christian and Jewish Narrative*. Edited by Jo-Ann A. Brant, Charles W. Hedrick, and Chris Shea. SBLSymS 32. Atlanta: SBL, 2005.

Hachlili, "Architecture." Hachlili, Rachel. "Art and Architecture: Jewish." *DNTB* 125–29.

Hachlili, "Goliath Family." Hachlili, Rachel. "The Goliath Family in Jericho: Funerary Inscriptions from a First-Century A.D. Jewish Monumental Tomb." *BASOR* 235 (Summer 1979): 31–65.

Hachlili, "Jericho." Hachlili, Rachel. "Herodian Jericho." *OEANE* 3:16–18.

Hachlili, "Necropolis." Hachlili, Rachel. "A Second Temple Period Jewish Necropolis in Jericho." *BA* 43 (1980): 235–40.

Hachlili, "Origin." Hachlili, Rachel. "The Origin of the Synagogue: A Re-assessment." *JSJ* 28 (1, 1997): 34–47.

Hachlili, "Torah Shrine." Hachlili, Rachel. "Torah Shrine and Ark in Ancient Synagogues: A Re-evaluation." *ZDPV* 116 (2, 2000): 146–83.

Hachlili, "Zodiac." Hachlili, Rachel. "The Zodiac in Ancient Jewish Synagogue Art: A Review." *JSQ* 9 (3, 2002): 219–58.

Hachlili, "Zodiac in Art." Hachlili, Rachel. "The Zodiac in Ancient Jewish Art: Representation and Significance." *BASOR* 228 (Dec. 1977): 61–77.

Hachlili and Killebrew, "Byt glyt." Hachlili, Rachel, and Ann Killebrew. "Byt glyt—msphh byryhw bm'h h' lsh-n." *Qad* 14 (3–4, 1981): 118–22.

Hachlili and Killebrew, "Customs." Hachlili, Rachel, and Ann Killebrew. "Jewish Funerary Customs during the Second Temple Period, in the Light of the Excavations at the Jericho Necropolis." *PEQ* 115 (1983): 109–39.

Hachlili and Killebrew, "Saga." Hachlili, Rachel, and Ann Killebrew. "The Saga of the Goliath Family." *BAR* 9 (1, 1983): 44–53.

Hadas, *Aristeas*. Hadas, Moses, ed. and trans. *Aristeas to Philocrates (Letter of Aristeas)*. New York: Harper & Brothers, 1951. Repr., New York: KTAV, 1973.

Hadas, "Introduction." Hadas, Moses. Introduction. Pages ix–xxiii in *The Complete Works of Tacitus*. Edited by Moses Hadas. Translated by Alfred John Church and William Jackson Brodribb. New York: Random House, 1942.

Hadas, "Routes." Hadas, Gideon. "Dead Sea Sailing Routes during the Herodian Period." *BAIAS* 26 (2008): 31–36.

Hadas and Smith, *Heroes*. Hadas, Moses, and Morton Smith. *Heroes and Gods: Spiritual Biographies in Antiquity*. Religious Perspectives 13. New York: Harper & Row, 1965.

Hadas-Lebel, "Jacob et Esaü." Hadas-Lebel, Mireille. "Jacob et Esaü ou Israël et Rome dans le Talmud et le Midrash." *RHR* 201 (4, 1984): 369–92.

Hadas-Lebel, "Mariages mixtes." Hadas-Lebel, Mireille. "Les mariages mixtes dans la famille d'Hérode et la *halakha* pré-talmudique sur la patrilinéarité." *REJ* 152 (3–4, 1993): 397–404.

Hadidian, "Philonism." Hadidian, Yervant H. "Philonism in the Fourth Gospel." Pages 211–22 in *The MacDonald Presentation Volume: A Tribute to Duncan Black MacDonald, Consisting of Articles by Former Students, Presented to Him on His Seventieth Birthday, April 9, 1933*. Princeton: Princeton University Press, 1933.

Hadjiev, "Honor." Hadjiev, Tchavdar S. "Honor and Shame." Pages 333–38 in *Dictionary of the Old Testament Prophets*. Edited by Mark J. Boda and J. Gordon McConville. Downers Grove, Ill.: IVP Academic, 2012.

Haenchen, *Acts*. Haenchen, Ernst. *The Acts of the Apostles: A Commentary*. Philadelphia: Westminster, 1971.

Haenchen, "Acts as Source Material." Haenchen, Ernst. "The Book of Acts as Source Material for the History of Early Christianity." Pages 258–78 in *Studies in Luke-Acts: Essays in Honor of Paul Schubert*. Edited by Leander E. Keck and J. Louis Martyn. Nashville: Abingdon, 1966.

Haenchen, *John*. Haenchen, Ernst. *John: A Commentary on the Gospel of John*. Edited by Robert W. Funk with Ulrich Busse. Translated by Robert W. Funk. 2 vols. Hermeneia. Philadelphia: Fortress, 1984.

Haenchen, "'We' in Acts." Haenchen, Ernst. "'We' in Acts and the Itinerary." *JTC* 1 (1965): 65–99.

Haensch, "Inscriptions." Haensch, Rudolf. "Inscriptions as Sources of Knowledge for Religions and Cults in the Roman World of Imperial Times." Pages 176–87 in *A Companion to Roman Religion*. Edited by Jörg Rüpke. BCompAW. Oxford: Blackwell, 2011.

Hafemann, *2 Corinthians*. Hafemann, Scott J. *2 Corinthians*. NIVAC. Grand Rapids: Zondervan, 2000.

Hafemann, *Suffering*. Hafemann, Scott J. *Suffering and Ministry in the Spirit: Paul's Defense of His Apostolic Ministry in II Corinthians 2:14–3:3*. Grand Rapids: Eerdmans, 1990.

Hafemann, "Triumph." Hafemann, Scott J. "Roman Triumph." *DNTB* 1004–8.

Hagner, *Hebrews*. Hagner, Donald A. *Hebrews: A Good News Commentary*. San Francisco: Harper & Row, 1983.

Hagner, *Introduction*. Hagner, Donald A. *The New Testament: A Historical and Theological Introduction*. Grand Rapids: Baker Academic, 2012.

Hagner, "Judaism." Hagner, Donald A. "Paul and Judaism: Testing the New Perspective." Pages 75–105 in *Revisiting Paul's Doctrine of Justification: A Challenge to the New Perspective*. By Peter Stuhlmacher. Downers Grove, Ill.: InterVarsity, 2001.

Hagner, "Matrix." Hagner, Donald A. "Paul and Judaism—The Jewish Matrix of Early Christianity: Issues in the Current Debate." *BBR* 3 (1993): 111–30.

Hagner, *Matthew*. Hagner, Donald A. *Matthew*. 2 vols. WBC 33AB. Dallas: Word, 1993–95.

Hagner, "Vision." Hagner, Donald A. "The Vision of God in Philo and John: A Comparative Study." *JETS* 14 (2, 1971): 81–93.

Hahn, "Alms." Hahn, Johannes. "Alms." *BrillPauly* 1:522–23.

Hahn, "Beggars." Hahn, Johannes. "Beggars." *BrillPauly* 2:578–80.

Hahn, "Entwicklung." Hahn, Ferdinand. "Gibt es eine Entwicklung in den Aussagen über die Rechtfertigung bei Paulus?" *EvT* 53 (4, 1993): 342–66.

Hahn, "Kingdom." Hahn, Scott W. "Kingdom and Church in Luke-Acts: From Davidic Christology to Kingdom Ecclesiology." Pages 294–321 in *Reading Luke: Interpretation, Reflection, Formation*. Grand Rapids: Zondervan, 2005.

Hahn, "Prayers." Hahn, Frances Hickson. "Performing the Sacred: Prayers and Hymns." Pages 235–48 in *A Companion to Roman Religion*. Edited by Jörg Rüpke. BCompAW. Oxford: Blackwell, 2011.

Hahn, "Simony." Hahn, Johannes. "Simony." *BrillPauly* 13:489–90.

Hahn, "Überlieferungen." Hahn, Ferdinand. "Das Problem alter christologischer Überlieferungen in der Apostelgeschichte unter besonderer Berücksichtigung von Act 3,19–21." Pages 129–54 in *Les Actes des apôtres: Traditions, rédaction, théologie*. Edited by Jacob Kremer. BETL 48. Gembloux, Belg.: J. Duculot; Leuven: Leuven University Press, 1979.

Hair, "Witches." Hair, P. E. H. "Heretics, Slaves, and Witches—as Seen by Guinea Jesuits c. 1610." *JRelAf* 28 (2, 1998): 131–44.

Hakem, "Napata and Meroe." Hakem, A. A., with I. Hrbek and J. Vercoutter. "The Civilization of Napata and Meroe." Pages 298–321 in *Ancient Civilizations of Africa*. Edited by G. Mokhtar. General History of Africa 2. Berkeley: University of California Press; London: Heinemann Educational Books; Paris: United Nations Educational, Scientific and Cultural Organization, 1981.

Hakola, "Pharisees." Hakola, Raimo. "'Friendly' Pharisees and Social Identity in Acts." Pages 181–200 in *Contemporary Studies in Acts*. Edited by Thomas E. Phillips. Macon, Ga.: Mercer University Press, 2009.

Halberstam, "Peace." Halberstam, David. "When 'Civil Rights' and 'Peace' Join Forces." Pages 187–211 in *Martin Luther King, Jr.: A Profile*. Edited by C. Eric Lincoln. Rev. ed. New York: Hill & Wang, 1984.

Halcolm, "Agent." Halcomb, T. Michael W. "Paul the Change Agent: The Context Aims and Implications of an Apostolic Innovator." PhD diss., Asbury Theological Seminary, 2013.

Haley, "Hadrian." Haley, Evan. "Hadrian as Romulus, or the Self-Representation of a Roman Emperor." *Latomus* 64 (4, 2005): 969–80.

Haliburton, *Harris*. Haliburton, Gordon Mackay. *The Prophet Harris*. London: Longmans, 1973.

Hall, "Antonia." Hall, John F. "Antonia, Tower of." *ABD* 1:274.

Hall, "Chrysostom." Hall, Christopher A. "John Chrysostom." Pages 39–58 in *Reading Romans through the Centuries: From the Early Church to Karl Barth*. Edited by Jeffrey P. Greenman and Timothy Larsen. Grand Rapids: Brazos, 2005.

Hall, "Cicero and Quintilian." Hall, Jon. "Cicero and Quintilian on the Oratorical Use of Hand Gestures." *CQ* 54 (1, 2004): 143–60.

Hall, "Circumcision in Reverse." Hall, Robert G. "Epispasm: Circumcision in Reverse." *BRev* 8 (4, 1992): 52–57.

Hall, "Delivery." Hall, Jon. "Oratorical Delivery and the Emotions: Theory and Practice." Pages 218–34 in *A Companion to Roman Rhetoric*. Edited by William Dominik and Jon Hall. Oxford: Blackwell, 2007.

Hall, "Epispasm and Dating." Hall, Robert G. "Epispasm and the Dating of Ancient Jewish Writings." *JSP* 2 (1988): 71–86.

Hall, *Histories*. Hall, Robert G. *Revealed Histories: Techniques for Ancient Jewish and Christian Historiography*. JSPSup 6. Sheffield, U.K.: JSOT Press, 1991.

Hall, "History." Hall, Robert G. "Revealed History: A Jewish and Christian Technique of Interpreting the Past." PhD diss., Duke University, 1986.

Hall, "Inference." Hall, Robert G. "Historical Inference and Rhetorical Effect: Another Look at Galatians 1 and 2." Pages 308–20 in *Persuasive Artistry: Studies in New Testament Rhetoric in Honor of George A. Kennedy*. Edited by Duane F. Watson. JSNTSup 50. Sheffield, U.K.: Sheffield Academic, 1991.

Hall, *Reading Scripture*. Hall, Christopher A. *Reading Scripture with the Church Fathers*. Downers Grove, Ill.: InterVarsity, 1998.

Hallett, "Authors." Hallett, Judith. "Women Authors: Rome." *BrillPauly* 15:713–17.

Hallett, *Nude*. Hallett, Christopher H. *The Roman Nude*. Oxford Studies in Ancient Culture and Representation. Oxford: Oxford University Press, 2005.

Hallett, "Role." Hallett, Judith P. "The Role of Women in Roman Elegy: Countercultural Feminism." Pages 241–62 in *Women in the Ancient World: The Arethusa Papers*. Edited by John Peradotto and J. P. Sullivan. SSCS. Albany: State University of New York Press, 1984.

Hallett, "*Same* and *Other*." Hallett, Judith P. "Women as *Same* and *Other* in Classical Roman Elite." *Helios* 16 (1, 1989): 59–78.

Hallevy, "Mhsbt." Hallevy, A. A. "Mhsbt ysr'l wmhsbt ywn (Jewish Thought and Greek Thought)." *JerSJT* 2 (4, 1982–83): 497–514.

Halperin, "Ascension." Halperin, David J. "Ascension or Invasion: Implications of the Heavenly Journey in Ancient Judaism." *Religion* 18 (1, 1988): 47–67.

Halperin, "Merkabah Midrash." Halperin, David J. "Merkabah Midrash in the Septuagint." *JBL* 101 (3, 1982): 351–63.

Halpern-Amaru, "Joy." Halpern-Amaru, Betsy. "Joy as Piety in the 'Book of Jubilees.'" *JJS* 56 (2, 2005): 185–205.

Halton, "Law." Halton, J. Charles. "Law." Pages 493–501 in *Dictionary of the Old Testament Prophets*. Edited by Mark J. Boda and J. Gordon McConville. Downers Grove, Ill.: IVP Academic, 2012.

Halusza, "Statues." Halusza, Adria. "Sacred Signified: The Semiotics of Statues in the Greek Magical Papyri." *Arethusa* 41 (3, 2008): 479–94.

Halverson, "Dynamics." Halverson, John. "Dynamics of Exorcism: The Sinhalese Sanniyakuma." *HR* 10 (1971): 334–59.

Hamblin, "Miracles." Hamblin, R. L. "Miracles in the Book of Acts." *SWJT* 17 (1, 1974): 19–34.

Hamel, "Argo to Nineveh." Hamel, Gildas. "Taking the Argo to Nineveh: Jonah and Jason in a Mediterranean Context." *Judaism* 44 (3, 1995): 341–59.

Hamerton-Kelly, *Pre-existence*. Hamerton-Kelly, R. G. *Pre-existence, Wisdom, and the Son: A Study of the Idea of Pre-existence in the New Testament*. Cambridge: Cambridge University Press, 1973.

Hamidovic, "Halakhah." Hamidovic, David. "La Halakhah chez les Esséniens et son rôle dans la question messianique." *REJ* 167 (3–4, 2008): 345–65.

Hamidovic, "Remarque." Hamidovic, D. "La remarque énigmatique d'Ac 5,4 dans la légende d'Ananias et Saphira." *Bib* 86 (3, 2005): 407–15.

Hamilton, "Bootstraps." Hamilton, James M. "N. T. Wright and Saul's Moral Bootstraps: Newer Light on 'the New Perspective.'" *TJ* 25 (2, 2004): 139–55.

Hamilton, *Revolt*. Hamilton, Kenneth. *Revolt against Heaven: An Enquiry Into Anti-supernaturalism*. Grand Rapids: Eerdmans, 1965.

Hamilton, *Spirit and Eschatology*. Hamilton, Neill Q. *The Holy Spirit and Eschatology in Paul*. SJTOP 6. Edinburgh: Oliver & Boyd, 1957.

Hamilton, "Theology of Spirit." Hamilton, James M. "Rushing Wind and Organ Music: Toward Luke's Theology of the Spirit in Acts." *RTR* 65 (1, 2006): 15–33.

Hamm, *Acts*. Hamm, M. Dennis. *The Acts of the Apostles*. New Collegeville Bible Commentary, New Testament 5. Collegeville, Minn.: Liturgical Press, 2005.

Hamm, "Acts 3:12–26." Hamm, M. Dennis. "Acts 3:12–26: Peter's Speech and the Healing of the Man Born Lame." *PRSt* 11 (3, 1984): 199–217.

Hamm, "Blindness and Healing." Hamm, M. Dennis. "Paul's Blindness and Its Healing: Clues to Symbolic Intent (Acts 9; 22 and 26)." *Bib* 71 (1, 1990): 63–72.

Hamm, "Paradigm." Hamm, M. Dennis. "Acts 4:23–31—A Neglected Biblical Paradigm of Christian Worship (Especially in Troubled Times)." *Worship* 77 (3, 2003): 225–37.

Hamm, "Service." Hamm, M. Dennis. "The Tamid Service in Luke-Acts: The Cultic Background behind Luke's Theology of Worship (Luke 1:5–25; 18:9–14; 24:50–53; Acts 3:1; 10:3, 30)." *CBQ* 65 (2, 2003): 215–31.

Hamm, "Sign of Healing." Hamm, M. Dennis. "The Sign of Healing." PhD diss., Saint Louis University, 1975.

Hammel, "Change." Hammel, E. A. "Economic Change, Social Mobility, and Kinship in Serbia." *SWJA* 25 (2, Summer 1969): 188–97.

Hammond, "Patterns." Hammond, Philip C. "Nabataean Settlement Patterns inside Petra." *AHB* 5 (1–2, 1991): 36–46.

Hammond, "Speeches." Hammond, Nigel G. L. "The Speeches in Arrian's *Indica* and *Anabasis*." *CQ* 49 (1, 1999): 238–53.

Hammond, "Western Part of Via Egnatia." Hammond, Nigel G. L. "The Western Part of the Via Egnatia." *JRS* 64 (1974): 185–94 and plates 9–10.

Hammond and Price, "Ruler-cult." Hammond, Mason, and Simon R. F. Price. "Ruler-cult: Roman." *OCD*[3] 1338–39.

Hammond-Tooke, "Aetiology." Hammond-Tooke, W. D. "The Aetiology of Spirit in Southern Africa." Pages 43–65 in *Afro-Christian Religion and Healing in Southern Africa*. Edited by G. C. Oosthuizen, S. D. Edwards, W. H. Wessels, and I. Hexham. AfSt 8. Lewiston, N.Y.: Edwin Mellen, 1989.

Han, "Prayer." Han, Kyu Sam. "Theology of Prayer in the Gospel of Luke." *JETS* 43 (4, 2000): 675–93.

Hanciles, *Beyond Christendom*. Hanciles, Jehu J. *Beyond Christendom: Globalization, African Migration, and the Transformation of the West*. Maryknoll, N.Y.: Orbis, 2008.

Hanfmann, "Campaign." Hanfmann, George M. A. "The Tenth Campaign at Sardis." *BASOR* 191 (Oct. 1968): 2–41.

Hanfmann, *Sardis*. Hanfmann, George M. A., assisted by William E. Mierse.

Sardis from Prehistoric to Roman Times: Results of the Archaeological Exploration of Sardis, 1958–1975. Cambridge, Mass.: Harvard University Press, 1983.

Hanfmann and Waldbaum, "Kybele and Artemis." Hanfmann, George M. A., and Jane C. Waldbaum. "Kybele and Artemis." *Archaeology* 22 (1969): 264–69.

Hang, *Crushing*. Hang, Tsang To. *Crushing the Wall*. Surabaya, Indonesia: Gereja Kristen Abdiel Gloria, 2011.

Hankinson, *Sceptics*. Hankinson, R. J. *The Sceptics*. London: Routledge, 1995.

Hansberger, "Mose." Hansberger, Therese. "'Mose segnete Israel mit 'sryk, und David segnete Israel mit 'sry (MTeh 1,2): Psalm 1 und der Psalter im rabbinischen Midrash zu den Psalmen (MTeh 1)." *BZ* 46 (1, 2002): 25–47.

Hansberry, *Africa*. Hansberry, William Leo. *Africa and Africans as Seen by Classical Writers*. Edited by Joseph E. Harris. William Leo Hansberry African History Notebook 2. Washington, D.C.: Howard University Press, 1977. Repr., 1981.

Hansberry, *Pillars*. Hansberry, William Leo. *Pillars in Ethiopian History*. Edited by Joseph E. Harris. William Leo Hansberry African History Notebook 1. Washington, D.C.: Howard University Press, 1974. Repr., 1981.

Hansen, "Galatia." Hansen, G. Walter. "Galatia." Pages 377–95 in *The Book of Acts in Its Graeco-Roman Setting*. Edited by David W. J. Gill and Conrad Gempf. Vol. 2 of *The Book of Acts in Its First Century Setting*. Edited by Bruce W. Winter. Grand Rapids: Eerdmans; Carlisle, U.K.: Paternoster, 1994.

Hansen, *Galatians*. Hansen, G. Walter. *Galatians*. Downers Grove, Ill.: InterVarsity, 1994.

Hansen, "Galatians." Hansen, G. Walter. "Galatians, Letter to the." *DPL* 323–34.

Hansen, "Preaching." Hansen, G. Walter. "The Preaching and Defence of Paul." Pages 295–324 in *Witness to the Gospel: The Theology of Acts*. Edited by I. Howard Marshall and David Peterson. Grand Rapids: Eerdmans, 1998.

Hansen, "Update." Hansen, Mogens Herman. "An Update on the Shotgun Method." *GRBS* 48 (3, 2008): 259–86.

Hanson, *Acts*. Hanson, R. P. C. *The Acts in the Revised Standard Version, with Introduction and Commentary*. Oxford: Clarendon, 1967.

Hanson, "Dreams and Visions." Hanson, John S. "Dreams and Visions in the Graeco-Roman World and Early Christianity." *ANRW* 23.2.1395–1427. Part 2, *Principat*, 23.2. Edited by H. Temporini and W. Haase. Berlin: de Gruyter, 1980.

Hanson, "Exodus." Hanson, Anthony. "John I.14–18 and Exodus XXXIV." *NTS* 23 (1, 1976): 90–101.

Hanson, "Herodians and Kinship." Hanson, K. C. "The Herodians and Mediterranean Kinship, Part I: Genealogy and Descent." *BTB* 19 (3, 1989): 75–84.

Hanson, *Influence*. Hanson, Richard A. *Tyrian Influence in the Upper Galilee*. Meiron Excavation Project 2. Cambridge, Mass.: American Schools of Oriental Research, 1980.

Hanson, "Journey of Nikias." Hanson, R. P. C. "The Journey of Paul and the Journey of Nikias: An Experiment in Comparative Historiography." *SE* 4 (1968): 315–18.

Hanson, *Unity*. Hanson, Stig. *The Unity of the Church in the New Testament: Colossians and Ephesians*. Lexington, Ky.: American Theological Library Association, 1963.

Hanson, *Utterances*. Hanson, Anthony Tyrrell. *The Living Utterances of God: The New Testament Exegesis of the Old*. London: Darton, Longman & Todd, 1983.

Hanson and Oakman, *Palestine*. Hanson, K. C., and Douglas E. Oakman. *Palestine in the Time of Jesus: Social Structures and Social Conflicts*. Minneapolis: Fortress, 1998.

Haraguchi, "Call for Repentance." Haraguchi, Takaaki. "A Call for Repentance to the Whole Israel—A Rhetorical Study of Acts 3:12–26." *AJT* 18 (2, 2004): 267–82.

Haraguchi, "Farewell Discourse." Haraguchi, Takaaki. "A Tragic Farewell Discourse? In Search of a New Understanding of Paul's Miletus Speech (Acts 20:18–35)." *AJBI* 30–31 (2004–5): 137–53.

Haran, "Continuity and Change." Haran, Menahem. "From Early to Classical Prophecy: Continuity and Change." *VT* 27 (Oct. 1977): 385–97.

Haran, "Image." Haran, Menahem. "The Priestly Image of the Tabernacle." *HUCA* 36 (1965): 191–226.

Haran, *Temples*. Haran, Menahem. *Temples and Temple-Service in Ancient Israel*. Oxford: Clarendon, 1978.

Harari, "Moses." Harari, Yuval. "Moses, the Sword, and *The Sword of Moses*: Between Rabbinical and Magical Traditions." *JSQ* 12 (4, 2005): 293–329.

Harden, *Phoenicians*. Harden, Donald. *The Phoenicians*. New York: Praeger, 1962.

Harder, "Defixio." Harder, Ruth Elisabeth. "Defixio." *BrillPauly* 4:175–78.

Harder, "Scylla." Harder, Ruth Elisabeth. "Scylla." *BrillPauly* 13:146.

Hardesty, *Faith Cure*. Hardesty, Nancy A. *Faith Cure: Divine Healing in the Holiness and Pentecostal Movements*. Peabody, Mass.: Hendrickson, 2003.

Hardie, "Epic." Hardie, Philip Russell. "Epic." *OCD³* 530.

Hardie, "*Locus amoenus*." Hardie, Philip Russell. "*Locus amoenus*." *OCD³* 880.

Hardin, "Decrees." Hardin, Justin K. "Decrees and Drachmas at Thessalonica: An Illegal Assembly in Jason's House (Acts 17.1–10a)." *NTS* 52 (1, 2006): 29–49.

Harding, *Androtion*. Harding, Phillip. *Androtion and the Atthis: The Fragments Translated with Introduction and Commentary*. New York: Oxford University Press, 1994. Introduction, 1–52; commentary, 78–197.

Harding, "*Atthis*." Harding, Phillip Edward. "*Atthis*." *OCD³* 211–12.

Harding, "Historicity of Acts." Harding, Mark. "On the Historicity of Acts: Comparing Acts 9.23–5 with 2 Corinthians 11.32–3." *NTS* 39 (4, 1993): 518–38.

Harding, "Local History." Harding, Phillip. "Local History and Atthidography." Pages 180–88 in *A Companion to Greek and Roman Historiography*. Edited by John Marincola. 2 vols. Oxford: Blackwell, 2007.

Harding, "Prayer." Harding, Mark. "A Hebrew Congregational Prayer from Egypt." Pages 145–47, §11, in *A Review of the Greek Inscriptions and Papyri Published 1984–85*. By S. R. Llewelyn, with the collaboration of R. A. Kearsley. Vol. 8 of *New Documents Illustrating Early Christianity*. North Ryde, N.S.W.: Ancient History Documentary Research Centre, Macquarie University; Grand Rapids: Eerdmans, 1998.

Hardman, *Awakeners*. Hardman, Keith J. *The Spiritual Awakeners: American Revivalists from Solomon Stoddard to D. L. Moody*. Chicago: Moody, 1983.

Hardon, "Miracle Narratives." Hardon, John A. "The Miracle Narratives in the Acts of the Apostles." *CBQ* 16 (3, 1954): 303–18.

Hardy, "Priestess." Hardy, Edward R. "The Priestess in the Greco-Roman World." *Chm* 84 (4, 1970): 264–70.

Hardy, *World*. Hardy, W. G. *The Greek and Roman World*. Cambridge, Mass.: Schenkman, 1962.

Hare, *Euthyphro*. Hare, John E. *Plato's Euthyphro*. Bryn Mawr Commentaries. Bryn Mawr, Pa.: Thomas Library, Bryn Mawr College, 1985.

Hare, *Persecution*. Hare, Douglas R. A. *The Theme of Jewish Persecution of Christians in the Gospel according to St. Matthew*. Cambridge: Cambridge University Press, 1967.

Hare, "Rejection in Gospels and Acts." Hare, Douglas R. A. "The Rejection of the Jews in the Synoptic Gospels and Acts." Pages 27–47 in *Antisemitism and the Foundations of Christianity*. Edited by Alan T. Davies. New York: Paulist, 1979.

Hare, "Relationship." Hare, Douglas R. A. "The Relationship between Jewish and Gentile Persecution of Christians." *JES* 4 (3, 1967): 446–56.

Harich-Schwarzbauer, "Philosophers." Harich-Schwarzbauer, Henriette. "Women Philosophers." *BrillPauly* 15:718–21.

Harland, *Associations*. Harland, Philip A. *Associations, Synagogues, and Congregations: Claiming a Place in Ancient Mediterraean Society*. Minneapolis: Fortress, 2003.

Harland, "Dimensions." Harland, Philip A. "Familial Dimensions of Group Identity: 'Brothers' (ἀδελφοί) in Associations of the Greek East." *JBL* 124 (3, 2005): 491–513.

Harland, "Honours." Harland, Philip A. "Honours and Worship: Emperors, Imperial Cults, and Associations at Ephesus (First to Third Centuries C.E.)." *SR/SR* 25 (3, 1996): 319–34.

Harland, "'Mothers' and 'Fathers.'" Harland, Philip A. "Familial Dimensions of Group Identity (II): 'Mothers' and 'Fathers' in Associations and Synagogues of the Greek World." *JSJ* 38 (1, 2007): 57–79.

Härle, "Paulus und Luther." Härle, Wilfried. "Paulus und Luther: Ein kritischer Blick auf die 'New Perspektive.'" *ZTK* 103 (3, 2006): 362–93.

Harmon, "Introduction," Harmon, A. M. Introduction to *Charon*. Page 395 in vol. 2 of *Lucian*. Edited by A. M. Harmon, K. Kilburn, and M. D. Macleod. 8 vols. LCL. Cambridge, Mass.: Harvard University Press, 1913–67.

Harmon, "Musicians." Harmon, Roger. "Musicians (Female)." *BrillPauly* 9:364–69.

Harmon, "Technitai." Harmon, Roger. "Technitai." *BrillPauly* 14:201–2.

Harms, *Paradigms*. Harms, Richard B. *Paradigms from Luke-Acts for Multicultural Communities*. AUSt, series 7, Theology and Religion 216. New York; Bern: Lang, 2001.

Harms, "Tradition." Harms, Robert. "Oral Tradition and Ethnicity." *JIHist* 10 (1, 1979): 61–85.

Harnack, *Acts*. Harnack, Adolf von. *The Acts of the Apostles*. Translated by J. R. Wilkinson. New Testament Studies 3. New York: G. P. Putnam's Sons; London: Williams & Norgate, 1909.

Harner, *Shaman*. Harner, Michael. *The Way of the Shaman: A Guide to Power and Healing*. San Francisco: Harper & Row, 1980.

Harper, *Amos*. Harper, William Rainey. *A Critical and Exegetical Commentary on Amos and Hosea*. ICC. Edinburgh: T&T Clark, 1905.

Harper, "Census Inscriptions." Harper, Kyle. "The Greek Census Inscriptions of Late Antiquity." *JRS* 98 (2008): 83–119.

Harper, "Women in Philosophy." Harper, Victoria Lynn. "Women in Philosophy." *OCD³* 1625–26.

Harpur, *Touch*. Harpur, Tom. *The Uncommon Touch: An Investigation of Spiritual Healing*. Toronto: McClelland & Stewart, 1994.

Harrauer, "Agnostos Theos." Harrauer, Christine. "Agnostos Theos." *BrillPauly* 1:346–47.

Harrell, *Divorce*. Harrell, Pat Edwin. *Divorce and Remarriage in the Early Church: A History of Divorce and Remarriage in the Ante-Nicene Church*. Austin, Tex.: R. B. Sweet, 1967.

Harrell, "Final Blow." Harrell, James A. "Final Blow to IAA Report: Flawed Geochemistry Used to Condemn James Inscription." *BAR* 30 (1, 2004): 38–41.

Harrell, *Possible*. Harrell, David Edwin, Jr. *All Things Are Possible: The Healing and Charismatic Revivals in Modern America*. Bloomington: Indiana University Press, 1975.

Harrelson, *Cult*. Harrelson, Walter. *From Fertility Cult to Worship*. Garden City, N.Y.: Doubleday, 1969.

Harries, "Trends." Harries, J. G. "Early Trends in Biblical Commentaries as Reflected in Some Qumran Texts." *EvQ* 36 (2, 1964): 100–105.

Harrill, "Asia Minor." Harrill, J. Albert. "Asia Minor." *DNTB* 130–36.

Harrill, "Dramatic Function." Harrill, J. Albert. "The Dramatic Function of the Running Slave Rhoda (Acts 12.13–16): A Piece of Greco-Roman Comedy." *NTS* 46 (1, 2000): 150–57.

Harrill, "Functionaries." Harrill, J. Albert. "Servile Functionaries or Priestly Leaders? Roman Domestic Religion, Narrative Intertextuality, and Pliny's Reference to Slave Christian *ministrae* (Ep. 10,96,8)." *ZNW* 97 (1, 2006): 111–30.

Harrill, "Paul and Slavery." Harrill, J. Albert. "Paul and Slavery." Pages 575–607 in *Paul in the Greco-Roman World: A Handbook*. Edited by J. Paul Sampley. Harrisburg, Pa.: Trinity Press International, 2003.

Harrill, "Physics." Harrill, J. Albert. "Stoic Physics, the Universal Conflagration, and the Eschatological Destruction of the 'Ignorant and Unstable' in 2 Peter." Pages 115–40 in *Stoicism in Early Christianity*. Edited by Tuomas Rasimus, Troels Engberg-Pedersen, and Ismo Dunderberg. Grand Rapids: Baker Academic, 2010.

Harrill, "Slavery." Harrill, J. Albert. "Slavery." *DNTB* 1124–28.

Harrill, *Slaves*. Harrill, J. Albert. *Slaves in the New Testament: Literary, Social, and Moral Dimensions*. Minneapolis: Fortress, 2006.

Harrington, "Abraham Traditions." Harrington, Daniel J. "Abraham Traditions in the Testament of Abraham and in the 'Rewritten Bible' of the Intertestamental Period." Pages 165–72 in *Studies on the Testament of Abraham*. Edited by George W. E. Nickelsburg. SBLSCS 6. Missoula, Mont.: Scholars Press, 1976.

Harrington, "Bible." Harrington, Daniel J. "The Bible Rewritten (Narratives)." Pages 239–47 in *Early Judaism and Its Modern Interpreters*. Edited by Robert A. Kraft and George W. E. Nickelsburg. SBLBMI 2. Atlanta: Scholars Press, 1986.

Harrington, "Collaborative Nature." Harrington, Daniel J. "The Collaborative Nature of the Pauline Mission." *BibT* 42 (4, 2004): 201–6.

Harrington, "Co-workers." Harrington, Daniel J. "Paul and His Co-workers." *P&P* 17 (8, 2003): 320–25.

Harrington, *God's People*. Harrington, Daniel J. *God's People in Christ*. Philadelphia: Fortress, 1980.

Harrington, "Holiness." Harrington, Hannah K. "Holiness and Law in the Dead Sea Scrolls." *DSD* 8 (2, 2001): 124–35.

Harrington, *Matthew*. Harrington, Daniel J. *The Gospel according to Matthew*. Collegeville, Minn.: Liturgical Press, 1982.

Harrington, "Paul the Jew." Harrington, Daniel J. "Paul the Jew." *CathW* 235 (1406, 1992): 68–73.

Harrington, "Prayers." Harrington, Daniel J. "Prayers in Tobit." *BibT* 37 (2, 1999): 86–90.

Harrington, "Pseudo-Philo." Harrington, Daniel J. "Pseudo-Philo." *DNTB* 864–68.

Harrington, "Purity." Harrington, Hannah K. "Purity and the Dead Sea Scrolls—Current Issues." *CBR* 4 (3, 2006): 397–428.

Harris, *Acts Today*. Harris, Ralph W. *Acts Today: Signs and Wonders of the Holy Spirit*. Springfield, Mo.: Gospel, 1995.

Harris, *Art*. Harris, J. R. *Egyptian Art*. London: Spring Books, 1966.

Harris, "Dead." Harris, Murray J. "'The Dead Are Restored to Life': Miracles of Revivification in the Gospels." Pages 295–326 in *The Miracles of Jesus*. Edited by David Wenham and Craig Blomberg. Gospel Perspectives 6. Sheffield, U.K.: JSOT Press, 1986.

Harris, "Demography." Harris, William V. "Demography, Geography, and the Sources of Roman Slaves." *JRS* 89 (1999): 62–75.

Harris, "Did Paul Quote Euripides?" Harris, Rendel. "Did St. Paul Quote Euripides?" *ExpT* 31 (1, 1919): 36–37.

Harris, "Infanticide." Harris, William V. "The Theoretical Possibility of Extensive Infanticide in the Graeco-Roman World." *CQ* 32 (1, 1982): 114–16.

Harris, *Jesus as God*. Harris, Murray J. *Jesus as God: The New Testament Use of* Theos *in Reference to Jesus*. Grand Rapids: Baker, 1992.

Harris, *Literacy*. Harris, William V. *Ancient Literacy*. Cambridge, Mass.: Harvard University Press, 1989.

Harris, "Oaths." Harris, B. F. "Oaths of Allegiance to Caesar." *Prudentia* 14 (2, 1982): 109–22.

Harris, "Opinions." Harris, William V. "Roman Opinions about the Truthfulness of Dreams." *JRS* 93 (2003): 18–34.

Harris, *Origin*. Harris, J. Rendel. *The Origin of the Prologue to St. John's Gospel*. Cambridge: Cambridge University Press, 1917.

Harris, "Paul on Map." Harris, Judith. "Putting Paul on the Map." *BAR* 26 (1, 2000): 14.

Harris, "Possession 'Hysteria.'" Harris, Grace. "Possession 'Hysteria' in a Kenya Tribe." *AmAnth* 59 (6, 1957): 1046–66.

Harris, "References." Harris, Murray J. "References to Jesus in Early Classical Authors." Pages 343–68 in *The Jesus Tradition outside the Gospels*. Edited by David Wenham. Gospel Perspectives 5. Sheffield, U.K.: JSOT Press, 1984.

Harris, *Restraining Rage*. Harris, William V. *Restraining Rage: The Ideology of Anger Control in Classical Antiquity*. Cambridge, Mass.: Harvard University Press, 2001.

Harris, *Scylla*. Harris, J. Rendel. *Scylla and Charybdis*. Manchester: University Press; London: Longmans, Green, 1925.

Harris, "ΣΥΝΕΙΔΗΣΙΣ." Harris, Bruce F. "ΣΥΝΕΙΔΗΣΙΣ (Conscience) in the Pauline Writings." *WTJ* 24 (2, 1962): 173–86.

Harris, *Testimonies*. Harris, J. Rendel. *Testimonies*. 2 vols. Cambridge: Cambridge University Press, 1916–20.

Harris, "Titus 2:13." Harris, Murray J. "Titus 2:13 and the Deity of Christ." Pages 262–77 in *Pauline Studies: Essays Presented to Professor F. F. Bruce on His 70th Birthday*. Edited by Donald A. Hagner and Murray J. Harris. Exeter, U.K.: Paternoster; Grand Rapids: Eerdmans, 1980.

Harris and Schuster, "Lap of Luxury." Harris, Judith, and Angela M. H. Schuster. "The Lap of Luxury." *Archaeology* 54 (3, 2001): 30–32.

Harrison, "Acts 22:3." Harrison, Everett F. "Acts 22:3—A Test Case for Luke's Reliability." Pages 251–60 in *New Dimensions in New Testament Study*. Edited by Richard N. Longenecker and Merrill C. Tenney. Grand Rapids: Zondervan, 1974.

Harrison, *Authorities*. Harrison, James R. *Paul and the Imperial Authorities at Thessalonica and Rome*. WUNT 273. Tübingen: Mohr Siebeck, 2011.

Harrison, "Benefaction Ideology." Harrison, James R. "Benefaction Ideology and Christian Responsibility for Widows." Pages 106–16, §7, in *A Review of the Greek Inscriptions and Papyri Published 1984–85*. By S. R. Llewelyn, with the collaboration of R. A. Kearsley. Vol. 8 of *New Documents Illustrating Early Christianity*. North Ryde, N.S.W.: Ancient History Documentary Research Centre, Macquarie University, 1998.

Harrison, "Disease." Harrison, Roland K. "Disease." *ISBE* 1:953–60.

Harrison, "Ecloga." Harrison, Stephen J. "Ecloga." *OCD*³ 502.

Harrison, "Ephesian Theory." Harrison, P. N. "The Pastoral Epistles and Duncan's Ephesian Theory." *NTS* 2 (4, 1956): 250–61.

Harrison, *Grace*. Harrison, James R. *Paul's Language of Grace in Its Graeco-Roman Context*. WUNT 2.172. Tübingen: J. C. B. Mohr, 2003.

Harrison, "Hypotheses." Harrison, Percy N. "Important Hypotheses Reconsidered, III: The Authorship of the Pastoral Epistles." *ExpT* 67 (3, 1955): 77–81.

Harrison, "Imitation." Harrison, James R. "The Imitation of the 'Great Man' in Antiquity: Paul's Inversion of a Cultural Icon." Pages 213–54 in *Christian Origins and Greco-Roman Culture: Social and Literary Contexts for the New Testament*. Edited by Stanley Porter and Andrew W. Pitts. Vol. 1 of Early Christianity in Its Hellenistic Context. Vol. 9 in Texts and Editions for New Testament Study. Leiden: Brill, 2013.

Harrison, *Introduction*. Harrison, Roland K. *Introduction to the Old Testament*. Grand Rapids: Eerdmans, 1969.

Harrison, "John 1:14." Harrison, Everett F. "A Study of John 1:14." Pages 23–36 in *Unity and Diversity in New Testament Theology: Essays in Honor of G. E. Ladd*. Edited by Robert A. Guelich. Grand Rapids: Eerdmans, 1978.

Harrison, "Miracles." Harrison, Peter. "Miracles, Early Modern Science, and Rational Religion." *CH* 75 (3, 2006): 493–510.

Harrison, "Paul." Harrison, James R. "Paul among the Romans." Pages 143–76 in *All Things to All Cultures: Paul among Jews, Greeks, and Romans*. Edited by Mark Harding and Alanna Nobbs. Grand Rapids: Eerdmans, 2013.

Harrison, "Rites." Harrison, R. K. "The Rites and Customs of the Qumran Sect." Pages 26–36 in *The Scrolls and Christianity:*

Historical and Theological Significance. Edited by Matthew Black. London: SPCK, 1969.

Harrison and Yamauchi, "Census." Harrison, Roland K., and Edwin M. Yamauchi. "Census." Pages 262–71 in vol. 1 of *Dictionary of Daily Life in Biblical and Post-Biblical Antiquity.* Edited by Edwin M. Yamauchi and Marvin R. Wilson. Peabody, Mass.: Hendrickson, 2014.

Harrison and Yamauchi, "Cities." Harrison, Roland K., and Edwin M. Yamauchi. "Cities." Pages 290–305 in vol. 1 of *Dictionary of Daily Life in Biblical and Post-Biblical Antiquity.* Edited by Edwin M. Yamauchi and Marvin R. Wilson. Peabody, Mass.: Hendrickson, 2014.

Harrison et al., *Criticism.* Harrison, R. K., et al. *Biblical Criticism: Historical, Literary, and Textual.* Grand Rapids: Zondervan, 1978.

Harris-Shapiro, *Messianic Judaism.* Harris-Shapiro, Carol. *Messianic Judaism: A Rabbi's Journey through Religious Change in America.* Boston: Beacon, 1999.

Harrisville, "ΠΙΣΤΙΣ ΧΡΙΣΤΟΥ." Harrisville, Roy A. "ΠΙΣΤΙΣ ΧΡΙΣΤΟΥ: Witness of the Fathers." *NovT* 36 (3, 1994): 233–41.

Harrop, "Stephen." Harrop, Clayton K. "Stephen and Paul." Pages 179–201 in *With Steadfast Purpose: Essays on Acts in Honor of Henry Jackson Flanders, Jr.* Edited by Naymond H. Keathley. Waco: Baylor University Press, 1990.

Harstine, "Imitate." Harstine, Stan. Review of Dennis R. MacDonald, *Does the New Testament Imitate Homer? Four Cases from the Acts of the Apostles. JBL* 124 (2, 2005): 383–85.

Hart, "Baptism." Hart, Larry. "Spirit Baptism: A Dimensional Charismatic Perspective." Pages 105–69 in *Perspectives on Spirit Baptism: Five Views.* Edited by Chad Owen Brand. Nashville: Broadman & Holman, 2004.

Hart, *Delusions.* Hart, David Bentley. *Atheist Delusions: The Christian Revolution and Its Fashionable Enemies.* New Haven: Yale University Press, 2009.

Harter et al., "Toilet Practices." Harter, Stephanie, et al. "Toilet Practices among Members of the Dead Sea Scrolls Sect at Qumran (100 BCE–68 CE)." *RevQ* 21 (84, 2004): 579–84.

Hartley, "Atonement." Hartley, John E. "Atonement, Day of." *DOTP* 54–61.

Hartman, "Name of Jesus." Hartman, Lars. "'Into the Name of Jesus.'" *NTS* 20 (4, 1974): 432–40.

Hartman, "*Psychae.*" Hartman, Lars. "*Psychae*—'själ'? Att läsa Septuaginta som grekisk text." *SEÅ* 70 (2005): 89–99.

Hartman, "Thoughts." Hartman, Thomas C. "Some Thoughts on the Sumerian King List and Genesis 5 and 11 B." *JBL* 91 (1, 1972): 25–32.

Hartmann, "Homosexuality." Hartmann, Elke. "Homosexuality." *BrillPauly* 6:468–72.

Hartmann, "Kanttekeningen." Hartmann, B. "Kanttekeningen bij Herodotus de godsdiensthistoricus." *NedTT* 33 (4, 1979): 265–74.

Hartsock, "Blindness." Hartsock, J. Chad. "Blindness and Deafness." Pages 90–91 in *Dictionary of Jesus and the Gospels.* 2nd ed. Edited by Joel B. Green, Jeannine K. Brown, and Nicholas Perrin. Downers Grove, Ill.: IVP Academic, 2013.

Hartsock, *Sight.* Hartsock, Chad. *Sight and Blindness in Luke-Acts: The Use of Physical Features in Characterization.* BIS 94. Leiden: Brill, 2008.

Harun, "Überschreitung." Harun, Martin. "Überschreitung religiöser und kultureller Grenzen: Reflexion über die Apostelgeschichte." *BK* 59 (1, 2004): 18–24.

Harvey, *History.* Harvey, A. E. *Jesus and the Constraints of History.* Philadelphia: Westminster, 1982.

Harvey, *Listening.* Harvey, John D. *Listening to the Text: Oral Patterning in Paul's Letters.* Foreword by Richard N. Longenecker. Grand Rapids: Baker; Leicester, U.K.: Apollos, 1998.

Harvey, "Torah." Harvey, Warren. "Torah." *EncJud* 14:1239–46.

Harwood, *Spiritist.* Harwood, Alan. *Rx—Spiritist as Needed: A Study of a Puerto Rican Community Mental Health Resource.* New York: Wiley, 1977. Repr., Ithaca, N.Y.: Cornell University Press, 1987.

Hasel, *Amos.* Hasel, Gerhard F. *Understanding the Book of Amos.* Grand Rapids: Baker, 1991.

Hasel, "Identity." Hasel, Gerhard F. "The Identity of 'the Saints of the Most High' in Daniel 7." *Bib* 56 (2, 1975): 173–92.

Hasel, *New Testament Theology.* Hasel, Gerhard F. *New Testament Theology: Basic Issues in the Current Debate.* Grand Rapids: Eerdmans, 1978.

Hasel, *Old Testament Theology.* Hasel, Gerhard F. *Old Testament Theology: Basic Issues in the Current Debate.* Rev. ed. Grand Rapids: Eerdmans, 1972.

Hasel, *Remnant.* Hasel, Gerhard F. *The Remnant: The History and Theology of the Remnant Idea from Genesis to Isaiah.* 3rd ed. Berrien Springs, Mich.: Andrews University Press, 1980.

Hasitschka, "Frauen." Hasitschka, Marin. "'Die Frauen in den Gemeinden sollen schweigen': 1 Kor 14,33b-36—Anweisung des Paulus zur rechten Ordnung im Gottesdienst." *SNTSU* 22 (1997): 47–56.

Haslam, "Centurion." Haslam, J. A. G. "The Centurion at Capernaum: Luke 7:1–10." *ExpT* 96 (4, 1985): 109–10.

Hata, "Moses within Anti-Semitism." Hata, Gohei. "The Story of Moses Interpreted within the Context of Anti-Semitism." Pages 180–97 in *Josephus, Judaism and Christianity.* Edited by Louis H. Feldman and Gohei Hata. Detroit: Wayne State University Press, 1987.

Hata, "Version." Hata, Gohei. "Is the Greek Version of Josephus' *Jewish War* a Translation or a Rewriting of the First Version?" *JQR* 66 (2, 1975): 89–108.

Hatch, *Faith.* Hatch, William Henry Paine. *The Pauline Idea of Faith in Its Relation to Jewish and Hellenistic Religion.* HTS. Cambridge, Mass.: Harvard University Press, 1917. Repr., New York: Kraus, 1969.

Hatina, "Consolations." Hatina, Thomas R. "Consolations/Tanhumim (4Q176)." *DNTB* 226–27.

Hatina, "Context." Hatina, Thomas R. "John 20,22 in Its Eschatological Context: Promise or Fulfillment?" *Bib* 74 (2, 1993): 196–219.

Hatina, "Exile." Hatina, Thomas R. "Exile." *DNTB* 348–51.

Hatt, "Syncrétisme." Hatt, Jean Jacques. "Le syncrétisme gallo-romain." Pages 117–26 in *Mystères et syncrétismes.* Edited by M. Philonenko and M. Simon. EHRel 2. Paris: Librairie Orientaliste Paul Geuthner, 1975.

Hauck, "Μιαίνω." Hauck, Friedrich. "Μιαίνω." *TDNT* 4:644–47.

Hauerwas and Jones, *Narrative.* Hauerwas, Stanley, and L. Gregory Jones, eds. *Why Narrative? Readings in Narrative Theology.* Grand Rapids: Eerdmans, 1989.

Haught, *Atheism.* Haught, John F. *God and the New Atheism: A Critical Response to Dawkins, Harris, and Hitchens.* Louisville: Westminster John Knox, 2008.

Hauptman, "Haggadah." Hauptman, Judith. "How Old Is the Haggadah?" *Judaism* 51 (1, 2002): 5–18.

Hauser, *Strukturen.* Hauser, Hermann J. *Strukturen der Abschlusserzählung der Apostelgeschichte (Apg 28, 16–31).* AnBib 86. Rome: Biblical Institute Press, 1979.

Havelaar, "Acts 5.1–11 and Interpretations." Havelaar, Henriette. "Hellenistic Parallels to Acts 5.1–11 and the Problem of Conflicting Interpretations." *JSNT* 67 (1997): 63–82.

Havelock, *Aphrodite.* Havelock, Christine Mitchell. *The Aphrodite of Knidos and Her Successors: A Historical Review of the Female Nude in Greek Art.* Ann Arbor: University of Michigan Press, 1995.

Hawass, "Nubia." Hawass, Zahi. "Nubia." *OEANE* 4:170–71.

Hawkins, *Horae synopticae.* Hawkins, John C. *Horae synopticae.* Oxford: Clarendon, 1909.

Hawthorne, "Concept." Hawthorne, Gerald F. "The Concept of Faith in the Fourth Gospel." *BSac* 116 (462, 1959): 117–26.

Hawthorne, *Philippians.* Hawthorne, Gerald F. *Philippians.* WBC 43. Waco: Word, 1983.

Hay, "Extremism." Hay, David M. "Putting Extremism in Context: The Case of Philo, *De migratione* 89–93." *SPhilA* 9 (1997): 126–42.

Hay, *Glory at Right Hand.* Hay, David M. *Glory at the Right Hand: Psalm 110 in Early Christianity.* SBLMS 18. Nashville: Abingdon, 1973.

Haya-Prats, *Believers.* Haya-Prats, Gonzalo. *Empowered Believers: The Holy Spirit in the Book of Acts.* Edited by Paul Elbert. Translated by Scott A. Ellington. Eugene, Ore.: Cascade, 2011.

Hayes, "Converts." Hayes, Christine. "Do Converts to Judaism Require Purification? M. Pes. 8:8—An Interpretive Crux Solved." *JSQ* 9 (4, 2002): 327–52.

Hayes, "Intermarriage." Hayes, Christine. "Intermarriage and Impurity in Ancient Jewish Sources." *HTR* 92 (1, 1999): 3–36.

Hayes, "Mthembu." Hayes, Stephen. "Mthembu, Toitoi Smart." No pages. *DACB.* Online: http://www.dacb.org/stories/botswana/mthembu_toitoi smart.html.

Hayes, "Oracles." Hayes, John H. "The Usage of Oracles against Foreign Nations in Ancient Israel." *JBL* 87 (1, 1968): 81–92.

Hayes, "Prophetism." Hayes, John H. "Prophetism at Mari and Old Testament Parallels." *AThR* 49 (1967): 397–409.

Hayes, "Roman Pottery." Hayes, John W. "Roman Pottery from the South Stoa at Corinth." *Hesperia* 42 (1973): 416–70.

Hayles, "Correct." Hayles, D. J. "The Roman Census and Jesus' Birth: Was Luke Correct? Part 1: The Roman Census System." *BurH* 9 (4, 1973): 113–32. "Part II: Quirinius' Career and a Census in Herod's Day." *BurH* 10 (1, 1974): 16–31.

Hayman, "Fall." Hayman, A. P. "The Fall, Freewill, and Human Responsibility in Rabbinic Judaism." *SJT* 37 (1, 1984): 13–22.

Hayman, "Magician." Hayman, A. Peter. "Was God a Magician? Sefer Yesira and Jewish Magic." *JJS* 40 (2, 1989): 225–37.

Hayman, "Man from Sea." Hayman, A. P. "The 'Man from the Sea' in 4 Ezra 13." *JJS* 49 (1, 1998): 1–16.

Hayman, "Observations." Hayman, Peter. "Some Observations on Sefer Yesira: (2)

The Temple at the Centre of the Universe." *JJS* 37 (2, 1986): 176–82.

Hays, "Category or Methodology." Hays, Richard B. "Intertextuality: A Catchall Category or a Specific Methodology?" Paper presented at the annual meeting of the SBL, San Antonio, Tex., Nov. 21, 2004.

Hays, *Conversion.* Hays, Richard B. *The Conversion of the Imagination: Paul as Interpreter of Israel's Scripture.* Grand Rapids: Eerdmans, 2005.

Hays, "Cushites." Hays, J. Daniel. "The Cushites: A Black Nation in the Bible." *BSac* 153 (611, 1996): 270–80; (612, 1996): 396–409.

Hays, *Echoes.* Hays, Richard B. *Echoes of Scripture in the Letters of Paul.* New Haven: Yale University Press, 1989.

Hays, *Ethics.* Hays, Christopher M. *Luke's Wealth Ethics: A Study in Their Coherence and Character.* WUNT 2.275. Tübingen: Mohr Siebeck, 2010.

Hays, *Faith.* Hays, Richard B. *The Faith of Jesus Christ: An Investigation of the Narrative Substructure of Galatians 3:1–4:11.* SBLDS 56. Chico, Calif.: Scholars Press, 1983.

Hays, *First Corinthians.* Hays, Richard B. *First Corinthians.* IBC. Louisville: John Knox, 1997.

Hays, "Marcion." Hays, Christopher M. "Marcion vs. Luke: A Response to the Plädoyer of Matthias Klinghardt." *ZNW* 99 (2, 2008): 213–32.

Hays, *Moral Vision.* Hays, Richard B. *The Moral Vision of the New Testament: A Contemporary Introduction to New Testament Ethics.* San Francisco: HarperSanFrancisco, 1996.

Hays, "Perspective." Hays, J. Daniel. "A Biblical Perspective on Interracial Marriage." *CrisTR* n.s. 6 (2, 2009): 5–23.

Hayward, "Abraham as Proselytizer." Hayward, Robert. "Abraham as Proselytizer at Beer-Sheba in the Targums of the Pentateuch." *JJS* 49 (1, 1998): 24–37.

Hayward, "Chant." Hayward, Robert. "The Chant of the Seraphim and the Worship of the Second Temple." *PIBA* 20 (1997): 62–80.

Hayward, "Figure of Adam." Hayward, Robert. "The Figure of Adam in Pseudo-Philo's Biblical Antiquities." *JSJ* 23 (1, 1992): 1–20.

Hayward, "Jerome." Hayward, Robert. "Saint Jerome and the Aramaic Targumim." *JSS* 32 (1, 1987): 105–23.

Hayward, "Pseudo-Jonathan." Hayward, Robert. "Targum Pseudo-Jonathan to Genesis 27:31." *JQR* 84 (2–3, 1993): 177–88.

Hayward, "Sacrifice." Hayward, Robert. "The Sacrifice of Isaac and Jewish Polemic

against Christianity." *CBQ* 52 (2, 1990): 292–306.

Hayward, "State of Research." Hayward, Robert. "The Present State of Research into the Targumic Account of the Sacrifice of Isaac." *JJS* 32 (2, 1981): 127–50.

Head, "Letter-Carriers." Head, Peter M. "Named Letter-Carriers among the Oxyrhynchus Papyri." *JSNT* 31 (3, 2009): 279–99.

Head, "Nazi Quest." Head, Peter M. "The Nazi Quest for an Aryan Jesus." *JSHJ* 2 (1, 2004): 55–89.

Head, "Note on *Reading.*" Head, Peter M. "A Further Note on *Reading and Writing in the Time of Jesus.*" *EvQ* 75 (4, 2003): 343–45.

Head, "Texts." Head, Peter M. "Acts and the Problem of Its Texts." Pages 415–44 in *The Book of Acts in Its Ancient Literary Setting.* Edited by Bruce W. Winter and Andrew D. Clarke. Vol. 1 of *The Book of Acts in Its First Century Setting.* Edited by Bruce W. Winter. Grand Rapids: Eerdmans; Carlisle, U.K.: Paternoster, 1993.

Healey, "Aretas." Healey, John F. "Aretas." *OCD*[3] 153.

Healey, "Bostra." Healey, John F. "Bostra." *OCD*[3] 254–55.

Healey, "Ituraea." Healey, John F. "Ituraea." *OCD*[3] 776.

Healey, "Nabataeans." Healey, John F. "Nabataeans." *OCD*[3] 1021.

Healey, "Syrian Deities." Healey, John F. "Syrian Deities." *OCD*[3] 1465.

Heard, "Libya." Heard, Warren J., Jr. "Libya." *ABD* 4:324.

Heard and Evans, "Revolutionary Movements." Heard, Warren J., Jr., and Craig A. Evans, "Revolutionary Movements, Jewish." *DNTB* 936–47.

Heard and Yamazaki-Ransom, "Revolutionary Movements." Heard, Warren J., Jr., and Kazuhiko Yamazaki-Ransom, "Revolutionary Movements." Pages 789–99 in *Dictionary of Jesus and the Gospels.* 2nd ed. Edited by Joel B. Green, Jeannine K. Brown, and Nicholas Perrin. Downers Grove, Ill.: IVP Academic, 2013.

Hearon, "Read Ourselves." Hearon, Holly E. "To Read Ourselves as the 'Other.'" *Enc* 63 (1–2, 2002): 109–18.

Heath, *Hermogenes.* Heath, Malcolm, ed. and trans. *Hermogenes On Issues: Strategies of Argument in Later Greek Rhetoric.* Oxford: Clarendon, 1995.

Heath, "Homer." Heath, Jane. "Homer or Moses? A Hellenistic Perspective on Moses' Throne Vision in Ezekiel Tragicus." *JJS* 58 (1, 2007): 1–18.

Heath, "Invention." Heath, Malcolm. "Invention." Pages 89–119 in *Handbook of Classical Rhetoric in the Hellenistic Period,*

330 B.C.–A.D. 400. Edited by Stanley E. Porter. Leiden: Brill, 1997.

Heath, *Unity.* Heath, Malcolm. *Unity in Greek Poetics.* Oxford: Clarendon, 1989.

Heath, "Visuality." Heath, Jane. "Ezekiel Tragicus and Hellenistic Visuality: The Phoenix at Elim." *JTS* 57 (1, 2006): 23–41.

Hecht, "Kinship." Hecht, Irene W. D. "Kinship and Migration: The Making of an Oregon Isolate Community." *JIHist* 8 (1, Summer 1977): 45–67.

Hedges, "Prosperity Theology." Hedges, Daniel. "Prosperity Theology." Pages 348–49 in vol. 1 of *Encyclopedia of Religious Revivals in America.* Edited by Michael McClymond. 2 vols. Westport, Conn.: Greenwood, 2007.

Hedlun, "Reading." Hedlun, Randall J. "A New Reading of Acts 18:24–19:7: Understanding the Ephesian Disciples Encounter as Social Conflict." *R&T* 17 (1–2, 2010): 40–60.

Hedrick, "Paul's Conversion/Call." Hedrick, Charles W. "Paul's Conversion/Call: A Comparative Analysis of the Three Reports in Acts." *JBL* 100 (3, 1981): 415–32.

Hedrick, "Samaritan." Hedrick, Pamela. "The Good Samaritan, Cornelius, and the Just Use of Force." Pages 123–34 in *Acts and Ethics.* Edited by Thomas E. Phillips. NTMon 9. Sheffield, U.K.: Sheffield Phoenix, 2005.

Hedrick, "Secret Mark." Hedrick, Charles W. "'Secret Mark': A Modern Forgery?" *BAR* 35 (6, 2009): 43–61, 86, 88, 90, 92.

Hedrick, "Stalemate." Hedrick, Charles W. "The Secret Gospel of Mark: Stalemate in the Academy." *JECS* 11 (2, Summer 2003): 133–45.

Heen, "Patronage." Heen, Erik. "Radical Patronage in Luke-Acts." *CurTM* 33 (6, 2006): 445–58.

Hefley and Hefley, *Blood.* Hefley, James, and Marti Hefley. *By Their Blood: Christian Martyrs of the Twentieth Century.* 2nd ed. Grand Rapids: Baker, 1996.

Heger, "Exegesis." Heger, Paul. "Qumran Exegesis: 'Rewritten Torah' or Interpretation?" *RevQ* 22 (85, 2005): 61–87.

Heger, "Prayer." Heger, Paul. "Did Prayer Replace Sacrifice at Qumran?" *RevQ* 22 (86, 2005): 213–33.

Heid, "Romanness." Heid, Stefan. "The Romanness of Roman Christianity." Pages 406–26 in *A Companion to Roman Religion.* Edited by Jörg Rüpke. BCompAW. Oxford: Blackwell, 2011.

Heidel, *Genesis.* Heidel, Alexander. *The Babylonian Genesis.* 2nd ed. Chicago: University of Chicago Press, 1951.

Heider, "Molech." Heider, George C. "Molech." Pages 581–85 in *Dictionary of Deities and Demons in the Bible.* 2nd rev. ed. Edited by Karel van der Toorn, Bob Becking, and Pieter W. van der Horst. Leiden: Brill; Grand Rapids: Eerdmans, 1999.

Heijne, "Aqedat Isak." Heijne, Camilla von. "Aqedat Isak: Judisk tolkning av Genesis 22:1–19." *SEÅ* 62 (1997): 57–86.

Heil, "Arius Didymus." Heil, Christoph. "Arius Didymus and Luke-Acts." *NovT* 42 (4, 2000): 358–93.

Heil, "Believers." Heil, John Paul. "Paul and the Believers of Western Asia." Pages 79–92 in *The Blackwell Companion to Paul.* Edited by Stephen Westerholm. BCompRel. Oxford: Blackwell, 2011.

Heil, *Meal Scenes.* Heil, John Paul. *The Meal Scenes in Luke-Acts: An Audience-Oriented Approach.* SBLMS 52. Atlanta: SBL, 1999.

Heiligenthal, "Petrus und Jakobus." Heiligenthal, Roman. "'Petrus und Jakobus, der Gerechte': Gedanken zur Rolle der beiden Säulenapostel in der Geschichte des frühen Christentums." *ZNT* 2 (4, 1999): 32–40.

Heim, *Transformation.* Heim, Karl. *The Transformation of the Scientific World View.* New York: Harper & Brothers, 1953.

Heimgartner, "Mission." Heimgartner, Martin. "Mission." *BrillPauly* 9:63–65.

Heindl, "Rezeption." Heindl, Andreas. "Zur Rezeption der Gestalt des Judas Iskariot im Islam und im Judentum: Ein Versuch der Annäherung an heikles Thema (Teil II)." *PzB* 16 (1, 2007): 43–66.

Heine, *Women.* Heine, Susanne. *Women and Early Christianity: A Reappraisal.* Translated by John Bowden. Minneapolis: Augsburg; London: SCM, 1987.

Heinemann, "Profile." Heinemann, Joseph. "Profile of a Midrash: The Art of Composition in Leviticus Rabba." *JAAR* 39 (2, 1971): 141–50.

Heinen, "Ägyptische Grundlagen." Heinen, Heinz. "Ägyptische Grundlagen des antiken Antijudaismus, zum Judenexkurs des Tacitus, Historien V 2–13." *TTZ* 101 (2, 1992): 124–49.

Heininger, "Tarsus und zurück." Heininger, Bernhard. "Einmal Tarsus und zurück (Apg 9, 30; 11, 25–26): Paulus als Lehrer nach der Apostelgeschichte." *MTZ* 49 (2, 1998): 125–43.

Heinrichs, "Freedmen." Heinrichs, Johannes. "Freedmen: Rome." *BrillPauly* 5:541–45.

Heintz, *Magicien.* Heintz, Florent. *Simon "Le Magicien": Actes 8,5–25 et l'accusation de magie contre les prophètes thaumaturges dans l'antiquité.* CahRB 39. Paris: J. Gabalda, 1997.

Heinze, "Galli." Heinze, Theodor. "Galli." *BrillPauly* 5:668–69.

Heinze, "Teiresias." Heinze, Theodor. "Teiresias." *BrillPauly* 14:216–17.

Heinzel, "Kult der Artemis." Heinzel, Elma. "Zum Kult der Artemis von Ephesos." *JÖAI* 50 (1972–73): 243–51.

Heiskanan, "Structure." Heiskanan, Veronica Stolte. "Community Structure to Kinship Ties: Extended Family Relations in Three Finnish Communities." *IJComSoc* 10 (3–4, Sept. 1969): 251–62.

Hekman, "Power." Hekman, Donald. "'Power' in Luke and Acts." *NotesT* 13 (1, 1999): 17–41.

Hekster, "Epiphanies." Hekster, Olivier. "Reversed Epiphanies: Roman Emperors Deserted by Gods." *Mnemosyne* 63 (4, 2010): 601–15.

Heldman, "Axum." Heldman, Marilyn E. "Axum." *OEANE* 1:239–41.

Hellerman, "Humiliation." Hellerman, Joseph H. "The Humiliation of Christ in the Social World of Roman Philippi, Part 1." *BSac* 160 (639, 2003): 321–36.

Hellerman, "Purity." Hellerman, Joseph H. "Purity and Nationalism in Second Temple Literature: 1–2 Maccabees and Jubilees." *JETS* 46 (3, 2003): 401–21.

Hellerman, "Servants." Hellerman, Joseph H. "Vindicating God's Servants in Philippi and in Philippians: The Influence of Paul's Ministry in Philippi upon the Composition of Philippians 2:6–11." *BBR* 20 (1, 2010): 85–102.

Helly, "Thessaly." Helly, Bruno. "Thessaly." *OCD*³ 1511–12.

Hemelrijk, "Empresses." Hemelrijk, Emily Ann. "Local Empresses: Priestesses of the Imperial Cult in the Cities of the Latin West." *Phoenix* 61 (3–4, 2007): 318–49.

Hemelrijk, "Kinship." Hemelrijk, Emily A. "Fictive Kinship as a Metaphor for Women's Civic Roles." *Hermes* 138 (4, 2010): 455–69.

Hemelrijk, "Masculinity." Hemelrijk, Emily Ann. "Masculinity and Femininity in the *Laudatio Turiae.*" *CQ* 54 (1, 2004): 185–97.

Hemelrijk, *Matrona docta.* Hemelrijk, Emily Ann. *Matrona docta: Educated Women in the Roman Elite from Correlia to Julia Domna.* London: Routledge, 1999.

Hemelrijk, "Patronesses." Hemelrijk, Emily Ann. "City Patronesses in the Roman Empire." *Historia* 53 (2, 2004): 209–45.

Hemer, *Acts in History.* Hemer, Colin J. *The Book of Acts in the Setting of Hellenistic History.* Edited by Conrad H. Gempf. WUNT 49. Tübingen: Mohr Siebeck, 1989.

Hemer, "Address." Hemer, Colin J. "The Address of 1 Peter." *ExpT* 89 (8, 1978): 239–43."

Hemer, "Alexandria Troas." Hemer, Colin J. "Alexandria Troas." *TynBul* 26 (1975): 79–112.

Hemer, "Areopagus Address." Hemer, Colin J. "The Speeches of Acts, 2: The Areopagus Address." *TynBul* 40 (1989): 239–59.

Hemer, "Audeitorion." Hemer, Colin J. "Audeitorion." *TynBul* 24 (1973): 128.

Hemer, "Ephesian Elders." Hemer, Colin J. "The Speeches of Acts, 1: The Ephesian Elders at Miletus." *TynBul* 40 (1989): 77–85.

Hemer, "Euraquilo and Melita." Hemer, Colin J. "Euraquilo and Melita." *JTS*, n.s., 26 (1975): 100–111.

Hemer, "First Person Narrative." Hemer, Colin J. "First Person Narrative in Acts 27–28." *TynBul* 36 (1985): 79–109.

Hemer, "Further Note." Hemer, Colin J. "Phrygia: A Further Note." *JTS*, n.s., 28 (1, 1977): 99–101.

Hemer, *Letters*. Hemer, Colin J. *The Letters to the Seven Churches of Asia in Their Local Setting*. JSNTSup 11. Sheffield, U.K.: JSOT Press, 1986.

Hemer, "Name of Felix." Hemer, Colin J. "The Name of Felix Again." *JSNT* 31 (1987): 45–49.

Hemer, "Name of Paul." Hemer, Colin J. "The Name of Paul." *TynBul* 36 (1985): 179–83.

Hemer, "Observations." Hemer, Colin J. "Observations on Pauline Chronology." Pages 3–18 in *Pauline Studies: Essays Presented to Professor F. F. Bruce on His 70th Birthday*. Edited by Donald A. Hagner and Murray J. Harris. Exeter, U.K.: Paternoster; Grand Rapids: Eerdmans, 1980.

Hemer, "*Ostraka*." Hemer, Colin J. "The Edfu *ostraka* and the Jewish Tax." *PEQ* 105 (1, 1973): 6–12.

Hemer, "Paul at Athens." Hemer, Colin J. "Paul at Athens: A Topographical Note." *NTS* 20 (3, 1974): 341–50.

Hemer, "Phrygia." Hemer, Colin J. "The Adjective 'Phrygia.'" *JTS*, n.s., 27 (1, 1976): 122–26.

Hemer, "Three Taverns." Hemer, Colin J. "Three Taverns." *ISBE* 4:843–44.

Hempel, "Who Rebukes?" Hempel, Charlotte. "Who Rebukes in 4Q477?" *RevQ* 16 (4, 1995): 655–56.

Hendel, "Serpent." Hendel, Ronald S. "Serpent." Pages 744–47 in *Dictionary of Deities and Demons in the Bible*. 2nd rev. ed. Edited by Karel van der Toorn, Bob Becking, and Pieter W. van der Horst. Leiden: Brill; Grand Rapids: Eerdmans, 1999.

Henderson, "Baptized." Henderson, T. "'What Is to Prevent Me from Being Baptized?' Reading beyond the Readily Apparent." *CTSR* 93 (3, 2003): 14–22.

Henderson, *Prophets*. Henderson, Ebenezer. *The Twelve Minor Prophets*. London: Hamilton, Adams, 1858. Repr., Grand Rapids: Baker, 1980.

Hendrickson, "Ancient Reading." Hendrickson, G. L. "Ancient Reading." *CJ* 25 (1929): 182–96.

Hendrix, "Patron Networks." Hendrix, Holland L. "Benefactor/Patron Networks in the Urban Environment: Evidence from Thessalonica." *Semeia* 56 (1991): 39–58.

Hendrix, "Philippi." Hendrix, Holland L. "Philippi." *ABD* 5:313–17.

Hendrix, "Thessalonica." Hendrix, Holland L. "Thessalonica." *ABD* 6:523–27.

Hendrix, "Thessalonicans." Hendrix, Holland L. "Thessalonicans Honor Romans." ThD diss., Harvard University, 1984.

Hengel, *Acts and History*. Hengel, Martin. *Acts and the History of Earliest Christianity*. Translated by John Bowden. London: SCM, 1979; Philadelphia: Fortress, 1980.

Hengel, *Atonement*. Hengel, Martin. *The Atonement: The Origins of the Doctrine in the New Testament*. Translated by John Bowden. Philadelphia: Fortress, 1981.

Hengel, *Charismatic Leader*. Hengel, Martin. *The Charismatic Leader and His Followers*. Edited by John Riches. Translated by James Greig. New York: Crossroad, 1981.

Hengel, *Crucifixion*. Hengel, Martin. *Crucifixion in the Ancient World and the Folly of the Message of the Cross*. Philadelphia: Fortress, 1977.

Hengel, "Geography of Palestine." Hengel, Martin. "The Geography of Palestine in Acts." Pages 27–78 in *The Book of Acts in Its Palestinian Setting*. Edited by Richard Bauckham. Vol. 4 of *The Book of Acts in Its First Century Setting*. Edited by Bruce W. Winter. Grand Rapids: Eerdmans; Carlisle, U.K.: Paternoster, 1995.

Hengel, "Hellenismus." Hengel, Martin. "Qumran und der Hellenismus." Pages 333–72 in *Qumrân: Sa piété, sa théologie, et son milieu*. Edited by M. Delcor. BETL 46. Gembloux, Belg., and Paris: J. Duculot; Leuven: Leuven University Press, 1978.

Hengel, *Jesus and Paul*. Hengel, Martin. *Between Jesus and Paul: Studies in the History of Earliest Christianity*. Philadelphia: Fortress, 1983.

Hengel, *Judaism and Hellenism*. Hengel, Martin. *Judaism and Hellenism: Studies in Their Encounter in Palestine during the Early Hellenistic Period*. Translated by John Bowden. 2 vols. in 1. Philadelphia: Fortress, 1974.

Hengel, "List." Hengel, Martin. "Ἰουδαία in the Geographical List of Acts 2:9–11 and Syria as 'Greater Judea.'" *BBR* 10 (2, 2000): 161–80.

Hengel, "Liste." Hengel, Martin. "'Ἰουδαία in der geographischen Liste Apg 2,9–11 und Syrien als 'Grossjudäa.'" *RHPR* 80 (1, 2000): 51–68.

Hengel, *Mark*. Hengel, Martin. *Studies in the Gospel of Mark*. Translated by John Bowden. Philadelphia: Fortress, 1985.

Hengel, "Paul in Arabia." Hengel, Martin. "Paul in Arabia." *BBR* 12 (1, 2002): 47–66.

Hengel, *Peter*. Hengel, Martin. *Saint Peter: The Underestimated Apostle*. Translated by Thomas H. Trapp. Grand Rapids: Eerdmans, 2010.

Hengel, *Pre-Christian Paul*. Hengel, Martin. *The Pre-Christian Paul*. Valley Forge, Pa.: Trinity Press International, 1991.

Hengel, "Problems." Hengel, Martin. "Literary, Theological, and Historical Problems in the Gospel of Mark." Pages 209–51 in *The Gospel and the Gospels*. Edited by Peter Stuhlmacher. Grand Rapids: Eerdmans, 1991.

Hengel, *Property*. Hengel, Martin. *Property and Riches in the Early Church: Aspects of a Social History of Early Christianity*. Philadelphia: Fortress, 1974.

Hengel, *Son*. Hengel, Martin. *The Son of God*. Translated by John Bowden. Philadelphia: Fortress, 1976.

Hengel, *Zeloten*. Hengel, Martin. *Die Zeloten: Untersuchungen zur jüdischen Freiheitsbewegung in der Zeit von Herodes I. bis 70 n. Chr.* AGSU 1. Leiden and Cologne: Brill, 1961.

Hengel and Schwemer, *Between Damascus and Antioch*. Hengel, Martin, and Anna Maria Schwemer. *Paul between Damascus and Antioch: The Unknown Years*. Translated by John Bowden. London: SCM; Louisville: Westminster John Knox, 1997.

Henige, "History." Henige, David. "African History and the Rule of Evidence: Is Declaring Victory Enough?" Pages 91–104 in *African Historiographies: What History for Which Africa?* Edited by Bogumil Jewsiewicki and David Newbury. SSAMD 12. Beverly Hills, Calif.: Sage, 1986.

Henney, "Belief." Henney, Jeannette H. "Spirit-Possesion Belief and Trance Behavior in Two Fundamentalist Groups in St. Vincent." Pages 1–111 in *Trance, Healing, and Hallucination: Three Field Studies in Religious Experience*. By Felicitas D. Goodman, Jeannette H. Henney, and Esther Pressel. New York: Wiley, 1974.

Henrichs, "Atheism." Henrichs, Albert. "The Atheism of Prodicus." *Bolletino del Centro internazionale per lo studio dei papiri ercolanesi* 6 (1976): 15–21.

Henrichs, "Epiphany." Henrichs, Albert. "Epiphany." *OCD³* 546.

Henrichs, "Fasting." Henrichs, Albert. "Fasting." OCD^3 588–89.

Henrichs, "Identities." Henrichs, Albert. "Changing Dionysiac Identities." Pages 137–60 in *Self-Definition in the Greco-Roman World*. Edited by Ben F. Meyer and E. P. Sanders. Vol. 3 of *Jewish and Christian Self-Definition*. Edited by E. P. Sanders. Philadelphia: Fortress, 1982.

Henrichs, "Moira." Henrichs, Albert. "Moira." *BrillPauly* 9:124–26.

Henrichs, "Notes." Henrichs, Albert. "Two Doxographical Notes: Democritus and Prodicus on Religion." *HSCP* 79 (1975): 93–123.

Henrichs, "Oedipus." Henrichs, Albert. "Oedipus." *BrillPauly* 10:44–48.

Henrichs, "Zeus." Henrichs, Albert. "Zeus." *BrillPauly* 15:918–26.

Henriksén, "Earinus." Henriksén, Christer. "Earinus: An Imperial Eunuch in the Light of the Poems of Martial and Statius." *Mnemosyne* 50 (3, 1997): 281–94.

Henry, "*Hetairai*." Henry, Madeleine Mary. "*Hetairai*." OCD^3 702.

Henry, *Philodemus*. Henry, W. Benjamin. Notes to *Philodemus, On Death*. SBLW GRW 29. Atlanta: SBL, 2009.

Henshke, "Haggadah." Henshke, David. "'The Lord Brought Us Forth from Egypt': On the Absence of Moses in the Passover Haggadah." *AJSR* 31 (1, 2007): 61–73.

Hepner, "Tenth Commandment." Hepner, Gershon. "The Samaritan Version of the Tenth Commandment." *JSP* 20 (1, 2006): 147–52.

Hepper, *Plants*. Hepper, F. Nigel. *Baker Encyclopedia of Bible Plants*. Grand Rapids: Baker; Leicester, U.K.: InterVarsity, 1992.

Herbert, "Orientation." Herbert, Sharon C. "The Orientation of Greek Temples." *PEQ* 116 (1, 1984): 31–34.

Herbert, "Silk Road." Herbert, Kevin. "The Silk Road: The Link between the Classical World and Ancient China." *CBull* 73 (2, 1997): 119–24.

Herford, *Christianity*. Herford, R. Travers. *Christianity in Talmud and Midrash*. London: Williams & Norgate, 1903. Repr., Library of Philosophical and Religious Thought. Clifton, N.J.: Reference Book Publishers, 1966.

Herford, *Pharisees*. Herford, R. Travers. *The Pharisees*. Boston: Beacon, 1952.

Héring, *First Corinthians*. Héring, Jean. *The First Epistle of Saint Paul to the Corinthians*. Translated by A. W. Heathcote and P. J. Allcock. London: Epworth, 1962.

Héring, *Second Corinthians*. Héring, Jean. *The Second Epistle of Saint Paul to the Corinthians*. Translated by A. W. Heathcote and P. J. Allcock. London: Epworth, 1962.

Herman, "Gift." Herman, Gabriel. "Gift, Greece." OCD^3 637.

Herman, "Motifs." Herman, Geoffrey. "Iranian Epic Motifs in Josephus' Antiquities (XVIII, 314–370)." *JJS* 57 (2, 2006): 245–68.

Hernando, "Function." Hernando, James D. "Pneumatological Function in the Narrative of Acts: Drawing Foundational Insight for a Pentecostal Missiology." Pages 241–76 in *Trajectories in the Book of Acts: Essays in Honor of John Wesley Wyckoff*. Edited by Paul Alexander, Jordan Daniel May, and Robert G. Reid. Eugene, Ore.: Wipf & Stock, 2010.

Heron, *Channels*. Heron, Benedict. *Channels of Healing Prayer*. Foreword by Francis MacNutt. Notre Dame, Ind.: Ave Maria, 1992; London: Darton, Longman & Todd, 1989.

Herr, "Salt." Herr, Larry G. "Salt." *ISBE* 4:286–87.

Herr, "Sybwtyw." Herr, M. D. "Sybwtyw sl mrd br-kwkb.'" *Zion* 43 (1–2, 1978): 1–11.

Herr, "Window." Herr, Larry G. "Window." *ISBE* 4:1068.

Herrmann, "Bannoun." Herrmann, Léon. "Bannoun ou Ioannoun, Félix ou Festus? (Flavius Josèphe, *Vie*, 11 et 13)." *REJ* 135 (1–3, 1976): 151–55.

Herscher, "Archaeology." Herscher, Ellen. "Archaeology in Cyprus." *AJA* 102 (2, 1998): 309–54.

Hershkovitz, "Cremation." Hershkovitz, Israel. "Cremation, Its Practice and Identification: A Case Study from the Roman Period." *TA* 15–16 (1, 1988–89): 98–100, and plates 15–16. (Abstract: *NTA* 34:354.)

Herskovitz, *Life*. Herskovitz, Melville J. *Life in a Haitian Valley*. New York: Doubleday, 1971.

Hertig, "Cross-cultural Mediation." Hertig, Young Lee. "Cross-cultural Mediation: From Exclusion to Inclusion, Acts 6:1–7; also 5:33–42." Pages 59–72 in *Mission in Acts: Ancient Narratives in Contemporary Context*. Edited by Robert L. Gallagher and Paul Hertig. AmSocMissS 34. Maryknoll, N.Y.: Orbis, 2004.

Hertig, "Dynamics." Hertig, Paul. "Dynamics in Hellenism and the Immigrant Congregation, Acts 6:8–8:2." Pages 73–86 in *Mission in Acts: Ancient Narratives in Contemporary Context*. Edited by Robert L. Gallagher and Paul Hertig. AmSocMissS 34. Maryknoll, N.Y.: Orbis, 2004.

Hertig, "Mystery Tour." Hertig, Paul. "The Magical Mystery Tour: Philip Encounters Magic and Materialism in Samaria, Acts 8:4–25." Pages 103–13 in *Mission in Acts: Ancient Narratives in Contemporary Context*. Edited by Robert L. Gallagher and Paul Hertig. AmSocMissS 34. Maryknoll, N.Y.: Orbis, 2004.

Hertig and Gallagher, "Introduction." Hertig, Paul, and Robert L. Gallagher. "Introduction: Background to Acts." Pages 2–17 in *Mission in Acts: Ancient Narratives in Contemporary Context*. Edited by Robert L. Gallagher and Paul Hertig. AmSocMissS 34. Maryknoll, N.Y.: Orbis, 2004.

Herum, "Theology." Herum, Nathan M. "Augustine's Theology of the Miraculous." MDiv thesis, Beeson Divinity School, 2009.

Herwerden, *Lexicon*. Herwerden, Henricus van. *Lexicon graecum suppletorium et dialectium*. 2nd ed. 2 vols. Leiden: A. W. Sijthoff, 1910.

Herz, "Emperors." Herz, Peter. "Emperors: Caring for the Empire and Their Successors." Pages 304–16 in *A Companion to Roman Religion*. Edited by Jörg Rüpke. BCompAW. Oxford: Blackwell, 2011.

Herzfeld, "House." Herzfeld, Michael. "'As in Your Own House': Hospitality, Ethnography, and the Stereotype of Mediterranean Society." Pages 75–89 in *Honor and Shame and the Unity of the Mediterranean*. Edited by David D. Gilmore. AAAM 22. Washington, D.C.: American Anthropological Association, 1987.

Hes, "Role." Hes, Jozef P. "The Changing Social Role of the Yemenite *Mori*." Pages 364–83 in *Magic, Faith, and Healing: Studies in Primitive Psychiatry Today*. Edited by Ari Kiev. Foreword by Jerome D. Frank. New York: Free Press, 1964.

Heschel, "De-Judaization." Heschel, Susannah. "Redemptive Anti-Semitism: The De-Judaization of the New Testament in the Third Reich." Pages 235–63 in *Literary Studies in Luke-Acts: Essays in Honor of Joseph B. Tyson*. Edited by Richard P. Thompson and Thomas E. Phillips. Macon, Ga.: Mercer University Press, 1998.

Heschel, *Prophets*. Heschel, Abraham J. *The Prophets*. New York: Harper & Row, 1962.

Hess, "Joshua." Hess, Richard S. "Joshua." Pages 2–93 in vol. 2 of *Zondervan Illustrated Bible Backgrounds Commentary: Old Testament*. Edited by John Walton. 5 vols. Grand Rapids: Zondervan, 2009.

Hesse, "Miracles." Hesse, Mary. "Miracles and the Laws of Nature." Pages 33–42 in *Miracles: Cambridge Studies in Their Philosophy and History*. Edited by C. F. D. Moule. London: A. R. Mowbray; New York: Morehouse-Barlow, 1965.

Hesse, "Pigs." Hesse, Brian. "Pigs." *OEANE* 4:347–48.

Hesselgrave, *Movements*. Hesselgrave, David J. *Dynamic Religious Movements: Case Studies of Rapidly Growing Religious*

Movements around the World. Grand Rapids: Baker, 1978.

Hester, Inheritance. Hester, James D. Paul's Concept of Inheritance: A Contribution to the Understanding of Heilsgeschichte. SJTOP 14. Edinburgh: Oliver & Boyd, 1968.

Hester, "Queers." Hester (Amador), J. David. "Queers on account of the Kingdom of Heaven: Rhetorical Constructions of the Eunuch Body." Scriptura 90 (2005): 809–23.

Hester, "Unity." Hester (Amador), J. David. "The Unity of 2 Corinthians: A Test Case for a Re-discovered and Re-invented Rhetoric." Neot 33 (2, 1999): 411–32.

Heth, "Demonization." Heth, William A. "Demonization Then and Now: How Contemporary Cases Fill In the Biblical Data." Paper presented at the fifty-eighth annual meeting of the Evangelical Theological Society, Washington, D.C., Nov. 16, 2006.

Heusler, Kapitalprozesse. Heusler, Erika. Kapitalprozesse im lukanischen Doppelwerk: Die Verfahren gegen Jesus und Paulus in exegetischer und rechtshistorischer Analyse. NTAbh, neue Folge, 38. Münster: Aschendorff, 2000.

Heutger, "Paulus auf Malta." Heutger, Nicolaus. "Paulus auf Malta' im Lichte der maltesischen Topographie." BZ 28 (1, 1984): 86–88.

Heuthorst, "Apologetic Aspect." Heuthorst, G. "The Apologetic Aspect of Acts 2:1–13." Scripture 9 (6, 1957): 33–43.

Hexham, "Shembe." Hexham, Irving. "Shembe, Isaiah Mdliwamafa." No pages. DACB. Online: http://www.dacb.org/stories/southafrica/shembe2_isaiah.html.

Heye, Sabbath in Ethiopia. Heye, Bekele. The Sabbath in Ethiopia: An Exploration of Christian Roots. Foreword by Charles E. Bradford. Lincoln, Neb.: Center for Creative Ministry, 2003.

Heyob, Isis. Heyob, Sharon Kelly. The Cult of Isis among Women in the Graeco-Roman World. ÉPROER 51. Leiden: Brill, 1975.

Heyworth and Wilson, "Editions, Second." Heyworth, Stephen, and Nigel Wilson. "Editions, Second." BrillPauly 4:809–12.

Heyworth and Wilson, "Variants." Heyworth, Stephen, and Nigel Wilson. "Author's Variants." BrillPauly 2:403–5.

Hezser, "Impact." Hezser, Catherine. "The Impact of Household Slaves on the Jewish Family in Roman Palestine." JSJ 34 (4, 2003): 375–424.

Hezser, "Literacy." Hezser, Catherine. Jewish Literacy in Roman Palestine. Tübingen: Mohr Siebeck, 2001.

Hezser, Slavery. Hezser, Catherine. Jewish Slavery in Antiquity. Oxford: Oxford University Press, 2005.

Hickling, "Portrait in Acts 26." Hickling, C. J. A. "The Portrait of Paul in Acts 26." Pages 499–503 in Les Actes des apôtres: Traditions, rédaction, théologie. Edited by Jacob Kremer. BETL 48. Gembloux, Belg.: J. Duculot; Leuven: Leuven University Press, 1979.

Hicks, "Demetrius the Silversmith." Hicks, E. L. "Demetrius the Silversmith: An Ephesian Study." Exp, 4th ser., 1 (1890): 401–22.

Hicks, "Postscript." Hicks, E. L. "Ephesus: A Postscript." Exp, 4th ser., 2 (1890): 144–49.

Hickson, "Augustus triumphator." Hickson, Frances V. "Augustus triumphator: Manipulation of the Triumphal Theme in the Political Program of Augustus." Latomus 50 (1, 1991): 124–38.

Hickson, Heal. Hickson, James Moore. Heal the Sick. 2nd ed. London: Methuen, 1924.

Hidal, "Rombilden." Hidal, Sten. "Rombilden i 1 Makkabeerboken 8." SEÅ 70 (2005): 101–5.

Hiebert, "Excluded Middle." Hiebert, Paul G. "The Flaw of the Excluded Middle." Missiology 10 (1, Jan. 1982): 35–47.

Hiebert, "Power Encounter." Hiebert, Paul. "Power Encounter in Folk Islam." Pages 45–61 in Muslims and Christians on the Emmaus Road. Edited by J. Dudley Woodberry. Monrovia, Calif.: MARC, 1989.

Hien, "Yin Illness." Hien, Nguyen Thi. "Yin Illness: Its Diagnosis and Healing Within Lên Dông (Spirit Possession) Rituals of the Viêt." AsEthn 67 (2, 2008): 305–21.

Hiers, "Problem of Delay." Hiers, Richard H. "The Problem of the Delay of the Parousia in Luke-Acts." NTS 20 (2, 1974): 145–55.

Hiesel, "Minoan Culture." Hiesel, Gerhard. "Minoan Culture and Archaeology." Brill Pauly 9:12–23.

Higgins, "Belief." Higgins, A. J. B. "Jewish Messianic Belief in Justin Martyr's Dialogue with Trypho." NovT 9 (4, 1967): 298–305.

Higgins, "Messiah." Higgins, A. J. B. "The Priestly Messiah." NTS 13 (3, 1967): 211–39.

Higgins, "Preface and Kerygma." Higgins, A. J. B. "The Preface to Luke and the Kerygma in Acts." Pages 78–91 in Apostolic History and the Gospel: Biblical and Historical Essays Presented to F. F. Bruce on His 60th Birthday. Edited by W. Ward Gasque and Ralph P. Martin. Exeter, U.K.: Paternoster; Grand Rapids: Eerdmans, 1970.

Higgins, "Priest." Higgins, A. J. B. "Priest and Messiah." VT 3 (4, 1953): 321–36.

Higgins, Son of Man. Higgins, A. J. B. Jesus and the Son of Man. Philadelphia: Fortress, 1964.

Highet, "Reciprocity." Highet, Gilbert. "Reciprocity (Greece)." OCD³ 1295.

Hilbert, "Enemies." Hilbert, Benjamin D. H. "185,000 Slain Maccabean Enemies (Times Two): Hyperbole in the Books of Maccabees." ZAW 122 (1, 2010): 102–6.

Hilborn, "Glossolalia." Hilborn, David. "Glossolalia as Communication: A Linguistic-Pragmatic Perspective." Pages 111–46 in Speaking in Tongues: Multidisciplinary Perspectives. Edited by Mark J. Cartledge. SPCI. Waynesboro, Ga., and Bletchley, Milton Keynes, U.K.: Paternoster, 2006.

Hild, "Aphrodisias." Hild, Friedrich. "Aphrodisias (2)." BrillPauly 1:830.

Hild, "Tarsus." Hild, Friedrich. "Tarsus." BrillPauly 14:155–56.

Hild and Hellenkemper, Kilikien. Hild, Friedrich, and Hansgerd Hellenkemper. Kilikien und Isaurien. Tabula Imperii Byzanti 5. Wien: Österreichische Akademie der Wissenschaften, 1990.

Hill, "Division." Hill, Craig C. "Acts 6.1–8.4: Division or Diversity?" Pages 129–53 in History, Literature, and Society in the Book of Acts. Edited by Ben Witherington III. Cambridge: Cambridge University Press, 1996.

Hill, Gospels. Hill, C. E. Who Chose the Gospels? Probing the Great Gospel Conspiracy. Oxford: Oxford University Press, 2010.

Hill, Hellenists. Hill, Craig C. Hellenists and Hebrews: Reappraising Division within the Earliest Church. Minneapolis: Fortress, 1992.

Hill, Matthew. Hill, David. The Gospel of Matthew. NCBC. Grand Rapids: Eerdmans; London: Marshall, Morgan & Scott, 1972.

Hill, Polycarp. Hill, Charles E. From the Lost Teaching of Polycarp: Identifying Irenaeus' Apostolic Presbyter and the Author of Ad Diognetum. WUNT 186. Tübingen: Mohr Siebeck, 2006.

Hill, Prophecy. Hill, David. New Testament Prophecy. NFTL. Atlanta: John Knox, 1979.

Hill, "Prophecy in Revelation." Hill, David. "Prophecy and Prophets in the Revelation of St. John." NTS 18 (4, 1972): 401–18.

Hill, "Temple." Hill, Andrew E. "The Temple of Asclepius: An Alternative Source for Paul's Body Theology?" JBL 99 (3, 1980): 437–39.

Hill and James, Glory. Hill, Charles E., and Frank A. James, III, eds. The Glory of the Atonement: Biblical, Theological & Practical Perspectives. Downers Grove, Ill.: InterVarsity, 2004.

Hillard, Nobbs, and Winter, "Corpus." Hillard, T., A. Nobbs, and B. Winter. "Acts and the Pauline Corpus, I: Ancient Literary Parallels." Pages 183–213 in *The Book of Acts in Its Ancient Literary Setting*. Edited by Bruce W. Winter and Andrew D. Clarke. Vol. 1 of *The Book of Acts in Its First Century Setting*. Edited by Bruce W. Winter. Grand Rapids: Eerdmans; Carlisle, U.K.: Paternoster, 1993.

Hillgarth, *Paganism*. Hillgarth, J. N. *Christianity and Paganism, 350–750: The Conversion of Western Europe*. Rev. ed. Philadelphia: University of Pennsylvania Press, 1986.

Hills, "Acts and Acts." Hills, Julian V. "The Acts of the Apostles and the *Acts of Paul*." Pages 24–54 in *SBL Seminar Papers, 1994*. Edited by Eugene H. Lovering Jr. SBLSP 33. Atlanta: Scholars Press, 1994.

Hills, "*Acts of Paul*." Hills, Julian V. "The *Acts of Paul* and the Legacy of the Lukan Acts." Pages 145–58 in *The Apocryphal Acts of the Apostles in Intertextual Perspectives*. Edited by Robert F. Stoops. Semeia 80. Atlanta: Scholars Press, 1997.

Hills, "Equal Justice." Hills, Julian V. "Equal Justice under the (New) Law: The Story of Ananias and Sapphira in Acts 5." *Forum* 3 (1, 2000): 105–20.

Hiltner, "Theology." Hiltner, Seward. "Toward a Theology of Conversion in the Light of Psychology." Pages 179–90 in *Conversion: Perspectives on Personal and Social Transformation*. Edited by Walter E. Conn. New York: Alba House, 1978.

Hilton, "Family." Hilton, Anne. "Family and Kinship Among the Kongo South of the Zaïre River from the Sixteenth to the Nineteenth Centuries." *JAfrHist* 24 (2, 1983): 189–206.

Hilton, "Introduction." Hilton, John. "Introduction" (to *Florida*). Pages 123–36 in Apuleius, *Rhetorical Works*. Translated and annotated by Stephen Harrison, John Hilton, and Vincent Hunink. Edited by Stephen Harrison. Oxford: Oxford University Press, 2001.

Hilton and Marshall, *Gospels and Judaism*. Hilton, Michael, with Gordian Marshall. *The Gospels and Rabbinic Judaism: A Study Guide*. Hoboken, N.J.: KTAV, 1988.

Himbaza, "Décalogue." Himbaza, Innocent. "La Décalogue de Papyrus Nash, Philon, 4Qphyl G, 8Qphyl 3, et 4Qmez A." *RevQ* 20 (79, 2002): 411–28.

Himes, "Peter." Himes, Paul A. "Peter and the Prophetic Word: The Theology of Prophecy Traced through Peter's Sermons and Epistles." *BBR* 21 (2, 2011): 227–44.

Himmelfarb, "Ascent." Himmelfarb, Martha. "Heavenly Ascent and the Relationship of the Apocalypses and the *hekhalot* Literature." *HUCA* 59 (1988): 73–100.

Himmelfarb, "Impurity and Sin." Himmelfarb, Martha. "Impurity and Sin in 4QD, 1QS, and 4Q512." *DSD* 8 (1, 2001): 9–37.

Himmelfarb, "Levi." Himmelfarb, Martha. "Levi, Phinehas, and the Problem of Intermarriage at the Time of the Maccabean Revolt." *JSQ* 6 (1, 1999): 1–24.

Hindley, "Date." Hindley, J. C. "Towards a Date for the Similitudes of Enoch: An Historical Approach." *NTS* 14 (4, 1968): 551–65.

Hinds, "Martial's Ovid." Hinds, Stephen E. "Martial's Ovid/Ovid's Martial." *JRS* 97 (2007): 113–54.

Hinds, "Ovid." Hinds, Stephen E. "Ovid." *OCD*³ 1084–87.

Hine, "Glossolalia." Hine, Virginia H. "Pentecostal Glossolalia: Toward a Functional Interpretation." *JSSR* 8 (2, 1969): 211–36.

Hinkle, "Preaching." Hinkle, Mary E. "Preaching for Mission: Ancient Speeches and Postmodern Sermons, Acts 7:2–53; 13:16–41; 14:15–17." Pages 87–102 in *Mission in Acts: Ancient Narratives in Contemporary Context*. Edited by Robert L. Gallagher and Paul Hertig. AmSocMissS 34. Maryknoll, N.Y.: Orbis, 2004.

Hinnells, "Reflections." Hinnells, John R. "Reflections on the Bull-Slaying Scene." Pages 290–312 in vol. 2 of *Mithraic Studies: Proceedings of the First International Congress of Mithraic Studies*. Edited by John R. Hinnells. 2 vols. Manchester, U.K.: Manchester University Press, 1975.

Hinson, "History of Glossolalia." Hinson, E. Glenn. "A Brief History of Glossolalia." Pages 45–75 in *Glossolalia: Tongue Speaking in Biblical, Historical, and Psychological Perspective*. By Frank Stagg, E. Glenn Hinson, and Wayne E. Oates. Nashville: Abingdon, 1967.

Hinson, "Worshiping." Hinson, E. Glenn. "Worshiping like Pagans?" *ChH* 37 (1993): 16–20.

Hintermaier, "Grundlage." Hintermaier, Johann. "Grundlage und Entwicklung der paulinischen Mission am Beispiel von Apg 16,11–40." *SNTSU* 25 (2000): 152–75.

Hirsch, *Literacy*. Hirsch, E. D. *Cultural Literacy*. Boston: Houghton Mifflin, 1987.

Hirsch, *Validity*. Hirsch, E. D. *Validity in Interpretation*. New Haven: Yale University Press, 1967.

Hirschberg and Barasch, *Recovery*. Hirschberg, Caryle, and Marc Ian Barasch, *Remarkable Recovery: What Extraordinary Healings Tell Us about Getting Well and Staying Well*. New York: Riverhead, 1995.

Hirschfeld, "En-Gedi." Hirschfeld, Yizhar. "En-Gedi: 'A Very Large Village of Jews.'"

SBFLA 55 (2005): 327–54 and plates 11–34.

Hirschfeld, "History and Town-Plan." Hirschfeld, Yizhar. "The History and Town-Plan of Ancient *Hammat Gader*." *ZDPV* 103 (1987): 101–16 and plates 12–14.

Hirschfeld, "Ramat Hanadiv." Hirschfeld, Yizhar. "Ramat Hanadiv and Ein Gedi: Property versus Poverty in Judea before 70." Pages 384–92 in *Jesus and Archaeology*. Edited by James H. Charlesworth. Grand Rapids: Eerdmans, 2006.

Hirschfeld, "Ship of Paul." Hirschfeld, Nicolle. "The Ship of Saint Paul, Part I: Historical Background." *BA* 53 (1, 1990): 25–30.

Hirschfeld and Birger-Calderon, "Estates near Caesarea." Hirschfeld, Yizhar, and R. Birger-Calderon, "Early Roman and Byzantine Estates near Caesarea." *IEJ* 41 (1–3, 1991): 81–111.

Hirschfeld and Peleg, "Gemstone." Hirschfeld, Yizhar, and Orit Peleg. "An Early Roman Gemstone Depicting Apollo Found at *Rāmat ha-Nādīv*." *ZDPV* 121 (1, 2005): 59–66.

Hirschfeld and Solar, "Baths." Hirschfeld, Yizhar, and Giora Solar. "Sumptuous Roman Baths Uncovered near Sea of Galilee: Hot Springs Drew the Afflicted from around the World." *BAR* 10 (1984): 22–40.

Hirschfeld and Solar, "Hmrhs'wt." Hirschfeld, Yizhar, and Giora Solar. "Hmrhs'wt hrwmyym sl hmt-gdr—slws 'wnwt-hpyrh (The Roman Thermae at Hammath-Gader—Three Seasons of Excavations)." *Qad* 13 (1980): 66–70.

Hirschfeld and Vamosh, "Estate." Hirschfeld, Yizhar, with Miriam Feinberg Vamosh. "A Country Gentleman's Estate: Unearthing the Splendors of Ramat Hanadiv." *BAR* 31 (2, 2005): 18–31.

Hirshman, "Jewish Universalism." Hirshman, Marc. "Rabbinic Universalism in the Second and Third Centuries." *HTR* 93 (2, 2000): 101–15.

Hirth, "Königin von Saba." Hirth, Volkmar. "Die Königin von Saba und der Kämmerer aus dem Mohrenland oder das Ende menschlicher Weisheit vor Gott." *BN* 83 (1996): 13–15.

Hitchcock and Jones, *Spirit Possession*. Hitchcock, John T., and Rex L. Jones, eds. *Spirit Possession in the Nepal Himalayas*. New Delhi: Vikas, 1976. Repr., 1994.

Hjelm, "Samaritans." Hjelm, Ingrid. "What Do Samaritans and Jews Have in Common? Recent Trends in Samaritan Studies." *CBR* 3 (1, 2004): 9–59.

Hoare, "Approach." Hoare, Frank. "A Pastoral Approach to Spirit Possession and

Witchcraft Manifestations among the Fijian People." *MissSt* 21 (1, 2004): 113–37.

Hobart, *Medical Language*. Hobart, William Kirk. *The Medical Language of St. Luke.* Dublin: Hodges, Figgis, 1882. Repr., Grand Rapids: Baker, 1954.

Hobsbawm, *Bandits*. Hobsbawm, Eric J. *Bandits*. 2nd ed. Hammondsworth, U.K.: Penguin, 1985.

Hock, "Curriculum." Hock, Ronald F. "The Educational Curriculum in Chariton's *Callirhoe.*" Pages 15–36 in *Ancient Fiction: The Matrix of Early Christian and Jewish Narrative.* Edited by Jo-Ann A. Brant, Charles W. Hedrick, and Chris Shea. SBLSymS 32. Atlanta: SBL, 2005.

Hock, "Cynics and Rhetoric." Hock, Ronald F. "Cynics and Rhetoric." Pages 755–73 in *Handbook of Classical Rhetoric in the Hellenistic Period, 330 B.C.–A.D. 400.* Edited by Stanley E. Porter. Leiden: Brill, 1997.

Hock, "Ethnography." Hock, Ronald F. "The Greek Novel and Literary Ethnography: The Household in the World of the New Testament." Pages 106–17 in *Text, Image, and Christians in the Graeco-Roman World: A Festschrift in Honor of David Lee Balch.* Edited by Aliou Cissé Niang and Carolyn Osiek. PrTMS 176. Eugene, Ore.: Pickwick, 2012.

Hock, "Experience." Hock, Ronald F. "Social Experience and the Beginning of the Gospel of Mark." Pages 311–26 in *Reimagining Christian Origins: A Colloquium Honoring Burton L. Mack.* Edited by Elizabeth Castelli and Hal Taussig. Valley Forge, Pa.: Trinity, 1996.

Hock, "Novel." Hock, Ronald F. "The Greek Novel." Pages 127–46 in *Greco-Roman Literature and the New Testament: Selected Forms and Genres.* Edited by David E. Aune. SBLSBS 21. Atlanta: Scholars Press, 1988.

Hock, "Paul and Education." Hock, Ronald F. "Paul and Greco-Roman Education." Pages 198–227 in *Paul in the Greco-Roman World: A Handbook.* Edited by J. Paul Sampley. Harrisburg, Pa.: Trinity Press International, 2003.

Hock, "Rhetoric of Romance." Hock, Ronald F. "The Rhetoric of Romance." Pages 445–65 in *Handbook of Classical Rhetoric in the Hellenistic Period, 330 B.C.–A.D. 400.* Edited by Stanley E. Porter. Leiden: Brill, 1997.

Hock, "Social Class." Hock, Ronald F. "Paul's Tentmaking and the Problem of His Social Class." *JBL* 97 (4, 1978): 555–64.

Hock, *Social Context*. Hock, Ronald F. *The Social Context of Paul's Ministry: Tentmaking and Apostleship.* Philadelphia: Fortress, 1980.

Hock, "Why Read." Hock, Ronald F. "Why New Testament Scholars Should Read

Ancient Novels." Pages 121–38 in *Ancient Fiction and Early Christian Narrative.* Edited by Ronald F. Hock, J. Bradley Chance, and Judith Perkins. SBLSymS 6. Atlanta: SBL, 1998.

Hock, "Workshop." Hock, Ronald F. "The Workshop as a Social Setting for Paul's Missionary Preaching." *CBQ* 41 (3, 1979): 438–50.

Höcker, "Door." Höcker, Christoph. "Door: Graeco-Roman Antiquity." *BrillPauly* 4:671–72.

Höcker, "Ephesus: Archaeology." Höcker, Christoph. "Ephesus: Archaeology." *Brill Pauly* 4:1030–32.

Höcker, "Forum." Höcker, Christoph. "Forum: Archaeology and Urban Studies." *BrillPauly* 5:510–19.

Höcker, "House." Höcker, Christoph. "House: Greece, Etruria, Rome." *Brill Pauly* 6:539–49.

Höcker, "Insula." Höcker, Christoph. "Insula." *BrillPauly* 6:838–40.

Höcker, "Lararium." Höcker, Christoph. "Lararium." *BrillPauly* 7:244–45.

Höcker, "Parthenon." Höcker, Christoph. "Parthenon." *BrillPauly* 10:566–70.

Höcker, "Prostitution." Höcker, Christoph. "Prostitution. II. Classical Antiquity." *BrillPauly* 12:58–61.

Höcker, "Stairs." Höcker, Christoph. "Stairs, Stairways: Graeco-Roman Antiquity." *BrillPauly* 13:781–82.

Höcker, "Temple." Höcker, Christoph. "Temple: Greece." *BrillPauly* 14:249–55.

Höcker, "Villa." Höcker, Christoph. "Villa." *BrillPauly* 15:411–19.

Höcker, "Window." Höcker, Christoph. "Window." *BrillPauly* 15:647–52.

Höcker, "Wonders." Höcker, Christoph. "Wonders of the World." *BrillPauly* 15:724–25.

Höcker and Hurschmann, "Forum." Höcker, Christoph, and Rolf Hurschmann. "Forum: Roman Forums." *BrillPauly* 5:521–30.

Höcker and Prayon, "Altar." Höcker, Christoph, and Friedhelm Prayon. "Altar." *Brill Pauly* 1:543–49.

Höckmann, "Harbours." Höckmann, Olaf. "Harbours, Docks." *BrillPauly* 5:1135–40.

Höckmann, "Inland Navigation." Höckmann, Olaf. "Inland Navigation." *Brill Pauly* 6:815–17.

Hodge, "Apostle to Gentiles." Hodge, C. Johnson. "Apostle to the Gentiles: Constructions of Paul's Identity." *BibInt* 13 (3, 2005): 270–88.

Hodges, *Indigenous Church*. Hodges, Melvin L. *The Indigenous Church.* Springfield, Mo.: Gospel, 1976.

Hodges, *Theology of Mission*. Hodges, Melvin L. *A Theology of the Church and Its Mission: A Pentecostal Perspective.* Springfield, Mo.: Gospel, 1977.

Hodges, "Tongues." Hodges, Zane C. "The Purpose of Tongues." *BSac* 120 (1963): 226–33.

Hodgson, "Tribulation Lists." Hodgson, Robert. "Paul the Apostle and First Century Tribulation Lists." *ZNW* 74 (1–2, 1983): 59–80.

Hoehner, *Antipas*. Hoehner, Harold W. *Herod Antipas.* SNTSMS 17. Cambridge: Cambridge University Press, 1972.

Hoehner, *Ephesians*. Hoehner, Harold W. *Ephesians: An Exegetical Commentary.* Grand Rapids: Baker, 2002.

Hoehner, "Herod." Hoehner, Harold W. "Herod." *ISBE* 2:688–98.

Hoehner, "Herodian Dynasty." Hoehner, Harold W. "Herodian Dynasty." *DNTB* 485–94.

Hoenig, "Conversion." Hoenig, Sidney B. "Conversion during the Talmudic Period." Pages 33–66 in *Conversion to Judaism: A History and Analysis.* Edited by David Max Eichhorn. New York: KTAV, 1965.

Hoenig, "Kinds of Labor." Hoenig, Sidney B. "The Designated Number of Kinds of Labor Prohibited on the Sabbath." *JQR* 68 (4, 1978): 193–208.

Hoenig, "Sicarii in Masada." Hoenig, Sidney B. "The Sicarii in Masada—Glory or Infamy?" *Tradition* 11 (1, 1970): 5–30.

Hoerber, "Decree of Claudius." Hoerber, Robert O. "The Decree of Claudius in Acts 18:2." *CTM* 31 (11, 1960): 690–94.

Hoerber, "Galatians and Acts." Hoerber, Robert G. "Galatians 2:1–10 and the Acts of the Apostles." *CTM* 31 (8, 1960): 482–91.

Hoeree and Hoogbergen, "History." Hoeree, Joris, and Wim Hoogbergen. "Oral History and Archival Data Combined: The Removal of the Saramakan Granman Kofi Bosuman as an Epistemological Problem." *CommCog* 17 (2–3, 1984): 245–89.

Hoffeditz, "*Divus*." Hoffeditz, D. M. "*Divus* of Augustus: The Influence of the Trials of *maiestas* upon Pontius Pilate's Coins." *IsNumR* 1 (2006): 87–96.

Hoffer, "Manasseh's Repentance." Hoffer, Victoria. "And He Prayed to Him: Manasseh's Repentance and Its Reception in the Midrash." *Hermenêutica* 1 (2001): 55–78.

Höffken, "Elischa." Höffken, Peter. "Elischa in seinem Verhältnis zu Elija bei Josephus." *ETL* 81 (4, 2005): 477–86.

Höffken, "Hiskija." Höffken, Peter. "Hiskija und Jesaja bei Josephus." *JSJ* 29 (1, 1998): 37–48.

Höffken, "Reichsteilung." Höffken, Peter. "Eine Reichsteilung bei Josephus Flavius: Beobachtungen zu seiner Auffassung von Daniel 5." *JSJ* 36 (2, 2005): 197–205.

Höffken, "Rolle." Höffken, Peter. "Zur Rolle der Davidsverheissung bei Josephus Flavius." *ZAW* 114 (4, 2002): 577–93.

Höffken, "Überlegungen." Höffken, Peter. "Überlegungen zum Leserkreis der 'Antiquitates' des Josephus." *JSJ* 38 (3, 2007): 328–41.

Höffken, "Weltreiche." Höffken, Peter. "Weltreiche und Prophetie Israels bei Flavius Josephus." *TZ* 55 (1, 1999): 47–56.

Hoffman, "Baths." Hoffman, Daniel L. "Baths and Bathing." Pages 146–56 in vol. 1 of *Dictionary of Daily Life in Biblical and Post-Biblical Antiquity*. Edited by Edwin M. Yamauchi and Marvin R. Wilson. Peabody, Mass.: Hendrickson, 2014.

Hoffman, *Berakhah*. Hoffman, Lawrence A. "Rabbinic *berakhah* and Jewish Spirituality." *Concilium* 26 (3, 1990): 18–30.

Hoffman, "Ordination juive." Hoffman, Lawrence A. "L'ordination juive à la veille du christianisme." *MaisD* 138 (1979): 7–47.

Hoffman, "Torah Service." Hoffman, Jeffrey. "The Ancient Torah Service in Light of the *realia* of the Talmudic Era." *ConsJud* 42 (2, 1989–90): 41–48.

Hoffman and Kurzenberger, "Miraculous." Hoffman, Louis, and Marika Kurzenberger. "The Miraculous and Mental Illness." Pages 65–93 in *Parapsychological Perspectives*. Vol. 3 of *Miracles: God, Science, and Psychology in the Paranormal*. Edited by J. Harold Ellens. Westport, Conn.; London: Praeger, 2008.

Hoffmann, *Porphyry's Against Christians*. *Porphyry's Against the Christians: The Literary Remains*. Edited and translated by R. Joseph Hoffmann. Amherst, N.Y.: Prometheus, 1994.

Hoffmeier, *Israel in Egypt*. Hoffmeier, James K. *Israel in Egypt: The Evidence for the Authenticity of the Exodus Tradition*. New York: Oxford University Press, 1997.

Hofius, "Sayings." Hofius, Otfried. "Unknown Sayings of Jesus." Pages 336–60 in *The Gospel and the Gospels*. Edited by Peter Stuhlmacher. Grand Rapids: Eerdmans, 1991.

Hofmann, "Novels: Christian." Hofmann, Heinz. "Novels: Christian." *BrillPauly* 9:846–49.

Hofmann, "Novels: Latin." Hofmann, Heinz. "Novels: Latin." *BrillPauly* 9:843–46.

Hofmann, "Square." Hofmann, Heinz. "Sator Square." *BrillPauly* 13:17–19.

Hogan, "Defense." Hogan, Derek. "Paul's Defense: A Comparison of the Forensic Speeches in Acts, *Callirhoe*, and *Leucippe and Clitophon*." *PRSt* 29 (1, 2002): 73–87.

Hohlfelder, "Caesarea." Hohlfelder, Robert L. "Caesarea Beneath the Sea." Pages 124–29 in *Archaeology in the World of Herod, Jesus and Paul*. Edited by Hershel Shanks and Dan P. Cole. Vol. 2 in Archaeology and the Bible: The Best of BAR. Washington, D.C.: Biblical Archaeology Society, 1990.

Hohlfelder, *Coins*. Hohlfelder, Robert L. *The Coins*. Vol. 3 of *Kenchreai, Eastern Port of Corinth: Results of Investigations by the University of Chicago and Indiana University for the American School of Classical Studies at Athens*. Leiden: Brill, 1978.

Hölbl, "Kunstelemente." Hölbl, Gunther. "Ägyptische Kunstelemente im phönikischen Kulturkries des I. Jahrtausends v. Chr.: Zur Methodik ihrer Verwendung." *Or* 58 (1989): 318–25.

Holder, "Hume." Holder, Rodney D. "Hume on Miracles: Bayesian Interpretation, Multiple Testimony, and the Existence of God." *BJPhilSc* 49 (1, Mar. 1998): 49–65.

Holder, "Revival." Holder, Ralph R. "Revival in China." *PentEv* 1814 (Feb. 12, 1949): 7.

Holford-Strevens, "Archaism." Holford-Strevens, Leofranc Adrian. "Archaism in Latin." *OCD*³ 143.

Holgate, "Connections." Holgate, David. "Connections and Collisions: Acts 16." Pages 145–53 in *Acts in Practice*. Edited by John Vincent. Practice Interpretation 2. Blandford Forum, Dorset UK: Deo Publishing, 2012.

Holladay, "Acts and Fragments." Holladay, Carl R. "Acts and the Fragments of Hellenistic Jewish Historians." Pages 171–98 in *Jesus and the Heritage of Israel: Luke's Narrative Claim upon Israel's Legacy*. Edited by David P. Moessner. Luke the Interpreter of Israel 1. Harrisburg, Pa.: Trinity Press International, 1999.

Holladay, "Background." Holladay, William L. "The Background of Jeremiah's Self-Understanding." *JBL* 83 (1964): 153–64.

Holladay, "House." Holladay, John S., Jr. "House: Syro-Palestinian Houses." *OEANE* 3:94–114.

Holladay, "Jeremiah." Holladay, William L. "Jeremiah and Moses: Further Observations." *JBL* 85 (1, 1966): 17–27.

Holladay, "Statecraft." Holladay, John S. "Assyrian Statecraft and the Prophets of Israel." *HTR* 63 (Jan. 1970): 29–51.

Holladay, *Theios aner*. Holladay, Carl R. "*Theios aner*" in Hellenistic Judaism: A Critique of the Use of This Category in New Testament Christology. SBLDS 40. Missoula, Mont.: Scholars Press, 1977.

Hollan, "Culture." Hollan, Douglas. "Culture and Dissociation in Toraja." *TranscPsyc* 37 (2000): 545–59.

Holland, "Jericho." Holland, Thomas A. "Jericho." *OEANE* 3:220–24.

Hollander, "Bekering." Hollander, Harm W. "De bekering van Paulus (The Apostle Paul's Conversion)." *NedTT* 56 (1, 2002): 27–38.

Hollander and van der Hout, "Abortion." Hollander, Harm W., and Gijsbert E. van der Hout. "The Apostle Paul Calling Himself an Abortion: 1 Cor. 15:8 within the Context of 1 Cor. 15:8–10." *NovT* 38 (3, 1996): 224–36.

Hollenbach, "Demoniacs." Hollenbach, Paul W. "Jesus, Demoniacs, and Public Authorities: A Socio-historical Study." *JAAR* 49 (1981): 567–88.

Hollenbach, "Roundel." Hollenbach, George M. "The Qumran Roundel: An Equatorial Sundial?" *DSD* 7 (2, 2000): 123–29.

Hollenback, "Irony." Hollenback, Bruce. "Lest They Should Turn and Be Forgiven: Irony." *BTr* 34 (1983): 312–21.

Hollenweger, "Dialogue." Hollenweger, Walter J. "The Pentecostal Elites and the Pentecostal Poor: A Missed Dialogue?" Pages 200–214 in *Charismatic Christianity as a Global Culture*. Edited by Karla Poewe. SCR. Columbia: University of South Carolina Press, 1994.

Hollenweger, *Pentecostals*. Hollenweger, Walter J. *The Pentecostals*. London: SCM, 1972. Repr., Peabody, Mass.: Hendrickson, 1988.

Holloway, "Beguile." Holloway, Paul A. "'Beguile Your Soul' (Sir xiv 16; xxx 23): An Epicurean Theme in Ben Sira." *VT* 58 (2, 2008): 219–34.

Holloway, "Enthymeme." Holloway, Paul A. "The Enthymeme as an Element of Style in Paul." *JBL* 120 (2, 2001): 329–39.

Holloway, "Paul." Holloway, Paul A. "Paul as a Hellenistic Philosopher: The Evidence of Philippians." Pages 52–68 in *Paul and the Philosophers*. Edited by Ward Blanton and Hent de Vries. New York: Fordham University Press, 2013.

Holloway, "Prose." Holloway, Paul A. "Paul's Pointed Prose: The *sententia* in Roman Rhetoric and Paul." *NovT* 40 (1, 1998): 32–53.

Holloway, "Truths." Holloway, Paul A. "Inconvenient Truths: Early Jewish and Christian History Writing and the Ending of Luke-Acts." Pages 418–33 in *Die Apostelgeschichte im Kontext antiker und frühchristlicher Historiographie*. Edited by Jörg Frey, Clare K. Rothschild, and Jens Schröter, with Bettina Rost. BZNWK 162. Berlin: de Gruyter, 2009.

Holm, "Role Theory." Holm, Nils G. "Sunden's Role Theory and Glossolalia." *JSSR* 26 (3, 1987): 383–89.

Holman, "Spirit-Filled." Holman, Charles L. "What Does It Mean Today to Be Spirit-Filled? Ephesians and Ecumenism (or Ecumenical Pneumatology)." *SpCh* 4 (2, 2002): 151–60.

Holmås, "House." Holmås, Geir Otto. "'My House Shall Be a House of Prayer': Regarding the Temple as a Place of Prayer in Acts within the Context of Luke's Apologetical Objective." *JSNT* 27 (4, 2005): 393–416.

Holmberg, "Methods." Holmberg, Bengt. "The Methods of Historical Reconstruction in the Scholarly 'Recovery' of Corinthian Christianity." Pages 255–71 in *Christianity at Corinth: The Quest for the Pauline Church*. Edited by Edward Adams and David G. Horrell. Louisville: Westminster John Knox, 2004.

Holmberg, *Sociology*. Holmberg, Bengt. *Sociology and the New Testament, An Appraisal*. Minneapolis: Fortress, 1990.

Holmén, *Covenant Thinking*. Holmén, Tom. *Jesus and Jewish Covenant Thinking*. BIS 55. Leiden: Brill, 2001.

Holmén, "Doubts about Dissimilarity." Holmén, Tom. "Doubts about Double Dissimilarity: Restructuring the Main Criterion of Jesus-of-History Research." Pages 47–80 in *Authenticating the Words of Jesus*. Edited by Bruce Chilton and Craig A. Evans. NTTS 28.1. Leiden: Brill, 1999.

Holmén, "Introduction." Holmén, Tom. "An Introduction to the Continuum Approach." Pages 1–16 in *Jesus from Judaism to Christianity: Continuum Approaches to the Historical Jesus*. Edited by Tom Holmén. EurSCO. LNTS 352. London: T&T Clark, 2007.

Holmén and Porter, *Handbook*. Tom Holmén and Stanley E. Porter, eds. *Handbook for the Study of the Historical Jesus*. 4 vols. Boston: Brill, 2010.

Holmes, "Wisdom." Holmes, S. "Wisdom of Solomon." *APOT* 1:518–68.

Holmyard, "Prophesying." Holmyard, Harold R. "Does 1 Corinthians 11:2–16 Refer to Women Praying and Prophesying in Church?" *BSac* 154 (616, 1997): 461–72.

Holowchak, "Lucretius." Holowchak, M. Andrew. "Lucretius on the Gates of Horn and Ivory: A Psychophysical Challenge to Prophecy by Dreams." *JHistPhil* 42 (4, 2004): 355–68.

Holte, "Logos." Holte, Ragnar. "Logos Spermatikos: Christianity and Ancient Philosophy according to St. Justin's Apologies." *ST* 12 (1958): 109–68.

Holtz, "Geschichte und Verheissung." Holtz, T. "Geschichte und Verheissung: 'Auferstanden nach der Schrift.'" *EvT* 57 (3, 1997): 179–96.

Holtzmann, "Actes." Holtzmann, H. "Les Actes des apôtres." *RevThéol* 6 (1868): 283–301.

Holtzmann, *Synoptiker–Apostelgeschichte*. Holtzmann, Heinrich Julius. *Die Synoptiker–Die Apostelgeschichte*. Vol. 1 of *Handcommentar zum Neuen Testament*. By Heinrich Julius Holtzmann et al. Freiburg im Breisgau: J. C. B. Mohr, 1889.

Holum, "Building Power." Holum, Kenneth G. "Building Power: The Politics of Architecture." *BAR* 30 (5, 2004): 36–45, 57.

Holum, "Caesarea." Holum, Kenneth G. "Caesarea." *OEANE* 1:399–404.

Holum, "New Dig." Holum, Kenneth G. "Starting a New Dig." *BAR* 17 (1, 1991): 34–39.

Holum, "Temple Hill." Holum, Kenneth G. "Caesarea's Temple Hill: The Archaeology of Sacred Space in an Ancient Mediterranean City." *NEA* 67 (4, 2004): 184–99.

Holwerda, *Spirit*. Holwerda, David Earl. *The Holy Spirit and Eschatology in the Gospel of John: A Critique of Rudolf Bultmann's Present Eschatology*. Kampen, Neth.: J. H. Kok, 1959. Distributed by Eerdmans, Grand Rapids.

Holzhausen, "Silvanus." Holzhausen, Jens. "Silvanus." *BrillPauly* 13:468–70.

Holzhausen, "Simon Magus." Holzhausen, Jens. "Simon Magus." *BrillPauly* 13:484–85.

Hong, "Leadership." Hong, Young-gi. "Social Leadership and Church Growth." Pages 221–51 in *David Yonggi Cho: A Close Look at His Theology and Ministry*. Edited by Wonsuk Ma, William W. Menzies, and Hyeon-sung Bae. AJPS Series 1. Baguio City, Philippines: APTS; Kyunggi-do, Korea: Hansei University Press, 2004.

Honigman, "Philon." Honigman, Sylvie. "Philon, Flavius Josèphe, et la citoyenneté alexandrine: Vers une utopie politique." *JJS* 48 (1, 1997): 62–90.

Honoré, "Aquil(l)ius Gallus." Honoré, Tony. "Aquil(l)ius Gallus, Gaius." *OCD*³ 134.

Honoré, "Law and Procedure." Honoré, Tony. "Law and Procedure, Roman: 1. Civil Law." *OCD*³ 827–29.

Honoré, "Lawyers." Honoré, Tony. "Lawyers, Roman." *OCD*³ 835–36.

Hoof, "Differences." Hoof, L. van. "Strategic Differences: Seneca and Plutarch on Controlling Anger." *Mnemosyne* 60 (1, 2007): 59–86.

Hooff, "Image." Hooff, Anton J. L. van. "The Image of Ancient Suicide." *SyllClass* 9 (1998): 47–69.

Hook, "Oedipus." Hook, Brian S. "Oedipus and Thyestes among the Philosophers: Incest and Cannibalism in Plato, Diogenes, and Zeno." *CP* 100 (1, 2005): 17–40.

Hooker, "Adam." Hooker, Morna D. "Adam in Romans I." *NTS* 6 (4, 1960): 297–306.

Hooker, "Artemis." Hooker, Morna D. "Artemis of Ephesus." *JTS* 64 (1, 2013): 37–46.

Hooker, *Message*. Hooker, Morna D. *The Message of Mark*. London: Epworth, 1983.

Hooker, "Philippians." Hooker, Morna D. "The Letter to the Philippians." Pages 497–549 in vol. 11 of *The New Interpreter's Bible*. Edited by Leander Keck. Nashville: Abingdon, 2000.

Hooker, "ΠΙΣΤΙΣ ΧΡΙΣΤΟΥ." Hooker, Morna D. "ΠΙΣΤΙΣ ΧΡΙΣΤΟΥ." *NTS* 35 (3, 1989): 321–42.

Hooker, *Preface*. Hooker, Morna D. *A Preface to Paul*. New York: Oxford University Press, 1980.

Hooker, *Servant*. Hooker, Morna D. *Jesus and the Servant*. London: SPCK, 1959.

Hooley, "Rhetoric." Hooley, Dan. "Rhetoric and Satire: Horace, Persius, and Juvenal." Pages 396–412 in *A Companion to Roman Rhetoric*. Edited by William Dominik and Jon Hall. Oxford: Blackwell, 2007.

Hooper, "Awakening." Hooper, Emmanuel. "The Great Awakening of 1905: The Welsh Revival and Its Influence on the American Revival." Pages 222–32 in *Revival, Renewal, and the Holy Spirit*. Edited by Dyfed Wyn Roberts. SEHT. Eugene, Ore.: Wipf & Stock, 2009.

Hoover, "Coinage." Hoover, O. D. "A Late Hellenistic Lead Coinage from Gaza." *IsNumR* 1 (2006): 25–35 and plates 4–5.

Hope, "Trophies." Hope, Valerie M. "Trophies and Tombstones: Commemorating the Roman Soldier." *WArch* 35 (1, 2003): 79–97.

Hopkins, "Age at Marriage." Hopkins, M. Keith. "The Age of Roman Girls at Marriage." *PopSt* 18 (1964–65): 309–27.

Hopkins, "Cereals." Hopkins, David C. "Cereals." *OEANE* 1:479–81.

Hopkins, *Conquerors*. Hopkins, Keith. *Conquerors and Slaves*. Cambridge: Cambridge University Press, 1978.

Hopkins, "Status." Hopkins, Jamal-Dominique. "The Authoritative Status of *Jubilees* at Qumran." *Hen* 31 (1, 2009): 97–104.

Hopman, *Scylla*. Hopman, Marianne Govers. *Scylla: Myth, Metaphor, Paradox*. Cambridge: Cambridge University Press, 2012.

Horbury, "Benediction." Horbury, William. "The Benediction of the *minim* and Early Jewish-Christian Controversy." *JTS* 33 (1, 1982): 19–61.

Horbury, "Brigand." Horbury, William. "Christ as Brigand in Ancient Anti-Christian Polemic." Pages 183–95 in *Jesus and the Politics of His Day*. Edited by Ernst

Bammel and C. F. D. Moule. Cambridge: Cambridge University Press, 1984.

Horbury, "Inscription." Horbury, William. "A Proselyte's Heis Theos Inscription Near Caesarea." *PEQ* 129 (2, 1997): 133–37.

Horbury, "Ossuaries." Horbury, William. "The 'Caiaphas' Ossuaries and Joseph Caiaphas." *PEQ* 126 (1, 1994): 32–48.

Horgan, "Prophecies." Horgan, Maurya P. "The Bible Explained (Prophecies)." Pages 247–53 in *Early Judaism and Its Modern Interpreters*. Edited by Robert A. Kraft and George W. E. Nickelsburg. SBLBMI 2. Atlanta: Scholars Press, 1986.

Horn, "Gütergemeinschaft." Horn, Friedrich Wilhelm. "Die Gütergemeinschaft der Urgemeinde." *EvT* 58 (5, 1998): 370–83.

Horn, "Haltung." Horn, Friedrich Wilhelm. "Die Haltung des Lukas zum römischen Staat im Evangelium und in der Apostelgeschichte." Pages 203–24 in *The Unity of Luke-Acts*. Edited by Joseph Verheyden. BETL 142. Leuven: Leuven University Press, 1999.

Horn, "Kollektenthematik." Horn, Friedrich Wilhelm. "Die Kollektenthematik in der Apostelgeschichte." Pages 135–56 in *Die Apostelgeschichte und die hellenistische Geschichtsschreibung: Festschrift für Eckhard Plümacher zu seinem 65. Geburtstag*. Edited by Cilliers Breytenbach and Jens Schröter. Leiden: Brill, 2004.

Horn, "Nasiräat." Horn, Friedrich Wilhelm. "Paulus, das Nasiräat, und die Nasiräer." *NovT* 39 (2, 1997): 117–37.

Horn, "Speaking in Tongues." Horn, William M. "Speaking in Tongues: A Retrospective Appraisal." *LQ* 17 (4, 1965): 316–29.

Horn, "Tempel." Horn, Friedrich Wilhelm. "Paulus und der herodianische Tempel." *NTS* 53 (2, 2007): 184–203.

Horn, "Verzicht." Horn, Friedrich Wilhelm. "Der Verzicht auf die Beschneidung im frühen Christentum." *NTS* 42 (4, 1996): 479–505.

Hornblower, "Aspasia." Hornblower, Simon. "Aspasia." *OCD*³ 192.

Hornblower, "Bribery." Hornblower, Simon. "Bribery, Greek." *OCD*³ 259–60.

Hornblower, "Demagogues." Hornblower, Simon. "Demagogues, Demagogy." *OCD*³ 446.

Hornblower, "Introduction." Hornblower, Simon. "Introduction." Pages 1–72 in *Greek Historiography*. Edited by Simon Hornblower. New York: Oxford University Press, 1994.

Hornblower, "Thucydides." Hornblower, Simon. "Thucydides." *BrillPauly* 14:631–37.

Horne, "Phrase." Horne, Charles M. "The Meaning of the Phrase 'And Thus All Israel Will Be Saved' (Romans 11:26)." *JETS* 21 (4, 1978): 329–34.

Hornik and Parsons, "Perspectives." Hornik, Heidi J., and Mikeal C. Parsons. "Philological and Performative Perspectives on Pentecost." Pages 137–53 in *Reading Acts Today: Essays in Honour of Loveday C. A. Alexander*. Edited by Steve Walton et al. LNTS 427. London: T&T Clark, 2011.

Horowitz and Hurowitz, "Urim." Horowitz, Wayne, and Victor Hurowitz. "Urim and Thummim in Light of a Psephomancy Ritual from Assur (LKA 137)." *JANESCU* 21 (1992): 95–115.

Horrell, "Ἀδελφοί." Horrell, David G. "From ἀδελφοί to οἶκος θεοῦ: Social Transformation in Pauline Christianity." *JBL* 120 (2, 2001): 293–311.

Horrell, *Approaches*. Horrell, David G., ed. *Social-Scientific Approaches to New Testament Interpretation*. Edinburgh: T&T Clark, 1999.

Horrell, "Label." Horrell, David G. "The Label Χριστιανός: 1 Peter 4:16 and the Formation of Christian Identity." *JBL* 126 (2, 2007): 361–81.

Horrell, "Space." Horrell, David G. "Domestic Space and Christian Meetings at Corinth: Imagining New Contexts and the Buildings East of the Theatre." *NTS* 50 (2004): 349–69.

Horrell, "Studies." Horrell, David G. "Recent Pauline Studies." *EpwRev* 32 (3, 2005): 65–74.

Horrell and Adams, "Introduction." Horrell, David G., and Edward Adams. "Introduction: The Scholarly Quest for Paul's Church at Corinth: A Critical Survey." Pages 1–43 in *Christianity at Corinth: The Quest for the Pauline Church*. Edited by Edward Adams and David G. Horrell. Louisville: Westminster John Knox, 2004.

Horrell and Adams, Introduction to Murphy-O'Connor's essay. Horrell, David G., and Edward Adams. Introduction to Murphy-O'Connor's essay. Pages 129–30 in *Christianity at Corinth: The Quest for the Pauline Church*. Edited by Edward Adams and David G. Horrell. Louisville: Westminster John Knox, 2004.

Horsfall, "Statistics." Horsfall, Nicholas. "Statistics or States of Mind?" Pages 59–76 in *Literacy in the Roman World*. Edited by Mary Beard et al. JRASS 3. Ann Arbor: Journal of Roman Archaeology, University of Michigan, 1991.

Horsley, "Assembly." Horsley, Richard A. "Paul's Assembly in Corinth: An Alternative Society." Pages 371–95 in *Urban Religion in Roman Corinth: Interdisciplinary Approaches*. Edited by Daniel N. Schowalter and Steven J. Friesen. HTS 53. Cambridge, Mass.: Harvard University Press, 2005.

Horsley, *Corinthians*. Horsley, Richard A. *1 Corinthians*. ANTC. Nashville: Abingdon, 1998.

Horsley, *Documents*, 1. Horsley, G. H. R. *A Review of the Greek Inscriptions and Papyri Published in 1976*. Vol. 1 of *New Documents Illustrating Early Christianity*. North Ryde, N.S.W.: Ancient History Documentary Research Centre, Macquarie University, 1981.

Horsley, *Documents*, 2. Horsley, G. H. R. *A Review of the Greek Inscriptions and Papyri Published in 1977*. Vol. 2 of *New Documents Illustrating Early Christianity*. North Ryde, N.S.W.: Ancient History Documentary Research Centre, Macquarie University, 1982.

Horsley, *Documents*, 3. Horsley, G. H. R. *A Review of the Greek Inscriptions and Papyri Published in 1978*. Vol. 3 of *New Documents Illustrating Early Christianity*. North Ryde, N.S.W.: Ancient History Documentary Research Centre, Macquarie University, 1983.

Horsley, *Documents*, 4. Horsley, G. H. R. *A Review of the Greek Inscriptions and Papyri Published in 1979*. Vol. 4 of *New Documents Illustrating Early Christianity*. North Ryde, N.S.W.: Ancient History Documentary Research Centre, Macquarie University, 1987.

Horsley, *Documents*, 5. Horsley, G. H. R. *Linguistic Essays*. Vol. 5 of *New Documents Illustrating Early Christianity*. North Ryde, N.S.W.: Ancient History Documentary Research Centre, Macquarie University, 1989.

Horsley, "Ethics." Horsley, Richard A. "Ethics and Exegesis: 'Love Your Enemies' and the Doctrine of Non-violence." *JAAR* 54 (1986): 3–31.

Horsley, "Formula." Horsley, Richard A. "The Background of the Confessional Formula in I Kor 8:6." *ZNW* 69 (1–2, 1978): 130–35.

Horsley, *Galilee*. Horsley, Richard A. *Galilee: History, Politics, People*. Valley Forge, Pa.: Trinity Press International, 1995.

Horsley, "High Priests." Horsley, Richard A. "High Priests and the Politics of Roman Palestine: A Contextual Analysis of the Evidence in Josephus." *JSJ* 17 (1986): 23–55.

Horsley, "Inscriptions of Ephesos." Horsley, G. H. R. "The Inscriptions of Ephesos and the New Testament." *NovT* 34 (2, 1992): 105–68.

Horsley, "Introduction." Horsley, Richard A. "General Introduction." Pages 1–8 in *Paul and Empire: Religion and Power in Roman Imperial Society*. Edited by Richard A. Horsley. Harrisburg, Penn.: Trinity Press International, 1997.

Horsley, "Jewish 'Terrorists.'" Horsley, Richard A. "The Sicarii: Ancient Jewish 'Terrorists.'" *JR* 59 (4, 1979): 435–58.

Horsley, "Law of Nature." Horsley, Richard A. "The Law of Nature in Philo and Cicero." *HTR* 71 (1–2, 1978): 35–59.

Horsley, "Marriage." Horsley, Richard A. "Spiritual Marriage with Sophia." *VC* 33 (1, 1979): 30–54.

Horsley, "Movements." Horsley, Richard A. "Early Christian Movements: Jesus Movements and the Renewal of Israel." *HTS/TS* 62 (4, 2006): 1201–25.

Horsley, "Name Change." Horsley, G. H. R. "Name Change as an Indication of Religious Conversion in Antiquity." *Numen* 34 (1, 1987): 1–17.

Horsley, *Paul and Empire*. Horsley, Richard A., ed. *Paul and Empire: Religion and Power in Roman Imperial Society*. Harrisburg, Penn.: Trinity Press International, 1997.

Horsley, "Paul and Slavery." Horsley, Richard A. "Paul and Slavery: A Critical Alternative to Recent Readings." *Semeia* 83–84 (1998): 153–200.

Horsley, "Politarchs." Horsley, G. H. R. "The Politarchs." Pages 419–31 in *The Book of Acts in Its Graeco-Roman Setting*. Edited by David W. J. Gill and Conrad Gempf. Vol. 2 of *The Book of Acts in Its First Century Setting*. Edited by Bruce W. Winter. Grand Rapids: Eerdmans; Carlisle, U.K.: Paternoster, 1994.

Horsley, *Religion and Empire*. Horsley, Richard A. *Religion and Empire: People, Power, and the Life of the Spirit*. Minneapolis: Fortress, 2003.

Horsley, "Society." Horsley, Richard A. "1 Corinthians: A Case Study of Paul's Assembly as an Alternative Society." Pages 242–52 in *Paul and Empire: Religion and Power in Roman Imperial Society*. Edited by Richard A. Horsley. Harrisburg, Penn.: Trinity Press International, 1997.

Horsley, "Speeches." Horsley, G. H. R. "Speeches and Dialogue in Acts." *NTS* 32 (4, 1986): 609–14.

Horsley and Hanson, *Bandits*. Horsley, Richard A., and John S. Hanson. *Bandits, Prophets, and Messiahs: Popular Movements in the Time of Jesus*. Minneapolis: Winston, 1985.

Horster, "Professionals." Horster, Marietta. "Living on Religion: Professionals and Personnel." Pages 331–41 in *A Companion to Roman Religion*. Edited by Jörg Rüpke. BCompAW. Oxford: Blackwell, 2011.

Hort, *Judaistic Christianity*. Hort, Fenton John Anthony. *Judaistic Christianity*. Edited by J. O. F. Murray. 1894. Repr., Grand Rapids: Baker, 1980.

Horton, *Acts*. Horton, Stanley M. *Acts: A Logion Press Commentary*. Springfield: Gospel Publishing House, 2001.

Horton, "Baptism." Horton, Stanley M. "Spirit Baptism: A Pentecostal Perspective." Pages 47–94 in *Perspectives on Spirit Baptism: Five Views*. Edited by Chad Owen Brand. Nashville: Broadman & Holman, 2004.

Horton, *Corinthians*. Horton, Stanley M. *I and II Corinthians: A Logion Press Commentary*. Springfield, Mo.: Gospel, 1999.

Horton, *Death*. Horton, Dennis J. *Death and Resurrection: The Shape and Function of a Literary Motif in the Book of Acts*. Eugene, Ore.: Pickwick, 2009.

Horton, "Possession." Horton, Robin. "Types of Spirit Possession in Kalabari Religion." Pages 14–49 in *Spirit Mediumship and Society in Africa*. Edited by John Beattie and John Middleton. Foreword by Raymond Firth. New York: Africana, 1969.

Horton, "Semitisms." Horton, Fred L. "Reflections on the Semitisms of Luke-Acts." Pages 1–23 in *Perspectives on Luke-Acts*. ABPRSSS 5. Edited by Charles H. Talbert. Danville, Va.: Association of Baptist Professors of Religion; Edinburgh: T&T Clark, 1978.

Horton, *Spirit*. Horton, Stanley M. *What the Bible Says about the Holy Spirit*. Springfield, Mo.: Gospel, 1976.

Horton and Blakely, "Behold, Water!" Horton, Fred L., and Jeffrey A. Blakely. "'Behold, Water! Tell el-Hesi and the Baptism of the Ethiopian Eunuch (Acts 8:26–40)." *RB* 107 (1, 2000): 56–71.

Horwitz, "Ru'ah." Horwitz, Riska G. "Ru'ah ha-Kodesh." *EncJud* 14:364–68.

Hose, "Cassius Dio." Hose, Martin. "Cassius Dio: A Senator and Historian in the Age of Anxiety." Pages 461–67 in *A Companion to Greek and Roman Historiography*. Edited by John Marincola. 2 vols. Oxford: Blackwell, 2007.

Hose, "Historiography: Rome." Hose, Martin. "Historiography: Rome." *BrillPauly* 6:422–26.

Hoskyns, *Gospel*. Hoskyns, Edwyn Clement. *The Fourth Gospel*. Edited and completed by Francis Noel Davey. 2nd rev. ed. London: Faber & Faber, 1947.

Hoss, "Mikwen." Hoss, Stefanie. "Die Mikwen der späthellenistischen bis byzantinischen Zeit in Palästina." *ZDPV* 123 (1, 2007): 49–79.

Hossenfelder, "Ataraxia." Hossenfelder, Malte. "Ataraxia." *BrillPauly* 2:218–19.

Hossenfelder, "Happiness." Hossenfelder, Malte. "Happiness." *BrillPauly* 5:1132–35.

Hossenfelder, "Oikeiosis." Hossenfelder, Malte. "Oikeiosis." *BrillPauly* 10:68–69.

Hotze, "Zeugen." Hotze, G. "Christi Zeugen bis an die Grenzen der Erde—Die Apostelsgeschichte (Teil 1)." *BL* 72 (1, 1999): 29–35.

Houlden, "Purpose." Houlden, James L. "The Purpose of Luke." *JSNT* 21 (1984): 53–65.

Houlden, "Review." Houlden, James L. Review of M. D. Goulder, *Type and History in Acts*. *JTS* 17 (1966): 143–45.

Hounsa, *Figure*. Hounsa, Kponjesu Amos. *La figure d'Ananias dans la conversion-vocation de Paul à partir des Actes 9:1–31*. Yaoundé, Cameroon: CLÉ, 2011.

House, "Defilement by Association." House, Colin. "Defilement by Association: Some Insights from the Usage of κοινός/κοινόω in Acts 10 and 11." *AUSS* 21 (1983): 143–53.

House, "Suffering and Purpose." House, Paul R. "Suffering and the Purpose of Acts." *JETS* 33 (3, 1990): 317–30.

Houston, "Evidence." Houston, George W. "Papyrological Evidence for Book Collections and Libraries in the Roman Empire." Pages 233–67 in *Ancient Literacies: The Culture of Reading in Greece and Rome*. Edited by William A. Johnson and Holt N. Parker. Oxford: Oxford University Press, 2009.

Houston, "Foods." Houston, Walter J. "Foods, Clean and Unclean." *DOTP* 326–36.

Houston, "Library." Houston, G. W. "How Did You Get Hold of a Book in a Roman Library? Three Second-Century Scenarios." *CBull* 80 (1, 2004): 5–13.

Houston, *Miracles*. Houston, J. *Reported Miracles: A Critique of Hume*. Cambridge: Cambridge University Press, 1994.

Houtman, "Lijdende." Houtman, Alberdina. "Wat is er met de lijdende knecht gebeurd? De lezing van Jesaja 52:13–53:12 volgens Targoem Jonathan." *NedTT* 59 (3, 2005): 235–51.

Houtman, "Pentateuch." Houtman, Cornelis. "The Pentateuch." Pages 166–205 in *The World of the Old Testament*. Edited by A. S. van der Woude. Translated by Sierd Woudstra. Grand Rapids: Eerdmans, 1989.

Howard, *Amos*. Howard, J. K. *Amos among the Prophets*. Grand Rapids: Baker, 1968.

Howard, "Beginnings in Rome." Howard, George. "The Beginnings of Christianity in Rome: A Note on Suetonius, Life of Claudius XXV.4." *ResQ* 24 (3, 1981): 175–77.

Howard, *Crisis in Galatia*. Howard, George. *Paul: Crisis in Galatia (A Study in Early Christian Theology)*. Cambridge: Cambridge University Press, 1979.

Howard, *Criticism*. Howard, Wilbert Francis. *The Fourth Gospel in Recent Criticism and Interpretation*. 3rd ed. London: Epworth, 1945.

Howard, "End." Howard, George E. "Christ the End of the Law: The Meaning of Romans 10 4ff." *JBL* 88 (3, 1969): 331–37.

Howard, "Septuagint of Amos." Howard, George E. "Some Notes on the Septuagint of Amos." *VT* 20 (1, 1970): 108–12.

Howard, "Source." Howard, Paul Edward. "The Book of Acts as a Source for the Study of the Life of Paul." PhD diss., University of Southern California, 1959.

Howard, *Student Power*. Howard, David M. *Student Power in World Missions*. 2nd ed. Downers Grove, Ill.: InterVarsity, 1979.

Howard, *Tetragram*. Howard, George. "The Tetragram and the New Testament." *JBL* 96 (1, 1977): 63–83.

Howell, "Authority." Howell, Justin R. "The Imperial Authority and Benefaction of Centurions and Acts 10.34–43: A Response to C. Kavin Rowe." *JSNT* 31 (1, 2008): 25–51.

Howell, "Dualism." Howell, Don N. "Pauline Eschatological Dualism and Its Resulting Tensions." *TJ* 14 (1, 1993): 3–24.

Howell, "Embedded Letter." Howell, Justin R. "Embedded Letter as Rhetorical Exornatio in Acts 23:26–30." Paper presented at the annual meeting of the SBL, Washington, D.C., Nov. 20, 2006.

Howell, "Interchange." Howell, Don N. "God-Christ Interchange in Paul: Impressive Testimony to the Deity of Jesus." *JETS* 36 (4, 1993): 467–79.

Howell, "Letters." Howell, Justin R. "Embedded Letters and Rhetorical αὔξησις." Pages 154–80 in *Contemporary Studies in Acts*. Edited by Thomas E. Phillips. Macon, Ga.: Mercer University Press, 2009.

Howes, "Handelinge." Howes, Llewellyn. "Handelinge se uitbeelding van die rol van vroue in die vroeë kerk." *HTS/TS* 61 (4, 2005): 1183–1208.

Howson, *Value*. Howson, J. S. *The Evidential Value of the Acts of the Apostles*. New York: E. P. Dutton, 1880.

Hoyt, "Poor in Luke-Acts." Hoyt, Thomas, Jr. "The Poor in Luke-Acts." PhD diss., Duke University, 1974.

Hoyt, "Romans." Hoyt, Thomas, Jr. "Romans." Pages 249–75 in *True to Our Native Land: An African American New Testament Commentary*. Edited by Brian K. Blount, with Cain Hope Felder, Clarice J. Martin, and Emerson Powery. Minneapolis: Fortress, 2007.

Hruby, "Exégèse." Hruby, Kurt. "Exégèse rabbinique et exégèse patristique." *RevScRel* 47 (2–4, 1973): 341–72.

Hruby, "Horas de oración." Hruby, Kurt. "Las horas de oración en el judaísmo de la epoca de Jesús." *RivB* 34 (1, 1972): 55–72.

Hruby, "Ordination." Hruby, Kurt. "La notion d'ordination dans la tradition juive." *MaisD* 102 (1970): 30–56.

Hruska, "Plough." Hruska, Blahoslav. "Plough. I. Ancient Near East and Egypt." *BrillPauly* 11:405–6.

Hsu, "Effect." Hsu, Francis L. K. "The Effect of Dominant Kinship Relationships on Kin and Non-kin Behavior: A Hypothesis." *AmAnth* 67 (June 1965): 638–61.

Hubbard, "Commissioning Accounts." Hubbard, Benjamin J. "The Role of Commissioning Accounts in Acts." Pages 187–98 in *Perspectives on Luke-Acts*. ABPRSSS 5. Edited by Charles H. Talbert. Danville, Va.: Association of Baptist Professors of Religion; Edinburgh: T&T Clark, 1978.

Hubbard, *Joshua*. Hubbard, Robert L. *Joshua*. NIVAC. Grand Rapids: Zondervan, 2009.

Hubbard, "Out of Mind." Hubbard, Moyer V. "Was Paul out of His Mind? Re-reading 2 Corinthians 5.13." *JSNT* 70 (1998): 39–64.

Hubbard, *Redaction*. Hubbard, Benjamin Jerome. *The Matthean Redaction of a Primitive Apostolic Commissioning: An Exegesis of Matthew 28:16–20*. SBLDS 19. Missoula, Mont.: SBL, 1974.

Hubbard, "Urban Uprisings." Hubbard, Moyer V. "Urban Uprisings in the Roman World: The Social Setting of the Mobbing of Sosthenes." *NTS* 51 (3, 2005): 416–28.

Huber, Huber, "Psychology." Huber, Stefan, and Odilo W. Huber. "Psychology of Religion." Pages 133–55 in *Studying Global Pentecostalism: Theories and Methods*. Edited by Allan Anderson, Michael Bergunder, André Droogers, and Cornelis van der Laan. Berkeley: University of California, 2010.

Hübner, "Constellations." Hübner, Wolfgang. "Constellations: Classical Antiquity." *BrillPauly* 4:1188–94.

Hübner, "Eclipses." Hübner, Wolfgang. "Eclipses." *BrillPauly* 4:790–92.

Hübner, *Gesetz*. Hübner, Hans. *Das Gesetz bei Paulus: Ein Beitrag zum Werden der paulinischen Theologie*. FRLANT 119. Göttingen: Vandenhoeck & Ruprecht, 1978.

Hübner, "Necessity." Hübner, Wolfgang. "Necessity." *BrillPauly* 9:587–89.

Hübner, "Ptolemaic View." Hübner, Wolfgang. "The Ptolemaic View of the Universe." *GRBS* 41 (1, 2000): 59–93.

Hübner, *Theologie*. Hübner, Hans. *Biblische Theologie des Neues Testaments*. 3 vols. Göttingen: Vandenhoeck & Ruprecht, 1990–95.

Hübner, "Weather Portents." Hübner, Wolfgang. "Weather Portents and Signs." *Brill Pauly* 15:603–5.

Hübner, "Zodiac." Hübner, Wolfgang. "Zodiac." *BrillPauly* 15:938–46.

Hübner, "Zölibat." Hübner, Hans. "Zölibat in Qumran?" *NTS* 17 (2, 1971): 153–67.

Hudson, "Principal Family." Hudson, Egbert C. "The Principal Family at Pisidian Antioch." *JNES* 15 (2, 1956): 103–7.

Hudson, *Religion*. Hudson, Winthrop S. *Religion in America: An Historical Account of the Development of American Religious Life*. 3rd ed. New York: Scribner's, 1981.

Hudson, "Strange Words." Hudson, Neil. "Strange Words and Their Impact on Early Pentecostals: A Historical Perspective." Pages 52–80 in *Speaking in Tongues: Multidisciplinary Perspectives*. Edited by Mark J. Cartledge. SPCI. Waynesboro, Ga., and Bletchley, Milton Keynes, U.K.: Paternoster, 2006.

Huebner, "Marriage." Huebner, S. R. "'Brother-Sister' Marriage in Roman Egypt: A Curiosity of Humankind or a Widespread Family Strategy?" *JRS* 97 (2007): 21–49.

Huffmon, "Oracular Process." Huffmon, Herbert B. "The Oracular Process: Delphi and the Near East." *VT* 57 (4, 2007): 449–60.

Huffmon, "Prophecy." Huffmon, Herbert B. "Prophecy in the Mari Letters." *BA* 31 (Dec. 1968): 101–24.

Hughes, *Acts*. Hughes, R. Kent. *Acts: The Church Afire*. Wheaton, Ill.: Crossway, 1996.

Hughes, "Rhetoric." Hughes, Frank Witt. "The Rhetoric of Reconciliation: 2 Corinthians 1.1–2.13 and 7.5–8.24." Pages 246–61 in *Persuasive Artistry: Studies in New Testament Rhetoric in Honor of George A. Kennedy*. Edited by Duane F. Watson. JSNTSup 50. Sheffield, U.K.: Sheffield Academic, 1991.

Hughes, "View." Hughes, Jack. "The New Perspective's View of Paul and the Law." *MSJ* 16 (2, 2005): 261–76.

Huizenga, "Battle." Huizenga, Leroy Andrew. "The Battle for Isaac: Exploring the Composition and Function of the *aqedah* in the Book of Jubilees." *JSP* 13 (1, 2002): 33–59.

Hulen, "Dialogues." Hulen, Amos B. "The 'Dialogues with the Jews' as Sources for the Early Jewish Argument against Christianity." *JBL* 51 (1932): 58–70.

Hull, *Spirit in Acts*. Hull, J. H. E. *The Holy Spirit in the Acts of the Apostles*. London: Lutterworth, 1967; Cleveland: World, 1968.

Hull, "Yoke." Hull, Gretchen Gaebelein. "Under the Yoke: Facing the Challenge of Global Oppression." Pages 16–19 in *World Christian Summer Reader, 1990.* Pasadena, Calif.: World Christian, 1990.

Hultgren, "Formulation." Hultgren, Arland J. "The *pistis Christou* Formulation in Paul." *NovT* 22 (3, 1980): 248–63.

Hultgren, "Origin." Hultgren, Stephen. "The Origin of Paul's Doctrine of the Two Adams in 1 Corinthians 15.45–49." *JSNT* 25 (3, 2003): 343–70.

Hultgren, *Romans.* Hultgren, Arland J. *Paul's Letter to the Romans: A Commentary.* Grand Rapids: Eerdmans, 2011.

Hultgren, "Stories." Hultgren, Arland J. "The Miracle Stories in the Gospels: The Continuing Challenge for Interpreters." *WW* 29 (2, Spring 2009): 129–35.

Hultkrantz, *Healing.* Hultkrantz, Åke. *Shamanic Healing and Ritual Drama: Health and Medicine in Native North American Religious Traditions.* HMFT. New York: Crossroad Herder, 1997. Original copyright, Lutheran General Health System, 1992.

Humbert, "Objections." Humbert of Romans. "Objections to Crusades Answered." *ChH* 40 (1993): 20–21.

Humble, "*Mebaqqer.*" Humble, Bill J. "The *mebaqqer* in the Dead Sea Scrolls." *ResQ* 7 (1–2, 1963): 33–38.

Hume, *Ancestral Power.* Hume, Lynne. *Ancestral Power: The Dreaming, Consciousness, and Aboriginal Australians.* 2nd ed. Edinburgh: T&T Clark, 1998.

Hume, *Community.* Hume, Douglas A. *The Early Christian Community: A Narrative Analysis of Acts 2:41–47 and 4:32–35.* WUNT 2.298. Tübingen: Mohr Siebeck, 2011.

Hume, *Miracles.* Hume, David. *Of Miracles.* Introduction by Antony Flew. La Salle, Ill.: Open Court, 1985.

Hummel, "Factum et fictum." Hummel, Adrian. "Factum et fictum: Literarische und theologische Erwägungen zur Romreise des Paulus in der Apostelgeschichte (Apg 27,1–28,16)." *BN* 105 (2000): 39–53.

Humphrey, "Collision." Humphrey, Edith M. "Collision of Modes? Vision and Determining Argument in Acts 10:1–11:18." *Semeia* 71 (1995): 65–84.

Humphrey, *Ecstasy.* Humphrey, Edith M. *Ecstasy and Intimacy: When the Holy Spirit Meets the Human Spirit.* Foreword by Eugene H. Peterson. Grand Rapids and Cambridge: Eerdmans, 2006.

Humphrey, *Joseph and Aseneth.* Humphrey, Edith M. *Joseph and Aseneth.* Sheffield, U.K.: Sheffield Academic, 2000.

Humphrey, *Voice.* Humphrey, Edith M. *And I Turned to See the Voice: The Rhetoric of Vision in the New Testament.* StTheolInt. Grand Rapids: Baker Academic, 2007.

Hünemörder, "Gazelle." Hünemörder, Christian. "Gazelle." *BrillPauly* 5:716–17.

Hünemörder, "Laurel." Hünemörder, Christian. "Laurel." *BrillPauly* 7:300–302.

Hünemörder, "Mosquito." Hünemörder, Christian. "Mosquito." *BrillPauly* 9:234–35.

Hünemörder, "Notos." Hünemörder, Christian. "Notos: Meteorology." *BrillPauly* 9:831.

Hünemörder, "Peacock." Hünemörder, Christian. "Peacock." *BrillPauly* 10:661–62.

Hünemörder, "Purple." Hünemörder, Christian. "Purple." *BrillPauly* 12:231–33.

Hünemörder, "Snake." Hünemörder, Christian. "Snake: Zoology." *BrillPauly* 13:553–56.

Hünemörder, "Winds." Hünemörder, Christian. "Winds: Meteorology." *BrillPauly* 15:652–54.

Hünemörder, "Wolf." Hünemörder, Christian. "Wolf." *BrillPauly* 15:690–93.

Hünemörder, "Worms." Hünemörder, Christian. "Worms." *BrillPauly* 15:760–62.

Hunink, "Introduction." Hunink, Vincent. "Introduction" to Apuleius *Apology.* Pages 11–24 in Apuleius, *Rhetorical Works.* Translated and annotated by Stephen Harrison, John Hilton, and Vincent Hunink. Edited by Stephen Harrison. Oxford: Oxford University Press, 2001.

Hunn, "Πίστις Χριστοῦ." Hunn, Debbie. "Πίστις Χριστοῦ in Galatians 2:16: Clarification from 3:1–6." *TynBul* 57 (1, 2006): 23–33.

Hunt, "Eunuchs." Hunt, E. David. "Eunuchs: Secular." *OCD*³ 569.

Hunt, *History and Legacy.* Hunt, Rosalie Hall. *Bless God and Take Courage: The Judson History and Legacy.* Valley Forge, Pa.: Judson, 2005.

Hunt, "Murmuring." Hunt, Joel H. "Murmuring." *DOTP* 579–82.

Hunt, "Sociology." Hunt, Stephen. "Sociology of Religion." Pages 179–201 in *Studying Global Pentecostalism: Theories and Methods.* Edited by Allan Anderson, Michael Bergunder, André Droogers, and Cornelis van der Laan. Berkeley: University of California, 2010.

Hunter, "Aspects." Hunter, Harold D. "Aspects of Initial-Evidence Dogma: A European-American Holiness Perspective." *AJPS* 1 (2, 1998): 185–202.

Hunter, "Genre." Hunter, Richard. "Literary Genre." *BrillPauly* 7:652–55.

Hunter, *Gospel according to Paul.* Hunter, Archibald M. *The Gospel according to St. Paul.* Philadelphia: Westminster, 1966.

Hunter, "Incantation Bowls." Hunter, Erica C. D. "Incantation Bowls: A Mesopotamian Phenomenon?" *Or* 65 (3, 1996): 220–33 and plates 3–4.

Hunter, *John.* Hunter, Archibald M. *The Gospel according to John.* CBC. Cambridge: Cambridge University Press, 1965.

Hunter, *Message.* Hunter, Archibald M. *The Message of the New Testament.* Philadelphia: Westminster, 1944.

Hunter, "Portrait." Hunter, Harold D. "A Portrait of How the Azusa Doctrine of Spirit Baptism Shaped American Protestantism." *Enr* 11 (2, 2006): 79–90.

Hunter, *Predecessors.* Hunter, Archibald M. *Paul and His Predecessors.* Rev. ed. Philadelphia: Westminster; London: SCM, 1961.

Hunter, *Romans.* Hunter, Archibald M. *The Epistle to the Romans.* London: SCM, 1955.

Hunter and Chan, *Protestantism.* Hunter, Alan, and Kim-Kwong Chan. *Protestantism in Contemporary China.* Cambridge: Cambridge University Press, 1993.

Huntingford, "Takla." Huntingford, G. W. B. "The Lives of Takla Hāymānot." *JEthS* 4 (July 1966): 35–40.

Hur, *Reading.* Hur, Ju. *A Dynamic Reading of the Holy Spirit in Luke-Acts.* JSNTSup 211. Sheffield, U.K.: Sheffield Academic, 2001.

Hurd, "I Thess. 2:13–16." Hurd, John Coolidge. "Paul ahead of His Time: I Thess. 2:13–16." Pages 21–36 in vol. 1 of *Anti-Judaism in Early Christianity.* Edited by Peter Richardson. Waterloo, Ont.: Wilfred Laurier University Press, 1986.

Hurd, "Chronology and Theology." Hurd, John Coolidge. "Pauline Chronology and Pauline Theology." Pages 225–48 in *Christian History and Interpretation: Studies Presented to John Knox.* Edited by W. R. Farmer, C. F. D. Moule, and R. R. Niebuhr. Cambridge: Cambridge University Press, 1967.

Hurd, "Reflections." Hurd, John C. "Reflections concerning Paul's 'Opponents' in Galatia." Pages 129–48 in *Paul and His Opponents.* Edited by Stanley E. Porter. PAST 2. Leiden: Brill, 2005.

Hurreiz, "Zar." Hurreiz, Sayyid. "Zar as a Ritual Psychodrama: From Cult to Club." Pages 147–55 in *Women's Medicine: The zar-bori Cult in Africa and Beyond.* Edited by I. M. Lewis, Ahmed Al-Safi, and Sayyid Hurreiz. Edinburgh: International African Institute, Edinburgh University Press, 1991.

Hurschmann, "Acclamatio." Hurschmann, Rolf. "Acclamatio." *BrillPauly* 1:64–65.

Hurschmann, "Advertizing." Hurschmann, Rolf. "Advertizing." *BrillPauly* 15:978–79.

Hurschmann, "Curtain." Hurschmann, Rolf. "Curtain." *BrillPauly* 4:1200.

Hurschmann, "Fasciae." Hurschmann, Rolf. "Fasciae." *BrillPauly* 5:360.

Hurschmann, "Furniture." Hurschmann, Rolf. "Furniture: Classical Antiquity." *BrillPauly* 5:622–24.

Hurschmann, "Gestures." Hurschmann, Rolf. "Gestures: Greece and Rome." *BrillPauly* 5:832–39.

Hurschmann, "Greeting." Hurschmann, Rolf. "Greeting." *BrillPauly* 5:1022–24.

Hurschmann, "Household Equipment." Hurschmann, Rolf. "Household Equipment." *BrillPauly* 6:549–51.

Hurschmann, "Hygiene, Personal." Hurschmann, Rolf. "Hygiene, Personal." *BrillPauly* 6:604–5.

Hurschmann, "Kalathos." Hurschmann, Rolf. "Kalathos." *BrillPauly* 7:8.

Hurschmann, "Kanoun." Hurschmann, Rolf. "Kanoun." *BrillPauly* 7:17.

Hurschmann, "Kiss." Hurschmann, Rolf. "Kiss: Visual Representations." *BrillPauly* 7:62–63.

Hurschmann, "Litter." Hurschmann, Rolf. "Litter, Sedan Chair." *BrillPauly* 7:727–28.

Hurschmann, "Lock." Hurschmann, Rolf. "Lock, Key: Classical Antiquity." *Brill Pauly* 7:766–68.

Hurschmann, "Mourning Dress." Hurschmann, Rolf. "Mourning Dress." *BrillPauly* 9:246–47.

Hurschmann, "Nudity." Hurschmann, Rolf. "Nudity: Everyday Life and Sport." *Brill Pauly* 9:874.

Hurschmann, "Plate." Hurschmann, Rolf. "Plate." *BrillPauly* 11:337.

Hurschmann, "Scissors." Hurschmann, Rolf. "Scissors." *BrillPauly* 13:96–97.

Hurschmann, "Swaddling Clothes." Hurschmann, Rolf. "Swaddling Clothes." *Brill Pauly* 13:972.

Hurschmann, "Table." Hurschmann, Rolf. "Table." *BrillPauly* 14:80–81.

Hurschmann, "Tainia." Hurschmann, Rolf. "Tainia." *BrillPauly* 14:117.

Hurschmann, "Throne." Hurschmann, Rolf. "Throne: Graeco-Roman Antiquity." *Brill Pauly* 14:628–29.

Hurst, "Platonic." Hurst, Lincoln D. "How 'Platonic' Are Heb. viii.5 and ix.23?" *JTS* 34 (1, 1983): 156–68.

Hurtado, *Become God*. Hurtado, Larry W. *How on Earth Did Jesus Become a God? Historical Questions about Earliest Devotion to Jesus*. Grand Rapids: Eerdmans, 2005.

Hurtado, "Collection." Hurtado, Larry W. "The Jerusalem Collection and the Book of Galatians." *JSNT* 1 (5, 1979): 46–62.

Hurtado, "Convert." Hurtado, Larry W. "Convert, Apostate, or Apostle to the Nations? The 'Conversion' of Paul in Recent Scholarship." *SR/SR* 22 (3, 1993): 273–84.

Hurtado, "Fixation." Hurtado, Larry W. "Oral Fixation and New Testament Studies? 'Orality', 'Performance' and Reading Texts in Early Christianity." *NTS* 60 (3, July 2014): 321–40.

Hurtado, "Homage." Hurtado, Larry W. "Homage to the Historical Jesus and Early Christian Devotion." *JSHJ* 1 (2, 2003): 131–46.

Hurtado, "Lord." Hurtado, Larry W. "Lord." *DPL* 560–69.

Hurtado, *Lord Jesus Christ*. Hurtado, Larry W. *Lord Jesus Christ: Devotion to Jesus in Earliest Christianity*. Grand Rapids: Eerdmans, 2003.

Hurtado, "Monotheism." Hurtado, Larry W. "First-Century Jewish Monotheism." *JSNT* 71 (1998): 3–26.

Hurtado, *One God*. Hurtado, Larry W. *One God, One Lord: Early Christian Devotion and Ancient Jewish Monotheism*. Philadelphia: Fortress, 1988.

Hurtado, "Signs." Hurtado, Larry W. "The Function and Pattern of Signs and Wonders in the Apostolic and Subapostolic Period." MA thesis, Trinity Evangelical Divinity School, 1967.

Hurtado, "Son." Hurtado, Larry W. "Son of God." *DPL* 900–6.

Hus, "Résistance des Étrusques." Hus, Alain. "Résistance et assimilation des Étrusques à la culture grecque." Pages 151–59 in *Assimilation et résistance à la culture gréco-romaine dans le monde ancien: Travaux du VIe Congrès international d'études classiques*. Edited by D. M. Pippidi. FIAEC. Paris: Belles Lettres, 1976.

Huss, "Africa: Discovery." Huss, Werner. "Africa: History of Africa's Discovery." *BrillPauly* 1:291–94.

Huss, "Africa: Roman Province." Huss, Werner. "Africa: Roman Province." *BrillPauly* 1:295–98.

Huss, "Cyrenaica." Huss, Werner. "Cyrenaica." *BrillPauly* 4:2–3.

Huss, "Cyrene: History." Huss, Werner. "Cyrene: History." *BrillPauly* 4:6–10.

Huss, "Mauretania." Huss, Werner. "Mauretania." *BrillPauly* 8:493–96.

Huss, "Meninx." Huss, Werner. "Meninx." *BrillPauly* 8:688.

Huss, "Niger." Huss, Werner. "Niger." *Brill Pauly* 9:749.

Huss, "Syrtis." Huss, Werner. "Syrtis." *Brill Pauly* 14:73–74.

Husser, *Dreams*. Husser, Jean-Marie. *Dreams and Dream Narratives in the Biblical World*. Biblical Seminar 63. Sheffield: Sheffield Academic Press, 1999.

Hutchinson, "Instructions." Hutchinson, Gregory O. "Read the Instructions: Didactic Poetry and Didactic Prose." *CQ* 59 (1, 2009): 196–211.

Hutson, "Timid." Hutson, Christopher R. "Was Timothy Timid? On the Rhetoric of Fearlessness (1 Corinthians 16:10–11) and Cowardice (2 Timothy 1:7)." *BR* 42 (1997): 58–73.

Hutter, "Earth." Hutter, Manfred. "Earth." Pages 272–73 in *Dictionary of Deities and Demons in the Bible*. 2nd rev. ed. Edited by Karel van der Toorn, Bob Becking, and Pieter W. van der Horst. Leiden: Brill; Grand Rapids: Eerdmans, 1999.

Huttner, "Zivilisationskritik." Huttner, Ulrich. "Zur Zivilisationskritik in der frühen Kaiserzeit: Die Diskreditierung der *Pax romana*." *Historia* 49 (4, 2000): 446–66.

Hutton, "Introduction." Hutton, Maurice. Introduction to *Agricola*. Pages 149–60 in Tacitus, *Dialogus, Agricola, Germania*. Translated by William Peterson and Maurice Hutton. LCL. New York: G. P. Putnam's Sons, 1914.

Huttungen, "Stoic Law." Huttungen, Niko. "Stoic Law in Paul?" Pages 39–58 in *Stoicism in Early Christianity*. Edited by Tuomas Rasimus, Troels Engberg-Pedersen, and Ismo Dunderberg. Grand Rapids: Baker Academic, 2010.

Hvalvik, "Believer." Hvalvik, Reider. "Paul as a Jewish Believer—According to the Book of Acts." Pages 121–53 in *Jewish Believers in Jesus: The Early Centuries*. Edited by Oskar Skarsaune and Reidar Hvalvik. Peabody, Mass.: Hendrickson, 2007.

Hvalvik, "Jøde." Hvalvik, Reidar. "'For jøde først og så for greker.' Til betydningen av Rom 1,16b." *TTKi* 60 (3, 1989): 189–96.

Hvalvik, "Stadig." Hvalvik, Reidar. "'Stadig har jeg måttet reise omkring . . .' Om Paulus' reisevirksomhet og reisen i antikken." *TTKi* 80 (1, 2009): 27–47.

Hyldahl, *Chronologie*. Hyldahl, Niels. *Die paulinische Chronologie*. ATDan 19. Leiden: Brill, 1986.

Hyldahl, "En ny Paulus?" Hyldahl, Niels. "En ny Paulus?" *DTT* 67 (2, 2004): 150–54.

Ibba, "Spirits." Ibba, Giovanni. "The Evil Spirits in Jubilees and the Spirit of the Bastards in 4Q510 with Some Remarks on Other Qumran Manuscripts." *Hen* 31 (1, 2009): 111–16.

Idel, "Magic." Idel, Moshe. "Jewish Magic from the Renaissance Period to Early Hasidism." Pages 82–117 in *Religion, Science, and Magic: In Concert and in Conflict*. Edited by Jacob Neusner, Ernest S. Frerichs, and Paul Virgil McCracken Flesher. Oxford: Oxford University Press, 1989.

Igenoza, "Hypothesis." Igenoza, O. A. "The *vaticinia ex eventu* Hypothesis and the Fall of Jerusalem: The Perspectives of Luke Acts and African Culture." *AfThJ* 24 (1, 2001): 3–16.

Iglesias, "Reflexoes." Iglesias, Esther. "Reflexoes sobre o quefazer da historia oral no mundo rural." *Dados* 27 (1, 1984): 59–70.

Iglesias-Zoido, "Speeches." Iglesias-Zoido, Juan Carlos. "The Pre-Battle Speeches of Alexander at Issus and Gaugamela." *GRBS* 50 (2, 2010): 215–41.

Ikeobi, "Healing." Ikeobi, Goddy. "Healing and Exorcism: The Nigerian Pastoral Experience." Pages 55–104 in *Healing and Exorcism—The Nigerian Experience: Proceedings, Lectures, Discussions, and Conclusions of the First Missiology Symposium on Healing and Exorcism, Organised by the Spiritan International School of Theology, Attakwu, Enugu, May 18–20, 1989*. Edited by Chris U. Manus, Luke N. Mbefo, and E. E. Uzukwu. Enugu, Nigeria: Snapp, 1992.

Ilan, "Frauen." Ilan, Tal. "Jüdische Frauen in der Spätantike: Ein Überblick." *KuI* 15 (1, 2000): 7–15.

Ilan, "Lhbdly ktyb." Ilan, Tal. "Lhbdly ktyb sl smwt btqwpt byt sny." *Leš* 52 (1987): 3–7. (Abstract: *NTA* 34:87.)

Ilan, "Quest for Beruriah." Ilan, Tal. "The Quest for the Historical Beruriah, Rachel, and Imma Shalom." *AJSR* 22 (1, 1997): 1–17.

Ilan, "Torah." Ilan, Tal. "The Torah of the Jews of Ancient Rome." *JSQ* 16 (4, 2009): 363–95.

Ilan, *Women*. Ilan, Tal. *Jewish Women in Greco-Roman Palestine*. Tübingen: J. C. B. Mohr; Peabody, Mass.: Hendrickson, 1996.

Ilan, "Women to Pharisaism." Ilan, Tal. "The Attraction of Aristocratic Women to Pharisaism during the Second Temple Period." *HTR* 88 (1, 1995): 1–33.

Ilan, "Women's Studies." Ilan, Tal. "Women's Studies and Jewish Studies—When and Where Do They Meet?" *JSQ* 3 (2, 1996): 162–73.

Ingalls, "Demography." Ingalls, Wayne. "Demography and Dowries: Perspectives on Female Infanticide in Classical Greece." *Phoenix* 56 (3–4, 2002): 246–54.

"Inn: Antiquity." "Inn: Classical Antiquity." *BrillPauly* 6:818–21.

Inowlocki, "*Interpretatio*." Inowlocki, Sabrina. "Eusebius of Caesarea's *interpretatio christiana* of Philo's *De vita contemplativa*." *HTR* 97 (3, 2004): 305–28.

Inowlocki, "Neither Adding nor Omitting." Inowlocki, Sabrina. "'Neither Adding nor Omitting Anything': Josephus' Promise Not to Modify the Scriptures in Greek and Latin Context." *JJS* 56 (1, 2005): 48–65.

Inowlocki, "Rewriting." Inowlocki, Sabrina. "Josephus' Rewriting of the Babel Narrative (Gen 11:1–9)." *JSJ* 37 (2, 2006): 169–91.

Instone and Spawforth, "Agōnes." Instone, Stephen J., and Antony J. S. Spawforth. "Agōnes." *OCD*³ 41–42.

Instone-Brewer, "Infanticide." Instone-Brewer, David. "Infanticide and the Apostolic Decree of Acts 15." *JETS* 52 (2, June 2009): 301–21.

Instone-Brewer, "Psychiatrists." Instone-Brewer, David. "Jesus and the Psychiatrists." Pages 133–48 in *The Unseen World: Christian Reflections on Angels, Demons, and the Heavenly Realm*. Edited by Anthony N. S. Lane. Grand Rapids: Baker; Carlisle, U.K.: Paternoster, 1996.

Instone-Brewer, *Traditions*. Instone-Brewer, David. *Traditions of the Rabbis from the Era of the New Testament*. Grand Rapids: Eerdmans, 2004–.

Instone-Brewer and Harland, "Associations." Instone-Brewer, David, and Philip A. Harland. "Jewish Associations in Roman Palestine: Evidence from the Mishnah." *JGRCJ* 5 (2008): 200–221.

"Interest." "Interest: Classical Antiquity." *BrillPauly* 6:851–54.

Inwood, "Mnesarchus." Inwood, Brad. "Mnesarchus." *BrillPauly* 9:98.

Inwood, "Natural Law." Inwood, Brad. "Natural Law in Seneca." *SPhilA* 15 (2003): 81–99.

Inwood, "Stoicism." Inwood, Brad. "Stoicism." *BrillPauly* 13:852–57.

Irudaya, "Samaritans." Irudaya, Raj. "Who Are the Samaritans?" *Vid* 68 (8, 2004): 579–94.

Irvin and Sunquist, *Earliest Christianity*. Irvin, Dale T., and Scott W. Sunquist. *Earliest Christianity to 1453*. Vol. 1 of *History of the World Christian Movement*. Markynoll, N.Y.: Orbis, 2001.

Irvin and Sunquist, *History*. Irvin, Dale T., and Scott W. Sunquist. *Modern Christianity from 1454–1800*. Vol. 2 of *History of the World Christian Movement*. Markynoll, N.Y.: Orbis, 2012.

Irwin, *Philosophy*. Irwin, Terence, ed. *Classical Philosophy*. Oxford Readers. New York: Oxford University Press, 1999.

Irwin, "Stoic Inhumanity." Irwin, Terence H. "Stoic Inhumanity." Pages 219–41 in *The Emotions in Hellenistic Philosophy*. Edited by Juha Sihvola and Troels Engberg-Pedersen. TSHP 46. Dordrecht, Neth.: Kluwer Academic, 1998.

Isaac, "Ethiopia." Isaac, Ephraim. "Ethiopia." *OEANE* 2:273–78.

Isaac, "Identity." Isaac, Ephraim. "The Question of Jewish Identity and Ethiopian Jewish Origins." *Midstream* 51 (5, 2005): 29–34.

Isaac, *Invention of Racism*. Isaac, Benjamin. *The Invention of Racism in Classical Antiquity*. Princeton: Princeton University Press, 2004.

Isaac, "Latin and Greek." Isaac, B. "Latin and Greek in the Inscriptions of Caesarea Maritima." *JRA* 16 (2003): 665–68.

Isaac, "Proto-racism." Isaac, Benjamin. "Proto-racism in Graeco-Roman Antiquity." *WArch* 38 (1, 2006): 32–47.

Isaacs, "Disorder." Isaacs, T. Craig. "The Possessive States Disorder: The Diagnosis of Demonic Possession." *PastPsy* 35 (4, Summer 1987): 263–73.

Isaacs, *Spirit*. Isaacs, Marie E. *The Concept of Spirit: A Study of Pneuma in Hellenistic Judaism and Its Bearing on the New Testament*. Heythrop Monographs 1. London: Heythrop College Press, 1976.

Isbell, *Bowls*. Isbell, Charles D. *Corpus of the Aramaic Incantation Bowls*. SBLDS 17. Missoula, Mont.: Scholars Press, 1975.

Isbell, "Story." Isbell, Charles D. "The Story of the Aramaic Magical Incantation Bowls." *BA* 41 (1, 1978): 5–16.

Isenberg, "Polemic." Isenberg, Sheldon R. "An Anti-Sadducee Polemic in the Palestinian Targum Tradition." *HTR* 63 (3, 1970): 433–44.

Isenberg, "Sale." Isenberg, M. "The Sale of Sacrificial Meat." *CP* 70 (4, 1975): 271–73.

Isichei, *History*. Isichei, Elizabeth. *A History of Christianity in Africa from Antiquity to the Present*. Lawrenceville, N.J.: Africa World; Grand Rapids: Eerdmans, 1995.

Ising, *Blumhardt*. Ising, Dieter. *Johann Christoph Blumhardt, Life and Work: A New Biography*. Translated by Monty Ledford. Eugene, Ore.: Cascade, 2009. Translated from *Johann Christoph Blumhardt: Leben und Werk*. Göttingen: Vandenhoeck & Ruprecht, 2002.

Isizoh, "Areopagus Speech." Isizoh, Chidi Denis. "A Reading of the Areopagus Speech (Acts 17, 22–31) from the African Traditional Religious Perspective." *AfCS* 14 (2, 1998): 1–25.

Isler, "Theatre." Isler, Hans-Peter. "Theatre: Architecture." *BrillPauly* 14:383–90.

Issar and Yakir, "Isotopes." Issar, Arie S., and Dan Yakir. "Isotopes from Wood Buried in the Roman Siege Ramp of Masada: The Roman Period's Colder Climate." *BA* 60 (2, 1997): 101–6.

Issler, "Prototype." Issler, Klaus. "Jesus' Example: Prototype of the Dependent,

Spirit-Filled Life." Pages 189–24 in *Jesus in Trinitarian Perspective: An Introductory Christology*. Edited by Fred Sanders and Klaus Issler. Foreword by Gerald Bray. Nashville: Broadman & Holman, 2007.

Ito, "Authenticity." Ito, Akio. "The Question of the Authenticity of the Ban on Swearing (Matthew 5.33–37)." *JSNT* 43 (1991): 5–13.

Iverson, "Orality." Iverson, Kelly R. "Orality and the Gospels: A Survey of Recent Research." *CBR* 8 (1, 2009): 71–106.

Ivey, "Discourses." Ivey, Gavin. "Diabolical Discourses: Demonic Possession and Evil in Modern Psychopathology." *SAJPsyc* 32 (4, 2002): 54–59.

Izard, "Relationships." Izard, Carroll E. "Emotion-Cognition Relationships and Human Development." Pages 17–37 in *Emotions, Cognition, and Behaviour*. Edited by Carroll E. Izard, Jerome Kagan, and Robert B. Zajonc. Cambridge: Cambridge University Press, 1984.

Jackson, "Churches." Jackson, William Charles. "Breakthrough Churches Then and Now: Using a Conflict Model to Interpret Acts." DMiss diss., Fuller Theological Seminary School of Intercultural Studies, 2011.

Jackson, "Conventions." Jackson, Howard M. "Ancient Self-Referential Conventions and Their Implications for the Authorship and Integrity of the Gospel of John." *JTS* 50 (1, 1999): 1–34.

Jackson, "Family Law." Jackson, Bernard S. "How Jewish Is Jewish Family Law?" *JJS* 55 (2, 2004): 201–29.

Jackson, *Quest*. Jackson, Bill. *The Quest for the Radical Middle: A History of the Vineyard*. Foreword by Todd Hunter. Cape Town: Vineyard International, 1999.

Jackson, "Roman Influence." Jackson, Bernard S. "On the Problem of Roman Influence on the Halakah and Normative Self-Definition in Judaism." Pages 157–203 in *Aspects of Judaism in the Graeco-Roman Period*. Edited by E. P. Sanders with A. I. Baumgarten and Alan Mendelson. Vol. 2 of *Jewish and Christian Self-Definition*. Edited by E. P. Sanders. Philadelphia: Fortress, 1981.

Jackson-McCabe, "Implanted Preconceptions." Jackson-McCabe, Matt. "The Stoic Theory of Implanted Preconceptions." *Phronesis* 49 (4, 2004): 323–47.

Jacobs, *Exegesis*. Jacobs, Louis. *Jewish Biblical Exegesis*. New York: Behrman House, 1973.

Jacobs, "Leadership." Jacobs, Mignon R. "Leadership, Elders." *DOTP* 515–18.

Jacobs, "Love." Jacobs, Louis. "Greater Love Hath No Man . . .: The Jewish Point of View of Self-Sacrifice." *Judaism* 6 (Winter 1957): 41–47.

Jacobs, "Motifs." Jacobs, Irving. "Literary Motifs in the *Testament of Job*." *JJS* 21 (1–4, 1970): 1–10.

Jacobs, "Possession." Jacobs, Donald R. "Possession, Trance State, and Exorcism in Two East African Communities." Pages 175–87 in *Demon Possession: A Medical, Historical, Anthropological, and Theological Symposium*. Edited by John Warwick Montgomery. Minneapolis: Bethany House, 1976.

Jacobs, "Sanction for Martyrdom." Jacobs, Irving. "Eleazar ben Yair's Sanction for Martyrdom." *JSJ* 13 (1–2, 1982): 183–86.

Jacobs, "When Rabbis Cry." Jacobs, Jill. "When the Rabbis Cry: Talmudic Responses to Injustice in the Biblical Text." *Reconstructionist* 66 (2, 2002): 37–41.

Jacobsen, *Thinking in Spirit*. Jacobsen, Douglas. *Thinking in the Spirit: Theologies of the Early Pentecostal Movement*. Bloomington: Indiana University Press, 2003.

Jacobsen and Wasserberg, *Preaching*. Jacobsen, David Schnasa, and Gunter Wasserberg. *Preaching Luke-Acts*. Nashville: Abingdon, 2001.

Jacobson, "Adoptive Parents." Jacobson, Howard. "Adoptive Parents in Rabbinic Exegesis of the Bible." *VT* 49 (2, 1999): 261–62.

Jacobson, "Anchor." Jacobson, David M. "The Anchor on the Coins of Judaea." *BAIAS* 18 (2000): 73–81.

Jacobson, "Apion and Sacrifice." Jacobson, Howard. "Apion, the Jews, and Human Sacrifice." *CQ* 51 (1, 2001): 318–19.

Jacobson, "Artapanus." Jacobson, Howard. "Artapanus Judaeus." *JJS* 57 (2, 2006): 210–21.

Jacobson, "Colors." Jacobson, David M. "Herod the Great Shows His True Colors." *NEA* 64 (3, 2001): 100–104.

Jacobson, "Helmet." Jacobson, David M. "Military Helmet or Dioscuri Motif on Herod the Great's Largest Coin?" *IsNumR* 2 (2007): 93–101.

Jacobson, "Kings." Jacobson, David M. "Three Roman Client Kings: Herod of Judaea, Archelaus of Cappadocia, and Juba of Mauretania." *PEQ* 133 (1, 2001): 22–38.

Jacobson, "Palestine and Israel." Jacobson, David M. "Palestine and Israel." *BASOR* 313 (Feb. 1999): 65–74.

Jacobson, "Palestine Meant Israel." Jacobson, David M. "When Palestine Meant Israel." *BAR* 27 (3, 2001): 42–47, 57.

Jacobson, "Rejection." Jacobson, Howard. "A Philonic Rejection of Plato." *Mnemosyne* 57 (4, 2004): 488.

Jacobson, "Roman Temple." Jacobson, David. "Herod's Roman Temple." *BAR* 28 (2, 2002): 18–27, 60–61.

Jacobson, "Shoes." Jacobson, Howard. "Shoes and Jews." *REJ* 161 (1–2, 2002): 233.

Jacobson, "Vision." Jacobson, Howard. "Samuel's Vision in Pseudo-Philo's *Liber antiquitatum biblicarum*." *JBL* 112 (2, 1993): 310–11.

Jacobson, "Visions of Past." Jacobson, Howard. "Visions of the Past: Jews and Greeks." *Judaism* 35 (4, 1986): 467–82.

Jacobson and Weitzman, "Alloy." Jacobson, David M., and M. P. Weitzman. "Black Bronze and the 'Corinthian Alloy.'" *CQ* 45 (2, 1995): 580–83.

Jacobson and Weitzman, "Bronze." Jacobson, David M., and M. P. Weitzman. "What Was Corinthian Bronze?" *AJA* 96 (2, 1992): 237–47.

Jacobus, "Curse." Jacobus, Helen R. "The Curse of Cainan (*Jub.* 8.1–5): Genealogies in Genesis 5 and Genesis 11 and a Mathematical Pattern." *JSP* 18 (3, 2009): 207–32.

Jacquette, "Divinity." Jacquette, Dale. "Zeno of Citium on the Divinity of the Cosmos." *SR/SR* 24 (4, 1995): 415–31.

Jacquin, "Worte in der Erziehung." Jacquin, Françoise. "Die Zehn Worte in der jüdischen Erziehung." *IKaZ/Communio* 22 (1, 1993): 23–35.

Jaeger, *Christianity and Paideia*. Jaeger, Werner. *Early Christianity and Greek Paideia*. Cambridge, Mass.: Harvard University Press, 1961.

Jaffé, "'Amei-ha-ares.'" Jaffé, Dan. "Les 'amei-ha-ares durant le IIe et le IIIe siècle: État des sources et des recherches." *REJ* 161 (1–2, 2002): 1–40.

Jaillard, "Plutarque et divination." Jaillard, Dominique. "Plutarque et la divination: La piété d'un prêtre philosophe." *RHR* 224 (2, 2007): 149–69.

Jaki, *Miracles and Physics*. Jaki, Stanley. *Miracles and Physics*. Front Royal, Va.: Christendom, 1989.

Jakobielski, "Christian Nubia." Jakobielski, S. "Christian Nubia at the Height of Its Civilization." Pages 194–223 in *Ancient Civilizations of Africa*. Edited by G. Mokhtar. General History of Africa 2. Berkeley: University of California Press; London: Heinemann Educational; Paris: United Nations Educational, Scientific and Cultural Organization, 1981.

Jakobsson, "Founded." Jakobsson, Jens. "Who Founded the Indo-Greek Era of 186/5 B.C.E.?" *CQ* 59 (2, 2009): 505–10.

James, "Constructions." James, Sharon Lynn. "Introduction: Constructions of Gender and Genre in Roman Comedy and Elegy." *Helios* 25 (1, 1998): 3–16.

James, *Egypt*. James, T. G. H. *Ancient Egypt: The Land and Its Legacy*. Austin: University of Texas, 1988.

James, "God Came to England." James, Frank A., III. "When God Came to England." *ChH* 72 (2001): 16–19.

James, "Self." James, William. "The Divided Self and Conversion." Pages 121–36 in *Conversion: Perspectives on Personal and Social Transformation*. Edited by Walter E. Conn. New York: Alba House, 1978.

Jameson, "Sicily." Jameson, Michael H. "Sicily." *OCD*³ 1401–3.

Jameson, "Sicily Cults." Jameson, Michael H. "Sicily and Magna Graecia, Cults and Mythology." *OCD*³ 1403.

Jameson, "Soteria." Jameson, Michael H. "Soteria." *OCD*³ 1428.

Jankowski, "Messianische Realpolitik?" Jankowski, G. "Messianische Realpolitik? Anmerkungen zu Apostelgeschichte 21–22." *T&K* 22 (81–82, 1999): 65–85.

Janne, "Impulsore Chresto." Janne, H. "Impulsore Chresto." "Mélanges Bidez." *AIPHOS* 2 (1934): 531–53.

Janowski, "Satyrs." Janowski, Bernd. "Satyrs." Pages 732–33 in *Dictionary of Deities and Demons in the Bible*. 2nd rev. ed. Edited by Karel van der Toorn, Bob Becking, and Pieter W. van der Horst. Leiden: Brill; Grand Rapids: Eerdmans, 1999.

Jansen, "Distinctions." Jansen, G. C. M. "Social Distinctions and Issues of Privacy in the Toilets of Hadrian's Villa." *JRA* 16 (203): 137–52.

Jansen-Winkeln, "Alexandria." Jansen-Winkeln, Karl. "Alexandria in Egypt." *BrillPauly* 1:496–98.

Jansen-Winkeln, "Healing Deities." Jansen-Winkeln, Karl. "Healing Deities, Healing Cults: Egypt." *BrillPauly* 6:21–22.

Janzen, "Land." Janzen, Waldemar. "Land." *ABD* 4:143–54.

Jaquette, "Life and Death." Jaquette, James L. "Life and Death, *adiaphora*, and Paul's Rhetorical Strategies." *NovT* 38 (1, 1996): 30–54.

Jas, "Hénoch." Jas, Michel. "Hénoch et le fils de l'homme: Datation du livre des paraboles pour une situation de l'origine du gnosticisme." *RRéf* 30 (3, 1979): 105–19.

Jassen, "Presentation." Jassen, Alex P. "The Presentation of the Ancient Prophets as Lawgivers at Qumran." *JBL* 127 (2, 2008): 307–37.

Jastram, "Comparison." Jastram, Nathan. "A Comparison of Two 'Proto-Samaritan' Texts from Qumran: 4QpaleoExodᵐ and 4QNumᵇ." *DSD* 5 (3, 1998): 264–89.

Jastrow, *Dictionary*. Jastrow, Marcus. *Dictionary of the Targumim, Talmud Babli, Yerushalmi, and Midrashic Literature*. New York: Judaica, 1971.

Jaubert, "Pays de Damas." Jaubert, A. "'Le pays de Damas.'" *RB* 65 (2, 1958): 214–48.

Jáuregui, "Panorama." Jáuregui, José Antonio. "Panorama de la evolución de los estudios lucanos." *EstBib* 61 (3, 2003): 351–98.

Jayakumar, "Circumcision." Jayakumar, Kamalakar. "'Circumcision' in Jewish Religion." *BangTF* 33 (2, 2001): 21–37.

Jeffers, "Families." Jeffers, James S. "Jewish and Christian Families in First-Century Rome." Pages 128–50 in *Judaism and Christianity in First-Century Rome*. Edited by Karl P. Donfried and Peter Richardson. Grand Rapids: Eerdmans, 1998.

Jeffers, personal correspondence. Jeffers, James S. Personal correspondence with the author, Dec. 19, 2005.

Jeffers, *World*. Jeffers, James S. *The Greco-Roman World of the New Testament Era: Exploring the Background of Early Christianity*. Downers Grove, Ill.: InterVarsity, 1999.

Jeffery, *Secret Gospel*. Jeffery, Peter. *The Secret Gospel of Mark Unveiled: Imagined Rituals of Sex, Death, and Madness in a Biblical Forgery*. New Haven: Yale University Press, 2007.

Jefford, "Acts 15 and Didache 6." Jefford, Clayton N. "Tradition and Witness in Antioch: Acts 15 and Didache 6." *PRSt* 19 (4, 1992): 409–19.

Jeffries, "Healing." Jeffries, M. D. "Miraculous Healing, as Recorded in the Scriptures, and as Claimed Since That Day." *RevExp* 19 (1, Jan. 1922): 64–73.

Jellicoe, "Seventy(-Two)." Jellicoe, Sidney. "St Luke and the 'Seventy(-Two).'" *NTS* 6 (4, 1960): 319–21.

Jenkins, "Livia." Jenkins, Thomas E. "Livia the Princeps: Gender and Ideology in the Consolatio ad Liviam." *Helios* 36 (1, 2009): 1–25.

Jenkins, *New Faces*. Jenkins, Philip. *The New Faces of Christianity: Believing the Bible in the Global South*. New York and Oxford: Oxford University Press, 2006.

Jenkins, *Next Christendom*. Jenkins, Philip. *The Next Christendom: The Coming of Global Christianity*. New York: Oxford University Press, 2002.

Jenkins, "Reading." Jenkins, Philip. "Reading the Bible in the Global South." *IBMR* 30 (2, 2006): 67–73.

Jenkins, "Reindorf." Jenkins, Paul. "Reindorf, Carl Christian." No pages. *DACB*. Online: http://www.dacb.org/stories/ghana/reindorf2_carl.html.

Jennings, *Good News*. Jennings, Theodore W., Jr. *Good News to the Poor: John Wesley's Evangelical Economics*. Nashville: Abingdon, 1990.

Jensen, *Antipas*. Jensen, Morten Hørning. *Herod Antipas in Galilee: The Literary and Archaeological Sources on the Reign of Herod Antipas and Its Socio-Economic Impact on Galilee*. 2nd ed. WUNT 2.215. Tübingen: Mohr Siebeck, 2010.

Jensen, "Binding." Jensen, Robin M. "The Binding or Sacrifice of Isaac: How Jews and Christians See Differently." *BRev* 9 (5, 1993): 42–51.

Jensen, "Nudity." Jensen, Robin M. "Nudity in Early Christian Art." Pages 296–319 in *Text, Image, and Christians in the Graeco-Roman World: A Festschrift in Honor of David Lee Balch*. Edited by Aliou Cissé Niang and Carolyn Osiek. PrTMS 176. Eugene, Ore.: Pickwick, 2012.

Jensen, "Royal Purple." Jensen, Lloyd B. "Royal Purple of Tyre." *JNES* 22 (2, 1963): 104–18.

Jeremias, *Briefe*. Jeremias, Joachim. *Die Briefe an Timotheus und Titus*. Göttingen: Vandenhoeck & Ruprecht, 1949.

Jeremias, *Eucharistic Words*. Jeremias, Joachim. *The Eucharistic Words of Jesus*. Translated by Norman Perrin. Philadelphia: Fortress, 1966.

Jeremias, "Γωνία." Jeremias, Joachim. "Γωνία, ἀκρογωνιαῖος, κεφαλὴ γωνίας." *TDNT* 1:791–93.

Jeremias, *Jerusalem*. Jeremias, Joachim. *Jerusalem in the Time of Jesus*. Philadelphia: Fortress; London: SCM, 1969.

Jeremias, *Message*. Jeremias, Joachim. *The Central Message of the New Testament*. New York: Scribner's, 1965.

Jeremias, "Μωυσῆς." Jeremias, Joachim. "Μωυσῆς." *TDNT* 4:848–73.

Jeremias, "Παῖς." Jeremias, Joachim. "Παῖς θεοῦ in Later Judaism in the Period after the LXX." *TDNT* 5:677–700.

Jeremias, "Pap. Egerton." Jeremias, Joachim. Introduction to "Pap. Egerton 2." Pages 94–96 in *Gospels and Related Writings*. Vol. 1 of *New Testament Apocrypha*. Edited by Edgar Hennecke, Wilhelm Schneemelcher, and R. McL. Wilson. Philadelphia: Westminster, 1963.

Jeremias, *Parables*. Jeremias, Joachim. *The Parables of Jesus*. 2nd rev. ed. New York: Scribner's, 1972.

Jeremias, "Paulus als Hillelit." Jeremias, Joachim. "Paulus als Hillelit." Pages 88–94 in *Neotestamentica et Semitica: Studies in Honour of Matthew Black*. Edited by E. E. Ellis and M. Wilcox. Edinburgh: T&T Clark, 1969.

Jeremias, *Prayers*. Jeremias, Joachim. *The Prayers of Jesus*. Philadelphia: Fortress, 1964.

Jeremias, *Promise*. Jeremias, Joachim. *Jesus' Promise to the Nations*. Translated by S. H. Hooke. SBT 24. London: SCM, 1958.

Jeremias, "Qumran Texts." Jeremias, Joachim. "The Qumran Texts and the New Testament." *ExpT* 70 (3, 1958): 68–69.

Jeremias, *Sermon*. Jeremias, Joachim. *The Sermon on the Mount*. Translated by Norman Perrin. Philadelphia: Fortress, 1963.

Jeremias, *Theology*. Jeremias, Joachim. *New Testament Theology*. New York: Scribner's, 1971.

Jeremias, *Unknown Sayings*. Jeremias, Joachim. *Unknown Sayings of Jesus*. Translated by Reginald H. Fuller. 2nd ed. London: SPCK, 1964.

Jeremias, "Untersuchungen." Jeremias, Joachim. "Untersuchungen zum Quellenproblem der Apostelgeschichte." *ZNW* 36 (1937): 205–21.

Jervell, *Apostelgeschichte*. Jervell, Jacob. *Die Apostelgeschichte*. 17th ed. KEKNT 3. Göttingen: Vandenhoeck & Ruprecht, 1998.

Jervell, "Church." Jervell, Jacob. "The Church of Jews and Godfearers." Pages 11–20 in *Luke-Acts and the Jewish People: Eight Critical Perspectives*. Edited by Joseph B. Tyson. Minneapolis: Augsburg, 1988.

Jervell, "Faithfulness." Jervell, Jacob. "God's Faithfulness to the Faithless People: Trends in Interpretation of Luke-Acts." *WW* 12 (1, 1992): 29–36.

Jervell, "Future." Jervell, Jacob. "The Future of the Past: Luke's Vision of Salvation History and Its Bearing on His Writing of History." Pages 104–26 in *History, Literature, and Society in the Book of Acts*. Edited by Ben Witherington III. Cambridge: Cambridge University Press, 1996.

Jervell, "Israel und Heidenvölken." Jervell, Jacob. "Das gespaltene Israel und die Heidenvölken: Zur Motivierung der Heidenmission in der Apostelgeschichte." *ST* 19 (1–2, 1965): 68–96.

Jervell, *Luke and People of God*. Jervell, Jacob. *Luke and the People of God: A New Look at Luke-Acts*. Minneapolis: Augsburg, 1972.

Jervell, "Paul in Acts: Theology." Jervell, Jacob. "Paul in the Acts of the Apostles: Tradition, History, Theology." Pages 297–306 in *Les Actes des apôtres: Traditions, rédaction, théologie*. Edited by Jacob Kremer. BETL 48. Gembloux, Belg.: J. Duculot; Leuven: Leuven University Press, 1979.

Jervell, *Theology*. Jervell, Jacob. *The Theology of the Acts of the Apostles*. New Testament Theology. Cambridge and New York: Cambridge University Press, 1996.

Jervell, *Unknown Paul*. Jervell, Jacob. *The Unknown Paul: Essays on Luke-Acts and Early Christian History*. Minneapolis: Augsburg, 1984.

Jervis, "Law." Jervis, L. Ann. "Law/Nomos in Greco-Roman World." *DNTB* 631–36.

Jervis, "Reconsideration." Jervis, L. Ann. "1 Corinthians 14.34–35: A Reconsideration of Paul's Limitation of the Free Speech of Some Corinthian Women." *JSNT* 58 (1995): 51–74.

Jeska, "Stephanus." Jeska, Joachim. "Stephanus—zentrale Gestalt oder Randfigur der Apostelgeschichte?" *BK* 55 (2, 2000): 68–73.

Jeske, "Luke and Paul on Paul." Jeske, Richard. "Luke and Paul on the Apostle Paul." *CurTM* 4 (1977): 28–38.

Jeste et al., "Schizophrenia." Jeste, Dilip V., et al. "Did Schizophrenia Exist before the Eighteenth Century?" *ComPsy* 26 (6, 1985): 493–503.

Jesudasan, "Prayer." Jesudasan, Ignatius. "Prayer in the Acts of the Apostles." *JDharm* 28 (4, 2003): 543–48.

Jewett, "Agitators." Jewett, Robert. "The Agitators and the Galatian Congregation." *NTS* 17 (2, 1971): 198–212.

Jewett, *Chronology*. Jewett, Robert. *A Chronology of Paul's Life*. Philadelphia: Fortress, 1979.

Jewett, *Hebrews*. Jewett, Robert. *Letter to Pilgrims: A Commentary on the Epistle to the Hebrews*. New York: Pilgrim, 1981.

Jewett, *Male*. Jewett, Paul K. *Man as Male and Female: A Study in Sexual Relationships from a Theological Point of View*. Grand Rapids: Eerdmans, 1975.

Jewett, "Mapping 'Missionary Journey.'" Jewett, Robert. "Mapping the Route of Paul's 'Second Missionary Journey' from Dorylaeum to Troas." *TynBul* 48 (1, 1997): 1–22.

Jewett, *Romans*. Jewett, Robert, assisted by Roy D. Kotansky. *Romans: A Commentary*. Edited by Eldon Jay Epp. Hermeneia. Minneapolis: Fortress, 2007.

Jewett, "Shame." Jewett, Robert. "Paul, Shame, and Honor." Pages 551–74 in *Paul in the Greco-Roman World: A Handbook*. Edited by J. Paul Sampley. Harrisburg, Pa.: Trinity Press International, 2003.

Jewett, *Thessalonian Correspondence*. Jewett, Robert. *The Thessalonian Correspondence: Pauline Rhetoric and Millenarian Piety*. Philadelphia: Fortress, 1986.

Jiménez, "Spirit." Jiménez, Pablo A. "The Spirit Told Me to Go: A Hispanic Homiletic Reading of Acts 11:12." *Apuntes* 23 (1, 2003): 28–34.

Jipp, "Messiah." Jipp, Joshua W. "Luke's Scriptural Suffering Messiah: A Search for Precedent, a Search for Identity." *CBQ* 72 (2, 2010): 255–74.

Jipp, "Speech." Jipp, Joshua W. "Paul's Areopagus Speech of Acts 17:16–34 as Both Critique and Propaganda." *JBL* 131 (3, 2012): 567–88.

Jipp, *Visitations*. Jipp, Joshua W. *Divine Visitations and Hospitality to Strangers in Luke-Acts: An Interpretation of the Malta Episode in Acts 28:1–10*. NovTSup 153. Leiden: Brill, 2013.

Jobes, "Relevance Theory." Jobes, Karen H. "Relevance Theory and the Translation of Scripture." *JETS* 50 (4, 2007): 773–97.

Jocelyn, "Lucretius." Jocelyn, H. D. "Lucretius, His Copyists and the Horrors of the Underworld (*De rerum natura* 3.978–1023)." *ACl* 29 (1986): 43–56.

Jochim, *Religions*. Jochim, Christian. *Chinese Religions: A Cultural Perspective*. Prentice-Hall Series in World Religions. Englewood Cliffs, N.J.: Prentice-Hall, 1986.

Jocz, *People*. Jocz, Jakob. *The Jewish People and Jesus Christ: The Relationship Between Church and Synagogue*. 3rd ed. Grand Rapids: Baker, 1979.

Jóczwiak, "Mesjanizm." Jóczwiak, F. "Mesjanizm w literaturze z Qumran (Le messianisme dans les textes de Qumran)." *RocTK* 10 (1, 1963): 35–42.

Johanson, "Alternative View." Johanson, Ernest. "An Alternative View of Baptism in the Holy Spirit." ThM thesis, Fuller Theological Seminary, 1994.

Johns, "New Directions." Johns, Donald A. "Some New Directions in the Hermeneutics of Classical Pentecostalism's Doctrine of Initial Evidence." Pages 145–67 in *Initial Evidence: Historical and Biblical Perspectives on the Pentecostal Doctrine of Spirit Baptism*. Edited by Gary B. McGee. Peabody, Mass.: Hendrickson, 1991.

Johnson, *Acts*. Johnson, Luke Timothy. *The Acts of the Apostles*. SP 5. Collegeville, Minn.: Liturgical Press, 1992.

Johnson, "Alone." Johnson, Gerald. "Alone in the Mountains." *MounM* (Nov. 1995): 20–21.

Johnson, "Antioch." Johnson, Sherman E. "Antioch, the Base of Operations." *LTQ* 18 (2, 1983): 64–73.

Johnson, "Authority." Johnson, Harmon A. "Authority over the Spirits: Brazilian Spiritism and Evangelical Church Growth." MA thesis, Fuller Theological Seminary, 1969.

Johnson, "*Delatorum*." Johnson, Gary J. "*De conspiratione delatorum*: Pliny and the Christians Revisited." *Latomus* 47 (2, 1988): 417–22.

Johnson, "Faith of Jesus." Johnson, Luke Timothy. "Rom 3:21–26 and the Faith of Jesus." *CBQ* 44 (1, 1982): 77–90.

Johnson, "Fictions." Johnson, Sara. "Third Maccabees: Historical Fictions and the Shaping of Jewish Identity in the Hellenistic Period." Pages 185–97 in *Ancient Fiction: The Matrix of Early Christian and Jewish Narrative*. Edited by Jo-Ann A. Brant, Charles W. Hedrick, and Chris Shea. SBLSymS 32. Atlanta: SBL, 2005.

Johnson, *Function*. Johnson, Luke Timothy. *The Literary Function of Possessions in Luke-Acts*. SBLDS 39. Missoula, Mont.: SBL, 1977.

Johnson, *Genealogies*. Johnson, Marshall D. *The Purpose of the Biblical Genealogies: With Special Reference to the Setting of the Genealogies of Jesus*. 2nd ed. SNTSMS 8. Cambridge: Cambridge University Press, 1988.

Johnson, "Growing Church." Johnson, Harmon A. "The Growing Church in Haiti." Coral Gables, Fla.: West Indies Mission, 1970.

Johnson, *History in Philippines*. Johnson, David M. *Led by the Spirit: The History of the American Assemblies of God Missionaries in the Philippines*. Foreword by L. John Bueno. Manila: ICI Ministries, 2009.

Johnson, *Hume*. Johnson, David. *Hume, Holism, and Miracles*. Cornell Studies in the Philosophy of Religion. Ithaca, N.Y.: Cornell University Press, 1999.

Johnson, "Imitate." Johnson, Luke Timothy. "Does the New Testament Imitate Homer? Four Cases from the Acts of the Apostles." *TS* 66 (3, 2005): 489–90.

Johnson, "Jesus against Idols." Johnson, Dennis E. "Jesus against the Idols: The Use of Isaianic Servant Songs in the Missiology of Acts." *WTJ* 52 (2, 1990): 343–53.

Johnson, "Knowledge." Johnson, S. Lewis, Jr. "Paul and the Knowledge of God." *BSac* 129 (513, 1972): 61–74.

Johnson, "Literary Criticism." Johnson, Luke Timothy. "Literary Criticism of Luke-Acts: Is Reception-History Pertinent?" *JSNT* 28 (2, 2005): 159–62.

Johnson, "Luke-Acts." Johnson, Luke Timothy. "Luke-Acts, Book of." *ABD* 4:403–20.

Johnson, *Mind*. Johnson, Bill. *The Supernatural Power of a Transformed Mind: Access to a Life of Miracles*. Shippensburg, Pa.: Destiny Image, 2005.

Johnson, "Neurotheology." Johnson, Ron. "Neurotheology: The Interface of Neuropsychology and Theology." Pages 207–29 in *Psychodynamics*. Vol. 3 of *The Healing Power of Spirituality: How Faith Helps Humans Thrive*. Edited by J. Harold Ellens. Santa Barbara, Calif.: Praeger, 2010.

Johnson, "Paul and Riot." Johnson, Sherman E. "The Apostle Paul and the Riot in Ephesus." *LTQ* 14 (4, 1979): 79–88.

Johnson, "Possession." Johnson, Walter C. "Demon Possession and Mental Illness." *JASA* 34 (3, 1982): 149–54.

Johnson, *Prayer*. Johnson, Norman B. *Prayer in the Apocrypha and Pseudepigrapha*. JBLMS 2. Philadelphia: Society of Biblical Literature and Exegesis, 1948.

Johnson, *Prophetic Jesus*. Johnson, Luke Timothy. *Prophetic Jesus, Prophetic Church: The Challenge of Luke-Acts to Contemporary Christians*. Grand Rapids: Eerdmans, 2011.

Johnson, *Real Jesus*. Johnson, Luke Timothy. *The Real Jesus: The Misguided Quest for the Historical Jesus and the Truth of the Traditional Gospels*. San Francisco: HarperSanFrancisco, 1996.

Johnson, *Revelation*. Johnson, Alan F. *Revelation*. ExpBC. Grand Rapids: Zondervan, 1996.

Johnson, *Romans*. Johnson, Luke Timothy. *Reading Romans: A Literary and Theological Commentary*. Macon, Ga.: Smyth & Helwys, 2001.

Johnson, "Sabaoth/Sabazios." Johnson, Sherman E. "Sabaoth/Sabazios: A Curiosity in Ancient Religion." *LTQ* 13 (4, 1978): 97–103.

Johnson, *Sharing Possessions*. Johnson, Luke Timothy. *Sharing Possessions: Mandate and Symbol of Faith*. Philadelphia: Fortress, 1981.

Johnson, "Slander." Johnson, Luke Timothy. "The New Testament's Anti-Jewish Slander and Conventions of Ancient Rhetoric." *JBL* 108 (3, 1989): 419–41.

Johnson, "Sociology of Reading." Johnson, William A. "Toward a Sociology of Reading in Classical Antiquity." *AJP* 121 (4, 2000): 593–627.

Johnson, "Taciturnity." Johnson, Luke Timothy. "Taciturnity and True Religion: James 1:26–27." Pages 329–39 in *Greeks, Romans, and Christians: Essays in Honor of Abraham J. Malherbe*. Edited by David L. Balch, Everett Ferguson, and Wayne A. Meeks. Minneapolis: Fortress, 1990.

Johnson, *Timothy*. Johnson, Luke Timothy. *1 Timothy, 2 Timothy, Titus*. Know Preaching Guides. Atlanta: John Knox, 1987.

Johnson, "Tongues." Johnson, S. L. "The Gift of Tongues and the Book of Acts." *BSac* 120 (1963): 309–11.

Johnson, *Writings*. Johnson, Luke Timothy. *The Writings of the New Testament: An Interpretation*. Philadelphia: Fortress, 1986.

Johnson and Butzen, "Prayer." Johnson, Judith L., and Nathan D. Butzen. "Intercessory Prayer, Group Psychology, and Medical Healing." Pages 249–61 in *Medical and Therapeutic Events*. Vol. 2 of *Miracles: God, Science, and Psychology in the Paranormal*. Edited by J. Harold Ellens. 3 vols. Westport, Conn.: Praeger, 2008.

Johnson and Ross, *Atlas*. Johnson, Todd M., and Kenneth R. Ross, eds. *Atlas of Global Christianity, 1910–2010*. Edinburgh: Center for the Study of Global Christianity, 2009.

Johnson, Barrett, and Crossing, "Christianity 2010." Johnson, Todd M., David B. Barrett, and Peter F. Crossing. "Christianity 2010: A View from the *New Atlas of Global Christianity*." *IBMR* 34 (1, Jan. 2010): 29–36.

Johnston, "Archegos." Johnston, George. "Christ as Archegos." *NTS* 27 (3, 1981): 381–85.

Johnston, "Commandments." Johnston, Robert Morris. "'The Least of the Commandments': Deuteronomy 22:6–7 in Rabbinic Judaism and Early Christianity." *AUSS* 20 (1982): 205–15.

Johnston, "Dead, Cult of." Johnston, Sarah Iles. "Dead, Cult of the: Greece." *Brill Pauly* 4:113–14.

Johnston, *Ephesians*. Johnston, George. *Ephesians, Philippians, Colossians, and Philemon*. Century Bible. Greenwood, S.C.: Attic, 1967.

Johnston, "Gates." Johnston, Sarah Iles. "Gates, Deities Associated with." *Brill Pauly* 5:705–6.

Johnston, "Interpretations." Johnston, Robert Morris. "Parabolic Interpretations Attributed to Tannaim." PhD diss., Hartford Seminary Foundation, 1977.

Johnston, "Leadership." Johnston, Robert M. "Leadership in the Early Church During Its First Hundred Years." *JATS* 17 (2, Autumn 2006): 2–17.

Johnston, "Spirit." Johnston, George. "'Spirit' and 'Holy Spirit' in the Qumran Literature." Pages 27–42 in *New Testament Sidelights: Essays in Honor of Alexander Converse Purdy*. Edited by Harvey K. McArthur. Hartford: Hartford Seminary Foundation Press, 1960.

Johnston, "Statues." Johnston, Sarah Iles. "Animating Statues: A Case Study in Ritual." *Arethusa* 41 (3, 2008): 445–77.

Johnston, "Underworld." Johnston, Sarah Iles. "Underworld." *Brill Pauly* 15:107–9.

"Jokes." "Jokes." *Brill Pauly* 6:1200–1202.

Jokinen, "Gospels." Jokinen, Mark. "The Four Canonical Gospels Were Never Anonymous." *McMaster Journal of Theology and Ministry* 15 (2012–13): 3–16.

Jonas, *Religion*. Jonas, Hans. *The Gnostic Religion: The Message of the Alien God and the Beginnings of Christianity*. 2nd rev. ed. Boston: Beacon, 1963.

Jones, "Apion." Jones, Kenneth R. "The Figure of Apion in Josephus' *Contra Apionem*." *JSJ* 36 (3, 2005): 278–315.

Jones, "Apollonius' Passage." Jones, C. P. "Apollonius of Tyana's Passage to India." *GRBS* 42 (2, 2001): 185–99.

Jones, "Army." Jones, James L. "The Roman Army." Pages 187–217 in *The Catacombs and the Colosseum: The Roman Empire as the Setting of Primitive Christianity*. Edited by Stephen Benko and John J. O'Rourke. Valley Forge, Pa.: Judson, 1971.

Jones, *Bankers*. Jones, David. *The Bankers of Puteoli: Finance, Trade, and Industry in the Roman World*. Stroud: Tempus, 2006.

Jones, "*Christos* in Luke-Acts." Jones, Donald L. "The Title *Christos* in Luke-Acts." *CBQ* 32 (1970): 69–76.

Jones, *Chrysostom*. Jones, C. P. *The Roman World of Dio Chrysostom*. Cambridge, Mass.: Harvard University Press, 1978.

Jones, *Cities of Provinces*. Jones, A. H. M. *The Cities of the Eastern Roman Provinces*. Oxford: Clarendon, 1937.

Jones, "Claudius and Question." Jones, H. Stuart. "Claudius and the Jewish Question at Alexandria." *JRS* 16 (1926): 27–28.

Jones, "Cocktail." Jones, Prudence J. "Cleopatra's Cocktail." *CW* 103 (2, 2010): 207–20.

Jones, "Cremation." Jones, David W. "To Bury or Burn? Toward an Ethic of Cremation." *JETS* 53 (2, June 2010): 335–47.

Jones, "Dinner Theater." Jones, C. P. "Dinner Theater." Pages 185–98 in *Dining in a Classical Context*. Edited by William J. Slater. Ann Arbor: University of Michigan Press, 1991.

Jones, *Empire*. Jones, A. M. H. *The Empire*. Vol. 2 of *A History of Rome through the Fifth Century*. New York: Walker, Macmillan, 1970.

Jones, "Epigram." Jones, C. P. "An Epigram on Apollonius of Tyana." *JHS* 100 (1980): 190–94.

Jones, "Fire." Jones, Arun. "Playing with Fire." Pages 209–24 in *A New Day: Essays on World Christianity in Honor of Lamin Sanneh*. Edited by Akintunde E. Akinade. Foreword by Andrew F. Walls. New York: Peter Lang, 2010.

Jones, "Holds Power." Jones, Christine. "Who Holds the Power? Acts 25.23–26." Pages 165–69 in *Acts in Practice*. Edited by John Vincent. Practice Interpretation 2. Blandford Forum, Dorset UK: Deo Publishing, 2012.

Jones, "Last Apostle." Jones, Paul R. "1 Corinthians 15:8: Paul the Last Apostle." *TynBul* 36 (1985): 3–34.

Jones, "Meaning." Jones, Brice C. "The Meaning of the Phrase 'And the Witnesses Laid Down Their Cloaks' in Acts 7:58." *ExpT* 123 (3, 2011): 113–18.

Jones, "Names." Jones, Meriel. "Heavenly and Pandemic Names in Heliodorus' *Aethiopica*." *CQ* 56 (2, 2006): 548–62.

Jones, *Parables*. Jones, Ivor H. *The Matthean Parables: A Literary and Historical Commentary*. NovTSup 80. Leiden: Brill, 1995.

Jones, "Parmenides." Jones, Barrington. "Parmenides' 'The Way of Truth.'" *JHistPhil* 11 (1973): 287–98.

Jones, "Passage." Jones, C. P. "Apollonius of Tyana's Passage to India." *GRBS* 42 (2, 2001): 185–99.

Jones, "Petra Inscription." Jones, Richard N. "A New Reading of the Petra Temple Inscription." *BASOR* 275 (Aug. 1989): 41–46.

Jones, "Polybius of Sardis." Jones, C. P. "Polybius of Sardis." *CP* 91 (3, 1996): 247–53.

Jones, "Rejoinder." Jones, F. Stanley. "An Ancient Jewish Christian Rejoinder to Luke's Acts of the Apostles: Pseudo-Clementine *Recognitions* 1.27–71." *Semeia* 80 (1997): 223–45.

Jones, *Roman Government*. Jones, A. H. M. *Studies in Roman Government and Law*. Oxford: Blackwell, 1960.

Jones, "Rumors." Jones, Timothy. "Rumors of Angels?" *CT* (Apr. 5, 1993): 18–22.

Jones, "'Servant' in Luke-Acts." Jones, Donald L. "The Title 'Servant' in Luke-Acts." Pages 148–65 in *Luke-Acts: New Perspectives from the Society of Biblical Literature Seminar*. Edited by Charles H. Talbert. New York: Crossroad, 1984.

Jones, *Stigma*. Jones, C. P. "*Stigma*: Tattooing and Branding in Graeco-Roman Antiquity." *JRS* 77 1987): 139–55.

Jones, *Wonders*. Jones, Philip Hanson. *Wonders, Signs, Miracles . . . Why Not? Tales of a Missionary in China*. New York: Exposition Press, 1966.

Jones and Jones, *Women*. Jones, Violet Rhoda, and L. Bevan Jones. *Women in Islam*. Lucknow, India: Lucknow, 1941.

Jones and Mitchell, "Lycaonia." Jones, A. H. M., and Stephen Mitchell. "Lycaonia." *OCD*³ 894.

Jones and Mitchell, "Tarsus." Jones, A. H. M., and Stephen Mitchell. "Tarsus." *OCD*³ 1476.

Jones and Rhodes, "*Epistatēs*." Jones, A. H. M., and P. J. Rhodes. "*Epistatēs*." *OCD*³ 547.

Jones and Rhodes, "Liturgy." Jones, A. H. M., and P. J. Rhodes. "Liturgy: Greek." *OCD*³ 875.

Jones and Salles, "Sidon." Jones, A. H. M., and Jean-François Salles. "Sidon." *OCD*³ 1404.

Jones and Spawforth, "Liturgy." Jones, A. H. M., and Antony J. S. Spawforth. "Liturgy: Roman and Greco-Roman Egyptian." *OCD*³ 875–76.

Jones, Kuhrt, and Spawforth, "Damascus." Jones, A. H. M., Amélie Kuhrt, and Antony J. S. Spawforth. "Damascus." *OCD*³ 427.

Jones, Seyrig, and Salles, "Tyre." Jones, A. H. M., Henri Seyrig, and Jean-François Salles. "Tyre." *OCD*³ 1568.

Jones, Seyrig, and Sherwin-White, "Seleucia." Jones, A. H. M., Henri Seyrig, and Susan Mary Sherwin-White. "Seleucia (2) in Pieria." *OCD*³ 1380.

Jones, Seyrig, Liebeschuetz, and Sherwin-White, "Antioch." Jones, A. H. M., Henri Seyrig, W. Liebeschuetz, and Susan Mary Sherwin-White. "Antioch (1)." *OCD*³ 107.

Jones, Seyrig, Sherwin-White, and Liebeschuetz, "Syria." Jones, A. H. M., Henri Seyrig, Susan Mary Sherwin-White, and W. Liebeschuetz. "Syria." *OCD*³ 1464–65.

Jong, *Rasputin*. Jong, Alex de. *The Life and Times of Grigorii Rasputin*. London: Collins, 1982.

Jonge, "Anointed." Jonge, Marinus de. "The Use of the Word 'Anointed' in the Time of Jesus." *NovT* 8 (2–4, 1966): 132–48.

Jonge, "Behavior." Jonge, Marinus de. "Rachel's Virtuous Behavior in the *Testament of Issachar*." Pages 340–52 in *Greeks, Romans, and Christians: Essays in Honor of Abraham J. Malherbe*. Edited by David L. Balch, Everett Ferguson, and Wayne A. Meeks. Minneapolis: Fortress, 1990.

Jonge, "Chronology." Jonge, Henk Jan de. "The Chronology of the Ascension Stories in Luke and Acts." *NTS* 59 (2, 2013): 151–71.

Jonge, *Jesus*. Jonge, Marinus de. *Jesus: Stranger from Heaven and Son of God*. Edited and translated by John E. Steely. Missoula, Mont.: Scholars Press, 1977.

Jonge, "New Testament." Jonge, Marinus de. "The New Testament." *JPFC* 37–43.

Jonge and van der Woude, "11QMelchizedek." Jonge, Marinus de, and A. S. van der Woude. "11QMelchizedek and the New Testament." *NTS* 12 (4, 1966), 301–26.

Jongkind, "Another Class." Jongkind, Dirk. "Corinth in the First Century AD: The Search for Another Class." *TynBul* 52 (1, 2001): 139–48.

Jonquière, *Prayer in Josephus*. Jonquière, Tessel M. *Prayer in Josephus*. AJEC 70. Leiden: Brill, 2007.

Jordan, *Burden*. Jordan, Winthrop D. *The White Man's Burden: Historical Origins of Racism in the United States*. New York: Oxford University Press, 1974.

Jordan, *Egypt*. Jordan, Paul. *Egypt the Black Land*. Oxford: Phaidon; New York: E. P. Dutton, 1976.

Jordan, "Erotic Spell." Jordan, David R. "P.Duk.inv. 230, an Erotic Spell." *GRBS* 40 (2, 1999): 159–70.

Jordan, "Formulae." Jordan, David R. "P.Duk. inv. 729, Magical Formulae." *GRBS* 46 (2, 2006): 159–73.

Jordan, "New Curse Tablets." Jordan, David R. "New Greek Curse Tablets (1985–2000)." *GRBS* 41 (1, 2000): 5–46.

Jørgensen, "ACTA 15:22–29." Jørgensen, T. "ACTA 15:22–29: Historiske og eksegetiske problemer." *NTT* 90 (1, 1989): 31–45.

Joseph, "Remapping." Joseph, Palolil V. "Remapping Mission: A North Indian Mission Paradigm." Pages 1–21 in *Remapping Mission Discourse: A Festschrift in Honor of the Rev. George Kuruvila Chavanikamannil*. Edited by Simon Samuel and P. V. Joseph. Dehradun, India: New Theological College Press; Delhi: ISPCK, 2008.

Joshel, "Nurturing." Joshel, Sandra R. "Nurturing the Master's Child: Slavery and the Roman Child-Nurse." *Signs* 12 (1, 1986): 3–22.

Jost, "Hermes." Jost, Madeleine. "Hermes." *OCD*³ 690–91.

Joubert, "Dionisius." Joubert, S. J. "Dionisius van Halikarnassus en die oorsprong van weldoenerskap." *SK* 21 (3, 2000): 583–91.

Joubert, "Exchange." Joubert, Stephan J. "One Form of Social Exchange or Two? 'Euergetism,' Patronage, and New Testament Studies." *BTB* 31 (1, 2001): 17–25.

Joubert, "Gesigpunt." Joubert, S. J. "Die gesigpunt van die verteller en die funksie van die Jerusalemgemeente binne die 'opsommings' in Handelinge." *SK* 10 (1, 1989): 21–35.

Joubert, "*Patronus*." Joubert, Stephan J. "*Patronus* as dominante sosiale sisteem in die Romeinse wêreld gedurende die Nuwe-Testamentiese era." *SK* 21 (1, 2000): 66–78.

Joubert, "Shifting Styles." Joubert, Stephan J. "Shifting Styles of Church Leadership: Paul's Pragmatic Leadership Style in 1 and 2 Corinthians during the Organization of the Collection for Jerusalem." *VerbEc* 23 (3, 2002): 678–88.

Joukowsky, "Petra Great Temple." Joukowsky, Martha S. "The Petra Great Temple: A Nabataean Architectural Miracle." *NEA* 65 (4, 2002): 235–48.

Joy, "Transitions." Joy, C. I. D. "Transitions and Trajectories in the Early Christian Community in the Context of Pluralism and Mission in Acts: A Postcolonial Reading." *BiBh* 32 (4, 2006): 326–41.

Ju, "Immortality." Ju, A. E. "Stoic and Posidonian Thought on the Immortality of the Soul." *CQ* 59 (1, 2009): 112–24.

Judge, "Ancient Beginnings." Judge, Edwin A. "Ancient Beginnings of the Modern World." Pages 468–82 in vol. 2 of *Ancient History in a Modern University*. Edited by T. W. Hillard et al. 2 vols. Grand Rapids: Eerdmans, 1998.

Judge, *Athens*. Judge, Edwin A. *Jerusalem and Athens: Cultural Transformation in Late Antiquity*. Edited by Alanna Nobbs. Tübingen: Mohr Siebeck, 2010.

Judge, "Boasting." Judge, Edwin A. "Paul's Boasting in Relation to Contemporary Professional Practice." *ABR* 16 (1968): 37–50.

Judge, "Cilicia." Judge, Edwin A. "Cilicia." *ISBE* 1:698–99.

Judge, "Decrees." Judge, Edwin A. "The Decrees of Caesar at Thessalonica." *RTR* 30 (1, 1971): 1–7.

Judge, *First Christians*. Judge, Edwin A. *The First Christians in the Roman World: Augustan and New Testament Essays*. Edited by James R. Harrison. WUNT 229. Tübingen: Mohr Siebeck, 2008.

Judge, "Judaism and Rise." Judge, Edwin A. "Judaism and the Rise of Christianity: A Roman Perspective." *TynBul* 45 (2, 1994): 355–68.

Judge, "Magical Use." Judge, Edwin A. "The Magical Use of Scripture in the Papyri." Pages 198–208 in *Jerusalem and Athens: Cultural Transformation in Late Antiquity*, by Edwin A. Judge. Edited by Alanna Nobbs. Tübingen: Mohr Siebeck, 2010. First published as "The Magical Use of Scripture in the Papyri." Pages 339–49 in *Perspectives on Language and Text: Essays and Poems in Honor of Francis I. Anderson's Sixtieth Birthday, July 28, 1985*. Edited by Edgar W. Conrad and Edward G. Newing. Winona Lake, Ind.: Eisenbrauns, 1987.

Judge, *Pattern*. Judge, Edwin A. *The Social Pattern of the Christian Groups in the First Century: Some Prolegomena to the Study of New Testament Ideas of Social Obligation*. London: Tyndale, 1960.

Judge, "Paul and Socrates." Judge, Edwin A. "St Paul and Socrates." Pages 670–83 in *The First Christians in the Roman World: Augustan and New Testament Essays*. Edited by James R. Harrison. WUNT 229. Tübingen: Mohr Siebeck, 2008. First published as "St Paul and Socrates," *Interchange* 14 (1973): 106–16.

Judge, "Perga." Judge, Edwin A. "Perga." *ISBE* 3:767–68.

Judge, *Rank*. Judge, Edwin A. *Rank and Status in the World of the Caesars and St Paul*. Broadhead Memorial Lecture, 1981. University of Canterbury Publications 29. [Christchurch, N.Z.]: University of Canterbury Press, 1982.

Judge, "Rhetoric of Inscriptions." Judge, Edwin A. "The Rhetoric of Inscriptions." Pages 807–28 in *Handbook of Classical Rhetoric in the Hellenistic Period, 330 B.C.–A.D. 400*. Edited by Stanley E. Porter. Leiden: Brill, 1997.

Judge, "Roman Base." Judge, Edwin A. "The Roman Base of Paul's Mission." *TynBul* 56 (1, 2005): 103–17.

Judge, "Scholastic Community." Judge, Edwin A. "The Early Christians as a Scholastic Community." *JRH* 1 (1, 1960): 4–15; (3): 125–37. Reprinted in Judge, *First Christians*, 526–52.

Judge, "Sources." Judge, Edwin A. "Biblical Sources of Historical Method." Pages 276–81 in *Jerusalem and Athens: Cultural Transformation in Late Antiquity*. Edited by Alanna Nobbs. Tübingen: Mohr Siebeck, 2010.

Judge, "Toleration." Judge, Edwin A. "Synagogue and Church in the Roman Empire. The Insoluble Problem of Toleration." *RTR* 68 (1, 2009): 29–45.

Judge and Thomas, "Origin." Judge, Edwin A., and G. S. R. Thomas. "The Origin of the Church at Rome: A New Solution?" *RTR* 25 (3, 1966): 81–94.

Juel, *Messianic Exegesis*. Juel, Donald. *Messianic Exegesis: Christological Interpretation of the Old Testament in Early Christianity*. Philadelphia: Fortress, 1988.

Juel, *Promise*. Juel, Donald. *Luke-Acts: The Promise of History*. Atlanta: John Knox, 1983.

Juel, "Use of Psalm 16." Juel, Donald. "Social Dimensions of Exegesis: The Use of Psalm 16 in Acts 2." *CBQ* 43 (1981): 543–56.

Jules-Rosette, "Healers." Jules-Rosette, Bennetta. "Faith Healers and Folk Healers: The Symbolism and Practice of Indigenous Therapy in Urban Africa." *Religion* 11 (1981): 127–49.

Jules-Rosette, "Spirituality." Jules-Rosette, Bennetta. "Creative Spirituality from Africa to America: Cross-cultural Influences in Contemporary Religious Forms." *WJBlSt* 4 (4, 1980): 273–85.

Juncker, "Christ as Angel." Juncker, Gunther. "Christ as Angel: The Reclamation of a Primitive Title." *TJ* 15 (2, 1994): 221–50.

Jung, *Language*. Jung, Chang-Wook. *The Original Language of the Lukan Infancy Narrative*. JSNTSup 267. London: T&T Clark, 2004.

Jung, *Symbolic Life*. Jung, Carl G. *The Symbolic Life*. Vol. 18 of *The Collected Works of C. G. Jung*. 20 vols. Princeton, N.J.: Princeton University Press, 1977.

Junk, "Peirene." Junk, Tim. "Peirene. I. Mythology." *BrillPauly* 10:680.

Junk, "Python." Junk, Tim. "Python." *Brill Pauly* 12:298.

Just, *Luke*. Just, Arthur A., Jr., ed. *Luke*. ACCS: New Testament 3. Downers Grove, Ill.: InterVarsity, 2003.

Kadetotad, "Practices." Kadetotad, N. K. "Religious Practices of a Mysore Village." Pages 379–87 in *The Realm of the Extra-human: Ideas and Actions*. Edited by Agehananda Bharati. The Hague and Paris: Mouton, 1976. Distributed by Aldine, Chicago.

Kadushin, *Mind*. Kadushin, Max. *The Rabbinic Mind*. 3rd ed. New York: Bloch, 1972.

Kaenel, "Minting." Kaenel, Hans-Markus von. "Minting." *BrillPauly* 9:28–32.

Kaeppler, "Rank." Kaeppler, Adrienne L. "Rank in Tonga." *Ethnology* 10 (2, 1971): 174–93.

Kaesser, "Tweaking." Kaesser, Christian. "Tweaking the Real: Art Theory and the Borderline between History and Morality in Plutarch's *Lives*." *GRBS* 44 (4, 2004): 361–74.

Kahana, "Zar Spirits." Kahana, Yael. "The Zar Spirits, a Category of Magic in the System of Mental Health Care in Ethiopia." *IJSocPsyc* 31 (Summer 1985): 125–43.

Kahl, *Galatians Re-Imagined*. Kahl, Brigitte. *Galatians Re-Imagined: Reading with the Eyes of the Vanquished*. Paul in Critical Contexts. Minneapolis: Fortress, 2010.

Kahle, "Karaites." Kahle, P. "The Karaites and the Manuscripts from the Cave." *VT* 3 (1953): 82–84.

Kahn, "Anaximander." Kahn, Charles H. "Anaximander." *OCD³* 86.

Kahn, "Anaximenes." Kahn, Charles H. "Anaximenes." *OCD³* 86.

Kahn, "Herodian Innovation." Kahn, Lisa C. "Herodian Innovation: The Glass Industry." *NEA* 77 (2, June 2014): 129–39.

Kahn, "Thales." Kahn, Charles H. "Thales." *OCD³* 1491.

Kahn, "Xenophanes." Kahn, Charles H. "Xenophanes." *OCD³* 1628.

Kaiser, "Baptism." Kaiser, Walter C., Jr. "The Baptism in the Holy Spirit as the Promise of the Father: A Reformed Perspective." Pages 15–37 in *Perspectives on Spirit Baptism: Five Views*. Edited by Chad Owen Brand. Nashville: Broadman & Holman, 2004.

Kaiser, "Centre." Kaiser, Walter C., Jr. "The Centre of Old Testament Theology: The Promise." *Them* 10 (1974): 1–10.

Kaiser, "Inclusion of Gentiles." Kaiser, Walter C., Jr. "The Davidic Promise and the Inclusion of the Gentiles (Amos 9:91–5 and Acts 15:13–18): A Test Passage for Theological Systems." *JETS* 20 (2, 1977): 97–111.

Kaiser, "Matters." Kaiser, Walter C., Jr. "The Weightier and Lighter Matters of the Law: Moses, Jesus, and Paul." Pages 176–92 in *Current Issues in Biblical and Patristic Interpretation: Studies in Honor of Merrill C. Tenney Presented by His Former Students*. Edited by Gerald F. Hawthorne. Grand Rapids: Eerdmans, 1975.

Kaiser, "Pantheon." Kaiser, Walter C., Jr. "The Ugaritic Pantheon." PhD diss., Brandeis University, 1973.

Kaiser, "Promise in Psalm 16." Kaiser, Walter C., Jr. "The Promise to David in Psalm 16 and Its Application in Acts 2:25–33 and 13:32–37." *JETS* 23 (3, 1980): 219–29.

Kaiser, "Rezeption." Kaiser, Otto. "Die Rezeption der stoischen Providenz bei Ben Sira." *JNSL* 24 (1, 1998): 41–54.

Kaiser, *Theology*. Kaiser, Walter C., Jr. *Toward an Old Testament Theology*. Grand Rapids: Zondervan, 1978.

Kákosy, "Egypt." Kákosy, László. "Egypt in Ancient Greek and Roman Thought." Pages 3–14 in vol. 1 of *Civilizations of the Ancient Near East*. Edited by Jack M. Sasson. 4 vols. New York: Scribner's, 1995.

Kalcyk, "Delos." Kalcyk, Hansjörg. "Delos." *BrillPauly* 4:210–15.

Kalcyk and Niemeyer, "Melite." Kalcyk, Hansjörg, and Hans Georg Niemeyer. "Melite (7)." *BrillPauly* 8:638.

Kaler, "Letter." Kaler, Michael. "The Letter of Peter to Philip and Its Message of Gnostic Revelation and Christian Unity." *VC* 63 (3, 2009): 264–95.

Kaletsch, "Aphrodisias." Kaletsch, Hans. "Aphrodisias (1)." *BrillPauly* 1:828–29.

Kaletsch, "Lydia." Kaletsch, Hans. "Lydia." *BrillPauly* 8:2–11.

Kalimi, "Born Circumcised." Kalimi, Isaac. "'He Was Born Circumcised': Some Midrashic Sources, Their Concept, Roots, and Presumably Historical Context." *ZNW* 93 (1–2, 2002): 1–12.

Kalimi, "Episoden." Kalimi, Isaac. "Episoden aus dem Neuen Testament und ihr Ursprung in der Hebräischen Bibel/dem Alten Testament." *SNTSU* 36 (2011): 93–110.

Kalimi, "Esther." Kalimi, Isaac. "The Book of Esther and the Dead Sea Scrolls' Community." *TZ* 60 (2, 2004): 101–6.

Kalimi, "Geboren." Kalimi, Isaac. "Geboren als ein Beschnittener: Eine Betrachtung zum Konzept der Vollkommenheit im historischen Kontext einiger jüdischer Quellen." *BN* 123 (2004): 75–91.

Kalimi, "Josef." Kalimi, Isaac. ". . . Und Josef verleumdete seine Brüder: Josefs Verrat in den Midraschim als Beitrag zur zeitgenössischen jüdisch-christlichen Kontroverse." *ZRGG* 54 (1, 2002): 23–31.

Kalimi, "Murders." Kalimi, Isaac. "The Murders of the Messengers: Stephen versus Zechariah and the Ethical Values of 'New' versus 'Old' Testament." *ABR* 56 (2008): 69–73.

Kalimi and Purvis, "Hiding." Kalimi, Isaac, and James D. Purvis. "The Hiding of the Temple Vessels in Jewish and Samaritan Literature." *CBQ* 56 (4, 1994): 679–85.

Kallas, *View*. Kallas, James. *The Satanward View: A Study in Pauline Theology*. Philadelphia: Westminster, 1966.

Kalu, *African Pentecostalism*. Kalu, Ogbu. *African Pentecostalism: An Introduction*. Oxford: Oxford University Press, 2008.

Kalu, "Lijadu." Kalu, Ogbu U. "Lijadu, Emmanuel Moses." No pages. *DACB*. Online: http://www.dacb.org/stories/nigeria/lijadu2_emmanuel.html.

Kamesar, "Endiathetos." Kamesar, Adam. "The *logos endiathetos* and the *logos prophorikos* in Allegorical Interpretation: Philo and the D-Scholia to the *Iliad*." *GRBS* 44 (2, 2004): 163–81.

Kampen, "Cult." Kampen, John. "The Cult of Artemis and the Essenes in Syro-Palestine." *DSD* 10 (2, 2003): 205–20.

Kampling, "Freude." Kampling, Rainer. "Freude bei Paulus." *TTZ* 101 (1, 1992): 69–79.

Kamsler, "Philo." Kamsler, Harold M. "Philo Judaeus: Linking Biblical Judaism and Hellenistic Beliefs." *JBQ* 26 (2, 1998): 111–15.

Kamtekar, "ΑΙΔΩΣ." Kamtekar, Rachana. "ΑΙΔΩΣ in Epictetus." *CP* 93 (2, 1998): 136–60.

Kanavou, "Names." Kanavou, Nikoletta. "Personal Names in the *Vita Aesopi* (*Vita G or Perriana*)." *CQ* 56 (1, 2006): 208–19.

Kanda, "Form." Kanda, Shigeo Harold. "The Form and Function of the Petrine and Pauline Miracle Stories in the Acts of the Apostles." PhD diss., Claremont Graduate School, 1973.

Kane, "Cult Meal." Kane, J. P. "The Mithraic Cult Meal in Its Greek and Roman Environment." Pages 313–51 in vol. 2 of *Mithraic Studies: Proceedings of the First International Congress of Mithraic Studies*. Edited by John R. Hinnells. 2 vols. Manchester, U.K.: Manchester University Press, 1975.

Kanellopoulos, "Plan." Kanellopoulos, Chrysanthos. "A New Plan of Petra's City Center." *NEA* 65 (4, 2002): 251–54.

Kant, "Inscriptions." Kant, Laurence H. "Jewish Inscriptions in Greek and Latin." *ANRW* 20.2:671–713. Part 2, *Principat*, 20.2. Edited by H. Temporini and W. Haase. Berlin: de Gruyter, 1987.

Kantowicz, *Rage of Nations*. Kantowicz, Edward R. *The Rage of Nations*. World in the Twentieth Century 1. Grand Rapids: Eerdmans, 1999.

Kantzios, "Pan." Kantzios, Ippokratis. "'Old' Pan and 'New' Pan in Menander's *Dyskolos*." *CJ* 106 (1, 2010): 23–42.

Kany, "Bericht." Kany, R. "Der lukanische Bericht von Tod und Auferstehung Jesu aus der Sicht eines hellenistichen Romanlesers." *NovT* 28 (1, 1986): 75–90.

Kany, "Warum." Kany, Roland. "Warum fand die Apostelgeschichte keine Fortsetzung in der Antike? Elf Thesen zu einem ungelösten Problem." Pages 327–48 in *Die Apostelgeschichte im Kontext antiker und frühchristlicher Historiographie*. Edited by Jörg Frey, Clare K. Rothschild, and Jens Schröter, with Bettina Rost. BZNWK 162. Berlin: de Gruyter, 2009.

Kanyoro, "Mission." Kanyoro, Musimbi. "Thinking Mission in Africa." Pages 61–70 in *The Feminist Companion to the Acts of the Apostles*. Edited by Amy-Jill Levine with Marianne Blickenstaff. Cleveland: Pilgrim; Edinburgh: T&T Clark, 2004.

Kapera, "Administration." Kapera, Zdzislaw J. "The Roman Administration of Cyprus in the Time of Paul's Visit (Concerning Acts 13,4–12)." *PJBR* 8 (1, 2009): 17–30.

Kapfer, "Attitudes." Kapfer, Hilary Evans. "The Relationship between the Damascus Document and the Community Rule: Attitudes toward the Temple as a Test Case." *DSD* 14 (2, 2007): 152–77.

Kapferer, *Exorcism*. Kapferer, Bruce. *A Celebration of Demons: Exorcism and the Aesthetics of Healing in Sri Lanka*. 2nd ed. Oxford: Berg, 1991.

Kapic and Vander Lugt, "Ascension." Kapic, Kelly M., and Wesley Vander Lugt. "The Ascension of Jesus and the Descent of the Holy Spirit in Patristic Perspective: A Theological Reading." *EvQ* 79 (1, 2007): 23–33.

Kaplan and Johnson, "Navajo Psychopathology." Kaplan, Bert, and Dale Johnson. "The Social Meaning of Navajo Psychopathology and Psychotherapy." Pages 203–29 in *Magic, Faith, and Healing: Studies in Primitive Psychiatry Today*. Edited by Ari Kiev. Foreword by Jerome D. Frank. New York: Free Press, 1964.

Kaplan and Sadock, *Psychiatry*. Kaplan, Harold I., and Benjamin J. Sadock. *Comprehensive Textbook of Psychiatry*. 4th ed. Baltimore: Williams & Wilkins, 1985.

Kapolyo, *Condition*. Kapolyo, Joe M. *The Human Condition: Christian Perspectives through African Eyes*. Downers Grove, Ill.: InterVarsity, 2005.

Käppel, "Manto." Käppel, Lutz. "Manto." *BrillPauly* 8:261.

Käppel, "Monsters." Käppel, Lutz. "Monsters: Classical Antiquity." *BrillPauly* 9:183–84.

Käppel, "Notos." Käppel, Lutz. "Notos: Myth." *BrillPauly* 9:831.

Käppel, "Nymphs." Käppel, Lutz. "Nymphs." *BrillPauly* 9:928.

Käppel, "Phoenix." Käppel, Lutz. "Phoenix [5]." *BrillPauly* 11:171–72.

Käppel, "Themis." Käppel, Lutz. "Themis." *BrillPauly* 14:424–25.

Käppel, "Underworld." Käppel, Lutz. "Underworld." *BrillPauly* 15:109–10.

Karakolis, "Schlugen." Karakolis, C. "'Alle schlugen Sosthenes, Gallio aber kümmerte sich nicht darum' (Apg 18,17). Zur Bedeutung eines narrativen Details." *ZNW* 99 (2, 2008): 233–46.

Karanika, "Songs." Karanika, Andromache. "Inside Orpheus' Songs: Orpheus as an Argonaut in Apollonius Rhodius' *Argonautica*." *GRBS* 50 (3, 2010): 391–419.

Kariamadam, "Council." Kariamadam, Paul. "The Jerusalem Council (Acts 15:1–35)—An Indian Re-reading." *Jeev* 34 (200, 2004): 162–73.

Karmon and Spanier, "Remains." Karmon, Nira, and Ehud Spanier. "Remains of a Purple Dye Industry Found at Tel Shiqmona." *IEJ* 38 (1988): 184–86 and plates 27 B, C, D.

Karris, *Invitation*. Karris, Robert J. *Invitation to Acts: A Commentary on the Acts of the Apostles with Complete Text from the Jerusalem Bible*. Garden City, N.Y.: Image Books, Doubleday, 1978.

Karris, "Poor." Karris, Robert J. "Poor and Rich: The Lukan *Sitz im Leben*." Pages 112–25 in *Perspectives on Luke-Acts*. ABPRSSS 5. Edited by Charles H. Talbert. Danville, Va.: Association of Baptist Professors of Religion; Edinburgh: T&T Clark, 1978.

Karris, *Saying*. Karris, Robert J. *What Are They Saying about Luke and Acts? A Theology of the Faithful God*. New York: Paulist, 1979.

Karttunen, "India." Karttunen, Klaus. "India." *BrillPauly* 6:769–73.

Karttunen, "Taprobane." Karttunen, Klaus. "Taprobane." *BrillPauly* 14:136–37.

Käsemann, *Romans*. Käsemann, Ernst. *Commentary on Romans*. Edited and translated by Geoffrey W. Bromiley. Grand Rapids: Eerdmans, 1980.

Käsemann, *Testament*. Käsemann, Ernst. *The Testament of Jesus*. Translated by Gerhard Krodel. Philadelphia: Fortress, 1978.

Kasher, "M'srt." Kasher, A. "M'srt hprwst'ts bqhylwt ysr'l btpwsh hhlnyst't-hrwmyt." *Zion* 47 (4, 1982): 399–406.

Kashtan, "Akko-Ptolemais." Kashtan, Nadav. "Akko-Ptolemais: A Maritime Metropolis in Hellenistic and Early Roman Times, 332 BCE–70 CE, as Seen through the Literary Sources." *MHR* 3 (1, 1988): 37–53.

Kassimir, "Politics." Kassimir, Ronald. "The Politics of Popular Catholicism in Uganda." Pages 248–74 in *East African Expressions of Christianity*. Edited by Thomas Spear and Isaria N. Kimambo. EAfSt. Athens, Ohio: Ohio University Press; Oxford: James Currey; Dar es Salaam: Mkuki na Nyota; Nairobi: East African Educational Publishers, 1999.

Kaster, "*Grammaticus*." Kaster, Robert A. "*Grammaticus*." *OCD*³ 646.

Kaster, "Scholarship." Kaster, Robert A. "Scholarship, Ancient: Latin." *OCD*³ 1364–65.

Kaster, "Shame." Kaster, Robert A. "The Shame of the Romans." *TAPA* 127 (1997): 1–19.

Katterjohn and Fackler, *People*. Katterjohn, Arthur D., with Mark Fackler. *The Tribulation People*. Carol Stream, Ill.: Creation House, 1976.

Katz, "Healing." Katz, Richard. "Healing and Transformation: Perspectives from !Kung Hunter-Gatherers." Pages 207–27 in *Altered States of Consciousness and Mental Health: A Cross-Cultural Perspective*. Edited by Colleen A. Ward. CCRMS 12. Newbury Park, Calif.: Sage, 1989.

Katz, "Issues." Katz, Stephen T. "Issues in the Separation of Judaism and Christianity after 70 C.E.: A Reconsideration." *JBL* 103 (1, 1984): 43–76.

Katzenstein, "Tyre." Katzenstein, H. J. "Tyre." *ABD* 6:686–92.

Katzin, "Testing." Katzin, David. "'The Time of Testing': The Use of Hebrew Scriptures in 4Q171's Pesher of Psalm 37." *HS* 45 (2004): 121–62.

Katzoff, "Edicts and Ta'anit." Katzoff, Ranon. "Roman Edicts and Ta'anit 29A." *CP* 88 (2, 1993): 141–44.

Katzoff, "Purchase." Katzoff, Louis. "Purchase of the Machpelah." *Dor le Dor* 16 (1987–88): 29–31.

Katzoff, "*Suffragium*." Katzoff, Ranon. "*Suffragium* in Exodus Rabbah 37.2." *CP* 81 (3, 1986): 235–40.

Kauffman, "Introduction." Kauffman, Richard A. "Introduction." Pages 6–9 in *Essays on Spiritual Bondage and Deliverance*. Edited by Willard M. Swartley. Occasional Papers 11. Elkhart, Ind.: Institute of Mennonite Studies, 1988.

Kaufman, "Eastern Wall." Kaufman, Asher S. "The Eastern Wall of the Second Temple at Jerusalem Revealed." *BA* 44 (1981): 108–15.

Kaufman, "Temple." Kaufman, Asher S. "Where the Ancient Temple of Jerusalem Stood." *BAR* 9 (2, 1983): 42–59.

Kaufmann, "Idea." Kaufmann, Yehezkel. "The Messianic Idea: The Real and the

Hidden Son-of-David." *JBQ* 22 (3, 1994): 141–50.

Kaufmann, "Underworld." Kaufmann, Helen. "Virgil's Underworld in the Mind of Roman Late Antiquity." *Latomus* 69 (1, 2010): 150–60.

Kaufmann-Heinimann, "Religion." Kaufmann-Heinimann, Annemarie. "Religion in the House." Pages 188–201 in *A Companion to Roman Religion*. Edited by Jörg Rüpke. BCompAW. Oxford: Blackwell, 2011.

Kaunfer and Kaunfer, "Time and Torah." Kaunfer, Alvan, and Elie Kaunfer. "Time and Torah: A Curious Concept Revisited." *ConsJud* 54 (4, 2002): 15–32.

Kauppi, *Gods*. Kauppi, Lynn Allan. *Foreign but Familiar Gods: Greco-Romans Read Religion in Acts*. LNTS 277. London: T&T Clark, 2006.

Kavanagh, "Identity." Kavanagh, Bernard J. "The Identity and Fate of Caligula's Assassin, Aquila." *Latomus* 69 (4, 2010): 1007–17.

Kay, "Glossolalia." Kay, William K. "The Mind, Behaviour, and Glossolalia: A Psychological Perspective." Pages 174–205 in *Speaking in Tongues: Multi-disciplinary Perspectives*. Edited by Mark J. Cartledge. SPCI. Waynesboro, Ga., and Bletchley, Milton Keynes, U.K.: Paternoster, 2006.

Kayama, "Israel." Kayama, Hisao. "Luke's Understanding of Israel: A Sequential Reading of Luke-Acts." *AJBI* 25–26 (2000): 21–48.

Kaye, *Apology*. Kaye, John, *The First Apology of Justin Martyr*. Edinburgh: John Grant, 1912.

Kaye, "Portrait of Silas." Kaye, B. N. "Acts' Portrait of Silas." *NovT* 21 (1, 1979): 13–26.

Kazen, "Son of Man." Kazen, Thomas. "Son of Man as Kingdom Imagery: Jesus between Corporate Symbol and Individual Redeemer Figure." Pages 87–108 in *Jesus from Judaism to Christianity: Continuum Approaches to the Historical Jesus*. Edited by Tom Holmén. EurSCO. LNTS 352. London: T&T Clark, 2007.

Kea, "Septuagint." Kea, Perry V. "The Septuagint as a Source for Acts 6:8–8:1." *Forum* 5 (1, 2002): 95–104.

Kea, "Source Theories." Kea, Perry. "Source Theories for the Acts of the Apostles." *Forum* 4 (1, 2001): 7–26.

Keane, "Cave-Women." Keane, Catherine C. "Juvenal's Cave-Woman and the Programmatics of Satire." *CBull* 78 (1, 2002): 5–20.

Keane, "Satiric Memories." Keane, Catherine. "Satiric Memories: Autobiography and the Construction of Genre." *CJ* 97 (3, 2002): 215–31.

Kearns, "Autochthons." Kearns, Emily. "Autochthons." *OCD*³ 224.

Kearns, "Hero-cult." Kearns, Emily. "Hero-cult." *OCD*³ 693–94.

Kearns, "Religion, Greek." Kearns, Emily. "Religion, Greek." *OCD*³ 1300–1301.

Kearns, "Talos." Kearns, Emily. "Talos." *OCD*³ 1472.

Kearns, "Women in Cult." Kearns, Emily. "Women in Cult." *OCD*³ 1624–25.

Kearsley, "Acts 14.13." Kearsley, R. A. "Acts 14.13: The Temple Just outside the City." Pages 209–10, §32, in *A Review of the Greek Inscriptions and Papyri Published in 1980–81*. By S. R. Llewelyn, with the collaboration of R. A. Kearsley. Vol. 6 of *New Documents Illustrating Early Christianity*. North Ryde, N.S.W.: Ancient History Documentary Research Centre, Macquarie University, 1992.

Kearsley, "Angels." Kearsley, R. A. "Angels in Asia Minor: The Cult of Hosios and Dikaios." Pages 206–9, §31, in *A Review of the Greek Inscriptions and Papyri Published in 1980–81*. By S. R. Llewelyn, with the collaboration of R. A. Kearsley. Vol. 6 of *New Documents Illustrating Early Christianity*. North Ryde, N.S.W.: Ancient History Documentary Research Centre, Macquarie University, 1992.

Kearsley, "Asiarchs (1994)." Kearsley, R. A. "The Asiarchs." Pages 363–76 in *The Book of Acts in Its Graeco-Roman Setting*. Edited by David W. J. Gill and Conrad Gempf. Vol. 2 of *The Book of Acts in Its First Century Setting*. Edited by Bruce W. Winter. Grand Rapids: Eerdmans; Carlisle, U.K.: Paternoster, 1994.

Kearsley, "Asiarchs (*ABD*)." Kearsley, R. A. "Asiarchs." *ABD* 1:495–97.

Kearsley, "Asiarchs, *archiereis*." Kearsley, R. A. "Asiarchs, *archiereis*, and the *archiereiai* of Asia." *GRBS* 27 (2, 1986): 183–92.

Kearsley, "Benefactor." Kearsley, R. A. "A Civic Benefactor of the First Century in Asia Minor." Pages 233–41, §10, in *A Review of the Greek Inscriptions and Papyri Published in 1982–83*. By S. R. Llewelyn, with the collaboration of R. A. Kearsley. Vol. 7 of *New Documents Illustrating Early Christianity*. North Ryde, N.S.W.: Ancient History Documentary Research Centre, Macquarie University, 1994.

Kearsley, "Neokoros." Kearsley, R. A. "Ephesus: *Neokoros* of Artemis." Pages 203–6, §30, in *A Review of the Greek Inscriptions and Papyri Published in 1980–81*. By S. R. Llewelyn, with the collaboration of R. A. Kearsley. Vol. 6 of *New Documents Illustrating Early Christianity*. North Ryde, N.S.W.: Ancient History Documentary Research Centre, Macquarie University, 1992.

Kearsley, "Octavian." Kearsley, R. A. "Octavian and Augury: The Years 30–27 B.C." *CQ* 59 (1, 2009): 147–66.

Keathley, *Mission*. Keathley, Naymond H. *The Church's Mission to the Gentiles: Acts of the Apostles, Epistles of Paul*. All the Bible. Macon, Ga.: Smyth & Helwys, 1999.

Keay, "Work." Keay, Simon. "Recent Archaeological Work in Roman Iberia (1990–2002)." *JRS* 93 (2003): 146–211.

Kechagia, "Rivalry." Kechagia, Eleni. "Rethinking a Professional Rivalry: Early Epicureans against the Stoa." *CQ* 60 (1, 2010): 132–55.

Keck, "Ethos." Keck, Leander E. "On the Ethos of Early Christians." *JAAR* 42 (1974): 435–52.

Keck, "Images." Keck, Leander E. "Images of Paul in the New Testament." *Interpretation* 43 (4, 1989): 341–51.

Keck, *Jesus*. Keck, Leander E. *Who Is Jesus? History in the Perfect Tense*. Minneapolis: Fortress, 2001.

Keck, *Mandate*. Keck, Leander E. *Mandate to Witness: Studies in the Book of Acts*. Valley Forge, Pa.: Judson, 1964.

Keck, "*Pathos*." Keck, Leander E. "*Pathos* in Romans? Mostly Preliminary Remarks." Pages 71–96 in *Paul and Pathos*. Edited by Thomas H. Olbricht and Jerry L. Sumney. SBLSymS 16. Atlanta: SBL, 2001.

Keck, *Paul*. Keck, Leander E. *Paul and His Letters*. ProcC. Philadelphia: Fortress, 1979.

Keck, "Poor." Keck, Leander E. "The Poor among the Saints in Jewish Christianity and Qumran." *ZNW* 57 (1–2, 1966): 54–78.

Keck, *Romans*. Keck, Leander E. *Romans*. ANTC. Nashville: Abingdon, 2005.

Kee, "Central Authority." Kee, Howard Clark. "Central Authority in Second-Temple Judaism and Subsequently: From Synedrion to Sanhedrin." *ARJ* 2 (1999): 51–63.

Kee, *Community*. Kee, Howard Clark. *Community of the New Age: Studies in Mark's Gospel*. Philadelphia: Westminster, 1977.

Kee, *Every Nation*. Kee, Howard Clark. *To Every Nation under Heaven: The Acts of the Apostles*. Harrisburg, Pa.: Trinity Press International, 1997.

Kee, "Hippocratic Letters." Kee, Howard Clark. "Hippocratic Letters." *DNTB* 498–99.

Kee, *Miracle*. Kee, Howard Clark. *Miracle in the Early Christian World: A Study in Sociohistorical Method*. New Haven: Yale University Press, 1983.

Kee, *Origins*. Kee, Howard Clark. *Christian Origins in Sociological Perspective: Methods and Resources*. Philadelphia: Westminster, 1980.

Kee, "Quests." Kee, Howard Clark. "A Century of Quests for the Culturally Compatible Jesus." *ThTo* 52 (1, 1995): 17–28.

Kee, "Reassessing Evidence from Gospels." Kee, Howard Clark. "Early Christianity in the Galilee: Reassessing the Evidence from the Gospels." Pages 3–22 in *The Galilee in Late Antiquity*. Edited by L. I. Levine. New York: Jewish Theological Seminary of America Press, 1992.

Kee, "Response to Oster." Kee, Howard Clark. "The Changing Meaning of Synagogue: A Response to Richard Oster." *NTS* 40 (2, 1994): 281–83.

Kee, "Self-Definition." Kee, Howard Clark. "Self-Definition in the Asclepius Cult." Pages 118–36 in *Self-Definition in the Greco-Roman World*. Edited by Ben F. Meyer and E. P. Sanders. Vol. 3 of *Jewish and Christian Self-Definition*. Edited by E. P. Sanders. Philadelphia: Fortress, 1982.

Kee, "Tell-Er-Ras." Kee, Howard Clark. "Tell-Er-Ras and the Samaritan Temple." *NTS* 13 (4, 1967): 401–2.

Kee, "Terminology." Kee, Howard Clark. "The Terminology of Mark's Exorcism Stories." *NTS* 14 (2, 1968): 232–46.

Kee, "Transformation." Kee, Howard Clark. "The Transformation of the Synagogue after 70 C.E.: Its Import for Early Christianity." *NTS* 36 (1, 1990): 1–24.

Keedy, "Leadership." Keedy, John L. "Examining Teacher Instructional Leadership within the Small Group Dynamics of Collegial Groups." *TTEd* 15 (7, 1999): 785–99.

Keen, *Medieval Europe*. Keen, Maurice. *The Penguin History of Medieval Europe*. Harmondsworth, U.K.: Penguin, 1991. Rev. from London: Routledge & Kegan Paul, 1968.

Keener, *Acts*. Keener, Craig S. *Acts: An Exegetical Commentary*. 4 vols. Grand Rapids: Baker Academic, 2012–15.

Keener, "Acts 2:1–21." Keener, Craig S. "Day of Pentecost, Years A, B, C: First Lesson—Acts 2:1–21." Pages 524–28 in *The First Readings: The Old Testament and Acts*. Vol. 1 of *The Lectionary Commentary: Theological Exegesis for Sunday's Texts*. Edited by Roger E. Van Harn. Grand Rapids: Eerdmans; London: Continuum, 2001.

Keener, "Acts as Historiography." Keener, Craig S. "Acts as Ancient Historiography." Paper presented at the Divinity School of Vanderbilt University, Nashville, Tennessee, Nov. 29, 2012.

Keener, *Acts Studies*. Keener, Craig S. *Acts*. ImBSt. Nashville: Abingdon, 2011.

Keener, "Adultery." Keener, Craig S. "Adultery, Divorce." *DNTB* 6–16.

Keener, "Aftermath of Eunuch." Keener, Craig S. "The Aftermath of the Ethiopian Eunuch." *AMECR* 118 (385, 2003): 112–24.

Keener, "Apologetic." Keener, Craig S. "Paul and Sedition: Pauline Apologetic in Acts." *BBR* 22 (2, 2012): 201–24.

Keener, "Asia and Europe." Keener, Craig S. "Between Asia and Europe: Postcolonial Mission in Acts 16:8–10." *AJPS* 11 (1–2, 2008): 3–14.

Keener, "Asiarchs." Keener, Craig S. "Paul's 'Friends' the Asiarchs (Acts 19.31)." *JGRCJ* 3 (2006): 134–41.

Keener, "Assumptions." Keener, Craig S. "Assumptions in Historical Jesus Research: Using Ancient Biographies and Disciples' Traditioning as a Control." *JSHJ* 9 (1, 2011): 26–58.

Keener, "Athens." Keener, Craig S. "Note on Athens: Do 1 Corinthians 16.15 and Acts 17.34 Conflict?" *JGRCJ* 7 (2010): 137–39.

Keener, *Background Commentary*. Keener, Craig S. *The IVP Bible Background Commentary: New Testament*. Downers Grove, Ill.: InterVarsity, 1993.

Keener, "Beheld." Keener, Craig S. "'We Beheld His Glory': John 1:14." Pages 15–25 in *Aspects of Historicity in the Fourth Gospel*. Edited by Paul N. Anderson, Felix Just, and Tom Thatcher. Vol. 2 of *John, Jesus and History*. SBL Early Christianity and Its Literature 2. Atlanta: SBL, 2009.

Keener, "Biographies." Keener, Craig S. "Reading the Gospels as Biographies of a Sage." *BurH* 47 (2011): 59–66.

Keener, "Brood of Vipers." Keener, Craig S. "'Brood of Vipers' (Mt. 3.7; 12.34; 23.33)." *JSNT* 28 (1, 2005): 3–11.

Keener, "Case." Keener, Craig S. "A Reassessment of Hume's Case against Miracles in Light of Testimony from the Majority World Today." *PRSt* 38 (3, Fall 2011): 289–310.

Keener, "Cave." Keener, Craig S. "The Nativity Cave and Gentile Myths." *JGRCJ* 7 (2010): 59–67.

Keener, "Claims." Keener, Craig S. "First-Person Claims in Some Ancient Historians and Acts." *JGRCJ* 10 (2014): 9–23.

Keener, "Comparisons." Keener, Craig S. "Cultural Comparisons for Healing and Exorcism Narratives in Matthew's Gospel." *HTS/TS* 66 (1, 2010).

Keener, "Corinthian Believers." Keener, Craig S. "Paul and the Corinthian Believers." Pages 46–62 in *The Blackwell Companion to Paul*. Edited by Stephen Westerholm. Oxford: Blackwell, 2011.

Keener, *Corinthians*. Keener, Craig S. *1 and 2 Corinthians*. NCamBC. Cambridge: Cambridge University Press, 2005.

Keener, "Did Not Know." Keener, Craig S. "We Cannot Say We Did Not Know." *Prism* 11 (2, Mar. 2004): 14–15.

Keener, "Diversity." Keener, Craig S. "Embracing God's Passion for Diversity: A Theology of Racial and Ethnic Plurality." *Enr* 12 (3, 2007): 20–28.

Keener, "Edict." Keener, Craig S. "Edict of Claudius." In *Brill Encyclopedia of Early Christianity*. Leiden: Brill, forthcoming.

Keener, "Education." Keener, Craig S. "Women's Education and Public Speech in Antiquity." *JETS* 50 (4, 2007): 747–59.

Keener, "Epicureans." Keener, Craig S. "Epicureans." In *Brill Encyclopedia of Early Christianity*. Leiden: Brill, forthcoming.

Keener, "Eyes." Keener, Craig S. "A Note on Figurative Eyes in Galatians 4:15." *JGRCJ* 5 (2008): 47–49.

Keener, "Family." Keener, Craig S. "Family and Household." *DNTB* 353–68.

Keener, "Festivals." Keener, Craig S. "Festivals in John's Gospel and the Book of Acts." Seminar paper presented in the Johannine Writings Seminar, Society for New Testament Studies, Bard College, Aug. 3, 2011.

Keener, "Fever." Keener, Craig S. "Fever and Dysentery in Acts 28:8 and Ancient Medicine." *BBR* 19 (3, 2009): 393–402.

Keener, "Foundation." Keener, Craig S. "Building a Biblical Foundation for Worldwide Mission." Paper presented at the meeting of the Institute for Biblical Research, Orlando, Fla., Nov. 21, 1998.

Keener, "Friendship." Keener, Craig S. "Friendship." *DNTB* 380–88.

Keener, *Gift*. Keener, Craig S. *Gift and Giver: The Holy Spirit for Today*. Grand Rapids: Baker, 2001.

Keener, "Gifts." Keener, Craig S. "Gifts (Spiritual)." Pages 155–61 in *The Westminster Theological Wordbook of the Bible*. Edited by Donald E. Gowan. Louisville: Westminster John Knox, 2003.

Keener, "Head Coverings." Keener, Craig S. "Head Coverings." *DNTB* 442–47.

Keener, "Heavenly Court." Keener, Craig S. "Matthew 5:22 and the Heavenly Court." *ExpT* 99 (2, 1987): 46.

Keener, "Heavenly Mindedness." Keener, Craig S. "Heavenly Mindedness and Earthly Good: Contemplating Matters Above in Colossians 3.1–2." *JGRCJ* 6 (2009): 175–90.

Keener, *Historical Jesus*. Keener, Craig S. *The Historical Jesus of the Gospels*. Grand Rapids: Eerdmans, 2009.

Keener, "Holy Spirit." Keener, Craig. "The Holy Spirit." Pages 158–73 in *The Oxford Handbook of Evangelical Theology*. Edited by Gerald R. McDermott. New York: Oxford University Press, 2010.

Keener, "Human Stones." Keener, Craig S. "Human Stones in a Greek Setting—Luke 3.8; Matthew 3.9; Luke 19.40." *JGRCJ* 6 (2009): 28–36.

Keener, "Husband." Keener, Craig S. "Husband of One Wife." *AMEZQR* 109 (1, 1997): 5–24.

Keener, "Interethnic Marriages." Keener, Craig S. "Interethnic Marriages in the New Testament (Matt 1:3–6; Acts 7:29; 16:1–3; 1 Cor 7:14)." *CrisTR* n.s. 6 (2, 2009): 25–43.

Keener, "Interracial Marriage." Keener, Craig S. "The Bible and Interracial Marriage." Pages 2–27 in *Just Don't Marry One: Interracial Dating, Marriage, and Parenting*. Edited by George A. Yancey and Sherelyn Whittum Yancey. Valley Forge, Pa.: Judson, 2002.

Keener, "Inverted Guilt." Keener, Craig S. "A Note on Inverted Guilt in Acts 7:55–60." *JGRCJ* 5 (2008): 41–44.

Keener, "Invitations." Keener, Craig S. "Some New Testament Invitations to Ethnic Reconciliation." *EvQ* 75 (3, 2003): 195–213.

Keener, *John*. Keener, Craig S. *The Gospel of John: A Commentary*. 2 vols. Peabody, Mass.: Hendrickson; Grand Rapids: Baker Academic, 2003.

Keener, "John." Keener, Craig S. "John, Gospel of." Pages 419–36 in *Dictionary of Jesus and the Gospels*. 2nd ed. Edited by Joel B. Green, Jeannine K. Brown, and Nicholas Perrin. Downers Grove, Ill.: IVP Academic, 2013.

Keener, "Kiss." Keener, Craig S. "Kiss, Kissing." *DNTB* 628–29.

Keener, "Learning." Keener, Craig S. "Learning in the Assemblies: 1 Corinthians 14:34–35." Pages 161–71 in *Discovering Biblical Equality: Complementarity without Hierarchy*. Edited by Ronald W. Pierce, Rebecca Merrill Groothuis, and Gordon D. Fee. Downers Grove, Ill.: InterVarsity, 2004.

Keener, "Luke-Acts and Historical Jesus." Keener, Craig S. "Luke-Acts and Historical Jesus." Paper presented at the second Princeton-Prague Symposium on Jesus: Methodological Approaches to the Historical Jesus, Princeton, Apr. 19, 2007. Pages 600–623 in *Jesus Research: New Methodologies and Perceptions; The Second Princeton-Prague Symposium on Jesus Research*. Edited by James H. Charlesworth. Grand Rapids: Eerdmans, 2014.

Keener, "Luke's Pneumatology." Keener, Craig S. "Luke's Pneumatology in Acts for the 21st Century." Pages 205–22 in *Contemporary Issues in Pneumatology: Festschrift in Honor of George M. Flattery*. Edited by James E. Richardson. Springfield, Mo.: Global University, 2009.

Keener, "Madness." Keener, Craig S. "Paul's Positive Madness in Acts 26:24–25." In *Zur Kultur einer Religionsgeschichte*. Edited by Manfred Lang and Joseph Verheyden. Forthcoming.

Keener, "Man and Woman." Keener, Craig S. "Man and Woman." *DPL* 583–92.

Keener, "Marriage." Keener, Craig S. "Marriage." *DNTB* 680–93.

Keener, "Marriage, Divorce." Keener, Craig S. "Marriage, Divorce, and Adultery." *DLNTD* 712–17.

Keener, *Marries Another*. Keener, Craig S. *. . . And Marries Another: Divorce and Remarriage in the Teaching of the New Testament*. Peabody, Mass.: Hendrickson; Grand Rapids: Baker Academic, 1991.

Keener, *Matthew*. Keener, Craig S. *The Gospel of Matthew: A Socio-Rhetorical Commentary*. Grand Rapids: Eerdmans, 2009. Rev. version of *A Commentary on the Gospel of Matthew*. Grand Rapids: Eerdmans, 1999.

Keener, *Matthew* (1997). Keener, Craig S. *Matthew*. IVPNTC. Downers Grove, Ill.: InterVarsity, 1997.

Keener, "Matthew's Missiology." Keener, Craig S. "Matthew's Missiology: Making Disciples of the Nations (Matt 28:19–20)." *AJPS* 12 (1, Jan. 2009): 3–20.

Keener, "Mayhem." Keener, Craig S. "Mutual Mayhem: A Plea for Peace and Truth in the Madness of Nigeria." *CT* (Nov. 2004): 60–64.

Keener, "Milk." Keener, Craig S. "Milk." *DNTB* 707–9.

Keener, "Miracle Reports in Gospels and Today." Keener, Craig S. "Miracle Reports in the Gospels and Today." Plenary address for "Special Divine Action," 2014 conference for the Ian Ramsey Centre for Science and Religion, Oxford University, Oxford, U.K., July 14, 2014.

Keener, "Miracle Reports: Perspectives." Keener, Craig S. "Miracle Reports: Perspectives, Analogies, Explanations." Pages 53–65 in *Hermeneutik der frühchristlichen Wundererzählungen: Historiche, literarische und rezeptionsästhetische Aspekte*. Edited by Bernd Kollmann and Ruben Zimmermann. WUNT 339. Tübingen: Mohr Siebeck, 2014.

Keener, *Miracles*. Keener, Craig S. *Miracles: The Credibility of the New Testament Accounts*. Grand Rapids: Baker Academic, 2011.

Keener, "Miracles." Keener, Craig S. "Miracles." Pages 101–7 in vol. 2 of *The Oxford Encyclopedia of Bible and Theology*. 2 vols. Edited by Samuel E. Balentine. New York: Oxford University Press, 2015.

Keener, "Miracles: Dictionary." Keener, Craig S. "Miracles." In *Dictionary of Christianity and Science*. Edited by Paul Copan et al. Grand Rapids: Zondervan, forthcoming.

Keener, "Monotheism." Keener, Craig S. "The Exhortation to Monotheism in Acts 14:15–17." Pages 47–70 in *Kingdom Rhetoric: New Testament Explorations in Honor of Ben Witherington III*. Edited by T. Michael W. Halcomb. Eugene, Ore.: Wipf & Stock, 2013.

Keener, "Ndoundou." Keener, Médine Moussounga. "Daniel Ndoundou." No pages. *DACB*. Online: http://www.dacb .org/stories/congo/ndoundou_daniel .html.

Keener, "Official." Keener, Craig S. "Novels' 'Exotic' Places and Luke's African Official (Acts 8:27)." *AUSS* 46 (1, 2008): 5–20.

Keener, "Otho." Keener, Craig S. "Otho: A Targeted Comparison of Suetonius' Biography and Tacitus' History, with implications for the Gospels' Historical Reliability." *BBR* 21 (3, 2011): 331–55.

Keener, "Parallel Figures." Keener, Craig S. "Jesus and Parallel Jewish and Greco-Roman Figures." Pages 85–111 in *Christian Origins and Greco-Roman Culture: Social and Literary Contexts for the New Testament*. Edited by Stanley Porter and Andrew W. Pitts. Vol. 1 of *Early Christianity in Its Hellenistic Context*. Vol. 9 in Texts and Editions for New Testament Study. Leiden: Brill, 2013.

Keener, *Paul*. Keener, Craig S. *Paul, Women, and Wives: Marriage and Women's Ministry in the Letters of Paul*. Peabody, Mass.: Hendrickson; Grand Rapids: Baker Academic, 1992.

Keener, "Pentecost." Keener, Craig S. "Pentecost." Pages 360–61 in *The Westminster Theological Wordbook of the Bible*. Edited by Donald E. Gowan. Louisville: Westminster John Knox, 2003.

Keener, "Perspective." Keener, Craig S. "Women in Ministry: Another Egalitarian Perspective." Pages 203–48 in *Two Views on Women in Ministry*. Edited by James R. Beck. Rev. ed. Grand Rapids: Zondervan, 2005.

Keener, "Pillars." Keener, Craig S. "The Pillars and the Right Hand of Fellowship in Galatians 2:9." *JGRCJ* 7 (2010): 51–58.

Keener, "Plausibility." Keener, Craig S. "The Plausibility of Luke's Growth Figures in Acts 2.41; 4.4; 21.20." *JGRCJ* 7 (2010): 140–63.

Keener, "Pneumatology." Keener, Craig S. "The Function of Johannine Pneumatology in the Context of Late First-Century Judaism." PhD diss., Duke University, 1991.

Keener, "Possession." Keener, Craig S. "Spirit Possession as a Cross-Cultural Experience." *BBR* 20 (2010): 215–36.

Keener, "Power." Keener, Craig S. "Power of Pentecost: Luke's Missiology in Acts 1–2." *AJPS* 12 (1, Jan. 2009): 47–73.

Keener, *Questions.* Keener, Craig S. *3 Crucial Questions about the Holy Spirit.* Grand Rapids: Baker, 1996.

Keener, "Raising." Keener, Craig S. "'The Dead Are Raised' (Matthew 11:5// Luke 7:22): Resuscitation Accounts in the Gospels and Eyewitness Testimony." *BBR* 25 (1, 2015): 55–79.

Keener, "Reconciliation." Keener, Craig S. "The Gospel and Racial Reconciliation." Pages 117–30 in *The Gospel in Black and White: Theological Resources for Racial Reconciliation.* Edited by Dennis L. Ockholm. Downers Grove, Ill.: InterVarsity, 1997.

Keener, "Reply." Keener, Craig S. "A Brief Reply to Robert Miller and Amy-Jill Levine." *JSHJ* 9 (2011): 112–17.

Keener, "Reports and Analogy." Keener, Craig S. "Miracle Reports and the Argument from Analogy." *BBR* 25 (4, 2015): forthcoming.

Keener, "Reports Today." Keener, Craig S. "Miracle Reports in the Gospels and Today." Plenary address, "Special Divine Action," 2014 conference for the Ian Ramsey Centre for Science and Religion, Oxford University, Oxford, U.K., July 14, 2014.

Keener, *Revelation.* Keener, Craig S. *Revelation.* NIVAC. Grand Rapids: Zondervan, 2000.

Keener, "Review of *Acts in Setting.*" Keener, Craig S. Review of vols. 1–2 of *The Book of Acts in Its First Century Setting. JETS* 39 (4, 1996): 692–94.

Keener, "Review of Gaventa." Keener, Craig S. Review of Beverly Roberts Gaventa, *Acts. RBL* 8 (2006): 456–58. Online, Nov. 2005. http://www.bookreviews.org/pdf/4040_5058.pdf.

Keener, "Review of Jipp." Keener, Craig S. Review of Joshua W. Jipp, *Divine Visitation and Hospitality to Strangers in Luke-Acts. BBR,* forthcoming.

Keener, "Review of Lincoln." Keener, Craig S. Review of Andrew T. Lincoln, *The Gospel according to Saint John. RBL* 8 (2006): 430–35. Online May 27, 2006: http://www.bookreviews.org/pdf/5024_5292.pdf.

Keener, "Review of Pervo." Keener, Craig S. Review of Richard I. Pervo, *Acts. JETS* 52 (2, June 2009): 386–89.

Keener, "Review of Peterson." Keener, Craig S. Review of David G. Peterson, *The Acts of the Apostles. BBR* 20 (2010): 126–28.

Keener, "Review of *Preaching Matthew.*" Keener, Craig S. Review of Mike Graves and David M. May, *Preaching Matthew: Interpretation and Proclamation. RBL*

(June 14, 2008). Online: http://www.bookreviews.org/pdf/6164_6590.pdf.

Keener, "Review of *Windows.*" Keener, Craig S. Review of Bruce J. Malina, *Windows on the World of Jesus: Time Travel to Ancient Judea. CRBR* 7 (1994): 225–27.

Keener, "Rhetorical Techniques." Keener, Craig S. "Some Rhetorical Techniques in Acts 24:2–21." Pages 221–51 in *Paul's World.* Edited by Stanley E. Porter. PAST 4. Leiden: Brill, 2008.

Keener, *Romans.* Keener, Craig S. *Romans.* NCCS 6. Eugene, Ore.: Wipf & Stock, 2009.

Keener, "Sent." Keener, Craig S. "Sent Like Jesus: Johannine Missiology (Jn 20:21–22)." *AJPS* 12 (1, Jan. 2009): 21–45.

Keener, "Shepherd." Keener, Craig S. "Shepherd, Flock." *DLNTD* 1090–93.

Keener, "Spirit." Keener, Craig S. "Spirit, Holy Spirit, Advocate, Breath, Wind." Pages 484–96 in *The Westminster Theological Wordbook of the Bible.* Edited by Donald E. Gowan. Louisville: Westminster John Knox, 2003.

Keener, *Spirit.* Keener, Craig S. *The Spirit in the Gospels and Acts: Divine Purity and Power.* Peabody, Mass.: Hendrickson, 1997. Repr., Grand Rapids: Baker Academic, 2010.

Keener, "Spirit Perspectives." Keener, Craig S. "'Fleshly' versus Spirit Perspectives in Romans 8:5–8." Pages 211–29 in *Paul: Jew, Greek, and Roman.* Edited by Stanley Porter. PAST 5. Leiden: Brill, 2008.

Keener, "Study of Rhetoric." Keener, Craig S. "Suggestions for Future Study of Rhetoric and Matthew's Gospel." *HTS/TS* 66 (1, 2010).

Keener, "Subordination." Keener, Craig S. "Is Subordination within the Trinity Really Heresy? A Study of John 5:18 in Context." *TJ,* n.s., 20 (1, 1999): 39–51.

Keener, "Subversive Conservative." Keener, Craig S. "Subversive Conservative: How Could Paul Communicate His Radical Message to Those Threatened by It?" *ChH* 47 (1995): 35–37.

Keener, "Tabernacle." Keener, Craig S. "Tabernacle." Pages 837–40 in *Dictionary of Biblical Imagery.* Edited by Leland Ryken, James C. Wilhoit, and Tremper Longman III. Downers Grove, Ill.: InterVarsity, 1998.

Keener, "Teaching Ministry." Keener, Craig S. "A Spirit-Filled Teaching Ministry in Acts 19:9." Pages 46–58 in *Trajectories in the Book of Acts: Essays in Honor of John Wesley Wyckoff.* Edited by Jordan May, Paul Alexander, and Robert G. Reid. Eugene, Ore.: Wipf & Stock, 2010.

Keener, "Temple." Keener, Craig S. "One New Temple in Christ (Ephesians

2:11–22; Acts 21:27–29; Mark 11:17; John 4:20–24)." *AJPS* 12 (1, 2009): 75–92.

Keener, "Tongues." Keener, Craig S. "Why Does Luke Use Tongues as a Sign of the Spirit's Empowerment?" *JPT* 15 (2, 2007): 177–84.

Keener, "Transformation." Keener, Craig S. "Transformation through Divine Vision in 1 John 3:2–6." *F&M* 23 (1, 2005): 13–22.

Keener, "Troops." Keener, Craig S. "Acts 10: Were Troops Stationed in Caesarea During Agrippa's Rule?" *JGRCJ* 7 (2010): 164–76.

Keener, "Truth." Keener, Craig S. "'What Is Truth?': Pilate's Perspective on Jesus in John 18:33–38." In *Glimpses of Jesus through the Johannine Lens.* Vol. 3 of *John, Jesus and History.* Atlanta: Scholars Press, 2014.

Keener, "Vigor." Keener, Craig S. "Youthful Vigor and the Maturity of Age: Peter and the Beloved Disciple in John 20–21." In *Rediscovering John: Essays on the Fourth Gospel in Honour of Frédéric Manns.* Edited by L. Daniel Chrupcala. Studium Biblicum Franciscanum Analecta 80. Milan: Edizioni Terra Santa, 2013.

Keener, "Vote." Keener, Craig S. "A Note on Paul's Figurative Vote in Acts 26:10." *JGRCJ* 5 (2008): 44–46.

Keener, "Warfare." Keener, Craig S. "Paul and Spiritual Warfare." Pages 107–23 in *Paul's Missionary Methods in His Time and Ours.* Edited by Robert Plummer and John Mark Terry. Downers Grove, Ill.: IVP Academic, 2012.

Keener, "Woman." Keener, Craig S. "Woman and Man." *DLNTD* 1205–15.

Keener, "Worship." Keener, Craig S. "The Tabernacle and Contextual Worship." *Asbury Journal* 67 (1, 2012): 127–38.

Keener and Carroll, *Reading.* Keener, Craig S., and M. Daniel Carroll R., eds. *Global Voices: Reading the Bible in the Majority World.* Foreword by Edwin M. Yamauchi. Peabody, Mass.: Hendrickson, 2013.

Keener and Usry, *Faith.* Keener, Craig S., and Glenn Usry. *Defending Black Faith.* Downers Grove, Ill.: InterVarsity, 1997.

Keesing, "Shrines." Keesing, Roger M. "Shrines, Ancestors, and Cognatic Descent: The Kwaio and Tallensi." *AmAnth* 72 (4, 1970): 755–75.

Keesmat, "Capital." Keesmat, Sylvia C. "Reading Romans in the Capital of the Empire." Pages 47–64 in *Reading Paul's Letter to the Romans.* Edited by Jerry L. Sumney. SBLRBS 73. Atlanta: SBL, 2012.

Kehne, "Legatio." Kehne, Peter. "Legatio." *BrillPauly* 7:351–52.

Keil, *Ephesos*. Keil, Josef. *Ephesos: Ein Führer durch die Ruinenstätte und ihre Geschichte*. 5th ed. Vienna: Österreichisches Archäologisches Institut, 1964.

Keil and Delitzsch, *Exodus*. Keil, C. F., and F. Delitzsch. *The Second Book of Moses (Exodus)*. Translated by James Martin. Vol. 2 of *Biblical Commentary on the Old Testament*. Edinburgh: T&T Clark, n.d. Repr., Grand Rapids: Eerdmans, 1980.

Keil and Delitzsch, *Samuel*. Keil, C. F., and F. Delitzsch. *The Books of Samuel*. Translated by James Martin. Vol. 5 of *Biblical Commentary on the Old Testament*. Edinburgh, n.d. Repr., Grand Rapids: Eerdmans, 1980.

Keitel, "Non-appearance." Keitel, Elizabeth. "The Non-appearance of the Phoenix at Tacitus *Annals* 6.28." *AJP* 120 (3, 1999): 429–42.

Keitel, "Vitellius." Keitel, Elizabeth. "Feast Your Eyes on This: Vitellius as a Stock Tyrant (Tac. *Hist.* 3.36–39)." Pages 441–46 in *A Companion to Greek and Roman Historiography*. Edited by John Marincola. 2 vols. Oxford: Blackwell, 2007.

Keith, "Claim." Keith, Chris. "The Claim of John 7.15 and the Memory of Jesus' Literacy." *NTS* 56 (1, Jan. 2010): 44–63.

Keith, "Grapho-Literacy." Keith, Chris. "'In My Own Hand': Grapho-Literacy and the Apostle Paul." *Bib* 89 (1, 2008): 39–58.

Keith, "Lay of Land." Keith, Alison M. "The Lay of the Land in Ovid's 'Perseid' (Met. 4.610–5.249)." *CW* 102 (3, 2009): 259–72.

Kelber, "Imperialism." Kelber, Werner H. "Roman Imperialism and Early Christian Scribality." Pages 135–53 in *Orality, Literacy, and Colonialism in Antiquity*. SBLSemS 47. Atlanta: SBL, 2004.

Kelber, "Work." Kelber, Werner H. "The Work of Birger Gerhardsson in Perspective." Pages 173–206 in *Jesus in Memory: Traditions in Oral and Scribal Perspectives*. Edited by Werner H. Kelber and Samuel Byrskog. Waco: Baylor University Press, 2009.

Kelhoffer, "The Maccabees at Prayer." Kelhoffer, James A. "The Maccabees at Prayer: Pro- and Anti-Hasmonean Tendencies in the Prayers of First and Second Maccabees." *Early Christianity* 2 (2, 2011): 198–218.

Kelhoffer, "Paul and Justin." Kelhoffer, James A. "The Apostle Paul and Justin Martyr on the Miraculous: A Comparison of Appeals to Authority." *GRBS* 42 (2, 2001): 163–84.

Keller, "Disease Concept." Keller, Mark. "The Disease Concept of Alcoholism Revisited." *JSAlc* 37 (11, 1976): 1694–1717.

Keller, *Hammer*. Keller, Mary. *The Hammer and the Flute: Women, Power, and Spirit Possession*. Baltimore: Johns Hopkins University Press, 2002.

Kelley, "Perspective." Kelley, Nicole. "The Cosmopolitan Expression of Josephus' Prophetic Perspective in the *Jewish War*." *HTR* 97 (3, 2004): 257–74.

Kelly, "Ammianus Marcellinus." Kelly, Gavin. "Ammianus Marcellinus: Tacitus' Heir and Gibbon's Guide." Pages 348–61 in *The Cambridge Companion to the Roman Historians*. Edited by Andrew Feldherr. Cambridge: Cambridge University Press, 2009.

Kelly, "Approches." Kelly, Douglas. "Nouvelles approches à la théologie biblique de la justification." *RésCon* 55–56 (2005): 9–21.

Kelly, "Corruption." Kelly, Christopher M. "Corruption." *OCD*³ 402–3.

Kelly, "Forge Tongues." Kelly, Gavin. "'To Forge Their Tongues to Grander Styles': Ammianus' Epilogue." Pages 474–80 in *A Companion to Greek and Roman Historiography*. Edited by John Marincola. 2 vols. Oxford: Blackwell, 2007.

Kelly, *Pastoral Epistles*. Kelly, J. N. D. *A Commentary on the Pastoral Epistles*. London: Adam & Charles Black; New York: Harper & Row, 1963.

Kelly, *Peter*. Kelly, J. N. D. *A Commentary on the Epistles of Peter and Jude*. Thornapple Commentaries. Grand Rapids: Baker, 1981.

Kelly, "Riot Control." Kelly, Benjamin. "Riot Control and Imperial Ideology in the Roman Empire." *Phoenix* 61 (1–2, 2007): 150–76.

Kelsey, *Healing*. Kelsey, Morton T. *Healing and Christianity in Ancient Thought and Modern Times*. New York: Harper & Row, 1973.

Kemezis, "Absence." Kemezis, Adam M. "Lucian, Fronto, and the Absence of Contemporary Historiography under the Antonines." *AJP* 131 (2, 2010): 285–325.

Kemp, "Flattery." Kemp, Jerome. "Flattery and Frankness in Horace and Philodemus." *GR* 57 (1, Apr. 2010): 65–76.

Kendall, "Ethnoarchaeology." Kendall, Timothy. "Ethnoarchaeology in Meroitic Studies." Pages 625–745 in *Studia Meroitica, 1984*. Edited by Sergio Donadoni and Steffen Wenig. Meroitica 10. Berlin: Akademie, 1989.

Kendler et al., "Dimensions." Kendler, Kenneth S., et al. "Dimensions of Religiosity and Their Relationship to Lifetime Psychiatric and Substance Use Disorders." *AmJPsyc* 160 (3, 2003): 496–503.

Kennedy, *Art of Rhetoric*. Kennedy, George A. *The Art of Rhetoric in the Roman World: 300 B.C.–A.D. 300*. Princeton: Princeton University Press, 1972.

Kennedy, *Classical Rhetoric*. Kennedy, George A. *Classical Rhetoric and Its Christian and Secular Tradition from Ancient to Modern Times*. Chapel Hill: University of North Carolina Press, 1980.

Kennedy, "Demography." Kennedy, David. "Demography, the Population of Syria, and the Census of Q. Aemilius Secundus." *Levant* 38 (2006): 109–24.

Kennedy, *Epistles*. Kennedy, H. A. A. *The Theology of the Epistles*. New York: Scribner's, 1920.

Kennedy, "Genres." Kennedy, George A. "The Genres of Rhetoric." Pages 43–50 in *Handbook of Classical Rhetoric in the Hellenistic Period 330, B.C.–A.D. 400*. Edited by Stanley E. Porter. Leiden: Brill, 1997.

Kennedy, *New Testament Interpretation*. Kennedy, George A. *New Testament Interpretation through Rhetorical Criticism*. Chapel Hill: University of North Carolina Press, 1984.

Kennedy, "Source Criticism." Kennedy, George A. "Classical and Christian Source Criticism." Pages 125–55 in *The Relationships among the Gospels: An Interdisciplinary Dialogue*. Edited by William O. Walker Jr. San Antonio: Trinity University Press, 1978.

Kennedy, "Survey of Rhetoric." Kennedy, George A. "Historical Survey of Rhetoric." Pages 3–41 in *Handbook of Classical Rhetoric in the Hellenistic Period, 330 B.C.–A.D. 400*. Edited by Stanley E. Porter. Leiden: Brill, 1997.

Kennedy, "*Zar* Ceremonies." Kennedy, John G. "Nubian *Zar* Ceremonies as Psychotherapy." *Human Organization* 26 (1967): 185–94.

Kennerly, "*Sermo*." Kennerly, Michele. "*Sermo* and Stoic Sociality in Cicero's *De Officiis*." *Rhetorica* 28 (2, 2010): 119–37.

Kent, *Inscriptions*. Kent, John Harvey. *The Inscriptions, 1926–1950*. Vol. 8, part 3, of *Corinth: Results of Excavations Conducted by the American School of Classical Studies at Athens*. Princeton: American School of Classical Studies at Athens, 1966.

Kent, *Jerusalem to Rome*. Kent, Homer A. *Jerusalem to Rome: Studies in the Book of Acts*. Grand Rapids: Baker, 1972.

Kenyon, *Archaeology*. Kenyon, Kathleen M. *Archaeology in the Holy Land*. 2nd ed. New York and Washington, D.C.: Frederick A. Praeger, 1965.

Kenyon, "Case." Kenyon, Susan M. "The Case of the Butcher's Wife: Illness, Possession and Power in Central Sudan." Pages 89–108 in *Spirit Possession, Modernity and Power in Africa*. Edited by Heike Behrend and Ute Luig. Madison: University of Wisconsin Press, 1999.

Kenyon, "*Zar*." Kenyon, Susan M. "The Story of a Tin Box: *Zar* in the Sudanese Town of Sennar." Pages 100–117 in *Women's Medicine: The zar-bori Cult in Africa and Beyond*. Edited by I. M. Lewis, Ahmed Al-Safi, and Sayyid Hurreiz. Edinburgh: International African Institute, Edinburgh University Press, 1991.

Keown, *Evangelism*. Keown, Mark J. *Congregational Evangelism in Philippians: The Centrality of an Appeal for Gospel Proclamation to the Fabric of Philippians*. PBMon. Milton Keynes: Paternoster, 2008.

Keown, "Evangelism." Keown, Mark J. "Congregational Evangelism in Paul: The Paul of Acts." *Colloq* 42 (2, 2010): 231–51.

Kepple, "Analysis." Kepple, Robert J. "An Analysis of Antiochene Exegesis of Galatians 4:24–26." *WTJ* 39 (1976–77): 239–49.

Ker, "Missionary Activity." Ker, Donald P. "Jewish Missionary Activity under Review." *IBS* 18 (4, 1996): 205–16.

Ker, "Nocturnal Writers." Ker, James. "Nocturnal Writers in Imperial Rome: The Culture of *lucubratio*." *CP* 99 (3, 2004): 209–42.

Kerferd, "Reason." Kerferd, G. B. "Reason as a Guide to Conduct in Greek Thought." *BJRL* 64 (1981): 141–64.

Kerin, *Touch*. Kerin, Dorothy. *The Living Touch*. Kent: Courier, 1914.

Kerkeslager, "Absence." Kerkeslager, Allen. "The Absence of Dionysios, Lampo, and Isidoros from the Violence in Alexandria in 38 C.E." *SPhilA* 17 (2005): 49–94.

Kerkeslager, "Agrippa." Kerkeslager, Allen. "Agrippa I and the Judeans of Alexandria in the Wake of the Violence in 38 CE." *REJ* 168 (1–2, 2009): 1–49.

Kerkeslager, "Identity." Kerkeslager, Allen. "Maintaining Jewish Identity in the Greek Gymnasium: A 'Jewish Load' in *CPJ* 3.519 (= P. Schub. 37 = P. Berol. 13406)." *JSJ* 28 (1, 1997): 12–33.

Kern, "Conversion." Kern, Philip H. "Paul's Conversion and Luke's Portrayal of Character in Acts 8–10." *TynBul* 54 (2, 2003): 63–80.

Kern-Ulmer, "Bewertung." Kern-Ulmer, Brigitte. "Die Bewertung der Proselyten in rabbinischen Schrifttum." *Judaica* 50 (1, 1994): 1–17.

Kern-Ulmer, "Depiction of Magic." Kern-Ulmer, Brigitte. "The Depiction of Magic in Rabbinic Texts: The Rabbinic and the Greek Concept of Magic." *JSJ* 27 (3, 1996): 289–303.

Kern-Ulmer, "Evil Eye." Kern-Ulmer, Brigitte. "The Power of the Evil Eye and the Good Eye in Midrashic Literature." *Judaism* 40 (3, 1991): 344–53.

Kern-Ulmer, "Vorlage und Rezeption." Kern-Ulmer, Brigitte. "Zwischen ägyptischer

Vorlage und talmudischer Rezeption: Josef und die Ägypterin." *Kairos* 34–35 (1992–93): 75–90.

Kessler, "Conflict." Kessler, Clive S. "Conflict and Sovereignty in Kelantanese Malay Spirit Seances." Pages 295–332 in *Case Studies in Spirit Possession*. Edited by Vincent Crapanzaro and Vivian Garrison. New York: Wiley, 1977.

Kessler, "Paul the Jew." Kessler, Edward. "Year of Paul 13: St Paul the Jew." *Past Rev* 5 (3, 2009): 16–22.

Keyes, "Letter of Introduction." Keyes, Clinton W. "The Greek Letter of Introduction." *AJP* 56 (1935): 28–44.

Keylock, "Distinctness." Keylock, Leslie R. "Bultmann's Law of Increasing Distinctness." Pages 193–210 in *Current Issues in Biblical and Patristic Interpretation: Studies in Honor of Merrill C. Tenney Presented by His Former Students*. Edited by Gerald F. Hawthorne. Grand Rapids: Eerdmans, 1975.

Keyser, "Cometary Theory." Keyser, Paul T. "On Cometary Theory and Typology from Nechepso-Petosiris through Apuleius to Servius." *Mnemosyne* 47 (5, 1994): 625–51.

Khai, *Cross*. Khai, Chin Khua. *The Cross among Pagodas: A History of the Assemblies of God in Myanmar*. Baguio City, Philippines: Asia Pacific Theological Seminary, 2003.

Khai, "Pentecostalism." Khai, Chin Khua. "The Assemblies of God and Pentecostalism in Myanmar." Pages 261–80 in *Asian and Pentecostal: The Charismatic Face of Christianity in Asia*. Edited by Allan Anderson and Edmond Tang. Foreword by Cecil M. Robeck. RStMiss, AJPS 3. Oxford: Regnum; Baguio City, Philippines: APTS, 2005.

Khalifeh, "Sarepta." Khalifeh, Issam Ali. "Sarepta." *OEANE* 4:488–90.

Khalifeh, "Sidon." Khalifeh, Issam Ali. "Sidon." *OEANE* 5:38–41.

Kibicho, "Continuity." Kibicho, Samuel G. "The Continuity of the African Conception of God into and through Christianity: A Kikuyu Case-Study." Pages 370–88 in *Christianity in Independent Africa*. Edited by Edward Fasholé-Luke et al. Bloomington: Indiana University Press, 1978.

Kidd, *Awakening*. Kidd, Thomas S. *The Great Awakening: The Roots of Evangelical Christianity in Colonial America*. New Haven: Yale University Press, 2007.

Kidd, "Healing." Kidd, Thomas S. "The Healing of Mercy Wheeler: Illness and Miracles among Early American Evangelicals." *WMQ* 63 (1, Jan. 2006): 149–70.

Kidwell, "Law." Kidwell, Robert Brian. "Luke, Paul, and the Law." Pages 71–85

in *Kingdom Rhetoric: New Testament Explorations in Honor of Ben Witherington III*. Edited by T. Michael W. Halcomb. Eugene, Ore.: Wipf & Stock, 2013.

Kiedzik, "Bibliografia." Kiedzik, M. "Ewangelia i Dzieje Apostolskie św. Łukasza—bibliografia publikacji w Polsce za lata 1986(85)–97." *ColT* 69 (4, 1999): 117–38.

Kiel, "Blindness." Kiel, Micah D. "Tobit's Theological Blindness." *CBQ* 73 (2, 2011): 281–98.

Kienast, "Eutychus." Kienast, Dietmar. "Eutychus." *BrillPauly* 5:241.

Kierdorf, "Annales maximi." Kierdorf, Wilhelm. "Annales maximi." *BrillPauly* 1:702–3.

Kierdorf, "Annalists." Kierdorf, Wilhelm. "Annalists." *BrillPauly* 1:703.

Kierdorf, "Burial." Kierdorf, Wilhelm. "Burial." *BrillPauly* 2:829–34.

Kierdorf, "Consolatio." Kierdorf, Wilhelm. "Consolatio as a literary genre." *BrillPauly* 3:704–6.

Kierdorf, "Laudatio funebris." Kierdorf, Wilhelm. "Laudatio funebris." *BrillPauly* 7:297–99.

Kierdorf, "Lot." Kierdorf, Wilhelm. "Lot, election by: Rome." *BrillPauly* 7:817–19.

Kierdorf, "Praetor." Kierdorf, Wilhelm. "Praetor." *BrillPauly* 11:771–73.

Kierdorf, "Propraetor." Kierdorf, Wilhelm. "Propraetor." *BrillPauly* 12:37.

Kierdorf, "Proquaestor." Kierdorf, Wilhelm. "Proquaestor." *BrillPauly* 12:38.

Kiev, *Magic*. Kiev, Ari, ed. *Magic, Faith, and Healing: Studies in Primitive Psychiatry Today*. Foreword by Jerome D. Frank. New York: Free Press, 1964.

Kiev, "Value." Kiev, Ari. "The Psychotherapeutic Value of Spirit-Possession in Haiti." Pages 143–48 in *Trance and Possession States: Proceedings of the Second Annual Conference, R. M. Bucke Memorial Society, March 4–6, 1966*. Edited by Raymond Prince. Montreal: R. M. Bucke Memorial Society, 1968.

Kilgallen, "Acceptable." Kilgallen, John J. "Clean, Acceptable, Saved: Acts 10." *ExpT* 109 (10, 1998): 301–2.

Kilgallen, "Acts 17,22b–31." Kilgallen, John J. "Acts 17,22b–31—What Kind of Speech Is This?" *RB* 110 (3, 2003): 417–24.

Kilgallen, "Acts 28,28." Kilgallen, John J. "Acts 28,28—Why?" *Bib* 90 (2, 2009): 176–87.

Kilgallen, "Assumptions." Kilgallen, John J. "'With Many Other Words' (Acts 2,40): Theological Assumptions in Peter's Pentecost Speech." *Bib* 83 (1, 2002): 71–87.

Kilgallen, "Chose." Kilgallen, John J. "'The Apostles Whom He Chose because of the

Holy Spirit': A Suggestion regarding Acts 1,2." *Bib* 81 (3, 2000): 414–17.

Kilgallen, *Commentary*. Kilgallen, John J. *A Brief Commentary on the Acts of the Apostles*. New York: Paulist, 1988.

Kilgallen, "Difference." Kilgallen, John J. "A Major Difference between Law and Faith, in Luke and His Traditions." *ExpT* 116 (2, 2004): 37–41.

Kilgallen, "Ephesian Elders." Kilgallen, John J. "Paul's Speech to the Ephesian Elders: Its Structure." *ETL* 70 (1, 1994): 112–21.

Kilgallen, "Function of Speech." Kilgallen, John J. "The Function of Stephen's Speech (Acts 7,2–53)." *Bib* 70 (2, 1989): 173–93.

Kilgallen, "Heal." Kilgallen, John J. "'. . . And I Will Heal Them' (Acts 28:27)." *PIBA* 28 (2005): 87–105.

Kilgallen, "Hostility." Kilgallen, John J. "Hostility to Paul in Pisidian Antioch (Acts 13,45)—Why?" *Bib* 84 (1, 2003): 1–15.

Kilgallen, "Pentecost." Kilgallen, John J. "Luke Speaks to Theophilus about Pentecost." *PIBA* 27 (2004): 40–43.

Kilgallen, "Persecution." Kilgallen, John J. "Persecution in the Acts of the Apostles." Pages 143–60 in *Luke and Acts*. Edited by Gerald O'Collins and Gilberto Marconi. Translated by Matthew J. O'Connell. New York: Paulist, 1993.

Kilgallen, "Role of *magos*." Kilgallen, John J. "Acts 13:4–12: The Role of the *magos*." *EstBib* 55 (2, 1997): 223–37.

Kilgallen, "Rome." Kilgallen, John J. "Luke Wrote to Rome—A Suggestion." *Bib* 88 (2, 2007): 251–55.

Kilgallen, "Servant You Anointed." Kilgallen, John J. "Your Servant Jesus Whom You Anointed (Acts 4, 27)." *RB* 105 (2, 1998): 185–201.

Kilgallen, *Speech*. Kilgallen, John. *The Stephen Speech: A Literary and Redactional Study of Acts 7,2–53*. AnBib 67. Rome: Biblical Institute Press, 1976.

Kilgallen, "Speech of Stephen." Kilgallen, John J. "The Speech of Stephen, Acts 7:2–53." *ExpT* 115 (9, 2004): 293–97.

Kilgallen, "Thucydides 2.97.4." Kilgallen, John J. "Acts 20:35 and Thucydides 2.97.4." *JBL* 112 (2, 1993): 312–14.

Kilgallen, "Turning Points." Kilgallen, John J. "Acts: Literary and Theological Turning Points." *BTB* 7 (1977): 177–80.

Kilgallen, "Use of Psalm 16:8–11." Kilgallen, John J. "The Use of Psalm 16:8–11 in Peter's Pentecost Speech." *ExpT* 113 (2, 2001): 47–50.

Killebrew, "Baths." Killebrew, Ann. "Baths." *OEANE* 1:283–85.

Killebrew, "Furniture." Killebrew, Ann. "Furniture and Furnishings: Hellenistic, Roman, and Byzantine Periods." *OEANE* 2:358–62.

Killgrove, "Response." Killgrove, Kristina. "Response to C. Bruun, 'Water, oxygen isotopes and immigration to Ostia-Portus.'" *JRA* 23 (2010): 133–36.

Kilpatrick, "Quotations in Acts." Kilpatrick, G. D. "Some Quotations in Acts." Pages 81–97 in *Les Actes des apôtres: Traditions, rédaction, théologie*. Edited by Jacob Kremer. BETL 48. Gembloux, Belg.: J. Duculot; Leuven: University Press, 1979.

Kilpatrick, "Style." Kilpatrick, G. D. "Two Studies of Style and Text in the Greek New Testament." *JTS* 41 (1, 1990): 94–98.

Kim, "Atonement." Kim, Jintae. "The Concept of Atonement in Early Rabbinic Thought and the New Testament Writings." *JGRCJ* 2 (2001–5): 117–45.

Kim, *Bread*. Kim, Dong-sun. *The Bread for Today and the Bread for Tomorrow: The Ethical Significance of the Lord's Supper in the Korean Context*. Asian Thought and Culture 49. New York, Bern: Lang, 2001.

Kim, *Caesar*. Kim, Seyoon. *Christ and Caesar: The Gospel and the Roman Empire in the Writings of Paul and Luke*. Grand Rapids: Eerdmans, 2008.

Kim, "Cain." Kim, Angela Y. "Cain and Abel in the Light of Envy: A Study in the History of the Interpretation of Envy in Genesis 4.1–16." *JSP* 12 (1, 2001): 65–84.

Kim, "Complexity." Kim, See Nan. "The Complexity of False Prophecy." *STJ* 11 (1, 2003): 21–39.

Kim, "Concept of Atonement." Kim, Jintae. "The Concept of Atonement in 1 John: A Redevelopment of the Second Temple Concept of Atonement." PhD diss., Westminster Theological Seminary, 2003.

Kim, "Dream." Kim, Tae Hun. "The Dream of Alexander in Josephus *Ant.* 11.325–39." *JSJ* 34 (4, 2003): 425–42.

Kim, "Fellowship." Kim, Ho Kyung. "The Table Fellowship as the Symbol of the Temple in Lukan Community." *YonsRTC* 5 (1999): 91–101.

Kim, "Healing." Kim, Sean C. "Reenchanted: Divine Healing in Korean Protestantism." Pages 267–85 in *Global Pentecostal and Charismatic Healing*. Edited by Candy Gunther Brown. Foreword by Harvey Cox. Oxford: Oxford University Press, 2011.

Kim, "Hellenistic Thought." Kim, Jintae. "The Concept of Atonement in Hellenistic Thought and 1 John." *JGRCJ* 2 (2001–5): 100–116.

Kim, "Influence." Kim, Kwan Soo. "A Study of the Influence of Healing Ministry to Church Growth with Reference to Korea Evangelical Church." DMin diss., Fuller Theological Seminary and Asian Center for Theological Studies and Mission, Seoul, 1987.

Kim, *Introduction*. Kim, Yung Suk. *A Theological Introduction to Paul's Letters: Exploring a Threefold Theology of Paul*. Eugene, Ore.: Cascade, 2011.

Kim, "Jesus, Sayings of." Kim, Seyoon. "Jesus, Sayings of." *DPL* 475–92.

Kim, *Letter of Recommendation*. Kim, Chan-Hie. *Form and Structure of the Familiar Greek Letter of Recommendation*. SBLDS 4. Missoula, Mont.: SBL, 1972.

Kim, "Mission." Kim, Sung Hwan. "The Holy Spirit's Mission in the Book of Acts: Its Repetition and Continuation." ThM thesis, Fuller School of World Mission, 1993.

Kim, "Montanism." Kim, Lucien Jinkwang. "Is Montanism a Heretical Sect or Pentecostal Antecedent?" *AJPS* 12 (1, 2009): 113–24.

Kim, *New Perspective*. Kim, Seyoon. *Paul and the New Perspective: Second Thoughts on the Origin of Paul's Gospel*. Grand Rapids: Eerdmans, 2002.

Kim, *Origin*. Kim, Seyoon. *The Origin of Paul's Gospel*. Tübingen: J. C. B. Mohr, 1981.

Kim, "Pentecostalism." Kim, Sung-Gun. "Pentecostalism, Shamanism, and Capitalism within Contemporary Korean Society." Pages 23–38 in *Spirits of Globalization: The Growth of Pentecostalism and Experiential Spiritualities in a Global Age*. Edited by Sturla J. Stålsett. London: SCM, 2006.

Kim, "Prominent Woman." Kim, Ig-Jin. "A Prominent Woman in Early Korean Pentecostal Movement: Gui-Im Park (1912–1994)." *AJPS* 9 (2, July 2006): 199–218.

Kim, "Quotations." Kim, J.-W. "Explicit Quotations from Genesis within the Context of Stephen's Speech in Acts." *Neot* 41 (2, 2007): 341–60.

Kim, "Reenchanted." Kim, Sean C. "Reenchanted: Divine Healing in Korean Protestantism." Pages 267–85 in *Global Pentecostal and Charismatic Healing*. Edited by Candy Gunther Brown. Foreword by Harvey Cox. Oxford: Oxford University Press, 2011.

Kim, *Stewardship and Almsgiving*. Kim, Kyoung-Jin. *Stewardship and Almsgiving in Luke's Theology*. JSNTSup 155. Sheffield, U.K.: Sheffield Academic, 1998.

Kim, "Targum Isaiah 53." Kim, Jintae. "Targum Isaiah 53 and the New Testament Concept of Atonement." *JGRCJ* 5 (2008): 81–98.

Kimball, "Learning." Kimball, Solon T. "Learning a New Culture." Pages 182–92 in *Crossing Cultural Boundaries: The*

Anthropological Experience. Edited by Solon T. Kimball and James B. Watson. San Francisco: Chandler, 1972.

Kimbrough, "Sabbath." Kimbrough, S. T. "The Concept of Sabbath at Qumran." *RevQ* 5 (4, 1966): 483–502.

Kimelman, "Evidence." Kimelman, Reuven. "*Birkath Ha-Minim* and the Lack of Evidence for an Anti-Christian Jewish Prayer in Late Antiquity." Pages 226–44 in *Aspects of Judaism in the Graeco-Roman Period*. Edited by E. P. Sanders with A. I. Baumgarten and Alan Mendelson. Vol. 2 of *Jewish and Christian Self-Definition*. Edited by E. P. Sanders. Philadelphia: Fortress, 1981.

King, "Amos 9:11–12." King, David M. "The Use of Amos 9:11–12 in Acts 15:16–18." *AshTJ* 21 (1989): 8–13.

King, "Anthropology." King, Helen. "Anthropology and the Classics." *OCD*³ 103.

King, *Believer*. King, Paul L. *A Believer with Authority: The Life and Message of John A. MacMillan*. Camp Hill, Pa.: Christian Publications, 2001.

King, "Body." King, Helen. "Body." *OCD*³ 245–46.

King, "Chastity." King, Helen. "Chastity: Before Christianity." *OCD*³ 319–20.

King, "Circumcision." King, Philip J. "Circumcision—Who Did It, Who Didn't, and Why." *BAR* 32 (4, 2006): 48–55.

King, "Diet." King, Anthony. "Diet in the Roman World: A Regional Inter-site Comparison of the Mammal Bones." *JRA* 12 (1999): 168–202.

King, "Gender Roles: Medicine." King, Helen. "Gender Roles: Medicine." *Brill Pauly* 5:744–46.

King, "Midwives." King, Helen. "Midwives." *OCD*³ 979.

King, *Mountains*. King, Paul L. *Moving Mountains: Lessons in Bold Faith from Great Evangelical Leaders*. Grand Rapids: Chosen, 2004.

King, "Women." King, Helen. "Women." *OCD*³ 1623–24.

Kingdon, "Zealots." Kingdon, H. Paul. "The Origin of the Zealots." *NTS* 19 (1, 1972): 74–81.

Kinghorn *Story*. Kinghorn, Kenneth Cain. *The Story of Asbury Theological Seminary*. Lexington, Ky.: Emeth, 2010.

Kingsbury, *Christology*. Kingsbury, Jack Dean. *The Christology of Mark's Gospel*. Philadelphia: Fortress, 1983.

Kingsbury, "Pharisees in Luke-Acts." Kingsbury, J. D. "The Pharisees in Luke-Acts." Pages 1497–1512 in vol. 2 of *The Four Gospels, 1992: Festschrift Frans Neirynck*. Edited by F. van Segbroek. BETL 100. Leuven: Leuven University Press, 1992.

Kinnear, *Tide*. Kinnear, Angus. *Against the Tide: The Story of Watchman Nee*. Wheaton, Ill.: Tyndale House, 1978.

Kinsella, "Transformation." Kinsella, Sean E. "The Transformation of the Jewish Passover in an Early Christian Liturgy: The Influence of the Passover *haggadah* in the *Apostolic Tradition*." *ScEs* 52 (2, 2000): 215–28.

Kinzing, "Non-Separation.'" Kinzig, Wolfram. "'Non-Separation': Closeness and Co-operation between Jews and Christians in the Fourth Century." *VC* 45 (1, 1991): 27–53.

Kippenberg, "Magic." Kippenberg, Hans G. "Magic in Roman Civil Discourse: Why Rituals Could Be Illegal." Pages 137–63 in *Envisioning Magic: A Princeton Seminar and Symposium*. Edited by Peter Schäfer and Hans G. Kippenberg. SHR 75. Leiden: Brill, 1997.

Kirby, *Ephesians*. Kirby, John C. *Ephesians: Baptism and Pentecost (An Inquiry into the Structure and Purpose of the Epistle to the Ephesians)*. Montreal: McGill University Press, 1968.

Kirchschläger, "Exorzismus." Kirchschläger, Walter. "Exorzismus in Qumran?" *Kairos* 18 (1976): 135–53.

Kirchschläger, "Fieberheilung." Kirchschläger, W. "Fieberheilung in Apg 28 und Lk 24." Pages 509–21 in *Les Actes des apôtres: Traditions, rédaction, théologie*. Edited by Jacob Kremer. BETL 48. Gembloux, Belg.: J. Duculot; Leuven: Leuven University Press, 1979.

Kirk, "Apostleship." Kirk, J. Andrew. "Apostleship since Rengstorf: Towards a Synthesis." *NTS* 21 (2, 1975): 249–64.

Kirk, "Memory." Kirk, Alan. "Memory." Pages 155–72 in *Jesus in Memory: Traditions in Oral and Scribal Perspectives*. Edited by Werner H. Kelber and Samuel Byrskog. Waco: Baylor University Press, 2009.

Kirk, *Vision*. Kirk, Kenneth E. *The Vision of God—The Christian Doctrine of the Summum Bonum: The Bampton Lectures for 1928*. Abridged ed. London: Longmans, Green, & Company, 1934.

Kirner, "Apostolat." Kirner, Guido O. "Apostolat und Patronage (I): Methodischer Teil und Forschungsdiskussion." *ZAC/JAC* 6 (1, 2002): 3–37.

Kirschner, "Imitatio." Kirschner, Robert. "Imitatio rabbini." *JSJ* 17 (1986): 70–79.

Kisau, "Acts." Kisau, Paul Mumo. "Acts of the Apostles." Pages 1297–1348 in *Africa Bible Commentary*. Edited by Tokunboh Adeyemo. Grand Rapids: Zondervan; Nairobi: WordAlive, 2006.

Kisau, "Sharing." Kisau, Paul Mumo. "The Sharing of Goods with the Poor

Is a Christian Imperative." *AfET* 19 (1, 2000): 25–36.

Kisirinya, "Re-interpreting." Kisirinya, S. K. "Re-interpreting the Major Summaries (Acts 2:42–46; 4:32–35; 5:12–16)." *AfCS* 18 (1, 2002): 67–74.

Kislev, "Vocabulary." Kislev, Itamar. "The Vocabulary of the Septuagint and Literary Criticism: The Case of Numbers 27,15–23." *Bib* 90 (1, 2009): 59–67.

Kistemaker, *Acts*. Kistemaker, Simon J. *Exposition of the Acts of the Apostles*. Grand Rapids: Baker, 1990.

Kistemaker, "Speeches in Acts." Kistemaker, Simon J. "The Speeches in Acts." *CrisTR* 5 (1, 1990): 31–41.

Kister, "Fragment." Kister, Menahem. "On a New Fragment of the Damascus Covenant." *JQR* 84 (2–3, 1993–94): 249–51.

Kister, "Parallel." Kister, Menahem. "A Qumranic Parallel to 1 Thess 4:4? Reading and Interpretation of 4Q416 2 II 21." *DSD* 10 (3, 2003): 365–70.

Kitaoji, "Structure." Kitaoji, Hironobu. "The Structure of the Japanese Family." *AmAnth* 73 (Oct. 1971): 1036–57.

Kitchen, "Background." Kitchen, Kenneth A. "Some Egyptian Background to the Old Testament." *TynBul* 5 (16, 1960): 4–18.

Kitchen, "Egypt." Kitchen, Kenneth A. "Egypt, Egyptians." *DOTP* 207–14.

Kitchen, *Orient*. Kitchen, Kenneth A. *Ancient Orient and the Old Testament*. Downers Grove, Ill.: InterVarsity, 1966.

Kitchen, *Reliability*. Kitchen, Kenneth A. *On the Reliability of the Old Testament*. Grand Rapids: Eerdmans, 2003.

Kitchen, *World*. Kitchen, Kenneth A. *The Bible in Its World*. Downers Grove, Ill.: InterVarsity, 1978.

Kitz, "Terminology." Kitz, Anne Marie. "The Hebrew Terminology of Lot Casting and Its Ancient Near Eastern Context." *CBQ* 62 (2000): 207–14.

Klassen, "Fire." Klassen, J. P. "Fire in the Pararno." MA thesis, Fuller Theological Seminary, 1975.

Klassen, "King." Klassen, William. "The King as 'Living Law' with Particular Reference to Musonius Rufus." *SR/SR* 14 (1, 1985): 63–71.

Klassen, "Kiss." Klassen, William. "Kiss (NT)." *ABD* 4:89–92.

Klauck, "Accuser." Klauck, Hans-Josef. "Accuser, Judge, and Paraclete—On Conscience in Philo of Alexandria." *SK* 20 (1, 1999): 107–18.

Klauck, "Ärzten." Klauck, Hans-Josef. "Von Ärzten und Wundertätern: Heil und Heilung in der Antike." *BK* 61 (2, 2006): 94–98.

Klauck, *Context*. Klauck, Hans-Josef. *The Religious Context of Early Christianity: A Guide to Graeco-Roman Religions*. Translated by Brian McNeil. Minneapolis: Fortress, 2003.

Klauck, "Gütergemeinschaft." Klauck, Hans-Josef. "Gütergemeinschaft in der klassischen Antike, in Qumran, und im Neuen Testament." *RevQ* 11 (1, 1982): 47–79.

Klauck, *Letters*. Klauck, Hans-Josef, with Daniel P. Bailey. *Ancient Letters and the New Testament: A Guide to Context and Exegesis*. Waco: Baylor University Press, 2006.

Klauck, *Magic*. Klauck, Hans-Josef. *Magic and Paganism in Early Christianity: The World of the Acts of the Apostles*. Translated by Brian McNeil. Minneapolis: Fortress, 2003.

Klauck, "Pantheisten." Klauck, Hans-Josef. "Pantheisten, Polytheisten, Monotheisten—Eine Reflexion zur griechisch-römischen und biblischen Theologie." Pages 3–56 in *Religion und Gesellschaft im frühen Christentum: Neutestamentliche Studien*. WUNT 152. Tübingen: Mohr Siebeck, 2003.

Klauck, "Paphos and Lystra." Klauck, Hans-Josef. "With Paul in Paphos and Lystra: Magic and Paganism in the Acts of the Apostles." *Neot* 28 (1, 1994): 93–108.

Klauck, "Presence." Klauck, Hans-Josef. "Presence in the Lord's Supper: 1 Corinthians 11:23–26 in the Context of Hellenistic Religious History." Pages 57–74 in *One Loaf, One Cup—Ecumenical Studies of 1 Cor 11 and Other Eucharistic Texts: The Cambridge Conference on the Eucharist, August 1988*. Edited by Ben F. Meyer. New Gospel Studies 6. Macon, Ga.: Mercer University Press, 1993.

Klauck, "Rhetorik: Exordium." Klauck, Hans-Josef. "Hellenistische Rhetorik im Diasporajudentum: Das Exordium des vierten Makkabäerbuchs (4 Makk 1.1–12)." *NTS* 35 (3, 1989): 451–65.

Klauck, "Sacrifice." Klauck, Hans-Josef. "Sacrifice and Sacrificial Offerings: New Testament." *ABD* 5:886–91.

Klauck, "Urbane Frömmigkeit." Klauck, Hans-Josef. "'Urbane Frömmigkeit' in den paulinischen Gemeinden?" *LebSeel* 43 (1, 1992): 20–26.

Klauck, "Von Kassandra." Klauck, Hans-Josef. "Von Kassandra bis zur Gnosis: Im Umfeld der frühchristlichen Glossalalie." *ThQ* 179 (4, 1999): 289–312.

Klaus, "Global Culture." Klaus, Byron D. "Pentecostalism as a Global Culture: An Introductory Overview." Pages 127–30 in *The Globalization of Pentecostalism: A Religion Made to Travel*. Edited by Murray W. Dempster, Byron D. Klaus, and Douglas Petersen. Foreword by Russell P. Spittler. Carlisle, U.K.: Paternoster; Oxford: Regnum, 1999.

Klaus, "Mission." Klaus, Byron D. "The Mission of the Church." Pages 567–95 in *Systematic Theology: A Pentecostal Perspective*. Edited by Stanley M. Horton. Springfield, Mo.: Logion, 1994.

Klausner, *Jesus of Nazareth*. Klausner, Joseph. *Jesus of Nazareth: His Life, Times, and Teaching*. Translated by Herbert Danby. Foreword by Sidney B. Hoenig. New York: Macmillan, 1925. Repr., New York: Menorah, 1979.

Klausner, *Jesus to Paul*. Klausner, Joseph. *From Jesus to Paul*. Translated by W. Stinespring. Foreword by Sidney Hoenig. London: Macmillan, 1943. Repr., New York: Menorah, 1979.

Klausner, *Messianic Idea*. Klausner, Joseph. *Messianic Idea in Israel*. Translated by W. F. Stinespring. London: Allen & Unwin, 1956.

Klawans, "Fate." Klawans, Jonathan. "Josephus on Fate, Free Will, and Ancient Jewish Types of Compatibilism." *Numen* 56 (1, 2009): 44–90.

Klawans, "Gentile Impurity." Klawans, Jonathan. "Notions of Gentile Impurity in Ancient Judaism." *AJSR* 20 (2, 1995): 285–312.

Klawans, "Idolatry." Klawans, Jonathan. "Idolatry, Incest, and Impurity: Moral Defilement in Ancient Judaism." *JSJ* 29 (4, 1998): 391–415.

Klawans, "Impurity." Klawans, Jonathan. "The Impurity of Immorality in Ancient Judaism." *JJS* 48 (1, 1997): 1–16.

Klawans, "Purity." Klawans, Jonathan. "Moral and Ritual Purity." Pages 266–84 in *The Historical Jesus in Context*. Edited by Amy-Jill Levine, Dale C. Allison Jr., and John Dominic Crossan. PrRR. Princeton: Princeton University Press, 2006.

Kleberg, *Hôtels*. Kleberg, Tönnes. *Hôtels, restaurants, et cabarets dans l'antiquité romaine*. BEURU 61. Uppsala: Almquist & Wiksells, 1957.

Klein, "Messianism." Klein, Ralph W. "Aspects of Intertestamental Messianism." Pages 191–203 in *The Bible in Its Literary Milieu*. Edited by Vincent L. Tollers and John R. Maier. Grand Rapids: Eerdmans, 1979.

Klein, "Purpose." Klein, Günter. "Paul's Purpose in Writing the Epistle to the Romans." Pages 32–49 in *The Romans Debate*. Edited by Karl P. Donfried. Minneapolis: Augsburg, 1977.

Klein, "Romfan." Klein, Hans. "Wie wird aus Kaiwan ein Romfan? Eine textkritische Miszelle zu Apg 7,42f." *ZNW* 97 (1, 2006): 139–40.

Kleiner, "Women." Kleiner, Diana E. E. "Women and Family Life on Roman Imperial Funerary Altars." *Latomus* 46 (3, 1987): 545–54.

Kleinman, *Healers*. Kleinman, Arthur. *Patients and Healers in the Context of Culture*. CSHSMC 3. Berkeley: University of California Press, 1980.

Kleve, "Daimon." Kleve, K. "The Daimon of Socrates." *SIFC* 4 (1986): 5–18.

Klijn, "Stephen's Speech." Klijn, A. F. J. "Stephen's Speech—Acts VII.2–53." *NTS* 4 (1, 1957): 25–31.

Kline, "Sayings." Kline, Leslie L. "Harmonized Sayings of Jesus in the Pseudo-Clementine Homilies and Justin Martyr." *ZNW* 66 (3–4, 1975): 223–41.

Kline, *Treaty*. Kline, Meredith G. *Treaty of the Great King—The Covenant Structure of Deuteronomy: Studies and Commentary*. Grand Rapids: Eerdmans, 1963.

Klingbeil, "Animal Imagery." Klingbeil, Gerald A. "Animal Imagery." Pages 29–36 in *Dictionary of the Old Testament Prophets*. Edited by Mark J. Boda and J. Gordon McConville. Downers Grove, Ill.: IVP Academic, 2012.

Klingbeil, "Historical Criticism." Klingbeil, Gerald A. "Historical Criticism." *DOTP* 401–20.

Klingbeil, *Ordination*. Klingbeil, Gerald A. *A Comparative Study of the Ritual of Ordination as Found in Leviticus 8 and Emar 369*. Lewiston, N.Y.: Edwin Mellen, 1998.

Klinger, "Statuette." Klinger, Sonia. "A Terracotta Statuette of Artemis with a Deer at the Israel Museum." *IEJ* 51 (2, 2001): 208–24.

Kloner and Eisenberg, "M'rt." Kloner, Amos, and E. Eisenberg. "M'rt qbwrh mymy byt sny b'yzwr kpr s'wl, yrwslym." '*Atiqot* 21 (1992): 55–51.

Kloppenborg, "Associations." Kloppenborg, John S. "Associations in the Ancient World." Pages 323–38 in *The Historical Jesus in Context*. Edited by Amy-Jill Levine, Dale C. Allison Jr., and John Dominic Crossan. PrRR. Princeton: Princeton University Press, 2006.

Kloppenborg, "Dating Theodotos." Kloppenborg, John S. "Dating Theodotos (CIJ II 1404)." *JJS* 51 (2, 2000): 243–80.

Kloppenborg, "Theodotus Synagogue Inscription." Kloppenborg, John S. "The Theodotus Synagogue Inscription and the Problem of First-Century Synagogue Buildings." Pages 236–82 in *Jesus and Archaeology*. Edited by James H. Charlesworth. Grand Rapids: Eerdmans, 2006.

Klose, "Minting." Klose, Dietrich. "Minting: The Orient." *BrillPauly* 9:32–33.

Klutz, *Exorcism Stories*. Klutz, Todd. *The Exorcism Stories in Luke-Acts: A Sociostylistic*

Reading. SNTSMS 129. Cambridge: Cambridge University Press, 2004.

Knapp, "Aegean Islands." Knapp, A. Bernard. "Aegean Islands." *OEANE* 1:17–22.

Knapstad, "Power." Knapstad, Bård Løkken. "Show Us the Power! A Study of the Influence of Miracles on the Conversion Process from Islam to Christianity in an Indonesian Context." ThM thesis, Norwegian Lutheran School of Theology, 2005.

Knauf, "Ethnarchen." Knauf, Ernst Axel. "Zum Ethnarchen des Aretas 2 Kor 11:32." *ZNW* 74 (1–2, 1983): 145–47.

Knibb, *Esdras*. Knibb, Michael A. *The First and Second Books of Esdras*. Cambridge: Cambridge University Press, 1979.

Knibb, "Introduction." Knibb, Michael A. Introduction to "Martyrdom and Ascension of Isaiah." *OTP* 2:143–55.

Knibbe, "Via Sacra." Knibbe, Dieter. "*Via Sacra Ephesiaca*: New Aspects of the Cult of Artemis Ephesia." Pages 141–55 in *Ephesos, Metropolis of Asia: An Interdisciplinary Approach to Its Archaeology, Religion, and Culture*. Edited by Helmut Koester. HTS. Valley Forge, Pa.: Trinity Press International, 1995.

Knight, *Psalms*. Knight, George A. F. *Psalms*. 2 vols. Philadelphia: Westminster, 1982–83.

Knight, *Sayings*. Knight, George W., III. *The Faithful Sayings in the Pastoral Epistles*. Grand Rapids: Baker, 1979.

Knoll, *Denkmäler*. Knoll, Fritz, Heinrich Swoboda, and Josef Keil. *Denkmäler aus Lykaonien, Pamphylien, und Isaurien*. Deutsche Gesellschaft der Wissenschaften und Künste für die Tschechoslowakische Republik in Prag. Brno, Czech.: Rohrer, 1935.

Knoppers, "Gerizim." Knoppers, Garry N. "Mt. Gerizim and Mt. Zion: A Study in the Early History of the Samaritans and Jews." *SR/SR* 34 (3–4, 2005): 309–38.

Knoppers, "Problem." Knoppers, Gerald N. "The Synoptic Problem? An Old Testament Perspective." *BBR* 19 (1, 2009): 11–34.

Knowling, "Acts." Knowling, R. J. "The Acts of the Apostles." Pages 1–554 in vol. 2 of *The Expositor's Greek Testament*. Edited by W. Robertson Nicoll. 5 vols. New York: Hodder & Stoughton, 1897–1910. Repr., Grand Rapids: Eerdmans, 1979.

Knox, *Acts*. Knox, Wilfred L. *The Acts of the Apostles*. Cambridge: Cambridge University Press, 1948.

Knox, "Acts and Corpus." Knox, John. "Acts and the Pauline Letter Corpus." Pages 279–87 in *Studies in Luke-Acts*. Edited by Leander E. Keck and J. Louis Martyn. Nashville: Abingdon, 1966.

Knox, "Evidence of Acts." Knox, John. "The Evidence of Acts." Pages 43–52 in *Chapters in a Life of Paul*. New York: Abingdon, 1950.

Knox, *Gentiles*. Knox, Wilfred L. *St. Paul and the Church of the Gentiles*. Cambridge: Cambridge University Press, 1939.

Knox, *Jerusalem*. Knox, Wilfred L. *St. Paul and the Church of Jerusalem*. Cambridge University Press, 1925.

Knox, "Reflections." Knox, John. "Reflections." Pages 107–14 in *Cadbury, Knox, and Talbert: American Contributions to the Study of Acts*. Edited by Mikeal C. Parsons and Joseph B. Tyson. SBLBSNA 18. SBLCP. Atlanta: Scholars Press, 1992.

Knox, "Serpent." Knox, Peter E. "The Serpent in the Augustan Garden: Horace's First Epode and the Ara Pacis." *CJ* 107 (1, 2011): 65–71.

Knuuttila and Sihvola, "Emotions." Knuuttila, Simo, and Juha Sihvola. "How the Philosophical Analysis of the Emotions Was Introduced." Pages 1–19 in *The Emotions in Hellenistic Philosophy*. Edited by Juha Sihvola and Troels Engberg-Pedersen. TSHP 46. Dordrecht, Neth.: Kluwer Academic, 1998.

Kobelski, "Melchizedek." Kobelski, P. J. "Melchizedek and Melchiresa: The Heavenly Prince of Light and the Prince of Darkness in the Qumran Literature." PhD diss., Fordham University, 1978.

Koch, "Border." Koch, Dietrich-Alex. "Crossing the Border: The 'Hellenists' and Their Way to the Gentiles." *Neot* 39 (2, 2005): 289–312.

Koch, *Gifts*. Koch, Kurt. *Charismatic Gifts*. Quebec: Association for Christian Evangelism, 1975.

Koch, "God-Fearers." Koch, Dietrich-Alex. "The God-Fearers between Facts and Fiction: Two Theosebeis-Inscriptions from Aphrodisias and Their Bearing for the New Testament." *ST* 60 (1, 2006): 62–90.

Koch, "*Macella*." Koch, Dietrich-Alex. "'Alles, was ἐν μακέλλῳ verkauft wird, esst . . .': Die *macella* von Pompeji, Gerasa, und Korinth und ihre Bedeutung für die Auslegung von 1Kor 10,25." *ZNW* 90 (3–4, 1999): 194–219.

Koch, "Menschensohn." Koch, Klaus. "Der 'Menschensohn' in Daniel." *ZAW* 119 (3, 2007): 369–85.

Koch, "Messias." Koch, Klaus. "Messias und Sündenvergebung in Jesaja 53-Targum: Ein Beitrag zur Praxis der aramäischen Bibelübersetzung." *JSJ* 3 (2, 1972): 117–48.

Koch, "Proselyten." Koch, Dietrich-Alex. "Proselyten und Gottesfürchtige als Hörer der Reden von Apostelgeschichte 2,14–39 und 13,16–41." Pages 83–107 in *Die Apostelgeschichte und die hellenistische

Geschichtsschreibung: Festschrift für Eckhard Plümacher zu seinem 65. Geburtstag*. Edited by Cilliers Breytenbach and Jens Schröter. Leiden: Brill, 2004.

Koch, *Revival*. Koch, Kurt. *The Revival in Indonesia*. Baden: Evangelization Publishers; Grand Rapids: Kregel, 1970.

Koch, "Völkertafel." Koch, Dietrich-Alex. "Die Völkertafel von Josephus, Antiquitates Iudaicae I und das 'Galatien' des Paulus." *ZNW* 103 (1, 2012): 136–41.

Koch, *Zulus*. Koch, Kurt E. *God Among the Zulus*. Translated by Justin Michell and Waldemar Engelbrecht. Natal, R.S.A.: Mission Kwa Sizabanu, 1981.

Kochavi, "Antipatris." Kochavi, Moshe. "Antipatris." *ABD* 1:272–74.

Kochavi, "Aphek." Kochavi, Moshe. "Aphek." *OEANE* 1:147–51.

Kodell, *Luke*. Kodell, Jerome. *The Gospel according to Luke*. Collegeville Bible Commentary. Collegeville, Minn.: Liturgical Press, 1983.

Koenig, *Hospitality*. Koenig, John. *New Testament Hospitality: Partnership with Strangers as Promise and Mission*. OBT 17. Philadelphia: Fortress, 1985.

Koenig, *Medicine*. Koenig, Harold G. *Medicine, Religion, and Health: Where Science and Spirituality Meet*. Templeton Science and Religion Series. West Conshohocken, Pa.: Templeton Foundation, 2008.

Koester, "Being." Koester, Helmut. "The Divine Human Being." *HTR* 78 (3–4, 1985): 243–52.

Koester, *Ephesos*. Koester, Helmut, ed. *Ephesos, Metropolis of Asia: An Interdisciplinary Approach to Its Archaeology, Religion, and Culture*. HTS. Valley Forge, Pa.: Trinity Press International, 1995.

Koester, "Ephesos in Literature." Koester, Helmut. "Ephesos in Early Christian Literature." Pages 119–40 in *Ephesos, Metropolis of Asia: An Interdisciplinary Approach to Its Archaeology, Religion, and Culture*. Edited by Helmut Koester. HTS. Valley Forge, Pa.: Trinity Press International, 1995.

Koester, "Eschatology." Koester, Helmut. "From Paul's Eschatology to the Apocalyptic Schemata of 2 Thessalonians." Pages 441–58 in *The Thessalonian Correspondence*. Edited by Raymond F. Collins. BETL 87. Leuven: Leuven University Press, 1990.

Koester, "Heroes." Koester, Helmut. "On Heroes, Tombs, and Early Christianity: An Epilogue." Pages 257–64 in *Flavius Philostratus: Heroikos*. Edited and translated by Jennifer K. Berenson Maclean and Ellen Bradshaw Aitken. SBLWGRW 1. Atlanta: SBL, 2001.

Koester, *Introduction*. Koester, Helmut. *Introduction to the New Testament*. 2 vols. Philadelphia: Fortress, 1982.

Koester, "Melikertes." Koester, Helmut. "Melikertes at Isthmia: A Roman Mystery Cult." Pages 355–66 in *Greeks, Romans, and Christians: Essays in Honor of Abraham J. Malherbe*. Edited by David L. Balch, Everett Ferguson, and Wayne A. Meeks. Minneapolis: Fortress, 1990.

Koester, *Paul and World*. Koester, Helmut. *Paul and His World: Interpreting the New Testament in Its Context*. Minneapolis: Fortress, 2007.

Koester, "Silence." Koester, Helmut. "The Silence of the Apostle." Pages 339–49 in *Urban Religion in Roman Corinth: Interdisciplinary Approaches*. Edited by Daniel N. Schowalter and Steven J. Friesen. HTS 53. Cambridge, Mass.: Harvard University Press, 2005.

Koester, "Spectrum." Koester, Craig R. "The Spectrum of Johannine Readers." Pages 5–19 in *"What Is John?" Readers and Reading of the Fourth Gospel*. Edited by Fernando F. Segovia. SBLSymS 3. Atlanta: Scholars Press, 1996.

Koester, "Structure." Koester, Helmut. "The Structure and Criteria of Early Christian Beliefs." Pages 205–31 in *Trajectories through Early Christianity*. By James M. Robinson and Helmut Koester. Philadelphia: Fortress, 1971.

Koester, *Symbolism*. Koester, Craig R. *Symbolism in the Fourth Gospel: Meaning, Mystery, Community*. Minneapolis: Fortress, 1995.

Koet, "Díptico." Koet, Bart J. "Lucas 10,38–42 y Hch 6,1–7: Un díptico lucano acerca de diakonia." *Mayéutica* 37 (83, 2011): 5–24.

Koet, "Divine Communication." Koet, Bart J. "Divine Communication in Luke-Acts." Pages 745–57 in *The Unity of Luke-Acts*. Edited by Joseph Verheyden. BETL 142. Leuven: Leuven University Press, 1999.

Koet, "Droomuitleg." Koet, Bart J. "Droomuitleg van de Rabbijnen." *Coll* 29 (1, 1999): 27–47.

Koet, "Poglądy." Koet, Bart J. "Poglądy św. Łukasza na Żydów—odrzucenie czy polemika?" *ColT* 64 (2, 1994): 53–66.

Koet, *Studies*. Koet, Bart J. *Five Studies on Interpretation of Scripture in Luke-Acts*. SNTA 14. Leuven: Leuven University Press, 1989.

Koets, *Deisidaimonia*. Koets, Peter John. *Deisidaimonia: A Contribution to the Knowledge of Religious Terminology in Greek*. Purmerend, Neth.: J. Mussies, 1929.

Koger, *Slaveowners*. Koger, Larry. *Black Slaveowners: Free Black Slave Masters in South Carolina, 1790–1860*. Jefferson, N.C.: McFarland, 1985.

Kohler, *Theology*. Kohler, K. *Jewish Theology*. New York: Macmillan, 1923.

Kohn, "Plays." Kohn, Thomas D. "Who Wrote Seneca's Plays?" *CW* 96 (3, 2003): 271–80.

Kokkinos, "Gentilicium." Kokkinos, Nikos. "A Fresh Look at the *gentilicium* of Felix, Procurator of Judaea." *Latomus* 49 (1, 1990): 126–41.

Kokkinos, "Herod's Death." Kokkinos, Nikos. "Herod's Horrid Death." *BAR* 28 (2, 2002): 28–35, 62.

Kolb, "Agora." Kolb, Frank. "Agora." *Brill Pauly* 1:349–55.

Kolb, "Mansion." Kolb, Bernhard. "Excavating a Nabataean Mansion." *NEA* 65 (4, 2002): 260–64.

Kolb, "Newspaper." Kolb, Anne. "Newspaper." *BrillPauly* 9:698–99.

Kolb, "Postal Services." Kolb, Anne. "Postal Services." *BrillPauly* 11:689–91.

Kolb, "Telegraphy." Kolb, Anna. "Telegraphy." *BrillPauly* 14:223–24.

Kolenkow, "Role." Kolenkow, Anitra Bingham. "What Is the Role of Testament in the Testament of Abraham?" *HTR* 67 (2, 1974): 182–84.

Kolenkow, "Testament." Kolenkow, Anitra Bingham. "The Literary Genre 'Testament.'" Pages 259–67 in *Early Judaism and Its Modern Interpreters*. Edited by Robert A. Kraft and George W. E. Nickelsburg. SBLBMI 2. Atlanta: Scholars Press, 1986.

Kolitz, "Masada." Kolitz, Zvi. "Masada—Suicide or Murder?" *Tradition* 12 (1, 1971): 5–26.

Kollmann, "Offenbarung." Kollmann, Bernd. "Göttliche Offenbarung magisch-pharmakologischer Heilkunst im Buch Tobit." *ZAW* 106 (2, 1994): 289–99.

Kollmann, "Philippus." Kollmann, Bernd. "Philippus der Evangelist und die Anfänge der Heidenmission." *Bib* 81 (4, 2000): 551–65.

Kollmann, "Schwurverbot." Kollmann, Bernd. "Das Schwurverbot Mt 5, 33–37/Jak 5, 12 im Spiegel antiker Eidkritik." *BZ* 40 (2, 1966): 179–93.

Koloski-Ostrow, "Latrines." Koloski-Ostrow, Ann O. "Roman Latrines." *ArchOd* 7 (3, 2004): 48–55.

Koltun-Fromm, "Sexuality." Koltun-Fromm, Naomi. "Sexuality and Holiness: Semitic Christian and Jewish Conceptualizations of Sexual Behavior." *VC* 54 (4, 2000): 375–95.

Konen, "Shipwrecks." Konen, Heinrich. "Shipwrecks, Exploration of." *BrillPauly* 13:392–403.

Konings and Carmo, "Querigma." Konings, Johan, and Solange Maria do Carmo. "Marcos, Lucas e o *querigma* de salvação universal." *REB* 69 (273, 2009): 103–19.

Konkel, *Kings*. Konkel, August H. *1 and 2 Kings*. NIVAC. Grand Rapids: Zondervan, 2006.

Konradt, "Datierung." Konradt, Matthias. "Zur Datierung des sogenannten antiochenischen Zwischenfalls." *ZNW* 102 (1, 2011): 19–39.

Konstan, "*Apollonius* and Novel." Konstan, David. "*Apollonius, King of Tyre* and the Greek Novel." Pages 173–82 in *The Search for the Ancient Novel*. Edited by James Tatum. Baltimore: Johns Hopkins University Press, 1994.

Konstan, "Clemency." Konstan, David. "Clemency as a Virtue." *CP* 100 (4, 2005): 337–46.

Konstan, "Friendship." Konstan, David. "Greek Friendship." *AJP* 117 (1, 1996): 71–94.

Konstan, "Introduction." Konstan, David. "Introduction." Pages xi–xxx in *Heraclitus: Homeric Problems*. Edited and translated by Donald A. Russell and David Konstan. SBLWGRW 14. Atlanta: SBL, 2005.

Konstan, "Invention." Konstan, David. "The Invention of Fiction." Pages 3–17 in *Ancient Fiction and Early Christian Narrative*. Edited by Ronald F. Hock, J. Bradley Chance, and Judith Perkins. SBLSymS 6. Atlanta: SBL, 1998.

Konstan, "Patrons." Konstan, David. "Patrons and Friends." *CP* 90 (4, 1995): 328–42.

Konstan, *Symmetry*. Konstan, David. *Sexual Symmetry: Love in the Ancient Novel and Related Genres*. Princeton: Princeton University Press, 1994.

Konstan et al., "Introduction." Konstan, David, et al., "Introduction." Pages 1–24 in *Philodemus: On Frank Criticism*. Edited and translated by David Konstan et al. SBLTT 43. Graeco-Roman Series 13. Atlanta: Scholars Press, 1998.

Koons, *Realism*. Koons, Robert C. *Realism Regained: An Exact Theory of Causation, Teleology, and the Mind*. Oxford: Oxford University Press, 2000.

Kooten, "Church." Kooten, George H. van. "Ἐκκλησία τοῦ θεοῦ: The 'Church of God' and the Civic Assemblies (ἐκκλησίαι) of the Greek Cities in the Roman Empire: A Response to Paul Trebilco and Richard A. Horsley." *NTS* 58 (4, 2012): 522–48.

Kopaska and Liston, *Afterburn*. Kopaska, Kc, and Carole Liston. *Afterburn: The Kc Kopaska Story. A Story of Tragedy, Redemption, and Transformation*. Bloomington, Ind.: Westbow/Nelson, 2011.

Koperski, "Women and Discipleship." Koperski, Veronica. "Luke 10,38–42 and Acts 6,1–7: Women and Discipleship in the Literary Context of Luke-Acts." Pages 517–44 in *The Unity of Luke-Acts*.

Edited by Joseph Verheyden. BETL 142. Leuven: Leuven University Press, 1999.

Koren and Nevo, "Approaches." Koren, J., and Y. D. Nevo. "Methodological Approaches to Islamic Studies." *Der Islam* 68 (1991): 87–107.

Korfmann, "Troy." Korfmann, Manfred. "Troy: Archaeology." *BrillPauly* 14:973–78.

Korostelina, "Insults." Korostelina, Karina. "Intergroup Identity Insults: A Social Identity Theory Perspective." *Identity: An International Journal of Theory and Research* 14 (3, 2014): 214–29.

Körting, "Theology of Atonement." Körting, Corinna. "Theology of Atonement in the Feast Calendar of the Temple Scroll: Some Observations." *JSP* 18 (2, 2004): 232–47.

Koschorke, Ludwig, and Delgado, *History.* Koschorke, Klaus, Frieder Ludwig, and Mariano Delgado, eds., with Roland Spliesgart. *A History of Christianity in Asia, Africa, and Latin America, 1450–1990: A Documentary Sourcebook.* Grand Rapids: Eerdmans, 2007.

Koskenniemi, "Apollonius." Koskenniemi, Erkki. "Apollonius of Tyana: A Typical θεῖος ἀνήρ?" *JBL* 117 (3, 1998): 455–67.

Koskenniemi, "Background." Koskenniemi, Erkki. "The Religious-Historical Background of the New Testament Miracles." Pages 103–16 in *Religious and Spiritual Events.* Vol. 1 of *Miracles: God, Science, and Psychology in the Paranormal.* Edited by J. Harold Ellens. 3 vols. Westport, Conn.; London: Praeger, 2008.

Koskenniemi, *Miracle-Workers.* Koskenniemi, Erkki. *The Old Testament Miracle-Workers in Early Judaism.* WUNT 2.206. Tübingen: Mohr Siebeck, 2005.

Koskenniemi, "Moses." Koskenniemi, Erkki. "Moses—A Well-Educated Man: A Look at the Educational Idea in Early Judaism." *JSP* 17 (4, 2008): 281–96.

Kosman, "Definition." Kosman, L. A. "Charmides' First Definition: Sophrosyne as Quietness." Pages 203–16 in vol. 2 of *Essays in Ancient Greek Philosophy.* Edited by J. P. Anton, G. L. Kustas, and A. Preus. Albany: State University of New York Press, 1971–.

Kosman, "Story." Kosman, Admiel. "The Story of a Giant Story: The Winding Way of Og King of Bashan in the Jewish Haggadic Tradition." *HUCA* 73 (2002): 157–90.

Koss, "Spirits." Koss, Joan D. "Spirits as Socializing Agents: A Case Study of a Puerto Rican Girl Reared in a Matrocentric Family." Pages 365–82 in *Case Studies in Spirit Possession.* Edited by Vincent Crapanzaro and Vivian Garrison. New York: Wiley, 1977.

Köstenberger and O'Brien, *Salvation.* Köstenberger, Andreas J., and Peter T. O'Brien. *Salvation to the Ends of the Earth: A Biblical Theology of Mission.* Downers Grove, Ill.: InterVarsity, 2001.

Kotansky, "Amulet." Kotansky, Roy. "An Inscribed Copper Amulet from 'Evron." *'Atiqot* 20 (1991): 81–87.

Kotansky, "Demonology." Kotansky, Roy. "Demonology." *DNTB* 269–73.

Kotansky, "Remnants." Kotansky, Roy. "Remnants of a Liturgical Exorcism on a Gem." *Mus* 108 (1995): 143–56.

Kotlar, "Mikveh." Kotlar, David. "Mikveh." Pages 1534–44 in vol. 11 of *Encyclopaedia Judaica.* 16 vols. Jerusalem: Keter, 1972.

Kottak, "Adaptation." Kottak, Conrad P. "Cultural Adaptation, Kinship, and Descent in Madagascar." *SWJA* 27 (2, Summer 1971): 129–47.

Kottak, "Kinship." Kottak, Conrad Phillip. "Kinship and Class in Brazil." *Ethnology* 6 (4, 1967): 427–43.

Kovacs, *Corinthians.* Kovacs, Judith L., trans. and ed. *1 Corinthians: Interpreted by Early Christian Commentators.* The Church's Bible. Grand Rapids: Eerdmans, 2005.

Kovacs, "Introduction to *Cyclops.*" Kovacs, David. Introduction to *Cyclops.* Pages 53–58 in Euripides, *Cyclops, Alcestes, Medea.* Edited by David Kovacs. LCL. Cambridge, Mass.: Harvard University Press, 1994.

Kovacs, "Introduction to *Medea.*" Kovacs, David. Introduction to *Medea.* Pages 285–91 in Euripides, *Cyclops, Alcestes, Medea.* Edited by David Kovacs. LCL. Cambridge, Mass.: Harvard University Press, 1994.

Kovelman, "Farce." Kovelman, Arkadi. "Farce in the Talmud." *RRJ* 5 (1, 2002): 86–92.

Kowalski, "Exegese." Kowalski, Beate. "'Verstehst du denn auch, was du liest?' (Apg 8,30). Wege der Exegese und Bibeldidaktik heute." *TGl* 99 (2, 2009): 129–46.

Kowalski, "Fenstersturz." Kowalski, Beate. "Der Fenstersturz des Eutychus in Troas (Apg 20,7–12)." *SNTSU* 30 (2005): 19–37.

Kowalski, "Widerstände." Kowalski, Beate. "Widerstände, Visionen, und Geistführung bei Paulus." *ZKT* 125 (4, 2003): 387–410.

Kraabel, "Disappearance." Kraabel, Alf Thomas. "The Disappearance of the 'God-Fearers.'" *Numen* 28 (2, 1981): 113–26.

Kraabel, "Evidence." Kraabel, Alf Thomas. "New Evidence of the Samaritan Diaspora Has Been Found on Delos." *BA* 47 (1, 1984): 44–46.

Kraabel, "Hypsistos." Kraabel, Alf Thomas. "Hypsistos and the Synagogue at Sardis." *GRBS* 10 (1, 1969): 81–93.

Kraabel, "Jews in Rome." Kraabel, Alf Thomas. "Jews in Imperial Rome: More Archaeological Evidence from an Oxford Collection." *JJS* 30 (1, 1979): 41–58.

Kraabel, "Judaism in Asia Minor." Kraabel, Alf Thomas. "Judaism in Western Asia Minor under the Roman Empire, with a Preliminary Study of the Jewish Community at Sardis, Lydia." ThD diss., Harvard Divinity School, 1968.

Kraabel, "Lutherans in Acts." Kraabel, Alf Thomas. "Greeks, Jews, and Lutherans in the Middle Half of Acts." *HTR* 79 (1–3, 1986): 147–57.

Kraabel, "Synagogue and Community." Kraabel, Alf Thomas. "The Synagogue and the Jewish Community: Impact." Pages 178–90 in *Sardis from Prehistoric to Roman Times: Results of the Archaeological Exploration of Sardis, 1958–1975.* Edited by George M. A. Hanfmann, assisted by William E. Mierse. Cambridge, Mass.: Harvard University Press, 1983.

Kraeling, "Jewish Community at Antioch." Kraeling, Carl H. "The Jewish Community at Antioch." *JBL* 51 (1932): 130–60.

Kraeling, *John the Baptist.* Kraeling, Carl H. *John the Baptist.* New York: Scribner's, 1951.

Kraemer, *Aseneth.* Kraemer, Ross Shepard. *When Aseneth Met Joseph: A Late Antique Tale of the Biblical Patriarch and His Egyptian Wife, Reconsidered.* New York: Oxford University Press, 1998.

Kraemer, "Doctor." Kraemer, David. "Why Your Son (or Daughter), the Doctor, Really Is God." *ConsJud* 59 (1, 2006): 72–79.

Kraemer, "Ecstasy." Kraemer, Ross Shepard. "Ecstasy and Possession: The Attraction of Women to the Cult of Dionysus." *HTR* 72 (1, 1979): 55–80.

Kraemer, "Ecstatics." Kraemer, Ross Shepard. "Ecstatics and Ascetics: Studies in the Functions of Religious Activities for Women in the Greco-Roman World." PhD diss., Princeton University, 1976.

Kraemer, "Euoi." Kraemer, Ross Shepard. "'Euoi saboi' in Demosthenes de Corona: In Whose Honor Were the Women's Rites?" Pages 229–36 in *SBL Seminar Papers, 1981.* Edited by Kent Harold Richards. SBLSP 20. Chico, Calif.: Scholars Press, 1981.

Kraemer, "Evidence." Kraemer, Ross Shepard. "Non-literary Evidence for Jewish Women in Rome and Egypt." *Helios* 13 (2, 1986): 85–101.

Kraemer, "Inscription from Malta." Kraemer, Ross Shepard. "A New Inscription from Malta and the Question of Women Elders in the Diaspora Jewish Communities." *HTR* 78 (3–4, 1985): 431–38.

Kraemer, *Maenads*. Kraemer, Ross Shepard. *Maenads, Martyrs, Matrons, Monastics: A Sourcebook on Women's Religions in the Greco-Roman World*. Philadelphia: Fortress, 1988.

Kraemer, "Meaning of 'Jew.'" Kraemer, Ross Shepard. "On the Meaning of the Term 'Jew' in Greco-Roman Inscriptions." *HTR* 82 (1, 1989): 35–53.

Kraemer, "Monastic Women." Kraemer, Ross Shepard. "Monastic Jewish Women in Greco-Roman Egypt: Philo Judaeus on the Therapeutrides." *Signs* 14 (2, 1989): 342–70.

Krafft, "Earthquake." Krafft, Fritz. "Earthquake: Greco-Roman World." *BrillPauly* 4:767–69.

Krafft et al., "Astronomy." Krafft, Fritz, et al. "Astronomy." *BrillPauly* 2:199–210.

Kraft, *Christianity in Culture*. Kraft, Charles H. *Christianity in Culture: A Study in Dynamic Biblical Theologizing in Cross-cultural Perspective*. Foreword by Bernard Ramm. Maryknoll, N.Y.: Orbis, 1981.

Kraft, "Judaism on Scene." Kraft, Robert A. "Judaism on the World Scene." Pages 81–98 in *The Catacombs and the Colosseum: The Roman Empire as the Setting of Primitive Christianity*. Edited by Stephen Benko and John J. O'Rourke. Valley Forge, Pa.: Judson, 1971.

Kraft, "Reassessing." Kraft, Robert A. "Reassessing the 'Recensional Problem' in Testament of Abraham." Pages 121–37 in *Studies on the Testament of Abraham*. Edited by George W. E. Nickelsburg. SBLSCS 6. Missoula, Mont.: Scholars Press, 1976.

Kraftchick, "Πάθη." Kraftchick, Steven J. "Πάθη in Paul: The Emotional Logic of 'Original Argument.'" Pages 39–68 in *Paul and Pathos*. Edited by Thomas H. Olbricht and Jerry L. Sumney. SBLSymS 16. Atlanta: SBL, 2001.

Kragelund, "Nero's *luxuria*." Kragelund, Patrick. "Nero's *luxuria*, in Tacitus and in the *Octavia*." *CQ* 50 (2, 2000): 494–515.

Kramer, "Literature." Kramer, Samuel Noah. "Sumerian Literature in the Bible." Pages 272–84 in *The Bible in Its Literary Milieu*. Edited by Vincent L. Tollers and John R. Maier. Grand Rapids: Eerdmans, 1979.

Kramer, "Variation." Kramer, Samuel Noah. "'Man and His God': A Sumerian Variation on the 'Job' Motif." Pages 170–82 in *Wisdom in Israel and in the Ancient Near East; Presented to Professor Harold Henry Rowley for His 65th Birthday*. Edited by Martin Noth and D. Winton Thomas. VTSup 3. Leiden: Brill, 1960.

Krampe, "Fenus nauticum." Krampe, Christoph. "Fenus nauticum." *BrillPauly* 5:381–82.

Krampe, "Naufragium." Krampe, Christoph. "Naufragium." *BrillPauly* 9:541–42.

Krasser, "Reading." Krasser, Helmut. "Light Reading." *BrillPauly* 7:553–55.

Kratz, *Rettungswunder*. Kratz, Reinhard G. *Rettungswunder. Motiv-, traditions- und formkritische Aufarbeitung einer biblischen Gattung*. EurH 23.123. Frankfurt: Lang, 1979.

Kraus, "(Il)literacy." Kraus, Thomas J. "(Il)literacy in Non-literary Papyri from Graeco-Roman Egypt: Further Aspects of the Educational Ideal in Ancient Literary Sources and Modern Times." *Mnemosyne* 53 (3, 2000): 322–42.

Kraus, "Illiterate." Kraus, Thomas J. "'Uneducated,' 'Ignorant,' or even 'Illiterate'? Aspects and Background for an Understanding of ἀγράμματοι (and ἰδιῶται) in Acts 4.13." *NTS* 45 (3, 1999): 434–49.

Krause, "Colonatus." Krause, Jens-Uwe. "Colonatus." *BrillPauly* 3:538–41.

Krause, "Exploring." Krause, Neal. "Exploring the Stress-Buffering Effects of Church-Based and Secular Social Support on Self-Rated Health in Late Life." *JGPSSS* 61 (1, 2006): S35–43.

Krause, "Honestiores." Krause, Jens-Uwe. "Honestiores/Humiliores." *BrillPauly* 6:472–74.

Krause, "Patrocinium." Krause, Jens-Uwe. "Patrocinium." *BrillPauly* 10:618–20.

Krause, "Support." Krause, Neal. "Church-Based Social Support and Mortality." *JGPSSS* 61 (3, 2006): S140–46.

Krause, *Witwen und Waisen*. Krause, Jens-Uwe. *Witwen und Waisen im römischen Reich*. 4 vols. HABES 16–19. Stuttgart: Steiner, 1994–95.

Krauter, *Bürgerrecht*. Krauter, Stefan. *Bürgerrecht und Kultteilnahme: politische und kultische Rechte und Pflichten in griechischen Poleis, Rom und antikem Judentum*. BZNWK 127. Berlin, New York: de Gruyter, 2004.

Krauter, "Epos." Krauter, Stefan. "Vergils Evangelium und das lukanische Epos? Überlegungen zu Gattung und Theologie des lukanischen Doppelwerkes." Pages 214–43 in *Die Apostelgeschichte im Kontext antiker und frühchristlicher Historiographie*. Edited by Jörg Frey, Clare K. Rothschild, and Jens Schröter, with Bettina Rost. BZNWK 162. Berlin: de Gruyter, 2009.

Kraybill, *Cult and Commerce*. Kraybill, J. Nelson. *Imperial Cult and Commerce in John's Apocalypse*. JSNTSup 132. Sheffield, U.K.: Sheffield Academic, 1996.

Kraybill and Sweetland, "Sociological Perspective." Kraybill, Donald B., and Dennis M. Sweetland. "Possessions in Luke-Acts: A Sociological Perspective." *PRSt* 10 (3, 1983): 215–39.

Krebs, "Conversation." Krebs, Christopher B. "A Seemingly Artless Conversation: Cicero's De Legibus (1.1–5)." *CP* 104 (1, 2009): 90–106.

Kreiser, "Devils." Kreiser, B. Robert. "The Devils of Toulon: Demonic Possession and Religious Politics in Eighteenth-Century Provence." Pages 63–111 in *Possession and Exorcism*. Vol. 9 of *Articles on Witchcraft, Magic, and Demonology: A Twelve-Volume Anthology of Scholarly Articles*. Edited by Brian P. Levack. New York: Garland, 1992. Reprinted from pages 173–221 in *Church, State, and Society under the Bourbon Kings of France*. Edited by Richard M. Golden. Lawrence, Kans.: Coronado Press, 1982.

Kreiser, *Miracles*. Kreiser, B. Robert. *Miracles, Convulsions, and Ecclesiastical Politics in Early Eighteenth-Century Paris*. Princeton: Princeton University Press, 1978.

Kreitzer, "Clue to Acts 19.23–41." Kreitzer, Larry J. "A Numismatic Clue to Acts 19.23–41: The Ephesian Cistophori of Claudius and Agrippina." *JSNT* 30 (1987): 59–70.

Kreitzer, *Corinthians*. Kreitzer, Larry J. *2 Corinthians*. Sheffield, U.K.: Sheffield Academic, 1996.

Kreitzer, "Rome." Kreitzer, Larry J. "Nero's Rome: Images of the City on Imperial Coinage." *EvQ* 61 (4, 1989): 301–9.

Kreitzer, "Travel." Kreizer, Larry J. "Travel." *DPL* 945–46.

Kremer, *Pfingstbericht*. Kremer, Jacob. *Pfingstbericht und Pfingstgeschehen: Eine exegetische Untersuchung zu Apg 2,1–13*. SBS 63/64. Stuttgart: KBW (Katholisches Bibelwerk) Verlag, 1973.

Kremer, "Wiedergabe." Kremer, Jacob. "Die dreifache Wiedergabe des Damaskuserlebnisses Pauli in der Apostelgeschichte: Eine Hilfe für das rechte Verständnis der lukanischen Osterevangelien." Pages 329–55 in *The Unity of Luke-Acts*. Edited by Joseph Verheyden. BETL 142. Leuven: Leuven University Press, 1999.

Krentz, "All Things." Krentz, Edgar. "Paul: All Things to All People—Flexible and Welcoming." *CurTM* 24 (3, 1997): 238–44.

Krentz, "Down." Krentz, Edgar. "Turning the World Upside Down—Preaching Luke's Story." *CurTM* 36 (6, 2009): 434–39.

Krentz, "Games." Krentz, Edgar. "Paul, Games, and the Military." Pages 344–83 in *Paul in the Greco-Roman World: A Handbook*. Edited by J. Paul Sampley. Harrisburg, Pa.: Trinity Press International, 2003.

Krentz, "Necessity." Krentz, Edgar. "Necessity Is Laid on Me: The Birth of Mission in Paul." *CurTM* 33 (1, 2006): 5–21.

Krentz, "Oxymora." Krentz, Edgar. "The Sense of Senseless Oxymora." *CurTM* 28 (6, 2001): 577–84.

Krieger, "Abendmahlsgemeinschaft." Krieger, Klaus-Stefan. "Die erste Abendmahlsgemeinschaft: Das Apostelkonzil-Modell einer Verständigung." *BK* 55 (2, 2000): 79–82.

Krieger, "Hauptquelle." Krieger, Klaus-Stefan. "Zur Frage nach der Hauptquelle über die Geschichte der Provinz Judäa in den Antiquitates judaicae des Flavius Josephus." *BN* 63 (1992): 37–41.

Krieger, "Judenfeind." Krieger, Klaus-Stefan. "Pontius Pilate—ein Judenfeind? Zur Problematik einer Pilatus-Biographie." *BN* 78 (1995): 63–83.

Krieger, "Paul and Torah." Krieger, L. "Paul and Torah." *CHSP* 60 (1990): 41–47.

Krieger, "Priester." Krieger, Klaus-Stefan. "Priester, Bandenchef, Geschichtsschreiber: Leben und Werk des Flavius Josephus." *BK* 53 (2, 1998): 50–54.

Krieger, "Problematik." Krieger, Klaus-Stefan. "Die Problematik chronologischer Rekonstruktionen zur Amtszeit des Pilatus." *BN* 61 (1992): 27–32.

Krieger, "Schwester." Krieger, Klaus-Stefan. "Berenike, die Schwester König Agrippas II., bei Flavius Josephus." *JSJ* 28 (1, 1997): 1–11.

Krieger, "Verwandter." Krieger, Klaus-Stefan. "War Flavius Josephus ein Verwandter des hasmonäischen Königshauses?" *BN* 73 (1994): 58–65.

Krings, "History." Krings, Matthias. "On History and Language of the 'European' *Bori* Spirits of Kano, Nigeria." Pages 53–67 in *Spirit Possession, Modernity and Power in Africa*. Edited by Heike Behrend and Ute Luig. Madison: University of Wisconsin Press, 1999.

Krippner, "Disorders." Krippner, Stanley. "Cross-cultural Treatment Perspectives on Dissociative Disorders." Pages 338–61 in *Dissociation: Clinical and Theoretical Perspectives*. Edited by S. J. Lynn and J. W. Rhue. New York: Guilford, 1994.

Krippner, "Perspectives." Krippner, Stanley C. "Conflicting Perspectives on Shamans and Shamanism: Points and Counterpoints." *AmPsyc* (Nov. 2002): 962–77.

Krippner and Achterberg, "Experiences." Krippner, Stanley, and Jeanne Achterberg. "Anomalous Healing Experiences." Pages 353–96 in *Varieties of Anomalous Experience: Examining the Scientific Evidence*. Edited by Etzel Cardeña, Steven Jay Lynn, and Stanley Krippner. Washington,

D.C.: American Psychological Association, 2000.

Krodel, *Acts*. Krodel, Gerhard A. *Acts*. AugCNT. Minneapolis: Augsburg, 1986.

Kroeber, *Anthropology*. Kroeber, A. L. *Anthropology: Culture Patterns and Processes*. New York: Harcourt Brace Jovanovich, 1948.

Kroeger, "Classicist's View." Kroeger, Catherine Clark. "1 Timothy 2:12—A Classicist's View." Pages 225–44 in *Women, Authority, and the Bible*. Edited by Alvera Mickelsen. Downers Grove, Ill.: InterVarsity, 1986.

Kroeger, "Cults." Kroeger, Catherine Clark. "The Apostle Paul and the Greco-Roman Cults of Women." *JETS* 30 (1, 1987): 25–38.

Kroeger and Kroeger, *Woman*. Kroeger, Richard Clark, and Catherine Clark Kroeger. *I Suffer Not a Woman: Rethinking 1 Timothy 2:11–15 in Light of Ancient Evidence*. Grand Rapids: Baker, 1992.

Kroeker, "Messianic Ethics." Kroeker, P. Travis. "Whither Messianic Ethics? Paul as Political Theorist." *JSCE* 25 (2, 2005): 37–58.

Kroll, "Greek Inscriptions." Kroll, John H. "The Greek Inscriptions of the Sardis Synagogue." *HTR* 94 (1, 2001): 5–55.

Kron, "Anthropometry." Kron, Geoffrey. "Anthropometry, Physical Anthropology, and the Reconstruction of Ancient Health, Nutrition, and Living Standards." *Historia* 54 (1, 2005): 68–83.

Kruse, "Persecution." Kruse, Colin. "Persecution." *DNTB* 775–78.

Kruse, *Romans*. Kruse, Colin G. *Paul's Letter to the Romans*. PillNTC. Grand Rapids: Eerdmans, 2012.

Krygier, "Extermination." Krygier, Rivon. "Did God Command the Extermination of the Canaanites? The Rabbis' Encounter with Genocide." *ConsJud* 57 (2, 2005): 78–94.

Kselman, *Miracles*. Kselman, Thomas A. *Miracles and Prophecies in Nineteenth-Century France*. New Brunswick, N.J.: Rutgers University Press, 1983.

Kuck, "Preaching." Kuck, David W. "Preaching on Acts for Mission Formation." *CurTM* 31 (1, 2004): 32–39.

Kugel and Greer, *Interpretation*. Kugel, James L., and Rowan A. Greer. *Early Biblical Interpretation*. LEC 3. Philadelphia: Westminster, 1986.

Kugler, "Evidence." Kugler, Robert A. "Some Further Evidence for the Samaritan Provenance of *Aramaic Levi* (1QTestLevi; 4QTestLevi)." *RevQ* 17 (65–68, 1996): 351–58.

Kügler, "König." Kügler, Joachim. "Der andere König: Religionsgeschichtliche

Anmerkungen zum Jesusbild des Johannesevangeliums." *ZNW* 88 (3–4, 1997): 223–41.

Kugler, "Reconstruction." Kugler, Robert. "4Q225 2 i 1–2: A Possible Reconstruction and Explanation." *JBL* 126 (1, 2007): 172–81.

Kuhlman, *Miracles*. Kuhlman, Kathryn. *I Believe in Miracles*. New York: Prentice-Hall, 1962.

Kuhn, "Gekreuzigten." Kuhn, Heinz-Wolfgang. "Zum Gekreuzigten von Giv'at ha-Mivtar: Korrektur eines Versehens in der Erstveröffentlichung." *ZNW* 69 (1978): 118–22.

Kuhn, "Messias." Kuhn, Heinz-Wolfgang. "Die beiden Messias in den Qumrantexten und die Messiasvorstellung in der rabbinischen Literatur." *ZAW* 70 (1958): 200–208.

Kuhn, "Son of God." Kuhn, Karl A. "The 'One like a Son of Man' Becomes the 'Son of God.'" *CBQ* 69 (1, 2007): 22–42.

Kuhn, *Structure*. Kuhn, Thomas S. *The Structure of Scientific Revolutions*. 2nd ed. Chicago: University of Chicago Press, 1970.

Kuhrt, "Mesopotamia." Kuhrt, Amélie. "Ancient Mesopotamia in Classical Greek and Hellenistic Thought." Pages 55–66 in vol. 1 of *Civilizations of the Ancient Near East*. Edited by Jack M. Sasson. 4 vols. New York: Scribner's, 1995.

Külling, *Geheimnis*. Külling, Heinz. *Geoffenbartes Geheimnis: eine Auslegung von Apostelgeschichte 17,16–34*. ATANT 79. Zürich: Theologischer Verlag, 1993.

Kulp, "Origins." Kulp, Joshua. "The Origins of the Seder and Haggadah." *CBR* 4 (1, 2005): 109–34.

Kulp, "Patterns." Kulp, Joshua. "Organisational Patterns in the Mishnah in Light of Their Toseftan Parallels." *JJS* 58 (1, 2007): 52–78.

Külzer, "Geography." Külzer, Andreas. "Samothrace. I. Geography and History." *BrillPauly* 12:937–38.

Kümmel, *Introduction*. Kümmel, Werner George. *Introduction to the New Testament*. London: SCM, 1965.

Kümmel, *Promise*. Kümmel, Werner Georg. *Promise and Fulfilment: The Eschatological Message of Jesus*. SBT 23. Naperville, Ill.: Alec R. Allenson, 1957.

Kümmel, *Römer 7*. Kümmel, Werner Georg. *Römer 7 und die Bekehrung des Paulus*. Leipzig: Hinrichs, 1929.

Kümmel, *Theology*. Kümmel, Werner Georg. *The Theology of the New Testament according to Its Major Witnesses—Jesus, Paul, John*. Translated by John E. Steely. Nashville: Abingdon, 1973.

Kundert, "Bindung Isaaks." Kundert, Lukas. "Die 'Bindung Isaaks' im frühen

Judentum—und ihre Wirkung auf das Neue Testament." *BL* 72 (3, 1999): 135–54.

Kunin, "Proselytes." Kunin, David A. "Proselytes, a Scab or a Blessing? Rabbinic Attitudes to Converts." *JPJ* 5 (1995): 96–112.

Kunkel, *Introduction*. Kunkel, Wolfgang. *An Introduction to Roman Legal and Constitutional History*. 2nd ed. Oxford: Clarendon, 1973.

Kunst, "Privatbibliotheken." Kunst, Christiane. "Römische Privatbibliotheken: Zur Selbstinszenierung der römischen Aristokratie." *ZRGG* 57 (1, 2005): 48–59.

Kuper, "Kinship." Kuper, Hilda. "Kinship among the Swazi." Pages 86–110 in *African Systems of Kinship and Marriage*. Edited by A. R. Radcliffe-Brown and Daryll Forde. New York: Oxford University Press, 1950.

Kurek-Chomycz, "Tendency." Kurek-Chomycz, D. A. "Is There an 'Anti-Priscan' Tendency in the Manuscripts? Some Textual Problems with Prisca and Aquila." *JBL* 125 (1, 2006): 107–28.

Kurichianil, "Orderly Account." Kurichianil, John. "The Acts of the Apostles—'An Orderly Account' (An Examination of the Plan of the Acts)." *BiBh* 34 (2, 2008): 150–82.

Kurichianil, "Paul." Kurichianil, John. "Paul in the Acts of the Apostles." *ITS* 45 (3, 2008): 255–93.

Kurichianil, "Speeches." Kurichianil, John. "The Speeches in Acts and the Old Testament." *ITS* 17 (2, 1980): 181–86.

Kurz, *Acts*. Kurz, William S. *Acts of the Apostles*. CCSS. Grand Rapids: Baker Academic, 2013.

Kurz, "Approaches." Kurz, William S. "Narrative Approaches to Luke-Acts." *Bib* 68 (1987): 195–220.

Kurz, "Effects of Variant Narrators." Kurz, William S. "Effects of Variant Narrators in Acts 10–11." *NTS* 43 (4, 1997): 570–86.

Kurz, "Luke 22:14–38." Kurz, William S. "Luke 22:14–38 and Greco-Roman and Biblical Farewell Addresses." *JBL* 104 (2, 1985): 251–68.

Kurz, "Models." Kurz, William S. "Narrative Models for Imitation in Luke-Acts." Pages 171–89 in *Greeks, Romans, and Christians: Essays in Honor of Abraham J. Malherbe*. Edited by David L. Balch, Everett Ferguson, and Wayne A. Meeks. Minneapolis: Fortress, 1990.

Kurz, "Promise and Fulfillment." Kurz, William. "Promise and Fulfillment in Hellenistic Jewish Narratives and in Luke and Acts." Pages 147–70 in *Jesus and the Heritage of Israel: Luke's Narrative Claim upon Israel's Legacy*. Edited by David P. Moessner. Luke the Interpreter of Israel

1. Harrisburg, Pa.: Trinity Press International, 1999.

Kurz, *Reading Luke-Acts*. Kurz, William S. *Reading Luke-Acts: Dynamics of Biblical Narrative*. Louisville: Westminster John Knox, 1993.

Kurz, "Rhetoric in Christological Proof." Kurz, William S. "Hellenistic Rhetoric in the Christological Proof of Luke-Acts." *CBQ* 42 (2, 1980): 171–95.

Kurzinger, *Apostelgeschichte*. Kurzinger, Joseph. *Die Apostelgeschichte*. Würzburg: Echter-Verlag, 1951.

Kushnir-Stein, "City Goddess." Kushnir-Stein, Alla. "The City Goddess on the Weights of Ascalon." *IsNumR* 1 (2006): 117–22 and plates 15–17.

Kushnir-Stein, "Weights." Kushnir-Stein, Alla. "Two Lead Weights from the Colony of Caesarea Maritima." *IsNumR* 2 (2007): 137–41.

Kustas, "Diatribe." Kustas, George L. "Diatribe in Ancient Rhetorical Theory." *CHSP* 22 (1976): 1–15.

Kuznecov, "Typology." Kuznecov, A. M. "On the Typology of the Semantic Field of Kinship Terms." *Ling* 125 (Apr. 1, 1974): 5–14.

Kvalbein, "Wonders." Kvalbein, Hans. "The Wonders of the End-Time: Metaphoric Language in 4Q521 and the Interpretation of Matthew 11.5 par." *JSP* 18 (1998): 87–110.

Kvalbein, "Wunder." Kvalbein, Hans. "Die Wunder der Endzeit: Beobachtungen zu 4Q521 und Matth 11,5p." *ZNW* 88 (1–2, 1997): 111–25.

Kwan, "Argument." Kwan, Kai-Man. "The Argument from Religious Experience." Pages 498–552 in *The Blackwell Companion to Natural Theology*. Edited by William Lane Craig and J. P. Moreland. Oxford: Blackwell, 2009.

Kwon, *Corinthians*. Kwon, Oh-Young. *1 Corinthians 1–4: Reconstructing Its Social and Rhetorical Situation and Re-Reading It Cross-Culturally for Korean-Confucian Christians Today*. Eugene, Ore.: Wipf & Stock, 2010.

Kwon, "Foundations." Kwon, Tack Joe. "The Theoretical Foundations of Healing Ministry and the Applications to Church Growth." DMin diss., Fuller Theological Seminary, 1985.

Kydd, *Gifts*. Kydd, Ronald A. N. *Charismatic Gifts in the Early Church*. Peabody, Mass.: Hendrickson, 1984.

Kydd, *Healing*. Kydd, Ronald A. N. *Healing through the Centuries: Models for Understanding*. Peabody, Mass.: Hendrickson, 1998.

Kyomo, "Healing." Kyomo, Andrew A. "Faith and Healing in the African

Context." Pages 145–56 in *Charismatic Renewal in Africa: A Challenge for African Christianity*. Edited by Mika Vähäkangas and Andrew A. Kyomo. Nairobi: Acton, 2003.

Kypriou and Zapheiropoulou, ΡΟΔΟΣ. Kypriou, Euangelia, and Diana Zapheiropoulou. ΡΟΔΟΣ 2.400 ΧΡΟΝΙΑ. 2 vols. Athens: Hypourgeio Politismou, 1999. (Proceedings of Oct. 24–29, 1993, conference in Rhodes.)

Kyrychenko, "Old Slavonic Acts." Kyrychenko, Alexander. "The Old Slavonic Acts in *apparatus critici* of the Greek NT: Observations and Suggestions." *NovT* 47 (1, 2005): 69–74.

Kysar, *Maverick Gospel*. Kysar, Robert. *John, The Maverick Gospel*. Atlanta: John Knox, 1976.

Kytzler, "Utopia." Kytzler, Bernhard. "Utopia." *BrillPauly* 15:145–48.

Laansma, "Mysticism." Laansma, Jon C. "Mysticism." *DNTB* 725–37.

Labendz, "Epicurean." Labendz, Jenny R. "'Know What to Answer the Epicurean': A Diachronic Study of the *'apiqoros* in Rabbinic Literature." *HUCA* 74 (2003): 175–214.

La Bua, "Obscuritas." La Bua, Giuseppe. "*Obscuritas* e *dissimulatio* nella *Pro Tulio* di Cicerone." *Rhetorica* 23 (3, 2005): 261–80.

Lacey, "Patria potestas." Lacey, W. K. "*Patria potestas*." Pages 121–44 in *The Family in Ancient Rome: New Perspectives*. Edited by Beryl Rawson. Ithaca, N.Y.: Cornell University Press, 1986.

Lach, "Zrzeszenia." Lach, J. "Uczta Zrzeszenia z Qumran a Ostatnia Wieczerza (Convivium congregationis quomranensis cum ultima cena comparatur)." *RuBL* 11 (1958): 489–97.

Lachs, *Commentary*. Lachs, Samuel Tobias. *A Rabbinic Commentary on the New Testament: The Gospels of Matthew, Mark, and Luke*. Hoboken, N.J.: KTAV; New York: Anti-Defamation League of B'Nai B'Rith, 1987.

Lachs, "Matthew 23:27–28." Lachs, Samuel Tobias. "On Matthew 23:27–28." *HTR* 68 (1975): 385–88.

Lachs, "Pharisees and Sadducees on Angels." Lachs, Samuel Tobias. "The Pharisees and Sadducees on Angels: A Reexamination of Acts XXIII.8." *GCAJS* 6 (1977): 35–42.

Lacomara, "Deuteronomy." Lacomara, Aelred. "Deuteronomy and the Farewell Discourse (Jn 13:31–16:33)." *CBQ* 36 (1, 1974): 65–84.

La Croce, "Concepto." La Croce, Ernesto. "El concepto de locure en Grecia clasica." *APsPSAL* 27 (4–5, 1981): 285–91.

Ladd, *Criticism*. Ladd, George Eldon. *The New Testament and Criticism*. Grand Rapids: Eerdmans, 1967.

Ladd, *Hope*. Ladd, George Eldon. *The Blessed Hope*. Grand Rapids: Eerdmans, 1956.

Ladd, *Kingdom*. Ladd, George Eldon. *The Gospel of the Kingdom*. London: Paternoster, 1959. Repr., Grand Rapids: Eerdmans, 1978.

Ladd, "Israel." Ladd, George Eldon. "Israel and the Church." *EvQ* 36 (4, 1964): 206–13.

Ladd, *Last Things*. Ladd, George Eldon. *The Last Things*. Grand Rapids: Eerdmans, 1978.

Ladd, "Pensée de Paul." Ladd, George Eldon. "Introduction à la pensée de Paul." *Hok* 10 (1979): 18–36.

Ladd, "Righteousness." Ladd, George Eldon. "Righteousness in Romans." *SWJT* 19 (1, 1976): 6–17.

Ladd, *Theology*. Ladd, George Eldon. *A Theology of the New Testament*. Grand Rapids: Eerdmans, 1974.

Ladd, *Young Church*. Ladd, George Eldon. *The Young Church*. New York: Abingdon, 1964.

Ladouceur, "Josephus and Masada." Ladouceur, David J. "Josephus and Masada." Pages 95–113 in *Josephus, Judaism, and Christianity*. Edited by Louis H. Feldman and Gohei Hata. Detroit: Wayne State University Press, 1987.

Ladouceur, "Masada: Consideration." Ladouceur, David J. "Masada: A Consideration of the Literary Evidence." *GRBS* 21 (3, 1980): 245–60.

Ladouceur, "Shipwreck and Pollution." Ladouceur, David. "Hellenistic Preconceptions of Shipwreck and Pollution as a Context for Acts 27–28." *HTR* 73 (3–4, 1980): 435–49.

Laes, "Midwives." Laes, Christian. "Midwives in Greek Inscriptions in Hellenistic and Roman Antiquity." *ZPE* 176 (2011): 154–62.

Laetsch, *Prophets*. Laetsch, Theodore. *The Minor Prophets*. St. Louis: Concordia, 1970.

Lafargue, "Orphica." Lafargue, M. "Orphica." *OTP* 2:795–97.

Lafond, "Gallia." Lafond, Yves. "Gallia/Gaul." *BrillPauly* 5:669–73.

Laguna, "Childhood." Laguna, Frederica de. "Childhood among the Yakutat Tlingit." Pages 3–23 in *Culture and Meaning in Cultural Anthropology: In Honor of A. Irving Hallowell*. Edited by Melford E. Spiro. New York: Free Press; London: Collier-Macmillan, 1965.

Laidlaw, Nixon, and Price, "Crete." Laidlaw, William Allison, Lucia F. Nixon, and Simon R. F. Price. "Crete, Greek and Roman." *OCD*³ 408–9.

Laidlaw and Sherwin-White, "Cos." Laidlaw, William Allison, and Susan Mary Sherwin-White. "Cos." *OCD*³ 403–4.

Laing, "Collection." Laing, Mark. "The Pauline Collection for the 'Poor' in Jerusalem: An Examination of Motivational Factors Influencing Paul." *BangTF* 34 (1, 2002): 83–92.

Laing, "Consequences." Laing, Mark. "The Consequences of the 'Mass Movements.'" *IndCHR* 35 (2, 2001): 91–104.

Laird, "Rhetoric." Laird, Andrew. "The Rhetoric of Roman Historiography." Pages 197–213 in *The Cambridge Companion to the Roman Historians*. Edited by Andrew Feldherr. Cambridge: Cambridge University Press, 2009.

Laird, "Speech Presentation." Laird, Andrew J. W. "Speech Presentation." *OCD*³ 1434.

Laistner, *Historians*. Laistner, M. L. W. *The Greater Roman Historians*. Berkeley: University of California Press; London: Cambridge University Press, 1947.

Lake, "Ascension." Lake, Kirsopp. "The Ascension." *BegChr* 5:16–22.

Lake, "Chronology." Lake, Kirsopp. "The Chronology of Acts." *BegChr* 5:445–67.

Lake, "Communism." Lake, Kirsopp. "The Communism of Acts II. and IV.–VI. and the Appointment of the Seven." *BegChr* 5:140–51.

Lake, "Conversion." Lake, Kirsopp. "The Conversion of Paul and the Events Immediately Following It." *BegChr* 5:188–95.

Lake, "Death of Judas." Lake, Kirsopp. "The Death of Judas." *BegChr* 5:22–30.

Lake, *Healer*. Lake, Robert G. (Medicine Grizzlybear Lake). *Native Healer: Initiation into an Ancient Art*. Wheaton: Quest Books, Theosophical Publishing House, 1991.

Lake, "Localities." Lake, Kirsopp. "Localities in and near Jerusalem Mentioned in Acts." *BegChr* 5:474–79.

Lake, "Poets." Lake, Kirsopp. "Your Own Poets." *BegChr* 5:246–57.

Lake, "Proselytes." Lake, Kirsopp. "Proselytes and God-Fearers." *BegChr* 5:74–96.

Lake, "Route." Lake, Kirsopp. "Paul's Route in Asia Minor." *BegChr* 5:224–39.

Lake, "Spirit." Lake, Kirsopp. "The Holy Spirit." *BegChr* 5:96–111.

Lake, "Twelve." Lake, Kirsopp. "The Twelve and the Apostles." *BegChr* 5:37–59.

Lake, "Unknown God." Lake, Kirsopp. "The Unknown God." *BegChr* 5:240–46.

Lake and Cadbury, *Commentary*. Lake, Kirsopp, and Henry J. Cadbury. *English Translation and Commentary*. Vol. 4 of *The Beginnings of Christianity: The Acts of the Apostles*. Edited by F. J. Foakes-Jackson and Kirsopp Lake. London: Macmillan, 1933. Repr., Grand Rapids: Baker Book House, 1979.

Lalleman, "Apocryphal Acts." Lalleman, Pieter J. "Apocryphal Acts and Epistles." *DNTB* 66–69.

Lamb, "Introduction." Lamb, W. R. M. Introduction to *Theages*. Pages 342–45 in vol. 12 of *Plato*. Translated by Harold North Fowler et al. 12 vols. LCL. Cambridge, Mass.: Harvard University Press, 1914–26.

Lambek, "Disease." Lambek, Michael. "From Disease to Discourse: Remarks on the Conceptualization of Trance and Spirit Possession." Pages 36–61 in *Altered States of Consciousness and Mental Health: A Cross-Cultural Perspective*. Edited by Colleen A. Ward. CCRMS 12. Newbury Park, Calif.: Sage, 1989.

Lambek, *Knowledge*. Lambek, Michael. *Knowledge and Practice in Mayotte: Local Discourses of Islam, Sorcery, and Spirit Possession*. Toronto: University of Toronto Press, 1993.

Lambert, "Couple." Lambert, Frank. "The Religious Odd Couple." *ChH* 38 (1993): 30–32,

Lambert, *Millions*. Lambert, Tony. *China's Christian Millions: The Costly Revival*. London: Monarch, 1999.

Lambert, "Redemption." Lambert, David. "Did Israel Believe That Redemption Awaited Its Repentance? The Case of *Jubilees* 1." *CBQ* 68 (4, 2006): 631–50.

Lambert, "Regulations." Lambert, Stephen D. "Athenian State Laws and Decrees, 352/1–322/1: II Religious Regulations." *ZPE* 154 (2005): 125–59.

Lambert, "Testaments." Lambert, David. "Last Testaments in the Book of Jubilees." *DSD* 11 (1, 2004): 82–107.

Lamboley, "Palici." Lamboley, Jean-Luc. "Palici." *BrillPauly* 10:386–87.

Lambrecht, "Farewell Address." Lambrecht, J. "Paul's Farewell Address at Miletus (Acts 20,17–38)." Pages 307–37 in *Les Actes des apôtres: Traditions, rédaction, théologie*. Edited by Jacob Kremer. BETL 48. Gembloux, Belg.: J. Duculot; Leuven: Leuven University Press, 1979.

Lambrecht, *Second Corinthians*. Lambrecht, Jan. *Second Corinthians*. SP 8. Collegeville, Minn.: Liturgical Press, 1999.

Lamoreaux, "Identity." Lamoreaux, Jason T. "Social Identity, Boundary Breaking, and Ritual: Saul's Recruitment on the Road to Damascus." *BTB* 38 (3, 2008): 122–34.

Lamour, "Organisation." Lamour, Denis. "L'organisation du récit dans l'*Autobiographie* de Flavius Josèphe." *BAGB* 55 (2, 1996): 141–50.

Lampe, "Acta 19." Lampe, Peter. "Acta 19 im Spiegel der ephesischen Inschriften." *BZ* 36 (1, 1992): 59–76.

Lampe, *Christen.* Lampe, Peter. *Die stadtrömischen Christen in den ersten beiden Jahrhunderten: Untersuchungen zur Sozialgeschichte.* 2nd ed. WUNT 18. Tübingen: Mohr, 1989.

Lampe, "Einsichten." Lampe, Peter. "Psychologische Einsichten Quintilians in der *Institutio oratoria.*" *NTS* 52 (4, 2006): 533–54.

Lampe, *Lexicon.* Lampe, Geoffrey W. H. *A Patristic Greek Lexicon.* Oxford: Clarendon, 1961.

Lampe, "Lucan Portrait of Christ." Lampe, G. W. H. "The Lucan Portrait of Christ." *NTS* 2 (3, 1956): 160–75.

Lampe, "Miracles." Lampe, G. W. H. "Miracles in the Acts of the Apostles." Pages 163–78 in *Miracles: Cambridge Studies in Their Philosophy and History.* Edited by C. F. D. Moule. London: A. R. Mowbray; New York: Morehouse-Barlow, 1965.

Lampe, "Patrons." Lampe, Peter. "Paul, Patrons, and Clients." Pages 488–523 in *Paul in the Greco-Roman World: A Handbook.* Edited by J. Paul Sampley. Harrisburg, Pa.: Trinity Press International, 2003.

Lampe, *Paul to Valentinus.* Lampe, Peter. *From Paul to Valentinus: Christians at Rome in the First Two Centuries.* Edited by Marshall D. Johnson. Translated by Michael Steinhauser. Minneapolis: Fortress, 2003.

Lampe, "Paulus-Zeltmacher." Lampe, Peter. "Paulus-Zeltmacher." *BZ* 31 (2, 1987): 256–61.

Lampe, *Seal.* Lampe, G. W. H. *The Seal of the Spirit.* New York: Longmans, Green, 1951.

Lampe, "Spirit in Luke." Lampe, G. W. H. "The Holy Spirit in the Writings of St. Luke." Pages 159–200 in *Studies in the Gospels: Essays in Memory of R. H. Lightfoot.* Edited by D. E. Nineham. Oxford: Blackwell, 1957.

Lampe, "Wolves." Lampe, G. W. H. "'Grievous Wolves' (Acts 20:29)." Pages 253–68 in *Christ and Spirit in the New Testament: Studies in Honor of C. F. D. Moule.* Edited by Barnabas Lindars and Stephen S. Smalley. Cambridge: Cambridge University Press, 1973.

Lamprecht, "Heating." Lamprecht, Heinz-Otto. "Heating." *BrillPauly* 6:27–29.

Lanci, "Stones." Lanci, John R. "The Stones Don't Speak and the Texts Tell Lies: Sacred Sex at Corinth." Pages 205–20 in *Urban Religion in Roman Corinth: Interdisciplinary Approaches.* Edited by Daniel N. Schowalter and Steven J. Friesen. HTS 53. Cambridge, Mass.: Harvard University Press, 2005.

Land, *Diffusion.* Land, Darin H. *The Diffusion of Ecclesiastical Authority: Sociological Dimensions of Leadership in the Book of Acts.* PrTMS 90. Eugene, Ore.: Pickwick, 2008.

Landau, "Unknown Apostle." Landau, Brent. "The Unknown Apostle: A Pauline *Agraphon* in Clement of Alexandria's *Stromateis.*" *ASDE* 25 (2, 2008): 117–27.

Landman, "Traditions." Landman, H. Leo. "Some Aspects of Traditions Received from Moses at Sinai: *Halakhah le-Mosheh mi-Sinai.*" *JQR* 67 (2–3, 1976–77): 111–28.

Landon, "Beyond Peirene." Landon, Mark E. "Beyond Peirene: Toward a Broader View of Corinthian Water Supply." Pages 43–62 in *Corinth: The Centenary, 1896–1996.* Edited by Charles K. Williams II and Nancy Bookidis. Vol. 20 of *Corinth: Results of Excavations Conducted by the American School of Classical Studies at Athens.* Princeton: American School of Classical Studies at Athens, 2003.

Landscape Survey. U.S. *Religious Landscape Survey: Religious Beliefs and Practices—Diverse and Politically Relevant.* Washington, D.C.: Pew Forum on Religion and Public Life, June 2008. Online: http://religions .pewforum.org/pdf/report2-religious -landscape-study-full.pdf.

Lane, *Gentile Mission.* Lane, Thomas J. *Luke and the Gentile Mission: Gospel Anticipates Acts.* EUSTS 571. Frankfurt and New York: Peter Lang, 1996.

Lane, *Hebrews.* Lane, William L. *Hebrews.* 2 vols. WBC 47A, B. Dallas: Word, 1991.

Lane, "Legacy." Lane, William L. "Paul's Legacy from Pharisaism: Light from the Psalms of Solomon." *ConcJ* 8 (4, 1982): 130–38.

Lane, *Mark.* Lane, William L. *The Gospel according to Mark.* NICNT. Grand Rapids: Eerdmans, 1974.

Lane, "Sabazius and Jews." Lane, Eugene N. "Sabazius and the Jews in Valerius Maximus: A Re-examination." *JRS* 69 (1979): 35–38.

Lane, "Social Perspectives." Lane, William L. "Social Perspectives of Roman Christianity during the Formative Years from Nero to Nerva: Romans, Hebrews, *1 Clement.*" Pages 196–244 in *Judaism and Christianity in First-Century Rome.* Edited by Karl P. Donfried and Peter Richardson. Grand Rapids: Eerdmans, 1998.

Lane, "*Theios anēr.*" Lane, William L. "*Theios anēr* Christology and the Gospel of Mark." Pages 144–61 in *New Dimensions in New Testament Study.* Edited by Richard N. Longenecker and Merrill C. Tenney. Grand Rapids: Zondervan, 1974.

Lang, "Abschiedsreden." Lang, Manfred. "Johanneische Abschiedsreden und Senecas Konsolationsliteratur: Wie konnte

ein Römer Joh 13,31–17,26 lesen?" Pages 365–411 in *Kontexte des Johannesevangeliums: Das vierte Evangelium in religions- und traditionsgeschichtlicher Perspektive.* Edited by Jörg Frey and Udo Schnelle, in collaboration with Juliane Schlegel. WUNT 75. Tübingen: Mohr Siebeck, 2004.

Lang, "*Dux.*" Lang, Manfred. "Der *bonus dux.* Tacitus' Agricola und der lukanische Paulus." Pages 244–76 in *Die Apostelgeschichte im Kontext antiker und frühchristlicher Historiographie.* Edited by Jörg Frey, Clare K. Rothschild, and Jens Schröter, with Bettina Rost. BZNWK 162. Berlin: de Gruyter, 2009.

Lang, *Kunst.* Lang, Manfred. *Die Kunst des christlichen Lebens: Rezeptionsästhetische Studien zum lukanischen Paulusbild.* ABIG 29. Lepizig: Evangelische Verlagsanstalt, 2008.

Lang, "Neues." Lang, Friedrich Gustav. "Neues über Lydia? Zur Deutung von 'Purpurhändlerin' in Apg 16,14." *ZNW* 100 (1, 2009): 29–44.

Lang, "Oppression." Lang, Graeme. "Oppression and Revolt in Ancient Palestine: The Evidence in Jewish Literature from the Prophets to Josephus." *SocAnal* 49 (4, 1989): 325–42.

Lang, "Self." Lang, Manfred. "The Christian and the Roman Self: The Lukan Paul and a Roman Reading." Pages 151–73 in *Christian Body, Christian Self: Concepts of Early Christian Personhood.* Edited by Clare K. Rothschild and Trevor W. Thompson, with the assistance of Robert S. Kinney. Tübingen: Mohr Siebeck, 2011.

Langdon, "Hills." Langdon, Merle K. "Classifying the Hills of Rome." *Eranos* 97 (1–2, 1999): 98–107.

Lange, "Daughters." Lange, Armin. "Your Daughters Do Not Give to Their Sons and Their Daughters Do Not Take for Your Sons (Ezra 9,12): Intermarriage in Ezra 9–10 and in the Pre-Maccabean Dead Sea Scrolls, Teil 1." *BN* 137 (2008): 17–39.

Lange, "Intermarriage." Lange, Armin. "Your Daughters Do Not Give to Their Sons and Their Daughters Do Not Take for Your Sons (Ezra 9,12). Intermarriage in Ezra 9–10 and in the Pre-Maccabean Dead Sea Scrolls. Teil 2." *BN* 139 (2008): 79–98.

Lange, "Physiognomie." Lange, Armin. "Physiognomie oder Gotteslob? 4Q301 3." *DSD* 4 (3, 1997): 282–96.

Lange, "Revival." Lange, Nicholas de. "The Revival of the Hebrew Language in the Third Century CE." *JSQ* 3 (4, 1996): 342–58.

Lange, "Seers." Lange, Armin. "Greek Seers and Israelite-Jewish Prophets." *VT* 57 (4, 2007): 461–82.

Langer, "Study." Langer, Ruth. "From Study of Scripture to a Reenactment of Sinai: The Emergence of the Synagogue Torah Service." *Worship* 72 (1, 1998): 43–67.

Langer, "Vermögensrecht." Langer, Gerhard. "Zum Vermögensrecht von Frauen in der Ehe am Beispiel des Mischna- und Tosefta-Traktates Ketubbot." *Kairos* 34–35 (1992–93): 27–63.

Langner, *Hechos.* Langner, Córdula. *Evangelio de Lucas. Hechos de los Apóstoles.* Biblioteca Bíblica Básica 16. Navarra, Spain: Editorial Verbo Divino, 2008.

Langton, "Identity." Langton, Daniel R. "Modern Jewish Identity and the Apostle Paul: Pauline Studies as an Intra-Jewish Ideological Battleground." *JSNT* 28 (2, 2005): 217–58.

Langton, "Myth." Langton, Daniel R. "The Myth of the 'Traditional View of Paul' and the Role of the Apostle in Modern Jewish-Christian Polemics." *JSNT* 28 (1, 2005): 69–104.

Lanier, "Review." Lanier, David E. Review of *The IVP Bible Background Commentary.* *F&M* 12 (1, 1994): 96–97.

Lanternari, "Dreams." Lanternari, Vittorio. "Dreams as Charismatic Significants: Their Bearing on the Rise of New Religious Movements." Pages 321–35 in *The Realm of the Extra-human: Ideas and Actions.* Edited by Agehananda Bharati. The Hague and Paris: Mouton, 1976. Distributed by Aldine, Chicago.

Laperrousaz, "Dépôts." Laperrousaz, Ernest-Marie. "À propos des dépôts d'ossements d'animaux trouvés à Qoumrân." *RevQ* 9 (4, 1978): 569–73.

Lapide, *Hebrew.* Lapide, Pinchas E. *Hebrew in the Church: The Foundations of Jewish-Christian Dialogue.* Translated by Erroll F. Rhodes. Grand Rapids: Eerdmans, 1984.

Lapin, "Rabbis and Cities." Lapin, Hayim. "Rabbis and Cities in Later Roman Palestine: The Literary Evidence." *JJS* 50 (2, 1999): 187–207.

LaPoorta, "Unity." LaPoorta, Jappie. "Unity or Division." Pages 151–69 in *The Globalization of Pentecostalism: A Religion Made to Travel.* Edited by Murray W. Dempster, Byron D. Klaus, and Douglas Petersen. Foreword by Russell P. Spittler. Carlisle: Paternoster; Oxford: Regnum, 1999.

Lapp, *Archaeology.* Lapp, Paul W. *Biblical Archaeology and History.* New York: World, 1969.

Larbi, "Anim." Larbi, E. Kingsley. "Peter Newman Anim." No pages. *DACB.* Online: http://www.dacb.org/stories /ghana/anim_peter.html.

Lardner, *Works. Works of Nathaniel Lardner, D.D., with a life by Dr. Kippis.* 10 vols. London: William Ball, 1838. (First published in 1788.)

Larkin, *Acts.* Larkin, William J., Jr. *Acts.* IVPNTC. Downers Grove, Ill.: Inter-Varsity, 1995.

Larkin, "Old Testament as Key." Larkin, William J., Jr. "Luke's Use of the Old Testament as a Key to His Soteriology." *JETS* 20 (1977): 325–35.

Larkin, "Recovery of Luke-Acts." Larkin, William J., Jr. "The Recovery of Luke-Acts as 'Grand Narrative' for the Church's Evangelistic and Edification Tasks in a Postmodern Age." *JETS* 43 (3, 2000): 405–15.

Larkin, "Spirit and Jesus." Larkin, William J., Jr. "The Spirit and Jesus 'on Mission' in the Postresurrection and Postascension Stages of Salvation History: The Impact of the Pneumatology of Acts on Its Christology." Pages 121–39 in *New Testament Greek and Exegesis: Essays in Honor of Gerald F. Hawthorne.* Edited by Amy M. Donaldson and Timothy B. Sailors. Grand Rapids and Cambridge: Eerdmans, 2003.

Larmer, *Water.* Larmer, Robert A. *Water into Wine? An Investigation of the Concept of Miracle.* Kingston, Ont., and Montreal: McGill-Queen's University Press, 1988.

Laroche, "Numbers." Laroche, Roland A. "Popular Symbolic/Mystical Numbers in Antiquity." *Latomus* 54 (3, 1995): 568–76.

Larson, "Migration." Larson, Peter A. "Migration and Church Growth in Argentina." DMiss diss., Fuller Theological Seminary, 1973.

Larsson, "Apostlagärningarna." Larsson, Edwin. "Om apostlagärningarna inte fanns." *TTKi* 64 (1, 1993): 1–19. (Abstract: *NTA* 38:45.)

Larsson, "Hellenisten und Urgemeinde." Larsson, Edwin. "Die Hellenisten und die Urgemeinde." *NTS* 33 (2, 1987): 205–25.

Larsson, "Paul: Law and Salvation." Larsson, Edwin. "Paul: Law and Salvation." *NTS* 31 (3, 1985): 425–36.

Larsson, "Septuagint." Larsson, Gerhard. "Septuagint versus Masoretic Chronology." *ZAW* 114 (4, 2002): 511–21.

Larsson, "Synpunkter." Larsson, Edwin. "Apostlagärningarnas historiska värde: Synpunkter på den aktuella debatten." *STK* 65 (4, 1989): 145–55.

Larsson, "Temple-Criticism." Larsson, Edwin. "Temple-Criticism and the Jewish Heritage: Some Reflections on Acts 6–7." *NTS* 39 (3, 1993): 379–95.

Laskaris, "Mothers." Laskaris, Julie. "Nursing Mothers in Greek and Roman Medicine." *AJA* 112 (3, 2008): 459–64.

LaSor, "Egypt." LaSor, William Sanford. "Egypt." *ISBE* 2:29–47.

LaSor, *Knew.* LaSor, William Sanford. *Men Who Knew Christ.* Glendale, Calif.: Regal, 1971.

LaSor, "Messiahs." LaSor, William Sanford. "'The Messiahs of Aaron and Israel.'" *VT* 6 (4, 1956): 425–29.

LaSor, "Miqva'ot." LaSor, William Sanford. "Discovering What Jewish Miqva'ot Can Tell Us about Christian Baptism." *BAR* 13 (1, 1987): 52–59.

LaSor, "Mysia." LaSor, William Sanford. "Mysia." *ISBE* 3:451.

LaSor, "Palestine." LaSor, William Sanford. "Palestine." *ISBE* 3:632–49.

LaSor, *Scrolls.* LaSor, William Sanford. *The Dead Sea Scrolls and the Christian Faith.* Chicago: Moody, 1962.

LaSor, Hubbard, and Bush, *Survey.* LaSor, William Sanford, David Allan Hubbard, and Frederic W. Bush. *Old Testament Survey: The Message, Form, and Background of the Old Testament.* 2nd ed. Grand Rapids: Eerdmans, 1996.

Last, "Bori." Last, Murray. "Spirit Possession as Therapy: *Bori* among Non-Muslims in Nigeria." Pages 49–63 in *Women's Medicine: The zar-bori Cult in Africa and Beyond.* Edited by I. M. Lewis, Ahmed Al-Safi, and Sayyid Hurreiz. Edinburgh: International African Institute, Edinburgh University Press, 1991.

Last, "Social Policy." Last, Hugh. "The Social Policy of Augustus." Pages 425–64 in *The Augustan Empire: 44 B.C.–A.D. 70.* Edited by S. A. Cook, F. E. Adcock, and M. P. Charlesworth. CAH 10. Cambridge: Cambridge University Press, 1934. Repr., 1966.

Latacz, "Epic: Antiquity." Latacz, Joachim. "Epic: Classical Antiquity." *BrillPauly* 4:1040–48.

Latacz, "Epic: Literature." Latacz, Joachim. "Epic: Greek Literature (From Homer to Nonnus)." *BrillPauly* 4:1048–50.

Lateiner, "Contest." Lateiner, Donald. "Contest (*Agōn*) in Thucydides." Pages 336–41 in *A Companion to Greek and Roman Historiography.* Edited by John Marincola. 2 vols. Oxford: Blackwell, 2007.

Lateiner, "Gestures." Lateiner, Donald. "Gestures." *OCD*[3] 635–36.

Lateiner, "Mothers." Lateiner, Donald. "*Procul este parentes*: Mothers in Ovid's *Metamorphoses*." *Helios* 33 (2, 2006): 189–201.

Latourette, *First Five Centuries.* Latourette, Kenneth Scott. *The First Five Centuries.* Vol. 1 of *A History of the Expansion of Christianity.* New York: Harper & Row, 1970.

Latourette, *To A.D. 1500.* Latourette, Kenneth Scott. *To A.D. 1500.* Vol. 1 of

A History of Christianity. San Francisco: HarperSanFrancisco, 1975.

Lau, "Gasthäuser." Lau, Markus. "Gasthäuser im Urchristentum: Eine Spurensuche im lukanischen Doppelwerk." *Diakonia* 44 (1, 2013): 8–13.

Laub, "Gewalt." Laub, Franz. "Der Christ und die staatliche Gewalt—zum Verständnis der 'politischen' Paränese Röm 13,1–7 in der gegenwärtigen Diskussion." *MTZ* 30 (4, 1979): 257–65.

Laubscher, "Angel of Truth." Laubscher, Frans du T. "God's Angel of Truth and Melchizedek: A Note on 11QMelch 13b." *JSJ* 3 (1, 1972): 45–51.

Laurence and Newsome, *Rome, Ostia, Pompeii*. Laurence, Ray, and David Newsome. *Rome, Ostia, Pompeii: Movement and Space*. Oxford: Oxford University Press, 2011.

Laurentin, *Miracles*. Laurentin, René. *Miracles in El Paso?* Ann Arbor: Servant, 1982.

Laurentin, "Traces d'allusions." Laurentin, René. "Traces d'allusions étymologiques en Luc 1–2." *Bib* 37 (1956): 435–56; 38 (1, 1957): 1–23.

Laurin, "Immortality." Laurin, Robert B. "The Question of Immortality in the Qumran Hodayot." *JSS* 3 (1958): 344–55.

Laurin, "Messiahs." Laurin, Robert B. "The Problem of Two Messiahs in the Qumran Scrolls." *RevQ* 4 (13/1, 1963): 39–52.

Lavan, "Slaves." Lavan, Myles. "Slaves to Rome: The Rhetoric of Mastery in Titus' Speech to the Jews (Bellum Judaicum 6.328–50)." *Ramus* 36 (1, 2007): 25–38.

LaVerdiere, "Breaking of Bread." LaVerdiere, Eugene. "The Breaking of the Bread." *Emmanuel* 105 (1, 1999): 39–44.

Lavery, "Never Seen." Lavery, Gerald B. "Never Seen in Public: Seneca and the Limits of Cosmopolitanism." *Latomus* 56 (1, 1997): 3–13.

LaViolette and Fleisher, "Archaeology." LaViolette, Adria, and Jeffrey Fleisher. "The Archaeology of Sub-Saharan Urbanism: Cities and Their Consequences." Pages 327–52 in *African Archaeology*. Edited by Ann Brower Stahl. BSGA. Oxford: Blackwell, 2005.

Lawlor, *Nabataeans*. Lawlor, John Irving. *The Nabataeans in Historical Perspective*. Baker Studies in Biblical Archaeology. Grand Rapids: Baker, 1974.

Lawrence, *Atlas*. Lawrence, Paul. *The IVP Atlas of Bible History*. Edited by Alan Millard, Heinrich von Siebenthal, and John Walton. Downers Grove, Ill.: IVP Academic, 2006.

Lawrence, *Revolt*. Lawrence, T. E. *Revolt in the Desert*. New York: Doran, 1927.

Lawrence, "Roots of Divination." Lawrence, John M. "Ancient Near Eastern Roots of Graeco-Roman Sacrificial Divination." *NEASB* 15–16 (Summer–Fall 1980): 51–71.

Laws, *James*. Laws, Sophie. *A Commentary on the Epistle of James*. HNTC. San Francisco: Harper & Row, 1980.

Lawton, *Miracles*. Lawton, John Stewart. *Miracles and Revelation*. New York: Association, 1960.

Laytner, "Suffering." Laytner, Anson. "Suffering in the *Sifrei*: Akiba's Lesson on Menasheh." *JRefJud* 37 (2, 1990): 47–51.

Lazar, "Aggression." Lazar, Ineke Maria. "Management of Aggression in a Male-Dominated Culture: Samoan Migrant Women in Distress." Paper presented at the National Women's Studies Association Conference, Arcata, Calif., June 1982.

Lazenby, "Archers." Lazenby, John F. "Archers (Greek and Hellenistic)." *OCD*³ 144–45.

Lazenby, "Logistics." Lazenby, John F. "Logistics (Greek, Military)." *OCD*³ 881–82.

Lazenby, "Military Training." Lazenby, John F. "Military Training (Greek)." *OCD*³ 980–81.

Leach, "Essays." Leach, Edmund. "Two Essays concerning the Symbolic Representation of Time." Pages 108–16 in *Reader in Comparative Religion: An Anthropological Approach*. Edited by William A. Lessa and Evon Z. Vogt. 3rd ed. New York: Harper & Row, 1972.

Leahy, "Diversity." Leahy, Anthony. "Ethnic Diversity in Ancient Egypt." Pages 225–34 in vol. 1 of *Civilizations of the Ancient Near East*. Edited by Jack M. Sasson. 4 vols. New York: Scribner's, 1995.

Leaney, *Luke*. Leaney, A. R. C. *A Commentary on the Gospel according to St. Luke*. London: Adama & Charles Black, 1958.

Leaney, "Significance." Leaney, A. R. C. "The Eschatological Significance of Human Suffering in the Old Testament and the Dead Sea Scrolls." *SJT* 16 (3, 1963): 286–96.

Leaney, "Text." Leaney, Robert. "The Lucan Text of the Lord's Prayer (Lk. xi.2–4)." *NovT* 1 (1956): 103–11.

Leary, "Aprons." Leary, T. J. "The 'Aprons' of St Paul—Acts 19:12." *JTS* 41 (2, 1990): 527–29.

Leary, "Improper Name." Leary, T. J. "Paul's Improper Name." *NTS* 38 (3, 1992): 467–69.

Leary, "Pork and Proselytes." Leary, T. J. "Of Paul and Pork and Proselytes." *NovT* 35 (3, 1993): 292–93.

Lease, "Caesarea Mithraeum." Lease, Gary. "The Caesarea Mithraeum: A Preliminary Announcement." *BA* 38 (1, 1975): 2–10.

Leavitt, "Trance." Leavitt, Johan. "Are Trance and Possession Disorders?" *TranscPsycRR* 30 (1993): 51–57.

Le Bohec, "Contubernium." Le Bohec, Yann. "Contubernium." *BrillPauly* 3:757.

Le Bohec, "Decimatio." Le Bohec, Yann. "Decimatio." *BrillPauly* 4:150–51.

Le Bohec, "Desertor." Le Bohec, Yann. "Desertor." *BrillPauly* 4:315.

Le Bohec, "Disciplina." Le Bohec, Yann. "Disciplina militaris." *BrillPauly* 4:537–39.

Le Bohec, "Ensigns." Le Bohec, Yann. "Ensigns." *BrillPauly* 4:992–97.

Le Bohec, "Prisoners of War." Le Bohec, Yann. "Prisoners of War. III. Rome." *BrillPauly* 11:877–78.

Le Bohec, "Soldiers' Pay." Le Bohec, Yann. "Soldiers' Pay: Rome." *BrillPauly* 13:612–13.

Le Bohec, "Tabernaculum." Le Bohec, Yann. "Tabernaculum." *BrillPauly* 14:79.

Le Bohec, "Vigiliae." Le Bohec, Yann. "Vigiliae." *BrillPauly* 15:408.

Lebra, *Patterns*. Lebra, Takie Sugiyama. *Japanese Patterns of Behavior*. Honolulu: University Press of Hawaii, 1976.

Lebram, "Literarische Form." Lebram, J. C. H. "Die literarische Form des vierten Makkabäerbuches." *VC* 28 (2, 1974): 81–96.

Lebrun, "Asianisme." Lebrun, René. "Asianisme et monde biblique." *RTL* 24 (3, 1993): 373–76.

Leclaire, "Cardiologist." Leclaire, Jennifer. "Florida Cardiologist Documents Miracles." *Charisma* (May 2008): 38.

Leclant, "Napata and Meroe." Leclant, J. "The Empire of Kush: Napata and Meroe." Pages 278–95 in *Ancient Civilizations of Africa*. Edited by G. Mokhtar. General History of Africa 2. Berkeley: University of California Press; London: Heinemann Educational; Paris: United Nations Educational, Scientific and Cultural Organization, 1981.

Le Cornu, *Acts*. Le Cornu, Hilary, with Joseph Shulam. *A Commentary on the Jewish Roots of Acts*. 2 vols. Jerusalem: Academon, 2003.

Le Cornu, *Galatians*. Le Cornu, Hilary, with Joseph Shulam. *A Commentary on the Jewish Roots of Galatians*. Jerusalem: Academon, 2005.

Le Déaut, "Intercession." Le Déaut, Roger. "Aspects de l'intercession dans le judaïsme ancien." *JSJ* 1 (1, 1970): 35–57.

Le Déaut, "Savu'ot." Le Déaut, Roger. "Savu'ot och den kristna pingsten i NT." *SEÅ* 44 (1979): 148–70. Abstract: *NTA* 24:250.

Lederle, "Evidence." Lederle, Henry I. "Initial Evidence and the Charismatic Movement: An Ecumenical Appraisal." Pages 131–41 in *Initial Evidence: Historical and Biblical Perspectives on the Pentecostal Doctrine of Spirit Baptism.* Edited by Gary B. McGee. Peabody, Mass.: Hendrickson, 1991.

Lederle, *Treasures.* Lederle, Henry I. *Treasures Old and New: Interpretations of "Spirit-Baptism" in the Charismatic Renewal Movement.* Peabody, Mass.: Hendrickson, 1988.

Le Donne, *Historiographical Jesus.* Le Donne, Anthony. *The Historiographical Jesus: Memory, Typology, and the Son of David.* Waco: Baylor University Press, 2009.

Le Donne, "Offering." Le Donne, Anthony. "The Improper Temple Offering of Ananias and Sapphira." *NTS* 59 (3, 2013): 346–64.

Lee, "Against." Lee, Jae Hyun. "Against Richard B. Hays's 'Faith of Jesus Christ.'" *JGRCJ* 5 (2008): 51–80.

Lee, "Erastus." Lee, Gary A. "Erastus." *ISBE* 2:126.

Lee, "Korean Pentecost." Lee, Young-Hoon. "Korean Pentecost: The Great Revival of 1907." *AJPS* 4 (1, 2001): 73–83.

Lee, "Movement." Lee, Young-Hoon. "The Korean Holy Spirit Movement in Relation to Pentecostalism." Pages 509–26 in *Asian and Pentecostal: The Charismatic Face of Christianity in Asia.* Edited by Allan Anderson and Edmond Tang. Foreword by Cecil M. Robeck. RStMiss, AJPS 3. Oxford: Regnum; Baguio City, Philippines: APTS, 2005.

Lee, "Parchments." Lee, G. M. "The Books and the Parchments—Studies in Texts: II Tim. 4:13." *Theology* 74 (610, 1971): 168–69.

Lee, "Possession." Lee, S. G. "Spirit Possession among the Zulu." Pages 128–56 in *Spirit Mediumship and Society in Africa.* Edited by John Beattie and John Middleton. Foreword by Raymond Firth. New York: Africana, 1969.

Lee, "Powers." Lee, Jung Young. "Interpreting the Demonic Powers in Pauline Thought." *NovT* 12 (1, 1970): 54–69.

Lee, "Self-Presentation." Lee, Raymond L. M. "Self-Presentation in Malaysian Spirit Seances: A Dramaturgical Perspective on Altered States of Consciousness in Healing Ceremonies." Pages 251–66 in *Altered States of Consciousness and Mental Health: A Cross-Cultural Perspective.* Edited by Colleen A. Ward. CCRMS 12. Newbury Park, Calif.: Sage, 1989.

Lee, "Sociology." Lee, Richard B. "The Sociology of !Kung Bushman Trance Performances." Pages 35–54 in *Trance and Possession States: Proceedings of the Second Annual Conference, R. M. Bucke Memorial Society, March 4–6, 1966.* Edited by Raymond Prince. Montreal: R. M. Bucke Memorial Society, 1968.

Lee, "Tension." Lee, H.-S. "Biblical, Theological Reflections on the Tension between Divine Sovereignty and Human Responsibility in Paul's Letters." *ChongTJ* 6 (2, 2001): 50–72.

Lee, "Translations: Greek." Lee, John A. L. "Translations of the Old Testament: I. Greek." Pages 775–83 in *Handbook of Classical Rhetoric in the Hellenistic Period, 330 B.C.–A.D. 400.* Edited by Stanley E. Porter. Leiden: Brill, 1997.

Lee, "Unrest." Lee, Clarence L. "Social Unrest and Primitive Christianity." Pages 121–38 in *The Catacombs and the Colosseum: The Roman Empire as the Setting of Primitive Christianity.* Edited by Stephen Benko and John J. O'Rourke. Valley Forge, Pa.: Judson, 1971.

Leeman, "Antieke." Leeman, A. D. "Antieke en moderne geschiedschrijving. Een misleidende Cicero-interpretatie." *Hermeneus* 61 (1989): 235–41.

Leeper, "Gift." Leeper, Gregory J. "The Nature of the Pentecostal Gift with Special Reference to Numbers 11 and Acts 2." *AJPS* 6 (1, 2003): 23–38.

Lees and Fiddes, "Healed." Lees, Bill, and Paul Fiddes. "How Are People Healed Today? The Relationship between the 'Medical' and the 'Spiritual' in Healing." Pages 5–30 in *Christian Healing: What Can We Believe?* Edited by Ernest Lucas. London: Lynx Communications, SPCK, 1997.

Lefebvre, "Diffusion." Lefebvre, Ludovic. "La diffusion du culte de Sarapis en Grèce continentale et dans les îles de l'Égée au IIIᵉ siècle avant J.-C." *RHPR* 88 (4, 2008): 451–67.

Lefkowitz, *Women in Myth.* Lefkowitz, Mary R. *Women in Greek Myth.* Baltimore: Johns Hopkins University Press, 1986.

Lefkowitz and Fant, *Life.* Lefkowitz, Mary R., and Maureen B. Fant. *Women's Life in Greece and Rome.* Baltimore: Johns Hopkins University Press; London: Gerald Duckworth, 1982.

Légasse, "Apologétique." Légasse, Simon. "L'apologétique à l'égard de Rome dans le process de Paul: Actes 21,27–26,32." *RSR* 69 (2, 1981): 249–55.

Légasse, "Baptême." Légasse, Simon. "Baptême juif des prosélytes et baptême chrétien." *BLE* 77 (1, 1976): 3–40.

Légasse, "Career." Légasse, Simon. "Paul's Pre-Christian Career according to Acts." Pages 365–90 in *The Book of Acts in Its Palestinian Setting.* Edited by Richard Bauckham. Vol. 4 of *The Book of Acts in Its First Century Setting.* Edited by Bruce W. Winter. Grand Rapids: Eerdmans; Carlisle, U.K.: Paternoster, 1995.

Légasse, "Encore ἑστῶτα." Légasse, Simon. "Encore ἑστῶτα en Actes 7,55–56." *Fil Neot* 3 (5, 1990): 63–66.

Legrand, "Apostle to Pastor." Legrand, Lucien. "From Apostle to Pastor: St. Paul's Pastoral Itinerary." *ITS* 26 (2, 1989): 152–70.

Legrand, "Review." Legrand, Lucien. "Review of Philippe 'l'évangéliste' au tournant de la mission dans les Actes des apôtres." *ITS* 49 (1, 2012): 83–92.

Lehmann, "Light on Astrology." Lehmann, Manfred R. "New Light on Astrology in Qumran and the Talmud." *RevQ* 8 (32/4, 1975): 599–602.

Lehmann, *Struggle.* Lehmann, David. *Struggle for the Spirit: Religious Transformation and Popular Culture in Brazil and Latin America.* Cambridge, Mass.: Polity (with Blackwell), 1996.

Lehmann and Lehmann, *Samothrace: Excavations.* Lehmann, Karl, and Phyllis Williams Lehmann, eds. *Samothrace: Excavations Conducted by the Institute of Fine Arts of New York University.* 11 vols. BollS 60. New York: Pantheon; Princeton: Princeton University Press, 1958–98.

Lehnardt, *Ta'aniyot.* Lehnardt, Andreas. *Ta'aniyot—Fasten.* Übersetzung des Talmud Yerushalmi 2/9. Tübingen: Mohr Siebeck, 2008.

Lehnert, "Absage." Lehnert, Volker A. "Absage an Israel oder offener Schluss? Apg 28,25–28 als paradoxe Intervention." *TBei* 29 (6, 1998): 315–23.

Lehnert, "Verstockung." Lehnert, Volker A. "Die 'Verstockung Israels' und biblische Hermeneutik: Ein exegetisches Kabinettstückchen zur Methodenfrage." *ZNT* 8 (16, 2005): 13–19.

Lehoux, "Drugs." Lehoux, Daryn. "Drugs and the Delphic Oracle." *CW* 101 (1, 2007): 41–56.

Lehtinen, "Petra Papyri." Lehtinen, Marjo. "The Petra Papyri." *NEA* 65 (4, 2002): 277–78.

Leibowitz, "Heroes." Leibowitz, Shira. "Heroes, Scholars, and School Teachers: The Education of Jewish Babylonian Children." *ConsJud* 53 (4, 2001): 44–51.

Leicht, "Mashbia'." Leicht, Reimund. "Mashbia' Ani 'Alekha: Types and Patterns of Ancient Jewish and Christian Exorcism Formulae." *JSQ* 13 (4, 2006): 319–43.

Leicht, "Version." Leicht, Reimund. "A Newly Discovered Hebrew Version of the Apocryphal 'Prayer of Manasseh.'" *JSQ* 3 (4, 1996): 359–73.

Leidwanger, personal correspondence. Leidwanger, Justin. Personal correspondence with the author, October 7 and 9, 2014.

Leigh, "Early Roman Epic." Leigh, Matthew. "Early Roman Epic and the Maritime Moment." *CP* 105 (3, 2010): 265–80.

Leigh, "Emotions." Leigh, Matthew. "Quintilian on the Emotions (*Institutio oratoria* 6 preface and 1–2)." *JRS* 94 (2004): 122–40.

Leigh, "Epic." Leigh, Matthew. "Epic and Historiography at Rome." Pages 483–92 in *A Companion to Greek and Roman Historiography*. Edited by John Marincola. 2 vols. Oxford: Blackwell, 2007.

Leigh, "Forgiveness." Leigh, David J. "Forgiveness, Pity, and Ultimacy in Ancient Greek Culture." *UltRM* 27 (2, 2004): 152–61.

Leiman, "Josephus and Canon." Leiman, Sid Z. "Josephus and the Canon of the Bible." Pages 50–58 in *Josephus, the Bible, and History*. Edited by Louis H. Feldman and Gohei Hata. Detroit: Wayne State University Press, 1989.

Leineweber, *Witwen*. Leineweber, Matthias. *Lukas und die Witwen: Eine Botschaft an die Gemeinden in der hellenistisch-römischen Gesellschaft*. Europäische Hochschulschriften, Reihe 23 Theologie 915. Frankfurt; Bern: Lang, 2011.

Leiris, *Possession*. Leiris, Michel. *La possession et ses aspects theatreaux chez les Ethiopiens de Gender*. Paris: Plon, 1958.

Leisegang, *Ursprung*. Leisegang, Hans. *Pneuma hagion: Der Ursprung des Geistbegriffs der synoptischen Evangelien aus der griechischen Mystik*. VFVRUL 4. Leipzig: J. C. Hinrichs, 1922. Repr., Hildesheim: Georg Olms, 1970.

Leivestad, "Dogma." Leivestad, Ragnar. "Das Dogma von der prophetenlosen Zeit." *NTS* 19 (3, 1973): 288–99.

Leivestad, "Exit." Leivestad, Ragnar. "Exit the Apocalyptic Son of Man." *NTS* 18 (3, 1972): 243–67.

Lejeune, "Phrygian Language." Lejeune, Michel. "Phrygian Language." *OCD*[3] 1177.

Lemaire, "Engraved." Lemaire, André. "Engraved in Memory: Diaspora Jews Find Eternal Rest in Jerusalem." *BAR* 32 (3, 2006): 52–57.

Lemaire, "Evaluation." Lemaire, André. "Critical Evaluation of the IAA Committee Reports regarding the Ossuary Inscription." *PJBR* 2 (2, 2003): 29–60.

Lemaire, "Flawed." Lemaire, André. "Israel Antiquities Authority's Report on the James Ossuary Deeply Flawed." *BAR* 29 (6, 2003): 50–59, 67, 70.

Lemaire, "Ossuaire." Lemaire, André. "L'ossuaire de 'Jacques fils de Joseph, le frère de Jésus': Une brève réponse." *PJBR* 2 (2, 2003): 81–87.

Lemaire, "Rejoinder." Lemaire, André. "The 'James Ossuary on Trial': A Short Rejoinder." *BAIAS* 22 (2004): 35–36.

Lemaire, "Scepter." Lemaire, André. "Probable Head of Priestly Scepter from Solomon's Temple Surfaces in Jerusalem." *BAR* 10 (1, 1984): 24–29.

LeMarquand, "African Readings." LeMarquand, Grant. "African Readings of Paul." Pages 488–503 in *The Blackwell Companion to Paul*. Edited by Stephen Westerholm. BCompRel. Oxford: Blackwell, 2011.

Leme Lopes, "Diagnostico." Leme Lopes, José. "Diagnostico diferencial das psicoses afetivas e suas implicacoes terapeuticas." *JBPsi* 33 (3, 1984): 201–5.

Lemerle, *Philippes*. Lemerle, Paul. *Philippes et la Macédoine orientale à l'époque chrétienne et byzantine*. BEFAR 158. Paris: E. de Boccard, 1945.

Lemmer, "Strategist." Lemmer, H. R. "Paul, Misogynist or Strategist?" *TheolEv* 26 (2, 1993): 103–20.

Lémonon, "Christianismes." Lémonon, Jean-Pierre. "Les christianismes à Éphèse au Ier siècle." Pages 85–119 in *Les Actes des apôtres—Histoire, récit, théologie: XXe congrès de l'Association catholique française pour l'étude de la Bible (Angers, 2003)*. Edited by Michel Berder. LD 199. Paris: Cerf, 2005.

Lempp, "Nations." Lempp, Walter. "Nations in Amos." *SEAJT* 1 (3, 1960): 20–33.

Lendon, "Historians." Lendon, J. E. "Historians without History: Against Roman Historiography." Pages 41–61 in *The Cambridge Companion to the Roman Historians*. Edited by Andrew Feldherr. Cambridge: Cambridge University Press, 2009.

Lenfant, "Historians." Lenfant, Dominique. "Greek Historians of Persia." Pages 200–209 in *A Companion to Greek and Roman Historiography*. Edited by John Marincola. 2 vols. Oxford: Blackwell, 2007.

Lennartsson, *Refreshing*. Lennartsson, Göran. *Refreshing and Restoration: Two Eschatological Motifs in Acts 3:19–21*. Lund: Lund University, Centre for Theology and Religious Studies, 2007.

Lennon, "Pollution." Lennon, Jack T. "Pollution and Ritual Impurity in Cicero's *De domo sua*." *CQ* 60 (2, 2010): 427–45.

Lenski, *Acts*. Lenski, R. C. H. *The Interpretation of the Acts of the Apostles*. Columbus, Ohio: Lutheran Book Concern, 1934. Repr., Minneapolis: Augsburg, 1961.

Lenski, "Status Crystallization." Lenski, Gerhard E. "Status Crystallization: A Non-vertical Dimension of Social Status." *AmSocRev* 19 (1954): 405–13.

Lentz, *Luke's Portrait*. Lentz, John Clayton, Jr. *Luke's Portrait of Paul*. SNTSMS 77. Cambridge: Cambridge University Press, 1993.

Lentzen-Deis, "Motiv." Lentzen-Deis, Fritzleo. "Das Motiv der 'Himmelsöffnung' in verschiedenen Gattungen der Umweltliteratur des Neuen Testaments." *Bib* 50 (3, 1969): 301–27.

Leon, *Jews of Rome*. Leon, Harry J. *The Jews of Ancient Rome*. Morris Loeb Series. Philadelphia: Jewish Publication Society of America, 1960.

Leonard, "Spirit Mediums." Leonard, Anne P. "Spirit Mediums in Palau: Transformations in a Traditional System." Pages 129–77 in *Religion, Altered States of Consciousness, and Social Change*. Edited by Erika Bourguignon. Columbus: Ohio State University Press, 1973.

Leonard, "Status." Leonard, Eugenie Andruss. "St. Paul on the Status of Women." *CBQ* 12 (3, 1950): 311–20.

Leonardi, "Ecclesiologia." Leonardi, Giovanni. "Ecclesiologia narrativa e dinamica di Luca (Vangelo e Atti): Un tentativo di sintesi." *StPat* 50 (3, 2003): 925–57.

Léonas, "Note." Léonas, Alexis. "A Note on Acts 3,25–26: The Meaning of Peter's Genesis Quotation." *ETL* 76 (1, 2000): 149–61.

Léon-Dufour, "Approches." Léon-Dufour, Xavier. "Approches diverses du miracle." Pages 11–39 in *Les Miracles de Jésus selon le Nouveau Testament*, by J.-N. Aletti et al. Edited by Xavier Léon-Dufour. Paris: Éditions du Seuil, 1977.

Leonhard, "Älteste Haggada." Leonhard, Clemens. "Die älteste Haggada: Übersetzung der Pesachhaggada nach dem palästinischen Ritus und Vorschläge zu ihrem Ursprung und ihrer Bedeutung für die Geschichte der christlichen Liturgie." *ALW* 45 (2, 2003): 201–31.

Leoni, "Incendio." Leoni, Tommaso. "Tito e l'incendio del tempio di Gerusalemme: Repressione o clemenza disubbiditia?" *Ostraka* 9 (2, 2000): 455–70.

Leoni, "Wishes." Leoni, Tommaso. "'Against Caesar's Wishes': Flavius Josephus as a Source for the Burning of the Temple." *JJS* 58 (1, 2007): 39–51.

Lerstrom, "Transitions." Lerstrom, Alan C. "International Study Transitions: Creating and Leading a Reentry Workshop." Paper presented at the eighty-first annual meeting of the Speech Communication Association, San Antonio, Tex., Nov. 18–21, 1995.

Lesko, "Death." Lesko, Leonard H. "Death and Afterlife in Ancient Egyptian Thought." Pages 1763–74 in *Civilizations of the Ancient Near East*. Edited by Jack M. Sasson. 4 vols. New York: Scribner's, 1995.

Lessa and Vogt, *Reader*. William A. Lessa and Evon Z. Vogt, eds. *Reader in Comparative Religion: An Anthropological Approach.* 4th ed. New York: Harper & Row, 1979.

Lesses, "Sorceresses." Lesses, Rebecca. "Exe(o)rcising Power: Women as Sorceresses, Exorcists, and Demonesses in Babylonian Jewish Society of Late Antiquity." *JAAR* 69 (2, 2001): 343–75.

Lesses, "Speaking with Angels." Lesses, Rebecca. "Speaking with Angels: Jewish and Greco-Egyptian Revelatory Adjurations." *HTR* 89 (1, 1996): 41–60.

Lesswing, "Aphrodite." Lesswing, Laura Marian. "The Aphrodite of Knidos: Sex Toy or Civic Symbol?" MA thesis, Williams College, 2010.

Lestang, *Annonce*. Lestang, François. *Annonce et Accueil de L'Évangile: Les figures individuelles de croyants dans le deuxième voyage missionaire de Paul (Ac 16,6–18,18).* EtBib 63. Pendé: J. Gabalda, 2012.

Lestang, "Louange." Lestang, François. "À la louange du dieu inconnu: Analyse rhétorique de Ac 17.22–31." *NTS* 52 (3, 2006): 394–408.

Lester, "Galatians 2:1–10." Lester, Russell. "Galatians 2:1–10 and Acts: An Old Problem Revisited." Pages 217–38 in *With Steadfast Purpose: Essays on Acts in Honor of Henry Jackson Flanders, Jr.* Edited by Naymond H. Keathley. Waco: Baylor University Press, 1990.

Lev, "'Aylonit." Lev, Sarra. "How the *'aylonit* Got Her Sex." *AJSR* 31 (2, 2007): 297–316.

Levang, "Content." Levang, Raymond K. "The Content of an Utterance in Tongues." *Paraclete* 23 (1, 1989): 14–20.

Levene, "Heal." Levene, Dan. "Heal O' Israel: A Pair of Duplicate Magic Bowls from the Pergamon Museum in Berlin." *JJS* 54 (1, 2003): 104–21.

Levene, "Inscription." Levene, Dan. "Rare Magic Inscription on Human Skull." *BAR* 35 (2, 2009): 46–50, 68.

Levene, "Name." Levene, Dan. "'. . . And by the name of Jesus . . .': An Unpublished Magic Bowl in Jewish Aramaic." *JSQ* 6 (4, 1999): 283–308.

Levene, "Roman Historiography." Levene, D. S. "Roman Historiography in the Late Republic." Pages 275–89 in *A Companion to Greek and Roman Historiography.* Edited by John Marincola. 2 vols. Oxford: Blackwell, 2007.

Levene and Rothenberg, "Evidence." Levene, Dan, and Beno Rothenberg. "Early Evidence for Steelmaking in the Judaic Sources." *JQR* 92 (1–2, 2001): 105–27.

Levick, "Careers." Levick, Barbara M. "Careers." *OCD*³ 290–91.

Levick, *Claudius*. Levick, Barbara M. *Claudius.* New Haven: Yale University Press, 1990.

Levick, "Economy." Levick, Barbara M. "The Roman Economy: Trade in Asia Minor and the Niche Market." *GR* 51 (2, 2004): 180–98.

Levick, *Roman Colonies*. Levick, Barbara M. *Roman Colonies in Southern Asia Minor.* Oxford: Clarendon, 1967.

Levine, "Beth-She'arim." Levine, Lee I. "Beth-She'arim." *OEANE* 1:309–11.

Levine, *Caesarea*. Levine, Lee I. *Caesarea under Roman Rule.* SJLA 7. Leiden: Brill, 1975.

Levine, "First-Century Synagogue." Levine, Lee I. "The First-Century Synagogue: New Perspectives." *STK* 77 (1, 2001): 22–30.

Levine, *Hellenism*. Levine, Lee I. *Judaism and Hellenism in Antiquity: Conflict or Confluence?* Peabody, Mass.: Hendrickson, 1998.

Levine, "Introduction to *Companion*." Levine, Amy-Jill. Introduction. Pages 1–21 in *The Feminist Companion to the Acts of the Apostles.* Edited by Amy-Jill Levine with Marianne Blickenstaff. Cleveland: Pilgrim; Edinburgh: T&T Clark, 2004.

Levine, "Introduction to *Historical Jesus*." Levine, Amy-Jill. Introduction. Pages 1–39 in *The Historical Jesus in Context.* Edited by Amy-Jill Levine, Dale C. Allison Jr., and John Dominic Crossan. PrRR. Princeton: Princeton University Press, 2006.

Levine, "Letters." Levine, Nachman. "Reading Crowned Letters and Semiotic Silences in Menachot 29b." *JJS* 53 (1, 2002): 35–48.

Levine, *Misunderstood Jew*. Levine, Amy-Jill. *The Misunderstood Jew: The Church and the Scandal of the Jewish Jesus.* San Francisco: HarperSanFrancisco, 2006.

Levine, "Nature and Origin." Levine, Lee I. "The Nature and Origin of the Palestinian Synagogue Reconsidered." *JBL* 115 (3, 1996): 425–48.

Levine, "Purification." Levine, Lee I. "R. Simeon b. Yohai and the Purification of Tiberias: History and Tradition." *HUCA* 49 (1978): 143–85.

Levine, "Responsibility." Levine, Amy-Jill. "Discharging Responsibility: Matthean Jesus, Biblical Law, and Hemorrhaging Woman." Pages 379–97 in *Treasures New and Old: Recent Contributions to Matthean Studies.* Edited by David R. Bauer and Mark Allan Powell. SBLSymS 1. Atlanta: Scholars Press, 1996.

Levine, "Synagogue." Levine, Lee I. "The Second Temple Synagogue: The Formative Years." Pages 7–31 in *The Synagogue in Late Antiquity.* Edited by Lee I. Levine. Philadelphia: American Schools of Oriental Research, 1986.

Levine, "Theory." Levine, Amy-Jill. "Theory, Apologetic, History: Reviewing Jesus' Jewish Context." *ABR* 55 (2007): 57–78.

Levine, "Twice." Levine, Nachman. "Twice as Much of Your Spirit: Pattern, Parallel and Paronomasia in the Miracles of Elijah and Elisha." *JSOT* 85 (1999): 25–46.

Levine, "Women in Tobit." Levine, Amy-Jill. "Women in Tobit." *BibT* 37 (2, 1999): 80–85.

Levinskaya, "Cohort." Levinskaya, Irina. "The Italian Cohort in Acts 10:1." Pages 106–25 in *The New Testament in Its First Century Setting: Essays on Context and Background in Honour of B. W. Winter on His 65th Birthday.* Edited by P. J. Williams et al. Grand Rapids and Cambridge, U.K.: Eerdmans, 2004.

Levinskaya, *Diaspora Setting*. Levinskaya, Irina. *The Book of Acts in Its Diaspora Setting.* Vol. 5 of *The Book of Acts in Its First Century Setting.* Edited by Bruce W. Winter. Grand Rapids: Eerdmans; Carlisle, U.K.: Paternoster, 1996.

Levinskaya, "Gentile Prayer House?" Levinskaya, Irina. "A Jewish or Gentile Prayer House? The Meaning of ΠΡΟΣΕΥΧΗ." *TynBul* 41 (1, 1990): 154–59.

Levinskaya, "Inscription and Problem." Levinskaya, Irina. "The Inscription from Aphrodisias and the Problem of God-Fearers." *TynBul* 41 (2, 1990): 312–18.

Levinsohn, *Connections*. Levinsohn, Stephen H. *Textual Connections in Acts.* SBLMS 31. Atlanta: Scholars Press, 1987.

Levinson, "Gbwlwt." Levinson, J. "Gbwlwt wmkspwt: sypry 'ymwt byn rbnym lmkspwt bsprwt hz"l." *Tarbiz* 75 (3–4, 2006): 295–328 (Abstract: *NTA* 53:120).

Levison, "Adam." Levison, John R. "Early Judaism Looks at Adam." *BibT* 30 (6, 1992): 372–77.

Levison, "Adam and Eve." Levison, John R. "Adam and Eve, Literature Concerning." *DNTB* 1–6.

Levison, "Character." Levison, John R. "The Roman Character of Funerals in the Writings of Josephus." *JSJ* 33 (3, 2002): 245–77.

Levison, *Filled*. Levison, John R. *Filled with the Spirit.* Grand Rapids: Eerdmans, 2009.

Levison, "Interpretation." Levison, John R. "Josephus' Interpretation of the Divine Spirit." *JJS* 47 (2, 1996): 234–55.

Levison, "Rhetoric." Levison, John R. "Did the Spirit Inspire Rhetoric? An Exploration of George Kennedy's Definition of

Early Christian Rhetoric." Pages 25–40 in *Persuasive Artistry: Studies in New Testament Rhetoric in Honor of George A. Kennedy*. Edited by Duane F. Watson. JSNTSup 50. Sheffield, U.K.: Sheffield Academic, 1991.

Levison, "Ruth." Levison, John R. "Josephus's Version of Ruth." *JSP* 8 (1991): 31–44.

Levison, "Types of Prophecy." Levison, John R. "Two Types of Ecstatic Prophecy according to Philo." *SPhilA* 6 (1994): 83–89.

Levison, "Withdraw." Levison, John R. "Did the Spirit Withdraw from Israel? An Evaluation of the Earliest Jewish Data." *NTS* 43 (1, 1997): 35–57.

Levy, "Bad Timing." Levy, Abraham. "Bad Timing." *BAR* 24 (4, 1998): 18–23.

Lévy, "Conversation." Lévy, Carlos. "La conversation à Rome à la fin de la république: Des pratiques sans théorie?" *Rhetorica* 11 (4, 1993): 399–414.

Levy, Krey, and Ryan, *Romans*. Levy, Ian Christopher, Philip D. W. Krey, and Thomas Ryan. *The Letter to the Romans*. The Bible in Medieval Tradition. Grand Rapids: Eerdmans, 2013.

Lewin, "Implications." Lewin, Linda. "Some Historical Implications of Kinship Organization for Family-Based Politics in the Brazilian Northeast." *CSSH* 21 (Apr. 1979): 262–92.

Lewis, *Ancient Malta*. Lewis, Harrison Adolphus. *Ancient Malta: A Study of Its Antiquities*. Gerrards Cross: Smythe, 1977.

Lewis, "Deprivation Cults." Lewis, I. M. "Spirit Possession and Deprivation Cults." Pages 311–33 in *Possession and Exorcism*. Vol. 9 of *Articles on Witchcraft, Magic, and Demonology: A Twelve-Volume Anthology of Scholarly Articles*. Edited by Brian P. Levack. New York: Garland, 1992. Reprinted from *Man* 1 (1966): 307–29.

Lewis, *Ecstatic Religion*. Lewis, I. M. *Ecstatic Religion: An Anthropological Study of Spirit Possession and Shamanism*. Pelican Anthropology Library. Harmondsworth, U.K., and Baltimore: Penguin, 1971.

Lewis, *Healing*. Lewis, David C. *Healing: Fiction, Fantasy, or Fact?* London: Hodder & Stoughton, 1989.

Lewis, *History*. Lewis, Bernard. *History Remembered, Recovered, Invented*. New York: Simon & Schuster, 1975.

Lewis, "Horoscope." Lewis, A.-M. "Augustus and His Horoscope." *Phoenix* 62 (3–4, 2008): 308–37.

Lewis, "Ignatius." Lewis, R. B. "Ignatius and the 'Lord's Day.'" *AUSS* 6 (1, 1968): 46–59.

Lewis, "Intercessio." Lewis, Andrew Dominic Edwards. "Intercessio." *OCD*³ 760.

Lewis, "Introduction." Lewis, I. M. "Introduction: *Zar* in Context—The Past, the Present, and Future of an African Healing Cult." Pages 1–16 in *Women's Medicine: The zar-bori Cult in Africa and Beyond*. Edited by I. M. Lewis, Ahmed Al-Safi, and Sayyid Hurreiz. Edinburgh: International African Institute, Edinburgh University Press, 1991.

Lewis, *Life*. Lewis, Naphtali. *Life in Egypt under Roman Rule*. Oxford: Clarendon, 1983.

Lewis, *Literary Sources*. Lewis, Naphtali, ed. *The Ancient Literary Sources*. Vol. 1 of *Samothrace: Excavations Conducted by the Institute of Fine Arts of New York University*. Edited by Karl Lehmann and Phyllis Williams Lehmann. BollS 60. New York: Pantheon; Princeton: Princeton University Press, 1958.

Lewis, "Mark 10:14." Lewis, Jack P. "Mark 10:14, *koluein*, and *baptizein*." *ResQ* 21 (3, 1978): 129–34.

Lewis, *Miracles*. Lewis, C. S. *Miracles: A Preliminary Study*. New York: Macmillan, 1948.

Lewis, *Paths*. Lewis, Harrison Adolphus. *A Guide to the Remote Paths and Lanes of Ancient Malta*. Gerrards Cross: Smythe, 1974.

Lewis, "Possession." Lewis, I. M. "Spirit Possession in Northern Somaliland." Pages 188–219 in *Spirit Mediumship and Society in Africa*. Edited by John Beattie and John Middleton. Foreword by Raymond Firth. New York: Africana, 1969.

Lewis, *Prophets*. Lewis, Jack P. *The Minor Prophets*. Grand Rapids: Baker, 1966.

Lewis, *Public Services*. Lewis, Naphtali. *The Compulsory Public Services of Roman Egypt*. Papyrologica florentina 11. Florence: Gonnelli, 1982.

Lewis, *Race and Slavery*. Lewis, Bernard. *Race and Slavery in the Middle East: An Historical Enquiry*. New York: Oxford University Press, 1990.

Lewis, "Signs." Lewis, David C. "Appendix F: Signs and Wonders in Sheffield, U.K.—A Social Anthropologist's Analysis of Words of Knowledge, Manifestations of the Spirit, and the Effectiveness of Divine Healing." Pages 248–69 in *Power Healing*. By John Wimber, with Kevin Springer. San Francisco: Harper & Row, 1987.

Lewis, "Spirits and Sex War." Lewis, I. M. "Correspondence: Spirits and the Sex War." *Man*, n.s., 2 (4, Dec. 1967): 626–28.

Lewis, *Transposition*. Lewis, C. S. *Transposition and Other Addresses*. London: Geoffrey Bles, 1949.

Lewis, Al-Safi, and Hurreiz, *Medicine*. Lewis, I. M., Ahmed Al-Safi, and Sayyid Hurreiz, eds. *Women's Medicine: The zar-bori Cult in Africa and Beyond*. Edinburgh: International African Institute, Edinburgh University Press, 1991.

Lewis and Reinhold, *Empire*. Lewis, Naphtali, and Meyer Reinhold. *Roman Civilization, Sourcebook II: The Empire*. New York: Harper & Row, 1955.

Ley, "Hermes." Ley, Anne. "Hermes: Iconography." *BrillPauly* 6:220–21.

Leyrer, "Πίστις Χριστοῦ." Leyrer, Daniel P. "Πίστις Χριστοῦ: Faith in or Faithfulness of Christ?" *WLQ* 104 (2, 2007): 152–54.

Liardon, *Generals*. Liardon, Roberts. *God's Generals: Why Some Succeeded and Why Some Failed*. New Kensington, Pa.: Whitaker House, 1996.

Libero, "Disability." Libero, Loretana de. "Disability." *BrillPauly* 4:534–36.

Libero, "Fasces." Libero, Loretana de. "Fasces." *BrillPauly* 5:359–60.

Libero, "Provocatio." Libero, Loretana de. "Provocatio." *BrillPauly* 12:87.

Licauco, "Psychic Healing." Licauco, Jaime. "Psychic Healing in the Philippines." Pages 93–96 in *Proceedings of the Fourth International Conference on the Study of Shamanism and Alternate Modes of Healing, Held at the St. Sabina Center, San Rafael, California, September 5–7, 1987*. Edited by Ruth-Inge Heinze. N.p.: Independent Scholars of Asia; Madison, Wis.: A-R Editions, 1988.

Lichtenberger, *Baupolitik*. Lichtenberger, Achim. *Die Baupolitik Herodes des Grossen*. ADPV 26. Wiesbaden: Harrassowitz, 1999.

Lichtenberger, "Foundation Legends." Lichtenberger, Achim. "City Foundation Legends in the Decapolis." *BAIAS* 22 (2004): 23–34.

Lichtenberger, "Lebenskraft." Lichtenberger, Hermann. "Dass du nicht vergisst (Devarim-Dtn 4,9): Von der Lebenskraft der Tora." *TBei* 21 (4, 1990); 196–204.

Lichtenberger, "Spirits." Lichtenberger, Hermann. "Spirits and Demons in the Dead Sea Scrolls." Pages 14–21 in *The Holy Spirit and Christian Origins: Essays in Honor of James D. G. Dunn*. Edited by Graham N. Stanton, Bruce W. Longenecker, and Stephen C. Barton. Grand Rapids: Eerdmans, 2004.

Licona, "Biographies." Licona, Michael R. "Using Plutarch's Biographies to Help Resolve Differences in Parallel Gospel Accounts." Paper presented in the New Testament Backgrounds section at the Evangelical Theological Society, Baltimore, Nov. 21, 2013.

Licona, "Historicity of Resurrection." Licona, Michael R. "The Historicity of the Resurrection of Christ: Historiographical Considerations in the Light of Recent Debates." PhD diss., University of Pretoria, 2008.

Licona, *Resurrection*. Licona, Michael R. *The Resurrection of Jesus: A New Historiographical Approach*. Downers Grove, Ill.: InterVarsity; Nottingham, U.K.: Apollos, 2010.

LiDonnici, "Artemis and Worship." LiDonnici, Lynn. "The Images of Artemis Ephesia and Greco-Roman Worship: A Reconsideration." *HTR* 85 (4, 1992): 389–415.

LiDonnici, "Burning." LiDonnici, Lynn. "Burning for It: Erotic Spells for Fever and Compulsion in the Ancient Mediterranean World." *GRBS* 39 (1, 1998): 63–98.

LiDonnici, "Megabyzos Priesthood." LiDonnici, Lynn. "The Ephesian Megabyzos Priesthood and Religious Diplomacy at the End of the Classical Period." *Religion* 29 (3, 1999): 201–14.

Liébaert and Bernard, "Dieu et prochain." Liébaert, Jacques, and Jacques Bernard. "Dieu et le prochain dans le judaïsme ancient." *MScRel* 60 (2, 2003): 7–21.

Lieber, "Angels." Lieber, Andrea. "Angels That Kill: Mediation and the Threat of Bodily Destruction in *hekhalot* Narratives." *StSpir* 14 (2004): 17–35.

Lieber, "Table." Lieber, Andrea. "I Set a Table before You: The Jewish Eschatological Character of Aseneth's Conversion Meal." *JSP* 14 (1, 2004): 63–77.

Lieberman, *Hellenism*. Lieberman, Saul. *Hellenism in Jewish Palestine: Studies in the Literary Transmission, Beliefs, and Manners of Palestine in the I Century B.C.E.–IV Century C.E.* 2nd ed. TSJTSA 18. New York: Jewish Theological Seminary of America Press, 1962.

Lieberman, "Light." Lieberman, Saul. "Light on the Cave Scrolls from Rabbinic Sources." *PAAJR* 20 (1951): 395–404.

Liebeschuetz, "Influence." Liebeschuetz, Wolf. "The Influence of Judaism among Non-Jews in the Imperial Period." *JJS* 52 (2, 2001): 235–52.

Liefeld, *Acts*. Liefeld, Walter Lewis. *Interpreting the Book of Acts*. Grand Rapids: Baker, 1995.

Liefeld, "Preacher." Liefeld, Walter Lewis. "The Wandering Preacher as a Social Figure in the Roman Empire." PhD diss., Columbia University, 1967.

Lienau and Meyer, "Peirene." Lienau, Cay, and Ernst Meyer. "Peirene. II. Topography." *BrillPauly* 10:680–81.

Lienau and Olshausen, "Isthmus." Lienau, Cay, and Eckart Olshausen. "Isthmus." *BrillPauly* 6:990–91.

Lienhardt, "Death." Lienhardt, Godfrey. "The Situation of Death: An Aspect of Anuak Philosophy." *AnthrQ* 35 (2, 1962): 74–85.

Lieu, "Attraction." Lieu, Judith M. "The 'Attraction of Women' in/to Early Judaism and Christianity: Gender and the Politics of Conversion." *JSNT* 72 (1998): 5–22.

Lieven, "Moon Deities." Lieven, Alexandra von. "Moon Deities: Egypt." *BrillPauly* 9:201–2.

Lieven, "Underworld." Lieven, Alexandra von. "Underworld." *BrillPauly* 15:104–6.

Lifshitz, *Donateurs et fondateurs*. Lifshitz, Baruch. *Donateurs et fondateurs dans les synagogues juives: Répertoire des dédicaces grecques relatives à la réflection des synagogues*. CahRB. Paris: Gabalda, 1967.

Lifshitz, "Sympathisants." Lifshitz, Baruch. "Du nouveau sur les 'sympathisants.'" *JSJ* 1 (1, 1970): 77–84.

Lifshitz and Schiby, "Synagogue samaritaine." Lifshitz, B., and J. Schiby. "Une synagogue samaritaine à Théssalonique." *RB* 75 (1968): 368–78.

"Light." "Light." Pages 509–12 in *Dictionary of Biblical Imagery*. Edited by Leland Ryken, James C. Wilhoit, and Tremper Longman III. Downers Grove, Ill.: InterVarsity, 1998.

Lightfoot, *Acts*. Lightfoot, J. B. *The Acts of the Apostles: A Newly Discovered Commentary*. Vol. 1 of The Lightfoot Legacy Set. Edited by Ben Witherington III and Todd D. Still. Downers Grove, Ill.: IVP Academic, 2014.

Lightfoot, *Colossians*. Lightfoot, J. B. *Saint Paul's Epistles to the Colossians and to Philemon*. 3rd ed. London.: Macmillan, 1879. Repr., Grand Rapids: Zondervan, 1959.

Lightfoot, *Galatians*. Lightfoot, J. B. *Saint Paul's Epistle to the Galatians*. 3rd ed. London: Macmillan, 1869.

Lightfoot, *Gospel*. Lightfoot, R. H. *St. John's Gospel: A Commentary*. Edited by C. F. Evans. London: Oxford University Press, 1960.

Lightfoot, *Notes*. Lightfoot, J. B. *Notes on the Epistles of St. Paul*. 2nd ed. London: Macmillan, 1904. Repr., Winona Lake, Ind.: Alpha, n.d.

Lightfoot, *Philippians*. Lightfoot, J. B. *St. Paul's Epistle to the Philippians*. London: Macmillan, 1913. Repr., Grand Rapids: Zondervan, 1953.

Lightfoot, *Talmud*. Lightfoot, John. *A Commentary on the New Testament from the Talmud and Hebraica*. 4 vols. Oxford: Oxford University Press, 1859. Repr., Grand Rapids: Baker, 1979. (Originally

published as *Horae hebraicae et talmudicae*.)

Lightfoot, "Third Notebook on Acts." Lightfoot, J. B. Unpublished material transcribed and shared with the author by Ben Witherington III.

Lightman and Zeisel, "Univira." Lightman, Marjorie, and William Zeisel. "Univira: An Example of Continuity and Change in Roman Society." *CH* 46 (1, 1977): 19–32.

Lightstone, "Diaspora Judaism." Lightstone, Jack. "Roman Diaspora Judaism." Pages 345–77 in *A Companion to Roman Religion*. Edited by Jörg Rüpke. BCompAW. Oxford: Blackwell, 2011.

Lignée, "Soixante-douze." Lignée, H. "La mission des soixante-douze: Lc 10,1–12, 17–20." *AsSeign* 45 (1974): 64–74.

Lim, "Critique." Lim, David S. "An Evangelical Critique of 'Initial Evidence' Doctrine." *AJPS* 1 (2, 1998): 219–29.

Lim, "Evaluation." Lim, David S. "A Missiological Evaluation of David Yonggi Cho's Church Growth." Pages 181–207 in *David Yonggi Cho: A Close Look at His Theology and Ministry*. Edited by Wonsuk Ma, William W. Menzies, and Hyeonsung Bae. AJPS Series 1. Baguio City, Philippines: APTS; Kyunggi-do, Korea: Hansei University Press, 2004.

Lim, "Evangelism." Lim, David S. "Evangelism in the Early Church." *DLNTD* 353–59.

Lim, "Orientation." Lim, Timothy H. "Eschatological Orientation and the Alteration of Scripture in the Habakkuk Pesher." *JNES* 49 (2, 1990): 185–94.

Lim, "Reference." Lim, Timothy H. "The Alleged Reference to the Tripartite Division of the Hebrew Bible." *RevQ* 20 (77, 2001): 23–37.

Lim, "Reflection." Lim, David. "A Reflection on the 'Initial Evidence' Discussion from a Pentecostal Pastor's Perspective." *AJPS* 2 (2, 1999): 223–32.

Limbeck, "Lobpreis." Limbeck, Meinrad. "Der Lobpreis Gottes als Sinn des Daseins." *ThQ* 150 (3, 1970): 349–57.

Limbeck, *Ordnung*. Limbeck, Meinrad. *Die Ordnung des Heils: Untersuchungen zum Gesetzesverständnis des Frühjudentums*. KBANT. Düsseldorf: Patmos, 1971.

Limberis, "Ambiguities." Limberis, Vasiliki. "Ecclesiastical Ambiguities: Corinth in the Fourth and Fifth Centuries." Pages 443–57 in *Urban Religion in Roman Corinth: Interdisciplinary Approaches*. Edited by Daniel N. Schowalter and Steven J. Friesen. HTS 53. Cambridge, Mass.: Harvard University Press, 2005.

Lincicum, "Apotropaism." Lincicum, David. "Scripture and Apotropaism in the Second Temple Period." *BN* 138 (2008): 63–87.

Lincicum, "Fever." Lincicum, David. "Greek Deuteronomy's 'Fever and Chills' and Their Magical Afterlife." *VT* 58 (4–5, 2008): 544–49.

Lincoln, "Banditry." Lincoln, Levi R. "Jewish Banditry and Peasant Protest Movements 6–66 CE: A Comparative Approach." *JS/TS* 17 (1, 2008): 219–39.

Lincoln, *Ephesians*. Lincoln, Andrew T. *Ephesians*. WBC 42. Dallas: Word, 1990.

Lincoln, "Interpetation of Luke's Pentecost." Lincoln, Andrew T. "Theology and History in the Interpretation of Luke's Pentecost." *ExpT* 96 (7, 1985): 204–9.

Lincoln, *John*. Lincoln, Andrew T. *The Gospel according to Saint John*. BNTC. Peabody, Mass.: Hendrickson; London: Continuum, 2005.

Lincoln, *Paradise*. Lincoln, Andrew T. *Paradise Now and Not Yet: Studies in the Role of the Heavenly Dimension in Paul's Thought with Special Reference to His Eschatology*. SNTSMS 43. Cambridge: Cambridge University Press, 1981.

Lind, "Abstraction." Lind, L. R. "Roman Religion and Ethical Thought: Abstraction and Personification." *CJ* 69 (2, 1973–74): 108–19.

Lindars, *Apologetic*. Lindars, Barnabas. *New Testament Apologetic*. London: SCM, 1961.

Lindars, *Behind*. Lindars, Barnabas. *Behind the Fourth Gospel: Studies in Creative Criticism*. London: Talbot Press, 1971.

Lindars, "Re-enter." Lindars, Barnabas. "Reenter the Apocalyptic Son of Man." *NTS* 22 (1, 1975): 52–72.

Lindars, *Son of Man*. Lindars, Barnabas. *Jesus Son of Man: A Fresh Examination of the Son of Man Sayings in the Gospels in the Light of Recent Research*. Grand Rapids: Eerdmans, 1983.

Lindblom, *Prophecy*. Lindblom, J. *Prophecy in Ancient Israel*. Philadelphia: Fortress, 1962.

Lindboe, "Samfunnsvitenskapene." Lindboe, I. M. "Samfunnsvitenskapene og Det nye testamente: Interessante modellermetodiske svakheter." *NTT* 93 (3, 1992): 167–74.

Lindemann, "Anfänge." Lindemann, Andreas. "Der 'äthiopische Eunuch' und die Anfänge der Mission unter den Völkern nach Apg 8–11." Pages 109–33 in *Die Apostelgeschichte und die hellenistische Geschichtsschreibung: Festschrift für Eckhard Plümacher zu seinem 65. Geburtstag*. Edited by Cilliers Breytenbach and Jens Schröter. Leiden: Brill, 2004.

Lindemann, "Einheit." Lindemann, Andreas. "Einheit und Vielfalt im lukanischen Doppelwerk: Beobachtungen zu Reden, Wundererzählungen, und Mahlberichten." Pages 225–53 in *The Unity of Luke-Acts*. Edited by Joseph Verheyden. BETL 142. Leuven: Leuven University Press, 1999.

Lindemann, "Samaritaner." Lindemann, Andreas. "Samaria und Samaritaner im Neuen Testament." *WD* 22 (1993): 51–76.

Lindemann, "Unborn Babe." Lindemann, Andreas. "'Do Not Let a Woman Destroy the Unborn Babe in Her Belly': Abortion in Ancient Judaism and Christianity." *ST* 49 (2, 1995): 253–71.

Linden, "Cities." Linden, Eugene. "The Exploding Cities of the Developing World." Pages 406–15 in *Globalization and the Challenges of a New Century: A Reader*. Edited by Patrick O'Meara, Howard D. Mehlinger, and Matthew Krain. Bloomington: Indiana University Press, 2000.

Linderski, "Palladium." Linderski, Jerzy. "Palladium." *OCD³* 1100–1101.

Lindner, "Frau und Beruf." Lindner, Ruth. "Frau und Beruf in der frühen römischen Kaiserzeit." *BK* 57 (3, 2002): 153–57.

Lindner, "Geschichtsauffassung." Lindner, Helgo. "Die Geschichtsauffassung des Flavius Josephus im Bellum judaicum: Gleichzeitig ein Beitrag zur Quellenfrage, Diss., Tübingen 1970." *TLZ* 96 (12, 1971): 953–54.

Lindner, "Heiligtum." Lindner, Manfred. "Ein nabatäisches Heiligtum oberhalb der Nischenklamm (*Sidd el-Maʿāğīn*) von Petra (Jordanien)." *ZDPV* 106 (1990): 145–54 and plates 14–19.

Lindner, "Water Supply." Lindner, Manfred. "Water Supply and Water Management at Ancient Sabra (Jordan)." *PEQ* 137 (1, 2005): 33–52.

Lindner and Hübl, "Daughter." Lindner, Manfred, and H. Hübl. "Where Pharao's Daughter Got Her Drinking Water From: The *ʿÊn Brāk* Conduit to Petra." *ZDPV* 113 (1997): 61–67 and plates 1–12A.

Lindsay, *Golden Ass*. Lindsay, Jack, trans. *The Golden Ass by Apuleius*. Bloomington: Indiana University Press, 1960.

Lindsay, *Lake*. Lindsay, Gordon. *John G. Lake: Apostle to Africa*. Dallas: Christ for the Nations, 1981.

Lindsey, *Jesus*. Lindsey, Robert L. *Jesus, Rabbi and Lord. The Hebrew Story of Jesus behind Our Gospels*. Oak Creek, Wis.: Cornerstone, 1990.

Lindstrøm, "Animals." Lindstrøm, Torill Christine. "The Animals of the Arena: How and Why Could Their Destruction and Death Be Endured and Enjoyed?" *World Archaeology* 42 (2, 2010): 310–23.

Linforth, *Arts of Orpheus*. Linforth, Ivan M. *The Arts of Orpheus*. Berkeley: University of California Press, 1941.

Ling, "Response." Ling, Tan May. "A Response to Frank Macchia's 'Groans Too Deep for Words: Towards a Theology of Tongues as Initial Evidence.'" *AJPS* 1 (2, 1998): 175–83.

Ling, "Stranger in Town." Ling, Roger. "A Stranger in Town: Finding the Way in an Ancient City." *GR* 37 (2, 1990): 204–14.

Link, "Slinger." Link, Stefan. "Slinger." *Brill Pauly* 13:544.

Link, "Staff Sling." Link, Stefan. "Staff Sling." *BrillPauly* 13:778.

Linss, "Humor." Linss, Wilhelm C. "The Hidden Humor of St. Paul." *CurTM* 25 (3, 1998): 195–99.

Linthicum, "Acts of Power." Linthicum, Robert C. "The Apostle Paul's Acts of Power, Acts 22–28." Pages 297–312 in *Mission in Acts: Ancient Narratives in Contemporary Context*. Edited by Robert L. Gallagher and Paul Hertig. AmSocMissS 34. Maryknoll, N.Y.: Orbis, 2004.

Linton, "Aspect." Linton, Olof. "The Third Aspect—A Neglected Point of View: A Study in Gal. i–ii and Acts ix and xv." *ST* 3 (1951): 79–95.

Lintott, "Ambitus." Lintott, Andrew William. "Ambitus." *OCD³* 70–71.

Lintott, "Cliens." Lintott, Andrew W. "Cliens, Clientes." *BrillPauly* 3:450–52.

Lintott, "Dionysius." Lintott, Andrew William. "Dionysius the Areopagite." *OCD³* 477–78.

Lintott, "Equites." Lintott, Andrew William. "Equites Romani." *BrillPauly* 5:1–4.

Lintott, "Freedmen and Slaves." Lintott, Andrew. "Freedmen and Slaves in the Light of Legal Documents from First-Century A.D. Campania." *CQ* 52 (2, 2002): 555–65.

Lintott, "Provocatio." Lintott, Andrew William. "Provocatio: From the Struggle of the Orders to the Principate." *ANRW* 2:226–67. Part 1, *Republik*, 2. Edited by H. Temporini and W. Haase. Berlin: de Gruyter, 1972.

Lintott, "Punishment." Lintott, Andrew William. "Punishment, Greek and Roman Practice." *OCD³* 1278–79.

Lintott, *Romans*. Lintott, Andrew. *The Romans in the Age of Augustus*. Malden, Mass.: Wiley-Blackwell, 2010.

Lintott, "Torture." Lintott, Andrew William. "Torture." *OCD³* 1535.

Lipka, "Domestic Cults." Lipka, Michael. "Notes on Pompeian Domestic Cults." *Numen* 53 (3, 2006): 327–58.

Litewski, "Appellation." Litewski, Wieslaw. "Die römische Appellation in

Zivilsachen: Ein Abriss, I. Prinzipat." *ANRW* 2 (14, 1982): 60–96.

Litfin, *Theology*. Litfin, Duane. *St. Paul's Theology of Proclamation: 1 Corinthians 1–4 and Greco-Roman Rhetoric*. SNTSMS 83. Cambridge: Cambridge University Press, 1994.

Litke, "Samaritan Chronology." Litke, Wayne. "Acts 7.3 and Samaritan Chronology." *NTS* 42 (1, 1996): 156–60.

Littauer and Crouwel, "Chariots." Littauer, Mary Aiken, and J. H. Crouwel. "Chariots." *ABD* 1:888–92.

Litwak, *Echoes*. Litwak, Kenneth Duncan. *Echoes of Scripture in Luke-Acts: Telling the History of God's People Intertextually.* JSNTSup 282. London: T&T Clark, 2005.

Litwak, "Prophets." Litwak, Kenneth D. "Israel's Prophets Meet Athens' Philosophers: Scriptural Echoes in Acts 17,22–31." *Bib* 85 (2, 2004): 199–216.

Litwak, "Views." Litwak, Kenneth D. "One or Two Views of Judaism: Paul in Acts 28 and Romans 11 on Jewish Unbelief." *TynBul* 57 (2, 2006): 229–49.

Liu, "Nature." Liu, Irene. "Nature and Knowledge in Stoicism: On the Ordinariness of the Stoic Sage." *Apeiron* 41 (4, 2008): 247–75.

Liver, "Offering." Liver, Jacob. "The Half-Shekel Offering in Biblical and Post-biblical Literature." *HTR* 56 (1963): 173–98.

Liverani, "Tyre." Liverani, M. "Tyre." Translated by William Sanford LaSor. *ISBE* 4:932–34.

Livingston, "Seven." Livingston, Michael. "The Seven: Hebrews, Hellenists, and Heptines." *JHC* 6 (1, 1999): 32–63.

Livingstone, *Defenders*. Livingstone, David N. *Darwin's Forgotten Defenders: The Encounter between Evangelical Theology and Evolutionary Thought*. Grand Rapids: Eerdmans; Edinburgh: Scottish Academic, 1987.

Liwak, "Tyrus." Liwak, Rüdinger. "Tyrus." *BrillPauly* 15:71–74.

Llewellyn, "Events." Llewellyn, Russ. "Religious and Spiritual Miracle Events in Real-Life Experience." Pages 241–63 in *Religious and Spiritual Events*. Vol. 1 of *Miracles: God, Science, and Psychology in the Paranormal*. Edited by J. Harold Ellens. 3 vols. Westport, Conn.; London: Praeger, 2008.

Llewellyn-Jones, *Tortoise*. Llewellyn-Jones, Lloyd. *Aphrodite's Tortoise: The Veiled Woman of Ancient Greece*. Swansea: The Classical Press of Wales, 2003.

Llewellyn-Jones and Robson, *Ctesias*. Llewellyn-Jones, Lloyd, and James Robson. *Ctesias' History of Persia: Tales of the Orient*. New York: Routledge, 2010.

Llewelyn, *Documents*, 6. Llewelyn, S. R., with the collaboration of R. A. Kearsley. *A Review of the Greek Inscriptions and Papyri Published in 1980–81*. Vol. 6 of *New Documents Illustrating Early Christianity*. North Ryde, N.S.W.: Ancient History Documentary Research Centre, Macquarie University, 1992.

Llewelyn, *Documents*, 7. Llewelyn, S. R., with the collaboration of R. A. Kearsley. *A Review of the Greek Inscriptions and Papyri Published in 1982–83*. Vol. 7 of *New Documents Illustrating Early Christianity*. North Ryde, N.S.W.: Ancient History Documentary Research Centre, Macquarie University, 1994.

Llewelyn, *Documents*, 8. Llewelyn, S. R. *A Review of the Greek Inscriptions and Papyri Published 1984–85*. Vol. 8 of *New Documents Illustrating Early Christianity*. Ancient History Documentary Research Centre, Macquarie University, N.S.W. Australia; Grand Rapids: Eerdmans, 1998.

Llewelyn and Beek, "Reading." Llewelyn, Stephen R., and Dionysia van Beek. "Reading the Temple Warning as a Greek Visitor." *JSJ* 42 (1, 2011): 1–22.

Lloyd-Jones, *Christianity*. Lloyd-Jones, Martyn. *Authentic Christianity. Studies in the Book of Acts 1*. Wheaton, Ill.: Crossway, 2000.

Loader, "Christ at Right Hand." Loader, W. R. G. "Christ at the Right Hand—Ps. CX.1 in the New Testament." *NTS* 24 (2, 1978): 199–217.

Lobell, "Talk." Lobell, J. A. "Trash Talk." *Archaeology* 62 (2, 2009): 20–25.

Lock, *Pastoral Epistles*. Lock, Walter. *A Critical and Exegetical Commentary on the Pastoral Epistles*. ICC. Edinburgh: T&T Clark, 1924.

Lockwood, "Exclude." Lockwood, Peter F. "Does 1 Corinthians 14:34–35 Exclude Women from the Pastoral Office?" *LTJ* 30 (1, 1996): 30–38.

Lockwood, "House Church." Lockwood, G. "The House Church: From Acts to Constantine." *LTJ* 43 (2, 2009): 97–100.

Lockwood, Browning, and Wilson, "Aristarchus." Lockwood, John Francis, Robert Browning, and Nigel Guy Wilson. "Aristarchus (2)." *OCD*[3] 159.

Lodge, *Ethics*. Lodge, R. C. *Plato's Theory of Ethics: The Moral Criterion and the Highest Good*. New York: Harcourt, Brace; London: Kegan Paul, Trench, Trubner, 1928.

Lodge, "Salvation Theologies." Lodge, John G. "The Salvation Theologies of Paul and Luke." *ChicSt* 22 (1, 1983): 35–52.

Loewen, "Possession." Loewen, Jacob A. "Demon Possession and Exorcism in Africa, in the New Testament Context, and in North America; or: Toward a Western

Scientific Model of Demon Possession and Exorcism." Pages 118–45 in *Essays on Spiritual Bondage and Deliverance*. Edited by Willard M. Swartley. Occasional Papers 11. Elkhart, Ind.: Institute of Mennonite Studies, 1988.

Loewenstamm, *Evolution*. Loewenstamm, Samuel E. *The Evolution of the Exodus Tradition*. Translated by Baruch J. Schwartz. Perry Foundation for Biblical Research, Hebrew University, Jerusalem. Jerusalem: Magnes, 1992.

Lofland and Stark, "Conversion." Lofland, John, and Rodney Stark. "Becoming a World Saver: A Theory of Conversion from a Deviant Perspective." *AmSocRev* 30 (1965): 862–75.

Lofthouse, "Spirit in Acts and Fourth Gospel." Lofthouse, W. F. "The Holy Spirit in the Acts and the Fourth Gospel." *ExpT* 52 (9, 1941): 334–36.

Loftus, "Note." Loftus, Francis. "A Note on *syntagma tōn Galilaiōn* B.J. iv 558." *JQR* 65 (3, 1975): 182–83.

Loftus, "Revolts." Loftus, Francis. "The Anti-Roman Revolts of the Jews and the Galileans." *JQR* 68 (2, 1977): 78–98.

Lohfink, "Taten Gottes." Lohfink, Gerhard. "Gibt es noch Taten Gottes?" *Orientierung* 42 (11, 1978): 124–26.

Lohmann, "Diolkos." Lohmann, Hans. "Diolkos, Diholkos." *BrillPauly* 4:460–61.

Lohmann, "Milesia." Lohmann, Hans. "Milesia." *BrillPauly* 8:877–79.

Lohmeyer, "Abendmahl." Lohmeyer, Ernst. "Das Abendmahl in der Urgemeinde." *JBL* 56 (3, 1937): 217–52.

Lohse, "Apostleship." Lohse, Eduard. "St. Peter's Apostleship in the Judgment of St. Paul, the Apostle to the Gentiles: An Exegetical Contribution to an Ecumenical Debate." *Greg* 72 (3, 1991): 419–35.

Lohse, *Colossians*. Lohse, Eduard. *Colossians and Philemon*. Translated by William R. Poehlmann and Robert J. Karris. Edited by Helmut Koester. Hermeneia. Philadelphia: Fortress, 1971.

Lohse, *Environment*. Lohse, Eduard. *The New Testament Environment*. Translated by John E. Steely. Nashville: Abingdon, 1976.

Lohse, *Mark's Witness*. Lohse, Eduard. *Mark's Witness to Jesus Christ*. New York: Association, 1955.

Lohse, "Theologie." Lohse, Eduard. "Christus, des Gesetzes Ende? Die Theologie des Apostels Paulus in kritischer Perspektive." *ZNW* 99 (1, 2008): 18–32.

Lohwasser, "Kandake." Lohwasser, Angelika. "Kandake." *BrillPauly* 7:15.

Lohwasser, "Meroe." Lohwasser, Angelika. "Meroe." *BrillPauly* 8:717–18.

Lohwasser, "Meroitic." Lohwasser, Angelika. "Meroitic." *BrillPauly* 8:718.

Loisy, *Actes.* Loisy, Alfred. *Les Actes des apôtres.* Paris: Émile Nourry, 1920.

Lolos, "Via Egnatia." Lolos, Yannis. "Via Egnatia after Egnatius: Imperial Policy and Inter-regional Contacts." *MHR* 22 (2, 2007): 273–93.

Loman, "No Women." Loman, Pasi. "No Women, No War: Women's Participation in Ancient Greek Warfare." *GR* 51 (1, 2004): 34–54.

Lomas, "Neapolis." Lomas, H. Kathryn. "Neapolis." *OCD³* 1031–32.

Lomas, "Puteoli." Lomas, H. Kathryn. "Puteoli." *OCD³* 1280–81.

Lomas, "Rhegium." Lomas, H. Kathryn. "Rhegium." *OCD³* 1312.

Lomax, "Nonviolence." Lomax, Louis. "When 'Nonviolence' Meets 'Black Power.'" Pages 157–80 in *Martin Luther King, Jr.: A Profile.* Edited by C. Eric Lincoln. Rev. ed. New York: Hill & Wang, 1984.

Long, "Allegory." Long, A. A. "Allegory in Philo and Etymology in Stoicism: A Plea for Drawing Distinctions." *SPhilA* 9 (1997): 198–210.

Long, "Divination." Long, Burke O. "The Effect of Divination upon Israelite Literature." *JBL* 92 (4, 1973): 489–97.

Long, "Freedom." Long, A. A. "Freedom and Determinism in the Stoic Theory of Human Action." Pages 173–99 in *Problems in Stoicism.* Edited by A. A. Long. London: Athlone, 1971.

Long, *Philosophy.* Long, A. A. *Hellenistic Philosophy: Stoics, Epicureans, Sceptics.* New York: Scribner's, 1974.

Long, "Political Theology." Long, Frederick J. "Ephesians: Paul's Political Theology in Greco-Roman Political Context." Pages 255–309 in *Christian Origins and Greco-Roman Culture: Social and Literary Contexts for the New Testament.* Edited by Stanley Porter and Andrew W. Pitts. Vol. 1 of Early Christianity in Its Hellenistic Context. Vol. 9 in Texts and Editions for New Testament Study. Leiden: Brill, 2013.

Long, "Samuel." Long, V. Phillips. "1 Samuel." Pages 267–411 in vol. 2 of *Zondervan Illustrated Bible Backgrounds Commentary: Old Testament.* Edited by John Walton. 5 vols. Grand Rapids: Zondervan, 2009.

Long, "2 Samuel." Long, V. Phillips. "2 Samuel." Pages 412–91 in vol. 2 of *Zondervan Illustrated Bible Backgrounds Commentary: Old Testament.* Edited by John Walton. 5 vols. Grand Rapids: Zondervan, 2009.

Long and McMurry, *Collapse.* Long, Zeb Bradford, and Douglas McMurry. *The Collapse of the Brass Heaven.* Grand Rapids: Baker, 1994.

Longenecker, *Acts.* Longenecker, Richard N. *Acts.* ExpBC. Grand Rapids: Zondervan, 1995.

Longenecker, "Amanuenses." Longenecker, Richard N. "Ancient Amanuenses and the Pauline Epistles." Pages 281–97 in *New Dimensions in New Testament Study.* Edited by Richard N. Longenecker and Merrill C. Tenney. Grand Rapids: Zondervan, 1974.

Longenecker, "Aversion." Longenecker, Bruce W. "Lukan Aversion to Humps and Hollows: The Case of Acts 11.27–12.25." *NTS* 50 (2, 2004): 185–204.

Longenecker, "Character." Longenecker, Bruce W. "Moral Character and Divine Generosity: Acts 13:13–52 and the Narrative Dynamics of Luke-Acts." Pages 141–65 in *New Testament Greek and Exegesis: Essays in Honor of Gerald F. Hawthorne.* Edited by Amy M. Donaldson and Timothy B. Sailors. Grand Rapids and Cambridge: Eerdmans, 2003.

Longenecker, "Christological Motifs." Longenecker, Richard N. "Some Distinctive Early Christological Motifs." *NTS* 14 (4, 1968): 529–45.

Longenecker, *Christology.* Longenecker, Richard N. *The Christology of Early Jewish Christianity.* London: SCM, 1970. Repr., Grand Rapids: Baker, 1981.

Longenecker, "Contours." Longenecker, Bruce W. "Contours of Covenant Theology in the Post-conversion Paul." Pages 125–46 in *The Road from Damascus: The Impact of Paul's Conversion on His Life, Thought, and Ministry.* Edited by Richard N. Longenecker. Grand Rapids: Eerdmans, 1997.

Longenecker, "Critiquing." Longenecker, Bruce W. "On Critiquing the 'New Perspective' on Paul: A Case Study." *ZNW* 96 (3–4, 2005): 263–71.

Longenecker, *Exegesis.* Longenecker, Richard N. *Biblical Exegesis in the Apostolic Period.* Grand Rapids: Eerdmans, 1975.

Longenecker, "Good News." Longenecker, Bruce W. "Good News to the Poor: Jesus, Paul, and Jerusalem." Pages 37–65 in *Jesus and Paul Reconnected: Fresh Pathways into an Old Debate.* Edited by Todd D. Still. Grand Rapids: Eerdmans, 2007.

Longenecker, "Hope." Longenecker, Richard N. "A Realized Hope, a New Commitment, and a Developed Proclamation: Paul and Jesus." Pages 18–42 in *The Road from Damascus: The Impact of Paul's Conversion on His Life, Thought, and Ministry.* Edited by Richard N. Longenecker. Grand Rapids: Eerdmans, 1997.

Longenecker, *Introducing Romans.* Longenecker, Richard N. *Introducing Romans:*

Critical Issues in Paul's Most Famous Letter. Grand Rapids: Eerdmans, 2011.

Longenecker, "Melchizedek Argument." Longenecker, Richard N. "The Melchizedek Argument of Hebrews." Pages 161–85 in *Unity and Diversity in New Testament Theology: Essays in Honor of George E. Ladd.* Edited by Robert A. Guelich. Grand Rapids: Eerdmans, 1978.

Longenecker, "Middle." Longenecker, Bruce W. "Exposing the Economic Middle: A Revised Economy Scale for the Study of Early Urban Christianity." *JSNT* 31 (3, 2009): 243–78.

Longenecker, *Ministry and Message.* Longenecker, Richard N. *The Ministry and Message of Paul.* Grand Rapids: Zondervan, 1971.

Longenecker, *Paul.* Longenecker, Richard N. *Paul, Apostle of Liberty.* New York: Harper & Row, 1964. Repr., Grand Rapids: Baker, 1976.

Longenecker, *Remembering the Poor.* Longenecker, Bruce W. *Remembering the Poor: Paul, Poverty, and the Greco-Roman World.* Grand Rapids: Eerdmans, 2010.

Longenecker, *Social Ethics.* Longenecker, Richard N. *New Testament Social Ethics for Today.* Grand Rapids: Eerdmans, 1984.

Longenecker, *Wine.* Longenecker, Richard N. *New Wine into Fresh Wineskins: Contextualizing the Early Christian Confessions.* Peabody, Mass.: Hendrickson, 1999.

Longkumer, "Study." Longkumer, Akumla. "A Study of the Revival Movement in Nagaland." MTh thesis, Fuller Theological Seminary, 1981.

Longstaff, *Conflation.* Longstaff, Thomas R. W. *Evidence of Conflation in Mark? A Study in the Synoptic Problem.* SBLDS 28. Missoula, Mont.: Scholars Press, 1977.

Lönnermark, "Frågan." Lönnermark, L.-G. "Till frågan om romarbrevets integritet." *SEÅ* 33 (1968): 141–48.

Lönnqvist and Lönnqvist, "Emergence." Lönnqvist, Minna, and Kenneth Lönnqvist. "The Emergence of a New Archaeological Theory on the Qumran Community." *QC* 12 (2–4, 2004): 81–107.

Lönnqvist and Lönnqvist, "Phenomena." Lönnqvist, Kenneth, and Minna Lönnqvist. "Reconstructing Some Palaeoenvironmental Phenomena and Geoarchaeological Processes at Qumran, Israel." *QC* 14 (1–2, 2006): 1–35.

Lopez, *Apostle.* Lopez, Davina C. *Apostle to the Conquered: Reimagining Paul's Mission.* Paul in Critical Contexts. Minneapolis: Fortress, 2008.

Lopez, "Visualizing." Lopez, Davina C. "Visualizing Significant Otherness: Reimagining Paul(ine Studies) through Hybrid Lenses." Pages 74–94 in *The Colonized*

Apostle: Paul through Postcolonial Eyes. Edited by Christopher D. Stanley. Minneapolis: Fortress, 2011.

Lopez and Penner, "Houses." Lopez, Davina C., and Todd Penner. "'Houses Made with Hands': The Triumph of the Private in New Testament Scholarship." Pages 89–105 in *Text, Image, and Christians in the Graeco-Roman World: A Festschrift in Honor of David Lee Balch*. Edited by Aliou Cissé Niang and Carolyn Osiek. PrTMS 176. Eugene, Ore.: Pickwick, 2012.

López Barja de Quiroga, "Mobility." López Barja de Quiroga, Pedro. "Freedmen Social Mobility in Roman Italy." *Historia* 44 (3, 1995): 326–48.

López Fernández, "Yugo." López Fernández, Enrique. "El yugo de Jesús (Mt 11,28–30): Historia y sentido de una metáfora." *StOv* 11 (1983): 65–118.

Loraux, *Funeral Oration*. Loraux, Nicole. *The Invention of Athens: The Funeral Oration in the Classical City*. Cambridge, Mass.: Harvard University Press, 1986.

Lord, "Introduction." Lord, Louis E. Introduction to *Pro Flacco*. Pages 357–59 in Cicero, *The Speeches: In Catalinam I–IV, Pro Mureno, Pro Sulla, Pro Flacco*. Translated by Louis E. Lord. LCL. Cambridge, Mass.: Harvard University Press, 1946.

Lord, *Singer*. Lord, Albert B. *The Singer of Tales*. New York: Atheneum, 1965.

Losch, "Kämmerer der Königen." Losch, Stephan. "Der Kämmerer der Königin Kandake (Apg. 8,27)." *ThQ* 111 (1930): 477–519.

Losie, "Speech on Areopagus." Losie, Lynn Allan. "Paul's Speech on the Areopagus: A Model of Cross-cultural Evangelism, Acts 17:16–34." Pages 221–38 in *Mission in Acts: Ancient Narratives in Contemporary Context*. Edited by Robert L. Gallagher and Paul Hertig. AmSocMissS 34. Maryknoll, N.Y.: Orbis, 2004.

Lotufo-Neto, "Influences." Lotufo-Neto, Francisco. "Religious Influences on Psychotherapy in Brazil." Pages 192–206 in *Psychodynamics*. Vol. 3 of *The Healing Power of Spirituality: How Faith Helps Humans Thrive*. Edited by J. Harold Ellens. Santa Barbara, Calif.: Praeger, 2010.

Loubser, "Media Criticism." Loubser, J. A. "Media Criticism and the Myth of Paul, the Creative Genius, and His Forgotten Co-workers." *Neot* 34 (2, 2000): 329–45.

Loubser, "Possession." Loubser, J. A. "Possession and Sacrifice in the New Testament and African Traditional Religion: The Oral Forms and Conventions behind the Literary Genres." *Neot* 37 (2, 2003): 221–45.

Lövestam, "Address." Lövestam, Evald. "Paul's Address at Miletus." *ST* 41 (1987): 1–10.

Lövestam, "Apostlagärningarnas ärende." Lövestam, E. "Apostlagärningarnas ärende." *STK* 64 (1, 1988): 1–6. (Abstract: *NTA* 34:44.)

Lövestam, "Nyckel." Lövestam, Evald. "En gammaltestamentlig nyckel till Paulustalet i Miletos (Apg 20:18–35)." *SEÅ* 51–52 (1986–87): 137–47.

Lövestam, *Son and Saviour*. Lövestam, Evald. *Son and Saviour: A Study of Acts 13, 32–37*. Translated by Michael J. Petry. Coniectanea neotestamentica 18. Lund, Swed.: C. W. K. Gleerup; Copenhagen: Ejnar Munksgaard, 1961.

Lovett, "Holiness-Pentecostalism." Lovett, Leonard. "Black Holiness-Pentecostalism." *DPCM* 76–84.

Lowe, "IOYΔAIOI." Lowe, Malcolm. "Who Were the IOYΔAIOI?" *NovT* 18 (1976): 101–30.

Lowe, "Rethinking." Lowe, Stephen D. "Rethinking the Female Status/Function Question: The Jew/Gentile Relationship as Paradigm." *JETS* 34 (1, 1991): 59–75.

Lowe, "Scylla." Lowe, Dunstan. "Scylla, the Diver's Daughter: Aeschrion, Hedyle, and Ovid." *CP* 106 (3, 2011): 260–64.

Lowe and Flusser, "Theory." Lowe, Malcolm, and David Flusser. "Evidence Corroborating a Modified Proto-Matthean Synoptic Theory." *NTS* 29 (1, 1983): 25–47.

Lown, "Miraculous." Lown, John S. "The Miraculous in the Greco-Roman Historians." *Forum* 2 (4, 1986): 36–42.

Lozano, "*Divi Augusti*." Lozano, Fernando. "*Divi Augusti* and *theoi sebastoi*: Roman Initiatives and Greek Answers." *CQ* 57 (1, 2007): 139–52.

Lucas, "Influence." Lucas, Rex A. "The Influence of Kinship upon Perception of an Ambiguous Stimulus." *AmSocRev* 31 (1966): 227–36.

Lucas, "Origin." Lucas, Ernest C. "The Origin of Daniel's Four Empires Scheme Re-examined." *TynBul* 40 (2, 1989): 185–202.

Luce, *Livy*. Luce, T. James. *Livy: The Composition of His History*. Princeton: Princeton University Press, 1977.

Luciani, "Sorte." Luciani, F. "La sorte di Enoch in un ambiguo passo targumico." *BeO* 22 (2, 1980): 125–58.

Lüdemann, *Acts*. Lüdemann, Gerd, assisted by Tom Hall. *The Acts of the Apostles: What Really Happened in the Earliest Days of the Church*. Amherst, N.Y.: Prometheus, 2005.

Lüdemann, "Acts as Source." Lüdemann, Gerd. "Acts of the Apostles as a Historical Source." Pages 109–25 in *The Social World of Formative Christianity and Judaism: Essays in Tribute to Howard Clark Kee*. Edited by Jacob Neusner et al. Philadelphia: Fortress, 1988.

Lüdemann, *Christianity*. Lüdemann, Gerd. *Early Christianity according to the Traditions in Acts: A Commentary*. Minneapolis: Fortress, 1989.

Lüdemann, "Impropriety." Lüdemann, Gerd. "Acts of Impropriety: The Imbalance of History and Theology in Luke-Acts." *TJT* 24 (1, 2008): 65–79.

Lüdemann, *Paul*. Lüdemann, Gerd. *Paul: The Founder of Christianity*. Amherst, N.Y.: Prometheus, 2002.

Lüdemann, "Successors." Lüdemann, Gerd. "The Successors of Pre-70 Jerusalem Christianity: A Critical Evaluation of the Pella-Tradition." Pages 161–73 in *The Shaping of Christianity in the Second and Third Centuries*. Vol. 1 of *Jewish and Christian Self-Definition*. Edited by E. P. Sanders. Philadelphia: Fortress, 1980.

Lüdemann, "Tale." Lüdemann, Gerd. "A Tale with a Spin: A Tailspin for Truth." *FourR* 22 (2, 2009): 15, 18.

Lüdemann, *Two Thousand Years*. Lüdemann, Gerd, with contributions by Frank Schleritt and Martina Janssen. *Jesus after Two Thousand Years: What He Really Said and Did*. Amherst, N.Y.: Prometheus, 2001.

Ludlam, "'Lwhy." Ludlam, Ivor. "'lwhy msh 'sl str'bwn." *Tarbiz* 66 (3, 1997): 337–49.

Ludlow, "Recension." Ludlow, Jared W. "The *Testament of Abraham*: Which Came First—Recension A or Recension B?" *JSP* 13 (1, 2002): 3–15.

Ludwig, "Altered States." Ludwig, Arnold M. "Altered States of Consciousness." Pages 69–95 in *Trance and Possession States: Proceedings of the Second Annual Conference, R. M. Bucke Memorial Society, March 4–6, 1966*. Edited by Raymond Prince. Montreal: R. M. Bucke Memorial Society, 1968.

Ludwig, *Order Restored*. Ludwig, Garth D. *Order Restored: A Biblical Interpretation of Health, Medicine, and Healing*. St. Louis: Concordia Academic, 1999.

Lugt, "Incubus." Lugt, Maaike van der. "The *Incubus* in Scholastic Debate: Medicine, Theology and Popular Belief." Pages 175–200 in *Religion and Medicine in the Middle Ages*. Edited by Peter Biller and Joseph Ziegler. YSMT 3. Woodbridge, Suffolk: York Medieval Press, The University of York (with Boydell Press), 2001.

Lührmann, "Beginnings. Lührmann, Dieter. "The Beginnings of the Church at Thessalonica." Pages 237–49 in *Greeks, Romans, and Christians: Essays in Honor of Abraham J. Malherbe*. Edited by David L. Balch, Everett Ferguson, and Wayne A. Meeks. Minneapolis: Fortress, 1990.

Lührmann, "Pharisaic Tradition." Lührmann, Dieter. "Paul and the Pharisaic Tradition." *JSNT* 36 (1989): 75–94.

Luig, "Worlds." Luig, Ute. "Constructing Local Worlds: Spirit Possession in the Gwembe Valley, Zambia." Pages 124–41 in *Spirit Possession, Modernity and Power in Africa*. Edited by Heike Behrend and Ute Luig. Madison: University of Wisconsin Press, 1999.

Luke, "Enoch's Ascension." Luke, K. "Enoch's Ascension: The Apocalyptic Tradition." *ITS* 25 (3, 1988): 236–52.

Luke, "Ideology." Luke, Trevor. "Ideology and Humor in Suetonius' *Life of Vespasian* 8." *CW* 103 (4, 2010): 511–27.

Luke, "Society Divided." Luke, K. "Society Divided by Religion: The Jewish World of Jesus' Time." *BiBh* 1 (3, 1975): 195–209.

Luke, "Son of Man." Luke, K. "Enoch and the Son of Man." *ITS* 37 (1, 2000): 46–64.

Luke, "Touch." Luke, Trevor S. "A Healing Touch for Empire: Vespasian's Wonders in Domitianic Rome." *GR* 57 (1, 2010): 77–106.

Luling, "Possession Cults." Luling, Virginia. "Some Possession Cults in Southern Somalia." Pages 167–77 in *Women's Medicine: The* zar-bori *Cult in Africa and Beyond*. Edited by I. M. Lewis, Ahmed Al-Safi, and Sayyid Hurreiz. Edinburgh: International African Institute, Edinburgh University Press, 1991.

Lull, "Servant-Benefactor." Lull, David J. "The Servant-Benefactor as a Model of Greatness (Luke 22:24–30)." *NovT* 28 (4, 1986): 289–305.

Lull, *Spirit in Galatia*. Lull, David John. *The Spirit in Galatia: Paul's Interpretation of Pneuma as Divine Power*. SBLDS 49. Chico, Calif.: Scholars Press, 1980.

Luna, "Reflections." Luna, Miguel. "Reflections on Organizational Patterns among Pauline Congregations." *JATS* 18 (1, 2007): 2–14.

Lund, "Verbrennung." Lund, Allan A. "Zur Verbrennung der sogenanten *Chrestiani* (Tac. Ann. 15,44)." *ZRGG* 60 (3, 2008): 253–61.

Lundquist, "Biblical Temple." Lundquist, John M. "Biblical Temple." *OEANE* 1:324–30.

Lung-Kwong, *Purpose*. Lung-Kwong, Lo. *Paul's Purpose in Writing Romans: The Upbuilding of a Jewish and Gentile Christian Community in Rome*. Edited by Philip P. Chia and Yeo Khiok-khng. Jian Dao DS 6. Bible and Literature 4. Hong Kong: Alliance Bible Seminary Press, 1998.

Lunn, "Allusions." Lunn, Nicholas P. "Allusions to the Joseph Narrative in the Synoptic Gospels and Acts: Foundations of a Biblical Type." *JETS* 55 (1, 2012): 27–41.

Lurker, *Symbols*. Lurker, Manfred. *The Gods and Symbols of Ancient Egypt: An Illustrated Dictionary*. London: Thames & Hudson, 1980.

Luter, "Deep." Luter, A. Boyd. "Deep and Wide: Education Overflowing as Evangelism from Ephesus." *F&M* 19 (1, 2001): 34–49.

Luter, "Savior (*DLNTD*)." Luter, A. Boyd, Jr. "Savior." *DLNTD* 1082–84.

Luter, "Savior (*DPL*)." Luter, A. Boyd, Jr. "Savior." *DPL* 867–69.

Luther, *Selections*. Luther, Martin. *Selections from His Writings*. Edited by John Dillenberger. New York: Anchor, 1962.

Lutz, "Musonius." Lutz, Cora E. "Musonius Rufus: The Roman Socrates." *YCS* 10 (1947): 3–147.

Luwel, "Begrip." Luwel, Andre. "Het economisch begrip van de techniek in Oudheid en Middeleeuwen." *TijSW* 28 (2, 1983): 148–58.

Luz, "Masada." Luz, Menahem. "Eleazar's Second Speech on Masada and Its Literary Precedents." *RMPhil* 126 (1, 1983): 25–43.

Luz, *Matthew*. Luz, Ulrich. *Matthew 1–7: A Commentary*. CC. Translated by Wilhelm C. Linss. Minneapolis: Augsburg Fortress, 1989.

Luzbetak, *Church and Cultures*. Luzbetak, Louis J. *The Church and Cultures*. Techny, Ill.: Divine Word, 1970. Repr., Pasadena, Calif.: William Carey Library, 1976.

Lyall, "Law." Lyall, Francis. "Roman Law in the Writings of Paul—Adoption." *JBL* 88 (4, 1969): 458–66.

Lyall, "Slave and Freedman." Lyall, Francis. "Roman Law in the Writings of Paul—The Slave and the Freedman." *NTS* 17 (1, 1970): 73–79.

Lyall, *Slaves*. Lyall, Francis. *Slaves, Citizens, Sons: Legal Metaphors in the Epistles*. Grand Rapids: Zondervan, 1984.

Lygunda li-M, "Pelendo." Lygunda li-M, Fohle. "Pelendo, Isaac." No pages. *DACB*. Online: http://www.dacb.org/stories/demrepcongo/f-pelendo_isaac.html.

Lynch-Watson, *Robe*. Lynch-Watson, Janet. *The Saffron Robe: A Life of Sadhu Sundar Singh*. London: Hodder & Stoughton, 1975.

Lyons, *Autobiography*. Lyons, George. *Pauline Autobiography: Toward a New Understanding*. SBLDS 73. Atlanta: Scholars Press, 1985.

Lys, *Rûach*. Lys, Daniel. *Rûach—Le souffle dans l'Ancien Testament: Enquête anthropologique à travers l'histoire théologique d'Israël*. EHPR 56. Paris: Presses Universitaires de France, 1962.

Ma, "Challenges." Ma, Jungja. "Pentecostal Challenges in East and South-East Asia." Pages 183–202 in *The Globalization of Pentecostalism: A Religion Made to Travel*. Edited by Murray W. Dempster, Byron D. Klaus, and Douglas Petersen. Foreword by Russell P. Spittler. Carlisle, U.K.: Paternoster; Oxford: Regnum, 1999.

Ma, "Empowerment." Ma, Wonsuk. "The Empowerment of the Spirit of God in Luke-Acts: An Old Testament Perspective." Pages 28–40 in *The Spirit and Spirituality: Essays in Honor of Russell P. Spittler*. Edited by Wonsuk Ma and Robert P. Menzies. JPTSup 24. London: T&T Clark, 2004.

Ma, "Encounter." Ma, Julie C. "'A Close Encounter with the Transcendental': Proclamation and Manifestation in Pentecostal Worship in Asian Context." Pages 127–45 in *Asian Church and God's Mission: Studies Presented in the International Symposium on Asian Mission in Manila, January 2002*. Edited by Wonsuk Ma and Julie C. Ma. Manila: OMF Literature; West Caldwell, N.J.: MWM, 2003.

Ma, "Eschatology." Ma, Wonsuk. "Pentecostal Eschatology: What Happened When the Wave Hit the West End of the Ocean." *AJPS* 12 (1, Jan. 2009): 95–112.

Ma, "Manifestations." Ma, Julie C. "Manifestations of Supernatural Power in Luke-Acts and the Kankana-eys Tribe of the Philippines." *SpCh* 4 (2, 2002): 109–28.

Ma, *Mission*. Ma, Julie C. *Mission Possible: The Biblical Strategy for Reaching the Lost*. RStMiss. Foreword by Walter C. Kaiser, Jr. Eugene, Ore.: Wipf and Stock, 2005.

Ma, "Mission." Ma, Julie C. "Pentecostalism and Asian Mission." *Missiology* 35 (1, Jan. 2007): 23–37.

Ma, "Santuala." Ma, Julie C. "Santuala: A Case of Pentecostal Syncretism." *AJPS* 3 (1, 2000): 61–82.

Ma, "Sign." Ma, Wonsuk. "'If It Is a Sign': An Old Testament Reflection on the Initial Evidence Discussion." *AJPS* 2 (2, 1999): 163–75.

Ma, *Spirit*. Ma, Wonsuk. *Until the Spirit Comes: The Spirit of God in the Book of Isaiah*. JSOTSup 271. Sheffield, U.K.: Sheffield Academic, 1999.

Ma, *Spirits*. Ma, Julie C. *When the Spirit Meets the Spirits: Pentecostal Ministry among the Kankana-ey Tribe in the Philippines*. SICHC 118. Frankfurt: Peter Lang, 2000.

Ma, "Studies." Ma, Wonsuk. "Biblical Studies in the Pentecostal Tradition: Yesterday, Today, and Tomorrow." Pages 52–69 in *The Globalization of Pentecostalism: A Religion Made to Travel*. Edited by Murray W. Dempster, Byron D. Klaus, and Douglas Petersen. Foreword by Russell P. Spittler. Carlisle, U.K.: Paternoster; Oxford: Regnum, 1999.

Ma, "Theology." Ma, Wonsuk. "Asian (Classical) Pentecostal Theology in Context." Pages 59–91 in *Asian and Pentecostal: The*

Charismatic Face of Christianity in Asia. Edited by Allan Anderson and Edmond Tang. Foreword by Cecil M. Robeck. RSt Miss, AJPS 3. Oxford: Regnum; Baguio City, Philippines: APTS, 2005.

Ma, "Vanderbout." Ma, Julie C. "Elva Vanderbout: A Woman Pioneer of Pentecostal Mission among Igorots." *JAM* 3 (1, 2001): 121–40.

Ma, "Veneration." Ma, Wonsuk. "Three Types of Ancestor Veneration in Asia: An Anthropological Analysis." Pages 163–77 in *Asian Church and God's Mission: Studies Presented in the International Symposium on Asian Mission in Manila, January 2002.* Edited by Wonsuk Ma and Julie C. Ma. Manila: OMF Literature; West Caldwell, N.J.: MWM, 2003.

Ma, "Women." Ma, Julie. "Asian Women and Pentecostal Ministry." Pages 129–46 in *Asian and Pentecostal: The Charismatic Face of Christianity in Asia.* Edited by Allan Anderson and Edmond Tang. Foreword by Cecil M. Robeck. RStMiss, AJPS 3. Oxford: Regnum; Baguio City, Philippines: APTS, 2005.

Maass, "Delphi: Topography." Maass, Michael. "Delphi: Topography and Archaeology." *BrillPauly* 4:216–23.

MacArthur, *Chaos.* MacArthur, John F., Jr. *Charismatic Chaos.* Grand Rapids: Zondervan, 1992.

Macaulay-Lewis, "Pots." Macaulay-Lewis, E. R. "Planting Pots at Petra: A Preliminary Study of *ollae perforatae* at the Petra Garden Pool Complex and at the 'Great Temple.'" *Levant* 38 (2006): 159–70.

Macchi, "Sacrifice samaritain." Macchi, Jean-Daniel. "Le sacrifice samaritain de la Pâque." *FoiVie* 95 (4, 1996): 67–76.

Macchia, "Babel." Macchia, Frank D. "Babel and the Tongues of Pentecost—Reversal or Fulfilment? A Theological Perspective." Pages 34–51 in *Speaking in Tongues: Multi-disciplinary Perspectives.* Edited by Mark J. Cartledge. SPCI. Waynesboro, Ga., and Bletchley, Milton Keynes, U.K.: Paternoster, 2006.

Macchia, *Baptized.* Macchia, Frank D. *Baptized in the Spirit: A Global Pentecostal Theology.* Grand Rapids: Zondervan, 2006.

Macchia, "Groans." Macchia, Frank D. "Groans Too Deep for Words: Towards a Theology of Tongues as Initial Evidence." *AJPS* 1 (2, 1998): 149–73.

Macchia, *Spirituality.* Macchia, Frank D. *Spirituality and Social Liberation: The Message of the Blumhardts in the Light of Wuerttemburg Pietism.* PWS 4. Metuchen, N.J.: Scarecrow, 1993.

Maccini, *Women as Witnesses.* Maccini, Robert Gordon. *Her Testimony Is True: Women as Witnesses according to John.*

JSNTSup 125. Sheffield, U.K.: Sheffield Academic, 1996.

Maccoby, "Corpse." Maccoby, Hyam. "The Corpse in the Tent." *JSJ* 28 (2, 1997): 195–209.

Maccoby, "Rejoinder." Maccoby, Hyam. "Paul and Circumcision: A Rejoinder." *JQR* 82 (1–2, 1991): 177–80.

MacDonald, "Acts 12:1–17 and Iliad 24." MacDonald, Dennis R. "Luke's Emulation of Homer: Acts 12:1–17 and Iliad 24." *Forum* 3 (1, 2000): 197–205.

MacDonald, "Categorization." MacDonald, Dennis R. "A Categorization of Antetextuality in the Gospels and Acts: A Case for Luke's Imitation of Plato and Xenophon to Depict Paul as a Christian Socrates." Pages 211–25 in *The Intertextuality of the Epistles: Explorations of Theory and Practice.* Edited by Thomas L. Brodie, Dennis R. MacDonald and Stanley E. Porter. NTMon 16. Sheffield: Sheffield Phoenix, 2006.

MacDonald, *Epics.* MacDonald, Dennis R. *The Homeric Epics and the Gospel of Mark.* New Haven: Yale University Press, 2000.

MacDonald, "Eutychus and Elpenor." MacDonald, Dennis R. "Luke's Eutychus and Homer's Elpenor: Acts 20:7–12 and Odyssey 10–12." *JHC* 1 (1994): 5–24.

MacDonald, "Farewell." MacDonald, Dennis R. "Paul's Farewell to the Ephesian Elders and Hector's Farewell to Andromache: A Strategic Imitation of Homer's *Iliad*." Pages 189–203 in *Contextualizing Acts: Lukan Narrative and Greco-Roman Discourse.* Edited by Todd Penner and Caroline Vander Stichele. SBLSymS 20. Atlanta: SBL, 2003.

MacDonald, "Glossolalia." MacDonald, William G. "Glossolalia in the New Testament." *BETS* 7 (2, 1964): 59–68.

MacDonald, *Imitate Homer.* MacDonald, Dennis R. *Does the New Testament Imitate Homer? Four Cases from the Acts of the Apostles.* New Haven: Yale University Press, 2003.

MacDonald, "Lydia." MacDonald, Dennis R. "Lydia and Her Sisters as Lukan Fictions." Pages 105–10 in *The Feminist Companion to the Acts of the Apostles.* Edited by Amy-Jill Levine with Marianne Blickenstaff. Cleveland: Pilgrim; Edinburgh: T&T Clark, 2004.

MacDonald, "Married to Unbelievers." MacDonald, Margaret Y. "Early Christian Women Married to Unbelievers." *SR/SR* 19 (2, 1990): 221–34.

MacDonald, "Papias." MacDonald, Dennis R. "Luke's Use of Papias for Narrating the Death of Judas." Pages 43–62 in *Reading Acts Today: Essays in Honour of Loveday C. A. Alexander.* Edited by Steve Walton

et al. LNTS 427. London: T&T Clark, 2011.

MacDonald, *Pauline Churches.* MacDonald, Margaret Y. *The Pauline Churches: A Socio-historical Study of Institutionalisation in the Pauline and Deutero-Pauline Writings.* Cambridge: Cambridge University Press, 1988.

MacDonald, "Poetry." MacDonald, Dennis R. "Classical Greek Poetry and the Acts of the Apostles: Imitations of Euripides' *Bacchae.*" Pages 463–96 in *Christian Origins and Greco-Roman Culture: Social and Literary Contexts for the New Testament.* Edited by Stanley Porter and Andrew W. Pitts. Vol. 1 of *Early Christianity in Its Hellenistic Context.* Vol. 9 in *Texts and Editions for New Testament Study.* Leiden: Brill, 2013.

MacDonald, "Reading." MacDonald, Margaret Y. "Reading 1 Corinthians 7 through the Eyes of Families." Pages 38–52 in *Text, Image, and Christians in the Graeco-Roman World: A Festschrift in Honor of David Lee Balch.* Edited by Aliou Cissé Niang and Carolyn Osiek. PrTMS 176. Eugene, Ore.: Pickwick, 2012.

MacDonald, "Relationships." MacDonald, Dennis R. "Which Came First? Intertextual Relationships among the Apocryphal Acts of the Apostles." Pages 11–41 in *The Apocryphal Acts of the Apostles in Intertextual Perspectives.* Edited by Robert F. Stoops. *Semeia* 80. Atlanta: Scholars Press, 1997.

MacDonald, "Review." MacDonald, Dennis R. Review of Karl Olav Sandnes, *The Gospel "According to Homer and Virgil": Cento and Canon.* RBL 9 (2011). Online: http://www.bookreviews.org /pdf/7971_8718.pdf.

MacDonald, "Role of Women." MacDonald, Margaret Y. "Was Celsus Right? The Role of Women in the Expansion of Early Christianity." Pages 157–84 in *Early Christian Families in Context: An Interdisciplinary Dialogue.* Edited by David L. Balch and Carolyn Osiek. Grand Rapids and Cambridge: Eerdmans, 2003.

MacDonald, *Samaritans.* MacDonald, John. *The Theology of the Samaritans.* Philadelphia: Westminster, 1964.

MacDonald, "Shipwrecks." MacDonald, Dennis R. "The Shipwrecks of Odysseus and Paul." *NTS* 45 (1, 1999): 88–107.

MacDonald, "Women in Churches." MacDonald, Margaret Y. "Women in the Pauline Churches." Pages 268–84 in *The Blackwell Companion to Paul.* Edited by Stephen Westerholm. BCompRel. Oxford: Blackwell, 2011.

Macdonald, *Worship.* Macdonald, Alexander B. *Christian Worship in the Primitive Church.* Edinburgh: T&T Clark, 1934.

MacDowell, "*Ankhisteia*." MacDowell, Douglas Maurice. "*Ankhisteia*." *OCD*³ 94.

MacDowell, "Antidosis." MacDowell, Douglas Maurice. "Antidosis." *OCD*³ 104.

MacDowell, "Eleven." MacDowell, Douglas Maurice. "Eleven." *OCD*³ 520.

MacDowell, "Introduction." MacDowell, Douglas Maurice. Introduction. Pages 9–19 in Gorgias, *Encomium of Helen*. Edited and translated by Douglas Maurice MacDowell. Bristol, U.K.: Bristol Classical Press, 1982.

MacDowell, "*Nomothetai*." MacDowell, Douglas Maurice. "*Nomothetai*." *OCD*³ 1047–48.

MacDowell, "Ostracism." MacDowell, Douglas Maurice. "Ostracism." *OCD*³ 1083.

MacDowell, "*Paragraphē*." MacDowell, Douglas Maurice. "*Paragraphē*." *OCD*³ 1112.

MacDowell, "*Stratēgoi*." MacDowell, Douglas Maurice. "*Stratēgoi*." *OCD*³ 1447–48.

MacDowell, "Sycophants." MacDowell, Douglas Maurice. "Sycophants." *OCD*³ 1459.

MacDowell, "*Tamiai*." MacDowell, Douglas Maurice. "*Tamiai*." *OCD*³ 1472.

MacGaffey, "Epistemological Ethnocentrism." MacGaffey, Wyatt. "Epistemological Ethnocentrism in African Studies." Pages 42–48 in *African Historiographies: What History for Which Africa?* Edited by Bogumil Jewsiewicki and David Newbury. SSAMD 12. Beverly Hills, Calif.: Sage, 1986.

MacGaffey, "Ideology." MacGaffey, Wyatt. "African Ideology and Belief: A Survey." *AfSR* 24 (2–3, 1981): 227–74.

MacGaffey, "Structure." MacGaffey, Wyatt. "Lineage Structure, Marriage, and the Family amongst the Central Bantu." *JAfrHist* 24 (2, 1983): 173–87.

MacGillivray, "Patronage." MacGillivray, Erlend D. "Re-evaluating Patronage and Reciprocity in Antiquity and New Testament Studies." *JGRCJ* 6 (2009): 37–81.

MacGregor, "Principalities." MacGregor, G. H. C. "Principalities and Powers: The Cosmic Background of Paul's Thought." *NTS* 1 (1, 1954): 17–28.

Machinist, "Voice." Machinist, Peter. "The Voice of the Historian in the Ancient Near Eastern and Mediterranean World." *Interpretation* 57 (2, 2003): 117–37.

Maciel del Río, "Pedro dormía." Maciel del Río, C. "Pedro dormía en medio de dos soldados (Análisis narrativo estilístico de Act 12, 1–23)." *EfMex* 13 (37, 1995): 27–46.

Mack, *Lost Gospel*. Mack, Burton L. *The Lost Gospel: The Book of Q and Christian Origins*. San Francisco: HarperSanFrancisco, 1993.

Mack, *Myth*. Mack, Burton L. *A Myth of Innocence: Mark and Christian Origins*. Philadelphia: Fortress, 1988.

Mack, *Race*. Mack, Raymond W., ed. *Race, Class, and Power*. 2nd ed. New York: D. Van Nostrand, 1968.

Mack and Murphy, "Wisdom Literature." Mack, Burton L., and Roland E. Murphy. "Wisdom Literature." Pages 371–410 in *Early Judaism and Its Modern Interpreters*. Edited by Robert A. Kraft and George W. E. Nickelsburg. SBLBMI 2. Atlanta: Scholars Press, 1986.

Mack and Robbins, *Patterns*. Mack, Burton L., and Vernon K. Robbins. *Patterns of Persuasion in the Gospels*. Sonoma, Calif.: Polebridge, 1989.

Mackay, "Plutarch." Mackay, Barry S. "Plutarch and the Miraculous." Pages 93–112 in *Miracles: Cambridge Studies in Their Philosophy and History*. Edited by C. F. D. Moule. London: A. R. Mowbray; New York: Morehouse-Barlow, 1965.

MacKendrick, *Stones*. MacKendrick, Paul. *The Greek Stones Speak: The Story of Archaeology in Greek Lands*. New York: St. Martin's, 1962.

Mackie, "Seeing God." Mackie, Scott D. "Seeing God in Philo of Alexandria: The Logos, the Powers, or the Existent One?" *SPhilA* 21 (2009): 25–47.

MacKinnon, "Hog." MacKinnon, Michael. "High on the Hog: Linking Zooarchaeological, Literary, and Artistic Data for Pig Breeds in Roman Italy." *AJA* 105 (4, 2001): 649–73.

Macklin, "Yankee." Macklin, June. "A Connecticut Yankee in Summer Land." Pages 41–86 in *Case Studies in Spirit Possession*. Edited by Vincent Crapanzaro and Vivian Garrison. New York: Wiley, 1977.

Maclean and Aitken, *Heroikos*. Maclean, Jennifer K. Berenson, and Ellen Bradshaw Aitken, eds. and trans. *Flavius Philostratus: Heroikos*. SBLWGRW 1. Atlanta: SBL, 2001.

MacLennan and Kraabel, "Invention." MacLennan, Robert S., and A. Thomas Kraabel. "The God-Fearers—A Literary and Theological Invention." *BAR* 12 (5, 1986): 46–53, 64.

Macleod, "Introduction to *Gout*." Macleod, M. D. Introduction to *Gout and Swift-of-Foot*. Pages 319–22 in vol. 8 of *Lucian*. Translated by A. M. Harmon, K. Kilburn, and M. D. Macleod. 8 vols. LCL. Cambridge, Mass.: Harvard University Press, 1913–67.

Macleod, "Introduction to *Lucius*." Macleod, M. D. Introduction to *Lucius or Ass*. Pages 47–51 in vol. 8 of *Lucian*. Translated by A. M. Harmon, K. Kilburn, and M. D. Macleod. 8 vols. LCL. Cambridge, Mass.: Harvard University Press, 1913–67.

Macleod, "Perspective." Macleod, David. "The New Perspective: Paul, Luther, and Judaism." *SBET* 22 (1, 2004): 4–31.

MacMullen, *Christianizing*. MacMullen, Ramsay. *Christianizing the Roman Empire*. New Haven: Yale University Press, 1984.

MacMullen, "Conversion." MacMullen, Ramsay. "Conversion: A Historian's View." *SecCent* 5 (2, 1985–86): 67–81.

MacMullen, *Enemies*. MacMullen, Ramsay. *Enemies of the Roman Order: Treason, Unrest, and Alienation in the Empire*. Cambridge, Mass.: Harvard University Press, 1966.

MacMullen, "Hellenizing." MacMullen, Ramsay. "Hellenizing the Romans (2nd Century B.C.)." *Historia* 40 (4, 1991): 419–38.

MacMullen, *Paganism*. MacMullen, Ramsay. *Paganism in the Roman Empire*. New Haven: Yale University Press, 1981.

MacMullen, *Second Church*. MacMullen, Ramsay. *The Second Church: Popular Christianity A.D. 200–400*. SBLWGRW Sup 1. Atlanta: SBL, 2009.

MacMullen, *Social Relations*. MacMullen, Ramsay. *Roman Social Relations: 50 B.C. to A.D. 284*. New Haven: Yale University Press, 1974.

MacMullen, "Women in Public." MacMullen, Ramsay. "Women in Public in the Roman Empire." *Historia* 29 (1980): 209–18.

MacNutt, *Angels*. MacNutt, Judith. *Angels Are for Real: Inspiring, True Stories and Biblical Answers*. Minneapolis: Chosen, 2012.

MacNutt, *Crime*. MacNutt, Francis. *The Nearly Perfect Crime: How the Church Almost Killed the Ministry of Healing*. Grand Rapids: Chosen, 2005.

MacNutt, *Healing*. MacNutt, Francis. *Healing*. Notre Dame, Ind.: Ave Maria, 1974.

MacNutt, *Power*. MacNutt, Francis. *The Power to Heal*. Notre Dame, Ind.: Ave Maria, 1977.

MacPhail, "Path." MacPhail, Richard D. "Finding a Path in Others' Worlds—The Emic Challenges of Exorcism." *BangTF* 31 (1, 1999): 168–204.

MacRae, "Miracle." MacRae, George W. "Miracle in *The Antiquities* of Josephus." Pages 127–48 in *Miracles: Cambridge Studies in Their Philosophy and History*. Edited by C. F. D. Moule. London: A. R. Mowbray; New York: Morehouse-Barlow, 1965.

MacRae, "Temple." MacRae, George W. "Heavenly Temple and Eschatology in the Letter to the Hebrews." *Semeia* 12 (1978): 179–99.

Macro, "Cities." Macro, Anthony D. "The Cities of Asia Minor under the Roman

Imperium." *ANRW* 7.2:658–97. Part 2, *Principat*, 7.2. Edited by H. Temporini and W. Haase. Berlin: de Gruyter, 1980.

Macurdy, "Julia Berenice." Macurdy, Grace Harriet. "Julia Berenice." *AJP* 56 (1935): 246–53.

Maddocks, *Ministry*. Maddocks, Morris. *The Christian Healing Ministry*. 3rd ed. London: SPCK, 1995.

Maddox, *Purpose*. Maddox, Robert. *The Purpose of Luke-Acts*. Studies of the New Testament and Its World. Edinburgh: T&T Clark, 1982. FRLANT. Göttingen: Vandenhoeck & Ruprecht, 1982.

Mader, "Pursuit." Mader, Gottfried. "Programming Pursuit: Apollo and Daphne at Ovid, *Met*. 1.490–542." *CBull* 84 (1, 2009): 16–26.

Maehler, "Books." Maehler, Herwig. "Books, Greek and Roman." *OCD*³ 249–52.

Maehler, "Tachygraphy." Maehler, Herwig. "Tachygraphy." *OCD*³ 1468–69.

Magaji and Danmallam, "Magaji." Magaji, Sule, and Galadima Danmallam. "Magaji, Sule." No pages. *DACB*. Online: http://www.dacb.org/stories/nigeria/magaji1_sule.html.

Magen, "Bty-knst." Magen, I. "Bty-knst swmrynym." *Qad* 25 (3–4, 1992): 66–90.

Magen, "Yrwslym." Magen, Y. "Yrwslym kmrkz sl t'syyt kly-'bn btqwpt hwrdws." *Qad* 17 (4, 1984): 124–27.

Magen, Zionit, and Sirkis, "Qryt-spr." Magen, Y., Y. Zionit, and E. Sirkis. "Qryt-spr-'yyrh yhwdyt wbyt-knst mymy hbyt hsny (Kiryat Sefer—A Jewish Village and Synagogue of the Second Temple Period)." *Qad* 32 (117, 1999): 25–32.

Maggay, "Issues." Maggay, Melba Padilla. "Early Protestant Missionary Efforts in the Philippines: Some Intercultural Issues." Pages 29–41 in *Asian Church and God's Mission: Studies Presented in the International Symposium on Asian Mission in Manila, January 2002*. Edited by Wonsuk Ma and Julie C. Ma. Manila: OMF Literature; West Caldwell, N.J.: MWM, 2003.

Magie, *Roman Rule*. Magie, David. *Roman Rule in Asia Minor*. 2 vols. Princeton: Princeton University Press, 1950.

Magness, "Cults." Magness, Jodi. "The Cults of Isis and Kore at Samaria-Sebaste in the Hellenistic and Roman Periods." *HTR* 94 (2, 2001): 157–77.

Magness, "Observations." Magness, Jodi. "Some Observations on the Roman Temple at Kedesh." *IEJ* 40 (1990): 173–81.

Magness, "Ossuaries." Magness, Jodi. "Ossuaries and the Burials of Jesus and James." *JBL* 124 (1, 2005): 121–54.

Magness, "Qumran." Magness, Jodi. "Qumran, the Site of the Dead Sea Scrolls: A Review Article." *RevQ* 22 (88, 2006): 640–64.

Magness, *Sense*. Magness, J. Lee. *Sense and Absence: Structure and Suspension in the Ending of Mark's Gospel*. SBLSemS. Atlanta: SBL, 1986.

Magness, "Synagogue." Magness, Jodi. "The Date of the Sardis Synagogue in Light of the Numismatic Evidence." *AJA* 109 (3, 2005): 443–75.

Magness, "Toilet Practices." Magness, Jodi. "Toilet Practices at Qumran: A Response." *RevQ* 22 (86, 2005): 277–78.

Magness-Gardiner, "Cilicia." Magness-Gardiner, Bonnie. "Cilicia." *OEANE* 2:8–11.

Magruder, "Reading." Magruder, Jeff C. "What Simon Saw but Luke Didn't Say: A Pentecostal Reading of the Samaritan Revival in Acts 8.9–24." Pages 290–99 in *Trajectories in the Book of Acts: Essays in Honor of John Wesley Wyckoff*. Edited by Paul Alexander, Jordan Daniel May, and Robert G. Reid. Eugene, Ore.: Wipf & Stock, 2010.

Maharam, "Genius." Maharam, Wolfram-Aslan. "Genius." *BrillPauly* 5:756–58.

Maher, "God as Judge." Maher, Michael. "God as Judge in the Targums." *JSJ* 29 (1, 1998): 49–62.

Maher, "Humble." Maher, Michael. "Humble of Heart: The Virtue of Humility in Rabbinic Literature." *MilS* 11 (1983): 25–43.

Maher, *Targum*. Maher, Michael, trans. *Targum Pseudo-Jonathan: Exodus*. With *Targum Neofiti 1: Exodus*. Translated by Martin McNamara, with notes by Robert Hayward. Aramaic Bible 2. Collegeville, Minn.: Liturgical Press, 1994.

Maher, "Yoke." Maher, Michael. "'Take My Yoke upon You' (Matt. XI.29)." *NTS* 22 (1, 1975): 97–103.

Mahoney, *History*. Mahoney, Leonard. *A History of Maltese Architecture: From Ancient Times up to 1800*. Zabbar: Veritas Press, 1988.

Maier, "Historian." Maier, Paul L. "Luke as a Hellenistic Historian." Pages 413–34 in *Christian Origins and Greco-Roman Culture: Social and Literary Contexts for the New Testament*. Edited by Stanley Porter and Andrew W. Pitts. Vol. 1 of Early Christianity in Its Hellenistic Context. Vol. 9 in Texts and Editions for New Testament Study. Leiden: Brill, 2013.

Maier, "Kult." Maier, Johann. "Zu Kult und Liturgie der Qumrangemeinde." *RevQ* 14 (4, 1990): 543–86.

Maier, "Paphos." Maier, Franz Georg. "Paphos." *OEANE* 4:245–46.

Maier, *Temple Scroll*. Maier, Johann. *The Temple Scroll: An Introduction, Translation, and Commentary*. JSOTSup 34. Sheffield, U.K.: JSOT Press, 1985.

Maier, "Torah." Maier, Johann. "La Torah di purità nel Levitico e sua trattazione nella letteratura giudaica del periodo del secondo tempio e nei primi secoli cristiani." *ASDE* 13 (1, 1996): 39–66.

Mainville, "Jésus et l'Esprit." Mainville, Odette. "Jésus et l'Esprit dans l'oeuvre de Luc: Éclairage à partir d'Ac 2,33." *ScEs* 42 (2, 1990): 193–208.

Mainville, "Liberté." Mainville, Odette. "La question de la liberté en Luc-Actes: Une question impertinente." *Theof* 32 (1, 2001): 45–62.

Mainville, "Messianisme." Mainville, Odette. "Le messianisme de Jésus: Le rapport annonce/accomplissement entre Lc 1,35 et Ac 2,33." Pages 313–27 in *The Unity of Luke-Acts*. Edited by Joseph Verheyden. BETL 142. Leuven: Leuven University Press, 1999.

Makarius, "Violation." Makarius, Laura. "The Violation of Taboo and Magical Power." Pages 231–35 in *The Realm of the Extra-human: Ideas and Actions*. Edited by Agehananda Bharati. The Hague and Paris: Mouton, 1976. Distributed by Aldine, Chicago.

Makris and Al-Safi, "Spirit Possession Cult." Makris, Gerasimos P., and Ahmad Al-Safi. "The *tumbura* Spirit Possession Cult of the Sudan." Pages 118–36 in *Women's Medicine: The zar-bori Cult in Africa and Beyond*. Edited by I. M. Lewis, Ahmed Al-Safi, and Sayyid Hurreiz. Edinburgh: International African Institute, Edinburgh University Press, 1991.

Makris and Natvig, "Bibliography." Makris, G. P., and Richard Natvig. "The *zar, tumbura*, and *bori* Cults: A Select Annotated Bibliography." Pages 233–82 in *Women's Medicine: The zar-bori Cult in Africa and Beyond*. Edited by I. M. Lewis, Ahmed Al-Safi, and Sayyid Hurreiz. Edinburgh: International African Institute, Edinburgh University Press, 1991.

Malamat, "Revelations." Malamat, Abraham. "Prophetic Revelations in New Documents from Mari and the Bible." Pages 207–27 in *Volume du Congrès: Genève, 1965*. VTSup 15. Leiden: Brill, 1966.

Malan, "Apostolate." Malan, F. S. "The Relationship between Apostolate and Office in the Theology of Paul," in "Ministry in the Pauline Letters: Proceedings of the Twelfth Meeting of 'Die Nawe-Testamentiese-Werkgemeenskap van Suid-Afrika.'" Special Issue, *Neot* 10 (1976): 53–68.

Malatesta, *Interiority*. Malatesta, Edward. *Interiority and Covenant: A Study of* einai en *and* menein en *in the First Letter of Saint John*. AnBib 69. Rome: Biblical Institute Press, 1978.

Malbon, "Importance of Minor Characters." Malbon, Elizabeth Struthers. "The Major

Importance of the Minor Characters in Mark." Pages 58–86 in *The New Literary Criticism and the New Testament*. Edited by Edgar V. McKnight and Elizabeth Struthers Malbon. Valley Forge, Pa.: Trinity Press International; Sheffield, U.K.: JSOT Press, 1994.

Malcolm, "Conversion." Malcolm, Lois. "Conversion, Conversation, and Acts 15." *WW* 22 (3, 2002): 246–54.

Malek, "Stranger." Malek, Jeri Sue. "The Kind, Quiet Stranger." *MounM* (Oct. 1994): 16–17.

Malherbe, "Antisthenes." Malherbe, Abraham J. "Antisthenes and Odysseus, and Paul at War." *HTR* 76 (2, 1983): 143–73.

Malherbe, "Beasts." Malherbe, Abraham J. "The Beasts at Ephesus." *JBL* 87 (1, 1968): 71–80.

Malherbe, "Epicureans." Malherbe, Abraham J. "Self-Definition among Epicureans and Cynics." Pages 46–59 in *Self-Definition in the Greco-Roman World*. Edited by Ben F. Meyer and E. P. Sanders. Vol. 3 of *Jewish and Christian Self-Definition*. Edited by E. P. Sanders. Philadelphia: Fortress, 1982.

Malherbe, "Gentle as Nurse." Malherbe, Abraham J. "'Gentle as a Nurse': The Cynic Background to I Thess ii." *NovT* 12 (2, 1970): 203–17.

Malherbe, "Life." Malherbe, Abraham J. "Life in the Graeco-Roman World." Pages 4–36 in *The World of the New Testament*. Edited by Abraham J. Malherbe. Austin, Tex.: R. B. Sweet, 1967.

Malherbe, *Moral Exhortation*. Malherbe, Abraham J. *Moral Exhortation, a Greco-Roman Sourcebook*. LEC 4. Philadelphia: Westminster, 1986.

Malherbe, "Not in a Corner." Malherbe, Abraham J. "Not in a Corner: Early Christian Apologetic in Acts 26:26." *SecCent* 5 (4, 1986): 193–210.

Malherbe, "Overseers." Malherbe, Abraham J. "Overseers as Household Managers in the Pastoral Epistles." Pages 72–88 in *Text, Image, and Christians in the Graeco-Roman World: A Festschrift in Honor of David Lee Balch*. Edited by Aliou Cissé Niang and Carolyn Osiek. PrTMS 176. Eugene, Ore.: Pickwick, 2012.

Malherbe, "Paul as Pastor." Malherbe, Abraham J. "The Apostle Paul as a Pastor." Pages 98–138 in *Jesus, Paul, and John*. By C. K. Barrett et al. ChuenKLS 1. Hong Kong: Theology Division, Chung Chi College, Chinese University of Hong Kong, 1999.

Malherbe, "Philosopher." Malherbe, Abraham J. "Paul: Hellenistic Philosopher or Christian Pastor?" *AThR* 68 (1, 1986): 3–13.

Malherbe, *Philosophers*. Malherbe, Abraham J. *Paul and the Popular Philosophers*. Philadelphia: Fortress, 1989.

Malherbe, "Physical Description." Malherbe, Abraham J. "A Physical Description of Paul." *HTR* 79 (1–3, 1986): 170–75.

Malherbe, *Social Aspects*. Malherbe, Abraham J. *Social Aspects of Early Christianity*. 2nd ed. Philadelphia: Fortress, 1983.

Malherbe, "Theorists." Malherbe, Abraham J. "Ancient Epistolary Theorists." *OJRS* 5 (2, 1977): 3–77.

Malherbe, *Thessalonians*. Malherbe, Abraham J. *The Letters to the Thessalonians*. AB 32B. New York: Doubleday, 2000.

Malick, "Contribution." Malick, D. E. "The Contribution of Codex Bezae Cantabrigiensis to an Understanding of Women in the Book of Acts." *JGRCJ* 4 (2007): 158–83.

Malina, *Anthropology*. Malina, Bruce J. *The New Testament World: Insights from Cultural Anthropology*. Atlanta: John Knox, 1981.

Malina, "Criticism." Malina, Bruce J. "Rhetorical Criticism and Social-Scientific Criticism: Why Won't Romanticism Leave Us Alone?" Pages 72–101 in *Rhetoric, Scripture, and Theology: Essays from the 1994 Pretoria Conference*. Edited by Stanley E. Porter and Thomas H. Olbricht. JSNTSup 131. Sheffield, U.K.: Sheffield Academic, 1996.

Malina, *Social Gospel*. Malina, Bruce J. *The Social Gospel of Jesus: The Kingdom of God in Mediterranean Perspective*. Minneapolis: Fortress, 2001.

Malina, *Windows*. Malina, Bruce J. *Windows on the World of Jesus: Time Travel to Ancient Judea*. Louisville: Westminster John Knox, 1993.

Malina and Neyrey, "Honor and Shame." Malina, Bruce J., and Jerome H. Neyrey. "Honor and Shame in Luke-Acts: Pivotal Values of the Mediterranean World." Pages 25–65 in *The Social World of Luke-Acts: Models for Interpretation*. Edited by Jerome H. Neyrey. Peabody, Mass.: Hendrickson, 1991.

Malina and Neyrey, "Personality." Malina, Bruce J., and Jerome H. Neyrey. "First-Century Personality: Dyadic, Not Individual." Pages 67–96 in *The Social World of Luke-Acts: Models for Interpretation*. Edited by Jerome H. Neyrey. Peabody, Mass.: Hendrickson, 1991.

Malina and Neyrey, *Portraits*. Malina, Bruce J., and Jerome H. Neyrey. *Portraits of Paul: An Archaeology of Ancient Personality*. Louisville: Westminster John Knox, 1996.

Malina and Pilch, *Acts*. Malina, Bruce J., and John J. Pilch. *Social-Science Commentary on the Book of Acts*. Minneapolis: Fortress, 2008.

Malina and Pilch, *Letters*. Malina, Bruce J., and John J. Pilch. *Social-Science Commentary on the Letters of Paul*. Minneapolis: Fortress, 2006.

Malina and Rohrbaugh, *Gospels*. Malina, Bruce J., and Richard L. Rohrbaugh. *Social-Science Commentary on the Synoptic Gospels*. Minneapolis: Fortress, 1992.

Malina and Rohrbaugh, *John*. Malina, Bruce J., and Richard L. Rohrbaugh. *Social-Science Commentary on the Gospel of John*. Minneapolis: Fortress, 1998.

Malinowski, "Tendencies." Malinowski, Francis X. "Torah Tendencies in Galilean Judaism according to Flavius Josephus with Gospel Comparisons." *BTB* 10 (1, 1980): 30–36.

Malipurathu, "Mission." Malipurathu, Thomas. "Mission as Witnessing: A Biblical Reflection." *Vid* 70 (11, 2006): 807–26.

Malkin, *Greek Ethnicity*. Malkin, Irad, ed. *Ancient Perceptions of Greek Ethnicity*. CHSC 5. Cambridge, Mass.: Harvard University Press, 2001.

Malkin, "*Temenos*." Malkin, Irad. "*Temenos*." *OCD*³ 1481.

Malkin, "Votive Offerings." Malkin, Irad. "Votive Offerings." *OCD*³ 1612–13.

Mallen, *Reading*. Mallen, Peter. *The Reading and Transformation of Isaiah in Luke-Acts*. LNTS 367. London; New York: T&T Clark, 2008.

Maloney, "Authorship." Maloney, Elliott C. "Biblical Authorship and the Pastoral Letters." *BibT* 24 (2, 1986): 119–23.

Maloney, "Cultures." Maloney, Elliott. "Cultures in Conflict." *BibT* 33 (5, 1995): 276–80.

Maloney, *Narration of Works*. Maloney, Linda M. *"All That God Had Done with Them": The Narration of the Works of God in the Early Christian Community as Described in the Acts of the Apostles*. AUSt 7, Theology and Religion, 91. New York: Peter Lang, 1991.

Malony, "Debunking." Malony, H. Newton. "Debunking Some of the Myths about Glossolalia." Pages 102–10 in *Charismatic Experiences in History*. Edited by Cecil M. Robeck Jr. Peabody, Mass.: Hendrickson, 1985.

Malony and Lovekin, *Glossolalia*. Malony, H. Newton, and A. Adams Lovekin. *Glossolalia: Behavioral Science Perspectives on Speaking in Tongues*. New York: Oxford University Press, 1985.

Maly, "Women and Luke." Maly, Eugene H. "Women and the Gospel of Luke." *BTB* 10 (3, 1980): 99–104.

Manana, "Kitonga." Manana, Francis. "Kitonga, Arthur." No pages. *DACB*.

Online: http://www.dacb.org/stories /kenya/kitonga_arthur.html.

Manana, "Magaji." Manana, Francis. "Magaji, Sule." No pages. *DACB*. Online: http:// www.dacb.org/stories/nigeria/magaji _sule.html.

Manana, "Ndaruhutse." Manana, Francis. "Ndaruhutse, David." No pages. *DACB*. Online: http://www.dacb.org/stories /burundi/ndaruhutse_david.html.

Mancini, *Discoveries*. Mancini, Ignazio. *Archaeological Discoveries Relative to the Judaeo-Christians: Historical Survey*. Translated by G. Bushell. Jerusalem: Studium Biblicum Franciscan Printing Press, 1970.

Mandel, "Exegesis." Mandel, Paul. "Midrashic Exegesis and Its Precedents in the Dead Sea Scrolls." *DSD* 8 (2, 2001): 149–68.

Mandouze, "Donatisme." Mandouze, André. "Le donatisme représente-t-il la résistance à Rome de l'Afrique tardive?" Pages 357–66 in *Assimilation et résistance à la culture gréco-romaine dans le monde ancien: Travaux du VIe Congrès international d'études classiques*. Edited by D. M. Pippidi. FIAEC. Paris: Belles Lettres, 1976.

Mandryk, *Operation World*. Mandryk, Jason. *Operation World*. 7th ed. Colorado Springs: Biblica, 2010.

Mangatt, "Believing Community." Mangatt, George. "Believing Community according to the Acts of the Apostles." *BiBh* 16 (3, 1990): 173–81.

Mangatt, "Spirit and Church." Mangatt, George. "The Holy Spirit and the Apostolic Church." *BiBh* 18 (1, 1992): 34–54.

Manning, "Seneca." Manning, C. E. "Seneca and the Stoics on the Equality of the Sexes." *Mnemosyne* 26 (1973): 170–77.

Manns, "Ante lucem." Manns, Frédéric. "'Ante lucem' dans la lettre de Pline le Jeune à Trajan (Ep. X, 96)." *Antonianum* 62 (2–3, 1987): 338–43.

Manns, "Femme." Manns, Frédéric. "La femme et la synagogue à l'époque de Jésus." *EphLit* 109 (2, 1995): 159–65.

Manns, "Galilée." Manns, Frédéric. "La Galilée dans le quatrieme évangile." *Antonianum* 72 (3, 1997): 351–64.

Manns, "Jacob." Manns, Frédéric. "Jacob, le Min, selon la Tosephta Hulin 2,22–24: Contribution à l'étude du christianisme primitif." *CNS* 10 (3, 1989): 449–65.

Manns, "Jacques 2, 24–26." Manns, Frédéric. "Jacques 2, 24–26 à la lumière du judaïsme." *BeO* 26 (3, 1984): 143–49.

Manns, "Mort de Judas." Manns, Frédéric. "Un midrash chrétien: Le récit de la mort de Judas." *RevScRel* 54 (3, 1980): 197–203.

Manns, "Pâque." Manns, Fréderic. "Pâque juive et Pâque chrétienne." *EphLit* 113 (1, 1999): 31–46.

Manns, "Source de l'aggadah." Manns, Frédéric. "Une source de l'aggadah juive: La littérature grecque." *SBFLA* 29 (1979): 111–44.

Mannsperger, "Troy." Mannsperger, Dietrich. "Troy." *BrillPauly* 14:968–73.

Mansfield, *Pentecost*. Mansfield, Patti Gallagher. *As by a New Pentecost: The Dramatic Beginning of the Catholic Charismatic Renewal*. Foreword by Léon-Joseph Cardinal Suenens. Steubenville, Ohio: Franciscan University Press, 1992.

Mansfield, *Spirit and Gospel*. Mansfield, M. Robert. *"Spirit and Gospel" in Mark*. Peabody, Mass.: Hendrickson, 1987.

Manson, *Design*. Manson, Neil, ed. *God and Design: The Teleological Argument and Modern Science*. London: Routledge, 2003.

Manson, *Hebrews*. Manson, William. *The Epistle to the Hebrews: An Historical and Theological Reconsideration*. Baird Lecture, 1949. London: Hodder & Stoughton, 1951.

Manson, "Letter." Manson, T. W. "St Paul's Letter to the Romans—and Others." Pages 1–16 in *The Romans Debate*. Edited by Karl P. Donfried. Minneapolis: Augsburg, 1977.

Manson, *Paul and John*. Manson, T. W. *On Paul and John: Some Selected Theological Themes*. SBT 38. London: SCM, 1963.

Manson, *Sayings*. Manson, T. W. *The Sayings of Jesus*. London: SCM, 1957. Repr., Grand Rapids: Eerdmans, 1979.

Manson, *Servant-Messiah*. Manson, T. W. *The Servant-Messiah*. Cambridge: Cambridge University Press, 1961.

Mantel, "Dichotomy." Mantel, Hugo. "The Dichotomy of Judaism during the Second Temple." *HUCA* 44 (1973): 55–87.

Mantel, *History of Sanhedrin*. Mantel, Hugo. *Studies in the History of the Sanhedrin*. HSS 17. Cambridge, Mass.: Harvard University Press, 1961.

Mantel, "Nature of Synagogue." Mantel, Hugo. "The Nature of the Great Synagogue." *HTR* 60 (1, 1967): 69–91.

Mantey, "Causal Use of *eis*." Mantey, Julius R. "The Causal Use of *eis* in the New Testament." *JBL* 70 (1951): 45–48.

Mantey, "*Eis* Again." Mantey, Julius R. "On Causal *eis* Again." *JBL* 70 (1951): 309–11.

Mantle, "Addendum." Mantle, Inga C. "Addendum: The Religious Roles of Children in the Provinces." *GR* 57 (1, 2010): 117–21.

Mantle, "Roles." Mantle, Inga C. "The Roles of Children in Roman Religion." *GR* 49 (1, 2002): 85–106.

Manuwald, "Humans." Manuwald, Gesine. "What Do Humans Get to Know about the Gods and Their Plans? On Prophecies and Their Deficiencies in Valerius Flaccus' Argonautica." *Mnemosyne* 62 (4, 2009): 586–608.

Ma'oz, "Synagogue from Second Temple." Ma'oz, Zvi Uri. "A Synagogue from the Time of the Second Temple." *IsLN* 3 (1978): 138–42.

Ma'oz, "Synagogues." Ma'oz, Zvi Uri. "Ancient Synagogues and the Golan." *BA* 51 (2, 1988): 116–28.

Maquet, "Shaman." Maquet, Jacques. "Introduction: Scholar and Shaman." Pages 1–6 in *Ecstasy and Healing in Nepal: An Ethnopsychiatric Study of Tamang Shamanism*. By Larry Peters. Malibu, Calif.: Undena, 1981.

Marböck, "Herz." Marböck, Johannes. "Mit Hand und Herz. Der schriftgelehrte Weise und das Handwerk in Sir 38,24–34." *BN* 139 (2008): 39–60.

March, "Rhadamanthys." March, Jennifer R. "Rhadamanthys." *OCD³* 1311.

Marchant, "Introduction." Marchant, E. C. Introduction to *Memorabilia* and *Oeconomicus*. Pages vii–xxvii in vol. 4 of *Xenophon*. Translated by Carleton L. Brownson, O. J. Todd, and E. C. Marchant. 4 vols. LCL. New York: G. P. Putnam's Sons, 1918–23.

Marchetti, "Words." Marchetti, S. C. "Words and Silence: Atticus as the Dedicatee of de Amicitia." *CW* 103 (1, 2009): 93–99.

Marconi, "Interpretation." Marconi, Gilberto. "History as a Hermeneutical Interpretation of the Difference between Acts 3:1–10 and 4:8–12." Pages 167–80 in *Luke and Acts*. Edited by Gerald O'Collins and Gilberto Marconi. Translated by Matthew J. O'Connell. New York: Paulist, 1993.

Marcus, "Alexander." Marcus, Ralph. "Alexander the Great and the Jews." Pages 512–32 in vol. 6 of *Josephus*. Translated by H. St. J. Thackeray, Ralph Marcus, and L. H. Feldman. 9 vols. LCL. Cambridge, Mass.: Harvard University Press, 1926–65.

Marcus, "*Eis*." Marcus, Ralph. "On Causal *eis*." *JBL* 70 (1951): 129–30.

Marcus, "Elusive *eis*." Marcus, Ralph. "The Elusive Causal *eis*." *JBL* 71 (1952): 43–44.

Marcus, "Names and Attributes." Marcus, Ralph. "Divine Names and Attributes in Hellenistic Jewish Literature." *PAAJR* 3 (1931–32): 43–120.

Marcus, "Schism." Marcus, Ralph. "Josephus on the Samaritan Schism." Pages 498–511 in vol. 6 of *Josephus*. Translated by H. St. J. Thackeray, Ralph Marcus, and L. H. Feldman. 9 vols. LCL. Cambridge, Mass.: Harvard University Press, 1926–65.

Marcus, "Scrolls." Marcus, Ralph. "The Qumran Scrolls and Early Judaism." *BR* 1 (1956): 9–47.

Mare, "Acts 7." Mare, W. Harold. "Acts 7: Jewish or Samaritan in Character?" *WTJ* 34 (1, 1971): 1–21.

Mare, *Archaeology.* Mare, W. Harold. *The Archaeology of the Jerusalem Area.* Grand Rapids: Baker, 1987.

Mare, "Bed." Mare, W. Harold. "Bed." *ISBE* 1:445–47.

Marek, "Patara." Marek, Christian. "Patara." *BrillPauly* 10:594–95.

Margel, "Religio/superstitio." Margel, Serge. "Religio/superstitio: La crise des institutions, de Cicéron à Augustin." *RTP* 138 (3, 2006): 193–207.

Marguerat, *Actes.* Marguerat, Daniel. *Les Actes des apôtres (1–12).* CNT, 2e série, 5 A. Geneva: Labor et Fides, 2007.

Marguerat, "Actes de Paul." Marguerat, Daniel. "Actes de Paul et Actes canoniques: Un phénomène de relecture." *Apocrypha* 8 (1997): 207–24.

Marguerat, "Acts of Paul." Marguerat, Daniel. "The Acts of Paul and the Canonical Acts: A Phenomenon of Rereading." Pages 169–83 in *The Apocryphal Acts of the Apostles in Intertextual Perspectives.* Edited by Robert F. Stoops. *Semeia* 80. Atlanta: Scholars Press, 1997.

Marguerat, "Avenir." Marguerat, Daniel. "L'avenir de la loi: Matthieu à l'épreuve de Paul." *ETR* 57 (3, 1982): 361–73.

Marguerat, "Enigma of Closing." Marguerat, Daniel. "The Enigma of the Silent Closing of Acts (28:16–31)." Pages 284–304 in *Jesus and the Heritage of Israel: Luke's Narrative Claim upon Israel's Legacy.* Edited by David P. Moessner. Luke the Interpreter of Israel 1. Harrisburg, Pa.: Trinity Press International, 1999.

Marguerat, "Énigme." Marguerat, Daniel. "'Et quand nous sommes entrés dans Rome': L'énigme de la fin du livre des Actes (28,16–31)." *RHPR* 73 (1, 1993): 1–21.

Marguerat, "Héritage." Marguerat, Daniel. "L'héritage de Paul en débat: Actes des apôtres et Actes de Paul." *FoiVie* 94 (4, 1995): 87–97.

Marguerat, *Histoire.* Marguerat, Daniel. *La première histoire du christianisme (les Actes des apôtres).* LD 180. Paris: Cerf, 1999.

Marguerat, *Historian.* Marguerat, Daniel. *The First Christian Historian: Writing the "Acts of the Apostles."* Translated by Ken McKinney, Gregory J. Laughery, and Richard Bauckham. SNTSMS 121. Cambridge: Cambridge University Press, 2002.

Marguerat, "Image de Paul." Marguerat, Daniel. "L'image de Paul dans les Actes des apôtres." Pages 121–54 in *Les Actes des apôtres—Histoire, récit, théologie: XXe congrès de l'Association catholique française pour l'étude de la Bible (Angers, 2003).* Edited by Michel Berder. LD 199. Paris: Cerf, 2005.

Marguerat, "Magie, guérison, et parole." Marguerat, Daniel. "Magie, guérison, et parole dans les Actes des apôtres." *ETR* 72 (2, 1997): 197–208.

Marguerat, "Mort d'Ananias." Marguerat, Daniel. "La mort d'Ananias et Saphira (Ac 5.1–11) dans la stratégie narrative de Luc." *NTS* 39 (2, 1993): 209–26.

Marguerat, "Pionnier." Marguerat, Daniel. "Luc, pionnier de l'historiographie chrétienne." *RSR* 92 (4, 2004): 513–38.

Marguerat, "Réception." Marguerat, Daniel. "Paul après Paul: Une histoire de réception." *NTS* 54 (3, 2008): 317–37.

Marguerat, "Resurrection." Marguerat, Daniel. "The Resurrection and Its Witnesses in the Book of Acts." Pages 171–85 in *Reading Acts Today: Essays in Honour of Loveday C. A. Alexander.* Edited by Steve Walton et al. LNTS 427. London: T&T Clark, 2011.

Marguerat, "Terreur dans l'Église." Marguerat, Daniel. "Terreur dans l'Église: Le drame d'Ananias et Saphira (Actes 5,1–11)." *FoiVie* 91 (5, 1992): 77–88.

Marguerat, "Unité." Marguerat, Daniel. "Luc-Actes: Une unité à construire." Pages 57–81 in *The Unity of Luke-Acts.* Edited by Joseph Verheyden. BETL 142. Leuven: Leuven University Press, 1999.

Marguerat, "Voyageurs." Marguerat, Daniel. "Voyages et voyageurs dans le livre des Actes et la culture gréco-romaine." *RHPR* 78 (1, 1998): 33–59.

Marguerat, "Wie historisch?" Marguerat, Daniel. "Wie historisch ist die Apostelgeschichte?" *ZNT* 9 (18, 2006): 44–51.

Marguerat and Steffek, "Naissance." Marguerat, Daniel, and Emmanuelle Steffek. "Luc-Actes et la naissance du Dieu universel." *ETR* 87 (1, 2012): 35–55.

Marin et al., "Scale." Marin, Gerardo, et al. "Development of a Short Acculturation Scale for Hispanics." *HisJBehSc* 9 (1987): 183–205.

Marincola, "Audiences." Marincola, John. "Ancient Audiences and Expectations." Pages 11–23 in *The Cambridge Companion to the Roman Historians.* Edited by Andrew Geldherr. Cambridge: Cambridge University Press, 2009.

Marincola, *Authority.* Marincola, John. *Authority and Tradition in Ancient Historiography.* New York: Cambridge University Press, 1997.

Marincola, "Genre." Marincola, John. "Genre, Convention and Innovation in Greco-Roman Historiography." Pages 281–324 in *The Limits of Historiography: Genre and Narrative in Ancient Historical Texts.* Mnemosyne Supplement 191. Edited by Christina Shuttleworth Kraus. Leiden: Brill, 1999.

Marincola, "Introduction." Marincola, John. "Introduction." Pages 1–9 in *A Companion to Greek and Roman Historiography.* Edited by John Marincola. 2 vols. Oxford: Blackwell, 2007.

Marincola, "Looking to End." Marincola, John. "Looking to the End: Structure and Meaning in Greco-Roman Historiography." *Papers of the Langford Latin Seminar* 12 (2005): 285–320.

Marincola, "Speeches." Marincola, John. "Speeches in Classical Historiography." Pages 118–32 in *A Companion to Greek and Roman Historiography.* Edited by John Marincola. 2 vols. Oxford: Blackwell, 2007.

Marincola, "Tacitus' Prefaces." Marincola, John. "Tacitus' Prefaces and the Decline of Imperial Historiography." *Latomus* 58 (2, 1999): 391–404.

Marincola, "Universal History." Marincola, John. "Universal History from Ephorus to Diodorus." Pages 171–79 in *A Companion to Greek and Roman Historiography.* Edited by John Marincola. 2 vols. Oxford: Blackwell, 2007.

Mariz, *Coping.* Mariz, Cecília Loreto. *Coping with Poverty: Pentecostals and Christian Base Communities in Brazil.* Philadelphia: Temple University Press, 1994.

Mark, "Marriage." Mark, Linda Li. "Patrilateral Cross-Cousin Marriage among the Magpie Miao: Preferential or Prescriptive." *AmAnth* 69 (1967): 55–62.

Markle, "Body." Markle, George B., IV. "Body, Mind, and Faith." Pages 15–20 in *Faith Healing: Finger of God? Or, Scientific Curiosity?* Compiled by Claude A. Frazier. New York: Thomas Nelson, 1973.

Markschies, "Schlafkulte." Markschies, Christoph. "Gesund werden im Schlaf? Die antiken Schlafkulte und das Christentum." *TLZ* 131 (12, 2006): 1233–44.

Marlow, "Land." Marlow, Hilary F. "The Land." Pages 489–93 in *Dictionary of the Old Testament Prophets.* Edited by Mark J. Boda and J. Gordon McConville. Downers Grove, Ill.: IVP Academic, 2012.

Marmorstein, *Anthropomorphism.* Marmorstein, A. *Essays in Anthropomorphism.* Vol. 2 of *The Old Rabbinic Doctrine of God.* London: Oxford University Press, 1937. Reprinted in *The Doctrine of Merits in Old Rabbinical Literature; and The Old Rabbinic Doctrine of God: I, The Names and Attributes of God; II, Essays in Anthropomorphism.* 3 vols. in 1. New York: KTAV, 1968.

Marmorstein, "Attitude." Marmorstein, A. "The Attitude of the Jews Towards Early Christianity." *Exp* 49 (155, Nov. 1923): 383–89.

Marmorstein, *Merits*. Marmorstein, A. *The Doctrine of Merits in Old Rabbinical Literature*. London: [Oxford University Press], 1920. Reprinted in *The Doctrine of Merits in Old Rabbinical Literature; and The Old Rabbinic Doctrine of God: I, The Names and Attributes of God; II, Essays in Anthropomorphism*. 3 vols. in 1. New York: KTAV, 1968.

Marmorstein, *Names*. Marmorstein, A. *The Names and Attributes of God*. Vol. 1 of *The Old Rabbinic Doctrine of God*. London: Oxford University Press, 1927. Reprinted in *The Doctrine of Merits in Old Rabbinical Literature; and The Old Rabbinic Doctrine of God: I, The Names and Attributes of God; II, Essays in Anthropomorphism*. 3 vols. in 1. New York: KTAV, 1968.

Marnham, *Lourdes*. Marnham, Patrick. *Lourdes: A Modern Pilgrimage*. New York: Coward, McCann & Geoghegan, 1981.

Marostica, "Learning." Marostica, Matthew. "Learning from the Master: Carlos Annacondia and the Standardization of Pentecostal Practices in and beyond Argentina." Pages 207–27 in *Global Pentecostal and Charismatic Healing*. Edited by Candy Gunther Brown. Foreword by Harvey Cox. Oxford: Oxford University Press, 2011.

Marrou, *Education*. Marrou, Henri Irenee. *A History of Education in Antiquity*. Translated by G. Lamb. New York: Sheed & Ward, 1956.

Marsden, *Outrageous Idea*. Marsden, George M. *The Outrageous Idea of Christian Scholarship*. New York: Oxford University Press, 1997.

Marsden, *Soul of University*. Marsden, George M. *The Soul of the American University: From Protestant Establishment to Established Nonbelief*. New York and Oxford: Oxford University Press, 1994.

Marsella, Friedman, and Spain, "Aspects." Marsella, Anthony J., Matthew J. Friedman, and E. Huland Spain. "Ethnocultural Aspects of PTSD: An Overview of Research and Research Directions." Pages 105–29 in *Ethnocultural Aspects of Posttraumatic Stress Disorder: Issues, Research, and Clinical Applications*. Edited by Anthony J. Marsella et al. Washington, D.C.: American Psychological Association, 1996.

Marsh, *Amos*. Marsh, John. *Amos and Micah*. TBC. London: SCM, 1959.

Marshall, *Acts*. Marshall, I. Howard. *The Acts of the Apostles: An Introduction and Commentary*. TNTC. Grand Rapids: Eerdmans, 1980.

Marshall, "Acts." Marshall, I. Howard. "Acts." Pages 513–606 in *Commentary on the New Testament Use of the Old Testament*. Edited by G. K. Beale and D. A. Carson. Grand Rapids: Baker Academic, 2007.

Marshall, "Acts 20.28." Marshall, I. Howard. "The Place of Acts 20.28 in Luke's Theology of the Cross." Pages 154–70 in *Reading Acts Today: Essays in Honour of Loveday C. A. Alexander*. Edited by Steve Walton et al. LNTS 427. London: T&T Clark, 2011.

Marshall, *Blood*. Marshall, Paul A. *Their Blood Cries Out: The Worldwide Tragedy of Modern Christians Who Are Dying for Their Faith*. Dallas: Word, 1997.

Marshall, "Conclusion." Marshall, I. Howard. "Romans 16:25–27—An Apt Conclusion." Pages 170–86 in *Romans and the People of God: Essays in Honor of Gordon D. Fee on the Occasion of His 65th Birthday*. Edited by Sven K. Soderlund and N. T. Wright. Grand Rapids: Eerdmans, 1999.

Marshall, "Current Study." Marshall, I. Howard. "Acts in Current Study." *ExpT* 115 (2, 2003): 49–52.

Marshall, *Enmity*. Marshall, Peter. *Enmity in Corinth: Social Conventions in Paul's Relations with the Corinthians*. WUNT 2.23. Tübingen: Mohr Siebeck, 1987.

Marshall, "Hellenistic Christianity." Marshall, I. Howard. "Palestinian and Hellenistic Christianity: Some Critical Comments." *NTS* 19 (3, 1973): 271–87.

Marshall, *Historian and Theologian*. Marshall, I. Howard. *Luke: Historian and Theologian*. Exeter, U.K.: Paternoster, 1970.

Marshall, "Historical Criticism." Marshall, I. Howard. "Historical Criticism." Pages 126–38 in *New Testament Interpretation: Essays on Principles and Methods*. Edited by I. Howard Marshall. Grand Rapids: Eerdmans, 1977.

Marshall, *Kept*. Marshall, I. Howard. *Kept by the Power of God: A Study in Perseverance and Falling Away*. London: Epworth, 1969. Repr., Minneapolis: Bethany Fellowship, 1974.

Marshall, "Lord's Supper." Marshall, I. Howard. "Lord's Supper." *DPL* 569–75.

Marshall, *Luke*. Marshall, I. Howard. *The Gospel of Luke: A Commentary on the Greek Text*. NIGTC. Grand Rapids: Eerdmans; Exeter, U.K.: Paternoster, 1978.

Marshall, "Luke and 'Gospel.'" Marshall, I. Howard. "Luke and His 'Gospel.'" Pages 273–92 in *The Gospel and the Gospels*. Edited by Peter Stuhlmacher. Grand Rapids: Eerdmans, 1991.

Marshall, "Luke as Theologian." Marshall, I. Howard. "Luke as Theologian." *ABD* 4:402–3.

Marshall, "Luke's View of Paul." Marshall, I. Howard. "Luke's View of Paul." *SWJT* 33 (1990): 41–51.

Marshall, *Origins*. Marshall, I. Howard. *The Origins of New Testament Christology*. 2nd ed. Downers Grove, Ill.: InterVarsity, 1990.

Marshall, *Pastoral Epistles*. Marshall, I. Howard, with Philip H. Towner. *A Critical and Exegetical Commentary on the Pastoral Epistles*. Edinburgh: T&T Clark, 1999.

Marshall, "Pastoral Epistles." Marshall, I. Howard. "The Pastoral Epistles." Pages 108–23 in *The Blackwell Companion to Paul*. Edited by Stephen Westerholm. BCompRel. Oxford: Blackwell, 2011.

Marshall, "Reading." Marshall, I. Howard. "Reading the Book, 7: Luke-Acts." *ExpT* 108 (7, 1997): 196–200.

Marshall, "Resurrection." Marshall, I. Howard. "The Resurrection in the Acts of the Apostles." Pages 92–107 in *Apostolic History and the Gospel: Biblical and Historical Essays Presented to F. F. Bruce on His 60th Birthday*. Edited by W. Ward Gasque and Ralph P. Martin. Exeter, U.K.: Paternoster; Grand Rapids: Eerdmans, 1970.

Marshall, "Shame." Marshall, Peter. "A Metaphor of Social Shame: *Thriambeuein* in 2 Cor. 2:14." *NovT* 25 (4, 1983): 302–17.

Marshall, "Significance of Pentecost." Marshall, I. Howard. "The Significance of Pentecost." *SJT* 30 (4, 1977): 347–69.

Marshall, "Son of Man Sayings." Marshall, I. Howard. "The Synoptic Son of Man Sayings in Recent Discussion." *NTS* 12 (4, 1966): 327–51.

Marshall, "Son or Servant?" Marshall, I. Howard. "Son of God or Servant of Yahweh? A Reconsideration of Mark i.11." *NTS* 15 (3, 1969): 326–36.

Marshall, "Theme in Parts." Marshall, I. Howard. "'Israel' and the Story of Salvation: One Theme in Two Parts." Pages 340–57 in *Jesus and the Heritage of Israel: Luke's Narrative Claim upon Israel's Legacy*. Edited by David P. Moessner. Luke the Interpreter of Israel 1. Harrisburg, Pa.: Trinity Press International, 1999.

Marshall, *Theology*. Marshall, I. Howard. *New Testament Theology: Many Witnesses, One Gospel*. Downers Grove, Ill.: InterVarsity, 2004.

Marshall, "Theology." Marshall, I. Howard. "How Does One Write on the Theology of Acts?" Pages 3–16 in *Witness to the Gospel: The Theology of Acts*. Edited by I. Howard Marshall and David Peterson. Grand Rapids: Eerdmans, 1998.

Marshall, *Thessalonians*. Marshall, I. Howard. *1 and 2 Thessalonians*. NCBC. Grand Rapids: Eerdmans, 1983.

Marshall, "Treatise." Marshall, I. Howard. "Acts and the 'Former Treatise.'" Pages 163–82 in *The Book of Acts in Its Ancient Literary Setting*. Edited by Bruce W. Winter and Andrew D. Clarke. Vol. 1 of *The Book of Acts in Its First Century Setting*. Edited by Bruce W. Winter. Grand Rapids: Eerdmans; Carlisle, U.K.: Paternoster, 1993.

Marshall, "Works." Marshall, I. Howard. "Salvation, Grace, and Works in the Later Writings in the Pauline Corpus." *NTS* 42 (3, 1996): 339–58.

Marshall and Peterson, *Witness*. Marshall, I. Howard, and David Peterson, eds. *Witness to the Gospel: The Theology of Acts*. Grand Rapids: Eerdmans, 1998.

Marshall and Shea, *Silenced*. Marshall, Paul, and Nina Shea. *Silenced: How Apostasy and Blasphemy Codes Are Choking Freedom Worldwide*. New York: Oxford University Press, 2011.

Martell-Otero, "Satos." Martell-Otero, Loida I. "Of Satos and Saints: Salvation from the Periphery." *Perspectivas: Hispanic Theological Initiative Occasional Paper Series* 4 (Summer 2001): 7–33. Edited by Renata Furst-Lambert.

Martens, "Unwritten Law." Martens, John W. "Unwritten Law in Philo: A Response to Naomi G. Cohen." *JJS* 43 (1, 1992): 38–45.

Martin, *Acts*. Martin, Francis, ed., in collaboration with Evan Smith. *Acts*. ACCS: New Testament 5. Downers Grove, Ill.: InterVarsity, 2006.

Martin, "Anti-individualistic Ideology." Martin, Luther H. "The Anti-individualistic Ideology of Hellenistic Culture." *Numen* 41 (2, 1994): 117–40.

Martin, "Approaches." Martin, Ralph P. "Approaches to New Testament Exegesis." Pages 220–51 in *New Testament Interpretation: Essays on Principles and Methods*. Edited by I. Howard Marshall. Grand Rapids: Eerdmans, 1977.

Martin, "Areopagus." Martin, Hubert M., Jr. "Areopagus." *ABD* 1:370–72.

Martin, "Artemidorus." Martin, Luther H. "Artemidorus: Dream Theory in Late Antiquity." *SecCent* 8 (1991): 97–108.

Martin, "Athens." Martin, Hubert M., Jr. "Athens." *ABD* 1:513–18.

Martin, "Barnabas and Paul in Lystra." Martin, Luther H. "Gods or Ambassadors of God? Barnabas and Paul in Lystra." *NTS* 41 (1, 1995): 152–56.

Martin, *Bede*. Martin, Lawrence T., ed. and trans. *Venerable Bede: Commentary on the Acts of the Apostles*. Kalamazoo, Mich.: Cistercian, 1989.

Martin, *Body*. Martin, Dale B. *The Corinthian Body*. New Haven: Yale University Press, 1995.

Martin, "Chamberlain's Journey." Martin, Clarice J. "A Chamberlain's Journey and the Challenge of Interpretation for Liberation." *Semeia* 47 (1989): 105–35.

Martin, "Christianity." Martin, David. "Evangelical and Charismatic Christianity in Latin America." Pages 73–86 in *Charismatic Christianity as a Global Culture*. Edited by Karla Poewe. SCR. Columbia: University of South Carolina Press, 1994.

Martin, "Chronos Myth." Martin, Troy W. "The Chronos Myth in Cynic Philosophy." *GRBS* 38 (1, 1997): 85–108.

Martin, *Colossians*. Martin, Ralph P. *Colossians and Philemon*. NCBC. Grand Rapids: Eerdmans, 1978.

Martin, "Construction." Martin, Dale B. "The Construction of the Ancient Family: Methodological Considerations." *JRS* 86 (1996): 40–60.

Martin, *Corinthians*. Martin, Ralph P. *2 Corinthians*. WBC 40. Waco: Word, 1986.

Martin, "Dichotomy." Martin, Dale B. "Paul and the Judaism/Hellenism Dichotomy: Toward a Social History of the Question." Pages 29–62 in *Paul beyond the Judaism/Hellenism Divide*. Edited by Troels Engberg-Pedersen. Louisville: Westminster John Knox, 2001.

Martin, "Evidence." Martin, R. A. "Syntactical Evidence of Aramaic Sources in Acts i–xv." *NTS* 11 (1, 1964): 38–59.

Martin, *Foundations*. Martin, Ralph P. *The Acts, The Letters, The Apocalypse*. Vol. 2 of *New Testament Foundations: A Guide for Christian Students*. Grand Rapids: Eerdmans; Exeter, U.K.: Paternoster, 1978.

Martin, *Glossolalia*. Martin, Ira Jay. *Glossolalia in the Apostolic Church*. Berea, Ky.: Berea College Press, 1960.

Martin, "*Heimarmene*." Martin, Luther H. "Josephus' Use of *heimarmene* in the Jewish Antiquities XIII, 171–3." *Numen* 28 (2, 1981): 127–37.

Martin, "Hermes." Martin, Luther H. "Hermes." Pages 405–11 in *Dictionary of Deities and Demons in the Bible*. 2nd rev. ed. Edited by Karel van der Toorn, Bob Becking, and Pieter W. van der Horst. Leiden: Brill; Grand Rapids: Eerdmans, 1999.

Martin, "Hymns." Martin, Ralph P. "Hymns, Hymn Fragments, Songs, Spiritual Songs." *DPL* 419–23.

Martin, "*Imperitia*." Martin, Susan D. "*Imperitia*: The Responsibility of Skilled Workers in Classical Roman Law." *AJP* 122 (1, 2001): 107–29.

Martin, "Interpretations." Martin, Clarice J. "Womanist Interpretations of the New Testament: The Quest for Holistic and Inclusive Translation and Interpretation." Pages 225–44 in vol. 2 of *Black Theology: A Documentary History*. Edited by James H. Cone and Gayraud S. Wilmore. 2 vols. Maryknoll, N.Y.: Orbis, 1993.

Martin, "Introduction to Acts." Martin, Francis. "Introduction to the Acts of the Apostles." Pages xvii–xxvi in *Acts*. Edited by Francis Martin, with Evan Smith. ACCS 5. Downers Grove, Ill.: InterVarsity, 2006.

Martin, "Introduction to Bede." Martin, Lawrence T. "Introduction." Pages xv–xxxv in *The Venerable Bede: Commentary on the Acts of the Apostles*. Kalamazoo, Mich.: Cistercian Publications, 1989.

Martin, *James*. Martin, Ralph P. *James*. WBC 48. Waco: Word, 1988.

Martin, "Language." Martin, Clarice J. "'Somebody Done Hoodoo'd the Hoodoo Man': Language, Power, Resistance, and the Effective History of Pauline Texts in American Slavery." *Semeia* 83–84 (1998): 203–33.

Martin, *Lecture sémiotique*. Martin, François. *Actes des apôtres: Lecture sémiotique*. Lyon: Profac-Cadir, 2002.

Martin, "Life-Setting." Martin, Ralph P. "The Life-Setting of the Epistle of James in the Light of Jewish History." Pages 97–103 in *Biblical and Near Eastern Studies: Essays in Honor of William Sanford LaSor*. Edited by Gary A. Tuttle. Grand Rapids: Eerdmans, 1978.

Martin, "Mithraism." Martin, Luther H. "Roman Mithraism and Christianity." *Numen* 36 (1, 1989): 2–15.

Martin, "Pericope." Martin, Ralph P. "The Pericope of the Healing of the Centurion's Servant/Son (Matt 8:5–13 par. Luke 7:1–10): Some Exegetical Notes." Pages 14–22 in *Unity and Diversity in New Testament Theology: Essays in Honor of George E. Ladd*. Edited by Robert A. Guelich. Grand Rapids: Eerdmans, 1978.

Martin, "Philo's Use." Martin, Michael. "Philo's Use of Syncrisis: An Examination of Philonic Composition in the Light of the Progymnasmata." *PRSt* 30 (3, 2003): 271–97.

Martin, *Prophet*. Martin, William. *A Prophet with Honor: The Billy Graham Story*. New York: William Morrow, 1991.

Martin, *Reconciliation*. Martin, Ralph P. *Reconciliation: A Study of Paul's Theology*. Atlanta: John Knox, 1981.

Martin, *Religions*. Martin, Luther H. *Hellenistic Religions: An Introduction*. New York: Oxford University Press, 1987.

Martin, "Resisting." Martin, Dennis. "Resisting the Devil in the Patristic, Medieval, and Reformation Church." Pages 46–71 in *Essays on Spiritual Bondage and*

Deliverance. Edited by Willard M. Swartley. Occasional Papers 11. Elkhart, Ind.: Institute of Mennonite Studies, 1988.

Martin, "Review of Meggitt." Martin, Dale B. Review of Justin J. Meggitt, *Paul, Poverty, and Survival*. *JSNT* 84 (2001): 51–64.

Martin, "Slave Families." Martin, Dale B. "Slave Families and Slaves in Families." Pages 207–30 in *Early Christian Families in Context: An Interdisciplinary Dialogue*. Edited by David L. Balch and Carolyn Osiek. Grand Rapids and Cambridge: Eerdmans, 2003.

Martin, *Slavery*. Martin, Dale B. *Slavery as Salvation: The Metaphor of Slavery in Pauline Christianity*. New Haven: Yale University Press, 1990.

Martin, "Slavery." Martin, Dale B. "Ancient Slavery, Class, and Early Christianity." *FidHist* 23 (2, 1991): 105–13.

Martin, "Syntax Criticism." Martin, R. A. "Syntax Criticism of the Testament of Abraham." Pages 95–120 in *Studies on the Testament of Abraham*. Edited by George W. E. Nickelsburg. SBLSCS 6. Missoula, Mont.: Scholars Press, 1976.

Martin, "Tacitus." Martin, Ronald Haithwaite. "Tacitus." *OCD*[3] 1469–71.

Martin, "Theodotus Inscription." Martin, Matthew J. "Interpreting the Theodotus Inscription: Some Reflections on a First Century Jerusalem Synagogue Inscription and E. P. Sanders's 'Common Judaism.'" *ANES* 39 (2002): 160–81.

Martin, "Topic Lists." Martin, Michael W. "Progymnastic Topic Lists: A Compositional Template for Luke and Other *Bioi*?" *NTS* 54 (2008): 18–41.

Martin, "Voice of Emotion." Martin, Troy W. "The Voice of Emotion: Paul's Pathetic Persuasion (Gal 4:12–20)." Pages 181–202 in *Paul and Pathos*. Edited by Thomas H. Olbricht and Jerry L. Sumney. SBLSymS 16. Atlanta: SBL, 2001.

Martin, *Worship*. Martin, Ralph P. *The Worship of God*. Grand Rapids: Eerdmans, 1982.

Martín-Asensio, *Foregrounding*. Martín-Asensio, Gustavo. *Transitivity-Based Foregrounding in the Acts of the Apostles: A Functional-Grammatical Approach to the Lukan Perspective*. JSNTSup 202, Studies in New Testament Greek 8. Sheffield, U.K.: Sheffield Academic Press, 2000.

Martindale, "Translation." Martindale, Charles Anthony. "Translation." *OCD*[3] 1545–46.

Martínez, "Pablo." Martínez, A. E. "Pablo, el obrero: Oficio y opción a favor de 'los trabajadores.'" *Apuntes* 23 (2, 2003): 44–64.

Martínez, "Reevaluación." Martínez, A. E. "Reevaluación crítica del 'testimonio' de Flavio Josefo acerca de Jesús." *Apuntes* 25 (3, 2005): 84–118.

Martinez and Wetli, "Santeria." Martinez, Rafael, and Charles V. Wetli. "Santeria: A Magico-religious System of Afro-Cuban Origin." *AmJSocPsyc* 2 (3, 1982): 32–38.

Martínez-Taboas, "Seizures." Martínez-Taboas, Alfonso. "Psychogenic Seizures in an Espiritismo Context: The Role of Culturally Sensitive Psychotherapy." *PsycTRPT* 42 (1, 2005): 6–13.

Martínez-Taboas, "World." Martínez-Taboas, Alfonso. "The Plural World of Culturally Sensitive Psychotherapy: A Response to Castro-Blanco's (2005) Comments." *PsycTRPT* 42 (1, 2005): 17–19.

Martini, "Pamphylia." Martini, Wolfram. "Pamphylia." *BrillPauly* 10:415–17.

Martini, "Tendances." Martini, C. "La tradition textuelle des Actes des apôtres et les tendances de l'Église ancienne." Pages 21–35 in *Les Actes des apôtres: Traditions, rédaction, théologie*. Edited by Jacob Kremer. BETL 48. Gembloux, Belg.: J. Duculot; Leuven: Leuven University Press, 1979.

Martín-Moreno, "Alegría." Martín-Moreno, Juan Manuel. "Alegría y experiencia de Dios en la obra lucana." *Manresa* 75 (294, 2003): 51–68.

Martins Terra, "Milagres." Martins Terra, J. E. "Os milagres helenisticos." *RCB* 4 (15–16, 1980): 229–62.

Martinson, "Ending." Martinson, Paul Varo. "The Ending Is Prelude: Discontinuities Lead to Continuities, Acts 1:1–11 and 28:23–31." Pages 313–23 in *Mission in Acts: Ancient Narratives in Contemporary Context*. Edited by Robert L. Gallagher and Paul Hertig. AmSocMissS 34. Maryknoll, N.Y.: Orbis, 2004.

Martitz, "Υἱός." Martitz, Wülfing von. "Υἱός in Greek." *TDNT* 8:335–40.

Martone, "Septuagint." Martone, Corrado. "Qumran Readings in Agreement with the Septuagint against the Masoretic Text, Part One: The Pentateuch." *Hen* 27 (1–2, 2005): 53–113.

Martone, "Testo." Martone, Corrado. "Un testo qumranico che narra la morte del Messia? A propositio del recente dibattito su 4Q285." *RivB* 42 (3, 1994): 329–36.

Martyn, "Glimpses." Martyn, J. Louis. "Glimpses into the History of the Johannine Community." Pages 149–76 in *L'Évangile de Jean: Sources, rédaction, théologie*. Edited by Marinus de Jonge. BETL 45. Gembloux, Belg.: J. Duculot; Leuven: University Press, 1977.

Martyn, "Mission." Martyn, J. Louis. "A Law-Observant Mission to the Gentiles: The Background of Galatians." *SJT* 38 (3, 1985): 307–24.

Martyn, *Theology*. Martyn, J. Louis. *History and Theology in the Fourth Gospel*. Nashville: Abingdon, 1968.

Marx, *Manifesto*. Marx, Karl. *Manifesto of the Communist Party*. GBWW 50. Chicago: Encyclopedia Britannica, 1952.

Marx, "New Theophilus." Marx, Werner G. "A New Theophilus." *EvQ* 52 (1, 1980): 17–26.

Marx, "Physician." Marx, Werner G. "Luke, the Physician, Re-examined." *ExpT* 91 (6, 1980): 168–72.

Marx, "Prédestination." Marx, Alfred. "Y a-t-il une prédestination à Qumran?" *RevQ* 6 (2, 1967): 163–81.

Marx, "Racines." Marx, Alfred. "Les racines du célibat essénien." *RevQ* 7 (3, 1970): 323–42.

Marxsen, *Mark*. Marxsen, Willi. *Mark the Evangelist: Studies on the Redaction History of the Gospel*. Translated by James Boyce, Donald Juel, and William Poehlmann, with Roy A. Harrisville. Nashville: Abingdon, 1969.

Mary, *Mysticism*. Mary, Sylvia. *Pauline and Johannine Mysticism*. London: Darton, Longman & Todd, 1964.

Maser, "Synagoge und Ecclesia." Maser, Peter. "Synagoge und Ecclesia—Erwägungen zur Frühgeschichte des Kirchenbaus und der christlichen Bildkunst." *Kairos* 32–33 (1990–91): 9–26.

Masland et al., "Slavery." Masland, Tom, et al. "Slavery." *Newsweek* (May 4, 1992): 30–39.

Mason, "Chief Priests." Mason, Steve. "Chief Priests, Sadducees, Pharisees, and Sanhedrin in Acts." Pages 115–78 in *The Book of Acts in Its Palestinian Setting*. Edited by Richard Bauckham. Vol. 4 of *The Book of Acts in Its First Century Setting*. Edited by Bruce W. Winter. Grand Rapids: Eerdmans; Carlisle, U.K.: Paternoster, 1995.

Mason, "Contradiction." Mason, Steven. "Contradiction or Counterpoint? Josephus and Historical Method." *RRJ* 6 (2–3, 2003): 145–88.

Mason, "Dominance." Mason, Steven. "Pharisaic Dominance before 70 CE and the Gospels' Hypocrisy Charge (Matt 23:2–3)." *HTR* 83 (1990): 363–81.

Mason, "Jews." Mason, Steve. "Jews, Judaeans, Judaizing, Judaism: Problems of Categorization in Ancient History." *JSJ* 38 (4–5, 2007): 457–512.

Mason, *Josephus and New Testament*. Mason, Steven. *Josephus and the New Testament*. Peabody, Mass.: Hendrickson, 1992.

Mason, *Ko Thah Byu*. Mason, Francis. *The Karen Apostle; or, Memoir of Ko Thah Byu*. Bassein, Burma: SGAU Karen Press, 1884.

Mason, *Pharisees*. Mason, Steven. *Flavius Josephus on the Pharisees*. StPB 39. Leiden: Brill, 1991.

Mason, "Value for Study." Mason, Steven. "Josephus: Value for New Testament Study." *DNTB* 596–600.

Mason, "Was Josephus a Pharisee?" Mason, Steven. "Was Josephus a Pharisee? A Reexamination of Life 10–12." *JJS* 40 (1, 1989): 31–45.

Masquelier, "Invention." Masquelier, Adeline. "The Invention of Anti-Tradition: Dodo Spirits in Southern Nigeria." Pages 34–49 in *Spirit Possession, Modernity and Power in Africa*. Edited by Heike Behrend and Ute Luig. Madison: University of Wisconsin Press, 1999.

Massa, *Pompeii*. Massa, Aldo. *The World of Pompeii*. Geneva: Minerva, 1972.

Massey, "Disagreement." Massey, Preston T. "Disagreement in the Greco-Roman Literary Tradition and the Implications for Gospel Research." *BBR* 22 (1, 2012): 51–80.

Masson, "Grecs et Libyens." Masson, Olivier. "Grecs et Libyens en Cyrénaïque, d'après les témoignages de l'épigraphie." Pages 377–87 in *Assimilation et résistance à la culture gréco-romaine dans le monde ancien: Travaux du VIe Congrès international d'études classiques*. Edited by D. M. Pippidi. FIAEC. Paris: Belles Lettres, 1976.

Mastin, "Scaeva." Mastin, B. A. "Scaeva the Chief Priest." *JTS* 27 (2, 1976): 405–12.

Mastrocinque, "Choices." Mastrocinque, Attilio. "Creating One's Own Religion: Intellectual Choices." Pages 378–91 in *A Companion to Roman Religion*. Edited by Jörg Rüpke. BCompAW. Oxford: Blackwell, 2011.

Mastrocinque, "Lares." Mastrocinque, Attilio. "Lares." *BrillPauly* 7:247–49.

Matassa, "Myth." Matassa, Lidia. "Unravelling the Myth of the Synagogue on Delos." *BAIAS* 25 (2007): 81–115.

Matera, *Kingship*. Matera, Frank J. *The Kingship of Jesus: Composition Theology in Mark 15*. SBLDS 66. Chico, Calif.: Scholars Press, 1982.

Matera, "Luke 22, 66–71." Matera, Frank J. "Luke 22,66–71: Jesus before the ΠΡΕΣΒΥΤΕΡΙΟΝ." Pages 517–33 in *L'Évangile de Luc: The Gospel of Luke*. Edited by F. Neirynck. Rev. ed. BETL 32. Leuven: Leuven University Press, 1989.

Matera, "Luke 23,1–25." Matera, Frank J. "Luke 23,1–25: Jesus before Pilate, Herod, and Israel." Pages 535–51 in *L'Évangile de Luc: The Gospel of Luke*. Edited by F. Neirynck. Rev. ed. BETL 32. Leuven: Leuven University Press, 1989.

Matera, "Responsibility for Death." Matera, Frank J. "Responsibility for the Death of Jesus according to the Acts of the Apostles." *JSNT* 39 (1990): 77–93.

Matera, *Romans*. Matera, Frank J. *Romans*. PNTC. Grand Rapids: Baker Academic, 2010.

Matera, *II Corinthians*. Matera, Frank J. *II Corinthians: A Commentary*. NTL. Louisville: Westminster John Knox, 2003.

Matera, *Theology*. Matera, Frank J. *New Testament Theology: Exploring Diversity and Unity*. Louisville: Westminster John Knox, 2007.

Mates, *Stoic Logic*. Mates, Benson. *Stoic Logic*. UCPP 26. Berkeley: University of California Press, 1953.

Matheson, *Epictetus*. Matheson, P. E., ed. and trans. *Epictetus: The Discourses and Manual Together with Fragments of His Writings*. 2 vols. Oxford: Clarendon, 1916.

Mathews, "Hospitality." Mathews, J. B. "Hospitality and the New Testament Church: An Historical and Exegetical Study." ThD diss., Princeton Theological Seminary, 1965.

Matlock, "Detheologizing." Matlock, R. Barry. "Detheologizing the πίστις Χριστοῦ Debate: Cautionary Remarks from a Lexical Semantic Perspective." *NovT* 42 (1, 2000): 1–23.

Matlock, "Πίστις Χριστοῦ." Matlock, R. Barry. "'Even the Demons Believe': Paul and πίστις Χριστοῦ." *CBQ* 64 (2, 2002): 300–318.

Matlock, "Road." Matlock, R. Barry. "Does the Road to Damascus Run through the Letters of Paul?" Pages 81–100 in *Reading Acts Today: Essays in Honour of Loveday C. A. Alexander*. Edited by Steve Walton et al. LNTS 427. London: T&T Clark, 2011.

Matson, *Conversion Narratives*. Matson, David Lertis. *Household Conversion Narratives in Acts: Pattern and Interpretation*. JSNTSup 123. Sheffield, U.K.: Sheffield Academic, 1996.

Matson, "Death." Matson, Mark. "The Death of Jesus in John and Luke: Theological Convergences." Seminar paper for the Johannine Writings Seminar, Society for New Testament Studies, Bard College, Aug. 4, 2011.

Matson, *Dialogue*. Matson, Mark A. *In Dialogue with Another Gospel? The Influence of the Fourth Gospel on the Passion Narrative of the Gospel of Luke*. SBLDS 178. Atlanta: SBL, 2001.

Matsuoka, "Fox Possession." Matsuoka, Etsuko. "The Interpretations of Fox Possession: Illness as Metaphor." *CMPsy* 15 (1991): 453–77.

Matthews, "Clemency." Matthews, Shelly. "Clemency as Cruelty: Forgiveness and Force in the Dying Prayers of Jesus and Stephen." *BibInt* 17 (1–2, 2009): 118–46.

Matthews, *Converts*. Matthews, Shelly. *First Converts: Rich Pagan Women and the Rhetoric of Mission in Early Judaism and Christianity*. Stanford, Calif.: Stanford University Press, 2001.

Matthews, "Elite Women." Matthews, Shelly. "Elite Women, Public Religion, and Christian Propaganda in Acts 16." Pages 111–33 in *The Feminist Companion to the Acts of the Apostles*. Edited by Amy-Jill Levine with Marianne Blickenstaff. Cleveland: Pilgrim; Edinburgh: T&T Clark, 2004.

Matthews, "Emperor and Historians." Matthews, John. "The Emperor and His Historians." Pages 290–304 in *A Companion to Greek and Roman Historiography*. Edited by John Marincola. 2 vols. Oxford: Blackwell, 2007.

Matthews, "Eunapius." Matthews, John F. "Eunapius." *OCD*[3] 568–69.

Matthews, *Faith Factor*. Matthews, Dale A., with Connie Clark. *The Faith Factor: Proof of the Healing Power of Prayer*. New York: Viking, 1998.

Matthews, "Hellenists." Matthews, Shelly. "Hellenists, History, Ethics." Paper presented at the annual meeting of the SBL, Washington, D.C., Nov. 20, 2006.

Matthews, "Ladies' Aid." Matthews, Shelly. "Ladies' Aid: Gentile Noblewomen as Saviors and Benefactors in the *Antiquities*." *HTR* 92 (2, 1999): 199–218.

Matthews, "Making Your Point." Matthews, Victor H. "Making Your Point: The Use of Gestures in Ancient Israel." *BTB* 42 (1, 2012): 18–29.

Matthews, "Names, Greek." Matthews, Elaine. "Names, Personal, Greek." *OCD*[3] 1022–24.

Matthews, "Review." Matthews, Christopher R. Review of Samuel Byrskog, *Story as History—History as Story*. *RBL* (July 17, 2001). Online: http://www.bookreviews.org/pdf/1085_270.pdf.

Matthews, "Stoning." Matthews, Shelly. "The Need for the Stoning of Stephen." Pages 124–39 in *Violence in the New Testament*. Edited by Shelly Matthews and E. Leigh Gibson. New York: T&T Clark, 2005.

Matthiae, "Nabatäer." Matthiae, Karl. "Die Nabatäer: Ein antikes Handelsvolk in der Wüste." *Altertum* 35 (4, 1989): 222–31.

Mattila, "Ben Sira." Mattila, Sharon Lea. "Ben Sira and the Stoics: A Reexamination of the Evidence." *JBL* 119 (3, 2000): 473–501.

Mattila, "Wisdom." Mattila, Sharon Lea. "Wisdom, Sense Perception, Nature, and Philo's Gender Gradient." *HTR* 89 (2, 1996): 103–29.

Mattill, "Date and Purpose." Mattill, A. J., Jr. "The Date and Purpose of Luke-Acts: Rackham Reconsidered." *CBQ* 40 (1978): 335–50.

Mattill, *Last Things*. Mattill, A. J., Jr. *Luke and the Last Things: A Perspective for the Understanding of Lukan Thought*. Dillsboro: Western North Carolina Press, 1979.

Mattill, "*Naherwartung*." Mattill, A. J., Jr. "*Naherwartung, Fernerwartung*, and the Purpose of Luke-Acts: Weymouth Reconsidered." *CBQ* 34 (1972): 276–93.

Mattill, "Purpose." Mattill, A. J., Jr. "The Purpose of Acts: Schneckenburger Reconsidered." Pages 108–22 in *Apostolic History and the Gospel: Biblical and Historical Essays Presented to F. F. Bruce on His 60th Birthday*. Edited by W. W. Gasque and R. P. Martin. Exeter, U.K.: Paternoster; Grand Rapids: Eerdmans, 1970.

Mattill, "Value." Mattill, A. J., Jr. "The Value of Acts as a Source for the Study of Paul." Pages 76–98 in *Perspectives on Luke-Acts*. ABPRSSS 5. Edited by Charles H. Talbert. Danville, Va.: Association of Baptist Professors of Religion; Edinburgh: T&T Clark, 1978.

Mattill, "'Way of Tribulation.'" Mattill, A. J., Jr. "'The Way of Tribulation.'" *JBL* 98 (4, 1979): 531–46.

Mattill and Mattill, *Bibliography*. Mattill, A. J., Jr., and Mary Bedford Mattill. *A Classified Bibliography of Literature on the Acts of the Apostles*. NTTS 7. Leiden: Brill, 1966.

Mattingly, *Christianity*. Mattingly, Harold. *Christianity in the Roman Empire*. New York: W. W. Norton, 1967.

Mattingly and Hitchner, "Roman Africa." Mattingly, David J., and R. Bruce Hitchner. "Roman Africa: An Archaeological Review." *JRS* 85 (1995): 165–213.

Mattioli, "Ironia di Paolo." Mattioli, Anselmo. "La sorridente ironia di Paolo: Frasi e espressioni argute negli Atti e nelle Lettere." *Teresianum* 46 (2, 1995): 367–411.

Mattusch, "Corinthian Bronze." Mattusch, Carol C. "Corinthian Bronze: Famous, but Elusive." Pages 219–32 in *Corinth: The Centenary, 1896–1996*. Edited by Charles K. Williams II and Nancy Bookidis. Vol. 20 of *Corinth: Results of Excavations Conducted by the American School of Classical Studies at Athens*. Princeton: American School of Classical Studies at Athens, 2003.

Mauchline, "Persistent Belief." Mauchline, John. "Implicit Signs of a Persistent Belief in the Davidic Empire." *VT* 20 (3, 1970): 287–303.

Mauck, *Trial*. Mauck, John W. *Paul on Trial: The Book of Acts as a Defense of Christianity*. Foreword by Donald A. Hagner. Nashville: Nelson, 2001.

Maull, "Stream." Maull, Georgia. "Stream, Stone, Oikos, Polis: Sacred Space and Ancient Mystery Cult Sanctuaries." *CurTM* 39 (2, 2012): 151–55.

Maurizio, "Pythia's Role." Maurizio, Lisa. "Anthropology and Spirit Possession: A Reconsideration of the Pythia's Role at Delphi." *JHS* 115 (1995): 69–86.

Mauser, *Christ in Wilderness*. Mauser, Ulrich. *Christ in the Wilderness*. SBT 39. London: SCM, 1963.

Maxwell, *African Gifts*. Maxwell, David. *African Gifts of the Spirit: Pentecostalism and the Rise of a Zimbabwean Transnational Religious Movement*. Oxford: James Currey; Harare, Zimbabwe: Weaver; Athens: Ohio University Press, 2006.

Maxwell, "Audience." Maxwell, Kathy R. "The Role of the Audience in Ancient Narrative: Acts as a Case Study." *ResQ* 48 (3, 2006): 171–80.

Maxwell, "Witches." Maxwell, David. "Witches, Prophets, and Avenging Spirits: The Second Christian Movement in North-East Zimbabwe." *JRelAf* 25 (3, 1995): 309–39.

May, "Reader-Response Critic." May, Jordan Daniel. "Is Luke a Reader-Response Critic? Luke's Aesthetic Trajectory of Isaiah 49.6 in Acts 13.47." Pages 59–86 in *Trajectories in the Book of Acts: Essays in Honor of John Wesley Wyckoff*. Edited by Paul Alexander, Jordan Daniel May, and Robert G. Reid. Eugene, Ore.: Wipf & Stock, 2010.

May, "Synagogues." May, Herbert Gordon. "Synagogues in Palestine." *BA* 7 (1, 1944): 1–20.

May, *Witnesses to Pentecost*. May, Jordan Daniel. *Global Witnesses to Pentecost: The Testimony of "Other Tongues."* Cleveland, Tenn.: CPT Press, 2013.

May and Stark, "Reconstruction." May, Natalia N., and Stas I. Stark. "Reconstruction of the Architectural Decor of the Major Synagogue at Korazim." *'Atiqot* 43 (2002): 207–52.

Mayer, "Abrahambildes." Mayer, Günter. "Aspekte des Abrahambildes in der hellenistisch-jüdischen Literatur." *EvT* 32 (2, 1972): 118–27.

Mayer, "Anfang." Mayer, Reinhold. "Der Anfang des Evangeliums in Galiläa." *BK* 36 (2, 1981): 213–21.

Mayer and Rühle, "Salomo." Mayer, Reinhold, and Inken Rühle. "Salomo als Prototyp eines Weisen? Die Weisheit Salomos—einmal anders." *BK* 52 (4, 1997): 193–99.

Mayers, *Christianity Confronts Culture*. Mayers, Marvin K. *Christianity Confronts Culture: A Strategy for Cross-cultural Evangelism*. Grand Rapids: Zondervan, 1974.

Mayer-Schärtel, "Frauenbild." Mayer-Schärtel, Bärbel. "Das Frauenbild des Josephus." *BK* 53 (2, 1998): 84–86.

Mayerson, "Translations." Mayerson, Philip. "Translations Involving γλεῦκος/μοῦστος: Must or Wine? Or Must Wine?" *BASP* 36 (1–4, 1999): 123–28.

Maynard-Reid, "Samaria." Maynard-Reid, Pedrito U. "Samaria." *DLNTD* 1075–77.

Maynard-Reid, *Worship*. Maynard-Reid, Pedrito U. *Diverse Worship: African-American, Caribbean, and Hispanic Perspectives*. Downers Grove, Ill.: InterVarsity, 2000.

Mayor, *James*. Mayor, Joseph B. *The Epistle of St. James*. 3rd rev. ed. London: Macmillan, 1913. Repr., Minneapolis: Klock & Klock, 1977.

Mays, *Amos*. Mays, James Luther. *Amos: A Commentary*. Philadelphia: Westminster, 1969.

Mazar, "Bull." Mazar, Amihai. "Bronze Bull Found in Israelite 'High Place' from the Time of the Judges." *BAR* 9 (5, 1983): 34–40.

Mazar, "Excavations." Mazar, Benjamin. "Excavations near Temple Mount Reveal Splendors of Herodian Jerusalem." *BAR* 6 (4, 1980): 44–59.

Mazar, "Josephus and Excavations." Mazar, Benjamin. "Josephus Flavius and the Archaeological Excavations in Jerusalem." Pages 325–29 in *Josephus, the Bible, and History*. Edited by Louis H. Feldman and Gohei Hata. Detroit: Wayne State University Press, 1989.

Mazar, Avi-Yonah, and Malamat, *Views*. Mazar, Benjamin, Michael Avi-Yonah, and Abraham Malamat, eds. *Views of the Biblical World*. 5 vols. New York: Arco, 1959.

Mazich, "Geography." Mazich, Edward. "Geography as Narrative in Luke-Acts." *BibT* 41 (2, 2003): 95–101.

Mben, "Women." Mben, J. Loic. "Women in Pauline Corpus." *HekRev* 37 (2007): 7–20.

Mbiti, *Religions*. Mbiti, John S. *African Religions and Philosophies*. Garden City, N.Y.: Doubleday, 1970.

McAll, "Deliverance." McAll, R. Kenneth. "The Ministry of Deliverance." *ExpT* 86 (10, July 1975): 296–98.

McAll, "Taste." McAll, R. Kenneth. "Taste and See." Pages 269–78 in *Demon Possession: A Medical, Historical, Anthropological, and Theological Symposium*. Edited by John Warwick Montgomery. Minneapolis: Bethany House, 1976.

McArthur, "Celibacy." McArthur, Harvey. "Celibacy in Judaism at the Time of Christian Beginnings." *AUSS* 25 (1987): 163–81.

McCane, "Bones." McCane, Byron R. "Bones of Contention? Ossuaries and

Reliquaries in Early Judaism and Christianity." *SecCent* 8 (4, 1991): 235–46.

McCane, "Burial Practices." McCane, Byron R. "Burial Practices, Jewish." *DNTB* 173–75.

McCane, "Shame." McCane, Byron R. "'Where No One Had Yet Been Laid': The Shame of Jesus' Burial." Pages 431–52 in *Authenticating the Activities of Jesus*. Edited by Bruce Chilton and Craig A. Evans. NTTS 28.2. Leiden: Brill, 1999.

McCann and Freed, *Archaeology*. McCann, Anna Marguerite, and Joann Freed. *Deep Water Archaeology: A Late-Roman Ship from Carthage and an Ancient Trade Route near Skerki Bank off Northwest Sicily*. JRASS 13. Ann Arbor, Mich.: Journal of Roman Archaeology, 1994.

McCann and Oleson, *Shipwrecks*. McCann, Anna Marguerite, and John Peter Oleson. *Deep-Water Shipwrecks off Skerki Bank: The 1997 Survey*. JRASS 58. Portsmouth, R.I.: Journal of Roman Archaeology, 2004.

McCant, *2 Corinthians*. McCant, J. W. *2 Corinthians*. Readings. Sheffield, U.K.: Sheffield Academic, 1999.

McCasland, *Finger*. McCasland, Selby Vernon. *By the Finger of God: Demon Possession and Exorcism in Early Christianity in the Light of Modern Views of Mental Illness*. Introduction by David Cole Wilson. New York: Macmillan, 1951.

McCasland, "Way." McCasland, Selby Vernon. "'The Way.'" *JBL* 77 (3, 1958): 222–30.

McClenon, *Events*. McClenon, James. *Wondrous Events: Foundations of Religious Belief*. Philadelphia: University of Pennsylvania Press, 1994.

McClenon, *Healing*. McClenon, James. *Wondrous Healing: Shamanism, Human Evolution, and the Origin of Religion*. DeKalb, Ill.: Northern Illinois University Press, 2002.

McClenon and Nooney, "Experiences." McClenon, James, and Jennifer Nooney. "Anomalous Experiences Reported by Field Anthropologists: Evaluating Theories Regarding Religion." *AnthCons* 13 (2, 2002): 46–60.

McClymond, *Encyclopedia of Revivals*. McClymond, Michael, ed. *Encyclopedia of Religious Revivals in America*. 2 vols. Westport, Conn.: Greenwood, 2007.

McClymond, *Stranger*. McClymond, Michael J. *Familiar Stranger: An Introduction to Jesus of Nazareth*. Grand Rapids: Eerdmans, 2004.

McComiskey and Longman, "Amos." McComiskey, Thomas E., and Tremper Longman III. "Amos." Pages 349–420 in vol. 8 of *The Expositor's Bible Commentary*. Rev. ed. Grand Rapids: Zondervan, 2008.

McConnell, *Testimony*. McConnell, James R., Jr. *The Topos of Divine Testimony in Luke-Acts*. Eugene, Ore.: Pickwick, 2014.

McConvery, "Ancient Physicians." McConvery, Brendan. "Ancient Physicians and Their Art." *BibT* 36 (5, 1998): 306–12.

McConvery, "Praise." McConvery, Brendan. "Ben Sira's 'Praise of the Physician' (Sir 38:1–15) in the Light of Some Hippocratic Writings." *PIBA* 21 (1998): 62–86.

McCoskey, "Imperative." McCoskey, Denise Eileen. "Answering the Multicultural Imperative: A Course on Race and Ethnicity in Antiquity." *CW* 92 (6, 1999): 553–61.

McCoskey, *Race*. McCoskey, Denise Eileen. *Race: Antiquity and Its Legacy*. New York: Oxford University Press, 2012.

McCown, "Ephesia Grammata." McCown, Chester C. "The Ephesia Grammata in Popular Belief." *TPAPA* 54 (1923): 128–31.

McCown, *Genesis*. McCown, Chester Charlton. *The Genesis of the Social Gospel*. New York and London: Alfred A. Knopf, 1929.

McCoy, "Shadow of Thucydides." McCoy, W. J. "In the Shadow of Thucydides." Pages 3–22 in *History, Literature, and Society in the Book of Acts*. Edited by Ben Witherington III. Cambridge: Cambridge University Press, 1996.

McCracken, "Interpretation." McCracken, Victor. "The Interpretation of Scripture in Luke-Acts." *ResQ* 41 (4, 1999): 193–210.

McCullough, "Gladiators." McCullough, Anna. "Female Gladiators in Imperial Rome: Literary Context and Historical Fact." *CW* 101 (2, 2008): 197–209.

McDonald, "Antioch." McDonald, Lee Martin. "Antioch (Syria)." *DNTB* 34–37.

McDonald, "Athens." McDonald, William A. "Archaeology and St. Paul's Journeys in Greek Lands, Part II: Athens." *BA* 4 (1, 1941): 1–10.

McDonald, "Ephesus." McDonald, Lee Martin. "Ephesus." *DNTB* 318–21.

McDonald, "Herodotus." McDonald, A. H. "Herodotus on the Miraculous." Pages 81–92 in *Miracles: Cambridge Studies in Their Philosophy and History*. Edited by C. F. D. Moule. London: A. R. Mowbray; New York: Morehouse-Barlow, 1965.

McDonald, "Philippi." McDonald, Lee Martin. "Philippi." *DNTB* 787–89.

McDonald, "Romans XVI." McDonald, J. I. H. "Was Romans XVI a Separate Letter?" *NTS* 16 (4, 1970): 369–72.

McDonald, *Story*. McDonald, Lee Martin. *The Story of Jesus in History and Faith: An Introduction*. Grand Rapids: Baker Academic, 2013.

McDonnell, *Renewal*. McDonnell, Kilian. *Charismatic Renewal and the Churches*. New York: Seabury, 1976.

McDonnell, "Writing." McDonnell, Myles. "Writing, Copying, and Autograph Manuscripts in Ancient Rome." *CQ* 46 (2, 1996): 469–91.

McDonnell and Akallo, *Girl Soldier*. McDonnell, Faith J. H., and Grace Akallo. *Girl Soldier: A Story of Hope for Northern Uganda's Children*. Grand Rapids: Chosen, 2007.

McDonnell and Montague, *Initiation*. McDonnell, Kilian, and George T. Montague. *Christian Initiation and Baptism in the Holy Spirit: Evidence from the First Eight Centuries*. Collegeville, Minn.: Liturgical Press, 1991.

McDonough, "Small Change." McDonough, Sean M. "Small Change: Saul to Paul, Again." *JBL* 125 (2, 2006): 390–91.

McEleney, "Conversion." McEleney, Neil J. "Conversion, Circumcision, and the Law." *NTS* 20 (3, 1974): 319–41.

McGavran, "Healing and Evangelization." McGavran, Donald. "Healing and the Evangelization of the World." Pages 289–99 in *1979 Brasilia Church Growth Seminar*. Brazil: Sevic, 1979.

McGee, "Calcutta Revival." McGee, Gary B. "The Calcutta Revival of 1907 and the Reformulation of Charles F. Parham's 'Bible Evidence' Doctrine." *AJPS* 6 (1, 2003): 123–43.

McGee, "Dilemma." McGee, Gary B. "The Dilemma over the Apostolic Nature of Mission in Modern Missions." Pages 47–66 in *He Gave Apostles: Apostolic Ministry in the 21st Century*. Edited by Edgar R. Lee. Springfield, Mo.: Assemblies of God Theological Seminary Press, 2005.

McGee, "Hermeneutics." McGee, Gary B. "Early Pentecostal Hermeneutics: Tongues as Evidence in the Book of Acts." Pages 96–118 in *Initial Evidence: Historical and Biblical Perspectives on the Pentecostal Doctrine of Spirit Baptism*. Edited by Gary B. McGee. Peabody, Mass.: Hendrickson, 1991.

McGee, "Logic." McGee, Gary B. "Taking the Logic 'a Little Further': Late Nineteenth-Century References to the Gift of Tongues in Mission-Related Literature and Their Influence on Early Pentecostalism." *AJPS* 9 (1, 2006): 99–125.

McGee, *Miracles*. McGee, Gary B. *Miracles, Missions, & American Pentecostalism*. Am SocMissS 45. Maryknoll, N.Y.: Orbis, 2010.

McGee, "Miracles." McGee, Gary B. "Miracles." Pages 252–54 in *Encyclopedia of Mission and Missionaries*. Edited by Jonathan J. Bonk. New York: Routledge, 2007.

McGee, "Miracles and Mission." McGee, Gary B. "Miracles and Mission Revisited." *IBMR* 25 (Oct. 2001): 146–56.

McGee, *People of Spirit*. McGee, Gary B. *People of the Spirit: The Assemblies of God*. Springfield, Mo.: Gospel, 2004.

McGee, "Possessions." McGee, Daniel B. "Sharing Possessions: A Study in Biblical Ethics." Pages 163–78 in *With Steadfast Purpose: Essays on Acts in Honor of Henry Jackson Flanders, Jr.* Edited by Naymond H. Keathley. Waco: Baylor University Press, 1990.

McGee, *Preached*. McGee, Gary B. *This Gospel Shall Be Preached: A History and Theology of Assemblies of God Foreign Missions to 1959*. Springfield, Mo.: Gospel Publishing House, 1986.

McGee, "Radical Strategy." McGee, Gary B. "The Radical Strategy in Modern Mission: The Linkage of Paranormal Phenomena with Evangelism." Pages 69–95 in *The Holy Spirit and Mission Dynamics*. Edited by C. Douglas McConnell. Evangelical Missiological Society Series 5. Pasadena, Calif.: William Carey, 1997.

McGee, "Regions Beyond." McGee, Gary B. "To the Regions Beyond: The Global Expansion of Pentecostalism." Pages 69–95 in *The Century of the Holy Spirit: 100 Years of Pentecostal and Charismatic Renewal, 1901–2001*. Edited by Vinson Synan. Nashville: Thomas Nelson, 2001.

McGee, "Revivals in India." McGee, Gary B. "Pentecostal Phenomena and Revivals in India: Implications for Indigenous Church Leadership." *IBMR* 20 (July 1996): 112–17.

McGee, "Shortcut." McGee, Gary B. "Shortcut to Language Preparation? Radical Evangelicals, Missions, and the Gift of Tongues." *IBMR* 25 (July 2001): 118–23.

McGee, "Strategies." McGee, Gary B. "Strategies for Global Mission." Pages 203–24 in *Called and Empowered: Global Mission in Pentecostal Perspective*. Edited by Murray A. Dempster, Byron D. Klaus, and Douglas Petersen. Peabody, Mass.: Hendrickson, 1991.

McGee, "Strategy." McGee, Gary B. "The Radical Strategy." Pages 47–59 in *Signs and Wonders in Ministry Today*. Edited by Benny C. Aker and Gary B. McGee. Foreword by Thomas E. Trask. Springfield, Mo.: Gospel, 1996.

McGill, "Seneca on Plagiarizing." McGill, Scott. "Seneca the Elder on Plagiarizing Cicero's *Verrines*." *Rhetorica* 23 (4, 2005): 337–46.

McGing, "Bandits." McGing, Brian C. "Bandits, Real and Imagined, in Greco-Roman Egypt." *BASP* 35 (3–4, 1998): 159–83.

McGinn, "Brothel." McGinn, Thomas A. J. "How to Find a Brothel in Pompeii." *Arch Od* 7 (1, 2004): 18–25, 62.

McGinn, "Co-workers." McGinn, Sheila E. "Women Co-workers of Paul." *BibT* 42 (4, 2004): 213–17.

McGinn, "*Feminae probrosae*." McGinn, Thomas A. J. "*Feminae probrosae* and the Litter." *CJ* 93 (3, 1998): 241–50.

McGinn, "Missing Females?" McGinn, Thomas A. J. "Missing Females? Augustus' Encouragement of Marriage between Freeborn Males and Freedwomen." *Historia* 53 (2, 2004): 200–208.

McGinn, "Palatine." McGinn, Thomas A. J. "Caligula's Brothel on the Palatine." *EMC* 17 (1, 1998): 95–107.

McGinn, "Taxation." McGinn, Thomas A. J. "The Taxation of Roman Prostitutes." *Helios* 16 (1, 1989): 79–110.

McGinn, "Widows." McGinn, Thomas A. J. "Widows, Orphans, and Social History." *JRA* 12 (1999): 617–32.

McGinnis, "Center." McGinnis, Ernest B. "Delphi's Influence on the World of the New Testament, Part 1: Delphi: Center of the World." *BibSp* 20 (1, 2007): 25–32.

McGinnis, "Faults." McGinnis, Ernest B. "Delphi's Influence on the World of the New Testament, Part 3: Faults, Fumes, and Visions." *BibSp* 21 (3, 2008): 65–69.

McGinnis, "Oracles." McGinnis, Ernest B. "Delphi's Influence on the World of the New Testament, Part 2: The Oracles of Delphi." *BibSp* 20 (2, 2007): 61–64.

McGrath, "Apologetics." McGrath, Alister E. "Apologetics to the Romans." *BSac* 155 (620, 1998): 387–93.

McGrath, "Cross." McGrath, Alister E. "Cross, Theology of the." *DPL* 192–97.

McGrath, *Dialogue*. McGrath, Alister E. *The Foundations of Dialogue in Science and Religion*. Oxford: Blackwell, 1998.

McGrath, "Justification." McGrath, Alister E. "Justification." *DPL* 517–23.

McGrath, *Science and Religion*. McGrath, Alister E. *Science and Religion: An Introduction*. Oxford: Blackwell, 1999.

McGrath, *Universe*. McGrath, Alister E. *A Fine-Tuned Universe: The Quest for God in Science and Theology*. Louisville: Westminster John Knox, 2009.

McGraw, "Corinth." McGraw, Larry. "The City of Corinth." *SWJT* 32 (1, 1989): 5–10.

McGrew, "Argument." McGrew, Timothy. "The Argument from Miracles: A Cumulative Case for the Resurrection of Jesus of Nazareth." Pages 593–662 in *The Blackwell Companion to Natural Theology*. Edited by J. P. Moreland and William Lane Craig. Oxford: Blackwell, 2009.

McGrew, "Miracles." McGrew, Timothy. "Miracles." *The Stanford Encyclopedia of Philosophy*. Winter 2010 Edition. Edited by Edward N. Zalta. http://plato.stanford.edu/entries/miracles/.

Mchami, "Possession." Mchami, R. E. K. "Demon Possession and Exorcism in Mark 1:21–28." *AfThJ* 24 (1, 2001): 17–38.

McInerney, "Arrian and Romance." McInerney, Jeremy. "Arrian and the Greek Alexander Romance." *CW* 100 (4, 2007): 424–30.

McIntyre, "Baptism and Forgiveness." McIntyre, Luther B. "Baptism and Forgiveness in Acts 2:38." *BSac* 153 (609, 1996): 53–62.

McIver, "Eyewitnesses." McIver, Robert K. "Eyewitnesses as Guarantors of the Accuracy of the Gospel Traditions in the Light of Psychological Research." *JBL* 131 (3, 2012): 529–46.

McKay, "Foreign Gods?" McKay, K. L. "Foreign Gods Identified in Acts 17:18?" *TynBul* 45 (2, 1994): 411–12.

McKay, *Houses*. McKay, Alexander G. *Houses, Villas, and Palaces in the Roman World*. Ithaca, N.Y.: Cornell University Press, 1975.

McKeating, *Amos*. McKeating, Henry. *The Books of Amos, Hosea, and Micah*. CBC. Cambridge: Cambridge University Press, 1971.

McKechnie, "Embassies." McKechnie, Paul R. "Judaean Embassies and Cases before Roman Emperors, AD 44–66." *JTS* 56 (2, 2005): 339–61.

McKechnie, "Paul." McKechnie, Paul. "Paul among the Jews." Pages 103–23 in *All Things to All Cultures: Paul among Jews, Greeks, and Romans*. Edited by Mark Harding and Alanna Nobbs. Grand Rapids: Eerdmans, 2013.

McKelvey, "Cornerstone." McKelvey, R. J. "Christ the Cornerstone." *NTS* 8 (4, 1962): 352–59.

McKenna, *Miracles*. McKenna, Briege, with Henry Libersat. *Miracles Do Happen*. New York: St. Martin's Press, 1987.

McKenzie, "Glimpsing Alexandria." McKenzie, Judith S. "Glimpsing Alexandria from Archaeological Evidence." *JRA* 16 (2003): 35–63.

McKenzie, "Historiography." McKenzie, Steven L. "Historiography, Old Testament." *DOTHB* 418–25.

McKenzie, *Isaiah*. McKenzie, John L. *Second Isaiah: Introduction, Translation, and Notes*. AB 20. New York: Doubleday, 1968.

McKenzie, "Sculpture." McKenzie, Judith S. "The Development of Nabataean Sculpture at Petra and Khirbet Tannur." *PEQ* 120 (2, 1988): 81–107.

McKenzie, Gibson, and Reyes, "Reconstruction." McKenzie, Judith S., Sheila Gibson, and A. T. Reyes. "Reconstruction of the Nabataean Temple Complex at Khirbet et-Tannur." *PEQ* 134 (1, 2002): 44–83.

McKenzie, Gibson, and Reyes, "Serapeum." McKenzie, Judith S., Sheila Gibson, and A. T. Reyes. "Reconstructing the Serapeum in Alexandria from Archaeological Evidence." *JRS* 94 (2004): 73–121.

McKeown, "Blessings." McKeown, James. "Blessings and Curses." *DOTP* 83–87.

McKeown, "Land." McKeown, James. "Land, Fertility, Famine." *DOTP* 487–91.

McKim, "Self-Knowledge." McKim, Richard. "Socratic Self-Knowledge and 'Knowledge of Knowledge' in Plato's *Charmides*." *TAPA* 115 (1985): 59–77.

McKirahan, "Protagoras." McKirahan, Richard D., Jr. "Socrates and Protagoras on *sophrosyne* and Justice: *Protagoras* 333–334." *Apeiron* 18 (1984): 19–25.

McKnight, *Community*. McKnight, Scot. *A Community Called Atonement*. Nashville: Abingdon, 2007.

McKnight, *James*. McKnight, Scot. *The Letter of James*. NICNT. Grand Rapids: Eerdmans, 2011.

McKnight, *Light among Gentiles*. McKnight, Scot. *A Light among the Gentiles: Jewish Missionary Activity in the Second Temple Period*. Minneapolis: Fortress, 1991.

McKnight, "Proselytism." McKnight, Scot. "Proselytism and Godfearers." *DNTB* 835–47.

McKnight and Malbon, "Introduction." McKnight, Edgar V., and Elizabeth Struthers Malbon. Introduction. Pages 15–26 in *The New Literary Criticism and the New Testament*. Edited by Edgar V. McKnight and Elizabeth Struthers Malbon. Valley Forge, Pa.: Trinity Press International; Sheffield, U.K.: JSOT Press, 1994.

McKnight and Modica, *Caesar*. McKnight, Scot, and Joseph B. Modica. *Jesus Is Lord, Caesar Is Not: Evaluating Empire in New Testament Studies*. Downers Grove, Ill.: InterVarsity, 2013.

McLaren, "Ananus, James, and Christianity." McLaren, James S. "Ananus, James, and Earliest Christianity: Josephus' Account of the Death of James." *JTS* 52 (1, 2001): 1–25.

McLaren, "Jews and Cult." McLaren, James S. "Jews and the Imperial Cult: From Augustus to Domitian." *JSNT* 27 (3, 2005): 257–78.

McLaren, "Josephus' Summary Statements." McLaren, James S. "Josephus' Summary Statements regarding the Essenes, Pharisees, and Sadducees." *ABR* 48 (2000): 31–46.

McLaughlin, *Ethics*. McLaughlin, Raymond W. *The Ethics of Persuasive Preaching*. Grand Rapids: Baker, 1979.

McLean, "Correct View of Kingdom?" McLean, John A. "Did Jesus Correct the Disciples' View of the Kingdom?" *BSac* 151 (2, 1994): 215–27.

McNally, "Maenad." McNally, Sheila. "The Maenad in Early Greek Art." Pages 107–41 in *Women in the Ancient World: The Arethusa Papers*. Edited by John Peradotto and J. P. Sullivan. SSCS. Albany: State University of New York Press, 1984.

McNamara, *Judaism*. McNamara, Martin. *Palestinian Judaism and the New Testament*. GNS 4. Wilmington, Del.: Michael Glazier, 1983.

McNamara, "Melchizedek." McNamara, Martin. "Melchizedek: Gen 14,17–20 in the Targums, in Rabbinic and Early Christian Literature." *Bib* 81 (1, 2000): 1–31.

McNamara, "NovT." McNamara, Martin. "NovT et Targum Palaestinense ad Pentateuchum." *VD* 43 (6, 1965): 288–300.

McNamara, "Review." McNamara, Martin. Review of 2nd ed. of Joseph Fitzmyer, *The Genesis Apocryphon of Qumran Cave 1: A Commentary*. *ITQ* 40 (3, 1973): 283–85.

McNamara, *Targum*. McNamara, Martin. *Targum and Testament*. Grand Rapids: Eerdmans, 1972.

McNaughton, *Blacksmiths*. McNaughton, Patrick R. *The Mande Blacksmiths: Knowledge, Power, and Art in West Africa*. Bloomington: Indiana University Press, 1988.

McNelis, "Grammarians." McNelis, Charles. "Grammarians and Rhetoricians." Pages 285–96 in *A Companion to Roman Rhetoric*. Edited by William Dominik and Jon Hall. Oxford: Blackwell, 2007.

McNicol, "Temple." McNicol, Allan J. "The Eschatological Temple in the Qumran Pesher 4QFlorilegium 1:1–7." *OJRS* 5 (1977): 133–41.

McRay, "Antioch." McRay, John R. "Antioch on the Orontes." *DPL* 23–25.

McRay, *Archaeology*. McRay, John R. *Archaeology and the New Testament*. Grand Rapids: Baker, 1991.

McRay, "Archaeology and NT." McRay, John R. "Archaeology and the NT." *DNTB* 93–100.

McRay, "Athens." McRay, John R. "Athens." *DNTB* 139–40.

McRay, "Authorship." McRay, John. "The Authorship of the Pastoral Epistles: A Consideration of Certain Adverse Arguments to Pauline Authorship." *ResQ* 7 (1–2, 1963), 2–18.

McRay, "Caesarea Maritima." McRay, John R. "Caesarea Maritima." *DNTB* 176–77.

McRay, "Corinth." McRay, John R. "Corinth." *DNTB* 227–31.

McRay, "Cyprus." McRay, John R. "Cyprus." *ABD* 1:1228–30.

McRay, "Ephesus." McRay, John R. "Ephesus and the New Testament." *ABW* 1 (2, 1991): 8–9.

McRay, "Miletus." McRay, John. "Miletus." *ABD* 4:825–26.

McRay, "Thessalonica." McRay, John R. "Thessalonica." *DNTB* 1231–33.

McTavish, "Priest." McTavish, James. "The Priest and the Art of Ancient Rhetoric: Moral Character and the Practice of Rhetoric." *East Asian PastRev* 46 (3, 2009): 269–84.

McVeigh, "Possession." McVeigh, Brian. "Spirit Possession in Sukyo, Mahikari: A Variety of Sociopsychological Experience." *JapRel* 21 (2, 1996): 283–98.

McWhirter, *Prophets*. McWhirter, Jocelyn. *Rejected Prophets: Jesus and His Witnesses in Luke-Acts*. Minneapolis: Fortress, 2013.

Mead, "Opinion." Mead, Richard T. "A Dissenting Opinion about Respect for Context in Old Testament Quotations." *NTS* 10 (1, 1963): 279–89.

Meagher, "Paul's Experience." Meagher, P. M. "Paul's Experience of the Risen Lord: Reflections on Mission, Persecution, and Religio-cultural Loyalty." *Jeev* 34 (200, 2004): 146–61.

Meagher, "Pentecost Spirit." Meagher, P. M. "Pentecost Spirit: To Witness." *Vid* 62 (4, 1998): 273–79.

Meagher, "Twig." Meagher, John C. "As the Twig Was Bent: Antisemitism in Greco-Roman and Earliest Christian Times." Pages 1–26 in *Antisemitism and the Foundations of Christianity*. Edited by Alan T. Davies. New York: Paulist, 1979.

Mealand, "Close and Vocabulary." Mealand, David L. "The Close of Acts and Its Hellenistic Greek Vocabulary." *NTS* 36 (4, 1990): 583–97.

Mealand, "Community of Goods at Qumran." Mealand, David L. "Community of Goods at Qumran." *TZ* 31 (3, 1975): 129–39.

Mealand, "Dissimilarity Test." Mealand, David L. "Dissimilarity Test." *SJT* 31 (1978): 41–50.

Mealand, "Extent." Mealand, David L. "The Extent of the Pauline Corpus: A Multivariate Approach." *JSNT* 59 (1995): 61–92.

Mealand, "Historians and Style." Mealand, David L. "Hellenistic Historians and the Style of Acts." *ZNW* 82 (1–2, 1991): 42–66.

Mealand, "Many Proofs." Mealand, David L. "The Phrase 'Many Proofs' in Acts 1,3 and in Hellenistic Writers." *ZNW* 80 (1–2, 1989): 134–35.

Mealand, "Not Many Days." Mealand, David L. "'After Not Many Days' in Acts 1.5 and Its Hellenistic Context." *JSNT* 42 (1991): 69–77.

Mealand, "Paradox." Mealand, David L. "The Paradox of Philo's Views on Wealth." *JSNT* 24 (1985): 111–15.

Mealand, "Philo's Attitude." Mealand, David L. "Philo of Alexandria's Attitude to Riches." *ZNW* 69 (1978): 258–64.

Mealand, "Utopian Allusions." Mealand, David L. "Community of Goods and Utopian Allusions in Acts II–IV." *JTS,* n.s., 28 (1, 1977): 97–99.

Mealand, "Verbs." Mealand, David L. "Luke-Acts and the Verbs of Dionysius of Halicarnassus." *JSNT* 63 (1996): 63–86.

Meban, "Eclogues." Meban, David. "Virgil's Eclogues and Social Memory." *AJP* 130 (1, 2009): 99–130.

Mediavilla, "Oración de Jesús." Mediavilla, R. "La oración de Jesús en el tercer evangelio." *Mayéutica* 4 (10, 1978): 5–34. (Abstract: *NTA* 24:135–36.)

Mee and Rice, "Rhodes." Mee, Christopher B., and Ellen E. Rice. "Rhodes." *OCD*³ 1315–16.

Meek, *Mission*. Meek, James A. *The Gentile Mission in Old Testament Citations in Acts: Text, Hermeneutic and Purpose.* LNTS 385. New York: T&T Clark, 2008.

Meeks, "Agent." Meeks, Wayne A. "The Divine Agent and His Counterfeit in Philo and the Fourth Gospel." Pages 43–67 in *Aspects of Religious Propaganda in Judaism and Early Christianity.* Edited by Elisabeth Schüssler Fiorenza. UNDCSJCA 2. Notre Dame, Ind.: University of Notre Dame Press, 1976.

Meeks, "Aliens." Meeks, Wayne A. "Corinthian Christians as Artificial Aliens." Pages 129–38 in *Paul beyond the Judaism/Hellenism Divide.* Edited by Troels Engberg-Pedersen. Louisville: Westminster John Knox, 2001.

Meeks, "Androgyne." Meeks, Wayne A. "The Image of the Androgyne: Some Uses of a Symbol in Earliest Christianity." *HR* 13 (3, 1974): 165–208.

Meeks, "Birth." Meeks, Wayne A. "Judaism, Hellenism, and the Birth of Christianity." Pages 17–27 in *Paul beyond the Judaism/Hellenism Divide.* Edited by Troels Engberg-Pedersen. Louisville: Westminster John Knox, 2001.

Meeks, "Foreword." Meeks, Wayne A. Foreword. Pages 9–10 in *From the Maccabees to the Mishnah.* By Shaye J. D. Cohen. LEC 7. Philadelphia: Westminster, 1987.

Meeks, "Hypomnēmata." Meeks, Wayne A. "Hypomnēmata from an Untamed Sceptic: A Response to George Kennedy." Pages 157–72 in *The Relationships among the Gospels: An Interdisciplinary Dialogue.* Edited by William O. Walker Jr. San Antonio: Trinity University Press, 1978.

Meeks, "Jew." Meeks, Wayne A. "'Am I a Jew?'—Johannine Christianity and Judaism." Pages 163–86 in vol. 1 of *Christianity, Judaism, and Other Greco-Roman Cults: Studies for Morton Smith at Sixty.* Edited by Jacob Neusner. 4 vols. SJLA 12. Leiden: Brill, 1975.

Meeks, *Moral World.* Meeks, Wayne A. *The Moral World of the First Christians.* LEC 6. Philadelphia: Westminster, 1986.

Meeks, *Prophet-King.* Meeks, Wayne A. *The Prophet-King: Moses Traditions and the Johannine Christology.* NovTSup 14. Leiden: Brill, 1967.

Meeks, *Urban Christians.* Meeks, Wayne A. *The First Urban Christians: The Social World of the Apostle Paul.* New Haven: Yale University Press, 1983.

Meeks, "Why Study?" Meeks, Wayne A. "Why Study the New Testament?" *NTS* 51 (2, 2005): 155–70.

Meeks and Fitzgerald, *Writings.* Meeks, Wayne A., and John T. Fitzgerald, eds. *The Writings of St. Paul: Annotated Texts, Reception, and Criticism.* 2nd ed. NortCE. New York: W. W. Norton, 2007.

Meeks and Wilken, *Antioch.* Meeks, Wayne A., and Robert L. Wilken. *Jews and Christians in Antioch in the First Four Centuries of the Common Era.* SBLSBS 13. Missoula, Mont.: Scholars Press, 1978.

Meester, "Pèlerin d'Éthiopie." Meester, Paul de. "Le pèlerin d'Éthiopie: Essai d'une interprétation 'africaine' des Actes 8,26–40." *Telema* 18 (1979): 5–18.

Meester, "Philippe et l'eunuque." Meester, Paul de. "'Philippe et l'eunuque éthiopien' ou 'Le baptême d'un pèlerin de Nubie'?" *NRTh* 103 (3, 1981): 360–74.

Meggitt, "Madness." Meggitt, Justin J. "The Madness of King Jesus: Why Was Jesus Put to Death, but His Followers Were Not?" *JSNT* 29 (4, 2007): 379–413.

Meggitt, "Meat Consumption." Meggitt, Justin J. "Meat Consumption and Social Conflict in Corinth." *JTS* 45 (1, 1994): 137–41.

Meggitt, *Poverty.* Meggitt, Justin J. *Paul, Poverty, and Survival.* Edinburgh: T&T Clark, 1998.

Meggitt, "Status of Erastus." Meggitt, Justin J. "The Social Status of Erastus (Rom. 16:23)." *NovT* 38 (3, 1996): 218–23.

Mehl, "Asiarchy." Mehl, Andreas. "Asiarchy." *BrillPauly* 2:157.

Meier, "Angels." Meier, Samuel A. "Angels, Messengers, Heavenly Beings." Pages 24–29 in *Dictionary of the Old Testament Prophets.* Edited by Mark J. Boda and J. Gordon McConville. Downers Grove, Ill.: IVP Academic, 2012.

Meier, "Circle of Twelve." Meier, John P. "The Circle of the Twelve: Did It Exist during Jesus' Public Ministry?" *JBL* 116 (3, 1997): 635–72.

Meier, "Halaka." Meier, John P. "Is There *halaka* (the Noun) at Qumran?" *JBL* 122 (1, 2003): 150–55.

Meier, "Jesus in Josephus." Meier, John P. "Jesus in Josephus: A Modest Proposal." *CBQ* 52 (1, 1990): 76–103.

Meier, "John the Baptist." Meier, John P. "John the Baptist in Josephus: Philology and Exegesis." *JBL* 111 (2, 1992): 225–37.

Meier, *Marginal Jew.* Meier, John P. *A Marginal Jew: Rethinking the Historical Jesus.* 4 vols. ABRL. New York: Doubleday, 1991–.

Meier, *Matthew.* Meier, John P. *Matthew.* NTM 3. Wilmington, Del.: Michael Glazier, 1980.

Meier, "Quest." Meier, John P. "The Quest for the Historical Jesus as a Truly Historical Project." *Grail* 12 (3, 1996): 43–52.

Meier, "Reflections." Meier, John P. "Reflections on Jesus-of-History Research Today." Pages 84–107 in *Jesus' Jewishness: Exploring the Place of Jesus within Early Judaism.* Edited by James H. Charlesworth. Philadelphia: American Interfaith Institute; New York: Crossroad, 1991.

Meier, "Samaritans." Meier, John P. "The Historical Jesus and the Historical Samaritans: What Can Be Said?" *Bib* 81 (2, 2000): 202–32.

Meier, "Signs." Meier, Samuel A. "Signs and Wonders." *DOTP* 755–62.

Meier, "Testimonium." Meier, John P. "The Testimonium, Evidence for Jesus outside the Bible." *BRev* 7 (3, 1991): 20–25, 45.

Meier, "Third Quest." Meier, John P. "The Present State of the 'Third Quest' for the Historical Jesus: Loss and Gain." *Bib* 80 (4, 1999): 459–87.

Meier, *Vision.* Meier, John P. *The Vision of Matthew: Christ, Church, and Morality in the First Gospel.* Theological Inquiries. New York: Paulist, 1979.

Meiggs, Gallina, and Claridge, *Roman Ostia.* Meiggs, Russell, Anna Gallina, and Amanda Claridge. *"Roman Ostia" Revisited: Archaeological and Historical Papers in Memory of Russell Meiggs.* London: British School at Rome, in collaboration with the Soprintendenza archeologica di Ostia, 1996.

Meijer, "Philosophers." Meijer, P. A. "Philosophers, Intellectuals, and Religion in Hellas." Pages 216–62 in *Faith, Hope, and Worship: Aspects of Religious Mentality in the Ancient World.* Edited by H. S. Versnel. SGRR 2. Leiden: Brill, 1981.

Meinardus, "Shipwrecked in Dalmatia." Meinardus, Otto F. A. "St. Paul Shipwrecked in Dalmatia." *BA* 39 (4, 1976): 145–47.

Meinardus, "Traditions." Meinardus, Otto F. A. "Dalmatian and Catalanian Traditions about St. Paul's Journeys." *EkkPhar* 61 (1–4, 1979): 221–30.

Meinwald, "Ignorance." Meinwald, Constance. "Ignorance and Opinion in Stoic Epistemology." *Phronesis* 50 (3, 2005): 215–31.

Meirovich, "Crisis." Meirovich, Harvey. "Handling Crisis: An Aggadic Response." *ConsJud* 49 (2, 1997): 56–67.

Meiser, "Gattung." Meiser, Martin. "Gattung, Adressaten und Intention von Philos 'In Flaccum.'" *JSJ* 30 (4, 1999): 418–30.

Meister, "Ephorus." Meister, Klaus. "Ephorus." *BrillPauly* 4:1035–36.

Meister, "Genealogy." Meister, Klaus. "Genealogy: Greece." *BrillPauly* 5:747.

Meister, "Herodotus." Meister, Klaus. "Herodotus." *BrillPauly* 6:265–71.

Meister, "Historiography: Greece." Meister, Klaus. "Historiography: Greece." *BrillPauly* 6:418–21.

Meister, "Lindian Chronicle." Meister, Klaus. "Lindian Chronicle." *BrillPauly* 7:607–8.

Meister, "Local Chronicles." Meister, Klaus. "Local Chronicles, Local History." *BrillPauly* 7:762–63.

Meister, "Theopompus." Meister, Klaus. "Theopompus." *OCD*³ 1505–6.

Meister, "Thermae." Meister, Klaus. "Thermae." *BrillPauly* 14:536–49.

Mekacher and van Haeperen, "Choix." Mekacher, Nina, and Françoise van Haeperen. "Le choix des vestales, miroir d'une société en évolution (IIIe s. a. C.–Ier s. p. C.)." *RHR* 220 (1, 2003): 63–80.

Mekkattukunnel, *Blessing*. Mekkattukunnel, Andrews George. *Priestly Blessing of the Risen Christ: An Exegetico-theological Analysis of Luke 24,50–53*. New York: Peter Lang, 2001.

Mekkattukunnel, "Proof for Unity." Mekkattukunnel, Andrews George. "Further Proof for the Unity of Luke-Acts." *BiBh* 29 (3, 2003): 221–29.

Melbourne, "Acts 1:8." Melbourne, Bertram L. "Acts 1:8 Re-examined: Is Acts 8 Its Fulfillment?" *JRT* 57 (2, 2001)/58 (1–2, 2005): 1–18.

Melbourne, "End of Earth." Melbourne, Bertram L. "Acts 1:8: Where on Earth Is the End of the Earth?" Pages 1–14 in *2000 Years of Christianity in Africa*. Edited by Emory J. Tolbert. N.p.: Sabbath in Africa Study Group, 2005.

Melbourne, "Gospel in Africa." Melbourne, Bertram L. "Acts 1:8 and the Gospel in Africa." Pages 15–28 in *2000 Years of Christianity in Africa*. Edited by Emory J. Tolbert. N.p.: Sabbath in Africa Study Group, 2005.

Melchert, "Lycian Language." Melchert, H. Craig. "Lycian Language." *OCD*³ 895.

Melchior, "Pompey." Melchior, Aislinn. "What Would Pompey Do? *Exempla* and Pompeian Failure in the *Bellum Africum*." *CJ* 104 (3, 2009): 241–57.

Mellor, *Tacitus*. Mellor, Ronald. *Tacitus*. London: Routledge, 1993.

Melzer-Keller, "Frauen." Melzer-Keller, Helga. "Frauen in der Apostelgeschichte." *BK* 55 (2, 2000): 87–91.

Mena, Padilla, and Maldonado, "Stress." Mena, Francisco J., Amado M. Padilla, and Margarita Maldonado. "Acculturative Stress and Specific Coping Strategies among Immigrant and Later Generation College Students." *HisJBehSc* 9 (1987): 207–25.

Mena Salas, "Condiciones." Mena Salas, Enrique. "Condiciones para una misión cristiana a los gentiles en el entorno sirio: El ejemplo de Antioquía." *EstBib* 64 (2, 2006): 163–99.

Ménard, "Messianic Title." Ménard, Jacques E. "*Pais Theou* as Messianic Title in the Book of Acts." *CBQ* 19 (1957): 83–92.

Ménard, "Self-Definition." Ménard, Jacques E. "Normative Self-Definition in Gnosticism." Pages 134–50 in *The Shaping of Christianity in the Second and Third Centuries*. Vol. 1 of *Jewish and Christian Self-Definition*. Edited by E. P. Sanders. Philadelphia: Fortress, 1980.

Menberu, "Abraham." Menberu, Dirshaye. "Emmanuel Abraham." No pages. *DACB*. Online: http://www.dacb.org/stories /ethiopia/emmanuel_abraham.html.

Menberu, "Estifanos." Menberu, Dirshaye. "Abba Estifanos." No pages. *DACB*. Online: http://www.dacb.org/stories /ethiopia/estifanos_.html.

Menberu, "Mekonnen Negera." Menberu, Dirshaye. "Mekonnen Negera." No pages. *DACB*. Online: http://www.dacb.org /stories/ethiopia/mekonnen_negera .html.

Menberu, "Regassa Feysa." Menberu, Dirshaye. "Regassa Feysa." No pages. *DACB*. Online: http://www.dacb.org/stories /ethiopia/regassa_feysa.html.

Mendell, *Tacitus*. Mendell, C. W. *Tacitus: The Man and His Work*. New Haven: Yale University Press, 1957.

Mendels, "Five Empires." Mendels, Doron. "The Five Empires: A Note on a Propagandistic *topos*." *AJP* 102 (3, 1981): 330–37.

Mendels, "Rejection." Mendels, Doron. "Was the Rejection of Gifts One of the Reasons for the Outbreak of the Maccabean Revolt? A Preliminary Note on the Role of Gifting in the Book of 1 Maccabees." *JSP* 20 (4, 2011): 243–56.

Mendels, "Revolt." Mendels, Doron. "First Jewish Revolt." *OEANE* 2:313–15.

Mendels, "Utopia and Essenes." Mendels, Doron. "Hellenistic Utopia and the Essenes." *HTR* 72 (3–4, 1979): 207–22.

Mendelsohn, "Slavery." Mendelsohn, Isaac. "Slavery in the Ancient Near East." *BA* 9 (3, 1946): 78–88.

Mendenhall, "Covenant Forms." Mendenhall, George E. "Covenant Forms in Israelite Traditions." *BA* 17 (3, 1954): 50–76.

Mendenhall, "Mari." Mendenhall, George E. "Mari." *BA* 11 (1, 1948): 1–19.

Méndez-Moratalla, *Paradigm*. Méndez-Moratalla, Fernando. *The Paradigm of Conversion in Luke*. JSNTSup 252. London: T&T Clark, 2004.

Menken, *Techniques*. Menken, M. J. J. *Numerical Literary Techniques in John: The Fourth Evangelist's Use of Numbers of Words and Syllables*. NovTSup 55. Leiden: Brill, 1985.

Menoud, "Actes et l'Eucharistie." Menoud, Philippe-Henri. "Les Actes des apôtres et l'Eucharistie." *RHPR* 33 (1953): 21–36.

Menoud, "Pentecôte." Menoud, Philippe-Henri. "La Pentecôte lucanienne et l'histoire." *RHPR* 42 (2–3, 1962): 141–47.

Menoud, "Plan des Actes." Menoud, Philippe-Henri. "Le plan des Actes des apôtres." *NTS* 1 (1, 1954): 44–51.

Mensah, "Basis." Mensah, Felix Augustine. "The Spiritual Basis of Health and Illness in Africa." Pages 171–80 in *Health Knowledge and Belief Systems in Africa*. Edited by Toyin Falola and Matthew M. Heaton. Durham, N.C.: Carolina Academic Press, 2008.

Menzies, *Anointed*. Menzies, William W. *Anointed to Serve: The Story of the Assemblies of God*. Springfield, Mo.: Gospel, 1971.

Menzies, *Development*. Menzies, Robert P. *The Development of Early Christian Pneumatology with Special Reference to Luke-Acts*. JSNTSup 54. Sheffield, U.K.: Sheffield Academic, 1991.

Menzies, *Empowered*. Menzies, Robert P. *Empowered for Witness: The Spirit in Luke-Acts*. London: T&T Clark, 2004.

Menzies, "Issue." Menzies, William W. "The Initial Evidence Issue: A Pentecostal Response." *AJPS* 2 (2, 1999): 261–78.

Menzies, "John's Place." Menzies, Robert P. "John's Place in the Development of Early Christian Pneumatology." Pages 41–52 in *The Spirit and Spirituality: Essays in Honor of Russell P. Spittler*. Edited by Wonsuk Ma and Robert P. Menzies. JPTSup 24. London: T&T Clark, 2004.

Menzies, "Occurrences." Menzies, Glen. "Pre-Lukan Occurrences of the Phrase 'Tongue(s) of Fire.'" *Pneuma* 22 (1, 2000): 27–60.

Menzies, "Paradigm." Menzies, Robert P. "Acts 2.17–21: A Paradigm for Pentecostal Mission." *JPT* 17 (2, 2008): 200–218.

Menzies, "Power." Menzies, Robert P. "Spirit and Power in Luke-Acts: A Response to Max Turner." *JSNT* 49 (1993): 11–20.

Menzies, "Sending." Menzies, Robert P. "The Sending of the Seventy and Luke's Purpose." Pages 87–113 in *Trajectories in the Book of Acts: Essays in Honor of John Wesley Wyckoff.* Edited by Paul Alexander, Jordan Daniel May, and Robert G. Reid. Eugene, Ore.: Wipf & Stock, 2010.

Menzies, "Tongues." Menzies, Robert P. "Evidential Tongues: An Essay on Theological Method." *AJPS* 1 (2, 1998): 111–23.

Menzies, "Universality." Menzies, Robert P. "Paul and the Universality of Tongues: A Response to Max Turner." *AJPS* 2 (2, 1999): 283–95.

Merenlahti, *Poetics.* Merenlahti, Petri. *Poetics for the Gospels? Rethinking Narrative Criticism.* Studies of the New Testament and Its World. New York and London: T&T Clark, 2002.

Merenlahti and Hakola, "Reconceiving." Merenlahti, Petri, and Raimo Hakola. "Reconceiving Narrative Criticism." Pages 13–48 in *Characterization in the Gospels: Reconceiving Narrative Criticism.* Edited by David Rhoads and K. Syreeni. JSNTSup 184. Sheffield, U.K.: Sheffield Academic, 1999.

Meritt, *Inscriptions.* Meritt, Benjamin Dean. *Greek Inscriptions, 1896–1927.* Vol. 8, part 1, of *Corinth: Results of Excavations Conducted by the American School of Classical Studies at Athens.* Cambridge, Mass.: Harvard University Press, 1931.

Merkelbach, *Inschriften von Assos.* Merkelbach, Reinhold, ed. *Die Inschriften von Assos.* IGSK 4. Bonn: Rudolf Habelt, 1976.

Merkelbach, *Mysterium.* Merkelbach, Reinhold. *Roman und Mysterium in der Antike.* Munich: Beck, 1962.

Merkelbach, "Novel and Aretalogy." Merkelbach, Reinhold. "Novel and Aretalogy." Pages 283–95 in *The Search for the Ancient Novel.* Edited by James Tatum. Baltimore: Johns Hopkins University Press, 1994.

Merkelbach, "Osiris-Fest." Merkelbach, Reinhold. "Das Osiris-Fest des 24./25. Dezember in Rom." *Aeg* 49 (1–4, 1969): 89–91.

Merker, *Sanctuary.* Merker, Gloria S. *The Sanctuary of Demeter and Kore: Terracotta Figurines of the Classical, Hellenistic, and Roman Periods.* Vol. 18, part 4, of *Corinth: Results of Excavations Conducted by the American School of Classical Studies at Athens.* Princeton: American School of Classical Studies at Athens, 2000.

Merkle, *Elder.* Merkle, Benjamin L. *The Elder and Overseer: One Office in the Early Church.* Studies in Biblical Literature 57. New York: Lang, 2003.

Merkle, "True Story." Merkle, Stefan. "Telling the True Story of the Trojan War: The Eyewitness Account of Dictys of Crete." Pages 183–96 in *The Search for the Ancient Novel.* Edited by James Tatum. Baltimore: Johns Hopkins University Press, 1994.

Merola, "Letters." Merola, Marco. "Letters to the Crocodile God." *Archaeology* 60 (6, 2007): 22–27.

Merriam, *Anthropology of Music.* Merriam, Alan P. *The Anthropology of Music.* Chicago: Northwestern University Press, 1964.

Merrill, "450 Years." Merrill, Eugene H. "Paul's Use of 'About 450 Years' in Acts 13:20." *BSac* 138 (551, 1981): 246–57.

Merrill, "Image." Merrill, Eugene H. "Image of God." *DOTP* 441–45.

Merritt, "Barabbas." Merritt, Robert L. "Jesus Barabbas and the Paschal Pardon." *JBL* 104 (1, 1985): 57–68.

Merz, "Importunate Widow." Merz, Annette. "How a Woman Who Fought Back and Demanded Her Rights Became an Importunate Widow: The Transformations of a Parable of Jesus." Pages 49–86 in *Jesus from Judaism to Christianity: Continuum Approaches to the Historical Jesus.* Edited by Tom Holmén. EurSCO. LNTS 352. London: T&T Clark, 2007.

Merz, "Witch." Merz, Johannes. "'I Am a Witch in the Holy Spirit': Rupture and Continuity of Witchcraft Beliefs in African Christianity." *Missiology* 36 (2, Apr. 2008): 201–17.

Meshel, "Rock." Meshel, Ze'ev. "The Nabataean 'Rock' and the Judaean Desert Fortresses." *IEJ* 50 (1–2, 2000): 109–15.

Meshorer, "Sacrifice." Meshorer, Ya'akov. "A Samaritan Syncretistic Passover Sacrifice on a Coin of Neapolis." *IsNumJ* 14 (2000–2002): 194–95 and plate 21.

Messineo and Borgia, *Ancient Sicily.* Messineo, G., and E. Borgia. *Ancient Sicily: Monuments Past and Present.* Rome: Vision, 2005.

Messing, "Zar Cult." Messing, Simon D. "Group Therapy and Social Status in the *zar* Cult of Ethiopia." *AmAnth* 60 (6, 1958): 1120–47.

Messner, "Soteriologie." Messner, S. "Paulinischer Soteriologie und die 'Aqedat Jitzschaq." *Judaica* 51 (1, 1995): 33–49.

Metaxas, *Grace.* Metaxas, Eric. *Amazing Grace: William Wilberforce and the Heroic Campaign to End Slavery.* Foreword by Floyd H. Flake. San Francisco: HarperSanFrancisco, 2007.

Méthy, "Monde." Méthy, Nicole. "Le monde romain dans les lettres de Pline le Jeun: espace et valeurs." *Mnemosyne* 62 (2, 2009): 237–49.

Metzger, "Antioch-on-Orontes." Metzger, Bruce M. "Antioch-on-the-Orontes." *BA* 11 (4, 1948): 69–88.

Metzger, "Astrological Geography." Metzger, Bruce M. "Ancient Astrological Geography and Acts 2:9–11." Pages 123–33 in *Apostolic History and the Gospel: Biblical and Historical Essays Presented to F. F. Bruce on His 60th Birthday.* Grand Rapids: Eerdmans; Exeter, U.K.: Paternoster, 1970. Repr., pages 46–56 in *New Testament Studies: Philological, Versional, and Patristic.* NTTS 10. Leiden: Brill, 1980.

Metzger, "Considerations." Metzger, Bruce M. "Considerations of Methodology in the Study of the Mystery Religions and Early Christianity." *HTR* 48 (1, 1955): 1–20.

Metzger, "Forgeries." Metzger, Bruce M. "Literary Forgeries and Canonical Pseudepigrapha." *JBL* 91 (1, 1972): 3–24.

Metzger, *Outline.* Metzger, Ernest. *A New Outline of the Roman Civil Trial.* Oxford: Clarendon, 1997.

Metzger, "Papyri." Metzger, Bruce M. "Recently Published Greek Papyri of the New Testament." *BA* 10 (2, May 1947): 25–44.

Metzger, "Reconsideration." Metzger, Bruce M. "A Reconsideration of Certain Arguments against the Pauline Authorship of the Pastoral Epistles." *ExpT* 70 (3, 1958): 91–94.

Metzger, *Revelation.* Metzger, Bruce M. *Breaking the Code: Understanding the Book of Revelation.* Nashville: Abingdon, 1993.

Metzger, "Seventy." Metzger, Bruce M. "Seventy or Seventy-Two Disciples?" *NTS* 5 (4, 1959): 299–306.

Metzger, *Text.* Metzger, Bruce M. *The Text of the New Testament.* New York: Oxford University Press, 1968.

Metzger, *Textual Commentary.* Metzger, Bruce M. *A Textual Commentary on the Greek New Testament.* Corrected ed. New York: United Bible Societies, 1975.

Metzger, "Translation." Metzger, Bruce M. "On the Translation of John i.1." *ExpT* 63 (4, 1952): 125–26.

Meunier, "Dieu chrétien." Meunier, Bernard. "Le dieu chrétien et le divin païen dans l'antiquité." *LumVie* 49 (245, 2000): 59–67.

Mews, "Revival." Mews, Stuart. "The Revival of Spiritual Healing in the Church of England, 1920–26." Pages 299–331 in *The Church and Healing: Papers Read* at the Twentieth Summer Meeting and the Twenty-First Winter Meeting of the Ecclesiastical History Society. Edited by W. J. Sheils. Oxford: Blackwell, 1982.

Meyer, "Evidence." Meyer, Stephen C. "Evidence for Design in Physics and Biology: From the Origin of the Universe to the Origin of Life." Pages 53–111 in Science and Evidence for Design in the Universe. By Michael J. Behe, William A. Dembski, and Stephen C. Meyer. Proceedings of the Wethersfield Institute 9. San Francisco: Ignatius, 2000.

Meyer, Realism. Meyer, Ben F. Critical Realism and the New Testament. PrTMS 17. Allison Park, Penn.: Pickwick, 1989.

Meyer, "Scientific Status." Meyer, Stephen C. "The Scientific Status of Intelligent Design: The Methodological Equivalence of Naturalistic and Non-naturalistic Origins Theories." Pages 151–211 in Science and Evidence for Design in the Universe. By Michael J. Behe, William A. Dembski, and Stephen C. Meyer. Proceedings of the Wethersfield Institute 9. San Francisco: Ignatius, 2000.

Meyer, Ursprung. Meyer, Eduard. Ursprung und Anfänge des Christentums. 3 vols. Stuttgart: J. G. Cotta, 1921–23.

Meyers, "Challenge." Meyers, Eric M. "The Challenge of Hellenism for Early Judaism and Christianity." BA 55 (2, 1992): 84–91.

Meyers, "Gendered Space." Meyers, Eric M. "The Problem of Gendered Space in Syro-Palestinian Domestic Architecture: The Case of Roman-Period Galilee." Pages 44–69 in Early Christian Families in Context: An Interdisciplinary Dialogue. Edited by David L. Balch and Carolyn Osiek. Grand Rapids and Cambridge: Eerdmans, 2003.

Meyers, "Judaism and Christianity." Meyers, Eric M. "Early Judaism and Christianity in the Light of Archaeology." BA 51 (2, 1988): 69–79.

Meyers, "Regionalism." Meyers, Eric M. "Galilean Regionalism as a Factor in Historical Reconstruction." BASOR 221 (Feb. 1976): 93–101.

Meyers, "State." Meyers, Eric M. "The Current State of Galilean Synagogues Studies." Pages 127–37 in The Synagogue in Late Antiquity. Edited by Lee I. Levine. Philadelphia: American Schools of Oriental Research, 1986.

Meyers, "Synagogue." Meyers, Eric M. "Synagogue." ABD 6:251–60.

Meyers, "Synagogues." Meyers, Eric M. "Ancient Synagogues in Galilee: Their Religious and Cultural Setting." BA 43 (2, 1980): 97–108.

Meyers and Kraabel, "Remains." Meyers, Eric M., and A. Thomas Kraabel. "Archaeology, Iconography, and Nonliterary Written Remains." Pages 175–210 in Early Judaism and Its Modern Interpreters. Edited by Robert A. Kraft and George W. E. Nickelsburg. SBLBMI 2. Atlanta: Scholars Press, 1986.

Meyers and Meyers, "Sepphoris." Meyers, Carol L., and Eric M. Meyers. "Sepphoris." OEANE 4:527–36.

Meyers and Strange, Archaeology. Meyers, Eric M., and James F. Strange. Archaeology, the Rabbis, and Early Christianity. Nashville: Abingdon, 1981.

Meyer-Schwelling, "Light." Meyer-Schwelling, Stefan. "Light, Metaphysics of." BrillPauly 7:550.

Meyshan, "Coin Type of Agrippa." Meyshan, Joseph. "A New Coin Type of Agrippa II and Its Meaning." IEJ 11 (4, 1961): 181–83.

Meyshan, "Coins." Meyshan, Joseph. "Jewish Coins in Ancient Historiography: The Importance of Numismatics for the History of Israel." PEQ 96 (1964): 46–52.

Miccoli, "Spirito festivo." Miccoli, Paolo. "Lo spirito festivo della religione greco-romana." EunDoc 55 (3, 2002): 125–27.

Michael, "Gäbrä-Seyon." Michael, Belaynesh. "Gäbrä-Seyon." No pages. DACB. Online: http://www.dacb.org/stories/ethiopia/gabra_seyon.html.

Michael, Philippians. Michael, J. Hugh. The Epistle of Paul to the Philippians. MNTC. London: Hodder & Stoughton, 1928.

Michaels, "Evidences." Michaels, J. Ramsey. "Evidences of the Spirit, or the Spirit as Evidence? Some Non-Pentecostal Reflections." Pages 202–18 in Initial Evidence: Historical and Biblical Perspectives on the Pentecostal Doctrine of Spirit Baptism. Edited by Gary B. McGee. Peabody, Mass.: Hendrickson, 1991.

Michaels, John. Michaels, J. Ramsey. John. GNC. San Francisco: Harper & Row, 1984.

Michaels, "Pairs and Parallels." Michaels, J. Ramsey. "Pairs and Parallels: Jesus and Inclusive Language." DaughSar 11 (2, 1985): 7–10.

Michaels, "Paul and Baptist." Michaels, J. Ramsey. "Paul and John the Baptist: An Odd Couple?" TynBul 42 (2, 1991): 245–60.

Michaels, "Paul in Tradition." Michaels, J. Ramsey. "Paul in Early Church Tradition." DPL 692–95.

Michaels, Revelation. Michaels, J. Ramsey. Revelation. IVPNTC. Downers Grove, Ill.: InterVarsity, 1997.

Michaels, Servant. Michaels, J. Ramsey. Servant and Son: Jesus in Parable and Gospel. Atlanta: John Knox, 1981.

Michaelsen, "Ecstasy." Michaelsen, Peter. "Ecstasy and Possession in Ancient Israel. A Review of Some Recent Contributions." SJOT 2 (1989): 28–54.

Michalopoulos, "Attempts." Michalopoulos, Andreas N. "Lucius' Suicide Attempts in Apuleius' Metamorphoses." CQ 52 (2, 2002): 538–48.

Michalowski, "Christianity in Nubia." Michalowski, K. "The Spreading of Christianity in Nubia." Pages 326–40 in Ancient Civilizations of Africa. Edited by G. Mokhtar. General History of Africa 2. Berkeley: University of California Press; London: Heinemann Educational; Paris: United Nations Educational, Scientific and Cultural Organization, 1981.

Michel, Abschiedsrede. Michel, Hans-Joachim. Die Abschiedsrede des Paulus an die Kirche Apg 20 17–38. SANT 35. Munich: Kösel, 1973.

Michel, "Annäherungen." Michel, Karl-Heinz. "'In keinem andern ist das Heil' (Apg 4,12): Annäherungen an eine christologische Spitzenaussage des Neuen Testament." TBei 43 (2, 2012): 129–36.

Michel, "Eutyches." Michel, Simone. "Eutyches (1)." BrillPauly 5:240.

Michel, Maître. Michel, A. Le maître de justice d'après les documents de la mer Morte, la littérature apocryphe et rabbinique. Avignon: Aubanel Père, 1954.

Michel, Bellegarde-Smith, and Racine-Toussaint, "Mouths." Michel, Claudine, Patrick Bellegarde-Smith, and Marlène Racine-Toussaint. "From the Horses' Mouths: Women's Words/Women's Worlds." Pages 70–83 in Haitian Vodou: Spirit, Myth, and Reality. Edited by Patrick Bellegarde-Smith and Claudine Michel. Bloomington: Indiana University Press, 2006.

Mickelsen, Interpreting. Mickelsen, A. Berkeley. Interpreting the Bible. Grand Rapids: Eerdmans, 1963.

"Midas: Historical." "Midas: Historical." BrillPauly 8:856–57.

Middleton, "Growth." Middleton, V. J. "Church Growth in Tribal India." MA thesis, Fuller Theological Seminary, 1972.

Middleton, "Possession." Middleton, John. "Spirit Possession among the Lugbara." Pages 220–32 in Spirit Mediumship and Society in Africa. Edited by John Beattie and John Middleton. Foreword by Raymond Firth. New York: Africana, 1969.

Midelfort, "Possession." Midelfort, H. C. Erik. "The Devil and the German People: Reflections on the Popularity of Demon Possession in Sixteenth-Century Germany." Pages 113–33 in Possession and Exorcism. Edited by Brian P. Levack. Articles on Witchcraft, Magic, and Demonology 9. New York: Garland, 1992.

Mielcarek, "Język." Mielcarek, Krzysztof. "Język Septuaginty i jego wpływ na autora Trzeciej Ewangelii." *RocT* 49 (1, 2002): 33–47.

Mierse, "Architecture." Mierse, William Edwin. "The Architecture of the Lost Temple of Hercules Gaditanus and Its Levantine Associations." *AJA* 108 (4, 2004): 545–75.

Miesner, "Narrative." Miesner, Donald A. "The Missionary Journeys Narrative: Patterns and Implications." Pages 199–214 in *Perspectives on Luke-Acts*. ABPRSSS 5. Edited by Charles H. Talbert. Danville, Va.: Association of Baptist Professors of Religion; Edinburgh: T&T Clark, 1978.

Míguez-Bonino, "Acts 2." Míguez-Bonino, José. "Acts 2:1–42: A Latin American Perspective." Pages 161–65 in *Return to Babel: Global Perspectives on the Bible*. Edited by John R. Levison and Priscilla Pope-Levison. Louisville: Westminster John Knox, 1999.

Mihaila, "Relationship." Mihaila, Corin. "The Paul-Apollos Relationship and Paul's Stance Toward Greco-Roman Rhetoric: An Exegetical and Socio-Historical Study of 1 Corinthians 1–4." PhD diss., Southeastern Baptist Theological Seminary, 2006.

Mijoga, "Merit." Mijoga, Hilary B. P. "The Use of the Term 'Merit' in Connection with Paul's Phrase ἔργα νόμου (*erga nomou*, 'Deeds of the Law')." *JTSA* 100 (1998): 20–35.

Mikalson, "Festivals." Mikalson, Jon D. "Festivals: Greek." *OCD³* 593.

Mikalson, "Oaths." Mikalson, Jon D. "Oaths." *OCD³* 1057.

Mikalson, "*Pannychis*." Mikalson, Jon D. "*Pannychis*." *OCD³* 1106.

Milazzo, "Sermone." Milazzo, Vincenza. "'Etsi imperitus sermone . . .': Girolamo e i solecismi di Paolo nei commentari alle epistole paoline." *ASDE* 12 (2, 1995): 261–77.

Milbank, *Social Theory*. Milbank, John. *Theology and Social Theory*. Cambridge, Mass.: Blackwell, 1991.

Miles and Trompf, "Luke and Antiphon." Miles, Gary B., and Garry Trompf. "Luke and Antiphon: The Theology of Acts 27–28 in the Light of Pagan Beliefs about Divine Retribution, Pollution, and Shipwreck." *HTR* 69 (3–4, 1976): 259–67.

"Milesian Tales." "Milesian Tales." *BrillPauly* 8:880–81.

Milgrom, "Custody." Milgrom, Jacob. "The Shared Custody of the Tabernacle and a Hittite Analogy." *JAOS* 90 (1970): 204–9.

Milgrom, *Leviticus*. Milgrom, Jacob. *Leviticus: A New Translation with Introduction and Commentary*. AB 3. 3 vols. New York: Doubleday, 1991–2001.

Milgrom, "Prolegomenon." Milgrom, Jacob. "A Prolegomenon to Lev. 17:11." *JBL* 90 (1971): 149–56.

Milgrom, *Studies*. Milgrom, Jacob. *Studies in Levitical Terminology*. Berkeley: University of California Press, 1970.

Milik, *Discovery*. Milik, J. T. *Ten Years of Discovery in the Wildernes of Judaea*. London: SCM, 1959.

Milik, "Écrits préésséniens." Milik, J. T. "Écrits préésséniens de Qumrân: D'Hénoch à Amram." Pages 91–106 in *Qumrân: Sa piété, sa théologie, et son milieu*. Edited by M. Delcor. BETL 46. Gembloux, Belg., and Paris: J. Duculot; Leuven: Leuven University Press, 1978.

Milik, "Testament de Lévi." Milik, J. T. "Le Testament de Lévi en araméen: Fragment de la grotte 4 de Qumrân (Pl. IV)." *RB* 62 (3, 1955): 398–406.

Milikowski, "Again: *Damascus*." Milikowski, Chaim. "Again: *Damascus* in Damascus Document and in Rabbinic Literature." *RevQ* 11 (1, 1982): 97–106.

Milikowski, "Gehenna." Milikowsky, Chaim. "Which Gehenna? Retribution and Eschatology in the Synoptic Gospels and in Early Jewish Texts." *NTS* 34 (2, 1988): 238–49.

Milikowsky, "'Lyhw." Milikowsky, C. "'lyhw whsyh (Elijah and the Messiah)." *JerSJT* 2 (4, 1982–83): 491–96.

Milikowsky, "Midrash." Milikowsky, Chaim. "Midrash as Fiction and Midrash as History: What Did the Rabbis Mean?" Pages 117–27 in *Ancient Fiction: The Matrix of Early Christian and Jewish Narrative*. Edited by Jo-Ann A. Brant, Charles W. Hedrick, and Chris Shea. SBLSymS 32. Atlanta: SBL, 2005.

Millanao T., "Comprensión." Millanao T., Pablo. "Una comprensión de la expresión 'Palabra de Dios' en los Evangelios y en los Hechos de los Apóstoles." *DavLog* 8 (1, 2009): 1–15.

Millar, "Community and Culture." Millar, Fergus. "Empire, Community, and Culture in the Roman Near East: Greeks, Syrians, Jews, and Arabs." *JJS* 38 (2, 1987): 143–64.

Millar, *Empire and Neighbours*. Millar, Fergus. *The Roman Empire and Its Neighbours*. New York: Dell, 1967.

Millar, "Ishmael." Millar, Fergus. "Hagar, Ishmael, Josephus, and the Origins of Islam." *JJS* 44 (1, 1993): 23–45.

Millar, *Near East*. Millar, Fergus. *The Roman Near East, 31 B.C.–A.D. 337*. Cambridge, Mass.: Harvard University Press, 1993.

Millar, "World of *Ass*." Millar, Fergus. "The World of the *Golden Ass*." *JRS* 71 (1981): 63–75.

Millar and Burton, "Equites." Millar, Fergus, and Graham Paul Burton. "Equites." *OCD³* 550–52.

Millard, "Duma." Millard, J. A. "Duma, William." No pages. *DACB*. Online: http://www.dacb.org/stories/southafrica/duma_william.html.

Millard, "Kain." Millard, Matthias. "Kain—Ethische Evidenz in der Genesis: Ein Element biblischer Ethik in auslegungsgeschichtlicher Perspektive." *T&K* 22 (83, 1999): 3–13.

Millard, "Gebote." Millard, Matthias. "Die rabbinischen noachidischen Gebote und das biblische Gebot Gottes an Noah: Ein Beitrag zur Methodendiskussion." *WD* 23 (1995): 71–90.

Millard, "Literacy." Millard, Alan. "Literacy in the Time of Jesus." *BAR* 29 (4, 2003): 36–45.

Millard, "Methods." Millard, A. R. "Methods of Studying the Patriarchal Narratives as Ancient Texts." Pages 43–58 in *Essays on the Patriarchal Narratives*, by A. R. Millard and D. J. Wiseman. Leicester: Inter-Varsity, 1980.

Millard, *Reading and Writing*. Millard, Alan. *Reading and Writing in the Time of Jesus*. Biblical Seminar 69. Sheffield, U.K.: Sheffield Academic, 2000.

Millard, Hoffmeier, and Baker, *Historiography in Context*. Millard, Alan, James K. Hoffmeier, and David W. Baker, eds. *Faith, Tradition, and History: Old Testament Historiography in Its Near Eastern Context*. Winona Lake, Ind.: Eisenbrauns, 1994.

Millay, "Time Travel." Millay, Jean. "Time Travel: A Guide for the Guide." Pages 100–106 in *Proceedings of the Fourth International Conference on the Study of Shamanism and Alternate Modes of Healing, Held at the St. Sabina Center, San Rafael, California, September 5–7, 1987*. Edited by Ruth-Inge Heinze. N.p.: Independent Scholars of Asia; Madison, Wis.: A-R Editions, 1988.

Miller, "Adam." Miller, Robert J. "Adam and Edom: The Costs and Benefits of Monotheism." *FourR* 20 (3, 2007): 8–10, 20.

Miller, "Apollo Lairbenos." Miller, Kevin M. "Apollo Lairbenos." *Numen* 32 (1, 1985): 46–70.

Miller, "Context." Miller, James C. "The Jewish Context of Paul's Gentile Mission." *TynBul* 58 (1, 2007): 101–15.

Miller, *Convinced*. Miller, John B. F. *Convinced That God Had Called Us: Dreams, Visions, and the Perception of God's Will in Luke-Acts*. BIS 85. Leiden: Brill, 2007.

Miller, "Dogs." Miller, Geoffrey D. "Attitudes toward Dogs in Ancient Israel: A Reassessment." *JSOT* 32 (4, 2008): 487–500.

Miller, "Dream." Miller, John B. F. "Paul's Dream at Troas: Reconsidering the Interpretations of Characters and Commentators." Pages 138–53 in *Contemporary Studies in Acts*. Edited by Thomas E. Phillips. Macon, Ga.: Mercer University Press, 2009.

Miller, *Empowered for Mission* Miller, Denzil R. *Empowered for Global Mission: A Missionary Look at the Book of Acts*. Foreword by John York. [Springfield, Mo.]: Life Publishers International, 2005.

Miller, "Ethnicity." Miller, David M. "Ethnicity Comes of Age: An Overview of Twentieth-Century Terms for *Ioudaios*." *CBR* 10 (2, 2012): 293–311.

Miller, "Exploring." Miller, John B. F. "Exploring the Function of Symbolic Dream-Visions in the Literature of Antiquity, with Another Look at 1 QapGen 19 and Acts 10." *PRSt* 37 (4, 2010): 441–55.

Miller, "Fragments." Miller, Robert D. "The Greek Biblical Fragments from Qumran in Text-Critical Perspective." *BeO* 48 (4, 2001): 235–48.

Miller, "Idolatry." Miller, Isaac. "Idolatry and the Polemics of World-Formation from Philo to Augustine." *JRH* 28 (2, 2004): 126–45.

Miller, "Image." Miller, J. Maxwell. "In the 'Image' and 'Likeness' of God." *JBL* 91 (3, 1972): 289–304.

Miller, "Imperial Cult." Miller, Colin. "The Imperial Cult in the Pauline Cities of Asia Minor and Greece." *CBQ* 72 (2, 2010): 314–32.

Miller, "Introduction." Miller, Walter. Introduction. Pages vii–xiii in vol. 1 of Xenophon, *Cyropaedia*. Translated by Walter Miller. 2 vols. LCL. Cambridge, Mass.: Harvard University Press, 1914.

Miller, "*Ioudaios*." Miller, David M. "The Meaning of *Ioudaios* and Its Relationship to Other Group Labels in Ancient 'Judaism.'" *CBR* 9 (1, 2010): 98–126.

Miller, "*Minim*." Miller, Stuart S. "The *minim* of Sepphoris Reconsidered." *HTR* 86 (4, 1993): 377–402.

Miller, "Number in Cities." Miller, Stuart S. "On the Number of Synagogues in the Cities of 'Erez Israel." *JJS* 49 (1, 1998): 51–66.

Miller, "Rabbis." Miller, Stuart S. "'Epigraphical' Rabbis, Helios, and Psalm 19: Were the Synagogues of Archaeology and the Synagogues of the Sages One and the Same?" *JQR* 94 (1, 2003): 27–76.

Miller, "Redaction of Tobit." Miller, James E. "The Redaction of Tobit and the Genesis Apocryphon." *JSP* 8 (1991): 53–61.

Miller, "Review of Keown." Miller, James C. Review of Mark J. Keown, *Congregational Evangelism in Philippians. RBL* 7 (2009).

Miller, *Seminar*. Miller, Robert J. *The Jesus Seminar and Its Critics*. Santa Rosa, Calif.: Polebridge, 1999.

Miller, "Targum." Miller, Merrill P. "Targum, Midrash, and the Use of the Old Testament in the New Testament." *JSJ* 2 (1, 1971): 29–82.

Miller, "Vision." Miller, Chris A. "Did Peter's Vision in Acts 10 Pertain to Men or the Menu?" *BSac* 159 (635, 2002): 302–17.

Miller, *Wesley*. Miller, Basil. *John Wesley: The World His Parish*. 2nd ed. Grand Rapids: Zondervan, 1943.

Miller and Yamamori, *Pentecostalism*. Miller, Donald E., and Tetsunao Yamamori. *Global Pentecostalism: The New Face of Christian Social Engagement*. Berkeley: University of California Press, 2007.

Millett, "Banks." Millett, Paul C. "Banks." *OCD³* 232–33.

Millett, "Finance." Millett, Paul C. "Finance, Greek and Hellenistic." *OCD³* 595–96.

Millett, "Maritime Loans." Millett, Paul C. "Maritime Loans." *OCD³* 924.

Milligan, *Thessalonians*. Milligan, George. *St Paul's Epistles to the Thessalonians: The Greek Text with Introduction and Notes*. London: Macmillan, 1908.

Millis, "Origins." Millis, Benjamin W. "The Social and Ethnic Origins of the Colonists in Early Roman Corinth." Pages 13–36 in *Corinth in Context: Comparative Studies on Religion and Society*. Edited by Steven J. Friesen et al. NovTSup 134. New York: Brill, 2010.

Mills, *Acts* (1996). Mills, Watson E. *The Acts of the Apostles*. Bibliographies for Biblical Research. New Testament Series. Lewiston, N.Y.: Mellen Biblical Press, 1996.

Mills, *Bibliography on Acts*. Mills, Watson E. *A Bibliography of the Periodical Literature on the Acts of the Apostles, 1962–1984*. NovTSup 58. Leiden: Brill, 1986.

Mills, *Glossolalia: Bibliography*. Mills, Watson E. *Glossolalia: A Bibliography*. Studies in the Bible and Early Christianity. New York: Edwin Mellen, 1985.

Mills, *Index*. Mills, Watson E. *Index to Periodical Literature on Christ and the Gospels*. NTTS 27. Leiden: Brill, 1998.

Mills, "Utterances and Glossolalia." Mills, Watson E. "Early Ecstatic Utterances and Glossolalia." *PRSt* 24 (1, 1997): 29–40.

Milnor, "Literacy." Milnor, Kristina. "Literary Literacy in Roman Pompeii: The Case of Vergil's *Aeneid*." Pages 288–319 in *Ancient Literacies: The Culture of Reading in Greece and Rome*. Edited by William A. Johnson and Holt N. Parker. New York: Oxford University Press, 2009.

Milnor, "Women." Milnor, Kristina. "Women in Roman Historiography." Pages 276–87 in *The Cambridge Companion to the Roman Historians*. Edited by Andrew Feldherr. Cambridge: Cambridge University Press, 2009.

Milojčić et al., *Samos*. Milojčić, Vladimir, et al. *Samos*. DeutsArcIns. Bonn: Rudolf Habelt, 1961–.

Milson, "Design." Milson, David. "The Design of the Royal Gates at Megiddo, Hazor, and Gezer." *ZDPV* 102 (1986): 87–92.

Miltner, *Ephesos*. Miltner, Franz. *Ephesos: Stadt der Artemis und des Johannes*. Vienna: Franz Deuticke, 1958.

Min, *Solidarity*. Min, Anselm Kyongsuk. *The Solidarity of Others in a Divided World: A Postmodern Theology after Postmodernism*. New York and London: T&T Clark, 2004.

Minar, *Politics*. Minar, Edwin L., Jr. *Early Pythagorean Politics in Practice and Theory*. ConnCMon 2. Baltimore: Waverly, 1942.

Minear, "Cosmology." Minear, Paul S. "The Cosmology of the Apocalypse." Pages 23–37 in *Current Issues in New Testament Interpretation*. Edited by W. Klassen and G. F. Snyder. New York: Harper, 1962.

Minear, *Hope*. Minear, Paul S. *Christian Hope and the Second Coming*. Philadelphia: Westminster, 1954.

Minear, *Images*. Minear, Paul S. *Images of the Church in the New Testament*. Philadelphia: Westminster, 1960.

Minear, *Kingdom*. Minear, Paul S. *The Kingdom and the Power: An Exposition of the New Testament Gospel*. Philadelphia: Westminster, 1950.

Mingo, "Mujeres." Mingo, Alberto de. "San Pablo y las mujeres." *Moralia* 26 (1, 2003): 7–29.

Minnen, "Roman Citizen." Minnen, Peter van. "Paul the Roman Citizen." *JSNT* 56 (1994): 43–52.

Minnen, "Women." Minnen, Peter van. "Did Ancient Women Learn a Trade outside the Home? Note on SB XVIII 13305." *ZPE* 123 (1998): 199–203.

Minns, *Scythians*. Minns, Ellis H. *Scythians and Greeks: A Survey of Ancient History and Archaeology on the North Coast of the Euxine from the Danube to the Caucasus*. Cambridge: Cambridge University Press, 1913.

"Miracle Woman." "Miracle Woman." *Time* (Sept. 14, 1970): 62, 64.

"Miracles, Miracle-workers." "Miracles, Miracle-workers: Biblical–Early Christian." *BrillPauly* 9:53–56.

Miranda, "Chiamata di Paolo." Miranda, Americo. "La chiamata di Paolo nella comunità cristiana nelle tre narrazioni degli Atti dell'episodio di Demasco (At

9,1–19a; 22,3–21; 26,9–23)." *RivB* 46 (1, 1998): 61–88.

Miranda, "Schicksal." Miranda, Peter. "Das Schicksal des Gerechten in der biblischen Tradition." *BK* 52 (4, 1997): 187–90.

Mira Seo, "Plagiarism." Mira Seo, Joanne. "Plagiarism and Poetic Identity in Martial." *AJP* 130 (4, 2009): 567–93.

Miskov, personal correspondence. Miskov, Jennifer. Personal correspondence with the author, May 22–23, 2014.

Mitchell, "Aborted Apostle." Mitchell, Matthew W. "Reexamining the 'Aborted Apostle': An Exploration of Paul's Self-Description in 1 Corinthians 15.8." *JSNT* 25 (4, 2003): 469–85.

Mitchell, "Accommodation." Mitchell, Margaret M. "Pauline Accommodation and 'Condescension' (συγκατάβασις): 1 Cor 9:19–23 and the History of Influence." Pages 197–214 in *Paul beyond the Judaism/Hellenism Divide*. Edited by Troels Engberg-Pedersen. Louisville: Westminster John Knox, 2001.

Mitchell, *Anatolia*. Mitchell, Stephen. *Anatolia: Land, Men, and Gods in Asia Minor*. 2 vols. Oxford: Clarendon, 1993.

Mitchell, "Antioch (*OCD*)." Mitchell, Stephen. "Antioch (2)." *OCD*³ 107.

Mitchell, "Antioch of Pisidia." Mitchell, Stephen. "Antioch of Pisidia." *ABD* 1:264–65.

Mitchell, "Archaeology." Mitchell, Stephen. "Archaeology in Asia Minor, 1990–1998." *ArchRep* 45 (1998–99): 125–92.

Mitchell, "Asia Minor." Mitchell, Stephen. "Asia Minor." *OCD*³ 190–91.

Mitchell, "Assos." Mitchell, Stephen. "Assos." *OCD*³ 194–95.

Mitchell, "Atonement." Mitchell, David C. "Messiah ben Joseph: A Sacrifice of Atonement for Israel." *RRJ* 10 (1, 2007): 77–94.

Mitchell, "Cilician Gates." Mitchell, Stephen. "Cilician Gates." *OCD*³ 331.

Mitchell, "Deliverer." Mitchell, David C. "The Fourth Deliverer: A Josephite Messiah in 4QTestimonia." *Biblica* 86 (2005): 545–53.

Mitchell, "Family Matters." Mitchell, Margaret M. "Why Family Matters for Early Christian Literature." Pages 345–58 in *Early Christian Families in Context: An Interdisciplinary Dialogue*. Edited by David L. Balch and Carolyn Osiek. Grand Rapids and Cambridge: Eerdmans, 2003.

Mitchell, "Friends by Name." Mitchell, Alan C. "'Greet the Friends by Name': New Testament Evidence for the Greco-Roman *topos* on Friendship." Pages 225–62 in *Greco-Roman Perspectives on Friendship*. Edited by John T. Fitzgerald. SBLRBS 34. Atlanta: Scholars Press, 1997.

Mitchell, "Friendship in Acts 2:44–47." Mitchell, Alan C. "The Social Function of Friendship in Acts 2:44–47 and 4:32–37." *JBL* 111 (2, 1992): 255–72.

Mitchell, "Galatia." Mitchell, Stephen. "Galatia." *ABD* 2:870–72.

Mitchell, "Homer." Mitchell, Margaret M. "Homer in the New Testament?" *JR* 83 (2, 2003): 244–60.

Mitchell, "Iconium and Ninica." Mitchell, Stephen. "Iconium and Ninica: Two Double Communities in Roman Asia Minor." *Historia* 28 (1979): 435–78.

Mitchell, "Lycia." Mitchell, Stephen. "Lycia." *OCD*³ 894–95.

Mitchell, "Many-Sorted Man." Mitchell, Margaret M. "'A Variable and Many-Sorted Man': John Chrysostom's Treatment of Pauline Inconsistency." *JECS* 6 (1, 1998): 93–111.

Mitchell, "Messiah in Targums." Mitchell, David C. "Messiah bar Ephraim in the Targums." *AramSt* 4 (2, 2006): 221–41.

Mitchell, "Myra." Mitchell, Stephen. "Myra." *OCD*³ 1016.

Mitchell, "Palimpsests." Mitchell, Margaret M. "Pauline Palimpsests and the Protestant-Catholic Divide." *HDBull* 30 (1, 2001): 9–16.

Mitchell, "Pamphylia." Mitchell, Stephen. "Pamphylia." *OCD*³ 1102–3.

Mitchell, "Perspective." Mitchell, Margaret M. "A Patristic Perspective on Pauline περιαυτολογία." *NTS* 47 (3, 2001): 354–71.

Mitchell, "Pessinus." Mitchell, Stephen. "Pessinus." *OCD*³ 1148.

Mitchell, "Phrygia." Mitchell, Stephen. "Phrygia." *OCD*³ 1176.

Mitchell, "Pisidia." Mitchell, Stephen. "Pisidia." *OCD*³ 1186.

Mitchell, "Population and Land." Mitchell, Stephen. "Population and the Land in Roman Galatia." *ANRW* 7.2:1073–75. Part 2, *Principat*, 7.2. Edited by H. Temporini and W. Haase. Berlin: de Gruyter, 1980.

Mitchell, *Rhetoric of Reconciliation*. Mitchell, Margaret M. *Paul and the Rhetoric of Reconciliation: An Exegetical Investigation of the Language and Composition of 1 Corinthians*. Louisville: Westminster John Knox, 1991.

Mitchell, "Rich." Mitchell, Alan C. "Rich and Poor in the Courts of Corinth: Litigiousness and Status in 1 Corinthians 6.1–11." *NTS* 39 (4, 1993): 562–86.

Mitchell, "Via Sebaste." Mitchell, Stephen. "Via Sebaste." *OCD*³ 1595–96.

Mitescu, "Sull'ipotesi." Mitescu, Adriana. "Sull'ipotesi del 'monoteismo pagano': Mithra e la preghiera precristiana." *Teresianum* 53 (2, 2002): 453–76.

Mitford, "Cyprus." Mitford, Terence B. "Roman Cyprus." *ANRW* 7.2.1286–1384. Part 2, *Principat*, 7.2. Edited by H. Temporini and W. Haase. Berlin: de Gruyter, 1995.

"Mithras." "Mithras." *BrillPauly* 9:73–77.

Mitsis, "Stoics and Aquinas." Mitsis, Phillip. "The Stoics and Aquinas on Virtue and Natural Law." *SPhilA* 15 (2003): 35–53.

Mittag, "Unruhen." Mittag, Peter Franz. "Unruhen im hellenistischen Alexandreia." *Historia* 52 (2, 2003): 161–208.

Mittelstadt, *Spirit*. Mittelstadt, Martin William. *The Spirit and Suffering in Luke-Acts: Implications for a Pentecostal Pneumatology*. JPTSup 26. London: T&T Clark, 2004.

Mittelstaedt, *Historiker*. Mittelstaedt, Alexander. *Lukas als Historiker: Zur Datierung des lukanischen Doppelwerkes*. TANZ 43. Tübingen: Francke, 2006.

Mitten, "Sardis." Mitten, David Gordon. "A New Look at Ancient Sardis." *BA* 24 (2, 1966): 38–68.

Mitton, *Ephesians*. Mitton, C. Leslie. *Ephesians*. NCBC. Greenwood, S.C.: Attic, 1976.

Miura, *David*. Miura, Yuzuru. *David in Luke-Acts: His Portrayal in the Light of Early Judaism*. WUNT 2.232. Tübingen: Mohr Siebeck, 2007.

Miura, "David as Prophet." Miura, Yuzuru. "David as Prophet: The Use of Ps 15 (LXX) in Acts 2:25–31." [In Japanese.] *Exegetica* 18 (2007): 21–46.

Mlasowsky, "Axum." Mlasowsky, Alexander. "Axum, Axomis (Aksum)." *BrillPauly* 2:432–34.

Moazami, "Evil Animals." Moazami, Mahnaz. "Evil Animals in the Zoroastrian Religion." *HR* 44 (4, 2005): 300–317.

Moberly, "Planned and Shaped." Moberly, Robert B. "When Was Acts Planned and Shaped?" *EvQ* 65 (1, 1993): 5–26.

Moda, "Paolo prigioniero." Moda, A. "Paolo prigioniero e martire: Premessa-introduzione." *BeO* 34 (3, 1992): 179–88.

Modarressi, "Zar Cult." Modarressi, Taghi. "The Zar Cult in South Iran." Pages 149–55 in *Trance and Possession States: Proceedings of the Second Annual Conference, R. M. Bucke Memorial Society, March 4–6, 1966*. Edited by Raymond Prince. Montreal: R. M. Bucke Memorial Society, 1968.

Moehring, "Acts IX 7." Moehring, Horst R. "The Verb *akouein* in Acts IX, 7 and XXII, 9." *NovT* 3 (1–2, 1959): 80–99.

Moehring, "Persecution in A.D. 19." Moehring, Horst R. "The Persecution of the Jews and the Adherents of the Isis Cult at Rome A.D. 19." *NovT* 3 (1959): 293–304.

Moessner, "Arrangement." Moessner, David P. "Dionysius's Narrative 'Arrangement' (οἰκονομία) as the Hermeneutical Key to Luke's Re-vision of the 'Many.'" Pages 149–64 in *Paul, Luke, and the Graeco-Roman World*. Edited by Alf Christophersen et al. JSNTSup 217. Sheffield, U.K.: Sheffield Academic, 2002; London: T&T Clark, 2003.

Moessner, "Christ." Moessner, David P. "'The Christ Must Suffer,' the Church Must Suffer: Rethinking the Theology of the Cross in Luke-Acts." Pages 165–95 in *SBL Seminar Papers, 1990*. Edited by David J. Lull. SBLSP 29. Atlanta: Scholars Press, 1990.

Moessner, "End(s)ings." Moessner, David P. "'Completed End(s)ings' of Historiographical Narrative: Diodorus Siculus and the End(ing) of Acts." Pages 193–221 in *Die Apostelgeschichte und die hellenistische Geschichtsschreibung: Festschrift für Eckhard Plümacher zu seinem 65. Geburtstag*. Edited by Cilliers Breytenbach and Jens Schröter. Leiden: Brill, 2004.

Moessner, "Fulfillment." Moessner, David P. "The Ironic Fulfillment of Israel's Glory." Pages 35–50 in *Luke-Acts and the Jewish People: Eight Critical Perspectives*. Edited by Joseph B. Tyson. Minneapolis: Augsburg, 1988.

Moessner, "Luke 9:1–50." Moessner, David P. "Luke 9:1–50: Luke's Preview of the Journey of the Prophet like Moses of Deuteronomy." *JBL* 102 (4, 1983): 575–605.

Moessner, "Poetics." Moessner, David P. "The Appeal and Power of Poetics (Luke 1:1–4): Luke's Superior Credentials (παρηκολουθηκότι), Narrative Sequence (καθεξῆς), and Firmness of Understanding (ἡ ἀσφάλεια) for the Reader." Pages 84–123 in *Jesus and the Heritage of Israel: Luke's Narrative Claim upon Israel's Legacy*. Edited by David P. Moessner. Luke the Interpreter of Israel 1. Harrisburg, Pa.: Trinity Press International, 1999.

Moessner, "Prologues." Moessner, David P. "The Lukan Prologues in the Light of Ancient Narrative Hermeneutics: Παρηκολουθηκότι and the Credentialed Author." Pages 399–417 in *The Unity of Luke-Acts*. Edited by Joseph Verheyden. BETL 142. Leuven: Leuven University Press, 1999.

Moessner, "Re-reading." Moessner, David P. "Re-reading Talbert's Luke: The *bios* of 'Balance' or the 'Bias' of History?" Pages 203–28 in *Cadbury, Knox, and Talbert: American Contributions to the Study of Acts*. Edited by Mikeal C. Parsons and Joseph B. Tyson. Atlanta: Scholars Press, 1992.

Moessner, "Script." Moessner, David P. "The 'Script' of the Scriptures in Acts: Suffering as God's 'Plan' (βουλή) for the World for the 'Release of Sins.'" Pages 218–50 in *History, Literature, and Society in the Book of Acts*. Edited by Ben Witherington III. Cambridge: Cambridge University Press, 1996.

Moessner, "Synergy." Moessner, David P. "The Triadic Synergy of Hellenistic Poetics in the Narrative Epistemology of Dionysius of Halicarnassus and the Authorial Intent of the Evangelist Luke (Luke 1:1–4; Acts 1:1–8)." *Neot* 42 (2, 2008): 289–303.

Moessner and Tiede, "Introduction." Moessner, David P., and David L. Tiede. "Introduction: Two Books but One Story?" Pages 1–4 in *Jesus and the Heritage of Israel: Luke's Narrative Claim upon Israel's Legacy*. Edited by David P. Moessner. Luke the Interpreter of Israel 1. Harrisburg, Pa.: Trinity Press International, 1999.

Moffatt, *First Corinthians*. Moffatt, James D. *The First Epistle of Paul to the Corinthians*. MNTC. London: Hodder & Stoughton, 1938.

Moffatt, *General Epistles*. Moffatt, James D. *The General Epistles: James, Peter, and Judas*. MNTC. Garden City, N.Y.: Doubleday, Doran, 1928.

Moffatt, *Hebrews*. Moffatt, James D. *A Critical and Exegetical Commentary on the Epistle to the Hebrews*. ICC. Edinburgh: T&T Clark, 1924.

Moffatt, *Introduction*. Moffatt, James. *An Introduction to the Literature of the New Testament*. 3rd ed. International Theological Library. New York: Scribner's, 1918.

Mohr et al., "Integration." Mohr, S., P. Y. Brandt, L. Borras, C. Gillieron, and P. Huguelet. "Toward an Integration of Spirituality and Religiousness into the Psychosocial Dimension of Schizophrenia." *AmJPsyc* 163 (11, 2006): 1952–59.

Molassiotis et al., "Medicine." Molassiotis, Alexander, et al. "Complementary and Alternative Medicine Use in Lung Cancer Patients in Eight European Countries." *Complementary Therapies in Clinical Practice* 12 (1, 2006): 34–39.

Moles, "Cynics." Moles, John L. "Cynics." *OCD*³ 418–19.

Moles, "Time." Moles, John. "Time and Space Travel in Luke-Acts." Pages 101–22 in *Engaging Early Christian History: Reading Acts in the Second Century*. Edited by Rubén R. Dupertuis and Todd Penner. Bristol, Conn.: Acumen, 2013.

Moll et al., "Networks." Moll, Jorge, et al. "Human Fronto-mesolimbic Networks Guide Decisions about Charitable Donation." *PNAS* 103 (42, 2006): 15623–28.

Möller, "Amos." Möller, Karl. "Amos, Book of." Pages 5–16 in *Dictionary of the Old Testament Prophets*. Edited by Mark J. Boda and J. Gordon McConville. Downers Grove, Ill.: IVP Academic, 2012.

Molthagen, "Geschichtsschreibung." Molthagen, Joachim. "Geschichtsschreibung und Geschichtsverständnis in der Apostelgeschichte im Vergleich mit Herodot, Thukydides und Polybios." Pages 159–81 in *Die Apostelgeschichte im Kontext antiker und frühchristlicher Historiographie*. Edited by Jörg Frey, Clare K. Rothschild, and Jens Schröter, with Bettina Rost. BZNWK 162. Berlin: de Gruyter, 2009.

Molthagen, "Konflikte." Molthagen, Joachim. "Die ersten Konflikte der Christen in der griechisch-römischen Welt." *Historia* 40 (1, 1991): 42–76.

Moltmann, "Blessing." Moltmann, Jürgen. "The Blessing of Hope: The Theology of Hope and the Full Gospel of Life." *JPT* 13 (2, 2005): 147–61.

Moltmann, *Place*. Moltmann, Jürgen. *A Broad Place: An Autobiography*. Translated by Margaret Kohl. Minneapolis: Fortress, 2008.

Momigliano, *Biography*. Momigliano, Arnaldo. *The Development of Greek Biography*. Carl Newell Jackson Lectures. Cambridge, Mass.: Harvard University Press, 1993.

Momigliano, *Historiography*. Momigliano, Arnaldo. *Essays in Ancient and Modern Historiography*. Middletown, Conn.: Wesleyan University Press; Oxford: Blackwell, 1977.

Momigliano, "Nero." Momigliano, Arnaldo. "Nero." Pages 702–42 in *The Augustan Empire: 44 B.C.–A.D. 70*. Edited by S. A. Cook, F. E. Adcock, and M. P. Charlesworth. CAH 10. Cambridge: Cambridge University Press, 1934. Repr., 1966.

Momigliano, "Rhetoric." Momigliano, Arnaldo. "The Rhetoric of History and the History of Rhetoric: On Hayden White's Tropes." Pages 49–59 in *Settimo contributo alla storia degli studi classici e del mondo antico*. Rome: Edizioni di Storia e letteratura, 1984.

Momigliano, "Theological Efforts." Momigliano, Arnaldo. "The Theological Efforts of the Roman Upper Classes in the First Century B.C." *CP* 79 (3, 1984): 199–211.

Momigliano and Griffin, "Burrus." Momigliano, Arnaldo, and Miriam T. Griffin. "Afranius Burrus, Sextus." *OCD*³ 33.

Momigliano and Spawforth, "Cyrene." Momigliano, Arnaldo, and Antony J. S. Spawforth. "Cyrene, Edicts of." *OCD*³ 422.

Mommsen, *History*. Mommsen, Theodor. *The History of Rome: The Conquest of Carthage to the End of the Republic*. Edited by Dero A. Saunders and John H. Collins. New York: Meridian, 1958.

Mommsen, "Rechtverhältnisse." Mommsen, Theodor. "Die Rechtverhältnisse des Apostels Paulus." *ZNW* 2 (1901): 81–96.

Mondin, "Esistenza." Mondin, Battista. "Esistenza, natura, inconoscibilità, e ineffabilità di Dio nel pensiero di Filone Alessandrino." ScC 95 (5, 1967): 423–47.

Moniot, "Historiography." Moniot, Henri. "Profile of a Historiography: Oral Tradition and Historical Research in Africa." Pages 50–58 in African Historiographies: What History for Which Africa? Edited by Bogumil Jewsiewicki and David Newbury. SSAMD 12. Beverly Hills, Calif.: Sage, 1986.

Monson, "Kings." Monson, John. "1 Kings." Pages 2–109 in vol. 3 of Zondervan Illustrated Bible Backgrounds Commentary: Old Testament. Edited by John Walton. 5 vols. Grand Rapids: Zondervan, 2009.

Monson, Map Manual. Monson, J., ed. Student Map Manual: Historical Geography of the Bible Lands. Grand Rapids: Zondervan; Jerusalem: Pictorial Archive (Near Eastern History), 1979.

Montague, "Prayer." Montague, George T. "Prayer in the Pauline Letters." BibT 32 (3, 1994): 156–60.

Montague, Timothy. Montague, George T. First and Second Timothy, Titus. CCSS. Grand Rapids: Baker Academic, 2008.

Montanari, "Artemidorus." Montanari, Franco. "Artemidorus of Tarsus." Brill Pauly 2:59–60.

Montanari, "Hypomnema." Montanari, Franco. "Hypomnema." BrillPauly 6:641–43.

Montefiore, Gospels. Montefiore, C. G. The Synoptic Gospels. 2 vols. 2nd ed. London: Macmillan, 1927. Repr., Library of Biblical Studies. New York: KTAV, 1968.

Montefiore, Hebrews. Montefiore, Hugh. A Commentary on the Epistle to the Hebrews. BNTC. London: Adam & Charles Black, 1964.

Montefiore, Judaism and Paul. Montefiore, C. G. Judaism and St. Paul: Two Essays. London: Max Goschen, 1914. Repr., New York: Arno, 1973.

Montefiore, Miracles. Montefiore, Hugh. The Miracles of Jesus. London: SPCK, 2005.

Montefiore, "Spirit of Judaism." Montefiore, C. G. "Spirit of Judaism." BegChr 1:35–81.

Montefiore and Loewe, Anthology. Montefiore, C. G., and Herbert Loewe, eds. and trans. A Rabbinic Anthology. London: Macmillan, 1938. Reprinted with a new prolegomenon by Raphael Loewe. New York: Schocken, 1974.

Montes Peral, "Dios." Montes Peral, Luis Angel. "El Dios Trinidad de la primera iglesia, en la experiencia religiosa de María, guiada por el Espíritu Santo, en el acontecimiento de Pentecostés (Hch 1,14)." EphMar 59 (2, 2009): 251–72.

Montevecchi, "Samaria e Samaritani." Montevecchi, Orsolina. "Samaria e Samaritani in Egitto." Aeg 76 (1–2, 1996): 81–92.

Montgomery, "Comfort." Montgomery, Gary T. "Comfort with Acculturation Status among Students from South Texas." HisJBehSc 14 (2, 1992): 201–23.

Montiglio, "Travel." Montiglio, Silvia. "Should the Aspiring Wise Man Travel? A Conflict in Seneca's Thought." AJP 127 (4, 2006): 553–86.

Montiglio, "Wandering Philosophers." Montiglio, Silvia. "Wandering Philosophers in Classical Greece." JHS 120 (2000): 86–105.

Montilus, "Vodun." Montilus, Guérin C. "Vodun and Social Tranformation in the African Diasporic Experience: The Concept of Personhood in Haitian Vodun Religion." Pages 1–6 in Haïtian Vodou: Spirit, Myth, and Reality. Edited by Patrick Bellegarde-Smith and Claudine Michel. Bloomington: Indiana University Press, 2006.

Moo, Letters. Moo, Douglas J. The Letters to the Colossians and to Philemon. PillNTC. Grand Rapids: Eerdmans, 2008.

Moo, "Paul and Law." Moo, Douglas J. "Paul and the Law in the Last Ten Years." SJT 40 (2, 1987): 287–307.

Moo, Romans. Moo, Douglas J. The Epistle to the Romans. Grand Rapids and Cambridge: Eerdmans, 1996.

Moody, "Chronology." Moody, Dale. "A New Chronology for the Life and Letters of Paul." Pages 223–40 in Chronos, Kairos, Christos: Nativity and Chronological Studies Presented to Jack Finegan. Edited by Jerry Vardaman and Edwin M. Yamauchi. Winona Lake, Ind.: Eisenbrauns, 1989.

Moolenburgh, Meetings. Moolenburgh, H. C. Meetings with Angels: One Hundred and One Real-Life Encounters. Translated by Tony Langham and Plym Peters. New York: Barnes & Noble; C. W. Daniel, 1995.

Moon, "Nudity." Moon, Warren G. "Nudity and Narrative: Observations on the Frescoes from the Dura Synagogue." JAAR 60 (4, 1992): 587–658.

Mooneyham, "Demonism." Mooneyham, W. Stanley. "Demonism on the Mission Field: Problems of Communicating a Difficult Phenomenon." Pages 209–19 in Demon Possession: A Medical, Historical, Anthropological, and Theological Symposium. Edited by John Warwick Montgomery. Minneapolis: Bethany House, 1976.

Moore, "Canon." Moore, George Foot. "The Definition of the Jewish Canon and the Repudiation of the Christian Scriptures." Pages 99–125 in Essays in Modern Theology and Related Subjects: Gathered and Published as a Testimonial to Charles Augustus Briggs on the Completion of His Seventieth Year, January 15, 1911. New York: Scribner's, 1911.

Moore, "Δικαιοσύνη." Moore, Richard K. "Δικαιοσύνη and Cognates in Paul: The Semantic Gulf between Two Major Lexicons (Bauer-Arndt-Gingrich-Danker and Louw-Nida)." Colloq 30 (1, 1998): 27–43.

Moore, "Empire." Moore, Stephen D. "Paul after Empire." Pages 9–23 in The Colonized Apostle: Paul through Postcolonial Eyes. Edited by Christopher D. Stanley. Minneapolis: Fortress, 2011.

Moore, "End of Earth." Moore, Thomas S. "'To the End of the Earth': The Geographical and Ethnic Universalism of Acts 1:8 in Light of Isaianic Influence on Luke." JETS 40 (3, 1997): 389–99.

Moore, "Introduction." Moore, Clifford H. "Introduction: Life and Works of Tacitus." Pages vii–xiii in vol. 1 of Tacitus. Translated by Clifford H. Moore and John Jackson. 4 vols. LCL. London: Heinemann; Cambridge, Mass.: Harvard University Press, 1931–37.

Moore, Judaism. Moore, George Foot. Judaism in the First Centuries of the Christian Era. 3 vols. Cambridge, Mass.: Harvard University Press, 1927–30. Repr., 3 vols. in 2. New York: Schocken, 1971.

Moore, "Life." Moore, Clifford H. "Life in the Roman Empire at the Beginning of the Christian Era." BegChr 1:218–62.

Moore, "Quakerism." Moore, Rosemary. "Late Seventeenth-Century Quakerism and the Miraculous: A New Look at George Fox's 'Book of Miracles.'" Pages 335–44 in Signs, Wonders, Miracles: Representations of Divine Power in the Life of the Church. Papers Read at the 2003 Summer Meeting and the 2004 Winter Meeting of the Ecclesiastical History Society. Edited by Kate Cooper and Jeremy Gregory. Rochester, N.Y.: Boydell & Brewer, for the Ecclesiastical History Society, 2005.

Moore, "Villages." Moore, A. M. T. "Villages." OEANE 5:301–3.

Moore and Anderson, "Masculinity." Moore, Stephen D., and Janice Capel Anderson. "Taking It Like a Man: Masculinity in 4 Maccabees." JBL 117 (2, 1998): 249–73.

Moore and Segovia, Criticism. Moore, Stephen D., and Fernando F. Segovia. Postcolonial Biblical Criticism: Interdisciplinary Intersections. London: T&T Clark, 2005.

Mor and Rappaport, Bibliography. Mor, Menahem, and Uriel Rappaport. Bibliography of Works on Jewish History in the Hellenistic and Roman Period, 1976–1980. Jerusalem: Zalman Shazar Center for the Furtherance of the Study of Jewish History, Historical Society of Israel, 1982.

Moran, "Prophecy." Moran, William L. "New Evidence from Mari on the History of Prophecy." *Bib* 50 (1969): 15–56.

Moreau, "Right Thing." Moreau, A. Scott. "Do the Right Thing—but Results Are Not Guaranteed, Acts 21:17–22:36; 24:10–21." Pages 274–82 in *Mission in Acts: Ancient Narratives in Contemporary Context*. Edited by Robert L. Gallagher and Paul Hertig. AmSocMissS 34. Maryknoll, N.Y.: Orbis, 2004.

Morel-Vergniol, "Ève . . . et Lilith?" Morel-Vergniol, Danielle. "Adam, Ève . . . et Lilith?" *FoiVie* 99 (4, 2000): 39–51.

Moreland, "Mythmaking." Moreland, Milton. "The Jerusalem Community in Acts: Mythmaking and the Sociorhetorical Functions of a Lukan Setting." Pages 285–310 in *Contextualizing Acts: Lukan Narrative and Greco-Roman Discourse*. Edited by Todd Penner and Caroline Vander Stichele. SBLSymS 20. Atlanta: SBL, 2003.

Moreland, *Triangle*. Moreland, J. P. *Kingdom Triangle: Recover the Christian Mind, Renovate the Soul, Restore the Spirit's Power*. Grand Rapids: Zondervan, 2007.

Moreland and Issler, *Faith*. Moreland, J. P., and Klaus Issler. *In Search of a Confident Faith: Overcoming Barriers to Trusting God*. Downers Grove, Ill.: InterVarsity, 2008.

Morgado, "Paul in Jerusalem." Morgado, Joe. "Paul in Jerusalem: A Comparison of His Visits in Acts and Galatians." *JETS* 37 (1, 1994): 55–68.

Morgan, "*Achilleae comae*." Morgan, Llewelyn. "*Achilleae comae*: Hair and Heroism according to Domitian." *CQ* 47 (1, 1997): 209–14.

Morgan, "Fiction." Morgan, J. R. "Fiction and History: Historiography and the Novel." Pages 553–64 in *A Companion to Greek and Roman Historiography*. Edited by John Marincola. 2 vols. Oxford: Blackwell, 2007.

Morgan, "Impasse." Morgan, Timothy C. "Egypt's Identity Impasse." *CT* 52 (4, 2008): 60–61.

Morgan, "Luc-Actes." Morgan, J. "Luc-Actes: un tour de force littéraire et théologique." *Hok* 103 (2013): 9–29.

Morgan, "Review." Morgan, M. Gwyn. Review of A. J. Woodman, *Rhetoric in Classical Historiography*. *Ploutarchos* 9 (1992–93): 34–37.

Morgan, Hornblower, and Spawforth, "Delphi." Morgan, Catherine A., Simon Hornblower, and Antony J. S. Spawforth. "Delphi." *OCD*[3] 444–45.

Morgan-Wynne, "Traditionsgrundlage." Morgan-Wynne, John E. "2 Corinthians VIII.18f. and the Question of a Traditionsgrundlage for Acts." *JTS* 30 (1, 1979): 172–73.

Morgenstern, "Ark." Morgenstern, Julian. "The Ark, the Ephod, and the 'Tent of Meeting.'" *HUCA* 17 (1942–43): 153–265.

Morgenstern, "Magic Bowl." Morgenstern, Matthew. "The Jewish Babylonian Aramaic Magic Bowl BM 91767 Reconsidered." *Mus* 120 (1–2, 2007): 5–27.

Morgenthaler, *Lukas und Quintilian*. Morgenthaler, Robert. *Lukas und Quintilian: Rhetorik als Erzählkunst*. Zurich: Gotthelf, 1993.

Morisi, "Origine." Morisi, Marzia. "Per l'origine dell'apocalittica: Dall'ambivalenza delle nozze miste greche all'ambiguità delle nozze miste guidaiche." *Antonianum* 73 (3, 1998): 483–504.

Morkot, "Axumis." Morkot, Robert G. "Axumis." *OCD*[3] 227.

Morkot, "Ethiopia." Morkot, Robert G. "Ethiopia." *OCD*[3] 558.

Morkot, "Meroe." Morkot, Robert G. "Meroe." *OCD*[3] 962.

Morkot, "Nubia." Morkot, Robert G. "Nubia." *OCD*[3] 1052.

Morkot, "Trogodytae." Morkot, Robert G. "Trogodytae." *OCD*[3] 1555.

Moro, "Mosè." Moro, Caterina. "Mosè nell'Egitto greco-romano: tradizioni in conflitto." *ASDE* 26 (1, 2009): 165–70.

Morphew, *Breakthrough*. Morphew, Derek J. *Breakthrough: Discovering the Kingdom*. Cape Town: Vineyard International, 1991.

Morrall, "Marx and Weber." Morrall, John. "Marx and Weber Ride Again: Some Recent Interpretations of Graeco-Roman Politics and Society." *PolSt* 31 (2, 1983): 312–19.

Morray-Jones, "Mysticism." Morray-Jones, Christopher R. A. "Transformational Mysticism in the Apocalyptic-Merkabah Tradition." *JJS* 43 (1, 1992): 1–31.

Morray-Jones, "Paradise." Morray-Jones, Christopher R. A. "Paradise Revisited (2 Cor 12:1–12)—The Jewish Mystical Background of Paul's Apostolate, Part 2: Paul's Heavenly Ascent and Its Significance." *HTR* 86 (3, 1993): 265–92.

Morrice, "Joy." Morrice, William G. "Joy." *DPL* 511–12.

Morris, *Apocalyptic*. Morris, Leon. *Apocalyptic*. Grand Rapids: Eerdmans, 1972.

Morris, "Cemeteries." Morris, Ian. "Cemeteries." *OCD*[3] 307.

Morris, *Cross in New Testament*. Morris, Leon. *The Cross in the New Testament*. Grand Rapids and Cambridge: Eerdmans, 1965.

Morris, "Dead." Morris, Ian. "Dead, Disposal of." *OCD*[3] 431–32.

Morris, "Faith." Morris, Leon. "Faith." *DPL* 285–91.

Morris, *John*. Morris, Leon. *The Gospel according to John: The English Text with Introduction, Exposition, and Notes*. NICNT. Grand Rapids: Eerdmans, 1971.

Morris, *Judgment*. Morris, Leon. *The Biblical Doctrine of Judgment*. Grand Rapids: Eerdmans, 1960.

Morris, *Lectionaries*. Morris, Leon. *The New Testament and the Jewish Lectionaries*. London: Tyndale, 1964.

Morris, "Lectionaries." Morris, Leon. "The Gospels and the Jewish Lectionaries." Pages 129–56 in *Studies in Midrash and Historiography*. Edited by R. T. France and David Wenham. Gospel Perspectives 3. Sheffield, U.K.: JSOT Press, 1983.

Morris, *Luke*. Morris, Leon. *The Gospel according to St. Luke*. TNTC. Grand Rapids: Eerdmans, 1974.

Morris, *Preaching*. Morris, Leon. *The Apostolic Preaching of the Cross*. 3rd ed. Grand Rapids: Eerdmans, 1965.

Morris, *Romans*. Morris, Leon. *The Epistle to the Romans*. Grand Rapids: Eerdmans; Leicester, U.K.: Inter-Varsity, 1988.

Morris, *Studies*. Morris, Leon. *Studies in the Fourth Gospel*. Grand Rapids: Eerdmans, 1969.

Morris, *Thessalonians*. Morris, Leon. *The First and Second Epistles to the Thessalonians*. NICNT. Grand Rapids: Eerdmans, 1959.

Morsy, "Possession." Morsy, Soheir A. "Spirit Possession in Egyptian Ethnomedicine: Origins, Comparison, and Historical Specificity." Pages 189–208 in *Women's Medicine: The zar-bori Cult in Africa and Beyond*. Edited by I. M. Lewis, Ahmed Al-Safi, and Sayyid Hurreiz. Edinburgh: International African Institute, Edinburgh University Press, 1991.

Morton, "Dawit." Morton, Alice. "Dawit: Competition and Integration in an Ethiopian Wuqabi Cult Group." Pages 193–234 in *Case Studies in Spirit Possession*. Edited by Vincent Crapanzaro and Vivian Garrison. New York: Wiley, 1977.

Morton and MacGregor, *Structure*. Morton, A. Q., and G. H. C. MacGregor. *The Structure of Luke and Acts*. New York: Harper & Row, 1964.

Morwood, "Cupid." Morwood, James. "Cupid Grows Up." *GR* 57 (1, 2010): 107–16.

Moscati, *Phoenicians*. Moscati, Sabatino. *The World of the Phoenicians*. Translated by Alastair Hamilton. New York: Praeger, 1968.

Moses, *Transfiguration Story*. Moses, A. D. A. *Matthew's Transfiguration Story and*

Jewish-Christian Controversy. JSNTSup 122. Sheffield, U.K.: Sheffield Academic, 1996.

Mosher and Jacobs, "Seminar." Mosher, Lucinda A., and Claude Jacobs. "The Worldviews Seminar: An Intensive Survey of American Urban Religious Diversity." Pages 261–75 in *Teaching Religion and Healing.* Edited by Linda L. Barnes and Inés Talamantez. AARTRSS. Oxford: Oxford University Press, 2006.

Mosley, "Reporting." Mosley, A. W. "Historical Reporting in the Ancient World." *NTS* 12 (1, 1965): 10–26.

Moss, "Sect." Moss, Gloria. "The Essenes' Sister Sect in Egypt: A Meeting between Paganism and Judaism?" *FaithFreed* 54 (1, 2001): 58–76.

Mosser, "City." Mosser, Carl. "No Lasting City: Rome, Jerusalem, and the Place of Hebrews in the History of Earliest 'Christianity.'" PhD diss., University of St. Andrews, 2004.

Mossman, "Plutarch and Biography." Mossman, Judith. "Plutarch and English Biography." *Herm* 183 (2007): 75–100.

Mossman, "Plutarch on Animals." Mossman, Judith. "Plutarch on Animals: Rhetorical Strategies in *De sollertia animalium.*" *Herm* 179 (2005): 141–63.

Most, "Imitate Septuagint?" Most, William G. "Did St. Luke Imitate the Septuagint?" *JSNT* 15 (1982): 30–41.

Motto, "Progress." Motto, Anna Lydia. "The Idea of Progress in Senecan Thought." *CJ* 79 (3, 1984): 225–40.

Motyer, *Lion.* Motyer, J. A. *The Day of the Lion.* Downers Grove, Ill.: InterVarsity, 1974.

Moucarry, *Prophet.* Moucarry, Chawkat. *The Prophet and the Messiah: An Arab Christian's Perspective on Islam and Christianity.* Downers Grove, Ill.: InterVarsity, 2001.

Moule, *Birth.* Moule, C. F. D. *The Birth of the New Testament.* New York: Harper & Row, 1962.

Moule, "Christology of Acts." Moule, C. F. D. "The Christology of Acts." Pages 159–85 in *Studies in Luke-Acts: Essays in Honor of Paul Schubert.* Edited by Leander E. Keck and J. Louis Martyn. Nashville: Abingdon, 1966.

Moule, "Circumstances." Moule, C. F. D. "The Influence of Circumstances on the Use of Christological Terms." *JTS* 10 (1959): 247–63.

Moule, "Classification." Moule, C. F. D. "Excursus 2: The Classification of Miracle Stories." Pages 239–43 in *Miracles: Cambridge Studies in Their Philosophy and History.* Edited by C. F. D. Moule. London: A. R. Mowbray; New York: Morehouse-Barlow, 1965.

Moule, "Factor." Moule, C. F. D. "A Neglected Factor in the Interpretation of Johannine Eschatology." Pages 155–60 in *Studies in John: Presented to Professor Dr. J. N. Sevenster on the Occasion of His Seventieth Birthday.* Edited by W. C. van Unnik. NovTSup 24. Leiden: Brill, 1970.

Moule, *Idiom Book.* Moule, C. F. D. *An Idiom Book of New Testament Greek.* 2nd ed. Cambridge: Cambridge University Press, 1959.

Moule, *Mark.* Moule, C. F. D. *The Gospel according to Mark.* Cambridge: Cambridge University Press, 1965.

Moule, *Messengers.* Moule, C. F. D. *Christ's Messengers: Studies in the Acts of the Apostles.* New York: Association, 1957.

Moule, "Obligation." Moule, C. F. D. "Obligation in the Ethic of Paul." Pages 389–406 in *Christian History and Interpretation: Studies Presented to John Knox.* Edited by W. R. Farmer, C. F. D. Moule, and R. R. Niebuhr. Cambridge: Cambridge University Press, 1967.

Moule, "Once More, Hellenists." Moule, C. F. D. "Once More, Who Were the Hellenists?" *ExpT* 70 (4, 1959): 100–102.

Moulton, *Grammar.* Moulton, James Hope. *A Grammar of New Testament Greek.* 4 vols. Edinburgh: T&T Clark, 1908.

Moulton and Milligan, *Vocabulary.* Moulton, James Hope, and George Milligan. *The Vocabulary of the Greek Testament: Illustrated from the Papyri and Other Non-literary Sources.* Grand Rapids: Eerdmans, 1930.

Mounce, "Eschatology." Mounce, Robert H. "Pauline Eschatology and the Apocalypse." *EvQ* 46 (1974): 164–66.

Mounce, *Pastoral Epistles.* Mounce, William D. *Pastoral Epistles.* WBC 46. Nashville: Nelson, 2000.

Mounce, *Peter.* Mounce, Robert H. *A Living Hope: A Commentary on 1 and 2 Peter.* Grand Rapids: Eerdmans, 1982.

Mounce, *Revelation.* Mounce, Robert H. *The Book of Revelation.* NICNT. Grand Rapids: Eerdmans, 1977.

Mount, "Investigation." Mount, Christopher. "Luke-Acts and the Investigation of Apostolic Tradition: From a Life of Jesus to a History of Christianity." Pages 380–92 in *Die Apostelgeschichte im Kontext antiker und frühchristlicher Historiographie.* Edited by Jörg Frey, Clare K. Rothschild, and Jens Schröter, with Bettina Rost. BZNWK 162. Berlin: de Gruyter, 2009.

Mount, *Pauline Christianity.* Mount, Christopher. *Pauline Christianity: Luke-Acts and the Legacy of Paul.* NovTSup 104. Leiden, Köln: Brill, 2002.

Mountford and Winterbottom, "Aquila Romanus." Mountford, James Frederick, and Michael Winterbottom. "Aquila Romanus." *OCD*³ 133.

Mourelatos, "Alternatives." Mourelatos, Alexander P. D. "Some Alternatives in Interpreting Parmenides." *Monist* 62 (1979): 3–14.

Mouritsen, *Freedman.* Mouritsen, Henrik. *The Freedman in the Roman World.* Cambridge: Cambridge University Press, 2011.

Mourlon Beernaert, "Collaboratrices." Mourlon Beernaert, Pierre. "Les collaboratrices de saint Paul. Annonce de la Parole et labeur apostolique." *LumVie* 50 (2, 1995): 169–83.

Mowery, "Caristanius." Mowery, Robert L. "Paul and Caristanius at Pisidian Antioch." *Bib* 87 (2, 2006): 223–42.

Mowery, "God the Father." Mowery, Robert L. "God the Father in Luke-Acts." Pages 124–32 in *New Views on Luke and Acts.* Edited by Earl Richard. Collegeville, Minn.: Liturgical Press, 1990.

Mowvley, "Exodus." Mowvley, Henry. "John 1.14–18 in the Light of Exodus 33.7–34.35." *ExpT* 95 (5, 1984): 135–37.

Moxnes, "Construction." Moxnes, Halvor. "The Construction of Galilee as a Place for the Historical Jesus—Part I." *BTB* 31 (1, 2001): 26–37.

Moxnes, "Social Relations." Moxnes, Halvor. "Social Relations and Economic Interaction in Luke's Gospel: A Research Report." Pages 58–75 in *Luke-Acts: Scandinavian Perspectives.* Edited by Petri Luomanen. PFES 54. Helsinki: Finnish Exegetical Society; Göttingen: Vandenhoeck & Ruprecht, 1991.

Moyer, "Practices." Moyer, James C. "Hittite and Israelite Cultic Practices: A Selected Comparison." Pages 19–38 in *Scripture in Context II: More Essays on the Comparative Method.* Edited by William W. Hallo, James C. Moyer, and Leo G. Perdue. Winona Lake, Ind.: Eisenbrauns, 1983.

Moyer, "Purity." Moyer, James C. "The Concept of Ritual Purity among the Hittites." PhD diss., Brandeis University, 1969.

Mozley, "Introduction." Mozley, J. H. Introduction. Pages vii–xx in Valerius Flaccus, *Argonautica.* Translated by J. H. Mozley. Rev. ed. LCL. Cambridge, Mass.: Harvard University Press, 1936.

Mthethwa, "Music." Mthethwa, B. N. "Music and Dance as Therapy in African Traditional Societies with Special Reference to the iBlandla lamaNazaretha (the Church of the Nazarites)." Pages 241–56 in *Afro-Christian Religion and Healing in Southern Africa.* Edited by G. C. Oosthuizen, S. D. Edwards, W. H. Wessels, and I. Hexham. AfSt 8. Lewiston, N.Y.: Edwin Mellen, 1989.

Muckensturm-Poulle, "Gymnosophists." Muckensturm-Poulle, Claire. "Gymnosophists." *BrillPauly* 5:1060.

Mueller, "Faces of Lust." Mueller, Celeste DeSchryver. "Two Faces of Lust." *BibT* 41 (5, 2003): 308–14.

Mueller, "Single Women." Mueller, Ilse. "Single Women in the Roman Funerary Inscriptions." *ZPE* 175 (2010): 295–303.

Mufwata, *Extrémités*. Mufwata, Albert Kaumba. *Jusqu'aux Extrémités de la Terre: La référence aux prophètes comme fondement de l'ouverture universaliste aux chapitres 2 et 13 des Actes des Apôtres*. CahRB 67. Paris: Gabalda, 2006.

Muggia, "Regium." Muggia, Anna. "Regium." *BrillPauly* 12:441–43.

Muhly, "Cyprus." Muhly, J. D. "Cyprus." *OEANE* 2:89–96.

Muhly, "Homer and Phoenicians." Muhly, James D. "Homer and the Phoenicians: The Relations between Greece and the Near East in the Late Bronze and Early Iron Ages." *Berytus* 19 (1970): 19–64.

Muir, "Education." Muir, J. V. "Education, Roman." *OCD*³ 509–10.

Müller, "Abraham-Gestalt." Müller, Mogens. "Die Abraham-Gestalt im Jubiläenbuch: Versuch einer Interpretation." *JSP* 10 (2, 1996): 238–57.

Müller, "Entscheidung." Müller, P. G. "Die jüdische Entscheidung gegen Jesus nach der Apostelgeschichte." Pages 523–31 in *Les Actes des apôtres: Traditions, rédaction, théologie*. Edited by Jacob Kremer. BETL 48. Gembloux, Belg.: J. Duculot; Leuven: Leuven University Press, 1979.

Müller, "Leben." Müller, K. "'Denn das Leben ist in ihm': Erwägungen zum Bluttabu im rabbinischen und frühchristlichen Denken." *T&K* 23 (88, 2000): 3–15.

Müller, "Möglichkeit." Müller, Karlheinz. "Möglichkeit und Vollzug jüdischer Kapitalgerichtsbarkeit im Prozess gegen Jesus von Nazareth." Pages 41–83 in *Der Prozess gegen Jesus: Historische Rückfrage und theologische Deutung*. QDisp 112. Freiburg im Breisgau: Herder, 1988.

Müller, "Palaestina." Müller, Mogens. "Hvad blev Palaestina kaldt i antikken?" *DTT* 68 (2, 2005): 139–44.

Müller, "Parakletenvorstellung." Müller, Ulrich B. "Die Parakletenvorstellung im Johannesevangelium." *ZTK* 71 (1, 1974): 31–78.

Müller, "Priska." Müller, Christoph G. "Priska und Aquila: Der Weg eines Ehepaares und die paulinische Mission." *MTZ* 54 (3, 2003): 195–210.

Müller, "Reception." Müller, Mogens. "The Reception of the Old Testament in Matthew and Luke-Acts: From Interpretation to Proof from Scripture." *NovT* 43 (4, 2001): 315–30.

Müller, "Rezeption." Müller, Andreas. "Eusebs Rezeption der Apostelgeschichte in der *Vita Constantini*." Pages 393–417 in *Die Apostelgeschichte im Kontext antiker und frühchristlicher Historiographie*. Edited by Jörg Frey, Clare K. Rothschild, and Jens Schröter, with Bettina Rost. BZNWK 162. Berlin: de Gruyter, 2009.

Müller, "Sandon." Müller, Hans-Peter. "Sandon." *BrillPauly* 12:954–55.

Müller, "Schriftstellerische Plural." Müller, Markus. "Der sogenannte 'schriftstellerische Plural'—neu betrachtet: Zur Frage der Mitarbeiter als Mitverfasser der Paulusbriefe." *BZ* 42 (2, 1998): 181–201.

Müller-Kessler, Mitchell, and Hockey, "Amulet." Müller-Kessler, C., T. C. Mitchell, and M. I. Hockey. "An Inscribed Silver Amulet from Samaria." *PEQ* 139 (1, 2007): 5–19.

Mullin, *History*. Mullin, Robert Bruce. *A Short World History of Christianity*. Louisville: Westminster John Knox, 2008.

Mullin, *Miracles*. Mullin, Robert Bruce. *Miracles and the Modern Religious Imagination*. New Haven: Yale University Press, 1996.

Mullins, "Commissioning Forms." Mullins, Terence Y. "New Testament Commissioning Forms, Especially in Luke-Acts." *JBL* 95 (4, 1976): 603–14.

Mullins, "Formulas." Mullins, Terence Y. "Formulas in New Testament Epistles." *JBL* 91 (1972): 380–90.

Mullins, "Religious Roles." Mullins, Patrick. "The Religious Roles of Women among Israel's Neighbors." *MilS* 45 (2000): 81–111.

Mullins, "Secular Roles." Mullins, Patrick. "The Public, Secular Roles of Women in Biblical Times." *MilS* 43 (1999): 79–111.

Mulloor, "Ascension." Mulloor, Augustine. "Ascension (Acts 1:1–11): A Challenge of the Indian Church to Start Afresh." *Jeev* 34 (200, 2004): 101–7.

"Multilingualism." "Multilingualism." *Brill Pauly* 9:269–73.

Mumcuoglu and Zias, "De-loused." Mumcuoglu, Kostas Y., and Joseph Zias. "How the Ancients De-loused Themselves." *BAR* 15 (6, 1989): 66–69.

Munck, *Acts*. Munck, Johannes. *The Acts of the Apostles*. Revised by W. F. Albright and C. S. Mann. AB 31. Garden City, N.Y.: Doubleday, 1967.

Munck, *Israel*. Munck, Johannes. *Christ and Israel: An Interpretation of Romans 9–11*. Foreword by Krister Stendahl. Philadelphia: Fortress, 1967.

Munck, "Jewish Christianity." Munck, Johannes. "Jewish Christianity in Post-Apostolic Times." *NTS* 6 (2, Jan. 1960): 103–16.

Munck, *Salvation*. Munck, Johannes. *Paul and the Salvation of Mankind*. Richmond, Va.: John Knox, 1959.

Mundhenk, "Invisible Man." Mundhenk, Norman A. "The Invisible Man (Acts 4.9–10)." *BTr* 57 (4, 2006): 203–6.

Mundhenk, "Note." Mundhenk, Norman A. "A Note on Acts 17.24." *BTr* 53 (4, 2002): 441–42.

Muñiz Grijalvo, "Elites." Muñiz Grijalvo, Elena. "Elites and Religious Change in Roman Athens." *Numen* 52 (2, 2005): 255–82.

Munoa, "*Merkavah*." Munoa, Phillip B. "Jesus, the *merkavah*, and Martyrdom in Early Christian Tradition." *JBL* 121 (2, 2002): 303–25.

Muñoz-Larrondo, *Postcolonial Reading*. Muñoz-Larrondo, Rubén. *A Postcolonial Reading of the Acts of the Apostles*. StBibLit 147. New York: Peter Lang, 2012.

Munteanu, "*Misericordia*." Munteanu, Dana LaCourse. "*Qualis Tandem Misericordia in Rebus Fictis*? Aesthetic and Ordinary Emotion." *Helios* 36 (2, 2010): 117–47.

Muntz, "Diodorus Siculus." Muntz, Charles E. "Diodorus Siculus and Megasthenes: A Reappraisal." *CP* 107 (1, 2012): 21–37.

Muntz, "Sources." Muntz, Charles E. "The Sources of Diodorus Siculus, Book 1." *CQ* 61 (2, 2011): 574–94.

Muraoka, "Separate Unit." Muraoka, Takamitsu. "Is the Septuagint Amos VIII 12–IX 10 a Separate Unit?" *VT* 20 (4, 1970): 496–500.

Murdock, "Patterns." Murdock, George Peter. "Patterns of Sibling Terminology." *Ethnology* 7 (1, 1968): 1–24.

Murdock, *Theories*. Murdock, George Peter. *Theories of Illness: A World Survey*. Pittsburgh: University of Pittsburgh Press, 1980.

Murgatroyd, "Ending." Murgatroyd, P. "The Ending of Apuleius' *Metamorphoses*." *CQ* 54 (1, 2004): 319–21.

Murison, "Death of Titus." Murison, Charles Leslie. "The Death of Titus: A Reconsideration." *AHB* 9 (3–4, 1995): 135–42.

Murphy, "Aspects of Shamanism." Murphy, Jane M. "Psychotherapeutic Aspects of Shamanism on St. Lawrence Island, Alaska." Pages 53–83 in *Magic, Faith, and Healing: Studies in Primitive Psychiatry Today*. Edited by Ari Kiev. Foreword by Jerome D. Frank. New York: Free Press, 1964.

Murphy, "Disposition." Murphy, Catherine M. "The Disposition of Wealth in the *Damascus Document* Tradition." *RevQ* 19 (73, 1999): 83–129.

Murphy, "Idolatry." Murphy, Frederick J. "Retelling the Bible: Idolatry in Pseudo-Philo." *JBL* 107 (2, 1988): 275–87.

Murphy, "Perspectives." Murphy, Edward Francis. "Church Growth Perspectives from the Book of Acts." DMiss diss., Fuller School of World Mission, 1979.

Murphy, "Relationship." Murphy, Roland E. "The Relationship between the Testaments." *CBQ* 26 (1964): 349–59.

Murphy, "Role of Barnabas." Murphy, S. Jonathan. "The Role of Barnabas in the Book of Acts." *BSac* 167 (667, 2010): 319–41.

Murphy, "Social Science." Murphy, Nancey. "Social Science, Ethics, and the Powers." Pages 29–38 in *Transforming the Powers: Peace, Justice, and the Domination System*. Edited by Ray Gingerich and Ted Grimsrud. Minneapolis: Fortress, 2006.

Murphy, "Understanding." Murphy, Roland E. "Christian Understanding of the Old Testament." *TD* 18 (1970): 321–32.

Murphy and Ellis, *Nature*. Murphy, Nancey, and George F. R. Ellis. *On the Moral Nature of the Universe: Theology, Cosmology, and Ethics*. Minneapolis: Fortress, 1996.

Murphy and Kasdan, "Agnation." Murphy, Robert F., and Leonard Kasdan. "Agnation and Endogamy: Some Further Considerations." *SWJA* 23 (1967): 1–14.

Murphy-O'Connor, "Antonia." Murphy-O'Connor, Jerome. "Where Was the Antonia Fortress?" *RB* 111 (1, 2004): 78–89.

Murphy-O'Connor, "Bronze." Murphy-O'Connor, Jerome. "Corinthian Bronze." *RB* 90 (1, 1983): 80–93.

Murphy-O'Connor, "Cenacle." Murphy-O'Connor, Jerome. "The Cenacle—Topographical Setting for Acts 2:44–45." Pages 303–21 in *The Book of Acts in Its Palestinian Setting*. Edited by Richard Bauckham. Vol. 4 of *The Book of Acts in Its First Century Setting*. Edited by Bruce W. Winter. Grand Rapids: Eerdmans; Carlisle, U.K.: Paternoster, 1995.

Murphy-O'Connor, "Character." Murphy-O'Connor, Jerome. "The Non-Pauline Character of 1 Corinthians 11:2–16?" *JBL* 95 (4, 1976): 615–21.

Murphy-O'Connor, "Co-authorship." Murphy-O'Connor, Jerome. "Co-authorship in the Corinthian Correspondence." *RB* 100 (4, 1993): 562–79.

Murphy-O'Connor, *Corinth*. Murphy-O'Connor, Jerome. *St. Paul's Corinth: Texts and Archaeology*. Introduction by John H. Elliott. GNS 6. Wilmington, Del.: Michael Glazier, 1983.

Murphy-O'Connor, "Corinth." Murphy-O'Connor, Jerome. "Corinth." *ABD* 1:1134–39.

Murphy-O'Connor, *Corinthians*. Murphy-O'Connor, Jerome. *1 Corinthians: The People's Bible Commentary*. Rev. ed. Oxford: Bible Reading Fellowship, 1999.

Murphy-O'Connor, "Doing in 'Arabia'?" Murphy-O'Connor, Jerome. "What Was Paul Doing in 'Arabia'?" *BRev* 10 (5, 1994): 46–47.

Murphy-O'Connor, "Jewish Mission?" Murphy-O'Connor, Jerome. "A First-Century Jewish Mission to Gentiles?" *Pacifica* 5 (1, 1992): 32–42.

Murphy-O'Connor, "Judah." Murphy-O'Connor, Jerome. "Judah the Essene and the Teacher of Righteousness." *RevQ* 10 (4, 1981): 579–85.

Murphy-O'Connor, "Lots of God-Fearers?" Murphy-O'Connor, Jerome. "Lots of God-Fearers? *Theosebeis* in the Aphrodisias Inscription." *RB* 99 (2, 1992): 418–24.

Murphy-O'Connor, *Paul*. Murphy-O'Connor, Jerome. *Paul: His Story*. Oxford: Oxford University Press, 2004.

Murphy-O'Connor, "Paul and Gallio." Murphy-O'Connor, Jerome. "Paul and Gallio." *JBL* 112 (2, 1993): 315–17.

Murphy-O'Connor, "Paul in Arabia." Murphy-O'Connor, Jerome. "Paul in Arabia." *CBQ* 55 (4, 1993): 732–37.

Murphy-O'Connor, "Prisca." Murphy-O'Connor, Jerome. "Prisca and Aquila." *BRev* 8 (6, 1992): 40–51, 62.

Murphy-O'Connor, "Promoter." Murphy-O'Connor, Jerome. "St Paul: Promoter of the Ministry of Women." *P&P* 6 (8–9, 1992): 307–11.

Murphy-O'Connor, "Remarques." Murphy-O'Connor, Jerome. "Remarques sur l'exposé du professeur Y. Yadin." *RB* 79 (1, 1972): 99–100.

Murphy-O'Connor, "What Paul Knew." Murphy-O'Connor, Jerome. "What Paul Knew of Jesus." *ScrB* 12 (2, 1981): 35–40.

Murphy-O'Connor, "Where?" Murphy-O'Connor, Jerome. "Where Was James Buried?" *BRev* 19 (3, 2003): 34–42.

Murray, "Conflator." Murray, A. Gregory. "Mark the Conflator." *DRev* 102 (1984): 157–62.

Murray, "Convivium." Murray, Oswyn. "Convivium." *OCD*³ 387.

Murray, "Evangelism." Murray, George W. "Paul's Corporate Evangelism in the Book of Acts." *BSac* 155 (618, 1998): 189–200.

Murray, "Magical Female." Murray, Michele. "The Magical Female in Graeco-Roman Rabbinic Literature." *R&T* 14 (3–4, 2007): 284–309.

Murray, *Philosophy*. Murray, Gilbert. *The Stoic Philosophy*. New York: G. P. Putnam's Sons, 1915.

Murray, *Romans*. Murray, John. *The Epistle to the Romans: The English Text with Introduction, Exposition, and Notes*. 2 vols. NICNT. Grand Rapids: Eerdmans, 1965.

Murray, *Splendor*. Murray, Margaret A. *The Splendor That Was Egypt*. New York: Hawthorn, 1963.

Murray, *Stages*. Murray, Gilbert. *Five Stages of Greek Religion*. New York: Columbia University Press, 1925. Repr., Westport, Conn.: Greenwood, 1976.

Murray, *Temples*. Murray, Margaret A. *Egyptian Temples*. London: Sampson Low, Marston, [1931].

Murray, Gordon, and Simpson, *Healing*. Murray, Andrew, A. J. Gordon, and A. B. Simpson. *Healing: The Three Great Classics on Divine Healing*. Compiled and edited by Jonathan L. Graf. Camp Hill, Pa.: Christian, 1992. (Includes Andrew Murray, *Divine Healing*; A. J. Gordon, *The Ministry of Healing*; A. B. Simpson, *The Gospel of Healing*.)

Musk, "Popular Islam." Musk, Bill A. "Popular Islam: The Hunger of the Heart." Pages 208–15 in *The Gospel and Islam: A 1978 Compendium*. Edited by Don M. McCurry. Monrovia, Calif.: MARC, 1979.

Mussies, "Artemis." Mussies, Gerard. "Artemis." Pages 91–97 in *Dictionary of Deities and Demons in the Bible*. 2nd rev. ed. Edited by Karel van der Toorn, Bob Becking, and Pieter W. van der Horst. Leiden: Brill; Grand Rapids: Eerdmans, 1999.

Mussies, "Greek." Mussies, G. "Greek in Palestine and in the Diaspora." *JPFC* 1040–64.

Mussies, "Variation." Mussies, Gerard. "Variation in the Book of Acts." *FilNeot* 4 (8, 1991): 165–82.

Mussies, "Vehicle." Mussies, Gerard. "Greek as the Vehicle of Early Christianity." *NTS* 29 (3, 1983): 356–69.

Mussies, "Wind-Gods." Mussies, Gerard. "Wind-Gods." Pages 898–900 in *Dictionary of Deities and Demons in the Bible*. 2nd rev. ed. Edited by Karel van der Toorn, Bob Becking, and Pieter W. van der Horst. Leiden: Brill; Grand Rapids: Eerdmans, 1999.

Mutafian, *La Cilicie*. Mutafian, Claude. *La Cilicie au carrefour des empires*. Paris: Belles Lettres, 1988.

Muth, "Pax Augusta." Muth, Susanne. "Pax Augusta: Die Politisierung des Friedens im antiken Rom." *BK* 61 (3, 2006): 130–37.

Muthuraj, "Mission." Muthuraj, J. G. "Mission in Early Christianity: A Re-reading of Acts of the Apostles." *BangTF* 32 (2, 2000): 1–17.

Myllykoski, "Luke and John." Myllykoski, Matti. "The Material Common to Luke and John: A Sketch." Pages 115–56 in *Luke-Acts: Scandinavian Perspectives*.

Edited by Petri Luomanen. PFES 54. Helsinki: Finnish Exegetical Society; Göttingen: Vandenhoeck & Ruprecht, 1991.

Mylonas, *Eleusis*. Mylonas, George E. *Eleusis and the Eleusinian Mysteries*. Princeton: Princeton University Press, 1961.

Myre, "Loi." Myre, André. "La loi dans l'ordre cosmique et politique selon Philon d'Alexandrie." *ScEs* 24 (2, 1972): 217–47.

Myrou, "Sosthenes." Myrou, Augustine. "Sosthenes: The Former Crispus (?)." *GOTR* 44 (1–4, 1999): 207–12.

"Mystery of Horses." "The Mystery of the Horses of the Sun at the Temple Entrance." *BAR* 4 (2, June 1978): 8–9.

Nadal, "Descent." Nadal, S. F. "Dual Descent in the Nuba Hills." Pages 333–59 in *African Systems of Kinship and Marriage*. Edited by A. R. Radcliffe-Brown and Daryll Forde. New York: Oxford University Press, 1950.

Naden, "Another Stor[e]y." Naden, Tony. "Another Stor[e]y . . ." *BTr* 41 (2, 1990): 243.

Nádor, "Sophismus." Nádor, Georg. "Sophismus und seine Beurteilung im Talmud." *Sefarad* 55 (2, 1995): 327–33.

Naeh, "Ποτήριον." Naeh, Shlomo. "Ποτήριον ἐν χειρὶ κυρίου: Philo and the Rabbis on the Powers of God and the Mixture in the Cup." *SCI* 16 (1997): 91–101.

Nagar and Torgeë, "Characteristics." Nagar, Yossi, and Hagit Torgeë. "Biological Characteristics of Jewish Burial in the Hellenistic and Early Roman Periods." *IEJ* 53 (2, 2003): 164–71.

Nagel, "Lyrics." Nagel, Rebecca. "Statius' Horatian Lyrics, Silvae 4.5 and 4.7." *CW* 102 (2, 2009): 143–57.

Nagel, "Twelve." Nagel, Norman. "The Twelve and the Seven in Acts 6 and the Needy." *ConcJ* 31 (2, 2005): 113–26.

Nagy, "Prologue." Nagy, Gregory. "The Sign of the Hero: A Prologue." Pages xi–xxxv in *Flavius Philostratus: Heroikos*. Edited and translated by Jennifer K. Berenson Maclean and Ellen Bradshaw Aitken. SBLWGRW 1. Atlanta: SBL, 2001.

Nagy, "*Superstitio*." Nagy, Àgnes A. "*Superstitio* et *coniuratio*." *Numen* 49 (2, 2002): 178–92.

Naipaul, *Masque*. Naipaul, V. S. *The Masque of Africa: Glimpses of African Belief*. New York: Alfred A. Knopf, 2010.

Najman, "Authority." Najman, Hindy. "The Law of Nature and the Authority of Mosaic Law." *SPhilA* 11 (1999): 55–73.

Najman, "Wilderness." Najman, Hindy. "Towards a Study of the Uses of the Concept of Wilderness in Ancient Judaism." *DSD* 13 (1, 2006): 99–113.

Najman, "Written Copy." Najman, Hindy. "A Written Copy of the Law of Nature: An Unthinkable Paradox?" *SPhilA* 15 (2003): 54–63.

Nanan, "Sorcerer." Nanan, Madame. "The Sorcerer and Pagan Practices." Pages 81–87 in *Our Time Has Come: African Christian Women Address the Issues of Today*. Edited by Judy Mbugua. Grand Rapids: Baker; Carlisle, U.K.: Paternoster, 1994.

Nanos, "Churches." Nanos, Mark D. "To the Churches within the Synagogues of Rome." Pages 11–28 in *Reading Paul's Letter to the Romans*. Edited by Jerry L. Sumney. SBLRBS 73. Atlanta: SBL, 2012.

Nanos, *Mystery*. Nanos, Mark D. *The Mystery of Romans: The Jewish Context of Paul's Letter*. Minneapolis: Fortress, 1996.

Nanos, "Paul's Judaism." Nanos, Mark D. "Paul and Judaism: Why Not Paul's Judaism?" Pages 117–60 in *Paul Unbound: Other Perspectives on the Apostle*. Edited by Mark D. Given. Peabody, Mass.: Hendrickson, 2010.

Nanos, "Spies." Nanos, Mark D. "Intruding 'Spies' and 'Pseudo-brethren': The Jewish Intra-group Politics of Paul's Jerusalem Meeting (Gal 2:1–10)." Pages 59–97 in *Paul and His Opponents*. Edited by Stanley E. Porter. PAST 2. Leiden: Brill, 2005.

Narayanan, "Shanti." Narayanan, Vasudha. "Shanti: Peace for the Mind, Body, and Soul." Pages 61–82 in *Teaching Religion and Healing*. Edited by Linda L. Barnes and Inés Talamantez. AARTRSS. Oxford: Oxford University Press, 2006.

Nardoni, "Concept." Nardoni, Enrique. "The Concept of Charism in Paul." *CBQ* 55 (1, 1993): 68–80.

Narducci, "Rhetoric." Narducci, Emanuele. "Rhetoric and Epic: Vergil's *Aeneid* and Lucan's *Bellum Civile*." Pages 382–95 in *A Companion to Roman Rhetoric*. Edited by William Dominik and Jon Hall. Oxford: Blackwell, 2007.

Narkiss, "Elements." Narkiss, Bezalel. "Pagan, Christian, and Jewish Elements in the Art of Ancient Synagogues." Pages 183–88 in *The Synagogue in Late Antiquity*. Edited by Lee I. Levine. Philadelphia: American Schools of Oriental Research, 1986.

Nash and Schaw, "Achievement." Nash, Dennison, and Louis C. Schaw. "Achievement and Acculturation: A Japanese Example." *Context and Meaning in Cultural Anthropology*. Edited by Melford E. Spiro. New York: Free Press, 1965.

Nasrallah, "Cities." Nasrallah, Laura. "The Acts of the Apostles, Greek Cities, and Hadrian's Panhellenion." *JBL* 127 (3, 2008): 533–66.

Nassif, "Body." Nassif, Bradley. "The Starving Body of Christ." *CHB* 94 (2007): 11–13.

Natvig, "Zar Cult." Natvig, Richard. "Some Notes on the History of the *zar* Cult in Egypt." Pages 178–88 in *Women's Medicine: The zar-bori Cult in Africa and Beyond*. Edited by I. M. Lewis, Ahmed Al-Safi, and Sayyid Hurreiz. Edinburgh: International African Institute, Edinburgh University Press, 1991.

Natvig, "*Zar* Spirits." Natvig, Richard. "Oromos, Slaves, and the *zar* Spirits: A Contribution to the History of the *zar* Cult." *IJAHS* 20 (4, 1987): 669–89.

Nauck, "Komposition der Areopagrede." Nauck, Wolfgang. "Die Tradition und Komposition der Areopagrede." *ZTK* 53 (1956): 11–52.

Nave, *Repentance*. Nave, Guy D., Jr. *The Role and Function of Repentance in Luke-Acts*. SBLABib 4. Atlanta: SBL, 2002.

Naveh, "Fragments." Naveh, Joseph. "Fragments of an Aramaic Magic Book from Qumran." *IEJ* 48 (3–4, 1998): 252–61.

Naveh and Magen, "Inscriptions." Naveh, Joseph, and Yitzhak Magen. "Aramaic and Hebrew Inscriptions of the Second Century BCE at Mount Gerizim." *'Atiqot* 32 (1997): 9–17.

Navone, "Empire." Navone, John. "Luke-Acts and the Roman Empire." *BibT* 42 (4, 2004): 230–34.

Ndofunsu, "Prayer." Ndofunsu, Diakanua. "The Role of Prayer in the Kimbanguist Church." Pages 577–96 in *Christianity in Independent Africa*. Edited by Edward Fasholé-Luke et al. Bloomington: Indiana University Press, 1978.

Neagoe, *Trial*. Neagoe, Alexandru. *The Trial of the Gospel: An Apologetic Reading of Luke's Trial Narratives*. SNTSMS 116. Cambridge: Cambridge University Press, 2002.

Neal, *Smoke*. Neal, Emily Gardiner. *Where There's Smoke: The Mystery of Christian Healing*. New York: Morehouse-Barlow, 1967.

Neale, *None but Sinners*. Neale, David A. *None but the Sinners: Religious Categories in the Gospel of Luke*. JSNTSup 58. Sheffield, U.K.: JSOT Press, 1991.

Needham, "Kinship." Needham, Rodney. "Remarks on the Analysis of Kinship and Marriage." Pages 1–34 in *Rethinking Kinship and Marriage*. Edited by Rodney Needham. ASAMS 11. New York: Tavistock, 1971.

Needham, *Rethinking*. Needham, Rodney, ed. *Rethinking Kinship and Marriage*. ASAMS 11. New York: Tavistock, 1971.

Negash, "Demelash." Negash, Teshome. "Damtew Demelash." No pages. *DACB*.

Online: http://www.dacb.org/stories/ethiopia/demelash_damtew.html.

Negbi, *Gods*. Negbi, Ora. *Canaanite Gods in Metal: An Archaeological Study of Ancient Syro-Palestinian Figurines*. Publications of the Institute of Archaeology. Tel Aviv: Tel Aviv University Press, 1976.

Negev, "Caesarea." Negev, Abraham. "Caesarea." Pages 270–85 in vol. 1 of *Encyclopedia of Archaeological Excavations in the Holy Land*. Edited by Michael Avi-Yonah. Englewood Cliffs, N.J.: Prentice-Hall, 1975.

Negev, "Nabatean Inscriptions." Negev, Avraham. "Nabatean Inscriptions." *OEANE* 4:81–82.

Negev, "Understanding Nabateans." Negev, Avraham. "Understanding the Nabateans." *BAR* 14 (6, 1988): 26–45.

Neil, *Acts*. Neil, William. *The Acts of the Apostles*. NCBC. London: Marshall, Morgan & Scott; Grand Rapids: Eerdmans, 1973.

Neil, *Thessalonians*. Neil, William. *The Epistle of Paul to the Thessalonians*. MNTC. London: Hodder & Stoughton, 1950.

Neill, "Demons." Neill, Stephen. "Demons, Demonology." Pages 161–62 in *Concise Dictionary of the Christian World Mission*. Edited by Stephen Neill, Gerald H. Anderson, and John Goodwin. Nashville: Abingdon, 1971.

Neill, *History of Missions*. Neill, Stephen. *A History of Christian Missions*. Harmondsworth, U.K.: Penguin, 1964.

Neirynck, "Luke 4,16–30." Neirynck, Frans. "Luke 4,16–30 and the Unity of Luke-Acts." Pages 357–95 in *The Unity of Luke-Acts*. Edited by Joseph Verheyden. BETL 142. Leuven: Leuven University Press, 1999.

Neirynck, "Miracle Stories." Neirynck, Frans. "The Miracle Stories in the Acts of the Apostles: An Introduction." Pages 169–213 in *Les Actes des apôtres: Traditions, rédaction, théologie*. Edited by Jacob Kremer. BETL 48. Gembloux, Belg.: J. Duculot; Leuven: Leuven University Press, 1979.

Nell, "Leadership." Nell, Ian A. "Leadership in Acts through a Social Capital Lens." *VerbEc* 30 (2, 2009): art. #87, 7 pages. doi: 10.4102/ve.v30i2.87.

Nellessen, "Gemeinden." Nellessen, E. "Die Presbyter der Gemeinden in Lykaonien und Pisidien (Apg 14,23)." Pages 493–98 in *Les Actes des apôtres: Traditions, rédaction, théologie*. Edited by Jacob Kremer. BETL 48. Gembloux, Belg.: J. Duculot; Leuven: Leuven University Press, 1979.

Nelson, "Fish." Nelson, M. "A Note on Apuleius's Magical Fish." *Mnemosyne* 54 (1, 2001): 85–86.

Nelson, "Leadership." Nelson, Peter K. "Leadership and Discipleship: A Study of Luke 22:24–30." PhD diss., Trinity College, Bristol, U.K., 1991.

Nelson, "Temple." Nelson, Harold H. "The Egyptian Temple." Pages 147–58 in *The Biblical Archaeologist Reader*. Edited by G. Ernest Wright and David Noel Freedman. Chicago: Quadrangle, 1961.

Nepper-Christensen, "Apostelmodet." Nepper-Christensen, Poul. "Apostelmodet i Jerusalem." *DTT* 56 (3, 1993): 169–88.

Nerlove and Romney, "Sibling Terminology." Nerlove, Sara, and A. Kimball Romney. "Sibling Terminology and Cross-Sex Behavior." *AmAnth* 69 (Apr. 1967): 179–87.

Ness, "Astrology." Ness, Lester. "Astrology." *ABW* 2 (1, 1992): 44–53.

Netzer, *Architecture*. Netzer, Ehud. *The Architecture of Herod, the Great Builder*. Tübingen: Mohr Siebeck, 2006; Grand Rapids: Baker Academic, 2008.

Netzer, "Jericho." Netzer, Ehud. "A Synagogue from the Hasmonean Period Recently Exposed in the Western Plain of Jericho." *IEJ* 49 (3–4, 1999): 203–21.

Netzer, "Kysd." Netzer, Ehud. "Kysd nr'w wtpqdw h'zrwt, hlskwt whs'rym shqypw 't byt hmqds hsny." *Qad* 38 (130, 2005): 97–106.

Netzer, "Masada." Netzer, Ehud. "Masada." *NEAEHL* 3:973–85.

Netzer, "Mqww'wt." Netzer, Ehud. "Mqww'wt-hthrh mymy byt sny byryhw" [Miqvaot of the Second Temple Period at Jericho]. *Qad* 11 (2–3, 1978): 54–59.

Netzer, "Promontory Palace." Netzer, Ehud. "The Promontory Palace." Pages 149–59 in *Excavations at Caesarea Maritima 1975, 1976, 1979—Final Report*. Edited by Lee Levine and Ehud Netzer. Qedem 21. Jerusalem: Hebrew University of Jerusalem Press, 1986.

Netzer, "Reconstruction." Netzer, Ehud. "A New Reconstruction of Paul's Prison." *BAR* 35 (1, Jan. 2009): 44–51, 71.

Neubrand, *Völker*. Neubrand, Maria. *Israel, die Völker und die Kirche: Eine exegetische Studie zu Apg 15*. SBB 55. Stuttgart: Verlag Katholisches Bibelwerk, 2006.

Neudecker, "Eutychides." Neudecker, Richard. "Eutychides." *BrillPauly* 5:241.

Neudecker, "Iniquity." Neudecker, Reinhard. "Does God Visit the Iniquity of the Fathers upon Their Children? Rabbinic Commentaries on Exod 20,5b (Deut 5,9b)." *Greg* 81 (1, 2000): 5–24.

Neudecker, "Kolossos." Neudecker, Richard. "Kolossos." *BrillPauly* 7:87.

Neudecker, "Phidias." Neudecker, Richard. "Phidias." *BrillPauly* 11:3–5.

Neudecker, "Relationship." Neudecker, Reinhard. "Master-Disciple/Disciple-Master Relationship in Rabbinic Judaism and in the Gospels." *Greg* 80 (2, 1999): 245–61.

Neudecker, "Volk." Neudecker, Reinhard. "'Das ganze Volk sah die Stimmen . . .': Haggadische Auslegung und Pfingstbericht." *Bib* 78 (3, 1997): 329–49.

Neudorfer, "Speech." Neudorfer, Heinz-Werner. "The Speech of Stephen." Pages 275–94 in *Witness to the Gospel: The Theology of Acts*. Edited by I. Howard Marshall and David Peterson. Grand Rapids: Eerdmans, 1998.

Neuhaus, "Rencontre." Neuhaus, David M. "À la rencontre de Paul. Connaître Paul aujourd'hui—un changement de paradigme?" *RSR* 90 (3, 2002): 353–76.

Neumann, "Gewinn." Neumann, Nils. "Kein Gewinn = Gewinn: Die kynisch geprägte Struktur der Argumentation in 1 Tim 6:3–12." *NovT* 51 (2, 2009): 127–47.

Neumann, "Trilingual Inscriptions." Neumann, Günter. "Trilingual Inscriptions: General; Trilingual Inscriptions with Greek and Latin Text." *BrillPauly* 14:921–22.

Neusner, "Approaches." Neusner, Jacob. "Scriptural, Essenic, and Mishnaic Approaches to Civil Law and Government: Some Comparative Remarks." *HTR* 73 (3–4, 1980): 419–34.

Neusner, *Beginning*. Neusner, Jacob. *Judaism in the Beginning of Christianity*. Philadelphia: Fortress, 1984.

Neusner, *Christianity*. Neusner, Jacob, ed. *Christianity, Judaism, and Other Greco-Roman Cults: Studies for Morton Smith at Sixty. Part One: New Testament*. SJLA 12.1. Leiden: Brill, 1975.

Neusner, "Comparing Judaisms." Neusner, Jacob. "Comparing Judaisms." *HR* 18 (2, 1978): 177–91.

Neusner, *Connection*. Neusner, Jacob. *Canon and Connection: Intertextuality in Judaism*. Lanham, Md.: University Press of America, 1987.

Neusner, "Conversion." Neusner, Jacob. "The Conversion of Adiabene to Judaism." *JBL* 83 (1, 1964): 60–66.

Neusner, *Crisis*. Neusner, Jacob. *First-Century Judaism in Crisis: Yohanan ben Zakkai and the Renaissance of Torah*. Nashville: Abingdon, 1975.

Neusner, "Foreword." Neusner, Jacob. Foreword. Pages xxv–xlvi in *Memory and Manuscript: Oral Tradition and Written Transmission in Rabbinic Judaism and Early Christianity; Tradition and Transmission in Early Christianity*. By Birger Gerhardsson. Grand Rapids: Eerdmans, 1998.

Neusner, "Gamaliel." Neusner, Jacob. "From Biography to Theology: Gamaliel and the Patriarchate." *JHC* 12 (1, 2006): 29–62.

Neusner, "History." Neusner, Jacob. "The Idea of History in Rabbinic Judaism. What Kinds of Questions Did the Ancient Rabbis Answer?" *NBf* 90 (1027, 2009): 277–94.

Neusner, "Kingdom." Neusner, Jacob. "The Kingdom of Heaven in Kindred Systems, Judaic and Christian." *BBR* 15 (2, 2005): 279–305.

Neusner, "*Merkavah* Tradition." Neusner, Jacob. "The Development of the *merkavah* Tradition." *JSJ* 2 (2, 1971): 149–60.

Neusner, *New Testament*. Neusner, Jacob. *Rabbinic Literature and the New Testament: What We Cannot Show, We Do Not Know*. Valley Forge, Pa.: Trinity Press International, 1994.

Neusner, "Pharisees." Neusner, Jacob. "Josephus' Pharisees: A Complete Repertoire." Pages 274–92 in *Josephus, Judaism, and Christianity*. Edited by Louis H. Feldman and Gohei Hata. Detroit: Wayne State University Press, 1987.

Neusner, *Politics to Piety*. Neusner, Jacob. *From Politics to Piety: The Emergence of Pharisaic Judaism*. 2nd ed. New York: KTAV, 1979.

Neusner, *Purities*. Neusner, Jacob. *A History of the Mishnaic Law of Purities*. 22 vols. Leiden: Brill, 1974–77.

Neusner, "Sacrifice." Neusner, Jacob. "Sacrifice in Rabbinic Judaism: The Presentation of the Atonement-rite of Sacrifice in Tractate Zebahim, in the Mishnah, Tosefta, Bavli, and Yerushalmi." *ASDE* 18 (1, 2001): 225–53.

Neusner, *Sat*. Neusner, Jacob. *There We Sat Down: Talmudic Judaism in the Making*. Nashville: Abingdon, 1972.

Neusner, "Sin, Repentance." Neusner, Jacob. "Sin, Repentance, Atonement, and Resurrection: The Perspective of Rabbinic Theology on the Views of James 1–2 and Paul in Romans 3–4." *ASDE* 18 (2, 2001): 409–31.

Neusner, "Testimony." Neusner, Jacob. "'By the Testimony of Two Witnesses' in the Damascus Document IX, 17–22 and in Pharisaic-Rabbinic Law." *RevQ* 8 (30/2, 1973): 197–217.

Neusner, *Traditions*. Neusner, Jacob. *The Rabbinic Traditions about the Pharisees before 70*. 3 vols. Leiden: Brill, 1971.

Nevius, *Possession*. Nevius, John L. *Demon Possession and Allied Themes*. Chicago: Fleming H. Revell, 1894.

New, "Name." New, Silva. "The Name, Baptism, and the Laying on of Hands." *BegChr* 5:121–40.

Newlands, "Mothers." Newlands, Carole. "Mothers in Statius's Poetry: Sorrows and Surrogates." *Helios* 33 (2, 2006): 203–26.

Newlands, "Ovid." Newlands, Carole. "Select Ovid." *CW* 102 (2, 2009): 173–77.

Newman, "*Sandak*." Newman, Hillel I. "*Sandak* and Godparent in Midrash and Medieval Practice." *JQR* 97 (1, 2007): 1–32.

Newman and Nida, *Acts*. Newman, Barclay M., and Eugene A. Nida. *A Translator's Handbook on the Acts of the Apostles*. Stuttgart: United Bible Societies, 1972.

Newmyer, "Climate." Newmyer, Stephen. "Climate and Health: Classical and Talmudic Perspective." *Judaism* 33 (4, 1984): 426–38.

Newmyer, "Medicine." Newmyer, Stephen. "Talmudic Medicine: A Classicist's Perspective." *Judaism* 29 (3, 1980): 360–67.

Newport, "Seat of Moses." Newport, Kenneth G. C. "A Note on the 'Seat of Moses' (Matthew 23:2)." *AUSS* 28 (1990): 53–58.

Newsom, "Songs." Newsom, Carol A. "Songs of the Sabbath Sacrifice (4Q400–407, 11Q17, Mas 1K)." *DNTB* 1137–39.

Newton, *Observations*. Newton, Sir Isaac. *Observations upon the Prophecies of Daniel and the Apocalypse of St. John: In Two Parts*. London: J. Darby and T. Browne, 1733.

Neyrey, "Benefactor." Neyrey, Jerome H. "God, Benefactor and Patron: The Major Cultural Model for Interpreting the Deity in Greco-Roman Antiquity." *JSNT* 27 (4, 2005): 465–92.

Neyrey, "Ceremonies." Neyrey, Jerome H. "Ceremonies in Luke-Acts: The Case of Meals and Table Fellowship." Pages 361–87 in *The Social World of Luke-Acts: Models for Interpretation*. Edited by Jerome H. Neyrey. Peabody, Mass.: Hendrickson, 1991.

Neyrey, "Epicureans and Theodicy." Neyrey, Jerome H. "Acts 17, Epicureans, and Theodicy: A Study in Stereotypes." Pages 118–34 in *Greeks, Romans, and Christians: Essays in Honor of Abraham J. Malherbe*. Edited by David L. Balch et al. Minneapolis: Fortress, 1990.

Neyrey, "Forensic Defense Speech." Neyrey, Jerome H. "The Forensic Defense Speech and Paul's Trial Speeches in Acts 22–26: Form and Function." Pages 210–24 in *Luke-Acts: New Perspectives from the Society of Biblical Literature Seminar*. Edited by Charles H. Talbert. New York: Crossroad, 1984.

Neyrey, "Location of Paul." Neyrey, Jerome H. "Luke's Social Location of Paul: Cultural Anthropology and the Status of Paul in Acts." Pages 251–79 in *History, Literature, and Society in the Book of Acts*. Edited by Ben Witherington III. Cambridge: Cambridge University Press, 1996.

Neyrey, "Lost." Neyrey, Jerome H. "Lost in Translation: Did It Matter If Christians 'Thanked' God or 'Gave God Glory'?" *CBQ* 71 (1, 2009): 1–23.

Neyrey, "Miracles." Neyrey, Jerome H. "Miracles, In Other Words: Social Science Perspectives on Healings." Pages 19–56 in *Miracles in Jewish and Christian Antiquity: Imagining Truth*. Edited by John C. Cavadini. NDST 3. Notre Dame, Ind.: University of Notre Dame, 1999.

Neyrey, *Passion*. Neyrey, Jerome H. *The Passion according to Luke: A Redaction Study of Luke's Soteriology*. Theological Inquiries. New York: Paulist, 1985.

Neyrey, "Polemic." Neyrey, Jerome H. "The Form and Background of the Polemic in 2 Peter." *JBL* 99 (3, 1980): 407–31.

Neyrey, "Shame of Cross." Neyrey, Jerome H. "'Despising the Shame of the Cross': Honor and Shame in the Johannine Passion Narrative." *Semeia* 68 (1994): 113–37.

Neyrey, *Social World*. Neyrey, Jerome H., ed. *The Social World of Luke-Acts: Models for Interpretation*. Peabody, Mass.: Hendrickson, 1991.

Neyrey, "Teaching." Neyrey, Jerome H. "'Teaching You in Public and from House to House' (Acts 20.20): Unpacking a Cultural Stereotype." *JSNT* 26 (1, 2003): 69–102.

Newell, "Suicide Accounts." Newell, Raymond R. "The Forms and Historical Value of Josephus' Suicide Accounts." Pages 278–94 in *Josephus, the Bible, and History*. Edited by Louis H. Feldman and Gohei Hata. Detroit: Wayne State University Press, 1989.

Ng, "Guardians." Ng, Esther Yue L. "Mirror Reading and Guardians of Women in the Early Roman Empire." *JTS* 59 (2, 2008): 679–95.

Nguyen, "Asian View." Nguyen, vanThanh. "An Asian View of Biblical Hospitality." *Vid* 74 (6, 2010): 445–59.

Nguyen, *Peter*. Nguyen, vanThanh. *Peter and Cornelius: A Story of Conversion and Mission*. AmSocMissS 15. Eugene, Ore.: Pickwick, 2012.

Niang, *Faith*. Niang, Aliou Cissé. *Faith and Freedom in Galatia and Senegal: The Apostle Paul, Colonists and Sending Gods*. BIS 97. Leiden: Brill, 2009.

Niang, "Seeing." Niang, Aliou Cissé. "Seeing and Hearing Jesus Christ Crucified in Galatians 3:1 under Watchful Imperial Eyes." Pages 160–82 in *Text, Image, and Christians in the Graeco-Roman World: A Festschrift in Honor of David Lee Balch*. Edited by Aliou Cissé Niang and Carolyn

Osiek. PrTMS 176. Eugene, Ore.: Pickwick, 2012.

Niccum, "Voice." Niccum, Curt. "The Voice of the Manuscripts on the Silence of Women: The External Evidence for 1 Cor 14.34–5." NTS 43 (2, 1997): 242–55.

Nicholas, "Centumviri." Nicholas, Barry. "Centumviri." OCD³ 309–10.

Nicholas, "Edict." Nicholas, Barry. "Edict." OCD³ 505–6.

Nicholas, "Evidence." Nicholas, Barry. "Evidence, Roman." OCD³ 579.

Nichols, Ctesias. Nichols, Andrew G. Ctesias: On India and Fragments of His Minor Works; Introduction, Translation and Commentary. London: Bristol Classics, 2011.

Nichols, "Miracles." Nichols, Terence. "Miracles in Science and Theology." Zyg 37 (3, 2002): 703–15.

Nicholson, "Confidentiality." Nicholson, John. "The Delivery and Confidentiality of Cicero's Letters." CJ 90 (1, 1994): 33–63.

Nicholson, Death. Nicholson, Godfrey C. Death as Departure: The Johannine Descent-Ascent Schema. SBLDS 63. Chico, Calif.: Scholars Press, 1983.

Nicholson, "Expression." Nicholson, E. W. "The Meaning of the Expression 'm h'rs in the Old Testament." JSS 10 (1, 1965): 59–66.

Nickbackht, "Aemulatio." Nickbackht, Mehran A. "Aemulatio in Cold Blood: A Reading of the End of the Aeneid." Helios 37 (1, 2010): 49–80.

Nickelsburg, "Apocalyptic." Nickelsburg, George W. E. "Apocalyptic and Myth in 1 Enoch 6–11." JBL 96 (3, 1977): 383–405.

Nickelsburg, "Ektrōma." Nickelsburg, George W. E. "An ektrōma, Though Appointed from the Womb: Paul's Apostolic Self-Description in 1 Corinthians 15 and Galatians 1." HTR 79 (1–3, 1986): 198–205.

Nickelsburg, "Eschatology." Nickelsburg, George W. E. "Eschatology in the Testament of Abraham: A Study of the Judgment Scene in the Two Recensions." Pages 23–64 in Studies on the Testament of Abraham. Edited by George W. E. Nickelsburg. SBLSCS 6. Missoula, Mont.: Scholars Press, 1976.

Nickelsburg, "Genre." Nickelsburg, George W. E. "The Genre and Function of the Markan Passion Narrative." HTR 73 (1980): 153–84.

Nickelsburg, Literature. Nickelsburg, George W. E. Jewish Literature between the Bible and the Mishnah. Philadelphia: Fortress, 1981.

Nickelsburg, "Review." Nickelsburg, George W. E. "Review of the Literature." Pages 9–22 in Studies on the Testament of Abraham. Edited by George W. E. Nickelsburg. SBLSCS 6. Missoula, Mont.: Scholars Press, 1976.

Nickelsburg, "Son of Man." Nickelsburg, George W. E. "Son of Man." Pages 800–804 in Dictionary of Deities and Demons in the Bible. 2nd rev. ed. Edited by Karel van der Toorn, Bob Becking, and Pieter W. van der Horst. Leiden: Brill; Grand Rapids: Eerdmans, 1999.

Nickelsburg, "Structure and Message." Nickelsburg, George W. E. "Structure and Message in the Testament of Abraham." Pages 85–94 in Studies on the Testament of Abraham. Edited by George W. E. Nickelsburg. SBLSCS 6. Missoula, Mont.: Scholars Press, 1976.

Nicklas and Tilly, Acts as Church History. Nicklas, Tobias, and Michael Tilly, eds. The Book of Acts as Church History: Text, Textual Traditions and Ancient Interpretations/Apostelgeschichte als Kirchengeschichte: Text, Texttraditionen und antike Auslegungen. Berlin: de Gruyter, 2003.

Nickle, Collection. Nickle, Keith F. The Collection: A Study in Biblical Theology. SBT 48. Naperville, Ill.: Alec R. Allenson, 1966.

Nicolai, "Place of History." Nicolai, Roberto. "The Place of History in the Ancient World." Pages 13–26 in A Companion to Greek and Roman Historiography. Edited by John Marincola. 2 vols. Oxford: Blackwell, 2007.

Nicolini, "Notes." Nicolini, Beatrice. "Notes on Magical Practices in Zanzibar and Pemba. The Role of the Waganga During Colonial Times." Pages 115–26 in Studies in Witchcraft, Magic, War, and Peace in Africa. Edited by Beatrice Nicolini. Lewiston, N.Y.: Edwin Mellen, 2006.

Niditch, "Adam." Niditch, Susan. "The Cosmic Adam: Man as Mediator in Rabbinic Literature." JJS 34 (2, 1983): 137–46.

Niehaus, Themes. Niehaus, Jeffrey J. Ancient Near Eastern Themes in Biblical Theology. Grand Rapids: Kregel Academic, 2008.

Niehoff, "Circumcision." Niehoff, Maren R. "Circumcision as a Marker of Identity: Philo, Origen, and the Rabbis on Gen 17:1–14." JSQ 10 (2, 2003): 89–123.

Niehoff, "Exegesis in Alexandria." Niehoff, Maren R. "Homeric Scholarship and Bible Exegesis in Ancient Alexandria: Evidence from Philo's 'Quarrelsome' Colleagues." CQ 57 (1, 2007): 166–82.

Niehoff, "Identity." Niehoff, Maren R. "Jewish Identity and Jewish Mothers: Who Was a Jew according to Philo?" SPhilA 11 (1999): 31–54.

Niehoff, "Mother." Niehoff, Maren R. "Mother and Maiden, Sister and Spouse: Sarah in Philonic Midrash." HTR 97 (4, 2004): 413–44.

Niehoff, "Phoenix." Niehoff, Maren R. "The Phoenix in Rabbinic Literature." HTR 89 (3, 1996): 245–65.

Niehoff, "Two Examples." Niehoff, Maren R. "Two Examples of Josephus' Narrative Technique in His 'Rewritten Bible.'" JSJ 27 (1, 1996): 31–45.

Nielsen, "Amphitheatre." Nielsen, Inge. "Amphitheatre." BrillPauly 1:608–13.

Nielsen, Fulfilled. Nielsen, Anders Eyvind. Until It Is Fulfilled: Lukan Eschatology according to Luke 22 and Acts 20. WUNT 2.126. Tübingen: Mohr Siebeck, 2000.

Nielsen, "Library." Nielsen, Inge. "Library." BrillPauly 7:498–503.

Nielsen, "Purpose." Nielsen, Anders E. "The Purpose of the Lucan Writings with Particular Reference to Eschatology." Pages 76–93 in Luke-Acts: Scandinavian Perspectives. Edited by Petri Luomanen. PFES 54. Helsinki: Finnish Exegetical Society; Göttingen: Vandenhoeck & Ruprecht, 1991.

Nielsen, "Temple." Nielsen, Inge. "Temple: Rome." BrillPauly 14:258–61.

Niemand, "Testimonium." Niemand, C. "Das Testimonium Flavianum: Befunde, Diskussionsstand, Perspektiven." PzB 17 (1, 2008): 45–71.

Niemandt, "Missional Church." Niemandt, Cornelius J. P. "Acts for Today's Missional Church." HTS/TS 66 (1, 2010) Art. #336, 8 pages. doi: 10.4102/hts.v66i1.336.

Niemeyer, "Cyrene: Archaeology." Niemeyer, Hans Georg. "Cyrene: Archaeology." BrillPauly 4:10.

Niemeyer, "Mauretania: Archaeology." Niemeyer, Hans Georg. "Mauretania: Archaeology." BrillPauly 8:496–97.

Niemeyer, Röllig, and Eder, "Phoenicians." Niemeyer, Hans Georg, Wolfgang Röllig, and Walter Eder. "Phoenicians, Poeni." BrillPauly 11:147–68.

Nienkirchen, "Visions." Nienkirchen, Charles. "Conflicting Visions of the Past: The Prophetic Use of History in the Early American Pentecostal-Charismatic Movements." Pages 119–33 in Charismatic Christianity as a Global Culture. Edited by Karla Poewe. SCR. Columbia: University of South Carolina Press, 1994.

Nietmann, "Seneca." Nietmann, W. D. "Seneca on Death: The Courage to Be or Not to Be." International Philosophical Quarterly 6 (1966): 81–89.

Nieto Ibáñez, "Grove." Nieto Ibáñez, Jesús-María. "The Sacred Grove of Scythopolis (Flavius Josephus, Jewish War II 466–471)." IEJ 49 (3–4, 1999): 260–68.

Nigdelis, "Associations." Nigdelis, Pantelis M. "Voluntary Associations in Roman Thessalonike: In Search of Identity and

Support in a Cosmopolitan Society." Pages 13–47 in *From Roman to Early Christian Thessalonike*. Edited by Laura Nasrallah, Charalambos Bakirtzis, and Steven J. Friesen. HTS 64. Cambridge, Mass.: Harvard University Press, 2010.

Nikiprowetzky, "Josephus and Parties." Nikiprowetzky, Valentin. "Josephus and the Revolutionary Parties." Translated by Angela Armstrong. Pages 216–36 in *Josephus, the Bible, and History*. Edited by Louis H. Feldman and Gohei Hata. Detroit: Wayne State University Press, 1989.

Nikiprowetzky, "Sabbat." Nikiprowetzky, Valentin. "Le sabbat et les armes dans l'histoire ancienne d'Israël." *REJ* 159 (1–2, 2000): 1–17.

Nikiprowetzky, *Sibylle*. Nikiprowetzky, Valentin. *La troisième Sibylle*. Études juives 9. Paris: La Haye, 1970.

Nikolsky, "Epicurus." Nikolsky, Boris. "Epicurus on Pleasure." *Phronesis* 46 (4, 2001): 440–65.

Nikopoulou-de Sike, *Delphi*. Nikopoulou-de Sike, Yvonne. *Delphi*. Athens: A&C Publications, 1978.

Nilson, "Addressed." Nilson, Jon. "To Whom Is Justin's *Dialogue with Trypho* Addressed?" *TS* 38 (3, Sept. 1977): 538–46.

Nilsson, *Cults*. Nilsson, Martin Persson. *Cults, Myths, Oracles, and Politics in Ancient Greece*. SUSIA 8°, 1. Lund, Swed.: C. W. K. Gleerup, 1951.

Nilsson, *Folk Religion*. Nilsson, Martin P. *Greek Folk Religion*. Foreword by Arthur Darby Nock. New York: Columbia University Press, 1940; rev. ed. New York: Harper, 1961.

Nilsson, *Piety*. Nilsson, Martin Persson. *Greek Piety*. Translated by Herbert Jennings Rose. Oxford: Clarendon, 1948.

Ní-Mheallaigh, "Pseudo-Documentarism." Ní-Mheallaigh, Karen. "Pseudo-Documentarism and the Limits of Ancient Fiction." *AJP* 129 (3, 2008): 403–31.

Nineham, "Authorship." Nineham, D. E. "The Case against the Pauline Authorship." Pages 21–35 in *Studies in Ephesians*. Edited by F. L. Cross. London: A. R. Mowbray, 1956.

Nineham, *Mark*. Nineham, D. E. *Gospel of Saint Mark*. Baltimore: Penguin, 1963. Repr., Philadelphia: Westminster, 1977.

Nippel, "Police." Nippel, Wilfried. "Police." *BrillPauly* 11:463–64.

Niskanen, "Kingdoms." Niskanen, Paul. "Kingdoms, Dominions, and the Reign of God." *BibT* 42 (6, 2004): 343–48.

Nissen, "Pigs." Nissen, Hans Jörg. "Pigs. I. Near East and Egypt." *BrillPauly* 11:244–45.

Nissen, "Ptolemais." Nissen, Hans Jörg. "Ptolemais." *BrillPauly* 12:174.

Nissen and Oelsner, "Mesopotamia." Nissen, Hans Jörg, and Joachim Oelsner. "Mesopotamia." *BrillPauly* 8:727–46.

Nix, "Caesar." Nix, Sarah A. "Caesar as Jupiter in Lucan's Bellum Civile." *CJ* 103 (3, 2008): 281–94.

Njoroge wa Ngugi, "Catechetical Discourse." Njoroge wa Ngugi, J. "Stephen's Speech as Catechetical Discourse." *LivL* 33 (4, 1997): 64–71.

Njoroge wa Ngugi, "Stephen's Speech." Njoroge wa Ngugi, J. "Stephen's Speech in Acts 7:1–53 as a Challenge for Enculturation in Catechesis." *AfCS* 18 (1, 2002): 34–66.

Noack, *Jesus Ananiassøn*. Noack, Bent. *Jesus Ananiassøn og Jesus fra Nasaret: En drøptelse af Josefus, Bellum judaicum VI 5, 3*. Tekst og Tolkning 6. Copenhagen: Gyldendal, 1975.

Noack, "Pentecost in Jubilees." Noack, Bent. "The Day of Pentecost in Jubilees, Qumran, and Acts." *ASTI* 1 (1962): 73–95.

Noack, "Qumran and Jubilees." Noack, Bent. "Qumran and the Book of Jubilees." *SEÅ* 22–23 (1957–58): 191–207.

Nobbs, "Brothers." Nobbs, Alanna. "'Beloved Brothers' in the New Testament and Early Christian World." Pages 143–50 in *The New Testament in Its First Century Setting: Essays on Context and Background in Honour of B. W. Winter on His 65th Birthday*. Edited by P. J. Williams et al. Grand Rapids and Cambridge, U.K.: Eerdmans, 2004.

Nobbs, "Cyprus." Nobbs, Alanna. "Cyprus." Pages 279–89 in *The Book of Acts in Its Graeco-Roman Setting*. Edited by David W. J. Gill and Conrad Gempf. Vol. 2 of *The Book of Acts in Its First Century Setting*. Edited by Bruce W. Winter. Grand Rapids: Eerdmans; Carlisle, U.K.: Paternoster, 1994.

Nobbs, "Historians." Nobbs, Alanna. "What Do Ancient Historians Make of the New Testament?" *TynBul* 57 (2, 2006): 285–90.

Nobbs, "Histories." Nobbs, Alanna. "Acts and Subsequent Ecclesiastical Histories." Pages 153–62 in *The Book of Acts in Its Ancient Literary Setting*. Edited by Bruce W. Winter and Andrew D. Clarke. Vol. 1 of *The Book of Acts in Its First Century Setting*. Edited by Bruce W. Winter. Grand Rapids: Eerdmans; Carlisle, U.K.: Paternoster, 1993.

Noble, "Possession." Noble, D. A. "Demoniacal Possession among the Giryama." *Man* 61 (1961): 50–52.

Nock, *Christianity*. Nock, Arthur Darby. *Early Gentile Christianity and Its Hellenistic Background*. New York: Harper & Row, 1964.

Nock, *Conversion*. Nock, Arthur Darby. *Conversion: The Old and the New in Religion from Alexander the Great to Augustine of Hippo*. Oxford: Clarendon, 1933.

Nock, "Developments." Nock, Arthur Darby. "Religious Developments from the Close of the Republic to the Death of Nero." Pages 465–511 in *The Augustan Empire: 44 B.C.–A.D. 70*. Edited by S. A. Cook, F. E. Adcock, and M. P. Charlesworth. CAH 10. Cambridge: Cambridge University Press, 1934. Repr., 1966.

Nock, *Essays*. Nock, Arthur Darby. *Essays on Religion and the Ancient World*. Edited by Zeph Stewart. 2 vols. Cambridge, Mass.: Harvard University Press, 1972.

Nock, "Genius of Mithraism." Nock, Arthur Darby. "The Genius of Mithraism." *JRS* 27 (1937): 108–13.

Nock, "Gnosticism." Nock, Arthur Darby. "Gnosticism." *HTR* 57 (4, Oct. 1964): 255–79.

Nock, "Magus." Nock, Arthur Darby. "Paul and the Magus." *BegChr* 5:164–88.

Nock, *Paul*. Nock, Arthur Darby. *St. Paul*. New York: Harper and Brothers, 1938. Repr., New York: Harper & Row, 1963.

Nock, "Vocabulary." Nock, Arthur Darby. "The Vocabulary of the New Testament." *JBL* 52 (2–3, 1933): 131–39.

Nodet, "Humanity." Nodet, Étienne. "The Emphasis on Jesus' Humanity in the Earliest Kerygma." Paper presented at the second Princeton-Prague Symposium on Jesus: Methodological Approaches to the Historical Jesus, Princeton, Apr. 19, 2007.

Nodet, "Théophile." Nodet, Étienne. "Théophile (Lc 1,1–4; Ac 1,1)." *RB* 119 (4, 2012): 585–95.

Nolan, "Stoic Gunk." Nolan, Daniel. "Stoic Gunk." *Phronesis* 51 (2, 2006): 162–83.

Nolen, *Healing*. Nolen, William A. *Healing: A Doctor in Search of a Miracle*. New York: Random House, 1974.

Nolen, "Woman." Nolen, William A. "The Woman Who Said No to Cancer." *Science Digest* (Dec. 1982): 34–37.

Noll, *History*. Noll, Mark A. *A History of Christianity in the United States and Canada*. Grand Rapids: Eerdmans, 1992.

Noll, *Rise*. Noll, Mark A. *The Rise of Evangelicalism: The Age of Edwards, Whitefield, and the Wesleys*. A History of Evangelicalism 1. Downers Grove, Ill.: InterVarsity, 2003.

Noll, *Shape*. Noll, Mark A. *The New Shape of World Christianity: How American Experience Reflects Global Faith*. Downers Grove, Ill.: IVP Academic, 2009.

Noll and Nystrom, *Clouds*. Noll, Mark A., and Carolyn Nystrom. *Clouds of Witnesses: Christian Voices from Africa and Asia*. Downers Grove, Ill.: InterVarsity, 2011.

Nolland, *Luke*. Nolland, John. *Luke 1–9:20*. WBC 35A. Waco: Word, 1989.

Nolland, "Luke's Readers." Nolland, John. "Luke's Readers—A Study of Luke 4.22–8; Acts 13.46; 18.6; 28.28 and Luke 21.5–36." PhD diss., University of Cambridge, 1977.

Nolland, "Misleading Statement." Nolland, John. "A Misleading Statement of the Essene Attitude to the Temple (Josephus, *Antiquities*, XVIII, I, 5, 19)." *RevQ* 9 (4, 1978): 555–62.

Nolland, "Parallels to 'Physician.'" Nolland, John. "Classical and Rabbinic Parallels to 'Physician, Heal Yourself' (Lk. iv 23)." *NovT* 21 (3, 1979): 193–209.

Nolland, "Proselytes." Nolland, John. "Uncircumcised Proselytes?" *JSJ* 12 (2, 1981): 173–94.

Nolland, "Salvation-History." Nolland, John. "Salvation-History and Eschatology." Pages 63–81 in *Witness to the Gospel: The Theology of Acts*. Edited by I. Howard Marshall and David Peterson. Grand Rapids: Eerdmans, 1998.

Nolland, "Words." Nolland, John. "Words of Grace (Luke 4.22)." *Bib* 65 (1, 1984): 44–60.

Nollé, "Lot." Nollé, Johannes. "Lot, Election by: Religious." *BrillPauly* 7:819–20.

Noorda, "Scene." Noorda, S. J. "Scene and Summary. A Proposal for Reading Acts 4,32–5,16." Pages 475–83 in *Les Actes des apôtres: Traditions, rédaction, théologie*. Edited by Jacob Kremer. BETL 48. Gembloux, Belg.: J. Duculot; Leuven: Leuven University Press, 1979.

Norden, *Agnostos theos*. Norden, Eduard. *Agnostos theos: Untersuchungen zur Formengeschichte religiöser Rede*. Leipzig: Teubner, 1913.

Noreña, "Economy." Noreña, Carlos F. "The Social Economy of Pliny's Correspondence with Trajan." *AJP* 128 (2, 2007): 239–77.

Norris, "Antioch." Norris, Frederick W. "Antioch of Syria." *ABD* 1:265–69.

Norris, "Christians Only." Norris, Frederick W. "'Christians Only, but Not the Only Christians' (Acts 19:1–7)." *ResQ* 28 (2, 1985–86): 97–105.

Norris, "Isis, Sarapis, and Demeter." Norris, Frederick W. "Isis, Sarapis, and Demeter in Antioch of Syria." *HTR* 75 (2, 1982): 189–207.

Norris and Inglehart, *Sacred*. Norris, Pippa, and Ronald Inglehart. *Sacred and Secular: Religion and Politics Worldwide*. Cambridge: Cambridge University Press, 2004.

North, "Bona Dea." North, J. A. "Bona Dea." *OCD*³ 249.

North, "Damascus." North, Robert. "The Damascus of Qumran Geography." *PEQ*, 87 (1955): 34–48.

North, "IDEIN PERI." North, J. L. "Is IDEIN PERI (Acts 15.6, cf. 18.15) a Latinism?" *NTS* 29 (2, 1983): 264–66.

North, "Liber Pater." North, J. A. "Liber Pater." *OCD*³ 854.

North, "Mare." North, Helen F. "The Mare, the Vixen, and the Bee: *Sophrosyne* as the Virtue of Women in Antiquity." *ICS* 2 (1977): 35–48.

North, "Priests." North, J. A. "Priests (Greek and Roman)." *OCD*³ 1245–46.

North, *Sophrosyne*. North, Helen F. *Sophrosyne: Self-Knowledge and Self-Restraint in Greek Literature*. Ithaca, N.Y.: Cornell, 1966.

North, "'Sophrosyne' in Criticism." North, Helen F. "The Concept of 'Sophrosyne' in Greek Literary Criticism." *CP* 43 (1948): 1–17.

North, "Temple Officials." North, J. A. "Temple Officials." *OCD*³ 1482–83.

North, "War." North, Robert. "'Kittim' War or 'Sectaries' Liturgy?" *Bib* 39 (1958): 84–93.

Northwood, "*De Oratore*." Northwood, S. J. "Cicero *de Oratore* 2.51–64 and Rhetoric in Historiography." *Mnemosyne* 61 (2, 2008): 228–44.

Norwood, "Colloquium." Norwood, Douglass Paul. "A Reconciliation Colloquium for Church Leaders in Suriname." DMin diss., Assemblies of God Theological Seminary, 2001.

Norwood, *Greek Tragedy*. Norwood, Gilbert. *Greek Tragedy*. New York: Hill & Wang, [1960].

Noth, *History*. Noth, Martin. *The History of Israel*. 2nd ed. New York: Harper & Row, 1960.

Nothomb, "Juifs." Nothomb, Paul. "Nouveau Regard Sur <<Les Juifs>> de Jean." *FoiVie* 71 (4, 1972): 65–69.

Nötscher, "Schicksalsglaube." Nötscher, Friedrich. "Schicksalsglaube in Qumran und Umwelt (2. Teil)." *BZ* 4 (1, 1960): 98–121.

Novak, *Suicide and Morality*. Novak, David. *Suicide and Morality: The Theories of Plato, Aquinas, and Kant and Their Relevance for Suicidology*. New York: Scholars Studies Press, 1975.

Novello, "Nature." Novello, Henry L. "The Nature of Evil in Jewish Apocalyptic: The Need for 'Integral' Salvation." *Colloq* 35 (1, 2003): 47–63.

Nowacki, *Argument*. Nowacki, Mark R. *The Kalam Cosmological Argument for God*. New York: Prometheus Books, 2007.

Noy, "Half Burnt." Noy, David. "'Half Burnt in an Emergency Pyre': Roman Cremations Which Went Wrong." *GR* 47 (2, 2000): 186–96.

Noy, *Inscriptiones*. Noy, David, et al. *Inscriptiones Judaicae Orientis*. Vol. 1: *Eastern Europe*. TSAJ 101. Tübingen: Mohr Siebeck, 2004.

Noy, "Inscriptions." Noy, David. "Inscriptions and Papyri: Jewish." *DNTB* 539–41.

Noy, "Writing." Noy, David. "Writing in Tongues: The Use of Greek, Latin, and Hebrew in Jewish Inscriptions from Roman Italy." *JJS* 48 (2, 1997): 300–311.

Noyes, "Seneca." Noyes, Russell. "Seneca on Death." *JRelHealth* 12 (1973): 223–40.

Nsenga, "Fuisa." Nsenga, Fidèle Bavuidinsi. "Joseph Fuisa Mbuku." No pages. *DACB*. Online: http://www.dacb.org/stories/demrepcongo/f-fuisa_joseph.html.

Ntumba, "Ananie." Ntumba, Valentin Kapambu. "Ac 5, 1–11—Ananie et Saphire: Lecture exégètique et réflexions théologiques." *HekRev* 34 (2005): 43–55.

Ntumba, "Mort." Ntumba, Valentin Kapambu. "La mort d'Ananie et de Saphire—le Dieu de la Bible cautionne-t-il la mort d'un être humain? De la nécessité de mieux lire Ac 5,1–11." *Teresianum* 57 (1, 2006): 115–34.

Nukunya, *Kinship*. Nukunya, G. K. *Kinship and Marriage among the Anlo Ewe*. LSE MSA 37. New York: Humanities, 1969.

Numbere, *Vision*. Numbere, Nonyem E. *A Man and a Vision: A Biography of Apostle Geoffrey D. Numbere*. Diobu, Nigeria: Greater Evangelism Publications, 2008.

Nun, "Fishing." Nun, Mendel. "Fishing." *OEANE* 2:315–17.

Nünlist, "Eris." Nünlist, René. "Eris." *Brill Pauly* 5:36.

Nünlist, "Teichoscopy." Nünlist, René. "Teichoscopy." *BrillPauly* 14:216.

Nunnally, *Acts*. Nunnally, Wave. *The Book of Acts: An Independent-Study Textbook*. Springfield, Mo.: Global University, 2007.

Nussbaum, "Phenomena." Nussbaum, Kurt. "Abnormal Mental Phenomena in the Prophets." *JRelHealth* 13 (3, 1974): 194–200.

Nussbaum, *Therapy*. Nussbaum, Martha C. *The Therapy of Desire: Theory and Practice in Hellenistic Ethics*. Martin Classical Lectures, n.s. 2. Princeton: Princeton University Press, 2009.

Nutton, "Epidemic Diseases." Nutton, Vivian. "Epidemic Diseases." *BrillPauly* 4:1092–94.

Nutton, "Epilepsy." Nutton, Vivian. "Epilepsy." *BrillPauly* 4:1109.

Nutton, "Fever." Nutton, Vivian. "Fever." *BrillPauly* 5:409–10.

Nutton, "Hospital." Nutton, Vivian. "Hospital." *BrillPauly* 6:523–27.

Nutton, "Medical Ethics." Nutton, Vivian. "Medical Ethics." *BrillPauly* 8:553–56.

Nutton, "Medicine." Nutton, Vivian. "Medicine." *BrillPauly* 8:569–82.

Nutton, "Phlebotomy." Nutton, Vivian. "Phlebotomy." *BrillPauly* 11:131–32.

Nutton, "Training." Nutton, Vivian. "Training (Medical)." *BrillPauly* 14:840–41.

Nygren, *Romans*. Nygren, Anders. *Commentary on Romans*. 3rd paperback ed. Philadelphia: Fortress, 1975.

Oakes, *Philippians*. Oakes, Peter. *Philippians: From People to Letter*. SNTSMS 110. Cambridge: Cambridge University Press, 2001.

Oakes, "Weber's *Sociology*." Oakes, Guy. "On Max Weber's *Agrarian Sociology of Ancient Civilizations*." *BJSoc* 28 (2, 1977): 242–43.

Oakley, *Commentary*. Oakley, Stephen P. *A Commentary on Livy Books VI–X*. 4 vols. Oxford: Clarendon, 1997–2005.

Oakman, "Countryside." Oakman, Douglas E. "The Countryside in Luke-Acts." Pages 151–79 in *The Social World of Luke-Acts: Models for Interpretation*. Edited by Jerome H. Neyrey. Peabody, Mass.: Hendrickson, 1991.

Oakman, "Economics." Oakman, Douglas E. "Economics of Palestine." *DNTB* 303–8.

Oakman, "Peasant." Oakman, Douglas E. "Was Jesus a Peasant? Implications for Reading the Samaritan Story." *BTB* 22 (1992): 117–25.

Oates, "Conversion." Oates, Wayne E. "Conversion: Sacred and Secular." Pages 149–68 in *Conversion: Perspectives on Personal and Social Transformation*. Edited by Walter E. Conn. New York: Alba House, 1978.

Oates, "Study." Oates, Wayne E. "A Sociopsychological Study of Glossolalia." Pages 76–99 in *Glossolalia: Tongue Speaking in Biblical, Historical, and Psychological Perspective*. By Frank Stagg, E. Glenn Hinson, and Wayne E. Oates. Nashville: Abingdon, 1967.

Obbink, "Atheism of Epicurus." Obbink, Dirk. "The Atheism of Epicurus." *GRBS* 30 (1989): 187–223.

Obed, "House Fellowship." Obed, Uzodinma. "House Fellowship." Page 1336 in *Africa Bible Commentary*. Edited by Tokunboh Adeyemo. Grand Rapids: Zondervan; Nairobi: WordAlive, 2006.

Oberhelman, "Dreams." Oberhelman, Steven. "A Survey of Dreams in Ancient Greece." *CBull* 55 (1979): 36–40.

Oberleitner, *Funde aus Ephesos*. Oberleitner, Wolfgang. *Funde aus Ephesos und Samothrake*. Kunsthistorisches Museum, Wien, Katalog der Antikensammlung 2. Wien: Kunsthistorisches Museum, 1978.

Obeyesekere, "Idiom." Obeyesekere, Gananath. "The Idiom of Demonic Possession: A Case Study." *SSMed* 4 (1970): 97–111.

Obeyesekere, "Possession." Obeyesekere, Gananath. "Psychocultural Exegesis of a Case of Spirit Possession in Sri Lanka." Pages 235–94 in *Case Studies in Spirit Possession*. Edited by Vincent Crapanzaro and Vivian Garrison. New York: Wiley, 1977.

Obijole, "Influence of Conversion." Obijole, Olubayo. "The Influence of the Conversion of St. Paul on His Theology of the Cross." *EAfrJET* 6 (2, 1987): 27–36.

Oblau, "Christianity in China." Oblau, Gotthard. "Pentecostal by Default? Contemporary Christianity in China." Pages 411–36 in *Asian and Pentecostal: The Charismatic Face of Christianity in Asia*. Edited by Allan Anderson and Edmond Tang. Foreword by Cecil M. Robeck. RSt Miss, AJPS 3. Oxford: Regnum; Baguio City, Philippines: APTS, 2005.

Oblau, "Healing." Oblau, Gotthard. "Divine Healing and the Growth of Practical Christianity in China." Pages 307–27 in *Global Pentecostal and Charismatic Healing*. Edited by Candy Gunther Brown. Foreword by Harvey Cox. Oxford: Oxford University Press, 2011.

O'Brien, *Colossians, Philemon*. O'Brien, Peter T. *Colossians, Philemon*. WBC 44. Waco: Word, 1982.

O'Brien, *Philippians*. O'Brien, Peter T. *The Epistle to the Philippians: A Commentary on the Greek Text*. NIGTC. Grand Rapids: Eerdmans, 1991.

O'Brien, "Prayer in Luke-Acts." O'Brien, Peter T. "Prayer in Luke-Acts." *TynBul* 24 (1973): 111–27.

O'Brien and Rickenbacker, "Alcoholism." O'Brien, John Maxwell, and Barney L. Rickenbacker. "Alcoholism." *OCD*³ 56.

Ockinga, "Divinity." Ockinga, Boyo. "Thoughts on the Nature of the Divinity of the Ruler in Ancient Egypt and Imperial Rome." *Prudentia* 26 (1, 1994): 17–34.

O'Collins, "Closing of Appearances." O'Collins, Gerald. "Luke on the Closing of the Easter Appearances." Pages 161–66 in *Luke and Acts*. Edited by Gerald O'Collins and Gilberto Marconi. Translated by Matthew J. O'Connell. New York: Paulist, 1993.

O'Collins and Kendall, "Joseph of Arimathea." O'Collins, Gerald O., and Daniel Kendall. "Did Joseph of Arimathea Exist?" *Bib* 75 (1994): 235–41.

O'Connell, "Hallucinations." O'Connell, Jake. "Jesus' Resurrection and Collective Hallucinations." *TynBul* 60 (1, 2009): 69–105.

O'Connor, *Healing Traditions*. O'Connor, Bonnie Blair. *Healing Traditions: Alternative Medicine and the Health Professions.* Philadelphia: University of Pennsylvania, 1995.

O'Connor, "Meroë." O'Connor, David. "Meroë." *OEANE* 3:472–73.

O'Connor, *Movement*. O'Connor, Edward D. *The Pentecostal Movement in the Catholic Church*. Notre Dame, Ind.: Ave Maria, 1971.

O'Connor, "Nubia." O'Connor, David. "Nubia before the New Kingdom." Pages 46–61 in vol. 1 of *Africa in Antiquity: The Arts of Ancient Nubia and the Sudan*. 2 vols. Brooklyn, N.Y.: Brooklyn Museum, 1978.

O'Connor, *Theism*. O'Connor, Timothy. *Theism and Ultimate Explanation*. Oxford: Blackwell, 2008.

O'Day, "Acts." O'Day, Gail R. "Acts." Pages 305–12 in *The Women's Bible Commentary*. Edited by Carol A. Newsom and Sharon H. Ringe. London: SPCK; Louisville: Westminster John Knox, 1992.

O'Day, "John." O'Day, Gail R. "The Gospel of John: Introduction, Commentary, and Reflections." *NIB* 9:491–865.

O'Day, *Revelation*. O'Day, Gail R. *Revelation in the Fourth Gospel: Narrative Mode and Theological Claim*. Philadelphia: Fortress, 1986.

Odeberg, *Gospel*. Odeberg, Hugo. *The Fourth Gospel Interpreted in Its Relation to Contemporaneous Religious Currents in Palestine and the Hellenistic-Oriental World*. Uppsala: Almqvist & Wiksells, 1929. Repr., Amsterdam: B. R. Grüner; Chicago: Argonaut, 1968.

Odeberg, *Pharisaism*. Odeberg, Hugo. *Pharisaism and Christianity*. Translated by J. M. Moe. St. Louis: Concordia, 1964.

Odell-Scott, "Dilemma." Odell-Scott, David W. "Editorial Dilemma: The Interpolation of 1 Cor 14:34–35 in the Western Manuscripts of D, G, and 88." *BTB* 30 (2, 2000): 68–74.

Oden, *Christianity*. Oden, Thomas C. *Early Libyan Christianity: Uncovering a North African Tradition*. Downers Grove, Ill.: IVP Academic, 2011.

Oden, "Persistence." Oden, Robert A., Jr. "The Persistence of Canaanite Religion." *BA* 39 (1, 1976): 31–36.

Oden and Hall, *Mark*. Oden, Thomas C., and Christopher A. Hall, eds. *Mark*. ACCS: New Testament 2. Downers Grove, Ill.: InterVarsity, 1998.

Oderberg, "Argument." Oderberg, David S. "Traversal of the Infinite, the 'Big Bang,' and the Kalam Cosmological Argument." *Philosophia Christi* 4 (2002); 305–36.

Odili, "Agents." Odili, Jones Ugochukwu. "The Role of Indigenous Agents in the Advent and Growth of the Anglican Church in Emu Clan of Delta State, 1911–2002." Master's thesis, University of Port Harcourt, Choba, Rivers State, Nigeria.

Odili, "Okeriaka." Odili, Jones Ugochukwu. "Godwin Ikwuasum Okeriaka." No pages. *DACB.* Online: http://www.dacb.org/stories/nigeria/okeriaka_godwin.html.

Odili, "Osaele." Odili, Jones Ugochukwu. "Abraham Osuam Osaele." No pages. *DACB.* Online: http://www.dacb.org/stories/nigeria/osaele_abraham.html.

Oduyoye, *Hearing.* Oduyoye, Mercy Amba. *Hearing and Knowing: Theological Reflections on Christianity in Africa.* CTAfS. Maryknoll, N.Y.: Orbis, 1986. Repr., Nairobi: Acton, 2000.

Oegema, "Gebot." Oegema, Gerbern S. "Das Gebot der Nächstenliebe im lukanischen Doppelwerk." Pages 507–16 in *The Unity of Luke-Acts.* Edited by Joseph Verheyden. BETL 142. Leuven: Leuven University Press, 1999.

Oeming, "Glaube." Oeming, Manfred. "Der Glaube Abrahams: Zur Rezeptionsgeschichte von Gen 15,6 in der Zeit des zweiten Tempels." *ZAW* 110 (1, 1998): 16–33.

Oepke, "ὄναρ." Oepke, Albrecht. "ὄναρ." *TDNT* 5:220–38.

Oesterley, *Liturgy.* Oesterley, William Oscar Emil. *The Jewish Background of the Christian Liturgy.* Oxford: Clarendon, 1925.

Oesterreich, *Possession.* Oesterreich, T. K. *Possession: Demoniacal and Other among Primitive Races, in Antiquity, the Middle Ages, and Modern Times.* Translated by D. Ibberson. New Hyde Park, N.Y.: University Books, 1966.

Ó Fearghail, *Introduction.* Ó Fearghail, Fearghus. *The Introduction to Luke-Acts: A Study of the Role of Lk 1,1–4,44 in the Composition of Luke's Two-Volume Work.* AnBib 126. Rome: Pontificio Istituto Biblico, 1991.

Offermann, "Apollos." Offermann, Henry. "Apollos, Apelles, Apollonius." *LCR* 38 (1919): 145–50.

Ogereau, "Κοινωνία." Ogereau, Julien M. "Paul's κοινωνία with the Philippians: *Societas* as a Missionary Funding Strategy." *NTS* 60 (3, July 2014): 360–78.

Ogilbee and Riess, *Pilgrimage.* Ogilbee, Mark, and Jana Riess. *American Pilgrimage: Sacred Journeys and Spiritual Destinations.* Brewster, Mass: Paraclete, 2006.

Ogilvie, "Phoenix." Ogilvie, R. M. "Phoenix." *JTS,* n.s., 9 (1958): 308–14.

O'Gorman, "Intertextuality." O'Gorman, Ellen. "Intertextuality and Historiography." Pages 231–42 in *The Cambridge Companion to the Roman Historians.* Edited by Andrew Feldherr. Cambridge: Cambridge University Press, 2009.

O'Gorman, "Politics." O'Gorman, Ellen. "The Politics of Sallustian Style." Pages 379–84 in *A Companion to Greek and Roman Historiography.* Edited by John Marincola. 2 vols. Oxford: Blackwell, 2007.

O'Grady, "Review." O'Grady, John F. Review of Craig S. Keener, *The Gospel of John: A Commentary. TS* 65 (3, 2004): 631–33.

O'Hagan, "Pentecost." O'Hagan, Angelo P. "The First Christian Pentecost (Acts 2:1–13)." *SBFLA* 23 (1973): 50–66.

Ohana, "Prosélytisme." Ohana, Moise. "Prosélytisme et Targum palestinien: Données nouvelles pour la datation de Néofiti 1." *Bib* 55 (1974): 317–32.

O'Hea, "Note." O'Hea, Margaret. "Note on a Roman Milestone from Gadora (al-Salt) in the Jordan Valley." *Levant* 34 (2002): 235–38.

Öhler, *Barnabas.* Öhler, Markus. *Barnabas: Die historische Person und ihre Rezeption in der Apostelgeschichte.* WUNT 156. Tübingen: Mohr Siebeck, 2003.

Öhler, "Urgemeinde." Öhler, Markus. "Die Jerusalemer Urgemeinde im Spiegel des antiken Vereinswesens." *NTS* 51 (3, 2005): 393–415.

Ohnuki-Tierney, "Shamanism." Ohnuki-Tierney, Emiko. "Shamanism and World View: The Case of the Ainu of the Northwest Coast of Southern Sakhalin." Pages 175–200 in *The Realm of the Extra-human: Ideas and Actions.* Edited by Agehananda Bharati. The Hague and Paris: Mouton, 1976. Distributed by Aldine, Chicago.

O'Keefe, "Lucretius." O'Keefe, Tim. "Lucretius on the Cycle of Life and the Fear of Death." *Apeiron* 36 (1, 2003): 43–66.

Okoronkwo, *Compromise.* Okoronkwo, Michael Enyinwa. *The Jerusalem Compromise as a Conflict-Resolution Model: A Rhetoric-Communicative Analysis of Acts 15 in the Light of Modern Linguistics.* ArbInt 1. Bonn: Borengässer, 2001.

Oksenberg Rorty, "Faces." Oksenberg Rorty, Amélie. "The Two Faces of Stoicism: Rousseau and Freud." Pages 243–70 in *The Emotions in Hellenistic Philosophy.* Edited by Juha Sihvola and Troels Engberg-Pedersen. TSHP 46. Dordrecht, Neth.: Kluwer Academic, 1998.

Olapido, *Development.* Olapido, Caleb Oluremi. *The Development of the Doctrine of the Holy Spirit in the African Indigenous Christian Movement.* New York: Peter Lang, 1996.

Olbricht, "Delivery and Memory." Olbricht, Thomas H. "Delivery and Memory." Pages 159–67 in *Handbook of Classical Rhetoric in the Hellenistic Period, 330 B.C.–A.D. 400.* Edited by Stanley E. Porter. Leiden: Brill, 1997.

Olbricht, "*Pathos* as Proof." Olbricht, Thomas H. "*Pathos* as Proof in Greco-Roman Rhetoric." Pages 7–22 in *Paul and Pathos.* Edited by Thomas H. Olbricht and Jerry L. Sumney. SBLSymS 16. Atlanta: SBL, 2001.

Oldfather, "Introduction to Diodorus Siculus." Oldfather, C. H. Introduction. Pages vii–xxvii in vol. 1 of *Diodorus Siculus.* Translated by C. H. Oldfather et al. 12 vols. LCL. London: Heinemann; Cambridge, Mass.: Harvard University Press, 1933–67.

Oldfather, "Introduction to Epictetus." Oldfather, W. A. Introduction. Pages vii–xxxviii in vol. 1 of *Epictetus.* Translated by W. A. Oldfather. 2 vols. LCL. London: Heinemann; New York: G. P. Putnam's Sons, 1926–28.

Oliver, "Epistle of Claudius." Oliver, James H. "The Epistle of Claudius Which Mentions the Proconsul Junius Gallio." *Hesperia* 40 (Apr. 1971): 239–40.

Oliver, "Insignificance." Oliver, Isaac W. "Simon Peter Meets Simon the Tanner: The Ritual Insignificance of Tanning in Ancient Judaism." *NTS* 59 (1, 2013): 50–60.

Oliver and Fage, *History of Africa.* Oliver, Roland, and J. D. Fage. *A Short History of Africa.* Oxford: Facts on File, 1989.

Olmedo, Martinez, and Martinez, "Acculturation." Olmedo, Esteban L., Joe L. Martinez Jr., and Sergio R. Martinez. "Measure of Acculturation for Chicano Adolescents." *PsycRep* 42 (1978): 159–70.

Olmstead, *Persian Empire.* Olmstead, A. T. *History of the Persian Empire.* Chicago: University of Chicago Press, 1959.

Olsen, "Nubia." Olsen, Glenn W. "Early Christian Nubia: Progress and Prospects of Research." *Proceedings of the PMR Conference* 6 (1981): 74–77.

Olsen, "Race." Olsen, Edward G. "What Shall We Teach about Race and Racism?" Pages 356–60 in *Teaching in the Inner City: A Book of Readings.* Vol. 3 of *Commitment to Teaching.* Edited by James C. Stone and Frederick W. Schneider. New York: Thomas Y. Crowell, 1970.

Olshausen, "Achaia." Olshausen, Eckart. "Achaia [Roman Province]." *BrillPauly* 1:80, 83.

Olshausen, "Europe." Olshausen, Eckart. "Europe/Europa." *BrillPauly* 5:206–10.

Olshausen, "Incorporation." Olshausen, Eckart. "Incorporation into the Roman Empire." *BrillPauly* 6:398–400.

Olshausen, "Pontos Euxeinos." Olshausen, Eckart. "Pontos Euxeinos." *BrillPauly* 11:599–607.

Olshausen, "Pontus." Olshausen, Eckart. "Pontus." *BrillPauly* 11:607–9.

Olshausen, "Sicily." Olshausen, Eckart. "Sicily: History." *BrillPauly* 13:422–25.

Olshausen, "Taurus." Olshausen, Eckart. "Taurus." *BrillPauly* 14:172.

Olshausen and Sauer, "Propontis." Olshausen, Eckart, and Vera Sauer. "Propontis." *BrillPauly* 12:31–32.

Olson, *Bruchko.* Olson, Bruce. *Bruchko.* Rev. ed. Lake Mary: Creation House, 1995.

Olson, "Eusebius." Olson, Ken A. "Eusebius and the *Testimonium Flavianum.*" *CBQ* 61 (2, 1999): 305–22.

Olson, "Expressions of Confidence." Olson, Stanley N. "Pauline Expressions of Confidence in His Addressees." *CBQ* 47 (1985): 282–95.

Olson, "Pentecost." Olson, Mark J. "Pentecost." *ABD* 5:222–23.

Olssen, Mitternacht, and Brandt, *Synagogue.* Olssen, Birger, Dieter Mitternacht, and Olof Brandt. *The Synagogue of Ancient Ostia and the Jews of Rome: Interdisciplinary Studies.* Jonsered, Sweden: Paul Åströms Förlag, 2001.

Olsson, *Structure.* Olsson, Birger. *Structure and Meaning in the Fourth Gospel: A Text Linguistic Analysis of John 2:1–11 and 4:1–42.* Translated by Jean Gray. Lund, Swed.: Gleerup, 1974.

Olyan, "Dimensions." Olyan, Saul M. "The Exegetical Dimensions of Restrictions on the Blind and the Lame in Texts from Qumran." *DSD* 8 (1, 2001): 38–50.

Omanson, "Identifying." Omanson, Roger L. "Who's Who in Romans 16? Identifying Men and Women among the People Paul Sent Greetings To." *BTr* 49 (4, 1998): 430–36.

Omerzu, "Angeklagter." Omerzu, Heike. "Der Apostel als Angeklagter—juristische Verfahren gegen Paulus in der Apostelgeschichte des Lukas." *Jahrbuch der Akademie der Wissenschaften zu Göttingen* (2002): 126–37.

Omerzu, "Apologetik." Omerzu, Heike. "Das Imperium schlägt zurück: Die Apologetik der Apostelgeschichte auf dem Prüfstand." *ZNT* 9 (18, 2006): 26–36.

Omerzu, "Darstellung." Omerzu, Heike. "Die Darstellung der Römer in der Textüberlieferung der Apostelgeschichte." Pages 147–81 in *The Book of Acts as Church History: Text, Textual Traditions and Ancient Interpretations/Apostelgeschichte als Kirchengeschichte: Text, Texttraditionen und antike Auslegungen.* Edited by Tobias Nicklas and Michael Tilly. Berlin: de Gruyter, 2003.

Omerzu, "Emancipation." Omerzu, Heike. "Women, Magic, and Angels: On the Emancipation of Job's Daughters in the Apocryphal Testament of Job." Pages 85–103 in *Bodies in Question: Gender, Religion, Text.* Edited by Darlene Bird and Yvonne Sherwood. Burlington, Vt.: Ashgate, 2005.

Omerzu, "Fallstudie." Omerzu, Heike. "Fallstudie: Der Prozess des Paulus." Pages 247–52 in *Prolegomena–Quellen–Geschichte.* Edited by Kurt Erlemann and Karl Leo Noethlichs. Vol. 1 of *Neues Testament und Antike Kultur.* Edited by Kurt Erlemann et al. Neukirchen-Vluyn: Neukirchener Verlag, 2004.

Omerzu, *Prozess.* Omerzu, Heike. *Der Prozess des Paulus: Eine exegetische und rechtshistorische Untersuchung der Apostelgeschichte.* BZNW 115. Berlin: de Gruyter, 2002.

Omerzu, "Schweigen." Omerzu, Heike. "Das Schweigen des Lukas: Überlegungen zum offenen Ende der Apostelgeschichte." Pages 127–56 in *Das Ende des Paulus: Historische, theologische, und literaturgeschichtliche Aspekte.* Edited by Friedrich Wilhelm Horn. BZNW 106. Berlin: de Gruyter, 2001.

Omerzu, "Spurensuche." Omerzu, Heike. "Spurensuche: Apostelgeschichte und Paulusbriefe als Zeugnisse einer ephesischen Gefangenschaft des Paulus." Pages 295–326 in *Die Apostelgeschichte im Kontext antiker und frühchristlicher Historiographie.* Edited by Jörg Frey, Clare K. Rothschild, and Jens Schröter, with Bettina Rost. BZNWK 162. Berlin: de Gruyter, 2009.

Omerzu, "Verhältnis." Omerzu, Heike. "Das traditionsgeschichtliche Verhältnis der Begegnungen von Jesus mit Herodes Antipas und Paulus mit Agrippa II." *SNTSU* 28 (2003): 121–45.

O'Neal, "Delation." O'Neal, William J. "Delation in the Early Empire." *CBull* 55 (2, 1978): 24–28.

O'Neil, "Plutarch on Friendship." O'Neil, Edward N. "Plutarch on Friendship." Pages 105–22 in *Greco-Roman Perspectives on Friendship.* Edited by John T. Fitzgerald. SBLRBS 34. Atlanta: Scholars Press, 1997.

O'Neill, *Theology.* O'Neill, J. C. *The Theology of Acts in Its Historical Setting.* 2nd ed. London: SPCK, 1970.

Ong, *Orality and Literacy.* Ong, Walter J. *Orality and Literacy: The Technologizing of the Word.* London: Methuen, 1982.

Ong, *Spirits.* Ong, Aihwa. *Spirits of Resistance and Capitalist Discipline.* Albany: State University of New York Press, 1987.

Onken, "Rural Exodus." Onken, Björn. "Rural Exodus." *BrillPauly* 12:785–87.

Onken and Umbach, "Espionage." Onken, Björn, and Kathrin Umbach. "Espionage." *BrillPauly* 5:67–68.

Onwu, "Acts 17:16–34 in Africa." Onwu, Nlenanya. "Ministry to the Educated: Reinterpreting Acts 17:16–34 in Africa." *AfCS* 4 (4, 1988): 61–71.

Oosthuizen, *Healer-Prophet.* Oosthuizen, G. C. *The Healer-Prophet in Afro-Christian Churches.* Studies in Christian Mission 3. Leiden: Brill, 1992.

Oosthuizen, "Healing." Oosthuizen, G. C. "Indigenous Healing within the Context of African Independent Churches." Pages 71–90 in *Afro-Christian Religion and Healing in Southern Africa.* Edited by G. C. Oosthuizen et al. African Studies 8. Lewiston, N.Y.: Edwin Mellen, 1989.

Oosthuizen et al., "Introduction." Oosthuizen, G. C., et al. Introduction. Pages 5–8 in *Afro-Christian Religion and Healing in Southern Africa.* Edited by G. C. Oosthuizen et al. African Studies 8. Lewiston, N.Y.: Edwin Mellen, 1989.

Opp, *Lord for Body.* Opp, James. *The Lord for the Body: Religion, Medicine, and Protestant Faith Healing in Canada, 1880–1930.* Montreal: McGill-Queen's University Press, 2005.

Oppenheimer, "Jewish Lydda." Oppenheimer, Aharon. "Jewish Lydda in the Roman Era." *HUCA* 59 (1988): 115–36.

Oppermann, "Rider-gods." Oppermann, Manfred. "Rider-gods and Heroes." *OCD*³ 1317–18.

Oquendo, Horwath, and Martinez, "Ataques." Oquendo, Maria, Ewald Horwath, and Abigail Martinez. "Ataques de nervios: Proposed Diagnostic Criteria for a Culture Specific Syndrome." *CMPsy* 16 (1992): 367–76.

Orchard, "Ellipsis." Orchard, Bernard. "The Ellipsis between Galatians 2,3 and 2,4." *Bib* 54 (4, 1973): 469–81.

O'Reilly, *Victims.* O'Reilly, A. J. *The Victims of the Mamertine: Scenes from the Early Church.* Montreal: D. & J. Sadlier, 1875.

Orejas and Sánchez-Palencia, "Mines." Orejas, Almudena, and F. Javier Sánchez-Palencia. "Mines, Territorial Organization, and Social Structure in Roman Iberia: Carthago Noua and the Peninsular Northwest." *AJA* 106 (4, 2002): 581–99.

Orenstein, "Death." Orenstein, Henry. "Death and Kinship in Hinduism: Structural and Functional Interpretations." *AmAnth* 72 (Dec. 1970): 1357–77.

Orlin, "Boundaries." Orlin, Eric M. "Octavian and Egyptian Cults: Redrawing the Boundaries of Romanness." *AJP* 129 (2, 2008): 231–53.

Orlin, "Religion." Orlin, Eric. "Urban Religion in the Middle and Late Republic." Pages 58–70 in *A Companion to Roman Religion.* Edited by Jörg Rüpke. BComp AW. Oxford: Blackwell, 2011.

Orlinsky, "Text Studies." Orlinsky, Harry M. "Qumran and the Present State of Old Testament Text Studies: The Septuagint Text." *JBL* 78 (1, 1959): 26–33.

Orlov, "Brother." Orlov, Andrei A. "Noah's Younger Brother Revisited: Anti-Noachic Polemics and the Date of 2 (Slavonic) Enoch." *Hen* 26 (2, 2004): 172–87.

Orlov, "Origin." Orlov, Andrei A. "The Origin of the Name 'Metatron' and the Text of 2 (Slavonic Apocalypse of) Enoch." *JSP* 21 (2000): 19–26.

Orme, "Antioquía." Orme, John H. "Antioquía: Paradigma para la Iglesia y la misión." *Kairós* 25 (1999): 29–36.

O'Rourke, "Law." O'Rourke, John J. "Roman Law and the Early Church." Pages 165–86 in *The Catacombs and the Colosseum: The Roman Empire as the Setting of Primitive Christianity*. Edited by Stephen Benko and John J. O'Rourke. Valley Forge, Pa.: Judson, 1971.

O'Rourke, "Rom 1, 20." O'Rourke, John J. "Romans 1, 20 and Natural Revelation." *CBQ* 23 (3, 1961): 301–6.

Orth, *Logios*. Orth, Emil. *Logios*. Leipzig: Teubner, 1926.

Ortiz, "Archaeology of Israel." Ortiz, Steven M. "Archaeology of the Land of Israel." *DNTB* 100–111.

Ortlund, "Justified." Ortlund, Dane C. "Justified by Faith, Judged according to Works: Another Look at a Pauline Paradox." *JETS* 52 (2, June 2009): 323–39.

Orton, *Scribe*. Orton, David E. *The Understanding Scribe: Matthew and the Apocalyptic Ideal*. JSNTSup 25. Sheffield, U.K.: Sheffield Academic, 1989.

Osborn, *Justin*. Osborn, Eric Francis. *Justin Martyr*. BHT 47. Tübingen: J. C. B. Mohr, 1973.

Osborn and Osborn, *Evangelism*. Osborn, T. L., and Daisy Osborn. *Faith Library in 23 volumes—20th Century Legacy of Apostolic Evangelism: Autobiographical Anthology*. 24 vols. Tulsa, Okla.: Osfo International, 1923–97.

Osborne, "Farmers." Osborne, Robin. "Farmers: Greece." *BrillPauly* 5:354–56.

Osborne, "Hermeneutics." Osborne, Grant R. "Hermeneutics/Interpreting Paul." *DPL* 388–97.

Osborne, "History and Theology." Osborne, Grant R. "History and Theology in the Synoptic Gospels." *TJ* 24 (1, 2003): 5–22.

Osborne, *Matthew*. Osborne, Grant R. *Matthew*. ZECNT. Grand Rapids: Zondervan, 2010.

Osborne, "Neighbours." Osborne, Robin. "Neighbours." *BrillPauly* 9:617–18.

Osborne, "Peter?" Osborne, Robert E. "Where Did Peter Go?" *CJT* 14 (1968): 274–77.

Osborne, "Prayer." Osborne, Grant R. "Moving Forward on Our Knees: Corporate Prayer in the New Testament." *JETS* 53 (2, June 2010): 243–67.

Osborne, "Resurrection." Osborne, Grant R. "Resurrection." *DNTB* 930–36.

Osborne, "Wild Beasts." Osborne, Robert E. "Paul and the Wild Beasts." *JBL* 85 (2, 1966): 225–30.

Osburn, "Historical Present." Osburn, Carroll D. "The Historical Present in Mark as a Text-Critical Criterion." *Bib* 64 (4, 1983): 486–500.

Osgood, "Caesar." Osgood, Josiah. "Caesar and the Pirates: Or How to Make (and Break) an Ancient Life." *GR* 57 (2, 2010): 319–36.

Osgood, "Vox." Osgood, Josiah. "The *vox* and *verba* of an Emperor: Claudius, Seneca, and *le prince idéal*." *CJ* 102 (4, 2007): 329–53.

Osiek, "City." Osiek, Carolyn. "The City: Center of Early Christian Life." *BibT* 31 (1, 1993): 17–21.

Osiek, "Diakonos." Osiek, Carolyn. "Diakonos and Prostatis: Women's Patronage in Early Christianity." *HTS/TS* 61 (1–2, 2005): 347–70.

Osiek, "Female Slaves." Osiek, Carolyn. "Female Slaves, *porneia*, and the Limits of Obedience." Pages 255–74 in *Early Christian Families in Context: An Interdisciplinary Dialogue*. Edited by David L. Balch and Carolyn Osiek. Grand Rapids and Cambridge: Eerdmans, 2003.

Osiek, "Handmaid." Osiek, Carolyn. "The New Handmaid: The Bible and the Social Sciences." *TS* 50 (1989): 260–78.

Osiek, *Saying*. Osiek, Carolyn. *What Are They Saying about the Social Setting of the New Testament?* Rev. ed. New York: Paulist, 1992.

Osiek and Balch, *Families*. Osiek, Carolyn, and David L. Balch. *Families in the New Testament World: Households and House Churches*. Louisville: Westminster John Knox, 1997.

Osiek and MacDonald, *Place*. Osiek, Carolyn, and Margaret Y. MacDonald, with Janet H. Tulloch. *A Woman's Place: House Churches in Earliest Christianity*. Minneapolis: Augsburg Fortress, 2006.

Oss, "View." Oss, Douglas A. "A Pentecostal/Charismatic View." Pages 239–83 in *Are Miraculous Gifts for Today? Four Views*. Edited by Wayne A. Grudem. Grand Rapids: Zondervan, 1996.

Osten-Sacken, "Bücher der Tora." Osten-Sacken, Peter von der. "Die Bücher der Tora als Hütte der Gemeinde: Amos 5:26f. in der Damaskusschrift." *ZAW* 91 (3, 1979): 423–35.

Osten-Sacken, "Geist." Osten-Sacken, Peter von der. "Geist im Buchstaben: Vom Glanz des Mose und des Paulus." *EvT* 41 (3, 1981): 230–35.

Oster, "Acts 19:23–41 and Inscription." Oster, Richard. "Acts 19:23–41 and an Ephesian Inscription." *HTR* 77 (2, 1984): 233–37.

Oster, "Artemis as Opponent." Oster, Richard. "The Ephesian Artemis as an Opponent of Early Christianity." *JAC* 19 (1976): 24–44.

Oster, *Bibliography*. Oster, Richard. *A Bibliography of Ancient Ephesus*. ATLA Bibliography Series 19. Metuchen, N.J.: Scarecrow, 1987.

Oster, "Commentary." Oster, Richard. "A Historical Commentary on the Missionary Success Stories in Acts 19:11–40." PhD diss., Princeton Theological Seminary, 1974.

Oster, *Corinthians*. Oster, Richard. *1 Corinthians*. College Press NIV Commentary. Joplin, Mo.: College Press, 1995.

Oster, "Emperor Veneration." Oster, Richard. "Christianity and Emperor Veneration in Ephesus: Iconography of a Conflict." *ResQ* 25 (3, 1982): 143–49.

Oster, "Ephesus." Oster, Richard. "Ephesus." *ABD* 2:542–49.

Oster, "Ephesus as Center." Oster, Richard. "Ephesus as a Religious Center under the Principate, I: Paganism before Constantine." *ANRW* 18.3:1661–1728. Part 2, *Principat*, 18.3. Edited by H. Temporini and W. Haase. Berlin: de Gruyter, 1990.

Oster, "Misuse." Oster, Richard. "Use, Misuse, and Neglect of Archaeological Evidence in Some Modern Works on 1 Corinthians (1 Cor 7,1–5; 8,10; 11,2–16; 12,14–26)." *ZNW* 83 (1–2, 1992): 52–73.

Oster, "Rejoinder to Kee." Oster, Richard. "Supposed Anachronism in Luke-Acts' Use of ΣΥΝΑΓΩΓΗ: A Rejoinder to H. C. Kee." *NTS* 39 (2, 1993): 178–208.

Oster, "Windows." Oster, Richard. "Numismatic Windows into the Social World of Early Christianity: A Methodological Inquiry." *JBL* 101 (2, 1982): 195–223.

Ostmeyer, "Sexualethik." Ostmeyer, Karl-Heinrich. "Die Sexualethik des antiken Judentums im Licht des Babylonischen Talmuds." *BTZ* 12 (2, 1995): 167–85.

Ostrow, "Problems." Ostrow, Steven E. "Problems in the Topography of Roman Puteoli." PhD diss., University of Michigan, 1977.

O'Sullivan, "Mind." O'Sullivan, Timothy M. "The Mind in Motion: Walking and Metaphorical Travel in the Roman Villa." *CP* 101 (2, 2006): 133–52.

Oswald, "Exposure." Oswald, Renate. "Exposure, Myths and Legends of." *BrillPauly* 5:278–80.

Oswalt, *Isaiah.* Oswalt, John N. *Isaiah.* NIVAC. Grand Rapids: Zondervan, 2003.

Oswalt, *Isaiah 1–39.* Oswalt, John N. *The Book of Isaiah: Chapters 1–39.* NICOT. Grand Rapids: Eerdmans, 1986.

Oswalt, *Isaiah 40–66.* Oswalt, John N. *The Book of Isaiah: Chapters 40–66.* NICOT. Grand Rapids: Eerdmans, 1998.

O'Toole, "Acts 13,13–52." O'Toole, Robert F. "Christ's Resurrection in Acts 13,13–52." *Bib* 60 (3, 1979): 361–72.

O'Toole, *Acts 26.* O'Toole, Robert F. *Acts 26: The Christological Climax of Paul's Defense (Ac 22:1–26:36).* AnBib 78. Rome: Biblical Institute Press, 1978.

O'Toole, "Αὐθεντια." O'Toole, Robert F. "ἡ αὐθεντια στην εκκλησια κατα τα κειμενα Λουκας-Πραξεις." *DBM* 25 (2, 1996): 10–47.

O'Toole, *Christology.* O'Toole, Robert F. *Luke's Presentation of Jesus: A Christology.* SubBi 25. Rome: Pontificio Istituto Biblico, 2004.

O'Toole, "Davidic Covenant of Pentecost." O'Toole, Robert F. "Acts 2:30 and the Davidic Covenant of Pentecost." *JBL* 102 (2, 1983): 245–58.

O'Toole, "Εἰρήνη." O'Toole, Robert F. "Εἰρήνη, an Underlying Theme in Acts 10, 34–43." *Bib* 77 (4, 1996): 461–76.

O'Toole, "Not to Us but to God." O'Toole, Robert F. " 'You Did Not Lie to Us (Human Beings) but to God' (Acts 5, 4c)." *Bib* 76 (2, 1995): 182–209.

O'Toole, "Notion of 'Imitators.'" O'Toole, Robert F. "'Luke's Notion of 'Be Imitators of Me as I Am of Christ' in Acts 25–26." *BTB* 8 (4, 1978): 155–56.

O'Toole, "Observations on *anistēmi.*" O'Toole, Robert F. "Some Observations on *anistēmi,* 'I raise,' in Acts 3:22, 26." *ScEs* 31 (1, 1979): 85–92.

O'Toole, "Parallels between Jesus and Disciples." O'Toole, Robert F. "Parallels between Jesus and His Disciples in Luke-Acts: A Further Study." *BZ,* n.s., 27 (2, 1983): 195–212.

O'Toole, "Philip and Eunuch." O'Toole, Robert F. "Philip and the Ethiopian Eunuch (Acts VIII 25–40)." *JSNT* 17 (1983): 25–34.

O'Toole, "Poverty." O'Toole, Robert F. "Poverty and Wealth in Luke-Acts." *ChicSt* 30 (1, 1991): 29–41.

O'Toole, "Servant." O'Toole, Robert F. "How Does Luke Portray Jesus as Servant of YHWH?" *Bib* 81 (3, 2000): 328–46.

O'Toole, "Treatment of Jews." O'Toole, Robert F. "Reflections on Luke's Treatment of Jews in Luke-Acts." *Bib* 74 (4, 1993): 529–55.

O'Toole, *Unity of Theology.* O'Toole, Robert F. *The Unity of Luke's Theology.* Wilmington, Del.: Glazier, 1984.

Ott, "Röm. 1, 19ff." Ott, Heinrich. "Röm. 1, 19ff. als dogmatisches Problem." *TZ* 15 (1, 1959): 40–50.

Ott and Netland, *Globalizing Theology.* Ott, Craig, and Harold A. Netland, eds. *Globalizing Theology: Belief and Practice in an Era of World Christianity.* Grand Rapids: Baker Academic, 2006.

Ottenberg, *Double Descent.* Ottenberg, Simon. *Double Descent in an African Society: The Afikpo Village-Group.* Seattle: University of Washington Press, 1968.

Otto, *Dionysus.* Otto, Walter F. *Dionysus: Myth and Cult.* Translated by Robert B. Palmer. Bloomington: Indiana University Press, 1965.

Oursler, *Power.* Oursler, Will. *The Healing Power of Faith.* New York: Hawthorn, 1957.

Outler, *Wesley.* Outler, Albert C., Jr., ed. *John Wesley.* New York: Oxford University Press, 1964.

Ovadiah, "Pavements." Ovadiah, Asher. "Mosaic Pavements of the Herodian Period in Israel." *MHR* 5 (2, 1990): 207–21.

Ovadiah and Mucznik, "Zodiac." Ovadiah, Asher, and Sonia Mucznik. "A Fragmentary Roman Zodiac and Horoscope from Caesarea Maritima." *SBFLA* 46 (1996): 375–80 and plates 31–32.

Overman, "Archaeology." Overman, John Andrew. "Recent Advances in the Archaeology of the Galilee in the Roman Period." *CurBS* 1 (1993): 35–57.

Overman, *Crisis.* Overman, John Andrew. *Church and Community in Crisis: The Gospel according to Matthew.* NTIC. Valley Forge, Pa.: Trinity Press International, 1996.

Overman, "Deciphering." Overman, John Andrew. "Deciphering the Origins of Christianity" (review of Burton L. Mack, *A Myth of Innocence: Mark and Christian Origins*). *Interpretation* 44 (1990): 193–95.

Overman, *Gospel and Judaism.* Overman, John Andrew. *Matthew's Gospel and Formative Judaism: The Social World of the Matthean Community.* Minneapolis: Fortress, 1990.

Overman, "Judaism: A Study." Overman, John Andrew. "Matthew's Gospel and Formative Judaism: A Study of the Social World of the Matthean Community." PhD diss., Boston University Graduate School, 1989.

Overman, "Neglected Features." Overman, John Andrew. "The God-Fearers: Some Neglected Features." *JSNT* 32 (1988): 17–26.

Overstreet, "Concept." Overstreet, R. Larry. "The Greek Concept of the 'Seven Stages of Life' and Its New Testament Significance." *BBR* 19 (4, 2009): 537–63.

Owczarek, *Sons.* Owczarek, Christopher. *Sons of the Most High: Love of Enemies in Luke-Acts: Teaching and Practice.* Nairobi: Paulines Publications Africa, 2002.

Owen, "4QDeut[n]." Owen, Elizabeth. "4QDeut[n]: A Pre-Samaritan Text?" *DSD* 4 (2, 1997): 162–78.

Owen, "Scope." Owen, H. P. "The Scope of Natural Revelation in Rom. I and Acts XVII." *NTS* 5 (2, 1959): 133–43.

Owen, "Stephen's Vision." Owen, H. P. "Stephen's Vision in Acts VII.55–6." *NTS* 1 (3, 1955): 224–26.

Owens, *City.* Owens, E. J. *The City in the Greek and Roman World.* London: Routledge, 1991.

Oxley, "Certainties." Oxley, Simon. "Certainties Transformed: Jonah and Acts 10:9–35." *EcRev* 56 (3, 2004): 322–26.

Oyen, "Criteria." Oyen, Geert van. "How Do We Know (What There Is to Know)? Criteria for Historical Jesus Research." *LouvS* 26 (3, 2001): 245–67.

Pabel, "Retelling." Pabel, Hilmar M. "Retelling the History of the Early Church: Erasmus' Paraphrase on Acts." *CH* 69 (1, 2000): 63–85.

Packer, *Acts.* Packer, J. W. *Acts of the Apostles.* CBC. Cambridge: Cambridge University Press, 1966.

Packer, "Housing." Packer, J. E. "Housing and Population in Imperial Ostia and Rome." *JRS* 57 (1967): 80–95.

Paczkowski, "Ombelico." Paczkowski, Mieczyslaw Celestyn. "Gerusalemme— 'Ombelico del mondo' nella tradizione cristiana antica." *SBFLA* 55 (2005): 165–202.

Paddock, "Family Language." Paddock, Alisha. "Putting Family Language Back into the Family of God." *SCJ* 11 (1, 2008): 83–91.

Padgett, "Rationale." Padgett, Alan. "The Pauline Rationale for Submission: Biblical Feminism and the *hina* Clauses of Titus 2:1–10." *EvQ* 59 (1, 1987): 39–52.

Padgug, "Problems." Padgug, Robert A. "Problems in the Theory of Slavery and Slave Society." *ScSoc* 40 (1, 1976): 3–27.

Padilla, "Παιδεία." Padilla, Osvaldo. "Hellenistic παιδεία and Luke's Education: A Critique of Recent Approaches." *NTS* 55 (4, 2009): 416–37.

Padilla, *Speeches.* Padilla, Osvaldo. *The Speeches of Outsiders in Acts: Poetics, Theology, and Historiography.* SNTSMS

144. Cambridge: Cambridge University Press, 2008.

Paffenroth, "Famines." Paffenroth, Kim. "Famines in Luke-Acts." *ExpT* 112 (12, 2001): 405–7.

Pagels, *Paul*. Pagels, Elaine Hiesey. *The Gnostic Paul: Gnostic Exegesis of the Pauline Letters*. Philadelphia: Fortress, 1975.

Paget, "Observations." Paget, James Carleton. "Some Observations on Josephus and Christianity." *JTS* 52 (2, 2001): 539–624.

Paget, "Proselytism." Paget, James Carleton. "Jewish Proselytism at the Time of Christian Origins: Chimera or Reality?" *JSNT* 62 (1996): 65–103.

Pahl, "Gospel." Pahl, M. W. "The 'Gospel' and the 'Word': Exploring Some Early Christian Patterns." *JSNT* 29 (2, 2006): 211–27.

Pahlitzsch, "Arabia." Pahlitzsch, Johannes. "Arabia." *BrillPauly* 1:939–41.

Pahlitzsch, "Lydda." Pahlitzsch, Johannes. "Lydda." *BrillPauly* 8:1.

Paige, "Demons." Paige, Terence. "Demons and Exorcism." *DPL* 209–11.

Paige, "Matrix." Paige, Terence. "The Social Matrix of Women's Speech at Corinth: The Context and Meaning of the Command to Silence in 1 Corinthians 14:33b–36." *BBR* 12 (2, 2002): 217–42.

Paige, "Spirit." Paige, Terence. "Holy Spirit." *DPL* 404–13.

Paige, "Stoicism." Paige, Terence. "Stoicism, ἐλευθερία and Community at Corinth." Pages 180–93 in *Worship, Theology and Ministry in the Early Church: Essays in Honor of Ralph P. Martin*. Edited by Michael J. Wilkins and Terence Paige. JSNTSup 87. Sheffield: Sheffield Academic Press, 1992.

Paimoen, "Missionary Team." Paimoen, Eddy. "The Importance of Paul's Missionary Team." *STJ* 4 (2, 1996): 157–73.

Painter, "Caesarea." Painter, R. Jackson. "East Meets West: Caesarea Maritima in Josephus and the Acts of the Apostles." Paper presented at the annual meeting of the SBL, Washington, D.C., Nov. 20, 2006.

Painter, *James*. Painter, John. "James." Pages 1–174 in *James and Jude*. By John Painter and David A. deSilva. Paideia. Grand Rapids: Baker Academic, 2012.

Painter, *John*. Painter, John. *John: Witness and Theologian*. Foreword by C. K. Barrett. London: SPCK, 1975.

Palatty, "Ascension." Palatty, Paul. "The Ascension of Christ in Lk-Acts (An Exegetical Critical Study of Lk 24,50–53 and Acts 1,2–3, 9–11)." *BiBh* 12 (2, 1986): 100–117.

Pally, *Evangelicals*. Pally, Marcia. *The New Evangelicals: Expanding the Vision of the Common Good*. Foreword by John Milbank. Grand Rapids: Eerdmans, 2011.

Palma, "Ἀποφθέγγομαι." Palma, Anthony. "'Ἀποφθέγγομαι: Declare under Inspiration." *Advance* (Feb. 1978): 31.

Palma, "Glossolalia." Palma, Anthony. "Glossolalia in the Light of the New Testament and Subsequent History." Bachelor of Theology thesis, Biblical Seminary in New York, April 1960.

Palma, *Spirit*. Palma, Anthony D. *The Holy Spirit: A Pentecostal Perspective*. Foreword by George O. Wood. Springfield, Mo.: Logion, 2001.

Palmer, "Monograph (1992)." Palmer, Darryl W. "Acts and the Historical Monograph." *TynBul* 43 (2, 1992): 373–88.

Palmer, "Monograph (1993)." Palmer, Darryl W. "Acts and the Ancient Historical Monograph." Pages 1–29 in *The Book of Acts in Its Ancient Literary Setting*. Edited by Bruce W. Winter and Andrew D. Clarke. Vol. 1 of *The Book of Acts in Its First Century Setting*. Edited by Bruce W. Winter. Grand Rapids: Eerdmans; Carlisle, U.K.: Paternoster, 1993.

Palmer, "Vow." Palmer, D. "Defining a Vow of Abstinence." *Colloq* 5 (1973): 38–41.

Pancaro, *Law*. Pancaro, Severino. *The Law in the Fourth Gospel*. Leiden: Brill, 1975.

Panier, "Récit." Panier, Louis. "Récit—discours. De l'explication des causes à l'enchaînement des figures: Lecture de Actes 2–4." *SémBib* 134 (2009): 4–16.

Panikulam, *Koinōnia*. Panikulam, George. *Koinōnia in the New Testament: A Dynamic Expression of Christian Life*. AnBib 85. Rome: Biblical Institute Press, 1979.

Pankau and Siemon-Netto, "Revolution." Pankau, Matthias, and Uwe Siemon-Netto. "The Other Iranian Revolution." *CT* (July 2012): 44–47.

Pankhurst, *Chronicles*. Pankhurst, Richard K. P., ed. *The Ethiopian Royal Chronicles*. Addis Ababa: Oxford University Press, 1967.

Pannenberg, "History." Pannenberg, Wolfhart. "History and the Reality of the Resurrection." Pages 62–72 in *Resurrection Reconsidered*. Edited by Gavin D'Costa. Oxford: Oneworld, 1996.

Pannenberg, *Jesus*. Pannenberg, Wolfhart. *Jesus—God and Man*. Translated by L. L. Wilkins and D. A. Priebe. Philadelphia: Westminster, 1974.

Panning, "Acts 6." Panning, Armin J. "Acts 6: The 'Ministry' of the Seven." *WLQ* 93 (1, 1996): 11–17.

Pantelis, "Etnias e iglesias." Pantelis, J. "Etnias e iglesias en Hechos de los apóstoles." *Apuntes* 24 (3, 2004): 109–18.

Pao, *Isaianic Exodus*. Pao, David W. *Acts and the Isaianic New Exodus*. WUNT 2.130. Tübingen: Mohr Siebeck, 2000. Repr., Grand Rapids: Baker, 2002.

Papadopoulos, "Σαύλος." Papadopoulos, C. "Ο Σαύλος τυφλός." *DBM* 28 (2, 1999): 35–37.

Paparazzo, "Metals." Paparazzo, Ernesto. "Pliny the Elder on Metals: Philosophical and Scientific Issues." *CP* 103 (1, 2008): 40–54.

Park, "Barriers." Park, James H. "Overcoming Internal Barriers: The 'Conversion' of Ananias and Peter in Acts 9–10." *JAAS* 12 (1, 2009): 19–35.

Park, "Berichte." Park, Chan Woong. "Summarische Berichte über das Leben Jesu: Die Darstellungen im lukanischen Doppelwerk und sogenannten *Testamentum Flavianum* (Ant 18,63–64)." *YonsRTC* 5 (1999): 193–211.

Park, "Berufung." Park, Heon-wook. "Die Berufung des Paulus zur Völkermission—im Hinblick auf die Tempelvision von Jerusalem in Apg. 22,17–21." *AJBI* 23 (1997): 46–63.

Park, *Healing*. Park, Andrew Sung. *Racial Conflict and Healing: An Asian-American Theological Perspective*. Maryknoll, N.Y.: Orbis, 1996.

Park, *Herem*. Park, Hyung Dae. *Finding Herem? A Study in the Light of* Herem. LNTS 357. New York: T&T Clark, 2007.

Park, *Hurt to Healing*. Park, Andrew Sung. *From Hurt to Healing: A Theology of the Wounded*. Nashville: Abingdon, 2004.

Park, *Jew or Gentile*. Park, Eung Chun. *Either Jew or Gentile: Paul's Unfolding Theology of Inclusivity*. Louisville: Westminster John Knox, 2003.

Park, "Principles." Park, Hyung Dae. "Drawing Ethical Principles from the Process of the Jerusalem Council: A New Approach to Acts 15:4–29." *TynBul* 61 (2, 2010): 271–91.

Park, "Spirituality." Park, Myung Soo. "Korean Pentecostal Spirituality as Manifested in the Testimonies of Members of Yoido Full Gospel Church." Pages 43–67 in *David Yonggi Cho: A Close Look at His Theology and Ministry*. Edited by Wonsuk Ma, William W. Menzies, and Hyeonsung Bae. AJPSS 1. Baguio City, Philippines: APTS Press, Hansei University Press, 2004.

Park, "Survey." Park, Timothy Kiho. "A Survey of the Korean Missionary Movement." *JAM* 4 (1, 2002): 111–19.

Park, "Untersuchung." Park, Chan-Woong. "Eine Untersuchung zum Bild Johannes des Täufers bei Josephus und Lukas: Ihre Darstellungen im Blick auf politische Zusammenhänge." *YonsJT* 4 (1999): 59–83.

Parke, *Oracle*. Parke, H. W. *A History of the Delphic Oracle*. Oxford: Blackwell, 1939.

Parke, *Oracles*. Parke, H. W. *The Oracles of Zeus: Dodona, Olympia, Ammon*. Oxford: Blackwell, 1967.

Parke, *Sibyls*. Parke, H. W. *Sibyls and Sibylline Prophecy in Classical Antiquity*. Edited by B. C. McGing. New York: Routledge, 1988.

Parker, "Angel." Parker, Floyd. "The Terms 'Angel' and 'Spirit' in Acts 23,8." *Bib* 84 (3, 2003): 344–65.

Parker, "Apokatastasis." Parker, James, III. "The Concept of Apokatastasis in Acts: A Study in Primitive Christian Theology." DTh diss., University of Basil, 1978.

Parker, "Attic Cults." Parker, Robert C. T. "Attic Cults and Myths." *OCD³* 212.

Parker, "Bendis." Parker, Robert C. T. "Bendis." *OCD³* 238–39.

Parker, "Boedromia." Parker, Robert C. T. "Boedromia." *OCD³* 246.

Parker, "Books." Parker, Holt N. "Books and Reading Latin Poetry." Pages 186–229 in *Ancient Literacies: The Culture of Reading in Greece and Rome*. Edited by William A. Johnson and Holt N. Parker. New York: Oxford University Press, 2009.

Parker, "Campaigns." Parker, Victor L. "Judas Maccabaeus' Campaigns against Timothy." *Bib* 87 (4, 2006): 457–76.

Parker, "Decapolis." Parker, S. Thomas. "Decapolis." *OEANE* 2:127–30.

Parker, "Dioscuri." Parker, Robert C. T. "Dioscuri." *OCD³* 484.

Parker, "Divination." Parker, Robert C. T. "Divination: Greek." *OCD³* 487–88.

Parker, "Epimenides." Parker, Robert. "Epimenides." *BrillPauly* 4:1112–13.

Parker, "Hymns." Parker, Robert C. T. "Hymns (Greek)." *OCD³* 735–36.

Parker, "Hypsistos." Parker, Robert C. T. "Hypsistos." *OCD³* 739.

Parker, "Letters." Parker, Victor. "The Letters in II Maccabees: Reflexions on the Book's Composition." *ZAW* 119 (3, 2007): 386–402.

Parker, "Oracles." Parker, Robert C. T. "Oracles." *OCD³* 1071–72.

Parker, "*Patrōoi theoi*." Parker, Robert C. T. "*Patrōoi theoi*." *OCD³* 1127.

Parker, "Pollution." Parker, Robert C. T. "Pollution, the Greek Concept of." Pages 553–54 in *The Oxford Companion to Classical Civilization*. Edited by Simon Hornblower and Antony Spawforth. Oxford: Oxford University Press, 1998.

Parker, "Possession Trance." Parker, Simon B. "Possession Trance and Prophecy in Pre-exilic Israel." *VT* 28 (July 1978): 271–85.

Parker, *Prison*. Parker, John Henry. *The Ancient Prison of the Kings of Rome, Commonly Called the Mamertine Prison*. Rome: Piale and Co., 1879.

Parker, "Sabazius." Parker, Robert C. T. "Sabazius." *OCD³* 1341.

Parker, "Sacrifice." Parker, Robert C. T. "Sacrifice, Greek." *OCD³* 1344–45.

Parker, "Shipwrecks." Parker, A. J. "Shipwrecks, Ancient." *OCD³* 1400.

Parker, *Shipwrecks*. Parker, A. J. *Ancient Shipwrecks of the Mediterranean and the Roman Provinces*. British Archaeological Reports, International series 580. Oxford: Tempus Reparatum, 1992.

Parker, "Sons of Gods." Parker, Simon B. "Sons of (the) God(s)." Pages 794–800 in *Dictionary of Deities and Demons in the Bible*. 2nd rev. ed. Edited by Karel van der Toorn, Bob Becking, and Pieter W. van der Horst. Leiden: Brill; Grand Rapids: Eerdmans, 1999.

Parker, "Suffering." Parker, Paul P. "Suffering, Prayer, and Miracles." *JRelHealth* 36 (3, 1997): 205–19.

Parker, "Transjordan." Parker, S. Thomas. "Transjordan in the Persian through Roman Period." *OEANE* 5:235–38.

Parker, "Treatise." Parker, Pierson. "The 'Former Treatise' and the Date of Acts." *JBL* 84 (1965): 52–58.

Parker, "Vestals." Parker, Holt N. "Why Were the Vestals Virgins? Or the Chastity of Women and the Safety of the Roman State." *AJP* 125 (4, 2004): 563–601.

Parker and Watson, "*Centurio*." Parker, Henry Michael Denne, and George Ronald Watson. "*Centurio*." *OCD³* 310–11.

Parker, Watson, and Coulston, "*Cohors*." Parker, Henry Michael Denne, George Ronald Watson, and Jonathan C. N. Coulston. "*Cohors*." *OCD³* 356.

Parkes, *Conflict*. Parkes, James. *The Conflict of the Church and the Synagogue: A Study in the Origins of Antisemitism*. New York: Atheneum, 1979.

Parmentier, "Zungenreden." Parmentier, Martin. "Das Zungenreden bei den Kirchenvätern." *Bijdr* 55 (4, 1994): 376–98.

Paroschi, "Baptism." Paroschi, Wilson. "Acts 19:1–7 Reconsidered in Light of Paul's Theology of Baptism." *AUSS* 47 (1, 2009): 73–100.

Parr, "Arabian Peninsula." Parr, Peter J. "The Arabian Peninsula before the Time of Islam." *OEANE* 160–64.

Parr, "Dating." Parr, Peter J. "Dating the Hydraulic Installations in the Siq at Petra." *PEQ* 140 (2, 2008): 81–86.

Parrot, *Temple*. Parrot, Andre. *The Temple of Jerusalem*. London: SCM, 1957.

Parry, "Retelling *Samuel*." Parry, Donald W. "Retelling *Samuel*: Echoes of the *Books of Samuel* in the Dead Sea Scrolls." *RevQ* 17 (65–68, 1996): 293–306.

Parshall, *Bridges*. Parshall, Phil. *Bridges to Islam: A Christian Perspective on Folk Islam*. Grand Rapids: Baker, 1983.

Parshall, "Lessons." Parshall, Phil. "Lessons Learned in Contextualization." Pages 251–72 in *Muslims and Christians on the Emmaus Road*. Edited by J. Dudley Woodberry. Monrovia, Calif.: MARC, 1989.

Parsons, *Acts*. Parsons, Mikeal C. *Acts*. PCNT. Grand Rapids: Baker Academic, 2008.

Parsons, *Body*. Parsons, Mikeal C. *Body and Character in Luke and Acts: The Subversion of Physiognomy in Early Christianity*. Grand Rapids: Baker Academic, 2006.

Parsons, "Character." Parsons, Mikeal C. "The Character of the Lame Man in Acts 3–4." *JBL* 124 (2, 2005): 295–312.

Parsons, "Defiled AND Unclean." Parsons, Mikeal C. "'Nothing Defiled AND Unclean': The Conjunction's Function in Acts 10:14." *PRSt* 27 (3, 2000): 263–74.

Parsons, *Departure*. Parsons, Mikeal C. *The Departure of Jesus in Luke-Acts: The Ascension Narratives in Context*. JSNTSup 21. Sheffield, U.K.: JSOT Press, 1987.

Parsons, "Kinship." Parsons, Talcott. "Kinship and the Associational Aspect of Social Structure." Pages 409–38 in *Kinship and Culture*. Edited by Francis L. K. Hsu. Chicago: Aldine, 1971.

Parsons, *Luke*. Parsons, Mikeal C. *Luke: Storyteller, Interpreter, Evangelist*. Peabody, Mass.: Hendrickson, 2007.

Parsons, "Place of Jerusalem." Parsons, M. C. "The Place of Jerusalem on the Lukan Landscape: An Exercise in Symbolic Cartography." Pages 155–71 in *Literary Studies in Luke-Acts: Essays in Honor of Joseph B. Tyson*. Edited by Richard P. Thompson and Thomas E. Phillips. Macon, Ga.: Mercer University Press, 1998.

Parsons, "*Progymnasmata*." Parsons, Mikeal C. "Luke and the *progymnasmata*: A Preliminary Investigation into the Preliminary Exercises." Pages 43–63 in *Contextualizing Acts: Lukan Narrative and Greco-Roman Discourse*. Edited by Todd Penner and Caroline Vander Stichele. SBLSymS 20. Atlanta: SBL, 2003.

Parsons, "Unity: Rethinking." Parsons, Mikeal C. "The Unity of Luke-Acts: Rethinking the *opinio communis*." Pages 29–53 in *With Steadfast Purpose: Essays on Acts in Honor of Henry Jackson Flanders Jr.* Edited by N. H. Keathley. Waco: Baylor University Press, 1990.

Parsons and Culy, *Acts*. Parsons, Mikeal C., and Martin M. Culy. *Acts: A Handbook on the Greek Text*. Waco: Baylor University Press, 2003.

Parsons and Gorman, "Unity." Parsons, Mikeal C., and Heather M. Gorman. "The Assumed Authorial Unity of Luke and Acts: A Review Essay." *Neot* 46 (1, 2012): 139–52.

Parsons and Pervo, *Rethinking*. Parsons, Mikeal C., and Richard I. Pervo. *Rethinking the Unity of Luke and Acts*. Minneapolis: Fortress, 1993.

Parvis, "Ephesus." Parvis, Merrill M. "Archaeology and St. Paul's Journeys in Greek Lands, Part IV: Ephesus." *BA* 8 (3, 1945): 62–73.

Paschalis, "Afterlife." Paschalis, Michael. "The Afterlife of Emperor Claudius in Seneca's *Apocolocyntosis*." *Numen* 56 (2–3, 2009): 198–216.

Pascuzzi, "Battle." Pascuzzi, Maria. "The Battle of the Gospels: Paul's Anti-imperial Message and Strategies Past and Present for Subverting the Empire." *PIBA* 30 (2007): 34–53.

Pasquier, "Experience." Pasquier, Jacques. "Experience and Conversion." Pages 191–200 in *Conversion: Perspectives on Personal and Social Transformation*. Edited by Walter E. Conn. New York: Alba House, 1978.

Passamaneck, "Mandate." Passamaneck, Stephen M. "The Jewish Mandate of Martyrdom: Logic and Illogic in the *halakhah*." *HUCA* 74 (2003): 215–41.

Pasternak, "Atrophy." Pasternak, Burton. "Agnatic Atrophy in a Formosan Village." *AmAnth* 70 (1, Feb. 1968): 93–96.

Pastor, "Strata." Pastor, Jack. "Josephus and Social Strata: An Analysis of Social Attitudes." *Hen* 19 (3, 1997): 295–312.

Pate, "Missions." Pate, Larry D. "Pentecostal Missions from the Two-Thirds World." Pages 242–58 in *Called and Empowered: Global Mission in Pentecostal Perspective*. Edited by Murray A. Dempster, Byron D. Klaus, and Douglas Petersen. Peabody, Mass.: Hendrickson, 1991.

Pate et al., *Story*. Pate, C. Marvin, et al. *The Story of Israel: A Biblical Theology*. Downers Grove, Ill.: InterVarsity; Leicester, U.K.: Apollos, 2004.

Patella, "Caesarea Maritima." Patella, Michael. "Caesarea Maritima." *BibT* 45 (1, 2007): 35–38.

Patella, "Damascus." Patella, Michael. "Paul's Damascus." *BibT* 47 (2, 2009): 107–11.

Patella, "Edom." Patella, Michael. "Land of Edom." *BibT* 45 (4, 2007): 233–36.

Patella, "Gaza." Patella, Michael. "Seers' Corner: Gaza." *BibT* 45 (3, 2007): 162–66.

Patella, "Headquarters." Patella, Michael. "Paul's Headquarters." *BibT* 45 (5, 2007): 299–303.

Patella, "Travels." Patella, Michael. "Saint Paul's Travels, Part I: By Land." *BibT* 46 (4, 2008): 236–40.

Paterson, "Elections." Paterson, Jeremy James. "Elections and Voting: Roman." *OCD*[3] 516–17.

Paterson, "Wine." Paterson, Jeremy James. "Wine (Greek and Roman)." *OCD*[3] 1622–23.

Paterson and Spawforth, "Negotiatores." Paterson, Jeremy James, and Antony J. S. Spawforth. "Negotiatores." *OCD*[3] 1032.

Pathrapankal, "Way." Pathrapankal, J. "Christianity as a 'Way' according to the Acts of the Apostles." Pages 533–39 in *Les Actes des apôtres: Traditions, rédaction, théologie*. Edited by Jacob Kremer. BETL 48. Gembloux, Belg.: J. Duculot; Leuven: Leuven University Press, 1979.

Patrich, *Carceres*. Patrich, Joseph. "The *carceres* of the Herodian Hippodrome/Stadium at Caesarea Maritima and Connections with the Circus Maximus." *JRA* 14 (2001): 269–83.

Patrich, "Chapel." Patrich, Joseph. "A Chapel of St. Paul at Caesarea Maritima?" *SBFLA* 50 (2000): 363–82 and plates 27–30.

Patrich, "Temple." Patrich, Joseph. "Reconstructing the Magnificent Temple Herod Built." *BRev* 4 (5, 1988): 16–29.

Patte, *Hermeneutic*. Patte, Daniel. *Early Jewish Hermeneutic in Palestine*. SBLDS 22. Missoula, Mont.: Scholars Press, 1975.

Patte, *Matthew*. Patte, Daniel. *The Gospel according to Matthew: A Structural Commentary on Matthew's Faith*. Philadelphia: Fortress, 1987.

Pattengale, "Achaia." Pattengale, Jerry A. "Achaia." *ABD* 1:53.

Pattengale, "Berea." Pattengale, Jerry A. "Berea." *ABD* 1:675.

Patterson, *Immortality*. Patterson, Robert Leet. *Plato on Immortality*. University Park: Pennsylvania State University Press, 1965.

Patterson, "Slavery." Patterson, Orlando. "Paul, Slavery, and Freedom: Personal and Socio-historical Reflections." *Semeia* 83–84 (1998): 263–79.

Patterson, *Theories*. Patterson, C. H. *Theories of Counseling and Psychotherapy*. New York: Harper & Row, 1980.

Pattison, "Research on Glossolalia." Pattison, E. Mansell. "Behavioral Science Research on the Nature of Glossolalia." *JASA* (Sept. 1968): 73–86.

Patton, "Correction." Patton, Kimberley C. "'Great and Strange Correction': Intentionality, Locality, and Epiphany in the Category of Dream Incubation." *HR* 43 (3, 2004): 194–223.

Patzia, *Emergence*. Patzia, Arthur G. *The Emergence of the Church: Context, Growth, Leadership, and Worship*. Downers Grove, Ill.: InterVarsity, 2001.

Paul, "Diction." Paul, Shalom M. "Sargon's Administrative Diction in II Kings 17[27]." *JBL* 88 (1, 1969): 73–74.

Paul, "Prophets." Paul, Shalom M. "Prophets and Prophecy (In the Bible)." *EncJud* 13:1160–64.

Paul, "Wine." Paul, Shalom M. "Classifications of Wine in Mesopotamian and Rabbinic Sources." *IEJ* 25 (1, 1975): 42–45.

Paulsen, "Competitions." Paulsen, Thomas. "Competitions, Artistic: Literary Competitions: Greece." *BrillPauly* 4:1182–84.

Paulus, "Advocatus." Paulus, Christoph Georg. "Advocatus." *BrillPauly* 1:162–63.

Paulus, "Appellatio." Paulus, Christoph Georg. "Appellatio." *BrillPauly* 1:894–95.

Pauw, "Influence of Emotions." Pauw, D. A. "The Influence of Emotions upon Events in the *Acts of the Apostles*." *EkkPhar* 77 (1, 1995): 39–56.

Pawlikowski, "Pharisees." Pawlikowski, John T. "The Pharisees and Christianity." *BibT* 49 (1970): 47–53.

Payne, "Fuldensis." Payne, Philip Barton. "Fuldensis, Sigla for Variants in Vaticanus, and 1 Cor 14.34–5." *NTS* 41 (2, 1995): 240–62.

Payne, "MS. 88." Payne, Philip Barton. "MS. 88 as Evidence for a Text without 1 Cor 14.34–5." *NTS* 44 (1, 1998): 152–58.

Payne, "Semitisms." Payne, D. F. "Semitisms in the Book of Acts." Pages 134–50 in *Apostolic History and the Gospel: Biblical and Historical Essays Presented to F. F. Bruce on His 60th Birthday*. Edited by W. Ward Gasque and Ralph P. Martin. Grand Rapids: Eerdmans; Exeter, U.K.: Paternoster, 1970.

Payne-Jackson, "Illness." Payne-Jackson, Arvilla. "Spiritual Illness and Healing: 'If the Lord Wills.'" Pages 55–64 in *Faith, Health, and Healing in African-American Life*. Edited by Stephanie Y. Mitchem and Emilie M. Townes. RelHHeal. Westport, Conn.: Praeger, 2008.

Peake, "Colossians." Peake, A. S. "Colossians." Pages 477–547 in vol. 3 of *The Expositor's Greek Testament*. Edited by W. Robertson Nicoll. 5 vols. New York: Hodder & Stoughton, 1897–1910. Repr., Grand Rapids: Eerdmans, 1979.

Pearce, "Council of Seven." Pearce, Sarah J. K. "Flavius Josephus as Interpreter of Biblical Law: The Council of Seven and the Levitical Servants in *Jewish Antiquities* 4.214." *HeyJ* 36 (4, 1995): 477–92.

Pearcy, "Galen." Pearcy, Lee T. "Galen and Stoic Rhetoric." *GRBS* 24 (3, 1983): 259–72.

Pearl, *Theology*. Pearl, Chaim. *Theology in Rabbinic Stories*. Peabody, Mass.: Hendrickson, 1997.

Pearlman, *Zealots*. Pearlman, Moshe. *The Zealots of Masada*. New York: Scribner's, 1967.

Pearson, "Alexander." Pearson, Brook W. R. "Alexander the Great." *DNTB* 20–23.

Pearson, "Alexandria." Pearson, Birger A. "Alexandria." *OEANE* 1:65–69.

Pearson, "Antioch." Pearson, Brook W. R. "Antioch (Pisidia)." *DNTB* 31–34.

Pearson, "Associations." Pearson, Brook W. R. "Associations." *DNTB* 136–38.

Pearson, "Christians." Pearson, Birger A. "Christians and Jews in First-Century Alexandria." *HTR* 79 (1986): 206–16.

Pearson, "Civic Cults." Pearson, Brook W. R. "Civic Cults." *DNTB* 218–20.

Pearson, "Domestic Religion." Pearson, Brook W. R. "Domestic Religion and Practices." *DNTB* 298–302.

Pearson, "Gymnasia." Pearson, Brook W. R. "Gymnasia and Baths." *DNTB* 435–36.

Pearson, "Idolatry, Jewish Conception." Pearson, Brook W. R. "Idolatry, Jewish Conception of." *DNTB* 526–29.

Pearson, "Polytheism." Pearson, Brook W. R. "Polytheism." *DNTB* 815–18.

Pearson, *Terminology*. Pearson, Birger A. *The Pneumatikos-Psychikos Terminology in 1 Corinthians: A Study in the Theology of the Corinthian Opponents of Paul and Its Relation to Gnosticism*. SBLDS 12. Missoula, Mont.: Scholars Press, 1973.

Pease, "Book Burning." Pease, A. S. "Notes on Book Burning." Pages 145–60 in *Munera studiosa*. Edited by M. H. Shepperd. Cambridge, Mass.: Episcopal Theological School Press, 1946.

Peat, "Science." Peat, F. David. "Science as Story." Pages 53–62 in *Sacred Stories: A Celebration of the Power of Story to Transform and Heal*. Edited by Charles and Anne Simpkinson. San Francisco: HarperSanFrancisco, 1993.

Peck, *Glimpses*. Peck, M. Scott. *Glimpses of the Devil: A Psychiatrist's Personal Accounts of Possession, Exorcism, and Redemption*. New York: Free Press, 2005.

Peckham, "Phoenicia." Peckham, Brian. "Phoenicia." *ABD* 5:349–57.

Peckham, *Sounds*. Peckham, Colin and Mary. *Sounds from Heaven: The Revival on the Isle of Lewis, 1949–1952*. Fearn, Ross-shire, Scotland: Christian Focus, 2004.

Peel, "Christianization." Peel, J. D. Y. "The Christianization of African Society: Some Possible Models." Pages 443–54 in *Christianity in Independent Africa*. Edited by Edward Fasholé-Luke et al. Bloomington: Indiana University Press, 1978.

Peever, "Tent-Making." Peever, Elizabeth Ruth. "Asian Missionaries and Tent-Making." Pages 257–65 in *Asian Church and God's Mission: Studies Presented in the International Symposium on Asian Mission in Manila, January 2002*. Edited by Wonsuk Ma and Julie C. Ma. Manila: OMF Literature; West Caldwell, N.J.: MWM, 2003.

Peilstöcker, "Archaeology." Peilstöcker, Martin. "Urban Archaeology in Yafo (Jaffa): Preliminary Planning for Excavations and Research of a Mediterranean Port City." *PEQ* 139 (3, 2007): 149–65.

Peinador, "Protoevangelio." Peinador, M. "El protoevangelio (Gen III,15) en la exposición de Flión y en un poema de Prudencio." *EphMar* 39 (3–4, 1989): 455–65.

Peirano, "Hellenized Romans." Peirano, Irene. "Hellenized Romans and Barbarized Greeks: Reading the End of Dionysius of Halicarnassus, *Antiquitates Romanae*." *JRS* 100 (2010): 32–53.

Peisker, "Konsekutives." Peisker, Carl Heinz. "Konsekutives ἵνα in Markus 4:12." *ZNW* 59 (1968): 126–27.

Pekridou-Gorecki, "Dyeing." Pekridou-Gorecki, Anastasia. "Dyeing." *BrillPauly* 4:756–57.

Pekridou-Gorecki, "Fulling." Pekridou-Gorecki, Anastasia. "Fulling, Fuller." *BrillPauly* 5:576–77.

Pekridou-Gorecki, "Linen." Pekridou-Gorecki, Anastasia. "Linen, Flax." *BrillPauly* 7:620–21.

Pekridou-Gorecki, "Silk." Pekridou-Gorecki, Anastasia. "Silk." *BrillPauly* 13:462–64.

Pekridou-Gorecki, "Textiles." Pekridou-Gorecki, Anastasia. "Textiles, Production of: Classical Antiquity." *BrillPauly* 14:342–46.

Pélaez del Rosal, "Reanimación." Pélaez del Rosal, Jésus. "'La reanimación de un cadáver': Un problema de fuentes y géneros." *Alfinge* 1 (1983): 151–73.

Peleg, "Gender and Ossuaries." Peleg, Yifat. "Gender and Ossuaries: Ideology and Meaning." *BASOR* 325 (Feb. 2002): 65–73.

Peleg and Amit, "Another *miqveh*." Peleg, Yuval, and David Amit. "Another *miqveh* near Alon Shevut." *'Atiqot* 48 (2004): 95–98.

Pelikan, *Acts*. Pelikan, Jaroslav. *Acts*. BTCB. Grand Rapids: Brazos, 2005.

Pelletier, "Josèphe." Pelletier, André. "Ce que Josèphe a dit de Jésus (*Ant.* XVIII, 63–64)." *REJ* 124 (January–June 1965): 9–21.

Pelling, "Commentarii." Pelling, C. B. R. "*Commentarii*." *OCD*[3] 373.

Pelling, "Historians of Rome." Pelling, Christopher. "The Greek Historians of Rome." Pages 244–58 in *A Companion to Greek and Roman Historiography*. Edited by John Marincola. 2 vols. Oxford: Blackwell, 2007.

Pelling, "Historiography." Pelling, C. B. R. "Historiography, Roman." *OCD*[3] 716–17.

Pelling, "Plutarch's Method in Roman Lives." Pelling, C. B. R. "Plutarch's Method of Work in the Roman Lives." *JHS* 99 (1979): 74–96.

Pelling, "Plutarch's Socrates." Pelling, C. B. R. "Plutarch's Socrates." *Herm* 179 (2005): 105–39.

Pelser, "Women." Pelser, G. M. M. "Women and Ecclesiastical Ministries in Paul," in "Ministry in the Pauline Letters: Proceedings of the Twelfth Meeting of 'Die Nawe-Testamentiese-Werkgemeenskap van Suid-Afrika.'" Special Issue, *Neot* 10 (1976): 92–109.

Pembroke, "Prostitution." Pembroke, Simon Geoffrey. "Prostitution, Sacred." *OCD*[3] 1263–64.

Penna, "Juifs à Rome." Penna, Romano. "Les juifs à Rome au temps de l'apôtre Paul." *NTS* 28 (3, 1982): 321–47.

Penna, "Motivo." Penna, Romano. "Il motivo della *'aqedah* sullo sfondo di *Rom.* 8,32." *RivB* 33 (4, 1985): 425–60.

Penner, "Contextualizing." Penner, Todd. "Contextualizing Acts." Pages 1–21 in *Contextualizing Acts: Lukan Narrative and Greco-Roman Discourse*. Edited by Todd Penner and Caroline Vander Stichele. SBLSymS 20. Atlanta: SBL, 2003.

Penner, "Discourse." Penner, Todd. "Civilizing Discourse: Acts, Declamation, and the Rhetoric of the *polis*." Pages 65–104 in *Contextualizing Acts: Lukan Narrative and Greco-Roman Discourse*. Edited by Todd Penner and Caroline Vander Stichele. SBLSymS 20. Atlanta: SBL, 2003.

Penner, "Madness." Penner, Todd. "Madness in the Method? The Acts of the Apostles in Current Study." *CBR* 2 (2, 2004): 223–93.

Penner, *Praise*. Penner, Todd. *In Praise of Christian Origins: Stephen and the Hellenists in Lukan Apologetic Historiography*. Foreword by David L. Balch. New York and London: T&T Clark, 2004.

Penner, "Reading." Penner, Todd. "Reading Acts in the Second Century: Reflections on Method, History, and Desire." Pages 1–15 in *Engaging Early Christian History: Reading Acts in the Second Century*. Edited by Rubén R. Dupertuis and Todd Penner. Durham, UK: Acumen, 2013.

Penner, "Reconfiguring." Penner, Todd. "Reconfiguring the Rhetorical Study of Acts: Reflections on the Method in and the Learning of a Progymnastic Poetics." *PRSt* 30 (4, 2003): 425–39.

Penner and Vander Stichele, *Contextualizing Acts*. Todd Penner and Caroline Vander

Stichele, eds. *Contextualizing Acts: Lukan Narrative and Greco-Roman Discourse*. SBLSymS 20. Atlanta: SBL, 2003.

Penner and Vander Stichele, "Point de Vue." Penner, Todd, and Caroline Vander Stichele. "Le territoire corinthien: Point de vue et poétique dans les Actes des Apôtres." Pages 197–204 in *Regards croisés sur la Bible: Études sur le point de vue. Actes du IIIe colloque international du Réseau de recherche en narrativité biblique, Paris, 8–10 juin 2006*. Préface par Daniel Marguerat. Lectio divina. Paris: Les Éditions du Cerf, 2007.

Penney, "Devil." Penney, Douglas L. "Finding the Devil in the Details: Onomastic Exegesis and the Naming of Evil in the World of the New Testament." Pages 37–52 in *New Testament Greek and Exegesis: Essays in Honor of Gerald F. Hawthorne*. Edited by Amy M. Donaldson and Timothy B. Sailors. Grand Rapids and Cambridge: Eerdmans, 2003.

Penney, *Missionary Emphasis*. Penney, John Michael. *The Missionary Emphasis of Lukan Pneumatology*. JPTSup 12. Sheffield, U.K.: Sheffield Academic, 1997.

Penney and Wise, "Beelzebub." Penney, Douglas L., and Michael O. Wise. "By the Power of Beelzebub: An Aramaic Incantation Formula from Qumran (4Q 560)." *JBL* 113 (4, 1994): 627–50.

Pennington, "Relationship." Pennington, John E., Jr. "The Relationship of the Human Spirit to the Holy Spirit in the Process of Healing." Pages 156–63 in *Healing and Religious Faith*. Edited by Claude A. Frazier. Philadelphia: United Church Press, 1974.

Peppard, *Son of God*. Peppard, Michael. *The Son of God in the Roman World: Divine Sonship in Its Social and Political Contexts*. New York: Oxford University Press, 2011.

Peradotto and Sullivan, "Introduction." Peradotto, John, and J. P. Sullivan. Introduction. Pages 1–6 in *Women in the Ancient World: The Arethusa Papers*. Edited by John Peradotto and J. P. Sullivan. SSCS. Albany: State University of New York Press, 1984.

Perdue, "Rhetoric." Perdue, Leo G. "Rhetoric and the Art of Persuasion in the Wisdom of Solomon." Pages 183–98 in *Text, Image, and Christians in the Graeco-Roman World: A Festschrift in Honor of David Lee Balch*. Edited by Aliou Cissé Niang and Carolyn Osiek. PrTMS 176. Eugene, Ore.: Pickwick, 2012.

Perdue, "Sage." Perdue, Leo G. "The Death of the Sage and Moral Exhortation: From Ancient Near Eastern Instructions to Graeco-Roman Paraenesis." *Semeia* 50 (1990): 81–109.

Pereira, "Persecution." Pereira, F. "Persecution in Acts." *BiBh* 4 (2, 1978): 131–55.

Pereira de Queiroz, "Myths." Pereira de Queiroz, Maria Isaura. "Messianic Myths and Movements." *Diogenes* 90 (Summer 1975): 78–99.

Perelmuter, "Strength." Perelmuter, Hayim Goren. "The Strength of the Elders." *BibT* 30 (6, 1992): 347–52.

Peretz, "Development." Peretz, David. "Development, Object-Relationships, and Loss." Pages 3–19 in *Loss and Grief: Psychological Management in Medical Practice*. Edited by Bernard Schoenberg et al. New York: Columbia University Press, 1970.

Peretz, "Interpreter." Peretz, Daniel. "The Roman Interpreter and His Diplomatic and Military Roles." *Historia* 55 (4, 2006): 451–70.

Pereyra, "Significado." Pereyra, Rúben. "El significado de IOUDAIOI en el Evangelio de Juan." *Theo* 3 (2, 1988): 116–36.

Perkin, "Money." Perkin, Hazel W. "Money." *ISBE* 3:402–9.

Perkins, *Corinthians*. Perkins, Pheme. *First Corinthians*. PCNT. Grand Rapids: Baker Academic, 2012.

Perkins, "Fictive *Scheintod*." Perkins, Judith. "Fictive *Scheintod* and Christian Resurrection." *R&T* 13 (3–4, 2006): 396–418.

Perkins, "John." Perkins, Pheme. "The Gospel according to John." Pages 942–85 in *The New Jerome Biblical Commentary*. Edited by Raymond E. Brown, Joseph A. Fitzmyer, and Roland E. Murphy. Englewood Cliffs, N.J.: Prentice Hall, 1990.

Perkins, *Justice*. Perkins, John. *Let Justice Roll Down*. Ventura, Calif.: Regal, 1976.

Perkins, *Reading*. Perkins, Pheme. *Reading the New Testament: An Introduction*. 2nd ed. New York: Paulist, 1988.

Perkins, "This World." Perkins, Judith B. "This World or Another? The Intertextuality of the Greek Romances, the Apocryphal Acts, and Apuleius' *Metamorphoses*." Pages 247–60 in *The Apocryphal Acts of the Apostles in Intertextual Perspectives*. Edited by Robert F. Stoops. Semeia 80. Atlanta: Scholars Press, 1997.

Perkins, "World of *Acts of Peter*." Perkins, Judith. "The Social World of the *Acts of Peter*." Pages 296–307 in *The Search for the Ancient Novel*. Edited by James Tatum. Baltimore: Johns Hopkins University Press, 1994.

Pernot, "Rendez-vous." Pernot, Laurent. "Un rendez-vous manqué." *Rhetorica* 11 (4, 1993): 421–34.

Pernot, "Rhetoric." Pernot, Laurent. "The Rhetoric of Religion." *Rhetorica* 24 (3, 2006): 235–54.

Perrin, *Bultmann*. Perrin, Norman. *The Promise of Bultmann*. Philadelphia: Fortress, 1969.

Perrin, *Kingdom*. Perrin, Norman. *The Kingdom of God in the Teaching of Jesus*. Philadelphia: Westminster, 1963.

Perrin, *Language*. Perrin, Norman. *Jesus and the Language of the Kingdom: Symbol and Metaphor in New Testament Interpretation*. Philadelphia: Fortress, 1976.

Perrin, *Thomas*. Perrin, Nicholas. *Thomas and Tatian: The Relationship between the Gospel of Thomas and the Diatessaron*. SBLABib 5. Atlanta: SBL, 2002.

Perrot, "Lecture de la Bible." Perrot, C. "La lecture de la Bible dans les synagogues au premier siècle de notre ère." *MaisD* 126 (1976): 24–41.

Perry, "Aliens." Perry, John. "Are Christians the 'Aliens Who Live in Your Midst'? Torah and the Origins of Christian Ethics in Acts 10–15." *JSCE* 29 (2, 2009): 157–74.

Perry, "Diligentia." Perry, Ellen E. "Notes on *diligentia* as a Term of Roman Art Criticism." *CP* 95 (4, 2001): 445–58.

Perry, "Life and Death." Perry, Megan A. "Life and Death in Nabataea: The North Ridge Tombs and Nabataean Burial Practices." *NEA* 65 (4, 2002): 265–70.

Perry, "Paul in Acts." Perry, Gregory R. "Paul in Acts and the Law in the Prophets." *HBT* 31 (2, 2009): 160–77.

Perry, *Sources*. Perry, Alfred Morris. *The Sources of Luke's Passion Narrative*. Chicago: University of Chicago Press, 1920.

Persinger, "EEG profiles." Persinger, Michael A. "Striking EEG Profiles from Single Episodes of Glossolalia and Transcendental Meditation." *PerMS* 58 (1, 1984): 127–33.

Person, "Analysis." Person, Raymond F., Jr. "Conversation Analysis." Pages 86–90 in *Dictionary of the Old Testament Prophets*. Edited by Mark J. Boda and J. Gordon McConville. Downers Grove, Ill.: IVP Academic, 2012.

Person, "Scribe as Performer." Person, Raymond F. "The Ancient Israelite Scribe as Performer." *JBL* 117 (4, 1998): 601–9.

Pervo, *Acts*. Pervo, Richard I. *Acts: A Commentary*. Minneapolis: Fortress, 2009.

Pervo, "Converting." Pervo, Richard I. "Converting Paul: The Call of the Apostle in Early Christian Literature." *Forum* 7 (2, 2004): 127–58.

Pervo, *Dating Acts*. Pervo, Richard I. *Dating Acts: Between the Evangelists and the Apologists*. Santa Rosa, Calif.: Polebridge, 2006.

Pervo, "Dating Acts." Pervo, Richard I. "Dating Acts." *Forum* 5 (1, 2002): 53–72.

Pervo, "Direct Speech." Pervo, Richard I. "Direct Speech in Acts and the Question of Genre." *JSNT* 28 (3, 2006): 285–307.

Pervo, "Dying." Pervo, Richard I. "Dying and Rising with Paul." *FourR* 23 (1, 2010): 3–8.

Pervo, "Egging." Pervo, Richard I. "Egging On the Chickens: A Cowardly Response to Dennis MacDonald and Then Some." Pages 43–56 in *The Apocryphal Acts of the Apostles in Intertextual Perspectives*. Edited by Robert F. Stoops. *Semeia* 80. Atlanta: Scholars Press, 1997.

Pervo, "Entführung." Pervo, Richard I. "Die Entführung in das Serail: Aspasia—A Female Aesop?" Pages 61–88 in *Ancient Fiction: The Matrix of Early Christian and Jewish Narrative*. Edited by Jo-Ann A. Brant, Charles W. Hedrick, and Chris Shea. SBLSymS 32. Atlanta: SBL, 2005.

Pervo, "Fabula." Pervo, Richard I. "A Nihilist Fabula: Introducing *The Life of Aesop*." Pages 77–120 in *Ancient Fiction and Early Christian Narrative*. Edited by Ronald F. Hock, J. Bradley Chance, and Judith Perkins. SBLSymS 6. Atlanta: SBL, 1998.

Pervo, "Flattery." Pervo, Richard I. "Flattery in Its Sincerest Manifestation." *FourR* 22 (5, 2009): 11–14, 28.

Pervo, "Friends." Pervo, Richard I. "With Lucian—Who Needs Friends? Friendship in the *Toxaris*." Pages 163–80 in *Greco-Roman Perspectives on Friendship*. Edited by John T. Fitzgerald. SBLRBS 34. Atlanta: Scholars Press, 1997.

Pervo, "Gates." Pervo, Richard I. "The Gates Have Been Closed (Acts 21:30): The Jews in Acts." *JHC* 11 (2, 2005): 128–49.

Pervo, "Hard Act." Pervo, Richard I. "A Hard Act to Follow: The Acts of Paul and the Canonical Acts." *JHC* 2 (2, 1995): 3–32.

Pervo, "Heritage and Claims." Pervo, Richard I. "Israel's Heritage and Claims upon the Genre(s) of Luke and Acts: The Problems of a History." Pages 127–43 in *Jesus and the Heritage of Israel: Luke's Narrative Claim upon Israel's Legacy*. Edited by David P. Moessner. Luke the Interpreter of Israel 1. Harrisburg, Pa.: Trinity Press International, 1999.

Pervo, "Meet Right." Pervo, Richard I. "Meet Right—and Our Bounden Duty: Community Meetings in Acts." *Forum* 4 (1, 2001): 45–62.

Pervo, *Mystery*. Pervo, Richard I. *The Mystery of Acts: Unraveling Its Story*. Santa Rosa, Calif.: Polebridge, 2008.

Pervo, "Perilous Things." Pervo, Richard I. "'On Perilous Things': A Response to Beverly R. Gaventa." Pages 37–44 in *Cadbury, Knox, and Talbert: American Contributions to the Study of Acts*. Edited by Mikeal C. Parsons and Joseph B. Tyson. Atlanta: Scholars Press, 1992.

Pervo, *Profit*. Pervo, Richard I. *Profit with Delight: The Literary Genre of the Acts of the Apostles*. Philadelphia: Fortress, 1987.

Pervo, "Rhetoric in Apocrypha." Pervo, Richard I. "Rhetoric in the Christian Apocrypha." Pages 793–805 in *Handbook of Classical Rhetoric in the Hellenistic Period, 330 B.C.–A.D. 400*. Edited by Stanley E. Porter. Leiden: Brill, 1997.

Pervo, "Same Genre?" Pervo, Richard I. "Must Luke and Acts Belong to the Same Genre?" Pages 309–16 in *SBL Seminar Papers, 1989*. Edited by D. J. Lull. SBLSP 28. Atlanta: Scholars Press, 1989.

Pervo, *Story*. Pervo, Richard I. *Luke's Story of Paul*. Minneapolis: Augsburg Fortress, 1990.

Pesch, *Apostelgeschichte*. Pesch, Rudolf. *Die Apostelgeschichte*. 2 vols. EKKNT 5. Zurich: Benziger, 1986.

Peskowitz, "Textiles." Peskowitz, Miriam. "Textiles in the Classical Period." *OEANE* 5:195–97.

Peterman, "Giving." Peterman, G. W. "Giving and Receiving in Paul's Epistles." DPhil thesis, King's College, London, 1992.

Peterman, "Marriage." Peterman, G. W. "Marriage and Sexual Fidelity in the Papyri, Plutarch, and Paul." *TynBul* 50 (2, 1999): 163–72.

Peterman, "Suicide." Peterman, John E. "The Socratic Suicide." Pages 3–15 in *New Essays on Socrates*. Edited by Eugene Kelly. Lanham, Md.: University Press of America, 1984.

Peters, *Healing in Nepal*. Peters, Larry. *Ecstasy and Healing in Nepal: An Ethnopsychiatric Study of Tamang Shamanism*. Malibu, Calif.: Undena, 1981.

Petersen, *Freedman*. Petersen, Lauren Hackworth. *The Freedman in Roman Art and Art History*. Cambridge: Cambridge University Press, 2006.

Petersen, "Genre." Petersen, Norman R. "Can One Speak of a Gospel Genre?" *Neot* 28 (3, 1994): 137–58.

Petersen, "Kin Research." Petersen, Karen Kay. "Kin Network Research: A Plea for Comparability." *JMFam* 31 (2, May 1969): 271–80.

Petersen, "Latin American Pentecostalism." Petersen, Douglas. "The Azusa Street Mission and Latin American Pentecostalism." *IBMR* 30 (2, 2006): 66–67.

Petersen, *Literary Criticism*. Petersen, Norman R. *Literary Criticism for New Testament Critics*. Philadelphia: Fortress Press, 1978.

Petersen, *Might*. Petersen, Douglas. *Not by Might nor by Power: A Pentecostal Theology of Social Concern in Latin America*. Preface by Jose Miguez Bonino. Oxford: Regnum; Carlisle, U.K.: Paternoster, 1996.

Petersen, *Sociology*. Petersen, Norman R. *The Gospel of John and the Sociology of Light: Language and Characterization in the Fourth Gospel*. Valley Forge, Pa.: Trinity Press International, 1993.

Peterson, *Acts*. Peterson, David. *The Acts of the Apostles*. PillNTC. Grand Rapids: Eerdmans; Nottingham, U.K.: Apollos, 2009.

Peterson, "Atonement Theology." Peterson, David. "Atonement Theology in Luke-Acts: Reflections on Its Background." Pages 56–71 in *The New Testament in Its First Century Setting: Essays on Context and Background in Honour of B. W. Winter on His 65th Birthday*. Edited by P. J. Williams et al. Grand Rapids and Cambridge, U.K.: Eerdmans, 2004.

Peterson, *Eloquence*. Peterson, Brian K. *Eloquence and the Proclamation of the Gospel in Corinth*. SBLDS 163. Atlanta: Scholars Press, 1998.

Peterson, "Enterprise." Peterson, David. "Luke's Theological Enterprise: Integration and Intent." Pages 521–44 in *Witness to the Gospel: The Theology of Acts*. Edited by I. Howard Marshall and David Peterson. Grand Rapids: Eerdmans, 1998.

Peterson, "Extent." Peterson, Jeffrey. "The Extent of Christian Theological Diversity: Pauline Evidence." *ResQ* 47 (1, 2005): 1–12.

Peterson, "Fulfilment and Purpose." Peterson, David. "The Motif of Fulfilment and the Purpose of Luke-Acts." Pages 83–104 in *The Book of Acts in Its Ancient Literary Setting*. Edited by Bruce W. Winter and Andrew D. Clarke. Vol. 1 of *The Book of Acts in Its First Century Setting*. Edited by Bruce W. Winter. Grand Rapids: Eerdmans; Carlisle, U.K.: Paternoster, 1993.

Peterson, "Introduction." Peterson, William. "Introduction to Dialogus." Pages 3–16 in *Tacitus, Dialogus, Agricola, Germania*. Translated by William Peterson and Maurice Hutton. LCL. New York: G. P. Putnam's Sons, 1914.

Peterson, *Perfection*. Peterson, David. *Hebrews and Perfection: An Examination of the Concept of Perfection in the "Epistle to the Hebrews."* SNTSMS 47. Cambridge: Cambridge University Press, 1982.

Peterson, "Worship." Peterson, David. "The Worship of the New Community." Pages 373–96 in *Witness to the Gospel: The Theology of Acts*. Edited by I. Howard Marshall and David Peterson. Grand Rapids: Eerdmans, 1998.

Petit, "Traversée exemplaire." Petit, Madeleine. "À propos d'une traversée exemplaire du désert du Sinaï selon Philon (*Hypothetica* VI, 2–3.8): Texte biblique et apologétique concernant Moïse chez quelques écrivains juifs." *Sem* 26 (1976): 137–42.

Pettinato, *Archives*. Pettinato, Giovanni. *The Archives of Ebla: An Empire Inscribed in the Clay*. Garden City, N.Y.: Doubleday, 1981.

Pettis, "Fourth Pentecost." Pettis, Stephen J. "The Fourth Pentecost: Paul and the Power of the Holy Spirit, Acts 19:1–22." Pages 248–56 in *Mission in Acts: Ancient Narratives in Contemporary Context*. Edited by Robert L. Gallagher and Paul Hertig. AmSocMissS 34. Maryknoll, N.Y.: Orbis, 2004.

Petuchowski, "Teshuvah." Petuchowski, Jacob J. "The Concept of 'Teshuvah' in the Bible and the Talmud." *Judaism* 17 (2, 1968): 175–85.

Petuchowski and Brocke, *Liturgy*. Petuchowski, Jacob J., and Michael Brocke, eds. *The Lord's Prayer and Jewish Liturgy*. New York: Seabury, 1978.

Petzel, "Bürgschaft." Petzel, Paul. "Bürgschaft der Kommentare: Zur Autorität im rabbinischen Judentum." *Orientierung* 70 (19, 2006): 207–9; (20, 2006): 219–23; (21, 2006): 231–35.

Petzer, "Reconsidering." Petzer, Jacobus H. "Reconsidering the Silent Women of Corinth—A Note on 1 Corinthians 14:34–35." *TheolEv* 26 (2, 1993): 132–38.

Petzl, "Men." Petzl, Georg. "Men." *BrillPauly* 8:656–58.

Pfandl, "Interpretations." Pfandl, Gerhard. "Interpretations of the Kingdom of God in Daniel 2:44." *AUSS* 34 (2, 1996): 249–68.

Pfann, "Coinage." Pfann, Stephen J. "Dated Bronze Coinage of the Sabbatical Years of Release and the First Jewish City Coin." *BAIAS* 24 (2006): 101–13.

Pfeiffer, *Ras Shamra*. Pfeiffer, Charles F. *Ras Shamra and the Bible*. Grand Rapids: Baker, 1962.

Pfeiffer, *Scrolls*. Pfeiffer, Charles F. *The Dead Sea Scrolls and the Bible*. Grand Rapids: Baker, 1969.

Pfeiffer, *Tell el Amarna*. Pfeiffer, Charles F. *Tell el Amarna and the Bible*. Grand Rapids: Baker, 1963.

Pfeiffer, *World*. Pfeiffer, Charles F. *The Biblical World: A Dictionary of Biblical Archaeology*. Grand Rapids: Baker, 1966.

Pfitzner, *Agon Motif*. Pfitzner, Victor C. *Paul and the Agon Motif: Traditional Athletic Imagery in the Pauline Literature*. NovTSup 16. Leiden: Brill, 1967.

Pfitzner, "School." Pfitzner, Victor C. "The School of Jesus: Jesus-Traditions in Pauline Paraenesis." *LTJ* 13 (2–3, 1979): 22–36.

Philip, "Growth." Philip, Puthvaíl Thomas. "The Growth of the Baptist Churches of Tribal Nagaland." MA thesis, Fuller School of World Mission, 1972.

Philip, *Pneumatology*. Philip, Finny. *The Origins of Pauline Pneumatology: The Eschatological Bestowal of the Spirit upon Gentiles in Judaism and in the Early Development of Paul's Theology*. Tübingen: Mohr Siebeck, 2005.

Philip, "Quelques notes." Philip, Maertens. "Quelques notes sur πνικτός." *NTS* 45 (4, 1999): 593–96.

Philip, "Revolution." Philip, Finny. "The Thomas Mathews Revolution." *C&C* 36 (1, 2005): 18–23.

Phillips, "Balance." Phillips, Elaine A. "The Tilted Balance: Early Rabbinic Perceptions of God's Justice." *BBR* 14 (2, 2004): 223–40.

Phillips, "Genre." Phillips, Thomas E. "The Genre of Acts: Moving toward a Consensus?" *CBR* 4 (3, 2006): 365–96.

Phillips, "Lares." Phillips, C. Robert, III. "Lares." *OCD*³ 815–16.

Phillips, "Lemures." Phillips, C. Robert, III. "Lemures." *OCD*³ 843.

Phillips, *Paul and Acts*. Phillips, Thomas E. *Paul, His Letters, and Acts*. LPSt. Peabody, Mass.: Hendrickson, 2009.

Phillips, "Prophets." Phillips, Thomas E. "Prophets, Priests, and Godfearing Readers: The Priestly and Prophetic Traditions in Luke-Acts." Pages 222–39 in *Contemporary Studies in Acts*. Edited by Thomas E. Phillips. Macon, Ga.: Mercer University Press, 2009.

Phillips, "Revisiting Philo." Phillips, Thomas E. "Revisiting Philo: Discussions of Wealth and Poverty in Philo's Ethical Discourse." *JSNT* 83 (2001): 111–21.

Phillips, "Role Model." Phillips, Thomas E. "Paul as a Role Model in Acts: The 'We' Passages in Acts 16 and Beyond." Pages 49–63 in *Acts and Ethics*. Edited by Thomas E. Phillips. NTMon 9. Sheffield, U.K.: Sheffield Phoenix, 2005.

Phillips, "Twelve Gods." Phillips, C. Robert III. "Twelve (Olympian) Gods." *BrillPauly* 15:47–48.

Phillips, Van Vorhees, and Ruth, "Birthday." Phillips, D. P., C. A. Van Voorhees, and T. E. Ruth. "The Birthday: Lifeline or Deadline?" *Psychosomatic Medicine* 54 (1992): 532–42.

Philonenko, "Ossements desséchés." Philonenko, Marc. "De Qoumrân à Doura-Europos: La vision des ossements desséchés (*Ézéchiel* 37,1–4)." *RHPR* 74 (1, 1994): 1–12.

Phinney, "Narratives." Phinney, D. N. "Call/Commission Narratives." Pages 65–71 in *Dictionary of the Old Testament Prophets*. Edited by Mark J. Boda and J. Gordon McConville. Downers Grove, Ill.: IVP Academic, 2012.

Phiri, "System." Phiri, Kings M. "Some Changes in the Matrilineal Family System among the Chewa of Malawi since the Nineteenth Century." *JAfrHist* 24 (2, 1983): 257–74.

Pichler, "Anliegen." Pichler, Josef. "Das theologische Anliegen der Paulusrezeption im lukanischen Werk." Pages 731–43 in *The Unity of Luke-Acts*. Edited by Joseph Verheyden. BETL 142. Leuven: Leuven University Press, 1999.

Pichler, *Paulusrezeption*. Pichler, Josef. *Paulusrezeption und Paulusbild in der Apostelgeschichte 13,16–52*. InnTStud 50. Innsbruck: Tyrolia, 1997.

Pienaar, "Sondaars." Pienaar, Henk. "'Sondaars' in die tyd van Jesus ('Sinners' in the Time of Jesus)." *HvTS* 53 (3, 1997): 751–72.

Pierce, "Faith." Pierce, Larry. "Where There's Faith, There's Hope for Boys." *CT* (Sept. 13, 1993): 80.

Pierce, Groothuis, and Fee, *Equality*. Pierce, Ronald W., Rebecca Merrill Groothuis, and Gordon D. Fee, eds. *Discovering Biblical Equality: Complementarity without Hierarchy*. Downers Grove, Ill.: InterVarsity, 2004.

Pieris, "Humour." Pieris, Aloysius. "Prophetic Humour and the Exposure of Demons: Christian Hope in the Light of a Buddhist Exorcism." *VidJTR* 60 (5, 1996): 311–22.

Pigeaud, *Sibylles*. Pigeaud, Jackie, ed. *Les Sibylles: Actes des VIIIèmes entretiens de la Garenne Lemot, 18 au 20 octobre 2001*. Nantes: Université de Nantes, 2005.

Pikaza, "Jesús histórico." Pikaza, Xabier. "El Jesús histórico: Nota bibliográfico-temática." *IgViv* 210 (2002): 85–90.

Pike, "Congregation." Pike, Dana M. "The 'Congregation of YHWH' in the Bible and at Qumran." *RevQ* 17 (65–68, 1996): 233–40.

Pilch, "Anthropology." Pilch, John J. "Insights and Models from Medical Anthropology for Understanding the Healing Activity of the Historical Jesus." *HTS/TS* 51 (2, 1995): 314–37.

Pilch, "Apostle." Pilch, John J. "Paul's Call to Be an Apostle." *BibT* 41 (6, 2003): 377–81.

Pilch, "Beat." Pilch, John J. "'Beat His Ribs While He Is Young' (Sir 30:12): A Window on the Mediterranean World." *BTB* 23 (3, 1993):101–13.

Pilch, "Call." Pilch, John J. "Paul's Call to Be a Holy Man (Apostle): In His Own Words and in Other Words." *HTS/TS* 61 (1–2, 2005): 371–83.

Pilch, "Colors." Pilch, John J. "Colors and Dyes." *BibT* 37 (2, 1999): 102–6.

Pilch, "Desert." Pilch, John J. "Desert and Wilderness." *BibT* 37 (4, 1999): 247–51.

Pilch, "Dreams." Pilch, John J. "Dreams." *BibT* 38 (3, 2000): 174–78.

Pilch, "Eye." Pilch, John J. "The Evil Eye." *BibT* 42 (1, 2004): 49–53.

Pilch, *Flights.* Pilch, John J. *Flights of the Soul: Visions, Heavenly Journeys, and Peak Experiences in the Biblical World.* Grand Rapids: Eerdmans, 2011.

Pilch, *Healing.* Pilch, John J. *Healing in the New Testament: Insights from Medical and Mediterranean Anthropology.* Minneapolis: Fortress, 2000.

Pilch, "Healing." Pilch, John J. "Healing in Luke-Acts." Pages 203–19 in *The Social World of the New Testament: Insights and Models.* Edited by Jerome H. Neyrey and Eric C. Stewart. Peabody, Mass.: Hendrickson, 2008.

Pilch, "Insult." Pilch, John J. "The Art of Insult." *BibT* 36 (3, 1998): 179–84.

Pilch, "Jews and Christians." Pilch, John J. "Are There Jews and Christians in the Bible?" *HvTS* 53 (1997): 1–7.

Pilch, "Lying." Pilch, John J. "Lying and Deceit in the Letters to the Seven Churches." *BTB* 22 (1992): 126–35.

Pilch, "Naming." Pilch, John J. "Naming the Nameless in the Bible." *BibT* 44 (5, 2006): 315–20.

Pilch, "Samaritans." Pilch, John J. "Jesus and the Samaritans." *BibT* 40 (3, 2002): 172–77.

Pilch, "Sickness." Pilch, John J. "Sickness and Healing in Luke-Acts." Pages 181–209 in *The Social World of Luke-Acts: Models for Interpretation.* Edited by Jerome H. Neyrey. Peabody, Mass.: Hendrickson, 1991.

Pilch, "Sky Journeys." Pilch, John J. "The Holy Man, Enoch, and His Sky Journeys." Pages 103–11 in *Shamans Unbound.* Edited by Mihály Hoppál and Zsuzsanna Simonkay, with Kornélia Buday and Dávid Somfai Kara. BibSham 14. Budapest: Akadémiai Kiadó, 2008.

Pilch, "Trance Experience." Pilch, John J. "Paul's Ecstatic Trance Experience near Damascus in Acts of the Apostles." *HvTS* 58 (2, 2002): 690–707.

Pilch, *Visions.* Pilch, John J. *Visions and Healing in the Acts of the Apostles: How the Early Believers Experienced God.* Collegeville, Minn.: Liturgical Press, 2004.

Pilgaard, "*Theios aner.*" Pilgaard, Aage. "The Hellenistic *theios aner*—A Model for Early Christian Christology?" Pages 101–22 in *The New Testament and Hellenistic Judaism.* Edited by Peder Borgen and Søren Giversen. Peabody, Mass.: Hendrickson, 1997.

Pilgrim, "Creation." Pilgrim, Walter E. "Luke-Acts and a Theology of Creation." *WW* 12 (1, 1992): 51–58.

Pilhofer, *Philippi.* Pilhofer, Peter. *Philippi. Band I: Die erste christliche Gemeinde Europas. Band II: Katalog der Inschriften von Philippi.* WUNT 87, 119. Tübingen: Mohr Siebeck, 1995–2000.

Pillai, *Interpretation.* Pillai, C. A. Joachim. *Apostolic Interpretation of History: A Commentary on Acts 13:16–41.* Hicksville, N.Y.: Exposition, 1980.

Pillai, *Preaching.* Pillai, C. A. Joachim. *Early Missionary Preaching: A Study of Luke's Report in Acts 13.* Hicksville, N.Y.: Exposition, 1979.

Piñero, "Mediterranean View." Piñero, Antonio. "A Mediterranean View of Prophetic Inspiration: On the Concept of Inspiration in the *Liber antiquitatum biblicarum* by Pseudo-Philo." *MHR* 6 (1, 1991): 5–34.

Pines, "Darkness." Pines, Shlomo. "From Darkness into Great Light." *Imm* 4 (1974): 47–51.

Pines, "Model." Pines, Shlomo. "A Platonistic Model for Two of Josephus' Accounts of the Doctrine of the Pharisees concerning Providence and Man's Freedom of Action." *Imm* 7 (1977): 38–43.

Pinkster, "Present Tense." Pinkster, Harm. "The Present Tense in Virgil's Aeneid." *Mnemosyne* 52 (6, 1999): 705–17.

Pinnock, "Foreword." Pinnock, Clark H. Foreword. Pages vii–viii in *The Charismatic Theology of Saint Luke.* By Roger Stronstad. Peabody, Mass.: Hendrickson, 1984.

Pinson, "Kinship." Pinson, Ann. "Kinship and Economy in Modern Iceland: A Study in Social Continuity." *Ethnology* 18 (2, Apr. 1979): 183–97.

Piper, "Demonstration." Piper, John. "The Demonstration of the Righteousness of God in Romans 3:25,26." *JSNT* 2 (7, 1980): 2–32.

Piper, *Justification.* Piper, John. *The Justification of God: An Exegetical and Theological Study of Romans 9:1–23.* Grand Rapids: Baker, 1983.

Piper, "Righteousness." Piper, John. "The Righteousness of God in Romans 3,1–8." *TZ* 36 (1, 1980): 3–16.

Pirolo, *Reentry Team.* Pirolo, Neal. *The Reentry Team: Caring for Your Returning Missionaries.* San Diego, Calif.: Emmaus Road International, 2000.

Pitard, "Damascus." Pitard, Wayne T. "Damascus." *OEANE* 2:103–6.

Pitcher, "Characterization." Pitcher, L. V. "Characterization in Ancient Historiography." Pages 102–17 in *A Companion to Greek and Roman Historiography.* Edited

by John Marincola. 2 vols. Oxford: Blackwell, 2007.

Pitigliani, "Catacombs." Pitigliani, Letizia. "A Rare Look at the Jewish Catacombs of Rome." *BAR* 6 (3, 1980): 32–43.

Pitre, *Tribulation.* Pitre, Brant. *Jesus, the Tribulation, and the End of the Exile: Restoration Eschatology and the Origin of the Atonement.* Tübingen: Mohr Siebeck; Grand Rapids: Baker Academic, 2005.

Pitto, "Señor." Pitto, A. "Jesucristo proclamado Señor en la Iglesia: Pablo y las primeras profesiones de fe." *ScrTh* 40 (2, 2008): 385–403.

Pitt-Rivers, "Kith." Pitt-Rivers, Julian. "The Kith and the Kin." Pages 89–105 in *The Character of Kinship.* Edited by Jack Goody. New York: Cambridge University Press, 1973.

Pitts, "Citation." Pitts, Andrew W. "Source Citation in Greek Historiography and in Luke(-Acts)." Pages 349–88 in *Christian Origins and Greco-Roman Culture: Social and Literary Contexts for the New Testament.* Edited by Stanley Porter and Andrew W. Pitts. Vol. 1 of Early Christianity in Its Hellenistic Context. Vol. 9 in Texts and Editions for New Testament Study. Leiden: Brill, 2013.

Pixner, "Church of the Apostles." Pixner, Bargil. "Church of the Apostles Found on Mt. Zion." *BAR* 16 (3, 1990): 16–35, 60.

Pixner, "Gate." Pixner, Bargil. "The History of the 'Essene Gate' Area." *ZDPV* 105 (1989): 96–104 and plates 8–16a.

Pixner, "Gateway." Pixner, Bargil. "Jerusalem's Essene Gateway: Where the Community Lived in Jesus' Time." *BAR* 23 (3, 1997): 22–31, 64, 66.

Pixner, "Zion." Pixner, Bargil. "Mount Zion, Jesus, and Archaeology." Pages 309–22 in *Jesus and Archaeology.* Edited by James H. Charlesworth. Grand Rapids: Eerdmans, 2006.

Pixner, Chen, and Margalit, "Zion." Pixner, Bargil, Doron Chen, and Shlomo Margalit. "Mount Zion: The 'Gate of the Essenes' Reexcavated." *ZDPV* 105 (1989): 85–95 and plates 8–16a.

Pizzuto-Pomaco, "Shame." Pizzuto-Pomaco, Julia. "From Shame to Honour: Mediterranean Women in Romans 16." PhD diss., University of St. Andrews, 2003.

Plantinga, *Minds.* Plantinga, Alvin. *God and Other Minds: A Study of the Rational Justification of Belief in God.* Rev. ed. Ithaca, N.Y.: Cornell University Press, 1990.

Plantinga, "Science." Plantinga, Alvin. "Science and Religion: Why Does the Debate Continue?" Pages 93–123 in *The Religion and Science Debate: Why Does It Continue?* Edited by Harold W. Attridge. New Haven: Yale University Press, 2009.

Plath, "Ellipsis." Plath, Robert. "Ellipsis." *BrillPauly* 4:926.

Plath, "Polysyndeton." Plath, Robert. "Poly-syndeton." *BrillPauly* 11:534.

Plath, "Prolepsis." Plath, Robert. "Prolepsis." *BrillPauly* 12:1.

Platvoet, "Rule." Platvoet, Jan G. "The Rule and Its Exceptions: Spirit Possession in Two African Societies." *JStRel* 12 (1, 1999): 5–51.

Platz-Horster, "Techniques." Platz-Horster, Gertrud. "Early Techniques of Producing Glass Objects." *BrillPauly* 5:861–64.

Pleket, "Elites and Business." Pleket, H. W. "Urban Elites and Business in the Greek Part of the Roman Empire." Pages 131–44 in *Trade in the Ancient Economy*. Edited by Peter Garnsey, Keith Hopkins, and C. R. Whittaker. Berkeley: University of California Press, 1983.

Plevnik, "Authenticity." Plevnik, Joseph. "1 Thessalonians 5,1–11: Its Authenticity, Intention, and Message." *Bib* 60 (1979): 71–90.

Plevnik, "Destination." Plevnik, Joseph. "The Destination of the Apostle and of the Faithful: Second Corinthians 4:13b–14 and First Thessalonians 4:14." *CBQ* 62 (1, 2000): 83–95.

Plümacher, "Acta-Forschung." Plümacher, Eckhard. "Acta-Forschung, 1974–1982." *TRu* 48 (1983): 1–56; 49 (1984): 105–69.

Plümacher, "Cicero und Lukas." Plümacher, Eckhard. "Cicero und Lukas: Bemerkungen zu Stil und Zweck der historischen Monographie." Pages 759–75 in *The Unity of Luke-Acts*. Edited by Joseph Verheyden. BETL 142. Leuven: Leuven University Press, 1999.

Plümacher, "Fiktion und Wunder." Plümacher, Eckhard. "ΤΕΡΑΤΕΙΑ: Fiktion und Wunder in der hellenistisch-römischen Geschichtsschreibung und in der Apostelgeschichte." *ZNW* 89 (1–2, 1998): 66–90.

Plümacher, *Geschichte*. Plümacher, Eckhard. *Geschichte und Geschichten: Aufsätze zur Apostelgeschichte und zu den Johannesakten*. Edited by Jens Schröter and Ralph Brucker. WUNT 170. Tübingen: Mohr Siebeck, 2004.

Plümacher, "Griechischer Historiker." Plümacher, Eckhard. "Lukas als griechischer Historiker." *PWSup* 14 (1974): 235–64.

Plümacher, "Historiker." Plümacher, Eckhard. "Stichwort: Lukas, Historiker." *ZNT* 9 (18, 2006): 2–8.

Plümacher, *Lukas*. Plümacher, Eckhard. *Lukas als hellenistischer Schriftsteller: Studien zur Apostelgeschichte*. SUNT 9. Göttingen: Vandenhoeck & Ruprecht, 1972.

Plümacher, "Luke as Historian." Plümacher, Eckhard. "Luke as Historian." Translated by Dennis Martin. *ABD* 4:398–402.

Plümacher, "Mission Speeches." Plümacher, Eckhard. "The Mission Speeches in Acts and Dionysius of Halicarnassus." Pages 251–66 in *Jesus and the Heritage of Israel: Luke's Narrative Claim upon Israel's Legacy*. Edited by David P. Moessner. Luke the Interpreter of Israel 1. Harrisburg, Pa.: Trinity Press International, 1999.

Plümacher, "Missionsreden." Plümacher, Eckhard. "Die Missionsreden der Apostelgeschichte und Dionys von Halikarnass." *NTS* 39 (2, 1993): 161–77.

Plümacher, "Monographie." Plümacher, Eckhard. "Die Apostelgeschichte als historiche Monographie." Pages 457–66 in *Les Actes des apôtres: Traditions, rédaction, théologie*. Edited by Jacob Kremer. BETL 48. Gembloux, Belg.: J. Duculot; Leuven: Leuven University Press, 1979.

Plümacher, "Thukydidesreminiszenz." Plümacher, Eckhard. "Eine Thukydidesreminiszenz in der Apostelgeschichte (Ac 20, 33–35—Thuk. II 97, 3f.)." *ZNW* 83 (3–4, 1992): 270–75.

Plümacher, "Wirklichkeitserfahrung." Plümacher, Eckhard. "Wirklichkeitserfahrung und Geschichtsschreibung bei Lukas: Erwägungen zu den Wir-Stücken der Apostelgeschichte." *ZNW* 68 (1977): 2–22.

Plüss, "Evidence." Plüss, Jean-Daniel. "Initial Evidence or Evident Initials? A European Point of View on a Pentecostal Distinctive." *AJPS* 2 (2, 1999): 213–22.

Plymale, *Prayer Texts*. Plymale, Steven F. *The Prayer Texts of Luke-Acts*. AUSt 7, Theology and Religion, 118. New York: Peter Lang, 1991.

Pocock, Van Rheenen, and McConnell, *Face*. Pocock, Michael, Gailyn Van Rheenen, and Douglas McConnell. *The Changing Face of World Missions: Engaging Contemporary Issues and Trends*. Grand Rapids: Baker Academic, 2005.

Podella, "King's Highway." Podella, Thomas. "King's Highway." *BrillPauly* 7:48.

Poewe, *Religions*. Poewe, Karla. *New Religions and the Nazis*. New York and London: Routledge, 2006.

Poewe, "Rethinking." Poewe, Karla. "Rethinking the Relationship of Anthropology to Science and Religion." Pages 234–58 in *Charismatic Christianity as a Global Culture*. Edited by Karla Poewe. SCR. Columbia: University of South Carolina Press, 1994.

Pogoloff, "Isocrates." Pogoloff, Stephen Mark. "Isocrates and Contemporary Hermeneutics." Pages 338–62 in *Persuasive Artistry: Studies in New Testament Rhetoric in Honor of George A. Kennedy*. Edited by Duane F. Watson. JSNTSup 50. Sheffield, U.K.: Sheffield Academic, 1991.

Pogoloff, *Logos*. Pogoloff, Stephen Mark. *Logos and Sophia: The Rhetorical Situation of 1 Corinthians*. SBLDS 134. Atlanta: Scholars Press, 1992.

Pohor, "Slavery." Pohor, Rubin. "Slavery." Page 89 in *Africa Bible Commentary*. Edited by Tokunboh Adeyemo. Grand Rapids: Zondervan; Nairobi: WordAlive, 2006.

Poirier, "Callings." Poirier, John C. "Spirit-Gifted Callings in the Pauline Corpus, Part I: The Laying On of Hands." *JBPRes* 1 (Fall 2009): 83–99.

Poirier, "Generational Reckoning." Poirier, John C. "Generational Reckoning in Hesiod and in the Pentateuch." *JNES* 62 (3, 2003): 193–99.

Poirier, "Linguistic Situation." Poirier, John C. "The Linguistic Situation in Jewish Palestine in Late Antiquity." *JGRCJ* 4 (2007): 55–134.

Poirier, "Narrative Role." Poirier, John C. "The Narrative Role of Semitic Languages in the Book of Acts." *FilNeot* 16 (31–32, 2003): 107–16.

Poirier, "Purity." Poirier, John C. "Purity beyond the Temple in the Second Temple Era." *JBL* 122 (2, 2003): 247–65.

Poirier, "Return." Poirier, John C. "The Endtime Return of Elijah and Moses at Qumran." *DSD* 10 (2, 2003): 221–42.

Poirier and Frankovic, "Celibacy." Poirier, John C., and Joseph Frankovic. "Celibacy and Charism in 1 Cor 7:5–7." *HTR* 89 (1, 1996): 1–18.

Pokorny, "Romfahrt." Pokorny, Petr. "Die Romfahrt des Paulus und der antike Roman." *ZNW* 64 (1973): 233–44.

Poland, *Criticism*. Poland, Lynn M. *Literary Criticism and Biblical Hermeneutics*. AARAS 48. Atlanta: Scholars Press, 1985.

Polanyi, *Knowledge*. Polanyi, Michael. *Personal Knowledge: Towards a Post-critical Philosophy*. Rev. ed. Chicago: University of Chicago Press, 1962.

Polaski, "Taming Tamar." Polaski, D. C. "On Taming Tamar: Amram's Rhetoric and Women's Roles in Pseudo-Philo's *Liber antiquitatum biblicarum* 9." *JSP* 13 (1995): 79–99.

Polhill, *Acts*. Polhill, John B. *Acts*. NAC 26. Nashville: Broadman, 1992.

Polignac, "Argos." Polignac, François de. "Argos entre centre et périphérie: L'espace cultuel de la cité grecque." *ASSR* 30 (59/1, 1985): 55–63.

"Politics of Thirst." "The New Politics of Thirst." *WPR* (Nov. 1992): 18–20.

Polkinghorne, *Belief*. Polkinghorne, John. *Belief in God in an Age of Science*. Terry

Lectures. New Haven: Yale University Press, 1998.

Polkinghorne, *Faith*. Polkinghorne, John. *The Faith of a Physicist: Reflections of a Bottom-Up Thinker*. Gifford Lectures, 1993–94. Minneapolis: Fortress, 1994.

Polkinghorne, *Quarks*. Polkinghorne, John. *Quarks, Chaos, and Christianity: Questions to Science and Religion*. New York: Crossroad, 1994.

Polkinghorne and Beale, *Questions*. Polkinghorne, John, and Nicholas Beale. *Questions of Truth: Fifty-One Responses to Questions about God, Science, and Belief*. Louisville: Westminster John Knox, 2009.

Pollard, "Covenant." Pollard, Edward Bagby. "Covenant of Salt." *ISBE* 1:794.

Pollard and Reid, *Rise and Fall*. Pollard, Justin, and Howard Reid. *The Rise and Fall of Alexandria: Birthplace of the Modern World*. New York: Penguin, 2007.

Poloma, "Glossolalia." Poloma, Margaret M. "Glossolalia, Liminality, and Empowered Kingdom Building: A Sociological Perspective." Pages 147–73 in *Speaking in Tongues: Multi-disciplinary Perspectives*. Edited by Mark J. Cartledge. SPCI. Waynesboro, Ga., and Bletchley, Milton Keynes, U.K.: Paternoster, 2006.

Pomeroy, *Goddesses*. Pomeroy, Sarah B. *Goddesses, Whores, Wives, and Slaves: Women in Classical Antiquity*. New York: Schocken, 1975.

Pomeroy, "Introduction." Pomeroy, Arthur J. Introduction. Pages 1–8 in Arius Didymus, *Epitome of Stoic Ethics*. Edited by Arthur J. Pomeroy. SBLTT 44. Graeco-Roman Series 14. Atlanta: SBL, 1999.

Pomeroy, "Women in Egypt." Pomeroy, Sarah B. "Women in Roman Egypt: A Preliminary Study Based on Papyri." Pages 303–22 in *Reflections of Women in Antiquity*. Edited by Helene P. Foley. New York: Gordon & Breach Science, 1981.

Poniży, "Recognition." Poniży, Bogdan. "Recognition of God according to the Book of Wisdom 13:1–9." *PJBR* 1 (2, 2001): 201–6.

Ponsot, "Israël." Ponsot, Hervé. "Et ainsi tout Israël sera sauvé: Rom., xi, 26a." *RB* 89 (3, 1982): 406–17.

Pont, "Fondateur." Pont, A.-V. "L'empereur 'fondateur': Enquête sur les motifs de la reconnaisance civique." *REG* 120 (2, 2007): 526–52.

Pope-Levison, *Pulpit*. Pope-Levison, Priscilla. *Turn the Pulpit Loose: Two Centuries of American Women Evangelists*. New York: Palgrave Macmillan, 2004.

Popkes, "Worte." Popkes, Enno Edzard. "Die letzten Worte des lukanischen Paulus: Zur Bedeutung von Acts 28,25–28 für das Paulusbild der Apostelgeschichte."

Pages 605–25 in *Die Apostelgeschichte im Kontext antiker und frühchristlicher Historiographie*. Edited by Jörg Frey, Clare K. Rothschild, and Jens Schröter, with Bettina Rost. BZNWK 162. Berlin: de Gruyter, 2009.

Popovic, "Physiognomic Knowledge." Popovic, Mladen. "Physiognomic Knowledge in Qumran and Babylonia: Form, Interdisciplinarity, and Secrecy." *DSD* 13 (2, 2006): 150–76.

Popper, *Historicism*. Popper, Karl R. *The Poverty of Historicism*. 3rd ed. New York, Evanston: Harper & Row; London: Routledge & Kegan Paul, 1961.

Porath, "Hmnhrh." Porath, Yosef. "Hmnhrh sl 'mt hmym hgbwhh lqysryh brks hkwrkr (g'sr'-zrq)' (The Tunnel of Caesarea Maritima's High Level Aqueduct at the Kurkar Ridge [Jisr ez-Zarqa])." *'Atiqot* 30 (1996): 23–43, 126–27. (Abstract: *NTA* 42:529.)

Porciani, "Enigma." Porciani, Leone. "The Enigma of Discourse: A View of Thucydides." Pages 328–35 in *A Companion to Greek and Roman Historiography*. Edited by John Marincola. 2 vols. Oxford: Blackwell, 2007.

Porras, "Return." Porras, Eliud. "The Return of the Hero: Notes on the Use of Disguise, Compositional Patterns, and the New Heroic Quest in the *Odyssey*." Homer Seminar thesis, Department of Classics, Birkbeck College, University of London, 1990.

Porter, "Acco." Porter, H. "Acco." *ISBE* 1:23–24.

Porter, "Census." Porter, Stanley E. "The Reasons for the Lukan Census." Pages 165–88 in *Paul, Luke, and the Graeco-Roman World*. Edited by Alf Christophersen et al. JSNTSup 217. Sheffield, U.K.: Sheffield Academic, 2002; London: T&T Clark, 2003.

Porter, "Chronology." Porter, Stanley E. "Chronology, New Testament." *DNTB* 201–8.

Porter, "Comment(ary)ing." Porter, Stanley E. "Comment(ary)ing on Acts." Paper presented at the annual meeting of the SBL, Philadelphia, Nov. 21, 2005.

Porter, "Creeds." Porter, Wendy J. "Creeds and Hymns." *DNTB* 231–38.

Porter, *Criteria*. Porter, Stanley E. *The Criteria for Authenticity in Historical-Jesus Research: Previous Discussions and New Proposals*. JSNTSup 91. Sheffield: Sheffield Academic Press, 2000.

Porter, "Developments." Porter, Stanley E. "Developments in the Text of Acts before the Major Codices." Pages 31–67 in *The Book of Acts as Church History: Text, Textual Traditions and Ancient Interpretations/ Apostelgeschichte als Kirchengeschichte:*

Text, Texttraditionen und antike Auslegungen. Edited by Tobias Nicklas and Michael Tilly. Berlin: de Gruyter, 2003.

Porter, "Diatribe." Porter, Stanley E. "Diatribe." *DNTB* 296–98.

Porter, "Efforts." Porter, Stanley E. "Recent Efforts to Reconstruct Early Christianity on the Basis of Its Papyrological Evidence." Pages 71–84 in *Christian Origins and Greco-Roman Culture: Social and Literary Contexts for the New Testament*. Edited by Stanley Porter and Andrew W. Pitts. Vol. 1 of Early Christianity in Its Hellenistic Context. Vol. 9 in Texts and Editions for New Testament Study. Leiden: Brill, 2013.

Porter, "Genre and Ethics." Porter, Stanley E. "The Genre of Acts and the Ethics of Discourse." Pages 1–15 in *Acts and Ethics*. Edited by Thomas E. Phillips. NTMon 9. Sheffield, U.K.: Sheffield Phoenix, 2005.

Porter, "Greek in Galilee." Porter, Stanley E. "Jesus and the Use of Greek in Galilee." Pages 123–54 in *Studying the Historical Jesus: Evaluations of the State of Current Research*. Edited by Bruce Chilton and Craig A. Evans. NTTS 19. Leiden: Brill, 1994.

Porter, "Greek of New Testament." Porter, Stanley E. "Greek of the New Testament." *DNTB* 426–35.

Porter, *Idioms*. Porter, Stanley E. *Idioms of the Greek New Testament*. 2nd ed. Biblical Languages: Greek 2. Sheffield, U.K.: JSOT Press, 1994.

Porter, "Inscriptions." Porter, Stanley E. "Inscriptions and Papyri: Greco-Roman." *DNTB* 529–39.

Porter, "Introduction to Opponents." Porter, Stanley E. "Introduction to the Study of Paul's Opponents." Pages 1–5 in *Paul and His Opponents*. Edited by Stanley E. Porter. PAST 2. Leiden: Brill, 2005.

Porter, "Latin Language." Porter, Stanley E. "Latin Language." *DNTB* 630–31.

Porter, "Papyri, Palestinian." Porter, Stanley E. "Papyri, Palestinian." *DNTB* 764–66.

Porter, "Paul and Letters." Porter, Stanley E. "Paul of Tarsus and His Letters." Pages 533–85 in *Handbook of Classical Rhetoric in the Hellenistic Period, 330 B.C.–A.D. 400*. Edited by Stanley E. Porter. Leiden: Brill, 1997.

Porter, *Paul in Acts*. Porter, Stanley E. *Paul in Acts*. LPSt. Peabody, Mass.: Hendrickson, 2001. Reprint of *The Paul of Acts: Essays in Literary Criticism, Rhetoric, and Theology*. WUNT 115. Tübingen: Mohr Siebeck, 1999.

Porter, "Portrait." Porter, Stanley E. "The Portrait of Paul in Acts." Pages 124–38 in *The Blackwell Companion to Paul*. Edited by Stephen Westerholm. BCompRel. Oxford: Blackwell, 2011.

Porter, "Speak Latin." Porter, Stanley E. "Did Paul Speak Latin?" Pages 289–308 in *Paul: Jew, Greek, and Roman.* Edited by Stanley Porter. PAST 5. Leiden: Brill, 2008.

Porter, "Teach." Porter, Stanley E. "Did Jesus Ever Teach in Greek?" *TynBul* 44 (1993): 199–235.

Porter, "Thucydidean View?" Porter, Stanley E. "Thucydides 1.22.1 and Speeches in Acts: Is There a Thucydidean View?" *NovT* 32 (2, 1990): 121–42.

Porter, "'We' Passages." Porter, Stanley E. "Excursus: The 'We' Passages." Pages 545–74 in *The Book of Acts in Its Graeco-Roman Setting.* Edited by David W. J. Gill and Conrad Gempf. Vol. 2 of *The Book of Acts in Its First Century Setting.* Edited by Bruce W. Winter. Grand Rapids: Eerdmans; Carlisle, U.K.: Paternoster, 1994.

Porter and Westfall, "Cord." Porter, Stanley E., and Cynthia Long Westfall. "A Cord of Three Strands: Mission in Acts." Pages 108–34 in *Christian Mission: Old Testament Foundations and New Testament Developments.* Edited by Stanley E. Porter and Cynthia Long Westfall. Eugene, Ore.: Pickwick, 2010.

Porterfield, *Healing.* Porterfield, Amanda. *Healing in the History of Christianity.* New York and Oxford: Oxford University Press, 2005.

Porton, "Diversity." Porton, Gary G. "Diversity in Postbiblical Judaism." Pages 57–80 in *Early Judaism and Its Modern Interpreters.* Edited by Robert A. Kraft and George W. E. Nickelsburg. SBLBMI 2. Atlanta: Scholars Press, 1986.

Porton, "Midrash." Porton, Gary G. "Rabbinic Midrash: Public or Private." *RRJ* 5 (2, 2002): 141–69.

Porton, "Pronouncement Story." Porton, Gary G. "The Pronouncement Story in Tannaitic Literature: A Review of Bultmann's Theory." *Semeia* 20 (1981): 81–99.

Porton, "Sadducees." Porton, Gary G. "Sadducees." *DNTB* 1050–52.

Postell, *Adam as Israel.* Postell, Seth D. *Adam as Israel: Genesis 1–3 as the Introduction to the Torah and Tanakh.* Eugene, Ore.: Pickwick, 2011.

Poster, "Affections." Poster, Carol. "The Affections of the Soul: *Pathos,* Protreptic, and Preaching in Hellenistic Thought." Pages 23–37 in *Paul and Pathos.* Edited by Thomas H. Olbricht and Jerry L. Sumney. SBLSymS 16. Atlanta: SBL, 2001.

Pothecary, "Strabo." Pothecary, Sarah. "Strabo the Geographer: His Name and Its Meaning." *Mnemosyne* 52 (6, 1999): 691–704.

Pothen, "Missions." Pothen, Abraham T. "Indigenous Cross-cultural Missions in India and Their Contribution to Church Growth: With Special Emphasis on Pentecostal-Charismatic Missions." PhD diss., Fuller Theological Seminary, 1990.

Potin, *Fête de la Pentecôte.* Potin, Jean. *La fête juive de la Pentecôte: Étude des textes liturgiques.* 2 vols. LD 65. Paris: Cerf, 1971.

Potin, "Fête de la Pentecôte." Potin, Jean. "Approches de la fête juive de la Pentecôte." *FoiVie* 80 (1, 1981): 91–95.

Potter, "Claros." Potter, David S. "Claros." *OCD³* 335.

Potter, "Didyma." Potter, David S. "Didyma." *OCD³* 467.

Potter, "Lystra." Potter, David S. "Lystra." *ABD* 4:426–27.

Potter, *Prophets.* Potter, David S. *Prophets and Emperors: Human and Divine Authority from Augustus to Theodosius.* Cambridge, Mass.: Harvard University Press, 1994.

Potts, "Piety." Potts, Charlotte R. "The Art of Piety and Profit at Pompeii: A New Interpretation of the Painted Shop Façade at IX.7.1–2." *GR* 56 (1, 2009): 55–70.

Pouderon, "Alexandrie." Pouderon, Bernard. "Alexandrie du IIIᵉ siècle avant au IIIᵉ siècle après J.-C." *FoiVie* 107 (4, 2008): 5–22.

Poulin, "Loving-Kindness." Poulin, Joan. "Loving-Kindness towards Gentiles according to the Early Jewish Sages." *Théologiques* 11 (1–2, 2003): 89–112.

Poulos, "Pronouncement Story." Poulos, Paula Nassen. "Form and Function of the Pronouncement Story in Diogenes Laertius' *Lives.*" *Semeia* 20 (1981): 53–63.

Powell, *Acts.* Powell, Mark Allan. *What Are They Saying about Acts?* New York: Paulist, 1991.

Powell, "Salvation." Powell, Mark Allan. "Salvation in Luke-Acts." *WW* 12 (1, 1992): 5–10.

Powell, "Table Fellowship." Powell, Mark Allan. "Table Fellowship." Pages 925–31 in *Dictionary of Jesus and the Gospels.* 2nd ed. Edited by Joel B. Green, Jeannine K. Brown, and Nicholas Perrin. Downers Grove, Ill.: IVP Academic, 2013.

Power, "Galba." Power, Tristan J. "Suetonius Galba 1: Beginning or Ending?" *CP* 104 (2, 2009): 216–20.

Power, "Taunt." Power, Tristan J. "The Servants' Taunt: Homer and Suetonius' Galba." *Historia* 58 (2, 2009): 242–45.

"Power of Prayer." "The Power of Prayer." *C&C* 36 (2, 2007): 21.

Powers, "Daughters." Powers, Janet Everts. "'Your Daughters Shall Prophesy': Pentecostal Hermeneutics and the Empowerment of Women." Pages 313–37 in *Globalization of Pentecostalism: A Religion Made to Travel.* Edited by Murray W. Dempster, Byron D. Klaus, and Douglas Petersen. Foreword by Russell P. Spittler. Carlisle, U.K.: Paternoster; Oxford: Regnum, 1999.

Powers, "Treasures." Powers, Tom. "Treasures in the Storeroom." *BAR* 29 (4, 2003): 46–51.

Powlison, "Model." Powlison, David. "The Classical Model." Pages 89–111 in *Understanding Spiritual Warfare: Four Views.* Edited by James K. Beilby and Paul Rhodes Eddy. Grand Rapids: Baker Academic, 2012.

Poythress, "Analyses of Modern Tongues-Speaking." Poythress, Vern S. "Linguistic and Sociological Analyses of Modern Tongues-Speaking: Their Contributions and Limitations." *WTJ* 42 (1979): 367–98.

Poythress, "Holy Ones." Poythress, Vern S. "The Holy Ones of the Most High in Daniel VII." *VT* 26 (2, 1976): 208–13.

Poythress, "Romans 1:3–4." Poythress, Vern S. "Is Romans 1:3–4 a *Pauline* Confession after All?" *ExpT* 87 (6, 1976): 180–83.

Praeder, "Acts 27:1–28:16." Praeder, Susan Marie. "Acts 27:1–28:16: Sea Voyages in Ancient Literature and the Theology of Luke-Acts." *CBQ* 46 (4, 1984): 683–706.

Praeder, "First Person Narration." Praeder, Susan Marie. "The Problem of First Person Narration in Acts." *NovT* 29 (3, 1987): 193–218.

Praeder, "Luke-Acts and Novel." Praeder, Susan Marie. "Luke-Acts and the Ancient Novel." Pages 269–92 in *SBL Seminar Papers, 1981.* Edited by K. H. Richards. SBLSP 20. Chico, Calif.: Scholars Press, 1981.

Praeder, "Parallels." Praeder, Susan Marie. "Jesus-Paul, Peter-Paul, and Jesus-Peter Parallels in Luke-Acts: A History of Reader Response." Pages 23–39 in *SBL Seminar Papers, 1984.* Edited by K. H. Richards. SBLSP 23. Chico, Calif.: Scholars Press, 1984.

Praet, Demoen, and Gyselinck, "Domitian." Praet, Danny, Kristoffel Demoen, and Wannes Gyselinck. "Domitian and Pentheus, Apollonius and Dionysos: Echoes of Homer and Euripides' Bacchae in Philostratus' *Vita Apollonii.*" *Latomus* 70 (4, 2011): 1059–67.

Prather, *Miracles.* Prather, Paul. *Modern-Day Miracles: How Ordinary People Experience Supernatural Acts of God.* Kansas City, Mo.: Andrews and McMeel, 1996.

Prato, "Idolatry." Prato, Gian Luigi. "Idolatry Compelled to Search for Its Gods: A Peculiar Agreement between Textual Tradition and Exegesis (Amos 5:25–27 and Acts 7:42–43)." Pages 181–96 in *Luke and Acts.* Edited by Gerald O'Collins and Gilberto Marconi. Translated by

Matthew J. O'Connell. New York: Paulist, 1993.

Prema, "Paradigm." Prema, Sr. "Acts 2:17–21: A Paradigm for a Collaborative Mission." *Jeev* 34 (200, 2004): 122–36.

Prescendi, "Deuil." Prescendi, Francesca. "Le deuil à Rome: Mise en scène d'une émotion." *RHR* 225 (2, 2008): 297–313.

Prescendi, "Fides." Prescendi, Francesca. "Fides: Religion." *BrillPauly* 5:414–15.

Prescendi, "Numen." Prescendi, Francesca. "Numen." *BrillPauly* 9:893–95.

Prescendi, "Pales." Prescendi, Francesca. "Pales." *BrillPauly* 10:385.

Pressel, "Possession." Pressel, Esther. "Negative Spirit Possession in Experienced Brazilian Umbanda Spirit Mediums." Pages 333–64 in *Case Studies in Spirit Possession.* Edited by Vincent Crapanzaro and Vivian Garrison. New York: Wiley, 1977.

Pressel, "Trance." Pressel, Esther. "Umbanda Trance and Possession in São Paulo, Brazil." Pages 113–225 in *Trance, Healing, and Hallucination: Three Field Studies in Religious Experience.* By Felicitas D. Goodman, Jeannette H. Henney, and Esther Pressel. New York: Wiley, 1974.

Pressel, "Umbanda." Pressel, Esther. "Umbanda in São Paulo: Religious Innovation in a Developing Society." Pages 264–318 in *Religion, Altered States of Consciousness, and Social Change.* Edited by Erika Bourguignon. Columbus: Ohio State University Press, 1973.

Prestel, "Erprobung." Prestel, Peter. "Die Erprobung des Abraham: Zur Gestaltung der Aqedah bei Flavius Josephus." *WD* 25 (1999): 93–112.

Pretzler, "Pausanias and Tradition." Pretzler, Maria. "Pausanias and Oral Tradition." *CQ* 55 (1, 2005): 235–49.

Preus, "Tongues." Preus, Klemet. "Tongues: An Evaluation from a Scientific Perspective." *CTQ* 46 (4, 1982): 277–93.

Preuschen, *Apostelgeschichte.* Preuschen, Erwin. *Die Apostelgeschichte.* HNT 4.1. Tübingen: Mohr-Siebeck, 1913.

Price, "Dreams." Price, Simon R. F. "Dreams." *OCD³* 496–97.

Price, "Easters." Price, Robert M. "Brand X Easters." *FourR* 20 (6, 2007): 13–15, 18–19, 23.

Price, "Evolution of Genres." Price, Robert M. "Implied Reader Response and the Evolution of Genres: Transitional Stages between the Ancient Novels and the Apocryphal Acts." *HvTS* 53 (4, 1997): 909–38.

Price, "Failure." Price, Jonathan J. "The Failure of Rhetoric in Josephus' Bellum Judaicum." *Ramus* 36 (1, 2007): 6–24.

Price, "Light from Qumran." Price, James L. "Light from Qumran upon Some Aspects of Johannine Theology." Pages 9–37 in *John and Qumran.* Edited by James H. Charlesworth. London: Geoffrey Chapman, 1972.

Price, "Man and God." Price, Simon R. F. "Between Man and God: Sacrifice in the Roman Imperial Cult." *JRS* 70 (1980): 28–43.

Price, "Neōkoros." Price, Simon R. F. "Neōkoros." *OCD³* 1034.

Price, "Paulus absconditus (2002)." Price, Robert M. "Paulus absconditus: Paul versus John in Ephesian Tradition." *Forum* 5 (1, 2002): 87–94.

Price, "Paulus absconditus (2003)." Price, Robert M. "Paulus absconditus: Paul versus John in Ephesian Tradition." *JHC* 10 (1, 2003): 100–109.

Price, "Procession." Price, Simon R. F. "Procession." *BrillPauly* 11:905–9.

Price, "Rhoda." Price, Robert M. "Rhoda and Penelope: Two More Cases of Luke's Suppression of Women." Pages 98–104 in *The Feminist Companion to the Acts of the Apostles.* Edited by Amy-Jill Levine with Marianne Blickenstaff. Cleveland: Pilgrim; Edinburgh: T&T Clark, 2004.

Price, *Rituals.* Price, S. R. F. *Rituals and Power: The Roman Imperial Cult in Asia Minor.* Cambridge and New York: Cambridge University Press, 1984.

Price, *Son of Man.* Price, Robert M. *The Incredible Shrinking Son of Man: How Reliable Is the Gospel Tradition?* Amherst, N.Y.: Prometheus, 2003.

Price, *Widow Traditions.* Price, Robert M. *The Widow Traditions in Luke-Acts: A Feminist-Critical Study.* SBLDS 155. Atlanta: Scholars Press, 1997.

Prickett, *Origins of Narrative.* Prickett, Stephen. *Origins of Narrative: The Romantic Appropriation of the Bible.* Cambridge: Cambridge University Press, 1996.

Priest, "Mebaqqer." Priest, John F. "Mebaqqer, Paqid, and the Messiah." *JBL* 81 (1, 1962): 55–61.

Priest, "Messiah." Priest, John F. "The Messiah and the Meal in 1QSa." *JBL* 82 (1, 1963): 95–100.

Prieur, "Actes 2,42 et culte réformé." Prieur, Jean-Marc. "Actes 2,42 et le culte réformé." *FoiVie* 94 (2, 1995): 61–72.

Prince, "EEG." Prince, Raymond. "Can the EEG Be Used in the Study of Possession States?" Pages 121–37 in *Trance and Possession States: Proceedings of the Second Annual Conference, R. M. Bucke Memorial Society, March 4–6, 1966.* Edited by Raymond Prince. Montreal: R. M. Bucke Memorial Society, 1968.

Prince, "Foreword." Prince, Raymond. Foreword. Pages xi–xvi in *Case Studies in Spirit Possession.* Edited by Vincent Crapanzaro and Vivian Garrison. New York: Wiley, 1977.

Prince, "Possession Cults." Prince, Raymond. "Possession Cults and Social Cybernetics." Pages 157–65 in *Trance and Possession States: Proceedings of the Second Annual Conference, R. M. Bucke Memorial Society, March 4–6, 1966.* Edited by Raymond Prince. Montreal: R. M. Bucke Memorial Society, 1968.

Prince, "Review." Prince, Deborah Thompson. Review of William Sanger Campbell, *The "We" Passages in the Acts of the Apostles: The Narrator as Narrative Character.* *RBL* (Jan. 17, 2009): 4–5. http://www.bookreviews.org/pdf/6149_6568.pdf.

Prince, "Variations." Prince, Raymond. "Variations in Psychotherapeutic Procedures." Pages 291–349 in vol. 6 of *Handbook of Cross-cultural Psychology: Psychopathology.* Edited by H. C. Triandis and J. G. Draguns. Boston: Allyn & Bacon, 1980.

Prince, "Yoruba Psychiatry." Prince, Raymond. "Indigenous Yoruba Psychiatry." Pages 84–120 in *Magic, Faith, and Healing: Studies in Primitive Psychiatry Today.* Edited by Ari Kiev. Foreword by Jerome D. Frank. New York: Free Press, 1964.

Pritchard, *East.* Pritchard, James B., ed. *The Ancient Near East.* 2 vols. Princeton: Princeton University Press, 1973.

Pritchard, *Solomon.* Pritchard, James B., ed. *Solomon and Sheba.* London: Phaidon, 1974.

Pritchard, "Textiles." Pritchard, Frances. "The Use of Textiles, c. 1000–1500." Pages 355–78 in *The Cambridge History of Western Textiles.* Edited by David Jenkins. 2 vols. Cambridge: Cambridge University Press, 2003.

Pritz, *Nazarene Christianity.* Pritz, Ray A. *Nazarene Jewish Christianity: From the End of the New Testament Period until Its Disappearance in the Fourth Century.* StPB 37. Jerusalem: Magnes; Leiden: Brill, 1988.

Procopé, "Epicureans." Procopé, John. "Epicureans on Anger." Pages 171–96 in *The Emotions in Hellenistic Philosophy.* Edited by Juha Sihvola and Troels Engberg-Pedersen. TSHP 46. Dordrecht, Neth.: Kluwer Academic, 1998.

Propp, "Demons." Propp, William H. C. "Exorcising Demons." *BRev* 20 (5, 2004): 14–21, 47.

"Prosecutor Repudiates Report." "Israeli Prosecutor Repudiates IAA Report on Forgery." *BAR* 31 (3, 2005): 46–47.

Protus, "Chukwu." Protus, Kemdirim O. "John (Nwagwu) Chukwu." No pages. *DACB.* Online: http://www.dacb.org/stories/nigeria/chukwu_john.html.

Protus, "Latunde." Protus, Kemdirim O. "Elija Titus Latunde." No pages. *DACB.*

Online: http://www.dacb.org/stories/nigeria/latunde_.html.

Provan, "Kings." Provan, Iain. "2 Kings." Pages 110–219 in vol. 3 of *Zondervan Illustrated Bible Backgrounds Commentary: Old Testament*. Edited by John Walton. 5 vols. Grand Rapids: Zondervan, 2009.

Prowse et al., "Isotopic Evidence." Prowse, Tracy L., et al. "Isotopic Evidence for Age-Related Immigration to Imperial Rome." *American Journal of Physical Anthropology* 132 (2007): 510–19.

Pryce and Gill, "Lighting." Pryce, Frederick Norman, and David W. J. Gill. "Lighting." *OCD³* 861.

Pryce, Lang, and Vickers, "Measures." Pryce, Frederick Norman, Mabel L. Lang, and Michael Vickers. "Measures." *OCD³* 942–43.

Pryke, "Eschatology." Pryke, John. "Eschatology in the Dead Sea Scrolls." Pages 45–57 in *The Scrolls and Christianity: Historical and Theological Significance*. Edited by Matthew Black. London: SPCK, 1969.

Pryke, "Identity." Pryke, E. J. "The Identity of the Qumran Sect: A Reconsideration." *NovT* 10 (1, 1968): 43–61.

Pryke, "John." Pryke, John. "John the Baptist and the Qumran Community." *RevQ* 4 (4, 1964): 483–96.

Pryke, "Spirit." Pryke, John. "'Spirit' and 'Flesh' in the Qumran Documents and Some New Testament Texts." *RevQ* 5 (3, 1965): 345–60.

Pryzwansky, "Cornelius Nepos." Pryzwansky, Molly M. "Cornelius Nepos: Key Issues and Critical Approaches." *CJ* 105 (2, 2009): 97–108.

Przybylski, *Righteousness*. Przybylski, Benno. *Righteousness in Matthew and His World of Thought*. SNTSMS 41. Cambridge: Cambridge University Press, 1980.

Pucci, "Arenas." Pucci, Michael. "Arenas." *DNTB* 111–14.

Pucci, "Circuses." Pucci, Michael. "Circuses and Games." *DNTB* 209–12.

Pucci, "Pottery." Pucci, Giuseppe. "Pottery and Trade in the Roman Period." Pages 105–17 in *Trade in the Ancient Economy*. Edited by Peter Garnsey, Keith Hopkins, and C. R. Whittaker. Berkeley: University of California Press, 1983.

Puech, "Apocalypse." Puech, Émile. "Une apocalypse messianique (4Q521)." *RevQ* 15 (4, 1992): 475–522 and plates 1–3.

Puech, *Données qumraniennes*. Puech, Émile. *Les données qumraniennes et classiques*. Vol. 2 of *La croyance des esséniens en la vie future—immortalité, resurrection, vie éternelle? Histoire d'un croyance dans le judaïsme ancien*. EtBib, n.s., 22. Paris: Gabalda, 1993.

Puech, "Esprit." Puech, Émile. "L'Esprit saint à Qumrân." *SBFLA* 49 (1999): 283–97.

Puech, "Gospels." Puech, Henri-Charles. "Gnostic Gospels and Related Documents." Pages 231–362 in *Gospels and Related Writings*. Vol. 1 of *New Testament Apocrypha*. Edited by Edgar Hennecke, Wilhelm Schneemelcher, and R. McL. Wilson. Philadelphia: Westminster, 1963.

Puech, "James." Puech, Émile. "James the Just, or Just James? The 'James Ossuary' on Trial." *BAIAS* 21 (2003): 45–53.

Puech, "Manuscrit." Puech, Émile. "Notes sur le manuscrit de 11QMelchîsédeq." *RevQ* 12 (4, 1987): 483–513.

Puech, "Messianisme." Puech, Émile. "Messianisme, eschatologie, et résurrection dans les manuscrits de la mer Morte." *RevQ* 18 (70, 1997): 255–98.

Puech, "Nécropoles." Puech, Émile. "Les nécropoles juives palestiniennes au tournant de notre ère." *QF* 15–16 (1982): 35–55.

Puigdollers i Noblom, "Grans sacerdots." Puigdollers i Noblom, Rodolf. "Els grans sacerdots jueus des de l'època d'Herodes el Gran fins a la guerra jueva." *RCT* 30 (1, 2005): 49–89.

Puiggali, "Démonologie." Puiggali, J. "La démonologie de Philostrate." *RSPT* 67 (1983): 117–30.

Puig i Tàrrech, "Voyages à Jérusalem." Puig i Tàrrech, Armand. "Les voyages à Jérusalem (Lc 9,51; Ac 19,21)." Pages 493–505 in *The Unity of Luke-Acts*. Edited by Joseph Verheyden. BETL 142. Leuven: Leuven University Press, 1999.

Pulleyn, "Power of Names." Pulleyn, Simon. "The Power of Names in Classical Greek Religion." *CQ* 44 (1, 1994): 17–25.

Pullinger, *Dragon*. Pullinger, Jackie, with Andrew Quicke. *Chasing the Dragon*. London: Hodder & Stoughton, 1980.

Pummer, "Offshoot." Pummer, Reinhard. "The Samaritans—A Jewish Offshoot or a Pagan Cult?" *BRev* 7 (5, 1991): 22–29, 40.

Pummer, "Samaritan Pentateuch." Pummer, Reinhard. "The Samaritan Pentateuch and the New Testament." *NTS* 22 (4, 1976): 441–43.

Pummer, "Samaritanism." Pummer, Reinhard. "Samaritanism in Caesarea Maritima." Pages 181–202 in *Religious Rivalries and the Struggle for Success in Caesarea Maritima*. Edited by Terence L. Donaldson. SChrJud 8. Waterloo, Ont.: Wilfrid Laurier University Press, 2000.

Pummer, "Samaritans." Pummer, Reinhard. "Samaritans." *OEANE* 4:469–72.

Pummer, "Synagogue." Pummer, Reinhard. "How to Tell a Samaritan Synagogue from a Jewish Synagogue." *BAR* 24 (3, 1998): 24–35.

Pummer, "Tabernacle." Pummer, Reinhard. "The Tabernacle in the Samaritan Tradition." *Theof* 37 (1, 2006): 45–64.

Punnoose, "Filadelfia Church." Punnoose, Joy. "Filadelfia Fellowship Church of India." *C&C* 36 (1, 2005): 32–33.

Punt, "Agency." Punt, Jeremy. "Pauline Agency in Postcolonial Perspective: Subverter of or Agent for Empire?" Pages 53–61 in *The Colonized Apostle: Paul through Postcolonial Eyes*. Edited by Christopher D. Stanley. Minneapolis: Fortress, 2011.

Purcell, "Castor." Purcell, Nicholas. "Castor and Pollux." *OCD³* 301–2.

Purcell, "Concordia." Purcell, Nicholas. "Concordia." *OCD³* 375–76.

Purcell, "Consentes Di." Purcell, Nicholas. "Consentes Di." *OCD³* 377.

Purcell, "Economy." Purcell, Nicholas. "Economy, Roman." *OCD³* 504–5.

Purcell, "Fortuna/Fors." Purcell, Nicholas. "Fortuna/Fors." *OCD³* 606.

Purcell, "Geography." Purcell, Nicholas. "Geography." *OCD³* 632–33.

Purcell, "Houses, Italian." Purcell, Nicholas. "Houses, Italian." *OCD³* 731–32.

Purcell, "Itineraries." Purcell, Nicholas. "Itineraries." *OCD³* 775.

Purcell, "Lighthouses." Purcell, Nicholas. "Lighthouses." *OCD³* 861.

Purcell, "Maps." Purcell, Nicholas. "Maps." *OCD³* 920.

Purcell, "Periploi." Purcell, Nicholas. "Periploi." *OCD³* 1141–42.

Purcell, "Postal Service." Purcell, Nicholas. "Postal Service." *OCD³* 1233–34.

Purcell, "Syrtes." Purcell, Nicholas. "Syrtes." *OCD³* 1466.

Purcell, "Travel." Purcell, Nicholas. "Travel." *OCD³* 1547–48.

Purcell, "Vicus." Purcell, Nicholas. "Vicus." *OCD³* 1598.

Purcell, "Vigiles." Purcell, Nicholas. "Vigiles." *OCD³* 1598.

Purvis, "Samaritans." Purvis, James D. "The Fourth Gospel and the Samaritans." *NovT* 17 (3, 1975): 161–98.

Pusey, "Baptism." Pusey, Karen. "Jewish Proselyte Baptism." *ExpT* 95 (4, 1984): 141–45.

Puskas, "Conclusion: Investigation." Puskas, Charles B. "The Conclusion of Luke-Acts: An Investigation of the Literary Function and Theological Significance of Acts 28:16–31." PhD diss., St. Louis University, 1980.

Puskas, *Conclusion: Significance*. Puskas, Charles B. *The Conclusion of Luke-Acts: The Significance of Acts 28:16–31*. Eugene, Or.: Pickwick, 2009.

Puskas and Crump, *Introduction*. Puskas, Charles B., and David Crump. *An Introduction to the Gospels and Acts*. Grand Rapids: Eerdmans, 2008.

Pytches, "Anglican." Pytches, David. "Fully Anglican, Fully Renewed." Pages 186–97 in *Power Encounters among Christians in the Western World*. Edited by Kevin Springer. Introduction and afterword by John Wimber. San Francisco: Harper & Row, 1988.

Pytches, *Come*. Pytches, David. *Come Holy Spirit: Learning How to Minister in Power*. London: Hodder & Stoughton, 1985.

Pythian-Adams, "'Deserted' Gaza." Pythian-Adams, W. J. "The Problem of 'Deserted' Gaza." *PEFQS* 55 (1923): 30–36.

Quack, "Efficacy." Quack, Joachim Friedrich. "Postulated and Real Efficacy in Late Antique Divination Rituals." *Journal of Ritual Studies* 24 (1, 2010): 45–60.

Quack, "Mages égyptianisés?" Quack, Joachim Friedrich. "Les mages égyptianisés? Remarks on Some Surprising Points in Supposedy Magusean Texts." *JNES* 65 (4, 2006): 267–82.

Quarles, "Lord." Quarles, Charles L. "Lord or Legend: Jesus as the Messianic Son of Man." Paper presented at the 2011 Greer-Heard Point Counterpoint Forum, New Orleans, Feb. 26, 2011.

Quarles, "Perspective." Quarles, Charles L. "The New Perspective and Means of Atonement in Jewish Literature of the Second Temple Period." *CrisTR* n.s. 2 (2, 2005): 39–56.

Quarles, "Soteriology." Quarles, Charles L. "The Soteriology of R. Akiba and E. P. Sanders' *Paul and Palestinian Judaism*." *NTS* 42 (2, 1996): 185–95.

Quast, *Corinthian Correspondence*. Quast, Kevin. *Reading the Corinthian Correspondence: An Introduction*. New York: Paulist, 1994.

Quesnel, "Analyse rhétorique." Quesnel, Michel. "Analyse rhétorique des discours d'apologie de Paul: Ac 22 et 26." Pages 155–76 in *Les Actes des apôtres—Histoire, récit, théologie: XXe congrès de l'Association catholique française pour l'étude de la Bible (Angers, 2003)*. Edited by Michel Berder. LD 199. Paris: Cerf, 2005.

Quesnel, "Critère." Quesnel, Michel. "Le critère de la fidélité à l'Esprit." *Christus* 179 (1998): 293–301.

Quesnel, "Naufrage." Quesnel, Michel. "Le naufrage de saint Paul." *Transversalités* 69 (1999): 47–57.

Quesnel, "Paul prédicateur." Quesnel, Michel. "Paul prédicateur dans les Actes des apôtres." *NTS* 47 (4, 2001): 469–81.

Quinn, "Kivebulaya." Quinn, Frederick. "Apolo Kivebulaya." No pages. *DACB*. Online: http://www.dacb.org/stories/demrepcongo/kivebulaya3_apollo.html.

Quinn, "Volume." Quinn, Jerome D. "The Last Volume of Luke: The Relation of Luke-Acts to the Pastoral Epistles." Pages 62–75 in *Perspectives on Luke-Acts*. AB PRSSS 5. Edited by Charles H. Talbert. Danville, Va.: Association of Baptist Professors of Religion; Edinburgh: T&T Clark, 1978.

Quinn and Wacker, *Letters*. Quinn, Jerome D., and William C. Wacker. *The First and Second Letters to Timothy: A New Translation with Notes and Commentary*. Grand Rapids: Eerdmans, 2000.

Quirke and Spencer, *Museum Book*. Quirke, Stephen, and Jeffrey Spencer, eds. *The British Museum Book of Ancient Egypt*. London: Thames & Hudson, 1992.

Raban et al., "Harbours." Raban, A., et al. "Caesarea and Its Harbours: A Preliminary Report of the 1988 Season." *IEJ* 40 (4, 1990): 241–56 and plates 25–27.

Rabbie, "Wit and Humor." Rabbie, Edwin. "Wit and Humor in Roman Rhetoric." Pages 207–17 in *A Companion to Roman Rhetoric*. Edited by William Dominik and Jon Hall. Oxford: Blackwell, 2007.

Rabe, "Prophecy." Rabe, Virgil W. "Origins of Prophecy." *BASOR* 221 (Feb. 1976): 125–28.

Rabello, "Condition." Rabello, Alfredo Mordechai. "The Legal Condition of the Jews in the Roman Empire." *ANRW* 13:662–762. Part 2, *Principat*, 13. Edited by H. Temporini and W. Haase. Berlin: de Gruyter, 1980.

Rabey, "Prophet." Rabey, Steve. "The People's Prophet." *CHB* 79 (2003): 32–34.

Rabin, "Imperative." Rabin, Chaim. "L-with Imperative (Gen. XXIII)." *JSS* 13 (1, 1968): 113–24.

Rabin, "Jannaeus." Rabin, Chaim. "Alexander Jannaeus and the Pharisees." *JJS* 7 (1–2, 1956): 3–11.

Rabinovitch, "Parallels." Rabinovitch, Nachum L. "Damascus Document IX, 17–22 and Rabbinic Parallels." *RevQ* 9 (1, 1977): 113–16.

Rabinowitz, "Reconsideration of 'Damascus.'" Rabinowitz, Isaac. "A Reconsideration of 'Damascus' and '390 Years' in the 'Damascus' ('Zadokite') Fragments." *JBL* 73 (1954): 11–35.

Raboteau, *Slave Religion*. Raboteau, Albert J. *Slave Religion: The "Invisible Institution" in the Antebellum South*. Oxford: Oxford University Press, 1978.

Race, "Influence." Race, Marianne. "Galilee's Influence on Jesus." *BibT* 41 (2, 2003): 73–79.

Race, "Introduction." Race, William H. Introduction. Pages 1–41 in vol. 1 of Pindar, *Odes*. Translated by William H. Race. 2 vols. LCL. Cambridge, Mass.: Harvard University Press, 1997.

Race, "Journeys." Race, Marianne. "Missionary Journeys: A Hazardous Adventure." *BibT* 37 (5, 1999): 281–87.

Racine, "Review." Racine, Jean-François. Review of William Sanger Campbell, *The "We" Passages in the Acts of the Apostles: The Narrator as Narrative Character*. *RBL* (Oct. 4, 2008). http://www.bookreviews.org/pdf/6149_6569.pdf.

Rack, "Healing." Rack, Henry D. "Doctors, Demons, and Early Methodist Healing." Pages 137–52 in *The Church and Healing: Papers Read at the Twentieth Summer Meeting and the Twenty-First Winter Meeting of the Ecclesiastical History Society*. Edited by W. J. Sheils. Oxford: Blackwell, 1982.

Rackham, *Acts*. Rackham, Richard Belward. *The Acts of the Apostles*. 14th ed. London: Methuen, 1951. Repr., Grand Rapids: Baker, 1964.

Rackham, "Greece (Geography)." Rackham, Oliver. "Greece (Geography)." *OCD*³ 648.

Rad, *Theology*. Rad, Gerhard von. *The Theology of Israel's Historical Traditions*. Vol. 1 of *Old Testament Theology*. Translated by D. M. G. Stalker. New York: Harper & Row, 1962.

Rad, "Verheissung." Rad, Gerhard von. "Verheissung." *EvT* 13 (1953): 406–13.

Radcliffe-Brown, "Taboo." Radcliffe-Brown, A. R. "Taboo." Pages 72–83 in *Reader in Comparative Religion: An Anthropological Approach*. Edited by William A. Lessa and Evon Z. Vogt. 3rd ed. New York: Harper & Row, 1965.

Radcliffe-Brown and Forde, *Systems*. *African Systems of Kinship and Marriage*. Edited by A. R. Radcliffe-Brown and Daryll Forde. New York: Oxford University Press, 1950.

Radet and Paris, "Inscriptions de Pisidie." Radet, G., and P. Paris. "Inscriptions de Pisidie de Lycaonie et d'Isaurie." *BullCorr Hell* 10 (1886): 500–514.

Radice, "Introduction." Radice, Betty. Introduction. Pages 11–33 in *The Letters of the Younger Pliny*. Translated by Betty Radice. Baltimore: Penguin, 1963.

Radl, "Beziehungen." Radl, Walter. "Die Beziehungen der Vorgeschichte zur Apostelgeschichte, dargestellt an Lk 2,22–39." Pages 297–312 in *The Unity of Luke-Acts*. Edited by Joseph Verheyden. BETL 142. Leuven: Leuven University Press, 1999.

Radl, *Paulus*. Radl, Walter. *Paulus und Jesus im Lukanischen Doppelwerk: Untersuchungen zu Parallelmotiven im Lukasevangelium und in der Apostelgeschichte*. Europäische Hochschulschriften 23.49. Bern: Lang, 1975.

Raepsaet, "Donkey." Raepsaet, Georges. "Donkey." BrillPauly 4:664–70.

Raepsaet, "Land Transport." Raepsaet, Georges. "Land Transport." BrillPauly 7:200–209.

Raguraman, Vijaysagar, and Chandrasekaran, "Presentation." Raguraman, Janakiraman, K. John Vijaysagar, and R. Chandrasekaran. "An Unusual Presentation of PTSD." ANZJPsyc 38 (9, 2004): 760.

Raharimanantsoa, Mort. Raharimanantsoa, Mamy. Mort et Espérance selon la Bible Hébraïque. ConBOT 53. Stockholm: Almqvist & Wiksell, 2006.

Rahim, "Zar." Rahim, S. I. "Zar among Middle-Aged Female Psychiatric Patients in the Sudan." Pages 137–46 in Women's Medicine: The zar-bori Cult in Africa and Beyond. Edited by I. M. Lewis, Ahmed Al-Safi, and Sayyid Hurreiz. Edinburgh: International African Institute, Edinburgh University Press, 1991.

Rahmani, "Amulet." Rahmani, L. Y. "A Magic Amulet from Nahariyya." HTR 74 (1981): 387–90.

Rahmani, "Cameo." Rahmani, L. Y. "An Ancient Cast of a Cameo." IEJ 28 (1–2, 1978): 83–85 and plate 21B.

Rahmani, "Customs." Rahmani, L. Y. "Ancient Jerusalem's Funerary Customs and Tombs, Part Four." BA 45 (1982): 109–19.

Rahmani, "Glwsqmwt." Rahmani, L. Y. "Glwsqmwt wlyqwt 'snwt bslhy tqwpt byt sny." Qad 11 (1978): 102–12.

Rahmani, "Remarks." Rahmani, L. Y. "Some Remarks on R. Hachlili's and A. Killebrew's 'Jewish Funerary Customs.'" PEQ 118 (1986): 96–100.

Rahmani, "Synagogue Chairs." Rahmani, L. Y. "Stone Synagogue Chairs: Their Identification, Use, and Significance." IEJ 40 (1990): 192–214 and plates 19–21.

Rahnenführer, "Testament des Hiob." Rahnenführer, Dankwort. "Das Testament des Hiob und das Neue Testament." ZNW 62 (1–2, 1971): 68–93.

Rainbow, "Christology." Rainbow, Paul A. "Logos Christology." DNTLD 665–67.

Rainbow, "Justification." Rainbow, Paul A. "Justification according to Paul's Thessalonian Correspondence." BBR 19 (2, 2009): 249–74.

Rainbow, "Melchizedek." Rainbow, Paul A. "Melchizedek as a Messiah at Qumran." BBR 7 (1997): 179–94.

Rainer, "Church Growth and Evangelism." Rainer, Thom S. "Church Growth and Evangelism in the Book of Acts." CrisTR 5 (1, 1990): 57–68.

Rainey, "Gaza." Rainey, Anson F. "Gaza." ISBE 2:415–18.

Rainey, "Herodotus' Description." Rainey, Anson F. "Herodotus' Description of the East Mediterranean Coast." BASOR 321 (Feb. 2001): 57–63.

Rainey, "Kingdom." Rainey, Anson F. "The Kingdom of Ugarit." BA 28 (Dec. 1965): 102–25.

Räisänen, "Conversion and Development." Räisänen, Heikki. "Paul's Conversion and the Development of His View of the Law." NTS 33 (3, 1987): 404–19.

Räisänen, "Marcion." Räisänen, Heikki. "Marcion." Pages 301–15 in The Blackwell Companion to Paul. Edited by Stephen Westerholm. BCompRel. Oxford: Blackwell, 2011.

Räisänen, Mutter. Räisänen, Heikki. Die Mutter Jesu im Neuen Testament. 2nd ed. AASF B 247. Helsinki: Suomalainen Tiedeakatemia, 1989.

Räisänen, Paul and Law. Räisänen, Heikki. Paul and the Law. WUNT 29. Tübingen: Mohr (Siebeck), 1983.

Räisänen, "Redemption." Räisänen, Heikki. "The Redemption of Israel: A Salvation-Historical Problem in Luke-Acts." Pages 94–114 in Luke-Acts: Scandinavian Perspectives. Edited by Petri Luomanen. PFES 54. Helsinki: Finnish Exegetical Society; Göttingen: Vandenhoeck & Ruprecht, 1991.

Rajak, "Charter." Rajak, Tessa. "Was There a Roman Charter for the Jews?" JRS 74 (1984): 107–23.

Rajak, "Community and Boundaries." Rajak, Tessa. "The Jewish Community and Its Boundaries." Pages 9–28 in The Jews among Pagans and Christians in the Roman Empire. Edited by Judith Lieu, John North, and Tessa Rajak. London: Routledge, 1992.

Rajak, "Gaius." Rajak, Tessa. "Gaius (1)." OCD³ 619–20.

Rajak, "Jewish-Greek Literature." Rajak, Tessa. "Jewish-Greek Literature." OCD³ 795–96.

Rajak, "Jews." Rajak, Tessa. "Jews." OCD³ 796–98.

Rajak, Josephus. Rajak, Tessa. Josephus: The Historian and His Society. Philadelphia: Fortress, 1984; London: Gerald Duckworth, 1983.

Rajak, "Justus of Tiberias." Rajak, Tessa. "Josephus and Justus of Tiberias." Pages 81–94 in Josephus, Judaism, and Christianity. Edited by Louis H. Feldman and Gohei Hata. Detroit: Wayne State University Press, 1987.

Rajak, "Location." Rajak, Tessa. "The Location of Cultures in Second Temple Palestine: The Evidence of Josephus." Pages 1–14 in The Book of Acts in Its Palestinian Setting. Edited by Richard Bauckham.

Vol. 4 of The Book of Acts in Its First Century Setting. Edited by Bruce W. Winter. Grand Rapids: Eerdmans; Carlisle, U.K.: Paternoster, 1995.

Rajak, "Moses in Ethiopia." Rajak, Tessa. "Moses in Ethiopia: Legend and Literature." JJS 29 (2, 1978): 111–22.

Rajak, "Ptolemais." Rajak, Tessa. "Ptolemais." OCD³ 1271.

Rajak, "Synagogue within City." Rajak, Tessa. "The Synagogue within the Greco-Roman City." Pages 161–73 in Jews, Christians, and Polytheists in the Ancient Synagogue: Cultural Interaction in the Greco-Roman Period. Edited by Steven Fine. London: Routledge, 1999.

Rajak and Noy, "Office and Status." Rajak, Tessa, and David Noy. "Archisynagogos: Office and Social Status in the Graeco-Roman World." JRS 83 (1993): 75–93.

Rakocy, "Akwila." Rakocy, Waldemar. "Akwila i Pryscylla: wspólpracownicy apostola Pawla i wczesnochrzescijanscy misjonarze." RocT 55 (1, 2008): 125–41.

Rakocy, "Problem datacji." Rakocy, W. "Problem datacji i kolokacji w misji Pawła tzw. Soboru Jerosolimskiego." ColT 72 (2, 2002): 31–44.

Rakocy, "Struktura Ap 12, 1–19." Rakocy, W. "Struktura literacka Dz Ap 12, 1–19 (La struttura letteraria di Atti 12, 1–19)." ColT 64 (4, 1994): 39–45.

Rakocy, "Tradycja." Rakocy, W. "Tradycja i redakcja przekazu o pośpiechu Pawla na święta Pięćdziesiątnicy (Dz 20, 16) (Tradition and Redaction of the Record about Paul's Hurry for the Day of Pentecost [Acts 20,16])." RocT 46 (1, 1999): 149–69.

Rakotojoelinandrasana, "Gospel in Adversity." Rakotojoelinandrasana, Daniel. "The Gospel in Adversity: Reading Acts 16:16–34 in African Context." WW 21 (2, 2001): 191–97.

Ramaroson, "Études." Ramaroson, Leonard. "Trois études récentes sur 'la foi de Jésus' dans saint Paul." ScEs 40 (3, 1988): 365–77.

Ramelli, "Discours." Ramelli, Ilaria L. E. "Dieu et la philosophie: Le discours de Paul à Athènes dans trois 'actes apocryphes' et dans la philosophie patristique." Greg 93 (1, 2012): 75–90.

Ramelli, Hierocles. Ramelli, Ilaria. Introduction and Commentary. Hierocles the Stoic: Elements of Ethics, Fragments, and Excerpts. Translated (from Ramelli's work) by David Konstan. SBLWGRW 28. Atlanta: SBL, 2009.

Ramirez, "Faiths." Ramirez, Daniel. "Migrating Faiths: A Social and Cultural History of Pentecostalism in the U.S.-Mexico Borderlands." PhD diss., Duke University, 2005.

Ramsaran, "Paul and Maxims." Ramsaran, Rollin A. "Paul and Maxims." Pages 429–56 in *Paul in the Greco-Roman World: A Handbook*. Edited by J. Paul Sampley. Harrisburg, Pa.: Trinity Press International, 2003.

Ramsay, *Bethlehem*. Ramsay, William M. *Was Christ Born at Bethlehem? A Study in the Credibility of St. Luke*. London: Hodder & Stoughton, 1898. Repr., Grand Rapids: Baker, 1979.

Ramsay, *Church in Empire*. Ramsay, William M. *The Church in the Roman Empire*. 5th ed. London: Hodder & Stoughton, 1897. Repr., Grand Rapids: Baker, 1979.

Ramsay, *Cities of Paul*. Ramsay, William M. *The Cities of St. Paul: Their Influence on His Life and Thought*. London: Hodder & Stoughton, 1907. Repr., Grand Rapids: Baker, 1979.

Ramsay, "Derbe." Ramsay, William M. "Derbe." *Exp*, 7th ser., 1 (1906): 544–60.

Ramsay, *Discovery*. Ramsay, William M. *The Bearing of Recent Discovery on the Trustworthiness of the New Testament*. London: Hodder & Stoughton, 1915. Repr., Grand Rapids: Baker, 1979.

Ramsay, *Galatia*. Ramsay, William M. "The Galatia of Saint Paul and the Galatic Territory of the Book of Acts." Pages 15–58 in vol. 4 of *Studia biblica et ecclesiastica: Essays Chiefly in Biblical and Patristic Criticism*. Oxford: Clarendon; New York: Macmillan, 1896. Reprinted as *The Galatia of Saint Paul and the Galatic Territory of the Book of Acts*. Analecta Gorgiana 10. Piscataway, N.J.: Gorgias, 2006.

Ramsay, *Galatians*. Ramsay, William M. *A Historical Commentary on St. Paul's Epistle to the Galatians*. New York: G. P. Putnam's Sons, 1900. Repr., Grand Rapids: Baker, 1979.

Ramsay, *Letters*. Ramsay, William M. *The Letters to the Seven Churches of Asia*. London: Hodder & Stoughton, 1904. Repr., Grand Rapids: Baker, 1979.

Ramsay, *Luke the Physician*. Ramsay, William M. *Luke the Physician and Other Studies in the History of Religion*. London: Hodder & Stoughton, 1908. Repr., Grand Rapids: Baker, 1979.

Ramsay, *Other Studies*. Ramsay, William M. *Pauline and Other Studies in Early Church History*. New York: A. C. Armstrong and Son, 1906. Repr., Grand Rapids: Baker, 1979.

Ramsay, "Paul at Ephesus." Ramsay, William M. "Saint Paul at Ephesus." *Exp*, 4th ser., 2 (1890): 1–22.

Ramsay, *Pictures*. Ramsay, William M. *Pictures of the Apostolic Church: Studies in the Book of Acts*. London: Hodder & Stoughton, 1910. Repr., Grand Rapids: Baker, 1959.

Ramsay, "Pisidian Antioch." Ramsay, William M. "Pisidian Antioch." *Exp*, 7th ser., 3 (1907): 72–87, 271–88, 338–59.

Ramsay, "Roads and Travel." Ramsay, William M. "Roads and Travel (in NT)." Pages 375–402 in vol. 5 of *Dictionary of the Bible*. Edited by James Hastings. 5 vols. Edinburgh: T&T Clark; New York: Scribner's, 1898–1923.

Ramsay, "Sketches." Ramsay, William M. "Sketches in the Religious Antiquities of Asia Minor." *Annual of the British School at Athens* 18 (1911–12): 37–79 and plates.

Ramsay, "Tarsian Citizenship." Ramsay, William M. "The Tarsian Citizenship of St. Paul." *ExpT* 16 (1, 1904): 18–21.

Ramsay, *Teaching*. Ramsay, William M. *The Teaching of St. Paul in Terms of the Present Day*. 2nd ed. London: Hodder & Stoughton, 1913. Repr., Grand Rapids: Baker, 1979.

Ramsay, *Traveler*. Ramsay, William M. *St. Paul the Traveler and Roman Citizen*. Revised by Mark Wilson. Rev. and updated ed. London: Angus Hudson; Grand Rapids: Kregel, 2001.

Ramsay, *Traveller and Citizen*. Ramsay, William M. *St. Paul the Traveller and the Roman Citizen*. 3rd ed. London: Hodder & Stoughton, 1897.

Ramsby and Severy-Hoven, "Gender." Ramsby, Teresa R., and Beth Severy-Hoven. "Gender, Sex, and the Domestication of the Augustan Age." *Arethusa* 40 (1, 2007): 43–71.

Ramsey, "Amos 4 12." Ramsey, George W. "Amos 4 12—A New Perspective." *JBL* 89 (2, 1970): 187–91.

Ramsey, "Speech-Forms." Ramsey, George W. "Speech-Forms in Hebrew Law and Prophetic Oracles." *JBL* 96 (1, 1977): 45–58.

Rance, "*Simulacra pugnae*." Rance, Philip. "*Simulacra pugnae*: The Literary and Historical Tradition of Mock Battles in the Roman and Early Byzantine Army." *GRBS* 41 (3, 2000): 223–75.

Ranger, "Dilemma." Ranger, Terence. "Medical Science and Pentecost: The Dilemma of Anglicanism in Africa." Pages 333–65 in *The Church and Healing: Papers Read at the Twentieth Summer Meeting and the Twenty-First Winter Meeting of the Ecclesiastical History Society*. Edited by W. J. Sheils. Oxford: Blackwell, 1982.

Ranger, "Religion." Ranger, Terence. "African Religion, Witchcraft, and the Liberation War in Zimbabwe." Pages 351–78 in *Studies in Witchcraft, Magic, War, and Peace in Africa*. Edited by Beatrice Nicolini. Lewiston, N.Y.: Edwin Mellen, 2006.

Rapa, "Galatians." Rapa, Robert K. "Galatians." Pages 549–640 in vol. 11 (*Romans–Galatians*) of *The Expositor's Bible Commentary*. Rev. ed. Edited by Tremper Longman III and David E. Garland. Grand Rapids: Zondervan, 2008.

Rapallo, "Umorismo." Rapallo, Umberto. "L'umorismo fra antichità e tardo-antico: Una prospettiva interdisciplinare." *Orpheus* 25 (1–2, 2004): 22–63.

Raphael, "Travail." Raphael, Freddy. "Le travail de la memoire et les limites de l'histoire orale." *Annales* 35 (1, 1980): 127–45.

Rappaport, "Yhsy." Rappaport, Uriel. "Yhsy yhwdym wl'-yhwdym b'rs-'sr'l whmrd hgdwl brwmy" [The Relations between Jews and Non-Jews and the Great War against Rome]. *Tarbiz* 47 (1–2, 1978): 1–14.

Rapske, "Citizenship." Rapske, Brian. "Citizenship, Roman." *DNTB* 215–18.

Rapske, *Custody*. Rapske, Brian M. *The Book of Acts and Paul in Roman Custody*. Vol. 3 of *The Book of Acts in Its First Century Setting*. Edited by Bruce W. Winter. Grand Rapids: Eerdmans; Carlisle, U.K.: Paternoster, 1994.

Rapske, "Defense of Prisoner." Rapske, Brian M. "The Lukan Defense of the Missionary Prisoner Paul." *TynBul* 44 (1993): 193–96.

Rapske, "Exiles." Rapske, Brian Mark. "Exiles, Islands, and the Identity and Perspective of John in Revelation." Pages 311–46 in *Christian Origins and Greco-Roman Culture: Social and Literary Contexts for the New Testament*. Edited by Stanley Porter and Andrew W. Pitts. Vol. 1 of Early Christianity in Its Hellenistic Context. Vol. 9 in Texts and Editions for New Testament Study. Leiden: Brill, 2013.

Rapske, "Opposition." Rapske, Brian M. "Opposition to the Plan and Persecution." Pages 235–56 in *Witness to the Gospel: The Theology of Acts*. Edited by I. Howard Marshall and David Peterson. Grand Rapids: Eerdmans, 1998.

Rapske, "Pauline Imprisonment." Rapske, Brian M. "Pauline Imprisonment and the Lukan Defense of the Missionary Prisoner Paul in the Light of Greco-Roman Sources." PhD diss., University of Aberdeen, 1992.

Rapske, personal correspondence. Rapske, Brian. Personal correspondence, Oct. 13, 2014.

Raspke, "Prison." Rapske, Brian M. "Prison, Prisoner." *DNTB* 827–30.

Rapske, "Travel and Shipwreck." Rapske, Brian M. "Acts, Travel, and Shipwreck." Pages 1–47 in *The Book of Acts in Its Graeco-Roman Setting*. Edited by David W. J. Gill and Conrad Gempf. Vol. 2 of *The Book of Acts in Its First Century Setting*. Edited by Bruce W. Winter. Grand

Rapids: Eerdmans; Carlisle, U.K.: Paternoster, 1994.

Rapske, "Travel and Trade." Rapske, Brian M. "Travel and Trade." *DNTB* 1245–50.

Rapuano, "Ein Yael?" Rapuano, Yehudah. "Did Philip Baptize the Eunuch at Ein Yael?" *BAR* 16 (6, 1990): 44–49.

Rashidi, "Africans in Civilizations." Rashidi, Runoko. "Africans in Early Asian Civilizations: A Historical Overview." Pages 15–52 in *African Presence in Early Asia*. Edited by Ivan Van Sertima and Runoko Rashidi. New Brunswick, N.J.: Transactions Books (Rutgers)/Journal of African Civilizations, 1988.

Rasmussen, "Shaman's Journey." Rasmussen, Knud. "A Shaman's Journey to the Sea Spirit." Pages 123–29 in *Intellectual Culture of the Hudson Bay Eskimos*. 3 vols. in 1. Report of the Fifth Thule Expedition, 1921–24, 7.1. Copenhagen: Gyldendal, 1930. Reprinted in abridged form, pages 308–11 in *Reader in Comparative Religion: An Anthropological Approach*. Edited by William A. Lessa and Evon Z. Vogt. 4th ed. New York: Harper & Row, 1979.

Raspe, "Manetho on Exodus." Raspe, Lucia. "Manetho on the Exodus." *JSQ* 5 (2, 1998): 124–54.

Rathbone, "Alexandria." Rathbone, Dominic W. "Alexandria." *OCD*³ 61–62.

Rathbone, "Egypt." Rathbone, Dominic W. "Egypt." *OCD*³ 511–12.

Rathbone, "Famine." Rathbone, Dominic W. "Famine." *OCD*³ 586.

Rathbone, "Farmers." Rathbone, Dominic W. "Farmers: Rome." *BrillPauly* 5:356–58.

Rathbone, "Food Supply." Rathbone, Dominic W. "Food Supply: Roman." *OCD*³ 604.

Rathbone, "Latifundia." Rathbone, Dominic W. "Latifundia/Large Estates." *BrillPauly* 7:270–75.

Rathbone, "*Navicularii*." Rathbone, Dominic W. "*Navicularii*." *OCD*³ 1030.

Rathmann, "Roads." Rathmann, Michael. "Roads. V. Roman Empire." *BrillPauly* 12:622–47.

Rathmann, "Via Appia." Rathmann, Michael. "Via Appia." *BrillPauly* 15:368–69.

Rathmann, "Via Egnatia." Rathmann, Michael. "Via Egnatia." *BrillPauly* 15:370.

Rauh, *Merchants*. Rauh, Nicholas K. *Merchants, Sailors, and Pirates in the Roman World*. Stroud: Tempus, 2003.

Raurell, "Gift." Raurell, F. "Righteousness' Gift of Immortality (Wis 1,1–15)." *Laur* 40 (3, 1999): 417–36.

Rausch, *Messianic Judaism*. Rausch, David A. *Messianic Judaism: Its History, Theology and Polity*. Texts and Studies in Religion 14. New York: Mellen, 1982.

Raveh and Kingsley, "Status of Dor." Raveh, Kurt, and Sean A. Kingsley. "The Status of Dor in Late Antiquity: A Maritime Perspective." *BA* 54 (4, 1991): 198–207.

Ravens, *Restoration*. Ravens, David. *Luke and the Restoration of Israel*. JSNTSup 119. Sheffield, U.K.: Sheffield Academic, 1995.

Rawson, "Children." Rawson, Beryl. "Children in the Roman *familia*." Pages 170–200 in *The Family in Ancient Rome: New Perspectives*. Edited by Beryl Rawson. Ithaca, N.Y.: Cornell University Press, 1986.

Rawson, "Death." Rawson, Beryl. "Death, Burial, and Commemoration of Children in Roman Italy." Pages 277–97 in *Early Christian Families in Context: An Interdisciplinary Dialogue*. Edited by David L. Balch and Carolyn Osiek. Grand Rapids and Cambridge: Eerdmans, 2003.

Rawson, "Family." Rawson, Beryl. "The Roman Family." Pages 1–57 in *The Family in Ancient Rome: New Perspectives*. Edited by Beryl Rawson. Ithaca, N.Y.: Cornell University Press, 1986.

Ray, *Irony*. Ray, Jerry Lynn. *Narrative Irony in Luke-Acts: The Paradoxical Interaction of Prophetic Fulfillment and Jewish Rejection*. MBPS 28. Lewiston, N.Y.: Mellen Biblical Press, 1996.

Raynor, "Moeragenes and Philostratus." Raynor, D. H. "Moeragenes and Philostratus: Two Views of Apollonius of Tyana." *CQ* 34 (1, 1984): 222–26.

Read, "Spirit." Read, James. "More than the Spirit of Mission? Revisiting the Work of the Spirit in the Book of Acts." *SBET* 27 (1, 2009): 24–49.

Read, Monterroso, and Johnson, *Growth*. Read, William R., Victor M. Monterroso, and Harmon A. Johnson. *Latin American Church Growth*. Grand Rapids: Eerdmans, 1969.

Read-Heimerdinger, *Bezan Text*. Read-Heimerdinger, Jenny. *The Bezan Text of Acts. A Contribution of Discourse Analysis to Textual Criticism*. JSNTSup 236. London: Sheffield Academic, 2002.

Read-Heimerdinger, "Simeon." Read-Heimerdinger, Jenny. "Who Is 'Simeon' in James' Speech to the Jerusalem Meeting (Acts 15.14)?" *EstBib* 64 (3–4, 2006): 631–45.

Reardon, "Homing to Rome." Reardon, Patrick Henry. "Homing to Rome: The *Aeneid* and the Acts of the Apostles." *OiC* 38 (1, 2003): 45–55.

Reasoner, *Full Circle*. Reasoner, Mark. *Romans in Full Circle: A History of Interpretation*. Louisville: Westminster John Knox, 2005.

Reasoner, "Theme." Reasoner, Mark. "The Theme of Acts: Institutional History or Divine Necessity in History?" *JBL* 118 (4, 1999): 635–59.

Rebenich, "Historical Prose." Rebenich, Stefan. "Historical Prose." Pages 265–337 in *Handbook of Classical Rhetoric in the Hellenistic Period, 330 B.C.–A.D. 400*. Edited by Stanley E. Porter. Leiden: Brill, 1997.

"Records 2002." "Voting Records: Fall 2002." *Forum* 5 (1, 2002): 117–20.

Reddish, *Revelation*. Reddish, Mitchell G. *Revelation*. SHBC. Macon, Ga.: Smyth & Helwys, 2001.

Redditt, "*Nomos*." Redditt, Paul L. "The Concept of *nomos* in Fourth Maccabees." *CBQ* 45 (2, 1983): 249–70.

Reden, "Market." Reden, Sitta von. "Market: Classical Antiquity." *BrillPauly* 8:374–77.

Reden, "Money." Reden, Sitta von. "Money, Money Economy: Greece." *BrillPauly* 9:147–50.

Reden, "Unemployment." Reden, Sitta von. "Unemployment." *BrillPauly* 15:111–12.

Reden, "Work." Reden, Sitta von. "Work: Greece and Rome." *BrillPauly* 15:739–44.

Reden, "Working Hours." Reden, Sitta von. "Working Hours." *BrillPauly* 15:746–47.

Redford, "Contextualization." Redford, Shawn B. "The Contextualization and Translation of Christianity, Acts 9:1–9; 22:3–33; 26:2–23." Pages 283–96 in *Mission in Acts: Ancient Narratives in Contemporary Context*. Edited by Robert L. Gallagher and Paul Hertig. AmSocMissS 34. Maryknoll, N.Y.: Orbis, 2004.

Redman, "Eyewitnesses." Redman, Judith C. S. "How Accurate Are Eyewitnesses? Bauckham and the Eyewitnesses in the Light of Psychological Research." *JBL* 129 (1, 2010): 177–97.

Reed, "Acts 17:16–34." Reed, David. "Acts 17:16–34 in an African Context (An Assessment from a N. Atlantic/Western Perspective)." *AfET* 22 (1, 2003): 87–101.

Reed, *Archaeology*. Reed, Jonathan L. *Archaeology and the Galilean Jesus: A Reexamination of the Evidence*. Harrisburg, Pa.: Trinity Press International, 2000.

Reed, "Case History." Reed, William Standish. "Case History and Opinion or Four Steps to Wholeness." Pages 38–43 in *Faith Healing: Finger of God? Or, Scientific Curiosity?* Compiled by Claude A. Frazier. New York: Thomas Nelson, 1973.

Reed, "Construction." Reed, Annette Yoshiko. "The Construction and Subversion of Patriarchal Perfection: Abraham and Exemplarity in Philo, Josephus, and the *Testament of Abraham*." *JSJ* 40 (2, 2009): 185–212.

Reed, "Contributions." Reed, Jonathan L. "Archaeological Contributions to the Study of Jesus and the Gospels." Pages 40–54 in *The Historical Jesus in Context*.

Edited by Amy-Jill Levine, Dale C. Allison Jr., and John Dominic Crossan. PrRR. Princeton: Princeton University Press, 2006.

Reed, "Epistle." Reed, Jeffrey T. "The Epistle." Pages 171–93 in *Handbook of Classical Rhetoric in the Hellenistic Period, 330 B.C.–A.D. 400*. Edited by Stanley E. Porter. Leiden: Brill, 1997.

Reeder, "Mother of Gods." Reeder, Ellen D. "The Mother of the Gods and the Hellenistic Bronze Matrix." *AJA* 91 (3, 1987): 423–40.

Reekmans, "Views." Reekmans, Tony. "Juvenal's Views on Social Change." *AncSoc* 2 (1971): 117–61.

Rees, "Panegyric." Rees, Roger. "Panegyric." Pages 136–48 in *A Companion to Roman Rhetoric*. Edited by William Dominik and Jon Hall. Oxford: Blackwell, 2007.

Reeves, "Chaplain." Reeves, Robert B., Jr. "The Hospital Chaplain Looks at Grief." Pages 362–72 in *Loss and Grief: Psychological Management in Medical Practice*. Edited by Bernard Schoenberg et al. New York: Columbia University Press, 1970.

Reeves, "Eunuch." Reeves, Keith H. "The Ethiopian Eunuch: A Key Transition from Hellenist to Gentile Mission, Acts 8:26–40." Pages 114–22 in *Mission in Acts: Ancient Narratives in Contemporary Context*. Edited by Robert L. Gallagher and Paul Hertig. AmSocMissS 34. Maryknoll, N.Y.: Orbis, 2004.

Refoulé, "Discours de Pierre." Refoulé, F. "Le discours de Pierre à l'assemblée de Jérusalem." *RB* 100 (2, 1993): 239–51.

Regev, "Abominated Temple." Regev, Eyal. "Abominated Temple and a Holy Community: The Formation of the Notions of Purity and Impurity in Qumran." *DSD* 10 (2, 2003): 243–78.

Regev, "Baths." Regev, Eyal. "The Ritual Baths near the Temple Mount and Extrapurification before Entering the Temple Courts." *IEJ* 55 (2, 2005): 194–204.

Regev, "Cherchez." Regev, Eyal. "Cherchez les femmes: Were the *yahad* Celibates?" *DSD* 15 (2, 2008): 253–84.

Regev, "Concerns." Regev, Eyal. "Temple Concerns and High-Priestly Prosecutions from Peter to James: Between Narrative and History." *NTS* 56 (1, 2010): 64–89.

Regev, "Family Burial." Regev, Eyal. "Family Burial, Family Structure, and the Urbanization of Herodian Jerusalem." *PEQ* 136 (2, 2004): 109–31.

Reggy-Mamo, "Widows." Reggy-Mamo, Mae Alice. "Widows and Orphans." Page 817 in *Africa Bible Commentary*. Edited by Tokunboh Adeyemo. Grand Rapids: Zondervan; Nairobi: WordAlive, 2006.

Reibnitz, "Friendship." Reibnitz, Barbara von. "Friendship: Philosophy." *BrillPauly* 5:555–57.

Reich, "Baths." Reich, Ronny. "They Are Ritual Baths." *BAR* 28 (2, 2002): 50–55.

Reich, "Inscriptions." Reich, Ronny. "Ossuary Inscriptions from the Caiaphas Tomb." *JerPersp* 4 (4–5, 1991): 13–22.

Reich, "'Isawiya." Reich, R. "A *miqweh* at 'Isawiya near Jerusalem." *IEJ* 34 (4, 1984): 220–23.

Reich, "Jars." Reich, Ronny. "6 Stone Water Jars." *JerPersp* 48 (1995): 30–33.

Reich, "Miqweh." Reich, Ronny. "A Miqweh at 'Isawiya near Jerusalem." *IEJ* 34 (4, 1984): 220–23.

Reich, "Mqww'wt." Reich, Ronny. "Mqww'wt-thrh yhwdyym btl gzr." *Qad* 15 (2–3, 1982): 74–76.

Reich, "Name." Reich, Ronny. "Caiaphas Name Inscribed on Bone Boxes." *BAR* 18 (5, 1992): 38–44.

Reich, "Possible *miqwa'ot*." Reich, Ronny. "Two Possible *miqwa'ot* on the Temple Mount." *IEJ* 39 (1–2, 1989): 63–65.

Reich and Billig, "Theatre Seats." Reich, Ronny, and Ya'akov Billig, "A Group of Theatre Seats Discovered near the South-Western Corner of the Temple Mount." *IEJ* 50 (3–4, 2000): 175–84.

Reich and Shukron, "Brykt hsylwh." Reich, Ronny, and E. Shukron. "Brykt hsylwh mymy hbyt hsny byrwslym." *Qad* 38 (130, 2005): 91–96.

Reicke, "Caesarea." Reicke, Bo. "Caesarea, Rome, and the Captivity Epistles." Pages 277–86 in *Apostolic History and the Gospel: Biblical and Historical Essays Presented to F. F. Bruce on His 60th Birthday*. Edited by W. Ward Gasque and Ralph P. Martin. Exeter, U.K.: Paternoster; Grand Rapids: Eerdmans, 1970.

Reicke, *Epistles*. Reicke, Bo. *The Epistles of James, Peter, and Jude*. AB 37. Garden City, N.Y.: Doubleday, 1964.

Reicke, *Era*. Reicke, Bo. *The New Testament Era: The World of the Bible from 500 B.C. to A.D. 100*. Translated by David E. Green. Philadelphia: Fortress, 1974.

Reicke, "God of Abraham." Reicke, Bo. "The God of Abraham, Isaac, and Jacob in New Testament Theology." Pages 186–94 in *Unity and Diversity in New Testament Theology: Essays in Honor of George E. Ladd*. Edited by Robert A. Guelich. Grand Rapids: Eerdmans, 1978.

Reicke, "Lord and Church." Reicke, Bo. "The Risen Lord and His Church: The Theology of Acts." *Interpretation* 13 (2, 1959): 156–69.

Reicke, "Theologie." Reicke, Bo. "Natürliche Theologie nach Paulus." *SEÅ* 22–23 (1957–58): 154–67.

Reid, *Choosing*. Reid, Barbara E. *Choosing the Better Part? Women in the Gospel of Luke*. Collegeville, Minn.: Liturgical Press, 1996.

Reid, "Model." Reid, Patrick V. "Paul as a Model for Evangelization." *List* 30 (2, 1995): 83–93.

Reid, "Power." Reid, Barbara E. "The Power of the Widows and How to Suppress It (Acts 6.1–7)." Pages 71–88 in *The Feminist Companion to the Acts of the Apostles*. Edited by Amy-Jill Levine with Marianne Blickenstaff. Cleveland: Pilgrim; Edinburgh: T&T Clark, 2004.

Reid, "Purple." Reid, Barbara E. "What's Biblical about . . . the Color Purple?" *BibT* 44 (5, 2006): 313–14.

Reid, "Resistance Discourse." Reid, Robert G. "Spirit-Empowerment as Resistance Discourse: An Imperial-Critical Reading of Acts 2." Pages 21–45 in *Trajectories in the Book of Acts: Essays in Honor of John Wesley Wyckoff*. Edited by Paul Alexander, Jordan Daniel May, and Robert G. Reid. Eugene, Ore.: Wipf & Stock, 2010.

Reid, "Sacrifice." Reid, Daniel G. "Sacrifice and Temple Service." *DNTB* 1036–50.

Reid, "Strategies." Reid, Robert Stephen. "Ad Herennium Argument Strategies in 1 Corinthians." *JGRCJ* 3 (2006): 192–22.

Reider, "MSHTY." Reider, Joseph. "On MSHTY in the Qumran Scrolls." *BASOR* 134 (Apr. 1954): 27.

Reif, "Review." Reif, S. C. Review of P. Schäfer, *Die Vorstellung vom heiligen Geist*. *JSS* 18 (1, 1973): 156–62.

Reifenberg, "Beziehungen." Reifenberg, A. "Das antike zyprische Judentum und seine Beziehungen zu Palästina." *JPOS* 12 (1932): 209–13.

Reiling, *Hermas*. Reiling, J. *Hermas and Christian Prophecy: A Study of the Eleventh Mandate*. NovTSup 37. Leiden: Brill, 1973.

Reilly, *Slaves*. Reilly, Linda Collins. *Slaves in Ancient Greece—Slaves from Greek Manumission Inscriptions*. Chicago: Ares, 1978.

Reim, "Joh. 8.44." Reim, Günter. "Joh. 8.44—Gotteskinder/Teufelskinder: Wie antijudaistisch ist 'Die wohl antijudaistischste Äusserung des NT'?" *NTS* 30 (4, 1984): 619–24.

Reimer, "Biography." Reimer, Andy M. "A Biography of a Motif: The Empty Tomb in the Gospels, the Greek Novels, and Shakespeare's *Romeo and Juliet*." Pages 297–316 in *Ancient Fiction: The Matrix of Early Christian and Jewish Narrative*. Edited by Jo-Ann A. Brant, Charles W. Hedrick, and Chris Shea. SBLSymS 32. Atlanta: SBL, 2005.

Reimer, *Miracle*. Reimer, Andy M. *Miracle and Magic: A Study in the Acts of the*

Apostles and the "Life of Apollonius of Tyana." JSNTSup 235. London: Sheffield Academic, 2002.

Reimer, *Women*. Reimer, Ivoni Richter. *Women in the Acts of the Apostles: A Feminist Liberation Perspective*. Translated by Linda M. Maloney. Minneapolis: Fortress, 1995.

Reinbold, "Hellenisten." Reinbold, Wolfgang. "Die 'Hellenisten': Kritische Anmerkungen zu einem Fachbegriff der neutestamentlichen Wissenschaft." *BZ* 42 (1, 1998): 96–102.

Reiner, "Fortune-Telling." Reiner, Erica. "Fortune-Telling in Mesopotamia." *JNES* 19 (1, 1960): 23–85.

Reines, "Laughter." Reines, Chaim W. "Laughter in Biblical and Rabbinic Literature." *Judaism* 21 (2, 1972): 176–83.

Reinhardt, "Population Size." Reinhardt, Wolfgang. "The Population Size of Jerusalem and the Numerical Growth of the Jerusalem Church." Pages 237–65 in *The Book of Acts in Its Palestinian Setting*. Edited by Richard Bauckham. Vol. 4 of *The Book of Acts in Its First Century Setting*. Edited by Bruce W. Winter. Grand Rapids: Eerdmans; Carlisle, U.K.: Paternoster, 1995.

Reinhold, *Diaspora*. Reinhold, Meyer. *Diaspora: The Jews among the Greeks and Romans*. Sarasota, Fla., and Toronto: Samuel Stevens, 1983.

Reinhold, *History of Purple*. Reinhold, Meyer. *The History of Purple as a Status Symbol in Antiquity*. CollLat 116. Brussels: Revue d'Études Latines, 1970.

Reinmuth, "Beobachtungen." Reinmuth, Eckart. "Beobachtungen zur Rezeption der Genesis bei Pseudo-Philo (LAB 1–8) und Lukas (Apg 7.2–17)." *NTS* 43 (4, 1997): 552–69.

Reinmuth, "Perspektive." Reinmuth, Eckart. "Paulus in jüdischer Perspektive—aktuelle Stimmen aus Exegese und Philosophie." *BTZ* 25 (1, 2008): 117–42.

Reinmuth, "Zwischen Investitur und Testament." Reinmuth, Eckart. "Zwischen Investitur und Testament: Beobachtungen zur Rezeption des Josuabuches im Liber antiquitatum biblicarum." *JSP* 16 (1, 2002): 24–43.

Reis, "Areopagus." Reis, David M. "The Areopagus as Echo Chamber: *Mimesis* and Intertextuality in Acts 17." *JHC* 9 (2, 2002): 259–77.

Reiser, "Charakter." Reiser, Marius. "Von Caesarea nach Malta: Literarischer Charakter und historische Glaubwürdigkeit von Act 27." Pages 49–74 in *Das Ende des Paulus: Historische, theologische und literaturgeschichtliche Aspekte*. Edited by F. W. Horn. BZNW 106. Berlin: de Gruyter, 2001.

Reiser, "Erkenne." Reiser, Marius. "Erkenne dich selbst! Selbsterkenntnis in Antike und Christentum." *TTZ* 101 (2, 1992): 81–100.

Reiser, "Heiden." Reiser, Marius. "Hat Paulus Heiden bekehrt?" *BZ* 39 (1, 1995): 76–91.

Reiter et al., "Diabetes and Fasting." Reiter, J., et al. "Type 1 Diabetes and Prolonged Fasting." *DiabMed* 24 (4, 2007): 436–39.

Reitz, "Catalogue." Reitz, Christiane. "Catalogue." *BrillPauly* 3:6–8.

Reitz, "Ekphrasis." Reitz, Christiane. "Ekphrasis: Latin." *BrillPauly* 4:875–77.

Reitzel, "Luke's Temple Image." Reitzel, Frank X. "St. Luke's Use of the Temple Image." *RB* 38 (4, 1979): 520–39.

Reitzenstein, *Mystery-Religions*. Reitzenstein, Richard. *Hellenistic Mystery-Religions: Their Basic Ideas and Significance*. Translated by John E. Steeley. PTMS 15. Pittsburgh: Pickwick, 1978.

Remijsen, "Introduction." Remijsen, Sofie. "The Introduction of the Antiochene Olympics: A Proposal for a New Date." *GRBS* 50 (3, 2010): 411–36.

Remijsen, "Postal Service." Remijsen, Sofie. "The Postal Service and the Hour as a Unit of Time in Antiquity." *Historia* 56 (2, 2007): 127–40.

Remijsen and Clarysse, "Incest." Remijsen, Sofie, and Willy Clarysse. "Incest or Adoption? Brother-Sister Marriage in Roman Egypt Revisited." *JRS* 98 (2008): 53–61.

Remus, "Authority." Remus, Harold. "Authority, Consent, Law: *Nomos, physis*, and the Striving for a 'Given.'" *SR/SR* 13 (1, 1984): 5–18.

Remus, *Conflict*. Remus, Harold. *Pagan-Christian Conflict over Miracle in the Second Century*. Cambridge, Mass.: Philadelphia Patristic Foundation, 1983.

Remus, *Healer*. Remus, Harold. *Jesus as Healer*. UJT. Cambridge: Cambridge University Press, 1997.

Remus, "'Magic or Miracle?'" Remus, Harold. "'Magic or Miracle'? Some Second-Century Instances." *SecCent* 2 (3, 1982): 127–56.

Remus, "Moses." Remus, Harold. "Moses and the Thaumaturges: Philo's *De vita Mosis* as a Rescue Operation." *LTP* 52 (3, 1996): 665–80.

Remus, "Paganism." Remus, Harold. "The End of 'Paganism'?" *SR/SR* 33 (2, 2004): 191–208.

Remus, "Terminology." Remus, Harold. "Does Terminology Distinguish Early Christian from Pagan Miracles?" *JBL* 101 (4, 1982): 531–51.

Renehan, "Acts 17.28." Renehan, Robert. "Acts 17.28." *GRBS* 20 (4, 1979): 347–53.

Renehan, "Quotations." Renehan, Robert. "Classical Greek Quotations in the New Testament." Pages 17–46 in *The Heritage of the Early Church: Essays in Honor of the Very Reverend Georges Vasilievich Florovsky*. OrChrAn 195. Rome: Pontificium Institutum Studiorum Orientalium, 1973.

Renfrew and Bahn, *Archaeology*. Renfrew, Colin, and Paul Bahn. *Archaeology: Theories, Methods, and Practice*. London: Thames & Hudson, 1991.

Renger, "Hieros Gamos." Renger, Johannes. "Hieros Gamos: Ancient Orient." *Brill Pauly* 6:321.

Renger, "Inns." Renger, Johannes. "Inns: Ancient Orient." *BrillPauly* 6:817–18.

Renger, "Votive Offerings." Renger, Johannes. "Votive Offerings: Ancient Near East and Egypt." *BrillPauly* 15:525–26.

Rengstorf, *Apostolate*. Rengstorf, Karl Heinrich. *Apostolate and Ministry*. St. Louis: Concordia, 1969.

Rengstorf, "ἀπόστολος." Rengstorf, Karl Heinrich. "ἀπόστολος." *TDNT* 1:398–447.

Rengstorf, "Election of Matthias." Rengstorf, Karl Heinrich. "The Election of Matthias." Pages 178–92 in *Current Issues in New Testament Interpretation: Essays in Honor of Otto A. Piper*. Edited by William Klassen and Graydon F. Snyder. New York: Harper & Row, 1962.

Reniers, "L'épopée." Reniers, Dominique. "L'épopée ou du voyage comme condition à l'héroïsme dans l'instauration du patriarcat dans la Grèce archaïque." *MScRel* 66 (3, 2009): 5–29.

Repath, "*Leucippe*." Repath, Ian D. "Achilles Tatius' *Leucippe and Cleitophon*: What Happened Next?" *CQ* 55 (1, 2005): 250–65.

Repschinski, "Hananias." Repschinski, Boris. "Warum mussten Hananias und Saphira sterben?" *PzB* 18 (1, 2009): 49–61.

Rese, "Funktion." Rese, Martin. "Die Funktion der alttestamentlichen Zitate und Anspielungen in den Reden der Apostelgeschichte." Pages 61–79 in *Les Actes des apôtres: Traditions, rédaction, théologie*. Edited by Jacob Kremer. BETL 48. Gembloux, Belg.: J. Duculot; Leuven: Leuven University Press, 1979.

Rese, "Second Thoughts." Rese, Martin. "The Jews in Luke-Acts: Some Second Thoughts." Pages 185–202 in *The Unity of Luke-Acts*. Edited by Joseph Verheyden. BETL 142. Leuven: Leuven University Press, 1999.

Retzleff, "Group." Retzleff, Alexandra. "The Dresden Type Satyr-Hermaphrodite Group in Roman Theaters." *AJA* 111 (3, 2007): 459–72.

Retzleff, "Theatres." Retzleff, Alexandra. "Near Eastern Theatres in Late Antiquity." *Phoenix* 57 (1–2, 2003): 115–38.

"Review of *Tarsus*." Review of W. C. van Unnik, *Tarsus or Jerusalem*, in "Notes of Recent Exposition." *ExpT.* 74 (8, 1963): 225–28.

Reviv, "Elements." Reviv, Hanoch. "Early Elements and Late Terminology in the Descriptions of the Non-Israelite Cities in the Bible." *IEJ* 27 (4, 1977): 189–96.

Rexine, *Religion in Plato and Cicero*. Rexine, John E. *Religion in Plato and Cicero*. New York: Philosophical Library, 1959.

Reydams-Schils, "Stoicized Readings." Reydams-Schils, Gretchen. "Stoicized Readings of Plato's *Timaeus* in Philo of Alexandria." *SPhilA* 7 (1995): 85–102.

Reyes, "Remembering." Reyes, Carlito D. "Remembering Paul, Remembering the Poor." *Diwa* 33 (2, 2008): 211–24.

Reymond, "Paul sur le chemin." Reymond, Sophie. "Paul sur le chemin de Damas (*Ac 9, 22 et 26*): Temps et espace d'une expérience." *NRTh* 118 (4, 1996): 520–38.

Reynier, *Recherches*. Reynier, Chantal. *Paul de Tarse en Méditerranée: Recherches autour de la navigation dans l'antiquité (Ac 27–28,16)*. LD 206. Paris: Cerf, 2006.

Reynier, "Voyages." Reynier, Chantal. "Les voyages de Paul vus à travers les déplacements dans l'antiquité." *Didaskalia* 38 (1, 2008): 51–68.

Reynolds, "Africa." Reynolds, Joyce Maire. "Africa (Libya), Exploration." *OCD*[3] 33.

Reynolds, "Antioch." Reynolds, H. R. "Antioch, the Birthplace of Christianity." *The Thinker* 3 (1893): 134–38.

Reynolds, "Aphrodisias." Reynolds, Joyce Maire. "Aphrodisias." *OCD*[3] 119–20.

Reynolds, "Cyrene." Reynolds, Joyce Maire. "Cyrene." *OCD*[3] 421–22.

Reynolds, "Libya." Reynolds, Joyce Maire. "Libya." *OCD*[3] 855–56.

Reynolds, *Magic*. Reynolds, Barrie. *Magic, Divination and Witchcraft among the Barotse of Northern Rhodesia*. Berkeley: University of California Press, 1963.

Reynolds, "Son of Man." Reynolds, Benjamin E. "The 'One like a Son of Man' according to the Old Greek of Daniel 7,13–14." *Bib* 89 (1, 2008): 70–80.

Rhoads and Michie, *Mark*. Rhoads, David, and Donald Michie. *Mark as Story: An Introduction to the Narrative of a Gospel*. Philadelphia: Fortress, 1982.

Rhoads, Esterline, and Lee, *Empire*. Rhoads, David, David Esterline, and Jae Won Lee. *Luke-Acts and Empire: Essays in Honor of Robert L. Brawley*. PrTMS 151. Eugene, Ore.: Pickwick, 2011.

Rhodes, "Areopagus." Rhodes, Peter J. "Areopagus." *BrillPauly* 1:1046–47.

Rhodes, "Bureaucracy." Rhodes, P. J. "Bureaucracy (Greek)." *OCD*[3] 265.

Rhodes, "Diet." Rhodes, James N. "Diet and Desire: The Logic of the Dietary Laws according to Philo." *ETL* 79 (1, 2003): 122–33.

Rhodes, "Documents." Rhodes, P. J. "Documents and the Greek Historians." Pages 56–66 in *A Companion to Greek and Roman Historiography*. Edited by John Marincola. 2 vols. Oxford: Blackwell, 2007.

Rhodes, "Ekklesia." Rhodes, Peter J. "Ekklesia." *BrillPauly* 4:868–70.

Rhodes, "Ekklesiasterion." Rhodes, Peter J. "Ekklesiasterion." *BrillPauly* 4:870.

Rhodes, "Elections." Rhodes, P. J. "Elections and Voting: Greek." *OCD*[3] 516.

Rhodes, "Epigamia." Rhodes, Peter J. "Epigamia." *BrillPauly* 4:1095–96.

Rhodes, "Episkopos." Rhodes, Peter J. "Episkopos, Episkopoi." *BrillPauly* 4:1127.

Rhodes, "Katacheirotonia." Rhodes, Peter J. "Katacheirotonia." *BrillPauly* 7:30.

Rhodes, "Lot." Rhodes, Peter J. "Lot, Election by: Greece." *BrillPauly* 7:816–17.

Rhodes, "Psephisma." Rhodes, Peter J. "Psephisma." *BrillPauly* 12:110–11.

Rhodes, "Stasis." Rhodes, P. J. "Stasis." *OCD*[3] 1438.

Rhodes, "Synhedrion." Rhodes, Peter J. "Synhedrion: Greek." *BrillPauly* 14:26–27.

Rhodes, "Tabernacle." Rhodes, James N. "Tabernacle and Temple." Pages 119–37 in *Contemporary Studies in Acts*. Edited by Thomas E. Phillips. Macon, Ga.: Mercer University Press, 2009.

Rhodes, "Triakonta." Rhodes, Peter J. "Triakonta." *BrillPauly* 14:897–98.

Rhodes, "Triakosioi." Rhodes, Peter J. "Triakosioi." *BrillPauly* 14:898.

Rhyne, *Faith*. Rhyne, C. Thomas. *Faith Establishes the Law*. SBLDS 55. Chico, Calif.: Scholars Press, 1981.

Rhyne, "Nomos." Rhyne, C. Thomas. "*Nomos dikaiosynēs* and the Meaning of Romans 10:4." *CBQ* 47 (3, 1985): 486–99.

Ricciardi, "Henoc." Ricciardi, Alberto. "1 Henoc 70–71: ¿Es Henoc el hijo del hombre?" *CuadTeol* 17 (1998): 129–46.

Rice, "Lindus." Rice, Ellen E. "Lindus." *OCD*[3] 862–63.

Rice, "Roots." Rice, Gene. "The African Roots of the Prophet Zephaniah." *JRT* 36 (1979): 21–31.

Rice and Stacey, "Dynamics." Rice, Dale, and Kathleen Stacey. "Small Group Dynamics as a Catalyst for Change: A Faculty Development Model for Academic Service-Learning." *MJCSL* 4 (Fall 1997): 64–71.

Richard, "Acts 15." Richard, Earl. "The Divine Purpose: The Jews and the Gentile Mission (Acts 15)." Pages 188–209 in *Luke-Acts: New Perspectives from the Society of Biblical Literature Seminar*. Edited by Charles H. Talbert. New York: Crossroad, 1984.

Richard, "Author." Richard, Earl. "Luke: Author and Thinker." Pages 15–32 in *New Views on Luke and Acts*. Edited by Earl Richard. Collegeville, Minn.: Liturgical Press, 1990.

Richard, *Composition*. Richard, Earl. *Acts 6:1–8:4: The Author's Method of Composition*. SBLDS 41. Missoula, Mont.: Scholars Press, 1978.

Richard, "Experiences." Richard, Pablo. "The Pluralistic Experiences of the First Christian Communities according to the Acts of the Apostles." *DVerb* 62–63 (2002): 24–31.

Richard, "Joseph Episode." Richard, Earl. "The Polemical Character of the Joseph Episode in Acts 7." *JBL* 98 (2, 1979): 255–67.

Richard, "Pentecost." Richard, Earl. "Pentecost as a Recurrent Theme in Luke-Acts." Pages 133–49 in *New Views on Luke and Acts*. Edited by Earl Richard. Collegeville, Minn.: Liturgical Press, 1990.

Richard, "Pluralistic Experiences." Richard, Pablo. "The Pluralistic Experiences of the First Christian Communities according to the Acts of the Apostles." *Word & Worship* 35 (3, 2002): 192–206.

Richard, "Samaritan Evidence." Richard, Earl. "Acts 7: An Investigation of the Samaritan Evidence." *CBQ* 39 (2, 1977): 190–208.

Richards, "Chronological Relationship." Richards, J. R. "Romans and I Corinthians: Their Chronological Relationship and Comparative Dates." *NTS* 13 (1, 1966): 14–30.

Richards, "Factors." Richards, Wes. "An Examination of Common Factors in the Growth of Global Pentecostalism: Observed in South Korea, Nigeria, and Argentina." *JAM* 7 (1, 2005): 85–106.

Richards, *Letter Writing*. Richards, E. Randolph. *Paul and First-Century Letter Writing: Secretaries, Composition, and Collection*. Downers Grove, Ill.: InterVarsity, 2004.

Richards, "Romans and Corinthians." Richards, J. R. "Romans and I Corinthians: Their Chronological Relationship and Comparative Dates." *NTS* 13 (1, 1966): 14–30.

Richardson, "Debate." Richardson, Neil. "The Debate about God: Acts 17." Pages 155–63 in *Acts in Practice*. Edited by John Vincent. Practice Interpretation 2. Blandford Forum, Dorset UK: Deo Publishing, 2012.

Richardson, *Eternity*. Richardson, Don. *Eternity in Their Hearts*. Ventura, Calif.: Regal, 1981.

Richardson, "Inconsistency." Richardson, Peter. "Pauline Inconsistency: I Corinthians 9:19–23 and Galatians 2:11–14." *NTS* 26 (3, 1980): 347–62.

Richardson, *Israel*. Richardson, Peter. *Israel in the Apostolic Age*. SNTSMS 10. Cambridge: Cambridge University Press, 1969.

Richardson, "Khirbet Qana." Richardson, Peter. "Khirbet Qana (and Other Villages) as a Context for Jesus." Pages 120–44 in *Jesus and Archaeology*. Edited by James H. Charlesworth. Grand Rapids: Eerdmans, 2006.

Richardson, "Order and Glossolalia." Richardson, William. "Liturgical Order and Glossolalia in 1 Corinthians 14.26c–33a." *NTS* 32 (1, 1986): 144–53.

Richardson, "SKT." Richardson, H. Neil. "SKT (Amos 9:11): 'Booth' or 'Succoth'?" *JBL* 92 (3, 1973): 375–81.

Richardson, "Synagogues." Richardson, Peter. "Augustan-Era Synagogues in Rome." Pages 17–29 in *Judaism and Christianity in First-Century Rome*. Edited by Karl P. Donfried and Peter Richardson. Grand Rapids: Eerdmans, 1998.

Richardson, *Theology*. Richardson, Alan. *An Introduction to the Theology of the New Testament*. New York: Harper and Brothers, 1958.

Richardson and Gooch, "Logia." Richardson, Peter, and Peter Gooch, "Logia of Jesus in 1 Corinthians." Pages 39–62 in *The Jesus Tradition outside the Gospels*. Edited by David Wenham. Gospel Perspectives 5. Sheffield, U.K.: JSOT Press, 1984.

Richlin, "Adultery." Richlin, Amy. "Approaches to the Sources on Adultery at Rome." *WomSt* 8 (1–2, 1981): 225–50.

Richmond, "Spies." Richmond, J. A. "Spies in Ancient Greece." *GR* 45 (1, 1998): 1–18.

Richmond, Strong, and DeLaine, "Rostra." Richmond, Ian Archibald, Donald Emrys Strong, and Janet DeLaine. "Rostra." *OCD*[3] 1336.

Richmond, Strong, and Patterson, "Forum Romanum." Richmond, Ian Archibald, Donald Emrys Strong, and John Robert Patterson. "Forum Romanum." *OCD*[3] 607–8.

Rickman, "Grain Trade." Rickman, Geoffrey E. "The Grain Trade under the Roman Empire." Pages 261–75 in *The Seaborne Commerce of Ancient Rome: Studies in Archaeology and History*. Edited by J. H. D'Arms and E. C. Kopff. MAAR 36. Rome: American Academy, 1980.

Ridderbos, *Galatia*. Ridderbos, Herman N. *The Epistle of Paul to the Churches of Galatia*. Grand Rapids: Eerdmans, 1953.

Ridderbos, *Paul: Outline*. Ridderbos, Herman N. *Paul: An Outline of His Theology*. Translated by John Richard De Witt. Grand Rapids: Eerdmans, 1975.

Ridderbos, *Paul and Jesus*. Ridderbos, Herman N. *Paul and Jesus*. Translated by David H. Freeman. Philadelphia: Presbyterian and Reformed, 1974.

Ridderbos, "Speeches of Peter." Ridderbos, Herman N. *The Speeches of Peter in the Acts of the Apostles*. Tyndale New Testament Lecture, 1961. London: Tyndale, 1962.

Riddle, "Hospitality." Riddle, Donald W. "Early Christian Hospitality: A Factor in the Gospel Transmission." *JBL* 57 (2, 1938): 141–54.

Ridgeway, "Sculpture." Ridgeway, Brunilde S. "Sculpture from Corinth." *Hesperia* 50 (1981): 422–48.

Riederer, "Extraction." Riederer, Josef. "The Extraction of Silver." *BrillPauly* 13:475–76.

Riederer, "Iron: Greece." Riederer, Josef. "Iron: Greece; Italy; Central Europe; Myth and Philosophy." *BrillPauly* 6:940–43.

Riederer, "Ores." Riederer, Josef. "Iron: Iron and Iron Ores." *BrillPauly* 6:938–40.

Riederer, "Silver." Riederer, Josef. "Silver: Greece; Rome." *BrillPauly* 13:473–74.

Riederer and Wartke, "Iron." Riederer, Josef, and Ralf-B. Wartke. "Iron: Ancient Orient." *BrillPauly* 6:940.

Riesenfeld, "Background." Riesenfeld, Harald. "The Mythological Background of New Testament Christology." Pages 81–95 in *The Background of the New Testament and Its Eschatology: Essays in Honor of Charles Harold Dodd*. Edited by W. D. Davies and D. Daube. Cambridge: Cambridge University Press, 1964.

Riesenfeld, *Tradition*. Riesenfeld, Harald. *The Gospel Tradition*. Philadelphia: Fortress, 1970.

Riesner, "Amphipolis." Riesner, Rainer. "Amphipolis: Eine übersehene Paulus-Station." *BK* 44 (2, 1989): 79–81.

Riesner, *Early Period*. Riesner, Rainer. *Paul's Early Period: Chronology, Mission Strategy, Theology*. Translated by Doug Stott. Grand Rapids: Eerdmans, 1998.

Riesner, "Education élémentaire." Riesner, Rainer. "Education élémentaire juive et tradition évangélique." *Hok* 21 (1982): 51–64.

Riesner, "Familiengrab." Riesner, Rainer. "Wurde das Familiengrab des Hohenpriesters Kajaphas entdeckt?" *BK* 46 (2, 1991): 82–84.

Riesner, "Gate." Riesner, Rainer. "Josephus' 'Gate of the Essenes' in Modern Discussion." *ZDPV* 105 (1989): 105–9 and plates 8–16a.

Riesner, "House Churches." Riesner, Rainer. "What Does Archaeology Teach Us about Early House Churches?" *TTKi* 78 (3–4, 2007): 159–85.

Riesner, "Hymn." Riesner, Rainer. "James's Speech (Acts 15:13–21), Simeon's Hymn (Luke 2:29–32), and Luke's Sources." Pages 263–78 in *Jesus of Nazareth, Lord and Christ: Essays on the Historical Jesus and New Testament Christology*. Edited by Joel B. Green and Max Turner. Grand Rapids: Eerdmans; Carlisle, U.K.: Paternoster, 1994.

Riesner, *Jesus*. Riesner, Rainer. *Jesus als Lehrer: Eine Untersuchung zum Ursprung der Evangelien-Überlieferung*. 2nd ed. WUNT 2.7. Tübingen: J. C. B. Mohr, 1984.

Riesner, "Pauline Chronology." Riesner, Rainer. "Pauline Chronology." Pages 9–29 in *The Blackwell Companion to Paul*. Edited by Stephen Westerholm. BCompRel. Oxford: Blackwell, 2011.

Riesner, "Rückkehr." Riesner, Rainer. "Die Rückkehr der Augenzeugen: Eine neue Entwicklung in der Evangelienforschung." *TBei* 38 (6, 2007): 337–52.

Riesner, "Synagogues in Jerusalem." Riesner, Rainer. "Synagogues in Jerusalem." Pages 179–211 in *The Book of Acts in Its Palestinian Setting*. Edited by Richard Bauckham. Vol. 4 of *The Book of Acts in Its First Century Setting*. Edited by Bruce W. Winter. Grand Rapids: Eerdmans; Carlisle, U.K.: Paternoster, 1995.

Riesner, "Zuverlässigkeit." Riesner, Rainer. "Die historische Zuverlässigkeit der Apostelgeschichte." *ZNT* 9 (18, 2006): 38–43.

Rife et al., "Cemetery Project." Rife, Joseph L., et al. "Life and Death at a Port in Roman Greece: The Kenchreai Cemetery Project, 2002–2006." *Hesperia* 76 (1, 2007): 143–81.

Rifkin, "Ekphrasis." Rifkin, Adrian. "Addressing Ekphrasis: A Prolegomenon to the Next." *CP* 102 (1, 2007): 72–82.

Rigato, "Donna." Rigato, Maria Luisa. "La donna valorizzata nell'opera di s. Luca," in "La teologia narrativa di san Luca," *Credere oggi* 119–20 (Sept.–Dec. 2000): 111–20.

Rigato, "Evento." Rigato, Maria Luisa. "L'evento della Pentecoste secondo At 2,3–4 alla luce di Is 6,5–8." *RivB* 48 (4, 2000): 443–51.

Rigato, "Valore inclusivo." Rigato, Maria Luisa. "Il valore inclusivo di πάντες nella narrazione dell'evento di Pentecoste in Luca (At 2,3–4): Apostoli-testimoni pentecostali." *RivB* 48 (2, 2000): 129–50.

Riggsby, "Memoir." Riggsby, Andrew M. "Memoir and Autobiography in Republican Rome." Pages 266–74 in *A Companion to Greek and Roman Historiography*. Edited by John Marincola. 2 vols. Oxford: Blackwell, 2007.

Riggsby, "'Public' and 'Private.'" Riggsby, Andrew M. "'Public' and 'Private' in Roman Culture: The Case of the *cubiculum*." *JRA* 10 (1997): 36–56.

Riggsby, "Verdicts." Riggsby, Andrew M. "Did the Romans Believe in Their Verdicts?" *Rhetorica* 15 (3, 1997): 235–51.

Rigsby, "Hauranus." Rigsby, Kent J. "Hauranus the Epicurean." *CJ* 104 (1, 2008): 19–22.

Rigsby, "Sarapeum." Rigsby, Kent J. "Founding a Sarapeum." *GRBS* 42 (1, 2001): 117–24.

Riley, "Demon." Riley, Greg J. "Demon." Pages 235–40 in *Dictionary of Deities and Demons in the Bible*. 2nd rev. ed. Edited by Karel van der Toorn, Bob Becking, and Pieter W. van der Horst. Leiden: Brill; Grand Rapids: Eerdmans, 1999.

Riley, "Devil." Riley, Greg J. "Devil." Pages 244–50 in *Dictionary of Deities and Demons in the Bible*. 2nd rev. ed. Edited by Karel van der Toorn, Bob Becking, and Pieter W. van der Horst. Leiden: Brill; Grand Rapids: Eerdmans, 1999.

Rinaldi, "Note prosopografiche." Rinaldi, Giancarlo. "Procuratore Felix: Note prosopografiche in margine ad una rilettura di At 24." *RivB* 39 (4, 1991): 423–66.

Rincón Alvarez, "Mensajes." Rincón Alvarez, Manuel. "Mensajes cristianos en las Epístolas morales a Lucilio y otros escritos de Séneca." *Ciudad de Dios* 222 (3, 2009): 697–747.

Ringe, *Liberation*. Ringe, Sharon H. *Jesus, Liberation, and the Biblical Jubilee: Images for Ethics and Christology*. OBT 19. Philadelphia: Fortress, 1985.

Ringe, *Luke* Ringe, Sharon H. *Luke*. WestBC. Louisville: Westminster John Knox, 1995.

Ringgren, *Faith*. Ringgren, Helmer. *The Faith of Qumran*. Philadelphia: Fortress, 1963.

Ringgren, *Religion*. Ringgren, Helmer. *Israelite Religion*. Translated by David E. Green. Philadelphia: Fortress, 1966.

Ringgren, *Word*. Ringgren, Helmer. *Word and Wisdom: Studies in the Hypostatization of Divine Qualities and Functions in the Ancient Near East*. Lund, Swed.: Häkan Ohlsson, 1947.

Ripat, "Language." Ripat, Pauline. "The Language of Oracular Inquiry in Roman Egypt." *Phoenix* 60 (3–4, 2006): 304–28.

Ripat, "Omens." Ripat, Pauline. "Roman Omens, Roman Audiences, and Roman History." *GR* 53 (2, 2006): 155–74.

Rissi, *Time*. Rissi, Mathias. *Time and History: A Study on the Revelation*. Translated by Gordon C. Winsor. Richmond, Va.: John Knox, 1966.

Rist, *Epicurus*. Rist, John M. *Epicurus: An Introduction*. Cambridge: Cambridge University Press, 1972.

Rist, "Monism." Rist, John M. "Monism: Plotinus and Some Predecessors." *HSCP* 69 (1965): 329–44.

Rist, "Seneca and Orthodoxy." Rist, John M. "Seneca and Stoic Orthodoxy." *ANRW* 36.3:1993–2012. Part 2, *Principat*, 36.3. Edited by H. Temporini and W. Haase. Berlin: de Gruyter, 1989.

Rist, *Terminology*. Rist, John M. *The Use of Stoic Terminology in Philo's Quod Deus immutabilis sit 33–50*. PSCC 23. Berkeley, Calif.: Center for Hermeneutical Studies in Hellenistic and Modern Culture, 1976.

Ritchie, *Spirit*. Ritchie, Mark Andrew. *Spirit of the Rainforest: A Yanomamö Shaman's Story*. 2nd ed. Chicago: Island Lake, 2000.

Ritmeyer and Ritmeyer, "Akeldama." Ritmeyer, Leen, and Kathleen Ritmeyer. "Akeldama: Potter's Field or High Priest's Tomb?" *BAR* 20 (6, 1994): 22–35, 76, 78.

Ritner, *Mechanics*. Ritner, Robert Kriech. *The Mechanics of Ancient Egyptian Magical Practice*. SAOC 54. Chicago: Oriental Institute of the University of Chicago, 1993.

Rius-Camps, "Confrontación." Rius-Camps, Josep. "Confrontación en la iglesia primitiva: Los círculos hebreos y helenistas en la obra de Lucas (Evangelio y Hechos de los apóstoles." *FilNeot* 18 (35–36, 2005): 45–84.

Rius-Camps, "Maria en Hechos." Rius-Camps, Josep. "Maria, la madre de Jesús, en los Hechos de los apóstoles." *EphMar* 43 (2, 1993): 263–75.

Rius-Camps and Read-Heimerdinger, "Readings XIV." Rius-Camps, Josep, and Jenny Read-Heimerdinger. "The Variant Readings of the Western Text of the Acts of the Apostles (XIV) (Acts 8:1b-40)." *FilNeot* 15 (29–30, 2002): 111–32.

Rius-Camps and Read-Heimerdinger, "Readings XV." Rius-Camps, Josep, and Jenny Read-Heimerdinger. "The Variant Readings of the Western Text of the Acts of the Apostles (XV) (Acts 9:1–30)." *Fil Neot* 16 (31–32, 2003): 133–45.

Rius-Camps and Read-Heimerdinger, "Readings XVI." Rius-Camps, Josep, and Jenny Read-Heimerdinger. "The Variant Readings of the Western Text of the Acts of the Apostles (XVI) (Acts 9:31–11:18)." *FilNeot* 17 (33–34, 2004): 44–88.

Rius-Camps and Read-Heimerdinger, "Readings XVII." Rius-Camps, Josep, and Jenny Read-Heimerdinger. "The Variant Readings of the Western Text of the Acts of the Apostles (XVII) (Acts 11:19–12:25)." *FilNeot* 18 (35–36, 2005): 135–65.

Rius-Camps and Read-Heimerdinger, "Readings XVIII." Rius-Camps, Josep, and Jenny Read-Heimerdinger. "The Variant Readings of the Western Text of the Acts of the Apostles (XVIII)." *FilNeot* 16 (37–38, 2006): 99–112.

Rius-Camps and Read-Heimerdinger, "Reconsideration." Rius-Camps, Josep, and Jenny Read-Heimerdinger. "After the Death of Judas: A Reconsideration of the Status of the Twelve Apostles." *RCT* 29 (2, 2004): 305–34.

Rivera-Pagán, "Transformation." Rivera-Pagán, Luis N. "Pentecostal Transformation in Latin America." Pages 190–210 in *Twentieth-Century Global Christianity*. Edited by Mary Farrell Bednarowski. A People's History of Christianity 7. Philadelphia: Fortress, 2008.

Rives, "Interpretatio Romana." Rives, James B. "*Interpretatio Romana*." *OCD*[3] 761.

Rives, "Magic in XII Tables." Rives, James B. "Magic in the XII Tables Revisited." *CQ* 52 (1, 2002): 270–90.

Rives, "Phrygian Tales." Rives, James B. "Phrygian Tales." *GRBS* 45 (3, 2005): 223–44.

Rives, "Popular." Rives, James B. "How Popular Were the 'Oriental Cults'?" Paper presented at the annual meeting of the SBL, Orlando, Fla., 1998.

Rives, *Religion*. Rives, James B. *Religion in the Roman Empire*. Oxford: Blackwell, 2007.

Rives, "Silvanus." Rives, James B. "Silvanus." *OCD*[3] 1408.

Rives, "Venus." Rives, James B. "Venus." *BrillPauly* 15:284–87.

Rivkin, "Meaning." Rivkin, Ellis. "The Meaning of Messiah in Jewish Thought." *USQR* 26 (4, 1971): 383–406.

Rivkin, "Messiah." Rivkin, Ellis. "The Meaning of Messiah in Jewish Thought." Pages 54–75 in *Evangelicals and Jews in Conversation on Scripture, Theology, and History*. Edited by Marc H. Tanenbaum, Marvin R. Wilson, and James A. Rudin. Grand Rapids: Baker, 1978.

Rivkin, "Pharisees." Rivkin, Ellis. "Defining the Pharisees: the Tannaitic Sources." *HUCA* 40–41 (1969–70): 205–49.

Rikvin, "Pseudepigraph." Rivkin, Ellis. "The Book of Jubilees—An Anti-Pharisaic Pseudepigraph?" *ErIsr* 16 (1982): 193–98.

Rivkin, *Revolution*. Rivkin, Ellis. *A Hidden Revolution*. Nashville: Abingdon, 1978.

Rix, "Supernomen." Rix, Helmut. "Supernomen." *BrillPauly* 13:952.

Rizakis, "Elites." Rizakis, Athanasios. "Urban Elites in the Roman East: Enhancing

Regional Positions and Social Superiority." Pages 317–30 in *A Companion to Roman Religion*. Edited by Jörg Rüpke. BCompAW. Oxford: Blackwell, 2011.

Ro, *Alternatives*. Ro, Bong Rin, ed. *Christian Alternatives to Ancestor Practices*. Taichung, Taiwan: Asia Theological Association, 1985.

Roach, "Choice." Roach, David. "From Free Choice to God's Choice: Augustine's Exegesis of Romans 9." *EvQ* 80 (2, 2008): 129–41.

Roaf, *Atlas*. Roaf, Michael. *Cultural Atlas of Mesopotamia and the Ancient Near East*. New York: Facts on File, 1990.

Robbins, *Beyond*. Robbins, Vernon K. *Sea Voyages and Beyond: Emerging Strategies in Socio-Rhetorical Interpretation*. ESEC. Blandford Forum, Dorset: Deo Publishing, 2010.

Robbins, "Claims of Prologues." Robbins, Vernon K. "The Claims of the Prologues and Greco-Roman Rhetoric: The Prefaces to Luke and Acts in Light of Greco-Roman Rhetorical Strategies." Pages 63–83 in *Jesus and the Heritage of Israel: Luke's Narrative Claim upon Israel's Legacy*. Edited by David P. Moessner. Luke the Interpreter of Israel 1. Harrisburg, Pa.: Trinity Press International, 1999.

Robbins, "Embaterion." Robbins, Emmet. "Embaterion." *BrillPauly* 4:937.

Robbins, "Introduction." Robbins, Vernon K. "Introduction." Pages vii–xvii in *The Rhetoric of Pronouncement*. Edited by Vernon K. Robbins. Semeia 64. Atlanta: Scholars Press, 1994.

Robbins, *Jesus the Teacher*. Robbins, Vernon K. *Jesus the Teacher: A Socio-rhetorical Interpretation of Mark*. Minneapolis: Augsburg Fortress, 1992.

Robbins, "Kastoreion." Robbins, Emmet. "Kastoreion." *BrillPauly* 7:26.

Robbins, "Land and Sea." Robbins, Vernon K. "By Land and by Sea: The We-Passages and Ancient Sea Voyages." Pages 215–42 in *Perspectives on Luke-Acts*. ABPRSSS 5. Edited by Charles H. Talbert. Danville, Va.: Association of Baptist Professors of Religion; Edinburgh: T&T Clark, 1978.

Robbins, "Location." Robbins, Vernon K. "The Social Location of the Implied Author of Luke-Acts." Pages 305–32 in *The Social World of Luke-Acts: Models for Interpretation*. Edited by Jerome H. Neyrey. Peabody, Mass.: Hendrickson, 1991.

Robbins, "Meal." Robbins, Vernon K. "Last Meal: Preparation, Betrayal, and Absence (Mark 14:12–25)." Pages 21–40 in *The Passion in Mark: Studies in Mark 14–16*. Edited by Werner H. Kelber. Philadelphia: Fortress, 1976.

Robbins, "Prefaces." Robbins, Vernon K. "Prefaces in Greco-Roman Biography and Luke-Acts." *PRSt* 6 (2, Summer 1979): 94–108.

Robbins, "Prefaces in Biography." Robbins, Vernon K. "Prefaces in Greco-Roman Biography and Luke-Acts." Pages 198–207 in vol. 2 of *SBL Seminar Papers, 1978*. Edited by P. J. Achtemeier. 2 vols. SBLSP 14. Missoula, Mont.: Scholars Press, 1978.

Robbins, "Pronouncement Stories." Robbins, Vernon K. "Classifying Pronouncement Stories in Plutarch's *Parallel Lives*." *Semeia* 20 (1981): 29–52.

Robbins, "Propemptikon." Robbins, Emmet. "Propemptikon." *BrillPauly* 12:20–21.

Robbins, *Quotes*. Robbins, Vernon K. *Ancient Quotes and Anecdotes: From Crib to Crypt*. Sonoma, Fla.: Polebridge, 1989.

Robbins, *Rhetoric*. Robbins, Vernon K. *The Rhetoric of Pronouncement*. Semeia 64. Atlanta: Scholars Press, 1994.

Robbins, "Test Case." Robbins, Vernon K. "Socio-rhetorical Criticism: Mary, Elizabeth, and the Magnificat as a Test Case." Pages 164–209 in *The New Literary Criticism and the New Testament*. Edited by Edgar V. McKnight and Elizabeth Struthers Malbon. Valley Forge, Pa.: Trinity Press International; Sheffield, U.K.: JSOT Press, 1994.

Robbins, *Texture*. Robbins, Vernon K. *Exploring the Texture of Texts: A Guide to Socio-Rhetorical Interpretation*. Valley Forge, Pa.: Trinity Press International, 1996.

Robbins, "We-Passages and Sea Voyages." Robbins, Vernon K. "The We-Passages in Acts and Ancient Sea Voyages." *BR* 20 (1975): 5–18.

Robbins, "Work Songs." Robbins, Emmet. "Work Songs." *BrillPauly* 15:745–46.

Robbins, "Writing." Robbins, Vernon K. "Writing as a Rhetorical Act in Plutarch and the Gospels." Pages 142–68 in *Persuasive Artistry: Studies in New Testament Rhetoric in Honor of George A. Kennedy*. Edited by Duane F. Watson. JSNTSup 50. Sheffield, U.K.: Sheffield Academic, 1991.

Robeck, "Charismata." Robeck, Cecil M., Jr. "Origen's Treatment of the Charismata in 1 Corinthians 12:8–10." Pages 111–25 in *Charismatic Experiences in History*. Edited by Cecil M. Robeck Jr. Peabody, Mass.: Hendrickson, 1985.

Robeck, "Charismatic Movements." Robeck, Cecil M., Jr. "Charismatic Movements." *GDT* 145–54.

Robeck, *Mission*. Robeck, Cecil M., Jr. *The Azusa Street Mission and Revival: The Birth of the Global Pentecostal Movement*. Nashville: Thomas Nelson, 2006.

Robeck, "Seymour." Robeck, Cecil M., Jr. "William J. Seymour and 'The Bible Evidence.'" Pages 72–95 in *Initial Evidence: Historical and Biblical Perspectives on the Pentecostal Doctrine of Spirit Baptism*. Edited by Gary B. McGee. Peabody, Mass.: Hendrickson, 1991.

Robeck, "Tongues." Robeck, Cecil M., Jr. "Tongues." *DPL* 939–43.

Robert, "Avenir." Robert, Philippe de. "L'avenir d'un oracle: Citations et relectures bibliques de 2 Samuel 7." *ETR* 73 (4, 1998): 483–90.

Robert, *Croyances*. Robert, J. M. *Croyances et coutumes magico-religieuses des Wafipa païens*. Tabora, Tanzania: Tanganyika Mission Press, 1949.

Robert, *Décrets*. Robert, Jeanne, and Louis Robert. *DécHell*. Vol. 1 of *Claros*. Paris: Éditions de Recherche sur les Civilisations, 1989.

Robert, "Introduction." Robert, Dana L. "Introduction: Historical Themes and Current Issues." Pages 1–28 in *Gospel Bearers, Gender Barriers: Missionary Women in the Twentieth Century*. Edited by Dana L. Robert. Maryknoll, N.Y.: Orbis, 2002.

Roberto, "History." Roberto, Umberto. "From Hellenistic to Christian Universal History: Julius Africanus and the Atthidographers on the Origins of Athens." *ZAC/JAC* 14 (3, 2010): 525–39.

Roberts, "Closure." Roberts, Deborah H. "Closure." *OCD³* 351.

Roberts, *Fragment*. Roberts, C. H. *An Unpublished Fragment of the Fourth Gospel*. Manchester: Manchester University Press, 1935.

Roberts, "New Parallel." Roberts, J. J. M. "A New Parallel to I Kings 18_{28-29}." *JBL* 89 (1, 1970): 76–77.

Roberts, "Reception." Roberts, Deborah H. "The Reception of Classical Mythology in Modern Handbooks and Collections." *CBull* 84 (1, 2009): 57–99.

Roberts, "Resources." Roberts, Andrew. "The Acts of the Apostles: Resourcing and Developing Fresh Expressions of Church." *EpwRev* 36 (3, 2009): 26–43.

Roberts, *Revival*. Roberts, Dyfed Wyn, ed. *Revival, Renewal, and the Holy Spirit*. SEHT. Eugene, Ore.: Wipf & Stock, 2009.

Roberts, "Seers." Roberts, P. "Seers or Overseers?" *ExpT* 108 (10, 1997): 301–5.

Roberts, "Sphragis." Roberts, Deborah H. "Sphragis." *OCD³* 1435.

Robertson, *Conversations*. Robertson, C. K. *Conversations with Scripture: The Acts of the Apostles*. New York: Morehouse, 2010.

Robertson, "Epidauros to Lourdes." Robertson, David. "From Epidauros to Lourdes: A History of Healing by Faith." Pages 179–89 in *Faith Healing: Finger of God? Or, Scientific Curiosity?* Compiled by Claude A. Frazier. New York: Thomas Nelson, 1973.

Robertson, *Grammar*. Robertson, A. T. *A Grammar of the Greek New Testament in the Light of Historical Research*. Nashville: Broadman, 1934.

Robertson, *Greek and Roman Architecture*. Robertson, D. S. *Greek and Roman Architecture*. 2nd ed. Cambridge: Cambridge University Press, 1943.

Robertson, "Limits." Robertson, C. K. "The Limits of Leadership: Challenges to Apostolic Homeostasis in Luke-Acts." *AThR* 87 (2, 2005): 273–90.

Robertson, *Luke*. Robertson, A. T. *Luke the Historian in the Light of Research*. New York: Scribner's, 1923.

Robertson, *Word*. Robertson, O. Palmer. *The Final Word*. Carlisle, Pa.: Banner of Truth, 1993.

Robertson and Dietrich, "Fate." Robertson, Noel, and B. C. Dietrich. "Fate." *OCD*[3] 589–90.

Robertson and Dietrich, "Tyche." Robertson, Noel, and B. C. Dietrich. "Tyche." *OCD*[3] 1566.

Robertson and Plummer, *First Corinthians*. Robertson, Archibald, and Alfred Plummer. *A Critical and Exegetical Commentary on the First Epistle of St Paul to the Corinthians*. 2nd ed. ICC. Edinburgh: T&T Clark, 1914.

Robichaux, "Incorporation." Robichaux, Kerry S. "The Spirit's Incorporation of the Operations of Christ in Acts through Jude." *AfCrit* 13 (1, 2008): 48–66.

Robinson, "Ardua." Robinson, Matthew. "Ardua et Astra: On the Calculation of the Dates of the Rising and Setting of Stars." *CP* 104 (3, 2009): 354–75.

Robinson, "Ascendancy." Robinson, John A. T. "Ascendancy." *ANQ* 5 (2, 1964): 5–9.

Robinson, *Body*. Robinson, John A. T. *The Body: A Study in Pauline Theology*. London: SCM, 1957.

Robinson, "Challenge." Robinson, Bernard. "The Challenge of the Gospel Miracle Stories." *NBf* 60 (1979): 321–34.

Robinson, *Coming*. Robinson, John A. T. *Jesus and His Coming*. 2nd ed. Philadelphia: Westminster, 1979.

Robinson, *Criminal Law*. Robinson, O. F. *The Criminal Law of Ancient Rome*. London: Duckworth; Baltimore: Johns Hopkins University Press, 1995.

Robinson, "Destination." Robinson, John A. T. "The Destination and Purpose of St. John's Gospel." *NTS* 6 (2, 1960): 117–31.

Robinson, *Ephesians*. Robinson, J. Armitage. *St Paul's Epistle to the Ephesians*. 2nd ed. London: James Clarke, 1904.

Robinson, "Fountains." Robinson, Betsey A. "Fountains and the Formation of Cultural Identity at Roman Corinth." Pages 111–40 in *Urban Religion in Roman Corinth: Interdisciplinary Approaches*. Edited by Daniel N. Schowalter and Steven J. Friesen. HTS 53. Cambridge, Mass.: Harvard University Press, 2005.

Robinson, "Paul in Cyprus." Robinson, Bernard P. "Paul and Barnabas in Cyprus." *ScrB* 26 (2, 1996): 69–72.

Robinson, *Personality*. Robinson, H. Wheeler. *Corporate Personality in Ancient Israel*. Rev. ed. Introduction by Gene M. Tucker. Philadelphia: Fortress, 1980.

Robinson, "Primitive Christology." Robinson, John A. T. "The Most Primitive Christology of All?" *JTS* 7 (1956): 177–89.

Robinson, *Problem of History*. Robinson, James M. *The Problem of History in Mark and Other Marcan Studies*. Philadelphia: Fortress, 1982.

Robinson, *Redating*. Robinson, John A. T. *Redating the New Testament*. Philadelphia: Westminster; London: SCM, 1976.

Robinson, "ΣΠΕΡΜΟΛΟΓΟΣ." Robinson, Maurice A. "ΣΠΕΡΜΟΛΟΓΟΣ: Did Paul Preach from Jesus' Parables?" *Bib* 56 (2, 1975): 231–40.

Robinson, *Studies*. Robinson, John A. T. *Twelve New Testament Studies*. SBT 34. London: SCM, 1962.

Robinson, "Testament." Robinson, Stephen E. "The Testament of Adam and the Angelic Liturgy." *RevQ* 12 (1, 1985): 105–10.

Robinson, *Trust*. Robinson, John A. T. *Can We Trust the New Testament?* Grand Rapids: Eerdmans, 1977.

Robinson and Wall, *Called*. Robinson, Anthony B., and Robert W. Wall. *Called to Be Church: The Book of Acts for a New Day*. Grand Rapids: Eerdmans, 2006.

Rocchi, "Delphi: Organization." Rocchi, Giovanna Daviero. "Delphi: Organization and History." *BrillPauly* 4:223–26.

Rochberg-Halton, "Elements." Rochberg-Halton, Francesca. "Elements of the Babylonian Contribution to Hellenistic Astrology." *JAOS* 108 (1, 1988): 51–62.

Rochberg-Halton, "Horoscopes." Rochberg-Halton, Francesca. "Babylonian Horoscopes and Their Sources." *Or* 58 (1, 1989): 102–23 and plates 1–2.

Rochberg-Halton, "New Evidence." Rochberg-Halton, Francesca. "New Evidence for the History of Astrology." *JNES* 43 (2, 1984): 115–40.

Rochette, "Bilingualisme." Rochette, Bruno. "Sur le bilingualisme dans l'Égypte gréco-romaine." *ChrÉg* 71 (141, 1996): 153–68.

Rochette, "Juifs et Romains." Rochette, Bruno. "Juifs et Romains: Y a-t-il eu un antijudaïsme romain?" *REJ* 160 (1–2, 2001): 1–31.

Rochette, "Papyrologica bilinguia." Rochette, Bruno. "Papyrologica bilinguia graeco-latina." *Aeg* 76 (1–2, 1996): 57–79.

Rochette, "Tibère." Rochette, Bruno. "Tibère, les cultes étrangers, et les astrologues (Suétone, Vie de Tibère, 36)." *ÉtudClass* 69 (2, 2001): 189–94.

Rochette, "Trimalchion." Rochette, Bruno. "Trimalchion ou l'antijudaïsme de Pétrone." *REJ* 157 (3–4, 1998): 359–69.

Rodd, "Finger." Rodd, Cyril S. "Spirit or Finger." *ExpT* 72 (5, 1961): 157–58.

Roddy, "Two Parts." Roddy, Nicolae. "'Two Parts: Weeks of Seven Weeks': The End of the Age as *terminus ad quem* for 2 Baruch." *JSP* 14 (1996): 3–14.

Rodríguez, *Call Yourself*. Rodríguez, Rafael. *If You Call Yourself a Jew: Reappraising Paul's Letter to the Romans*. Eugene, Ore.: Cascade, 2014.

Rodríguez Ruiz, "Composición." Rodríguez Ruiz, Miguel. "El lugar de composición del cuarto evangelio: Exposición y valoración de las diversas opiniones." *EstBib* 57 (1–4, 1999): 613–41.

Rodríguez Ruiz, "Discurso misionero." Rodríguez Ruiz, Miguel. "Hacia una definición del 'discurso misionero': Los discursos misioneros de los Hechos de los apóstoles a la luz de la retórica antigua." *EstBib* 49 (4, 1991): 425–50.

Roduit, "Discours." Roduit, Alexandre. "Le discours d'Agrippa II dans *La guerre juive* de Flavius Josèphe." *REJ* 162 (3–4, 2003): 365–402.

Roebuck, *Asklepieion*. Roebuck, Carl. *The Asklepieion and Lerna*. Vol. 14 of *Corinth: Results of Excavations Conducted by the American School of Classical Studies at Athens*. Princeton: American School of Classical Studies at Athens, 1951.

Roeder, "Geschichte Nubiens." Roeder, Günther. "Die Geschichte Nubiens und des Sudans." *Klio* 12 (1912): 51–82.

Roessli, "Vies." Roessli, Jean-Michel. "Vies et métamorphoses de la Sibylle: Notes critiques." *RHR* 224 (2, 2007): 253–71.

Roetzel, *Paul*. Roetzel, Calvin J. *Paul: A Jew on the Margins*. Louisville: Westminster John Knox, 2003.

Rofé, "Slave-Girl." Rofé, Alexander. "Moses' Mother and Her Slave-Girl according to 4QExod[b]." *DSD* 9 (1, 2002): 38–43.

Rogers, "Background." Rogers, Cleon L. "The Dionysian Background of Ephesians 5:18." *BSac* 136 (543, 1979): 249–57.

Rogers, *Ministry*. Rogers, Glenn. *Holistic Ministry and Cross-cultural Mission in Luke-Acts*. N.p.: Mission and Ministry Resources, 2004.

Rogers, "Pastoral Epistles." Rogers, Patrick. "The Pastoral Epistles as

Deutero-Pauline." *ITQ* 45 (4, 1978): 248–60.

Rogers, "Tongues." Rogers, Cleon L. "The Gift of Tongues in the Post Apostolic Church (A.D. 100–400)." *BSac* 122 (486, 1965): 134–43.

Rogers, "Wisdom." Rogers, Jessie. "Wisdom—Woman or Angel in Sirach 24?" *JNSL* 27 (1, 2001): 71–80.

Rohrbacher, "Digressions." Rohrbacher, David. "Ammianus' Roman Digressions and the Audience of the *Res Gestae*." Pages 468–73 in *A Companion to Greek and Roman Historiography*. Edited by John Marincola. 2 vols. Oxford: Blackwell, 2007.

Rohrbaugh, "Pre-industrial City." Rohrbaugh, Richard L. "The Pre-industrial City in Luke-Acts: Urban Social Relations." Pages 125–49 in *The Social World of Luke-Acts: Models for Interpretation*. Edited by Jerome H. Neyrey. Peabody, Mass.: Hendrickson, 1991.

Rokéah, "Proselytism." Rokéah, David. "Ancient Jewish Proselytism in Theory and in Practice." *TZ* 52 (3, 1996): 206–24.

Rokéah, "Tacitus and Antisemitism." Rokéah, David. "Tacitus and Ancient Antisemitism." *REJ* 154 (3–4, 1995): 281–94.

Rolfe, "Introduction." Rolfe, J. C. Introduction to *The Lives of the Caesars*. Pages xvii–xxxi in vol. 1 of *Suetonius*. Translated by J. C. Rolfe. 2 vols. LCL. London: Heinemann; New York: Macmillan; Cambridge, Mass.: Harvard University Press, 1914.

Rolin, "Pierre." Rolin, Patrice. "Pierre, Paul, Jacques à Jérusalem." *FoiVie* 96 (4, 1997): 99–114.

Roll, "Roads." Roll, Israel. "Imperial Roads across and Trade Routes beyond the Roman Province of *Judaea-Palaestina* and *Arabia*: The State of Research." *TA* 32 (1, 2005): 107–18.

Roll and Tal, "Villa." Roll, I., and O. Tal. "A Villa of the Early Roman Period at Apollonia-Arsuf." *IEJ* 58 (2, 2008): 132–49.

Roller, "Great Mother." Roller, Lynn E. "The Great Mother at Gordion: The Hellenization of an Anatolian Cult." *JHS* 111 (1991): 128–43 and plates 3–4.

Roller, "Horizontal Women." Roller, Matthew. "Horizontal Women: Posture and Sex in the Roman *convivium*." *AJP* 124 (3, 2003): 377–422, figs. a–d.

Roller, "Past." Roller, Matthew. "The Exemplary Past in Roman Historiography and Culture." Pages 214–30 in *The Cambridge Companion to the Roman Historians*. Edited by Andrew Feldherr. Cambridge: Cambridge University Press, 2009.

Röllig, "Moon Deities." Röllig, Wolfgang. "Moon Deities: Ancient Orient." *Brill Pauly* 9:200–201.

Rollins, "Miracles." Rollins, Wayne G. "Jesus and Miracles in Historical, Biblical, and Psychological Perspective." Pages 36–56 in *Religious and Spiritual Events*. Vol. 1 of *Miracles: God, Science, and Psychology in the Paranormal*. Edited by J. Harold Ellens. Westport, Conn.; London: Praeger, 2008.

Rollinson, "*Mythos* and *mimesis*." Rollinson, Philip. "*Mythos* and *mimesis* in Humanist Critical Theory." *CBull* 73 (2, 1997): 149–53.

Roloff, *Apostelgeschichte*. Roloff, Jürgen. *Die Apostelgeschichte*. Göttingen: Vandenhoeck, 1981.

Romaniuk, "Crainte." Romaniuk, Kazimierz. "La crainte de Dieu à Qumran et dans le Nouveau Testament." *RevQ* 4 (1, 1963): 29–38.

Romano, "City Planning." Romano, David Gilman. "City Planning, Centuriation, and Land Division in Roman Corinth: Colonia Laus Iulia Corinthiensis and Colonia Iulia Flavia Augusta Corinthiensis." Pages 279–301 in *Corinth: The Centenary, 1896–1996*. Edited by Charles K. Williams II and Nancy Bookidis. Vol. 20 of *Corinth: Results of Excavations Conducted by the American School of Classical Studies at Athens*. Princeton: American School of Classical Studies at Athens, 2003.

Romano, "Folk-Healing." Romano, Octavio I. "Charismatic Medicine, Folk-Healing, and Folk-Sainthood." *AmAnth* 67 (1965): 1151–73.

Romano, "Planning." Romano, David Gilman. "Urban and Rural Planning in Roman Corinth." Pages 25–59 in *Urban Religion in Roman Corinth: Interdisciplinary Approaches*. Edited by Daniel N. Schowalter and Steven J. Friesen. HTS 53. Cambridge, Mass.: Harvard University Press, 2005.

Römer, "Vie de Moïse." Römer, Thomas C. "La construction d'une 'vie de Moïse' dans la Bible hébraïque et chez quelques auteurs hellénistiques." *Transversalités* 85 (2003): 13–30.

Romm, *Edges*. Romm, James S. *The Edges of the Earth in Ancient Thought: Geography, Exploration, and Fiction*. Princeton: Princeton Unversity Press, 1994.

Roncace, "Portraits." Roncace, Mark. "Josephus' (Real) Portraits of Deborah and Gideon: A Reading of *Antiquities* 5.198–232." *JSJ* 31 (3, 2000): 247–74.

Roncace, "Samson." Roncace, Mark. "Another Portrait of Josephus' Portrait of Samson." *JSJ* 35 (2, 2004): 185–207.

Rondholz, "Rubicon." Rondholz, Anke. "Crossing the Rubicon. A Historio-

graphical Study." *Mnemosyne* 62 (3, 2009): 432–50.

Rood, "Christ comme *dynamis*." Rood, L. A. "Le Christ comme *dynamis Theou*." Pages 93–108 in *Littérature et théologie pauliniennes*. By A. Descamps et al. Paris: Desclée de Brouwer, 1960.

Rood, "Development." Rood, Tim. "The Development of the War Monograph." Pages 147–58 in *A Companion to Greek and Roman Historiography*. Edited by John Marincola. 2 vols. Oxford: Blackwell, 2007.

Rook, "Boanerges." Rook, John T. "'Boanerges, Sons of Thunder' (Mark 3:17)." *JBL* 100 (1, 1981): 94–95.

Rook, "Names." Rook, John T. "The Names of the Wives from Adam to Abraham in the Book of *Jubilees*." *JSP* 7 (1990): 105–17.

Rook, "Tradition." Rook, John T. "A Twenty-Eight-Day Month Tradition in the Book of *Jubilees*." *VT* 31 (1, 1981): 83–87.

Rook, "Women in Acts." Rook, John T. "Women in Acts: Are They Equal Partners with Men in the Earliest Church?" *McMJT* 2 (2, 1991): 29–41.

Rooker, "Blasphemy." Rooker, Mark F. "Blasphemy." *DOTP* 80–83.

Roon, *Authenticity*. Roon, A. van. *The Authenticity of Ephesians*. NovTSup 39. Leiden: Brill, 1974.

Ropes, *Galatians*. Ropes, James Hardy. *The Singular Problem of the Epistle to the Galatians*. HTS 14. Cambridge, Mass.: Harvard University Press, 1929. Repr., New York: Kraus, 1969.

Ropes, *James*. Ropes, James Hardy. *A Critical and Exegetical Commentary on the Epistle of St. James*. ICC. Edinburgh: T&T Clark, 1916.

Ropes, *Text*. Ropes, James Hardy. *The Text of Acts*. Vol. 3 of *The Beginnings of Christianity: The Acts of the Apostles*. Edited by F. J. Foakes-Jackson and Kirsopp Lake. London: Macmillan, 1926. Repr., Grand Rapids: Baker Book House, 1979.

Rordorf, "Conversion." Rordorf, Willy. "Paul's Conversion in the Canonical Acts and in the *Acts of Paul*." Translated by Peter W. Dunn. Pages 137–44 in *The Apocryphal Acts of the Apostles in Intertextual Perspectives*. Edited by Robert F. Stoops. Semeia 80. Atlanta: Scholars Press, 1997.

Rordorf, "Sonntagnachtgottesdienste." Rordorf, Willy. "Sonntagnachtgottesdienste der christlichen Frühzeit?" *ZNW* 68 (1977): 138–41.

Rordorf, "Theology." Rordorf, W. "The Theology of Rudolf Bultmann and Second-Century Gnosis." *NTS* 13 (4, 1967): 351–62.

Røsaeg, "Blinding." Røsaeg, Nils A. "The Blinding of Paul: Observations to a Theme." *SEÅ* 71 (2006): 159–85.

Roschke, "Healing." Roschke, Ronald W. "Healing in Luke, Madagascar, and Elsewhere." *CurTM* 33 (6, 2006): 459–71.

Rose, *Faith Healing.* Rose, Louis. *Faith Healing.* Edited by Bryan Morgan. Rev. ed. Baltimore and Harmondsworth, U.K.: Penguin, 1971.

Rose, "Hope." Rose, Mark. "New Hope for a Forgotten City." *Archaeology* 61 (2, 2008): 36–39.

Rose, "Music." Rose, Herbert Jennings. "Music in Worship." *OCD*³ 1012.

Rose, "Parthians." Rose, Charles Brian. "The Parthians in Augustan Rome." *AJA* 109 (1, 2005): 21–75.

Rose, "Pax." Rose, Herbert Jennings. "Pax." *OCD*³ 1129.

Rose, "Praxidikai." Rose, Herbert Jennings. "Praxidikai." *OCD*³ 1242.

Rose, "Return to Cyrene." Rose, Mark. "Return to Cyrene." *Archaeology* 58 (5, 2005): 16–23.

Rose, "Seneca." Rose, A. R. "Seneca and Suicide: The End of the *Hercules furens.*" *ClassO* 60 (1983): 109–11.

Rose and Dietrich, "Rhodes." Rose, Herbert Jennings, and B. C. Dietrich. "Rhodes, Cults and Myths." *OCD*³ 1316–17.

Rose and Hornblower, "Charybdis." Rose, Herbert Jennings, and Simon Hornblower. "Charybdis." *OCD*³ 319.

Rose and Hornblower, "Euhemerus." Rose, Herbert Jennings, and Simon Hornblower. "Euhemerus." *OCD*³ 567.

Rose and March, "Memnon." Rose, Herbert Jennings, and Jennifer R. March. "Memnon (1)." *OCD*³ 955.

Rose and North, "*Libri pontificales.*" Rose, Herbert Jennings, and J. A. North. "*Libri pontificales.*" *OCD*³ 855.

Rose et al., "Minos." Rose, Herbert Jennings, et al. "Minos." *OCD*³ 987.

Rose, Parke, and DeLaine, "Monotheism." Rose, Herbert Jennings, Herbert William Parke, and Janet DeLaine. "Monotheism." *OCD*³ 994.

Rose and Scheid, "Iustitia." Rose, Herbert Jennings, and John Scheid. "Iustitia." *OCD*³ 791.

Rösel, "Theologie." Rösel, Martin. "Theologie der griechischen Bibel zur Wiedergabe der Gottesaussagen im LXX-Pentateuch." *VT* 48 (1, 1998): 49–62.

Rösel, "Translation of Name." Rösel, Martin. "The Reading and Translation of the Divine Name in the Masoretic Tradition and the Greek Pentateuch." *JSOT* 31 (4, 2007): 411–28.

Roselaar, "Assidui." Roselaar, Saskia T. "*Assidui* or *proletarii*? Property in Roman Citizen Colonies and the *vacatio militiae.*" *Mnemosyne* 62 (4, 2009): 609–23.

Rosen, "Psychopathology." Rosen, George. "Psychopathology in the Social Process—Dance Frenzies, Demonic Possession, Revival Movements, and Similar So-Called Psychic Epidemics: An Interpretation." Pages 219–50 in *Possession and Exorcism.* Edited by Brian P. Levack. Articles on Witchcraft, Magic, and Demonology 9. New York: Garland, 1992.

Rosen, "Sophrosyne." Rosen, Stanley. "Sophrosyne and Selbstbewusstsein." *RevMet* 26 (1973): 617–42.

Rosenberg, "Messiah." Rosenberg, Roy A. "The Slain Messiah in the Old Testament." *ZAW* 99 (2, 1987): 259–61.

Rosenberg, "Moreh." Rosenberg, Roy A. "Who Is the Moreh hasSedeq?" *JAAR* 36 (2, 1968): 118–22.

Rosenberger, "*Nobiles.*" Rosenberger, Veit. "Republican *Nobiles*: Controlling the *Res Publica.*" Pages 292–303 in *A Companion to Roman Religion.* Edited by Jörg Rüpke. BCompAW. Oxford: Blackwell, 2011.

Rosenberger, "Omen." Rosenberger, Veit. "Omen." *BrillPauly* 10:122–23.

Rosenberger, "Rites." Rosenberger, Veit. "Expiatory Rites." *BrillPauly* 5:275–76.

Rosenberger, "Temple Economy." Rosenberger, Veit. "Temple Economy: Classical Antiquity." *BrillPauly* 14:263–65.

Rosenblatt, "Narration." Rosenblatt, Marie Eloise. "Recurring Narration as a Lukan Literary Convention in Acts: Paul's Jerusalem Speech in Acts 22:1–22." Pages 94–105 in *New Views on Luke and Acts.* Edited by Earl Richard. Collegeville, Minn.: Liturgical Press, 1990.

Rosenblatt, *Paul the Accused.* Rosenblatt, Marie-Eloise. *Paul the Accused: His Portrait in the Acts of the Apostles.* ZSNT. Collegeville, Minn.: Liturgical Press, 1994.

Rosenfeld, "Culture." Rosenfeld, Ben-Zion. "Inland Culture versus Coastal Culture in Roman Palestine—A Perspective of Jewish Society." *REJ* 169 (3–4, 2010): 349–73.

Rosenfeld, "Josephus and Coast." Rosenfeld, Ben-Zion. "Flavius Josephus and His Portrayal of the Coast (Paralia) of Contemporary Roman Palestine: Geography and Ideology." *JQR* 91 (1–2, 2000): 143–83.

Rosenfeld, "M'mdw." Rosenfeld, Ben-Zion. "M'mdw wpw'lw sl rbn gmly'l lpny hlyktw lybnh." *Zion* 55 (2, 1990): 151–69.

Rosenfeld, "Sage and Temple." Rosenfeld, Ben-Zion. "Sage and Temple in Rabbinic Thought after the Destruction of the Second Temple." *JSJ* 28 (4, 1997): 437–64.

Rosenfeld, "Simeon b. Yohai." Rosenfeld, Ben-Zion. "R. Simeon b. Yohai—Wonder Worker and Magician, Scholar, *saddiq*, and Hasid." *REJ* 158 (3–4, 1999): 349–84.

Rosenfeld and Menirav, "Synagogue." Rosenfeld, Ben-Zion, and Joseph Menirav. "The Ancient Synagogue as an Economic Center." *JNES* 58 (4, 1999): 259–76.

Rosenmeyer, *Fictions.* Rosenmeyer, Patricia A. *Ancient Epistolary Fictions: The Letter in Greek Literature.* Cambridge: Cambridge University Press, 2001.

Rosenstein, "Sorting Out the Lot." Rosenstein, Nathan. "Sorting Out the Lot in Republican Rome." *AJP* 116 (1, 1995): 43–75.

Rosen-Zvi, "Bilhah." Rosen-Zvi, Ishay. "Bilhah the Temptress: The Testament of Reuben and 'The Birth of Sexuality.'" *JQR* 96 (1, 2006): 65–94.

Rosen-Zvi, "Yeser." Rosen-Zvi, Ishay. "Ysr hr' bsprwt h'mwr'yt bhynh mhds." *Tarbiz* 77 (1, 2007): 71–107.

Roshwald, "Ben Zoma." Roshwald, Mordecai. "The Teaching of Ben Zoma." *Judaism* 42 (1, 1993): 14–28.

Rosivach, "*Anus.*" Rosivach, Vincent. "*Anus*: Some Older Women in Latin Literature." *CW* 88 (2, 1994): 107–17.

Rosner, "Biblical History." Rosner, Brian S. "Acts and Biblical History." Pages 65–82 in *The Book of Acts in Its Ancient Literary Setting.* Edited by Bruce W. Winter and Andrew D. Clark. Vol. 1 of *The Book of Acts in Its First Century Setting.* Edited by Bruce W. Winter. Grand Rapids: Eerdmans; Carlisle, U.K.: Paternoster, 1993.

Rosner, *Ethics.* Rosner, Brian S. *Paul, Scripture, and Ethics: A Study of 1 Corinthians 5–7.* Leiden: Brill, 1994. Repr., Grand Rapids: Baker, 1999.

Rosner, "Judges." Rosner, Brian S. "Moses Appointing Judges: An Antecedent to 1 Cor 6,1–6?" *ZNW* 82 (3–4, 1991): 275–78.

Rosner, *Law.* Rosner, Brian S. *Paul and the Law: Keeping the Commandments of God.* New Studies in Biblical Theology 31. Downers Grove, Ill.: InterVarsity, 2013.

Rosner, "Progress." Rosner, Brian S. "The Progress of the Word." Pages 215–34 in *Witness to the Gospel: The Theology of Acts.* Edited by I. Howard Marshall and David Peterson. Grand Rapids: Eerdmans, 1998.

Rosny, *Healers.* Rosny, Eric de. *Healers in the Night.* Translated by Robert R. Barr. Maryknoll, N.Y.: Orbis, 1985.

Rosól, "Etymology." Rosól, Rafal. "The Etymology of Greek συβάκχος." *Mnemosyne* 63 (3, 2010): 445–49.

Ross, "Extra Words in 18:21." Ross, J. M. "The Extra Words in Acts 18:21." *NovT* 34 (3, 1992): 247–49.

Ross, "Floating Words." Ross, J. M. "Floating Words: Their Significance for Textual Criticism." *NTS* 38 (1, 1992): 153–56.

Ross, "Miracle." Ross, John P. "Some Notes on Miracle in the Old Testament." Pages 43–60 in *Miracles: Cambridge Studies in Their Philosophy and History*. Edited by C. F. D. Moule. London: A. R. Mowbray; New York: Morehouse-Barlow, 1965.

Ross, "Prophecy." Ross, James F. "Prophecy in Hamath, Israel, and Mari." *HTR* 63 (Jan. 1970): 1–28.

Ross, "Revelation." Ross, Jacob Joshua. "Revelation: In Talmudic Literature." *EncJud* 14:119–22.

Ross, "Spelling of Jerusalem." Ross, J. M. "The Spelling of Jerusalem in Acts." *NTS* 38 (3, 1992): 474–76.

Ross, "Thessalonians." Ross, J. M. "1 Thessalonians 3.13." *BTr* 26 (4, 1975): 444.

Rossano, "Note archeologiche." Rossano, Piero. "Note archeologiche sulla antica Tessalonica." *RivB* 6 (3, 1958): 242–47.

Rossum, "Pentecost." Rossum, Joost van. "The 'Johannine Pentecost': John 20:22 in Modern Exegesis and in Orthodox Theology." *SVTQ* 35 (2–3, 1991): 149–67.

Rost, "Aposteldekret." Rost, Bettina. "Das Aposteldekret im Verhältnis zur Mosetora." Pages 563–604 in *Die Apostelgeschichte im Kontext antiker und frühchristlicher Historiographie*. Edited by Jörg Frey, Clare K. Rothschild, and Jens Schröter, with Bettina Rost. BZNWK 162. Berlin: de Gruyter, 2009.

Rost, *Judaism*. Rost, Leonhard. *Judaism outside the Hebrew Canon: An Introduction to the Documents*. Translated by David E. Green. Nashville: Abingdon, 1976.

Roth, *Blind, Lame, Poor*. Roth, S. John. *The Blind, the Lame, and the Poor: Character Types in Luke-Acts*. JSNTSup 144. Sheffield, U.K.: Sheffield Academic, 1997.

Roth, *Encyclopedia*. Roth, Cecil, ed. *The Concise Jewish Encyclopedia*. New York: New American Library, 1980.

Roth, "Food." Roth, Ulrike. "Food, Status, and the *peculium* of Agricultural Slaves." *JRA* 18 (2005): 278–92.

Roth, "Legion." Roth, Jonathan. "The Size and Organization of the Imperial Roman Legion." *Historia* 43 (3, 1994): 346–62.

Roth, *Looms*. Roth, Henry Ling. *Ancient Egyptian and Greek Looms*. Bankfield Museum Notes, 2nd ser., 2. Halifax, U.K.: F. King and Sons, 1913.

Roth, "Marcion's Gospel." Roth, Dieter T. "Marcion's Gospel and Luke: The History

of Research in Current Debate." *JBL* 127 (3, 2008): 513–27.

Roth, "Pray-er." Roth, S. John. "Jesus the Pray-er." *CurTM* 33 (6, 2006): 488–500.

Roth, "Reference." Roth, Cecil. "A Talmudic Reference to the Qumran Sect?" *RevQ* 2 (2, 1960): 261–65.

Roth, "Subject Matter of Exegesis." Roth, Cecil. "The Subject Matter of Qumran Exegesis." *VT* 10 (1, 1960): 51–68.

Roth, "Teacher." Roth, Cecil. "The Teacher of Righteousness." *Listener* 57 (June 27, 1957): 1037–41.

Rothaus, *Corinth*. Rothaus, Richard M. *Corinth—The First City of Greece: An Urban History of Late Antique Cult and Religion*. RGRW 139. Leiden: Brill, 2000.

Rothschild, "Irony." Rothschild, Clare K. "Irony and Truth: The Value of *De Historia Conscribenda* for Understanding Hellenistic and Early Roman Period Historiographical Method." Pages 277–91 in *Die Apostelgeschichte im Kontext antiker und frühchristlicher Historiographie*. Edited by Jörg Frey, Clare K. Rothschild, and Jens Schröter, with Bettina Rost. BZNWK 162. Berlin: de Gruyter, 2009.

Rothschild, *Paul in Athens*. Rothschild, Clare K. *Paul in Athens: The Popular Religious Context of Acts 17*. WUNT 341. Tübingen: Mohr Siebeck, 2014.

Rothschild, *Rhetoric of History*. Rothschild, Clare K. *Luke-Acts and the Rhetoric of History: An Investigation of Early Christian Historiography*. WUNT 2.175. Tübingen: Mohr Siebeck, 2004.

Rothstein, "Pedagogue." Rothstein, David. "Joseph as Pedagogue: Biblical Precedents for the Depiction of Joseph in *Aramaic Levi* (4Q213)." *JSP* 14 (3, 2005): 223–29.

Rothstein, "Testimony." Rothstein, David. "Women's Testimony at Qumran: The Biblical and Second Temple Evidence." *RevQ* 21 (84, 2004): 597–614.

Rountree, "Genre." Rountree, Clarke. "The (Almost) Blameless Genre of Classical Greek Epideictic." *Rhetorica* 19 (3, 2001): 293–305.

Rouse, "Introduction." Rouse, W. H. D. Introduction. Pages vii–xix in Lucretius, *De rerum natura*. Translated by W. H. D. Rouse. 3rd ed. LCL. Cambridge, Mass.: Harvard University Press, 1937.

Rousseau, "Asceticism." Rousseau, Philip. "Asceticism." *OCD*³ 186–87.

Rousseau, "Conversion." Rousseau, Philip. "Conversion." *OCD*³ 386–87.

Rousselle, "Cults." Rousselle, Robert. "Healing Cults in Antiquity: The Dream Cures of Asclepius of Epidaurus." *JPsycHist* 12 (3, 1985): 339–52.

Rousselle, "Snake-Handling." Rousselle, Robert. "Comparative Psychohistory: Snake-Handling in Hellenistic Greece and the American South." *JPsycHist* 11 (4, 1984): 477–89.

Roux, "Style and Text." Roux, L. V. le. "Style and Text of Acts 4:25 (a)." *Neot* 25 (1, 1991): 29–32.

Rovner, "Corrigenda." Rovner, Jay. "An Early Passover Haggadah: Corrigenda." *JQR* 91 (3–4, 2001): 429.

Rovner, "Haggadah." Rovner, Jay. "An Early Passover Haggadah according to the Palestinian Rite." *JQR* 90 (3–4, 2000): 337–96.

Rowe, "Authority." Rowe, C. Kavin. "Authority and Community: Lukan *dominium* in Acts." Pages 96–108 in *Acts and Ethics*. Edited by Thomas E. Phillips. NTMon 9. Sheffield, U.K.: Sheffield Phoenix, 2005.

Rowe, "Continuity." Rowe, C. Kavin. "Acts 2.36 and the Continuity of Lukan Christology." *NTS* 53 (1, 2007): 37–56.

Rowe, "Cult." Rowe, C. Kavin. "Luke-Acts and the Imperial Cult: A Way through the Conundrum?" *JSNT* 27 (3, 2005): 297–300.

Rowe, "Grammar." Rowe, C. Kavin. "The Grammar of Life: The Areopagus Speech and Pagan Tradition." *NTS* 57 (1, Jan. 2011): 31–50.

Rowe, "Hermeneutics." Rowe, C. Kavin. "History, Hermeneutics, and the Unity of Luke-Acts." *JSNT* 28 (2, 2005): 131–57.

Rowe, "Reception History." Rowe, C. Kavin. "Literary Unity and Reception History: Reading Luke-Acts as Luke and Acts." *JSNT* 29 (4, 2007): 449–57.

Rowe, "Style." Rowe, Galen O. "Style." Pages 121–57 in *Handbook of Classical Rhetoric in the Hellenistic Period, 330 B.C.–A.D. 400*. Edited by Stanley E. Porter. Leiden: Brill, 1997.

Rowe, "Trinity." Rowe, C. Kavin. "Luke and the Trinity: An Essay in Ecclesial Biblical Theology." *SJT* 56 (1, 2003): 1–26.

Rowe, *World*. Rowe, C. Kavin. *World Upside Down: Reading Acts in the Graeco-Roman Age*. New York: Oxford University Press, 2009.

Rowe and Hays, "Commentary." Rowe, C. Kavin, and Richard B. Hays. "What Is a Theological Commentary?" *ProEccl* 16 (1, 2007): 26–32.

Rowland, "Paul." Rowland, Christopher C. "Paul, St." *OCD*³ 1128.

Rowland, "Visions." Rowland, Christopher C. "Apocalyptic Visions and the Exaltation of Christ in the Letter to the Colossians." *JSNT* 19 (1983): 73–83.

Rowland, "Visions in Apocalyptic Literature." Rowland, Christopher C. "The

Visions of God in Apocalyptic Literature." *JSJ* 10 (2, 1979): 137–54.

Rowlandson and Takahashi, "Marriage." Rowlandson, Jane, and Ryosuke Takahashi. "Brother-Sister Marriage and Inheritance Strategies in Greco-Roman Egypt." *JRS* 99 (2009): 104–39.

Rowley, "4QpNahum." Rowley, H. H. "4QpNahum and the Teacher of Righteousness." *JBL* 75 (3, 1956): 188–93.

Rowley, "Baptism." Rowley, H. H. "Jewish Proselyte Baptism and the Baptism of John." *HUCA* 15 (1940): 313–34.

Rowley, "Kittim." Rowley, H. H. "The Kittim and the Dead Sea Scrolls." *PEQ* 88 (1956): 92–109.

Roxburgh, "Impact." Roxburgh, Kenneth. "The Impact of the Welsh Revival on Baptist Churches in Scotland." Pages 185–207 in *Revival, Renewal, and the Holy Spirit*. Edited by Dyfed Wyn Roberts. SEHT. Eugene, Ore.: Wipf & Stock, 2009.

Royer, "God Who Surprises." Royer, L. "The God Who Surprises." *BibT* 33 (5, 1995): 298–302.

Royse, "Heraclitus." Royse, James R. "Heraclitus B 118 in Philo of Alexandria." *SPhilA* 9 (1997): 211–16.

Royse, "Papyrus." Royse, James R. "The Oxyrhynchus Papyrus of Philo." *BASP* 17 (3–4, 1980): 155–65.

Royse, "Philo's Division." Royse, James R. "Philo's Division of His Works into Books." *SPhilA* 13 (2001): 59–85.

Roysircar-Sodowsky, "Acculturation." Roysircar-Sodowsky, Gargi. "Counseling and Psychotherapy for Acculturation and Ethnic Identity Concerns with Immigrant and International Students." Pages 248–68 in *Practicing Multiculturalism: Affirming Diversity in Counseling and Psychology*. Boston: Allyn & Bacon, 2004.

Roysircar-Sodowsky and Lai, "Variables." Roysircar-Sodowsky, Gargi, and Edward Wai Ming Lai. "Asian Immigrant Variables and Structural Models of Cross-cultural Distress." Pages 211–34 in *International Migration and Family Change: The Experience of U.S. Immigrants*. Edited by Alan Booth, Ann C. Crouter, and Nancy Landale. Mahwah, N.J.: Lawrence Erlbaum, 1997.

Roysircar-Sodowsky, Lai, and Plake, "Effects." Roysircar-Sodowsky, Gargi, Edward Wai Ming Lai, and Barbara S. Plake. "Moderating Effects of Socio-cultural Variables on Acculturation Attitudes of Hispanics and Asian Americans." *JCouns Dev* 70 (1991): 194–204.

Roysircar-Sodowsky and Maestas, "Acculturation." Roysircar-Sodowsky, Gargi, and Michael V. Maestas. "Acculturation, Ethnic Identity, and Acculturative Stress: Theory, Research, and Measurement."

Pages 131–72 in *Handbook of Cross-cultural and Multicultural Assessment*. Edited by R. H. Dana. Hillsdale, N.J.: Erlbaum, 2000.

Roysircar-Sodowsky and Maestas, "Assessment." Roysircar-Sodowsky, Gargi, and Michael V. Maestas. "Assessment of Acculturation and Cultural Variables." Pages 77–94 in *Asian American Mental Health: Assessment Theories and Methods*. Dordrecht, Neth.: Kluwer Academic, 2002.

Roysircar-Sodowsky and Plake, "Differences." Roysircar-Sodowsky, Gargi, and Barbara S. Plake. "A Study of Acculturation Differences among International People and Suggestions for Sensitivity to Within-Group Differences." *JCounsDev* 71 (1992): 53–59.

Rubenstein, "Gittin." Rubenstein, Jeffrey L. "Bavli Gittin 55b–56b: An Aggadic Narrative in Its Halakhic Context." *HS* 38 (1997): 21–45.

Rubenstein, *Paul*. Rubenstein, Richard L. *My Brother Paul*. New York: Harper & Row, 1972.

Rubincam, "Numbers." Rubincam, Catherine. "Numbers in Greek Poetry and Historiography: Quantifying Fehling." *CQ* 53 (2, 2003): 448–63.

Ruble, "Tongues." Ruble, R. L. "A Scriptural Evaluation of Tongues in Contemporary Theology." ThD diss., Dallas Theological Seminary, 1964.

Ruck, "Mystery." Ruck, Carl A. P. "Solving the Eleusinian Mystery." Pages 35–50 in *The Road to Eleusis: Unveiling the Secret of the Mysteries*. By Robert Gordon Wasson, Albert Hofmann, and Carl A. P. Ruck. New York: Harcourt Brace Jovanovich, 1978.

Rudhardt, "Attitude des Grecs." Rudhardt, Jean. "De l'attitude des Grecs à l'égard des religions étrangères." *RHR* 209 (3, 1992): 219–38.

Rudolph, "Jew to Jews." Rudolph, David Jacob. "A Jew to the Jews: Jewish Contours of Pauline Flexibility in 1 Corinthians 9:19–23." PhD diss., Cambridge University, 2006.

Rudolph and Willitts, *Introduction*. Rudolph, David, and Joel Willitts, eds. *Introduction to Messianic Judaism: Its Ecclesial Context and Biblical Foundations*. Grand Rapids: Zondervan, 2013.

Ruffing, "Plough." Ruffing, Kai. "Plough. II. Classical Antiquity." *BrillPauly* 11:406–7.

Ruffing, "Sheep." Ruffing, Kai. "Sheep: Rome." *BrillPauly* 13:381–84.

Ruffle, *Egyptians*. Ruffle, John. *The Egyptians: An Introduction to Egyptian Archaeology*. Ithaca, N.Y.: Cornell University Press, 1977.

Rüger, "ΝΑΖΑΡΕΘ." Rüger, Hans Peter. "ΝΑΖΑΡΕΘ/ΝΑΖΑΡΑ ΝΑΖΑΡΗΝΟΣ/ΝΑΖΩΡΑΙΟΣ." *ZNW* 72 (3–4, 1981): 257–63.

Rumph, *Signs*. Rumph, Jane. *Signs and Wonders in America Today: Amazing Accounts of God's Power*. Ann Arbor: Servant, 2003.

Rundin, "Pozo Moro." Rundin, John S. "Pozo Moro, Child Sacrifice, and the Greek Legendary Tradition." *JBL* 123 (3, 2004): 425–47.

Runesson, "Oldest Building." Runesson, Anders. "The Oldest Original Synagogue Building in the Diaspora: A Response to L. Michael White." *HTR* 92 (4, 1999): 409–33.

Runesson, "Synagogue." Runesson, Anders. "A Monumental Synagogue from the First Century: The Case of Ostia." *JSJ* 33 (2, 2002): 171–220.

Runia, "Atheists." Runia, David T. "Atheists in Aëtius: Text, Translation and Comments on *De placitis* 1.7.1–10." *Mnemosyne* 49 (5, 1996): 542–76.

Runia, "City." Runia, David T. "The Idea and the Reality of the City in the Thought of Philo of Alexandria." *JHI* 61 (3, 2000): 361–79.

Runia, "*Hairesis*-Model." Runia, David T. "Philo of Alexandria and the Greek *hairesis*-Model." *VC* 53 (2, 1999): 117–47.

Runia, "Middle Platonist?" Runia, David T. "Was Philo a Middle Platonist? A Difficult Question Revisited." *SPhilA* 5 (1993): 112–40.

Runnalls, "Ethiopian Campaign." Runnalls, Donna. "Moses' Ethiopian Campaign." *JSJ* 14 (2, 1983): 135–56.

Runnalls, "Rhetoric." Runnalls, Donna R. "The Rhetoric of Josephus." Pages 737–54 in *Handbook of Classical Rhetoric in the Hellenistic Period, 330 B.C.–A.D. 400*. Edited by Stanley E. Porter. Leiden: Brill, 1997.

Rüpke, "Commentarii." Rüpke, Jörg. "Commentarii." *BrillPauly* 3:628–29.

Rüpke, "Ephemeris." Rüpke, Jörg. "Ephemeris." *BrillPauly* 4:1022.

Rüpke, "Kult." Rüpke, Jörg. "Kult jenseits der Polisreligion: Polemiken und Perspektiven." *JAC* 47 (2004): 5–15.

Rüpke, "Religion." Rüpke, Jörg. "Roman Religion—Religions of Rome." Pages 1–9 in *A Companion to Roman Religion*. Edited by Jörg Rüpke. BCompAW. Oxford: Blackwell, 2011.

Rüpke, *Religion*. Rüpke, Jörg. *Religion: Antiquity and Its Legacy*. Ancients and Moderns. New York: Oxford University Press, 2013.

Rüpke, "Triumphator." Rüpke, Jörg. "Triumphator and Ancestor Rituals between Symbolic Anthropology and Magic." *Numen* 53 (3, 2006): 251–89.

Rupp, "Salamis." Rupp, David W. "Salamis." *OEANE* 4:456–58.

Rupprecht, "Attitudes." Rupprecht, Arthur W. "Attitudes on Slavery among the Church Fathers." Pages 261–77 in *New Dimensions in New Testament Study*. Edited by Richard N. Longenecker and Merrill C. Tenney. Grand Rapids: Zondervan, 1974.

Rusam, "Πίστις." Rusam, Dietrich. "Was versteht Paulus unter der πίστις ('Ιησοῦ Χριστοῦ (Röm 3,22.26; Gal 2,16.20; 3,22; Phil 3,9)?" *PzB* 11 (1, 2002): 47–70.

Ruscillo, "Gluttony." Ruscillo, Deborah. "When Gluttony Ruled!" *Archaeology* 54 (6, 2001): 20–25.

Rusecki, "Kryteria." Rusecki, Marian. "Kryteria historyczności cudów Jezusa." *RocT* 54 (6, 2007): 317–34.

Russell, "Anointing." Russell, Walt. "The Anointing with the Holy Spirit in Luke-Acts." *TJ* 7 (1, 1986): 47–63.

Russell, *Apocalyptic*. Russell, D. S. *The Method and Message of Jewish Apocalyptic*. Philadelphia: Westminster, 1964.

Russell, "Believed Philip Preaching." Russell, E. A. " 'They Believed Philip Preaching' (Acts 8.12)." *IBS* 1 (3, 1979): 169–76.

Russell, *Declamation*. Russell, Donald Andrew Frank Moore. *Greek Declamation*. Cambridge University Press, 1983.

Russell, "Emasculation." Russell, Brigette Ford. "The Emasculation of Antony: The Construction of Gender in Plutarch's *Life of Antony*." *Helios* 25 (2, 1998): 121–37.

Russell, "Epicedion." Russell, Donald Andrew Frank Moore. "Epicedion." *OCD*³ 531–32.

Russell, "*Propemptikon*." Russell, Donald Andrew Frank Moore. "*Propemptikon*." *OCD*³ 1258.

Russell, "Rhetoric, Greek." Russell, Donald Andrew Frank Moore. "Rhetoric, Greek." *OCD*³ 1312–14.

Russell, "Virtue." Russell, Daniel C. "Virtue as 'Likeness to God' in Plato and Seneca." *JHistPhil* 42 (3, 2004): 241–60.

Russell and Konstan, *Heraclitus*. Russell, Donald A., and David Konstan, eds. and trans. *Heraclitus: Homeric Problems*. SBLWGRW 14. Atlanta: SBL, 2005.

Rusten, "*Ekphrasis*." Rusten, Jeffrey Stuart. "*Ekphrasis*." *OCD*³ 515.

Rusten, "Paradoxographers." Rusten, Jeffrey Stuart. "Paradoxographers." *OCD*³ 1112.

Rutenber, *Doctrine*. Rutenber, Culbert Gerow. *The Doctrine of the Imitation of God in Plato*. New York: King's Crown, Columbia University Press, 1946.

Rutgers, "Evidence." Rutgers, Leonard Victor. "Archaeological Evidence for the Interaction of Jews and Non-Jews in Late Antiquity." *AJA* 96 (1, 1992): 101–18.

Rutgers, "Interaction." Rutgers, Leonard Victor. "Interaction and Its Limits: Some Notes on the Jews of Sicily in Late Antiquity." *ZPE* 115 (1997): 245–56.

Rutgers, "Policy." Rutgers, Leonard Victor. "Roman Policy toward the Jews: Expulsions from the City of Rome during the First Century C.E." Pages 93–116 in *Judaism and Christianity in First-Century Rome*. Edited by Karl P. Donfried and Peter Richardson. Grand Rapids: Eerdmans, 1998.

Rutherford, "*Boukoloi*." Rutherford, Ian. "The Genealogy of the *boukoloi*: How Greek Literature Appropriated an Egyptian Narrative-Motif." *JHS* 120 (2000): 106–21.

Rutherford, "Silence." Rutherford, R. B. "Silence." *OCD*³ 1406–7.

Rutherford, "Tragedy." Rutherford, Richard. "Tragedy and History." Pages 504–14 in *A Companion to Greek and Roman Historiography*. Edited by John Marincola. 2 vols. Oxford: Blackwell, 2007.

Ruthven, *Cessation*. Ruthven, Jon. *On the Cessation of the Charismata: The Protestant Polemic on Postbiblical Miracles*. JPTSup 3. Sheffield, U.K.: Sheffield Academic, 1993.

Ruthven, "Covenant." Ruthven, Jon. "'This Is My Covenant with Them': Isaiah 59.19–21 as the Programmatic Prophecy of the New Covenant in the Acts of the Apostles." *JPT* 17 (1, 2008): 32–47; (2, 2008): 219–37.

Ruthven, "Miracle." Ruthven, Jon. "Miracle." *GDT* 546–50.

Rutledge, "*Delatores*." Rutledge, Steven H. "*Delatores* and the Tradition of Violence in Roman Oratory." *AJP* 120 (4, 1999): 555–73.

Rutledge, "Oratory." Rutledge, Steven H. "Oratory and Politics in the Empire." Pages 108–21 in *A Companion to Roman Rhetoric*. Edited by William Dominik and Jon Hall. Oxford: Blackwell, 2007.

Rutledge, "Philhellenism." Rutledge, Steven H. "Tiberius' Philhellenism." *CW* 101 (4, 2008): 453–67.

Rutschowscaya et al., "Textiles." Rutschowscaya, Marie-Hélène, et al. "Textiles, Coptic." *CE* 7:2210–30.

Rutz, *Megashift*. Rutz, James. *Megashift: Igniting Spiritual Power*. Colorado Springs, Colo.: Empowerment, 2005.

Ruzer, "Unhappy." Ruzer, Serge. "Who Is Unhappy with the Davidic Messiah? Notes on Biblical Exegesis in 4Q161, 4Q174, and the Book of Acts." *CNS* 24 (2, 2003): 229–55.

Ryan, "Lydia." Ryan, Rosalie. "Lydia, a Dealer in Purple Goods." *BibT* 22 (5, 1984): 285–89.

Rycroft, *Innocence*. Rycroft, Charles. *The Innocence of Dreams*. London: Hogarth; New York: Pantheon, 1979.

Saarinen, "Luther." Saarinen, Risto. "How Luther Got Paul Right." *Dial* 46 (2, 2007): 170–73.

Sabbe, "Saying." Sabbe, M. "The Son of Man Saying in Acts 7,56." Pages 241–79 in *Les Actes des apôtres: Traditions, rédaction, théologie*. Edited by Jacob Kremer. BETL 48. Gembloux, Belg.: J. Duculot; Leuven: Leuven University Press, 1979.

Sabourin, *Miracles*. Sabourin, Leopold. *The Divine Miracles Discussed and Defended*. Rome: Officium Libri Catholici, 1977.

Sabugal, "1QRegla." Sabugal, S. "1QRegla de la comunidad IX, 11: Dos ungidos, un mesías." *RevQ* 8 (3, 1974): 417–23.

Sabugal, "Areópago." Sabugal, S. "El kerygma de Pablo en el Areópago ateniense (Act 17, 22–31): Análisis histórico-tradicional." *RevAg* 31 (95, 1990): 505–34.

Sabugal, "Curación." Sabugal, S. "La curación del 'cojo de nacimiento' por Pedro (Act 3,1–11): Análisis histórico-tradicional." *RevAg* 32 (98, 1991): 595–613.

Sabugal, "Dios cumplió." Sabugal, S. "'¡Dios cumplió la promesa' patriarcal 'resucitando a Jesús!' (Act 13, 16–41): Análisis redaccional e histórico-tradicional." *EstAg* 24 (3, 1989): 549–83.

Sabugal, "Exégesis de Aristóbulo." Sabugal, S. "La exégesis bíblica de Aristóbulo y del seudo-Aristeas." *RevAgEsp* 20 (61–62, 1979): 195–202.

Sabugal, "Kérygmas de Pedro." Sabugal, S. "Los kérygmas de Pedro ante el Sanedrín judaico (Act 4, 8–12; 5, 29–32): Análisis histórico-tradicional." *EstAg* 25 (1, 1990): 3–14.

Sacks, "Historiography." Sacks, Kenneth S. "Historiography, Hellenistic." *OCD*³ 715–16.

Sacks, "Mnaseas." Sacks, Kenneth S. "Mnaseas." *OCD*³ 992.

Saddington, "Note." Saddington, Denis. "A Note on the Number of Troops Stationed in the Antonia in Jerusalem." *ExpT* 116 (12, 2005): 431.

Saddington, "Rhetoric." Saddington, Denis. "A Note on the Rhetoric of Four Speeches in Josephus." *JJS* 58 (2, 2007): 228–35.

Saffrey, "Aphrodite à Corinthe." Saffrey, Henri Dominique. "Aphrodite à Corinthe: Réflexions sur une idée reçue." *RB* 92 (3, 1985): 359–74.

Saffrey, "Juif." Saffrey, Henri Dominique. "Paul (Saül), un juif de la diaspora." *RSPT* 91 (2, 2007): 313–21.

Safrai, "Abraham und Sara." Safrai, Chana. "Abraham und Sara—Spender des Lebens." *EvT* 62 (5, 2002): 348–62.

Safrai, "Description in Works." Safrai, Zeev. "The Description of the Land of Israel in Josephus' Works." Pages 295–324 in *Josephus, the Bible, and History*. Edited by Louis H. Feldman and Gohei Hata. Detroit: Wayne State University Press, 1989.

Safrai, "Education." Safrai, Shemuel. "Education and the Study of the Torah." *JPFC* 945–70.

Safrai, "Hebrew Sources." Safrai, Shemuel. "Hebrew and Aramaic Sources." *JPFC* 1–18.

Safrai, "Hkl." Safrai, Shemuel, and C. Safrai, "Hkl 'wlyn lmnyyn sb'h (All Are Invited to Read)." *Tarbiz* 66 (3, 1997): 395–401.

Safrai, "Home." Safrai, Shemuel. "Home and Family." *JPFC* 728–92.

Safrai, "Insulting High Priest." Safrai, Shemuel. "Insulting God's High Priest." *JerPersp* 55 (1999): 34–36.

Safrai, "Literary Languages." Safrai, Shemuel. "Literary Languages in the Time of Jesus." *JerPersp* 4 (2, 1991): 3–9.

Safrai, "Pilgrimage to Jerusalem." Safrai, Shemuel. "Pilgrimage to Jerusalem at the End of the Second Temple Period." Pages 12–21 in *Studies in the Jewish Background of the New Testament*. Edited by O. Michel et al. Assen, Neth.: Van Gorcum, 1969.

Safrai, "Place of Women." Safrai, Shemuel. "The Place of Women in First-Century Synagogues." *JerPersp* 40 (1993): 3–6, 14.

Safrai, "Relations." Safrai, Shemuel. "Relations between the Diaspora and the Land of Israel." *JPFC* 184–215.

Safrai, "Religion." Safrai, Shemuel. "Religion in Everyday Life." *JPFC* 793–833.

Safrai, "Segregated." Safrai, Shemuel. "Were Women Segregated in the Ancient Synagogue?" *JerPersp* 52 (1997): 24–36.

Safrai, "Self-Government." Safrai, Shemuel. "Jewish Self-Government." *JPFC* 377–419.

Safrai, "Spoken Languages." Safrai, Shemuel. "Spoken Languages in the Time of Jesus." *JerPersp* 4 (1, 1991): 3–8, 13.

Safrai, "Synagogue." Safrai, Shemuel. "The Synagogue." *JPFC* 908–44.

Safrai, "Temple." Safrai, Shemuel. "The Temple." *JPFC* 865–907.

Sagona, *Archaeology*. Sagona, Claudia. *The Archaeology of Punic Malta*. Ancient Near Eastern Studies Supplement 9. Leuven: Peeters, 2002.

Sagona, Gregory, and Bugeja, *Antiquities*. Sagona, Claudia, Isabelle Vella Gregory, and Anton Bugeja. *Punic Antiquities of Malta and Other Ancient Artefacts Held in Ecclesiastic and Private Collections*. Ancient Near Eastern Studies Supplement 18. Leuven: Peeters, 2003–6.

Sahin, *Inschriften von Perge*. Sahin, Sencer, ed. *Die Inschriften von Perge*. IGSK 54. Bonn: Rudolf Hablet, 1999–.

Saïd, "City." Saïd, Suzanne. "The City in the Greek Novel." Pages 216–36 in *The Search for the Ancient Novel*. Edited by James Tatum. Baltimore: Johns Hopkins University Press, 1994.

Saïd, "Myth." Saïd, Suzanne. "Myth and Historiography." Pages 76–88 in *A Companion to Greek and Roman Historiography*. Edited by John Marincola. 2 vols. Oxford: Blackwell, 2007.

Salamone, "Bori." Salamone, Frank. "The Bori and I: Reflections of a Mature Anthropologist." *AnthHum* 20 (1995): 15–19.

Saldarini, *Community*. Saldarini, Anthony J. *Matthew's Christian-Jewish Community*. CSHJ. Chicago: University of Chicago Press, 1994.

Saldarini, "Conflict." Saldarini, Anthony J. "The Gospel of Matthew and Jewish-Christian Conflict." Pages 38–61 in *Social History of the Matthean Community: Cross-disciplinary Approaches*. Edited by David L. Balch. Minneapolis: Fortress, 1991.

Saldarini, "Deathbed Scenes." Saldarini, Anthony J. "Last Words and Deathbed Scenes in Rabbinic Literature." *JQR* 68 (1, 1977): 28–45.

Salisbury, "Possession." Salisbury, R. F. "Possession among the Siane (New Guinea)." *TranscPsycRR* 3 (1966): 108–16.

Sallaberger and Felber, "Purification." Sallaberger, Walther, and Heinz Felber. "Purification. B. Religious. I. Ancient Orient and Egypt." *BrillPauly* 12:225–26.

Sallares, "Disease." Sallares, J. Robert. "Disease." *OCD*³ 486.

Sallares, "Grain." Sallares, Robert. "Grain: Graeco-Roman Antiquity." *BrillPauly* 5:966–74.

Sallares, "Grain Trade." Sallares, Robert. "Grain Trade, Grain Import." *BrillPauly* 5:976–81.

Sallares, "Infanticide." Sallares, J. Robert. "Infanticide." *OCD*³ 757.

Sallares, "Meals." Sallares, J. Robert. "Meals." *OCD*³ 942.

Sallares, "Plague." Sallares, J. Robert. "Plague." *OCD*³ 1188.

Saller, "Age." Saller, Richard P. "Men's Age at Marriage and Its Consequences in the Roman Family." *CP* 82 (1, 1987): 21–34.

Saller, *Mater familias*. Saller, Richard P. "*Pater familias, mater familias*, and the Gendered Semantics of the Roman Household." *CP* 94 (2, 1999): 182–97.

Saller, *Patronage*. Saller, Richard P. *Personal Patronage under the Early Empire*. Cambridge: Cambridge University Press, 1982.

Saller, "Poverty." Saller, Richard P. "Poverty, Honor, and Obligation in Imperial Rome." *Criterion* 37 (2, 1998): 12–20.

Saller, "Women." Saller, Richard P. "Women, Slaves, and the Economy of the Roman Household." Pages 185–204 in *Early Christian Families in Context: An Interdisciplinary Dialogue*. Edited by David L. Balch and Carolyn Osiek. Grand Rapids and Cambridge: Eerdmans, 2003.

Saller and Shaw, "Tombstones." Saller, Richard P., and Brent D. Shaw. "Tombstones and Roman Family Relations in the Principate: Civilians, Soldiers, and Slaves." *JRS* 74 (1984): 124–56.

Salles, "Diversité." Salles, Catherine. "La diversité de la situation des femmes dans l'empire romain aux 1er et 2e siècles." *FoiVie* 88 (5, 1989): 43–48.

Salles, "Ἐκπύρωσις." Salles, Ricardo. "Ἐκπύρωσις and the Goodness of God in Cleanthes." *Phronesis* 50 (1, 2005): 56–78.

Salles, "Pythies et sibylles." Salles, Catherine. "Pythies et sibylles contre augures et haruspices: La divination en Grèce et à Rome." *FoiVie* 98 (4, 1999): 63–74.

Salles, "Sarepta." Salles, Jean-François. "Sarepta." *OCD*³ 1357.

Salles, "Société interculturelle." Salles, Catherine. "Le monde gréco-romain du 1er siècle: Une société interculturelle?" *Supplément* 156 (1986): 15–28.

Sallmann, "Technical Literature." Sallmann, Klaus. "Technical Literature." *BrillPauly* 14:195–201.

Salmeier, *Restoring*. Salmeier, Michael A. *Restoring the Kingdom: The Role of God as the "Ordainer of Times and Seasons" in the Acts of the Apostles*. PrTMS 165. Eugene, Ore.: Pickwick, 2011.

Salmon, "Diolkos." Salmon, John B. "Diolkos." *OCD*³ 475.

Salmon, "Insider." Salmon, Marilyn. "Insider or Outsider? Luke's Relationship with Judaism." Pages 76–82 in *Luke-Acts and the Jewish People: Eight Critical Perspectives*. Edited by Joseph B. Tyson. Minneapolis: Augsburg, 1988.

Salmon, "Lechaeum." Salmon, John B. "Lechaeum." *OCD*³ 837.

Salmon and Potter, "Pomptine Marshes." Salmon, Edward Togo, and T. W. Potter. "Pomptine Marshes." *OCD*³ 1219.

Salmon and Potter, "Via Appia." Salmon, Edward Togo, and T. W. Potter. "Via Appia." *OCD*³ 1594.

Salmon, Boardman, and Potter, "Melita." Salmon, Edward Togo, John Boardman, and T. W. Potter. "Melita." *OCD*³ 954.

Salomonsen, "Debat." Salomonsen, Børge. "Nogle synspunkter fra den nyere debat omkring zeloterne." *DTT* 27 (1964): 149–62.

Salomonsen, "Methods." Salomonsen, Jane. "Methods of Compassion or Pretension? Conducting Anthropological Fieldwork in Modern Magical Communities." *Pom* 8 (1999): 4–13.

Salomonsen, "Remarks." Salomonsen, Børge. "Some Remarks on the Zealots with Special Regard to the Term 'Qannaim' in Rabbinic Literature." *NTS* 12 (2, 1966): 164–76.

Salway, "Onomastic Practice." Salway, Benet. "What's in a Name? A Survey of Roman Onomastic Practice from c. 700 B.C. to A.D. 700." *JRS* 84 (1994): 124–45.

Salzman, "Introduction." Salzman, Michele Renee. "Introduction." Pages xiii–lxxii in *The Letters of Symmachus: Book 1*. Translated by Michele Renee Salzman and Michael Roberts. Introduction and commentary by Michele Renae Salzman. SBLWGRW 30. Atlanta: SBL, 2011.

Samarin, "Explanations." Samarin, William J. "Sociolinguistic vs. Neurophysiological Explanations for Glossolalia: Comment on Goodman's Paper." *JSSR* 11 (3, 1972): 293–96.

Samarin, "Making Sense." Samarin, William J. "Making Sense of Glossolalic Nonsense." *SocRes* 46 (1, 1979): 88–105.

Samarin, "Variation." Samarin, William J. "Variation and Variables in Religious Glossolalia." *LangSoc* 1 (1, 1972): 121–30.

Sambursky, "Gematria." Sambursky, Shmuel. "On the Origin and Significance of the Term Gematria." *JJS* 29 (1, 1978): 35–38.

Samkutty, *Samaritan Mission*. Samkutty, V. J. *The Samaritan Mission in Acts*. LNTS 328. London: T&T Clark, 2006.

Sammut, *Monuments*. Sammut, Edward. *The Monuments of Mdina: The Ancient Capital City of Malta and Its Art Treasures*. Malta: Progress Press Co., Ltd., 1960.

Sampathkumar, "Aquila and Priscilla." Sampathkumar, P. A. "Aquila and Priscilla: A Family at the Service of the Word." *ITS* 34 (1–3, 1997): 185–201.

Sampathkumar, "Bandits." Sampathkumar, P. A. "Bandits and Messiahs: Social Revolts in the Time of Jesus." *Jeev* 30 (175, 2000): 72–89.

Sampathkumar, "Rich and Poor." Sampathkumar, P. A. "The Rich and the Poor in Luke-Acts." *BiBh* 22 (4, 1996): 175–89.

Sampley, "Frank Speech." Sampley, J. Paul. "Paul and Frank Speech." Pages 293–318 in *Paul in the Greco-Roman World: A Handbook*. Edited by J. Paul Sampley. Harrisburg, Pa.: Trinity Press International, 2003.

Sampley, "Introduction." Sampley, J. Paul. "Introduction." Pages 1–15 in *Paul in the Greco-Roman World: A Handbook*. Edited by J. Paul Sampley. Harrisburg, Pa.: Trinity Press International, 2003.

Sampley, *Paul*. Sampley, J. Paul, ed. *Paul in the Greco-Roman World: A Handbook*. Harrisburg, Pa.: Trinity Press International, 2003.

Samuel, "Acts of Philip." Samuel, Simon. "The Acts of Philip and the τινες ανδρες (Certain Men) of Cyprus and Cyrene: A Remapping of Early Christian Mission Frontiers." Pages 42–71 in *Remapping Mission Discourse: A Festschrift in Honor of the Rev. George Kuruvila Chavanikamannil*. Edited by Simon Samuel and P. V. Joseph. Dehradun, India: New Theological College; Delhi: ISPCK, 2008.

Samuel, "Mission." Samuel, Simon. "Mission amidst Affluence and Affliction." *Doon Theological Journal* 5 (1, 2008): 21–42.

Samuel, "Paul on Areopagus." Samuel, S. J. "Paul on the Areopagus: A Mission Perspective." *BangTF* 18 (1, 1986): 17–32.

Samuel, *Reading*. Samuel, Simon. *A Postcolonial Reading of Mark's Story of Jesus*. LNTS 340. London: T&T Clark, 2007.

Samuel and Joseph, *Remapping*. Samuel, Simon, and P. V. Joseph, eds. *Remapping Mission Discourse: A Festschrift in Honor of the Rev. George Kuruvila Chavanikamannil*. Dehradun, India: New Theological College; Delhi: ISPCK, 2008.

Sánchez, "Daimones." Sánchez, S. "Los 'daimones' del mundo helénico." *ByF* 2 (4, 1976): 47–59.

Sánchez Cañizares, "Filosofia." Sánchez Cañizares, Javier. "Filosofia griega y revelación cristiana: La recepción patrística del discurso del Areópago." *ScrTh* 39 (1, 2007): 185–201.

Sánchez de Toca, "Μεσημβρίαν." Sánchez de Toca, M. "Πορεύου κατὰ μεσημβρίαν (Hch 8, 26)." *EstBib* 55 (1, 1997): 107–15.

Sánchez Walsh, *Identity*. Sánchez Walsh, Arlene M. *Latino Pentecostal Identity: Evangelical Faith, Self, and Society*. New York: Columbia University Press, 2003.

Sanday, *Criticism*. Sanday, William. *The Criticism of the Fourth Gospel*. Oxford: Clarendon, 1905.

Sanday and Headlam, *Romans*. Sanday, William, and Arthur Headlam. *A Critical and Exegetical Commentary on the Epistle to the Romans*. 5th ed. ICC. Edinburgh: T&T Clark, 1902.

Sanders, "Authorship." Sanders, J. N. "The Case for the Pauline Authorship." Pages 9–20 in *Studies in Ephesians*. Edited by F. L. Cross. London: A. R. Mowbray, 1956.

Sanders, "Between Jews and Gentiles." Sanders, Jack T. "Paul between Jews and Gentiles in Corinth." *JSNT* 65 (1997): 67–83.

Sanders, "Biblical Perspective." Sanders, Cheryl Jeanne. "Black Women in Biblical Perspective: Resistance, Affirmation, and Empowerment." 121–43 in *Living the Intersection: Womanism and Afrocentrism in Theology*. Minneapolis: Fortress, 1995.

Sanders, "Birth Certificate." Sanders, Henry A. "The Birth Certificate of a Roman Citizen." *CP* 22 (4, 1927): 409–13.

Sanders, *Crete*. Sanders, Ian F. *Roman Crete: An Archaeological Survey and Gazetteer of Late Hellenistic, Roman, and Early Byzantine Crete*. Warminster, Wilts., U.K.: Aris & Phillips, 1982.

Sanders, *Ethics*. Sanders, Cheryl J. *Empowerment Ethics for a Liberated People: A Path to African American Social Transformation*. Minneapolis: Fortress, 1995.

Sanders, "Evidence." Sanders, G. D. R. "Archaeological Evidence for Early Christianity and the End of Hellenic Religion in Corinth." Pages 419–42 in *Urban Religion in Roman Corinth: Interdisciplinary Approaches*. Edited by Daniel N. Schowalter and Steven J. Friesen. HTS 53. Cambridge, Mass.: Harvard University Press, 2005.

Sanders, *Figure*. Sanders, E. P. *The Historical Figure of Jesus*. New York: Penguin, 1993.

Sanders, *Hymns*. Sanders, Jack T. *The New Testament Christological Hymns: Their Historical Religious Background*. Cambridge: Cambridge University Press, 1971.

Sanders, "Isaiah 61 to Luke 4." Sanders, J. A. "From Isaiah 61 to Luke 4." Pages 75–106 in vol. 1 of *Christianity, Judaism, and Other Greco-Roman Cults: Studies for Morton Smith at Sixty*. Edited by Jacob Neusner. 4 vols. SJLA 12. Leiden: Brill, 1975.

Sanders, *Jesus and Judaism*. Sanders, E. P. *Jesus and Judaism*. Philadelphia: Fortress, 1985.

Sanders, *Jesus to Mishnah*. Sanders, E. P. *Jewish Law from Jesus to the Mishnah: Five Studies*. London: SCM; Philadelphia: Trinity Press International, 1990.

Sanders, "Jewish People." Sanders, Jack T. "The Jewish People in Luke-Acts." Pages 51–75 in *Luke-Acts and the Jewish People: Eight Critical Perspectives*. Edited by Joseph B. Tyson. Minneapolis: Augsburg, 1988.

Sanders, *John*. Sanders, J. N. *A Commentary on the Gospel according to St. John*. Edited and completed by B. A. Mastin. HNTC. New York: Harper & Row, 1968.

Sanders, *Judaism*. Sanders, E. P. *Judaism: Practice and Belief, 63 BCE–66 CE*. London: SCM; Philadelphia: Trinity Press International, 1992.

Sanders, *Law and People*. Sanders, E. P. *Paul, the Law, and the Jewish People*. Philadelphia: Fortress, 1983.

Sanders, *Margins*. Sanders, Cheryl J. *Ministry at the Margins: The Prophetic Mission of Women, Youth and the Poor*. Downers Grove, Ill.: InterVarsity, 1997.

Sanders, "Nomism." Sanders, E. P. "Covenantal Nomism Revisited." *JSQ* 16 (1, 2009): 25–55.

Sanders, "Notion." Sanders, Kirk R. "On a Causal Notion in Philodemus' On Anger." *CQ* 59 (2, 2009): 642–47.

Sanders, "Parable and Anti-Semitism." Sanders, Jack T. "The Parable of the Pounds and Lucan Anti-Semitism." *TS* 42 (1981): 660–68.

Sanders, *Paul and Judaism*. Sanders, E. P. *Paul and Palestinian Judaism: A Comparison of Patterns of Religion*. Philadelphia: Fortress, 1977.

Sanders, "Redaction in Luke XV.11–32." Sanders, Jack T. "Tradition and Redaction in Luke XV.11–32." *NTS* 15 (4, 1969): 433–38.

Sanders, "Salvation of Jews." Sanders, Jack T. "The Salvation of the Jews in Luke Acts." Pages 104–28 in *Luke-Acts: New Perspectives from the Society of Biblical Literature Seminar*. Edited by Charles H. Talbert. New York: Crossroad, 1984.

Sanders, *Schismatics*. Sanders, Jack T. *Schismatics, Sectarians, Dissidents, Deviants: The First One Hundred Years of Jewish-Christian Relations*. Valley Forge, Pa.: Trinity Press International, 1993.

Sanders, "Slavery and Conversion." Sanders, Cheryl Jeanne. "Slavery and Conversion: An Analysis of Ex-Slave Testimony." ThD diss., Harvard University, 1985.

Sanders, "Suffering." Sanders, E. P. "R. Akiba's View of Suffering." *JQR* 63 (4, 1973): 332–51.

Sanders, *Tendencies*. Sanders, E. P. *The Tendencies of the Synoptic Tradition*. SNTSMS 9. Cambridge: Cambridge University Press, 1969.

Sanders, "Urban Corinth." Sanders, G. D. R. "Urban Corinth: An Introduction." Pages 11–24 in *Urban Religion in Roman Corinth: Interdisciplinary Approaches*. Edited by Daniel N. Schowalter and Steven J. Friesen. HTS 53. Cambridge, Mass.: Harvard University Press, 2005.

Sanders, "What We Know." Sanders, E. P. "How Do We Know What We Know about Jesus?" Pages 38–61 in *Jesus Two Thousand Years Later*. Edited by James H. Charlesworth and Walter P. Weaver. FSCS. Harrisburg, Pa.: Trinity Press International, 2000.

Sanders, "Who Is a Jew?" Sanders, Jack T. "Who Is a Jew and Who Is a Gentile in the Book of Acts?" *NTS* 37 (3, 1991): 434–55.

Sandmel, *Anti-Semitism*. Sandmel, Samuel. *Anti-Semitism in the New Testament?* Philadelphia: Fortress, 1978.

Sandmel, *Genius of Paul*. Sandmel, Samuel. *The Genius of Paul*. New York: Farrar, Straus & Cudahy, 1958.

Sandmel, "Hellenistic Judaism." Sandmel, Samuel. "Palestinian and Hellenistic Judaism and Christianity: The Question of the Comfortable Theory." *HUCA* 50 (1979): 137–48.

Sandmel, *Judaism*. Sandmel, Samuel. *Judaism and Christian Beginnings*. New York: Oxford University Press, 1978.

Sandmel, *Scriptures*. Sandmel, Samuel. *The Hebrew Scriptures: An Introduction to Their Literature and Religious Ideas*. New York: Alfred A. Knopf, 1963.

Sandner, "Psychology." Sandner, Donald. "Analytical Psychology and Shamanism." Pages 277–83 in *Proceedings of the Fourth International Conference on the Study of Shamanism and Alternate Modes of Healing, Held at the St. Sabina Center, San Rafael, California, September 5–7, 1987*. Edited by Ruth-Inge Heinze. N.p.: Independent Scholars of Asia; Madison, Wis.: A-R Editions, 1988.

Sandnes, *Challenge*. Sandnes, Karl Olav. *The Challenge of Homer: School, Pagan Poets and Early Christianity*. LNTS 400. New York: T&T Clark, 2009.

Sandnes, *Gospel*. Sandnes, Karl Olav. *The Gospel "According to Homer and Virgil": Cento and Canon*. Leiden: Brill, 2011.

Sandnes, "Idolatry and Virtue." Sandnes, Karl O. "Between Idolatry and Virtue: Paul and Hellenistic Religious Environment." *Mishkan* 38 (2003): 4–14.

Sandnes, "Imitatio." Sandnes, Karl O. "*Imitatio Homeri*? An Appraisal of Dennis R. MacDonald's 'Mimesis Criticism.'" *JBL* 124 (4, 2005): 715–32.

Sandnes, "Paul and Socrates." Sandnes, Karl O. "Paul and Socrates: The Aim of Paul's Areopagus Speech." *JSNT* 50 (1993): 13–26.

Sandnes, "Stendahl's Exegesis of 4:12." Sandnes, Karl O. "Beyond 'Love Language': A Critical Examination of Krister Stendahl's Exegesis of Acts 4:12." *ST* 52 (1, 1998): 43–56.

Sandy, "Hellenistic Egypt." Sandy, D. Brent. "Hellenistic Egypt." *DNTB* 473–77.

Sanneh, *Disciples*. Sanneh, Lamin. *Disciples of All Nations: Pillars of World Christianity*. New York and Oxford: Oxford University Press, 2008.

Sanneh, *West African Christianity*. Sanneh, Lamin. *West African Christianity: The Religious Impact*. Maryknoll, N.Y.: Orbis, 1983.

Sanneh, *Whose Religion?* Sanneh, Lamin. *Whose Religion Is Christianity? The Gospel beyond the West*. Grand Rapids and Cambridge, U.K.: Eerdmans, 2003.

Sant and Sammut, "Doch auf Malta." Sant, C., and J. Sammut. "Paulus war doch auf Malta!" *TGl* 80 (3, 1990): 327–32.

Santala, "Messiah." Santala, Risto. "The Despised Messiah and His Despised People." *Mishkan* 43 (2005): 16–24.

Santer, "Text." Santer, Mark. "The Text of Ephesians I.1." *NTS* 15 (2, 1969): 247–48.

Saoût, "Annonce." Saoût, Yves. "Annonce de l'Évangile et libertés humaines dans l'oeuvre de Luc." *Spiritus* 192 (2008): 299–312.

Saoyao, "Practices." Saoyao, Emilia M. "The Peculiar Cultural Practices of the Taloy Ibaloys." MA thesis, University of Baguio, Philippines, 1989.

Sarason, "Intersections." Sarason, Richard S. "The 'Intersections' of Qumran and Rabbinic Judaism: The Case of Prayer Texts and Liturgies." *DSD* 8 (2, 2001): 169–81.

Sargunam, "Churches." Sargunam, Ezra. "Multiplying Churches in Urban India." MA thesis, Fuller Theological Seminary, 1973.

Särkiö, "Versöhnung." Särkiö, Riita. "Die Versöhnung mit Gott—und mit Paulus: Zur Bedeutung der Gemeindesituation in Korinth für 2 Kor 5.14–21." *ST* 52 (1, 1998): 29–42.

Sarna, *Exodus*. Sarna, Nahum M. *Exploring Exodus: The Heritage of Biblical Israel*. New York: Schocken, 1986.

Sarna, *Genesis*. Sarna, Nahum M. *Understanding Genesis: The Heritage of Biblical Israel*. New York: Schocken, 1966.

Sarthou-Lajus, "Goût." Sarthou-Lajus, Nathalie. "Du goût pour les stoïciens." *Études* 410 (6, 2009): 775–86.

Sassi, "Physiognomy." Sassi, Maria Michela. "Physiognomy." *OCD*³ 1181.

Sasson, "Circumcision." Sasson, Jack M. "Circumcision in the Ancient Near East." *JBL* 85 (4, 1966): 473–76.

Satake, "1Kr 15,3." Satake, Akira. "1Kr 15,3 und das Verhalten von Paulus den Jerusalemern gegenüber." *AJBI* 16 (1990): 100–111.

Satlow, "Construction of Masculinity." Satlow, Michael L. "'Try to Be a Man': The Rabbinic Construction of Masculinity." *HTR* 89 (1, 1996): 19–40.

Satlow, "Constructions." Satlow, Michael L. "Jewish Constructions of Nakedness in Late Antiquity." *JBL* 116 (3, 1997): 429–54.

Satlow, "Love." Satlow, Michael L. "'One Who Loves His Wife like Himself': Love in Rabbinic Marriage." *JJS* 49 (1, 1998): 67–86.

Satlow, "Philosophers." Satlow, Michael L. "Theophrastus's Jewish Philosophers." *JJS* 59 (1, 2008): 1–20.

Satterthwaite, "Acts." Satterthwaite, Philip E. "Acts against the Background of Classical Rhetoric." Pages 337–79 in *The Book of Acts in Its Ancient Literary Setting*. Edited by Bruce W. Winter and Andrew D. Clark. Vol. 1 of *The Book of Acts in Its First Century Setting*. Edited by Bruce W. Winter. Grand Rapids: Eerdmans; Carlisle, U.K.: Paternoster, 1993.

Satyavrata, "Perspectives." Satyavrata, Ivan M. "Contextual Perspectives on Pentecostalism as a Global Culture." Pages 203–21 in *The Globalization of Pentecostalism: A Religion Made to Travel*. Edited by Murray W. Dempster, Byron D. Klaus, and Douglas Petersen. Foreword by Russell P. Spittler. Carlisle, U.K.: Paternoster; Oxford: Regnum, 1999.

Saucy, "View." Saucy, Robert L. "An Open but Cautious View." Pages 95–148 in *Are Miraculous Gifts for Today? Four Views*. Edited by Wayne A. Grudem. Grand Rapids: Zondervan, 1996.

Sauer, "Passes." Sauer, Vera. "Mountain Passes." *BrillPauly* 9:242–43.

Saulnier, "Josèphe." Saulnier, Christiane. "Flavius Josèphe et la propagande flavienne." *RB* 96 (4, 1989): 545–62.

Saunders, "Synagogues." Saunders, Ernest W. "Christian Synagogues and Jewish-Christianity in Galilee." *Explor* 3 (1, 1977): 70–77.

Saunders, "Zar Experience." Saunders, Lucie Wood. "Variants in Zar Experience in an Egyptian Village." Pages 177–92 in *Case Studies in Spirit Possession*. Edited by Vincent Crapanzaro and Vivian Garrison. New York: Wiley, 1977.

Savage, *Power*. Savage, Timothy B. *Power through Weakness: Paul's Understanding of the Christian Ministry in 2 Corinthians*. SNTSMS 86. Cambridge: Cambridge University Press, 1996.

Savelle, "Reexamination." Savelle, Charles H. "A Reexamination of the Prohibitions in Acts 15." *BSac* 161 (644, 2004): 449–68.

Savona-Ventura, *Medicine in Malta*. Savona-Ventura, Charles. *Ancient and Medieval Medicine in Malta: Before 1600 AD*. San Gwann, SGN, Malta: Publishers Enterprises Group (PEG), 2004.

Sawicki, *Crossing Galilee*. Sawicki, Marianne. *Crossing Galilee: Architectures of Contact in the Occupied Land of Jesus*. Harrisburg, Pa.: Trinity Press International, 2000.

Sawyer, "Judith's Performance." Sawyer, Deborah F. "Gender Strategies in Antiquity: Judith's Performance." *FemTheol* 28 (2001): 9–26.

Sawyer and Wallace, *Afraid*. Sawyer, M. James, and Daniel B. Wallace, eds. *Who's Afraid of the Holy Spirit? An Investigation into the Ministry of the Spirit of God Today*. Dallas: Biblical Studies Press, 2005.

Say, "History." Say, Saw Doh. "A Brief History and Development Factors of the Karen Baptist Church of Burma (Myanma)." ThM thesis, Fuller School of World Mission, 1990.

Scaer, "Foundations." Scaer, Peter J. "Luke and the Foundations of the Church." *CTQ* 76 (1–2, 2012): 57–72.

Schachter, "Cabiri." Schachter, Albert. "Cabiri." *OCD*[3] 267.

Schachter, "Charites." Schachter, Albert. "Charites (Graces)." *BrillPauly* 3:197–99.

Schachter, "Corinthian Cults." Schachter, Albert. "Corinthian Cults and Myths." *OCD*[3] 391.

Schachter, "Omphalos." Schachter, Albert. "Omphalos." *OCD*[3] 1067.

Schachter, "Springs." Schachter, Albert. "Springs, Sacred." *OCD*[3] 1436–37.

Schäfer, "Entertainers." Schäfer, Alfred. "Entertainers." *BrillPauly* 4:997–1000.

Schäfer, "Funktion." Schäfer, Jan. "Zur Funktion der Dionysosmysterien in der Apostelgeschichte. Eine intertextuelle Betrachtung der Berufungs- und Befreiungserzählungen in der Apostelgeschichte und der Bakchen des Euripides." *TZ* 66 (3, 2010): 199–222.

Schäfer, "Geist." Schäfer, Peter. "Die Termini 'Heiliger Geist' und 'Geist der Prophetie' im den Targumim und das Verhältnis der Targumim zueinander." *VT* 20 (3, 1970): 304–14.

Schäfer, "Journey." Schäfer, Peter. "New Testament and Hekhalot Literature: The Journey into Heaven in Paul and in Merkavah Mysticism." *JJS* 35 (1, 1984): 19–35.

Schäfer, "Magic and Religion." Schäfer, Peter. "Magic and Religion in Ancient Judaism." Pages 19–43 in *Envisioning Magic: A Princeton Seminar and Symposium*. Edited by Peter Schäfer and Hans G. Kippenberg. SHR 75. Leiden: Brill, 1997.

Schäfer, "Magic Literature." Schäfer, Peter. "Jewish Magic Literature in Late Antiquity and Early Middle Ages." *JJS* 41 (1, 1990): 75–91.

Schäfer, "Schöpfung." Schäfer, Peter. "Tempel und Schöpfung: Zur Interpretation einiger Heiligtums-traditionen in der rabbinischen Literatur." *Kairos* 16 (2, 1974): 122–33.

Schäfer, "Torah." Schäfer, Peter. "Die Torah der messianischen Zeit." *ZNW* 65 (1–2, 1974): 27–42.

Schäfer, *Vorstellung*. Schäfer, Peter. *Die Vorstellung vom Heiligen Geist in der rabbinischen Literatur*. SANT 28. München: Kösel, 1972.

Schaffner, "Fames." Schaffner, Brigitte. "Fames." *BrillPauly* 5:331.

Schaffner, "Febris." Schaffner, Brigitte. "Febris." *BrillPauly* 5:376–77.

Schaffner, "Felicitas." Schaffner, Brigitte. "Felicitas." *BrillPauly* 5:377–78.

Schapera, "Kinship." Schapera, Isaac. "Kinship and Marriage among the Tswana." Pages 140–65 in *African Systems of Kinship and Marriage*. Edited by A. R. Radcliffe-Brown and Daryll Forde. New York: Oxford University Press, 1950.

Schapera, *Life*. Schapera, Isaac. *Married Life in an African Tribe*. Evanston, Ill.: Northwestern University Press, 1966.

Scharf, "Expository Preachers." Scharf, Greg R. "Were the Apostles Expository Preachers? Old Testament Exposition in the Book of Acts." *TJ* 31 (1, 2010): 65–93.

Scharlemann, "Speech: Lucan Creation?" Scharlemann, Martin H. "Acts 7:2–53—Stephen's Speech: A Lucan Creation?" *ConcJ* 4 (2, 1978): 52–57.

Scharlemann, *Stephen*. Scharlemann, Martin H. *Stephen: A Singular Saint*. AnBib 34. Rome: Pontifical Biblical Institute, 1968.

Schart, "Twelve." Schart, Aaron. "Twelve, Book of the: History of Interpretation." Pages 806–17 in *Dictionary of the Old Testament Prophets*. Edited by Mark J. Boda and J. Gordon McConville. Downers Grove, Ill.: IVP Academic, 2012.

Schatzmann, *Charismata*. Schatzmann, Siegfried. *A Pauline Theology of Charismata*. Peabody, Mass.: Hendrickson, 1987.

Schazmann, *Asklepieion*. Schazmann, Paul, with Rudolf Herzog. *Asklepieion*. Kos 1. Berlin: Heinrich Keller, 1932.

Schechter, *Aspects*. Schechter, Solomon. *Some Aspects of Rabbinic Theology*. New York: Macmillan, 1909. Reprinted as *Aspects of Rabbinic Theology*. New York: Schocken, 1961.

Schechter, "Parallels." Schechter, Solomon. "Some Rabbinic Parallels to the New Testament." *JQR* 12 (1900): 415–33.

Schedl, "Ehebruchklausel." Schedl, Claus. "Zur Ehebruchklausel der Bergpredigt im Lichte der neu gefundenen Tempelrolle." *TPQ* 130 (1982): 362–65.

Schedl, *History*. Schedl, Claus. *History of the Old Testament*. 5 vols. Staten Island, N.Y.: Alba House, 1972.

Scheer, "Dioscuri." Scheer, Tanja. "Dioscuri: Religion." *BrillPauly* 4:518–20.

Scheid, "Africa: Religion." Scheid, John. "Africa: Religion." *BrillPauly* 1:294–95.

Scheid, "Febris." Scheid, John. "Febris." *OCD*[3] 591.

Scheid, "Sacrifice." Scheid, John. "Sacrifice, Roman." *OCD*³ 1345–46.

Scheid, "Superstitio." Scheid, John. "Superstitio." *OCD*³ 1456.

Scheidel, "Age Structure." Scheidel, Walter. "Roman Age Structure: Evidence and Models." *JRS* 91 (2001): 1–26.

Scheidel, "Death Declarations." Scheidel, Walter. "The Death Declarations of Roman Egypt. A Re-appraisal." *BASP* 36 (1–4, 1999): 53–70.

Scheidel, "Finances." Scheidel, Walter. "Finances, Figures, and Fiction." *CQ* 46 (1, 1996): 222–38.

Scheidel, "Incest Revisited." Scheidel, Walter. "Incest Revisited: Three Notes on the Demography of Sibling Marriage in Roman Egypt." *BASP* 32 (3–4, 1995): 143–55.

Scheidel, "Mobility." Scheidel, Walter. "Human Mobility in Roman Italy, II: The Slave Population." *JRS* 95 (2005): 64–79.

Scheidel, "Quantifying." Scheidel, Walter. "Quantifying the Sources of Slaves in the Early Roman Empire." *JRS* 87 (1997): 156–69.

Scheidel, "Women." Scheidel, Walter. "The Most Silent Women of Greece and Rome: Rural Labour and Women's Life in the Ancient World (II)." *GR* 43 (1, 1996): 1–10.

Scheidel and Friesen, "Size." Scheidel, Walter, and Steven J. Friesen. "The Size of the Economy and the Distribution of Income in the Roman Empire." *JRS* 99 (2009): 61–91.

Schenker, "Martyrium." Schenker, Adrian. "Das fürbittend sühnende Martyrium 2 Makk 7,37–38 und das Kelchwort Jesu." *FZPhTh* 50 (3, 2003): 283–92.

Schenkeveld, "Philosophical Prose." Schenkeveld, Dirk M. "Philosophical Prose." Pages 195–264 in *Handbook of Classical Rhetoric in the Hellenistic Period, 330 B.C.–A.D. 400*. Edited by Stanley E. Porter. Leiden: Brill, 1997.

Schepens, "Aspects." Schepens, Guido. "Some Aspects of Source Theory in Greek Historiography." Pages 100–118 in *Greek and Roman Historiography*. Oxford Readings in Classical Studies. Edited by John Marincola. New York: Oxford University Press, 2011.

Schepens, "History." Schepens, Guido. "History and *Historia*: Inquiry in the Greek Historians." Pages 39–55 in *A Companion to Greek and Roman Historiography*. Edited by John Marincola. 2 vols. Oxford: Blackwell, 2007.

Scherberger, "Shaman." Scherberger, Laura. "The Janus-Faced Shaman: The Role of Laughter in Sickness and Healing Among the Makushi." *AnthHum* 30 (1, 2005): 55–69.

Scherberich, "Sueton und Josephus." Scherberich, Klaus. "Sueton und Josephus über die Ermorderung des Caligula." *RMPhil* 142 (1, 1999): 74–83.

Scherf, "Memnon." Scherf, Johannes. "Memnon." *BrillPauly* 8:649–50.

Scherf, "Memnonides." Scherf, Johannes. "Memnonides." *BrillPauly* 8:652–53.

Scherf, "Midas." Scherf, Johannes. "Midas: Graeco-Roman Literature." *BrillPauly* 8:857–58.

Scherrer, "Ephesos from Roman Period." Scherrer, Peter. "The City of Ephesos from the Roman Period to Late Antiquity." Pages 1–25 in *Ephesos, Metropolis of Asia: An Interdisciplinary Approach to Its Archaeology, Religion, and Culture*. Edited by Helmut Koester. HTS. Valley Forge, Pa.: Trinity Press International, 1995.

Scherrer, "Ephesus: History." Scherrer, Peter. "Ephesus: History." *BrillPauly* 4:1024–29.

Scheuer, "Fama." Scheuer, Hans Jürgen. "Fama." *BrillPauly* 5:330–31.

Schiemann, "Abolitio." Schiemann, Gottfried. "Abolitio." *BrillPauly* 1:24.

Schiemann, "Communio." Schiemann, Gottfried. "Communio." *BrillPauly* 3:670–72.

Schiemann, "Concubinatus." Schiemann, Gottfried. "Concubinatus." *BrillPauly* 3:682–83.

Schiemann, "Contumacia." Schiemann, Gottfried. "Contumacia." *BrillPauly* 3:758.

Schiemann, "Conubium." Schiemann, Gottfried. "Conubium." *BrillPauly* 3:758–59.

Schiemann, "Death Penalty." Schiemann, Gottfried. "Death Penalty: Graeco-Roman." *BrillPauly* 4:137.

Schiemann, "Decollatio." Schiemann, Gottfried. "Decollatio." *BrillPauly* 4:156.

Schiemann, "Deportatio." Schiemann, Gottfried. "Deportatio." *BrillPauly* 4:306.

Schiemann, "Effractor." Schiemann, Gottfried. "Effractor." *BrillPauly* 4:838.

Schiemann, "Fides." Schiemann, Gottfried. "Fides: Law." *BrillPauly* 5:415–17.

Schiemann, "Furor." Schiemann, Gottfried. "Furor." *BrillPauly* 5:625–26.

Schiemann, "Furtum." Schiemann, Gottfried. "Furtum." *BrillPauly* 5:626–27.

Schiemann, "Indulgentia." Schiemann, Gottfried. "Indulgentia." *BrillPauly* 6:793–94.

Schiemann, "Intestabilis." Schiemann, Gottfried. "Intestabilis." *BrillPauly* 6:875–76.

Schiemann, "Ius iurandum." Schiemann, Gottfried. "Ius iurandum." *BrillPauly* 6:1134–35.

Schiemann, "Libel." Schiemann, Gottfried. "Libel." *BrillPauly* 7:483.

Schiemann, "Manumission." Schiemann, Gottfried. "Manumission." *BrillPauly* 8:263–66.

Schiemann, "Minores." Schiemann, Gottfried. "Minores." *BrillPauly* 9:23–24.

Schiemann, "Torture." Schiemann, Gottfried. "Torture." *BrillPauly* 14:794–96.

Schierling and Schierling, "Influence of Romances." Schierling, Stephen P., and Marla J. Schierling. "The Influence of the Ancient Romances on Acts of the Apostles." *CBull* 54 (1978): 81–88.

Schiesaro, "Laudatio funebris." Schiesaro, Alessandro. "Laudatio funebris." *OCD*³ 822.

Schiff, "Shadow." Schiff, Miriam. "Living in the Shadow of Terrorism: Psychological Distress and Alcohol Use among Religious and Non-Religious Adolescents in Jerusalem." *SSMed* 62 (9, 2006): 2301–12.

Schiffman, "Communal Meals." Schiffman, Lawrence H. "Communal Meals at Qumran." *RevQ* 10 (1, 1979): 45–56.

Schiffman, "Crossroads." Schiffman, Lawrence H. "At the Crossroads: Tannaitic Perspectives on the Jewish Christian Schism." Pages 115–56 in *Aspects of Judaism in the Graeco-Roman Period*. Edited by E. P. Sanders with A. I. Baumgarten and Alan Mendelson. Vol. 2 of *Jewish and Christian Self-Definition*. Edited by E. P. Sanders. Philadelphia: Fortress, 1981.

Schiffman, "House of Adiabene." Schiffman, Lawrence H. "The Conversion of the Royal House of Adiabene in Josephus and Rabbinic Sources." Pages 293–312 in *Josephus, Judaism, and Christianity*. Edited by Louis H. Feldman and Gohei Hata. Detroit: Wayne State University Press, 1987.

Schiffman, "Israel." Schiffman, Lawrence H. "Israel, Land of." *DNTB* 554–58.

Schiffman, *Jew*. Schiffman, Lawrence H. *Who Was a Jew? Rabbinic and Halakhic Perspectives on the Jewish Christian Schism*. Hoboken, N.J.: KTAV, 1985.

Schiffman, *Law*. Schiffman, Lawrence H. *Sectarian Law in the Dead Sea Scrolls: Courts, Testimony, and the Penal Code*. BJS 33. Chico, Calif.: Scholars Press, 1983.

Schiffman, "Miqsat." Schiffman, Lawrence H. "Miqsat Ma'aseh ha-Torah and the Temple Scroll." *RevQ* 14 (3, 1990): 435–57.

Schiffman, "Scroll." Schiffman, Lawrence H. "The Unfinished Scroll: A Reconsideration of the End of the Temple Scroll." *DSD* 15 (1, 2008): 67–78.

Schiffman, "Scrolls." Schiffman, Lawrence H. "The Dead Sea Scrolls and the Early History of Jewish Liturgy." Pages 33–48 in *The Synagogue in Late Antiquity*. Edited by Lee I. Levine. Philadelphia: American Schools of Oriental Research, 1986.

Schille, *Apostelgeschichte*. Schille, Gottfried. *Die Apostelgeschichte des Lukas*. THKNT

5. Berlin: Evangelische Verlagsanstalt, 1983.

Schipper, "Mattatias." Schipper, Friedrich T. "Mattatias und Josua: Eine Beobachtung zur Typologie in der jüdisch-hellenistischen Geschichtsschreibung." *BN* 125 (2005): 95–96.

Schlapbach, "Providentia." Schlapbach, Karin. "Providentia." *BrillPauly* 12:82.

Schlatter, *Romans*. Schlatter, Adolf. *Romans: The Righteousness of God*. Translated by Siegfried S. Schatzmann. Foreword by Peter Stuhlmacher. Peabody, Mass.: Hendrickson, 1995.

Schlegel, *Dominance*. Schlegel, Alice. *Male Dominance and Female Autonomy: Domestic Authority in Matrilineal Societies*. Foreword by Raoul Naroll. [New Haven, Conn.]: Human Relations Area Files Press, 1972.

Schlier, "ἀνέχω." Schlier, Heinrich. "ἀνέχω." *TDNT* 1:359–60.

Schlier, *Principalities*. Schlier, Heinrich. *Principalities and Powers in the New Testament*. New York: Herder & Herder, 1961.

Schlink, *World*. Schlink, Basilea. *The Unseen World of Angels and Demons*. Old Tappan, N.J.: Fleming H. Revell, 1985.

Schloen, "Ashkelon." Schloen, David. "Ashkelon." *OEANE* 1:220–23.

Schlueter, *Measure*. Schlueter, Carol J. *Filling Up the Measure: Polemical Hyperbole in 1 Thessalonians 2.14–16*. Sheffield, U.K.: JSOT Press, 1994.

Schluntz, "Protectress." Schluntz, Erika L. "'Protectress of Petra': Isis and Popular Cult in Nabataean Petra." Paper presented at the annual meeting of the SBL, Orlando, Fla., Nov. 1998.

Schmeling, "Spectrum." Schmeling, Gareth. "The Spectrum of Narrative: Authority of the Author." Pages 19–29 in *Ancient Fiction and Early Christian Narrative*. Edited by Ronald F. Hock, J. Bradley Chance, and Judith Perkins. SBLSymS 6. Atlanta: SBL, 1998.

Schmeller, "Gegenwelten." Schmeller, Thomas. "Gegenwelten: Zum Vergleich zwischen paulinischen Gemeinden und nichtchristlichen Gruppen." *BZ* 47 (2, 2003): 167–85.

Schmeller, "Weg der Jesusbotschaft." Schmeller, Thomas. "Der Weg der Jesusbotschaft in die Städte." *BK* 47 (1, 1992): 18–24.

Schmid, "Eklektische Textkonstitution." Schmid, Ulrich. "Eklektische Textkonstitution als theologische Rekonstruktion: Zur Heilsbedeutung des Todes Jesu bei Lukas (Lk 22,15–20 und Apg 20,28)." Pages 577–84 in *The Unity of Luke-Acts*. Edited by Joseph Verheyden. BETL 142. Leuven: Leuven University Press, 1999.

Schmid, "Geistwirkungen." Schmid, H. H. "Ekstatische und charismatische Geistwirkungen im Alten Testament." Pages 83–99 in *Erfahrung und Theologie des Heiligen Geistes*. Edited by Claus Heitmann and Heribert Mühlen. Hamburg: Agentur des Rauhen Hauses, 1974.

Schmid, "Moderation." Schmid, W. Thomas. "Socratic Moderation and Self-Knowledge." *JHistPhil* 21 (1983): 339–48.

Schmid, "Sünde." Schmid, J. "Sünde und Sühne im Judentum." *BibLeb* 6 (1, 1965): 16–26.

Schmid, "Wadi Farasa Project." Schmid, Stephan G. "The International Wadi Farasa Project (IWFP): Between Microcosm and Macroplanning—A First Synthesis." *PEQ* 133 (2, 2001): 159–97.

Schmidt, "Abkehr." Schmidt, Karl Matthias. "Abkehr von der Rückkehr: Aufbau und Theologie der Apostelgeschichte im Kontext des lukanischen Diasporaverständnisses." *NTS* 53 (3, 2007): 406–24.

Schmidt, "Astrologie." Schmidt, Francis. "Astrologie juive ancienne: Essai d'interprétation de *4QCryptique (4Q186)*." *RevQ* 18 (69, 1997): 125–41.

Schmidt, "Bekehrung." Schmidt, Karl Matthias. "Bekehrung zur Zerstreuung: Paulus und der äthiopische Eunuch im Kontext der lukanischen Diasporatheologie." *Bib* 88 (2, 2007): 191–213.

Schmidt, "Circles, Literary." Schmidt, Peter Lebrecht. "Circles, Literary." *BrillPauly* 3:350–51.

Schmidt, "Competitions." Schmidt, Peter Lebrecht. "Competitions, Artistic: Literary Competitions: Rome." *BrillPauly* 3:1185–88.

Schmidt, "Einweihung in Mysterien." Schmidt, Victor. "Apuleius *Met.* III.15f.: Die Einweihung in die falschen Mysterien (Apuleiana Groningana VII)." *Mnemosyne* 35 (3–4, 1982): 269–82.

Schmidt, "Friede." Schmidt, Karl Matthias. "Die Friede von Cäsarea: Apg 12,20–22 und die Krönung des armenischen Königs Tiridates." *BZ* 52 (1, 2008): 110–17.

Schmidt, "Historiography of Acts." Schmidt, Daryl D. "The Historiography of Acts: Deuteronomistic or Hellenistic?" Pages 417–27 in *SBL Seminar Papers, 1985*. Edited by K. H. Richards. SBLSP 24. Atlanta: Scholars Press, 1985.

Schmidt, *Hostility to Wealth*. Schmidt, Thomas E. *Hostility to Wealth in the Synoptic Gospels*. JSNTSup 15. Sheffield, U.K.: JSOT Press, 1987.

Schmidt, "Hostility to Wealth." Schmidt, Thomas E. "Hostility to Wealth in Philo of Alexandria." *JSNT* 19 (1983): 85–97.

Schmidt, "Influences." Schmidt, Daryl D. "Rhetorical Influences and Genre: Luke's Preface and the Rhetoric of Hellenistic Historiography." Pages 27–60 in *Jesus and the Heritage of Israel: Luke's Narrative Claim upon Israel's Legacy*. Edited by David P. Moessner. Luke the Interpreter of Israel 1. Harrisburg, Pa.: Trinity Press International, 1999.

Schmidt, "Letter." Schmidt, Peter Lebrecht. "Letter." *BrillPauly* 7:436–38.

Schmidt, "Linguistic Evidence." Schmidt, Daryl. "1 Thess 2:13–16: Linguistic Evidence for an Interpolation." *JBL* 102 (2, 1983): 269–79.

Schmidt, "Psychiatry." Schmidt, K. E. "Folk Psychiatry in Sarawak: A Tentative System of Psychiatry of the Iban." Pages 139–55 in *Magic, Faith, and Healing: Studies in Primitive Psychiatry Today*. Edited by Ari Kiev. Foreword by Jerome D. Frank. New York: Free Press, 1964.

Schmidt, "Public Recital." Schmidt, Peter Lebrecht. "Public Recital." *BrillPauly* 12:178–81.

Schmidt, "Recensions." Schmidt, Francis. "The Two Recensions of the Testament of Abraham: In Which Way Did the Transformation Take Place?" Pages 65–84 in *Studies on the Testament of Abraham*. Edited by George W. E. Nickelsburg. SBLSCS 6. Missoula, Mont.: Scholars Press, 1976.

Schmidt, "Stellung." Schmidt, K. L. "Die Stellung der Evangelien in der allgemeinen Literaturgeschichte." Pages 59–60 in vol. 1 of ΕΥΧΑΡΙΣΤΗΡΙΟΝ: *Studien zur Religion und Literatur des Alten und Neuen Testaments, Festschrift für Hermann Gunkel*. Edited by Hans Schmidt. 2 vols. in 1. FRLANT 19. Göttingen: Vandenhoeck & Ruprecht, 1923.

Schmidt, "Sturz des Serapis." Schmidt, Stefan. "Der Sturz des Serapis: Zur Bedeutung paganer Götterbilder im spätantiken Alexandria." *BN* 147 (2010): 127–46.

Schmidt, "Translating Faith." Schmidt, Daryl D. "Translating Paul's Faith." *FourR* 18 (3, 2005): 17–19.

Schmidt, "Weg." Schmidt, Karl Matthias. "Der weite Weg vom Saulus zum Paulus: Anmerkungen zur narrativen Funktion der ersten Missionsreise." *RB* 119 (1, 2012): 77–109.

Schmithals, "Abfassung." Schmithals, Walter. "Zur Abfassung und ältesten Sammlung der paulinischen Hauptbriefe." *ZNW* 51 (3–4, 1960): 225–45.

Schmithals, *Apostle*. Schmithals, Walter. *The Office of Apostle in the Early Church*. Translated by John E. Steely. Nashville: Abingdon, 1969.

Schmithals, *Gnosticism in Corinth*. Schmithals, Walter. *Gnosticism in Corinth: An Investigation of the Letters to* the Corinthians. Translated by John E. Steely. Nashville: Abingdon, 1971.

Schmithals, *Paul and Gnostics*. Schmithals, Walter. *Paul and the Gnostics*. Translated by John E. Steely. Nashville: Abingdon, 1972.

Schmitt, "Kerygme." Schmitt, J. "Kerygme pascal et lecture scripturaire dans l'instruction d'Antioche (Act. 13,23–37)." Pages 155–67 in *Les Actes des apôtres: Traditions, rédaction, théologie*. Edited by Jacob Kremer. BETL 48. Gembloux, Belg.: J. Duculot; Leuven: Leuven University Press, 1979.

Schmitt, "Zeugnis der Auferstehung." Schmitt, Armin. "Ps 16,8–11 als Zeugnis der Auferstehung in der Apg." *BZ* 17 (2, 1973): 229–48.

Schmitz, "Eisphora." Schmitz, Winfried. "Eisphora." *BrillPauly* 4:865–66.

Schmitz, "Loan." Schmitz, Winfried. "Loan." *BrillPauly* 7:757–60.

Schmitz, "Naukleros." Schmitz, Winfried. "Naukleros." *BrillPauly* 9:542.

Schmitz, "Sidon." Schmitz, Philip C. "Sidon." *ABD* 6:17–18.

Schmitzer, "Copyright." Schmitzer, Ulrich. "Copyright." *BrillPauly* 3:778–79.

Schnabel, *Acts*. Schnabel, Eckhard J. *Acts*. ZECNT. Grand Rapids: Zondervan, 2012.

Schnabel, "Beginnings." Schnabel, Eckhard J. "Jesus and the Beginnings of the Mission to the Gentiles." Pages 37–58 in *Jesus of Nazareth, Lord and Christ: Essays on the Historical Jesus and New Testament Christology*. Edited by Joel B. Green and Max Turner. Grand Rapids: Eerdmans; Carlisle, U.K.: Paternoster, 1994.

Schnabel, *Brief des Paulus an die Korinther*. Schnabel, Eckhard J. *Der erste Brief des Paulus an die Korinther*. Historisch Theologische Auslegung Neues Testament. Wuppertal: R. Brockhaus, 2006.

Schnabel, *Mission*. Schnabel, Eckhard J. *Early Christian Mission*. 2 vols. Downers Grove, Ill.: InterVarsity; Leicester, U.K.: Apollos, 2004.

Schnabel, "Mission." Schnabel, Eckhard J. "Mission, Early Non-Pauline." *DLNTD* 752–75.

Schnabel, *Missionary*. Schnabel, Eckhard J. *Paul the Missionary: Realities, Strategies and Methods*. Downers Grove, Ill.: InterVarsity; Leicester, U.K.: Apollos, 2008.

Schnabel, "Paul in Athens." Schnabel, Eckhard J. "Contextualising Paul in Athens: The Proclamation of the Gospel before Pagan Audiences in the Graeco-Roman World." *R&T* 12 (2, 2005): 172–90.

Schnabel, "Reading Acts." Schnabel, Eckhard. "Fads and Common Sense: Reading Acts in the First Century and Reading Acts Today." *JETS* 54 (2, June 2011): 251–78.

Schnackenburg, *John*. Schnackenburg, Rudolf. *The Gospel according to St. John*. Translated by Kevin Smyth. 3 vols. Vol. 1: New York: Herder & Herder, 1968. Vol. 2: New York: Seabury, 1980. Vol. 3: New York: Crossroad, 1982.

Schneckenburger, *Apostelgeschichte*. Schneckenburger, Matthias. *Über den Zweck der Apostelgeschichte: Zugleich eine Ergänzung der neueren Commentare*. Bern: Fischer, 1841.

Schneemelcher, "Introduction." Schneemelcher, Wilhelm. "General Introduction." Translated by George Ogg. Pages 19–68 in *Gospels and Related Writings*. Vol. 1 of *New Testament Apocrypha*. Edited by Edgar Hennecke, Wilhelm Schneemelcher, and R. McL. Wilson. Philadelphia: Westminster, 1963.

Schneider, *Apostelgeschichte*. Schneider, Gerhard. *Die Apostelgeschichte*. HTKNT 5. Freiburg im Breisgau: Herder, 1980–.

Schneider, "Castration." Schneider, Helmuth. "Castration of Animals." *Brill Pauly* 2:1188–89.

Schneider, "Ivory." Schneider, Helmuth. "Ivory." *BrillPauly* 6:1153.

Schneider, "Nutrition." Schneider, Helmuth. "Nutrition: Greece and Rome." *BrillPauly* 9:916–21.

Schneider, "Pigs." Schneider, Helmuth. "Pigs. III. Classical Antiquity." *BrillPauly* 11:246–47.

Schneider, "Reflections." Schneider, H. P. "Some Reflections on the Dialogue of Justin Martyr with Trypho." *SJT* 15 (2, 1962): 164–75.

Schneider, "Rigging." Schneider, Helmuth. "Rigging." *BrillPauly* 12:592–93.

Schneider, "Stephanus." Schneider, Gerhard. "Stephanus, die Hellenisten, und Samaria." Pages 215–40 in *Les Actes des apôtres: Traditions, rédaction, théologie*. Edited by Jacob Kremer. BETL 48. Gembloux, Belg.: J. Duculot; Leuven: Leuven University Press, 1979.

Schneider, "Traffic." Schneider, Helmuth. "Traffic: Classical Antiquity." *BrillPauly* 14:822–23.

Schneider, "Univira." Schneider, Helmuth. "Univira." *BrillPauly* 15:116.

Schneider, "Veterans." Schneider, Helmuth. "Veterans." *BrillPauly* 15:350–54.

Schneider, "Zweck." Schneider, Gerhard. "Der Zweck des Lukanischen Doppelwerks." *BZ* 21 (1, 1977): 45–66.

Schniedewind, "1QSa." Schniedewind, William M. "Rule of the Congregation/Messianic Rule (1QSa)." *DNTB* 1024–26.

Schniedewind, "King." Schniedewind, William M. "King and Priest in the Book of Chronicles and the Duality of Qumran Messianism." *JJS* 45 (1, 1994): 71–78.

Schniedewind, "Melchizedek." Schniedewind, William M. "Melchizedek, Traditions of." *DNTB* 693–95.

Schniedewind, "*Tendenz* in Greek Text." Schniedewind, William M. "Textual Criticism and Theological Interpretation: The Pro-temple *Tendenz* in the Greek Text of Samuel-Kings." *HTR* 87 (1, 1994): 107–16.

Schoedel, "Ambassadorial Activities." Schoedel, William R. "Apologetic Literature and Ambassadorial Activities." *HTR* 82 (1, 1989): 55–78.

Schoeneberger et al., "Abuse." Schoeneberger, Marlies L., et al. "Substance Abuse among Rural and Very Rural Drug Users at Treatment Entry." *American Journal of Drug and Alcohol Abuse* 32 (1, 2006): 87–110.

Schoeps, *Argument*. Schoeps, Hans Joachim. *The Jewish-Christian Argument: A History of Theologies in Conflict*. Translated by David E. Green. New York: Holt, Rinehart & Winston; London: Faber & Faber, 1965.

Schoeps, "Ebionitische Apokalyptik." Schoeps, Hans Joachim. "Ebionitische Apokalyptik im Neuen Testament." *ZNW* 51 (1960): 101–11.

Schoeps, *Paul*. Schoeps, Hans Joachim. *Paul: The Theology of the Apostle in the Light of Jewish Religious History*. Translated by Harold Knight. Philadelphia: Westminster, 1961.

Schoeps, "Prophetenmorde." Schoeps, Hans Joachim. "Die jüdischen Prophetenmorde." Pages 126–43 in *Aus frühchristlichen Zeit: Religionsgeschichtliche Untersuchungen*. Tübingen: J. C. B. Mohr, 1950.

Schofer, "Cosmology." Schofer, Jonathan Wyn. "Theology and Cosmology in Rabbinic Ethics: The Pedagogical Significance of Rainmaking Narratives." *JSQ* 12 (3, 2005): 227–59.

"Schola." "Schola." *BrillPauly* 13:64–67.

Scholem, *Gnosticism*. Scholem, Gershom G. *Jewish Gnosticism, Merkabah Mysticism, and Talmudic Tradition*. New York: Jewish Theological Seminary of America Press, 1965.

Scholem, "Luria." Scholem, Gershom G. "Luria, Isaac ben Solomon." Page 578 in vol. 11 of *Encylopaedia Judaica*. 16 vols. Jerusalem: Keter, 1971.

Scholem, *Sabbatai Sevi*. Scholem, Gershom G. *Sabbatai Sevi: The Mystical Messiah*. Princeton: Princeton University Press, 1973.

Scholem, *Trends*. Scholem, Gershom G. *Major Trends in Jewish Mysticism*. 3rd rev. ed. New York: Schocken, 1971.

Scholer, "Co-Workers." Scholer, David M. "Paul's Women Co-Workers in the Ministry of the Church." *DaughSar* 6 (4, 1980): 3–6.

Scholer, "Writing." Scholer, David M. "Writing and Literature: Greco-Roman." *DNTB* 1282–89.

Scholl, *Apostelgeschichte*. Scholl, Norbert. *Lukas und seine Apostelgeschichte: Die Verbreitung des Glaubens*. Darmstadt: Wissenschaftliche Buchgesellschaft, 2007.

Scholtus, "Problemas." Scholtus, Silvia C. "Problemas eclesiásticos: Respuesta bíblica según Hechos 1–15." *DavLog* 5 (2, 2006): 135–49.

Schönberger, "Stephanus." Schönberger, Rolf. "Der heilige Stephanus. Was bezeugt der erste Märtyrer?" *Geist und Leben* 83 (6, 2010): 464–72.

Schöpflin, "Heilung." Schöpflin, Karin. "Naaman: Seine Heilung und Bekehrung im Alten und im Neuen Testament." *BN* 141 (2009): 35–56.

Schorch, "Bedeutung." Schorch, Stefan. "Die Bedeutung der samaritanischen mündlichen Tradition für die Exegese des Pentateuch." *WD* 25 (1999): 77–91.

Schorch, "Hellenizing Women." Schorch, Stefan. "Hellenizing Women in the Biblical Tradition: The Case of LXX Genesis." *BIOSCS* 41 (2008): 3–16.

Schottroff, "Aspects." Schottroff, Luise. "Important Aspects of the Gospel for the Future." Pages 205–10 in *Readers and Reading of the Fourth Gospel*. Vol. 1 of *What Is John?* Edited by Fernando F. Segovia. SBLSymS 3. Atlanta: Scholars Press, 1996.

Schoville, "Glass." Schoville, Keith N. "Bottles and Glass." Pages 208–16 in vol. 1 of *Dictionary of Daily Life in Biblical and Post-Biblical Antiquity*. Edited by Edwin M. Yamauchi and Marvin R. Wilson. Peabody, Mass.: Hendrickson, 2014.

Schowalter, "Seeking Shelter." Schowalter, Daniel N. "Seeking Shelter in Roman Corinth: Archaeology and the Placement of Paul's Communities." Pages 327–41 in *Corinth in Context: Comparative Studies on Religion and Society*. Edited by Steven J. Friesen et al. NovTSup 134. Leiden: Brill, 2010.

Schreck, "Nazareth Pericope." Schreck, Christopher J. "The Nazareth Pericope: Luke 4,16–30 in Recent Study." Pages 399–471 in *L'Évangile de Luc: The Gospel of Luke*. Edited by F. Neirynck. Rev. ed. BETL 32. Leuven: Leuven University Press, 1989.

Schreiber, "Aktualisierung." Schreiber, Stefan. "Aktualisierung göttlichen Handelns am Pfingsttag: Das frühjüdische Fest in Apg 2,1." *ZNW* 93 (1–2, 2002): 58–77.

Schreiber, "Berufen." Schreiber, Stefan. "Berufen als erster Apostel für Israel und die Völker: Petrus im lukanischen Doppelwerk." *BK* 67 (4, 2012): 215–20.

Schreiber, "König." Schreiber, Stefan. "König JHWH und königlicher Gesalbter: Das Repräsentanzverhältnis in 4Q174." *SNTSU* 26 (2001); 205–19.

Schreiber, "Menschensohn." Schreiber, Stefan. "Henoch als Menschensohn: Zur problematischen Schlussidentifikation in den Bilderreden des äthiopischen Henochbuches (äthHen 71,14)." *ZNW* 91 (1–2, 2000): 1–17.

Schreiber, "Verstehst du denn?" Schreiber, Stefan. "'Verstehst du denn, was du liest?' Beobachtungen zur Begegnung von Philippus und dem äthiopischen Eunuchen (Apg 8,26–40)." *SNTSU* 21 (1996): 42–72.

Schreiner, *Romans*. Schreiner, Thomas R. *Romans*. BECNT. Grand Rapids: Baker, 1998.

Schreiner, "Works of Law." Schreiner, Thomas R. "'Works of Law' in Paul." *NovT* 33 (3, 1991): 217–44.

Schremer, "Boethusians." Schremer, Adiel. "The Name of the Boethusians: A Reconsideration of Suggested Explanations and Another One." *JJS* 48 (2, 1997): 290–99.

Schröder, "History." Schröder, Volker. "Rewriting History for the Early Modern Stage: Racine's Roman Tragedies." Pages 380–93 in *The Cambridge Companion to the Roman Historians*. Edited by Andrew Feldherr. Cambridge: Cambridge University Press, 2009.

Schroeder, "Friendship." Schroeder, Frederic M. "Friendship in Aristotle and Some Peripatetic Philosophers." Pages 35–57 in *Greco-Roman Perspectives on Friendship*. Edited by John T. Fitzgerald. SBLRBS 34. Atlanta: Scholars Press, 1997.

Schröter, "Actaforschung 1." Schröter, Jens. "Actaforschung seit 1982: I. Forschungsgeschichte und Kommentare." *TRu* 72 (2, 2007): 179–230.

Schröter, "Actaforschung 2." Schröter, Jens. "Actaforschung seit 1982: II. Sammelbände. Text- und Rezeptionsgeschichte." *TRu* 72 (3, 2007): 293–345.

Schröter, "Actaforschung 3." Schröter, Jens. "Actaforschung seit 1982: III. Die Apostelgeschichte als Geschichtswerk." *TRu* 72 (4, 2007): 383–419.

Schröter, "Actaforschung 4." Schröter, Jens. "Actaforschung seit 1982: IV. Israel, die Juden, und das Alte Testament—Paulusrezeption." *TRu* 73 (1, 2008): 1–59.

Schröter, "Actaforschung 5." Schröter, Jens. "Actaforschung seit 1982: V. Theologische Einzelthemen." *TRu* 73 (2, 2008): 150–96.

Schröter, "Actaforschung 6." Schröter, Jens. "Actaforschung seit 1982. VI. Gestalten und Gruppen. Einzelthemen. Bilanz und Perspektive." *TRu* 73 (3, 2008): 282–333.

Schröter, "Heiden." Schröter, Jens. "Heil für die Heiden und Israel: Zum Zusammenhang von Christologie und Volk Gottes bei Lukas." Pages 285–308 in *Die Apostelgeschichte und die hellenistische Geschichtsschreibung: Festschrift für Eckhard Plümacher zu seinem 65. Geburtstag*. Edited by Cilliers Breytenbach and Jens Schröter. Leiden: Brill, 2004.

Schröter, "Modell." Schröter, Jens. "Paulus als Modell christlicher Zeugenschaft: Apg 9,15f. und 28,30f. als Rahmen der lukanischen Paulusdarstellung und Rezeption des 'historischen' Paulus." Pages 53–80 in *Reception of Paulinism in Acts. Réception du Paulinisme dans les Actes des Apôtres*. Edited by Daniel Marguerat. BETL 229. Leuven: Peeters, 2009.

Schröter, "Paulusrezeption." Schröter, Jens. "Kirche im Anschluss an Paulus: Aspekte der Paulusrezeption in der Apostelgeschichte und in den Pastoralbriefen." *ZNW* 98 (1, 2007): 77–104.

Schröter, "Stellung." Schröter, Jens. "Zur Stellung der Apostelgeschichte im Kontext der antiken Historiographie." Pages 27–47 in *Die Apostelgeschichte im Kontext antiker und frühchristlicher Historiographie*. Edited by Jörg Frey, Clare K. Rothschild, and Jens Schröter, with Bettina Rost. BZNWK 162. Berlin: de Gruyter, 2009.

Schubert, "Ehescheidung." Schubert, Kurt. "Ehescheidung im Judentum zur Zeit Jesu." *ThQ* 151 (1, 1971): 23–27.

Schubert, "Final Cycle." Schubert, Paul. "The Final Cycle of Speeches in the Book of Acts." *JBL* 87 (1, 1968): 1–16.

Schubert, *Kommunismus*. Schubert, Hans von. *Der Kommunismus der Widertäufer in Münster und seine Quellen*. Heidelberg: Winter, 1911.

Schubert, "Sacra Sinagoga." Schubert, Kurt. "Sacra Sinagoga—zur Heiligkeit der Synagoge in der Spätantike." *BL* 54 (1, 1981): 27–34.

Schuler, "Politarchs." Schuler, Carl. "The Macedonian Politarchs." *CP* 55 (1960): 90–100.

Schuller, "4Q372." Schuller, Eileen. "4Q372 1: A Text about Joseph." *RevQ* 14 (3, 1990): 349–76.

Schuller, "Resurrection." Schuller, Eileen. "Ideas of Resurrection in Intertestamental Sources." *BibT* 27 (3, 1989): 140–45.

Schuller, "Thanksgiving Hymns." Schuller, Eileen. "Thanksgiving Hymns (1QH)." *DNTB* 1214–18.

Schultz, "Angelic Opposition." Schultz, Joseph P. "Angelic Opposition to the Ascension of Moses and the Revelation of the Law." *JQR* 61 (4, 1971): 282–307.

Schultz, "Cemetery." Schultz, Brian. "The Qumran Cemetery: 150 Years of Research." *DSD* 13 (2, 2006): 194–228.

Schultz, "Murder." Schultz, Celia E. "The Romans and Ritual Murder." *JAAR* 78 (2, 2010): 516–41.

Schultz, "Prejudice." Schultz, Celia E. "Modern Prejudice and Ancient Praxis: Female Worship of Hercules at Rome." *ZPE* 133 (2000): 291–97.

Schultz, "Qumran." Schultz, Brian. "Who Lived at Qumran?" *BAR* 33 (5, 2007): 58–59.

Schultz, "Registers." Schultz, Fritz. "Roman Registers of Births and Birth Certificates." *JRS* 32 (1942): 78–91; 33 (1943): 55–64.

Schultz, "Views of Patriarchs." Schultz, Joseph P. "Two Views of the Patriarchs: Noahides and Pre-Sinai Israelites." Pages 43–59 in *Texts and Responses: Studies Presented to Nahum N. Glatzner on the Occasion of His Seventieth Birthday by His Students.* Edited by Michael A. Fishbane and Paul R. Flohr. Leiden: Brill, 1975.

Schultze, "Cincinnatus." Schultze, Clemence. "Clothing Cincinnatus: Dionysius of Halicarnassus." Pages 404–10 in *A Companion to Greek and Roman Historiography.* Edited by John Marincola. 2 vols. Oxford: Blackwell, 2007.

Schulz, "Junia." Schulz, Ray R. "Junia Reinstated: Her Sisters Still Waiting." *LTJ* 38 (3, 2004): 129–43.

Schulz, "Look." Schulz, Ray R. "Another Look at the Text of 1 Corinthians 14:33–35." *LTJ* 32 (3, 1998): 128–31.

Schulze, "Intoxicating Substances." Schulze, Christian. "Intoxicating Substances." *Brill Pauly* 6:877–80.

Schulzki, "Kypros." Schulzki, Heinz-Joachim. "Kypros." *BrillPauly* 7:118–25.

Schumaker, "Suggestibility." Schumaker, J. F. "The Adaptive Value of Suggestibility and Dissociation." Pages 108–31 in *Human Suggestibility: Advances in Theory, Research, and Application.* Edited by J. F. Schumaker. Florence, Ky.: Taylor & Francis/Routledge, 1991.

Schürer, *Age of Jesus Christ.* Schürer, Emil. *The History of the Jewish People in the Age of Jesus Christ (175 B.C.–A.D. 135).* Revised and edited by Geza Vermes, Fergus Millar, and Martin Goodman. 3 vols. in 4. Edinburgh: T&T Clark, 1973–87.

Schürer, *Time of Jesus.* Schürer, Emil. *A History of the Jewish People in the Time of Jesus.* Edited by Nahum N. Glatzer. New York: Schocken, 1961. Abridged from vols. 1–2 of *The History of the Jewish People in the Age*

of Jesus Christ. 5 vols. Edinburgh: T&T Clark, 1886–90.

Schusky, *Manual.* Schusky, Ernest L. *Manual for Kinship Analysis.* 2nd ed. SAnthM. New York: Holt, Rinehart and Winston, 1972.

Schusky, *Variation.* Schusky, Ernest L. *Variation in Kinship.* New York: Holt, Rinehart & Winston, 1974.

Schüssler Fiorenza, "Criteria." Schüssler Fiorenza, Elisabeth. "Theological Criteria and Historical Reconstruction: Martha and Mary, Luke 10:38–42." *CHSP* 53 (1987): 1–12.

Schüssler Fiorenza, "Interpretation." Schüssler Fiorenza, Elisabeth. "A Feminist Critical Interpretation for Liberation: Martha and Mary, Lk. 10:38–42." *RelIntL* 3 (2, 1986): 21–36.

Schüssler Fiorenza, *Memory.* Schüssler Fiorenza, Elisabeth. *In Memory of Her: A Feminist Theological Reconstruction of Christian Origins.* New York: Crossroad, 1983.

Schüssler Fiorenza, *Revelation.* Schüssler Fiorenza, Elisabeth. *The Book of Revelation: Justice and Judgment.* Philadelphia: Fortress, 1985.

Schüssler Fiorenza, "Revelation." Schüssler Fiorenza, Elisabeth. "The Revelation to John." Pages 99–120 in *Hebrews–James–1 and 2 Peter–Jude–Revelation.* Edited by Gerhard Krodel. ProcC. Philadelphia: Fortress, 1977.

Schüssler Fiorenza, "Women." Schüssler Fiorenza, Elisabeth. "Women in the Pre-Pauline and Pauline Churches." *USQR* 33 (3–4, 1978): 153–66.

Schütz, "Prédication." Schütz, Pierre-André. "La prédication de Paul à Athènes (Actes 17,16–34) et la nôtre en contexte postmoderne." *Hok* 93 (2008): 20–37.

Schwab, "Psychosomatic Medicine." Schwab, John J. "Psychosomatic Medicine: Its Past and Present." *Psychosomatics* 26 (7, 1985): 583–93.

Schwank, "Berg." Schwank, Benedikt. "Grabungen auf 'diesem Berg' (Joh 4,20–21): Der archäologische Beitrag." *BK* 47 (4, 1992): 220–21.

Schwank, "Grabungen." Schwank, Benedikt. "Die neuen Grabungen in Sepphoris." *ErAuf* 63 (1987): 222–25; *BK* 42 (2, 1987): 75–79.

Schwank, "Nacht." Schwank, Benedikt. "'Als wir schon die vierzehnte Nacht auf der Adria trieben' (Apg 27,27)." *ErAuf* 66 (1, 1990): 44–49.

Schwank, "Spurensuche auf Kefalonia." Schwank, Benedikt. "Also doch Malta? Spurensuche auf Kefalonia." *BK* 45 (1, 1990): 43–46.

Schwank, "Wasserkrüge." Schwank, Benedikt. "'Sechs steinerne Wasserkrüge' (Joh 2,6)." *ErAuf* 73 (4, 1997): 314–16.

Schwank, "Wort." Schwank, Benedikt. "'Das Wort des Herrn geht aus von Jerusalem' (Jes 2,3): Warum wurde das Apostelkonzil nach vorn gezogen? (Apg 15)." Pages 619–25 in *The Unity of Luke-Acts.* Edited by Joseph Verheyden. BETL 142. Leuven: Leuven University Press, 1999.

Schwankl, "Lauft." Schwankl, Otto. "'Lauft so, dass ihr gewinnt': Zur Wettkampfmetaphorik in 1 Kor 9." *BZ* 41 (2, 1997): 174–91.

Schwartz, "Antonia." Schwartz, Daniel R. "'Stone House,' *birah*, and Antonia during the Time of Jesus." Pages 341–48 in *Jesus and Archaeology.* Edited by James H. Charlesworth. Grand Rapids: Eerdmans, 2006.

Schwartz, "Ben Stada and Peter." Schwartz, Joshua. "Ben Stada and Peter in Lydda." *JSJ* 21 (1, 1990): 1–18.

Schwartz, "Birah." Schwartz, Joshua. "The Temple in Jerusalem: Birah and Baris in Archaeology and Literature." Pages 29–49 in *The Centrality of Jerusalem: Historical Perspectives.* Edited by Marcel Poorthuis and Chana Safrai. Kampen, Neth.: Kok Pharos, 1996.

Schwartz, "Callirhoe's Choice." Schwartz, Saundra. "Callirhoe's Choice: Biological *vs* Legal Paternity." *GRBS* 40 (1, 1999): 23–5.

Schwartz, "Dogs." Schwartz, Joshua. "Dogs in Jewish Society in the Second Temple Period and in the Time of the Mishnah and Talmud." *JJS* 55 (2, 2004): 246–77.

Schwartz, "Futility." Schwartz, Daniel R. "Futility of Preaching Moses (Acts 15,21)." *Bib* 67 (2, 1986): 276–81.

Schwartz, "Infant Exposure." Schwartz, Daniel R. "Did the Jews Practice Infant Exposure and Infanticide in Antiquity?" *SPhilA* 16 (2004): 61–95.

Schwartz, "Inscription in Library." Schwartz, Seth. "A Greek Inscription in the Library of the Annenberg Research Institute." *JQR* 80 (1–2, 1989): 87–91.

Schwartz, "Judaisms." Schwartz, Seth. "How Many Judaisms Were There? A Critique of Neusner and Smith on Definition and Mason and Boyarin on Categorization." *Journal of Ancient Judaism* 2 (2, 2011): 208–38.

Schwartz, "Maccabees and Acts." Schwartz, Daniel R. "On 1–2 Maccabees and Acts." Pages 119–29 in *Die Apostelgeschichte im Kontext antiker und frühchristlicher Historiographie.* Edited by Jörg Frey, Clare K. Rothschild, and Jens Schröter, with Bettina Rost. BZNWK 162. Berlin, New York: de Gruyter, 2009.

Schwartz, "Nicanor Gate." Schwartz, Joshua. "Once More on the Nicanor Gate." *HUCA* 62 (1991): 245–83.

Schwartz, "Peter." Schwartz, Joshua. "Peter and Ben Stada in Lydda." Pages 391–414 in *The Book of Acts in Its Palestinian Setting*. Edited by Richard Bauckham. Vol. 4 of *The Book of Acts in Its First Century Setting*. Edited by Bruce W. Winter. Grand Rapids: Eerdmans; Carlisle, U.K.: Paternoster, 1995.

Schwartz, "Priests in *Ep. Arist.*" Schwartz, Daniel R. "The Priests in *Ep. Arist.* 310." *JBL* 97 (4, 1978): 567–71.

Schwartz, "Rome in Novel." Schwartz, Saundra. "Rome in the Greek Novel: Images and Ideas of Empire in Chariton's Persia." *Arethusa* 36 (3, 2003): 375–94.

Schwartz, "Sympathizers." Schwartz, Daniel R. "Non-joining Sympathizers (Acts 5, 13–14)." *Bib* 64 (4, 1983): 550–55.

Schwartz, "Temples." Schwartz, Daniel R. "The Three Temples of 4QFlorilegium." *RevQ* 10 (1979): 83–91.

Schwartz, "Trial Scenes." Schwartz, Saundra. "The Trial Scenes in the Greek Novels and in Acts." Pages 105–37 in *Contextualizing Acts: Lukan Narrative and Greco-Roman Discourse*. Edited by Todd Penner and Caroline Vander Stichele. SBLSymS 20. Atlanta: SBL, 2003.

Schwartz et al., "Behaviors." Schwartz, Carolyn, et al. "Altruistic Social Interest Behaviors Are Associated with Better Mental Health." *Psychosomatic Medicine* 65 (5, 2003): 778–85.

Schweitzer, *Quest*. Schweitzer, Albert. *The Quest of the Historical Jesus*. Translated by W. Montgomery. Introduction by James M. Robinson. New York: Macmillan, 1968.

Schweizer, *Colossians*. Schweizer, Eduard. *The Letter to the Colossians: A Commentary*. Translated by Andrew Chester. Minneapolis: Augsburg, 1982.

Schweizer, "Concerning Speeches." Schweizer, Eduard. "Concerning the Speeches in Acts." Pages 208–16 in *Studies in Luke-Acts: Essays in Honor of Paul Schubert*. Edited by Leander E. Keck and J. Louis Martyn. Nashville: Abingdon, 1966.

Schweizer, "Davidic 'Son.'" Schweizer, Eduard. "The Concept of the Davidic 'Son of God' in Acts and Its Old Testament Background." Pages 186–93 in *Studies in Luke-Acts: Essays in Honor of Paul Schubert*. Edited by Leander E. Keck and J. Louis Martyn. Nashville: Abingdon, 1966.

Schweizer, *Jesus*. Schweizer, Eduard. *Jesus*. Translated by David E. Green. NTL. London: SCM, 1971.

Schweizer, *Mark*. Schweizer, Eduard. *The Good News according to Mark*. Translated by Donald H. Madvig. Atlanta: John Knox, 1970.

Schweizer, *Matthew*. Schweizer, Eduard. *The Good News according to Matthew*. Translated by David E. Green. Atlanta: John Knox, 1975.

Schweizer, *Parable*. Schweizer, Eduard. *Jesus the Parable of God: What Do We Really Know about Jesus?* PrTMS 37. Allison Park, Pa.: Pickwick, 1994.

Schweizer, "Son of Man Again." Schweizer, Eduard. "The Son of Man Again." *NTS* 9 (3, 1963): 256–61.

Schweizer, *Spirit*. Schweizer, Eduard. *The Holy Spirit*. Translated by Reginald H. Fuller and Ilse Fuller. Philadelphia: Fortress, 1980.

Schwemer, "Gründungslegenden." Schwemer, Anna Maria. "Die griechischen und jüdischen Gründungslegenden Alexandrias." *BN* 148 (2011): 3–18.

Schwemer, "Weather Gods." Schwemer, Daniel. "Weather Gods." *BrillPauly* 15:601–2.

Schwentzel, "Images." Schwentzel, Christian-Georges. "Images grecques de Souverains Juifs (63 av. J.-C.–44 apr. J.-C.)." *RB* 117 (4, 2010): 528–49.

Schwertheim, "Assos." Schwertheim, Elmar. "Assos." *BrillPauly* 2:184–86.

Schwertheim, "Lampsacus." Schwertheim, Elmar. "Lampsacus." *BrillPauly* 7:190–91.

Schwertheim, "Mysia." Schwertheim, Elmar. "Mysia." *BrillPauly* 9:426–28.

Schwertheim, "Troad." Schwertheim, Elmar. "Troad." *BrillPauly* 14:955–56.

Schwindt, "Anthology." Schwindt, Jürgen Paul. "Anthology." *BrillPauly* 1:726–31.

"Science or Miracle." "Science or Miracle? Holiday Season Survey Reveals Physicians' Views of Faith, Prayer, and Miracles." *Business Wire*, Dec. 20, 2004. http://www.businesswire.com/portal/site/google/index.jsp?ndmViewID=news_view&news&newsID=20041220005244&newsLang=en.

Scobie, "Origins and Development." Scobie, Charles H. H. "The Origins and Development of Samaritan Christianity." *NTS* 19 (4, 1973): 390–414.

Scobie, "Source Material." Scobie, Charles H. H. "The Use of Source Material in the Speeches of Acts III and IV." *NTS* 25 (4, 1979): 399–421.

Scodel, "Drama and Rhetoric." Scodel, Ruth. "Drama and Rhetoric." Pages 489–504 in *Handbook of Classical Rhetoric in the Hellenistic Period, 330 B.C.–A.D. 400*. Edited by Stanley E. Porter. Leiden: Brill, 1997.

Scott, "Acts 10:34." Scott, J. Julius, Jr. "Acts 10:34, a Text for Racial and Cultural Reconciliation among Christians." Pages 131–39 in *The Gospel in Black and White: Theological Resources for Racial Reconciliation*. Edited by Dennis L. Ockholm. Downers Grove, Ill.: InterVarsity, 1997.

Scott, "Ascent." Scott, James M. "Heavenly Ascent in Jewish and Pagan Traditions." *DNTB* 447–52.

Scott, "Attitudes." Scott, David. "Buddhist Attitudes to Hellenism: A Review of the Issue." *SR/SR* 15 (4, 1986): 433–41.

Scott, "Binitarian Nature." Scott, Steven Richard. "The Binitarian Nature of the Book of Similitudes." *JSP* 18 (1, 2008): 55–78.

Scott, *Corinthians*. Scott, James M. *2 Corinthians*. NIBCNT. Peabody, Mass.: Hendrickson, 1998.

Scott, "Cornelius Incident." Scott, J. Julius, Jr. "The Cornelius Incident in the Light of Its Jewish Setting." *JETS* 34 (4, 1991): 475–84.

Scott, *Customs*. Scott, J. Julius, Jr. *Customs and Controversies: Intertestamental Jewish Backgrounds of the New Testament*. Grand Rapids: Baker, 1995.

Scott, "Deuteronomic Tradition." Scott, James M. "Paul's Use of Deuteronomic Tradition." *JBL* 112 (4, 1993): 645–65.

Scott, "Galatia." Scott, James M. "Galatia, Galatians." *DNTB* 389–91.

Scott, "Geographical Perspectives." Scott, James M. "Geographical Perspectives in Late Antiquity." *DNTB* 411–14.

Scott, "Horizon." Scott, James M. "Luke's Geographical Horizon." Pages 483–544 in *The Book of Acts in Its Graeco-Roman Setting*. Edited by David W. J. Gill and Conrad Gempf. Vol. 2 of *The Book of Acts in Its First Century Setting*. Edited by Bruce W. Winter. Grand Rapids: Eerdmans; Carlisle, U.K.: Paternoster, 1994.

Scott, "Local Responses." Scott, Sarah. "Local Responses to Roman Imperialism." *AJA* 114 (3, 2010): 557–61.

Scott, *Nations*. Scott, James M. *Paul and the Nations: The Old Testament and Jewish Background of Paul's Mission to the Nations with Special Reference to the Destination of Galatians*. WUNT 84. Tübingen: J. C. B. Mohr, 1995.

Scott, *Parable*. Scott, Bernard Brandon. *Hear Then the Parable: A Commentary on the Parables of Jesus*. Minneapolis: Augsburg Fortress, 1989.

Scott, *Pastoral Epistles*. Scott, E. F. *The Pastoral Epistles*. MNTC. London: Hodder & Stoughton, 1936.

Scott, *Relevance*. Scott, R. B. Y. *The Relevance of the Prophets*. New York: Macmillan, 1954.

Scott, *Spirit*. Scott, Ernest F. *The Spirit in the New Testament*. London: Hodder & Stoughton; New York: George H. Doran, 1923.

Scott, "Stephen's Speech." Scott, J. Julius, Jr. "Stephen's Speech: A Possible Model for Luke's Historical Method?" *JETS* 17 (2, 1974): 91–97.

Scott, "Tabernacle." Scott, John Atwood. "The Pattern of the Tabernacle." PhD diss., University of Pennsylvania, 1965.

Scott, "Triumph." Scott, James M. "The Triumph of God in 2 Cor 2:14: Additional Evidence of Merkabah Mysticism in Paul." *NTS* 42 (2, 1996): 260–81.

Scott, "World Mission." Scott, J. Julius. "Stephen's Defense and the World Mission of the People of God." *JETS* 21 (2, 1978): 131–41.

Scourfield, "Chaereas." Scourfield, J. H. D. "Chaereas, Hippolytus, Theseus: Tragic Echoes, Tragic Potential in Chariton." *Phoenix* 64 (3–4, 2010): 291–313.

Scourfield, "Consolation." Scourfield, J. H. D. "Consolation." *OCD*³ 378.

Scramuzza, *Sicily*. Scramuzza, Vincent Mary. *Roman Sicily*. Baltimore: Johns Hopkins Press, 1937.

Scranton, "Commercial Features." Scranton, Robert. "The Harbor-Side Commercial Features." Pages 39–52 in *Topography and Architecture*. By Robert Scranton, Joseph W. Shaw, and Leila Ibrahim. Vol. 1 of *Kenchreai, Eastern Port of Corinth: Results of Investigations by the University of Chicago and Indiana University for the American School of Classical Studies at Athens*. Leiden: Brill, 1978.

Scranton, "Harbor-Side Sanctuaries." Scranton, Robert. "The Harbor-Side Sanctuaries." Pages 53–90 in *Topography and Architecture*. By Robert Scranton, Joseph W. Shaw, and Leila Ibrahim. Vol. 1 of *Kenchreai, Eastern Port of Corinth: Results of Investigations by the University of Chicago and Indiana University for the American School of Classical Studies at Athens*. Leiden: Brill, 1978.

Scroggs, *Adam*. Scroggs, Robin. *The Last Adam: A Study in Pauline Anthropology*. Philadelphia: Fortress, 1966.

Scroggs, *Homosexuality*. Scroggs, Robin. *The New Testament and Homosexuality: Contextual Background for Contemporary Debate*. Philadelphia: Fortress, 1983.

Scroggs, "Present State." Scroggs, Robin. "The Sociological Interpretation of the New Testament: The Present State of Research." *NTS* 26 (2, 1980): 164–79.

Scroggs, "Woman." Scroggs, Robin. "Paul and the Eschatological Woman." *JAAR* 40 (3, 1972): 283–303.

Scullard, "Gessius Florus." Scullard, Howard Hayes. "Gessius Florus." *OCD*³ 635.

Scurlock, "Death." Scurlock, JoAnn. "Death and the Afterlife in Ancient Mesopotamian Thought." Pages 1883–93 in *Civilizations of the Ancient Near East*. Edited by Jack M. Sasson. 4 vols. New York: Scribner's, 1995.

Scurlock, "Ghosts." Scurlock, JoAnn. "Ghosts in the Ancient Near East: Weak or Powerful?" *HUCA* 68 (1997): 77–96.

Seaford, "Thunder." Seaford, Richard. "Thunder, Lightning, and Earthquake in the *Bacchae* and the Acts of the Apostles." Pages 139–48 in *Studies in the Nature of Greek Divinity*. Edited by Alan B. Lloyd. London: Duckworth, 1997.

Seager, "Synagogue." Seager, Andrew R. "The Synagogue and the Jewish Community: The Building." Pages 168–77 in *Sardis from Prehistoric to Roman Times: Results of the Archaeological Exploration of Sardis, 1958–1975*. Edited by George M. A. Hanfmann, assisted by William E. Mierse. Cambridge, Mass.: Harvard University Press, 1983.

Seager and Kraabel, "Synagogue." Seager, Andrew R., and A. Thomas Kraabel, "The Synagogue and the Jewish Community." Pages 168–90 in *Sardis from Prehistoric to Roman Times: Results of the Archaeological Exploration of Sardis, 1958–1975*. Edited by George M. A. Hanfmann, assisted by William E. Mierse. Cambridge, Mass.: Harvard University Press, 1983.

Seagrave, "Natural Law Theory." Seagrave, S. Adam. "Cicero, Aquinas, and Contemporary Issues in Natural Law Theory." *RevMet* 62 (3, 2009): 491–523.

Seale, "Collaboration." Seale, J. Paul. "Christian Missionary Medicine and Traditional Healers: A Case Study in Collaboration from the Philippines." *Missiology* 21 (3, 1993): 311–20.

Sears, "View." Sears, Robert T. "A Catholic View of Exorcism and Deliverance." Pages 100–114 in *Essays on Spiritual Bondage and Deliverance*. Edited by Willard M. Swartley. Occasional Papers 11. Elkhart, Ind.: Institute of Mennonite Studies, 1988.

Sebald, "Witchcraft." Sebald, Hans. "Franconian Witchcraft: The Demise of a Folk Magic." *AnthrQ* 53 (3, 1980): 173–87.

Seccombe, "Luke and Isaiah." Seccombe, David. "Luke and Isaiah." *NTS* 27 (2, 1981): 252–59.

Seccombe, "Organized Charity." Seccombe, David. "Was There Organized Charity in Jerusalem before the Christians?" *JTS* 29 (1, 1978): 140–43.

Seccombe, "People." Seccombe, David. "The New People of God." Pages 349–72 in *Witness to the Gospel: The Theology of Acts*. Edited by I. Howard Marshall and David Peterson. Grand Rapids: Eerdmans, 1998.

Sechrest, *Jew*. Sechrest, Love L. *A Former Jew: Paul and the Dialectics of Race*. LNTS 410. London: T&T Clark, 2009.

Séd, "Traditions secrètes." Séd, Nicholas. "Les traditions secrètes et les disciples de Rabban Yohanan ben Zakkai." *RHR* 184 (1, 1973): 49–66.

Seeley, "Cynics." Seeley, David. "Jesus and the Cynics Revisited." *JBL* 116 (4, 1997): 704–12.

Seeligmann, "Phōs." Seeligmann, I. "Deixai autō phōs." [In Hebrew.] *Tarbiz* 27 (2–3, 1958): 127–41.

Seely, "Heart." Seely, David Rolph. "The 'Circumcised Heart' in 4Q434 *Barki Nafshi*." *RevQ* 17 (65–68, 1996): 527–35.

Seesengood, "Rules." Seesengood, Robert P. "Rules for an Ancient Philadelphian Religious Organization and Early Christian Ethical Teaching." *SCJ* 5 (2, 2002): 217–33.

Segal, "Acts 15." Segal, Alan F. "Acts 15 as Jewish and Christian History." *Forum* 4 (1, 2001): 63–87.

Segal, "Ascent in Judaism." Segal, Alan F. "Heavenly Ascent in Hellenistic Judaism, Early Christianity, and Their Environment." *ANRW* 23.2:1333–94. Part 2, *Principat*, 23.2. Edited by H. Temporini and W. Haase. Berlin: de Gruyter, 1980.

Segal, *Convert*. Segal, Alan F. *Paul the Convert: The Apostolate and Apostasy of Paul the Pharisee*. New Haven: Yale University Press, 1990.

Segal, "Covenant." Segal, Alan F. "Covenant in Rabbinic Writings." *SR/SR* 14 (1, 1985): 53–62.

Segal, "Death Penalty." Segal, Peretz. "The 'Divine Death Penalty' in the Hatra Inscriptions and the Mishnah." *JJS* 40 (1, 1989): 46–52.

Segal, "Exégètes juifs." Segal, Alan F. "Paul et ses exégètes juifs contemporains." *RSR* 94 (3, 2006): 413–41.

Segal, "Few Contained Many." Segal, Eliezer. "'The Few Contained the Many': Rabbinic Perspectives on the Miraculous and the Impossible." *JJS* 54 (2, 2003): 273–82.

Segal, "Menace." Segal, Charles. "The Menace of Dionysus: Sex Roles and Reversals in Euripides' Bacchae." Pages 195–212 in *Women in the Ancient World: The Arethusa Papers*. Edited by John Peradotto and J. P. Sullivan. SSCS. Albany: State University of New York Press, 1984.

Segal, *Passover*. Segal, J. B. *The Hebrew Passover from the Earliest Times to A.D. 70*. LOS 12. New York: Oxford University Press, 1963.

Segal, "Penalty." Segal, Peretz. "The Penalty of the Warning Inscription from the Temple of Jerusalem." *IEJ* 39 (1–2, 1989): 79–84.

Segal, "Presuppositions." Segal, Alan F. "Paul's Jewish Presuppositions." Pages 159–72 in *The Cambridge Companion* to *St Paul*. Edited by James D. G. Dunn. Cambridge: Cambridge University Press, 2003.

Segal, "Resurrection." Segal, Alan F. "Paul's Thinking about Resurrection in Its Jewish Context." *NTS* 44 (3, 1998): 400–419.

Segal, "Revolutionary." Segal, Alan F. "Jesus, the Jewish Revolutionary." Pages 199–225 in *Jesus' Jewishness: Exploring the Place of Jesus within Early Judaism*. Edited by James H. Charlesworth. Philadelphia: American Interfaith Institute; New York: Crossroad, 1991.

Segal, "Ruler." Segal, Alan F. "Ruler of This World: Attitudes about Mediator Figures and the Importance of Sociology for Self-Definition." Pages 245–68 in *Aspects of Judaism in the Graeco-Roman Period*. Edited by E. P. Sanders with A. I. Baumgarten and Alan Mendelson. Vol. 2 of *Jewish and Christian Self-Definition*. Edited by E. P. Sanders. Philadelphia: Fortress, 1981.

Segal, "Studying." Segal, Alan F. "Studying Judaism with Christian Sources." *USQR* 44 (3–4, 1991): 267–86.

Segal, "Theaters." Segal, Arthur. "Theaters." *OEANE* 5:199–202.

Segal and Eisenberg, "Sussita-Hippos." Segal, Arthur, and Michael Eisenberg. "Sussita-Hippos of the Decapolis: Town Planning and Architecture of a Roman Byzantine City." *NEA* 70 (2, 2007): 86–107.

Segalla, "Problema." Segalla, Giuseppe. "Il problema della volontà libera nell'apocalittica ebràica e nei 'Testamenti dei 12 patrìarchi.'" *DivThom* 70 (1–2, 1967): 108–16.

Seger, "Shechem." Seger, Joe D. "Shechem." *OEANE* 5:19–23.

Segert, "Languages." Segert, Stanislav. "The Languages of Historical Jesus." *CV* 44 (2, 2002): 161–73.

Segert, "Review (1968)." Segert, Stanislav. Review of J. A. Fitzmyer, *The Genesis Apocryphon of Qumran Cave I, a Commentary* (1966). *JSS* 13 (2, 1968): 281–82.

Segert, "Review (1972)." Segert, Stanislav. Review of J. A. Fitzmyer, *The Genesis Apocryphon of Qumran Cave I, A Commentary* (2nd rev. ed., 1971). *JSS* 17 (2, 1972): 273–74.

Segovia, *Farewell*. Segovia, Fernando F. *The Farewell of the Word: The Johannine Call to Abide*. Minneapolis: Fortress, 1991.

Seidler, "Kant." Seidler, Michael J. "Kant and the Stoics on Suicide." *JHI* 44 (1983): 429–54.

Seidlmayer, "Nubia." Seidlmayer, Stephan Johannes. "Nubia." *BrillPauly* 9:867–70.

Seifrid, *Justification*. Seifrid, Mark A. *Justification by Faith: The Origin and Development*

of a Central Pauline Theme*. NovTSup 68. Leiden: Brill, 1992.

Seifrid, "Problems." Seifrid, Mark A. "The 'New Perspective on Paul' and Its Problems." *Them* 25 (2, 2000): 4–18.

Seim, *Double Message*. Seim, Turid Karlsen. *The Double Message: Patterns of Gender in Luke and Acts*. Nashville: Abingdon, 1994.

Seiter and Waddell, "Reentry Process." Seiter, John S., and Debra Waddell. "The Intercultural Reentry Process: Reentry Shock, Locus of Control, Satisfaction, and Interpersonal Uses of Communication." Paper presented at the annual meeting of the Western Speech Communication Association, Spokane, Wash., Feb. 17–21, 1989.

Seitz, "Two Spirits." Seitz, Oscar J. F. "Two Spirits in Man: An Essay in Biblical Exegesis." *NTS* 6 (1, 1959): 82–95.

Seland, *Violence*. Seland, Torrey. *Establishment Violence in Philo and Luke: A Study of Non-conformity to the Torah and Jewish Vigilante Reactions*. BIS 15. Leiden: Brill, 1995.

Selden, "Genre." Selden, Daniel L. "Genre of Genre." Pages 39–64 in *The Search for the Ancient Novel*. Edited by James Tatum. Baltimore: Johns Hopkins University Press, 1994.

"Seleucia Pieria." "Seleucia Pieria." *BrillPauly* 13:213.

Selinger, "Demetriosunruhen." Selinger, Reinhard. "Die Demetriosunruhen (Apg. 19,23–40): Eine Fallstudie aus rechtshistorischer Perspektive." *ZNW* 88 (3–4, 1997): 242–59.

Selkin, "Exegesis." Selkin, Carol Barbara. "Exegesis and Identity: The Hermeneutics of *miqwa'ot* in the Greco-Roman Period." PhD diss., Duke University, 1993.

Sell, "Seven." Sell, Phillip W. "The Seven in Acts 6 as a Ministry Team." *BSac* 167 (665, 2010): 58–67.

Sellers, "*Zar*." Sellers, Barbara. "The *zar*: Women's Theatre in the Southern Sudan." Pages 156–64 in *Women's Medicine: The zar-bori Cult in Africa and Beyond*. Edited by I. M. Lewis, Ahmed Al-Safi, and Sayyid Hurreiz. Edinburgh: International African Institute, Edinburgh University Press, 1991.

Seltman, "Wardrobe of Artemis." Seltman, Charles. "The Wardrobe of Artemis." *NumC*, 6th ser., 12 (1952): 33–51.

Selwyn, *Peter*. Selwyn, Edward Gordon. *The First Epistle of St. Peter: The Greek Text with Introduction, Notes, and Essays*. 2nd ed. New York: Macmillan, 1947.

Senior and Stuhlmueller, *Foundation for Mission*. Senior, Donald P., and Carroll Stuhlmueller. *The Biblical Foundation for Mission*. Maryknoll, N.Y.: Orbis, 1983.

Sensing, "Paraenesis." Sensing, Timothy. "Towards a Definition of Paraenesis." *ResQ* 38 (3, 1996): 145–58.

Seow, "Context." Seow, Choon Leong. "The Syro-Palestinian Context of Solomon's Dream." *HTR* 77 (1984): 141–52.

Sequeira, "Prayer." Sequeira, T. d'A. "Prayer: A Pauline Perspective." *Jeev* 33 (194, 2003): 142–51.

Serban and Baluta, "Mithraism." Serban, Ioan, and Closca L. Baluta. "On Mithraism in the Army of Dacia Superior." Pages 573–78 in *Mysteria Mithrae*. Edited by Ugo Bianchi. ÉPROER 80. Leiden: Brill, 1979.

Setzer, *Responses*. Setzer, Claudia J. *Jewish Responses to Early Christians: History and Polemics, 30–150 C.E.* Minneapolis: Fortress, 1994.

Setzer, "Resurrection." Setzer, Claudia J. "Resurrection of the Dead as Symbol and Strategy." *JAAR* 69 (1, 2001): 65–101.

Seul, *Rettung*. Seul, Peter. *Rettung für alle: Die Romreise des Paulus nach Apg 27,1–28, 16*. BBB 146. Berlin: Philo, 2003.

Sevenster, *Anti-Semitism*. Sevenster, J. N. *The Roots of Pagan Anti-Semitism in the Ancient World*. NovTSup 41. Leiden: Brill, 1975.

Sevenster, *Greek*. Sevenster, J. N. *Do You Know Greek? How Much Greek Could the First Jewish Christians Have Known?* NovTSup 19. Leiden: Brill, 1968.

Sevenster, *Seneca*. Sevenster, J. N. *Paul and Seneca*. NovTSup 4. Leiden: Brill, 1961.

Shaked, "Jesus." Shaked, Shaul. "Jesus in the Magic Bowls: A propos Dan Levene's '. . . and by the name of Jesus . . .'" *JSQ* 6 (4, 1999): 309–19.

Shank, "Prophet." Shank, David A. "A Prophet of Modern Times: The Thought of William Wadé Harris." 3 vols. PhD diss., University of Aberdeen, 1980.

Shanks, "*BAR* Interviews Yadin." Shanks, Hershel. "*BAR* Interviews Yigael Yadin." *BAR* 9 (1, 1983): 16–23.

Shanks, "Channels." Shanks, Hershel. "The Puzzling Channels in Ancient Latrines." *BAR* 28 (5, 2002): 48–51, 70.

Shanks, "Destruction." Shanks, Hershel. "The Destruction of Pompeii: God's Revenge?" *BAR* 36 (4, 2010): 60–67, 77.

Shanks, "Inscription." Shanks, Hershel. "Inscription Reveals Roots of Maccabean Revolt." *BAR* 34 (6, 2008): 56–59.

Shanks, "Is It a Synagogue?" Shanks, Hershel. "Is It or Isn't It—a Synagogue?" *BAR* 27 (6, 2001): 51–57.

Shanks, "Sample." Shanks, Hershel. "The Seventh Sample: IAA Report Shows Evidence for Authenticity of 'Jesus.'" *BAR* 30 (2, 2004): 44–47.

Shanks, "Who Lies?" Shanks, Hershel. "Who Lies Here? Jordan Tombs Match

Those at Qumran." *BAR* 25 (5, 1999): 48–53, 76.

Shanks, "Zodiac." Shanks, Hershel. "Synagogue Excavation Reveals Stunning Mosaic of Zodiac and Torah Ark." *BAR* 10 (3, 1984): 32–44.

Shapiro, "Wisdom." Shapiro, David S. "Wisdom and Knowledge of God in Biblical and Talmudic Thought." *Tradition* 12 (2, 1971): 70–89.

Sharp, "Miracles." Sharp, John C. "Miracles and the 'Laws of Nature.'" *SBET* 6 (1988): 1–19.

Sharp, *Possessed*. Sharp, Lesley A. *The Possessed and the Dispossessed: Spirits, Identity, and Power in a Madagascar Migrant Town*. CSHSMC. Berkeley: University of California Press, 1993.

Sharp, "Possessed." Sharp, Lesley A. "Possessed and Dispossessed Youth: Spirit Possession of School Children in Northwest Madagascar." *CMPsy* 14 (1990): 339–64.

Sharp, "Power of Possession." Sharp, Lesley A. "The Power of Possession in Northwest Madagascar: Contesting Colonial and National Hegemonies." Pages 3–19 in *Spirit Possession, Modernity and Power in Africa*. Edited by Heike Behrend and Ute Luig. Madison: University of Wisconsin Press, 1999.

Sharp, "Zeal." Sharp, Carolyn J. "Phinehan Zeal and Rhetorical Strategy in 4QMMT." *RevQ* 18 (70, 1997): 207–22.

Sharpe, "Adam." Sharpe, John L., III. "The Second Adam in the Apocalypse of Moses." *CBQ* 35 (1, 1973): 35–46.

Sharples, *Stoics, Epicureans, and Sceptics*. Sharples, Robert W. *Stoics, Epicureans, and Sceptics: An Introduction to Hellenistic Philosophy*. London: Routledge, 1996.

Sharvit, "Hkhn." Sharvit, Baruch. "Hkhn bkt mdbr yhwdh." *BMik* 70 (1977): 313–20.

Shaub, "Analysis." Shaub, Robert William. "An Analysis of the Healing Ministries Conducted in Three Contemporary Churches." DMin diss., Eastern Baptist Theological Seminary, 1980.

Shauf, "Eunuch." Shauf, Scott. "Locating the Eunuch: Characterization and Narrative Context in Acts 8:26–40." *CBQ* 71 (4, 2009): 762–75.

Shauf, *Theology*. Shauf, Scott. *Theology as History, History as Theology: Paul in Ephesus in Acts 19*. BZNW 133. Berlin: de Gruyter, 2005.

Shaw, "Age." Shaw, Brent D. "The Age of Roman Girls at Marriage: Some Reconsiderations." *JRS* 77 (1987): 30–46.

Shaw, *Awakening*. Shaw, Mark. *Global Awakening: How 20th-Century Revivals Triggered a Christian Revolution*. Downers Grove, Ill.: IVP Academic, 2010.

Shaw, "Brigandry." Shaw, Brent D. "Brigandry." *BrillPauly* 2:768–72.

Shaw, "Brotherhood." Shaw, Brent D. "Ritual Brotherhood in Roman and Post-Roman Societies." *Traditio* 52 (1997): 327–55.

Shaw, "Harborage." Shaw, Joseph. "The Harborage." Pages 13–38 in *Topography and Architecture*. By Robert Scranton, Joseph W. Shaw, and Leila Ibrahim. Vol. 1 of *Kenchreai, Eastern Port of Corinth: Results of Investigations by the University of Chicago and Indiana University for the American School of Classical Studies at Athens*. Leiden: Brill, 1978.

Shaw, "Raising." Shaw, Brent D. "Raising and Killing Children: Two Roman Myths." *Mnemosyne* 54 (1, 2001): 31–77.

Shaya, "Temple." Shaya, Josephine. "The Greek Temple as Museum: The Case of the Legendary Treasure of Athena from Lindos." *AJA* 109 (3, 2005): 423–42.

Shea, "Azazel." Shea, William H. "Azazel in the Pseudepigrapha." *JATS* 13 (1, 2002): 1–9.

Shea, "Educating." Shea, Chris. "Educating Paul." *Forum* 5 (2, 2002): 225–34.

Shea, "Imitating." Shea, Chris. "Imitating Imitation: Vergil, Homer, and Acts 10:1–11:18." Pages 37–59 in *Ancient Fiction: The Matrix of Early Christian and Jewish Narrative*. Edited by Jo-Ann A. Brant, Charles W. Hedrick, and Chris Shea. SBLSymS 32. Atlanta: SBL, 2005.

Shea, "Pieces of Epic." Shea, Chris. "Pieces of Epic in the Shipwreck in Acts 27." *Forum* 5 (1, 2002): 73–86.

Shea, "Stage." Shea, Chris. "Setting the Stage for Romances: Xenophon of Ephesus and the Ecphrasis." Pages 61–76 in *Ancient Fiction and Early Christian Narrative*. Edited by Ronald F. Hock, J. Bradley Chance, and Judith Perkins. SBLSymS 6. Atlanta: SBL, 1998.

Sheeley, *Asides*. Sheeley, Steven M. *Narrative Asides in Luke-Acts*. JSNTSup 72. Sheffield, U.K.: Sheffield Academic, 1992.

Sheeley, "Narrative Presence." Sheeley, Steven M. "Getting into the Act(s): Narrative Presence in the 'We' Sections." *PRSt* 26 (2, 1999): 203–20.

Sheldon, *Mystery Religions*. Sheldon, Henry C. *The Mystery Religions and the New Testament*. New York: Abingdon, 1918.

Sheler, *True*. Sheler, Jeffrey L. *Is the Bible True? How Modern Debates and Discoveries Affirm the Essence of the Scriptures*. New York: HarperCollins, 1999.

Shelley, *History*. Shelley, Bruce L. *Church History in Plain Language*. 2nd ed. Nashville: Thomas Nelson, 1995.

Shelton, "Boldness." Shelton, James B. "Holy Boldness in Acts with Special Reference to Pauline-Lukan Intertextuality." Pages 300–320 in *Trajectories in the Book of Acts: Essays in Honor of John Wesley Wyckoff*. Edited by Paul Alexander, Jordan Daniel May, and Robert G. Reid. Eugene, Ore.: Wipf & Stock, 2010.

Shelton, "Epistemology." Shelton, James B. "Epistemology and Authority in the Acts of the Apostles: An Analysis and Test Case Study of Acts 15:1–29." *SpCh* 2 (2, 2000): 231–47.

Shelton, *Mighty in Deed*. Shelton, James B. *Mighty in Word and Deed: The Role of the Holy Spirit in Luke-Acts*. Peabody, Mass.: Hendrickson, 1991.

Shelton, *Romans*. Shelton, Jo-Ann. *As the Romans Did: A Sourcebook in Roman Social History*. 2nd ed. New York and Oxford: Oxford University Press, 1998.

Shelton, "Used to Be?" Shelton, James B. "'Not like It Used to Be?': Jesus, Miracles, and Today." *JPT* 14 (2, 2006): 219–27. (Response to Keith Warrington, "Healing Narratives.")

Shemesh, "Angels." Shemesh, Aharon. "'The Holy Angels Are in Their Council': The Exclusion of Deformed Persons from Holy Places in Qumranic and Rabbinic Literature." *DSD* 4 (2, 1997): 179–206.

Shemesh, "Note on 4Q339." Shemesh, Aharon. "A Note on 4Q339: 'List of False Prophets.'" *RevQ* 20 (78, 2001): 319–20.

Shemesh, "Vegetarian Ideology." Shemesh, Yael. "Vegetarian Ideology in Talmudic Literature and Traditional Biblical Exegesis." *RRJ* 9 (2006): 141–66.

Shenk and Stutzman, *Communities*. Shenk, David W., and Ervin R. Stutzman. *Creating Communities of the Kingdom: New Testament Models of Church Planting*. Foreword by Myron S. Augsburger. Scottsdale, Pa.: Herald, 1988.

Shepherd, *Narrative Function*. Shepherd, William H., Jr. *The Narrative Function of the Holy Spirit as a Character in Luke-Acts*. SBLDS 147. Atlanta: Scholars Press, 1994.

Shepherd, "Targums." Shepherd, Michael B. "Targums, the New Testament, and Biblical Theology of the Messiah." *JETS* 51 (1, 2008): 45–58.

Sheppard, "Bithynia." Sheppard, Anthony. "Bithynia." *ABD* 1:750–53.

Sherif, "Nubia before Napata." Sherif, N. M. "Nubia before Napata (-3100 to -750)." Pages 245–74 in *Ancient Civilizations of Africa*. Edited by G. Mokhtar. General History of Africa 2. Berkeley: University of California Press; London: Heinemann Educational; Paris: United Nations Educational, Scientific and Cultural Organization, 1981.

Sheriffs, "Testing." Sheriffs, Deryck C. T. "Testing." *DOTP* 830–34.

Sherk, *Empire*. Sherk, Robert K., ed. and trans. *The Roman Empire: Augustus to Hadrian*. Translated Documents of Greece and Rome 6. New York: Cambridge University Press, 1988.

Sherrill, *Tongues*. Sherrill, John L. *They Speak with Other Tongues*. Old Tappan, N.J.: Fleming H. Revell, 1965.

Sherwin-White, "Pilate." Sherwin-White, A. N. "Pilate, Pontius." *ISBE* 4:867–69.

Sherwin-White, *Society*. Sherwin-White, A. N. *Roman Society and Roman Law in the New Testament*. Oxford: Clarendon, 1963.

Sherwin-White, "Trial." Sherwin-White, A. N. "The Trial of Christ." Pages 97–116 in *Historicity and Chronology in the New Testament*. Essays by D. E. Nineham et al. London: SPCK, 1965.

Sherwin-White and Lintott, "*Peregrini*." Sherwin-White, A. N., and Andrew William Lintott. "*Peregrini*." *OCD*³ 1138.

Sherwin-White, Jones, and Honoré, "*Decuriones*." Sherwin-White, A. N., A. H. M. Jones, and Tony Honoré. "*Decuriones*." *OCD*³ 437–38.

Sherwin-White, Levick, and Bispham, "Colonization." Sherwin-White, A. N., Barbara M. Levick, and Edward Henry Bispham. "Colonization, Roman." *OCD*³ 364–65.

Shibata, "Ineffable." Shibata, You. "On the Ineffable—Philo and Justin." Pages 19–47 in supplementary vol. 1 of *Patristica: Proceedings of the Colloquia of the Japanese Society for Patristic Studies*. Tokyo: Japanese Society for Patristic Studies, 2001–.

Shields, "Areopagus Sermon and Romans." Shields, Bruce E. "The Areopagus Sermon and Romans 1:18ff: A Study in Creation Theology." *ResQ* 20 (1977): 23–40.

Shiell, *Reading Acts*. Shiell, William David. *Reading Acts: The Lector and the Early Christian Audience*. BIS 70. Boston: Brill Academic, 2004.

Shillington, *Introduction*. Shillington, V. George. *An Introduction to the Study of Luke-Acts*. TTCABS. New York: T&T Clark, 2007.

Shinan, "Sermons." Shinan, Avigdor. "Sermons, Targums, and the Reading from Scriptures in the Ancient Synagogue." Pages 97–110 in *The Synagogue in Late Antiquity*. Edited by Lee I. Levine. Philadelphia: American Schools of Oriental Research, 1986.

Shinde, "Animism." Shinde, Benjamin Prasad. "Animism in Popular Hinduism." DMiss diss., Fuller Theological Seminary, 1975.

Shipley, "Chios." Shipley, D. Graham J. "Chios." *OCD*³ 322–23.

Shipley, *History of Samos*. Shipley, D. Graham J. *A History of Samos, 800–188 BC*. Oxford: Clarendon, 1987.

Shipley, "Imbros." Shipley, D. Graham J. "Imbros." *OCD*³ 749.

Shipley, "Samos." Shipley, D. Graham J. "Samos." *OCD*³ 1351.

Shipley and Rouaché, "Mytilene." Shipley, D. Graham J., and Charlotte Rouaché. "Mytilene." *OCD*³ 1020.

Shirock, "Exorcists." Shirock, Robert J., Jr. "Whose Exorcists Are They? The Referents of οἱ υἱοὶ ὑμῶν at Matthew 12.27/ Luke 11.19." *JSNT* 46 (1992): 41–51.

Shogren, "Prophecy." Shogren, Gary Steven. "Christian Prophecy and Canon in the Second Century: A Response to B. B. Warfield." *JETS* 40 (4, 1997): 609–26.

Shoko, *Religion*. Shoko, Tabona. *Karanga Indigenous Religion in Zimbabwe: Health and Well-Being*. VitIndRel. Foreword by James L. Cox. Burlington, Vt.: Ashgate, 2007.

Shorter, "Possession and Healing." Shorter, Aylward. "Spirit Possession and Christian Healing in Tanzania." *African Affairs* 79 (314, 1980): 45–53.

Shorter, "Spirit Possession." Shorter, Aylward. "The *migawo*: Peripheral Spirit Possession and Christian Prejudice." *Anthrop* 65 (1970): 110–26.

Shorter, *Witchdoctor*. Shorter, Aylward. *Jesus and the Witchdoctor: An Approach to Healing and Wholeness*. London: Geoffrey Chapman; Maryknoll, N.Y.: Orbis, 1985.

Shortt, *Christianophobia*. Shortt, Rupert. *Christianophobia: A Faith under Attack*. Grand Rapids: Eerdmans, 2012.

Shotter, "Agrippina." Shotter, David C. A. "Agrippina the Elder—A Woman in a Man's World." *Historia* 49 (3, 2000): 341–57.

Shotwell, *Exegesis*. Shotwell, Willis A. *The Biblical Exegesis of Justin Martyr*. London: SPCK, 1965.

Shuler, *Genre*. Shuler, Philip L. *A Genre for the Gospels: The Biographical Character of Matthew*. Philadelphia: Fortress, 1982.

Shuler, "Genre(s)." Shuler, Philip L. "The Genre(s) of the Gospels." Pages 459–83 in *The Interpretations of the Gospels*. Edited by D. L. Dungan. BETL 95. Leuven: Leuven University Press, 1990.

Shupak, "Learning Methods." Shupak, Nili. "Learning Methods in Ancient Israel." *VT* 53 (3, 2003): 416–26.

Shutt, "Aristeas." Shutt, R. J. H. Introduction to "Letter of Aristeas." *OTP* 2:7–11.

Shutt, "Concept." Shutt, R. J. H. "The Concept of God in the Works of Flavius Josephus." *JJS* 31 (2, 1980): 171–89.

Sicre Díaz, "Tradiciones." Sicre Díaz, José Luis. "Las tradiciones de Jacob: Búsqueda y rechazo de la propia identidad." *EstBib* 60 (4, 2002): 443–78.

Sidebottom, *James*. Sidebottom, E. M. *James, Jude, and 2 Peter*. NCBC. Greenwood, S.C.: Attic, 1967.

Sider, *Christians*. Sider, Ronald J. *Rich Christians in an Age of Hunger*. Foreword by Kenneth Kantzer. Dallas: Word, 1990.

Sider, *Killing*. Sider, Ronald J., ed. *The Early Church on Killing: A Comprehensive Sourcebook on War, Abortion, and Capital Punishment*. Grand Rapids: Baker Academic, 2012.

Sider, *Scandal*. Sider, Ronald J. *The Scandal of the Evangelical Conscience: Why Are Christians Living Just like the Rest of the World?* Grand Rapids: Baker, 2005.

Sidwell, "Mental Illness." Sidwell, Barbara. "Gaius Caligula's Mental Illness." *CW* 103 (2, 2010): 183–206.

Siebert, "Immolatio." Siebert, Anne Viola. "Immolatio." *BrillPauly* 6:744–46.

Siegel, "Employment." Siegel, Jonathan P. "The Employment of Palaeo-Hebrew Characters for the Divine Names at Qumran in the Light of Tannaitic Sources." *HUCA* 42 (1971): 159–72.

Siegel, "Israel." Siegel, Seymour. "The Meaning of Israel in Jewish Thought." Pages 98–118 in *Evangelicals and Jews in Conversation on Scripture, Theology, and History*. Edited by Marc H. Tanenbaum, Marvin R. Wilson, and James A. Rudin. Grand Rapids: Baker, 1978.

Siegel, "References." Siegel, Jonathan P. "Two Further Medieval References to the Teacher of Righteousness." *RevQ* 9 (3, 1978): 437–40.

Siegert, "Gottesfürchtige." Siegert, Folker. "Gottesfürchtige und Sympathisanten." *JSJ* 4 (2, 1973): 109–64.

Siegert, "Homily." Siegert, Folker. "Homily and Panegyrical Sermon." Pages 421–43 in *Handbook of Classical Rhetoric in the Hellenistic Period, 330 B.C.–A.D. 400*. Edited by Stanley E. Porter. Leiden: Brill, 1997.

Siegert, "Vérité." Siegert, Folker. "L'antiquité a-t-elle connu la notion de vérité historique? Quelques extraits de Polybe." *ASDE* 22 (2, 2005): 455–64.

Sievers, "Name." Sievers, Joseph. "What's in a Name? Antiochus in Josephus' '*Bellum judaicum*.'" *JJS* 56 (1, 2005): 34–47.

Sievers, "Women in Hasmonean Dynasty." Sievers, Joseph. "The Role of Women in the Hasmonean Dynasty." Pages 132–46 in *Josephus, the Bible, and History*. Edited by Louis H. Feldman and Gohei Hata. Detroit: Wayne State University Press, 1989.

Siffer, "Annonce." Siffer, Nathalie. "L'annonce du vrai Dieu dans les discours missionnaires aux païens: Actes 14,15–17 et 17,22–31." *RevScRel* 81 (4, 2007): 523–44.

Siffer, "Proclamation du Royaume." Siffer, Nathalie. "La proclamation du Royaume de Dieu comme marqueur de continuité entre Jésus et l'Église dans l'ouvre de Luc." *RSR* 99 (3, 2011): 349–69.

Sigal, *Halakah*. Sigal, Phillip. *The Halakah of Jesus of Nazareth according to the Gospel of Matthew*. Lanham, Md.: University Press of America, 1986.

Signer, "Balance." Signer, Michael A. "Restoring the Balance: Musings on Miracles in Rabbinic Judaism." Pages 111–26 in *Miracles in Jewish and Christian Antiquity: Imagining Truth*. Edited by John C. Cavadini. NDST 3. Notre Dame, Ind.: University of Notre Dame, 1999.

Sigountos and Shank, "Public Roles." Sigountos, James G., and Myron Shank. "Public Roles for Women in the Pauline Church: A Reappraisal of the Evidence." *JETS* 26 (3, 1983): 283–95.

Siker, "Abraham." Siker, Jeffrey S. "Abraham in Graeco-Roman Paganism." *JSJ* 18 (2, 1987): 188–208.

Silberman, "Challenge." Silberman, Lou H. "Challenge and Response: Pesiqta Derab Kahana, Chapter 26 as an Oblique Reply to Christian Claims." *HTR* 79 (1–3, 1986): 247–53.

Silberman, "Language." Silberman, Lou H. "Language and Structure in the Hodayot (1QH 3)." *JBL* 75 (2, 1956): 96–106.

Silberman, "Messiahs." Silberman, Lou H. "The Two 'Messiahs' of the Manual of Discipline." *VT* 5 (1, 1955): 77–82.

Silberman, "Ossuary." Silberman, Neil Asher. "Ossuary: A Box for Bones." *BAR* 17 (3, 1991): 73–74.

Silberman, "Paul's Viper." Silberman, Lou H. "Paul's Viper: Acts 28:3–6." *Forum* 8 (3–4, 1992): 247–53.

Silberman, "Queen of Sheba." Silberman, Lou H. "The Queen of Sheba in Judaic Tradition." Pages 65–84 in *Solomon and Sheba*. Edited by J. B. Pritchard. London: Phaidon, 1974.

Silberman, "Unriddling." Silberman, Lou H. "Unriddling the Riddle: A Study in the Structure and Language of the Habakkuk Pesher." *RevQ* 3 (1961–62): 323–64.

Silberman and Goren, "Faking." Silberman, Neil Asher, and Yuval Goren. "Faking Biblical History." *Archaeology* 56 (5, 2003): 20–29.

Silk, "*Gnōmē*." Silk, Michael S. "*Gnōmē*." *OCD³* 640.

Silver, "Moses and Birds." Silver, Daniel J. "Moses and the Hungry Birds." *JQR* 64 (2, 1973): 123–53.

Silvoso, *Perish*. Silvoso, Ed. *That None Should Perish: How to Reach Entire Cities for Christ through Prayer Evangelism*. Foreword by C. Peter Wagner. Ventura, Calif.: Regal, 1994.

Sim, "Appearances." Sim, David C. "The Appearances of the Risen Christ to Paul: Identifying Their Implications and Complications." *ABR* 54 (2006): 1–12.

Sim, "Παλιγγενεσία." Sim, David C. "The Meaning of παλιγγενεσία in Matthew 19.28." *JSNT* 50 (1993): 3–12.

Sim, "Relevance Theoretic Approach." Sim, Margaret Gavin. "A Relevance Theoretic Approach to the Particle ἵνα in Koine Greek." PhD diss., University of Edinburgh, 2006.

Simfukwe, "Rites." Simfukwe, Joe. "Funeral and Burial Rites." Page 1462 in *Africa Bible Commentary*. Edited by Tokunboh Adeyemo. Grand Rapids: Zondervan; Nairobi: WordAlive, 2006.

Simkovich, "Greek Influence." Simkovich, Malka Zeiger. "Greek Influence on the Composition of 2 Maccabees." *JSJ* 42 (3, 2011): 293–310.

Simon, "Causes." Simon, Stephen J. "Women Who Pleaded Causes before the Roman Magistrates." *CBull* 66 (3–4, 1990): 79–81.

Simon, "Identität." Simon, Marie. "Das Problem der jüdischen Identität in der Literatur des jüdischen Hellenismus." *Kairos* 30–31 (1988–89): 41–52.

Simon, "Jupiter-Yahvé." Simon, Marcel. "Jupiter-Yahvé: Sur un essai de théologie pagano-juive." *Numen* 23 (1, 1976): 40–66.

Simon, "Priestesses." Simon, Stephen J. "The Functions of Priestesses in Greek Society." *CBull* 67 (2, 1991): 9–13.

Simon, *Sects*. Simon, Marcel. *Jewish Sects at the Time of Jesus*. Philadelphia: Fortress, 1967.

Simon, *Stephen and Hellenists*. Simon, Marcel. *St Stephen and the Hellenists in the Primitive Church*. Haskell Lectures, 1956. New York: Longmans, Green, 1958.

Simon, "Synkretismus." Simon, Marie. "Zum Problem des jüdisch-griechischen Synkretismus." *Kairos* 17 (2, 1975): 89–99.

Simonsohn, *Jews in Sicily*. Simonsohn, Shlomo. *Between Scylla and Charybdis: The Jews in Sicily*. Brill's Series in Jewish Studies 43. Leiden: Brill, 2011.

Simonson, *Jews in Sicily*. Simonson, Shelomoh. *The Jews in Sicily*, vol. 1, *383–1300*. A Documentary History of the Jews in Italy 13. StPB 48.3. Leiden: Brill, 1997.

Simpson, "Bone." Simpson, St. John. "Bone, Ivory, and Shell: Artifacts of the Persian through Roman Periods." *OEANE* 1:343–48.

Simpson, *Church*. Simpson, A. B. *The Spirit-Filled Church in Action: The Dynamics of Evangelism from the Book of Acts*. Camp Hill, Pa.: Christian Publications, 1996.

Simpson, "Investigation." Simpson, Leon Dennis. "An Investigation into the Jewish Character of Paul's Letter to the Romans." ThD diss., Southwestern Baptist Theological Seminary, 1973.

Simpson, *Literature of Egypt*. Simpson, William Kelly, ed. *The Literature of Ancient Egypt: An Anthology of Stories, Instructions, Stelae, Autobiographies, and Poetry*. 3rd ed. New Haven: Yale University Press, 2003.

Simshäuser, "Behandlung." Simshäuser, Wilhelm. "Die Behandlung der Abtreibung in der antiken römischen Rechts-und Gesellschaftsordnung." *ForKathTheol* 8 (3, 1992): 174–86.

Sinaiko, *Love*. Sinaiko, Herman L. *Love, Knowledge, and Discourse in Plato: Dialogue and Dialectic in Phaedrus, Republic, Parmenides*. Chicago: University of Chicago Press, 1965.

Sinclair, "*Sententia*." Sinclair, Patrick. "The *sententia* in *Rhetorica ad Herennium*: A Study in the Sociology of Rhetoric." *AJP* 114 (4, 1993): 561–80.

Sinclair, "Temples." Sinclair, Patrick. "'These Are MY Temples in Your Hearts' (Tac. *Ann*. 4.38.2)." *CP* 86 (4, 1991): 333–35.

Singer, "Hills." Singer, Suzanne. "'From These Hills . . .'" *BAR* 4 (2, 1978): 16–25.

Singer and Greenstone, "Noachian Laws." Singer, I., and J. H. Greenstone. "Noachian Laws." Pages 648–50 in vol. 7 of *The Jewish Encyclopedia*. Edited by Isidore Singer. 12 vols. New York: Funk & Wagnalls, 1901–6.

Singer and Nutton, "Surgery." Singer, Charles Joseph, and Vivian Nutton. "Surgery." *OCD³* 1457–58.

Singleton, "Spirits." Singleton, Michael. "Spirits and 'Spiritual Direction': The Pastoral Counselling of the Possessed." Pages 471–78 in *Christianity in Independent Africa*. Edited by Edward Fasholé-Luke et al. Bloomington: Indiana University Press, 1978.

Sirat and Woog, "Maître." Sirat, René-Samuel, and Agnès Woog. "Moïse 'notre maître,' prince des prophètes." *VSpir* 146 (702, 1992): 625–32.

Sithole, *Voice*. Sithole, Surprise, with David Wimbish. *Voice in the Night*. Minneapolis: Chosen, 2012.

Sivan, "Rabbinics." Sivan, Hagith. "Rabbinics and Roman Law: Jewish-Gentile/Christian Marriage in Late Antiquity." *REJ* 156 (1–2, 1997): 59–100.

Sjoberg, *Preindustrial City*. Sjoberg, Gideon. *The Preindustrial City: Past and Present*. New York: Free Press, 1960.

Skarsaune, *Shadow*. Skarsaune, Oskar. *In the Shadow of the Temple: Jewish Influences on*

Early Christianity. Downers Grove, Ill.: InterVarsity, 2002.

Skarsaune and Hvalvik, *Believers*. Skarsaune, Oskar, and Reidar Hvalvik, eds. *Jewish Believers in Jesus: The Early Centuries*. Peabody, Mass.: Hendrickson, 2007.

Skeat, "Cheap." Skeat, T. C. "Was Papyrus Regarded as 'Cheap' or 'Expensive' in the Ancient World?" *Aeg* 75 (1–2, 1995): 75–93.

Skeat, "Parchments." Skeat, T. C. "'Especially the Parchments': A Note on 2 Timothy IV.13." *JTS* 30 (1, 1979): 173–77.

Skehan, "Exodus." Skehan, Patrick W. "Exodus in the Samaritan Recension from Qumran." *JBL* 74 (3, 1955): 182–87.

Skemp, "Ἀδελφός." Skemp, Vincent. "Ἀδελφός and the Theme of Kinship in Tobit." *ETL* 75 (1, 1999): 92–103.

Skinner, "Dames." Skinner, Marilyn B. "Des bonnes dames et méchantes." *CJ* 83 (1987): 69–74.

Skinner, *Locating Paul*. Skinner, Matthew L. *Locating Paul: Places of Custody as Narrative Settings in Acts 21–28*. SBLABib 13. Atlanta: SBL, 2003.

Skinner, "Review of Fieger." Skinner, Matthew L. Review of Michael Fieger, *Im Schatten der Artemis*. *RelSRev* 27 (1, 2001): 79.

Skinner, "Unchained Ministry." Skinner, Matthew L. "Unchained Ministry: Paul's Roman Custody (Acts 21–28) and the Sociopolitical Outlook of the Book of Acts." Pages 79–95 in *Acts and Ethics*. Edited by Thomas E. Phillips. NTMon 9. Sheffield, U.K.: Sheffield Phoenix, 2005.

Slane, *Sanctuary*. Slane, Kathleen Warner. *The Sanctuary of Demeter and Kore: The Roman Pottery and Lamps*. Vol. 18, part 2, of *Corinth: Results of Excavations Conducted by the American School of Classical Studies at Athens*. Princeton: American School of Classical Studies at Athens, 1990.

Slater, *Dining*. Slater, W. J. *Dining in a Classical Context*. Ann Arbor: University of Michigan Press, 1991.

Slater, "Emergence." Slater, Jonathan P. "The Emergence of the Matrilineal Principle in Judaism." *ConsJud* 55 (1, 2002): 15–29.

Slater, "Exodus 20:11." Slater, Thomas B. "The Possible Influence of LXX Exodus 20:11 on Acts 14:15." *AUSS* 30 (2, 1992): 151–52.

Slater, "Introduction." Slater, William J. Introduction. Pages 1–5 in *Dining in a Classical Context*. Edited by William J. Slater. Ann Arbor: University of Michigan Press, 1991.

Slater, "Kiddush." Slater, Herbert Tarr, Jr. "Does the Kiddush Precede Christianity?" *AUSS* 7 (1, 1969): 57–68.

Slater, "Presentation of Paul." Slater, Thomas B. "The Presentation of Paul in Acts." *BiBh* 19 (1, 1993): 19–46.

Sleeman, *Geography*. Sleeman, Matthew. *Geography and the Ascension Narrative in Acts*. SNTSMS 146. Cambridge: Cambridge University Press, 2009.

Sleeper, "Pentecost and Resurrection." Sleeper, C. F. "Pentecost and Resurrection." *JBL* 84 (4, 1965): 389–99.

Slingerland, "Acts 18:1–17 and Luedemann's Chronology." Slingerland, Dixon. "Acts 18:1–17 and Luedemann's Pauline Chronology." *JBL* 109 (4, 1990): 686–90.

Slingerland, "Gallio Inscription." Slingerland, Dixon. "Acts 18:1–18, the Gallio Inscription, and Absolute Pauline Chronology." *JBL* 110 (3, 1991): 439–49.

Slingerland, "'Jews' in Pauline Portion." Slingerland, Dixon. "'The Jews' in the Pauline Portion of Acts." *JAAR* 54 (2, 1986): 305–21.

Slingerland, "Orosius' *Historiarum*." Slingerland, Dixon. "Suetonius *Claudius* 25.4, Acts 18, and Paulus Orosius' *Historiarum adversum paganos libri VII*: Dating the Claudian Expulsion(s) of Roman Jews." *JQR* 83 (1–2, 1992): 127–44.

Slingerland, "Suetonius and Cassius Dio." Slingerland, Dixon. "Suetonius *Claudius* 25.4 and the Account in Cassius Dio." *JQR* 79 (4, 1989): 305–22.

Sloan, "Paul and Law." Sloan, Robert B. "Paul and the Law: Why the Law Cannot Save." *NovT* 33 (1, 1991): 35–60.

Sloan, "Signs." Sloan, Robert B. "'Signs and Wonders': A Rhetorical Clue to the Pentecost Discourse." Pages 145–62 in *With Steadfast Purpose: Essays on Acts in Honor of Henry Jackson Flanders, Jr.* Edited by Naymond H. Keathley. Waco: Baylor University Press, 1990.

Slomovic, "Understanding." Slomovic, Elieser. "Toward an Understanding of the Exegesis in the DSS." *RevQ* 7 (1, 1969): 3–15.

Slootjes, "Potentes." Slootjes, Daniëlle. "Local Potentes in the Roman Empire: A New Approach to the Concept of Local Elites." *Latomus* 68 (2, 2009): 416–32.

Sloyan, "Concepts." Sloyan, Gerard S. "'Primitive' and 'Pauline' Concepts of the Eucharist." *CBQ* 23 (1961): 1–13.

Sloyan, "James." Sloyan, Gerard S. "The Letter of James." Pages 28–49 in *Hebrews–James–1 and 2 Peter–Jude–Revelation*. Edited by Gerhard Krodel. ProcC. Philadelphia: Fortress, 1977.

Sloyan, "Samaritans." Sloyan, Gerard S. "The Samaritans in the New Testament." *Horizons* 10 (1983): 7–21.

Sluiter, "Homer." Sluiter, Ineke. "Homer in the Dining Room: An Ancient Rhetorical

Interpretation of the Duel between Paris and Menelaus (Plut. *Quaest. Conv.* 9.13)." *CW* 98 (4, 2005): 379–96.

Slusser, "Reading Silently." Slusser, Michael. "Reading Silently in Antiquity." *JBL* 111 (3, 1992): 499.

Sly, *Perception*. Sly, Dorothy. *Philo's Perception of Women*. BJS 209. Atlanta: Scholars Press, 1990.

Small, "Memory." Small, Jocelyn Penny. "Artificial Memory and the Writing Habits of the Literate." *Helios* 22 (2, 1995): 159–66.

Small, "Orator." Small, Jocelyn Penny. "Memory and the Roman Orator." Pages 195–206 in *A Companion to Roman Rhetoric*. Edited by William Dominik and Jon Hall. Oxford: Blackwell, 2007.

Small, *Wax Tablets*. Small, Jocelyn Penny. *Wax Tablets of the Mind: Cognitive Studies of Memory and Literacy in Classical Antiquity*. London: Routledge, 1997.

Smalley, "Christology Again." Smalley, Stephen S. "The Christology of Acts Again." Pages 79–93 in *Christ and the Spirit in the New Testament: Studies in Honour of Charles Francis Digby Moule*. Edited by Barnabas Lindars and Stephen S. Smalley. Cambridge: Cambridge University Press, 1973.

Smalley, "Christology of Acts." Smalley, Stephen S. "The Christology of Acts." *ExpT* 73 (12, 1962): 358–62.

Smalley, *John*. Smalley, Stephen S. *John: Evangelist and Interpreter*. Exeter, U.K.: Paternoster, 1978.

Smalley, "Spirit, Kingdom, and Prayer." Smalley, Stephen S. "Spirit, Kingdom, and Prayer in Luke-Acts." *NovT* 15 (1973): 59–71.

Smallwood, "High Priests." Smallwood, E. Mary. "High Priests and Politics in Roman Palestine." *JTS* 13 (1962): 14–34.

Smallwood, *Jews*. Smallwood, E. Mary. *The Jews under Roman Rule: From Pompey to Diocletian*. SJLA 20. Leiden: Brill, 1976.

Smallwood and Griffin, "Berenice." Smallwood, E. Mary, and Miriam T. Griffin. "Berenice (4)." *OCD³* 239.

Smallwood and Rajak, "Caesarea." Smallwood, E. Mary, and Tessa Rajak. "Caesarea (2) in Palestine." *OCD³* 272.

Smallwood and Rajak, "Josephus." Smallwood, E. Mary, and Tessa Rajak. "Josephus." *OCD³* 798–99.

Smaltz, "Peter." Smaltz, Warren. "Did Peter Die in Jerusalem?" *JBL* 71 (1952): 211–16.

Smarczyk, "Phyle." Smarczyk, Bernhard. "Phyle." *BrillPauly* 11:210–13.

Smelik, "Language." Smelik, Willem F. "Language, Locus, and Translation between the Talmudim." *JAramB* 3 (1–2, 2001): 199–224.

Smelik, "Witch." Smelik, K. A. D. "The Witch of Endor: 1 Samuel 28 in Rabbinic and Christian Exegesis till 800 A.D." *VC* 33 (2, 1979): 160–79.

Smidt, *Evangelicals*. Smidt, Corwin E. *American Evangelicals Today*. Lanham, Md.: Rowman & Littlefield, 2013.

Smit, "Self-Praise." Smit, Peter-Ben. "Paul, Plutarch and the Problematic Practice of Self-Praise (περιαυτολογία): The Case of Phil 3.2–21." *NTS* 60 (3, July 2014): 341–59.

Smit, "Tongues." Smit, Joop F. M. "Tongues and Prophecy: Deciphering 1 Cor 14,22." *Bib* 75 (2, 1994): 175–90.

Smit Sibinga, "*Serta Paulina*." Smit Sibinga, Joost. "*Serta Paulina*: On Composition Technique in Paul." *FilNeot* 10 (19–20, 1997): 35–54.

Smith, "Acts Seminar." Smith, Dennis E. "Introducing the Acts Seminar." *FourR* 13 (3, 2000): 6–10.

Smith, *Animals*. Smith, Christian. *Moral, Believing Animals: Human Personhood and Culture*. Oxford: Oxford University Press, 2003.

Smith, "Aphrodisias." Smith, R. R. R. "Aphrodisias." *OEANE* 1:151–52.

Smith, *Art and Architecture*. Smith, W. Stevenson. *The Art and Architecture of Ancient Egypt*. Pelican History of Art 14. Baltimore: Penguin, 1958.

Smith, "Back Together." Smith, Abraham. "Putting 'Paul' Back Together Again: William Wells Brown's *Clotel* and Black Abolitionist Approaches to Paul." *Semeia* 83–84 (1998): 251–62.

Smith, "Banquet." Smith, Dennis E. "The Messianic Banquet Reconsidered." Pages 64–73 in *The Future of Early Christianity: Essays in Honor of Helmut Koester*. Philadelphia: Augsburg Fortress, 1991.

Smith, "Baptism." Smith, Derwood. "Jewish Proselyte Baptism and the Baptism of John." *ResQ* 25 (1, 1982): 13–32.

Smith, "Begetting." Smith, Morton. "'God's Begetting the Messiah' in 1QSa." *NTS* 5 (3, 1959): 218–24.

Smith, "Bir Madhkur Project." Smith, Andrew M. "Bir Madhkur Project: A Preliminary Report on Recent Fieldwork." *BASOR* 340 (Nov. 2005): 57–75.

Smith, "Caesar's Decree." Smith, Robert. "Caesar's Decree (Luke 2:1–2): Puzzle or Key?" *CurTM* 7 (6, 1980): 343–51.

Smith, "Chronology." Smith, Robert W. "New Evidence regarding Early Christian Chronology: A Reconsideration." Pages 133–39 in *Chronos, Kairos, Christos, II: Chronological, Nativity, and Religious Studies in Memory of Ray Summers*. Edited by E. Jerry Vardaman. Macon: Mercer University Press, 1998.

Smith, "Comparison of Tradition." Smith, Morton. "A Comparison of Early Christian and Early Rabbinic Tradition." *JBL* 82 (2, 1963): 169–76.

Smith, "Correspondence." Smith, Murray J. "The Thessalonian Correspondence." Pages 269–301 in *All Things to All Cultures: Paul among Jews, Greeks, and Romans*. Edited by Mark Harding and Alanna Nobbs. Grand Rapids: Eerdmans, 2013.

Smith, "Coworkers." Smith, Susan. "Women: Coworkers and Apostles with Paul." *BibT* 46 (2, 2008): 93–98.

Smith, *Education*. Smith, William A. *Ancient Education*. New York: Philosophical Library, 1955.

Smith, "Egyptian Cults at Corinth." Smith, Dennis E. "The Egyptian Cults at Corinth." *HTR* 70 (3–4, 1977): 201–31.

Smith, "Epicurean Priest." Smith, Martin F. "An Epicurean Priest from Apamea in Syria." *ZPE* 112 (1996): 120–30.

Smith, "Fall 2007." Smith, Dennis E. "Fall Meeting, 2007: Report on the Acts Seminar." *FourR* 21 (1, 2008): 19–21.

Smith, "Fall 2008." Smith, Dennis E. "Fall Meeting 2008. On the Voting Results for the Acts Seminar." *FourR* 22 (2, 2009): 19–20.

Smith, "Fellowship." Smith, Dennis E. "Table Fellowship as a Literary Motif in the Gospel of Luke." *JBL* 106 (4, 1987): 613–38.

Smith, "Function of Refutation." Smith, Julien C. H. "The Rhetorical Function of Refutation in Acts 6–7 and 10–15." Pages 103–18 in *Contemporary Studies in Acts*. Edited by Thomas E. Phillips. Macon, Ga.: Mercer University Press, 2009.

Smith, "Glossolalia." Smith, Dwight Moody. "Glossolalia and Other Spiritual Gifts in a New Testament Perspective." *Interpretation* 28 (1974): 307–20.

Smith, *Gnostic Origins*. Smith, Carl B., II. *No Longer Jews: The Search for Gnostic Origins*. Peabody, Mass.: Hendrickson, 2004.

Smith, "Gospels." Smith, D. Moody. "When Did the Gospels Become Scripture?" *JBL* 119 (1, 2000): 3–20.

Smith, "History." Smith, Robert H. "History and Eschatology in Acts." *CTM* 29 (1958): 881–901.

Smith, "Hope after Babel?" Smith, David. "What Hope after Babel? Diversity and Community in Gen 11:1–9; Exod 1:1–14; Zeph 3:1–13; and Acts 2:1–13." *HBT* 18 (2, 1996): 169–91.

Smith, *Hosea, Amos, Micah*. Smith, Gary V. *Hosea, Amos, Micah*. NIVAC. Grand Rapids: Zondervan, 2001.

Smith, "House Church." Smith, Dennis E. "The House Church as Social Environment." Pages 3–21 in *Text, Image, and Christians in the Graeco-Roman World: A Festschrift in Honor of David Lee Balch*. Edited by Aliou Cissé Niang and Carolyn Osiek. PrTMS 176. Eugene, Ore.: Pickwick, 2012.

Smith, "Jerusalem Church." Smith, Dennis E. "Was There a Jerusalem Church? Christian Origins according to Acts and Paul." *Forum* 3 (1, 2000): 57–74.

Smith, *John*. Smith, D. Moody. *John*. ANTC. Nashville: Abingdon, 1999.

Smith, *John among Gospels*. Smith, D. Moody. *John among the Gospels: The Relationship in Twentieth-Century Research*. Minneapolis: Fortress, 1992.

Smith, "Letters." Smith, Ian K. "The Later Pauline Letters: Ephesians, Philippians, Colossians, and Philemon." Pages 302–27 in *All Things to All Cultures: Paul among Jews, Greeks, and Romans*. Edited by Mark Harding and Alanna Nobbs. Grand Rapids: Eerdmans, 2013.

Smith, *Magician*. Smith, Morton. *Jesus the Magician*. San Francisco: Harper & Row, 1978.

Smith, "Meeting 2006." Smith, Dennis E. "Fall Meeting, 2006: Report on the Acts Seminar." *FourR* 20 (1, 2007): 21–22.

Smith, "Meeting 2007." Smith, Dennis E. "Spring Meeting, 2007: Report from the Acts Seminar." *FourR* 20 (3, 2007): 11–14.

Smith, "Metaphilosophy." Smith, Quentin. "The Metaphilosophy of Naturalism." *Philo* 4 (2, 2001): 195–215. Online: http://www.philoonline.org/library/smith_4_2.

Smith, "Occult in Josephus." Smith, Morton. "The Occult in Josephus." Pages 236–56 in *Josephus, Judaism, and Christianity*. Edited by Louis H. Feldman and Gohei Hata. Detroit: Wayne State University Press, 1987.

Smith, *Parallels*. Smith, Morton. *Tannaitic Parallels to the Gospels*. Philadelphia: SBL, 1951.

Smith, "Pauline Worship." Smith, Morton. "Pauline Worship as Seen by Pagans." *HTR* 73 (1–2, 1980): 241–49.

Smith, "Portrait of Stephen." Smith, Abraham. "'Full of Spirit and Wisdom': Luke's Portrait of Stephen (Acts 6:1–8:1a) as a Man of Self-Mastery." Pages 97–114 in *Asceticism and the New Testament*. Edited by Leif Eric Vaage and Vincent L. Wimbush. London: Routledge, 1999.

Smith, "Possession." Smith, James H. "Of Spirit Possession and Structural Adjustment Programs: Government Downsizing, Education and Their Enchantments in Neo-Liberal Kenya." *JRelAf* 31 (4, 2001): 427–56.

Smith, "Refutation." Smith, Julien C. H. "The Rhetorical Function of Refutation in Acts 6–7, 10–15." Paper presented at the annual meeting of the SBL, Washington, D.C., Nov. 20, 2006.

Smith, "Resistance Discourse." Smith, James K. A. "Tongues as 'Resistance Discourse': A Philosophical Perspective." Pages 81–110 in Speaking in Tongues: Multidisciplinary Perspectives. Edited by Mark J. Cartledge. SPCI. Waynesboro, Ga., and Bletchley, Milton Keynes, U.K.: Paternoster, 2006.

Smith, "Rethinking Secularization." Smith, Christian. "Introduction: Rethinking the Secularization of American Public Life." Pages 1–96 in The Secular Revolution: Power, Interests, and Conflict in the Secularization of American Public Life. Edited by Christian Smith. Berkeley: University of California Press, 2003.

Smith, "Rewriting." Smith, Dennis E. "The Acts of the Apostles and the Rewriting of Christian History: On the Critical Study of Acts." Forum 5 (1, 2002): 7–32.

Smith, Rhetoric in Alexandria. Smith, Robert W. The Art of Rhetoric in Alexandria: Its Theory and Practice in the Ancient World. The Hague: Martinus Nijhoff, 1974.

Smith, Rhetoric of Interruption. Smith, Daniel Lynwood. The Rhetoric of Interruption: Speech-Making, Turn-Taking, and Rule-Breaking in Luke-Acts and Ancient Greek Narrative. BZNW 193. Berlin: de Gruyter, 2012.

Smith, "Sarcophagus." Smith, Robert Houston. "A Sarcophagus from Pella: New Light on Earliest Christianity." Archaeology 26 (4, 1973): 250–56.

Smith, "Sect." Smith, Morton. "The Dead Sea Sect in Relation to Ancient Judaism." NTS 7 (1961): 347–60.

Smith, "Secularizing Education." Smith, Christian. "Secularizing American Higher Education: The Case of Early American Sociology." Pages 97–159 in The Secular Revolution: Power, Interests, and Conflict in the Secularization of American Public Life. Edited by Christian Smith. Berkeley: University of California Press, 2003.

Smith, T., "Sources." Smith, T. C. "The Sources of Acts." Pages 55–75 in With Steadfast Purpose: Essays on Acts in Honor of Henry Jackson Flanders Jr. Edited by N. H. Keathley. Waco: Baylor University Press, 1990.

Smith, "Spring 2008." Smith, Dennis E. "Spring Meeting 2008: Report on the Acts Seminar." FourR 21 (1, 2008): 13–15.

Smith, "Spring 2009." Smith, Dennis E. "Spring Meeting 2009. On the Voting Results for the Acts Seminar." FourR 22 (4, 2009): 19–21.

Smith, "Structure." Smith, David E. "Acts and the Structure of the Christian Bible." Pages 93–102 in Contemporary Studies in Acts. Edited by Thomas E. Phillips. Macon, Ga.: Mercer University Press, 2009.

Smith, Studies. Smith, T. C. Studies in Acts. Greenville, S.C.: Smyth & Helwys, 1991.

Smith, Symposium. Smith, Dennis E. From Symposium to Eucharist: The Banquet in the Early Christian World. Minneapolis: Augsburg Fortress, 2003.

Smith, Thinking. Smith, James K. A. Thinking in Tongues: Outline of a Pentecostal Philosophy. Grand Rapids: Eerdmans, 2010.

Smith, "Translation." Smith, Yancy W. "Bible Translation and Ancient Visual Culture: Divine Nakedness and the 'Circumcision of Christ' in Colossians 2:11." Pages 320–41 in Text, Image, and Christians in the Graeco-Roman World: A Festschrift in Honor of David Lee Balch. Edited by Aliou Cissé Niang and Carolyn Osiek. PrTMS 176. Eugene, Ore.: Pickwick, 2012.

Smith, "Understand." Smith, Abraham. "'Do You Understand What You Are Reading?': A Literary Critical Reading of the Ethiopian (Kushite) Episode (Acts 8:26–40)." JITC 22 (1, 1994): 48–70.

Smith, "Variety." Smith, Morton. "What Is Implied by the Variety of Messianic Figures?" JBL 78 (1, 1959): 66–72.

Smith, "Visit." Smith, Eli. "A Visit to Antipatris." BSac 1 (1843): 478–96.

Smith, Voyage. Smith, James. The Voyage and Shipwreck of St. Paul (with Dissertations on the Life and Writings of St. Luke, and the Ships and Navigation of the Ancients. Revised and corrected by Walter E. Smith. 4th ed. Longmans, Green, 1880. Repr., Grand Rapids: Baker, 1978.

Smith, "Wide Angles." Smith, James D., III. "Wide Angles and Zoom Lenses." ChH 72 (2001): 20–21.

Smith, "Zealots." Smith, Morton. "Zealots and Sicarii, Their Origins and Relation." HTR 64 (1, 1971): 1–19.

Smith and Hoppe, "Seleucia." Smith, Robert W., and Leslie J. Hoppe. "Seleucia." ABD 5:1074–76.

Smyth, "Scrolls and Messiah." Smyth, Kevin. "The Dead Sea Scrolls and the Messiah." Studies 45 (1956): 1–14.

Snaith, Amos, Hosea, Micah. Snaith, Norman H. Amos, Hosea, and Micah. Epworth Preacher's Commentaries. London: Epworth, 1956.

Snodgrass, Stories. Snodgrass, Klyne R. Stories with Intent: A Comprehensive Guide to the Parables of Jesus. Grand Rapids: Eerdmans, 2008.

Snow and Phillips, "Model." Snow, David A., and Cynthia Phillips. "The Lofland-Stark Conversion Model: A Critical Reassessment." Social Problems 27 (1980): 430–47.

Snowden, Blacks in Antiquity. Snowden, Frank M., Jr. Blacks in Antiquity: Ethiopians in the Greco-Roman Experience. Cambridge, Mass.: Harvard University Press, 1970.

Snowden, "Black-White Relations." Snowden, Frank M. "Black-White Relations in the Ancient Greek and Roman Worlds." MedQ 1 (2, 1990): 72–92.

Snowden, Color Prejudice. Snowden, Frank M. Before Color Prejudice: The Ancient View of Blacks. Cambridge, Mass.: Harvard University Press, 1983.

Snyder, Corinthians. Snyder, Graydon F. First Corinthians: A Faith Community Commentary. Macon, Ga.: Mercer University Press, 1992.

Snyder, "Gifts." Snyder, Howard A. "Spiritual Gifts." Pages 325–38 in The Oxford Handbook of Evangelical Theology. Edited by Gerald R. McDermott. Oxford: Oxford University Press, 2010.

Snyder, "Interaction." Snyder, Graydon F. "The Interaction of Jews with Non-Jews in Rome." Pages 69–90 in Judaism and Christianity in First-Century Rome. Edited by Karl P. Donfried and Peter Richardson. Grand Rapids: Eerdmans, 1998.

Snyder, "Naughts and Crosses." Snyder, H. Gregory. "Naughts and Crosses: Pesher Manuscripts and Their Significance for Reading Practices at Qumran." DSD 7 (1, 2000): 26–48.

Soards, "Review." Soards, Marion L. Review of Richard Pervo, Profit with Delight. JAAR 58 (2, 1990): 307–10.

Soards, "Setting." Soards, Marion L. "The Historical and Cultural Setting of Luke-Acts." Pages 33–47 in New Views on Luke and Acts. Edited by Earl Richard. Collegeville, Minn.: Liturgical Press, 1990.

Soards, Speeches. Soards, Marion L. The Speeches in Acts: Their Content, Context, and Concerns. Louisville: Westminsster John Knox, 1994.

Soards, "Speeches in Relation to Literature." Soards, Marion L. "The Speeches in Acts in Relation to Other Pertinent Ancient Literature." ETL 70 (1, 1994): 65–90.

Soares Prabhu, Quotations. Soares Prabhu, George M. The Formula Quotations in the Infancy Narrative of Matthew: An Enquiry into the Tradition History of Mt 1–2. Rome: Biblical Institute Press, 1976.

Sobol, Amazons. Sobol, Donald J. The Amazons of Greek Mythology. South Brunswick, N.J., and New York: A. S. Barnes, 1972.

Söding, "Widerspruch." Söding, Thomas. "Widerspruch und Leidensnachfolge: Neutestamentliche Gemeinden im

Konflikt mit der paganen Gesellschaft." *MTZ* 41 (2, 1990): 137–55.

Sofowora, *Traditional Medicine*. Sofowora, Abayomi. *Medicinal Plants and Traditional Medicine in Africa*. New York: John Wiley & Sons, 1982.

Soggin, *Introduction*. Soggin, J. Alberto. *Introduction to the Old Testament*. Philadelphia: Westminster, 1980.

Sohm, *Institutes*. Sohm, Rudolph. *The Institutes of Roman Law*. Translated by James Crawford Ledlie. Oxford: Clarendon, 1892.

Sokolowski, "Sarapis in Greece." Sokolowski, Franciszek. "Propagation of the Cult of Sarapis and Isis in Greece." *GRBS* 15 (4, 1974): 441–48.

Sokolowski, "Testimony on Cult." Sokolowski, Franciszek. "A New Testimony on the Cult of Artemis of Ephesus." *HTR* 58 (4, 1965): 427–31.

Sole, "Rapporto." Sole, Luciano. "Quale il rapporto che lega la persecuzione alla Chiesa? Suggerimenti e spunti dagli Atti degli apostoli." *Divinitas* 46 (3, 2003): 257–88.

Solin, "Names, Roman." Solin, Heikki. "Names, Personal, Roman." *OCD*[3] 1024–26.

Solivan, *Spirit*. Solivan, Samuel. *The Spirit, Pathos, and Liberation: Toward an Hispanic Pentecostal Theology*. JPTSup 14. Sheffield, U.K.: Sheffield Academic, 1998.

Soll, "Acrostics." Soll, William Michael. "Babylonian and Biblical Acrostics." *Bib* 69 (1988): 305–23.

Solomon, "Healing." Solomon, Robert. "Healing and Deliverance." *GDT* 361–68.

Solomon, "Kinship." Solomon, Michael. "Kinship and the Transmission of Religious Charisma: The Case of Honganji." *JAS* 33 (3, 1974): 403–13.

Sommer, "Prophecy." Sommer, Benjamin D. "Did Prophecy Cease? Evaluating a Reevaluation." *JBL* 115 (1, 1996): 31–47.

Sonnabend, "Catastrophes." Sonnabend, Holger. "Catastrophes." *BrillPauly* 9:522–27.

Sonnabend, "Cos." Sonnabend, Holger. "Cos." *BrillPauly* 3:856–59.

Sonnabend, "Crete." Sonnabend, Holger. "Crete." *BrillPauly* 3:934–38.

Sonnabend, "Ida." Sonnabend, Holger. "Ida." *BrillPauly* 6:709.

Sonnabend, "Lindus." Sonnabend, Holger. "Lindus." *BrillPauly* 7:609–12.

Sonnabend, "Mytilene." Sonnabend, Holger. "Mytilene." *BrillPauly* 9:471–74.

Sonnabend, "Phoenix." Sonnabend, Holger. "Phoenix [8]." *BrillPauly* 11:173.

Sonnabend, "Rhodos." Sonnabend, Holger. "Rhodos." *BrillPauly* 12:570–74.

Sonnabend, "Samos." Sonnabend, Holger. "Samos." *BrillPauly* 12:930–37.

Sonne, "Use." Sonne, Isaiah. "The Use of Rabbinic Literature as Historical Sources." *JQR* 36 (1945–46): 147–69.

Sorabji, "Chrysippus." Sorabji, Richard. "Chrysippus–Posidonius–Seneca: A High-Level Debate on Emotion." Pages 149–69 in *The Emotions in Hellenistic Philosophy*. Edited by Juha Sihvola and Troels Engberg-Pedersen. TSHP 46. Dordrecht, Neth.: Kluwer Academic, 1998.

Sorabji, *Emotion*. Sorabji, Richard. *Emotion and Peace of Mind: From Stoic Agitation to Christian Temptation*. Oxford: Oxford University Press, 2000.

Soramuzza, "Policy." Soramuzza, Vincent M. "The Policy of the Early Roman Emperors towards Judaism." *BegChr* 5:277–97.

Sosa, "Pureza." Sosa, Carlos R. "Pureza e impureza en la narrativa de Pedro, Cornelio, y el Espíritu Santo en Hechos 10." *Kairós* 41 (2007): 55–78.

Sosin, "Word for Woman?" Sosin, Joshua D. "A Word for Woman?" *GRBS* 38 (1, 1997): 75–83.

Sourbut, "Philippi." Sourbut, Catherine. "Paul in Philippi: Reflections on Mission in the Light of the Apostle's Hermeneutics." *ExpT* 120 (11, 2009): 534–40.

Sourvinou-Inwood, "Artemis." Sourvinou-Inwood, Christiane. "Artemis." *OCD*[3] 182–84.

Sourvinou-Inwood, "Delphic Oracle." Sourvinou-Inwood, Christiane. "Delphic Oracle." *OCD*[3] 445–46.

Sousa, "Women." Sousa, Alexandra O. de. "Defunct Women: Possession among the Bijagós Islanders." Pages 81–88 in *Spirit Possession, Modernity and Power in Africa*. Edited by Heike Behrend and Ute Luig. Madison: University of Wisconsin Press, 1999.

Southall, "Ideology." Southall, Aidan. "Ideology and Group Composition in Madagascar." *AmAnth* 73 (1971): 144–64.

Southall, "Possession." Southall, Aidan. "Spirit Possession and Mediumship among the Alur." Pages 232–72 in *Spirit Mediumship and Society in Africa*. Edited by John Beattie and John Middleton. Foreword by Raymond Firth. New York: Africana, 1969.

Southern, *Army*. Southern, Pat. *The Roman Army: A Social and Institutional History*. New York: Oxford, 2007.

Souza, "Harbours." Souza, Philip de. "Harbours." *OCD*[3] 666–67.

Souza, "Navigation." Souza, Philip de. "Navigation." *OCD*[3] 1030–31.

Souza, "Piracy." Souza, Philip de. "Piracy." *OCD*[3] 1184–85.

Souza, "Pirates." Souza, Philip de. "Ancient Rome and the Pirates." *HT* 51 (7, 2001): 48–53.

Souza, "Ships." Souza, Philip de. "Ships." *OCD*[3] 1400.

Souza, "Triremes." Souza, Philip de. "Triremes." *OCD*[3] 1553.

Sowers, "Circumstances." Sowers, Sidney. "The Circumstances and Recollection of the Pella Flight." *TZ* 26 (1970): 305–20.

Spahlinger, "Sueton-Studien II." Spahlinger, Lothar. "Sueton-Studien, II: Der wundertätige Kaiser Vespasian (Sueton, Vesp. 7,2–3)." *Phil* 148 (2, 2004): 325–46.

Spangler, "Criticism." Spangler, G. A. "Aristotle's Criticism of Parmenides in *Physics* I." *Apeiron* 13 (1979): 92–103.

Spanos et al., "Learned Behavior." Spanos, Nicholas P., et al. "Glossolalia as Learned Behavior: An Experimental Demonstration." *JAbnPsy* 95 (1, 1986): 21–23.

Spawforth, "Achaia." Spawforth, Antony J. S. "Achaia." *OCD*[3] 6.

Spawforth, "Artisans." Spawforth, Antony J. S. "Artisans and Craftsmen." *OCD*[3] 185.

Spawforth, "Brigandage." Spawforth, Antony J. S. "Brigandage." *OCD*[3] 260–61.

Spawforth, "Corinth." Spawforth, Antony J. S. "Corinth: Roman." *OCD*[3] 391.

Spawforth, "Euergetism." Spawforth, Antony J. S. "Euergetism." *OCD*[3] 566.

Spawforth, "Free Cities." Spawforth, Antony J. S. "Free Cities." *OCD*[3] 609.

Spawforth, "Homonoia." Spawforth, Antony J. S. "Homonoia." *OCD*[3] 720.

Spawforth, "Nationalism." Spawforth, Antony J. S. "Nationalism: Hellenistic and Roman." *OCD*[3] 1027–28.

Spawforth, "Phaleron." Spawforth, Antony J. S. "Phaleron." *OCD*[3] 1153.

Spawforth, "Race." Spawforth, Antony J. S. "Race." *OCD*[3] 1293.

Spawforth, "Roman Corinth." Spawforth, Antony J. S. "Roman Corinth: The Formation of a Colonial Elite." Pages 167–82 in *Roman Onomastics in the Greek East*. Edited by A. D. Rizakis. Athens: de Boccard, 1996.

Spawforth, "Tourism." Spawforth, Antony J. S. "Tourism." *OCD*[3] 1535.

Speckman, "Beggars." Speckman, McGlory T. "Beggars and Gospel in Luke-Acts: Preliminary Observations on an Emerging Model in the Light of Recent Developmental Theories." *Neot* 31 (2, 1997): 309–37.

Speckman, "Healing." Speckman, McGlory T. "Healing and Wholeness in Luke-Acts as Foundation for Economic Development: A Particular Reference to ὁλοκληρία in Acts 3:16." *Neot* 36 (1–2, 2002): 97–109.

Speidel, "Army." Speidel, Michael P. "The Roman Army in Judaea under the Procurators: The Italian and the Augustan Cohort in the Acts of the Apostles." *AncSoc* 13–14 (1982–83): 233–40.

Speidel, "Pay Scales." Speidel, M. Alexander. "Roman Army Pay Scales." *JRS* 82 (1992): 87–106 and plate 1.

Spence, *Palace.* Spence, Jonathan D. *The Memory Palace of Matteo Ricci.* New York: Viking Penguin, 1984.

Spencer, *Acts.* Spencer, F. Scott. *Acts.* Sheffield, U.K.: Sheffield Academic, 1997.

Spencer, "Approaches." Spencer, F. Scott. "Acts and Modern Literary Approaches." Pages 381–414 in *The Book of Acts in Its Ancient Literary Setting.* Edited by Bruce W. Winter and Andrew D. Clarke. Vol. 1 of *The Book of Acts in Its First Century Setting.* Edited by Bruce W. Winter. Grand Rapids: Eerdmans; Carlisle, U.K.: Paternoster, 1993.

Spencer, *Beyond Curse.* Spencer, Aida Besançon. *Beyond the Curse: Women Called to Ministry.* Nashville: Thomas Nelson, 1985.

Spencer, "Cloth." Spencer, F. Scott. "Women of 'the Cloth' in Acts: Sewing the Word." Pages 134–54 in *The Feminist Companion to the Acts of the Apostles.* Edited by Amy-Jill Levine with Marianne Blickenstaff. Cleveland: Pilgrim; Edinburgh: T&T Clark, 2004.

Spencer, *Foundations.* Spencer, Metta, with Alex Inkeles. *Foundations of Modern Sociology.* 3rd ed. Englewood Cliffs, N.J.: Prentice-Hall, 1982.

Spencer, *Gospel and Acts.* Spencer, F. Scott. *The Gospel of Luke and Acts of the Apostles.* IBT. Nashville: Abingdon, 2008.

Spencer, "Neglected Widows." Spencer, F. Scott. "Neglected Widows in Acts 6:1–7." *CBQ* 56 (4, 1994): 715–33.

Spencer, "Odyssey in Acts." Spencer, F. Scott. "Paul's Odyssey in Acts: Status Struggles and Island Adventures." *BTB* 28 (4, 1998): 150–59.

Spencer, *Philip.* Spencer, F. Scott. *The Portrait of Philip in Acts: A Study of Role and Relations.* JSNTSup 67. Sheffield, U.K.: Sheffield Academic, 1992.

Spencer, "Scared to Death." Spencer, F. Scott. "Scared to Death: The Rhetoric of Fear in the 'Tragedy' of Ananias and Sapphira." Pages 63–80 in *Reading Acts Today: Essays in Honour of Loveday C. A. Alexander.* Edited by Steve Walton et al. LNTS 427. London: T&T Clark, 2011.

Spencer, *Timothy.* Spencer, Aída Besançon. *1 Timothy.* NCCS. Eugene, Ore.: Cascade, 2013.

Spencer, "Voice." Spencer, F. Scott. "Out of Mind, out of Voice: Slave-Girls and Prophetic Daughters in Luke-Acts." *BibInt* 7 (2, 1999): 133–55.

Spencer, "Waiter." Spencer, F. Scott. "A Waiter, a Magician, a Fisherman, and a Eunuch: The Pieces and Puzzles of Acts 8." *Forum* 3 (1, 2000): 155–78.

Spencer, "Young Man." Spencer, F. Scott. "Wise Up, Young Man: The Moral Vision of Saul and Other νεανίσκοι in Acts." Pages 34–48 in *Acts and Ethics.* Edited by Thomas E. Phillips. NTMon 9. Sheffield, U.K.: Sheffield Phoenix, 2005.

Spencer Kennard, "Provincial Assembly." Spencer Kennard, J., Jr. "The Jewish Provincial Assembly." *ZNW* 53 (1–2, 1962): 25–51.

Sperber, "Note." Sperber, Daniel. "A Note on Some Shi'urim and Graeco-Roman Measurements." *JJS* 20 (1–4, 1969): 81–86.

Sperber and Wilson, "Précis." Sperber, Dan, and Deirdre Wilson. "Précis of Relevance: Communication and Cognition." *BehBrSc* 10 (1987): 697–754.

Sperber and Wilson, *Relevance.* Sperber, Dan, and Deirdre Wilson. *Relevance: Communication and Cognition.* Oxford: Blackwell, 1986.

Spero, "Judgments." Spero, Shubert. "'And These Are the Judgments That You Shall Set before Them' (Ex. 21:1): 'As a Set Table' (Mekhilta)." *JBQ* 32 (1, 2004): 16–19.

Spero, "Tabernacle." Spero, Shubert. "From Tabernacle (*mishkan*) and Temple (*mikdash*) to Synagogue (*bet keneset*)." *Tradition* 38 (3, 2004): 60–85.

Spicer, "Acculturation." Spicer, Edward H. "Acculturation." Pages 21–27 in vol. 1 of *International Encyclopedia of the Social Sciences.* Edited by David L. Sills. 17 vols. New York: Macmillan; Free Press, 1968.

Spickard and Cragg, *Global History.* Spickard, Paul R., and Kevin M. Cragg. *A Global History of Christians.* Grand Rapids: Baker, 2003. Originally published as *God's Peoples: A Social History of Christians.* Grand Rapids: Baker, 1994.

Spieckermann, "Stadtgott." Spieckermann, Hermann. "Stadtgott und Gottesstadt: Beobachtungen im alten Orient und im Alten Testament." *Bib* 73 (1992): 1–31.

Spigel, "Reconsidering." Spigel, Chad S. "Reconsidering the Question of Separate Seating in Ancient Synagogues." *JJS* 63 (1, 2012): 62–83.

Spilsbury, "Josephus on Rise." Spilsbury, Paul. "Flavius Josephus on the Rise and Fall of the Roman Empire." *JTS* 54 (1, 2003): 1–24.

Spinks, "Growth." Spinks, Bryan D. "The Growth of Liturgy and the Church Year."

Pages 601–17 in *Constantine to c. 600.* Edited by Augustine Casiday and Frederick W. Norris. Vol. 2 of *The Cambridge History of Christianity.* 9 vols. Cambridge: Cambridge University Press, 2007.

Spiro, "Samaritan Background." Spiro, Abram. "Appendix V: Stephen's Samaritan Background." Pages 285–300 in *The Acts of the Apostles.* By Johannes Munck. Revised by W. F. Albright and C. S. Mann. AB 31. Garden City, N.Y.: Doubleday, 1967.

Spitaler, "Doubting." Spitaler, Peter. "'Doubting' in Acts 10:20?" *FilNeot* 20 (39–40, 2007): 81–93.

Spitaler, "Shift." Spitaler, Peter. "*Diakrinesthai* in Mt. 21:21, Mk. 11:23, Acts 10:20, Rom. 4:20; 14:23, Jas. 1:6, and Jude 22—The 'Semantic Shift' That Went Unnoticed by Patristic Authors." *NovT* 49 (1, 2007): 1–39.

Spittler, *Corinthian Correspondence.* Spittler, Russell P. *The Corinthian Correspondence.* Springfield, Mo.: Gospel, 1976.

Spittler, "Glossolalia." Spittler, Russell P. "Glossolalia." *DPCM* 335–41.

Spittler, "Introduction." Spittler, Russell P. Introduction to "Testament of Job." *OTP* 1:829–38.

Spittler, "Limits." Spittler, Russell P. "The Limits of Ecstasy: An Exegesis of 2 Corinthians 12:1–10." Pages 259–66 in *Current Issues in Biblical and Patristic Interpretation: Studies in Honor of Merrill C. Tenney Presented by His Former Students.* Edited by Gerald F. Hawthorne. Grand Rapids: Eerdmans, 1975.

Spittler, "Testament of Job." Spittler, Russell P. "Testament of Job." *DNTB* 1189–92.

Spitzer, *Proofs.* Spitzer, Robert J. *New Proofs for the Existence of God: Contributions of Contemporary Physics and Philosophy.* Grand Rapids: Eerdmans, 2010.

Spivey, Smith, and Black, *Anatomy.* Spivey, Robert A., D. Moody Smith, and C. Clifton Black. *Anatomy of the New Testament.* 6th ed. Upper Saddle River, N.J.: Pearson Prentice Hall, 2007.

Spooner, "Politics." Spooner, Brian. "Politics, Kinship, and Ecology in Southeast Persia." *Ethnology* 8 (2, 1969): 139–52.

Sprinkle, "Law." Sprinkle, Joe M. "Law." *DOTHB* 643–50.

Sprinkle, "'Pre-Sanders' Thinkers." Sprinkle, Preston M. "The Old Perspective on the New Perspective: A Review of Some 'Pre-Sanders' Thinkers." *Them* 30 (2, 2005): 21–31.

Spurgeon, *Autobiography.* Spurgeon, Charles H. *The Autobiography of Charles H. Spurgeon.* 4 vols. London and Cincinnati: Curts & Jennings, 1899.

Squires, "Acts 8.4–12.25." Squires, John T. "The Function of Acts 8.4–12.25." *NTS* 44 (4, 1998): 608–17.

Squires, *Plan*. Squires, John T. *The Plan of God in Luke-Acts*. SNTSMS 76. Cambridge: Cambridge University Press, 1993.

Squires, "Plan." Squires, John T. "The Plan of God." Pages 19–39 in *Witness to the Gospel: The Theology of Acts*. Edited by I. Howard Marshall and David Peterson. Grand Rapids: Eerdmans, 1998.

Stabell, "Modernity." Stabell, Timothy D. "'The Modernity of Witchcraft' and the Gospel in Africa." *Missiology* 38 (4, Oct. 2010): 460–74.

Stachowiak, "Pouczenia." Stachowiak, Lech. "Pouczenia etyczne w literaturze międzytestamentalnej (Die sittlichen Mahnungen in der intertestamentlichen Literatur)." *ColT* 48 (3, 1978): 43–62.

Staden, "Erasistratus." Staden, Heinrich von. "Erasistratus." *OCD*[3] 552–53.

Staden, "Hairesis and Heresy." Staden, Heinrich von. "Hairesis and Heresy: The Case of the *haireseis iatrikai*." Pages 76–100 in *Self-Definition in the Greco-Roman World*. Edited by Ben F. Meyer and E. P. Sanders. Vol. 3 of *Jewish and Christian Self-Definition*. Edited by E. P. Sanders. Philadelphia: Fortress, 1982.

Stadter, "Biography." Stadter, Philip. "Biography and History." Pages 528–40 in *A Companion to Greek and Roman Historiography*. Edited by John Marincola. 2 vols. Oxford: Blackwell, 2007.

Stager, "Eroticism at Ashkelon." Stager, Lawrence E. "Eroticism and Infanticide at Ashkelon." *BAR* 17 (4, 1991): 34–53, 72.

Stager and Wolff, "Sacrifice." Stager, Lawrence E., and Samuel R. Wolff. "Child Sacrifice at Carthage—Religious Rite or Population Control; Archaeological Evidence Provides Basis for a New Analysis." *BAR* 10 (1, Jan. 1984): 30–51.

Stagg, *Acts*. Stagg, Frank. *The Book of Acts: The Early Struggle for an Unhindered Gospel*. Nashville: Broadman, 1955.

Stagg, "Glossolalia." Stagg, Frank. "Glossolalia in the New Testament." Pages 20–44 in *Glossolalia: Tongue Speaking in Biblical, Historical, and Psychological Perspective*. By Frank Stagg, E. Glenn Hinson, and Wayne E. Oates. Nashville: Abingdon, 1967.

Stagg, "Mission." Stagg, Frank. "Paul's Final Mission to Jerusalem." Pages 259–78 in *With Steadfast Purpose: Essays on Acts in Honor of Henry Jackson Flanders, Jr.* Edited by Naymond H. Keathley. Waco: Baylor University Press, 1990.

Stagg, "Unhindered Gospel." Stagg, Frank. "The Unhindered Gospel." *RevExp* 71 (4, 1974): 451–62.

Stählin, *Apostelgeschichte*. Stählin, G. *Die Apostelgeschichte überstezt und erklärt*. 16th ed. NTD 5. Göttingen: Vandenhoeck & Ruprecht, 1980.

Stählin, "Apostelgeschichte 16:7." Stählin, G. "Τὸ πνεῦμα Ἰησοῦ (Apostelgeschichte 16:7)." Pages 229–52 in *Christ and Spirit in the New Testament: Studies in Honor of C. F. D. Moule*. Edited by Barnabas Lindars and Stephen S. Smalley. Cambridge: Cambridge University Press, 1973.

Stahlmann, "Brothels." Stahlmann, Ines. "Brothels." *BrillPauly* 2:790–91.

Stahlmann, "Gender Roles." Stahlmann, Ines. "Gender Roles: Rome." *BrillPauly* 5:743–44.

Stalder, "Geist." Stalder, Kurt. "Der Heilige Geist in der lukanischen Ekklesiologie." *UnS* 30 (1975): 287–93.

Stallsmith, "Thesmophoria." Stallsmith, Allaire Brisbane. "Interpreting the Athenian Thesmophoria." *CBull* 84 (1, 2009): 28–45.

Stallsmith, "Thesmophoros." Stallsmith, Allaire B. "The Name of Demeter Thesmophoros." *GRBS* 48 (2, 2008): 115–31.

Stambaugh, *City*. Stambaugh, John E. *The Ancient Roman City*. Baltimore: Johns Hopkins University Press, 1988.

Stambaugh and Balch, *Environment*. Stambaugh, John E., and David L. Balch. *The New Testament in Its Social Environment*. LEC 2. Philadelphia: Westminster, 1986.

Stampp, *Institution*. Stampp, Kenneth M. *The Peculiar Institution: Slavery in the Ante-bellum South*. New York: Alfred A. Knopf, 1956.

Stamps, "Children." Stamps, D. L. "Children in Late Antiquity." *DNTB* 197–201.

Stamps, "Rhetoric." Stamps, D. L. "Rhetoric." *DNTB* 953–59.

Stancil, "Evaluation." Stancil, Theron. "A Text-Critical Evaluation of Acts 2:42." *F&M* 23 (3, 2006): 17–36.

Stang, "Dionysius." Stang, Charles M. "Dionysius, Paul, and the Significance of the Pseudonym." *Modern Theology* 24 (4, 2008): 541–55.

Stange, "Configurations." Stange, Paul D. "Configurations of Javanese Possession Experience." *RelT* 2 (2, Oct. 1979): 39–54.

Stanley, "4QTanhumim." Stanley, Christopher D. "The Importance of 4QTanhumim (4Q176)." *RevQ* 15 (1992): 569–82.

Stanley, *Apostle*. Stanley, Christopher D., ed. *The Colonized Apostle: Paul through Postcolonial Eyes*. Minneapolis: Fortress, 2011.

Stanley, *Diffusion*. Stanley, Brian. *The Global Diffusion of Evangelicalism: The Age of Billy Graham and John Stott*. A History of Evangelicalism 5. Downers Grove, Ill.: InterVarsity, 2013.

Stanley, "Hybrid." Stanley, Christopher D. "Paul the Ethnic Hybrid? Postcolonial Perspectives on Paul's Ethnic Categorizations." Pages 110–26 in *The Colonized Apostle: Paul through Postcolonial Eyes*. Edited by Christopher D. Stanley. Minneapolis: Fortress, 2011.

Stanley, "Jew nor Greek." Stanley, Christopher D. "'Neither Jew nor Greek': Ethnic Conflict in Graeco-Roman Society." *JSNT* 64 (1996): 101–24.

Stanley, *Language of Scripture*. Stanley, Christopher D. *Paul and the Langage of Scripture: Citation Technique in the Pauline Epistles and Contemporary Literature*. SNTSMS 69. Cambridge: Cambridge University Press, 1992.

Stanley, "Paul and Homer." Stanley, Christopher D. "Paul and Homer: Greco-Roman Citation Practice in the First Century CE." *NovT* 32 (1, 1990): 48–78.

Stanley, "Pearls." Stanley, Christopher D. "'Pearls before Swine': Did Paul's Audiences Understand His Biblical Quotations?" *NovT* 41 (2, 1999): 124–44.

Stanley, *Resurrection*. Stanley, David Michael. *Christ's Resurrection in Pauline Soteriology*. AnBib 13. Rome: Pontifical Biblical Institute, 1961.

Stanton, "Communities." Stanton, Graham N. "The Communities of Matthew." *Interpretation* 46 (1992): 379–91.

Stanton, *Gospel Truth?* Stanton, Graham N. *Gospel Truth? New Light on Jesus and the Gospels*. Valley Forge, Pa.: Trinity Press International, 1995.

Stanton, *Gospels*. Stanton, Graham N. *The Gospels and Jesus*. Oxford Bible Series. Oxford: Oxford University Press, 1989.

Stanton, "Hellenism." Stanton, Greg R. "Hellenism." *DNTB* 464–73.

Stanton, *Jesus of Nazareth*. Stanton, Graham N. *Jesus of Nazareth in New Testament Preaching*. Cambridge: Cambridge University Press, 1974.

Stanton, "Magician." Stanton, Graham N. "Jesus of Nazareth: A Magician and a False Prophet Who Deceived God's People?" Pages 164–80 in *Jesus of Nazareth, Lord and Christ: Essays on the Historical Jesus and New Testament Christology*. Edited by Joel B. Green and Max Turner. Grand Rapids: Eerdmans; Carlisle, U.K.: Paternoster, 1994.

Stanton, "Message and Miracles." Stanton, Graham N. "Message and Miracles." Pages 56–71 in *The Cambridge Companion to Jesus*. Edited by Markus Bockmuehl. Cambridge: Cambridge University Press, 2001.

Stanton, *New People*. Stanton, Graham N. *A Gospel for a New People: Studies in Matthew*. Edinburgh: T&T Clark, 1992; Louisville: Westminster John Knox, 1993.

Starcky, "Texte messianique." Starcky, J. "Une texte messianique araméen de la grotte 4 de Qumrân." Pages 51–66 in *Mémorial du cinquantenaire, 1914–1964, École des langues orientales anciennes de l'Institut catholique de Paris.* Travaux de l'Instut catholique de Paris 10. Paris: Bloud et Gay, 1964.

Stark, "Antioch." Stark, Rodney. "Antioch as the Social Situation for Matthew's Gospel." Pages 189–210 in *Social History of the Matthean Community: Cross-disciplinary Approaches.* Minneapolis: Fortress, 1991.

Stark, "Christianizing the Empire." Stark, Rodney. "Christianizing the Urban Empire: An Analysis Based on 22 Greco-Roman Cities." *SocAnal* 52 (1, 1991): 77–88.

Stark, *Cities.* Stark, Rodney. *Cities of God: The Real Story of How Christianity Became an Urban Movement and Conquered Rome.* New York: HarperCollins, 2006.

Stark, *Ionia.* Stark, Freya. *Ionia: A Quest.* London: John Murray, 1954.

Stark, *Rise.* Stark, Rodney. *The Rise of Christianity: A Sociologist Reconsiders History.* Princeton: Princeton University Press, 1996.

Stark and Bainbridge, *Religion.* Stark, Rodney, and William Sims Bainbridge. *Religion, Deviance, and Social Control.* London: Routledge, 1996.

Starner, "Co-Laborers." Starner, Rob. "Luke and Paul: Co-Laborers . . . and Collaborators?" Pages 194–240 in *Trajectories in the Book of Acts: Essays in Honor of John Wesley Wyckoff.* Edited by Paul Alexander, Jordan Daniel May, and Robert G. Reid. Eugene, Ore.: Wipf & Stock, 2010.

Starner, *Kingdom.* Starner, Rob. *Kingdom of Power, Power of Kingdom: The Opposing World Views of Mark and Chariton.* Foreword by Mikeal C. Parsons. Eugene, Ore.: Pickwick, 2011.

Starner, "Review." Starner, Rob. Review of *The IVP Bible Background Commentary.* *BA* 58 (3, 1995): 174–75.

Starr, "Flexibility." Starr, Raymond J. "The Flexibility of Literary Meaning and the Role of the Reader in Roman Antiquity." *Latomus* 60 (2, 2001): 433–45.

Starr, "*Pater patriae.*" Starr, Raymond J. "Augustus as *Pater patriae* and Patronage Decrees." *ZPE* 172 (2010): 296–98.

Starr, "Reading Aloud." Starr, Raymond J. "Reading Aloud: *Lectores* and Roman Reading." *CJ* 86 (4, 1991): 337–43.

Stauffer, *Jesus and Story.* Stauffer, Ethelbert. *Jesus and His Story.* Translated by Richard Winston and Clara Winston. New York: Alfred A. Knopf, 1960.

Staveley and Lintott, "*Lictores.*" Staveley, Eastland Stuart, and Andrew William Lintott. "*Lictores.*" *OCD*[3] 860.

Staveley and Lintott, "*Provocatio.*" Staveley, Eastland Stuart, and Andrew William Lintott. "*Provocatio.*" *OCD*[3] 1267–68.

Steck, "'Zeugen' und 'Tora-Sucher.'" Steck, Odil Hannes. "Die getöteten 'Zeugen' und die verfolgten 'Tora-Sucher' in Jub 1,12: Ein Beitrag zur Zeugnis-Terminologie der Jubiläenbuches (I)." *ZAW* 107 (3, 1995): 445–65.

Steel, "Archaeology." Steel, Louise. "Archaeology in Cyprus, 1997–2002." *ArchRep* 50 (2004): 93–111.

Stefaniak, "Poglądy." Stefaniak, L. "Poglądy mesjańskie czy eschatologiczne sekty z Qumran? (Les opinions de la secte de Qumrân, sont-elles messianiques ou eschatologiques?)" *RocTK* 9 (4, 1962): 59–73.

Steffek, "Juifs et païens." Steffek, Emmanuelle. "Quand juifs et païens se mettent à table (Ac 10)." *ETR* 80 (1, 2005): 103–11.

Stegeman, "Faith." Stegeman, John. "A Woman's Faith." Pages 35–37 in *Faith Healing: Finger of God? Or, Scientific Curiosity?* Compiled by Claude A. Frazier. New York: Thomas Nelson, 1973.

Stegemann, "Römischer Bürger." Stegemann, Wolfgang. "War der Apostel Paulus ein römischer Bürger?" *ZNW* 78 (3, 1987): 200–229.

Stegemann, Malina, and Theissen, *Setting.* Stegemann, Wolfgang, Bruce J. Malina, and Gerd Theissen, eds. *The Social Setting of Jesus and the Gospels.* Minneapolis: Fortress, 2002.

Stegner, "Homily." Stegner, William Richard. "The Ancient Jewish Synagogue Homily." Pages 51–69 in *Greco-Roman Literature and the New Testament: Selected Forms and Genres.* Edited by David E. Aune. SBLSBS 21. Atlanta: Scholars Press, 1988.

Stegner, "Jew, Paul the." Stegner, William R. "Jew, Paul the." *DPL* 503–11.

Stegner, "Jewish Paul." Stegner, William R. "A Jewish Paul." *AsTJ* 47 (1, 1992): 89–95.

Stegner, "Temptation Narrative." Stegner, William R. "The Temptation Narrative: A Study in the Use of Scripture by Early Jewish Christians." *BR* 35 (1990): 5–17.

Stehly, "Upanishads." Stehly, Ralph. "Une citation des Upanishads dans Joseph et Aséneth." *RHPR* 55 (2, 1975): 209–13.

Steimle, *Religion.* Steimle, Christopher. *Religion im römischen Thessaloniki. Sakraltopographie, Kult und Gesellschaft 168 v. Chr.—324 n. Chr.* Studien und Texte zu Antike und Christentum 47. Tübingen: Mohr Siebeck, 2008.

Stein, "'Criteria.'" Stein, Robert H. "The 'Criteria' for Authenticity." Pages 225–63 in vol. 1 of *Studies of History and Tradition in the Four Gospels.* Edited by R. T. France and David Wenham. 2 vols. Gospel Perspectives 1–2. Sheffield, U.K.: JSOT Press, 1980–81.

Stein, "Galatians 2:1–10 and Acts 15:1–35." Stein, Robert H. "The Relationship of Galatians 2:1–10 and Acts 15:1–35: Two Neglected Arguments." *JETS* 17 (1974): 239–42.

Stein, *Messiah.* Stein, Robert H. *Jesus the Messiah: A Survey of the Life of Christ.* Downers Grove, Ill.: InterVarsity, 1996.

Stein, *Method and Message.* Stein, Robert H. *The Method and Message of Jesus' Teachings.* Philadelphia: Westminster, 1978.

Stein, "Reading." Stein, Dominique. "Is a Psycho-analytical Reading of the Bible Possible?" *Concilium* 138 (1980): 24–32.

Steiner, "Incomplete Circumcision." Steiner, Richard C. "Incomplete Circumcision in Egypt and Edom: Jeremiah (9:24–25) in the Light of Josephus and Jonckheere." *JBL* 118 (3, 1999): 497–505.

Steiner, "*Laissez-passer.*" Steiner, Richard C. "A Jewish Aramaic (or Hebrew) *laissez-passer* from the Egyptian Port of Berenike." *JNES* 63 (4, 2004): 277–81.

Steiner, "*Mbqr.*" Steiner, Richard C. "The *mbqr* at Qumran, the *episkopos* in the Athenian Empire, and the Meaning of *lbqr'* in Ezra 7:14: On the Relation of Ezra's Mission to the Persian Legal Project." *JBL* 120 (4, 2001): 623–46.

Steiner, "Rise." Steiner, Richard C. "On the Rise and Fall of Canaanite Religion at Baalbek: A Tale of Five Toponyms." *JBL* 128 (3, 2009): 507–25.

Steiner, "Warum asketisch?" Steiner, A. "Warum lebten die Essener asketisch?" *BZ* 15 (1, 1971): 1–28.

Stem, "Lessons." Stem, Rex. "The Exemplary Lessons of Livy's Romulus." *TAPA* 137 (2007): 435–71.

Stem, "Stoic." Stem, Rex. "The First Eloquent Stoic: Cicero on Cato the Younger." *CJ* 101 (1, 2005): 37–49.

Stemberger, "Auferstehungslehre." Stemberger, Günter. "Zur Auferstehungslehre in der rabbinschen Literatur." *Kairos* 15 (1973): 238–66.

Stemberger, "Bedeutung des 'Landes." Stemberger, Günter. "Die Bedeutung des 'Landes Israel' in der rabbinischen Tradition." *Kairos* 25 (3–4, 1983): 176–99.

Stemberger, "Hermeneutik." Stemberger, Günter. "Griechisch-römische und rabbinische Hermeneutik." *CV* 41 (2, 1999): 101–15.

Stemberger, "Pesachhaggada." Stemberger, Günter. "Pesachhaggada und Abendmahlsberichte des Neuen Testaments." *Kairos* 29 (3–4, 1987): 147–58.

Stempvoort, "Interpretation of Ascension." Stempvoort, P. A. van. "The Interpretation of the Ascension in Luke and Acts." *NTS* 5 (1, 1958): 30–42.

Stendahl, "Hate." Stendahl, Krister. "Hate, Non-retaliation, and Love: 1QS x,17–20 and Rom. 12:19–21." *HTR* 55 (4, 1962): 343–55.

Stendahl, *Paul.* Stendahl, Krister. *Paul among Jews and Gentiles and Other Essays.* Philadelphia: Fortress, 1976.

Stendahl, *School of Matthew.* Stendahl, Krister. *The School of St. Matthew and Its Use of the Old Testament.* Philadelphia: Fortress, 1968.

Stenger, "Apophthegma." Stenger, Jan. "Apophthegma, Gnome, und Chrie: Zum Verhältnis dreier literarischer Kleinformen." *Phil* 150 (2, 2006): 203–21.

Stenger, "Minos." Stenger, Jan. "Minos." *BrillPauly* 9:24–26.

Stenger, "Minotaurus." Stenger, Jan. "Minotaurus." *BrillPauly* 9:26–27.

Stenger, "Nemesis." Stenger, Jan. "Nemesis." *BrillPauly* 9:629–30.

Stenger, "Peleus." Stenger, Jan. "Peleus." *BrillPauly* 10:694–96.

Stenger, "Troy." Stenger, Jan. "Troy: Mythology: The Trojan Cycle." *BrillPauly* 14:979–81.

Stenschke, *Gentiles.* Stenschke, Christoph W. *Luke's Portrait of Gentiles prior to Their Coming to Faith.* WUNT 2.108. Tübingen: Mohr Siebeck, 1999.

Stenschke, "Hinweise." Stenschke, Christoph W. "Hinweise zu einem wiederentdeckten Gebiet der Actaforschung (I) und zu zwei bemerkenwerten Monographien zu Apostelgeschichte 13f und zum Galaterbrief (II)." *CV* 41 (1, 1999): 65–91.

Stenschke, "Salvation." Stenschke, Christoph W. "The Need for Salvation." Pages 125–44 in *Witness to the Gospel: The Theology of Acts.* Edited by I. Howard Marshall and David Peterson. Grand Rapids: Eerdmans, 1998.

Stephen, "Church." Stephen, Anil. "The Church at the Top of the World." *CT* (Apr. 3, 2000): 56–59.

Stephens, *Annihilation.* Stephens, Mark B. *Annihilation or Renewal? The Meaning and Function of New Creation in the Book of Revelation.* WUNT 307. Tübingen: Mohr Siebeck, 2011.

Stephens, "Destroyers." Stephens, Mark B. "Destroying the Destroyers of the Earth: The Meaning and Function of New Creation in the Book of Revelation." PhD diss., Macquarie University, Sydney, Australia, 2009.

Stephens, *Family.* Stephens, William N. *The Family in Cross-cultural Perspective.* New York: Holt, Rinehart & Winston, 1963.

Stephens, "Who Read Novels?" Stephens, Susan A. "Who Read Ancient Novels?" Pages 405–18 in *The Search for the Ancient Novel.* Edited by James Tatum. Baltimore: Johns Hopkins University Press, 1994.

Sterck-Degueldre, *Frau.* Sterck-Degueldre, Jean-Pierre. *Eine Frau namens Lydia: Zur Geschichte und Komposition in Apostelgeschichte 16,11–15,40.* WUNT 2.176. Tübingen: Mohr Siebeck, 2004.

Sterck-Degueldre, "Frau." Sterck-Degueldre, Jean-Pierre. "Eine Frau namens Lydia. Erstbekehrte nach dem Apostelkonvent." *BK* 64 (1, 2009): 39–43.

Sterling, *Ancestral Philosophy.* Sterling, Gregory E., ed. *The Ancestral Philosophy: Hellenistic Philosophy in Second Temple Judaism: Essays of David Winston.* BJS 331. SPhilMon 4. Providence: Brown University Press, 2001.

Sterling, "Apostle." Sterling, Gregory E. "From Apostle to the Gentiles to Apostle of the Church: Images of Paul at the End of the First Century." *ZNW* 99 (1, 2008): 74–98.

Sterling, "Appropriation." Sterling, Gregory E. "The Jewish Appropriation of Hellenistic Historiography." Pages 231–43 in *A Companion to Greek and Roman Historiography.* Edited by John Marincola. 2 vols. Oxford: Blackwell, 2007.

Sterling, "Athletes of Virtue." Sterling, Gregory E. "'Athletes of Virtue': An Analysis of the Summaries in Acts (2:41–47; 4:32–35; 5:12–16)." *JBL* 113 (4, 1994): 679–96.

Sterling, "Historians." Sterling, Gregory E. "Historians, Greco-Roman." *DNTB* 499–504.

Sterling, *Historiography.* Sterling, Gregory E. *Historiography and Self-Definition: Josephos, Luke-Acts, and Apologetic Historiography.* NovTSup 64. Leiden: Brill, 1992.

Sterling, "Legitimation." Sterling, Gregory E. "'Opening the Scriptures': The Legitimation of the Jewish Diaspora and the Early Christian Mission." Pages 199–225 in *Jesus and the Heritage of Israel: Luke's Narrative Claim upon Israel's Legacy.* Edited by David P. Moessner. Luke the Interpreter of Israel 1. Harrisburg, Pa.: Trinity Press International, 1999.

Sterling, "Platonizing Moses." Sterling, Gregory E. "Platonizing Moses: Philo and Middle Platonism." *SPhilA* 5 (1993): 96–111.

Sterling, "Queen of Virtues." Sterling, Gregory E. "'The Queen of the Virtues': Piety in Philo of Alexandria." *SPhilA* 18 (2006): 103–23.

Sterling, "Recherché." Sterling, Gregory E. "Recherché or Representative? What Is the Relationship between Philo's Treatises and Greek-Speaking Judaism?" *SPhilA* 11 (1999): 1–30.

Sterling, "School." Sterling, Gregory E. "'The School of Sacred Laws': The Social Setting of Philo's Treatises." *VC* 53 (2, 1999): 148–64.

Sterling, *Sisters.* Sterling, Dorothy, ed. *We Are Your Sisters: Black Women in the Nineteenth Century.* New York: W. W. Norton, 1984.

Sterling, "Understanding." Sterling, Gregory E. "'Do You Understand What You Are Reading?' The Understanding of the LXX in Luke-Acts." Pages 101–18 in *Die Apostelgeschichte im Kontext antiker und frühchristlicher Historiographie.* Edited by Jörg Frey, Clare K. Rothschild, and Jens Schröter, with Bettina Rost. BZNWK 162. Berlin: de Gruyter, 2009.

Sterling, "Universalizing the Particular." Sterling, Gregory E. "Universalizing the Particular: Natural Law in Second Temple Jewish Ethics." *SPhilA* 15 (2003): 64–80.

Stern, "Aspects." Stern, Menahem. "Aspects of Jewish Society: The Priesthood and Other Classes." *JPFC* 561–630.

Stern, *Authors.* Stern, Menahem, ed. *Greek and Latin Authors on Jews and Judaism.* 3 vols. Jerusalem: Israel Academy of Sciences and Humanities, 1974–84.

Stern, "Chronology." Stern, M. "Chronology." *JPFC* 62–77.

Stern, "Diaspora." Stern, M. "The Jewish Diaspora." *JPFC* 117–83.

Stern, "Greek and Latin Literature." Stern, M. "The Jews in Greek and Latin Literature." *JPFC* 1101–59.

Stern, "Herod." Stern, M. "The Reign of Herod and the Herodian Dynasty." *JPFC* 216–307.

Stern, "Josephus and Empire." Stern, Menahem. "Josephus and the Roman Empire as Reflected in *The Jewish War.*" Pages 71–80 in *Josephus, Judaism, and Christianity.* Edited by Louis H. Feldman and Gohei Hata. Detroit: Wayne State University Press, 1987.

Stern, "Limitations." Stern, Karen B. "Limitations of 'Jewish' as a Label in Roman North Africa." *JSJ* 39 (3, 2008): 307–36.

Stern, *Parables in Midrash.* Stern, David. *Parables in Midrash: Narrative and Exegesis in Rabbinic Literature.* Cambridge, Mass.: Harvard University Press, 1991.

Stern, "Province." Stern, M. "The Province of Judaea." *JPFC* 308–76.

Stern and Magen, "Temple." Stern, Ephraim, and Yitzhak Magen, "Archaeological Evidence for the First Stage of the Samaritan Temple on Mount Gerizim." *IEJ* 52 (1, 2002): 49–57.

Stern and Schlick-Nolte, *Early Glass*. Stern, E. Marianne, and Birgit Schlick-Nolte. *Early Glass of the Ancient World, 1600 B.C.–A.D. 50: Ernesto Wolf Collection*. Ostfildern, Ger.: Gerd Hatje, 1994.

Stern, Berg, and Sharon, "Tel Dor." Stern, E., J. Berg, and I. Sharon. "Tel Dor, 1988–1989: Preliminary Report." *IEJ* 41 (1–3, 1991): 46–61.

Sternberg, *Poetics*. Sternberg, Meir. *The Poetics of Biblical Narrative*. Bloomington: Indiana University Press, 1985.

Steuernagel, "ΑΚΟΥΟΝΤΕΣ." Steuernagel, Gert. "ΑΚΟΥΟΝΤΕΣ ΜΕΝ ΤΗΣ ΦΩΝΗΣ (Apg. 9.7): Ein Genitiv in der Apostelgeschichte." *NTS* 35 (4, 1989): 619–24.

Stevens, *Theology*. Stevens, George B. *The Johannine Theology: A Study of the Doctrinal Contents of the Gospel and Epistles of the Apostle John*. New York: Scribner's, 1894.

Stevens, "Warrior." Stevens, Bruce A. "'Why "Must" the Son of Man Suffer?' The Divine Warrior in the Gospel of Mark." *BZ* 31 (1, 1987): 101–10.

Stevens and Drinkwater, "Forum Iulii." Stevens, Courtenay Edward, and John Frederick Drinkwater. "Forum Iulii." *OCD*[3] 607.

Stevenson, "Army." Stevenson, G. H. "The Army and Navy." Pages 218–38 in *The Augustan Empire: 44 B.C.–A.D. 70*. Edited by S. A. Cook, F. E. Adcock, and M. P. Charlesworth. CAH 10. Cambridge: Cambridge University Press, 1934. Repr., 1966.

Stevenson, "Rise of Eunuchs." Stevenson, Walter. "The Rise of Eunuchs in Greco-Roman Antiquity." *JHistSex* 5 (4, 1995): 495–511.

Stevenson, "Women in Livy." Stevenson, Tom. "Women of Early Rome as Exempla in Livy, *Ab Urbe Condita*, Book 1." *CW* 104 (2, 2011): 175–89.

Stevenson and Lintott, "Clubs." Stevenson, George Hope, and Andrew William Lintott. "Clubs, Roman." *OCD*[3] 352–53.

Stewart, "Guardian Angel." Stewart, Lois. "Rice Straw and a Guardian Angel." *MounM* (Mar. 1995): 12–13.

Stewart, "Procedure." Stewart, Roy A. "Judicial Procedure in New Testament Times." *EvQ* 47 (1975): 94–109.

Stewart, *Pyramids*. Stewart, Desmond. *The Pyramids and Sphinx*. New York: Newsweek, 1971.

Stewart, "Retrospective Styles." Stewart, Andrew F. "Retrospective Styles." *OCD*[3] 1309–10.

Stewart, "Synagogue." Stewart, Roy A. "The Synagogue." *EvQ* 43 (1, 1971): 36–46.

Steyn, "Ἐκχεῶ." Steyn, Gert J. "Ἐκχεῶ ἀπὸ τοῦ πνεύματος . . . (Ac 2:17, 18): What Is

Being Poured Out?" *Neot* 33 (2, 1999): 365–71.

Steyn, "Γλῶσσαι." Steyn, Gert J. "A Note on Translating and Interpreting . . . γλῶσσαι ὡσεὶ πυρός . . . (Acts 2:3)." *EkkPhar* 80 (1, 1998): 21–27.

Steyn, "*LXX-Sitate*." Steyn, Gert J. "*LXX-Sitate* in die Petrus- en Paulusredes van Handelinge." *SK* 16 (1, 1995): 125–41.

Steyn, *Septuagint Quotations*. Steyn, Gert J. *Septuagint Quotations in the Context of the Petrine and Pauline Speeches of the Acta apostolorum*. CBET 12. Kampen, Neth.: Kok Pharos, 1995.

Steyn, "*Vorlage* of Quotations." Steyn, Gert J. "Notes on the *Vorlage* of the Amos Quotations in Acts." Pages 60–81 in *Die Apostelgeschichte und die hellenistische Geschichtsschreibung: Festschrift für Eckhard Plümacher zu seinem 65. Geburtstag*. Edited by Cilliers Breytenbach and Jens Schröter. Leiden: Brill, 2004.

Steyne, *Gods of Power*. Steyne, Philip M. *Gods of Power: A Study of the Beliefs and Practices of Animists*. Houston: Touch, 1990.

Stibbe, *Gospel*. Stibbe, Mark W. G. *John's Gospel*. New Testament Readings. London: Routledge, 1994.

Stibbe, *Prophetic Evangelism*. Stibbe, Mark W. G. *Prophetic Evangelism: When God Speaks to Those Who Don't Know Him*. Bletchley, Milton Keynes, U.K.: Authentic Media, 2004.

Stieglitz, "Names." Stieglitz, Robert R. "The Hebrew Names of the Seven Planets." *JNES* 40 (2, 1981): 135–37.

Stigers, "World." Stigers, Eva Stehle. "Sappho's Private World." *WomSt* 8 (1–2, 1981): 47–63.

Still, *Jesus and Paul*. Still, Todd D., ed. *Jesus and Paul Reconnected: Fresh Pathways into an Old Debate*. Grand Rapids: Eerdmans, 2007.

Still, "Loathe Labor." Still, Todd D. "Did Paul Loathe Manual Labor? Revisiting the Work of Ronald F. Hock on the Apostle's Tentmaking and Social Class." *JBL* 125 (4, 2006): 781–95.

Still, "Macedonian Believers." Still, Todd D. "Paul and the Macedonian Believers." Pages 30–45 in *The Blackwell Companion to Paul*. Edited by Stephen Westerholm. BCompRel. Oxford: Blackwell, 2011.

Still, "Paul's Aims." Still, E. Coye. "Paul's Aims regarding εἰδωλόθυτα: A New Proposal for Interpreting 1 Corinthians 8:1–11:1." *NovT* 44 (4, 2002): 333–43.

Still, "Slavery." Still, Todd D. "Pauline Theology and Ancient Slavery: Does the Former Support or Subvert the Latter?" *HBT* 27 (2, 2005): 21–34.

Stinton, *Jesus of Africa*. Stinton, Diane B. *Jesus of Africa: Voices of Contemporary African Christology*. Maryknoll, N.Y.: Orbis, 2004.

Stipp, "Vier Gestalten." Stipp, Hermann-Josef. "Vier Gestalten einer Totenerweckungserzählung (1 Kön 17,17–24; 2 Kön 4,8–37; Apg 9,36–42; Apg 20,7–12)." *Bib* 80 (1, 1999): 43–77.

Stirrat, "Possession." Stirrat, Richard L. "Demonic Possession in Roman Catholic Sri Lanka." *JAnthRes* 33 (1977): 122–57.

Stock, "Berufung." Stock, Klemens. "Die Berufung Marias (Lk 1,26–38)." *Bib* 61 (4, 1980): 457–91.

Stock, "Chiastic Awareness." Stock, Augustine. "Chiastic Awareness and Education in Antiquity." *BTB* 14 (1, 1984): 23–27.

Stöger, *Rethinking Ostia*. Stöger, Hanna. *Rethinking Ostia: A Spatial Enquiry into the Urban Society of Rome's Imperial Port-Town*. Leiden: Leiden University Press, 2011.

Stogiannos, "Πνευμα Πυθωνα." Stogiannos, V. P. "'Πνευμα Πυθωνα' (Pr. 16, 16): Ἡ συντάντηση του ἀρχεγονου χριστιανισμου με τη μαντικη." *DBM* 9 (2, 1980): 99–114. (Abstract: *NTA* 26:261.)

Stokes, *One and Many*. Stokes, Michael C. *One and Many in Presocratic Philosophy*. Cambridge, Mass.: Harvard University Press, 1971.

Stökl Ben Ezra, "Weighing." Stökl Ben Ezra, Daniel. "Weighing the Parts: A Papyrological Perspective on the Parting of the Ways." *NovT* 51 (2, 2009): 168–86.

Stol, "Kaiwan." Stol, M. "Kaiwan." Page 478 in *Dictionary of Deities and Demons in the Bible*. 2nd rev. ed. Edited by Karel van der Toorn, Bob Becking, and Pieter W. van der Horst. Leiden: Brill; Grand Rapids: Eerdmans, 1999.

Stoller, "Change." Stoller, Paul. "Stressing Social Change and Songhay Possession." Pages 267–84 in *Altered States of Consciousness and Mental Health: A Cross-Cultural Perspective*. Edited by Colleen A. Ward. CCRMS 12. Newbury Park, Calif.: Sage, 1989.

Stoller, "Eye." Stoller, Paul. "Eye, Mind, and Word in Anthropology." *L'Homme* 24 (3–4, 1984): 91–114.

Stoller and Olkes, *Shadow*. Stoller, Paul, and Cheryl Olkes. *In Sorcery's Shadow: A Memoir of Apprenticeship among the Songhay of Niger*. Chicago: University of Chicago Press, 1987.

Stonehouse, *Areopagus*. Stonehouse, N. B. *Paul before the Areopagus and Other New Testament Studies*. Grand Rapids: Eerdmans, 1957.

Stoneman, "Traditions." Stoneman, Richard. "Jewish Traditions on Alexander the Great." *SPhilA* 6 (1994): 37–53.

Stoops, "*Acts of Peter*." Stoops, Robert F., Jr. "The *Acts of Peter* in Intertextual Context." Pages 57–86 in *The Apocryphal Acts of the Apostles in Intertextual Perspectives*. Edited by Robert F. Stoops. *Semeia* 80. Atlanta: Scholars Press, 1997.

Stoops, "Riot." Stoops, Robert F. "Riot and Assembly: The Social Context of Acts 19:23–41." *JBL* 108 (1, 1989): 73–91.

Storey, "Insulae." Storey, Glenn R. "Regionaries-Type Insulae 2: Architectural/Residential Units at Rome." *AJA* 106 (3, 2002): 411–34.

Storey, "Population." Storey, Glenn R. "The Population of Ancient Rome." *Antiquity* 71 (274, 1997): 966–78.

Storey, "Skyscrapers." Storey, Glenn R. "The 'Skyscrapers' of the Ancient Roman World." *Latomus* 62 (1, 2003): 3–26.

Storey, "Units at Ostia." Storey, Glenn R. "Regionaries-Type Insulae 1: Architectural/Residential Units at Ostia." *AJA* 105 (3, 2001): 389–401.

Storms, *Convergence*. Storms, Sam. *Convergence: Spiritual Journeys of a Charismatic Calvinist*. Kansas City, Mo.: Enjoying God Ministries, 2005.

Storms, *Guide*. Storms, Sam. *The Beginner's Guide to Spiritual Gifts*. Ventura, Calif.: Regal, 2002.

Storms, "View." Storms, Sam. "A Third Wave View." Pages 175–223 in *Are Miraculous Gifts for Today? Four Views*. Edited by Wayne A. Grudem. Grand Rapids: Zondervan, 1996.

Stothers, "Objects." Stothers, Richard. "Unidentified Flying Objects in Classical Antiquity." *CJ* 103 (1, 2007): 79–92.

Stothers, "Optics." Stothers, Richard. "Ancient Meteorological Optics." *CJ* 105 (1, 2009): 27–42.

Stott, "Response." Stott, John. "John Stott's Response to Chapter 6." Pages 306–31 in *Evangelical Essentials: A Liberal-Evangelical Dialogue*. By David L. Edwards and John Stott. Downers Grove, Ill.: InterVarsity, 1988.

Stoutenburg, "Review." Stoutenburg, Dennis. Review of *The IVP Bible Background Commentary*. *JETS* 39 (1, 1996): 152–53.

Stover, "Apollonius." Stover, Timothy. "Apollonius, Valerius Flaccus, and Statius: Argonautic Elements in Thebaid 3.499–647." *AJP* 130 (3, 2009): 439–55.

Stowasser, "Überlegungen." Stowasser, Martin. "Am 5,25–27; 9,11f. in der Qumranüberlieferung und in der Apostelgeschichte: Text- und traditionsgeschichtliche Überlegungen zu 4Q174 (Florilegium) III 12/CD VII 16/Apg

7,42b-43; 15,16–18." *ZNW* 92 (1–2, 2001): 47–63.

Stowers, *Diatribe*. Stowers, Stanley K. *The Diatribe and Paul's Letter to the Romans*. SBLDS 57. Chico, Calif.: Scholars Press, 1981.

Stowers, "Diatribe." Stowers, Stanley K. "The Diatribe." Pages 71–83 in *Greco-Roman Literature and the New Testament: Selected Forms and Genres*. Edited by David E. Aune. SBLSBS 21. Atlanta: Scholars Press, 1988.

Stowers, *Letter Writing*. Stowers, Stanley K. *Letter Writing in Greco-Roman Antiquity*. LEC 5. Philadelphia: Westminster, 1986.

Stowers, *Rereading of Romans*. Stowers, Stanley K. *A Rereading of Romans: Justice, Jews, and Gentiles*. New Haven: Yale University Press, 1994.

Stowers, "Resemble Philosophy?" Stowers, Stanley K. "Does Pauline Christianity Resemble a Hellenistic Philosophy?" Pages 81–102 in *Paul beyond the Judaism/Hellenism Divide*. Edited by Troels Engberg-Pedersen. Louisville: Westminster John Knox, 2001.

Stowers, "Self-Mastery." Stowers, Stanley K. "Paul and Self-Mastery." Pages 524–50 in *Paul in the Greco-Roman World: A Handbook*. Edited by J. Paul Sampley. Harrisburg, Pa.: Trinity Press International, 2003.

Stowers, "Status, Speaking, and Teaching." Stowers, Stanley K. "Social Status, Public Speaking, and Private Teaching: The Circumstances of Paul's Preaching Activity." *NovT* 26 (1, 1984): 59–82.

Stowers, "Synagogue in Theology of Acts." Stowers, Stanley K. "The Synagogue in the Theology of Acts." *ResQ* 17 (3, 1974): 129–43.

Strachan, *Gospel*. Strachan, Robert Harvey. *The Fourth Gospel: Its Significance and Environment*. London: Student Christian Movement, 1917.

Strachan, *Second Corinthians*. Strachan, Robert Harvey. *The Second Epistle of Paul to the Corinthians*. MNTC. London: Hodder & Stoughton, 1935.

Strachan, *Theology of Irving*. Strachan, Gordon. *The Pentecostal Theology of Edward Irving*. Peabody, Mass.: Hendrickson, 1973.

Strack, *Introduction*. Strack, Hermann L. *Introduction to the Talmud and Midrash*. Philadelphia: Jewish Publication Society of America, 1931. Repr., New York: Atheneum, 1969.

Strack and Billerbeck, *Kommentar*. Strack, Hermann L., and Paul Billerbeck. *Kommentar zum Neuen Testament aus Talmud und Midrasch*. 6 vols. Munich: Beck, 1956.

Straight, *Miracles*. Straight, Bilinda. *Miracles and Extraordinary Experience in Northern

Kenya*. Philadelphia: University of Pennsylvania Press, 2007.

Strait, "King." Strait, Drew J. "Proclaiming Another King Named Jesus? The Acts of the Apostles and the Roman Imperial Cult(s)." Pages 130–45 in *Jesus Is Lord, Caesar Is Not: Evaluating Empire in New Testament Studies*. Edited by Scot McKnight and Joseph B. Modica. Downers Grove, Ill.: IVP Academic, 2013.

Strand, "Day." Strand, Kenneth A. "Another Look at 'Lord's Day' in the Early Church and in Rev. I.10." *NTS* 13 (2, 1967): 174–81.

Strange, "Galilee." Strange, James F. "Galilee." *DNTB* 391–98.

Strange, "Jesus-Tradition." Strange, W. A. "The Jesus-Tradition in Acts." *NTS* 46 (1, 2000): 59–74.

Strange, "Nazareth." Strange, James F. "Nazareth." *OEANE* 4:113–14.

Strange, *Problem*. Strange, W. A. *The Problem of the Text of Acts*. SNTSMS 71. Cambridge: Cambridge University Press, 1992.

Strange and Shanks, "House in Capernaum." Strange, James F., and Hershel Shanks. "Has the House Where Jesus Stayed in Capernaum Been Found?" *BAR* 8 (6, 1982): 26–37.

Strange and Shanks, "Synagogue." Strange, James F., and Hershel Shanks. "Synagogue Where Jesus Preached Found at Capernaum." *BAR* 9 (6, 1983): 25–31.

Strasburger, "Umblick." Strasburger, Hermann. "Umblick in Trümmerfeld der griechischen Geschichtsschreibung." Pages 3–52 in *Historiographia Antiqua. Commentationes Lovanienses editae in honorem W. Peremans septuagenarii*. Symbolae Facultatis litterarum et philosophiae Lovaniensis A, 6. Leuven: University Press, 1977.

Stratton, "Imagining Power." Stratton, Kimberly. "Imagining Power: Magic, Miracle, and the Social Context of Rabbinic Self-Representation." *JAAR* 73 (2, 2005): 361–93.

Strauch, "Community." Strauch, Judith. "Community and Kinship in Southeastern China: The View from the Multilineage Villages of Hong Kong." *JAS* 43 (1, 1983): 21–50.

Strauss, *Messiah*. Strauss, Mark L. *The Davidic Messiah in Luke-Acts: The Promise and Its Fulfillment in Lukan Christology*. JSNTSup 110. Sheffield, U.K.: Sheffield Academic, 1995.

Stravinskas, "Role of Spirit." Stravinskas, Peter M. J. "The Role of the Spirit in Acts 1 and 2." *BibT* 18 (4, 1980): 263–68.

Strawn, "Pharaoh." Strawn, Brent A. "Pharaoh." *DOTP* 631–36.

Štrba, "Miqveh." Štrba, Blažej. "Miqveh—rituálne vodné zariadenie na očišťovanie v ranom judaizme." StBibSlov (2006): 79–106.

Streeter, Gospels. Streeter, Burnett Hillman. The Four Gospels: A Study of Origins Treating of the Manuscript Tradition, Sources, Authorship, and Dates. Rev. ed. London: Macmillan, 1930.

Streeter and Picton-Turbervill, Woman. Streeter, Burnett Hillman, and Edith Picton-Turbervill. Woman and the Church. London: F. Fisher Unwin, 1917.

Strelan, "Acts 19:12." Strelan, Rick. "Acts 19:12: Paul's 'Aprons' Again." JTS 54 (1, 2003): 154–57.

Strelan, Artemis. Strelan, Rick. Paul, Artemis, and the Jews in Ephesus. BZNWK 80. New York and Berlin: de Gruyter, 1996.

Strelan, "Gamaliel's Hunch." Strelan, Rick. "Gamaliel's Hunch." ABR 47 (1999): 53–69.

Strelan, "Holy Spirit." Strelan, Rick. "What Might a Pagan Have Understood by 'Holy Spirit'?" Colloq 42 (2, 2010): 151–72.

Strelan, "Recognizing." Strelan, Rick. "Recognizing the Gods (Acts 14.8–10)." NTS 46 (4, 2000): 488–503.

Strelan, "Running Prophet." Strelan, Rick. "The Running Prophet (Acts 8:30)." NovT 43 (1, 2001): 31–38.

Strelan, "Stares." Strelan, Rick. "Strange Stares: Atenizein in Acts." NovT 41 (3, 1999): 235–55.

Strelan, Strange Acts. Strelan, Rick. Strange Acts: Studies in the Cultural World of the Acts of the Apostles. BZNW 126. Berlin: de Gruyter, 2004.

Strelan, "Tabitha." Strelan, Rick. "Tabitha: The Gazelle of Joppa (Acts 9:36–41)." BTB 39 (2, 2009): 77–86.

Stricher, "Parallels." Stricher, J. "The Men-Women Parallels in the Work of Luke." BDV 53 (1999): 14–17.

Striker, "Sceptics." Striker, Gisela. "Sceptics." OCD³ 1362–63.

Strobel, "Galatia." Strobel, Karl. "Galatia: Roman Province." BrillPauly 5:650–51.

Strobel, "Hauses." Strobel, August. "Der Begriff des 'Hauses' im griechischen und römischen Privatrecht." ZNW 56 (1965): 91–100.

Strobel, "Passa-Symbolik." Strobel, August. "Passa-Symbolik und Passa-Wunder in Act. XII. 3ff." NTS 4 (3, 1958): 210–15.

Strobel, "Pessinus." Strobel, Karl. "Pessinus." BrillPauly 10:861–63.

Strobel, "Region." Strobel, Karl. "Galatia: Region." BrillPauly 5:648–50.

Strom, "Background to Acts 12." Strom, Mark R. "An Old Testament Background to Acts 12.20–23." NTS 32 (2, 1986): 289–92.

Strombeck, Rapture. Strombeck, J. F. First the Rapture. Foreword by Warren W. Wiersbe. Eugene, Ore.: Harvest House, 1982.

Strong, "Jerusalem Council." Strong, David K. "The Jerusalem Council: Some Implications for Contextualization, Acts 15:1–35." Pages 196–208 in Mission in Acts: Ancient Narratives in Contemporary Context. Edited by Robert L. Gallagher and Paul Hertig. AmSocMissS 34. Maryknoll, N.Y.: Orbis, 2004.

Stronstad, Baptized. Stronstad, Roger. Baptized and Filled with the Holy Spirit. Springfield, Mo.: Africa's Hope, 2004.

Stronstad, "Baptized." Stronstad, Roger. "On Being Baptized in the Holy Spirit: A Lukan Emphasis." Pages 160–93 in Trajectories in the Book of Acts: Essays in Honor of John Wesley Wyckoff. Edited by Paul Alexander, Jordan Daniel May, and Robert G. Reid. Eugene, Ore.: Wipf & Stock, 2010.

Stronstad, Charismatic Theology. Stronstad, Roger. The Charismatic Theology of St. Luke. Peabody, Mass.: Hendrickson, 1984.

Stronstad, Prophethood. Stronstad, Roger. The Prophethood of All Believers: A Study in Luke's Charismatic Theology. JPTSup 16. Sheffield, U.K.: Sheffield Academic, 1999.

Stronstad, Scripture. Stronstad, Roger, ed. Spirit, Scripture, and Theology: A Pentecostal Perspective. Baguio City, Philippines: Asian Pacific Theological Seminary Press, 1995.

Stronstad et al., "Review." Stronstad, Roger, et al. "Review of Prophetic Jesus, Prophetic Church: The Challenge of Luke-Acts." JPT 22 (1, 2013): 1–36.

Strouch and Höcker, "Dodona." Strouch, Daniel, and Christoph Höcker. "Dodona, Dodone: Archaeological Finds." Brill Pauly 5:606.

Stroud, Demeter. Stroud, Ronald S. Demeter and Persephone in Ancient Corinth. Princeton: American School of Classical Studies at Athens, 1987.

Stroumsa, "Form(s)." Stroumsa, Gedaliahu G. "Form(s) of God: Some Notes on Metatron and Christ." HTR 76 (3, 1983): 269–88.

Stroumsa, "Testimony." Stroumsa, Guy G. "Comments on Charles Hedrick's Article: A Testimony." JECS 11 (2, Summer 2003): 147–53.

Strubbe, "Young Magistrates." Strubbe, Johan H. M. "Young Magistrates in the Greek East." Mnemosyne 68 (1, 2005): 88–111.

Strugnell, "Flavius Josephus." Strugnell, John. "Flavius Josephus and the Essenes: Antiquities XVIII, 18–22." JBL 77 (2, 1958): 106–15.

Strugnell, "Wives." Strugnell, John. "More on Wives and Marriage in the Dead Sea Scrolls: (4Q416 2 ii 21 and 4QMMT §B)." RevQ 17 (65–68, 1996): 537–47.

Stuart, "Textual Criticism." Stuart, Douglas. "Inerrancy and Textual Criticism." Pages 97–117 in Inerrancy and Common Sense. Edited by Roger R. Nicole and J. Ramsey Michaels. Preface by Harold J. Ockenga. Grand Rapids: Baker, 1980.

Stubbs, "Shape." Stubbs, David L. "The Shape of Soteriology and the pistis Christou Debate." SJT 61 (2, 2008): 137–57.

Stuckenbruck, "Angels of Nations." Stuckenbruck, Loren T. "Angels of the Nations." DNTB 29–31.

Stuehrenberg, "Reformation." Stuehrenberg, Paul F. "The Study of Acts before the Reformation: A Bibliographic Introduction." NovT 29 (2, 1987): 100–136.

Stuhlmacher, "Genre(s)." Stuhlmacher, Peter. "The Genre(s) of the Gospels: Response to P. L. Shuler." Pages 484–94 in The Interrelations of the Gospels. Edited by D. L. Dungan. BETL 95. Leuven: Leuven University Press, 1990.

Stuhlmacher, Justification. Stuhlmacher, Peter. Revisiting Paul's Doctrine of Justification: A Challenge to the New Perspective. Downers Grove, Ill.: InterVarsity, 2001.

Stuhlmacher, "Pauline Gospel." Stuhlmacher, Peter. "The Pauline Gospel." Pages 149–72 in The Gospel and the Gospels. Edited by Peter Stuhlmacher. Grand Rapids: Eerdmans, 1991.

Stuhlmacher, Romans. Stuhlmacher, Peter. Paul's Letter to the Romans: A Commentary. Translated by Scott J. Hafemann. Louisville: Westminster John Knox, 1994.

Stuhlmacher, "Theme." Stuhlmacher, Peter. "The Theme: The Gospel and the Gospels." Pages 1–25 in The Gospel and the Gospels. Edited by Peter Stuhlmacher. Grand Rapids: Eerdmans, 1991.

Stumpf, "Tessera." Stumpf, Gerd. "Tessera." BrillPauly 14:313–14.

Sturgeon, "Amazon." Sturgeon, Mary C. "The Corinth Amazon: Formation of a Roman Classical Sculpture." AJA 99 (3, 1995): 483–505.

Stylianopoulis, Justin. Stylianopoulis, Theodore. Justin Martyr and the Mosaic Law. SBLDS 20. Missoula, Mont.: Scholars Press, 1975.

Suazo, "Poder." Suazo, David. "El poder de la verdad para transformar culturas: El evangelio transforma a individuos, estruturas, y sociedades (Hechos 16:11–40)." Kairós 37 (2005): 97–110.

"Sudan: Caught." "Sudan: Caught in a Vicious Cycle of Human Rights Abuses,

Poverty, and Political Turmoil." *Amnesty Action* (Winter 1995): 1, 3.

"Sudan—Ravages." "Sudan—The Ravages of War: Political Killings and Humanitarian Disaster." London: Amnesty International, Sept. 29, 1993. Amnesty International Index: AFR 54/29/93.

Suder, "Age Classification." Suder, Wieslaw. "On Age Classification in Roman Imperial Literature." *CBull* 55 (1, 1978): 5–9.

Suhl, "Seeweg." Suhl, Alfred. "Zum Seeweg Alexandrien-Rom." *TZ* 47 (3, 1991): 208–13.

Suhl, "Titel." Suhl, Alfred. "Zum Titel πρῶτος τῆς νήσου (Erster der Insel) Apg 28,7." *BZ* 36 (2, 1992): 220–26.

Sukenik, "Records." Sukenik, Eleazar Lipa. "The Earliest Records of Christianity." *AJA* 51 (1947): 351–65.

Sukenik, *Synagogues.* Sukenik, Eleazar Lipa. *Ancient Synagogues in Palestine and Greece.* London: Oxford University Press, 1934.

Sullivan, "Cappadocia." Sullivan, Richard D. "Cappadocia." *ABD* 1:870–72.

Sullivan, "Pontus." Sullivan, Richard D. "Pontus." *ABD* 5:401–2.

Sultana and Falzon, *Wildlife.* Sultana, Joe, and Victor Falzon, eds. *Wildlife of the Maltese Islands.* Floriana, Malta: Environmental Protection Department, 1996.

Sulzbach, "Geography." Sulzbach, Carla. "The Function of the Sacred Geography in the Book of Jubilees." *JS/TS* 14 (2, 2005): 283–305.

Sumi, "Impersonating." Sumi, Geoffrey S. "Impersonating the Dead: Mimes at Roman Funerals." *AJP* 123 (4, 2002): 559–85.

Sumi, "Monuments." Sumi, Geoffrey S. "Monuments and Memory: The Aedes Castoris in the Formation of Augustan Ideology." *CQ* 59 (1, 2009): 167–86.

Summers, "Approach." Summers, Steve. "'Out of My Mind for God': A Social-Scientific Approach to Pauline Pneumatology." *JPT* 13 (1998): 77–106.

Sumney, *Opponents.* Sumney, Jerry L. *Identifying Paul's Opponents: The Question of Method in 2 Corinthians.* JSNTSup 40. Sheffield, U.K.: JSOT Press, 1990.

Sumney, "Πάθος." Sumney, Jerry L. "Paul's Use of πάθος in His Argument against the Opponents of 2 Corinthians." Pages 147–60 in *Paul and Pathos.* Edited by Thomas H. Olbricht and Jerry L. Sumney. SBLSymS 16. Atlanta: SBL, 2001.

Sumney, "Rationalities." Sumney, Jerry L. "Alternative Rationalities in Paul: Expanding Our Definition of Argument." *ResQ* 46 (1, 2004): 1–9.

Sumney, "Studying Opponents." Sumney, Jerry L. "Studying Paul's Opponents: Advances and Challenges." Pages 7–58 in

Paul and His Opponents. Edited by Stanley E. Porter. PAST 2. Leiden: Brill, 2005.

Sunderland, *Manual.* Sunderland, La Roy. *Anti-Slavery Manual, Containing a Collection of Facts and Arguments on American Slavery.* New York: S. W. Benedict, 1837. Repr., Detroit: Negro History Press, 1969.

Sunderland, *Testimony.* Sunderland, La Roy. *The Testimony of God against Slavery; or, A Collection of Passages from the Bible Which Show the Sin of Holding Property in Man, with Notes.* Boston: Webster & Southard, 1835.

Sundkler, *Bantu Prophets.* Sundkler, Bengt. *Bantu Prophets in South Africa.* 2nd ed. London: Oxford University Press, 1961.

Sundkler, *Bara Bukoba.* Sundkler, Bengt. *Bara Bukoba: Church and Community in Tanzania.* London: C. Hurst, 1980.

Sundkler, "Worship." Sundkler, Bengt. "Worship and Spirituality." Pages 545–53 in *Christianity in Independent Africa.* Edited by Edward Fasholé-Luke et al. Bloomington: Indiana University Press, 1978.

Sundwall, "Ammianus Geographicus." Sundwall, Gavin A. "Ammianus Geographicus." *AJP* 117 (4, 1996): 619–43.

Sung, *Diaries.* Sung, John (Song, Shangchieh). *The Diaries of John Sung: An Autobiography.* Translated by Stephen L. Sheng. Brighton, Mich.: Luke H. Sheng, Stephen L. Sheng, 1995.

Surgy, *Église.* Surgy, Albert de. *L'Église du christianisme céleste: Un exemple d'église prophétique au Bénin.* Paris: Karthala, 2001.

Susaimanickam, "Name." Susaimanickam, J. "By the Name of Jesus Christ: Reflections on Acts 4:8–12." *ITS* 43 (3–4, 2006): 309–24.

Sussman, "Binding." Sussman, Varda. "The Binding of Isaac as Depicted on a Samaritan Lamp." *IEJ* 48 (3–4, 1998): 183–89.

Sussman, "Cave." Sussman, Varda. "A Burial Cave on Mount Scopus." '*Atiqot* 21 (1992): 89–96.

Sussman, "Lighting." Sussman, Varda. "Lighting the Way through History: The Evolution of Ancient Oil Lamps." *BAR* 11 (2, 1985): 42–56.

Sussman, "Oil-Lamp." Sussman, Varda. "A Giant Cretan Oil-Lamp from Herod's Seaside Palace at Caesarea." *IEJ* 45 (4, 1995): 278–82.

Sussman, "Workers." Sussman, Linda S. "Workers and Drones; Labor, Idleness, and Gender Definition in Hesiod's Beehive." Pages 79–93 in *Women in the Ancient World: The Arethusa Papers.* Edited by John Peradotto and J. P. Sullivan. SSCS. Albany: State University of New York Press, 1984.

Sutcliffe, "Baptism." Sutcliffe, Edmund Felix. "Baptism and Baptismal Rites at Qumran?" *HeyJ* 1 (3, 1960): 179–88.

Sutcliffe, "Meals." Sutcliffe, Edmund Felix. "Sacred Meals at Qumran?" *HeyJ* 1 (1960): 48–65.

Sutcliffe, "Review." Sutcliffe, E. F. Review of H. Mantel, *Studies in the History of the Sanhedrin. HeyJ* 4 (3, 1963): 283–87.

Swain, "Culture." Swain, Simon C. R. "Hellenic Culture and the Roman Heroes of Plutarch." *JHS* 110 (1990): 126–45.

Swain, "Plutarch." Swain, Simon. "Plutarch: Chance, Providence, and History." *AJP* 110 (2, 1989): 272–302.

Swan, *Desert Mothers.* Swan, Laura. *The Forgotten Desert Mothers: Sayings, Lives, and Stories of Early Christian Women.* New York: Paulist, 2001.

Swanson, "4Q534." Swanson, Cara A. "Birth of the Chosen One (4Q534)." *DNTB* 170–71.

Swanson, "Bibliography." Swanson, Dennis M. "Bibliography of Works on the New Perspective on Paul." *MSJ* 16 (2, 2005): 317–24.

Swartz, "Angels." Swartz, Michael D. "'Like the Ministering Angels': Ritual and Purity in Early Jewish Mysticism and Magic." *AJSR* 19 (2, 1994): 135–67.

Swartz, "Ritual Procedures." Swartz, Michael D. "Ritual Procedures in Magical Texts from the Cairo Genizah." *JSQ* 13 (4, 2006): 305–18.

Sweeney, *Story.* Sweeney, Douglas A. *The American Evangelical Story: A History of the Movement.* Grand Rapids: Baker Academic, 2005.

Sweeney, "Twelve." Sweeney, Marvin A. "Twelve, Book of the." Pages 788–806 in *Dictionary of the Old Testament Prophets.* Edited by Mark J. Boda and J. Gordon McConville. Downers Grove, Ill.: IVP Academic, 2012.

Sweetland, "Luke the Christian." Sweetland, Dennis M. "Luke the Christian." Pages 48–63 in *New Views on Luke and Acts.* Edited by Earl Richard. Collegeville, Minn.: Liturgical Press, 1990.

Sweetman, "Knossos." Sweetman, Rebecca J. "Roman Knossos: The Nature of a Globalized City." *AJA* 111 (1, 2007): 61–81.

Swetnam, "Bestowal." Swetnam, James. "Bestowal of the Spirit in the Fourth Gospel." *Bib* 74 (4, 1993): 556–76.

Swetnam, *Jesus and Isaac.* Swetnam, James. *Jesus and Isaac: A Study in the Epistle to the Hebrews in the Light of the Aqedah.* AnBib 94. Rome: Pontifical Biblical Institute, 1981.

Swidler, *Women.* Swidler, Leonard. *Women in Judaism: The Status of Women in Formative*

Judaism. Metuchen, N.J.: Scarecrow, 1976.

Swinburne, *Existence*. Swinburne, Richard. *The Existence of God*. 2nd ed. New York: Oxford University Press, 2004.

Swinburne, *Miracle*. Swinburne, Richard. *The Concept of Miracle*. New Studies in the Philosophy of Religion. London: Macmillan, 1970.

Swiny, "Research Institute." Swiny, Stuart. "Cyprus American Archaeological Research Institute." *OEANE* 96–97.

Swiny and Katzev, "Shipwreck." Swiny, Helena Wylde, and Michael L. Katzev. "The Kyrenia Shipwreck: A Fourth-Century B.C. Greek Merchant Ship." Pages 339–55 in *Marine Archaeology: Proceedings of the Twenty-third Symposium of the Colston Research Society, University of Bristol, April 4–8, 1971*. Edited by D. J. Blackman. Hamden, Conn.: Archon Books; London: Butterworths, 1973.

Syme, "Pallas." Syme, Ronald. "Antonius Pallas, Marcus." *OCD*³ 116–17.

Synan, "Legacies." Synan, Vinson. "The Lasting Legacies of the Azusa Street Revival." *Enr* 11 (2, 2006): 142–52.

Synan, *Movement*. Synan, Vinson. *The Holiness-Pentecostal Movement in the United States*. Grand Rapids: Eerdmans, 1971.

Synan, *Power*. Synan, Vinson. *The Old-Time Power: A History of the Pentecostal Holiness Church*. Franklin Springs, Ga.: Advocate, 1973.

Synan, "Seymour." Synan, Vinson. "Seymour, William Joseph." *DPCM* 778–81.

Synan, *Voices*. Synan, Vinson. *Voices of Pentecost: Testimonies of Lives Touched by the Holy Spirit*. Ann Arbor: Servant, 2003.

Syon, "Evidence." Syon, Danny. "Numismatic Evidence of Jewish Presence in Galilee before the Hasmonean Annexation?" *IsNumR* 1 (2006): 21–24.

Syon, "Gamla." Syon, Danny. "Gamla: Portrait of a Rebellion." *BAR* 18 (1, 1992): 20–37, 72.

Syreeni, "Paradigms." Syreeni, Kari. "The Gospel in Paradigms: A Study in the Hermeneutical Space of Luke-Acts." Pages 36–57 in *Luke-Acts: Scandinavian Perspectives*. Edited by Petri Luomanen. PFES 54. Helsinki: Finnish Exegetical Society; Göttingen: Vandenhoeck & Ruprecht, 1991.

Szesnat, "Homoeroticism." Szesnat, Holger. "Philo and Female Homoeroticism: Philo's Use of γύνανδρος and Recent Work on *tribades*." *JSJ* 30 (2, 1999): 140–47.

Szesnat, "Σκηνοποιός." Szesnat, Holger. "What Did the σκηνοποιός Paul Produce?" *Neot* 27 (2, 1993): 391–402.

Szesnat, "Virgins." Szesnat, Holger. "'Mostly Aged Virgins': Philo and the Presence of the Therapeutrides at Lake Mareotis." *Neot* 32 (1, 1998): 191–201.

Tabb, "Salvation." Tabb, Brian J. "Salvation, Spreading, and Suffering: God's Unfolding Plan in Luke-Acts." *JETS* 58 (1, 2015): 43–61.

Tabor, "Divinity." Tabor, James D. "'Returning to the Divinity': Josephus's Portrayal of the Disappearances of Enoch, Elijah, and Moses." *JBL* 108 (2, 1989): 225–38.

Tabor, "Messiah." Tabor, James D. "A Pierced or Piercing Messiah?—The Verdict Is Still Out." *BAR* 18 (6, 1992): 58–59.

Tabor, "Resurrection." Tabor, James D. "4Q521 'On Resurrection' and the Synoptic Gospel Tradition: A Preliminary Study." *JSP* 10 (1992): 149–62.

Tait, "Banquet." Tait, Michael. "The Last 'Last Supper': The Messianic Banquet in the Pseudepigrapha." *ScrB* 37 (2, 2007): 77–86.

Tait, "End of Law." Tait, Michael. "The End of the Law: The Messianic Torah in the Pseudepigrapha." *NBf* 89 (1024, 2008): 691–701.

Tajra, "Appel à César." Tajra, Harry W. "L'appel à César: Séparation d'avec le christianisme?" *ETR* 56 (4, 1981): 593–98.

Tajra, *Trial*. Tajra, Harry W. *The Trial of St. Paul: A Juridical Exegesis of the Second Half of the Acts of the Apostles*. WUNT 2. Tübingen: J. C. B. Mohr, 1989.

Takacs and Haase, "Isis." Takacs, Sarolta A., and Mareile Haase. "Isis: Greece and Rome." *BrillPauly* 6:966–72.

Takmer and Önen, "Surveys." Takmer, Burak, and Nihal Tüner Önen. "Surveys of the Route-Network in West Pamphylia: A New Portion of the Via Sebaste Extending Between Perge and Klimax." *Adalya* 11 (2008): 109–32.

Tal, "Raison d'Être." Tal, Abraham. "Is There a Raison d'Être for an Aramaic Targum in a Hebrew-Speaking Society?" *REJ* 160 (3–4, 2001): 357–78.

Tal, "Traditions." Tal, Abraham. "Divergent Traditions of the Samaritan Pentateuch as Reflected by Its Aramaic Targum." *JAramB* 1 (2, 1999): 297–314.

Talbert, *Acts*. Talbert, Charles H. *Reading Acts: A Literary and Theological Commentary on the Acts of the Apostles*. Rev. ed. Macon, Ga.: Smyth & Helwys, 2005.

Talbert, "Again: Mission." Talbert, Charles H. "Once Again: The Gentile Mission in Luke-Acts." Pages 99–109 in *Der Treue Gottes trauen: Beiträge zum Werk des Lukas für Gerhard Schneider*. Edited by C. Bussmann and W. Radl. Freiburg im Breisgau: Herder, 1991.

Talbert, *Apocalypse*. Talbert, Charles H. *The Apocalypse: A Reading of the Revelation of John*. Louisville: Westminster John Knox, 1994.

Talbert, *Barrington Atlas*. Talbert, Richard J. A., ed. *Barrington Atlas of the Greek and Roman World*. Princeton: Princeton University Press, 2000.

Talbert, "Cartography." Talbert, Richard. "Cartography." *BrillPauly* 2:1138–43.

Talbert, "Chance." Talbert, Charles H. "Reading Chance, Moessner, and Parsons." Pages 229–40 in *Cadbury, Knox, and Talbert: American Contributions to the Study of Acts*. Edited by Mikeal C. Parsons and Joseph B. Tyson. Atlanta: Scholars Press, 1992.

Talbert, "Concept of Immortals." Talbert, Charles H. "The Concept of Immortals in Mediterranean Antiquity." *JBL* 94 (3, 1975): 419–36.

Talbert, "Conversion in Acts." Talbert, Charles H. "Conversion in the Acts of the Apostles: Ancient Auditors' Perceptions." Pages 141–53 in *Literary Studies in Luke-Acts: Essays in Honor of Joseph B. Tyson*. Edited by Richard P. Thompson and Thomas E. Phillips. Macon, Ga.: Mercer University Press, 1998.

Talbert, *Corinthians*. Talbert, Charles H. *Reading Corinthians: A Literary and Theological Commentary on 1 and 2 Corinthians*. New York: Crossroad, 1987.

Talbert, *Delay*. Talbert, Charles H. "II Peter and the Delay of the Parousia." *VC* 20 (3, 1966): 137–45.

Talbert, *Ephesians*. Talbert, Charles H. *Ephesians and Colossians*. PCNT. Grand Rapids: Baker Academic, 2007.

Talbert, "Geography." Talbert, Richard. "Geography: Greece and Rome." *BrillPauly* 5:773–76.

Talbert, *Gospel*. Talbert, Charles H. *What Is a Gospel? The Genre of the Canonical Gospels*. Philadelphia: Fortress, 1977.

Talbert, *John*. Talbert, Charles H. *Reading John: A Literary and Theological Commentary on the Fourth Gospel and the Johannine Epistles*. New York: Crossroad, 1992.

Talbert, *Luke and Gnostics*. Talbert, Charles H. *Luke and the Gnostics: An Examination of the Lucan Purpose*. New York: Abingdon, 1966.

Talbert, *Matthew*. Talbert, Charles H. *Matthew*. PCNT. Grand Rapids: Baker Academic, 2010.

Talbert, *Mediterranean Milieu*. Talbert, Charles H. *Reading Luke-Acts in Its Mediterranean Milieu*. NovTSup 107. Leiden: Brill, 2003.

Talbert, "Monograph." Talbert, Charles H. "The Acts of the Apostles: Monograph or *bios*?" Pages 58–72 in *History, Literature, and Society in the Book of Acts*. Edited by

Ben Witherington III. Cambridge: Cambridge University Press, 1996.

Talbert, "Myth." Talbert, Charles H. "The Myth of a Descending-Ascending Redeemer in Mediterranean Antiquity." *NTS* 22 (4, 1976): 418–40.

Talbert, *Patterns.* Talbert, Charles H. *Literary Patterns, Theological Themes, and the Genre of Luke-Acts.* SBLMS 20. Missoula, Mont.: Scholars Press, 1974.

Talbert, "Promise and Fulfillment." Talbert, Charles H. "Promise and Fulfillment in Lucan Theology." Pages 91–103 in *Luke-Acts: New Perspectives from the Society of Biblical Literature Seminar.* Edited by Charles H. Talbert. New York: Crossroad, 1984.

Talbert, *Reading Luke.* Talbert, Charles H. *Reading Luke: A Literary and Theological Commentary on the Third Gospel.* New York: Crossroad, 1982.

Talbert, "Review." Talbert, Charles H. Review of Richard A. Burridge, *What Are the Gospels? JBL* 112 (4, 1993): 714–15.

Talbert, "Revisionists." Talbert, Charles H. "Paul, Judaism, and the Revisionists." *CBQ* 63 (1, 2001): 1–22.

Talbert, *Romans.* Talbert, Charles H. *Romans.* SHBC. Macon, Ga.: Smyth & Helwys, 2002.

Talbert, "Small-Town Sources." Talbert, Richard J. A. "Small-Town Sources of Geographic Information in the World of Imperial Rome." *CBull* 80 (1, 2004): 15–25.

Talbert, "Worship." Talbert, Charles H. "Worship in the Fourth Gospel and in Its Milieu." Pages 337–56 in *Perspectives on John: Method and Interpretation in the Fourth Gospel.* Edited by Robert B. Sloan and Mikeal C. Parsons. NABPRSS 11. Lewiston, N.Y.: Edwin Mellen, 1993.

Talbert and Hayes, "Sea Storms." Talbert, Charles H., and J. H. Hayes. "A Theology of Sea Storms in Luke-Acts." Pages 267–83 in *Jesus and the Heritage of Israel: Luke's Narrative Claim upon Israel's Legacy.* Edited by David P. Moessner. Luke the Interpreter of Israel 1. Harrisburg, Pa.: Trinity Press International, 1999.

Taliaferro and Hendrickson, "Racism." Taliaferro, Charles, and Anders Hendrickson. "Hume's Racism and His Case against the Miraculous." *Philosophia Christi* 4 (2, 2002): 427–41.

Talib, "Diaspora." Talib, Y., with F. Samir. "The African Diaspora in Asia." Pages 704–33 in *Africa from the Seventh to the Eleventh Century.* Edited by M. El Fasi, with I. Hrbek. General History of Africa 3. Berkeley: University of California Press; London: Heinemann Educational; Paris: United Nations Educational, Scientific and Cultural Organization, 1988.

Tallman, *Shakarian.* Tallman, Matthew W. *Demos Shakarian: The Life, Legacy, and Vision of a Full Gospel Business Man.* ATSSWCRMPCS 2. Lexington, Ky.: Emeth, 2010.

Talmon, "Institutionalized Prayer." Talmon, Shemaryahu. "The Emergence of Institutionalized Prayer in Israel in the Light of the Qumran Literature." Pages 265–84 in *Qumrân: Sa piété, sa théologie, et son milieu.* Edited by M. Delcor. BETL 46. Gembloux, Belg., and Paris: J. Duculot; Leuven: Leuven University Press, 1978.

Talmon, "Link." Talmon, Shemaryahu. "A Further Link between the Judean Covenanters and the Essenes." *HTR* 56 (4, 1963): 313–19.

Tammuz, "Mare clausum?" Tammuz, Oded. "Mare clausum? Sailing Seasons in the Mediterranean in Early Antiquity." *MHR* 20 (2, 2005): 145–62.

Tan, *Zion Traditions.* Tan, Kim Huat. *The Zion Traditions and the Aims of Jesus.* SNTSMS 91. Cambridge: Cambridge University Press, 1997.

Tang, "Healers." Tang, Edmond. "'Yellers' and Healers—Pentecostalism and the Study of Grassroots Christianity in China." Pages 467–86 in *Asian and Pentecostal: The Charismatic Face of Christianity in Asia.* Edited by Allan Anderson and Edmond Tang. Foreword by Cecil M. Robeck. RStMiss, *AJPS* 3. Oxford: Regnum; Baguio City, Philippines: APTS, 2005.

Tångberg, "Justification." Tångberg, Arvid. "The Justification of the Servant of the Lord: Light from Qumran on the Interpretation of Isaiah 53:11aβ." *TTKi* 72 (1–2, 2001): 31–36.

Tannehill, *Acts.* Tannehill, Robert C. *The Acts of the Apostles.* Vol. 2 of *The Narrative Unity of Luke-Acts: A Literary Interpretation.* Minneapolis: Fortress, 1990.

Tannehill, "Ethics." Tannehill, Robert C. "Do the Ethics of Acts Include the Ethical Teaching in Luke?" Pages 109–22 in *Acts and Ethics.* Edited by Thomas E. Phillips. NTMon 9. Sheffield, U.K.: Sheffield Phoenix, 2005.

Tannehill, "Functions of Peter's Speeches." Tannehill, Robert C. "The Functions of Peter's Mission Speeches in the Narrative of Acts." *NTS* 37 (3, 1991): 400–414.

Tannehill, *Luke.* Tannehill, Robert C. *The Gospel according to Luke.* Vol. 1 of *The Narrative Unity of Luke-Acts: A Literary Interpretation.* Philadelphia: Fortress, 1986.

Tannehill, "Paul's Defense." Tannehill, Robert C. "The Narrator's Strategy in the Scenes of Paul's Defense: Acts 21:27–26:32." *Forum* 8 (3–4, 1992): 255–69.

Tannehill, "Rejection." Tannehill, Robert C. "Rejection by Jews and Turning to Gentiles: The Pattern of Paul's Mission in Acts." Pages 83–101 in *Luke-Acts and the Jewish People: Eight Critical Perspectives.* Edited by Joseph B. Tyson. Minneapolis: Augsburg, 1988.

Tannehill, *Shape.* Tannehill, Robert C. *The Shape of Luke's Story: Essays on Luke-Acts.* Eugene, Ore.: Cascade Books, 2005.

Tannehill, "Story of Israel." Tannehill, Robert C. "The Story of Israel within the Lukan Narrative." Pages 325–39 in *Jesus and the Heritage of Israel: Luke's Narrative Claim upon Israel's Legacy.* Edited by David P. Moessner. Luke the Interpreter of Israel 1. Harrisburg, Pa.: Trinity Press International, 1999.

Tannehill, *Sword.* Tannehill, Robert C. *The Sword of His Mouth.* SBLSemSup 1. Missoula, Mont.: Scholars Press, 1975.

Tannehill, "Tragic Story." Tannehill, Robert C. "Israel in Luke-Acts: A Tragic Story." *JBL* 104 (1, 1985): 69–85.

Tannenbaum, "God-Fearers." Tannenbaum, Robert F. "Jews and God-Fearers in the Holy City of Aphrodite." *BAR* 12 (5, 1986): 54–57.

Tanner, "China." Tanner, Jeremy. "Ancient Greece, Early China: Sino-Hellenic Studies and Comparative Approaches to the Classical World: A Review Article." *JHS* 129 (2009): 89–109.

Tanner, "Quotation." Tanner, J. Paul. "James's Quotation of Amos 9 to Settle the Jerusalem Council Debate in Acts 15." *JETS* 55 (1, 2012): 65–85.

Tanner, "Theory." Tanner, R. E. S. "The Theory and Practice of Sukuma Spirit Mediumship." Pages 273–89 in *Spirit Mediumship and Society in Africa.* Edited by John Beattie and John Middleton. Foreword by Raymond Firth. New York: Africana, 1969.

Tantlevskij, "Melchizedek." Tantlevskij, Igor R. "Melchizedek *redivivus* in Qumran: Some Peculiarities of Messianic Ideas and Elements of Mysticism in the Dead Sea Scrolls." *QC* 12 (1, 2004): 3–80.

Tantlevskij, "Wisdom." Tantlevskij, Igor R. "The Wisdom of Solomon, the Therapeutae, and the Dead Sea Scrolls." *QC* 11 (1–4, 2003): 107–15.

Tanton, "Gospel and Baptism: Acts 2:38." Tanton, Lanny Thomas. "The Gospel and Water Baptism: A Study of Acts 2:38." *JGES* 3 (1, 1990): 27–52.

Tanton, "Gospel and Baptism: Acts 22:16." Tanton, Lanny T. "The Gospel and Water Baptism: A Study of Acts 22:16." *JGES* 4 (1, 1991): 23–40.

Tappy, "Samaria." Tappy, Ron. "Samaria." *OEANE* 4:463–67.

Taran, "Plato." Taran, Leonardo. "Plato, *Phaedo,* 62A." *AJP* 87 (1966): 326–36.

Tari, *Wind*. Tari, Mel, with Cliff Dudley. *Like a Mighty Wind*. Carol Stream, Ill.: Creation House, 1971.

Tari and Tari, *Breeze*. Tari, Mel, and Nona Tari. *The Gentle Breeze of Jesus*. Harrison, Ark.: New Leaf, 174.

Tarn, *Civilisation*. Tarn, William Woodthorpe. *Hellenistic Civilisation*. Revised by W. W. Tarn and G. T. Griffith. 3rd rev. ed. New York: New American Library, 1974.

Tarn, Gray, and Spawforth, "Arabia." Tarn, William Woodthorpe, Eric William Gray, and Antony J. S. Spawforth. "Arabia." *OCD*³ 134–35.

Tarr, *Foolishness*. Tarr, Del. *The Foolishness of God: A Linguist Looks at the Mystery of Tongues*. Foreword by Jack Hayford. Springfield, Mo.: Access, 2010.

Tarr, "Power." Tarr, Del. "The Church and the Spirit's Power." Pages 9–20 in *Signs and Wonders in Ministry Today*. Edited by Benny C. Aker and Gary B. McGee. Foreword by Thomas E. Trask. Springfield, Mo.: Gospel, 1996.

"Tarry." "Tarry Until." *Tongues of Fire* (June 15, 1898): 93.

Tasca, "Pia disobbedienza." Tasca, Francesca. "La pia disobbedienza: L'esegesi di *Atti* 5,29 dalla patristica latina ai *libelli de lite*." *ASDE* 22 (1, 2005): 223–54.

Tassin, "Foi et violence." Tassin, Claude. "Foi et violence: Traditions juives sur Pinhas (Nb 25)." *Spiritus* 182 (2006): 69–78.

Tate, "Antioch on Orontes." Tate, Georges. "Antioch on Orontes." *OEANE* 1:144–45.

Tatje and Hsu, "Variations." Tatje, Terrence, and Francis L. K. Hsu. "Variations in Ancestor Worship Beliefs and Their Relation to Kinship." *SWJA* 25 (2, 1969): 153–72.

Tatum, "Epoch." Tatum, W. Barnes. "The Epoch of Israel: Luke I–II and the Theological Plan of Luke-Acts." *NTS* 13 (2, 1967): 184–95.

Tatum, "Galatians 2." Tatum, Gregory. "Galatians 2:1–14/Acts 15 and Paul's Ministry in 1 Thessalonians and 1 Corinthians." *RB* 116 (1, 2009): 70–81.

Tatum, "Second Commandment." Tatum, W. Barnes. "The LXX Version of the Second Commandment (Ex. 20,3–6=Deut 5,7–10): A Polemic against Idols, Not Images." *JSJ* 17 (2, 1986): 177–95.

Taubenschlag, *Law of Egypt*. Taubenschlag, Raphael. *The Law of Greco-Roman Egypt in the Light of the Papyri, 332 B.C.–640 A.D.* 2nd ed. Warsaw: Panstwowe Wydawnictwo Naukowe, 1955.

Täuber, "Cilicia." Täuber, Hans. "Cilicia." *BrillPauly* 3:329–30.

Taussig, "Melancholy." Taussig, Hal. "Melancholy, Colonialism, and Complicity: Complicating Counterimperial Readings of Aphrodisias's Sebasteion." Pages 280–95 in *Text, Image, and Christians in the Graeco-Roman World: A Festschrift in Honor of David Lee Balch*. Edited by Aliou Cissé Niang and Carolyn Osiek. PrTMS 176. Eugene, Ore.: Pickwick, 2012.

Taylor, "Artemis." Taylor, Lily Ross. "Artemis of Ephesus." *BegChr* 5:251–56.

Taylor, "Asiarchs." Taylor, Lily Ross. "The Asiarchs." *BegChr* 5:256–62.

Taylor, *Atonement*. Taylor, Vincent. *The Atonement in New Testament Teaching*. London: Epworth, 1945.

Taylor, "Baptism." Taylor, T. M. "The Beginnings of Jewish Proselyte Baptism." *NTS* 2 (3, 1956): 193–98.

Taylor, "Beautiful." Taylor, Justin. "The Gate of the Temple Called 'the Beautiful' (Acts 3:2, 10)." *RB* 106 (4, 1999): 549–62.

Taylor, "Cemeteries." Taylor, Joan E. "The Cemeteries of Khirbet Qumran and Women's Presence at the Site." *DSD* 6 (3, 1999): 285–323.

Taylor, "'Christians' at Antioch." Taylor, Justin. "Why Were the Disciples First Called 'Christians' at Antioch? (Ac 11, 26)." *RB* 101 (1, 1994): 75–94.

Taylor, "Community of Disciples." Taylor, Justin. "The Community of Jesus' Disciples." *PIBA* 21 (1998): 25–32.

Taylor, "Decrees." Taylor, Justin. "The Jerusalem Decrees (Acts 15.20, 29 and 21.25) and the Incident at Antioch (Gal 2.11–14)." *NTS* 47 (3, 2001): 372–80.

Taylor, *Egypt and Nubia*. Taylor, John H. *Egypt and Nubia*. Cambridge, Mass.: Harvard University Press; Trustees of the British Museum, 1991.

Taylor, "Ethnarch." Taylor, Justin. "The Ethnarch of King Aretas at Damascus: A Note on 2 Cor 11,32–33." *RB* 99 (4, 1992): 719–28.

Taylor, "Family." Taylor, Donald L. "The Changing German Family." *IJComSoc* 10 (3–4, Sept. 1969): 299–302.

Taylor, *Formation*. Taylor, Vincent. *The Formation of the Gospel Tradition*. 2nd ed. London: Macmillan, 1935. Repr., 1960.

Taylor, "Fraction du pain." Taylor, Justin. "La fraction du pain en Luc-Actes." Pages 281–95 in *The Unity of Luke-Acts*. Edited by Joseph Verheyden. BETL 142. Leuven: Leuven University Press, 1999.

Taylor, "History and Tradition." Taylor, Nicholas H. "Stephen in History and Tradition." *ScrB* 37 (1, 2007): 21–29.

Taylor, *Hume*. Taylor, A. E. *David Hume and the Miraculous*. The Leslie Stephen Lecture, Cambridge University, 1927. Cambridge: Cambridge University Press, 1927.

Taylor, "Identity." Taylor, Nicholas H. "Apostolic Identity and the Conflicts in Corinth and Galatia." Pages 99–127 in *Paul and His Opponents*. Edited by Stanley E. Porter. PAST 2. Leiden: Brill, 2005.

Taylor, *Immerser*. Taylor, Joan E. *The Immerser: John the Baptist within Second Temple Judaism*. Grand Rapids: Eerdmans, 1997.

Taylor, "Jerusalem and Temple." Taylor, Nicholas H. "Jerusalem and the Temple in Early Christian Life and Teaching." *Neot* 33 (2, 1999): 445–61.

Taylor, "Jerusalem Temple." Taylor, Nicholas H. "The Jerusalem Temple in Luke-Acts." *HTS/TS* 60 (1–2, 2004): 459–85.

Taylor, "List." Taylor, Justin. "The List of the Nations in Acts 2:9–11." *RB* 106 (3, 1999): 408–20.

Taylor, *Mark*. Taylor, Vincent. *The Gospel according to St. Mark*. London: Macmillan, 1952.

Taylor, *Missiology*. Taylor, William D., ed. *Global Missiology for the 21st Century: The Iguassu Dialogue*. Foreword by Ravi Zacharias. Globalization of Mission Series. Grand Rapids: Baker, 2000.

Taylor, *Party Politics*. Taylor, Lily Ross. *Party Politics in the Age of Caesar*. Berkeley: University of California Press, 1966.

Taylor, "Paul's Missionfield." Taylor, Justin. "St Paul's Missionfield: The World of Acts 13–28." *PIBA* 21 (1998): 9–24.

Taylor, "Pilate." Taylor, Joan E. "Pontius Pilate and the Imperial Cult in Roman Judaea." *NTS* 52 (4, 2006): 555–82.

Taylor, "Reciprocity." Taylor, Walter F. "Reciprocity, Siblings, and Paul: Why Act Ethically?" *LTJ* 39 (2–3, 2005): 181–95.

Taylor, "Stephen." Taylor, Nicholas H. "Stephen, the Temple, and Early Christian Eschatology." *RB* 110 (1, 2003): 62–85.

Taylor, "Subcultures." Taylor, Rabun. "Two Pathic Subcultures in Ancient Rome." *JHistSex* 7 (3, 1997): 319–71.

Taylor, "Temple." Taylor, Nicholas H. "Luke-Acts and the Temple." Pages 709–21 in *The Unity of Luke-Acts*. Edited by Joseph Verheyden. BETL 142. Leuven: Leuven University Press, 1999.

Taylor, "Texts and Critics." Taylor, Justin. "Ancient Texts and Modern Critics: Acts 15, 1–34." *RB* 99 (2, 1992): 373–78.

Taylor, "Virgin Mothers." Taylor, Joan E. "Virgin Mothers: Philo on the Women Therapeutae." *JSP* 12 (1, 2001): 37–63.

Taylor, "Witness." Taylor, Justin. "Witness in the Book of Acts." *P&P* 16 (4, 2002): 129–33.

Taylor et al., "Textiles." Taylor, Joan E., et al. "Qumran Textiles in the Palestine Exploration Fund, London: Radiocarbon Dating Results." *PEQ* 137 (2, 2005): 159–67.

Taylor and Davies, "Therapeutae." Taylor, Joan E., and Philip R. Davies, "The So-Called Therapeutae of *De vita contemplativa*: Identity and Character." *HTR* 91 (1, 1998): 3–24.

Tcherikover, *Civilization*. Tcherikover, Victor. *Hellenistic Civilization and the Jews*. Translated by S. Applebaum. Philadelphia: Magnes, 1961.

Tcherikover, "Ideology." Tcherikover, Victor. "The Ideology of the Letter of Aristeas." *HTR* 51 (1958): 59–85.

Tchernia, "Wine." Tchernia, André. "Italian Wine in Gaul at the End of the Republic." Pages 87–104 in *Trade in the Ancient Economy*. Edited by Peter Garnsey, Keith Hopkins, and C. R. Whittaker. Berkeley: University of California Press, 1983.

Tedlock, "Observation." Tedlock, Barbara. "From Participant Observation to the Observation of Participation: The Emergence of Narrative Ethnography." *JAnthRes* 47 (1991): 69–94.

Teeple, *Prophet*. Teeple, Howard M. *The Mosaic Eschatological Prophet*. JBLMS 10. Philadelphia: SBL, 1957.

Tell, "Wisdom." Tell, Håkan. "Wisdom for Sale? The Sophists and Money." *CP* 104 (1, 2009): 13–33.

Telò, "Gaze." Telò, Mario. "The Eagle's Gaze in the Opening of Heliodorus' *Aethiopica*." *AJP* 132 (4, 2011): 581–613.

Temin, "Market Economy." Temin, Peter. "A Market Economy in the Early Roman Empire." *JRS* 91 (2001): 169–81.

Temmerman, "Beauty." Temmerman, Koen de. "Blushing Beauty: Characterizing Blushes in Chariton's *Callirhoe*." *Mnemosyne* 60 (2, 2007): 235–52.

Temmerman, "Revisited." Temmerman, Koen de. "Chaereas Revisited: Rhetorical Control in Chariton's 'Ideal' Novel Callirhoe." *CQ* 59 (1, 2009): 247–62.

Temmerman, "Rhetoric." Temmerman, Koen de. "Ancient Rhetoric as a Hermeneutical Tool for the Analysis of Characterization in Narrative Literature." *Rhetorica* 28 (1, 2010): 23–51.

Temporini–Gräfin Vitzthum, "Family." Temporini–Gräfin Vitzthum, Hildegard. "Imperial Family, Women of the." *BrillPauly* 6:751–53.

Ten, "Racism." Ten, C. L. "Hume's Racism and Miracles." *JValInq* 36 (2002): 101–7.

Tennant, *Miracle*. Tennant, F. R. *Miracle and Its Philosophical Presuppositions: Three Lectures Delivered in the University of London 1924*. Cambridge: Cambridge University Press, 1925.

Tennant, *Theology*. Tennant, F. R. *Philosophical Theology*. 2 vols. Cambridge: Cambridge University Press, 1928–30. Vol. 1: *The Soul and Its Faculties*, 1928. Vol. 2: *The World, the Soul, and God*, 1930.

Tenney, "Antioch." Tenney, Merrill C. "The Influence of Antioch on Apostolic Christianity." *BSac* 107 (1950): 298–310.

Tenney, *Galatians*. Tenney, Merrill C. *Galatians: The Charter of Christian Liberty*. Grand Rapids: Eerdmans, 1951.

Teugels, "Kuise." Teugels, G. "De kuise Jozef: De receptie van een bijbels modl." *NedTT* 45 (3, 1991): 193–203.

Thackeray, *Josephus*. Thackeray, H. St. John. *Josephus: The Man and the Historian*. New York: Jewish Institute of Religion Press, 1929. Repr., New York: KTAV, 1967.

Thapar, *History*. Thapar, Romila. *A History of India*. Vol. 1. Baltimore: Penguin, 1965–66.

Tharekadavil, "Gerizim." Tharekadavil, Antony. "Samaritans' Mount Gerizim and Pentateuch." *BiBh* 32 (1, 2006): 42–64.

Thatcher, "Pilate." Thatcher, Tom. "Philo on Pilate: Rhetoric or Reality?" *ResQ* 37 (4, 1995): 215–18.

Thayer, "Discussions." Thayer, J. Henry. "Recent Discussions respecting the Lord's Supper." *JBL* 18 (1899): 110–31.

Theissen, *Erleben*. Theissen, Gerd. *Erleben und Verhalten der ersten Christen: Eine Psychologie des Urchristentums*. Munich: Gütersloh, 2007.

Theissen, *Gospels*. Theissen, Gerd. *The Gospels in Context: Social and Political History in the Synoptic Tradition*. Translated by Linda M. Maloney. Minneapolis: Fortress, 1991.

Theissen, *Miracle Stories*. Theissen, Gerd. *The Miracle Stories of the Early Christian Tradition*. Edited by John Riches. Translated by Francis McDonagh. Philadelphia: Fortress, 1983.

Theissen, "Nasir Khusraw." Theissen, Gerd. "La conversion de Paul et celle de Nasir Khusraw: Une rencontre au musée imaginaire de l'histoire." *ETR* 83 (4, 2008): 507–27.

Theissen, "Nouvelle perspective." Theissen, Gerd. "La nouvelle perspective sur Paul et ses limites. Quelques réflexions psychologiques." *ETR* 83 (4, 2008): 529–51.

Theissen, "Schichtung." Theissen, Gerd. "Soziale Schichtung in der korinthischen Gemeinde: Ein Beitrag zur Soziologie des hellenistischen Urchristentums." *ZNW* 65 (3–4, 1974): 232–72.

Theissen, *Setting*. Theissen, Gerd. *The Social Setting of Pauline Christianity: Essays on Corinth*. Philadelphia: Fortress, 1982.

Theissen, "Social Conflicts." Theissen, Gerd. "Social Conflicts in the Corinthian Community: Further Remarks on J. J. Meggitt, *Paul, Poverty and Survival*." *JSNT* 25 (3, 2003): 371–91.

Theissen, "Social Setting." Theissen, Gerd. "The Social Setting of Pauline Communities." Pages 248–67 in *The Blackwell Companion to Paul*. Edited by Stephen Westerholm. BCompRel. Oxford: Blackwell, 2011.

Theissen, *Sociology*. Theissen, Gerd. *Sociology of Early Palestinian Christianity*. Translated by John Bowden. Philadelphia: Fortress, 1978.

Theissen, "Structure." Theissen, Gerd. "The Social Structure of the Pauline Communities: Some Critical Remarks on J. J. Meggitt, *Paul, Poverty and Survival*." *JSNT* 84 (2001): 65–84.

Theissen, *Writing and Politics*. Theissen, Gerd. *Gospel Writing and Church Politics: A Socio-rhetorical Approach*. ChuenKLS 3. Hong Kong: Theology Division, Chung Chi College, Chinese University of Hong Kong, 2001.

Theissen and Merz, *Guide*. Theissen, Gerd, and Annette Merz. *The Historical Jesus: A Comprehensive Guide*. Translated by John Bowden. Minneapolis: Fortress, 1998.

Thekkekara and Punnapadam, "Growth." Thekkekara, M., and T. Punnapadam. "The Growth of the Community through Struggles (Acts 2:42–4:37): Challenges of the Church in India." *Jeev* 34 (200, 2004): 137–45.

Theobald, "Allen." Theobald, Michael. "'Allen bin ich alles geworden . . .' (1 Kor 9,22b): Paulus und das Problem der Inkulturation des Glaubens." *ThQ* 176 (1, 1996): 1–6.

Theron, "Motivation." Theron, S. W. "Motivation of Paraenesis in 'The Testaments of the Twelve Patriarchs.'" *Neot* 12 (1978): 133–50.

Thesleff, *Texts*. Thesleff, Holger. *The Pythagorean Texts of the Hellenistic Period*. AAAH 30.1. Åbo, Finland: Åbo Akademi, 1965.

Thiede, "Conflagration." Thiede, Carsten Peter. "A Pagan Reader of 2 Peter: Cosmic Conflagration in 2 Pet 3 and the *Octavius* of Minucius Felix." *JSNT* 26 (1986): 79–96.

Thielman, "Law." Thielman, Frank. "Law." *DPL* 529–42.

Thielman, *Paul and Law*. Thielman, Frank. *Paul and the Law: A Contextual Approach*. Downers Grove, Ill.: InterVarsity, 1994.

Thielman, "Plight to Solution." Thielman, Frank. "From Plight to Solution: A Framework for Understanding Paul's View of the Law in Romans and Galatians against a Jewish Background." PhD diss., Duke University, 1987.

Thielman, "Style of Fourth Gospel." Thielman, Frank. "The Style of the Fourth Gospel and Ancient Literary Critical Concepts of Religious Discourse." Pages 169–83 in *Persuasive Artistry: Studies in New Testament Rhetoric in Honor of George A. Kennedy*. Edited by Duane F. Watson.

JSNTSup 50. Sheffield, U.K.: Sheffield Academic, 1991.

Thielman, *Theology*. Thielman, Frank. *Theology of the New Testament*. Grand Rapids: Zondervan, 2005.

Thiering, "Cleansing." Thiering, Barbara E. "Inner and Outer Cleansing at Qumran as a Background to New Testament Baptism." *NTS* 26 (2, 1980): 266–77.

Thiering, *Gospels and Qumran*. Thiering, Barbara E. *The Gospels and Qumran: A New Hypothesis*. ANZSTR. Sydney: Theological Explorations, 1981.

Thiering, "Initiation." Thiering, Barbara E. "Qumran Initiation and New Testament Baptism." *NTS* 27 (5, 1981): 615–31.

Thiering, "*Mebaqqer*." Thiering, Barbara E. "*Mebaqqer* and *episkopos* in the Light of the Temple Scroll." *JBL* 100 (1, 1981): 59–74.

Thiering, "Source." Thiering, Barbara E. "The Biblical Source of Qumran Asceticism." *JBL* 93 (3, 1974): 429–44.

Thiering, "Suffering." Thiering, Barbara E. "Suffering and Asceticism at Qumran, as Illustrated in the Hodayot." *RevQ* 8 (3, 1974): 393–405.

Thiering, "Wicked Priest." Thiering, Barbara E. "Once More the Wicked Priest." *JBL* 97 (2, 1978): 191–205.

Thiessen, *Christen in Ephesus*. Thiessen, Werner. *Christen in Ephesus: Die historische und theologische Situation in vorpaulinischer und paulinischer Zeit und zur Zeit der Apostelgeschichte und der Pastoralbriefe*. Tübingen: Francke, 1995.

Thiselton, *Corinthians*. Thiselton, Anthony C. *The First Epistle to the Corinthians: A Commentary on the Greek Text*. Grand Rapids: Eerdmans; Carlisle, U.K.: Paternoster, 2000.

Thiselton, *Horizons*. Thiselton, Anthony C. *The Two Horizons: New Testament Hermeneutics and Philosophical Description*. Grand Rapids: Eerdmans, 1980.

Thiselton, "Semantics." Thiselton, Anthony C. "Semantics and New Testament Interpretation." Pages 75–104 in *New Testament Interpretation: Essays on Principles and Methods*. Edited by I. Howard Marshall. Grand Rapids: Eerdmans, 1977.

Thiselton, *Spirit*. Thiselton, Anthony C. *The Holy Spirit—In Biblical Teaching, through the Centuries, and Today*. Grand Rapids: Eerdmans, 2013.

Thissen, "Namen." Thissen, Heinz J. "Zum Namen 'Moses.'" *RMPhil* 147 (1, 2004): 55–62.

Thollander, *Mathews*. Thollander, Jon. *He Saw a Man Named Mathews: A Brief Testimony of Thomas and Mary Mathews, Pioneer Missionaries to Rajasthan*. Udaipur,

Rajasthan, India: Native Missionary Movement, Cross & Crown, 2000.

Thom, "*Akousmata*." Thom, Johan C. "'Don't Walk on the Highways': The Pythagorean *akousmata* and Early Christian Literature." *JBL* 113 (1, 1994): 93–112.

Thom, "Equality." Thom, Johan C. "'Harmonious Equality': The *topos* of Friendship in Neopythagorean Writings." Pages 77–103 in *Greco-Roman Perspectives on Friendship*. Edited by John T. Fitzgerald. SBLRBS 34. Atlanta: Scholars Press, 1997.

Thoma, "Death Penalty." Thoma, Clemens. "The Death Penalty and Torture in the Jewish Tradition." *Concilium* 120 (1979): 64–74.

Thoma, "Frühjüdische Martyrer." Thoma, Clemens. "Frühjüdische Martyrer: Glaube an Auferstehung und Gericht." *FreiRund* 11 (2, 2004): 82–93.

Thoma, "Priesthood." Thoma, Clemens. "The High Priesthood in the Judgment of Josephus." Pages 196–215 in *Josephus, the Bible, and History*. Edited by Louis H. Feldman and Gohei Hata. Detroit: Wayne State University Press, 1989.

Thomas, "Archives." Thomas, Rosalind. "Archives." *OCD*[3] 149–50.

Thomas, "Bilingualism." Thomas, Rosalind. "Bilingualism." *OCD*[3] 240–41.

Thomas, "Canon and Antitype." Thomas, Christine M. "Canon and Antitype: The Relationship between the *Acts of Peter* and the New Testament." *Semeia* 80 (1997): 185–205.

Thomas, "Charismatic Structure." Thomas, John Christopher. "The Charismatic Structure of Acts." *JPT* 13 (1, 2004): 19–30.

Thomas, "Church at Antioch." Thomas, Norman E. "The Church at Antioch: Crossing Racial, Cultural, and Class Barriers, Acts 11:19–30; 13:1–3." Pages 144–56 in *Mission in Acts: Ancient Narratives in Contemporary Context*. Edited by Robert L. Gallagher and Paul Hertig. AmSoc MissS 34. Maryknoll, N.Y.: Orbis, 2004.

Thomas, "Dead." Thomas, Christine M. "Placing the Dead: Funerary Practice and Social Stratification in the Early Roman Period at Corinth and Ephesos." Pages 281–304 in *Urban Religion in Roman Corinth: Interdisciplinary Approaches*. Edited by Daniel N. Schowalter and Steven J. Friesen. HTS 53. Cambridge, Mass.: Harvard University Press, 2005.

Thomas, *Deliverance*. Thomas, John Christopher. *The Devil, Disease, and Deliverance: Origins of Illness in New Testament Thought*. JPTSup 13. Sheffield, U.K.: Sheffield Academic, 1998.

Thomas, "Fluidity." Thomas, Christine M. "Stories without Texts and without Authors: The Problem of Fluidity in Ancient

Novelistic Texts and Early Christian Literature." Pages 273–91 in *Ancient Fiction and Early Christian Narrative*. Edited by Ronald F. Hock, J. Bradley Chance, and Judith Perkins. SBLSymS 6. Atlanta: SBL, 1998.

Thomas, *Footwashing*. Thomas, John Christopher. *Footwashing in John 13 and the Johannine Community*. JSNTSup 61. Sheffield, U.K.: JSOT Press, 1991.

Thomas, "Hermeneutics." Thomas, Robert L. "Hermeneutics of the New Perspective on Paul." *MSJ* 16 (2, 2005): 293–316.

Thomas, "Literacy." Thomas, Rosalind. "Literacy." *OCD*[3] 868–69.

Thomas, "Records." Thomas, Rosalind. "Records and Record-keeping, Attitudes to." *OCD*[3] 1296.

Thomas, "Religion in Ephesos." Thomas, Christine M. "At Home in the City of Artemis: Religion in Ephesos in the Literary Imagination of the Roman Period." Pages 81–117 in *Ephesos, Metropolis of Asia: An Interdisciplinary Approach to Its Archaeology, Religion, and Culture*. Edited by Helmut Koester. HTS. Valley Forge, Pa.: Trinity Press International, 1995.

Thomas, "Report." Thomas, Harold. "Report on the Chorti-Maya Indians of Guatemala." MA thesis, Fuller Theological Seminary, 1973.

Thomas, *Revelation 19*. Thomas, David A. *Revelation 19 in Historical and Mythological Context*. StBibLit 118. New York: Peter Lang, 2008.

Thomas, "Suffering." Thomas, Heath A. "Suffering." Pages 757–66 in *Dictionary of the Old Testament Prophets*. Edited by Mark J. Boda and J. Gordon McConville. Downers Grove, Ill.: IVP Academic, 2012.

Thomas, "Tongues." Thomas, R. L. "Tongues . . . Will Cease." *JETS* 17 (1974): 81–89.

Thomas, "Upside-Down." Thomas, Michael D. "The World Turned Upside-Down: Carnivalesque and Satiric Elements in Acts." *PRSt* 31 (4, 2004): 453–65.

Thomas, *Walls*. Thomas, Sandy. *Beyond Jungle Walls: Bringing Hope to the Forgotten Congo*. Springfield, Mo.: 21st Century Press, 2005.

Thomas, "Worshiping." Thomas, Nancy J. "Worshiping, Working, and Waiting: Exploring Paul's Call to Mission, Acts 9:1–22." Pages 123–32 in *Mission in Acts: Ancient Narratives in Contemporary Context*. Edited by Robert L. Gallagher and Paul Hertig. AmSocMissS 34. Maryknoll, N.Y.: Orbis, 2004.

Thomas, "Writing." Thomas, Rosalind. "Writing, Reading, Public and Private 'Literacies': Functional Literacy and Democratic Literacy in Greece." Pages 13–45 in *Ancient Literacies: The Culture *of Reading in Greece and Rome.* Edited by William A. Johnson and Holt N. Parker. New York: Oxford University Press, 2009.

Thomas and van Aarde, "Samaria." Thomas, A., and Andries van Aarde. "Samaria as belangeruimte in Lukas-Handelinge." *HTS/TS* 54 (3–4, 1998): 760–88.

Thompson, "Accusations." Thompson, Richard P. "'Say It Ain't So, Paul!' The Accusations against Paul in Acts 21 in Light of His Ministry in Acts 16–20." *BR* 45 (2000): 34–50.

Thompson, *Archaeology.* Thompson, J. Arthur. *The Bible and Archaeology.* Grand Rapids: Eerdmans, 1962.

Thompson, "Background." Thompson, R. W. "The Alleged Rabbinic Background of Rom 3,31." *ETL* 63 (1, 1987): 136–48.

Thompson, *Church.* Thompson, Richard P. *Keeping the Church in Its Place: The Church as Narrative Character in Acts.* New York: T&T Clark, 2006.

Thompson, *Clothed.* Thompson, Michael B. *Clothed with Christ: The Example and Teaching of Jesus in Romans 12.1–15.13.* JSNTSup 59. Sheffield, U.K.: JSOT Press, 1991.

Thompson, "Contrasting Portraits." Thompson, Richard P. "Believers and Religious Leaders in Jerusalem: Contrasting Portraits of Jews in Acts 1–7." Pages 327–44 in *Literary Studies in Luke-Acts: Essays in Honor of Joseph B. Tyson.* Edited by Richard P. Thompson and Thomas E. Phillips. Macon, Ga.: Mercer University Press, 1998.

Thompson, "Covenant." Thompson, J. Arthur. "Covenant (OT)." *ISBE* 1:790–93.

Thompson, "Dalman." Thompson, Steven. "Gustaf Dalman, Anti-Semitism, and the Language of Jesus Debate." *JRH* 34 (1, 2010): 36–54.

Thompson, *Debate.* Thompson, William M. *The Jesus Debate: A Survey and Synthesis.* New York: Paulist, 1985.

Thompson, "Diadochi." Thompson, Glen L. "Diadochi." *DNTB* 278–81.

Thompson, "Ephesians iii.13." Thompson, G. H. P. "Ephesians iii.13 and 2 Timothy ii.10 in the Light of Colossians i.24." *ExpT* 71 (6, 1960): 187–89.

Thompson, "Ethics." Thompson, Richard P. "'What Do You Think You Are Doing, Paul?': Synagogues, Accusations, and Ethics in Paul's Ministry in Acts 16–21." Pages 64–78 in *Acts and Ethics.* Edited by Thomas E. Phillips. NTMon 9. Sheffield, U.K.: Sheffield Phoenix, 2005.

Thompson, "Hairstyles." Thompson, Cynthia L. "Hairstyles, Head-Coverings, and St. Paul: Portraits from Roman Corinth." *BA* 51 (2, 1988): 101–15.

Thompson, "Idealization." Thompson, Alan J. "Unity in Acts: Idealization or Reality?" *JETS* 51 (3, 2008): 523–42.

Thompson, "Internet." Thompson, Michael B. "The Holy Internet: Communication between Churches in the First Christian Generation." Pages 49–70 in *The Gospels for All Christians: Rethinking the Gospel Audiences.* Edited by Richard Bauckham. Grand Rapids: Eerdmans, 1998.

Thompson, "Military." Thompson, Glen L. "Roman Military." *DNTB* 991–95.

Thompson, *One People.* Thompson, Alan J. *One Lord, One People: The Unity of the Church in Acts in Its Literary Setting.* LNTS. London: T&T Clark, 2008.

Thompson, "Paul in Acts." Thompson, Michael B. "Paul in the Book of Acts: Differences and Distance." *ExpT* 122 (9, June 2011): 425–36.

Thompson, *Responsibility.* Thompson, Alden Lloyd. *Responsibility for Evil in the Theodicy of IV Ezra: A Study Illustrating the Significance of Form and Structure for the Meaning of the Book.* SBLDS 29. Missoula, Mont.: Scholars Press, 1977.

Thompson, "Son of Man." Thompson, G. H. P. "The Son of Man: The Evidence of the Dead Sea Scrolls." *ExpT* 72 (4, 1961): 125.

Thompson, *Unfolding Plan.* Thompson, Alan J. *The Acts of the Risen Lord Jesus: Luke's Account of God's Unfolding Plan.* New Studies in Biblical Theology 27. Downers Grove, Ill.: InterVarsity; Nottingham: Apollos, 2011.

Thompson, "Unity." Thompson, Alan J. "The Unity of the Church in Acts in Its Literary Setting." PhD diss., Trinity Evangelical Divinity School, 2004.

Thompson, Wenger, and Bartling, "Recall." Thompson, Charles P., Steven K. Wenger, and Carl A. Bartling. "How Recall Facilitates Subsequent Recall: A Reappraisal." *JExpPsyc* 4 (3, 1978): 210–21.

Thorburn, "Lixae." Thorburn, John E. "*Lixae* and *calones*: Following the Roman Army." *CBull* 79 (1, 2003): 47–61.

Thorburn, "Tiberius." Thorburn, John E. "Suetonius' Tiberius: A Proxemic Approach." *CP* 103 (4, 2008): 435–48.

Thorion, "'dm." Thorion, Yohanan. "'dm und bn 'dm in den Qumrantexten." *RevQ* 10 (2, 1980): 305–8.

Thorley, "Census." Thorley, John. "The Nativity Census: What Does Luke Actually Say?" *GR* 26 (1, 1979): 81–84.

Thornton, "Anti-Samaritan Exegesis." Thornton, T. C. G. "Anti-Samaritan Exegesis Reflected in Josephus' Retelling of Deuteronomy, Joshua, and Judges." *JTS* 47 (1, 1996): 125–30.

Thornton, "Bachelors." Thornton, T. C. G. "Jewish Bachelors in New Testament Times." *JTS* 23 (2, 1972): 444–45.

Thornton, "Calendar." Thornton, T. C. G. "The Samaritan Calendar: A Source of Friction in New Testament Times." *JTS* 42 (2, 1991): 577–80.

Thornton, "Continuing Steadfast." Thornton, T. C. G. "'Continuing Steadfast in Prayer'—New Light on a New Testament Phrase." *ExpT* 83 (1, 1971): 23–24.

Thornton, "End of the Earth." Thornton, T. C. G. "To the End of the Earth: Acts 1:8." *ExpT* 89 (12, 1978): 374–75.

Thornton, *Zeuge.* Thornton, Claus-Jürgen. *Der Zeuge des Zeugen: Lukas als Historiker der Paulusreisen.* WUNT 56. Tübingen: Mohr Siebeck, 1991.

Thorsen, "Samothrace." Thorsen, Donald A. D. "Samothrace." *ABD* 5:949.

Thorsteinsson, "Paul." Thorsteinsson, Runar M. "Paul and Roman Stoicism: Romans 12 and Contemporary Stoic Ethics." *JSNT* 29 (2, Dec. 2006): 139–61.

Thorsteinsson, "Stoicism." Thorsteinsson, Runar M. "Stoicism as a Key to Pauline Ethics in Romans." Pages 15–38 in *Stoicism in Early Christianity.* Edited by Tuomas Rasimus, Troels Engberg-Pedersen, and Ismo Dunderberg. Grand Rapids: Baker Academic, 2010.

Thouless, "Psychology." Thouless, Robert H. "The Psychology of Conversion." Pages 137–47 in *Conversion: Perspectives on Personal and Social Transformation.* Edited by Walter E. Conn. New York: Alba House, 1978.

Thrall, *2 Corinthians.* Thrall, Margaret E. *A Critical and Exegetical Commentary on the Second Epistle to the Corinthians.* 2 vols. Edinburgh: T&T Clark, 1994–2000.

Thrall, *Letters.* Thrall, Margaret E. *The First and Second Letters of Paul to the Corinthians.* CBC. Cambridge: Cambridge University Press, 1965.

Thrall, "Origin." Thrall, Margaret E. "The Origin of Pauline Christology." Pages 304–16 in *Apostolic History and the Gospel: Biblical and Historical Essays Presented to F. F. Bruce on His 60th Birthday.* Edited by W. Ward Gasque and Ralph P. Martin. Exeter, U.K.: Paternoster; Grand Rapids: Eerdmans, 1970.

Thrall, "ΣΥΝΕΙΔΗΣΙΣ." Thrall, Margaret E. "The Pauline Use of ΣΥΝΕΙΔΗΣΙΣ." *NTS* 14 (1, 1967): 118–25.

Throckmorton, "Shipwrecks, Anchors, and Paul." Throckmorton, Peter. "Shipwrecks, Anchors, and St Paul." *History from the Sea: Shipwrecks and Archaeology.* Edited by Peter Throckmorton. London: Mitchell Beazley, 1987.

Thür, "Embateuein." Thür, Gerhard. "Embateuein." *BrillPauly* 4:937.

Thür, "Epobelia." Thür, Gerhard. "Epobelia." *BrillPauly* 4:1158–59.

Thür, "Kakegoria." Thür, Gerhard. "Kakegoria." *BrillPauly* 7:5.

Thür, "Kakosis." Thür, Gerhard, "Kakosis." *BrillPauly* 7:6.

Thür, "Katalysis." Thür, Gerhard. "Katalysis." *BrillPauly* 7:32.

Thür, "Kategoros." Thür, Gerhard. "Kategoros." *BrillPauly* 7:34–35.

Thür, "Katengyan." Thür, Gerhard. "Katengyan." *BrillPauly* 7:35.

Thür, "Menysis." Thür, Gerhard. "Menysis." *BrillPauly* 8:706.

Thür, "Misthosis." Thür, Gerhard. "Misthosis." *BrillPauly* 9:68–72.

Thür, "Prodosia." Thür, Gerhard. "Prodosia." *BrillPauly* 11:933.

Thür, "Prosklesis." Thür, Gerhard. "Prosklesis." *BrillPauly* 12:49–50.

Thür, "Pseudokleteias graphe." Thür, Gerhard. "Pseudokleteias graphe." *BrillPauly* 12:116–17.

Thür, "Synegoros." Thür, Gerhard. "Synegoros." *BrillPauly* 14:23–24.

Thür, "Way." Thür, Hike. "The Processional Way in Ephesos as a Place of Cult and Burial." Pages 157–99 in *Ephesos, Metropolis of Asia: An Interdisciplinary Approach to Its Archaeology, Religion, and Culture*. Edited by Helmut Koester. HTS. Valley Forge, Pa.: Trinity Press International, 1995.

Thurén, "Chrysostom." Thurén, Lauri. "John Chrysostom as a Rhetorical Critic: The Hermeneutics of an Early Father." *BibInt* 9 (2, 2001): 180–218.

Thurén, "Writings." Thurén, Lauri. "The General New Testament Writings." Pages 587–607 in *Handbook of Classical Rhetoric in the Hellenistic Period, 330 B.C.–A.D. 400*. Edited by Stanley E. Porter. Leiden: Brill, 1997.

Thurman, *Disinherited*. Thurman, Howard. *Jesus and the Disinherited*. New York: Abingdon-Cokesbury, 1949. Repr., Richmond, Ind.: Friends United, 1981.

Thurs, "Quantum Physics." Thurs, Daniel Patrick. "That Quantum Physics Demonstrated the Doctrine of Free Will." Pages 196–205 in *Galileo Goes to Jail and Other Myths about Science and Religion*. Edited by Ronald L. Numbers. Cambridge, Mass.: Harvard University Press, 2009.

Thurston, "Midrash." Thurston, Robert W. "Midrash and 'Magnet' Words in the New Testament." *EvQ* 51 (1, 1979): 22–39.

Thurston, *Widows*. Thurston, Bonnie Bowman. *The Widows: A Women's Ministry in the Early Church*. Minneapolis: Fortress, 1989.

Thuruthumaly, "Mysticism." Thuruthumaly, Joseph. "Mysticism in Pauline Writings." *BiBh* 18 (3, 1992): 140–52.

Tiede, "Contending." Tiede, David L. "Contending with God: The Death of Jesus and the Trial of Israel in Luke-Acts." Pages 301–8 in *The Future of Early Christianity: Essays in Honor of Helmut Koester*. Philadelphia: Augsburg Fortress, 1991.

Tiede, "Conversion." Tiede, David L. "The Conversion of the Church." *CurTM* 33 (1, 2006): 42–51.

Tiede, *Figure*. Tiede, David L. *The Charismatic Figure as Miracle Worker*. SBLDS 1. Missoula, Mont.: SBL, 1972.

Tiede, "Glory." Tiede, David L. "'Glory to Thy People Israel': Luke-Acts and the Jews." Pages 21–34 in *Luke-Acts and the Jewish People: Eight Critical Perspectives*. Edited by Joseph B. Tyson. Minneapolis: Augsburg, 1988.

Tiede, *Prophecy*. Tiede, David L. *Prophecy and History in Luke-Acts*. Philadelphia: Fortress, 1980.

Tiede, "World." Tiede, David L. "The God Who Made the World." *CurTM* 33 (1, 2006): 52–62.

Tigchelaar, "Names of Spirits." Tigchelaar, Eibert J. C. "'These Are the Names of the Spirits of . . .': A Preliminary Edition of *4Qcatalogue of Spirits (4Q230)* and New Manuscript Evidence for the *Two Spirits Treatise (4Q257 and 1Q29a)*." *RevQ* 21 (84, 2004): 529–47.

Tigchelaar, "Sabbath Halakha." Tigchelaar, Eibert J. C. "Sabbath Halakha and Worship in *4QWays of Righteousness: 4Q421 11 and 13 + 2 + 8 par 4Q264a 1–2*." *RevQ* 18 (71, 1998): 359–72.

Tigerstedt, "Idea." Tigerstedt, Eugene N. "Plato's Idea of Poetical Inspiration." *Commentationes Humanarum Litterarum (Societas Scientiarum Fennica)* 44 (2, 1969): 5–76.

Tilborg, "Acts 17:27." Tilborg, Sjef van. "Acts 17:27—'That They Might Feel after Him and Find . . .'" *HvTS* 57 (1–2, 2001): 86–104.

Tilborg, *Ephesus*. Tilborg, Sjef van. *Reading John in Ephesus*. NovTSup 83. Leiden: Brill, 1996.

Tilborg, *Leaders*. Tilborg, Sjef van. *The Jewish Leaders in Matthew*. Leiden: Brill, 1972.

Tilborg, *Love*. Tilborg, Sjef van. *Imaginative Love in John*. BIS 2. Leiden: Brill, 1993.

Tilborg and Counet, *Appearances*. Tilborg, Sjef van, and Patrick Chatelion Counet. *Jesus' Appearances and Disappearances in Luke 24*. BIS 45. Leiden: Brill, 2000.

Tilley, "Phenomenology." Tilley, James A. "A Phenomenology of the Christian Healer's Experience." PhD diss., Fuller Graduate School of Psychology, 1989.

Tilley, "Trireme." Tilley, Alec F. "Trireme: History of the Trireme." *BrillPauly* 14:937–38.

Timmer, "Nomism." Timmer, Daniel C. "Variegated Nomism Indeed: Multiphase Eschatology and Soteriology in the Qumranite *Community Rule* (1QS) and the New Perspective on Paul." *JETS* 52 (2, June 2009): 341–56.

Tinh, "Sarapis and Isis." Tinh, Tran Tam. "Sarapis and Isis." Pages 101–17 in *Self-Definition in the Greco-Roman World*. Edited by Ben F. Meyer and E. P. Sanders. Vol. 3 of *Jewish and Christian Self-Definition*. Edited by E. P. Sanders. Philadelphia: Fortress, 1982.

Tipei, "Speech." Tipei, John F. "Paul's Areopagus Speech: A Lesson on Creation as an Evangelistic Tool." *Sacra Scripta* 8 (1, 2010): 96–115.

Tippett, *People Movements*. Tippett, Alan R. *People Movements in Southern Polynesia: Studies in the Dynamics of Church-Planting and Growth in Tahiti, New Zealand, Tonga, and Samoa*. Chicago: Moody, 1971.

Tippett, "Possession." Tippett, Alan R. "Spirit Possession as It Relates to Culture and Religion: A Survey of Anthropological Literature." Pages 143–74 in *Demon Possession: A Medical, Historical, Anthropological, and Theological Symposium*. Edited by John Warwick Montgomery. Minneapolis: Bethany House, 1976.

Tippett, *Solomon Islands Christianity*. Tippett, Alan R. *Solomon Islands Christianity: A Study in Growth and Obstruction*. WSCM. London: Lutterworth, 1967.

Tippett, *Verdict Theology*. Tippett, Alan R. *Verdict Theology in Missionary Theory*. South Pasadena, Calif.: William Carey Library, 1973.

Tiwald, "Archäologie." Tiwald, Markus. "Biblische Archäologie im Schwerefeld von Geisteswissenschaften, Politik, und Theologie." *PzB* 13 (2, 2004): 69–82.

Tobin, "Philo and Sibyl." Tobin, Thomas H. "Philo and the Sibyl: Interpreting Philo's Eschatology." *SPhilA* 9 (1997): 84–103.

Tobin, *Rhetoric in Contexts*. Tobin, Thomas H. *Paul's Rhetoric in Its Contexts: The Argument of Romans*. Peabody, Mass.: Hendrickson, 2004.

Tod and Hornblower, "Clubs." Tod, Marcus Niebuhr, and Simon Hornblower. "Clubs, Greek." *OCD*[3] 351–52.

Todd, "Evidence." Todd, Stephen C. "Evidence, Ancient Attitudes to." *OCD*[3] 578–799.

Todd, "Hibernia." Todd, Malcolm. "Hibernia (Ireland)." *BrillPauly* 6:298–99.

Todd, "Introduction." Todd, O. J. Introduction. Pages 376–79 in vol. 3 of *Xenophon*. Translated by O. J. Todd. 4 vols. LCL. New York: G. P. Putnam's Sons, 1918–23.

Todd, "Monism." Todd, Robert B. "Monism and Immanence: The Foundations of Stoic Physics." Pages 137–60 in *The Stoics*. Edited by John M. Rist. Berkeley: University of California Press, 1978.

Todd, "Thule." Todd, Malcolm. "Thule." *BrillPauly* 14:638–39.

Tödt, *Son of Man*. Tödt, Heinz Eduard. *The Son of Man in the Synoptic Tradition*. Philadelphia: Westminster, 1965.

Toepel, "Planetary Demons." Toepel, Alexander. "Planetary Demons in Early Jewish Literature." *JSP* 14 (3, 2005): 231–38.

Tolbert, "Roots." Tolbert, Emory J. "The Search for African Roots and the Biblical Sabbath." Pages 29–44 in *2000 Years of Christianity in Africa*. Edited by Emory J. Tolbert. N.p.: Sabbath in Africa Study Group, 2005.

Tomes, "Heroism." Tomes, Roger. "Heroism in 1 and 2 Maccabees." *BibInt* 15 (2, 2007): 171–99.

Tomkins, *History*. Tomkins, Stephen. *A Short History of Christianity*. Grand Rapids: Eerdmans, 2005.

Tomkins, *Wesley*. Tomkins, Stephen. *John Wesley: A Biography*. Grand Rapids: Eerdmans, 2003.

Tomkins, *Wilberforce*. Tomkins, Stephen. *William Wilberforce: A Biography*. Grand Rapids and Cambridge: Eerdmans, 2007.

Tomlin, "Epicureans." Tomlin, Graham. "Christians and Epicureans in 1 Corinthians." *JSNT* 68 (1997): 51–72.

Tomlin, "Vicarius." Tomlin, R. S. O. "Vicarius." *OCD*³ 1597.

Tomlinson, "Agora." Tomlinson, Richard Allan. "Agora." *OCD*³ 42–43.

Tomlinson, "Odeum." Tomlinson, Richard Allan. "Odeum." *OCD*³ 1060.

Tomlinson, "Temple." Tomlinson, Richard Allan. "Temple." *OCD*³ 1482.

Tomlinson, "Theatres." Tomlinson, Richard Allan. "Theatres (Greek and Roman), Structure." *OCD*³ 1495.

Tomson, "Centrality." Tomson, Peter J. "The Centrality of Jerusalem and Its Temple as Viewed by Clement of Rome, Luke, and Jesus." *AnBrux* 5 (2000): 97–112.

Tomson, "Counsel." Tomson, Peter J. "Gamaliel's Counsel and the Apologetic Strategy of Luke-Acts." Pages 585–604 in *The Unity of Luke-Acts*. Edited by Joseph Verheyden. BETL 142. Leuven: Leuven University Press, 1999.

Tomson, "Israel." Tomson, Peter J. "The Names Israel and Jew in Ancient Judaism and in the New Testament, I." *Bijdr* 47 (2, 1986): 120–40.

Tomson, "Scriptures." Tomson, Peter J. "Luke-Acts and the Jewish Scriptures." *AnBrux* 7 (2002): 164–83.

Tomson, "Tradycje." Tomson, P. J. "Tradycje Jezusowe a chrystologia Pawla Apostola (Jesus Traditions and Christology in Paul's Letters)." *ColT* 63 (2, 1993): 27–43.

Toner, *Culture*. Toner, Jerry. *Popular Culture in Ancient Rome*. Malden, Mass.; Cambridge, U.K.: Polity, 2009.

Tonlieu, "Family." Tonlieu, Lado L. "The Church as Family of God in the Pauline Corpus." *HekRev* 24 (2000): 16–27.

Tonquédec, *Miracles*. Tonquédec, Joseph de. *Miracles*. Translated by Frank M. Oppenheim. West Baden Springs, Ind.: West Baden College, 1955. Translated from "Miracle." Pages 517–78 in vol. 3 of *Dictionnaire Apologétique de la Foi Catholique*. Edited by A. d'Alès. Paris: Beauchesne, 1926.

Tonstad, *Meaning*. Tonstad, Sigve K. *The Lost Meaning of the Seventh Day*. Berrien Springs, Mich.: Andrews University Press, 2009.

Tonstad, "Πίστις Χριστοῦ." Tonstad, Sigve. "Πίστις Χριστοῦ: Reading Paul in a New Paradigm." *AUSS* 40 (1, 2002): 37–59.

Tooley, "Shepherd." Tooley, Wilfred. "The Shepherd and Sheep Image in the Teaching of Jesus." *NovT* 7 (1, 1964): 15–25.

Toomer, "Aratus." Toomer, G. J. "Aratus." *OCD*³ 136–37.

Toomer, "Aristarchus." Toomer, G. J. "Aristarchus (1)." *OCD*³ 159.

Toomer, "Clocks." Toomer, G. J. "Clocks." *OCD*³ 350.

Toomer, "Constellations." Toomer, G. J. "Constellations and Named Stars." *OCD*³ 381–83.

Toral-Niehoff, "Mission: Islam." Toral-Niehoff, Isabel. "Mission: Islam." *Brill Pauly* 8:65–66.

Tornos, "Fecha del hambre." Tornos, Andrés M. "La fecha del hambre de Jerusalén, aludida por Act 11, 28–30." *EstEcl* 33 (130, 1959): 303–16.

Torr, *Rhodes*. Torr, Cecil. *Rhodes in Ancient Times*. Cambridge: Cambridge University Press, 1885.

Torrance, "Baptism." Torrance, T. F. "Proselyte Baptism." *NTS* 1 (2, 1954): 150–54.

Torrance, "Origins." Torrance, T. F. "The Origins of Baptism." *SJT* 11 (June 1958): 158–71.

Torrance, "Probability." Torrance, Alan J. "The Lazarus Narrative, Theological History, and Historical Probability." Pages 245–62 in *The Gospel of John and Christian Theology*. Edited by Richard Bauckham and Carl Mosser. Grand Rapids and Cambridge: Eerdmans, 2008.

Torrey, *Composition*. Torrey, Charles C. *The Composition and Date of Acts*. HTS 1. Cambridge, Mass.: Harvard University Press, 1916. Repr., New York: Kraus, 1969.

Torrey, "Fragment." Torrey, Charles C. "A Hebrew Fragment of Jubilees." *JBL* 71 (1, 1952): 39–41.

Torrey, "Messiah." Torrey, Charles C. "The Messiah Son of Ephraim." *JBL* 66 (3, 1947): 253–77.

Tosi, "Lexicography." Tosi, Renzo. "Lexicography." *BrillPauly* 7:468–71.

Tournay, "Polémique." Tournay, Raymond Jacques. "Polémique antisamaritaine et le feu du *TOFET*." *RB* 104 (3, 1997): 354–67.

Toussaint, "Tongues." Toussaint, Stanley D. "First Corinthians Thirteen and the Tongues Question." *BSac* 120 (1963): 311–16.

Touwaide, "Disease." Touwaide, Alain. "Disease." *BrillPauly* 4:543–54.

Touwaide, "Malaria." Touwaide, Alain. "Malaria." *BrillPauly* 8:195–96.

Touwaide, "Medicinal Plants." Touwaide, Alain. "Medicinal Plants." *BrillPauly* 8:558–68.

Touwaide, "Methodists." Touwaide, Alain. "Methodists." *BrillPauly* 8:801–2.

Touwaide, "Poisons." Touwaide, Alaine. "Poisons." *BrillPauly* 11:450–52.

Tov, "Compositions." Tov, Emanuel. "Rewritten Bible Compositions and Biblical Manuscripts, with Special Attention to the Samaritan Pentateuch." *DSD* 5 (3, 1998): 334–54.

Towey, "Damascus." Towey, Anthony. "'Damascus' and Pastoral Ministry." *PastRev* 5 (4, 2009): 22–27.

Towner, "Practice." Towner, Philip H. "Mission Practice and Theology under Construction (Acts 18–20)." Pages 417–36 in *Witness to the Gospel: The Theology of Acts*. Edited by I. Howard Marshall and David Peterson. Grand Rapids: Eerdmans, 1998.

Townsend, "Acts 9:1–29." Townsend, John T. "Acts 9:1–29 and Early Church Tradition." Pages 87–98 in *Literary Studies in Luke-Acts: Essays in Honor of Joseph B. Tyson*. Edited by Richard P. Thompson and Thomas E. Phillips. Macon, Ga.: Mercer University Press, 1998.

Townsend, "Date." Townsend, John T. "The Date of Luke-Acts." Pages 47–62 in *Luke-Acts: New Perspectives from the Society of Biblical Literature Seminar*. Edited by Charles H. Talbert. New York: Crossroad, 1984.

Townsend, "Education." Townsend, John T. "Ancient Education in the Time of the Early Roman Empire." Pages 139–63 in

The Catacombs and the Colosseum: The Roman Empire as the Setting of Primitive Christianity. Edited by Stephen Benko and John J. O'Rourke. Valley Forge, Pa.: Judson, 1971.

Townsend, "Journeys and Missionary Societies." Townsend, John T. "Missionary Journeys in Acts and European Missionary Societies." *AThR* 68 (2, 1986): 99–104.

Townsend, "Speeches." Townsend, John T. "The Speeches in Acts." *AThR* 42 (1960): 150–59.

Toynbee, *Thought.* Toynbee, Arnold J. *Greek Historical Thought.* New York: New American Library, 1952.

Tracey, "Syria." Tracey, Robyn. "Syria." Pages 223–78 in *The Book of Acts in Its Graeco-Roman Setting.* Edited by David W. J. Gill and Conrad Gempf. Vol. 2 of *The Book of Acts in Its First Century Setting.* Edited by Bruce W. Winter. Grand Rapids: Eerdmans; Carlisle, U.K.: Paternoster, 1994.

"Trade Routes." "Trade Routes in Imperial Roman Times, according to Ancient Sources (1st–3rd cents. AD)." *BrillPauly* 4:1179–80.

Trapp, "Letters." Trapp, Michael B. "Letters, Greek." *OCD*³ 846–47.

Trapp, *Maximus.* Trapp, Michael B., ed. and trans. *Maximus of Tyre: The Philosophical Orations.* Oxford: Clarendon, 1997.

Travis, "Judgment." Travis, Stephen H. "Judgment." *DPL* 516–17.

Trebilco, "Asia." Trebilco, Paul R. "Asia." Pages 291–362 in *The Book of Acts in Its Graeco-Roman Setting.* Edited by David W. J. Gill and Conrad Gempf. Vol. 2 of *The Book of Acts in Its First Century Setting.* Edited by Bruce W. Winter. Grand Rapids: Eerdmans; Carlisle, U.K.: Paternoster, 1994.

Trebilco, "Call Themselves." Trebilco, Paul R. "Why Did the Early Christians Call Themselves ἡ ἐκκλησία?" *NTS* 57 (3, 2011): 440–60.

Trebilco, *Communities.* Trebilco, Paul R. *Jewish Communities in Asia Minor.* SNTSMS 69. Cambridge: Cambridge University Press, 1991.

Trebilco, "Communities." Trebilco, Paul R. "Jewish Communities in Asia Minor." *DNTB* 562–69.

Trebilco, *Ephesus.* Trebilco, Paul R. *The Early Christians in Ephesus from Paul to Ignatius.* Grand Rapids: Eerdmans, 2007. Originally published in WUNT 166. Tübingen: Mohr Siebeck, 2004.

Trebilco, "Self-Designations." Trebilco, Paul. "The Significance of the Distribution of Self-Designations in Acts." *NovT* 54 (2012): 30–49.

Trebilco, "Servants of Most High God." Trebilco, Paul R. "Paul and Silas—'Servants of the Most High God' (Acts 16.16–18)." *JSNT* 36 (1989): 51–73.

Trebilco and Evans, "Diaspora Judaism." Trebilco, Paul R., and Craig A. Evans. "Diaspora Judaism." *DNTB* 281–96.

Treggiari, *Freedmen.* Treggiari, Susan. *Roman Freedmen during the Late Republic.* Oxford: Clarendon, 1969.

Treggiari, "Jobs for Women." Treggiari, Susan. "Jobs for Women." *AJAH* 1 (1976): 76–104.

Treggiari, "Jobs in Household." Treggiari, Susan. "Jobs in the Household of Livia." *PBSR* 43 (1975): 48–77.

Treggiari, *Marriage.* Treggiari, Susan. *Roman Marriage: Iusti coniuges from the Time of Cicero to the Time of Ulpian.* Oxford: Clarendon, 1991.

Treggiari, "Marriage." Treggiari, Susan. "Marriage." *BrillPauly* 8:385–91.

Treggiari, "Marriage and Family." Treggiari, Susan. "Marriage and Family in Roman Society." Pages 132–82 in *Marriage and Family in the Biblical World.* Edited by Ken M. Campbell. Downers Grove, Ill.: InterVarsity, 2003.

Treggiari, "Symbol." Treggiari, Susan. "The Upper-Class House as Symbol and Focus of Emotion in Cicero." *JRA* 12 (1999): 33–56.

Treidler, "Ionische Meer." Treidler, Hans. "Das Ionische Meer im Altertum." *Klio* 22 (1928): 86–91.

Trelenberg, "Märtyrer." Trelenberg, Jörg. "Der frühchristliche Märtyrer und der stoische Weise: Eine topologische Untersuchung." *ZAC/JAC* 14 (2, 2010): 328–55.

Trell, "Architecture on Coins." Trell, Bluma L. "Architecture on Ancient Coins." *Archaeology* 29 (1976): 6–15.

Trémel, "Actes 20,7–12." Trémel, Yves-Bernard. "À propos d'Actes 20,7–12: Puissance du thaumaturge ou du témoin?" *RTP* 30 (4, 1980): 359–69.

Trémel, "Risque de paganisation." Trémel, Yves-Bernard. "Voie du salut et religion populaire: Paul et Luc face au risque de paganisation." *LumVie* 30 (153–54, 1981): 87–108.

Tremolada, "Gesù e lo Spirito." Tremolada, Pierantonio. "Gesù e lo Spirito nel Vangelo di Luca: Annotazioni esegetiche per una cristologia secondo lo Spirito." *ScC* 130 (1, 2002): 117–60.

Trever, "Covenanters." Trever, John C. "The Qumran Covenanters and Their Use of Scripture." *Personalist* 39 (2, 1958): 127–38.

Treves, "Date." Treves, Marco. "The Date of the War of the Sons of Light." *VT* 8 (1958): 419–24.

Treves and Cornell, "*Tumultus.*" Treves, Piero, and Tim J. Cornell. "*Tumultus.*" *OCD*³ 1564–65.

Treves and Levick, "Suffect." Treves, Piero, and Barbara M. Levick. "Suffect, *suffectio.*" *OCD*³ 1453.

Treves and Lintott, "Coercitio." Treves, Piero, and Andrew William Lintott. "Coercitio." *OCD*³ 355.

Treves and Lintott, "*Viatores.*" Treves, Piero, and Andrew William Lintott. "*Viatores.*" *OCD*³ 1596.

Tribulato, *Language.* Tribulato, Olga. *Language and Linguistic Contact in Ancient Sicily.* Cambridge Classical Studies. Cambridge: Cambridge University Press, 2012.

Trifon, "Msmrwt." Trifon, Dalia. "H'm 'brw msmrwt hkwhnym myhwdh lglyl 'hry mrd br-kwkb'?" *Tarbiz* 59 (1–2, 1989–90): 77–93.

Trifon, "Qt' mmsnh." Trifon, D. "Qt' mmsnh k'dwt lm'mdw sl hmlk 'gryps hsny." *Cathedra* 53 (1989): 27–48.

Trigg, "Tales." Trigg, R. "Tales Artfully Spun." Pages 117–32 in *The Bible as Rhetoric: Studies in Biblical Persuasion and Credibility.* Edited by M. Warner. WSPL. London: Routledge, 1990.

Trigger, "Ballana Culture." Trigger, Bruce G. "The Ballana Culture and the Coming of Christianity." Pages 106–19 in vol. 1 of *Africa in Antiquity: The Arts of Ancient Nubia and the Sudan.* 2 vols. Brooklyn, N.Y.: Brooklyn Museum, 1978.

Trigger, "Nubian, Nilotic?" Trigger, Bruce G. "Nubian, Negro, Black, Nilotic?" Pages 26–35 in vol. 1 of *Africa in Antiquity: The Arts of Ancient Nubia and the Sudan.* 2 vols. Brooklyn, N.Y.: Brooklyn Museum, 1978.

Trimble, "Masada." Trimble, Virginia L. "Masada, Suicide, and Halakhah." *ConsJud* 31 (2, 1977): 45–55.

Trites, "Church Growth." Trites, Allison A. "Church Growth in the Acts of the Apostles." *McMJT* 1 (1, 1990): 1–18.

Trites, "Prayer Motif." Trites, Allison A. "The Prayer Motif in Luke-Acts." Pages 168–86 in *Perspectives on Luke-Acts.* ABPRSSS 5. Edited by Charles H. Talbert. Danville, Va.: Association of Baptist Professors of Religion; Edinburgh: T&T Clark, 1978.

Trites, *Witness.* Trites, Allison A. *The New Testament Concept of Witness.* SNTSMS 31. Cambridge: Cambridge University Press, 1977.

Trobisch, "Narrative Welt." Trobisch, David. "Die narrative Welt der Apostelgeschichte." *ZNT* 9 (18, 2006): 9–14.

Trocmé, "Apôtre et Rome." Trocmé, Étienne. "L'apôtre Paul et Rome: Réflexions sur une fascination." *RHPR* 72 (1, 1992): 41–51.

Trocmé, "Beginnings of Historiography." Trocmé, Étienne. "The Beginnings of Christian Historiography and the History of Early Christianity." *ABR* 31 (1983): 1–13.

Trocmé, *Esprit-Saint.* Trocmé, Étienne. *L'Esprit-Saint et l'Église.* Paris: Fayard, 1969.

Trocmé, "Rempart." Trocmé, Etienne. "Le rempart de Damas: Un faux pas de Paul?" *RHPR* 69 (4, 1989): 475–79.

Troeltsch, *Social Teaching.* Troeltsch, Ernst. *The Social Teaching of the Christian Churches.* Translated by Olive Wyon. Introductory note by Charles Gore. 2 vols. Halley Stewart Publications 1. London: George Allen & Unwin; New York: Macmillan, 1931.

Troftgruben, *Conclusion.* Troftgruben, Troy M. *A Conclusion Unhindered: A Study of the Ending of Acts within Its Literary Environment.* WUNT 2.280. Tübingen: Mohr Siebeck, 2010.

Troftgruben, "Ending." Troftgruben, Troy M. "Ending 'in an Unhindered Manner' (Acts 28:31): The Ending of Acts within Its Literary Environment." PhD diss., Princeton Theological Seminary, 2009.

Trompf, "Attitudes." Trompf, G. W. "On Attitudes toward Women in Paul and Paulinist Literature: 1 Corinthians 11:3–16 and Its Context." *CBQ* 42 (2, 1980): 196–215.

Trompf, "Death of Paul." Trompf, G. W. "On Why Luke Declined to Recount the Death of Paul: Acts 27–28 and Beyond." Pages 225–39 in *Luke-Acts: New Perspectives from the Society of Biblical Literature Seminar.* Edited by Charles H. Talbert. New York: Crossraod, 1984.

Trompf, *Historical Recurrence.* Trompf, G. W. *The Idea of Historical Recurrence in Western Thought.* Berkeley: University of California Press, 1979.

Trompf, *Retributive Justice.* Trompf, G. W. *Early Christian Historiography: Narratives of Retributive Justice.* London: Continuum, 2000.

Tronier, "Spørgsmålet." Tronier, Henrik. "Spørgsmålet om hermeneutisk kongruens i Pauluseksegesen, 2. del: Allegorisk og typologisk hermeneutic i eksegesen." *DTT* 55 (3, 1992): 191–208.

Tropper, "Children." Tropper, Amram. "Children and Childhood in Light of the Demographics of the Jewish Family in Late Antiquity." *JSJ* 37 (3, 2006): 299–343.

Tröster, "Hegemony." Tröster, Manuel. "Roman Hegemony and Non-State Violence: A Fresh Look at Pompey's Campaign against the Pirates." *GR* 56 (1, 2009): 14–33.

Troster, "Quest." Troster, Lawrence. "Journey to the Center of the Earth: *Birkat Ha-Mazon* and the Quest for Holiness." *ConsJud* 47 (2, 1995): 3–16.

Trousdale, *Movements.* Trousdale, Jerry. *Miraculous Movements.* Nashville: Thomas Nelson, 2012.

Trudinger, "Damascus Road." Trudinger, Paul. "St. Paul, the Damascus Road, 'My Gospel,' and Jesus." *FaithFreed* 59 (2, 2006): 102–7.

Trudinger, "Milieu." Trudinger, Paul. "The Ephesus Milieu." *DRev* 106 (365, 1988): 286–96.

Trull, "Interpretation." Trull, Gregory V. "Peter's Interpretation of Psalm 16:8–11 in Acts 2:25–32." *BSac* 161 (644, 2004): 432–48.

Trumbower, "Jesus and Speech." Trumbower, Jeffrey A. "The Historical Jesus and the Speech of Gamaliel (Acts 5.35–9)." *NTS* 39 (4, 1993): 500–517.

Trump, "Malta." Trump, D. H. "Malta." *OEANE* 3:402–5.

Trümper, "Environment of Households." Trümper, Monika. "Material and Social Environment of Greco-Roman households in the East: The Case of Hellenistic Delos." Pages 19–43 in *Early Christian Families in Context: An Interdisciplinary Dialogue.* Edited by David L. Balch and Carolyn Osiek. Grand Rapids and Cambridge: Eerdmans, 2003.

Trzaskoma, "Chariton and Tragedy." Trzaskoma, Stephen M. "Chariton and Tragedy: Reconsiderations and New Evidence." *AJP* 131 (2, 2010): 219–31.

Trzaskoma, "Echoes." Trzaskoma, Stephen Michael. "Echoes of Thucydides' Sicilian Expedition in Three Greek Novels." *CP* 106 (1, 2011): 61–66.

Trzaskoma, "Miletus." Trzaskoma, Stephen Michael. "Why Miletus? Chariton's Choice of Setting and Xenophon's *Anabasis.*" *Mnemosyne* 65 (2, 2012): 300–307.

Trzaskoma, "Novelist Writing 'History.'" Trzaskoma, Stephen M. "A Novelist Writing 'History': Longus' Thucydides Again." *GRBS* 45 (1, 2005): 75–90.

Tsirkin, "Canaan." Tsirkin, Juri B. "Canaan; Phoenicia; Sidon." *AuOr* 19 (2, 2001): 271–79.

Tsochos, "Religion." Tsochos, Charalampos. "Samothrace. II. Religion." *BrillPauly* 12:938–42.

Tsuchido, "Anti-Semitism." Tsuchido, Kiyoshi. "Is There Anti-Semitism in the Fourth Gospel? An Exegetical Study of John 11:45–54." *AJBI* 21 (1995): 57–72.

Tsuk, "Aqueduct." Tsuk, Tsvika. "The Aqueduct to Legio and the Location of the Camp of the VIth Roman Legion." *TA* 15–16 (1, 1988–89): 92–97 and plates 13–14.

Tubiana, "Zar." Tubiana, Joseph. "Zar and buda in Northern Ethiopia." Pages 19–33 in *Women's Medicine: The zar-bori Cult in Africa and Beyond.* Edited by I. M. Lewis, Ahmed Al-Safi, and Sayyid Hurreiz. Edinburgh: International African Institute, Edinburgh University Press, 1991.

Tuchelt, "Didyma (*BrillPauly*)." Tuchelt, Klaus. "Didyma." *BrillPauly* 4:390–95.

Tuchelt, "Didyma (*OEANE*)." Tuchelt, Klaus. "Didyma." *OEANE* 2:159–61.

Tucker, "History." Tucker, Aviezer. "The Future of Philosophy of History." *HistTh* 40 (1, 2001): 37–56.

Tucker, *Jerusalem.* Tucker, Ruth. *From Jerusalem to Irian Jaya: A Biographical History of Christian Missions.* Grand Rapids: Zondervan, 1983.

Tucker, *Knowledge.* Tucker, Aviezer. *Our Knowledge of the Past: A Philosophy of Historiography.* Cambridge: Cambridge University Press, 2004.

Tucker, "Legal Background." Tucker, Gene M. "The Legal Background of Genesis 23." *JBL* 85 (1, 1966): 77–84.

Tucker, "Prophetic Speech." Tucker, Gene M. "Prophetic Speech." *Interpretation* 32 (Jan. 1978): 31–45.

Tucker, "Sins." Tucker, Aviezer. "Sins of Our Fathers: A Short History of Religious Child Sacrifice." *ZRGG* 51 (1, 1999): 30–47.

Tuckett, "Christology." Tuckett, Christopher M. "The Christology of Luke-Acts." Pages 133–64 in *The Unity of Luke-Acts.* Edited by Joseph Verheyden. BETL 142. Leuven: Leuven University Press, 1999.

Tuckett, *History.* Tuckett, Christopher M. *Q and the History of Early Christianity: Studies on Q.* Peabody, Mass.: Hendrickson, 1996.

Tuckett, *Luke.* Tuckett, Christopher M. *Luke.* NTG. Sheffield, U.K.: Sheffield Academic, 1996.

Tuckett, "Paul and Ethics." Tuckett, Christopher M. "Paul, Scripture, and Ethics: Some Reflections." *NTS* 46 (3, 2000): 403–24.

Tuckett, "Review." Tuckett, Christopher. Review of Richard Bauckham, *Jesus and the Eyewitnesses.* RBL (Dec. 15, 2007). Online: http://www.bookreviews.org /pdf/5650_6184.pdf.

Tuckett, "Sources." Tuckett, Christopher M. "Sources and Methods." Pages 121–37 in *The Cambridge Companion to Jesus.* Edited by Markus Bockmuehl. Cambridge: Cambridge University Press, 2001.

Tully, "Στρατάρχης." Tully, Geoffrey D. "The στρατάρχης of *Legio* VI Ferrata and the Employment of Camp Prefects as Vexillation Commanders." *ZPE* 120 (1998): 226–32.

Tuplin, "Hellenica." Tuplin, Christopher. "Continuous Histories (*Hellenica*)." Pages 159–70 in *A Companion to Greek and Roman Historiography*. Edited by John Marincola. 2 vols. Oxford: Blackwell, 2007.

Turaki, "Legacy." Turaki, Yusufu. "The British Colonial Legacy in Northern Nigeria." PhD diss., Boston University, 1982.

Turner, "Actuality." Turner, Edith. "Psychology, Metaphor, or Actuality? A Probe into Iñupiat Eskimo Healing." *AnthConsc* 3 (1–2, 1992): 1–8.

Turner, "Advances." Turner, Edith. "Advances in the Study of Spirit Experience: Drawing Together Many Threads." *Anth Consc* 17 (2, 2006): 33–61.

Turner, "Anthropology." Turner, Edith. "The Anthropology of Experience: The Way to Teach Religion and Healing." Pages 193–205 in *Teaching Religion and Healing*. Edited by Linda L. Barnes and Inés Talamantez. AARTRSS. Oxford: Oxford University Press, 2006.

Turner, "Authoritative Preaching." Turner, Max. "The Spirit of Prophecy and the Power of Authoritative Preaching in Luke-Acts: A Question of Origins." *NTS* 38 (1, 1992): 66–88.

Turner, "Challenge." Turner, Max. "The Spirit in Luke-Acts: A Support or a Challenge to Classical Pentecostal Paradigms?" *VE* 27 (1997): 75–101.

Turner, "Concept." Turner, M. M. B. "The Concept of Receiving the Spirit in John's Gospel." *VE* 10 (1976): 24–42.

Turner, "'Divine' Christology." Turner, Max. "The Spirit of Christ and 'Divine' Christology." Pages 413–36 in *Jesus of Nazareth, Lord and Christ: Essays on the Historical Jesus and New Testament Christology*. Edited by Joel B. Green and Max Turner. Grand Rapids: Eerdmans; Carlisle, U.K.: Paternoster, 1994.

Turner, *Drums*. Turner, V. W. *The Drums of Affliction: A Study of Religious Processes among the Ndembu of Zambia*. Oxford: Clarendon; London: International African Institute, 1968.

Turner, "Empowerment." Turner, Max. "'Empowerment for Mission'? The Pneumatology of Luke-Acts: An Appreciation and Critique of James B. Shelton's *Mighty in Word and Deed*." *VE* 24 (1994): 103–22.

Turner, "Every Believer as Witness?" Turner, Max. "Every Believer as a Witness in Acts?—In Dialogue with John Michael Penney." *AshTJ* 30 (1998): 57–71.

Turner, "Experience." Turner, Max. "Early Christian Experience and Theology of 'Tongues'—A New Testament Perspective." Pages 1–33 in *Speaking in Tongues: Multi-disciplinary Perspectives*. Edited by Mark J. Cartledge. SPCI. Waynesboro, Ga., and Bletchley, Milton Keynes, U.K.: Paternoster, 2006.

Turner, *Experiencing Ritual*. Turner, Edith, with William Blodgett, Singleton Kahoma, and Fideli Benwa. *Experiencing Ritual: A New Interpretation of African Healing*. SCEthn. Philadelphia: University of Pennsylvania Press, 1992.

Turner, *Gifts*. Turner, Max. *The Holy Spirit and Spiritual Gifts in the New Testament Church and Today*. Rev. ed. Peabody, Mass.: Hendrickson, 1998.

Turner, *Grammatical Insights*. Turner, Nigel. *Grammatical Insights into the New Testament*. Edinburgh: T&T Clark, 1965.

Turner, *Hands*. Turner, Edith. *The Hands Feel It: Healing and Spirit Presence among a Northern Alaskan People*. DeKalb, Ill.: Northern Illinois University Press, 1996.

Turner, *Healers*. Turner, Edith. *Among the Healers: Stories of Spiritual and Ritual Healing around the World*. Religion, Health, and Healing. Westport, Conn.: Praeger, 2006.

Turner, "Hebraic Sources." Turner, Nigel. "The Relation of Luke I and II to Hebraic Sources and to the Rest of Luke-Acts." *NTS* 2 (2, 1955): 100–109.

Turner, *Insights*. Turner, Nigel. *Grammatical Insights into the New Testament*. Edinburgh: T&T Clark, 1965.

Turner, "Interpreting." Turner, Max. "Interpreting the Samaritans of Acts 8: The Waterloo of Pentecostal Soteriology and Pneumatology." *Pneuma* 23 (2, 2001): 265–86.

Turner, "Jesus and Spirit in Perspective." Turner, M. Max B. "Jesus and the Spirit in Lucan Perspective." *TynBul* 32 (1981): 3–42.

Turner, "Paul and Globalisation." Turner, Geoffrey. "Paul and the Globalisation of Christianity." *NBf* 86 (1002, 2005): 165–71.

Turner, *Power*. Turner, Max. *Power from on High: The Spirit in Israel's Restoration and Witness in Luke-Acts*. Sheffield, U.K.: Sheffield Academic, 1996.

Turner, "Reality." Turner, Edith. "The Reality of Spirits." *ReVision* 15 (1, 1992): 28–32.

Turner, "Reality of Spirits." Turner, Edith. "The Reality of Spirits." *Shamanism* 10 (1, Spring–Summer 1997).

Turner, "Responses." Turner, Max. "A Response to the Responses of Menzies and Chan." *AJPS* 2 (2, 1999): 297–308.

Turner, "Review." Turner, Max. Review of Craig S. Keener, *The Spirit in the Gospels and Acts*. *Them* 23 (2, 1998): 69–71.

Turner, "Significance of Receiving." Turner, M. M. B. "The Significance of Receiving the Spirit in Luke-Acts: A Survey of Modern Scholarship." *TJ* 2 (2, 1981): 131–58.

Turner, "Spirit and Miracles." Turner, Max. "The Spirit and the Power of Jesus' Miracles in the Lucan Conception." *NovT* 33 (2, 1991): 124–52.

Turner, "'Spirit' as Power." Turner, Max. "The 'Spirit of Prophecy' as the Power of Israel's Restoration and Witness." Pages 327–48 in *Witness to the Gospel: The Theology of Acts*. Edited by I. Howard Marshall and David Peterson. Grand Rapids: Eerdmans, 1998.

Turner, "Spirit Endowment." Turner, M. M. B. "Spirit Endowment in Luke-Acts: Some Linguistic Considerations." *VE* 12 (1981): 45–63.

Turner, "Spirit of Christ and Christology." Turner, M. M. B. "The Spirit of Christ and Christology." Pages 168–90 in *Christ the Lord*. Edited by H. H. Rowdon. Leicester, U.K.: Inter-Varsity, 1982.

Turner, "Testament of Abraham." Turner, Nigel. "The 'Testament of Abraham': Problems in Biblical Greek." *NTS* 1 (3, 1955): 219–23.

Turner, "Thoughts." Turner, Nigel. "Second Thoughts, VII: Papyrus Finds." *ExpT* 76 (2, 1964): 44–48.

Turner, "Tongues." Turner, Max. "Tongues: An Experience for All in the Pauline Churches?" *AJPS* 1 (2, 1998): 231–53.

Turner, "Work." Turner, Max. "The Work of the Holy Spirit in Luke-Acts." *WW* 23 (2, 2003): 146–53.

Tuttle, *Riot*. Tuttle, William M., Jr. *Race Riot: Chicago in the Red Summer of 1919*. New York: Atheneum, 1977.

Tuttle, *Wesley*. Tuttle, Robert G., Jr. *John Wesley: His Life and Theology*. Grand Rapids: Zondervan, 1978.

Twaissi, "Edom." Twaissi, Saad. "Nabataean Edom: A Demographic and Archaeological Sedentarisation and Regional Dynamics." *Levant* 39 (2007): 143–63.

Twelftree, "ΕΚΒΑΛΛΩ." Twelftree, Graham H. "'ΕΙ ΔΕ . . . ΕΓΩ ΕΚΒΑΛΛΩ ΤΑ ΔΑΙΜΟΝΙΑ . . .'" Pages 361–400 in *The Miracles of Jesus*. Edited by David Wenham and Craig Blomberg. Gospel Perspectives 6. Sheffield, U.K.: JSOT Press, 1986.

Twelftree, *Exorcist*. Twelftree, Graham H. *Jesus the Exorcist: A Contribution to the Study of the Historical Jesus*. Peabody, Mass.: Hendrickson; Tübingen: J. C. B. Mohr, 1993.

Twelftree, "Healing." Twelftree, Graham H. "Healing, Illness." *DPL* 378–81.

Twelftree, "Historian and Miraculous." Twelftree, Graham. "The Historian and the Miraculous." Plenary address for

"Special Divine Action," the 2014 conference for the Ian Ramsey Centre for Science and Religion, Oxford University, Oxford, U.K., July 13, 2014.

Twelftree, "Jesus in Traditions." Twelftree, Graham H. "Jesus in Jewish Traditions." Pages 289–341 in *The Jesus Tradition outside the Gospels*. Edited by David Wenham. Gospel Perspectives 5. Sheffield, U.K.: JSOT Press, 1984.

Twelftree, *Miracle Worker*. Twelftree, Graham H. *Jesus the Miracle Worker: A Historical and Theological Study*. Downers Grove, Ill.: InterVarsity, 1999.

Twelftree, "Miracles." Twelftree, Graham H. "The Miracles of Jesus: Marginal or Mainstream?" *JSHJ* 1 (1, 2003): 104–24.

Twelftree, *Name*. Twelftree, Graham H. *In the Name of Jesus: Exorcism among Early Christians*. Grand Rapids: Baker Academic, 2007.

Twelftree, *Paul*. Twelftree, Graham H. *Paul and the Miraculous: A Historical Reconstruction*. Grand Rapids: Baker Academic, 2013.

Twelftree, *People*. Twelftree, Graham H. *People of the Spirit: Exploring Luke's View of the Church*. Grand Rapids: Baker Academic, 2009.

Twelftree, "Prayer." Twelftree, Graham H. "Prayer and the Coming of the Spirit in Acts." *ExpT* 117 (7, 2006): 271–76.

Twelftree, "Sanhedrin." Twelftree, Graham H. "Sanhedrin." *DNTB* 1061–65.

Twelftree, "Scribes." Twelftree, Graham H. "Scribes." *DNTB* 1086–89.

Twelftree, "Signs." Twelftree, Graham H. "Signs, Wonders, Miracles." *DPL* 875–77.

Twelftree, *Triumphant*. Twelftree, Graham H. *Christ Triumphant: Exorcism Then and Now*. London: Hodder & Stoughton, 1985.

"Twins." "Twins." *BrillPauly* 15:49–51.

Tyler, "Context." Tyler, Stephen A. "Context and Variation in Koya Kinship Terminology." *AmAnth* 68 (June 1966): 693–707.

Tyson, "Authority in Acts." Tyson, Joseph B. "Authority in Acts." *BibT* 30 (5, 1992): 279–83.

Tyson, "Coming to Dinner." Tyson, Joseph B. "Guess Who's Coming to Dinner: Peter and Cornelius in Acts 10:1–11:18." *Forum* 3 (1, 2000): 179–96.

Tyson, "Date of Acts." Tyson, Joseph B. "The Date of Acts: A Reconsideration." *Forum* 5 (1, 2002): 33–51.

Tyson, "Dates." Tyson, Joseph B. "Why Dates Matter: The Case of the Acts of the Apostles." *FourR* 18 (2, 2005): 8–11, 14, 17–18.

Tyson, "History to Rhetoric." Tyson, Joseph B. "From History to Rhetoric and Back: Assessing New Trends in Acts Studies." Pages 23–42 in *Contextualizing Acts: Lukan Narrative and Greco-Roman Discourse*. Edited by Todd Penner and Caroline Vander Stichele. SBLSymS 20. Atlanta: SBL, 2003.

Tyson, *Images of Judaism*. Tyson, Joseph B. *Images of Judaism in Luke-Acts*. Columbia: University of South Carolina Press, 1992.

Tyson, "Jewish Public." Tyson, Joseph B. "The Jewish Public in Luke-Acts." *NTS* 30 (4, 1984): 574–83.

Tyson, "Legacy." Tyson, Joseph B. "The Legacy of F. C. Baur and Recent Studies of Acts." *Forum* 4 (1, 2001): 125–44.

Tyson, *Luke, Judaism, and Scholars*. Tyson, Joseph B. *Luke, Judaism, and the Scholars: Critical Approaches to Luke-Acts*. Columbia: University of South Carolina Press, 1999.

Tyson, *Marcion*. Tyson, Joseph B. *Marcion and Luke-Acts: A Defining Struggle*. Columbia: University of South Carolina Press, 2006.

Tyson, "Opponents." Tyson, Joseph B. "Paul's Opponents in Galatia." *NovT* 10 (4, 1968): 241–54.

Tyson, "Opposition in Luke." Tyson, Joseph B. "The Opposition to Jesus in the Gospel of Luke." *PRSt* 5 (3, 1978): 144–50.

Tyson, "Problem." Tyson, Joseph B. "The Problem of Jewish Rejection in Acts." Pages 124–37 in *Luke-Acts and the Jewish People: Eight Critical Perspectives*. Edited by Joseph B. Tyson. Minneapolis: Augsburg, 1988.

Tyson, "Reading as Godfearer." Tyson, Joseph B. "Jews and Judaism in Luke-Acts: Reading as a Godfearer." *NTS* 41 (1, 1995): 19–38.

Tyson, "Source Criticism." Tyson, Joseph B. "Source Criticism of the Gospel of Luke." Pages 24–39 in *Perspectives on Luke-Acts*. ABPRSSS 5. Edited by Charles H. Talbert. Danville, Va.: Association of Baptist Professors of Religion; Edinburgh: T&T Clark, 1978.

Tyson, "Themes." Tyson, Joseph B. "Themes at the Crossroads: Acts 15 in Its Lukan Setting." *Forum* 4 (1, 2001): 105–24.

Tyson, "Wrestling." Tyson, Joseph B. "Wrestling with and for Paul: Efforts to Obtain Pauline Support by Marcion and the Author of Acts." Pages 13–28 in *Contemporary Studies in Acts*. Edited by Thomas E. Phillips. Macon, Ga.: Mercer University Press, 2009.

Tzaferis, "Crucifixion." Tzaferis, Vassilios. "Crucifixion—The Archaeological Evidence." *BAR* 11 (1, 1985): 44–53.

Tzaferis, "Cults." Tzaferis, Vassilios. "Cults and Deities Worshipped at Caesarea Philippi-Banias." Pages 190–201 in *Priests, Prophets, and Scribes: Essays on the Formation and Heritage of Second Temple Judaism in Honour of Joseph Blenkinsopp*. Edited by Eugene Ulrich et al. JSOTSup 149. Sheffield, U.K.: JSOT Press, 1992.

Tzaferis, "Inscribed." Tzaferis, Vassilios. "Inscribed 'to God Jesus Christ.'" *BAR* 33 (2, 2007): 38–49.

Tzaferis and Avner, "Hpyrwt." Tzaferis, Vassilios, and R. Avner. "Hpyrwt b'ny's." *Qad* 23 (3–4, 1990): 110–14.

Tzeng, Osgood, and May, "Differences." Tzeng, Oliver C. S., Charles E. Osgood, and William H. May. "Idealized Cultural Differences in Kincept Conceptions." *Ling* 172 (May 5, 1976): 51–77.

Tzounakas, "Peroration." Tzounakas, Spyridon. "The Peroration of Cicero's Pro Milone." *CW* 102 (2, 2009): 129–41.

Uchelen, "Halacha." Uchelen, Nico Adriaan van. "Halacha in het Nieuwe Testament?" *NedTT* 49 (3, 1995): 177–89.

Udoh, "Plain." Udoh, Fabian E. "Jewish Antiquities XIV.205, 207–08 and 'The Great Plain.'" *PEQ* 134 (2, 2002): 130–43.

Udoh, "Views on the Law." Udoh, Fabian E. "Paul's Views on the Law: Questions about Origin (Gal. 1:6–2:21; Phil. 3:2–11)." *NovT* 42 (3, 2000): 214–37.

Uggeri, "Mater Magna." Uggeri, Giovanni. "Mater Magna." *BrillPauly* 8:458–59.

Uggeri, "Tres Tabernae." Uggeri, Giovanni. "Tres Tabernae (1)." *BrillPauly* 14:890.

Uhlig, "Pseudepigraphischer Actaschluss." Uhlig, Siegbert. "Ein pseudepigraphischer Actaschluss in der äthiopischen Version." *OrChr* 73 (1989): 129–36.

Ukachukwu Manus, "Areopagus Speech." Ukachukwu Manus, Chris. "The Areopagus Speech (Acts 17:16–34): A Study of Luke's Approach to Evangelism and Its Significance in the African Context." *AfThJ* 14 (1, 1985): 3–18.

Ukachukwu Manus, "Community of Love." Ukachukwu Manus, Chris. "The Community of Love in Luke's Acts: A Sociological Exegesis of Acts 2:41–47 in the African Context." *WAfJES* 2 (1, 1990): 11–37.

Ukachukwu Manus, "Conversion Narratives." Ukachukwu Manus, Chris. "Conversion Narratives in the Acts: A Study on Lukan Historiography." *ITS* 22 (2, 1985): 172–95.

Ukachukwu Manus, "Healing." Ukachukwu Manus, Chris. "Healing and Exorcism: The Scriptural Viewpoint." Pages 84–104 in *Healing and Exorcism—The Nigerian Experience: Proceedings, Lectures, Discussions, and Conclusions of the First Missiology Symposium on Healing and Exorcism, Organised by the Spiritan International School of Theology, Attakwu, Enugu, May 18–20, 1989*. Edited by Chris

Ukachukwu Manus, Luke N. Mbefo, and E. E. Uzukwu. Attakwu, Enugu, Nigeria: Spiritan International School of Theology, 1992.

Ukachukwu Manus, "Hypothesis." Ukachukwu Manus, Chris. "'Amanuensis Hypothesis': A Key to the Understanding of Paul's Epistles in the New Testament." *BiBh* 10 (3, 1984): 160–74.

Ukachukwu Manus, "Miracle-Workers." Ukachukwu Manus, Chris. "Miracle-Workers/Healers as Divine Men: Their Role in the Nigerian Church and Society." *AJT* 3 (2, 1989): 658–69.

Ulfgard, "Bibelutläggning." Ulfgard, Hakan. "'Realistisk bibelutläggning' efter Qumranfynden: Telningen i den yttersta tiden—det nya förbundet fore och efter Jesus." *SEÅ* 63 (1998): 147–66.

Ullendorff, "Candace and the Queen of Sheba." Ullendorff, Edward. "Candace (Acts VIII.27) and the Queen of Sheba." *NTS* 2 (1, Sept. 1955): 53–56.

Ullucci, "Sacrifice." Ullucci, Daniel. "Before Animal Sacrifice: A Myth of Innocence." *R&T* 15 (3–4, 2008): 357–74.

Ulmer, "Advancement." Ulmer, Rivka. "The Advancement of Arguments in Exegetical Midrash Compared to That of the Greek ΔΙΑΤΡΙΒΗ." *JSJ* 28 (1, 1997): 48–91.

Ulrich, "Non-attestation." Ulrich, Eugene. "The Non-attestation of a Tripartite Canon in 4QMMT." *CBQ* 65 (2, 2003): 202–14.

Ulrich, "Text for Samuel." Ulrich, Eugene. "Josephus' Biblical Text for the Books of Samuel." Pages 81–96 in *Josephus, the Bible, and History*. Edited by Louis H. Feldman and Gohei Hata. Detroit: Wayne State University Press, 1989.

Ulrichs, "Ears." Ulrichs, Karl Friedrich. "Some Notes on Ears in Luke-Acts, especially in Lk. 4.21." *BN* 98 (1999): 28–31.

Ulrichsen, "Troen." Ulrichsen, Jarl H. "Troen på et liv etter døden i Qumranteksten." *NTT* 78 (1977): 151–63.

Umeh, *Dibia*. Umeh, John Anenechukwu. *After God Is Dibia*. Vol. 2 of Igbo Cosmology, Healing, Divination & Sacred Science in Nigeria. London: Karnak House, 1999.

Umurhan and Penner, "Crossroads." Umurhan, Osman, and Todd Penner. "Luke and Juvenal at the Crossroads: Space, Movement, and Morality in the Roman Empire." Pages 165–93 in *Christian Origins and Greco-Roman Culture: Social and Literary Contexts for the New Testament*. Edited by Stanley Porter and Andrew W. Pitts. Vol. 1 of Early Christianity in Its Hellenistic Context. Vol. 9 in Texts and Editions for New Testament Study. Leiden: Brill, 2013.

Unger, "Pisidian Antioch." Unger, Merrill F. "Pisidian Antioch and Gospel Penetration of the Greek World." *BSac* 118 (1961): 46–53.

Ungern-Sternberg, "Proletarii." Ungern-Sternberg, Jürgen von. "Proletarii." *Brill Pauly* 12:1–2.

Ungern-Sternberg, "Seditio." Ungern-Sternberg, Jürgen von. "Seditio." *Brill Pauly* 13:195–96.

Ungern-Sternberg, "Tradition." Ungern-Sternberg, Jürgen von. "The Tradition on Early Rome and Oral History." Pages 119–49 in *Greek and Roman Historiography*. Oxford Readings in Classical Studies. Translated by Mark Beck. Edited by John Marincola. New York: Oxford University Press, 2011.

Unseth, "Semantic Shift." Unseth, Peter. "Semantic Shift on a Geographical Term." *BTr* 49 (3, 1998): 323–31.

Unsok Ro, "Context." Unsok Ro, Johannes. "Socio-Economic Context of Post-Exilic Community and Literacy." *ZAW* 120 (4, 2008): 597–611.

Untermann, "Hispania." Untermann, Jürgen. "Hispania, Iberia: Languages." *BrillPauly* 6:392, 395.

Uprichard, "Baptism." Uprichard, R. E. Henry. "The Baptism of Jesus." *IBS* 3 (1981): 187–202.

Upton, "Potter's Field." Upton, John A. "The Potter's Field and the Death of Judas." *ConcJ* 8 (1982): 213–19.

Urbach, *Sages*. Urbach, Ephraim E. *The Sages: Their Concepts and Beliefs*. Translated by Israel Abrahams. 2 vols. 2nd ed. Jerusalem: Magnes, 1979.

Urbach, "Self-Isolation." Urbach, Ephraim E. "Self-Isolation or Self-Affirmation in Judaism in the First Three Centuries: Theory and Practice." Pages 269–98 in *Aspects of Judaism in the Graeco-Roman Period*. Edited by E. P. Sanders with A. I. Baumgarten and Alan Mendelson. Vol. 2 of *Jewish and Christian Self-Definition*. Edited by E. P. Sanders. Philadelphia: Fortress, 1981.

Urbainczyk, *Revolts*. Urbainczyk, Theresa. *Slave Revolts in Antiquity*. Berkeley: University of California, 2008.

Urban and Henry, "Abraham." Urban, Linwood, and Patrick Henry. "'Before Abraham Was I Am': Does Philo Explain John 8:56–58?" *Studia philonica* 6 (1979–80): 157–95.

Urbanz, "Gebet." Urbanz, Werner. "Das Gebet bei Flavius Josephus: Das Werk von Tessel Jonquière und weitere Überlegungen." *PzB* 17 (1, 2008): 15–28.

Ure et al., "Miletus." Ure, Percy Neville, et al. "Miletus." *OCD*³ 980.

Uribe Ulloa, "Syneídēsis." Uribe Ulloa, Pablo. "Syneídēsis en la Biblia griega y mada' en la Biblia hebrea. Implicaciones para una valoración del término 'conciencia' al interior del Antiguo Testamento." *Moralia* 32 (121, 2009): 7–17.

Urman, "House of Assembly." Urman, Dan. "The House of Assembly and the House of Study: Are They One and the Same?" *JJS* 44 (2, 1993): 236–57.

Uscatescu and Martín-Bueno, "Macellum." Uscatescu, Alexandra, and Manuel Martín-Bueno, "The *macellum* of Gerasa (Jerash, Jordan): From a Market Place to an Industrial Area." *BASOR* 307 (Aug. 1997): 67–88.

Usher, "Apostrophe." Usher, Stephen. "Apostrophe in Greek Oratory." *Rhetorica* 28 (4, 2010): 351–62.

Usher, "Doggerel." Usher, M. D. "Diogenes' Doggerel: *Chreia* and Quotation in Cynic Performance." *CJ* 104 (3, 2009): 207–23.

Usher, "Introduction to Dinarchus." Usher, Stephen. "Introduction" to *Dinarchus*. Pages 246–49 in vol. 2 of Dionysius of Halicarnassus. *Critical Essays*. 2 vols. Translated by Stephen Usher. LCL. Cambridge, Mass.: Harvard University Press, 1974.

Usher, "Oratio Recta." Usher, Stephen. "Oratio Recta and Oratio Obliqua in Polybius." *GRBS* 49 (4, 2009): 487–514.

Usry and Keener, *Religion*. Usry, Glenn, and Craig S. Keener. *Black Man's Religion: Can Christianity Be Afrocentric?* Downers Grove, Ill.: InterVarsity, 1996.

Ustinova, *Supreme Gods*. Ustinova, Yulia. *The Supreme Gods of the Bosporan Kingdom: Celestial Aphrodite and the Most High God*. RGRW 135. Leiden: Brill, 1999.

Ustinova, "Theos Hypsistos." Ustinova, Yulia. "The *thiasoi* of Theos Hypsistos in Tanais." *HR* 31 (2, 1991): 150–80.

Uval, "Streams." Uval, Beth. "Streams of Living Water: The Feast of Tabernacles and the Holy Spirit." *JerPersp* 49 (1995): 22–23, 37.

Uytanlet, *Historiography*. Uytanlet, Samson. *Luke-Acts and Jewish Historiography: A Study on the Theology, Literature, and Ideology of Luke-Acts*. WUNT 2.366. Tübingen: Mohr Siebeck, 2014.

Uzukwu, "Address." Uzukwu, E. E. "Opening Address." Pages 7–10 in *Healing and Exorcism—The Nigerian Experience: Proceedings, Lectures, Discussions, and Conclusions of the First Missiology Symposium on Healing and Exorcism, Organised by the Spiritan International School of Theology, Attakwu, Enugu, May 18–20, 1989*. Edited by Chris U. Manus, Luke N. Mbefo, and E. E. Uzukwu. Enugu, Nigeria: Snapp, 1992.

Vaage, "Barking." Vaage, Leif E. "Like Dogs Barking: Cynic *parrēsia* and Shameless Asceticism." *Semeia* 57 (1992): 25–39.

Vadakkedom, "Work." Vadakkedom, Jose. "The Work of the Holy Spirit: The Universalistic Approach in Acts 6–12." *Jeev* 34 (200, 2004): 174–83.

Vakayil, "Dialogue." Vakayil, Prema. "Paul's Dialogue with the Athenian Intellectuals in Acts 17:16–34." *ITS* 45 (4, 2008): 449–59.

Valantasis, "Musonius." Valantasis, Richard. "Musonius Rufus and Roman Ascetical Theory." *GRBS* 40 (3, 1999): 207–31.

Vale, "Sources." Vale, Ruth. "Literary Sources in Archaeological Description: The Case of Galilee, Galilees, and Galileans." *JSJ* 18 (2, 1987): 209–26.

Valentino, "Homiletical Charge." Valentino, Timothy R. "The Homiletical Charge in the Book of Acts: Does Luke Reveal Any Anti-Semitism?" *EvJ* 14 (2, 1996): 62–76.

Vallance, "Anatomy." Vallance, J. T. "Anatomy and Physiology." *OCD³* 82–85.

Vallance, "Medicine." Vallance, J. T. "Medicine." *OCD³* 945–49.

Vallance, "*Pneuma*." Vallance, J. T. "*Pneuma*." *OCD³* 1202.

Vallance, "Pneumatists." Vallance, J. T. "Pneumatists." *OCD³* 1202–3.

Valler, "Talk." Valler, Shulamit. "Women's Talk—Men's Talk: Babylonian Talmud *Erubin* 53a–54a." *REJ* 162 (3–4, 2003): 421–45.

Vallet, "Elam." Vallet, François. "Elam." Translated by Stephen Rosoff. *ABD* 2:423–29.

Vallet, *Rhégion*. Vallet, Georges. *Rhégion et Zancle; histoire, commerce et civilisation des cités chalcidiennes du détroit de Messine*. BEFAR 189. Paris: É. de Boccard, 1958.

Van Dam, "Divination." Van Dam, Cornelis. "Divination, Magic." Pages 159–62 in *Dictionary of the Old Testament Prophets*. Edited by Mark J. Boda and J. Gordon McConville. Downers Grove, Ill.: IVP Academic, 2012.

Van de Bunt–van den Hoek, "Aratus' Phainomena." Van de Bunt–van den Hoek, Annewies. "Aristobulos, Acts, Theophilus, Clement—Making Use of Aratus' Phainomena: A Peregrination." *Bijdr* 41 (3, 1980): 290–99.

Van den Berghe, "Institution." Van den Berghe, Pierre L. "The Peculiar Institution: Patterson and Foner on Slavery and Abolition." *EthRacSt* 7 (2, 1984): 301–5.

Van den Brink, "Burial Ground." Van den Brink, Edwin C. M. "A 'Provincial' Roman-Period Samaritan Burial Ground in Pardes Ha-Gedud, Netanya." *'Atiqot* 47 (2004): 131–54.

Van den Broek, *Myth of Phoenix*. Van den Broek, R. *The Myth of the Phoenix*. Leiden: Brill, 1972.

Van den Broek, "Phoenix." Van den Broek, Roelof. "Phoenix." Pages 655–57 in *Dictionary of Deities and Demons in the Bible*. 2nd rev. ed. Edited by Karel van der Toorn, Bob Becking, and Pieter W. van der Horst. Leiden: Brill; Grand Rapids: Eerdmans, 1999.

Van den Eynde, "Children." Van den Eynde, Sabine. "Children of the Promise: On the διαθήκη-Promise to Abraham in Lk 1,72 and Acts 3,25." Pages 469–82 in *The Unity of Luke-Acts*. Edited by Joseph Verheyden. BETL 142. Leuven: Leuven University Press, 1999.

Van den Heever, "Novel." Van den Heever, Gerhard. "Novel and Mystery: Discourse, Myth, and Society." Pages 89–114 in *Ancient Fiction: The Matrix of Early Christian and Jewish Narrative*. Edited by Jo-Ann A. Brant, Charles W. Hedrick, and Chris Shea. SBLSymS 32. Atlanta: SBL, 2005.

Van der Ben, *Charmides*. Van der Ben, Nico. *The Charmides of Plato: Problems and Interpretations*. Amsterdam: B. R. Grüner, 1985.

Vander Broek, "Sitz." Vander Broek, Lyle D. "The Markan Sitz im Leben: A Critical Investigation." PhD diss., Drew University, 1983.

Van der Horst, "Amazons." Van der Horst, Pieter W. "Amazons." Pages 27–28 in *Dictionary of Deities and Demons in the Bible*. 2nd rev. ed. Edited by Karel van der Toorn, Bob Becking, and Pieter W. van der Horst. Leiden: Brill; Grand Rapids: Eerdmans, 1999.

Van der Horst, "Aphrodisias." Van der Horst, Pieter W. "Jews and Christians in Aphrodisias in the Light of Their Relations in Other Cities of Asia Minor." *NedTT* 43 (2, 1989): 106–21.

Van der Horst, "Beobachtungen." Van der Horst, Pieter W. "Einige Beobachtungen zum Thema Frauen im antiken Judentum." *BTZ* 10 (1, 1993): 77–93.

Van der Horst, "Bibliomancy." Van der Horst, Pieter W. "Ancient Jewish Bibliomancy." *JGRCJ* 1 (2000): 9–17.

Van der Horst, "Celibacy." Van der Horst, Pieter W. "Celibacy in Early Judaism." *RB* 109 (3, 2002): 390–402.

Van der Horst, *Chaeremon*. Van der Horst, Pieter W. *Chaeremon, Egyptian Priest and Stoic Philosopher*. Leiden: Brill, 1984.

Van der Horst, "Cornutus." Van der Horst, Pieter W. "Cornutus and the New Testament." *NovT* 23 (2, 1981): 165–72.

Van der Horst, "Cosmic Conflagration." Van der Horst, Pieter W. "'The Elements Will Be Dissolved with Fire': The Idea of Cosmic Conflagration in Hellenism, Ancient Judaism, and Early Christianity." Pages 271–92 in *Hellenism–Judaism–Christianity: Essays on Their Interaction*, by P. W. van der Horst. 2nd ed. Leuven: Peeters, 1994.

Van der Horst, "Diaspora." Van der Horst, Pieter W. "De Samaritaanse diaspora in de oudheid." *NedTT* 42 (2, 1988): 134–44.

Van der Horst, "Dike." Van der Horst, Pieter W. "Dike." Pages 250–52 in *Dictionary of Deities and Demons in the Bible*. 2nd rev. ed. Edited by Karel van der Toorn, Bob Becking, and Pieter W. van der Horst. Leiden: Brill; Grand Rapids: Eerdmans, 1999.

Van der Horst, "Egerton 5." Van der Horst, Pieter W. "Papyrus Egerton 5: Christian or Jewish?" *ZPE* 121 (1998): 173–82.

Van der Horst, "Elements." Van der Horst, Pieter W. "Greek Philosophical Elements in Some Judaeo-Christian Prayers." *Sacra Scripta: Journal of the Centre for Biblical Studies* 7 (1, 2009): 55–64.

Van der Horst, "Funerary Inscriptions." Van der Horst, Pieter W. "Jewish Funerary Inscriptions: Most Are in Greek." *BAR* 18 (5, 1992): 46–57.

Van der Horst, "Graf." Van der Horst, Pieter W. "Het graf van de profetes Hulda in de joodse traditie" [The Grave of Hulda, the Prophetess, in Jewish Tradition]. *NedTT* 55 (2, 2001): 91–96.

Van der Horst, "Grafschrift." Van der Horst, Pieter W. "Het grafschrift van Jakobus, de broer van Jezus?" [The Epitaph of James, the Brother of Jesus?] *NedTT* 57 (1, 2003): 1–9.

Van der Horst, "Greek Evidence." Van der Horst, Pieter W. "Neglected Greek Evidence for Early Jewish Liturgical Prayer." *JSJ* 29 (3, 1998): 278–96.

Van der Horst, "Hierocles." Van der Horst, Pieter W. "Hierocles the Stoic and the New Testament." *NovT* 17 (2, 1975): 156–60.

Van der Horst, "Jews of Crete." Van der Horst, Pieter W. "The Jews of Ancient Crete." *JJS* 39 (2, 1988): 183–200.

Van der Horst, "Judaism." Van der Horst, Pieter W. "Judaism in Asia Minor." Pages 321–40 in *The Cambridge History of Religions in Antiquity, Volume II: From the Hellenistic Age to Late Antiquity*. Edited by M. R. Salzman and W. Adler. Cambridge: Cambridge University Press, 2013.

Van der Horst, "Languages." Van der Horst, Pieter W. "The Samaritan Languages in the Pre-Islamic Period." *JSJ* 32 (2, 2001): 178–92.

Van der Horst, "Macrobius." Van der Horst, Pieter W. "Macrobius and the New Testament: A Contribution to the Corpus hellenisticum." *NovT* 15 (3, 1973): 220–32.

Van der Horst, "Maria." Van der Horst, Pieter W. "Maria the Jewish Alchemist." *DNTB* 679–80.

Van der Horst, "Maximus van Tyrus." Van der Horst, Pieter W. "Maximus van Tyrus over het gebed: Een geannoteerde vertaling van Εἰ δεῖ εὔχεσθαι." *NedTT* 49 (1, 1995): 12–23.

Van der Horst, "Musonius." Van der Horst, Pieter W. "Musonius Rufus and the New Testament." *NovT* 16 (4, 1974): 306–15.

Van der Horst, "New Altar?" Van der Horst, Pieter W. "A New Altar of a Godfearer?" *JJS* 43 (1, 1992): 32–37.

Van der Horst, "Nogmaals." Van der Horst, Pieter W. "Nogmaals: Het grafschrift van Jakobus, de broervan Jezus (Once More: The Epitaph of James, Brother of Jesus)." *NedTT* 58 (1, 2004): 18–27.

Van der Horst, "Not Revile." Van der Horst, Pieter W. "'Thou Shalt Not Revile the Gods': The LXX Translation of Ex. 22:28 (27), Its Background and Influence." *SPhilA* 5 (1993): 1–8.

Van der Horst, "Parallels to Acts." Van der Horst, Pieter W. "Hellenistic Parallels to the Acts of the Apostles." *JSNT* 8 (25, 1985): 49–60.

Van der Horst, "Platonist." Van der Horst, Pieter W. "A Pagan Platonist and a Christian Platonist on Suicide (Macrobius and St. Augustine)." *VC* 25 (1971): 282–88.

Van der Horst, "Prayer." Van der Horst, Pieter W. "Silent Prayer in Antiquity." *Numen* 41 (1, 1994): 1–25.

Van der Horst, "Pseudo-Phocylides." Van der Horst, Pieter W. Introduction to "Pseudo-Phocylides." *OTP* 2:565–73.

Van der Horst, "Samaritans and Hellenism." Van der Horst, Pieter W. "Samaritans and Hellenism." *SPhilA* 6 (1994): 28–36.

Van der Horst, "Seven Months' Children." Van der Horst, Pieter W. "Seven Months' Children in Jewish and Christian Literature from Antiquity." *ETL* 54 (4, 1978): 346–60.

Van der Horst, "Shadow." Van der Horst, Pieter W. "Peter's Shadow: The Religio-Historical Background of Acts v.15." *NTS* 23 (2, 1977): 204–12.

Van der Horst, "Unknown God." Van der Horst, Pieter W. "The Altar of the 'Unknown God' in Athens (Acts 17.23) and the Cults of 'Unknown Gods' in the Graeco-Roman World." Pages 165–202 in *Hellenism–Judaism–Christianity: Essays on Their Interaction*, by P. W. van der Horst. 2nd ed. Kampen: Kok Pharos, 1994.

Van der Horst, "Unknown God (2)." Van der Horst, Pieter W. "Unknown God." Pages 882–85 in *Dictionary of Deities and Demons in the Bible*. 2nd rev. ed. Edited by Karel van der Toorn, Bob Becking, and

Pieter W. van der Horst. Leiden: Brill; Grand Rapids: Eerdmans, 1999.

Van der Horst, "Waarachtige." Van der Horst, Pieter W. "'De waarachtige en niet met handen gemaakte God.'" *NedTT* 45 (3, 1991): 177–82.

Van der Horst, "Women in *Liber*." Van der Horst, Pieter W. "Portraits of Biblical Women in Pseudo-Philo's *Liber antiquitatum biblicarum*." *JSP* 5 (1989): 29–46.

Van der Horst, "Women in Testament of Job." Van der Horst, Pieter W. "The Role of Women in the Testament of Job." *NedTT* 40 (4, 1986): 273–89.

Van der Horst, "Zult." Van der Horst, Pieter W. "'Gij zult van goden geen kwaad spreken': De Septuaginta vertaling van Exodus 22:27 (28), haar achtergrond en invloed." *NedTT* 46 (3, 1992): 192–98.

Van der Horst and Newman, *Prayers*. Van der Horst, Pieter W., and Judith H. Newman. *Early Jewish Prayers in Greek*. Commentaries on Early Jewish Literature. Berlin: de Gruyter, 2008.

VanderKam, "Author." VanderKam, James C. "The Putative Author of the Book of Jubilees." *JSS* 26 (2, 1981): 209–17.

VanderKam, "Covenant." VanderKam, James C. "Covenant and Pentecost." *CTJ* 37 (2, 2002): 239–54.

VanderKam, "People." VanderKam, James C. "The People of the Dead Sea Scrolls: Essenes or Sadducees?" *BRev* 7 (2, 1991): 42–47.

VanderKam, "Pronouncement Stories." VanderKam, James C. "Intertestamental Pronouncement Stories." *Semeia* 20 (1981): 65–72.

VanderKam, *Studies in Jubilees*. VanderKam, James C. *Textual and Historical Studies in the Book of Jubilees*. HSM 14. Missoula, Mont.: Scholars Press, 1977.

VanderKam, "Traditions." VanderKam, James C. "Enoch Traditions in Jubilees and Other Second-Century Sources." Pages 229–51 in vol. 1 of *SBL Seminar Papers, 1978*. Edited by Paul J. Achtemeier. 2 vols. SBLSP 13. Missoula, Mont.: Scholars Press, 1978.

VanderKam, "Wisdom." VanderKam, James C. "Mantic Wisdom in the Dead Sea Scrolls." *DSD* 4 (3, 1997): 336–53.

Van der Kooij, "Death of Josiah." Van der Kooij, Arie. "The Death of Josiah according to 1 Esdras." *Textus* 19 (1998): 97–109.

Van der Laan, "Approaches." Van der Laan, Cornelis. "Historical Approaches." Pages 202–19 in *Studying Global Pentecostalism: Theories and Methods*. Edited by Allan Anderson, Michael Bergunder, André Droogers, and Cornelis van der Laan. Berkeley: University of California, 2010.

Van der Loos, *Miracles*. Van der Loos, Hendrik. *The Miracles of Jesus*. NovTSup 9. Leiden: E. J. Brill, 1965.

Vandermarck, "Natural Knowledge." Vandermarck, William. "Natural Knowledge of God in Romans: Patristic and Medieval Interpretation." *TS* 34 (1, 1973): 36–52.

Van der Meer, *Ostia Speaks*. Van der Meer, L. Bouke. *Ostia Speaks: Inscriptions, Buildings and Spaces in Rome's Main Port*. Leeuven: Peeters, 2012.

Van der Minde, "Absonderung." Van der Minde, Hans-Jürgen. "Die Absonderung der Frommen: Die Qumrangemeinschaft als Heiligtum Gottes." *BL* 61 (3, 1988): 190–97.

Van der Ploeg, "Meals." Van der Ploeg, J. "The Meals of the Essenes." *JSS* 2 (1957): 163–75.

Van der Ploeg, *Rouleau*. Van der Ploeg, J., ed. *Le rouleau de la guerre: Traduit et annoté avec une introduction*. STDJ 2. Leiden: Brill, 1959.

Van der Poel, "Use." Van der Poel, Marc. "The Use of *exempla* in Roman Declamation." *Rhetorica* 27 (3, 2009): 332–53.

Vanderpool, "Portraiture." Vanderpool, Catherine de Grazia. "Roman Portraiture: The Many Faces of Corinth." Pages 369–84 in *Corinth: The Centenary, 1896–1996*. Edited by Charles K. Williams II and Nancy Bookidis. Vol. 20 of *Corinth: Results of Excavations Conducted by the American School of Classical Studies at Athens*. Princeton: American School of Classical Studies at Athens, 2003.

Vander Stichele, "Gender." Vander Stichele, Caroline. "Gender and Genre: Acts in/of Interpretation." Pages 311–29 in *Contextualizing Acts: Lukan Narrative and Greco-Roman Discourse*. Edited by Todd Penner and Caroline Vander Stichele. SBLSymS 20. Atlanta: SBL, 2003.

Vander Stichele, "Silence." Vander Stichele, Caroline. "Is Silence Golden? Paul and Women's Speech in Corinth." *LouvS* 20 (2–3, 1995): 241–53.

Van der Stockt, "Hypomnema." Van der Stockt, Luc. "A Plutarchan Hypomnema on Self-Love." *AJP* 120 (4, 1999): 575–99.

Van der Toorn, "Cybele." Van der Toorn, Karel. "Cybele." Pages 214–15 in *Dictionary of Deities and Demons in the Bible*. 2nd rev. ed. Edited by Karel van der Toorn, Bob Becking, and Pieter W. van der Horst. Leiden: Brill; Grand Rapids: Eerdmans, 1999.

Van der Toorn, "Oracle de victoire." Van der Toorn, Karel. "L'oracle de victoire comme expression prophétique au Proche-Orient ancien." *RB* 94 (1987): 63–97.

Van der Toorn, *Religion*. Van der Toorn, Karel. *Family Religion in Babylonia, Syria and Israel: Continuity and Change in the*

Forms of Religious Life. Studies in the History and Culture of the Ancient Near East 7. Leiden: Brill, 1996.

Van der Toorn, "Shepherd." Van der Toorn, Karel. "Shepherd." Pages 770–71 in *Dictionary of Deities and Demons in the Bible*. 2nd rev. ed. Edited by Karel van der Toorn, Bob Becking, and Pieter W. van der Horst. Leiden: Brill; Grand Rapids: Eerdmans, 1999.

Van der Waal, "Temple in Luke." Van der Waal, C. "The Temple in the Gospel according to Luke." *Neot* 7 (1973): 44–59.

Vander Waerdt, "Theory." Vander Waerdt, Paul A. "The Original Theory of Natural Law." *SPhilA* 15 (2003): 17–34.

Van der Woude, "Wicked Priests." Van der Woude, A. S. "Wicked Priest or Wicked Priests? Reflections on the Identification of the Wicked Priest in the Habakkuk Commentary." *JJS* 33 (1–2, 1982): 349–59.

Van de Sandt, "Acts 13, 32–52." Van de Sandt, Huub. "The Quotations in Acts 13, 32–52 as a Reflection of Luke's LXX Interpretation." *Bib* 75 (1, 1994): 26–58.

Van de Sandt, "Acts 15.6–21." Van de Sandt, Huub. "An Explanation of Acts 15.6–21 in the Light of Deuteronomy 4.29–35 (LXX)." *JSNT* 46 (1992): 73–97.

Van de Sandt, "Amos 5, 25–27." Van de Sandt, Huub. "Why Is Amos 5, 25–27 Quoted in Acts 7, 42f.?" *ZNW* 82 (1–2, 1991): 67–87.

Van de Sandt, "Fate of Gentiles." Van de Sandt, Huub. "The Fate of the Gentiles in Joel and Acts 2: An Intertextual Study." *ETL* 66 (1, 1990): 56–77.

Van de Sandt, "No Salvation." Van de Sandt, Huub. "Acts 28,28—No Salvation for the People of Israel? An Answer in the Perspective of the LXX." *ETL* 70 (4, 1994): 341–58.

Van de Sandt, "Presence." Van de Sandt, Huub. "The Presence and Transcendence of God: An Investigation of Acts 7,44–50 in the Light of the LXX." *ETL* 80 (1, 2004): 30–59.

Van de Water, "Moses' Exaltation." Van de Water, Rick. "Moses' Exaltation: Pre-Christian?" *JSP* 21 (2000): 59–69.

Van de Water, "Punishment." Van de Water, Rick. "The Punishment of the Wicked Priest and the Death of Judas." *DSD* 10 (3, 2003): 395–419.

Van Elderen, "Archaeological Observations." Van Elderen, Bastiaan. "Some Archaeological Observations on Paul's First Missionary Journey." Pages 151–61 in *Apostolic History and the Gospel: Essays Presented to F. F. Bruce*. Edited by W. W. Gasque and R. P. Martin. Grand Rapids: Eerdmans, 1970.

Van Elderen, "Glossolalia." Van Elderen, Bastiaan. "Glossolalia in the New Testament." *BETS* 7 (2, 1964): 53–58.

Van Engen, "Peter's Conversion." Van Engen, Charles E. "Peter's Conversion: A Culinary Disaster Launches the Gentile Mission, Acts 10:1–11:18." Pages 133–43 in *Mission in Acts: Ancient Narratives in Contemporary Context*. Edited by Robert L. Gallagher and Paul Hertig. AmSocMissS 34. Maryknoll, N.Y.: Orbis, 2004.

Van Gelder, "Possession." Van Gelder, David W. "A Case of Demon Possession." *JPast Care* 41 (2, 1987): 151–61.

Van Halsema, "Betrouwbaarheid." Van Halsema, J. H. "De historische betrouwbaarheid van het Pinksterverhaal." *NTT* 20 (2, 1966): 218.

Van Henten, "Moses as Messenger." Van Henten, Jan Willem. "Moses as Heavenly Messenger in Assumptio Mosis 10:2 and Qumran Passages." *JJS* 54 (1, 2003): 216–27.

Van Henten, "Prolegomena." Van Henten, Jan Willem. "Einige Prolegomena zum Studien der jüdischen Martyrologie." *Bijdr* 46 (1985): 381–90.

Van Henten, "Python." Van Henten, Jan Willem. "Python." Pages 669–71 in *Dictionary of Deities and Demons in the Bible*. 2nd rev. ed. Edited by Karel van der Toorn, Bob Becking, and Pieter W. van der Horst. Leiden: Brill; Grand Rapids: Eerdmans, 1999.

Van Henten, "Ruler Cult." Van Henten, Jan Willem. "Ruler Cult." Pages 711–16 in *Dictionary of Deities and Demons in the Bible*. 2nd rev. ed. Edited by Karel van der Toorn, Bob Becking, and Pieter W. van der Horst. Leiden: Brill; Grand Rapids: Eerdmans, 1999.

Vanhoozer, *Meaning*. Vanhoozer, Kevin J. *Is There a Meaning in This Text? The Bible, the Reader, and the Morality of Literary Knowledge*. Grand Rapids: Zondervan, 1998.

Vanhoozer, "Meaning." Vanhoozer, Kevin J. "Augustinian Inerrancy: Literary Meaning, Literal Truth, and Literate Interpretation in the Economy of Biblical Discourse." Pages 199–235 in *Five Views on Biblical Inerrancy*. Edited by J. Merrick and Stephen M. Garrett. Grand Rapids: Zondervan, 2013.

Vanhoozer, *Postmodern Theology*. Vanhoozer, Kevin J., ed. *The Cambridge Companion to Postmodern Theology*. Cambridge: Cambridge University Press, 2003.

Vanhoye, "Πίστις Χριστοῦ." Vanhoye, Albert. "Πίστις Χριστοῦ: Fede in Cristo o affidabilità di Cristo?" *Bib* 80 (1, 1999): 1–21.

Vanhoye, "Validità." Vanhoye, Albert. "Salvezza universale nel Cristo e validità dell'antica alleanza." *CCl* 145 (3467, 1994): 433–45.

Vanhoye, "Validité." Vanhoye, Albert. "Salut universel par le Christ et validité de l'ancienne alliance." *NRTh* 116 (6, 1994): 815–35.

Van Koppen and van der Toorn, "Holy One." Van Koppen, Frans, and Karel van der Toorn, "Holy One." Pages 415–18 in *Dictionary of Deities and Demons in the Bible*. 2nd rev. ed. Edited by Karel van der Toorn, Bob Becking, and Pieter W. van der Horst. Leiden: Brill; Grand Rapids: Eerdmans, 1999.

Vann, "Construction." Vann, Lindley. "Herod's Harbor Construction Recovered Underwater." Pages 130–35 in *Archaeology in the World of Herod, Jesus and Paul*. Edited by Hershel Shanks and Dan P. Cole. Vol. 2 in Archaeology and the Bible: The Best of BAR. Washington, D.C.: Biblical Archaeology Society, 1990.

Vanni, "Giorno." Vanni, Ugo. "Il 'giorno del Signore' in Apoc. 1,10, giorno di purificazione e di discernimento." *RivB* 26 (2, 1978): 187–99.

Van Seters, "Historiography." Van Seters, John. "Is There Any Historiography in the Hebrew Bible? A Hebrew-Greek Comparison." *JNSL* 28 (2, 2002): 1–25.

Van Seters, "Primeval Histories." Van Seters, John. "The Primeval Histories of Greece and Israel Compared." *ZAW* 100 (1988): 1–22.

Van Seters, *Search*. Van Seters, John. *In Search of History: Historiography in the Ancient World and the Origins of Biblical History*. New Haven: Yale University Press, 1983.

Vansina, "Afterthoughts." Vansina, Jan. "Afterthoughts on the Historiography of Oral Tradition." Pages 105–10 in *African Historiographies: What History for Which Africa?* Edited by Bogumil Jewsiewicki and David Newbury. SSAMD 12. Beverly Hills, Calif.: Sage, 1986.

Vansina, "Knowledge." Vansina, Jan. "Knowledge and Perceptions of the African Past." Pages 28–41 in *African Historiographies: What History for Which Africa?* Edited by Bogumil Jewsiewicki and David Newbury. SSAMD 12. Beverly Hills, Calif.: Sage, 1986.

Vanstiphout, "Memory." Vanstiphout, Herman. "Memory and Literacy in Ancient Western Asia." Pages 2181–96 in vol. 4 of *Civilizations of the Ancient Near East*. Edited by Jack M. Sasson. 4 vols. New York: Scribner's, 1995.

Van Til, "Credo." Van Til, Cornelius. "My Credo." Pages 1–21 in *Jerusalem and Athens: Critical Discussions on the Theology and Apologetics of Cornelius Van Til*. Edited by E. R. Geehan. Nutley, N.J.: Presbyterian and Reformed, 1971.

Van Unnik, "'Acts' and Confirmation." Van Unnik, W. C. "The 'Book of Acts' and the

Confirmation of the Gospel." *NovT* 4 (1, 1960): 26–59.

Van Unnik, "Anathema." Van Unnik, W. C. "Jesus: Anathema or Kyrios (1 Cor. 12:3)." Pages 113–26 in *Christ and Spirit in the New Testament: Studies in Honor of C. F. D. Moule*. Edited by Barnabas Lindars and Stephen S. Smalley. Cambridge: Cambridge University Press, 1973.

Van Unnik, "Befehl an Philippus." Van Unnik, W. C. "Der Befehl an Philippus." *ZNW* 47 (1956): 181–91. Repr., pages 328–39 in vol. 1 of *Sparsa collecta: The Collected Essays of W. C. van Unnik*. 3 vols. NovTSup 29–31. Leiden: Brill, 1973–83.

Van Unnik, "Book and Historiography." Van Unnik, W. C. "Luke's Second Book and the Rules of Hellenistic Historiography." Pages 37–60 in *Les Actes des apôtres: Traditions, rédaction, théologie*. Edited by Jacob Kremer. BETL 48. Gembloux, Belg.: J. Duculot; Leuven: Leuven University Press, 1979.

Van Unnik, "Once More Prologue." Van Unnik, W. C. "Once More St. Luke's Prologue." *Neot* 7 (1973): 7–26.

Van Unnik, "Storm Center." Van Unnik, W. C. "Luke-Acts, a Storm Center in Contemporary Scholarship." Pages 15–32 in *Studies in Luke-Acts: Essays in Honor of Paul Schubert*. Edited by Leander E. Keck and J. Louis Martyn. Nashville: Abingdon, 1966.

Van Unnik, *Tarsus*. Van Unnik, W. C. *Tarsus or Jerusalem: The City of Paul's Youth*. Translated by George Ogg. London: Epworth, 1962.

Van Unnik, "Teaching of Good Works." Van Unnik, W. C. "The Teaching of Good Works in 1 Peter." *NTS* 1 (2, 1954): 92–110.

Van Veldhuizen, "Model of Philanthropia." Van Veldhuizen, Milo. "Moses: A Model of Hellenistic Philanthropia." *RefR* 38 (3, 1985): 215–24.

Van Voorst, *Jesus*. Van Voorst, Robert E. *Jesus outside the New Testament: An Introduction to the Ancient Evidence*. Grand Rapids: Eerdmans, 2000.

Van Wickevoort Crommelin, "Euphrates." Van Wickevoort Crommelin, Bernhard. "Euphrates Frontier (Roman)." *BrillPauly* 5:188–89.

Vardaman, "Chronology." Vardaman, E. Jerry. "A Provisional Chronology of the New Testament: Jesus through Paul's Early Years." Pages 313–19 in *Chronos, Kairos, Christos, II: Chronological, Nativity, and Religious Studies in Memory of Ray Summers*. Edited by E. Jerry Vardaman. Macon, Ga.: Mercer University Press, 1998.

Vardaman, "Lectures." Vardaman, E. Jerry. "Chronology and Early Church History

in the New Testament." Three lectures, Hong Kong Baptist Theological Seminary, June 15–29, 1998. (Cited by lecture and pages.)

Vardaman, "Life." Vardaman, E. Jerry. "Jesus' Life: A New Chronology." Pages 55–82 in *Chronos, Kairos, Christos: Nativity and Chronological Studies Presented to Jack Finegan*. Edited by Jerry Vardaman and Edwin M. Yamauchi. Winona Lake, Ind.: Eisenbrauns, 1989.

Vardaman, "Solution." Vardaman, E. Jerry. "Lysanias and Quirinius: A New Solution through Micrographics." Unpublished paper sent to Jack Finegan, Jan. 29, 1975.

Varickasseril, "Portrait." Varickasseril, Jose. "The Lukan Portrait of the Early Church: A Study of the Major Summaries in the Acts of the Apostles." *MissT* 7 (1, 2005): 40–50.

Varickasseril, "Prayer." Varickasseril, Jose. "Prayer and Ministry in the Acts of the Apostles." *MissT* 10 (4, 2008): 300–321.

Varickasseril, "Shepherding." Varickasseril, Jose. "Shepherding through Teaching: Pastoral Reflections on the Acts of the Apostles." *MissT* 8 (3, 2006): 214–26.

Varo Pineda, "Hacia." Varo Pineda, Francisco. "Hacia una 'nueva' lectura cristiana de la Biblia." *EstBib* 66 (1–4, 2008): 195–215.

Vasaly, "Characterization." Vasaly, Ann. "Characterization and Complexity: Caesar, Sallust, and Livy." Pages 245–60 in *The Cambridge Companion to the Roman Historians*. Edited by Andrew Feldherr. Cambridge: Cambridge University Press, 2009.

Vassiliadis, "Equality." Vassiliadis, Petros. "Equality and Justice in Classical Antiquity and in Paul: The Social Implications of the Pauline Collection." *SVTQ* 36 (1–2, 1992): 51–59.

Vattuone, "Historiography." Vattuone, Riccardo. "Western Greek Historiography." Pages 189–99 in *A Companion to Greek and Roman Historiography*. Edited by John Marincola. 2 vols. Oxford: Blackwell, 2007.

Vatuk, "Reference." Vatuk, Sylvia. "Reference, Address, and Fictive Kinship in Urban North India." *Ethnology* 8 (3, 1969): 255–72.

Vatuk, "Trends." Vatuk, Sylvia J. "Trends in North Indian Urban Kinship: The 'Matrilateral Assymetry' Hypothesis." *SWJA* 27 (3, Autumn 1971): 287–307.

Veenhof, "Libraries." Veenhof, Klaas R. "Libraries and Archives." *OEANE* 3:351–57.

Veghazi, "Imitación." Veghazi, Esteban N. "La idea de la 'imitación de Dios' en el judaísme." *RevistB* 41 (1979): 91–95.

Velankanni, "Eucharist." Velankanni, Francis. "The Eucharist and Table Fellowship in the New Testament." *East Asian PastRev* 44 (2, 2007): 147–64.

Veldkamp, *Farmer*. Veldkamp, Herman. *The Farmer from Tekoa*. Saint Catherines, Ont.: Paideia, 1977.

Vellanickal, *Sonship*. Vellanickal, Matthew. *The Divine Sonship of Christians in the Johannine Writings*. AnBib 72. Rome: Biblical Institute Press, 1977.

Veltman, "Defense Speeches." Veltman, Fred. "The Defense Speeches of Paul in Acts." Pages 243–56 in *Perspectives on Luke-Acts*. ABPRSSS 5. Edited by Charles H. Talbert. Danville, Va.: Association of Baptist Professors of Religion; Edinburgh: T&T Clark, 1978.

Veltri, "Loanwords." Veltri, Giuseppe. "Greek Loanwords in the Palestinian Talmud: Some New Suggestions." *JSS* 47 (2, 2002): 237–40.

Venetz, "Frauen." Venetz, Hermann-Josef. "Frauen von Rang und Namen: Ein anderer Blick in paulinische Gemeinden." *BK* 57 (3, 2002): 127–33.

Venit, "Tomb." Venit, Marjorie Susan. "The Stagni Painted Tomb: Cultural Interchange and Gender Differentiation in Roman Alexandria." *AJA* 103 (4, 1999): 641–69.

Venter, *Reconciliation*. Venter, Alexander. *Doing Reconciliation: Racism, Reconciliation, and Transformation in the Church and World*. Cape Town: Vineyard International, 2004.

Venter, "Reviewing History." Venter, P. M. "Reviewing History in Apocalyptic Literature as Ideological Strategy." *HTS/TS* 60 (3, 2004): 703–23.

Verbaal, "End of Liberty." Verbaal, Wim. "Cicero and Dionysios the Elder, or the End of Liberty." *CW* 99 (2, 2006): 145–56.

Verger, "Trance." Verger, Pierre. "Trance and Convention in Nago-Yoruba Spirit Mediumship." Pages 50–66 in *Spirit Mediumship and Society in Africa*. Edited by John Beattie and John Middleton. Foreword by Raymond Firth. New York: Africana, 1969.

Verheyden, "Source(s) of Luke 21." Verheyden, Joseph. "The Source(s) of Luke 21." Pages 491–516 in *L'Évangile de Luc: The Gospel of Luke*. Edited by F. Neirynck. Rev. ed. BETL 32. Leuven: Leuven University Press, 1989.

Verheyden, *Unity*. Verheyden, Joseph, ed. *The Unity of Luke-Acts*. BETL 142. Leuven: Leuven University Press, 1999.

Verheyden, "Unity." Verheyden, Joseph. "The Unity of Luke-Acts." *ETL* 74 (4, 1998): 516–26.

Verheyden, "Unity of Luke-Acts." Verheyden, Joseph. "The Unity of Luke-Acts." *HTS/TS* 55 (4, 1999): 964–79.

Verheyden, "What Are We Up To?" Verheyden, Joseph. "The Unity of Luke-Acts: What Are We Up To?" Pages 3–56 in *The Unity of Luke-Acts*. Edited by Joseph Verheyden. BETL 142. Leuven: Leuven University Press, 1999.

Verhoef, "Paulines." Verhoef, Eduard. "Pseudepigraphic Paulines in the New Testament." *HTS/TS* 59 (3, 2003): 991–1005.

Verhoef, "Pseudepigraphy." Verhoef, Eduard. "Pseudepigraphy and Canon." *BN* 106 (2001): 90–98.

Verhoef, "Reacted." Verhoef, Eduard. "Christians Reacted Differently to Non-Christian Cults." *HTS/TS* 67 (1, 2011): 804, seven pages.

Verhoef, "Syncretism." Verhoef, Eduard. "Syncretism in the Church of Philippi." *HTS/TS* 64 (2, 2008): 697–714.

Verlaguet, "Mystique." Verlaguet, Waltraud. "La mystique de Paul—le Paul des mystiques." *FoiVie* 105 (4, 2006): 53–70.

Verman and Adler, "Path Jumping." Verman, Mark, and Shulamit H. Adler. "Path Jumping in the Jewish Magical Tradition." *JSQ* 1 (2, 1993–94): 131–48.

Vermaseren, *Corpus*. Vermaseren, Maarten J. *Corpus cultus Cybelae Attidisque*. Leiden: Brill, 1977.

Vermaseren, *Cybele*. Vermaseren, Maarten J. *Cybele and Attis: The Myth and the Cult*. Translated by A. H. H. Lemmers. London: Thames & Hudson, 1977.

Vermes, "Elements." Vermes, Geza. "Historiographical Elements in the Qumran Writings: A Synopsis of the Textual Evidence." *JJS* 58 (1, 2007): 121–39.

Vermes, "Forum." Vermes, Geza. "The Oxford Forum for Qumran Research: Seminar on the Rule of War from Cave 4 (4Q285)." *JJS* 43 (1, 1992): 85–94.

Vermes, "Halakah." Vermes, Geza. "Sectarian Matrimonial Halakah in the Damascus Rule." *JJS* 25 (1, 1974): 197–202.

Vermes, "Hanina." Vermes, Geza. "Hanina ben Dosa: A Controversial Galilean Saint from the First Century of the Christian Era." *JJS* 23 (1, 1972): 28–50; 24 (1, 1973): 51–64.

Vermes, "Interpretation." Vermes, Geza. "The Qumran Interpretation of Scripture in Its Historical Setting." *ALUOS* 6 (1966–68): 84–97.

Vermes, *Jesus and Judaism*. Vermes, Geza. *Jesus and the World of Judaism*. London: SCM, 1983. Philadelphia: Fortress, 1984.

Vermes, *Jesus the Jew*. Vermes, Geza. *Jesus the Jew: A Historian's Reading of the Gospels*. Philadelphia: Fortress, 1973.

Vermes, "Jesus the Jew." Vermes, Geza. "Jesus the Jew." Pages 108–22 in *Jesus' Jewishness: Exploring the Place of Jesus within Early Judaism*. Edited by James H. Charlesworth. Philadelphia: American Interfaith Institute; New York: Crossroad, 1991.

Vermes, "Notice." Vermes, Geza. "The Jesus Notice of Josephus Re-examined." *JJS* 38 (1, 1987): 1–10.

Vermes, "Pierced Messiah." Vermes, Geza. "The 'Pierced Messiah' Text—An Interpretation Evaporates." *BAR* 18 (4, 1992): 80–82.

Vermes, *Religion*. Vermes, Geza. *The Religion of Jesus the Jew*. Minneapolis: Augsburg Fortress, 1993.

Vermes, *Scrolls*. Vermes, Geza, ed. *The Dead Sea Scrolls in English*. 2nd ed. New York: Penguin, 1981.

Vermes, *Scrolls in Perspective*. Vermes, Geza, with Pamela Vermes. *The Dead Sea Scrolls: Qumran in Perspective*. Rev. ed. Philadelphia: Fortress, 1977.

Vermeule, *Art*. Vermeule, Cornelius C. *Roman Imperial Art in Greece and Asia Minor*. Cambridge, Mass.: Harvard University Press, 1968.

Verner, *Household*. Verner, David C. *The Household of God: The Social World of the Pastoral Epistles*. SBLDS 71. Chico, Calif.: Scholars Press, 1983.

Versnel, "Amulets." Versnel, H. S. "Amulets." *OCD³* 78.

Versnel, "Deisidaimonia." Versnel, H. S. "Deisidaimonia." *OCD³* 441.

Versnel, "Devotio." Versnel, H. S. "Devotio." *BrillPauly* 4:327–29.

Versnel, "Devotio 1." Versnel, H. S. "Devotio 1." *OCD³* 460.

Versnel, "Herring?" Versnel, H. S. "Red (Herring?): Comments on a New Theory concerning the Origin of the Triumph." *Numen* 53 (3, 2006): 290–326.

Versnel, "Miracles." Versnel, H. S. "Miracles." *OCD³* 989.

Versnel, "Prayer." Versnel, H. S. "Prayer." *OCD³* 1242–43.

Versnel, "Sin." Versnel, H. S. "Sin." *OCD³* 1410–11.

Versnel, "Votum." Versnel, H. S. "Votum." *OCD³* 1613.

Verstraete, "Slavery." Verstraete, Beert C. "Slavery and the Social Dynamics of Male Homosexuality Relations in Ancient Rome." *JHom* 5 (3, 1980): 227–36.

Vervenne, "Blood." Vervenne, Marc. "'The Blood Is the Life and the Life Is the Blood': Blood as Symbol of Life and Death in Biblical Tradition (Gen. 9,4)." Pages 451–70 in *Ritual and Sacrifice in the Ancient Near East*. Edited by Jan Quaegebeur. OLA 55. Leuven: Peeters, 1993.

Via, *Kerygma and Comedy*. Via, Dan O. *Kerygma and Comedy in the New Testament: A Structuralist Approach to Hermeneutic*. Philadelphia: Fortress, 1975.

Via, "Moses and Meaning." Via, Jane E. "Moses and Meaning in Luke-Acts: A Redaction-Critical Analysis of Acts 7:35–37." PhD diss., Marquette University, 1976.

Vicastillo, "Hermanos." Vicastillo, Salvador. "Los hermanos de Jesús en el testimonio de Tertuliano." *RevAg* 47 (144, 2006): 621–23.

Vicent Cernuda, "Desvaído." Vicent Cernuda, A. "El desvaído Lázaro y el deslumbrador discípulo amado." *EstBib* 52 (4, 1994): 453–516.

Vickers, "Hellenistic Thessaloniki." Vickers, Michael J. "Hellenistic Thessaloniki." *JHS* 92 (1972): 156–70.

Victor, "Testimonium." Victor, Ulrich. "Das Testimonium Flavianum: Ein authentischer Text des Josephus." *NovT* 52 (1, 2010): 72–82.

Victor, "Wechsel der Tempora." Victor, Ulrich. "Der Wechsel der Tempora in griechischen erzählenden Texten mit besonderer Berücksichtigung der Apostelgeschichte." Pages 27–57 in *Die Apostelgeschichte und die hellenistische Geschichtsschreibung: Festschrift für Eckhard Plümacher zu seinem 65. Geburtstag*. Edited by Cilliers Breytenbach and Jens Schröter. Leiden: Brill, 2004.

Vidler, *Revolution*. Vidler, Alec R. *The Church in an Age of Revolution: 1789 to the Present Day*. Penguin History of the Church 5. London: Penguin, 1974.

Vielhauer, "Paulinism." Vielhauer, Philipp. "On the 'Paulinism' of Acts." Pages 33–50 in *Studies in Luke-Acts: Essays in Honor of Paul Schubert*. Edited by Leander E. Keck and J. Louis Martyn. Nashville: Abingdon, 1966.

Vilbert, "Origines." Vilbert, Jean-Claude. "Aux origines d'une condamnation: L'homosexualité dans la Rome antique et l'Église des premiers siècles." *LVit* 29 (147, 1980): 15–28.

Viljoen, "Intercessor." Viljoen, François P. "Jesus as Intercessor in Luke-Acts." *APB* 19 (2008): 329–49.

Villalón, "Deux messies." Villalón, José R. "Sources vétéro-testamentaires de la doctrine qumranienne des deux messies." *RevQ* 8 (29/1, 1972): 53–63.

Villemin, "Ecclésiologie." Villemin, Laurent. "Les Actes des apôtres dans l'ecclésiologie de Vatican II." Pages 213–30 in *Les Actes des apôtres—Histoire, récit, théologie: XXe congrès de l'Association catholique française pour l'étude de la Bible (Angers, 2003)*. Edited by Michel Berder. LD 199. Paris: Cerf, 2005.

Villiers, "Church Rule." Villiers, J. L. de. "Indications of Church Rule or Government in Pauline Parenetic Material," in "Ministry in the Pauline Letters: Proceedings of the Twelfth Meeting of 'Die Nawe-Testamentiese-Werkgemeenskap van Suid-Afrika.'" Special Issue, *Neot* 10 (1976): 69–80.

Villiers, "Peace." Villiers, Pieter G. R. de. "Peace in Luke and Acts: A Perspective on Biblical Spirituality." *APB* 19 (2008): 110–34.

Villiers and Germiquet, *"Religio."* Villiers, Pieter G. R. de, and Eddie A. Germiquet. *"Religio* and *superstitio* in Early Christianity and Graeco-Roman Society: Christian Perspectives on Paganism." *APB* 9 (1998): 52–69.

Villiers and Germiquet, "Superstition." Villiers, Pieter G. R. de, and Eddie A. Germiquet. "Paul and Paganism in Acts 17: Superstition in Early Christianity and Graeco-Roman Society." *APB* 9 (1998): 35–51.

Vinagre, "Terminologie." Vinagre, Miguel A. "Die griechische Terminologie der Traumdeutung." *Mnemosyne* 49 (3, 1996): 257–82.

Vincent, *Philippians, Philemon.* Vincent, Marvin R. *A Critical and Exegetical Commentary on the Epistles to the Philippians and to Philemon.* ICC. Edinburgh: T&T Clark, 1897.

Vincent, "Sociology." Vincent, Mike. "How God Shapes Society: The Sociology of Miracles in Modern Christianity." Bachelor of Arts in sociology senior thesis, Princeton University, 2010.

Vine, "Purpose and Date." Vine, Victor E. "The Purpose and Date of Acts." *ExpT* 96 (2, 1984): 45–48.

Vinson, "Enthymemes." Vinson, Richard B. "A Comparative Study of the Use of Enthymemes in the Synoptic Gospels." Pages 119–41 in *Persuasive Artistry: Studies in New Testament Rhetoric in Honor of George A. Kennedy.* Edited by Duane F. Watson. JSNTSup 50. Sheffield, U.K.: Sheffield Academic, 1991.

Vinson, "Touch." Vinson, Richard B. "The Minas Touch: Anti-Kingship Rhetoric in the Gospel of Luke." *PRSt* 35 (1, 2008): 69–86.

Visser, "Lycaon." Visser, Edzard. "Lycaon." *BrillPauly* 7:909–10.

Vivante, "Authors." Vivante, Bella Zweig. "Women Authors: Greece." *BrillPauly* 15:710–13.

Vivian, "Movimenti." Vivian, A. "I movimenti che si oppongono al tempio: Il problema del sacerdozio di Melchisedeq." *Hen* 14 (1–2, 1992): 97–112.

Viviano, "Beatitudes." Viviano, Benedict T. "Beatitudes Found among Dead Sea Scrolls." *BAR* 18 (6, 1992): 53–55, 66.

Viviano, "Publication." Viviano, Benedict T. "Eight Beatitudes at Qumran and in Matthew? A New Publication from Cave Four." *SEÅ* 58 (1993): 71–84.

Viviano, "Qumran." Viviano, Benedict T. "Eight Beatitudes from Qumran." *BibT* 31 (4, 1993): 219–24.

Viviano, "State." Viviano, Benedict Thomas. "The Christian and the State in Acts and Paul (Acts 25,16 and Rom 13,1–7): Roman Fairness Revisited." Pages 227–38 in *Reception of Paulinism in Acts. Réception du Paulinisme dans les Actes des Apôtres.* Edited by Daniel Marguerat. BETL 229. Leuven: Peeters, 2009.

Viviano and Taylor, "Sadducees, Angels, and Resurrection." Viviano, Benedict T., and Justin Taylor. "Sadducees, Angels, and Resurrection (Acts 23:8–9)." *JBL* 111 (3, 1992): 496–98.

Vivier, "Glossolalic." Vivier, Lincoln M. "The Glossolalic and His Personality." Pages 153–75 in *Beiträge zur Ekstase.* Edited by Theodor Spoerri. BPN 134. Basel: S. Karger, 1968.

Vliet, *No Single Testimony.* Vliet, Hendrik van. *No Single Testimony: A Study of the Adoption of the Law of Deut. 19:5 par. into the New Testament.* Utrecht, Neth.: Kemink, 1958.

Vogel, *Contra Apionem."* Vogel, Manuel. "Josephus' *Contra Apionem* und der antike Antijudaismus." *BK* 53 (2, 1998): 79–83.

Vogel, *Pythagoras.* Vogel, Cornelia J. de. *Pythagoras and Early Pythagoreanism: An Interpretation of Neglected Evidence on the Philosopher Pythagoras.* Assen, Neth.: Van Gorcum, 1966.

Vogel, "Traumdarstellungen." Vogel, Manuel. "Traumdarstellungen bei Josephus und Lukas." Pages 130–56 in *Die Apostelgeschichte im Kontext antiker und frühchristlicher Historiographie.* Edited by Jörg Frey, Clare K. Rothschild, and Jens Schröter, with Bettina Rost. BZNWK 162. Berlin: de Gruyter, 2009.

Vogel, "Vita 64–69." Vogel, Manuel. "Vita 64–69, das Bilderverbot, und die Galiläapolitik des Josephus." *JSJ* 30 (1, 1999): 65–79.

Vogt, "Brutes." Vogt, Katja Maria. "Sons of the Earth: Are the Stoics Metaphysical Brutes?" *Phronesis* 54 (2, 2009): 136–54.

Vogt, "Tempel." Vogt, Ernest. "Vom Tempel zum Felsendom." *Bib* 55 (1, 1974): 23–64.

Völkl, "Lapidation." Völkl, Artur. "Lapidation." *BrillPauly* 7:239.

Völkl, "Perjury." Völkl, Artur. "Perjury." *BrillPauly* 10:805.

Vorster, "Blessedness." Vorster, Willem S. "Stoics and Early Christians on Blessedness." Pages 38–51 in *Greeks, Romans, and Christians: Essays in Honor of Abraham J. Malherbe.* Edited by David L. Balch, Everett Ferguson, and Wayne A. Meeks. Minneapolis: Fortress, 1990.

Vos, "Apis." Vos, Richard L. "Apis." Pages 68–72 in *Dictionary of Deities and Demons in the Bible.* 2nd rev. ed. Edited by Karel van der Toorn, Bob Becking, and Pieter W. van der Horst. Leiden: Brill; Grand Rapids: Eerdmans, 1999.

Vos, "Change." Vos, Craig S. de. "The Significance of the Change from οἶκος to οἰκία in Luke's Account of the Philippian Gaoler (Acts 16:30–4)." *NTS* 41 (2, 1995): 292–96.

Vos, "Charge." Vos, Craig S. de. "Finding a Charge That Fits: The Accusation against Paul and Silas at Philippi (Acts 16.19–21)." *JSNT* 74 (1999): 51–63.

Vos, *Conflicts.* Vos, Craig S. de. *Church and Community Conflicts: The Relationships of the Thessalonian, Corinthian, and Philippian Churches with Their Wider Civic Communities.* SBLDS 168. Atlanta: Scholars Press, 1999.

Vos, "Cos." Vos, Howard F. "Cos." *ISBE* 1:785–86.

Voss, "Consilium." Voss, Wulf Eckart. "Consilium." *BrillPauly* 3:702–3.

Vössing, "Archive." Vössing, Konrad. "Archive." *BrillPauly* 1:1023–27.

Vössing, "Libraries." Vössing, Konrad. "Libraries: Greece, Rome, Christian Libraries." *BrillPauly* 7:504–11.

"Voting Records." "Voting Records." *Forum* 3 (1, 2000): 207–15.

Vouga, "Paradoxie." Vouga, François. "Die Paradoxie des Evangeliums in der modernen Kultur: Apg 17,22–31." Pages 171–91 in *Die Apostelgeschichte und die hellenistische Geschichtsschreibung: Festschrift für Eckhard Plümacher zu seinem 65. Geburtstag.* Edited by Cilliers Breytenbach and Jens Schröter. Leiden: Brill, 2004.

Vout, "Emperor." Vout, Caroline. "Representing the Emperor." Pages 261–75 in *The Cambridge Companion to the Roman Historians.* Edited by Andrew Feldherr. Cambridge: Cambridge University Press, 2009.

Vout, "Myth." Vout, Caroline. "The Myth of the Toga: Understanding the History of Roman Dress." *GR* 43 (2, 1996): 204–20.

Waard, "Acts 3, 22.23 and Text." Waard, Jan de. "The Quotation from Deuteronomy in Acts 3, 22.23 and the Palestinian Text: Additional Arguments." *Bib* 52 (4, 1971): 537–40.

Waard and Smalley, *Handbook*. Waard, Jan de, and William Smalley. *A Translator's Handbook on the Book of Amos.* New York: United Bible Societies, 1979.

Waardt, "Witchcraft." Waardt, Hans de. "Dutch Witchcraft in the Sixteenth and Seventeenth Centuries." *SocG* 36 (3–4, 1989): 224–44.

Wacholder, "Nicolaus." Wacholder, Ben Zion. "Josephus and Nicolaus of Damascus." Pages 147–72 in *Josephus, the Bible, and History.* Edited by Louis H. Feldman and Gohei Hata. Detroit: Wayne State University Press, 1989.

Wacholder, "Teacher." Wacholder, Ben Zion. "Who Is the Teacher of Righteousness?" *BRev* 15 (2, 1999): 26–29.

Wachsmann and Haldane, "Anchors." Wachsmann, Shelley, and Douglas Haldane. "Anchors." *OEANE* 1:137–40.

Wacht, "Gütergemeinschaft." Wacht, Manfred. "Gütergemeinschaft." Pages 1–59 in vol. 13 of *Reallexikon für Antike und Christentum.* Edited by Franz Dolger et al. Stuttgart: Hiersemann, 1950–.

Wächter, "Astrologie." Wächter, Ludwig. "Astrologie und Schicksalsglaube im rabbinischen Judentum." *Kairos* 11 (3, 1969): 181–200.

Wächter, "Messianismus." Wächter, Ludwig. "Jüdischer und christlichen Messianismus." *Kairos* 18 (2, 1976): 119–34.

Wackenheim, "Babel." Wackenheim, Charles. "De Babel à Pentecôte." *LumVie* 58 (281, 2009): 47–56.

Wacker, *Heaven.* Wacker, Grant. *Heaven Below: Early Pentecostals and American Culture.* Cambridge, Mass.: Harvard University Press, 2001.

Wacker, "Living." Wacker, Grant. "Living with Signs and Wonders: Parents and Children in Early Pentecostal Culture." Pages 423–42 in *Signs, Wonders, Miracles: Representations of Divine Power in the Life of the Church. Papers Read at the 2003 Summer Meeting and the 2004 Winter Meeting of the Ecclesiastical History Society.* Edited by Kate Cooper and Jeremy Gregory. Rochester, N.Y.: Boydell & Brewer, for the Ecclesiastical History Society, 2005.

Wade, "Gods." Wade, Martha. "Beware of Multiple Gods—A Note on Acts 3.13." *BTr* 58 (4, 2007): 200–202.

Wade, "Son of Man." Wade, Loron. "'Son of Man' Comes to the Judgment in Daniel 7:13." *JATS* 11 (1–2, 2000): 277–81.

Wade, "Translating." Wade, Martha L. "'We Did What?': Problems in Translating the 'We' Passages of Acts in the Apal Language." *BTr* 60 (2, 2009): 93–99.

Wade-Gery, "Thucydides." Wade-Gery, Henry Theodore. "Thucydides." *OCD³* 1516–19.

Wagenaar, "Kumba." Wagenaar, Hinne. "Babel, Jerusalem, and Kumba: Missiological Reflections on Genesis 11:1–9 and Acts 2:1–13." *IntRevMiss* 92 (366, 2003): 406–21.

Wagner, *Acts.* Wagner, C. Peter. *The Acts of the Holy Spirit: A Modern Commentary on the Book of Acts.* Ventura, Calif.: Regal, 2000.

Wagner, *Baptism.* Wagner, Günter. *Pauline Baptism and the Pagan Mysteries: The Problem of the Pauline Doctrine of Baptism in Romans VI.1–11, in Light of Its Religiohistorical "Parallels."* Translated by J. P. Smith. Edinburgh: Oliver & Boyd, 1967.

Wagner, *Bibliography.* Wagner, Günter. *An Exegetical Bibliography of the New Testament: Luke and Acts.* Macon, Ga.: Mercer University Press, 1985.

Wagner, "Divine Femaleness." Wagner, Walter. "Divine Femaleness: Two Second-Century Contributions." *JRelS* 17 (1–2, 1991): 19–43.

Wagner, *Heralds.* Wagner, J. Ross. *Heralds of the Good News: Isaiah and Paul "In Concert" in the Letter to the Romans.* Leiden: Brill, 2002.

Wagner, "Paul and Scripture." Wagner, J. Ross. "Paul and Scripture." Pages 154–71 in *The Blackwell Companion to Paul.* Edited by Stephen Westerholm. BCompRel. Oxford: Blackwell, 2011.

Wagner, "Perspective." Wagner, C. Peter. "A Church Growth Perspective on Pentecostal Missions." Pages 265–84 in *Called and Empowered: Global Mission in Pentecostal Perspective.* Edited by Murray A. Dempster, Byron D. Klaus, and Douglas Petersen. Peabody, Mass.: Hendrickson, 1991.

Wagner, *Wave.* Wagner, C. Peter. *The Third Wave of the Holy Spirit.* Ann Arbor: Vine, 1988.

Wagner and Lotfi, "Learning." Wagner, Daniel A., and Abdelhamid Lotfi. "Learning to Read by 'Rote.'" *IJSocLang* 42 (1983): 111–21.

Wagner-Hasel, "Hospitality." Wagner-Hasel, Beate. "Hospitality: Greece and Rome." *BrillPauly* 6:529–32.

Wagner-Hasel, "Roles: Greece." Wagner-Hasel, Beate. "Gender Roles: Greece." *BrillPauly* 5:740–43.

Wahlde, "Acts 4, 24–31." Wahlde, Urban C. von. "Acts 4,24–31: The Prayer of the Apostles in Response to the Persecution of Peter and John—and Its Consequences." *Bib* 77 (2, 1996): 237–44.

Wahlde, "Archaeology." Wahlde, Urban C. von. "Archaeology and John's Gospel." Pages 523–86 in *Jesus and Archaeology.*

Edited by James H. Charlesworth. Grand Rapids: Eerdmans, 2006.

Wahlde, "Assessment of Persecution." Wahlde, Urban C. von. "The Theological Assessment of the First Christian Persecution: The Apostles' Prayer and Its Consequences in Acts 4, 24–31." *Bib* 76 (4, 1995): 523–31.

Wahlde, "Jews." Von Wahlde, Urban C. "The Johannine 'Jews': A Critical Survey." *NTS* 28 (1, Jan. 1982): 33–60.

Wahlen, "Vision." Wahlen, Clinton. "Peter's Vision and Conflicting Definitions of Purity." *NTS* 51 (4, 2005): 505–18.

Währisch-Oblau, "Healthy." Währisch-Oblau, Claudia. "God Can Make Us Healthy Through and Through: On Prayers for the Sick and the Interpretation of Healing Experiences in Christian Churches in China and African Immigrant Congregations in Germany." *Int RevMiss* 90 (356–57, 2001): 87–102.

Wainwright, "Pyramid." Wainwright, J. A. "Zoser's Pyramid and Solomon's Temple." *ExpT* 91 (5, 1980): 137–40.

Wainwright, "Silas." Wainwright, Allan. "Where Did Silas Go? (And What Was His Connection with *Galatians*?)" *JSNT* 8 (1980): 66–70.

Walaskay, *Acts.* Walaskay, Paul W. *Acts.* WestBC. Louisville: Westminster John Knox, 1998.

Walaskay, *Came to Rome.* Walaskay, Paul W. *"And So We Came to Rome": The Political Perspective of St Luke.* SNTSMS 49. Cambridge: Cambridge University Press, 1983.

Walbank, "Aspects of Coinage." Walbank, Mary E. Hoskins. "Aspects of Corinthian Coinage in the Late 1st and Early 2nd Centuries A.C." Pages 337–48 in *Corinth: The Centenary, 1896–1996.* Edited by Charles K. Williams II and Nancy Bookidis. Vol. 20 of *Corinth: Results of Excavations Conducted by the American School of Classical Studies at Athens.* Princeton: American School of Classical Studies at Athens, 2003.

Walbank, "Fortune." Walbank, Frank W. "Fortune (*tychē*) in Polybius." Pages 349–55 in *A Companion to Greek and Roman Historiography.* Edited by John Marincola. 2 vols. Oxford: Blackwell, 2007.

Walbank, "Foundation." Walbank, Mary E. Hoskins. "The Foundation and Planning of Early Roman Corinth." *JRA* 10 (1997): 95–130.

Walbank, "Graves." Walbank, Mary E. Hoskins. "Unquiet Graves: Burial Practices of the Roman Corinthians." Pages 249–80 in *Urban Religion in Roman Corinth: Interdisciplinary Approaches.* Edited by Daniel N. Schowalter and

Steven J. Friesen. HTS 53. Cambridge, Mass.: Harvard University Press, 2005.

Walbank, *Papers*. Walbank, Frank W. *Selected Papers: Studies in Greek and Roman History and Historiography*. Cambridge: Cambridge University Press, 1985.

Walbank, *Speeches*. Walbank, F. W. *Speeches in Greek Historians*. J. L. Myres Memorial Lecture 3. Oxford: Blackwell, 1965.

Walbank, "Tragedy." Walbank, Frank W. "History and Tragedy." *Historia* 9 (1960): 216–34.

Walcot, "Widows." Walcot, Peter. "On Widows and Their Reputation in Antiquity." *SO* 66 (1991): 5–26.

Walde, "Dreams." Walde, Christine. "Dreams, Interpretation of Dreams: Classical Antiquity." *BrillPauly* 4:715–19.

Walde, "Irony." Walde, Christine. "Irony: Rhetoric." *BrillPauly* 6:943–44.

Walde, "Metamorphosis." Walde, Christine. "Metamorphosis." *BrillPauly* 8:783–85.

Walde, "Mnemonics." Walde, Christine. "Mnemonics." *BrillPauly* 9:96–97.

Walde, "Muses." Walde, Christine. "Muses." *BrillPauly* 9:322–25.

Walde, "Nyx." Walde, Christine. "Nyx." *BrillPauly* 9:931–32.

Walde, "Pathos." Walde, Christine. "Pathos." *BrillPauly* 10:599–600.

Walker, "Acts and Corpus Reconsidered." Walker, William O., Jr. "Acts and the Pauline Corpus Reconsidered." *JSNT* 24 (1985): 3–23.

Walker, "Acts and Corpus Revisited." Walker, William O., Jr. "Acts and the Pauline Corpus Revisited: Peter's Speech at the Jerusalem Conference." Pages 77–86 in *Literary Studies in Luke-Acts: Essays in Honor of Joseph B. Tyson*. Edited by Richard P. Thompson and Thomas E. Phillips. Macon, Ga.: Mercer University Press, 1998.

Walker, "Benefactor." Walker, Donald D. "Benefactor." *DNTB* 157–59.

Walker, "Concept." Walker, William O., Jr. "The Origin of the Son of Man Concept as Applied to Jesus." Pages 156–65 in *The Bible in Its Literary Milieu*. Edited by Vincent L. Tollers and John R. Maier. Grand Rapids: Eerdmans, 1979.

Walker, "Disagion." Walker, Norman. "Disagion versus Trisagion, a Copyist Defended." *NTS* 7 (2, 1961): 170–71.

Walker, "*Enargeia*." Walker, Andrew D. "*Enargeia* and the Spectator in Greek Historiography." *TAPA* 123 (1993): 353–77.

Walker, "Harrist Church." Walker, Sheila Suzanne. "Christianity African Style: The Harrist Church of the Ivory Coast." PhD diss., University of Chicago, 1976.

Walker, "Hours." Walker, Norman. "The Reckoning of Hours in the Fourth Gospel." *NovT* 4 (1, 1960): 69–73.

Walker, "Origin of Concept." Walker, William O., Jr. "The Origin of the Son of Man Concept as Applied to Jesus." *JBL* 91 (4, 1972): 482–90.

Walker, "Pauline Letters." Walker, William O. "Acts and the Pauline Letters: A Select Bibliography with Introduction." *Forum* 5 (1, 2002): 105–15.

Walker, "Paulinization." Walker, William O., Jr. "The 'Paulinization' of Peter in the Book of Acts." *FourR* 22 (3, 2009): 9–12, 14.

Walker, "Paul's Views." Walker, William O., Jr. "1 Corinthians 11:2–16 and Paul's Views regarding Women." *JBL* 94 (1, 1975): 94–110.

Walker, "Portrayal." Walker, William O., Jr. "The Portrayal of Aquila and Priscilla in Acts: The Question of Sources." *NTS* 54 (4, 2008): 479–95.

Walker, "Propaganda." Walker, D. P. "Demonic Possession Used as Propaganda in the Later 16th Century." Pages 283–94 in *Possession and Exorcism*. Vol. 9 of *Articles on Witchcraft, Magic, and Demonology: A Twelve-Volume Anthology of Scholarly Articles*. Edited by Brian P. Levack. New York: Garland, 1992. Reprinted from pages 237–48 in *Scienze, Credenze Occulte Livelli di Cultura*. Florence: Olschki, 1982.

Walker, *Revolution*. Walker, Sheila Suzanne. *The Religious Revolution in the Ivory Coast: The Prophet Harris and His Church*. Chapel Hill: University of North Carolina Press, 1983.

Walker, "Thrice-Holy." Walker, Norman. "The Origin of the 'Thrice-Holy.'" *NTS* 5 (2, 1959), 132–33.

Walker and Dickerman, "Influence." Walker, Anita M., and Edmund H. Dickerman. "'A Woman under the Influence': A Case of Alleged Possession in Sixteenth-Century France." Pages 183–202 in *Possession and Exorcism*. Vol. 9 of *Articles on Witchcraft, Magic, and Demonology: A Twelve-Volume Anthology of Scholarly Articles*. Edited by Brian P. Levack. New York: Garland, 1992.

Wall, "Acts." Wall, Robert W. "The Acts of the Apostles." *NIB* 10:1–368.

Wall, "Canonical Context." Wall, Robert W. "The Acts of the Apostles in Canonical Context." *BTB* 18 (1988): 16–24.

Wall, "Comment(ary)ing." Wall, Robert W. "Comment(ary)ing on Acts." Paper presented at the annual meeting of the SBL, Philadelphia, Nov. 21, 2005.

Wall, "Function." Wall, Robert W. "The Function of LXX Habakkuk 1:5 in the Book of Acts." *BBR* 10 (2, 2000): 247–58.

Wall, "Intertextuality." Wall, Robert W. "Intertextuality, Biblical." *DNTB* 541–51.

Wall, "'Son' of Jonah." Wall, Robert W. "Peter, 'Son' of Jonah: The Conversion of Cornelius in the Context of the Canon." *JSNT* 29 (1987): 79–90.

Wall, "Successors to 'Twelve.'" Wall, Robert W. "Successors to 'the Twelve' according to Acts 12:1–17." *CBQ* 53 (4, 1991): 628–43.

Wall, "Waiting." Wall, Robert W. "Waiting on the Holy Spirit (Acts 1.4): Extending a Metaphor to Biblical Interpretation." *JPT* 22 (1, 2013): 37–53.

Wallace, *Grammar*. Wallace, Daniel B. *Greek Grammar beyond the Basics: An Exegetical Syntax of the New Testament*. Grand Rapids: Zondervan, 1996.

Wallace, *Miracles*. Wallace, Ronald S. *The Gospel Miracles: Studies in Matthew, Mark, and Luke*. Grand Rapids: Eerdmans, 1960.

Wallace, *Urban Environment*. Wallace, Samuel E. *The Urban Environment*. Homewood, Ill.: Dorsey, 1980.

Wallace and Williams, *Acts*. Wallace, Richard, and Wynne Williams. *The Acts of the Apostles: A Companion*. Bristol: Bristol Classical, 1993.

Wallace and Williams, *Worlds*. Wallace, Richard, and Wynne Williams. *The Three Worlds of Paul of Tarsus*. London: Routledge, 1998.

Wallace-Hadrill, "*Domus*." Wallace-Hadrill, Andrew. "*Domus* and *insulae* in Rome: Families and Housefuls." Pages 3–18 in *Early Christian Families in Context: An Interdisciplinary Dialogue*. Edited by David L. Balch and Carolyn Osiek. Grand Rapids and Cambridge: Eerdmans, 2003.

Wallace-Hadrill, *Houses*. Wallace-Hadrill, Andrew. *Houses and Society in Pompeii and Herculaneum*. Princeton: Princeton University Press, 1994.

Wallinga, "Poseidonios." Wallinga, H. T. "Poseidonios on Beating to Windward (*FGH* 87F46 and Related Passages)." *Mnemosyne* 53 (4, 2000): 431–47.

Wallis, "Conscience." Wallis, Richard T. "The Idea of Conscience in Philo of Alexandria." *Studia philonica* 3 (1974–75): 27–40.

Wallis, *Conscience in Philo*. Wallis, Richard T. *The Idea of Conscience in Philo of Alexandria*. PSCC 13. Berkeley, Calif.: Center for Hermeneutical Studies in Hellenistic and Modern Culture, 1975.

Walsh, *Dictionary*. Walsh, Michael, ed. *Dictionary of Christian Biography*. Collegeville, Minn.: Liturgical Press, 2001.

Walsh, *Livy*. Walsh, P. G. *Livy: Historical Aims and Methods*. Cambridge: Cambridge University Press, 1961.

Walsh, "Reconstructing." Walsh, Richard. "Reconstructing the New Testament Churches: The Place of Acts." Pages 309–25 in *With Steadfast Purpose: Essays on Acts in Honor of Henry Jackson Flanders, Jr.* Edited by Naymond H. Keathley. Waco: Baylor University Press, 1990.

Walsh, *Shamanism*. Walsh, Roger. *The World of Shamanism: New Views of an Ancient Tradition*. Woodbury, Minn.: Llewellyn Publications, 2007.

Walsh, "Signs." Walsh, Tim. "'Signs and Wonders That Lie': Unlikely Polemical Outbursts Against the Early Pentecostal Movement in Britain." Pages 410–22 in *Signs, Wonders, Miracles: Representations of Divine Power in the Life of the Church. Papers Read at the 2003 Summer Meeting and the 2004 Winter Meeting of the Ecclesiastical History Society*. Edited by Kate Cooper and Jeremy Gregory. Rochester, N.Y.: Boydell & Brewer, for the Ecclesiastical History Society, 2005.

Walsh et al., "Transcendence." Walsh, James W., et al. "Spiritual Transcendence and Religious Practices in Recovery from Pathological Gambling: Reducing Pain or Enhancing Quality of Life?" *RSSSR* 18 (2007): 155–75.

Walter, "Apostelgeschichte 6.1" Walter, Nikolaus. "Apostelgeschichte 6.1 und die Anfänge der Urgemeinde in Jerusalem." *NTS* 29 (3, 1983): 370–93.

Walter, "Periods." Walter, Uwe. "Periods, division into." *BrillPauly* 10:791–96.

Walter, "Proselyt aus Antiochien." Walter, Nikolaus. "Nikolaos, Proselyt aus Antiochien, und die Nikolaiten in Ephesus und Pergamon: Ein Beitrag auch zum Thema Paulus und Ephesus." *ZNW* 93 (3–4, 2002): 200–226.

Walters, "Adoption." Walters, James C. "Paul, Adoption, and Inheritance." Pages 42–76 in *Paul in the Greco-Roman World: A Handbook*. Edited by J. Paul Sampley. Harrisburg, Pa.: Trinity Press International, 2003.

Walters, "Civic Identity." Walters, James C. "Civic Identity in Roman Corinth and Its Impact on Early Christians." Pages 397–417 in *Urban Religion in Roman Corinth: Interdisciplinary Approaches*. Edited by Daniel N. Schowalter and Steven J. Friesen. HTS 53. Cambridge, Mass.: Harvard University Press, 2005.

Walters, "Egyptian Religions." Walters, James C. "Egyptian Religions in Ephesos." Pages 281–309 in *Ephesos, Metropolis of Asia: An Interdisciplinary Approach to Its Archaeology, Religion, and Culture*. Edited by Helmut Koester. HTS. Valley Forge, Pa.: Trinity Press International, 1995.

Walters, "Impact." Walters, James C. "Romans, Jews, and Christians: The Impact of the Romans on Jewish/Christian Relations in First-Century Rome." Pages 175–95 in *Judaism and Christianity in First-Century Rome*. Edited by Karl P. Donfried and Peter Richardson. Grand Rapids: Eerdmans, 1998.

Walters, *Unity*. Walters, Patricia. *The Assumed Authorial Unity of Luke and Acts. A Reassessment of the Evidence*. SNTSMS 145. Cambridge: Cambridge University Press, 2009.

Walton, "Acts." Walton, Steve. "Acts." Pages 27–31 in *Dictionary for the Theological Interpretation of the Bible*. Edited by Kevin J. Vanhoozer. London: SPCK; Grand Rapids: Baker Academic, 2005.

Walton, "Acts of God." Walton, Steve. "The Acts—of God? What Is the 'Acts of the Apostles' All About?" *EvQ* 80 (4, 2008): 291–306.

Walton, "Beginning." Walton, Steve. "Where Does the Beginning of Acts End?" Pages 447–67 in *The Unity of Luke-Acts*. Edited by Joseph Verheyden. BETL 142. Leuven: Leuven University Press, 1999.

Walton, "Communism." Walton, Steve. "Primitive Communism in Acts? Does Acts Present the Community of Goods (2:44–45; 4:32–35) as Mistaken?" *EvQ* 80 (2, 2008): 99–111.

Walton, *Genesis*. Walton, John H. *Genesis*. NIVAC. Grand Rapids: Zondervan, 2001.

Walton, "Genesis." Walton, John H. "Genesis." Pages 2–159 in vol. 1 of *Zondervan Illustrated Bible Backgrounds Commentary: Old Testament*. Edited by John Walton. 5 vols. Grand Rapids: Zondervan, 2009.

Walton, *Leadership*. Walton, Steve. *Leadership and Lifestyle: The Portrait of Paul in the Miletus Speech and 1 Thessalonians*. SNTSMS 108. Cambridge: Cambridge University Press, 2000.

Walton, "Mission." Walton, Steve. "What Does 'Mission' in Acts Mean in Relation to the 'Powers That Be'?" *JETS* 55 (3, Sept. 2012): 537–56.

Walton, "Ὁμοθυμαδόν." Walton, Steve. "Ὁμοθυμαδόν in Acts: Co-location, Common Action, or 'of One Heart and Mind'?" Pages 89–105 in *The New Testament in Its First Century Setting: Essays on Context and Background in Honour of B. W. Winter on His 65th Birthday*. Edited by P. J. Williams et al. Grand Rapids: Eerdmans, 2004.

Walton, "Perspectives." Walton, Steve. "A Tale of Two Perspectives? The Place of the Temple in Acts." Pages 135–49 in *Heaven on Earth: The Temple in Biblical Theology*. Edited by T. Desmond Alexander and Simon Gathercole. Waynesboro, Ga.: Paternoster, 2004.

Walton, "Sandas." Walton, Francis Redding. "Sandas." *OCD³* 1353.

Walton, "Spirituality." Walton, Steve. "A Spirituality of Acts?" Pages 186–200 in *Reading Acts Today: Essays in Honour of Loveday C. A. Alexander*. Edited by Steve Walton et al. LNTS 427. London: T&T Clark, 2011.

Walton, "State." Walton, Steve. "The State They Were In: Luke's View of the Roman Empire." Pages 1–41 in *Rome in the Bible and the Early Church*. Edited by Peter Oakes. Carlisle, U.K.: Paternoster; Grand Rapids: Baker, 2002.

Walton, "Suicide." Walton, Richard E. "Socrates' Alleged Suicide." *JValInq* 14 (1980): 287–300.

Walton, "Trying Paul." Walton, Steve. "Trying Paul or Trying Rome? Judges and Accused in the Roman Trials of Paul in Acts." Pages 122–41 in *Luke-Acts and Empire: Essays in Honor of Robert L. Brawley*. Edited by David Rhoads, David Esterline, and Jae Won Lee. PrTMS 151. Eugene, Ore.: Pickwick, 2011.

Walton and Sandy, *World*. Walton, John H., and D. Brent Sandy. *The Lost World of Scripture: Ancient Literary Culture and Biblical Authority*. Downers Grove, Ill.: IVP Academic, 2013.

Walton, Matthews, and Chavalas, *Background Commentary*. Walton, John H., Victor H. Matthews, and Mark W. Chavalas. *The IVP Bible Background Commentary: Old Testament*. Downers Grove, Ill.: InterVarsity, 2000.

Walvoord, *Revelation*. Walvoord, John F. *The Revelation of Jesus Christ: A Commentary*. Chicago: Moody, 1966.

Walz, "Cursing." Walz, Craig A. "The Cursing Paul: Magical Contexts in Acts 13 and the New Testament Apocrypha, Acts 13:6–12." Pages 167–82 in *Mission in Acts: Ancient Narratives in Contemporary Context*. Edited by Robert L. Gallagher and Paul Hertig. AmSocMissS 34. Maryknoll, N.Y.: Orbis, 2004.

Wambacq, "Possibilité." Wambacq, B. N. "Matthieu 5,31–32: Possibilité de divorce ou obligation de rompre une union illégitime." *NRTh* 104 (1982): 34–49.

Wanamaker, "Agent." Wanamaker, Charles A. "Christ as Divine Agent in Paul." *SJT* 39 (4, 1986): 517–28.

Wanamaker, *Thessalonians*. Wanamaker, Charles A. *The Epistles to the Thessalonians*. NIGTC. Grand Rapids: Eerdmans, 1990.

Wandrey, "Iosephus." Wandrey, Irina. "Iosephus Flavius." *BrillPauly* 6:920–22.

Wandrey, "Literature: Jewish-Hellenistic." Wandrey, Irina. "Literature: Jewish-Hellenistic." *BrillPauly* 7:694–99.

Wansink, "Law." Wansink, Craig S. "Roman Law and Legal System." *DNTB* 984–91.

Ward, *Amos*. Ward, James M. *Amos and Isaiah: Prophets of the Word of God.* Nashville: Abingdon, 1969.

Ward, "Baths." Ward, Roy Bowen. "Women in Roman Baths." *HTR* 85 (2, 1992): 125–47.

Ward, "Believing." Ward, Keith. "Believing in Miracles." *Zyg* 37 (3, 2002): 741–50.

Ward, "Latinisms." Ward, J. S. "Roman Greek: Latinisms in the Greek of Flavius Josephus." *CQ* 57 (2, 2007): 632–49.

Ward, "Miracles and Testimony." Ward, Keith. "Miracles and Testimony." *RelS* 21 (1985): 134–45.

Ward, "Musonius." Ward, Roy Bowen. "Musonius and Paul on Marriage." *NTS* 36 (2, 1990): 281–89.

Ward, "Possession." Ward, Colleen A. "Possession and Exorcism: Psychopathology and Psychotherapy in a Magico-Religious Context." Pages 125–44 in *Altered States of Consciousness and Mental Health: A Cross-Cultural Perspective.* Edited by Colleen A. Ward. CCRMS 12. Newbury Park, Calif.: Sage, 1989.

Ward, "Tyre." Ward, William A. "Tyre." *OEANE* 5:247–50.

Ward and Beaubrun, "Possession." Ward, Colleen, and Michael H. Beaubrun. "Spirit Possession and Neuroticism in a West Indian Pentecostal Community." *BSClinPsyc* 20 (4, 1981): 295–96.

Ward and Beaubrun, "Psychodynamics." Ward, Colleen, and Michael H. Beaubrun. "The Psychodynamics of Demon Possession." *JSSR* 19 (1980): 201–7.

Wardle, "Blame Game." Wardle, David. "The Blame Game: An Aspect of Handling Military Defeat in the Early Principate." *Hermes* 139 (1, 2011): 42–50.

Wardle, "Caligula and Client Kings." Wardle, David. "Caligula and the Client Kings." *CQ* 42 (2, 1992): 437–43.

Wardle, *Valerius Maximus*. David Wardle, ed. and trans. *Valerius Maximus: Memorable Deeds and Sayings.* Oxford: Clarendon, 1998.

Wardy, "Eleatic Pluralism." Wardy, Robert B. B. "Eleatic Pluralism." *AGP* 70 (1988): 125–46.

Ware, *Synopsis*. Ware, James P. *Synopsis of the Pauline Letters in Greek and English.* Grand Rapids: Baker Academic, 2010.

Warmington, "Taurus Range." Warmington, Eric Herbert. "Taurus Mountain Range." *OCD*³ 1477.

Warmington and Hornblower, "Europe." Warmington, Eric Herbert, and Simon Hornblower. "Europe." *OCD*³ 574.

Warmington and Millett, "Thule." Warmington, Eric Herbert, and Martin J. Millett. "Thule." *OCD*³ 1521–22.

Warmington and Salles, "Red Sea." Warmington, Eric Herbert, and Jean-François Salles. "Red Sea." *OCD*³ 1296–97.

Warmington and Wilson, "Africa, Roman." Warmington, Brian Herbert, and Roger J. A. Wilson. "Africa, Roman." *OCD*³ 34–35.

Warnecke, *Romfahrt des Paulus*. Warnecke, Heinz. *Die tatsächliche Romfahrt des Apostels Paulus.* SBS 127. Stuttgart: Katholisches Bibelwerk, 1987.

Warner, *Evangelist*. Warner, Wayne E. *The Woman Evangelist: The Life and Times of Charismatic Evangelist Maria B. Woodworth-Etter.* Studies in Evangelicalism 8. Metuchen, N.J.: Scarecrow, 1986.

Warner, *Kuhlman*. Warner, Wayne E. *Kathryn Kuhlman: The Woman behind the Miracles.* Ann Arbor: Servant, 1993.

Warner, "Living by Faith." Warner, Wayne E. "'Living by Faith': A Story of Paul and Betty Wells." *Assemblies of God Heritage* 16 (4, 1996–97): 3–4, 24.

Warner, "Still Healed." Warner, Wayne E. "Still Healed of TB—after 52 years." *Pentecostal Evangel* (July 8, 2001): 28.

Warner, "Witchcraft." Warner, Richard. "Witchcraft and Soul Loss: Implications for Community Psychiatry." *HCPsy* 28 (9, 1977): 686–90.

Warren, "Diogenes *Epikourios*." Warren, James. "Diogenes *Epikourios*: Keep Taking the Tablets." *JHS* 120 (2000): 144–48.

Warren, "Lucretius." Warren, James. "Lucretius, Symmetry Arguments, and Fearing Death." *Phronesis* 46 (4, 2001): 466–91.

Warren, "Pleasure." Warren, James. "Pleasure, Plutarch's *Non posse* and Plato's *Republic*." *CQ* 61 (1, 2011): 278–93.

Warren, "Trisagion." Warren, A. L. "A Trisagion Inserted in the 4QSamª Version of the Song of Hannah, 1 Sam. 2:1–10." *JJS* 45 (2, 1994): 278–85.

Warrington, *Discovering*. Warrington, Keith. *Discovering the Holy Spirit in the New Testament.* Peabody, Mass.: Hendrickson, 2005.

Warrington, *Healer*. Warrington, Keith. *Jesus the Healer: Paradigm or Unique Phenomenon?* Carlisle, U.K., and Waynesboro, Ga.: Paternoster, 2000.

Warrington, "Healing." Warrington, Keith. "Healing and Suffering in the Bible." *Int RevMiss* 95 (376–77, 2006): 154–65.

Warrington, "Healing Narratives." Warrington, Keith. "Acts and the Healing Narratives: Why?" *JPT* 14 (2, 2006): 189–217.

Warrington, "Response." Warrington, Keith. "A Response to James Shelton concerning Jesus and Healing: Yesterday and Today." *JPT* 15 (2, 2007): 185–93.

Warrington, "Suffering." Warrington, Keith. "Suffering and the Spirit in Luke-Acts." *JBPRes* 1 (Fall 2009): 15–32.

"Wars over Water?" "Next, Wars over Water?" *WPR* (Nov. 1995): 8–13.

Wartke, "Pitch." Wartke, Ralf-B. "Pitch: I. Ancient Orient and Egypt." *BrillPauly* 11:303–4.

Washington, *Fellowship*. Washington, James Melvin. *Frustrated Fellowship: The Black Baptist Quest for Social Power.* Macon, Ga.: Mercer University Press, 1986.

Wasserberg, "Lk-Apg als Paulusapologie." Wasserberg, Günter. "Lk-Apg als Paulusapologie." Pages 723–29 in *The Unity of Luke-Acts.* Edited by Joseph Verheyden. BETL 142. Leuven: Leuven University Press, 1999.

Wasserstein, "Non-hellenized Jews." Wasserstein, Abraham. "Non-hellenized Jews in the Semi-hellenized East." *SCI* 14 (1995): 111–37.

Wasson, Hofmann, and Ruck, *Eleusis*. Wasson, Robert Gordon, Albert Hofmann, and Carl A. Ruck. *The Road to Eleusis: Unveiling the Secret of the Mysteries.* New York: Harcourt Brace Jovanovich, 1978.

"Water: Medicine." "Water: The First and Best Medicine." *World Vision Partners* (Spring 1994).

Waterman, "Sources." Waterman, G. Henry. "The Sources of Paul's Teaching on the Second Coming of Christ in 1 and 2 Thessalonians." *JETS* 18 (2, 1975): 105–13.

Waters, *Justification*. Waters, Guy Prentiss. *Justification and the New Perspectives on Paul: A Review and Response.* Phillipsburg, N.J.: P&R, 2004.

Watson, "Bathe." Watson, Nigel M. "'The Philosopher Should Bathe and Brush His Teeth'—Congruence between Word and Deed in Graeco-Roman Philosophy and Paul's Letters to the Corinthians." *ABR* 42 (1994): 1–16.

Watson, "Blastus." Watson, Jo Ann Ford. "Blastus." *ABD* 1:753.

Watson, "Boasting." Watson, Duane F. "Paul and Boasting." Pages 77–100 in *Paul in the Greco-Roman World: A Handbook.* Edited by J. Paul Sampley. Harrisburg, Pa.: Trinity Press International, 2003.

Watson, "Cities." Watson, Duane F. "Cities, Greco-Roman." *DNTB* 212–15.

Watson, "Collection." Watson, Deborah Elaine. "Paul's Collection in Light of Motivations and Mechanisms for Aid to the Poor in the First-Century World." PhD diss., University of Durham, 2006.

Watson, "Diatribe." Watson, Duane F. "Diatribe." *DPL* 213–14.

Watson, "Education." Watson, Duane F. "Education: Jewish and Greco-Roman." *DNTB* 308–13.

Watson, "Faith." Watson, Francis. "By Faith (of Christ): An Exegetical Dilemma and Its Scriptural Solution." Pages 147–63 in *The Faith of Jesus Christ: Exegetical, Biblical, and Theological Studies*. Edited by Michael F. Bird and Preston M. Sprinkle. Foreword by James D. G. Dunn. Milton Keynes: Paternoster; Peabody, Mass.: Hendrickson, 2009.

Watson, *Gentiles*. Watson, Francis. *Paul, Judaism, and the Gentiles: Beyond the New Perspective*. Rev. ed. Grand Rapids: Eerdmans, 2007.

Watson, "Greece and Macedon." Watson, Duane F. "Greece and Macedon." *DNTB* 421–26.

Watson, "Identity." Watson, Francis. "The Triune Divine Identity: Reflections on Pauline God-Language, in Disagreement with J. D. G. Dunn." *JSNT* 80 (2000): 99–124.

Watson, "Invective." Watson, Lindsay Cameron. "Invective." *OCD*³ 762.

Watson, "Natural Law." Watson, Gerard. "The Natural Law and Stoicism." Pages 216–38 in *Problems in Stoicism*. Edited by A. A. Long. London: Athlone, 1971.

Watson, "Painful Letter." Watson, Francis. "2 Cor. x–xiii and Paul's Painful Letter to the Corinthians." *JTS* 35 (2, 1984): 324–46.

Watson, "Rhetorical Questions." Watson, Duane F. "1 Corinthians 10:23–11:1 in the Light of Greco-Roman Rhetoric: The Role of Rhetorical Questions." *JBL* 108 (2, 1989): 301–18.

Watson, *Second Corinthians*. Watson, Nigel. *The Second Epistle to the Corinthians*. Epworth Commentaries. London: Epworth, 1993.

Watson, "Slave Law." Watson, Alan. "Roman Slave Law and Romanist Ideology." *Phoenix* 37 (1, 1983): 53–65.

Watson, "Speech." Watson, Duane F. "Paul's Speech to the Ephesian Elders (Acts 20.17–38): Epideictic Rhetoric of Farewell." Pages 184–208 in *Persuasive Artistry: Studies in New Testament Rhetoric in Honor of George A. Kennedy*. Edited by Duane F. Watson. JSNTSup 50. Sheffield, U.K.: Sheffield Academic, 1991.

Watson and Spawforth, "Sacramentum." Watson, George Ronald, and Antony J. S. Spawforth. "Sacramentum (Military)." *OCD*³ 1343.

Watts, "Exodus Imagery." Watts, Rikk E. "Exodus Imagery." Pages 205–14 in *Dictionary of the Old Testament Prophets*. Edited by Mark J. Boda and J. Gordon McConville. Downers Grove, Ill.: IVP Academic, 2012.

Watts, "Seneca on Slavery." Watts, William. "Seneca on Slavery." *DRev* 90 (300, 1972): 183–95.

Wayman, "Meaning." Wayman, Alex. "The Religious Meaning of Possession States (with Indo-Tibetan Emphasis)." Pages 167–79 in *Trance and Possession States: Proceedings of the Second Annual Conference, R. M. Bucke Memorial Society, March 4–6, 1966*. Edited by Raymond Prince. Montreal: R. M. Bucke Memorial Society, 1968.

Wcela, "Messiah(s)." Wcela, Emil A. "The Messiah(s) of Qumrân." *CBQ* 26 (3, 1964): 340–49.

Weatherly, "Purpose." Weatherly, Jon A. "The Writer's versus the Reader's Purpose: Interpreting Acts Theologically." *SCJ* 5 (1, 2002): 93–113.

Weatherly, *Responsibility*. Weatherly, Jon A. *Jewish Responsibility for the Death of Jesus in Luke-Acts*. JSNTSup 106. Sheffield, U.K.: JSOT Press, 1994.

Weaver, *Epiphany*. Weaver, John B. *Plots of Epiphany: Prison-Escape in Acts of the Apostles*. BZNW 131. Berlin: de Gruyter, 2004.

Weaver, *Familia*. Weaver, P. R. C. *Familia Caesaris: A Social Study of the Emperor's Freedmen and Slaves*. Cambridge: Cambridge University Press, 1972.

Weaver, "P. Oxy. 3312." Weaver, Paul. "P. Oxy. 3312 and Joining the Household of Caesar." *ZPE* 149 (2004): 196–204.

Weaver, "Status." Weaver, P. R. C. "The Status of Children in Mixed Marriages." Pages 145–69 in *The Family in Ancient Rome: New Perspectives*. Edited by Beryl Rawson. Ithaca, N.Y.: Cornell University Press, 1986.

Webb, *Baptizer*. Webb, Robert L. *John the Baptizer and Prophet: A Socio-historical Study*. JSNTSup 62. Sheffield, U.K.: JSOT Press, 1991.

Webb, "John." Webb, Robert L. "John the Baptist and His Relationship to Jesus." Pages 179–229 in *Studying the Historical Jesus: Evaluations of the State of Current Research*. Edited by Bruce Chilton and Craig A. Evans. NTTS 19. Leiden: Brill, 1994.

Webb, *Slaves*. Webb, William J. *Slaves, Women, and Homosexuals: Exploring the Hermeneutics of Cultural Analysis*. Foreword by Darrell L. Bock. Downers Grove, Ill.: InterVarsity, 2001.

Webber, "Heathen So Arrogant." Webber, Randall C. "'Why Were the Heathen So Arrogant?' The Socio-rhetorical Strategy of Acts 3–4." *BTB* 22 (1, 1992): 19–25.

Webber, "Note." Webber, Randall C. "A Note on 1 Corinthians 15:3–5." *JETS* 26 (3, 1983): 265–69.

Weber, *Sociology*. Weber, Max. *The Agrarian Sociology of Ancient Civilizations*. Translated by R. I. Frank. London: New Left, 1976.

Webster, "Creolizing." Webster, Jane. "Creolizing the Roman Provinces." *AJA* 105 (2, 2001): 209–25.

Webster, "Terrors." Webster, Robert. "'Those Distracting Terrors of the Enemy': Demonic Possession and Exorcism in the Thought of John Wesley." *BJRL* 85 (2/3, 2003): 373–85.

Wedderburn, "'Apostolic Decree': Redaction." Wedderburn, A. J. M. "The 'Apostolic Decree': Tradition and Redaction." *NovT* 35 (4, 1993): 362–89.

Wedderburn, *Beyond Resurrection*. Wedderburn, A. J. M. *Beyond Resurrection*. London: SCM; Peabody, Mass.: Hendrickson, 1999.

Wedderburn, "Collection." Wedderburn, A. J. M. "Paul's Collection: Chronology and History." *NTS* 48 (1, 2002): 95–110.

Wedderburn, "Redaction in Acts 2.1–13." Wedderburn, A. J. M. "Traditions and Redaction in Acts 2.1–13." *JSNT* 55 (1994): 27–54.

Wedderburn, "'We'-Passages." Wedderburn, A. J. M. "The 'We'-Passages in Acts: On the Horns of a Dilemma." *ZNW* 93 (1–2, 2002): 78–98.

Weeber, "Environment." Weeber, Karl-Wilhelm. "Environment, Environmental Behavior." *BrillPauly* 4:1002–8.

Weeber, "Travels." Weeber, Karl-Wilhelm. "Travels." *BrillPauly* 14:869–79.

Weeden, *Mark*. Weeden, Theodore J., Sr. *Mark—Traditions in Conflict*. Philadelphia: Fortress, 1971.

Weeden, "Theory." Weeden, Theodore J. "Kenneth Bailey's Theory of Oral Tradition: A Theory Contested by Its Evidence." *JSHJ* 7 (1, 2009): 3–43.

Weeks, "Medicine." Weeks, Kent. "Medicine, Surgery, and Public Health in Ancient Egypt." Pages 1787–98 in vol. 3 of *Civilizations of the Ancient Near East*. Edited by Jack M. Sasson. 4 vols. New York: Scribner's, 1995.

Weems, "Reflections." Weems, Renita J. "Womanist Reflections on Biblical Hermeneutics." Pages 216–24 in vol. 2 of *Black Theology: A Documentary History*. Edited by James H. Cone and Gayraud S. Wilmore. 2 vols. Maryknoll, N.Y.: Orbis, 1993.

Wegner, *Chattel*. Wegner, Judith Romney. *Chattel or Person? The Status of Women in the Mishnah*. New York: Oxford University Press, 1988.

Wegner, "Tragelaphos." Wegner, Judith Romney. "Tragelaphos Revisted: The

Anomaly of Woman in the Mishnah." *Judaism* 37 (2, 1988): 160–72.

Wehnert, "Gestrandet." Wehnert, Jürgen. "Gestrandet: Zu einer neuen These über den Schiffbruch des Apostels Paulus auf dem Wege nach Rom (Apg 27–28)." *ZTK* 87 (1, 1990): 67–99.

Wehnert, "Insel Kephallenia." Wehnert, Jürgen. "'. . . Und da erfuhren wir, dass die Insel Kephallenia heisst': Zur neuesten Auslegung von Apg 27–28 und ihrer Methode." *ZTK* 88 (2, 1991): 169–80.

Wehnert, *Wir-Passagen*. Wehnert, Jürgen. *Die Wir-Passagen der Apostelgeschichte: Ein lukanisches Stilmittel aus jüdischer Tradition*. Göttingen: Vandenhoeck & Ruprecht, 1989.

Weima, "Aristotle." Weima, Jeffrey A. D. "What Does Aristotle Have to Do with Paul? An Evaluation of Rhetorical Criticism." *CTJ* 32 (2, 1997): 458–68.

Weima, *Endings*. Weima, Jeffrey A. D. *Neglected Endings: The Significance of the Pauline Letter Closings*. JSNTSup 101. Sheffield, U.K.: JSOT Press, 1994.

Weima, "Evaluation." Weima, Jeffrey A. D. "The Function of the Law in Relation to Sin: An Evaluation of the View of H. Räisänen." *NovT* 32 (3, 1990): 219–35.

Weima, "Letters." Weima, Jeffrey A. D. "Letters, Greco-Roman." *DNTB* 640–44.

Weima, "Peace." Weima, Jeffrey D. "'Peace and Security' (1 Thess 5.3): Prophetic Warning or Political Propaganda?" *NTS* 58 (2012): 331–59.

Weima, "Theory." Weima, Jeffrey A. D. "Epistolary Theory." *DNTB* 327–30.

Weima, *Thessalonians*. Weima, Jeffrey A. D. *1–2 Thessalonians*. BECNT. Grand Rapids: Baker Academic, 2014.

Weinert, "Luke, Stephen, and Temple." Weinert, Francis D. "Luke, Stephen, and the Temple in Luke-Acts." *BTB* 17 (3, 1987): 88–90.

Weinert, "Meaning of Temple." Weinert, Francis D. "The Meaning of the Temple in Luke-Acts." *BTB* 11 (3, 1981): 85–89.

Weinfeld, "Covenant Making." Weinfeld, Moshe. "Covenant Making in Anatolia and Mesopotamia." *JANESCU* 22 (1993): 135–39.

Weinfeld, "Giving of Law." Weinfeld, Moshe. "Pentecost as a Festival of the Giving of the Law." *Imm* 8 (1978): 7–18.

Weinfeld, "Grace." Weinfeld, Moshe. "Grace after Meals in Qumran." *JBL* 111 (3, 1992): 427–40.

Weinfeld, "Patterns." Weinfeld, Moshe. "Ancient Near Eastern Patterns in Prophetic Literature." *VT* 27 (Apr. 1977): 178–95.

Weisberg, "Desirable but Dangerous." Weisberg, Dvora. "Desirable but Dangerous:

Rabbis' Daughters in the Babylonian Talmud." *HUCA* 75 (2004): 121–61.

Weiser, *Apostelgeschichte*. Weiser, Alfons. *Die Apostelgeschichte*. 2 vols. ÖKTNT 5. Gütersloh: Mohn, 1981–85.

Weiser, *Psalms*. Weiser, Artur. *The Psalms: A Commentary*. Translated by Herbert Hartwell. Philadelphia: Westminster, 1962.

Weisgerber, "Mining." Weisgerber, Gerd. "Mining." *BrillPauly* 9:5–9.

Weisman and Hackett, "Predilection." Weisman, Avery D., and Thomas P. Hackett. "Predilection to Death: Death and Dying as a Psychiatric Problem." *Psychosomatic Medicine* 23 (1961): 232–56.

Weiss, "Antioch." Weiss, Peter. "Antioch πρὸς Πισιδίᾳ." *BrillPauly* 1:760.

Weiss, "Aufruhr." Weiss, Alexander. "Der Aufruhr der Silberschmiede (Apg 19,23–40) und das Edikt des Paullus Fabius Persicus (I. Ephesos 17–19)." *BZ* 53 (1, 2009): 69–81.

Weiss, "Buildings." Weiss, Zeev. "Buildings for Mass Entertainment: Tradition and Innovation in Herodian Construction." *NEA* 77 (2, June 2014): 98–107.

Weiss, "Donativum." Weiss, Peter. "Donativum." *BrillPauly* 4:659–60.

Weiss, "Herrenmahl." Weiss, Johannes. "Das Herrenmahl der Urgemeinde." *ProtMon* 16 (1912): 53–60.

Weiss, *History*. Weiss, Johannes. *The History of Primitive Christianity*. Edited by F. C. Grant. London: Macmillan, 1937.

Weiss, "Mosaic." Weiss, Zeev. "The Sepphoris Synagogue Mosaic." *BAR* 26 (5, 2000): 48–61, 70.

Weiss, "Quästoren." Weiss, Alexander. "Keine Quästoren in Korinth: Zu Goodrichs (und Theißens) These über das Amt des Erastos (Röm 16.23)." *NTS* 56 (4, Oct. 2010): 576–81.

Weiss, "Sabbath among Samaritans." Weiss, Herold. "The Sabbath among the Samaritans." *JSJ* 25 (2, 1994): 252–73.

Weiss, "Sabbath in Corpus." Weiss, Herold. "The Sabbath in the Pauline Corpus." *SPhilA* 9 (1997): 287–315.

Weiss, "Sabbath in Josephus." Weiss, Herold. "The Sabbath in the Writings of Josephus." *JSJ* 29 (4, 1998): 363–90.

Weiss, "Sepphoris." Weiss, Zeev. "Sepphoris." *NEAEHL* 4:1324–28.

Weiss, *Zeichen*. Weiss, Wolfgang. *"Zeichen und Wunder": Eine Studie zu der Sprachtradition und ihrer Verwendung im Neuen Testament*. WMANT 67. Neukirchen-Vluyn: Neukirchener Verlag, 1995.

Weißenberger, "Tyrannus." Weißenberger, Michael. "Tyrannus." *BrillPauly* 15:66.

Weissenrieder, *Images*. Weissenrieder, Annette. *Images of Illness in the Gospel of Luke:*

Insights of Ancient Medical Texts. WUNT 2.164. Tübingen: Mohr Siebeck, 2003.

Weitzman, "Feasts." Weitzman, Steven. "From Feasts into Mourning: The Violence of Early Jewish Festivals." *JR* 79 (4, 1999): 545–65.

Weitzman, "Josephus." Weitzman, Steven. "Josephus on How to Survive Martyrdom." *JJS* 55 (2, 2004): 230–45.

Welborn, "Correspondence." Welborn, L. L. "The Corinthian Correspondence." Pages 205–42 in *All Things to All Cultures: Paul among Jews, Greeks, and Romans*. Edited by Mark Harding and Alanna Nobbs. Grand Rapids: Eerdmans, 2013.

Welborn, "Discord." Welborn, L. L. "On the Discord in Corinth: 1 Corinthians 1–4 and Ancient Politics." *JBL* 106 (1, 1987): 85–111.

Welborn, *Politics*. Welborn, L. L. *Politics and Rhetoric in the Corinthian Epistles*. Macon, Ga.: Mercer University Press, 1997.

Welborn, "Runaway Paul." Welborn, L. L. "The Runaway Paul." *HTR* 92 (2, 1999): 115–63.

Welbourn, "Healing." Welbourn, F. B. "Healing as a Psychosomatic Event." Pages 351–68 in *Afro-Christian Religion and Healing in Southern Africa*. Edited by G. C. Oosthuizen et al. African Studies 8. Lewiston, N.Y.: Edwin Mellen, 1989.

Welbourn, "Spirit Initiation." Welbourn, F. B. "Spirit Initiation in Ankole and a Christian Spirit Movement in Western Kenya." Pages 290–306 in *Spirit Mediumship and Society in Africa*. Edited by John Beattie and John Middleton. Foreword by Raymond Firth. New York: Africana, 1969.

Welch, "Miracles." Welch, John W. "Miracles, *maleficium*, and *maiestas* in the Trial of Jesus." Pages 349–83 in *Jesus and Archaeology*. Edited by James H. Charlesworth. Grand Rapids: Eerdmans, 2006.

Welch, "Statue Head." Welch, Katherine. "A Statue Head of the 'Great Mother' from Samothrace." *Hesperia* 65 (4, 1996): 467–73 and plates 89–92.

Wells, "Characterization." Wells, Lola M. "Peter's Characterization in Luke-Acts." *RevRel* 51 (3, 1992): 397–402.

Wells, "Exodus." Wells, Bruce. "Exodus." Pages 160–283 in vol. 1 of *Zondervan Illustrated Bible Backgrounds Commentary: Old Testament*. Edited by John Walton. 5 vols. Grand Rapids: Zondervan, 2009.

Wells, "Impiety." Wells, Jack. "Impiety in the Middle Republic: The Roman Response to Temple Plundering in Southern Italy." *CJ* 105 (3, 2010): 229–43.

Welsby, *Kingdom of Kush*. Welsby, Derek A. *The Kingdom of Kush: The Napatan and Meroitic Empires*. London: British

Museum, 1996. Repr., Princeton: Markus Wiener, 1998.

Welwei, "Gerousia." Welwei, Karl-Wilhelm. "Gerousia: Graeco-Roman." *BrillPauly* 5:817–18.

Wendl, "Slavery." Wendl, Tobias. "Slavery, Spirit Possession and Ritual Consciousness: The *Tchamba* Cult among the Mina of Togo." Pages 111–23 in *Spirit Possession, Modernity and Power in Africa*. Edited by Heike Behrend and Ute Luig. Madison: University of Wisconsin Press, 1999.

Wendland, *Cultural Factor*. Wendland, Ernst R. *The Cultural Factor in Bible Translation: A Study of Communicating the Word of God in a Central African Cultural Context*. London: United Bible Societies, 1987.

Wendt, *Apostelgeschichte*. Wendt, Hans Hinrich. *Die Apostelgeschichte*. 9th ed. KEKNT 3. Göttingen: Vandenhoeck & Ruprecht, 1913.

Wendt, "Trustworthiness." Wendt, Hans Hinrich. "The Historical Trustworthiness of the Book of Acts." *HibJ* 12 (1913–14): 141–61.

Wengst, *Pax*. Wengst, Klaus. *Pax Romana and the Peace of Jesus Christ*. Philadelphia: Fortress, 1987.

Wenham, "Apocalypse." Wenham, David. "Paul and the Synoptic Apocalypse." Pages 345–75 in vol. 2 of *Studies of History and Tradition in the Four Gospels*. Edited by R. T. France and David Wenham. 2 vols. Gospel Perspectives 1–2. Sheffield, U.K.: JSOT Press, 1980–81.

Wenham, *Bible*. Wenham, John W. *Christ and the Bible*. Downers Grove, Ill.: InterVarsity, 1977.

Wenham, "Corpus." Wenham, David. "Acts and the Pauline Corpus, II: The Evidence of Parallels." Pages 215–58 in *The Book of Acts in Its Ancient Literary Setting*. Edited by Bruce W. Winter and Andrew D. Clarke. Vol. 1 of *The Book of Acts in Its First Century Setting*. Edited by Bruce W. Winter. Grand Rapids: Eerdmans; Carlisle, U.K.: Paternoster, 1993.

Wenham, *Leviticus*. Wenham, Gordon J. *The Book of Leviticus*. Grand Rapids: Eerdmans, 1979.

Wenham, "Numbers." Wenham, John. "The Large Numbers in the Bible." *JBQ* 21 (1993): 116–20.

Wenham, "Paulinism of Acts Again." Wenham, David. "The Paulinism of Acts Again." *Them* 13 (1988): 53–55.

Wenham, "Paul's Use." Wenham, David. "Paul's Use of the Jesus Tradition: Three Samples." Pages 7–37 in *The Jesus Tradition outside the Gospels*. Edited by David Wenham. Gospel Perspectives 5. Sheffield, U.K.: JSOT Press, 1984.

Wenham, "Peter to Rome?" Wenham, John W. "Did Peter Go to Rome in A.D. 42?" *TynBul* 23 (1972): 94–102.

Wenham, *Rediscovery*. Wenham, David. *The Rediscovery of Jesus' Eschatological Discourse*. Gospel Perspectives 4. Sheffield, U.K.: JSOT Press, 1984.

Wenham, "Source Criticism." Wenham, David. "Source Criticism." Pages 139–52 in *New Testament Interpretation: Essays on Principles and Methods*. Edited by I. Howard Marshall. Grand Rapids: Eerdmans, 1977.

Wenham, "Story." Wenham, David. "The Story of Jesus Known to Paul." Pages 297–311 in *Jesus of Nazareth, Lord and Christ: Essays on the Historical Jesus and New Testament Christology*. Edited by Joel B. Green and Max Turner. Grand Rapids: Eerdmans; Carlisle, U.K.: Paternoster, 1994.

Wenham, "Tension." Wenham, David. "The Christian Life—A Life of Tension? A Consideration of the Nature of Christian Experience in Paul." Pages 80–94 in *Pauline Studies: Essays Presented to Professor F. F. Bruce on His 70th Birthday*. Edited by Donald A. Hagner and Murray J. Harris. Exeter, U.K.: Paternoster; Grand Rapids: Eerdmans, 1980.

Wenham and Walton, *Guide*. Wenham, David, and Steve Walton. *A Guide to the Gospels and Acts*. Vol. 1 of Exploring the New Testament. 2nd ed. Downers Grove, Ill.: IVP Academic, 2011.

Wenk, *Power*. Wenk, Matthias. *Community-Forming Power: The Socio-ethical Role of the Spirit in Luke-Acts*. JPTSup 19. Sheffield, U.K.: Sheffield Academic, 2000.

Wenk, "Power." Wenk, Matthias. "Community Forming Power: Reconciliation and the Spirit in Acts." *JEurPentTA* 19 (1999): 17–33.

Wenkel, "Speech-Acts." Wenkel, David H. "Imprecatory Speech-Acts in the Book of Acts." *AsTJ* 63 (2, 2008): 81–93.

Wenz, "Fatale Argumentation." Wenz, H. "'Fatale Argumentation des Paulus'?" *ELKZ* 15 (Sept. 15, 1961): 304–6.

Werbner, "Truth." Werbner, Richard. "Truth-on-Balance: Knowing the Opaque Other in Tswapong Wisdom Divination." Pages 190–211 in *Witchcraft Dialogues: Anthropological and Philosophical Exchanges*. Edited by George Clement Bond and Diane M. Ciekawy. Athens, Ohio: Center for International Studies, Ohio University, 2001.

Werman, "*Jubilees* 30." Werman, Cana. "*Jubilees* 30: Building a Paradigm for the Ban on Intermarriage." *HTR* 90 (1, 1997): 1–22.

Wernicke, "Artemis." Wernicke, K. "Artemis." Pages 1336–1440 in vol. 2 of *Realencyclopädie der classischen Altertumswissenschaft*. Edited by August Pauly and Georg Wissowa. 49 vols. in 58. Stuttgart: J. B. Metzler, 1894–1980.

Wescoat, "Assos." Wescoat, Bonna D. "Assos." *OEANE* 1:223–25.

Wesley, *Church*. Wesley, Luke. *The Church in China: Persecuted, Pentecostal, and Powerful*. Baguio City, Philippines: AJPS Books, 2004.

Wesley, *Journal*. Wesley, John. *The Journal of the Rev. John Wesley*. Edited by Nehemiah Curnock. 8 vols. London: Epworth, 1938.

Wesley, *Notes*. Wesley, John. *Explanatory Notes upon the New Testament*. London: Epworth, 1966; originally 1754.

Wesley, *Stories*. Wesley, Luke. *Stories from China: Fried Rice for the Soul*. Milton Keynes, U.K., and Waynesboro, Ga.: Authentic Media, 2005.

Wessels, "Doctrine." Wessels, Roland Heinrich. "The Doctrine of the Baptism in the Holy Spirit among the Assemblies of God." ThD diss., Pacific School of Religion, 1966.

Wessels, "Empowered." Wessels, Wilhelm J. "Empowered by the Spirit of Yahweh: A Study of Micah 3:8." *JBPRes* 1 (Fall 2009): 33–47.

West, "Baby." West, Stephanie. "Whose Baby? A Note on P. Oxy. 744." *ZPE* 121 (1998): 167–72.

West, *Inscriptions*. West, Allen Brown. *Latin Inscriptions, 1896–1926*. Vol. 8, part 2, of *Corinth: Results of Excavations Conducted by the American School of Classical Studies at Athens*. Cambridge, Mass.: Harvard University Press, 1931.

West, "Introduction." West, Martin L. Introduction. Pages 2–37 in *Greek Epic Fragments from the Seventh to the Fifth Centuries BC*. Translated by Martin L. West. LCL. Cambridge, Mass.: Harvard University Press, 2003.

West, "*Joseph and Asenath*." West, Stephanie. "*Joseph and Asenath*: A Neglected Greek Romance." *CQ* 24 (1, 1974): 70–81.

West, "Plato." West, Elinor Jane Maddock. "Plato and Socrates: The Men and Their Methods." Pages 131–36 in *New Essays on Socrates*. Edited by Eugene Kelly. Lanham, Md.: University Press of America, 1984.

West, "Rhampsinitos." West, Stephanie. "Rhampsinitos and the Clever Thief (Herodotus 2.121)." Pages 322–27 in *A Companion to Greek and Roman Historiography*. Edited by John Marincola. 2 vols. Oxford: Blackwell, 2007.

West, "Rhapsodes." West, Martin Litchfield. "Rhapsodes." OCD^3 1311–12.

West, *Sorcery*. West, Harry G. *Ethnographic Sorcery*. Chicago: University of Chicago Press, 2007.

Westcott, *Epistles*. Westcott, Brooke Foss. *The Epistles of John: The Greek Text with Notes and Essays*. 4th ed. London: Macmillan, 1902. Repr., Grand Rapids: Eerdmans, 1966.

Westcott, *Gospel*. Westcott, Brooke Foss. *The Gospel according to St. John: The Authorized Version with Introduction and Notes*. London: John Murray, 1882. Repr., Grand Rapids: Eerdmans, 1950.

Westerholm, "Introduction." Westerholm, Stephen. "Introduction." Pages 1–5 in *The Blackwell Companion to Paul*. Edited by Stephen Westerholm. BCompRel. Oxford: Blackwell, 2011.

Westerholm and Evans, "Sabbath." Westerholm, Stephen, and Craig A. Evans. "Sabbath." *DNTB* 1031–35.

Westermann, "Promise." Westermann, Claus. "The Way of Promise through the Old Testament." Pages 200–224 in *The Old Testament and the Christian Faith*. Edited by Bernhard W. Anderson. New York: Harper & Row, 1963.

Westermann, *Slave Systems*. Westermann, William L. *Slave Systems of Greek and Roman Antiquity*. Philadelphia: American Philosophical Society, 1955.

Westgate, "House." Westgate, Ruth. "House and Society in Classical and Hellenistic Crete: A Case Study in Regional Variation." *AJA* 111 (3, 2007): 423–57.

Wevers, "Scrolls." Wevers, John W. "The Dead Sea Scrolls and the Septuagint." *BIOSCS* 38 (2005): 1–24.

Whalin, *Samuel Morris*. Whalin, W. Terry. *Samuel Morris: The Apostle of Simple Faith*. Uhrichsville, Ohio: Barbour, 1996.

Wharton, "Tacitus' Tiberius." Wharton, David B. "Tacitus' Tiberius: The State of the Evidence for the Emperor's *ipsissima verba* in the *Annals*." *AJP* 118 (1, 1997): 119–25.

Whately, *Doubts*. Whately, Richard. *Historic Doubts Relative to Napoleon Bonaparte*. Andover: Warren F. Draper, 1874.

Whealey, "Josephus." Whealey, Alice. "Josephus on Jesus: Evidence from the First Millennium." *TZ* 51 (4, 1995): 285–304.

Whealey, "Testimonium." Whealey, Alice. "The Testimonium Flavianum in Syriac and Arabic." *NTS* 54 (4, 2008): 573–90.

Wheeler, *Beyond Frontiers*. Wheeler, Sir Mortimer. *Rome beyond the Imperial Frontiers*. London: G. Bell & Sons, 1954. Repr., Westport, Conn.: Greenwood, 1971.

Wheelock, "Spirit Baptism." Wheelock, Donald Ray. "Spirit Baptism in American Pentecostal Thought." PhD diss., Emory University, 1983.

Whisson, "Disorders." Whisson, Michael G. "Some Aspects of Functional Disorders among the Kenyan Luo." Pages 283–304

in *Magic, Faith, and Healing: Studies in Primitive Psychiatry Today*. Edited by Ari Kiev. Foreword by Jerome D. Frank. New York: Free Press, 1964.

Whitacre, *John*. Whitacre, Rodney A. *John*. IVPNTC. Downers Grove, Ill.: InterVarsity, 1999.

White, *Artemidorus*. White, Robert J., ed. and trans. *Artemidorus: The Interpretation of Dreams (Oneirocritica)*. NCS. Park Ridge, N.J.: Noyes, 1975.

White, "Cyrene." White, Donald. "Cyrene." *OEANE* 2:97–98.

White, "Development." White, L. Michael. "Urban Development and Social Change." Pages 27–79 in *Ephesos, Metropolis of Asia: An Interdisciplinary Approach to Its Archaeology, Religion, and Culture*. Edited by Helmut Koester. HTS. Valley Forge, Pa.: Trinity Press International, 1995.

White, "Finances." White, William, Jr. "Finances." Pages 218–36 in *The Catacombs and the Colosseum: The Roman Empire as the Setting of Primitive Christianity*. Edited by Stephen Benko and John J. O'Rourke. Valley Forge, Pa.: Judson, 1971.

White, "First Christians." White, L. Michael. "The First Christians: What Did the Neighbors Think?" *Forum* 3 (1, 2000): 9–29.

White, "Image." White, J. L. "Paul's Image of God." *Forum* 5 (2, 2002): 235–44.

White, *Initiation*. White, R. E. O. *The Biblical Doctrine of Initiation*. Grand Rapids: Eerdmans, 1960.

White, "Jews." White, Martin Christopher. "The Identity and Function of the Jews and Related Terms in the Fourth Gospel." PhD diss., Emory University, 1972.

White, "Lady." White, John. "Young Lady, Old Hag." Pages 69–86 in *Power Encounters among Christians in the Western World*. Edited by Kevin Springer. Introduction and afterword by John Wimber. San Francisco: Harper & Row, 1988.

White, "Meteorological Appraisal." White, R. W. "A Meteorological Appraisal of Acts 27:5–26." *ExpT* 113 (12, 2002): 403–7.

White, "Oration." White, L. Michael. "Favorinus's 'Corinthian Oration': A Piqued Panorama of the Hadrianic Forum." Pages 61–110 in *Urban Religion in Roman Corinth: Interdisciplinary Approaches*. Edited by Daniel N. Schowalter and Steven J. Friesen. HTS 53. Cambridge, Mass.: Harvard University Press, 2005.

White, *Origins of Architecture*. White, L. Michael. *The Social Origins of Christian Architecture*. 2 vols. HTS 42. Valley Forge, Pa.: Trinity Press International, 1996–97.

White, "*Pater familias*." White, L. Michael. "Paul and *pater familias*." Pages 457–87 in *Paul in the Greco-Roman World: A*

Handbook. Edited by J. Paul Sampley. Harrisburg, Pa.: Trinity Press International, 2003.

White, "Peace and Security." White, Joel R. "'Peace and Security' (1 Thessalonians 5.3): Is It Really a Roman Slogan?" *NTS* 59 (3, July 2013): 382–95.

White, "Pentecost Event." White, L. Michael. "The Pentecost Event: Lukan Redaction and Themes in Acts 2." *Forum* 3 (1, 2000): 75–103.

White, "Revisited." White, L. Michael. "The Delos Synagogue Revisited: Recent Fieldwork in the Graeco-Roman Diaspora." *HTR* 80 (2, 1987): 133–60.

White, "Revival." White, Eryn. "Revival and Renewal Amongst the Eighteenth-Century Welsh Methodists." Pages 1–12 in *Revival, Renewal, and the Holy Spirit*. Edited by Dyfed Wyn Roberts. SEHT. Eugene, Ore.: Wipf & Stock, 2009.

White, "Synagogue and Society." White, L. Michael. "Synagogue and Society in Imperial Ostia: Archaeological and Epigraphic Evidence." *HTR* 90 (1, 1997): 23–58.

White, "Synagogue in Ostia." White, L. Michael. "Synagogue and Society in Imperial Ostia: Archaeological and Epigraphic Evidence." Pages 30–68 in *Judaism and Christianity in First-Century Rome*. Edited by Karl P. Donfried and Peter Richardson. Grand Rapids: Eerdmans, 1998.

White, "Tradition." White, John L. "The Greek Documentary Letter Tradition, Third Century B.C.E. to Third Century C.E." *Semeia* 22 (1982): 89–106.

White and Frend, "Bithynia." White, George E., and W. H. C. Frend. "Bithynia." *ISBE* 1:520.

Whitefield, *Journals*. Whitefield, George. *Journals*. Carlisle, Pa., and Edinburgh: Banner of Truth Trust, 1960.

Whitehouse, "Glass." Whitehouse, David. "Glass." *OEANE* 2:413–15.

Whitehouse, "Shipwreck on Nile." Whitehouse, Helen. "Shipwreck on the Nile: A Greek Novel on a 'Lost' Roman Mosaic?" *AJA* 89 (1, 1985): 129–34 and plate 28.

Whitman, *Homer*. Whitman, Cedric H. *Homer and the Heroic Tradition*. Cambridge, Mass.: Harvard University Press, 1967.

Whitmarsh, "Titles." Whitmarsh, Tim. "The Greek Novel: Titles and Genre." *AJP* 126 (4, 2005): 587–611.

Whittaker, "Introduction." Whittaker, C. R. Introduction. Pages ix–lxxxvii in vol. 1 of Herodian, *History*. Translated by C. R. Whittaker. 2 vols. LCL. Cambridge, Mass.: Harvard University Press, 1969.

Whittaker, *Jews and Christians*. Whittaker, Molly. *Jews and Christians: Graeco-Roman*

Views. CCWJCW 6. Cambridge: Cambridge University Press, 1984.

Whittaker, "Roman Trade." Whittaker, C. R. "Late Roman Trade and Traders." Pages 163–80 in *Trade in the Ancient Economy.* Edited by Peter Garnsey, Keith Hopkins, and C. R. Whittaker. Berkeley: University of California Press, 1983.

Whitters, "Observations." Whitters, Mark F. "Some New Observations about Jewish Festal Letters." *JSJ* 32 (2001): 272–88.

Whybray, *Isaiah.* Whybray, R. N. *Isaiah 40–66.* NCBC. Grand Rapids: Eerdmans; London: Marshall, Morgan & Scott, 1975.

Whybray, *Making.* Whybray, R. N. *The Making of the Pentateuch: A Methodological Study.* JSOTSup 53. Sheffield, U.K.: JSOT Press, 1987.

Wicker, "Defectu." Wicker, Kathleen O'Brien. "De defectu oraculorum (Moralia 409E–438E)." Pages 131–80 in *Plutarch's Theological Writings and Early Christian Literature.* Edited by Hans Dieter Betz. SCHNT 3. Leiden: Brill, 1975.

Wickkiser, "Asklepios." Wickkiser, Bronwen. "Asklepios Appears in a Dream: Antiquity's Greatest Healer." *ArchOd* 8 (4, 2005): 14–25, 48–49.

Wieder, "'Damascus' and Redemption." Wieder, Naphtali. "The 'Land of Damascus' and Messianic Redemption." *JJS* 20 (1–4, 1969): 86–88.

Wieder, "Exegesis among Karaites." Wieder, Naphtali. "The Dead Sea Scrolls Type of Biblical Exegesis among the Karaites." Pages 75–105 in *Between East and West: Essays Dedicated to the Memory of Bela Horovitz.* Edited by Alexander Altmann. London: East and West Library, 1958.

Wieder, "Messiahs." Wieder, Naphtali. "The Doctrine of the Two Messiahs among the Karaites." *JJS* 6 (1, 1953): 14–23.

Wieder, "Notes." Wieder, Naphtali. "Notes on the New Documents from the Fourth Cave of Qumran." *JJS* 7 (1–2, 1956): 71–76.

Wieder, "Sectaries and Karaites." Wieder, Naphtali. "The Qumran Sectaries and the Karaites." *JQR* 47 (1956–57): 269–92.

Wiefel, "Community." Wiefel, Wolfgang. "The Jewish Community in Ancient Rome and the Origins of Roman Christianity." Pages 100–119 in *The Romans Debate.* Edited by Karl P. Donfried. Minneapolis: Augsburg, 1977.

Wiens, *Sermon.* Wiens, Delbert. *Stephen's Sermon and the Structure of Luke-Acts.* North Richland Hills, Tex.: BIBAL, 1996.

Wiersma, "Novel." Wiersma, S. "The Ancient Greek Novel and Its Heroines: A Female Paradox." *Mnemosyne* 43 (1–2, 1990): 109–23.

Wiesehöfer, "Exposure." Wiesehöfer, Josef. "Child Exposure." *BrillPauly* 3:224–25.

Wiesehöfer, "Hospitality." Wiesehöfer, Josef. "Hospitality: Iran." *BrillPauly* 6:529.

Wiesehöfer, "Marriage, Age." Wiesehöfer, Josef. "Marriage, Age at." *BrillPauly* 8:393–95.

Wiesehöfer, "Mortality." Wiesehöfer, Josef. "Mortality." *BrillPauly* 9:214–15.

Wiesehöfer, "Proskynesis." Wiesehöfer, Josef. "Proskynesis." *BrillPauly* 12:50–51.

Wiesehöfer, "Pubertas." Wiesehöfer, Josef. "Pubertas." *BrillPauly* 12:177–78.

Wiesehöfer, "Youth." Wiesehöfer, Josef. "Youth." *BrillPauly* 15:853–56.

Wiest, "Stephen." Wiest, Stephen. R. "The Story of Stephen in Acts 6:1–8:4: History Typologized or Typology Historicized?" *Forum* 3 (1, 2000): 121–53.

Wigger, *Saint.* Wigger, John. *American Saint: Francis Asbury and the Methodists.* Oxford: Oxford University Press, 2009.

Wightman, "Fortresses in Jerusalem." Wightman, Gregory J. "Temple Fortresses in Jerusalem, Part II: The Hasmonean Baris and Herodian Antonia." *BAIAS* 10 (1990–91): 7–35.

Wikenhauser, *Apostelgeschichte.* Wikenhauser, Alfred. *Die Apostelgeschichte.* 4th ed. RNT 5. Regensburg: Pustet, 1961.

Wikenhauser, "Doppelträume." Wikenhauser, Alfred. "Doppelträume." *Bib* 29 (1948): 100–111.

Wikenhauser, *Geschichtswert.* Wikenhauser, Alfred. *Apostelgeschichte und ihr Geschichtswert.* Münster: Aschendorff, 1921.

Wikenhauser, *Mysticism.* Wikenhauser, Alfred. *Pauline Mysticism: Christ in the Mystical Teaching of St. Paul.* New York: Herder & Herder, 1960.

Wilch, "Jewish Guilt." Wilch, John R. "Jewish Guilt for the Death of Jesus—Anti-Judaism in the Acts of the Apostles?" *LTJ* 18 (2, 1984): 49–58.

Wilcken, *Alexander.* Wilcken, Ulrich. *Alexander the Great.* Translated by G. C. Richards. New York: W. W. Norton, 1967.

Wilckens, "Interpreting." Wilckens, Ulrich. "Interpreting Luke-Acts in a Period of Existentialist Theology." Pages 60–83 in *Studies in Luke-Acts: Essays in Honor of Paul Schubert.* Edited by Leander E. Keck and J. Louis Martyn. Nashville: Abingdon, 1966.

Wilckens, "Kerygma und Evangelium." Wilckens, Ulrich. "Kerygma und Evangelium bei Lukas (Beobachtungen zu Acta 10:34–43)." *ZNW* 49 (3–4, 1958): 223–37.

Wilckens, *Missionsreden.* Wilckens, Ulrich. *Die Missionsreden der Apostelgeschichte: Form- und traditionsgeschichtliche Unter-*

suchungen. 3rd ed. WMANT 5. Neukirchen-Vluyn: Neukirchener Verlag, 1974.

Wilcox, "Blind." Wilcox, David. "How Blind the Watchmaker?" Pages 168–81 in *Evidence of Purpose: Scientists Discover the Creator.* Edited by John Marks Templeton. New York: Continuum, 1994.

Wilcox, "Dualism." Wilcox, Max. "Dualism, Gnosticism, and Other Elements in the Pre-Pauline Tradition." Pages 83–96 in *The Scrolls and Christianity: Historical and Theological Significance.* Edited by Matthew Black. London: SPCK, 1969.

Wilcox, "Foreword to Speeches." Wilcox, Max. "A Foreword to the Study of the Speeches in Acts." Pages 206–25 in vol. 1 of *Christianity, Judaism, and Other Greco-Roman Cults: Studies for Morton Smith at Sixty.* Edited by Jacob Neusner. 4 vols. SJLA 12. Leiden: Brill, 1975.

Wilcox, "God-Fearers—Reconsideration." Wilcox, Max. "The 'God-Fearers' in Acts—A Reconsideration." *JSNT* 13 (1981): 102–22.

Wilcox, "Grief." Wilcox, Amanda. "Exemplary Grief: Gender and Virtue in Seneca's Consolations to Women." *Helios* 33 (1, 2006): 73–100.

Wilcox, "Influence." Wilcox, Max. "Semitic Influence on the New Testament." *DNTB* 1093–98.

Wilcox, "Pattern." Wilcox, Max. "'According to the Pattern *(tbnyt)* . . .': Exodus 25, 40 in the New Testament and Early Jewish Thought." *RevQ* 13 (1988): 647–56.

Wilcox, "Rivals." Wilcox, Amanda. "Sympathetic Rivals: Consolation in Cicero's Letters." *AJP* 126 (2, 2005): 237–55.

Wilcox, *Semitisms of Acts.* Wilcox, Max. *The Semitisms of Acts.* Oxford: Clarendon, 1965.

Wilcox, "Tree." Wilcox, Max. "'Upon the Tree'—Deut 21:22–23 in the New Testament." *JBL* 96 (1, 1977): 85–99.

Wild, "Dyeing." Wild, John Peter. "Dyeing." *OCD*[3] 499.

Wild, "Linen." Wild, John Peter. "Linen." *OCD*[3] 863.

Wild, *Water.* Wild, Robert A. *Water in the Cultic Worship of Isis and Sarapis.* ÉPROER 87. Leiden: Brill, 1981.

Wiles, *Gospel.* Wiles, Maurice F. *The Spiritual Gospel: The Interpretation of the Fourth Gospel in the Early Church.* Cambridge: Cambridge University Press, 1960.

Wiles, "Miracles." Wiles, Maurice F. "Miracles in the Early Church." Pages 219–34 in *Miracles: Cambridge Studies in Their Philosophy and History.* Edited by C. F. D. Moule. London: A. R. Mowbray; New York: Morehouse-Barlow, 1965.

Wiles, *Prayers*. Wiles, Gordon P. *Paul's Intercessory Prayers: The Significance of the Intercessory Prayer Passages in the Letters of St Paul*. SNTSMS 24. Cambridge: Cambridge University Press, 1974.

Wilk, "Apg 10,1–11,18." Wilk, Florian. "Apg 10,1–11,18 im Licht der lukanischen Erzählung vom Wirken Jesu." Pages 605–17 in *The Unity of Luke-Acts*. Edited by Joseph Verheyden. BETL 142. Leuven: Leuven University Press, 1999.

Wilken, "Christians." Wilken, Robert L. "The Christians as the Romans (and Greeks) Saw Them." Pages 100–125 in *The Shaping of Christianity in the Second and Third Centuries*. Vol. 1 of *Jewish and Christian Self-Definition*. Edited by E. P. Sanders. Philadelphia: Fortress, 1980.

Wilken, "Collegia." Wilken, Robert. "Collegia, Philosophical Schools, and Theology." Pages 268–91 in *The Catacombs and the Colosseum: The Roman Empire as the Setting of Primitive Christianity*. Edited by Stephen Benko and John J. O'Rourke. Valley Forge, Pa.: Judson, 1971.

Wilken, *Judaism*. Wilken, Robert L. *Judaism and the Early Christian Mind: A Study of Cyril of Alexandria's Exegesis and Theology*. YPR 15. New Haven: Yale University Press, 1971.

Wilken, "Social Interpretation of Apologetics." Wilken, Robert. "Toward a Social Interpretation of Early Christian Apologetics." *CH* 39 (4, 1970): 437–58.

Wilkerson, *Beyond*. Wilkerson, Ralph. *Beyond and Back: Those Who Died and Lived to Tell It!* Anaheim, Calif.: Melodyland Productions, 1977.

Wilkerson, *Cross*. Wilkerson, David, with John Sherrill and Elizabeth Sherrill. *The Cross and the Switchblade*. New York: Pyramid, 1962.

Wilkie, "Imagination." Wilkie, Rab. "Spirited Imagination: Ways of Approaching the Shaman's World." Pages 135–64 in *Being Changed: The Anthropology of Extraordinary Experience*. Edited by David Young and Jean-Guy Goulet. Petersborough, Ont.: Broadview, 1994.

Wilkins, *Discipleship*. Wilkins, Michael J. *Discipleship in the Ancient World and Matthew's Gospel*. 2nd ed. Grand Rapids: Baker, 1995. First ed.: Leiden: Brill, 1988.

Wilkinson, *Healing*. Wilkinson, John. *The Bible and Healing: A Medical and Theological Commentary*. Edinburgh: Handsel; Grand Rapids: Eerdmans, 1998.

Wilkinson, *Health*. Wilkinson, John. *Health and Healing: Studies in New Testament Principles and Practice*. Edinburgh: Handsel Press, 1980.

Wilkinson, *Jerusalem*. Wilkinson, John. *Jerusalem as Jesus Knew It: Archaeology as Evidence*. London: Thames & Hudson, 1978.

Wilkinson, "Orientation." Wilkinson, J. "Orientation, Jewish and Christian." *PEQ* 116 (1, 1984): 16–30.

Wilkinson, "Population." Wilkinson, John. "Ancient Jerusalem: Its Water Supply and Population." *PEQ* 106 (1, 1974): 33–51 and plates VII–XII.

Willcock, "Homer." Willcock, M. M. "Homer." *OCD*[3] 718–20.

Williams, "Acts." Williams, Demetrius K. "The Acts of the Apostles." Pages 213–48 in *True to Our Native Land: An African American New Testament Commentary*. Edited by Brian K. Blount, with Cain Hope Felder, Clarice J. Martin, and Emerson Powery. Minneapolis: Fortress, 2007.

C. Williams, *Acts*. Williams, C. S. C. *A Commentary on the Acts of the Apostles*. New York: Harper & Row, 1957.

D. Williams, *Acts*. Williams, David J. *Acts*. NIBCNT. Peabody, Mass.: Hendrickson, 1990. Repr., Carlisle, U.K.: Paternoster, 1995.

R. Williams, *Acts*. Williams, R. R. *Acts of the Apostles: "Nothing Can Stop the Gospel."* TBC. London: SCM, 1965.

Williams, "Alternative Names." Williams, Margaret H. "The Use of Alternative Names by Diaspora Jews in Graeco-Roman Antiquity." *JSJ* 38 (3, 2007): 307–27.

Williams, "Answer." Williams, Timothy. "Pentecostalism's Answer to Indonesia's Unreached Muslims." *JAM* 5 (1, 2003): 93–118.

Williams, "Bubularius." Williams, Margaret H. "*Alexander, bubularius de macello*: Humble Sausage-seller or Europe's First Identifiable Purveyor of Kosher Beef?" *Latomus* 61 (1, 2002): 122–33.

Williams, "Bwaya." Williams, Mark S. "*Bwaya* as Spirit-Being: Filipino Islam and the Supernatural." *JAM* 7 (1, 2005): 119–31.

Williams, "Case." Williams, Margaret H. "The Case for Jewish Use of Moses as a Personal Name in Greco-Roman Antiquity." *ZPE* 140 (2002): 279–83.

Williams, "Catechesis." Williams, R. R. "The Pauline Catechesis." Pages 89–96 in *Studies in Ephesians*. Edited by F. L. Cross. London: A. R. Mowbray, 1956.

Williams, "Catena." Williams, Tyler F. "Catena (4Q177)." *DNTB* 195–96.

Williams, "Christianity." Williams, D. H. "The Earliest 'Mere Christianity.'" *CHB* 96 (2007): 23–26.

Williams, "Coins." Williams, Jonathan. "Religion and Roman Coins." Pages 143–63 in *A Companion to Roman Religion*. Edited by Jörg Rüpke. BCompAW. Oxford: Blackwell, 2011.

Williams, "Corinth and Domestic Religion." Williams, Charles K. "The City of Corinth and Its Domestic Religion." *Hesperia* 50 (1981): 408–21.

Williams, "Ecstaticism." Williams, Cyril G. "Ecstaticism in Hebrew Prophecy and Christian Glossolalia." *SR/SR* 3 (4, 1973): 320–38.

Williams, "Exarchon." Williams, Margaret H. "Exarchon: An Unsuspected Jewish Liturgical Title from Ancient Rome." *JJS* 51 (1, 2000): 77–87.

Williams, "Expulsion in A.D. 19." Williams, Margaret H. "The Expulsion of the Jews from Rome in A.D. 19." *Latomus* 48 (4, 1989): 765–84.

Williams, "Germanicus." Williams, Kathryn F. "Tacitus' Germanicus and the Principate." *Latomus* 68 (1, 2009): 117–30.

Williams, "Glossolalia as Phenomenon." Williams, Cyril G. "Glossolalia as a Religious Phenomenon: 'Tongues' at Corinth and Pentecost." *Religion* 5 (1, 1975): 16–32.

Williams, "Greek Love." Williams, Craig A. "Greek Love at Rome." *CQ* 45 (2, 1995): 517–39.

Williams, *Homosexuality*. Williams, Craig A. *Roman Homosexuality*. 2nd ed. Foreword by Martha Nussbaum. New York: Oxford University Press, 2010.

Williams, "Image and Text." Williams, Margaret H. "Image and Text in the Jewish Epitaphs of Late Ancient Rome." *JSJ* 42 (3, 2011): 328–50.

Williams, "Ioudaios." Williams, Margaret H. "The Meaning and Function of *Ioudaios* in Greco-Roman Inscriptions." *ZPE* 116 (1997): 249–62.

Williams, "Jews of Corycus." Williams, Margaret H. "The Jews of Corycus—A Neglected Diasporan Community from Roman Times." *JSJ* 25 (2, 1994): 274–86.

Williams, "Josephus on Pharisees." Williams, David S. "Josephus or Nicolaus on the Pharisees?" *REJ* 156 (1–2, 1997): 43–58.

Williams, *Justin Martyr*. Williams, A. Lukyn, ed. and trans. *Justin Martyr: The Dialogue with Trypho*. Translations of Christian Literature. New York: Macmillan, 1930.

Williams, *Lamps*. Williams, Hector. *The Lamps*. Vol. 5 of *Kenchreai, Eastern Port of Corinth: Results of Investigations by the University of Chicago and Indiana University for the American School of Classical Studies at Athens*. Leiden: Brill, 1981.

Williams, *Miracle Stories*. Williams, Benjamin E. *Miracle Stories in the Biblical Book Acts of the Apostles*. MBPS 59. Lewiston, N.Y.: Edwin Mellen, 2001.

Williams, *Miraculous*. Williams, T. C. *The Idea of the Miraculous: The Challenge to Science and Religion*. New York: St. Martin's, 1990.

Williams, "Moses." Williams, Margaret H. "Jewish Use of Moses as a Personal Name in Graeco-Roman Antiquity—A Note." *ZPE* 118 (1997): 274.

Williams, "Names." Williams, Margaret H. "Palestinian Jewish Personal Names in Acts." Pages 79–114 in *The Book of Acts in Its Palestinian Setting*. Edited by Richard Bauckham. Vol. 4 of *The Book of Acts in Its First Century Setting*. Edited by Bruce W. Winter. Grand Rapids: Eerdmans; Carlisle, U.K.: Paternoster, 1995.

Williams, "Neokoros." Williams, Jonathan. "Neokoros." *BrillPauly* 9:639–40.

Williams, "Old Testament Pentecost." Williams, David T. "Old Testament Pentecost." *Scriptura* 84 (2003): 498–511.

Williams, *Radical Reformation*. Williams, George Huntston. *The Radical Reformation*. Philadelphia: Westminster, 1962.

Williams, "Refounding." Williams, Charles K., II. "The Refounding of Corinth: Some Roman Religious Attitudes." Pages 26–37 in *Roman Architecture in the Greek World*. Edited by S. Macready and F. S. Thompson. London: Society of Antiquaries, 1987.

Williams, *Renewal Theology*. Williams, J. Rodman. *Renewal Theology*. 3 vols. Grand Rapids: Zondervan, 1990.

Williams, "Righteousness." Williams, Sam K. "The 'Righteousness of God' in Romans." *JBL* 99 (2, 1980): 241–90.

Williams, "Roman Corinth." Williams, Charles K., II. "Roman Corinth: The Final Years of Pagan Cult Facilities along East Theater Street." Pages 221–47 in *Urban Religion in Roman Corinth: Interdisciplinary Approaches*. Edited by Daniel N. Schowalter and Steven J. Friesen. HTS 53. Cambridge, Mass.: Harvard University Press, 2005.

Williams, "Seismology." Williams, Gareth D. "Greco-Roman Seismology and Seneca on Earthquakes in *Natural Questions* 6." *JRS* 96 (2006): 124–46.

Williams, *Shame*. Williams, Bernard. *Shame and Necessity*. Berkeley: University of California Press, 1993.

Williams, *Signs*. Williams, Don. *Signs, Wonders, and the Kingdom of God: A Biblical Guide for the Reluctant Skeptic*. Ann Arbor: Servant, 1989.

Williams, "Smith on Pharisees." Williams, David S. "Morton Smith on the Pharisees in Josephus." *JQR* 84 (1, 1993): 29–41.

Williams, "Structure Re-considered." Williams, Margaret H. "The Structure of Roman Jewry Re-considered—Were the Synagogues of Ancient Rome Entirely Homogeneous?" *ZPE* 104 (1994): 129–41.

Williams, *Systematic Theology*. Williams, Ernest S. *Systematic Theology*. 3 vols. Springfield, Mo.: Gospel, 1953.

Williams, "Theology of Amos." Williams, Donald L. "The Theology of Amos." *Rev Exp* 63 (Fall 1966): 393–403.

Williams, "Θεοσεβὴς." Williams, Margaret H. "'Θεοσεβὴς γὰρ ἦν'—The Jewish Tendencies of Poppaea Sabina." *JTS* 39 (1, 1988): 97–111.

Williams, *Tongues*. Williams, Cyril G. *Tongues of the Spirit: A Study of Pentecostal Glossolalia and Related Phenomena*. Cardiff: University of Wales Press, 1981.

Williams, "Winds." Williams, Gareth. "Seneca on Winds: The Art of Anemology in *Natural Questions* 5." *AJP* 126 (3, 2005): 417–50.

Williamson, *Chronicles*. Williamson, H. G. M. *1 and 2 Chronicles*. NCBC. Grand Rapids: Eerdmans; London: Marshall, Morgan & Scott, 1982.

Williamson, "Land." Williamson, Paul R. "Land." *DOTHB* 638–43.

Williamson, "Tradition." Williamson, Clark M. "The 'Adversus Judaeos' Tradition in Christian Theology." *Enc* 39 (Summer 1978): 273–96.

Williamson, "Triumph." Williamson, Lamar, Jr. "Led in Triumph: Paul's Use of *thriambeuō*." *Interpretation* 22 (3, 1968): 317–32.

Williamson, *World of Josephus*. Williamson, G. A. *The World of Josephus*. London: Secher & Warburg, 1964.

Willimon, *Acts*. Willimon, William H. *Acts*. IBC. Louisville: John Knox, 1988.

Willis, "Banquets." Willis, Wendell L. "Banquets." *DNTB* 143–46.

Willis, "Corinthusne?" Willis, Wendell L. "Corinthusne deletus est?" *BZ* 35 (2, 1991): 233–41.

Willis, *Idol Meat*. Willis, Wendell L. *Idol Meat in Corinth: The Pauline Argument in 1 Corinthians 8 and 10*. SBLDS 68. Chico, Calif.: Scholars Press, 1985.

Willis, "Networking." Willis, Wendell. "The Networking of the Pauline Churches: An Exploratory Essay." *ResQ* 50 (2, 2008): 69–78.

Willitts, "Messianism." Willitts, Joel. "Matthew and Psalms of Solomon's Messianism: A Comparative Study in First-Century Messianology." *BBR* 22 (1, 2012): 27–50.

Willner, "Definition." Willner, Dorothy. "Definition and Violation: Incest and the Incest Taboos." *Man* 18 (1983): 134–59.

Willner, "Oedipus Complex." Willner, Dorothy. "The Oedipus Complex, Antigone, and Electra: The Woman as Hero and Victim." *AmAnth* 84 (1, 1982): 58–78.

Willoughby, *Initiation*. Willoughby, Harold R. *Pagan Initiation: A Study of Mystery Initiations in the Graeco-Roman World*. Chicago: University of Chicago Press, 1929.

Wills, "Aesop Tradition." Wills, Lawrence M. "The Aesop Tradition." Pages 222–37 in *The Historical Jesus in Context*. Edited by Amy-Jill Levine, Dale C. Allison Jr., and John Dominic Crossan. PrRR. Princeton: Princeton University Press, 2006.

Wills, "Depiction of Jews." Wills, Lawrence M. "The Depiction of the Jews in Acts." *JBL* 110 (4, 1991): 631–54.

Wills, "Form of Sermon." Wills, Lawrence M. "The Form of the Sermon in Hellenistic Judaism and Early Christianity." *HTR* 77 (3–4, 1984): 277–99.

Wills, *Quest*. Wills, Lawrence M. *The Quest of the Historical Gospel: Mark, John, and the Origins of the Gospel Genre*. London: Routledge, 1997.

Wills, Yaeger, and Sandy, "Effect." Wills, Thomas Ashby, Alison M. Yaeger, and James M. Sandy. "Buffering Effect of Religiosity for Adolescent Substance Use." *Psychology of Addictive Behaviors* 17 (1, 2003): 24–31.

Wilmore, *Religion*. Wilmore, Gayraud S. *Black Religion and Black Radicalism: An Interpretation of the Religious History of Afro-American People*. 2nd rev. ed. Maryknoll, N.Y.: Orbis, 1989.

Wilshire, "Servant-City." Wilshire, Leland Edward. "The Servant-City: A New Interpretation of the 'Servant of the Lord' in the Servant Songs of Deutero-Isaiah." *JBL* 94 (3, Sept. 1975): 356–67.

Wilson, "Apostle Apollos." Wilson, Andrew. "Apostle Apollos?" *JETS* 56 (2, June 2013): 325–35.

Wilson, *Approaches*. Wilson, Robert R. *Sociological Approaches to the Old Testament*. Philadelphia: Fortress, 1984.

Wilson, "Barbers." Wilson, Marvin R. "Barbers and Beards." Pages 136–45 in vol. 1 of *Dictionary of Daily Life in Biblical and Post-Biblical Antiquity*. Edited by Edwin M. Yamauchi and Marvin R. Wilson. Peabody, Mass.: Hendrickson, 2014.

Wilson, "Bribery." Wilson, Marvin R. "Bribery." Pages 217–25 in vol. 1 of *Dictionary of Daily Life in Biblical and Post-Biblical Antiquity*. Edited by Edwin M. Yamauchi and Marvin R. Wilson. Peabody, Mass.: Hendrickson, 2014.

Wilson, "Cilicia." Wilson, Mark. "Cilicia: The First Christian Churches in Anatolia." *TynBul* 54 (1, 2003): 15–30.

Wilson, *Culture of Egypt*. Wilson, John A. *The Culture of Ancient Egypt*. Chicago: University of Chicago Press, 1951.

Wilson, "Date." Wilson, Gerald H. "A First Century C.E. Date for the Closing of the Book of Psalms?" *JBQ* 28 (2, 2000): 102–10.

Wilson, "Early Prophecy." Wilson, Robert R. "Early Israelite Prophecy." *Interpretation* 32 (Jan. 1978): 3–16.

Wilson, "Ecstasy." Wilson, Robert R. "Prophecy and Ecstasy: A Reexamination." *JBL* 98 (3, 1979): 321–37.

Wilson, *Editing of Psalter.* Wilson, Gerald H. *The Editing of the Hebrew Psalter.* Chico, Calif.: Scholars Press, 1985.

Wilson, "*Fullonica.*" Wilson, Andrew. "The Archaeology of the Roman *fullonica.*" *JRA* 16 (2003): 442–46.

Wilson, *Gentile Mission.* Wilson, Stephen G. *The Gentiles and the Gentile Mission in Luke-Acts.* SNTSMS 23. Cambridge: Cambridge University Press, 1973.

Wilson, *Gnosis and New Testament.* Wilson, R. McL. *Gnosis and the New Testament.* Philadelphia: Fortess; Oxford: Blackwell, 1968.

Wilson, *Gnostic Problem.* Wilson, R. McL. *The Gnostic Problem.* London: A. R. Mowbray, 1958.

Wilson, "Hellenistic Judaism." Wilson, Walter T. "Hellenistic Judaism." *DNTB* 477–82.

Wilson, *Hungry.* Wilson, Carol B. *For I Was Hungry and You Gave Me Food: Pragmatics of Food Access in the Gospel of Matthew.* Eugene, Ore: Pickwick, 2014.

Wilson, "Hysteria." Wilson, William P. "Hysteria and Demons, Depression and Oppression, Good and Evil." Pages 223–31 in *Demon Possession: A Medical, Historical, Anthropological, and Theological Symposium.* Edited by John Warwick Montgomery. Minneapolis: Bethany House, 1976.

Wilson, *Leaving.* Wilson, Stephen G. *Leaving the Fold: Apostates and Defectors in Antiquity.* Minneapolis: Fortress, 2004.

Wilson, "Lukan Eschatology." Wilson, Stephen G. "Lukan Eschatology." *NTS* 16 (4, 1970): 330–47.

Wilson, *Luke and Law.* Wilson, Stephen G. *Luke and the Law.* SNTSMS 50. Cambridge: Cambridge University Press, 1983.

Wilson, "Miracle Events." Wilson, William P. "How Religious or Spiritual Miracle Events Happen Today." Pages 264–79 in *Religious and Spiritual Events.* Vol. 1 of *Miracles: God, Science, and Psychology in the Paranormal.* Edited by J. Harold Ellens. 3 vols. Westport, Conn.; London: Praeger, 2008.

Wilson, *Pastoral Epistles.* Wilson, Stephen G. *Luke and the Pastoral Epistles.* London: SPCK, 1979.

Wilson, personal correspondence. Wilson, Mark. Personal correspondence, Nov. 25, 2011; Oct. 13, 2014.

Wilson, "Philo and Gnosticism." Wilson, R. McL. "Philo of Alexandria and Gnosticism." *Kairos* 14 (3, 1972): 213–19.

Wilson, "Philo and Gospel." Wilson, R. McL. "Philo and the Fourth Gospel." *ExpT* 65 (2, 1953): 47–49.

Wilson, *Psalms.* Wilson, Gerald H. *Psalms: Volume 1.* NIVAC. Grand Rapids: Zondervan, 2002.

Wilson, "Rhetoric." Wilson, Marcus. "Rhetoric and the Younger Seneca." Pages 425–38 in *A Companion to Roman Rhetoric.* Edited by William Dominik and Jon Hall. Oxford: Blackwell, 2007.

Wilson, *Rituals of Kinship.* Wilson, Monica. *Rituals of Kinship among the Nyakyusa.* London: Oxford University Press, 1957.

Wilson, "Route." Wilson, Mark. "The Route of Paul's First Journey to Pisidian Antioch." *NTS* 55 (4, 2009): 471–83.

Wilson, "Scholarship." Wilson, Nigel Guy. "Scholarship, Ancient: Greek." *OCD*³ 1363–64.

Wilson, *Sicily.* Wilson, Roger John Anthony. *Sicily under the Roman Empire: The Archaeology of a Roman Province, 36 BC–AD 535.* Archaeologists' Guides to the Roman Empire. Warminster, England: Aris & Phillips, 1990.

Wilson, "Simon." Wilson, R. McL. "Simon and Gnostic Origins." Pages 485–91 in *Les Actes des apôtres: Traditions, rédaction, théologie.* Edited by Jacob Kremer. BETL 48. Gembloux, Belg.: J. Duculot; Leuven: Leuven University Press, 1979.

Wilson, "Spirit." Wilson, R. McL. "The Spirit in Gnostic Literature." Pages 345–55 in *Christ and Spirit in the New Testament: Studies in Honour of C. F. D. Moule.* Edited by Barnabas Lindars and Stephen S. Smalley. Cambridge: Cambridge University Press, 1973.

Wilson, "Urban Legends." Wilson, Walter T. "Urban Legends: Acts 10:1–11:18 and the Strategies of Greco-Roman Foundation Narratives." *JBL* 120 (1, 2001): 77–99.

Wilson and Sperber, "Outline." Wilson, Deirdre, and Dan Sperber. "An Outline of Relevance Theory." Pages 21–41 in *Encontro de linguistas: Actas.* Edited by H. O. Alves. UCPLA. Minho, Port.: Universidade do Minho, 1985.

Wilson and Sperber, "Representation." Wilson, Deirdre, and Dan Sperber. "Representation and Relevance." Pages 133–53 in *Mental Representations: The Interface between Language and Reality.* Edited by Ruth M. Kempson. Cambridge: Cambridge University Press, 1988.

Wilson and Tzaferis, "Banias Dig." Wilson, John F., and Vassilios Tzaferis. "Banias Dig Reveals King's Palace." *BAR* 24 (1, 1998): 54–61, 85.

Wilt, "Appealing to Context." Wilt, Timothy. "On Appealing to Context." *BTr* 42 (2, 1991): 234–36.

Wimber, *Healing.* Wimber, John, with Kevin Springer. *Power Healing.* San Francisco: Harper & Row, 1987.

Wimber, *Power Evangelism.* Wimber, John, with Kevin Springer. *Power Evangelism.* San Francisco: Harper & Row, 1986.

Wimmer, *Fasting.* Wimmer, Joseph F. *Fasting in the New Testament: A Study in Biblical Theology.* New York: Paulist, 1982.

Wimsatt and Beardsley, "Intentional Fallacy." Wimsatt, W. K., and Monroe C. Beardsley. "The Intentional Fallacy." Pages 3–18 in *The Verbal Icon: Studies in the Meaning of Poetry.* Edited by W. K. Wimsatt. Lexington: University of Kentucky, 1954.

Winandy, "Finale des Actes." Winandy, Jacques. "La finale des Actes: Histoire ou théologie." *ETL* 73 (1, 1997): 103–6.

Winckler, "Gardens." Winckler, Jack. "Gardens of Nymphs: Public and Private in Sappho's Lyrics." *WomSt* 8 (1–2, 1981): 65–91.

Winckley, "Ministry." Winckley, Edward. "The Church's Ministry of Healing." Pages 175–81 in *Healing and Religious Faith.* Edited by Claude A. Frazier. Philadelphia: United Church, 1974.

Windisch, "Christusepiphanie." Windisch, Hans. "Die Christusepiphanie vor Damascus (Act 9, 22 und 26) und ihre religionsgeschichtlichen Parallelen." *ZNW* 31 (1962): 1–23.

Windisch, "Tradition." Windisch, Hans. "The Case against the Tradition." *Beg Chr* 2:298–348.

Wineland, "Amphipolis." Wineland, John D. "Amphipolis." *ABD* 1:216–17.

Wineland, "Attalia." Wineland, John D. "Attalia." *ABD* 1:523.

Wineland, "Derbe." Wineland, John D. "Derbe." *ABD* 2:144–45.

Wineland, "Patara." Wineland, John D. "Patara." *ABD* 5:177–78.

Wineland, "Samos." Wineland, John D. "Samos." *ABD* 5:948.

Winger, "Grace." Winger, Michael. "From Grace to Sin: Names and Abstractions in Paul's Letters." *NovT* 41 (2, 1999): 145–75.

Winiarczyk, "Altertum?" Winiarczyk, Marek. "Wer galt im Altertum als Atheist?" *Phil* 128 (2, 1984): 157–83.

Wink, "Model." Wink, Walter. "The World Systems Model." Edited by Gareth Higgins. Pages 47–71 in *Understanding Spiritual Warfare: Four Views.* Edited by

James K. Beilby and Paul Rhodes Eddy. Grand Rapids: Baker Academic, 2012.

Wink, "Stories." Wink, Walter. "Our Stories, Cosmic Stories, and the Biblical Story." Pages 209–22 in *Sacred Stories: A Celebration of the Power of Story to Transform and Heal*. Edited by Charles and Anne Simpkinson. San Francisco: HarperSanFrancisco, 1993.

Wink, "Worldview." Wink, Walter. "The New Worldview: Spirit at the Core of Everything." Pages 17–28 in *Transforming the Powers: Peace, Justice, and the Domination System*. Edited by Ray Gingerich and Ted Grimsrud. Minneapolis: Fortress, 2006.

Wink, "Write." Wink, Walter. "Write What You See." *FourR* 7 (3, May 1994): 3–9.

Winkelman, "Spirituality." Winkelman, Michael. "Spirituality and the Healing of Addictions: A Shamanic Drumming Approach." Pages 455–70 in *Religion and Healing in America*. Edited by Linda L. Barnes and Susan S. Sered. New York: Oxford University Press, 2005.

Winkelman and Carr, "Approach." Winkelman, Michael, and Christopher Carr. "Teaching about Shamanism and Religious Healing: A Cross-cultural, Biosocial-Spiritual Approach." Pages 171–90 in *Teaching Religion and Healing*. Edited by Linda L. Barnes and Inés Talamantez. AARTRSS. Oxford: Oxford University Press, 2006.

Winslow, "Religion." Winslow, Donald. "Religion and the Early Roman Empire." Pages 237–54 in *The Catacombs and the Colosseum: The Roman Empire as the Setting of Primitive Christianity*. Edited by Stephen Benko and John J. O'Rourke. Valley Forge, Pa.: Judson, 1971.

Winston, "Determinism." Winston, David S. "Freedom and Determinism in Greek Philosophy and Jewish Hellenistic Wisdom." *Studia philonica* 2 (1973): 40–50.

Winston, *Freedom*. Winston, David. *Freedom and Determinism in Philo of Alexandria*. PSCC 20. Berkeley, Calif.: Center for Hermeneutical Studies in Hellenistic and Modern Culture, 1976.

Winston, "Freedom." Winston, David S. "Freedom and Determinism in Philo of Alexandria." *Studia philonica* 3 (1974–75): 47–70.

Winston, "Philo's Mysticism." Winston, David. "Philo's Mysticism." *SPhilA* 8 (1996): 74–82.

Winston, "Types of Prophecy." Winston, David. "Two Types of Mosaic Prophecy according to Philo." *JSP* 4 (1989): 49–67.

Winter, "Antioch." Winter, S. C. "Antioch in Acts and Maccoby's 'Two-Tiered' Christianity." *Forum* 4 (1, 2001): 27–44.

Winter, "Athenians." Winter, Bruce W. "Introducing the Athenians to God: Paul's Failed Apologetic in Acts 17?" *Them* 31 (1, 2005): 38–59.

Winter, "Bibliography." Winter, P. "Bibliography to Josephus, *Antiquitates judaicae*, XVIII, 63, 64." *JHistS* 2 (4, 1969–70): 292–96.

Winter, "*Captatio benevolentiae*." Winter, Bruce W. "The Importance of the *captatio benevolentiae* in the Speeches of Tertullus and Paul in Acts 24:1–21." *JTS* 42 (2, 1991): 505–31.

Winter, "Gallio." Winter, Bruce W. "Rehabilitating Gallio and His Judgement in Acts 18:14–15." *TynBul* 57 (2, 2006): 291–308.

Winter, "Gallio's Ruling." Winter, Bruce W. "Gallio's Ruling on the Legal Status of Early Christianity (Acts 18:14–15)." *TynBul* 50 (2, 1999): 213–24.

Winter, "Imperial Cult." Winter, Bruce W. "The Imperial Cult." Pages 93–103 in *The Book of Acts in Its Graeco-Roman Setting*. Edited by David W. J. Gill and Conrad Gempf. Vol. 2 of *The Book of Acts in Its First Century Setting*. Edited by Bruce W. Winter. Grand Rapids: Eerdmans; Carlisle, U.K.: Paternoster, 1994.

Winter, "Imperial Cult: Corinthian Church." Winter, Bruce W. "The Achaean Federal Imperial Cult, II: The Corinthian Church." *TynBul* 46 (1, 1995): 169–78.

Winter, "Introducing Gods." Winter, Bruce W. "On Introducing Gods to Athens: An Alternative Reading of Acts 17:18–20." *TynBul* 47 (1, 1996): 71–90.

Winter, *Left Corinth*. Winter, Bruce W. *After Paul Left Corinth: The Influence of Secular Ethics and Social Change*. Grand Rapids and Cambridge: Eerdmans, 2001.

Winter, "Litigation." Winter, Bruce W. "Civil Litigation in Secular Corinth and the Church: The Forensic Background to 1 Corinthians 6.1–8." *NTS* 37 (4, 1991): 559–72.

Winter, "Observations." Winter, Paul. "Some Observations on the Language in the Birth and Infancy Stories of the Third Gospel." *NTS* 1 (2, 1954): 111–21.

Winter, "Official Proceedings." Winter, Bruce W. "Official Proceedings and the Forensic Speeches in Acts 24–26." Pages 305–36 in *The Book of Acts in Its Ancient Literary Setting*. Edited by Bruce W. Winter and Andrew D. Clark. Vol. 1 of *The Book of Acts in Its First Century Setting*. Edited by Bruce W. Winter. Grand Rapids: Eerdmans; Carlisle, U.K.: Paternoster, 1993.

Winter, "Philo among Sophists." Winter, Bruce W. "Philo and Paul among the Sophists." PhD diss., Macquarrie University, 1989.

Winter, *Philo and Paul*. Winter, Bruce W. *Philo and Paul among the Sophists*. SNTSMS 96. Cambridge: Cambridge University Press, 1997.

Winter, "Public." Winter, Bruce W. "In Public and in Private: Early Christians and Religious Pluralism." Pages 125–48 in *One God, One Lord: Christianity in a World of Religious Pluralism*. Edited by A. D. Clarke and B. W. Winter. 2nd ed. Grand Rapids: Baker, 1992.

Winter, "Shortages." Winter, Bruce W. "Acts and Food Shortages." Pages 59–78 in *The Book of Acts in Its Graeco-Roman Setting*. Edited by David W. J. Gill and Conrad Gempf. Vol. 2 of *The Book of Acts in Its First Century Setting*. Edited by Bruce W. Winter. Grand Rapids: Eerdmans; Carlisle, U.K.: Paternoster, 1994.

Winter, *Trial*. Winter, Paul. *On the Trial of Jesus*. SJFWJ 1. Berlin: de Gruyter, 1961.

Winter, *Welfare*. Winter, Bruce W. *Seek the Welfare of the City: Christians as Benefactors and Citizens*. First-Century Christians in the Graeco-Roman World. Grand Rapids: Eerdmans; Carlisle, U.K.: Paternoster, 1994.

Winter, *Wives*. Winter, Bruce W. *Roman Wives, Roman Widows: The Appearance of New Women and the Pauline Communities*. Grand Rapids: Eerdmans, 2003.

Winterbottom, "Asianism." Winterbottom, Michael. "Asianism and Atticism." *OCD*[3] 191.

Winterbottom, "*Recitatio*." Winterbottom, Michael. "*Recitatio*." *OCD*[3] 1295–96.

Winterbottom, "Rhetoric." Winterbottom, Michael. "Rhetoric, Latin." *OCD*[3] 1314.

Wintermute, "Introduction." Wintermute, Orval S. Introduction to "Jubilees." *OTP* 2:35–50.

Wire, *Prophets*. Wire, Antoinette Clark. *The Corinthian Women Prophets: A Reconstruction through Paul's Rhetoric*. Minneapolis: Fortress, 1990.

Wirgin, *Jubilees*. Wirgin, Wolf. *The Book of Jubilees and the Maccabaean Era of Shmittah Cycles*. LUOSM Series 7. [Leeds: Leeds University Oriental Society, 1965.]

Wischmeyer, "ΘΕΟΣ ΥΨΙΣΤΟΣ." Wischmeyer, Wolfgang. "ΘΕΟΣ ΥΨΙΣΤΟΣ: Neues zu einer alten Debatte." *ZAC/JAC* 9 (1, 2005): 149–68.

Wise, "4Q318." Wise, Michael O. "Thunder Text (4Q318)." *DNTB* 1233–35.

Wise, "11QTemple." Wise, Michael O. "Temple Scroll (11QTemple)." *DNTB* 1183–86.

Wise, "General Introduction." Wise, Michael O. "Dead Sea Scrolls: General Introduction." *DNTB* 252–66.

Wise, "Introduction to 4Q158." Wise, Michael O. Introduction to 4Q158. *DSSNT* 199–200.

Wise, "Introduction to 4Q242." Wise, Michael O. Introduction to 4Q242. *DSSNT* 265–66.

Wise, "Introduction to 4Q370." Wise, Michael O. Introduction to 4Q370. *DSSNT* 330.

Wise, "Introduction to 4Q374." Wise, Michael O. Introduction to 4Q374. *DSSNT* 335.

Wise, "Introduction to 4Q377." Wise, Michael O. Introduction to 4Q377. *DSSNT* 337–38.

Wise, "Introduction to 4Q470." Wise, Michael O. Introduction to 4Q470. *DSSNT* 403.

Wise, "Introduction to Apocryphal Psalms." Wise, Michael O. Introduction to the Apocryphal Psalms. *DSSNT* 198.

Wise, "Palestinian Aramaic." Wise, Michael O. "Palestinian Aramaic." *OEANE* 4:237–38.

Wise, "To Know." Wise, Michael O. "To Know the Times and the Seasons: A Study of the Aramaic Chronograph 4Q559." *JSP* 15 (1997): 3–51.

Wise and Tabor, "Messiah." Wise, Michael O., and James D. Tabor. "The Messiah at Qumran." *BAR* 18 (6, 1992): 60–63, 65.

Wiseman, "Abraham." Wiseman, D. J. "Abraham Reassessed." Pages 139–56 in *Essays on the Patriarchal Narratives*. Edited by A. R. Millard and D. J. Wiseman. Leicester, England: Inter-Varsity, 1980.

Wiseman, "Decree." Wiseman, T. P. "'There Went Out a Decree from Caesar Augustus . . .'" *NTS* 33 (3, 1987): 479–80.

Wiseman, "Gymnasium Area." Wiseman, James A. "The Gymnasium Area at Corinth, 1969–70." *Hesperia* 41 (1972): 1–42.

Wiseman, *Historiography.* Wiseman, T. P. *Historiography and Imagination: Eight Essays on Roman Culture.* Exeter: University of Exeter Press, 1994.

Wiseman, "Lying Historians." Wiseman, T. P. "Lying Historians: Seven Types of Mendacity." Pages 314–36 in *Greek and Roman Historiography.* Oxford Readings in Classical Studies. Edited by John Marincola. New York: Oxford University Press, 2011.

Wiseman, "Macedonian Family." Wiseman, James. "A Distinguished Macedonian Family of the Roman Imperial Period." *AJA* 88 (1984): 567–82.

Wiseman, "Prehistory." Wiseman, T. P. "The Prehistory of Roman Historiography." Pages 67–75 in *A Companion to Greek and Roman Historiography.* Edited by John Marincola. 2 vols. Oxford: Blackwell, 2007.

Wiseman, *Records.* Wiseman, P. J. *Ancient Records and the Structure of Genesis: A Case for Literary Unity.* Edited by D. J. Wiseman. Nashville: Thomas Nelson, 1985.

Wiseman, "Tents." Wiseman, D. J. "They Lived in Tents." Pages 195–200 in *Biblical and Near Eastern Studies: Essays in Honor of William Sanford Lasor.* Edited by Gary A. Tuttle. Grand Rapids: Eerdmans, 1978.

Witcher, "Extended Metropolis." Witcher, Rob. "The Extended Metropolis: *Urbs, suburbium,* and Population." *JRA* 18 (2005): 120–38.

Witetschek, "Christus und Caesar." Witetschek, Stephan. "Christus und Caesar bei Lukas und Johannes: Der Kaiserkult in Ephesos und das Neue Testament." *MTZ* 60 (1, 2009): 51–61.

Witetschek, "Color." Witetschek, Stephan. "Artemis and Asiarchs: Some Remarks on Ephesian Local Colour in Acts 19." *Bib* 90 (3, 2009): 334–55.

Witherington, *Acts.* Witherington, Ben, III. *The Acts of the Apostles: A Socio-rhetorical Commentary.* Grand Rapids: Eerdmans, 1998.

Witherington, "Addendum." Witherington, Ben, III. "Editor's Addendum" to W. J. McCoy, "In the Shadow of Thucydides." Pages 23–32 in *History, Literature, and Society in the Book of Acts.* Edited by Ben Witherington III. Cambridge: Cambridge University Press, 1996.

Witherington, "Anti-feminist Tendencies." Witherington, Ben, III. "The Anti-feminist Tendencies of the 'Western' Text in Acts." *JBL* 103 (1, 1984): 82–84.

Witherington, "Christology." Witherington, Ben, III. "Christology." *DPL* 100–115.

Witherington, *Christology of Jesus.* Witherington, Ben, III. *The Christology of Jesus.* Minneapolis: Augsburg Fortress, 1990.

Witherington, *Corinthians.* Witherington, Ben, III. *Conflict and Community in Corinth: A Socio-rhetorical Commentary on 1 and 2 Corinthians.* Grand Rapids: Eerdmans, 1995.

Witherington, *Doctor.* Witherington, Ben, III. *Is There a Doctor in the House?* Grand Rapids: Zondervan, 2011.

Witherington, "Editing." Witherington, Ben, III. "Editing the Good News: Some Synoptic Lessons for the Study of Acts." Pages 324–47 in *History, Literature, and Society in the Book of Acts.* Edited by Ben Witherington III. Cambridge: Cambridge University Press, 1996.

Witherington, *End.* Witherington, Ben, III. *Jesus, Paul, and the End of the World: A Comparative Study in New Testament Eschatology.* Downers Grove, Ill.: Inter-Varsity, 1992.

Witherington, "Exception." Witherington, Ben, III. "Matthew 5.32 and 19.9—Exception or Exceptional Situation?" *NTS* 31 (4, 1985): 571–76.

Witherington, *Galatia.* Witherington, Ben, III. *Grace in Galatia: A Commentary on Paul's Letter to the Galatians.* Edinburgh: T&T Clark; Grand Rapids: Eerdmans, 1998.

Witherington, *Meal.* Witherington, Ben, III. *Making a Meal of It: Rethinking the Theology of the Lord's Supper.* Waco: Baylor University Press, 2007.

Witherington, *Philemon, Colossians, and Ephesians.* Witherington, Ben, III. *The Letters to Philemon, the Colossians, and the Ephesians: A Socio-Rhetorical Commentary on the Captivity Epistles.* Grand Rapids: Eerdmans, 2007.

Witherington, *Romans.* Witherington, Ben, III, with Darlene Hyatt. *Paul's Letter to the Romans: A Socio-rhetorical Commentary.* Grand Rapids: Eerdmans, 2004.

Witherington, "Salvation." Witherington, Ben, III. "Salvation and Health in Christian Antiquity: The Soteriology of Luke-Acts in Its First-Century Setting." Pages 145–66 in *Witness to the Gospel: The Theology of Acts.* Edited by I. Howard Marshall and David Peterson. Grand Rapids: Eerdmans, 1998.

Witherington, *Sage.* Witherington, Ben, III. *Jesus the Sage: The Pilgrimage of Wisdom.* Minneapolis: Fortress, 1994.

Witherington, *Story.* Witherington, Ben, III. *The New Testament Story.* Grand Rapids: Eerdmans, 2004.

Witherington, "Thoughts." Witherington, Ben, III. "Not So Idle Thoughts about *eidolothuton.*" *TynBul* 44 (2, 1993): 237–54.

Witherington, *Titus, Timothy, John.* Witherington, Ben, III. *A Socio-rhetorical Commentary on Titus, 1–2 Timothy, and 1–3 John.* Vol. 1 of *Letters and Homilies for Hellenized Christians.* Downers Grove, Ill.: IVP Academic; Nottingham, U.K.: Apollos, 2006.

Witherington, "Why Not Eat?" Witherington, Ben, III. "Why Not Eat Idol Meat? Is It What You Eat or Where You Eat It?" *BRev* 10 (3, 1994): 38–43, 54–55.

Witherington, *Wisdom.* Witherington, Ben, III. *John's Wisdom: A Commentary on the Fourth Gospel.* Louisville: Westminster John Knox, 1995.

Witherington, *Women.* Witherington, Ben, III. *Women in the Ministry of Jesus: A Study of Jesus' Attitudes to Women and Their Roles as Reflected in His Earthly Life.* SNTSMS 51. Cambridge: Cambridge University Press, 1984.

Witherup, "Cornelius Over Again." Witherup, Ronald D. "Cornelius Over and Over and Over Again: 'Functional Redundancy' in the Acts of the Apostles." *JSNT* 49 (1993): 45–66.

Witherup, "Functional Redundancy." Witherup, Ronald D. "Functional Redundancy in the Acts of the Apostles: A Case Study." *JSNT* 48 (1992): 67–86.

Wittke, "Antioch on Orontes." Wittke, Anne-Maria. "Antioch on the Orontes." *BrillPauly* 1:758.

Wittkowsky, "Zitate." Wittkowsky, Vadim. "'Pagane' Zitate im Neuen Testament." *NovT* 51 (2, 2009): 107–26.

Wittlieb, "Bedeutung." Wittlieb, Marian. "Die theologische Bedeutung der Erwähnung von 'Māšîah/Christós' in den Pseudepigraphen des Alten Testaments palästinischen Ursprungs." *BN* 50 (1989): 26–33.

Witulski, "Erzählstrategien." Witulski, Thomas. "Apologetische Erzählstrategien in der Apostelgeschichte—ein neuer Blick auf Acts 15:36–19:40." *NovT* 48 (4, 2006): 329–52.

Wiyono, "Timor Revival." Wiyono, Gani. "Timor Revival: A Historical Study of the Great Twentieth-Century Revival in Indonesia." *AJPS* 4 (2, 2001): 269–93.

Wodi, "Wodi." Wodi, Sam. "Wodi, Herbert Nyemahame Amadi." No pages. *DACB*. Online: http://www.dacb.org/stories/nigeria/wodi_amadi.html.

Woerther, "Origines." Woerther, Frédérique. "Aux origines de la notion rhétorique d'*èthos*." *REG* 118 (1, 2005): 79–116.

Wohl, "Scenes." Wohl, Victoria. "Scenes from a Marriage: Love and *logos* in Plutarch's *Coniugalia praecepta*." *Helios* 24 (2, 1997): 170–92.

Wojciechowski, "Aesopic Tradition." Wojciechowski, Michael. "Aesopic Tradition in the New Testament." *JGRCJ* 5 (2008): 99–109.

Wojciechowski, "Boasting." Wojciechowski, Michal. "Paul and Plutarch on Boasting." *JGRCJ* 3 (2006): 99–109.

Wojciechowski, "Don." Wojciechowski, Michal. "Le don de l'Esprit Saint dans Jean 20.22 selon Tg. Gn. 2.7." *NTS* 33 (2, 1987): 289–92.

Wojciechowski, "Vocabulary." Wojciechowski, Michal. "Philosophical Vocabulary of Arius Didymus and the New Testament." *RocT* 53 (1, 2006): 25–34.

Woldering, *Art.* Woldering, Irmgard. *The Art of Egypt: The Time of the Pharaohs.* New York: Greystone, 1963.

Wolf, "Virgin of Guadalupe." Wolf, Eric. "The Virgin of Guadalupe: A Mexican National Symbol." *JAmFolk* 71 (1958): 34–39. Repr., pages 112–15 in *Reader in Comparative Religion: An Anthropological Approach.* Edited by William A. Lessa and Evon Z. Vogt. 4th ed. New York: Harper & Row, 1979.

Wolfe, "Structure." Wolfe, Kenneth R. "The Chiastic Structure of Luke-Acts and Some Implications for Worship." *SWJT* 22 (2, 1980): 60–71.

Wolff, *Amos.* Wolff, Hans Walter. *Joel and Amos.* Hermeneia. Philadelphia: Fortress, 1977.

Wolff, "Λαλεῖν γλώσσαις." Wolff, Christian. "Λαλεῖν γλώσσαις in the Acts of the Apostles." Pages 189–99 in *Paul, Luke, and the Graeco-Roman World.* Edited by Alf Christophersen et al. JSNTSup 217. Sheffield, U.K.: Sheffield Academic, 2002; London: T&T Clark, 2003.

Wolffe, "Dismantling." Wolffe, John. "Dismantling Discrimination." *ChH* 53 (1997): 37–39.

Wolffe, *Expansion.* Wolffe, John. *The Expansion of Evangelicalism: The Age of Wilberforce, More, Chalmers, and Finney.* Downers Grove, Ill.: InterVarsity, 2007.

Wolfson, *Philo.* Wolfson, Harry Austryn. *Philo: Foundations of Religious Philosophy in Judaism, Christianity, and Islam.* 2 vols. 4th rev. ed. Cambridge, Mass.: Harvard University Press, 1968.

Wolter, "Apollos und Johannesjünger." Wolter, Michael. "Apollos und die ephesinischen Johannesjünger (Acts 18:24–19:7)." *ZNW* 78 (1–2, 1987): 49–73.

Wolter, "Epochengeschichte." Wolter, Michael. "Das lukanische Doppelwerk als Epochengeschichte." Pages 253–84 in *Die Apostelgeschichte und die hellenistische Geschichtsschreibung: Festschrift für Eckhard Plümacher zu seinem 65. Geburtstag.* Edited by Cilliers Breytenbach and Jens Schröter. Leiden: Brill, 2004.

Wolter, "Israel's Future and Delay." Wolter, Michael. "Israel's Future and the Delay of the Parousia, according to Luke." Pages 307–24 in *Jesus and the Heritage of Israel: Luke's Narrative Claim upon Israel's Legacy.* Edited by David P. Moessner. Luke the Interpreter of Israel 1. Harrisburg, Pa.: Trinity Press International, 1999.

Wolter, "Proömien." Wolter, Michael. "Die Proömien des lukanischen Doppelwerks (Lk 1,1–4 und Apg 1,1–2)." Pages 437–94 in *Die Apostelgeschichte im Kontext antiker und frühchristlicher Historiographie.* Edited by Jörg Frey, Clare K. Rothschild, and Jens Schröter, with Bettina Rost. BZNWK 162. Berlin: de Gruyter, 2009.

Womack, "Coprolalia." Womack, Sheila A. "From Coprolalia to Glossolalia: Structural Similarities Between Gilles de la Tourette Syndrome and Speaking in Tongues." *JMBeh* 3 (1, Winter 1982): 75–88.

Wood, "Dip." Wood, Bryant G. "To Dip or Sprinkle? The Qumran Cisterns in Perspective." *BASOR* 256 (Fall 1984): 45–60.

Wood, "Ethics." Wood, John A. "The Ethics of the Jerusalem Council." Pages 239–58 in *With Steadfast Purpose: Essays on Acts in Honor of Henry Jackson Flanders, Jr.* Edited by Naymond H. Keathley. Waco: Baylor University Press, 1990.

Wood, "Marxism and Greece." Wood, Ellen. "Marxism and Ancient Greece." *HistW* 11 (Spring 1981): 3–22.

Wood, "Typology." Wood, J. Edwin. "Isaac Typology in the New Testament." *NTS* 14 (4, 1968): 583–89.

Wood and Wood, "Preparation." Wood, R. Paul, and Wardine Wood. "Preparation for Signs and Wonders." Pages 60–73 in *Signs and Wonders in Ministry Today.* Edited by Benny C. Aker and Gary B. McGee. Foreword by Thomas E. Trask. Springfield, Mo.: Gospel, 1996.

Woodberry, "Roots." Woodberry, Robert D. "The Missionary Roots of Liberal Democracy." *American Political Science Review* 106 (2, May 2012): 244–74.

Woodhead and Wilson, "Syracuse." Woodhead, Arthur Geoffrey, and Roger J. A. Wilson. "Syracuse." *OCD³* 1463–64.

Woodman, "Cicero." Woodman, A. J. "Cicero on Historiography: *De Oratore* 2.51–64." *CJ* 104 (1, 2008): 23–31.

Woodman, *Rhetoric.* Woodman, A. J. *Rhetoric in Classical Historiography: Four Studies.* London: Croom Helm, 1988.

Woodman, *Tacitus.* Woodman, Anthony J. *Tacitus: The Annals.* Indianapolis: Hackett, 2004.

Woods, "Caligula." Woods, David. "Caligula on Augustus' Alleged Incest with Julia." *RMPhil* 152 (3–4, 2009): 400–404.

Woodward, "Angels." Woodward, Kenneth. "Angels." *Newsweek* (Dec. 27, 1993): 52–57.

Woodward, *Career.* Woodward, C. Vann. *The Strange Career of Jim Crow.* New York: Oxford University Press, 1957.

Woodward, *Miracles.* Woodward, Kenneth L. *The Book of Miracles: The Meaning of the Miracle Stories in Christianity, Judaism, Buddhism, Hinduism, Islam.* New York: Simon & Schuster, 2000.

Woodworth-Etter, *Diary.* Woodworth-Etter, Maria. *Signs and Wonders God Wrought in the Ministry for Forty Years.* Indianapolis: M. B. W. Etter, 1916. Reprinted as *A Diary of Signs and Wonders: A Classic.* Tulsa, Okla.: Harrison House, 1980.

Woodworth-Etter, *Miracles.* Woodworth-Etter, Maria. *Miracles, Signs, and Wonders Wrought in the Life and Ministry of Mrs. Woodworth-Etter from 1844–1916.* Portland, Ore.: Apostolic, 1984.

Woolf, "Becoming Roman." Woolf, Greg. "Becoming Roman, Staying Greek: Culture, Identity, and the Civilizing Process in the Roman East." *Proceedings of the Cambridge Philological Society* 40 (1995): 116–43.

Woolf, "Hedonist." Woolf, Raphael. "What Kind of Hedonist Was Epicurus?" *Phronesis* 49 (4, 2004): 302–22.

Woolf, "Literacy." Woolf, Greg. "Literacy or Literacies in Rome?" Pages 46–68 in *Ancient Literacies: The Culture of Reading in Greece and Rome*. Edited by William A. Johnston and Holt N. Parker. New York: Oxford University Press, 2009.

Woolf, "Romans and Natives." Woolf, Greg. "Beyond Romans and Natives." *WArch* 28 (3, 1997): 339–50.

Woolley, *Exorcism*. Woolley, Reginald Maxwell. *Exorcism and the Healing of the Sick*. London: SPCK, 1932.

Wordelman, "Divides." Wordelman, Amy L. "Cultural Divides and Dual Realities: A Greco-Roman Context for Acts 14." Pages 205–32 in *Contextualizing Acts: Lukan Narrative and Greco-Roman Discourse*. Edited by Todd Penner and Caroline Vander Stichele. SBLSymS 20. Atlanta: SBL, 2003.

Workman, "Date." Workman, W. P. "A New Date-Indication in Acts." *ExpT* 11 (7, 1900): 316–19.

Wormell and Mitchell, "Lampsacus." Wormell, Donald E. W., and Stephen Mitchell. "Lampsacus." *OCD*³ 813.

Worsfold, *Virgins*. Worsfold, T. Cato. *The History of the Vestal Virgins of Rome*. 2nd ed. London: Rider, 1934.

Wotschitzky, "Ephesus." Wotschitzky, Alfons. "Ephesus: Past, Present, and Future of a Great Metropolis." *Archaeology* 14 (1961): 205–12.

Wrede, *Secret*. Wrede, William. *The Messianic Secret*. Translated by J. C. G. Greig. Cambridge, U.K.: James Clarke, 1971.

Wright, *Acts*. Wright, N. T. *Acts for Everyone*. Part One: Chapters 1–12. Louisville: Westminster John Knox, 2008.

Wright, *Archaeology*. Wright, G. Ernest. *Biblical Archaeology*. Philadelphia: Westminster, 1962.

Wright, "Birth." Wright, N. T. "A New Birth? An Article Review of John Dominic Crossan's *The Birth of Christianity: Discovering What Happened in the Years Immediately after the Execution of Jesus*." *SJT* 53 (1, 2000): 72–91.

Wright, "Building Materials." Wright, G. R. H. "Building Materials and Techniques: Persian through Roman Periods." *OEANE* 1:367–79.

Wright, "Day of Atonement." Wright, David P. "Day of Atonement." *ABD* 2:72–76.

Wright, "'Ebed/Doulos." Wright, Benjamin G. "'Ebed/Doulos: Terms and Social Status in the Meeting of Hebrew Biblical

and Hellenistic Roman Culture." *Semeia* 83–84 (1998): 83–111.

Wright, *Ethics*. Wright, Christopher J. *Old Testament Ethics for the People of God*. Downers Grove, Ill.: InterVarsity, 2004.

Wright, *Founder*. Wright, N. T. *What Saint Paul Really Said: Was Paul of Tarsus the Real Founder of Christianity?* Grand Rapids: Eerdmans, 1997.

Wright, "Interpretations." Wright, Nigel G. "Charismatic Interpretations of the Demonic." Pages 149–63 in *The Unseen World: Christian Reflections on Angels, Demons, and the Heavenly Realm*. Edited by Anthony N. S. Lane. Grand Rapids: Baker; Carlisle, U.K.: Paternoster, 1996.

Wright, *Justification*. Wright, N. T. *Justification: God's Plan and Paul's Vision*. Downers Grove, Ill.: IVP Academic, 2009.

Wright, "Justin Martyr's Testimony." Wright, David F. "Christian Faith in the Greek World: Justin Martyr's Testimony." *EvQ* 54 (2, 1982): 77–87.

Wright, "Midrash." Wright, Addison G. "The Literary Genre Midrash." *CBQ* 28 (2, 1966): 105–38; (4, 1966): 417–57.

Wright, *Miracle*. Wright, C. J. *Miracles in History and in Modern Thought or Miracle and Christian Apologetic*. New York: Henry Holt, 1930.

Wright, *Mission*. Wright, Christopher J. H. *The Mission of God: Unlocking the Bible's Grand Narrative*. Downers Grove, Ill.: IVP Academic, 2006.

Wright, *Mission of People*. Wright, Christopher J. H. *The Mission of God's People: A Biblical Theology of the Church's Mission*. Grand Rapids: Zondervan, 2010.

Wright, *Paul*. Wright, N. T. *Paul and the Faithfulness of God*. 2 vols. Vol. 4 of *Christian Origins and the Question of God*. Minneapolis: Fortress, 2013.

Wright, "Paul and Empire." Wright, N. T. "Paul and Empire." Pages 285–97 in *The Blackwell Companion to Paul*. Edited by Stephen Westerholm. BCompRel. Oxford: Blackwell, 2011.

Wright, *People of God*. Wright, N. T. *The New Testament and the People of God*. Vol. 1 of *Christian Origins and the Question of God*. Minneapolis: Fortress; London: SPCK, 1992.

Wright, "Perspective on Paul." Wright, N. T. "A Fresh Perspective on Paul?" *BJRL* 83 (1, 2001): 21–39.

Wright, *Perspectives*. Wright, N. T. *Pauline Perspectives: Essays on Paul, 1978–2013*. Minneapolis: Fortress, 2013.

Wright, *Process*. Wright, J. Stafford. *Man in the Process of Time: A Christian Assessment of the Powers and Functions of Human Personality*. Grand Rapids: Eerdmans, 1955.

Wright, "Response." Wright, N. T. "In Grateful Dialogue: A Response." Pages 244–77 in *Jesus and the Restoration of Israel: A Critical Assessment of N. T. Wright's Jesus and the Victory of God*. Edited by Carey C. Newman. Downers Grove, Ill.: InterVarsity, 1999.

Wright, *Resurrection*. Wright, N. T. *The Resurrection of the Son of God*. Vol. 3 of *Christian Origins and the Question of God*. Minneapolis: Fortress, 2003.

Wright, "Seminar." Wright, N. T. "Five Gospels but No Gospel: Jesus and the Seminar." Pages 83–120 in *Authenticating the Activities of Jesus*. Edited by Bruce Chilton and Craig A. Evans. NTTS 28.2. Leiden: Brill, 1999.

Wright, *Spirit through Old Testament*. Wright, Christopher J. H. *Knowing the Holy Spirit through the Old Testament*. Downers Grove, Ill.: IVP Academic, 2006.

Wright, "Temple." Wright, G. Ernest. "The Temple in Palestine-Syria." Pages 169–84 in *The Biblical Archaeologist Reader*. Edited by G. Ernest Wright and David Noel Freedman. Garden City, N.Y.: Doubleday, 1961.

Wright, *Victory*. Wright, N. T. *Jesus and the Victory of God*. Vol. 2 of *Christian Origins and the Question of God*. Minneapolis: Fortress, 1996.

Wright and Hübner, "Unclean and Clean." Wright, David P., and Hans Hübner. "Unclean and Clean." *ABD* 6:729–45.

Wuellner, "Arrangement." Wuellner, Wilhelm. "Arrangement." Pages 51–87 in *Handbook of Classical Rhetoric in the Hellenistic Period, 330 B.C.–A.D. 400*. Edited by Stanley E. Porter. Leiden: Brill, 1997.

Wuthnow, *Heaven*. Wuthnow, Robert. *After Heaven: Spirituality in America Since the 1950s*. Berkeley: University of California Press, 1998.

Wyatt, "Calf." Wyatt, Nicolas. "Calf." Pages 180–82 in *Dictionary of Deities and Demons in the Bible*. 2nd rev. ed. Edited by Karel van der Toorn, Bob Becking, and Pieter W. van der Horst. Leiden: Brill; Grand Rapids: Eerdmans, 1999.

Wycherley, "Athens." Wycherley, R. E. "St. Paul at Athens." *JTS* 19 (2, 1968): 619–21.

Wyckoff, "Baptism." Wyckoff, John W. "The Baptism in the Holy Spirit." Pages 423–55 in *Systematic Theology: A Pentecostal Perspective*. Edited by Stanley M. Horton. Springfield, Mo.: Logion, 1994.

Wykstra, "Problem." Wykstra, Stephen J. "The Problem of Miracle in the Apologetic from History." *JASA* 30 (4, 1978): 154–63.

Wyllie, "Effutu." Wyllie, Robert W. "Do the Effutu Really Believe That the Spirits

Cause Illness? A Ghanaian Case Study." *JRelAf* 24 (33, 1994): 228–40.

Wyllie, "Views." Wyllie, Robert. "Views on Suicide and Freedom in Stoic Philosophy and Some Related Contemporary Points of View." *Prudentia* 5 (1973): 15–32.

Wyschogrod, "Christianity and Law." Wyschogrod, Michael. "Christianity and Mosaic Law." *ProEccl* 2 (4, 1993): 451–59.

Wyschogrod, "Judaism and Christianity." Wyschogrod, Michael. "Judaism and Evangelical Christianity." Pages 34–52 in *Evangelicals and Jews in Conversation on Scripture, Theology, and History*. Edited by Marc H. Tanenbaum, Marvin R. Wilson, and James A. Rudin. Grand Rapids: Baker, 1978.

Xavier, "Faith." Xavier, Aloysius. "Faith vs. Law: A Cultural Identity Crisis in Pauline Theology." *BiBh* 27 (1, 2001): 5–18.

Xenakis, "Suicide Therapy." Xenakis, Jason. "Stoic Suicide Therapy." *Sophia* 40 (1972): 88–99.

Xeravits, "Moses Redivivus." Xeravits, Géza G. "Moses Redivivus in Qumran?" *QC* 11 (1–4, 2003): 91–105.

Yadin, "Attitude." Yadin, Yigael. "L'attitude essénienne envers la polygamie et le divorce." *RB* 79 (1, 1972): 98–99.

Yadin, *Masada*. Yadin, Yigael. *Masada: Herod's Fortress and the Zealots' Last Stand*. New York: Random House, 1966.

Yadin, "Melchizedek." Yadin, Yigael. "A Note on Melchizedek and Qumran." *IEJ* 15 (3, 1965): 152–54.

Yadin, *Scroll of War*. Yadin, Yigael. *The Scroll of the War of the Sons of Light against the Sons of Darkness*. Translated by Batya and Chaim Rabin. Oxford: Oxford University Press, 1962.

Yadin, "Temple Scroll." Yadin, Yigael. "The Temple Scroll." *BAR* 10 (5, 1984): 32–49.

Yahalom, "Angels." Yahalom, Joseph. "Angels Do Not Understand Aramaic: On the Literary Use of Jewish Palestinian Aramaic in Late Antiquity." *JJS* 47 (1, 1996): 33–44.

Yalman, "Healing Rituals." Yalman, Nur. "The Structure of Sinhalese Healing Rituals." Pages 115–50 in *Religion in South Asia*. Edited by Edward B. Harper. Seattle: University of Washington Press, 1964.

Yalman, "Structure." Yalman, Nur. "The Structure of the Sinhalese Kindred: A Re-Examination of the Dravidian Terminology." *AmAnth* 64 (June 1962): 548–75.

Yamamori and Chan, *Witnesses*. Yamamori, Tetsunao, and Kim-kwong Chan. *Witnesses to Power: Stories of God's Quiet Work in a Changing China*. Waynesboro, Ga., and Carlisle, U.K.: Paternoster, 2000.

Yamauchi, *Africa*. Yamauchi, Edwin M. *Africa and the Bible*. Foreword by Kenneth A. Kitchen. Grand Rapids: Baker, 2004.

Yamauchi, "Archives." Yamauchi, Edwin M. "Archives." Pages 75–81 in vol. 1 of *Dictionary of Daily Life in Biblical and Post-Biblical Antiquity*. Edited by Edwin M. Yamauchi and Marvin R. Wilson. Peabody, Mass.: Hendrickson, 2014.

Yamauchi, *Cities*. Yamauchi, Edwin M. *The Archaeology of New Testament Cities in Western Asia Minor*. Grand Rapids: Baker, 1980.

Yamauchi, "Concord." Yamauchi, Edwin M. "Concord, Conflict, and Community: Jewish and Evangelical Views of Scripture." Pages 154–96 in *Evangelicals and Jews in Conversation on Scripture, Theology, and History*. Edited by Marc H. Tannenbaum, Marvin R. Wilson, and James A. Rudin. Grand Rapids: Baker, 1978.

Yamauchi, "Crucifixion." Yamauchi, Edwin M. "The Crucifixion and Docetic Christology." *CTQ* 46 (1982): 1–20.

Yamauchi, "Cyrene in Libya." Yamauchi, Edwin M. "The Archaeology of Biblical Africa: Cyrene in Libya." *ABW* 2 (1, 1992): 6–18.

Yamauchi, *Gnosticism*. Yamauchi, Edwin M. *Pre-Christian Gnosticism: A Survey of the Proposed Evidences*. Grand Rapids: Eerdmans, 1973.

Yamauchi, "Homer." Yamauchi, Edwin M. "Historic Homer: Did It Happen?" *BAR* 33 (2, 2007): 28–37, 76.

Yamauchi, "Magic?" Yamauchi, Edwin M. "Magic or Miracle? Diseases, Demons, and Exorcisms." Pages 89–183 in *The Miracles of Jesus*. Edited by David Wenham and Craig Blomberg. Gospel Perspectives 6. Sheffield, U.K.: JSOT Press, 1986.

Yamauchi, "Magic in World." Yamauchi, Edwin M. "Magic in the Biblical World." *TynBul* 34 (1983): 169–200.

Yamauchi, *Persia*. Yamauchi, Edwin M. *Persia and the Bible*. Foreword by Donald J. Wiseman. Grand Rapids: Baker, 1990.

Yamauchi, "Qumran and Colosse." Yamauchi, Edwin M. "Qumran and Colosse." *BSac* 121 (482, 1964): 141–52.

Yamauchi, "Scythians." Yamauchi, Edwin M. "The Scythians—Who Were They? And Why Did Paul Include Them in Colossians 3:11?" *Priscilla Papers* 21 (4, 2007): 15–17.

Yamauchi, *Stones*. Yamauchi, Edwin M. *The Stones and the Scriptures: An Introduction to Biblical Archaeology*. Grand Rapids: Baker, 1972.

Yamauchi, "Troas." Yamauchi, Edwin M. "Troas." *ABD* 6:666–67.

Yamauchi, "Tyrannus." Yamauchi, Edwin M. "Tyrannus." *ABD* 6:686.

Yamazaki-Ransom, "Antiochus." Yamazaki-Ransom, Kazuhiko. "Paul, Agrippa I, and Antiochus IV: Two Persecutors in Acts in Light of 2 Maccabees 9." Pages 107–21 in *Luke-Acts and Empire: Essays in Honor of Robert L. Brawley*. Edited by David Rhoads, David Esterline, and Jae Won Lee. PrTMS 151. Eugene, Ore.: Pickwick, 2011.

Yancey, *Scholarship*. Yancey, George. *Compromising Scholarship: Religious and Political Bias in American Higher Education*. Waco: Baylor University Press, 2011.

Yao, "Barriers." Yao, Santos. "Dismantling Social Barriers through Table Fellowship, Acts 2:42–47." Pages 29–36 in *Mission in Acts: Ancient Narratives in Contemporary Context*. Edited by Robert L. Gallagher and Paul Hertig. AmSocMissS 34. Maryknoll, N.Y.: Orbis, 2004.

Yap, "Syndrome." Yap, P. M. "The Possession Syndrome: A Comparison of Hong Kong and French Findings." *JMenSc* 106 (Jan. 1960): 114–37.

Yarbrough, "Paul." Yarbrough, O. Larry. "Paul, Marriage, and Divorce." Pages 404–28 in *Paul in the Greco-Roman World: A Handbook*. Edited by J. Paul Sampley. Harrisburg, Pa.: Trinity Press International, 2003.

Yardeni, "Scroll." Yardeni, Ada. "A New Dead Sea Scroll in Stone? Bible-like Prophecy Was Mounted in a Wall 2,000 Years Ago." *BAR* 34 (1, 2008): 60–61.

Yarnell, "Bridges." Yarnell, Malcolm B., III. "Shall We 'Build Bridges' or 'Pull Down Strongholds'?" *SWJT* 47 (1, 2009): 73–100.

Yates, *Expansion*. Yates, Timothy. *The Expansion of Christianity*. Downers Grove, Ill.: InterVarsity, 2004.

Yates, "Worship." Yates, Roy. "'The Worship of Angels' (Col 2:18)." *ExpT* 97 (1, 1985): 12–15.

Yavetz, "Authors." Yavetz, Zvi. "Latin Authors on Jews and Dacians." *Historia* 47 (1, 1998): 77–107.

Yavetz, "Judeophobia." Yavetz, Zvi. "Judeophobia in Classical Antiquity: A Different Approach." *JJS* 44 (1, 1993): 1–22.

Yegül, "Complex." Yegül, F. Kret K. "The Bath-Gymnasium Complex." Pages 148–61 in *Sardis from Prehistoric to Roman Times: Results of the Archaeological Exploration of Sardis, 1958–1975*. Edited by George M. A. Hanfmann, assisted by William E. Mierse. Cambridge, Mass.: Harvard University Press, 1983.

Yener, "Taurus Mountains." Yener, K. Aslihan. "Taurus Mountains." *OEANE* 5:155–56.

Yeo, "Response." Yeo, K. K. "Response: Multicultural Readings: A Biblical Warrant and an Eschatological Vision."

Pages 27–37 in *Global Voices: Reading the Bible in the Majority World*. Edited by Craig Keener and M. Daniel Carroll R. Foreword by Edwin Yamauchi. Peabody, Mass.: Hendrickson, 2013.

Yeomans, *Healing*. Yeomans, Lilian B. *Healing from Heaven*. Springfield, Mo.: Gospel, 1935.

Ying, "Ruler." Ying, Lin. "Ruler of the Treasure Country: The Image of the Roman Empire in Chinese Society from the First to the Fourth Century AD." *Latomus* 63 (2, 2004): 327–39.

Yoder, "Exodus." Yoder, James D. "The Exodus of Jerusalem." *EvJ* 4 (2, 1986): 51–69.

Yohannan, *Revolution*. Yohannan, K. P. *Revolution in World Missions*. Carrollton, Tex.: Gospel for Asia, 2004.

Yong, *Spirit Poured*. Yong, Amos. *The Spirit Poured Out on All Flesh: Pentecostalism and the Possibility of Global Theology*. Grand Rapids: Baker, 2005.

Yoo, "Entretien." Yoo, S-H. "L'entretien de Paul avec les personages royaux." *YonsJT* 4 (1999): 47–58.

Yoo, "Paul et Festus." Yoo, S.-H. "Paul et Festus." *YonsJT* 2 (1997): 51–65.

Yoo, "Sens." Yoo, S.-H. "Le sens du parcours juridique de Paul." *YonsJT* 5 (2000): 17–36.

York, "Indigenous Missionaries." York, Ted E. "Indigenous Missionaries—A Fruit of Revival: Lessons from the Indonesian Revival of 1965 to 1971." *JAM* 5 (2, 2003): 243–58.

York, *Missions*. York, John V. *Missions in the Age of the Spirit*. Foreword by Byron D. Klaus. Springfield, Mo.: Logion, 2000.

Young, "Aphrodite Cult." Young, Philip H. "The Cypriote Aphrodite Cult: Paphos, Rantidi, and Saint Barnabas." *JNES* 64 (1, 2005): 23–44.

Young, "Commandment." Young, Norman H. "The Commandment to Love Your Neighbor as Yourself and the Parable of the Good Samaritan (Luke 10:25–37)." *AUSS* 21 (3, 1983): 265–72.

Young, "Israelite Literacy." Young, Ian M. "Israelite Literacy: Interpreting the Evidence." *VT* 48 (2, 1998): 239–53; (3, 1998): 408–22.

Young, *Jewish Theologian*. Young, Brad H. *Jesus the Jewish Theologian*. Forewords by Marvin R. Wilson and Rabbi David Wolpe. Peabody, Mass.: Hendrickson. 1995.

Young, "Media." Young, T. Cuyler, Jr. "Media." *ABD* 4:658–59.

Young, "Miracles in History." Young, William. "Miracles in Church History." *Chm* 102 (2, 1988): 102–21.

Young, "Motif." Young, Brad H. "The Ascension Motif of 2 Corinthians 12 in Jewish, Christian, and Gnostic Texts." *GTJ* 9 (1, 1988): 73–103.

Young, *Parables*. Young, Brad H. *Jesus and His Jewish Parables: Rediscovering the Roots of Jesus' Teaching*. New York: Paulist, 1989.

Young and Ford, *Meaning*. Young, Frances, and David F. Ford. *Meaning and Truth in 2 Corinthians*. Grand Rapids: Eerdmans, 1987.

Youngblood, "Amos 4:12." Youngblood, Ronald. "לקראת in Amos 4:12." *JBL* 90 (1, 1971): 98.

Youngblood, "Embalming Process." Youngblood, Clark R. "The Embalming Process in Ancient Egypt." *BI* 14 (2, 1988): 80–83.

Youngblood, "Ethiopia." Youngblood, Ronald F. "Ethiopia." *ISBE* 2:193–97.

Youngblood, "Gamaliel." Youngblood, Ronald F. "Gamaliel." *ISBE* 2:393–94.

Younger, *Conquest Accounts*. Younger, K. Lawson. *Ancient Conquest Accounts: A Study in Ancient Near Eastern and Biblical History Writing*. JSOTSup 98. Sheffield, U.K.: Sheffield Academic, 1990.

Young-Widmaier, "Representation." Young-Widmaier, Michael R. "Quintilian's Legal Representation of Julia Berenice." *Historia* 51 (1, 2002): 124–29.

Yoyotte, "Egypt." Yoyotte, J. "Pharaonic Egypt: Society, Economy, and Culture." Pages 112–35 in *Ancient Civilizations of Africa*. Edited by G. Mokhtar. General History of Africa 2. Berkeley: University of California Press; London: Heinemann Educational; Paris: United Nations Educational, Scientific and Cultural Organization, 1981.

Yrigoyen, *Acts*. Yrigoyen, Charles, Jr. *Acts for Our Time*. Nashville: Abingdon, 1992.

Ytterbrink, *Biography*. Ytterbrink, Maria. *The Third Gospel for the First Time: Luke within the Context of Ancient Biography*. Lund, Swed.: Lund University—Centrum för teologi och religionsvetenskap, 2004.

Yun, "Baptism." Yun, K. D. "Baptism in the Holy Spirit." *GDT* 95–97.

Yun, *Heavenly Man*. Yun, Brother, with Paul Hattaway. *The Heavenly Man: The Remarkable True Story of Chinese Christian Brother Yun*. London: Monarch, 2002.

Yung, "Case Studies." Yung, Hwa. "Case Studies in Spiritual Warfare from East Asia." Pages 138–45 in *Deliver Us from Evil: An Uneasy Frontier in Christian Mission*. Edited by A. Scott Moreau, Tokunboh Adeyemo, David G. Burnett, Bryant L. Myers, and Hwa Yung. Monrovia, Calif.: Lausanne Committee for World Evangelization, 2002.

Yung, "Integrity." Yung, Hwa. "The Integrity of Mission in the Light of the Gospel: Bearing the Witness of the Spirit." *MissSt* 24 (2007): 169–88.

Yung, "Pentecostalism." Yung, Hwa. "Pentecostalism and the Asian Church." Pages 37–57 in *Asian and Pentecostal: The Charismatic Face of Christianity in Asia*. Edited by Allan Anderson and Edmond Tang. Foreword by Cecil M. Robeck. RStMiss, AJPS 3. Oxford: Regnum; Baguio City, Philippines: APTS, 2005.

Yung, *Quest*. Yung, Hwa. *Mangoes or Bananas? The Quest for an Authentic Asian Christian Theology. Biblical Theology in an Asian Context*. Oxford: Regnum, 1997.

Zabehlicky, "Harbor." Zabehlicky, Heinrich. "Preliminary Views of the Ephesian Harbor." Pages 201–15 in *Ephesos, Metropolis of Asia: An Interdisciplinary Approach to Its Archaeology, Religion, and Culture*. Edited by Helmut Koester. HTS. Valley Forge, Pa.: Trinity Press International, 1995.

Zabehlicky-Scheffenegger, "Factories." Zabehlicky-Scheffenegger, Susanne. "Subsidiary Factories of Italian Sigillata Potters." Pages 217–28 in *Ephesos, Metropolis of Asia: An Interdisciplinary Approach to Its Archaeology, Religion, and Culture*. Edited by Helmut Koester. HTS. Valley Forge, Pa.: Trinity Press International, 1995.

Zadorojnyi, "Cato's Suicide." Zadorojnyi, Alexei V. "Cato's Suicide in Plutarch." *CQ* 57 (1, 2007): 216–30.

Zahl, "Mistakes." Zahl, Paul F. M. "Mistakes of the New Perspective on Paul." *Them* 27 (1, 2001): 5–11.

Zahn, *Apostelgeschichte*. Zahn, Theodor. *Die Apostelgeschichte des Lucas*. 2 vols. Kommentar zum Neuen Testament 5. 4th ed. Leipzig: Deichert, 1927.

Zahn, *Introduction*. Zahn, Theodor. *Introduction to the New Testament*. Edinburgh: T&T Clark, 1909.

Zalcman, "Eternal City." Zalcman, Lawrence. "The Eternal City: Rome or Jerusalem?" *JJS* 48 (2, 1997): 312–13.

Zambrini, "Historians." Zambrini, Andrea. "The Historians of Alexander the Great." Pages 210–20 in *A Companion to Greek and Roman Historiography*. Edited by John Marincola. 2 vols. Oxford: Blackwell, 2007.

Zaminer, "Chorus." Zaminer, Frieder. "Chorus." *BrillPauly* 3:247–50.

Zangenberg, "Farewell." Zangenberg, Jürgen. "The 'Final Farewell': A Necessary Paradigm Shift in the Interpretation of the Qumran Cemetery." *QC* 8 (3, 1999): 213–18.

Zangenberg, "Samaria." Zangenberg, Jürgen. "Between Jerusalem and the Galilee: Samaria in the Time of Jesus." Pages 393–433 in *Jesus and Archaeology*. Edited by James H. Charlesworth. Grand Rapids: Eerdmans, 2006.

Zangenberg, "Simon Magus." Zangenberg, Jürgen. "Simon Magus." Pages 519–40 in *Religionsgeschichte des Neuen Testaments: Festschrift für Klaus Berger zum 60. Geburtstag.* Edited by Axel von Dobbeler, Kurt Erlemann, and Roman Heiligenthal. Tübingen: Francke, 2000.

Zanker, "Lyric." Zanker, Andreas T. "Late Horatian Lyric and the Virgilian Golden Age." *AJP* 131 (3, 2010): 495–516.

Zarecki, "Duet." Zarecki, Jonathan P. "A Duet of Praise: Horace, Vergil and the Subject of Canemus in *Carm.* 4.15.32." *CJ* 105 (3, 2010): 245–63.

Zarrow, "Coins." Zarrow, Edward M. "Imposing Romanisation: Flavian Coins and Jewish Identity." *JJS* 57 (1, 2006): 44–55.

Zechariah, "Factors." Zechariah, Chelliah. "Factors Affecting the Growth of the Protestant Churches in Tamil Nadu and Kerala." MTh thesis, Fuller Theological Seminary, 1980.

Zehetbauer, "Stephanus." Zehetbauer, Markus. "Stephanus—der erste Heidentäufer?" *BZ* 57 (1, 2013): 82–96.

Zehnle, *Pentecost Discourse.* Zehnle, Richard F. *Peter's Pentecost Discourse: Tradition and Lukan Reinterpretation in Peter's Speeches of Acts 2 and 3.* SBLMS 15. Nashville: Abingdon, 1971.

Zehnle, "Salvific Character." Zehnle, Richard F. "The Salvific Character of Jesus' Death in Lucan Soteriology." *TS* 30 (1969): 420–44.

Zeichmann, "Location." Zeichmann, Christopher B. "Οἱ στρατηγοί τοῦ ἱεροῦ and the Location of Luke-Acts' Composition." *Early Christianity* 3 (2, 2012): 172–87.

Zeigan, "Wachstumsnotizen." Zeigan, Holger. "Die Wachstumsnotizen der Acta: Ein Vorschlag zur Gliederung des lukanischen Werks." *BN* 131 (2006): 65–78.

Zeigler, "Lake." Zeigler, James R. "Lake, John Graham." *DPCM* 531.

Zeitlin, "Dreams." Zeitlin, Solomon. "Dreams and Their Interpretation from the Biblical Period to the Tannaitic Time: An Historical Study." *JQR* 66 (1975): 1–18.

Zeitlin, "Galileans." Zeitlin, Solomon. "Who Were the Galileans? New Light on Josephus' Activities in Galilee." *JQR* 64 (3, 1974): 189–203.

Zeitlin, "Inscription." Zeitlin, Solomon. "The Warning Inscription of the Temple." *JQR* 38 (1947–48): 111–16.

Zeitlin, "'Jubilees' and Pentateuch." Zeitlin, Solomon. "The Book of 'Jubilees' and the Pentateuch." *JQR* 48 (1957–58): 218–35.

Zeitlin, "Jubilees, Character." Zeitlin, Solomon. "The Book of Jubilees, Its Character and Its Significance." *JQR* 30 (1, 1939): 1–31.

Zeller, "Elija." Zeller, Dieter. "Elija und Elischa im Frühjudentum." *BK* 41 (4, 1986): 154–60.

Zeller, "Front." Zeller, Dieter. "Die angebliche enthusiastische oder spiritualistische Front in 1 Kor 15." *SPhilA* 13 (2001): 176–89.

Zeller, "Parallele." Zeller, Eduard. "Eine griechische Parallele zu der Erzählung Apostelgesch. 16:19ff." *Zeitschrift für wissenschaftliche Theologie* 8 (1865): 101–8.

Zempleni, "Symptom." Zempleni, Andras. "From Symptom to Sacrifice: The Story of Khady Fall." Translated by Karen Merveille. Pages 87–140 in *Case Studies in Spirit Possession.* Edited by Vincent Crapanzaro and Vivian Garrison. New York: Wiley, 1977.

Zerbe, "Constructions." Zerbe, Gordon. "Constructions of Paul in Filipino Theology of Struggle." Pages 236–55 in *The Colonized Apostle: Paul through Postcolonial Eyes.* Edited by Christopher D. Stanley. Minneapolis: Fortress, 2011.

Zerbe, "Politics." Zerbe, Gordon. "The Politics of Paul: His Supposed Social Conservatism and the Impact of Postcolonial Readings." Pages 62–73 in *The Colonized Apostle: Paul through Postcolonial Eyes.* Edited by Christopher D. Stanley. Minneapolis: Fortress, 2011.

Zerhusen, "Judean *diglossia* in Acts 2?" Zerhusen, Bob. "An Overlooked Judean *diglossia* in Acts 2?" *BTB* 25 (3, 1995): 118–30.

Zerhusen, "Tongues in 1 Cor 14." Zerhusen, Bob. "The Problem Tongues in 1 Cor 14: A Reexamination." *BTB* 27 (4, 1997): 139–52.

Zeron, "Swansong." Zeron, Alexander. "The Swansong of Edom." *JJS* 31 (2, 1980): 190–98.

Zetterholm, "Judar." Zetterholm, Magnus. "Judar och hedningar i den tidiga kritendomen." *STK* 79 (1, 2003): 22–30.

Zetterholm, "Kontinuitet." Zetterholm, Karin Hedner. "Kontinuitet och förändring i judendomen: Den muntliga Torahs roll." *SEÅ* 71 (2006): 209–30.

Zettner, *Amt.* Zettner, Christoph. *Amt, Gemeinde und kirchliche Einheit in der Apostelgeschichte des Lukas.* EurH 23.423. Frankfurt am Main: Lang, 1991.

Zevi and Jodice, *Puteoli.* Zevi, Fausto, and Mimmo Jodice. *Puteoli.* Naples, Italy: Banco di Napoli, 1993.

Zhang, *Paul Among Jews.* Zhang, Wenxi. *Paul Among Jews: A Study of the Meaning and Significance of Paul's Inaugural Sermon in the Synagogue of Antioch in Pisidia (Acts 13:16–41) for His Missionary Work among the Jews.* Eugene, Ore.: Wipf & Stock, 2011.

Zhaoming, "Chinese Denominations." Zhaoming, Deng. "Indigenous Chinese Pentecostal Denominations." Pages 437–66 in *Asian and Pentecostal: The Charismatic Face of Christianity in Asia.* Edited by Allan Anderson and Edmond Tang. Foreword by Cecil M. Robeck. RStMiss, AJPS 3. Oxford: Regnum; Baguio City, Philippines: APTS, 2005.

Zias, "Bones." Zias, Joseph E. "Whose Bones?" *BAR* 24 (6, 1998): 40–45, 64–66.

Zias, "Cemeteries." Zias, Joseph E. "The Cemeteries of Qumran and Celibacy: Confusion Laid to Rest?" *DSD* 7 (2, 2000): 220–53.

Zias, "Confusion." Zias, Joseph E. "The Cemeteries of Qumran and Celibacy: Confusion Laid to Rest?" Pages 444–71 in *Jesus and Archaeology.* Edited by James H. Charlesworth. Grand Rapids: Eerdmans, 2006.

Zias, "Mount Scopus Tomb." Zias, Joseph E. "Human Skeletal Remains from the Mount Scopus Tomb." *'Atiqot* 21 (1992): 97–103.

Zias, "Remains from 'Caiaphas' Tomb." Zias, Joseph E. "Human Skeletal Remains from the 'Caiaphas' Tomb." *'Atiqot* 21 (1992): 78–80.

Zias, Tabor, and Harter-Lailheugue, "Toilets." Zias, Joseph E., James D. Tabor, and Stephainie Harter-Lailheugue. "Toilets at Qumran, the Essenes, and the Scrolls: New Anthropological Data and Old Theories." *RevQ* 22 (88, 2006): 631–40.

Ziderman, "Identification." Ziderman, Irving. "First Identification of Authentic *Tekelet.*" *BASOR* 265 (1987): 25–33.

Ziderman, "Purple Dyeing." Ziderman, I. Irving. "Seashells and Ancient Purple Dyeing." *BA* 53 (1990): 98–101.

Ziegler, *Dionysos.* Ziegler, Detlef. *Dionysos in der Apostelgeschichte—eine intertextuelle Lektüre.* RelBiog 18. Berlin: LIT Verlag, 2008.

Ziesler, "Justification." Ziesler, John A. "Justification by Faith in the Light of the 'New Perspective' on Paul." *Theology* 94 (759, 1991): 188–94.

Ziesler, "Luke and Pharisees." Ziesler, John A. "Luke and the Pharisees." *NTS* 25 (2, 1979): 146–57.

Ziesler, "Name in Acts." Ziesler, John A. "The Name of Jesus in the Acts of the Apostles." *JSNT* 4 (1979): 28–41.

Ziesler, "Vow." Ziesler, John A. "The Vow of Abstinence Again." *Colloq* 6 (1973): 49–50.

Ziller, "Dialectics." Ziller, Robert C. "Group Dialectics: The Dynamics of Groups over Time." *HumDev* 20 (5, 1977): 293–308.

Zimbrich, "Mimesis." Zimbrich, Ulrike. "Mimesis." *BrillPauly* 8:926–28.

Zimmerli, "Promise." Zimmerli, Walther. "Promise and Fulfillment." Pages 89–122 in *Essays in Old Testament Hermeneutics*. Edited by Claus Westermann. Richmond: John Knox, 1963.

Zimmerli and Jeremias, *Servant*. Zimmerli, Walther, and Joachim Jeremias. *The Servant of God*. Naperville, Ill.: Alec R. Allenson, 1957.

Zimmerman, "Libyes." Zimmerman, Klaus. "Libyes, Libye." *BrillPauly* 7:515–16.

Zimmerman, "Messenger Scenes." Zimmerman, Bernhard. "Messenger Scenes." *BrillPauly* 8:765–66.

Zimmermann, "Deus ex machina." Zimmermann, Bernhard. "Deus ex machina." *BrillPauly* 4:323–24.

Zimmermann, "Hinführung." Zimmermann, Ruben. "Hinführung." Pages 513–25 in *Die Wunder Jesu*. Edited by Ruben Zimmermann. Vol. 1 in *Kompendium der frühchristlichen Wundererzählungen*. München: Gütersloh, 2013.

Zimmermann, *Iniuria*. Zimmermann, Reinhard. "*Iniuria* and Defamation." *OCD*³ 759.

Zimmermann, "Lycia." Zimmerman, Martin. "Lycia et Pamphylia." *BrillPauly* 7:915.

Zimmermann, "Myra." Zimmerman, Martin. "Myra." *BrillPauly* 9:412–13.

Zimmermann, "Prologue." Zimmermann, Bernhard. "Prologue." *BrillPauly* 12:2–4.

Zimmermann, "Restitution." Zimmermann, Reinhard. "Restitution." *OCD*³ 1309.

Zimmermann, "Theft." Zimmermann, Reinhard. "Theft." *OCD*³ 1496.

Zimmern, *Commonwealth*. Zimmern, Alfred. *The Greek Commonwealth: Politics and Economics in Fifth-Century Athens*. 5th ed. Oxford: Oxford University Press, 1931.

Zingerman, "Name." Zingerman, Yevgeniy Y. "'What's in a Name?': Hellenistic and Rabbinic Techniques of Proper Names' Interpretation." *Hen* 33 (2, 2011): 297–315.

Zipor, "Talebearers." Zipor, Moshe A. "Talebearers, Peddlers, Spies, and Converts: The Adventures of the Biblical and Post-biblical Roots *rg"l* and *rk"l*." *HS* 46 (2005): 129–44.

Zissu, "Graves." Zissu, Boaz. "'Qumran Type' Graves in Jerusalem: Archaeological Evidence of an Essene Community?" *DSD* 5 (2, 1998): 158–71.

Zissu, "Tomb." Zissu, Boaz. "Odd Tomb Out: Has Jerusalem's Essene Cemetery Been Found?" *BAR* 25 (2, 1999): 50–55, 62.

Zissu and Ganor, "Horvat 'Ethri." Zissu, Boaz, and Amir Ganor. "Horvat 'Ethri—A Jewish Village from the Second Temple Period and the Bar Kokhba Revolt in the Judean Foothills." *JJS* 60 (1, 2009): 90–136.

Zissu and Goren, "Ossuary." Zissu, Boaz, and Yuval Goren. "The Ossuary of 'Miriam Daughter of Yeshua Son of Caiaphas, Priests [of] Ma'aziah from Beth 'Imri.'" *IEJ* 61 (2011): 74–95.

Zissu, Tepper, and Amit, "Miqwa'ot." Zissu, Boaz, Yotam Tepper, and David Amit. "*Miqwa'ot* at Kefar 'Othnai near Legio." *IEJ* 56 (1, 2006): 57–66.

Zlotnick, "Memory." Zlotnick, Dov. "Memory and the Integrity of the Oral Tradition." *JANESCU* 16–17 (1984–85): 229–41.

Zmijewski, "Pastoralbriefe." Zmijewski, Josef. "Die Pastoralbriefe als pseudepigraphische Schriften-Beschreibung, Erklärung, Bewertung." *SNTSU* 4 (1979): 97–118.

Zon, "Droga." Zon, A. "Droga w Regule Wspólnoty. 1QS 9.18." *RuBL* 16 (4, 1963): 187–96. (Abstract: *NTA* 8:430.)

Zugmann, "Judentum." Zugmann, Michael. "Philo Iudaeo-Hellenisticus: Judentum und Hellenismus in der Sicht des alexandrinischen Gelehrten." *SNTSU* 35 (2010): 189–229.

Zuiderhoek, "Centralization." Zuiderhoek, Arjan. "Government Centralization in Late Second and Third Century A.D. Asia Minor: A Working Hypothesis." *CW* 103 (1, 2009): 39–51.

Zuiderhoek, "Munificence." Zuiderhoek, Arjan. "The Ambiguity of Munificence." *Historia* 56 (2, 2007): 196–213.

Zuiderhoek, "Sociology." Zuiderhoek, Arjan. "On the Political Sociology of the Imperial Greek City." *GRBS* 48 (4, 2008): 417–45.

Zuntz, *Persephone*. Zuntz, Günther. *Persephone: Three Essays on Religion and Thought in Magna Graecia*. Oxford: Clarendon, 1971.

Zweck, "Areopagus Speech." Zweck, Dean. "The Areopagus Speech of Acts 17." *LTJ* 21 (3, 1987): 111–22.

Zweck, "Exordium." Zweck, Dean "The Exordium of the Areopagus Speech, Acts 17.22, 23." *NTS* 35 (1, 1989): 94–103.

Zweck, "Wright." Zweck, Dean. "Wright or Wrong? A Perspective on the New Perspective on Paul." *LTJ* 41 (1, 2007): 16–26.

Zwiep, *Ascension*. Zwiep, Arie W. *The Ascension of the Messiah in Lukan Christology*. NovTSup 87. Leiden: Brill, 1997.

Zwiep, *Community*. Zwiep, Ari W. *Christ, the Spirit and the Community of God*. WUNT 2.293. Tübingen: Mohr Siebeck, 2010.

Zwiep, *Judas*. Zwiep, Arie W. *Judas and the Choice of Matthias: A Study on Context and Concern of Acts 1:15–26*. WUNT 2.187. Tübingen: Mohr Siebeck, 2004.

Zwiep, "Text." Zwiep, A. W. "The Text of the Ascension Narratives (Luke 24, 50–3; Acts 1, 1–2, 9–11." *NTS* 42 (2, 1996): 219–44.

Zyl, "Meaning." Zyl, Hermie C. van. "The Soteriological Meaning of Jesus' Death in Luke-Acts: A Survey of Possibilities." *VerbEc* 23 (2, 2002): 533–57.

Zywica, "Odpowiedzialnosc." Zywica, Z. "Odpowiedzialnosc Zydow jerozolimskich za utrate godnosci synow Abrahama I laski usprawiedliwienia w Jezusie (Dz 13,13–41)." *ColT* 78 (2, 2008): 31–49.

INDEX OF SELECT SUBJECTS

Note: Because most subjects receive comment at relevant passages, primarily large treatments in excursuses or the introduction are indexed here.

abandoned cases, 3418–20
abridgment and expansion, 143–47
acculturation, 3130
Adam theology, Jewish, 2645–47
Adriatic Sea, 3635–36
advocates, 3355–58, 3387–89
agent, agency, 1619–21, 3510–11, 3516–17
Agrippa I, see esp. 1867–69
Agrippa II, see esp. 3473, 3477–79
Alexandria, 848, 1307–8, 1344, 1387–88, 1834, 2310, 2476–77, 2566, 2800–2807, 2812, 2834, 2864, 3582–84, 3617, 3650, 3694
allegory, 59, 157n80, 259n14, 487–90, 616, 631–32, 1344, 1369, 1415, 2051, 2151, 2160–61, 2594, 2609n3093, 2632n3299, 2633, 2655, 2656n3561, 2689n3918, 2799, 2812, 3568–69
alms, 1059–60, 3408–9
Amazons, 1557–60
amulets, charms, 2436, 2454, 2844, 2854, 2856–57, 2883
anger, 2308–9
anonymity, 411–12, 2367
anthropology, 11–12, 364–65, 367, 591n92, 1803nn741–742, 2441–47, 2851, and passim
anti-Judaism (and pro-Judaism), 460–77, 2472–77, 3718–19
Antioch on the Orontes (Syrian Antioch), 1834–40, 1983–84, 1995
Antioch, Pisidian, 2032–44
antithesis, 3406n477, 3526
apartments, 2716–17, 2973–74, 3728–31
Aphrodite, 2573, 2575, 2655, 2689, 2693, 2696, 2718, 2788–89, 2877, 2893, 2931
Apollo, 326, 328, 329n74, 657, 805, 809nn260–261, 853, 883, 897n361, 900n410, 901, 909, 919n630, 1071, 1097, 1141n947, 1278n293, 1383, 1397, 1511, 1514, 1647, 1836, 1842, 1889, 1976, 2007, 2147n1571, 2148n1575, 2148n1577, 2150n1594, 2152, 2161n1733, 2166, 2335, 2395,

2422–29, 2429n1328, 2435, 2457–59, 2461, 2493, 2495n2018, 2575–78, 2590n2895, 2629, 2632n3299, 2650n3494, 2662, 2695, 2718, 2754, 2759n4633, 2872n5649, 2878, 2879n5740, 2892, 2893n5866, 2897n5908, 2930n6203, 2934, 2935, 2936n6253, 2963n126, 2979n282, 2984, 2986n372, 2987, 3077, 3078, 3097, 3149
Apollonius of Tyana, 53, 64, 83, 329–34, 381, 432, 454n138, 546, 584, 588n67, 589n75, 593, 663, 669n204, 705n491, 706n518, 720, 756n210, 776n425, 809, 868, 928n738, 1016, 1063, 1081, 1154, 1209, 1388, 1500, 1508, 1640, 1648n462, 1650n488, 1723, 1784, 1850n181, 2135, 2160, 2352n521, 2429n1325, 2437–38, 2464, 2475, 2491n1978, 2598, 2605n3052, 2615n3147, 2677, 2751n4540, 2758n4625, 2830n5282, 2835n5333, 2842–43, 2887n5821, 3012, 3055, 3058, 3107n1606, 3171n456, 3196, 3199n698, 3329n1734
apologetic
  in Acts generally, 427–28, 438, 441–58, 498–99
  for Paul, 223–24, 434, 436, 445–49, 3377–78
  speeches, 266–67, 302, 304, 306, 3197–98. See also defense speeches in Acts 22–26
apologetic historiography, 161–63
apostasy, 2180–81, 3125–31, 3198
apostleship, Lukan meaning of, 642n4, 645, 749, 752–53, 768–69, 1977n19, 2124–25, 2222–23n182, 2223. See also Twelve, the, background for significance of
appeals in Roman law, 3464–67, 3553
Aramaic language, use of in Judea and Galilee, 1255–57, 3191–95
Areopagus, 2600–2602
ascension, Jesus's, 711–32

ascension narratives, ancient, 717–19, 731
astrology in antiquity, 837–39, 931–32
atheism, 2587–89, 2591n2903, 2592–93, 2597, 2610, 2643n3420
Athena, 2573–77, 2605, 2892, 2931, 2934
Athens, 2565–67, 2572–80. See also Areopagus
Attalia, 2027–29, 2032, 2034, 2189–90
audience, 423–34
author of Acts, 402–22. See also "we" narratives

banishment, exile, 2699–2700
baptism, ritual washings, ancient settings for, 977–82
"barbarians," views of, 2114, 2123, 2156, 2169, 2337–38, 3665–67, 3680–81
baths in Greco-Roman antiquity, 2513, 2751–54, 2821; cf. 2385
begging in antiquity, 1061–62
benefactors and patrons, 2408–13, 3692. See also philanthropia
Berenice, see esp. 3473–76
bilingualism, 643, 1255–57, 1288, 2694, 3112, 3168–70, 3191n623, 3193, 3195
biography, ancient, 54–61
Bithynia, 2330–31
black, dark colors, 728–30
blended genres, 61, 114n178, 139n213
blindness, figurative, 1640–42
brevity, conciseness, 3367–69
bribery, corruption, 3437–42
burden of proof, 201n302, 203
burial customs, 1471–77

Caesarea Maritima, 1692–93, 1732–36, 1786, 1795, 1815–16, 1833–34, 1875–76, 1957–58, 1960–61, 1966–67
castration, 1567–71
celibacy in antiquity, 3098–3101
centurions, 1742–44, 3162–63, 3248, 3250, 3253, 3313, 3316, 3320, 3347, 3570–71, 3574, 3604, 3683

INDEX OF AUTHORS
AND SELECT NAMES

Bruce, J., 1551
Bruce, S., 1616n163
Brucker, R., 334n137
Bruckner, L. I., 1519n600
Brueggemann, W. A., 1346n493,
    2249n420, 2249n422
Brug, J. F., 34n175, 777n440
Bruggen, J. van, 177n84, 186n166,
    3122n72
Bruner, F. D., 681n295, 811n289,
    814n312, 1522n620, 1523nn626–627
Bruni, G., 520n183
Bruns, J. E., 1642n414
Brunt, P. A., 118n11, 1142n961,
    2766n4718
Brusco, E. E., 884n230
Bruun, C., 3702n1516
Bryan, C., 442n40, 874n139, 1103n625,
    1324n308, 3514n1354
Bryce, D. W., 602n36
Bryce, T. R., 591n94, 2152n1624,
    3078n1320, 3581n253, 3581n255
Bryen, A. Z., 1503n391, 2173n1875,
    2777n4818
Bryne, T. de, 691n372
Bryson, S., 1884n174
Buber, M., 890n285
Buchanan, G. W., 157n83, 464n38,
    755n204, 784n24, 808n249,

960n1085, 1112n715, 1373n764,
    1413n1145, 1451n1507, 1612n132,
    1939nn936–937, 3368n178
Bucher, G. S., 563n80
Büchler, A., 1031n415, 1588n1303,
    3035n820
Buchler, I. R., 1663n616
Büchli, J., 1100n590, 2412n1144
Büchner, D., 1892n243
Büchsel, D. F., 529n241, 531nn253–254,
    531n259, 531n261, 537n317,
    799n161, 903n442
Buckingham, J., 375n504, 1708n46
Buckland, W. W., 607n80, 607n82,
    712n582, 768n335, 1145n990,
    1304n87, 1305n93, 1305n108,
    1385n890, 1386n896, 1474n83,
    1747n201, 1747n204, 1748nn205–
    206, 1906n414, 1913n523, 1914n532,
    1915n543, 1916n565, 1923n682,
    1924n694, 1928n756, 1932nn820–
    821, 2318n202, 2406n1055,
    2411n1119, 3315n1613, 3468n999,
    3531n1532
Buckwalter, H. D., 500n31, 503n44,
    555n43, 958n1070, 963n1121,
    1934n860
Budin, S. L., 1516n558, 2007n250
Buell, D. K., 1560n1002
Bugeja, A., 3663n1073
Bulgakov, S., 373n479
Bull, D. L., 2455n1654
Bull, R. J., 1492n268, 1492n270,
    1513n524, 1733n44, 1733n51,
    1753n266, 1786n583, 1786n585,
    3327n1722
Bullinger, E. W., 863n13
Bullock, J. D., 1603n53
Bultmann, R., 135n167, 139n211,
    144n260, 198n279, 228, 228n46,
    330n91, 336n153, 337n162,
    360n379, 361, 361nn383–384, 363,
    519, 519n177, 519n179, 530n246,
    536n315, 673n236, 767n320,
    793n102, 922n668, 978n1258,
    983n1315, 1007n141, 1010n176,
    1066n275, 1388n925, 1404n1058,
    1498n329, 1516n557, 1593n1351,
    1605n67, 1672n695, 1696n889,
    1722n187, 1829n937, 1832,
    2079n951, 2089n1055, 2184n1984,
    2456n1664, 2460, 2470n1785,
    2673n3760, 2833, 2842n5400,
    2846n5431, 3039n863
Bundy, D. D., 826n407
Bunine, A., 1861n298, 2195n5,
    3444n815, 3746n343
Bünker, M., 302n377
Bunyan, J., 2976n254
Burchard, C., 1008n159, 1102nn615–
    616, 1608nn104–105, 1801n721,
    3227n937, 3518n1389
Burckhardt, L., 3584n287
Buresch, K., 2427n1309
Burfeind, C., 1583n1251, 1583n1257,
    2861n5575, 3749n361
Burford, A., 2723n4274

4103

INDEX OF OTHER ANCIENT SOURCES

Note: The authorship of many ancient sources is uncertain to various degrees; for ease of reference, sources are cited under their traditional authors or collections even when (as in many cases) the sources are considered pseudonymous or misattributed or the collections are simply a matter of historical convention.

Old Testament Apocrypha

2 Maccabees

18:20–21 2671n3733
18:22 953n1022

19:2 2224n187
19:4 932n800

19:7 1401n1035
19:9 1073n347

19:13 666n172
19:14 1146n998

19:18 802n187
19:22 1086n471

Old Testament Pseudepigrapha

Lives of the Prophets

Martyrdom of Isaiah

Memar Marqah (Samaritan)

Odes of Solomon

Orphica

Paraphrase of Shem

Philo the Poet

Prayer of Jacob

Prayer of Joseph

Psalms of Solomon

15:4 1353n600
16:2 3532n1539
16:3 2462n1712
17 687n343
17:11 255n200,
  1025n347,
  1130n851,
  2269n624,
  2273n670
18:2–9 967n1155
18:4 3229n948,
  3511n1317
18:7 2462n1712
18:9 1219n106
18:10–12 879n179,
  1111n704
19:2 3128n118
19:5 1371n746

Naphtali
1:2 856n718
1:6 2641n3401
1:6–12 3192n633
2:2 1655n535
2:2–3 949n990
2:4–5 772n374
2:5 2665n3681
2:9–10 1636n364
3:1 1183n92
3:3 2622n3215,
  2683n3846
3:5 2147n1562

4:1 475n129,
  512n105, 719n633,
  877n163, 2030n508,
  3273n1293
5:1 734n9
5:3–5 966n1151
5:8 846n586,
  3501n1233
6:1–10 3567n110
6:6 3657n1017
6:8 1479n130
6:8–9 3633n812
7:1 913n564
8:2 966n1151
8:8 3097n1512,
  3435n720
9:1 1371n746

Reuben
1:6 1103, 1450n1490
1:6–10 2272n660
1:9 973n1211
1:10 1993n115
2:1 973n1211,
  1189n142, 3029n752
2:1–2 2433n1377
2:3–4 1189n142
2:8 2594n2932
2:9 1103, 1450n1490
3:3 2273n672
3:3ff. 2433n1377
3:8 1103, 1450n1490
3:11–12 617n253

3:15 3631n794
4:1 2273n672,
  3060n1105
4:3 3267n1232
4:6 1450n1490,
  2273n672
4:8 1217n99,
  2273n673,
  3060n1105,
  3238n1003
4:9 335n138,
  1504n393
4:11 1189n148,
  2273n672
5:1–5 617n253
5:3 1546n808,
  3631n794
5:6 2146n1562
6:1 617n253,
  1773n445
6:1–2 604n48
6:1–3 2273n672,
  3060n1105
6:5–12 967n1155
6:8 966n1150
7:2 1371n746

Simeon
1:2 3071n1233
2:5 949n990,
  2462n1712
2:6–7 1364n686

2:7 1190n154,
  2433n1379
2:11 1364n686
2:13 973n1211
2:14 1364n686
3 1207n23
3:1 1189n142
3:2–3 1364n686
3:3 1312n176
3:4 1992n103,
  2237n301
4:3 1689n838
4:4 534, 1845n141
4:4–9 1364n686
4:8 949n990
5:4 31n156, 719n633
5:5 966n1150
6:2 1423n1220
6:6 2434n1389
7:2 693n386
8:2 1371n746

Zebulun
1:5–7 146n283,
  1368n716
2:2 1217n96,
  1364n687
3:3 913n564
3:4 767n319,
  2227n208
4:1–3 899n399, 1991
5:1 3489n1146
5:2 772n374

6:2 1766n374
8:2 877n161
9:5 877nn161–163
9:7 973n1211,
  1106n649,
  1107n651
9:8 513n110,
  2100n1141,
  3525n1489
10:1–2 1480n144
10:2 3286n1390
10:6 1463n1630
10:6/7 1371n746

Treatise of Shem
in toto: 774n397,
  838n499
2:5 1855n231
2:9 2434n1387,
  2436n1430
4:5 3583n285
6:1 585n31,
  1580n1224
6:16 3583n285
7:15 2273n670
7:19 2496n2032
7:20 585n31,
  1580n1224
9:9 2273n670
10:16 2273n670
11:6 3583n285

Dead Sea Scrolls and Related Texts

1Q19bis
2 4 1884n170

1Q20
1 I, 7 1090n505
II, 1 3053n1030
II, 14 1090n505
V, 23 1800n714
VI, 13 1090n505
VI, 15 1090n505
VI, 20 3053n1030
VII, 7 1090n505
XII, 17 1090n505
XV, 9 475n129
XX, 18 1620n214
XX, 28 2850n5485

1Q21
in toto: 255n197

1Q22
in toto: 475n129,
  802n195, 2180n1938
I, 5 2169n1835

I, 7–8 737n33,
  877nn162–163
I, 11–12 967n1161
II, 8 1626n272

1Q27
1 I, 5–6 3524n1471,
  3526
I, 9–11 512n105

**1Q28a (see also
1QSa)**
I, 7–11 755n204
I, 11 2257n503
I, 16 778n441
II, 11–12 1672n696
II, 19–20 967n1161

1Q29
in toto: 778n443
1 2010n280,
  2013n326
1 3 802n195, 802n197
2 2 802n197

2 3 802n195

1Q31
1 1 1187n127

1Q34
in toto: 784n27,
  937n871, 3036n831,
  3053n1032,
  3598n454

1Q34bis
1 + 2 6 1755n278,
  3598n454
3 II, 5 937n871
3 II, 6 3053n1032
3 II, 7 535n301,
  2332n317,
  2818n5178
3 II, 8 3036n831

1Q39
1 6 2332n317,
  2818n5178

**1Qap Gen^{ar}/Genesis
Apocryphon**
in toto: 2353n528,
  3193n646
II 1383, 1631n324,
  3229n948
II, 1 3053n1030
II, 4 2462n1708
II, 14 1091n515
II, 15–16 2438n1454
II, 19 894n333
II, 19–25 719n633
V 719n633
XII, 17 1091n515,
  2462n1708
XIX 3779n8
XIX, 14–23 914n572
XX 2439n1463
XX, 2–8 614n195
XX, 10–11 146n284,
  1368n717
XX, 12 2462n1708
XX, 16 1067n286,
  2462n1708

XX, 16–17
  2434n1403
XX, 19–20
  2439n1468
XX, 19–29
  2439n1468
XX, 21–22
  3684n1302
XX, 21–29
  2438n1457,
  2441n1489
XX, 22 1288,
  1528n667
XX, 28–29 1067n286,
  3684n1302
XX, 29 1288,
  1528n667
XX, 31 2402n1018
XXI, 2 2462n1708
XXI, 17–18 1401
XXI, 20 2462n1708
XXI, 20–22 1008n153
XXII, 15–16
  2462n1708
XXII, 21 2462n1708

4Q375–376

in toto: 802n195

4Q376

in toto: 778n443,
2010n280,
2013n326
1 I, 1 967n1161
1 II, 1 802n197

4Q377

1 II, 5 967n1161,
1079n394,
1115n743
1 II, 10 726n693
2 II, 5 3088n1419
2 II, 7–8 1631n324,
1885n176
2 II, 11 1245n347,
1397n999,
2143n1528,
3088n1419

4Q378

22 2 885n241,
1084n446,
2065n846

4Q380

in toto: 2070n881,
2493n2008
I, 2–6 1350

4Q381

in toto: 2070n881,
2493n2008
15 7 966n1146
46 5 937n869
69 4 535n301,
894n335
76–77 12 1442n1413

4Q382

Frg. 1 717n616
Frg. 3 717n616
Frg. 9 717n616
16 2 966n1146
Frg. 31 717n616

4Q385

2 802n185
2 7–8 802n185
3 3 683n304
3 3–5 688n349
3 4–5 682n298
4 1606n84
4 11 804n212

4Q385–386

in toto: 783n14

4Q386

in toto: 802n185
1 III, 1–2 1412n1132,
1682n777

4Q387

Frg. 2–3 1130n851
Frg. 2.4 1130n851
Frg. 3.6 1130n851

4Q388

in toto: 802n185

4Q388a

6 2 1109n681

4Q389

Frg. 2 1115n751,
3177n502
E.2 3048n957
4 2060n801

4Q390

1 7–9 475n129,
877n163
1 9 1109n681

4Q392

Frg. 1 3524n1475
1 4–6 3526n1498

4Q393

in toto: 1460n1608
3 5 2234n269
3 7 752n185
4 5 1083n429

4Q400

1 I, 4–5 1991n92
1 I, 14 1626nn271–
272
1 I, 16 973n1209
1 I, 19–20 808n249

4Q400–407

in toto: 807n243,
1046n37, 1278n298

4Q402

3–4 7–10 1408n1100

4Q403

1 I, 1 808n247
1 I, 1–3 808n246
1 I, 5–6 808n246
1 I, 6–29 1277n284
1 I, 21 808n247
1 I, 22 1627n273,
1627n281
1 I, 23 808n249
1 I, 26 808n247
1 I, 31 808n247,
3053n1030, 3527
1 I, 39–40 1034n443,
1757n293,
2643n3424
1 II, 10 2040n623
1 II, 11 808n247
1 II, 15 1035n456
1 II, 19–20 808n249
1 II, 20 808n247
1 II, 22 808n249
1 II, 24 808n247,
808n249

4Q404

2 3 1627n273

4Q405

3 II, 1–15 1277n284
3 II, 13 1627n273
13 6 1627n273
15 II, 2–3 804n212
19 1035n456
20 II 1035n456,
1827n918
20 II, 7–11 808n245
20 II, 10 804n212
20 II + 21–22
1441n1407,
1441n1410
20–22 12 1090n505
21–22 1035n456
21–22 13 1827n918
23 I, 8–10 1035n456
23 I, 11 1626n272

4Q409

1 I 2965n140
1 I, 8 1800n714

4Q412

Frg. 1 2269n621
1 10 3048n957

4Q414

12 979n1284
2269n621

4Q416

1 838n510

2 (+4Q417) I, 17
1939n942
2 II, 6 2332n317,
2818n5179
2 II, 13 1671n684
2 II, 19–20 855n702,
1024n326
2 II, 21 625n357,
1655n535
2 III, 8–12 1025n349
2 III, 14 1627n275
2 III, 20–IV, 2
625n369
2 III, 20–IV, 6
625n370
2 III, 20–IV, 7
625n371

4Q417

in toto: 625n357,
625nn369–371,
855n702, 1024n326,
1025n349, 1671n684
1 I 3277
1 I, 17–22 1025n352
2 [+ 4Q418] II, 12
1450n1496

4Q418

8 4 533
8 6 2332n317,
2818n5179
9 15 1627n275
55 4 3030n755
55 7 3030n755
55 9 3030n755
69 II, 13 3054n1035
81 5 1671n684
81 14 3054n1034
127 3 2632n3299

4Q421

in toto: 2048n710
11 2001n195
13 2001n195

4Q422

in toto: 268n99
I, 7 2332n317,
2818n5178
II, 2–6 2146n1562
III, 4–5 335n147,
349n280
III, 7 2826n5232
III, 11 2826n5232

4Q424

in toto: 2269n621
1 3 1642n417,
3755n419
1 3–4 3275n1308
1 6 2547n2506

1 10 1276n268, 1277
3 3 3520n1409

4Q427

2 + 3 II, 13 1310n165
8 I, 10 3233n968
8 II, 18 2818n5178

4Q429

1 IV, 3 943n935
4 I, 10 1626n272

4Q430

1 4 2010n278

4Q434

1 I, 3–4 1642n417,
3755n419
1 I, 4 1424n1231
1 II, 3 1426n1252
1 II, 3–4 2394n903,
3520n1410

4Q435

1 I, 1 1424n1231

4Q436

1 II, 1 2818n5179

4Q440

3 I, 16 1798n695

4Q444

1 I 676n260
1 I, 1 534, 2332n317,
2818n5178
1 I, 2–4 534
1 I, 4 1803n737
1 1, 3 1310n165
1 3–4 + 2 I 4 1203n302

4Q448

in toto: 2070n881,
2493n2008
II, 1 1090n505
II, 3–6 836n473

4Q451

24 7 2100n1141,
3525n1489

4Q458

in toto: 1672n697
2 II, 6 966n1146

Cambridge Geniza Text

Oxford Geniza Text

Josephus

Against Apion

Jewish War

Philo of Alexandria

Targumic Texts

Mishnah, Talmud, and Related Literature

Other Rabbinic Works

Esther Rabbah

1:4 1632n331
1:5 1854n219
1:17 1346n501
2:4 1789n607,
 3011n597,
 3544n1652
2:13 854n681
4:12 3513n1346
7:11 778n443
8:3 2314n152
9:2 2258n514
10:5 537n320,
 873n122, 946n954,
 2332n318

Exodus Rabbah

1:1 986n1337,
 1346n503,
 1659n570
1:4 1353n595,
 2082n985
1:5 1115n751,
 3178n503
1:9 512n102, 1052n99
1:12 614n196,
 1353n593,
 2082n983
1:13 613n186,
 1139n933,
 1381n853
1:20 1383, 2072n902,
 2100n1135,
 3525n1482
1:22 1393n968,
 2100n1135,
 3525n1482
1:23 1386n899
1:24 2100n1135,
 3525n1482
1:26 874n138, 1388,
 2254n480
1:28 1353n593,
 2082n983
1:28–29 1392
1:29 1394n983,
 3224n921
1:30 1066, 1394n982
1:31 1395n986
1:35 2082n982
2:2 2081n972,
 3036n831
2:4 1353n593,
 1872n56, 2082n983
2:5 1884n170
2:6 1113n727,
 3054n1035,
 3178n503
3:4 716n611,
 1115n751
3:13 3125n93
4:2 1393n968
4:3 906n497,
 1053n107
5:8 2215n130

5:9 803n204, 807n241
5:12 1143n965,
 3264n1212,
 3266n1218,
 3297n1477
5:14 3523n1463
5:20 522n197,
 536n312, 895n341,
 1220n114,
 3036n832,
 3043n906
6:1 1317n215,
 3679n1248
6:3 1109n675,
 1620n210,
 3679n1248
6:4 1620n210
7:4 879n179
8:1 537n320, 677n266
8:2 1191n168,
 1784n562
9:2 1766n378
9:3 1765n367,
 3671n1160
9:6 1505n416,
 2009n276,
 2845n5427
10:1 3670n1155
10:4 146n277
12:4 1139n933,
 1442n1412
14:3 772n376,
 2100n1141,
 3525n1477,
 3525n1489
15:3 1353n593,
 2082n983
15:4 1353n595,
 2082n985
15:5 1348n522
15:6 2100n1132,
 3525n1478
15:10 1353n593,
 2082n983
15:11 1070n319,
 1115n751,
 1361n661,
 2236n288,
 3178n503
15:12 3038n858
15:16 1632n330
15:17 537n320
15:20 1139n931
15:22 1070n319
15:24 1655n530
15:27 804n206
15:29 1422n1207
15:30 1671n683
15:31 3054n1034
16:1 1353n593,
 2082n983
17:2 844n573,
 1119n782
17:3 2216n137
17:4 1442n1416
18:3 1386n898

18:5 1189n147,
 1884n170
18:11 3525nn1476–
 1477
18:12 716n612,
 874n138
19:2 1189n148
19:4 514n127,
 514n130, 2216n138
19:5 2216n137,
 3072n1247
19:6 1115n751,
 3011n597,
 3178n503,
 3544n1652
20:4 3054n1035
20:5 906n497
20:6 2258n514
20:8 838n512
20:10 939n897
20:19 1505n416,
 2009n276,
 2845n5427
21 1938n918
21:3 772n374
21:5 731n744,
 2344n435
21:7 421n175,
 1189n147
21:11 1282n341
22:3 2385n806
23:5 1353n593,
 2082n983
23:6 874n138
24:3 3036n843,
 3037n851
25:10 1968n1184
25:12 687n343,
 688n350, 736n22,
 1107n655,
 1108n664
27:3 906n497
27:5 514n127
27:9 537n320,
 1318n242,
 3020n683
28:1 959n1076,
 959n1079,
 1005n122,
 1113n729
28:5 1317n219
29:4 1318n238,
 1318n240
29:9 808n245
30:3 1318n242,
 2646n3453
30:9 512n103,
 737n38, 844n573,
 1119n782,
 2264n565
30:12 1627n277,
 2217n145
30:13 1659n571
30:16 2665n3681,
 2668n3709
30:18 1139n933,
 1442n1412

30:19 784n21,
 803n201,
 2649n3490,
 3127n104
30:20 906n497,
 1642n417,
 3755n419
30:21 2113n1253
30:24 585n31,
 1580n1224
31:1 973n1210
31:2 1189n147
31:3 957n1058,
 1025n345,
 1025n351
31:5 1025n351,
 1435n1352
31:6 3675n1211
31:14 1025n351, 1058
31:16 785n37
31:17 1412n1134
32:3 897n358,
 906n497, 2344n433
32:4 667n176
32:9 1115n751
33:1 1318n238
33:5 537n320
33:7 1317n218
34:1 803n204
34:2 1282n344
34:3 3036n841
35:5 1412n1134
36:3 3525n1491
37:2 2409n1098
38:6 839n517,
 936n858
38:8 2216n137
41:1 1408
41:5 959n1076
41:7 870n86,
 1189n148,
 1317n233,
 1409n1111,
 2237n302,
 2591n2897,
 3235n989
42:4 908n502,
 1404n1055,
 1606n80
42:6 1407n1088
42:7 1407
42:9 1261n108,
 1424n1227,
 2004n220
43:1 1189n147
43:3 772n374
44:5 989n1363,
 1353n595,
 2082n985
45:2 839n515
45:5 727n705,
 896n349, 1632n338
45:6 3679n1248
46:3 772n374
46:4–5 1671n683
47:3 784n21,
 2649n3490

47:5 517n158,
 675n246, 871n107,
 957n1058,
 959n1076,
 1693n868,
 2158n1681,
 2322, 2322n233,
 2979n288,
 3048n957,
 3049n964
48:2 1407n1090
48:4 802n185,
 3500n1225
48:6 537n320
50:1 2100n1141,
 3524n1474.
 3525n1489
51:2 1178n39,
 1276n269,
 3057n1070,
 3132n159
51:5 465n52
51:6 1276n269,
 3057n1070
51:7 954n1029
51:8 2237n302
52:2 975n1229
52:3 636n515,
 1025n351,
 1058n195,
 1069n307,
 3568n113
On Exod 1:22
 1380n851
On Exod 24:7
 3523n1460

Genesis Rabbah

in toto: 2220n164
1:1 2668n3709
1:4 767n320,
 937n874, 973n1210,
 1951n1035
1:5 908n505,
 956n1050,
 1086n470,
 1110n691,
 1271n212,
 3011n597,
 3544n1653
1:6 2100n1132,
 2100n1137,
 3525n1478,
 3525n1485
1:10 784n20,
 908n505,
 2649n3490,
 3011n597,
 3544n1653
1:13 1111n702
1:15 615n201, 653n58
2:2 675n246
2:3 1352n577,
 2100n1133,
 2646n3459,
 3525n1480

Apostolic Fathers

3.15 389n36, 652n53
3.15–16 1403n1053
3.16 2310n115
4.2 1806n763
5.1 398n98,
1403n1053
5.2 2222n182
6 1723n205, 3093
6.1 1403n1053
7.2 398
12.2 186n167
18 762n280
18.1 763n283

21.1 1853n209
24 761
26.1 1848n163,
1849n173
28.1 394n63

Polycarp

Letter to the Philippians
in toto: 223n11
1.2 396–97, 944n942,
944n944, 3777n1

2.1 1807, 1887n199,
3528n1512, 3777n1
2.2 401n120, 2260
2.3 3047n951, 3777n1
3.2 394n63, 430n54
4.1 401n120
4.3 401n120,
1011n193
5.2 401n120, 1217n99
5.2–3 1940n949
5.3 2260
6.1 401n120,
1217n99, 2260,

3132n159,
3405n470
6.2 1807n779
6.3 397, 2260n526
7.2 1992n107
8.1 1588n1300
8.2 401n120
9.1 394n63, 430n54,
2222n182
9.1–2 401n120, 431,
1282n337
10.2 401n120
11.1 233n87

11.1–2 401n120,
1276n277
11.2–3 394n63
11.3 430n54
11.4 233n87
12.1 2309n106
12.2 2308n98
12.3 401n120, 431,
3457n895
13.2 233n87,
2492n1990,
3429n672

Patristic and Other Early Christian Sources

Ambrose

Concerning Repentance
2.4.23 1532n705

De Nabuthae historia
1 1055n134

De officiis ministrorum
1.18.79 1457n1567

Epistulae
39 1479n135

The Holy Spirit
2.150 812

Letters to Priests
59 2581n2795

Ambrosiaster

Commentary on Paul's Epistles
81:11–12 983n1314
81:12–13 1815n835
81:31–32 2181n1944
81:34 1528n665,
1814n829
81:169–79 7n18
81:190 769n337
Rom 1:16 691n372
Rom 6 3747n351
Rom 16:7 1613n142
Rom 16:16
3073n1268
Those cited instead by
Vogels reference:
Vogels, 3–4
2683n3848,
2685n3856

Vogels, 12–13
2671n3728
Vogels, 18–19
2671n3728
Vogels, 39 2622n3217
Vogels, 41 2622n3217
Vogels, 96 2270n632
Vogels, 118 3646n919
Vogels, 209–10
3710n1592
Vogels, 292–93
2829n5275
Vogels, 293 3560n49
Vogels, 294–95
3653n987
Vogels, 295–96
3669n1145
Vogels, 296
2736n4410,
3048n956

Ammonius

Catena in Acta
3.16 1099n584
3.39 2084n1014
16.23 2487n1933
16.31–32 2486n1923
18.25 2808n5098,
2811n5126
27.10 3598n456
28.9 544n366

Anglo-Saxon Chronicle
in toto: 3589n356

Anti-Marcionite Prologue to Luke
in toto: 88n309, 410,
645n29

Aphrahat

Demonstrations
21.9 1362n672

Apollinaris of Laodicea

in toto: 761n270,
762n280, 763n283
Rom 12:6 906n477
Rom 13:1–7
1231n214
Pauluskommentare 59
2622n3217

Arator

On the Acts of the Apostles
1 666n174, 774n397,
842n553, 1279n304,
1768n393, 1942n959
2 1639n389,
2457n1668,
2976n254,
3230n955,
3674n1201

Aristides the Philosopher

Apology to Hadrian
in toto: 2678n3799
15.2 708n543
15.7–8 1028n385

Athanasius

Discourses against Arians
1.43 2162–63n1752

Festal Letters
19.5 1541n769,
1585n1276
42 2854n5512

Homilies
TLG 2035.669
2966n148

On the Incarnation
48 2440n1481
54.3 1782n520

Vita Antonii/On the Life of Anthony
63 2440n1481
80 372, 2440n1477

Athenagoras

A Plea for Christians
1 2910n6022
3 2551n2546,
2589n2876,
3073n1268,
3125n89,
3480n1086
4 2378n729,
2578n2766,
2597n2971,
2639n3377
5 2656n3572
6 2656n3572
7 535n303, 807n237,
1161n1161
12.2 3031n770
13 2663n3662
20–22 2161n1735,
2162n1751
26 2432n1360
27 2663n3662
27.3 3277n1325
30.3 3503n1244
32 1516n559,
2272n661, 3073
33.1–2 1380n841
35 2904n5978
35.6 1380nn841–842

Augustine

Advantage of Believing
16.34 373n479

Against the Two Letters of the Pelagians
1.19.37 1599n13

Baptism
2.16.21 828
3.16 1528n669
4.22.30 828

City of God
6.5.1–3 2589n2878,
2589n2882
14.8 3599n463
14.8.1 3627n755
22.8 373nn480–481,
1712n70

Confessions
6.3 1583
8.12 885n235,
1239n291
8.12.29 1599n13
9.7.16 373n479
9.9 610n125, 623n324
10.35 2613n3134

De doctrina christiana
4.41 142n234

Enarrations on the Psalms
96.15 2646n3460

Epistles
22 1599n13
41.1 3007n551

Nag Hammadi Texts

(besides those arranged elsewhere; see apocryphal gospels and acts)

New Testament Apocrypha and Pseudepigrapha

Other Greek and Latin Works and Authors

4 (to Delos), 184
2117n1295,
2119n1317
4 (to Delos), 301
1166n1211
5 (to the Baths of
Pallas), 98–102
1398n1004
5 (to the Baths of
Pallas), 111–16
1398n1004
5 (to the Baths of
Pallas), 131–36
3390n346
6 (to Demeter), 56
2102n1153
6 (to Demeter),
59 1634n348,
2177n1904
6 (to Demeter), 63
1766n379
6 (to Demeter), 72–73
2991n417

Iambi

3.193 902n434
4.194.106 2166n1806
6 3067n1182
12.202.70 3041n890

Minor Poems

380 1766n379

Callistratus

Descriptions

2 852n658, 2391n881
4 1562n1030,
1562n1034
9 1554n898

In *Digest* **of
Justinian**

47.21.2 446n68,
2678n3802,
2699n4030,
3198n688

Calpurnius Flaccus

Declamations

40 2415n1184

Calpurnius Siculus

1.42–45 878, 1110,
1111n705

Catasterisms

15 1576n1184
17 1576n1184

Cato/Dionysius Cato

*Collection of
Distichs* (**Dicta
Catonis**)

1–57 2269n621
10 1390n943,
1390n946,
2185n1995
20 624n350
25 2274n687

Disticbs

2.10 3325n1708
3.12 622n312
3.20 622n312
3.21 1024n339
4.1 1023n320

Cato the Elder

*De agricultura
(De re rustica)*

59 1913n519
120 859n781

Origins

Frg. 77 174n57

Catullus

Carmina

1.3–4 655
3.5 225n26,
3279n1339
4.25–27 3695n1422
5.7–13 3120n55
7.3 3120n55
10.7–13 1170n1246,
3439
11.2–3 704
11.6 3325n1705
13.1–8 1010n184
14 2858n5558
14.1–3 225n26,
3279n1339
27 860n789
27.1 854n673,
854n677
32.10 2829n5278,
3512n1324
34.21–22 1070n313,
2632n3302
36.6–8 2858
36.18–20 2858
37.1 2416n1190
37.9–10 2416n1190
44.10–21 2858n5558
45.11–12 225n26
48.1 225n26
48.3 3120n55
49.5–7 1388n923,
2101n1150

52.1 670n210, 863n6,
3772n575
52.4 670n210, 863n6,
3772n575
55.17 1577n1190
57.1 670n210, 863n6,
3772n575
57.10 670n210,
863n6, 3772n575
61.4–5 993n19,
1290n429,
2899n5927
61.4–62.66
2492n1993
61.15 2969n169
61.39–40 993n19,
1290n429,
2899n5927
61.49–50 993n19,
1290n429,
2899n5927
61.59–60 993n19,
1290n429,
2899n5927
61.77–78 2969n169
61.94–95 2969n169
61.96 993n19,
1290n429
61.106 993n19,
1290n429
61.113 993n19,
1290n429
61.114 2969n169
61.117–18 993n19,
1290n429,
2899n5927
61.137–38 993n19,
1290n429,
2899n5927
61.142–43 993n19,
1290n429,
2899n5927
61.147–48 993n19,
1290n429,
2899n5927
61.152–53 993n19,
1290n429,
2899n5927
61.154–56 622n314
61.157–58 993n19,
1290n429,
2899n5927
61.162–63 993n19,
1290n429,
2899n5927
61.167–68 993n19,
1290n429,
2899n5927
61.172–73 993n19,
1290n429,
2899n5927
61.177–78 993n19,
1290n429,
2899n5927
61.182–83 993n19,
1290n429,
2899n5927

62.4–5 993n19,
1290n429, 1601n37,
2899n5927
62.10 993n19,
1290n429, 1601n37,
2899n5927
62.19 993n19,
1290n429, 1601n37,
2899n5927
62.25 993n19,
1290n429, 1601n37,
2899n5927
62.31 993n19,
1290n429, 1601n37,
2899n5927
62.34–35 586n35,
1683n790,
2177n1909,
2559n2622,
3324n1698
62.38 993n19,
1290n429,
2899n5927
62.48 993n19,
1290n429,
2899n5927
62.59–65 622n314
62.66 993n19,
1290n429,
2899n5927
63 627n395
63.4 627n395
63.4–6 2167n1809
63.5 1569n1097
63.6 1569n1101
63.7 1577n1191
63.8 1577n1191
63.8–9 2166n1806
63.9 2166n1796
63.12 1569n1097
63.27 1569n1101
63.29 2166n1806
63.34 1569n1097
64 1768n392
64.21 2661n3626
64.25 2969n169
64.48 705n497,
1573n1145
64.156 3614n629,
3615n633
64.176 757n231,
2418, 2418n1213
64.202–6 1174n8,
3390n346
64.207–9 1642n414
64.241–45 2500n2073
64.298 2662n3629
64.302 2969n169
64.327 993n19,
1290n429
64.333 993n19,
1290n429
64.337 993n19,
1290n429
64.342 993n19,
1290n429

64.347 993n19,
1290n429
64.352 993n19,
1290n429
64.356 993n19,
1290n429
64.361 993n19,
1290n429
64.365 993n19,
1290n429
64.371 993n19,
1290n429
64.375 993n19,
1290n429
64.381 993n19,
1290n429
64.387 2662n3629
66.79 2969n169
67.23–24 2272n661
67.29–30 2272n661
68.19–26 3009n572
68A.65 3696n1440
70.4 800, 800n173
76.8 653n56
78.1–6 2272n661
82.1–4 225n26,
3279n1339
86.1 1577n1190,
1577n1193
90.1–4 1681n767,
2272n659
90.2 1501n357
96.1–6 1477n108,
3067n1183

Celsus, Aulus Cornelius

De medicina

3.14 3687

Cercidas

Frg. 1 730n742,
2134n1432,
2505n2128
38–41 1185n114

Chaeremon Stoicus

Frg. 10 1036n458

Chariton

*Chaereas and
Callirhoe*

in toto: 53, 64n114,
64n120, 599,
670n210, 1143,
2502n2095
1.1.1 53n12
1.1.3 925n696
1.1.4 604n51
1.1.4–5 2879n5739,
2969n171

Chrysippus

De Fato

Cicero

Academica

Against Caecilius

Brutus, or De claris oratoribus

3.15.39 1782n521
3.6.14 897n370
3.16.42 172n40
3.20–24 2637n3372
3.24 3689n1374

De officiis

in toto: 2267n591
1.1.1 2566
1.1.3–4 2583n2814
1.4.11 1767n380,
  2904n5981
1.47–48 3314n1611
1.16.50 2267n592,
  2621–22n3210
1.16.51 1015n227
1.17.54 447n73,
  624n348, 1015n229,
  1031n409
1.17.56 1176n25
1.22.77 3568n119
1.23 2412n1144
1.26.90 1024n328
1.26.91 1153n1085
1.28.100 2267n591
1.29.102 2237n300,
  2308n96
1.33.120 928n736,
  930n767
1.38.136 2237n300,
  2308n96
1.40.142 175n70
1.128 2134n1442
1.148 2134n1442
1.42.150–51
  2723n4270
2.5.18 2237n300,
  2308n96
2.16.55–57 609n121,
  613n171, 1942n957
2.18.64 2414n1164
2.21.75 1276n269
3.6.28 2648
3.10.41 1365n698
3.17.71 1642n414
3.17.72 2267n591
3.26.99 3666n1108
3.28.101 2267n591
3.113 123n55
43.1.5 1015n227

De optimo genere oratorum

6.17 1784n551
14 2143n1526

De oratore

in toto: 118n11
1.10.40 1783n538,
  1962
1.31.143 2626n3249,
  3361n93,
  3545n1660
1.38.172 1783n538,
  1962

1.142 296n328
1.158 132n131
1.187 3211n792
1.196 3181n539
1.45.199 2423n1259
1.47 2617n3168
1.231 2607n3066,
  3352n15
1.251 255n192
1.260–61 3190n620
2.11.46 3050n975,
  3060n1108
2.15.62–63 120n33
2.43.182 3055n1044
2.185–90 2891n5860
2.45.189 135n172,
  145n264, 2076n936
2.45.191 3009n575
2.46.189 3009n575
2.46.189–90
  3051n1007
2.51–53 110n143
2.51–54 98n70
2.51–64 98n70
2.55–58 118n11
2.55.225 3265n1217
2.57 132n129
2.57.270–71 866n34
2.58.236 70n165,
  867n53, 3274n1301
2.61.251 70n165
2.253–63 3274n1301
2.62 118n11, 155n65,
  695n406
2.62–64 118n11
2.63 98n70, 119n27,
  155n65
2.63–64 118n11
2.64 67n140, 118n11
2.80 2626n3249
2.80.325 3010n592
2.326–28 3202n721,
  3367n163
2.81.333–37
  970n1187
2.84.343–44
  2996n463,
  3050n975,
  3060n1108
2.85.346 2996,
  2996n463,
  3050n975
2.85.347 2996,
  3021n689
2.94 132n129
2.133–47 708n546
2.185–90 1312n181
2.216–89 869n77
2.250–54 2629n3277
2.264 3203n726
2.266 225n23
2.321 869n78
2.351 291n282,
  296n328
3.9.37–39 285n231
3.10.39 2654
3.11.43 2566

3.14.55 2583n2812
3.20.75 2578n2767
3.27.104–5 195n257,
  1668n666, 2304n64
3.34.137 2767n4724
3.168 1101n607,
  3754n411
3.198 2285n797
3.52.199 285n231
3.53.202–3 195n257,
  1668n666, 2304n64
3.53.203 3049n966
3.53.204 3133n167,
  3242n1022,
  3414n537
3.53.205 869n77,
  3053n1026
3.214 2802n5054
3.58.217–18
  2893n5870,
  3272n1280
3.220 255n192

De partitione oratoria

8.28 3018n652
15.52–17.28
  3054n1036
15.53 1517n577,
  3022n708
16.55 3053n1026
16.55–56 3054n1036
17.58 3054n1037
21.71 3060
21.73 2996, 3017n642
22 146n283
23.80 2414n1164
72 800n174

De provinciis consularibus

in toto: 3180n533
1.1 1354n604
1.2 2237n300,
  2254n481, 2308n91
2.3 1354n604
4.8 1354n604
5.11 1354n604
7.15 3165n408
8.18 269n106,
  851n650, 970n1192,
  1354n604,
  1811n807
9.23 1354n604,
  3180n533
10.25 1354n604
12.30 1354n604
12.31 1799n708
13.32 1354n604
16.38 1354n604,
  2914n6062
16.39 1354n604

De re publica

1.43 3198n688

2.7 2685n3858
2.7–8 2688nn3907–
  3908
2.27 123n55
3.9.15 720n651,
  1376n788,
  2117n1297,
  2631n3297
3.25.37 1636n364
3.36 157n75
5.1 1319n251
5.1.2 1319n254,
  2474n1815, 3128
6.14.14 730n742
6.15.15 1408n1098,
  1413n1144,
  1947n1001,
  2503n2111,
  2505, 3293n1446,
  3528n1510
6.16.16 1319n256,
  3131n156
6.17.17 918n630,
  3528n1510
6.19.20 3528n1510
6.24.26 1319n256,
  1784n558
6.26.29 730n742,
  1605n76,
  1947n1005,
  3528n1510
9.571d–572a
  2347n459

De senectute (Cato Major)

in toto: 656
1.1 656
12.40 986n1336
13.45 1007n144
14.47 1450n1493,
  2237n300
17.59 2402n1017
20.78 949n986

Epistulae ad familiares/Letters to Friends

in toto: 232
1.1.1 3437
1.1.4 2410n1101,
  3444n810
1.2.2 2777
1.2.3 1133n878,
  1778n484, 1820,
  2979n287
1.2.4 869n80,
  1213n65,
  2516n2235,
  2830n5278
1.3.2 1305n95,
  1623n243,
  1911n495
1.6.1 1654n523,
  3089n1423

1.7.1 2283n774
1.7.2 1206n13, 1207
1.8.1–2 2222,
  2287n814,
  2913n6049
1.9.1 3052n1020
1.9.9 2410n1101,
  3444n810
1.9.11 1037n469,
  3680n1262
1.9.15 605n55,
  626n388, 2389n852,
  2799n5022
1.10.1 2991
2.1.1 2283n777,
  2991n421
2.1.1–2 3052n1020
2.2.1 2283n777,
  3052n1020
2.3.2 3052n1020
2.4.1 1654n522,
  2291n857,
  3089n1423,
  3483n1105,
  3759n451
2.4.2 3364n128
2.5.1 2291n857,
  3759n451
2.6.1 3415n551
2.10.1 2283n777,
  2991n421,
  3052n1020
2.11.1 3483n1105
2.12.1 2291n857,
  3759n451
2.13.1 2283n777,
  2991n421
2.14.1 3594n410
2.17.1 1649n475
3.1.1 1654n523,
  2291n857,
  3089n1423,
  3759n451
3.1.2 1305n93,
  2283n771
3.1.3 1624n246
3.3.2 234n96,
  2292n869,
  3333n1775,
  3660n1038
3.8.6 1649n475
3.8.10 706n524,
  845n584, 1649n475
3.10.7 3209n774
3.11.1 1649n475,
  2283n776
3.11.2 2554n2566,
  3067n1187,
  3439n768,
  3440n779
4.1.2 3376n250
4.4.1 2283n777,
  2991n421
4.4.2 2291n857,
  3759n451
4.5.4 2685n3858

Dio Chrysostom

Diodore

History

Diomedes

Ars Grammatica

Diodorus Siculus

Library of History

20 1062n232,
1155n1114

The Dance

25 2605n3051
37 777n431,
2167n1818,
2650n3496
38 2423n1257
42 2696n3997
45 326n42, 1723n196
54 2985n362
63 135n174
65 284n215, 285n221
68 2167n1806
76 1835

**The Dead Come
to Life, or The
Fisherman**

in toto: 1152n1069,
2134n1435,
2135n1453
1 1454n1538
2 941n916,
2505n2129
3 1152n1069
4 1916n574
5 1145n990,
1804n747,
1916n575,
2411n1117,
3315n1613,
3407n488
6 480n170,
2660n3614
9 3391, 3438n758
10 3370n191
11 3508n1295
13 2718n4220
15 2134n1435,
2135n1453,
2600n2997
17 1152n1069,
3397n409
31 1483n182
33 818n335,
3544n1651
37 2134n1435,
2135n1453
42 1062n232,
1156n1115,
2134n1435,
2135n1453,
2140n1506,
2483n1898,
2541n2443,
2569n2693,
2583n2816,
2614n3142,
3055n1048,
3133n162
43 2582n2796,
2582n2806
44 2137, 2140n1504
51 2593n2920

Demonax

in toto: 44n10
1 2012n316
1–2 3047n948
2 148n2, 1618n183
3 1153n1074,
1181n75, 2012n316
5 2135n1446,
2137n1474, 2606
7 416n103,
2135n1446,
2137n1474,
2309n102
9 1394n980
11 868, 1453,
1757n295, 2154,
2578n2766,
2605n3054, 2606,
2643n3429,
3665n1090
12 1570n1118,
3754n411
13 1156n1115,
2140n1506
13ff. 1388n921
14 269n106, 851n650,
971, 1811n807,
1960n1115,
2094n1093,
2388n836
15 1570n1118
16 1453
18 1570n1118
19 1577n1191
19–20 1243n325,
1499n337,
2113n1252,
2586n2848
21 2134
23 1504n400
27 327n46,
2426n1289
31 2009n269
34 516n151,
2578n2767,
3666n1101
35 3593n400,
3596n435,
3628n762
37 897n361,
1853n213
40 3170, 3666n1114
44 3274n1299
48 1155n1114,
2134n1435,
2140n1503,
3223n907
50 1570n1118,
2487n1934, 2769
51 2308n95
54 1052n89,
2012n316,
2056n769
55 2141nn1509–
1510, 3099n1530

57 2695n3983,
3181n544
61 2134, 2137n1465
63 1693n863,
2224n187,
2991n419
65 2505n2128
66 1474
67 1474

Demosthenes

43–50 3019

**Dialogues of
Courtesans**

in toto: 177n85
1 (Glycera and Thais),
281 1594n1357,
2009n276,
2274n677
4 (Melitta and Bacchis
1), 286 1505n416,
2009n276,
2274n677
6 (Crobyle and
Corinna ¶4), 295
2679n3816
7 (Musarium and Her
Mother ¶1), 295–96
2679n3816
7 (Musarium and Her
Mother ¶2), 296
3640n868
7 (Musarium and Her
Mother ¶2), 296–97
2601n3014,
2678n3803
10 (Chelidonium and
Drosis ¶4), 307
1557n940
12 (Joessa, Pythias,
and Lysias ¶1), 310–
11 2679n3816
12 (Joessa, Pythias,
and Lysias ¶1), 311
3640n868
12 (Joessa, Pythias,
and Lysias ¶5), 314
2783n4865
12 (Joessa, Pythias,
and Lysias ¶5), 315
2783n4865
13 (Leontichus, Che-
nidas, and Hymnis),
315–19 2679n3816
14 (Dorio and Myrtale
1) 1178n37
14 (Dorio and Myrtale
1), 319 2679n3816
14 (Dorio and Myrtale
2), 320 3640n868
14 (Dorio and Myrtale
3), 320 3640n868
14 (Dorio and Myrtale
3), 321 3696n1431
288 1852n200

**Dialogues of
the Dead**

328–29 (1/1, Diogenes
1) 3697n1452
329 (1/1, Diogenes 1)
2134n1432,
2583n2816,
2685n3856,
2688n3901,
2746n4497
332 (1/1, Diogenes 2)
2583n2816,
2685n3856
336 (3/2, Dead to
Pluto against Menip-
pus the Cynic 1)
1024n330,
2134n1432,
2490n1969
336–37 (3/2, Dead
to Pluto against
Menippus the Cynic
1–2) 1016n236,
3009n572
337 (3/2, Dead to
Pluto against Menip-
pus the Cynic 2)
1024n330
340 (10/3, Menippus,
Amphilocus, and
Trophonius 2)
1783n521,
1783n527
341–43 (14/1, Hermes
and Charon 1–2)
2151n1614
344–45 (15/5, Pluto
and Hermes 1)
1962n1136
347 (16/6, Terp-
sion and Pluto 1)
1962n1136
356–57 (17/7, Ze-
nophantus and
Callidemides 2–3)
1962n1136
358–59 (18/8, Cne-
mon and Damnippus
1) 1962n1136
363–64 (20/10,
Charon and Hermes
1) 1024n330
364–65 (20/10,
Charon and Hermes
2) 1155n1114,
2140nn1503–1504
365 (20/10, Charon
and Hermes 2)
3071n1238
370 (20/10, Charon
and Hermes 8)
2010n291
371–72 (20/10,
Charon and Hermes
9) 1156n1115,
2140n1506

374 (20/10, Charon
and Hermes 10)
1530n681,
2134n1436,
3055n1048
375 (20/10, Charon
and Hermes 12–13)
1472n52
380–89 (25/12, Al-
exander, Hannibal,
Minos, and Scipio
1–7) 1807n775
390 (13/13, Diogenes
and Alexander 1)
1785n566
395 (12/14, Philip
and Alexander 1)
849n626, 1785n566
397–98 (12/14, Philip
and Alexander 1) ¶5
1785n566
402–3 (11/16, Dio-
genes and Heracles
1–2) 667n178
408 (5/18, Menip-
pus and Hermes 1)
2151n1614
410–11 (27/19, Aeacus
and Protesilaus 1–2)
930n770
414 (6/20, Menippus
and Aeacus 2)
611n137, 1483n182
415 (6/20, Menippus
and Aeacus 3)
1770n416
416 (6/20, Menippus
and Aeacus 4)
1278n287,
2502n2098,
2505n2129
419 (6/20, Menippus
and Aeacus ¶6)
2606n3058,
2606n3064
420 (4/21, Menippus
and Cerberus 1)
2134n1432
421 (4/21, Menippus
and Cerberus 1–2)
3628n764
422 (4/21, Menippus
and Cerberus 1–2)
3628n764
423 (2/22, Charon and
Menippus 1)
1016n236,
3622n714
424 (2/22, Charon
and Menippus 1)
2151n1614
425 (2/22, Charon
and Menippus 3)
2134n1432
429–31 (29/24, Dio-
genes and Mausolus
1–3) 1024n330

Minucius Felix

Octavius

Modestinus

Digest

Moretum

Musaeus

Hero and Leander

Musonius Rufus (Lutz)

Nemesius

De Natura hominis

Nicolaus of Damascus

History

Vitae Caesaris

Tristia

Panyassis

Papinianus

Digest

Parthenius

Love Romance

Paul of Aegina

Paulus, Julius

Digest

*Sententiae/
Opinions*

Pausanias

*Collected Attic
Words*

*Description
of Greece*

Pliny the Younger

Epistles

Quintus Curtius Rufus

History of Alexander

Quintus of Smyrna

Posthomerica

Res gestae divi Augusti

Rhetorica ad Alexandrum

Synesius

On Dio

Epistles

Syrianus

Commentary on Hermogenes's "On Issues"

Tabula Peutingeriana

Tacitus

Agricola

Annals

7.388 2969n169
7.415–16 667n186,
2148n1577
7.415–20 913n560
7.428 2150n1597
7.641–817 741n70
7.770 2150n1597,
2661n3626,
2860n5570
8 1731n31
8.124 3317n1640
8.398 2150n1597,
2661n3626,
2860n5570
8.407–15 620n286
8.523–26 1174n8
8.680–81 800n167
9.16 1436n1359
9.20–21 1436n1364
9.247 1082n427,
1083n429
9.282 931n776
9.297 1663n613
9.314–66 1885n178,
1954n1064,
2977n265,
3030n758
9.375–445 1885n178,
1954n1064,
2977n265,
3030n758
9.465–67 1872n55,
1874n70
9.485 1474n80
9.487 1716nn117–
118
9.495 2662n3629
9.525–29 536n305,
2493n2000
9.566 3042n894,
3042n897
9.617 1483n182
9.625 2150n1597,
2860n5570
9.630–31 1174n8
9.638 2141n1507
9.641 730n742,
1947n1005
9.642 1785n572
9.646–52 667n186,
2148n1577
9.657–58 667n186,
723n673
9.658 2148n1577
10.2 2662n3631
10.100 2150n1597,
2662n3626,
2860n5570
10.100–103 1827n918
10.116 954n1025
10.120–45 741n70
10.138 1577n1189
10.220 2166n1795
10.234 2166n1795
10.471–72 3016n639
10.495–96 962n1107

10.503 3016n639,
3017n643
10.517 3317n1640
10.517–20 1478n116,
2631n3297
10.668 2150n1597,
2860n5570
10.681–82 2500n2079
10.729–41 3016n632
11.43 929n740
11.122–31 1093n531,
1166n1213
11.148–50 1477n106
11.165 3317n1641
11.178 3317n1641
11.241 1827n918,
3188n609
11.243–95 1229
11.292 3317n1641
11.300 1827n918,
3188n609
11.321 1959n1109,
2914n6063
11.342 866n42,
1212n60, 1229
11.470 3017n643
11.570–72 1380n849
11.734 610n136,
1484n191,
1559n994
12.6 3043n914
12.52–53 611n137,
1483n182,
1593n1347,
1890n229
12.67–69 1577n1190
12.99 1570n1113
12.99–100 2114n1271
12.150 3017n643
12.178 2150n1597,
2662n3626,
2860n5570
12.195 1436n1356,
1436n1359
12.407–8 918n618
12.416 1593n1347,
1890n229
12.433–35 2995n452
12.434 3072n1259
12.438–43 2995n452
12.463 918n618
12.468ff. 3231n959
12.600–603
2500n2072
12.606 1577n1190
12.778 1069n310,
1071n321,
2162n1749
12.784–85 667n186
12.791 2150n1597,
2860n5570
12.843 2662n3626

Ciris

480 3595n431

Copa

1–6 588n56
33 2416
38 1424n1229

Culex

246 2969n169

Eclogues

in toto: 3035n821
1.1–5 3034n806
2.15–17 1577n1190
2.63 3041n890
3.3–6 3035n823
3.34 3030n763
3.41–42 838n499
3.80 3042n894
4.4–25 878
4.61 1384n880
5.56–57 730n742,
1947n1005
5.60 3042n894
5.64 730n742
8.27–28 878n169
8.29 2969n169
8.47–50 2550n2531,
2696n3994
8.52 3042n894
8.75 1774n448,
2436n1424
9.47 730n743,
1947n1005

Georgics

1.121 2661n3626
1.125–29 1014n219
1.130 3041n890
1.204–58 838n499
1.276–86 3099n1534
1.283 2661n3626
1.297–98 1547n828
1.328 2661n3626
1.353 2661n3626
2.116–17 1552n881
2.325 2150n1597,
2661n3626,
2860n5570
2.523 3071n1233
2.535 3722n86
3.17 2401n1000
3.284 20n109, 554
3.295–96 3595n417
3.307 2401n1000
3.331–34 1547n826
3.341 3049n965
3.349–83 1555n915
3.406–8 3030n765,
3042n900
4.155–57 1015
4.221–22 2165,
2637n3370,
2659n3595
4.225 2637n3370

4.226–27 730n742,
1947n1005
4.405–14 667n186,
2149n1582
4.440–42 667n186,
2149n1582
4.561 845n582

Vita Aesopi/Life of Aesop/Aesop Romance

in toto: 57n56, 65n124,
66n132, 114,
129n110, 635n508,
769n343, 1801n725
1 226n27
6 1762n339,
3512n1325
6–8 1665n646
33 915n588,
2350n496
33–55 1926n728
36 2569n2695
51 2271n649
101 2985n361
124 1062n234
124–42 2424n1273
125–26 1062n234
126 1916n573
127 1312n179
127–28 2934n6230
128 2935nn6243–
6244, 3461n931
130 1916n573
132 1475n93,
2935n6243
133 1460n1602
134 2906n5986
135 2847n5450
138 2847n5450
139 2416n1198,
2906n5986
140 1916n573
142 1460n1602,
2631n3296
end 1422n1212

Vitruvius

On Architecture
1.pref. 1 516n144,
3376n249
1.pref. 2 1442n1412
1.1.5 1914n530,
3710n1590
1.2.7 327n48,
2752n4551,
2972n200
1.6.4 2577n2750
2.1.8 193n234
2.8.17 2973n224
3 2897n5900
5.pref. 3 3367n160
5.1 2764n4697

5.2.1 1884,
2484n1906
5.3.1 2901n5951
5.3.3 2902n5958
5.3.4–8 2926n6160
5.5 2926n6160
5.5.1 2926n6160
5.5.7 2926n6160
5.6.1–2 2902n5954,
2903n5965,
2926n6162
5.7.1 2902n5954
5.8 2926n6160
5.10.1 2751n4542
5.10.1–5 2751n4537
5.10.2 1593n1342,
2751n4541
5.10.4 2751n4534
5.12.1 2376n711
5.12.1–2 1733n46,
3590n373
5.12.2 2376n711
6.pref. 1 3077n1307
6.pref. 1–2 1025n354,
1065n261,
3691n1388
6.pref. 2 3181n541
6.pref. 3 2729n4337
6.pref. 4 2729n4337
6.pref. 5 1275n256
6.3.9 2972n200
6.3.10 2972n200
6.4.1 870n89,
871n105,
2752n4551
6.5.1–3 425n15,
1786n587,
1901n360
6.6.6–7 2972n200
6.7.2 706n523
6.7.4 604n53
6.7.4–5 1006n134,
1945n988
7.pref. 10–17 176n82,
659
7.pref. 18 660
7.10.1–4 729n725
7.11.1 2401n1002
7.13.1 2402
7.13.1–2 2401n997
7.13.3 2400
7.14.1 2401n997
8 2751n4536
8.pref. 1 531n251
8.2.5–6 800n164,
3608n556
8.2.6 1551n873
8.2.7 1552n880
8.3.4 327n49,
1593n1342,
2752n4547,
2979n283
8.6.1–15 2751n4536

Other Ancient and Medieval Sources

Papyri, Inscriptions, and Fragment Collections

108 2874n5677
109 2874n5677
132 2929n6183
143.36a–d 2929n6183
212 2929n6183
215 2942n6310
233 2929n6183
236 2929n6183
241 2929n6183
295.9 3021n693
300 2930n6194
304 2930n6194
304a 2930n6194
424a 2394
425.10 2884n5784
426 2827n5243,
2828n5258
442 3021n693
444 2828
454 2888
504 2874n5679
505 2874n5679
508 2878n5734
2.508–9 2891n5852
515 2893
516A 2893
520 2893
547 2828, 2886,
2900n5940, 2903
547 (1) 2884n5784
547 (2) 2884n5784
554 2885n5790
585–86 2884n5784
586 2884n5786
597 2920n6122
599 3720n53
611 2827n5244
614.18 2920n6123
621 3021n693
627A/B 2827n5241
633 3021n693
633.3 3021n693
636 2828n5262
636.9–10 2884,
2884n5784
639.9–10 2884n5784
644 3021n693
646 2828n5262
661.19 3021n693
666a.9 3021n693
676A 2827n5241
678A 2827n5241
680 2523n2306
684A 2523n2306
702 3021n693
724.3 3021n693
727 2828n5262
728 2888n5828
735 2827n5241
740 2930n6194
803 2881n5750
811 2827n5241,
2831n5297
824 3021n693
833 3021n693
876 2885n5801
898 2885n5801

898.3 2920n6122
898.4 2920n6122
904a.7 2885n5801
924a 3021n693
938a 3021n693
941 1559n986,
2878n5725
946 2881n5750
980 3021n693
984 2827n5242,
2831n5297,
2881n5750
994 3021n693
1001 2829
1001.5 2829n5268
1003–4 2943
1008 2881n5750
1009 2943
1012 2829
1012.4 2829n5268
1017 2523n2306
1020.7 2920n6123
1029 2829
1042 3021n693
1047 2523n2306
1060 3021n693
1203 2892
1210 2874n5677,
2892
1211 627n392, 2893
1212 2893
1213 2791, 2893
1214–27 2874
1217 2874
1218 2874
1225 2874
1228 2874n5677
1229 2893
1230 2893n5867
1230–32 2791
1234–35 2894n5874
1237 929n750, 2893
1238 929n750, 2873,
2956n72
1239–41 2892n5865
1239–43 328n64,
2839n5370
1240.1 1166n1216
1242 2892n5865
1243 2873,
2892n5865
4.1251 2792
1252 2892n5866
1253–54 328n64,
2839, 2892
1255 2430n1339,
2843, 2843n5405,
2873
1260 2892
1261 2885n5801
1262 2860n5570,
2892n5865
1264 2288n832
1265 2873, 2878
1267–68 2893
1269 2874
1270 2893

1377 2829
1382a 3021n693
1387 2881n5750
1487–88 2881n5750,
2943n6323
1539 2827n5244
1548 2827n5244
1552 3021n693
1577A 2888
1578a 2885
1578a.11–12
2885n5798
1587 3021n693
1601A 2523n2306
1603 3021n693
5.1676–77 2792n4968
1722 3021n693
1882 3021n693
1910 2930n6194
1944 658n98,
3021n693
1977a 2920n6122
1987 2920n6122
2018 2920n6122
2039.8–9 2907n6003
2040.4–5 2930n6194
2065 2829n5272,
2911n6035
2069 3021n693
2076 2888n5828
2076–80 2828
2100 2827n5241
2101 2834n5324
2202 2834n5324
2211 2834n5324
2212 2881n5750,
2884n5784
2212.a6–7
2884n5784,
2884n5786,
2885n5799
2212.17 2884n5784
2260A 2523n2306
2441 2884n5784
2446 2881n5750
2948a 3021n693
2950f 3021n693
3016 3021n693
3025 2828n5262
3029 2827n5241
3031 2920n6122
3047 2827n5243,
2831n5297
3050 2888
3051 2827n5241
3053 2523n2306
3058 3021n693
3062 2831n5297,
3021n693
3065 2888
3071 3021n693
3080–81 2827n5241
3224 2523n2306
3258 2885n5801
1.3263.7–9
2891n5852
3417 2829

3422 3021n693
3429 2920n6122
3429.25 2920n6122
3803 frg. b.9
2907n6003
3817.1 929n750
3817A.2 2844n5418
3817A.6 2844n5418
3817A.8 2844n5418
3820C 2844n5418
3901 2827n5244
4336 2930n6194
4340 2827n5244

IG/Inscriptiones
graecae

1².73.9 3615n634
2.1097 2584
2.1099 2584
2².1553–78
2714n4166
2².1945 2864n5597
2².1968 2864n5597
2².1973 2864n5597
2².1985 2864n5597
2².1990 2864n5597
2².2030 2864n5597
2².2059 2864n5597
2².3250 2577n2747
2².3269 2578
2².3271 2578
2².3271.4–5
2576n2739
2².3274 2578
2².3277 453n125,
776n414, 2578,
2602n3025
2².3278 2578
2².3449 776n414,
2569n2696
2².7931 2579n2768
2².8934 2579n2768
2².12609 2579n2768
3.1.706 2600n2993
3.2.2395 2954n54
4.128 1069n303,
2978n275,
3627n753
4.951.107ff. 1498n329
4.951.110ff. 1498n329
4.951.113ff. 1498n329
4.951.120–21
1665n648
4.952.86ff. 1498n329
4.952.110ff. 1498n329
4.952.132–33
1498n329
5.1.961 2315n167
7.2713 453n125
9².670 627n393
10.2.1.291 2396
10.2.31 2555n2576
12.1.11 3078
12.1.531 2325n251
12.1.532 2325n251
12.1.534 2325n251

12.1.593 3078
12.1.677 3149n292
12.1.895 2325n251
12.3.178 2292n864
12.3.420 2153n1633
12.3.522 2153n1633
12.5.891 2577n2750
12.8.186.9 2906n5988
14.24 588n56,
2416n1192
14.601 3682
14.830 3703
14.1308 3605n525
14.1976 624n349
14.2548 3346n1884
126 2551
127 2551n2544
133 2551
137 2551

IGBulg/
Inscriptiones grae-
cae in Bulgaria
repertae

4.2263 2386n813

IGLS/Inscriptions
grecques et latines
de la Syrie

5.1998 442n50,
3574n178

IGRR

1.177 3605n525
1.417 1923n673
1.467 2882n5767,
2883n5775
1.512 3682
1.1110 1147n1014
1.1183 1747n192,
1747n195,
2274n685
3.137 3020n674,
3302n1512,
3303n1532
3.262 2110n1224
3.263 2115n1279
3.930 2014
3.933 2015n347
3.935 2014
3.971 2015n347
3.978 2015n347
3.1474 2110n1224
4.788.10 2938n6270
4.836.8 1136n896
4.1406 2153n1633
4.1415 2153n1633
4.1431.29 2924n6149

I. Ital./
Inscriptiones Italiae

13.1.187 2501n2088
13.1.189 2501n2088
13.2 p. 187 1385n893

7.320 2690n3933
7.321 2027n468, 2037
7.330 2027n468, 2037
7.331 2037
7.359 2150n1600
7.406 2150n1600
7.432 2150nn1599–
  1600
7.453 2150n1600
7.454 2150n1600
7.476 2150n1600
7.486 2027n468,
  2037, 2041n638
7.495 2150n1600
7.521 2150nn1599–
  1600
8.1 2150n1592, 2152
8.4 2122
8.5 2131n1416
8.8 2131n1416
8.12 2175n1892, 2312
8.26 2122

Meritt, *Inscriptions*

14.2 2691
16.2–6 2691
19.2 2691
19.5–6 2691
57.76.7 1138n915
57.86.1 1138n916
57.107.2 1138n916
75.3–4 2691
118 326n37

Mesha Inscription

in toto: 1390n940,
  1618n188

**Mount Athos
Manuscript**

in toto: 979n1284

**OGIS/*Orientis
graeci inscriptiones
selectae***

90 1147n1017
96 2804n5070
101 2804n5070
129 2804n5070
134 2804n5070
138 2804n5070
329.51 3483n1108
339.31 3363n114
419 3477
421 3571
432 2804n5070
455 2899
480.8–9 2902n5954
483.181 2488n1947
494.13 2906n5988
494.13–14 2906n5987
509.18 3254n1122

528 2909n6020,
  3682n1282
532 3020n674,
  3302n1512,
  3303n1532
544 2909n6020
544–45 3682n1282
545 2909n6020
549 2909n6020,
  3682n1282
572 3580n242
578.7–8 3183
595 3702n1516
598 3149
599 1048n57
652 2909n6020,
  3682n1282
666 1147n1014
666.4–7 3363n118
667.3–4 3336n1797
669.17 3505n1266
674 1747n195,
  2274n685
726 2804n5069

**P.Amh./*The
Amherst Papyri***

2.141 611n140
62.6–7 1986n48

**P.Beatty/*Chester
Beatty Biblical
Papyri***

3 recto 2349n492
4 906n483, 909n510
16 728n715

P.Bour.

20 3359n72

P.Cair.

49359 1856n248
49360 1856n248

P.Cair.Masp.

3.67325.verso
  1968n1181
67353 2301n26

**P.Cair.Zen./*Zenon
Papyri***

25004 3086n1398
59001.48–52 775n410
59003.11–22
  1915n543
59015 verso 5
  1936n897
59029 3596n440
59060.1 2283nn787–
  788
59154.1 2283n787

59426.1 2283n787
59192.1 2283n787
59251.1 2283n787

**P.Col./*Columbia
Papyri***

1.4.1 3583n281
27.1.25–28 419n149
27.1.26 419n149
27.1.28 419n149
270.1.25–28 775n410

P.Col. inv.

480 1915n547

**P.Coll.Youtie/
Collectanea papy-
rologica**

2.92 2405n1053
66.28 3333n1776
66.32 3333n1776

**PDM/*Papyri de-
moticae magicae***

in toto: 1500n343,
  1505n416,
  1510n487
14.68 2438n1453
14.74–91 664n147
14.95 664n147
14.98–102 664n147
14.169 664n147
14.287 2438n1453
14.574–85 417n119
14.1061–62 1506n422
61.197–216 623n324,
  2274n677
190 2166n1788

PDM Supplement

117–30 913n567
131–32 1636n362
131–34 2167n1818
163 1636n362
183 1636n362
183–84 837n495,
  1505n411

**P.Duk./*Duke
University papyrus
collection***

5 inv. 729 2274n677

P.Egerton

5 1045n30

**P.Eleph./
*Elephantine Papyri***

in toto: 3194n655

1.3–4 2274n678
1.6 1275n264
1.6–7 2510n2185,
  3290n1417
1.16–18 775n410
13.1 2284n787
13.1–2 2284n788

P.Enteux.

26 1267n165

P.Fam.Teb.

19 3387n326

P.Fay.

91 2713n4157
93.7 2422n1247

**P.Flor./*Papyri
greco-egizii, Papiri
Fiorentini***

1.58 611n140
61 2479n1864,
  3387n326
61.59ff. 1095n553

**P.Fouad/*Les
Papyrus Fouad I***

1.21 3655n999
8 501n36, 849n626,
  1147n1017
21 3359n71
26 3361, 3363n117
26.13 3527n1507
26.21–24 2548
26.25 3363n119
26.49–50 3363n119
26.55–56 3531n1529

**P.Giss./*Griechische
Papyri im Museum
des Oberhessischen
Geschichtsvereins
zu Giessen***

11 3583n281
17 1925n713,
  2991n420
17.4 2284n788
19.18 2292n866
21 621n301
40.2.27–29
  2803n5061
41 2805
43 400n117
80.13 2284n788

**P.Giss.Univ./*Mit-
teilungen aus der
Papyrussammlung
der Giessener Uni-
versitätsbibliothek***

20.38 2284n788
21.2 2284n787
21.11 501n35,
  623n332, 1637n370,
  2284n788

**PGM/*Papyri grae-
cae magicae***

in toto: 547n391,
  1500n343,
  1505n416,
  1506n423,
  1506n428,
  2441n1491,
  2854n5514, 2857,
  2876n5705
1.77–78 1638n377,
  3518n1388
1.80–81 2010n282
1.80–82 2847n5451
1.86 2438n1453
1.88–89 1504n402
1.88–90 2010n282
1.114 1531n694
1.130–32 2855n5521
1.160–61 1066n265,
  2846
1.164–66 1504n402,
  2010n282
1.165 1066n265
1.167 2846,
  2847n5451
1.168–72 1066n267
1.171–92 2846
1.172 2915n6074
1.172–90 1066n268
1.175–77 1191n163,
  2850n5479
1.178–81 1636n362,
  1782n520,
  1784n557
1.179–80 731n744
1.179–81 2436n1429
1.179–85 1504n402
1.181–85 2010n282
1.186–87 1805
1.190–91 2915n6074,
  3680n1257
1.192–94 2855n5521
1.216–17 1066n265,
  2846n5440
1.222–31 1327n339,
  1504n398,
  1805n759,
  1890n229
1.247–62 1327n339,
  1504n398,
  1805n759
1.248–49 1503n385,
  2847n5452